AGE, WEIGHT & DISTANCE TABLE
For use with Chase and Hurdle races

Distance	Age	Jan	Feb	Mar	Apr	May	June
2m	5	12—7	12—7	12—7	12—7	12—7	12—7
	4	11—13	12—0	12—1	12—2	12—3	12—4
2¼m	5	12—7	12—7	12—7	12—7	12—7	12—7
	4	11—12	11—13	12—0	12—1	12—2	12—3
2½m	5	12—7	12—7	12—7	12—7	12—7	12—7
	4	11—11	11—12	11—13	12—0	12—1	12—2
2¾m	5	12—6	12—7	12—7	12—7	12—7	12—7
	4	11—10	11—11	11—12	11—13	12—0	12—1
3m	5	12—6	12—6	12—7	12—7	12—7	12—7
	4	11—8	11—10	11—11	11—12	11—13	12—0

Distance	Age	July	Aug	Sep	Oct	Nov	Dec
2m	5	12—7	12—7	12—7	12—7	12—7	12—7
	4	12—4	12—5	12—5	12—6	12—6	12—7
	3	11—5	11—6	11—8	11—9	11—11	11—12
2¼m	5	12—7	12—7	12—7	12—7	12—7	12—7
	4	12—3	12—4	12—5	12—5	12—6	12—6
	3	11—4	11—5	11—7	11—8	11—9	11—10
2½m	5	12—7	12—7	12—7	12—7	12—7	12—7
	4	12—2	12—3	12—4	12—5	12—6	12—6
	3		11—4	11—6	11—7	11—8	11—9
2¾m	5	12—7	12—7	12—7	12—7	12—7	12—7
	4	12—2	12—3	12—4	12—5	12—5	12—6
	3					11—7	11—8
3m	5	12—7	12—7	12—7	12—7	12—7	12—7
	4	12—1	12—2	12—3	12—4	12—5	12—5
	3				11—5	11—6	11—7

For 6-y-o's and older, use 12-7 in all cases

Note Race distances in the above tables are shown only at ¼-mile intervals. For races of 2m1f use the 2¼-mile table weights; for races of 2m3f use 2½ miles; and so forth. For races over odd distances, the nearest distance shown in the table should be used. Races over distances longer than 3 miles should be treated as 3-mile races.

National Hunt Flat races A separate age, weight & distance table is used for NH Flat races but there is no weight-for-age allowance for 5-y-o's; over 2 miles from January to November the allowance for 4-y-o's is 1 lb less than it is over jumps.

CHASERS & HURDLERS 2018/19

Price £75.00

A TIMEFORM PUBLICATION

A Timeform Publication

Compiled and produced by

Geoff Greetham (Publishing Editor), Paul Muncaster (Managing Editor),
John Ingles (Senior Editor, 'Top Horses In France' & Editor for pedigrees),
Phil Turner (Handicapper and Essays), Dan Barber (Handicapper and noteforms),
Martin Rigg, Paul Goodenough (Handicappers), David Cleary (Essays),
Kris Hilliam, Jake Price (noteforms), David Holdsworth, Wendy Muncaster,
Rachel Todd, Chris Wright, Ivan Gardiner, Michael Williamson (Production)

CONTENTS

The age, weight and distance table, for use in applying the ratings in races involving horses of different ages, appears on the end paper at the front of the book

Chasers & Hurdlers 2018/19

Introduction

A century ago, like the rest of the nation, racing was attempting to return to normal after the ravages of the Great War. Jumping had soldiered on in 1918 with a handful of courses staging racing in a season restricted to the early months of the year, with the prospects for the following winter initially looking bleaker still. A ban on racing under National Hunt Rules was announced in June 1918 with the transportation of horses putting too much additional strain on railways struggling with the war effort. The restriction was lifted within days of the Armistice and, by the end of November, the *Racing Calendar* was announcing fixtures for the following January at Manchester, Wolverhampton, Gatwick, Sandown and Windsor. In March, Aintree staged the Grand National for the first time since the 'Khaki Grand National' of 1915 in front of packed stands. 'We thus had the first revelation of the racing boom which came with the end of the war,' reported *The Bloodstock Breeders' Review*. The large crowds had a popular winner to cheer as the favourite Poethlyn won at 11/4, still the shortest odds of any winner in the race's history. The field of twenty-two was small by modern standards, but accounts vary as to how many actually finished. According to *The Bloodstock Breeders' Review*, 'a remarkable feature of the contest was the comparatively large number of horses that went the two rounds and passed the judge', noting that 'the management very sensibly built the fences a shade lower than usual, and perhaps a little thinner' to allow for the lack of Aintree experience among most of the field. While that publication and T. H. Bird's *A Hundred Grand Nationals* put the number of finishers at eleven, Reg Green's *A Race Apart* records only seven who completed.

Poethlyn (a first-fence faller when returning to Aintree a year later) had also won the last of three substitute races for the Grand National, run over the same trip at Gatwick during the war years, the last two of which were run as 'The War National'. Among Poethlyn's rivals at Gatwick were two others, Shaun Spadah and Sergeant Murphy, who went on to win the Grand National in the following decade. Aintree was not the only racecourse requisitioned by the military during the war. Cheltenham was used as a Voluntary Aid Hospital for wounded soldiers which was one of the beneficiaries from money raised from the sale of race cards at the 1918 War National. Cheltenham was among the racecourses to mark the centenary of the Armistice in the latest season, doing so on the Sunday of its November meeting. Poethlyn was partnered to his wins at Gatwick and Aintree by Ernie Piggott, champion jump jockey and later grandfather of Lester. Another of Lester's relatives, his uncle Fred Rickaby, who won the One Thousand Guineas four times as well as an Oaks, never had the chance to become a champion. Serving as a private in the Tank Corps, he died in France aged twenty-three just a month before the Armistice. Lester Piggott's mother Iris—Rickaby's sister—gave her son Rickaby's middle name in his memory. One of the early casualties of the war with a racing connection was Major Arthur Hughes-Onslow, 'Junks' to his friends,

'It's very unlikely he'll come back and run in it a third time.' Although Tiger Roll's trainer has announced a light campaign leading to another tilt at the Grand National, owner Michael O'Leary seems to have ruled out an attempt by Tiger Roll to try to equal Red Rum's three Grand National victories (first or second in the race five years running); whether or not he goes for a third win, Tiger Roll's successive victories have been a boon for the organisers of Aintree's great race as it goes through another period of change; runner-up Magic of Light carved a huge chunk out of the last fence, taking the sort of liberty that would have put her on the deck in former years

an all-round sportsman and the leading military rider of his day, who was a three-times winner of Sandown's Grand Military Gold Cup, a race which, by its nature, soon counted other war dead among its past winners.

The huge human losses of the Great War are well documented but the sacrifices that horses made in the conflict have only become more widely acknowledged in recent years in commemorations of the war's centenary. The notion of the *War Horse* has been popularised by the Steven Spielberg film (based on Michael Morpurgo's novel of the same name), and by the stage version featuring the life-sized puppet Joey familiar from ITV Racing's opening titles. It was only in 2014 that the Dickin Medal, the 'animal Victoria Cross', was awarded posthumously, in recognition of the wider contribution made by animals in wartime, to a real 'war horse', Warrior, the mount during World War I of General Jack Seely, the grandfather of Brough Scott. Warrior survived the war against all odds (he became known as 'the horse the Germans couldn't kill') and went on to win a point-to-point on the Isle of Wight in peacetime. Millions of other equines, thoroughbreds among them, were less fortunate. If not direct casualties of warfare, they succumbed to disease, exhaustion or starvation. Britain's losses amounted to nearly half a million animals, many of them remounts imported from overseas to replenish the supply of horses whose life expectancy at the front at the height of the conflict was put at ten days. The war in total was reckoned to have claimed the lives of half of the sixteen million animals estimated to have been used by all sides.

The last War National at Gatwick in 1918 was won by Poethlyn, the best steeplechaser during the war years; he started favourite for the National the following year when the race moved back to Aintree and carried 12-7 to an impressive victory in front of packed stands

The Sporting Life did its bit for the war effort by raising money for ambulances for the Allied front, but it was also at the forefront of the defence of racing, criticising those who wanted to stop it for 'depriving our soldiers of sport, which is their favourite topic of conversation in the trenches'; Aintree was one of the racecourses taken over by the military but films of the substitute Nationals at Gatwick were sent out to France to be shown to the troops

Poethlyn and the other horses who kept racing going in Britain through the war years can therefore be considered the lucky ones given the fates that befell so many of their contemporaries. Seen from a historical perspective, too, the twenty-first century thoroughbred leads a pampered existence compared to vast numbers of horses who have gone before them, and not just those caught up in war. Hell for Horses is the title of an early chapter in Ulrich Raulff's 2015 book *Farewell to the Horse*, source of the statistics quoted above, which explores, as the subtitle says, 'the final century of our relationship [with the horse].' In the days before the invention of the combustion engine, the horse transported people and goods in the world's rapidly developing cities of the late nineteenth century such as Paris, London and New York. 'For the horses living in and consumed by the nineteenth-century city, seized by the storm of mechanisation, it was no healthy environment. Their muscles, tendons, hooves and joints could only endure the harsh work of providing draught power for the urban modes of transport for a few years,' says Raulff. Omnibus and tram horses had short working lives, though 'for many the end came even sooner by way of permanent lameness, a sad fate concluded with the veterinarian's bullet.' Twenty six thousand horses each year in London ended their lives at the knacker's yard to be turned into cat food and fertilizer.

As well as the war horse, the working horse has all but disappeared over the course of the twentieth century, not just from farms and fields but from city streets where they were once a daily sight for urban dwellers, as much for those living in the country. London's horse population, for example, at the end of the nineteenth century, stood at three hundred thousand. Mechanisation should be something to celebrate for all who care about horse welfare. But the loss of man's daily working relationship with the horse has resulted in a section of the population wanting to confine the racing thoroughbred to the 'safety' of a stable or a paddock. Racing, formerly well down the list of hazardous occupations for a horse, has been left by default standing virtually alone as an activity in which the horse runs the risk of injury—or worse—even if those risks are small compared to what has been asked of horses in the past.

The 'social contract', the unwritten permission that allows racing to take place (and has consigned blood sports to history, or at least outlawed them), came up for discussion in the House of Commons in October after a public petition, supported by an animal rights group, reached the required hundred thousand signatures to force a debate. Those behind the petition called for the setting up of a new independent body for the protection of racehorses. The accusation levelled at the BHA was that their remit to promote the sport represented a conflict of interest with their responsibility for animal welfare. 'Without [the best possible welfare practice], the integrity, veracity and legitimacy of racing fall at the first hurdle,' it was claimed. 'Sadly, racing has fallen at that hurdle and is stricken by its own ineptness at getting up to the task in hand and protecting horses from harm.' How an independent body would be any more successful than the BHA in eliminating risk from the sport was not made clear. Another 'damning indictment of the BHA's failings' was supposedly the five hundred or so whip offences each year (another interpretation of such figures might be that the tighter the whip rules, the more likely it is that jockeys fall foul of them).

The reports of the debate made interesting reading, though, alarmingly, they also revealed—through misconceptions, ignorance or plain hostility—a lack of 'racing literacy' among some MPs. The portrayal, for example, of racing's governing body as 'an exclusive old boys' club run like a masonic lodge' sounds suspiciously like a description of the old Jockey Club, not the BHA. It was also claimed 'horses are trained to jump and race—those things do not exactly come to a horse naturally.' The horse would have become extinct millennia ago if the ability to outrun predators and clear obstacles in its path had not become part of its natural make-up! There were references to 'the barbaric use of the whip' and 'the tide of death and abuse in the horse racing industry.' Perhaps the most bizarre statement in the debate concerned racehorse fatalities: 'We have to ask whether, if we applied the same standards to animal welfare as we do to human welfare…we would accept the same number of deaths in cricketers and rugby players.'

Fortunately for racing, it does still have some friends in the House of Commons who were able to put forward a robust and informed defence of the sport's welfare record and the importance of the sport remaining in its own hands. Among those to speak up for racing were Tewkesbury's Conservative MP Laurence Robertson and St Helens North's Labour MP Conor McGinn, the co-chairmen of the all-party parliamentary racing and bloodstock industries group, whose constituencies include Cheltenham and Haydock respectively. McGinn told the House that the ultimate aim of those behind the petition was 'to get rid of British horse racing', before making the point that the BHA has a proven track record of improving equine welfare, that breaches of rules relating to equine welfare are dealt with by a fully independent panel, and that it was impractical to try to separate such an integral principle as welfare from the rest of the BHA's powers. 'Every rule and regulation in British racing, enforced by the BHA's stewarding, course inspectorate, stable inspection and veterinary teams has the welfare of the thoroughbred racehorse at its heart.'

It was McGinn who used the term 'racing literacy' in a guest column, shortly after the debate, in the *Racing Post* in which he expressed his disappointment that 'so few pro-racing MPs were in the chamber to challenge the ill-informed rhetoric.' 'Sadly', he wrote, 'most of my parliamentary colleagues have little regard for racing and even less experience of it', before he went on to express his fear that such lack of understanding could have 'dire consequences for our sport'. McGinn also highlighted the lack of appreciation by many of his Parliamentary colleagues that racing and gambling, whilst having a relationship with each other, are nonetheless distinct. 'MPs no longer just equate the two, they think they are one and the same. It isn't hard to see how in that context politicians—most of whom haven't had an each-way bet on the Grand National, never mind been to visit their local racecourse—think that if betting is bad then racing must be bad too.'

The House of Commons debate was concluded by the Minister for Animal Welfare David Rutley, representing the Government, who welcomed the BHA's ongoing work in the area of welfare and rejected the need for a new body to be created. But his speech came with a clear message for the BHA to do more to reduce fatality rates, his final words being 'I hope that the BHA is listening to this debate.' The message was received loud and clear. BHA chief executive Nick Rust referred to Parliament's demands for more ambitious welfare standards when the BHA published its review into the fatalities at the 2018 Cheltenham Festival in December. When the BHA's 2019 business plan was published later the same month, equine welfare was made the priority. In March, a new Horse Welfare Board was created with the remit of developing an industry-wide welfare strategy. Its recommendations are expected by the end of the year, while it will also look at how racing's welfare standards are communicated.

In the circumstances, the BHA could have done without a series of incidents which swayed the tightrope along which it must feel it is being made to tread. An outbreak of equine flu and a highly controversial National Hunt Chase at the Cheltenham Festival tested the BHA's surefootedness, while in January it published figures revealing that fatalities on racecourses in 2018 were at their highest since 2014. The size of that increase hardly warranted the headlines and attendant bad publicity generated by the BHA's press release which should have given more emphasis to attempting to put the increase into some kind of perspective. Fatality rates are extremely low, and inevitably there are small fluctuations, up or down, in the fatality rate from one year to the next. The latest increase was from 0.18% to 0.22%. In other words, it needed two decimal places to register any kind of variation at all. Four *hundredths* of a per cent! These are annual figures, combining Flat and jump racing, and most of the increase was down to, proportionally, a greater increase in the number of deaths on the Flat. The long-term trend has seen fatality rates fall to the current five-year average of 0.2% (that particular figure given only to one decimal place), a message which ought to take precedence over minimal annual fluctuations. The BHA pledged to 'stay ahead of public opinion' in the wake of the latest increase, chief executive Nick Rust being acutely aware of the power of social media (a point developed in the essay on Le Breuil). That said, if the BHA feels and acts as if public opinion is snapping at its heels, it runs the risk of being chased into a corner from which there is no escape. Rather than running ahead of public opinion, the BHA perhaps needs to do more to 'protect the brand' and even try to change public opinion. There is a lobby, including in Parliament, which will not be satisfied with anything greater than a fatality rate of zero, in which case the BHA is on a hiding to nothing. The increase in the fatality rate should also serve as a reminder that statistics can be a strong ally when they support your case, but too much reliance on them can backfire if circumstances change. It is tempting fate, in a sport with inherent risks, to make too strong, or too simplistic, a link between welfare measures and favourable outcomes.

As the BHA is pressured to 'stay ahead of public opinion', it runs a growing risk of alienating racing's participants, particularly its trainers and jockeys. Details of the BHA review into the 2018 Festival are given in the extended essay on **Le Breuil**, winner of the National Hunt Chase for amateur riders, in which there were only four finishers—if the Cheltenham stewards were correct in handing out punishments for riders continuing on tired horses, there should have been even fewer finishers. The essay summarises other areas of tension between racing's administrators and its participants, the fallout from 'the four-miler' (a misnomer in future following a reduction in the race's distance) bringing matters to something of a head. The outbreak of equine flu in February, which some initially feared might jeopardise the Festival, was another episode which caused friction as detailed in the essay on the winner of the rearranged Betfair Hurdle **Al Dancer**. The National Hunt Chase was additionally marred by one of the latest Festival's three fatalities, Ballyward's owners Andrea and Graham Wylie also losing Invitation Only in the Cheltenham Gold Cup, while their wretched luck persisted at Aintree where Up For Review was fatally injured when brought down at the first in the Grand National, the first fatality in that race since the changes made to the course in 2012. The highest profile death at the Festival, and one that animal rights groups tried to capitalise on, was that of **Sir Erec** who started a hot favourite for the Triumph Hurdle. His essay highlights the transparency over fatality rates that has long existed in horse racing. The same approach has now been adopted by greyhound racing, another sport facing increased hostility from animal welfare groups.

The latest running of the National Hunt Chase was not the first to prompt a review of the race's conditions, an earlier revamp resulting in better fields and an illustrious roll call of recent winners and placed horses that includes Cheltenham Gold Cup winner Native River, the Grand National third Rathvinden, and the National Hunt Chase's most notable winner **Tiger Roll**, the first since Red Rum to win consecutive Grand Nationals. In a National notable for its lack of incident, the 4/1 favourite Tiger Roll became the shortest-priced winner since Poethlyn a hundred years earlier and became the eighth horse in the race's history to win the Grand National more than once, a claim Poethlyn doesn't legitimately share due to his first success coming in a substitute event. The resumption of racing at Aintree after World War I was not the last time the great race staged a revival—comebacks are a theme of Tiger Roll's essay—Red Rum's popularity helping to resurrect the fortunes of the Grand National after it was on its knees in the 'seventies. Tiger Roll was partnered again by Davy Russell who enjoyed a largely armchair ride to win his second Grand National before going on win the following month's Grand Steeple-Chase de Paris (see 'Top Horses in France') on Carriacou on his very first ride over fences at Auteuil. With an earlier Cheltenham Gold Cup win to his name on Lord Windermere, Russell has now matched Fred Winter's riding achievement of winning all three of steeplechasing's greatest prizes, though Winter achieved the treble in the same year, 1962, when he won the Grand National on Kilmore and both the Gold Cup and Grand Steeple-Chase de Paris on Mandarin. Winter also won the Grand National on Sundew in 1957 and the Gold Cup in 1961 on Saffron Tartan.

Whether Russell partners Tiger Roll in a hat-trick bid at Aintree looked far from certain at one stage, though if he doesn't bid to emulate Red Rum, Tiger Roll's essay has a proposal for how he could make history at Cheltenham instead. With Rule The World winning the 2016 Grand National, Michael O'Leary's Gigginstown House Stud has now won three of the last four Grand Nationals and there is time yet for further success in the race, with or without Tiger Roll. But as covered in the essay on novice hurdler **Battleoverdoyen**, the days of the Gigginstown cavalry pitching up with a rainbow of distinguishing caps in the top staying chases are numbered as O'Leary has announced the

Within a month of Tiger Roll's second Grand National victory, Michael O'Leary announced his intention to scale back and eventually wind up his dominant Gigginstown House Stud operation; Gigginstown House has won seven owners' championships in Ireland and the maroon, white star and armlets has been carried to three Grand National wins at Aintree and two Cheltenham Gold Cup successes (War of Attrition and Don Cossack). Gigginstown House Stud will still have well over a hundred horses in training in the next season. 'Next season will see the last of the bumper horses, the one after that will be the last for the novice hurdlers, the following the last for the novice chasers and so on,' said O'Leary who is spending more time on his teenage children's activities

bet365 Celebration Chase, Sandown—
a record-breaking nineteenth consecutive win for Timeform Horse of the Year Altior

gradual winding down of his racing empire, which won a seventh owners' championship in Ireland. The mixed fortunes of the Gigginstown novice hurdlers are covered in the essay on Punchestown winner **Felix Desjy**.

Tiger Roll had earlier won his second Cross-Country Chase at the Cheltenham Festival to join a select group of horses with four Festival wins that also now includes **Altior** after his second victory in the Queen Mother Champion Chase earlier in the afternoon. Altior was one of three Festival winners for his jockey Nico de Boinville, the meeting's leading rider for the first time. Top two-mile chasers struggle for wider recognition compared to Grand National heroes, but Altior joins Istabraq and Kauto Star in Timeform's pantheon of three-times Horse of the Year award winners and stands one short of matching Desert Orchid's four titles (contrasts with the Desert Orchid era feature in the essay on Altior). In winning his third Celebration Chase at Sandown at the end of the season, Altior broke the record of another former Timeform Horse of the Year, Big Buck's, by extending his unbeaten record over jumps to nineteen races. Big Buck's also dominated for season after season in another of jumping's divisions in which fame is hard to come by, the staying hurdlers. The unheralded star staying hurdler of the latest season was **Paisley Park**, who not only has similar potential to have a lasting hold on the

Thursday's card at the Cheltenham Festival produced a 'golden hour' for the sport; Frodon's victory under champion conditional Bryony Frost and the victory of Paisley Park forty minutes later in the Stayers' Hurdle, for owner Andrew Gemmell who has been blind from birth, made the front pages, as well as the sports pages

division but provided one of the human stories of the jumping year, as his essay recounts. The third day of the Festival often pales beside Cheltenham's other highlights (the Ryanair Chase is the day's official feature nowadays ahead of the more established Stayers' Hurdle) but the joy of Paisley Park's blind owner Andrew Gemmell and of Bryony Frost, rider of the Ryanair winner Frodon, and the warmth with which the record crowd of 67,821 greeted both winners, provided the best possible advertisement for jumping (each day of the Festival had record attendances totalling 266,779 for the four days).

Frost, who in November became only the second female jockey in Britain after Lucy Alexander to ride out her claim, has the gift of turning the normally banal post-race interview into a compelling account of the partnership of horse and rider, speaking as much for her mounts as for herself. 'Don't you dare not send me into the last, I want this more than you, now come on!' was Frost's interpretation of the message she was getting from the bold-jumping Frodon in the closing stages of the Ryanair. A year after Katie Walsh's win on Relegate in the Champion Bumper, Frost became the first female jockey to win a Grade 1 over jumps at the Festival, an achievement soon matched the following day by Rachael Blackmore on **Minella Indo** in the Spa (Albert Bartlett) Novices' Hurdle, the second winner of the week after A Plus Tard in the novices' handicap chase for the jockey who battled for the Irish championship for much of the season. Like Paisley Park, Frodon had finished last at the previous year's Festival, but he, along with other young stablemates **Cyrname** and **Clan des Obeaux**, formed a trio of Grade 1-winning chasers who helped Paul Nicholls to the trainers' title for the first time since 2015/16. While Frodon was in his element around Cheltenham, winning three times there (he also beat the Welsh Grand National winner **Elegant Escape** in the Cotswold Chase), Cyrname was not even entered for the Festival due to his apparent need to race right-handed. He was the surprise package of the season among the leading chasers,

After two seasons in which he had to settle for second behind Nicky Henderson, Paul Nicholls regained the trainers' title in Britain; it was the eleventh time Nicholls has been champion and he has been either first or second in the table in each of the last twenty-one seasons

Espoir d'Allen's fifteen-length triumph in the Champion Hurdle is the greatest winning margin in the race's history; triple champion Istabraq and the first double champion back in the 'thirties Insurance were the joint holders, both recording twelve-length wins; Dorothy Paget, most successful owner in the race with four wins before she was overtaken by J. P. McManus, the owner of Istabraq and Espoir d'Allen, is pictured leading in Insurance who landed the odds in small fields in 1932 and 1933 on his only two starts in the race

much improved to win twice at Ascot after the turn of the year, with a wide-margin success in the Ascot Chase earning him a BHA handicap mark superior to Altior's. A first meeting between the two is eagerly awaited. As for Clan des Obeaux, he won at Ascot on the same day as Cyrname in the rearranged Denman Chase (the stable had five winners on the card among a total of eight on the day), but his biggest win came when providing Nicholls with a tenth win in the King George VI Chase. Clan des Obeaux's essay examines the fortunes of Nicholls' stable since setting a record prize money total in 2007/8, a season in which Denman, Kauto Star (winner of the second of his five King Georges that season) and future Grand National winner Neptune Collonges took the first three places in the Gold Cup, and Master Minded won the Queen Mother Champion Chase. The stable's jockeys are covered in the essay on novice chaser **Dynamite Dollars**, the first big winner as stable jockey for Harry Cobden who also partnered Clan des Obeaux and Cyrname. Clan des Obeaux was a non-staying fifth in the Cheltenham Gold Cup, but the stable has a big Gold Cup hope—in more ways than one—in the imposing form of the RSA Chase winner **Topofthegame**, like Clan des Obeaux part-owned by Paul Barber, as was Denman, himself a former RSA winner.

Richard Johnson received an OBE in the New Year's Honours and went on to win his fourth jockeys' championship, reaching 200 winners with a double at Perth on the penultimate day of the season; Harry Cobden slotted in well as first jockey at Manor Farm Stables and would have been champion jockey if the title had been decided on 1,2,3 prize-money earnings

Mullins was champion trainer in Ireland for the thirteenth time, seeing off the challenge of Gordon Elliott much more comfortably than in recent seasons. Taking on Ireland's top trainers on their own turf can seem like a David and Goliath struggle at times for smaller British yards, but there were some notable success stories for those willing to take a shot. Among them was **Simply Ned**'s Grade 1 victory at Leopardstown at Christmas for trainer Nicky Richards who also gained 'a triumph for the North' when winning the Scottish Grand National with **Takingrisks** (whose essay returns to the subject of northern jumping). Besides Nicky Henderson's successes at Punchestown already mentioned, others who made the trip worthwhile were Harry Fry, who won the Champion Stayers' Hurdle with veteran **Unowhatimeanharry** for the second time, and Colin Tizzard, whose novice hurdler **Reserve Tank** added a second Grade 1 win to his earlier success at Aintree. Tizzard also won the Tolworth Hurdle with **Elixir de Nutz** and the Ladbrokes Trophy with **Sizing Tennessee** but says his 'next good one' is **Lostintranslation** who had some good tussles with Defi du Seuil before beating Topofthegame in the Mildmay Novices' Chase at Aintree.

The colours of the late Ann and Alan Potts, carried prominently in the latest season by Magic of Light and Supasundae, as well as by Sizing Tennessee, like those of Gigginstown eventually, will become rarer sights on racecourses in future. J. P. McManus, champion owner in Britain again (as well as owner of **Champ** who is named after A. P. McCoy) and the Cheltenham Festival's most successful owner (see Defi du Seuil's essay), is ever present in the ranks of leading owners, but the ownership landscape is an ever-changing one. Paul and Clare Rooney, whose Cheltenham 'boycott' made headlines and is covered on their Liverpool Hurdle winner **If The Cap Fits**, are to halve their jumping string for the season ahead, while Mike Grech and Stuart Parkin, who had horses with Henderson among other yards, sold their jointly-owned string of around thirty horses at Doncaster in May. Another big-spending owner,

Noel Fehily headed the season's retirements at the age of forty-three, announcing he would be quitting after partnering 50/1-shot Eglantine du Seuil to victory at the Cheltenham Festival where his career wins included the Champion Hurdle on Buveur d'Air and the Queen Mother Champion Chase on Special Tiara in 2017 (Buveur d'Air gave him his second Champion Hurdle win after Rock On Ruby and he also won two King George VI Chases on Silviniaco Conti); in Ireland, Rachael Blackmore battled it out with Paul Townend and Davy Russell for the jockeys' title, eventually coming second with 90 winners, just two years after being the first woman to become champion conditional

Darren Yates, snapped up winning pointer Interconnected from that dispersal for £620,000, a record price for a jumper at auction. The booming market in Irish pointers was evident from some of the purchases that marked a significant increase in the jumping interests of 'Flat' owners Cheveley Park Stud, though the essay on their Champion Bumper winner **Envoi Allen** (their other Festival winner was A Plus Tard) gives a reminder that their involvement in the winter game dates back a while. **Getaway Trump** is another promising young performer for the Owners Group syndicates, in addition to Triumph Hurdle winner Pentland Hills, while an owner and sponsor who made a comeback in the latest season was Irish property developer Sean Mulryan, his wife's colours carried to victory by **City Island** in the Baring Bingham, now run once again in the name of Mulryan's company Ballymore.

While owners come and go, jump jockeys just seem to keep going, or at least for much longer than they once did. Ruby Walsh retired at thirty-nine, while Noel Fehily, who rode another of Mullins' winners at Cheltenham, Eglantine du Seuil, and is another in the all-time top ten of jump jockeys by number of wins, announced his retirement at the age of forty-three, his career touched on in the essay on If The Cap Fits. Walsh says he marvels at the longevity of his British counterpart Richard Johnson, still going strongly at forty-two. Johnson was champion for the fourth time in a season that brought him two hundred winners, as well as an OBE, and is summarised in the entry on La Bague Au Roi. Barry Geraghty, forty in September 2019, broke a leg in the Topham late in the season but had earlier moved into fourth place in the all-time jump jockeys list at Cheltenham in January. Meanwhile, in France, the Prix Merci Jacques Ricou at Auteuil in November marked the retirement at the age of thirty-eight of the five-times French champion who made a name for himself in Britain early this century thanks principally to his partnership with the top-class Jair du Cochet, their wins including inflicting a defeat ('regicide' in the words of his rather embarrassed trainer Guillaume Macaire) on the odds-on Best Mate in the Peterborough Chase. The North's top jockey Brian Hughes, third in the jockeys' championship in the latest season, reached the milestone of a thousand winners in January. A notable career achievement from the pointing field was Will Biddick breaking the record for the most number of wins by a British rider in that sphere when recording his four hundred and fifteenth victory in April, beating Richard Burton's record set in 2011. Gina Andrews set a new seasonal record in points for a female rider with a forty-first success earlier the same month.

To return briefly to an earlier topic, racing's enemies should note that some of the most passionate supporters of horse welfare are those who have made careers in broadcasting and writing about the sport. When he died in 2015, Sir Peter O'Sullevan held the position of Vice President of World Horse Welfare (formerly the International League for the Protection of Horses), which described him as 'the greatest champion of the horse in living memory' and credited him with 'leaving an extraordinary legacy of improved welfare for millions of horses worldwide.' Racing lost another vocal supporter of horse welfare when John McCririck, for many the 'face of racing', died in July at the age of seventy-nine. His colourful career, dating back to well before he became a television personality, is reviewed in the essay on **Delta Work** whose only defeat over fences came when third to Topofthegame in the RSA before establishing himself as the season's leading staying novice chaser at Punchestown. Richard Barber, brother of Topofthegame's co-owner, died in June aged seventy-seven. The last of Richard Barber's four victories in the Foxhunter Chase came with Earthmover who later became the first of Paul Nicholls' four successes in the same race. Nicholls described Barber as 'a massive influence' on his career; among well over a thousand winners trained by Barber 'between the flags' was See More Business, a horse he bought for just 5,600 guineas, who went on to become Nicholls' first winner of the Gold Cup, as well as winning his first two King Georges. Silver Streak's essay remembers Sam Morshead, who died in September 2018 at the age of just sixty-three. Best known in his riding days for partnering big-race winners for the Rimells, including on the brothers Gaye Brief and Gaye Chance, Morshead, awarded an MBE for services to racing and charity, was one of the first professional jockeys to go into racecourse administration, with Perth flourishing under his management for more than twenty years before ill-health forced him to retire in 2015. As *Chasers & Hurdlers* was going to press, the news came that the former stalwart of northern racing Ferdy Murphy had died in France, aged seventy. His career is touched on in the essay on Takingrisks.

As usual, the names of horses highlighted in this Introduction are among those covered in essay form. They form part of the comprehensive A to Z of all the horses which ran in Britain during the season, as well as the pick of those from Ireland who didn't, totalling 9,132. There will be fewer than usual references from the latest season to performances at Towcester which has staged no racing since May 2018 and went into administration in August of that year. With talks over the future of the Northamptonshire course still ongoing, it has not been allocated any dates on the 2020 fixture list. Some of the essays and individual commentaries cover performances that took place outside the British season, either at the Punchestown Festival (held the week after the season ended in Britain) or in France which has its own review 'Top Horses in France' at the back of this Annual.

October 2019

TIMEFORM CHAMPIONS OF 2018/19

Altior joins Istabraq and Kauto Star as a three-time winner of the Timeform Horse of the Year award, just one short of equalling Desert Orchid's four titles; Nico de Boinville has ridden Altior to sixteen of his record-breaking nineteen consecutive wins

HORSE OF THE YEAR
& BEST TWO-MILE CHASER
RATED AT 180p

ALTIOR

9 b.g High Chaparral – Monte Solaro (Key of Luck)

Owner Mrs Patricia Pugh   Trainer Nicky Henderson

BEST STAYING CHASER – RATED AT 176
KEMBOY
7 b. g. Voix du Nord – Vitora (Victory Note)
Owner Supreme Horse Racing Club & Brett T Graham & Ken Sharp
Trainer W. P. Mullins

BEST NOVICE CHASER – RATED AT 169p
CHACUN POUR SOI
7 b. g. Policy Maker – Kruscyna (Ultimately Lucky)
Owner Mrs S. Ricci   Trainer W. P. Mullins

BEST HUNTER CHASER – RATED AT 137
HAZEL HILL
11 b. g. Milan – Resenting (Presenting)
Owner Mrs D. Williams   Trainer Philip Rowley

BEST TWO-MILE HURDLER – RATED AT 170
ESPOIR D'ALLEN
5 b. g. Voix du Nord – Quadanse (Maille Pistol)
Owner Mr John P. McManus   Trainer Gavin Patrick Cromwell

BEST STAYING HURDLER – RATED AT 166p
PAISLEY PARK
7 b. g. Oscar – Presenting Shares (Presenting)
Owner Mr Andrew Gemmell   Trainer Emma Lavelle

BEST NOVICE HURDLER – RATED AT 157p
KLASSICAL DREAM
5 b. g. Dream Well – Klassical Way (Septieme Ciel)
Owner Mrs Joanne Coleman   Trainer W. P. Mullins

BEST JUVENILE HURDLER – RATED AT 147p
FUSIL RAFFLES
4 b. g. Saint des Saints – Tali des Obeaux (Panoramic)
Owner Simon Munir & Isaac Souede   Trainer Nicky Henderson

BEST BUMPER PERFORMER – RATED AT 125
ENVOI ALLEN
5 b. g. Muhtathir – Reaction (Saint des Saints)
Owner Cheveley Park Stud   Trainer Gordon Elliott

THE TIMEFORM 'TOP 100'
CHASERS AND HURDLERS

Hurdlers

170	Espoir d'Allen
166p	Paisley Park
163	Buveur d'Air
162	Apple's Jade (f)
160+	Presenting Percy
159+	If The Cap Fits
159	Benie des Dieux (f)
159	Samcro
159	Verdana Blue (f)
158	Master Dino
158	Sam Spinner
157p	Klassical Dream
157+	Sharjah
157	Supasundae
156	Bapaume
156	Bedrock
156	Mr Adjudicator
156§	Wicklow Brave
155	Ch'tibello
155	Darasso
155	Petit Mouchoir
155	We Have A Dream
155x	Melon
154	Aux Ptits Soins
154	Call Me Lord
154	Faugheen
154	Laurina (f)
154	Midnight Shadow
154	Silver Streak
154	Tiger Roll
154	William Henry
153p	Getaway Trump
153	Global Citizen
153	Wholestone
153	Younevercall
152	Early Doors
152	Jezki
152	Summerville Boy
151+	Saldier
151	City Island
151	Off You Go
151	Sire du Berlais
151	Unowhatimeanharry
150p	Reserve Tank
150	Ballyandy
150	Old Guard
150	Sams Profile
150	Shaneshill
150§	West Approach
149p	Champ
149	Black Op
149	Brain Power
149	Roksana (f)
148	Minella Awards
148	Vision des Flos
147p	Fusil Raffles
147	Agrapart
147	Bacardys
147	Ballymoy
147	Killultagh Vic
147	Le Prezien
147	Lil Rockerfeller
147	Minella Indo
147	Mohaayed
147	Not Many Left
147	On The Blind Side
147	Thomas Darby
147	Tobefair
147	Tombstone
146p	Bright Forecast
146p	Emitom
146p	Pentland Hills
146	A Toi Phil
146	Bleu Berry
146	Brio Conti
146	Cracking Smart
146	Felix Desjy
146	Nautical Nitwit
146	Scarpeta
146	Shades of Midnight
146	Yorkhill
146§	Rashaan
145	Aramon
145	Commander of Fleet
145	Dallas des Pictons
145	Ivanovich Gorbatov
145	Pic d'Orhy
145	Quick Grabim
145	Saglawy
145	Stratum
145	Voix du Reve
144	Al Dancer
144	Asthuria (f)
144	Bachasson
144	Brewin'upastorm
144	Davids Charm
144	Grand Sancy
144	Itchy Feet
144	Ronald Pump
143p	Mister Fisher
143	De Name Escapes Me
143	Keeper Hill
143	Le Patriote
143	Thomas Campbell
143	Walk To Freedom

Chasers

180p	Altior
176	Kemboy
174	Al Boum Photo
174	Min
173+	Cyrname
170	Un de Sceaux
169p	Chacun Pour Soi
169x	Bristol de Mai
167	Anibale Fly
167	Frodon
167	Tiger Roll
166	Aso
166	Clan des Obeaux
166	Politologue
165+	Native River
165+	Presenting Percy
165	Bellshill
165	Monalee
165	Road To Respect
164p	Defi du Seuil
164	Balko des Flos
164	Fox Norton
164	Sceau Royal
164	Thistlecrack
163p	Delta Work
163	Definitly Red
162p	Topofthegame
162+	Duc des Genievres
162	Rathvinden
162	Simply Ned
162	Top Notch
161p	Santini
161	Alpha des Obeaux
161	Elegant Escape
161	Footpad
161	Janika
160p	Lostintranslation
160	Ballyoisin
160	Black Corton
160	The Storyteller
160§	Outlander
159p	Real Steel
159	God's Own
159	Invitation Only
158p	Le Richebourg
158	Hell's Kitchen
158	Terrefort
157	A Plus Tard
157	Cadmium
157	Charbel
157	Coneygree
157	Hammersly Lake
157	Lake View Lad
157	Sizing Tennessee
157§	Beware The Bear
156+	Voix du Reve
156	Castlegrace Paddy
156	Cloudy Dream
156	Great Field
156	Jury Duty
156	Saint Calvados
156	Shattered Love (f)
156	Snow Falcon
156	Sub Lieutenant
155	Acapella Bourgeois
155	Coney Island
155	Double Shuffle
155	Gold Present
155	Kildisart
155	Magic of Light (f)
155	Ordinary World
155	Ozzie The Oscar
155	Pairofbrowneyes
155	Sizing Codelco
155	Talkischeap
155	Valtor
155	Virgilio
155	Yala Enki

154p	Burrows Saint	154	O O Seven	153	Mister Whitaker
154p	Cilaos Emery	154	Waiting Patiently	153	San Benedeto
154p	Kalashnikov	153p	Kaiser Black	153	Total Recall
154p	Tout Est Permis	153+	Dynamite Dollars	152	Dounikos
154	A Toi Phil	153	Baron Alco	152	Isleofhopendreams
154	Dolos	153	Clarcam	152	Otago Trail
154	Edwulf	153	Forest Bihan	152	Ramses de Teillee
154	Go Conquer	153	Hardline	152	Robinsfirth

THE TIMEFORM TOP JUVENILES, NOVICES, HUNTER CHASERS AND NH FLAT HORSES

Juvenile Hurdlers
147p Fusil Raffles
146p Pentland Hills
145 Pic d'Orhy
143 Fakir d'Oudairies
143 Sir Erec
142p Gardens of Babylon
142 French Made (f)
141 Coeur Sublime
139 Band of Outlaws
138 Chief Justice
135 Quel Destin
134 Cracker Factory
134 Tiger Tap Tap
133 Christopher Wood
132 Nelson River
132 Rocky Blue
131 Coko Beach
131 Way Back Home
130 Adjali
130 Havingagoodtime (f)
129p Ecco
129p Lucky Lover Boy
129 Fanfan du Seuil
129 Surin (f)
128 Chica Buena (f)
128 Naturelle (f)
127p Morosini
127p Vision du Puy (f)
127 Got Trumped
127 Torpillo

Novice Hurdlers
157p Klassical Dream
153p Getaway Trump
151 City Island
150p Reserve Tank
150 Sams Profile
149p Champ
147 Minella Indo
147 Thomas Darby
146p Bright Forecast
146p Emitom
146 Felix Desjy
145 Aramon
145 Commander of Fleet
145 Dallas des Pictons
145 Quick Grabim
144 Al Dancer
144 Brewin'upastorm

144 Grand Sancy
144 Itchy Feet
144 Ronald Pump
143p Mister Fisher
142p Battleoverdoyen
142 Canardier
142 Rouge Vif
141p Tornado Flyer
141 Dorrells Pierji
141 Eglantine du Seuil (f)
141 Elixir de Nutz
141 Rhinestone
141 Triplicate

Novice Chasers
169p Chacun Pour Soi
164p Defi du Seuil
163p Delta Work
162p Topofthegame
162+ Duc des Genievres
161p Santini
160p Lostintranslation
159p Real Steel
158p Le Richebourg
157 A Plus Tard
156+ Voix du Reve
155 Kildisart
155 Talkischeap
154p Burrows Saint
154p Cilaos Emery
154p Kalashnikov
153p Kaiser Black
153+ Dynamite Dollars
153 Hardline
151p La Bague Au Roi (f)
151 Ballyward
151 Mengli Khan
151 Ornua
150p Master Dino
150 Getabird
150 Glen Forsa
150 Spiritofthegames
150 Top Ville Ben
150 Us And Them
149§ Duca de Thaix

National Hunt Flat Horses
125 Envoi Allen
121+ Blue Sari
121 Thyme Hill

119 Get In The Queue
118 Abacadabras
117 Gypsy Island (f)
117p Beacon Edge
117p Malone Road
116p King Roland
116 Embittered
116 McFabulous
115p Festival d'Ex
113 Colreevy (f)
113 Sempo
112 Eden du Houx
112 Stick With Bill
111p Thatsy
111 December Second
110p Longhouse Poet
110 Imperial Alcazar
110 Meticulous
110 The Glancing Queen (f)
109 Daylight Katie (f)
109 Enrilo
109 Flic Ou Voyou
109 Master Debonair
109 Midnight Run
109 Nobby
108+ Enemy Coast Ahead
108 Montego Grey
108 Santa Rossa (f)

Hunter Chasers
137 Hazel Hill
136+ Caid du Berlais
135 Burning Ambition
134 Road To Rome
134 Top Wood
133+ Shantou Flyer
133 Risk A Fine
132 Sizing Rome
131 Monsieur Gibraltar
131§ Wonderful Charm
130 Mr Mercurial
130 Virak
129 Bishops Road
129 Fenno's Storm
129 Ucello Conti
128 Seefood
128 Stand Up And Fight
128 The Last But One
127 Mendip Express
127 Sizing Coal

2018/19 STATISTICS

The following tables show the leading owners, trainers, jockeys, sires of winners and horses over jumps in Britain during 2018/19. The prize-money statistics, compiled by *Timeform*, relate to win-money and to first-three prize money. Win money has traditionally been used to decide the trainers' championship, though since 1994 the BHB (now the BHA) and the National Trainers' Federation have recognised championships decided by total prize money as determined by the *Racing Post*. The jockeys' championship has traditionally been decided by the number of wins.

OWNERS (1,2,3 earnings)	Horses	Wnrs	Indiv'l Races Won	Runs	%	Stakes £
1 Mr John P. McManus	161	64	94	489	19.2	1,991,604
2 Mr Simon Munir & Mr Isaac Souede	40	20	31	158	19.6	975,622
3 Gigginstown House Stud	45	2	3	57	5.3	846,376
4 Ann & Alan Potts Limited	22	8	11	103	10.7	786,520
5 Paul & Clare Rooney	66	27	47	211	22.3	644,870
6 Mrs Patricia Pugh	3	2	7	14	50.0	581,534
7 Mr P. J. Vogt	6	2	5	21	23.8	453,707
8 Mrs J. Donnelly	2	1	1	3	33.3	447,088
9 Mr Trevor Hemmings	63	20	27	205	13.2	426,319
10 Mrs Johnny de la Hey	18	6	7	68	10.3	375,802
11 Mr Andrew Gemmell	1	1	5	5	100.0	347,744
12 Mr J. Hales	5	4	5	20	25.0	267,281

OWNERS (win money)	Horses	Wnrs	Indiv'l Races Won	Runs	%	Stakes £
1 Mr John P. McManus	161	64	94	489	19.2	1,406,414
2 Mr Simon Munir & Mr Isaac Souede	40	20	31	158	19.6	601,420
3 Gigginstown House Stud	45	2	3	57	5.3	597,025
4 Mrs Patricia Pugh	3	2	7	14	50.0	571,048
5 Paul & Clare Rooney	66	27	47	211	22.3	468,504
6 Ann & Alan Potts Limited	22	8	11	103	10.7	429,027
7 Mr P. J. Vogt	6	2	5	21	23.8	403,071
8 Mrs J. Donnelly	2	1	1	3	33.3	351,688
9 Mr Andrew Gemmell	1	1	5	5	100.0	347,744
10 Mr Trevor Hemmings	63	20	27	205	13.2	274,126
11 Mrs Johnny de la Hey	18	6	7	68	10.3	248,208
12 Sullivan Bloodstock Limited	18	6	7	37	18.9	198,428

TRAINERS (1,2,3 earnings)	Horses	Wnrs	Indiv'l Races Won	Runs	%	Stakes £
1 Paul Nicholls	161	76	135	589	22.9	3,158,852
2 Nicky Henderson	174	89	141	544	25.9	2,836,312
3 Dan Skelton	244	118	205	988	20.7	2,216,846
4 Colin Tizzard	129	51	77	600	12.8	1,753,171
5 W. P. Mullins, Ireland	63	8	8	74	10.8	1,336,423
6 Gordon Elliott, Ireland	120	35	55	206	26.7	1,309,852
7 Philip Hobbs	143	66	106	560	18.9	1,246,651
8 Alan King	139	57	91	499	18.2	1,202,795
9 Nigel Twiston-Davies	128	43	63	529	11.9	1,134,609
10 Tom George	103	38	52	377	13.8	803,454
11 Harry Fry	74	30	47	242	19.4	769,519
12 Evan Williams	117	36	53	507	10.5	757,710

TRAINERS (by win money)	Horses	Wnrs	Indiv'l Races Won	Runs	%	Stakes £
1 Paul Nicholls	161	76	135	589	22.9	2,267,392
2 Nicky Henderson	174	89	141	544	25.9	2,238,302
3 Dan Skelton	244	118	205	988	20.7	1,598,088
4 Colin Tizzard	129	51	77	600	12.8	1,063,199
5 Gordon Elliott, Ireland	120	35	55	206	26.7	1,055,630
6 Philip Hobbs	143	66	106	560	18.9	944,867
7 W. P. Mullins, Ireland	63	8	8	74	10.8	932,879
8 Nigel Twiston-Davies	128	43	63	529	11.9	762,634
9 Alan King	139	57	91	499	18.2	756,857
10 Harry Fry	74	30	47	242	19.4	623,562
11 Peter Bowen	82	34	64	368	17.4	560,920
12 Emma Lavelle	77	23	35	263	13.3	547,636

TRAINERS (with 100+ winners)	Horses	Wnrs	Indiv'l Races Won	2nd	3rd	Runs	%
1 Dan Skelton	244	118	205	146	116	988	20.7
2 Nicky Henderson	174	89	141	89	56	544	25.9
3 Paul Nicholls	161	76	135	111	67	589	22.9
4 Philip Hobbs	143	66	106	75	70	560	18.9

JOCKEYS (by wins)	1st	2nd	3rd	Unpl	Mts	%
1 Richard Johnson	200	152	134	493	980	20.5
2 Harry Skelton	178	122	102	343	745	23.9
3 Brian Hughes	146	143	128	471	888	16.4
4 Harry Cobden	109	93	55	261	518	21.0
5 Sam Twiston-Davies	105	86	78	412	681	15.4
6 Aidan Coleman	95	68	90	329	582	16.3
7 Sean Bowen	91	79	65	360	595	15.3
8 Wayne Hutchinson	88	64	48	213	413	21.3
9 Nico de Boinville	86	56	32	207	381	22.6
10 Tom Scudamore	82	83	75	445	685	12.0
11 Tom O'Brien	77	65	74	332	548	14.1
12 James Bowen	72	58	56	295	481	15.0

JOCKEYS (1,2,3 earnings)	Races Won	Rides	%	Stakes £
1 Harry Cobden	109	518	21.0	2,207,952
2 Richard Johnson	200	980	20.5	2,124,087
3 Harry Skelton	178	745	23.9	2,016,944
4 Nico de Boinville	86	381	22.6	1,742,226
5 Brian Hughes	146	888	16.4	1,408,156
6 Sam Twiston-Davies	105	681	15.4	1,342,334
7 Sean Bowen	91	595	15.3	1,320,980
8 Aidan Coleman	95	582	16.3	1,171,395
9 Tom Scudamore	82	685	12.0	1,121,544
10 Daryl Jacob	58	370	15.7	1,115,977
11 Tom O'Brien	77	548	14.1	1,060,680
12 Barry Geraghty	35	150	23.3	1,025,040

JOCKEYS (by win money)	Races Won	Rides	%	Stakes £
1 Harry Cobden	109	518	21.0	1,488,727
2 Harry Skelton	178	745	23.9	1,465,617
3 Richard Johnson	200	980	20.5	1,453,896
4 Nico de Boinville	86	381	22.6	1,447,853

CONDITIONAL JOCKEYS	1st	2nd	3rd	Unpl	Mts	%
1 Bryony Frost	50	43	30	184	307	16.3
2 Ross Chapman	36	41	33	233	343	10.5
3 Rex Dingle	32	20	28	107	187	17.1
4 Jonjo O'Neill Jr	30	23	27	114	194	15.5

AMATEUR RIDERS	1st	2nd	3rd	Unpl	Mts	%
1 Mr David Maxwell	15	14	8	26	63	23.8
2 Mr Sam Waley-Cohen	10	5	3	14	32	31.2
3 Miss Becky Smith	9	11	9	61	90	10.0

SIRES OF WINNERS (1,2,3 earnings)	Races Won	Runs	%	Stakes £
1 Flemensfirth (by Alleged)	83	640	13.0	1,478,239
2 Midnight Legend (by Night Shift)	123	748	16.4	1,440,832
3 Oscar (by Sadler's Wells)	92	690	13.3	1,429,805
4 King's Theatre (by Sadler's Wells)	92	540	17.0	1,382,778
5 Beneficial (by Top Ville)	93	685	13.6	1,159,298
6 Milan (by Sadler's Wells)	86	754	11.4	1,139,814
7 Westerner (by Danehill)	90	638	14.1	1,046,231
8 Kayf Tara (by Sadler's Wells)	68	758	9.0	1,042,281
9 Presenting (by Mtoto)	91	770	11.8	970,521
10 Stowaway (by Slip Anchor)	94	599	15.7	909,941
11 Getaway (by Monsun)	76	483	15.7	899,357
12 Authorized (by Montjeu)	37	213	17.4	817,371
13 Mahler (by Galileo)	72	439	16.4	760,180
14 Voix du Nord (by Valanour)	24	114	21.1	743,692
15 Yeats (by Sadler's Wells)	81	503	16.1	733,918

SIRES OF WINNERS (by win money)	Horses	Indiv'l Wnrs	Races Won	Stakes £
1 Oscar (by Sadler's Wells)	187	59	92	1,135,920
2 Midnight Legend (by Night Shift)	164	73	123	1,049,570
3 King's Theatre (by Sadler's Wells)	127	52	92	1,005,939
4 Flemensfirth (by Alleged)	187	58	83	897,550
5 Beneficial (by Top Ville)	156	53	93	780,363
6 Authorized (by Montjeu)	57	23	37	735,192
7 Milan (by Sadler's Wells)	208	60	86	723,295
8 Getaway (by Monsun)	130	47	76	718,295
9 Westerner (by Danehill)	150	58	90	705,825
10 Voix du Nord (by Valanour)	23	14	24	678,071

LEADING HORSES (1,2,3 earnings)	Won	Runs	£
1 Altior 9 b.g High Chaparral–Monte Solaro	5	5	562,145
2 Tiger Roll 9 b.g Authorized–Swiss Roll	2	3	540,235
3 Frodon 7 b.g Nickname–Miss Country	4	5	408,516
4 Al Boum Photo 7 b.g Buck's Boum–Al Gane	1	1	351,688
5 Paisley Park 7 b.g Oscar–Presenting Shares	5	5	347,744
6 Magic of Light 8 b.m Flemensfirth–Quest of Passion	2	5	261,939
7 Espoir d'Allen 5 b.g Voix du Nord–Quadanse	1	1	254,745
8 Clan des Obeaux 7 b.g Kapgarde–Nausicaa des Obeaux	2	5	215,080
9 If The Cap Fits 7 b.g Milan–Derravaragh Sayra	2	5	201,812
10 Silver Streak 6 gr.g Dark Angel–Happy Talk	2	7	199,755
11 Verdana Blue 7 b.m Getaway–Blue Gallery	4	6	192,525
12 Bristol de Mai 8 gr.g Saddler Maker–La Bole Night	1	4	183,512

EXPLANATORY NOTES

'Chasers & Hurdlers 2018/19' deals individually, in alphabetical sequence, with every horse that ran over jumps or in National Hunt Flat races in Britain during the 2018/19 season, plus a number of foreign-trained horses that did not race here. For each of these horses is given (1) its age, colour and sex, (2) its breeding and, where this information has not been given in a previous Chasers & Hurdlers or Racehorses Annual, usually a family outline, (3) a form summary giving its Timeform rating—or ratings—at the end of the previous season, followed by the details of all its performances during the past season, (4) a Timeform rating—or ratings—of its merit (which appears in the margin), (5) a Timeform commentary on its racing or general characteristics as a racehorse, with some suggestions, perhaps, regarding its prospects for 2019/20 and (6) the name of the trainer in whose charge it was on the last occasion it ran.

The book is published with a twofold purpose. Firstly, it is intended to have permanent value as a review of the exploits and achievements of the more notable of our chasers and hurdlers in the 2018/19 season. Thus, while the commentaries upon the vast majority of the horses are, of necessity, in note form, the best horses are more critically examined. The text is illustrated by posed portraits of the most notable horses (where these are available) and photographs of the major races. Secondly, the book is designed to help the punter to analyse races, and the notes which follow contain instructions for using the data.

TIMEFORM RATINGS

The Timeform Rating of a horse is simply the merit of the horse expressed in pounds and is arrived at by careful examination of its running against other horses using a scale of weight for distance beaten. Timeform maintains a 'running' handicap of all horses in training throughout the season.

THE LEVEL OF THE RATINGS

At the close of each season the ratings of all the horses that have raced are re-examined which explains why some of the ratings may be different from those in the final issue of the 2018/19 Timeform Chasing Black Book series. The 'Chasers & Hurdlers' figure is the definitive Timeform Rating.

RATINGS AND WEIGHT-FOR-AGE

The reader has, in the ratings in this book, a universal handicap embracing all the horses in training it is possible to weigh up, ranging from tip-top performers, with ratings from 170 upwards, down to those rated around the 60 mark. All the ratings are at weight-for-age, so that equal ratings mean horses of equal merit. In using Timeform to assess the prospects of various runners, allowance should be made for any difference specified by the Age, Weight and Distance Table at the front.

Steeplechase ratings, preceded by c, should not be confused with hurdle ratings, preceded by h. Where a horse has raced over fences and also over hurdles its ratings as a chaser and hurdler are printed one above the other, the steeplechase rating (c) being placed above the hurdle rating (h).

Thus with REGALITY c157

h143

the top figure, 157, is the rating to be used in steeplechases, and the one below, 143, is for use only in hurdle races. Where a horse has a rating based on its performance in a bumper it is preceded by 'b'. The procedure for making age and weight adjustments to the ratings (i.e. for the calculation of Race Ratings) is as follows:

A. Horses of the Same Age

If the horses all carry the same weight there are no adjustments to be made, and the horses with the highest ratings have the best chances. If the horses carry different weights, jot down their ratings, and to the rating of each horse add one point for every pound the horse is set to carry less than 12st 7lb, or subtract one point for every pound it has to carry more than 12st 7lb. When the ratings have been adjusted in this way the highest resultant figure indicates the horse with the best chance at the weights.

Example (any distance: any month of the season)

Teucer	5 yrs (11-0) ..	Rating 140 ..	add 21	....	161
Kiowa	5 yrs (10-7) ..	Rating 125 ..	add 28	....	153
Golden Age	5 yrs (10-4) ..	Rating 120 ..	add 31	....	151

Teucer has the best chance, and Golden Age the worst

B. Horses of Different Ages

In this case, reference must be made to the Age, Weight and Distance Table at the front. Use the Table for steeplechasers and hurdlers alike. Treat each horse separately, and compare the weight it has to carry with the weight prescribed for it in the table, according to the age of the horse, the distance of the race and the month of the year. Then, add one point to the rating for each pound the horse has to carry less than the weight given in the table: or, subtract one point from the rating for every pound it has to carry more than the weight prescribed by the table. The highest resultant figure indicates the horse most favoured by the weights.

Example (2¾m steeplechase in January)

(Table Weights: 8-y-o 12-7; 7-y-o 12-7; 5-y-o 12-6)

Black Book	8 yrs (12-8) ..	Rating 140 ..	subtract 1	....	139
Pressman	7 yrs (12-3) ..	Rating 132 ..	add 4	....	136
Copyright	5 yrs (12-7) ..	Rating 150 ..	subtract 1	....	149

Copyright has the best chance, and Pressman the worst

Example (3m hurdle race in March)

(Table Weights: 9-y-o 12-7; 5-y-o 12-7; 4-y-o 11-11)

Oxer	9 yrs (10-12) ..	Rating 110 ..	add 23	....	133
Clairval	5 yrs (10-7) ..	Rating 119 ..	add 28	....	147
Gallette	4 yrs (10-7) ..	Rating 128 ..	add 18	....	146

Clairval has the best chance, and Oxer the worst

C. Horses in bumpers

The procedure for calculating Race Ratings in bumpers is precisely the same as in (A) or (B).

Example (2m bumper in February)

(Table Weights: 6-y-o 12-7; 5-y-o 12-7; 4-y-o 12-1)

Squall	6 yrs (10-12) ..	Rating 88 ..	add 23	....	111
Lupin	5 yrs (11-3) ..	Rating 97 ..	add 18	....	115
Chariot	4 yrs (10-9) ..	Rating 84 ..	add 20	....	104

Lupin has the best chance, and Chariot the worst

The bumper ratings can be used not only within the context of bumper races themselves, but also as an indication of the potential form of such horses in their first few starts over jumps.

JOCKEYSHIP AND RIDERS' ALLOWANCES

For the purposes of rating calculations it should, in general, be assumed that the allowance the rider is able to claim (3 lb, 5 lb, or 7 lb) is nullified by his or her inexperience. Therefore, the weight adjus*tments to the ratings should be calculated on the weight allotted by the handicapper, or determined by the conditions of the race*, and no extra addition should be made to a rating because the horse's rider claims an allowance. This is the general routine procedure; but, of course, after the usual adjustments have been made the quality of jockeyship is still an important factor to be considered when deciding between horses with similar chances.

WEIGHING UP A RACE

The ratings tell which horses in a particular race are most favoured by the weights; but complete analysis demands that the racing character of each horse is also studied carefully to see if there is any reason why the horse might be expected not to run up to its rating. It counts for little that a horse is thrown in at the weights if it has no pretensions whatever to staying the distance, or is unable to act on the prevailing going. Suitability of distance and going are no doubt the most important points to be considered, but there are others. For example, the ability of a horse to accommodate itself to the conformation of the track. There is also the matter of a horse's ability and dependability as a jumper and of its temperament: nobody would be in a hurry to take a short price about a horse with whom it is always an even chance whether it will get round or not, or whether it will consent to race.

A few minutes spent checking up on these matters in the commentaries upon the horses concerned will sometimes put a very different complexion on a race from that which is put upon it by the ratings alone. We repeat, therefore, that the correct way to use Timeform, or this annual volume, in the analysis of individual races is, first to use the ratings to discover which horses are most favoured by the weights, and second, to check through the comments on the horses to see what factors other than weight might also affect the outcome of the race.

THE FORM SUMMARIES

The form summaries enclosed in the brackets list each horse's performances in the last season in sequence, showing, for each race, its distance in furlongs, the state of the going and the horse's placing at the finish. Steeplechase form figures are prefixed by the letter 'c', hurdle form figures by the letter 'h' and bumper form figures by the letter 'b'.

The going is symbolised as follows: f–firm, m–good to firm, g–good, d–good to soft/dead, s–soft, v–heavy.

Placings are indicated up to sixth place, by superior figures, an asterisk denoting a win; and superior letters are used to convey what happened to the horse during the race: F–fell (F^3 denotes remounted and finished third); pu–pulled up; ur–unseated rider; bd–brought down; R–refused; rr–refused to race; su–slipped up; ro–ran out; co–carried out; d–disqualified

Thus, [2018/19 h82, b80: h16g h16s* c18g^{pu} h16f^2 c20v^F Apr 10] states that the horse was rated 82 over hurdles and 80 in bumpers at the end of the previous season. In the 2018/19 jumping season the horse ran five times; unplaced in a 2m hurdle race on good going, winning a 2m hurdle race on soft going, being pulled up in a 2¼m steeplechase on good going, running second in a 2m hurdle race on firm going and falling in a 2½m steeplechase on heavy going. Its last race was on April 10th.

Where sale prices are given they are in guineas unless otherwise stated. The prefix \$ refers to American dollars and € indicates the euro. Any other currencies are converted into pounds sterling at the prevailing exchange rate.

THE RATING SYMBOLS

The following symbols, attached to the ratings, are to be interpreted as stated:-

p   likely to improve.

P   capable of *much* better form.

+   the horse may be better than we have rated it.

d   the horse appears to have deteriorated, and might no longer be capable of running to the rating given.

§   unreliable (for temperamental or other reasons).

§§   so temperamentally unsatisfactory as to be not worth a rating.

x   poor jumper.

xx   a very bad jumper, so bad as to be not worth a rating.

?   the horse's rating is suspect or, used without a rating, the horse can't be assessed with confidence or, if used in the in-season Timeform publications, that the horse is out of form.

CHASERS & HURDLERS 2018/19

Horse	Commentary	Rating

AAH PAT (IRE) 5 b.g. Arcadio (GER) – She My Belle (IRE) (Dr Massini (IRE)) [2018/19 **b64**
b16.8m⁴ b16.5g⁶ Nov 3] poor form in bumpers. *Stuart Crawford, Ireland*

AARDWOLF (USA) 5 b.g. Cape Cross (IRE) – Desert Gazelle (USA) (Smart Strike **h113**
(CAN)) [2018/19 h102: h16.7g² h16.7g² h16.3g* h16g* h16m³ h16g³ h18g⁶ h18g⁶ Apr 27]
fair hurdler: won novices at Stratford and Worcester in June: left Warren Greatrex after
sixth start: likely to prove best around 2m: acts on heavy and good to firm going: races
prominently. *Elizabeth Voss Murray, USA*

AARON LAD (IRE) 8 b.g. Daylami (IRE) – Borntobepampered (Entrepreneur) [2018/19 **h134**
h117: h23.9d⁶ h23.1g* h24g* h24d h24g⁶ Apr 17] angular gelding: useful handicap
hurdler: won at Market Rasen in November and Cheltenham (by 3 lengths from Keeper
Hill) in December: stays 3m: acts on heavy going. *Dr Richard Newland*

AARYAM (FR) 7 b.g. Dylan Thomas (IRE) – Selinea (FR) (Keltos (FR)) [2018/19 h–: **h–**
h16.8g h20g h18.7m h21.6g⁶ Jul 6] little form: wore headgear/tongue tie: dead. *John Flint*

AASLEAGH DAWN (IRE) 6 b.m. Milan – Aasleagh Lady (IRE) (Presenting) [2018/19 **c113**
h19g h16.5g h16.5g h18.8g* h20g* h20g h17.3g⁶ h21.2m⁴ h21.9s h22d* h21g h20d c20d⁶ **h110**
h24s³ h18.9m Apr 20] market leggy mare: first foal: dam unraced half-sister to fairly useful
hurdler/useful chaser (stayed 3¼m) Mostly Bob and fairly useful 2½m hurdle winner
Hannibal The Great (by Milan): fair hurdler: won mares maiden at Downpatrick in July and
handicap at Navan in November: 25/1, similar form when sixth in novice at Navan (16¾
lengths behind He's No Molly) on chasing debut: stays 3m: acts on soft going: tried in
cheekpieces: usually races off pace. *Gavin Patrick Cromwell, Ireland*

ABACADABRAS (FR) 5 b.g. Davidoff (GER) – Cadoubelle des As (FR) (Cadoudal **b118**
(FR)) [2018/19 b16.3d* b16g^{ro} b16.4s⁴ Mar 13] €14,000 3-y-o: useful-looking gelding:
third foal: half-brother to French 19f hurdle winner Tequilas (by Voix du Nord): dam
French maiden (placed up to 2¼m over hurdles): smart form in bumpers: won maiden at
Galway (by short head from Kerrkenny Gold) in October: length second of 10 to Colreevy
in Champion INH Flat Race at Punchestown shortly after end of British season, hanging
left/carrying head awkwardly: not straightforward (ran out second outing). *Gordon Elliott,
Ireland*

ABBEYGREY (IRE) 10 b.g. Generous (IRE) – Garw Valley (Mtoto) [2018/19 c104, h–: **c97 §**
c20g² c25.2g⁶ c25.2d⁵ c23.6d c26.1d⁴ c27.5g Apr 14] winning hurdler: modest handicap **h–**
chaser: stays 3¼m: acts on heavy going: has worn headgear: tried in tongue tie:
untrustworthy. *Evan Williams*

ABBEY STREET (IRE) 8 b.g. Asian Heights – Cnocbui Cailin (IRE) (Moscow Society **h98**
(USA)) [2018/19 h98: h24g² h23.3g² May 27] compact gelding: maiden pointer: modest
maiden hurdler: stays 3m: acts on soft going: in hood last 2 starts: races towards rear.
Paul Henderson

ABBEYVIEW (IRE) 12 b.g. Misternando – Castle Spirit (IRE) (Clearly Bust) [2018/19 **c103**
c103: c25.5g² May 30] multiple winning pointer, including in 2019: fair hunter chaser:
stays 25f: acts on good to firm going. *Mrs S. Fenwick*

ABBREVIATE (GER) 8 b.g. Authorized (IRE) – Azalee (GER) (Lando (GER)) [2018/19 **c123 §**
c128, h–: c25.1m² c23.8g^{pu} c25.1m⁶ c24.2s² c24.2d⁵ Jan 4] good-topped gelding: winning **h–**
hurdler: fairly useful maiden chaser: stays 25f: acts on soft and good to firm going: wears
headgear: temperamental. *Kim Bailey*

ABLAZE 5 ch.m. Arcano (IRE) – Angry Bark (USA) (Woodman (USA)) [2018/19 h16v⁶ **h–**
h21d^{pu} Jan 28] half-sister to fairly useful hurdler Arthurs Secret (2½m-3m winner, by
Sakhee's Secret) and fair hurdler Mattoral (2m winner, by High Chaparral): modest on Flat,
stays 16.5f: no form over hurdles. *Laura Mongan*

ABLAZING (IRE) 8 b.g. Mastercraftsman (IRE) – Moore's Melody (IRE) (Marju (IRE)) **h100**
[2018/19 h–: h19.9d⁵ h21.2d⁶ Dec 19] fairly useful handicap hurdler, lightly raced and not
knocked about only completed start after 2016/17: stayed 2½m: acted on good to soft
going: wore headgear: dead. *Johnny Farrelly*

A BOLD MOVE (IRE) 9 b.g. Shantou (USA) – Sprint For Gold (USA) (Slew O' Gold (USA)) [2018/19 c–, h108: h15.8d⁵ h16.7g³ h19.5sᵖᵘ h21.2dᵖᵘ Dec 19] has had breathing operation: winning pointer: maiden hurdler, largely out of sorts in 2018/19: pulled up only chase start: stays 2½m: acts on good to soft going: often wears cheekpieces: usually races prominently. *Alastair Ralph* **c–** **h96**

ABOLITIONIST (IRE) 11 b.g. Flemensfirth (USA) – All The Roses (IRE) (Roselier (FR)) [2018/19 h24.7g* c26d⁵ h24dᵖᵘ Mar 14] workmanlike gelding: fairly useful handicap hurdler: won at Aintree in November: smart handicap chaser: encouraging fifth in veterans event at Newbury (18 lengths behind Carole's Destrier) in March: left Ellmarie Holden after only start in 2017/18: stays 29f: acts on soft and good to firm going: has worn headgear, including final start. *Dr Richard Newland* **c132** **h126**

A BOOK OF INTRIGUE 6 b.g. Alflora (IRE) – Kahlua Cove (Karinga Bay) [2018/19 b78: b15.8d* Mar 3] well-made gelding: fair form in bumpers: won at Huntingdon on sole start in 2018/19: will be suited by further than 2m: has joined John O'Shea. *Fergal O'Brien* **b92**

ABOUT GLORY 5 b.g. Nayef (USA) – Lemon Rock (Green Desert (USA)) [2018/19 h–: h19.6gᵖᵘ Aug 31] fair at best on Flat: no form over hurdles: tried in cheekpieces. *John David Riches* **h–**

ABOVE BOARD (IRE) 8 b.g. Mahler – Blackwater Babe (IRE) (Arctic Lord) [2018/19 c124, h–: c24m* c24.1g³ c23d² c25g c23.8g⁶ c23.8d⁶ Dec 19] rangy gelding: has had breathing operation: winning hurdler: useful handicap chaser: won at Uttoxeter in May: stays 3m: acts on soft and good to firm going: usually races towards rear. *Jonjo O'Neill* **c131** **h–**

ABRICOT DE L'OASIS (FR) 9 b.g. Al Namix (FR) – La Normandie (FR) (Beyssac (FR)) [2018/19 c110, h108: c26.3gꟳ c22.6g³ Apr 14] winning hurdler: fair chaser nowadays: stays 3m: acts on soft and good to firm going: wears headgear. *J. H. Henderson* **c112** **h–**

ABSOLUTE JAFFA 4 ch.f. Lucarno (USA) – Reverse Swing (Charmer) [2018/19 b12.4s⁶ h16.7g⁴ h15.8m⁴ Apr 1] tall filly: sixth foal: half-sister to fairly useful hurdler/useful chaser Monbeg Legend (2½m-2¾m winner, by Midnight Legend) and modest hurdler/poor chaser Cleve Cottage (23f-3¼m winner, by Presenting): dam (c92/h77) 2m-3m hurdle/chase winner: showed a bit only bumper start: modest form over hurdles: better effort when fourth in novice at Market Rasen in February: will stay 2½m: in hood last 2 starts: remains capable of better. *Oliver Greenall* **h96 p** **b–**

ABSOLUTELY DYLAN (IRE) 6 b.g. Scorpion (IRE) – Cash Customer (IRE) (Bob Back (USA)) [2018/19 h107, b83: c19.3g* c19.4g³ c22.9v* c23.4s⁴ c20s c23.9dᵖᵘ c21.3g⁵ Mar 29] fair hurdler: fair chaser: won maiden at Sedgefield in October and handicap at Haydock in December: stays 23f: acts on heavy going: has hinted at temperament. *Sue Smith* **c110** **h–**

ABSOLUTE POWER 8 b.g. Flemensfirth (USA) – Crystal Ballerina (IRE) (Sadler's Wells (USA)) [2018/19 h107: c22.4d⁶ c20.9s³ c23.4s² Dec 19] twice-raced hurdler: fairly useful form over fences: best effort when second in novice handicap at Newbury in December: will stay beyond 23f: acts on soft going. *Rebecca Curtis* **c127** **h–**

ACACIA DREAM (IRE) 5 b.m. Mahler – Paumafi (IRE) (Shardari) [2018/19 b14g⁶ Jan 17] €2,200 3-y-o: seventh foal: dam (h96), 2¼m-2½m hurdle winner, half-sister to Grand National winner Comply Or Die: tailed off in bumper. *Martin Keighley* **b–**

ACAPELLA BOURGEOIS (FR) 9 ch.g. Network (GER) – Jasmine (FR) (Valanjou (FR)) [2018/19 c150, h–: h20.3d c20g* c29d³ Apr 22] lengthy gelding: useful hurdler: very smart chaser: won minor event at Clonmel (by 8½ lengths from Yorkhill) in March: third in Irish Grand National Chase at Fairyhouse (7¼ lengths behind Burrows Saint) month later: stays 29f: acts on heavy going: has worn hood, including all starts in 2018/19: tried in tongue tie: usually races close up. *W. P. Mullins, Ireland* **c155** **h–**

ACARO (FR) 5 b.g. Sinndar (IRE) – Accusation (IRE) (Barathea (IRE)) [2018/19 h103: c18mᵖᵘ h20.5g³ h19.2d h19.2v* h19.5d Mar 20] good-topped gelding: fair handicap hurdler: won at Fontwell in March: pulled up in novice handicap on chasing debut: stays 21f: acts on heavy going: tried in tongue tie: usually races off pace. *Robert Walford* **c–** **h112**

ACCESSALLAREAS (IRE) 14 ch.g. Swift Gulliver (IRE) – Arushofgold (IRE) (Alphabatim (USA)) [2018/19 c82§, h–: c16g⁶ c17m⁵ c15.7g⁵ c16.3m⁵ c16.5g³ c17.2g c17g⁴ c16g⁶ c16g³ c23.9s⁴ Dec 6] workmanlike gelding: very lightly raced over hurdles: poor handicap chaser: stays 21f: acts on soft and good to firm going: wears headgear: has worn tongue tie: usually races close up: unreliable. *Sarah-Jayne Davies* **c67 §** **h–**

ACCOMPLICE (FR) 5 gr.g. Network (GER) – Miss Vitoria (FR) (Kaldounevees (FR)) **h111 p**
[2018/19 h17.6s* h18.5d Feb 22] second foal: dam, French maiden (placed up to 19f over
hurdles), half-sister to smart French hurdler (placed at 2¼m/19f) Blue Bresil: fair form
over hurdles: won 4-y-o event at Fontainebleau in November: left A. Adeline de Boisbrunet
after: remains open to improvement. *Paul Nicholls*

ACCORDING TO ALEX (FR) 4 gr.g. Al Namix (FR) – Go Lison (FR) (Turgeon **b–**
(USA)) [2018/19 b15.8d Mar 13] well beaten in bumper. *Henry Daly*

ACCORDINGTOGINO (IRE) 6 ch.g. Perugino (USA) – Accordintomags (IRE) **h105**
(Accordion) [2018/19 h20.5g² h20.7d⁵ h20.3s³ Mar 18] €4,800 3-y-o: first foal: dam
unraced: won sole start in Irish points: fair form over hurdles: best effort when second in
maiden at Leicester in December. *Dan Skelton*

ACCORDING TO HARRY (IRE) 10 b.g. Old Vic – Cassilis (IRE) (Persian Bold) **c106**
[2018/19 c102, h–: c20.3g⁴ c21.6gᵖᵘ Jun 5] winning hurdler: fairly useful handicap chaser, **h–**
below best since 2016/17: stays 3m: acts on soft and good to firm going: usually races
prominently. *Nicky Martin*

ACCORDINI 7 b.g. Dr Massini (IRE) – Haveyoubeen (IRE) (Accordion) [2018/19 b16g⁶ **c70**
b16.2g⁵ b16.2m c23.6g⁴ Apr 26] point winner: modest form in bumpers for Donald **b78**
Whillans: well beaten in novice hunter on chasing debut (tongue tied). *Gareth Moore*

ACCORD (IRE) 9 b.g. Arcadio (GER) – Detente (Medicean) [2018/19 c120, h–: h18.7g² **c–**
h25gᵖᵘ c26m³ c24mᵖᵘ Oct 21] sturdy, workmanlike gelding: maiden hurdler: fairly useful **h97**
handicap chaser at best, has lost his way: stays 19f: acts on heavy going: has worn
headgear: tried in tongue tie. *David Bridgwater*

ACCOST (IRE) 6 b.m. Ask – Minora (IRE) (Cataldi) [2018/19 b–: b16.2g May 27] no **b–**
form in bumpers: in tongue tie last 2 starts. *N. W. Alexander*

ACDC (IRE) 9 b.g. King's Theatre (IRE) – Always Alert (IRE) (Slip Anchor) [2018/19 **c131**
c127, h–: c19.4m* c21.5d⁴ c25s³ c23.4d⁴ c31.8mᵖᵘ Apr 13] has had breathing operation: **h–**
winning hurdler: useful handicap chaser: won at Wetherby (by 3 lengths from Willie Boy)
in October: stays 3m: acts on good to firm and heavy going: wears hood/tongue tie: usually
races off pace. *Chris Grant*

ACE CHEETAH (USA) 5 b.g. Kitten's Joy (USA) – Imagistic (USA) (Deputy Minister **b62**
(CAN)) [2018/19 b74: b15.8g⁶ b16.3m⁵ b16.7m⁴ Aug 5] poor form in bumpers (little better
on Flat): tried in tongue tie. *J. R. Jenkins*

ACE COMBAT 4 b.g. Shamardal (USA) – Require (Montjeu (IRE)) [2018/19 h16gᵖᵘ **h80**
h16m³ Apr 25] good-bodied gelding: has had breathing operation: fair at best on Flat, stays
10.5f: little show over hurdles: in tongue tie first start. *Michael Madgwick*

ACERTAIN CIRCUS 9 ch.g. Definite Article – Circus Rose (Most Welcome) [2018/19 **h111**
h104: h20.6d h23.1g⁴ h23.1g* h23.4m² Apr 22] well-made gelding: fair handicap hurdler:
won at Market Rasen in March: stays 23f: acts on soft and good to firm going: has worn
tongue tie. *Pam Sly*

ACE VENTURA 4 b.g. Mayson – Ventura Highway (Machiavellian (USA)) [2018/19 **h103**
h16.7d³ h15.7m h15.8g⁶ Mar 19] fairly useful on Flat, stays 1¼m: fair form over hurdles:
best effort when third in juvenile at Market Rasen in February. *Oliver Greenall*

ACEY MILAN (IRE) 5 b.g. Milan – Strong Wishes (IRE) (Strong Gale) [2018/19 b118: **h120**
h20v² h20.5s⁵ h15.9s* h15.9v³ Mar 16] rather unfurnished gelding: multiple bumper
winner: fairly useful form over hurdles: won novice at Plumpton in February: wears tongue
tie. *Anthony Honeyball*

ACHILLE (FR) 9 gr.g. Dom Alco (FR) – Hase (FR) (Video Rock (FR)) [2018/19 c113, **c131**
h–: c24s² c24.2d* c24.2d* c28.4dᵖᵘ c23.8s* Apr 7] lengthy gelding: winning hurdler: **h–**
useful handicap chaser: won at Exeter in January, Sandown in February and Ffos Las (by
head from Ami Desbois) in April: stays 3m: acts on heavy going: wears cheekpieces: front
runner/races prominently. *Venetia Williams*

ACHILL ROAD BOY (IRE) 10 b.g. Morozov (USA) – Presenting Katie (IRE) **c108**
(Presenting) [2018/19 c98, h91: c26.2gᵘʳ c24.1g³ c24.5v³ h23.3v⁴ c25.2g² c23.4g* c26.3s² **h90**
c26.2g² c30.6dᵘʳ Apr 26] fair handicap hurdler/chaser: won over fences at Kelso in January:
stays 3¼m: acts on heavy going: in blinkers 3 of last 4 starts. *Stuart Coltherd*

ACKER BILK (IRE) 5 ch.g. Rip Van Winkle (IRE) – Portentous (Selkirk (USA)) **h104**
[2018/19 h16d* h16.8dᵖᵘ Sep 21] fairly useful on Flat, stays 1½m: fair form over hurdles:
won maiden at Worcester in August: went as if amiss next time: wears cheekpieces/tongue
tie. *David Pipe*

ACLASSAGOLD (IRE) 6 b.g. Gold Well – Midnight Classic (IRE) (Classic Cliche **h88** (IRE)) [2018/19 b16g h20g h16s h16.5d h19.5d⁵ h21.2v⁵ h20.3d Apr 9] €2,500 3-y-o, **b–** £43,000 5-y-o: good-topped gelding: second foal: dam unraced: won completed start in Irish points: well beaten in bumper: modest form over hurdles. *Deborah Faulkner*

ACQUIRER (IRE) 4 b.g. Zoffany (IRE) – See Emily Play (IRE) (Galileo (IRE)) [2018/19 **h107** h17.7g³ Sep 9] fair maiden on Flat, stays 16.5f: 33/1, third in juvenile at Fontwell (3 lengths behind Twenty Twenty) on hurdling debut: will be suited by further than 2¼m. *Richard Hughes*

ACROSS THE PARK (IRE) 5 b.g. Presenting – Miss Baresi (IRE) (Milan) [2018/19 **h78** b16.8g⁶ b16.8s h15.3g⁶ h16.5d³ h18.5d Jan 1] well held in bumpers: poor form over **b–** hurdles. *Linda Blackford*

ACT ALONE 10 b.g. Act One – Figlette (Darshaan) [2018/19 h21sᵖᵘ h23.1g h26.4gᵖᵘ Apr **h–** 14] leggy, close-coupled gelding: fairly useful hurdler at best, no form in 2018/19 when tongue tied. *Jennifer Mason*

ACTINPIECES 8 gr.m. Act One – Bonnet's Pieces (Alderbrook) [2018/19 c143, h–: c24d **c125** c24.2mᶠ c23.9g⁴ c28.8vᵖᵘ Dec 8] workmanlike mare: winning hurdler: useful handicap **h–** chaser, well below best in 2018/19: stays 25f: acts on soft going. *Pam Sly*

ACTION REPLAY (IRE) 8 b.g. Milan – Mary Connors (IRE) (Mandalus) [2018/19 **c116** c–p, h96: c19.4d⁴ c20g⁶ Jun 24] maiden hurdler: fairly useful form over fences: best effort **h–** when fourth in novice handicap at Ffos Las in May: stays 19f: acts on heavy going. *Philip Hobbs*

ACTIVIAL (FR) 9 gr.g. Lord du Sud (FR) – Kissmirial (FR) (Smadoun (FR)) [2018/19 **c149** c–, h–: h22.8g h25g³ c19.4g² c21.6g* c21s³ c20.6d⁶ c25s⁶ c21.1d Apr 5] angular gelding: **h133** useful handicap hurdler: third at Warwick (5¼ lengths behind Black Sam Bella) in May: smart chaser: won graduation event at Haydock (by 16 lengths from Magic Saint) in November: second in similar event at Ascot (short head behind Kildisart) in December and sixth in Ultima Handicap Chase at Cheltenham (7 lengths behind Beware The Bear) in March: left Neil Mulholland after second start: stays 25f: acts on heavy going: has worn hood/tongue tie. *Tom George*

ACT OF SUPREMACY (IRE) 9 b.g. Presenting – Supreme Touch (IRE) (Supreme **c–** Leader) [2018/19 h19.6g⁵ h23.3g h18.5g Oct 1] good-topped gelding: maiden hurdler, **h83** modest at best: pulled up only start over fences: stays 2¼m: acts on soft going. *Emma Lavelle*

ACT OF VALOUR 5 b.g. Harbour Watch (IRE) – B Berry Brandy (USA) (Event of The **h133** Year (USA)) [2018/19 h132: h15.7gᶠ May 12] strong gelding: useful handicap hurdler: raced around 2m: acted on heavy going: often raced prominently/travelled strongly: dead. *Paul Nicholls*

ACTONETAKETWO 9 b.m. Act One – Temple Dancer (Magic Ring (IRE)) [2018/19 **h– §** h–§: h16.5g Jan 9] sturdy mare: no form over hurdles: in cheekpieces last 5 starts: temperamental. *Derrick Scott*

ADAM DU BRETEAU (FR) 9 ch.g. Network (GER) – Odelie de Fric (FR) (April Night **c– §** (FR)) [2018/19 c125§, h–: c26.1g c22.6mᵖᵘ c25.5mᵖᵘ Jul 1] maiden hurdler: fairly useful **h–** chaser at best, no form in 2018/19: usually wore headgear: front runner/raced prominently: unreliable: dead. *Jonjo O'Neill*

ADAMS PARK 4 b.g. Mastercraftsman (IRE) – Ile Deserte (Green Desert (USA)) **h114** [2018/19 h16.7m³ h16.3m* h15.8s⁴ Jul 29] half-brother to modest hurdler Havisham (2½m winner, by Mount Nelson): fairly useful maiden on Flat, stays 1½m: fair form over hurdles: won juvenile at Stratford in July: will be suited by 2½m: acts on good to firm going: wears headgear. *Dr Richard Newland*

ADELPHI PRINCE 6 b.g. Schiaparelli (GER) – Cailin Na Ri (IRE) (King's Theatre **h72** (IRE)) [2018/19 b70: b16.8d⁴ h20.5d h16.4s h16.6g⁵ Feb 20] poor form in bumpers/over **b74** hurdles. *Philip Kirby*

ADHERENCE 6 b.g. Sir Percy – Straight Laced (Refuse To Bend (IRE)) [2018/19 h96: **h99** h19s* h19.5g³ Apr 26] modest handicap hurdler: won at Taunton in March after year off: should stay 3m: acts on heavy going: has worn cheekpieces. *Tim Vaughan*

ADJALI (GER) 4 b.g. Kamsin (GER) – Anabasis (GER) (High Chaparral (IRE)) [2018/19 **h130** h17.4s³ h16.7s* h16s² h16.8d³ h16.8d h17d⁴ Apr 4] sturdy gelding: third foal: half-brother to smart German/US 1m/9f winner A Raving Beauty (by Mastercraftsman): dam ran twice on Flat in Germany: useful hurdler: won juvenile at Market Rasen in December. second in Finale Juvenile Hurdle at Chepstow (neck behind Quel Destin) later in December and fourth in Anniversary Hurdle at Aintree (6½ lengths behind Pentland Hills) in April: left Guillaume Macaire after first start: raced around 2m: acts on soft going: usually front runner/races prominently. *Nicky Henderson*

ADJOURNED 4 gr.g. Rip Van Winkle (IRE) – Bite of The Cherry (Dalakhani (IRE)) **b90**
[2018/19 b15.7g⁴ b15.3g⁴ Apr 14] close-coupled gelding: first foal: dam useful 13f winner: fair form in bumpers: won maiden at Southwell in October: left James Bethell after. *Kim Bailey*

ADJUTANT 4 b.g. Champs Elysees – Jubilee (Selkirk (USA)) [2018/19 h16.3g Mar 30] **h105 p**
fairly useful on Flat, stays 8.5f: 12/1, some encouragement when seventh in novice at Stratford (5 lengths behind Petit Palais) on hurdling debut: open to improvement. *Olly Murphy*

ADMIRAL BARRATRY (FR) 6 b.g. Soldier of Fortune (IRE) – Haskilclara (FR) **h125**
(Green Tune (USA)) [2018/19 h116: h21m² h18.9g⁶ h19.6d* h21.6d⁴ h24.3g h19.8s⁶ h20d Apr 5] useful-looking gelding: fairly useful hurdler: won novice at Huntingdon in December: sixth in EBF 'National Hunt' Novices' Handicap Hurdle Final at Sandown in March: left Mrs Jane Williams after second start: stays 2¾m: acts on soft going: tried in cheekpieces. *Lucy Wadham*

ADMIRAL BLAKE 12 b.g. Witness Box (USA) – Brenda Bella (FR) (Linamix (FR)) **c–**
[2018/19 c–, h79: h24g⁵ h23s May 25] poor handicap hurdler: maiden chaser: stays 3m: **h59**
raced mostly on soft/heavy going: tried in blinkers: in tongue tie last 5 starts. *Laura Young*

ADMIRAL KID (IRE) 8 b.g. Mythical Kid (USA) – English Clover (Tina's Pet) **c95**
[2018/19 h–: h15.7g⁴ h16.8g⁶ c20.9m² c19.4mᵖᵘ Jul 15] lengthy gelding: bumper winner: **h87**
maiden hurdler: modest form on completed start over fences: stayed 21f: acted on soft and good to firm going: in hood/tongue tie last 4 starts: dead. *Neil Mulholland*

ADMIRAL SPICE (IRE) 4 gr.g. Lethal Force (IRE) – Rustam (Dansili) [2018/19 **h74**
h15.8m⁵ h15.8g h16d h15.8s h16.6g⁶ Jan 25] modest maiden on Flat, stays 1½m: poor form over hurdles: tried in cheekpieces. *Sophie Leech*

ADMIRAL'S SECRET 8 b.g. Kayf Tara – Bobs Bay (IRE) (Bob's Return (IRE)) **c124 §**
[2018/19 c118, h–: c17.5s² c15.7d* c16.3dʳʳ c15.7gᶠ c16.4d³ Mar 1] rangy gelding: lightly- **h–**
raced maiden hurdler: fairly useful handicap chaser: won at Wincanton in December: bred to be suited by further than 2m: acts on heavy going: wears tongue tie: best treated with caution (has refused to race). *Victor Dartnall*

ADMIRAL'S SUNSET 6 b.m. Mount Nelson – Early Evening (Daylami (IRE)) [2018/19 **h107**
h15.3m⁵ h15.8g⁴ h16.8g³ h16g⁵ h16.2g* h16.2g³ h16.3s⁵ h19d² Apr 24] tall, rather unfurnished mare: half-sister to fair hurdler Early Applause (17f winner, by Royal Applause): fairly useful on Flat, stays 13.5f: fair hurdler: won 3-runner mares handicap at Hereford in November: unproven beyond 17f: acts on soft going. *David Weston*

ADRENALIN FLIGHT (IRE) 13 b.g. Dr Massini (IRE) – Chapel Queen (IRE) (Jolly **c102**
Jake (NZ)) [2018/19 c27.7g³ May 17] lengthy gelding: winning pointer: winning hurdler: **h–**
fairly useful chaser at best, third in hunter only start under Rules since 2015/16: stays 4m: acts on good to firm and heavy going: usually wears headgear. *Mrs Sally Rawlins*

ADRIEN DU PONT (FR) 7 b.g. Califet (FR) – Santariyka (FR) (Saint des Saints (FR)) **c149**
[2018/19 c143, h–: c23.8m⁴ c22.4s c24g² c24g³ c21.1d Apr 5] well-made gelding: winning **h–**
hurdler: smart handicap chaser: won at Kempton (by 3½ lengths from Just A Sting) in December: third in Grade 3 at same course (5 lengths behind Walt) in February: stays 3m, at least as effective at shorter: acts on good to firm and heavy going: tried in hood: wears tongue tie: often travels strongly. *Paul Nicholls*

ADRRASTOS (IRE) 7 b.g. Areion (GER) – Laren (GER) (Monsun (GER)) [2018/19 **c131**
c131, h115: c16d* c15.8d⁴ Apr 4] lengthy gelding: fairly useful hurdler: useful form over **h–**
fences: won handicap at Hereford in March after lengthy absence: unproven beyond 17f: acts on good to firm and heavy going: has worn hood: usually leads. *Jamie Snowden*

AENGUS (IRE) 9 b.g. Robin des Champs (FR) – Which Thistle (IRE) (Saddlers' Hall **c–**
(IRE)) [2018/19 c–, h121: c26.1gᵖᵘ c24gᵖᵘ c20v c26.2gᵖᵘ c23.4vᵖᵘ Mar 16] fairly useful **h–**
hurdler: no form over fences: usually wears headgear. *Jennie Candlish*

AERODROME 4 b.f. Nathaniel (IRE) – Westerly Air (USA) (Gone West (USA)) **b78**
[2018/19 b13.7m² Oct 4] half-sister to 3 winners on Flat, including 11.7f/13f winner Windshield (by Montjeu): dam 9.4f winner: 7/1, second in junior bumper at Huntingdon (1¾ lengths behind Carry On). *Henry Spiller*

AERO MAJESTIC (IRE) 6 b.g. Arcadio (GER) – So Pretty (IRE) (Presenting) [2018/19 **c–**
c–, h100, b85: c21.6sᵖᵘ h25d Feb 17] angular gelding: winning pointer: maiden hurdler: no **h–**
form in chases: usually wears cheekpieces. *Sean Conway*

AERTON BRAE 6 b.m. Bahri (USA) – Roadworthy (IRE) (Lord Americo) [2018/19 **b–** b16.2g[pu] Apr 15] third foal: dam (h74) ungenuine 2m hurdle winner (stayed 3m): pulled up in bumper. *William Young Jnr*

A FALLING STAR 6 bl.g. Aeroplane – Westendview (Alleging (USA)) [2018/19 b15.8g[5] **b–** Jul 27] tailed off in bumper. *Alan Phillips*

AFFAIRE D'HONNEUR (FR) 8 ch.g. Shirocco (GER) – Affaire de Moeurs (FR) **c–** (Kaldounevees (FR)) [2018/19 c–, h88: h24g h16m c21.4g[pu] h18.7m[2] h23g* h15.5g[6] **h101** h24.2d[6] h20.1d[5] Mar 26] leggy gelding: has had breathing operation: fair hurdler: won seller at Worcester in September: no form over fences: left Kevin Frost after fifth start: stays 23f: acts on soft going: tried in headgear: usually in tongue tie in 2018/19. *Tony Carroll*

AFFLUENCE (IRE) 4 b.g. Thewayyouare (USA) – Castalian Spring (IRE) (Oasis **h82 p** Dream) [2018/19 h15.8g[4] Mar 19] fair on Flat, stays 11f: 14/1, some encouragement when fourth in maiden at Huntingdon (27¾ lengths behind Locker Room Talk) on hurdling debut: should do better. *Martin Smith*

AFOREMENTIONED (FR) 6 b.g. Zanzibari (USA) – Parcelle de Sou (FR) (Ajdayt **h131** (USA)) [2018/19 h16d* h16g h20d[4] h21.6v[3] h24d[4] Apr 23] €35,000 3-y-o: fifth foal: half-brother to 3 winners, including useful hurdler/chaser Darwins Fox (2m-2½m winner, by Kahyasi): dam (h119), French 15f hurdle winner, half-sister to smart French chaser (2¼m-21f winner) Geluroni: useful form over hurdles: won conditionals maiden at Limerick in November: fourth in novice handicap at Fairyhouse (4½ lengths behind Ronald Pump) final start: stays 3m: acts on heavy going: wears tongue tie. *Joseph Patrick O'Brien, Ireland*

AFTER ASPEN (IRE) 9 b.g. Mountain High (IRE) – None The Wiser (IRE) (Dr Massini **c– §** (IRE)) [2018/19 c111, h115: c24v[pu] h26d Dec 31] has had breathing operation: fairly useful **h– §** hurdler/fair chaser at best, no form in 2018/19: stays 3m: acts on heavy going: usually wears headgear: tried in tongue tie: temperamental. *Olly Murphy*

AFTERCLASS (IRE) 11 b.g. Stowaway – Afsana (IRE) (Bluebird (USA)) [2018/19 **c–** c23.8g[pu] May 16] winning pointer: maiden hurdler: no form in chases: has worn headgear/ **h–** tongue tie. *Mrs E. Mercy McEwen*

AGAINN DUL AGHAIDH 8 b.g. Black Sam Bellamy (IRE) – Star Ar Aghaidh (IRE) **c70 x** (Soviet Star (USA)) [2018/19 c85: c23.6g[4] c25.2s[6] c20v[6] c20.3d c19.9g[pu] c24.2d[pu] Mar 26] multiple point winner: poor maiden chaser: not a fluent jumper. *Alan Jones*

AGAMEMMON (IRE) 7 b.g. Getaway (GER) – Oscar Road (IRE) (Oscar (IRE)) **c113** [2018/19 c113, h–: c23.9d* c24g[3] c25.6g[4] c23d[6] c19.4g[4] Jan 12] maiden hurdler: fair **h–** handicap chaser: won at Market Rasen in May: stays 3m: acts on soft going: has worn headgear, including last 2 starts: has joined Henry Oliver. *Tom George*

AGENTLEMAN (IRE) 9 b.g. Trans Island – Silvine (IRE) (Shernazar) [2018/19 c82§, **c91 §** h–: c17.2g[2] c15.6g[2] c17.2g* Jul 8] maiden hurdler: modest handicap chaser: won novice **h–** event at Market Rasen in July: stays 21f: acts on heavy going: has worn cheekpieces: tried in tongue tie: strong traveller who usually finds little. *Peter Winks*

AGENT LOUISE 11 b.m. Alflora (IRE) – Oso Special (Teenoso (USA)) [2018/19 h80§: **h– §** h22.8v h23.3v[6] h25g[pu] Feb 18] modest hurdler at best, no form in 2018/19: usually wears headgear: unreliable. *Mike Sowersby*

AGENT MEMPHIS (IRE) 7 b.m. Scorpion (IRE) – Forces of Destiny (IRE) (Luso) **c102** [2018/19 h–: h20g h16g[6] h19.9g[5] c20d[2] c23.8g[pu] c19.4v[3] c19.2s[F] c23.6g[5] Mar 19] modest **h91** form over hurdles: fair form over fences: stays 2½m: acts on heavy going: in headgear last 5 starts: usually races close up. *Kim Bailey*

AGENT VALDEZ 6 b.m. Arvico (FR) – Soleil Sauvage (Loup Sauvage (USA)) [2018/19 **b79** b16g[4] b15.8d[5] Mar 30] £3,500 3-y-o, £20,000 5-y-o: third foal: half-sister to fairly useful hurdler/chaser Bandsman (2m-2½m winner, by Bandmaster): dam unraced half-sister to fairly useful 2m hurdle winner Bien Bronze: off mark in Irish points at second attempt: modest form in bumpers. *Fergal O'Brien*

AGENT WESTY (IRE) 5 b.g. Fame And Glory – Isis du Berlais (FR) (Cadoudal (FR)) **h78** [2018/19 b16.5m[4] h15.8v h15.8d h16.5g[6] h16d h15.8d Mar 30] €20,000 3-y-o: half-brother **b65** to several winners, including useful but unreliable hurdler/chaser Ipsos du Berlais (2½m-23f winner, by Poliglote), stayed 29f, and fair hurdler Bradford Bridge (2½m-23f winner, by Milan): dam French 15f-2¼m hurdle/chase winner: well beaten in maiden bumper: poor form over hurdles: will stay at least 2½m: tried in tongue tie. *Evan Williams*

AGE OF GLORY 10 b.g. Zamindar (USA) – Fleeting Moon (Fleetwood (IRE)) [2018/19 h100: h17g Feb 18] fair hurdler at best, lame only start in 2018/19: stays 2½m: acts on heavy going. *Barbara Butterworth*   h–

AGE OF WISDOM (IRE) 6 ch.g. Pivotal – Learned Friend (GER) (Seeking The Gold (USA)) [2018/19 h66p: h16d h16.3s^{ur} h16d h20.7g h20.5g* h20.5g^2 Apr 21] well-made gelding: fair hurdler: won handicap at Plumpton in April: stays 21f: best form on good going: usually wears cheekpieces. *Gary Moore*   h107

AGGRESSIVE (IRE) 4 b.g. Declaration of War (USA) – Three Moons (IRE) (Montjeu (IRE)) [2018/19 b13.7m* h17f* Mar 30] fourth foal: half-brother to smart 1m-1½m winner Tashaar (by Sea The Stars): dam useful 9.7f winner: impressive winner of junior bumper at Huntingdon in October: left David Elsworth, won maiden at Camden on hurdling debut by length from Demonstration: should progress. *Katherine Neilson, USA*   h104 p
b96

AGGY WITH IT (IRE) 5 b.m. Presenting – Agathe du Berlais (FR) (Poliglote) [2018/19 b17g^5 b16.7g* Mar 20] €50,000 3-y-o: second foal: dam French maiden half-sister to high-class hurdler (stays 3m) Agrapart and very smart hurdler/winning chaser (2m/17f winner) Afsoun: fair form in bumpers: won 4-runner maiden at Market Rasen in March, hard held: open to further improvement. *Dan Skelton*   b92 p

AGINCOURT REEF (IRE) 10 b.g. Gold Well – Hillside Native (IRE) (Be My Native (USA)) [2018/19 c–§, h91§: h21.2g^5 h20.7g^{pu} h20g^5 h20.3g^6 h25.5g^3 h23.8g* h19.7s^3 h23s h21.7d^6 h24.2d Mar 22] good-topped gelding: fair handicap hurdler: won at Ludlow (conditionals) in November: winning chaser: stays 3¼m: acts on good to firm and heavy going: wears headgear: one to treat with caution (races lazily). *Roger Teal*   c– §
h100 §

AGRAPART (FR) 8 b.g. Martaline – Afragha (IRE) (Darshaan) [2018/19 h160: h20g^4 h24.4s h24d^{pu} h24.7g Apr 6] good-topped gelding: high-class hurdler: largely out of form in 2018/19 (raced on Flat shortly after end of season): stays 3m: best form on soft/heavy going. *Nick Williams*   h147

AGREEMENT (IRE) 9 b.g. Galileo (IRE) – Cozzene's Angel (USA) (Cozzene (USA)) [2018/19 c83, h–: c22.6g Sep 4] lengthy gelding: winning hurdler: maiden chaser, well held only jumps start in 2018/19: probably stays 23f: acts on soft going: usually wears headgear. *Nikki Evans*   c–
h–

AGUSTA GOLD (IRE) 6 b.m. Gold Well – Chloes Choice (IRE) (Presenting) [2018/19 h22.2m^4 h20.4m^2 h22.4m^2 h18.8d* h24s^2 h20d* h18g^3 h22v^3 h20.3g^2 Apr 18] €17,500 3-y-o: second foal: sister to fairly useful 2½m hurdle winner Stick To The Plan: dam unraced half-sister to fairly useful hurdler/high-class chaser (stayed 3m) Farmer Jack: bumper winner: fairly useful hurdler: won mares maiden at Downpatrick in August and handicap at Navan in January: third in Kerry Group EBF Shannon Spray Mares Novices' Hurdle at Limerick (4½ lengths behind Robin de Carlow) in March and second in listed mares handicap at Cheltenham (beaten 3½ lengths by Sunshade) in April: stays 3m: acts on good to firm and heavy going: often travels strongly. *Ms Margaret Mullins, Ireland*   h126

A HARE BREATH (IRE) 11 b.g. Alkaadhem – Lady Willmurt (IRE) (Mandalus) [2018/19 c–, h138: c15.9g^5 h16.8g h20.5d h19.8g Apr 27] well-made gelding: useful hurdler/chaser, disappointing in 2018/19: stays 21f: acts on soft going: in cheekpieces last 2 starts: often races towards rear. *Ben Pauling*   c–
h100

AHEAD OF THE CURVE (FR) 7 b.g. Ballingarry (IRE) – Jasla (FR) (Highest Honor (FR)) [2018/19 h133: h23.9g Sep 26] sturdy gelding: winning pointer: useful hurdler at best, well held in handicap only start in 2018/19: stays 3m: acts on heavy going: usually wears headgear: wears tongue tie. *Susan Corbett*   h–

AHEAD OF THE GAME (IRE) 5 b.g. Westerner – Kildea Cailin (IRE) (Anshan) [2018/19 b16.5m^3 b16g b16g Apr 25] €20,000 3-y-o: third foal: brother to fairly useful hurdler/useful chaser Kupatana (2¼m-21f winner): dam unraced: fair form in bumpers: better effort when third in maiden at Taunton in November. *Johnny Farrelly*   b89

AH LITTLELUCK (IRE) 9 b.g. Mahler – Star of Hope (IRE) (Turtle Island (IRE)) [2018/19 h132: c25.1m^2 c22.5d c22.7g^{ur} c20g^3 c21g^4 c24d* c28.4g^{ur} c26d Mar 14] compact gelding: useful hurdler: fairly useful chaser: won maiden at Navan in January: stays 3m: acts on heavy going: wears tongue tie. *T. Gibney, Ireland*   c127
h–

AHORSEWITHNONAME 4 b.f. Cacique (IRE) – Sea of Galilee (Galileo (IRE)) [2018/19 b13.7g^4 b13m^3 b16.8d* Apr 23] third foal: half-sister to French 13f winner Resurrection (by Manduro): dam, 1¼m winner, out of useful French hurdler/fairly useful chaser up to 19f Mesange Royale: fairly useful form in bumpers: won mares event at Sedgefield in April, suited by emphasis on speed. *Brian Ellison*   b97

AH WELL (IRE) 7 b.g. Gold Well – Valentina Gaye (IRE) (Snurge) [2018/19 h20.8g³ **h108** h20.7d³ Mar 13] €16,500 3-y-o: first foal: dam unraced half-sister to fair hurdler/useful chaser (stays 25f) Full Cry out of half-sister to high-class staying chaser Kingsmark: fair form over hurdles: better effort when third in maiden at Doncaster in January: will stay 3m. *Thomas Gallagher*

AIMEE DE SIVOLA (FR) 5 ch.m. Network (GER) – Neva de Sivola (FR) (Blushing **h116** Flame (USA)) [2018/19 b98: h15.8d⁴ h16.3d⁵ h19.5d³ h18.5d² h18.9m Apr 20] rather unfurnished mare: bumper winner: fairly useful form over hurdles: best effort when second in mares handicap at Exeter in February: will stay at least 2½m: acts on good to soft going: usually races prominently. *Nick Williams*

AINE'S CHOICE (IRE) 8 b.m. Darsi (FR) – Karlybelle (FR) (Sandhurst Prince) **h–** [2018/19 h15.8g h16g h16m h16g⁶ h23g Aug 15] €9,000 3-y-o: half-sister to 3 winners by Shernazar, including bumper winner/fairly useful hurdler Primroseandblue (2m-2¾m winner), and a winning pointer by Classic Cliche: dam French maiden: point winner: well held in Irish bumpers and over hurdles: tried in cheekpieces. *Richenda Ford*

AINMISFEARR (IRE) 4 b.f. Famous Name – Virevolle (FR) (Kahyasi) [2018/19 b14g **h–** h16g h16s⁶ h16g h16d Jan 27] lengthy filly: half-sister to several winners on Flat abroad: **b–** dam unraced half-sister to fairly useful French hurdler up to 19f Verdoro: little show in bumper/over hurdles: wears tongue tie. *Gavin Patrick Cromwell, Ireland*

AINT DUNNE YET (IRE) 8 b.g. Flemensfirth (USA) – Merry Batim (IRE) (Alphabatim **c131** (USA)) [2018/19 c17.5d⁰ c21.3s* c21.5p⁰ Apr 21] winning hurdler: useful form over **h–** fences: won maiden at Leopardstown (in control when left clear last) in March: went wrong next time: stays 21f: acts on heavy going: front runner/races prominently, often travels strongly. *Noel Meade, Ireland*

AIN'T MY FAULT (IRE) 6 b.g. Beneficial – Coolnasneachta (IRE) (Old Vic) [2018/19 **h109** h20.1s⁵ h20v⁴ h17s² h15.7d h19.3d⁶ Mar 24] €21,000 3-y-o: second foal: half-brother to fairly useful/ungenuine hurdler Lion In His Heart (2m winner, by Westerner): dam, unraced, out of sister to top-class staying chaser Life of A Lord: winning Irish pointer: fair form over hurdles: in tongue tie last 3 starts: front runner. *Lucinda Russell*

AINTREE MY DREAM (FR) 9 b.g. Saint des Saints (FR) – Pretty Melodie (FR) **c136** (Lesotho (USA)) [2018/19 c132p, h–: c23.4d⁶ c20s² c20d⁶ c24vp⁰ c19.4g* Apr 14] lengthy **h–** gelding: winning hurdler: useful form over fences: won handicap at Stratford (in hood, by 3¼ lengths from Western Miller) in April: left Dan Skelton after fourth start: best form up to 21f: acts on heavy going: wears tongue tie. *Milton Harris*

AIR DE ROCK (FR) 7 b.g. High Rock (IRE) – Onciale (FR) (Ultimately Lucky (IRE)) **c120** [2018/19 c90, h–: c16v⁶ c16d² c16d² c19.9g* c20.3g³ c19.4g⁰ Apr 26] maiden hurdler: **h–** fairly useful handicap chaser: won at Huntingdon in February: stays 2½m: acts on heavy going: tried in cheekpieces: usually races prominently. *Venetia Williams*

AIRDRIGH (IRE) 7 b.g. Winged Love (IRE) – Maolisa (IRE) (Jamesmead) [2018/19 **c74 x** h74x: h23.9g⁵ h23.9g⁶ c20.1g⁵ c20.1g⁴ c23.5s h24g h20.1s⁴ h20.6d⁴ h16.6d h24.3d² **h77 x** c24.1d⁶ h23.9g Apr 24] poor maiden hurdler: similar form over fences: stays 3m: acts on soft going: wears cheekpieces/tongue tie: often let down by jumping. *Stuart Crawford, Ireland*

AIR GLIDER (IRE) 9 b.g. Mountain High (IRE) – California Blue (FR) (Pebble (FR)) **h–** [2018/19 h23.3dp⁰ h21.2dp⁰ Apr 23] winning pointer: maiden hurdler, no form in 2018/19: has worn blinkers: tried in tongue tie. *Sean Conway*

AIR HORSE ONE 8 gr.g. Mountain High (IRE) – Whisky Rose (IRE) (Old Vic) [2018/19 **h133** h144: h15.3g h20.5s h19d² h19.3d⁶ h19.9vp⁰ Mar 16] sturdy gelding: useful handicap hurdler: standout effort in 2018/19 when second at Taunton (5 lengths behind Unison) in January: stays 21f: acts on heavy going. *Harry Fry*

AIR NAVIGATOR 8 b.g. Yeats (IRE) – Lox Lane (IRE) (Presenting) [2018/19 h107, **c126** b105: c20.9s* c19.2v c20.2g² c19.9d⁶ c23.4d³ c19.9m⁶ Apr 20] big, rangy gelding: dual **h–** bumper winner: maiden hurdler: fairly useful form over fences: won novice handicap at Ffos Las in November: stays 23f: acts on soft going. *Tom George*

AIRTON 6 b.g. Champs Elysees – Fly In Style (Hernando (FR)) [2018/19 h16.5g* h19d² **h122** h16.3g³ h16g h16g Apr 27] close-coupled gelding: fairly useful on Flat, stays 16.5f: fairly useful form over hurdles: won novice at Taunton in February: tried in blinkers. *David Pipe*

AKARITA LIGHTS (IRE) 5 b.g. Arctic Cosmos (USA) – Akarita (IRE) (Akarad (FR)) **b98** [2018/19 b91: b16.2g* b16.7m² Apr 21] fairly useful form in bumpers: won at Kelso in May: left John Quinn after. *Alan King*

AKKAPENKO (FR) 5 b.g. Archipenko (USA) – Akka (Hernando (FR)) [2018/19 h–: **h83** h16g h16.3g² h16.8g³ h16.8m h16.5d⁵ Apr 24] poor maiden hurdler: raced around 2m: best form on good going: tried in cheekpieces. *Tim Vaughan*

ALADDIN SANE (IRE) 5 b.g. Teofilo (IRE) – Aqua Aura (USA) (Distorted Humor **h–** (USA)) [2018/19 h–: h16.7gᵖᵘ h15.7gᵘʳ h16.7g h16.8m h16.8dᶠ Apr 23] has had breathing operation: no form over hurdles: has worn hood: in tongue tie last 5 starts. *Henry Hogarth*

ALANJOU (FR) 9 b.g. Maresca Sorrento (FR) – Partie Time (FR) (Nononito (FR)) **c83 §** [2018/19 c20.5m⁴ c23.8g⁵ h23g c25.8m² c25.8gᵖᵘ c23m⁴ c24g c28.5d c24.2v⁶ Dec 20] **h–** close-coupled gelding: maiden hurdler: poor handicap chaser: stays 3¼m: acts on good to firm and heavy going: wears headgear: has joined Barry Brennan: temperamental. *Henry Tett*

ALBERTA (IRE) 10 ch.g. Choisir (AUS) – Akita (IRE) (Foxhound (USA)) [2018/19 **h–** h113: h19.6gᶠ May 22] fair hurdler: raced mainly at 2m: acted on soft going: wore visor: often raced towards rear: dead. *Suzi Best*

ALBERT D'OLIVATE (FR) 9 b.g. Alberto Giacometti (IRE) – Komunion (FR) **c–** (Luchiroverte (IRE)) [2018/19 c–, h110§: h23.6dᵖᵘ Nov 21] good-topped gelding: fair **h– §** hurdler: maiden chaser: stayed 3¼m: best form on good/heavy going: usually wore headgear: in tongue tie last 5 starts: temperamental: dead. *Neil Mulholland*

ALBERT GEORGE 5 ch.g. Paco Boy (IRE) – Avonrose (Avonbridge) [2018/19 b15.8v⁵ **b–** b16g Apr 25] no form in bumpers. *Sarah-Jayne Davies*

ALBERTO'S DREAM 10 b.g. Fantastic Spain (USA) – Molly's Folly (My Lamb) **c99** [2018/19 c117, h–: c25.2s c23.6d⁵ Mar 21] winning hurdler: fairly useful handicap chaser, **h–** below form in 2018/19: stays 29f: acts on heavy going: has worn headgear. *Tom Lacey*

ALBERT'S BACK 5 b.g. Champs Elysees – Neath (Rainbow Quest (USA)) [2018/19 **h130** h128p: h16.4g² Feb 23] useful form over hurdles: second in handicap at Newcastle (4 lengths behind Joke Dancer) on sole outing in 2018/19. *Michael Easterby*

AL BOUM PHOTO (FR) 7 b.g. Buck's Boum (FR) – Al Gane (FR) (Dom Alco **c174** (FR)) [2018/19 c161+, h–: c21.5s* c26.3d* Mar 15] **h–**

Twenty years after his first tilt at the Cheltenham Gold Cup with Florida Pearl, a steeplechaser saddled at the time with the tag of being a 'second Arkle', master trainer Willie Mullins finally broke a so-called 'Gold Cup hoodoo' when 12/1-shot Al Boum Photo took the latest edition. Mullins has had charge of some of the finest staying chasers trained in Ireland in recent times when he has dominated the Irish jumping scene—he was champion in Ireland for the thirteenth time in the latest season—and Al Boum Photo's success followed no fewer than six second places for Mullins in Cheltenham's blue riband event. The top-class Florida Pearl won four Irish Hennessy Gold Cups and a King George VI Chase, as well as recording Cheltenham Festival wins in the Champion Bumper and the SunAlliance, and his three Gold Cup appearances yielded a best-placed runner-up spot, behind Looks Like Trouble on his second try. The stable's Grand National winner Hedgehunter and Sir des Champs, a dual Festival winner whom Mullins described at the time as being 'right up there with Florida Pearl', were his next Gold Cup runners-up, before 16/1-shot On His Own nearly pulled it off in 2014. On His Own went down by a short head to another outsider Lord Windermere, almost getting back up in the last few strides after making much of the running. On His Own suffered interference from the winner but the Cheltenham stewards allowed the result to stand after an inquiry lasting nearly fifteen minutes; Mullins considered an appeal but that was quickly ruled out by On His Own's owners Andrea and Graham Wylie ('It was a long inquiry and you've got to respect the stewards' decision'), though there must have been a fair prospect of the Cheltenham stewards' decision being overturned, given the marked deviation on the run-in by the winner and the fact that On His Own was beaten only a couple of inches. Two second places followed for Closutton in 2015 and 2016, both with Djakadam who was also fourth when starting favourite in 2017 on the third of his four appearances in the race.

The quartet which represented the Mullins stable in the latest Cheltenham Gold Cup (the first one under the sponsorship of Magners) didn't include any of the three runners at the head of the betting, the previous season's RSA Chase winner Presenting Percy, who started 100/30 favourite although he hadn't run over fences since, the King George VI Chase winner Clan des Obeaux, a 5/1-shot, and the King

Magners Cheltenham Gold Cup, Cheltenham—reigning title-holder Native River (white face and noseband) is swallowed up at the second last, where Al Boum Photo takes over from the grey Bristol de Mai, Clan des Obeaux (spots) and 2018 third Anibale Fly (hoops) ...

George third Native River who was sent off at 6/1 to become the first to win the Gold Cup in successive years since Best Mate (Kauto Star's two wins were interrupted by his defeat by Denman). According to the betting, fourth was the best the Mullins stable could expect, with the Savills Chase (formerly the Lexus) winner Kemboy the shortest-priced of its four runners at 8/1, just ahead of 9/1-shot Bellshill, the choice of stable number-one Ruby Walsh who had partnered him to victory in an Irish Gold Cup that had been reduced to a field of four after six of the intended runners were among a spate of ground-related withdrawals on the second day of the Dublin Racing Festival. The second and third from the previous year's Cheltenham Gold Cup were back again. Might Bite, a 14/1-shot, had been running as if he had developed a persistent problem after a tough campaign in which his memorable Gold Cup battle with Native River had been his only defeat, while Anibale Fly (22/1), who had gone on to reach the frame in the Grand National after his Gold Cup third, had been running over shorter distances in the latest season. Also in a representative line-up at Cheltenham were the dual Betfair Chase winner Bristol de Mai, the former King George VI Chase winner Thistlecrack, who had finished a good second to Clan des Obeaux in his bid to win that race again after coming third in the Betfair, the previous year's Golden Miller winner Shattered Love (a rare appearance by a mare in the field) and the progressive Welsh Grand National winner Elegant Escape.

Al Boum Photo went into the Cheltenham Gold Cup as the third in line in the Mullins contingent, having had just seven outings over fences and been beaten once in his four completed starts. The three chases in which he had not completed had been a Grade 2 novice event at Limerick, where he fell when in front at the last, the RSA Chase at the Cheltenham Festival, where he was held in third behind Presenting Percy at the second last when taking a heavy fall that ended Ruby Walsh's season, and the Champion Novices' at Punchestown where, in bizarre circumstances, Paul Townend steered him sharply to the right on the approach to the final fence, where he looked in command, and Al Boum Photo crashed through the wing, unseated his rider and carried out his closest challenger Finian's Oscar. Al Boum Photo, like a number of his stable companions, was held up in the latest season by the persistent dry conditions and he missed the Savills Chase at Leopardstown's Christmas meeting because there wasn't deemed to be enough give in the ground (he hasn't been risked so far over fences on going any less yielding than the good to soft he encountered in the Gold Cup). Al Boum Photo eventually made his seasonal debut five days later, on New Year's Day, at Tramore, which has the smallest circuit—

just under a mile, with a run-in of one hundred and sixty yards—of any track in Britain and Ireland. The tight layout didn't affect Al Boum Photo who faced no easy task under a Grade 1 penalty (for winning the Ryanair Gold Cup at the Fairyhouse Easter meeting), conceding weight all round in the listed Savills Chase to others who wouldn't have looked out of place in the Leopardstown Grade 1 of the same name. Al Boum Photo led home a one, two, three for his stable on the soft ground, travelling well all the way and staying on strongly to win by six lengths and sixteen from Total Recall and Invitation Only, both also making their belated reappearance. Al Boum Photo and Anibale Fly were among the ground-related, late withdrawals from the Irish Gold Cup but, while Anibale Fly was rerouted to finish second in the Red Mills Chase over two and a half miles at Gowran, Al Boum Photo lined up for the Cheltenham Gold Cup without another run, though Ruby Walsh, who partnered him to victory at Tramore, overlooked him at Cheltenham where he was reunited with Paul Townend who can now claim to have had both his best and his worst moments in the saddle on the same horse!

Al Boum Photo, whose Savills Chase victory at Tramore was his first over fences at beyond two and a half miles, was the only one of the Mullins-trained quartet to complete the course in the Gold Cup. The race was run for the three others before it was a third over, with Kemboy unseating his jockey at the first, Bellshill's jumping letting him down badly before he was pulled up, while 33/1-shot Invitation Only, who made the early running, fell fatally at the tenth, contributing to a miserable week for his and Bellshill's owners Andrea and Graham Wylie who had also lost the promising novice Ballyward in the National Hunt Chase on the opening afternoon. Soon after Invitation Only's exit, the latest Gold Cup began to evoke memories of the previous year's drawn-out struggle as the always prominent Might Bite and Native River, who recovered from a sluggish start to work his way into his customary position, battled it out at the head of affairs. There was to be no repeat of twelve months earlier, however, when the pair made the race almost entirely their own from a long way out before Native River finally outstayed his rival. Native River was headed in the latest edition by the patiently ridden Al Boum Photo approaching the second last (where Might Bite was pulled up after folding

... master trainer Willie Mullins' Gold Cup drought is finally over as Paul Townend and Al Boum Photo have matters firmly under control at the last

Mrs J. Donnelly's "Al Boum Photo"

tamely entering the final straight), while Bristol de Mai and Clan des Obeaux were still there with every chance and Anibale Fly was making ground under pressure. Al Boum Photo was untidy at the second last but he kept on well when shaken up and had a decisive advantage over Bristol de Mai at the final fence. Ridden out, Al Boum Photo won by two and a half lengths and three and three quarters from Anibale Fly (who took second up the steep climb to the finish) and Bristol de Mai. Native River plugged on for fourth, ahead of the weakening Clan des Obeaux, who failed to stay the extra distance in the conditions, while Presenting Percy was never really travelling as well as he can and managed only eighth, found to be lame afterwards. Thistlecrack jumped poorly and was pulled up while Shattered Love reportedly suffered post-race ataxia.

Too many in the field failed to run to form for the latest Gold Cup to be regarded as an exceptional renewal, but Al Boum Photo is still only seven and could well make an impact in the race again another year. He lost little in defeat when beaten two lengths by Kemboy (the pair well clear of a good field) in the Punchestown Gold Cup on his only subsequent appearance. Not jumping quite so well as he had at Cheltenham, Al Boum Photo held every chance from three out and stuck to his task well, finding Kemboy just too strong on the day. Nine Cheltenham Festival winners were turned out again at the Punchestown Festival—which took place shortly after the end of the British season—but only two of them, Klassical Dream and Minella Indo, managed to follow up. The opportunity to complete the Cheltenham Gold Cup and Punchestown Gold Cup double has existed since 1998/9 when the latter was instituted, and the double has been achieved in the same season only by Kicking King, War of Attrition and Sizing John (who completed a notable treble which included the Irish Gold Cup). Kicking King, War of Attrition and Sizing John were all seven-year-olds, incidentally.

44

			Cadoudal	Green Dancer
	Buck's Boum (FR)		(br 1979)	Come To Sea
	(b 2005)	Buck's		Le Glorieux
Al Boum Photo (FR)			(b 1993)	Buckleby
(b.g. 2012)		Dom Alco		Dom Pasquini
	Al Gane (FR)		(gr 1987)	Alconaca
	(b 2005)	Magic Spring		True Brave
			(b 1997)	Carama

The tall Al Boum Photo was one of two winners at the Cheltenham Festival (Arkle winner Duc des Genievres being the other) for his French sire Buck's Boum, a brother to four-times World [Stayers'] Hurdle winner Big Buck's. It was the third year in a row that the Cheltenham World Cup had been won by a horse whose sire raced over jumps (Buck's Boum was one of the leading juvenile hurdlers of his year in France). Like Indian River, the sire of Native River, Buck's Boum is by Cadoudal who was the leading sire of thoroughbred jumpers in France on numerous occasions and the sire of Cheltenham Gold Cup winner and dual King George winner Long Run (a contemporary of Buck's Boum whom he beat in the Prix Cambaceres, the top autumn hurdle race for three-year-olds in France). Cadoudal sired another champion juvenile hurdler in France in Saint des Saints, the sire of Djakadam. Al Boum Photo's dam, the unraced Al Gane, has also produced a winning chaser in France, Diteou, a sister to Al Boum Photo, and there is a two-year-old brother in the pipeline, as well as a yearling filly by Cokoriko. Al Gane is from a family that has had some notable winners in Britain, details of which appeared in the essay on Al Boum Photo in *Chasers & Hurdlers 2017/18*. Al Boum Photo stays three and a quarter miles well and acts on heavy going (his Gold Cup and Punchestown Gold Cup performances came on good to soft and he has yet to encounter good going or firmer over fences). He usually travels strongly in his races and has worn ear plugs on his two Cheltenham Festival appearances. *W. P. Mullins, Ireland*

ALCALA (FR) 9 gr.g. Turgeon (USA) – Pail Mel (FR) (Sleeping Car (FR)) [2018/19 **c148** c151, h–: c21g⁴ c21g² c21.4m⁶ Jul 21] tall gelding: winning hurdler: smart handicap **h–** chaser: second at Newton Abbot (3½ lengths behind Bagad Bihoue) in June: has won at 3¼m, usually races over shorter: acts on good to firm and heavy going: has worn hood: wears tongue tie: often races towards rear/travels strongly. *Paul Nicholls*

ALCANAR (USA) 6 ch.g. Teofilo (IRE) – Badalona (Cape Cross (IRE)) [2018/19 h16v⁵ **h94** Dec 17] workmanlike gelding: maiden on Flat: fair form over hurdles: likely to stay further than 2m. *Tony Carroll*

ALCHIMIX (FR) 9 b.g. Al Namix (FR) – Julie Noire (FR) (Agent Bleu (FR)) [2018/19 **c– §** c75§, h–: h20.6gᵖᵘ May 11] maiden hurdler/chaser: usually wears cheekpieces: tried in **h–** tongue tie: temperamental. *John Wainwright*

ALCOCK AND BROWN (IRE) 7 b.g. Oasis Dream – Heart Stopping (USA) (Chester **h122** House (USA)) [2018/19 h–: h16g⁶ h20g* h20g* Jul 4] fairly useful handicap hurdler: won at Worcester in June and July: stays 2½m: acts on soft and good to firm going. *Dan Skelton*

AL CO (FR) 14 ch.g. Dom Alco (FR) – Carama (FR) (Tip Moss (FR)) [2018/19 c123, h–: **c113** c32.5g³ c27.7g² c24.2m⁵ h23.3g⁶ c24.1gᵖᵘ Aug 20] smallish, angular gelding: winning **h81** hurdler: fair chaser nowadays: stays 4m: acts on any going: has worn headgear. *Peter Bowen*

AL DANCER (FR) 6 gr.g. Al Namix (FR) – Steel Dancer (FR) (Kaldounevees (FR)) **h144** [2018/19 b105: h17.1d* h15.8s* h16.8g* h15.7d* h16.4s Mar 12]

During its days under the sponsorship of Schweppes and then the Tote, Britain's richest handicap hurdle, originally known as the Gold Trophy, often fell victim to the winter weather. Only six renewals took place during the 'eighties, for example, but there is a more flexible approach these days by the BHA in saving and rescheduling big races from meetings that would simply have been abandoned in the past, resulting in the 2011 and 2012 editions being postponed to a slightly later date. 2009 was therefore the last time the weather put paid to the race but, ten years later, Newbury's meeting, featuring what is now the Betfair Hurdle, was the highest-profile casualty of what ostensibly looked, briefly at least, a far more serious threat to racing than either frost or snow. On a Saturday when the important Betfair Hurdle card, also featuring the Game Spirit Chase and Denman Chase, should have been the main attraction, ITV4, scheduled to be covering Warwick as well as Newbury,

Betfair Hurdle, Ascot—
Al Dancer becomes the eighth novice winner from the last ten renewals as he pulls clear of outsider
Magic Dancer (cheekpieces) in a race rerouted from Newbury as a result of the equine flu shutdown

showed five live races from Naas instead, starting with a twenty-five-runner maiden hurdle, while the *Racing Post* carried cards and form for two South African meetings and Cagnes-sur-Mer as well as Naas. An outbreak of equine flu led to a shutdown of racing in Britain—which lasted for six days and resulted in the loss of twenty-three meetings—but the Betfair Hurdle was salvaged and run a week later at Ascot. Disruption to the racing programme, however, was slight compared with the time British racing's biosecurity had been threatened by the 2001 outbreak of foot and mouth disease which resulted in eighty-two meetings being lost by the end of that season, including the Cheltenham Festival. In response to the growing foot and mouth epidemic, the British Horseracing Board, as it then was, announced a self-imposed seven-day suspension of racing, but thereafter the Board made strenuous efforts to keep racing's show on the road by rearranging fixtures in the face of pressure from the National Farmers' Union for racing to cease and also criticism from sections of the media for carrying on. At the same time, racing in Ireland was suspended indefinitely even though there had been no outbreak of the disease there.

The British Horseracing Authority responded to the equine flu outbreak with a similar self-imposed suspension of racing, which took immediate effect forty-eight hours before Newbury's Betfair Hurdle meeting, after three horses in Donald McCain's Cheshire stable tested positive for the virus the previous evening after the trainer became concerned about their health and contacted the BHA. Quarantine restrictions were initially placed on more than a hundred stables that had runners at meetings earlier the same week at Ayr, Ludlow and Wolverhampton where they could have come into contact with runners from McCain's yard, though the number of stables placed in isolation—or under 'lockdown' as it came to be known—soon rose to one hundred and seventy-four after an unconfirmed case in the stable of Rebecca Menzies in the North East, with no connection to the McCain runners, came to light. An outbreak in Australia in 2007 had wrought havoc over a period of more than three months, but that was in a population of unvaccinated thoroughbreds. Since 1981, all racehorses in Britain have been required to be vaccinated against equine flu, which is highly contagious, though the current vaccine was shown not to be fully effective against the latest strain which was first detected in Europe late in 2018 and subsequently identified as an American variant of the virus. Racing in Ireland continued, with Irish trainers who had runners at the three British meetings in question having time to isolate their horses—something British trainers had not been able to do—before returning to their yards. Ireland had its own case of flu in January which was contained without racing being halted, though a temporary ban on entries from Britain was put in place after Britain's outbreak because the Irish authorities 'didn't know the extent of the problem in Britain.' A warning about equine flu had been given towards the end of January and British trainers had been told to report any suspicious cases, which should have given the BHA something to go on, but the British authorities still took a 'belt, button and braces' approach which led to the sport remaining in limbo while the BHA's veterinary team set about gathering information from tests ordered on all the horses in the stables involved in the 'lockdown.' The disease, apparently, can take three days before symptoms appear which led to the BHA announcing that it 'will take until Sunday before all the required information can be gathered [some of the tests were done too early and needed taking again]'. By the Saturday, the BHA had had the results of seven hundred tests, as its vets worked round the clock, with a further five thousand swabs distributed to the targeted stables but not yet returned. Some of the biggest stables caught up in the shutdown had not even received the swabs, including those of Richard Hannon and Richard Fahey, each of whom train more than two hundred and fifty horses ('If you don't live in Newmarket, you can't get the testing kits, my vet asked for a thousand for me and his other clients and at the moment he has got thirty,' said Fahey).

With Cheltenham only weeks away, the National Trainers Federation initially supported the BHA's action to test all horses in the 'lockdown' stables, as the best hope of containing the potential spread and any potentially more serious long-term consequences. Despite being in charge of the racecourse group which suffered most from lost fixtures, Arena Racing Company chief executive Martin Cruddace thought the BHA had 'excelled' with its handling of the situation. However, support for the BHA was by no means unanimous, with others finding the measures disproportionate. As well as having the Betfair Hurdle favourite Al Dancer, Nigel Twiston-Davies needed his Grand National hope Ballyhill to finish in the first four in the Denman Chase as a last chance to qualify for Aintree before the weights were published. Describing the BHA's response as 'a total knee-jerk reaction', Twiston-Davies said 'I should think every trainer in Britain has a horse with a snotty nose… Flu is endemic in the whole horse population…We all have bugs and treat them as they come.' Al Dancer's trainer, joined by Colin Tizzard who had been due to run Native River against Clan des Obeaux in the Denman Chase, might have been speaking as one with more to lose than most from Newbury being cancelled, but the opinions were shared by at least one leading vet. Piet Ramzan, a fellow of the Royal College of Veterinary Surgeons, echoed Twiston-Davies' and Tizzard's comments, saying 'To some degree it looks an overreaction and isn't necessarily justified by the circumstances, given flu is endemic in the UK.'

While vaccinated thoroughbreds might have had nothing worse than 'a snotty nose', the wider horse population was at greater risk from what the BHA's director of equine health and welfare David Sykes described as 'not a common cold, it is a highly contagious and potentially serious disease.' Endemic it may be, but other than three further positive cases at McCain's yard and another four (who displayed no clinical symptoms) from Simon Crisford's Kremlin House Stables in Newmarket (the Menzies case turned out to be a false alarm), no other signs of flu had been detected from swabs taken across the country. With a decision on a resumption due on Monday evening from the BHA's veterinary committee, the announcement on Sunday evening of the Kremlin House cases was a blow to hopes. 'Sources' at the BHA reportedly told the *Daily Mail* that the aim of restarting racing on the Wednesday looked unrealistic, with the following Monday a more likely date.

That prospect led to a growing clamour for the BHA to push ahead with at least a partial resumption (the Irish authorities had already lifted their ban on British entries). Racing could, in any event, initially have continued without a wholesale shutdown (with surveillance and testing taking place at the isolated yards) and it was frustrating that stables not affected, or which had returned clear tests, were left kicking their heels. The reigning champion trainer Nicky Henderson, a cautious supporter initially of the BHA's 'better safe than sorry' approach, led the way with a forceful call for a return in an interview in the *Racing Post* on the Monday. 'It's like a school in which little Johnny has a runny nose or Freddie is under the weather. Do you send those two home, or do you close the school? If we don't race on Wednesday, there's a chance we won't race at Cheltenham [four weeks away]. We have to start racing again. What is going to happen otherwise? What circumstances are suddenly going to come into play to let us race again?'

Henderson's intervention, along with others from leading trainers, was probably decisive. The swabbing programme was nowhere near completed (thousands remained to be done, begging the question about how prepared the BHA had been for a situation that it had warned about in January), while some swabbings had not been carried out correctly and others sent back for re-testing. It was clear that the sport could not wait for the BHA's veterinary team to make absolutely sure every yard was clear and common sense prevailed. When it met on the Monday evening, the BHA's veterinary committee sanctioned a resumption of racing on the Wednesday while keeping in 'lockdown' some stables considered as possible risks (the isolated stables of McCain and Crisford, meanwhile, faced being closed for several more weeks). For BHA chief executive Nick Rust, his organisation's prompt and decisive action had been fully justified. 'The fact that it's argued that this is prevalent in all yards most of the time has been put to sleep by the testing we've done,' he claimed. 'This is something that can potentially kill horses if they have not been vaccinated properly or recently.' Rust added that he was pleased that the crisis—which made headlines in the national news—had had the effect of generating wider interest in racing though, as Alastair Down put it in the *Racing Post*, that was 'rather like London Zoo announcing their delight at the public interest shown since all our lions escaped into Regent's Park.'

While there was general relief when racing therefore resumed immediately after six days, without an extension to the shutdown (twenty-two stables which had runners at the Ayr meeting where McCain had an infected runner were barred from having runners for an extra day), some trainers were less supportive of the more stringent vaccination protocols which accompanied the restart. Instead of the need to vaccinate annually, a change to the rules now required a horse to have been vaccinated within the last six months before being allowed to race. This made no difference to a trainer like Paul Nicholls, who routinely vaccinates his string in January, but overnight it had a far bigger impact on others, including on Nicky Henderson whose horses had last had their jabs the previous summer. As a result, one of the horses Henderson was unable to run was Countister in the rescheduled Betfair Hurdle at Ascot (the Denman Chase was also added to Ascot's card which already featured the Ascot Chase under Betfair sponsorship), while Jane Williams, whose husband Nick called the new rule 'absolutely ridiculous', was prevented from running another of the original leading Betfair Hurdle fancies Monsieur Lecoq. Nick Williams asked why races like the Betfair Hurdle had not been rescheduled to a later date so that horses originally targeted at them, but not eligible under the new vaccination rules, would have time to meet the new criteria. Six extra fixtures in late-February were added to provide opportunities for horses denied a run earlier in the month. To avoid horses needing to be vaccinated in mid-season in future, the BHA has changed to an eight-month renewal period, rather than six, to take effect from January 1st 2020.

It was therefore a smaller than usual field of fourteen which lined up for a smaller than usual prize for the Betfair Hurdle which was worth £47,829 to the winner, considerably less than the £88,272 Kalashnikov had picked up at Newbury the year before. Al Dancer headed the betting at 5/2 ahead of fellow novice Getaway Trump for Paul Nicholls at 4/1. Al Dancer had a similar profile to this stable's recent winners of the race Splash of Ginge and Ballyandy who had been among the other novices to dominate the Betfair Hurdle over the last decade. After a win at Bangor, Al Dancer had finished fourth in the Grade 2 bumper at Aintree the previous season and had begun the latest campaign with wins at short odds in ordinary novice hurdles at Carlisle and Ffos Las. Those wins got him into a handicap at Cheltenham in December off what proved a wholly inadequate mark as he drew right away after leading approaching the last to win what looked a competitive event beforehand by eleven lengths. A mark 12 lb higher in the Betfair did nothing to check Al Dancer's progress through the hurdling ranks. As at Cheltenham, Al Dancer didn't settle fully in a hood, racing just behind the leaders, but he saved ground round the inner all the way and was produced to lead at the last before quickening clear without Sam Twiston-Davies having to ask too much of him. Al Dancer won by three and three quarter lengths, with long-priced pair Magic Dancer and Blu Cavalier taking the places and Getaway Trump, who was caught further back than ideal, completing the frame. Two years earlier, Ballyandy had gone on to start joint favourite for the Supreme Novices' Hurdle in which he finished fourth. Ballyandy went closest to giving the Twiston-Davies stable a winner at the latest Festival when third in the

Coral Cup, while Al Dancer, also sent off joint favourite for the Supreme, proved a big disappointment in a race in which his owner Dai Walters' other well-fancied runner Angels Breath, trained by Nicky Henderson, also failed to meet expectations.

Al Dancer (FR) (gr.g. 2013)	Al Namix (FR) (gr 1997)	Linamix (gr 1987)	Mendez
			Lunadix
		Dirigeante (b 1991)	Lead On Time
			Daytona
	Steel Dancer (FR) (b 2002)	Kaldounevees (gr 1991)	Kaldoun
			Safaroa
		Hero's Dancer (b 1992)	Hero's Honor
			Disco Dancer

The well-made Al Dancer is by Al Namix who has already sired the high-class jumpers Grandouet, Petit Mouchoir and Saphir du Rheu. Al Dancer's unraced dam Steel Dancer has had three other winners in France, including Steely Dancer (by Until Sundown), a middle-distance stayer on the Flat and Set Dancer (by Irish Wells), a winning chaser at around twenty-one furlongs. The pick of her French winners was Tzar's Dancer (by Tzar Rodney) who won thirteen races in a lengthy career, notably the top French handicap chase the Prix du President de La Republique, and finished fourth in the Grand Steeple-Chase de Paris. Al Dancer's grandam Hero's Dancer failed to win from numerous attempts on the Flat and over jumps and great grandam Disco Dancer was another who never ran. However, Disco Dancer is the grandam of Sir d'Orton and Logans Run who were fairly useful chasers in Britain. Al Dancer has raced mainly on ground softer than good and is likely to be best at around two miles for the time being. He wore a hood on his final start in bumpers, as well as for both his wins in handicaps in the latest season. The hood was left off at Cheltenham (he wore ear plugs there), though that alone cannot have accounted for how he ran. Al Dancer's first two starts in bumpers had come for Christian Williams before he joined Nigel Twiston-Davies. Al Dancer looks likely to be seen over fences in the next season. *Nigel Twiston-Davies*

ALDERBROOK LAD (IRE) 13 ch.g. Alderbrook – Alone Tabankulu (IRE) (Phardante (FR)) [2018/19 c121x, h–: c21.2g* c21.2m³ c25.5g⁴ c21.2s c20g⁶ Sep 23] winning hurdler: fairly useful handicap chaser: won at Cartmel (fourth success there) in May: stays 25f: acts on good to firm and heavy going: has worn headgear: tried in tongue tie: front runner/races prominently: often let down by jumping. *Micky Hammond* — **c119 x** **h–**

AL DESTOOR 9 ch.g. Teofilo (IRE) – In A Silent Way (IRE) (Desert Prince (IRE)) [2018/19 h110: h20.5v² h19.6v² h20.1s² Dec 12] close-coupled gelding: fair maiden hurdler: stays 2½m: acts on heavy going: wears tongue tie. *Jennie Candlish* — **h110**

ALDRIN (FR) 6 b.g. New Approach (IRE) – Trip To The Moon (Fasliyev (USA)) [2018/19 h103: h16.8gᵖᵘ h16g* h15.8g⁶ h18.6g* Nov 8] has had breathing operation: fair handicap hurdler: won at Worcester in September and Market Rasen in November: stays 19f: best form on good going: wears tongue tie: often races towards rear. *David Pipe* — **h114**

ALEXANDERTHEGREAT (FR) 4 b.g. Redoute's Choice (AUS) – Garota da Ipanema (FR) (Sillery (USA)) [2018/19 h16dᵘʳ Nov 28] fair on Flat, stays 1¾m: went as if amiss on hurdling debut. *John Quinn* — **h–**

ALEXANDER THE GREY 8 gr.g. Fair Mix (IRE) – Cadourova (FR) (Cadoudal (FR)) [2018/19 h101: h16mᵖᵘ h16.2g c20g⁶ c19.4m² c22.6m³ c17mᶠ Sep 8] has had breathing operation: maiden hurdler: fair form over fences: stays 19f: acts on good to firm and good to soft going: has worn hood: usually wears tongue tie: usually travels strongly. *Graeme McPherson* — **c106** **h62**

ALF 'N' DOR (IRE) 8 ch.g. Flemensfirth (USA) – Greenflag Princess (IRE) (Executive Perk) [2018/19 c108§, h90: c20g² c20g³ c19.4d² c20.3g⁶ c16v² c20.2g⁶ c20.3s⁵ c19.7d* c20.2m³ c16s⁴ c19.4g* Apr 21] sturdy gelding: winning hurdler: fair handicap chaser: won at Plumpton in January and Ffos Las in April: stays 3m: acts on heavy going: usually wears headgear/tongue tie: usually races prominently: temperamental. *Peter Bowen* — **c108 §** **h–**

ALFIBOY 9 b.g. Alflora (IRE) – Cloudy Pearl (Cloudings (IRE)) [2018/19 c–, h94: c20.1g h16.2g Apr 15] workmanlike gelding: has had breathing operation: maiden hurdler: no form in chases: should stay beyond 2m: acts on heavy going: has worn hood: usually races off pace. *Sue Smith* — **c–** **h–**

ALFIE CORBITT (IRE) 6 b.g. Arakan (USA) – Millanymare (IRE) (Old Vic) [2018/19 **h95 p** h20v h20.8g h18.5d h24.1g² Apr 11] €11,000 3-y-o, £68,000 5-y-o: has had breathing operation: third foal: half-brother to 2¼m bumper winner Westinmare (by Definite Article): dam (c107/h110), 2¾m-3m hurdle/chase winner, sister to useful hurdler/chaser (winner up to 3m) Glasker Mill: off mark in Irish points at third attempt: modest form over hurdles: tried in tongue tie: open to further improvement. *Kim Bailey*

ALFIE'S CHOICE (IRE) 7 b.g. Shantou (USA) – Bally Bolshoi (IRE) (Bob Back **h121** (USA)) [2018/19 h112: h22.1g* h25.4g* h20.9m⁵ h20.1g* Oct 5] fairly useful hurdler: won novice at Cartmel in May, and handicaps at same course in July and Hexham in October: stays 25f: acts on soft going: has worn cheekpieces: usually races prominently. *Keith Dalgleish*

ALFIE SPINNER (IRE) 14 b.g. Alflora (IRE) – Little Red Spider (Bustino) [2018/19 **c–** c134, h–: c23.6v Dec 8] good-topped gelding: has had breathing operation: winning **h–** hurdler: useful chaser, well held only start in 2018/19: stays 4m: acts on heavy going: wears cheekpieces/tongue tie: front runner/races prominently. *Kerry Lee*

ALIANDY (IRE) 8 b.g. Presenting – Water Rock (El Conquistador) [2018/19 h–: h19.6g³ **h116** h24.1s⁴ h19.9s² Dec 31] good-topped gelding: fairly useful handicap hurdler: second at Uttoxeter in December: best up to 3m: acts on soft going: signs of temperament (has played up at start). *Kim Bailey*

ALICE LISLE 5 ch.m. Flemensfirth (USA) – Twilight Affair (Dansili) [2018/19 h–, b60: **h79** h21.2g³ h19.9s⁵ h19.9sᵖᵘ Mar 21] poor form over hurdles: tried in blinkers: in tongue tie last 4 starts. *Tim Easterby*

ALICES MAN (IRE) 9 b.g. Golan (IRE) – Awbeg Flower (IRE) (Alphabatim (USA)) **c–** [2018/19 c73, h80: c26m⁴ Dec 1] workmanlike gelding: poor handicap hurdler/maiden **h–** chaser: stays 3m: acts on soft going: wears blinkers: often in tongue tie. *Hugh Beggs, Ireland*

ALISIER D'IRLANDE (FR) 9 br.g. Kapgarde (FR) – Isati's (FR) (Chamberlin (FR)) **c146** [2018/19 c144, h–: c20.6m² c20sᵖᵘ Sep 14] good sort: winning hurdler: smart chaser: **h–** second in Grade 3 event at Killarney (9½ lengths behind Ballyoisin) in May: stayed 21f: acted on good to firm and heavy going: tried in headgear: wore tongue tie: front runner/raced prominently: dead. *Henry de Bromhead, Ireland*

ALI THE HUNTER (IRE) 6 ch.m. Papal Bull – Polish Spring (IRE) (Polish Precedent **h91** (USA)) [2018/19 h72: h15.3d³ h19.5d h16.5s⁵ h15.3gᵖᵘ h16g⁶ Apr 10] modest form over hurdles: should stay beyond 2m: acts on good to soft pace: temperament under suspicion. *Johnny Farrelly*

A LITTLE CHAOS (IRE) 5 b.m. Yeats (IRE) – Marias Dream (IRE) (Desert Sun) **h111** [2018/19 b17.7s⁵ b13.7m⁵ h15.8g⁴ h16.7v h16d* h16.7g* h20.5d⁶ Mar 23] sturdy mare: **b78** third foal: dam (h78), lightly raced over hurdles, 1m/9f winner on Flat: third in Irish point on debut: unplaced in bumpers: fair form over hurdles: won novices at Fakenham (mares) in December and Market Rasen in February: unproven beyond 17f: acts on good to soft going. *Stuart Edmunds*

A LITTLE EARLY (IRE) 5 gr.g. Carlotamix (FR) – Bid At Dawn (IRE) (Saddlers' Hall **b56** (IRE)) [2018/19 b16s Nov 7] little show in bumper/point. *Harry Whittington*

A LITTLE MAGIC (IRE) 8 b.g. Kayf Tara – Debut (IRE) (Presenting) [2018/19 c139, **c94** h–: c16.2g⁴ Mar 28] winning hurdler: useful handicap chaser, well beaten only start in **h–** 2018/19 after long absence: stays 21f: acts on good to firm and good to soft going: wears hood: in tongue tie last 5 starts. *Jonjo O'Neill*

ALIZEE DE JANEIRO (FR) 9 b.m. Network (GER) – Katana (GER) (Funambule **c123** (USA)) [2018/19 c–, h107: c16g* c20.1gᵖᵘ c17.1d* h18.1g* c17.1g³ c17.1d* c17.1g* **h116** c16.3gᵖᵘ Apr 18] fairly useful handicap hurdler: won mares event at Kelso in December: fairly useful handicap chaser: won at Perth (novice) in May and Kelso in November and March (twice, another novice event on first occasion): stays 19f: acts on heavy going: wears cheekpieces. *Lucinda Russell*

ALIZEE JAVILEX (FR) 9 b.m. Le Fou (IRE) – Etoile du Lion (FR) (New Target) **h85** [2018/19 h71: h20.6g⁴ h18.6m² h21.6g³ h24gᵘʳ h24dᵖᵘ Oct 28] modest maiden hurdler: left Lucy Wadham after first start, Dan Skelton after third: stays 21f: acts on good to firm going, probably on heavy: tried in cheekpieces: in tongue tie last 4 starts. *Paul O'Flynn, Ireland*

AL KHERB 4 b.g. Al Kazeem – Perfect Spirit (IRE) (Invincible Spirit (IRE)) [2018/19 **h111** h16.7s³ h15.6g⁵ h15.7m* h15.7m h16.7m³ Apr 21] fairly useful 1¼m/1½m winner on Flat: fair form over hurdles: won maiden at Catterick in February: raced around 2m: acts on soft and good to firm going. *John Quinn*

ALKOPOP (GER) 5 gr.g. Jukebox Jury (IRE) – Alkeste (GER) (Nebos (GER)) [2018/19 **h–**
h21.6s^{pu} h23.1s Mar 5] rather unfurnished gelding: no promise either start over hurdles.
David Arbuthnot

ALL ABOUT YOU (IRE) 5 b.g. Thewayyouare (USA) – Fake Tan (IRE) (Eagle Eyed **b86**
(USA)) [2018/19 b17s^2 b16g Mar 29] £8,000 3-y-o: eighth foal: half-brother to a winning
pointer by Flemensfirth: dam, maiden on Flat, half-sister to dam of fairly useful hurdler/
smart chaser (stays 3½m) Royal Vacation: fair form in bumpers: much better effort when
second at Carlisle in March. *Nigel Twiston-Davies*

ALLAHO (FR) 5 b.g. No Risk At All (FR) – Idaho Falls (FR) (Turgeon (USA)) [2018/19 **h138**
b16g^4 h24d* h24d^3 Mar 15] good-topped gelding: will make a chaser: fourth foal: half- **b95**
brother to 2 winners, including useful 2m hurdle winner Shanning (by Spanish Moon): dam
unraced sister to useful staying chaser Tarquinius: fourth at Leopardstown only start in
bumpers: useful form over hurdles: ran once in 2017/18 for G. Cherel in France: won
Surehaul Mercedes-Benz Novices' Hurdle at Clonmel (by 4 lengths from Minella Indo) in
February: progressed further when placed behind same horse in Albert Bartlett Novices'
Hurdle (Spa) at Cheltenham and Irish Daily Mirror Novices' Hurdle (War of Attrition) at
Punchestown, latter shortly after end of British season. *W. P. Mullins, Ireland*

ALLART (IRE) 5 b.g. Shantou (USA) – The Adare Woman (IRE) (Oscar (IRE)) [2018/19 **b95 p**
b16.3d^3 Nov 8] second foal: half-brother to bumper winner Sweet Adare (by Getaway):
dam (b87), promoted third in bumper on only start, sister to useful hurdler/smart chaser
(stayed 2½m) William's Wishes and fair hurdler/useful chaser (stays 21f) Beggar's
Wishes: 7/2, shaped with promise when third in bumper at Newbury (3¼ lengths behind
Drunken Pirate) on debut: open to improvement. *Nicky Henderson*

ALLBARNONE 11 b.g. Alflora (IRE) – What A Gem (Karinga Bay) [2018/19 c–, h108: **c–**
h25.4g* May 28] good-topped gelding: fair handicap hurdler: won at Cartmel only start in **h108**
2018/19: maiden chaser: stays 25f: acts on soft and good to firm going. *Gary Hanmer*

ALL CHANGE 6 b.m. Motivator – Polly Flinders (Polar Falcon (USA)) [2018/19 b80: **h–**
b15.8g^3 b16g h16d h15.5g^{pu} h21.2g^{pu} Jan 17] poor form in bumpers: none over hurdles. **b61**
Paul Webber

ALLCHILLEDOUT 10 b.g. Alflora (IRE) – Miss Chinchilla (Perpendicular) [2018/19 **c– §**
c104§, h–: c23.8v^{pu} Nov 11] sturdy gelding: has had breathing operation: winning hurdler: **h–**
fair handicap chaser, seemed to down tools only start in 2018/19: stays 3¼m: best form on
soft/heavy going: wears blinkers: usually in tongue tie: one to avoid. *Colin Tizzard*

ALL CURRENCIES (IRE) 7 b.m. Getaway (GER) – Splendid Presence (IRE) **c120**
(Presenting) [2018/19 h120: c17.4d^4 c20d^3 c20s^3 c19.7s^2 c20d^3 Mar 10] sturdy mare: **h–**
winning hurdler: fairly useful hurdler: similar form when placed over fences: stayed 21f:
acted on soft going: tried in hood: dead. *Gary Moore*

ALLDUCKORNODINNER (IRE) 9 b.g. Robin des Pres (FR) – Inforthenight (IRE) **c91**
(Simply Great (FR)) [2018/19 h20v h19d c20d* c21.5s^5 h22g^3 c20d c19.2g^2 h21g^2 h23.9g **h99**
h20.2d^2 Apr 26] modest maiden hurdler: similar form over fences: won handicap at Down
Royal in December: stays 2¾m: acts on soft going: usually leads. *Gavin Patrick Cromwell,
Ireland*

AL LE GONE (FR) 8 b.g. Al Namix (FR) – Applepom (FR) (Apple Tree (FR)) [2018/19 **c63**
c19.3g^3 Apr 23] unplaced in point: poor form in maiden hurdle/novice hunter chase nearly **h–**
3 years apart. *Miss C. Walton*

ALLELU ALLELUIA (GER) 8 b.g. Doyen (IRE) – Anna Spectra (IRE) (Spectrum **c136**
(IRE)) [2018/19 h116: c19.4m* c19.4g^{pu} c21.4g^3 h23.1g^3 h23m^3 c23g* c25.1g c20d^2 **h113**
c26g^{pu} Apr 17] has had breathing operation: fairly useful handicap hurdler: useful handicap
chaser: won novice events at Stratford in May and Worcester (with plenty in hand) in
October: stays 23f: acts on good to firm and good to soft going: in blinkers 3 of last 4 starts:
races off pace. *Jonjo O'Neill*

ALLETRIX (IRE) 6 b.m. Flemensfirth (USA) – Miracle Trix (IRE) (Old Vic) [2018/19 **c111 p**
c20d^6 h18g^4 h20.2d^4 h19.9s Mar 12] €15,000 3-y-o: close-coupled mare: second foal: dam **h131**
unraced half-sister to fairly useful hurdler/very smart chaser (stayed 25f) Aces Four and
fairly useful hurdler (2m-2½m winner) Hell Cat Maggie (by Flemensfirth): useful hurdler:
fourth in mares handicap at Leopardstown (3¼ lengths behind Sassy Diva) in February:
9/2, shaped as if needing run when sixth of 7 in novice at Punchestown (19½ lengths
behind Judgement Day) on chasing debut: stays 2½m: acts on heavy going: wears hood:
races towards rear: should do better over fences. *Mrs J. Harrington, Ireland*

51

ALLEZ COOL (IRE) 10 ch.g. Flemensfirth (USA) – La Fisarmonica (IRE) (Accordion)   **c86**
[2018/19 c80, h–: c20.1d⁴ Mar 26] winning hurdler: fair handicap chaser, very lightly raced   **h–**
nowadays: stays 25f: acts on heavy going: wears headgear. *George Bewley*

ALLEZ DANCE (FR) 5 b.m. Great Pretender (USA) – Comedie Divine (FR) (Lesotho   **h118**
(USA)) [2018/19 h16.5d* h16.8d Mar 14] unfurnished mare: sister to 2 winners in France,
including winning hurdler/fairly useful cross-country chaser Amazing Comedy (17f-27f
winner), and half-sister to 3 winners, including fairly useful French 17f hurdle winner
Un Comedien (by Poliglote): dam French 15f hurdle winner: fairly useful hurdler: trained
prior to 2018/19 by R. Collet in France: won maiden at Punchestown by 2¾ lengths from
Galilean) in February: best effort when 13¼ lengths third to Elfile in listed mares novice at
same course shortly after end of British season: unproven beyond 2m: acts on soft going.
W. P. Mullins, Ireland

ALLEZ JACQUES (IRE) 7 b.g. Robin des Champs (FR) – Crystal Stream (IRE) (Dr   **c110**
Massini (IRE)) [2018/19 h109: h21.9g⁴ c22.6mᶠ c25.8dᵖᵘ c23.9gᵖᵘ Nov 8] compact   **h106**
gelding: fair maiden hurdler: failed to complete all 3 starts over fences: third when fell last
in novice handicap at Stratford in July: stays 2¾m: acts on good to firm and heavy going:
often races towards rear: has bled. *Emma Lavelle*

ALLEZ KARAKOZ 7 b.g. Great Pyramid (IRE) – Fleur A Lay (USA) (Mr Greeley   **b86**
(USA)) [2018/19 b16g² b16g⁵ Jun 27] third foal: half-brother to 2 winners, including 2¼m
bumper winner Cullentry Royal (by Royal Applause): dam maiden on Flat: fair form in
bumpers: better effort when second at Worcester in June: behind both starts on Flat in
France. *Ms N. M. Hugo*

ALL FOR THE BEST (IRE) 7 b.g. Rip Van Winkle (IRE) – Alleluia (Caerleon (USA))   **h118**
[2018/19 h117: h22.1g² May 26] fairly useful handicap hurdler: had breathing operation
before second at Cartmel, only start in 2018/19: stays 2¾m: acts on good to firm and good
to soft going: has worn cheekpieces: in tongue tie last 4 starts. *Robert Stephens*

ALLFREDANDNOBELL (IRE) 6 b.g. Alfred Nobel (IRE) – Its In The Air (IRE)   **h103**
(Whipper (USA)) [2018/19 h101: h22.1g* h22.1m² Jul 1] fair handicap hurdler: won at
Cartmel in May: stayed 2¾m: acted on soft and good to firm going: in visor last 4 starts:
dead. *Micky Hammond*

ALL GOOD THINGS (IRE) 7 b.g. Dahjee (USA) – Material Lady (IRE) (Barathea   **c98**
(IRE)) [2018/19 h16s⁵ h17g⁴ h19.5g h24d c19.2s⁴ c22.5sᵘʳ c19d h24d h15.8s⁶ h15.7s⁵   **h99**
h16d⁵ c19.4gᶠ Apr 14] seventh foal: half-brother to 3 winners on Flat, including 7.5f-8.6f
winner Cape Velvet (by Cape Cross): dam, maiden (stayed 1¼m), ran once over hurdles:
modest handicap hurdler: similar form on first of 2 completed starts over fences: left James
A. Nash after eighth start: stays 19f: acts on heavy going: usually wears headgear: in
tongue tie last 3 starts. *Matt Sheppard*

ALL HAIL CAESAR (IRE) 5 b.g. Nathaniel (IRE) – Ragiam (ITY) (Martino Alonso   **h108**
(IRE)) [2018/19 b86p: b16.4d b15.6g² b16.4d² h19.7g⁵ Feb 19] strong gelding: fair form in   **b88**
bumpers: 50/1, fifth in novice at Wetherby (11¾ lengths behind Schiehallion Munro) on
hurdling debut. *Rebecca Menzies*

ALL HANDS ON DECK (IRE) 6 b.m. Flemensfirth (USA) – On Galley Head (IRE)   **h85**
(Zaffaran (USA)) [2018/19 b82: b15.3m⁶ h16g⁴ h18.5g h16d⁶ h19.7g² h18.5m Nov 6]   **b72**
sparely-made mare: modest form in bumpers/over hurdles: left Harry Fry after second
start: best effort at 2½m: sometimes in hood: in tongue tie last 2 starts: dead. *Neil Mulholland*

ALL HELL LET LOOSE 10 b.g. Shantou (USA) – Gan Ainm (IRE) (Mujadil   **c130**
(USA)) [2018/19 c26m⁵ c19.9g c22g² c20g⁵ c24sᶠ Sep 12] useful-looking gelding: **h–**
winning hurdler: useful chaser: second in minor event at Tramore (½ length behind Ask
Susan) in August: placed in points in 2019: stays 3¼m: acts on good to firm and heavy
going: has worn headgear: wears tongue tie: usually races prominently: has joined
T. E. Hyde. *Henry de Bromhead, Ireland*

ALLIE BEAG (IRE) 8 b.m. Gold Well – Donishallprincess (IRE) (Safety Catch (USA))   **c85**
[2018/19 c21.2m³ Apr 22] £16,000 5-y-o: third foal: dam (c84), winning pointer, half-sister
to fairly useful hurdler/chaser (2½m-25f winner) Netminder: point winner: in cheekpieces/
tongue tie, 9/1, last of 3 in novice hunter at Fakenham on chasing debut. *Alan Hill*

ALL IS GOOD (IRE) 7 b.g. Scorpion (IRE) – Peinture Rose (IRE) (Marathon (USA))   **c109 §**
[2018/19 h110: c16.2m⁴ c16.5g² c16.2g³ c15.7g⁶ c16.5d³ c15.9f² c18.2dᵖᵘ c16m² Apr 23]   **h–**
sturdy gelding: has had breathing operation: fair hurdler/maiden chaser: unproven beyond
17f: acts on firm and soft going: has worn headgear, including final start when also tongue
tied: unreliable. *Robin Dickin*

ALLITERATION 4 ch.g. Poet's Voice – Duo de Choc (IRE) (Manduro (GER)) [2018/19 **h97**
h15.8g⁵ h16m⁶ h16d² h15.8s³ h16s h21.7d⁶ Feb 24] fair maiden on Flat, stayed 1m: modest
form over hurdles: dead. *Jo Hughes*

ALL KINGS (IRE) 10 b.g. Milan – Rilmount (IRE) (Roselier (FR)) [2018/19 c109§, **c109 §**
h105§; c25.8g³ c25.8g² c26.2g⁴ c23.6s⁵ c25.1g^ur c16.1d³ c20.2g⁴ c21.7g^ur c16.1d c19.2s⁵ **h– §**
Apr 16] lengthy gelding: maiden hurdler: fair maiden chaser: stays 3¼m: acts on soft
going: usually in headgear: tried in tongue tie: one to treat with caution. *Bob Buckler*

ALL MY LOVE (IRE) 7 b.m. Lord Shanakill (USA) – Afilla (Dansili) [2018/19 h117: **h122**
h20d^ur h16v* h16d³ h20.6g Apr 3] fairly useful handicap hurdler: won mares event at
Lingfield in February: probably stays 2½m: acts on heavy going. *Pam Sly*

ALLNITE (IRE) 4 b.g. Arcano (IRE) – Paint The Town (IRE) (Sadler's Wells (USA)) **h–**
[2018/19 h15.8g⁶ h16.7d h15.7g h21.2d^pu Jan 21] has had breathing operation: poor
maiden on Flat, stays 1½m: no form over hurdles: wears hood. *Marjorie Fife*

ALLONOK 6 b.g. Kalanisi (IRE) – Isabello (IRE) (Presenting) [2018/19 b16d b16d⁵ **h–**
h17g⁶ h16d^pu Mar 20] mid-division on second start in bumpers, only sign of ability: tried **b78**
in hood. *Dan Skelton*

ALLOW DALLOW (IRE) 12 b.g. Gold Well – Russland (GER) (Surumu (GER)) **c–**
[2018/19 c–, h–: c16g May 8] maiden hurdler: fairly useful chaser at best, lightly raced and **h–**
no form since 2016/17: stays 3m: acts on heavy going: wears headgear: has worn tongue
tie. *Nikki Evans*

ALL RILED UP 11 b.m. Dr Massini (IRE) – Martha Reilly (IRE) (Rainbows For Life **h–**
(CAN)) [2018/19 h19.5d^pu h19.6d^pu Apr 26] modest hurdler at best, no form in 2018/19
after long lay-off. *Harry Chisman*

ALL SET TO GO (IRE) 8 gr.g. Verglas (IRE) – Firecrest (IRE) (Darshaan) [2018/19 **c132**
h124: h15.7g⁵ h18.5g^pu h16.3g* h17.2m h16.7m^pu c15.7g* c16.5g* c15.9g³ c16.3d^pu **h128 §**
h16.5g Apr 6] angular gelding: fairly useful but unreliable handicap hurdler: won at
Stratford in June: useful form over fences: won novices at Southwell in August and
Worcester (closing when left clear last) in September: unproven beyond 17f: acts on good
to firm and heavy going: often in headgear: wears tongue tie. *Kevin Frost*

ALLTHATGLISTENS (IRE) 6 b.m. Gold Well – Avenging Angel (IRE) (Heron Island **b–**
(IRE)) [2018/19 b15.3m May 15] £8,000 4-y-o: third foal: dam unraced half-sister to
useful hurdler (stayed 3¼m) Melody Maid, herself dam of useful hurdler/chaser up to 21f
Black Jack Blues: runner-up in point on debut: well held in mares bumper. *Paul Nicholls*

ALL THE ANSWERS 8 br.g. Kayf Tara – Shatabdi (IRE) (Mtoto) [2018/19 c16.7s* **c131**
c16.5g⁴ Dec 1] winning hurdler: useful form over fences: won handicap at Cork in **h–**
November with plenty in hand: unproven beyond 17f: acts on soft going: has worn hood:
usually in tongue tie. *Joseph Patrick O'Brien, Ireland*

ALL THE COLOURS 8 b.g. Rainbow High – Stephanie (Shernazar) [2018/19 b–: **h–**
h19.2g^ur h16g h15.7g^pu Jul 15] no form. *Phil York*

ALLTHEGEAR NO IDEA (IRE) 12 b.g. Sayarshan (FR) – All The Gear (IRE) **c– x**
(Nashamaa) [2018/19 c111x, h110: h26.4m^pu May 20] fairly useful hurdler at best, went **h–**
wrong only start in 2018/19: maiden chaser: stays 27f: acts on heavy going: has worn
headgear, including last 4 starts: often let down by jumping over fences. *Nigel Twiston-
Davies*

ALLTIMEGOLD (IRE) 6 b.g. Gold Well – Carryonharriet (IRE) (Norwich) [2018/19 **c86**
h75, b–: h21.7g h18.5m⁵ c20d c16d³ c16.3d² Apr 6] sturdy gelding: has had breathing **h–**
operation: maiden hurdler: modest form over fences: unproven beyond 2m: acts on good to
soft going: has worn headgear: in tongue tie last 3 starts: usually races prominently.
Tim Vaughan

ALL TOGETHER (FR) 8 ch.g. Zambezi Sun – Mareha (IRE) (Cadeaux Genereux) **c107**
[2018/19 c–, h112: h18.6g c19.9g² h18.9s* h18.9d⁴ h20.4v⁴ c17.9s³ Mar 4] compact **h135**
gelding: useful hurdler: won minor event at Pau in December: similar standard at one time
over fences, just fair form in 2018/19: left Johnny Farrelly after first start: stays 2½m: acts
on heavy going. *David Cottin, France*

ALL YOURS (FR) 8 ch.g. Halling (USA) – Fontaine Riant (FR) (Josr Algarhoud (IRE)) **c–**
[2018/19 h16s^pu Mar 9] smallish, workmanlike gelding: smart hurdler at best, pulled up in **h–**
handicap only start since 2016/17: once-raced chaser: raced around 2m: acts on heavy
going: usually wears hood/tongue tie. *Sean Curran*

ALLYSSON MONTERG (FR) 9 b.g. Network (GER) – Mellyssa (FR) (Panoramic) **c142** [2018/19 c142, h–: c26s c24.2s^pu c25.3d^4 Jan 26] strong gelding, lightly raced: winning **h–** hurdler: useful chaser: stays 25f: acts on heavy going: tried in cheekpieces: wears tongue tie: usually races prominently. *Richard Hobson*

ALMAZHAR GARDE (FR) 4 ch.g. Kapgarde (FR) – Loin de Moi (FR) (Loup Solitaire **b72** (USA)) [2018/19 b16d^5 Mar 19] 3/1, fifth in bumper at Wetherby (13¼ lengths behind Sheshoon Sonny). *Charlie Longsdon*

ALMINAR (IRE) 6 b.g. Arakan (USA) – Classic Magic (IRE) (Classic Cliche (IRE)) **c109** [2018/19 h93, b–: c20s c19.2d^4 c23.6d^3 c23.8s* Feb 26] maiden hurdler: fair form over **h–** fences: won novice handicap at Ffos Las (dead-heated with Top And Drop) in February: stays 3m: acts on soft going: in cheekpieces last 2 starts: in tongue tie in 2018/19. *Nigel Hawke*

ALMONTASER (FR) 5 ch.g. Manduro (GER) – Mamitador (Anabaa (USA)) [2018/19 **h–** h15.8v h18.6s^5 h15.8m Apr 23] poor maiden on Flat: well held in novice hurdles. *Nikki Evans*

ALMOST GOLD (IRE) 6 b.g. Gold Well – Shining Lights (IRE) (Moscow Society **h110** (USA)) [2018/19 h87p: h19.7g^3 h19.4g* h23.5s h23.1d^4 h24.2d^3 h23.1d^3 Mar 24] good- topped gelding: fair handicap hurdler: won novice event at Doncaster in November: stays 3m: acts on good to soft going. *Ian Williams*

ALOHAMORA (IRE) 5 ch.m. English Channel (USA) – America Alone (Dalakhani **h106** (IRE)) [2018/19 h107: h15.8v^4 h20g h16d h20.2d^6 h20d^5 h24d^3 Mar 4] fair handicap hurdler: stays 3m: acts on soft going. *James A. Nash, Ireland*

ALONE NO MORE (IRE) 7 b.g. Gold Well – Cherry In A Hurry (IRE) (Be My Native **h87** (USA)) [2018/19 h16.2g h16.2g h22s^pu h23.9g Apr 24] €35,000 3-y-o, £21,000 5-y-o: brother to a winning pointer, and half-brother to fair hurdler/fairly useful chaser Jump Jet (19f/2½m winner, by Beneficial) and a winning pointer by Snurge: dam, winning pointer, out of half-sister to smart staying chaser Omerta: off mark in Irish points at tenth attempt: modest form over hurdles. *Rose Dobbin*

ALONG CAME THEO (IRE) 9 b.g. Vertical Speed (FR) – Kachina (IRE) (Mandalus) **c79 §** [2018/19 h98§: h19.4g^2 h23.3s h21.4d^3 c19.2m^2 c20.9v^pu Mar 7] modest maiden hurdler: **h92 §** poor form over fences: stays 21f: acts on good to firm and heavy going: in cheekpieces last 5 starts: usually races towards rear: temperamental. *Andrew Crook*

ALPHABETICAL ORDER 11 b.g. Aflora (IRE) – Lady Turk (FR) (Baby Turk) **h112** [2018/19 h115: h16.2g^3 h16m Apr 12] fair handicap hurdler nowadays: stays 21f: acts on heavy going. *R. Mike Smith*

ALPHA DES OBEAUX (FR) 9 b.g. Saddler Maker (IRE) – Omega des Obeaux (FR) **c161** (Saint Preuil (FR)) [2018/19 c156, h143: c24g^5 c20g^2 c22m* c21.5s^4 c25s^2 c25d^2 Feb 23] **h–** lengthy gelding: high-class hurdler at best: as good over fences: won 3-runner listed event at Thurles (by 1¼ lengths from Valseur Lido) in November: second in Clonmel Oil Chase (3 lengths behind Kemboy) earlier in November, Thyestes Handicap Chase at Gowran (1¼ lengths behind Invitation Only) in January and Bobbyjo Chase at Fairyhouse (3½ lengths behind Rathvinden) in February: stays 25f: acts on good to firm and heavy going: wears headgear: has worn tongue tie, including last 5 starts: usually leads. *Gordon Elliott, Ireland*

ALPH (IRE) 5 b.g. Gold Well – She's Our Banker (IRE) (Hawk Wing (USA)) [2018/19 **b88** b15.8m^2 b16.3s b15.8d^6 b16.3g^6 Mar 30] €42,000 3-y-o: rather unfurnished gelding: has had breathing operation: first foal: dam, well beaten in bumper/on Flat, half-sister to useful 2m hurdler Tudor City out of smart She's Our Mare: fair form in bumpers, best effort on debut: in hood last 2 starts. *Nicky Henderson*

ALPINE SECRET (IRE) 7 br.g. Stowaway – Squaw Valley (IRE) (Saddlers' Hall (IRE)) **c–** [2018/19 c97, h–: c16.5g May 10] maiden hurdler/chaser: little show in 2018/19, including **h–** in points. *Ben Pauling*

ALRIGHTJACK (IRE) 5 b.g. Stowaway – Brogella (IRE) (King's Theatre (IRE)) **h117** [2018/19 b95p: b16d^5 b17.7g* h15.3g h16v* h20.5s^2 h19.9g^2 h19.5g^2 Apr 26] fairly useful **b100** form in bumpers: won at Fontwell in November: fairly useful form over hurdles: won maiden at Lingfield in February: second in 3 novices after: stays 21f: acts on heavy going: front runner/races prominently. *Jamie Snowden*

ALRIGHT SUNSHINE (IRE) 4 b.g. Casamento (IRE) – Miss Gibraltar (Rock of **b106** Gibraltar (IRE)) [2018/19 b14g* b14.6s^2 b15.6g* b15.6m* Feb 28] half-brother to several winners on Flat, including useful 10.4f-1¾m winner Jaameh (by Iffraaj): dam ran once on Flat: useful form in bumpers: won at Carlisle (junior) in November and 4-runner events at Musselburgh in January and February (by 8 lengths from Book of Invasions). *Keith Dalgleish*

ALSA MIX (FR) 7 gr.m. Al Namix (FR) – Lady Tsana (FR) (True Brave (USA)) [2018/19 **h122**
b16g* h18.5g* h19.8v* h20.5d⁶ h24dᵖᵘ Mar 15] €10,000 4-y-o, £65,000 6-y-o: lengthy **b90**
mare: fourth foal: dam unraced half-sister to winning hurdler/fairly useful chaser (stayed
19f) Lady An Co: won Irish mares maiden point on debut: also won mares bumper at
Worcester (by 5 lengths from Freedom Run) in September: fairly useful form over hurdles:
won mares novice at Exeter in November and Winter Novices' Hurdle at Sandown (by 3½
lengths from Darlac) in December: should stay beyond 2½m: best effort on heavy going:
wears hood. *Alan King*

AL SHAHIR (IRE) 7 b.g. Robin des Champs (FR) – Sarah Massini (IRE) (Dr Massini **c112**
(IRE)) [2018/19 h122: c20g⁴ c16.4dᵖᵘ Nov 30] useful-looking gelding: fairly useful **h–**
hurdler: found little when fourth in novice handicap at Carlisle on chasing debut: bled next
time: should stay beyond 2m: acts on soft going: in tongue tie last 2 starts. *Dan Skelton*

ALTIEPIX (FR) 9 ch.g. Fragrant Mix (IRE) – Naltiepy (FR) (Dom Alco (FR)) [2018/19 **c118 §**
c125, h–: c16m³ c19.4mᵖᵘ c22.6g c19.4dᵖᵘ Oct 20] good-topped gelding: has had breathing **h–**
operation: winning hurdler: fairly useful handicap chaser: has won over 3m, just as
effective around 2m: acts on good to firm and heavy going: has worn headgear, including
last 2 starts: wears tongue tie: unreliable. *Kerry Lee*

ALTIOR (IRE) 9 b.g. High Chaparral (IRE) – Monte Solaro (IRE) (Key of Luck **c180 p**
(USA)) [2018/19 c179g, h–: c15.5v* c16g* c16.8d* c15.9s* c15.5g* Apr 27] **h–**

In the manner of his name, Altior's reputation just soars higher and higher.
With due respect to Tiger Roll and his monumental achievement in winning a second
Grand National (commemorated on the cover of this edition), and to the BHA's
handicapping team which has Cyrname—not Altior—at the head of its list of the top
jumpers in Britain, there could be only one recipient of the Timeform Horse of the
Year award. Altior joins Istabraq and Kauto Star as a three-times winner and now
stands on the brink of equalling Desert Orchid's four such titles. Kept to two miles,
Altior won five more races in the latest season, four of them at Grade 1 level, again
establishing himself as the undisputed champion in that division and stretching his
unblemished record over jumps to nineteen (the first five over hurdles), the longest
winning sequence in history by a jumper, beating by one the run of victories by the
champion staying hurdler Big Buck's earlier in the century. The option of stepping
Altior up to three miles was apparently considered in the latest season—he was
given an entry in the King George VI Chase at Kempton—but, although his trainer
admitted to being 'very tempted', Altior's connections eventually stuck to the tried
and tested route. Altior's tendency to do just as much as he has to in his races, and
occasionally to give the impression he might be in some trouble, has perhaps resulted
in his reputation relying more on his amazing unbroken sequence of victories than
on the style, or the substance, of those victories.

Altior is certainly enjoyed and valued by the jumping public but, at present,
he arguably has some way to go to match the form and charisma of his former
stablemate Sprinter Sacre, for example, whose best displays are still fresh enough to
be compared directly with those of Altior. Sprinter Sacre's imperious performances
in 2012/13 saw him win the Tingle Creek by fifteen lengths, the Clarence House
by fourteen and the Queen Mother Champion Chase by nineteen, followed by an
easy win over Cue Card in the Melling Chase before completing a victory in the
Champion Chase at Punchestown that extended his unbeaten start over fences to ten.
Those performances earned Sprinter Sacre a Timeform rating of 192p, the highest
awarded to any horse in the *Chasers & Hurdlers* era, ahead of Kauto Star (191)
and Desert Orchid (187). The longevity and enduring brilliance shown by Kauto
Star and Desert Orchid undoubtedly contributed to their making bigger names for
themselves than Sprinter Sacre outside the narrow confines of the sport, but there
is no doubt that Sprinter Sacre would have been somewhere up with them in the
eyes of the wider sporting public if his career had not been interrupted by a lengthy
spell on the sidelines with a heart condition. The fact that he recovered to put up
further top-class performances in another unbeaten campaign in 2015/16—including
victories over Un de Sceaux in both the Queen Mother Champion Chase and the
Celebration Chase (by fifteen lengths)—means that Sprinter Sacre's status in the
annals of steeplechasing is assured, at least among the sport's followers.

Betfair Tingle Creek Chase, Sandown—2016 winner Un de Sceaux is in his element with the mud flying, yet still proves no match for the peerless Altior (right), the pair pictured taking the second last

As with Altior, Sprinter Sacre became known for his achievements in the 'cinderella' two-mile division which tends to be overshadowed in public estimation by the staying races. Top two-mile steeplechasers don't always get the wider recognition their performances deserve and it is probably significant that both Desert Orchid and Kauto Star, who were champions at two miles, became household names largely because of their performances at three miles plus (Sprinter Sacre won the Melling Chase over two and a half). Desert Orchid and Kauto Star were Cheltenham Gold Cup winners and won nine editions of the King George VI Chase between them (Kauto Star's five victories in Kempton's mid-season staying championship equalled Golden Miller's five in the Cheltenham Gold Cup in the 'thirties, making that pair the only horses to have won the same top-level championship race over jumps in Britain five times). Altior's connections now seem set to campaign him over further than two miles, dangling the tantalising prospect of running him in the King George VI Chase in which he will almost certainly come up against a field with more strength in depth than most of those he has faced in his races at two miles. Altior's trainer Nicky Henderson admits that 'It's fair to say that a lot of people won't call him a great horse until he can prove himself over a different distance… and that time has come.' Altior's jockey Nico de Boinville sounded similarly bullish when interviewed after Altior had won the Celebration Chase at Sandown—'Racing needs to see the best against the best and this fellow is ready to step up in trip. Ascot, two and three quarter miles [1965 Chase in November] against Cyrname—bring it on!'

There is no reason, of course, why Altior should not be the champion at two miles, as well as over staying distances. Desert Orchid, for example, was champion two-miler and champion staying chaser for three years concurrently, including in his Cheltenham Gold Cup-winning year, the thirtieth anniversary of which was celebrated in the latest season. Desert Orchid was regarded as a two-mile specialist for long enough (he was untried at three miles before the first of his four victories in the King George VI Chase) and in the 1988/9 season he won not only the King George VI Chase and the Cheltenham Gold Cup, but also two of the season's biggest two-mile chases, the Tingle Creek at Sandown and the Victor Chandler (now the Clarence House) at Ascot. Both those races were among Altior's Grade 1 victories in the latest season but they were handicaps back in Desert Orchid's day, before jumping began the process of framing more of its major races as conditions events to mirror the programme on the Flat. Apart from the Queen Mother Champion Chase, there wasn't a single weight-for-age race of status for the two-mile chasers at that time, but Desert Orchid's performances under top weight of 12-0 in the Tingle Creek and the Victor Chandler were clearly superior to any others among the two-milers that season (his stablemate Barnbrook Again won the Queen Mother Champion Chase). Desert Orchid conceded between 18 lb and 28 lb to his five rivals at Sandown where he made all for an easy twelve-length win; he showed tremendous courage when pushed to the limit at Ascot where he prevailed by a head in a driving finish with Panto Prince, to whom he was conceding 22 lb (Desert Orchid also had his Gold Cup warm-up in a handicap, the Gainsborough at Sandown, warding off another spirited challenge, this time from Pegwell Bay who had landed both of Cheltenham's signature pre-Christmas handicaps and was in receipt of 18 lb from Desert Orchid). Winning championship races at both two miles and three miles demands different qualities in a horse and few are capable of showing the versatility required, though the portents are good for Altior who has looked for the last two seasons as if he will get further than two and a quarter miles (the longest distance over which he has run). Indeed, he looked in the latest season as if he might well benefit from racing over longer distances. Desert Orchid, incidentally, extended the variety of distances over which he himself was successful even further by winning a Whitbread Gold Cup over three miles five furlongs (he also won an Irish Grand National under 12-0, conceding between 26 lb and 28 lb all round, his connections having considered running him under 12-2 in the Grand National at Aintree that season before public pressure not to risk him resulted in his owners deciding he should be withdrawn at the first forfeit stage to end the clamour).

Altior's second season over fences in 2017/18 had not begun until mid-February, after he was found to need an operation for a breathing problem (he has reportedly had his palate cauterised again over the latest summer), but everything seemed to go more smoothly for him in the latest season. He looked likely to reappear in the Shloer Chase at Cheltenham but, in the end, connections waited for the Betfair Tingle Creek Chase at Sandown in early-December when he came up against a previous winner of the race, Irish-trained Un de Sceaux, as genuine and consistent performer as you could find, with a superb record over fences. Timeform's top-rated two-mile chaser in his outstanding novice season, Un de Sceaux wasn't beaten in his completed starts over fences until those two seconds, mentioned earlier, to a rejuvenated Sprinter Sacre in the Queen Mother Champion Chase and the Celebration Chase, since when he had recorded a string of top-class performances, suffering his only defeat the previous season when producing a rare below-form effort when odds-on to gain a second success in the Ryanair Chase at the Cheltenham Festival. When the paths of Altior and Un de Sceaux finally crossed in the latest Tingle Creek, the prevailing conditions were right up Un de Sceaux's street, the going turning very heavy after a torrential downpour in the half hour or so immediately preceding the race. Altior started at 13/8-on and Un de Sceaux at 7/2 in a four-runner line-up completed by two of the previous season's smartest novices, Sceau Royal and Saint Calvados, winners respectively on their reappearance of the Shloer Chase at Cheltenham and the Poplar Square Chase at Naas (in which Saint Calvados looked in control when left clear by the fall of Arkle winner Footpad at the last). The two second-season chasers were left behind from three out as Un de

Matchbook Clarence House Chase, Ascot—a change of tactics as Altior makes all, with a pair of Grade 1 winners in Fox Norton (right) and Diego du Charmil eventually proving no opposition to him at all

Betway Queen Mother Champion Chase, Cheltenham—all to play for at the last, before Altior's trademark late surge sees off the grey Politologue and Sceau Royal (just in front), with a change of tactics backfiring on fifth-placed Min (white face)

Sceaux, jumping superbly, drew clear with Altior. Apart from an uncharacteristic mistake at the second, Altior was also foot perfect and he began his challenge in earnest early in the home straight. The race was still in the balance at the last, where Altior edged ahead and then stayed on strongly on the run-in to beat Un de Sceaux fairly and squarely by four lengths, with fifteen lengths back to third-placed Saint Calvados. Altior's performance was outstanding, bettered in the Tingle Creek this century only in 2012, by Sprinter Sacre, and in the epic renewal of 2004 featuring Moscow Flyer, Azertyuiop and Well Chief.

For Altior's trainer, the extreme conditions for the Tingle Creek had been a worry beforehand. 'The ground was horrible and I think it really tested him, if he was going to get beaten it would have been today.' The relatively short gap between the Tingle Creek and the King George VI Chase—eighteen days—swayed connections against running Altior in the Christmas highlight ('He must have come out of Sandown not a little bruised after such a battle'). He did appear twenty-four hours after the King George, though, in the Unibet Desert Orchid Chase over the two-mile course at Kempton. He made short work of his four rivals, landing odds of 8/1-on by nineteen lengths from Diego du Charmil and producing a performance that was hard to fault, jumping splendidly and leading on the bridle three out and soon being well clear.

Altior's next assignment was the Matchbook Clarence House Chase at Ascot in January. With Un de Sceaux, winner of the last three editions, an absentee, Altior faced a very straightforward task against Fox Norton, returning from a lengthy absence, and Diego du Charmil. Whether the Clarence House is worth its place in the programme as a Grade 1 is debatable, though no such debate would have taken place had Un de Sceaux not missed the race because connections believed he needed more give in the ground. Un de Sceaux started odds-on for each of his victories and Altior was the ninth odds-on favourite in the twelve runnings since it was turned into a conditions event. The race hasn't had a double-figure field since its days as a handicap and the three-runner line-up for the latest edition was the smallest in its history (Desert Orchid was its first winner when it was the Victor Chandler, after two earlier scheduled runnings, in 1987 and 1988, were lost to the weather). In addition to Desert Orchid, a number of established top-class performers contested the Victor Chandler when it was a handicap, including Viking Flagship, Martha's Son, Waterloo Boy, Call Equiname, Azertyuiop and Well Chief, but it must be doubted—given the easier opportunities available now—whether the race would have attracted Altior had it still been a handicap. In what was virtually a lap of honour, Altior beat

Fox Norton and Diego du Charmil by seven lengths and thirty-four, making all and never being in the slightest danger of defeat, his performance marred only by a series of jumps to the left, some of them markedly so.

Altior equalled a long-standing record with his facile victory in the Clarence House, his twelfth consecutive win over fences matching a sequence first achieved towards the end of the nineteenth century by Game Hen, then equalled by Gangbridge (whose successes included the 1901 Welsh National) and by Pride of Ivanhoe who set his sequence in hunter chases in 1961 and 1962 (he fell when a short-priced favourite to make it thirteen in the Foxhunters' at Aintree). Altior broke the record in the Betway Queen Mother Champion Chase on his next start when he also drew level with Big Buck's on eighteen successive victories over jumps (Big Buck's achieved his eighteen record-breaking wins over hurdles between 2009 and 2012, beating the previous record of sixteen by three-times Champion Hurdle winner Sir Ken). Altior had already beaten the record—set at thirteen by another Champion Hurdle winner Bula—of the longest winning sequence from the beginning of a career over jumps, and he started at 11/4-on to maintain his unbroken run in the Betway Queen Mother Champion Chase. Altior would have been odds on the year before—he was sent off at evens—but for a late scare in which he suffered some lameness in his near-fore two days before that race and had to pass an examination by a racecourse vet on raceday before being deemed fit to run. There were no such hiccups before the latest running for Altior who was described by his trainer as having been 'frighteningly quick' when schooled over five fences on the Friday before Cheltenham.

If things looked rosy for Altior, that could not be said early in the week for the prospects of the race itself taking place as scheduled. The threat of high winds on Wednesday, Queen Mother Champion Chase day, evoked memories of 2008 when the same card had to be cancelled with near fifty miles an hour gales making the temporary tented village unsafe. On that occasion, the Cheltenham executive rescheduled the races to produce a ten-race programme on Thursday and a nine-race programme on Friday, Cheltenham Gold Cup day. The provision of emergency services was an obstacle to postponing Wednesday's card to Saturday on that occasion, but, if the Wednesday card had been lost at the latest Festival, contingency plans were in place for a 'People's Saturday' (all money for tickets sold for Wednesday would have been refunded). The more substantial nature of the hospitality areas in Cheltenham's temporary village means they are now able to withstand all but the most inhospitable conditions and, after an early-morning inspection, with the precise wind strength not so strong as predicted, the course was passed fit for racing (plans had been put in place earlier in the week for some Irish challengers to be stabled at Aintree racecourse in the days leading up to Cheltenham to ensure that normal plans to travel from Ireland by ferry were not compromised by the forecast high winds on Wednesday).

bet365 Celebration Chase, Sandown—a record-breaking nineteenth straight win for Altior, as he again proves too strong for Sceau Royal and God's Own (checks)

Altior faced nine opponents in the Queen Mother Champion Chase in what shaped up into looking like largely a re-run of twelve months earlier. Saint Calvados, a 25/1-shot, was the only runner who had contested the previous year's Arkle Trophy, the top race for the two-mile novice chasers and often a significant pointer to the following year's Champion Chase (Sprinter Sacre—who was paraded on Champion Chase day—and Altior had been the two most recent chasers to win the races in successive years). The second, third, fourth and fifth—Min, God's Own, Politologue and Ordinary World—were back again, while the Shloer winner and Tingle Creek fourth Sceau Royal was another who renewed rivalry with Altior. Sceau Royal had been forced to miss the previous year's Arkle but showed his aptitude for Cheltenham by stepping up on his performance in the autumn in the Shloer and outrunning odds of 16/1 in the Champion Chase. Saint Calvados and Altior stole a bit of a march on the rest at the start and Altior tracked Saint Calvados, several lengths clear of the main body of the field. Altior jumped superbly until making a mistake at the water (later described by his jockey as a result of 'miscommunication, he was winging the fences but I felt there wasn't a stride there, you don't want to be too extravagant in those tacky conditions').

Altior's jumping towards the end of the race was not so fluent as usual and he was untidy at both of the fences in the home straight after taking over in front three from the finish. Min had got Altior off the bridle in the race twelve months earlier, before being overpowered to finish seven lengths second, but he looked beaten some way out this time after being shuffled back before the home turn and it was Politologue and Sceau Royal who gave Altior most to do. That pair pounced on Altior at the last, where both held every chance, with the patiently-ridden Sceau Royal actually heading Altior, although the champion quickly rallied to regain the lead. Typically finding plenty in the closing stages, Altior stayed on up the hill to win by a length and three quarters and the same from Politologue and Sceau Royal, with 25/1-shot Hell's Kitchen a creditable fourth, just ahead of 7/2 second favourite Min who clearly failed to give his running. Saint Calvados was seventh while God's Own, running in the race for the fourth time, was still in contention for a place in the frame when pulled up sharply before the last, reportedly found afterwards to be lame. Altior didn't reproduce his best in the Queen Mother Champion Chase but his performance, highlighted by his usual strong finish, pulling it out when needed on the run-in, showed just why he has been so hard to beat. As soon as Nico de Boinville shook him up, Altior responded and found more. 'He has toughed it out,' said the jockey. 'They gave it a good go but he has found that extra gear, I don't know where it comes from, he is just a fabulous racehorse who can do anything, although he has pulled up a tired horse today.' Altior's winning margin, incidentally, was the narrowest in any of his races over fences so far.

In winning the Queen Mother Chase for the second time—joining this century's other dual winners Moscow Flyer, Master Minded and Sprinter Sacre— Altior took his successes at the Cheltenham Festival to four in as many years (his first triumph, in the Supreme Novices' Hurdle of 2016, marks the last occasion that Altior started at odds against). Altior's feat of four Cheltenham Festival wins was matched forty minutes later by Tiger Roll who won the Cross Country Chase. Altior and Tiger Roll became the eleventh and twelfth horses to have won at least four times at the meeting. The mare Quevega won six times, all over hurdles, while Golden Miller's five Gold Cups means that he holds the record for a chaser. Dudley, the best specialist two-mile chaser between the wars was the first to win four times at what was then the National Hunt meeting which, at that time, had no championship event for two-mile chasers, two of Dudley's victories coming in the Grand Annual, the second of them under 12-7. Other chasers who have recorded four victories at what is now the Festival are the war-time Gold Cup winner Medoc II, the hunter chaser Baulking Green and the mighty Arkle. Sir Ken completed his four-timer when he won the Cotswold Chase, while the staying handicapper Willie Wumpkins, Istabraq and Big Buck's achieved all four of their victories over hurdles. Dudley, by the way, once enjoyed a winning streak of seventeen, though his victories came in a variety of races, ten of which were over jumps. More recent two-mile champions Pendil (a rarity like Desert Orchid and Kauto Star in being equally as good, if not better, at three miles), Badsworth Boy and Moscow Flyer also compiled notable sequences over fences. Pendil lost just two of his first twenty races over fences, and when Badsworth Boy won his third Queen Mother Champion Chase it was his seventeenth win in eighteen completed steeplechases (his low jumping style left little room for error and he had also fallen three times and unseated his rider once in a twenty-two-race sequence). Moscow Flyer wasn't beaten in his first nineteen completed steeplechases, which included his two successes in the Queen Mother Champion Chase, but two falls and three unseated riders were interspersed in that sequence.

    Altior's record-breaking nineteenth consecutive win came in the five-runner bet365 Celebration Chase at Sandown's Finale meeting where it was mooted at one time that he might meet Cyrname who was eventually ruled out of contention with the prospect of drying ground. Up against some of the 'usual suspects', Altior duly completed his third successive win in the season's final Grade 1, starting at 6/1-on and scoring in now customary fashion, coming under pressure briefly in the home straight and offering a moment of hope again to the stronger travelling Sceau Royal who put in a challenge to Altior at the last before being left behind as Altior stayed on strongly on the run-in to beat him by two and a half lengths this time. God's Own, recovered from his injury at Cheltenham, finished a further three lengths back in third without ever landing a blow, while 33/1 outsider Vosne Romanee seemed to excel himself in finishing just another two lengths away in fourth, his proximity to the first three limiting the view that could be taken of the bare form.

Altior (IRE) (b.g. 2010)	High Chaparral (IRE) (b 1999)	Sadler's Wells (b 1981)	Northern Dancer Fairy Bridge
		Kasora (b 1993)	Darshaan Kozana
	Monte Solaro (IRE) (br 2000)	Key of Luck (b 1991)	Chief's Crown Balbonella
		Footsteps (br 1991)	Broken Hearted Remoosh

Mrs Patricia Pugh's "Altior"

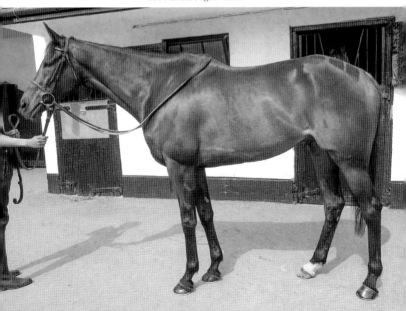

The good-topped Altior is one of four winners produced so far by the fair winning two-mile hurdler Monte Solaro, none of which has been successful beyond two and a half miles (she is also the dam of Altior's close relative—by another Sadler's Wells stallion Milan—who made a record €365,000 as a three-year-old at the 2018 Derby Sale and has yet to race). Monte Solaro's other winners have all been at least fairly useful, the useful two-mile hurdler Princess Leya and the now-deceased fairly useful hurdler/chaser Silverhow, successful four times including twice over fences at two and a half miles, both also being by sons of Sadler's Wells with a good record for imparting stamina, Old Vic and Yeats respectively. Monte Solaro's other winner Key To The West (by another staying influence Westerner) was a fairly useful hurdler and a useful chaser who won five times at up to two and a half miles. Altior's sire the Derby and Irish Derby winner High Chaparral was one of the best sons of Sadler's Wells and he attracted jumps breeders late in his career. He sired a Sandown Gold Cup winner for Seven Barrows in Hadrian's Approach, who was from a family on the distaff side that had produced some good staying chasers over the years. Influences for stamina don't exactly jump out in Altior's pedigree, though his grandam the winning two-year-old Footsteps (a half-sister to the Triumph Hurdle and Haydock Premier Long Distance Hurdle runner-up Moorish) was by Broken Hearted, sire of Grand National winner Numbersixvalverde. Altior's great grandam Remoosh showed little on the track but was a half-sister to the high-class sprinting two-year-old Nomination who went on to sire winners over jumps including Bold Boss, a prolific winning juvenile hurdler who also won the Gerry Feilden at Newbury. Altior, who has worn ear plugs, including in the last two runnings (removed at the start in the latest edition) of the Queen Mother Champion Chase, is no certainty on pedigree to stay three miles but he will definitely stay beyond two and a quarter. He acts on heavy going but doesn't need the mud and, despite a tendency to sometimes go left, he is a very good jumper. Notably genuine and reliable, he still doesn't seem to have reached his limit and is sure to win more top races. *Nicky Henderson*

ALTO DES MOTTES (FR) 9 b.g. Dream Well (FR) – Omance (FR) (Video Rock (FR)) **c86**
[2018/19 c–, h–: c24.2d⁶ c24.2g h23.3g c31.9s³ c26m² c24.2s⁶ c25.2g⁶ c26.3s c31.9vᵖᵘ **h–**
c24.2g⁴ Apr 15] rather sparely-made gelding: winning hurdler: poor handicap chaser nowadays: stays 3¾m: acts on good to firm and heavy going: wears headgear: tried in tongue tie. *Henry Hogarth*

ALTRUISM (IRE) 9 b.g. Authorized (IRE) – Bold Assumption (Observatory (USA)) **c–**
[2018/19 c–, h135: h16.4g h16.4d² Apr 6] workmanlike gelding: useful hurdler/chaser at **h125** best, lightly raced: stays 2¾m: acts on soft and good to firm going: tried in headgear. *James Moffatt*

ALVARADO (IRE) 14 ch.g. Goldmark (USA) – Mrs Jones (IRE) (Roselier (FR)) **c111**
[2018/19 c129§, h–: c23.6d c28.4g³ c26.3d⁶ Jan 1] tall gelding: winning hurdler: useful **h–** handicap chaser at best, in frame twice in Grand National at Aintree and Scottish Grand National at Ayr: thorough stayer: acted on good to firm and heavy going: retired. *Fergal O'Brien*

ALWAYS LION (IRE) 9 b.g. Let The Lion Roar – Addie's Choice (IRE) (Norwich) **c102**
[2018/19 c122, h–: c23.8g⁴ h23.8m* Feb 28] lightly-raced gelding: fairly useful form over **h122** hurdles: won 4-runner handicap at Musselburgh (visored) in February: similar form when winning first of 2 starts over fences: stays 3m: acts on good to firm and good to soft going. *Iain Jardine*

ALWAYS ON THE BALL (FR) 6 ch.g. Kapgarde (FR) – Etoile des Iles (FR) **c–**
(Starborough) [2018/19 h96: h24.5g³ h20.3gᵖᵘ c19.9dᵖᵘ Dec 26] runner-up twice in Irish **h92** points: modest form over hurdles: pulled up in novice handicap on chasing debut: in cheekpieces last 2 starts: tried in tongue tie. *Charlie Longsdon*

ALWAYS ON THE RUN (IRE) 9 br.g. Robin des Pres (FR) – Kerrys Cottage (IRE) **c110**
(Leading Counsel (USA)) [2018/19 h133, h–: c20.3g⁵ c23.8gᵖᵘ c23.8d³ c24.2g² Mar 29] **h–** has had breathing operation: winning hurdler: fair chaser nowadays: barely stays 3m: acts on soft and good to firm going: normally wears hood: usually leads. *Tom George*

ALWAYS RESOLUTE 8 b.g. Refuse To Bend (IRE) – Mad Annie (USA) (Anabaa (USA)) [2018/19 h106: h17.2g³ h16.7g h17.2d² h19.7d* h21.6s⁶ h19.4g* h15.7m² h16.5gᵘʳ Apr 6] compact gelding: fairly useful handicap hurdler: won at Wetherby in November and Doncaster in January: left Brian Ellison after third start: stays 2½m: acts on good to firm and heavy going: has worn headgear, including last 2 starts. *Ian Williams* **h120**

ALWAYS TIPSY 10 b.g. Dushyantor (USA) – French Pick (USA) (Johannesburg (USA)) [2018/19 c107, h–: c21.6g⁶ c23.4g⁴ h22.8d⁶ h22.7d⁴ h23.9g⁴ Apr 24] smallish, lengthy gelding: fair handicap hurdler/chaser: stays 3m: acts on heavy going: front runner/races prominently. *N. W. Alexander* **c95 h100**

ALYS ROCK (IRE) 10 gr.m. Medaaly – Rock Slide (IRE) (Bob Back (USA)) [2018/19 c71, h69: c16.5g* c17.3g⁴ c16.5g c15.7gᵖᵘ h16.8g⁶ Nov 1] rather sparely-made mare: modest hurdler at best: similar standard over fences: won handicap at Worcester in June: stays 21f, raced mainly at shorter: acts on soft and good to firm going: tried in cheekpieces/tongue tie: inconsistent. *Laura Morgan* **c93 h–**

AMALFI DOUG (FR) 9 gr.g. Network (GER) – Queissa (FR) (Saint Preuil (FR)) [2018/19 c–, h95: c16.3m³ Aug 6] has had breathing operation: maiden hurdler: little form in chases: won on point debut in April: tried in hood: in tongue tie last 3 starts. *Dan Skelton* **c64 h–**

AMANTO (GER) 9 b.g. Medicean – Amore (GER) (Lando (GER)) [2018/19 c–, h108: h19.3m³ h15.5g⁴ h20d³ h16.3d³ Jan 16] good-topped gelding: fairly useful maiden hurdler: lightly-raced chaser: stays 2½m: acts on soft and good to firm going: has worn headgear: usually tongue tied. *Ali Stronge* **c– h116**

AMARONE GENTLEMAN (IRE) 7 b.g. Oscar (IRE) – Tigrera (IRE) (Helissio (FR)) [2018/19 b–: b16.2g h20.2gᵖᵘ Jul 5] has had breathing operation: no form in bumpers/maiden hurdle: wears tongue tie. *Susan Corbett* **h– b–**

AMATEUR (IRE) 6 ch.g. Giant's Causeway (USA) – Adja (IRE) (Rock of Gibraltar (IRE)) [2018/19 h19.9g⁶ h19.8vᵖᵘ Dec 7] good-topped gelding: bumper winner: modest form over hurdles: better effort when sixth in maiden at Uttoxeter: tried in cheekpieces. *John Flint* **h93**

AMAULINO (FR) 6 b.g. Saint des Saints (FR) – Sea Well (FR) (Pistolet Bleu (IRE)) [2018/19 c23d* c20g⁵ c22.7g⁶ h21.9s c24g⁵ c21g c25.5d c20.5g c24d⁴ c21.3s* c28.5g* c25gᵖᵘ Apr 6] compact gelding: second foal: half-brother to French 1m/9f winner Sea Flower (by My Risk): dam, placed up to 19f over hurdles in France, 1¼m/11f winner on Flat: fairly useful hurdler at best: as good over fences: won maiden at Tipperary in May, and handicap at Leopardstown (conditionals) and Ulster National at Downpatrick (by 3½ lengths from School Lane) in March: left Colin Bowe after sixth start: stays 29f: acts on heavy going: often wears headgear: in tongue tie last 4 starts: races off pace. *R. K. Watson, Ireland* **c126 h103**

AMAZING COMEDY (FR) 9 b.g. Great Pretender (IRE) – Comedie Divine (FR) (Lesotho (USA)) [2018/19 c23.9d⁵ c25.8d² c22.9g c25.8g² c23.4g² c26.8s* c30.2g* c24.9dᵘʳ c30.2s c23.4s² Apr 9] good-topped gelding: winning hurdler: fairly useful cross-country chaser: won at Compiegne in November: fourth at Cheltenham (handicap) next time: stays 3¼m: acts on good going: wears headgear: has worn tongue tie. *David Cottin, France* **c128 h–**

AMBER FLUSH 10 b.m. Sir Harry Lewis (USA) – Sari Rose (FR) (Vertical Speed (FR)) [2018/19 c–, h81: h25g⁶ h23g⁶ h23.3g³ h24gᵖᵘ h23g⁶ h22.1g h25.8gᵖᵘ h23.3g Sep 23] poor handicap hurdler: lightly-raced chaser: stays 25f: acts on good to firm and good to soft going: wears headgear: tried in tongue tie. *Clare Ellam* **c– h68**

AMBER GAMBLER (GER) 9 b.g. Doyen (IRE) – Auenglocke (GER) (Surumu (GER)) [2018/19 c116, h–: c20g⁶ c17.2sᵖᵘ c22.6g⁶ Mar 30] workmanlike gelding: winning hurdler: fairly useful handicap chaser, below form in 2018/19: stays 3m, effective at much shorter: acts on soft going: in cheekpieces last 2 starts. *Ian Williams* **c83 h–**

AMBEROSE 6 ch.m. Sulamani (IRE) – Miss Nellie (IRE) (Presenting) [2018/19 b16.2g³ h16d⁶ h16.4d h17s⁵ h21.4d² h21.4d⁶ h17d* h20.2g² Apr 25] second foal: sister to bumper winner Rubytwo: dam unraced half-sister to fairly useful hurdler/chaser (stayed 3½m) Aldertune: tailed off in bumper: fair handicap hurdler: won mares event at Carlisle in March: stays 21f: acts on soft going. *Nicky Richards* **h104 b–**

AMBION HILL (IRE) 4 b.g. Getaway (GER) – Vertality (IRE) (Vertical Speed (FR)) [2018/19 b16.8d b16.8d⁴ Mar 24] €22,000 3-y-o: second foal: dam unraced half-sister to fairly useful hurdler/useful chaser (stayed 2¾m) Macs Flamingo and fairly useful hurdler (stayed 3m) Parish Business: fair form in bumpers: better effort when fourth at Exeter. *Colin Tizzard* **b85**

AMBITIOUS PURSUIT (IRE) 11 b.g. Cloudings (IRE) – Gladriels Jem (IRE) (Mister **c– §**
Lord (USA)) [2018/19 c25.8g^{pu} May 16] multiple point winner: little impact in hunter
chases: in cheekpieces last 3 starts: temperamental. *Mrs L. Glanville*

AMBLE INN 7 b.m. Sulamani (IRE) – Distant Florin (Medicean) [2018/19 h82: h20.3g⁴ **h85**
h23.4g⁴ h24g Jun 25] modest maiden hurdler: stays 23f: best form on good going: front
runner/races prominently. *Anthony Carson*

AMBRE DES MARAIS (FR) 9 ch.m. Network (GER) – Fee des Marais (FR) **h109**
(Chamberlin (FR)) [2018/19 h108: h16d² h16.7g² h21.6g Oct 1] fair handicap hurdler:
stays 2½m: acts on heavy going: held up. *Johnny Farrelly*

AMENHOTEPTHETHIRD 4 b.g. Motivator – Autumn Wealth (IRE) (Cadeaux **h–**
Genereux) [2018/19 h17.7m⁶ Oct 5] no form on Flat: well beaten in juvenile hurdle: dead.
Mark Gillard

AMERICAN CRAFTSMAN (IRE) 5 gr.g. Mastercraftsman (IRE) – Quiet Mouse **h105**
(USA) (Quiet American (USA)) [2018/19 h112: h16.7g h15.8g⁵ h16.2g⁴ h16.6g Dec 29]
fair handicap hurdler: raced mainly at 2m: acts on soft going: tried in cheekpieces.
Henry Oliver

AMERICAN (FR) 9 b.g. Malinas (GER) – Grande Sultane (FR) (Garde Royale) [2018/19 **c–**
c153+, h–: c26s^{pu} c34v^{pu} Mar 16] tall, useful-looking gelding: winning hurdler: very smart **h–**
chaser at best, no show either start in 2018/19: stays 25f: acts on heavy going. *Harry Fry*

AMERICAN HISTORY (USA) 5 b.g. High Chaparral (IRE) – Spinning Time (USA) **h101**
(Giant's Causeway (USA)) [2018/19 h16g⁴ h16g² h18.5g⁴ h20g Oct 11] fair on Flat, stays
1¾m: fair form over hurdles: in tongue tie first 3 starts: sold 9,500 gns in November.
William Muir

AMERICAN LIFE (FR) 12 b.g. American Post – Poplife (FR) (Zino) [2018/19 h98§, **h82 §**
h23.3g h23.1g h23s⁶ h25d⁴ h23.6d³ h23.1d⁵ Apr 9] close-coupled gelding: poor handicap
hurdler nowadays: left Oliver Greenall after second start: stays 27f: acts on heavy going:
wears headgear/tongue tie: usually races off pace: temperamental. *Milton Harris*

AMERICAN TOM (FR) 8 b.g. American Post – Kirkla (FR) (Bikala) [2018/19 c139, h–: **c–**
c20.6m⁵ h16.3g³ h16d² h18.7g⁴ h19.7g^F Apr 11] fairly useful form over hurdles: useful **h122**
chaser at best: left W. P. Mullins after second start: stays 2½m: acts on heavy going: in hood
last 3 starts: has worn tongue tie, including in 2018/19. *Olly Murphy*

AMETHEA (IRE) 5 b.m. Yeats (IRE) – Moricana (GER) (Konigsstuhl (GER)) [2018/19 **h79**
b15.8g b15.7g h20.5g h19.5d⁶ h19.2v h19d^{pu} Dec 31] €26,000 3-y-o: close-coupled mare: **b77**
sister to fair hurdler/useful chaser Reikers Island (2¾m-25f winner) and closely related/
half-sister to numerous winners, including hurdler Modesto (winner up to 21f in Europe,
by Platini): dam German 9.5f/1¼m winner: mid-field at best in bumpers: poor form over
hurdles: tried in cheekpieces: usually races prominently. *Ben Pauling*

AMI DESBOIS (FR) 9 b.g. Dream Well (FR) – Baroya (FR) (Garde Royale) [2018/19 **c137**
c136, h–: c23.4d^{ur} c23.6v³ c27.3s⁴ c24.2s² c24.2s⁶ c23.8s² Apr 7] good-topped gelding: **h–**
winning hurdler: useful handicap chaser: second at Ffos Las (head behind Achille) in April:
stays 3m: acts on heavy going: wears tongue tie: front runner/races prominently, often
travels strongly. *Graeme McPherson*

AMILLIONTIMES (IRE) 11 b.g. Olden Times – Miss Million (IRE) (Roselier (FR)) **c111**
[2018/19 c116, h–: c26.2g² c23.4g⁵ c24.2m c23.8g⁵ c23.8g⁴ c23.8g³ c26.2g⁵ c26.2g⁴ **h–**
Dec 29] winning hurdler: fair handicap chaser: will stay extreme distances: acts on good to
firm and good to soft going: wears tongue tie: usually races towards rear. *Jackie Stephen*

AMIRAL COLLONGES (FR) 9 ch.g. Dom Alco (FR) – Idole Collonges (FR) (Brezzo **c89 §**
(FR)) [2018/19 c114§, h–: c25.5g⁵ c30.7d^{pu} c23.6d⁵ Apr 6] lengthy gelding: winning **h–**
hurdler: fair handicap chaser, below form in 2018/19: stays 29f: acts on soft and good to
firm going: wears cheekpieces: temperamental. *James Evans*

AMIRR (IRE) 9 b.g. New Approach (IRE) – Dress Uniform (USA) (Red Ransom (USA)) **c–**
[2018/19 h102: h15.3m⁴ h15.8g* h16g h19.9g^F c15.7g^{pu} c16g^{pu} h15.3g Nov 22] fair **h100**
hurdler: won maiden at Uttoxeter in June: no show over fences: unproven beyond 2m: acts
on good to firm going: tried in visor. *Seamus Mullins*

AMLOVI (IRE) 6 b.m. Court Cave (IRE) – Portanob (IRE) (Be My Native (USA)) **b–**
[2018/19 b–: b16g b16d Mar 21] no form in bumpers: tried in hood. *Adrian Wintle*

A MONTMARTRE (FR) 7 b.m. Montmartre (FR) – Stefania (IRE) (Monsun (GER)) **c95**
[2018/19 h–: c15.7m⁴ c16.5g⁴ c20g³ c21g⁵ Jul 22] winning hurdler: modest form over **h–**
fences: stays 2½m: acts on soft and good to firm going. *Nick Mitchell*

AMOOLA GOLD (GER) 6 b.g. Mamool (IRE) – Aughamore Beauty (IRE) (Dara Monarch) [2018/19 b–: h16m² h19.9g⁵ h16.4g c16g* c18.2d³ Dec 13] rangy gelding: fair form over hurdles: second in maiden at Warwick in May: fairly useful form over fences: won novice handicap at Hereford in November: finished lame next time: stays 2¼m: acts on good to firm and good to soft going: often races prominently: remains with potential as a chaser. *Dan Skelton* **c125 p / h111**

AMORE ALATO 10 b.g. Winged Love (IRE) – Sardagna (FR) (Medaaly) [2018/19 c125, h–: c24d c21.4m⁵ c23.8m Jul 13] strong gelding: has had breathing operation: winning hurdler: fairly useful handicap chaser: folded all starts in 2018/19: stays 3m: acts on soft going: tried in cheekpieces. *Dan Skelton* **c121 / h–**

AMORLETTE 5 b.m. Fair Mix (IRE) – Amaretto Rose (Alflora (IRE)) [2018/19 b15.7v b16g Feb 22] sixth foal: half-sister to bumper winner Belle Amis (by Black Sam Bellamy): dam (h141) bumper/2m hurdle winner: no form in bumpers. *Jamie Snowden* **b–**

AMOR VERDADERO (IRE) 5 b.m. Jeremy (USA) – Blanchfield (IRE) (Luso) [2018/19 b17.3g b16.6d h20.5vᵖᵘ Nov 14] €10,000 3-y-o: third foal: dam (h96), bumper/2½m hurdle winner, half-sister to very smart hurdler/smart chaser (stayed 25f) Bensalem and smart hurdler/useful chaser (21f-3m winner) Court In Motion: no show in bumpers/maiden hurdle: has joined Gordon Elliott. *Liam Lennon, Ireland* **h– / b–**

AMOUR DE NUIT (IRE) 7 b.g. Azamour (IRE) – Umthoulah (IRE) (Unfuwain (USA)) [2018/19 h137: c20.5g* c16g* c18.8m⁵ c19.1g* c20.2m² c20.5g⁴ c17.8d² Feb 24] good-bodied gelding: useful hurdler: similar standard over fences: won novice at Kempton in May, novice handicap at Ludlow (finished alone) in October and handicap at Doncaster (by 5 lengths from The Unit) in December, all small-field events: stays 2½m: acts on good to firm and good to soft going: tried in hood: usually races prominently. *Paul Nicholls* **c138 / h–**

AMOUR D'OR 8 b.m. Winged Love (IRE) – Diletia (Dilum (USA)) [2018/19 h90: h18.5g* h21.6g* h21.6g h21.6v c23.6g⁵ c23.8sᵖᵘ Nov 23] sturdy mare: modest handicap hurdler: won at Newton Abbot in May and June: no form over fences: stays 2¾m: acts on heavy going: in cheekpieces last 3 starts: usually wears tongue tie. *Gail Haywood* **c– / h92**

AMRON KALI (IRE) 9 b.m. Kalanisi (IRE) – Glacial Snowboard (IRE) (Glacial Storm (USA)) [2018/19 h104: h20g² h26d h25.8gᵖᵘ h26.5g³ Jul 6] sturdy mare: has had breathing operation: fair handicap hurdler: stays 3¼m: acts on good to firm and heavy going: tried in cheekpieces: wears tongue tie: usually races nearer last than first. *Paul Henderson* **h98**

AMUSE ME 13 gr.g. Daylami (IRE) – Have Fun (Indian Ridge) [2018/19 c77, h–: c20.1d c21.4g c25.5m⁵ h22.1g Jul 23] sturdy gelding: fairly useful hurdler/fair chaser at best, no form in 2018/19: usually in headgear/tongue tie. *Lucinda Egerton* **c– / h–**

AMZAC MAGIC 7 b.g. Milan – Queen's Banquet (Glacial Storm (USA)) [2018/19 h84: h19.5s h21.6v⁴ h19.2v³ h19.8s* Mar 7] point winner: modest form over hurdles: won handicap at Wincanton in March: stays 2½m: acts on heavy going: in hood last 5 starts. *Jack R. Barber* **h98**

ANAHLINE 4 b.f. Rail Link – Al Rayanah (Almushtarak (IRE)) [2018/19 b15.8d b16m Apr 22] third foal: dam 1m winner: no form in bumpers. *Paul Howling* **b–**

ANAX (IRE) 5 b.g. Oscar (IRE) – Limetree Leader (IRE) (Supreme Leader) [2018/19 b15.8s⁵ b16.7g⁶ Apr 13] third foal: dam unraced half-sister to Irish Grand National winner Thunder And Roses: fair form in bumpers: better effort when fifth at Ffos Las in February. *Rebecca Curtis* **b92**

ANCIENT SANDS (IRE) 11 b.g. Footstepsinthesand – Antiguan Wells (IRE) (Sadler's Wells (USA)) [2018/19 h20g h16g* c17gᵖᵘ h16g Dec 27] useful handicap hurdler: won at Listowel (by 2½ lengths from Beau Et Sublime) in June: maiden chaser, often let down by jumping: unproven beyond 17f: acts on good to firm and heavy going: has worn tongue tie. *John E. Kiely, Ireland* **c– x / h138**

ANDANOTHER 5 b.g. And Beyond (IRE) – Catriona (Bustino) [2018/19 b16.2s b17s Nov 12] no form in bumpers. *Harriet Graham* **b–**

ANDAPA (FR) 5 br.m. Kapgarde (FR) – Daniety (FR) (Bonbon Rose (FR)) [2018/19 b17.7g* b16g* h21.7gᶠ h20.5g⁶ h15.9g³ Apr 7] £1,200 3-y-o: first foal: dam, French maiden (second in 17f hurdle), closely related to very smart French chaser Lagunak (stayed 27f) and to dam of Irish Grand National winner Burrows Saint: fairly useful form in bumpers: won at Plumpton in May and Worcester (conditionals/amateurs) in June: failed to match that over hurdles: best effort when third in maiden at Plumpton. *Michael Roberts* **h91 / b98**

ANDHAAR 13 b.g. Bahri (USA) – Deraasaat (Nashwan (USA)) [2018/19 h73§: h23.3g **h73 §** h23.3g* h23.3g h23.9g³ h23.3g h23.9g⁶ h24.3g³ h22g⁴ h23.8gᵖᵘ h23.9g Apr 24] rather leggy gelding: poor handicap hurdler: won at Hexham in May: stays 3m: acts on soft and good to firm going: usually wears headgear: tried in tongue tie: unreliable. *N. W. Alexander*

ANDOK (IRE) 5 b.g. Elzaam (AUS) – My Causeway Dream (IRE) (Giant's Causeway **h–** (USA)) [2018/19 h15.8m⁶ Oct 4] fairly useful on Flat, stays 10.5f: well beaten in novice on hurdling debut. *Richard Fahey*

ANDORNS LEGACY 4 b.f. Andorn (GER) – Cayman Sound (Turtle Island (IRE)) **b–** [2018/19 b12.4g b15.7m b15.7d⁶ Mar 6] half-sister to several winners, including fairly useful hurdler Norfolk Sky (2m-2¼m winner, by Haafhd): dam 1½m winner: no form in bumpers: has worn hood. *Philip Kirby*

AND THE NEW (IRE) 8 b.g. Kalanisi (IRE) – Wheredidthemoneygo (IRE) (Anshan) **h129** [2018/19 h128: h21g h17.7d² h21g h21m h18.5d⁴ Mar 24] lengthy gelding: has had breathing operation: fairly useful handicap hurdler: second at Fontwell in November: stays 19f: acts on soft going: has worn hood, including usually in 2018/19: in tongue tie last 3 starts. *Johnny Farrelly*

ANDY DUFRESNE (IRE) 5 b.g. Doyen (IRE) – Daytona Lily (IRE) (Beneficial) **b106 P** [2018/19 b16d* Jan 29] £330,000 4-y-o: fourth foal: half-brother to fair chaser Clondaw Rigger (3m/2½f winner, by Stowaway): dam, 2m hurdle winner, sister to fairly useful hurdler/chaser (stayed 3m) Its Crucial: won maiden point on debut in March 2018: 8/15, also won maiden bumper at Down Royal impressively by 10 lengths from Golden Spread: exciting prospect. *Gordon Elliott, Ireland*

ANEMOI (FR) 5 b.g. Manduro (GER) – Recambe (IRE) (Cape Cross (IRE)) [2018/19 **h127** b95: h15.7m* h16.6m* h20.3d³ h16.5g³ h16m Apr 13] tall, rather unfurnished gelding: bumper winner: fairly useful form over hurdles: won novices at Ascot in November and Doncaster in December: had breathing operation before running poorly final start: should stay beyond 17f: acts on good to firm going. *Harry Whittington*

AN FEAR CIUIN (IRE) 8 b.g. Galileo (IRE) – Potion (Pivotal) [2018/19 h105: h16g³ **h102** h16.2g⁴ h16.2g² h20.2g h16.2g* h16.2g⁵ h15.6g⁵ h15.6g⁴ h16.2g² Apr 24] fair handicap hurdler: won at Kelso in October: stays 2½m: acts on good to firm going: has worn cheekpieces, including in 2018/19. *R. Mike Smith*

ANGE DES MALBERAUX (FR) 9 b.g. Michel Georges – Petite Baie (FR) (Alamo **c120** Bay (USA)) [2018/19 h95: h21.4g h18.5m* c24g* h23.1m⁴ c23.8g* c26.2g c27.6s* **h103** c25.5s* c32.6g Feb 23] fair handicap hurdler: won at Newton Abbot in July: fairly useful handicap chaser: won at Uttoxeter later in July and Perth in September, both novice events, and at Market Rasen in December and Warwick in January: left James Ewart after first start: stays 3½m: acts on good to firm and heavy going: usually wore headgear for previous yard: normally tongue tied in 2018/19: travels strongly held up. *Dan Skelton*

ANGEL MOON 6 gr.m. Fair Mix (IRE) – Pougatcheva (FR) (Epervier Bleu) [2018/19 **h–** b68: b16g⁵ h19.6gᵖᵘ Aug 3] poor form in bumpers: pulled up in mares maiden on hurdling **b–** debut. *Fergal O'Brien*

ANGEL OF HARLEM 6 b.m. Presenting – Whoops A Daisy (Definite Article) [2018/19 **h121** h96: h20.6g* h20.3g² h21.6m³ h20.6g* h20.3g* h24g² h23.9d h24.3m⁴ Apr 12] fairly useful hurdler: won handicap at Market Rasen (conditionals) in July, and novices at same course in August and Southwell in September: fourth in mares handicap at Ayr in April: stays 3m: acts on good to firm going: in cheekpieces last 5 starts: wears tongue tie. *Olly Murphy*

ANGEL OF THE NORTH (IRE) 4 gr.f. Dark Angel (IRE) – Kay Es Jay (FR) (Xaar) **h80** [2018/19 h17.7g⁶ h16.7g⁶ h16d⁶ h16g h16g Apr 10] modest on Flat, stays 9.5f: poor form over hurdles: tried in cheekpieces. *Dan Skelton*

ANGELS ANTICS 6 b.m. Schiaparelli (GER) – Safari Run (IRE) (Supreme Leader) **c110 x** [2018/19 h122, b78: c20.9d c20.5gᵖᵘ c24.2d⁶ c22.5v³ c24s³ c29.6d⁴ Apr 26] strong mare: **h–** fairly useful hurdler: held back by attitude/jumping over fences: stays 3m: acts on heavy going: in visor last 2 starts: has joined Samuel Drinkwater. *Nigel Twiston-Davies*

ANGELS BREATH (IRE) 5 gr.g. Shantou (USA) – Mystic Masie (IRE) (Turgeon **h140** (USA)) [2018/19 h15.7s* h16m² h16.4s h20g³ Apr 6] €85,000 3-y-o: useful-looking gelding: third foal: brother to bumper/fairly useful 21f hurdle winner Outofthisworld: dam unraced half-sister to useful hurdler/smart chaser (2m winner) Toubab: easy winner of Irish point on debut: useful form over hurdles: won Kennel Gate Novices' Hurdle at Ascot (by

4½ lengths from Danny Kirwan) in December: second in Dovecote Novices' Hurdle at Kempton (¾ length behind Southfield Stone) and third in Mersey Novices' Hurdle at Aintree (5½ lengths behind Reserve Tank, racing keenly): should be suited by further than 2m. *Nicky Henderson*

ANGEL'S ENVY 7 b.m. Yeats (IRE) – Caoba (Hernando (FR)) [2018/19 h80: h19.9g³ **h83** h20.6g h20.2g⁵ h23.9g³ h23.9g³ h20.2d⁶ Apr 26] has had breathing operation: poor maiden hurdler: stays 3m: has worn headgear, including in 2018/19: tried in tongue tie. *Iain Jardine*

ANGUINO (FR) 6 b.g. Lucarno (USA) – Anguilla (GER) (Trempolino (USA)) [2018/19 **c–** c–, h98: h16.4s Dec 22] maiden hurdler, well held only start in 2018/19: once-raced chaser: **h–** raced mainly around 2m. *Andrew Crook*

ANGUS MILAN (IRE) 10 b.g. Milan – Lasado (IRE) (Jurado (USA)) [2018/19 c121, **c117** h–: c20.5g³ c20.1g c24gᵖᵘ c24.1s³ c19.1g³ c21.5d² c17sᵖᵘ Mar 18] winning hurdler: fairly **h–** useful handicap chaser: stays 3m: acts on heavy going: tried in cheekpieces: wears tongue tie: usually races off pace, often travels strongly. *Noel C. Kelly, Ireland*

ANIBALE FLY (FR) 9 b.g. Assessor (IRE) – Nouba Fly (FR) (Chamberlin (FR)) **c167** [2018/19 c164, h–: c16.7v⁶ c20d² c26.3d² c34.3g⁵ Apr 6] lengthy gelding: winning hurdler: **h–** top-class chaser: second in Red Mills Chase at Gowran (2 lengths behind Monalee) in February and Cheltenham Gold Cup (career-best effort, 2½ lengths behind Al Boum Photo) in March: stayed on all too gradually under top weight when fifth to Tiger Roll in Grand National at Aintree: stays 4¼m: acts on heavy going: wears tongue tie. *A. J. Martin, Ireland*

ANIGHTINLAMBOURN (IRE) 5 b.m. Gold Well – Madgehil (IRE) (Anshan) **b87** [2018/19 b16g³ b16d Nov 28] €35,000 3-y-o: fifth foal: half-sister to useful hurdler Hunters Hoof (2m-2½m winner) and bumper winner Huntress (both by Flemensfirth): dam, well held in bumpers, half-sister to smart 2m hurdler Kilcash and useful hurdler/fairly useful chaser (2m-2¼m winner) Snow Dragon: fair form in bumpers: better effort when third in mares event at Warwick (hooded). *Ben Pauling*

Mr John P. McManus' "Anibale Fly"

ANIMATED HERO 6 b.g. Sakhee's Secret – Society (IRE) (Barathea (IRE)) [2018/19 **h–** h–, b85: h17.2g^{pu} May 28] tall, narrow gelding: fair form in bumpers: no show in novice hurdles/on Flat: in tongue tie last 4 starts. *Rebecca Menzies*

ANIMORE 6 b.m. Sulamani (IRE) – More Likely (Shambo) [2018/19 b16g^4 b16.2d^4 **h100** b16d^3 h19.8m^2 h19.8m^5 Mar 22] third foal: sister to bumper winner/fair 2½m hurdle **b80** winner Tokaramore and half-sister to bumper winner Shambougg (by Tobougg): dam (c125/h97) 2m-25f hurdle/chase winner: modest form in bumpers: fair form over hurdles: better effort when second in maiden at Musselburgh: wears hood. *Iain Jardine*

ANIS DES MALBERAUX (FR) 9 b.g. Reste Tranquille (FR) – Scavenger (FR) **h67** (Nashamaa) [2018/19 h21.6g^5 h16.8s h25g^{pu} h23.9d Mar 11] poor form over hurdles: tried in cheekpieces. *Chris Down*

ANJILINA (IRE) 5 b.m. Yeats (IRE) – Whisky (IRE) (Supreme Leader) [2018/19 b16.6s^5 **h100** b16d^4 h19.9v^2 h23.3d^6 Mar 26] €37,000 3-y-o: eighth foal: dam unraced sister to useful 2m **b70** hurdler Spirit Leader, herself dam of high-class staying hurdler Prince of Scars and useful hurdler/smart staying chaser Folsom Blue: poor form in bumpers: fair form over hurdles: much better effort when second in mares novice at Sedgefield: in hood last 3 starts. *Mrs Caroline McCaldin, Ireland*

AN LAOCH (IRE) 7 b.g. Flemensfirth (USA) – Petite Ballerina (IRE) (Oscar (IRE)) **c83 §** [2018/19 c108, h–: c23.4g^{pu} c19.4g^4 Apr 21] has had breathing operation: point winner: **h–** lightly-raced hurdler: fair maiden chaser, below form in 2018/19: left Chris Grant after first start: stays 3¼m: acts on good to soft going: tried in cheekpieces: wears tongue tie: temperamental. *Tim Vaughan*

ANNAJEMIMA 5 b.m. Firebreak – Leaping Flame (USA) (Trempolino (USA)) [2018/19 **b–** ab16g^6 ab16g^6 Nov 27] lengthy, rather unfurnished mare: half-sister to several winners on Flat, including useful winners up to 2m Ascalon (by Galileo) and Captain John Nixon (by Beat Hollow): dam French 7f winner: behind in bumpers. *Suzi Best*

ANNDARROW (IRE) 6 b.m. Beat Hollow – Kim Hong (IRE) (Charnwood Forest **h84** (IRE)) [2018/19 h88: h23.9d^4 h23.3g Jun 14] has had breathing operation: poor maiden hurdler: stays 3m: acts on good to firm and good to soft going: tried in tongue tie: usually races towards rear. *Philip Hobbs*

ANNIE ANGEL (IRE) 8 b.m. King's Theatre (IRE) – Lady Rene (IRE) (Leading Counsel **c91 p** (USA)) [2018/19 h102, b89: c22.4d c23.6g^6 Mar 19] won Irish point on debut: lightly- **h–** raced hurdler: modest form in novice handicap chases: remains open to improvement over fences. *Amanda Perrett*

ANNIE BONNY 6 b.m. Black Sam Bellamy (IRE) – Queenoz (IRE) (Oscar (IRE)) **h110** [2018/19 h15.8d^5 h21.2g^3 h16d^4 h15.5d^6 h16d^5 h21.2d^4 h16.8v* h19s Mar 19] £1,200 3-y-o, £30,000 5-y-o: first foal: dam unraced half-sister to fairly useful hurdler (stayed 19f) Casper King out of sister to useful hurdler/smart chaser (stayed 3m) Supreme Prince: won Irish point on debut: fair handicap hurdler: won novice event at Sedgefield in March: should stay 2½m: acts on heavy going. *Evan Williams*

ANNIE MC (IRE) 5 b.m. Mahler – Classic Mari (IRE) (Classic Cliche (IRE)) [2018/19 **h135** h19.5d^3 h20.6g^2 h23.5s^4 h19.5d* h18.5d^5 h20.5d* Mar 23] £20,000 4-y-o: good-topped mare: second foal: dam lightly-raced half-sister to Stayers' Hurdle winner Princeful: runner-up both starts in Irish points: useful form over hurdles: won mares handicap at Chepstow in January and Mares 'National Hunt' Novices' Hurdle Final at Newbury (by 8 lengths from Sixty's Belle) in March: stays 3m: acts on soft going: usually races towards rear. *Jonjo O'Neill*

ANNIVERSARY GIFT 6 b.g. Sulamani (IRE) – Methodical (Lujain (USA)) [2018/19 **h–** b15.8d h16.5d h16.3d h20.5d^{pu} Mar 22] lengthy, rather unfurnished gelding: no form in **b–** bumper/over hurdles. *Colin Tizzard*

ANNSAM 4 b.g. Black Sam Bellamy (IRE) – Bathwick Annie (Sula Bula) [2018/19 **h91 p** h16.3d^5 h16.5d^3 Mar 11] strong, lengthy gelding: sixth foal: closely related to bumper winner/fairly useful hurdler Massannie (19f-2¾m winner, by Dr Massini) and half-brother to fair hurdler Courtlands Prince (2m/17f winner, by Presenting), stays 21f: dam (c127/ h95) 2½m-25f chase winner: modest form over hurdles: better effort when third in maiden at Taunton: open to further improvement. *Evan Williams*

ANNY'S LAND 9 ch.m. Millkom – Whisplan (Genuine Gift (CAN)) [2018/19 h16.2g **h–** May 12] first foal: dam unraced: point winner in 2017: well held in mares novice on hurdling debut. *Rose Dobbin*

ANOLYSSE MORINIERE (FR) 9 b.g. Network (GER) – Onolyssa (FR) (Nononito (FR)) [2018/19 c16.1dᵖᵘ Feb 28] failed to complete in points: winning hurdler: twice-raced chaser, pulled up in hunter in 2018/19: usually wears headgear. *Mrs Janet Ackner* **c– h–**

ANOTHER CRICK 6 b.g. Arcadio (GER) – Suetsu (IRE) (Toulon) [2018/19 h109, b88: h16m c16s² c15.7s² c16.4d* c20.5g* Feb 23] lengthy gelding: maiden hurdler: useful form over fences: won novice handicap at Newbury (by 3¼ lengths from Early du Lemo) in December and handicap at Kempton in February: stays 2½m: acts on heavy going: has worn hood: usually races towards rear: sure to progress further as a chaser. *Noel Williams* **c136 p h80**

ANOTHER DAY DONE (IRE) 8 b.g. Davorin (JPN) – Perfect Memory (IRE) (Nashwan (USA)) [2018/19 b73: h24g h19.7m⁶ h16.2g c19.4s² c24.2sᵖᵘ c22.7mᵖᵘ Jan 22] maiden pointer: little impact in novice hurdles: modest form in chases: best effort when second in novice handicap at Wetherby: stays 2½m: acts on soft going: wears hood: tried in tongue tie: often races towards rear. *Mark Walford* **c98 h–**

ANOTHER DRAMA (IRE) 7 b.g. Gamut (IRE) – Rachrush (IRE) (Sadler's Wells (USA)) [2018/19 h16g⁶ h16.3m h16d Aug 29] €7,000 4-y-o, £6,000 6-y-o: half-brother to 2 winners, including smart hurdler Jack Cool (2m/17f winner, by One Cool Cat): dam unraced: point winner: poor form over hurdles: will be suited by 2½m+: remains open to improvement. *Noel Williams* **h77 p**

ANOTHER EMOTION (FR) 7 gr.g. Turgeon (USA) – Line Perle (FR) (Gold And Steel (FR)) [2018/19 h113p: h23.4v² h23.6s⁴ h23.5d Feb 16] sturdy gelding: runner-up on completed start in Irish points: fairly useful form over hurdles: second in handicap at Sandown in December: stays 23f: acts on heavy going: tried in cheekpieces: usually front runner/races prominently. *Warren Greatrex* **h115**

ANOTHER FRONTIER (IRE) 8 b.g. Darsi (FR) – Scent With Love (IRE) (Winged Love (IRE)) [2018/19 c116, h114: c24g* c25gᵘʳ c26.1g² c24gᵖᵘ c23.4dᵖᵘ c25.5dᵖᵘ h26g c29.6dᵖᵘ Apr 26] sturdy gelding: winning hurdler: fairly useful handicap chaser: won at Uttoxeter in October: lost form later in season: stays 3¼m: acts on heavy going: wears headgear. *Nigel Twiston-Davies* **c117 d h–**

ANOTHER GO (IRE) 6 gr.g. Strategic Prince – Golden Rose (GER) (Winged Love (IRE)) [2018/19 h68: h15.7g h19.8vᵖᵘ h15.8d h15.3g h17.7g Apr 22] lengthy gelding: little form over hurdles. *Ralph Smith* **h–**

ANOTHER HERO (IRE) 10 b.g. Kalanisi (IRE) – Storm Front (IRE) (Strong Gale) [2018/19 c136, h–: c25g⁴ c26.1mᵖᵘ Jul 1] workmanlike gelding: winning hurdler: useful handicap chaser: stayed 3¼m: acted on good to firm and heavy going: tried in cheekpieces/ tongue tie: dead. *Jonjo O'Neill* **c124 h–**

ANOTHER MATTIE (IRE) 12 b.g. Zagreb (USA) – Silver Tassie (FR) (Kaldounevees (FR)) [2018/19 c–, h109: h19.5v⁵ h24.6v h24s⁴ h24.3s⁴ h20.2d³ Apr 26] workmanlike gelding: modest handicap hurdler nowadays: maiden chaser: stays 3m: acts on heavy going: has worn headgear, including final start: wears tongue tie. *N. W. Alexander* **c– h96**

EBF TBA Mares' National Hunt Novices' Hurdle Final (Limited Handicap), Newbury—a wide-margin win for Annie Mc on a red letter day for promising conditional Jonjo O'Neill Jr

*Fulke Walwyn Kim Muir Challenge Cup Amateur Riders' Handicap Chase, Cheltenham—
a first win in the race for Mr Derek O'Connor as he produces Any Second Now (hoops) with a
well-timed run to overhaul the grey Kilfilum Cross*

ANOTHER STOWAWAY (IRE) 7 b.g. Stowaway – Another Pet (IRE) (Un Desperado (FR)) [2018/19 h122: c20.5g² c22.5gᵖᵘ c22.7m* c24.2d³ c19.2d⁶ Mar 24] well-made gelding: has had breathing operations: maiden hurdler: useful form over fences: won novice handicap at Leicester (by 10 lengths from Forth Bridge) in January: stays 3m: acts on good to firm and good to soft going: wears tongue tie. *Tom George* **c135 h–**

ANOTHER THEATRE (IRE) 6 b.m. Shantou (USA) – Whats Another One (IRE) (King's Theatre (IRE)) [2018/19 h16g⁴ h16.2g³ h15.7g* h16.4s* h19.9d⁴ Feb 25] €12,000 3-y-o: fourth foal: half-sister to fairly useful hurdler/chaser Okotoks (2m winner, by Gamut), stays 2½m: dam lightly raced in bumpers/over hurdles: placed in Irish points: fairly useful form over hurdles: won mares novice at Catterick in December and mares handicap at Newcastle in January: should be suited by further than 2m: acts on soft going: usually races prominently. *Henry Oliver* **h118**

ANOTHER VENTURE (IRE) 8 ch.g. Stowaway – Hard Luck (IRE) (Old Vic) [2018/19 c132, h–: c23.6v⁵ c27.3s⁶ c30.7d⁵ c25.7d* c23.4d⁴ Apr 8] tall, strong gelding: winning hurdler: useful handicap chaser: won at Plumpton in March: stays 3¼m: acts on heavy going: usually in headgear nowadays. *Kim Bailey* **c132 h–**

AN SCAIRP (IRE) 7 b.g. Scorpion (IRE) – Stepping Out Well (IRE) (Zaffaran (USA)) [2018/19 h22.2g Jul 10] multiple point winner: well held in bumpers/maiden hurdle. *Jennifer Mason* **h–**

ANTEROS (IRE) 11 b.g. Milan – Sovereign Star (IRE) (Taufan (USA)) [2018/19 c111§, h127§: h25g³ h26.5v⁴ h23.9gᶠ h23.6v⁶ h23.6s⁵ c25.7s⁴ h16s Feb 15] lengthy gelding: fairly useful handicap hurdler: maiden chaser: stays 3¼m: acts on heavy going: usually in headgear: wears tongue tie: races towards rear: unreliable. *Sophie Leech* **c79 § h124 §**

ANTI COOL (IRE) 10 b.g. Heron Island (IRE) – Youngborogal (IRE) (Anshan) [2018/19 c17g⁶ c16.3d⁶ c17sᵖᵘ c16d c15.7g² c15.7d³ Apr 24] has had breathing operation: maiden hurdler: poor handicap chaser nowadays: best form on good going: wears headgear: tried in tongue tie. *Robin Dickin* **c77 h–**

ANTON CHIGURH 10 b.g. Oasis Dream – Barathiki (Barathea (IRE)) [2018/19 h–: h19.5sᵖᵘ Nov 21] modest on Flat, stays 9.5f: maiden hurdler, pulled up both starts in handicaps: tried in hood. *Nikki Evans* **h–**

ANTON DOLIN (IRE) 11 ch.g. Danehill Dancer (IRE) – Ski For Gold (Shirley Heights) **h83**
[2018/19 h89§: h15.8g³ h15.8g³ h18.7m² h15.8m⁶ h18.6m⁶ h18.6gᵖᵘ h16.7g h15.8g h15.5g
Dec 6] poor handicap hurdler nowadays: stays 2½m: acts on soft and good to firm going:
has worn headgear, including final start: often races towards rear. *Michael Mullineaux*

ANTONY (FR) 9 b.g. Walk In The Park (IRE) – Melanie du Chenet (FR) (Nikos) [2018/19 **c130**
c131, h–: c26m² c21.6m³ Oct 5] good-topped gelding: winning hurdler: useful handicap **h–**
chaser: stays 3¼m: acts on soft and good to firm going: tried in cheekpieces. *Gary Moore*

ANTUNES 5 b.g. Nathaniel (IRE) – Aigrette Garzette (IRE) (Peintre Celebre (USA)) **h120**
[2018/19 h107: h16.4g h15.8s* h15.5g⁵ h16.3d³ h16d² Mar 20] big, well-made gelding:
has had breathing problems: fairly useful handicap hurdler: won at Uttoxeter in December:
third in novice event at Newbury in March: raced at 2m: acts on soft going: usually races
off pace. *Dan Skelton*

ANY DRAMA (IRE) 8 b.g. Gamut (IRE) – Oak Lodge (IRE) (Roselier (FR)) [2018/19 **c115 p**
c20sᶠ Dec 11] medium-sized gelding: useful form over hurdles: off 21 months, 7/1, **h–**
keeping on just outside frame when hampered and fell 2 out in maiden won by Crucial Role
at Uttoxeter on chasing debut: should stay 3m: acts on soft going: in headgear last 2 starts:
open to improvement over fences. *Harry Fry*

ANY SECOND NOW (IRE) 7 b.g. Oscar (IRE) – Pretty Neat (IRE) (Topanoora) **c148**
[2018/19 c144, h–: c19d⁵ c21.2g² c24.5g⁵ c24d³ c26d* c29dᶠ Apr 22] rangy gelding: **h–**
winning hurdler: smart chaser: won Fulke Walwyn Kim Muir Chase at Cheltenham by 3¾
lengths from Kilfilum Cross) in March: third in Ten Up Novices' Chase at Navan (4 lengths
behind Chris's Dream) previous month: will stay beyond 3¼m: acts on heavy going: in
blinkers last 4 starts. *T. M. Walsh, Ireland*

ANYTIME NOW (IRE) 7 b.g. Beneficial – Rag's Lady (IRE) (King's Ride) [2018/19 **h110**
h20g h21.8g⁴ h20.2g² h20.2g³ h20m³ h19.5g h21.5g⁵ h20.5v⁶ Nov 14] €10,000 3-y-o:
brother to fairly useful hurdler/useful chaser Avondhu Lady (2m-2½m winner) and half-
brother to a winning pointer by Milan: dam unraced: bumper winner: fair maiden hurdler:
stays 21f: acts on good to soft going. *Gordon Elliott, Ireland*

ANYTIME WILL DO (IRE) 6 b.g. Scorpion (IRE) – Pellerossa (IRE) (Good Thyne **h131 p**
(USA)) [2018/19 b103p: h15.8g* h16.7g* h15.8g⁵ Feb 21] fell in point: bumper winner:
useful form over hurdles: won maiden at Uttoxeter (with plenty in hand) and novice at
Bangor in October: keeping on 2 lengths down when bad mistake last in novice won by
Hes No Trouble at Huntingdon final start: likely to be suited by further than 17f: remains
with potential. *Dan Skelton*

APACHEE PRINCE (IRE) 10 b.g. Indian Danehill (IRE) – Wheredidthemoneygo **c85**
(IRE) (Anshan) [2018/19 c–, h88: h22.1m c19.4mᵖᵘ c23.9g³ h25.8s² c25.7m⁴ h25.5g⁵ **h83**
c25.6s³ c21.2dᵖᵘ Jan 1] rather leggy gelding: modest handicap hurdler/maiden chaser:
unplaced in points in 2019: stays 3¼m: acts on soft going: wears headgear/tongue tie.
Olly Murphy

APACHE JACK (IRE) 11 b.g. Oscar (IRE) – Cailin Supreme (IRE) (Supreme Leader) **c–**
[2018/19 c111, h126: h22.1g h23.9g h24.3d h20.2gᵖᵘ h16s** Jan 8] fairly useful handicap **h120**
hurdler: back to form when won at Ayr in January: winning chaser: stays 3m: acts on heavy
going: wears headgear. *Stuart Crawford, Ireland*

APACHE PILOT 11 br.g. Indian Danehill (IRE) – Anniejo (Presenting) [2018/19 c88, h–: **c94**
c20.1d³ c24.2g* c24.1g³ c24.2g⁴ c24.1g⁶ c31.9sᵖᵘ c23.9s³ c23.4gᵘʳ c26.3s c24.2d³ c24.2g³ **h–**
Apr 15] maiden hurdler: modest handicap chaser: won at Hexham in May: stays 25f: acts
on soft going: often in headgear: wears tongue tie. *Maurice Barnes*

APACHE SONG 6 ch.m. Mount Nelson – Pantita (Polish Precedent (USA)) [2018/19 **h122**
h124: h20g* h20.6g May 20] sturdy mare: fairly useful handicap hurdler: won mares event
at Fakenham in May: stays 2½m: acts on heavy going. *James Eustace*

APACHE VALLEY 4 b.f. Sleeping Indian – Vallani (IRE) (Vettori (IRE)) [2018/19 b17g **h–**
h20.1g Apr 15] first foal: dam (h94) 3m hurdle winner: little show in bumper/novice **b–**
hurdle. *James Ewart*

A PERFECT GIFT (IRE) 5 br.m. Presenting – Keyras Choice (IRE) (Flemensfirth **b92**
(USA)) [2018/19 b15.8s* b16.7d⁴ Jan 17] €30,000 3-y-o: second foal: dam unraced half-
sister to top-class hurdler/chaser (best efforts around 2m) Sizing Europe: fair form in
bumpers: won maiden at Uttoxeter in December: likely to stay 2½m. *Olly Murphy*

Close Brothers Novices' Handicap Chase, Cheltenham—a first Cheltenham Festival success for jockey Rachael Blackmore as A Plus Tard storms clear of fellow Irish raider Tower Bridge

A PLACE APART (IRE) 5 b.g. Power – Simadartha (USA) (Gone West (USA))   **c111** [2018/19 h16.5g h16.7g h20.1d h16g² h18.8s* c18m* h16.6g⁴ h16d⁴ c19.9s³ c19.9mᵖᵘ Apr   **h108** 20] close-coupled gelding: half-brother to French 2¼m chase winner Paradise City (by Danehill Dancer): fair maiden on Flat, stays 1¾m: fair hurdler: won maiden at Downpatrick in October: similar form over fences: won novice handicap at Kempton later in October: stays 19f: acts on good to firm and heavy going: has worn cheekpieces, including final start. *Gavin Patrick Cromwell, Ireland*

A PLUS TARD (FR) 5 b.g. Kapgarde (FR) – Turboka (FR) (Kahyasi) [2018/19 c20d²   **c157** c19d* c20d² c20.2s* Mar 12] rather unfurnished gelding: fourth foal: dam, French   **h–** 17f-2½m hurdle/chase winner, half-sister to useful French chaser (2½m-2¾m winner) Dottore: useful hurdle winner in France for D. Bressou: very smart form over fences: won maiden at Naas (by 3¼ lengths from Duc des Genievres) in December and Close Brothers Novices' Handicap Chase at Cheltenham (much improved, by 16 lengths from Tower Bridge) in March: stamina seemed stretched when third in Champion Novices' Chase won by Delta Work at Punchestown shortly after end of British season: stays 2½m: acts on soft going: usually travels strongly. *Henry de Bromhead, Ireland*

APPLAUS (GER) 7 b.g. Tiger Hill (IRE) – All About Love (GER) (Winged Love (IRE))   **c– §** [2018/19 c119, h99: c17.1g May 9] winning hurdler: fairly useful chaser at best: pulled up   **h–** both starts in points in 2019: unproven beyond 2m: acts on heavy going: wears headgear: tried in tongue tie: temperamental. *Micky Hammond*

APPLE MACK 6 b.g. Apple Tree (FR) – Allerford Annie (IRE) (Oscar (IRE)) [2018/19   **h105** b16.7g h19.5s h16.8s h21.4g³ h21.7d² h23.1d h26.5g Apr 20] second foal: brother to fairly   **b–** useful 3m hurdle winner/winning pointer Applesolutely: dam unraced: fell in point: well beaten in bumper: fair form over hurdles: stays 2¾m: acts on good to soft going: usually front runner/races prominently. *Richard Mitford-Slade*

APPLE OF OUR EYE 9 b.g. Passing Glance – Apple Anthem (True Song) [2018/19   **c–** c118, h121: h21g May 12] sturdy gelding: fairly useful hurdler at best: has lost his way: **h–** running to similar level when falling on first of 2 starts over fences: stays 21f: acts on soft going: in blinkers last 2 starts. *Charlie Longsdon*

APPLESANDPIERRES (IRE) 11 b.g. Pierre – Cluain Chaoin (IRE) (Phardante (FR))   **c126** [2018/19 c–, h125: h16.2d² h17.2g* h17.2m⁶ c21.2g² c21m³ c17.3sᵖᵘ Aug 27] lengthy   **h131** gelding: winning pointer: useful handicap hurdler: won at Cartmel in May: fairly useful form when placed in chases: left Dan Skelton after first start: stays 21f: acts on good to firm and heavy going: wears headgear. *Sophie Leech*

APPLE'S JADE (FR) 7 b.m. Saddler Maker (IRE) – Apple's For Ever (FR) (Nikos) **h162**
[2018/19 h156: h20d* h20g* h24g* h16g* h16.4s^6 h24.7g^3 Apr 6]

How long before another mare wins the Champion Hurdle? Annie Power had
been only the fourth of her sex to win the Champion Hurdle when successful in 2016,
and the first for more than twenty years. It seems unlikely that there will be a similar
wait until the race falls to a mare again, and it was short odds about that happening
in the latest season. Despite the presence of Buveur d'Air, bidding to make his own
piece of history by winning the Champion Hurdle for the third year running, he was
only third choice in the betting at the off behind the mares Apple's Jade and Laurina.
Another of the season's best mares, Buveur d'Air's stable-companion Verdana Blue,
was also in the line-up, her odds of 33/1 more a reflection of the fact that the soft
ground was all against her, rather than her chances strictly on form. Both Apple's
Jade and Laurina were past winners of the two mares races which have been added
to the Festival programme during the last ten years or so. Apple's Jade had won the
David Nicholson Mares' Hurdle in 2017 (Annie Power had looked sure to collect in
the same contest two years earlier when falling at the last), while Laurina, who was
still unbeaten for Willie Mullins going into the Champion Hurdle, had won the third
running of the Dawn Run Mares' Novices Hurdle in 2018.

The David Nicholson Mares' Hurdle, first run in 2008 and promoted
to Grade 1 the year Annie Power fell, handing victory to stablemate Glens Melody,
represents the pinnacle of the mares jumping programme, at least on the British side
of the Irish Sea. Britain had some catching up to do compared with Ireland, where
there were already more extensive opportunities for mares over both hurdles and
fences. Ireland already had two Grade 1 hurdles for mares only, one restricted to
novices at Fairyhouse's Easter meeting, and the other the Mares Champion Hurdle
at the Punchestown Festival. Annie Power had won both those races in her novice
season when they were run as Grade 1 contests for the first time. Annie Power,
whose name now appears in the race title, won the Punchestown race again a year
later, since when it had also gone to Apple's Jade who followed up her Cheltenham
win in 2017. Introducing mares races to the Cheltenham Festival (which will have a
mares chase in 2021, about which there is more in the essay on La Bague Au Roi),
and the ongoing expansion of the 'black type' programme of mares races over jumps
more generally, has not been universally popular, but the presence of three top mares
in the latest Champion Hurdle field was surely evidence of the scheme starting to
pay dividends. There were thirty-five 'black type' races for mares in Britain in the
latest season, twenty-five more than ten years previously.

Mares have long accounted for around a fifth of the population of jumpers
in training, a proportion that has tended to vary little, though in 2018 that increased
to nearer a quarter for the first time. Ruth Quinn, who has been behind the project at
the BHA, believes an increase to twenty-five per cent is feasible over the next five
years and thirty per cent in another ten. Motivation for improving opportunities for
mares over jumps came in part from the need to improve the value of filly foals to
National Hunt breeders. The better programme for mares has meant that not only are
more being put into training, but they are also making more money than previously
in the sale-ring, including as part of the currently booming market in Irish pointers.
Maire Banrigh fetched £320,000 at the Cheltenham Festival Sales in 2017 before
going on to win both her starts over hurdles in the latest season for Dan Skelton in
the colours of John Hales. That record for a jumping filly was broken at the same

*baroneracing.com Hatton's Grace Hurdle, Fairyhouse—a third straight win in the race for
Apple's Jade, who already has matters sewn up on the run to the final flight*

sale during the latest Festival when My Whirlwind joined another trainer who has enjoyed plenty of success with mares, Nicky Henderson, for £400,000, topping the sale. 'We like mares and we like mares races,' said Verdana Blue's trainer. 'There is a good programme for them now.'

Whilst benefiting the majority of the population of jumping mares as a whole, the expanded mares programme has been criticised for the easier options it affords at the top to the very best mares who are good enough to be competing in open company, with the 7-lb sex allowance, against male rivals. It's a valid point, though in such cases connections are arguably open to as much as criticism as the architects of the programme book. Quevega won six consecutive David Nicholson Mares' Hurdles at Cheltenham so never crossed swords with Big Buck's who won his four World Hurdles during the same period, though at Punchestown Quevega won four World Series Hurdles against all-comers. Annie Power did run in the World Hurdle (a year when the Mullins stable had Quevega going for her sixth win in the David Nicholson Mares' Hurdle, and Hurricane Fly bidding for a third Champion Hurdle). It was only a twist of fate that led to her contesting, and then winning, the Champion Hurdle two years later. Annie Power was not even entered for the race that January, only supplemented later when connections' main hope Faugheen had to miss the Champion Hurdle through injury. Annie Power was just one good horse among several in the Ricci string, just like Apple's Jade among the even more powerful Gigginstown operation. Bigger owners with several options in a number of Festival races are inevitably going to need a good reason not to run a mare in a mares race when they have other horses available for the top open races. As Gigginstown's racing manager Eddie O'Leary put it, 'We'll go to the Champion Hurdle [with Apple's Jade] if you will allow us to run a gelding in the mares race.'

O'Leary was speaking straight after Apple's Jade had routed her rivals by upwards of sixteen lengths in the Irish Champion Hurdle at Leopardstown in February—a good enough reason, it turned out, to go for the Champion Hurdle at Cheltenham after all. Until then, a third attempt at the David Nicholson Mares' Hurdle had been Apple's Jade's stated aim all season. The Irish Champion Hurdle was Apple's Jade's first start at two miles for some time, after being campaigned with great success over two and a half and three miles for the best part of three seasons.

Squared Financial Christmas Hurdle, Leopardstown—Faugheen's fall at the second last leaves not a challenger in sight, the winning margin for Apple's Jade twenty-six lengths this time

BHP Insurance Irish Champion Hurdle, Leopardstown—
the drop back to two miles poses no problems for Apple's Jade, who is clear on the extended run-in
of 2018 winner Supasundae and 2017 winner Petit Mouchoir

Her latest campaign began in identical fashion to the previous one as she again completed a hat-trick before the turn of the year in the Lismullen Hurdle at Navan, the Hatton's Grace Hurdle at Fairyhouse and the Christmas Hurdle at Leopardstown. After easily beating Jezki by eleven lengths at Navan (the Lismullen was marred by a fatal injury to her main rival Identity Thief), Apple's Jade demolished her field with a high-class performance to win the baroneracing.com Hatton's Grace for the third year. Travelling strongly behind Wicklow Brave, as the pair raced clear of their seven rivals almost from the off, Apple's Jade took up the running three out and had the race sewn up before the next, passing the post twenty lengths clear of second favourite Supasundae. Another mare, Limini, was a further two lengths back in third, faring best of Willie Mullins' four runners. Apple's Jade had won her first Hatton's Grace as a four-year-old by just a short head in a thriller with the older mare Vroum Vroum Mag, while her 2017 win had been gained more easily after she had stormed clear to beat the Stayers' Hurdle winner Nichols Canyon by nine lengths with Supasundae back in third. Twenty lengths, though, was a record winning margin for the Hatton's Grace which has had two other triple winners in its twenty-five history. Limestone Lad's first win in 1999 came when inflicting a shock defeat on Istabraq who was himself going for a third consecutive win in the race that year. Limestone Lad went chasing the following season, but won two more Hatton's Graces after that before passing the baton to his stable-companion Solerina who proceeded to win the next three editions for their trainer James Bowe. Solerina won nineteen of her twenty-seven completed starts (none of her starts were in races confined to mares, by the way), though she only competed once outside Ireland, finishing fourth in 2004 to Iris's Gift in one of the best editions of the Stayers' Hurdle.

Apple's Jade's performance in the Hatton's Grace inevitably heightened interest in connections' plans for her at Cheltenham, though Gordon Elliott reaffirmed that the David Nicholson Mares' Hurdle was still the target, being the race she had the best chance of winning. Elliott provided the same response after the outcome of her next race made the question more pertinent still. She had won her first Squared Financial Christmas Hurdle at Leopardstown twelve months earlier in gutsy fashion by half a length from Supasundae, but her second win in the race was gained by a still wider margin than the Hatton's Grace. It would have been closer if her main rival Faugheen had not fallen heavily two out when still in touch, but that left Apple's Jade a long way clear to come home by twenty-six lengths from Early Doors who had been beaten a similar distance when fifth behind her in the Hatton's Grace. 'About three and a half' was Michael O'Leary's answer when asked to rate the chances, on a scale of one to ten, of Apple's Jade running in the Stayers' Hurdle but some bookmakers were taking no chances, making her the 4/1 favourite for that race.

The option of the Champion Hurdle still wasn't on the table. Apple's Jade thrives on her racing, and her trainer blamed her lack of a run between the Christmas Hurdle and Cheltenham the previous season for her disappointing performance when she finished only third in her bid to win the David Nicholson Mares' Hurdle again, though she was also reported as having come into season. Therefore, Apple's

Gigginstown House Stud's "Apple's Jade"

Jade's next run was in the BHP Insurance Irish Champion Hurdle at Leopardstown in February, back at two miles in a bid to emulate Supasundae who successfully dropped back in trip to win the race twelve months earlier after being beaten by Apple's Jade in the Christmas Hurdle. Supasundae and Melon were Apple's Jade's main rivals, both starting at 4/1 as Apple's Jade was sent off the 11/8-on favourite, with Gigginstown's 2017 winner Petit Mouchoir on 12/1 and Elliott fielding two more Gigginstown runners, Farclas and Tombstone, both outsiders. While the distances of her races had varied, Apple's Jade's style of running remained constant, and the tenth Grade 1 of her career (her fifth under Jack Kennedy) was gained in typical fashion, though the familiarity of how she went about things, travelling strongly in the lead and jumping well in the main, if slightly to her right as usual, did nothing to detract from how impressive she was once again. Supasundae was left trailing as Apple's Jade drew clear approaching the home turn, with Petit Mouchoir eventually beaten a further five lengths back in third, ahead of the disappointing Melon and the two outsiders. Apple's Jade provided her trainer with his first win in the race, and she became the first mare to be successful since Like-A-Butterfly beat Limestone Lad in 2003.

A top-class performance over two miles promptly banished thoughts of a Stayers' Hurdle challenge as the more appealing alternative to another David Nicholson Mares' Hurdle for Apple's Jade; now it was the Champion Hurdle (she had been given entries in all three races) that was the race in which most commentators wanted to see her at Cheltenham, even if Eddie O'Leary, who has been quoted earlier, seemingly wasn't prepared to change his mind. 'Her ideal trip is two and a half miles, and Cheltenham is the wrong way round for her,' he added. 'You'd be taking on a serious horse in Buveur d'Air, and she would be giving him a length at every hurdle.' But twenty-four hours later, his brother Michael, 'genuinely surprised' by her performance after saying he had expected Melon to be too quick for her, put her chances of running in the Champion Hurdle at '75-25'.

Apple's Jade had been doubly declared at the 2018 Festival for both the David Nicholson Mares' Hurdle and the Stayers' Hurdle (even though there had never seemed much doubt that she would be running in the former), resulting in a £500 fine for Elliott (also imposed on Willie Mullins for doubly declaring Min at the meeting). That practice was ended by a change to the rules for the latest Festival which meant that Apple's Jade's declaration for the Champion Hurdle finally ended any speculation about which race she would be running in. It was clear a long way from home that she wouldn't be winning it, her defeat coming in such a way as to leave no regrets about her not going for the Mares' Hurdle instead, as she wouldn't have won that either. An unsatisfactory scope later explained her performance. As Michael O'Leary had said after the Irish Champion Hurdle 'If you're going to lose, I'd rather lose trying to win a Champion Hurdle than a Mares' Hurdle.' Never travelling with her usual zest, Apple's Jade trailed home sixth of the seven finishers behind the other two mares, Laurina also disappointing in fourth and Verdana Blue, as expected, inconvenienced by the ground in fifth.

It was the first time in her career that Apple's Jade had finished out of the first three. She is nothing if not tough, though, and her campaign was far from over. Indeed, she has now run at both the Cheltenham and Punchestown Festivals in each of the last four years, additionally taking in Aintree in between in the latest season, as she had done as a juvenile hurdler for Willie Mullins when she was such an impressive winner of the Anniversary Hurdle. She performed better on her last two starts in the latest season, but without recapturing her brilliance from earlier in the season. Back over three miles in the Liverpool Hurdle and odds-on to land a race sponsored by her owner (run as the Ryanair Stayers' Hurdle), Apple's Jade came off worst in a three-way finish with If The Cap Fits and the latest David Nicholson Mares' Hurdle winner Roksana. Apple's Jade then started joint favourite with Buveur d'Air for the Punchestown Champion Hurdle but could manage only fifth behind him in the seven-runner field.

Apple's Jade (FR) (b.m. 2012)	Saddler Maker (IRE) (b 1998)	Sadler's Wells (b 1981)	Northern Dancer Fairy Bridge
		Animatrice (b 1985)	Alleged Alexandrie
	Apple's For Ever (FR) (b 2000)	Nikos (b or br 1981)	Nonoalco No No Nanette
		Apple's Girl (b 1989)	Le Pontet Silver Girl

Another benefit of more mares being encouraged to race over jumps is that it gives breeders greater opportunity to use broodmares who have proven their ability and soundness on the track. That, you would think, can only be good for the breed. It was baffling, therefore, to read the opinions of former trainers Henrietta Knight and Charles Egerton, along with Mick Channon, whose wide-ranging criticism of the BHA in a letter to the *Racing Post* in the wake of the Cheltenham Festival included a rant about 'the plethora of mares-only races that will weaken the breed and distort pedigrees.' As for the 'plethora' of races for mares, they still constitute less than ten per cent of the race programme despite having almost doubled in number since the 2005/06 season. Apple's Jade is herself the product of a mare who had twenty races over jumps in France from the ages of three to seven, Apple's For Ever winning five times at up to two and a half miles over both hurdles and fences. Apple's Jade's grandam Apple's Girl enjoyed a still longer career, covering more than forty starts which included wins in major races at Auteuil such as the Prix Renaud du Vivier and the Prix La Barka. Apple's Jade's younger sister Apple's Shakira, a hot favourite when fourth in the 2018 Triumph Hurdle, ran only twice for Nicky Henderson in the latest season but wasn't beaten far when sixth in the Coral Cup. Apple's For Ever's latest foal to reach the racecourse is the four-year-old Grisy Apple's (by Montmartre) whose win over fences at Compiegne in May surely won't have gone unnoticed by would-be purchasers in Britain or Ireland. The tall Apple's Jade, usually an enthusiastic front runner, is versatile as well as tough, effective at two to three miles, and she acts on heavy ground. She is tongue tied nowadays and has reportedly had a breathing operation over the summer. Only the Grand National runner-up Magic of Light earned more prize money than Apple's Jade among mares in the latest season, while the others whose earnings topped £100,000 and made important contributions to the season were Verdana Blue, La Bague Au Roi, Lady Buttons, Camelia de Cotte (who made hay in mares novice chases in Ireland for Willie Mullins) and Roksana. *Gordon Elliott, Ireland*

APPLE'S SHAKIRA (FR) 5 b.m. Saddler Maker (IRE) – Apple's For Ever (FR) (Nikos) **h140**
[2018/19 h137: h16v[pu] h21s[6] Mar 13] lengthy mare: useful hurdler: back on track when sixth in Coral Cup at Cheltenham (2½ lengths behind William Henry) in March, finishing well: will stay beyond 21f: raced only on soft/heavy going: in hood last 3 starts. *Nicky Henderson*

APPLETREE LANE 9 b.m. Croco Rouge (IRE) – Emmasflora (Alflora (IRE)) [2018/19 **c–**
c80, h83: h22.1g[pu] May 30] maiden hurdler: poor form over fences: stays 2½m: acts on soft **h–**
going: tried in headgear. *Tom Gretton*

APRES LE DELUGE (FR) 5 gr.g. Stormy River (FR) – Ms Cordelia (USA) (Anabaa **h108 p**
(USA)) [2018/19 b91p: h16.8s[4] h15.5g[4] Dec 28] bumper winner: fair form over hurdles: better effort when fourth in novice at Exeter in December: should still improve. *Hughie Morrison*

APTERIX (FR) 9 b.g. Day Flight – Ohe Les Aulmes (FR) (Lute Antique (FR)) [2018/19 **c–**
c–, h113: h17.2m[5] h17.2g[4] h19.9m* h16.8m[2] h16m[3] h19.7g[3] h16.8s[pu] h16g[3] h16.8v[4] Jan **h113**
27] workmanlike gelding: fair handicap hurdler nowadays: won at Sedgefield in August: winning chaser: stays 2½m: acts on soft and good to firm going: tried in cheekpieces. *Brian Ellison*

APTLY PUT (IRE) 7 b.g. Yeats (IRE) – Versatile Approach (IRE) (Topanoora) [2018/19 **h107**
h110, b81: h21.4g h20.7d[4] h23.4d[3] h25.3m[2] Feb 26] point winner: fair maiden hurdler: stays 25f: acts on soft and good to firm going: in tongue tie last 4 starts: has joined James Moffatt. *Richard Spencer*

AQUARIAN (IRE) 5 b.g. Rock of Gibraltar (IRE) – Inchina (Montjeu (IRE)) [2018/19 **c96**
h16m h21.5g[5] h19.5g[6] h22g[5] h20g h19.5g[4] h25g* h25d[5] h27s[3] h22g[5] c20.9m[3] Apr 20] first **h96**
foal: dam 1¼m winner: modest handicap hurdler: won at Huntingdon in November: similar form when third in novice handicap at Carlisle (3¼ lengths behind Roll of Thunder) on chasing debut: left Joseph Patrick O'Brien after fourth start: stays 27f: acts on soft and good to firm going: usually wears headgear: often races towards rear. *Jonjo O'Neill*

Paddy Power Future Champions Novices' Hurdle, Leopardstown—a fourth straight win in the race for Willie Mullins as Aramon starts to pull clear of stable-companion Sancta Simona (hoops)

Supreme Horse Racing Club & Michael Songer's "Aramon"

AQUITAINE BOY (FR) 4 b.g. Walk In The Park (IRE) – Dolce Vita Yug (Emperor **b68**
Jones (USA)) [2018/19 b14.6s⁴ Dec 22] 9/1, fourth in junior bumper at Newcastle (18
lengths behind Lossiemouth). *James Ewart*

ARABIAN FAIRYTALE 4 b.f. Mawatheeq (USA) – Tattercoats (FR) (Whywhywhy **h–**
(USA)) [2018/19 h15.8g Nov 24] no form on Flat: well beaten in maiden on hurdling debut
(hooded). *Adam West*

ARAMON (GER) 6 b.g. Monsun (GER) – Aramina (GER) (In The Wings) [2018/19 **h145**
h19.8g* h16s² h16d* h16g³ h16g* h16g² h16.4s⁶ h16.5d² Apr 5] compact gelding: fair on
Flat in Germany, stays 1½m: smart hurdler: won maiden at Kilbeggan in August, For
Auction Novices' Hurdle at Navan in November and Future Champions Novices' Hurdle
at Leopardstown (by 10 lengths from Sancta Simona) in December: also second in
Chanelle Pharma Novices' Hurdle at Leopardstown (beaten head by Klassical Dream) and
Top Novices' Hurdle at Aintree (beaten 1½ lengths by Felix Desjy): well below form in
Champion Novices' Hurdle at Punchestown shortly after end of British season: won at
2½m on hurdling debut but raced at 2m otherwise: acts on soft going: usually races off
pace. *W. P. Mullins, Ireland*

A RATED (IRE) 8 b.g. Flemensfirth (USA) – Dawn Court (Rakaposhi King) [2018/19 **c144**
c141, h–: c19g c22.5d² c24s Sep 12] maiden hurdler: useful handicap chaser: second at **h–**
Galway (length behind Snugsborough Benny) in August: stays 2¾m: acts on heavy going:
usually leads. *Henry de Bromhead, Ireland*

ARBORETUM 11 b.g. Kayf Tara – Step Lively (Dunbeath (USA)) [2018/19 c–, h89: **c71** h20.3g^{pu} c24g c21.4g^6 h19.3s^{pu} h25.3g c19.2m^3 h24g h24.1g c23.6g* Apr 22] good-bodied **h56** gelding: poor handicap hurdler/chaser: won over fences at Huntingdon in April: stays easy 3m: best form on good going: in blinkers last 4 starts: has worn tongue tie: usually races towards rear. *Mike Sowersby*

ARCADE ATTRACTION (IRE) 5 b.g. Arcadio (GER) – Tobetall (Tobougg (IRE)) **h106** [2018/19 h16.2g h15.8d^3 h16.5g^3 Jan 9] €12,000 3-y-o: second foal: dam, third in bumper (no other form), half-sister to smart hurdler (stayed 3m) Attaglance: fair form over hurdles: best effort when third in maiden at Taunton: will stay 2½m. *Evan Williams*

ARCADIAN SEA (IRE) 5 b.g. Born To Sea (IRE) – Drombeg Dawn (IRE) (Orpen **h–** (USA)) [2018/19 h15.8g h20m^4 Apr 22] modest on Flat, stays 1¾m: last in maiden/novice hurdles: in hood first start: wears tongue tie. *Sarah Humphrey*

ARCANJA (IRE) 5 gr.g. Arcadio (GER) – Nanja Monja (IRE) (Bering) [2018/19 ab16.3s^6 **b55** Feb 23] 25/1, sixth in bumper at Newcastle. *George Bewley*

ARCHER'S UP 6 ch.g. Archipenko (USA) – Nadeszhda (Nashwan (USA)) [2018/19 **h111** h16.7m^5 h16g^5 h16.7d h17g^2 h19.5g^2 h16.7g Sep 29] fair on Flat, stays 13f: fair form over hurdles: stays 19f. *Gavin Patrick Cromwell, Ireland*

ARCHIE BROWN (IRE) 5 b.g. Aizavoski (IRE) – Pure Beautiful (IRE) (Un Desperado **b88 p** (FR)) [2018/19 b16.2d^3 Apr 26] €11,000 3-y-o: fifth foal: half-brother to fairly useful 19f hurdle winner Mentor and fair chaser Only Gorgeous (19f-31f winner) (both by Vertical Speed): dam winning pointer: 2/1, shaped well when third in bumper at Perth (6¾ lengths behind Equus Dancer): likely to improve. *Stuart Crawford, Ireland*

ARCHIE RICE (USA) 13 b.g. Arch (USA) – Gold Bowl (USA) (Seeking The Gold **c–** (USA)) [2018/19 c–, h94: h16.8g^{pu} Aug 15] good-topped gelding: multiple point winner: **h–** fair hurdler at best: well held only chase start: stayed 3¼m: acted on soft and good to firm going: dead. *Jimmy Frost*

ARCHIPPOS 6 b.g. Archipenko (USA) – Sparkling Clear (Efisio) [2018/19 h16d h16g^6 **h99** h19.7g h16g Apr 11] fairly useful on Flat, stays 16.5f: modest form over hurdles: should stay 2½m. *Philip Kirby*

ARCHIRONDEL (IRE) 5 b.g. Kalanisi (IRE) – Izind An Affair (IRE) (Zindabad (FR)) **h–** [2018/19 b16s b16.8s h20.5g Dec 28] little show in bumpers/maiden hurdle: won first **b71** completed start in points shortly after end of season. *Philip Hobbs*

ARCH MY BOY 5 b.g. Archipenko (USA) – Fairy Slipper (Singspiel (IRE)) [2018/19 **h130 p** b92: h16d* h15.8g* Apr 22] sturdy gelding: 1¾m winner on Flat: useful form over hurdles: won maiden at Fakenham (by 9 lengths from Zanzi Win) in March and novice at Huntingdon (by 30 lengths from Takbeer) in April: remains with potential. *Martin Smith*

ARCHVIEW SUNSHINE (IRE) 10 ch.m. Medaaly – Singing Winds (IRE) (Turtle **c–** Island (IRE)) [2018/19 h21.8g h20.1s h21.2g h20.6g* c24s^{pu} Dec 4] sixth foal: half-sister **h95** to a winner on Flat in Italy by Cape Cross: dam placed at 7f/1m: maiden pointer: 80/1, made all in mares maiden hurdle at Newcastle in November, only form under Rules: left Liam Lennon after first start. *Kenny Johnson*

ARCTIC CHIEF 9 b.g. Sleeping Indian – Neiges Eternelles (FR) (Exit To Nowhere **h90** (USA)) [2018/19 h78: h15.8g^5 h19.6m^6 Oct 4] modest form over hurdles: may prove best around 2m: acts on good to firm going: sometimes in tongue tie. *Richard Phillips*

ARCTIC FIRE (GER) 10 b.g. Soldier Hollow – Adelma (GER) (Sternkoenig (IRE)) **c94** [2018/19 h20m^3 h24d* h16g^4 h20d^4 c16s c20g^4 c20d^F Apr 21] rather leggy gelding: useful **h133** hurdler nowadays: won minor event at Cork in August: well held on completed starts over fences: stays 3m: acts on heavy going: wears hood. *Denis W. Cullen, Ireland*

ARCTIC FOOTPRINT 5 br.m. Blueprint (IRE) – Arctic Flow (Alflora (IRE)) [2018/19 **h–** b16.8s b16.8s h16.8d Feb 22] first foal: dam (c74/h83), 21f hurdle winner (stayed 3m), **b–** half-sister to Midlands Grand National winner Regal Flow: little promise in bumpers/ novice hurdle. *Chris Down*

ARCTIC GOLD (IRE) 8 b.g. Gold Well – Arctic Warrior (IRE) (Arctic Lord) [2018/19 **c121 x** c133x, h123: c23g^2 c24.4g^5 c21.4d^5 c20.6s h23.6d Feb 23] good-topped gelding: has had **h–** breathing operation: useful hurdler/maiden chaser at best, went wrong way in 2018/19: stays 3m: acts on heavy going: front runner/races prominently: often let down by jumping over fences. *Nigel Twiston-Davies*

ARCTIC ROAD 6 b.g. Flemensfirth (USA) – Arctic Actress (King's Theatre (IRE)) **h105**
[2018/19 h15.8g h16.4d h16.7s h23.3s⁶ h21.4d* h20.6d h20.6v* h23d* Apr 26] €58,000
3-y-o, £28,000 5-y-o: first foal: dam (h102), bumper/19f hurdle winner, half-sister to fairly
useful hurdlers/useful chasers up to 3m Wee Robbie and Isn't That Lucky: Irish point
winner: fair handicap hurdler: won at Ayr (conditionals) in February, Newcastle in March
and Bangor in April: stays 23f: acts on heavy going: in cheekpieces last 3 starts: wears
tongue tie. *Oliver Greenall*

ARCTIC VODKA 7 gr.g. Black Sam Bellamy (IRE) – Auntie Kathleen (Terimon) **c–**
[2018/19 h122: h23.3sᵖᵘ h19.3g⁶ c20s h21.4vᵖᵘ Nov 29] fair hurdler at best: no form in **h–**
2018/19, including on chasing debut: tried in cheekpieces: often leads. *Sharon Watt*

ARDAMIR (FR) 7 b.g. Deportivo – Kiss And Cry (FR) (Nikos) [2018/19 h–: h15.8g³ **h115**
h16d Jan 15] good-topped gelding: fairly useful handicap hurdler: fit from Flat, third at
Huntingdon in October: raced around 2m: acts on good to firm going: quirky. *Laura Mongan*

ARD CHROS (IRE) 7 b.g. Publisher (USA) – Threecrossmammies (IRE) (Be My Native **h110 p**
(USA)) [2018/19 h23.3d³ Mar 26] £1,800 3-y-o, £32,000 6-y-o: seventh foal: brother to
fairly useful hurdler/chaser Cross of Honour (2½m/21f winner) and half-brother to winning
pointers by Gothland and Brian Boru: dam placed in points: dual Irish point winner: 33/1,
promising third in novice at Hexham (12 lengths behind Captain CJ) on hurdling debut:
open to improvement. *Stuart Coltherd*

ARDEA (IRE) 11 b.g. Millenary – Dark Dame (IRE) (Norwich) [2018/19 c122: c22.2g⁶ **c–**
Feb 16] multiple point winner: fairly useful hunter chaser at best, well beaten only outing
in 2018/19: stays 3¼m: acts on soft going. *Justin Landy*

ARDERA CROSS (IRE) 8 ch.g. Shantou (USA) – Fair Maid Marion (IRE) (Executive **c115**
Perk) [2018/19 h19.7g h21mᶠ c22g⁶ c25g⁵ h20.7d³ h21.2d³ h24g³ h23.1g² h18.7g² h19.7g² **h116**
c16.2g* Apr 25] has had breathing operation: fairly useful handicap hurdler/chaser: won
over fences at Warwick in April: left Eoin Doyle after fourth start: stays 21f: acts on heavy
going: has worn headgear, including last 5 starts: wears tongue tie nowadays. *Dan Skelton*

ARDGLASS STAR (IRE) 5 b.g. Arctic Cosmos (USA) – Verney Roe (IRE) (Vinnie Roe **h–**
(IRE)) [2018/19 h16.8g³ b17s h16.2g Dec 9] £10,000 3-y-o: second foal: dam unraced **b90**
half-sister to fairly useful hurdler/chaser (2m-2½m winner) Noras Fancy: fair form in
bumpers: better effort when third at Sedgefield in October: well beaten in maiden on
hurdling debut. *Rose Dobbin*

ARDKILLY WITNESS (IRE) 13 b.g. Witness Box (USA) – Ardkilly Angel (IRE) **c–**
(Yashgan) [2018/19 c26.3dᵘʳ Mar 15] strong gelding: multiple point winner: winning **h–**
hurdler: useful chaser at best: unseated fifteenth in Foxhunter at Cheltenham only start
under Rules in 2018/19: stays 25f: acts on heavy going: has worn headgear/tongue tie. *Miss
K. L. Smith*

ARDLETHEN (IRE) 6 ch.g. Arakan (USA) – Itsafamilyaffair (IRE) (Oscar (IRE)) **h131**
[2018/19 h23d³ h23.3s* h23.3d* h24.7d Apr 5] workmanlike gelding: second foal: dam
unraced sister to fairly useful hurdler/chaser (stayed 2½m) Baltiman: won Irish point on
debut: useful form over hurdles: won maiden at Uttoxeter in December and novice at same
course (by 7 lengths from The Cashel Man) in February. *Dan Skelton*

ARDMAYLE (IRE) 7 ch.g. Whitmore's Conn (USA) – Welsh Connection (IRE) (Welsh **c132**
Term) [2018/19 c–, h116: h16v⁴ h17.7v⁴ c15.5d³ c15.5d* Mar 8] compact gelding: fairly **h100**
useful handicap hurdler: below form first 2 starts in 2018/19: useful form over fences: won
handicap at Sandown (by 16 lengths from Lickpenny Larry, avoiding mistakes) in March:
stays 2½m: acts on heavy going. *Ali Stronge*

ARDMILLAN (IRE) 11 b.g. Golan (IRE) – Black Gayle (IRE) (Strong Gale) [2018/19 **c91**
c93, h96: c23.8g⁴ h23g Jun 11] maiden hurdler: modest handicap chaser: left Stuart **h–**
Crawford after first start: stays 3m: acts on heavy going: tried in cheekpieces/tongue tie:
often races towards rear. *David Pipe*

ARDVIEW BOY (IRE) 10 b.g. Tamayaz (CAN) – Cill Uird (IRE) (Phardante (FR)) **c86**
[2018/19 h91: h16g h16m h16m h19.8g c19.2d⁴ c15.6g³ c23.5g c23.5s⁵ h16d Oct 28] **h69**
modest maiden hurdler, below form in 2018/19: modest form in chases: won twice in
points soon after start of season: unproven beyond 17f: acts on heavy and good to firm
going. *J. J. Lambe, Ireland*

ARGANTE (FR) 10 b.g. Singspiel (IRE) – Abyaan (IRE) (Ela-Mana-Mou) [2018/19 h–: **h–**
h20g Nov 20] sturdy gelding: fairly useful 2½m hurdle winner, lightly raced and no form
since 2016/17: tried in cheekpieces. *Henry Spiller*

ARGENT KNIGHT 9 gr.g. Sir Percy – Tussah (Daylami (IRE)) [2018/19 h101: h25m⁶ **h86** May 7] compact gelding: maiden hurdler, fair form at best in 2014/15: tried in headgear. *Christopher Kellett*

ARGOT 8 b.g. Three Valleys (USA) – Tarot Card (Fasliyev (USA)) [2018/19 c114, h–: **c89** c17dᵖᵘ c15.9g⁴ Mar 8] lengthy gelding: multiple point winner: winning hurdler: fairly **h–** useful chaser at best, below form in hunters in 2018/19: stays 21f: acts on heavy going: wears headgear. *J. R. Barlow*

ARGYLE (IRE) 6 gr.g. Lawman (FR) – All Hallows (IRE) (Dalakhani (IRE)) [2018/19 **c–** h108: c17.8gᵘʳ h16s² h15.9d⁵ h16sᵘʳ c17.8vᵖᵘ Mar 16] sturdy gelding: fair handicap **h105** hurdler: failed to complete both starts over fences: unproven beyond 2m: acts on heavy going: wears visor. *Gary Moore*

ARIAN (IRE) 7 b.m. King's Theatre (IRE) – Brave Betsy (IRE) (Pistolet Bleu (IRE)) **c116** [2018/19 h109: h18.5g³ h21.9g c16v² c15.9m⁴ c16.5d⁵ Feb 17] strong mare: has had **h103** breathing operation: fair handicap hurdler: fairly useful form over fences: easily best effort when second in novice at Hereford in December: unproven beyond 2m: best form on soft/heavy going: wears cheekpieces nowadays: in tongue tie last 3 starts: front runner/races prominently. *John Flint*

ARION SKY (IRE) 5 b.m. Jeremy (USA) – Dream Function (IRE) (King's Theatre **b95** (IRE)) [2018/19 b16v³ b16d⁶ b16d* b16d⁶ Feb 25] first foal: dam (c117/h127), 19f hurdle/chase winner, sister to top-class chaser (stayed 3m) Captain Chris out of high-class chaser (best up to 2½m) Function Dream: fairly useful form in bumpers: won mares event at Ayr in February. *Gordon Elliott, Ireland*

ARISTOCLES (IRE) 6 b.g. High Chaparral (IRE) – Amathusia (Selkirk (USA)) **h–** [2018/19 h–: h23.8gᵖᵘ Nov 26] maiden hurdler, lightly raced and no form since 2016/17: wears cheekpieces. *Nikki Evans*

ARISTOCRACY 8 b.g. Royal Applause – Pure Speculation (Salse (USA)) [2018/19 h87: **c–** h23.1gᵖᵘ h23.3g⁵ h23.1m³ h25.5g h23.3s h21.9vᵖᵘ c24gᵖᵘ Apr 25] good-topped gelding: **h81** poor handicap hurdler: pulled up in novice handicap on chasing debut: left Fergal O'Brien after fourth start: stays 27f: acts on good to firm and good to soft going: has worn headgear: tried in tongue tie. *John O'Shea*

ARISTO DU PLESSIS (FR) 9 b.g. Voix du Nord (FR) – J'aime (FR) (Royal Charter **c– §** (FR)) [2018/19 c–, h138: h16m⁵ c17.1dᵖᵘ h16s* h15.7v⁶ h15.6g h20.9g⁴ h16.4g⁵ h16.2g **h130 §** h16.4d⁵ Apr 6] angular gelding: useful handicap hurdler: won at Wetherby (by 1¼ lengths from Cornerstone Lad) in December: largely below form after: no aptitude for chasing: stays 2½m: acts on heavy going: has worn headgear: front runner/races prominently: unreliable. *James Ewart*

ARIZONA BOUND (IRE) 7 b.g. Presenting – Loyal Gesture (IRE) (Darazari (IRE)) **c95** [2018/19 h93, b94: h23.9g c20.1g⁶ c24g³ c23.8g* c23.8gᵖᵘ c24.2g² c23.4gᶠ c24.2g⁶ **h–** c23.4g³ c23.8m⁴ c24.2v² c24.2d⁵ h23.9g Apr 24] maiden hurdler: modest handicap chaser: won at Perth in August: stays 3m: acts on heavy going: wears cheekpieces. *Lucinda Russell*

ARKWRISHT (FR) 9 b.g. Lavirco (GER) – Latitude (FR) (Kadalko (FR)) [2018/19 **c119** c141, h–: c16d³ c24dᵖᵘ c24.5g c28.7dᵘʳ c26dᶠ c29d Apr 22] well-made gelding: winning **h–** hurdler: useful chaser at best, disappointing in 2018/19: stays 29f: acts on heavy going: tried in cheekpieces: usually wears tongue tie. *Joseph Patrick O'Brien, Ireland*

ARKYN (FR) 4 ch.g. Champs Elysees – Fever Fever (USA) (Elusive Quality (USA)) **b91** [2018/19 b13.1g⁵ b14d³ ab16s* ab16g⁵ Feb 18] compact gelding: sixth foal: closely related to French/US 7f/1m winner Hijra (by Oratorio) and half-brother to fairly useful French hurdler Hot Motive (17f/2¼m winner, by Motivator): dam French 1m winner: fair form in bumpers: won at Lingfield in January. *Alan King*

ARMAANS WISH (IRE) 8 ch.g. Presenting – Pretty Puttens (IRE) (Snurge) [2018/19 **h106** h16g² bal 4] bumper winner: off 2 years, 13/8, second in novice at Worcester (4½ lengths behind Robin des Mana) on hurdling debut: dead. *Nicky Henderson*

ARMATTIEKAN (IRE) 5 b.g. Arakan (USA) – Serpentine Mine (IRE) (Rashar (USA)) **h93** [2018/19 b16.7g h18.6g⁶ h16.2g⁵ h15.8d h19.6g³ h19.6d³ Apr 26] €6,800 3-y-o, £15,000 **b–** 4-y-o: second foal: half-brother to modest hurdler Maureen's Star (3m winner, by Gold Well): dam unraced half-sister to dams of useful hurdlers/smart chasers Spiritofthegames (stays 21f) and Breedsbreeze (stayed 3m): fourth in Irish point: well beaten in bumper: modest form over hurdles: stays 2½m: acts on good to soft going. *Donald McCain*

ARMEDANDBEAUTIFUL 11 b.m. Oscar (IRE) – Grey Mistral (Terimon) [2018/19 **c–** c84, h90: c23.9g c22.6gᵖᵘ Sep 4] angular mare: maiden hurdler/chaser, no form over fences **h–** in 2018/19: wears headgear nowadays: tried in tongue tie. *Tom Gretton*

AR MEST (FR) 6 bl.g. Diamond Boy (FR) – Shabada (FR) (Cadoudal (FR)) [2018/19 **h125**
h113, b91: h16v h19.5d³ h15.5g* h16.3d* h15.7d⁵ Feb 16] close-coupled gelding: fairly
useful handicap hurdler: won at Leicester in December and Newbury in January: stays 19f:
acts on heavy going. *Gary Moore*

ARMOROUS 8 b.g. Generous (IRE) – Armorine (FR) (Jeune Homme (USA)) [2018/19 **h–**
h–: h21.7g h19.5g Oct 30] failed to complete in 3 points: little form over hurdles: has worn
hood. *Tom Weston*

ARMY BOOTS 6 b.g. Great Palm (USA) – Cool Katrina (Karinga Bay) [2018/19 **b–**
b16.7mᵘʳ Aug 5] tailed off when saddle slipped and rider unseated around 4f out in bumper
at Market Rasen. *Steve Gollings*

ARNICA 6 b.g. Champs Elysees – Cordoba (Oasis Dream) [2018/19 b16s⁵ b16d⁴ b16.4m³ **b82**
Mar 28] 14,000 3-y-o: third foal: brother to fair hurdler Included (2m/17f winner): dam 11f
winner: modest form in bumpers. *N. W. Alexander*

ARQALINA (IRE) 7 b.m. Arcano (IRE) – Pride Celebre (IRE) (Peintre Celebre (USA)) **h83**
[2018/19 h19.6vᵖᵘ h18.5v h19.7d³ h19.5d⁶ h23.9s* h23.1s Mar 18] ex-French mare: poor
handicap hurdler: won novice event at Ffos Las in February: stays 3m: acts on soft going.
Venetia Williams

ARQUEBUSIER (FR) 9 br.g. Discover d'Auteuil (FR) – Djurjura (FR) (Akarad (FR)) **c89**
[2018/19 c94, h–: c20g⁵ c21.6d⁶ c20d* c21.6s³ c22.7g⁵ c19.4d⁶ Apr 6] sturdy gelding: has **h–**
had breathing operation: winning hurdler: modest handicap chaser: won at Warwick in
December: stays 21f: acts on heavy going: wears headgear/tongue tie: usually races close
up. *Emma-Jane Bishop*

ARRIVEDERCI (FR) 4 gr.g. Martaline – Etoile d'Ainay (FR) (Dom Alco (FR)) **b94**
[2018/19 b16.2v* b16.8d⁴ Feb 22] sixth foal: dam, useful French hurdler/fairly useful
chaser (17f-3¼m winner), closely related to high-class hurdler/useful chaser (stayed 29f)
Crystal d'Ainay: fair form in bumpers: won junior event at Hereford in December. *Jonjo
O'Neill*

ARTFUL ARTIST (IRE) 10 b.g. Excellent Art – Silly Goose (IRE) (Sadler's Wells **h117**
(USA)) [2018/19 h16g² h15.7g* h16.7m Jul 21] fairly useful hurdler: won maiden at
Southwell in June: left A. J. Martin after final 2017/18 start: stays 2¼m: acts on good to soft
going: usually tongue tied prior to 2018/19. *Dr Richard Newland*

ARTHINGTON 6 b.g. Haafhd – Pequenita (Rudimentary (USA)) [2018/19 h127: h19.2s⁵ **h134**
h16v h15.3g h16s* h17.7s² h15.9g² h15.7m² Apr 20] compact gelding: useful handicap
hurdler: won at Lingfield in January: second at Haydock (head behind Cubswin) in April:
stays 2¼m: acts on good to firm and heavy going. *Seamus Mullins*

ARTHUR MAC (IRE) 6 ch.g. Getaway (GER) – Orchardstown Moss (IRE) (Lord of **h128**
Appeal) [2018/19 b101: h20.1s⁴ h16.7v⁴ h19.3g* h22s² h19.9s* h24.7d⁵ Apr 5] sturdy
gelding: bumper winner: fairly useful form over hurdles: won maiden at Catterick in
December and novice at Sedgefield in March: left Philip Hobbs after first start: stays 25f:
acts on heavy going. *Henry Oliver*

ARTHUR'S GIFT (IRE) 8 b.g. Presenting – Uncertain Affair (IRE) (Darshaan) [2018/19 **c133**
h130: c25g⁴ c19.2s c24.5s* c34vᵖᵘ Mar 16] rangy gelding: useful hurdler: similar form **h–**
over fences: won handicap at Carlisle (by 5 lengths from Len Brennan) in February: stays
25f: acts on soft and good to firm going. *Nigel Twiston-Davies*

ARTHUR'S QUEEN (FR) 8 b.m. Soldier of Fortune (IRE) – Tintagel (Oasis Dream) **h–**
[2018/19 h–: h16.8m h18.5g Jun 4] little form over hurdles. *Carroll Gray*

ARTHUR'S REUBEN 6 b.g. Malinas (GER) – Ambitious Annie (Most Welcome) **c90**
[2018/19 h89: h24gᵖᵘ h23.4g⁴ h25g³ c23.6d³ c23.6g* c23.6d³ c23.6d³ c24gꟳ Mar 28] **h77**
lengthy gelding: has had breathing operation: poor maiden hurdler: modest form over
fences: won maiden at Huntingdon in January: stays 25f: acts on good to soft going:
wears cheekpieces/tongue tie. *Jennie Candlish*

ARTHURS SECRET 9 ch.g. Sakhee's Secret – Angry Bark (USA) (Woodman (USA)) **h121**
[2018/19 h116: h20.1g h25.4g⁶ h21.4v² h23.8g² h21.4s⁴ h25.8g⁵ h24.3d* h25.8g³ h24.3m⁶
Apr 12] fairly useful handicap hurdler: won at Ayr in February: stays 3¼m: acts on good to
firm and heavy going: has worn headgear, including last 3 starts. *Sandy Thomson*

ARTHUR'S SECRET (FR) 9 b.g. Secret Singer (FR) – Luna Park (FR) (Cyborg (FR)) **c126**
[2018/19 c23s* c22.6dᵖᵘ c23.8g* c20d* c22.6gᵖᵘ Apr 14] multiple point winner: winning **h–**
hurdler: fairly useful hunter chaser: won at Worcester in May, and at Ludlow in February
and March: stays 3m: acts on soft going: has worn hood: tried in tongue tie: usually leads,
often travels strongly. *Martin Weston*

ARTHUR'S SIXPENCE 5 b.g. Vinnie Roe (IRE) – Loose Change (IRE) (Snurge) **h86**
[2018/19 h19.6g⁴ h19.9gᵖᵘ h15.8d² h21.3gᵖᵘ Apr 11] rather unfurnished gelding: has had breathing operation: first foal: dam, maiden pointer, half-sister to fairly useful hurdler (stayed 2½m) Regal Diamond (by Vinnie Roe): point winner: modest form over hurdles: should be suited by 2½m+: tried in tongue tie. *Kim Bailey*

ARTICHOKE HEART 4 b.f. Shantou (USA) – Seedless (Mtoto) [2018/19 b12.4s² **b77**
b12.4g⁵ b16.7d⁶ Apr 26] second foal: dam (c118/h119), 2½m-3m hurdle/chase winner, half-sister to useful hurdler (2m/17f winner) Seedling: modest form in bumpers. *Donald McCain*

ARTICLE FIFTY (IRE) 6 b.g. Doyen (IRE) – Annie Go (IRE) (Golan (IRE)) [2018/19 **h78**
h111, b96: h18.5d h19.7g Feb 19] sturdy gelding: has had breathing operation: point/bumper winner: maiden hurdler, well held both starts in 2018/19: usually front runner/races prominently. *Warren Greatrex*

ARTICLE OF WAR (IRE) 6 b.g. Definite Article – Form A Circle (IRE) (Topanoora) **h–**
[2018/19 b15.7g h20.6m⁶ Apr 21] tailed off in bumper/maiden hurdle. *Louise Allan* **b–**

ARTIC NEL 5 ch.m. Haafhd – Artic Bliss (Fraam) [2018/19 h15.8g⁴ Oct 16] has had **h93**
breathing operation: dam, 2m hurdle winner, half-sister to useful hurdler (stayed 3m) Mexican Pete: modest on Flat, stays 2m: 66/1, fourth in novice at Huntingdon (18¼ lengths behind Denmead) on hurdling debut. *Ian Williams*

ARTICULUM (IRE) 9 b.g. Definite Article – Lugante (IRE) (Luso) [2018/19 h132: **c140**
c16d² c16d* c15.9s³ Mar 12] sturdy gelding: useful hurdler: useful form over fences: won **h–**
3-runner novice at Naas (by 7½ lengths from Campeador) in January: third in Arkle Chase at Cheltenham (16¼ lengths behind Duc des Genievres) in March: unproven beyond 2m: acts on heavy going: wears tongue tie: usually races close up. *Terence O'Brien, Ireland*

ARTISTE DU GOUET (FR) 9 b.g. Lavirco (GER) – Newhaven (FR) (Subotica (FR)) **c–**
[2018/19 h19.5s h15.5g⁵ Dec 2] big, lengthy, workmanlike gelding: maiden hurdler: no **h–**
show over fences: tried in tongue tie. *Barry Brennan*

ART MAURESQUE (FR) 9 b.g. Policy Maker (IRE) – Modeva (FR) (Valanour (IRE)) **c148**
[2018/19 c155, h–: c19.4d c23.8m² c19.9d c24g⁵ c23.8dᶠ Feb 16] rangy gelding: has **h–**
reportedly had breathing operation: winning hurdler: smart handicap chaser: second in Sodexo Gold Cup at Ascot (½ length behind Traffic Fluide) in November: barely stays 3m: acts on good to firm and heavy going: has worn headgear. *Paul Nicholls*

ARTOFF (IRE) 4 ch.g. Notnowcato – Be Airlie (IRE) (Lord Americo) [2018/19 b16m Apr **b–**
13] runner-up in point on debut: little impression in bumper. *Keith Dalgleish*

ART OF SECURITY (IRE) 9 b.g. High Chaparral (IRE) – Irish Wedding (IRE) (Bob **c–**
Back (USA)) [2018/19 h20g* h22.8d⁶ c17dᵘʳ c21.2g c16d c19d c20s c20g Feb 24] fairly **h132**
useful on Flat, stays 17f: useful handicap hurdler: won at Ballinrobe (by 11 lengths from Bargy Lady) in May: no form over fences: stays 2½m: acts on soft going: has worn tongue tie, including last 6 starts. *Noel Meade, Ireland*

ART OF SUPREMACY (IRE) 7 b.g. Milan – Marble Desire (IRE) (Un Desperado **c–**
(FR)) [2018/19 c–, h103: h19.7s Dec 26] maiden hurdler, modest at best: pulled up only **h–**
chase start: dead. *Micky Hammond*

ARTY CAMPBELL (IRE) 9 b.g. Dylan Thomas (IRE) – Kincob (USA) (Kingmambo **h105**
(USA)) [2018/19 h100: h20g h21.6g⁶ h21.7g* h21.4f² Oct 28] workmanlike gelding: fair handicap hurdler: won at Hereford in October: stays 2¾m: acts on firm and soft going: normally wears cheekpieces: usually races towards rear. *Bernard Llewellyn*

ARVERNE (FR) 4 b.g. Doctor Dino (FR) – Argovie (FR) (Alberto Giacometti (IRE)) **h112**
[2018/19 h17.4s³ h17.4s* h16s³ Dec 27] second foal: dam (h112), French 2m/2¼m hurdle winner (also 11.5f winner on Flat), half-sister to fairly useful French hurdler/smart chaser up to 2¾m Parigny: fourth over 15f only start on Flat: fair form over hurdles: won juvenile at Auteuil in November: 10/1, 22¼ lengths third of 5 to Quel Destin in Finale Juvenile Hurdle at Chepstow next time. *A. Lacombe, France*

ARVICO BLEU (IRE) 7 b.g. Arvico (FR) – Sharifa (GER) (King's Theatre (IRE)) **c139**
[2018/19 h16v⁶ c17g⁴ c17d² c16g² c16.5g² c16d³ c16.3gᶠ Feb 7] third foal: dam, ran twice **h–**
on Flat, closely related to smart bumper winner Samain: fairly useful hurdler: useful form over fences, placed 4 times: just in front when fell last in maiden at Thurles final start: best form around 2m: acts on soft going: tried in tongue tie: front runner/races prominently. *Henry de Bromhead, Ireland*

ARVICO'S LIGHT 5 b.g. Arvico (FR) – Miss Lightning (Mujahid (USA)) [2018/19 **b–**
b16d Apr 6] tailed off in bumper. *Sarah-Jayne Davies*

ASANGY (ITY) 7 b.g. Gentlewave (IRE) – Art Naif (IRE) (Desert King (IRE)) [2018/19 **c101** c21.2g³ c22.6d^{pu} c20.2f* c20.9s² Mar 11] dam half-sister to fairly useful hurdler (stayed **h–** 2¾m) Universal Truth: fairly useful on Flat, stays 1½m: winning pointer: twice-raced hurdler: fair form in chases: won hunter at Leicester in February: stays 21f: acts on firm and soft going: usually races off pace. *Richard Edwards*

ASCENDANT 13 ch.g. Medicean – Ascendancy (Sadler's Wells (USA)) [2018/19 c–, **c–** h118: h16g⁸ May 8] well-made gelding: fairly useful hurdler: won conditionals seller at **h114** Fakenham only start in 2018/19: unseated early sole outing over fences: stays 21f: acts on good to firm and heavy going: has worn blinkers/tongue tie. *Johnny Farrelly*

ASCOT DE BRUYERE (FR) 9 b.g. Kapgarde (FR) – Quid de Neuville (FR) (Le **c134** Balafre (FR)) [2018/19 c114, h–: h24.3g c32.4g⁶ c23.4g* c20.1g* c23.4m² Mar 28] **h–** winning hurdler: fairly useful handicap chaser: won at Newcastle in January and February (by 18 lengths from Cave Top): best form up to 23f: acts on heavy going: wears headgear: often leads. *James Ewart*

AS DE PIQUE (IRE) 14 b.g. Woods of Windsor (USA) – Casheral (Le Soleil) [2018/19 **c108 x** c124x, h–: c24d c25g h20m⁶ h24m⁵ h24.3g Aug 5] modest form over hurdles: fairly useful **h94** handicap chaser, below best first 2 starts in 2018/19: stays 31f: acts on soft going: has worn headgear: wears tongue tie: often races towards rear: often let down by jumping over fences. *Gavin Patrick Cromwell, Ireland*

ASHES CORNER (IRE) 9 b.g. Marienbard (IRE) – Up Thyne Girl (IRE) (Good Thyne **c–** (USA)) [2018/19 h20.6d^{pu} c24.1d^{pu} c24.2d^{pu} Mar 26] maiden hurdler: no form in 2018/19 **h–** (including over fences) after long absence: tried in cheekpieces. *Julia Brooke*

ASHKOUL (FR) 6 b.g. Tamayuz – Asharna (IRE) (Darshaan) [2018/19 h125: h15.7g³ **h121** h16.3g³ h17.2m Jul 1] smallish gelding: fairly useful handicap hurdler: third to Silver Streak in Swinton Handicap at Haydock in May: raced around 2m: acts on soft going: wears tongue tie. *Dan Skelton*

ASHOKA (IRE) 7 gr.g. Azamour (IRE) – Jinskys Gift (IRE) (Cadeaux Genereux) **c127** [2018/19 c122, h107: c18g² May 7] well-made gelding: winning hurdler: fairly useful **h–** handicap chaser: stays 19f: acts on good to firm and heavy going: usually in cheekpieces: wears tongue tie: usually races nearer last than first. *Dan Skelton*

ASH PARK (IRE) 11 b.g. Milan – Distant Gale (IRE) (Strong Gale) [2018/19 c125, h–: **c117** c26.9d³ c24.5s^{pu} Feb 18] winning hurdler: fairly useful handicap chaser: third at Ayr in **h–** January after 15 months off: stays 27f: acts on soft and good to firm going: often races in rear. *Stuart Coltherd*

ASHUTOR (FR) 5 gr.g. Redoute's Choice (AUS) – Ashalanda (FR) (Linamix (FR)) **h112** [2018/19 h15.8d² h19.2d² h16s^F h16.7s³ Mar 23] useful on Flat in France for A. de Royer Dupre, stays 1¾m: fair form over hurdles: temperament under suspicion. *Paul Nicholls*

ASK ALICE 6 b.m. Robin des Champs (FR) – Viva Victoria (Old Vic) [2018/19 h–, b72: **h–** h15.7g May 6] poor form in bumpers: none over hurdles: tried in hood. *Martin Keighley*

ASKARI 6 b.g. Sea The Stars (IRE) – Loulwa (IRE) (Montjeu (IRE)) [2018/19 h18.8d **h118** h16.5d h23.1g³ h21.3m³ h19.6g³ h22.7g² h22d* h21s* Jan 1] fairly useful handicap hurdler: won at Navan in December and Tramore in January: stayed 23f: acted on soft going: in blinkers last 3 starts: dead. *Gordon Elliott, Ireland*

ASK BEN (IRE) 6 b.g. Ask – Decheekymonkey (IRE) (Presenting) [2018/19 h22d* **h128** h24.3d* h24.3g² h24d Mar 15] €6,000 3-y-o, £30,000 5-y-o: fourth foal: half-brother to fair chaser Goodgirlteresa (19f winner, by Stowaway): dam placed in point: runner-up on second of 2 starts in Irish points: fairly useful form over hurdles: won novices at Newcastle in December and Ayr in January: second in Prestige Novices' Hurdle at Haydock (10 lengths behind Lisnagar Oscar) next time: will stay beyond 3m. *Graeme McPherson*

ASK CATKIN (IRE) 7 b.m. Ask – Simple Reason (IRE) (Snurge) [2018/19 h95: h19.9g³ **c60** c20d⁶ c20d h23.9g c20.9g^{pu} Mar 26] has had breathing operations: modest maiden hurdler: **h94** well held both starts over fences: should stay 25f: acts on soft going: tried in hood/tongue tie: usually races in rear. *Tom Symonds*

ASK DILLON (IRE) 6 b.g. Ask – Mum's Miracle (IRE) (Luso) [2018/19 h15.7g² h16d² **h129** b16.4g⁵ h21.6s* h18.5d² h21s h21.6s* Apr 16] £40,000 5-y-o: good-topped gelding: **b100** closely related to modest chaser Dushy Valley (3¼m winner, by Dushyantor) and half-brother to fair hurdler Miracle House (2¾m winner, by Carroll House): dam, unraced, half-sister to useful chaser (stayed 3m) Patricksnineteenth: off mark in points at second attempt: fairly useful form in bumpers: likewise over hurdles: won maiden at Ascot in December and novice at Exeter (by 8 lengths from Boldmere) in April: will be suited by 3m. *Fergal O'Brien*

ASK FOR GLORY (IRE) 5 b.g. Fame And Glory – Ask Helen (IRE) (Pistolet Bleu **b107**
(IRE)) [2018/19 b16s* b16.4s Mar 13] £280,000 4-y-o: good-topped gelding: second foal:
dam, ran twice in bumpers, half-sister to fairly useful but temperamental hurdler/chaser
(stayed 3¼m) Montroe: easy winner of Irish point on debut: useful form in bumpers: won
at Chepstow (by 13 lengths from Imperial Esprit) in December. *Paul Nicholls*

ASK HIMSELF (IRE) 5 ch.g. Ask – Wintry Day (IRE) (Presenting) [2018/19 b16v² **b93**
b16.4v⁴ Mar 16] €21,000 3-y-o: fifth foal: closely related to bumper winner/useful
hurdler One For The Guv'nr (2m winner, by Oscar): dam, lightly raced over hurdles, half-
sister to fair hurdler/useful chaser (stayed 3m) Somemanforoneman: third in Irish point on
debut: fair form in bumpers: better effort when second at Chepstow in December. *Michael
Scudamore*

ASKING A LOT (IRE) 6 ch.m. Ask – Millbrook Marble (IRE) (Rudimentary (USA)) **h–**
[2018/19 h21.6gᵖᵘ h20g Aug 15] €5,000 3-y-o, £15,000 5-y-o: third foal: half-sister to
useful hurdler/chaser Woods Well (2½m-2¾m winner, by Fleetwood): dam maiden in
bumpers/over hurdles: off mark in Irish points at sixth attempt: little show over hurdles:
wears tongue tie. *Grace Harris*

ASKING FOR ANSWERS (IRE) 6 ch.g. Ask – Equation (IRE) (Lahib (USA)) **h88**
[2018/19 h17.1d h20.5vᵖᵘ h20.5s h20.5d h21.4d⁵ h24.3sᵘʳ Mar 9] €15,000 3-y-o: first foal:
dam (c97/h104), 2¼m hurdle winner (stayed 3m), half-sister to Scottish Grand National
winner Hello Bud: placed on second of 2 starts in Irish points: modest form over hurdles.
Martin Todhunter

ASKING QUESTIONS (IRE) 7 b.g. Ask – Just Sara (IRE) (Insan (USA)) [2018/19 **c109**
c113, h96: h20.3g² c25g c25.1g³ Nov 22] lengthy gelding: fair maiden hurdler: fair **h101**
handicap chaser: stays 25f: acts on heavy going: wears headgear/tongue tie: front runner/
races prominently. *Oliver Greenall*

ASK JILLY 6 b.m. Passing Glance – Heebie Jeebie (Overbury (IRE)) [2018/19 b15.7m **h–**
h15.8d h16d h15.3s Mar 7] second foal: dam (h84), maiden hurdler (stayed 19f), half-sister **b–**
to fairly useful hurdler (stayed 2¾m) Whistlejacquet: no form in bumper/over hurdles.
Martin Bosley

ASK LAUNA ESME (IRE) 6 ch.m. Ask – Nativebaltic (IRE) (Be My Native (USA)) **h–**
[2018/19 h16.8v Oct 12] seventh foal: half-sister to fairly useful hurdler Quickasyoucan
(3m winner, by Beneficial): dam unraced daughter of useful chaser up to 3m Baltic Brown:
unplaced in points: tailed off in novice on hurdling debut. *Jimmy Frost*

ASK MADGE (IRE) 7 ch.m. Ask – Wire Lady (IRE) (Second Set (IRE)) [2018/19 h16.2g **h–**
h22.1g⁵ May 30] €800 3-y-o: closely related to fairly useful hurdler One For Hocky (2m-
3m winner, by Brian Boru) and half-sister to bumper winner Lord Gale (by Bach): dam
unraced: little form over hurdles: tried in tongue tie. *Noel C. Kelly, Ireland*

ASKMEWHY (IRE) 5 b.g. Ask – Grey Clouds (Cloudings (IRE)) [2018/19 b16d Jan 4] **b–**
40/1, eighth in bumper at Wetherby. *Chris Grant*

ASK NILE (IRE) 7 b.g. Ask – Spirit of The Nile (FR) (Generous (IRE)) [2018/19 c131, **c133**
h95: h20s h24g³ c20d⁶ h16g⁴ h20g h16g² c20d³ c21.3s² h20.2s⁶ Apr 5] fairly useful **h125**
handicap hurdler: useful handicap chaser: second at Leopardstown (¾ length behind
Woods Well) in March: stays 3m: acts on heavy going: wears headgear: tried in tongue tie.
Seamus Neville, Ireland

ASKNOTWHAT (IRE) 8 ch.g. Dylan Thomas (IRE) – Princess Roseburg (USA) **c64**
(Johannesburg (USA)) [2018/19 c16s⁶ c17.8v⁴ c17.2dᵖᵘ h20.6g² h19.6g⁴ Apr 13] sturdy **h89**
gelding: modest maiden hurdler: little show over fences: left Kerry Lee after second start:
stays 21f: acts on good to firm going: has worn headgear, including in 2018/19: in tongue
tie last 3 starts. *Tom Gretton*

ASK PADDINGTON (IRE) 5 ch.g. Ask – Dual Obsession (Saddlers' Hall (IRE)) **h113**
[2018/19 b–: b15.7g³ b16.2g² b16.2g* h16.2g⁶ h16.2g³ h16.8g³ h21.2g* h20.9g* h21.3g⁶ **b96**
Apr 11] fairly useful form in bumpers: won 3-runner race at Perth in July: fair form over
hurdles: won maiden at Sedgefield in November and handicap at Kelso in March: stays
21f: best form on good going: usually wears hood: front runner/races prominently.
Micky Hammond

ASK PADDY (IRE) 7 ch.g. Ask – Dalzenia (FR) (Cadoudal (FR)) [2018/19 c103p, h–: **c99 p**
c19.2m² h24.1g Apr 11] sturdy gelding: fair hurdler at best: modest form both starts over **h–**
fences: stays 3¼m: acts on soft and good to firm going: tried in tongue tie: remains open to
improvement over fences. *Sam England*

ASK ROBIN (IRE) 7 b.g. Robin des Champs (FR) – Ask June (IRE) (Shernazar) **h91**
[2018/19 h20m⁴ Jul 9] half-brother to fair hurdler/fairly useful chaser Davinia's Tip
(2m/17f winner, by Presenting) and closely related/half-brother to 3 winning pointers: dam
(h108) 2½m bumper/2m hurdle winner: off mark in Irish points at third attempt: 7/2, some
encouragement when fourth of 5 in novice at Worcester (14 lengths behind Play The Ace)
on hurdling debut, but not seen out again. *Jamie Snowden*

ASKRUMOR (IRE) 6 b.m. Ask – Star of Hope (IRE) (Turtle Island (IRE)) [2018/19 **b–**
b16.3d Jun 8] fourth foal: half-sister to useful hurdler/fairly useful chaser Ah Littleluck
(2½m-3m winner, by Mahler): dam unraced half-sister to fairly useful hurdler/useful
chaser Scoop The Pot: maiden pointer: tailed off in bumper (wore cheekpieces/
tongue tie). *Mrs Sherree Lean*

ASK SHANROE (IRE) 7 b.g. Ask – Lady Quesada (IRE) (Alflora (IRE)) [2018/19 h–, **c–**
b–: c19.3g⁵ Oct 21] compact gelding: no form under Rules. *Mark Campion* **h–**

ASK THE TYCOON (IRE) 6 b.g. Ask – Mountainviewqueen (IRE) (Norwich) **h101**
[2018/19 h102, b90: h20.2g⁵ h19.5v³ h20.1s⁵ h24.3s⁶ h24.3dᵖᵘ Feb 25] off mark in Irish
points at third attempt: bumper winner: fair maiden hurdler: stays 2½m: acts on heavy
going: in visor last 4 starts: also in tongue tie last 2. *Lucinda Russell*

ASK THE WEATHERMAN 10 b.g. Tamure (IRE) – Whatagale (Strong Gale) [2018/19 **c122 §**
c134: h23.1v* c25.1g⁴ c23.8s Apr 7] sturdy gelding: has had breathing operation: fair form **h111**
when won novice at Exeter (by 2 lengths from Shamilan) in December, only outing over
hurdles: useful chaser at best: stays 3¼m: acts on heavy going: wears headgear: usually
races close up, but often lazily: temperamental. *Jack R. Barber*

ASOCKASTAR (IRE) 11 b.g. Milan – Baie Barbara (IRE) (Heron Island (IRE)) **c118**
[2018/19 c–§, h72§: c26.3g² c27.5d² c22.7m* c26.3d c21.1dᵖᵘ Apr 4] compact gelding: **h–**
winning hurdler: fairly useful chaser: won novice hunter at Leicester in February: second
in Stratford Champion Hunters' Chase 8 months earlier: stays 3½m: acts on soft and good
to firm going: wears headgear: tried in tongue tie: front runner/races prominently. *Daniel
John Bourne*

ASO (FR) 9 b.g. Goldneyev (USA) – Odyssee du Cellier (FR) (Dear Doctor (FR)) [2018/19 **c166**
c137, h–: c19.9d* c20.6d* c21d⁶ c20.6d² Mar 14] useful-looking gelding: winning hurdler: **h–**
top-class chaser, better than ever in 2018/19: won handicaps at Newbury (by 13 lengths
from Touch Kick) in November and Cheltenham (Grade 3, by 2 lengths from Happy Diva)
in January: second in Ryanair Chase (Festival Trophy) at Cheltenham (1¼ lengths behind
Frodon) in March: stays 3m: acts on heavy going: has worn cheekpieces. *Venetia Williams*

*Download The BetBright App Handicap Chase, Cheltenham—a fine weight-carrying performance
by Aso who keeps on too well for the smart mare Happy Diva*

ASPEN COLORADO (IRE) 7 b.g. Galileo (IRE) – St Roch (IRE) (Danehill (USA))   **c– x**
[2018/19 c19.7g^F h24g h24.3g h20d* h20g* h25s^5 h19.9v^{pu} h24d Mar 14] compact   **h128**
gelding: has had breathing operation: fairly useful handicap hurdler: won at Carlisle in
October and November: didn't take to chasing: left Joseph Patrick O'Brien after third start:
barely stays 25f: acts on soft going: has worn headgear/tongue tie: usually races towards
rear, often lazily. *Jonjo O'Neill*

ASTAROLAND (FR) 9 b.g. Astarabad (USA) – Orlandaise (FR) (Goldneyev (USA))   **h94**
[2018/19 h98: h21.2m^4 h20g^4 Jun 15] good-topped gelding: modest handicap hurdler:
barely stays 21f: tried in cheekpieces: has worn tongue tie, including last 5 starts. *Jennie Candlish*

AS THE CROW FLIES (IRE) 8 b.g. Presenting – Regle d'Or (FR) (Robin des Champs   **h–**
(FR)) [2018/19 h16s h20.5d h20d Apr 7] multiple point winner: no form over hurdles. *Sean McParlan, Ireland*

ASTHURIA (FR) 8 b.m. Sagacity (FR) – Baturia (FR) (Turgeon (USA)) [2018/19 c138,   **c131**
h131: c16g c19.5d* h19.4s^6 Jun 9] smallish mare: useful hurdler: useful chaser: won mares   **h144**
event at Limerick (by 2½ lengths from Teacher's Pet) in May: stays 2½m: acts on heavy
going: wears hood: usually leads. *W. P. Mullins, Ireland*

ASTIGOS (FR) 12 b.g. Trempolino (USA) – Astonishing (BRZ) (Vacilante (ARG))   **c86 §**
[2018/19 c88§, h–§: c24.1g^6 c23.8s^5 c25.3v^4 Dec 17] sturdy gelding: winning hurdler: **h– §**
fairly useful chaser at best: stayed 3¼m: acted on heavy going: often in headgear earlier in
career: tried in tongue tie: ungenuine: dead. *Lady Susan Brooke*

ASTRACAD (FR) 13 br.g. Cadoudal (FR) – Astre Eria (FR) (Garde Royale) [2018/19   **c107**
c120, h–: c23.8g^{pu} c20.2m^2 c19.4g^F c22.7m^3 c19.9d^2 c23.4d* c21.3g^6 c23.9m^2 Apr 21]   **h–**
sturdy gelding: winning hurdler: fair handicap chaser nowadays: won at Newcastle in
March: stays 23f: acts on soft and good to firm going: has worn headgear/tongue tie:
usually front runner/races prominently. *Nigel Twiston-Davies*

ASTRA VIA 4 b.f. Multiplex – Wou Oodd (Barathea (IRE)) [2018/19 h15.8g h16v^4 **h93**
h16.2d^2 h15.8v^2 Mar 16] fifth foal: sister to fairly useful hurdler/useful chaser Positively
Dylan (15f-2¾m winner): dam, maiden on Flat (stayed 1½m), half-sister to fairly useful
hurdler (2m-2½m winner) Elyaadi: modest form over hurdles. *Evan Williams*

ASTROFIRE 4 b.f. Kheleyf (USA) – Astromancer (USA) (Silver Hawk (USA)) [2018/19   **h–**
h16d^6 Nov 28] no form on Flat: tailed off in juvenile maiden on hurdling debut. *Mark H. Tompkins*

ASTUTE BOY (IRE) 5 b.g. Arcano (IRE) – Spa (Sadler's Wells (USA)) [2018/19   **h100**
h15.8g^5 h16d^2 h16.2g^4 h15.6g h15.6g Nov 26] fairly useful on Flat, stays 1¾m: fair form
over hurdles: left Harry Fry after second start: raced only at 2m: acts on good to soft going:
usually in tongue tie. *R. Mike Smith*

ASUM 8 b.g. Kayf Tara – Candy Creek (IRE) (Definite Article) [2018/19 h120: c16.2m   **c116**
c19.2m^{ur} c20.1g^{ur} c20.5g^3 c20.5v^2 c20.3g^5 Nov 26] fairly useful hurdler: similar form over   **h–**
fences: second in novice handicap at Ayr in November: will stay 2¾m+: acts on heavy
going: has worn hood: wears tongue tie: often leads. *Philip Kirby*

ASYLO (IRE) 7 b.g. Flemensfirth (USA) – Escrea (IRE) (Oscar (IRE)) [2018/19 h108, b–:   **h119**
h19.8v h19.9d* h19d^5 h19.9s^{pu} Dec 31] bumper winner: fairly useful form over hurdles:
won handicap at Uttoxeter in November: stays 2½m: acts on soft going: in cheekpieces last
3 starts. *Dr Richard Newland*

AS YOU LIKE (IRE) 8 b.g. Beneficial – Rubys Shadow (IRE) (Supreme Leader)   **c114**
[2018/19 c84, h110: c21.4g* c19.4m* c21g^2 c21g^2 Aug 21] fair hurdler: fair handicap   **h–**
chaser: won at Market Rasen and Ffos Las in June: stays 21f: acts on good to firm and good
to soft going: often travels strongly. *Jonjo O'Neill*

ATAGUISEAMIX (FR) 6 b.g. Al Namix (FR) – Olafane (FR) (Le Balafre (FR))   **h104 ?**
[2018/19 h–: h16.8m^3 h16.5d^5 h16.5d h23.1s^F Mar 5] lengthy gelding: has had breathing
operation: runner-up sole start in Irish points: easily best effort (fair form) over hurdles
when last of 9 finishers in novice at Exeter: tried in hood/tongue tie: usually races off pace,
often freely. *Susan Gardner*

A TAIL OF INTRIGUE (IRE) 11 b.g. Tillerman – Princess Commanche (IRE)   **c111 x**
(Commanche Run) [2018/19 c107x, h–: c24.2v^4 c26.3s^6 c24.2d^4 c24.2d Mar 8]   **h–**
workmanlike gelding: winning hurdler: fair chaser nowadays: left Katy Price after second
start: stays 3m: acts on good to firm and heavy going: has worn headgear: often let down
by jumping. *Joanne Priest*

ATALANTA'S GOLD (IRE) 6 b.m. Arcadio (GER) – Sandy Desert (Selkirk (USA)) **h99**
[2018/19 h82: h16g⁴ h15.7g* h20.6g² h19.2g Jun 16] modest handicap hurdler: won at
Towcester (conditionals) in May: stays 21f. *Gary Moore*

ATAMAN (IRE) 7 b.g. Sholokhov (IRE) – Diora (IRE) (Dashing Blade) [2018/19 h79: **h–**
h16.3g⁵ h17.7g⁶ Aug 30] sturdy gelding: poor maiden hurdler: in headgear last 2 starts: has
worn tongue tie, including last 4 starts: usually races towards rear. *Olly Murphy*

AT FIRST LIGHT 10 b.m. Echo of Light – Bisaat (USA) (Bahri (USA)) [2018/19 h59§: **h91**
h15.9s³ Feb 13] lengthy mare: modest handicap hurdler, very lightly raced nowadays: stays
2¾m: acts on heavy going: tried in hood: temperamental. *David Weston*

ATHREEOTHREE (IRE) 8 b.g. Presenting – Lucina (GER) (Groom Dancer (USA)) **c–**
[2018/19 h–: h21.4m³ h23s⁵ c20.9m c25.8gᵖᵘ Jul 6] multiple point winner: poor form over **h84**
hurdles: no show in 2 chases: wears blinkers: temperament under suspicion. *Jack R. Barber*

ATIRELARIGO (FR) 9 b.g. Puit d'Or (IRE) – Ouchka (FR) (April Night (FR)) [2018/19 **c112 x**
c19.4s⁴ c19.4v⁵ Dec 8] fairly useful handicap hurdler/chaser at best, off 20 months before **h–**
return: will stay 3m: acts on soft going: often let down by jumping over fences. *Philip Hobbs*

AT ITS OWN EXPENSE (IRE) 5 ch.g. Arakan (USA) – Blow A Gasket (IRE) **h118**
(Topanoora) [2018/19 b15.3g³ b16.2s³ h19d³ h19d* h19d³ Apr 4] €5,000 3-y-o: fifth foal: **b93**
dam unraced half-sister to fairly useful hurdler/fair chaser (stayed 2½m) Greenhall
Rambler: unplaced in Irish point: fair form in bumpers: better effort when third at Hereford:
fairly useful form over hurdles: won novice at Taunton in February: will stay 2½m.
Philip Hobbs

ATLANTA ABLAZE 8 b.m. Kayf Tara – Rocheflamme (FR) (Snurge) [2018/19 c–, h–: **c140**
c21.6g² c24g⁵ c20.9m³ c24.1g* c20.9g* c23.9g³ c20d* c20.5gᵘʳ c25.1g* c31.7sᶠ c23.8dᵖᵘ **h–**
Apr 26] well-made mare: has had breathing operation: winning hurdler: useful chaser: won
handicaps at Bangor in August and Hereford (mares) in October, and listed mares races at
Warwick (novice, by 19 lengths from Jester Jet) in December and Wincanton (by 15
lengths from Molly Childers) in February: stays 25f: acts on soft and good to firm going:
tried in tongue tie: usually races close up, often travels strongly. *Henry Daly*

ATLANTIC BREAKER (IRE) 9 b.g. Broadway Flyer (USA) – Alder Hall (IRE) **c–**
(Saddlers' Hall (IRE)) [2018/19 c21.4gᵖᵘ c16.4gᵖᵘ Apr 23] medium-sized gelding: winning **h–**
hurdler: maiden chaser, no form in 2018/19 after long absence: stays 2½m: acts on heavy
going: wears blinkers: in tongue tie last 2 starts: usually races off pace. *Sean Conway*

ATLANTIC GREY (IRE) 6 gr.g. Acambaro (GER) – Clooney Eile (IRE) (Definite **h93**
Article) [2018/19 h108: h21.2g h23.3g⁵ h18.5g* h21.6gᵖᵘ h16.3g⁵ h16.5d h16.8g Apr 20]
smallish, lengthy gelding: has had breathing operation: modest hurdler: won seller at
Newton Abbot in September: left Nigel Twiston-Davies after second start, Nigel Hawke
after third: stays 2½m: acts on good to soft going: has worn blinkers: tried in tongue tie.
Jimmy Frost

ATLANTIC STORM (IRE) 7 b.g. September Storm (GER) – Double Dream (IRE) **c117**
(Double Eclipse) [2018/19 c–p, h95: h16.7g² c15.7g* c16g² c17.2m² h16.7g³ **h110**
h16.3g⁴ c19.4g⁵ c16g⁵ c20d⁴ h16s³ Jan 21] good-topped gelding: fair hurdler: won seller
at Stratford in October: fairly useful handicap chaser: won at Southwell in June: left Dan
Skelton after fifth start, David Rees after sixth: unproven beyond 17f: acts on soft going:
has worn headgear: wears tongue tie: often races towards rear. *Rob Summers*

ATLANTIC SUNSHINE 4 b.f. Fight Club (GER) – Atlantic Lady (GER) (Dashing **b–**
Blade) [2018/19 b16.3d Mar 1] lengthy, unfurnished filly: third foal: dam (h84), lightly
raced over hurdles, 7.5f-1¼m winner on Flat in Germany: well beaten in mares bumper.
Nikki Evans

ATLAS (IRE) 6 b.g. Acclamation – Sheer Bliss (IRE) (Sadler's Wells (USA)) [2018/19 **h94**
h16g⁶ h16.7g Aug 31] half-brother to fairly useful hurdlers Gladiator King (2m winner, by
Dylan Thomas) and Rock Relief (2m-2½m winner, by Daylami): fairly useful on Flat, stays
1¼m: modest form over hurdles: raced around 2m: in headgear last 2 starts. *Denis Hogan,
Ireland*

ATLAS PEAK (IRE) 14 b.g. Namid – My Delilah (IRE) (Last Tycoon) [2018/19 h–: **h–**
h16.2d May 5] good-topped gelding: no longer of any account: has worn headgear.
Victor Thompson

A TOI PHIL (FR) 9 b.g. Day Flight – Lucidrile (FR) (Beyssac (FR)) [2018/19 c157, h–: **c154 d** c20m⁶ c20g³ c16.7v c17d^pu c20.5g⁵ h24d⁴ h24d⁵ c34.3g c29d Apr 22] well-made gelding: **h146** smart handicap hurdler: fifth in Pertemps Final at Cheltenham (8 lengths behind Sire du Berlais) in March: very smart chaser, largely disappointing in 2018/19: stays 25f: acts on heavy going: wears tongue tie: races towards rear. *Gordon Elliott, Ireland*

ATOMIC RUMBLE (IRE) 6 b.g. Oscar (IRE) – Atomic Betty (IRE) (Anshan) [2018/19 **h110** h95, b86: h21.9g* h20g* h19.3m h23s h20v⁶ h23.1s⁵ h26.4g³ Mar 30] fair handicap hurdler: won at Ffos Las in May and Aintree (conditionals) in June: stays 3¼m: acts on heavy going: wears tongue tie. *Peter Bowen*

ATTENTION PLEASE (IRE) 8 b.g. Kalanisi (IRE) – Dangerous Dolly (IRE) (Jurado **c98** (USA)) [2018/19 c97, h–: c26.2g³ c24.2s^pu c24.1g² c24.2g⁵ c23.8g* c24.2g^pu Feb 19] **h–** maiden hurdler: modest handicap chaser: won at Musselburgh in December: stays 27f: acts on soft and good to firm going: wears headgear. *Rose Dobbin*

ATTEST 6 b.g. Cacique (IRE) – Change Course (Sadler's Wells (USA)) [2018/19 h126: **c– p** c17s⁵ Dec 3] lengthy gelding: fairly useful hurdler: tailed off in novice on chasing debut: **h–** stays 19f: acts on soft and good to firm going: tried in cheekpieces: has joined Dr Richard Newland: should do better over fences. *Warren Greatrex*

AUBUSSON (FR) 10 b.g. Ballingarry (IRE) – Katioucha (FR) (Mansonnien (FR)) **c129** [2018/19 c134, h–: c21.9s⁵ c27.5g² c23g⁴ c23s⁵ h23.9s c32.4g^pu c30.2s c23.8m* Apr 23] **h–** tall, good-topped gelding: smart hurdler at best: fairly useful handicap chaser nowadays: won at Ludlow in April: stays 3¼m: acts on good to firm and heavy going: tried in cheekpieces. *Mrs Jane Williams*

AUDORA 8 b.m. Alflora (IRE) – Vixen Run (IRE) (Presenting) [2018/19 h–, b–: h21.6g³ **h93** h15.9s^pu Dec 3] modest form over hurdles: left Martin Hill after first start: should stay 3m. *Anthony Honeyball*

AUENWIRBEL (GER) 8 b.g. Sholokhov (IRE) – Auentime (GER) (Dashing Blade) **c91** [2018/19 c92, h–: c20g* c20g² c20g h16s c21.7d^ur h21d⁵ h23d² h25d⁵ Mar 3] angular **h85** gelding: modest handicap hurdler/chaser: won over fences at Worcester in June: stays 23f: acts on heavy going: tried in blinkers: usually wears tongue tie: usually races towards rear. *Laura Young*

AULD SOD (IRE) 6 b.g. Court Cave (IRE) – Didn't You Know (FR) (Trempolino (USA)) **h99** [2018/19 h19.9m⁶ h21.6m⁴ h18.5g³ h18.7g h16m⁵ h16.8d³ h16d⁶ h19.7g h16.8s⁶ h16.5d Apr 4] €9,500 3-y-o, £12,000 5-y-o: fourth foal: half-brother to 2 winning pointers by Tikkanen: dam (h81), maiden hurdler, sister to very smart hurdler/chaser (stayed 29f) Bounce Back: maiden pointer: modest maiden hurdler: left Ronald Harris after seventh start: stays 2¼m: wears headgear. *Milton Bradley*

AULDTHUNDER (IRE) 12 b.g. Oscar (IRE) – Jill's Girl (IRE) (Be My Native (USA)) **c–** [2018/19 c75, h–: h21.6g^pu Jul 6] has had breathing operation: poor hurdler/chaser **h–** nowadays: stays 3¼m: acts on heavy going: tried in cheekpieces: usually races prominently. *Ryan Chapman*

AUMIT HILL 6 b.g. Authorized (IRE) – Eurolinka (IRE) (Tirol) [2018/19 c19.2g⁶ **c–** h25.5s^pu Nov 28] maiden pointer: no form under Rules: tried in cheekpieces. *Laura Young* **h–**

AUNTIE MARY (IRE) 7 b.m. Scorpion (IRE) – Saucy Present (IRE) (Presenting) **b89** [2018/19 b16.2g² b16.7g² b16.2m* Sep 19] £36,000 5-y-o: fourth foal: half-sister to fairly useful hurdler/very smart chaser Ordinary World (2m winner, by Milan) and fair hurdler May Dullea (2½m winner, by King's Theatre): dam unraced: won completed start in points: fair form in bumpers: won at Kelso in September: wears hood: in tongue tie last 2 starts. *John McConnell, Ireland*

AUNTIE NEILA 4 ch.f. Intikhab (USA) – Storm Quest (Storming Home) [2018/19 **b–** b15.3g Dec 6] first foal: dam of no account: tailed off in junior bumper. *Paul George*

AUNTY ANN (IRE) 8 b.m. Vinnie Roe (IRE) – On Good Advise (IRE) (Taipan (IRE)) **c121** [2018/19 c115§, h109§: c23.9d³ c26.1g² c24s* c22.6g⁵ c25.8d⁵ c25.1m* c25.1g⁴ c26g^pu **h–** Apr 18] fair hurdler: fairly useful handicap chaser: won at Uttoxeter in July and Wincanton in October: stays 3¼m: acts on soft and good to firm going: tried in tongue tie: usually races prominently. *Charlie Longsdon*

AURELLO 5 b.m. Kayf Tara – Haudello (FR) (Marignan (USA)) [2018/19 b16.7d⁶ Jan 8] **b71**
closely related to bumper winner Mozo and a winning pointer (both by Milan) and half-
sister to 3 winners, including fairly useful hurdler/chaser Finney (2½m-3m winner, by
Supreme Leader) and fairly useful chaser Susie Sheep (3m winner, by Robin des Champs):
dam unraced: 20/1, sixth in bumper at Bangor. *Warren Greatrex*

AURILLAC (FR) 9 gr.g. Martaline – Ombrelle (FR) (Octagonal (NZ)) [2018/19 c26dᵖᵘ **c124 §**
c24.2s⁴ c30.7dᵖᵘ Feb 22] good-topped gelding: winning hurdler: useful maiden chaser at **h–**
best: stayed 3m: acted on soft going: usually wore headgear: temperamental: dead.
David Pipe

AURORA THUNDER 5 b.m. Malinas (GER) – Ninna Nanna (FR) (Garde Royale) **b81**
[2018/19 b16.2m⁶ b16.2d³ b15.6g⁴ b17g² Feb 24] £25,000 3-y-o: fifth foal: half-sister to 3
winners, including useful hurdler/fairly useful chaser Jacks Last Hope (2m-3m winner) and
useful/unreliable hurdler/chaser Ballycross (21f-3m winner) (both by King's Theatre): dam
second at 1¼m in France: modest form in bumpers. *Lucinda Russell*

AUSTIN FRIARS 7 b.g. New Approach (IRE) – My Luigia (IRE) (High Estate) [2018/19 **h– §**
h15.9g May 13] angular gelding: has had breathing operation: poor hurdler: raced only at
2m: tried in visor/tongue tie: temperamental. *Suzi Best*

AUTHORIZO (FR) 4 b.g. Authorized (IRE) – Street Lightning (FR) (Best of The Bests **h125**
(IRE)) [2018/19 h16s* h16d³ h16.8dᵖᵘ h16d Apr 22] good-topped gelding: dam half-sister
to fairly useful French hurdler/fair chaser (17f winner) Siena Serenade: fairly useful 11f
winner on Flat in France: fairly useful form over hurdles: won maiden at Fairyhouse in
January: third in Winning Fair Juvenile Hurdle at same course (5 lengths behind Way Back
Home) next time: wears tongue tie. *Gordon Elliott, Ireland*

AUTUMN SURPRISE (IRE) 6 b.m. Yeats (IRE) – Septembers Hawk (IRE) **h87**
(Machiavellian (USA)) [2018/19 h88: h19.9g* May 15] modest form over hurdles: won
mares novice at Sedgefield in May. *Tim Easterby*

AUVERGNAT (FR) 9 b.g. Della Francesca (USA) – Hesmeralda (FR) (Royal Charter **c140**
(FR)) [2018/19 c150, h119: c26m³ h21.9s h20d c24.5g* c30.2sᵖᵘ c29dᵖᵘ Apr 22] **h–**
workmanlike gelding: fairly useful hurdler at best: useful handicap chaser: won Paddy
Power Chase at Leopardstown (by 6½ lengths from Vieux Morvan) in December: stays
33f: acts on good to firm and heavy going: has worn headgear, including last 3 starts: tried
in tongue tie. *Enda Bolger, Ireland*

Paddy Power Chase, Leopardstown—a fourth win in seven years in this Christmas feature for
owner J. P. McManus as outsider Auvergnat (blinkers) fares best of the owner's eight-strong team

Mr J. Hales's "Aux Ptits Soins"

AUX PTITS SOINS (FR) 9 gr.g. Saint des Saints (FR) – Reflexion Faite (FR) (Turgeon (USA)) [2018/19 h24.2s⁵ h24d* h24d h24.7g* Apr 6] tall gelding: smart handicap hurdler: missed 2017/18: won at Cheltenham (by 7 lengths from De Name Evades Me) in January and Aintree (by 4½ lengths from Tommy Rapper) in April: winning chaser: stays 25f: acts on soft going. *Dan Skelton*   **c–** **h154**

AVANTGARDIST (GER) 5 ch.g. Campanologist (USA) – Avocette (GER) (Kings Lake (USA)) [2018/19 h16.7s h16d⁶ h16.3d⁶ h15.8d h21s* h24.2d³ Mar 22] leggy gelding: fair form over hurdles: won handicap at Warwick in March: stays 3m: acts on soft going. *Henry Oliver*   **h106**

AVARCHIE (FR) 5 b.g. Kentucky Dynamite (USA) – Teatime (FR) (Loup Solitaire (USA)) [2018/19 b71: b16m* Jul 9] tall gelding: fair form in bumpers: won at Worcester (hooded) in July. *John Butler*   **b92**

AVAST YE 6 ch.m. Native Ruler – Miss Hollybell (Umistim) [2018/19 b16g³ b16.3g⁴ h16.7g Sep 29] second foal: dam 6f winner: poor form in bumpers: tailed off in mares novice on hurdling debut. *Shaun Lycett*   **h–** **b72**

AVIATOR (GER) 11 br.g. Motivator – Amore (GER) (Lando (GER)) [2018/19 h–: h21g h25g* h24g Jun 12] fair handicap hurdler: won at Huntingdon in May: stayed 25f: acted on good to firm and good to soft going: in headgear last 3 starts: dead. *James Eustace*   **h108**

AVITHOS 9 b.m. Kayf Tara – Digyourheelsin (IRE) (Mister Lord (USA)) [2018/19 h–: h21.6v³ h23.1s⁶ h23.9dᵖᵘ h23.9g h23.1s* h23.1d³ Apr 9] modest handicap hurdler: won mares event at Exeter in March: stays 3m: acts on soft going: has worn blinkers, including last 3 starts. *Mark Gillard*   **h85**

AVOCADEAU (IRE) 8 b.g. Lawman (FR) – Christmas Cracker (FR) (Alhaarth (IRE)) [2018/19 h18.5g h18.5g⁵ h21.6g³ h23.9m⁵ Nov 15] modest on Flat, stays 1½m: modest form over hurdles: tried in cheekpieces. *Stuart Kittow*   **h90**

AVOCET (USA) 6 b.m. Artie Schiller (USA) – Striking Example (USA) (Empire Maker **h–**
(USA)) [2018/19 h15.8gᵖᵘ h15.8gᵖᵘ Apr 11] has had breathing operation: fair on Flat, stays
13.5f: pulled up both starts over hurdles: wears cheekpieces: in tongue tie first start.
Sarah Humphrey

AVOID DE MASTER (IRE) 5 b.g. Getaway (GER) – Tanit (Xaar) [2018/19 b16.5d⁵ **b75**
Apr 4] winning Irish pointer: 20/1, fifth in maiden bumper at Taunton. *David Dennis*

AVOIR DE SOINS (IRE) 5 ch.g. Flemensfirth (USA) – Garranlea Maree (IRE) (Presenting) **h–**
[2018/19 b15.8sᶠ h19.8sᵖᵘ Mar 7] no promise in bumper/maiden hurdle. *Anthony Honeyball* **b–**

AVONDHU PEARL (IRE) 8 ch.m. Beneficial – Ballinapierce Lady (IRE) (Glacial **c80**
Storm (USA)) [2018/19 c–, h82: c20.1d⁶ h20.2gᵖᵘ c21.6d h16.2g⁴ h19.7g⁵ h19.8m⁵ h19.8s **h76**
h19.9s² h17d³ Mar 24] winning pointer: poor maiden hurdler/chaser: stays 2½m: acts on
soft and good to firm going: has worn cheekpieces, including final start. *Stuart Coltherd*

AVONMORE 6 gr.m. Fair Mix (IRE) – Glenda Lough (IRE) (Supreme Leader) [2018/19 **h85**
b16gʳʳ b16.8g³ b17.7g⁴ b13.7g³ h15.9d³ Mar 18] third foal: half-sister to unreliable **b76 §**
bumper winner/fair hurdler Leaderofthedance (21f winner, by Norse Dancer): dam unraced
daughter of fairly useful hurdler/chaser up to 25f Garrylough: modest form in bumpers/
over hurdles: left Nicky Henderson after first start (hooded, refused to race): one to treat
with caution. *Barry Brennan*

AVORISK ET PERILS (FR) 4 b.f. No Risk At All (FR) – Pierre Azuree (FR) (Le **b74**
Glorieux) [2018/19 b12.6s b13.7v³ b16.5d b13.7g Apr 12] €14,000 3-y-o: fourth foal: half-
sister to bumper winner/fairly useful hurdler Puisque Tu Pars (2m winner, by Walk In The
Park): dam French maiden: poor form in bumpers. *Gary Moore*

AWAKE AT MIDNIGHT 7 b.g. Midnight Legend – Wakeful (Kayf Tara) [2018/19 **c122**
h113: h16g* c16s* c19.2s⁴ c20.5g c16.4d⁴ c19.2d² Apr 9] useful-looking gelding: fair **h112**
hurdler: won novice at Worcester in October: fairly useful form over fences: won novice
handicap at Chepstow in November: should stay beyond 19f: acts on soft going: usually
races off pace. *Philip Hobbs*

AWAY FOR SLATES (IRE) 9 b.g. Arcadio (GER) – Rumi (Nishapour (FR)) [2018/19 **c112**
h114d: h15.3g h21.4g h21.7sᵖᵘ c17s² c19.2m* c19.1d* c19.5v* c19.2d⁵ c20.1dᵖᵘ Apr 26] **h–**
fairly useful hurdler at best, no form in 2018/19: completed hat-trick in races over fences:
in handicaps at Catterick (novice) in February then Doncaster and Fontwell in March: stays
2½m: acts on good to firm and heavy going: wears headgear: tried in tongue tie.
Milton Harris

AWAYINTHEWEST (IRE) 7 b.m. Getaway (GER) – Sarah's Hall (IRE) (Saddlers' Hall **h124**
(IRE)) [2018/19 h16g² h16.5g* h20.7sᶠ h18.1g² h21.4s* h18g³ h22.5g² h18s h20d h16.8d
h20d Apr 7] smallish, plain mare: fairly useful hurdler: won mares handicap at Ballinrobe
in May and minor event at Galway in September: second in listed mares event at Limerick
(2 lengths behind Robin de Carlow) in October: stays 2¾m: acts on heavy going. *P. A. Fahy,
Ireland*

AWAYWITHTHEBLUES (IRE) 7 ch.g. Stowaway – Rhythm 'N' Blues (IRE) (Sinndar **h–**
(IRE)) [2018/19 h–, b–: h21.4g h19.5d Apr 6] little form over hurdles. *Robert Stephens*

AWESOMEDESTINATION (IRE) 6 ch.g. Dubai Destination (USA) – Don't Be Bleu **h–**
(IRE) (Pistolet Bleu (IRE)) [2018/19 b15.8d h19.5s h21d h15.8v Dec 17] placed twice in **b–**
points: well held in bumper/over hurdles. *Peter Bowen*

AWESOME ROCK (IRE) 10 ch.g. Rock of Gibraltar (IRE) – Dangerous Diva (IRE) **h73**
(Royal Academy (USA)) [2018/19 h15.9gᵖᵘ h15.9d⁴ h15.9g⁴ Apr 21] poor on Flat, stays
13.5f: poor form over hurdles: tried in hood. *Roger Ingram*

AWESOME ROSIE 8 b.m. Midnight Legend – Awesome Aunt (IRE) (Vestris Abu) **h105**
[2018/19 h117: h20.3g⁴ h18.5d⁶ h20.5s Mar 11] compact mare: fairly useful handicap
hurdler at best, disappointing in 2018/19: stays 21f: acts on heavy going: often travels
strongly. *Alan King*

AYALOR (FR) 9 b.g. Khalkevi (IRE) – Physicienne (FR) (Bonnet Rouge (FR)) [2018/19 **h–**
h20.6m Apr 21] fairly useful 19f hurdle winner, well held only start in 2018/19: tried in
tongue tie. *Joanne Thomason-Murphy*

AYE AYE CHARLIE 7 b.g. Midnight Legend – Trial Trip (Le Moss) [2018/19 h137: **h131**
h20g² h22.7d* h24s⁶ h24d⁶ h24d Mar 15] sturdy gelding: has had breathing operation:
useful hurdler: simple task in novice at Kelso in November: stays 23f: acts on soft going:
tried in cheekpieces: in tongue tie last 2 starts. *Fergal O'Brien*

AYELYA (IRE) 7 b.m. Nayef (USA) – Aliyama (IRE) (Red Ransom (USA)) [2018/19 **h67** h15.8g h16.8g⁵ h18.7m⁶ Sep 8] modest handicap hurdler at best, left John Joseph Hanlon after final start in 2017/18: stayed 21f: acted on good to soft going: sometimes in headgear/ tongue tie: front runner/raced prominently, tended to find little: dead. *Olly Murphy*

AYE RIGHT (IRE) 6 b.g. Yeats (IRE) – Gaybric (IRE) (Presenting) [2018/19 h117, b99: **h131** h20.9m* h20.9g* h21g⁶ h21.4s* h22.7g² h22.7J² h25.8g⁴ h24.3m* Apr 12] strong gelding: chasing type: useful hurdler: won novices at Kelso in September and October, and handicaps at Ayr in January and April (novice, by 3¾ lengths from Before Midnight): stays 3¼m: acts on soft and good to firm going: usually races close up. *Harriet Graham*

AYLA'S EMPEROR 10 b.m. Holy Roman Emperor (IRE) – Ayla (IRE) (Daylami (IRE)) **c– x** [2018/19 h100: h21.2g* h21.9g h23.9m h20m h20d c20m⁶ c20.3g^pu h19.9g^su h19.5s⁵ Nov **h99** 21] sturdy mare: modest handicap hurdler: won at Ludlow in May: no aptitude for chasing: stays 2¾m: acts on soft going: wears cheekpieces: often races towards rear. *John Flint*

AZA RUN (IRE) 9 b.g. Hurricane Run (IRE) – Aza Wish (IRE) (Mujadil (USA)) [2018/19 **c– §** c93§, h89§: c16.5g c16v h15.8s h16.8v h15.7g⁴ h16.8g^ur Apr 5] modest hurdler at best, no **h– §** form in 2018/19: little impact over fences: tried in tongue tie: untrustworthy. *Shaun Harris*

AZERT DE COEUR (FR) 9 b.g. Tiger Groom – Eden de Coeur (FR) (Lampon (FR)) **c–** [2018/19 c74, h–: h21.4g May 7] good-topped gelding: winning hurdler/chaser, retains **h–** little ability: in headgear last 2 starts. *Rebecca Menzies*

AZURE FLY (IRE) 11 br.g. Blueprint (IRE) – Lady Delight (IRE) (Be My Native (USA)) **c113 §** [2018/19 c121§, h–§: c24g⁴ c23.6g⁴ c25.6d² c26g³ Dec 14] good-topped gelding: has had **h– §** breathing operation: winning hurdler: fair handicap chaser: stays 33f: acts on good to firm and heavy going: usually in headgear: wears tongue tie: usually races close up: temperamental. *Charlie Longsdon*

AZURE GLAMOUR (IRE) 10 br.g. Golan (IRE) – Mirazur (IRE) (Good Thyne (USA)) **c–** [2018/19 c16.3g^pu May 4] winning hurdler: pulled up in points/hunter chase in 2018: has **h–** worn headgear: tried in tongue tie. *A. B. Leyshon*

AZZERTI (FR) 7 b.g. Voix du Nord (FR) – Zalagarry (FR) (Ballingarry (IRE)) [2018/19 **c137** h137: c20g⁴ h19.5d c18.8g³ c16.8s* c20.6d^F c20d* c20.6d c24.1m^pu Apr 13] rather leggy **h–** gelding: useful hurdler: useful chaser: won novice handicap at Ascot in December and 3-runner novice (10/1-on) at Ludlow in February: stays 2½m: acts on soft going: tried in hood. *Alan King*

AZZURI 7 b.g. Azamour (IRE) – Folly Lodge (Grand Lodge (USA)) [2018/19 c133, h121: **c146** c17g* c15.5s c15.7g⁴ c19.9d c16.5m* Apr 13] sturdy gelding: fairly useful hurdler: smart **h–** handicap chaser: won at Killarney (by 10 lengths from Our Dougal, only outing for Richard John O'Brien) in July and listed event at Ayr (after breathing operation, by 9 lengths from Vosne Romanee) in April: best form around 2m: acts on good to firm and heavy going: wears tongue tie: usually races close up. *Dan Skelton*

B

BABBLING STREAM 8 b.g. Authorized (IRE) – Elasouna (IRE) (Rainbow Quest **c110** (USA)) [2018/19 h20g³ h16g h20m* h22.4m⁴ h18.8d* h22g c20g⁴ c24.2m³ h19.3g⁶ Nov **h130** 24] lengthy gelding: useful hurdler: won handicap at Bellewstown in July and minor event at Downpatrick (by 3¾ lengths from Go Another One) in August: fair form over fences: left Henry de Bromhead after seventh start: stays 2¾m: acts on good to firm and heavy going: tried in cheekpieces: wears tongue tie nowadays. *Brian Barr*

BABOCHOFF 7 b.g. Babodana – Charm Offensive (Zieten (USA)) [2018/19 b16d Dec **b–** 31] tailed off in bumper. *Mark H. Tompkins*

BABY JAKE (IRE) 10 b.g. Morozov (USA) – Potters Dawn (IRE) (Talkin Man (CAN)) **c104** [2018/19 c123, h124: h16.8m⁴ h16g c16d⁵ c16.3s h16g h16s⁵ h16g c17s Jan 26] fairly **h105** useful handicap hurdler/maiden chaser, below form in 2018/19: stays 2½m: acts on good to firm and good to soft going: has worn headgear, including final start. *John Joseph Hanlon, Ireland*

BABY KING (IRE) 10 b.g. Ivan Denisovich (IRE) – Burn Baby Burn (IRE) (King's **c132** Theatre (IRE)) [2018/19 c136, h–: c15.8g⁶ c16.4s^bd c16d⁶ c16.2g³ c15.2g c16d^F c16m* **h–** Apr 23] good-topped gelding: has had breathing operation: winning hurdler: useful handicap chaser: won at Ludlow in April: stays 19f: acts on good to firm and heavy going: tried in cheekpieces: wears tongue tie. *Tom George*

BABYTAGGLE (IRE) 8 b.g. Brian Boru – Ardnataggle (IRE) (Aristocracy) [2018/19 **c92** h80: h20.6s c23.6d⁴ c24g^{ur} c26.1d c19.7s³ c19.2d⁶ c16s⁵ c17g² Apr 21] winning pointer: **h–** maiden hurdler: modest maiden chaser: stays 3m: acts on heavy going: wears hood. *Dai Williams*

BABY TED 6 ch.g. Pasternak – Dd's Glenalla (IRE) (Be My Native (USA)) [2018/19 h92, **h70** b81: h15.8g⁵ h18.7m^{ur} Aug 2] strong, compact gelding: placed in bumpers: modest form at best over hurdles. *Nigel Twiston-Davies*

BABY TICKER 10 ch.m. Endoli (USA) – Baby Gee (King Among Kings) [2018/19 h112: **h98** h17s⁵ h20v² Dec 2] fair handicap hurdler: should stay 2½m+: best form on soft/heavy going: tried in blinkers. *Donald Whillans*

BACARDYS (FR) 8 b.g. Coastal Path – Oasice (FR) (Robin des Champs (FR)) [2018/19 **c139** c136p, h155: c19d c21g^f h24d⁶ Mar 14] angular gelding: smart hurdler: 3 lengths second **h147** of 10 to Unowhatimeanharry in Champion Stayers' Hurdle at Punchestown shortly after end of British season: useful form over fences (fell on 2 of 4 starts): stays 3m: acts on heavy going. *W. P. Mullins, Ireland*

BACHASSON (FR) 8 gr.g. Voix du Nord (FR) – Belledonne (FR) (Shafoun (FR)) **c–** [2018/19 c159p, h–: h20g* h21d² Feb 17] smallish gelding: useful hurdler: won minor **h144** event at Punchestown (by 2¼ lengths from Darasso) in December: very smart chaser: should stay 3m: acts on heavy going. *W. P. Mullins, Ireland*

BACH DE CLERMONT (FR) 8 b.g. Della Francesca (USA) – Fleur de Princesse (FR) **c–** (Passing Sale (FR)) [2018/19 c119, h116: c20g⁴ c23.6g^{pu} May 28] well-made gelding: **h–** fairly useful hurdler: similar form at best over fences: stayed 2½m: acted on soft going: front runner/raced prominently: dead. *Evan Williams*

BACHELOR (IRE) 4 b.g. Holy Roman Emperor (IRE) – Shell Garland (USA) (Sadler's **h103** Wells (USA)) [2018/19 h16.6g⁵ h16d² h16g⁵ h16.5f⁵ Feb 5] fairly useful on Flat, stays 1m: fair form over hurdles: wears tongue tie. *Noel C. Kelly, Ireland*

BACHY BABY 7 b.g. Bach (IRE) – Bathwick Annie (Sula Bula) [2018/19 b77: b15.8m⁵ **h–** h16.3g^{pu} h16.3m^{pu} Jun 19] running to modest level when slipping up in bumper on debut **b–** in 2017/18, only sign of ability: in hood last 2 starts. *Michael Blake*

BACKINTHEOLDTIMES (IRE) 6 b.m. Olden Times – Tinas Friend (Environment **h–** Friend) [2018/19 h19.5d Oct 13] £12,500 5-y-o: fifth foal: half-sister to a winning pointer by Royal Storm: dam unraced: Irish point winner: 66/1, well held in mares novice hurdle. *Christian Williams*

BACKINTHESADDLE (IRE) 11 ch.g. Rudimentary (USA) – Grangeclare Lodge **c–** (IRE) (Top of The World) [2018/19 c85, h88: h19.2g May 9] modest hurdler, well held sole **h–** outing in 2018/19: lightly-raced chaser: stays 2½m: acts on good to soft going: tried in hood: wears tongue tie. *Daniel Steele*

BACKOFTHEROCK 10 b.g. Scorpion (IRE) – Oscars Vision (IRE) (Oscar Schindler **c72** (IRE)) [2018/19 c78, h81: c22.6g⁴ h25.8s^{pu} h25.5g⁶ Nov 5] raw-boned gelding: winning **h63** pointer: poor maiden hurdler/chaser: stays 3¼m: acts on good to soft going: wears hood: has worn tongue tie, including in 2018/19: usually races in rear. *David Rees*

BACK ON THE LASH 5 b.g. Malinas (GER) – Giovanna (Orpen (USA)) [2018/19 **h120** b15.8m* h16g³ h15.8g* h23.1g⁴ h20.3g^{pu} Apr 17] sturdy gelding: second foal: dam (h125) **b91** bumper/19f-27f hurdle winner: won maiden bumper at Ludlow (by 2½ lengths from Alph) in May on debut: fairly useful form over hurdles: won novice at Ludlow in January: fourth in handicap at Market Rasen next time. *Martin Keighley*

BACK TO BALLOO (IRE) 13 gr.g. Jimble (FR) – Fleur du Chenet (FR) (Northern **c–** Fashion (USA)) [2018/19 c–, h104: h16.7g h16.2g* h16.7g⁵ c16g⁵ h16m³ h16.2g Nov 9] **h91** modest handicap hurdler nowadays: won at Hexham in May: fairly useful chaser at best, last in handicap sole outing over fences in 2018/19: stays 2¼m: acts on good to firm and heavy going: has worn headgear/tongue tie: usually leads. *Peter Winks*

BACK TO THE THATCH (IRE) 7 b.g. Westerner – Melville Rose (IRE) (Phardante **c136** (FR)) [2018/19 c127p, h–: c24d c23.6v⁴ c27.3s² c34v^f Mar 16] winning hurdler: useful **h–** handicap chaser: second at Haydock (2¾ lengths behind Chef d'Oeuvre) in December: shaped well long way in Midlands Grand National final start: stays 27f: acts on heavy going. *Henry Daly*

BACT TO BLACK 7 b.g. Black Sam Bellamy (IRE) – Linagram (Classic Cliche (IRE)) **h95** [2018/19 h97: h23.1s⁶ h23s³ h23d* h23.1s⁶ Mar 5] sturdy gelding: modest handicap hurdler: won at Lingfield in January: stays 23f: acts on heavy going: in cheekpieces last 5 starts: races prominently. *Robert Walford*

888Sport Pendil Novices' Chase, Kempton—another fluent display from Bags Groove, who wins from the mare Castafiore (right)

BADDESLEY (IRE) 4 b.g. Presenting – Fox Theatre (IRE) (King's Theatre (IRE)) [2018/19 b17.7g² Apr 7] €35,000 3-y-o: fourth foal: brother to modest 2½m hurdle winner Fiesta Forever and half-brother to useful hurdler/chaser Valhalla (2m-23f winner, by Scorpion): dam unraced half-sister to fairly useful hurdler/smart chaser (stayed 21f) Sir Oj: 5/2, shaped well when second in bumper at Plumpton (2¾ lengths behind Strike The Flint). *Chris Gordon* **b97**

BADDESLEY KNIGHT (IRE) 6 b.g. Doyen (IRE) – Grangeclare Rhythm (IRE) (Lord Americo) [2018/19 b104: h16.3d⁴ h16v⁵ h15.9s* h15.9s³ Feb 13] tall gelding: bumper winner: fairly useful form over hurdles: won novice at Plumpton in January: likely to stay 2½m. *Chris Gordon* **h124**

BADDESLEY PRINCE (IRE) 5 b.g. Doyen (IRE) – Norabella (IRE) (Shantou (USA)) [2018/19 b15.7g⁵ h16.3d h16.7v h15.9d² h20.5dᶠ Mar 1] tall, rather unfurnished gelding: first foal: dam unraced half-sister to useful hurdler/smart chaser (2¾m-4m winner) Back In Focus: showed a bit in bumper: fairly useful form over hurdles: second in novice at Plumpton in January: will be suited by 2½m: remains open to improvement. *Chris Gordon* **h116 p b–**

BADEN (FR) 8 gr.g. Martaline – Ma Sonate (USA) (Val de L'Orne (FR)) [2018/19 c129, h–: c23.8m* c23gᵘʳ Oct 24] deep-girthed, well-made gelding: useful handicap chaser: won 3-runner novice event at Ludlow in May: stayed 25f: acted on soft and good to firm going: in cheekpieces last 4 starts: front runner/raced prominently: dead. *Nicky Henderson* **c131 h–**

BADILOU (FR) 8 b.g. Ballingarry (IRE) – Doumia (FR) (Dounba (FR)) [2018/19 c83, h–: c25.8gᵖᵘ May 16] angular gelding: winning hurdler: poor maiden chaser: stays 21f: acts on good to firm and good to soft going: wears headgear. *Martin Hill* **c– h–**

BAFANA BLUE 8 b.g. Blueprint (IRE) – Anniejo (Presenting) [2018/19 h95: h21.4g c20.1g* c22.5g⁶ c20.1g⁴ c24.2g* c23.4g⁵ c24.2g² c24.2s⁶ c25.2gᵖᵘ c23.8m³ c20.1m c24.2g* c23.8g⁴ Apr 24] compact gelding: modest maiden hurdler: fair handicap chaser: won at Hexham in May/October (novice events) and Wetherby in April: stays 3m: acts on good to firm and heavy going: wears tongue tie: temperamental. *Maurice Barnes* **c102 § h82**

BAGAD BIHOUE (FR) 8 b.g. Nickname (FR) – Lann Bihouee (FR) (Video Rock (FR)) **c141** [2018/19 c141, h–: c21g* c21.4m c23d Aug 29] useful-looking gelding: winning hurdler: **h–** useful handicap chaser: won at Newton Abbot (by 3½ lengths from Alcala) in June: stays 2¾m: acts on good to firm and good to soft going: usually races close up. *Paul Nicholls*

BAGAN 5 ch.g. Sulamani (IRE) – Aunt Rita (IRE) (Grand Lodge (USA)) [2018/19 b16.3g⁴ **h103** b15.8g^pu b16m⁴ h16m³ h16g⁴ h15.6g h18.6g³ Mar 27] angular gelding: tenth foal: dam, 6f **b88** winner, half-sister to fairly useful hurdler/very smart chaser (stayed 21f) Celibate: fair form in bumpers/over hurdles. *Tom Gretton*

BAGGING TURF (IRE) 9 b.m. Scorpion (IRE) – Monica's Story (Arzanni) [2018/19 **c–** c89, h–: h25m^ur h25.8g h21.6g² Jun 15] lengthy mare: fair hurdler: winning chaser: stays **h98** 2¾m: acts on heavy going: usually wears cheekpieces. *Gary Moore*

BAGS GROOVE (IRE) 8 b.g. Oscar (IRE) – Golden Moment (IRE) (Roselier (FR)) **c149** [2018/19 h141: c16d² c20.9d* c20.2g* c23.6d* c24g⁵ c20.5g* c19.9d⁴ Apr 4] good-topped **h–** gelding: winning hurdler: smart chaser: won novice at Ffos Las in October, Rising Star Novices' Chase at Wincanton (by 9 lengths from Secret Investor) in November, novice at Huntingdon (by 9 lengths from Thomas Campbell) in December and Pendil Novices' Chase at Kempton (by 1½ lengths from Castafiore) in February: stays 3m: acts on good to soft going: tried in cheekpieces: wears tongue tie: usually front runner/races prominently. *Harry Fry*

BAHAMA MOON (IRE) 7 b.g. Lope de Vega (IRE) – Bahama Bay (GER) (Dansili) **h102** [2018/19 h97: h17.1g³ h16.8s³ h19.7d² h15.7d³ h16s⁴ Mar 10] sturdy gelding: has had breathing operation: fair maiden hurdler: stays 2½m: acts on soft going. *Jonjo O'Neill*

BAHRIKATE 6 b.m. Bahri (USA) – Dispol Katie (Komaite (USA)) [2018/19 h96: **h97** h16.2g³ h16.2g³ h16.2g⁵ Jul 5] modest handicap hurdler: best at 2m: acts on soft going: wears tongue tie: usually races nearer last than first, often travels strongly. *Susan Corbett*

BAIE DES ILES (FR) 8 gr.m. Barastraight – Malownia (FR) (Smadoun (FR)) [2018/19 **c144** c144, h117: c21.9s* c27.3s c29.5s^pu c16d² c26.2v^F Mar 16] angular mare: winning hurdler: **h–** useful chaser: won Group 2 Prix des Drags at Auteuil in June: below form in latest renewal of race, and remained in France to join David Cottin: stays 29f: acts on heavy going: wears headgear. *Ross O'Sullivan, Ireland*

BAIHAS 9 b.g. Nayef (USA) – Allegretto (IRE) (Galileo (IRE)) [2018/19 h–: h21.6g^pu Jun **h–** 4] useful form on Flat at 3 yrs: no form over hurdles: tried in blinkers/tongue tie: dead. *Neil Mulholland*

BAILARICO (IRE) 6 b.g. Dubawi (IRE) – Baila Me (GER) (Samum (GER)) [2018/19 **h129** h20.5g^wo h20.5d³ h24.6g* h24.4g⁴ h23.1d Feb 22] tall, angular gelding: has had breathing operation: fairly useful on Flat, stays 16.5f: similar form over hurdles: won novice at Kempton in January: stays 25f: wears cheekpieces. *Warren Greatrex*

BAILEYS ARTIST 4 ch.g. Zoffany (IRE) – Marasima (IRE) (Barathea (IRE)) [2018/19 **h71** h16.4g⁴ h16.4s h16d h16g Feb 19] little impact on Flat/over hurdles. *Dianne Sayer*

BAILY SUNSET (IRE) 8 ch.g. Presenting – Kon Tiky (FR) (Perrault) [2018/19 h16m⁴ **c87** h19.7g³ h21.6m^pu c22.5g⁶ c19.7m² Oct 22] modest handicap hurdler: similar form over **h86** fences: left John Joseph Hanlon after second start: stayed 2½m: acted on good to firm and good to soft going: usually wore headgear: tried in tongue tie: dead. *Warren Greatrex*

BAJARDO (IRE) 11 b.g. Jammaal – Bit of Peace (IRE) (Le Bavard (FR)) [2018/19 c99, **c63** h–: c16g c16g c20.3s⁶ c19.4d c20.2g⁴ c19.5m⁴ Mar 29] raw-boned gelding: has had **h–** breathing operation: maiden hurdler: fair handicap chaser, well below form in 2018/19: stays 2¼m: acts on heavy going: tried in cheekpieces: wears tongue tie. *Emma-Jane Bishop*

BAKO DE LA SAULAIE (FR) 8 b.g. Balko (FR) – Krickette (FR) (Passing Sale (FR)) **c122** [2018/19 c122, h–: c20.1s³ c26.2g² c24.2s² Dec 8] winning hurdler: fairly useful maiden **h–** chaser: second in novice handicap at Wetherby in December: stays 3m: acts on soft going. *Rose Dobbin*

BALACH MOR (IRE) 7 b.g. Robin des Champs (FR) – Silver Skirt (IRE) (Silver **h–** Patriarch (IRE)) [2018/19 h–: h26g⁵ h25.5s^pu Nov 28] no solid form in bumper/over hurdles: in headgear last 2 starts. *Michael Scudamore*

BAL DE RIO (FR) 6 b.g. Vertigineux (FR) – Baldoranic (FR) (Panoramic) [2018/19 **h109** h112: h18.6m² h19.9m² Aug 30] fair maiden hurdler: stays 2½m: acts on soft going: tried in headgear. *Brian Ellison*

BALGEMMOIS (FR) 6 ch.g. Balko (FR) – Venise Doree (FR) (Starborough) [2018/19 **h104** h110: h19.6g⁵ May 10] rather unfurnished gelding: fair handicap hurdler: should stay further than 2m: best form on soft/heavy going: front runner/races prominently. *Ali Stronge*

BALIBOUR (FR) 7 b.g. Policy Maker (IRE) – Saintheze (FR) (Saint des Saints (FR)) **c113** [2018/19 h113, b70: c18m³ c16s c21.2d³ c20.2gᵖᵘ c21.4g⁴ Mar 27] good-topped gelding: **h–** fair maiden hurdler: similar form over fences: stays 2¾m: acts on good to firm and heavy going: tried in tongue tie. *Emma Lavelle*

BALKINSTOWN (IRE) 9 b.g. Westerner – Graffogue (IRE) (Red Sunset) [2018/19 **c92** h91: h23m² h23g² h23g³ h23.3g h23.9d⁴ h25.5g⁴ h25d* c23.8g³ Nov 26] modest handicap **h94** hurdler: won at Plumpton in November: 4/1, third in novice handicap at Ludlow on chasing debut: stays 25f: acts on good to firm and heavy going: usually in headgear: wears tongue tie. *Robert Stephens*

BALKO DES FLOS (FR) 8 ch.g. Balko (FR) – Royale Marie (FR) (Garde Royale) **c164** [2018/19 c166, h–: c24g⁴ c20.2d³ c24g c20.6d c25d³ Apr 4] good-topped gelding: winning **h–** hurdler: high-class chaser: third in John Durkan Memorial Punchestown Chase (4 lengths behind Min) in December and Bowl Chase at Aintree (9 lengths behind Kemboy) in April: stays 25f: acts on heavy going. *Henry de Bromhead, Ireland*

BALLASALLA (IRE) 7 br.g. Presenting – Papoose (IRE) (Little Bighorn) [2018/19 h88, **c111** b–: h17d⁴ c15.9s² c15.7g² c19.1g² c21.3dᵘʳ Mar 19] has had breathing operation: modest **h83** maiden hurdler: fair form over fences: should stay 21f: acts on soft going: in cheekpieces last 2 starts: wears tongue tie. *Donald McCain*

BALL D'ARC (FR) 8 b.g. Network (GER) – Pretty Moon (FR) (Moon Madness) **c135** [2018/19 c157, h–: h20d h20s c16s³ c24d³ Apr 21] sturdy gelding: useful hurdler at best, **h–** no form in 2018/19: useful chaser nowadays: third in Webster Cup Chase at Navan (21¼ lengths behind Darasso) in March and Imperial Call Chase at Cork (9 lengths behind Timeforwest) in April: stays 2½m: acts on heavy going: has worn hood. *Gordon Elliott, Ireland*

BALLELA'S DREAM 5 b.m. Josr Algarhoud (IRE) – Ballela Road (IRE) (Zaffaran **b63** (USA)) [2018/19 b17.1d b16s⁶ Jan 8] has had breathing operation: first foal: dam, winning pointer, half-sister to fairly useful hurdler (stays 25f) Clues And Arrows: poor form in bumpers: wears tongue tie. *John Dixon*

BALLETICON (IRE) 5 br.g. Arakan (USA) – Miss Garbo (IRE) (Bob Back (USA)) **b100** [2018/19 b15.7g² b16s² b16.7d⁵ Jan 8] €7,000 3-y-o, resold £10,500 3-y-o: second foal: dam, winning pointer, half-sister to fairly useful hurdlers/chasers Call Bewleys (2½m-2¾m winner) and Flinty Bay (2m-2½m winner): fairly useful form in bumpers: best effort when second at Chepstow in November. *Kim Bailey*

BALLI MARTINE (FR) 6 b.g. Ballingarry (IRE) – Miss Martine (FR) (Waki River **h109** (FR)) [2018/19 b90: b16g³ h15.7g³ h20g⁵ h19.6g³ Nov 4] rather unfurnished gelding: fairly **b95** useful form in bumpers: fair form over hurdles: best effort when third in novice at Huntingdon in November: stays 2½m: has worn hood. *Noel Williams*

BALLINAHINCH (IRE) 7 b.g. Oscar (IRE) – Before (IRE) (Ore) [2018/19 b95: **h106 p** h15.8m⁵ h19.9g³ Sep 12] lengthy gelding: in frame in bumpers: fair form over hurdles: better effort when third in maiden at Uttoxeter: open to further improvement. *Seamus Durack*

BALLINAHOW BILL (IRE) 7 b.g. Dubai Destination (USA) – Rainbow Lilly (IRE) **c101 x** (Beneficial) [2018/19 c24.2dᶠ c22.6d⁶ c25.2dᶠ Mar 6] first foal: dam (h75), maiden hurdler, **h–** half-sister to fairly useful hurdler/chaser (stayed 21f) Falcarragh and fairly useful hurdler (stays 2¾m) Champayne Lady: multiple point winner: maiden hurdler: fair form in chases: left Justin Landy after second start: stays 3m: acts on good to soft going: has worn hood: often races freely: often let down by jumping. *Miss C. R. Crane*

BALLINA LADY (IRE) 8 b.m. Royal Storm (IRE) – Tinas Friend (Environment Friend) **c–** [2018/19 c69, h–: c16.5gᵖᵘ c17.8m May 27] made frame in Irish points: little form under **h–** Rules: in headgear last 2 starts, tongue tied last 3: usually leads. *Graeme McPherson*

BALLINGARROW (IRE) 11 b.g. Heron Island (IRE) – Moss Abbey (Le Moss) [2018/19 **c–** c25.2g⁵ Mar 26] point winner: tailed off in novice on chasing debut. *Amaryllis Goschen*

BALLINTARA (IRE) 7 b.g. Getaway (GER) – Miltara (IRE) (Milan) [2018/19 h105: **h–** h25.8m⁶ May 27] workmanlike gelding: won point in February: modest maiden hurdler: stays 25f: acts on heavy going. *Diana Grissell*

BALLINURE (IRE) 9 b.g. Alkaadhem – Christy's Pride (IRE) (Kambalda) [2018/19 **c105 §** c128, h–: h19.2g* c20g⁴ h18.5s³ h21.6g c20.2gᵖᵘ Nov 10] compact gelding: has had **h119 §** breathing operation: fairly useful handicap hurdler in May: fairly useful handicap chaser, below form in 2018/19: stays 3m: acts on soft and good to firm going: has worn cheekpieces, including last 3 starts: unreliable. *Nicky Henderson*

BALLINVEGGA (IRE) 9 gr.g. Royal Anthem (USA) – Gill's Honey (IRE) (Celio Rufo) **c85** [2018/19 c23.8g⁵ c23.8g³ Jul 15] winning pointer/hurdler: modest maiden chaser: stayed **h–** 3m: best form on good going: in headgear last 3 starts: dead. *Jackie Stephen*

BALLON ONABUDGET (IRE) 6 b.g. Arcadio (GER) – Little Present (IRE) **h112** (Presenting) [2018/19 h16g h19d b16g* h15.8g² h16.7g Feb 17] €1,300 3-y-o; sturdy **b97** gelding: second foal: dam unraced: won ladies maiden bumper at Tramore (by 2¼ lengths from Owencurra Lass) in October: fair form over hurdles: left D. E. Fitzgerald after third start. *Tom George*

BALLOTIN (FR) 8 b.g. Enrique – Orphee de Vonnas (FR) (Jimble (FR)) [2018/19 c146, **c123** h–: c22.2g⁴ c15.9g* c20dᶠ Mar 21] winning hurdler: fairly useful hunter chaser nowadays: **h–** won at Leicester in March: stays 3m: acts on heavy going: wears headgear. *Philip Hobbs*

BALLYALTON (IRE) 12 b.g. Pierre – Almilto (IRE) (Mandalus) [2018/19 c139, h128: **c–** h24g³ c26.1m Jul 11] tall, good sort: fairly useful handicap hurdler nowadays: third at **h125** Southwell in June: smart chaser at best, well held sole outing over fences in 2018/19: stays 3m: acts on good to firm and heavy going: has worn cheekpieces, including in 2018/19. *Ian Williams*

BALLYANDREW (IRE) 8 b.g. Westerner – Royale Acadou (FR) (Cadoudal (FR)) **c–** [2018/19 c81, h85: h15.8m c19.4m Aug 2] maiden hurdler/chaser, no form in 2018/19: **h–** tried in hood. *Nigel Twiston-Davies*

BALLYANDY 8 b.g. Kayf Tara – Megalex (Karinga Bay) [2018/19 c139, h–: c19.4m³ **c137 x** c20.2gᵖᵘ h21g⁴ h19.9v* h19.3d³ h21s³ Mar 13] well-made gelding: smart handicap hurdler: **h150** won at Uttoxeter (by 4½ lengths from Burrows Park) in January: then third in Coral Cup at Cheltenham (½ length behind William Henry) in March: useful chaser: third in handicap at Wetherby (6 lengths behind Acdc) in October: will probably stay 3m: acts on heavy going: often travels strongly: often let down by jumping over fences. *Nigel Twiston-Davies*

BALLYANTICS (IRE) 8 b.g. Marienbard (IRE) – Ballindante (IRE) (Phardante (FR)) **c92** [2018/19 h88: h21.6g² c17.4g² c20.3g c21.6d h21.7v Dec 11] modest maiden hurdler: **h81** similar form over fences: stays 3m: acts on heavy going: tried in cheekpieces. *Neil Mulholland*

BALLYARTHUR (IRE) 9 b.g. Kayf Tara – Ariels Serenade (IRE) (Presenting) [2018/19 **c138** c137, h–: c20.6g⁵ c22.5gᵖᵘ c19.9d⁶ c22.9v² c25.6d⁴ c28.4gᶠ Feb 16] tall gelding: winning **h–** hurdler: useful handicap chaser: stayed 3¼m: acted on heavy going: often wore tongue tie: dead. *Nigel Twiston-Davies*

BALLYART (IRE) 6 b.g. Scorpion (IRE) – Candle Massini (IRE) (Dr Massini (IRE)) **h110** [2018/19 h19.9g⁴ h23.9d⁵ h23.6v² h23.5s h23.1d⁵ h24.2d Mar 22] tall gelding: sixth foal: half-brother to fair hurdler Wontbelongnow (2¾m winner, by Presenting) and a winning pointer by Flemensfirth: dam unraced: dead-heated for first in Irish point: fair form over hurdles: stays 3m: acts on heavy going: usually races close up. *Nigel Twiston-Davies*

BALLYBANE (IRE) 9 gr.g. Acambaro (GER) – Madam Sophie (IRE) (Moscow Society **c–** (USA)) [2018/19 c26gᵖᵘ May 4] long-backed gelding: unbeaten in 4 points: fair form on **h–** second of 2 starts over hurdles: pulled up in hunter on chasing debut: should stay 23f+: in cheekpieces last 2 starts: tried in tongue tie. *Miss Claire Harris*

BALLYBLAKE (IRE) 5 b.g. Arakan (USA) – Nonnetia (FR) (Trempolino (USA)) **h–** [2018/19 h19.9g Sep 23] pulled up in 2 Irish points: well beaten in novice hurdle. *Nigel Twiston-Davies*

BALLYBOKER BREEZE (IRE) 11 b.g. Gold Well – Ballyboker Lady (IRE) (Rashar **c138 x** (USA)) [2018/19 c24g² c25g* c23.8gᵖᵘ c23.8gᵘʳ c25gᶠ h24.4g³ Dec 29] fairly useful **h123** handicap hurdler: useful handicap chaser: won at Aintree (by 1¾ lengths from Petrou) in June: won points in March and April: stays 25f: acts on heavy going: often let down by jumping over fences. *Nicky Richards*

BALLYBOLLEY (IRE) 10 b.g. Kayf Tara – Gales Hill (IRE) (Beau Sher) [2018/19 **c–** c147, h–: c21g c21.4g⁵ c19.9d⁵ c20.2gᵖᵘ Feb 27] tall gelding: winning hurdler: smart **h–** chaser at best, no form in 2018/19: has worn hood: wears tongue tie. *Nigel Twiston-Davies*

BALLYBOUGH NORA (IRE) 6 b.m. Oscar (IRE) – Perspex Queen (IRE) (Presenting)   **h112**
[2018/19 h21g³ h21.4g⁴ h16.5s⁴ h21.4g³ h23.1d⁵ h21.6d⁴ h26.5g* Apr 20] £47,000 5-y-o:
rather unfurnished mare: sister to fairly useful hurdler Moonlight Drive (2¾m winner) and
2 winning pointers: dam winning pointer: point winner: fair handicap hurdler: won at
Newton Abbot in April: stays 3¼m: acts on good to soft going: hooded first 5 starts: usually
races off pace. *Jeremy Scott*

BALLYBREEN (IRE) 6 b.g. Gold Well – Miss Colclough (IRE) (Shernazar) [2018/19   **h63**
b16v⁵ h15.8v⁵ h18.5s h20s Apr 7] point winner: needed experience in bumper: poor form   **b–**
over hurdles. *Evan Williams*

BALLYCAINES (IRE) 4 ch.g. Finsceal Fior (IRE) – Annamanamoux (USA)   **h100**
(Leroidesanimaux (BRZ)) [2018/19 h15.3g⁵ Apr 14] compact gelding: has had breathing
operation: fair form on Flat: in tongue strap, 15/2, fifth in novice at Wincanton (7½ lengths
behind Highly Prized) on hurdling debut. *Nicky Henderson*

BALLYCAMP (IRE) 10 br.g. Kayf Tara – All Our Blessings (IRE) (Statoblest) [2018/19   **c101**
c107, h–: c20.5m³ c16.3g³ h15.7g⁶ c17.2m³ c21.4g⁶ c24g⁴ c19.2g c20.3g⁴ c23.9dᵖᵘ Nov   **h–**
22] lengthy gelding: fair maiden hurdler/chaser: stayed 21f: acted on good to firm and good
to soft going: tried in cheekpieces: wore tongue tie: dead. *Charles Pogson*

BALLYCASEY (IRE) 12 gr.g. Presenting – Pink Mist (IRE) (Montelimar (USA))   **c144**
[2018/19 c153d, h134: c21g³ c25g⁴ c30.2g⁵ c25d c30.2s⁴ Mar 13] good-topped gelding: **h–**
winning hurdler: useful chaser nowadays: third in minor event at Punchestown (12¼
lengths behind Ballyoisin) in June: stays 3¾m: acts on heavy going: has worn cheekpieces.
W. P. Mullins, Ireland

BALLYCOE 10 b.g. Norse Dancer (IRE) – Lizzy Lamb (Bustino) [2018/19 c–, h–:   **c90**
c19.7g³ c21.6g⁶ c23mᵖᵘ Jul 9] tall gelding: winning hurdler: fair handicap chaser, below   **h–**
form in 2018/19: stays 23f: acts on soft going: in cheekpieces last 3 starts: wears tongue tie.
Chris Gordon

BALLY CONOR (IRE) 6 b.g. Presenting – Soliya (FR) (Vaguely Pleasant (FR))   **h112**
[2018/19 b15.7g⁴ b16v* b16.4d³ h20.6d⁶ h20.6g² h20.6d⁵ Apr 6] first foal: dam (h125),   **b94**
2m-2¾m hurdle winner, half-sister to smart hurdler/chaser Solix (17f-21f winner) Solix: fair
form in bumpers: won at Ayr in November: fair form over hurdles: best effort when second
in novice at Newcastle in February. *Ruth Jefferson*

BALLYCROSS 8 b.g. King's Theatre (IRE) – Ninna Nanna (FR) (Garde Royale)   **c126 §**
[2018/19 c132§, h–: c23.8m² c25.5g⁴ c26.2g³ c23.6vᵖᵘ c27.3sᵖᵘ h23sᵖᵘ Mar 23] sturdy   **h– §**
gelding: fairly useful hurdler at best, pulled up final outing in 2018/19: useful handicap
chaser: stays 3m: acts on heavy going: wears cheekpieces: usually front runner/races
prominently: temperamental. *Nigel Twiston-Davies*

BALLYCRYSTAL COURT (IRE) 7 b.g. Court Cave (IRE) – Monavale (IRE) (Strong   **h109**
Gale) [2018/19 h107: h23.9g⁶ h19.8g² h23.8g⁵ h22.7g⁵ h19.8s³ Mar 10] has had breathing
operation: fair handicap hurdler: stays 2½m: acts on good to soft going: tried in tongue tie:
has joined Rebecca Menzies. *Nicky Richards*

BALLYCRYSTAL (IRE) 8 b.g. Oscar (IRE) – Musical Madam (IRE) (Musical Pursuit)   **c119**
[2018/19 c127, h–: c20.3g⁶ c21.4g c25.2g⁵ c25.2mᵖᵘ c26.3sᶠ Mar 3] useful-looking   **h–**
gelding: has had breathing operation: winning hurdler: fairly useful handicap chaser: stays
3m: acts on soft going: tried in cheekpieces/tongue tie. *Brian Ellison*

BALLYDARSI (IRE) 9 br.m. Darsi (FR) – Ballyday June (IRE) (Rock Hopper) [2018/19   **c63**
c22.5gᵖᵘ c23.6d c24d⁶ c20.9s³ c25.2d⁶ Jan 2] third foal: dam maiden pointer: point winner: **h–**
ran once over hurdles in Ireland for P. J. Rothwell: poor maiden chaser: usually wears
headgear: in tongue tie last 2 starts. *Matt Sheppard*

BALLYDINE (IRE) 9 ch.g. Stowaway – Bealaha Essie (IRE) (Denel (FR)) [2018/19   **c137**
c133p, h–: c23.4d⁵ c26d² c25.6d³ c34vᵖᵘ Mar 16] good-topped gelding: winning hurdler: **h–**
useful handicap chaser: third in Peter Marsh Chase at Haydock (4¼ lengths behind
Wakanda) in January: should stay long distances: acts on heavy going: in cheekpieces/
tongue tie last 2 starts. *Charlie Longsdon*

BALLYDUN OSCAR (IRE) 7 b.g. Oscar (IRE) – Calling Classy (IRE) (Good Thyne   **h101**
(USA)) [2018/19 h21.6g² h21.6g* h23.1g⁵ h23.1m⁵ Nov 6] sturdy gelding: has had
breathing operation: sixth foal: brother to fair 3m chase winner The Rockies, and closely
related to fair hurdler/fairly useful chaser Goodthynemilan (2½m-3m winner) and a
winning pointer (both by Milan): dam (h101) 2m-2½m hurdle winner: off mark in Irish
points at second attempt: fair form over hurdles: won maiden at Newton Abbot in July:
tongue tied first 3 starts. *Ben Pauling*

BALLYEGAN WARRIOR (IRE) 7 b.g. Getaway (GER) – Sweet Empire (IRE) **c–**
(Second Empire (IRE)) [2018/19 c–, h–: h19m⁰ᵖᵘ h21.6gᵖᵘ c24g Jul 18] maiden hurdler/ **h–**
chaser, no form in 2018/19: tried in visor: dead. *David Dennis*

BALLYELLIS (IRE) 6 b.g. Shantou (USA) – Chalice Wells (Sadler's Wells (USA)) **h109**
[2018/19 b–: h21g⁵ h23dᵖᵘ h15.8g⁴ h21.2d h16d⁶ h21.4g⁶ h21.2m Apr 23] fair maiden
hurdler: should stay 2½m+. *Nigel Twiston-Davies*

BALLYFARSOON (IRE) 8 ch.g. Medicean – Amzara (IRE) (Montjeu (IRE)) [2018/19 **h105**
h20g² h19.9m² h20g² h19.3m h15.7g² h19.4g³ h15.7g⁶ Jan 1] modest on Flat, stays 16.5f:
fair maiden hurdler: stays 2½m: acts on good to firm going: often wears visor: front runner/
races prominently. *Peter Winks*

BALLYGOWN BAY (IRE) 6 b.g. Flemensfirth (USA) – Star Shuil (IRE) (Soviet Star **h113**
(USA)) [2018/19 h108: h19m⁴ h19.7g⁴ h21d⁵ h23.5sᵖᵘ Dec 22] rather unfurnished gelding:
fair maiden hurdler: stays 2½m: acts on good to soft going. *Philip Hobbs*

BALLYHEIGUE BAY (IRE) 12 b.g. Rudimentary (USA) – Terinka (IRE) (Erins Isle) **c71**
[2018/19 c123, c123: c20v³ c24gᵖᵘ c25.7sᵖᵘ h20.5sᵘʳ h25s⁶ h23.5m² Mar 31] good-topped **h118**
gelding: fairly useful handicap hurdler: second at Ascot (conditionals) in March: fairly
useful handicap chaser, well below form in 2018/19: stays 31f: acts on good to firm and
heavy going: wears headgear/tongue tie: usually races close up. *Chris Gordon*

BALLYHILL (FR) 8 b.g. Al Namix (FR) – Laly Light (FR) (Start Fast (FR)) [2018/19 **c144**
c137x, h–: c19.4d h19.6d² c19.9s* c20.6d³ c20.6d³ c23.8d³ c21.1d Apr 5] good-topped **h130**
gelding: useful handicap hurdler: useful handicap chaser: won at Aintree in December:
third in Grade 3 events at Cheltenham (twice) in January: stays 21f: acts on heavy going.
Nigel Twiston-Davies

BALLYHOME (IRE) 8 b.g. Westerner – Nostra (FR) (Limnos (JPN)) [2018/19 h104p: **h120**
h21.3m* h21g⁵ h22.8s³ h23.1d² h23.1g* Mar 27] lengthy gelding: fairly useful handicap
hurdler: won at Wetherby (conditionals novice) in November and Market Rasen in March:
stays 23f: acts on soft and good to firm going: strong traveller. *Fergal O'Brien*

BALLYKAN 9 b.g. Presenting – La Marianne (Supreme Leader) [2018/19 c136, h–: **c124**
c24.2m² c24g⁴ c25.1g² c24.2d⁵ c23.8g⁴ Apr 24] lengthy, useful-looking gelding: winning **h–**
hurdler: fairly useful handicap chaser nowadays: stays 3¼m: acts on soft and good to firm
going: wears cheekpieces: usually tongue tied. *Nigel Twiston-Davies*

BALLYKNOCK CLOUD (IRE) 8 gr.g. Cloudings (IRE) – Ballyknock Present (IRE) **c105**
(Presenting) [2018/19 h110: c26.2g c23d c23d c25.1gᶠ Feb 16] has had breathing **h–**
operation: multiple point winner: fair form over hurdles: similar form over fences: stays
3m: acts on good to soft going: wears cheekpieces/tongue tie: usually races prominently.
Jack R. Barber

BALLY LAGAN (IRE) 11 gr.g. Kalanisi (IRE) – Rose Palma (FR) (Great Palm (USA)) **c82 §**
[2018/19 c99§, h–: c15.7g⁵ c20g⁶ c17.4g⁶ c21.7dᵖᵘ h19.7dᵖᵘ c20.5d c20.2g² c19.5m Mar **h–**
29] stocky gelding: has had breathing operation: maiden hurdler: poor handicap chaser
nowadays: stays 2¾m: acts on soft and good to firm going: wears headgear: has worn
tongue tie, including in 2018/19: unreliable. *Robin Dickin*

BALLY LONGFORD (IRE) 11 b.g. Gold Well – Stay On Line (IRE) (Over The River **c130 x**
(FR)) [2018/19 c136, h–: c25g⁴ c20v² c15.7d⁵ c24g² c24g⁴ h20.5d⁵ c20.2g² c20.2g⁵ Apr **h109**
14] lengthy gelding: fairly useful handicap hurdler, below form sole outing in 2018/19:
useful handicap chaser: stays 3¼m, fully effective over shorter: acts on soft and good to
firm going: has worn tongue tie: often let down by jumping over fences. *Colin Tizzard*

BALLYMAGROARTY BOY (IRE) 6 b.g. Milan – Glazed Storm (IRE) (Vinnie Roe **h119**
(IRE)) [2018/19 h97, b–: h22.8v* h23.3v h23.1dᶠ h25s² Mar 11] fairly useful handicap
hurdler: won at Haydock (conditionals) in December: stays 25f: best form on soft/heavy
going: tried in cheekpieces. *Nigel Hawke*

BALLYMALIN (IRE) 9 b.g. Presenting – Murrurundi (IRE) (Old Vic) [2018/19 c133, **c121 x**
h–: c26.2g c27.3s⁵ c28.8v² Feb 18] lengthy gelding: winning hurdler: fairly useful handicap **h–**
chaser nowadays: stays 4¼m: acts on heavy going: tried in visor: often let down by
jumping over fences. *Nigel Twiston-Davies*

BALLYMILAN 4 b.f. Milan – Ballyhoo (IRE) (Supreme Leader) [2018/19 b12.6s⁵ Dec **b79 p**
19] fourth foal: closely related to fair 3m chase winner Kilcrea Bridge (by Kayf Tara): dam
(h102) 21f-27f hurdle winner: 10/1, fifth in fillies junior bumper at Newbury (7½ lengths
behind Who What When), left poorly placed: should improve. *Neil Mulholland*

*Matchbook Holloway's Handicap Hurdle, Ascot—a sixth win in seven starts for Ballymoy,
who is chased home by Colonial Dreams (checked cap) and Seddon (centre)*

BALLYMOY (IRE) 6 b.g. Flemensfirth (USA) – John's Eliza (IRE) (Dr Massini (IRE)) **h147**
[2018/19 h136p, b92p: h16d* h16.3s⁴ h18.9v* h19.3d* h23.4s h19.2d⁶ Feb 24] sturdy
gelding: has had breathing operation: smart handicap hurdler: won at Chepstow in October,
Haydock (by 4½ lengths from Better Getalong) in December and Holloway's Handicap
Hurdle at Ascot (by 1¾ lengths from Colonial Dreams) in January: should stay at least
2½m: acts on heavy going: game and genuine. *Nigel Twiston-Davies*

BALLYNANTY (IRE) 7 gr.g. Yeats (IRE) – Reina Blanca (Darshaan) [2018/19 h15.6g⁵ **h112**
h15.6g⁵ h16.2gᵘʳ h19.8g³ h23.8g* h23.8mᵘʳ h20.9g² h24.3m Apr 12] fair handicap hurdler:
won at Musselburgh in January: stays 3m: best form on good going: tried in hood: wears
tongue tie: usually races in rear. *N. W. Alexander*

BALLYOISIN (IRE) 8 b.g. Presenting – Regal Force (IRE) (King's Ride) [2018/19 **c160**
c160, h129: c20.6m* c21g* h16s* c16d* c17g⁵ Dec 27] useful form over hurdles: won **h140 +**
handicap at Listowel (by length from Shanning) in September: high-class chaser:
won Grade 3 event at Killarney (by 9½ lengths from Alisier d'Irlande) in May, minor event
at Punchestown (by 8 lengths from Woodland Opera) in June and Fortria Chase at Navan
(by 23 lengths from Ordinary World) in November: stays 21f: acts on soft and good to firm
going: front runner/races prominently, usually travels strongly. *Enda Bolger, Ireland*

BALLYOPTIC (IRE) 9 b.g. Old Vic – Lambourne Lace (IRE) (Un Desperado (FR)) **c137**
[2018/19 c154, h147+: c25.9sᶠ c29.5s⁶ c28.4gᵖᵘ c34.3gᶠ Apr 6] well-made gelding: **h–**
winning hurdler: smart handicap chaser at best: sixth in Welsh Grand National at Chepstow
(26½ lengths behind Elegant Escape) in December, only completed start in 2018/19: stays
4m: acts on heavy going: has worn tongue tie, including in 2018/19. *Nigel Twiston-Davies*

BALLY RIVER BOY (IRE) 8 ch.g. Indian River (FR) – Maple River (IRE) (Over The **c101**
River (FR)) [2018/19 c26g* c27.5dᵖᵘ c24sᵖᵘ c20v³ Feb 18] multiple point winner: fair form
in hunter chases: won novice event at Fontwell in May: hooded first 3 starts. *David Thompson*

BALLYROCK (IRE) 13 b.g. Milan – Ardent Love (IRE) (Ardross) [2018/19 c–§, h111§: **c– §**
h23.1m May 8] useful-looking gelding: useful hurdler at best, well held sole outing in **h– §**
2018/19: winning chaser: stayed 3m: acted on heavy going: wore headgear/tongue tie:
usually raced close up: dead. *Tim Vaughan*

BALLYTHOMAS 12 b.g. Kayf Tara – Gregale (Gildoran) [2018/19 c–, h–: h20.3gᵖᵘ May **c–**
23] fair hurdler/chaser at best, no form since 2016/17: has worn cheekpieces, including **h–**
sole outing in 2018/19: usually leads. *David Thompson*

BALLYVIC BORU (IRE) 7 b.g. Brian Boru – Thedoublede (IRE) (Deploy) [2018/19 **c125**
h119: c16.4g² c17.1g* c21.4m² h20.6g c20.1g⁵ Apr 25] strong, lengthy gelding: winning **h–**
hurdler: fairly useful form over fences: won novice handicap at Kelso in May: stays 21f:
acts on good to firm going: tried in tongue tie: usually races close up. *Brian Ellison*

BALLYWARD (IRE) 7 b.g. Flemensfirth (USA) – Ifyoucouldseemenow (IRE) (Saddlers' Hall (IRE)) [2018/19 h145: c25.2g² c24d* c31.7sᶠ Mar 12] useful hurdler: smart form over fences: won Grade 3 novice at Naas (by 11 lengths from Chris's Dream) in January: stayed 3m: acted on heavy going: dead. *W. P. Mullins, Ireland* **c151 h–**

BALLYWOOD (FR) 5 b.g. Ballingarry (IRE) – Miss Hollywood (FR) (True Brave (USA)) [2018/19 c117p, h121: h16d⁴ h19.8v⁴ c18.2d* c16.4g* c16.4g² c16d* c20.5m⁴ Apr 13] fairly useful handicap hurdler: smart form over fences: won handicap at Taunton and novice handicap at Doncaster in December, and handicap at Ludlow (by ¾ length from Valseur du Granval) in March: second in Lightning Novices' Chase at Doncaster (3½ lengths behind Dynamite Dollars) in January: will prove best around 2m: acts on soft going: often travels strongly. *Alan King* **c146 h115**

BALNASLOW (IRE) 12 b.g. Presenting – Noble Choice (Dahar (USA)) [2018/19 c128, h–: c27.5d⁴ c26.3dᵖᵘ c21.1d Apr 4] tall gelding: winning pointer/hurdler: useful hunter chaser at best, below that level in 2018/19: stays 3¼m: acts on soft and good to firm going: tried in cheekpieces: has worn tongue tie. *Graham McKeever, Ireland* **c105 h–**

BALZAC TURGOT (FR) 8 b.g. Kapgarde (FR) – Perle d'Opale (FR) (Cyborg (FR)) [2018/19 c19.5g* c19.9m² c22.7gᵖᵘ Jul 17] winning hurdler: useful form over fences: won maiden at Ballinrobe in May: stayed 2½m: acted on soft and good to firm going: wore tongue tie: usually raced close up/travelled strongly: dead. *Henry de Bromhead, Ireland* **c135 h–**

BAMBI DU NOYER (FR) 8 b.g. Sageburg (IRE) – Zouk Wood (USA) (Woodman (USA)) [2018/19 c106, h108: c20.3g⁵ c17d⁴ c17.3m* c21.2g* h19.9d Mar 30] sturdy gelding: winning hurdler: fair chaser: won 2 handicaps at Cartmel in July, only starts for John Hodge: stays 21f: acts on soft and good to firm going: often in headgear: has worn tongue tie. *Sean Conway* **c114 h–**

BAMBYS GIRL 6 b.m. Kayf Tara – Bamby (IRE) (Glacial Storm (USA)) [2018/19 b16d Nov 28] second foal: half-sister to bumper winner Bambys Boy (by Lucarno): dam (c96/h89), 2m-2½m hurdle/chase winner, half-sister to fairly useful hurdler/fair chaser (stayed 3¼m) Mr Supreme: tailed off in mares bumper. *Micky Hammond* **b–**

BANANA JOE (IRE) 5 b.g. Getaway (GER) – Rosetiepy (FR) (Apple Tree (FR)) [2018/19 b15.8d b16.7s⁶ h19.8s Mar 7] little impact in bumpers: tailed off in maiden on hurdling debut. *Ben Pauling* **h– b–**

BANDITRY (IRE) 7 b.g. Iffraaj – Badalona (Cape Cross (IRE)) [2018/19 h117: h15.8g⁵ Nov 13] sturdy gelding: fairly useful hurdler, found little sole outing in sphere in 2018/19: may prove best at sharp 2m: acts on good to soft going: has worn hood. *Ian Williams* **h–**

BAND OF BLOOD (IRE) 11 b.g. King's Theatre (IRE) – Cherry Falls (IRE) (Ali-Royal (IRE)) [2018/19 c131, h–: c22.3g⁴ c24.2d Jan 5] sturdy gelding: winning hurdler: fairly useful handicap chaser nowadays: probably best around 3m: acts on heavy going: wears blinkers: has worn tongue tie. *Dr Richard Newland* **c122 h–**

BAND OF OUTLAWS (IRE) 4 b.g. Fast Company (IRE) – Band of Colour (IRE) (Spectrum (IRE)) [2018/19 h16v³ h16s* h16g* h16.4s* h17d⁵ Apr 4] strong, compact gelding: half-brother to modest 2m hurdle winner Smiling Lady (by Kris Kin): useful on **h139**

Boodles Juvenile Handicap Hurdle (Fred Winter), Cheltenham—J. J. Slevin produces hot favourite Band of Outlaws (white face) to overhaul fellow Irish raider Coko Beach (grey)

Mr Justin Carthy's "Band of Outlaws"

Flat, stays 1m: similar form over hurdles: won juvenile maiden at Limerick in December, novice at Naas in February and Fred Winter Juvenile Handicap Hurdle at Cheltenham (by 2 lengths from Coko Beach) in March: likely to prove best at 2m: acts on soft going: often travels strongly. *Joseph Patrick O'Brien, Ireland*

BANDON ROC 8 b.g. Shirocco (GER) – Azur (IRE) (Brief Truce (USA)) [2018/19   **c114 §**
c110§, h116: h25g c25.2s* c24v^pu c24.2v^6 Mar 18] winning hurdler: fair handicap chaser: **h–**
won at Hereford in December: stays 25f: acts on heavy going: wears headgear: temperamental. *Kim Bailey*

BANDSMAN 8 b.g. Bandmaster (USA) – Soleil Sauvage (Loup Sauvage (USA)) [2018/19   **c127**
h–: h16m* c20.5m* c21g^3 c16m^2 c20.5g c20s^pu c16.2g^2 c20g Apr 27] good-topped   **h123**
gelding: fairly useful handicap hurdler: won at Warwick in May: fairly useful handicap chaser: won novice event at Kempton later same month: stays 21f: acts on soft and good to firm going: tried in cheekpieces/tongue tie. *Dan Skelton*

BANFF (IRE) 6 b.g. Papal Bull – Hugs 'N Kisses (IRE) (Noverre (USA)) [2018/19 h98:   **h–**
h19.2g^pu May 14] modest on Flat, stays 2m: lightly-raced hurdler, pulled up sole outing in sphere in 2018/19: probably stays 2½m: in cheekpieces last 3 starts. *Olly Murphy*

BANG BANG ROSIE (IRE) 7 b.m. Stowaway – Restless Dreams (IRE) (Supreme   **c106 p**
Leader) [2018/19 h19g* h18.3g^2 h20g^3 h21g^4 c23d^2 h20d^4 h19.4g^3 h23.8g^4 h21.2d^6 Feb 6]   **h115**
€5,000 3-y-o: fourth foal: dam unraced sister to fairly useful hurdler/useful chaser (stayed 25f) Alright Now M'lad: runner-up both completed starts in points: bumper winner: fairly useful hurdler: won mares maiden at Limerick in May: second in maiden at Ballinrobe on chasing debut: left W. P. Mullins after fifth start: stays 23f: acts on good to soft going: in hood/tongue tie last 3 starts: usually races off pace: open to improvement as a chaser. *Peter Bowen*

BANG ON FRANKIE (IRE) 7 br.g. Kalanisi (IRE) – Shuil Abbey (IRE) (Saddlers' Hall (IRE)) [2018/19 h117: h16.4g³ h16.3s⁵ Nov 30] strong gelding: fairly useful form in bumpers/over hurdles: dead. *Nicky Martin* **h116**

BANG ON (IRE) 6 ch.g. Fracas (IRE) – Carramanagh Lady (IRE) (Anshan) [2018/19 b92: h16.7d⁴ h16.5d* h19d⁶ h19.2d h16s³ h18.5s⁴ Apr 16] fair form over hurdles: won novice at Taunton in November: should be suited by 2½m: acts on soft going: tried in hood: usually front runner/races prominently. *Jeremy Scott* **h112**

BANISH (USA) 6 b.g. Smart Strike (CAN) – Beyond Our Reach (IRE) (Danehill Dancer (IRE)) [2018/19 h16.3g h16g h15.7g⁴ h15.8g⁶ Oct 25] fairly useful on Flat, stays 1½m: poor form over hurdles: in hood last 3 starts. *Tom George* **h74**

BANKSY'S ART 4 b.g. Sixties Icon – Outside Art (Excellent Art) [2018/19 h16.7g³ h16.8s⁴ h16d⁴ Dec 4] fair maiden on Flat, stays 1½m: modest form over hurdles: best effort when third in juvenile at Market Rasen in November. *Mick Channon* **h96**

BANNY'S LAD 10 ch.g. Osorio (GER) – Skytrial (USA) (Sky Classic (CAN)) [2018/19 c109x, h–: h18.6g h22.1m⁵ c19.9m³ c20.3d^pu Nov 20] tall gelding: has had breathing operation: fair handicap hurdler/chaser, below form in 2018/19: stays 25f: acts on good to firm and heavy going: has worn cheekpieces, including in 2018/19. *Michael Easterby* **c83 h88**

BAPAUME (FR) 6 b.g. Turtle Bowl (IRE) – Brouhaha (FR) (American Post) [2018/19 h162: h25.4s² h19.4s* h20g⁴ h24g³ h24s² h24d⁴ Mar 14] useful-looking gelding: high-class hurdler: 3 lengths second to Mr Adjudicator in Prix La Barka at Auteuil after end of British season (won race in 2018): also placed 3 times in between, in Christmas Hurdle at Leopardstown, John Mulhern Galmoy Hurdle at Gowran (1¼ lengths behind Presenting Percy) and Champion Stayers' Hurdle at Punchestown: stays 25f: acts on soft going: usually races in rear. *W. P. Mullins, Ireland* **h156**

BARABOY (IRE) 9 b.g. Barathea (IRE) – Irina (IRE) (Polar Falcon (USA)) [2018/19 c–, h93: h16.8g May 15] modest hurdler at best, well held sole outing in 2018/19: winning chaser: unproven beyond 17f: acts on heavy going: wears headgear: has worn tongue tie. *Barry Murtagh* **c– h–**

BARACALU (FR) 8 gr.g. Califet (FR) – Myragentry (FR) (Myrakalu (FR)) [2018/19 h109: h20.1s⁴ h16.8s³ Dec 26] good-topped gelding: fair form at best over hurdles: tried in hood: has joined Tristan Davidson. *Sandy Thomson* **h92**

BARAROCCO 6 b.g. Shirocco (GER) – Behra (IRE) (Grand Lodge (USA)) [2018/19 b15.7g May 13] well held in bumper: dead. *Dan Skelton* **b–**

BARATINEUR (FR) 8 ch.g. Vendangeur (IRE) – Olmantina (FR) (Ragmar (FR)) [2018/19 h–: h15.8g h16.2g^pu h16s h19d⁵ h15.7g² h15.7g² h16.8v² h15.8s^pu Feb 26] modest handicap hurdler nowadays: left Kevin Bishop after fourth start, Sam England after seventh: stays 19f: acts on heavy going: tried in headgear/tongue tie: usually travels strongly. *Adrian Wintle* **h94**

BARBADOS BLUE (IRE) 5 b.m. Getaway (GER) – Buck's Blue (FR) (Epervier Bleu) [2018/19 b16g* h16d² h19d² Apr 4] €40,000 3-y-o: fourth foal: half-sister to fairly useful hurdler/useful chaser More Buck's (19f-3m winner, by Presenting): dam, French 19f hurdle winner, half-sister to Big Buck's: won conditionals/amateurs bumper at Warwick (by 15 lengths from Huntsmans Jog) on debut: fairly useful form over hurdles: better effort when second in novice at Taunton in April: will stay 2½m+: likely to progress further. *Nicky Henderson* **h115 p b94**

BARBARA VILLIERS 4 b.f. Champs Elysees – Frances Stuart (IRE) (King's Best (USA)) [2018/19 h16.8g³ h16.8g³ h16.7g⁵ Sep 29] fair maiden on Flat, stays 1½m: poor form over hurdles. *Evan Williams* **h70**

BARBROOK STAR (IRE) 7 b.g. Getaway (GER) – Fille de Robin (FR) (Robin des Champs (FR)) [2018/19 h110: h21g⁴ h20.3g⁴ c23.6s³ c24d³ c23.6d c25.1s* c23.6d Apr 6] useful-looking gelding: fair maiden hurdler: fairly useful form over fences: won handicap at Wincanton in March: stays 25f: acts on soft going: in cheekpieces last 2 starts. *Philip Hobbs* **c117 h107**

BARCALONA 7 gr.m. Sulamani (IRE) – Ruby Isabel (IRE) (Great Palm (USA)) [2018/19 b68: h19.5m⁴ Apr 22] little impact in bumpers/mares novice hurdle. *Colin Tizzard* **h–**

BARDD (IRE) 7 b.g. Dylan Thomas (IRE) – Zarawa (IRE) (Kahyasi) [2018/19 h104§: h15.8g^F h16.7g⁴ h16g⁴ h15.3m⁵ h20.5g⁵ h16s³ h16g² Apr 26] compact gelding: fair maiden hurdler: left Nicky Henderson after second start: raced mainly around 2m: acts on soft and good to firm going: front runner/races prominently: no battler. *Danni O'Neill* **h108 §**

BetVictor Gold Cup Handicap Chase, Cheltenham—
front runners dominate as Baron Alco holds off top-weight Frodon in an incident-packed race

BARD OF BRITTANY 5 b.g. Sayif (IRE) – Lily Le Braz (Montjeu (IRE)) [2018/19 h–, **h98** b–: h16d³ h16m⁴ h15.8g h18.6g⁶ Nov 8] angular gelding: modest form over hurdles: tried in hood: usually races towards rear. *Mick Channon*

BAREL OF LAUGHS (IRE) 13 b.g. Milan – Danette (GER) (Exit To Nowhere (USA)) **c126** [2018/19 c129, h–: c26.3g* May 4] workmanlike gelding: multiple point winner: maiden **h–** hurdler: useful hunter chaser: won at Cheltenham in May: stays 3¼m: acts on heavy going: wears cheekpieces: tried in tongue tie: usually responds generously to pressure. *Philip Rowley*

BARELY BLACK (IRE) 7 b.m. Urban Poet (USA) – Downtown Rosie (IRE) (Good **h74** Thyne (USA)) [2018/19 h84: h22.1g h23.3g² Jun 14] poor maiden hurdler: stays 23f: best form on good going: in cheekpieces last 3 starts. *Julia Brooke*

BARE NECESSITIES (IRE) 9 b.g. Sandmason – Marquante (IRE) (Brief Truce **c–** (USA)) [2018/19 h–: h25g h20.3s c20.3gᵖᵘ c15.7g⁶ Apr 3] maiden hurdler, no form since **h–** 2015/16, including over fences: tried in blinkers: in tongue tie last 2 starts. *Shaun Lycett*

BARFLY 5 gr.g. Fair Mix (IRE) – Just Smokie (Cloudings (IRE)) [2018/19 h22dᵖᵘ h20.1vᵖᵘ **h–** Dec 20] off mark in points at second attempt: no form over hurdles: in cheekpieces final start. *Chris Grant*

BARGY LADY (IRE) 7 b.m. Yeats (IRE) – Jolivia (FR) (Dernier Empereur (USA)) **c128 p** [2018/19 h17d h20g² h18.6m³ h22.4m* h22.8dF c17.4g⁴ c21g⁶ Oct 13] seventh foal: sister **h133** to bumper winner/fairly useful chaser (2½m/21f winner) Compadre, closely related to a winning pointer by Milan and half-sister to 2 winners, including useful hurdler/very smart chaser Sizing Tennessee (2m-3¼m winner, by Robin des Champs): dam (c109/h120), French 17f hurdle/chase winner, also 9f winner on Flat: useful handicap hurdler: won at Killarney (by 2¾ lengths from Lizzies Champ) in July: fairly useful form over fences: won mares maiden at Fairyhouse in October: stays 3m: acts on good to firm and heavy going: usually wears hood: open to further improvement as a chaser. *W. P. Mullins, Ireland*

BARKIS 10 ch.g. Selkirk (USA) – Batik (IRE) (Peintre Celebre (USA)) [2018/19 h106: **h110** h20.3g h18.5g* h15.8m⁶ Jul 13] fair handicap hurdler: won at Newton Abbot (conditionals) in July: stays 2½m: raced mainly on good going. *Nicky Henderson*

BARLEY HILL (IRE) 6 ch.g. Stowaway – Saysi (IRE) (Scribano) [2018/19 b86: **h86** h19.2g⁵ h15.8g⁶ h16.7gᵘʳ h16.3g h20.3s⁶ Dec 4] strong gelding: modest form over hurdles: should stay 2½m: acts on soft going. *Ben Pauling*

BARLOW (IRE) 12 br.g. Beneficial – Carrigeen Kerria (IRE) (Kemal (FR)) [2018/19 **c–** c87, h–: c26gᵖᵘ Jun 16] sturdy gelding: winning hurdler: fairly useful chaser at best, pulled **h–** up sole outing in 2018/19: stays 3¼m: acts on soft going: has worn cheekpieces, including in 2018/19: tried in tongue tie. *Emma Lavelle*

BARNAY 4 b.g. Nayef (USA) – Barnezet (GR) (Invincible Spirit (IRE)) [2018/19 h16.7d⁶ **h93** h15.6g⁴ h16d⁴ h19.9d⁵ h18.7sᵖᵘ h18.6g h16.8d⁵ Apr 23] fair on Flat, stays 1¼m: modest maiden hurdler: unproven beyond 2m: acts on good to soft going: in blinkers last 2 starts. *Clare Ellam*

BARNEY DWAN (IRE) 9 b.g. Vinnie Roe (IRE) – Kapricia Speed (FR) (Vertical Speed **c135** (FR)) [2018/19 c145, h–: c19.4d⁵ c24d³ c24g³ c26g⁶ h25g⁴ Apr 25] sturdy gelding: useful **h118** handicap hurdler, below form final outing in 2018/19: useful handicap chaser: stays 3m: acts on heavy going: in cheekpieces last 3 starts. *Fergal O'Brien*

BARNEY FROM TYANEE (IRE) 8 b.g. Milan – Miss Opera (Alflora (IRE)) [2018/19 c94, h92: h19.2g² h20g⁶ h23g c19.4mᵖᵘ Aug 2] modest handicap hurdler: maiden chaser, pulled up before outing in 2018/19: stays 2½m: acts on heavy going: in cheekpieces last 5 starts: tried in tongue tie. *Michael Blake* — **c–** **h92**

BARNEY'S CAULKER 8 b.g. Captain Gerrard (IRE) – Little Cascade (Forzando) [2018/19 h64: h16.2gʳᵒ h17.1d h16.2gᵘʳ h16.8dᵖᵘ Jan 21] small gelding: little form over hurdles: wears tongue tie. *Maurice Barnes* — **h–**

BARN HILL 7 b.g. Kayf Tara – Shuil Mavourneen (IRE) (Welsh Term) [2018/19 h–: h18.5m May 8] little show in novice hurdles: dead. *Philip Hobbs* — **h–**

BARON ALCO (FR) 8 ch.g. Dom Alco (FR) – Paula (FR) (Network (GER)) [2018/19 c19.4d² c20.2g* c20.6d⁴ Dec 15] sturdy gelding: winning hurdler: smart handicap chaser: won BetVictor Gold Cup at Cheltenham (by 2 lengths from Frodon) in November: stays 21f: acts on heavy going. *Gary Moore* — **c153** **h–**

BARON DU PLESSIS (FR) 8 b.g. Network (GER) – Larme A L'Oeil (FR) (Luchiroverte (IRE)) [2018/19 c103, h–: c24m³ c23.8g⁴ c20.2g⁴ c23.6d² c23.6d⁶ Jan 25] lengthy gelding: maiden hurdler: fair maiden chaser: stays 3m: acts on heavy going: in cheekpieces last 3 starts: unreliable. *Ian Williams* — **c100 §** **h–**

BARON VON CHILL 7 b.g. Sulamani (IRE) – Kings Maiden (IRE) (King's Theatre (IRE)) [2018/19 h16.7g* h15.8m³ h15.8m⁴ h15.7g² h16.7gᵖᵘ h18.6gᵖᵘ h20g Oct 11] has had breathing operation: trained in Ireland prior to 2018/19: modest handicap hurdler: won at Market Rasen in May: left Dan Skelton after fourth start: unproven beyond 17f: acts on good to firm going: usually wears headgear: often tongue tied in 2018/19: temperamental. *Adrian Wintle* — **h98 §**

BARRA (FR) 8 b.m. Vendangeur (IRE) – Oasaka (FR) (Robin des Champs (FR)) [2018/19 h139: c22g* c20d³ Apr 23] lengthy mare: useful hurdler: similar form over fences: won maiden at Kilbeggan in July: third in Grade 3 mares event at Fairyhouse (10½ lengths behind Camelia de Cotte) when next seen: stays 2¾m: acts on soft going: has worn cheekpieces: wears tongue tie: disappointed at Punchestown shortly after end of British season, but remains open to improvement as a chaser. *Gordon Elliott, Ireland* — **c130 p** **h–**

BARRAKILLA (IRE) 12 b.g. Milan – Kigali (IRE) (Torus) [2018/19 c126, h–: c20.9v⁴ Mar 7] good-topped gelding: winning hurdler: one-time useful chaser, well below best sole outing in 2018/19: stays 2½m: acts on heavy going. *Fergal O'Brien* — **c97** **h–**

BARRANCO VALLEY 8 b.g. Midnight Legend – Shali San (FR) (Saint des Saints (FR)) [2018/19 h18.5s⁴ Mar 18] fairly useful form when second on hurdling debut in 2015/16: fourth in maiden at Exeter on sole outing since. *David Pipe* — **h109**

BARRINGTON COURT (IRE) 5 ch.m. Mastercraftsman (IRE) – Arabian Hideway (IRE) (Desert Prince (IRE)) [2018/19 b16d* h16d³ h16d Jan 6] seventh foal: half-sister to 5f-7f winner Novay Essjay (by Noverre): dam unraced: useful form in bumpers: won listed mares event at Navan (by 10 lengths from Two Shoe Tom) in November: fairly useful form over hurdles: easily better effort when third in mares maiden at Naas in December. *Mrs J. Harrington, Ireland* — **h115** **b107**

BARRYS JACK (IRE) 9 b.g. Well Chosen – Theatre Fool (IRE) (King's Theatre (IRE)) [2018/19 c115, h107: h17.1g⁴ h17.1v³ Dec 2] fair handicap hurdler: winning chaser: stays 21f: acts on heavy going: usually races towards rear. *Brian Ellison* — **c–** **h101**

BARTERS HILL (IRE) 9 b.g. Kalanisi (IRE) – Circle The Wagons (IRE) (Commanche Run) [2018/19 c–, h–: h20.5sᵖᵘ Dec 1] strong, lengthy gelding: unbeaten in 4 bumpers: useful novice hurdler in 2015/16: no form after, including on chasing debut: stayed 3m: acted on soft going: retired. *Ben Pauling* — **c–** **h–**

BARTHOLOMEW J (IRE) 5 ch.g. Fast Company (IRE) – Mana (IRE) (Motivator) [2018/19 h16d h20.3s⁶ h20.6m³ Apr 21] fairly useful on Flat, stays 1½m: modest form over hurdles: may prove best at shorter than 2½m. *Lydia Pearce* — **h87**

BARTON KNOLL 7 b.g. Midnight Legend – Barton Flower (Danzero (AUS)) [2018/19 h110: h19.6g² h19.9g² h19.9g⁴ c19.2g² c19.1g* c20.2g³ c20d³ c20.3g² c19.4gᵖᵘ Apr 26] fair handicap hurdler: fairly useful form over fences: won novice at Doncaster in December: stays 2½m: acts on soft going: usually races close up. *John Mackie* — **c127** **h116**

BARTON ROSE 10 b.m. Midnight Legend – Barton Flower (Danzero (AUS)) [2018/19 c107, h–: c20.5m³ c20.3g³ c21g³ c21g³ c20g⁴ c23g⁴ c20.3d c19.9g³ c19.9g² Apr 11] rather leggy mare: winning hurdler: fair handicap chaser: best up to 21f: acts on good to firm and heavy going: has worn cheekpieces. *Charlie Longsdon* — **c103** **h–**

107

BASILDON 4 b.g. Champs Elysees – Casual (Nayef (USA)) [2018/19 ab16.3s* ab16.3s⁴ **b86** Feb 23] has had breathing operation: fifth foal: brother to very smart French/Australian 1¼m-1½m winner Harlem and half-brother to 2 winners, including bumper winner Shearling (by Rail Link): dam, 7f-1½m winner, half-sister to useful 2m hurdle winner Rich Coast: fair form in bumpers: won maiden event at Newcastle in January. *Brian Ellison*

BASSARABAD (FR) 8 b.g. Astarabad (USA) – Grivette (FR) (Antarctique (IRE)) **c113 §** [2018/19 c107§, h–: c24.5g³ c23g c24s² h26.4g³ c24gᵖᵘ Oct 7] tall, useful-looking gelding: **h98 §** has had breathing operation: modest handicap hurdler: fair handicap chaser: stays 3m: acts on heavy going: usually wears visor/tongue tie: temperamental. *Tim Vaughan*

BASTANTE (FR) 8 b.m. Khalkevi (IRE) – Pocahontas (FR) (Nikos) [2018/19 h21g **h–** h21.4g h19.4g⁴ Jan 9] £4,500 6-y-o: sixth foal: half-sister to useful chaser Tutchec (2½m-3¼m winner, by Turgeon): dam, French 17f-21f hurdle/chase winner (also 13.5f winner on Flat), half-sister to top-class 2m chaser Azertyuiop: off mark in points at eleventh attempt: no form over hurdles: wears tongue tie. *Richard Bandey*

BASTIEN (FR) 8 b.g. Panoramic – Que du Charmil (FR) (Grand Seigneur (FR)) [2018/19 **c123** h131: c23.6d⁴ c23.5s³ c23d⁴ Feb 28] sturdy gelding: useful hurdler: fairly useful form over **h–** fences: stays 3m: acts on heavy going. *Alan King*

BATCIO (FR) 7 gr.g. Montmartre (FR) – Besca Nueva (FR) (Lesotho (USA)) [2018/19 **h103** b16g⁴ b16.5g² b16g* h21.4s⁴ b16g* h16g⁶ b16d⁶ h16s⁶ h16g⁴ h19.4s Apr 26] half-brother **b108** to several winners in France, including hurdler/chaser Lheny (17f-19f winner, by Le Triton): dam French 1¼m-11.5f winner: won completed outing in points: useful bumper performer: won at Kilbeggan (maiden) in August and Down Royal (by 2¾ lengths from Multifactorial) in November: fair form over hurdles: raced mainly around 2m: acts on soft going: wears hood. *T. M. Walsh, Ireland*

BATTLEBRAVE (IRE) 6 b.g. Fracas (IRE) – Silly Mille (IRE) (Luso) [2018/19 b–: **h–** b16.7d h15.8dᵖᵘ h16s h16.7s⁴ Mar 23] workmanlike gelding: no form in bumpers/over **b–** hurdles. *John Groucott*

BATTLE DUST (IRE) 10 b.g. Portrait Gallery (IRE) – Katie O'Toole (IRE) (Commanche **c115** Run) [2018/19 c118§, h–§: c32.5g*ᵈ c31.9sᵖᵘ Nov 21] multiple point winner: winning **h–** hurdler: fairly useful chaser: first past post in hunter at Cheltenham (disqualified due to tack issues) in May: left Philip Rowley after: stays 3¾m: acts on heavy going: wears headgear. *Alastair Ralph*

BATTLE HARD (IRE) 7 ch.g. Presenting – Erintante (IRE) (Denel (FR)) [2018/19 **c–** h20.1s h16s h16.2g Jan 13] maiden pointer: fair form in Irish bumpers for Peter Fahey in **h–** 2017/18: no form over hurdles: pulled up on chasing debut: has worn hood, including in 2018/19. *Daragh Bourke*

BATTLE OF IDEAS (IRE) 6 ch.g. Fracas (IRE) – Haven't A Notion (Definite Article) **c100** [2018/19 h115: h19.9g⁵ c18m⁴ c23.6s c23dᵖᵘ c19.9dᵖᵘ Feb 17] lengthy gelding: fair **h99** handicap hurdler: similar form over fences: stays 21f: acts on heavy going: usually front runner/races prominently. *Colin Tizzard*

BATTLE OF MIDWAY (IRE) 5 b.g. Mahler – Womanofthemountain (IRE) **b106** (Presenting) [2018/19 b16s³ b16d³ b16s* b16d⁵ Apr 22] €50,000 3-y-o: fourth foal: half-brother to bumper winner/useful chaser Fact of The Matter (2½m-3¾m winner, by Brian Boru): dam ran once in bumper: well held completed start in points: useful form in bumpers: won maiden at Navan (by 2 lengths from Multifactorial) in March: will be suited by further than 2m. *Noel Meade, Ireland*

BATTLE OF SHILOH (IRE) 10 b.g. Shantou (USA) – Realt Na Ruise (IRE) (Soviet **c125** Star (USA)) [2018/19 c136, h–: c23.8g³ c24gᵖᵘ Dec 29] well-made gelding: winning **h–** hurdler: useful handicap chaser: third at Ascot in November: stays 23f: acts on heavy going: tried in cheekpieces. *Tom George*

BATTLEOFTHESOMME (IRE) 6 b.g. Mountain High (IRE) – Shannon Pearl (IRE) **h82** (Oscar (IRE)) [2018/19 b16.3g h21.4g⁴ h21.4g⁵ h21.4g h19.7gᵖᵘ h21.7gᵖᵘ Apr 12] big **b–** gelding: placed in point: tailed off in bumper: poor form over hurdles: tried in cheekpieces. *Kate Buckett*

BATTLEOVERDOYEN (IRE) 6 b.g. Doyen (IRE) – Battle Over (FR) (Sillery **h142 p** (USA)) [2018/19 b16g* h16d* h20d* h21sᵖᵘ Mar 13] **b107**

'There's always another billionaire.' That was the response of former Formula One supremo Bernie Ecclestone whenever long-time ally Max Mosley, in his role as president of motorsport's governing body the FIA, raised concerns about teams being forced to drop out of the sport due to spiralling costs. Mosley's plans to introduce a cap (limiting the amount each team could spend) were soon made to look prescient in the aftermath of the global recession towards the end of the last decade. In quick succession, major manufacturers Honda, Toyota and BMW all withdrew their Formula One teams as a direct result of the world's banking crisis (Ford had also dropped out a few years earlier). Ecclestone managed to keep the show on the road, however, and the void left by those departures was quickly filled, partly by attracting such as Tony Fernandes (of Air Asia), Richard Branson (Virgin empire) and Vijay Mallya (Indian drinks magnate) to support Formula One—although all three have since left the sport after their teams ran into financial troubles!

A similar scenario is being played out in horse racing. David Redvers, 2018 bloodstock agent of the year, warned in June that British racing may be 'teetering on the edge of oblivion' unless a plan is put into place similar to business models for Flat racing in such as Australia and Japan. Redvers complained that in Britain the sport was guilty of taking for granted the huge investment of a handful of mega-wealthy owners: 'At any moment our industry could be put in catastrophic peril through the loss of just one of the major players. Falling prize money, ill health or simply a change of heart could precipitate this at any time.' In truth, it is hard to argue with those concerns, though the National Hunt scene has thrown up some recent test cases which suggest there is enough money around to absorb the surprise departure of high-rollers. Big-spending Mike Grech and Stuart Parkin ended their brief dalliance when their string of twenty-nine active jumpers was entered for the Doncaster May Sales (twenty-eight were sold, one was withdrawn). Unlike those Formula One scenarios, the decision to dissolve the partnership had nothing to do with market forces and was reportedly prompted by a run of bad luck (notably injuries to their higher-rated performers) which saw Parkin 'fall out of love with the game'. Both Parkin and, in particular, Grech have indicated that they intend to return to ownership on their own at some stage, though neither bought back any of their existing stock. Bidding still proved fierce, however, with four horses reaching six-figure sums, notably the five-year-old Interconnected, who was sold for £620,000, the highest price paid at auction so far for a jumper in training, on the back of a promising second in a Newbury maiden hurdle less than three months earlier (he'd also run out a wide-margin winner of his only completed start in points prior to that). The successful bidder was Darren Yates, a property developer who made waves during the latest season in his bid to build up a select high quality string over both jumps (initially with North Yorkshire trainer Philip Kirby before switching most of his horses to Dan Skelton in the summer) and on the Flat. His quest to have a Grand National runner saw him shell out £360,000 (£300,000 purchase price plus VAT of £60,000) for the 2017 fourth Blaklion and, when the ten-year-old was forced to miss the race due to a late injury, a further £170,000 on Don Poli as a replacement at the select Aintree Sales forty-eight hours before the big race itself (66/1-shot Don Poli, also a ten-year-old, went on to finish last of nineteen finishers in the National).

Don Poli was one of two lots at the sale who had been left in the Grand National at the final declaration stage that morning, the other being the same connections' Outlander (who went on to finish ninth for new trainer Richard Spencer having also been sent off at 66/1), and the fact that Outlander also made a hefty sum (£165,000) is further evidence of the deep pockets of some of those involved in the sport at present. Both Don Poli and Outlander were offloaded by National Hunt racing's biggest spender Michael O'Leary, the CEO of Ryanair whose racing operation Gigginstown House Stud enjoyed arguably its finest hour forty-eight hours later when Tiger Roll won his second Grand National (Gigginstown's third). It therefore came as a major shock when, just over five weeks later, O'Leary announced that Gigginstown would not be buying any new horses, with the intention of phasing out its operation over the next five years. The potential fallout from this decision will have obvious repercussions for Irish racing. Two hundred and twenty-six individual horses carried the maroon, white star and armlets of Gigginstown during 2018/19, the huge string spread around seven yards—the bulk with Gordon Elliott (seventy-nine), Henry de Bromhead (thirty-five), Noel Meade (twenty-four) and Joseph O'Brien (twenty-one). It is estimated that Gigginstown has been splashing out approximately €6,000,000 a year on training fees, with its annual

Lawlor's of Naas Novices' Hurdle, Naas—Battleoverdoyen and Jack Kennedy already have matters firmly under control when untidy at the last

spending at British and Irish public auctions being around €5,000,000, not counting a further seven-figure sum every year on new stock sourced elsewhere (in France or through private purchases). The phrase 'spend more time with my family' has regularly been used down the years as an explanation whenever people (usually politicians) leave high profile positions, but O'Leary is adamant that spending more time with his four growing children is behind his decision—he remains CEO of the Ryanair group after stepping down from the day-to-day running of the airline itself in February. 'When the kids were smaller I went racing to get away from them! Now they are bigger and going in different directions, and they are at an age when I want to do things with them,' said O'Leary. 'I missed one day of the Dublin Racing Festival and I only attended one day of the Leopardstown Christmas Festival. For years I never had a horse run in England because I couldn't get to see them race. If I can't go to see them here (on Irish soil), why am I bothering?' It is also true that there isn't an awful lot left for Gigginstown to achieve—the chase-oriented operation can boast two Cheltenham Gold Cups (War of Attrition and Don Cossack) and four Irish Grand Nationals (Hear The Echo, Thunder And Roses, Rogue Angel and General Principle) to go with its trio of wins in the Aintree showpiece.

Gigginstown House Stud achieved its most successful season yet numerically in 2018/19, with a combined total of one hundred and sixty-two wins in Ireland and Britain (two more than in 2017/18). The O'Leary brothers won their fifth successive (seventh in total) owners' title on home soil, although it could be argued that—Tiger Roll aside—the Ryanair supremo and his brother Eddie won't have enjoyed their trips to the racecourse quite so much during the latest campaign, with many of their younger horses failing to meet expectations. Nascent superstar Samcro drew a blank from three starts and missed the big spring meetings with a lung infection, while the latest crop of Gigginstown novices didn't seem quite up to the usual high standards. Gigginstown managed just one winner (Tiger Roll in the Cross Country Chase) from a raiding party of thirty-seven at the 2019 Cheltenham Festival, compared to a record-breaking seven in 2018 and four in 2017, with eight of those eleven wins having been provided by novices or juveniles. There were six beaten favourites among the latest Gigginstown challengers, the most high profile of which was in the Champion Hurdle in which Apple's Jade ran no sort of race (she suffered other reverses at Aintree and Punchestown subsequently).

Arguably the most disappointing display by a Gigginstown favourite came twenty-four hours after the defeat of Apple's Jade when the highly regarded Battleoverdoyen was pulled up after being sent off a well-backed 3/1 favourite for the sixteen-runner Baring Bingham Novices' Hurdle (branded as the Ballymore). In truth, Battleoverdoyen never really looked like repeating Samcro's smooth victory in the 2018 edition, being on and off the bridle from a circuit out and never landing a serious blow, well held when his jockey eventually called it a day before the last (Gigginstown's two other runners Valdieu and Notebook trailed the field to finish tailed-off eleventh and twelfth respectively). A lost near-fore shoe may go some way to explaining Battleoverdoyen's laboured display which came after he had very much caught the eye beforehand, with Timeform's paddock representative that day summing him up as 'the most gorgeous-looking horse'. The chances are that his Cheltenham performance will prove to be a blip, as things have otherwise gone very well for Battleoverdoyen.

After landing a maiden bumper at Punchestown with the minimum of fuss in late-November Battleoverdoyen was warmed up for Cheltenham with wins over hurdles at Navan and Naas, recording good timeratings on both occasions. He made a big impression when he won a two-mile maiden at the former track in December, effortlessly pulling clear of a twenty-one-strong field to win by thirteen lengths from the consistent Momus (also owned by Gigginstown). There was more substance to his win at Naas the following month when he handled the step up to Grade 1 level in his stride to overcome more experienced rivals in a competitive renewal of the Lawlor's of Naas Novices' Hurdle. With his two nearest market rivals (the Willie Mullins-trained pair Tornado Flyer and Come To Me) both flopping, it was left to the outsider Sams Profile to push 2/1 favourite Battleoverdoyen closest, though Battleoverdoyen always had matters under control after jumping to the front with a fine leap two out, the longer trip suiting him well. Sams Profile managed only fifth in the Baring Bingham, but he did his bit for the Naas form when a fine second to Reserve Tank in the Champion Novices' Hurdle at Punchestown in May. Battleoverdoyen didn't get the chance to bounce back from Cheltenham, being a late non-runner from the same Punchestown contest after going lame on the morning of the race. Battleoverdoyen is a big, rangy, good sort, every inch a chaser on looks, and a novice chasing campaign beckons in 2019/20, when he will remain one of the most exciting prospects from within the Gigginstown ranks—'I have always thought that two and a half miles plus over fences would bring out the best in him,' enthused Elliott in May.

			Sadler's Wells	Northern Dancer
	Doyen (IRE)		(b 1981)	Fairy Bridge
	(b 2000)		Moon Cactus	Kris
Battleoverdoyen (IRE)			(b 1987)	Lady Moon
(b.g. 2013)			Sillery	Blushing Groom
	Battle Over (FR)		(b 1988)	Silvermine
	(b 1998)		Battle Quest	Noblequest
			(ch 1989)	Bathyale

Battleoverdoyen doesn't have the sort of jumps-overloaded pedigree that might be associated with an expensive recruit from the Irish pointing ranks, although his most immediate relatives are plying their trade under the National Hunt code. He is the eighth foal out of the French mare Battle Over, and one of only four to have reached the racecourse so far, though the family certainly made up for lost time in 2018/19. His year-older half-sister is the useful chaser Treackle Tart (by Winged Love), who won twice at around three miles for Somerset trainer Nicky Martin in the latest season, having won over hurdles earlier in her career. Battleoverdoyen's year-younger brother Swordsman looked a good prospect when winning a two and a half mile maiden hurdle at Fairyhouse for Gigginstown and Elliott in January, only to fluff his lines in graded company on both subsequent starts. Battle Over herself won both over hurdles and fences at up to eighteen furlongs in France as a four-year-old, though most of the other notable performers in the family made their mark on the Flat, including the useful French Group 3 mile and a quarter winner Hippy, who is out of a winning half-sister to Battle Over who won over the same trip herself before she went jumping. A career on the Flat was never an option for Battleoverdoyen, for whom current connections paid £235,000 at the Cheltenham April Sales in 2017. He had made a winning debut in a four-year-old maiden point earlier that month, chased home by another who went through the ring shortly after him at Cheltenham, Court Liability, who went on to win his first four starts under rules for Harry Whittington.

Spending on such a scale is a thing of the past now, of course, for the O'Learys and it will take a while before the full ramifications from Gigginstown's withdrawal from the sport can be assessed, particularly as its financial clout has bolstered all levels of the Irish racing industry in recent years. 'I think our decision will bring more people into racehorse ownership. I don't think it will have a huge impact on the sales, but it's likely that more of the better horses will finish up in England,' Michael O'Leary explained at the time. The first Goffs Land Rover Sale to be held without Gigginstown investment rather backed up the view that, although there may not be one of Bernie Ecclestone's billionaires waiting in the wings, there was still plenty of money to go around. The top lot of €185,000 (for a three-year-old Yeats half-brother to Gigginstown's smart hurdler Tombstone) was rather dwarfed by its equivalent (€325,000) from twelve months earlier, when four other lots topped that price, but the overall trade posted a healthier picture, with the average price rising by six per cent from a higher number of horses changing hands (419 compared to 393 in 2018). *Gordon Elliott, Ireland*

BATTLETANK (IRE) 6 b.g. Robin des Pres (FR) – Regal Brigade (IRE) (Anshan) **b–**
[2018/19 b16.7d Jan 8] tailed off in bumper. *John Groucott*

BATTYS DILEMMA (IRE) 7 b.g. Darsi (FR) – Rosetiepy (FR) (Apple Tree (FR)) **h–**
[2018/19 h19.3d^{pu} Mar 24] won Irish point on debut: pulled up in novice hurdle. *Ben Pauling*

BAWDEN ROCKS 10 b.g. Anabaa (USA) – Late Night (GER) (Groom Dancer (USA)) **c–**
[2018/19 c20.3g May 15] winning hurdler: fair maiden chaser, well beaten sole outing **h–** under Rules in 2018/19 (also well held in points): stays 2¾m: acts on heavy going: tried in cheekpieces: temperament under suspicion. *Mrs K. Lee*

BAY FORTUNA 10 b.g. Old Vic – East Rose (Keen) [2018/19 h89: h18.5g^2 h20g h21.6m **h93** Jul 14] sturdy gelding: modest handicap hurdler: stays 2½m: best form on good going: has worn cheekpieces, including final start. *Mark Usher*

BAYLEY'S DREAM 10 b.g. Presenting – Swaythe (USA) (Swain (IRE)) [2018/19 c23g^3 **c97 §** Jan 9] short-backed gelding: multiple point winner: winning hurdler: modest maiden **h– §** chaser nowadays: stays 3m: acts on good to firm and good to soft going: has worn headgear/ tongue tie: untrustworthy. *John Aprahamian*

BAY OF FREEDOM (IRE) 10 b.g. Heron Island (IRE) – Kate Gale (IRE) (Strong Gale) **c–**
[2018/19 c138, h107: h24g c24s^{pu} c30.2g c30.2g c25d c20s^{pu} Mar 17] angular gelding: **h–** winning hurdler: useful chaser at best, no form in 2018/19: tried in blinkers. *Peter Fahey, Ireland*

BAYSBROWN (IRE) 9 b.g. Fruits of Love (USA) – Whenever Wherever (IRE) **c–**
(Saddlers' Hall (IRE)) [2018/19 h23.9g^{ur} h23.9g^{pu} h23.9g^6 Aug 18] fair handicap hurdler, **h74** below form in 2018/19 after long absence: well held sole outing over fences: stays 25f: acts on soft and good to firm going: tried in blinkers. *Nicky Richards*

BAYWING (IRE) 10 br.g. Winged Love (IRE) – Cerise de Totes (FR) (Champ Libre **c112 x** (FR)) [2018/19 c149x, h–: c23.4d c24.2s^{pu} c32.6g^F Feb 23] winning hurdler: smart **h–** handicap chaser, below best in 2018/19: stayed 33f: best form on soft/heavy going: often let down by jumping: dead. *Nicky Richards*

BAZAROV (IRE) 6 br.g. Stowaway – Booley Bay (IRE) (Gulland) [2018/19 c22g^{pu} h20d **c–** h20d^5 h16s^6 h20v h21s^2 h19.3m^2 h16.8v^2 h19.7g* h20.5g^3 h23.4m* Apr 22] fair handicap **h105** hurdler: won at Hereford in March and Fakenham in April: pulled up in maiden on chasing debut: left John O. Clifford after sixth start: stays 23f: acts on soft and good to firm going: often in cheekpieces: has worn tongue tie, including in 2018/19: front runner. *Archie Watson*

BAZOOKA (IRE) 8 b.g. Camacho – Janadam (IRE) (Mukaddamah (USA)) [2018/19 **h107** h111: h16s^{pu} h15.5g* h19d^2 h15.7s^3 Mar 18] angular gelding: fair hurdler: won seller at Leicester in December: barely stays 19f: acts on heavy going: tried in cheekpieces: in tongue tie last 3 starts: often travels strongly. *David Flood*

BAZUKHOV (IRE) 7 ch.g. Stowaway – Boreen Perky (IRE) (Executive Perk) [2018/19 **h–** h20.3g^6 h16g h15.8g Oct 7] point winner: no form over hurdles: dead. *Fiona Kehoe*

BBOLD (IRE) 5 b.g. Aizavoski (IRE) – Molly Be (First Trump) [2018/19 b16.4d h16g^3 **h108** h19.9v^5 h15.8d^3 h15.8d^6 h21g* Apr 10] €6,000 3-y-o, resold £16,500 3-y-o, £40,000 4-y-o: **b77** seventh foal: half-brother to a winning pointer by Mahler and a winner on Flat abroad by Where Or When: dam, maiden on Flat (stayed 1¼m), half-sister to useful hurdler/chaser (stayed 2½m) Keltic Bard: runner-up sole start in Irish points: unplaced in bumper at Cheltenham: fair form over hurdles: won maiden at Warwick in April: stays 21f: acts on good to soft going. *Dan Skelton*

BEACH BREAK 5 b.g. Cacique (IRE) – Wemyss Bay (Sadler's Wells (USA)) [2018/19 **h122** h99: h16.8g^2 h17.2m^2 h16m^2 h17.2g* h16.7g* h16.3g* h16.8m^3 h16m^4 h16g^2 h15.8g h15.7m Apr 20] compact gelding: fairly useful hurdler: won maiden at Cartmel in July, and handicaps at Bangor in August and Stratford in September: raced around 2m: acts on good to firm and good to soft going: wears blinkers: front runner/races prominently. *Donald McCain*

BEACH DANCER (IRE) 5 b.g. Footstepsinthesand – All Night Dancer (IRE) (Danehill **h–** Dancer (IRE)) [2018/19 h15.8m^{pu} Oct 4] modest maiden on Flat, stays 7f: pulled up in novice on hurdling debut. *Nick Gifford*

BEACON EDGE (IRE) 5 b.g. Doyen (IRE) – Laurel Gift (IRE) (Presenting) [2018/19 **b117 p** b16g* b16g^4 Feb 2] €12,000 3-y-o: fifth foal: half-brother to fairly useful 2m hurdle winner Fridaynightlights (by Beneficial), stayed 21f: dam unraced sister to smart hurdler/chaser (stayed 3m) Jessies Dream: smart form in bumpers: won maiden at Ayr (by 4½ lengths from Soviet Castle) in October: best effort when 1¾ lengths third of 10 to Colreevy in Champion INH Flat Race at Punchestown shortly after end of British season: left Nicky Richards after first start: will go on improving. *Noel Meade, Ireland*

BEAKSTOWN (IRE) 6 b.g. Stowaway – Midnight Reel (IRE) (Accordion) [2018/19 **h132** b95p: h19.9g* h22d^2 h21g* h21s^{pu} Mar 13] rangy gelding: chasing type: has had breathing operation: won Irish point on debut: useful form over hurdles: won maiden at Uttoxeter in November and Leamington Novices' Hurdle at Warwick (by 3¾ lengths from Stoney Mountain) in January: wears tongue tie: usually races prominently, often travels strongly. *Dan Skelton*

BEALLANDENDALL (IRE) 11 b.g. Beneficial – Railstown Lady (IRE) (Supreme **c106** Leader) [2018/19 c107, h94: c20.5m^2 c19.4s^2 c19.4v^F c19.3d^3 c19.4s^{pu} c19.4d^{pu} **h–** Mar 20] compact gelding: winning hurdler: fair handicap chaser: stays 2½m: acts on good to firm and heavy going: has worn headgear: usually front runner/races prominently. *Deborah Faulkner*

BEA MY STAR (FR) 5 b.g. Sea's Legacy (IRE) – Lillibits (USA) (Kingmambo (USA)) **b–** [2018/19 b15.8g^5 Jun 6] tailed off in bumper. *Sue Smith*

BEAN IN TROUBLE 5 gr.g. Sulamani (IRE) – Bouncing Bean (M'bebe) [2018/19 **b95** b15.8d* Dec 26] third foal: dam (h84), lightly raced in bumpers/over hurdles, half-sister to Welsh Grand National winner Dream Alliance: 10/1, won bumper at Huntingdon (by neck from Fricka) on debut. *Alastair Ralph*

BEAN LIATH (IRE) 8 gr.m. Portrait Gallery (IRE) – Coolnasmear (IRE) (Flemensfirth **c–** (USA)) [2018/19 h75: h20g^5 h19.5d^{pu} h19.9s h19.5s h21.9v c24d^{ur} h25g^5 h23.6d^4 Mar 20] **h77** workmanlike mare: poor maiden hurdler: unseated third on chasing debut: stays 25f: acts on good to soft going. *Dai Williams*

BEARLY LEGAL (IRE) 13 b.g. Court Cave (IRE) – Fair Size (IRE) (Jurado (USA)) **c–** [2018/19 c–, h99: c25g^{pu} c25g^{pu} c21g^{pu} c23.5g^{pu} h27s^4 Mar 3] lengthy gelding: fairly **h–** useful hurdler/chaser at best, retains very little ability: tried in blinkers: wears tongue tie. *Karl Thornton, Ireland*

BEAR'S AFFAIR (IRE) 13 br.g. Presenting – Gladtogetit (Green Shoon) [2018/19 c126, **c114** h–: c20.8g⁶ c21.1dᵖᵘ Apr 4] sturdy gelding: point winner: winning hurdler: fairly useful **h–** hunter chaser: acts on heavy going. *Philip Rowley*

BEARS RAILS 9 b.g. Flemensfirth (USA) – Clandestine (Saddlers' Hall (IRE)) [2018/19 **c–** c116§, h–: c24.2g c21.6v c25.1d c23.6d Jan 18] big, workmanlike gelding: maiden hurdler: **h–** fairly useful chaser at best, no form in 2018/19: usually wears blinkers: has worn tongue tie, including in 2018/19: front runner/races prominently. *Colin Tizzard*

BEAST OF BELSTANE 4 b.g. Pivotal – Miss Corniche (Hernando (FR)) [2018/19 **b93** b13.7m⁶ b14g⁴ b14.6s⁶ b16.8d* Jan 11] half-brother to several winners, including fairly useful hurdler Italian Riviera (2¼m/19f winner, by Galileo): dam useful 7f-1¼m winner: fair form in bumpers: won at Sedgefield in January: tried in blinkers. *Keith Dalgleish*

BEAT THAT (IRE) 11 b.g. Milan – Knotted Midge (IRE) (Presenting) [2018/19 c136, **c140** h138: c25.8g* c24g* c23.6d⁴ c25g² c24g* Nov 21] tall gelding: winning hurdler: useful **h–** chaser: won novices at Newton Abbot in August and Southwell in September, and veterans handicap chaser at Warwick (by 7 lengths from Exitas) in November: stays 3¼m: acts on soft going. *Nicky Henderson*

BEAT THE JUDGE (IRE) 4 b.g. Canford Cliffs (IRE) – Charmingly (USA) (King of **h124** Kings (IRE)) [2018/19 h16g* h15.7d³ h16m² h17dᵖᵘ h15.9g⁵ Apr 21] good-topped gelding: fair maiden on Flat, stays 1¼m: fairly useful form over hurdles: won juvenile at Kempton in December: second in Adonis Juvenile Hurdle at same course (9 lengths behind Fusil Raffles) in February: raced around 2m: acts on good to firm going. *Gary Moore*

BEAU BAY (FR) 8 b.g. Bernebeau (FR) – Slew Bay (FR) (Beaudelaire (USA)) [2018/19 **c131** c130, h100: c18.2d⁶ c15.7d⁴ c15.2g* c16.4g⁶ c16d⁵ c16d⁵ c21.1d Apr 5] lengthy gelding: **h–** winning hurdler: useful handicap chaser: won at Wetherby (by 3¾ lengths from Nuts Well) in January: stays 2½m: acts on heavy going: wears headgear/tongue tie. *Dr Richard Newland*

BEAU DU BRIZAIS (FR) 7 gr.g. Kapgarde (FR) – Belle du Brizais (FR) (Turgeon **c129** (USA)) [2018/19 c123, h116: c22.6m⁶ c23.8m³ c24.2m² c23m³ c25.6s* c23.8d* c26g⁴ **h–** c31.8m Apr 13] compact gelding: winning hurdler: fairly useful handicap chaser: won at Ludlow (twice) in December: stays 3¼m: acts on soft and good to firm going. *Philip Hobbs*

BEAU ET SUBLIME (FR) 9 b.g. Saddler Maker (IRE) – Jolie Jouvencelle (FR) **c–** (Sandhurst Prince) [2018/19 h16g² h16.5m² h17d⁶ h16.2g h16d⁵ h16s h20.5d h20.5mᶠ Apr **h109** 13] has had breathing operation: fair handicap hurdler: winning chaser: left A. J. Martin after third start: stays 2½m: acts on soft and good to firm going: usually wears tongue tie. *R. Mike Smith*

BEAUFORT WEST (IRE) 5 b.g. Getaway (GER) – Blessingindisguise (IRE) (Luso) **h117** [2018/19 b16d h16.3s⁴ h16.3s⁶ h16s² h16.4sᵖᵘ Mar 12] second foal: dam unraced half- **b–** sister to Cheltenham Gold Cup winner Bobs Worth: runner-up in Irish point: well held in bumper: fairly useful form over hurdles: second in novice at Sandown in February: will stay beyond 2m. *Colin Tizzard*

BEAU HAZE 6 b.g. Black Sam Bellamy (IRE) – Bella Haze (Midnight Legend) [2018/19 **h86 p** b15.8v⁴ b15.8v h19.5d h16d⁴ h16g⁵ Apr 26] third foal: dam (h145) bumper/2m-2¾m **b65** hurdle winner: poor form in bumpers: modest form over hurdles: will stay 2½m+: open to further improvement. *Phillip Dando*

BEAU PHIL (FR) 8 ch.g. Cachet Noir (USA) – Neyrianne (FR) (Sheyrann) [2018/19 h–: **h98** h21.4m h15.8g³ h21.6gᵖᵘ h18.5m⁴ Jul 14] fair handicap hurdler: stays 2¾m: acts on soft and good to firm going: wears hood/tongue tie: temperament under suspicion. *Jeremy Scott*

BEAU SANCY (FR) 7 b.g. Blue Bresil (FR) – Touquette (FR) (Phantom Breeze) **c111** [2018/19 c86, h90, b–: c20.3g* c20.2m* c21.2g* c24.1s² c27.6s⁴ Dec 26] has had breathing **h–** operation: maiden hurdler: fair handicap chaser: completed hat-trick at Bangor, Wincanton and Fakenham in October: stays 3m: acts on soft and good to firm going: usually wears headgear/tongue tie: often travels strongly. *Olly Murphy*

BEAUTIFUL DRAMA (IRE) 5 b.m. Arcadio (GER) – Irish Mystics (IRE) (Ali-Royal **b–** (IRE)) [2018/19 b15.7d Apr 9] sixth foal: half-sister to useful hurdler/chaser Stowaway Magic (2m-21f winner, by Stowaway) and fairly useful chaser Minella For Me (2½m-3m winner, by King's Theatre): dam poor maiden hurdler: behind in bumper. *John McConnell, Ireland*

BEAUTIFUL PEOPLE (FR) 8 b.m. Early March – Night Fever (FR) (Garde Royale) **h93** [2018/19 h75: h24g² h24g* h21.2m h25.8s* h23.9dᵖᵘ Dec 13] lengthy mare: modest handicap hurdler: won at Southwell in August and Fontwell in October: stays 3¼m: acts on soft going: wears tongue tie: races towards rear. *Richard Phillips*

BEAUTY DRAGON (IRE) 7 b.g. Rip Van Winkle (IRE) – Turning Light (GER) h–
(Fantastic Light (USA)) [2018/19 b16.4g b16.4d h21.3d⁶ Jan 4] fifth foal: half-brother to 2 b–
winners on Flat, including smart winner up to 9f Surrey Star (by Dubawi): dam useful
German 1m-11f winner: well held in bumpers/maiden hurdle. *Gary Sanderson*

BECKY THE THATCHER 6 b.m. Mastercraftsman (IRE) – Fairmont (IRE) h124
(Kingmambo (USA)) [2018/19 h121: h24.1m⁶ h19.7g⁴ h18.9v² h21.3s h19.7g⁵ h20.1g²
Apr 15] close-coupled, rather lightly-built mare: fairly useful handicap hurdler: should stay
beyond 2½m: acts on heavy going: in cheekpieces last 5 starts. *Micky Hammond*

BE DARING (FR) 8 gr.g. Dom Alco (FR) – Quinine (FR) (Network (GER)) [2018/19 h88
h91: h19m⁴ h18.5d⁶ h21.7d³ Nov 18] good-topped gelding: modest maiden hurdler: stays
2¾m: acts on heavy going: usually wears hood: usually races nearer last than first.
Chris Gordon

BEDFORD FORREST (IRE) 10 br.g. Desert King (IRE) – Nadisha (IRE) (Rainbows c–
For Life (CAN)) [2018/19 c108: c25.2d^pu Mar 6] point winner: standout effort under Rules
when second in maiden chase at Cartmel in 2017/18. *Andrew Nicholls*

BEDROCK 6 b.g. Fastnet Rock (AUS) – Gemstone (IRE) (Galileo (IRE)) [2018/19 h144: h156
h16s⁴ h16g* h16g* Nov 2] sturdy gelding: very smart hurdler: won Grade 3 event at
Tipperary (by 4½ lengths from Plinth) in October and WKD Hurdle at Down Royal (by 1½
lengths from Samcro) in November: stays 19f: acts on soft going: in cheekpieces last 3
starts: wears tongue tie: often travels strongly: has joined Leslie F. Young in USA.
Iain Jardine

BEE AN ARISTOCRAT (IRE) 10 b.g. Flemensfirth (USA) – Windy Bee (IRE) h90
(Aristocracy) [2018/19 h87: h16.8g² h20g h16g* Jun 24] little impact in points: modest
handicap hurdler: won novice event at Worcester in June: seemed to stay 3m: acted on good
to firm going: tried in tongue tie: dead. *Jimmy Frost*

BEECHER (IRE) 4 ch.g. Shirocco (GER) – Roli Flight (IRE) (Roli Abi (FR)) [2018/19 h–
b15.3s h16d^pu h15.8g^pu Apr 21] no form in bumper/over hurdles. *Katy Price* b–

BEE CROSSING 8 b.m. Fair Mix (IRE) – Indeed To Goodness (IRE) (Welsh Term) h97
[2018/19 h109: h20.9g⁵ h19.6s³ Mar 23] lengthy mare: point winner: fair maiden hurdler,
below form both starts in 2018/19: stays 21f: acts on heavy going: tried in tongue tie.
Michael Scudamore

BEEHERE 7 ch.m. Nayef (USA) – Behra (IRE) (Grand Lodge (USA)) [2018/19 b16g Jun b–
2] half-sister to several winners, including smart hurdler Baradari (2m-23f winner, by
Manduro) and useful but temperamental hurdler/chaser Barizan (2m-2¼m winner, by
Kalanisi): dam, useful 1¼m winner, half-sister to very smart hurdler/top-class chaser
(winner up to 25f) Behrajan: tailed off in bumper. *Richard Price*

BEENO (IRE) 10 b.g. Exit To Nowhere (USA) – Kay Theatre (IRE) (King's Theatre h124
(IRE)) [2018/19 h131: h16.2g³ h17.2m² h22.1g³ h16.8m³ h20.9m⁶ h16g⁵ h16.2g h16.5g
h16.2g⁴ Apr 24] good-bodied gelding: fairly useful handicap hurdler nowadays: unproven
beyond 17f: acts on good to firm and heavy going: wears hood: usually leads. *Dianne Sayer*

BEET TOPPER (IRE) 6 b.g. Beat Hollow – What A Topper (IRE) (Petoski) [2018/19 h80
h20.5g h16d h15.9s⁴ h19.6d h19.2v^pu Feb 14] good-topped gelding: placed completed start
in Irish points: poor form over hurdles. *Anna Newton-Smith*

BEEVES (IRE) 12 b.g. Portrait Gallery (IRE) – Camas North (IRE) (Muharib (USA)) c145
[2018/19 c143, h–: c24d³ c23.8g² c26.1m c22.3g⁵ c23.8m² Jan 17] lengthy gelding: h–
winning hurdler: smart handicap chaser: placed at Uttoxeter (5 lengths behind
Minellacelebration) in May and Perth (2 lengths behind Henllan Harri) in June: stays 33f:
acts on good to firm and heavy going: wears headgear: front runner. *Jennie Candlish*

BEFORE MIDNIGHT 6 ch.g. Midnight Legend – Lady Samantha (Fraam) [2018/19 h125
b103: h19.6g² h19.5g^ur h21g² h19d* h19.8s h24.3m² Apr 12] good-topped gelding: bumper
winner: fairly useful form over hurdles: won novice at Taunton in January: second in
novice handicap at Ayr in April: stays 3m: acts on good to firm and good to soft going.
Nicky Henderson

BEGGARS CROSS (IRE) 9 b.g. Presenting – Ballygill Heights (IRE) (Symboli Heights c–
(FR)) [2018/19 c120, h–: c24g^pu May 7] sturdy gelding: winning hurdler: fairly useful h–
chaser, pulled up sole outing in 2018/19: stayed 3m: acted on soft going: tried in
cheekpieces/tongue tie: dead. *Jonjo O'Neill*

BEGGAR'S WISHES (IRE) 8 b.g. Oscar (IRE) – Strong Wishes (IRE) (Strong Gale) **c140**
[2018/19 c128, h–: c20.6g* c21v* c19.9d⁴ c19.9d c19.4s⁵ c21.6g³ c20.5m Apr 12] sturdy **h–**
gelding: winning hurdler: useful chaser: won handicap at Haydock in May and intermediate
event at Newton Abbot (by 1¼ lengths from Dolos) in October: stays 21f: acts on heavy
going: wears headgear/tongue tie. *Peter Bowen*

BEHINDTHELINES (IRE) 7 b.g. Milan – Sunset Leader (IRE) (Supreme Leader) **c–**
[2018/19 h115: c20.1gᵖᵘ Sep 27] has had breathing operation: runner-up on completed start **h–**
in Irish points: fairly useful hurdler: pulled up in novice on chasing debut: stays 3m: acts
on heavy going: wears tongue tie: front runner/races prominently. *Lucinda Russell*

BEHIND TIME (IRE) 8 b.g. Stowaway – She's Got To Go (IRE) (Glacial Storm (USA)) **c– §**
[2018/19 c124§, h–: c22.4sᵖᵘ c25dᶠ h22g Apr 12] good-topped gelding: winning hurdler: **h94**
fairly useful chaser at best: no form in 2018/19: left Harry Fry after first start: stays 3m: acts
on heavy going: often in cheekpieces: temperamental. *Enda Bolger, Ireland*

BEHOMEBYMIDNIGHT 7 b.m. Midnight Legend – Wise Little Girl (Singspiel (IRE)) **b–**
[2018/19 b17g May 18] third foal: half-sister to a winning pointer by Hurricane Run: dam
1¼m winner: well beaten completed start in points: in cheekpieces, tailed off in bumper.
S. Evans

BELAMI DES PICTONS (FR) 8 b.g. Khalkevi (IRE) – Nina des Pictons (FR) **c–**
(Denham Red (FR)) [2018/19 c150p, h–p: c24.2sᵖᵘ Feb 2] strong, compact gelding: **h–**
winning hurdler: smart chaser: reportedly bled sole outing in 2018/19: stays 3m: acts on
heavy going. *Venetia Williams*

BELARGUS (FR) 4 b.g. Authorized (IRE) – Belga Wood (USA) (Woodman (USA)) **h112**
[2018/19 h16v⁵ h16g⁶ h15.7d* Jan 19] good-topped gelding: fairly useful on Flat, stays
1½m: fair form over hurdles: won juvenile at Ascot in January: disappointed in handicap at
Punchestown shortly after end of British season. *Nick Gifford*

BEL ESPRIT (IRE) 10 b.m. Presenting – D Judge (IRE) (Strong Gale) [2018/19 h78: **c–**
c25.8gᶠ May 16] modest maiden hurdler: fell fifteenth on chasing debut: stays 23f: acts on **h–**
good to soft going. *Robert Stephens*

BELIZE 8 b.g. Rail Link – Costa Rica (IRE) (Sadler's Wells (USA)) [2018/19 h19d **h–**
h21.3gᶠ Apr 11] workmanlike gelding: has had breathing operation: fairly useful hurdler at
best, no form in 2018/19: stays 2¾m: acts on heavy going: in tongue tie last 2 starts.
Tim Vaughan

BELLA BEAU (IRE) 4 b.f. Jeremy (USA) – Bella Patrice (IRE) (Luso) [2018/19 b16.5d **b–**
b15.7d Mar 6] sixth foal: dam, lightly raced in bumpers/over hurdles, half-sister to smart
hurdler (2m-2½m) Davenport Milenium: no form in bumpers. *Nigel Hawke*

BELLAMY'S GREY 7 gr.g. Black Sam Bellamy (IRE) – Lambrini Queen (Environment **h68**
Friend) [2018/19 h96p, b75: h23.1s h19.5d h23.1s⁶ Mar 18] maiden hurdler, modest form
at best. *Carroll Gray*

BELLANEY KNIGHT (IRE) 9 bl.g. Marienbard (IRE) – Bellaney Jewel (IRE) **h–**
(Roselier (FR)) [2018/19 h99: h23.1g⁶ Aug 18] chasing sort: fair hurdler, well held sole
outing in 2018/19 following breathing operation: should be suited by 3m+: acts on good to
soft going: tried in tongue tie. *John Quinn*

BELLA'S VISION (FR) 6 ch.m. Vision d'Etat (FR) – Dalina (FR) (Trempolino (USA)) **h–**
[2018/19 h–, b–: h15.8s⁶ h15.7g h18.7g⁵ h23.3g h25g h21d⁵ h23.9dᵖᵘ Apr 24] little form:
in headgear/tongue tie last 4 starts. *Richard Phillips*

BELLE AMIS 6 ch.m. Black Sam Bellamy (IRE) – Amaretto Rose (Alflora (IRE)) **h94**
[2018/19 b93: h19.5d³ h19.9d⁵ h22.8d³ Mar 20] close-coupled mare: bumper winner:
modest form over hurdles. *Fergal O'Brien*

BELLE BELLA (IRE) 7 b.m. Kalanisi (IRE) – Reseda (GER) (Lavirco (GER)) [2018/19 **b68**
b15.8g⁶ May 28] fourth foal: sister to bumper winner Nana Joan: dam, (h100) 2m-19f
hurdle winner, half-sister to dual Velka Pardubicka winner Registana: 8/1, sixth in bumper
at Huntingdon (15½ lengths behind Westbury). *Ian Williams*

BELLE EMPRESS 8 b.m. Black Sam Bellamy (IRE) – Empress of Light (Emperor Jones **c111**
(USA)) [2018/19 h106: c20d⁵ c22.5v⁴ c22.6s³ Mar 11] fair form over hurdles: similar form **h–**
over fences: best effort when third in handicap at Stratford in March: stays 23f: acts on
heavy going: usually races towards rear. *Emma Lavelle*

BELLE EN NOIR 7 b.m. Black Sam Bellamy (IRE) – Miss Holly (Makbul) [2018/19 h–, **h–**
b64: h20g May 10] has had breathing operation: little impact in bumpers/over hurdles: has
worn tongue tie, including in 2018/19. *Steph Hollinshead*

BELLE'S SPIRIT 6 b.m. Kutub (IRE) – Dickies Girl (Saxon Farm) [2018/19 h–, b–: h20.3g Oct 10] no form: tried in cheekpieces. *David Bridgwater* — **h–**

BELL OF THE BALL (IRE) 9 b.m. Bachelor Duke (USA) – Grangehill Dancer (IRE) (Danehill Dancer (IRE)) [2018/19 h16.2g⁶ Jul 5] modest on Flat, stays 13f: modest hurdler at best, well held sole outing in 2018/19: stays 19f: acts on good to soft going: tried in blinkers. *Liam Lennon, Ireland* — **h–**

BELL OFTHE BONGATE (IRE) 5 b.m. Sakhee (USA) – Peace Lily (Dansili) [2018/19 b–: b16.2gᵖᵘ h20.9g h16.8d⁴ h16.4s Jan 29] has had breathing operation: no form: tried in tongue tie. *Harriet Graham* — **h– b–**

BELLOW MOME (FR) 8 b.g. Honolulu (IRE) – Oll Mighty Fellow (FR) (Ungaro (GER)) [2018/19 c25s c24d³ c29d⁵ Apr 22] useful-looking gelding: winning hurdler: useful handicap chaser: third in Leinster National Handicap Chase at Naas (9¾ lengths behind Pairofbrowneyes) in March: best up to 3m: acts on heavy going. *W. P. Mullins, Ireland* — **c133 h–**

BELLSHILL (IRE) 9 b.g. King's Theatre (IRE) – Fairy Native (IRE) (Be My Native (USA)) [2018/19 c168, h–: c24g⁴ c24g* c26.3dᵖᵘ Mar 15] — **c165 h–**

The new two-day Dublin Racing Festival in February, with its eight Grade 1 events, suffered something of a hiccup after the previous year's highly successful inaugural edition. The latest winter entered the record books as one of the driest on record in some places in Ireland, and the very unusual conditions presented problems for owners and trainers, many of whom were loath to risk their horses, which, in turn, meant that Ireland's racecourses sometimes struggled to offer enough good entertainment, especially in the higher-class races before the turn of the year. With the unseasonal weather continuing into January and early-February, Leopardstown faced an unfortunate situation as the Dublin Racing Festival loomed. There were those who felt the racetrack should have been watered, while the course executive was wary of taking that course because of the night-time freezing temperatures. In the event, with the going officially 'good, good to firm in places' (it had been soft twelve months earlier), there was a spate of non-runners, no fewer than twenty-six of them on the Sunday (nearly all due to the ground) and only four of the ten declared runners lined up in the feature event the Unibet Irish Gold Cup. The pick of Saturday's card—Irish Champion Hurdle day—was shown on ITV in Britain, after Musselburgh and Wetherby were lost to the weather, but Leopardstown was forced to take steps to ensure the meeting survived, moving the three steeplechases to the end of the seven-race card to counter the threat of overnight frost. In the event, Saturday's races were affected by low sun, with the final flight omitted in all the hurdle races, the final fence omitted on both circuits in the newly-promoted Grade 1 Dublin Chase, and the penultimate fence omitted on both circuits in the other Grade 1 chase on the day, the Arkle. The Saturday card was marred by a fatal accident to

Unibet Irish Gold Cup, Leopardstown—Bellshill (left) finds plenty for Ruby Walsh's urgings to edge out Road To Respect in a race decimated by non-runners

Andrea & Graham Wylie's "Bellshill"

the former Queen Mother Champion Chase winner Special Tiara who broke down in the Dublin Chase, something that might have played a part in the next day's mass withdrawals, along with the overnight frost which meant the track had to pass a precautionary inspection. Among those who were pulled out of the Irish Gold Cup were the previous year's winner Edwulf and three who had run well at the previous year's Cheltenham Festival, the Cheltenham Gold Cup third Anibale Fly, the Ryanair Chase winner Balko des Flos and the RSA Chase runner-up Monalee. One of the two Willie Mullins-trained challengers Al Boum Photo was also a late withdrawal on account of the going.

The two intended Mullins-trained runners in the Irish Gold Cup were fairly typical of the stable's good chasers in that they had been held up by the dry autumn. Neither Al Boum Photo nor Bellshill reached the racecourse until just after Christmas, both originally earmarked for a belated reappearance in the Savills Chase (formerly known as the Lexus) at Leopardstown on December 28th. However, even conditions that day (good) were deemed unsuitable for Al Boum Photo who was rerouted to a listed event at Tramore (where the ground was soft) on New Year's Day when he led home a one, two, three for the stable, beating two others also making their seasonal reappearance. Leopardstown enjoyed more luck with its Christmas meeting than with the Dublin Racing Festival and, allowing for the absence of Al Boum Photo, the Savills Chase attracted a cracking line-up, ten of the eleven runners having won at least once at Grade 1 level over fences. Bellshill had won the Punchestown Gold Cup in May from stablemate Djakadam, with Road To Respect third, in a line-up that included the winners of Ireland's three other Grade 1 open championship races for the staying chasers (Road To Respect had won what used to be the Lexus before finishing in the frame in the Cheltenham Gold Cup). It took a top-class performance from Bellshill to win at Punchestown and the stable's number-one Ruby Walsh preferred him to Kemboy (who had won the Clonmel Oil Chase in November) in the Savills Chase, for which Road To Respect started favourite after winning the JNwine.com Champion Chase at Down Royal on his reappearance. Bellshill finished a respectable fourth behind Kemboy (and a place behind Road To Respect) and shaped as if he would be all the better for the run, keeping on after losing his place early on the final circuit and not being unduly punished.

With an outing under his belt, Bellshill narrowly turned the tables on Road To Respect in the Irish Gold Cup, the pair dominating their two opponents, Outlander and The Storyteller who had finished fifth and sixth in the Savills Chase. Bellshill's sure-footed display contrasted with some uncharacteristically untidy jumping from Road To Respect as the pair served up a thrilling encounter, going toe-to-toe from some way out. Bellshill briefly showed in front three out but Road To Respect stuck to his task and the outcome was still in the balance at the final fence before Bellshill edged ahead near the line, responding well to strong driving to prevail by a short head, with seven and a half lengths back to The Storyteller in third. Bellshill gave his trainer his tenth success in the race and his first since Sir des Champs in 2013. Road To Respect went on to finish a good third in the Ryanair Chase at the Cheltenham Festival but the Irish Gold Cup effort seemed to leave its mark on Bellshill, who was pulled up in the Cheltenham Gold Cup after making a series of jumping mistakes and then ran below form in the Punchestown Gold Cup which took place shortly after the end of the British season. Ruby Walsh chose Bellshill ahead of Al Boum Photo and Kemboy at Cheltenham but he was on Kemboy at Punchestown where the Gold Cup winner Al Boum Photo disputed favouritism with him. Bellshill was sent off third favourite at 5/1 to repeat his victory of the previous year but he came under pressure on the home turn and found no extra from two out, eventually beaten over twenty-eight lengths into fourth behind Kemboy (Bellshill also well beaten by Al Boum Photo with 25/1-shot The Storyteller preventing a Mullins one, two, three).

Bellshill's Irish Gold Cup victory was the highlight of the season, along with that of the smart novice Voix du Reve in the Ryanair Gold Cup at Fairyhouse, for his owners Andrea and Graham Wylie who live in Britain but have all their horses with Willie Mullins. The campaign had its downs as well as its ups, unfortunately, with the Wylies losing two of their best horses at the Cheltenham Festival where their Thyestes Chase winner Invitation Only fell fatally in the Gold Cup after Ballyward had suffered a similar fate in the National Hunt Chase; the couple's Grand National runner, the smart Up For Review, sustained fatal injuries when brought down at the first in the Aintree showpiece.

		Sadler's Wells	Northern Dancer
Bellshill (IRE) (b.g. 2010)	King's Theatre (IRE) (b 1991)	(b 1981)	Fairy Bridge
		Regal Beauty	Princely Native
		(b 1981)	Dennis Belle
	Fairy Native (IRE) (b 1998)	Be My Native	Our Native
		(br 1979)	Witchy Woman
		Amy Fairy	The Parson
		(b 1981)	Copp On

Bellshill, who is workmanlike in appearance, is from one of the last few crops sired by King's Theatre who has been champion sire over jumps in Britain and Ireland five times (his final crop are now seven-year-olds and he slipped to sixth in the Anglo-Irish sires' table in the latest season). Bellshill is the seventh of twelve foals produced by the lightly-raced (bumpers and hurdles) performer Fairy Native. Bellshill is one of three winners produced by Fairy Native from matings with King's Theatre, following the fairly useful chaser Foxbridge, who stayed three miles, and Chieftain's Choice, who is fairly useful at up to two and a half miles and won over hurdles at Stratford and Doncaster in the latest season. Fairy Native has bred four winners in all, the ill-fated In The Zone (by Bob Back), who stayed three miles, proving fairly useful over fences after winning over hurdles. Presenting Leah (by Presenting) became the latest of Fairy Native's offspring to reach the racecourse, running twice in bumpers for Bellshill's trainer early in the latest season, finishing second at Kilbeggan in August. Fairy Native's 2017 colt by Walk In The Park made €70,000 as a foal. Fairy Native herself is from a family steeped in Irish jumping,

Bellshill's grandam Amy Fairy winning a bumper and going on to be successful both over hurdles and fences, while his great grandam Copp On also produced a half-sister to Amy Fairy, the unraced Steal On who became the dam of the most notable member of this family, the Queen Mother Champion Chase and dual King George VI Chase winner One Man. Copp On herself was a sister to the Powers Gold Cup (now Ryanair Gold Cup) winner Persian Wanderer and Bellshill's great great grandam Stroll On was a half-sister to the dam of notable Irish chaser Royal Bond and the successful mare Matchboard who went on to become the grandam of Champion Hurdle winners Morley Street and Granville Again. Interestingly, the first four dams on the bottom line of Bellshill's pedigree, Fairy Native, Amy Fairy, Copp On and Stroll On, are all by very successful jumping stallions—Be My Native, The Parson, Menelek and Vulgan respectively. Bellshill continues to do his family proud, his record including three victories at the Punchestown Festival as well as that Irish Gold Cup win (the best of four runs at the Cheltenham Festival was a third in Might Bite's RSA Chase). Bellshill stays extremely well and acts on heavy going, though he doesn't need the mud. *W. P. Mullins, Ireland*

BELLS 'N' BANJOS (IRE) 9 b.g. Indian River (FR) – Beechill Dancer (IRE) (Darnay) [2018/19 c125, h–: c24m⁴ c25g c24.2s⁶ c24d⁴ Apr 9] rangy gelding: winning hurdler: fairly useful handicap chaser: left Fergal O'Brien after third start: should stay beyond 3m: acts on heavy going: has worn cheekpieces, including in 2018/19: usually races close up: has suspect attitude (often races lazily). *Emma-Jane Bishop* c117 h–

BELLS OF PETERBORO (IRE) 4 gr.g. Carlotamix (FR) – Power of Future (GER) (Definite Article) [2018/19 b16.3s⁵ h19.9g⁵ h16g Apr 26] fourth foal: half-brother to fair hurdler Perfect Summer (2m-2½m winner, by High Chaparral) and bumper winner Ballinderry Moth (by Yeats): dam useful 1½m-1¾m winner: fifth in maiden bumper at Stratford (5¾ lengths behind Now Is The Winter): no form over hurdles. *Tim Vaughan* h– b85

BELLS OF WANSFORD 5 b.g. Multiplex – Et Voila (Alflora (IRE)) [2018/19 b15.7g Oct 10] 33/1, seventh in maiden bumper at Southwell. *Tim Vaughan* b–

BELMONT JEWEL (IRE) 7 b.m. Westerner – Maddy's Supreme (IRE) (Supreme Leader) [2018/19 h–p: h19.5d h20.6g h23vᵖᵘ h23.9gᵖᵘ h20.7d² h21.4g⁶ Mar 25] has had breathing operation: point winner: modest maiden hurdler: stays 21f: acts on good to soft going: in cheekpieces/tongue tie last 3 starts. *Michael Scudamore* h89

BELMONT PARK (FR) 8 br.g. Al Namix (FR) – Goldoulyssa (FR) (Cadoudal (FR)) [2018/19 c96, h–: c25.7s³ c19.7g³ Apr 21] maiden hurdler: modest maiden chaser: stays 2¾m: acts on good to soft going: usually in cheekpieces. *David Bridgwater* c89 h–

BELMOUNT (IRE) 10 b.g. Westerner – Artist's Jewel (Le Moss) [2018/19 c126x, h–: c24m³ c23.8g c23.8g* c23.8m* c24.2m² c25.1gᵖᵘ c26.7gᵖᵘ Jan 17] well-made gelding: winning hurdler: useful handicap chaser: won at Perth in September and Ludlow in October: stays 3¼m: acts on good to firm and heavy going: wears cheekpieces: often let down by jumping over fences. *Nigel Twiston-Davies* c131 x h–

BELTOR 8 b.g. Authorized (IRE) – Carahill (AUS) (Danehill (USA)) [2018/19 h16.5d* h19d h15.8d⁴ Mar 21] leggy gelding: fairly useful handicap hurdler: won at Taunton in December: raced mainly around 2m: acts on soft going: tried in hood. *Robert Stephens* h123

BEMPTON CLIFFS (IRE) 4 gr.g. Canford Cliffs (IRE) – Grand Lili (Linamix (FR)) [2018/19 b13m⁴ b14.6s⁵ Dec 22] poor form in bumpers/Flat maiden: wears hood. *Tony Coyle* b66

BEN ARTHUR (IRE) 9 b.g. Marienbard (IRE) – Oscartrainer (IRE) (Oscar (IRE)) [2018/19 c88, h100: c20.3d⁶ h25gᵖᵘ Feb 25] has had breathing operation: modest hurdler/ chaser at best, no form in 2018/19: stays 3m: best form on soft/heavy going: wears headgear/tongue tie: usually races prominently. *Kim Bailey* c– h–

BENARTY HILL (IRE) 9 b.g. September Storm (GER) – Crossmacahilly (IRE) (Executive Perk) [2018/19 h21.8g c25.5g h21.8d⁵ Aug 12] modest maiden hurdler, below form in 2018/19: winning chaser: stays 3m: acts on heavy going: has worn tongue tie: has joined Kenny Johnson. *Liam Lennon, Ireland* c– h78

BENATAR (IRE) 7 b.g. Beneficial – Carrigeen Lily (IRE) (Supreme Leader) [2018/19 c150p, h–: c21v⁴ c21g⁴ c23.8s³ c21d Jan 19] sturdy gelding: winning hurdler: smart chaser: third in Silver Cup at Ascot (8½ lengths behind Valtor) in December: stays 3m: acts on heavy going: usually races freely held up. *Gary Moore* c147 h–

BENBECULA 10 b.g. Motivator – Isle of Flame (Shirley Heights) [2018/19 c–, h91§: h21.4m⁴ h21.4m⁶ h21.6g⁴ h21.4mᵖᵘ Oct 19] angular gelding: poor handicap hurdler: maiden chaser: stays 21f: acts on heavy going: wears blinkers: often leads: untrustworthy. *Richard Mitchell* **c–**
h83 §

BEN BRODY (IRE) 9 b.g. Beneficial – Thethirstyscholars (IRE) (Be My Native (USA)) [2018/19 h21.2d⁶ Feb 20] fairly useful handicap hurdler in Ireland for Sean Byrne, below best sole outing in 2018/19: stays 3m: acts on heavy going: tried in cheekpieces. *Harry Chisman* **h103**

BEN BUIE (IRE) 5 br.g. Presenting – Change of Plan (IRE) (Alderbrook) [2018/19 b15.7m² b15.7s⁶ b16.3d Mar 23] £40,000 3-y-o: fifth foal: dam unraced half-sister to useful chaser (stayed 21f) Fairy Rath: fair form in bumpers: best effort when second at Ascot on debut: will stay beyond 2m. *Martin Keighley* **b90**

BENDOMINGO (IRE) 8 b.g. Beneficial – Bobbies Storm (IRE) (Bob Back (USA)) [2018/19 c72, h116: h21g¹ c20.9m² c19.4m c21.4gᶠ Aug 18] strong gelding: fair handicap hurdler, below form on return in 2018/19: fair form over fences: stayed 25f: acted on good to firm and good to soft going: wore tongue tie early in career: dead. *Nigel Twiston-Davies* **c103**
h83

BEN DUNDEE (IRE) 7 ch.g. Beneficial – Miss Dundee (IRE) (Bob Back (USA)) [2018/19 h136: c19.5g³ c20g⁴ c17dᵖᵘ c24gᶠ c20d⁶ c20.2s³ Mar 12] sturdy gelding: useful hurdler: similar form over fences: won maiden at Punchestown (by 6 lengths from Whisperinthebreeze) in November: stays 21f: acts on heavy going: wears tongue tie. *Gordon Elliott, Ireland* **c142**
h–

BENEAGLES (IRE) 7 b.g. Milan – Liss Rua (IRE) (Bob Back (USA)) [2018/19 h119: h23.9m² h23g* h26.5gᶠ Sep 10] useful-looking gelding: runner-up in Irish maiden point: useful handicap hurdler: won at Worcester (by length from Ennistown) in July: stays 25f: acts on soft and good to firm going: wears headgear. *Alan King* **h130**

BENECHENKO (IRE) 7 br.g. Beneficial – Beann Ard (IRE) (Mandalus) [2018/19 h112: h23.9g⁴ May 16] won Irish point on debut: fair maiden hurdler: will prove best at 3m+: acts on soft going: tried in cheekpieces. *Fergal O'Brien* **h105**

BENEFICIAL JOE (IRE) 9 b.g. Beneficial – Joleen (IRE) (Bob's Return (IRE)) [2018/19 c119, h123: c23.9dᵖᵘ c25.8gᵖᵘ Jul 22] sturdy gelding: fairly useful hurdler: maiden chaser, no form in 2018/19: little impact in points in March/April: stays 27f: acts on good to firm and good to soft going: wears hood: races towards rear. *Graeme McPherson* **c–**
h–

BENEMEADE (IRE) 11 b.g. Beneficial – Millicent Bridge (IRE) (Over The River (FR)) [2018/19 c17dᵖᵘ Jun 8] point winner: winning hurdler: fairly useful chaser at best for Noel Meade, pulled up in hunter sole outing under Rules in 2018/19: stays 3m: acts on soft and good to firm going: in blinkers last 5 starts. *Kieran Price* **c–**
h–

BENE REGINA (IRE) 7 b.m. Beneficial – Lareine d'Anjou (FR) (Panoramic) [2018/19 h19.7m⁴ h19.7g h24s⁵ Dec 16] €2,300 5-y-o, resold £5,000 5-y-o: seventh foal: half-sister to fair hurdler/chaser Cobbler's Queen (2½m-3m winner) and fair hurdler Representing (3m winner) (both by Presenting): dam French/Italian 15f-19f hurdle/chase winner: point winner: modest form over hurdles. *Nick Kent* **h86**

BENIE DES DIEUX (FR) 8 b.m. Great Pretender (IRE) – Cana (FR) (Robin des Champs (FR)) [2018/19 c148P, h151p: h19.9sᶠ Mar 12]
Different horse, but same jockey, same owner, same trainer, same race, same hurdle and same scenario. Whole books have been devoted to what academics call 'historic recurrence', a theory that has been around since ancient times which most know better as 'history repeating itself'. There can have been few better examples in racing than the closing stages of the latest David Nicholson Mares' Hurdle which must have had virtually everyone who witnessed them immediately thinking back to the uncannily similar events in the same race just four years earlier. On that occasion, odds-on Annie Power, trained by Willie Mullins and ridden by Ruby Walsh in the colours of Susannah Ricci, seemingly had the race at her mercy when falling at the final flight, an incident captured by a dramatic double-page photograph in *Chasers & Hurdlers* which shows Walsh still with his feet in the irons in a vain attempt to keep the partnership intact, though gravity had already won, with Annie Power's head buried in the Cheltenham turf. To everyone's relief, particularly her owners—Susannah Ricci's husband Rich said it was his best moment of the week—Annie Power got to her feet unscathed, as did Benie des Dieux who crumpled on landing in similar fashion at the same flight when four lengths up and still on the bridle in the latest renewal, after also being sent off at odds on. **c–**
h159

Dramatic though it was, it would be wrong to dwell too much on Benie des Dieux's Cheltenham mishap which is the only blemish on her record for current connections which otherwise consists of seven victories, three over fences and four at the top level over hurdles. The latest of those came after the end of the season in Britain and Ireland in the Grande Course de Haies d'Auteuil which provided a happier case of history repeating itself for Willie Mullins who landed his fifth edition of France's top hurdle. After his father Paddy won the race in 1984 with the great Dawn Run, it was another mare, Nobody Told Me, who provided Mullins with his first winner in 2003, with Rule Supreme winning a year later and Thousand Stars being successful in 2011 and 2012. Since Nobody Told Me, no mare had been successful until 2018 when De Bon Coeur had been a hugely impressive sixteen-length winner and she was the hot favourite to retain her title. De Bon Coeur came to the latest Grande Course de Haies as the winner of all but two of her fifteen starts. Like Benie des Dieux, she had a fall on her record which had cost her almost certain success in a big race—in the Prix Alain du Breil two years earlier—while she had the excuse of being in season when suffering her only defeat in completed starts. That had come in the Prix Leon Rambaud before her win in the Grande Course de Haies the year before, but she won that contest beforehand this time, one of just two starts in the current campaign after suffering a hairline fracture to a bone in her foot.

As has become usual with his Auteuil raids, Mullins was mob-handed, and while Benie des Dieux, ridden by Paul Townend following Walsh's retirement, stood out as the stable's main contender, she was accompanied by the same owners' Bapaume, runner-up twelve months earlier, dual Champion Hurdle runner-up Melon, recent Punchestown handicap winner Mr Adjudicator and the disappointing Yorkhill, a well-beaten sixth the year before. De Bon Coeur looked much the best of the home team in a field of twelve which also included her stable-companion Alex de Larredya, runner-up in a couple of past renewals and the only horse up until then to have beaten her. The two main contenders were among several still in contention on the home turn towards the end of a race in which the initial gallop had them well strung out before it steadied at around halfway. De Bon Coeur pressed on in the back straight on the final circuit and, having travelled fluently in fourth for much of the way,

Grande Course de Haies d'Auteuil, Auteuil—Benie des Dieux (right) and Paul Townend en route to providing Willie Mullins with his fifth win in France's premier hurdle race; the previous year's winner De Bon Coeur (stripes) is runner-up this time

Benie des Dieux improved to dispute the lead two out before going on at the final obstacle, not giving much room to De Bon Coeur on her inner who had to be steadied into it. De Bon Coeur had every chance to respond on the flat but was no match for Benie des Dieux who stretched away to win by six and a half lengths, De Bon Coeur rallying for second and getting the better of the Leon Rambaud runner-up Berjou, Bapaume, who briefly disputed second on the run-in, and the long-time leader Galop Marin. Mr Adjudicator was seventh while Yorkhill and Melon brought up the rear after pulling too hard. Unlike Melon, who gave himself no chance of seeing out the longer trip, Benie des Dieux stayed on strongly on her first attempt beyond two and a half miles. De Bon Coeur ran some way below her form of the previous year and was reported to have lost a shoe from the foot that had previously been injured. De Bon Coeur had, incidentally, been given a Royal Ascot entry in the Gold Cup despite never having run on the Flat, but her defeat quickly put paid to those plans and her retirement was announced later in the summer. Benie des Dieux's win came just two weeks after she had been successful for the second year running in the Irish Stallion Farms EBF Annie Power Mares Champion Hurdle at Punchestown where she started odds on in a field of five and beat her stable-companions Stormy Ireland and Good Thyne Tara, who had filled a creditable second and third after her departure in the David Nicholson Mares' Hurdle, by nine and a half lengths and fifteen.

A two-week gap between Punchestown and Auteuil was no doubt shorter than ideal, but it didn't deter her trainer who had been thwarted in his attempts to run Benie des Dieux before Cheltenham because of the unsuitably firmish ground that had prevailed for much of the season. The Grande Course de Haies also gave Benie des Dieux more of an opportunity to show how good she really is, something which contests restricted to her own sex had not fully revealed previously. She had had a below-par Apple's Jade back in third when winning the David Nicholson Mares' Hurdle on her return to hurdles at the 2018 Cheltenham Festival. The Grande Course de Haies was moved from its former date in June to be run on the same weekend as the top French chase, the Grand Steeple-Chase de Paris, the year before. On that occasion, both races were run on the Sunday of the two-day meeting, but in the latest season the Grande Course de Haies was given top billing as the highlight of the Saturday card. Fresh from winning his first Cheltenham Gold Cup and his first Irish Grand National, Mullins made a concerted effort to complete a famous double at Auteuil and win the Grand Steeple-Chase for the first time as well, sending no fewer than five of the stable's best staying chasers for the race. Mullins described the venture as 'very much a learning experience' after Rathvinden, Pleasant Company and Acapella Bourgeois trailed home as the last three finishers. Total Recall was another who failed to adapt well enough, but there was a much more encouraging performance from the Irish Grand National winner Burrows Saint in fifth who, despite being the youngest and least experienced chaser of the quintet, went round like an old hand, crucially, perhaps, unlike the others, having some experience of Auteuil's chase course from earlier in his career. There was some Irish success to celebrate after the Grand Steeple-Chase, however, a lack of experience over the varied obstacles proving no handicap to Davy Russell who came in for the winning ride on Carriacou.

Prior experience of Auteuil's hurdles is less important than it seems to be over fences, though Benie des Dieux was herself a dual course winner over hurdles when trained in France. A return to fences hasn't been ruled out for Benie des Dieux who could yet prove just as good over the larger obstacles. The pedigree of the angular Benie des Dieux was covered in *Chasers & Hurdlers 2017/18*. One point to add, though, is that she becomes the second winner of the Grande Course de Haies for her sire Great Pretender after Ptit Zig who won the 2016 renewal for Paul Nicholls.

Mrs S. Ricci's "Benie des Dieux"

Benie des Dieux stays twenty-five furlongs and acts on heavy going, and was tried in cheekpieces when trained in France. She has worn ear plugs in her two appearances in the David Nicholson Mares' Hurdle. Benie des Dieux has surely earned her place now alongside Quevega, Annie Power, Vroum Vroum Mag and Apple's Jade, the last-named handled by Mullins as a juvenile hurdler, among the most notable mares to have been through her trainer's hands. *W. P. Mullins, Ireland*

BENI LIGHT (FR) 8 b.g. Crossharbour – Or Light (FR) (Sleeping Car (FR)) [2018/19 c72, h–: c16.5g Jun 2] has had breathing operation: maiden hurdler: little form over fences: in hood last 3 starts: tried in tongue tie. *Tom George* — c– h–

BENIM 9 b.m. Authorized (IRE) – Princess Danah (IRE) (Danehill (USA)) [2018/19 h21.6gpu Jul 22] runner-up both starts in bumpers in 2014/15: pulled up in maiden on hurdling debut after very long absence: wears tongue tie. *Barry Brennan* — h–

BENISSIMO (IRE) 9 b.g. Beneficial – Fennor Rose (IRE) (Kotashaan (FR)) [2018/19 c–, h–: h19.9m³ h19.9g h15.8m⁶ c20gpu c15.7g⁵ Oct 25] poor handicap hurdler: poor maiden chaser: stays 21f: acts on heavy going: has worn cheekpieces, including in 2018/19: usually races nearer last than first. *Tony Forbes* — c62 h77

BENKEI (IRE) 9 b.g. Galileo (IRE) – Bywayofthestars (Danehill (USA)) [2018/19 h22.2m* h22.8d Aug 4] useful on Flat, stays 17f: useful handicap hurdler: won at Killarney (by 3¼ lengths from Just Get Cracking) in May: stays 2¾m: acts on good to firm and heavy going: has worn headgear, including final start: races prominently. *Harry Rogers, Ireland* — h132

BENNACHIE (IRE) 10 b.g. Milan – Stormy Lady (IRE) (Glacial Storm (USA)) [2018/19 c94§, h83§: c20.1gur c19.4mF Aug 2] workmanlike gelding: winning hurdler: modest handicap chaser: failed to complete both starts in 2018/19, though looked likely winner when falling 2 out on second occasion: stayed 2¾m: acted on soft and good to firm going: wore cheekpieces/tongue tie: temperamental: dead. *Tim Vaughan* — c95 § h– §

BENNY IN MILAN (IRE) 8 b.g. Milan – Chaparral Lady (IRE) (Broken Hearted) **h117**
[2018/19 h102: h16s h16g⁵ h16.6g h15.7gᵖᵘ h20.3g* h16m² h19.6g h16g h24d⁴ Apr 21]
fairly useful handicap hurdler: won at Southwell in October: second at Thurles in
November: left F. Flood after first start: stays 21f: acts on good to firm and good to soft
going: has worn headgear, including in 2018/19. *Denis Hogan, Ireland*

BENNY'S BRIDGE (IRE) 6 b.g. Beneficial – Wattle Bridge (IRE) (King's Theatre **h124**
(IRE)) [2018/19 b99: h16d² h15.7gᶠ h16.7s⁴ h16.8d⁴ h16s h16.7g* h16g Apr 27] good-
topped gelding: bumper winner: fairly useful hurdler: won handicap at Cheltenham in
January and novice at Market Rasen in March: raced around 2m: acts on good to soft
going: usually races off pace. *Fergal O'Brien*

BENNYS GIRL (IRE) 11 b.m. Beneficial – Be My Flower (IRE) (Be My Native (USA)) **c80**
[2018/19 c86, h–: c21.6g⁴ c25.2v³ c19.4v c20.9gᵖᵘ c29.2gᵖᵘ Apr 10] maiden hurdler: poor **h–**
handicap chaser: stays 3¼m: acts on good to firm and heavy going: usually front runner/
races prominently. *Dai Williams*

BENNYS KING (IRE) 8 b.g. Beneficial – Hellofafaithful (IRE) (Oscar (IRE)) [2018/19 **c141 p**
c–, h–: c19.4v* c21.4s* Dec 26] good-topped gelding: fairly useful hurdler: useful form **h–**
over fences: won handicap at Chepstow and novice handicap at Market Rasen in December:
will be suited by 3m: acts on heavy going: open to further improvement as a chaser.
Dan Skelton

BENNY'S SECRET (IRE) 9 br.g. Beneficial – Greenhall Rambler (IRE) (Anshan) **c99**
[2018/19 h103: h22.7g h20g h20.9d³ c19.4s⁵ c20.3g² c20.3m³ h20.9g² h22.7d⁷ Apr 8] **h106**
fair handicap hurdler: won at Kelso in April: similar form over fences: stays 23f: acts on
soft and good to firm going: wears hood: has worn tongue tie: usually races in rear.
N. W. Alexander

BENRUBEN (IRE) 6 b.g. Beneficial – Didinas (FR) (Kaldou Star) [2018/19 h24g³ h24gᵖᵘ **c142**
b16g* c16s c16.3g² c17s² c18gᶠ Mar 23] third foal: half-brother to useful bumper winner **h100**
Bordini (by Martaline) and a winning pointer by Astarabad: dam unraced half-sister to use- **b100**
ful French hurdler (winner up to 2¼m) Dallidas: unplaced both starts in points: won bumper
at Leopardstown (by ¾ length from Conflated) in December: fair form over hurdles: useful
form over fences: second in Grade 3 novice at Navan (8½ lengths behind Jetz) in March,
then would have won listed novice at Thurles but for falling heavily last: left Paul Nolan
after second start: best form around 2m: acts on soft going. *John W. Nicholson, Ireland*

BENSON 4 b.g. Beat Hollow – Karla June (Unfuwain (USA)) [2018/19 b15.8d⁵ Mar 21] **b84**
£14,000 3-y-o: closely related/half-brother to several winners, including fair hurdler Katie
Gale (2m winner, by Shirocco): dam US 1m winner: 40/1, fifth in bumper at Ludlow (5½
lengths behind Floressa). *Sarah-Jayne Davies*

BENTONS LAD 8 br.g. Bollin Eric – Spirit of Ecstasy (Val Royal (FR)) [2018/19 c78, **c79**
h92: h20.6g² h20.3g* h19.9g⁵ c21.2g⁵ h19.6g h18.6g h24.4g⁶ h19.6g⁵ h24g h19.7g Mar **h95**
26] has had breathing operation: modest handicap hurdler: won at Southwell in May: poor
maiden chaser on balance: left Mark Walford after fifth start: stays 21f: acts on good to soft
going: wears headgear: has worn tongue tie. *Graeme McPherson*

BE ONE 5 b.g. Multiplex – Riverside Bay (Karinga Bay) [2018/19 b16.2d⁵ Mar 26] point **b–**
winner: well beaten in maiden bumper. *Ann Hamilton*

BERBORU (IRE) 7 b.m. Brian Boru – Relic Hunter (IRE) (Presenting) [2018/19 b17.7s⁶ **h106**
h20.6g³ h24s⁴ h23.1s² Jan 20] fourth foal: dam (h78) maiden hurdler (stayed 2¾m): placed **b59**
in Irish points: well held in bumper: fair form over hurdles: best effort when second in
mares maiden at Exeter: tried in tongue tie. *Ben Pauling*

BERGAMOT (IRE) 4 b.f. Azamour (IRE) – Behrama (IRE) (Desert Style (IRE)) **b88**
[2018/19 b14g⁵ b14g³ b16.5d² b15.8m* Apr 23] good-topped filly: has had breathing
operation: first foal: dam (b88), bumper winner, out of half-sister to very smart hurdler/
top-class chaser up to 3¼m Behrajan: fair form in bumpers: won at Ludlow in April: will
stay further than 2m: wears tongue tie. *Dan Skelton*

BERLIEF ARAMIS 9 b.g. Bertolini (USA) – Kaylifa Aramis (Kayf Tara) [2018/19 h–: **h–**
h20gᵖᵘ Jun 2] little show over hurdles. *Alan Phillips*

BERMEO (IRE) 8 b.g. Definite Article – Miss Blueyes (IRE) (Dushyantor (USA)) **c94**
[2018/19 c–, h85: h23s⁵ h24g⁴ c25.8m⁶ c21g³ c25.8g* c23m* c26g* c28.5d² c26.7gᶠ **h74**
c24.2vᵖᵘ Dec 20] has had breathing operation: poor handicap hurdler: modest handicap
chaser: won at Newton Abbot (conditionals) and Worcester in September, and Fontwell in
November: stays 3½m: acts on good to firm and good to soft going: wears headgear/tongue
tie. *Johnny Farrelly*

BERMONDSEY BELLE (IRE) 5 b.m. Sir Percy – Bermondsey Girl (Bertolini (USA)) h–
[2018/19 h16.4v^pu Mar 16] sister to fair 2m hurdle winner Thames Knight: fair maiden on
Flat, stays 2m: pulled up in mares novice on hurdling debut. *Jackie Stephen*

BERNARDELLI (IRE) 11 b.g. Golan (IRE) – Beautiful Blue (IRE) (Xaar) [2018/19 **c111 x**
c127x, h–: c20.1g^5 Feb 23] winning hurdler: fairly useful handicap chaser, looked rusty h–
sole outing in 2018/19: stays 3m: acts on heavy going: wears headgear: often let down by
jumping. *Nicky Richards*

BERRY DE CARJAC (FR) 8 ch.g. Epalo (GER) – Miria Galanda (FR) (Chef de Clan c–
(FR)) [2018/19 c–, h98§: h16.8g^F h15.8g^5 May 31] workmanlike gelding: maiden on Flat: **h74 §**
fair hurdler, well below form in 2018/19: maiden chaser: stays 2½m: acts on good to firm
going: has worn headgear/tongue tie: has bled: temperamental. *Grace Harris*

BERRY POPPINS 5 b.m. Mawatheeq (USA) – Florie (Alflora (IRE)) [2018/19 b13.7d b–
Jan 25] sixth foal: half-sister to bumper winner/fairly useful 2m hurdle winner My Mate
Mark (by Sakhee) and bumper winner/fair hurdler Rafafie (2m-19f winner, by Kayf Tara):
dam unraced: well beaten in point/bumper. *Nick Littmoden*

BERTALUS (IRE) 10 b.g. City Honours (USA) – Deep Dalus (IRE) (Mandalus) c– §
[2018/19 c95§, h79§: h24.3d c31.9v^pu c24.2d^pu Mar 26] fair hurdler/modest chaser at best, h– §
no form in 2018/19: has worn headgear, including last 5 starts: one to treat with caution. *N.
W. Alexander*

BERTIE BARNES (IRE) 8 b.g. Craigsteel – Mahon Rose (IRE) (Roselier (FR)) h–
[2018/19 h106: h21m May 14] fair hurdler, well held sole outing in 2018/19: stayed 21f:
best form on soft/heavy going: dead. *Richard Phillips*

BERTIE BLAKE (IRE) 6 b.g. Beneficial – Diandrina (Mondrian (GER)) [2018/19 h86: **h79**
h19.9g h20.6g^pu h19.6g h19.9g^4 h19.9g^2 h24g^3 h24.1d h21.2d^2 h20.6g^4 Mar 14] poor
maiden hurdler: stays 3m: acts on good to soft going: wears cheekpieces: usually leads.
Philip Kirby

BERTIE BORU (IRE) 12 b.g. Brian Boru – Sleeven Lady (Crash Course) [2018/19 **c113 §**
c119§, h–: h23.1s c24.2d^4 c30.7s^pu Apr 16] strong, workmanlike gelding: maiden hurdler: h–
fairly useful handicap chaser: stays 3½m: acts on heavy going: has worn cheekpieces:
temperamental. *Carroll Gray*

BERTIELICIOUS 11 b.g. And Beyond (IRE) – Pennepoint (Pennekamp (USA)) **c56 x**
[2018/19 c16.4s^5 c15.6s^6 c16.4s^5 c16.5s^4 c16.4d^3 c19.3s^pu c16.4s c23.4d^pu Mar 5] maiden h–
hurdler: poor maiden chaser: unproven beyond 2m: acts on heavy going: wears headgear:
often let down by jumping. *Jonathan Haynes*

BERTIE LUGG 11 b.g. Beat All (USA) – Flakey Dove (Oats) [2018/19 c108, h–: c23.8g c–
c20.3g c24g^pu c24g^pu Oct 18] winning hurdler: fair chaser at best, no form in 2018/19: in h–
headgear last 3 starts: has worn tongue tie, including final start. *Tom Gretton*

BERTIE MOON 9 b.g. Bertolini (USA) – Fleeting Moon (Fleetwood (IRE)) [2018/19 h–
h20.3g h20.3s^pu Dec 16] fair hurdler at best, lightly raced and no form in sphere since
2015/16: has worn cheekpieces, including last 3 starts. *Tony Forbes*

BERTIMONT (FR) 9 gr.g. Slickly (FR) – Bocanegra (FR) (Night Shift (USA)) [2018/19 c–
c–, h111: h15.8m^3 h16.3m^3 Jun 19] smallish gelding: fair handicap hurdler: maiden chaser: **h113**
raced mainly around 2m: acts on soft and good to firm going: tried in cheekpieces: wears
tongue tie. *Dan Skelton*

BE SEEING YOU 8 ch.g. Medicean – Oshiponga (Barathea (IRE)) [2018/19 c–, h78: c–
c22.5g^F Jun 6] winning hurdler: maiden chaser, fell sole outing in 2018/19: stays 23f: acts h–
on good to firm going: has worn headgear: wears tongue tie. *Matt Sheppard*

BEST DIRECTOR (IRE) 11 b.g. Oscar (IRE) – Taneys Leader (IRE) (Supreme Leader) **c79**
[2018/19 c24.1g^3 May 19] multiple winning pointer: maiden hurdler: 40/1, third in novice h–
handicap at Bangor (24 lengths behind Nightline) on chasing debut. *John Groucott*

BEST PRACTICE (IRE) 8 br.g. Beneficial – Lemon Cello (IRE) (Accordion) [2018/19 **h96**
h101: h20.3g^6 Jun 12] fair maiden hurdler: probably stayed 2½m: best form on good going:
dead. *Jonjo O'Neill*

BEST TO COME (IRE) 6 b.g. Stowaway – Nippy Nora (IRE) (King's Theatre (IRE)) **c59**
[2018/19 b–p: h16.7g^5 h20g^5 h19.9g^4 h19.7s h19.9s^2 h19.9d^2 c19.2m^4 Feb 22] fair form **h105**
over hurdles: well beaten in novice handicap on chasing debut: left Tom George after
fourth start: stays 2½m: acts on soft going: tried in hood. *Keith Dalgleish*

BESTWORK (FR) 8 bl.g. Network (GER) – Harmony (FR) (Lute Antique (FR)) **c121 §**
[2018/19 c124, h–: c21g^{pu} c20.3g^3 c23g* c22.6g^2 c25.5g^{pu} c25.1g c20.5g^5 c19.9s^{pu} c19.4g^2 **h–**
c19.4g^F Apr 26] maiden hurdler: fairly useful handicap chaser: won at Worcester in July:
stays 23f: acts on soft and good to firm going: has worn headgear, including final start: tried
in tongue tie: front runner/races prominently: temperamental (possibly needs to dominate).
Charlie Longsdon

BETAMECHE (FR) 8 gr.g. Kapgarde (FR) – Kaldona (FR) (Kaldoun (FR)) [2018/19 **h126 p**
h16.3s h16d^2 h15.8v* h20.5d^2 Mar 2] well-made gelding: fairly useful form over hurdles:
won maiden at Uttoxeter in January: open to further improvement. *Dan Skelton*

BETANCOURT (IRE) 9 ch.g. Refuse To Bend (IRE) – Orinoco (IRE) (Darshaan) **c–**
[2018/19 c87, h92: h19.8s Mar 10] modest hurdler at best, found little sole outing in **h–**
2018/19: twice-raced chaser: stays 2½m: tried in cheekpieces. *Stef Keniry*

BET ON BETTY 6 b.m. Flying Legend (USA) – Cadourova (FR) (Cadoual (FR)) **b–**
[2018/19 b–: b16.7g May 19] no form in bumpers. *Oliver Greenall*

BETSALOTTIE 6 gr.g. Aqlaam (IRE) – Si Belle (IRE) (Dalakhani (IRE)) [2018/19 h16d Jan **h–**
15] fair on Flat, stays 2m: well beaten in novice hurdle. *John Bridger*

BETTER DAYS (IRE) 8 gr.g. Daylami (IRE) – Miss Edgehill (IRE) (Idris (IRE)) **c–**
[2018/19 c113, h–: c24.5g^{pu} c24s^{pu} c26g^5 Aug 30] workmanlike gelding: winning hurdler: **h–**
fair chaser at best, no form in 2018/19: has worn tongue tie. *Nigel Twiston-Davies*

BETTER GETALONG (IRE) 8 b.g. Gold Well – Arequipa (IRE) (Turtle Island (IRE)) **h131**
[2018/19 h131: h18.9v^2 h19.3d^6 h20.5s^5 Mar 9] good-topped gelding: useful handicap
hurdler: second at Haydock (4½ lengths behind Ballymoy) in December: stays 19f: acts on
heavy ground. *Nicky Richards*

BETTER NEWS 8 b.m. Fair Mix (IRE) – Welcome News (Bob Back (USA)) [2018/19 **h89**
h81p: h16s^5 h19.7s^{pu} h19d^{pu} h19g Feb 19] well held completed start in points: modest
maiden hurdler: unproven beyond 2m: acts on soft going: tried in hood/tongue tie.
Neil Mulholland

BETTY BATTENS 6 ch.m. Tobougg (IRE) – Where's My Slave (IRE) (Daylami (IRE)) **b–**
[2018/19 b16d b13.7g^6 Apr 24] first foal: dam (h107) maiden hurdler (stayed 3m)/winning
pointer: no form in bumpers. *Mike Hawker*

BETTY PETCH 5 ch.m. Schiaparelli (GER) – Perchance To Dream (Alflora (IRE)) **b67**
[2018/19 b16.8s^5 b15.8d b16s^6 Mar 9] £700 4-y-o: third foal: dam unraced half-sister to
useful hurdler/smart chaser (stayed 23f) Chilling Place: poor form in bumpers: wears
tongue tie. *Lucinda Egerton*

BETWEEN THE WATERS (IRE) 8 ch.g. Indian River (FR) – Catch Ball (Prince **c98**
Sabo) [2018/19 c96, h–: c22.5m^4 c21.6g^3 c17.2g c20.1g^2 c21.6g^3 c21.6s* c25.7m^2 c25.7g^2 **h–**
c20d^4 Nov 29] sturdy gelding: has had breathing operation: maiden hurdler: modest
handicap chaser: won at Fontwell (conditionals) in October: stays 3¼m: acts on firm and
soft going: wears headgear/tongue tie. *Jamie Snowden*

BEWARE THE BEAR (IRE) 9 b.g. Shantou (USA) – Native Bid (IRE) (Be My Native **c157 §**
(USA)) [2018/19 c147, h–: c26s^4 c26.3d* c25s* c28.8g^{pu} Apr 27] strong, workmanlike **h–**
gelding: has had breathing operation: winning hurdler: very smart handicap chaser: won at
Cheltenham (by 5 lengths from Shanroe Santos) in January and Ultima Handicap Chase
there (by 1¼ lengths from Vintage Clouds) in March: should stay 4m: acts on heavy going:
in headgear last 4 starts: usually races nearer last than first: temperamental. *Nicky Henderson*

*Ultima Handicap Chase, Cheltenham—Beware The Bear swoops to defeat the
Trevor Hemmings-owned greys Vintage Clouds (centre) and Lake View Lad (noseband)*

BEYEH (IRE) 11 b.m. King's Best (USA) – Cradle Rock (IRE) (Desert Sun) [2018/19 c106, h97: h20.3g May 15] small mare: fairly useful hurdler at best, behind sole outing in 2018/19: maiden chaser: stays 2¾m: acts on heavy going. *Michael Appleby*

c–
h–

BEYONDAPPROACH (IRE) 5 b.m. Jeremy (USA) – Gonebeyondajoke (IRE) (Footstepsinthesand) [2018/19 h19.5d⁵ Oct 13] €35,000 3-y-o: second foal: dam unraced half-sister to very smart/unreliable hurdler (stayed 3m) Won In The Dark: off mark in Irish points at second attempt: 14/1, fifth in mares novice at Chepstow (17¾ lengths behind Posh Trish) on hurdling debut: should improve. *Dan Skelton*

h91 p

BEYOND GOLD 9 b.g. And Beyond (IRE) – Senora d'Or (Le Coq d'Or) [2018/19 c26.2dᶠ Apr 8] third foal: half-brother to modest chaser Senora Moss (25f winner, by Le Moss): dam winning pointer: point winner: every chance when fell heavily 3 out in maiden hunter won by Longtymegone at Kelso on chasing debut. *C. Robson*

c93

BEYOND REDEMPTION (IRE) 5 b.g. Court Cave (IRE) – Hopeful Gleam (IRE) (Simply Great (FR)) [2018/19 b15.8d⁴ Mar 13] won Irish point on debut: 1/2, fourth in bumper at Huntingdon (15¾ lengths behind Sadlermor): has joined Gary Moore. *Nicky Henderson*

b71

BEYOND SUPREMACY (IRE) 7 ch.g. Beneficial – Slaney Athlete (IRE) (Warcraft (USA)) [2018/19 h88: h18.5m³ May 8] useful-looking gelding: modest form over hurdles. *Jack R. Barber*

h95

BEYONDTEMPTATION 11 ch.m. And Beyond (IRE) – Tempted (IRE) (Invited (USA)) [2018/19 h110: h16.2s h20.1sᵖᵘ h16.4g⁵ h16.8s* h16.4d² h20.1d h16.4d³ h18.9m Apr 20] fair handicap hurdler: won at Sedgefield in February: stays 23f, raced mainly at shorter: acts on heavy going: wears hood/tongue tie: front runner. *Jonathan Haynes*

h108

BEYONDTHEFLAME 9 b.m. And Beyond (IRE) – Flame of Zara (Blushing Flame (USA)) [2018/19 h70: h23.3g⁶ h23.3gᵖᵘ h16.2g⁴ h16.2m h16.2gᵖᵘ h20.1gᵖᵘ h19.9gᵖᵘ Nov 8] poor maiden hurdler: stays 23f: acts on good to soft going: wears headgear/tongue tie: front runner. *Jonathan Haynes*

h56

BEYOND THE GLEN 9 b.m. And Beyond (IRE) – Calabria (Neltino) [2018/19 h75: h22.1g c15.6m⁵ c15.7g⁶ c21.2d⁵ Aug 25] point winner: maiden hurdler: no form in chases: tried in tongue tie. *Chris Grant*

c–
h–

BEYOND THE LAW (IRE) 7 b.g. Westerner – Thegoodwans Sister (IRE) (Executive Perk) [2018/19 h123: c20gᶠ c19.7s⁵ c20d⁵ c21.5s² c20g⁶ c31.7sᶠ c24.5g⁵ c21.2v² c20d* Apr 21] lengthy gelding: has had breathing operation: winning hurdler: useful chaser: won maiden at Cork in April: stays 21f: acts on heavy going: tried in headgear: has worn tongue tie, including in 2018/19: front runner/races prominently. *M. F. Morris, Ireland*

c131
h–

BEYOND THE STARS 8 b.m. And Beyond (IRE) – Treasured Memories (Cloudings (IRE)) [2018/19 h–: h19.9g⁵ h23.3gᵖᵘ Jun 6] sparely-made mare: no form in points/over hurdles: in hood/tongue tie last 2 starts. *Maurice Barnes*

h–

BEYONDTHESTORM (IRE) 6 b.g. Flemensfirth (USA) – Blue Gale (IRE) (Be My Native (USA)) [2018/19 h20.5s⁶ Dec 19] €24,000 3-y-o, £150,000 4-y-o: sixth foal: half-brother to untrustworthy 25f/3¼m chase winner Kimora (by Bach): dam unraced half-sister to useful hurdler (stayed 2½m) Finns Cross: won Irish point on debut: 14/1, sixth in novice at Newbury (27¼ lengths behind Tidal Flow) on hurdling debut: likely to improve. *Nicky Henderson*

h86 p

BHUTAN (IRE) 6 gr.g. Galileo (IRE) – Ecology (USA) (Unbridled's Song (USA)) [2018/19 h17d⁴ h16g h20m² h16sᵖᵘ h21.4gᵖᵘ h16d³ h15.7m Apr 20] fairly useful 1¼m winner on Flat: fairly useful handicap hurdler: second at Bellewstown in July: left Joseph Patrick O'Brien after fourth start: stays 2½m: acts on soft and good to firm going: usually wears tongue tie. *Jonjo O'Neill*

h127

BIALCO (FR) 8 gr.g. Dom Alco (FR) – Lacanale (FR) (Kadalko (FR)) [2018/19 c125, h121: h20.5g² h22sᵖᵘ h22.7d* h22v² Mar 16] fairly useful hurdler: won handicap at Kelso in March: fairly useful chaser: stays 3m: acts on heavy going: has worn headgear: wears tongue tie. *Lucinda Russell*

c–
h129

BIBLICAL (FR) 4 ch.g. Harbour Watch (IRE) – Prophecie (FR) (Dansili) [2018/19 b16g² Mar 29] fifth foal: half-brother to French 7.5f-9.5f winner Panama (by Sholokhov): dam placed up to 1¼m in France: 3/1, second in bumper at Wetherby (head behind Old Jeroboam): has joined N. W. Alexander. *John Quinn*

b93

BIDDY BE (IRE) 6 b.m. Stowaway – Ballyoscar (IRE) (Oscar (IRE)) [2018/19 h20v^{pu} h16g h20.4g⁵ h21g⁴ h16.7g c17g^{pu} h16.4v^{pu} Apr 3] second foal: dam unraced half-sister to fairly useful hurdler (stayed 2¾m) Old Kilcash: poor maiden hurdler: pulled up in maiden on chasing debut: left Henry de Bromhead after sixth start: stays 2½m: acts on heavy going: often in tongue tie. *Mark Campion* — c– h83

BIDDY THE BOSS (IRE) 6 b.m. Doyen (IRE) – Thiarnathoir (IRE) (Gamut (IRE)) [2018/19 h19g² h16g⁴ h18.8g h16.5s h21g² h21.7d² h24d* h24d⁵ h22.5g⁴ h24g² h21g⁵ c20d⁴ c16g⁵ c19.6v* c24s⁵ c21.6m^{pu} Apr 20] €4,000 3-y-o: lengthy mare: first foal: dam, pulled up in point, half-sister to fairly useful hurdler/useful chaser (stayed 4m) Our Victoria out of half-sister to top-class chaser up to 3½m Our Vic: bumper winner: fairly useful hurdler: won mares maiden at Wexford in September: second in handicap at Clonmel in November: similar form over fences: won novice at Down Royal in March: stays 3m: acts on heavy going: has worn tongue tie, including last 3 starts. *Gavin Patrick Cromwell, Ireland* — c122 h116

BIENNIAL (IRE) 7 ch.g. Bienamado (USA) – Midnight Orchid (IRE) (Petardia) [2018/19 h97, b61: h16g⁴ h20.1g^{pu} h15.6g⁶ Nov 7] modest maiden hurdler: unproven beyond 2m: acts on heavy going: tried in tongue tie. *Ian Duncan* — h92

BIG BAD BEAR (IRE) 5 br.g. Jeremy (USA) – Our Polly (IRE) (Saint des Saints (FR)) [2018/19 b16.8s² b16d² b16.2g³ b16.2d* Apr 26] €55,000 3-y-o: first foal: dam unraced half-sister to useful hurdler/high-class chaser (stayed 25f) Invitation Only: fairly useful form in bumpers: won at Perth in April: will be suited by 2½m. *Nicky Richards* — b100

BIG BAD DOG (IRE) 5 b.g. Big Bad Bob (IRE) – Sunset Queen (IRE) (King's Theatre (IRE)) [2018/19 b–: b16.2g May 9] no form in bumpers. *Micky Hammond* — b–

BIG BAD DREAM (IRE) 7 b.g. Mountain High (IRE) – Stay At Home (IRE) (Blueprint (IRE)) [2018/19 b97: h20.5v h16.2g³ h16.2v³ Mar 14] placed in bumpers: fair form over hurdles: best effort when third in maiden at Kelso in December: should be suited by 2½m. *Donald Whillans* — h106

BIGBADJOHN (IRE) 10 br.g. Vinnie Roe (IRE) – Celtic Serenade (IRE) (Yashgan) [2018/19 c139, h–: c23.6d c26.7f* c25.1g^{pu} c23.8m⁵ Mar 31] tall gelding: winning hurdler: useful handicap chaser: won at Wincanton (by 1¾ lengths from Ridgeway Flyer) in October: stays 27f: acts on firm and soft going: in tongue tie last 3 starts: temperamental. *Nigel Twiston-Davies* — c135 § h–

BIG BAMBOO 7 ch.g. Kier Park (IRE) – Waheeba (Pivotal) [2018/19 b16.8s b15.3d h15.3g^{pu} Jan 17] no form in bumpers/novice hurdle: tried in hood. *Fiona Shaw* — h– b–

BIG BANG DE LOIRE (FR) 8 b.g. Califet (FR) – Grischa (FR) (Septieme Ciel (USA)) [2018/19 c91, h–: c24.2d^{pu} c21.6g⁶ c24d^{pu} c23.6d^{pu} c20.2g^{ur} Feb 27] point winner: lightly-raced hurdler: fair maiden chaser at best, little show under Rules in 2018/19: stays 2½m: acts on heavy going: has worn headgear, including in 2018/19: tried in tongue tie. *Giles Smyly* — c75 h–

BIG BOY BLUES (IRE) 6 ch.g. Resplendent Cee (IRE) – Lovely Pride (IRE) (Double Eclipse (IRE)) [2018/19 b15.3s Mar 7] tailed off in maiden bumper. *Nick Mitchell* — b–

BIG CHEVIOT 4 br.g. Bollin Eric – Miss Quickly (IRE) (Anshan) [2018/19 b16.4v⁶ Mar 16] tailed off in bumper. *Harriet Graham* — b–

BIGCHEXTOCASH (IRE) 7 b.g. Stowaway – Monakeeba (IRE) (Snurge) [2018/19 b–: h15.8d⁴ h19d⁶ h16s Mar 10] good-topped gelding: has had breathing operation: maiden Irish pointer: poor form over hurdles: tried in tongue tie. *Samuel Drinkwater* — h61

BIG CHIEF BENNY (IRE) 8 ch.g. Beneficial – Be Airlie (IRE) (Lord Americo) [2018/19 h20.5s h21g h19d⁴ Jan 19] stocky gelding: fairly useful handicap hurdler, below best in 2018/19 after long absence: stays 2½m: acts on soft going. *Alan King* — h113

BIG CHIP AND PIN 7 b.g. Generous (IRE) – Supreme Cove (Supreme Leader) [2018/19 h16.8s⁴ h16d⁴ h19.5d² c21g^{pu} Apr 20] modest maiden hurdler: well backed when pulled up in novice handicap on chasing debut: stays 19f: acts on good to soft going: should do better over fences. *Christian Williams* — c– p h94

BIG DATA (IRE) 5 br.g. Oscar (IRE) – Nolagh Supreme (IRE) (Supreme Leader) [2018/19 b16d⁴ Apr 6] €42,000 3-y-o: seventh foal: brother to a winning pointer, closely related to modest 23f hurdle winner Lawtop Legend (by Milan) and half-brother to fairly useful chaser Super Scorpion (3m winner, by Scorpion): dam unraced: 12/1, fourth in bumper at Chepstow (15 lengths behind One Touch). *Paul Webber* — b83

BIGDEAL (FR) 6 gr.g. Montmartre (FR) – Rauxa (Singspiel (IRE)) [2018/19 h–, b–: **h86** h20.5s⁵ h19.2d Jan 14] strong gelding: modest form over hurdles. *John E. Long*

BIG DIFFERENCE (IRE) 6 b.g. Presenting – Roque de Cyborg (IRE) (High Chaparral **h109** (IRE)) [2018/19 h105: h15.8d h23.1g h23.1g* Mar 14] placed in Irish points: fair form over hurdles: won handicap at Market Rasen in March: stays 23f: usually races prominently. *Ben Pauling*

BIG FIDDLE 6 b.m. Kayf Tara – Fiddling Again (Hernando (FR)) [2018/19 b15.8g b16d⁶ **h62** h21.2d h19.4d³ Mar 1] has had breathing operation: fifth foal: half-sister to 13f bumper **b73** winner Ifits A Fiddle (by Kalanisi): dam, bumper winner, half-sister to fairly useful hurdler/ useful chaser (17f-2½m winner) Classic Fiddle out of fairly useful hurdler/smart chaser (stayed 29f) Fiddling The Facts: poor form in bumpers/over hurdles: should prove suited by 2½m+. *Richard Phillips*

BIG FRED (IRE) 8 gr.g. Tikkanen (USA) – Whadouno (IRE) (Abednego) [2018/19 **h–** h100, b78: h15.8sᵖᵘ h18.5dᵖᵘ Apr 9] maiden hurdler, no form in 2018/19 (in headgear both starts). *Bernard Llewellyn*

BIG G 4 b.g. Cityscape – Crazy (GER) (Nicaron (GER)) [2018/19 b16.3s² Mar 11] first **b93** foal: dam (h94), 2m hurdle winner, also 1¼m/11f winner on Flat: 9/2, second in maiden bumper at Stratford (1½ lengths behind Hazm). *Dan Skelton*

BIG GEORGIE (IRE) 12 b.g. Exit To Nowhere (USA) – Afreen (IRE) (Entrepreneur) **c95** [2018/19 c23d³ Apr 4] multiple point winner: modest maiden chaser: stays 3¼m: best form on heavy going: tried in headgear. *J. M. Ridley*

BIGIRONONHISHIP (IRE) 8 b.g. Beneficial – Portobello Lady (IRE) (Broken **c117** Hearted) [2018/19 c125, h–: c22.9vᶠ c23.4s⁵ Jan 29] tall gelding: winning hurdler: fairly **h–** useful handicap chaser: best up to 3m: raced only on soft/heavy going: tried in tongue tie. *Rose Dobbin*

BIG MAN CLARENCE (IRE) 8 b.g. Golden Tornado (IRE) – Glens Lady (IRE) **h102** (Mister Lord (USA)) [2018/19 h20v h19.5v h23.5s² h23.5s² Jan 4] €17,000 3-y-o: workmanlike gelding: closely related to 2 winners by Dushyantor, including fairly useful 3m chase winner Glens Boy, and half-brother to 3 winners, including fairly useful hurdler/ chaser Glenwood Knight (23f/3m winner, by Presenting): dam unraced half-sister to Grand National winner Papillon: point winner: fair form over hurdles: stays 23f: acts on soft going. *Paul Henderson*

BIGMARTRE (FR) 8 b.g. Montmartre (FR) – Oh La Miss (FR) (Le Balafre (FR)) **c148** [2018/19 c149, h–: c15.9d⁶ c16.4sᵖᵘ c16d⁴ c15.7g³ c20.6d c21.1d c20.1g* Apr 25] lengthy **h–** gelding: winning hurdler: smart handicap chaser: won at Perth (by 16 lengths from Gardefort) in April: stays 2½m: acts on good to firm and heavy going: often in cheekpieces in 2018/19. *Harry Whittington*

BIG MEADOW (IRE) 8 br.g. Marienbard (IRE) – Lakyle Lady (IRE) (Bob Back **c110** (USA)) [2018/19 c120, h98: c30.7s³ c24.2dᵘʳ c28.5d⁵ c28.8vᵖᵘ c25.7g⁴ c25.7g⁴ Apr 7] **h–** well-made gelding: maiden hurdler: fairly useful handicap chaser, below form in 2018/19: stays 3m: acts on heavy going: wears headgear: tried in tongue tie. *Neil King*

BIG NASTY 6 b.g. Black Sam Bellamy (USA) – Hello My Lovely (Presenting) [2018/19 **h111 p** b15.7v³ b16s⁴ h24.1g² Apr 11] second foal: half-brother to bumper winner Harrisons **b86** Promise (by Westerner): dam (c85/h71), ungenuine 3m chase winner, sister to useful chaser (stayed 25f) Another Promise: fair form in bumpers: 6/1, showed plenty when second in novice at Wetherby (2½ lengths behind Trio For Rio) on hurdling debut: open to improvement. *Martin Keighley*

BIG 'N BETTER 7 b.g. Revoque (IRE) – Donastrela (IRE) (Tagula (IRE)) [2018/19 **h– p** b15.8d⁵ b16d⁵ b16.7v h16.3d Jan 16] second foal: dam, lightly raced over hurdles, 1¼m **b84** winner who stayed 2m on Flat, half-sister to useful hurdler/fairly useful chaser (stayed 23f) Kanpai: modest form in bumpers: well beaten in novice on hurdling debut: should do better. *Brendan Powell*

BIGNORM (IRE) 7 b.g. Mahler – Merry Heart (IRE) (Broken Hearted) [2018/19 b16g **h83** h16.7g h16.7g h19.5s h23.3s⁵ h24g⁴ h23.3d⁵ Mar 30] strong gelding: sixth foal: brother to **b66** useful hurdler/smart chaser (2m winner) Ornua and half-brother to a winning pointer by Moscow Society: dam unraced: unplaced in bumper: poor form over hurdles: stays 3m: acts on soft going. *Rosemary Gasson*

BIG PENNY (IRE) 7 b.m. Oscar (IRE) – Lady Marnay (IRE) (Darnay) [2018/19 h115: **c–** h23.3dᵖᵘ c24gᵖᵘ h19.8v⁴ h24gᵖᵘ h23.1g⁴ Apr 3] sturdy mare: has had breathing operations: **h106** fair handicap hurdler: pulled up in novice handicap on chasing debut: stays 25f: acts on soft and good to firm going: usually in headgear/tongue tie. *Jonjo O'Neill*

BIG PICTURE 7 b.g. Recharge (IRE) – Just Jenny (IRE) (King's Ride) [2018/19 h78: **c–** h23.9d³ h20.6g* h23.3g⁵ h23g h20g⁶ h18.5m⁶ h20v* h25g c19.4g^F Apr 14] compact **h86** gelding: modest handicap hurdler: won at Market Rasen (novice) in June and Ffos Las (conditionals) in December: fell first on chasing debut: stays 21f: acts on heavy going: wears headgear. *Johnny Farrelly*

BIG RIVER (IRE) 9 b.g. Milan – Call Kate (IRE) (Lord Americo) [2018/19 c144, h–: **c139** c23.4d^F h25s⁶ c25s⁴ c31.8m⁵ Apr 13] workmanlike gelding: winning hurdler: useful **h–** handicap chaser: fourth in Ultima Handicap Chase at Cheltenham (6½ lengths behind Beware The Bear) in March: stays 3¼m: acts on heavy going: wears tongue tie. *Lucinda Russell*

BIG SESS (IRE) 5 b.g. Flemensfirth (USA) – Akayid (Old Vic) [2018/19 b16.2g Apr 15] **b–** tailed off in bumper. *Tim Fitzgerald*

BIG STUART (IRE) 6 gr.g. Bushranger (IRE) – El Morocco (USA) (El Prado (IRE)) **b–** [2018/19 b16.8s⁵ b16d⁶ Mar 19] no form in bumpers. *Lynn Siddall*

BIG THUNDER 9 gr.g. Dalakhani (IRE) – Charlotte O Fraise (IRE) (Beat Hollow) **h–** [2018/19 h84: h22.1g⁵ h16.2g^pu Jun 16] maiden hurdler, no form in 2018/19: has worn cheekpieces, including in 2018/19. *Micky Hammond*

BIG TIME DANCER (IRE) 6 b.g. Zoffany (IRE) – Final Opinion (IRE) (King's **h128** Theatre (IRE)) [2018/19 h109: h16.2m* h15.8g⁴ h22.1s³ h16.2s⁶ h20.9g⁴ h19.7g² h19.4m* h21g* h20.3d h21.4m Apr 13] plain gelding: has had breathing operation: fairly useful hurdler: won maiden at Hexham in June, handicap at Doncaster in December and Lanzarote Hurdle at Kempton (by 1½ lengths from Solomon Grey) in January: stays 21f: acts on good to firm going: usually races nearer last than first, often travels strongly. *Jennie Candlish*

BIG TIME FRANK (IRE) 8 b.g. Bienamado (USA) – Pure Spirit (IRE) (Hubbly **c96 §** Bubbly (USA)) [2018/19 c82, h82: c23.5v² c24.2v² c20s² c24.2s² c23.5v² c24.2v² c26.2d⁵ **h–** c24.2d³ Apr 9] strong, workmanlike gelding: maiden hurdler: modest maiden chaser: stays 3m: acts on heavy going: wears headgear: no battler. *Polly Gundry*

BIGUNONTHEBALCONY 4 b.g. Fame And Glory – Zariyka (IRE) (Kalanisi (IRE)) **b87** [2018/19 b17.7g⁴ Apr 7] £30,000 3-y-o: fourth foal: half-brother to a winning pointer by Yeats: dam, unraced, closely related to useful hurdler (stayed 2½m) Zarinava: 11/2, fourth in bumper at Plumpton (11¼ lengths behind Strike The Flint). *Gary Moore*

BILLINGSLEY (IRE) 7 b.g. Millenary – Retain That Magic (IRE) (Presenting) **h101** [2018/19 h113p: h18.9v⁵ h23.5d h19.5d⁴ Mar 20] workmanlike gelding: fair hurdler: likely to prove best up to 2½m: acts on heavy going: usually front runner/races prominently. *Alastair Ralph*

BILLY BRONCO 8 ch.g. Central Park (IRE) – Nan (Buckley) [2018/19 c116g, h–: c23.6s **c115** c24s⁴ c24v^ro c24.2v* c24.2v⁴ Mar 18] winning hurdler: fairly useful handicap chaser: won **h–** novice chase at Exeter in March: probably stays 3¾m: best form on heavy going: in cheekpieces last 4 starts. *Evan Williams*

BILLY BROWN 7 b.g. Morpeth – Adalie (Absalom) [2018/19 b15.7g b16.5m⁶ Nov 15] **b–** unseated in Irish point: no form in 2 bumpers (hooded second one). *Alan Phillips*

BILLY FLIGHT (FR) 7 b.g. Walk In The Park (IRE) – Moon Flight (FR) (Saint Preuil **c– §** (FR)) [2018/19 c95§, h101§: c20.1g⁶ May 17] fair hurdler: little show over fences: stays **h– §** 25f: acts on good to firm going: has worn headgear: usually races towards rear: temperamental. *Noel Wilson*

BILLYGWYN TOO 6 b.g. Dr Massini (IRE) – Lady Prunella (IRE) (Supreme Leader) **b80** [2018/19 b100: b17g May 18] won bumper at Exeter in 2017/18: only eighth at Aintree on sole start under Rules in 2018/19: won for second time in points afterwards. *J. W. Tudor*

BILLY HICKS 8 b.g. Kayf Tara – Michelle's Ella (IRE) (Ela-Mana-Mou) [2018/19 h107: **c79** c24g⁴ c16v³ c21.6d c16m⁴ Apr 23] fair hurdler: poor form over fences: stays 19f: best form **h–** on soft/heavy going: has worn headgear, including in 2018/19. *Samuel Drinkwater*

BILLY MERRIOTT (IRE) 13 b.g. Dr Massini (IRE) – Hurricane Bella (IRE) (Taipan **c– §** (IRE)) [2018/19 c119, h–: c23d^pu Nov 29] sturdy gelding: point/hurdle winner: useful **h–** maiden chaser at best, pulled up sole outing in 2018/19: stays 23f: acts on soft going: has worn tongue tie: not one to trust. *Harry Fry*

BILLY MY BOY 10 b.g. Volochine (IRE) – Key West (FR) (Highest Honor (FR)) **c–**
[2018/19 c–, h104: h15.8g³ h16.8g⁴ h16g h18.5g⁰ʳ h16.8m² h16.8g* h16g⁵ Apr 26] fair **h104**
handicap hurdler: won at Newton Abbot in August: stays 19f: acts on
soft and good to firm going: wears headgear: tried in tongue tie. *Chris Down*

BILLY TEAL 14 ch.g. Keen – Morcat (Morston (FR)) [2018/19 c–, h–: h20.6g May 11] of **c–**
little account: tried in cheekpieces. *Lee James* **h–**

BILLY TWO TONGUES 11 b.g. Heron Island (IRE) – Ranahinch (IRE) (Persian **c–**
Mews) [2018/19 c116, h79: h22m⁴ h26.5g h24gᵖᵘ Aug 19] modest hurdler at best, no form **h–**
in 2018/19: fairly useful chaser at one time: stays 25f: acts on good to firm and heavy
going: tried in blinkers: has worn tongue tie, including final start. *Johnny Farrelly*

BINDON LANE 5 b.g. Arvico (FR) – Cuckoo Lane (IRE) (Midnight Legend) [2018/19 **h–**
b16.8s h18.5d h18.5s Mar 18] little impact in bumper/over hurdles. *Victor Dartnall* **b–**

BINGO D'OLIVATE (FR) 8 b.g. Laverock (IRE) – Ombrelle de L'Orme (FR) **c–**
(Marchand de Sable (USA)) [2018/19 c85, h90: h19.5v* h16.4s⁶ h17v³ h20.6dᶠ Apr 6] **h94**
angular gelding: modest handicap hurdler: won at Ayr in November: maiden chaser: stays
2½m: acts on heavy going: has worn headgear. *James Ewart*

BINN BORU 5 b.m. Brian Boru – Timoca (IRE) (Marju (IRE)) [2018/19 h15.8d⁶ h15.8m **h–**
h15.3g Apr 14] angular mare: first foal: dam (c92/h94), temperamental 2m hurdle winner
(stayed 2½m), also 10.7f winner on Flat: no form over hurdles. *Evan Williams*

BINT CHATTLEYA (FR) 4 b.f. Masterstroke (USA) – Chattleya (FR) (Desert King **h97**
(IRE)) [2018/19 h16g⁵ h16gˢᵘ h16.6g⁴ h16g Feb 13] fair maiden on Flat, stays 1½m:
modest form over hurdles. *James M. Barrett, Ireland*

BIRCH BANK 6 b.g. Multiplex – Dolly Duff (Alflora (IRE)) [2018/19 h80, b–: h20.3sᵖᵘ **h–**
h22gᵖᵘ Jan 15] has had breathing operation: maiden hurdler, no form in 2018/19: tried in
tongue tie. *Donald McCain*

BIRCHDALE (IRE) 5 b.g. Jeremy (USA) – Onewayortheother (IRE) (Presenting) **h138**
[2018/19 h21d* h20.3d* h24dᵖᵘ Mar 15] good sort: second foal: dam unraced sister to
useful hurdler/chaser (stays 3¼m) Some Invitation out of half-sister to top-class chaser up
to 3¼m Carlingford Lough: won Irish point on debut: useful form over hurdles: won
maiden at Warwick in December and Classic Novices' Hurdle at Cheltenham (by 18
lengths from Buster Valentine) in January: shaped as if amiss in Albert Bartlett Novices'
Hurdle (Spa) at Cheltenham final start: should stay 3m. *Nicky Henderson*

BIRCH HILL (IRE) 9 b.g. Kalanisi (IRE) – Miss Compliance (IRE) (Broken Hearted) **c118**
[2018/19 h118: c21.2g² c22.6m* c19.4mᵖᵘ Aug 2] well-made gelding: fairly useful hurdler: **h–**
similar form over fences: won novice handicap at Stratford in July: stays 23f: acts on soft
and good to firm going: tried in cheekpieces: wears tongue tie. *Sophie Leech*

BIRCH VALE (IRE) 7 br.m. Presenting – Oscar Rebel (IRE) (Oscar (IRE)) [2018/19 **h106**
h108, b88: h16.2g* h20.5v h15.7s³ h16.2v³ h18.9mᵘʳ Apr 20] fair hurdler: won mares
novice at Hexham in May: unproven beyond 17f: acts on heavy going: usually front
runner/races prominently. *Donald McCain*

BIRDS OF PREY (IRE) 5 b.g. Sir Prancealot (IRE) – Cute (Diktat) [2018/19 h16.5d² **h128**
h19d² h19.2s² h19s* h19d* h16g⁶ Apr 27] compact gelding: has had breathing operation:
useful on Flat, stays 1½m: fairly useful form over hurdles: won maiden at Taunton in
March and novice there in April: stays 19f: acts on soft going: wears tongue tie: usually
front runner/races prominently. *Paul Nicholls*

BISCAY BAY 4 ch.g. Champs Elysees – Cinnamon Bay (Zamindar (USA)) [2018/19 **h81**
h15.8mᵖᵘ h15.8g h15.8d⁶ h16d h19.5m⁵ Apr 22] poor form over hurdles: wears tongue tie.
Evan Williams

BISHOP OF BLING (IRE) 6 b.g. Big Bad Bob (IRE) – Convent Girl (IRE) (Bishop of **h–**
Cashel) [2018/19 h–: h16.7gᵖᵘ May 20] maiden hurdler, lightly raced and no form since
2016/17: in cheekpieces last 2 starts. *Alastair Ralph*

BISHOPS COURT 9 b.g. Helissio (FR) – Island of Memories (IRE) (Beneficial) **c118**
[2018/19 c133, h–: c20.3g⁴ c20.3g³ Oct 11] tall gelding: has had breathing operation: **h–**
maiden hurdler: useful handicap chaser, below form in 2018/19: stays 2½m: acts on heavy
going: wears headgear/tongue tie. *Neil Mulholland*

BISHOPSLOUGH (IRE) 11 b.g. Fruits of Love (USA) – Maid In Blue (IRE) (Bluebird **c–**
(USA)) [2018/19 h19.2vᵖᵘ Mar 6] point winner: fairly useful hurdler at best, lightly raced **h–**
and little form since 2015/16: winning chaser: stays 2¼m: acts on heavy going: has worn
tongue tie. *Danni O'Neill*

BISHOPS ROAD (IRE) 11 b.g. Heron Island (IRE) – Nice Resemblance (IRE) **c129** (Shernazar) [2018/19 c144, h–: c24s^{ur} c23.6d^6 c25g^3 c28.4g^2 c23.4d^{ur} c24.2d^{pu} c28.4g^6 **h–** c30.7d^3 Mar 3] compact gelding: winning hurdler: useful handicap chaser nowadays: second at Haydock in November: stays 3½m: acts on heavy going: wears headgear: often tongue tied in 2018/19. *Kerry Lee*

BISHOPSWOOD FLYER (IRE) 5 b.g. Arcadio (GER) – Catch The Class (IRE) **h–** (Flemensfirth (USA)) [2018/19 h23.9g^5 h23.3d^5 Mar 30] well held in novice hurdles. *Nigel Twiston-Davies*

BISOUBISOU 7 b.m. Champs Elysees – Marathea (FR) (Marathon (USA)) [2018/19 h82: **c–** h19.2g^3 h20g^4 h20g h19.6m^3 h20d* h19.3s h19.9s c19.3s^{pu} h20d^2 h20.7d Mar 13] angular **h79** mare: poor handicap hurdler: won at Fakenham in December: pulled up in novice handicap on chasing debut: left Olly Murphy after third start: stays 21f: acts on heavy going: wears headgear/tongue tie: temperament under suspicion. *Sarah Humphrey*

BIT MORE (IRE) 7 b.m. Brian Boru – Carmels Cottage (IRE) (Riberetto) [2018/19 **h–** b16.3d^6 h17.7g^6 h20g^{pu} Sep 28] runner-up on last of 3 starts in points: well beaten in **b–** bumper for David Phelan: no form over hurdles: dead. *Neil Mulholland*

BIT OF A CHARLIE 10 b.g. Emperor Fountain – Win A Hand (Nearly A Hand) [2018/19 **c–** h62: c25.8g^{pu} May 16] lengthy, angular gelding: little form over hurdles: pulled up in **h–** novice handicap on chasing debut: tried in tongue tie. *Robert Walford*

BIT OF A QUIRKE 6 ch.g. Monsieur Bond (IRE) – Silk (IRE) (Machiavellian (USA)) **h94** [2018/19 h96: h16.7g^5 h15.5d^4 h16g Feb 19] modest maiden hurdler: unproven beyond 17f: acts on good to soft going: usually races close up. *Mark Walford*

BITOFBLINDING (IRE) 5 b.g. Jeremy (USA) – Melodique (Kahyasi) [2018/19 **h–** b17.7g^6 b15.7m h19.2m Mar 29] £46,000 3-y-o: has had breathing operation: second foal: **b81** half-brother to fair hurdler/winning pointer Big Robin (19f winner, by Robin des Champs): dam unraced: modest form in bumpers: tailed off in maiden on hurdling debut. *Gary Moore*

BIT SPICY (IRE) 8 gr.m. Tikkanen (USA) – Like A Bolt (IRE) (Lahib (USA)) [2018/19 **h–** h–: h19.2s h15.9s^6 Feb 13] no form over hurdles: in blinkers last 2 starts. *Rebecca Woodman*

BITTER VIRTUE 8 b.m. Lucarno (USA) – Avoine (IRE) (Saddlers' Hall (IRE)) [2018/19 **h–** h100: h16.8g^{pu} Aug 21] rather leggy mare: fair hurdler at best, shaped as if amiss sole outing in 2018/19: stays 2½m: acts on good to firm going: tried in cheekpieces: has worn tongue tie. *Ian Williams*

BLACKADDER 7 b.g. Myboycharlie (IRE) – Famcred (Inchinor) [2018/19 h–x: h16g^4 **h62 x** h15.7g h15.7g^5 h17.7g^4 h16.8g h15.3m^{pu} Oct 19] poor maiden hurdler: will prove best at sharp 2m: acts on good to firm going: has worn headgear, including last 2 starts: often let down by jumping. *Mark Gillard*

BLACK ANTHEM 7 b.g. Royal Anthem (USA) – Rockababy (IRE) (King's **c83** Ride) [2018/19 h95: h21.7g^3 h20.3g h21.7m h21.2s^F h21.6v c20.2m^4 c20.2g* c23.6g **h88** h18.5d^3 Apr 9] modest maiden hurdler: similar form over fences: won handicap at Wincanton in February: stays 2½m: acts on soft going: tried in cheekpieces/tongue tie. *Brian Barr*

BLACK ART 7 ch.g. Black Sam Bellamy (IRE) – Art Series (Kalanisi (IRE)) [2018/19 **c–** h114: c16.4g^5 c19.3v^{pu} Mar 12] workmanlike gelding: fair hurdler: little show over fences: **h–** may prove best around 2m: best form on soft/heavy going. *Sue Smith*

BLACK BANJO (IRE) 10 br.g. Hawkeye (IRE) – Corkscrew Hill (IRE) (Golan (IRE)) **c–** [2018/19 c93?, h–: c19.9g^{pu} h23.1g Jun 5] maiden hurdler/chaser, no form in 2018/19: has **h–** worn headgear: wears tongue tie. *Claire Dyson*

BLACK BUBLE (FR) 6 b.g. Valanour (IRE) – Miss Bubble Rose (FR) (Sevres Rose **h121** (IRE)) [2018/19 h108: h19.6g^4 h23.3g^3 h19.9g h19.6g^6 h19.6g^5 h16g^5 h21d^3 h19.6g* h20.7d^5 h21.2d* h23.5m* h21m^2 Apr 25] fairly useful handicap hurdler: won at Huntingdon (conditionals) in January, Ludlow in February and Ascot (conditionals) in March: stays 3m: acts on soft and good to firm going: usually races off pace, often travels strongly. *Tony Carroll*

BLACK CENTAUR (IRE) 6 b.g. Oscar (IRE) – Arcanum (IRE) (Presenting) [2018/19 **h85** h19.5d h16s^5 h19.2d^5 Feb 24] £45,000 5-y-o: half-brother to several winners, including useful chaser Mr Mercurial (2½m-25f winner, by Westerner) and fairly useful chaser Black Scorpion (2½m-3m winner, by Scorpion): dam unraced: won Irish point on debut: modest form over hurdles. *Colin Tizzard*

bet365 Oaksey Chase, Sandown—Black Corton signs off 2018/19 with a win after several near-misses; Gold Present (right) and Cobra de Mai (noseband) fill the places

BLACK CORTON (FR) 8 br.g. Laverock (IRE) – Pour Le Meilleur (FR) (Video Rock (FR)) [2018/19 c151, h–: c24.2g² c26sᵖᵘ c20.5g² c23.8d² c23.4d² c22.7g* Apr 27] lengthy gelding: winning hurdler: high-class chaser: won Oaksey Chase at Sandown (by 11 lengths from Gold Present) in April: runner-up all other completed starts in 2018/19: stays 3m: acts on soft and good to firm going: has worn hood: wears tongue tie. *Paul Nicholls* **c160 h–**

BLACKDOWN HILLS 9 b.m. Presenting – Lady Prunella (IRE) (Supreme Leader) [2018/19 h107p: h20g* h15.7g* h20g c20gᵖᵘ c20.2d³ c15.9m³ c20.6g⁵ Apr 18] lengthy mare: fair hurdler: won mares maiden at Worcester in May and mares novice at Southwell in August: similar form over fences: stays 2½m: acts on good to firm going. *Seamus Mullins* **c107 h107**

BLACK EBONY 5 br.g. Malinas (GER) – Our Ethel (Be My Chief (USA)) [2018/19 b16.2g b16.2g² Apr 15] half-brother to several winners, including smart hurdler Attaglance (2m-2½m winner, by Passing Glance), stayed 3m, and fairly useful hurdler/useful chaser Hi George (2¼m-21f winner, by Doyen): dam bumper winner: fairly useful form in bumpers: better effort when second at Hexham in April: will be suited by 2½m. *Ruth Jefferson* **b94**

BLACKFINCH 4 ch.g. Black Sam Bellamy (IRE) – Grassfinch (Generous (IRE)) [2018/19 b15.8d² Mar 13] first foal: dam (h121) 23f/3m hurdle winner: 16/1, second in bumper at Huntingdon (2¼ lengths behind Sadlermor): will be suited by further than 2m. *Stuart Edmunds* **b87**

BLACKFYRE (IRE) 4 b.g. Redoute's Choice (AUS) – Hazarayna (Polish Precedent (USA)) [2018/19 h15.8m⁴ h16s⁵ h15.9s h20.7gᵖᵘ Apr 22] good-topped gelding: fair form when fourth in maiden, standout effort on Flat: modest form over hurdles: tried in cheekpieces: wears tongue tie. *Charlie Mann* **h87**

BLACKHILLSOFDAKOTA (IRE) 4 b.g. Galileo (IRE) – Aymara (Darshaan) [2018/19 b16g² b16d* b17d Apr 5] compact gelding: half-brother to numerous winners, including fairly useful hurdler Immortal Bridge (2½m/21f winner, by Fastnet Rock), stays 3m: dam 1½m winner: fair form in bumpers: won listed event at Limerick in March: likely to stay further than 2m. *John Halley, Ireland* **b94**

BLACK JACK JAXON 7 gr.g. Fair Mix (IRE) – No Virtue (Defacto (USA)) [2018/19 h–, b–: c24gᶠ c23g⁵ c24g h25.5g c25.2dᵖᵘ Jan 2] no form: often wore headgear/tongue tie: dead. *Steve Flook* **c– h–**

BLACKJACK KENTUCKY (IRE) 6 b.g. Oscar (IRE) – My Name's Not Bin (IRE) **h117**
(Good Thyne (USA)) [2018/19 h19.5s h23.6d³ h21.6s³ Apr 16] £100,000 4-y-o: seventh
foal: half-brother to fairly useful hurdler/winning pointer Champagne Present (3m winner,
by Presenting) and fair hurdler/chaser Thyne For Gold (19f-23f winner, by Robin des
Pres): dam (h108), 2¾m/3m hurdle winner, half-sister to fair hurdler/useful chaser (stayed
2½m) Clew Bay Cove: off mark in Irish points at second attempt: fairly useful form over
hurdles: best effort when third in novice at Chepstow in March. *Paul Nicholls*

BLACK JACK ROVER (IRE) 10 b.g. Vinnie Roe (IRE) – Kilgefin Tina (IRE) (City **c–**
Honours (USA)) [2018/19 c109, h–: c21.6g⁵ h23gᶠ Jul 31] point/hurdle winner: fair form **h–**
over fences: left Donald McCain after first start: stays 25f: acts on soft and good to firm
going. *Deborah Faulkner*

BLACKJACKTENNESSEE 5 b.g. Fair Mix (IRE) – No Virtue (Defacto (USA)) **c77**
[2018/19 h–, b72: h15.8g³ c20m⁴ c20.3gᶠ c17.4s Dec 14] leggy gelding: poor form over **h80**
hurdles/fences: often wears hood. *Steve Flook*

BLACK KALANISI (IRE) 6 b.g. Kalanisi (IRE) – Blackthorne Winter (IRE) (Old Vic) **h120**
[2018/19 b90: b15.8g² b16g* h20g* h21m² Apr 25] useful form in bumpers: won at **b106**
Worcester (by 14 lengths from Allez Karakoz) in June: fairly useful form over hurdles: won
maiden at same course later in June: will stay further than 2½m. *Joseph Tuite*

BLACK KETTLE (IRE) 9 b.g. Robin des Pres (FR) – Whistful Suzie (IRE) (Eurobus) **c–**
[2018/19 c95, h–: c15.6s c16.3g⁵ c20.1vᵖᵘ Mar 16] has had breathing operation: maiden **h–**
hurdler: modest chaser at best, no form in 2018/19: wears cheekpieces/tongue tie.
Micky Hammond

BLACK KEY 7 b.g. Authorized (IRE) – Pentatonic (Giant's Causeway (USA)) [2018/19 **h128**
h16g* h16m³ h21s* h15.7g⁴ h15.7d⁴ h16.8g Apr 17] fairly useful form: won maiden at
Listowel in June and handicap at Galway in August: left Henry de Bromhead after third
start: stays 21f: acts on good to firm and heavy going: tried in tongue tie: usually front
runner/races prominently. *Donald McCain*

BLACK LIGHTNING (IRE) 6 br.g. Whitmore's Conn (USA) – Annie May (IRE) **h84**
(Anshan) [2018/19 b94: b17.7g³ h21g⁵ h21d h20.5g⁶ h21.7s h22g Mar 30] fair form in **b86**
bumpers: poor form over hurdles: bred to be suited by 3m: sometimes in cheekpieces.
Nick Gifford

BLACKMILL (IRE) 8 b.g. Kalanisi (IRE) – Lady of The Mill (IRE) (Woods of Windsor **c92**
(USA)) [2018/19 c103, h98: c23.6d⁶ c24.2s c26.1d⁵ c26.2dᵖᵘ h23.1d* Apr 9] has had **h92**
breathing operation: modest hurdler: won handicap at Exeter in April: modest maiden
chaser: stays 23f: acts on heavy going: wears cheekpieces: has worn tongue tie, including
in 2018/19. *David Dennis*

BLACK MISCHIEF 7 b.g. Black Sam Bellamy (IRE) – Miss Mitch (IRE) (King's **h133**
Theatre (IRE)) [2018/19 h128: h20.6gᶠ h18.9g* h21.4d⁴ h24d Mar 14] workmanlike
gelding: useful handicap hurdler: won at Haydock (by ¾ length from Mr Antolini) in
November: stays 21f: acts on soft and good to firm going: wears cheekpieces/tongue tie.
Harry Fry

BLACK NARCISSUS (IRE) 10 b.m. Westerner – Arcanum (IRE) (Presenting) **c88 §**
[2018/19 c97§, h–§: c24.2s c28.8vᵖᵘ Feb 18] has had breathing operation: winning hurdler: **h– §**
modest handicap chaser: stays 3¼m: acts on heavy going: wears headgear/tongue tie: races
off pace: untrustworthy. *Alexandra Dunn*

BLACK N BLUE 7 ch.g. Galileo (IRE) – Coyote (Indian Ridge) [2018/19 b–: h20.2gᵖᵘ **h–**
May 16] no show in bumper/maiden hurdle. *R. Mike Smith*

BLACK OP (IRE) 8 br.g. Sandmason – Afar Story (IRE) (Desert Story (IRE)) [2018/19 **c143 +**
h152: c19.2s³ c20.6d³ h24d³ h24d h21.5g⁴ Apr 27] tall, good-topped gelding: smart **h149**
hurdler: third in Cleeve Hurdle at Cheltenham (14 lengths behind Paisley Park) in January:
useful form despite mistakes over fences: third in Dipper Novices' Chase (7¼ lengths
behind Lostintranslation) at same course earlier in month: stays 3m: acts on heavy going:
wears tongue tie. *Tom George*

BLACK OPIUM 5 b.m. Black Sam Bellamy (IRE) – Fragrant Rose (Alflora (IRE)) **b–**
[2018/19 b16g⁶ Mar 29] closely related to bumper winner/fairly useful 2½m/21f chase
winner Halo Moon and fair 21f hurdle winner Chantara Rose (both by Kayf Tara) and half-
sister to 2 winners: dam (c89/h104) bumper/17f-2½m hurdle winner: well beaten in
bumper. *Tina Jackson*

BLACK PRINCE (FR) 5 b.g. Falco (USA) – Thamara (USA) (Street Cry (IRE)) **h78**
[2018/19 h104: h19.9mᵖᵘ h23g³ Sep 2] has had breathing operation: fair form when second
in juvenile in 2017/18, easily best effort over hurdles: wears tongue tie. *Anthony Honeyball*

BLACK SAM BELLA 7 b.m. Black Sam Bellamy (IRE) – Newton Mo (Homo Sapien) **h127** [2018/19 h107: h23.3d* h24.7g* h25g* May 23] point winner: fairly useful form over hurdles: won all 3 starts in May, at Uttoxeter (mares), Aintree and Warwick: stays 25f: acts on good to soft going: held up: seemed sure to go on improving but not seen out again. *Dan Skelton*

BLACKSTAIRS LAD (IRE) 5 b.g. Flemensfirth (USA) – Blarney Kestrel (IRE) **h95** (Presenting) [2018/19 h15.8d⁶ h16s⁶ h16.3g Mar 30] placed in Irish points: modest form over hurdles: dead. *Jonjo O'Neill*

BLACK TEARS 5 b.m. Jeremy (USA) – Our Girl Salley (IRE) (Carroll House) [2018/19 **h133** h20g² h16.6d² h16g* h16.8d⁴ h20g⁵ Apr 21] €36,000 3-y-o: first foal: dam (c130/h135), bumper winner/2¼m-2½m hurdle winner (stayed 3m), half-sister to useful/ungenuine chaser (stayed 25f) Loch Ba: bumper winner: useful form over hurdles: won mares maiden at Fairyhouse in February: best effort when 2 lengths fourth of 22 to Eglantine du Seuil in Dawn Run Mares' Novices' Hurdle at Cheltenham: stays 2½m: acts on good to soft going: usually races prominently/travels strongly. *Gordon Elliott, Ireland*

BLACK TULIP 7 ch.m. Black Sam Bellamy (IRE) – Combe Florey (Alflora (IRE)) **c115** [2018/19 h117: c20g³ c20g² c20.6g² c22.5vᵖᵘ c24d⁵ c20.6g³ Apr 18] compact mare: fairly **h–** useful form over fences: similar form over fences: second in handicap at Warwick in November: stays 3m: acts on heavy going. *Henry Daly*

BLAGAPAR (FR) 8 b.g. Al Namix (FR) – Samarkand Bleue (FR) (Sleeping Car (FR)) **c118** [2018/19 h19.6g c24g² c22.5g* c23g Jul 4] fairly useful form over hurdles, shaped as if needing run **h86** on return: similar form over fences: won novice handicap at Uttoxeter in June: stays 3m: acts on good to firm and heavy going. *Dr Richard Newland*

BLAIRS COVE 7 b.g. Presenting – Raitera (FR) (Astarabad (USA)) [2018/19 h120: **c108 p** c17s⁶ c19.4g³ Mar 30] well-made gelding: fairly useful hurdler: fair form over fences: **h–** better effort when third in handicap at Stratford in March: stays 3m: best form on good going: wears tongue tie: open to further improvement over fences. *Dan Skelton*

BLAKEMOUNT (IRE) 11 br.g. Presenting – Smashing Leader (IRE) (Supreme Leader) **c102** [2018/19 c116, h–: c24.5d c26.2g⁵ c24.5s⁶ Feb 18] compact gelding: winning hurdler: **h–** useful handicap chaser at best, little impact in 2018/19: stays 33f: acts on heavy going. *Sue Smith*

BLAKERIGG (IRE) 8 b.g. Presenting – Azalea (IRE) (Marju (IRE)) [2018/19 c96, h–: **c117** c20.1dᵖᵘ c20.5d* c23.4d* c20v³ c23.8gᵖᵘ Apr 24] well-made gelding: has had breathing **h–** operation: lightly-raced hurdler: fairly useful handicap chaser: won at Ayr in November and Newcastle in December: stays 23f: acts on soft going (probably on heavy). *Nicky Richards*

BLAKLION 10 b.g. Kayf Tara – Franciscaine (FR) (Legend of France (USA)) [2018/19 **c–** c160, h–: c25.9s h25g h24.3g⁵ Feb 16] angular gelding: has had breathing operation: useful **h135** handicap hurdler: high-class chaser, behind sole outing over fences in 2018/19: stays 3½m: acts on heavy going: tried in hood: sold privately to join Philip Kirby £300,000 but missed Grand National due to injury. *Nigel Twiston-Davies*

BLAMEITALONMYROOTS (IRE) 9 b.m. Turtle Island (IRE) – Makingyourmindup **c99 §** (IRE) (Good Thyne (USA)) [2018/19 c119, h–: c26.1g⁶ c24.2dᵖᵘ c22.7mᵖᵘ Feb 14] angular **h–** mare: winning hurdler: fairly useful handicap chaser, well below form in 2018/19: stays 27f: acts on heavy going: has worn headgear, including final start: temperamental. *Oliver Sherwood*

BLAME IT ON ME (IRE) 4 br.g. Thewayyouare (USA) – Ma Nikitia (IRE) (Camacho) **h–** [2018/19 h15.7s Dec 18] modest maiden on Flat, stays 9.5f: tailed off in juvenile in hurdling debut. *Tim Easterby*

BLAME ME FOREVER (USA) 4 b.f. Blame (USA) – Empress Josephine (USA) **h–** (Empire Maker (USA)) [2018/19 h20.7g Feb 21] fair on Flat, stays 1¼m: in blinkers, tailed off in mares maiden on hurdling debut. *Don Cantillon*

BLAST OF KOEMAN (IRE) 8 ch.g. Shantou (USA) – Erintante (IRE) (Denel (FR)) **c134** [2018/19 c136, h–: c18.2g⁵ h24s⁴ c24gᶠ c16.7s³ c16.5g⁵ h20g* Dec 31] fairly useful **h123** handicap hurdler: won at Punchestown in December: useful handicap chaser: third at Cork (5¼ lengths behind All The Answers) in November: stays 21f: acts on heavy going: usually in headgear: wears tongue tie. *Robert Tyner, Ireland*

BLAYDON (IRE) 6 b.g. Milan – Pretty Impressive (IRE) (Presenting) [2018/19 b71: **h96** h23.9g⁴ h20.5v⁵ h20v h21.4s h24.3s² Mar 9] modest form over hurdles: stays 3m: best form on soft/heavy going: in cheekpieces last 4 starts. *Lucinda Russell*

BLAZER (FR) 8 ch.g. Network (GER) – Juppelongue (FR) (Trebrook (FR)) [2018/19 c137p, h–: h16s² c24s h16g c24.5g⁶ c17d³ h16g Feb 2] sturdy gelding: useful handicap hurdler: second in Galway Hurdle (3 lengths behind Sharjah) in August: useful handicap chaser: third in Dan Moore Memorial Handicap Chase at Fairyhouse (1¼ lengths behind Duca de Thaix) in January: effective from 2m to 3m: acts on heavy going. *W. P. Mullins, Ireland* **c143 h138**

BLAZER'S MILL (IRE) 5 b.g. Westerner – Creation (IRE) (Definite Article) [2018/19 b13.7v* Feb 14] £160,000 4-y-o: fifth foal: half-brother to bumper winner/fairly useful hurdler Taniokey (2m winner, stayed 21f) and bumper winner/fair hurdler War Creation (2m-19f winner), both by Scorpion: dam, ran once over hurdles, out of useful hurdler/chaser (stayed 3m) Palette: runner-up in Irish point: 1/6, won conditionals/amateurs bumper at Fontwell by 3½ lengths from Mount Windsor: open to improvement. *Olly Murphy* **b95 p**

BLAZING BUCK 13 ch.g. Fraam – Anapola (GER) (Polish Precedent (USA)) [2018/19 c32.5g⁶ May 4] small gelding: multiple point winner: fairly useful hurdler at best: tailed off in hunter on chasing debut: stays 3¼m: acts on heavy going: tried in cheekpieces/tongue tie: temperamental. *Gareth Moore* **c– h– §**

BLAZING GLEN (IRE) 11 ch.g. Beneficial – Kofiyah's Rose (IRE) (Roselier (FR)) [2018/19 c80§, h–: h19.6d h20.7d h19.2m⁶ Mar 29] maiden hurdler/chaser, no form in 2018/19: temperamental. *Alan Jessop* **c– § h– §**

BLAZING GOLD 6 b.m. Fair Mix (IRE) – Playing With Fire (IRE) (Witness Box (USA)) [2018/19 b58: b16g h18.7m Jun 19] unfurnished mare: little form in bumpers: tailed off in mares novice on hurdling debut. *Robin Dickin* **h– b–**

BLAZING TOM 8 b.g. Dr Massini (IRE) – Blazing Ember (Faustus (USA)) [2018/19 c26g May 4] multiple point winner: little impression in hunter at Cheltenham on chasing debut. *J. W. Tudor* **c–**

BLAZON 6 b.g. Dansili – Zante (Zafonic (USA)) [2018/19 h106: h15.8gᵖᵘ h15.8g h16g⁴ h15.7g³ c16.2g⁵ Sep 25] has had breathing operation: modest maiden hurdler: 4/1, fifth in novice handicap at Warwick (28¼ lengths behind Railroad Junkie) on chasing debut: raced mainly around 2m: acts on soft going: has worn headgear, including last 2 starts: tried in tongue tie. *Kim Bailey* **c– h96**

BLESS THE WINGS (IRE) 14 b.g. Winged Love (IRE) – Silva Venture (IRE) (Mandalus) [2018/19 c145, h–: c30.2g⁵ c30.2g⁶ h21d⁶ c30.2sᵖᵘ c34.3g Apr 6] sturdy gelding: winning hurdler: smart chaser, runs mainly in cross-country events nowadays: stays 4¼m: acts on good to firm and heavy going: wears headgear: has worn tongue tie. *Gordon Elliott, Ireland* **c145 h–**

BLETCHLEY CASTLE (IRE) 10 b.g. Dylan Thomas (IRE) – Zaafran (Singspiel (IRE)) [2018/19 c109, h–: c16.1d² c20.9sᵖᵘ Mar 11] multiple point winner: fair hurdler: lightly-raced chaser, better effort in 2018/19 when second in hunter at Taunton in February: stays 21f: acts on soft and good to firm going: wears tongue tie: front runner, usually races freely. *Miss H. Brookshaw* **c89 h–**

BLEU BERRY (FR) 8 b.g. Special Kaldoun (IRE) – Somosierra (FR) (Blushing Flame (USA)) [2018/19 h147: h19.4s h24s h21s Mar 13] well-made gelding: smart hurdler: stays 21f: best form on soft/heavy going: tried in cheekpieces: patiently ridden. *W. P. Mullins, Ireland* **h146**

BLEU ET NOIR 8 b.g. Enrique – Gastina (FR) (Pistolet Bleu (IRE)) [2018/19 h–: h16.8g³ h15.9gᵖᵘ Sep 23] fair handicap hurdler: stays 19f: acts on heavy going: wears hood. *Tim Vaughan* **h102**

BLEU ET OR (FR) 8 br.g. Maresca Sorrento (FR) – Panoplie (FR) (Arnaqueur (USA)) [2018/19 c22.6d⁵ c19.4m³ c21g⁵ Aug 15] point winner: twice-raced hurdler: poor form in chases: left Miss C. Packwood after first start: stays 21f: acts on good to soft going: in hood last 3 starts: tried in tongue tie. *Fergal O'Brien* **c84 h–**

BLEU ET ROUGE (FR) 8 gr.g. Charming Groom (FR) – Lady du Renom (FR) (Art Francais (USA)) [2018/19 c–, h151: h16.4dᶠ Dec 1] lengthy gelding: smart hurdler, fell fatally sole outing in 2018/19: winning chaser: stayed 19f: acted on heavy going: tried in tongue tie: usually raced towards rear. *Ben Haslam* **c– h–**

BLOODY NOSE (IRE) 7 b.g. Kalanisi (IRE) – Renvyle Society (IRE) (Moscow Society (USA)) [2018/19 h62: h23.3gᵖᵘ Jun 20] little form: tried in hood. *Mark Bradstock* **h–**

BLOTTOS (IRE) 7 b.g. Westerner – Autumn Beauty (IRE) (Darnay) [2018/19 h123: c15.9d c24.2s³ c24.2sᵖᵘ h21.3s h16.8s³ Feb 21] fair handicap hurdler: fairly useful form over fences: best effort when third in novice at Hexham in November: stays 3m: acts on heavy going. *Sue Smith* **c118 h110**

BLOW BY BLOW (IRE) 8 ch.g. Robin des Champs (FR) – Shean Rose (IRE) (Roselier **c143 §** (FR)) [2018/19 h149: c22.5s* c22.6g² c20g c24g³ c24dᵖᵘ c24d⁶ c24dᵖᵘ c34.3gᵖᵘ c29dᵖᵘ Apr **h–** 22] well-made gelding: has had breathing operation: smart hurdler: useful chaser: won maiden at Galway in October: placed after in Florida Pearl Novices' Chase at Punchestown (neck behind Some Neck) and Neville Hotels Novices' Chase at Leopardstown (18 lengths behind Delta Work): stays 23f: acts on heavy going: wears headgear/tongue tie: temperamental. *Gordon Elliott, Ireland*

BLUBERRY HIGH (IRE) 5 b.m. Getaway (GER) – Blu Louisiana (IRE) (Milan) **b88** [2018/19 b16.8g³ b16.7d² Apr 26] fourth foal: half-sister to bumper winner Peculiar Places (by Presenting): dam once-raced half-sister to very smart hurdler (stayed 21f) Dunguib: fair form in bumpers: better effort when second in mares event at Bangor in April. *Warren Greatrex*

BLU CAVALIER 9 b.g. Kayf Tara – Blue Ride (IRE) (King's Ride) [2018/19 h129: **c108 p** h16.8g² c20.3v³ h20d² h15.7d³ h21.5g⁵ Apr 27] well-made gelding: useful hurdler: third in **h134** Betfair Hurdle at Ascot (6¼ lengths behind Al Dancer) in February: 9/2, third in maiden at Bangor (28 lengths behind Jerrysback) on chasing debut: left Paul Nicholls after third start: stays 2½m: acts on heavy going: should do better over fences. *Ali Stronge*

BLUE APRIL (FR) 8 b.g. Blue Bresil (FR) – Royale Little (FR) (Garde Royale) [2018/19 **h82 §** h83§: h19m h17.7v² h15.8s⁶ h19s² h19.8s⁵ h19.6dᵖᵘ Apr 26] compact gelding: poor handicap hurdler: stays 19f: best form on soft/heavy going: wears headgear: one to treat with caution (has refused to race). *Jeremy Scott*

BLUE BALLERINA (IRE) 5 br.m. Fame And Glory – Peinture Rose (IRE) (Marathon **h54 p** (USA)) [2018/19 b–: h15.8g h16d h16.7s h15.8g h20.7dˢᵘ Mar 13] has had breathing operation: poor form over hurdles: tried in tongue tie: remains capable of better. *Oliver Greenall*

BLUE BATON (IRE) 6 b.m. Presenting – Blu Louisiana (IRE) (Milan) [2018/19 h–, b77: **h79** h16.2g² h16.2gᶠ h19.9g⁶ Jun 20] poor form over hurdles: should be suited by at least 2½m. *Lucinda Russell*

BLUE BULLET (FR) 8 b.g. Le Fou (IRE) – Jiletta (FR) (Passing Sale (FR)) [2018/19 **c96** h103: c20s⁴ c17.4sᵖᵘ c20.2m⁴ h15.8vᵖᵘ Jan 26] lengthy gelding: maiden hurdler: modest **h–** form over fences: best effort when fourth in novice handicap at Lingfield in November: stays 2½m: acts on heavy going: often in headgear/tongue tie: usually races close up: temperament under suspicion. *Jamie Snowden*

BLUE COMET 8 br.g. Blueprint (IRE) – Be My Valentine (IRE) (Be My Native (USA)) **c– p** [2018/19 h125: c23.8gᵖᵘ May 17] fairly useful hurdler: pulled up in novice on chasing **h–** debut: stays 23f: best form on good going: wears tongue tie: front runner/races prominently: should do better as a chaser. *Fergal O'Brien*

BLUE COVE 14 ch.g. Karinga Bay – Meadow Blue (Northern State (USA)) [2018/19 c–, **c–** h–: h23.3g c24.2gᵖᵘ Jun 16] workmanlike gelding: maiden hurdler/chaser, no form since **h–** 2016/17: has worn cheekpieces/tongue tie. *Lynn Siddall*

BLUE FLIGHT (FR) 6 b.g. Blue Bresil (FR) – Lover Flight (FR) (Saint Cyrien (FR)) **c147 p** [2018/19 h113, b97: h23.9gᵖᵘ c24.2d³ c18.8d* c23.4g* c23.4d* c26.2g² c31.8m⁴ Apr 13] **h–** big, strong gelding: winning hurdler: smart form over fences: won handicap at Ascot (amateurs, by 8 lengths from Ecu de La Noverie) in January, and at Kelso in novice handicap (by 3 lengths from My Old Gold) in February and listed event (by ½ length from Black Corton) in March: fourth in Scottish Grand National at Ayr (4¼ lengths behind Takingrisks) in April: stays 4m: acts on good to firm and heavy going: usually travels strongly: open to further improvement as a chaser. *Nigel Twiston-Davies*

BLUEFORTYTWO 6 gr.g. Overbury (IRE) – Celine Message (Silver Patriarch (IRE)) **h107** [2018/19 b92: h16v⁶ h20.5s² h20.6d Apr 6] placed in bumper: fair form over hurdles: best effort when second in novice at Ayr in March: tried in hood/tongue tie. *James Ewart*

BLUE HAVANA (IRE) 4 b.f. Havana Gold (IRE) – Labyrinthine (IRE) (Pivotal) **h–** [2018/19 h16.7g Sep 29] modest maiden on Flat, stayed 1½m: tailed off in juvenile on hurdling debut: dead. *John Quinn*

BLUE HUSSAR (IRE) 8 b.g. Montjeu (IRE) – Metaphor (USA) (Woodman (USA)) **h107** [2018/19 h108: h16m⁵ h19.7d³ h19.7g⁴ Jan 12] fair handicap hurdler: will be suited by 2½m+: acts on soft going: in cheekpieces last 3 starts. *Micky Hammond*

BLUE KASCADE (IRE) 12 ch.g. Kaieteur (USA) – Lydia Blue (IRE) (Eve's Error) **c118**
[2018/19 c117, h–: c24.2d c23.8g* c23.4g² c23.4g⁴ c24.1s^pu c24.2g² c30.6d^ur Apr 26] **h–**
winning hurdler: fairly useful handicap chaser: won at Perth in May: stays 3m: acts on
good to firm and heavy going: has worn headgear: front runner/races prominently.
Sandy Thomson

BLUE LOBSTER (IRE) 7 gr.m. Dilshaan – Miss Nova (Ra Nova) [2018/19 h16m **h–**
h15.8g^pu h18.5m Aug 6] €7,500 4-y-o: sixth foal: half-sister to 3 winners, including useful
hurdler/chaser Champers On Ice (2½m-3m winner, by Robin des Champs): dam (h86)
2½m hurdle winner: little show in bumpers/over hurdles (trained by P. A. Fahy prior to
2018/19): tried in tongue tie. *Matt Sheppard*

BLUE MERLIN 6 b.g. Fair Mix (IRE) – Mighty Merlin (Royal Applause) [2018/19 b–: **h54**
b16m⁴ h16g⁵ h16g h16.3m Sep 8] poor form in bumpers/novice hurdles. *Fergal O'Brien* **b65**

BLUE MONDAY (IRE) 6 b.g. Beneficial – Bradbury Baby (IRE) (Old Vic) [2018/19 **h–**
h23.8d h19.5g⁵ Apr 26] maiden pointer: no form over hurdles. *Fergal O'Brien*

BLUE MOUNTAIN BOY (IRE) 7 b.g. Blueprint (IRE) – Thegirlfromgalway (IRE) **c–**
(Royal Dane (IRE)) [2018/19 c–, b–: c20.2f⁵ Feb 26] multiple point winner: little impact
in 3 starts under Rules: tried in tongue tie. *T. Ellis*

BLUE N YELLOW (IRE) 6 b.g. Jeremy (USA) – Bluemamba (USA) (Kingmambo **h88**
(USA)) [2018/19 b96: h19g h15.8g² h16.5d⁴ h15.7d³ Apr 9] sturdy gelding: bumper
winner: modest form over hurdles: left Johnny Farrelly after second start. *Tom George*

BLUE PETAL (IRE) 4 ch.f. Haatef (USA) – Sapphire Spray (IRE) (Viking Ruler (AUS)) **h–**
[2018/19 h16.2g^F Jun 2] modest on Flat, stayed 7.5f: fell fatally on hurdling debut. *R. K.*
Watson, Ireland

BLUE RAMBLER 9 b.g. Monsun (GER) – La Nuit Rose (FR) (Rainbow Quest (USA)) **h126**
[2018/19 h24.4g² h19d⁵ h24.3g Feb 16] smallish, angular gelding: fairly useful handicap
hurdler: second at Doncaster in December: stays 3m: acts on soft going: in cheekpieces last
2 starts. *Ian Williams*

BLUE RHYTHM (IRE) 7 b.g. Milan – Madame Jean (FR) (Cricket Ball (USA)) **h90 §**
[2018/19 h91: h25m^pu h24g³ h23.1g h19.9v⁶ h24.3d⁶ h20.7g³ h20.3s⁴ h23.1d h19.6d Apr
26] fell in point: modest maiden hurdler: left Evan Williams after second start: stays 3m:
acts on heavy going: wears headgear: one to leave alone. *Alastair Ralph*

BLUE SARI (FR) 4 b.g. Saddex – Blue Aster (FR) (Astarabad (USA)) [2018/19 b16s* **b121**
b16.4s² Mar 13] rather unfurnished gelding: first foal: dam, ran once over hurdles in
France, out of half-sister to very smart chaser up to 4½m Royal Auclair: smart form in
bumpers: won maiden at Gowran (by 11 lengths from Front View) in January: second in
Champion Bumper at Cheltenham (¾ length behind Envoi Allen, going lame last strides) 7
weeks later. *W. P. Mullins, Ireland*

BLUE SKIMMER (IRE) 7 b.g. Arcano (IRE) – Cattiva Generosa (Cadeaux Genereux) **h90**
[2018/19 h18.8g³ h18.8d² h16m³ h16.5d h15.8s Dec 31] half-brother to useful French
hurdler/chaser Catmoves (2¼m-2¾m winner, by Medicean): fair maiden on Flat, stays
1½m: modest maiden hurdler: left J. J. Lambe after fourth start: stays 19f: acts on good to
firm and good to soft going. *Alastair Ralph*

BLUNDER BUSS (IRE) 6 b.g. Court Cave (IRE) – Shantou Rose (IRE) (Shantou **h111**
(USA)) [2018/19 h117, b85: h20.9g³ h20g⁵ h23.8g h19.9s⁴ h22.7d⁴ h20.9g⁵ h20.5m Apr
13] fair handicap hurdler: stays 21f: acts on soft going: tried in visor: temperament under
suspicion. *Chris Grant*

BLUSHING RED (FR) 5 ch.g. Le Havre (IRE) – Boliche (Key of Luck (USA)) [2018/19 **h114**
h67: h16m² h16.3m h16g³ h15.8m* h16g* h15.8d Dec 9] fair handicap hurdler: won
conditionals events at Ludlow in October and Kempton in November: raced around 2m:
acts on good to firm going: usually leads. *Emma Lavelle*

BOAGRIUS (IRE) 7 ch.g. Beneficial – Greenhall Rambler (IRE) (Anshan) [2018/19 **c127**
c117, h–: c20.9g³ c19.9g^ur c16.1d* c15.9f* c16.5m⁴ Apr 12] maiden hurdler: fairly useful **h–**
handicap chaser: won novice events at Taunton in January and Leicester in February: stays
21f: acts on firm and soft going: wears tongue tie. *Tom George*

BOA ISLAND (IRE) 9 b.g. Trans Island – Eskimo Kiss (IRE) (Distinctly North (USA)) **c88**
[2018/19 c–, h–: c21.2g^pu c26g² Feb 20] strong gelding: point winner, placed all 3 starts in **h–**
2018/19: maiden hurdler: fairly useful chaser at one time, nothing like force of old: left
James Moffatt after first start: stays 3m: acts on good to firm going: usually in headgear:
has worn tongue tie. *Miss G. Walton*

BOARD OF TRADE 8 ch.g. Black Sam Bellamy (IRE) – Realms of Gold (USA) (Gulch (USA)) [2018/19 h117: c24.2d⁵ c22.6s⁴ c24g³ Apr 10] fairly useful hurdler: fair form over fences: stays 3m: acts on soft going: tried in visor: usually races prominently. *Alan King* **c104 h–**

BOBBA TEE 7 b.g. Rail Link – Trompette (USA) (Bahri (USA)) [2018/19 b16.7m⁴ b16.3m⁵ Sep 8] poor form in bumpers. *Richard Whitaker* **b66**

BOBBIE THE DAZZLER (IRE) 5 b.m. Lawman (FR) – Fashion Statement (Rainbow Quest (USA)) [2018/19 h23.3g⁵ b16g h18.8g h18.8g⁶ h20.5g³ h20.5v* Nov 14] 800 3-y-o: fourth foal: half-sister to 2 winners on Flat, including 1¼m-1½m winner Mankini (by Dansili): dam, smart 1m-11f winner, half-sister to useful hurdler (stayed 2½m) Ruler of All: made frame in points: well held in bumper: fair form over hurdles: won maiden at Ayr in November: stays 2½m: acts on heavy going. *Liam Lennon, Ireland* **h105 b–**

BOBBLE EMERALD (IRE) 11 ch.g. Rudimentary (USA) – Aunt Emeralds (IRE) (Roselier (FR)) [2018/19 c–, h119: h16.8vᵖᵘ Jan 27] lengthy gelding: fairly useful hurdler, shaped as if amiss after long absence sole outing in 2018/19: once-raced chaser: has won over 3m, at least as effective at 2m: acts on good to firm and heavy going: has worn headgear: has worn tongue tie, including last 3 starts: front runner/races prominently. *Martin Keighley* **c– h–**

BOBESKA (IRE) 6 br.g. Big Bad Bob (IRE) – Roseska (USA) (Include (USA)) [2018/19 h16g h16g h19.3mᵖᵘ h16.2vᵖᵘ Mar 14] fair maiden on Flat, stays 1½m: no form over hurdles: left Kevin F. O'Donnell after second start: often in hood/tongue tie. *Mike Sowersby* **h–**

BOB FORD (IRE) 12 b.g. Vinnie Roe (IRE) – Polar Lamb (IRE) (Brush Aside (USA)) [2018/19 c128§, h–§: c23.6d c27.6s⁵ c20v² c28.8v⁵ c20v³ c22.9dᵖᵘ c29.6dᵖᵘ Apr 26] tall gelding: has had breathing operation: winning hurdler: fairly useful handicap chaser: stays 3½m: acts on heavy going: has worn headgear/tongue tie, including in 2018/19: front runner/races prominently: unreliable. *Alastair Ralph* **c115 § h– §**

BOB MAHLER (IRE) 7 b.g. Mahler – Cooladurragh (IRE) (Topanoora) [2018/19 h128§: c23.8g c23.6s² c24d³ c24.2s c23.4d* c25.3g* Apr 17] rangy, useful-looking gelding: has had breathing operation: fairly useful hurdler: useful form over fences: won novice handicaps at Newbury in March and Cheltenham (by 7 lengths from Little Bruce) in April: will stay long distances: acts on heavy going: has worn cheekpieces, including last 5 starts: usually races close up. *Warren Greatrex* **c136 h–**

BOB MAXWELL (IRE) 5 b.g. Big Bad Bob (IRE) – Catching Stars (IRE) (Halling (USA)) [2018/19 h16.3s h21.2g h21.2g h19.7g h15.7d⁴ Apr 9] fair maiden on Flat, stays 1¼m: poor form over hurdles. *Robin Dickin* **h74**

BOBNDAVE (IRE) 7 b.g. Brian Boru – Sidblack (IRE) (Turtle Island (IRE)) [2018/19 b15.8g⁴ b16.2m³ b15.7s⁶ h16.8s h16.7g⁴ h16.2g³ Apr 15] £2,500 3-y-o, £6,000 4-y-o: third foal: dam, unraced, half-sister to useful hurdler/smart chaser (stayed 3m) Bold Sir Brian (by Brian Boru): modest form in bumpers: similar form over hurdles: best effort when third in novice at Hexham in April: will stay 2½m+: better to come. *Sue Smith* **h75 p b80**

BOBO MAC (IRE) 8 gr.g. Whitmore's Conn (USA) – Blazing Love (IRE) (Fruits of Love (USA)) [2018/19 c122, h130: h24.2d² h24.2s h24d c24.2v⁵ Mar 5] sturdy gelding: has had breathing operation: fairly useful handicap hurdler: second at Newbury in November: fair form over fences: stays 25f: acts on heavy going: has worn cheekpieces, including in 2018/19. *Tom Symonds* **c107 h128**

BOBONYX 9 b.g. Phoenix Reach (IRE) – Twist The Facts (IRE) (Un Desperado (FR)) [2018/19 c78, h–: c23.8g⁴ c26g⁴ c17sᵖᵘ c23.8sᵖᵘ c25.7gᵖᵘ Apr 21] maiden hurdler: poor maiden chaser: stays 3¼m: acts on heavy going: has worn headgear, including in 2018/19: tried in tongue tie. *Dai Williams* **c74 h–**

BOCASIEN DESBOIS (FR) 8 gr.g. Smadoun (FR) – Quocasienne (FR) (Ungaro (GER)) [2018/19 c91, h89: c21.6g² c21.2gᵘʳ c20.1mᵖᵘ c21.6m³ c23.4g² h19.3m⁵ c20.1m⁴ Mar 28] has had breathing operation: poor maiden hurdler: modest handicap chaser: stays 3m: acts on soft going: tried in cheekpieces: usually races off pace. *Martin Todhunter* **c94 h64**

BODACIOUS NAME (IRE) 5 b.g. Famous Name – Nice Wee Girl (IRE) (Clodovil (IRE)) [2018/19 h–p: h16.2g² h22.7d⁴ h24.3v⁵ Nov 29] modest form over hurdles. *John Quinn* **h95**

BODEGA 11 b.g. Grape Tree Road – Gurleigh (IRE) (Pivotal) [2018/19 h25g⁶ h23.1g* h23.9m⁵ h26.5g h23.3sᶠ h26.5gᵖᵘ Aug 21] compact gelding: fairly useful handicap hurdler: won at Market Rasen in June: winning chaser: stays 3¼m: acts on good to firm and heavy going: usually wears headgear: has worn tongue tie, including in 2018/19. *Ian Williams* **c– h115**

BODEKIN POINT (IRE) 8 br.g. Robin des Pres (FR) – Countessdee (IRE) (Arctic Lord) [2018/19 c20d c21.7g³ Feb 19] poor maiden hurdler: similar form in chases: stays 2½m: acts on good to firm going. *Nicky Martin* **c65 h–**

BODES WELL (IRE) 4 b.g. Rock of Gibraltar (IRE) – Gypsie Queen (IRE) (Xaar) **h103**
[2018/19 h16.7m⁴ h17.7g⁴ h16.7g h17.7m* h15.8g⁶ h16g³ h16.5d h15.7g⁵ h16.5s⁶ h20.3d
Apr 24] fairly useful on Flat, stays 1m: fair hurdler: won juvenile at Fontwell in October:
stays 2¼m: acts on good to firm going: in headgear last 5 starts. *Warren Greatrex*

BOETHIUS 6 b.g. Manduro (GER) – Perfect Note (Shamardal (USA)) [2018/19 h–: **h92**
h21.7m h23g* h22m² h23gᵖᵘ Aug 22] modest handicap hurdler: won at Worcester in July:
stays 23f: acts on good to firm and heavy going: tried in headgear. *Tim Vaughan*

BOGARDUS (IRE) 8 b.g. Dalakhani (IRE) – Sugar Mint (IRE) (High Chaparral (IRE)) **h–**
[2018/19 h–: h16.2gᶠ Dec 9] fair form on Flat, stays 1½m: modest form when third in maiden in
2016/17, standout effort over hurdles. *Andrew Crook*

BOGOSS DU PERRET (FR) 8 b.g. Malinas (GER) – Lady Paques (FR) (Lights Out **c91**
(FR)) [2018/19 c93, h–: c20g⁶ c21g Aug 15] angular gelding: multiple point winner: **h–**
maiden hurdler: modest chaser: stays 3¼m: best form on good going: tried in blinkers.
Jimmy Frost

BOHERBUOY (IRE) 7 b.g. Galileo (IRE) – Potion (Pivotal) [2018/19 h131: h17d² **h132**
h20g⁴ May 29] useful form over hurdles: second in handicap at Killarney (1¾ lengths
behind Neverushacon) in May: unproven beyond 17f: acts on heavy going. *N. Madden,
Ireland*

BOHER CALL (IRE) 12 b.g. Indian River (FR) – Cill Fhair (IRE) (Naheez (USA)) **c88**
[2018/19 c111: c23g⁵ c20v⁶ c24.2d⁴ Mar 15] multiple point winner, including in March:
fair chaser, below form in 2018/19: stays 21f: acts on good to firm and heavy going: has
worn headgear: wears tongue tie: usually races close up. *Mrs K. Bandey*

BOHER LAD (IRE) 12 b.g. Gold Well – Shindeesharnick (IRE) (Roselier (FR)) **c–**
[2018/19 c–, h100: h24g h23.8d h26g h24g h23.6d⁵ h27g² h26.4g* Apr 14] smallish **h88**
gelding: point winner: modest handicap hurdler: won at Stratford in April: once-raced
chaser: stays 3¼m: acts on good to firm and heavy going: has worn headgear/tongue tie.
Alan Phillips

BOITE (IRE) 9 b.g. Authorized (IRE) – Albiatra (USA) (Dixieland Band (USA)) [2018/19 **c121**
h139: h21g⁵ h20.5s h16g⁵ h19.3d c15.9g² Mar 8] rather leggy gelding: has had breathing **h130**
operation: useful handicap hurdler: 5/4, second in maiden at Leicester (16 lengths behind
Hatcher) on chasing debut: stays 21f: acts on heavy going: has worn cheekpieces/tongue
tie. *Warren Greatrex*

BOKO FITTLEWORTH (IRE) 4 b.g. Most Improved (IRE) – Sycamores (FR) (Gold **h111**
Away (IRE)) [2018/19 h16.7m* h16.8g² Jul 22] modest maiden on Flat, stayed 1¼m: fair
form over hurdles: won juvenile at Market Rasen in June: dead. *Ben Pauling*

BOLAND'S MILL (IRE) 7 b.g. Winged Love (IRE) – Madam Rocher (IRE) (Roselier **h86**
(FR)) [2018/19 b16g h16.3d h16g h16.3s h15.9s h20.5g⁶ h21.2m Apr 23] rather sparely- **b–**
made gelding: sixth foal: brother to fairly useful hurdler/chaser Rowdy Rocher (2½m-3m
winner): dam unraced half-sister to fairly useful hurdler (2m-2¼m winner) Flynn:
placed in Irish points: last in bumper: modest form over hurdles: should stay 2½m: in
cheekpieces last 2 starts. *Thomas Gallagher*

BOLD EMPEROR (IRE) 6 b.g. Galileo (IRE) – Bastet (IRE) (Giant's Causeway **h110**
(USA)) [2018/19 h16s² Jan 8] fair maiden on Flat, stays 12.5f: similar form over hurdles:
won maiden in 2016/17: raced only at 2m: best form on soft/heavy going: in tongue tie last
2 starts. *John McConnell, Ireland*

BOLD IMAGE (IRE) 8 b.m. Milan – Golden Bay (Karinga Bay) [2018/19 h101: **h107**
h21.6m* h21.7g³ Sep 9] has had breathing operation: fair handicap hurdler: won at Newton
Abbot in August: stays 2¾m: acts on soft and good to firm going. *Dan Skelton*

BOLDMERE 6 b.g. Multiplex – Pugnacious Lady (Hernando (FR)) [2018/19 b95: h16s **h119**
h21d⁶ h20.6d⁴ h19.8s h21.6s² Apr 16] sturdy gelding: fairly useful form over hurdles: won
novice at Market Rasen in February: stays 2¾m: acts on soft going. *Graeme McPherson*

BOLD PLAN (IRE) 5 b.g. Jeremy (USA) – Kings Orchid (IRE) (King's Theatre (IRE)) **h126**
[2018/19 h103p: h16.3d³ h15.7s³ h19s* h19.9v² Mar 16] won Irish point on debut: fairly
useful form over hurdles: won novice at Taunton in February. *Evan Williams*

BOLD PRINCE RUPERT (IRE) 9 br.g. Royal Anthem (USA) – Fortune And Favour **h–**
(IRE) (Homo Sapien) [2018/19 h18.6m Aug 5] maiden hurdler, behind sole outing since
2016/17: has worn headgear. *Sara Ender*

BOLD REASON (GER) 4 b.g. Invincible Spirit (IRE) – Bufera (IRE) (King's Best **h110**
(USA)) [2018/19 h15.8g³ h16.7d⁵ h16d⁴ h15.7s² h15.7m⁴ h16m Apr 22] fairly useful on
Flat, stays 1m: fair form over hurdles: raced around 2m: acts on soft going: usually in
headgear. *Ben Pauling*

BOLISTER (FR) 8 b.g. Le Balafre (FR) – Girlish (FR) (Passing Sale (FR)) [2018/19 h–: c17s^F h17.7d^3 h16.6g^3 h15.9s^2 h18.6g^4 h17.7g^4 Apr 22] sturdy gelding: modest maiden hurdler: unseated first on chasing debut: unproven beyond 17f: acts on soft going. *Gary Moore* **c–ह92**

BOLTON BOY (IRE) 5 br.g. Arcadio (GER) – Peggy Maddock (IRE) (Oscar (IRE)) [2018/19 b15.7g^5 h19.5s h19.9s* h19.4g^5 h23.1d^F h23d^4 Apr 26] €30,000 3-y-o: fifth foal: half-brother to useful hurdler/chaser Marinero (2¼m-3m winner, by Presenting) and useful hurdler Tellthemnuttin (2½m-3m winner, by Shantou): dam, winning pointer, half-sister to useful hurdler/chaser (stayed 29f) Feathered Leader: fifth in maiden bumper at Southwell: fair form over hurdles: won maiden at Sedgefield in November: stays 2½m: acts on soft going. *Tim Vaughan* **h104 b76**

BOLVING (IRE) 8 b.g. Stowaway – Kiniohio (FR) (Script Ohio (USA)) [2018/19 h98: c20.3g^6 c20d^4 c23d^3 c25.1g^4 Feb 16] useful-looking gelding: maiden hurdler: fair form over fences: stays 23f: acts on soft going: has worn hood, including in 2018/19: has worn tongue tie. *Victor Dartnall* **c100 h–**

BOMBER'S MOON 8 b.g. Erhaab (USA) – Flaviola (IRE) (Moscow Society (USA)) [2018/19 h96, b84: h19.6g h19.7g h24.4g^3 h21d h21.7d h22g Mar 30] sturdy gelding: fair maiden hurdler: stays 3m: acts on good to soft going: wears tongue tie: usually races off pace. *Nigel Twiston-Davies* **h100**

BONBONNIERE 5 br.m. Martaline – La Bombonera (FR) (Mansonnien (FR)) [2018/19 h16d h17s^3 h16d h15.5d h20d^3 h25g^{pu} Apr 22] third foal: half-sister to useful hurdler/very smart chaser Burrows Saint (2½m-29f winner, including Irish Grand National, by Saint des Saints): dam (h126), French 2¼m hurdle winner, sister to very smart French chaser (stayed 27f) Lagunak: poor form over hurdles: stays 2½m: acts on good to soft going: tried in tongue tie. *Dan Skelton* **h67**

BON CALVADOS (FR) 5 b.g. Bonbon Rose (FR) – Lamorrese (FR) (Pistolet Bleu (IRE)) [2018/19 b16.4d^6 Dec 13] half-brother to 3 winners, notably useful hurdler/very smart chaser around 2m Saint Calvados (by Saint des Saints): dam lightly raced over hurdles in France: 11/10, sixth in bumper at Newcastle (18 lengths behind Corrieben Reiver): should do better. *Olly Murphy* **b65 p**

BON CHIC (IRE) 10 b.m. Presenting – Homebird (IRE) (Be My Native (USA)) [2018/19 c118§, h119: h25.4g^6 h22.1m h25.4g^4 h22.1d* h23.9g h24.7g h20.5v* h20v^6 Dec 2] useful-looking mare: fairly useful handicap hurdler: won mares events at Cartmel in August and Ayr in November: fairly useful chaser: stays 25f: acts on good to firm and heavy going: wears headgear: usually leads: unreliable. *James Moffatt* **c– § h122 §**

BONDS CONQUEST 10 ch.g. Monsieur Bond (IRE) – Another Conquest (El Conquistador) [2018/19 c78, h–: c20s^4 c19.4d c24.2v^5 c19.2d^3 Mar 24] strong gelding: maiden hurdler: poor handicap chaser: stays 21f: acts on heavy going: usually in headgear: usually front runner/races prominently. *Seamus Mullins* **c73 h–**

BON ENFANT (FR) 8 gr.g. Saint des Saints (FR) – Montanara Paris (FR) (Turgeon (USA)) [2018/19 h21g Nov 12] angular gelding: fairly useful hurdler, behind sole outing in 2018/19: stayed 3¼m: acted on soft going: tried in headgear: dead. *Warren Greatrex* **h–**

BONJOUR STEVE 8 b.g. Bahamian Bounty – Anthea (Tobougg (IRE)) [2018/19 h16.7g h15.8g h16.2g^5 h15.8g^6 h16.7s^4 Dec 14] has had breathing operation: fair on Flat, stays 8.5f: poor form over hurdles: likely to prove best at sharp 2m. *Richard Price* **h79**

BONNE NUIT 4 b.g. Arvico (FR) – Frosted Grape (IRE) (Kheleyf (USA)) [2018/19 b15.3g Apr 14] good-topped gelding: 50/1, well beaten in bumper at Wincanton. *Brian Barr* **b–**

BONNE QUESTION (FR) 10 gr.g. Tagula (IRE) – Amonita (GER) (Medaaly) [2018/19 h100: h18.6g h15.8s* h16s^2 h16d^5 Mar 19] sturdy gelding: fair handicap hurdler: won at Ffos Las in February: raced mainly around 2m: best form on soft/heavy going: often travels strongly. *Venetia Williams* **h114**

BONNET'S VINO 11 b.m. Grape Tree Road – Bonnet's Pieces (Alderbrook) [2018/19 c–, h107: h25g May 10] lengthy, medium-sized mare: fair hurdler, well held sole outing in 2018/19: fair chaser: stays 23f: acts on heavy going. *Pam Sly* **c– h–**

BONOBO (IRE) 12 b.g. Quws – Better Folly (IRE) (Rhoman Rule (USA)) [2018/19 c106x, h98: h15.8m^5 h16.8s^6 Jul 30] fair handicap hurdler: fair maiden chaser, often let down by jumping: stays 19f: acts on soft and good to firm going: has worn headgear, including in 2018/19: tried in tongue tie. *Evan Williams* **c– x h100**

BONZA GIRL 6 b.m. Midnight Legend – Purple Patch (Afzal) [2018/19 h82, b–: h19.2d* **h116**
h19d* h21.7v* h23s* h21.2d* h24.4g³ h20.3g⁶ Apr 18] fairly useful handicap hurdler:
completed 5-timer, winning at Fontwell/Taunton in November, Fontwell again (mares) in
December, Lingfield in January and Ludlow (mares) in February: stays 23f: acts on heavy
going: usually races prominently. *Jeremy Scott*

BOOBOROWIE (IRE) 6 b.g. Big Bad Bob (IRE) – Rejuvenation (IRE) (Singspiel **h90**
(IRE)) [2018/19 h69: h15.5g* Dec 2] lightly-made gelding: modest form over hurdles:
won handicap at Leicester only outing in 2018/19: raced around 2m: best form on good
going. *Ali Stronge*

BOOGIE LIFE 8 b.m. Tobougg (IRE) – Life Is Life (FR) (Mansonnien (FR)) [2018/19 **h79**
h81: h19.6g⁴ h23.3g⁵ h20.9g⁶ Oct 7] lengthy mare: poor maiden hurdler: in cheekpieces
last 2 starts: usually races prominently. *Donald McCain*

BOOK DIRECT (IRE) 8 b.g. Kayf Tara – Sinnaja (Sinndar (IRE)) [2018/19 h–: h19.9gᵖᵘ **h–**
Nov 17] third in Irish point: fair form when second in 2 novice hurdles in 2016/17, pulled
up both starts since. *Philip Hobbs*

BOOK OF DUST 5 ch.m. Pastoral Pursuits – Northern Bows (Bertolini (USA)) [2018/19 **h–**
h15.3d Dec 26] modest maiden on Flat, stays 8.5f: tailed off in mares novice on hurdling
debut. *Jamie Snowden*

BOOK OF GOLD (IRE) 7 b.g. Flemensfirth (USA) – Ballerina Queen (IRE) (Be My **c–**
Native (USA)) [2018/19 h118: c22.4d⁵ c23.6vᵖᵘ h26s⁶ h24.2d h21g³ Apr 10] sturdy **h105**
gelding: fair maiden hurdler: little impact over fences: stays 3m: acts on heavy going: has
worn cheekpieces: tried in tongue tie. *Oliver Sherwood*

BOOK OF INVASIONS (IRE) 4 ch.g. Declaration of War (USA) – Cedar Sea (IRE) **b91**
(Persian Bold) [2018/19 b14g² b13m* b14d³ b15.6m² b17d Apr 5] workmanlike gelding:
half-brother to several winners on Flat, including very smart 1m-13f winner Corsica (by
Cape Cross): dam French 1m winner: fair bumper performer: won junior event at Doncaster
in December: left K. J. Condon after first start. *John Ryan*

BOOK OF LOVE (IRE) 10 b.g. Kutub (IRE) – Love's Always Game (IRE) (Camden **c–**
Town) [2018/19 c–, h–: h20.2g h23.9g Aug 1] won sole start in Irish points: maiden **h–**
hurdler, no form since 2016/17: once-raced chaser: has worn headgear, including in
2018/19. *Martin Todhunter*

BOOLA RIVER (IRE) 9 b.m. Craigsteel – Hy Kate (IRE) (Over The River (FR)) **h–**
[2018/19 h60: h15.7g May 21] Irish point winner: little form over hurdles. *Seamus Mullins*

BOOMARANG 5 b.g. Passing Glance – Materiality (Karinga Bay) [2018/19 b15.8d⁴ **h117**
b16.8g* h16.6m³ h19.4g³ h18.5g⁴ Apr 20] £15,000 3-y-o: fifth foal: half-brother to modest **b92**
23f hurdle winner Mythical Legend (by Midnight Legend): dam, ran twice in bumpers,
sister to smart staying hurdler Material World: fair form in bumpers: won conditionals/
amateurs event at Newton Abbot in June: fairly useful form over hurdles: won maiden at
Newton Abbot in April. *Emma Lavelle*

BORAK (IRE) 7 b.g. Kodiac – Right After Moyne (IRE) (Imperial Ballet (IRE)) [2018/19 **h105**
h92: h15.3m⁴ h15.8g* h15.8m* h18.5m³ h16.7g⁶ h15.3f* h16.5m² h15.3g⁶ Dec 6] fair
handicap hurdler: won at Uttoxeter and Ffos Las in June, and Wincanton in October: stays
2¼m: acts on any going: has worn cheekpieces, including last 3 starts: has worn tongue tie.
Bernard Llewellyn

BORDEAUX BILL (IRE) 8 b.g. Craigsteel – Laura Croft (IRE) (Mister Lord (USA)) **c117 x**
[2018/19 c126, h–: c19.4g⁴ c24v⁵ h21.3s⁶ h19.7g³ h22.7g* h24.4g³ h19.9s* h26.6g Apr 25] **h128**
leggy, lengthy gelding: fairly useful handicap chaser: won at Kelso in February and
Sedgefield in March: fairly useful handicap hurdler, often let down by jumping: stays 3m:
acts on soft going. *Brian Ellison*

BORDER BREAKER (IRE) 10 br.g. Indian Danehill (IRE) – Flying Answer (IRE) **c112**
(Anshan) [2018/19 c97, h104: c21.2g* c20.1g³ c21.2s c20g³ c19.9m² Oct 4] angular **h–**
gelding: winning hurdler: fair handicap chaser: won at Cartmel in May: stays 3m: acts on
soft going: has worn headgear, including last 2 starts: wears tongue tie. *Sam England*

BORDERLINE CHATHO (FR) 8 b.g. Born King (JPN) – Nuance Bleue (FR) **c133**
(Epervier Bleu) [2018/19 h16.5m⁴ h19d* c21gᶠ Dec 28] fairly useful form over hurdles: **h128**
won maiden at Naas in November: just headed when fell last in maiden won by Gun Digger
at Leopardstown on chasing debut: dead. *Alan Fleming, Ireland*

BORDER VICTOR 7 b.g. Beat All (USA) – Sambara (IRE) (Shardari) [2018/19 h85§: **h98 §**
h23.9gᵖᵘ h23.3g⁵ h24.4g² h22.7g* h24.1d² h24.3d⁵ h19.3g² h24.1d* h24.1g Apr 11] has
had breathing operations: modest handicap hurdler: won novice events at Kelso in
December and Wetherby in March: stays 3m: acts on heavy going: wears headgear: has
looked reluctant. *Barry Murtagh*

BOREHAM BILL (IRE) 7 b.g. Tikkanen (USA) – Crimond (IRE) (Zaffaran (USA)) **c78**
[2018/19 h121: h20g⁴ h23.3g² c19.1m⁴ h23.3d³ h26.4g⁶ h24.3m Apr 20] workmanlike **h130**
gelding: has had breathing operation: fairly useful handicap hurdler: well beaten in novice
handicap on chasing debut: stays 23f: acts on heavy going: usually hooded in 2018/19:
usually races prominently: signs of temperament. *Emma Lavelle*

BORIC 11 b.g. Grape Tree Road – Petrea (St Ninian) [2018/19 c125, h–: c29.4g² c23.8g² **c118**
c29.2g³ Oct 21] maiden hurdler: fairly useful handicap chaser: stays 31f: acts on soft going: **h–**
wears headgear: usually races close up. *Simon Waugh*

BORICE (FR) 8 b.g. Network (GER) – Judice (FR) (Agent Bleu (FR)) [2018/19 c29.8s **c132**
c21.9s⁵ c24.5g c25s Jan 24] half-brother to several winners in France, including useful **h–**
hurdler/fairly useful chaser Visionice (17f-19f winner, by Dom Alco): dam, won French
1½m bumper, half-sister to Grand Steeple-Chase de Paris winner Arenice: lightly-raced
hurdler: useful chaser: left Francois Nicolle after second start: stays 27f: acts on soft going:
has worn cheekpieces/tongue tie, including in 2018/19. *Gordon Elliott, Ireland*

BORIS BORU (IRE) 8 b.g. Brian Boru – Gaye Roberta (IRE) (Bob Back (USA)) **h83**
[2018/19 h20g h24g h22dᶠ h16.6d h21.4s⁵ Jan 8] poor maiden hurdler: stays 3m: acts on
soft going: wears headgear. *Mrs Sarah Dawson, Ireland*

BORN A SAINT 6 ch.g. Phoenix Reach (IRE) – Kind Nell (Generous (IRE)) [2018/19 h–: **h–**
h20.3gᵖᵘ May 23] no show in 2 starts over hurdles, in cheekpieces second one. *Laura Morgan*

BORN AT MIDNIGHT 4 b.g. Midnight Legend – Wavet (Pursuit of Love) [2018/19 **h–**
b15.3g h17.7vˢᵘ h16.2d⁶ Jan 2] mid-field in junior bumper: no form over hurdles. *Bill Turner* **b68**

BORN FOR WAR (IRE) 7 ch.g. Wareed (IRE) – Oscar Bird (IRE) (Oscar (IRE)) **c115**
[2018/19 h90: h20.3g² c22.6m² c24.2s³ h23.8g⁴ c20.3g* c23.8g³ Jan 1] has had breathing **h104**
operation: fair form over hurdles: fairly useful form over fences: won novice handicap at
Musselburgh in November: left Tom George after third start: stays 3m: acts on good to firm
going: in visor last 2 starts. *Keith Dalgleish*

BORN LEGEND (IRE) 5 b.g. Born To Sea (IRE) – Hallowed Park (IRE) (Barathea **h–**
(IRE)) [2018/19 h98: h19mᵖᵘ h17f⁵ h16f³ h17f Apr 22] sturdy gelding, has had breathing
operation: winning hurdler: no form in 2018/19, leaving Oliver Sherwood after first start:
best effort at 17f: acts on soft going: wears headgear. *Mrs C. Gilbert, Jersey*

BORN SURVIVOR (IRE) 8 b.g. King's Theatre (IRE) – Bob's Flame (IRE) (Bob Back **c149**
(USA)) [2018/19 c139, h–: c20.3g* c20g c19.4m* c20.6d⁴ c20.5m* Apr 12] useful- **h–**
looking gelding: winning hurdler: smart handicap chaser: won at Southwell in May, and
listed events at Wetherby (by 3¼ lengths from Guitar Pete) in November and Ayr (by 7
lengths from Sizing Granite) in April: best up to 21f: acts on good to firm and heavy going:
tried in cheekpieces: races prominently. *Dan Skelton*

BORN TO BOOGIE 5 b.m. Bahri (USA) – Turtle Dove (Tobougg (IRE)) [2018/19 h–: **h–**
h16.5d Dec 13] modest on Flat, stays 6f: no show in 2 starts over hurdles. *Bill Turner*

BORN TO PLEASE 5 b.m. Stimulation (IRE) – Heart Felt (Beat Hollow) [2018/19 h16d **h92**
h16.3s h16.3d² h15.8d h20.7d Mar 13] sturdy mare: fair on Flat, stays 1¼m: modest form
over hurdles: best effort at 2m: acts on good to soft going. *Mark Usher*

BORN TO STING (IRE) 6 b.g. Scorpion (IRE) – Hatch Away (IRE) (Lord Americo) **h–**
[2018/19 b16s⁶ h16.3d h18.5dᵖᵘ Feb 22] no form in bumper/over hurdles. *Tom George* **b–**

BORUMA (IRE) 9 b.g. Brian Boru – Itlallendintears (IRE) (Lil's Boy (USA)) [2018/19 **c–**
c–, h118: h22.1g⁴ h22.1m³ h22.1g⁶ h25.4sᵖᵘ h23.3g⁵ h25.3gᶠ h25.3s³ h25.3g⁴ h25.3m⁴ Feb **h111**
26] rather leggy gelding: fair handicap hurdler: fell both starts over fences (likely to have
won both): stays 23f: acts on heavy going: wears headgear: usually races towards rear.
James Moffatt

BORU'S BROOK (IRE) 11 b.g. Brian Boru – Collybrook Lady (IRE) (Mandalus) **c–**
[2018/19 c–, h–: h19.2vᶠ Mar 6] good-topped gelding: fairly useful hurdler/chaser at best, **h–**
no form since 2015/16 (including on Flat): tried in blinkers. *Emma Owen*

BOSCO DI ALCO (FR) 8 gr.g. Dom Alco (FR) – Regate (FR) (Agent Bleu (FR)) **c113**
[2018/19 c19.9s⁶ c19.7g⁵ c23.5g³ c22.2m c23d⁵ c25m⁵ c24g⁴ c25gᵘʳ c22.6dᵖᵘ Nov 28] **h–**
sturdy gelding: winning hurdler: fair maiden chaser: stays 25f: acts on soft and good to firm
going: wears headgear/tongue tie. *Miss Elizabeth Doyle, Ireland*

BOSMAN RULE (IRE) 11 ch.g. Gamut (IRE) – Fairy Blaze (IRE) (Good Thyne (USA)) **c–**
[2018/19 c23.8m^{pu} Jan 17] winning hurdler: fair maiden chaser for W. P. Mullins: no show **h–**
in hunter/point in 2018/19 after long absence: stays 3m: acts on heavy going: has worn
cheekpieces: usually races prominently. *W. M. Wanless*

BOSS DES MOTTES (FR) 8 b.g. Califet (FR) – Puszta des Mottes (FR) (Useful (FR)) **c102**
[2018/19 c99, h–: c16.4g^4 c17.3g^2 c15.7g^2 c17.3m^4 h15.8g c17.2g* c16.4m^2 c19.2g **h–**
c19.2d^4 c15.2g^{pu} Mar 29] sparely-made gelding: winning hurdler: fair handicap chaser:
won at Market Rasen in August: stays 2¼m: acts on soft and good to firm going: often in
headgear: wears tongue tie. *Henry Hogarth*

BOSSINEY BAY (IRE) 4 b.f. Camelot – Ursula Minor (IRE) (Footstepsinthesand) **h97**
[2018/19 h15.8g^5 h15.8g^2 Apr 11] fairly useful on Flat, stays 11.5f: modest form over
hurdles: better effort when second in mares maiden at Huntingdon in April. *Oliver Greenall*

BOSS MANS LADDER (IRE) 7 b.g. Mahler – Glen Supreme (IRE) (Supreme Leader) **c79**
[2018/19 h107: h25m^4 h26d^3 h25.8g^4 c22.6m^4 c23g^{pu} Aug 15] fair handicap hurdler: poor **h104**
form over fences: stays 3¼m: acts on good to soft going: wears cheekpieces: usually races
prominently. *Ben Pauling*

BOSTIN (IRE) 11 ch.g. Busy Flight – Bustingoutallover (USA) (Trempolino (USA)) **h82**
[2018/19 h91: h20.5d h25g^3 h25g^6 Apr 22] sturdy gelding: poor handicap hurdler nowadays:
stays 3¼m: acts on soft and good to firm going: races towards rear. *Daniel O'Brien*

BOSTON HEATHER (IRE) 11 b.m. Elusive City (USA) – Colour's Red (IRE) (Red **c104**
Ransom (USA)) [2018/19 h23.3g* h23.9g^2 c23g^3 c23.6d^5 Oct 13] has had breathing **h102**
operation: placed in points: fair handicap hurdler: won novice event at Uttoxeter in July:
fair form in chases: better effort when third in novice at Worcester in September: stays 3m:
best form on good going: has worn headgear: in tongue tie last 4 starts. *Dan Skelton*

BOSTON SPRAY (IRE) 7 b.g. Presenting – Coonagh Cross (IRE) (Saddlers' Hall (IRE)) **c100 x**
[2018/19 h24g^2 h24g^3 h24m^3 c22g^{pu} c23d^F c21g^{pu} c21g^F c23.4d^6 Dec 13] first foal: dam, **h109**
bumper winner, half-sister to useful hurdler/chaser (2m-2½m winner) Sunset Lodge: point
winner: fair form over hurdles: similar form in chases, though often let down by jumping:
stays 3m: best form on good going: has worn headgear, including final start: wears tongue
tie. *Joseph Patrick O'Brien, Ireland*

BOSTON T PARTY 4 b.g. Declaration of War (USA) – Sri Kandi (Pivotal) [2018/19 **h73**
h16.2d^{pu} h16s h16.7d h16g Feb 22] modest form on Flat: little impact over hurdles: wears
cheekpieces. *Ben Case*

BOUDRY (FR) 8 b.g. Crossharbour – Lavande (FR) (Iris Noir (FR)) [2018/19 h101: **h–**
h20.6g^{pu} h21.7m Oct 24] workmanlike gelding: maiden hurdler, no form in 2018/19: left
Rose Dobbin after first start: has worn tongue tie. *John Butler*

BOUGGIETOPIECES 9 b.g. Tobougg (IRE) – Bonnet's Pieces (Alderbrook) [2018/19 **c– §**
c–§, h–: h19d^F h19.8s^{pu} h19s^4 h20.5g^4 Apr 21] poor handicap hurdler nowadays: winning **h79**
but temperamental chaser: stays 3m: acts on soft and good to firm going: has worn
headgear, including last 4 starts: has worn tongue tie, including last 2 starts. *Keiran Burke*

BOUGHTBEFORELUNCH (IRE) 6 b.g. Dubai Destination (USA) – Anie (IRE) **c116**
(Saffron Walden (FR)) [2018/19 h70: h19m h20.7g^3 h19.6m^5 c20.3g c20.3d* c23.6d^{ur} **h94**
c20d^3 c22.7m^2 c24g^2 Mar 28] lengthy gelding: modest form over hurdles: fairly useful
form over fences: won handicap at Southwell in November: second in novice handicap at
Warwick in March: stays 3m: acts on good to firm and good to soft going: in cheekpieces
last 5 starts: usually front runner/races prominently. *Paul Webber*

BOUNDERBY 5 b.g. Manduro (GER) – Most Charming (FR) (Darshaan) [2018/19 h16.7g^6 **h74**
h18.7g^{pu} Aug 28] fair maiden on Flat, stays 11.5f: poor form over hurdles. *Mark Loughnane*

BOUND FOR GLORY (IRE) 13 b.g. Witness Box (USA) – Musical View (IRE) **c93**
(Orchestra) [2018/19 c114, h–: c24.2g^4 May 8] multiple point winner: winning hurdler: fair **h–**
chaser: stayed 23f: acted on soft and good to firm going: tried in blinkers: in tongue tie last
4 starts: dead. *D. M. G. Fitch-Peyton*

BOUND HILL 10 b.g. Kayf Tara – Ardent Bride (Ardross) [2018/19 c88§, h–§: h19.2d^{pu} **c–**
c16.2d c24.2s^{pu} c21.6v^{pu} Feb 14] strong gelding: fair hurdler/modest chaser at best, no **h– §**
form in 2018/19: often wears headgear: temperamental. *Fiona Shaw*

BOURBON BORDERLINE (IRE) 5 b.g. Milan – Daraheen Diamond (IRE) (Husyan (USA)) [2018/19 b16d³ Mar 28] €57,000 3-y-o: brother to 2 winners, including bumper winner/useful hurdler Brewin'upastorm (2m winner), closely related to 2 winners by Dr Massini, including fairly useful hurdler/chaser Glam Gerry (2½m/21f winner), and half-brother to 2 winners, including useful hurdler/chaser Kimberlite King (2m-21f winner, by Good Thyne): dam unraced: off mark in Irish points at second attempt: in tongue strap, 5/4, shaped well when third in maiden bumper at Warwick (6½ lengths behind Welsh Saint): sure to progress. *Dan Skelton* **b96 p**

BOUTAN 6 gr.m. Tobougg (IRE) – High Tan (High Chaparral (IRE)) [2018/19 h84: h16g³ h15.8vᵘʳ h19s⁴ h15.8d h16d⁶ h21.2m⁴ Apr 23] poor maiden hurdler: stays 19f: acts on heavy going: has worn cheekpieces. *Grace Harris* **h84**

BOUVREUIL (FR) 8 b.g. Saddler Maker (IRE) – Madame Lys (FR) (Sheyrann) [2018/19 c122, h–: c15.2s* c15.2d⁶ c20.6d⁶ Mar 14] useful-looking gelding: has had breathing operation: winning hurdler: useful handicap chaser: won at Wetherby (by length from Movie Legend) in December: stays 21f: acts on heavy going: has worn hood, including last 3 starts: wears tongue tie: has high head carriage. *Ben Haslam* **c141 h–**

BOWIE (IRE) 12 br.g. Pelder (IRE) – La Fenice (IRE) (Krayyan) [2018/19 c–, h105: h18.6g h16.2g h18.6g h16.7g h18.6s² h17g⁵ h16.7g⁵ h18.6gᵖᵘ Apr 3] smallish gelding: modest handicap hurdler nowadays: once-raced chaser: stays 21f: acts on good to firm and heavy going: has worn cheekpieces, including last 4 starts: usually front runner/races prominently. *Nick Kent* **c– h89**

BOWLER BILL 6 gr.g. Great Palm (USA) – Overthrow (Overbury (IRE)) [2018/19 b–: b16.8g h20.3gᵖᵘ Jun 5] smallish gelding: no form in bumpers/maiden hurdle. *David Thompson* **h– b–**

BOW STREET RUNNER 4 b.g. Sixties Icon – Lakaam (Danzero (AUS)) [2018/19 h16.4gᵖᵘ h15.6gᵖᵘ h20.1vᵖᵘ Mar 14] little impact on Flat/over hurdles. *Victor Thompson* **h–**

BOXER BEAT (IRE) 12 b.g. Xaar – Pantoufle (Bering) [2018/19 c92, h–: c16g⁴ c20.3gᵖᵘ h22g⁵ c16.2g⁴ Apr 25] poor maiden hurdler/handicap chaser nowadays: stays 2½m: acts on soft and good to firm going: has worn headgear/tongue tie: usually races towards rear. *Lady Susan Brooke* **c82 h82**

BOX OFFICE (FR) 8 b.g. Great Pretender (IRE) – Quelle Mome (FR) (Video Rock (FR)) [2018/19 c110, h105: c17m³ c16g³ h15.7g⁵ c21.1m⁵ h15.7g³ h20.7d³ h15.5d c15.9g⁴ Mar 31] good-topped gelding: fair handicap hurdler/chaser: left Jonjo O'Neill before final outing: stays 21f: acts on soft going: tried in blinkers: has worn tongue tie: usually races towards rear. *C. von der Recke, Germany* **c102 h104**

BOYCHICK (IRE) 6 b.g. Holy Roman Emperor (IRE) – Al Saqiya (USA) (Woodman (USA)) [2018/19 h16.3g⁴ h16m² h16.8s⁴ h18.7g⁴ h16g⁶ h15.9m⁶ h15.8g⁶ Nov 17] has had breathing operation: closely related to a winning jumper in Japan by Rock of Gibraltar and half-brother to fairly useful hurdler Cashel Blue (3m-27f winner, by Aljabr): fair on Flat, stays 1½m: modest maiden hurdler: raced mainly around 2m: acts on good to firm going: tried in cheekpieces: front runner/races prominently. *Harry Whittington* **h97**

BOYFROMNOWHERE (IRE) 12 br.g. Old Vic – Eist Do Gale (IRE) (Strong Gale) [2018/19 c97§, h–: c24.1g May 19] sturdy gelding: winning hurdler: useful chaser at best, well held sole outing in 2018/19: stays 3¾m: acts on heavy going: has worn headgear, including last 2 starts: wears tongue tie: temperamental. *Adrian Wintle* **c– § h–**

BOYGOJUMPING 7 ch.g. Midnight Legend – Maisie Malone Vii (Damsire Unregistered) [2018/19 c–: c21.6g⁵ May 17] multiple point winner: poor form in chases: tried in tongue tie: dead. *Martin Peaty* **c78**

BOYHOOD (IRE) 8 b.g. Oscar (IRE) – Glen Dubh (IRE) (Supreme Leader) [2018/19 h135p: h23.9g² h23.1d³ h24d Mar 14] good-topped gelding: unplaced in Irish maiden point: useful handicap hurdler: third at Exeter (3¾ lengths behind Flemcara) in February: stays 3m: acts on soft going. *Tom George* **h137**

BOY IN A BENTLEY (IRE) 9 b.g. Kayf Tara – All Our Blessings (IRE) (Statoblest) [2018/19 c–, h107§: c20.5mᵘʳ c19.4mᵖᵘ c20.3g² c15.7m⁵ c20.3g² c19.7g² c19.9g² c20.2g² c23.6d Jan 7] lengthy gelding: fair hurdler: fair maiden chaser: stays easy 23f: acts on soft going: wears headgear/tongue tie: temperamental. *Neil Mulholland* **c106 § h– §**

BOY NAMED SIOUX 8 b.g. Indian Danehill (IRE) – Annie's Gift (IRE) (Presenting) [2018/19 h99, b–: h15.8g⁴ Nov 17] fair form over hurdles: dead. *Colin Tizzard* **h103**

BOY'S ON TOUR (IRE) 7 b.g. Beneficial – Galant Tour (IRE) (Riberetto) [2018/19 **c108** c95, h80, b78: c20.1g* c21.2m c20.1g* c15.8m³ c20.3mᵘʳ c20.1d² Apr 26] rather leggy **h–** gelding: maiden hurdler: fair handicap chaser: won at Perth in May and July: stays 2½m: acts on soft going: has worn hood: front runner/races prominently. *Lucinda Russell*

BRAAVOS 8 br.g. Presenting – Tatanka (IRE) (Lear Fan (USA)) [2018/19 c–, h128: **c108** c20.2m³ c21g⁵ c19.4m⁴ c19.2g² c26.3s⁵ c25.2g³ h19.7g c21.1s⁵ Feb 21] well-made **h–** gelding: winning hurdler: fair maiden chaser: left Philip Hobbs after third start: stays 3m: acts on heavy going: tried in cheekpieces: often in tongue tie in 2018/19. *Sam England*

BRACKA LILY (IRE) 7 b.m. Mahler – Hep To The Jive (FR) (Bahri (USA)) [2018/19 **h93** h82, b67: h21.4gᵖᵘ h16g h16.6d² h16.2g³ h21.4d⁶ h19.5v² h20d Apr 7] modest maiden hurdler: likely to prove best up to 2½m: acts on heavy going. *Noel C. Kelly, Ireland*

BRACKENMOSS RORY 7 b.g. Overbury (IRE) – Thorterdykes Lass (IRE) (Zaffaran **c– §** (USA)) [2018/19 c20sᵘʳ h20.1s² Nov 21] poor maiden hurdler: unseated third on chasing **h74 §** debut: stays 2½m: acts on soft going: tried in visor: temperamental. *Alistair Whillans*

BRADDAN HEAD 6 br.g. Recharge (IRE) – Solid Land (FR) (Solid Illusion (USA)) **h82** [2018/19 h97p, b–: h23gᵖᵘ h25.3g⁴ h19.9s⁵ h20.6dᵖᵘ h19.8m³ h20.2d Apr 26] sturdy gelding: poor maiden hurdler: left Charlie Longsdon after first start: in cheekpieces last 2 starts: tried in tongue tie. *Dianne Sayer*

BRADFORD BRIDGE (IRE) 7 b.g. Milan – Isis du Berlais (FR) (Cadoudal (FR)) **c–** [2018/19 c102, h–: h23.3g⁶ h21.6g² h20g* h23.1m* c22.6g h21.6s h21.4g Jan 5] well- **h115** made gelding: fairly useful handicap hurdler: won at Worcester and Exeter in October: maiden chaser: stays 23f: acts on good to firm and heavy going. *Philip Hobbs*

BRAES OF LOCHALSH 8 b.g. Tiger Hill (IRE) – Gargoyle Girl (Be My Chief (USA)) **h84** [2018/19 h82: h21.4g May 7] poor form over hurdles: in headgear last 2 starts. *Jim Goldie*

BRAID BLUE (IRE) 6 b.g. Gold Well – Outo'theblue (IRE) (Grand Lodge (USA)) **h120 p** [2018/19 b19.8g* b16.2g* h21.4s⁵ h16d⁵ h20d⁶ Apr 24] €8,500 4-y-o: sixth foal: **b101** half-brother to a winning pointer by Generous: dam unraced half-sister to smart hurdler (stayed 25f) Mistanoora: won bumpers at Kilbeggan and Perth early in season: fairly useful form over hurdles: won maiden at Perth in April: should stay 3m: remains with potential. *Gordon Elliott, Ireland*

BRAIN POWER (IRE) 8 b.g. Kalanisi (IRE) – Blonde Ambition (IRE) (Old Vic) **c136 +** [2018/19 c154, h–: c15.9g⁴ h21.4s⁵ h16.8s* h16.4sᵖᵘ h16mᵖᵘ Apr 13] rangy gelding: has had **h149** breathing operations: smart hurdler: won International Hurdle at Cheltenham (by 1¾ lengths from Silver Streak) in December: smart chaser at best, often let down by jumping: stays 2¼m: acts on soft going: has worn cheekpieces, including last 3 starts: tried in tongue tie: usually races towards rear. *Nicky Henderson*

Unibet International Hurdle, Cheltenham—
a successful return to hurdling for Brain Power, who is chased home by the grey Silver Streak

BRAMBLE BROOK 9 b.g. Kayf Tara – Briery Ann (Anshan) [2018/19 c117§, h–: **c120 §** c26.7m* c23.8g⁶ c26.1g³ c26v³ c23s⁴ c24.2d c25.8g³ Apr 20] strong gelding: maiden **h–** hurdler: fairly useful handicap chaser: won at Wincanton in May: stays 27f: acts on good to firm and heavy going: wears cheekpieces/tongue tie: usually front runner/races prominently: temperamental. *Colin Tizzard*

BRANDON CASTLE 7 b.g. Dylan Thomas (IRE) – Chelsey Jayne (IRE) (Galileo (IRE)) **h136** [2018/19 h15.9s* h15.9d* h15.9g* h16.4s^pu h15.9g Apr 21] sturdy gelding: useful on Flat, stays 14.5f: useful form over hurdles: won novices at Plumpton in December and January, and handicap at same course (by 9 lengths from Arthington) in February: raced only at 2m: acts on soft going: wears hood/tongue tie: front runner. *Neil King*

BRANDON HILL (IRE) 11 b.g. Beneficial – Annesbanker (IRE) (Anshan) [2018/19 **c131** c136, h–: c25g⁵ c21.1s² c24s³ Jan 21] lengthy gelding: has had breathing operation: **h–** winning hurdler: useful handicap chaser: second in Grand Sefton Chase at Aintree (1½ lengths behind Warriors Tale) in December: stays 3m: best form on soft/heavy going: bold-jumping front runner. *Tom George*

BRANDY AND RED (IRE) 10 b.g. Presenting – Mildan Grace (Afzal) [2018/19 c83: **c85** c24.2m³ c25.8g^pu c20g c21m³ c23g Jul 26] winning pointer: modest maiden chaser: left P. D. Rogers after second start: stays 3m: acts on good to firm going: in headgear last 2 starts: usually races prominently. *Jackie du Plessis*

BRANDY CROSS (IRE) 5 b.g. Le Fou (IRE) – Glenquin (IRE) (Supreme Leader) **h–** [2018/19 h20.5d h15.9g h20.5s⁶ Mar 11] strong gelding: maiden Irish pointer: no form over hurdles. *Zoe Davison*

BRANDY JAMES (GER) 4 b.g. Motivator – Bold Classic (USA) (Pembroke (USA)) **h106** [2018/19 h16d³ h16.2g² h15.8g² h16.3d⁴ h18.8d⁶ Mar 23] angular gelding: fair form on Flat: similar form over hurdles: should be suited by further than 2m: acts on good to soft going: in hood last 2 starts: usually races close up. *Harry Whittington*

BRAQUEUR D'OR (FR) 8 b.g. Epalo (GER) – Hot d'Or (FR) (Shafoun (FR)) [2018/19 **c135** c139, h112: c25g c23m* c25.6g^ur Nov 24] tall, angular gelding: has had breathing **h–** operation: maiden hurdler: useful handicap chaser: won at Taunton (by 6 lengths from Fox Appeal) in November: stays 3¼m: acts on good to firm and good to soft going. *Paul Nicholls*

BRAVANTINA 4 b.f. Trans Island – Falbrina (IRE) (Falbrav (IRE)) [2018/19 ab16.3g² **b75** b16.6g Jan 26] second foal: dam, ran once on Flat, half-sister to fairly useful hurdler (stayed 3m) Ameeq: modest form when runner-up on first of 2 starts in bumpers: wears tongue tie: little impact on Flat. *Mark Walford*

BRAVE DANCING 5 b.g. Mount Nelson – Purring (USA) (Mountain Cat (USA)) **c–** [2018/19 c101p, h115: c17.9s^F c16.5g^pu Oct 24] fairly useful form over hurdles: fair form **h–** only completed outing over fences: left David Cottin after first start: stays 2¼m: acts on heavy going: has worn cheekpieces, including in 2018/19: tried in tongue tie. *Ben Pauling*

BRAVE EAGLE (IRE) 7 b.g. Yeats (IRE) – Sinful Pleasure (IRE) (Sinndar (IRE)) **c143** [2018/19 h130: h20.5g* h24g* h23.1g² c23g* c21.6g* c23.6d³ Oct 13] lengthy gelding: **h137** useful handicap hurdler: won at Plumpton (conditionals) in May and Southwell in June: similar form over fences: won maiden at Worcester in July and novice at Fontwell in August: best effort when third in handicap at Chepstow (4½ lengths behind The Young Master) final start: stays 3m: acts on heavy going: tried in cheekpieces: usually responds generously to pressure. *Nicky Henderson*

BRAVE HELIOS 9 b.g. High Chaparral (IRE) – Renowned (IRE) (Darshaan) [2018/19 **c76** c93, h97: h20.7g² h24g^pu c22.6m⁶ Aug 2] rather leggy gelding: modest handicap hurdler: **h95** modest maiden chaser, below form final outing in 2018/19: stays 25f: acts on good going: has worn headgear, including in 2018/19: wears tongue tie. *Richard Phillips*

BRAVE JAQ (FR) 8 ch.g. Network (GER) – Galaxie (FR) (Useful (FR)) [2018/19 c–, h–: **c106** c16.3g⁶ c17.8g⁴ c17d² c20.2f³ c20.9s* c20g² Mar 28] maiden hurdler: fair hunter chaser: **h–** won novice event at Stratford in March: stays 21f: acts on soft going: wears hood/tongue tie: front runner/races prominently. *R. D. Potter*

BRAVENTARA 8 b.m. Kayf Tara – L'Aventure (FR) (Cyborg (FR)) [2018/19 h118: **c91** h23.6g⁵ h23.6v² c25.1g^ur c22.5v⁵ Jan 26] lengthy mare: fairly useful handicap hurdler: **h116** second at Chepstow in December: well below that level completed start over fences: stays 3¼m: acts on good to firm and heavy going. *Tom George*

BRAVE SEASCA (FR) 4 bl.g. Brave Mansonnien (FR) – Miss Laveron (FR) (Laveron) **b–** [2018/19 b16.4d Mar 5] tailed off in maiden bumper. *Thomas Cooper, Ireland*

BRAVE SPARTACUS (IRE) 13 b.g. Spartacus (IRE) – Peaches Polly (Slip Anchor) **c115**
[2018/19 c128, h105: c17.1g⁵ c21.2g³ c21.4mᵖᵘ c20.1g⁵ c21.2sᵖᵘ c19.3m² c19.4g⁴ c20.1g² **h–**
c19.2g⁶ c16.3g⁴ c19.2d* c19.2gᵖᵘ Mar 20] good-topped gelding: winning hurdler: fairly
useful handicap chaser: won at Market Rasen in February: stays 21f: acts on good to firm
and heavy going: has worn hood: front runner. *Gillian Boanas*

BRAW ANGUS 9 b.g. Alflora (IRE) – Suilven (Teenoso (USA)) [2018/19 h98: h19.5g **c–**
c19.9dᵖᵘ Dec 26] fair hurdler at best, no form in 2018/19 (including on chasing debut): **h–**
stays 21f: acts on soft going: has worn cheekpieces, inlcuding in 2018/19: temperament
under suspicion. *Kim Bailey*

BREAKEN (FR) 5 b.g. Sunday Break (JPN) – Kendoretta (FR) (Kendor (FR)) [2018/19 **h134 p**
h16d* Mar 31] half-brother to fairly useful hurdler Salsaretta (2m-2½m winner, by
Kingsalsa): lightly raced on Flat: useful form over hurdles: runner-up in juvenile at Auteuil
in 2017/18 for Mme P. Butel: much improved when won maiden at Limerick (by 17 lengths
from Calicojack) in March: in hood, raced too freely when 17½ lengths fourth to Gardens
of Babylon in novice at Punchestown shortly after end of British season: remains with
potential. *W. P. Mullins, Ireland*

BREAKFAST (IRE) 4 b.g. Kodiac – Pride Celebre (IRE) (Peintre Celebre (USA)) **h111**
[2018/19 h16.7m* h16.7g³ h16m³ Oct 17] fairly useful on Flat, stays 1¼m: fair form over
hurdles: won juvenile at Market Rasen in August: tried in tongue tie. *Donald McCain*

BREAKING GROUND (IRE) 7 b.g. Echo of Light – Mayfair (Green Desert (USA)) **h–**
[2018/19 h96, b–: h25mᵖᵘ May 7] Irish point winner: modest hurdler: stayed 23f: acted on
soft going: tried in headgear, including last 2 starts: wore tongue tie: dead. *Richenda Ford*

BREAKING WAVES (IRE) 5 b.g. Yeats (IRE) – Acoola (IRE) (Flemensfirth (USA)) **h121**
[2018/19 h102p: b16.4d³ h20.5s³ h19.5d⁶ h20.7d* h20.5d⁴ Mar 22] big, lengthy gelding: **b105**
has had breathing operation: useful form in bumpers: fairly useful form over hurdles: won
novice at Huntingdon in February: will stay 2¾m+. *Noel Williams*

BRECON HILL (IRE) 6 b.g. Arcano (IRE) – Bryanstown Girl (IRE) (Kalanisi (IRE)) **h122**
[2018/19 h107p, b102: h20.6g⁴ h15.8g* h15.8d² h15.5g* h16m⁴ h20dᵖᵘ Apr 5] close-
coupled gelding: bumper winner: fairly useful hurdler: won novices at Huntingdon in
November and Leicester in January: should be suited by 2½m: acts on good to soft going:
in tongue tie last 5 starts: front runner/races prominently. *Sarah Humphrey*

BREDON HILL LAD 12 ch.g. Kirkwall – Persian Clover (Abutammam) [2018/19 c106, **c92**
h–: c16v⁴ c21.6vᵖᵘ c16.2d c17.8s³ c20.2gᵖᵘ c17.8v* c17.5vᵖᵘ c17.8g⁴ Apr 12] lengthy **h–**
gelding: winning hurdler: modest handicap chaser nowadays: won at Fontwell in March:
stays 3m: acts on heavy going: wears headgear/tongue tie: front runner/races prominently:
temperament under suspicion. *Susan Gardner*

BREDON HILL LEO 7 b.g. Sulamani (IRE) – Persian Clover (Abutammam) [2018/19 **h–**
b67: h15.8v⁶ h15.8s h19.7sᵖᵘ h19.8sᵖᵘ Mar 7] poor form in bumpers: little show over
hurdles. *Susan Gardner*

BREEZE ALONG 9 ch.g. Denounce – Briery Breeze (IRE) (Anshan) [2018/19 c82, h58: **c–**
c16.5gᵖᵘ Sep 2] lengthy gelding: has had breathing operation: maiden hurdler: lightly- **h–**
raced chaser, amiss sole outing in 2018/19: in hood/tongue tie last 4 starts. *Dan Skelton*

BREEZEBLOCK (IRE) 6 b.g. Ask – Rose Island (Jupiter Island) [2018/19 b17.7s **h–**
h19.2mᵖᵘ Oct 24] no show in bumper/maiden hurdle. *Richenda Ford* **b–**

BREIZH ALKO (FR) 8 ch.g. Balko (FR) – Quisiera (FR) (Passing Sale (FR)) [2018/19 **h107**
h20.5d⁶ h22.8d* Mar 20] first foal: dam French 13f/1¾m bumper winner: fair form over
hurdles: won 4-y-o event in France in 2015/16: better for comeback when also won
handicap at Haydock in March. *Rebecca Menzies*

BRELAN D'AS (FR) 8 b.g. Crillon (FR) – Las de La Croix (FR) (Grand Tresor (FR)) **c138**
[2018/19 c123, h125: c16g² c22.4s² c15.7v* c20.6d⁵ c16.3g* c16.3d³ c15.8d⁵ Apr 4] good- **h–**
topped gelding: winning hurdler: useful chaser: won novices at Haydock in December and
Fakenham in February: stays 2¾m: acts on heavy going: has worn hood, including in
2018/19: wears tongue tie. *Paul Nicholls*

BRERETON (IRE) 8 b.g. Kalanisi (IRE) – Westgrove Berry (IRE) (Presenting) [2018/19 **c–**
c–, h–: h16gᵖᵘ Feb 15] useful-looking gelding: won point in May: little form under Rules: **h–**
tried in cheekpieces: has worn tongue tie. *Richard Harper*

Mrs Barbara Hester's "Brewin'upastorm"

BREWIN'UPASTORM (IRE) 6 b.g. Milan – Daraheen Diamond (IRE) (Husyan (USA)) [2018/19 b112p: h15.8d* h20.5d⁴ h20.3dᶠ h21s⁴ h20g² Apr 6] good-topped gelding: won point on debut: useful bumper performer: similar form over hurdles: won novice at Huntingdon in December: fourth in Ballymore Novices' Hurdle (Baring Bingham) at Cheltenham (5¾ lengths behind City Island) then second in Mersey Novices' Hurdle at Aintree (3¼ lengths behind Reserve Tank) last 2 starts: likely to prove best up to 2½m: acts on soft going: often travels strongly. *Olly Murphy* **h144**

BREX DRAGO (ITY) 7 b.g. Mujahid (USA) – Shibuni's Thea (IRE) (Barathea (IRE)) [2018/19 h16g h16g h16g h19d h16g h19.5g* h20d* h19.7d* h20d² h20s h16g h20s h19.4g⁵ h16.8d h22dᶠ Apr 22] useful on Flat, stays 10.5f: fairly useful hurdler: won handicaps at Kilbeggan (conditionals) and Listowel then conditionals novice at Clonmel, all in September: left David Peter Dunne after second start: stays 2½m: acts on good to soft going: sometimes in headgear. *Gavin Patrick Cromwell, Ireland* **h123**

BRIAC (FR) 8 b.g. Kapgarde (FR) – Jarwin Do (FR) (Grand Tresor (FR)) [2018/19 h96: h15.9g³ h15.9gᵖᵘ c16sᶠ h17.7v⁴ h21.9v* c19.3d* h16s³ c24s³ c19.4d³ Apr 6] sturdy gelding: fair handicap hurdler: won at Ffos Las in January: similar form over fences: won handicap at Sedgefield in January: left Mark Pattinson after second start: stays 2¾m: acts on heavy going: tried in headgear: usually races nearer last than first, often travels strongly. *Tim Vaughan* **c107 h108**

BRIAN BORANHA (IRE) 8 b.g. Brian Boru – Tapneiram (IRE) (Kahyasi) [2018/19 c121, h107: c24g* c21.4m c23.8g³ c29.2g* c24g c26g³ c31.8m Apr 13] rather lightly-built gelding: winning hurdler: useful handicap chaser: won at Southwell in May and Sedgefield (by 9 lengths from Mercers Court) in October: stays 29f: acts on soft going: usually races off pace. *Peter Niven* **c131 h–**

BRIANSTORM (IRE) 7 b.g. Brian Boru – Coco Moon (IRE) (Classic Cliche (IRE)) [2018/19 h121, b94: h15.7g⁶ c16.8s⁵ h19.9s⁴ Mar 21] well-made gelding: has had breathing operation: Irish point winner: fairly useful handicap hurdler, excuses in 2018/19: 5/2, fifth **c– p h111**

in novice handicap at Ascot (14½ lengths behind Azzerti) on chasing debut: unproven beyond 17f: acts on soft going: has worn hood, including in 2018/19: usually leads: should do better as a chaser. *Venetia Williams*

BRIDAL MARCH 5 ch.m. Casamento (IRE) – Exultate Jubilate (USA) (With Approval **h–** (CAN)) [2018/19 h15.8gᵖᵘ h15.8d Dec 5] sturdy mare: fair maiden on Flat, probably stays 1½m: no form over hurdles: wears cheekpieces. *John Mackie*

BRIDANE HIGH (IRE) 6 b.g. Mountain High (IRE) – Maylee (IRE) (Good Thyne **h–** (USA)) [2018/19 b16.2m⁵ h20.5v⁵ Nov 14] runner-up in Irish point: fifth in bumper at **b70** Kelso (17 lengths behind Auntie Mary): well beaten in maiden on hurdling debut. *Jackie Stephen*

BRIDEY'S LETTUCE (IRE) 7 b.g. Iffraaj – Its On The Air (IRE) (King's Theatre **h93** (IRE)) [2018/19 h88: h15.8gᵖᵘ h15.8g² Jun 6] modest form over hurdles: unproven beyond 2m: acts on soft going: tried in hood: often races freely. *Charles Pogson*

BRIERY BUNNY 7 b.m. Lucarno (USA) – Blackbriery Thyne (IRE) (Good Thyne **h93** (USA)) [2018/19 b15.8g h15.7d⁶ h16d Dec 18] has had breathing operation: third foal: **b–** half-sister to bumper winner/useful hurdler Meadowcroft Boy (2m/17f winner, by Kayf Tara): dam (h109), 2m hurdle winner, half-sister to useful hurdler/chaser (stayed 21f) Briery Queen: showed a bit in mares bumper: modest form over hurdles: better effort when sixth in mares novice at Southwell in November: in hood last 2 starts. *Oliver Sherwood*

BRIERY EXPRESS 6 b.m. Rail Link – Blackbriery Thyne (IRE) (Good Thyne (USA)) **b99** [2018/19 b86p: b17g* b15.8d⁵ b16s b17d Apr 4] good-topped mare: fairly useful bumper performer: won mares event at Aintree in October: will stay at least 2½m: wears hood. *Noel Williams*

BRIGADE OF GUARDS (IRE) 5 b.g. Presenting – Lasado (IRE) (Jurado (USA)) **h110** [2018/19 b87: h15.3g³ h16.3s h16.3s h19.2d h19.3m³ Mar 31] sturdy gelding: fair form over hurdles: bred to stay 2½m+: acts on soft and good to firm going: tried in visor. *Alan King*

BRIGADIER BOB (IRE) 6 b.g. Excellent Art – Plausabelle (Royal Applause) [2018/19 **h93** h88, b86: h15.8v² h20v h19.7g⁶ h19.5dᵖᵘ h19.6g⁵ Apr 13] good-topped gelding: modest maiden hurdler: best effort at 2m: acts on heavy going: tried in cheekpieces. *Kerry Lee*

BRIGADOON 12 b.g. Compton Place – Briggsmaid (Elegant Air) [2018/19 h15.8d **h77** h15.7g³ Mar 4] poor maiden hurdler nowadays: raced mainly around 2m: acts on good to firm going. *Michael Appleby*

BRIGHT ABBEY 11 ch.g. Halling (USA) – Bright Hope (IRE) (Danehill (USA)) **c–** [2018/19 h22.1gᵖᵘ May 26] fairly useful hurdler at best: in cheekpieces, pulled up sole **h–** outing in 2018/19 after long absence: lightly-raced chaser: stays 21f: acts on good to firm going. *Dianne Sayer*

BRIGHT FORECAST (IRE) 5 b.g. Arcadio (GER) – Check The Forecast (IRE) **h146 p** (Shernazar) [2018/19 h16.3s* h15.5g* h15.7d² h21s³ Mar 13] sturdy gelding: half-brother to 3 winners, including fairly useful hurdler/chaser Another Rebel (2m-2¾m winner, by Croco Rouge) and fairly useful hurdler Bitsandpieces (2m-3m winner, by Milan): dam unraced half-sister to useful hurdler/smart chaser (winner up to 3m) Southern Vic: last of 3 finishers in Irish point: smart form over hurdles: won maiden at Newbury (by neck from Sevarano) in November and novice at Leicester (by 3¼ lengths from Humble Hero) in December: second in Rossington Main Novices' Hurdle at Haydock (2½ lengths behind Mister Fisher) in January and third in Ballymore Novices' Hurdle (Baring Bingham) at Cheltenham (4¼ lengths behind City Island) in March: will stay beyond 21f: open to further improvement. *Ben Pauling*

BRIGHT NEW DAWN (IRE) 12 br.g. Presenting – Shuil Dorcha (IRE) (Bob Back **c– §** (USA)) [2018/19 c131§, h–§: c16.2g⁵ c16drr Feb 23] rangy, useful-looking gelding: **h– §** winning hurdler: smart chaser at best, has gone wrong way temperamentally (refused to race/virtually did so both starts in 2018/19): has worn headgear, including in 2018/19: has worn tongue tie: one to leave alone. *Olly Murphy*

BRIGHT PROSPECT (IRE) 10 b.g. Kutub (IRE) – Bright Future (IRE) (Satco (FR)) **c111** [2018/19 c112, h–: c20g⁵ c24.2g³ c32.4g c25.2m³ Feb 26] winning hurdler: fair handicap **h–** chaser: stays 25f: acts on soft and good to firm going: has worn cheekpieces, including last 3 starts: usually races close up. *Jackie Stephen*

BRIGHT SAFFRON 4 ch.f. Champs Elysees – Mercy Pecksniff (Shamardal (USA)) **h91 p** [2018/19 h15.8m⁵ h16g⁵ h16d³ Dec 13] fair on Flat, stays 1¾m: modest form over hurdles: best effort when third in juvenile maiden at Warwick in December: will be suited by 2½m: in cheekpieces last 2 starts: open to further improvement. *Clare Hobson*

BRIGHTS PARK (IRE) 7 b.g. Mahler – Ellesmere (IRE) (Turtle Island (IRE)) [2018/19   **h–** h95, b–: h24g^{pu} Jun 12] maiden hurdler. *Nick Kent*

BRIGHT TOMORROW (IRE) 8 b.g. Robin des Pres (FR) – Gweedara (IRE)   **c– x** (Saddlers' Hall (IRE)) [2018/19 c–x, h108: h21.4m^2 h20g h22m^2 h26.4m^6 Jul 22] fair   **h110** handicap hurdler: winning chaser (often let down by jumping): stayed 21f: acted on soft and good to firm going: wore cheekpieces: often tongue tied: dead. *Warren Greatrex*

BRILLARE MOMENTO (IRE) 8 b.m. Milan – Sunshine Leader (IRE) (Supreme   **c–** Leader) [2018/19 h134: h20g^3 h21g^{pu} h20.3s c20m^{pu} h24.4g^4 h20.3g Apr 18] well-made   **h130** mare: has had breathing operations: useful handicap hurdler: third at Worcester (5½ lengths behind Really Super) in September: pulled up in mares novice on chasing debut: stays 2¾m: acts on heavy going: has worn headgear, including last 5 starts: tried in tongue tie. *Martin Keighley*

BRINESTINE (USA) 10 b.g. Bernstein (USA) – Miss Zafonic (FR) (Zafonic (USA))   **c82** [2018/19 c77, h–: c16.5g^5 c20g^5 c19.4m* Jul 15] angular gelding: winning hurdler: poor   **h–** handicap chaser nowadays: won at Stratford in July: stays easy 19f: acts on good to firm going: wears headgear/tongue tie. *Emma-Jane Bishop*

BRING BACK CHARLIE 9 b.g. Green Card (USA) – Nafertiti (IRE) (Bob Back   **h78** (USA)) [2018/19 h89: h19m h15.8g^4 h15.8g^5 Jul 10] poor handicap hurdler: should stay 2½m: acts on good to firm and good to soft going: wears cheekpieces. *Nigel Twiston-Davies*

BRINGEWOOD BLUE (IRE) 12 br.m. Blueprint (IRE) – Carramore (IRE)   **c–** (Topanoora) [2018/19 h23.3g^{pu} c20.3d^R Jan 8] little form over hurdles: bled on chasing   **h–** debut. *John Needham*

BRIO CONTI (FR) 8 gr.g. Dom Alco (FR) – Cadoulie Wood (FR) (Cadoudal (FR))   **c–** [2018/19 c129P, h–: h23.4s^{pu} h19.3d* h21s^4 h20d^{pu} Apr 5] good-topped gelding: smart   **h146** handicap hurdler: won at Ascot (by head from Honest Vic) in February: fourth in Coral Cup at Cheltenham (2 lengths behind William Henry) next time: fairly useful form when successful sole outing over fences in 2017/18: stays 21f: acts on heavy going: travels strongly. *Paul Nicholls*

BRISTOL DE MAI (FR) 8 gr.g. Saddler Maker (IRE) – La Bole Night (FR) (April   **c169 x** Night (FR)) [2018/19 c165x, h–: c25.6g* c24g^F c26.3d^3 c25d^4 Apr 4]   **h–**

Nicknamed 'Haydock de Mai' by some, thanks to his impeccable record (four dominant wins from four starts) at the Lancashire track, Bristol de Mai nonetheless continues to show that he is no one-dimensional chaser. After adding his name to a short but distinguished list of chasers who have won the Betfair Chase more than once, Bristol de Mai emerged with credit after a ninth-fence fall in the King George VI Chase to finish third in the Cheltenham Gold Cup, coming out clear best of the British-trained runners, who included the first three in the King George. The form of the leading home-trained staying chasers was somewhat muddling in the latest season but, on balance, Bristol de Mai showed himself to be the best of them and undoubtedly has the ability to go close in the Gold Cup another year if things go his way. Most important among the things which would have to 'go his way' is his jumping. Bristol de Mai can be an unreliable jumper—although his fall in the King George is the only one on his record—and lapses in that department have become something of an unwelcome trademark. He made mistakes when finishing no better than a respectable fourth of six behind Kemboy in the Bowl at Aintree, a race in which he had run well when second to the King George winner and Cheltenham Gold Cup runner-up Might Bite twelve months earlier.

Bristol de Mai has won ten of his thirty races so far, his wins away from Haydock coming at six different tracks. He won a newcomers hurdle at Auteuil as a three-year-old for Guillaume Macaire before Simon Munir and Isaac Souede purchased him and sent him to Nigel Twiston-Davies, for whom he won over hurdles at Chepstow (the Grade 1 Finale Junior Hurdle) on his first start for the yard. His four other wins over fences have come at Warwick, Leicester, Sandown (the Grade 1 Scilly Isles Novices' Chase) and Wetherby (the Charlie Hall Chase), which, with his good placed efforts in Grade 1 company at Cheltenham (also second in the Golden Miller at the Festival) and Aintree (also third in the Anniversary Hurdle) illustrate that he has shown plenty of good form on a variety of courses, and cannot be labelled as simply a Haydock specialist.

If Bristol de Mai had demonstrated that he was capable of producing his best on different types of courses, he hadn't demonstrated the same versatility regarding ground conditions until the latest season. All his wins had been with give in the ground, the very best of his performances being achieved in the mud, among them his three victories at Haydock—in the Altcar Novices' Chase (by thirty-two lengths), the Peter Marsh Chase (by twenty-two) and the previous year's Betfair Chase (by fifty-seven, the record winning margin for any Grade 1 race over jumps in Britain). The going for the 2017 Betfair Chase was bottomless and front-running Bristol de Mai had his rivals well beaten a long way from home, the extreme conditions ultimately exaggerating his superiority in a race in which none of the five opponents could have given anything like their true running (three-times winner of the race Cue Card finished second). Bristol de Mai's subsequent performances seemed to bear out the conservative assessment of his Betfair Chase form and his sixth of seven in the King George VI Chase in particular, behind Might Bite, seemed to confirm that he was not the same horse away from the mud (although his jumping also let him down on that occasion). Bristol de Mai had gone on to run much better when second to Might Bite at Aintree where the soft-ground conditions had seemingly been much more in his favour.

An unseasonably dry autumn left conditions for the latest Betfair Chase (registered as the Lancashire Chase) much less testing than they usually are—the going was good (there were a couple of course records on the day)—and there was some speculation that Bristol de Mai might miss the race due to the ground. He started third favourite at 13/2 on the day in a five-runner field featuring a rematch between the Cheltenham Gold Cup first and second Native River and Might Bite, a rematch that dominated the pre-race previews at a time when both sets of connections were targeting the million-pound bonus for any horse completing the 'Classic Triple Crown' by adding the King George and then the Gold Cup, something previously achieved in the same season only by Kauto Star. Might Bite's reverse at the hands of Native River at Cheltenham had been the only defeat he had suffered since his debut over fences, apart from falling when well clear in the Kauto Star Novices' Chase. Under anything less extreme than the conditions he had encountered in the Gold Cup, Might Bite was probably the best staying chaser in training and he started at evens for the Betfair, with Native River at 5/2. Bristol de Mai was the only other runner at single-figure odds, the field being completed by the 2016 King George VI Chase winner Thistlecrack, a stablemate of Native River, and by Clan des Obeaux who had come third to Might Bite and Bristol de Mai in the Aintree Bowl. Bristol de Mai did not dominate his Betfair Chase rivals in the same way as he had done twelve months earlier and, although he travelled strongly, he actually surrendered the lead to Native River on occasions during the race before taking over again for the final time at the fourth last and asserting himself between the last two fences. Driven out, Bristol de Mai won by four lengths and a length and three quarters from Native River and Thistlecrack, with Clan des Obeaux three lengths further back in fourth and Might Bite a long way back in last.

As so often happens when there is a 'surprise' result to a big race, nearly as much attention was given afterwards to trying to account for Might Bite's abject display as was given to the winner. Before the race, TV cameras had captured Might Bite's trainer Nicky Henderson inspecting one of the fences at close hand and drawing a line from his shoulder as if measuring it. 'They've built some big fences for today,' said Henderson afterwards, and Might Bite's jockey Nico de Boinville went further, saying that the fences were 'not fair, very upright and too stiff and solid', which did not suit Might Bite's usually slick, flamboyant jumping style. Of the twenty-five runners in the four steeplechases on Betfair Chase day, six fell and one unseated its rider (there were two fallers and two jockeys unseated from a total of sixty-nine runners in the chases at the three other meetings on the day in Britain and Ireland). The Betfair Chase was the only one of the Haydock chases in which there wasn't a faller.

It was ironic that Haydock should find itself in the hot seat for producing fences that some participants found too big. When the permanent drop fences (regarded as among the stiffest in the country) were replaced by portable fences in

Betfair Chase (Lancashire), Haydock—Bristol de Mai repeats his 2017 win, chased home by the Colin Tizzard-trained pair Native River (noseband) and Thistlecrack; favourite Might Bite (left) wilts to finish last, his trainer Nicky Henderson (inset) having expressed concerns over the stiffness of Haydock's rebuilt fences

2007, there was criticism in the following years that the new fences were too easy, and 'jockeys were hurtling around here similar to a point-to-point', as clerk of the course Kirkland Tellwright described it. Having taken that lesson to heart, Haydock seemed to have found the right balance until the criticism on Betfair Chase day which focussed on the obstacles being a little too big and the top of them being too tightly packed, potentially catching out horses brushing through the top few inches, something they are usually able to do on most other courses. Haydock carried out remedial work before its next meeting, slightly reducing the height of the fences and making them a little less rigid. The Betfair Chase, of course, is one of Britain's premier staying chases and the fences for it should be stiff enough to provide a good test of jumping. That said, given the differences in the composition of fences from one track to another, perhaps information should be provided beforehand to trainers when a course makes material changes to its fences since the last time they were raced over. It would arguably be acceptable for the fences to be stiffer on Betfair

Chase day than on the rest of Haydock's racedays, but the participants are entitled to know about it in advance (and perhaps the course shouldn't stage a race for novices on that particular day, which is relatively early in the season). Incidentally, so far as Bristol de Mai was concerned, the fences presented not the slightest problem: he never put a foot wrong all the way, turning in a flawless round of jumping.

The five Betfair Chase runners met again in the King George VI Chase at Kempton on Boxing Day when Might Bite again started favourite. More widely, the King George betting seemed to ignore the result at Haydock, with Bristol de Mai an 8/1-shot, also behind both Native River and Thistlecrack in the betting. With habitual front runner Coneygree also in the line-up, Bristol de Mai seemed unlikely to get his own way up front and was ridden more patiently than usual. Unfortunately, Bristol de Mai didn't get the chance to show what he could do, falling at the ninth when in touch and hampering second favourite Waiting Patiently who unseated his rider. Not seen out between the King George and the Cheltenham Gold Cup,

Bristol de Mai went down by two and a half lengths and three and three quarters at Cheltenham to the Irish-trained pair Al Boum Photo and Anibale Fly, with the King George third Native River and the King George winner Clan de Obeaux following him home in fourth and fifth (King George runner-up Thistlecrack's jumping let him down and he was pulled up some way out). Bristol de Mai's jumping couldn't be criticised in the Gold Cup but, after again being ridden more patiently than usual and holding every chance from two out, he couldn't match Al Boum Photo and Anibale Fly up the steep climb from the last fence to the finish, a stretch where he lost second to Anibale Fly. Bristol de Mai's hard race at Cheltenham probably had a part to play in explaining his only subsequent performance, when beaten around ten lengths into fourth behind Kemboy in the Bowl at Aintree, although his jumping flaws returned on that occasion too, when he made serious mistakes at the seventh and the fourth last (Bristol de Mai held a Grand National entry at the Aintree meeting, set to race off a mark of 168 as opposed to his BHA mark of 173 at the time the weights were published).

Bristol de Mai (FR) (gr.g. 2011)	Saddler Maker (IRE) (b 1998)	Sadler's Wells (b 1981)	Northern Dancer / Fairy Bridge
		Animatrice (b 1985)	Alleged / Alexandrie
	La Bole Night (FR) (gr 1999)	April Night (gr 1986)	Kaldoun / My Destiny
		Grageline (b 1994)	Hellios / Rousseliere

The tall Bristol de Mai has been a grand servant to his owners who had another good year, finishing runner-up to J.P. McManus in the owners' table in Britain where forty horses ran in their colours, winning thirty-one races and £975,622 in first-

Mr Simon Munir & Mr Isaac Souede's "Bristol de Mai"

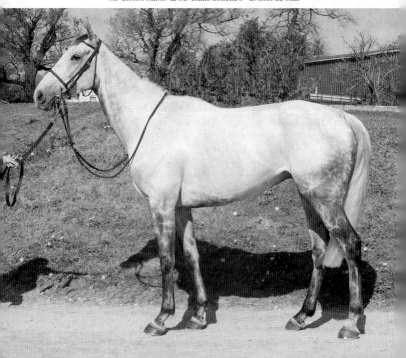

three prize money. The pair have, in one way, turned out to be victims of their own success. The fact that their operation has grown 'faster than expected' was given as the main reason for the dispersal of the collection of broodmares that they had been gradually acquiring. The draft of twenty-one mares, many of whom had been successful in their colours, grossed a total of €1,287,500 at Deauville in December. Among the star names in the sale were the Topham Chase winner Ma Filleule and the Scilly Isles Chase winner Gitane du Berlais who each fetched €220,000, both in foal to Martaline. The dispersal of the mares apparently signals no more than an intention by Munir and Souede to focus on their racing interests which have been the principal passion for them over the years. Nonetheless, with Gigginstown winding down and signs that some of jumping's other major owners are trimming their numbers, these are potentially worrying times for the sport.

To return to Bristol de Mai, his pedigree was covered in full detail in last year's Annual. His French sire Saddler Maker died in May 2016, his death, as so often, signalling a significant upturn in his reputation. His daughter Apple's Jade (who carries the Gigginstown colours) has continued to advertise the ability of her sire, as have Bristol de Mai and others, but his popularity had been growing at the time of his demise after the success at stud of his close relative Poliglote who had enjoyed a spell as champion sire of jumpers in France. The number of foals resulting from mares visiting Saddler Maker in his early years at stud could have been counted on the fingers of one hand, but the year he died (breaking a leg at exercise) he covered nearly one hundred and fifty mares. Like Bristol de Mai, most of Saddler Maker's progeny are AQPS (other than thoroughbred), and Bristol de Mai's selle francais dam La Bole Night showing nothing in three starts, but she has bred three winners, the others being Riva (by Winning Smile) and Ula de Mai (by Passing Sale), successful at a mile and a half and an extended mile and three quarters respectively. April Night, the sire of La Bole Night, is also the sire of the dam of both Clan des Obeaux and the redoubtable Un de Sceaux, among others. Bristol de Mai, who stays three and a quarter miles and acts on heavy going, has a justified reputation for performing particularly well after a break, which augurs well if his connections aim him at the Betfair Chase again on his reappearance. If he were to be successful, he would become the first horse to win three successive editions of that race (Kauto Star's four victories were achieved over a six-year period in which he also unseated his rider in the race, while Cue Card's winning sequence of three was interrupted by a below-par fourth behind Silviniaco Conti, the other horse who has won the Betfair more than once). Bristol de Mai wore ear plugs in the latest King George VI Chase and Cheltenham Gold Cup, as he had also done when winning the Charlie Hall Chase and the Betfair Chase the previous season. *Nigel Twiston-Davies*

BRITANIO BELLO (FR) 8 b.g. Irish Wells (FR) – Tchi Tchi Bang Bang (FR) (Perrault) [2018/19 c–, h–: c21.6s^{pu} c19.7m^5 c20s^5 c17s^4 Feb 13] tall, angular gelding: has had breathing operation: winning hurdler: poor maiden chaser: unproven beyond 2m: acts on heavy going: usually races freely, tends to find little. *Gary Moore*

c63
h–

BROADCLYST (IRE) 7 b.g. Ask – Broadcast (Broadsword (USA)) [2018/19 h23.8d^3 h23.1s h23.1s c23.6d^2 Apr 6] half-brother to fairly useful hurdler/chaser Kilronan High (19f-21f winner, by Mountain High), stayed 3m, and fair hurdler/fairly useful chaser Greyed A (19f-3¼m winner, by Daylami): dam (c65) temperamental maiden chaser: multiple point winner: fair form over hurdles: 33/1, did better when second in novice handicap at Chepstow (4½ lengths behind Pop Rockstar) on chasing debut. *Chris Down*

c115
h104

BROADWAY BELLE 9 b.m. Lucarno (USA) – Theatre Belle (King's Theatre (IRE)) [2018/19 h85: h23.3g^3 h23.3g* h27g^4 h24.6v h23.3v h27d^6 h27s^5 h23.3v^4 h27g Apr 5] poor handicap hurdler: won at Hexham (amateurs) in June: stays 27f: acts on good to firm and heavy going. *Chris Grant*

h84

BROADWAY DREAMS 5 b.g. Oasis Dream – Rosa Eglanteria (Nayef (USA)) [2018/19 h61: h18.7g^{pu} Oct 20] fair maiden on Flat, stays 1½m: little impact over hurdles. *Michael Blake*

h–

BROKE AWAY (IRE) 7 br.m. Stowaway – Not Broke Yet (IRE) (Broken Hearted) [2018/19 b81: h16.5g h16.5s h15.3g h15.3g^6 h19s h16.5d^3 Apr 24] poor form over hurdles: tried in hood. *Alexandra Dunn*

h76

BROMANCE 6 b.g. Showcasing – Romantic Destiny (Dubai Destination (USA)) **h97**
[2018/19 h16.7m³ Aug 5] modest on Flat, stays 12.5f: 28/1, third in maiden at Market
Rasen (6¼ lengths behind Fields of Fortune) on hurdling debut. *Peter Niven*

BRONCO BILLY (IRE) 9 b.g. Flemensfirth (USA) – La Fisarmonica (IRE) (Accordion) **c–**
[2018/19 c110, h–: c24.1gᵖᵘ Jun 5] well-made gelding: winning hurdler: fair chaser, badly **h–**
hampered sole outing in 2018/19: stays 25f: acts on heavy going: wears cheekpieces/
tongue tie: temperament under suspicion. *Jonjo O'Neill*

BRONZALLURE (IRE) 6 b.g. Dubai Destination (USA) – Satco Street (IRE) (Satco **h56 §**
(FR)) [2018/19 h72, b74: h25m h21.7g⁶ Oct 16] poor maiden hurdler: should be suited by
further stays than 17f: acts on soft and good to firm going: in headgear last 3 starts: wears tongue
tie: temperamental. *Oliver Greenall*

BROOKEVALE (IRE) 5 br.g. Kalanisi (IRE) – Railway House (IRE) (Ashkalani (IRE)) **b–**
[2018/19 b16.7v b16.6g⁵ Feb 20] beaten when fell in Irish point on debut: little impact in
bumpers. *Nigel Twiston-Davies*

BROOMEY ROAD 7 b.g. Bahri (USA) – Devinius (IRE) (Choisir (AUS)) [2018/19 **h–**
b16.2m b16.8m h16.2g⁶ h16.4g Nov 16] no form in bumpers/over hurdles: in hood last 2 **b–**
starts. *Harriet Graham*

BROOM TIP (IRE) 7 b.g. Flemensfirth (USA) – Norabelle (FR) (Alamo Bay (USA)) **c100**
[2018/19 c110, h107: c19.4d⁵ c24g⁴ Jun 14] fair form over hurdles: similar form over **h–**
fences: may prove best at short of 3m: acts on soft going: tried in tongue tie. *Tom George*

BROPHIES DOLL (IRE) 7 ch.m. Gamut (IRE) – Crossbar Lady (IRE) (Flemensfirth **h69 §**
(USA)) [2018/19 h21s⁶ h15.8dʳʳ Feb 20] fourth foal: half-sister to fairly useful hurdler/
chaser Storm of Swords (2m-2½m winner) and fair 2m hurdler Wild Fern (both by
Beneficial): dam unraced: Irish point winner: well beaten in bumper for James Albert
Jenkins in 2016/17 (wore hood): poor form completed start over hurdles, refused to race
other one. *Robert Stephens*

BROTHER BENNETT (FR) 9 gr.g. Martaline – La Gaminerie (FR) (Cadoudal (FR)) **c80 §**
[2018/19 c80§, h79: c17mᵖᵘ h16.3g⁵ h17.7g² h15.9s c19.7s⁴ c20s⁵ c17s³ c16.1d³ c16.5g³ **h75 §**
c17g* c17g² Apr 22] well-made gelding: has had breathing operation: poor maiden hurdler:
poor handicap chaser: won at Plumpton in April: stays 2¼m: acts on heavy going: wears
headgear/tongue tie: usually races off pace: temperamental. *Zoe Davison*

BROTHER SCOTT 12 b.g. Kirkwall – Crimson Shower (Dowsing (USA)) [2018/19 **c87**
c97, h–: c15.6g c15.6g c21.2m⁶ c21.6m³ Sep 19] smallish gelding: has had breathing **h–**
operation: winning hurdler: modest handicap chaser: stays 23f: acts on good to firm and
heavy going: usually races close up. *Barbara Butterworth*

BROTHER TEDD 10 gr.g. Kayf Tara – Neltina (Neltino) [2018/19 h136, h–: c20d² **c128**
c20.5s³ Mar 16] well-made gelding: winning hurdler: useful handicap chaser, lightly raced **h–**
in recent seasons: stays 2¾m: acts on good to firm and heavy going. *Philip Hobbs*

BROUGHTONS ADMIRAL 5 b.g. Born To Sea (IRE) – Chanter (Lomitas) [2018/19 **h120**
h113: h16g⁵ h21.2d h18.5s² h17g² h19.4d* h24g² Apr 17] neat gelding: fairly useful
handicap hurdler: won at Doncaster in March: second at Cheltenham in April: stays 3m:
acts on soft going: has worn headgear, including last 5 starts. *Alastair Ralph*

BROUGHTONS BANDIT 12 b.g. Kyllachy – Broughton Bounty (Bahamian Bounty) **c–**
[2018/19 c26gᵖᵘ c26m⁵ c19.7g⁴ c21.6dᵖᵘ Nov 18] winning hurdler: fairly useful chaser at **h–**
best, no form in 2018/19: tried in headgear: has worn tongue tie, including final start.
Phil York

BROUGHTONS RHYTHM 10 b.g. Araafa (IRE) – Broughton Singer (IRE) (Common **c107 §**
Grounds) [2018/19 c108, h107: c16sᵘʳ c17.4v⁴ c16.1d² c16.5d⁶ c15.7s² Mar 18] lengthy **h–**
gelding: winning hurdler: fair maiden chaser: unproven beyond 2m: acts on heavy going:
tried in hood: temperamental. *Oliver Sherwood*

BROWN BEAR (IRE) 8 b.g. Yeats (IRE) – Moray Firth (UAE) (Halling (USA)) **c100**
[2018/19 c104, h111: h21g⁶ c21.6g³ h25.8gᵖᵘ c21.6sᵖᵘ h23.4g³ h23.6g Apr 11] **h96**
useful-looking gelding: fair handicap hurdler/chaser: stays 2¾m: acts on good to firm and
good to soft going: has worn cheekpieces, including in 2018/19: usually races off pace.
Nick Gifford

BROWNDODD (IRE) 5 gr.g. Arcadio (GER) – Lady Greydoun (IRE) (Great Palm **c98**
(USA)) [2018/19 b16.3g⁶ h22.8v⁴ h23.1v h24.6g³ c15.9f⁵ c23.6g³ c23.8sᵖᵘ Apr 7] strong **h96**
gelding: unplaced in bumper : modest form over hurdles/fences: stayed 3m: acted on heavy **b–**
going: dead. *Nigel Twiston-Davies*

BROWN REVEL 10 b.m. Revoque (IRE) – Brown Seal (Arctic Lord) [2018/19 c–, h–: c24g^{pu} c20g c23g^{pu} c22.6g^{pu} c22.5g^{pu} Oct 7] winning pointer: little form under Rules: wears tongue tie. *Steve Flook* **c–**
h–

BRUMMIE BOYS (IRE) 4 b.g. Flemensfirth (USA) – Bobs Article (IRE) (Definite Article) [2018/19 b15.3g^3 Apr 14] €38,000 3-y-o: useful-looking gelding: sixth foal: half-brother to fairly useful but temperamental hurdler Towering (2m-23f winner, by Catcher In The Rye) and bumper winner/fairly useful hurdler Definitelyanoscar (2m winner, by Oscar): dam unraced sister to smart 2m hurdle winner Staying Article and half-sister to fairly useful hurdler/smart chaser (stayed 3m) Nunsback: 14/1, third in bumper at Wincanton (10 lengths behind Eritage): should do better. *Oliver Sherwood* **b80 p**

BRUNEL WOODS (IRE) 7 b.g. Oscar (IRE) – Golden Bay (Karinga Bay) [2018/19 h85p: h15.8d h15.5g h15.3g h19.7g^4 h19.6g^4 Apr 13] modest form over hurdles: stays 2½m: in tongue tie last 3 starts. *David Dennis* **h89**

BRYDEN BOY (IRE) 9 b.g. Craigsteel – Cailin Vic Mo Cri (IRE) (Old Vic) [2018/19 h126: h23.1g h23.3d h23.3v^2 h21.4s^6 h23.3d h24.1d^6 h23d^5 Apr 26] workmanlike gelding: fairly useful handicap hurdler: second at Uttoxeter in December: stays 3¼m: acts on heavy going: has worn cheekpieces, including in 2018/19: tried in tongue tie. *Jennie Candlish* **h119**

BRYNMAWR 9 b.g. Double Trigger (IRE) – Little Feat (Terimon) [2018/19 h120: c24.4g^F c23.6s^6 c24v^4 c22.4d^3 c24v^{pu} Mar 16] tall gelding: fairly useful hurdler: similar form over fences: third in novice handicap at Newbury in March: stays 2¾m: acts on heavy going: has worn cheekpieces, including last 4 starts: temperamental. *Colin Tizzard* **c116 §**
h–

BUACHAILL ALAINN (IRE) 12 b.g. Oscar (IRE) – Bottle A Knock (IRE) (Le Moss) [2018/19 c123§, h–: c29.4g* c27.5g* Jun 9] good-topped gelding: has had breathing operation: winning hurdler: useful handicap chaser: won at Cartmel (veterans) in May and Stratford (by 7 lengths from Aubusson) in June: stays 29f: acts on good to firm and heavy going: wears headgear/tongue tie: lazy/moody. *Peter Bowen* **c134 §**
h–

BUACHAILL BEAG 8 gr.g. And Beyond (IRE) – Bon Enfant (IRE) (Roselier (FR)) [2018/19 h16.8d^2 h15.8g h16g^F h18.6g^5 h15.9s^4 h21d h16.2g^{pu} Apr 25] fair maiden hurdler: has worn hood: has worn tongue tie, including in 2018/19: free-going front runner: temperamental. *Mark Rimell* **h100 §**

BUBBLE O'CLOCK (IRE) 6 ch.g. Robin des Champs (FR) – Flaithiuil (IRE) (Presenting) [2018/19 b–: h21.6g^5 h16d h21.6m^2 h21.4f^3 Oct 28] workmanlike gelding: has had breathing operation: fair form over hurdles: in hood last 4 starts: tried in tongue tie: often races freely. *Paul Nicholls* **h101**

BUBBLES ARCADE 7 b.m. Arkadian Hero (USA) – Alwariah (Xaar) [2018/19 b77: h15.3m h15.3m May 15] maiden pointer: bumper winner: little form on Flat/over hurdles. *Keiran Burke* **h–**

BUBBLES OF GOLD (IRE) 6 b.g. Gold Well – Bubble Bann (IRE) (Hubbly Bubbly (USA)) [2018/19 b15.8s^6 h22d^2 h23.3d^3 h20.6g^2 h21g* Apr 10] €25,000 3-y-o, £60,000 5-y-o: well-made gelding: fifth foal: dam unraced half-sister to fair hurdler/useful chaser (2m/17f winner) Vintage Treasure: won Irish point on debut: sixth in conditionals/amateurs bumper at Ffos Las: fairly useful form over hurdles: won maiden at Warwick in April: in cheekpieces last 2 starts. *Olly Murphy* **h115**
b78

BUBLE (IRE) 10 b.g. Milan – Glorious Moments (IRE) (Moonax (IRE)) [2018/19 c–, h109: h20.5g^5 h20.5s^4 h25.5d* c26m Mar 29] workmanlike gelding: fair handicap hurdler: won at Hereford in March: no form in chases: stays 3¼m: acts on soft and good to firm going: has worn cheekpieces. *David Bridgwater* **c–**
h108

BUCANEROS (IRE) 6 b.g. Stowaway – Silk Style (Polish Precedent (USA)) [2018/19 h16.3d h19.6v^{pu} h15.8g^6 h20.6d^{pu} h23.1g^5 Mar 27] lengthy gelding: half-brother to fairly useful hurdler Cajun Fiddle (2m winner, by Robin des Champs), stayed 19f, and modest hurdler/chaser Maid of Silk (2m-21f winner, by Blueprint): dam (h86) maiden hurdler (raced at 2m), out of half-sister to high-class hurdler/smart chaser up to 2½m Squire Silk: modest form over hurdles: tried in cheekpieces/tongue tie: usually races towards rear. *Olly Murphy* **h97**

BUCK BRAVO (IRE) 7 b.g. Mahler – Damoiselle (Sir Harry Lewis (USA)) [2018/19 h70: c25.8m c23.8s^3 c24.2v^{pu} Mar 5] has had breathing operation: point winner: maiden hurdler: poor form in chases: stays 3m: acts on soft going: in cheekpieces last 3 starts: has worn tongue tie. *David Rees* **c80**
h–

BUCK DANCING (IRE) 10 b.g. King's Theatre (IRE) – Polly Anthus (Kahyasi) **c101** [2018/19 h17.1v c24.5s³ c25.2dᵘʳ Mar 6] point winner: maiden hurdler: fair maiden chaser: **h–** left Patrick G. Kelly after second start: stays 25f: acts on heavy going: tried in blinkers: has worn tongue tie, including last 3 starts. *Miss J. I. Bedi*

BUCKEYE SHAN (IRE) 9 b.g. Darsi (FR) – Ballybeg Shan (IRE) (Zagreb (USA)) **c–** [2018/19 h16.3g h20g⁴ h21.7g⁴ h16.8m h16s h19.7s h20.5gᶠ Apr 21] pulled up in point: **h75** modest maiden hurdler at best for Vincent Laurence Halley: fell only chase start: left Sheila Lewis after sixth start: stays 2½m: acts on good to firm going: has worn hood: front runner/ races prominently. *Peter Bowen*

BUCKHORN TIMOTHY 10 b.g. Tamure (IRE) – Waimea Bay (Karinga Bay) [2018/19 **c–** c–, h130: h23.9v* h23.1d h19.9vᵖᵘ Mar 16] useful handicap hurdler: won at Ffos Las (by 5 **h134** lengths from Quiz Master) in November: winning chaser: stays 3¼m: acts on heavy going: usually races prominently. *Colin Tizzard*

BUCKLED 9 b.g. Midnight Legend – Mulberry Wine (Benny The Dip (USA)) [2018/19 **c97** c–, h119: c20.1d⁶ h20.2g⁶ h23.9g h20.9g⁵ h25.8d³ c20.3g³ h23.8gᵖᵘ h23.8m² Feb **h104** 28] fair handicap hurdler: modest form over fences: stays 3¼m: acts on firm and good to soft going: has worn headgear, including in 2018/19. *Sandy Thomson*

BUCKLE STREET 6 br.g. Cacique (IRE) – Rose Row (Act One) [2018/19 h130: **h122 §** h19.9gᵗᵗ h25g⁵ h22g⁴ h24.7g⁶ h23.9gᵗᵗ h23.6sᵗᵗ Dec 27] compact gelding: fairly useful handicap hurdler: stays 25f: acts on soft going: usually wears headgear: has worn tongue tie, including in 2018/19: one to avoid (refused to race 3 times in 2018/19). *Martin Keighley*

BUCK'S BEAUTIFUL (FR) 5 ch.m. Maresca Sorrento (FR) – Buck's Beauty (FR) – **b–** (Lyphard's Wish (FR)) [2018/19 b17.7g Feb 25] €12,000 3-y-o: seventh foal: half-sister to fair hurdler/fairly useful chaser Buck's Bond (3m-3¼m winner, by Turgeon) and French 21f chase winner Buck's Broker (by Nickname): dam, French 17f hurdle winner (also 1¼m winner on Flat), half-sister to Big Buck's: 50/1, behind in mares bumper at Plumpton. *Richard Bandey*

BUCK'S BIN'S (FR) 5 b.g. Khalkevi (IRE) – Buck's Bravo (FR) (Kapgarde (FR)) **h103 p** [2018/19 b14g³ h15.8g² Feb 28] €36,000 3-y-o, £60,000 4-y-o: first foal: dam, lightly raced **b82** over hurdles in France, out of half-sister to Big Buck's: Irish point winner: third in bumper at Ludlow (15 lengths behind Getariver): 6/1, second in novice at same course (10 lengths behind Snapdragon Fire) on hurdling debut: wears tongue tie: should improve. *Tom George*

BUDARRI 6 b.g. Supreme Sound – Amtaar (Nayef (USA)) [2018/19 h96: h16.2g² h20.2g² **c105** h20d h16.8g³ c15.6s³ h22.7g c19.2g² c16.3g³ c16.3s* c15.9g* c17.1g² c16.5m³ Apr 12] **h96** quite good-topped gelding: modest maiden hurdler: fair handicap chaser: won at Newcastle in January and Carlisle in February: stays 2½m: acts on good to firm and heavy going: wears headgear: usually front runner/races prominently. *Stuart Coltherd*

BUDDHA SCHEME (IRE) 5 b.g. Milan – Benefit Scheme (IRE) (Beneficial) [2018/19 **h85** b16d⁴ h22.8v⁵ h20.5s Jan 2] €40,000 3-y-o: first foal: dam fair 2m hurdle winner (stayed **b81** 3m): third in Irish point: fourth in bumper at Ayr (13¾ lengths behind Ribble Valley): modest form over hurdles: better effort when fifth in maiden at Haydock: wears tongue tie. *Lucinda Russell*

BUDDING ROBIN (IRE) 6 b.g. Robin des Pres (FR) – Another Vodka (IRE) (Moscow **h–** Society (USA)) [2018/19 b15.7g⁵ h20.8g Nov 30] fifth in bumper at Towcester (7 lengths **b80** behind Shaughnessy): well beaten in novice on hurdling debut. *Graeme McPherson*

BUDDY LIGHTNING 5 b.g. Multiplex – Love The Hat (Overbury (IRE)) [2018/19 **h–** b16.5g b16.5g h23g h16.2g⁵ h20gᵖᵘ Oct 24] no form in bumpers/over hurdles: left R. H. **b–** Lalor after second start. *Sheila Lewis*

BUFFALO BALLET 13 b.g. Kayf Tara – Minora (IRE) (Cataldi) [2018/19 c108, h–: **c99** c24.1s c24.1s³ c22.9dᵖᵘ Mar 20] has had breathing operation: winning hurdler: fair maiden **h–** chaser: stays 3¼m: best form on soft/heavy going: often in cheekpieces. *N. W. Alexander*

BUGSIE MALONE (IRE) 9 b.g. Mahler – The Irish Whip (Presenting) [2018/19 c118, **c118** h116: c24g* c26.1m h23g² h23g* h21.7g² h25g² h25.8m* h25m³ Oct 22] big gelding: **h121 §** fairly useful hurdler: won novice at Worcester in August and handicap at Fontwell in October: fairly useful handicap chaser: won at Kempton in May: thorough stayer: acts on soft and good to firm going: wears headgear: front runner: temperamental. *Chris Gordon*

BUILDING FUTURES (IRE) 6 b.g. Kalanisi (IRE) – Lady of The Mill (IRE) (Woods **h87** of Windsor (USA)) [2018/19 b–: h16v h19.6g⁴ h21d Dec 13] lengthy gelding: unplaced in bumpers: modest form over hurdles. *Jeremy Scott*

BUILDMEUPBUTTERCUP 5 ch.m. Sixties Icon – Eastern Paramour (IRE) (Kris Kin (USA)) [2018/19 b100: h16d* h16d⁵ h16.8d h20g Apr 21] workmanlike mare: dual bumper winner: fairly useful form over hurdles: won maiden at Navan in December: tried in hood. *W. P. Mullins, Ireland* **h123**

BULFIN ISLAND (IRE) 10 b.g. Milan – Tournore Court (IRE) (Insan (USA)) [2018/19 h–: h19gᶠ Feb 19] well-made gelding: Irish point winner: maiden hurdler, fell early sole outing in 2018/19: stays 3m: acts on soft going. *Kevin Bishop* **h–**

BULKOV (FR) 7 b.g. Zambezi Sun – Say Say (FR) (Garde Royale) [2018/19 c–, h129: c15.9d c16.4s⁶ c15.6v² c16.4s³ c21.1sᵖᵘ Mar 3] tall gelding: fairly useful hurdler/maiden chaser: raced mainly around 2m: acted on heavy going: in cheekpieces last 3 starts: dead. *Micky Hammond* **c121 h–**

BULLETPROOF (IRE) 13 b.g. Wareed (IRE) – Laura's Native (IRE) (Be My Native (USA)) [2018/19 c–, h100§: h16.8g h17.7g³ h18.5g h16.5dᵖᵘ Apr 24] poor handicap hurdler nowadays: once-raced chaser: stays 2¼m: acts on good to firm and good to soft going: wears headgear: has worn tongue tie: races off pace: unreliable. *Ken Cunningham-Brown* **c– h83 §**

BULLFROG (IRE) 6 b.m. Jeremy (USA) – Tramp Stamp (IRE) (King's Theatre (IRE)) [2018/19 b82: h16s³ h17.7v² Feb 14] rangy mare: bumper winner: fair form over hurdles: better effort when second in mares novice at Fontwell: open to further improvement. *Gary Moore* **h109 p**

BULLION (FR) 6 ch.g. Full of Gold (FR) – Ryde (FR) (Sillery (USA)) [2018/19 b83: h16.2g⁶ h16.2g⁵ h16.2g h20.9g⁶ h20.6d Apr 6] has had breathing operation: placed in bumper: poor form over hurdles: has worn hood. *James Ewart* **h83**

BULLS HEAD (IRE) 7 b.g. Darsi (FR) – Mrs Jenks (Gunner B) [2018/19 h108: h24.7g c20gᶠ c19.3sᵖᵘ c21.5dᵖᵘ Jan 20] third on completed start in points: fair hurdler at best, no form in 2018/19 (including in chases): usually races nearer last than first. *Martin Todhunter* **c– h–**

BUMBLE BAY 9 b.g. Trade Fair – Amica (Averti (IRE)) [2018/19 h–: h18.5m h16.7g⁶ h15.8g⁴ h15.8g² h15.8g⁵ Nov 2] sturdy gelding: poor handicap hurdler: raced mainly around 2m: acts on soft going: has worn headgear, including last 5 starts: wears tongue tie. *Robert Stephens* **h76**

BUNCH OF THYME (IRE) 4 b.g. Elzaam (AUS) – Goodie Goodie (Shirocco (GER)) [2018/19 h15.3f³ h15.8g⁵ h16.8s h17.7v⁶ Dec 11] little show on Flat: modest form over hurdles: tried in cheekpieces. *Bill Turner* **h89**

BUN DORAN (IRE) 8 b.g. Shantou (USA) – Village Queen (IRE) (King's Theatre (IRE)) [2018/19 c140, h–: c15.9g* c16.3d² c16.3d² Mar 15] useful-looking gelding: winning hurdler: smart handicap chaser: won at Cheltenham (by 8 lengths from Movie Legend) in November: second in Grand Annual there (1½ lengths behind Croco Bay) in March: effective from 2m-2½m: acts on heavy going: tried in tongue tie: often travels strongly. *Tom George* **c151 h–**

BUONAROTTI BOY (IRE) 7 b.g. Galileo (IRE) – Funsie (FR) (Saumarez) [2018/19 h107: h16.7g⁶ May 19] fair handicap hurdler: barely stays 2½m: acts on soft and good to firm going: wears headgear. *Sophie Leech* **h97**

BURBANK (IRE) 7 b.g. Yeats (IRE) – Spring Swoon (FR) (Highest Honor (FR)) [2018/19 c–p, h139: c15.9m² h21s h24.7g⁴ Apr 6] tall gelding: has had breathing operation: useful handicap hurdler: fourth at Aintree (13 lengths behind Aux Ptits Soins) in April: fairly useful form over fences: second in novice at Leicester on return: stays 21f: acts on heavy going: usually in headgear. *Nicky Henderson* **c117 h130**

BURDIGALA (FR) 6 b.g. Way of Light (USA) – Tiara (Risk Me (FR)) [2018/19 c18.9d* c19.9d c19.9g⁵ c18.9m² h21.3s Dec 8] maiden on Flat in France: fair maiden hurdler, laboured effort final outing in 2018/19: fair chaser: won minor event at Nancy in June: left G. Taupin after second start, S. Foucher after fourth: stays 19f: acts on soft and good to firm going: usually wears headgear. *Micky Hammond* **c108 h–**

BURGAS (FR) 8 b.g. Protektor (GER) – Tyrolienne Bleue (FR) (Sunshack) [2018/19 c19d² c20d⁵ c19.7s³ c21.5s³ Jan 26] winning hurdler: useful maiden chaser: placed 3 of 4 starts in 2018/19: stays 3m: acts on heavy going: has worn tongue tie, including last 2 starts: no battler. *Noel Meade, Ireland* **c132 § h–**

BURGESS DREAM (IRE) 10 b.g. Spadoun (FR) – Ennel Lady (IRE) (Erin's Hope) [2018/19 c80, h88: c25.7sᵖᵘ c23.5v* c26v* h23d c23.5vᵖᵘ Feb 18] tall, workmanlike gelding: poor handicap hurdler: poor handicap chaser: won at Lingfield and Fontwell in December: stays 3¼m: acts on heavy going: tried in cheekpieces. *Anna Newton-Smith* **c82 h70**

BURGESS VIEW (IRE) 9 b.g. Kayf Tara – Dahara (FR) (Take Risks (FR)) [2018/19 c–,   **c–**
h–: h23gᵖᵘ Sep 2] point winner: maiden hurdler: lightly-raced chaser: stays 3m: usually   **h–**
wears blinkers: has worn tongue tie. *Mike Hammond*

BURLINGTON BERT (FR) 8 b.g. Califet (FR) – Melhi Sun (FR) (Mansonnien (FR))   **h–**
[2018/19 h90: h20.2g⁵ Jul 31] tall, angular gelding: maiden hurdler, well held sole outing
in 2018/19: unproven beyond 17f: acts on soft and good to firm going: has worn tongue tie,
including last 3 starts. *Jean McGregor*

BURN BABY BYRNE 6 b.m. Malinas (GER) – Top of The Dee (Rakaposhi King)   **h120**
[2018/19 b15.8m³ h21.2g³ h21.2g⁴ h21.2g* h21.2d⁵ h19.5d² h21.2d³ h21.2d⁴ h21.2m*   **b87**
h18.9m Apr 20] £7,000 4-y-o: seventh foal: dam, winning pointer, half-sister to fairly
useful hurdler/chaser (stayed 21f) Senorita Rumbalita: Irish point winner: third in mares
bumper at Ludlow: fairly useful handicap hurdler: won at same course in November and
April (mares): will stay 3m: acts on good to firm and good to soft going: usually races in
rear. *Evan Williams*

BURNIEBOOZLE (IRE) 4 b.g. Frozen Power (IRE) – Tea Chest (IRE) (In The Wings)   **h–**
[2018/19 h16dᶠ Nov 28] modest maiden on Flat, stays 7f: fell fourth on hurdling debut.
John Quinn

BURNING AMBITION (IRE) 8 b.g. Scorpion (IRE) – Wyndham Miss Sally (IRE)   **c132**
(Flemensfirth (USA)) [2018/19 c132p: c19.6v* c21.1d² Apr 4] tall gelding: multiple point
winner: useful form in chases: won hunter at Down Royal in March: second in Foxhunters'
Chase at Aintree (2 lengths behind Top Wood) 3 weeks later: stays 25f: acts on heavy
going: strong traveller. *Pierce Michael Power, Ireland*

BURNING BRIGHT 6 gr.g. Fair Mix (IRE) – Cee Cee Rider (Classic Cliche (IRE))   **h–**
[2018/19 b–: h15.8g Nov 17] has had breathing operation: little show in bumper (wore
hood)/novice hurdle. *Ben Case*

BURNING ISSUES (IRE) 12 b.g. Gold Well – Jillie James (The Parson) [2018/19   **c94**
c19.2g c16g⁵ c20s⁶ c16d² c17g c18.2d c18g c18.5sᵖᵘ c21.3sᶠ c19.3g* Apr 23] winning   **h–**
hurdler: modest handicap chaser nowadays: won at Sedgefield in April: left P. J. Rothwell
after ninth start: stays 3¼m: acts on soft going: wears headgear: tried in tongue tie.
Joanne Foster

BURNING SANDS (IRE) 6 ch.g. Approve (IRE) – Innishmore (IRE) (Lear Fan (USA))   **c–**
[2018/19 b15.8g⁴ h18.5g⁵ h19.7g⁴ c19sᵖᵘ Dec 30] maiden pointer: well beaten in bumper/   **h–**
novice hurdles: pulled up in maiden on chasing debut: left Evan Williams after third start.   **b63**
Aytach Sadik

BURRENBRIDGE HOTEL (IRE) 8 b.g. Ivan Denisovich (IRE) – Hearthstead   **c117 §**
Dancer (USA) (Royal Academy (USA)) [2018/19 c122, h–: c16.5g⁴ c15.8g c17.4v³   **h–**
c17.2sᵖᵘ c20vᵖᵘ Jan 26] winning hurdler: fairly useful handicap chaser: unproven beyond
2m: acts on good to firm and heavy going: has worn headgear: moody. *Henry Oliver*

BURREN LIFE (IRE) 7 br.g. Pelder (IRE) – Burren Valley (IRE) (Phardante (FR))   **c133**
[2018/19 h131: c23g² c19d³ c20d⁴ c20d³ c19.7sᶠ Dec 27] point winner: useful hurdler: **h–**
similar form over fences: stayed 3m: acted on heavy going: retried in headgear last 2 starts:
dead. *Gordon Elliott, Ireland*

BURREN WALK 4 ch.f. Lucarno (USA) – Persian Walk (FR) (Persian Bold) [2018/19   **b83**
b16g³ Feb 22] £35,000 3-y-o: sister to 2 winners, including bumper winner/fairly useful
21f hurdle winner Persian Delight, and half-sister to several winners, including smart
hurdler/useful chaser Royal Shakespeare (2m-19f winner) and fair hurdler/fairly useful
chaser Safari Adventures (17f-2½m winner) (both by King's Theatre): dam French 1½m
winner: 6/1, third in mares bumper at Warwick (8 lengths behind Yeavering Belle).
Alan King

BURROWS EDGE (FR) 6 b.g. Martaline – La Vie de Boitron (FR) (Lavirco (GER))   **h130**
[2018/19 h126, b98: h21m² h21s³ Mar 16] good-topped gelding: will make a chaser:
placed both starts in Irish points: useful handicap hurdler: second at Kempton (neck behind
Erick Le Rouge) in February: will be suited by 3m: acts on good to firm and heavy going:
usually races prominently. *Nicky Henderson*

BURROWS LANE (FR) 8 b.g. Astarabad (USA) – Condoleezza (FR) (Mansonnien   **c87**
(FR)) [2018/19 h114: h21gᶠ h20g⁴ c22.6m³ c23g h23d⁶ Aug 29] lengthy gelding: fair   **h102**
handicap hurdler: modest form over fences: stays 3m: acts on good to firm and good to soft
going: wears cheekpieces/tongue tie: often flatters to deceive. *Charlie Longsdon*

BURROWS PARK (FR) 7 b.g. Astarabad (USA) – La Vie de Boitron (FR) (Lavirco **h132**
(GER)) [2018/19 h16.8s⁶ h21.2d* h19.9s* h19.9v² h24.3g³ h20.3d h25.8g* h24.7g Apr 6]
good-topped gelding: useful handicap hurdler: won at Ludlow (lady riders) and Uttoxeter
in December, and Kelso (by 3¼ lengths from Captain Drake) in March: stays 3¼m: acts on
heavy going. *Venetia Williams*

BURROWS SAINT (FR) 6 b.g. Saint des Saints (FR) – La Bombonera (FR) **c154 p**
(Mansonnien (FR)) [2018/19 c–, h134: c20d⁴ c20s* c24.5g* c29d* Apr 22] **h–**
   'Willie wasn't around when the entries were being made for the Irish
National, so we put him in, even though he'd only won a beginners chase. The
horses with experience usually have too much weight in those big handicaps and
Burrows Saint was going to be an improving novice running in a handicap for the
first time and we knew he would jump and stay.' Ruby Walsh's reasoning behind the
entry for six-year-old Burrows Saint in Ireland's richest and most competitive jumps
race proved inspired and led to the horse's trainer Willie Mullins enjoying a long
overdue success in one of the few big steeplechases he had still to win.
   Burrows Saint's maiden chase win had come at Gowran in early-March on
just his second start over fences for the Closutton yard (he had run in two chases as
a three-year-old in France). Burrows Saint started at odds on in a field of fifteen,
having matched some useful hurdles form when fourth behind Duc des Genievres in
a similar event on his reappearance over the course and distance the previous month.
There was nothing of the calibre of Duc des Genievres (a stablemate of Burrows
Saint) in the line-up when Burrows Saint got off the mark over fences, overcoming
a couple of fairly serious errors before confirming his promise with a six and a half
length victory over Rathnure Rebel, the first two having the race to themselves from
three out. Like a lot of the Mullins chasers, Burrows Saint had been kicking his heels
for most of the winter because of the unseasonably dry conditions but he made up
for lost time in the spring and followed up his Gowran victory three weeks later in
the Hugh McMahon Memorial Novices' Chase at Limerick where he was stepped up
to three miles for the first time. Burrows Saint relished the extra distance, jumping
better and looming up early in the home straight before forging clear, after being
joined at the last by stablemate Robin des Foret, to win by four lengths, with Roaring
Bull half a length away in third. Burrows Saint was clearly progressing well and
shaped as if he might prove even better as his stamina was tested.
   After some talk initially that Burrows Saint might be aimed instead at the
Ryanair Gold Cup, the two and a half mile Grade 1 for novices at the Irish Grand
National meeting, he took up his entry on Easter Monday in the big race itself,
which is run over three miles five furlongs. The 7-lb penalty picked up for the win
at Limerick had ensured that Burrows Saint would get a place in the maximum
thirty-strong line-up for the Boylesports Irish Grand National, in which he carried
10-8. Novices have a good record in the race, as alluded to by Ruby Walsh when
explaining how Burrows Saint originally came to be entered. Since the start of the

*Boylesports Irish Grand National, Fairyhouse—perennial champion trainer Willie Mullins breaks
his Irish National duck in no uncertain terms as the novice Burrows Saint leads home a stable
1, 2, 3 from 2018 runner-up Isleofhopendreams and Acapella Bourgeois*

century, Commanche Court, Davids Lad, Numbersixvalverde, Butler's Cabin, Niche Market, Lion Na Bearnai (a ten-year-old 33/1-shot), Shutthefrontdoor, Thunder And Roses and Our Duke had all been novices when successful in the Irish Grand National. Burrows Saint, partnered by Ruby Walsh who had the choice of the seven Mullins-trained runners, started 6/1 favourite at Fairyhouse where there were other novices prominent in the betting, notably Any Second Now (winner of the Kim Muir at Cheltenham and attempting a double last achieved by Omerta in 1991), Gun Digger (who had been going well in the National Hunt Chase when falling) and Whisperinthebreeze (also a faller in the National Hunt Chase after winning a good edition of the Leopardstown Chase). Gun Digger and Roaring Bull, two of the dozen runners carrying the Gigginstown colours, were among twelve (nine for Gigginstown) saddled by Gordon Elliott who had won his first Irish Grand National the previous year.

The stables of Willie Mullins and Gordon Elliott dominate the domestic jumping scene in Ireland and there were the usual murmurings that the monopoly of the Irish National was unfair, with the two yards responsible for nearly two thirds of the field (thirty-two were eliminated from the race at the final declaration stage). Among the other Mullins-trained runners were Pairofbrowneyes, the previous year's runner-up Isleofhopendreams and Bellow Mome who had filled the first three places in the latest Leinster National. That race had also been won the year before by Pairofbrowneyes who had missed the Grand National at Aintree to wait for Fairyhouse. Another of the Mullins contingent, Acapella Bourgeois, had returned to winning ways at Clonmel the previous month. The previous year's Irish National winner General Principle was in the line-up again but he was among a number who had run in the Grand National sixteen days earlier. Six of the Elliott contingent had been among the eleven from that stable that had contested the Aintree race which had been won again by the Elliott-trained Tiger Roll.

The same owner, trainer, jockey combination involved with the runner-up to Tiger Roll, the mare Magic of Light, also figured prominently for a long way at Fairyhouse, with Whisperinthebreeze taking over in front at around halfway and showing clear for a time. Whisperinthebreeze eventually paid the price and Burrows Saint, who was always travelling well, reeled him in on the home turn. Willie Mullins will have known the race was in the bag at the second last where Isleofhopendreams and Acapella Bourgeois were the only dangers to Burrows Saint who stayed on strongly to beat his stablemates by a length and three quarters and five and a half lengths, with Bellow Mome taking fifth place for good measure, passed only in the closing stages by the keeping-on Snugsborough Benny, who finished twenty-one lengths behind the third in an attritional race in which there were twelve finishers. The first of the Gigginstown runners to finish, Roaring Bull, fared best of the Elliott team, finishing sixth after being in contention briefly four out. Whisperinthebreeze eventually weakened into ninth, shaping much better than the bare result, while Pairofbrowneyes and Any Second Now were early fallers and Gun Digger was among those pulled up, as were the only two British-trained challengers Minella Rocco and Kimberlite Candy. Just a month after he had broken another so-called 'hoodoo' when sending out his first winner of the Cheltenham Gold Cup, Willie Mullins said that the victory of Burrows Saint meant just as much. 'The Irish National has been an unlucky race for us and it is nice to have finally cracked it. My father [Paddy] trained four winners of the race,' he said. It was the third Irish National win for Ruby Walsh who also rode Commanche Court and Numbersixvalverde.

Burrows Saint, who carried the colours of Mrs Susannah Ricci, went into the Irish National potentially unexposed—it was his first run in handicap company— and the evident feeling of his rider that he might prove to be the proverbial 'graded horse masquerading as a handicapper' was certainly borne out. For his much more experienced stablemate the ill-fated Isleofhopendreams (fatally injured in the Prix des Drags at Auteuil on his next start), it was the fourth time he had finished second in valuable handicap company (he had gone down in a photo in the previous year's Irish National and finished second in the Grand National Trial at Punchestown). The fact that the gallant Isleofhopendreams was thwarted at Fairyhouse by a stablemate who had been hard for the handicapper to assess led to a suggestion that novices should be barred from the major heritage handicaps. Novices also have a good record in the Scottish Grand National, for example, but such races are designed to be open to all-comers and good novices add to the quality of the fields, as well as adding to the interest, if not intrigue, for racegoers and punters.

Like Isleofhopendreams, Burrows Saint appeared again after the Irish Grand National, in a five-strong Willie Mullins challenge for France's top steeplechase, the Grand Steeple-Chase de Paris at Auteuil in May. He lacked the chasing experience of his older stable companions, the Grand National third Rathvinden, the very smart Pleasant Company (yet to be asked for an effort when unseating his jockey four out at Aintree), and Acapella Bourgeois and Total Recall (the last-named pulled up in the Irish National). However, Burrows Saint belied his inexperience by coming out best of the Mullins quintet, finishing a creditable fifth to the Davy Russell-ridden Carriacou who had himself finished third in the race as a five-year-old before being forced into a lengthy spell on the sidelines with injury. Burrows Saint jumped like an old hand at Auteuil and disputed the lead for a while before losing touch with the leaders from the second last. He should continue to progress and could well be aimed at the Grand National in the next season, his now-retired jockey urging the trainer to 'run him over hurdles now [to protect his handicap mark] and have a go at Tiger Roll!' Burrows Saint will be just seven when the next Grand National comes round and he is young enough to develop into a top-class performer over fences, perhaps even a Cheltenham Gold Cup contender (a future attempt to win a Grand Steeple-Chase de Paris also looks very much on the cards if all remains well with him).

Mrs S. Ricci's "Burrows Saint"

	Saint des Saints (FR) (b 1998)	Cadoudal (br 1979)	Green Dancer Come To Sea
Burrows Saint (FR) (b.g. 2013)		Chamisene (b 1980)	Pharly Tuneria
	La Bombonera (FR) (b or br 2006)	Mansonnien (ch 1984)	Tip Moss Association
		Bab Khaldoun (b 1998)	Kaldoun Brune Babe

Burrows Saint, whose useful efforts over hurdles included a third in the Champion Novices' Hurdle at Punchestown, always looked as if he would make a good chaser (he finished second to the very smart filly Dalia Grandchamp, a runner in the latest Grand Steeple-Chase on the second of his starts over fences before leaving Guillaume Macaire, for whom he had also run several times over hurdles). Burrows Saint is by the sire of the same connections' Djakadam who finished in the frame in the Cheltenham Gold Cup on three occasions for the Riccis before damaging a hock in the Grand Steeple-Chase de Paris which forced his retirement at the age of nine (he was also runner-up in four editions of the Punchestown Gold Cup). Saint des Saints was the leading juvenile hurdler of his year in France and also won his only completed start over fences. Burrows Saint's dam La Bombonera was a useful winner at two and a quarter miles over hurdles in France (no form in two races over hurdles in Britain for Venetia Williams) and also showed useful form over fences. Burrows Saint is her second foal and only winner so far, her third foal Bonbonniere (by Martaline) showing little over hurdles, including in handicaps, for Dan Skelton in the latest season. La Bombonera's fourth produce, a three-year-old filly by Martaline, made €45,000 at the latest Goffs Land Rover Sale and is to be trained by Oliver Sherwood. There is also a two-year-old filly by Montmartre and a yearling brother to Burrows Saint. The best performer in the immediate family before Burrows Saint came along was his dam's brother Lagunak who was a very smart staying chaser, winner of the Prix La Haye Jousselin, the most important steeplechase of the autumn in France. The genuine Burrows Saint stays twenty-nine furlongs and acts on soft going. He wears a tongue tie. *W. P. Mullins, Ireland*

BURST YA BUBBLE (IRE) 7 b.g. Spadoun (FR) – Accordian Lady (IRE) (Accordion) [2018/19 h115: h19.9g³ h20m⁶ c24g^ur Oct 25] rangy gelding: fairly useful handicap hurdler: held when unseated rider 3 out in novice handicap won by Rhaegar at Southwell on chasing debut: stays 2¾m: acts on good to firm and good to soft going: usually races nearer last than first. *Seamus Mullins*   **c99 h115**

BUSHMILL BOY 5 b.g. Malinas (GER) – Miss Holly (Makbul) [2018/19 b16s Jan 2] 7/2, seventh in bumper at Ayr (5½ lengths behind Curramore). *Donald Whillans*   **b80**

BUSTER EDWARDS (IRE) 6 b.g. Kalanisi (IRE) – Hot Oscar (IRE) (Oscar (IRE)) [2018/19 h104p: h23.1s h23.6d⁵ h21.3g⁴ Apr 11] placed in Irish point: fair form over hurdles: should stay 3m+. *David Pipe*   **h102**

BUSTER MOON (IRE) 7 b.g. Darsi (FR) – Orinocco Blue (IRE) (Pistolet Bleu (IRE)) [2018/19 h106: h18.5d⁶ h26.5g^pu Apr 20] unplaced on completed start in Irish points: fair form over hurdles in 2017/18, below that level both starts since. *Jeremy Scott*   **h90**

BUSTER THOMAS (IRE) 8 b.g. Westerner – Awesome Miracle (IRE) (Supreme Leader) [2018/19 c121, h–: c24g³ c21.4g⁵ c20.2g² c19.1g* Nov 30] winning hurdler: fairly useful handicap chaser: won at Doncaster in November: stays 3m: acts on heavy going: tried in tongue tie: usually races close up. *Emma Lavelle*   **c126 h–**

BUSTER VALENTINE (IRE) 6 b.g. Ask – Femme du Noir (IRE) (Supreme Leader) [2018/19 h16v* h20.6s* h20.3d² h20.5s^pu Mar 9] £100,000 5-y-o: tall gelding: first foal: dam (b86) made frame both starts in bumpers (one over 2½m): Irish point winner: fairly useful form over hurdles: won maiden at Ayr in November and novice at Newcastle in December: second in Classic Novices' Hurdle at Cheltenham (18 lengths behind Birchdale) in January: will stay beyond 21f. *Ruth Jefferson*   **h118**

BUSY LILLY 10 b.m. Bollin Eric – Princess Derry (Derrylin) [2018/19 h21s^pu h18.7g^pu Mar 30] of no account. *Charles Pogson*   **h–**

BUTLERGROVE KING (IRE) 10 b.g. King's Theatre (IRE) – Sanadja (IRE) (Slip Anchor) [2018/19 c101, h–: c21g⁴ c24g c24g² Apr 25] maiden hurdler: fair handicap chaser: left Dai Burchell after second start: stays 3m: acts on good to firm and heavy going: has worn cheekpieces/tongue tie, including in 2018/19. *Christian Williams*   **c97 h–**

BUVEUR D'AIR (FR) 8 b.g. Crillon (FR) – History (FR) (Alesso (USA)) [2018/19 **c–** c–, h167: h16.4d* h16g^2 h16s* h16.4s^F h20d^2 Apr 4] **h163**

There is often a very fine line between sporting success and failure. Champions are those who can tread closest to that line without going the wrong side of it. In tennis, it can be the difference between an ace and the serve going out. In motor racing, a split-second can be the difference between a race-winning overtaking manoeuvre or a race-ending crash. In jump racing, those margins are at their tightest in the top two-mile hurdles where quick but accurate jumping is key to success. In recent seasons, Buveur d'Air has been one of the finest exponents of getting from one side of a hurdle to the other. But at the third flight in the latest Champion Hurdle, his normally slick technique let him down and he paid the penalty. 'With his hurdling, there's such a fine margin, an inch every time, and you only have to get it wrong by half an inch,' said his trainer Nicky Henderson reflecting on his fall. 'If you're so slick and accurate, you're dangerously low, and the margin for error will always be there. He was an inch lower than he should have been I guess.'

Buveur d'Air's fall looked a heavy one but he was unscathed and soon on his feet, continuing riderless before accompanying winner Espoir d'Allen up the hill to the finish. Buveur d'Air's owner J. P. McManus had the consolation of winning the Champion Hurdle with his other runner, but the fall of his main contender cost Buveur d'Air much more than any chance he might have had of winning on the day. It also denied him the opportunity to join McManus's Istabraq, the Henderson-trained See You Then, and the earlier trio of Hatton's Grace, Sir Ken and Persian War, all triple winners of the Champion Hurdle. Five other dual winners of the Champion Hurdle have failed in their attempts to win it for a third year in succession. National Spirit came up against Hatton's Grace when fourth in 1949, Bula was odds on when only fifth to Comedy of Errors in 1973, Night Nurse came third to Monksfield in 1978, Monksfield was foiled in his own hat-trick bid only by Sea Pigeon in 1980, and Hardy Eustace was third to Brave Inca in 2006. All those bar Hardy Eustace had started favourite to win it for a third time.

The Champion Hurdle proved the low point of Buveur d'Air's season which had promised considerably more at the outset when he had looked as good as ever, at the very least. Before making his reappearance for the second season running in

BetVictor 'Fighting Fifth' Hurdle, Newcastle—a second successive win in the race for Buveur d'Air, who overcomes a final-flight blunder to thump young pretender Samcro

the 'Fighting Fifth' Hurdle at Newcastle at the beginning of December, Buveur d'Air was ante-post favourite to win the Champion Hurdle for a third time. Following the 'Fighting Fifth', he was a best-priced even money to complete the hat-trick after inflicting a surprisingly clear-cut defeat on the rival who began the season looking much his biggest threat on the Champion Hurdle scene. Despite a fall in the Punchestown Champion Hurdle on the final start of his otherwise faultless novice campaign, and then a shock defeat on his reappearance in a four-runner race at Down Royal when conceding weight to a race-fit rival, Samcro's stock was still as high as ever. So much so that Samcro marginally started favourite for the 'Fighting Fifth', at 6/5, with Buveur d'Air at 11/8. The five-runner field was completed by the Supreme Novices' winner Summerville Boy, another who began the season with Champion Hurdle aspirations, joined by another leading novice from the previous season Vision des Flos, who had been runner-up in Grade 1s at Aintree and Punchestown, and the 100/1 outsider Bleu Et Rouge—also carrying the McManus colours—who ended up sustaining a fatal injury in a fall four out. Having had a pre-season wind operation, Buveur d'Air landed his eleventh straight success in tremendously impressive style. Sauntering along behind Samcro, Buveur d'Air was still going strongly when taking over before the last, crashed through that flight without his momentum being halted, and then left Samcro for dead on the run-in, doubling his advantage in the last hundred yards to win by eight lengths without Barry Geraghty having to exert anything like full pressure.

Impressive though Buveur d'Air looked, subsequent events showed that the 'Fighting Fifth' form wasn't all it had seemed at the time. A third short-priced reverse for Samcro at Leopardstown just after Christmas effectively ended his season. Summerville Boy's second season over hurdles was equally one to forget, while Vision des Flos, third at Newcastle, finished well beaten at Cheltenham in the Coral Cup, albeit after winning the National Spirit at Fontwell. As for Buveur d'Air, a second Christmas Hurdle looked more or less a formality when he took on four rivals, including stable-companion Verdana Blue, at Kempton on Boxing Day. Again, Buveur d'Air wasn't foot perfect—he blundered three out—but his jumping wasn't to blame for his short-head defeat by Verdana Blue who had her ideal conditions and collared her stablemate on the line after stalking him for most of the way. It was another result which looks rather different now than it did at the time, the difference in ability between the pair in hindsight nowhere near so great as the betting suggested on the day, at least not under the sort of underfoot conditions which Verdana Blue clearly relishes, as she proved again when running away with the Scottish Champion Hurdle at Ayr on some of the firmest going encountered

Betdaq Punchestown Champion Hurdle, Punchestown—Davy Russell stands in for the injured Mark Walsh as Buveur d'Air regains the winning thread in a high-quality renewal

anywhere later in the season. Buveur d'Air's last defeat had also come at the hands of a stable companion when Altior beat him in the 2016 Supreme Novices'. Altior's own winning streak, now a record, remains intact. There were no upsets when Buveur d'Air met Vision des Flos again and beat him easily into second to win another Contenders Hurdle at Sandown in February, just as he had done prior to his two successful Champion Hurdle bids. However, Apple's Jade's impressive win in the Irish Champion Hurdle the same afternoon meant that it was her, rather than Buveur d'Air, who started favourite when he lined up for his hat-trick bid at Cheltenham.

The Champion Hurdle had been the final race of Buveur d'Air's previous campaign, with his trainer explaining before Cheltenham in the latest season that his neck win that day over Melon had taken a lot out of him. Henderson revealed that We Have A Dream in the next-door box to Buveur d'Air had a temperature at the time (he therefore missed the Triumph Hurdle but won at Aintree) and that Buveur d'Air was doubtless also under the weather, a factor which led Henderson to expect a better performance from Buveur d'Air in the latest Champion Hurdle, whilst acknowledging the field looked stronger. After his first Champion Hurdle victory, Buveur d'Air had easily followed up in the Aintree Hurdle. The same race was back on his agenda again in the latest season, and Buveur d'Air started odds-on to atone for his fall against the placed pair from the latest Champion Hurdle, Melon and Silver Streak. However, Buveur d'Air was beaten on merit, hampered by Melon's fall three out but held in the last fifty yards by the previous season's runner-up Supasundae who beat him by a length and a quarter. It would have been a tame way for the former champion to end his campaign but, far from being finished for the season, Buveur d'Air went into his summer break on the back of a win which looked as good a performance as any he has put up over the last two years.

In the Betdaq Punchestown Champion Hurdle, which took place shortly after the end of the British season, Buveur d'Air took on Apple's Jade, Supasundae and Melon again, with Wicklow Brave, Petit Mouchoir and Summerville Boy the three at longer odds. Back at two miles, Buveur d'Air started 2/1 joint favourite to turn the tables on 9/2 chance Supasundae whose win in the same race twelve months earlier had come in a dramatic renewal overshadowed by the falls of both Samcro and Melon. Apple's Jade was sent off the other joint favourite, also aiming to make up for disappointments at both Cheltenham and Aintree. Buveur d'Air might have lost his air of invincibility by the end of the latest season, but his smooth win under Davy Russell served as a reminder that he is still one of the best two-milers around. With Barry Geraghty having broken his leg in a fall later at the Grand National meeting, before his understudy Mark Walsh suffered a similar fate earlier on the Punchestown card, Russell took the ride on Buveur d'Air for the first time. Looming up to long-time leader Petit Mouchoir early in the straight with all the other riders hard at work, Russell asked Buveur d'Air to quicken clear going to the last before running out the two and a half length winner over the staying-on Supasundae. Wicklow Brave, runner-up twelve months earlier and the winner in 2017, was another length and a quarter back in third, ahead of Petit Mouchoir, a one-paced Apple's Jade, Summerville Boy and finally Melon, the last-named again well below the form that had seen him finish within a neck of Buveur d'Air at Cheltenham the previous spring.

Buveur d'Air (FR) (b.g. 2011)	Crillon (FR) (br 1996)	Saumarez (b or br 1987)	Rainbow Quest / Fiesta Fun
		Shangrila (b 1978)	Riverman / Garden Green
	History (FR) (b 1995)	Alesso (b or br 1983)	Alleged / Leandra
		Clair Deux Lune (ch 1990)	Altayan / Lili Dancer

The good-topped Buveur d'Air's AQPS pedigree was covered in his novice days in *Chasers & Hurdlers 2015/16* and there has been little to add since as his dam History has not produced any further foals. A reminder, though, that he is not the first top-class hurdler she has produced, or even the best strictly on Timeform ratings. Punchestowns won the 2008 Long Walk Hurdle for Nicky Henderson and

Mr John P. McManus' "Buveur d'Air"

was the only one to get anywhere near Big Buck's when he won the first of his four World Hurdles later that season. Punchestowns didn't reach the same heights over fences afterwards (he was rated 171 over hurdles), though his three wins in that sphere included the Scilly Isles Novices' Chase. Buveur d'Air gained his best annual rating over hurdles of 170 after his first win in the Champion Hurdle (he had begun the season by winning both his starts in novice chases), though his form as we saw it in the latest season fell short of that. In theory, it is not too late for Buveur d'Air to win a third Champion Hurdle (following the demise of Espoir d'Allen, he is around 7/1 second favourite behind Klassical Dream), but he would have to be back nearer his very best to do so, and only Comedy of Errors and Hurricane Fly have ever regained their Champion Hurdle crowns after losing them. Buveur d'Air stays two and a half miles, at least when conditions aren't testing, and he acts on heavy ground but doesn't need the mud. In line with the way he travels, he is a notably quick and, most of the time, accurate jumper. *Nicky Henderson*

BUYER BEWARE (IRE) 7 br.g. Big Bad Bob (IRE) – Adoring (IRE) (One Cool Cat (USA)) [2018/19 c–, h107: h20.3g⁴ c19.2g³ c15.7s⁴ c20.3g⁴ Jan 7] has had breathing operation: fair handicap hurdler at best: fair form over fences: left Lawrence Mullaney after first start: stays 2½m: acts on good to soft going: has worn hood: usually races close up. *Andrew Crook*   **c102 h92**

BUYWISE (IRE) 12 b.g. Tikkanen (USA) – Greenogue Princess (IRE) (Rainbows For Life (CAN)) [2018/19 c140, h–: c25g⁶ c25.6g⁴ h24g c24.2dᶠ h21.4gᵖᵘ h23.1dᵖᵘ Feb 22] lengthy gelding: useful hurdler at best: smart handicap chaser at one time: every chance when fell last in veterans event at Sandown in January, standout effort in 2018/19: stayed 25f: acted on good to firm and heavy going: tried in visor: usually raced towards rear: retired. *Evan Williams*   **c142 h–**

BUZZ DE TURCOING (FR) 5 b.g. Maresca Sorrento (FR) – Panora Night (FR) **h–**
(Panoramic) [2018/19 h20.3g⁶ Apr 17] fortunate winner of Irish point: in tongue strap,
100/1, well held in novice at Cheltenham on hurdling debut. *Samuel Drinkwater*

BYGONES FOR COINS (IRE) 11 ch.m. Danroad (AUS) – Reservation (IRE) **c–**
(Common Grounds) [2018/19 c–, h75: h19.5g 23.3g Sep 17] maiden hurdler, no form in **h–**
2018/19: once-raced chaser: stays 19f: acts on good to soft going: has worn cheekpieces:
wears tongue tie. *Kenny Johnson*

BY ORDER OF (IRE) 4 b.g. Shantou (USA) – Guydus (IRE) (Old Vic) [2018/19 h16.2g **h– p**
Mar 26] £40,000 3-y-o: second foal: half-brother to bumper winner/fairly useful hurdler
Dr Sanderson (2m-21f winner, by Jeremy): dam (c89/h98) ungenuine 2½m-3¼m hurdle/
chase winner: strong 3/1, well beaten in juvenile maiden hurdle at Hereford: clearly
thought capable of better. *Tom Lacey*

BY RAIL 5 br.g. Rail Link – Soldata (USA) (Maria's Mon (USA)) [2018/19 h–: h16.3m **c93**
h16g³ c16.5g² c16.2g² c17.4g⁴ c16.3d* c15.9m³ c16d⁵ Feb 20] poor form over hurdles: **h82**
modest form over fences: won handicap at Fakenham in December: raced around 2m: acts
on soft going: wears hood: usually leads. *Nick Littmoden*

BYRON BLUE (IRE) 10 br.g. Dylan Thomas (IRE) – High Society (IRE) (Key of Luck **h–**
(USA)) [2018/19 h107: h22mᶠ Jul 3] small gelding: fairly useful hurdler at best: stayed 3m:
acted on good to firm and good to soft going: hooded in 2016/17: wore tongue tie: usually
led: dead. *Brian Barr*

BYRONEGETONEFREE 8 b.g. Byron – Lefty's Dollbaby (USA) (Brocco (USA)) **h–**
[2018/19 h–: h17s⁴ h16.2g Apr 25] maiden hurdler: raced mainly at 2m: tried in headgear.
Stuart Coltherd

BYRON FLYER 8 b.g. Byron – Nursling (IRE) (Kahyasi) [2018/19 h20g⁶ Oct 28] **h120**
compact gelding: smart on Flat, stays 2m: useful handicap hurdler, excuses sole outing in
sphere in 2018/19: stays 21f: acts on heavy going. *Ian Williams*

BY THE BOARDWALK (IRE) 11 br.g. Presenting – Peripheral Vision (IRE) (Saddlers' **c109 §**
Hall (IRE)) [2018/19 c121, h–: c23.8g⁴ c24.5g⁵ c23.6g* Nov 13] strong gelding: has had **h–**
breathing operation: lightly-raced hurdler: fair handicap chaser nowadays: in cheekpieces,
won at Huntingdon in November: stays 3¼m: acts on good to firm and good to soft going:
usually wears tongue tie: unreliable. *Kim Bailey*

C

CABARET QUEEN 7 b.m. King's Theatre (IRE) – La Dame Brune (FR) (Mansonnien **c123**
(FR)) [2018/19 h108: h20g⁴ c24g* c23g* c21.6mᵖᵘ c33.8g⁵ c24gᵖᵘ c20d c26g⁴ Apr 18] **h105**
lengthy mare: has had breathing operation: fair hurdler: fairly useful handicap chaser: won
at Uttoxeter (novice) and Worcester in June: stays 3m: acts on good to soft going: wears
tongue tie: has been let down by jumping. *Dan Skelton*

CABERNET D'ALENE (FR) 7 b.g. Day Flight – Haifa du Noyer (FR) (Video Rock **h–**
(FR)) [2018/19 h117: h15.3m h15.5gᵘʳ h16sᵖᵘ h16m⁵ Apr 25] good-topped gelding: fairly
useful hurdler: well below form in 2018/19: left Nick Williams after second start: stays 19f:
acts on heavy and good to firm going: tried in cheekpieces. *Daniel O'Brien*

CABRAGH (IRE) 10 b.g. Old Vic – Satco Street (IRE) (Satco (FR)) [2018/19 c105, h–: **c105 §**
c24.2g⁵ c25.7s c25.3v⁶ c26d⁵ c24.2dᵘʳ c24.2d Mar 8] maiden hurdler: fair handicap **h–**
chaser: stays 3¼m: acts on soft going: wears headgear: tried in tongue tie: temperamental.
Charlie Mann

CADEAU DU BRESIL (FR) 7 b.g. Blue Bresil (FR) – Melanie du Chenet (FR) (Nikos) **c117**
[2018/19 c108, h–: c24.5g³ c25.7s⁴ c24d⁴ c25.5s c25.7s* c24s² c25.7g⁴ Apr 7] winning **h–**
hurdler: fairly useful handicap chaser: won at Plumpton in March and April: stays 3¼m:
acts on heavy going: has worn tongue tie: held up. *Grant Cann*

CADEAU GEORGE 10 b.g. Relief Pitcher – Sovereign's Gift (Elegant Monarch) [2018/19 **c– §**
c–§, h–: c23.4dᵖᵘ Mar 22] lengthy gelding: point winner: winning hurdler: useful chaser at **h–**
best: lightly raced and no form under Rules since 2016/17: stays 25f: acts on heavy going:
wears headgear: temperamental. *D. Gittins*

CADEAUX'S FIRE 6 ch.m. Major Cadeaux – Confetti (Groom Dancer (USA)) [2018/19 **h57**
h–, b–: h15.7g⁴ May 14] angular mare: has had breathing operation: well held in bumpers/
over hurdles: tried in tongue tie. *Charlie Longsdon*

CADELLIN 8 b.g. Black Sam Bellamy (IRE) – Clotted Cream (USA) (Eagle Eyed (USA))   **h81**
[2018/19 h98: h19.9v⁵ Mar 12] lightly-raced maiden hurdler: off 22 months before sole
outing in 2018/19: stays 21f: acts on good to firm and heavy going. *Donald McCain*

CADGERS HOLE 12 b.g. Helissio (FR) – Not So Prim (Primitive Rising (USA))   **h–**
[2018/19 h19.7g h19.9g⁴ Apr 5] poor maiden hurdler: best short of 3m: acts on good to soft
going: wears hood: has worn tongue tie. *Lynn Siddall*

CADMIUM (FR) 7 b.g. Early March – Mirquille (FR) (Passing Sale (FR)) [2018/19   **c157**
c148p, h–: c16g* c18.2d⁵ c16.5g² c18.6g* c16.2g³ c20g⁴ c21g⁴ c16g* c16s² c21.1d* Apr   **h–**
5] good-topped gelding: winning hurdler: very smart chaser: won novice at Roscommon in
June, Buck House Novices' Chase at Punchestown in October and Grade 3 event at Naas
(by 3 lengths from Doctor Phoenix) in February: well-backed 8/1, career-best effort when
also won 27-runner Topham Chase at Aintree final outing by 6 lengths from Sub Lieutenant,
jumping superbly and making most: stays 21f: acts on soft going: tried in cheekpieces:
often travels strongly: consistent. *W. P. Mullins, Ireland*

CADORE (IRE) 11 b.g. Hurricane Run (IRE) – Mansiya (Vettori (IRE)) [2018/19 h71:   **h57**
h20.2g h19.5v⁶ h20.6d⁵ h21.4d h19.8s Mar 10] leggy gelding: poor handicap hurdler: stays
easy 3m: acts on heavy going: wears headgear. *Lucy Normile*

CAFE AU LAIT (GER) 9 b.g. Nicaron (GER) – Cariera (GER) (Macanal (USA))   **c110 d**
[2018/19 h96: h20.6g³ c20.3g* h20.3g⁵ c20.9m* c19.2m⁴ h19d h19.5d⁵ c22.7m⁵ c19.2d³   **h93 d**
h19.2v⁴ Mar 6] sturdy gelding: modest handicap hurdler: fair form over fences: won novice
handicaps at Bangor in June and Ffos Las (left Dan Skelton after next outing) in July:
ended season out of sorts: stays 21f: acts on good to firm and heavy going: wears headgear/
tongue tie: normally waited with. *Milton Harris*

CAGE OF FEAR (IRE) 5 b.g. Milan – Baile An Droichid (IRE) (King's Ride) [2018/19   **b91**
b15.8s⁶ b16.2d³ Apr 26] €32,000 3-y-o, £50,000 4-y-o: half-brother to 3 winners, including
bumper winner/useful hurdler Gilt Shadow (2m-21f winner, by Beneficial) and modest
chaser Shanann Lady (2½m winner, by Anshan): dam winning pointer: runner-up in Irish
point: better effort in bumpers (fair form) when 4¼ lengths third at Perth, having run of
race. *Fergal O'Brien*

CAHILL (IRE) 7 b.g. Lawman (FR) – Malaspina (IRE) (Whipper (USA)) [2018/19 h17f*   **c–**
h17f* c17.4g c21.6gᵖᵘ h19.6m h21.4m³ h21.4f* h18.5m² h24d Nov 20] sturdy gelding: **h113**
fair hurdler: won at Les Landes in June (handicap) and July (minor event, final outing for
Mrs C. Gilbert) and handicap at Wincanton in October: little aptitude for chasing: stays
21f: acts on firm going: has worn headgear, including last 5 starts. *Warren Greatrex*

CAID DU BERLAIS (FR) 10 b.g. Westerner – Kenza du Berlais (FR) (Kahyasi)   **c136 +**
[2018/19 c133, h–: c26.3dᵖᵘ Mar 15] leggy gelding: unbeaten in points: winning hurdler: **h–**
useful hunter chaser nowadays: won Champion Hunters Chase at Punchestown (for second
year in row) shortly after end of British season by 28 lengths from Burning Ambition: stays
3¼m: acts on heavy going: wears tongue tie. *Mrs Rose Loxton*

*Randox Health Topham Handicap Chase, Aintree—bold-jumping Cadmium (left) is at the head of
affairs clearing the Canal Turn as trouble ensues in behind, Call It Magic unseating Mark Enright*

Supreme Horse Racing Club & Kenneth Sharp's "Cadmium"

CAID DU LIN (FR) 7 gr.g. Della Francesca (USA) – Asia du Lin (FR) (Agent Bleu (FR)) **c144**
[2018/19 h130: c16.5g* c16.4m² c15.9gᵖᵘ c18.8m² c16.8g* c16.3d c16.8m² c15.8g Apr 6] **h–**
sturdy gelding: useful hurdler: useful novice chaser: won at Worcester in September and
Ascot (Hurst Park Handicap Chase, by 1¼ lengths from Speredek) in November: stays
easy 19f: acts on soft and good to firm going: wears headgear/tongue tie. *Dr Richard Newland*

CAIRDE ARIS (IRE) 10 b.g. Definite Article – Avitta (IRE) (Pennekamp (USA)) **c–**
[2018/19 c21.6gᵖᵘ May 17] maiden pointer: winning hurdler: form in chases only when **h–**
second in maiden at Clonmel in 2015/16: stays 2½m: acts on heavy going: often in tongue
tie. *Miss Alexandra McAlpine*

CAIRNSHILL (IRE) 8 gr.g. Tikkanen (USA) – Ilikeyou (IRE) (Lord Americo) [2018/19 **h112**
h101: h20d h24.6g⁶ h24.8g⁵ h23.3g² h24g h23d⁵ h24s h25d² h25m* Apr 20] fair handicap
hurdler: won at Carlisle in April: left Mark McNiff after seventh start: barely stays 27f: acts
on soft and good to firm going: tongue tied for former yard: usually held up. *Kenny Johnson*

CAIUS MARCIUS (IRE) 8 b.g. King's Theatre (IRE) – Ain't Misbehavin (IRE) **c122**
(Trempolino (USA)) [2018/19 h122: h20g⁵ c16g² c15.6m² c16g² h16.2g* h16.7g* h15.7m³ **h137**
h16.4g h16m Apr 13] good-topped gelding: useful handicap hurdler: won at Perth in
August and Market Rasen (listed event, by 11 lengths from Theclockisticking) in
September: fairly useful form in novice chases, runner-up all 3 starts: unproven beyond
17f: acts on good to firm and heavy going: in cheekpieces last 5 starts. *Nicky Richards*

CAKE DE L'ISLE (FR) 7 b.g. Fragrant Mix (IRE) – Taiga de L'Isle (FR) (Ragmar (FR)) **c85**
[2018/19 h125: c20g c21.4sᵖᵘ Dec 26] rangy gelding: has had breathing operation: fairly **h–**
useful hurdler: promise on first of 2 starts in novice handicap chases: stays 21f: acts on
good to firm and good to soft going: in tongue tie last 4 starts. *Jonjo O'Neill*

CALACH (FR) 7 gr.g. Fragrant Mix (IRE) – Nobless d'Aron (FR) (Ragmar (FR)) **h102**
[2018/19 b85: h16.2g* h16.2s^{pu} Oct 13] fair form over hurdles: won novice at Hexham in
June: tried in hood: dead. *James Ewart*

CALARULES 6 gr.g. Aussie Rules (USA) – Ailincala (IRE) (Pursuit of Love) [2018/19 **h100**
h93: h19.6g^2 h22g^4 h23.3g^5 h23.3g^3 h19.5d^6 h21.2m^5 Apr 23] fair handicap hurdler: won
novice event at Stratford in June: stays 23f: acts on heavy going: has worn headgear: wears
tongue tie nowadays. *Tim Vaughan*

CA LE FERRA (FR) 9 b.g. Turgeon (USA) – Branceilles (FR) (Satin Wood) [2018/19 **c103**
h16v^5 c16.3s^{ur} c16.5s^4 c15.9g c20.1v^3 Mar 16] fair maiden hurdler: similar form in novice **h85**
events first 2 starts in handicap chases: should stay beyond 17f: acts on soft going: tried
hooded. *James Ewart*

CALETT MAD (FR) 7 b.g. Axxos (GER) – Omelia (FR) (April Night (FR)) [2018/19 c–, **c147**
h140: c21.4m c25g^4 c27.3g^5 c32.4g^2 c29.2g^2 Jan 12] tall gelding: has had breathing **h–**
operation: useful hurdler: smart handicap chaser: in frame 3 of 5 starts in 2018/19, running
particularly well when second in Classic Chase at Warwick (3¼ lengths behind Impulsive
Star) final outing: stays 4m: acts on heavy going: normally tongue tied. *Nigel Twiston-
Davies*

CALGARY TIGER 4 b.g. Tiger Groom – Sachiko (Celtic Swing) [2018/19 b14d b16.3s **b–**
b15.3s Mar 7] sturdy gelding: no form in bumpers. *William de Best-Turner*

CALIE DU MESNIL (FR) 7 b.m. Kapgarde (FR) – Perle du Mesnil (FR) (Villez (USA)) **h135**
[2018/19 h20g* h20.7s* h21.4s^3 h21g^2 h20d^{pu} h24g^2 h21s h20g Apr 21] compact mare:
second foal: half-sister to French 11f/1½m bumper winner Athena du Mesnil (by Al
Namix): dam lightly raced in French bumpers: useful hurdler: won mares maiden at
Tipperary in May and novice at Galway in August: best effort when seventh in handicap at
Punchestown (4½ lengths behind My Sister Sarah) shortly after end of British season: stays
3m: acts on soft going: has worn tongue tie. *W. P. Mullins, Ireland*

CALIN DU BRIZAIS (FR) 8 b.g. Loup Solitaire (USA) – Caline du Brizais (FR) **c121**
(Turgeon (USA)) [2018/19 c121, h98: c21g^4 h26d^2 h26.5m^{ur} h23.3g^4 c24.1g^4 c25.8d^3 **h108**
c25g^4 h27g^2 c28.5d^2 c30.7d c28.4s^{ur} c25.8g^2 Apr 20] good-topped gelding: fair handicap
hurdler: fairly useful handicap chaser: in frame 9 times in 2018/19: best up to 3½m: acts on
soft and good to firm going: tried in cheekpieces, normally blinkered: formerly tongue tied.
Nigel Hawke

CALINO D'AIRY (FR) 7 ch.g. Anzillero (GER) – Monita d'Airy (FR) (Oblat (FR)) **c–**
[2018/19 c145, h–: c22.5d c18.2g^F Aug 5] leggy gelding: winning hurdler: smart novice **h–**
chaser in 2017/18: stayed 2½m: acted on heavy going: dead. *Henry de Bromhead, Ireland*

CALIPSO COLLONGES (FR) 7 b.g. Crossharbour – Ivresse Collonges (FR) (Video **c130**
Rock (FR)) [2018/19 c–, h119: c20.3v^5 c20s* c23.8g^2 c26.2g^6 Mar 23] has had breathing **h–**
operation: fairly useful hurdler: useful form over fences: won novice handicap at Uttoxeter
in December: stays 3m: acts on heavy going: wears hood/tongue tie: has bled. *Olly Murphy*

CALIPTO (FR) 9 b.g. Califet (FR) – Peutiot (FR) (Valanour (IRE)) [2018/19 c140, h–: **c146 x**
c21.4g^{ur} c20.9g^5 c19.4s^{ur} c20.2g* c24g^3 c23.8d* c25s^{pu} Mar 12] tall gelding: has had **h–**
breathing operation: winning hurdler: smart handicap chaser: won at Wincanton in January
and Ascot (listed event, by 2¼ lengths from Black Corton) in February: stays 3m: acts on
heavy going: has worn hood/tongue tie (went without either in 2018/19): usually races off
pace: sketchy jumper. *Venetia Williams*

CALIVIGNY (IRE) 10 b.g. Gold Well – Summer Holiday (IRE) (Kambalda) [2018/19 **c106**
c112, h–: c16g^3 c20s^3 c20v* c26.2g* c21.5d^3 c26.2g^4 c22.4d^5 c30.6d^{pu} Apr 26] sturdy **h–**
gelding: has had breathing operation: winning hurdler: fair handicap chaser: won at
Carlisle and Kelso in December: stays 3¼m: acts on heavy going: wears headgear: tried in
tongue tie: patiently ridden. *N. W. Alexander*

CALIX DELAFAYETTE (FR) 7 b.g. Caballo Raptor (CAN) – Obepinedelafayette **h82**
(FR) (Sleeping Car (FR)) [2018/19 h117: h20.9g^3 May 9] sturdy gelding: has had breathing
operation: successful sole start in bumpers: fairly useful form over hurdles: won novice at
Kelso (by 18 lengths) in 2017/18: disappointing only appearance since: should stay 2½m:
wears hood. *James Ewart*

CALL CARLO 12 ch.g. Karinga Bay – Lady Widd (IRE) (Commanche Run) [2018/19 **c67**
c96, h–: c23.6d^3 c24.2v^F Mar 5] maiden hurdler: fair chaser: stayed 3m: acted on heavy **h–**
going: tried in blinkers: dead. *Venetia Williams*

CALLING DES BLINS (FR) 7 b.m. Konig Turf (GER) – Quelye des Blins (FR) (Silver Rainbow) [2018/19 c–, h94: h16g^pu Jun 24] modest maiden hurdler for Dan Skelton: pulled up only outing in 2018/19: last of 4 in novice handicap sole outing over fences: unproven beyond 2m: acts on good to firm going: wears tongue tie: takes strong hold. *Louise Davis* **c–**
h–

CALLIOPE 6 b.m. Poet's Voice – Costa Brava (IRE) (Sadler's Wells (USA)) [2018/19 h16.8g^3 h15.7g h19.3s^2 h19.9s^4 h20.1g^5 Apr 15] has had breathing operation: fair on Flat, stays 1¾m: modest form over hurdles: stays 2½m: acts on soft going: in hood last 4 starts. *Dianne Sayer* **h95**

CALL IT MAGIC (IRE) 9 ch.g. Indian River (FR) – Luas Luso (IRE) (Luso) [2018/19 c138, h109: c22.5g c24s c25.9s^4 c23.5g^2 c21.1d^ur c24d^6 Apr 21] raw-boned gelding: maiden hurdler: useful chaser: stays 3¼m: acts on heavy going: wears blinkers: usually front runner/races prominently. *Ross O'Sullivan, Ireland* **c135**
h–

CALL ME (IRE) 8 b.g. Craigsteel – Wake Me Gently (IRE) (Be My Native (USA)) [2018/19 h97: h23.9g^4 h23.9g^pu h23.9g^pu h24.3g h22g^5 Nov 7] angular gelding: Irish point winner: modest maiden hurdler: stays 3m: acts on good to firm: has worn headgear: usually races towards rear: lazy. *Lucy Normile* **h85**

CALL ME LORD (FR) 6 b.g. Slickly (FR) – Sosa (GER) (Cape Cross (IRE)) [2018/19 h154: h24.4s h16s^3 Mar 9] tall gelding: has scope: will make a chaser: smart hurdler: third in Imperial Cup at Sandown (5¼ lengths behind Malaya) in March: stays 21f, effective at shorter: acts on heavy going: travels strongly waited with. *Nicky Henderson* **h154**

CALL ME SID 7 b.g. Schiaparelli (GER) – Zolotaya (Kayf Tara) [2018/19 h115: c20v^pu c23d^3 c19.2d h21g^6 Apr 10] fairly useful hurdle winner: form in handicap chases only when third to Militarian in novice event at Taunton in November: stays 23f: acts on soft going: temperament under suspicion. *Jennifer Mason* **c118**
h109

CALL ME TJ 5 b.g. Mawatheeq (USA) – Silver Lily (IRE) (Gothland (FR)) [2018/19 b15.8g Nov 17] tailed off in bumper. *Sarah Humphrey* **b–**

CALL ME VIC (IRE) 12 b.g. Old Vic – Call Me Dara (IRE) (Arapahos (FR)) [2018/19 c132, h–: c24m c26.1g^4 c25.8g* c22.6m Sep 8] good-topped gelding: winning hurdler: fairly useful handicap chaser nowadays: won at Newton Abbot in July: successful twice in points in April: stays 3¼m: acts on good to firm and heavy going: tried in blinkers: races prominently. *Tom George* **c123**
h–

CALL ME WESTIE 7 b.g. Westerner – Popsie Hall (Saddlers' Hall (IRE)) [2018/19 h18.5d^pu Jan 1] no promise in bumper/maiden hurdle (mistakes). *Neil Mulholland* **h–**

CALL OFF THE DOGS (IRE) 4 ch.g. Bienamado (USA) – Lady Charmere (IRE) (Good Thyne (USA)) [2018/19 b16.3d Mar 23] 33/1, tailed off in Goffs UK Spring Sales Bumper at Newbury. *Gary Moore* **b–**

Keltbray Swinley Chase (Limited Handicap). Ascot—Calipto (right) comes late off a strong pace to beat Black Corton and 2018 winner Regal Encore (hoops)

CALL SIGN CHARLIE (IRE) 5 gr.m. Arakan (USA) – Ardea Brave (IRE) (Chester **h64**
House (USA)) [2018/19 b–: h15.7g^{ur} h16.3m^6 h21.4g^{pu} h15.3d^6 h16.8s^6 h15.9s h15.3g Feb
27] poor maiden hurdler: usually races freely. *Brian Barr*

CALLTHEBARMAN (IRE) 5 b.g. Lord Shanakill (USA) – African Scene (IRE) **c112 p**
(Scenic) [2018/19 h99: h16s* h16s h16.7m h16.2d h16.6s c21g^6 c20.5g* Oct 29] fair **h102**
handicap hurdler: won at Kilbeggan very early in season: similar form when winning
novice handicap at Ayr (comfortably) on second of 2 starts over fences: stays 2½m: acts on
soft going: tongue tied prior to Ayr: open to further improvement as a chaser. *Gavin Patrick
Cromwell, Ireland*

CALL THE COPS (IRE) 10 b.g. Presenting – Ballygill Heights (IRE) (Symboli Heights **c–**
(FR)) [2018/19 c–, h108: h16.8s h22g^2 h23.8m* h20.6v^3 Mar 16] sturdy gelding: fair **h101**
handicap hurdler nowadays: won at Musselburgh (by head from Triangle Rock) in
February: behind when refused last only chase outing: stays 3m: acts on good to firm and
heavy going: usually wears headgear: held up. *Ben Haslam*

CALL TO ORDER 9 b.g. Presenting – Theatre Girl (King's Theatre (IRE)) [2018/19 **c125**
c117p, h118: h25g^6 h23.1g^3 c20g^2 c19.2m* c25.5g^3 c19.7m^2 c23.8g^{pu} h23.8g^5 h21m Feb **h116**
23] well-made gelding: fairly useful handicap hurdler/chaser: won over fences at Market
Rasen in August: stayed 25f: acted on soft and good to firm going: wore headgear: dead.
Jonjo O'Neill

CALL ZAC (IRE) 10 b.g. Zerpour (IRE) – Dolly of Dublin (IRE) (Be My Native (USA)) **c–**
[2018/19 c85: c24.2d^{pu} May 5] maiden pointer: lightly-raced maiden chaser, modest form
at best: tried in visor: in tongue tie last 5 starts. *Mrs D. Walton*

CALTEX (FR) 7 bl.g. Network (GER) – Qomposita (FR) (Video Rock (FR)) [2018/19 **c131**
h20g c19.5g^4 c22.5d^2 c19.2d* c20s^F c19.9s^2 c20.2g^4 c22.5d^3 h20d Apr 5] tall, rather **h111**
sparely-made gelding: first foal: dam, unraced, closely related to smart hurdler/top-class
chaser (stayed 3m) Impek: fairly useful hurdler: useful chaser: won maiden at Downpatrick
in August: left Gordon Elliott, best effort when second in handicap at Aintree (3¼ lengths
behind Ballyhill) in December: stays 23f, effective at shorter: acts on heavy going: has
worn cheekpieces (including at Downpatrick): usually races prominently. *Henry Oliver*

CALUM GILHOOLEY (IRE) 5 br.g. Kalanisi (IRE) – Honeyed (IRE) (Persian Mews) **b94**
[2018/19 b16.7s* b15.8s Feb 26] €4,400 3-y-o: half-brother to several winners, including
fairly useful hurdler/useful chaser Gurkha Brave (2m-2½m winner, by Old Vic) and
fairly useful chaser Icing On The Cake (2m winner, by Spadoun), stayed 2½m: dam
unraced: fair form when winning at Bangor in December on first of 2 outings in bumpers.
Graeme McPherson

CALYPSO DELEGATOR (IRE) 6 b.g. Lilbourne Lad (IRE) – Amber Nectar (IRE) **h–**
(Barathea (IRE)) [2018/19 h87: h16.2g h16.2g Jun 16] poor maiden hurdler: raced only at
2m: acts on good to soft going: in headgear last 4 outings. *Micky Hammond*

CALYPSO JACK (IRE) 6 ch.g. Papal Bull – Miss Barbados (IRE) (Hawk Wing (USA)) **b–**
[2018/19 b17.7d Feb 24] tailed off in maiden bumper. *Linda Jewell*

CAMAPLU (FR) 7 gr.m. Turgeon (USA) – Line Tzigane (FR) (Bonnet Rouge (FR)) **h81**
[2018/19 h78: h15.9s^4 h15.9s^4 h16g^5 Apr 10] poor maiden hurdler: should stay beyond 2m:
acts on soft going: races freely. *David Bridgwater*

CAMELIA DE COTTE (FR) 7 b.m. Laveron – Traviata Valtat (FR) (Jimble (FR)) **c148**
[2018/19 c21g* c20g* c20g^4 c20g* c16.7v* c20.5g* c20d^2 c20d* Apr 23] first foal: dam, **h–**
French hurdle/chase winner around 19f, half-sister to fairly useful hurdler/useful chaser
(winner up to 21f) Edgbriar: fairly useful form over hurdles: took extremely well to
chasing in 2018/19, winning 6 times in mares company, including novice events at Cork
(Grade 3) in December and Thurles (Grade 2) in January and Grade 3 race at Fairyhouse
(smart form when beating stablemate Pravalaguna by 5½ lengths, dominating) in April:
stayed 21f: acted on heavy going: wore hood: enthusiastic front runner: retired (reportedly
in foal to Australia). *W. P. Mullins, Ireland*

CAMILE (IRE) 6 b.m. Captain Rio – Heroic Performer (IRE) (Royal Applause) [2018/19 **h103**
h16m h15.5g* h16.5d^2 h19.5d* Feb 6] half-sister to useful 2m hurdle winner MacNicholson
(by Definite Article), stays 2½m: fair on Flat (stays 1¼m): fair handicap hurdler: won
mares events at Leicester in December and, having left Joseph Patrick O'Brien, Ayr in
February: stays 19f: acts on good to soft going: has worn tongue tie. *Iain Jardine*

CAMILLAS WISH (IRE) 10 b.m. Presenting – Take Ine (FR) (Take Risks (FR)) **c82**
[2018/19 c112, h100: h25.4g^2 c25.5m^5 h25.4g^5 Jul 23] compact mare: fair handicap **h109**
hurdler/chaser: stays 3¼m: acts on good to firm and heavy going: has worn cheekpieces.
Micky Hammond

CAMLAD KINGFISHER 7 ch.g. Sulamani (IRE) – Val de Fleurie (GER) (Mondrian (GER)) [2018/19 b15.8m⁴ b16.7s h15.8g h15.8g h15.8d h19.6d Apr 26] stocky gelding: poor form on debut in bumpers: little show over hurdles, including in handicap. *Sarah-Jayne Davies*　**h–**
b74

CAMLANN (IRE) 8 b.g. Cape Cross (IRE) – Elle Galante (GER) (Galileo (IRE)) [2018/19 c19.9s* c19.9m³ c22.7g* Jul 17] sturdy gelding: fairly useful handicap hurdler: useful form over fences: won maiden at Kilbeggan very early in season and novice at Killarney (further progress when beating Le Martalin 4 lengths) in July: also first past post on Flat following month, but later disqualified due to prohibited substance: effective at 2m to easy 23f: acts on good to firm and heavy going: regularly hooded: tried in tongue tie: tough and consistent. *John Joseph Hanlon, Ireland*　**c132**
h–

CAMPEADOR (FR) 8 gr.g. Gris de Gris (IRE) – Royale Video (FR) (Video Rock (FR)) [2018/19 h151: c17dᶠ c16d* c16d² h16g h16d⁶ Apr 21] useful-looking gelding: smart hurdler at best: useful form both completed starts over fences, winning maiden at Fairyhouse in December: raced around 2m: acts on good to firm and heavy going: wears hood: tried in tongue tie: has found less than looked likely. *Gordon Elliott, Ireland*　**c138**
h–

CAMRON DE CHAILLAC (FR) 7 br.g. Laverock (IRE) – Hadeel (Polish Precedent (USA)) [2018/19 h116: h21g c23d⁶ c23.6d c21.6v⁴ Feb 14] close-coupled gelding: fair handicap hurdler: similar form first 2 outings in handicap chases: stays 3m: acts on heavy going, probably on good to firm: regularly in headgear. *Nigel Hawke*　**c108**
h–

CANADIAN GEORGE (FR) 4 b.g. George Vancouver (USA) – Connaissance (IRE) (Choisir (AUS)) [2018/19 h16m h15.8g h15.7g⁴ h15.7gᵘʳ Jan 10] fair maiden on Flat, stays 1¼m: mistakes when well held over hurdles. *Jennie Candlish*　**h78 x**

CANADIAN STEEL (IRE) 10 b.g. Craigsteel – Hil Rhapsody (Anshan) [2018/19 h23.3gᵖᵘ h19.5g c22.5gᵖᵘ h16g h16m h16d⁴ c20d⁵ c20dᵖᵘ Jan 29] winning pointer: poor maiden hurdler: some promise over fences: should stay beyond 2½m: acts on heavy going: has worn hood: normally tongue tied. *Noel C. Kelly, Ireland*　**c69**
h80

CANARDIER (FR) 7 b.g. Crillon (FR) – Idylle du Marais (FR) (Panoramic) [2018/19 h130p: h16m* h20g² h16.5d³ h24.4m³ h21g* h21s⁵ h20d³ Apr 5] angular gelding: useful hurdler: won maiden at Down Royal in May and novice at Cheltenham in October: shaped well in big-field handicaps at latter track (Coral Cup) and Aintree (Grade 3 event, 4 lengths third to Three Musketeers) after: stays easy 3m: acts on soft and good to firm going: usually hooded: travels strongly held up. *Dermot Anthony McLoughlin, Ireland*　**h142**

CAN CAN SIXTY TWO 4 b.f. Sixties Icon – Natalie Jay (Ballacashtal (CAN)) [2018/19 h16v⁶ h15.6g⁵ Dec 10] sister to fairly useful 2m hurdle winner Ingleby MacKenzie and half-sister to modest 2m hurdle winner Hoar Frost (by Fraam): fair on Flat, stays 11f: poor form over hurdles. *R. Mike Smith*　**h59**

CANDID COASTGUARD 4 ch.g. Harbour Watch (IRE) – Honesty Pays (Dr Fong (USA)) [2018/19 b16.2v⁶ Dec 15] tailed off in junior bumper. *David Dennis*　**b–**

CANDLELIGHT STORY 9 b.m. Kayf Tara – Foehn Gale (IRE) (Strong Gale) [2018/19 h–p: h15.8d⁶ h19.9g⁴ h19.9g h19.6g h23.3g⁴ Sep 23] modest maiden hurdler: stayed 23f: acted on good to soft going: wore cheekpieces/tongue tie last 2 starts: dead. *Jennie Candlish*　**h89**

CANDY BURG (FR) 6 b.g. Sageburg (IRE) – Candinie (USA) (Bernardini (USA)) [2018/19 h15.8m³ h17.2gᵖᵘ c21g* c21.4g c19.4d* c19.9gᶠ Nov 10] well-made gelding: fairly useful handicap hurdler: useful form over fences: won handicap at Newton Abbot in August and claimer at Ffos Las (final start for Olly Murphy) in October: stays 21f: acts on soft and good to firm going: wears tongue tie: prone to mistakes over fences. *Peter Bowen*　**c130**
h119

CANDYMAN CAN (IRE) 9 b.g. Holy Roman Emperor (IRE) – Palwina (FR) (Unfuwain (USA)) [2018/19 h94: h15.8g h16.5d⁵ h15.3d h19d⁵ Jan 19] lengthy, rather sparely-made gelding: poor maiden hurdler nowadays: stays 2½m: acts on good to soft going: has worn hood, including all 4 starts in 2018/19. *Laura Hurley*　**h80**

CANELIE (FR) 7 b.m. Gentlewave (IRE) – Medjie (FR) (Cyborg (FR)) [2018/19 h128: h20g h19.5sᵖᵘ Nov 13] has had breathing operation: fairly useful handicap hurdler: well below form both starts in 2018/19: stays 19f: acts on heavy going: tried in tongue tie: waited with. *Harry Fry*　**h102**

CANFORD THOMPSON 6 b.g. Canford Cliffs (IRE) – Sadie Thompson (IRE) (King's Best (USA)) [2018/19 h20g⁵ h20m⁴ h18.7m³ h18.6m³ h16.3g² h15.9g⁶ h16.3g* Oct 20] modest handicap hurdler: won lady riders event at Stratford in October: best around 2m: acts on good to firm going: tried in hood. *Neil King*　**h94**

CANGODEMAYO 7 b.m. Lucarno (USA) – Cadoutene (FR) (Cadoudal (FR)) [2018/19 **h–**
h79, b–: h16vᵖᵘ h19.7s h24.4gᵖᵘ Jan 9] winning Irish pointer: little form under Rules.
Ben Pauling

CANICALLYOUBACK 11 b.g. Auction House (USA) – Island Colony (USA) (Pleasant **c–**
Colony (USA)) [2018/19 c112, h102: c16.3g⁶ Jun 4] fair hurdler: useful novice handicap **h–**
chaser in 2016/17: deteriorated since: stays 19f: acts on good to firm and good to soft
going: tried in headgear/tongue tie. *Evan Williams*

CAN MESTRET (IRE) 12 b.g. Millenary – River Anita (IRE) (Riverhead (USA)) **c105**
[2018/19 c110: c24.2g² c21.6g² May 17] smallish gelding: multiple point winner: fair
hunter chaser: stays 21f: acts on heavy going: has worn hood. *S. R. Andrews*

CANNY STYLE 6 b.m. Canford Cliffs (IRE) – Stylish One (IRE) (Invincible Spirit (IRE)) **h101**
[2018/19 h108: h17.1d⁵ h16.8s* h15.7s⁴ h15.7dꟳ h19.9s h17d⁶ Mar 24] has had breathing
operation: fair handicap hurdler: left Kevin Ryan, won at Sedgefield in November:
unproven beyond 17f: acts on soft going: tongue tied 4 of last 5 outings. *Joanne Foster*

CANNY TOM (IRE) 9 b.g. Jimble (FR) – Tombazaan (IRE) (Good Thyne (USA)) **c112**
[2018/19 c114, h106: c20g h18.8g⁵ h24m² c20s³ h24.4g h21g h21g h19.9d h16s h21.4g³ **h109**
c19.4g⁶ c16.2g² Apr 25] sturdy gelding: has had breathing operation: fair handicap hurdler/
chaser: left Gordon Elliott, below par from autumn onwards: stays 3m, effective at shorter:
acts on good to firm and heavy going: tried in hood: regularly tongue tied. *Derek Frankland*

CANOODLE 7 b.m. Stimulation (IRE) – Flirtatious (Generous (IRE)) [2018/19 h114: **h117 §**
h16g* h16gᵀᵀ Sep 11] leggy mare: fairly useful handicap hurdler: won mares event at
Kempton in May: barely stays 19f: acts on soft and good to firm going: wears headgear:
best treated with caution (refused to race final outing). *Hughie Morrison*

CANTON PRINCE (IRE) 8 b.g. Shantou (USA) – Hasainm (IRE) (Grand Lodge **h128**
(USA)) [2018/19 h123: h21g* h21g h24.4g⁶ h21.7g⁵ Apr 24] fairly useful handicap
hurdler: won at Warwick on return in October: best around 2½m: acts on good to soft
going: usually waited with. *Tim Vaughan*

CANT PAY WONT PAY (IRE) 11 b.g. Flying Legend (USA) – Kadastrofs Prize (IRE) **c76**
(Kadastrof (FR)) [2018/19 c97, h–: c20.1d⁵ May 5] maiden hurdler: modest handicap **h–**
chaser: stays 3m: acts on heavy going: regularly wears headgear: tried in tongue tie.
Rose Dobbin

CANYON CITY 6 b.g. Authorized (IRE) – Colorado Dawn (Fantastic Light (USA)) **h132**
[2018/19 h114: h16m⁴ h15.8g h20m* h19.2m* h21g² h19.4g² h21g h21m³ h23.4d*
h24.7g⁶ Apr 6] good-topped gelding: useful handicap hurdler: significant progress in
2018/19, winning at Fakenham (twice) and Fontwell: should stay 3m+: acts on good to firm
and good to soft going: tried in visor: finds plenty. *Neil King*

CAN YOU BELIEVE IT (IRE) 6 br.g. Oscar (IRE) – Cassilis (IRE) (Persian Bold) **h94**
[2018/19 h20g h23g⁴ h23g h22g h16.8g² Apr 20] €47,000 3-y-o: closely related to fairly
useful hurdler/chaser According To Harry (19f-3m winner, by Old Vic) and half-brother to
3 winners, including fairly useful hurdler The Last Stand (2m winner, by Vettori): dam
unraced: modest form over hurdles: left Joseph Patrick O'Brien after debut: should stay
beyond 17f: tried in hood/tongue tie. *Nicky Martin*

CANYOUHEARMENOW (IRE) 8 b.g. Trans Island – First of April (IRE) (Presenting) **c–**
[2018/19 c72, h–: c21.6s⁵ c23.5vᵖᵘ c26vᵖᵘ⁵ Mar 16] has had breathing operation: well held **h–**
over hurdles: winning chaser: little form in 2018/19: wears headgear: has worn tongue tie.
Diana Grissell

CANYOURINGMEBACK (IRE) 7 b.g. Robin des Pres (FR) – Hunters Bar (IRE) **c113**
(Treasure Hunter) [2018/19 c82, h103: c23.6g² c19.9g* c19.9m* c25.1mᵘʳ c24.2mᵖᵘ **h–**
c25.1g c20.2m⁴ c20.2g⁵ c19.9dᵖᵘ Feb 17] maiden hurdler: fair handicap chaser: won at
Huntingdon in May and October: stayed 3m: acted on good to firm and heavy going: often
hooded: dead. *Nick Gifford*

CAPAC (IRE) 4 ch.g. Aizavoski (IRE) – Wigwam Mam (IRE) (Commanche Run) [2018/19 **b98 p**
b16.5d* Apr 4] half-brother to 3 winners, including bumper winner/top-class hurdler Brave
Inca (2m-2½m winner, including Champion Hurdle, by Good Thyne) and useful hurdler/
fairly useful chaser Yurok (2½m winner, by Alflora): dam unraced: 4/5, won maiden bumper
at Taunton (by 2½ lengths from Bergamot, plenty in hand) on debut: should progress.
Tom Lacey

CAPARD KING (IRE) 10 b.g. Beneficial – Capard Lady (IRE) (Supreme Leader) [2018/19 c121§, h–: c20g⁴ c26.1d⁵ c24dᶠ c24.1s² c26.2gᵘʳ c30.6dᵖᵘ Apr 26] sturdy gelding: winning hurdler: fairly useful handicap chaser: left Jonjo O'Neill after third start: stays 29f: acts on heavy going: has worn cheekpieces: one to treat with caution (last win April 2016). *Sandy Thomson* — **c121 §** **h–**

CAP DU NORD (FR) 6 br.g. Voix du Nord (FR) – Qualite Controlee (FR) (Poliglote) [2018/19 h105: c16.2g⁴ c16.5g⁵ c18m² c18g⁴ c19.2d² c21.1s* c21.1s* c21.2d* Mar 15] sturdy gelding: fair hurdler: fairly useful handicap chaser: completed hat-trick at Sedgefield (2) and Fakenham (improved again) in February/March: best up to 21f: acts on soft and good to firm going: in cheekpieces last 2 starts. *Christian Williams* — **c122** **h–**

CAPE BANJO (USA) 6 ch.g. Cape Blanco (IRE) – Magic of Love (Magic Ring (IRE)) [2018/19 h19.9g⁶ h16g⁶ Jul 31] fair on Flat (stayed 1½m): well held both starts over hurdles (in cheekpieces first one): dead. *Neil Mulholland* — **h–**

CAPE CASTER (IRE) 8 br.g. Cape Cross (IRE) – Playboy Mansion (IRE) (Grand Lodge (USA)) [2018/19 c117x, h–: h16.3g⁴ h16g⁴ h15.8m⁶ Oct 10] rather leggy gelding: fair handicap hurdler nowadays: fairly useful chaser: unproven beyond 17f: acts on good to firm and heavy going: tried in cheekpieces: tongue tied in 2018/19: waited with: not a fluent jumper of fences. *Evan Williams* — **c– x** **h102**

CAPE FAIR 6 b.m. Fair Mix (IRE) – Capania (IRE) (Cape Cross (IRE)) [2018/19 h19.6s⁴ h16g h16.7d⁴ Apr 26] third foal: half-sister to a winning pointer by Revoque: dam maiden on Flat (stayed 8.6f): well beaten completed start in points: fair form over hurdles. *Gary Hanmer* — **h104**

CAPE HIDEAWAY 7 b.g. Mount Nelson – Amiata (Pennekamp (USA)) [2018/19 h110: h20g² h21.2d h19.9d Mar 30] fair handicap hurdler: left Mark Walford after first start: stays easy 21f: acts on heavy going: wore cheekpieces prior to 2018/19. *Tim Vaughan* — **h108**

CAPELAND (FR) 7 b.g. Poliglote – Neiland (FR) (Cyborg (FR)) [2018/19 h127: c21g² c16.3g² c21.6m² c20.2g* c15.7g* c18.2d² c16d* c15.5d² c16d² c19.8d c16.8m⁴ Mar 31] good-topped gelding: has had breathing operation: fairly useful hurdler: quickly developed into much better chaser: won handicaps at Wincanton (2, conditionals race then novice event) in November and Ludlow in December: stays 2¾m, effective at shorter: acts on good to firm and good to soft going: has worn hood: wears tongue tie. *Paul Nicholls* — **c146** **h–**

CAP HORNER (FR) 7 gr.g. Apsis – Rapsodie Sea (FR) (April Night (FR)) [2018/19 c112, h108: c29.1g c27.7d⁵ c30.7sᵖᵘ c24d c26d c28.8vᵖᵘ c26v* c24.2d⁶ c25.1g² Apr 14] rather leggy gelding: maiden hurdler: modest handicap chaser: won at Fontwell in March: stays 3½m: acts on good to firm and heavy going: usually let down by jumping/attitude. *Seamus Mullins* — **c98 §** **h–**

CAPITAINE (FR) 7 gr.g. Montmartre (FR) – Patte de Velour (FR) (Mansonnien (FR)) [2018/19 c146, h131: h15.7g h16.3d⁴ h16.5g* h16.8d h19d² Apr 4] good-topped gelding: has had breathing operation: useful handicap hurdler: won at Taunton (by 1½ lengths from Sternrubin) in February: won both completed starts over fences in 2017/18: unproven beyond 17f: acts on any going: has worn hood: in tongue tie last 4 starts: usually races freely. *Paul Nicholls* — **c–** **h131**

CAPITAL FORCE (IRE) 8 b.g. Kayf Tara – Watson River (IRE) (Presenting) [2018/19 c19.9g³ c17m⁴ c17g³ c16g⁵ h16.5g² h16g h16g h16.8g⁵ Apr 17] useful-looking gelding: fairly useful hurdler: similar form over fences: left Henry de Bromhead after seventh start: stays 2¼m: acts on soft and good to firm going: tried in cheekpieces: usually in tongue tie. *Martin Keighley* — **c121** **h121**

CAPITOUL (FR) 7 b.g. Enrique – Ranavalo (FR) (Ungaro (GER)) [2018/19 c126p, h109: c16.5g* c16.2g⁴ c16.5g* c16.3g³ c16g⁵ Apr 25] neat gelding: has had breathing operation: fair hurdler: useful form over fences: won handicaps at Huntingdon (novice) in May and Worcester in June: free-going sort, best around 2m: acts on soft going: tried in hood. *Dr Richard Newland* — **c137** **h–**

CAPLA GREY 5 gr.g. Sir Percy – Great White Hope (IRE) (Noverre (USA)) [2018/19 b15.8g Apr 11] tailed off when collapsed 1f out in maiden bumper: dead. *Nick Littmoden* — **b–**

CAPMONFOR (FR) 6 b.g. Kap Rock (FR) – Fautine World (FR) (Lost World (IRE)) [2018/19 h17d h16.8s h16.7s h20.6dᵘʳ h24.1dᵖᵘ Mar 19] placed in Irish point: little form over hurdles: in cheekpieces last 2 starts. *Donald McCain* — **h–**

CAPONE (GER) 4 br.g. Nathaniel (IRE) – Codera (GER) (Zilzal (USA)) [2018/19 h16.6g⁴ h15.8g* h15.7g² h15.8g* h15.8g² Apr 21] half-brother to fairly useful hurdler Collodi (2m/17f winner, by Konigstiger) and fairly useful French hurdler/chaser Caritas (17f/2¼m — **h124**

winner, by Shirocco): useful maiden on Flat (stays 11f) in Germany: fairly useful form over hurdles: won juvenile at Ludlow in January and handicap at Huntingdon in March: likely to prove best around 2m: raced only on good going: usually held up. *Charlie Mann*

CAPPARATTIN 4 b.g. Universal (IRE) – Little Miss Prim (Gildoran) [2018/19 b14d h16.3d^{pu} Dec 29] workmanlike gelding: no promise in bumper/juvenile hurdle. *John O'Neill*   h– b–

CAPPAWAY (IRE) 6 b.g. Getaway (GER) – Cappa Or (IRE) (Oscar (IRE)) [2018/19 h–, b–: h16.7g^4 Oct 11] poor form over hurdles: dead. *Evan Williams*   h77

CAPPIELOW PARK 10 b.g. Exceed And Excel (AUS) – Barakat (Bustino) [2018/19 c–, h–: h17.7m c17.8v^{pu} c16d^5 c16.1d Mar 11] sturdy gelding: formerly fairly useful hurdler/chaser: lightly raced and little form since 2015/16: best around 2m: acts on heavy going: regularly wears headgear/tongue tie: races freely. *Tim Vaughan*   c81 h–

CAP SOLEIL (FR) 6 b.m. Kapgarde (FR) – Move Again (FR) (Noir Et Or) [2018/19 h132: h19.9s h20.3g Apr 18] good-topped mare: unbeaten in bumpers: useful novice hurdler in 2017/18: below best in David Nicholson Mares' Hurdle and listed mares handicap (both at Cheltenham) since: should stay 2½m: acts on heavy going. *Fergal O'Brien*   h116

CAP ST VINCENT (FR) 6 b.g. Muhtathir – Criquetot (FR) (Epervier Bleu) [2018/19 h97: h15.8g^5 h15.8d^6 c15.7g^3 c16g^4 c15.8g* c15.5s^3 Dec 7] workmanlike gelding: modest maiden hurdler: quickly proved much better over fences, winning handicaps at Ludlow (novice event) and Musselburgh in November: unproven beyond 2m: acts on soft going: waited with. *Tim Vaughan*   c116 h93

CAPSY DE MEE (FR) 7 b.g. Apsis – Koeur de Mee (FR) (Video Rock (FR)) [2018/19 c113, h–: h19.2g h21.6g^6 h15.9g Sep 23] modest maiden hurdler: lightly-raced maiden chaser: stays 19f: probably acts on soft going: tried in cheekpieces/tongue tie. *Jamie Snowden*   c– h86

CAPTAIN BROWN 11 b.g. Lomitas – Nicola Bella (IRE) (Sadler's Wells (USA)) [2018/19 c–x, h121: h16.2d h17.2g^{pu} h17.2m^{pu} h17.2m h17.2g^5 h17.2d^6 h16.8g^{bd} h15.6g Jan 7] rather leggy, lengthy gelding: formerly fairly useful handicap hurdler: regressed further in 2018/19: let down by jumping over fences: best around 2m: acts on soft and good to firm going: has worn headgear, including last 4 starts: tried in tongue tie. *James Moffatt*   c–x h88

CAPTAIN BUCK'S (FR) 7 b.g. Buck's Boum (FR) – Ombre Jaune (FR) (Brier Creek (USA)) [2018/19 c125, h118: c21g^4 c25.1m^3 c25.1g^6 c25.1g^5 c25.1d^5 c23.8d^3 Feb 20] fairly useful hurdler: fairly useful maiden chaser: stays 25f: acts on good to firm and heavy going: wears headgear/tongue tie: unreliable. *Paul Nicholls*   c120 § h–

CAPTAIN CARGO 7 b.g. Sulamani (IRE) – Raffles (FR) (Turgeon (USA)) [2018/19 h24g^3 h26g^2 h26d^2 h26s* Jan 21] unplaced in Irish points: fairly useful form over hurdles: won handicap at Warwick in January: stayed 3¼m well: dead. *Caroline Bailey*   h124

CAPTAIN CATTISTOCK 6 b.g. Black Sam Bellamy (IRE) – Pearl Buttons (Alflora (IRE)) [2018/19 h132: h19.5d^6 h24.3g^F c23.6d^3 c24.2d* c24v^3 c26g* Apr 12] useful handicap hurdler: quickly reached similar level in novice chases, winning at Exeter (handicap event) in February and Fontwell (in cheekpieces, landed odds despite idling run-in) in April: stays 3¼m: acts on heavy going: tried in cheekpieces: wears tongue tie: usually leads. *Paul Nicholls*   c139 h133

CAPTAIN CHAOS (IRE) 8 ch.g. Golan (IRE) – Times Have Changed (IRE) (Safety Catch (USA)) [2018/19 c141, h–: c23.6d c25g c19.9g c23.4d^2 c24.2s^2 c26d^6 Mar 14] lengthy, raw-boned gelding: winning hurdler: useful handicap chaser: second in Rehearsal Chase at Newcastle and Rowland Meyrick Chase at Wetherby (4 lengths behind Lake View Lad): likely to stay long distances: acts on heavy going: has worn blinkers, including last 3 starts: usually front runner/races prominently. *Dan Skelton*   c139 h–

CAPTAIN CJ (IRE) 8 b.g. Westerner – She's So Dainty (IRE) (Great Commotion (USA)) [2018/19 h23d^2 h22v^4 h23.3d* Mar 26] €5,200 3-y-o: fourth foal: closely related to bumper winner/modest hurdler Dainty Diva (19f winner, by Indian Danehill): dam (h93) 2m-19f hurdle winner: multiple winning pointer: fairly useful form over hurdles: landed odds in novice at Hexham in March with plenty in hand: likely to stay beyond 23f. *Dermot Anthony McLoughlin, Ireland*   h122

CAPTAIN CLAYTON (IRE) 12 b.g. Subtle Power (IRE) – Dont Hurry (IRE) (Muroto) [2018/19 h–: h16.4d h25d Mar 24] fair hurdler at best: lightly raced and little form since 2016/17: stays 2¾m: acts on heavy going: tried tongue tied. *Simon West*   h–

CAPTAIN COURAGEOUS (IRE) 6 b.g. Canford Cliffs (IRE) – Annacloy Pearl (IRE) **h102**
(Mull of Kintyre (USA)) [2018/19 h18g h20d h16g h16s h16g h16d⁵ h16.2g² Apr 25] fairly
useful on Flat (best short of 14.5f): fair maiden hurdler: unproven beyond 2m: acts on good
to soft going: tried in tongue tie: usually makes running/races prominently. *Gavin Patrick
Cromwell, Ireland*

CAPTAIN DRAKE (IRE) 6 b.g. Getaway (GER) – Julika (GER) (Nebos (GER)) **h128**
[2018/19 b98: h20g³ h21d⁵ h19.9v* h24g* h25.8g² Mar 23] has had breathing operation:
runner-up in Irish point: bumper winner: fairly useful form over hurdles: won maiden at
Uttoxeter in December and handicap at Southwell in March: stays 3¼m: acts on heavy
going: wears hood. *Harry Fry*

CAPTAIN FELIX 7 b.g. Captain Gerrard (IRE) – Sweet Applause (IRE) (Acclamation) **h116**
[2018/19 h16.7g* h16.7m⁴ h16.2g⁴ Aug 18] leggy gelding: fairly useful handicap hurdler:
won at Market Rasen in July: may prove best around 2m: acts on good to firm
going: front runner/races prominently. *James Eustace*

CAPTAIN HOX (IRE) 10 b.g. Danehill Dancer (IRE) – Shangri La (IRE) (Sadler's **c–**
Wells (USA)) [2018/19 c–§, h–: h18.9s c17s² Jan 26] fairly useful hurdler/chaser at best: **h–**
lightly raced and no form since 2016/17: stays 2½m: acts on heavy going: tried in headgear:
wears tongue tie: has hung right/looked half-hearted. *Patrick Griffin, Ireland*

CAPTAIN IVAN (IRE) 5 ch.g. Stowaway – Western Starlight (IRE) (Shahanndeh) **b77**
[2018/19 b15.8g⁵ Mar 19] 2/1, fifth in conditionals/amateurs bumper at Huntingdon (12¾
lengths behind Roque It). *Johnny Farrelly*

CAPTAIN JACK 6 b.g. Mount Nelson – Court Princess (Mtoto) [2018/19 h103: h16m⁶ **h76**
May 7] fair maiden hurdler: best around 2m: acts on heavy going. *Richard Price*

CAPTAIN KISSINGER 4 b.g. Captain Gerrard (IRE) – Nigella (Band On The Run) **h98**
[2018/19 h15.8m* h16m⁵ h15.8d⁶ Jan 28] modest maiden on Flat, stays 11f: similar form
over hurdles only when winning juvenile maiden at Ludlow in October. *Jo Hughes*

CAPTAIN KURT 5 b.g. Distant Peak (IRE) – Choral Singer (Daylami (IRE)) [2018/19 **h99**
b16.2g h16.2g⁴ h20.1s h22.7g³ h17s³ h20.9gᵖᵘ Mar 23] well held in bumper: modest form **b–**
over hurdles: stayed easy 23f: dead. *Jackie Stephen*

CAPTAIN MARMALADE (IRE) 7 gr.g. Duke of Marmalade (IRE) – Elisium **h55**
(Proclamation (IRE)) [2018/19 h16.3sᵖᵘ h16.5g Jan 9] modest on Flat, stays 8.5f: little
show in maiden hurdles: tried in hood. *Jimmy Fox*

CAPTAIN MCGARRY (IRE) 7 b.g. Oscar (IRE) – Garryduff Princess (IRE) (Husyan **h–**
(USA)) [2018/19 h15.8gᵖᵘ Mar 19] lengthy, useful-looking gelding: useful winner only
start in bumpers: 11/10, fatally injured in maiden at Huntingdon on hurdling debut 2 years
later. *Graeme McPherson*

CAPTAIN MOIRETTE (FR) 7 gr.g. Kap Rock (FR) – Rahana Moirette (FR) (Dom **h127**
Alco (FR)) [2018/19 h16d⁴ h15.7m* h15.7d* h16m Apr 12] rangy gelding: very much a
chasing type: fairly useful form over hurdles: won novices at Catterick in February and
Haydock in March: should be suited by further than 2m: smashing prospect for novice
chasing. *Sue Smith*

CAPTAIN MOWBRAY 8 ch.g. Shami – Some Like It Hot (Ashkalani (IRE)) [2018/19 **c113**
c108, h–: c24.2d² c24.2g³ c25.5g* c26.1g h25.8g⁶ c24.2g⁵ c26.3s² c23.4d c21.3d³ Mar 19] **h–**
maiden hurdler: fair handicap chaser: won at Cartmel in May: stays 3¼m: acts on soft
going: wears cheekpieces: dropped out. *Rebecca Menzies*

CAPTAIN PEACOCK 6 b.g. Champs Elysees – Blast Furnace (IRE) (Sadler's Wells **h124**
(USA)) [2018/19 h101: h19.6g* h19.6g* h20g² h20g h21g h24.2s⁶ Nov 30] strong,
compact gelding: fairly useful hurdler: won handicap and novice at Bangor in August:
stays 2½m: acts on good to soft going: tried in blinkers. *Oliver Sherwood*

CAPTAIN PUGWASH (IRE) 5 b.g. Sir Prancealot (IRE) – Liscoa (IRE) (Foxhound **h–**
(USA)) [2018/19 h16.2g Dec 29] fair on Flat, stays 11f: well beaten in novice on hurdling
debut. *Stef Keniry*

CAPTAIN REDBEARD (IRE) 10 ch.g. Bach (IRE) – Diesel Dancer (IRE) (Toulon) **c143**
[2018/19 c144, h141: h20g³ c25.6g³ c21.1s c25.6d⁶ c23.4g* c23.4d³ c34.3g Apr 6] sturdy **h137**
gelding: useful handicap hurdler/chaser: won minor event over fences at Kelso (beat sole
rival Definitly Red 2 lengths) in February: stays 3¼m (non-stayer in Grand National): acts
on heavy going. *Stuart Coltherd*

CAPTAIN REVELATION 7 ch.g. Captain Rio – Agony Aunt (Formidable (USA)) **h82**
[2018/19 h15.8g⁶ h16.7g h16.7g⁶ h15.8g⁶ h16.8m⁶ Oct 2] fair on Flat, stays 9.5f: poor form
over hurdles: raced around 2m: tried in cheekpieces. *Michael Mullineaux*

CAPTAIN SHARPE 11 ch.g. Tobougg (IRE) – Helen Sharp (Pivotal) [2018/19 c76§, h78§: c20.1d h23.3g^pu c24.2g^pu Jun 16] sturdy gelding: poor hurdler/chaser: wears headgear: regularly tongue tied: held up: unreliable. *Kenny Johnson* **c– §**
h– §

CAPTAIN SIMON (IRE) 7 b.g. Dubai Destination (USA) – Gayephar (Phardante (FR)) [2018/19 h–: h21.2g h20.3g^2 h23.1g c20d^pu Nov 29] well-made gelding: point/bumper winner: only modest form over hurdles: pulled up in novice handicap on chasing debut: stays 2½m: tried in cheekpieces. *Dan Skelton* **c–**
h97

CAPTAIN SPEAKING (FR) 4 ch.g. Linda's Lad – Hillflower (FR) (Sabrehill (USA)) [2018/19 h15.9d^4 h15.8m h16.3s h15.8g^6 h20.3s^pu h15.8g^3 Apr 11] fourth foal: half-brother to bumper winner Flic Ou Voyou (by Kapgarde): dam French 2m-19f hurdle winner: fair form over hurdles: standout effort in juvenile at Saint-Malo on first start, then left R. Chatel: has worn headgear. *Nick Littmoden* **h103**

CAPTAINS RUN (IRE) 7 ch.g. Curtain Time (IRE) – Sailors Run (IRE) (Roselier (FR)) [2018/19 h20.5s h20.5g^4 h19.5d^6 c23.6d^F Jan 25] workmanlike gelding: brother to 2 winners, including useful hurdler/very smart chaser Texas Jack (19f-25f winner), and half-brother to 2 winners, including fairly useful hurdler/useful chaser Drumconvis (19f-3m winner, by Taipan), stayed 4m: dam held both starts: placed once from 4 starts in Irish points: poor form over hurdles: held when fell heavily 2 out in novice handicap on chasing debut: bred to stay 3m+. *Philip Hobbs* **c–**
h84

CAPTAIN TOMMY (IRE) 5 b.g. Court Cave (IRE) – Freemantle Doctor (IRE) (Luso) [2018/19 b16.5m^5 h17.7v* h21.4g* h23.9g^2 Apr 24] €9,500 3-y-o, £15,000 4-y-o: third foal: half-brother to fairly useful hurdler Steamboat Bill (2½m-25f winner, by Kalanisi): dam (c98/h95), bumper winner, stayed 2½m over jumps: placed in Irish point: well beaten in maiden bumper (for Sam Thomas): fairly useful form over hurdles: won maiden at Fontwell in March and novice at Wincanton in April: further improvement when second in listed novice (4 lengths behind Go Another One) at Perth. *Harry Whittington* **h126**
b–

CAPTAIN WOODIE (IRE) 7 b.g. Presenting – Lasado (IRE) (Jurado (USA)) [2018/19 h15.8v Jan 26] dual bumper winner in 2016/17: off 23 months, well held in maiden at Uttoxeter on hurdling debut. *Nicky Henderson* **h91**

CAPTAIN ZEBO (IRE) 7 b.g. Brian Boru – Waydale Hill (Minster Son) [2018/19 h–, b92: h20d^3 h24g^4 h19.7g* h19.3s* h19.3d* Mar 24] bumper winner: useful form over hurdles: left M. F. Morris, won novices at Wetherby in November and Carlisle in December and March: should prove suited by 3m: acts on soft going: front runner/races prominently. *John Dixon* **h130**

CAPTIVA ISLAND (IRE) 6 b.g. Scorpion (IRE) – Sapphire Eile (Mujtahid (USA)) [2018/19 h110, b87: h16g^5 c20.3g^pu Jun 5] fair maiden hurdler: pulled up in novice handicap on chasing debut: likely to stay beyond 2¾m: acts on soft going: tried in cheekpieces: signs of temperament. *Olly Murphy* **c–**
h88

CAPTON 6 b.g. Cape Cross (IRE) – Flavian (Catrail (USA)) [2018/19 h16.4g h15.6g^3 h16.4m Mar 28] useful on Flat (stays 1¼m) at best: modest form over hurdles: best effort when third in maiden at Musselburgh in February. *Michael Easterby* **h98**

CAP YORK (FR) 7 b.g. Ballingarry (IRE) – Robbe (FR) (Video Rock (FR)) [2018/19 h23d^4 h24s^4 h24d* h24d h20d Apr 7] sturdy gelding: first foal: dam, lightly raced over hurdles in France (second at 17f), half-sister to fairly useful chaser up to 21f Sir Dream: useful hurdler: won maiden at Navan in December and handicap at Punchestown (by 3¼ lengths from Mormon) in February: stays 3m: acts on soft going: tried in headgear. *Noel Meade, Ireland* **h136**

CARALINE (FR) 8 b.m. Martaline – Vie Ta Vie (FR) (Villez (USA)) [2018/19 c128, h–: c20v^pu c19.4s^5 c15.2g^5 c15.2g c20.1d^3 c21.3d* c20.1d^5 Apr 6] winning hurdler: fairly useful handicap chaser: won at Wetherby in March: stays 21f: acts on heavy going: wears headgear/tongue tie: usually races prominently. *Micky Hammond* **c115**
h–

CARA'S WAY (IRE) 6 br.m. Robin des Champs (FR) – Dare To Venture (IRE) (Darazari (IRE)) [2018/19 b16.5d^5 b20g h16m^5 h20d^5 h19d^4 h19.4g* h21.2d^6 Jan 28] €85,000 3-y-o: sixth foal: half-sister to bumper winner/smart hurdler Movewiththetimes (15f-2¼m winner) and bumper winner/smart 2¼m hurdle winner Venture Capital (both by Presenting): dam unraced half-sister to fair hurdler/smart chaser up to 3m Horner Woods: pulled up on sole start in points: mid-field in 2 bumpers: fair form over hurdles: left Gordon Elliott, won mares handicap at Doncaster in January: stays 2½m: acts on good to soft going. *Philip Kirby* **h101**
b75

CARD GAME (IRE) 10 b.m. Scorpion (IRE) – Cardona (Dashing Blade) [2018/19 h120: **h127**
h16.2d* h16.2g³ h20.1g* h20.6m⁵ h20.6g⁵ h19.6d h19.4g⁴ Dec 14] small, compact mare:
fairly useful handicap hurdler: won at Hexham in May and June: stays 2½m: acts on soft
and good to firm going. *Ruth Jefferson*

CARDIGAN BAY (FR) 6 b.m. Turtle Bowl (IRE) – Nan's Catch (FR) (Loup Solitaire **h112**
(USA)) [2018/19 b16.2g⁶ b16g⁵ b17.7g* b16.4g h15.5d³ h15.5g² h15.8d³ h15.7d* **b85**
h19g⁵ Apr 25] lengthy mare: sixth foal: half-sister to 3 winners, including useful hurdler/
fairly useful chaser Catch One (17f–2½m winner, by Smadoun): dam (h116) French 2¼m
hurdle winner: fair form in bumpers: won mares event at Fontwell in September: similar
form over hurdles: improved when winning handicap at Southwell in April: should stay
beyond 2m: acts on good to soft going: wears hood/tongue tie: usually travels strongly.
Charlie Longsdon

CAREFULLY SELECTED (IRE) 7 b.g. Well Chosen – Knockamullen Girl (IRE) **h137 p**
(Alderbrook) [2018/19 b123: h22v* Mar 17] well-made gelding: winning pointer: smart
bumper performer in 2017/18: landed odds in maiden at Limerick on hurdling debut by ¾
length from Lord Schnitzel: useful form when 3½ lengths third of 12 to Minella Indo in
Irish Daily Mirror Novices' Hurdle at Punchestown shortly after end of British season:
stays 3m: exciting prospect. *W. P. Mullins, Ireland*

CAREYANNE 5 ch.m. Mount Nelson – Mayaar (USA) (Grand Slam (USA)) [2018/19 **h85**
h15.8d⁵ h16.7s⁶ h15.8m Apr 1] half-sister to fair hurdler Keep Calm (2½m winner, by War
Chant): fair on Flat, stays 1½m: form (modest) over hurdles only when fifth in maiden at
Ludlow. *David Loughnane*

CARIBERT (FR) 6 b.g. Ballingarry (IRE) – Cardamine (FR) (Garde Royale) [2018/19 **h114**
b112: h18.5d² Jan 1] well-made gelding: useful bumper winner: promising second in
maiden at Exeter (8 lengths behind Greeneteen) on hurdling debut: well beaten in minor
event at Punchestown shortly after end of British season. *Harry Fry*

CARLINGFORD LOUGH (IRE) 13 b.g. King's Theatre (IRE) – Baden (IRE) (Furry **c138**
Glen) [2018/19 c–, h–: c20sᶠ c24.5g Dec 27] lengthy gelding: winning hurdler: top-class **h–**
chaser in prime, winning 5 times at Grade 1 level (including 2 Irish Gold Cups and a
Punchestown Gold Cup): stayed 3¼m: acted on heavy going: tried in tongue tie: usually
raced towards rear: dead. *John E. Kiely, Ireland*

CARLINGFORD PRINCE (IRE) 10 ch.g. Definite Article – Castle Hope (IRE) (Old **c–**
Vic) [2018/19 h96: h21.4s c24.1d⁶ Feb 6] maiden pointer: modest form over hurdles, **h79**
lightly raced: well beaten in novice handicap on chasing debut: stays 2¾m: acts on good to
firm and heavy going: tried in hood. *Tim Reed*

CARLITA MORIVIERE (FR) 7 b.m. Balko (FR) – Halladine (FR) (Passing Sale (FR)) **h114**
[2018/19 h23g³ Apr 13] good-topped mare: modest form in bumpers: 28/1, showed more
when length third to Carrick Roads in maiden at Bangor on hurdling debut after 28-month
absence. *Ian Williams*

CARLO BIRAGHI (IRE) 4 ch.g. Galileo (IRE) – Kirinda (IRE) (Tiger Hill (IRE)) **h121 p**
[2018/19 h16g* Jan 14] useful 1¼m winner from just 3 outings on Flat: 12/1, looked good
prospect when won maiden at Punchestown by 7½ lengths from Pienta, forging clear) on
hurdling debut: sure to progress. *J. A. Stack, Ireland*

CARLO ROCKS (IRE) 9 b.g. Carlo Bank (IRE) – Rock Garden (IRE) (Bigstone (IRE)) **c98**
[2018/19 c24d⁵ c24v² c23.9d⁴ c24s³ Mar 23] compact gelding: winning hurdler: modest **h–**
form over fences: stays 3m: acts on heavy going: tried in headgear. *Caroline Bailey*

CARLOS DU FRUITIER (FR) 7 b.g. Diableneyev (USA) – Odyssee Madrik (FR) **c131**
(Antarctique (IRE)) [2018/19 h126: h22.8gur c21g² c20g c24.2mpu c24.2m³ c23.8g³ **h–**
c20.5g³ c23.4d² c24.2d* c24.2dpu Mar 8] useful-looking gelding: winning hurdler: useful
chaser: won Royal Artillery Gold Cup (Amateur Riders) at Sandown in February: stayed
3m: acted on soft and good to firm going: wore blinkers: usually raced prominently: dead.
Ben Pauling

CARNAGE 4 b.g. Holy Roman Emperor (IRE) – Sylvestris (IRE) (Arch (USA)) [2018/19 **h89**
h16gⁱ h16.2d⁴ h16s⁶ h16.2g³ Mar 26] well held on Flat: modest form over hurdles.
Nikki Evans

CARNSPINDLE (IRE) 7 b.m. Ask – Whistling Gypsy (IRE) (Good Thyne (USA)) **c123**
[2018/19 h126: c24g⁴ c24d⁴ c22.4d³ Mar 22] tall mare: fairly useful hurdler: similar form **h–**
over fences: will stay long distances: acts on heavy going: in cheekpieces 5 of last 6
outings: no easy ride (temperament under suspicion). *Warren Greatrex*

CARNTOP 6 b.g. Dansili – Milford Sound (Barathea (IRE)) [2018/19 h–p: h16.3m² h16g* h117
h16g* h19.9g³ h15.8m⁴ Oct 4] has had breathing operations: fairly useful form over
hurdles: won maiden in July and novice in August, both at Worcester: best around 2m: acts
on good to firm going: in tongue tie last 5 starts. *Jamie Snowden*

CARO DES FLOS (FR) 7 b.g. Tiger Groom – Royale Marie (FR) (Garde Royale) c–
[2018/19 h18.8g* h19.2m c20.3vᵖᵘ h19d h21.4g Apr 14] rather leggy gelding: fair hurdler: h111
won maiden at Downpatrick in May, then left W. P. Mullins: lost way after (pulled up in
maiden on chasing debut): stays 3m: acts on heavy going. *Julian Smith*

CAROLE'S DESTRIER 11 b.g. Kayf Tara – Barton May (Midnight Legend) [2018/19 c140
c127, h–: c23.6d³ c24.2vᵖᵘ c26d* c29.2g⁴ c28.4gᵖᵘ c26d* c31.8mᵖᵘ Apr 13] well- h–
made gelding: winning hurdler: useful handicap chaser nowadays: won at Newbury in
December and March (veterans race): stays 29f: acts on heavy going: wears cheekpieces.
Neil Mulholland

CAROLE'S VIGILANTE (IRE) 8 ch.g. Flemensfirth (USA) – Gotta Goa (IRE) c–
(Publisher (USA)) [2018/19 h110p: c20.9v⁶ c20v⁵ Jan 26] has had breathing operation: fair h–
form over hurdles: well held both outings in handicap chases: stays 21f: raced on soft/
heavy going: in hood last 2 starts. *Harry Whittington*

CAROLINES CHARM (IRE) 5 b.g. Masterofthehorse (IRE) – Truckers Princess (IRE) h–
(Beneficial) [2018/19 b16d b16.8s⁶ h15.8d h21gᵖᵘ Apr 10] has had breathing operation: in b80
front when fell last in Irish point: modest form in bumpers: little show in maiden hurdles:
tried in tongue tie. *Neil Mulholland*

CAROUSE (IRE) 4 b.g. Excelebration (IRE) – Terre du Vent (FR) (Kutub (IRE)) [2018/19 h97
h15.8m² h16gᵖᵘ h17.7v h15.8gᵖᵘ Jan 3] fairly useful on Flat, stays 1m: disappointing in
juvenile hurdles after close second in maiden event at Ludlow. *Evan Williams*

CARRAIGIN AONAIR (IRE) 7 b.m. Fastnet Rock (AUS) – Omanah (USA) h72
(Kayrawan (USA)) [2018/19 h17.7g⁵ h18.5m Jun 26] half-sister to fair 2m hurdle winner
Shan Dun Na Ngall (by Shantou): modest on Flat, stays 1½m: poor maiden hurdler: in
headgear last 3 starts. *Olly Murphy*

CARRICK ROADS (IRE) 5 ch.g. Robin des Champs (FR) – Jay Lo (IRE) (Glacial h122
Storm (USA)) [2018/19 b–: b17.7s h16.8d⁴ h19.2d² h23g* Apr 13] has had breathing b–
operation: well held in bumpers: fairly useful form over hurdles: further marked progress
when winning maiden at Bangor in April: will be suited by 3m+. *Colin Tizzard*

CARRIED AWAY 7 b.m. Trans Island – Carry Me (IRE) (Lafontaine (USA)) [2018/19 h–
h–: h21m⁶ h19.2g Jun 16] no show in point/over hurdles. *Phil York*

CARRIE DES CHAMPS (IRE) 5 b.m. Robin des Champs (FR) – Asturienne (Sleeping b101
Car (FR)) [2018/19 b16m⁴ b17.3g* b16.2g* b16.2g* b16g³ Oct 5] second foal: dam (c117/
h117), 2m-21f hurdle/chase winner, half-sister to high-class hurdler/useful chaser (stayed
25f) Lough Derg: fairly useful bumper performer: won at Downpatrick (mares maiden) in
June, and at Perth in August (mares race) and September: third in listed mares event at
Gowran (5½ lengths behind Yukon Lil) final outing: will be suited by further than 17f.
Gordon Elliott, Ireland

CARRIGDHOUN (IRE) 14 gr.g. Goldmark (USA) – Pet Tomjammar (IRE) (Accordion) c113
[2018/19 c122, h–: c24.5d⁶ c26.2g³ c24.1s⁶ c32.4g c26.9d c26.3sᵖᵘ c23.4d³ c30.6d⁶ h–
Apr 26] lengthy gelding: winning hurdler: formerly useful handicap chaser: just fair form
in 2018/19: stays 4m: acts on good to firm and heavy going: has worn headgear: wears
tongue tie: usually races prominently: no easy ride nowadays. *Maurice Barnes*

CARRIGMOORNA MATT (IRE) 8 b.g. Westerner – Carrigmorna Flyer (IRE) (Bob c–
Back (USA)) [2018/19 h23.3g⁵ h21d⁴ h19.5d² h23.9s⁴ h23.3v h18.7g* h19.7g* Apr 11] h123
runner-up in points: fairly useful hurdler: won sellers at Stratford in March and Wetherby
in April: thrice-raced maiden over fences: stays easy 3m, effective at much shorter: acts on
heavy going: wears cheekpieces: in tongue tie last 5 starts. *Neil Mulholland*

CARROLLS MILAN (IRE) 6 b.m. Milan – Native Crystal (IRE) (Be My Native h126
(USA)) [2018/19 h80: h20.2g² h20.6g⁴ h21.2s² h24.1d² h23.8g* h23.1g* h26.6g* Apr 25]
runner-up in Irish points: fairly useful handicap hurdler: won at Ludlow in February, and at
Market Rasen (both mares events) and Perth (conditionals) in April: stays 27f: acts on soft
going: front runner/races prominently, usually responds generously to pressure. *Fergal
O'Brien*

CARRY ON 4 b.g. Footstepsinthesand – Evening (Mark of Esteem (IRE)) [2018/19 b13.7m* Oct 4] fifth foal: half-brother to 3 winners, including bumper winner/useful 2m hurdler Beyond The Clouds (by Peintre Celebre): dam maiden (stayed 1¼m): 2/1, won junior bumper at Huntingdon by 1¾ lengths from Aerodrome, merely kept up to work: better to come. *Kevin Ryan* **b88 p**

CARRY ON ARCADIO (IRE) 7 b.g. Arcadio (GER) – Carryonharriet (IRE) (Norwich) [2018/19 h16d⁴ h20.5s Mar 9] in frame in bumper in 2016/17: modest form on first of 2 starts in novice hurdles at Ayr: should stay beyond 2m. *Nicky Richards* **h97**

CARRY ON SCORPION (IRE) 6 b.g. Scorpion (IRE) – All My Judges (Oscar (IRE)) [2018/19 h20.1vᵖᵘ Dec 20] placed in Irish points: pulled up in novice on hurdling debut: dead. *Daragh Bourke* **h–**

CARTA BLANCA (IRE) 6 gr.m. Authorized (IRE) – Alicante (Pivotal) [2018/19 h–: h17.2m⁶ Jul 1] compact mare: little form over hurdles: hooded first 3 outings. *Gemma Anderson* **h–**

CARTER MCKAY 8 gr.g. Martaline – Saxona (IRE) (Jade Robbery (USA)) [2018/19 h136: c19d c21.5s⁵ c20d⁶ c21.3s² c19.3g* Apr 23] workmanlike gelding: useful hurdler: fairly useful form over fences: left Gordon Elliott, won novice hunter at Sedgefield in April: stays 2¾m: acts on heavy going. *C. C. Pimlott* **c122 h–**

CARTWRIGHT 6 b.g. High Chaparral (IRE) – One So Marvellous (Nashwan (USA)) [2018/19 h133: h16s h18.8d⁵ h20d⁶ h16g h20.3d⁶ h21.4m⁴ Apr 13] useful handicap hurdler: stays 21f: acts on good to firm and heavy going: wears headgear. *Gordon Elliott, Ireland* **h135**

CARUMBA (IRE) 9 b.g. Gold Well – Sarah Marshall (IRE) (Flemensfirth (USA)) [2018/19 c–, h–: c20.9s⁵ Mar 11] winning pointer: no form in maiden hurdles/hunter chases: wears headgear. *Miss K. Frisby* **c– h–**

CARYTO DES BROSSES (FR) 7 b.g. Maresca Sorrento (FR) – Idole des Brosses (FR) (Port Etienne (FR)) [2018/19 c22.6d* Jun 8] €17,000 3-y-o: seventh foal: brother to fairly useful French/Swiss chaser Toscan des Brosses (2¼m-23f winner) and half-brother to 2 winners, including French hurdler/chaser Ryvalo des Brosses (17f-23f winner, by Passing Sale): dam French 11f/1¼m bumper winner: prolific winner in points, including in 2019: 3/1, looked good prospect when also won novice hunter at Stratford (by 6 lengths from Steeles Terrace) on chasing debut: sure to progress. *David Kemp* **c107 p**

CASABLANCA MIX (FR) 7 ch.m. Shirocco (GER) – Latitude (FR) (Kadalko (FR)) [2018/19 c141p, h–: c18m² c23.9g² c20.6d c19.9d³ h20.3g Apr 18] smallish, angular mare: fairly useful hurdler: useful chaser: placed 3 times in 2018/19, 5 lengths third to Happy Diva in listed mares event at Huntingdon final occasion: will prove best up to 3m: acts on good to firm and heavy going: tried in cheekpieces. *Nicky Henderson* **c139 h–**

CASA TALL (FR) 5 b.g. No Risk At All (FR) – Gribouille Parcs (FR) (Ungaro (GER)) [2018/19 h129: h15.3g⁵ h16d² h20.3d h15.7m⁴ Apr 20] fairly useful handicap hurdler: stays 2¼m: acts on soft and good to firm going: regularly hooded: usually races prominently. *Tom George* **h123**

CASCAYE (FR) 7 br.m. Merlino Mago – Castyana (IRE) (Anabaa (USA)) [2018/19 h–: h16g² May 7] fair handicap hurdler: unproven beyond 17f: acts on good to soft going, probably on heavy: normally in headgear: tried in tongue tie. *Kim Bailey* **h104**

CASCOVA (IRE) 4 b.g. Casamento (IRE) – Sina Cova (IRE) (Barathea (IRE)) [2018/19 b13.7g* b14d² b16.4s Mar 13] well-made gelding: fifth foal: half-brother to 2 winners on Flat, including smart 1½m-14.6f winner Cape Cova (by Cape Cross): dam, smart 1m-1½m winner, half-sister to smart hurdler/useful chaser (stayed 3m) Kadoun: fair form in bumpers: won junior event at Huntingdon on debut in November. *Martyn Meade* **b92**

CASEMATES SQUARE (IRE) 5 b.g. Casamento (IRE) – Marhaba (Nayef (USA)) [2018/19 h16d⁵ h19.9g⁸ h21g⁴ Oct 4] modest maiden on Flat, stays 16.5f: fair form over hurdles: in cheekpieces, improved again when fourth in maiden at Warwick. *Ian Williams* **h103**

CASEMENT (IRE) 5 b.g. Casamento (IRE) – Kirk Wynd (Selkirk (USA)) [2018/19 h16.8d Sep 21] fairly useful on Flat, stays 1¼m: 7/2, last of 7 finishers in novice at Newton Abbot on hurdling debut. *Alan King* **h–**

CASH AGAIN (FR) 7 br.g. Great Pretender (IRE) – Jeu de Lune (FR) (Useful (FR)) [2018/19 c112, h–: c21.4g⁵ c21.2g³ c21.2s⁶ c20.1g Oct 5] maiden hurdler: fair handicap chaser: stays 21f: acts on heavy going: races in rear. *Ben Haslam* **c100 h–**

CASH BACK (FR) 7 b.g. Linda's Lad – Holding (FR) (Useful (FR)) [2018/19 h16g* **h138** h16d² Apr 7] €1,000 4-y-o, resold €4,000 4-y-o: brother to smart hurdler Draconien (2m-19f winner) and half-brother to several winners, including fairly useful French chaser Nasthazya (2¼m-21f winner, by Rochesson): dam ran twice in French bumpers (second at 1¼m): useful form over hurdles: trained in 2017/18 by Y. Gourraud: won maiden at Thurles in March: easily best effort when second in novice at Fairyhouse (¾ length behind Mister Blue Sky) next time: usually in headgear. *W. P. Mullins, Ireland*

CASH IN MIND (FR) 8 b.g. Creachadoir (IRE) – Dynamic Dream (USA) (Dynaformer **h108** (USA)) [2018/19 h110: h16m h16g⁵ h16g² h16g⁴ h16d Sep 11] sturdy gelding: fair maiden hurdler: likely to prove best at 2m: acts on soft going: in blinkers last 2 starts: tongue tied second to fourth starts in 2018/19. *Des Donovan, Ireland*

CASH TO ASH (IRE) 6 b.g. Westerner – Knocklayde Rose (IRE) (Even Top (IRE)) **c106** [2018/19 h95: c24.2g⁵ c21.3d² c20.3s³ Dec 16] lightly-raced maiden hurdler: immediately **h–** better over fences, placed in handicaps at Wetherby and Southwell: stays 21f: acts on heavy going. *Mark Walford*

CASIMIR DU CLOS (FR) 7 b.g. Blue Bresil (FR) – Cyrienne du Maine (FR) (Saint **c78** Cyrien (FR)) [2018/19 h–: h19.7m h16d⁵ h20.6d h20.6dᵖᵘ c16.4s* c16.4g⁴ c15.6g⁵ Apr 15] **h–** poor form over hurdles: best effort over fences when winning novice handicap at Sedgefield in March: should stay beyond 2m: acts on soft going. *Stuart Coltherd*

CASINO MARKETS (IRE) 11 br.g. Fruits of Love (USA) – Vals Dream (IRE) (Pierre) **c123** [2018/19 c–, h126: c21g⁵ c19.4g⁴ c23g⁶ Jun 27] tall gelding: winning hurdler: fairly useful **h–** handicap chaser: has form at 3m, but races mainly around 2½m nowadays: acts on firm and soft going. *Emma Lavelle*

CASKO D'AIRY (FR) 7 b.g. Voix du Nord (FR) – Quaska d'Airy (FR) (Cachet Noir **h120 p** (USA)) [2018/19 h19.5s h20s⁵ h23.5s* h23.4s⁵ Feb 2] lengthy gelding: first foal: dam (c128/h119) French 17f-2½m hurdle/chase winner: fairly useful form over hurdles: won novice handicap at Ascot in December: stays 3m: acts on soft going: in tongue tie last 2 starts: remains with potential. *Paul Nicholls*

CASPER KING (IRE) 8 b.g. Scorpion (IRE) – Princess Supreme (IRE) (Supreme **c–** Leader) [2018/19 c–, h123: c19.2mᵖᵘ h24gᵖᵘ Mar 4] lengthy gelding: has had breathing **h–** operation: fairly useful hurdler at best: pulled up all 4 starts over fences: left Philip Hobbs after first start: stays 19f: acts on heavy going: in headgear last 3 starts: tried in tongue tie. *Lawney Hill*

CASPERS COURT (IRE) 5 gr.g. Court Cave (IRE) – Kindle Ball (FR) (Kaldounevees **h99** (FR)) [2018/19 b16.8s⁶ h18.5d h19s³ h19.8s Mar 7] £16,000 3-y-o: sixth foal: dam (h93), **b77** 2m/17f hurdle winner (stayed 21f), half-sister to winning hurdler/useful French chaser up to 21f Fire Ball: off mark in Irish points at second attempt: sixth in bumper at Exeter: modest form over hurdles. *Kayley Woollacott*

CASSE TETE (FR) 7 b.g. Poliglote – Ellapampa (FR) (Pampabird) [2018/19 c135, h–: **c102 x** c21gᵘʳ c20.5g³ c20.6dᵖᵘ Jan 26] lengthy gelding: maiden hurdler: useful handicap chaser: **h–** fatally injured in Grade 3 event at Cheltenham: best up to 21f: acted on soft going: usually held up: often let down by jumping. *Gary Moore*

CASSIS DE REINE 5 ch.m. Quatre Saisons – Reine de Violette (Olden Times) [2018/19 **h91** b85: h15.8dᵖᵘ h20.7g⁶ h19.8d⁴ Feb 28] lengthy, rather sparely-made mare: placed twice in bumpers: modest form over hurdles: in hood last 2 starts. *Bill Turner*

CASSIVELLAUNUS (IRE) 7 b.g. Danehill Dancer (IRE) – Celtic Heroine (IRE) **h91** (Hernando (FR)) [2018/19 h93: h25gᵖᵘ h15.9s h23.4d³ h19.2v² h23d³ h25s Feb 13] modest handicap hurdler: left Daniel Steele after first start: stays 23f: acts on heavy going: tried in visor. *Gary Moore*

CASTAFIORE (USA) 5 b.m. Street Cry (IRE) – Showlady (USA) (Theatrical) [2018/19 **c139** h121: h19.5d h16v⁴ c15.7s⁴ c20.2d* c19.9d* c20.5g² c19.8d c20.5m⁵ Apr 13] tall, angular **h114** mare: fair handicap hurdler: useful novice chaser: won mares race at Wincanton in December and Grade 2 event at Haydock (by 5 lengths from Jerrysback) in January: second in Pendil Novices' Chase at Kempton (1½ lengths behind Bags Groove) in February: stays 2½m: acts on good to firm and heavy going: wears headgear: usually races prominently. *Charlie Longsdon*

CASTALIERA (IRE) 8 b.m. Millenary – Castleknock (IRE) (Executive Perk) [2018/19 **h–** h21.4sᵖᵘ h19.9sᵖᵘ h17m Apr 20] second foal: dam unraced half-sister to useful hurdler (stayed 3m) Vast Consumption: lightly-raced maiden hurdler: left Ms M. M. Gannon, no promise in 2018/19 (bled second outing): tried in hood. *Iain Jardine*

CASTERLY ROCK (IRE) 7 b.g. King's Theatre (IRE) – Alderbrook Girl (IRE) **h115**
(Alderbrook) [2018/19 h111: h16g h19.6g² h16.8g^F Nov 14] tall gelding: fairly useful
maiden hurdler: stayed 2½m: acted on good to soft going: dead. *Philip Hobbs*

CASTLEBAWN WEST (IRE) 6 b.g. Westerner – Cooksgrove Lady (IRE) (Anshan) **h131**
[2018/19 h20s² h20g* h21s^pu h20d⁴ Apr 7] €24,000 3-y-o: sturdy gelding: first foal: dam
(h110) 2½m-3m hurdle winner: bumper winner: useful form over hurdles: won maiden
at Leopardstown in December: should stay beyond 2½m. *W. P. Mullins, Ireland*

CASTLEDHEM (IRE) 4 b.g. Alkaadhem – Castle Hope (IRE) (Old Vic) [2018/19 **b93**
b13.7g² Apr 24] €17,000 3-y-o: sixth foal: half-brother to bumper winners Soviet Castle
(by Soviet Star) and Sandanski (by Definite Article), latter stayed 3m over hurdles: dam
(h98), 2½m-3m hurdle winner, half-sister to useful hurdler (stayed 3m) Vast Consumption:
2/1, second in bumper at Fontwell (length behind Milkwood). *Nick Gifford*

CASTLEGRACE PADDY (IRE) 8 b.g. Flemensfirth (USA) – Thunder Road (IRE) **c156**
(Mtoto) [2018/19 c145p, h–: c16.7v* c17g⁴ c17g^F c15.9s⁶ Mar 13] tall gelding: winning **h–**
hurdler: very smart chaser: won Hilly Way Chase at Cork (by 16 lengths from Doctor
Phoenix) on reappearance in December: stays 2¼m: acts on heavy going: tried in tongue
strap. *P. A. Fahy, Ireland*

CASTLETOWN (FR) 7 gr.g. Poliglote – Message Personnel (FR) (Mansonnien (FR)) **c118 §**
[2018/19 c106§, h105§: c20.1g⁵ h17.1g c23.4g² c22.3g² c16.4d² c21.1s³ h20.5m* Apr 13] **h106 §**
fair handicap hurdler: won conditionals/amateurs event at Ayr in April: fairly useful
maiden chaser: seemingly stays 23f: acts on soft and good to firm going: wears headgear:
front runner/races prominently: travels strongly but no battler. *Pauline Robson*

CASUAL CAVALIER (IRE) 11 br.g. Presenting – Asklynn (IRE) (Beau Sher) [2018/19 **c112**
c105, h–: c20.9d⁴ c16.5v* c20.3s⁴ c20.5d² c20.1v* c23.4d⁴ Apr 6] maiden hurdler: fair **h–**
handicap chaser: won at Ayr in November and Newcastle in March: best short of 23f: acts
on heavy going: wears headgear. *Henry Oliver*

CASWELL BAY 4 b.g. Fame And Glory – Lauderdale (GER) (Nebos (GER)) [2018/19 **h105**
h15.8g³ h16v² h19.5d h15.7s⁴ Mar 18] €45,000 3-y-o: rather unfurnished gelding: closely
related to smart hurdler/useful chaser Zamdy Man (2m winner, by Authorized), and half-
brother to several winners, including smart hurdler Clyne (2m-2½m winner, by Hernando):
dam German 9.5f winner: fair form over hurdles. *Evan Williams*

CATACLYSM (IRE) 9 b.g. Captain Rio – Marilaya (IRE) (Shernazar) [2018/19 h17.1d^pu **h–**
h16.2g^pu Nov 9] lightly-raced maiden hurdler, of little account nowadays: tried in hood.
Kevin Hunter

CATAMARAN DU SEUIL (FR) 7 b.g. Network (GER) – Fleur du Tennis (FR) (Video **c139 x**
Rock (FR)) [2018/19 c133, h–: c19.4g* c21.1s^F c20.6d c20.2g² c24g c25s^pu Mar 12] good- **h–**
topped gelding: winning hurdler: useful handicap chaser: won at Wetherby (by 8 lengths
from Cracking Find) in November: mostly let down by jumping subsequently: stays 3m:
acts on heavy going: wears headgear. *Dr Richard Newland*

CATCHAMAT 10 b.m. Overbury (IRE) – More Flair (Alflora (IRE)) [2018/19 c–, h–: **c102**
c23.4g⁴ c15.6v³ c23.4g⁵ Jan 5] winning pointer: winning hurdler: seemingly fair form in **h–**
chases: should stay beyond 2¾m: acts on heavy going. *James Walton*

CATCHER ON THE GO (IRE) 9 b.g. Catcher In The Rye (IRE) – Suspicious Minds **h–**
(Anabaa (USA)) [2018/19 h107: h22m May 20] well held in point: fair handicap hurdler:
stays 2½m: best form on good going. tried in tongue tie. *Evan Williams*

CATCHIN TIME (IRE) 11 b.g. Chineur (FR) – Lady Dane (IRE) (Danetime (IRE)) **h95**
[2018/19 h89: h16g³ h15.8g² h15.8g² h16.5m³ h16.8s² h16.7s³ h15.3g⁴ h16.8s h15.8d²
h16.8d⁵ Apr 9] lengthy gelding: modest handicap hurdler: best around 2m: acts on heavy
and good to firm going: regularly in headgear: has worn tongue tie: races prominently.
Laura Hurley

CATCH THE SWALLOWS (IRE) 5 b.g. Masterofthehorse (IRE) – Nafrah (USA) **b97**
(Shamardal (USA)) [2018/19 b16.7d* Mar 10] €10,000 4-y-o: first foal: dam
unraced: runner-up in Irish point on debut: 5/1, overcame greenness when winning bumper
at Bangor by 1¼ lengths from Frenchy du Large. *David Pipe*

CATHAL'S STAR 6 ch.g. Malinas (GER) – Hand Inn Glove (Alflora (IRE)) [2018/19 **h96**
b66: h20.9g^pu h20.1g⁵ h16.2m² Jun 24] mid-field in bumper: modest form last 2 outings
over hurdles. *Ruth Jefferson*

CATLIN 4 b.f. Bollin Eric – Linen Line (Double Eclipse (IRE)) [2018/19 h16m h15.7m **h97** h20.6g² Mar 14] half-sister to fairly useful hurdler Silva Eclipse (2m winner, by Multiplex), stays 3m: dam unraced half-sister to fairly useful hurdler/chaser (stayed 25f) Rattlin (by Bollin Eric): well beaten on Flat: best effort over hurdles (modest form) when second in mares novice at Market Rasen: in hood last 2 starts. *Nick Kent*

CAULKIN (IRE) 16 b.g. King's Theatre (IRE) – Alice Brennan (IRE) (Good Thyne **c94 x** (USA)) [2018/19 c24.2g³ May 8] multiple winning pointer: winning hurdler: modest **h−** hunter chaser: stays easy 3m: acts on good to firm and good to soft going: prone to mistakes. *John Whyte*

CAUSE TOUJOURS (FR) 7 b.g. Khalkevi (IRE) – Viana (FR) (Signe Divin (USA)) **h125** [2018/19 h114p: h16m* h16.5g* h16.7g⁴ h17g² h15.7g² h17s² h15.7mF h16g Apr 27] compact gelding: has had breathing operation: fairly useful hurdler: won novice at Kempton in May and handicap at Aintree in June: runner-up 3 times subsequently: raced around 2m: acts on soft and good to firm going: has worn hood: wears tongue tie: strong-travelling sort who sometimes finds less than promised. *Ian Williams*

CAUTIOUS KATE (IRE) 12 b.m. Witness Box (USA) – Cautious Leader (Supreme **h−** Leader) [2018/19 h23.9d Dec 13] runner-up both completed starts in maiden points: lightly-raced maiden hurdler: little show in handicap only outing in 2018/19: stays 3m: acts on heavy going. *Carroll Gray*

CAUTORILLO 7 ch.m. Black Sam Bellamy (IRE) – Cent Prime (Hernando (FR)) **h85** [2018/19 h69, b80: h18.5g⁴ h16.7m⁵ h19.9g² h24gᵖᵘ Aug 19] modest form over hurdles: stays 2½m: tried in tongue tie. *Jamie Snowden*

CAVALRY SCOUT (IRE) 6 b.g. Mahler – Yourfinalanswer (IRE) (Supreme Leader) **h82** [2018/19 h23.1m⁵ h15.8g h24s h19.9v h24.3d⁴ h27s⁴ h24gᵖᵘ Mar 4] €19,000 3-y-o: third foal: dam, lightly raced over hurdles, half-sister to useful hurdler/top-class chaser (stayed 25f) Albertas Run: placed in Irish points: poor maiden hurdler: stays 3m: acts on good to soft going: in headgear last 3 starts: not a fluent jumper. *Laura Morgan*

CAVE HUNTER (IRE) 12 b.g. Court Cave (IRE) – Beasty Maxx (GER) (Keen) **c−** [2018/19 c−: c24.2gᵖᵘ Apr 15] multiple point winner: fairly useful hunter chaser at best: failed to complete since spring 2017: stays 3¼m: acts on good to firm and good to soft going: wears headgear: normally tongue tied. *Mrs Wendy Hamilton*

CAVENTARA 7 b.g. Kayf Tara – L'Aventure (FR) (Cyborg (FR)) [2018/19 h115p: **c99** c23.4dᵖᵘ c20.9s⁶ c26.2g⁵ c31.9vᵇᵈ Mar 14] fairly useful hurdler: only modest form over **h−** fences: bred to stay long distances: acts on heavy going: in cheekpieces last 3 starts. *Sandy Thomson*

CAVERNOUS (IRE) 6 br.g. Court Cave (IRE) – Willoughby Sue (IRE) (Dabali (IRE)) **b−** [2018/19 b−p: b16.3s Mar 11] down field in bumpers over 15 months apart. *Ben Pauling*

CAVE TOP (IRE) 7 b.g. Court Cave (IRE) – Cyrils Top Girl (IRE) (Top of The World) **c127** [2018/19 h127: c15.9d c19.9s⁶ c21.4s⁴ c20v* c20.1g² c20.6dF c20.1d⁶ Apr 6] sturdy **h−** gelding: maiden Irish pointer: fairly useful novice chaser: won handicap at Uttoxeter in January: stays 2½m: goes well on soft/heavy going. *Oliver Greenall*

CAVIAR D'ALLEN (FR) 7 b.g. Laveron – Quadanse (FR) (Maille Pistol (FR)) [2018/19 **c93** c−, h99: c21.2g² h15.8m c21g Jul 22] has had breathing operation: fair maiden hurdler: **h−** form (modest) in handicap chases only when second at Fakenham on return: won point in April: stays 21f: acts on heavy going: tried in hood/tongue tie. *Christian Williams*

CAVIAR ROYALE 4 b.g. Royal Applause – Precious Secret (IRE) (Fusaichi Pegasus **h−** (USA)) [2018/19 h16g⁶ h16s h19d Feb 28] modest maiden on Flat: tailed-off last all 3 starts over hurdles, hooded last 2. *Nikki Evans*

CAVICIANA 6 b.m. Court Cave (IRE) – Viciana (Sir Harry Lewis (USA)) [2018/19 **h−** b15.8m³ b16.5d h16d Apr 6] narrow, unfurnished mare: third foal: half-sister to fairly **b72** useful hurdler/chaser Holbrook Park (2½m-3¼m winner, by Midnight Legend) and fair hurdler Phoeniciana (2m winner, by Phoenix Reach): dam, (c102/h112) 2m-2½m winner, half-sister to fairly useful chaser (stayed 2½m) Terivic: some promise on first of 2 outings in bumpers: hooded, well beaten in novice at Chepstow on hurdling debut. *Neil Mulholland*

CAVOK (IRE) 7 b.m. Kayf Tara – Timon's Present (Presenting) [2018/19 b85: h19.5s³ **h98** h19.5vᵖᵘ h21.2d⁴ Feb 6] won Irish point on debut: placed in bumper: modest form over hurdles: will stay 3m. *Ben Pauling*

CAWDOR HOUSE BERT 12 b.g. Kayf Tara – Lady Shanan (IRE) (Anshan) [2018/19 **c−** c98, h−: c23.8gᵖᵘ c23.8sᵖᵘ Nov 23] winning hurdler: modest chaser: pulled up both outings **h−** in 2018/19: stays 21f: acts on heavy going: tried in cheekpieces: races in rear. *David Rees*

CEARA BE (IRE) 6 b.m. Oscar (IRE) – Pearl's A Singer (IRE) (Spectrum (IRE)) **h109**
[2018/19 b91: h16.3d⁶ h15.7d³ h15.5g² h20d* h18.6dᵖᵘ h20.3d² Apr 24] rather unfurnished
mare: bumper winner: fair form over hurdles: won handicap at Fakenham in January: stays
2½m: acts on good to soft going. *Alex Hales*

CEASE TO SURRENDER 8 b.g. Refuse To Bend (IRE) – Bel (Darshaan) [2018/19 **h79**
h20g⁴ h17.7mᵖᵘ May 27] some promise in seller on first of 2 starts over hurdles. *Henry Tett*

CECILATOR 5 b.m. Delegator – Cecily Parsley (Fantastic Light (USA)) [2018/19 h–: **h–**
h16.8g Jun 15] has had breathing operation: poor maiden on Flat: well beaten both outings
over hurdles: wears cheekpieces. *Noel Williams*

CECILE DE VOLANGES 11 ch.m. Kheleyf (USA) – Fyvie (Grand Lodge (USA)) **c–**
[2018/19 c–, h–: h24gᵘʳ c26g⁶ Jun 5] multiple point winner: little form under Rules: tried **h–**
in cheekpieces. *Mike Hawker*

CEDAR VALLEY (IRE) 5 b.m. Flemensfirth (USA) – Lunar Path (IRE) (Night Shift **h99**
(USA)) [2018/19 b92: b17.1d³ b16.4g⁵ h21.4g³ h21.7d³ h23.1s⁵ Jan 20] sturdy mare: **b94**
bumper winner: modest form over hurdles: will be suited by 3m: in cheekpieces last 2
starts. *Philip Hobbs*

CEEGEM (IRE) 7 b.g. Kalanisi (IRE) – Aboo Who (IRE) (Aboo Hom) [2018/19 c–, h85: **c–**
h21.4gᵖᵘ May 7] modest maiden hurdler: let down by jumping in novice handicap only **h–**
outing over fences: should stay 3m: acts on heavy going: in headgear last 3 starts.
Lucinda Russell

CELER ET AUDAX 7 b.m. Kayf Tara – Wannaplantatree (Niniski (USA)) [2018/19 h–, **h78**
b65: h15.8gᵖᵘ h23g h18.7g h19g⁴ h19.7g⁶ h23v⁴ h15.5d⁴ h19.5dᵖᵘ h23.9dᵖᵘ Apr 24] small,
leggy mare: poor maiden hurdler: stays 19f: acts on heavy going: has worn hood: prone to
bursting blood vessels. *John O'Shea*

CELESTIAL CHIMES (IRE) 8 ch.m. Mahler – Celestial Rose (IRE) (Roselier (FR)) **h75**
[2018/19 h60: h24g² h24g* Jun 25] poor handicap hurdler: won at Southwell in June:
thorough stayer: probably acts on heavy going: usually races nearer last than first.
Robin Dickin

CELESTIAL MAGIC 7 b.g. Black Sam Bellamy (IRE) – Mighty Merlin (Royal **c114**
Applause) [2018/19 c–, h112: c19.4m² c20gᵖᵘ Jun 14] fair hurdler: similar form when **h–**
second at Stratford sole completed start in novice handicap chases: stays 19f: acts on good
to firm and heavy going: races prominently. *Richard Phillips*

CELESTIAL PATH (IRE) 7 br.g. Footstepsinthesand – Miss Kittyhawk (IRE) (Hawk **h113**
Wing (USA)) [2018/19 h109: h21.4mᵖᵘ h16g* h15.8m* h16.8m⁶ h16g Nov 12] has had
breathing operation: fair handicap hurdler: won at Worcester (novice event) in June and
Uttoxeter in July: best at 2m: acts on good to firm going: wears headgear: tried in tongue
tie: usually races close up: has hinted at temperament/found little. *David Pipe*

CELLAR VIE 5 gr.g. Tikkanen (USA) – Branceilles (FR) (Satin Wood) [2018/19 b16.2g **b88**
b16.8s³ b16.2g⁵ Feb 14] half-brother to 3 winners, including useful hurdler/smart chaser Sa
Suffit (2m-2¾m winner, by Dolpour) and fair hurdler/fairly useful chaser Plus Jamais (2m-
3m winner, by Caballo Raptor): dam ran twice in France: easily best form in bumpers: best
effort when fifth at Kelso: in hood after debut. *James Ewart*

CELMA DES BOIS (FR) 7 b.g. Ballingarry (IRE) – Palafixe (FR) (Valanour (IRE)) **c100 p**
[2018/19 h84: h21m* c20s* Nov 13] well-made gelding: modest hurdler: won novice **h85**
handicap at Kempton in May: did well under circumstances (overcame jumping right)
when also won novice handicap at Lingfield on chasing debut by 5 lengths from Dalkadam:
stays 21f: acts on soft and good to firm going: open to improvement over fences. *Richard
Rowe*

CELTIC FLAMES (IRE) 9 gr.g. Celtic Swing – Don't Forget Shoka (IRE) (Don't **c104 x**
Forget Me) [2018/19 c110x, h101: c24.2d⁵ h23.9g⁴ h20.2g* Sep 10] fair form over hurdles: **h106**
won handicap at Perth in September: fair but error-prone handicap chaser: stays 3m: acts
on heavy going: has worn cheekpieces. *Lucinda Russell*

CELTIC JOY (IRE) 6 b.g. Kayf Tara – No Time For Tears (IRE) (Celtic Swing) [2018/19 **h111**
b83: h19.6g⁵ h20d⁵ h16d³ h15.8g h17.7m² Mar 29] fair form over hurdles: should stay
2½m: acts on good to firm going. *Emma Lavelle*

CELTIC LEGEND 6 b.m. Josr Algarhoud (IRE) – Celtic Flow (Primitive Rising (USA)) **b–**
[2018/19 b16.8d Apr 23] first foal: dam (c79/h65) ungenuine 27f/29f chase winner: tailed
off in mares bumper. *Philip Kirby*

CELTIC MONARCH (IRE) 10 b.g. Celtic Swing – Trim (IRE) (Ela-Mana-Mou) **h94**
[2018/19 h19.9g* h22.1g³ h19.8g⁶ h20.2s h19.9g⁶ h20.1s⁵ Nov 21] modest handicap
hurdler: won at Uttoxeter on reappearance in June: stays 2¾m: acts on soft and good to firm
going: tried in cheekpieces: in tongue tie last 5 starts: races in rear. *Mark McNiff, Ireland*

CELTIC SALLY (IRE) 7 b.m. Coroner (IRE) – Celtic Serenade (IRE) (Yashgan) **h85**
[2018/19 b–: b15.8m⁵ h19.9g² h20g⁵ Aug 22] maiden Irish pointer: well held in bumpers: **b–**
modest form over hurdles: in hood since debut. *Fergal O'Brien*

CELTIC STYLE (IRE) 6 b.m. Craigsteel – Kissangel (IRE) (Namaqualand (USA)) **h83**
[2018/19 b–: h16.8m⁴ h20m⁵ h21.6d⁶ h23.9d Oct 20] fourth in mares maiden at Exeter on
hurdling debut: no form otherwise. *Linda Blackford*

CELTIC TARA 5 b.m. Kayf Tara – Valdas Queen (GER) (Platini (GER)) [2018/19 b15.7d **b– p**
Apr 24] third foal: dam (b92), 1½m bumper winner, half-sister to useful hurdler/chaser
(stayed 3m) Victorias Groom: 13/8, held back by inexperience when seventh in bumper at
Southwell: clearly thought capable of better. *Olly Murphy*

CELTIC THUNDER (IRE) 10 b.g. Definite Article – Clash Princess (IRE) (Supreme **c– §**
Leader) [2018/19 c19.5g^pu c25.7g^pu Sep 23] multiple point winner: pulled up only hurdle **h–**
outing: maiden chaser, no form in 2018/19: wears headgear: has worn tongue tie:
ungenuine. *Olly Murphy*

CENTREOFEXCELLENCE (IRE) 8 b.g. Oscar (IRE) – Calm Approach (IRE) **c93**
(Anshan) [2018/19 h77: h16.8g⁴ h20g³ h18.7m h16.7g^pu h23g c20m⁵ c15.7g³ c17.4g* **h80**
c16g² c16s* Nov 28] sturdy gelding: has had breathing operation: poor handicap hurdler:
modest form over fences: won handicaps at Bangor in October and Hereford (novice
event) in November: best around 2m: acts on good to soft going: wears hood/tongue tie:
headstrong front runner. *Steve Flook*

CEPAGE (FR) 7 b.g. Saddler Maker (IRE) – Sience Fiction (FR) (Dom Alco (FR)) **c145**
[2018/19 c140x, h–: c20.6d² Dec 15] stocky gelding: winning hurdler: smart handicap **h–**
chaser: career-best effort when second in Caspian Caviar Gold Cup at Cheltenham (1¼
lengths behind Frodon) sole outing in 2018/19: stays 21f: acts on soft going: has won when
sweating badly. *Venetia Williams*

CEREAL KILLER (FR) 7 b.g. Buck's Boum (FR) – Dombrelle (FR) (Quart de Vin **h93**
(FR)) [2018/19 h104, b–: h21.2m³ May 13] tall gelding: won both starts in points: fair form
over hurdles. *Paul Nicholls*

CERNUNNOS 9 b.g. Della Francesca (USA) – Jackette (USA) (Mr Greeley (USA)) **c100 §**
[2018/19 c119§, h–: c22.6m c23.8m⁶ c20.3g c20g⁶ c22.5g² c20g³ c25.2g³ c20.2g³ **h–**
Dec 6] useful-looking gelding: winning hurdler: just fair handicap chaser in 2018/19:
barely stayed 27f: acted on soft going: regularly wore headgear: tongue tied: temperamental:
dead. *Tom George*

CERTAINLY RED 5 ch.g. Midnight Legend – Venetian Lass (First Trump) [2018/19 **b91**
b16s² Mar 16] second foal: dam unraced: 33/1, second in maiden bumper at Kempton (8
lengths behind easy winner Shishkin). *Lydia Richards*

CERVARO MIX (FR) 5 gr.g. Al Namix (FR) – Semiramiss (FR) (Pennekamp (USA)) **h116**
[2018/19 b17.7s² h16.7g⁵ h15.8g* h15.8d² h15.8d⁵ h15.7d* Apr 24] first foal: dam French **b92**
19f-3¼m hurdle/cross-country chase winner: pulled up in Irish point: second in bumper at
Fontwell: fairly useful form over hurdles: won maiden at Huntingdon in November and
novice at Southwell in April: will be suited by 2½m: acts on good to soft going: front
runner/races prominently. *Oliver Sherwood*

CESAR COLLONGES (FR) 7 ch.g. Fragrant Mix (IRE) – Prouesse Collonges (FR) **c123**
(Apple Tree (FR)) [2018/19 h112: c20.9s⁶ c17.2s* c15.5d Mar 8] fair hurdler: easily best **h–**
over fences (fairly useful form) when winning handicap at Market Rasen in
December: let down by jumping either side: unproven beyond 17f: acts on heavy going.
Evan Williams

CESAR ET ROSALIE (FR) 7 ch.g. Network (GER) – Regle de L'Art (FR) (Video **c119**
Rock (FR)) [2018/19 h115: c16s^pu c20.1d³ c25.1g⁴ c24v* c22.4d⁵ Mar 1] good-topped **h–**
gelding: fairly useful hurdler: similar form over fences: won novice handicap at Uttoxeter
in January: should prove suited by long distances: acts on good to firm and heavy going:
tried in hood: wears tongue tie. *Neil Mulholland*

C'EST JERSEY (FR) 7 b.g. Protektor (GER) – Myrtille Jersey (FR) (Murmure (FR)) **c136**
[2018/19 c136, h140: c25.2g³ c20d³ c29d^F Apr 22] smallish gelding: useful hurdler/maiden **h–**
chaser: stays 25f: acts on heavy going: often in headgear. *W. P. Mullins, Ireland*

C'EST LE BONHEUR (FR) 7 b.g. Laveron – Joie de La Vie (FR) (Quart de Vin (FR))   **b98**
[2018/19 b16.8m* Oct 2] closely related to bumper winner/useful hurdler Ainsi Va La Vie
(23f winner, by Lavirco) and half-brother to 3 winners, including bumper winner/useful
hurdler Sous Les Cieux (2m-2½m winner, by Robin des Champs): dam unraced: Irish point
winner: 15/8, won bumper at Sedgefield by ¾ length from Emma Lamb, battling well.
Dr Richard Newland

CEYHAN 7 ch.g. Rock of Gibraltar (IRE) – Alla Prima (IRE) (In The Wings) [2018/19   **h76**
h15.8g⁴ h16.8d⁴ Mar 24] fair on Flat, stays 13f: well held both starts over hurdles.
Barry Brennan

CHACUN POUR SOI (FR) 7 b.g. Policy Maker (IRE) – Kruscyna (FR) (Ultimately   **c169 p**
Lucky (IRE)) [2018/19 c16d* Mar 10]   **h–**
    The new kid on the block. When the final *Timeform Black Book* for the latest
season was published, straight after the end of the British season, Chacun Pour Soi
didn't even figure among the top twenty or so highest-rated novice chasers. His
name did, however, appear at the head of a list of 'large P' chasers, rated 148P
after a runaway win in a maiden chase at Naas in March on his first start for Willie
Mullins. That might have been that, for the time being at least, but connections
took a rather unorthodox route by throwing Chacun Pour Soi in at the deep end in a
red-hot Ryanair Novices' Chase at the Punchestown Festival. 'I thought we'd better
run him before he goes wrong again,' said his trainer Willie Mullins. The strapping
Chacun Pour Soi, an 'expensive purchase whom we've always thought the world
of' according to his owner before the Naas race, hadn't run since being acquired
from Emmanuel Clayeux three years earlier, since when he had been kept off the
course by a string of 'niggles and setbacks'. Chacun Pour Soi had won a juvenile
hurdle at Dieppe for the Clayeux stable, for whom his last appearance had come
when third over fences in a two-mile event for four-year-olds in March 2016, a race
won by King's Socks who went on to finish second to Footpad in the Prix Alain du
Breil at Auteuil before being transferred to David Pipe. Chacun Pour Soi's maiden
chase win was certainly expected—his home reputation preceded him and he started
at 9/4-on—but the manner of his victory must have taken even his connections
somewhat by surprise. It was exhilarating. Chacun Pour Soi travelled strongly in
front all the way and jumped superbly, being well clear entering the home straight
and winning hard held by thirty-one lengths from Portmore Lough. Chacun Pour Soi
was clearly out of the top drawer, a most exciting prospect who looked destined for
much better things.
    A superb field was assembled for the Ryanair Novices' Chase at Punchestown,
a week after the end of the British season (hence the absence of a form figure in
the summary at the start of this essay). It was a vintage edition, containing two
Cheltenham Festival winners, the Arkle winner Duc des Genievres and the Golden

*Ryanair Novices' Chase, Punchestown—a scintillating performance by the lightly-raced
Chacun Pour Soi who leaves Cheltenham Festival winners Defi du Seuil and
Duc des Genievres in his wake*

Mrs S. Ricci's "Chacun Pour Soi"

Miller winner Defi du Seuil, as well as Ornua, winner of the Maghull at Aintree, and Voix du Reve, who had also won a Grade 1, the Ryanair Gold Cup (former Powers Gold Cup) at Fairyhouse's Easter meeting. Us And Them, runner-up in four successive Grade 1s including the Arkle and the Maghull, was also in the line-up of seven. Facing four Grade 1 winners, including two from his own stable (Duc des Genievres and Voix du Reve), it was significant that Chacun Pour Soi started at only 3/1, third favourite behind Defi du Seuil and Duc des Genievres. Willie Mullins revealed afterwards details of the conversation that he had before the race with Chacun Pour Soi's jockey Robbie Power—an experienced rider Closutton might be using more in future. 'I told Robbie that we think he's a star and, if he's as good as we think, God knows what will happen!' What happened was spectacular. Ornua made the running from Duc des Genievres, with Chacun Pour Soi patiently ridden in a strongly-run race and kept towards the outside. Chacun Pour Soi was awkward four out, pitching on landing—he jumped well otherwise—but he pulled himself up to the leaders shortly afterwards and turned for home in front with the Arkle winner Duc des Genievres on his inside and the Golden Miller winner Defi du Seuil looming up on his outer. Chacun Pour Soi found plenty in the home straight and won going away in the end by four and a quarter lengths and sixteen from Defi du Seuil and Duc des Genievres, with Voix du Reve back in fourth (Ornua was pulled up, already beaten when blundering two out, and Us And Them unseated his jockey at the third). Such a clear-cut victory from two Grade 1 Cheltenham Festival winners marked Chacun Pour Soi as a tip-top novice worthy of mentioning in the same breath as some of the stable's best novice chasers of recent times, and a very exciting prospect for 2019/20.

		Policy Maker (IRE) (b 2000)	Sadler's Wells (b 1981)	Northern Dancer Fairy Bridge
Chacun Pour Soi (FR) (b.g. 2012)			Palmeraie (b 1993)	Lear Fan Petroleuse
		Kruscyna (FR) (b 2004)	Ultimately Lucky (b 1995)	Kris Oczy Czarnie
			Hanska (bl 1996)	Persian Combat Kiakhta

Chacun Pour Soi is by the smart middle-distance performer Policy Maker who was runner-up twice in the Grand Prix de Saint-Cloud. Policy Maker ran in the Wildenstein colours—he was home bred from the same family as Arc winner Peintre Celebre—and was retired to the Haras du Pin in France at the end of his six-year-old days. He was transferred to Blackrath Stud in County Kildare in 2015 after being purchased for just €25,000 at that year's Deauville December Sale. Policy Maker is probably best known in Britain as the sire of the smart handicap chaser Art Mauresque, while in France he sired a Prix Alain du Breil winner in Roll On Has. Policy Maker has been reasonably supported so far at his new base, with books of thirty-six, forty-six and twenty-six in his first three years, but with Chacun Pour Soi to represent him those numbers can only rise. Chacun Pour Soi's dam Kruscyna won five times at up to two and a quarter miles over jumps in France, showing useful form over hurdles—including when winning the Group 3 Prix Bournosienne—and winning over fences. Chacun Pour Soi is her second foal and her third Diva Reconce (by Kap Rock) is a bumper winner and has shown fair form over hurdles for Kim Bailey. Unproven beyond two miles, Chacun Pour Soi, who acts on soft going, looks tailor-made for the Queen Mother Champion Chase, though, given the horse's history, his trainer perhaps wisely refused to discuss plans after Punchestown, saying 'We'll plan next year when we get there.' *W. P. Mullins, Ireland*

CHAIN OF BEACONS 10 b.g. Midnight Legend – Millennium Girl (Skyliner) [2018/19 c112, h–: c17.1g⁴ c17.1g³ c17.1d⁴ c15.8g³ c15.8g² c15.9g Feb 24] workmanlike gelding: has had breathing operation: maiden hurdler: fair handicap chaser: stays 3m, but races mainly around 2m: acts on good to soft going: wears tongue tie: often travels strongly. *Katie Scott* **c106 h–**

CHAIN SMOKER 6 ch.g. Shantou (USA) – Handmemy Moneydown (IRE) (Saddlers' Hall (IRE)) [2018/19 h16v h15.9d h16d h25dᵖᵘ Mar 3] sturdy gelding: maiden Irish pointer: little show over hurdles, including in handicap (sent off favourite). *Gary Moore* **h–**

CHAMBARD (FR) 7 b.g. Gris de Gris (IRE) – Regina Park (FR) (Cadoudal (FR)) [2018/19 h16.7g h16.7sᵘʳ h15.8v² h16.8s* h15.8d² h19.3s² h15.7d³ Mar 20] second foal: dam, French maiden (third in 17f chase), half-sister to fair hurdler/fairly useful chaser (stays 3m) Arthur's Secret: fairly useful hurdler: won maiden at Exeter in January: will stay 2½m: acts on heavy going. *Venetia Williams* **h117**

CHAMERON (FR) 6 b.g. Laveron – Chamanka (FR) (Cadoudal (FR)) [2018/19 c132p, h–: c23.6dᶠ c20dᵘʳ h24d h24g Apr 17] angular gelding: has had breathing operation: fairly useful form over hurdles: useful form over fences, though let down by jumping: may prove best at shorter than 3m: acts on soft going: tried in blinkers. *Paul Nicholls* **c130 h127**

CHAMPAGNE AT TARA 10 gr.g. Kayf Tara – Champagne Lil (Terimon) [2018/19 c131§, h–§: c21.7g³ c15.8g* c16m* c16.8m² c16.8g⁶ c16.4g⁵ c16.3d c15.8d³ Apr 4] rangy gelding: has had breathing operation: winning hurdler: useful handicap chaser: won at Aintree in June and Uttoxeter in July: stays 2¾m, though all wins at 2m: acts on soft and good to firm going: has worn hood/tongue tie: held up: temperamental. *Jonjo O'Neill* **c141 § h– §**

CHAMPAGNE CHAMP 7 b.g. Champs Elysees – Maramba (Rainbow Quest (USA)) [2018/19 h122: h21m⁶ h21.4s⁴ h18.5d h21.4g² h20g* Apr 21] rather leggy gelding: has had breathing operation: useful handicap hurdler: won at Ffos Las (by 29 lengths from Never Equalled) in April: stays 21f: acts on soft and good to firm going: in blinkers last 2 starts: tried in tongue tie: has high head carriage. *Rod Millman* **h136**

CHAMPAGNE CHASER 9 b.g. Tobougg (IRE) – Champagne Lil (Terimon) [2018/19 c116, h107: h23.1g h23.1g h24s³ h25g Feb 18] lengthy gelding: fair handicap hurdler: maiden chaser, let down by jumping: stays 3m: acts on heavy going: tried in cheekpieces. *Tim Vaughan* **c– h99**

CHAMPAGNE CITY 6 ch.g. Tobougg (IRE) – City of Angels (Woodman (USA)) **h136**
[2018/19 h123: h15.8m⁴ h18.5g* h20.6m⁴ h16.8g³ h16.8d⁴ h16.3d² h16.2g² Mar 23] well-
made gelding: useful handicap hurdler: won at Newton Abbot in June: in frame all other
starts in 2018/19: stays easy 2¼m: acts on soft going. *Tom George*

CHAMPAGNE CLASSIC (IRE) 8 b.g. Stowaway – Classical Rachel (IRE) **c145 p**
(Shahanndeh) [2018/19 c24d³ c24d² Feb 17] point winner: winning hurdler: smart form **h–**
over fences, placed in Grade 3 novice at Naas (12¼ lengths third behind Ballyward) and
Ten Up Novices' Chase at Navan (close second to Chris's Dream): stays 3m: acts on heavy
going: open to further improvement as a chaser. *Gordon Elliott, Ireland*

CHAMPAGNE COURT (IRE) 6 b.g. Court Cave (IRE) – Lady Taipan (IRE) (Taipan **h120**
(IRE)) [2018/19 b16.4d⁴ h16d* h15.7s⁵ h21g⁵ h19.3g³ h20.3d⁴ h19.8g³ Apr 27] €12,000 **b94**
3-y-o: good-topped gelding: fifth foal: dam, placed in points, out of sister to Grand National
winner Royal Athlete: runner-up twice from 3 starts in Irish points: in frame in bumper at
Cheltenham: fairly useful novice hurdler: won at Lingfield in November: will prove suited
by further than 21f: acts on soft going: races prominently. *Jeremy Scott*

CHAMPAGNE EXPRESS 9 b.g. Kalanisi (IRE) – Marvellous Dream (FR) (Muhtathir) **h–**
[2018/19 h125: h23g⁶ Jul 17] well-made gelding: placed in Irish points: fairly useful
handicap hurdler, lightly raced: stays 21f: acts on soft going. *Nicky Henderson*

CHAMPAGNEFOROSCAR (IRE) 5 b.m. Oscar (IRE) – Creaking Step (IRE) **h–**
(Shernazar) [2018/19 b13.7m h19.5sᵖᵘ h16.5dᵖᵘ Dec 13] fifth foal: closely related to fairly **b–**
useful 2m hurdle winner Cracking Chap (by High Chaparral): dam unraced: no promise in
bumper/maiden hurdle. *Alexandra Dunn*

CHAMPAGNE GEORGE (IRE) 9 gr.g. Acambaro (GER) – Charannah (IRE) (Red **c–**
Sunset) [2018/19 h104: c26g⁵ c23.9mᵖᵘ c24gᵖᵘ Jul 15] fair hurdler: no form over fences: in **h–**
cheekpieces last 2 starts: has shaped as if amiss. *Neil Mulholland*

CHAMPAGNE IDEAS (IRE) 6 b.g. Acambaro (GER) – Charannah (IRE) (Red Sunset) **h93**
[2018/19 h20g⁴ h21.6d h16.8s h19.5d³ Apr 6] €9,000 5-y-o: fourth foal: brother to bumper
winner/fair 19f hurdle winner Champagne George: dam unraced half-sister to fair hurdler/
fairly useful chaser (stayed 3m) Fresh Air And Fun: placed in Irish points: off 4 months
(had breathing operation), first form over hurdles when 4¼ lengths third of 15 to Espalion
in novice handicap at Chepstow. *Chris Down*

CHAMPAGNE MIST (IRE) 7 b.g. Stowaway – Valentines Misty (IRE) (Presenting) **h98**
[2018/19 h16.3d⁵ h15.8v h19.7d Mar 9] €26,000 3-y-o, £22,500 5-y-o: fifth foal: dam
unraced daughter of fairly useful 19f-21f hurdle winner Jessica One: fourth on completed
start in points: modest form when fifth in introductory event at Newbury on hurdling debut:
well beaten subsequently: tried in hood. *Alastair Ralph*

CHAMPAGNE MYSTERY (IRE) 5 b.g. Shantou (USA) – Spanker (Suave Dancer **h125 p**
(USA)) [2018/19 h17sᵘʳ h16.7s² h21.4g² h16m² Apr 12] €33,000 3-y-o, £68,000 4-y-o:
brother to a winning pointer and half-brother to 3 winners, including fairly useful hurdler
First Trim (2m winner, by Acclamation): dam irresolute maiden (stayed 1½m): runner-up
completed start in Irish points: fairly useful form over hurdles, runner-up all 3 completed
starts: open to further improvement. *Nicky Henderson*

CHAMPAGNE PLATINUM (IRE) 5 gr.g. Stowaway – Saffron Holly (IRE) (Roselier **h121 p**
(FR)) [2018/19 h16.4d* h16.3d* Dec 29] €35,000 3-y-o, £250,000 4-y-o: well-made
gelding: sixth foal: half-brother to fairly useful hurdler/chaser The Chazer (2m-19f winner,
by Witness Box) and bumper winner/fair chaser Lismakeery (17f winner, by Beneficial),
stayed 2½m: dam unraced: won Irish point on debut: fairly useful form over hurdles: won
maiden at Newcastle and introductory event at Newbury (easily by 4½ lengths from
Percy's Word), both in December: off 4 months, only fifth of 6 to Klassical Dream in
Champion Novices' Hurdle at Punchestown shortly after end of British season: remains
open to improvement. *Nicky Henderson*

CHAMPAGNE POPPY (IRE) 6 b.m. Scorpion (IRE) – Princess Supreme (IRE) **h–**
(Supreme Leader) [2018/19 b–: h16spᵘ Mar 8] lengthy mare: no promise in bumper/novice
hurdle (mistakes). *Tom Lacey*

CHAMPAGNE TO GO (IRE) 9 b.m. Beneficial – Terre d'Orient (FR) (Kabool) **c–**
[2018/19 c–, h106: h22.7g² h25.4g³ h20.2g⁴ h20.1g³ h19.9g* h20vᵖᵘ h18.1g⁵ Dec 29] Irish **h104**
point winner: fair handicap hurdler: won mares event at Sedgefield in November: pulled up
in novice handicap only chase start: stays 25f: acts on heavy going: has worn cheekpieces:
usually held up. *Rebecca Menzies*

CHAMPAGNE WELL (IRE) 6 b.g. Gold Well – Perkanod (IRE) (Executive Perk) **h129**
[2018/19 b16s⁵ b16.8s* h19d³ h21.6d² h23.8d² h19.8s³ h24.7d⁶ Apr 5] €16,500 3-y-o, **b93**
€40,000 5-y-o: well-made gelding: will make a chaser: sixth foal: closely related to a
winning pointer by Oscar: dam, winning pointer, ran once over hurdles: off mark in Irish
points at third attempt: fair form in bumpers: won at Sedgefield in December: fairly useful
form over hurdles: first past post in maiden at Ludlow (demoted after causing interference
run-in) in February: third in EBF 'National Hunt' Novices' Handicap Hurdle Final at
Sandown next time: stays 25f: acts on soft going: races prominently. *Fergal O'Brien*

CHAMPAGNE WEST (IRE) 11 b.g. Westerner – Wyndham Sweetmarie (IRE) (Mister **c106**
Lord (USA)) [2018/19 c135, h–: c26m c21g⁵ c22.7f³ c21.1dᵖᵘ Apr 4] well-made gelding: **h–**
winning chaser: high-class chaser in prime: regressed plenty more in 2018/19, leaving
Henry de Bromhead after second start: stays 25f, effective at shorter: acts on heavy going:
tried in cheekpieces/tongue tie: usually makes running/races prominently, tends to find
little/make mistakes. *T. M. Frost*

CHAMPAYNE LADY (IRE) 7 ch.m. Robin des Champs (FR) – Maghereragh Lady **h125**
(IRE) (Old Vic) [2018/19 h114, b92: h19.9s³ h16d³ h22d⁵ Apr 22] rather sparely-made
mare: bumper winner: fairly useful hurdler: stays 2¾m: acts on heavy going: usually wears
tongue tie. *Alan Fleming, Ireland*

CHAMPERS ON ICE (IRE) 9 gr.g. Robin des Champs (FR) – Miss Nova (Ra Nova) **c–**
[2018/19 c–, h128: h24.3g⁴ h24dᵖᵘ Mar 14] tall, good-topped gelding: useful handicap **h124**
hurdler at best: off 14 months before 2018/19 return: winning chaser: stays 3m: acts on
heavy going: has worn headgear, including last 5 starts: tried in tongue tie. *David Pipe*

CHAMPION CHASE (FR) 7 b.g. Voix du Nord (FR) – Darling Frisco (FR) (Trebrook **c84**
(FR)) [2018/19 c93, h91: c20sᶠ c19.7s⁵ c16.4d⁶ c19.7s² c17g² Apr 7] maiden hurdler: **h–**
modest maiden chaser: stays 2½m: acts on heavy going: wears headgear: tried in tongue
tie: usually races close up. *Martin Bosley*

CHAMPIONE (IRE) 9 b.g. Tikkanen (USA) – Star Trix (IRE) (Peacock (FR)) [2018/19 **c–**
c16.3gᵖᵘ May 4] has had breathing operation: multiple point winner: modest maiden **h–**
hurdler: pulled up in hunter on chasing debut: stays 3m: acts on good to soft going: tried in
tongue tie. *J. W. Tudor*

CHAMPIONS CLUB (IRE) 5 b.g. Jeremy (USA) – Mrs Masters (IRE) (Un Desperado **h91**
(FR)) [2018/19 h15.9g h16.8s h16.8s Jan 20] €65,000 3-y-o: fourth foal: half-brother to
bumper winner/fairly useful hurdler Foggy's Wall (19f winner, by Golan) and bumper
winner Suncroft (by Flemensfirth): dam unraced half-sister to dams of smart chaser up to
3m Breedsbreeze and useful hurdler/smart chaser up to 21f Spiritofthegames: signs of
ability in maiden/novice hurdles. *Tim Vaughan*

CHAMP (IRE) 7 b.g. King's Theatre (IRE) – China Sky (IRE) (Definite Article) **h149 p**
[2018/19 h134p: h20.2g* h21d* h20.5s* h20.5d* h21s² h24.7d* Apr 5]

Sir Anthony McCoy OBE, the twenty-times champion jockey, was known
less formally during his riding career. To Billy Rock, the first to spot McCoy's
talent when he began riding out for his local trainer in Northern Ireland, the
teenager was 'Wee Anthony'. Years later, in November 2006, 'AP' won a handicap
chase at Lingfield on a Jonjo O'Neill-trained horse of that name in the colours of
J.P. McManus. Wee Anthony wasn't to be the last horse McManus named after his
retained rider who retired from the saddle at the end of the 2014/15 season, by which
time the perennial champion had simply become known as 'Champ' to many in
the sport. Wee Anthony was just a fair chaser, but calling a horse Champ put much
more of an onus on McManus to find a suitable candidate for such a name. The
early signs were very promising that he had made a good choice. Champ landed the
odds on his debut in a division of a maiden bumper at Southwell early in 2017 when
Timeform's report on the race called him 'as exciting a prospect as seen in British
bumpers this season.' A defeat at odds-on at Kempton next time ended any hopes
that he would be living up to his name in that particular sphere, but his longer-term
prospects as a jumper still looked very good and that was something he confirmed
in the latest season, not a 'champ' yet perhaps but certainly a horse who still has the
makings of one.

Champ was out in the early weeks of the season with his novice status still
intact after just one run the previous season when beaten a neck at Ascot by the smart
Vinndication. Champ landed the odds by ten lengths in both a maiden at Perth and
a novice at Warwick in May before being put away for bigger tests in the winter.

Betway Challow Novices' Hurdle, Newbury—Champ (right) quickens smartly at the end of a steadily-run race to see off Getaway Trump and the grey Kateson

Returning in a handicap at Newbury at the beginning of December and looking well ahead of his opening mark, Champ took a strong hold in mid-division before going on at the fifth flight and making the rest to beat Le Musee by four and a half lengths, conceding 19 lb to the runner-up. Champ looked the type for a bigger handicap, but at the end of the month he was returned to Newbury to take on six other last-time-out winners in the Betway Challow Novices' Hurdle, sent off the even-money favourite. In a steadily-run race, Champ didn't need to improve but won in most taking style, quickening to lead at the last and forging ahead to win by two and a half lengths from Getaway Trump who proved himself another top novice later in the season. Although beaten next time when contesting the Baring Bingham Novices' Hurdle (branded as the Ballymore) at Cheltenham, Champ improved again when finding only the Irish-trained City Island two lengths too good, having led from two out until approaching the last, and keeping on well (Brewin'upastorm was back in fourth as he had been in the Challow).

Doom Bar Sefton Novices' Hurdle, Aintree—Mark Walsh deputises for the injured Barry Geraghty at the eleventh hour as Champ copes splendidly with the step up in trip to record a second Grade 1 win of the season

Champ had been raced only at around two and a half miles over hurdles, either travelling strongly or sometimes taking a hold in his races, but he looked every bit as good when stepping up to an extended three miles in the Doom Bar Sefton Novices' Hurdle at Aintree. Connections had apparently been close to switching him to the Mersey Novices' instead over two and a half miles when the ground softened, though the longer option was chosen in the end with his future chasing career in mind. The way the race was run made the Sefton less of a test than it ought to have been. Indeed, most of the field of twelve were still closely grouped three out, but 9/4 favourite Champ had them well strung out at the line after he had made smooth headway to lead on the bridle two out under Mark Walsh, standing in for Barry Geraghty who had broken his leg in a fall in the Topham earlier on the card. Ridden after the last, Champ kept on well for a three-length win over the previously unbeaten Emitom, with a gap of seven to another of the leading contenders Lisnagar Oscar in third. The only disappointment among the market leaders was the Martin Pipe runner-up Dallas des Pictons who was beaten when making a mistake at the last and eased right off after reportedly losing his action. Champ was a second consecutive winner of the Sefton for his trainer Nicky Henderson after Santini, while Beat That was successful for Seven Barrows in 2014 and Rustle had won the first running of the race, which began life as the White Satin Novices' Hurdle, for Henderson in 1988. McCoy, incidentally, won the Sefton three times, including in the McManus silks on Black Jack Ketchum and At Fishers Cross.

Champ (IRE) (b.g. 2012)	King's Theatre (IRE) (b 1991)	Sadler's Wells (b 1981)	Northern Dancer / Fairy Bridge
		Regal Beauty (b 1981)	Princely Native / Dennis Belle
	China Sky (IRE) (b 2005)	Definite Article (b 1992)	Indian Ridge / Summer Fashion
		Katday (b 1987)	Miller's Mate / Kanara

There's every encouragement from Champ's pedigree that he will go further still in living up to his name as his dam is a half-sister to triple Gold Cup winner Best Mate. Champ's dam China Sky wasn't blessed with much ability herself and she made just three starts for Henderson, starting odds on for her debut in a bumper at Bangor with McCoy in the saddle and not offering much again in a couple of novice hurdles at Taunton and Wincanton for Geraghty. Champ is China Sky's first foal, while her next two foals, Track Mac (by Presenting) and Drury (a mare by Beat Hollow), made their first appearances in Irish bumpers in the spring without showing a great deal, though Track Mac has also finished second in his only completed point. Best Mate, whom McCoy partnered to success in the King George VI Chase, also showed plenty of promise in novice hurdles before making his name as a chaser and, like Champ, he too stepped up in trip to go one better at Aintree after finishing second at Cheltenham, though he won the Mersey Novices' after finishing second in the Supreme. Best Mate would have stood out in any broodmare's record, but his dam Katday produced some other good jumpers, with Best Mate's brother Cornish Rebel the pick of the rest. He wasn't alone among Katday's offspring in showing some temperament, but was a high-class staying chaser at his best, beaten a short head in the Scottish Grand National as a novice and finishing third in the following season's Hennessy Gold Cup and Welsh National. Cornish Rebel was also a former Challow winner, though there was an early indication that he had his quirks when he disappointed at odds of 5/4 in the Sefton. Champ is a tall gelding who looks the type to take very well to fences. He stays three miles but won't be at all inconvenienced if returned to a bit shorter to start with in novice chases. He acts on soft ground, probably on heavy. *Nicky Henderson*

CHANCEANOTHERFIVE (IRE) 7 b.g. Dubai Destination (USA) – Ryhall (IRE) **h94** (Saddlers' Hall (IRE)) [2018/19 b104: h20.2g⁴ h16.8m³ h16.2g⁴ h16.2g h20.1sᵖᵘ h23.8m⁴ h24.3s³ h23.8m² h27g³ Apr 5] sturdy gelding: point winner: dual bumper winner: disappointing maiden hurdler: left Keith Dalgleish after fifth start: stays 3m: acts on soft and good to firm going: in headgear 4 of last 5 outings: tried in tongue tie. *Stuart Coltherd*

CHANCE A TUNE (FR) 4 b.g. My Risk (FR) – Lyric Melody (FR) (Lyphard's Wish **b85**
(FR)) [2018/19 b15.3g² Dec 6] fifth foal: half-brother to French 17f chase winner Mister
Happy and modest/temperamental 2¾m chase winner Mister Dick (both by Great Journey):
dam, French 17f-19f hurdle/chase winner, also 1½m winner on Flat: 16/1, 2¾ lengths
second to Fearless in junior bumper at Wincanton. *Nigel Twiston-Davies*

CHANCE IT (IRE) 9 b.g. Tajraasi (USA) – Lafanta (IRE) (Oscar (IRE)) [2018/19 h16g **c–**
h16.8g h21.6gᵖᵘ h21.7g h15.9s⁶ Jan 16] maiden pointer: long-standing maiden hurdler: **h–**
twice-raced chaser: left P. Corkery after first start, Jimmy Frost after fourth: has worn
headgear: tried in tongue tie. *Jeremy Scott*

CHANCEITON (IRE) 8 b.g. Vinnie Roe (IRE) – Lissnabrucka (IRE) (Lord Americo) **c93**
[2018/19 c90, h–: h23.3g⁵ h23.3g⁶ c24.2g² c24.2mᵘʳ h23.9g³ h25.8g* h23.3g³ c31.9sᵖᵘ Nov **h92**
21] winning pointer: modest handicap hurdler: won at Kelso (conditionals) on heavy going:
similar form over fences: stays 3¼m: acts on heavy going: wears tongue tie. *Lucinda Russell*

CHANGEOFLUCK (IRE) 11 b.g. Gold Well – Sotattie (Teenoso (USA)) [2018/19 c96, **c102**
h–: c21.6g⁴ c27.5d³ c24gᵖᵘ c20.2f Feb 26] sturdy gelding: prolific point winner: maiden **h–**
hurdler/hunter chaser: has worn cheekpieces: wears tongue tie. *Alan Hill*

CHANGE UR TUNE (IRE) 7 br.g. Milan – Sunny Native (IRE) (Be My Native (USA)) **c89**
[2018/19 h–: h19.2g³ h20m h23.9dᵖᵘ h19.7s⁵ h21.6vᵖᵘ c20d³ c20.2gᵖᵘ c24g⁵ c24g* c24gᵖᵘ **h93**
Apr 25] modest maiden hurdler: modest form over fences: won novice handicap at Bangor
in April: stays 3m: probably acts on soft going: often in headgear: tongue tied last 2 starts.
Sheila Lewis

CHANGING THE GUARD 13 b.g. King's Best (USA) – Our Queen of Kings (Arazi **c– x**
(USA)) [2018/19 c96, h82§: c17.8m h16.8m⁶ c16.3m c19.4m Aug 2] sturdy gelding: **h– §**
winning hurdler/chaser, of little account nowadays: left Barry Brennan after first start:
wears headgear/tongue tie: temperamental. *Ryan Chapman*

CHANTARA ROSE 10 br.m. Kayf Tara – Fragrant Rose (Alflora (IRE)) [2018/19 c–, h–: **c102**
c21.6g³ c23.9dᵖᵘ c26g⁴ c25.5g⁴ h22.1d⁶ c22.5g Oct 7] fair handicap hurdler/maiden chaser: **h–**
stays 25f: acts on heavy going: usually in cheekpieces: wears tongue tie: usually races
nearer last than first. *Peter Bowen*

CHANTECLER (IRE) 8 b.g. Authorized (IRE) – Snow Goose (Polar Falcon (USA)) [2018/19 **h113**
h101x: h21.2m² h20.3g h18.5m⁶ h16.8m* h16.8g² h16.8g⁵ h15.8g⁵ Sep 23] lengthy
gelding: fair handicap hurdler: won at Newton Abbot in August: has form at 3¼m, effective
at much shorter: acts on good to firm and good to soft going: has worn headgear: tongue
tied: free-going front runner. *Neil Mulholland*

CHANTRY HOUSE (IRE) 5 br.g. Yeats (IRE) – The Last Bank (IRE) (Phardante (FR)) **b104 p**
[2018/19 b16s* Mar 10] €26,000 3-y-o, £295,000 4-y-o: closely related to fairly useful
hurdler/useful chaser The Last Day (2m winner, by Oscar) and half-brother to 2 winners by
Presenting, including fairly useful chaser On The Shannon (2½m/2¾m winner): dam, ran
once in bumper, sister to fair hurdler/fairly useful chaser (2m-2½m winner) Dantes Bank
and half-sister to useful hurdler (stayed 3m) Nancy Myles: off mark in Irish points at
second attempt: landed odds in 11-runner bumper at Warwick by 3½ lengths from
Edwardstone: exciting prospect. *Nicky Henderson*

CHAPARRAL PRINCE (IRE) 4 b.g. High Chaparral (IRE) – Snow Gretel (IRE) (Green **h111**
Desert (USA)) [2018/19 h17.7g h16g² h16g² h15.8g² h18.8d h16m⁴ Apr 12] lengthy
gelding: has had breathing operation: half-brother to fairly useful 2m hurdle winner
Mastermind (by Nathaniel): fair maiden on Flat, stays 1½m: similar form over hurdles:
should stay beyond 2m: acts on good to firm going: in blinkers last 3 starts. *Nicky Henderson*

CHAPEL ROCK 7 b.g. Baldhu Cavalier – North Coast Girl (Birthright) [2018/19 **b80**
b16.8m² Aug 6] 4/1, second in bumper at Newton Abbot. *Philip Hobbs*

CHAPMANSHYPE (IRE) 5 b.g. Aizavoski (IRE) – Call Her Something (IRE) (Heron **h103 p**
Island (IRE)) [2018/19 b16g* b15.7s h15.3g⁴ h16g² Apr 26] sturdy gelding: has had **b93**
breathing operation: first foal: dam unraced half-sister to fairly useful hurdler/useful chaser
(stayed 29f) Bowleaze: fair form in bumpers: won maiden event at Punchestown on debut
in October, then left Miss Elizabeth Doyle: tongue tied, fair form in frame both outings in
maiden hurdles: will be suited by 2½m: remains open to improvement. *Jamie Snowden*

CHARACTER ONESIE (IRE) 7 b.g. Dark Angel (IRE) – Flame Keeper (IRE) **h97**
(Pivotal) [2018/19 h99: h15.7g² h17.2gᵇᵈ May 26] fair maiden hurdler: raced around 2m:
acts on soft going. *Donald McCain*

Mrs Julie Martin and David R. Martin's "Charbel"

CHARBEL (IRE) 8 b.g. Iffraaj – Eoz (IRE) (Sadler's Wells (USA)) [2018/19 c157, h134: c20.1g³ c19.4d* c21g² c19.9d* c20.5g³ c21d⁵ c20.6dᵖᵘ c22.7g⁶ Apr 27] tall, useful-looking gelding: useful hurdler: high-class chaser: won handicap at Chepstow in October and Peterborough Chase at Huntingdon (by 8 lengths from God's Own) in December: placed either side of latter success in 1965 Chase at Ascot (½-length second to Politologue) and listed event at Kempton (5¼ lengths third behind Top Notch): stays 21f: acts on soft going: usually in cheekpieces: has worn tongue tie. *Kim Bailey* — **c157 h–**

CHARIN' CROSS 7 ch.g. Cockney Rebel (IRE) – Lush Lady (IRE) (Kris Kin (USA)) [2018/19 h–: h23.3g h23.3gᵖᵘ h23.3g⁵ h23.9gᵖᵘ Jul 5] poor maiden hurdler: stayed 23f: dead. *Micky Hammond* — **h64**

CHARLIE CHAPLIN (GER) 5 b.g. Lope de Vega (IRE) – Campina (Oasis Dream) [2018/19 h98: h15.8g h20g Jun 3] small, angular gelding: regressive maiden on Flat: likewise over hurdles: tried in blinkers. *Robert Eddery* — **h–**

CHARLIE COOK (IRE) 10 b.g. Royal Anthem (USA) – Supreme Baloo (IRE) (Supreme Leader) [2018/19 h–: h19.2g h24g⁴ Jul 15] well-made gelding: fair handicap hurdler, lightly raced: stays easy 23f: acts on good to firm and heavy going. *Graeme McPherson* — **h92**

CHARLIE MON (IRE) 10 ch.g. Presenting – Prowler (IRE) (Old Vic) [2018/19 c95§, h–: c24g⁴ c26.1g² c25.8g² c25.8g³ c25.8g⁴ Aug 21] lengthy, workmanlike gelding: maiden hurdler: modest handicap chaser: stays 3¼m: acts on firm and soft going: wears headgear: usually leads. *Mike Hammond* — **c97 h–**

CHARLIE PAPA LIMA (IRE) 8 b.g. Winged Love (IRE) – Fairylodge Scarlet (IRE) (Mister Lord (USA)) [2018/19 c105, h105: c19.9gᵖᵘ c21mᵖᵘ h21.6g c20s⁶ c21.7d² c20d c24.2s⁵ c25.1g³ Apr 14] angular gelding: Irish point winner: modest maiden hurdler/chaser: left Harry Whittington after second start: probably stays 3m: acts on soft and good to firm going: tried in hood: wears tongue tie. *Brian Barr* — **c93 h–**

CHARLIE'S LASS 6 b.m. Getaway (GER) – Oh So Beautiful (IRE) (Montjeu (IRE)) [2018/19 b16.2g³ b17.1d h15.6g⁴ h16.2gᶠ Dec 29] poor form in mares bumpers/novice hurdles: would have been suited by 2½m+: dead. *Lucinda Russell*　**h76 b72**

CHARLIE SNOW ANGEL 10 b.g. Overbury (IRE) – Sister Seven (IRE) (Henbit (USA)) [2018/19 c97, h–: c16gᵖᵘ c15.6s⁵ c15.8g⁵ c20.1sᵖᵘ c20.1g³ c16.3sʳʳ c21.6d² c20.1v² c21.6d³ c20.3d³ Apr 26] maiden hurdler: modest handicap chaser: stays 2¾m: acts on heavy going: tried in cheekpieces: wears tongue tie: one to treat with caution (has refused to race). *Sandy Forster*　**c97 § h–**

CHARLI PARCS (FR) 6 b.g. Anabaa Blue – Ella Parcs (FR) (Nikos) [2018/19 h142: h16.4g Nov 18] tall, useful-looking gelding: smart juvenile hurdler in 2016/17: in-and-out form since, down field in Greatwood Hurdle (Handicap) at Cheltenham sole start in 2018/19: raced around 2m: acts on soft going. *Nicky Henderson*　**h–**

CHARLOTTE DU BERRY 4 b.f. Black Sam Bellamy (IRE) – Fleet Footed (Fleetwood (IRE)) [2018/19 h16dᵘʳ Aug 29] fourth foal: dam, well held in bumpers/over hurdles, half-sister to high-class hurdler/useful chaser (stayed 25f) Lough Derg: hampered and unseated fourth in juvenile hurdle at Worcester. *Dai Burchell*　**h–**

CHARLOTTE'S CHUM (IRE) 10 b.m. Stowaway – Aunt Sue (IRE) (Shahanndeh) [2018/19 h17.3g h16.7m h21.8g⁵ h23.9g⁵ Aug 1] fifth foal: sister to fairly useful hurdler/ chaser (2m-2½m winner) Dazzling Susie: dam unraced: disappointing maiden hurdler/ chaser: often in headgear/tongue tie. *Gordon Elliott, Ireland*　**c– h70**

CHARMANT (FR) 7 b.g. Balko (FR) – Ravissante (FR) (Mad Tax (USA)) [2018/19 h115: c16.4g* c17.1g* c16.4s⁴ c16.5s* c20dᶠ Mar 24] fairly useful hurdler: useful form over fences: won handicaps at Sedgefield (novice) in November, Kelso in December and Ayr in March: unproven beyond 17f: acts on heavy going: hooded until reappearance: tried in tongue tie: travels strongly. *James Ewart*　**c139 h–**

CHARMING DREAM (FR) 5 b.g. Dream Well (FR) – Changing Times (FR) (Martaline) [2018/19 h16dᵖᵘ Nov 28] has had breathing operation: lightly-raced maiden hurdler: best effort when third in 3-y-o event at Fontainebleau in 2016/17 (for Guillaume Macaire): in tongue strap, pulled up in novice on British debut: has joined Rebecca Menzies. *Dan Skelton*　**h–**

CHARMING LAD (IRE) 14 b.g. Dushyantor (USA) – Glens Lady (IRE) (Mister Lord (USA)) [2018/19 c–, h–: c25.7gᵖᵘ May 13] rangy gelding: maiden hurdler/winning chaser, of no account nowadays: wears headgear/tongue tie. *Anthony Day*　**c– h–**

CHARMING ZEN (FR) 7 gr.g. Youmzain (IRE) – Nioumoun (FR) (Dadarissime (FR)) [2018/19 h–: c16d³ c16.4d² c16d⁴ c15.7d² c19.9g² Apr 22] workmanlike gelding: has had breathing operation: winning hurdler: fairly useful form over fences: best efforts around 2m: acts on good to soft going: in cheekpieces/tongue tie last 2 starts. *Olly Murphy*　**c127 h–**

CHARMIX (FR) 9 br.g. Laveron – Open Up (FR) (Fabulous Don (SPA)) [2018/19 c126, h107: c23.8g Jun 3] well-made gelding: winning hurdler: useful chaser at best: mostly well held since 2016/17: stays 3m: acts on heavy going: has worn headgear. *Sandy Thomson*　**c– h–**

CHASE END CHARLIE (IRE) 8 b.g. Scorpion (IRE) – Artist's Muse (IRE) (Cape Cross (IRE)) [2018/19 h23.3s h20gᵖᵘ h21.7g⁴ h20.6s² h25.5d³ h23.1d² h25.5d³ Mar 9] lengthy gelding: has had breathing operation: fair handicap hurdler: last of 3 on completed start over fences in 2016/17: stays 3¼m: acts on soft going: usually in cheekpieces. *Henry Oliver*　**c– h113**

CHASE ME (IRE) 8 b.g. Mahler – Collatrim Choice (IRE) (Saddlers' Hall (IRE)) [2018/19 c74p, h81: h19.9m² c20d² c16.5g⁴ c24g⁵ c22.7m³ Feb 14] strong, lengthy gelding: multiple point winner: poor maiden hurdler: modest form over fences: left Nigel Twiston-Davies after fourth start: probably stays 23f: acts on good to soft and good to firm going: often in headgear. *J. M. Ridley*　**c92 h78**

CHASE THE SPUD 11 b.g. Alflora (IRE) – Trial Trip (Le Moss) [2018/19 c145, h–: c28.8v c25.6dᵖᵘ Jan 19] workmanlike gelding: winning hurdler: smart chaser in prime: no form since winning reappearance in 2017/18: suited by extreme distances: acts on heavy going: tried in hood/tongue tie. *Fergal O'Brien*　**c– h–**

CHASE THE WIND (IRE) 10 ch.g. Spadoun (FR) – Asfreeasthewind (IRE) (Moscow Society (USA)) [2018/19 c24.1g⁶ c24g⁵ c20.3s⁶ c26.3d² c23.4d³ c26.2d⁵ c29.6d² Apr 26] lengthy gelding: has had breathing operation: winning hurdler: fair handicap chaser: stays 3¾m: acts on heavy and good to firm going: has worn hood: often tongue tied: front runner/ races prominently. *Joanne Foster*　**c105 h–**

CHASING HEADLIGHTS (IRE) 7 b.g. Getaway (GER) – Could Do (Cloudings (IRE)) [2018/19 h–, b–: h15.8s⁴ c19.7g⁵ c24g h20.5m³ c19.7g² h19d² c19.2gᵖᵘ h15.8d h20.5g h16.8g Apr 20] unplaced in point: poor maiden hurdler: similar form over fences: stays easy 21f: acts on good to firm and good to soft going: usually in headgear nowadays. *Alexandra Dunn* **c65 h79**

CHASMA 9 b.m. Kayf Tara – Luneray (FR) (Poplar Bluff) [2018/19 c104, h–: c20.3g⁶ h20.2g c20g³ c20g c20.3s⁵ h20.2g³ c20.1m* c21.1g* c19.3g³ Apr 23] winning hurdler: fair handicap chaser: won at Newcastle in March and Sedgefield (mares event) in April: stays 21f: acts on good to firm and heavy going: has worn cheekpieces, including last 4 starts: formerly tongue tied: usually held up. *Michael Easterby* **c107 h–**

CHASSEUR DE TETE (FR) 7 b.g. Coastal Path – Escomptee (FR) (Roi de Rome (USA)) [2018/19 h108: c20.1gᵘʳ c20.5v⁴ Nov 14] fair hurdler: let down by jumping both starts over fences: unproven beyond 2m: acted on heavy going: wore tongue tie last 5 starts: dead. *Lucinda Russell* **c107 h–**

CHATEAU CHINON (FR) 7 b.g. Dream Well (FR) – Liesse de Marbeuf (FR) (Cyborg (FR)) [2018/19 c–, h–: c20.3g⁴ c16g⁶ c15.6s⁶ c15.7gᶠ Oct 25] maiden hurdler: poor form over fences: unproven beyond 2m: acts on heavy going: has worn headgear. *Shaun Harris* **c80 h–**

CHATEAU CONTI (FR) 7 b.g. Vendangeur (IRE) – Regina Conti (FR) (Lavirco (GER)) [2018/19 h135: h20m³ c18.2dᵘʳ c18mᶠ c22.5s⁴ c17dᶠ h24sᵖᵘ Dec 6] useful hurdler: let down by jumping in maiden chases: stays 2½m: acts on good to firm and heavy going. *Joseph Patrick O'Brien, Ireland* **c110 x h138**

CHATEAU ROBIN (IRE) 8 br.g. Robin des Pres (FR) – Bella With A Zee (IRE) (Persian Bold) [2018/19 c106, h–: c19.9g³ c23.8m² Jun 21] sturdy gelding: lightly-raced maiden hurdler: fair maiden chaser: stays 3m: acts on good to firm and heavy going: in cheekpieces last 2 starts: races prominently. *Kim Bailey* **c104 h–**

CHATELIER (FR) 7 ch.g. Network (GER) – Elza III (FR) (Lazer (FR)) [2018/19 h80, b–: h19m* h19.9g h23gᵖᵘ c15.7g⁴ c20s³ Nov 13] modest handicap hurdler: won at Warwick (conditionals) in May: in frame both outings in handicap chases: stays 2½m: acts on heavy and good to firm going: tried in hood. *Samuel Drinkwater* **c83 h86**

CHATEZ (IRE) 8 b.g. Dandy Man (IRE) – Glory Days (GER) (Tiger Hill (IRE)) [2018/19 h99: h15.7g² h15.7s Dec 22] good-topped gelding: lightly-raced hurdler, fairly useful at best: much better on Flat, winning in April: raced around 2m: acts on heavy going. *Alan King* **h113**

CHATHAM STREET LAD (IRE) 7 br.g. Beneficial – Hearts Delight (IRE) (Broken Hearted) [2018/19 c17d⁶ c19.5d c19.5gᵘʳ h20s⁴ h16.3d h16v* h20s* h20d² h20d³ Feb 23] €30,000 3-y-o: second foal: dam (c92) 2¾m chase winner: useful handicap hurdler: won at Cork in December: running best race in maiden chases when hampered and unseated last in race won by Balzac Turgot at Ballinrobe: stays 2½m: acts on heavy going. *Michael Winters, Ireland* **c112 h133**

CHATO (FR) 7 ch.g. Malinas (GER) – Queen Bruere (FR) (Mansonnien (FR)) [2018/19 h99: h21.4m³ h23.3g³ h26.5g³ Jul 22] good-topped gelding: has had breathing operation: fair maiden hurdler: left Alan King after first start: stays up to 3m: acts on good to firm and heavy going: in cheekpieces last 2 starts: tried in tongue tie. *David Pipe* **h107**

CHAT TO CHARLIE (IRE) 5 ch.g. Stowaway – Miss Izzy (IRE) (Old Vic) [2018/19 b15.8d² b15.8s Apr 7] useful-looking gelding: first foal: dam unraced half-sister to fairly useful hurdler/smart chaser (stays 29f) Abolitionist: fair form when second at Huntingdon on first of 2 outings in bumpers: bred to be suited by 2½m+. *Graeme McPherson* **b91**

CHAUVET CAVE (IRE) 7 b.g. Court Cave (IRE) – Kindle Ball (FR) (Kaldounevees (FR)) [2018/19 b15.7s h19.9dᶠ h22sᵖᵘ Jan 29] tailed off in bumper: failed to complete in novice hurdles. *Jane Walton* **h– b–**

CHEAP AND CHEERFUL 6 b.g. Shirocco (GER) – Shayaza (Generous (IRE)) [2018/19 h16.5g h20.5g h16m⁴ h16g* h22g³ h19.8v Nov 11] fair form over hurdles: won maiden at Sligo in July: left Joseph Patrick O'Brien after fifth start: unproven beyond 2m: acted on good to firm going: usually wore tongue tie: dead. *Jonjo O'Neill* **h108**

CHEBSEY BEAU 9 b.g. Multiplex – Chebsey Belle (IRE) (Karinga Bay) [2018/19 c122, h–: c21.2s⁵ c21.4g h19.6g c22.4g h19.8g* h19.4g Jan 26] fairly useful handicap hurdler: won at Musselburgh in January: little show in handicap chases since winning novice event at Market Rasen in 2017/18: stays 21f: acts on good to firm and good to soft going: tried in visor: in tongue tie last 2 starts. *John Quinn* **c103 h110**

CHECKITOUT (IRE) 5 b.g. Salutino (GER) – Akasha (IRE) (Stowaway) [2018/19 **h104**
h19.5d⁴ h21d⁵ Mar 28] €19,000 3-y-o, £37,000 4-y-o: third foal: dam unraced: third in Irish
point in May 2018: better effort in maiden hurdles (fair form) when fourth at Chepstow.
Charlie Longsdon

CHEDDLETON 4 br.g. Shirocco (GER) – Over Sixty (Overbury (IRE)) [2018/19 **b93 p**
b15.7d⁴ Mar 20] €60,000 3-y-o: fourth foal: half-brother to bumper winner/useful hurdler
Spirit of Kayf (2m-2¾m winner, by Kayf Tara): dam (c128/h135), 2m-2¾m hurdle/chase
winner, half-sister to useful hurdler (stayed 3m) Diamant Noir: 9/2, won bumper at
Haydock on debut by 2 lengths from Foxey, travelling well to lead 2f out: should progress.
Jennie Candlish

CHEEKY CHICA (IRE) 6 bl.m. Stowaway – Hats And Heels (IRE) (Flemensfirth **b–**
(USA)) [2018/19 b82: b15.8gᵖᵘ May 8] modest form in bumpers only on debut: dead.
Neil Mulholland

CHEEKY RASCAL (IRE) 4 b.g. Most Improved (IRE) – Bessie Lou (IRE) (Montjeu **h94**
(IRE)) [2018/19 h15.3f* h17.7d h16.8s h15.8dᵖᵘ Feb 17] dam fairly useful 17f hurdle
winner: fair maiden on Flat, stays 1¾m: modest form when winning juvenile at Wincanton
on hurdling debut in October: regressed subsequently: in headgear last 2 starts. *Oliver
Sherwood*

CHEER'S DELBOY (IRE) 6 ch.g. Golan (IRE) – Lindy Lou (Hernando (FR)) [2018/19 **c100**
h102: h23.3g⁶ c20g⁵ Sep 11] workmanlike gelding: runner-up on second start in Irish **h76**
maiden points: maiden hurdler: some encouragement when fifth in novice handicap at
Worcester on chasing debut (finished lame): stays 23f: acts on soft going: tried in
cheekpieces. *Robin Dickin*

CHEF D'EQUIPE (FR) 7 b.g. Presenting – Millesimee (FR) (Video Rock (FR)) **c132**
[2018/19 c127, h110: c19.9d² c19.9s⁵ h19g* h20.5d² c20.2g³ h19.8g⁴ Mar 25] useful- **h127**
looking gelding: fairly useful hurdler: won novice at Taunton in January: useful handicap
chaser: stays 3m: acts on soft going: usually in hood: tried in tongue tie. *Philip Hobbs*

CHEF DES OBEAUX (FR) 7 b.g. Saddler Maker (IRE) – O Dame de Gene (FR) **c142**
(Passing Sale) [2018/19 h142: c20s³ c23.6dᵘʳ c26.2d⁴ c31.7sᵖᵘ Mar 12] tall gelding: **h–**
useful novice hurdler in 2017/18: similar form over fences only when winning 4-runner
novice at Chepstow (by 18 lengths) in February: stays 3¼m: acts on heavy going: in
cheekpieces last 2 starts. *Nicky Henderson*

CHEF DE TROUPE (FR) 6 b.g. Air Chief Marshal (IRE) – Tazminya (Fantastic Light **h–**
(USA)) [2018/19 h20gᵖᵘ h16m h16.3m⁵ Jul 22] useful on Flat (stays 1½m) in France for
Alain Couetil: well below that level all 3 outings over hurdles (5/4-favourite on debut).
Dr Richard Newland

CHEF D'OEUVRE (FR) 8 b.g. Martaline – Kostroma (FR) (Lost World (IRE)) [2018/19 **c132**
c–x, h118: c26.1g⁴ c26.2s³ c27.3s* c28.4g³ c34vᵖᵘ Mar 16] useful-looking gelding: **h–**
winning hurdler: useful handicap chaser: won at Haydock in December: also third in
Grand National Trial there (2 lengths behind Robinsfirth) later in winter: stays 3½m: acts
on heavy going: has worn headgear: usually races close up: signs of temperament.
Sam England

CHELSEA FLYER (IRE) 8 b.g. Westerner – Aktress (IRE) (Oscar (IRE)) [2018/19 **c123**
h115: h20d³ h20m⁵ c22.6gᶠ Aug 23] well-made gelding: fairly useful handicap hurdler: **h119**
keeping on (though still set to finish last of 3) when fell last in novice won by Golden
Birthday at Stratford on chasing debut: probably stays 23f: acts on good to firm and good
to soft going: tried in hood. *Emma Lavelle*

CHELTENAM DE VAIGE (FR) 7 b.g. Forestier (FR) – Ratina de Vaige (FR) (April **c67**
Night (FR)) [2018/19 h102: h21m⁴ c20.3g⁴ Jun 5] fair maiden hurdler: well beaten in **h85**
novice handicap on chasing debut: stays 21f: acts on heavy going. *Fergal O'Brien*

CHEQUE EN BLANC (FR) 7 b.g. Bernebeau (FR) – Necossaise (FR) (Michel **c105**
Georges) [2018/19 h102: c19.5s⁶ c28.5d* c25.7s⁶ c25.1g² Jan 5] lengthy gelding: fair **h–**
hurdler: fair form over fences: won handicap at Plumpton in November: will stay long
distances: acts on soft going: has worn headgear/tongue tie: held up. *Gary Moore*

CHEQUERED VIEW 6 b.m. Passing Glance – Blue Plaid (Clantime) [2018/19 b85: **c105 p**
h16g³ h15.7g* h19.3m h23.3d³ c21.2d* Dec 18] fair form over hurdles: won mares maiden **h100**
at Southwell in October: also won novice handicap at Fakenham on chasing debut
following month by 1¼ lengths from Thomas Todd: stays 23f: acts on good to soft going:
hooded prior to Fakenham: open to improvement over fences. *Martin Keighley*

CHERRY PRINCESS 9 gr.m. Act One – Francia (Legend of France (USA)) [2018/19 **h84** h74§: h16.2g³ h16.2g* h16.2g⁵ h16.2m² h16.2g⁶ Sep 17] poor handicap hurdler: won conditionals event at Hexham (little form elsewhere) in June: best around 2m: acts on good to firm and good to soft going: has worn cheekpieces: wears tongue tie: usually races in rear. *Barbara Butterworth*

CHESNEY BROWN (FR) 4 ch.g. Le Havre (IRE) – Jani's Queen (FR) (King's Best **b–** (USA)) [2018/19 b15.7m b15.8g Mar 19] last in bumpers. *Peter Niven*

CHESS PLAYER (IRE) 4 ch.g. No Risk At All (FR) – Merci Jandrer (FR) (Trempolino **b98 p** (USA)) [2018/19 b16m² Apr 13] sixth foal: half-brother to French 13f winner Merci Merci (by Full of Gold): dam unraced half-sister to useful hurdler/top-class chaser (stayed 3¼m) Djakadam: 11/4, showed plenty when 3¾ lengths second to promising December Second in bumper at Ayr: sure to progress and win races. *Ben Pauling*

CHESTERFIELD (IRE) 9 ch.g. Pivotal – Antique (IRE) (Dubai Millennium) [2018/19 **c138 p** h142: h15.7g² c16g² c15.9s³ c18g* Nov 26] compact gelding: useful handicap hurdler: **h142** second in Swinton Handicap at Haydock (¾ length behind Silver Streak) in May: useful form over fences: won maiden at Kempton in November: stays 2¼m: acts on heavy going: remains with potential as a chaser. *Seamus Mullins*

CHESTNUT PETE 4 ch.g. Native Ruler – Rabbit (Muhtarram (USA)) [2018/19 b15.8d⁶ **b–** b16d Apr 6] behind in bumpers. *Sophie Leech*

CHETSFORD WATER (IRE) 5 b.m. Yeats (IRE) – Courting Jenny (IRE) (Witness **h–** Box (USA)) [2018/19 b16.8s h19g Feb 19] has had breathing operation: second foal: dam **b–** unraced half-sister to fairly useful staying chasers Western Jo and Jepeck: well beaten in bumper and novice hurdle (tongue tied). *Harry Fry*

CHEZ HANS (IRE) 5 b.g. Aizavoski (IRE) – Hidden Reserve (IRE) (Heron Island **h111** (IRE)) [2018/19 b–: h15.8g⁵ h20.5g* h21.4gᵖᵘ h19.6g⁶ Apr 11] fair form over hurdles: won maiden at Leicester in December: disappointing both starts after, in cheekpieces final one. *Olly Murphy*

CHICA BUENA (IRE) 4 b.f. Thewayyouare (USA) – Easter Parade (Entrepreneur) **h128** [2018/19 h16.4g⁴ h17d⁶ h16g² h16.5s* h16.8g* h15.6g* h17s* h15.6g² h16.6g⁴ Jan 26] dam half-sister to fair hurdler/fairly useful chaser (stayed 21f) Undergraduate: modest form on Flat: fairly useful juvenile hurdler: won at Ballinrobe (maiden, then left Brendan Duke) in September, Sedgefield in October, Musselburgh (handicap) in November and Aintree (listed event, by 23 lengths from Liffeydale Dreamer) in December: will prove best around 2m: acts on good going: front runner/races prominently: travels strongly. *Keith Dalgleish*

CHICAGO LADY (IRE) 8 b.m. Stowaway – Gemmeus (IRE) (Bigstone (IRE)) **h90** [2018/19 h95: h23v³ h21.4d h19.3s⁵ Mar 7] runner-up in Irish point on debut: modest maiden hurdler: stays 23f: acts on heavy going. *Donald McCain*

CHICAGO OUTFIT (IRE) 14 b.g. Old Vic – Lambourne Lace (IRE) (Un Desperado **c92 §** (FR)) [2018/19 c100§, h–: c24.2g³ c24.2gⁿᵘ Jun 16] maiden hurdler: modest handicap **h–** chaser nowadays: stays 25f: acts on soft and good to firm going: wears headgear: usually leads: unreliable. *Leonard Kerr*

CHICA RAPIDA 7 ch.m. Paco Boy (IRE) – Tora Bora (Grand Lodge (USA)) [2018/19 **h–** h–: h15.8vᵘʳ h16sᵖᵘ Jan 21] lengthy mare: of no account: in cheekpieces last 2 starts. *Gail Haywood*

CHIC NAME (FR) 7 b.g. Nickname (FR) – Vuelta Al Ruedo (FR) (Ballingarry (IRE)) **c128** [2018/19 c137, h–: h19.5d c23.4d⁵ c24.2s⁶ c30.7d c26g* c31.8m Apr 13] good-topped **h–** gelding: winning hurdler: useful handicap chaser: won at Newbury in March: stays 31f: acts on heavy going: usually in headgear: tried in tongue tie. *Richard Hobson*

CHICORIA (IRE) 10 ch.g. Presenting – Coco Girl (Mystiko (USA)) [2018/19 c–§, **c– §** h110§: h24.6v⁶ h21.3s h22.7d⁶ Apr 8] sturdy gelding: fair handicap hurdler, disappointing **h94** in 2018/19: went wrong way over fences in 2015/16 after successful chasing debut: likely to stay beyond 3m: acts on heavy going: tried in cheekpieces: temperamental. *Tristan Davidson*

CHIDSWELL (IRE) 10 b.g. Gold Well – Manacured (IRE) (Mandalus) [2018/19 c130, **c131** h–: c21.5d⁵ c20.1s³ c23.4g* c26g* c31.8mᵖᵘ Apr 13] rangy gelding: winning hurdler: **h–** useful handicap chaser: won at Kelso in January and Grimthorpe Chase at Doncaster (by 9 lengths from Dingo Dollar) in March: bled final outing: stays 3¼m: acts on heavy going. *Nicky Richards*

CHIEF BRODY 8 b.g. Phoenix Reach (IRE) – Cherry Plum (Medicean) [2018/19 h107: **h109** h16g² h16v³ h20v h20.5d h18.6g² h19g Apr 25] rather sparely-made gelding: fair handicap hurdler: stays 19f: acts on heavy going: tried in cheekpieces. *William Muir*

CHIEF JUSTICE 4 b.g. Acclamation – Freedom Pass (USA) (Gulch (USA)) [2018/19 **h138** h16.5g² h16d* h16g* h16m* h16m² h16g* h16g² h16g⁵ h16.4s h16.5g* Apr 6] has had breathing operations: fairly useful maiden on Flat (likely to stay beyond 1m): useful juvenile hurdler: won at Worcester (left Richard Fahey after) in August, Listowel in September, Gowran in October, Bar One Racing Juvenile 3-Y-O Hurdle at Fairyhouse (by short head from Coeur Sublime) in December and conditionals/amateurs handicap at Aintree (by head from Thistimenextyear) in April: raced only at 2m: acts on good to firm and good to soft going (below form only outing on soft): wears tongue tie: waited with. *Gordon Elliott, Ireland*

CHIEFTAIN'S CHOICE (IRE) 10 b.g. King's Theatre (IRE) – Fairy Native (IRE) (Be **c–** My Native (USA)) [2018/19 c120, h114: h16m⁶ h16.7g h18.6g³ h18.7g* h20.3g² h21g³ **h118** h16.4g h16.6m* h16.6g⁴ h16.8d h16.5g h15.7m Apr 20] rather leggy gelding: fairly useful handicap hurdler: won at Stratford in August and Doncaster in December: in frame both outings in novice chases in 2017/18: placed at 2½m, at least as effective at 2m: acts on good to firm and heavy going: wears headgear. *Kevin Frost*

CHIKOKO TRAIL 4 ch.g. Sixties Icon – Search Party (Rainbow Quest (USA)) [2018/19 **h–** h16.3d⁶ Dec 29] lengthy, angular gelding: fair on Flat, stays 8.5f: tailed off in juvenile on hurdling debut. *Gary Moore*

CHILDRENS LIST (IRE) 9 b.g. Presenting – Snipe Hunt (IRE) (Stalker) [2018/19 **c132** c146p, h–: c24g² Jul 14] good-topped gelding: winning hurdler: smart chaser, lightly raced **h–** since 2015/16: best up to 25f: acts on heavy going. *W. P. Mullins, Ireland*

CHILLI FILLI 6 ch.m. Presenting – Daprika (FR) (Epervier Bleu) [2018/19 h120, b90: **h125** h21.2m* h24.6g⁴ h20.3g Apr 18] sturdy mare: bumper winner: fairly useful handicap hurdler: won mares event at Ludlow on reappearance in October: should stay further than 21f: acts on good to firm and good to soft going. *Henry Daly*

CHILL IN THE WOOD 10 br.m. Desert King – Zaffaranni (IRE) (Zaffaran **c96** (USA)) [2018/19 c88, h–: c26g² c23.8g c26g² c25.8g³ c23.6dᶠ c26m³ c25.2g⁵ c25.2s⁵ Nov **h–** 28] rather leggy mare: maiden hurdler: modest handicap chaser: stays 3¼m: acts on soft going: tried in cheekpieces: races in rear. *Dominic Ffrench Davis*

CHILLI ROMANCE (IRE) 8 b.m. Flemensfirth (USA) – Blue Romance (IRE) (Bob **h101** Back (USA)) [2018/19 h91: h16.3g⁴ h16g³ h15.3g³ h15.5g h15.5d* Dec 12] fair handicap hurdler: won novice event at Leicester in December: unproven beyond 2m: acts on soft going: has worn hood: wears tongue tie. *Fergal O'Brien*

CHIMES OF DYLAN (IRE) 6 b.g. Court Cave (IRE) – What A Princess (IRE) **h110** (Alderbrook) [2018/19 h110, b–: h20g⁴ h19.2g⁵ h19.9g h20g* h21.2v⁴ h19.5d Mar 20] has had breathing operation: in frame in Irish point: fair handicap hurdler: won novice event at Worcester (left Neil King after) in July: stays easy 2¾m: acts on good to soft going: tried in blinkers: in tongue tie last 4 starts: front runner. *Tim Vaughan*

CHINENSIS (IRE) 6 b.g. Well Chosen – Emily Vard (IRE) (Mr Combustible (IRE)) **h113** [2018/19 h23s³ h25.5d⁴ Mar 9] £82,000 5-y-o: lengthy, angular gelding: fifth foal: dam unraced half-sister to dam of fairly useful hurdler/useful chaser (stayed 2½m) Davenport Democrat: multiple Irish point winner: fair form in frame in novice hurdles at Lingfield and Hereford (bad mistake ninth). *Nigel Twiston-Davies*

CHINGACHGOOK 4 b.g. Al Kazeem – Natty Bumppo (IRE) (Kheleyf (USA)) [2018/19 **h109** h16d³ h16d⁴ h16.4s* Mar 10] fairly useful maiden on Flat, stays 10.5f: fair form over hurdles: improved when winning maiden at Musselburgh in March, despite hanging/jumping left: tried in hood. *Tristan Davidson*

CHIRICO VALLIS (FR) 7 b.g. Poliglote – Quora Vallis (FR) (Mansonnien (FR)) **c116** [2018/19 c130, h–: c17.3s³ c19.4dᵖᵘ Oct 14] well-made gelding: winning hurdler: useful **h–** novice chaser in 2017/18: below form both starts since: unproven beyond 17f: acts on heavy going: wears hood/tongue tie: signs of temperament (ran out once). *Neil Mulholland*

CHIVERS (IRE) 8 b.g. Duke of Marmalade (IRE) – Thara (USA) (Hennessy (USA)) **c95** [2018/19 h–: c17s⁴ c19.7s² c17.8v⁴ c20d³ c17.8s⁴ c16.1d⁴ c15.7g³ Apr 3] maiden hurdler: **h–** modest handicap chaser: won at Fontwell in December: effective at 2m to 2½m: acts on heavy going: has worn headgear. *Gary Moore*

CHLOE'S COURT (IRE) 6 br.m. Court Cave (IRE) – Howaya Pet (IRE) (Montelimar **h94** (USA)) [2018/19 h90, b66: h23.6d h21.7vᶠ h19.5d h20.5s⁵ Mar 11] modest maiden hurdler: should stay well beyond 21f: acts on heavy going. *Robert Walford*

CHOCOLATE BOX (IRE) 5 b.g. Zoffany (IRE) – Chocolate Mauk (USA) (Cozzene (USA)) [2018/19 h20.8g² Jan 9] half-brother to a winning jumper in USA by Posse: fairly useful on Flat, stays 16.5f: 13/2, 2¼ lengths second to De Forgotten One in maiden at Doncaster on hurdling debut: should do better. *Mark Loughnane* **h111 p**

CHOCOLATE DIAMOND (IRE) 8 ch.g. Intense Focus (USA) – Sagemacca (IRE) (Danehill Dancer (IRE)) [2018/19 h–: h21.7gᵖᵘ h21.7m May 27] no form over hurdles: in visor last 2 starts. *Daniel O'Brien* **h–**

CHOCOLAT NOIR (IRE) 6 b.m. Yeats (IRE) – Valrhona (IRE) (Spectrum (IRE)) [2018/19 h80: h22.7g⁶ h22.1g² h25.4g³ h22.1sꟳ h24.3g⁶ h23.3g h22.8v⁴ h22.7g³ h24.1d³ h24.3d Jan 20] modest maiden hurdler: stays 3m: acts on soft going: has worn headgear: usually races prominently. *Martin Todhunter* **h85**

CHOIX DES ARMES (FR) 7 b.g. Saint des Saints (FR) – Kicka (Shirley Heights) [2018/19 h114: h16g² h16d h18.5d⁵ h23.9d² Apr 4] good-topped gelding: has had breathing operation: fairly useful handicap hurdler: barely stays testing 19f: acts on heavy going: has worn hood. *Paul Nicholls* **h117**

CHOOCHOOBUGALOO 7 b.m. Rail Link – Charmante Femme (Bin Ajwaad (IRE)) [2018/19 h–: h19.9g² h19.5v³ h16.4d³ h16.2g* h15.8d c16.4g² Apr 5] lengthy mare: modest handicap hurdler: won mares event at Kelso in January: 11/2, neck second to Two Hoots in novice handicap at Sedgefield on chasing debut: stays 2½m: acts on heavy going: tried in hood: wears tongue tie: travels strongly, but has idled badly. *Sam England* **c93 h87**

CHOOKIE ROYALE 11 ch.g. Monsieur Bond (IRE) – Lady of Windsor (IRE) (Woods of Windsor (USA)) [2018/19 h99: h16.2g³ h16.8m* h16.2g⁴ h16.2g Oct 27] fair hurdler: won handicap at Sedgefield in August: raced around 2m: acts on soft and good to firm going: front runner/races prominently: one to treat with caution. *Keith Dalgleish* **h99 §**

CHORAL BEE 10 b.m. Oratorio (IRE) – Chief Bee (Chief's Crown (USA)) [2018/19 h60: h20.7dᵖᵘ h17.7mᵖᵘ Mar 29] of no account: has worn cheekpieces/tongue tie. *Alan Jessop* **h–**

CHORUS OF LIES 7 b.g. Teofilo (IRE) – Cherry Orchard (IRE) (King's Best (USA)) [2018/19 c16dꟳ Feb 20] has had breathing operation: fair form on hurdling debut in 2016/17: failed to progress: in cheekpieces/tongue tie, fell third on chasing debut: raced only at 2m: acts on good to firm going. *Alexandra Dunn* **c– h–**

CHOSEN DREAM (IRE) 11 b.g. Well Chosen – Peoples Dream (IRE) (Mandalus) [2018/19 c23m³ c27.5d* c23.7g⁴ c26.3dᵖᵘ c24.7d⁴ Apr 23] prolific winning pointer: maiden hurdler: fairly useful chaser: 66/1-winner of Stratford Champion Hunters' Chase in June: stays 3½m: acts on good to firm and good to soft going: tried in cheekpieces: wears tongue tie: usually races towards rear. *Graham McKeever, Ireland* **c123 h–**

CHOSEN FLAME (IRE) 7 b.g. Well Chosen – Flaming Misty (IRE) (Flemensfirth (USA)) [2018/19 h16.8s⁶ h17s⁶ h19.3g⁵ h16.8sᵖᵘ Feb 21] third foal: dam unraced half-sister to useful hurdler (stayed 3m) Busty Brown: off mark in points at fourth attempt: poor form over hurdles. *Rose Dobbin* **h82**

CHOSEN GINGER (IRE) 4 ch.g. Well Chosen – Shedan (IRE) (Perpendicular) [2018/19 b16.3g Mar 30] tailed off in bumper. *Sam Thomas* **b–**

CHOSEN MATE (IRE) 6 br.g. Well Chosen – Norwich Star (IRE) (Norwich) [2018/19 h16s* h16d² h16g* h20g⁵ Apr 6] £32,000 5-y-o: rather unfurnished gelding: first foal: dam unraced: winning pointer: useful novice hurdler: won maiden at Fairyhouse in January and Grade 2 event at Naas (by nose from Hannon) in February: remains with potential. *Gordon Elliott, Ireland* **h137 p**

CHOSEN PATH (IRE) 6 b.g. Well Chosen – Karsulu (IRE) (Mukaddamah (USA)) [2018/19 h128: c19.7g³ c23.4s* c23.9d² Feb 17] rather unfurnished gelding: fairly useful hurdler: better form over fences: won novice handicap at Newbury (by neck from Absolute Power) in December: jumped right/found little when disappointing final outing: stays 3m: acts on soft going. *Alan King* **c141 h–**

CHOSEN TRIBE (IRE) 7 ch.g. Stowaway – Native Kin (IRE) (Be My Native (USA)) [2018/19 h23.1gᵖᵘ h20.3gᵖᵘ Oct 10] maiden pointer: lightly-raced maiden hurdler, fair form at best: in tongue tie, pulled up both outings in 2018/19: stays 2¾m. *Julia Saunders* **h–**

CHOUNGAYA (FR) 6 b.g. Walk In The Park (IRE) – Autorite (FR) (Roakarad) [2018/19 b16.5g² b18m³ h16g* h16d³ h20d³ h20d⁵ h22g⁶ h24dꟳ h24d Apr 23] €165,000 3-y-o: first foal: dam, French maiden on Flat/over hurdles, out of Prix Ferdinand Dufaure winner Valdance: placed in bumpers: useful novice hurdler: won maiden at Tipperary in October: improved form in handicaps last 2 outings: stays 3m: acts on good to soft going: wears tongue tie: usually races prominently. *Joseph Patrick O'Brien, Ireland* **h137 b97**

CHOUQUETTE 5 b.m. Fame And Glory – Mille Et Une (FR) (Trempolino (USA)) **h60**
[2018/19 h86, b70: h16.2g⁵ h16d⁵ Nov 3] some promise in bumpers: modest form when
placed on hurdling debut: hooded, well held both outings in 2018/19. *Lucinda Russell*

CHOZEN (IRE) 7 b.g. Well Chosen – Kneeland Lass (IRE) (Bob Back (USA)) [2018/19 **c120**
h106: c15.7g⁴ c16.3gᵘʳ c16s⁴ c17.2m⁴ Apr 21] fair hurdler: fairly useful form over fences: **h–**
won handicaps at Southwell (novice) in October and Ffos Las in April: raced around 2m:
acts on soft going: wears hood: travels strongly: made running in 2018/19. *Tim Vaughan*

CHRIS'S DREAM (IRE) 7 b.g. Mahler – Janebailey (Silver Patriarch (IRE)) [2018/19 **c145**
h140, b85: c20d⁴ c24d² c24d⁴ c25d⁵ Apr 5] rangy gelding: useful hurdler: smart form over **h–**
fences: won maiden at Navan in December and Ten Up Novices' Chase at Navan (by ½
length from Champagne Classic) in February: stays 3m well: acts on heavy going. *Henry
de Bromhead, Ireland*

CHRISTMAS IN APRIL (FR) 7 b.g. Crillon (FR) – Similaresisoldofa (FR) (Kapgarde **c117**
(FR)) [2018/19 h111: h21g⁴ h21g³ h21g c23d c23.6d⁵ c20.1d³ Apr 26] good-topped **h113**
gelding: fair handicap hurdler: won at Warwick (left Nicky Henderson after) on
reappearance in May: best effort in novice handicap chases when close third at Perth final
outing: stays 3m: acts on good to soft going: has worn hood. *Colin Tizzard*

CHRISTMAS IN USA (FR) 7 b.g. Shaanmer (IRE) – Diamond of Diana (FR) **c–**
(Kapgarde (FR)) [2018/19 c–, h76: h16.2g⁶ h16.4d⁴ h16d* h17s* h16.4m² Mar 28] has had **h100**
breathing operation: fair handicap hurdler: won at Ayr in February and Carlisle (novice
event) in March: well held on completed start over fences in France in 2015/16: stays 2¼m:
acts on good to firm and heavy going: normally in headgear: wears tongue tie: usually front
runner/races prominently. *N. W. Alexander*

CHRISTMAS TWENTY (IRE) 9 br.g. Zagreb (USA) – Celestial Gale (IRE) **c92**
(Presenting) [2018/19 c95, h94: h22.7g³ h23.3g h23.3g² c24.2m⁴ h23.9g* h21.3gᵖᵘ Apr 11] **h102**
angular gelding: fair handicap hurdler: won at Perth in July: modest maiden chaser: stays
3m: acts on soft and good to firm going: regularly in headgear: usually races off pace.
Micky Hammond

CHRISTOPHER WOOD (IRE) 4 b.g. Fast Company (IRE) – Surf The Web (IRE) **h133**
(Ela-Mana-Mou) [2018/19 h17.7v* h16.3d* h17d³ Apr 4] strong, compact gelding: half-
brother to modest hurdler Kilshannig (2½m winner, by Galileo): dam half-sister to fair
hurdler/fairly useful chaser (2m-23f winner) Surfboard: fairly useful on Flat (should stay
beyond 1m): useful juvenile hurdler: won at Fontwell in February and Newbury (by 8
lengths from Zizaneur) in March: third in Anniversary Hurdle at Aintree (6¼ lengths
behind Pentland Hills) final outing. *Paul Nicholls*

CHTI BALKO (FR) 7 br.g. Balko (FR) – Ina Scoop (FR) (Murmure (FR)) [2018/19 **h140**
h138: h16d² h18.9g³ h18.9v³ h16.8d h16s Mar 9] angular gelding: placed on debut in Irish
point: useful handicap hurdler: stays easy 19f: acts on heavy going. *Donald McCain*

CH'TIBELLO (FR) 8 b.g. Sageburg (IRE) – Neicha (FR) (Neverneyev (USA)) **h155**
[2018/19 h150: h15.8d⁵ h20g⁶ h18.9g h20s² h16.8d* h20d³ Apr 4]
    Paul Nicholls has won the County Hurdle four times this century, a total
matched by Willie Mullins, but it is Nicholls' former assistant Dan Skelton who
has had the most success in the race in recent seasons. Ch'tibello's win in the
latest renewal was the third in four years for Skelton who was also successful with
Mohaayed twelve months earlier and Superb Story in 2016. Skelton has quickly
established an excellent record in some of the season's most competitive handicap
hurdles. The first big win of his career came in the 2013 Ladbroke at Ascot when
Willow's Saviour beat the Nicholls-trained Ptit Zig into second (Mohaayed won the
latest running, now the Betfair Exchange Hurdle), and since then Skelton has also
won a Greatwood Hurdle with North Hill Harvey and a 'Fixed Brush' Handicap
Hurdle at Haydock with Baradari, as well as the 2016 Scottish Champion Hurdle
which was the first major success of Ch'tibello's own career. Skelton also had the first
two in the Grade 3 staying handicap hurdle which opened the latest Grand National
card when Aux Ptits Soins beat stable-companion Tommy Rapper. Skelton's record
of three wins in the County Hurdle looks even better given that he has had runners in
just the last four renewals. He had three runners, including Mohaayed and North Hill
Harvey, when unsuccessful in 2017. Spiritofthegames was the stable's main hope in
2018, but he could finish only fifth behind 33/1-shot Mohaayed who was ridden by
Bridget Andrews. The latter partnership was reunited for the race again in March,

Randox Health County Handicap Hurdle, Cheltenham—a third County win in four years for trainer Dan Skelton as Ch'tibello (right) holds off the Nicky Henderson-trained pair We Have A Dream (centre) and Countister (hoops)

Mohaayed leading the field into the straight before finishing a creditable seventh under top weight at 40/1 behind 12/1-shot Ch'tibello ridden by Harry Skelton who had also been aboard Superb Story.

All three of Skelton's County Hurdle winners were laid out for the race after a break, Ch'tibello having already benefited from a similar approach when winning his Scottish Champion Hurdle after a five-month absence. Superb Story had not run since finishing second in the Greatwood the previous November, Mohaayed had been given a break since taking on Buveur d'Air and The New One in the Christmas Hurdle, while Ch'tibello had last been seen finishing second under top weight in a handicap over two and a half miles at Aintree's December meeting. In the meantime, he had undergone a wind operation. Ch'tibello's second to the previous season's Scottish Champion Hurdle winner Midnight Shadow at Aintree was his best run after three lesser efforts in handicaps at Ffos Las, Carlisle and Haydock. He didn't shape too badly in the first of those, the Welsh Champion Hurdle, but he was disappointing on his first attempt beyond two miles when strong in the betting at Carlisle and turned in a lacklustre effort at Haydock. But, as a result, Ch'tibello had dropped 8 lb in the weights between Ffos Las and Aintree. Ch'tibello had returned to handicap company on his final start the previous season when bidding to win his second Scottish Champion Hurdle, though he was well held at Ayr off a mark 19 lb higher than when successful in the race two years earlier. Ch'tibello had been highly tried in the interim, performing with credit to be placed in the Christmas Hurdle, the Champion Hurdle Trial at Haydock and the Kingwell Hurdle in which he was twice runner-up, but he faced a stiff task in the 2018 Champion Hurdle and was well held, reportedly finishing sore. Ch'tibello's County Hurdle win was his first success since winning the final edition of the valuable but short-lived Betfair Price Rush Hurdle at Haydock on the Betfair Chase card in 2016.

Like Mohaayed the year before, therefore, Ch'tibello apparently had little or nothing in hand of the handicapper when he lined up for the Randox Health County Hurdle. The same could also be said of the 5/1 favourite Whiskey Sour, third off a lower mark the year before and one of three in the race representing Willie Mullins. Less exposed was the Jane Williams-trained 13/2 second favourite Monsieur Lecoq, who had been runner-up in the Imperial Cup six days earlier, while Eclair de Beaufeu was another novice prominent in the betting and much the shortest-priced of Gordon Elliott's three runners. Unusually for a Festival handicap these days, the twenty-four runners were spread across the full weight range, from Mohaayed on 11-12 down to 100/1-shot Chieftain's Choice on 10-0 who was running from 4 lb out of the handicap. As Mohaayed led the field turning for home, Ch'tibello was hemmed in briefly on the inside coming from further back. After Eclair de Beaufeu had briefly gone clear on the run to the last (where he unseated), it was Ch'tibello who burst from the pack to lead over the final flight, not foot-perfect there himself before keeping on well to win by a length and a half from the Nicky Henderson pair

The Can't Say No Partnership's "Ch'tibello"

We Have A Dream and Countister who were separated by a head for the places and clear of Whiskey Sour in fourth. Ch'tibello ended his campaign with a still better run in defeat back in Grade 1 company, and back up in trip, when beaten less than two lengths into third behind Supasundae and Buveur d'Air in the Aintree Hurdle.

Ch'tibello (FR) (b.g. 2011)	Sageburg (IRE) (gr 2004)	Johannesburg (b 1999)	Hennessy Myth
		Sage Et Jolie (gr 1996)	Linamix Saganeca
	Neicha (FR) (b 1998)	Neverneyev (b 1990)	Nureyev River Rose
		Achdod (b 1993)	Assert Smiling

Ch'tibello ran twice in France before joining Skelton, unsuccessful on his debut on the Flat before winning a four-year-old contest over hurdles at Compiegne for Jean-Yves Artu. It didn't take him long to show plenty of ability for his new yard and, on just his second start in Britain, he was beaten little more than a length by Altior, no less, in a novice hurdle at Ascot. Ch'tibello is the best jumper sired by the Aga Khan's Prix d'Ispahan winner Sageburg and he is also the pick of a French family that has produced a variety of Flat and jumping winners. His dam Neicha was a maiden on the Flat, with her only placing coming over eleven furlongs at Mont-de-Marsan, but she has had a mix of winners at stud. Ch'tio Bilote (by Ultimately Lucky) was smart on the Flat, winning from a mile to a mile and a quarter and placed in Group 3 company, Fu Ji (by My Risk), another Flat winner, won three of his five races over middle distances in the Provinces, while Ch'tibello's younger brother J'Ai Oublie Nico won a two and a quarter mile chase. Ch'tibello's four-year-old half-sister Little Charlotte (by Diogenes) was well held in the latest season in a couple of bumpers at Warwick. Ch'tibello's grandam Achdod won over eleven and a half furlongs and bred three winners, including Achdir, a fairly useful hurdler at up to nineteen furlongs. Achdod was one of seven winners out of the maiden Smiling, the others including Ever Smile who became a fairly useful staying hurdler for Martin Pipe, winning seven races for him. The useful-looking Ch'tibello stays two and a half miles and acts on heavy ground. He has been tried once in a tongue tie. *Dan Skelton*

CHU CHU PERCY 8 b.g. Tobougg (IRE) – First Katoune (FR) (Poliglote) [2018/19 h107: c23.4g³ c23.8g* c23.8g⁶ c26.3m³ Aug 30] fair hurdler: fair form over fences: won novice handicap at Perth in July: should stay beyond 25f: acts on soft going: wears headgear: tried in tongue tie: usually races prominently: signs of temperament. *Alistair Whillans* **c111 h–**

CHUFFY CHUFFNELL (IRE) 5 b.g. Flemensfirth (USA) – Cathy Doun (IRE) (Spadoun (FR)) [2018/19 b15.7v⁴ h19.9v h21.2d h21.4g⁶ Feb 27] €64,000 3-y-o: first foal: dam unraced half-sister to Champion Bumper winner/fairly useful 2m hurdle winner Total Enjoyment (by Flemensfirth) and useful hurdler (stayed 2½m) Total Excitement: showed a bit in bumper and maiden/novice hurdles. *Ben Pauling* **h75 b75**

CHURCH HALL (IRE) 11 b.g. Craigsteel – Island Religion (IRE) (Religiously (USA)) [2018/19 c117, h105: h23g³ h21.9g c20d³ c23.6d* c22.6s⁶ c23.6d⁶ Apr 6] workmanlike gelding: fair handicap hurdler/chaser: won over fences at Chepstow in January: stays 3m: acts on soft going: wears tongue tie: usually races towards rear: sketchy jumper. *Emma-Jane Bishop* **c110 x h103**

CIAOIFSIN (IRE) 10 b.g. Indian Danehill (IRE) – Ciara's Surprise (IRE) (Norwich) [2018/19 h18.8g⁵ h20g⁴ h18.8d⁴ h20d⁴ h21.7g Oct 16] well beaten only outing on Flat: poor maiden hurdler: left Jarlath P. Fahey after fourth start: stayed 2½m: acted on good to firm and good to soft going: tried in hood: wore tongue tie last 5 starts: dead. *Matt Sheppard* **h82**

CIARABELLA (IRE) 6 b.m. Gold Well – Fancy Fashion (IRE) (Broken Hearted) [2018/19 b–: h16d h19.5d h20.5s h24d Apr 6] well beaten in bumpers (for R. Mike Smith) and over hurdles. *Ian Duncan* **h–**

CIBOIR (FR) 7 gr.g. Fragrant Mix (IRE) – Fleche Noir II (FR) (Quart de Vin (FR)) [2018/19 h–, b–: h18.6m⁴ Jul 21] no sign of ability: tried in hood. *Nick Kent* **h–**

CIEL DE NEIGE (FR) 4 b.g. Authorized (IRE) – In Caso di Neve (FR) (Country Reel (USA)) [2018/19 h16.9s⁵ h16.4s¹ Mar 13] first foal: dam French 1¼m winner: fairly useful form over hurdles: left G. Cherel/off 7 months, shaped well when 3¾ lengths third of 21 to Band of Outlaws in Fred Winter Juvenile Handicap Hurdle at Cheltenham: open to further improvement. *W. P. Mullins, Ireland* **h126 p**

CIGARISI (IRE) 7 b.g. Kalanisi (IRE) – Eileens Dream (IRE) (Oscar (IRE)) [2018/19 h16v⁶ h19.5vᵖᵘ h19.6g⁶ c18.2s⁴ Feb 4] lengthy gelding: fairly useful novice hurdler in 2016/17: disappointing since (well held in novice handicap on chasing debut): should stay 2½m: acts on heavy going. *Philip Hobbs* **c95 h94**

CILAOS EMERY (FR) 7 b.g. Califet (FR) – Queissa (FR) (Saint Preuil (FR)) [2018/19 h157: c16s* Jan 24] very smart hurdler: 11/8, promising start over fences when winning maiden at Gowran by 4 lengths from Impact Factor after 13-month absence: stays 2½m: acts on soft going: in hood last 5 starts: potentially high class as a chaser. *W. P. Mullins, Ireland* **c154 p h–**

CILAOS GLACE (FR) 6 br.g. Voix du Nord (FR) – Miss Glacee (FR) (Mister Mat (FR)) [2018/19 b–: h16s⁴ h16d h19.6d⁶ h17.7v* h16d⁴ Apr 6] well-made gelding: fairly useful form over hurdles: much improved when winning maiden at Fontwell in March and handicap at Chepstow in April: should stay beyond 2¼m: acts on heavy going: likely to progress further. *Oliver Sherwood* **h123 p**

CILLIAN'S WELL (IRE) 9 b.g. Trans Island – Live A Lot (IRE) (Saddlers' Hall (IRE)) [2018/19 h106: h16.8g⁴ h18.7g⁴ c20g c15.7g* c17g⁶ c16.4g³ c19.4g⁶ Apr 14] good-topped gelding: modest handicap hurdler: fair form over fences: won handicap at Southwell in October: stays 19f: acts on good to firm and good to soft going: wears headgear/tongue tie: often carries head awkwardly. *John Flint* **c104 h97**

CINDERFELLA 8 gr.g. Sagamix (FR) – Firecracker Lady (IRE) (Supreme Leader)   h–
[2018/19 h94: h23.3s h23.6d Mar 20] fair form in novice on hurdling debut in 2017/18:
lightly raced and disappointing since, leaving Kerry Lee after reappearance: bred to stay
3m+. *Nick Gifford*

CINEVATOR (IRE) 12 b.g. Dr Massini (IRE) – Hurricane Bella (IRE) (Taipan (IRE))   c– §
[2018/19 c–, h–: c23gpu c25.8mpu Sep 9] good-topped gelding: prolific point   h–
winner: winning hurdler/chaser: little form under Rules since 2014/15: usually in headgear:
moody. *Jeremy Scott*

CINTEX (FR) 7 b.g. Assessor (IRE) – Precieuze (FR) (Video Rock (FR)) [2018/19 h102,   c63
b68: h25.8g² h23.3gpu c25.7g³ c26v⁴ c23.6gpu c21.7g⁶ h22g⁶ h20.5g³ Apr 21] fair maiden   h102
hurdler: little form after reappearance, including in handicap chases: stays 3¼m: acts on
heavy going: in cheekpieces last 5 starts, also tongue tied 3 of last 4. *Neil Mulholland*

CIRCUIT COURT (IRE) 8 br.g. Court Cave (IRE) – Norwich Breeze (IRE) (Norwich)   h–
[2018/19 h–: h20.3gpu May 15] lengthy gelding: off mark in Irish points at fourth attempt:
little promise over hurdles. *Paul Webber*

CITADEL (FR) 7 b.g. Al Namix (FR) – Oreli (FR) (Robin des Pres (FR)) [2018/19 c–p,   c71
h–: c16.4gF c17.2gpu Jul 8] maiden hurdler: failed to complete all 6 outings over fences: left   h–
Dan Skelton after first start: tried in blinkers/tongue tie. *Laura Morgan*

CITY BREAK (IRE) 7 br.m. Getaway (GER) – Jane Hall (IRE) (Saddlers' Hall (IRE))   h–
[2018/19 h21.6dpu Nov 14] Irish point winner: pulled up in novice on hurdling debut: dead.
Michael Blake

CITY ISLAND (IRE) 6 b.g. Court Cave (IRE) – Victorine (IRE) (Un Desperado   h151
(FR)) [2018/19 b16g* h21s*d h16g* h19g* h21s* Mar 13]   b98

Balko des Flos' victory in the Gigginstown House Stud colours of Michael
O'Leary finally gave him a long-awaited first win in the 2018 running of the
Cheltenham Festival race he sponsors, the Ryanair Chase. A year later, another
Irish businessman was celebrating success in his own race when City Island won
the Ballymore Novices' Hurdle (Baring Bingham) for Ballymore's founder Sean
Mulryan and his wife Bernardine. Ballymore took over sponsorship of the Festival's
two mile five furlong Grade 1 novices' hurdle in 2007, but the first stint giving
their name to the race officially registered as the Baring Bingham lasted only three
seasons. Mulryan founded the Dublin-based property development company in 1982
but, after being one of the success stories of the 'Celtic Tiger' years, it was badly hit
by the financial crisis that followed which left it with around four billion euros of
debt to pay off. Now back in profit, Ballymore resumed sponsorship of the Baring
Bingham only in 2018 and a year later won the race with a horse named after one of
the company's developments in the docklands area of east London which it describes
as 'a cooler sibling to the mighty skyscrapers of Canary Wharf.' A photograph of the
Cheltenham Festival winner features proudly on the home page of the company's
web site. Ballymore have also resumed their sponsorship of the valuable two and a
half mile handicap hurdle on the final day of the Punchestown Festival in which the
Mulryan colours were carried in the latest edition by ninth-placed Take Revenge.
When the Saturday of the meeting became part of the Punchestown Festival proper
for the first time in 2008, the Ballymore Properties 25th Anniversary Hurdle, then
with a prize fund of €220,000, was the most valuable race on the card and briefly
became the richest handicap hurdle in either Ireland or Britain.

While Ballymore are back in the game as sponsors, City Island's Cheltenham
win marked the return of the Mulryan dark blue, yellow stripe to big-race success.
They had been carried into third place behind War of Attrition in the 2006
Cheltenham Gold Cup by the Irish chaser Forget The Past, but before the crash it
was in France where Mulryan built up the most successful string of jumpers of any
owner this century. In 2007, he completed a double in the top French chase and
hurdle when Mid Dancer won the Grand Steeple-Chase de Paris (his two later
wins in the race came after a change of ownership) and Zaiyad the Grande Course
de Haies d'Auteuil, Mid Dancer having also won the latter race the year before.
The remarkable record of the pair, along with stable-companions Cyrlight and Or
Noir de Somoza, a quartet trained for Mulryan by Arnaud Chaille-Chaille and who

Ballymore Novices' Hurdle (Baring Bingham), Cheltenham—a first Cheltenham Festival win for trainer Martin Brassil as City Island gets the better of a good duel with Champ (hoops)

between them had won fifty-two of their sixty-six starts in France over jumps by the end of June 2007, were detailed in the 'Top Horses In France' section of *Chasers & Hurdlers 2006/07*.

First past the post in all three of his starts over hurdles beforehand, City Island was an 8/1 chance at Cheltenham, though his form was hard to rate that highly after a much more low-key preparation than the three ahead of him in the betting. The 3/1 favourite Battleoverdoyen's two wins over hurdles for Gigginstown and Gordon Elliott included the Grade 1 Lawlor's of Naas Novices' Hurdle, 7/2-shot Champ's four-timer for Nicky Henderson had been completed in the Challow Novices' Hurdle at Newbury, while Easy Game, 7/1, had won a couple of graded novice hurdles at Navan on his last two starts for Willie Mullins. City Island's experience over hurdles amounted to two starts in maiden contests and then a comfortable win at odds of 5/1-on, conceding weight all round, in an auction novices hurdle at Naas in February. City Island's best piece of form prior to Cheltenham had come over two miles when beating Dallas des Pictons by three lengths at Leopardstown in December, with the runner-up going on to win a competitive handicap at the Dublin Racing Festival before finishing second in the final race at Cheltenham's four-day meeting, the Martin Pipe. City Island had been off the course for five months before that win, having already 'won' another maiden hurdle over the Baring Bingham trip at the Galway Festival. However, City Island subsequently lost that contest after testing positive for arsenic, a prohibited substance (only highly toxic in its inorganic form) which was traced to a seaweed-based feed supplement used by his stable. The IHRB waived the €1,000 fine set to be imposed on his trainer as they considered the substance had been administered unknowingly.

The Baring Bingham field of sixteen impressed as a good-looking bunch on the whole, City Island included; he's a strong type who will make a chaser in due course. Despite the big step up in grade, City Island looked very much at home, held up and travelling well, despite being inconvenienced by finding himself short of room a couple of times, as he made ground before joining the leaders jumping the second last. City Island turned for home upsides Champ on his outer, held a slight lead at the final flight and was driven out as he kept on to beat that rival by two lengths. The 25/1-chance Bright Forecast was beaten a further two and a quarter lengths after getting the better of a battle for third with the Challow fourth Brewin'upastorm, the first four finishing clear of the rest. Of the other leading contenders, Easy Game wasn't given a hard time once his chance had gone and was eighth of the twelve finishers, while Battleoverdoyen, another well-backed horse to disappoint, was pulled up after running no sort of race and was reported to have lost a shoe. The Festival's other Grade 1 novice hurdle winners Klassical Dream and Minella Indo followed up in equivalent contests at Punchestown, and the signs looked good for City Island doing the same, with Champ upholding the Baring Bingham form by winning the Sefton at Aintree. However, in the event, it seemed that maybe City Island's Cheltenham exertions had left their mark as he could finish

Sean & Bernardine Mulryan's "City Island"

only sixth, after going in snatches, in the Champion Novices' Hurdle behind Reserve Tank who had beaten Brewin'upastorm in the Mersey Novices' at Aintree, while the Baring Bingham fifth Sams Profile took second.

City Island (IRE) (b.g. 2013)	Court Cave (IRE) (b 2001)	Sadler's Wells (b 1981)	Northern Dancer / Fairy Bridge
		Wemyss Bight (b 1990)	Dancing Brave / Bahamian
	Victorine (IRE) (b 2001)	Un Desperado (b 1983)	Top Ville / White Lightning
		High Board (b 1977)	High Line / Matchboard

Like City Island's owner, his trainer Martin Brassil, who had not had a winner at the Cheltenham Festival before, had been away from the limelight since the first decade of the century. As well as the 2006 Grand National winner Numbersixvalverde, who won the Irish Grand National the year before as a novice, Brassil's best horse was the high-class chaser Nickname, a French import who went very well in the mud which meant all his runs for Brassil were confined to Ireland; he should have run in the 2007 Queen Mother Champion Chase but was withdrawn on the day when the ground dried out. Nickname was also one of the best entires to race over fences in the British Isles in recent times and went on to sire the likes of Cyrname and Frodon before he died in 2011, aged only twelve. Brassil bought City Island as an unbroken three-year-old at the Derby Sale for €31,000. He looks

212

well bought now and, while it's unusual for a top performer to be the product of two unraced horses, both his sire Court Cave and dam Victorine are proven producers, his dam having the added attraction of being a half-sister to the Champion Hurdle winners Morley Street and Granville Again. A brother to Beat Hollow, Court Cave also sired the 2017 Baring Bingham winner Willoughby Court and had a winner at the 2018 Festival as well with Mister Whitaker in the Close Brothers Novices' Handicap Chase. City Island is his dam's fifth winner. The mares Pink Hat (by Presenting) and Tasitiocht (by Oscar) were both fairly useful hurdlers at up to two and a half miles for Willie Mullins. Fort Worth (also by Presenting) also won over hurdles but made into a useful handicap chaser at around three miles for Jonjo O'Neill who also trained Easy Street (by High Chaparral), a fairly useful chaser who won at Warwick on his first start in the latest season before being fatally injured at Chepstow in April. Victorine's latest foal to reach the track is O'Connell Street (by Fame And Glory), who cost €125,000 as a three-year-old, and made the frame in a couple of bumpers in the spring for Nicky Henderson. Three of City Island's winning siblings were also successful in bumpers, as he was himself at Punchestown early in the season. He had made a promising debut when second at 33/1 in a similar contest for newcomers at the Punchestown Festival at the end of the previous season, a race in which Minella Indo finished third, incidentally (the Willie Mullins-trained Passageway, who beat the two future Cheltenham winners, hasn't raced since). City Island's grandam High Board was also unraced. Apart from breeding two Champion Hurdle winners (Morley Street, by the way, met with the first defeat of his career when fourth in the Sun Alliance Hurdle in the days before it had the registered title of the Baring Bingham), High Board was grandam of the Ascot Chase winner Hand Inn Hand, while more recently her great grandson Fagan was runner-up in the Spa Novices' Hurdle at the 2016 Festival. City Island, who wears a tongue tie, stays twenty-one furlongs and acts on soft ground. Despite his reverse at Punchestown he remains a good prospect for novice chases. *Martin Brassil, Ireland*

CITY LIMITS 5 ch.g. Nathaniel (IRE) – Wait It Out (USA) (Swain (IRE)) [2018/19 h16g h16.6d⁶ h16.5d³ h16g⁶ Mar 23] fair maiden on Flat, stays 2m: modest form last 2 outings over hurdles. *James A. Nash, Ireland* — **h99**

CITY NEVER SLEEPS (IRE) 7 b.g. Central Park (IRE) – Goodnightmrskelly (IRE) (Bigstone (IRE)) [2018/19 h20.3g² Sep 5] modest maiden hurdler: stays 2½m: acts on soft going: usually in headgear: tried in tongue tie. *Martin Keighley* — **h93**

CITY STAR 7 b.m. Black Sam Bellamy (IRE) – Danarama (Rock City) [2018/19 h58: h16m⁵ May 7] poor form over hurdles. *Ben Pauling* — **h63**

CITY SUPREME (IRE) 9 b.g. Milan – Run Supreme (IRE) (Supreme Leader) [2018/19 c95, h–: c95, h–: h23.1m May 8] good-topped gelding: fairly useful hurdler/novice chaser at best: lightly raced and well below form since 2016/17: stays 3¼m: acts on heavy going: often in headgear: wears tongue tie. *Anthony Honeyball* — **c–** **h–**

CIVIL UNREST (IRE) 13 ch.g. Blueprint (IRE) – Yore (IRE) (Ore) [2018/19 c101x, h103§: c15.6g³ c17.3g* c17.1g² c17.1d² c15.8g² c20.3g³ c15.8g⁴ c15.8m² c16.4g² Apr 23] fair hurdler: fair handicap chaser: won at Cartmel in May: stays 2½m: acts on soft and good to firm going: wears headgear: usually races close up. *James Ewart* — **c112** **h–**

CIVITESSES (FR) 7 b.m. Prince Kirk (FR) – Glenn Rose (FR) (Scooter Bleu (IRE)) [2018/19 h–: h15.7g h21.6g³ c16.3s⁴ c21gᵖᵘ Aug 15] maiden Irish pointer: poor maiden hurdler: little show in handicap chases: stays easy 2¾m: acts on soft going: usually in headgear: in tongue tie last 3 starts. *Brian Barr* — **c56** **h72**

CKALCO DES LOGES (FR) 7 b.g. Balko (FR) – Olla des Loges (FR) (Sleeping Car (FR)) [2018/19 c109, h108: c22.5dꟳ May 5] good-topped gelding: won maiden point on debut: fairly useful hurdler: only fair form over fences: stays 3m: acts on soft going: regularly in tongue tie. *Dan Skelton* — **c–** **h–**

CLAIMANTAKINFORGAN (FR) 7 b.g. Great Pretender (IRE) – Taquine d'Estrees (FR) (Take Risks (FR)) [2018/19 h147: c16g* c15.9g³ Nov 18] smart novice hurdler in 2017/18: useful form over fences, winning maiden at Uttoxeter (by 2½ lengths from Chesterfield) in November before 11 lengths third to Lalor in Grade 2 novice at Cheltenham: will be suited by 2½m: acts on soft going: remains open to improvement as a chaser. *Nicky Henderson* — **c139 p** **h–**

CLAN DES OBEAUX (FR) 7 b.g. Kapgarde (FR) – Nausicaa des Obeaux (FR) **c166**
(April Night (FR)) [2018/19 c162, h–: c25.6g⁴ c24g* c23.8d* c26.3d⁵ c25d² Apr 4]   **h–**

You can't keep a good man down. After two seasons in which he had to
settle for second place behind Nicky Henderson in the trainers' championship, Paul
Nicholls bounced back to regain the title. The competitive instincts of Nicholls have
seen him involved in some real scraps for the title over the years, most notably
with his great rival Martin Pipe whose record of fifteen championships is looking
increasingly within the reach of fifty-seven-year-old Nicholls who has now won the
trainers' title eleven times. Nicholls had won his tenth championship in the 2015/16
season after a thrilling battle with Willie Mullins which went down to the last day
of the season, but the latest championship, for which Henderson started at long
odds on, was gained more comfortably, thanks to the emergence of a wider spread
of Grade 1 talent at Manor Farm Stables. The yard had enjoyed only two Grade 1
wins in 2015/16—there were six in the latest season—when its success was built

*32Red King George VI Chase, Kempton—pace-setters Might Bite and Coneygree (right) have cried
enough as Clan des Obeaux (noseband) and Thistlecrack have matters to themselves approaching
two out, the fancied pair Bristol de Mai (grey) and the brought down Waiting Patiently (right)
having exited the race at halfway (inset photo) ...*

on a sustained flow of big weekend winners, many of them in handicaps. Over a decade has passed since Nicholls set a record in the 2007/08 season that still stands for the most prize money won in a British jumps season—£3,507,643 in first three earnings—with his stable's pre-eminence at around that time built on a magnificent team of steeplechasers which included Denman, Kauto Star and Neptune Collonges, who had filled the first three places in that season's Cheltenham Gold Cup, and the Queen Mother Champion Chase winner Master Minded. Celestial Halo also won the Triumph Hurdle for the yard in the same year and went on to put up a career-best effort twelve months later when going down by a neck to the Henderson-trained Punjabi in the Champion Hurdle. Nicholls-trained horses won the feature events on the three other days of that year's Festival, with Master Minded repeating his Queen Mother Champion Chase success, Big Buck's taking the first of his four World [Stayers'] Hurdles and Kauto Star regaining his Cheltenham Gold Cup crown with a crushing thirteen-length victory over Denman. Heady days for Manor Farm Stables

which Nicholls admits was 'incredibly lucky to have all those horses at the same time, each of them a horse of a lifetime really.' Paul Nicholls went on to be champion trainer for the fifth season in a row in 2009/10 but signs were emerging that the big races, usually so necessary for winning the trainers' title, were going to be harder for Manor Farm Stables (Celestial Halo managed only fourth in the Champion Hurdle, while Master Minded and Kauto Star were beaten at odds on in the Champion Chase and the Gold Cup—in which Denman was second—which left Big Buck's to put the stable's name in lights at the Cheltenham Festival). Nicholls took the title again in 2010/11 and 2011/12 (when Neptune Collonges won the Grand National and the stable also won the King George with Kauto Star and the Champion Hurdle with Rock On Ruby, as well as the World Hurdle). However, in recent seasons, Nicholls has faced a strong challenge from Nicky Henderson and Seven Barrows (the trainers' title has gone to the Henderson yard three times in the last seven years), while at the Cheltenham Festival the Irish challenge, particularly from the towering Mullins and Elliott stables, has been stronger than at any time in history (Mullins' and Elliott's 'offshore' earnings, mostly at the Festival, have seen them both finish well inside the top ten in the British domestic table in each of the last two years).

Manor Farm Stables has found it more difficult to source potential Grade 1 horses, partly in the wake of the much healthier Irish economy which has brought more prosperity to Irish jump racing. Many of the former Nicholls stars, including Kauto Star, Master Minded, Big Buck's and Neptune Collonges, were bought in France as young horses. 'At that time you could wait before you bought them—they were expensive but at least you knew they were good—but nowadays, because it is so competitive, you're forced into buying a horse that has finished second in a maiden hurdle at Auteuil for £300,000,' says Nicholls. 'You might then find the form is worthless—we've had a few of those here—so we have gone back to basics, buying stores for £60,000 to £100,000, but those horses need time. Looking at Ireland, if you want a winning pointer it could cost you £400,000. That's the market for you, it's hard to find value.' Nicholls reflects that there were occasions in the past when he 'had the trainers' title wrapped up by Christmas', which has engendered a feeling in some quarters that he has perhaps been gradually losing his edge. As Nicholls points out, however, he has been either first or second in the trainers' table in each of the last twenty-one seasons (including coming second to Martin Pipe on seven successive occasions before finally dethroning him in the 2005/6 season after losing nip-and-tuck battles on three different occasions that provided plenty of copy for the racing pages). The latest season saw Nicholls pass the 3,000-mark for wins over jumps in Britain, a milestone previously achieved only by Martin Pipe and Nicky Henderson, the last-named reaching 3,000 in August 2018. Pipe's 3,930 winners were notched over thirty-one seasons, while five-times champion Henderson took forty seasons to reach the same landmark. Nicholls has been training for twenty-eight years and has recorded over a hundred wins in a season nineteen times, including in each of the last eighteen seasons (his best was 171 wins in 2016/17). He won one hundred and thirty-five races in the latest season and took the championship with first three years' earnings of £3,158,852, his biggest total since those halcyon days in 2007/8 and 2008/9, seasons in which he recorded over one hundred and fifty wins.

Clan des Obeaux was one of the surprise packets of the latest season when he provided Paul Nicholls with his tenth victory in the King George VI Chase. He is a perfect example of his trainer's trademark patience ('Some owners are in too much of a hurry and that doesn't suit me, patience is the big thing and I want owners who understand and stick with it'). Clan des Obeaux arrived at Manor Farm Stables after winning a bumper at La Roche-sur-Yon on his only start in his native France for Nicolas Devilder in the 2014/15 season. Successful in a juvenile event at Newbury on his first start over hurdles, Clan des Obeaux made just three appearances in total in his first season with Nicholls, finishing second in the Finesse Hurdle and sixth in the Triumph Hurdle on two starts at Cheltenham after the turn of the year. Very much a chaser on looks and crying out for longer distances, Clan des Obeaux was sent straight over fences in his second season at Ditcheat and won twice in six outings at around two and a half miles, though he didn't run at the major spring festivals (his second win came in a novice at Exeter the week after the Cheltenham Festival).

... Clan des Obeaux has the measure of 2016 winner Thistlecrack (left) at the last; the latter's stable-companion Native River rallies into third

Reported problems with a splint interrupted Clan des Obeaux's next campaign after he had won a graduation chase at Haydock and finished second under top weight of 11-12 in the Caspian Caviar Gold Cup at Cheltenham just before Christmas. 'It did him good to have a little bit of time off,' says Nicholls who pitched him into Grade 1 company over fences for the first time on his return. Significantly, Clan des Obeaux was stepped up in trip, running over an extended three miles for the first time, and he finished a creditable third behind Might Bite and Bristol de Mai in the Bowl at Aintree. Clan des Obeaux was the youngest horse in the line-up, as he was in his first two races in the latest season when Might Bite and Bristol de Mai were again among his opponents.

Starting the outsider of five on his reappearance in the Betfair Chase at Haydock, Clan des Obeaux finished fourth, about nine lengths behind the winner Bristol de Mai, outpaced in the closing stages and seeming to be put in his place, although he was still very lightly raced and potentially not fully exposed over staying trips. Clan des Obeaux was one of two runners for his stable in the 32Red King George VI at Kempton on Boxing Day, the other being the grey Politologue, another patiently-trained French import who, like Clan des Obeaux, hadn't looked an obvious candidate to develop into a contender for the top races before stepping up the previous season to win the Tingle Creek and then the Melling Chase, successes that raised his profile considerably (he was an 11/1 underdog at Aintree where he beat Min in a close finish). Politologue won the 1965 Chase over twenty-one furlongs at Ascot on his reappearance on the same day that Clan des Obeaux ran in the Betfair Chase and he was sent off at odds of 5/1 at Kempton, fourth favourite behind Might Bite (3/1), Waiting Patiently (4/1) and Native River (9/2). Clan des Obeaux, on the other hand, was a 12/1-shot, the choice of young stable jockey Harry Cobden (promoted at the end of the previous season ahead of Sam Twiston-Davies).

Cobden apparently had no hesitation in choosing Clan des Obeaux over Politologue, according to Paul Nicholls, though one of the horse's owners, Sir Alex Ferguson, was conspicuous by his absence, choosing instead to watch Manchester United at Old Trafford. Ferguson saw the team win and must have been impressed from afar by the maturity shown by twenty-year-old Cobden on Clan des Obeaux who was one of only two King George runners who had not won in Grade 1 company over fences. The ten-strong line-up was thoroughly representative of the top domestic staying chasers (there was no challenger from Ireland) and included the last two winners of the race, Might Bite and Thistlecrack, the Cheltenham Gold Cup winners from 2015 and 2018 Coneygree and Native River, dual Betfair Chase winner Bristol de Mai and the unbeaten chaser Waiting Patiently, the best horse in the North. The King George was run at a sound gallop, set by Coneygree, and turned into a very good test of jumping and stamina, as it is designed to be. The departure at the ninth of Bristol de Mai, who brought down Waiting Patiently, took some gloss off the race, as did the tame performance of Might Bite who reportedly bled. Clan des Obeaux was fully deserving of his victory, though, always going well and ridden with plenty of confidence before looming up in the home straight to tackle the strong-travelling Thistlecrack and keeping on well, after leading at the last, to beat him by a length and a half, with Native River a further twelve lengths back in third. The first three had all contested the Betfair Chase, though they finished in reverse order at Kempton, with Politologue completing the frame while giving the impression that three miles stretched his stamina.

Two of the ten King George wins for Clan des Obeaux's trainer were recorded by Silviniaco Conti in 2013 and 2014 (Kauto Star won the race a record five times). In both those seasons, Silviniaco Conti contested all four of the open Grade 1s in Britain for staying chasers and Clan des Obeaux followed the same route, being the only one, apart from Bristol de Mai, to contest all four of the staying Grade 1s in the latest season. Neither Clan des Obeaux nor Bristol de Mai managed to add another Grade 1 to their records, though their reputations were still more or less intact following the spring festivals at Cheltenham and Aintree, after which the career 'match' score between them stood at three-two in Bristol de Mai's favour (two-two in the latest season).

Mr & Mrs P. K. Barber, G. Mason & Sir A. Ferguson's "Clan des Obeaux"

Clan des Obeaux completed his Cheltenham Gold Cup preparation with an impressive eleven-length victory over Terrefort in the Betfair Denman Chase, a race that had to be rescheduled when the BHA shut down the sport for six days in February in response to an outbreak of equine flu in the Cheshire stable of Donald McCain. Native River and Anibale Fly had been intended runners in the original Denman Chase at Newbury but both were absent when the race was restaged at Ascot a week later, along with the Betfair Hurdle, on what was dubbed 'Super Saturday'. With some trainers prevented from making entries, and others still having their entries kept under review and at risk of withdrawal, a further blow came with a stipulation that no horse could run if it had not been vaccinated against flu within the last six months (shortened from the existing twelve months). Several of Nicky Henderson's proposed runners were ruled out of their intended races (as were two of the leading Betfair Hurdle candidates Leoncavallo and Monsieur Lecoq). One yard not affected by the new rules was Manor Farm Stables (where the horses are vaccinated at the turn of the year) which enjoyed its own 'Super Saturday', extending its lead over Seven Burrows by sending out eight winners, five of them on the nine-race card at Ascot also including Cyrname in the feature Ascot Chase, on a day when the Nicholls horses won almost £250,000.

Clan des Obeaux had his ante-post odds for the Gold Cup shaved to around 6/1, making him third favourite behind Presenting Percy and Native River. Clan des Obeaux displaced Native River as second favourite on Gold Cup day but it was Bristol de Mai who came out best of the home-trained contenders, ahead of Native River and Clan des Obeaux, though the trio proved no match for two of the Irish challengers, Al Boum Photo and Anibale Fly. Clan des Obeaux travelled as well as any for a long way and had every chance before seemingly being found out in the softish conditions by the steep uphill finish, his performance emphasising that his speed, and slickness over the fences, are his strong suit. Clan des Obeaux turned the tables on Bristol de Mai in the Betway Bowl at Aintree where both nonetheless seemed to perform as if feeling the effects of hard races at Cheltenham. Clan des Obeaux came second to Al Boum Photo's stablemate Kemboy, a first-fence faller in the Gold Cup, but a nine-length defeat represented form some way below his best and Clan des Obeaux only just got the better of Balko des Flos in a race that turned into something of a tactical affair, with Kemboy dictating only a modest pace and having the run of things before quickening in striking fashion for a staying chaser from the second last.

The well-made Clan des Obeaux followed in something of a tradition of French-bred chasers who have won the King George VI Chase as six-year-olds since Francois Doumen began to target the race in the 'eighties, before which there hadn't been a French-trained winner of any sort over jumps in Britain for almost a quarter of a century. Doumen-trained chasers won five King Georges—as well as other major races in Britain— in the period up to the turn of the century, The Fellow gaining the first of his two victories in the race as a six-year-old, the age at which Algan also won the race for Doumen. The Doumen successes aroused more interest in French-bred jumpers among British stables and Kauto Star was six when he won his first King George, as was Long Run where he won his first of two for Nicky Henderson. French-bred chasers can often be a shade more precocious than their British- and Irish-bred counterparts and, like the Cheltenham Gold Cup winner Al Boum Photo, Clan des Obeaux is by a French stallion who raced over jumps. Kapgarde, also the sire of a Grand Steeple-Chase de Paris winner in Milord Thomas and a Cheltenham Festival winner in A Plus Tard, was successful over hurdles in France at three and four and went on to win over fences, finishing a close second in the Group 1 Prix Ferdinand Dufaure over an extended two and a half miles. Clan des Obeaux is the third foal and third winner produced by the April Night mare Nausicaa des Obeaux—Bristol de Mai's dam is also by April Night—who was placed at around two and a quarter miles over fences in France. Both her earlier foals were by Saddler Maker, the better of them being Bahia des Obeaux who won at up to nineteen furlongs over hurdles (the first foal was a filly, Varda des Obeaux, and she produced a colt to Kapgarde in 2018). Clan des Obeaux, who is possibly best at short of three and a quarter miles when the emphasis is on stamina, acts on heavy going but doesn't need the mud. He travels strongly in his races. *Paul Nicholls*

CLAN LEGEND 9 ch.g. Midnight Legend – Harrietfield (Nicholas Bill) [2018/19 c132, h124: c22.9v⁵ c20.1g⁴ c16.5s³ Mar 9] fairly useful hurdler/chaser: stays 21f: acts on heavy going: usually in tongue tie: used to make running, but ridden more patiently nowadays: strong-travelling sort. *N. W. Alexander* — **c123 h–**

CLARA SORRENTO (FR) 8 gr.g. Maresca Sorrento (FR) – Call Me Clara (FR) (Call Me Sam (FR)) [2018/19 h134: c25.1m⁴ c22g⁴ c21g* c20s² Nov 4] useful hurdler: useful form over fences: won maiden at Roscommon in October: much improved again when second in novice at Cork (6 lengths behind Winter Escape) final outing: stays 21f: acts on heavy going: formerly hooded: front runner/races prominently. *Noel Meade, Ireland* — **c139 h–**

CLARCAM (FR) 9 b.g. Califet (FR) – Rose Beryl (FR) (Lost World (IRE)) [2018/19 c145, h–: c22.5d* h19f h20d⁶ h21d h20d⁴ h20s⁶ Apr 20] good-topped gelding: formerly useful hurdler: smart handicap chaser: won Galway Plate (by 6 lengths from Patricks Park) on reappearance in August: left Gordon Elliott after fourth start: stays 23f: acts on good to firm and heavy going: wears headgear: has worn tongue tie. *Richard J. Hendriks, USA* — **c153 h122 +**

CLARENDON STREET (IRE) 6 b.g. Court Cave (IRE) – Carrigeen Kalmia (IRE) (Norwich) [2018/19 h21d² h21.3d* h20.6d⁵ Feb 5] €35,000 3-y-o: first foal: dam, (c141/h108) 2¼m/2½m chase winner, half-sister to dam of Irish Grand National winner Rogue Angel: fairly useful form over hurdles: won maiden at Wetherby (readily landed odds) in January. *Nicky Henderson* — **h121**

CLARET DABBLER 5 ch.g. Haafhd – Floreana (GER) (Acatenango (GER)) [2018/19 b16.2g b16.7g³ Mar 14] first foal: dam (c94/h115), 15f-3¼m hurdle/chase winner, half-sister to useful hurdler (stayed 2¾m) Fenix: fair form both outings in bumpers. *Gillian Boanas* — **b87**

CLASS CONTI (FR) 7 b.g. Poliglote – Gazelle Lulu (FR) (Altayan) [2018/19 c21.2v* Apr 14] half-brother to several winners, notably high-class hurdler/top-class chaser Silviniaco Conti (17f-25f winner, by Dom Alco) and useful hurdler/smart chaser Ucello Conti (17f-25f winner, by Martaline): dam French 11f/1½m winner: winning hurdler: useful chaser: off a year/left D. Sourdeau de Beauregard, won minor event at Tramore (by 23 lengths from Beyond The Law) in April: reportedly scoped unsatisfactorily when disappointing at Punchestown shortly after end of British season: stays 2¾m: acts on heavy going: in tongue tie both Irish starts. *W. P. Mullins, Ireland* — **c140 h–**

CLASSICAL MILANO (IRE) 8 b.g. Milan – Miss Baden (IRE) (Supreme Leader) [2018/19 c–, h–: c26.2g⁴ c23.4g² c24.2m* c23.8g c24.2g³ c24.2spu c26.2g c24.2g⁶ Nov 9] workmanlike gelding: winning hurdler: fair handicap chaser: won at Hexham in June: stays 3m: acts on good to firm going: has worn cheekpieces: front runner/races prominently. *George Bewley* — **c104 h–**

CLASSICAL ROCK (IRE) 5 b.g. Thewayyouare (USA) – Source of Light (IRE) (Diamond Green (FR)) [2018/19 h16g⁶ May 8] fair maiden on Flat, stays 1½m: little form over hurdles: tried in blinkers. *Denis Quinn* — **h–**

CLASSICAL SOUND (IRE) 7 b.g. Mahler – Sovienne (IRE) (Soviet Star (USA)) [2018/19 h78: h23.9g⁵ May 16] poor maiden hurdler: stays 27f: acts on heavy going. *Rose Dobbin* — **h63**

CLASSIC BEN (IRE) 6 b.g. Beneficial – Dark Daisy (IRE) (Kotashaan (FR)) [2018/19 h132, h102: c20g⁴ c23g² c23.8g⁵ c24g³ c24.2s* c26g⁴ Mar 23] lengthy gelding: useful hurdler: similar form over fences: won Masters Handicap Chase at Sandown in February: should stay beyond 3m: acts on soft going: has worn cheekpieces, including last 3 starts. *Stuart Edmunds* — **c133 h–**

CLASSIC JEWEL (IRE) 12 b.g. Classic Cliche (IRE) – Be My Libby (IRE) (Be My Native (USA)) [2018/19 c85§, h–: c24g² Jul 15] maiden hurdler: modest handicap chaser: stays 3m: acts on soft going: usually wears headgear/tongue tie: has been let down by attitude. *Evan Williams* — **c85 h–**

CLASSIC SENIORITY 7 b.g. Kyllachy – Dramatic Solo (Nayef (USA)) [2018/19 **h93**
h15.7g^6 h16d h16.2g h19.7g^{pu} h16.4m^{pu} Mar 22] useful on Flat, stays 7.5f: modest form
on hurdling debut: failed to progress: will prove best at 2m with emphasis on speed.
Marjorie Fife

CLASSIC TUNE 9 b.g. Scorpion (IRE) – Classic Fantasy (Classic Cliche (IRE)) [2018/19 **h100**
h–: h19.6g^{pu} h19g^4 h23.3s^{pu} h20.7d h23d h21s^4 h19.6g^2 Apr 13] lengthy gelding: fair
handicap hurdler: stays 21f: acts on soft going: in tongue tie last 2 starts. *Claire Dyson*

CLASSI MASSINI 8 b.m. Dr Massini (IRE) – Classi Maureen (Among Men (USA)) **h84**
[2018/19 h23.9d^4 Oct 20] modest maiden hurdler: stayed 3m: acted on good to soft going:
dead. *Peter Bowen*

CLASSULA 7 b.g. Sulamani (IRE) – Classic Fantasy (Classic Cliche (IRE)) [2018/19 h88, **h–**
b66: h24g^{pu} h21.7d h23.8g h19d^{pu} Dec 31] poor maiden hurdler: stays 21f: acts on soft **b66**
going: wears tongue tie: temperament under suspicion. *Claire Dyson*

CLASSY AFAIR 5 b.m. Fair Mix (IRE) – Classic Fantasy (Classic Cliche (IRE)) [2018/19 **h–**
b16d h21s^{pu} Apr 14] £1,200 3-y-o: fourth foal: half-sister to fair hurdler **b–**
Classic Tune (2½m winner, by Scorpion): dam (b93), lightly raced in bumpers, half-sister
to very smart chaser (best around 2m) Central House: no promise in bumper/over hurdles:
in tongue tie last 2 starts. *Claire Dyson*

CLAUD AND GOLDIE (IRE) 10 ch.g. Portrait Gallery (IRE) – Glacial Jewel (IRE) **c127**
(Glacial Storm (USA)) [2018/19 c20.1g^4 c20s^5 c23.4g^3 c23.4d* c26.2g^3 c24.1m^3 Apr 13]
sixth foal: dam unraced half-sister to fair hurdler/useful chaser (stayed 3m) Deciding
Moment: Irish point winner: fairly useful form in chases: won novice handicap at Kelso in
March: stays 3¼m: acts on good to soft and good to firm going: room for improvement in
jumping. *Sandy Forster*

CLAUDIO MONTEVERDI (IRE) 6 b.g. Galileo (IRE) – Dance For Fun (Anabaa **h–**
(USA)) [2018/19 h15.9g^{ur} Apr 21] little form on Flat since 2016: unseated second on
hurdling debut. *Adam West*

CLAYTON 10 b.g. Peintre Celebre (USA) – Blossom (Warning) [2018/19 h118: h16v **h118**
h16s^2 h16d^2 h16d* Mar 15] lengthy gelding: fairly useful hurdler: won seller at Fakenham
in March: unproven beyond 2m: acts on heavy going: usually in tongue tie: front runner/
races prominently. *Gary Moore*

*thetote.com Galway Plate Handicap Chase, Galway—an enterprising ride from Mark Enright
sees 33/1-shot Clarcam roll back the years on his final start on Irish soil*

CLAYTON HALL (IRE) 6 b.g. Lilbourne Lad (IRE) – Hawk Dance (IRE) (Hawk Wing (USA)) [2018/19 h–: h16.7g h22.1g⁶ h20g⁴ h17.2m Jun 29] sturdy gelding: poor maiden hurdler on balance: probably stays 2¾m: tried in tongue tie: temperamental. *John Wainwright*   **h73 §**

CLEARANCE 5 b.g. Authorized (IRE) – Four Miracles (Vettori (IRE)) [2018/19 h16.3d Jan 16] modest on Flat, stays 16.5f: well beaten in novice on hurdling debut. *Gary Moore*   **h–**

CLEARLY CAPABLE (IRE) 10 b.g. Bienamado (USA) – Spout Road (IRE) (Dr Massini (IRE)) [2018/19 c–, h91: h19m h21.6g h20g^F h21.6g² h21.6m² Aug 6] modest handicap hurdler: maiden chaser: left Brian Barr after fourth start: stays 2¾m: acts on good to firm going: usually in headgear/tongue tie: normally leads. *Dai Burchell*   **c– h93**

CLEMENTO (IRE) 5 b.g. Canford Cliffs (IRE) – Street Style (IRE) (Rock of Gibraltar (IRE)) [2018/19 h17.2g* h17.2d* Aug 25] half-brother to fair hurdler/chaser Moss Street (2m-2¼m winner, by Moss Vale): fair maiden on Flat, stays 13f: fairly useful form when winning novice hurdles at Cartmel in May and August. *John Quinn*   **h116**

CLEM (IRE) 5 b.m. Malinas (GER) – Glorybe (GER) (Monsun (GER)) [2018/19 b16.2g³ b16g⁴ Sep 2] second foal: dam (h103), 2m hurdle winner, also 11f winner on Flat in Germany, half-sister to useful hurdler/high-class chaser (stayed 21f) Ghizao: modest form on first of 2 outings in bumpers. *Laura Morgan*   **b75**

CLENI WELLS (FR) 8 b.g. Poliglote – Kailasa (FR) (R B Chesne) [2018/19 c–, h113: h16.8g⁴ h18.5g c16.3s⁴ h16.8g⁵ h18.7g⁶ h26.5d⁵ Sep 21] workmanlike gelding: fair handicap hurdler: maiden chaser: held both starts in Britain: stayed 19f: acted on soft and good to firm going: wore headgear: raced towards rear: inconsistent: dead. *Martin Hill*   **c81 h107**

CLEOFE 5 ch.m. Shirocco (GER) – Agnese (Abou Zouz (USA)) [2018/19 b16.2g b15.8g b15.7g Jul 15] fourth foal: half-sister to smart hurdler/fairly useful chaser Lieutenant Colonel (2m-3m winner, by Kayf Tara): dam bumper winner/maiden hurdler (stayed 3¼m): no form in bumpers: left Rebecca Menzies after first start: tried in hood. *Philip Kirby*   **b–**

CLICK AND COLLECT 7 b.g. Humbel (USA) – Galena (GER) (Lomitas) [2018/19 h19.9v^{pu} Mar 16] pulled up in novice hurdle. *Clare Ellam*   **h–**

CLIFF HOUSE (IRE) 9 b.g. Mustameet (USA) – Babble On (IRE) (Anita's Prince) [2018/19 c19.5d³ c19.5g⁴ c18.2g c16.5g⁶ c22g³ h20d h20g h16s* h16v⁶ Mar 18] useful handicap hurdler: won at Leopardstown in March: fairly useful form over fences: left John J. Walsh after third start: stays 2½m: acts on good to firm and heavy going: front runner/races prominently. *Mrs D. A. Love, Ireland*   **c118 h135**

CLIFFSIDE PARK (IRE) 10 b.g. Chevalier (IRE) – Lady Toulon (IRE) (Toulon) [2018/19 c104, h115: h20g² h16.7g⁵ h20d⁴ h19d⁶ h16d⁴ h18.7g^{pu} Mar 30] fair hurdler: won seller at Fakenham in January: lightly-raced maiden chaser: stays 2½m: acts on good to firm and heavy going: has worn headgear, including last 4 starts: tried tongue tied. *Olly Murphy*   **c– h110**

CLIFFS OF DOVER 6 b.g. Canford Cliffs (IRE) – Basanti (USA) (Galileo (IRE)) [2018/19 h–: h18.9g h16.6g³ h18.5d* Jan 1] useful handicap hurdler: at least as good as ever when winning at Exeter (by 6 lengths from Ebony Gale) in January: will probably stay 2½m: acts on good to firm and good to soft going. *Paul Nicholls*   **h138**

CLIVE CLIFTON (IRE) 6 b.g. Wootton Bassett – Dearest Daisy (Forzando) [2018/19 h17.7g h17.7g⁶ h19.2m⁵ h15.9g Nov 5] unseated in point: error-prone maiden hurdler. *Phil York*   **h– x**

CLOCK ON TOM 9 b.g. Trade Fair – Night Owl (Night Shift (USA)) [2018/19 h99: h15.7g⁵ h15.8g h15.8g⁶ h16.3g⁶ h15.8g⁵ Nov 17] compact gelding: modest handicap hurdler: unproven beyond 2m: acts on good to firm and heavy going: tried in cheekpieces: usually waited with. *Barry Leavy*   **h88**

CLOGHOUGE BOY (IRE) 9 b.g. Westerner – Back To Cloghoge (IRE) (Bob Back (USA)) [2018/19 h20.1s³ h20.1v⁵ h22s⁵ h23.1g h23.1g^{pu} Mar 20] point winner: fair form over hurdles: should stay beyond 2½m: acts on soft going: wears tongue tie. *Gillian Boanas*   **h107**

CLONDAW ACE (IRE) 6 b.g. Flemensfirth (USA) – Peace Time Beauty (IRE) (Saddlers' Hall (IRE)) [2018/19 b–: h19.5g⁶ h21.6g⁵ h20v⁶ c23.6g c23.8s^{pu} Apr 7] off mark in Irish points at third attempt: well held over hurdles: little aptitude for chasing: tried in visor. *Tim Vaughan*   **c– h–**

CLONDAW ANCHOR (IRE) 6 gr.g. Stowaway – Masiana (IRE) (Daylami (IRE)) **h113**
[2018/19 h19g² h17d* h16d³ h20.5d⁴ h21.4s Mar 7] tall, angular gelding: has had breathing
operation: second foal: half-brother to bumper winner/fairly useful hurdler The Welsh
Paddies (21f-3¼m winner, by Court Cave): dam (b86) second in bumper: runner-up in Irish
point: fair form over hurdles: won novice at Carlisle in November: should stay at least
2½m: acts on good to soft going: wears hood: tried in tongue tie. *Dan Skelton*

CLONDAW BANKER (IRE) 10 b.g. Court Cave (IRE) – Freya Alex (Makbul) **c57 x**
[2018/19 c119, h–: c17.3g⁵ c17.3mᵖᵘ h18.6m h22.1s⁴ h23.3g h19.3g⁶ Oct 25] useful- **h64**
looking gelding: has had breathing operation: poor handicap hurdler/maiden chaser
nowadays: stays 2½m: acts on soft going: wears cheekpieces: usually races towards rear:
prone to mistakes over fences. *Barry Murtagh*

CLONDAW BISTO (IRE) 8 b.g. September Storm (GER) – Solo Venture (IRE) **c104 §**
(Abednego) [2018/19 h108: c25.8v² c23.6s⁴ c25.7s² c25.7gᵖᵘ c26m⁵ Mar 29] has had **h–**
breathing operations: won Irish point on debut: fair maiden hurdler: similar form in
handicap chases only when second to The Tin Miner at Plumpton in December: stays 3¼m:
acts on soft going: has worn headgear/tongue tie: temperamental (often races lazily).
Suzy Smith

CLONDAW CASTLE (IRE) 7 b.g. Oscar (IRE) – Lohort Castle (IRE) (Presenting) **c146**
[2018/19 h129: c16.4d⁵ c16g² c15.9m* c16.5g* c15.9s⁴ c15.8g⁴ Apr 6] well-made gelding: **h–**
fairly useful hurdler: smart novice chaser: won at Leicester in January and Huntingdon
(handicap event, by 12 lengths from Peppay Le Pugh) in February: raced around 2m: acts
on soft and good to firm going: usually front runner/races prominently, strong traveller:
sound jumper. *Tom George*

CLONDAW CIAN (IRE) 9 br.g. Gold Well – Cocktail Bar (IRE) (Hubbly Bubbly **c111 §**
(USA)) [2018/19 c134§, h–: h26.5v³ h24.2d h24.2s c31.7s⁴ c25.3gᵖᵘ Apr 17] lengthy **h124 §**
gelding: fairly useful handicap hurdler: maiden chaser, fairly useful at best: left Suzy Smith
after third start: should stay beyond 3¼m: acts on heavy going: wears headgear: lazy and
unreliable. *Sophie Leech*

CLONDAW FIXER (IRE) 7 b.g. Court Cave (IRE) – The Millers Tale (IRE) (Rashar **h–**
(USA)) [2018/19 b–: h20.1gᵖᵘ h22sᵖᵘ Jan 29] tall gelding: has had breathing operation:
runner-up in Irish point: no form in bumper/over hurdles: tried in tongue tie. *George Bewley*

CLONDAW KAEMPFER (IRE) 11 b.g. Oscar (IRE) – Gra-Bri (IRE) (Rashar (USA)) **c112**
[2018/19 c–, h127: c24.1g² c20.1gᵖᵘ Aug 18] rangy gelding: useful hurdler at best: lightly- **h–**
raced maiden chaser: stayed 3m: acted on heavy going: regularly wore headgear: tongue
tied: usually raced prominently: dead. *Donald McCain*

CLONDAW NATIVE (IRE) 7 b.g. Golan (IRE) – Great Outlook (IRE) (Simply Great **c89 p**
(FR)) [2018/19 h128, b91: c23.6d⁶ h23.1g³ h24g Dec 14] won Irish point on debut: fairly **h118**
useful handicap hurdler: jumped right when well beaten in novice at Chepstow on chasing
debut (should do better): stays 3m: acts on good to soft going: tried in cheekpieces: races
prominently: temperament under suspicion. *Stuart Edmunds*

CLONDAW RIGGER (IRE) 7 b.g. Stowaway – Daytona Lily (IRE) (Beneficial) **c102**
[2018/19 c97, h74: c24g³ c23.6s⁴ c25.1g* Nov 22] maiden hurdler: fair handicap chaser: **h–**
won at Chepstow and Wincanton in November: stays 25f: acts on heavy going: wears
tongue tie. *Katy Price*

CLONDAW ROBIN (IRE) 6 ch.g. Robin des Champs (FR) – Old Town Queen (IRE) **c–**
(Bob's Return (IRE)) [2018/19 b16.7g b17.7s h20.5s h23s h16d c20.2mᵖᵘ Feb 14] good- **h–**
topped gelding: has had breathing operation: no form in varied company (including in **b–**
points): wears headgear. *Zoe Davison*

CLONDAW'S ANSWER (IRE) 6 b.g. Ask – Monabricka Lady (IRE) (Moscow **h–**
Society (USA)) [2018/19 b–: h19.5s h23.1s h19.8g⁵ Mar 25] off mark in Irish points at
third attempt: well held in bumper/over hurdles: tried in tongue tie. *Kayley Woollacott*

CLONDAW STORM (IRE) 5 gr.g. September Storm (GER) – Oh So Smart (IRE) **h98**
(Turgeon (USA)) [2018/19 b17s h16.7s h15.8g³ h15.8d⁴ h21.3g⁵ Apr 11] €21,000 3-y-o, **b–**
£42,000 4-y-o: second foal: brother to a winning pointer: dam, unraced, out of half-sister
to triple Grand Steeple-Chase de Paris winner Mid Dancer: runner-up in Irish point: tailed
off in bumper: modest form over hurdles. *Christopher Kellett*

CLONDAW WESTIE (IRE) 8 b.g. Westerner – You're A Native (IRE) (Saddlers' Hall **c122**
(IRE)) [2018/19 c122p, h88: c15.5s⁵ c19.5d⁴ c22.6s* c25gᵖᵘ Apr 6] smallish, angular **h–**
gelding: maiden hurdler: fairly useful handicap chaser: won at Stratford in March: stays
23f: acts on heavy going: wears cheekpieces/tongue tie: usually front runner/races
prominently. *Lawney Hill*

CLONDAW WHISPER (IRE) 6 b.g. Court Cave (IRE) – Whispering (IRE) (Royal Academy (USA)) [2018/19 b16d h15.3g h15.3g h15.3g Apr 3] little show in varied company: wears tongue tie. *Brian Barr* h– b–

CLONUSKER (IRE) 11 b.g. Fasliyev (USA) – Tamburello (IRE) (Roi Danzig (USA)) [2018/19 c15.7gᵖᵘ h20.5gᵖᵘ Apr 7] good-topped gelding: modest hurdler/chaser at best: off 2 years, pulled up both outings in 2018/19: stays 2½m: acts on heavy going: tried in cheekpieces: wears tongue tie. *Linda Jewell* c– h–

CLOONE LADY (IRE) 7 b.m. Milan – Cloone Leader (IRE) (Supreme Leader) [2018/19 h113p: c19.9g⁵ c20.5gᵖᵘ c25.2dᵖᵘ c24gᵖᵘ Apr 13] well-made mare: winning Irish pointer: lightly-raced maiden hurdler, runner-up final start in 2017/18: little promise in handicap chases: tried in cheekpieces: temperament under suspicion. *Kim Bailey* c– h–

CLOSEST FRIEND 10 b.g. Kayf Tara – Princess of War (Warrshan (USA)) [2018/19 c16.5g⁴ c19.4mᵖᵘ c21.4g² c24m⁴ Oct 21] lengthy gelding: winning hurdler: lightly-raced maiden chaser: form (fair) in 2018/19 only when runner-up in novice handicap at Market Rasen: stayed 21f: acted on good to firm and good to soft going: usually wore tongue tie: dead. *James Eustace* c103 h–

CLOSING CEREMONY (IRE) 10 b.g. Flemensfirth (USA) – Supreme Von Pres (IRE) (Presenting) [2018/19 c–, h119: h22.8v h24.3d* Jan 19] useful-looking gelding: fairly useful handicap hurdler nowadays: down in weights, won at Haydock in January: well held only outing over fences: stays 3¼m: acts on heavy going: makes running. *Emma Lavelle* c– h126

CLOTH CAP (IRE) 7 b.g. Beneficial – Cloth Fair (IRE) (Old Vic) [2018/19 h115: c19.9g³ c22.6g* c25.2g* c31.8m³ Apr 13] strong gelding: fairly useful hurdler: better over fences: won handicaps at Stratford and Catterick in November: off 5 months, shaped well when 4 lengths third of 23 to Takingrisks in Scottish Grand National at Ayr final start: stays 4m: acts on soft and good to firm going: usually travels strongly: sound jumper: likely to progress further. *Jonjo O'Neill* c134 p h–

CLOUD FORMATION 5 b.g. Cloudings (IRE) – Willowpattern (Young Buster (IRE)) [2018/19 b17.7g Apr 7] down field in bumper at Plumpton. *Martin Keighley* b–

CLOUD HOPPER (IRE) 5 gr.g. Dubai Destination (USA) – Drain Hopper (Cloudings (IRE)) [2018/19 h–, b–: h19.2vᵖᵘ h23dᵖᵘ h19s Feb 4] compact gelding: no solid form over hurdles: tried in cheekpieces/tongue tie. *Jamie Snowden* h–

CLOUDY DREAM (IRE) 9 gr.g. Cloudings (IRE) – Run Away Dream (IRE) (Acceglio) [2018/19 c157, h–: c19.9g³ Oct 28] good-topped gelding: winning hurdler: very smart handicap chaser: third in Old Roan Chase at Aintree (1¾ lengths behind Frodon) only outing in 2018/19: has form at 25f, but better at shorter: acts on heavy going: travels strongly held up: none too resolute. *Donald McCain* c156 h–

CLOUDY GLEN (IRE) 6 b.g. Cloudings (IRE) – Ribble (IRE) (Supreme Leader) [2018/19 h109, b–: h18.9s* h19.5d* h19.3d h19.3v* Mar 17] rather unfurnished gelding: fairly useful hurdler: won handicaps at Haydock (conditionals) in December and Chepstow in January, and novice at Carlisle in March: stays 19f: acts on heavy going: tried in hood: usually forces pace. *Venetia Williams* h124

CLUBS ARE TRUMPS (IRE) 10 b.g. Flemensfirth (USA) – Pairtree (Double Trigger (IRE)) [2018/19 c111§, h–: c23.9dᵖᵘ May 20] maiden hurdler: fair handicap chaser: stays 3¼m: acts on good to firm and good to soft going: wears headgear: tried in tongue tie: unreliable. *Jonjo O'Neill* c– § h–

CLUB TROPICANA 4 ch.f. Helmet (AUS) – Twenty Seven (IRE) (Efisio) [2018/19 h15.8dᵖᵘ Feb 6] dam half-sister to fairly useful 2m hurdle winner Artist's Muse: fair maiden on Flat, stays 8.5f: hooded, pulled up in juvenile on hurdling debut. *Richard Spencer* h–

CLUES AND ARROWS (IRE) 11 b.g. Clerkenwell (USA) – Ballela Girl (IRE) (Mandalus) [2018/19 c–, h–: c25.5g May 30] winning pointer/hurdler: maiden chaser: lightly raced and little form since 2016/17: tried in headgear. *Miss G. Walton* c– h–

CLYNE 9 b.g. Hernando (FR) – Lauderdale (GER) (Nebos (GER)) [2018/19 c134p, h145x: h24.2s² h20.3d⁵ h24.3g⁴ h24.7g Apr 6] tall, angular gelding: maiden hurdler: second in Long Distance Hurdle at Newbury (2½ lengths behind Unowhatimeanharry), best effort in 2018/19: useful form when runner-up in novice at Haydock on chasing debut in 2017/18, though made mistakes: stays 3m: goes well on soft/heavy going: usually races prominently. *Evan Williams* c– h140

CNOC SION (IRE) 9 b.g. Gold Well – Bondi Babe (IRE) (Meneval (USA)) [2018/19 h20g^{pu} c23g^6 c24g c20.3g* c20d^{pu} c19.4d^6 c20.2m^3 c18.2s^5 c24g^5 Apr 25] lightly-raced maiden hurdler: poor handicap chaser: won novice event at Bangor in October: stays 2½m: wears headgear: tried in tongue tie: temperamental. *Roy Brotherton* **c79 § h–**

COAL STOCK (IRE) 4 ch.g. Red Jazz (USA) – Scar Tissue (Medicean) [2018/19 h16.5d h16.3g^6 h15.9g^2 Apr 21] fair maiden on Flat, stays 11.5f: fair form over hurdles: improved further when second to The Flying Sofa in maiden at Plumpton final outing. *Sam Thomas* **h110**

COASTAL DRIFT 5 b.g. Black Sam Bellamy (IRE) – Absalom's Girl (Saddlers' Hall (IRE)) [2018/19 b–: h21.6d^5 h20.5s^{pu} h21.7d Feb 24] well held in bumper: best effort over hurdles (fair form) when 5 lengths third to Debestyman in novice at Plumpton: will stay 3m. *Colin Tizzard* **h107**

COASTAL TIEP (FR) 7 b.g. Coastal Path – Jaltiepy (FR) (Monjal (FR)) [2018/19 c136§, h–: c22d^5 c24d^2 c26.3d^{pu} c21.1d^4 c24.7d^3 Apr 23] good-topped gelding: winning hurdler: fairly useful hunter chaser nowadays: stays 3m: acts on good to soft going: usually in cheekpieces: tried in tongue tie: one to treat with caution. *Stuart Crawford, Ireland* **c126 § h–**

COASTLEY LANE 6 b.g. Bertolini (USA) – Miss Hermione (Bahamian Bounty) [2018/19 h16.2d h16.2g h17.2g Jul 23] tongue tied, well beaten over hurdles. *Maurice Barnes* **h–**

COBAJAYISLAND (IRE) 11 b.g. Heron Island (IRE) – Shinora (IRE) (Black Minstrel) [2018/19 c110, h–: c26.2g* c23.8g^{pu} May 31] maiden hurdler: fair handicap chaser: won at Kelso in May: stayed 3¼m: acted on heavy going: dead. *Michael Scudamore* **c114 h–**

COBOLOBO (FR) 7 br.g. Maresca Sorrento (FR) – Nanou des Brosses (FR) (Saint Cyrien (FR)) [2018/19 h120: c23.8v^2 c25.1g^3 c30.7d^{ur} Feb 22] good-topped gelding: has had breathing operation: fairly useful hurdler: better form when close second in novice at Ffos Las on chasing debut: let down by jumping both starts after: stays 3m: acts on soft going: tried in tongue tie: remains with potential as a chaser. *Jonjo O'Neill* **c129 p h–**

COBRA COMMANDER (IRE) 5 b.g. Beneficial – Run For Help (IRE) (Flemensfirth (USA)) [2018/19 h15.8v^{pu} h15.8d^5 h16s Mar 10] well-beaten third on debut in Irish point: little show over hurdles. *Tom Symonds* **h–**

COBRA DE MAI (FR) 7 b.g. Great Pretender (IRE) – Miria Galanda (FR) (Chef de Clan (FR)) [2018/19 c145, h120: c20g^4 c23.6d c19.4g* c21g^4 c20.6d^{pu} c20d c20.2g* c19.9g^5 c26g* c22.7g^4 Apr 27] angular gelding: has had breathing operation: fairly useful hurdler: smart handicap chaser: won at Stratford in November, Leicester in March and Cheltenham (by 13 lengths from Rocky's Treasure) in April: stays 3¼m, effective at shorter: acts on good to firm and heavy going: usually in cheekpieces: wears tongue tie. *Dan Skelton* **c148 h–**

COBY NINE (IRE) 6 b.g. Arcadio (GER) – Timing (Alhaarth (IRE)) [2018/19 b16.8v^5 h21.4g^3 h19.7s h16.8s h21.4g^2 h19s^3 Mar 19] second foal: dam (h96), 2m hurdle winner, also 1½m-2m winner on Flat, half-sister to useful hurdler/fairly useful chaser (stayed 19f) Fait Le Jojo: ran green in bumper: fair form over hurdles: stays 21f: acts on soft going. *Susan Gardner* **h101 b–**

COCK A DOODLE DOO (FR) 7 b.m. Della Francesca (USA) – Jiletta (FR) (Passing Sale (FR)) [2018/19 h16.5g h16g h16g^3 h16g* h16g h15.8g^4 h19.7g^6 h15.5d h20.6s h15.7d^5 h15.8m^2 Apr 23] has had breathing operation: fourth foal: half-sister to useful chaser Rileyev (2m/17f winner, by Goldneyev), stayed 2½m, and fairly useful French chaser Quakhdari (17f winner, by Akhdari): dam French 17f-19f chase winner: thrice-raced on Flat: modest hurdler: won mares maiden at Sligo in August: left James A. Nash after fifth start: unproven beyond 2m: best form on good going: tried in headgear: wears tongue tie. *Dan Skelton* **h96**

COCKER 7 b.g. Shirocco (GER) – Treble Heights (IRE) (Unfuwain (USA)) [2018/19 h73: h23.4g^6 h16m^4 Oct 19] maiden hurdler, poor nowadays: stays 2½m: acts on good to soft going: in cheekpieces last 3 starts. *Alan Blackmore* **h–**

COCKLEY BECK (IRE) 7 b.m. Westerner – Bobnval (IRE) (Bob Back (USA)) [2018/19 h100: h23.9g^3 h24.7g^4 h20d^5 h23.3g* h23.9g^2 Sep 27] has had breathing operation: fair handicap hurdler: won at Hexham in September: stays 3m: acts on heavy going: in cheekpieces last 5 starts: front runner/races prominently. *Nicky Richards* **h109**

COCKNEY SEAGULL (IRE) 6 br.g. Watar (IRE) – Acountry Lane (IRE) (Norwich) [2018/19 h–, b–: h20.7g^{pu} h19.6g^5 h21.7v h23d^6 h25s^{pu} c20.3g^{ur} h25g^5 Apr 22] little form over hurdles: unseated ninth on chasing debut: usually in headgear: tried in tongue tie: ungenuine. *Linda Jewell* **c– § h61 §**

CF Roberts 25 Years of Sponsorship Handicap Chase, Cheltenham—the durable Cogry (centre) outbattles Singlefarmpayment (right) and Rolling Dylan (left) in a three-way finish

COCKNEY WREN 6 b.m. Cockney Rebel (IRE) – Compose (Anabaa (USA)) [2018/19 h110: h15.8m⁶ May 13] rather sparely-made mare: has had breathing operation: fair form over hurdles in 2017/18, winning mares novice at Taunton: well held in handicap only outing since. *Harry Fry* **h–**

COCO LIVE (FR) 7 b.g. Secret Singer (FR) – Iona Will (FR) (Kadalko (FR)) [2018/19 c–, h–: c23d² Apr 4] multiple winning pointer: little form over hurdles: much better effort in chases when second in maiden hunter at Taunton: stays 23f: acts on good to soft going: tried in cheekpieces/tongue tie. *Mrs Harriet Waight* **c105 h–**

CODDINGTON BANKS 7 b.m. Fair Mix (IRE) – Coddington Girl (Green Adventure (USA)) [2018/19 h21.2dᵖᵘ h21sᵖᵘ Jan 21] fourth foal: half-sister to a winning pointer by Sir Harry Lewis: dam winning pointer: unplaced in points: pulled up in mares novice hurdles. *Sarah-Jayne Davies* **h–**

CODED MESSAGE 6 b.m. Oscar (IRE) – Ring Back (IRE) (Bob Back (USA)) [2018/19 b90: h15.8d³ h16v* h19.7s³ h16.5s³ h16.8d⁴ h23.1g² h20.3gᵖᵘ Apr 18] fairly useful hurdler: won mares novice at Lingfield in December: stays easy 23f: acts on heavy going. *Ben Case* **h117**

CODE OF LAW 9 ch.g. Papal Bull – Fyvie (Grand Lodge (USA)) [2018/19 c93§, h–: c20.5mᵖᵘ c17.8m* c17.3mᵖᵘ c17.2m⁵ c17.8g³ c19.5g³ c17.8g⁵ c20.3g⁵ Oct 3] maiden hurdler: modest handicap chaser: won at Fontwell in May: best up to 21f: acts on good to firm and good to soft going: wears headgear: temperamental. *Neil Mulholland* **c93 § h–**

CODESHARE 7 b.g. Dansili – Clepsydra (Sadler's Wells (USA)) [2018/19 h19.9v h19.3m⁴ h19.9v³ Mar 16] fairly useful on Flat, stays 14.5f: first form (modest) over hurdles when well-held third in novice at Uttoxeter final outing. *Peter Bowen* **h90**

COEUR BLIMEY (IRE) 8 b.g. Winged Love (IRE) – Eastender (Opening Verse (USA)) [2018/19 h126: h21g h19.7v* h20.5d h19.9v Mar 16] workmanlike gelding: fairly useful handicap hurdler: won at Hereford in December: also useful winner on Flat in April: stays 2½m: acts on heavy going: tried in cheekpieces: clumsy jumper. *Susan Gardner* **h129**

226

COEUR PENSIF (FR) 7 br.g. Laveron – Lady Easter (FR) (Cadoudal (FR)) [2018/19 **c–** h117: c24.1g⁶ h21g Nov 18] runner-up in Irish point: fair handicap hurdler: moody display **h104** in novice handicap on chasing debut: likely to stay beyond 25f: acts on soft going: tried in cheekpieces: temperament under suspicion. *Ben Pauling*

COEUR SUBLIME (IRE) 4 b.g. Elusive Pimpernel (USA) – Love Knot (IRE) **h141** (Lomitas) [2018/19 h16.5g* h16g² h16gᶠ h16d⁴ h16.8d² h16d³ Apr 22] sturdy gelding: dam half-sister to useful hurdler (stayed 3m) Sweetheart: successful in 1¼m maiden sole outing on Flat: useful juvenile hurdler: won at Down Royal in November: in frame all completed starts after, running especially well when 3 lengths second to Pentland Hills in Triumph Hurdle at Cheltenham in March: likely to stay beyond 17f: acts on good to soft going: races prominently/travels strongly. *Gordon Elliott, Ireland*

COEUR TANTRE (IRE) 8 ch.g. Fruits of Love (USA) – Ding Dong Belle (Minster **c106** Son) [2018/19 c125, h120: h20m³ c16.5g⁵ c19.4g³ h25mᵖᵘ Oct 22] fairly useful handicap **h121** hurdler: similar form in handicap chases: barely stays 2½m: acts on soft and good to firm going: has worn headgear: wears tongue tie. *Anthony Honeyball*

COGBURN 7 ch.g. Black Sam Bellamy (IRE) – Realms of Gold (USA) (Gulch (USA)) **h104** [2018/19 h110: h19g² h19dᵖᵘ Dec 13] useful-looking gelding: fair form over hurdles: sometimes wore eyeshields: dead. *Alan King*

COGRY 10 b.g. King's Theatre (IRE) – Wyldello (Supreme Leader) [2018/19 c137x, h–: **c140** c25g² c27.3g⁶ c26g* c29.2g c31.8mᵘʳ Apr 13] sturdy gelding: winning hurdler: useful **h–** handicap chaser: won Grade 3 event at Cheltenham in December: stays 4m: acts on heavy going: usually in headgear: usually leads. *Nigel Twiston-Davies*

COISA BLANCO (IRE) 6 b.g. Jeremy (USA) – Moon Legend (USA) (Gulch (USA)) **c– §** [2018/19 h–: h23s³ h23.3gᵖᵘ h20.6g⁶ h23g⁵ h24gᶠ h23g h24g⁴ h20.6d³ h19.7d h24.3dᵖᵘ **h87 §** h19g h20.6g⁵ c24g⁶ Apr 13] disappointing maiden hurdler: tailed off in novice handicap on chasing debut: left Jonjo O'Neill after sixth start: stays 23f: acts on soft going: wears headgear: tried in tongue tie: untrustworthy. *Oliver Greenall*

COJACK (IRE) 7 b.g. Presenting – In The Waves (IRE) (Winged Love (IRE)) [2018/19 **h–** h–: h22.2g⁶ Jul 10] good-topped gelding: lightly raced and little sign of ability. *Mark Bradstock*

COKO BEACH (FR) 4 gr.g. Cokoriko (FR) – Solana Beach (FR) (Take Risks (FR)) **h131** [2018/19 h17.4s* h16g h16.4s² Mar 13] fifth foal: half-brother to 3 winners in France, including fairly useful 15f hurdle winner Coastal Beach (by Coastal Path): dam, French 1¼m-12.5f winner, half-sister to fair French hurdler/useful chaser (stayed 27f) Top of The Sky: useful form over hurdles: won newcomers race at Nantes (left Francois Nicolle after) in October: much improved when second in Fred Winter Juvenile Handicap Hurdle at Cheltenham (2 lengths behind Band of Outlaws): shaped as if amiss at Punchestown shortly after end of British season. *Gordon Elliott, Ireland*

COLBY (IRE) 6 b.g. Witness Box (USA) – Wet And Dry (IRE) (Catcher In The Rye **h96** (IRE)) [2018/19 h101p, h90: h21.2g² h25.3s h23.8gᶠ Jan 7] modest form in maidens first 2 outings over hurdles: disappointing in handicaps both subsequent starts, in cheekpieces final one. *Chris Grant*

COLD AS ICE (FR) 7 gr.g. Montmartre (FR) – Turiama (FR) (Ashkalani (IRE)) [2018/19 **h110** h–: h21.2g⁴ h19.8s⁴ h19.8sᵖᵘ h19.5g Apr 26] easily best effort over hurdles (fair form) when 6½ lengths fourth to Smackwater Jack in maiden at Ludlow on return: disappointing in handicaps after: stays 21f: acts on good to soft going: usually front runner/races prominently. *Venetia Williams*

COLD FUSION (IRE) 6 b.m. Frozen Power (IRE) – Tuscania (USA) (Woodman (USA)) **h80 §** [2018/19 h23.1s⁶ h16.6g⁶ h19g⁵ h16.8d² h18.5d⁵ h23.9d⁴ Apr 24] poor maiden hurdler: stays 19f: acts on good to soft going: tried in headgear: temperamental. *Dai Williams*

COLDITZ CASTLE (IRE) 5 ch.g. Getaway (GER) – Stowaway Sue (IRE) (Stowaway) **h115** [2018/19 h73: h16.5dᵘʳ h15.3g³ h15.9s⁴ h19.8s² Mar 7] rather unfurnished gelding: fairly useful form over hurdles: will stay beyond 2½m. *Alan King*

COLD MARCH (FR) 9 b.g. Early March – Tumultueuse (FR) (Bering) [2018/19 c100, **c–** h115: c19.9g c24g⁵ Jan 12] good-topped gelding: maiden hurdler: smart handicap chaser at **h–** best for Venetia Williams: regressive since 2016/17: stays 2½m: acts on good to firm and heavy going: usually in headgear. *Harry Whittington*

Racing Post App Champion INH Flat, Punchestown—Mr Jamie Codd improvises after dropping his whip as Colreevy holds off the Gigginstown trio Abacadabras (star on cap), Beacon Edge and Embittered (hood)

COLD SHOULDER 5 b.g. Passing Glance – Averami (Averti (IRE)) [2018/19 h97: h20.2g⁶ h17.3g h16.7g* h19.5v* h20.1m⁶ h19.9v h15.8d h15.3gᶠ Mar 25] fair handicap hurdler: won at Bangor (conditionals event) in October and Ayr in November: left Gordon Elliott after fifth start: probably stays 2½m: acts on heavy going. *Tim Vaughan*   **h110**

COLD WESTON 6 ch.g. Malinas (GER) – Speed Bonnie Boat (Alflora (IRE)) [2018/19 b59: h15.8gᵖᵘ May 8] well held in bumpers: pulled up in novice on hurdling debut. *Henry Daly*   **h–**

COLLEGE OAK 4 ch.g. Norse Dancer (IRE) – Katmai (IRE) (Bob Back (USA)) [2018/19 b13.7g² Apr 12] £40,000 3-y-o: fifth foal: dam (b99), bumper winner, half-sister to triple Cheltenham Gold Cup winner Best Mate: 10/1 and hooded, 6 lengths second to Mount Windsor in bumper at Fontwell. *Jamie Snowden*   **b84**

COLLODI (GER) 10 b.g. Konigstiger (GER) – Codera (GER) (Zilzal (USA)) [2018/19 c–, h102: h16.8m³ h16.7g² h16.7m* h16.3g³ h16m* h15.8g⁵ h15.8d h15.5g h15.5g⁵ h15.8v³ h15.8dᵖᵘ h16.6g⁴ h16s² h15.9d² h15.8d² h16.8g* Apr 5] compact gelding: fair handicap hurdler: won at Market Rasen in July, Fakenham (conditionals selling event, final outing for Neil Mulholland) in October and Sedgefield in April: let down by jumping only start over fences: raced around 2m: acts on soft and good to firm going: has worn cheekpieces: tried in tongue tie: tough. *Conor Dore*   **c–** **h111**

COLLOONEY (IRE) 5 b.g. Yeats (IRE) – Amber Trix (IRE) (Scribano) [2018/19 b13.7g* h15.9s² h16.7d* h15.3g² h20.6g³ Apr 3] second foal: closely related to fairly useful hurdler/chaser Inaminna (19f winner, by Oscar): dam (h100) bumper winner/maiden hurdler (stayed 2½m): runner-up in Irish point on debut: won maiden bumper at Huntingdon (by 3¾ lengths from Simply Loveleh) in November: fairly useful form over hurdles: won novice at Bangor in January: tried in tongue tie: remains with potential. *Olly Murphy*   **h122 p** **b100**

COLMERS HILL 9 b.g. Crosspeace (IRE) – My Dancing Kin (Baryshnikov (AUS)) [2018/19 c101, h–: c23.8s* c24.2vᵖᵘ c23.8sᵖᵘ Feb 26] maiden hurdler: modest handicap chaser: won at Ffos Las on return in November: pulled up both starts after: stays 3¼m: acts on heavy going: in headgear last 5 starts: usually races close up: unreliable. *Jeremy Scott*   **c97 §** **h–**

COLMS DREAM (IRE) 10 ch.g. Beneficial – African Waters (IRE) (Be My Native (USA)) [2018/19 c25gᵖᵘ c22.6gᶠ Nov 18] winning hurdler: smart chaser at best: lightly raced and little form since spring 2016: stays 3m: acts on soft going: wears headgear/tongue tie. *Karl Thornton, Ireland*   **c–** **h–**

COLONEL CUSTARD (IRE) 6 ch.g. Mahler – Criaire Princess (IRE) (Tidaro (USA)) **h126**
[2018/19 b97: b16.8g* h16.8v* h16.4g⁵ h16.7s² h15.8v* h20g Apr 6] sturdy gelding: fair **b93**
form in bumpers: won at Newton Abbot in May: fairly useful form over hurdles: won
novices at same track in October and Ffos Las in January: should be suited by 2½m: acts
on heavy going: usually races prominently. *Nicky Martin*

COLONEL KEATING (IRE) 7 b.g. Yeats (IRE) – Jabroot (IRE) (Alhaarth (IRE)) **h103**
[2018/19 h20.5s h23s h19.2d⁶ h19.5d³ Mar 21] workmanlike gelding: second foal: dam
maiden (stayed 1½m): off mark in Irish points at second attempt: fair form over hurdles:
much improved when third in novice handicap at Chepstow final outing: should be suited
by 2½m+. *Richard Rowe*

COLONEL MILLER 5 b.g. Multiplex – Legion of Merit (Beat All (USA)) [2018/19 **h–**
b16.8g b16.3g⁵ ab16g³ h20.8g Jan 9] smallish gelding: first foal: dam unraced sister to **b84**
fairly useful hurdler (19f/2½m winner) Lieutenant Miller: modest form in bumpers: well
beaten in maiden on hurdling debut: should stay 2½m. *Alan King*

COLONIAL DREAMS (IRE) 7 b.g. Westerner – Dochas Supreme (IRE) (Supreme **h135**
Leader) [2018/19 h123: h21.2m² h21g⁶ h19.3d² h19d⁵ h19.8g* Apr 27] sturdy gelding:
useful handicap hurdler: won at Sandown (by length from Wait For Me) in April: stays 21f:
acts on good to firm and heavy going: free-going sort. *Nicky Henderson*

COLORADO GOLD 6 ch.m. Beat Hollow – Crevamoy (IRE) (Shardari) [2018/19 b–: **b77**
b17g⁵ b16.4m³ Mar 22] modest form in bumpers. *Daragh Bourke*

COLOUR ME IN (IRE) 4 b.f. Zoffany (IRE) – I Tilda (IRE) (Kris Kin (USA)) [2018/19 **h97**
h16d h16v⁴ h16s⁶ h16d h16vᵖᵘ h16.8g⁶ Apr 18] little form on Flat: modest juvenile hurdler:
should stay beyond 2m: acts on heavy going. *Thomas Mullins, Ireland*

COLREEVY (IRE) 6 b.m. Flemensfirth (USA) – Poetics Girl (IRE) (Saddlers' Hall **b113**
(IRE)) [2018/19 b107: b16d³ Apr 7] sturdy mare: close up when fell last in point: useful
bumper performer: won 10-runner Champion INH Flat Race at Punchestown shortly after
end of British season by length from Abacadabras, quickening clear entering straight and
battling well. *W. P. Mullins, Ireland*

COLT LIGHTNING (IRE) 6 b.g. Flemensfirth (USA) – Shannon Theatre (IRE) **h110**
(King's Theatre (IRE)) [2018/19 h108: h25g⁵ May 10] second in point: fair handicap
hurdler: stays 25f: acts on heavy going: front runner/races prominently. *Tom Lacey*

COLUMN OF FIRE (IRE) 5 b.g. Robin des Champs (FR) – Ghillie's Bay (IRE) **h119**
(King's Ride) [2018/19 b16d* h18g³ h20dᵇᵈ b16g² Feb 24] €115,000 3-y-o: brother to **b104**
bumper winner/fairly useful 2m hurdle winner Ladysingstheblues and half-brother to
several winners, including useful hurdler/smart chaser Tully East (2m-2½m winner, by
Shantou): dam unraced: fairly useful form in bumpers: won maiden event at Navan in
November: similar form when third of 20 to Lone Wolf on completed start in maiden
hurdles at Fairyhouse. *Gordon Elliott, Ireland*

COLWINSTON (IRE) 9 b.g. Mustameet (USA) – Miss Jeanney (IRE) (Topanoora) **h103**
[2018/19 h102: h16m³ h16.2g⁴ h20m² Aug 31] fair maiden hurdler: stays 2½m: acts on
good to firm and heavy going: wears tongue tie. *Miss Suzy Barkley, Ireland*

COMANCHE CHIEFTAIN (CAN) 7 b.g. Broken Vow (USA) – Platinum Preferred **c131**
(CAN) (Vindication (USA)) [2018/19 h124: c16.5g² c17.3g⁴ c16m⁶ c16.5g² c19.4m* **h114**
h20g⁵ c19.4g* c20g c24.2m² c19.4g⁶ c21.4mᶠ Apr 21] sturdy gelding: winning hurdler:
useful form over fences, winning handicaps at Stratford in August (novice event) in August
and September will prove best short of 3m: acts on good to firm and heavy going: formerly
hooded: front runner/races prominently. *Neil King*

COMBER MILL (FR) 7 ch.g. Le Fou (IRE) – Kalistina (FR) (Sillery (USA)) [2018/19 **c97**
h99: c16.5g² c16.5dᵘʳ c16gᵘʳ c17.4g c16gᵖᵘ h15.8vᶠ h15.8d⁶ h15.9s³ h16.7s* Mar 23] fair **h104**
handicap hurdler: won at Bangor in March: modest form when second in novice handicap
at Worcester on chasing debut: failed to complete 3 of 4 starts over fences after: unproven
beyond 17f: acts on heavy going: normally hooded: wears tongue tie: front runner/races
prominently. *Alastair Ralph*

COMBUSTIBLE GIRL (IRE) 6 b.m. Craigsteel – Slaney Legacy (IRE) (Mr **b–**
Combustible (IRE)) [2018/19 b16.8d b16.2g Feb 14] second foal: sister to poor 2¼m
hurdle winner Slaney Craiglegacy: dam placed in point: tailed off in bumpers. *Hugh Burns*

Gigginstown House Stud's "Commander of Fleet"

COMEHERE HI (IRE) 9 b.m. Gamut (IRE) – Dea Vesta (IRE) (Zieten (USA)) [2018/19 **c80** h16.5g⁶ h16g⁵ h18.8g⁶ h20.5gᶠ h20d h16g² c18m⁴ h15.5g⁵ c19.9s⁶ Apr 26] third foal: half- **h103** sister to a winning pointer by Whitmore's Conn: dam Italian 6f-1m winner: modest maiden on Flat (stays 1½m): fair handicap hurdler: mid-field both outings in maiden chases: stays 2¼m: acts on soft and good to firm going: formerly in hood. *James A. Nash, Ireland*

COMELY 7 b.m. Midnight Legend – Belle Magello (FR) (Exit To Nowhere (USA)) **h101** [2018/19 h104: h23.1m* Aug 5] sturdy mare: fair hurdler: won handicap at Market Rasen sole outing in 2018/19: stays 3m: acts on soft and good to firm going. *Nicky Henderson*

COME ON CHARLIE (FR) 7 b.g. Anzillero (GER) – End of Spring (FR) (Loup **c63** Solitaire (USA)) [2018/19 h96: h16.8gᵖᵘ h18.7g* h19.8g* h25.3g² c21.2d³ c18.2d³ **h99** c19.2sᵖᵘ Apr 16] workmanlike gelding: modest handicap hurdler: won at Stratford (novice event) in October and Musselburgh in December: let down by jumping/attitude in handicap chases: best short of 25f: acts on good to soft going. *Philip Hobbs*

COME ON LOUIS 11 b.g. Grape Tree Road – Seamill (IRE) (Lafontaine (USA)) **c61** [2018/19 h78: h19.6g⁶ c22.5g⁵ Jun 6] point winner: poor maiden hurdler: laboured fifth in **h–** novice handicap on chasing debut: stays 23f: acts on good to soft going: wears headgear/ tongue tie. *Oliver Greenall*

COME ON TEDDY (IRE) 5 b.g. Fame And Glory – Theatre View (IRE) (Old Vic) **h106** [2018/19 h92: h16.8s h18.5d³ Feb 22] runner-up in bumper: fair form when third to Umbrigado on second of 2 starts in novice hurdles at Exeter: will be suited by 2½m+. *Tom George*

COMEONTHEBULL (IRE) 7 ch.g. Papal Bull – Maratanas Gift (IRE) (Golan (IRE)) **h73** [2018/19 b16.3g² h22g⁵ b16.5g³ h16.8s h15.8v h19.5gᵖᵘ Apr 26] compact gelding: first **b87** foal: dam unraced: unplaced in Irish point: placed both outings in bumpers: only poor form over hurdles. *Robert Stephens*

COME TO ME (FR) 7 b.g. Spanish Moon (USA) – Hasta Manana (FR) (Useful (FR)) **h131**
[2018/19 h16g⁶ h16v* h20d h22gᵖᵘ Feb 2] €44,000 3-y-o: half-brother to several winners,
including smart hurdler/useful chaser Sweet My Lord (2m-2¾m winner, by Johann Quatz)
and useful hurdler/winning pointer Vivant Poeme (2¾m winner, by Early March): dam,
French 17f/2¼m hurdle/chase winner, also 1¼m-1¾m winner on Flat: bumper winner:
useful form over hurdles: won maiden at Cork (by 17 lengths from Lighthouse Warrier) in
December: off 3 months/tried again in hood, 18¾ lengths eighth to Reserve Tank in
Champion Novices' Hurdle at Punchestown shortly after end of British season.
W. P. Mullins, Ireland

COMMANCHE RED (IRE) 6 ch.g. Mahler – Auntie Bob (Overbury (IRE)) [2018/19 **h130**
b102: h19.2s* h15.7g⁵ h20.5s h20.5d³ h15.3g* h19.8gᵖᵘ Apr 27] strong gelding: bumper
winner: useful novice hurdler: won at Fontwell in October and Wincanton (handicap event,
by 1½ lengths from Ravenous) in March: likely to stay 2¾m+: acts on soft going: front
runner/races prominently. *Chris Gordon*

COMMANDER MILLER 5 b.g. Shirocco (GER) – Milliegait (Tobougg (IRE)) **h87**
[2018/19 b16g h19.7gᵖᵘ h19.6g h16.2g⁵ Apr 25] £22,000 3-y-o: rather unfurnished gelding: **b–**
has had breathing operation: fifth foal: half-brother to bumper winners/fairly useful 2m
hurdle winners Gaitway (by Medicean) and Diamond Gait (by Passing Glance): dam, 7f
winner (ran once over hurdles), half-sister to useful 2m hurdler Bold Gait out of half-sister
to Champion Hurdle winner Royal Gait: first form (including in bumper) when fifth in
novice hurdle at Perth. *Nicky Henderson*

COMMANDER OF FLEET (IRE) 5 b.g. Fame And Glory – Coonagh Cross (IRE) **h145**
(Saddlers' Hall (IRE)) [2018/19 b107p: h20.5g* h16g⁴ h22g* h24d² Mar 15] tall gelding:
point/bumper winner: smart novice hurdler: won at Punchestown (maiden) in November
and Nathaniel Lacy & Partners Solicitors Novices' Hurdle at Leopardstown (by ½ length
from Rhinestone) in February: further progress when 2 lengths second of 20 to Minella
Indo in Albert Bartlett Novices' Hurdle (Spa) at Cheltenham in March: lost action in
another Grade 1 event at Punchestown shortly after end of British season and is reportedly
to miss 2019/20 season: likely to stay beyond 3m. *Gordon Elliott, Ireland*

COMMIS D'OFFICE (FR) 7 b.g. Califet (FR) – Pas de Bal (FR) (Le Balafre (FR)) **c119**
[2018/19 c15.5sᵖᵘ c16d³ c15.7d² c17.4g⁴ Apr 13] good-topped gelding: has had breathing **h–**
operation: lightly-raced maiden hurdler: fairly useful handicap chaser: stays 2¼m: acts on
soft going: has worn hood: tried in tongue tie. *Venetia Williams*

COMMODORE BARRY (IRE) 6 br.g. Presenting – Specifiedrisk (IRE) (Turtle Island **h133**
(IRE)) [2018/19 b93: h20.7g³ h20s* h24g² h20g² h24s* h24.4g* h24.4g³ Jan 26] runner-
up on second start in Irish points: useful novice hurdler: won at Worcester in May,
Southwell in October (conditionals handicap) and December, and Doncaster (handicap,
typically dug deep when beating Blue Rambler a head) later in December: will stay beyond
3m: acts on soft going: wears tongue tie: tough front runner. *Kim Bailey*

COMMODORE (FR) 7 gr.g. Fragrant Mix (IRE) – Morvandelle (FR) (Video Rock **c126 p**
(FR)) [2018/19 c–, h106: c24d* c24.2s* Mar 9] compact gelding: maiden hurdler: fairly **h–**
useful form over fences: had breathing operation, vastly improved when winning handicaps
at Warwick in December and Sandown in March: stays 3m: acts on heavy going: strong-
galloping front runner: bold jumper: likely to progress further. *Venetia Williams*

COMPADRE (IRE) 8 b.g. Yeats (IRE) – Jolivia (FR) (Dernier Empereur (USA)) **c118**
[2018/19 c120, h–: c19.2dᵖᵘ c19.4m⁵ c24sᵖᵘ c24.1g⁵ c17.8g⁴ h23.3s⁶ h20.7d c21.4d* h25d² **h106**
c21.4d* Mar 14] useful-looking gelding: has had breathing operation: fair maiden hurdler:
fairly useful handicap chaser: won at Market Rasen in January and March: left Jonjo
O'Neill after fifth start: stays 25f: acts on soft going: usually wore hood/tongue tie for
former yard: travels strongly dropped out. *James Evans*

COMPATRIOT (IRE) 5 b.g. Pour Moi (IRE) – Wooded Glade (Oasis Dream) [2018/19 **h97**
h15.3m⁴ h16.7g⁵ h16.3m⁶ h15.8m h15.8sᵖᵘ h16.8m⁴ Oct 2] fair on Flat (stays
1½m): modest handicap hurdler: won novice event at Newton Abbot in September: raced
around 2m: probably acts on good to firm going: in tongue tie last 2 starts. *Olly Murphy*

COMPETITION 7 b.g. Multiplex – Compolina (Compton Place) [2018/19 h103p: **h116**
h15.8gᵖᵘ h15.8g* h15.8g* h17.7g² h16.3m³ Sep 8] has had breathing operation: fairly
useful form in novice hurdles: won twice at Uttoxeter in July: stays 2¼m: acts on good to
firm going: wears tongue tie. *Dr Richard Newland*

COMPLEX KID 7 b.g. Multiplex – Life Is Life (FR) (Mansonnien (FR)) [2018/19 b–: **b–**
b16.8g May 15] medium-sized gelding: well beaten in bumpers: dead. *Sandy Thomson*

COMPLYWITHME 5 b.m. Multiplex – Chico Time (IRE) (Presenting) [2018/19 b16g^{ro} **b60 §**
b16.2g^6 b16.8m^5 Oct 2] £7,000 4-y-o: first foal: dam (c96/h106), 25f-29f hurdle/chase
winner, half-sister to fairly useful hurdler/useful chaser (stayed 2¾m) Knock On The Head:
placed in point: showed more temperament than ability in bumpers: tried in headgear.
Laura Morgan

COMRADE CONRAD (IRE) 5 br.g. Canford Cliffs (IRE) – View (IRE) (Galileo **h115 §**
(IRE)) [2018/19 h114: h16d h16.8g h21d h21g* Apr 10] good-topped gelding: has had
breathing operation: fairly useful handicap hurdler: tongue tied, won at Warwick in April:
stays 21f: acts on soft going: usually in headgear: one to treat with caution. *Dan Skelton*

COMRAGH (IRE) 9 br.m. Desert King (IRE) – Akica (IRE) (Oscar (IRE)) [2018/19 h–: **h72**
h15.3m^6 h21.6g^{pu} Jun 15] lightly-raced winning hurdler: little form since 2015/16: stays
2½m: acts on soft going: in hood/tongue tie last 2 starts. *Jeremy Scott*

CONAS TAOI (IRE) 10 b.g. Exit To Nowhere (USA) – Zudika (IRE) (Ezzoud (IRE)) **c94**
[2018/19 c23.8v^{pu} c19.4v^{pu} c25.2s c25.1d^{pu} c26.3d^5 c24.2s c23.9s^2 c26.2g* c24.2g^3 **h–**
c26.2d^3 c29.2g^3 c26.2g^3 Apr 26] good-topped gelding: maiden hurdler: modest handicap
chaser nowadays: off almost 2 years before return: won at Carlisle in February: stays 29f:
acts on heavy going: wears cheekpieces. *Christian Williams*

CONCEALED AMBITION (IRE) 7 br.g. Stowaway – Clairefontaine (Alflora (IRE)) **c–**
[2018/19 h–: h20.3s c20d^{pu} Jan 15] poor form over hurdles: pulled up in novice handicap **h78**
on chasing debut. *Tim Vaughan*

CONCERTISTA (FR) 5 ch.m. Nathaniel (IRE) – Zagzig (Selkirk (USA)) [2018/19 **h136 p**
h16.8d^2 Mar 14] workmanlike mare: fairly useful on Flat (stays 1½m) in France for
Christophe Ferland: 66/1, shaped best when short-headed by stablemate Eglantine du Seuil
in 22-runner Dawn Run Mares' Novices' Hurdle at Cheltenham on hurdling debut: sure to
improve and win races. *W. P. Mullins, Ireland*

CONCHITA (GER) 4 b.f. Zoffany (IRE) – Cross Check (IRE) (Pivotal) [2018/19 b13.1g^3 **h84 p**
b14g^6 b12.4s* b13.7d^3 h15.8g^4 Apr 11] sixth foal: half-sister to 3 winners on Flat in Italy: **b80**
dam, Austrian 1m/9f winner, closely related to fairly useful hurdler (stayed 2½m)
Eyeballs Out: modest form in bumpers: won junior event at Wetherby (left Nigel Tinkler
after) in December: 5/2, weak-finishing fourth in mares maiden at Huntingdon on hurdling
debut (clearly thought capable of better): tried in cheekpieces. *Michael Roberts*

CONEYGREE 12 b.g. Karinga Bay – Plaid Maid (IRE) (Executive Perk) [2018/19 c–, h–: **c157**
c27.3g^3 c24g^{ur} c23.8d^{pu} Feb 16] strong gelding: had breathing operation: winning hurdler: **h–**
top-class chaser at best: won all 4 starts as a novice in 2014/15, including Cheltenham Gold
Cup: lightly raced and completed only once after 2016/17: stayed 27f: acted on heavy
going: tongued tied last 3 starts: forced pace: genuine: retired. *Mark Bradstock*

CONEY ISLAND (IRE) 8 b.g. Flemensfirth (USA) – Millys Gesture (IRE) (Milan) **c155**
[2018/19 c160, h–: h20d^3 c24g c20.6d^6 Mar 14] well-made gelding: useful hurdler: very **h134**
smart chaser: tongue tied, left plenty to do when 13½ lengths sixth of 12 to Frodon in
Ryanair Chase (Festival Trophy) at Cheltenham final outing: stays 3m: acts on heavy
going. *Edward P. Harty, Ireland*

CONFEY (IRE) 5 b.m. Morozov (USA) – Barbereilla (IRE) (City Honours (USA)) **h–**
[2018/19 b16g h16.8d^5 Mar 24] first foal: dam unraced half-sister to useful chaser (stayed **b–**
25f) Agus A Vic: tailed off in mares bumper/novice selling hurdle. *Seamus Mullins*

CONINGSBY 6 ch.g. Midnight Legend – Motcombe (IRE) (Carroll House) [2018/19 **c137**
h113: c20g^{ro} c20v^{pu} c24.5s^3 c24.2d* Mar 24] maiden hurdler: useful form over fences: **h–**
further marked progress when winning handicap at Exeter (by 13 lengths from Garrane) in
March: stays 3m: acts on heavy going: in headgear last 3 starts: usually races close up:
signs of temperament (ran out on reappearance). *Tom Lacey*

CONISTONE 5 ch.m. Poet's Voice – Protectress (Hector Protector (USA)) [2018/19 **h–**
h18.7m^F h16g h16g Jul 17] has had breathing operation: modest on Flat, stays 1½m: little
show over hurdles. *Dan Skelton*

CONKIES LAD (IRE) 13 b.g. Aahsaylad – King's Concubine (King's Ride) [2018/19 **c99**
c20v^2 Feb 18] multiple point winner: maiden hurdler, seemingly modest form at best: **h–**
runner-up in hunter at Lingfield (6 lengths behind Full Trottle) on chasing debut: stays
2½m: acts on heavy going: tried in cheekpieces. *Mrs F. Marshall*

CONNA CROSS (IRE) 8 b.g. Lecroix (GER) – Country Time (IRE) (Curtain Time **c126**
(IRE)) [2018/19 c125, h106: c20s^3 c20.9g^2 c19.2v^4 c23.4s^2 c20.5g^3 Feb 23] strong gelding: **h–**
fair hurdler: fairly useful handicap chaser: in frame all 5 outings in 2018/19: stays 23f: acts
on heavy going: tried in hood: usually races prominently. *Johnny Farrelly*

CONNECT FOUR 5 b.g. Midnight Legend – Sovereignsflagship (IRE) (Supreme Leader) [2018/19 b16d h19.5d h16g³ Apr 26] £82,000 3-y-o: eighth foal: dam unraced sister to useful hurdler/smart chaser (stayed 3¼m) Hell's Bay out of sister/half-sister to top-class 2m chasers Flagship Uberalles and Viking Flagship: green in bumper: better effort in maiden hurdles at Chepstow when 18 lengths third to Grey Diamond, finishing with running left: should be suited by further than 2m. *Tom George* **h95 b–**

CONNECTIVE (IRE) 4 ch.g. Dubawi (IRE) – Connecting (Singspiel (IRE)) [2018/19 b17m* Apr 20] £5,500 3-y-o: second foal: dam unraced: 5/2 and tongue tied, won 3-runner bumper at Carlisle by 2 lengths from Tonicngin. *Micky Hammond* **b90**

CONNETABLE (FR) 7 b.g. Saint des Saints (FR) – Montbresia (FR) (Video Rock (FR)) [2018/19 c–, h138: c20g c24.5d c23.8dᵖᵘ c24.2d³ Mar 15] compact gelding: useful hurdler: lightly-raced winning chaser: left Paul Nicholls, badly out of sorts in 2018/19, including in hunters: stays 3¼m: acts on heavy going: wears headgear. *James Evans* **c85 h–**

CONRAD HASTINGS (IRE) 8 b.g. Flemensfirth (USA) – Berkeley House (IRE) (Beneficial) [2018/19 c140, h–: c19.9m³ c22.5d c20g⁴ Sep 9] lengthy gelding: winning hurdler: useful handicap chaser: stays 23f, at least with emphasis on speed: acts on good to firm and heavy going. *Henry de Bromhead, Ireland* **c137 h–**

CONS AMIGO (IRE) 6 b.g. Blueprint (IRE) – Consproblem (IRE) (Mazaad) [2018/19 b16m h20.2g⁶ Apr 24] has had breathing operation: well-held third in Irish point: well beaten in bumper/maiden hurdle. *Leonard Kerr* **h– b–**

CONSTANCIO (IRE) 6 b.g. Authorized (IRE) – Senora Galilei (IRE) (Galileo (IRE)) [2018/19 h15.6g² h16.8s² h16g² h16.6g* h15.6mᵣₒ h16g³ h16.7d² Apr 26] has had breathing operation: fairly useful but quirky on Flat (stays 2m): fairly useful novice hurdler: won at Doncaster in January: raced around 2m: acts on good to soft going: tried in cheekpieces: front runner: ran out fifth outing (best efforts on left-handed courses). *Donald McCain* **h121**

CONSTANTINE BAY 8 b.g. Kayf Tara – Alina Rheinberg (GER) (Waky Nao) [2018/19 h25g⁵ Apr 25] well-made gelding: will make a chaser: winning pointer: smart novice hurdler in 2016/17: off over 2 years and left Nicky Henderson, not unduly punished in handicap at Warwick: stays 25f: acts on heavy going. *Ian Williams* **h–**

CONTENTED (IRE) 6 gr.g. Dalakhani (IRE) – Leo's Spirit (IRE) (Fantastic Light (USA)) [2018/19 h114: h23.1m⁴ c20g* c22.5g⁶ h19g⁵ Apr 27] fairly useful hurdler: similar form over fences: won novice handicap at Worcester in September: left Philip Hobbs after third outing: stays 2½m: acts on soft going: tried in blinkers. *Richard L. Valentine, USA* **c123 h118**

CONTINUUM 10 b.g. Dansili – Clepsydra (Sadler's Wells (USA)) [2018/19 h20.5s h16.3s h16g Apr 10] good-topped gelding: fair on Flat, stays 16.5f: little show over hurdles: tried in cheekpieces. *Peter Hedger* **h–**

CONTRE TOUS (FR) 7 b.g. Forestier (FR) – Orphee de Vonnas (FR) (Jimble (FR)) [2018/19 c119, h115: c15.7g⁶ h15.8g h16.2g c15.8g⁶ h15.7d⁶ h16.7g c15.8m⁴ h16.2g⁴ Apr 25] sturdy gelding: has had breathing operation: fair handicap hurdler: formerly fairly useful handicap chaser: well held in 2018/19: best around 2m: acts on good to firm and heavy going: usually in cheekpieces: wears tongue tie. *Brian Ellison* **c83 h97**

CONVIVIAL 4 b.f. Mount Nelson – Vino (Efisio) [2018/19 b13.1g⁶ Oct 20] fourth foal: sister to 1½m bumper winner Mountain Path and half-sister to 2 winners, including 1½m bumper winner Sherry (by Tobougg): dam, 7f winner, half-sister to fairly useful 2½m hurdle winner Ey Up Rocky: 16/1, held back by inexperience when sixth in junior bumper at Market Rasen. *Micky Hammond* **b70**

COOKING FAT 8 ch.g. Tobougg (IRE) – Ostfanni (IRE) (Spectrum (IRE)) [2018/19 c124, h100: c20.1g⁴ c23.8g* c24.5d³ c26.2g⁴ c23.4d⁵ c20.1dᵘʳ Apr 26] fair hurdler: fairly useful handicap chaser: won at Perth in July: stays 25f: acts on soft going: wears headgear: usually races off pace. *Pauline Robson* **c126 h–**

COOLANLY (IRE) 7 b.g. Flemensfirth (USA) – La Fisarmonica (IRE) (Accordion) [2018/19 h129, b99: h19.5dᶠ h21g* h20.5d⁵ h19.7g² h20.3d⁵ h24.7g h23.9g⁵ Apr 24] sturdy gelding: Irish point winner: bumper winner: useful novice hurdler: won Hyde Novices' Hurdle at Cheltenham (by 3¼ lengths from Pym) in November: stays 21f: acts on soft going. *Fergal O'Brien* **h131**

COOLANURE (IRE) 10 b.m. Portrait Gallery (IRE) – Aiguille (IRE) (Lancastrian) [2018/19 c64x, h–: c21.7gᵖᵘ Feb 19] maiden hurdler/error-prone maiden chaser. *Kevin Bishop* **c– x h–**

COOL ARTIST (IRE) 6 b.m. Vocalised (USA) – Langfuhrina (USA) (Langfuhr (CAN)) **h74**
[2018/19 h16.8g⁴ h16.5d⁴ Apr 24] half-sister to useful 2m hurdle winner Morga (by
Whipper): modest maiden on Flat (stays 10.5f): poor fourth both outings over hurdles.
Nigel Hawke

COOL DESTINATION (IRE) 6 ch.g. Dubai Destination (USA) – Coolafancy (IRE) **h114**
(Accordion) [2018/19 h21.2d⁶ h23.1s⁵ h21g² Apr 10] €17,500 3-y-o, £25,000 5-y-o: fifth
foal: half-brother to fairly useful hurdler/chaser Consharon Boy (2½m-25f winner) and a
winning pointer (both by Zagreb): dam, winning pointer, half-sister to fairly useful chaser
(stayed 25f) Silver Jack: Irish point winner: fair form over hurdles: much improved when
second in maiden at Warwick final outing: will be suited by 3m+. *Fergal O'Brien*

COOLE CODY (IRE) 8 b.g. Dubai Destination (USA) – Run For Cover (IRE) **c129**
(Lafontaine (USA)) [2018/19 h139: c20.9d⁴ c20.3vᵖᵘ h21.4d⁶ h23.4s² h24d h24.7g Apr 6] **h133**
lengthy gelding: Irish point winner: useful handicap hurdler: better effort over fences
(fairly useful form) when fourth to Bags Groove in novice at Ffos Las: stays 23f: acts on
heavy going: hooded prior to last 3 starts: wears tongue tie: usually races close up.
Michael Blake

COOLE HALL (IRE) 7 b.g. Flemensfirth (USA) – Coole Assembly (IRE) (Saddlers' **c–**
Hall (IRE)) [2018/19 h131: c24.2dᵖᵘ Dec 27] sturdy gelding: winning Irish pointer: useful **h–**
novice hurdler in 2017/18: off 10 months, not jump/travel well when pulled up in novice at
Wetherby on chasing debut: should be suited by 3m+: acts on heavy going. *Rose Dobbin*

COOLE WELL (IRE) 6 b.g. Gold Well – Bobs Lass (IRE) (Bob's Return (IRE)) **h120**
[2018/19 h92: h16.5dᵘʳ h15.9s* h17.7v² h16.6d² h19.6g⁵ Apr 11] has had breathing
operation: runner-up in Irish point: fairly useful novice hurdler: won at Plumpton in
December: may prove best around 2m: acts on heavy going: front runner. *Jamie Snowden*

COOLGREINE (IRE) 6 b.g. Definite Article – I Missed You (IRE) (Lord Americo) **h81 ?**
[2018/19 h20.6gᵖᵘ h16.8m⁴ Aug 30] first foal: dam placed in point: little impact in Irish
points: tongue tied, possibly flattered when front-running fourth at Sedgefield on completed
start in novice hurdles. *Jedd O'Keeffe*

COOLING 5 b.m. Firebreak – Esplanade (Danehill (USA)) [2018/19 b82: b16.7g h15.5g **h90**
h16.5g⁶ h15.8d³ h15.8g⁶ Feb 28] runner-up once in bumpers: modest form over hurdles. **b–**
John Flint

COOL MACAVITY (IRE) 11 b.g. One Cool Cat (USA) – Cause Celebre (IRE) (Peintre **h92**
Celebre (USA)) [2018/19 h125: h20.6gᵖᵘ h18.7m² h16.7g³ h18.5gᵖᵘ h16.5m⁶ h16.5d
h16.5d h19g Feb 19] sturdy gelding: modest handicap hurdler nowadays: left Nicky
Henderson after first start: best around 2m: acts on good to firm going: in headgear 4 of last
6 outings. *Alexandra Dunn*

COOLMEEN HILL (IRE) 8 b.g. Oscar (IRE) – Hazel's Tisrara (IRE) (Mandalus) **h–**
[2018/19 h108: h16.2g⁵ h16.5g Jun 15] has had breathing operation: maiden pointer:
bumper/hurdle winner: well beaten in handicaps in 2018/19: unproven beyond 17f: acts on
good to firm going: wears tongue tie. *Susan Corbett*

COOL MIX 7 gr.g. Fair Mix (IRE) – Lucylou (IRE) (Bob Back (USA)) [2018/19 h124: **c128**
c19.4m² c17.1d² c16.3d² c16.3g² c16.3g* c20.5m Apr 13] fairly useful hurdler: fairly **h–**
useful form over fences: runner-up 4 times prior to winning novice at Newcastle in
February: stays 2½m: acts on heavy going: normally hooded. *Iain Jardine*

COOLOGUE (IRE) 10 b.g. Helissio (FR) – Scolboa (IRE) (Bob's Return (IRE)) **c105**
[2018/19 c–, h–: h23.3g⁶ c20.3d³ c24vᵖᵘ Dec 1] good-topped gelding: has had breathing **h–**
operation: winning hurdler: smart handicap chaser at best: regressed markedly since
2016/17: stays 25f: acts on heavy going: tried in cheekpieces/tongue tie: usually leads.
Charlie Longsdon

COOL SKY 10 b.g. Millkom – Intersky High (USA) (Royal Anthem (USA)) [2018/19 **h121**
h117: h20g* h16.3m⁴ h20g Oct 28] angular gelding: fairly useful handicap hurdler: won at
Aintree in May: stays 2½m: acts on soft and good to firm going: in headgear 4 of last 6
starts. *Ian Williams*

COOL VALLEY (IRE) 10 b.g. Zerpour (IRE) – Jilly Jaffa Cake (IRE) (Waajib) [2018/19 **c96**
c16g³ c21.2g⁴ c16g⁴ c20.1g⁴ c25.5d⁶ c16.4m⁶ c15.6g² c21.6m⁴ c15.6s⁴ c21.6d² c15.8g⁴
c20.3g⁴ c16.5s³ c20.3g³ c17.1g⁴ c20.3g² c15.8m² c16.9s³ c15.2g⁵ c21.6d Apr 8] winning
pointer: modest maiden chaser: stays 2¾m: acts on soft and good to firm going: has worn
headgear. *William Young Jnr*

COOPERESS 6 b.m. Sixties Icon – Vilnius (Imperial Dancer) [2018/19 h79: h16.5d Dec **h–**
13] sturdy mare: modest on Flat (stays 9.5f): poor form over hurdles. *Dai Burchell*

COOPER'S FRIEND (IRE) 10 b.g. Kayf Tara – Graphic Lady (IRE) (Phardante (FR)) [2018/19 c107§, h–: c20.1g³ May 17] strong gelding: winning hurdler: fairly useful form over fences in 2016/17: regressive subsequently: best up to 2½m: acted on heavy going: usually wore headgear/tongue tie: temperamental: dead. *R. Mike Smith*   **c74 §**
h–

COOPERS SQUARE (IRE) 8 b.g. Mahler – Jessaway (IRE) (Dr Massini (IRE)) [2018/19 c–, h–: h16spu h19.7s c23.6d* c26.1d* c23.6dur h25g* c24g* c24.2d* c24g² Apr 25] modest handicap hurdler: won at Huntingdon in March: fair handicap chaser: successful at same track and Uttoxeter in February, Warwick (novice event) in March and Exeter in April: stays 3¼m: acts on good to soft going: has won with/without blinkers: open to further improvement. *Tom Weston*   **c108 p**
h86 p

COO STAR SIVOLA (FR) 7 b.g. Assessor (IRE) – Santorine (FR) (Della Francesca (USA)) [2018/19 c148, h–: c23.6d c24.2v³ c26g c25spu Mar 12] rangy gelding: winning hurdler: developed into smart chaser as a novice: disappointing in 2018/19: stays 25f: acts on heavy going. *Nick Williams*   **c139**
h–

COPAIN DE CLASSE (FR) 7 b.g. Enrique – Toque Rouge (FR) (Loup Solitaire (USA)) [2018/19 c130, h–: c18m* c19.4m⁴ c20.2g⁴ c15.5s⁶ c16.4g⁵ Mar 2] well-made gelding: has had breathing operation: winning hurdler: useful handicap chaser: won at Kempton (by 10 lengths from Casablanca Mix) on return in October: tame efforts after: stays 2¼m: acts on good to firm and good to soft going: tried in cheekpieces: wears tongue tie: weak finisher. *Paul Nicholls*   **c133 §**
h–

COPPER COIN 6 ch.g. Sulamani (IRE) – Silken Pearls (Leading Counsel (USA)) [2018/19 b98: h19.5gF Oct 30] in frame in bumpers: keeping on in close second when falling last in maiden won by Senior Citizen at Chepstow on hurdling debut: likely to be suited to 2½m+. *Michael Scudamore*   **h115**

COPPERFACEJACK (IRE) 9 b.g. Robin des Pres (FR) – Leone des Pres (FR) (Tip Moss (FR)) [2018/19 c109, h–: c24.5g⁴ c26.1g⁵ c24gpu c23.6gpu c25.2s* h25dpu c25.1g⁶ c24g⁵ Apr 25] workmanlike gelding: has had breathing operation: maiden hurdler: fair handicap chaser: won at Hereford in November: stays 29f: acts on soft and good to firm going: has worn cheekpieces: usually tongue tied: usually races close up. *Paul Webber*   **c105**
h–

COPPER GONE WEST (IRE) 6 b.m. Westerner – Copper Dusht (IRE) (Dushyantor (USA)) [2018/19 h20d² h21d h19.8g* h24.2d² h19.6s* h24gF Apr 17] £100,000 4-y-o: second foal: dam, ran once in bumper, half-sister to smart hurdler/chaser (stayed 21f) Copper Bleu and useful hurdler/chaser (winner up to 3m) Give Me A Copper: won Irish point on debut: fairly useful form over hurdles: won mares maiden at Musselburgh in February and novice at Bangor in March: stays 3m: acts on soft going. *Tim Vaughan*   **h124**

COPPERHEAD 5 ch.g. Sulamani (IRE) – How's Business (Josr Algarhoud (IRE)) [2018/19 b69: h16.3d h19.7s³ h20.5s h18.5s* h19.8s* Feb 15] sturdy gelding: fairly useful form over hurdles: much improved when winning handicaps at Exeter in January and Sandown (novice event) in February: likely to stay 3m: acts on soft going: open to further progress. *Colin Tizzard*   **h121 p**

COPPER PRINCE (IRE) 6 ch.g. Pelder (IRE) – Kora (IRE) (Mandalus) [2018/19 b–: b16g Jun 27] last in bumpers 5 months apart: tried in cheekpieces. *Laura Morgan*   **b–**

COPPER WEST (IRE) 8 b.g. Westerner – Printing Copper (IRE) (Blueprint (IRE)) [2018/19 h107, b84: c15.7g² c20.3g² c19.9g⁴ c19.4g² c20.1d⁴ c20.2m* c19.9m* Apr 20] strong, close-coupled gelding: has had breathing operation: maiden hurdler: fairly useful handicap chaser: won at Leicester (most fortunate) in December and Haydock in April: stays 2½m: acts on good to firm and good to soft going: has found less than looked likely. *Tom George*   **c124**
h–

COPT HILL 11 b.g. Avonbridge – Lalique (IRE) (Lahib (USA)) [2018/19 h–: h23.3g³ h24g² h23.9g h19.9g⁴ h19.5v⁵ h16.4d* h16.4s² h16.8v⁶ Jan 27] has had breathing operation: poor handicap hurdler: won at Newcastle in December: stays 2½m: acts on heavy going: wears headgear: tried in tongue tie: front runner/races prominently. *Julia Brooke*   **h75**

COQUIN MANS (FR) 7 b.g. Fragrant Mix (IRE) – Quissisia Mans (FR) (Video Rock (FR)) [2018/19 h153: h25.4spu h24s h21d⁵ h24d Mar 14] good-topped gelding: smart hurdler at best: disappointing in 2018/19: stays 3m, effective at much shorter: acts on heavy going: usually in hood. *W. P. Mullins, Ireland*   **h140**

CORA SUNDROP 6 b.m. Kayf Tara – L'Ultima (FR) (Verglas (IRE)) [2018/19 b75: b16.3g⁶ h16g² h17.7gpu Aug 23] modest form in bumpers: remote second on first of 2 starts in novice hurdles. *Warren Greatrex*   **h76**
b77

CORINDA 8 b.m. Midnight Legend – Conchita (St Ninian) [2018/19 h–: h20.9g Dec 9] **h–**
lightly raced: little promise in bumpers/over hurdles. *Philip Kirby*

CORINTO (IRE) 6 br.g. Flemensfirth (USA) – Fashion Target (IRE) (Broken Hearted) **h114**
[2018/19 h16.3d h19.6v⁵ h20d³ h18.6d⁴ h23.1d* h25.8v³ Mar 16] fifth foal: dam unraced
sister to useful hurdler/chaser (winner up to 2½m) Bedlam Boy: fair form over hurdles: won
handicap at Market Rasen in February: stays 23f: acts on good to soft going. *Olly Murphy*

CORNBOROUGH 8 ch.g. Sir Percy – Emirates First (IRE) (In The Wings) [2018/19 **h124**
h123: h17.2d⁵ h16m² h16g³ h16s⁵ h16.7g⁵ h19.7g³ h16.8g² Apr 17] compact gelding:
fairly useful handicap hurdler: won at Wetherby in November: probably stays easy 2½m:
acts on soft and good to firm going: has worn headgear. *Mark Walford*

CORNELIUS SOCKS (IRE) 9 b.g. Asian Heights – Delightful Choice (IRE) (Amoristic **h73**
(USA)) [2018/19 h21.6dᵘʳ h21.6g h18.5m⁵ h23.1v h16.8s h23.9s² Mar 20]
poor maiden hurdler: stays 3m: acts on soft going: in headgear 4 of last 5 outings. *Jackie
du Plessis*

CORNER CREEK (IRE) 9 b.g. Presenting – No Moore Bills (Nicholas Bill) [2018/19 **c96**
c95, h–: c24dᵖᵘ c24g* c24.2gᶠ c25.2s⁴ c25.6s⁴ Dec 16] lightly-raced maiden hurdler: **h–**
modest handicap chaser: won at Southwell in October: stays 3m: acts on good to soft
going: wears cheekpieces. *Michael Scudamore*

CORNERSTONE LAD 5 b.g. Delegator – Chapel Corner (IRE) (Alhaarth (IRE)) **h137**
[2018/19 h124: h16s² h15.7v* h18.1g³ h16.4d* Apr 6] useful handicap hurdler: won at
Haydock in December and Newcastle (career-best effort, by 2 lengths from Altruism) in
April: likely to stay 2½m: acts on heavy going: in cheekpieces 5 of last 6 outings: often
travels strongly. *Micky Hammond*

CORNISH BEAU (IRE) 12 ch.g. Pearl of Love (IRE) – Marimar (IRE) (Grand Lodge **h–**
(USA)) [2018/19 h21.6gᵖᵘ h20g h18.7m⁵ Jul 15] point winner: modest hurdler: left
Dr Richard Newland, no form in 2018/19: stays 2½m: best form on good going: wears
headgear. *Chris Down*

CORNISH WARRIOR (IRE) 8 b.g. Oscar (IRE) – Ballylooby Moss (IRE) (Supreme **c105**
Leader) [2018/19 h99: h21.4m c20.9g* c22.6g³ c24g* c25g c24d³ Apr 9] sturdy gelding: **h72**
modest handicap hurdler: fair form over fences: won handicaps at Ffos Las (novice) in May
and Southwell in October: should stay further than 3m: acts on soft going: wears
cheekpieces: usually front runner/races prominently. *Neil Mulholland*

CORONER'S REPORT (IRE) 6 b.g. Coroner (IRE) – My Linda (IRE) (Bob Back **h63**
(USA)) [2018/19 h20g h19.6g Aug 20] off mark in Irish points at second attempt: modest
maiden hurdler, off 18 months before return: stays 2½m: acts on heavy going: has worn
hood. *Rebecca Curtis*

CORRANY (IRE) 5 br.g. Court Cave (IRE) – Time For An Audit (Supreme Leader) **b89**
[2018/19 b17.7d³ b16.3d Mar 22] €48,000 3-y-o: seventh foal: half-brother to a winning
pointer by Presenting: dam (b85), ran twice in bumpers, half-sister to Hennessy Gold Cup
winner Trabolgan: fair form in bumpers at Fontwell and Newbury (listed event).
Nicky Henderson

CORRIEBEN REIVER 5 ch.g. Malinas (GER) – Wild Child Lucy (Karinga Bay) **b92**
[2018/19 b16d³ b16.4d* b16s⁴ b16s⁴ Mar 9] first foal: dam (b90), placed in bumpers, half-
sister to fairly useful chaser (stayed 25f) Cavers Glen: fair form in bumpers: won at
Newcastle in December: will be suited by 2¼m+. *Alistair Whillans*

CORRI LINDO (FR) 9 br.g. Corri Piano (FR) – Daresta (FR) (Ragmar (FR)) [2018/19 **c115**
h16s c16.3g⁶ c20.3d² Apr 26] winning pointer: maiden hurdler: left A. J. Martin, much **h–**
better effort in chases when nose second in conditionals handicap at Bangor: stays 2½m:
acts on heavy going: has worn hood: wears tongue tie. *Henry Oliver*

CORRUPTION 5 b.m. Malinas (GER) – Blue Ride (IRE) (King's Ride) [2018/19 b–: **b–**
b17g⁶ Nov 10] well held in bumpers. *Alexandra Dunn*

CORSECOMBE 7 ch.g. Norse Dancer (IRE) – Digyourheelsin (IRE) (Mister Lord **h–**
(USA)) [2018/19 b55: h23.6vᵖᵘ h18.5dᵖᵘ h19sᵖᵘ Feb 4] little sign of ability in bumpers/over
hurdles: tried in cheekpieces. *Mark Gillard*

COR WOT AN APPLE 8 b.g. Apple Tree (FR) – Chipewyas (FR) (Bering) [2018/19 c–, **c–**
h–: h17.7m⁵ h16g⁵ h16.8g⁵ h19.2g⁴ Aug 23] poor maiden hurdler nowadays: little show in **h74**
handicap chases: stays 2½m: acts on good to firm and good to soft going: has worn
cheekpieces: wears tongue tie. *Neil Mulholland*

CORZEAM (FR) 7 gr.g. Early March – Night Fever (FR) (Garde Royale) [2018/19 **h– §**
h103§: h19.3mᵖᵘ Nov 3] good-bodied gelding: fair but most ungenuine maiden hurdler:
wears hood: has worn tongue tie: one to leave alone. *Nigel Twiston-Davies*

COSETTE (IRE) 8 b.m. Champs Elysees – Luanas Pearl (IRE) (Bahri (USA)) [2018/19 **h97** h19.6g^2 Aug 3] fair on Flat (stays 17f): modest form over hurdles: wears cheekpieces. *Bernard Llewellyn*

COSHESTON 6 ch.g. Black Sam Bellamy (IRE) – Rare Ruby (IRE) (Dilshaan) [2018/19 **h87** b90p: b15.8g b16.7s^5 h17g^3 h19.3v^3 h16.7d Apr 26] modest form in bumpers: similar form **b82** over hurdles: likely to be suited by further than 19f. *Jennie Candlish*

COSMEAPOLITAN 6 b.g. Mawatheeq (USA) – Cosmea (Compton Place) [2018/19 **h119** h119p: h16.6m^3 Dec 1] good-topped gelding: useful on Flat (stays 1¾m): fairly useful form over hurdles: not seen to best effect when third in handicap at Doncaster on sole outing in 2018/19. *Alan King*

COSMIC DIAMOND 9 b.m. Multiplex – Lucy Glitters (Ardross) [2018/19 c–, h91: **c–** h24g^6 h23.9g^6 Feb 19] angular mare: modest handicap hurdler: left Paul Webber after **h87** reappearance: always behind sole outing over fences: stays 21f: acts on soft going: tried in visor: usually in tongue tie. *Nick Mitchell*

COSMIC KING (FR) 7 b.g. Kingsalsa (USA) – Kikinda (FR) (Daliapour (IRE)) **c111** [2018/19 h103: h15.8g* h16g h18.7g c16.5g* Apr 22] lengthy gelding: fair handicap **h102** hurdler: won novice event at Huntingdon in May: better form when winning 3-runner novice handicap at same track on chasing debut by 1½ lengths from Third Estate: probably stays 2½m: best form on good going: often hooded: usually races off pace. *Fergal O'Brien*

COSMIC TIGRESS 8 b.m. Tiger Hill (IRE) – Cosmic Case (Casteddu) [2018/19 h99: **h–** h16.2g h15.7g Aug 19] modest hurdler: well held in handicaps in 2018/19: raced around 2m: acts on soft and good to firm going. *John Quinn*

COSTANTE VIA (IRE) 8 b.m. Milan – Spirit Rock (IRE) (Rock Hopper) [2018/19 h81: **h100** h19.9s^3 h23.3s^2 h24g^2 Mar 4] fair maiden hurdler: stays 3m: acts on soft going: in tongue tie last 3 starts. *Nigel Twiston-Davies*

COSTA PERCY 5 b.g. Sir Percy – Costa Brava (IRE) (Sadler's Wells (USA)) [2018/19 **h–** h109: h19.9g h16.2g^{pu} Jun 23] fair juvenile hurdler in 2017/18: poor efforts in handicaps since: unproven beyond 17f: acts on good to soft going: front runner/races prominently. *Jennie Candlish*

COSTLY DREAM (IRE) 7 b.g. Yeats (IRE) – What Price Love (USA) (Repriced **c–** (USA)) [2018/19 h–: c26.2d^2 Apr 8] has had breathing operation: dual point winner: lightly **h–** raced and little form under Rules: tried in tongue tie. *J. Marshall*

COSY CLUB (IRE) 5 br.g. So You Think (NZ) – Bali Breeze (IRE) (Common Grounds) **h–** [2018/19 h101p: h16m^5 May 14] fair juvenile hurdler in 2017/18: possibly amiss only outing since: will prove best at easy 2m: acts on good to soft going: in tongue tie last 2 starts. *Dan Skelton*

COTSWOLD PRINCE (IRE) 4 b.g. Elzaam (AUS) – Kalinjara (IRE) (Sinndar (IRE)) **h115** [2018/19 b13.7g^6 b15.3g h19.4g^2 h20.3g Apr 17] has had breathing operation: sixth foal: **b73** dam unraced: poor form in 3-y-o bumpers: 66/1, showed much more when second to Manning Estate in novice at Doncaster on hurdling debut: out of depth only subsequent outing. *Martin Keighley*

COTSWOLD WAY (IRE) 6 b.g. Stowaway – Rosies All The Way (Robellino (USA)) **h135** [2018/19 h110, b80: h19.6g* h21.6m* h20.5d* h21g h19d* h20.3g^4 Apr 17] rather unfurnished gelding: useful hurdler: won at Huntingdon (maiden) in October, Exeter (novice) in November, Leicester (handicap) in December and Taunton (beating Capitaine 15 lengths in another handicap) in April: stays easy 2¾m: acts on good to firm and good to soft going. *Philip Hobbs*

COTTON CLUB (IRE) 8 b.g. Amadeus Wolf – Slow Jazz (USA) (Chief's Crown **h103** (USA)) [2018/19 h19.9g^3 h19.9m^2 h21.6g^2 h20g^5 h18.5g^4 h15.3f^4 h16.5d h21.4g h22g Mar 30] disappointing maiden hurdler: left Dr Richard Newland after fifth start: stays 2¾m: acts on good to firm going: has worn headgear. *Richard Mitchell*

COTTON JENNY (IRE) 8 br.m. Craigsteel – Rose N Alice (IRE) (Anshan) [2018/19 **c112** c22.5d^3 c21.7g^2 c16g^2 c25.1m^3 c17g^5 c19.4m^2 c20m^3 c17.5m^2 c20.5g^5 c16.3g^5 Apr 18] **h–** first foal: dam, 2m chase winner, half-sister to fairly useful hurdler/useful chaser (17f winner) Rocky Court: winning hurdler: fair maiden chaser: left Brian Jordan after fifth start: stays easy 2¾m: acts on good to firm and good to soft going: tried in tongue tie: usually races prominently. *Evan Williams*

COTTONVALE (IRE) 8 b.g. Touch of Land (FR) – Shuil Le Vic (IRE) (Old Vic) [2018/19 **h98** h20d^3 h19.7g^F h21g h24g^4 h22g^4 h21g h23.1m h19.8g^2 h23.3s^4 h19.7d^F h21.9v^2 h19.3g^F h20s^4 Apr 7] sturdy gelding: modest maiden hurdler: left Eoin Doyle after sixth start: stays 3m: acts on heavy going: has worn headgear, including last 4 starts. *Christian Williams*

COTTONWOOL BABY (IRE) 8 b.m. Gold Well – Golden Steppes (IRE) (Titus Livius   **c–§**
(FR)) [2018/19 c–, h74: c23.6d^{pu} c26.2g^{pu} Apr 26] in frame in Irish maiden points: lightly-   **h–**
raced maiden hurdler, modest at best: pulled up all 3 starts in handicap chases: should stay
3m+: has worn headgear/tongue tie: races off pace: temperamental. *Michael Scudamore*

COUGAR KID (IRE) 8 b.g. Yeats (IRE) – Western Skylark (IRE) (Westerner) [2018/19   **h108**
h111: h16.7g^5 h19.6g^2 h16.2g^3 h16.2g^2 h15.5d^3 h19.7v^3 h25.5d^5 h16d^3 h21s^6 h19.9d
h20.6m^4 Apr 21] lengthy gelding: fair handicap hurdler: stays 2¾m: acts on good to firm
and heavy going: regularly in headgear: usually races towards rear. *John O'Shea*

COUGAR'S GOLD (IRE) 8 b.g. Oscar (IRE) – Top Her Up (IRE) (Beneficial) [2018/19   **c117**
c98, h100: c26.2g^5 c23.8s^4 c20.9s* c20.9v^2 c24g* c21.6d^4 c20v* c20d^4 Mar 30] fair   **h–**
hurdler: fairly useful handicap chaser: won at Uttoxeter in December, Doncaster in January
and Uttoxeter in March: should stay 3¼m: acts on heavy going: wears cheekpieces/tongue
tie. *Peter Bowen*

COULBORN HOOD (IRE) 5 ch.g. Sans Frontieres (IRE) – Shy Sheila (IRE) (Rashar   **h–**
(USA)) [2018/19 h15.8g Oct 18] tailed off in novice hurdle on debut. *Henry Oliver*

COUNTERFEITER 9 b.g. Singspiel (IRE) – Grain of Truth (Gulch (USA)) [2018/19   **h86**
h15.8g^3 Nov 4] good-topped gelding: fair maiden hurdler: unproven beyond 2m: best
efforts on good going: wore blinkers once: dead. *Martin Bosley*

COUNTISTER (FR) 7 b.m. Smadoun (FR) – Tistairly (FR) (Fairly Ransom (USA))   **h136**
[2018/19 h121: h16.8d^3 h16d Apr 23] compact mare: useful form over hurdles: easily
better effort in 2018/19 when 1½ lengths third of 24 to Ch'tibello in County Hurdle at
Cheltenham: raced around 2m: acts on heavy going: often travels strongly. *Nicky Henderson*

COUNT MERIBEL 7 ch.g. Three Valleys (USA) – Bakhtawar (IRE) (Lomitas) [2018/19   **c145**
h130: c20g* c20.2g* c21s^4 c24.4s Mar 13] good-bodied gelding: useful hurdler: quickly   **h–**
proved even better in novice chases, winning at Carlisle (handicap event) and Cheltenham
(by neck from Le Breuil) in November: stays 2¾m: acts on heavy going. *Nigel Twiston-
Davies*

COUNTRY DELIGHTS (IRE) 6 b.m. Mahler – Nadwell (IRE) (Gold Well) [2018/19   **h–**
b–: h20.1g h20.2g h20.2g^6 h23.9g^{pu} h19.8s^{pu} h16.8g^{pu} Apr 5] well beaten in bumpers: poor
form over hurdles. *Hugh Burns*

COUNTRY'N'WESTERN (FR) 7 b.g. Samum (GER) – Cracking Melody (Shamardal   **h99 p**
(USA)) [2018/19 b69: h16d^4 Mar 4] bumper winner: fair on Flat, stays 16.5f: some
encouragement when fourth in maiden at Fakenham on hurdling debut: entitled to do
better. *Robert Eddery*

COUNT SIMON (IRE) 5 b.g. Rip Van Winkle (IRE) – Wedding Cake (IRE) (Groom   **h133**
Dancer (USA)) [2018/19 h18.8g^3 h16g^2 h17.3g* h16.7m^4 h17.5g^2 h19.8g^5 h16d^3
h19.5d^2 h19.5d^2 h18s^3 h19d^2 h18.8g^2 h20.2d* Apr 26] half-brother to fair 21f chase winner
Sposalizio (by Dr Fong): useful novice hurdler: won at Downpatrick in June and Perth
(handicap) in April: will be suited by further than 2½m: acts on soft and good to firm going:
wears headgear: tough and reliable. *Gordon Elliott, Ireland*

COUP DE PINCEAU (FR) 7 b.g. Buck's Boum (FR) – Castagnette III (FR) (Tin   **c136**
Soldier (FR)) [2018/19 h127: c24.2m* c23.8s* c24g^3 c23.8d^4 c24g^2 Mar 28] good-topped   **h–**
gelding: fairly useful hurdler: useful form over fences: won novices at Exeter in November
and Ludlow in December: in frame in better company all 3 starts after: stays 3m: acts on
soft and good to firm going: has worn headgear. *Paul Nicholls*

COURT AFFAIRS (IRE) 7 b.g. Court Cave (IRE) – Rock Money (IRE) (Deploy)   **h90**
[2018/19 h99: h23.1g^6 Jun 5] bumper winner: modest maiden hurdler: stays 2¾m: acts on
soft going. *Seamus Mullins*

COURT BALOO (IRE) 8 b.g. Court Cave (IRE) – Tremplin (IRE) (Tremblant) [2018/19   **c64**
c–, h82: h23.3g h25.4m^2 h23.9g^{pu} h27m h25.8g^5 h24g^2 c23.8g^5 h25.3g^{pu} Jan 1] sturdy   **h84**
gelding: has had breathing operation: poor handicap hurdler: little show in novice handicap
chases: stays 25f: acts on good to firm and heavy going: wears headgear. *Alistair Whillans*

COURT DANCER (IRE) 4 b.g. Court Cave (IRE) – Windsor Dancer (IRE) (Woods of   **h–**
Windsor (USA)) [2018/19 b15.8d h15.8g^F Apr 21] green in bumper: behind when fell last   **b–**
in novice on hurdling debut. *Evan Williams*

COURT DREAMING (IRE) 6 b.g. Court Cave (IRE) – Louis's Teffia (IRE) (Presenting)   **h121**
[2018/19 b81: h20.2g^2 h20.2g* h20.2g^4 h20.1g^2 h20.9d* h20.5m^3 Apr 13] fairly useful
form over hurdles: won novice at Perth in June and handicap at Kelso in November: stays
21f: acts on good to firm and good to soft going. *Nicky Richards*

COURT DUTY (IRE) 7 b.g. Court Cave (IRE) – Easter Duties (IRE) (Aristocracy) **c97**
[2018/19 h92, b–: h19.9g[4] h20g* h20m c23.6d c20.9g[6] c20d[3] c20.3g[4] Apr 13] fair handicap **h106**
hurdler: won at Worcester (conditionals) in July: modest form over fences: stays 2½m: acts
on heavy going. *John Flint*

COURT FRONTIER (IRE) 11 b.g. Court Cave (IRE) – Dame En Rouge (IRE) **c111 §**
(Imperial Frontier (USA)) [2018/19 c123, h112: c23.6d c26.7f[ur] c24.2v[3] c24.2s[5] **h–**
c24.2d[5] c28.8v[4] c31.9v c23.8s[pu] Apr 7] fair hurdler: fair handicap chaser nowadays: stays
31f: acts on good to firm and heavy going: has worn cheekpieces/tongue tie: unreliable.
Christian Williams

COURT IN MATERA (IRE) 5 b.g. Court Cave (IRE) – Orador Sur Glane (IRE) **h91**
(Shernazar) [2018/19 b17g h15.8g h17d[5] h15.8g h20.6s[pu] h20.3s[pu] h17m[2] Apr 20] £12,000 **b–**
3-y-o: fifth foal: brother to fair 23f hurdle winner Shepherd's Bight and half-brother to
fairly useful 2m hurdle winner King William (by Trans Island): dam winning pointer:
runner-up in point: well beaten in bumper for Edward Glassonbury: modest form over
hurdles: much improved when second in conditionals handicap at Carlisle final outing:
should stay beyond 17f: acts on good to firm going: tried in blinkers. *Oliver Greenall*

COURTINTHEMIDDLE (IRE) 8 b.g. Court Cave (IRE) – Kilmessan (IRE) **h75**
(Flemensfirth (USA)) [2018/19 h–: h21.2m[6] h23g[2] Jul 4] smallish gelding: runner-up in
Irish point: poor handicap hurdler: stays 23f: acts on good to firm going. *Deborah Faulkner*

COURT JURADO (IRE) 5 b.g. Court Cave (IRE) – Glen Eile (IRE) (Jurado (USA)) **h92**
[2018/19 h19.9s[4] h18.1d[4] h16.7d[5] Apr 26] €25,000 3-y-o, £25,000 4-y-o: seventh foal:
brother to bumper winner Timing'severything and half-brother to fairly useful hurdler/fair
chaser Profit Margin (2m-21f winner, by Presenting): dam unraced half-sister to useful
hurdler/fairly useful chaser (stayed 2½m) Glens Music, herself dam of smart hurdler
(stayed 2¾m) Glens Melody: won Irish point on debut: modest form over hurdles.
Donald McCain

COURT KING (IRE) 8 b.g. Indian River (FR) – Eliza Everett (IRE) (Meneval (USA)) **c112 §**
[2018/19 c123§, h120§: c29.1g[3] c23.8g h26.5m[pu] h25.4g[2] h25.4s[2] Aug 27] fairly useful **h119 §**
handicap hurdler/chaser: stayed 3¼m: acted on soft and good to firm going: usually wore
headgear: tried tongue tied: unreliable: dead. *Peter Bowen*

COURTLANDS PRINCE 10 b.g. Presenting – Bathwick Annie (Sula Bula) [2018/19 **c92**
h99: h23.1g h19.9m h20g[6] c21.4g[3] c22.6g[5] c20g Sep 25] fair handicap hurdler: well held **h75**
in 2018/19: modest form when third in novice handicap at Market Rasen on chasing debut:
failed to progress: stays 21f: acts on soft and good to firm going: in blinkers last 4 starts:
usually in tongue tie: front runner/races prominently. *Johnny Farrelly*

COURT LIABILITY (IRE) 6 b.g. Court Cave (IRE) – Whataliability (IRE) (Leading **h125**
Counsel (USA)) [2018/19 h120p, b102: h23.8g* h25d[4] h24.4g[pu] h24.3m Apr 20] runner-up
in Irish point: bumper winner: fairly useful form over hurdles: won handicap at
Musselburgh on return in December: stays 3m: acts on good to sort going: tried in
cheekpieces: usually races prominently. *Harry Whittington*

COURT MAID (IRE) 6 b.m. Court Cave (IRE) – She's A Venture (IRE) (Supreme **h125**
Leader) [2018/19 b20g[2] b16.7d* b17g[4] h16d[2] h20g* h24g* h16s* h18g h16.8d h20d[6] **b99**
h20g[6] Apr 21] sturdy mare: sixth foal: closely related to fairly useful hurdler/winning
pointer Wilcos Mo Chara (2m/17f winner, by Oscar), stayed 2½m, and half-sister to 2
winners by Definite Article, including bumper winner/smart 2½m hurdle winner Sheamus:
dam poor maiden hurdler: fairly useful bumper performer: won mares maiden event at
Galway in August: fairly useful form over hurdles: won mares maiden at Cork in October,
handicap at Punchestown in November and novice at Cork in January: effective at 2m to
3m: acts on soft going. *Thomas Mullins, Ireland*

COURT MASTER (IRE) 6 b.g. Court Cave (IRE) – Lusos Wonder (IRE) (Luso) **h109**
[2018/19 b93: h20v[4] h22d[3] h23s h24.2d[pu] Mar 22] sturdy gelding: has had breathing
operation: won Irish point on debut: runner-up in bumper: fair form over hurdles: should
be suited by 3m: tried in cheekpieces/tongue tie. *Michael Scudamore*

COURT MINSTREL (IRE) 12 b.g. Court Cave (IRE) – Theatral (Orchestra) [2018/19 **c–**
c–, h144: h18.5g h16.7m h16.8g h19.5d h21g Oct 26] lengthy gelding: very smart handicap **h125**
hurdler at best: never dangerous in 2018/19: stays 19f: has form on soft going, but better
under less testing conditions (acts on good to firm): dropped out. *Evan Williams*

COURT OUT (IRE) 6 b.g. Court Cave (IRE) – Madame Martine (IRE) (Spadoun (FR)) **h99**
[2018/19 b76: h15.7g[6] h20.3g[2] h20g h20.6m[pu] Apr 21] has had breathing operations:
modest form over hurdles: tried in tongue tie. *Jamie Snowden*

COURTOWN OSCAR (IRE) 10 b.g. Oscar (IRE) – Courtown Bowe VII (Damsire Unregistered) [2018/19 c131, h–: h24.3d c30.7d^pu Feb 22] fairly useful handicap hurdler/ useful handicap chaser at best: well below form both outings in 2018/19: stays 3½m: acts on heavy going: tried in cheekpieces: usually races close up. *Philip Kirby* **c–** **h–**

COURT PAINTER (IRE) 9 b.g. Court Cave (IRE) – Comings (IRE) (Grand Lodge (USA)) [2018/19 c80: c20.1d c21.4g^6 c20.1g^4 c20.1g^2 c20.1g^6 c23.8g c20.1s^6 c20.1v^pu c16.4d^5 Jan 11] point winner: poor maiden chaser: stays 21f: acts on soft going: wears cheekpieces: tried in tongue tie: temperamental. *Victor Thompson* **c74 §**

COURT ROYALE (IRE) 6 b.g. Court Cave (IRE) – Windsor Dancer (IRE) (Woods of Windsor (USA)) [2018/19 b95p: b15.8d^3 b16.3g^3 h20m^F h16.7g^3 h15.8g* h16.2g^4 h16.5d* h15.7s h16s^5 h16.5g^4 h15.8m* Apr 1] tall, angular gelding: fairly useful hurdler: won novice at Ludlow in October, and handicaps at Taunton in November and Ludlow again in April: best around 2m: acts on good to firm and good to soft going: travels smoothly waited with. *Evan Williams* **h124** **b89**

COURT TYCOON (IRE) 7 b.g. Court Cave (IRE) – Tycooness (IRE) (Last Tycoon) [2018/19 h16m h16g h16g^2 h16.5m^3 h20.4m* h22g^6 h24s h20g^3 h20g^2 h20g^2 h20g Dec 29] €31,000 3-y-o: half-brother to several winners, including fairly useful hurdler Tycoon Hall (2m/17f winner, by Halling) and fairly useful hurdler/chaser Jewel of The West (2m-2½m winner, by Desert Prince): dam 1½m winner: fairly useful hurdler: won maiden at Wexford in July: stays 2½m: acts on good to firm going. *Peter Fahey, Ireland* **h119**

COUSIN KHEE 12 b.g. Sakhee (USA) – Cugina (Distant Relative) [2018/19 c–, h115§: h19.8g^4 Apr 14] good-topped gelding: fair stayer on Flat: fair handicap hurdler nowadays: little aptitude for chasing sole try: stays 21f: acts on firm and soft going: tried in cheekpieces: temperamental. *Hughie Morrison* **c–** **h104 §**

COUSIN OSCAR (IRE) 7 b.g. Oscar (IRE) – On The Jetty (IRE) (Be My Native (USA)) [2018/19 c110, h100: h19.6g^4 h19.6g^4 c16.3g^2 h16.4s^2 Mar 10] sturdy gelding: has had breathing operations: fair handicap hurdler nowadays: similar form over fences: stays 2½m: acts on soft going: tried in headgear: tongue tied last 4 starts: usually front runner/ races prominently. *Donald McCain* **c110** **h113**

COUSIN PETE 11 b.g. Kayf Tara – Leachbrook Lady (Alderbrook) [2018/19 c129: c24s c26.3d^pu Mar 15] multiple point winner: fairly useful hunter chaser at best: poor efforts in 2018/19: stays 3¼m: acts on heavy going: wears tongue tie. *Mrs Elizabeth Brown* **c98**

COWSLIP 10 b.m. Tobougg (IRE) – Forsythia (Most Welcome) [2018/19 c–, h93: h22.1g May 28] modest handicap hurdler nowadays: little promise over fences: stays 3m: acts on soft going: wears cheekpieces. *Donald McCain* **c–** **h–**

CRACKER FACTORY 4 b.g. Poet's Voice – Pure Song (Singspiel (IRE)) [2018/19 h16.5g* h16.8g* h16.8g* h16.7g^2 h16m* h16.4g^2 h16.6g^5 h16.4s Mar 13] tall gelding: fair maiden on Flat, stays 1¼m: useful juvenile hurdler: won at Aintree in June, Newton Abbot in July and August, and Wetherby (Wensleydale Juvenile Hurdle, by 7 lengths from Chief Justice) in November: raced around 2m: acts on good to firm going: tried in cheekpieces. *Alan King* **h134**

CRACKER JAK (IRE) 5 b.g. September Storm (GER) – Princess Jaffa (IRE) (Zaffaran (USA)) [2018/19 b74: b16g^4 b16v^5 h16v h17.7v^6 h19.2d h21d^3 h21.7d^2 h24.2d* h21.6d* Apr 9] sturdy gelding: modest form in bumpers: fair handicap hurdler: won at Newbury in March and Exeter (novice event) in April: stays 3m: acts on good to soft going: usually races prominently. *Suzy Smith* **h108** **b78**

CRACKING DESTINY (IRE) 6 b.g. Dubai Destination (USA) – Cracking Gale (IRE) (Alderbrook) [2018/19 h–, b86: h16.7g^5 h16.7g h21.6s^3 c20.3d^2 c20.2g* c18.2s^3 c15.9g* c19.2d^4 c16.5g^3 Apr 11] good sort: modest form over hurdles (remains open to improvement): much better over fences: won handicaps at Wincanton (novice event) in January and Leicester in March: stays 2½m: best form on good going: formerly hooded: travels strongly held up. *Ian Williams* **c113** **h95 p**

CRACKING FIND (IRE) 8 b.g. Robin des Pres (FR) – Crack The Kicker (IRE) (Anshan) [2018/19 c128, h–: c20.6g^3 c15.2m^2 c19.4m^3 c19.4g^2 c15.2d* c16.4g* c16.4g^3 c15.8d^F Apr 4] lengthy gelding: winning hurdler: useful handicap chaser: won at Wetherby in December and Doncaster (by ½ length from Forest Bihan) in January: stays 2½m: acts on soft and good to firm going: usually front runner/races prominently. *Sue Smith* **c134** **h–**

CRACKING SMART (FR) 7 b.g. Great Pretender (IRE) – Maya du Frene (FR) (Le **h146**
Pommier d'Or) [2018/19 h150p: h24g⁶ h21d³ h21s Mar 13] tall gelding: smart hurdler:
shaped better than result when mid-field in Coral Cup at Cheltenham final outing: stays
3m: acts on heavy going: in cheekpieces last 4 starts: usually tongue tied: races prominently.
Gordon Elliott, Ireland

CRACKLE LYN ROSIE 5 b.m. Kayf Tara – Native Sunrise (IRE) (Definite Article) **b84**
[2018/19 b15.8g² b13.7m³ b15.8g⁵ b16.7d⁶ Jan 17] first foal: dam unraced half-sister to
useful hurdler/chaser (2m-2½m winner) The Jigsaw Man: modest form in bumpers.
Evan Williams

CRACK OF THUNDER (IRE) 10 b.g. September Storm (GER) – Keep Hunting (IRE) **c86 §**
(Nestor) [2018/19 c90, h–§: c20.1g⁵ c24.6g^F Aug 7] dual point winner: winning hurdler: **h– §**
maiden chaser, fair at best: probably stayed 29f: acted on soft going: wore headgear: tongue
tie last 2 starts: temperamental: dead. *Gordon Elliott, Ireland*

CRAFTY ROBERTO 11 ch.g. Intikhab (USA) – Mowazana (IRE) (Galileo (IRE)) **c–**
[2018/19 c101, h95: h15.8g h23.1g⁵ Jun 1] leggy gelding: fair handicap hurdler/maiden **h–**
chaser: stays 2½m: acts on good to firm and heavy going: regularly in headgear: usually
tongue tied. *Alex Hales*

CRAGGAKNOCK 8 b.g. Authorized (IRE) – Goodie Twosues (Fraam) [2018/19 h114: **h111 §**
h16.2d h18.6g² h20g h20d Oct 18] good-topped gelding: fair handicap hurdler nowadays:
should stay 2½m: acts on soft going: usually wears cheekpieces: temperamental. *Richard
Guest*

CRAIGANBOY (IRE) 10 b.g. Zagreb (USA) – Barnish River (IRE) (Riverhead (USA)) **c–**
[2018/19 c100, h104: c16.5v⁶ h24.3v* h24.3s² h24.3d² h24.3d⁴ c23.4v^F Mar 16] fair **h113**
handicap hurdler/chaser: won novice event over hurdles at Ayr in November: stays 3m: acts
on heavy going: usually hooded: wears tongue tie: races off pace. *N. W. Alexander*

CRAIGMOR (IRE) 7 b.g. Craigsteel – Twilight Princess (IRE) (Moscow Society **c112 p**
(USA)) [2018/19 h101, b–: h19.6g³ h20.3g² c19.4m* c24.1g^pu c21.2d* Jan 1] fair form **h101**
over hurdles: better over fences: won novice handicaps at Stratford in July and Fakenham
in January: should stay beyond 21f: acts on good to soft and good to firm going: in
cheekpieces last 3 starts: remains open to improvement as a chaser. *Olly Murphy*

CRAIG STAR (IRE) 9 b.g. Craigsteel – Different Dee (IRE) (Beau Sher) [2018/19 h118: **h107**
h16.2d h22.1g⁵ h20d h25.8d² h23.8g⁵ h22.7g⁵ h20.9g⁵ h20.9g Mar 23] fair handicap
hurdler: stays 25f: acts on heavy going: usually in headgear. *Donald McCain*

CRAKEHALL LAD (IRE) 8 ch.g. Manduro (GER) – My Uptown Girl (Dubai **h81**
Destination (USA)) [2018/19 h17.2g h16.7g⁶ h16.8m⁵ h18.6g h19.9g⁵ h24.1g Apr 11] poor
handicap hurdler nowadays: unproven beyond 17f: acts on soft going: wears headgear.
Andrew Crook

CRANBROOK CAUSEWAY (IRE) 7 b.g. Mohaajir (USA) – Kingarriff Bell (IRE) **c87**
(Mandalus) [2018/19 h–: c20.3g⁵ c25.2g⁴ c24.2s⁴ c20d^ur c23.9d⁵ c22.7f² Feb 26] has had **h–**
breathing operation: maiden hurdler: modest form over fences: barely stays 25f: acts on
firm going: wears headgear: tried in tongue tie: front runner/races prominently. *Graeme
McPherson*

CRANK EM UP (IRE) 8 b.g. Royal Anthem (USA) – Carrawaystick (IRE) (Old Vic) **c108 §**
[2018/19 c110§, h–: h27g³ c31.9s² c30.7s⁴ c26.3d³ Jan 11] fair handicap hurdler/chaser: **h105 §**
stays 4m: acts on heavy going: has worn headgear: lazy and temperamental. *Simon West*

CRAZY JACK (IRE) 11 b.g. Royal Anthem (USA) – Cindy's Fancy (IRE) (Shernazar) **c113**
[2018/19 c109, h–: c20.8g⁴ c20.9d⁴ c23.8m⁶ c21.1d^pu Apr 4] tall gelding: winning pointer/ **h–**
hurdler: fair hunter chaser: won handicap event at Stratford in June: stays 3m: acts on
heavy going: has worn cheekpieces. *Mrs A. R. Hewitt*

CREADAN BELLE (IRE) 6 b.m. Vinnie Roe (IRE) – Aliceaneileen (IRE) (Indian **b80**
Danehill (IRE)) [2018/19 b16g⁶ b16.2g⁴ b16.2s² b16d Dec 18] first foal: dam (h105)
unreliable maiden hurdler (stayed 2½m): modest form in bumpers: will prove suited by
further than 2m. *Gordon Elliott, Ireland*

CREADAN GRAE (IRE) 7 gr.g. Scorpion (IRE) – Tenerife Pearl (IRE) (Bravefoot) **c118**
[2018/19 h24g h20.5g⁴ c22g^pu h23.9g² c20.1g* c20.1s⁵ Oct 13] fifth foal: half-brother to **h105**
fair chaser October Revolution (23f winner, by Turtle Island) and a winning pointer by
Beneficial: dam, ran twice in points, half-sister to fair hurdler/fairly useful chaser (stayed
2½m) John James: fair maiden hurdler: better form when winning handicap at Perth in
September on second of 3 outings over fences: stays 3m: acts on soft going. *Gordon Elliott,
Ireland*

CREATIVE INERTA (IRE) 9 br.g. Balakheri (IRE) – Rambling Liss (IRE) (Presenting) **c106**
[2018/19 c97: c24.2m* c20.2g³ Feb 27] fair form in hunter chases: won at Exeter in May:
stays 3m: acts on soft and good to firm going: tried in hood: wears tongue tie. *B. Clarke*

CREEP DESBOIS (FR) 7 b.g. Great Pretender (IRE) – Brigade Mondaine (FR) **c116**
(Arnaqueur (USA)) [2018/19 c132, h–: c20.9gᵘʳ c19.9s⁴ c20d h24g² h24.3m Apr 20] good- **h116**
topped gelding: has had breathing operation: fairly useful handicap hurdler: useful form
over fences in 2017/18: rather disappointing since: stays 3m: acts on good to firm and
heavy going: tried in cheekpieces. *Ben Pauling*

CREEPY (IRE) 11 b.g. Westerner – Prowler (IRE) (Old Vic) [2018/19 c20.8gᵖᵘ May 4] **c–**
lengthy gelding: multiple winning pointer: formerly useful hurdler/chaser: retains little **h–**
ability: tried in headgear. *Mrs Claire Hardwick*

CREEVYTENNANT (IRE) 15 b.g. Bob's Return (IRE) – Northwood May (Teenoso **c126**
(USA)) [2018/19 c133, h113: c23.8g* c20.9dᵖᵘ c21.4g⁶ c23.8mᶠ Oct 10] rangy gelding: **h–**
maiden hurdler: fairly useful chaser: won hunter at Perth in May: stayed 25f: acted on good
to firm and heavy going: sometimes wore tongue tie: most tough and genuine: dead. *Fergal
O'Brien*

CREM FRESH 5 b.m. Malinas (GER) – Clotted Cream (USA) (Eagle Eyed (USA)) **b84**
[2018/19 ab16s b16.5d⁵ b16.5d⁵ b16m³ Apr 22] half-sister to 3 winners, including fairly
useful hurdler Maska Pony (2m-2½m winner, by Celtic Swing) and fair hurdler Revani
(17f winner, by Sulamani), stayed 21f: dam, 6f winner, half-sister to high-class 2m hurdler
Detroit City: modest form in bumpers. *Polly Gundry*

CRESSWELL LEGEND 8 b.g. Midnight Legend – Cresswell Willow (IRE) (Witness **c133**
Box (USA)) [2018/19 h127, b–: c20.1g² c25.2g² c23.8g c23.8m* Apr 1] sturdy gelding: **h–**
bumper winner: fairly useful hurdler: better over fences: won handicap at Ludlow in April:
stays 3¼m: acts on soft and good to firm going: wears tongue tie: usually leads. *Kim Bailey*

CREST 8 b.g. Kayf Tara – Maiden Voyage (Slip Anchor) [2018/19 c–, h–: c24.2d⁴ c24.2g² **c113**
c23.4g* c24.2sᵖᵘ c23.4sᵖᵘ c24.2d⁴ c24.2g⁶ c21.3g² Mar 29] has had breathing operation: **h–**
winning hurdler: fair handicap chaser: won novice event at Kelso in May: stays 25f: acts
on heavy going: wears cheekpieces/tongue tie: has shown temperament. *Micky Hammond*

Johnny Henderson Grand Annual Challenge Cup Handicap Chase, Cheltenham—
66/1-shot Croco Bay goes two places better than in 2015; Bun Doran (checks),
Brelan d'As (hoops, mainly hidden) and Forest Bihan (left) complete the frame

CREZIC (FR) 6 b.g. Califet (FR) – Valmasque (FR) (Start Fast (FR)) [2018/19 h16s* h16.5g[3] c16.5g[2] c17g[2] c19.9g[2] h16d[6] c19.2g[pu] Nov 23] well held only outing on Flat: fair hurdler: won maiden at Kilbeggan in April: better form when runner-up all 3 completed outings over fences (then left Gordon Elliott): stayed 2½m: acted on soft going: hooded prior to last 3 starts: dead. *Stef Keniry* **c122 h108**

CRIEVEHILL (IRE) 7 b.g. Arcadio (GER) – Ma Douce (IRE) (Mansonnien (FR)) [2018/19 c139, h–: c20g[2] c21.1s[6] c24.2s[6] c23.8d[4] c26d[4] Mar 14] lengthy gelding: winning hurdler: useful handicap chaser: probably stays 3¼m: acts on heavy going: has worn hood. *Nigel Twiston-Davies* **c138 h–**

CRIMSON SKIES (IRE) 4 ch.f. Declaration of War (USA) – Emily Blake (IRE) (Lend A Hand) [2018/19 h16.8s[5] h15.7d h16g Mar 29] fair maiden on Flat, stays 12.5f: poor form in novice hurdles. *John Davies* **h63**

CRINDLE CARR (IRE) 5 ch.g. Compton Place – Arley Hall (Excellent Art) [2018/19 h62: h19.5d Mar 20] modest on Flat, stays 2m: little show over hurdles. *John Flint* **h–**

CRIQ ROCK (FR) 8 ch.g. Kap Rock (FR) – Criquetot (FR) (Epervier Bleu) [2018/19 h117: h24.5g[bd] May 7] compact gelding: fairly useful maiden hurdler: stays 25f: acts on soft and good to firm going: races freely held up. *Alan King* **h–**

CRIQ SUN (FR) 7 ch.g. Zambezi Sun – Criquetot (FR) (Epervier Bleu) [2018/19 b16g h16g h16.3d b20g[3] h16d h19s* h16.6g[6] h19d[F] h23.9d* Apr 24] closely related to fair hurdler/fairly useful chaser Wake Board (2m-2½m winner, by Dansili) and half-brother to several winners, including fairly useful hurdler/useful chaser Criqtonic (17f-21f winner, by Green Tune): dam French 9f winner: modest form in bumpers: fair handicap hurdler: won at Limerick (left Mrs Lorna Fowler after) in December and Taunton (novice event) in April: stays 3m: acts on soft going: in hood last 2 starts. *Tim Vaughan* **h112 b77**

CRIXUS'S ESCAPE (IRE) 6 ch.g. Beneficial – Tierneys Choice (IRE) (Oscar (IRE)) [2018/19 h121p: h20g h23s[4] h16s[3] h20.5s* Mar 9] fairly useful form over hurdles: improved again when winning handicap at Ayr in March: should be suited by further than 2½m: acts on soft going. *Gillian Boanas* **h126**

CROCO BAY (IRE) 12 b.g. Croco Rouge (IRE) – April Thistle (IRE) (Alphabatim (USA)) [2018/19 c16.5g[2] c16.3d* Mar 15] close-coupled gelding: winning hurdler: useful handicap chaser nowadays: won Grand Annual at Cheltenham (66/1, always prominent, by 1½ lengths from Bun Doran) in March: unable to dominate when 19½ lengths third to Snugsborough Hall at Punchestown shortly after end of British season: stays 19f: acts on soft and good to firm going: in cheekpieces nowadays. *Ben Case* **c144 h–**

CROOKS PEAK 6 b.g. Arcadio (GER) – Ballcrina Girl (IRE) (Milan) [2018/19 b107: h16.8v[4] h16.8m* h16g* h16.3d* h16.8d Mar 15] useful-looking gelding: dual bumper winner: useful form over hurdles: won novices at Exeter and Kempton in November, and handicap at Newbury (by ¾ length from Champagne City) in March: raced around 2m: acts on good to firm and good to soft going. *Philip Hobbs* **h134**

CROPLEY (IRE) 10 gr.g. Galileo (IRE) – Niyla (IRE) (Darshaan) [2018/19 h84§: c20g* c19.4d[3] c23g[6] Jun 11] medium-sized gelding: winning but unreliable hurdler: modest form over fences: won novice handicap at Worcester in May: effective at much shorter: acts on soft going: has worn headgear, including last 3 starts. *Dai Burchell* **c97 h– §**

CROSSGALESFAMEGAME (IRE) 5 b.m. Mahler – Fame Forever (IRE) (King's Theatre (IRE)) [2018/19 b15.3d b16.7d[5] Jan 17] £22,000 4-y-o: first foal: dam, unraced, out of half-sister to useful hurdler/high-class chaser Noland: third both starts in Irish points: fair form in bumpers. *Fergal O'Brien* **b89**

CROSSHUE BOY (IRE) 9 b.g. Brian Boru – Gluais Linn (IRE) (Supreme Leader) [2018/19 c141p, h122: h21.9s c25.9s h20.3s[5] h20.2s[3] c20d[6] Mar 22] useful-looking gelding: fairly useful handicap hurdler: useful handicap chaser: below form both completed starts in 2018/19: should stay beyond 3m: acts on good to firm and heavy going: tried in cheekpieces: wears tongue tie. *Sean Thomas Doyle, Ireland* **c104 h118**

CROSSLEY TENDER 6 b.g. Sulamani (IRE) – Slow Starter (IRE) (Dr Massini (IRE)) [2018/19 h16.3d h19.2d[3] h17.7s[4] h21.4g[2] h21s[5] h21.6d Apr 9] €8,500 3-y-o: workmanlike gelding: seventh foal: brother to a winning pointer and half-brother to 2 others by Vinnie Roe and Loup Sauvage: dam unraced half-sister to useful hurdler/smart chaser (stayed 3m) Risk Accessor: winning pointer: fair form over hurdles: will stay 3m: acts on soft going: usually held up. *Paul Henderson* **h101**

CROSS OF STEEL (IRE) 6 b.g. Craigsteel – Gaelic Million (IRE) (Strong Gale) [2018/19 b–: h16.7g h21.2g h16.7s Dec 14] well held in bumper/over hurdles: tried in cheekpieces. *Jennie Candlish* **h–**

Vertem Eider Handicap Chase, Newcastle—
Crosspark edges out 2017 winner Mysteree (blinkers) in a ding-dong finish

CROSSPARK 9 b.g. Midnight Legend – Blue Shannon (IRE) (Be My Native (USA)) **c142**
[2018/19 c131, h–: c21.7g⁴ c26.1g⁴ c26.1g* h24s* c24.2s⁵ c29.2g³ c32.6g* c31.8m² **h130**
Apr 13] sturdy gelding: useful form over hurdles: won handicap at Southwell (by ½ length
from Wotzizname) in December: useful handicap chaser: won at Uttoxeter in November
and Eider (Handicap Chase) at Newcastle in February: also very good second to Takingrisks
in Scottish Grand National at Ayr final outing: stays 33f: acts on good to firm and heavy
going: tried in cheekpieces: often travels strongly: genuine. *Caroline Bailey*

CROWN HILL (IRE) 9 b.g. Definite Article – Silver Prayer (IRE) (Roselier (FR)) **c124**
[2018/19 c120, h109: c21.7g² h26d* May 30] good-topped gelding: fairly useful handicap **h115**
hurdler/chaser: won amateurs event over fences at Warwick in May: stays 3½m: acts on
heavy going: tried in hood. *Johnny Farrelly*

CROWN OF ROSES 5 b.m. Malinas (GER) – Ready To Crown (USA) (More Than **h–**
Ready (USA)) [2018/19 b16.3g b16g h16.3d h16d Apr 6] rather unfurnished mare: second **b–**
foal: half-sister to bumper winner/fairly useful hurdler Late Night Lily (2m-2½m winner,
by Midnight Legend): dam (h117) bumper/2m-19f hurdle winner: well held in bumpers/
novice hurdles. *Dan Skelton*

CROWN THEATRE (IRE) 10 b.g. King's Theatre (IRE) – Palesa's Legacy (IRE) **c–**
(Montelimar (USA)) [2018/19 c–, h–: c19.4dᵖᵘ c20.2gᵖᵘ Nov 10] rather leggy gelding: **h–**
winning chaser: useful chaser at best: lightly raced and no form since 2016/17: stays 2¼m:
acts on soft and good to firm going: tried in cheekpieces: wears tongue tie. *Jamie Snowden*

CROW STONE 5 b.g. Sulamani (IRE) – Merry Tina (Tina's Pet) [2018/19 b16.2d⁴ Mar **b65**
26] 50/1, fourth in maiden bumper at Hexham. *James Walton*

CRUACHAN (IRE) 10 b.g. Authorized (IRE) – Calico Moon (USA) (Seeking The Gold **c–**
(USA)) [2018/19 c–, h88: h20.2g h23.1g⁴ h20.2g h20.2g h19.5v Nov 14] poor handicap **h68**
hurdler: pulled up in novice only outing over fences: stays 2½m: acts on heavy going:
wears headgear. *Lucy Normile*

CRUCIAL ROLE 7 b.g. Westerner – The Lyme Volunteer (IRE) (Zaffaran (USA)) **c148**
[2018/19 h130: c21.6g³ c20s* c19.9d³ c22.5d* c25s c25dᶠ Apr 5] well-made gelding: **h–**
useful hurdler: smart form over fences: won maiden in December and novice handicap in
February (by 16 lengths from Rock My Style), both at Uttoxeter: would have stayed long
distances: acted on heavy going: made running/raced prominently: dead. *Dan Skelton*

CRUISEAWEIGH (IRE) 8 br.g. Oscar (IRE) – Triptoshan (IRE) (Anshan) [2018/19 c16.4d^{pu} c19.1d^2 Mar 1] deep-girthed, good sort: lightly-raced maiden hurdler: much better effort in handicap chases when second at Doncaster in March, though again found less than looked likely: stays 2½m: acts on heavy going: tried in tongue tie. *Tom George* **c116 h–**

CRUISING BYE 13 b.g. Alflora (IRE) – Althrey Flame (IRE) (Torus) [2018/19 c97x, h81: c23m^2 c23g* c23m^5 c28.5d^{pu} c24d^3 Apr 24] winning hurdler: modest handicap chaser: won at Worcester in July: stays 29f: acts on good to firm and heavy going: wears headgear/tongue tie: usually races lazily off pace: often let down by jumping. *Peter Bowen* **c99 x h–**

CRUMBS 5 gr.g. Fair Mix (IRE) – Granary House (Alflora (IRE)) [2018/19 b16s h16.2d^5 h18.1d^{pu} Apr 8] little show in bumper/novice hurdles. *Lucinda Russell* **h– b–**

CRUMPLEDANDCREASED (IRE) 7 br.m. Big Bad Bob (IRE) – Sunset Queen (IRE) (King's Theatre (IRE)) [2018/19 h16.7g h15.7g^F h17.2m^5 h15.8g Jul 27] €20,000 3-y-o: rather leggy mare: fifth foal: half-sister to fairly useful hurdler/useful chaser Definite Ruby (2¼m-23f winner, by Definite Article): dam unraced: placed 3 times in bumpers for W. P. Mullins: running best race over hurdles when falling 2 out in novice at Southwell in June: often hooded (has taken strong hold): usually in tongue strap. *Olly Murphy* **h89**

CRUSHED (IRE) 5 b.g. Beat Hollow – Sel (Salse (USA)) [2018/19 h–p: h15.9g* h17.2g^3 h16.2g^5 h16m h16m Nov 2] regressive on Flat: fair form over hurdles: won maiden at Plumpton in May: disappointing after next start, leaving Alan King prior to final one: raced around 2m: best form on good going: tried in cheekpieces: races prominently. *Mark Walford* **h111**

CRYPTO (IRE) 5 b.g. Gold Well – Top Lot (IRE) (Topanoora) [2018/19 b16.4d* Mar 5] €21,000 3-y-o: closely related to 2 winners, including fair hurdler/chaser (2½m-3m winner) Nicole's Milan (by Milan), and half-brother to several winners, including bumper winner/useful 2m hurdle winner Mumbo Jumbo (by Vinnie Roe): dam unraced: strong 11/2, looked good prospect when won maiden bumper at Newcastle by 16 lengths from Honda Fifty, forging clear. *Micky Hammond* **b103**

CRYSTAL LAD (FR) 7 ch.g. Kapgarde (FR) – Qrystale Mag (FR) (Vertical Speed (FR)) [2018/19 c122, h112+: h21g^{pu} h20.6d^2 h20.5d^6 h21s Mar 16] angular gelding: fairly useful handicap hurdler: similar form over fences in 2017/18: barely stays 3¼m: acts on soft going: usually races close up. *Gary Moore* **c– h115**

CRYSTAL SUNSTONE 5 b.g. Henrythenavigator (USA) – Crystal Power (USA) (Pleasant Colony (USA)) [2018/19 h16.3g^{pu} Jun 9] fair maiden on Flat (stays 1m) at 3 yrs for Eve Johnson Houghton: pulled up in novice on hurdling debut. *Alex Hales* **h–**

CRY WOLF 6 ch.g. Street Cry (IRE) – Love Charm (Singspiel (IRE)) [2018/19 h92§: h21.2m^5 May 13] workmanlike gelding: modest maiden handicap hurdler: mid-field only outing in 2018/19: developed into fairly useful performer back on Flat (stays 16.5f) subsequently: stays 2¾m: acts on soft going: wears headgear: temperamental. *James Evans* **h81 §**

CUBAN PETE (IRE) 7 b.g. Flemensfirth (USA) – Gee Whizz (FR) (Turgeon (USA)) [2018/19 h87, b–: h15.8v^6 h21.7d* Mar 9] fair form over hurdles: much improved when making all in handicap at Hereford in March: stays 2¾m: acts on heavy going. *Venetia Williams* **h104**

CUBOMANIA (IRE) 6 gr.g. Halling (USA) – Surrealism (Pivotal) [2018/19 h110: c20.1g* c19.2d^6 c17.1m* c20.1g* c18.6g^3 c19.8d* c22.6g^4 c20g^F c17g^2 c17d^2 c21g^5 c20.2s^{pu} c18g^4 c20g^F Apr 21] rather leggy gelding: fair hurdler: developed into useful novice chaser in 2018/19, winning 5 times, notably listed event at Thurles (by 22 lengths from Jetz) in March: stayed 21f: acted on good to firm and heavy going: wore tongue tie: dead. *Gordon Elliott, Ireland* **c144 h–**

CUBSWIN (IRE) 5 b.m. Zamindar (USA) – Moonlight Rhapsody (IRE) (Danehill Dancer (IRE)) [2018/19 h105: h15.7g* h16.7m^3 h17.7m^2 h15.3m^6 h16g^4 h15.8g^6 h16.6g^5 h15.3g* h15.7m* Apr 20] small mare: useful handicap hurdler: won mares events at Southwell in June and Wincanton in April, then successful again at Haydock later in April: stays easy 2¼m: acts on soft and good to firm going. *Neil King* **h131**

CUCKLINGTON 8 b.g. Kayf Tara – Ardrom (Ardross) [2018/19 c114, h–: c25g^{pu} c23.5d^3 c25.1d c26d^2 c25.1g^6 c29.2d^6 c25.1g^2 Apr 3] big, lengthy gelding: maiden hurdler: fair handicap chaser: stays 3¼m: acts on good to firm and heavy going: wears headgear: usually tongue tied. *Colin Tizzard* **c110 h–**

CUCKOO'S CALLING 5 b.m. So You Think (NZ) – Sinndarina (FR) (Sinndar (IRE)) [2018/19 b93: h15.6g^3 Nov 26] dual bumper winner: disappointing maiden on Flat: 6/5, close third in mares novice at Musselburgh on hurdling debut. *Keith Dalgleish* **h104**

CUCUMBER GIN (IRE) 5 b.m. Oscar (IRE) – Redwood Lady (IRE) (Presenting) **b–**
[2018/19 b15.7s Mar 18] €6,500 3-y-o: second foal: dam ran twice in points: tailed off in
bumper. *Nicky Martin*

CUDDLES MCGRAW (IRE) 6 b.g. Court Cave (IRE) – Stefphonic (IRE) (Orchestra) **c110**
[2018/19 h–, b–: h19.2g⁴ h20.2g³ c20.3g² c20d* c20v² c24gᵖᵘ Apr 10] modest form over **h99**
hurdles: better form in handicap chases: won novice event at Warwick in November: stayed
2½m: acted on heavy going: wore tongue tie: usually raced towards rear: dead. *Fergal
O'Brien*

CUDGEL 6 b.g. Sulamani (IRE) – Posh Stick (Rakaposhi King) [2018/19 h16.2d h20.1g **h54**
h16.2g h22.7g h23.3v⁵ h22g Jan 5] poor form over hurdles. *James Walton*

CUIRASSIER DEMPIRE (FR) 7 ch.g. Network (GER) – Juventhura (FR) (Video **c120**
Rock (FR)) [2018/19 c134p, h–: h23g⁵ c23d c21.4g⁶ c25.1m² Oct 19] lightly-raced maiden **h–**
hurdler: fairly useful handicap chaser: stays 25f: acts on good to firm and good to soft
going: weak finisher. *Tom George*

CUL DE POULE 7 b.g. Multiplex – Madam Blaze (Overbury (IRE)) [2018/19 h–, b83: **h112**
h20g* h23g³ Sep 11] promise in bumpers: fair form over hurdles: had breathing operation,
won maiden at Worcester on return in August: lame only subsequent outing: tongue tied
since debut. *Martin Keighley*

CULLY MAC (IRE) 8 b.g. Coroner (IRE) – Catch Those Kisses (Deploy) [2018/19 h–: **h69**
h16.2m⁶ h20.2gᵖᵘ h18.1m⁴ h20.9g h23.8g Nov 26] poor maiden hurdler: stays 21f: acts on
good to firm going: wears cheekpieces. *Andrew Wilson*

CULM COUNSELLOR 10 ch.g. Erhaab (USA) – Miss Counsel (Leading Counsel **c–**
(USA)) [2018/19 c85, h81: c24g c23m c23mᵖᵘ h26.4gᵖᵘ Apr 14] workmanlike gelding: has **h–**
had breathing operation: poor hurdler/chaser: stays 3¼m: acts on soft and good to firm
going: used to wear headgear: tried in tongue tie: races prominently. *Chris Down*

CULMINATION 7 b.g. Beat Hollow – Apogee (Shirley Heights) [2018/19 h92+: h16.8s² **h108**
h18.9sᵖᵘ h16.8v³ Jan 27] fair handicap hurdler: should stay beyond 17f: acts on heavy
going. *Donald McCain*

CULTIVATOR 8 b.g. Alflora (IRE) – Angie Marinie (Sabrehill (USA)) [2018/19 c132, **c135 x**
h–: h19g* h18.5g h21.6gᶠ c20m* c24.2mᵖᵘ Oct 19] useful handicap hurdler: won at **h135**
Warwick in May: useful form over fences: won maiden at Worcester in September, easily
better effort in 2018/19: stays 21f: acts on soft and good to firm going: has worn hood: none
too reliable (has made mistakes/shaped as if amiss). *Nicky Henderson*

CULTRAM ABBEY 12 br.g. Fair Mix (IRE) – Kansas City (FR) (Lute Antique (FR)) **c131**
[2018/19 c124, h–: c23.8g⁴ c22.3g⁴ c24.2dᵖᵘ c24.5sᵖᵘ c23.4d* Apr 8] big, lengthy gelding: **h–**
winning handicap chaser: useful handicap chaser: won at Kelso in December (veterans race) and
April: stays 27f: acts on heavy going: tried in cheekpieces. *Nicky Richards*

CULTURE DE SIVOLA (FR) 7 b.m. Assessor (IRE) – Neva de Sivola (FR) (Blushing **h135**
Flame (USA)) [2018/19 h128: h24.5g³ h24.6g* h23.5d⁵ h23.1d⁵ h24dᵖᵘ Mar 14] smallish,
sturdy mare: useful handicap hurdler: won mares event at Kempton in December: stays
3¼m: acts on heavy going. *Nick Williams*

CUNEO (FR) 7 b.g. Kapgarde (FR) – Mefertiti (FR) (Epervier Bleu) [2018/19 h22g³ **h138**
h20d⁵ h24g⁴ h24g⁵ h24d⁴ Mar 14] €40,000 3-y-o: good-topped gelding: fifth foal: dam
French bumper winner around 1½m: bumper winner: useful hurdler: first past post in
maiden at Punchestown (demoted after causing interference run-in) in November and
handicap at Leopardstown in December: further improvement when 3½ lengths fourth of
24 to Sire du Berlais in Pertemps Final at Cheltenham in March, bursting to front out wide
early in straight: stays 3m: acts on heavy going: tried in cheekpieces: usually races
prominently. *Henry de Bromhead, Ireland*

CUP OF GOLD 7 b.m. Midnight Legend – Cee Cee Rider (Classic Cliche (IRE)) [2018/19 **h–**
b–: h20g h19.9g⁵ May 27] little form in varied company. *Ben Case*

CURIOUS CARLOS 10 b.g. Overbury (IRE) – Classi Maureen (Among Men (USA)) **c129**
[2018/19 h131: c16.4g* c16g⁴ c20g⁵ h20g c16s⁴ c21.4d h16.2g⁶ Apr 24] stocky gelding: **h–**
useful hurdler: well held both outings in sphere in 2018/19: successful in early-season
novices at Sedgefield and Perth first 2 starts over fences, but disappointing in handicaps:
stays easy 2½m: acts on good to firm and heavy going: has worn hood/tongue tie (in latter
last 3 starts). *Peter Bowen*

CURRAGH HALL (IRE) 11 b.g. Saddlers' Hall (IRE) – Curragh Dane (IRE) (Danehill **c–**
Dancer (IRE)) [2018/19 c–, h–: c16.3gᵖᵘ c20.9dᵖᵘ c16.1dᵘʳ Feb 28] maiden pointer: **h–**
winning hurdler in 2013/14: no form in hunter chases: usually in headgear: wears tongue
tie. *L. Humphrey*

CURRAIGFLEMENS (IRE) 11 b.g. Flemensfirth (USA) – Curraig Monashee (IRE) **c105**
(Monashee Mountain (USA)) [2018/19 c106: c27.7g⁴ c20.9d^pu Jun 8] has had breathing
operation: multiple point winner: fair chaser: stays 3½m: acts on soft going: in headgear
last 3 starts: tried in tongue tie. *David Kemp*

CURRAMORE (IRE) 5 br.g. Arcadio (GER) – Beale Native (IRE) (Oscar (IRE)) **h103**
[2018/19 b16.6g⁶ b18g* b16s* h20.5s⁵ h18.1d³ h16.2g² Apr 25] first foal: dam (h76) **b95**
maiden hurdler: fairly useful form in bumpers: won at Sligo (maiden event) in August and,
having left Charles Byrnes, Ayr in January: fair form over hurdles. *Lucy Normile*

CUSHEEN BRIDGE (IRE) 11 b.g. Oscar (IRE) – One Hell Ofa Woman (IRE) **c114**
(Fourstars Allstar) [2018/19 c124, h–: c23.9d⁴ c23g c20.3g³ c22.6m c21.4g³ Sep **h–**
29] sturdy gelding: winning hurdler: fairly useful handicap chaser: not so good in 2018/19:
stays 3m: acts on heavy going: tried in cheekpieces: wears tongue tie. *Charles Pogson*

CUSHUISH 6 b.m. Yeats (IRE) – My Petra (Midnight Legend) [2018/19 b–: b15.3m **h94**
b15.3g⁴ h16.5d⁴ h16.5d⁶ h19d^ur h23.1s⁴ h19.7g h23.1d³ h23.9d^pu Apr 24] has had breathing **b69**
operation: poor form in bumpers: modest maiden hurdler: should stay at least 3m: acts on
soft going. *Bob Buckler*

CUSHY BUTTERFIELD (IRE) 7 b.m. Fruits of Love (USA) – Colleen Ard (IRE) **h–**
(Turtle Island (IRE)) [2018/19 h20.1g^pu h20.2g^pu h20.2g h20.1s^pu h20v^pu Dec 2] no sign of
ability: in tongue tie last 3 starts. *Sheena Walton*

CUT AND RUN 6 b.m. Getaway (GER) – Somethinaboutmolly (IRE) (Choisir (AUS)) **h97**
[2018/19 h–, b–: h15.8g⁵ h15.8g⁵ h15.5g^pu Dec 2] angular mare: well held in bumpers:
modest form over hurdles: in hood last 4 starts: often leads. *Martin Keighley*

CUT THE CORNER (IRE) 11 br.g. Vinnie Roe (IRE) – Snipe Victory (IRE) (Old Vic) **c141**
[2018/19 c133, h117: c21g* c20g c17g* c21.4m c16.5g⁴ h16.3m^pu c23.8m⁴ c16.4g⁶ **h–**
c22.6g³ c21g³ Apr 20] winning hurdler: useful handicap chaser: won at Newton Abbot in
May and Stratford in June: stays 3m, effective at much shorter: acts on good to firm and
good to soft going: has worn headgear: occasionally hangs/looks awkward. *Alastair Ralph*

CUT THE MUSTARD (FR) 7 br.m. Al Namix (FR) – Tadorna (FR) (Maresca Sorrento **h131**
(FR)) [2018/19 h112: h16g h16g² h18g² h16.8d h16d⁴ Apr 23] compact mare: useful
hurdler: runner-up 3 times in 2018/19: stays 2½m: acts on heavy going: in hood nowadays.
W. P. Mullins, Ireland

CYBALKO (FR) 6 b.g. Balko (FR) – Cybertina (FR) (Cyborg (FR)) [2018/19 b–: **c114 §**
h16.3m² h16g⁵ h16g⁵ h19.9g⁴ c15.7g² c15.9m² c19.7d⁵ c15.7g^F c17.8m⁴ h18.5d⁶ Apr 9] **h99 §**
workmanlike gelding: modest form over hurdles: better in handicap chases despite failing
to win: stays 2½m: acts on good to soft going: in headgear last 3 starts: usually front
runner/races prominently: unreliable. *David Bridgwater*

CYCLOP (IRE) 8 b.g. King's Theatre (IRE) – Tasmani (FR) (Turgeon (USA)) [2018/19 **c–**
c121, h94: c25.1s^pu c23.6d^pu Apr 6] good-topped gelding: winning hurdler: fairly useful **h–**
handicap chaser: pulled up both outings in 2018/19: stays 3½m: acts on heavy going: wears
headgear/tongue tie. *David Dennis*

CYDERCOURT (IRE) 6 b.g. Court Cave (IRE) – Lavender Track (IRE) (Pistolet Bleu **h84**
(IRE)) [2018/19 b80: h19.6g⁴ Oct 16] in frame first 2 outings in bumpers: let down by
jumping when remote fourth in maiden at Huntingdon on hurdling debut. *Nigel Twiston-
Davies*

CYPRUS AVENUE 7 b.m. Kayf Tara – Za Beau (IRE) (Beneficial) [2018/19 h90, b–: **h–**
h20.5g h20.5v h21.4s Jan 8] lengthy mare: has had breathing operation: modest maiden
hurdler: should stay beyond 2m: acts on heavy going: tried in tongue tie. *Ian Duncan*

CYRANO STAR (FR) 7 gr.g. Martaline – Quezac du Boulay (FR) (Useful (FR)) **h66**
[2018/19 h–: h24g^pu h18.6m⁶ h16.8s^pu h16.4s h16.8v⁴ h16g h16d^pu h17s² h17v Mar 17]
poor maiden hurdler: stays 2½m: acts on soft going: in cheekpieces last 3 starts: regularly
in tongue tie. *Andrew Crook*

CYRIEN STAR 12 b.g. Bollin Eric – Sainte Etoile (FR) (Saint Cyrien (FR)) [2018/19 **c– §**
c20.8g c23s^pu May 25] winning hurdler/chaser, retains little ability/enthusiasm: often in **h–**
headgear nowadays: one to leave alone. *R. D. Potter*

CYRIUS MORIVIERE (FR) 9 b.g. Vendangeur (IRE) – Sagesse Moriviere (FR) **c106**
(Vaguely Pleasant (FR)) [2018/19 c–, h124: h19g c20.9s^pu c21.2m² Apr 22] lengthy **h–**
gelding: winning pointer/hurdler: disappointing maiden chaser: left Ben Pauling after first
start: stays easy 21f: acts on good to firm and good to soft going: tried in cheekpieces:
wears tongue tie: normally makes running/races prominently. *Steve Barry*

CYRNAME (FR) 7 b.g. Nickname (FR) – Narquille (FR) (Passing Sale (FR))   **c173 +**
[2018/19 c156, h106: c20g^3 c16.8g c21d* c21d* Feb 16]   **h–**

Every season has its letdowns. Where were the likes of Samcro and Footpad
when the honours were handed out at the end of the latest campaign? Two of
jumping's most exciting prospects, the best novice hurdler and the best novice
chaser of 2017/18, had their problems and neither won a race in the latest season
or even came close to matching the level of form they had shown as novices. Might
Bite, unbeaten in 2017/18 except for a defeat in a stamina-sapping Cheltenham Gold
Cup in which he travelled like the best horse for most of the way, had looked all set
to make a bold bid for the million-pound bonus for the 'Classic Triple Crown'—
Betfair Chase, King George and Cheltenham Gold Cup—in the latest season but
folded tamely on all three of his starts. There were others too, as there always are,
whose performances failed to live up to expectations.

On the other side of the coin, the latest season produced some leading
performers whose success could hardly have been predicted before the campaign
opened. Chief among the gems unearthed was the front-running Cyrname whose
much improved performances convinced the BHA handicappers to put him at the top
of their list of the highest-rated steeplechasers in Britain, 1 lb ahead of Altior whose
brilliant achievements include setting the longest winning sequence by a jumper in
the history of the sport. Altior was the Timeform Horse of the Year—rated 7 lb ahead
of Cyrname—but there was no doubting the lasting impression made by Cyrname
in two scintillating victories at Ascot, a twenty-one-length demolition of nine rivals
in a competitive bet365 Handicap Chase in January being followed by an even more
striking seventeen-length rout of Waiting Patiently, Fox Norton, Politologue and
company in the Betfair Ascot Chase over the same course and distance a month later.

What was needed, of course, was for Cyrname and Altior to meet under
conditions which would establish an undisputed champion. Projected head-to-heads
between tip-top performers rarely materialise, however, whether they are between
boxing champions holding combinations of the four major belts who too often prefer
'routine' defences to unification fights, or connections of top racehorses. There
was talk for a time that Cyrname would take on Altior in the Celebration Chase
at Sandown's Finale meeting—he appeared among the six-day declarations—but,
in the end, ground conditions (the going was 'good') were cited as the reason for
Cyrname's absence, which left Altior with a straightforward task in the final Grade 1
of the season.

Cyrname, a French import as a four-year-old after winning a juvenile hurdle
at Pau for Patrice Quinton, failed to run up to expectations in Britain at first. He was
much too free in his races and sported a hood and a tongue tie from his British debut
onwards until the hood was finally dispensed with on his last two appearances in the
latest season (those breathtaking wide-margin wins at Ascot). Cyrname didn't win
over hurdles for Manor Farm Stables and was a little disappointing until proving
a completely different proposition when sent chasing. He started off by winning a

bet365 Handicap Chase, Ascot—Cyrname gets back on track with a vengeance
as he routs a competitive field under top weight

Betfair Ascot Chase, Ascot—another wide-margin win for the top-class Cyrname, who pulls seventeen lengths clear of 2018 winner Waiting Patiently from two out; Fox Norton (noseband) and Politologue (grey) complete the frame

novice handicap at Huntingdon as a five-year-old, leading all the way and jumping boldly in what has become his trademark style, and also won the Wayward Lad Novices' Chase at Christmas and the Pendil Novices' Chase, both at Kempton, to make it three wins from six starts over fences. He missed the Cheltenham Festival to wait for the Manifesto Novices' Chase at Aintree where he could manage only fourth behind Finian's Oscar, his jockey possibly overdoing the forcing tactics and Cyrname carrying his head awkwardly under pressure. On the face of it, Cyrname was just below the top drawer and wasn't going to be easy to place in his second season over fences. Two of his three defeats had come on his only appearances over fences at left-handed tracks—at Newbury, where he jumped right, as well as at Aintree—and all his races in the latest season were on right-handed courses, thought by connections to be a requirement for him nowadays (he was never a likely contender for the spring festivals at Cheltenham and Aintree, with Punchestown mentioned by his trainer as a possible alternative, along with Sandown's Finale meeting).

Cyrname reappeared in the latest season in an intermediate chase at Carlisle in early-November when he tried to make all, still holding a chance at the last before finishing a creditable third to the smart Mister Whitaker and the consistent mare Happy Diva. Cyrname looked likely to pay his way over the season, but he was a beaten favourite in the very valuable Hurst Park Handicap Chase over two miles at Ascot on his next appearance, not mixing it up front with Speredek in a thirteen-runner field on this occasion and fading to finish only seventh (three places behind his stablemate San Benedeto who had top weight). The transformation in Cyrname's next race, the bet365 Handicap Chase over two and a half miles at Ascot, was nothing short of remarkable. Mister Whitaker was top weight, conceding 2 lb to Cyrname and San Benedeto, in a field that also included Happy Diva and the less exposed Benatar who had finished third in the previous season's Golden Miller at Cheltenham and was sent off the 7/2 favourite, just preferred to Cyrname. Back up in trip and allowed to dominate, Cyrname kept up a good gallop all the way and just drew further and further clear of his rivals in the home straight to record a high-class effort on form that was confirmed by his timerating of 168 which instantly flagged him up as a genuine Grade 1 performer. Doitforthevillage stayed on to take second in the last fifty yards ahead of Happy Diva, with Mister Whitaker completing the frame (Benatar paid for trying to keep tabs on Cyrname—though he never got closer than ten lengths—and weakened from three out).

Twenty-length wins in competitive handicaps, when the winner shows apparently much improved form, can sometimes be filed in the 'too good to be true' category but Cyrname improved again in the Betfair Ascot Chase, back in Grade 1 company for the first time since his novice days when he had come second in the Scilly Isles Novices' Chase at Sandown as well as finishing fourth in the Manifesto.

Mrs Johnny de la Hey's "Cyrname"

Waiting Patiently had appeared just once in the latest season—when brought down in the King George VI Chase on Boxing Day—but he started 11/8 favourite for the six-runner Ascot Chase, with Cyrname at 3/1 and Cyrname's stablemate Politologue at 4/1 next in the betting, ahead of Queen Mother Champion Chase runner-up Fox Norton who had finished second to Altior in the Clarence House Chase at Ascot on his belated reappearance four weeks earlier. Cyrname turned the Ascot Chase into a procession, just as he had the bet365 Handicap. He put in a superb round of jumping and was always travelling well before quickening after the third last to put the race in safe keeping as he left the opposition trailing in his wake.

Staying on strongly, Cyrname won by the aforementioned seventeen lengths from Waiting Patiently who had been so impressive himself in beating Cue Card in the race twelve months earlier. Waiting Patiently never laid a glove on Cyrname and, although clearly not at his best on the day, would almost certainly have struggled to make a race of it with the winner even at his best. Fox Norton, possibly stretched by the trip, finished third, a further length and a quarter behind Waiting Patiently, while Politologue was another two lengths back in fourth, followed by the two outsiders Charbel and Aso. Once again, the clock provided independent confirmation of the value of Cyrname's outstanding effort, his timerating of 173 bettered in Britain and Ireland over the course of the season only by Min's 174 in another wide-margin winning performance in the Melling Chase at Aintree (where Politologue was second). Cyrname's display seemed to prompt thoughts among connections about supplementing him for the Ryanair Chase (he had no entries at the Cheltenham Festival), but, in the end, concerns about his likely effectiveness going left-handed persuaded them to stick to their original plan to bypass both Cheltenham and Aintree. Cyrname wasn't seen out again but his reappearance in the next season will be eagerly anticipated, as will any possible clash with Altior.

			Lost World		Last Tycoon
	Nickname (FR)		(b 1991)		Last Tango
	(b 1999)		Newness		Simply Great
Cyrname (FR)			(b 1988)		Neomenie
(b.g. 2012)			Passing Sale		No Pass No Sale
	Narquille (FR)		(b 1987)		Reachout And Touch
	(b 2001)		Quille III		Lee
			(b 1982)		Goelande

The good-topped Cyrname is the third Grade 1 winner trained at Manor Farm Stables to carry the royal blue, pink hoops, armlets and cap of Mrs Johnny de la Hey, following the Finale Junior Hurdle winner Adrien du Pont and the Maghull Novices' Chase winner Diego du Charmil. All three—foaled in the same year— were purchased out of French stables after catching the eye, Cyrname after he had accounted for sixteen rivals in that juvenile hurdle at Pau by nine lengths on his third start. Cyrname is by the same sire as that other Paul Nicholls-trained chasing star Frodon who is also from the final crop of Nickname whose demise at the age of twelve in 2011 is proving a blow for French breeders. Nickname, like some other popular French jumps sires at the moment (such as Saint des Saints, Balko, Buck's Boum and Kapgarde), made a name for himself over jumps, winning the Prix Alain du Breil before going on to make his mark as a top two-mile chaser for Martin Brassil in Ireland. Nickname was retired to stud in France where his three crops totalled fewer than two hundred foals (he never stood at more than €2,500).

Nickname and his half-brother the very smart Flat performer No Risk At All, the sire of the very useful novice hurdler Allaho who came third in the latest Spa Hurdle at the Cheltenham Festival, are products of the Wildenstein studs, out of the winning jumper Newness, now also deceased, who bred another Prix Alain du Breil winner in N'Avoue Jamais and a Prix Wild Monarch winner in Narkis, a brother to Nickname. No Risk At All, by the way, is now attracting three-figure books and more will surely be heard of him. On the distaff side, Cyrname is the best of the three winners, including the French seventeen-furlong hurdle winner Vakina (by Arvico), that Narquille has produced. An AQPS (other than thoroughbred), Narquille won at a mile and a half on the Flat and at seventeen furlongs over both hurdles and fences. Narquille's sire Passing Sale won the Gran Premio del Jockey Club and is best known in Britain as the sire of Grand National winner Mon Mome. He is also the sire of the dam of both Sire de Grugy and the Topham Chase winner Cadmium. Front-running Cyrname stays twenty-one furlongs and acts on soft going. He wears a tongue tie and was hooded until that equipment was dispensed with on his last two starts. He is regarded as being best suited by a right-handed track. *Paul Nicholls*

CYRUS DARIUS 10 b.g. Overbury (IRE) – Barton Belle (Barathea (IRE)) [2018/19   c– c143, h148: h18.9g h15.7s h20.3d⁶ h16.3d Mar 2] good-topped gelding: has had breathing   h– operation: very smart hurdler/useful chaser at best: left Ruth Jefferson, some promise but still well below par over hurdles in 2018/19: stays 2½m: acts on heavy going: in tongue tie last 2 starts. *Colin Tizzard*

CZECH HER OUT (IRE) 5 b.m. Fame And Glory – Molly Hussey (IRE) (Flemensfirth   **b90** (USA)) [2018/19 b15.8s⁵ b16.5d² b16.8g Apr 18] third foal: half-sister to fair hurdler/fairly useful chaser River of Intrigue (2½m-3¼m winner, by Indian River) and fair hurdler Shakeytry (19f winner, by Portrait Gallery): dam, poor maiden jumper, half-sister to fairly useful hurdler/fair chaser (winner around 2m) I Knew Well: fair form in bumpers: standout effort when second in mares event at Taunton. *Michael Scudamore*

D

DAARIO NAHARIS (IRE) 6 b.g. Winged Love (IRE) – Luck's A Lady (IRE) (Insan   **h112** (USA)) [2018/19 b15.8g³ b15.7s² h19.6d⁵ h19.4g² h21.2d⁴ Mar 21] €20,000 3-y-o,   **b99** £20,000 5-y-o: fourth foal: dam 2¼m bumper winner: in frame in Irish points: placed both outings in bumpers: fair form in novice hurdles: easily best effort when second at Doncaster in February, jumping fluently: usually leads. *Alastair Ralph*

DA BABA ELEPHANT (IRE) 10 b.g. Subtle Power (IRE) – Queenofbenitstown (IRE) **c109 p**
(Presenting) [2018/19 c102, h–: c20.1g³ c19.9g^pu c20s* c23.9g* c21.1m* Sep 6] big, **h–**
strong gelding: twice-raced hurdler: fair handicap chaser: completed hat-trick at Wexford
in July, Market Rasen in August and Sedgefield in September: stays 3m: acts on soft and
good to firm going: tried in cheekpieces: has worn tongue tie: front runner/races
prominently: open to further improvement over fences. *Ronan M. P. McNally, Ireland*

DABINETT MOON 11 b.m. Midnight Legend – Miss Crabapple (Sunyboy) [2018/19 **c98**
c104: c25.3g⁴ c22.6d^pu Jun 8] multiple point winner: fair hunter chaser: stays 3m: acts on
good to soft going. *Mrs F. J. Marriott*

DA DOU RON RON (FR) 6 b.m. Early March – I Am Free (FR) (Garde Royale) [2018/19 **h77**
b11.9m³ b13.9d⁵ h17.2m² h17.2g⁴ h17.2d h18.1m Sep 19] rather leggy mare: half-sister to **b?**
fairly useful French cross-country chaser Ray of Light (2¾m-3¼m winner, by Passing
Sale) and French 2¼m chase winner Paradize (by Johann Quatz): dam French maiden: in
frame on all bar one of 17 outings in French bumpers: poor form over hurdles: left
P. de Chevigny after second start: has worn headgear, including last 4 starts: has joined
Emmet Mullins. *Dianne Sayer*

DADSINLUCK 6 b.g. Presenting – Gemini Lucy (IRE) (Glacial Storm (USA)) [2018/19 **h87**
b17.7g b15.8g h19.3g^pu h16.5g h15.8d h19d⁴ Apr 4] compact gelding: has had breathing **b–**
operation: fourth foal: brother to useful hurdler Dadsintrouble (15f-23f winner) and half-
brother to useful hurdler/chaser Psychedelic Rock (2m-2½m winner, by Yeats): dam (c140/
h117) 2m-2½m hurdle/chase winner: no form in bumpers: modest form over hurdles: in
hood last 2 starts: in tongue tie last 4. *Tim Vaughan*

DAGIAN (IRE) 4 ch.g. Dawn Approach (IRE) – Hen Night (IRE) (Danehill Dancer **h110**
(IRE)) [2018/19 h15.7g⁵ h15.7s² h15.7g² h15.7m² Feb 26] fairly useful on Flat, stays 11.5f:
fair form over hurdles: tried in cheekpieces. *James Moffatt*

DAIM PIERJI (FR) 6 b.g. Coastal Path – Keensland (FR) (Le Balafre (FR)) [2018/19 **c108**
c19.9s⁶ c23s³ c23.4s⁴ Apr 9] fifth foal: half-brother to French 19f chase winner Veens **h–**
Pierji (by Alberto Giacometti): dam French 17f chase winner: has run only in France: well
held sole start over hurdles: fair maiden chaser: in frame in cross-country events in
2018/19: will stay 3m: acts on soft going. *Mrs Jane Williams*

DAISY CROCKETT (IRE) 5 b.m. Alamo Bay (USA) – Light of Dawn (USA) **b–**
(Dynaformer (USA)) [2018/19 b16.7m Jun 22] first foal: dam ran once on Flat: tailed off
in bumper/on Flat debut. *Conrad Allen*

DAKKAR COLLONGES (FR) 6 br.g. Network (GER) – Karesse Collonges (FR) **h111**
(Kadalko (FR)) [2018/19 h103: h21g⁶ h23.3g^F May 27] fair maiden hurdler: stayed 2¾m:
acted on soft going: dead. *Ben Case*

DAKLONDIKE (IRE) 7 b.g. Gold Well – Strong Irish (IRE) (Corrouge (USA)) [2018/19 **c146 §**
c132, h–: c27.3g^pu c22.9v* c25.6d^ur c32.6g^rr Feb 23] tall gelding: winning hurdler: smart **h–**
handicap chaser: won at Haydock (by length from Ballyarthur) in December, only completed
start in 2018/19: stays 3¼m: acts on heavy going: wears headgear: has worn tongue tie,
including last 2018/19: one to treat with caution (refused to race final start). *David Pipe*

DAKOTA GREY 8 gr.g. Fair Mix (IRE) – Miss Sassi (Terimon) [2018/19 c–, h102: c16g⁴ **c97**
c17.3g⁴ c16g^ur c23.8g³ c23.8g³ c20.1s⁶ Oct 13] modest hurdler: modest maiden chaser: **h–**
stays easy 3m: acts on heavy going: has worn headgear: tried in tongue tie. *Micky Hammond*

DALAMAN (IRE) 8 b.g. Duke of Marmalade (IRE) – Crimphill (IRE) (Sadler's Wells **c–**
(USA)) [2018/19 h105: c16s^F c20.3s^pu h20v³ h19.9s^pu h19.5g^pu Apr 26] lengthy gelding: **h103**
fair handicap hurdler: no aptitude for chasing: stays 2½m: acts on heavy going: tried in
cheekpieces: has worn tongue tie. *Neil Mulholland*

DALASIRI (IRE) 10 gr.g. Dylan Thomas (IRE) – Dalataya (IRE) (Sadler's Wells (USA)) **h–**
[2018/19 h19.6g Oct 30] fairly useful hurdler at best, well held sole start in sphere after
2015/16: stayed 21f: acted on heavy going: tried in headgear/tongue tie: dead. *Johnny
Farrelly*

DALE DOBACK 4 b.g. Medicean – Emulate (Alhaarth (IRE)) [2018/19 ab16s Jan 4] **b–**
lengthy gelding: well beaten in bumper. *Laura Mongan*

DALEELAK (IRE) 6 b.g. Arcano (IRE) – Alshamatry (USA) (Seeking The Gold (USA)) **h–**
[2018/19 h–: h17.7g h17.7m^pu May 27] no form over hurdles: tried in tongue tie. *Daniel
O'Brien*

DALILA DU SEUIL (FR) 6 gr.m. Bachir (IRE) – Misery (FR) (Baryshnikov (AUS)) **c132 p**
[2018/19 c17.5v* c20d^F Mar 10] rather unfurnished mare: fifth foal: dam, French maiden, **h–**
placed around 17f over hurdles: useful hurdler for M. Seror in France: similar form over

fences: won mares novice at Exeter (by 4½ lengths from Kalahari Queen) in December: stays 2¼m: acts on heavy going: usually wears hood: remains with potential as a chaser. *Harry Fry*

DALI MAIL (FR) 6 gr.g. Satri (IRE) – Queenly Mail (FR) (Medaaly) [2018/19 b98: h16v* h16s² h16.4v² Mar 16] workmanlike gelding: has had breathing operation: bumper winner: fairly useful form over hurdles: won maiden at Ayr in November: shaped well when second in handicap at Newcastle in March: wears tongue tie: usually races prominently/travels strongly: likely to improve further. *Donald Whillans*   **h124 p**

DALKADAM (FR) 8 gr.g. Martaline – Cadoudame (FR) (Cadoudal (FR)) [2018/19 c90, h–: c20.3g³ h23s c20g⁵ c20s² c23.6d⁴ c16s⁴ Jan 4] strong, workmanlike gelding: poor handicap hurdler: poor maiden chaser: stays 3m: acts on heavy going: has worn headgear, including last 4 starts: wears tongue tie. *J. R. Jenkins*   **c81 h69**

DALLAS COWBOY (IRE) 9 b.g. Beneficial – Watson River (IRE) (Presenting) [2018/19 c19.5dᵖᵘ c19.2g⁴ c16.4g⁴ c21.3d⁴ c19.2g⁵ c20.3gᵖᵘ c21.4g⁴ c17.2g² c21.4g³ c17.2m* Apr 21] good-bodied gelding: winning hurdler: fair handicap chaser: won at Market Rasen in April: left A. J. Martin after first start, John Wainwright after fifth: has form at 25f, raced mainly over shorter: acts on soft and good to firm going: has worn headgear/tongue tie: front runner/races prominently. *Tim Fitzgerald*   **c103 h–**

DALLAS DES PICTONS (FR) 6 b.g. Spanish Moon (USA) – Nadia des Pictons (FR) (Video Rock (FR)) [2018/19 b15.4g* h19d⁴ h16g² h20g* h24g* h20.3d² h24.7d Apr 5] rangy gelding: will make a chaser: third foal: half-brother to 2 French bumper winners, including 2m winner Univer des Pictons (by Nononito): dam unraced: won 2 bumpers in France for Alain Couetil, including at Le Pin Au Haras in May: smart form over hurdles: won maiden at Punchestown (by 10 lengths from Lighthouse Warrier) in January and handicap at Leopardstown (by neck from Calie du Mesnil) in February: second in Martin Pipe Conditional Jockeys' Handicap Hurdle at Cheltenham (1¼ lengths behind Early Doors) in March: stays 3m: acts on good to soft going. *Gordon Elliott, Ireland*   **h145 b?**

DALLUNA (FR) 4 b.g. Linda's Lad – Luna Sand (FR) (Footstepsinthesand) [2018/19 b13.7m⁵ h16g h16g h16d Nov 24] well beaten in junior bumper/over hurdles. *Eoin Griffin, Ireland*   **h– b–**

DAME DU SOIR (FR) 6 br.m. Axxos (GER) – Kassing (FR) (Passing Sale (FR)) [2018/19 h98p: h19.6g² h15.5d* h17.7v⁶ h16.8dᵖᵘ Mar 14] good-topped mare: bumper winner: fair form over hurdles: won mares novice at Leicester in January: unproven beyond 2m: acts on good to soft going. *David Bridgwater*   **h111**

DAMIENS DILEMMA (IRE) 11 b.g. Wareed (IRE) – Olympos Belle (IRE) (Shahrastani (USA)) [2018/19 c90: c26.2g⁴ c20.9d⁶ c25.5m* c25.5g⁵ c21.2d² c24.2g⁴ Apr 15] workmanlike gelding: multiple point winner: modest handicap chaser: won at Cartmel in June: stays 3¼m: acts on good to firm and good to soft going: in headgear last 4 starts: usually front runner/races prominently. *Mrs L. A. Coltherd*   **c99**

DAMIER (FR) 6 br.g. Network (GER) – Klassique (FR) (Lute Antique (FR)) [2018/19 h18.5g⁴ h23g⁵ h21g h25.5g h23.8g³ h24.4gᵖᵘ Jan 9] fell in Irish point: poor form over hurdles: best effort at 3m: raced only on good going: in cheekpieces last 3 starts: dead. *David Dennis*   **h80**

DAMUT I'M OUT (IRE) 9 b.g. Gamut (IRE) – Five Cents More (IRE) (Flemensfirth (USA)) [2018/19 h78: h23.3d³ h20m² h21.8g⁴ h21.2m³ h23.3g² Sep 17] multiple point winner: modest maiden hurdler: stays 23f: acts on good to firm and good to soft going: tried in cheekpieces: has joined Alastair Ralph. *Gavin Patrick Cromwell, Ireland*   **h96**

DANANDY (IRE) 12 b.g. Cloudings (IRE) – Tower Princess (IRE) (King's Ride) [2018/19 c120x, h–: c21.6g³ May 17] sturdy gelding: won twice in points: winning hurdler: fairly useful chaser at best: moody effort on hunter debut in May: stays 3¼m: acts on good to firm and heavy going: wears headgear: often let down by jumping. *Mrs K. Hobbs*   **c98 x h–**

DANBORU (IRE) 8 b.g. Brian Boru – Dandouce (Danzero (AUS)) [2018/19 c19.9s c20.6d² c19.3s² c21.7g² c24sᶠ Mar 23] won Irish point on debut: fair maiden chaser: left A. J. Martin after second start: stays 2¾m: acts on soft going: usually wears tongue tie. *Tim Vaughan*   **c104**

DANCE AVENUE (USA) 4 ch.f. Champs Elysees – Short Dance (USA) (Hennessy (USA)) [2018/19 b14g h16.4d⁵ Dec 1] strong, close-coupled filly: sister to 2 winners on Flat and half-sister to 3 winners, including Czech 2m hurdle winner Brisk Moos (by Galileo): dam useful 6f-1m winner: tailed off in junior bumper/juvenile hurdle: wears tongue tie. *Lucinda Russell*   **h– b–**

DANCECRAFT 5 b.m. Mastercraftsman (IRE) – Samba Chryss (IRE) (Galileo (IRE)) **h83**
[2018/19 h–, b72: h20.5g⁴ h17.7d h23.9g Feb 19] rather leggy mare: poor form over hurdles: in blinkers last 4 starts. *Gary Moore*

DANCED EVERY DANCE (IRE) 6 b.m. Oscar (IRE) – Kinnegads Pride (IRE) (Be **b74** My Native (USA)) [2018/19 b–: b16.8s³ b16.4m⁵ Mar 22] poor form in bumpers. *Donald Whillans*

DANCEINTOTHELIGHT 12 gr.g. Dansili – Kali (Linamix (FR)) [2018/19 c–, h107: **c–** h22.7g⁴ h19.6g⁴ h16.8m⁵ h19.6g³ h23.1g³ h22g⁴ h20g⁶ h19.3g³ h21.2g⁴ h19.3s² h19.9d³ **h101** h19.8s⁴ h19.6g² h19.6d Apr 26] sturdy gelding: fair handicap hurdler: fell both starts over fences: stays 21f: acts on good to firm and heavy going: tried in cheekpieces: wears tongue tie: front runner: amateur ridden. *Donald McCain*

DANCE OF FIRE 7 b.g. Norse Dancer (IRE) – Strictly Dancing (IRE) (Danehill Dancer **h82 §** (IRE)) [2018/19 h86: h15.6g⁶ h15.6g h18.1g h19.8s h16.4m⁴ h16.2g³ Apr 25] poor maiden hurdler: stays 19f: acts on good to soft going: tried in headgear: usually races off pace: temperamental. *N. W. Alexander*

DANCE OF TIME 12 b.g. Presenting – Northern Native (IRE) (Be My Native (USA)) **c93** [2018/19 c21.6g² c25.2d⁴ Mar 6] big gelding: prolific point winner: once-raced hurdler: **h–** modest form in hunter chases. *Miss H. J. Reveley*

DANCE TO PARIS 4 b.f. Champs Elysees – Riabouchinska (Fantastic Light (USA)) **h102** [2018/19 h16g* h17s⁶ h15.8g⁵ Jan 3] fairly useful on Flat, stays 2m: fair form over hurdles: won fillies juvenile at Fakenham in October: wears headgear: needs to improve jumping. *Lucy Wadham*

DANCE WITH KATE 8 b.m. Hamairi (IRE) – Vercheny (Petoski) [2018/19 h16d h16m **h–** Sep 17] no form on Flat/over hurdles: tried in cheekpieces. *Kevin Bishop*

DANCINGATDUNRAVEN (IRE) 6 b.g. Mahler – My Kit (IRE) (Be My Native **h–** (USA)) [2018/19 h21.4g Jan 5] won Irish maiden point on debut: in tongue tie, 2/1, tailed off in novice hurdle at Wincanton. *Philip Hobbs*

DANCING CONQUEST 9 b.m. Imperial Dancer – Another Conquest (El Conquistador) **c– x** [2018/19 c96x, h–: c25.8g⁵ May 16] strong mare: well held only hurdles outing: maiden **h–** chaser, usually let down by jumping. *Seamus Mullins*

DANCING DARCY (FR) 6 b.m. Shirocco (GER) – Polymiss (FR) (Poliglote) [2018/19 **b–** b15.7g b16m Apr 22] fourth foal: closely related to useful hurdler Whatmore (2m-2½m winner, by Schiaparelli): dam French 17f/2¼m hurdle/chase winner: well held in 2 bumpers. *Michael Appleby*

DANCING DORIS 4 b.f. Malinas (GER) – Peggies Run (Kayf Tara) [2018/19 b16m² Apr **b87 p** 22] £5,800 3-y-o: sixth foal: half-sister to bumper winner/fair hurdler Peggies Venture (2½m/21f winner, by Presenting): dam unraced half-sister to fair hurdler/useful chaser (stayed 3¼m) Latimer's Place and useful hurdler/fairly useful chaser (stayed 19f-2¾m winner) Penneyrose Bay: 7/1, promise when second in mares maiden bumper at Fakenham (4½ lengths behind Sopat, clear of rest): better to come. *Neil King*

DANCING DOUG (IRE) 6 br.g. Kalanisi (IRE) – Drumcay Polly (IRE) (Le Bavard **h106** (FR)) [2018/19 h103p, h87: h20gᶠ h21.2g³ h23.8d h17g³ h16.7g⁶ h21.2d² Apr 23] useful-looking gelding: fair maiden hurdler: left Sam Thomas after fifth start: stays 21f: acts on soft going. *Philip Kirby*

DANCING GREY 6 gr.m. Dream Eater (IRE) – State of Grace (Generous (IRE)) **h–** [2018/19 b16.8s⁵ b16.8g b16d³ b16.8v⁴ h19.5g h20sᵖᵘ Nov 23] fourth foal: dam, unraced, **b74** out of fairly useful hurdler/chaser up to 21f Vent d'Aout: poor form in bumpers: little show in 2 maiden hurdles: tried in cheekpieces. *Gail Haywood*

DANCING HEARTS 6 b.m. Makfi – Danceabout (Shareef Dancer (USA)) [2018/19 b–: **h–** b16.8g h18.5g h18.7m⁶ h19.7sᵖᵘ Dec 15] no form in bumpers/over hurdles: often wears **b–** hood. *Michael Scudamore*

DANCING ON MY OWN (IRE) 5 b.g. Milan – Morning Supreme (IRE) (Supreme **h134** Leader) [2018/19 h16s⁵ h16d² h16g³ h16g⁴ h21sᵖᵘ Mar 13] tall gelding: second foal: half-brother to 2¼m bumper winner You Raised Me Up (by Presenting); dam (c130/h142), 2m-2½m hurdle/chase winner, half-sister to useful hurdler (stayed 2¼m) Morning Run: useful form over hurdles: fourth in Chanelle Pharma Novices' Hurdle at Leopardstown (7¼ lengths behind Klassical Dream) in February: should stay beyond 2m: acts on good to soft going: front runner/races prominently. *Henry de Bromhead, Ireland*

DANCING SHADOW (IRE) 10 br.g. Craigsteel – Be My Shadow (IRE) (Torus) **c122 §** [2018/19 c–§, h116§: c25.1g c32.4g c26.7g⁴ c30.7d² c28.4s⁴ c30.7s⁴ Apr 16] tall, angular **h–** gelding: has had breathing operation: fair hurdler: fairly useful handicap chaser: second at Exeter in February and fourth at same course in April: stays 33f: acts on good to firm and heavy going: wears headgear: usually races close up: not one to trust. *Victor Dartnall*

DANCINGWITH STORMS (IRE) 5 ch.g. New Approach (IRE) – Mad About You **h113** (IRE) (Indian Ridge) [2018/19 h16s* h16.2g⁴ h17.7v h21.4s h19.9dᵘʳ h19.5m⁴ Apr 22] €12,000 3-y-o: third foal: half-brother to 2 winners on Flat, including 1¼m/11f winner Malinka (by Pivotal): dam smart 7f/1m winner who stayed 1¼m: unplaced in bumpers: fair form over hurdles: won maiden at Cork in May on final start for Ellmarie Holden: may prove best around 2m: acts on soft and good to firm going: in hood last 5 starts. *Warren Greatrex*

DANDOLO DU GITE (FR) 6 b.g. Khalkevi (IRE) – Lavande d'Eproniere (FR) (Saint **h116** Cyrien (FR)) [2018/19 h102: h15.7g² h22g* h18.6g³ h18.5d⁵ h19.5d⁶ Mar 20] has had breathing operations: runner-up in Irish point: bumper winner: fairly useful form over hurdles: won maiden at Stratford in October: third in novice at Market Rasen month later: stays 2¾m: wears tongue tie: usually races freely. *Neil Mulholland*

DANDRIDGE 10 ch.g. Doyen (IRE) – Arantxa (Sharpo) [2018/19 c–, h–: c20g³ c20.5g² **c127** c16.5m Apr 13] big, robust gelding: has had breathing operations: winning hurdler: fairly **h–** useful handicap chaser: second at Kempton in February: stays 2½m: acts on soft and good to firm going: has worn cheekpieces: wears tongue tie. *Charlie Longsdon*

DANDY DAN (IRE) 6 b.g. Midnight Legend – Playing Around (Act One) [2018/19 **c141** h126, b99: c20g² c27.5g³ c24.1g* c26.2g* c24.1d* c24.1m² Apr 13] fairly useful hurdle- **h–** useful form over fences: completed hat-trick in maiden at Bangor and handicap at Kelso in October, and novice at Ayr in February: stays 3¼m: acts on good to firm and good to soft going: tried in cheekpieces: wears tongue tie: usually front runner/races prominently. *Kim Bailey*

DAN EMMETT (USA) 9 ch.g. Flower Alley (USA) – Singing Dixie (USA) (Dixieland **c– x** Band (USA)) [2018/19 c–x, h–: c23.8vᶠ h22.8s⁶ h24.2d⁴ h26gᵖᵘ h24dᵖᵘ Apr 24] **h110** workmanlike gelding: fair handicap hurdler: let down by jumping over fences: stays 3¼m: acts on heavy going: has worn headgear, including last 4 starts: usually front runner/races prominently. *Michael Scudamore*

DAN GUN (IRE) 5 b.g. Intikhab (USA) – Lady Magdalena (IRE) (Invincible Spirit **h87** (IRE)) [2018/19 h79: h16m h16g h24g⁵ h27m h22g h24g⁶ h16.8s⁵ h17.7v h15.7d h20.2d Apr 26] modest maiden hurdler: left John Joseph Hanlon after sixth start: best effort at 3m: acts on soft going: tried in hood: usually races off pace. *Fergal O'Brien*

DAN MCGRUE (IRE) 7 b.g. Dansant – Aahsaypasty (IRE) (Aahsaylad) [2018/19 h118: **h112** h21.4gᵖᵘ h19.8s³ h19.8gᵖᵘ Apr 27] strong gelding: fairly useful novice hurdler in 2017/18, disappointing in handicaps since: stays 19f: acts on soft going: usually wears tongue tie: weak finisher. *Paul Nicholls*

DANNY KIRWAN (IRE) 6 b.g. Scorpion (IRE) – Sainte Baronne (FR) (Saint des Saints **h133 p** (FR)) [2018/19 h103P: h16g² h15.7s² Dec 21] tall gelding: easily won sole start in Irish points: bumper winner: useful form over hurdles: better effort when second in Kennel Gate Novices' Hurdle at Ascot (4½ lengths behind Angels Breath) in December: open to further improvement. *Paul Nicholls*

DANNY WHIZZBANG (IRE) 6 b.g. Getaway (GER) – Lakil Princess (IRE) (Bering) **h128 p** [2018/19 h25.5s* h23.1s* Mar 5] €40,000 3-y-o, €115,000 5-y-o: third foal: half-brother to 2 winners, including fairly useful hurdler/useful chaser Lastbutnotleast (2m-3m winner, by Flemensfirth): dam (c120/h115), 2m-2¼m hurdle/chase winner, half-sister to useful/ ungenuine hurdler/chaser (2m-3m winner) Moskova: Irish point winner: fairly useful form over hurdles: won both starts, maiden at Hereford in November and novice at Exeter in March: wears tongue tie: open to further improvement. *Paul Nicholls*

DANSE IDOL (IRE) 6 b.m. Dansant – Screen Idol (IRE) (Sadler's Wells (USA)) **h122** [2018/19 b16.4g⁶ h21.4g* h18.9v² h19.8s² h24.4g² h21.7g* Apr 12] strong mare: sister to **b86** a winning pointer and half-sister to 3 winners on Flat: dam 7f winner: point winner: fair form in bumpers: fairly useful form over hurdles: won mares maiden at Wincanton in December and novice at Fontwell in April: second in Jane Seymour Mares' Novices' Hurdle at Sandown (2¼ lengths behind Queenohearts) in February: stays 2¾m: acts on heavy going: usually travels strongly. *Paul Nicholls*

DANSEUR DU LARGE (FR) 6 gr.g. Martaline – Antagua (FR) (Cadoudal (FR)) **c96** [2018/19 h95: h24d^pu h23d^pu c23.6d^5 c23.5v^4 c24g^3 c24g* Apr 25] point winner: modest **h–** form over hurdles: similar form over fences: won novice handicap at Warwick in April: stays 3m: acts on heavy going. *Polly Gundry*

DANS LE VENT (FR) 6 b.g. Skins Game – Boreade (FR) (Lost World (IRE)) [2018/19 **h130** h129: h19.5d^4 h21g^4 h24g^4 h23.8g^4 h24.4g^2 h19.9s^3 h24g Apr 17] sturdy gelding: useful handicap hurdler: second to Skidoosh at Doncaster in February: stays 3m: acts on soft going: usually wears headgear: temperament under suspicion. *Jamie Snowden*

DAN'S QUEST 9 b.g. Kalanisi (IRE) – Piedmont (UAE) (Jade Robbery (USA)) [2018/19 **c–** h24g^pu h23s^pu c16.5g Jun 2] useful-looking gelding: has had breathing operation: poor **h–** maiden hurdler: well beaten in novice handicap on chasing debut: in headgear last 2 starts: tried in tongue tie. *Robin Dickin*

DAN'S WEE MAN 10 b.g. Kayf Tara – Hazel Bank Lass (IRE) (Insan (USA)) [2018/19 **c89** c24.2v^4 c23.6d^5 c25.7s^2 c24.2d^4 Mar 26] workmanlike gelding: point winner: maiden **h–** hurdler: modest maiden chaser nowadays: stays 3¼m: acts on heavy going: has worn headgear, including last 3 starts: tried in tongue tie. *Jennifer Mason*

DANVINNIE 10 b.g. Midnight Legend – Top Gale (IRE) (Topanoora) [2018/19 c102, h–: **c–** c20g^4 Mar 28] placed in points: maiden hurdler: fair form in chases, tailed off in hunter in **h–** 2018/19: stays 21f: acts on heavy going: often in headgear nowadays. *Mrs D. J. Treneer*

DAPHNE DU CLOS (FR) 6 b.m. Spanish Moon (USA) – Katarina du Clos (FR) **h100 P** (Panoramic) [2018/19 h15.8d^5 Jan 25] medium-sized mare: useful form in bumpers in 2016/17: off 24 months, evens, fifth in novice at Huntingdon (9¾ lengths behind Scarlet Dragon, not knocked about) on hurdling debut: ought to do much better. *Nicky Henderson*

DARA'S PRESENT (IRE) 8 b.g. Presenting – Ginandit (IRE) (Definite Article) **c90** [2018/19 h21d h15.8v^6 c23.8s c23.8s^pu Apr 7] has had breathing operation: off mark in **h88** Irish points at third attempt: modest form over hurdles/fences. *Harry Whittington*

DARASSO (FR) 6 br.g. Konig Turf (GER) – Nassora (FR) (Assessor (IRE)) [2018/19 **c150 p** h20g^2 h24s^5 h16d^4 c16s* Mar 18] fifth foal: half-brother to fair French hurdler/fairly useful **h155** chaser Urallia (17f-21f winner, by Califet): dam, French 2¼m hurdle/chase winner, half-sister to useful hurdler/smart staying chaser Ladalko and fairly useful hurdler/smart chaser (stayed 21f) Oumeyade: very smart hurdler: left G. Cherel after final start in 2017/18: won Red Mills Trial Hurdle at Gowran (by 11 lengths from Forge Meadow) in February: smart form over fences: won Webster Cup Chase at Navan (by 2¼ lengths from Cadmium) in March: stays 21f: acts on heavy going: open to further improvement as a chaser. *Joseph Patrick O'Brien, Ireland*

DARCEY'S PENNY 6 b.m. Bahri (USA) – Penteli (Double Trigger (IRE)) [2018/19 **b–** b16.8m b16.4d b16.2d Mar 26] third foal: dam (h83), 2¾m hurdle winner, also successful on Flat in Greece: well held in bumpers. *Susan Corbett*

DARCY WARD (FR) 6 b.g. Doctor Dino (FR) – Alzasca (FR) (Grape Tree Road) **c126 P** [2018/19 h124: h23.1g h21.4d^pu h17.7s^3 c19.2d* Apr 9] fair hurdler: 9/1, very good start **h111** over fences when won novice handicap at Exeter by 4½ lengths from Awake At Midnight: should be suited by at least 3m: acts on soft and good to firm going: in tongue tie last 2 starts: front runner/races prominently: capable of good deal better still as a chaser. *Jack R. Barber*

DAREBIN (GER) 7 ch.g. It's Gino (GER) – Delightful Sofie (GER) (Grand Lodge **c122** (USA)) [2018/19 c123, h–: c19.7g^2 c17.8s^3 c16.5g* c16.3g^2 c15.5s^4 c15.5d* c15.5s^5 **h–** c15.5d^2 c15.5d^3 c16.4g^6 c17g* Apr 22] lengthy gelding: winning hurdler: fairly useful handicap chaser: won at Huntingdon in November, Sandown in January and walked over at Plumpton in April: stays 2½m: acts on good to firm and heavy going: wears headgear: front runner/races prominently. *Gary Moore*

DARES TO DREAM (IRE) 5 br.m. Beneficial – Miss McGoldrick (IRE) (Kasakov) **b94** [2018/19 b–: b16.2d^2 b16.8s* b16.8d^2 b17d Apr 4] sturdy mare: fair bumper performer: won mares event at Sedgefield in December. *Philip Kirby*

DARE TO ENDEAVOUR 12 b.g. Alflora (IRE) – Miss Chinchilla (Perpendicular) **c–** [2018/19 h20s^5 h24s^4 h20g^4 c25.9s c27.3s Dec 30] tall gelding: poor hurdler (maiden)/ **h82** chaser nowadays: stays 3¼m: acts on heavy going: has worn headgear: sometimes in tongue tie in 2018/19. *Patrick Griffin, Ireland*

DARIUS DES BOIS (FR) 6 b.g. Great Pretender (IRE) – Palafixe (FR) (Valanour (IRE)) **c123** [2018/19 h123: c23.8s^2 c20d^2 c24.2d^pu c25.3g^pu Apr 17] tall gelding: has had breathing **h–** operation: fairly useful hurdler: similar form over fences: stays 3m: acts on soft going. *Nicky Henderson*

DARIUS DES SOURCES (FR) 6 gr.g. Irish Wells (FR) – Lionata (FR) (Lion Noir) **b92**
[2018/19 b16m⁶ Apr 13] €7,000 3-y-o, £38,000 6-y-o: third foal: dam French 11.5f winner:
off mark in Irish points at second attempt: 20/1, sixth in bumper at Ayr (9¾ lengths behind
December Second). *Chris Grant*

DARIYA (USA) 4 b.f. Include (USA) – Dubai (IRE) (Galileo (IRE)) [2018/19 h15.8d⁴ **h92**
h16.6d h15.8g³ Mar 19] fairly useful on Flat in France, stays 1¼m: modest form over
hurdles: best effort when third in fillies juvenile at Huntingdon (tongue tied).
Charlie Longsdon

DARK AND DANGEROUS (IRE) 11 b.g. Cacique (IRE) – Gilah (IRE) (Saddlers' **c–**
Hall (IRE)) [2018/19 c–, h97: h19.9s⁶ h22g h22g⁵ h19.9s² Mar 3] compact gelding: modest **h89**
handicap hurdler: winning chaser: best form around 2m: acts on heavy going: usually
wears headgear: tried in tongue tie. *Simon Waugh*

DARK EPISODE (IRE) 5 b.g. Getaway (GER) – No Moore Bills (Nicholas Bill) **h111**
[2018/19 b16.8v³ h16s³ h20.5d* h21.4gᵖᵘ h21.4g h19.5d h21g Apr 10] £50,000 3-y-o: half- **b90**
brother to several winners, including fairly useful hurdler Fionn Mac Cul (19f winner, by
Oscar) and fair hurdler/winning pointer Mtpockets (27f winner, by Deploy): dam (h75)
maiden hurdler (stayed 2½m): better than result when third in bumper at Newton Abbot:
fair form over hurdles: won conditionals novice at Leicester in December: disappointing
after: stays 2½m: acts on soft going: tried in hood: usually races off pace. *Philip Hobbs*

DARK FORCE (FR) 6 gr.g. Gris de Gris (IRE) – Maciga (FR) (Gunboat Diplomacy **h–**
(FR)) [2018/19 h76p: h15.8d May 5] showed a bit in bumper: well held in 2 maiden
hurdles. *Venetia Williams*

DARK INVADER (FR) 7 b.g. Saint des Saints (FR) – Minirose (FR) (Mansonnien (FR)) **c108 x**
[2018/19 h100: c20g⁶ c16.5g² c16m* c16.5g* c17.4g⁵ c17.3sᶠ c16.5d² c17.8g³ c16.5g⁵ **h–**
c15.7m* c17.5s⁵ h21.2s⁵ c16d⁴ c16d³ c17.2g⁵ c20.3g c19.4g⁵ Apr 21] sturdy gelding:
maiden hurdler: fair handicap chaser: won several events at Ffos Las in June, Worcester in
July and Wincanton in October: stays 2½m: acts on good to firm and heavy going: has worn
cheekpieces: sometimes let down by jumping. *Evan Williams*

DARK MAHLER (IRE) 8 b.g. Mahler – Aries Rambler (IRE) (Shernazar) [2018/19 **c–**
c111, h–: c19.2m⁶ May 8] has had breathing operation: maiden hurdler: fair form in chases, **h–**
well held sole start under Rules in 2018/19: won points in February and March: tried in
tongue tie. *Emma Lavelle*

DARK RULER (IRE) 10 b.g. Dark Angel (IRE) – Gino Lady (IRE) (Perugino (USA)) **h99**
[2018/19 h16.8g² h16v³ h16.2vᵖᵘ h16s⁵ h16.4g² h19.7gᵖᵘ h16.4s h16.4m Mar 28] fairly
useful on Flat, stays 1¾m: modest maiden hurdler: unproven beyond 17f: acts on heavy
going: tried in cheekpieces: usually leads. *Jason Ward*

DARKSIDEOFTARNSIDE (IRE) 5 b.g. Intense Focus (USA) – Beautiful Dancer **h–**
(IRE) (Danehill Dancer (IRE)) [2018/19 h15.7vᶠ h21.6s Dec 21] workmanlike gelding:
fairly useful on Flat, stays 13f: well held completed start over hurdles: in cheekpieces time
before. *Ian Williams*

DARK SUNSET (IRE) 8 b.m. Scorpion (IRE) – Wilmott's Fancy (Buckley) [2018/19 **h–**
h109: h20v h20.6sᵖᵘ Dec 22] runner-up in Irish maiden points: fair hurdler, no form in
2018/19: stays 25f: acts on heavy going: tried in cheekpieces. *Donald McCain*

DARK VALLEY (IRE) 9 b.g. Lend A Hand – Glorys Flame (IRE) (Flemensfirth (USA)) **c–**
[2018/19 c88?: c20s Nov 12] placed twice from 3 starts in Irish points: well held in 2
novice chases. *Micky Hammond*

DARLAC (FR) 6 b.g. Lucarno (USA) – Pail Mel (FR) (Sleeping Car (FR)) [2018/19 b83: **h125**
h19.2m* h21g⁴ h19.8v² h20.3d h24.3g h24dᵖᵘ Mar 15] good-topped gelding: runner-up on
second of 2 starts in Irish points: fairly useful form over hurdles: won maiden at Fontwell
in October: should stay beyond 21f: acts on good to firm and heavy going: tried in
cheekpieces: usually front runner/races prominently. *Colin Tizzard*

DARLING ALKO (FR) 6 b.g. Al Namix (FR) – Padalko Tatou (FR) (Kadalko (FR)) **b–**
[2018/19 b?: b15.8g b15.8g Mar 19] won maiden bumper at Senonnes-Pouance on debut
in 2017/18: well held all 3 starts in Britain. *Sam Thomas*

DARLING DU LARGE (FR) 6 b.m. Kapgarde (FR) – Dissidente (FR) (Double Bed **h99**
(FR)) [2018/19 b92: b16g h15.5d³ h16.8d³ h16.4v² h15.8m³ Apr 1] well-made mare: fair **b76**
form in bumpers/over hurdles. *Tom George*

DARLING MALTAIX (FR) 6 b.g. Voix du Nord (FR) – Rosalie Malta (FR) (Lavirco (GER)) [2018/19 h111, b–: h15.3m³ h19.3m⁴ h16.5d² h15.3g³ h21.6s* h21g⁵ h19.3d⁵ h21sᶠ Mar 16] good-topped gelding: has had breathing operation: fairly useful handicap hurdler: won at Ascot (conditionals) in December: stays 2¾m: acts on soft and good to firm going: wears hood: tried in tongue tie: usually races in rear. *Paul Nicholls* **h125**

DARLOA (IRE) 10 br.g. Darsi (FR) – Lady Lola (IRE) (Supreme Leader) [2018/19 c–, h73: c20.3gᵖᵘ h15.8m h15.8gᵖᵘ Jul 18] maiden hurdler: no form over fences: wears headgear/tongue tie. *Victor Dartnall* **c–**
h–

DARLYN 6 b.m. Authorized (IRE) – Darariyna (IRE) (Shirley Heights) [2018/19 b58: h15.8g⁴ h18.7mʳᵒ h16g⁴ h15.8g⁴ h15.8g* h15.7s* h16s⁴ h15.7s* Mar 18] fair handicap hurdler: won at Uttoxeter in November, and Southwell in December and March: will be suited by further than 2m: acts on soft going. *Henry Oliver* **h108**

DARRY DESBOIS (FR) 6 ch.g. Ballingarry (IRE) – Tiwa (FR) (Dom Pasquini (FR)) [2018/19 b–: b16.2g h16dᵖᵘ Nov 28] no show in bumpers/novice hurdle. *Martin Todhunter* **h–**
b–

DARSI IN THE PARK (IRE) 6 b.g. Darsi (FR) – Rock In The Park (IRE) (Rock Hopper) [2018/19 b–: h15.8g Oct 7] won completed start in Irish points: well beaten in bumper/maiden hurdle. *Jonjo O'Neill* **h–**

DARSI'S JEWEL (IRE) 6 b.g. Darsi (FR) – Bettys Daughter (IRE) (Supreme Leader) [2018/19 h20g h16.7sᵖᵘ h16.8s⁴ h15.7g⁶ h20.6g⁵ Mar 20] poor form over hurdles: left Norman Lee after first start: should be suited by 2½m+. *Sue Smith* **h76**

DARTAGNAN LE DUN (FR) 6 b.g. Kapgarde (FR) – Silvazeyra (FR) (Sheyrann) [2018/19 c105, h95: c16gᵘʳ h15.8s⁴ h15.9s h16d h19.6d Apr 26] has had breathing operation: modest maiden hurdler: fair form over fences, unseated rider on return: stays 2¼m: acts on soft going: wears tongue tie: usually races off pace. *Alex Hales* **c–**
h90

DARTFORD WARBLER (IRE) 12 b.g. Overbury (IRE) – Stony View (IRE) (Tirol) [2018/19 c96§, h100: c20.1d⁴ c20.1g c24.2g* c20g⁴ c24.2g³ c20.3s c24.2v³ c26.3s* c23.9s* c26.3s⁴ c22.9d³ c21.4g⁵ Apr 3] compact gelding: winning hurdler: fair handicap chaser: won at Hexham in June, Sedgefield in January and Market Rasen in February: stays 3¼m: acts on heavy going: tried in cheekpieces: usually front runner/races prominently: unreliable. *Sue Smith* **c100 §**
h–

DARTMOOR (FR) 4 b.g. Martaline – Danse du Soir (FR) (Nombre Premier) [2018/19 b17m³ Apr 20] €13,000 3-y-o, resold £32,000 3-y-o: closely related: half-brother to 2 winners in France, including hurdle/chase winner around 2m Dewsbury (by American Post): dam useful French 7.5f/1m winner: 5/4, last of 3 in bumper at Carlisle. *Jonjo O'Neill* **b81**

DARTMOOR GIRL (IRE) 5 b.m. So You Think (NZ) – Preveza (FR) (Dalakhani (IRE)) [2018/19 h–: h21.6vᵖᵘ h23.9dᵖᵘ h21.6vᵖᵘ h23.9g Feb 19] no form over hurdles: tried in blinkers/tongue tie. *Mark Gillard* **h–**

DARWINS THEORY (IRE) 11 b.g. Montjeu (IRE) – Thrift (IRE) (Green Desert (USA)) [2018/19 c–, h91: h15.3g h19.8sⁿᵒ Mar 7] fair hurdler, lightly raced and below best since 2016/17: maiden chaser: stays 2¼m: acts on good to firm and heavy going: has worn headgear: wears tongue tie. *Fiona Shaw* **c–**
h–

DASHEL DRASHER 6 b.g. Passing Glance – So Long (Nomadic Way (USA)) [2018/19 b98: h19.5s³ h16.3s³ h16.3s⁴ h19.5d* h19.3d* h20.5d* h20.3g* Apr 17] good-topped gelding: bumper winner: useful/progressive hurdler: completed 4-timer when winning novices at Chepstow in January, Ascot in February, Newbury in March and Cheltenham (by 3½ lengths from Thistle Do Nicely) in April: stays 21f: acts on heavy going: front runner. *Jeremy Scott* **h140**

DASHING OSCAR (IRE) 9 b.g. Oscar (IRE) – Be My Leader (IRE) (Supreme Leader) [2018/19 h133: c20g⁵ h19.5dᵖᵘ h19.6d Nov 14] lengthy gelding: useful hurdler, well below form in 2018/19: 11/4, fifth in maiden at Uttoxeter (23 lengths behind Mister Miyagi) on chasing debut: wears tongue tie. *Harry Fry* **c–**
h–

DASHING PERK 8 b.g. Kayf Tara – Dashing Executive (IRE) (Executive Perk) [2018/19 h118: c22.5g³ Oct 18] big, strong gelding: won Irish point on debut: fairly useful hurdler: 3/1, third in novice handicap at Uttoxeter (3 lengths behind Just A Sting) on chasing debut: stays 3m: acts on heavy going: tried in cheekpieces: front runner/races prominently: should improve over fences. *Dr Richard Newland* **c126 p**
h–

DASH OF BLUE 4 b.g. Great Pretender (IRE) – Madame Bleue (Sir Harry Lewis (USA)) [2018/19 b16s Mar 10] good-topped gelding: well beaten in bumper. *Ben Case* **b–**

DASSETT GOLD (FR) 6 b.g. Full of Gold (FR) – Marsavrile (FR) (April Night (FR)) [2018/19 h–, b–: h20.7gᵖᵘ May 10] compact gelding: modest form in bumpers: no form over hurdles: in cheekpieces last 2 starts. *Paul Webber* **h–**

DAUPHINE EREINE (FR) 7 b.m. Saint des Saints (FR) – Bellissima de Mai (FR) c123
(Pistolet Bleu (IRE)) [2018/19 c126, h–: c23.8g⁴ c26.2gᵖᵘ c25.6s⁴ c19.2vᵖᵘ c24s² c21.6mᵖᵘ h–
Apr 20] had breathing operation: maiden hurdler: fairly useful handicap chaser: second
at Bangor (mares event) in March: stays 3m: acts on soft going: in headgear last 4 starts:
often in tongue tie. *David Pipe*

DAUPHINESS 7 b.m. Lucarno (USA) – Princess Angelique (FR) (Sagacity (FR)) h–
[2018/19 h56, h–: h21dᵖᵘ h19.9s h24.4gᵖᵘ Jan 9] little promise in bumpers/over hurdles: in
cheekpieces final start. *Henry Daly*

DAVERON (IRE) 11 b.g. Winged Love (IRE) – Double Doc (IRE) (Moonax (IRE)) c67 §
[2018/19 c71, h63: c16g c20dᵖᵘ h21.7gᵖᵘ c16g⁶ c21.7d³ c19.9d⁵ c17.8sᵖᵘ c22.7f Feb 26] h–
workmanlike gelding: one-time fairly useful hurdler/chaser, retains little ability: stays 23f:
acts on heavy going: usually wears headgear. *Richard Price*

DAVID JOHN 8 b.g. Overbury (IRE) – Molly's Secret (Minshaanshu Amad (USA)) c106
[2018/19 c108, h–: h23.1g² h26.5m* c25.8s² h23.3g³ h23.3g⁵ h25.8g² h23.8g⁶ Nov 7] h105
sturdy gelding: fair handicap hurdler: won at Newton Abbot in June: fair chaser: left Tom
Lacey after fourth start: stays 3¼m: acts on soft and good to firm going: has worn headgear:
tried in tongue tie: front runner/races prominently. *Kevin Hunter*

DAVIDS CHARM (IRE) 8 b..Milan – Have More (Haafhd) [2018/19 h137p: h16s h144
h16s⁶ h16g Dec 2] useful handicap hurdler: stays 21f: acts on heavy going: has worn
headgear, including in 2018/19. *John J. Walsh, Ireland*

DAVID'S PHOEBE (IRE) 6 br.m. Dubai Destination (USA) – Miss Compliance (IRE) h113
(Broken Hearted) [2018/19 h107, b–: h19.6g³ h15.7g² h17.2g² h20d² Aug 29] fair handicap
hurdler: stays 2½m: acts on soft going. *Tom Lacey*

DAWERANN (IRE) 10 b.g. Medicean – Dawera (IRE) (Spinning World (USA)) c–
[2018/19 c111, h113: h23.9g⁴ c16gᵖᵘ Aug 16] fair handicap hurdler/maiden chaser: stays h107
3m: acts on good to firm and heavy going: wears headgear: has worn tongue tie, including
last 3 starts. *Gordon Elliott, Ireland*

DAWNIERIVER (IRE) 9 br.m. Indian River (FR) – In Sin (IRE) (Insan (USA)) c101
[2018/19 c106, h–: c23.9g⁴ c21.6g³ c23m⁶ c22.5g² c23.4g* c24.2g* c24s³ Dec 4] lengthy, h–
rather sparely-made mare: has had breathing operation: maiden hurdler: fair handicap
chaser: won 3-runner mares events at Newcastle and Fakenham in November: stays 3¼m:
acts on soft and good to firm going: wears cheekpieces. *Michael Scudamore*

DAWN RAIDER (IRE) 7 b.g. Mahler – Woodview Dawn (IRE) (Turtle Island (IRE)) h125
[2018/19 h24g h24g² h22.4m⁶ h21s³ h20.8g² h24s² h23.9d³ h20d h22.5g Mar 7] lengthy
gelding: first foal: dam unseated both starts in points: fairly useful handicap hurdler:
second at Sligo in August: stays 3m: acts on good to firm and heavy going: usually wears
tongue tie. *Patrick G. Kelly, Ireland*

DAWN'S LITTLE LADY 7 b.m. Dr Massini (IRE) – Kopylova (Moscow Society h–
(USA)) [2018/19 h–, b–: h18.5g h21.6gᵖᵘ Jul 6] no form in bumpers/over hurdles (lame
final outing). *Sarah Robinson*

DAWN SUNRISE (IRE) 6 ch.g. Mahler – Woodview Dawn (IRE) (Turtle Island (IRE)) h–
[2018/19 h19.5d h19.8sᵖᵘ h19.8g Mar 25] little impact in points/over hurdles. *Fiona Shaw*

DAWSON CITY 10 b.g. Midnight Legend – Running For Annie (Gunner B) [2018/19 c135
c132, h–: c28.4g² c32.4g⁵ c29.5s c30.7d* c34v⁵ c26g⁴ Apr 17] sturdy gelding: winning h–
hurdler: useful handicap chaser: won at Exeter (by 6 lengths from Dancing Shadow) in
February: out-and-out stayer: acts on heavy going: tried in cheekpieces. *Polly Gundry*

DAYBREAK BOY (IRE) 6 b.g. Kingsalsa (USA) – Aloisi (Kalanisi (IRE)) [2018/19 h126
h16g² h16g* h16d⁶ h19.5d* h20.3d Mar 15] half-brother to a winning hurdler in Australia
by Sinndar: useful on Flat, stays 13f: useful hurdler: won maiden at Navan in
September and minor event at Clonmel in January: stays 2½m: acts on soft going: usually
races prominently. *Henry de Bromhead, Ireland*

DAYDREAM AULMES (FR) 6 b.g. Linda's Lad – My Wish Aulmes (FR) (Lyphard's h121
Wish (FR)) [2018/19 b91: h15.7g⁴ h16s h16.2g⁶ h21d* h20.7d* h20.7d* h23.5d⁵ Feb 16]
lengthy gelding: runner-up in point: bumper winner: fairly useful handicap hurdler:
completed hat-trick at Warwick and Huntingdon (2) in December/January: threatening
when falling heavily 2 out at Ascot final outing: should stay beyond 21f: acts on good to
soft going: usually races towards rear/travels strongly. *Graeme McPherson*

DAYDREAM ISLAND (IRE) 9 b.g. Trans Island – Ring Hill (Bering) [2018/19 c70x, c62 x
h–: c24.1g⁴ c23.8g c20.1gᵖᵘ c23.8g⁴ c21.2mᵖᵘ c20gᵖᵘ Jul 10] strong gelding: maiden h–
hurdler: poor maiden handicap chaser: stays 3m: acts on heavy going: has worn headgear:
in tongue tie last 3 starts: prone to mistakes over fences. *Sheena Walton*

DAY IN PARADISE 8 b.m. Tobougg (IRE) – Sunnyland (Sovereign Water (FR)) **h–**
[2018/19 h67: h24g^{pu} Jun 25] little form over hurdles: dead. *Robert Stephens*

DAYLAMI KIRK (IRE) 8 b.g. Daylami (IRE) – Uptothefrontkirk (IRE) (Bob Back **c71**
(USA)) [2018/19 h74: h16m³ c20g^{pu} c17g c16g⁴ h21.4g Feb 27] tall, good-topped gelding: **h95**
modest form over hurdles: poor form over fences: left Ron Hodges after fourth start: best
effort at 2m: acts on good to firm going. *Paul Nicholls*

DAYLIGHT KATIE (FR) 6 b.m. Buonbon Rose (FR) – Sirani (FR) (Kapgarde (FR)) **b109**
[2018/19 b16d² b18g³ b17d* b17d³ Apr 4] €10,000 3-y-o, £110,000 4-y-o: smallish mare:
first foal: dam (h109), French maiden hurdler (stayed 19f), sister to fairly useful hurdler/
chaser (stayed 21f) Utopian: off mark in points on second attempt: useful form in bumpers:
won mares maiden at Gowran in February: placed after in Nickel Coin Mares' National
Hunt Flat Race at Aintree (2½ lengths behind The Glancing Queen) and EBF (Mares) INH
Flat Race at Punchestown, beaten 5 lengths by Gypsy Island at latter shortly after end of
British season: likely to stay at least 2½m: wears hood. *Gordon Elliott, Ireland*

DAY OF ROSES (IRE) 10 b.g. Acambaro (GER) – Dan's Choice (IRE) (Spanish Place **c98**
(USA)) [2018/19 c100, h–: c26v^{ro} c26d⁶ c19.2v^{pu} c27.5g* c26.2g⁴ Apr 26] maiden hurdler: **h–**
modest handicap chaser: won at Stratford in April: stays 3½m: acts on heavy going: hasn't
always looked straightforward (ran out on 2018/19 return). *Jeremy Scott*

DAYS OF HEAVEN (FR) 9 b.g. Saint des Saints (FR) – Daramour (FR) (Anabaa Blue) **c142**
[2018/19 c148, h–: c20g⁴ c21g^{pu} c21.4m h21d⁶ c21s* Apr 20] sturdy gelding: winning **h110**
hurdler: useful chaser: left Nicky Henderson after third start: won minor event at
Middleburg in April: stays 21f: acts on soft going: wears hood: signs of temperament (edgy
sort who has given trouble at start). *Jack O. Fisher, USA*

DAYTIME AHEAD (IRE) 8 gr.m. Daylami (IRE) – Bright Times Ahead (IRE) **h85**
(Rainbows For Life (CAN)) [2018/19 h109: h21.6v⁶ h21.2g Nov 15] fair handicap hurdler:
stays 2¾m: acts on heavy going: races towards rear. *Ron Hodges*

DEADLINE DIVA 4 b.f. Frankel – Hurry Home Hillary (USA) (Deputed Testamony **h111**
(USA)) [2018/19 h16.4g* h16g^F h16m h15.7m Mar 31] compact filly: fair on Flat in
France for N. Clement, stays 8.5f: fair form over hurdles: won newcomers race at Bordeaux
in September for Guillaume Macaire: well beaten both completed starts in Britain when
tongue tied. *Paul Nicholls*

DEADLY APPROACH 8 b.g. New Approach (IRE) – Speirbhean (IRE) (Danehill **c100**
(USA)) [2018/19 c111, h–: c16d^{ur} c16.3d³ c20d^{pu} c15.7s^{pu} c18.2d^{pu} Apr 4] maiden hurdler: **h–**
fair handicap chaser: raced mainly around 2m: acts on good to soft going: has worn
headgear, including last 4 starts: wears tongue tie: front runner. *Sarah-Jayne Davies*

DEADLY MOVE (IRE) 10 b.g. Scorpion (IRE) – Sounds Attractive (IRE) (Rudimentary **c96 §**
(USA)) [2018/19 c106§, h–: c21.6g^{pu} c19.4m³ c22.6m⁴ c25.8g^{pu} c25.5d⁵ c23.6s^{pu} Nov 7] **h–**
strong gelding: maiden hurdler: modest handicap chaser: stays 3m: acts on heavy going:
usually wears headgear: wears tongue tie: temperamental. *Peter Bowen*

DEADLY STING (IRE) 10 b.g. Scorpion (IRE) – Gaza Strip (IRE) (Hamas (IRE)) [2018/19 **c–**
c107, h–: c23.8m^{pu} Jan 17] lengthy gelding: has had breathing operation: little impact in 2 **h–**
points: winning hurdler: fairly useful chaser at one time, pulled up in hunter sole start in
2018/19: stays 23f: acts on heavy going: wears cheekpieces: in tongue tie last 5 starts. *Paul
H. Webb*

DEAD RIGHT 7 b.g. Alflora (IRE) – April Queen (Midnight Legend) [2018/19 h19g* **h120 p**
h19.9g* Apr 5] tall, useful-looking gelding: fairly useful form over hurdles: won novices
at Warwick in May and Sedgefield in April: will be suited by further than 2½m: open to
further improvement. *Neil Mulholland*

DEADRINGERFORLOVE 5 b.m. Black Sam Bellamy (IRE) – La Perrotine (FR) **h102 p**
(Northern Crystal) [2018/19 b16s⁴ b16d⁴ b15.7d h16d* Mar 21] good-topped mare: sixth **b88**
foal: closely related to bumper winner/fairly useful hurdler Scholastica (2m-2¾m winner,
by Old Vic) and half-sister to Cheltenham Gold Cup winner Sizing John (by Midnight
Legend): dam (h111) bumper/21f hurdle winner: fair form in bumpers: won mares novice
at Chepstow (by 3½ lengths from Fair Kate, readily) on hurdling debut: well held in listed
mares novice at Punchestown shortly after end of British season: will be suited by 2½m+:
remains open to improvement. *Harry Fry*

DEANS ROAD (IRE) 10 ch.g. Golan (IRE) – Close To Home (IRE) (Be My Native **c137**
(USA)) [2018/19 c138, h–p: c20g³ c16.7s^F c19.7s^{pu} Dec 27] workmanlike gelding: **h–**
winning hurdler: useful handicap chaser: third at Listowel (5¼ lengths behind Black
Scorpion) in September: likely to stay 3m: acts on heavy going: often races prominently.
Henry de Bromhead, Ireland

DEAR DORA (IRE) 5 gr.m. Dark Angel (IRE) – Lucky Flirt (USA) (Gulch (USA)) **b73**
[2018/19 b15.7g³ b16.2g Aug 18] £1,500 4-y-o: half-sister to several winners on Flat: dam
lightly raced on Flat in USA: poor form in bumpers. *Julia Brooke*

DEAR SIRE (FR) 7 gr.g. Al Namix (FR) – Polismith (FR) (Poliglote) [2018/19 h137: **c144**
h15.7g c21.2g* c21.2dᶠ c16.5g³ c16.4m* c15.9gᶠ Oct 26] tall gelding: useful hurdler: **h–**
similar form over fences: won maiden at Cartmel in July and novice at Sedgefield in
October: stays 21f: acts on soft and good to firm going: usually wears hood: usually races
prominently/travels strongly. *Donald McCain*

DEAUVILLE CRYSTAL (FR) 6 b.m. Raven's Pass (USA) – Top Crystal (IRE) **c129**
(Sadler's Wells (USA)) [2018/19 c112, h–: c23s* c23g* Jun 11] good-topped mare: has **h–**
had breathing operation: winning hurdler: fairly useful form over fences: won novices at
Worcester in May and Worcester in June: stays 3m: acts on heavy going: tried in visor:
wears tongue tie: usually races in mare. *Nigel Hawke*

DEAUVILLE DANCER (IRE) 8 b.g. Tamayuz – Mathool (IRE) (Alhaarth (IRE)) **c135**
[2018/19 c134, h100: c19.9g6 c21g5 c19.4g4 c20.5g4 c24g6 c20d4 c20.2g3 c20.2g* c21g2 **h–**
Apr 20] compact gelding: fair hurdler: useful handicap chaser: won at Kempton in
November and Wincanton in March: stays 21f: acts on heavy going: wears tongue tie.
David Dennis

DEBACLE 6 b.g. Bach (IRE) – De Blanc (IRE) (Revoque (IRE)) [2018/19 h–: h18.7g4 **c–**
h21.7m c25.7sᶠ c23.6gᶠ h23.8d Feb 20] sturdy gelding: poor form over hurdles: fell both **h72**
starts over fences: sometimes in headgear. *James Eustace*

DEBDEN BANK 5 b.g. Cacique (IRE) – Rose Row (Act One) [2018/19 b16.2s b16.3s **b–**
Mar 11] well held in 2 bumpers. *Martin Keighley*

DEBECE 8 b.g. Kayf Tara – Dalamine (FR) (Sillery (USA)) [2018/19 h137: h22.8gᶠ **c139**
c23.6d² c23.4g* c25.2g* c25g Apr 6] strong gelding: useful hurdler: similar form over **h–**
fences: won novices at Newcastle in January and Catterick in March: will stay 4m: acts on
soft going: front runner/races prominently. *Tim Vaughan*

DEBESTYMAN (IRE) 6 b.g. Mahler – Deise All Star (IRE) (Fourstars Allstar (USA)) **h113 p**
[2018/19 b17.7s5 b17.7s h20.5d4 h20.5s* Jan 16] £28,500 5-y-o: sturdy gelding: first foal: **b63**
dam winning pointer: off mark in Irish points at second attempt: poor form in bumpers: fair
form over hurdles: won novice at Plumpton in January: will stay 3m: remains open to
improvement. *Suzy Smith*

DEBROUILLARD (FR) 6 b.g. Irish Wells (FR) – Indecise (FR) (Cyborg (FR)) [2018/19 **h104**
b56: h19.7g6 h15.5d4 h20.8g4 h19.7g4 h21.3gᵖᵘ Apr 11] rather unfurnished gelding: fair
form over hurdles: best effort at 21f: wore hood in 2018/19. *Oliver Greenall*

DE BRUYNE HORSE 4 b.g. Showcasing – Right Rave (IRE) (Soviet Star (USA)) **h84**
[2018/19 h15.8g6 h17.7v5 h16s5 Dec 27] fairly useful on Flat, stays 7f: poor form over
hurdles: wears tongue tie: has joined Bernard Llewellyn. *Brendan Powell*

DEBT TO SOCIETY (IRE) 12 ch.g. Moscow Society (USA) – Nobody's Darling (IRE) **c– §**
(Supreme Leader) [2018/19 h24gᵖᵘ Aug 19] compact gelding: fair hurdler: pulled up sole **h– §**
start in 2018/19: winning chaser: stays 27f: acts on good to firm and heavy going: wears
headgear/tongue tie: unreliable. *Sam England*

DECEMBER SECOND (IRE) 5 b.g. Teofilo (IRE) – Bulbul (Shamardal (USA)) **b111**
[2018/19 b16m* Apr 13] £7,000 5-y-o: first foal: dam useful 6f winner: useful form in
bumpers: won at Ayr (by 3¾ lengths from Chess Player, impressively) on debut: 6 lengths
sixth of 10 to Colreevy in Champion INH Flat Race at Punchestown shortly after end of
British season. *Philip Kirby*

DECIMA (IRE) 5 b.m. Dream Ahead (USA) – Snowtime (IRE) (Galileo (IRE)) [2018/19 **h–**
h16.8sᵖᵘ Nov 2] fair on Flat, stays 11f: pulled up in novice on hurdling debut. *Michael
Easterby*

DECK OF CARDS (IRE) 7 br.g. Daylami (IRE) – Miss Edgehill (IRE) (Idris (IRE)) **h–**
[2018/19 b–: h16d May 30] workmanlike gelding: has had breathing operation: tailed off
in bumper/novice hurdle: pulled up all 3 starts in points. *Arthur Whiting*

DEDIGOUT (IRE) 13 b.g. Bob Back (USA) – Dainty Daisy (IRE) (Buckskin (FR)) **c–**
[2018/19 c–, h121: h24.1s Dec 8] big, deep-girthed gelding: high-class hurdler/smart **h–**
chaser at one time, no threat only start in 2018/19: stays 3m: acts on heavy going: wears
cheekpieces/tongue tie: signs of temperament. *Micky Hammond*

DE DOLLAR MAN (IRE) 8 ch.g. Vinnie Roe (IRE) – Dollar Bay (IRE) (Beau Sher) **c132**
[2018/19 c133, h–: c19.9d⁴ c18.8s^pu h16s^pu Feb 2] useful hurdler: useful chaser: fourth in **h–**
handicap at Newbury (2½ lengths behind Siruh du Lac) in November: stayed 2½m: acted
on heavy going: dead. *Evan Williams*

DEDUCE (FR) 6 b.m. Iffraaj – Count The Cost (USA) (Cozzene (USA)) [2018/19 h81: **h82**
h15.8g⁴ h16.7m^pu h21d^pu Nov 29] fair on Flat, stays 13.5f: poor maiden hurdler: tried in
tongue tie. *James Eustace*

DEEBAJ (IRE) 7 br.g. Authorized (IRE) – Athreyaa (Singspiel (IRE)) [2018/19 h109: **h118**
h16m h16v⁵ h19.5v* h23.3v³ h21m h21.7m² Mar 29] lengthy gelding: fairly useful
handicap hurdler: won at Lingfield in December: second at Fontwell in March: stays 23f:
acts on good to firm and heavy going: tried in visor/tongue tie: usually races off pace.
Gary Moore

DEEP RESOLVE (IRE) 8 b.g. Intense Focus (USA) – I'll Be Waiting (Vettori (IRE)) **h89**
[2018/19 h–: h15.8g h16.2g h15.8s⁴ h19.3s h20.6g³ Mar 20] modest handicap hurdler:
stays 21f: acts on heavy going. *Barry Leavy*

DEEPSAND (IRE) 10 br.g. Footstepsinthesand – Sinamay (USA) (Saint Ballado (CAN)) **h112**
[2018/19 h106: h16s⁶ h16.4d³ Mar 5] fair handicap hurdler: raced around 2m: acts on
heavy going: has worn headgear: wears tongue tie. *Lucinda Russell*

DEE STAR (IRE) 6 b.g. Shantou (USA) – Alicias Lady (IRE) (Bob Back (USA)) **h100**
[2018/19 b15.8g⁵ b16.3g⁵ h19.9g h24g⁴ h19.6g⁴ h23.3g h23.1s Dec 6] £12,000 4-y-o: first **b–**
foal: dam, lightly raced in points, out of sister to Grand National winner Royal Athlete: off
mark in points at fourth attempt: behind in bumpers/over hurdles: tried in cheekpieces.
Gary Hanmer

DEEWHY (IRE) 6 b.g. Papal Bull – Chanteuse de Rue (IRE) (Street Cry (IRE)) [2018/19 **h–**
h15.9s h20d^pu Mar 4] little impact in 2 novice hurdles. *Linda Jewell*

DEFI BLEU (FR) 6 b.g. Saddler Maker (IRE) – Glycine Bleue (FR) (Le Nain Jaune (FR)) **h139**
[2018/19 h16.5g² h20d* h20d³ h24s² h22g h20.3d³ Mar 15] €255,000 3-y-o: fourth foal:
half-brother to 3 winners, including useful hurdler/smart chaser Upsilon Bleu (2m-2½m
winner, by Panoramic): dam French 2½m-23f chase winner: runner-up in maiden point on
debut: bumper winner: useful hurdler: won maiden at Navan in November: placed in
Navan Novices' Hurdle and Grade 2 novice at Limerick in December, and Martin Pipe
Conditional Jockeys' Handicap Hurdle at Cheltenham in March: struck into himself at
Punchestown shortly after end of British season and will reportedly miss 2019/20 season:
stays 3m: acts on soft going: usually races prominently. *Gordon Elliott, Ireland*

DEFI DU SEUIL (FR) 6 b.g. Voix du Nord (FR) – Quarvine du Seuil (FR) (Lavirco **c164 p**
(GER)) [2018/19 h126: c15.9g⁵ c19.2s* c20.6d² c20s* c19.8d* Mar 14] **h–**

The 16/1 triumph of five-year-old Espoir d'Allen gave J. P. McManus his
eighth Champion Hurdle win in a renewal in which the same owner's Buveur d'Air
was a faller, foiled in his own attempt to win the championship for the third time.
Espoir d'Allen was the first of his age to win the race since Katchit eleven years
earlier, a record illustrating the uphill work that leading juveniles can face when
they come up against older opposition the following season. McManus himself had
had the experience the previous year with Defi du Seuil who had been unbeaten in
seven starts over hurdles as a juvenile, most notably landing the Triumph Hurdle/
Anniversary Hurdle double to establish himself as the clear leader of the four-year-
old generation.

Any hopes that Defi du Seuil might follow in the footsteps of Katchit (who
had landed the same double after a full juvenile campaign) by winning the
Champion Hurdle were dashed when he was seen out only twice in his second
season over hurdles (managing only fourth when odds-on for the Coral Hurdle at
Ascot and beating just one home behind Supasundae in the Irish Champion Hurdle).
Unlike Katchit, a Flat racer with lots of experience before being sent hurdling, Defi
du Seuil emanated from 'French bumpers', in which sphere he won the second of
his two starts for Emmanuel Clayeux before being purchased to join the McManus
battalions and sent into training with Philip Hobbs. Being a purpose-bred jumper
with an AQPS (other than thoroughbred) pedigree, Defi du Seuil was almost certainly
bought more with a chasing career in mind. A lengthy gelding with the size to make
a chaser (Katchit was only small), Defi du Seuil was put over fences in the latest
season and made a fine job of restoring his reputation by establishing himself as one

888Sport Scilly Isles Novices' Chase, Sandown—Defi du Seuil (hoops) reverses Dipper placings with Lostintranslation (right) back off level weights; the hitherto unbeaten Vinndication is back in third

of the best of the British-trained novice chasers, improving with virtually every race and being unlucky to catch a tartar in the shape of Chacun Pour Soi when trying to complete a Cheltenham Festival/Punchestown double in the Ryanair Novices' Chase at Ireland's big spring festival in May, shortly after the end of the British season (hence the absence of a form figure for that performance in the summary in the second line of this essay).

Defi du Seuil's debut over the larger obstacles gave no real clue that he would end up so near to the top of the tree in his new discipline. He seemed to lack confidence, making several mistakes including a particularly awkward leap at the last, when last of five behind Lalor in the November Novices' Chase at Cheltenham. If Lalor was the one that took the eye on that occasion, looking a likely contender even at such an early stage for the Arkle at the Festival, it didn't take long for Defi du Seuil to begin staking his own claims. Starting at 9/1, he looked a totally different proposition when winning the fairly valuable Heavitree Brewery Novices' Chase at Exeter in early-December, jumping much better and beating the 6/4 joint favourites Topofthegame and Black Op, two other smart recruits from hurdling, with something in hand by three and a half lengths and three quarters of a length. Back at Cheltenham on New Year's Day for the Dipper Novices' Chase, Defi du Seuil coped much better with the fences on the New Course than he had with those on the Old one on his debut. He looked sure to win when in control at the last (trading at 1.01 on the Betfair Exchange) but was headed in the final hundred yards by the rallying Lostintranslation who beat him by a length and a quarter, with Black Op a further six lengths back in third. Defi du Seuil wasn't found wanting for stamina in the Dipper over an extended two and a half miles and talk of his Cheltenham Festival target began to centre on the Golden Miller, rather than the Arkle. Before that, Defi du Seuil took his revenge on Lostintranslation when the pair met in the Grade 1 888Sport Scilly Isles Novices' Chase over two and a half miles at Sandown in early-February. Defi du Seuil had conceded 3 lb to his rival in the Dipper and at level weights he was entitled to turn the tables, which he did by three quarters of a length after taking the lead under pressure early on the run-in and being ridden right out, Lostintranslation finishing two and a half lengths ahead of third-placed Vinndication who started favourite.

The first three in the Scilly Isles Novices' Chase were among the home defence in the Golden Miller against a four-strong Irish challenge (three from the Mullins stable and Mengli Khan trained by Gordon Elliott). The Golden Miller, branded and more widely referred to nowadays as the JLT Novices' Chase, had its seventh running as a Grade 1 after being fast-tracked to championship status in only its third year in 2013. Vautour has been the outstanding winner in the race's relatively short history, in which Irish stables provided seven of the first eight winners. There are now five novice chases at the Cheltenham Festival meeting and the Golden Miller's intermediate distance and its Grade 1 status means that it tends to draw

JLT Novices' Chase (Golden Miller), Cheltenham—the rivals dominate once more as Defi du Seuil (hoops) again reels in Lostintranslation; Mengli Khan fares best of the Irish contingent in third

runners from both the Arkle and the 'novices' Gold Cup', the RSA Chase, the two long-standing Grade 1s for novice chasers at the meeting. The strength in depth of the three Grade 1s was less noticeably affected than it has been in some years, with all three races for the latest renewals attracting double-figure fields, though subsequent events did show that Defi du Seuil and Lostintranslation were significant losses from the fields for the Arkle and the RSA Chase respectively. As it was, the pair dominated the Golden Miller, Defi du Seuil taking his 'match' score with Lostintranslation to two-one. Heading the betting at 3/1 and 4/1 respectively, with Vinndication and the principal Mullins contender Real Steel next at 11/2 and 13/2, Defi du Seuil and Lostintranslation were separated by two and a quarter lengths at the line, clear of the rest, with the patiently-ridden Defi du Seuil showing the better turn of foot after challenging the sound-jumping front-running Lostintranslation at the final fence. Mengli Khan, third in the previous year's Supreme Novices' Hurdle, held every chance two out but was eventually beaten a further seven lengths into third in the Golden Miller, with the Timeform Novices' Handicap winner Kildisart fourth, Vinndication fifth (initially ruled out of the Festival before pleasing connections at home) and Real Steel sixth.

After a blank on the second day, Defi du Seuil was the second winner at the meeting for his owner J.P. McManus, following Espoir d'Allen. Sire du Berlais and Any Second Now went on to complete a treble in the famous emerald green, yellow hoops after Defi du Seuil's win, taking the Pertemps Final and the Fulke Walwyn Kim Muir Challenge Cup. Victory for Early Doors in the final race of the meeting on Friday, the Martin Pipe Conditional Jockeys' Handicap Hurdle, meant that J.P. McManus enjoyed five winners at the Cheltenham Festival for the third time, following his five-timers in 2012 and 2016 (on the last occasion following the very late promotion of Josies Orders in the Cross Country Chase). The Riccis had five winners at the 2016 Cheltenham Festival and they shared the Festival record for an owner with McManus until Gigginstown House Stud set a new mark with seven wins in 2018. The Cheltenham Festival has always been the highlight of the racing year for J.P. McManus who has now extended his record number of victories there to fifty-nine. A legendary high roller, McManus admits that his tilts in the betting ring have become less frequent over time. The enormous gamble on his first Festival winner, Mister Donovan in the Sun Alliance Novices' Hurdle in 1982, is said to have netted £250,000 and came at a time when his owner's fortunes were suffering badly, McManus admitting in an interview with the *Racing Post* in the latest season that 'But for Mister Donovan there might not have been any other horses or gambles, it was sink or swim day.' The McManus duels with the likes of Michael Simmonds of Heathorns and Scottish bookmaker Freddie Williams have entered the folklore of the Cheltenham betting ring, Williams' daughter reminiscing before the latest Festival (after she had sold the pitch she had operated since her father's death) about

Mr John P. McManus' "Defi du Seuil"

the Thursday of the Festival in 2006 when they laid McManus £100,000 at 6/1 about Reveillez and then £5,000 each-way on 50/1-shot Kadoun, the two wins costing Williams £900,000 after which ironically he was the victim of an armed robbery on his way back from the races, a robbery that would doubtless have been more lucrative for the perpetrators on almost any other day! 'Back then, the market was very strong and you could get on whatever you wanted with bookmakers who had their own opinions and would stand behind them, but those days are long gone,' said McManus who labels betting 'a young man's game'.

The huge McManus string of jumpers is spread around trainers in Britain and Ireland and, although he had to settle for second behind Gigginstown for the fifth season running in the owners' table in Ireland, he was leading owner in Britain for the twelfth time, with first three earnings of £1,991,604, over twice the total of his nearest rivals Simon Munir and Isaac Souede who were runners-up to him for the third year in succession. Defi du Seuil and Sire du Berlais were ridden at Cheltenham, by the way, by Barry Geraghty who rode his first Festival winner back in 2002 (Moscow Flyer in the Arkle) and went on to become the first jockey to ride winners of the four major championship events, the Champion Hurdle, the Queen Mother Champion Chase, the Stayers' Hurdle and the Gold Cup. Geraghty moved into fourth place in the latest season in the all-time list of top jump jockeys in Britain and Ireland, behind only Sir Anthony McCoy, Richard Johnson and Ruby Walsh. Geraghty was sidelined for the rest of the season after being injured in a fall in the Topham Chase at Aintree's Grand National meeting and Richard Johnson stood in for him on Defi du Seuil in the two-mile Ryanair Novices' Chase (there is no equivalent of the Golden Miller at the Punchestown Festival). The Arkle winner

Duc des Genievres was a second Grade 1 Cheltenham Festival winner in the Ryanair line-up but Defi du Seuil would have run out a comfortable winner (Duc des Genievres finished sixteen lengths down in third) had it not been for the unexposed Chacun Pour Soi who produced a devastating performance to prevent Defi du Seuil, who needed no excuses on the day for his four and a quarter length defeat, from joining Klassical Dream and Minella Indo as Cheltenham winners following up at Punchestown (nine Cheltenham winners made the attempt). Defi du Seuil was hampered briefly by a loose horse before the second last but it made no difference to the result, as he was outpaced by the winner late on after rallying to challenge at the last.

Defi du Seuil (FR) (b.g. 2013)	Voix du Nord (FR) (b 2001)	Valanour (b 1992)	Lomond / Vearia
		Dame Edith (b 1995)	Top Ville / Girl of France
	Quarvine du Seuil (FR) (b 2004)	Lavirco (bl or br 1993)	Konigsstuhl / La Virginia
		Fleur du Tennis (b 1993)	Video Rock / Via Tennise

Defi du Seuil's pedigree and background were covered in the essay on him in *Chasers & Hurdlers 2016/17*. More can be found about his now-deceased sire Voix du Nord in the entries on Espoir d'Allen and Kemboy, whose achievements in the latest season further emphasise Voix du Nord's loss to French jumping breeders. Defi du Seuil's dam Quarvine du Seuil won AQPS races on the Flat at a mile and a quarter and a mile and a half. Defi du Seuil's grandam Fleur du Tennis, who won six times on the Flat and finished second on her only start over hurdles, is a sister to the Reynoldstown Chase winner Jimmy Tennis and has produced numerous winners. Defi du Seuil, who often travels strongly, stays twenty-one furlongs and acts on soft going. He wore a hood in the parade ring before the Golden Miller. He will progress further as a chaser and should bridge the gap to open Grade 1 company in the next season. *Philip Hobbs*

DEFINATELY VINNIE 9 ch.g. Vinnie Roe (IRE) – Sohapara (Arapahos (FR)) [2018/19 **c96** h99: c23s⁴ c26.1g⁶ c26.2g⁶ c25.2sᵖᵘ c23.6d² c23.6d h26gᵘʳ c27.5g⁵ Apr 14] modest hurdler/ **h–** maiden chaser: stays 3¼m: acts on soft going: tried in blinkers. *Jane Mathias*

DEFINITELYANOSCAR (IRE) 6 b.m. Oscar (IRE) – Bobs Article (IRE) (Definite **h118** Article) [2018/19 b101: h19.5dᶠ h15.8g² h16d* h20.3sᵖᵘ h15.8d³ Mar 21] off mark in points at third attempt: bumper winner: fairly useful form over hurdles: won mares maiden at Warwick in November: second in similar event at Ludlow earlier in month: should stay 2½m: acts on good to soft going. *Harry Fry*

DEFINITE RIDGE (IRE) 12 ch.g. Definite Article – Do The Right Thing (Busted) **c65** [2018/19 h21.6g⁶ c22.6m⁴ Aug 2] workmanlike gelding: poor handicap hurdler/chaser: **h62** stays 3¼m: acts on soft and good to firm going: wears headgear: hard to catch right. *Alexandra Dunn*

DEFINITE WINNER (IRE) 8 b.m. Definite Article – Sindabezi (IRE) (Magical Strike **h87** (USA)) [2018/19 h–: h23s h21.6g h19.9g h23mᶠ h18.5mᵘʳ h19.8g* h19d³ h19.9s Dec 11] sturdy mare: has had breathing operation: modest handicap hurdler: standout effort when winning at Wincanton in November: stays 2½m: wears tongue tie. *Katy Price*

DEFINITE WISDOM (IRE) 6 b.g. Definite Article – Wisdom And Light (IRE) **h93** (Alderbrook) [2018/19 h16.2s h16.2g⁶ h24.3v⁴ h19.7s Dec 26] €22,000 3-y-o, £35,000 4-y-o: dam, little impact in points, half-sister to fairly useful chaser (stayed 2½m) Definite Dream (by Definite Article): runner-up on second start in Irish points: modest form over hurdles. *Rose Dobbin*

DEFINITELY GREY (IRE) 8 gr.g. Daylami (IRE) – Caroline Fontenail (IRE) **c–** (Kaldounevees (FR)) [2018/19 c114, h–: c24.5gᵖᵘ c26.1gᵖᵘ c24g⁵ h25g Oct 16] good- **h–** topped gelding: fair hurdler/chaser at best, no form in 2018/19: tried in headgear: wears tongue tie. *Charlie Longsdon*

DEFINITLY RED (IRE) 10 ch.g. Definite Article – The Red Wench (IRE) (Aahsaylad) **c163** [2018/19 c164, h–: c24.2g* c25s* c23.4g² c26.3dᵇᵈ Mar 15] sturdy gelding: winning **h–** hurdler: high-class chaser: won Charlie Hall Chase at Wetherby (by 2 lengths from Black Corton) in November and Many Clouds Chase at Aintree (by 4½ lengths from Double Shuffle) in December, both 4-runner events: should stay beyond 3¼m: acts on heavy going: front runner/races prominently. *Brian Ellison*

DEFI SACRE (FR) 6 b.g. Network (GER) – Iowa Sacree (FR) (Trebrook (FR)) [2018/19 **c–** h16.6g³ h19.4g⁵ h16.3d⁵ h19.9d h20.2g⁴ Apr 25] good-topped gelding: has had breathing **h113** operation: half-brother to several winners in France, including 17f-21f hurdle/chase winners Siowa Sacree (by Fragrant Mix) and Printemps Sacre (by Ragmar): dam, French 17f-21f hurdle/chase winner, half-sister to fair hurdler/fairly useful chaser (stayed 21f) Gazump: fair form over hurdles: won first of 2 starts over fences in France: stays 21f: acts on soft going: usually wears tongue tie: usually races close up. *Richard Hobson*

DE FORGOTTEN ONE 5 b.g. Malinas (GER) – As Was (Epalo (GER)) [2018/19 **h113** b15.7d⁶ h20.8g* h19.4g⁴ h21.3g⁶ Apr 11] third foal: half-brother to useful chaser The Two **b83** Amigos (3¼m-31f winner, by Midnight Legend): dam unraced half-sister to useful French hurdler/fairly useful chaser (17f-21f winner) Line Salsa: won Irish point on debut: promise when sixth in bumper at Ascot: fair form over hurdles: won maiden at Doncaster in January: likely to stay 2¾m+: tried in hood. *Tim Vaughan*

DE GOOD MAN LUKE (FR) 6 b.g. Noroit (GER) – Inedite II (FR) (Roi de Rome **h–** (USA)) [2018/19 b16.3s⁴ h21gᵖᵘ h16.7d Apr 26] €10,000 3-y-o: sixth foal: closely related **b82** to French hurdler/chaser Bouchat (17f-19f winner, by Network) and half-brother to 2 winners in France, including 17f/2¼m chase winner Saboum (by Robin des Champs): dam French 19f-21f chase winner: pulled up in Irish point: fourth in maiden bumper at Stratford: no threat both starts over hurdles: left Olly Murphy after second start. *Jake Thomas Coulson*

DEISE ABA (IRE) 6 b.g. Mahler – Kit Massini (IRE) (Dr Massini (IRE)) [2018/19 **h121 p** h19.5s* h19.3d⁴ h23.6d⁴ Mar 21] £66,000 5-y-o: tall, rather unfurnished gelding: third foal: dam, ran once in point, half-sister to fairly useful chaser (stayed 25f) Ibetellingyoualie: won Irish point over hurdles: fairly useful form over hurdles: won maiden at Chepstow in November: wears hood: remains open to improvement. *Philip Hobbs*

DEISE BLESS (IRE) 6 b.m. Scorpion (IRE) – Nighty Bless (IRE) (Executive Perk) **h79** [2018/19 b16d h16d h20.7gᵖᵘ h16d h20.6g⁴ Mar 14] half-sister to useful hurdler/chaser Sutton **b–** Manor (2¼m-3m winner, by Gold Well) and smart bumper winner Relic Rock (by Bienamado): dam unraced: unplaced in Irish point on debut: well beaten in mares bumper: poor form over hurdles: usually wears hood. *Kelly Morgan*

bet365 Charlie Hall Chase, Wetherby—the smallest field since 2000 helps Definitly Red go two places better than in 2017; Black Corton chases him home

DEISE VU (IRE) 11 b.g. Brian Boru – Deise Dreamer (IRE) (Beneficial) [2018/19 c100, **c106 §**
h–: c17m^{pu} c16.5g^{pu} c16.5g^6 c17g^2 c15.7g^{ur} c17g^2 c16g* c15.7g* c15.7s^3 Mar 18] maiden **h–**
hurdler: fair handicap chaser: won at Hereford in November and Southwell in March:
unproven beyond 17f: acts on heavy going: wears cheekpieces: tried in tongue tie: usually
leads: one to treat with caution. *Roy Brotherton*

DEJA BOUGG 8 b.m. Tobougg (IRE) – La Riveraine (USA) (Riverman (USA)) [2018/19 **h– x**
h105x: h21.9g^5 Apr 21] fair hurdler, well held sole start in 2018/19: stays 23f: acts on good
to firm and heavy going: usually in tongue tie: often let down by jumping. *Johnny Farrelly*

DEJA VUE (IRE) 5 b.m. Fame And Glory – Westgrove Berry (IRE) (Presenting) **h80 p**
[2018/19 h17.7v^5 Feb 14] €15,000 3-y-o, £82,000 4-y-o: fifth foal: half-sister to useful
hurdler/chaser Jetstream Jack (19f-23f winner, by Beneficial) and fair hurdler Nendrum
(2m winner, by Westerner), stayed 2½m: dam (h113), bumper/2m hurdle winner, half-sister
to useful hurdler/smart chaser (stays 3¼m) Mendip Express: won Irish point on debut:
11/4, fifth in mares novice at Fontwell (29½ lengths behind The Cull Bank) on hurdling
debut: better to come. *Anthony Honeyball*

DELAYED REACTION 7 b.m. Black Sam Bellamy (IRE) – J'arrive (Generous (IRE)) **h–**
[2018/19 b–: b15.8g b16g^4 h18.5g h19.2g^{pu} Jun 16] no form in bumpers/over hurdles. **b–**
Peter Hedger

DELEGATE 9 ch.g. Robin des Champs (FR) – As You Leave (FR) (Kaldounevees (FR)) **c116**
[2018/19 c135, h100: c20m^2 c20.3d^3 Apr 9] has had breathing operation: winning hurdler: **h–**
useful chaser: second in hunter at Ludlow in April: stays 21f: acts on good to firm
and heavy going: in cheekpieces last 2 starts: usually wears tongue tie: usually races close
up. *J. T. Guerriero*

DELFACE (FR) 6 b.g. Della Francesca (USA) – Septieme Face (USA) (Lit de Justice **h110**
(USA)) [2018/19 h108: h15.8m^6 h20g^6 h16.5d^6 h19.9v^3 h15.8s* h15.8v^2 h15.8s^3 h16g*
Apr 26] has had breathing operation: fair handicap hurdler: won at Uttoxeter in December
and Chepstow in April: stays 2½m: acts on heavy going: wears headgear: has worn tongue
tie: usually races prominently. *David Pipe*

DELIGHTFUL DAME (USA) 5 b.m. Lonhro (AUS) – Delighted (IRE) (Danehill **h81**
(USA)) [2018/19 b16g h16g h18.8g^5 h21g^{ur} h16.8m^6 Sep 6] half-sister to 3 winners on Flat **b–**
by Elusive Quality, including useful 6f winner Absent Pleasure: dam lightly raced on Flat:
tailed off in bumper: poor form over hurdles: in cheekpieces last 4 starts: wears tongue tie.
John Joseph Hanlon, Ireland

DELINEATE (IRE) 10 b.m. Definite Article – New Line (IRE) (Roselier (FR)) [2018/19 **c–**
c23.8d^6 Feb 6] point winner: maiden hurdler: tailed off in hunter on chasing debut. **h–**
Wyn Morris

DELIRANT (FR) 6 b.g. Khalkevi (IRE) – Kusea (FR) (Useful (FR)) [2018/19 h16.7g^4 **h101 p**
h18.5g* Aug 15] has had breathing operation: half-brother to several winners in France,
including 2½m chase winner Trotot (by Sleeping Car) and 17f hurdle winner Quimperial
(by April Night): dam, French 1½m/13f bumper winner, half-sister to fairly useful French
cross-country chaser Chriseti: won both starts in French bumpers in 2016/17,
including Group 1: fair form over hurdles: in hood, easily won maiden at Newton Abbot in
August: in tongue tie last 2 starts: should progress further. *David Pipe*

DELIRE D'ESTRUVAL (FR) 6 b.g. Youmzain (IRE) – Question d'Estruval (FR) **c136**
(Phantom Breeze) [2018/19 c–, h129: c15.9g* c16.4d^4 c20.5g c16.3g^2 c20s* Mar 9] sturdy **h–**
gelding: fairly useful hurdler: useful chaser: won maiden at Carlisle in October and novice
handicap at Sandown (by ¾ length from Volt Face) in March: stays 2½m: acts on heavy
going: in blinkers last 2 starts. *Ben Pauling*

DELIRIOUS LOVE (IRE) 7 b.g. Definite Article – Grangeclare Lark (IRE) (Old Vic) **h101**
[2018/19 b67: h16m^{ur} h20.3g^3 h17.7m^4 h15.7g^3 h16g^4 h20.3g^3 h21.4g h16.7g h21.2m
Apr 23] has had breathing operation: fair maiden hurdler: stays 2½m: acts on good to firm
going: has worn hood: wears tongue tie. *Graeme McPherson*

DELIVERANCE 4 b.g. Havana Gold (IRE) – Tentpole (USA) (Rainbow Quest (USA)) **h–**
[2018/19 h15.9g Sep 23] fair maiden on Flat, stays 1m: well beaten in juvenile on hurdling
debut. *Alexandra Dunn*

DELIVERINGPROMISES (IRE) 7 b.g. Oscar (IRE) – Monanore Music (IRE) (Needle **b–**
Gun (IRE)) [2018/19 b15.7g b16g^5 Jun 11] fell in point: little form in bumpers: tried in
tongue tie. *Joanne Thomason-Murphy*

DELL' ARCA (IRE) 10 b.g. Sholokhov (IRE) – Daisy Belle (GER) (Acatenango (GER)) **c140**
[2018/19 c139, h140: c25.8g⁴ h23.3s* c24s⁴ c25g h23.9g c27.3s³ c34vᵖᵘ Mar 16] **h141**
leggy gelding: useful handicap hurdler: won at Uttoxeter (by 5 lengths from Mr McGuiness)
in July: useful handicap chaser: fourth in Kerry National at Listowel (4¾ lengths behind
Snow Falcon) in September: stays 27f: acts on good to firm and heavy going: wears
headgear/tongue tie. *David Pipe*

DELLA SUN (FR) 13 b.g. Della Francesca (USA) – Algarve Sunrise (IRE) (Highest **c–**
Honor (FR)) [2018/19 h20g² h20gᵖᵘ Oct 11] workmanlike gelding: modest handicap hurdler **h94**
nowadays: once-raced over fences: stays 2½m: acts on firm and soft going: has worn
headgear. *Arthur Whitehead*

DELL ORO (FR) 6 b.g. Walk In The Park (IRE) – Kallistea (FR) (Sicyos (USA)) [2018/19 **c140**
h133: c18g² c20.5g⁴ c19.9g* c20sᵖᵘ c15.5d³ c20.2sᵖᵘ c16m³ Apr 1] tall gelding: useful **h–**
hurdler: useful handicap chaser: won novice event at Huntingdon in January: stays 21f:
acts on good to firm going: in headgear last 2 starts: temperament under suspicion. *Gary
Moore*

DELTA ROSE (IRE) 5 br.m. Robin des Champs (FR) – Cruising Katie (IRE) (Beneficial) **b72**
[2018/19 b16.3d Mar 1] €34,000 3-y-o: sturdy mare: second foal: dam fair hurdler/useful
chaser (2m-2½m winner): 16/1, seventh in mares bumper at Newbury. *Nick Gifford*

DELTA WORK (FR) 6 br.g. Network (GER) – Robbe (FR) (Video Rock (FR)) **c163 p**
[2018/19 h150: c19.5g* c20g* c24g* c24.4s³ Mar 13] **h–**

The essay on Delta Work in *Chasers & Hurdlers 2017/18* began with a
paragraph extolling the 'brave new world of outspoken sports broadcasting', quoting
examples from football and cricket of stinging criticism meted out by analysts Gary
Neville and Michael Vaughan, both of whom have made a successful switch to the
commentary box after being at the top of their respective sports and playing for their
country. The essay went on to comment on the fact that the same outspokenness
has not extended to horse racing, in which the participants are largely sheltered
from criticism nowadays, the defence of the ride by Barry Geraghty on the unlucky
Glenloe in the Pertemps Final by ex-jockey pundits Luke Harvey and Sir Anthony
McCoy quoted as an example. Matt Chapman, who now fills the role of bellowing
betting ring reporter for ITV, had broken ranks by suggesting that Geraghty should
have won by kicking for home earlier to nullify the risk of a mistake at the last
(Glenloe was travelling best when clouting the last where Delta Work took the lead
and went on to get the better of his rallying stablemate in a photo-finish).

The role now filled by Chapman was pioneered by another forceful
personality, John McCririck, who died in July 2019 at the age of seventy-nine.
Outspokenness in sports commentators, however, can be a two-edged sword,
balancing, on the one hand, the duty to raise matters that the watching audience
might find pertinent, while, on the other, being aware that criticism, particularly
if it is extreme and possibly unfair, can affect the livelihood of the person being
criticised. McCririck, with his deerstalker hat and mutton-chop whiskers, was never
afraid of expressing an opinion and became an instantly recognised public figure
thanks largely to the role he cultivated on television as a colourful, tic-tac waving
reporter ('Burlington Bertie', 100/30; 'Double Carpet', 33/1) in the 'betting jungle',
to use a phrase he himself coined. Over the years, he gradually became the 'face
of racing', called on by media outlets for an instant soundbite when racing issues
made the general news. 'Big Mac's' views did not always coincide with those of
the mainstream within the sport and he could be bombastic (as illustrated by his
remarks, quoted in the essay on Delta Work in last year's Annual, after widespread
criticism of Paul Carberry's ride on Harchibald in the 2005 Champion Hurdle).
McCririck was, however, a noted champion of the punter and a passionate supporter
of horse welfare (he wanted to ban the whip). His journalistic background included
winning awards in the 'seventies as specialist and campaigning journalist of the year
when he was with *The Sporting Life* (his work including the discovery that the Tote
was cooking its books in order to reduce payouts to winning punters, which led to
the Home Secretary at the time setting up an inquiry which almost led to the Tote's
chairman, Woodrow Wyatt, losing his job).

McCririck worked in his days at Channel 4 with a number of ex-performers in the sport who had taken up the microphone after hanging up their boots and saddles, and his journalistic insight often set him apart. He was frequently the pundit who asked the most pertinent questions, his thorough preparation—he always arrived for work with reams of notes—showing in his performances. 'My thought was always,' he said, 'to think about the viewer at home and what he might like to know, what bit of information from the racecourse might give him an insight.' Sadly, McCririck's reputation within racing suffered as his performances tended to become more eccentric, and his popularity in the corridors of power was affected by some demeaning appearances on reality TV programmes. He eventually found himself dropped in 2013 by Channel 4, against whom he took legal action claiming that he was a victim of age discrimination. When the case finally came to a tribunal, McCririck lost, the judgement concluding that the broadcaster was within its rights to sack him to avoid Channel 4 Racing being tarnished by 'his boorish, obnoxious and sexist' public image which was said to be putting off viewers. Ironically, viewing figures for Channel 4 Racing dropped—by up to a quarter, reportedly—when he was taken off, but he was never invited back and was largely ostracised by other media outlets on which he had sometimes appeared. He suffered poor health in his last few years when he claimed to have 'no purpose in life.'

'Come racing' was the evangelistic rallying cry of John McCririck to his TV audience and, as the growing attendances at the sport's major festivals testify, there are thousands who wouldn't trade a spot in the grandstand for keynote races at Cheltenham, Aintree or Punchestown in exchange for an armchair in front of the TV at home. Even in the harshest weather, it is a stirring feeling to be present on one of jumping's big days. Not even an overnight warning that racing might be cancelled on the Wednesday of the Festival meeting at Cheltenham because of high winds could deter a crowd of 59,209 (Wednesday's crowd is traditionally the smallest for the four days, as it was in the latest season when 71,849 packed in for the Gold Cup on Friday). Racing went ahead on the Wednesday after the course passed an 8am inspection, with the winds not so dangerous as forecast, and the main attraction—Altior's attempt to win his second Queen Mother Champion Chase and extend his

baroneracing.com Drinmore Novices' Chase, Fairyhouse—two of the best novice chasers of 2018/19, Delta Work and Le Richebourg (hoops), serve up a good finish

Dooley Insurance Group Champion Novices' Chase (Ellier), Punchestown—
Delta Work is more fluent than at Cheltenham and registers a most impressive win over
Discorama (virtually hidden) and A Plus Tard

winning sequence to a record-equalling eighteen—was supported superbly by Tiger Roll's runaway performance in the Cross Country Chase (both horses winning for the fourth time at the Festival). From the purists' point of view, however, perhaps the most satisfying race of the day was the RSA Insurance Novices' Chase, the race known colloquially as 'the novices' Gold Cup'. The race was widely expected to feature a close battle between Ireland's Delta Work, a stablemate of Tiger Roll and unbeaten over fences, and his two main British-trained rivals Santini and Topofthegame. The RSA did not disappoint with the trio that dominated the betting pulling well clear of their rivals, proving themselves well up to standard for the race and looking major contenders for top honours in the championship staying chases in the next season.

Topofthegame came out on top at Cheltenham from Santini and Delta Work, the distances only half a length and a length and three quarters (with Mister Malarky sixteen lengths further back in fourth). Connections of Delta Work will entertain hopes of turning the tables on the winner and runner-up another day, especially after his imperious twelve-length victory in the Dooley Insurance Group-sponsored Champion Novices' Chase (registered as the Ellier), the Grade 1 for staying novices at the Punchestown Festival, which took place shortly after the end of the British season. Delta Work resumed winning ways in exemplary fashion, jumping much more fluently than he had at Cheltenham where he made a couple of noticeable jumping errors. Taking over three out, Delta Work readily drew clear between the last two fences at Punchestown to win with plenty in hand from Discorama, narrowly beaten in the National Hunt Chase at Cheltenham, and A Plus Tard, who had won the novices' handicap chase at the same festival by sixteen lengths. It was a top-notch performance, one good enough, the way Timeform reads the form-book, to establish Delta Work as the season's leading staying novice chaser, ahead of Topofthegame, Santini and the Mildmay Novices' Chase winner Lostintranslation, all four of them giving the impression there is even better to come.

Delta Work's victory at Punchestown took his record over fences to four wins from five starts. The first of his three wins before Cheltenham was achieved in a maiden chase at Down Royal in November, when he had to scrap to beat Niven and Ben Dundee over two and a half miles, a distance which looked a bare minimum for him at the time. Delta Work left that form well behind, however, when beating Le Richebourg narrowly in the Grade 1 baroneracing.com Drinmore Novices' Chase over the same trip at Fairyhouse the following month. Delta Work won despite an uncharacteristic blunder at the last (he jumped well otherwise) which resulted in his rider losing an iron. Rallying well after losing the lead to Le Richebourg, Delta Work got back up on the run-in to win by half a length, the pair stretching eight lengths clear of third-placed Jetz, with Cadmium and Discorama fourth and fifth in a race that wasn't run at an end-to-end gallop. Delta Work still looked likely to benefit from a return to three miles—the distance of the War of Attrition Novices' Hurdle in which he had gone close, showing smart form, after winning the Pertemps Final—and he started at 15/8-on for the Grade 1 Neville Hotels Novices' Chase (registered

Gigginstown House Stud's "Delta Work"

as the Fort Leney) over the longer trip at Leopardstown's Christmas meeting. The Drinmore form had been given a boost when Le Richebourg won the Grade 1 Racing Post Novices' Chase at the meeting three days earlier, and Delta Work did his bit to advertise the Fairyhouse form with a straightforward eight-length victory from Mortal (who went on to finish fifth in the RSA). Mortal was upsides Delta Work at the last when he made a mistake but Delta Work's strong finish showed that he would still have won decisively even if Mortal had not made a hash of the final fence. Blow By Blow, a further ten lengths behind Mortal, completed a one, two, three for owners Gigginstown House Stud, who had five of the seven runners in the race. It had been intended that Delta Work would take in the Flogas Novices' Chase (the former Dr P. J. Moriarty) at the Dublin Racing Festival in February but he was a late withdrawal on account of the unseasonably dry conditions and wasn't seen out again until Cheltenham.

Delta Work (FR) (br.g. 2013)	Network (GER) (br 1997)	Monsun (br 1990)	Konigsstuhl
			Mosella
		Note (br 1977)	Reliance II
			Nicotiana
	Robbe (FR) (b 2005)	Video Rock (b 1984)	No Lute
			Pauvresse
		Hotesse du Bouille (b 1995)	Luchiroverte
			Kelinda

The good-topped Delta Work is by the now deceased Network, best known as the sire of Sprinter Sacre and also, incidentally, the sire of Le Richebourg who went on to win the Arkle at Leopardstown and would have started favourite for the Arkle at Cheltenham had he not been sidelined. Network was a smart middle-distance performer in Germany in his racing days and was the first son of Monsun to stand in France. He started by covering mostly non-thoroughbred mares (like Sprinter Sacre's dam Fatima III who ran just once) before making his name through the successes of such as dual Prix La Haye Jousselin winner and Grand Steeple-Chase de Paris runner-up Rubi Ball. Initially acquired by the French National Stud, Network was owned latterly by a syndicate of eighty breeders, which left little scope for anyone to use him who was not in the syndicate. Network's fertility declined in 2018 and he had only six foals in his latest crop, looking set for retirement (he covered just two mares in 2019 before breeders booked in to him were advised to use other stallions). Sadly, Network suffered a heart attack in July at Haras d'Enki, where he had stood for the last four seasons.

Delta Work's dam, the lightly-raced Video Rock mare Robbe, has had three winners so far, all of whom raced in the Gigginstown colours in the latest season. Cap York (by Ballingarry), who was bought after winning a bumper in France in 2016, has evidently had his training troubles but finally showed himself to be a useful staying hurdler in the latest season, winning twice at around three miles and finishing ninth in the Spa Novices' at Cheltenham. Delta Work's year-younger half-brother Elwood (by Martaline) was bought by Gigginstown for €170,000 at the Deauville May (2018) Sale and was also seen out over hurdles in Ireland, putting up his best effort when second in a handicap at Cork over three miles in March. The reliable Delta Work has now won a bumper (in France), over hurdles and over fences, and he has made the frame on all sixteen of his starts. He will stay further than three miles and acts on heavy going (though he doesn't need the mud). He wears a hood and a tongue tie and is a strong traveller in his races. He should continue to improve. *Gordon Elliott, Ireland*

DELUSIONOFGRANDEUR (IRE) 9 b.g. Mahler – Olivia Rose (IRE) (Mujadil (USA)) [2018/19 c141, h–: c19.4m⁵ c24d⁵ c25.6gᶠ Nov 24] winning hurdler: useful handicap chaser: stayed 29f: acted on soft going: usually raced close up: dead. *Sue Smith* **c120 h–**

DEMAND RESPECT 6 ch.g. Paco Boy (IRE) – Brilliance (Cadeaux Genereux) [2018/19 h–: h15.3m h15.3gᵖᵘ Nov 22] has had breathing operation: no form over hurdles: tried in tongue tie. *Laura Hurley* **h–**

DEMI SANG (FR) 6 b.g. Gris de Gris (IRE) – Morvandelle (FR) (Video Rock (FR)) [2018/19 c140, h116: c15.2d⁶ c15.8dᵖᵘ Apr 4] sturdy gelding: fairly useful hurdler: useful chaser for W. P. Mullins, well below form both starts in 2018/19: stays 19f: acts on heavy going: in tongue tie last 2 starts: usually races in rear. *Ben Haslam* **c106 h–**

DEMOGRAPHIC (USA) 10 b.g. Aptitude (USA) – Private Line (USA) (Private Account (USA)) [2018/19 h69: c22.5d c20.9gᵖᵘ May 31] winning hurdler: no form over fences: stays easy 3m: acts on soft and good to firm going: wears visor. *Emma Lavelle* **c– h–**

DEMON D'AUNOU (FR) 6 b.g. Martaline – Jimagine II (FR) (Video Rock (FR)) [2018/19 h125: h19g⁶ h18.5g⁶ h24g² h27m h16.3s⁴ Mar 11] sturdy gelding: has had breathing operations: fairly useful handicap hurdler: second at Southwell in August: may prove best at shorter than 3m: acts on soft going. *Jonjo O'Neill* **h121**

DEMON FOU (FR) 6 b.g. Le Fou (IRE) – Nevka (FR) (Astarabad (USA)) [2018/19 h16d h16.3g h19m* h20d² h23.9s⁵ h21.4g h17.7m³ Mar 29] €5,200 3-y-o: sturdy gelding: first foal: dam unraced: fair hurdler: won maiden at Taunton in November: stays 2½m: acts on good to firm and good to soft going: tried in hood. *Jeremy Scott* **h107**

DEMOPHON 5 b.g. Oasis Dream – Galatee (FR) (Galileo (IRE)) [2018/19 h15.8dᵖᵘ Feb 20] modest maiden on Flat, stays 2m: in cheekpieces, pulled up in maiden on hurdling debut. *Steve Flook* **h–**

DEMOPOLIS (FR) 5 b.g. Poliglote – Princess Demut (GER) (Tannenkonig (IRE)) [2018/19 h15.7v² h16s⁶ h16.8d h16d h16d Apr 6] lengthy gelding: third foal: half-brother to bumper winner Georgiator (by Simplex): dam, ran once on Flat in Germany, half-sister to Italian Group 1 2½m hurdle winner Prince Nico: fairly useful winner of juvenile at Auteuil on hurdling debut in 2017/18 for G.Cherel: disappointing in Britain: in hood last 2 starts: usually races freely. *Philip Hobbs* **h111**

DE NAME ESCAPES ME (IRE) 9 ch.g. Vinnie Roe (IRE) – Heartlight (IRE) **c128**
(Accordion) [2018/19 c112p, h133: h20d* h22.5d² c20d* c24.5g c24d⁵ Mar 10] sturdy **h143**
gelding: useful handicap hurdler: won at Naas in November: second at Navan (2½ lengths
behind Walk To Freedom) later in month: fairly useful handicap chaser: won at Navan in
December: stays 3m: acts on heavy going: has worn hood: usually wears tongue tie:
usually travels strongly. *Noel Meade, Ireland*

DE NAME EVADES ME (IRE) 7 b.g. Vinnie Roe (IRE) – Sound of The Crowd (IRE) **h123**
(Accordion) [2018/19 h115p: h23.9d² h26g* h24.2s³ h24d² Jan 1] workmanlike gelding:
Irish point winner: fairly useful form over hurdles: won novice at Warwick in November:
second in handicap at Cheltenham in January: will prove suited by extreme distances: acts
on soft going. *Fergal O'Brien*

DENILIQUIN (IRE) 4 gr.g. Mastercraftsman (IRE) – Bernie's Moon (USA) (Bernstein **h107**
(USA)) [2018/19 h17.4d* h16v⁴ Dec 7] useful-looking gelding: third foal: dam lightly
raced on Flat: fair form over hurdles: won maiden at Vichy in September for Gabriel
Leenders. *Paul Nicholls*

DENIS 4 b.g. Universal (IRE) – Exchanging Glances (Diktat) [2018/19 h16.3m h16.7m **h68**
h16.3g h15.8g⁵ Apr 22] rather unfurnished gelding: poor form over hurdles. *Paul Webber*

DENMEAD 6 b.g. Champs Elysees – Glorious Dreams (USA) (Honour And Glory (USA)) **h124**
[2018/19 h15.8g* h19.7m³ h15.7g³ h16g* h16d Apr 23] has had breathing operation: fairly
useful on Flat, stays 16.5f: fairly useful form over hurdles: won novices at Huntingdon in
October and Wetherby in March: unproven beyond 2m: best form on good going: wears
tongue tie. *Dan Skelton*

DENSFIRTH (IRE) 6 b.g. Flemensfirth (USA) – Denwoman (IRE) (Witness Box **h83**
(USA)) [2018/19 b88: h21.6d h23.6d⁶ Mar 21] fair form in bumpers: well held in 2 novice
hurdles: dead. *Paul Nicholls*

DENTLEY DE MEE (FR) 6 b.g. Lauro (GER) – Natty Twigy (FR) (Video Rock (FR)) **c128**
[2018/19 h123: h20.6g² c20v³ c19.1m² c20.6d⁴ c20.6d⁴ c20.2g² c16.8m³ c19.9m⁴ Apr 20] **h125**
useful-looking gelding: fairly useful handicap hurdler: second at Market Rasen in October:
fairly useful maiden chaser: third in novice handicap at Sandown in November: stays 21f:
acts on good to firm and heavy going: wears cheekpieces. *Nick Williams*

DE PLOTTING SHED (IRE) 9 b.g. Beneficial – Lady Willmurt (IRE) (Mandalus) **c120 §**
[2018/19 c139, h–: c22.5d^F c22.7g⁴ h24.4m⁴ h20.9m⁴ h20d h20g⁴ c17g Feb 2] useful- **h141 §**
looking gelding: useful hurdler: fourth in handicap at Kelso (5 lengths behind Go Another
One) in September: useful maiden chaser, below form in 2018/19: stays 3m: acts on good
to firm and heavy going: usually in blinkers in 2018/19: wears tongue tie: usually travels
strongly: has joined Suzi Best: irresolute. *Gordon Elliott, Ireland*

DEPUTY JONES (IRE) 6 b.m. Milan – Hudson Hope (IRE) (Topanoora) [2018/19 **h105 p**
h21.7g³ Apr 12] sixth foal: sister to a winning pointer and half-sister to fairly useful
hurdler/chaser Pass The Ball (2½m-3m winner, by Westerner): dam, lightly raced in
bumpers/over hurdles, half-sister to very smart staying chaser Cane Brake: won sole start
in Irish points: 10/1, third in novice at Fontwell (7 lengths behind Danse Idol) on hurdling
debut: sure to do better. *Neil Mulholland*

DEPUTY'S OSCAR (IRE) 6 b.m. Oscar (IRE) – Shesourpresent (IRE) (Presenting) **h79 p**
[2018/19 b18g b15.7d h15.8g³ Mar 19] sturdy mare: third foal: dam unraced sister to fairly **b75**
useful hurdler/chaser (stayed 25f) Coin Man: won mares maiden point on debut: modest
form in bumpers: 22/1, third in maiden at Huntingdon (26 lengths behind Locker Room
Talk) on hurdling debut: left M. P. Collins after first start: bred to be suited by 2½m+:
should improve over hurdles. *Stuart Edmunds*

DE RASHER COUNTER 7 b.g. Yeats (IRE) – Dedrunknmunky (IRE) (Rashar (USA)) **c145 p**
[2018/19 h126: c20g³ c20.9g^pu c19.2s c22.4d⁴ c23.6d² c24v* Mar 16] lengthy gelding: **h–**
fairly useful hurdler: smart form over fences: won novice handicaps at Newbury (by neck
from Walt) in December and Uttoxeter (by 6 lengths from Late Romantic) in March: will
probably stay beyond 3m: acts on heavy going: usually races off pace: likely to progress
further as a chaser. *Emma Lavelle*

DERINTOHER YANK (IRE) 8 b.g. Dubai Destination (USA) – Anns Present (IRE) **c– §**
(Presenting) [2018/19 c127§, h123§: c19g c17.4g⁶ Apr 13] fairly useful hurdler: fairly **h– §**
useful chaser, well below form both starts in 2018/19: stays 2½m: acts on soft going: wears
headgear: usually leads: has flashed tail/carried head awkwardly. *Donald McCain*

DERRIANA SPIRIT (IRE) 6 b.m. Flemensfirth (USA) – Distillery Lane (IRE) (Exit To **h111**
Nowhere (USA)) [2018/19 b97: h20.5v² h16.2s* h20.6g* h21.4s³ h24.3m⁶ Apr 12]
tall mare: bumper winner: fair form over hurdles: won mares novices at Hexham in
December and Newcastle in January: should stay 3m: acts on heavy going: front runner/
races prominently. *Nicky Richards*

DERRICK D'ANJOU (IRE) 8 b.g. Double Eclipse (IRE) – Belle d'Anjou (FR) (Saint **h91**
Cyrien (FR)) [2018/19 h23.9s³ Feb 26] modest maiden hurdler: placed on sole start in
2018/19 after missing previous season: stays 3¼m: acts on soft going: tried in blinkers:
wears tongue tie. *Graeme McPherson*

DERRINROSS (IRE) 8 b.g. Scorpion (IRE) – Cybele Eria (FR) (Johann Quatz (FR)) **h132**
[2018/19 h24v* h24s* h24d⁶ Mar 15] good-topped gelding: fourth foal: dam (c94/h112)
2m/17f hurdle/chase winner who stayed 2½m: winning pointer: useful form over hurdles:
won Kerry Group Stayers Novices' Hurdle at Cork (by 4 lengths from Sams Profile)
and Grade 2 novice at Limerick (by ¾ length from Defi Bleu) in December: stays 3m: acts
on heavy going: tried in cheekpieces: wears tongue tie: front runner/races prominently.
J. P. Dempsey, Ireland

DERRYFADDA(IRE) 10 b.g. Scorpion(IRE)–San Diego(IRE)(LeadingCounsel(USA)) **c–**
[2018/19 c–, h–: c21.4g May 11] maiden hurdler: fair chaser at best: stayed 27f: acted on **h–**
good to firm going: tried in tongue tie: dead. *Sam England*

DERRYNANE (IRE) 8 b.g. Oscar (IRE) – Tessano Queen (IRE) (Jurado (USA)) [2018/19 **h99**
h101: h16.7g* h15.8dᵖᵘ Mar 13] modest handicap hurdler: won at Market Rasen (lady
riders event) in November: stays 19f: acts on heavy going: wears tongue tie. *Donald McCain*

DESAI 5 br.g. Dansili – Arabesque (Zafonic (USA)) [2018/19 b16.8s⁵ Dec 7] tongue tied **b–**
when tailed off in bumper: modest maiden on Flat (refused to race on debut), best effort at
1m. *Noel Wilson*

DESARAY GIRL (FR) 4 gr.f. Montmartre (FR) – Feria To Bitch (FR) (Royal Charter **b68**
(FR)) [2018/19 b16.4d³ b16.8g Apr 18] €40,000 3-y-o: half-sister to fairly useful French
hurdler/fair chaser Brame de Nuit (15f-2¼m winner, by Sagacity) and French 17f-19f
hurdle/chase winner Arc des Taillons (by Sagamix): dam French 17f hurdle winner: poor
form in bumpers. *Philip Kirby*

DESERT DE BRUYERE (FR) 6 b.g. Great Pretender (IRE) – Quid de Neuville (FR) **h102**
(Le Balafre (FR)) [2018/19 b16g⁴ h20g⁶ h19.6g³ h19.9g³ h19.9d⁴ h23.3vᵖᵘ Dec 21] third **b93**
foal: half-brother to fair hurdler/useful chaser Ascot de Bruyere (2m-23f winner, by
Kapgarde): dam placed around 2¼m over jumps in France: placed in Irish point: fourth in
bumper at Worcester (4 lengths behind Fortunes Hiding) in June: fair form over hurdles:
best effort at 2½m: often races in rear/freely. *Rosemary Gasson*

DESERTER (IRE) 8 ch.g. Tagula (IRE) – Lady Van Gogh (Dubai Destination (USA)) **h–**
[2018/19 h20m Jul 13] fairly useful hurdler, well held sole start in 2018/19 after long
absence: stays 2½m: acts on good to firm and heavy going: tried in cheekpieces: wears
tongue tie. *Warren Greatrex*

DESERT ISLAND DUSK 8 b.g. Superior Premium – Desert Island Disc (Turtle Island **h111**
(IRE)) [2018/19 h104: h20.2g⁴ h20.1g* h20.1g⁶ h20.1g³ h16.2g h16.2g³ h20.9d⁴ h16g⁴
h16.8s² h19.8s² h19.7g⁶ h18.1dᶠ Apr 8] has had breathing operation: fair handicap hurdler:
won at Hexham in June: stays 2½m: acts on soft and good to firm going: has worn hood:
wears tongue tie. *Maurice Barnes*

DESERTMORE VIEW (IRE) 11 b.g. Fruits of Love (USA) – The Iron Lady (IRE) **c85**
(Polish Patriot (USA)) [2018/19 c59, h–: c19.2g⁵ Jul 8] multiple point winner: twice-raced **h–**
hurdler: winning chaser: stayed 3m: best form on good going: dead. *Kevin Bishop*

DESERT RETREAT (IRE) 8 b.g. Sandmason – Suny House (Carroll House) [2018/19 **c100 x**
h22.2g² h23.1m⁵ c26g³ c23.6g Oct 16] has had breathing operation: point winner: fair **h112 §**
maiden hurdler: similar form over fences (not a convincing jumper): stays 3¼m: acts on
soft going: wears blinkers: in tongue tie all 4 starts in 2018/19: temperamental. *Lawney Hill*

DESERT SENSATION (IRE) 7 b.g. Authorized (IRE) – Awwal Malika (USA) **c–**
(Kingmambo (USA)) [2018/19 c89, h108: h24.2d⁵ h21.3g³ h23.4m⁴ Apr 22] sturdy **h109**
gelding: fair handicap hurdler: little enthusiasm only try chasing: stays 3¼m: acts on soft
going: wears headgear/tongue tie. *Dr Richard Newland*

DESHAN (GER) 8 b.g. Soldier Hollow – Desimona (GER) (Monsun (GER)) [2018/19 **c–**
h94, b–: c16.5gᵖᵘ Jun 2] maiden hurdler: pulled up in novice handicap on chasing debut: **h–**
won on point debut in March: usually wears tongue tie. *Tim Vaughan*

DESILVANO 10 b.g. Desideratum – Cruz Santa (Lord Bud) [2018/19 h90: h26d May 30] **h–**
workmanlike gelding: point winner: poor hurdler nowadays: stays 25f: acts on heavy
going: often in cheekpieces. *James Evans*

DESIRABLE COURT (IRE) 6 b.m. Court Cave (IRE) – Desirable Rhythm (IRE) **c127**
(Hernando (FR)) [2018/19 h21.6g* h19.9g² h21.6m² h23g³ c16.2g* c20g⁵ c20.2m* **h120**
c15.9m* c20.6g⁴ Apr 18] £80,000 4-y-o: lengthy mare: has had breathing operations: fifth
foal: half-sister to a winning pointer by Tikkanen: dam bumper winner: fairly useful form
over hurdles: won mares novice at Newton Abbot early in season: similar form over fences:
walked over in maiden at Warwick in October, and won novice in December and listed
mares event in January (by ¾ length from Hope's Wishes), both at Leicester: left Alan King
after fourth start: stays 2¾m: acts on good to firm going: in tongue tie last 5 starts.
Dan Skelton

DESIREMOI D'AUTHIE (FR) 6 b.g. Cachet Noir (USA) – Toietmoi d'Authie (FR) **h108**
(Al Namix (FR)) [2018/19 h103: h16m⁵ h18.6g⁵ h17.7g² h19.3mᵖᵘ h16g³ h15.3d⁴ h15.3g²
h15.9g⁴ Feb 25] rather leggy gelding: fair maiden hurdler: left Alan King after second start:
unproven beyond 2m: acts on good to soft going: has worn hood, including in 2018/19.
Chris Gordon

DESSIE'S DIAMOND (IRE) 5 b.g. Dubai Destination (USA) – Diamond Katie (IRE) **h107**
(Night Shift (USA)) [2018/19 b16m³ b16g³ h16g⁶ h15.7s⁴ h16d⁵ h16v² Feb 18] compact **b90**
gelding: fourth foal: brother to fairly useful 2m hurdle winner Try Again: dam 5f winner:
fair form in bumpers/over hurdles. *Denis Coakley*

DESSINATEUR (FR) 6 b.g. Alberto Giacometti (IRE) – Castagnette III (FR) (Tin Soldier **c–**
(FR)) [2018/19 h101: c20.3gᶠ Oct 30] fair maiden hurdler: tailed off when fell fatally on **h–**
chasing debut. *Venetia Williams*

DESTINED TO SHINE (IRE) 7 b.g. Dubai Destination (USA) – Good Shine (IRE) **h114**
(Beneficial) [2018/19 h100: h19.7g² h19.7s* h21.2s³ h18.9sᵖᵘ h18.9d* Mar 20] sturdy
gelding: fair handicap hurdler: won at Hereford in November and Haydock (novice event)
in March: stays 2½m: acts on soft going: wears tongue tie: usually races towards rear.
Kerry Lee

DESTINEE ROYALE (FR) 6 b.m. Balko (FR) – Viana (FR) (Signe Divin (USA)) **h101 p**
[2018/19 b89: h19.5v³ Feb 18] has had breathing operation: bumper winner: 4/1, shaped
well when third in novice at Lingfield (5½ lengths behind Dominateur) on hurdling debut:
open to improvement. *Venetia Williams*

DESTINY AWAITS 10 b.g. Dubai Destination (USA) – Mellow Jazz (Lycius **h–**
(USA)) [2018/19 h23.9gᵖᵘ Aug 18] poor hurdler: stays 3m: acts on good to firm going: tried
in blinkers/tongue tie. *Andrew Hamilton*

DESTINYS CHOICE (IRE) 6 b.m. Dubai Destination (USA) – Leader's Hall (IRE) **b62**
(Saddlers' Hall (IRE)) [2018/19 b15.7s⁵ Mar 18] £70,000 5-y-o: sixth foal: half-sister to 3
winners by Presenting, including fairly useful hurdler/chaser Pressies Girl (2½m-2¾m
winner) and fairly useful hurdler/winning pointer She's Da One (19f-2¾m winner):
dam winning pointer: off mark in Irish points at second attempt: well held in bumper.
Michael Blake

DESTINY'S GOLD (IRE) 9 b.g. Millenary – Knockhouse Rose (IRE) (Roselier (FR)) **c109**
[2018/19 c–, h124: c19.4m⁵ c23g⁴ h20g* Jun 24] tall gelding: fair hurdler: won claimer at **h100**
Worcester in June: similar form over fences: pulled up on point debut: stays 23f: acts on
good to firm and good to soft going: wears headgear. *Dr Richard Newland*

DESTRIER (FR) 6 b.g. Voix du Nord (FR) – Razia (FR) (Robin des Champs (FR)) **c147**
[2018/19 h119: h16v³ c15.7s* c16.5d* c15.8g³ Apr 6] lengthy gelding: fairly useful form **h114**
over hurdles: smart form over fences: won novice handicap at Southwell (by ½ length from
Another Crick) in December and novice at Ayr (by 4½ lengths from Tonto's Spirit) in
January: best effort when third in Maghull Novices' Chase at Aintree (3 lengths behind
Ornua) in April: raced only at 2m: acts on heavy going: usually front runner/races
prominently. *Dan Skelton*

DETONATE (FR) 6 gr.g. Al Namix (FR) – Tadorna (FR) (Maresca Sorrento (FR)) **b–**
[2018/19 b63: b16.2g⁶ Jun 3] has had breathing operation: little show in bumpers: tried in
hood/tongue tie. *James Ewart*

DEVILS BRIDE (IRE) 12 b.g. Helissio (FR) – Rigorous (Generous (IRE)) [2018/19 **c131**
c154d, h–: c16g c17g⁴ c22.5d c22.5g c17d⁵ c25d c30.2sᵖᵘ Mar 13] winning hurdler: very **h–**
smart chaser at best, on downgrade: stays 23f: acts on soft and good to firm going: often
wears cheekpieces: wears tongue tie. *Henry de Bromhead, Ireland*

DEVILS WATER 8 b.g. Overbury (IRE) – Reel Charmer (Dancing High) [2018/19 h78: **h89**
h21.4g² May 7] modest maiden hurdler: stays 21f: in headgear last 4 starts: has worn
tongue tie. *Jane Walton*

DEVIOUS DICKS DAME 4 b.f. Dick Turpin (IRE) – Bridal White (Robellino (USA)) **h–**
[2018/19 b14g b12.6s b14d b17.7g h15.8gᵖᵘ h15.9g⁴ Apr 22] compact filly: sixth foal: dam **b–**
maiden on Flat/lightly raced over jumps: little show in bumpers/juvenile hurdles: wears
hood. *Zoe Davison*

DEVITO'SGOLDENGIRL (IRE) 8 b.m. Gold Well – Caracool (FR) (Cadoudal (FR)) **c73**
[2018/19 c–, h84: h20.2gᵖᵘ h18.1g h21.4d c20.3m⁶ c23.8s⁴ Mar 10] has had breathing **h–**
operation: Irish point winner: poor maiden hurdler: similar form over fences: should stay
2½m: acts on soft going: usually wears hood: wears tongue tie: front runner/races
prominently. *Lucinda Russell*

DEVITO'SREDROBIN (IRE) 6 b.m. Robin des Champs (FR) – Koko Rose (IRE) **h91**
(Beneficial) [2018/19 h16d h20.6g⁶ h19.9v⁵ h19.9s⁴ h19.6g⁶ Apr 13] €13,000 4-y-o, **b–**
£10,000 5-y-o: third foal: sister to fairly useful 2m hurdle winner Thirsty Work, stayed
2½m: dam unraced sister to top-class hurdler/very smart chaser (stayed 3¼m) More of
That: off mark in Irish points at third attempt: tailed off in mares bumper: modest form over
hurdles. *Donald McCain*

DEWCUP (IRE) 4 br.g. Finsceal Fior (IRE) – Elyaadi (Singspiel (IRE)) [2018/19 b16s³ **b107**
b16g⁸ b17d⁴ Apr 5] strong gelding: third foal: brother to fair 2m hurdle winner Minnie
Dahill, stays 2½m: dam (h125), fairly useful 2m-2½m hurdle winner, also useful 1½m-2m
winner on Flat: useful form in bumpers: won maiden at Thurles (by 3 lengths from
Blackhillsofdakota) in March: best effort when fourth in Grade 2 at Aintree (5¼ lengths
behind McFabulous) in April. *T. M. Walsh, Ireland*

DEW POND 7 b.g. Motivator – Rutland Water (IRE) (Hawk Wing (USA)) [2018/19 h16g⁵ **h99**
h16d⁵ h16.8s⁴ h20.6s⁴ h18.1g² h16g³ h16.7g⁴ Mar 20] modest maiden hurdler: stays 2¼m:
best form on good going: in blinkers last 4 starts: temperament under suspicion.
Tim Easterby

DEXCITE (FR) 8 b.g. Authorized (IRE) – Belle Alicia (FR) (Smadoun (FR)) [2018/19 **h104**
h109: h16gᵖᵘ h15.8g⁵ h16gᶠ h16.6gᵖᵘ Dec 29] well-made gelding: fair handicap hurdler:
left Tom George after first start: stays 19f: acts on soft going: tried in hood: usually races
towards rear: has joined Nick Kent: temperament under suspicion. *Alan King*

DE YOUNG WARRIOR 6 b.g. Schiaparelli (GER) – Nobratinetta (FR) (Celtic Swing) **b83**
[2018/19 b15.8g² Jul 18] seventh foal: half-brother to bumper winner Swinging Sultan (by
Sulamani) and fair hurdler Vinetta (19f winner, by Grape Tree Road): dam (b100), bumper
winner, also 1½m winner on Flat, half-sister to fairly useful hurdlers Bhutan (2m-2¼m
winner) and Cloth of Gold (stayed 3m): 10/1, second in bumper at Uttoxeter (17 lengths
behind Longhouse Sale): has joined L. Jefford. *Gillian Boanas*

DEYRANN DE CARJAC (FR) 6 b.g. Balko (FR) – Queyrann (FR) (Sheyrann) **h118**
[2018/19 h119p, b97: h16g⁸ h16d² h16.4gᶠ h19.6d² h18.6d² h16m⁵ Apr 12] rather
unfurnished gelding: fairly useful hurdler: won maiden at Warwick in May: stays 2½m:
acts on good to soft going. *Alan King*

D'GENTLE REFLEXION (FR) 6 b.g. Gentlewave (IRE) – Reflexion (FR) (Discover **c98**
d'Auteuil (FR)) [2018/19 b15.8m h18.5g c21.1g² c19.4v c20.4s⁶ c19.9g⁵ c21.4gᵖᵘ Mar 17] **h–**
modest at best in bumpers: well held in maiden only start over hurdles, then left Warren **b–**
Greatrex: modest form over fences: stays 21f. *David Cottin, France*

DHARMA RAIN (IRE) 4 b.f. High Chaparral (IRE) – Crazy Volume (IRE) **h90**
(Machiavellian (USA)) [2018/19 h16sᵖᵘ h15.8d⁶ h16g h16.3d h21.4g⁵ Mar 25] tall filly:
closely related to 2 winners over hurdles by Montjeu, including useful 2m-2¾m winner
Plinth: fair maiden on Flat, stays 1m: modest form over hurdles: tried in cheekpieces/
tongue tie. *Clare Hobson*

DHAROOS (IRE) 6 ch.g. New Approach (IRE) – Cailiocht (USA) (Elusive Quality **h–**
(USA)) [2018/19 h–: h15.3mᵖᵘ May 15] little show over hurdles. *Nigel Hawke*

DHOWIN (IRE) 5 b.g. Yeats (IRE) – On The Way Home (IRE) (Flemensfirth (USA)) **b91**
[2018/19 b16.8s⁵ b16d² Mar 19] €42,000 3-y-o: first foal: dam, ran twice over hurdles,
sister to useful hurdler Rock On The Moor and half-sister to high-class hurdler Get Me Out
of Here, both stayed 21f: fair form in bumpers: better effort when second at Wetherby in
March. *Jonjo O'Neill*

DIABLE DE SIVOLA (FR) 6 b.g. Noroit (GER) – Grande Route (IRE) (Lost World (IRE)) [2018/19 h130: c16d⁴ c20s⁵ c21.4m³ c20d² c19.2d² c20g³ Apr 27] rangy gelding: useful hurdler: similar form over fences: placed in novice handicaps at Exeter in March and Sandown in April: stays 21f: acts on soft and good to firm going. *Nick Williams*   c138 h–

DIABLERETS (FR) 6 ch.g. Vendangeur (IRE) – Lavande (FR) (Iris Noir (FR)) [2018/19 h–: h15.3m h16.8m c16.1m² c16sᵘʳ c16.1d⁶ h16.8sᵖᵘ Jan 20] lengthy gelding: little impact over hurdles or fences: usually wears hood: tried in tongue tie: hard ride. *Kayley Woollacott*   c64 h–

DIABLO DE ROUHET (FR) 6 b.g. Great Pretender (IRE) – Querelle d'Estruval (FR) (Panoramic) [2018/19 h121, b84: h23.6v³ c19s² Dec 30] plain gelding: maiden pointer: fairly useful form over hurdles: 11/4, second in maiden at Haydock (18 lengths behind Scorpion Sid) on chasing debut: stays 23f: acts on heavy going: has joined Nicky Henderson. *Jo Hughes*   c108 h115

DIAKALI (FR) 10 gr.g. Sinndar (IRE) – Diasilixa (FR) (Linamix (FR)) [2018/19 h106: c17.8g* c16.3g* c15.9g* c15.5sᵖᵘ c16g⁵ Dec 27] good-topped gelding: very smart hurdler at best: smart form over fences: completed hat-trick when winning novices at Fontwell (by 29 lengths from Our Three Sons) and Newton Abbot (by 23 lengths from Miss Night Owl) in June, and Cheltenham (by 9 lengths from Sister Sibyl) in October: has form at 25f, but effective at much shorter: acts on heavy going: wears headgear: usually leads. *Gary Moore*   c147 h–

DIAMOND BENNY (IRE) 7 b.g. Milan – Ben's Pride (Bollin Eric) [2018/19 h66: h25m⁵ May 7] little form over hurdles: tried in visor: in tongue tie last 2 starts. *Robert Stephens*   h–

DIAMOND CAUCHOIS (FR) 8 b.g. Crillon (FR) – Diamond Turtle (FR) (Limnos (JPN)) [2018/19 h151: h21sᵖᵘ Mar 13] rather leggy gelding: smart hurdler, pulled up sole start in 2018/19: stays 3m: acts on good to firm and heavy going: in tongue tie last 5 starts. *Gordon Elliott, Ireland*   h–

DIAMOND FORT (IRE) 7 ch.g. Gamut (IRE) – Ellie Forte (Alflora (IRE)) [2018/19 h124: h20g h18.5v⁴ h23.3d² h24.1d⁵ h24.3m⁵ Apr 20] unplaced in Irish points: fairly useful handicap hurdler: second at Uttoxeter in February: stays 23f: acts on heavy going: tried in cheekpieces: usually races off pace: temperament under suspicion. *Fergal O'Brien*   h125

DIAMOND GAIT 6 b.m. Passing Glance – Milliegait (Tobougg (IRE)) [2018/19 b98: h15.8g* h16.3s⁴ h16.6g* h16.8d Mar 14] sturdy mare: bumper winner: fairly useful form over hurdles: won mares maiden at Ludlow in November and novice at Doncaster in January: wears tongue tie. *Kim Bailey*   h123

DIAMOND GUY (FR) 6 b.g. Konig Turf (GER) – Unique Chance (FR) (Network (GER)) [2018/19 h115p: h15.8g* May 8] fair form over hurdles: won novice at Ludlow sole outing in 2018/19: usually wears tongue tie. *Paul Nicholls*   h108

DIAMOND KING (IRE) 11 b.g. King's Theatre (IRE) – Georgia On My Mind (FR) (Belmez (USA)) [2018/19 c–, h135: h16.2g⁴ Jan 13] useful-looking gelding: useful handicap hurdler for Gordon Elliott: well held sole start in sphere in 2018/19: winning chaser: stays 23f: acts on heavy going: tried in cheekpieces: wears tongue tie: won twice in points later in season. *Olly Murphy*   c– h85

DIAMOND REFLECTION (IRE) 7 b.g. Oasis Dream – Briolette (IRE) (Sadler's Wells (USA)) [2018/19 h–: h15.8m² h15.8g⁴ h16.8g⁵ Sep 10] poor maiden hurdler: best effort at 2m: acts on good to firm going: sometimes wears hood: wears tongue tie: modest on Flat. *Alexandra Dunn*   h66

DIAMOND ROCK 8 b.g. Kayf Tara – Crystal Princess (IRE) (Definite Article) [2018/19 c110, h–: c16gᵖᵘ c17g² c17.4gᶠ h16.3dᵖᵘ c17.1g⁶ Mar 23] sturdy gelding: fair handicap hurdler/chaser: left Henry Oliver after fourth start: stays 19f: acts on good to soft and good to firm going: tried in cheekpieces. *Sandy Thomson*   c102 h–

DIAMOND ROSE 7 b.m. Sagamix (FR) – Swiss Rose (Michelozzo (USA)) [2018/19 b15.8m⁵ b15.8g⁵ b13.7m h15.8d⁴ h21.2g h19.6d h19.6g Apr 13] smallish, angular mare: fourth foal: half-sister to 2 winners, including fair hurdler/fairly useful chaser Emerald Rose (21f-29f winner, by Sir Harry Lewis): dam no sign of ability: modest form in bumpers: poor form over hurdles: tried in hood. *Julian Smith*   h73 b75

DICA (FR) 13 ch.g. Kapgarde (FR) – Easy World (FR) (Lost World (IRE)) [2018/19 c120, h–: c15.6gᵖᵘ May 12] winning hurdler: fairly useful chaser, pulled up sole start in 2018/19: stays 3¼m, just as effective over much shorter: acts on any going: has worn tongue tie: usually leads. *Paul Collins*   c– h–

DICK DARSIE (IRE) 9 br.g. Darsi (FR) – Hurricane Jane (IRE) (Strong Gale) [2018/19 c94§, h–: c26.3s³ c24.2s⁵ Dec 12] maiden hurdler: modest handicap chaser: stays 3¼m: acts on heavy going: temperamental (usually soon off bridle). *Sue Smith*   c74 § h–

DICKIE DIVER (IRE) 6 b.g. Gold Well – Merry Excuse (IRE) (Flemensfirth (USA))   h136
[2018/19 h19.5d² h19.5d* h24d⁴ Mar 15] €12,000 3-y-o, £210,000 5-y-o: rangy gelding:
will make a chaser: first foal: dam, ran out only start in points, half-sister to useful chaser
around 2m Festive Affair out of half-sister to top-class chaser (winner up to 25f) Merry
Gale: easy winner on sole outing in Irish points: useful form over hurdles: won maiden at
Chepstow in February: best effort when fourth in Albert Bartlett Novices' Hurdle (Spa) at
Cheltenham (10¾ lengths behind Minella Indo) in March. *Nicky Henderson*

DICKY BOB 12 gr.g. Exit To Nowhere (USA) – She's A Gift (Bob's Return (IRE))   c104
[2018/19 c24.2d³ Apr 9] multiple point winner: fair form in hunter chases: third at Exeter
in April. *Miss V. J. Nicholls*

DICOSIMO (FR) 8 b.g. Laveron – Coralisse Royale (FR) (Tip Moss (FR)) [2018/19   c131
c137§, h137§: c19.9dᵖ° c16.4s⁵ c15.7d³ c16.3d* c16d⁴ c16d⁴ c16.4g³ c19.9g³ Apr 22]   h–
good-topped gelding: has had breathing operation: useful hurdler: useful handicap chaser:
won at Haydock (by 2 lengths from Zalvados) in January: third at Newbury (3¾ lengths
behind Lillington) in March: has won over 2¾m, at least as effective around 2m: acts on
heavy going: has worn hood: usually front runner/races prominently. *Warren Greatrex*

DIDERO VALLIS (FR) 6 b.g. Poliglote – Oreade Vallis (FR) (April Night (FR))   c133
[2018/19 h22.2m³ c23.4d c20.9s* c20.6s* c24g c20.6d⁵ Mar 14] strong gelding: first foal: h129
dam, French 19f/2½m chaser winner, half-sister to smart French chaser up to 23f Jerico
Vallis: fairly useful handicap hurdler: useful form over fences: won novice handicap at
Carlisle and handicap at Haydock (by 1¼ lengths from Gold Opera) in December: left W.
P. Mullins after first start: should stay 3m: acts on good to firm and heavy going: usually
front runner/races prominently. *Venetia Williams*

DIDNTITELLYA (IRE) 10 b.g. Presenting – Beauty Star (IRE) (Shalford (IRE)) [2018/19   c–
c23.8mᵘʳ Jan 17] point winner: maiden hurdler: little show in chases since winning maiden   h–
in 2013/14: stays 2½m: acts on heavy going: in cheekpieces last 3 starts: tried in tongue tie.
Major Harry Wallace

DIDO 9 b.g. Killer Instinct – Bowdlane Barb (Commanche Run) [2018/19 c16.3g⁵ c20.9sᵖᵘ   c93
Mar 11] workmanlike gelding: multiple point winner: maiden hurdler: modest form over   h–
fences. *D. Peters*

DIDTHEYLEAVEUOUTTO (IRE) 6 ch.g. Presenting – Pretty Puttens (IRE) (Snurge)   h125
[2018/19 b111+: h16g* h15.7g* h16g⁵ h15.7d Feb 16] sturdy gelding: useful bumper
performer: fairly useful form over hurdles: won maiden at Fakenham in October and
introductory event at Ascot in November. *Nick Gifford*

DIEG MAN (FR) 6 ch.g. Kapgarde (FR) – Majestic Card (FR) (Ultimately Lucky (IRE))   c121
[2018/19 h125: h22.1g* c21.2d* c22.5g Oct 18] has had breathing operation: fairly useful   h128
handicap hurdler: won at Cartmel early in season: similar form over fences: won novice at
same course in August with bit in hand: stays 2¾m: acts on soft going: tried in cheekpieces/
tongue tie. *Neil Mulholland*

DIEGO DU CHARMIL (FR) 7 b.g. Ballingarry (IRE) – Daramour (FR) (Anabaa Blue)   c150
[2018/19 c155p, h–: c17.5m⁵ c16g² c16.8d³ c15.5g⁵ Apr 27] tall, good-topped gelding: h–
winning chaser: smart chaser: second in Desert Orchid Chase at Kempton (19 lengths
behind Altior) in December: raced around 2m: acts on soft going: wears tongue tie.
Paul Nicholls

DIEU BENISSE (FR) 6 b.m. Blue Bresil (FR) – Flowerfull (FR) (Lightning (FR))   h114
[2018/19 h15.3dᶠ h15.8dᶠ h15.8m⁵ Apr 1] half-sister to French 17f hurdle winner Yo
Minfoutaie (by Saint des Saints) and fair French 2m-19f hurdle winner Hillflower (by
Sabrehill): fairly useful maiden on Flat, stays 12.5f: fair form over hurdles. *Nicky Henderson*

DIEU VIVANT (FR) 6 b.g. Network (GER) – Panique Pas (FR) (Video Rock (FR))   c135
[2018/19 h17.9d³ c22.4d* c21.9s⁶ c21.9s⁶ c21.9s⁶ h19.4s⁶ h21.4g Apr 14] strong, compact   h119
gelding: half-brother to several winners in France, including useful hurdler/smart chaser
Arry (17f-19f winner, by Boris de Deauville) and useful chaser Capferret (17f-2¾m
winner, by Day Flight): dam, French 11f bumper/2¼m hurdle winner, half-sister to smart
French chaser up to 23f Quart Monde (by Network): fairly useful maiden hurdler: useful
form over fences: won handicap at Clairefontaine in August: left Francois Nicolle after
sixth start: stays 2¾m: acts on soft going. *Oliver Greenall*

DIGER DAUDAIE (FR) 6 b.g. Tiger Groom – Stone Again (FR) (Passing Sale (FR))   h127
[2018/19 h19.5s⁵ h22d* h23s⁴ h23.6d³ h23.3v* Mar 16] €32,000 3-y-o, £48,000 5-y-o:
sturdy gelding: first foal: dam runner-up in French bumpers: winning pointer (dead-
heated): fairly useful form over hurdles: won novice at Newcastle in December and lady
riders handicap at Uttoxeter in March: likely to stay further than 3m: acts on heavy going:
in tongue tie last 2 starts. *Charlie Longsdon*

DIGGIN DEEP (IRE) 9 b.g. Royal Anthem (USA) – Lady Ramona (IRE) (Lord Americo) [2018/19 h20.4g h16g⁵ h22g h23.8g* h20.6d² h24.4g* h24g³ h24d Mar 4] maiden pointer: fair handicap hurdler: won at Musselburgh in November and Doncaster in January: maiden chaser: left R. Donohoe after third start: stays 3m: acts on good to soft going: has worn cheekpieces. *Stephen Michael Hanlon, Ireland* **c–** **h109**

DILIGENT (FR) 6 br.g. Kapgarde (FR) – Rapide (FR) (Assessor (IRE)) [2018/19 h21.6g³ h21.6d⁵ c21.6m⁵ c16.1dᵖᵘ c19.7dᵖᵘ Jan 6] has had breathing operation: first foal: dam (c107/h123), French 19f hurdle/chase winner, half-sister to smart French hurdler/fairly useful chaser (17f-21f winner) Vladimir: fair form over hurdles: fairly useful chaser for Guillaume Macaire, no form over fences in Britain: stays 2¾m: acts on soft going: tried in hood: in tongue tie last 5 starts. *Alexandra Dunn* **c–** **h101**

DILSON (IRE) 4 b.g. Sholokhov (IRE) – Diligent (Generous (IRE)) [2018/19 b13m⁶ h16s⁴ h16g h16.2g⁵ Mar 26] first foal: dam (b102), bumper winner, half-sister to useful 2m hurdle winner Jumps Road: well beaten in junior bumper: modest form over hurdles: will be suited by further than 2m. *Nick Williams* **h90** **b–**

DIMINPETE 6 ch.g. Geordieland (FR) – Sonoma (IRE) (Dr Devious (IRE)) [2018/19 h–, b–: h21.6gᵖᵘ h18.5m Aug 6] no form in bumpers/over hurdles: in cheekpieces last 2 starts. *Jeremy Scott* **h–** **b–**

DIMMESDALE 4 b.g. Nathaniel (IRE) – Diara Angel (IRE) (Hawk Wing (USA)) [2018/19 b15.3g Dec 6] well held in bumper: modest form for John O'Shea on Flat. *Tom Lacey* **b–**

DIMPLE (FR) 8 gr.g. Montmartre (FR) – Dynella (FR) (Sillery (USA)) [2018/19 c106, h–: c20.1d* h22.7g* c21.6g* h20.6g⁴ c20.5mᵖᵘ Apr 12] strong gelding: fairly useful hurdler: won handicap at Kelso (amateurs) in December: useful handicap chaser: won at Newcastle in December and again at Kelso (by 20 lengths from Mount Mews) in January: stays 23f: acts on good to soft going: has worn hood: front runner. *Sandy Thomson* **c132** **h115**

DINA MAKER (FR) 6 b.m. Policy Maker (IRE) – Kalinca de Thaix (FR) (Lights Out (FR)) [2018/19 h23.8d h15.8d h21.2dᵖᵘ c24gᵖᵘ c24gᵖᵘ Apr 25] €6,200 3-y-o: fifth foal: half-sister to fairly useful French hurdler/useful chaser Totem Flow (17f-21f winner, by With The Flow) and French 2¼m chase winner Alinea Tresor (by Califet): dam French maiden (third in 2m hurdle): off mark in points at fourth attempt (sole finisher): no form over hurdles/fences. *Tom Weston* **c–** **h–**

DINARIA DES OBEAUX (FR) 6 b.m. Saddler Maker (IRE) – Indiana Jaune (FR) (Le Nain Jaune (FR)) [2018/19 c137, h–: c23d² c20g³ h20d Dec 16] rather unfurnished mare: useful hurdler at best: second in listed event at Wexford (8 lengths behind Peregrine Run) in October: stays 23f: acts on heavy going: tried in cheekpieces: wears tongue tie: usually races prominently. *Gordon Elliott, Ireland* **c137** **h–**

DINEUR (FR) 13 ch.g. Discover d'Auteuil (FR) – Sky Rocket (FR) (Sky Lawyer (FR)) [2018/19 c22.2g c24.2dᵘʳ c21.1dᵖᵘ Apr 4] workmanlike gelding: winning hurdler: useful chaser at best, no form in hunters in 2018/19: has worn hood: wears tongue tie. *Mickey Bowen* **c–** **h–**

DING DING 8 ch.m. Winker Watson – Five Bells (IRE) (Rock of Gibraltar (IRE)) [2018/19 h107: h20.5g⁴ h25m⁴ h20.5g* h21d h21.7v⁵ h19.2d h20.5s³ h20.5g* Feb 25] short-backed mare: fair handicap hurdler: won at Plumpton in November and February (mares): stays 21f: acts on good to firm and heavy going: usually races close up. *Sheena West* **h111**

DINGO DOLLAR (IRE) 7 ch.g. Golden Lariat (USA) – Social Society (IRE) (Moscow Society (USA)) [2018/19 c147p, h–: h24.2d⁴ c26s³ c24g⁶ c26g² c26gᵖᵘ Apr 17] useful-looking gelding: useful form over hurdles: smart handicap chaser: second in Grimthorpe Chase at Doncaster (9 lengths behind Chidswell) in March: stays 3¼m: acts on heavy going: usually wears cheekpieces: front runner/races prominently. *Alan King* **c145** **h132 +**

DINNERLADY 6 b.m. Kirkwall – R Lillibet VII (Damsire Unregistered) [2018/19 b15.8g⁶ Apr 22] angular mare: first foal: dam unraced: in blinkers when tailed off in bumper. *Martin Bosley* **b–**

DINONS (FR) 6 b.g. Balko (FR) – Beni Abbes (FR) (Saint des Saints (FR)) [2018/19 b19.4s² b20g³ h24mᶠ h20.9g* h22g* h19.9m* h23.9g* h23.9d* h20d h24dᵖᵘ Mar 15] rather leggy gelding: fairly useful bumper performer: second in maiden at Kilbeggan very early in season: useful hurdler: completed 5-timer in maiden at Roscommon, and novices at Killarney, Sedgefield, Perth and Cheltenham between August-October: stays 3m: acts on good to firm and good to soft going. *Gordon Elliott, Ireland* **h132** **b97**

DINOS BENEFIT (IRE) 7 ch.m. Mr Dinos (IRE) – Beneficial Lady (IRE) (Beneficial) **c126**
[2018/19 h99, b83: c21.6g* c23.8g c17.5v^pu h21.2d² h18.5d* c19.2d³ Mar 24] fairly useful **h129**
form over hurdles: won mares handicap at Exeter in February: similar form over fences:
won mares maiden at Fontwell in November: stays 2¾m: acts on heavy going. *Colin Tizzard*

DINO VELVET (FR) 6 b.g. Naaqoos – Matgil (FR) (Grape Tree Road) [2018/19 h124: **h131**
h18.5g⁴ h15.3g h16g⁵ h16g⁵ h16.7g* h16.3s* h16m² Apr 13] sturdy gelding: useful
handicap hurdler: won at Market Rasen in February and Stratford (by 1¼ lengths from
Eceparti) in March: probably stays 2¼m: acts on soft and good to firm going. *Alan King*

DINSDALE 6 b.g. Cape Cross (IRE) – Emmy Award (IRE) (Sadler's Wells (USA)) **c126**
[2018/19 h111: h19.9g h20.3g⁵ h15.8m* c16.5d* c16.4m² c16.5m² Sep 17] good-topped **h107**
gelding: has had breathing operation: fair handicap hurdler: won at Ffos Las in July: fairly
useful form over fences: won novice handicap at Worcester in August: unproven beyond
2m: acts on soft and good to firm going: usually wears cheekpieces: wears tongue tie: has
joined Ben Pauling. *Michael Scudamore*

DIOCESE (FR) 6 b.g. Linda's Lad – Sempiternelle (FR) (Lavirco (GER)) [2018/19 **h107**
b12.9d* b14.9m* b11.9v² b11.9d³ h20.5v⁴ h15.7v³ h19.7s* h24.3d^F Jan 20] won bumpers **b?**
at Morlaix and Le Lion-d'Angers in May: fair form over hurdles: won novice handicap at
Wetherby in December: left J-F. Doucet after fourth start: dead. *R. Mike Smith*

DIOMEDE DES MOTTES (FR) 6 ch.g. Kapgarde (FR) – Nellyssa Bleu (FR) **h121**
(Epervier Bleu) [2018/19 h15.8g⁶ h21.6d² h20.5s³ h21.2d³ h19.8s h21d* Mar 28] £47,000
3-y-o, £25,000 5-y-o: well-made gelding: fifth foal: half-brother to 3 winners, including
bumper winner Babylone des Motte (by Blue Bresil) and French chaser Ulyssa des Mottes
(19f-2¾m winner, by Nononito): dam, French 1½m/13f bumper winner, half-sister to
useful hurdler (stayed 23f) Hulysse Royal: off mark in Irish points at third attempt: fairly
useful form over hurdles: won maiden at Warwick in March: stays 2¾m: acts on good to
soft going: tried in tongue tie. *Dan Skelton*

DIPLOMATE SIVOLA (FR) 6 ch.g. Noroit (GER) – None de Sivola (FR) (Cyborg **c134**
(FR)) [2018/19 c115, h112: c19.5s³ c21.6d² c23.5d* c23s² c25.2d* c24.2v^pu Mar 18] **h—**
compact gelding: winning hurdler in France: useful chaser: won intermediate handicap at
Lingfield in November and novice hunter at Catterick in March: second in handicap at
Taunton (short head behind Touch Kick) in between: stays 25f: acts on good to firm and
heavy going. *Philip Hobbs*

DIPLOMATICO (USA) 6 b.g. Ambassador (GER) – Dulcet Tone (USA) (Empire **c81**
Maker (USA)) [2018/19 h—: c20.9m⁵ c17.2g⁶ c16.3s² c21.6g c16.5g⁴ c20.3g⁴ c25.7m³ **h—**
c25.7g^pu Nov 5] has had breathing operations: maiden hurdler: poor maiden chaser:
probably stays 3¼m: acts on soft and good to firm going: has worn headgear/tongue tie: off
mark in points at second attempt in April. *David Bridgwater*

DIPPIN AND DIVING (IRE) 6 b.g. Kalanisi (IRE) – Supreme Dipper (IRE) (Supreme **b—**
Leader) [2018/19 b—: b15.7s Dec 18] well held in bumpers: tried in cheekpieces.
George Bewley

DISCAY 10 b.g. Distant Music (USA) – Caysue (Cayman Kai (IRE)) [2018/19 h20.3g* **c—**
h19.9g h19.9d⁶ h23.3s h24.1d* h20.7d² h20.5d⁴ h23.1g³ Mar 14] fair handicap hurdler: **h107**
won at Southwell in September and Wetherby in December: winning chaser: stays 3m: acts
on soft and good to firm going: has worn headgear: tried in tongue tie. *Philip Kirby*

DISCIPLE (IRE) 5 b.g. Fastnet Rock (AUS) – Gift From Heaven (IRE) (Excellent Art) **b—**
[2018/19 b16g⁶ Oct 11] tailed off in bumper. *Amy Murphy*

DISCKO DES PLAGES (FR) 6 b.g. Balko (FR) – Lady des Plages (FR) (Chamberlin **h94**
(FR)) [2018/19 b—: h16.3s h16.7s h16.3d h21s³ h21g Apr 10] tall, rather unfurnished
gelding: modest form over hurdles: stays 21f: acts on soft going: in hood last 2 starts: races
off pace. *Richard Hobson*

DISCORAMA (FR) 6 b.g. Saddler Maker (IRE) – Quentala (FR) (Lone Bid (FR)) **c149**
[2018/19 h136: c19d* c20g⁵ c24d^F c31.7s² Mar 12] lengthy, rather unfurnished gelding: **h—**
useful hurdler: smart form over fences: won maiden at Naas (by 1¼ lengths from Burgas)
in November: second in National Hunt Chase at Cheltenham (½ length behind Le Breuil) in
March and Champion Novices' Chase at Punchestown (12 lengths behind Delta Work)
shortly after end of British season: stays 4m: acts on heavy going: tried in hood: usually
races off pace. *Paul Nolan, Ireland*

DISCORDANTLY (IRE) 5 b.g. Salutino (GER) – Collinstown Queen (IRE) (King's **h128**
Ride) [2018/19 h20d h16s³ h20d³ h20d² h20.3d h20d* Apr 7] €26,000 3-y-o: half-brother
to 3 winners, including fairly useful hurdler/chaser Unowatimeen (2½m-3m winner, by
Supreme Leader) and fairly useful hurdler/winning pointer Front Man (2½m winner, by
Zaffaran): dam unraced: fairly useful form over hurdles: won maiden at Fairyhouse in
April: stays 2½m: acts on soft going. *Mrs J. Harrington, Ireland*

DISKO (FR) 8 gr.g. Martaline – Nikos Royale (FR) (Nikos) [2018/19 c164+, h–: c24gᶠ **c146**
Dec 28] useful-looking gelding: winning hurdler: high-class chaser, won 2 Grade 1 novices **h–**
in 2016/17: behind when falling heavily at last (in process of showing smart form) in
Savills Chase at Leopardstown sole start in 2018/19: stayed 25f: acted on soft going:
usually hooded: dead. *Noel Meade, Ireland*

DI'S PRIDE 6 b.m. Paco Boy (IRE) – Bramalea (Whitmore's Conn (USA)) [2018/19 **h–**
h18.7m Jun 19] poor maiden on Flat: tailed off in mares novice on hurdling debut.
David Bridgwater

DISSAVRIL (FR) 6 gr.m. Balko (FR) – Odile (FR) (Smadoun (FR)) [2018/19 b104: **h94**
h15.7g³ h16d⁵ h18.5vᶠ h16.5d⁵ h19g⁶ Feb 19] useful-looking mare: bumper winner:
modest form over hurdles. *Emma Lavelle*

DISSERTATION 7 b.m. Champs Elysees – Reel Style (Rainbow Quest (USA)) [2018/19 **c–**
c20d³ Mar 21] point winner: maiden hurdler: well beaten in hunter on chasing debut. **h–**
Andrew Quick

DISTANT HIGH 8 b.m. High Chaparral (IRE) – Distant Dreamer (USA) (Rahy (USA)) **h79**
[2018/19 h77: h16g² h23g h16.8g⁶ h16.8m⁴ h19.6g⁵ h18.7g⁴ Sep 4] poor maiden hurdler:
unproven beyond 2m: wears headgear: in tongue tie last 3 starts. *Richard Price*

DISTIME (IRE) 13 b.g. Flemensfirth (USA) – Technohead (IRE) (Distinctly North **c–**
(USA)) [2018/19 c103, h–: c20.8g May 4] workmanlike gelding: multiple point winner: **h–**
winning hurdler: fairly useful chaser at best, held in hunter in 2018/19: stays 25f: acts
on heavy going: tried in cheekpieces. *Mrs D. J. Ralph*

DISTINGO (IRE) 6 b.g. Smart Strike (CAN) – Distinctive Look (IRE) (Danehill (USA)) **h128**
[2018/19 h126: h15.8g² h15.7g³ h16g h15.7d h15.9gᶠ Feb 25] sturdy gelding: fairly useful
handicap hurdler: second at Huntingdon in November: stays 2¼m: acts on heavy going:
often wears headgear. *Gary Moore*

DISTRACTED (IRE) 11 b.m. Publisher (USA) – Richmond Usa (IRE) (Insan (USA)) **c76**
[2018/19 c86, h–: c23.8m³ c25.8gᵖᵘ c25.8g⁶ Sep 10] maiden hurdler: poor handicap chaser **h–**
nowadays: stays 27f: acts on good to firm and heavy going: wears headgear: tried in tongue
tie. *Robert Stephens*

DITES RIEN (IRE) 7 b.m. Kalanisi (IRE) – Our Soiree (IRE) (Milan) [2018/19 h83: **h70**
h23g⁶ Jul 26] poor maiden hurdler: stays 2¾m: best form on good going. *Neil Mulholland*

DIVA DU MAQUIS (FR) 6 b.m. Buck's Boum (FR) – Qualine du Maquis (FR) (Video **h91**
Rock (FR)) [2018/19 h93, b82: h21g h19.9s⁴ h23.3s h21.2d⁵ Jan 28] rather unfurnished
mare: modest maiden hurdler: should be suited by at least 3m: acts on soft going: in
cheekpieces last 3 starts. *Noel Williams*

DIVA RECONCE (FR) 6 b.m. Kap Rock (FR) – Kruscyna (FR) (Ultimately Lucky **h88**
(IRE)) [2018/19 h105p: h19.6vᵖᵘ h21d⁶ h21s⁴ Mar 10] sturdy mare: modest form over
hurdles. *Kim Bailey*

DIVIN BERE (FR) 6 b.g. Della Francesca (USA) – Mofa Bere (FR) (Saumarez) [2018/19 **h118**
h–: h15.7m⁵ h21g h23.1d Feb 22] good-topped gelding: fairly useful handicap hurdler:
fifth in listed event at Ascot in November: unproven beyond 17f: acts on soft going: tried
in blinkers/tongue tie: has joined Iain Jardine. *Paul Nicholls*

DIVINE PORT (USA) 9 b.g. Arch (USA) – Out of Reach (Warning) [2018/19 h101: **c109**
c15.9s* c16.5s³ c15.9g⁶ Feb 24] fair hurdler: similar form over fences: won novice **h–**
handicap at Carlisle in December: stays 2½m: acts on heavy going: tried in tongue tie.
Pauline Robson

DIVINE SPEAR (IRE) 8 b.g. Oscar (IRE) – Testaway (IRE) (Commanche Run) [2018/19 **c–**
c143p, h–: c20.6dᵖᵘ c24.2s c21.1dᶠ Apr 5] strong gelding: winning hurdler: useful chaser, **h–**
largely disappointing in 2018/19: stays 21f. *Nicky Henderson*

DIXIE LEE (IRE) 8 b.m. Holy Roman Emperor (IRE) – Ellazaria (Vettori (IRE)) **h130**
[2018/19 h16g³ h16.5m* h16.7m³ h17dᵖᵘ h16.5g Nov 3] third foal: dam (h110), French
2¼m hurdle winner (also 8.5f winner on Flat), closely related to fairly useful 2½m hurdle
winner Big Robert: useful hurdler: won minor event at Down Royal in June: third in
handicap at Bellewstown (1¾ lengths behind Monarch) in July: unproven beyond 17f: acts
on soft and good to firm going: has worn hood. *Dermot Anthony McLoughlin, Ireland*

DIZOARD 9 b.m. Desideratum – Riviere (Meadowbrook) [2018/19 h66: h23.3g h23.3g⁴ **h78** h23.3g h23.3g^{pu} h22g* h19.8s⁵ h23.8m⁶ Mar 22] poor handicap hurdler: won at Musselburgh in November: stays 2¾m: acts on soft going: has worn hood: usually races off pace. *Iain Jardine*

DIZZEY HEIGHTS (IRE) 7 b.m. Halling (USA) – Extreme Pleasure (IRE) (High **h84** Chaparral (IRE)) [2018/19 h86: h15.7g⁵ h20g² Jun 3] poor handicap hurdler: stays 2½m: best form on good going: wears hood: in tongue tie last 4 starts. *Neil King*

DJANGO DJANGO (FR) 6 gr.g. Voix du Nord (FR) – Lady Jannina (Sir Harry Lewis **h130** (USA)) [2018/19 h118, b89: h22g⁵ h23.6s* h24.3d h24.3m* Apr 20] sturdy gelding: useful handicap hurdler: won at Chepstow in November and Haydock (by 4 lengths from Skidoosh) in April: stays 3m: acts on soft and good to firm going. *Jonjo O'Neill*

DJARKEVI (FR) 6 b.g. Khalkevi (IRE) – Onvavoir (FR) (Diableneyev (USA)) [2018/19 **c103** h98p, b–: h15.8g² h19.6g h15.8m c19.4m^F c17.2g⁶ c16.5g⁵ c20g⁴ c20.2m³ c19.2g* Dec 28] **h96** has had breathing operation: modest maiden hurdler: fair form over fences: won handicap at Catterick in December: left Charlie Longsdon after eighth start: stays 2½m: best form on good going: usually wears hood/tongue tie: often races towards rear/freely. *Laura Morgan*

DJEBEL ROME (FR) 6 b.g. Voix du Nord (FR) – Precieuze (FR) (Video Rock (FR)) **b86** [2018/19 b17s³ b16.2d⁶ Mar 26] £14,000 5-y-o: fifth foal: half-brother to fairly useful French hurdler/chaser Voidirome (17f-19f winner, by Robin des Champs) and French chaser Be Work (2¼m-2¾m winner, by Network): dam unraced close relative to smart hurdler/top-class chaser (stayed 3m) Impek: in frame both starts in Irish points: fair form in bumpers: better effort when third at Carlisle in March. *Rebecca Menzies*

DJ HAVANA 4 b.g. Havana Gold (IRE) – Fantastic Santanyi (Fantastic Light (USA)) **b–** [2018/19 b15.7g Oct 10] well beaten in maiden bumper. *Shaun Lycett*

DJIN CONTI (FR) 6 b.g. Lucarno (USA) – Regina Conti (FR) (Lavirco (GER)) [2018/19 **c124** h99p: h15.3m* h16g h21.2g³ h25.3s² h24.4g⁶ c22.4d⁴ c24s* c26.3s² c24g* Apr 10] fair **h111** hurdler: won maiden at Wincanton in May: fairly useful form over fences: won handicap at Southwell in March and novice handicap at Warwick in April: stays 3¼m: acts on soft and good to firm going: tried in cheekpieces. *Harry Whittington*

DJINGLE (FR) 6 b.g. Voix du Nord (FR) – Jourie (FR) (Lute Antique (FR)) [2018/19 **c119** h129: c16.2g^{ur} h19.3d^{pu} Jan 19] tall gelding: fairly useful hurdler: raced freely/made **h–** mistakes and held when unseated last in novice won by Pacific de Baune at Warwick on chasing debut: stays 2¼m: acts on soft going: wears hood: has joined John Queally. *Paul Nicholls*

DOBITS SOCIETY (IRE) 5 b.g. Arcadio (GER) – Karinswift (Karinga Bay) [2018/19 **b–** b16.2g Aug 1] tailed off in bumper. *Olly Murphy*

DOC CARVER (IRE) 8 ch.g. Lakeshore Road (USA) – Tuney Tulip (IRE) (Taipan **c121** (IRE)) [2018/19 h117: c16s c15.7s³ c16d⁴ c15.9g² c20.9d⁴ c16s³ Apr 7] has had breathing **h–** operation: fairly useful maiden hurdler: similar form over fences: won handicap at Chepstow in January: bred to stay at least 2½m: acts on heavy going: has worn tongue tie. *Henry Oliver*

DOC PENFRO 7 b.g. Dr Massini (IRE) – Prescelli (IRE) (Snurge) [2018/19 b89: h20g² **h109** Jun 27] rangy gelding: in front when fell last in Irish point: fair form in bumpers: 9/2 and tongue tied, shaped well when second in maiden at Worcester (4½ lengths behind Black Kalanisi) on hurdling debut: seemed likely to progress but not seen out again. *Kevin Frost*

DOCTE DINA (FR) 5 ch.m. Doctor Dino (FR) – Artofmen (FR) (Lord of Men) [2018/19 **b79** b16.7d⁵ Apr 26] fifth foal: half-sister to French 2¼m/19f hurdle/chase winner La Henriade (by Turgeon): dam, French 17f-19f hurdle/chase winner (also 7.5f/1m winner on Flat), half-sister to fair hurdler/smart chaser (winner up to 21f) Something Wells: 9/2, fifth in mares bumper at Bangor (11¾ lengths behind The Milan Girl). *Nicky Henderson*

DOCTOR DEX (IRE) 6 b.g. Oscar (IRE) – Larnalee (IRE) (Presenting) [2018/19 b98: **h119** b16g² h15.6g² h16g* h19.4g* h20.3d h20d⁶ Apr 5] good-topped gelding: fair form in **b94** bumpers: fairly useful form over hurdles: won maiden at Wetherby in January and novice at Doncaster in February: stays 19f: temperament under suspicion. *Tom George*

DOCTOR HAZE 8 b.g. Dr Massini (IRE) – Gypsy Haze (Romany Rye) [2018/19 h101: **c–** c23.6g^{pu} May 22] winning pointer: maiden hurdler: pulled up in novice handicap on **h–** chasing debut: should be suited by 2½m+. *Kim Bailey*

DOCTOR JAZZ (IRE) 4 b.g. Most Improved (IRE) – Daliyana (IRE) (Cadeaux **h–** Genereux) [2018/19 h16d⁵ h16.4s h16.2g h16.7m⁵ Apr 21] fair on Flat, stays 11.5f: little form over hurdles. *Donald McCain*

DOCTOR PHOENIX (IRE) 11 br.g. Dr Massini (IRE) – Lowroad Cross (IRE)   **c144**
(Anshan) [2018/19 c162, h–: c20g⁵ c16.7v² c17g⁶ c20.5g⁶ c21g c16g² c18sᵖᵘ c20d⁵ Apr 22]   **h–**
winning hurdler: useful chaser nowadays, not force he was in 2017/18: second of 4
in Grade 3 event at Naas (3 lengths behind Cadmium) in February: stays 21f: acts on heavy
going: wears cheekpieces/tongue tie: usually races in rear. *Gordon Elliott, Ireland*

DOCTOR THEA 6 b.m. Multiplex – Kallithea (IRE) (Dr Fong (USA)) [2018/19 h79,   **h99**
h82: h20.6g* h22.1g⁵ h19.9m⁵ h23.1m³ h23.9d Feb 28] lengthy mare: modest handicap   **b82**
hurdler: won at Market Rasen early in season: left Jedd O'Keeffe after fourth start: stays
23f: acts on good to firm going: tried in visor. *Ryan Chapman*

DOCTOR WONG 7 b.g. Dr Massini (IRE) – Kitty Wong (IRE) (Supreme Leader)   **h–**
[2018/19 b–: h20.3gᵖᵘ Jun 5] placed in points: well held in bumper: pulled up in maiden on
hurdling debut. *Tom George*

DODGYBINGO (IRE) 6 b.g. Roderic O'Connor (IRE) – Happy Flight (IRE) (Titus   **h99**
Livius (FR)) [2018/19 h120: h17.2g h17.2m⁴ h17.2g³ h17.2d⁴ h20.2gᵖᵘ Sep 26] rather
leggy gelding: modest handicap hurdler: fatally injured at Perth: unproven beyond 17f:
acted on soft and good to firm going: wore headgear. *James Moffatt*

DOES IT IN STYLE (FR) 6 b.g. Balko (FR) – Malta de Ronceray (FR) (Dress Parade)   **h–**
[2018/19 h74: h18.5g May 16] poor maiden hurdler: will stay 2½m: in cheekpieces last 3
starts: no impact in points. *Dan Skelton*

DOESYOURDOGBITE (IRE) 7 b.g. Notnowcato – Gilah (IRE) (Saddlers' Hall (IRE))   **h109**
[2018/19 h116: h23.6d³ h23.3d h19.9d Mar 30] compact gelding: fair handicap hurdler:
stays 23f: acts on heavy going: wears headgear: temperament under suspicion. *Jonjo
O'Neill*

DOG OF WAR (FR) 5 b.g. Soldier of Fortune (IRE) – Zainzana (FR) (Green Desert   **b92**
(USA)) [2018/19 b16m b16g³ Mar 29] €95,000 3-y-o: lengthy, rather unfurnished gelding:
has had breathing operation: second foal: dam unraced half-sister to high-class hurdler/
smart chaser (stayed 21f) Zaynar and high-class hurdler (stayed 25f) Zaidpour: fair form
in bumpers: better effort when third at Wetherby in March: wears tongue tie. *Dan Skelton*

DOGON 4 b.g. Intello (GER) – Poppets Sweetlove (Foxhound (USA)) [2018/19 h17.9s³   **c127 p**
h16.9s² h16.9g³ c17.9s* h16.8dᵖᵘ h15.3g² h16.4sᵖᵘ Mar 13] closely related to smart 7f-9f   **h124**
winner Patentar (by Teofilo) and half-brother to 3 other winners on Flat: dam 7f/1m
winner: fairly useful maiden hurdler: placed in juveniles at Compiegne in September and
October: 3/10, won minor event at Fontainebleau (by 17 lengths) on chasing debut in
November: left Francois Nicolle after: stays 2¼m: acts on heavy going: in tongue tie final
start: should do better over fences. *Paul Nicholls*

DOING FINE (IRE) 11 b.g. Presenting – Howaya Pet (IRE) (Montelimar (USA))   **c124**
[2018/19 c136, h127: c25g c27.3g c29g⁵ c31.8m Apr 13] deep-girthed gelding: has had   **h–**
breathing operation: fairly useful handicap hurdler/chaser: stays 4m: has form on heavy
going, but races mainly under less testing conditions: wears headgear/tongue tie: usually
races off pace. *Neil Mulholland*

DOITFORJOE (IRE) 9 ch.g. Vinnie Roe (IRE) – Native Kin (IRE) (Be My Native   **c–**
(USA)) [2018/19 c108, h–: h25g c22.6mᶠ c22.6mᶠ c25.8sᵖᵘ c24gᵖᵘ Sep 5] winning hurdler: **h92**
fair chaser, no form in 2018/19: stays 3¼m: acts on good to firm going: in cheekpieces last
4 starts: wears tongue tie. *David Dennis*

DOITFORTHEVILLAGE (IRE) 10 b.g. Turtle Island (IRE) – Last Chance Lady   **c141**
(IRE) (Mister Lord (USA)) [2018/19 c138, h107: c15.9g⁶ c16.4s³ c19.4s* c21d³ c20d³   **h–**
c20.6d c21.1d³ Apr 5] angular gelding: maiden hurdler: useful handicap chaser: won at
Chepstow (by 7 lengths from Dusky Lark) in December: best up to 21f: acts on heavy
going: has worn hood: wears tongue tie: races off pace. *Paul Henderson*

DO IT FOR THY SEN (IRE) 5 ch.g. Mountain High (IRE) – Ashlings Princess (IRE)   **h–**
(Salford Express (IRE)) [2018/19 b16s h19.2s Jan 27] off mark in points at second attempt: **b–**
tailed off in bumper/maiden hurdle. *Kerry Lee*

DOLCIANO DICI (FR) 6 b.g. Assessor (IRE) – Louve Rina (FR) (Loup Solitaire   **c130**
(USA)) [2018/19 c17d⁴ c21.2g c17gᵖᵘ c16.3g⁵ c18s⁶ h16v⁴ Mar 21] third foal: half-brother   **h129**
to French 1½m winner Aprilia Dici (by Shaanmer): dam French 10.5f winner: fairly useful
form over hurdles: similar form over fences: standout effort when fourth in maiden at
Navan (12¾ lengths behind Us And Them) in November: unproven beyond 17f: acts on
heavy going. *W. P. Mullins, Ireland*

DOLLAR AND A DREAM (IRE) 10 b.g. Fruits of Love (USA) – Gorgeous Georgina (IRE) (Tirol) [2018/19 c–x, h87§: h16.8g⁵ h15.8gᵖᵘ h15.8g⁶ h15.8s h19.6g³ h19.6g⁶ h15.8g Sep 12] angular gelding: poor handicap hurdler: maiden chaser: stays 2½m: acts on soft and good to firm going: has worn headgear: usually wears tongue tie: has joined Ray Peacock: not one to trust. *Michael Mullineaux* **c– h69 §**

DOLLNAMIX (FR) 8 b.g. Al Namix (FR) – Sleeping Doll (FR) (Sleeping Car (FR)) [2018/19 h20m⁵ h23g⁴ h20.3g⁴ h20g h23.9d² h19d² h19sF h23.1d² Apr 9] sturdy gelding: has had breathing operation: fair maiden hurdler: stays 23f: acts on soft going: has worn tongue tie. *Emma Lavelle* **h103**

DOLLYS DESTINATION (IRE) 6 b.m. Dubai Destination (USA) – Rehill Lass (IRE) (Shernazar) [2018/19 h87: b16.2g* h16s⁴ h16d h17.6g⁶ Apr 12] placed in Irish point: fair bumper performer: won mares event at Hexham early in season: modest form over hurdles: left Noel C. Kelly after first start. *Gary McGill, Ireland* **h98 b91**

DOLLY'S DOT (IRE) 8 b.m. Vertical Speed (FR) – Our Dot (IRE) (Supreme Leader) [2018/19 h80: h16.2g h23.1s h20.6d⁴ h19.9d⁵ Jan 11] workmanlike mare: placed all 3 completed starts in points: poor handicap hurdler: stays 21f: acts on heavy going: front runner/races prominently. *Victor Thompson* **h57**

DOLOS (FR) 6 b.g. Kapgarde (FR) – Redowa (FR) (Trempolino (USA)) [2018/19 c150, h132: c21v² c15.9s² c21s³ c15.5s* c19.9d⁵ Mar 2] good-topped gelding: winning hurdler: smart chaser: won handicap at Sandown (by 4 lengths from Gino Trail) in February: stays 21f: acts on good to firm and heavy going: wears tongue tie: usually travels strongly: temperament under suspicion. *Paul Nicholls* **c154 h–**

DOLPHIN SQUARE (IRE) 5 b.g. Shantou (USA) – Carrig Eden Lass (IRE) (Luso) [2018/19 h18.5s* h21.6s⁴ Apr 16] €30,000 3-y-o, £80,000 5-y-o: fourth foal: brother to fairly useful hurdler/chaser Game of War (2m-19f winner): dam winning pointer: off mark in Irish points at fourth attempt: fairly useful form over hurdles: won maiden at Exeter in March. *Philip Hobbs* **h120**

DOMESDAY BOOK (USA) 9 br.g. Street Cry (IRE) – Film Script (Unfuwain (USA)) [2018/19 c–, h–: c25gᵖᵘ Oct 27] workmanlike gelding: winning hurdler: useful chaser, pulled up both starts since 2016/17: stays 3¼m: acts on heavy going: wears headgear. *Stuart Edmunds* **c– h–**

DOMESTIC DIVA (IRE) 8 b.m. Definite Article – Keep It Local (IRE) (Needle Gun (IRE)) [2018/19 h20g⁶ h19.9g h16.8s⁴ c15.7g³ c16.4d⁵ Jan 21] third foal: half-sister to winning pointers by Alderbrook and Beneficial: dam ran once in bumper: maiden pointer: poor maiden hurdler: modest form over fences: better effort when third in novice handicap at Catterick in December: left Sean P. Hennessy after first start: should stay beyond 2m: acts on soft going: in cheekpieces last 3 starts: usually wears tongue tie. *Jennie Candlish* **c90 h84**

DOM GARO CATELINE (FR) 6 b.g. Ungaro (GER) – Dame Jaune (FR) (Le Nain Jaune (FR)) [2018/19 ab16g⁴ h16.8sF Mar 21] sturdy gelding: well beaten in bumper: fell heavily second on hurdling debut. *Thomas Gallagher* **h– b–**

DOMINATEUR (FR) 6 b.g. Desir d'Un Soir (FR) – Sourya d'Airy (FR) (Sheyrann) [2018/19 h93p: h15.7g³ h19.5s² h19.5v³ h19.5v* h19.3s* Mar 7] fairly useful form over hurdles: won novices at Lingfield in February and Carlisle in March: likely to stay 3m: acts on heavy going. *Oliver Sherwood* **h118**

DOMINGO (FR) 6 b.g. Special Kaldoun (IRE) – Puligny Montrachet (FR) (Robin des Champs (FR)) [2018/19 c107, h–: c23.6dᵖᵘ c24gᵖᵘ Apr 25] maiden hurdler: fair chaser at best, pulled up both starts in 2018/19: stays 21f: acts on heavy going: has worn cheekpieces. *Venetia Williams* **c– h–**

DOMMAGE POUR TOI (FR) 6 b.g. Magadan (IRE) – Phenyl des Mottes (FR) (Bonnet Rouge (FR)) [2018/19 h16.6d³ h20s² h20d* Apr 7] €35,000 3-y-o: fourth foal: half-brother to a winning pointer by Malinas: dam, placed in 1½m bumpers in France, half-sister to dam of smart hurdler/very smart chaser around 2m Trifolium: pulled up in point on debut: useful form over hurdles: won Grade 2 novice at Fairyhouse (by ¾ length from Zero Ten) in April: improved further when 10 lengths fifth to Reserve Tank in Champion Novices' Hurdle at Punchestown shortly after end of British season. *Henry de Bromhead, Ireland* **h140**

DONA KATHARINA (IRE) 5 b.m. Stowaway – Western Whisper (IRE) (Supreme Leader) [2018/19 b16.2g⁵ b18g³ b16.5s² b16v² b16d⁵ b20d Apr 23] €70,000 3-y-o: sister to several winners, including very smart hurdler/top-class chaser Outlander (2m-3m winner) and useful hurdler/chaser Now McGinty (21f/3m winner): dam ran twice in bumpers: modest bumper performer. *Gordon Elliott, Ireland* **b83**

DONALD DUX (IRE) 5 b.g. Sholokhov (IRE) – Good Shine (IRE) (Beneficial) [2018/19 h– b15.7m h19.3v⁴ Mar 17] tailed off in bumper/novice hurdle. *Andrew Crook* **b–**

DONATELLO MAIL (FR) 6 ch.g. Zambezi Sun – Kestrel Mail (FR) (Cricket Ball **h–** (USA)) [2018/19 b15.8s h20.7d Feb 17] tailed off in bumper/novice hurdle. *David Dennis* **b–**

DON BERSY (FR) 6 b.g. Califet (FR) – Tropulka God (FR) (Tropular) [2018/19 h132: **c– §** c16dᵀᵀ h15.8gᵀᵀ Nov 13] good-topped gelding: fairly useful hurdler: refused to race both **h– §** starts under Rules in 2018/19, including on chasing debut: won twice in points in 2019: unproven beyond 17f: acts on soft going: tried in hood: one to leave alone. *Tom Symonds*

DONCESAR DE PRETOT (FR) 6 gr.g. Saddler Maker (IRE) – Kobila (FR) (Dom **h110** Alco (FR)) [2018/19 h20d² h20.3s⁴ Mar 18] has had breathing operation: fifth foal: half-brother to French cross-country chasers Capello de Pretot (2¾m winner, by Martaline) and Usagi (21f-3m winner, by Le Balafre): dam, French 19f/2½m hurdle/chase winner, half-sister to useful hurdler/chaser (17f-23f winner) Qozak: fair form over hurdles: trained in France before 2018/19: stays 2½m: acts on good to soft going: tried in cheekpieces. *Olly Murphy*

DON DES FOSSES (FR) 6 b.g. Denham Red (FR) – Sara des Fosses (FR) (Califet (FR)) **c99 §** [2018/19 h71p, b94: h20gᶠ h21.9d⁴ h19.6g⁵ h19.5d h20.3sᵖᵘ c20d c16.4s² c17s c19.7g⁴ **h106 §** c19.7g² Apr 21] sturdy gelding: has had breathing operations: won Irish point on debut: bumper winner: fair form over hurdles: modest form over fences: stays 2½m: acts on soft going: in headgear/tongue tie last 4 starts: temperamental. *Warren Greatrex*

DON HERBAGER (FR) 5 b.g. Saddler Maker (IRE) – Marie d'Altoria (FR) (Roi de **h67** Rome (USA)) [2018/19 h90: h16s h19.7s h19.7d h19.5dᵖᵘ Apr 6] largely poor form over hurdles. *Venetia Williams*

DON JUAN DU GOUET (FR) 6 b.g. Special Kaldoun (IRE) – Querida de Ferbet (FR) **h101** (Ragmar (FR)) [2018/19 b15.8s⁴ b15.8v⁵ h15.8g h15.8g⁵ h16.3g h21.2m Apr 23] third **b80** foal: dam, French maiden (placed in cross-country chases up to 23f), half-sister to smart hurdler/chaser (stays 25f) Val de Ferbet: modest form in bumpers: fair form over hurdles. *Henry Daly*

DONLADD (IRE) 5 b.g. Cloudings (IRE) – Kentford Serotina (Emperor Fountain) **b82** [2018/19 b16.7v⁵ b16d b16.3d Mar 23] £56,000 3-y-o: third foal: dam, of little account, half-sister to useful chaser up to 25f The Land Agent: modest form in bumpers. *Oliver Sherwood*

DON LAMI (FR) 6 ch.g. Honolulu (IRE) – Toutamie (FR) (Epalo (GER)) [2018/19 h109, **h118** b99: h25.8g* h25.8m² May 27] won Irish point on debut: bumper winner: fairly useful form over hurdles: won novice at Fontwell early in season: stays 3¼m: acts on good to firm and heavy going. *Anthony Honeyball*

DONNA'S DELIGHT (IRE) 8 b.g. Portrait Gallery (IRE) – Hot Lips (IRE) (Good **c120** Thyne (USA)) [2018/19 h120: c20g c23.4d³ c23.4g³ c24.5g³ Feb 24] fairly useful hurdler: **h–** similar form over fences: third in handicap at Newcastle in January: should be suited by long distances: acts on heavy going: in cheekpieces last 2 starts. *Sandy Thomson*

DONNA'S DIAMOND (IRE) 10 gr.g. Cloudings (IRE) – Inish Bofin (IRE) (Glacial **c121** Storm (USA)) [2018/19 c–, h144: c24.2s² h24.2g⁵ c22.3g⁴ c22.3g* h24.3g⁵ Feb 16] workmanlike **h–** gelding: useful hurdler: fairly useful form over fences: won novice at Kelso in December: stays 3¼m: acts on heavy going: usually races close up. *Chris Grant*

DONNAS DREAM (IRE) 6 b.m. Kalanisi (IRE) – Gerarda (IRE) (Toulon) [2018/19 **h102** b71: b17.1d h20.6g² h20.9g⁶ h19.9s³ h24s h19.8m³ h23.8m⁴ h19.7g⁴ Apr 11] poor form in **b–** bumpers: fair maiden hurdler: stays 21f: acts on soft and good to firm going: tried in cheekpieces: races off pace: has worn cheekpieces, including final start: has joined Mark Walford. *Chris Grant*

DO NOT DISTURB (IRE) 6 b.g. Mahler – Galbertstown Run (IRE) (Oscar (IRE)) **b–** [2018/19 b16v Nov 14] third in Irish point: 7/1, left behind straight in bumper at Ayr. *Rose Dobbin*

DON POLI (IRE) 10 b.g. Poliglote – Dalamine (FR) (Sillery (USA)) [2018/19 c25.9sᵖᵘ **c117** h24sᵖᵘ c26.2v³ c34.3g Apr 6] strong gelding: winning hurdler: top-class chaser at best, **h–** nothing like force of old: left Gordon Elliott after third start: stays 3¼m: acts on heavy going: has worn cheekpieces, including final start. *Philip Kirby*

DON'T ASK (IRE) 6 b.g. Ask – Outback Ivy (IRE) (Bob Back (USA)) [2018/19 h125, **h125** b91: h16v h19dᶠ Dec 13] fairly useful form over hurdles: third when fell last in handicap at Taunton in December: will prove suited by 2½m: acts on good to firm and heavy going: front runner/races prominently: has joined Sam Thomas. *Warren Greatrex*

DONT BE ROBIN (IRE) 7 b.g. Robin des Pres (FR) – Rainbow Times (IRE) (Jareer (USA)) [2018/19 h97, b61: h16.2g h19d h15.3d h19.7d⁶ h19d c16d⁴ c20.2g⁵ c17.5v³ c26.7g^ur c24.2d⁵ c26.2g* Apr 26] maiden Irish pointer: poor maiden hurdler: similar form over fences: won handicap at Chepstow in April: stays 3¼m: acts on heavy going: wears headgear. *Richenda Ford* **c82** **h82**

DONT CALL ME DORIS 9 b.m. Franklins Gardens – Grove Dancer (Reprimand) [2018/19 h–: h15.7g^pu h16.7g h16g^pu h17.7v^pu h16.5g^pu Jan 9] rather leggy mare: no form over hurdles: front runner/races prominently. *Sarah Robinson* **h–**

DONTCOUNTURCHIKENS (IRE) 5 b.g. Getaway (GER) – Stormy Breeze (IRE) (Glacial Storm (USA)) [2018/19 b81: b16s b16.6g² b18.5g³ Apr 20] has had breathing operation: fair form in bumpers: second in conditionals/amateurs event at Doncaster in March: 16/1, some encouragement when third in maiden at Newton Abbot (17¼ lengths behind Boomarang) on hurdling debut: wears tongue tie: entitled to do better. *David Dennis* **h98 p** **b87**

DON'T CRY ABOUT IT (IRE) 4 ch.g. Casamento (IRE) – Back At de Front (IRE) (Cape Cross (IRE)) [2018/19 h15.3f⁴ h16.7d Nov 14] modest maiden on Flat, stays 1¼m: poor form over hurdles. *Ali Stronge* **h70**

DONTDELAY (IRE) 9 b.g. Indian Danehill (IRE) – Garden Heaven (IRE) (Roselier (FR)) [2018/19 h23.3v* c24.2s⁴ h27s² h23.3v* h24d⁶ Apr 6] modest handicap hurdler: won at Hexham in December and March: 7/1, fourth in novice handicap at Wetherby (7¾ lengths behind Moving In Style) on chasing debut: stays 27f: acts on heavy going: sometimes in cheekpieces: tried in tongue tie: usually front runner/races prominently. *Micky Hammond* **c81** **h94**

DONT DO MONDAYS (IRE) 12 b.g. Rashar (USA) – Bit of A Chance (Lord Ha Ha) [2018/19 c–, h–: c21.6g² c26.3d Mar 15] multiple point winner: winning hurdler: fairly useful chaser: second in hunter at Fontwell early in season: stays 23f: acts on heavy going: usually wears headgear: tried in tongue tie. *Mrs Libby Lawson* **c117** **h–**

DON'T FENCE ME IN (IRE) 4 b.f. Fame And Glory – Great Idea (IRE) (Lion Cavern (USA)) [2018/19 h16d^pu Nov 28] modest form on Flat: pulled up in juvenile maiden on hurdling debut. *Paul Webber* **h–**

DONTMINDDBOYS (IRE) 10 gr.g. Portrait Gallery (IRE) – Native Ocean (IRE) (Be My Native (USA)) [2018/19 c102, h–: c25.2s^pu c24s³ c23.6d c22.7g^pu Mar 8] tall gelding: maiden hurdler: modest handicap chaser: stays 25f: acts on heavy going: has worn headgear, including last 3 starts: has worn tongue tie: often races lazily. *Robin Dickin* **c97** **h–**

DON'T SHOUT (IRE) 5 b.g. Oscar (IRE) – Asta Belle (FR) (Astarabad (USA)) [2018/19 b16s⁶ b16.7g² Apr 13] €110,000 3-y-o: lengthy gelding: has scope: fifth foal: brother to useful hurdler/winning pointer Lisnagar Oscar (19f-3m winner): dam unraced sister to high-class hurdler/top-class chaser (stays 3¼m) Whisper: fair form in bumpers: better effort when second in conditionals/amateurs event at Bangor. *Nigel Twiston-Davies* **b93**

DON'T TELL GEORGE (FR) 6 b.g. Enrique – Anowa (FR) (Lost World (IRE)) [2018/19 h87, b–: h19.5s h21.7d³ h19.2v⁴ Mar 16] has had breathing operation: modest form over hurdles: stays 2¾m: acts on heavy going: tried in hood/tongue tie. *Chris Gordon* **h95**

DONT TELL THE WIFE 5 b.g. Midnight Legend – Dizzy Frizzy (Loup Sauvage (USA)) [2018/19 b16g⁴ ab16.3s h16g Apr 10] modest form in bumpers: tailed off in novice on hurdling debut: tried in tongue tie. *Caroline Bailey* **h–** **b79**

DON'T THINK SO (IRE) 4 b.g. So You Think (NZ) – Lady Sefton (Oratorio (IRE)) [2018/19 b13.7g b14d b16g⁶ Feb 15] no form in bumpers: tried in cheekpieces: in tongue tie last 2 starts. *John Ryan* **b–**

DON'T TOUCH IT (IRE) 9 b.g. Scorpion (IRE) – Shandora (IRE) (Supreme Leader) [2018/19 c122, h–: h16g c17g⁵ h16s c17d³ c20s* c20m h16g⁴ Oct 16] fairly useful hurdler: useful chaser: won minor event at Listowel (by head from Listen Dear) in September: stays 2½m: acts on heavy going: usually wears cheekpieces nowadays: usually races towards rear. *Mrs J. Harrington, Ireland* **c141** **h126**

DORADO DOLLAR (IRE) 5 ch.g. Golden Lariat (USA) – Stability Treaty (IRE) (Old Vic) [2018/19 b16.2s ab16s h20.6m⁴ Apr 21] rather unfurnished gelding: well held in bumpers/maiden hurdle. *Ben Case* **h–** **b–**

DORANS RIVER (IRE) 9 br.g. Golan (IRE) – Inch Sunset (IRE) (Zaffaran (USA))   **c123**
[2018/19 h24g⁴ h21s⁴ h24g* h24s³ c22gᶠ c22.5sᵘʳ h24gᵖᵘ h24gᵖᵘ h24d h22.5g h22g² Apr   **h130**
12] useful handicap hurdler: won at Bellewstown in August: showing promise when stumbled
and fell after 2 out in maiden at Limerick on chasing debut: badly let down by jumping next
time: stays 3m: acts on soft and good to firm going: wears tongue tie. *S. J. Mahon, Ireland*

DORA'S FIELD (IRE) 6 b.m. Rip Van Winkle (IRE) – Rydal Mount (IRE) (Cape Cross   **h86**
(IRE)) [2018/19 h19m⁵ h18.5v⁶ h16d h16.8d³ h18.5d* Apr 9] fair on Flat, stays 1¼m:
modest form over hurdles: won novice seller at Exeter in April: stays 19f: acts on good to
firm and good to soft going: tried in blinkers: wears tongue tie: usually races towards rear.
Stuart Kittow

DORETTE (FR) 6 b.m. Kingsalsa (USA) – Ombrelle (FR) (Octagonal (NZ)) [2018/19   **b79**
b16.8m* b17.7g³ Sep 9] €6,500 3-y-o: fifth foal: half-sister to bumper winner/fairly useful
hurdler Aurillac (19f winner, by Martaline): dam lightly-raced half-sister to fairly useful
hurdler/smart chaser (2m-21f winner) Jim: modest form in bumpers: won at Newton Abbot
in August. *Olly Murphy*

DORKING BOY 5 ch.g. Schiaparelli (GER) – Megasue (Kayf Tara) [2018/19 b99: h19.5d   **h106**
h15.8d⁴ Feb 6] has had breathing operation: bumper winner: fair form over hurdles: better
effort when fourth in novice at Ludlow: usually in tongue tie. *Tom Lacey*

DORKING COCK (IRE) 5 b.g. Winged Love (IRE) – Kiss Jolie (FR) (Cadoudal (FR))   **h121**
[2018/19 b92: h19.2s³ h20g h15.7s h19.7s³ h16s* h17g* h17v² Mar 17] good-topped
gelding: will make a chaser: fairly useful handicap hurdler: won at Sandown (conditionals)
and Carlisle in February: stays 2½m: acts on heavy going: front runner/races prominently.
Tom Lacey

DORMOUSE 14 b.g. Medicean – Black Fighter (USA) (Secretariat (USA)) [2018/19   **h–**
h20.6g May 11] compact gelding: fair hurdler, well held sole start in 2018/19: stays 19f:
acts on good to firm and heavy going: wears cheekpieces: tried in tongue tie: usually races
towards rear. *Olly Murphy*

DOROTHY'S FLAME 7 ch.m. Black Sam Bellamy (IRE) – Flame of Zara (Blushing   **h–**
Flame (USA)) [2018/19 b16.2g b16.4d b16.8s h19.9v⁵ h19.9v⁶ h23.3d h24d Apr 6] third   **b–**
foal: dam placed in bumpers: no form in bumpers/over hurdles. *Jonathan Haynes*

DORRANA (IRE) 5 br.m. Darsi (FR) – Arts Theater (IRE) (King's Theatre (IRE))   **h–**
[2018/19 b16.8s⁵ b15.8s h18.5s Mar 18] half-sister to bumper winner/smart hurdler   **b73**
Shinrock Paddy (2m-2½m winner, by Deploy) and 2¼m bumper winner Spring Lane (by
Exit To Nowhere): dam unraced: poor form in bumpers: tailed off in maiden on hurdling
debut. *Kayley Woollacott*

DORRELLS PIERJI (FR) 6 br.g. Coastal Path – Playa Pierji (FR) (Sleeping Car (FR))   **h141**
[2018/19 b20g* b16g* h20s* h16g³ h20.7s* h24s⁶ h22g h24d Mar 15] €26,000 3-y-o: **b107**
angular gelding: fifth foal: half-brother to 3 winners in France, including fair hurdler/fairly
useful chaser Volnay Pierji (17f-19f winner, by Kotky Bleu): dam French 11f bumper
winner: winning pointer: useful form in bumpers: won at Wexford (maiden) in May and
Galway (by 2¾ lengths from Beautiful Citi) in August: useful form over hurdles: won
maiden at Listowel in September and novice at Galway in October: best effort when 1¼
lengths third of 25 to Mr Adjudicator in Ballymore Handicap Hurdle at Punchestown
shortly after end of British season: stays 21f: acts on soft going. *W. P. Mullins, Ireland*

DORTMUND PARK (FR) 6 b.g. Great Pretender (IRE) – Qena (FR) (Le Balafre (FR))   **h–**
[2018/19 h146: h20d⁵ h20g Dec 2] good-bodied gelding: has had breathing operation:
bumper winner: smart hurdler, disappointing since 2017/18: stays 2¾m: best form on soft/
heavy going: wears tongue tie. *Gordon Elliott, Ireland*

DORY (IRE) 6 br.m. Westerner – Papal Princess (IRE) (Revoque (IRE)) [2018/19 h105,   **h104**
b92: h20g² h19.9g* h19g² h20g h24.4g⁴ Nov 30] sturdy mare: bumper winner: fair hurdler:
won maiden at Uttoxeter in July: stays 2½m: acts on soft going: in cheekpieces last 2 starts:
front runner/races prominently. *Ian Williams*

DOSTAL PHIL (FR) 6 b.g. Coastal Path – Quiphile (FR) (Panoramic) [2018/19 h107p: **h120**
h15.8g² h16.4g h16.3d² h18.5s* Mar 18] useful-looking gelding: has had breathing
operation: fairly useful form over hurdles: won maiden at Exeter in March: stays 19f: acts
on soft going: in hood last 3 starts. *Philip Hobbs*

DO THE FANDANGO (IRE) 5 ch.m. Mahler – Stein Castle (IRE) (Shantou (USA))   **b–**
[2018/19 b17.1dᵖᵘ b16.2d Nov 10] second foal: dam unraced half-sister to smart hurdler/
high-class chaser (stayed 21f) Thisthatandtother, useful hurdler/very smart chaser (stayed
3¼m) The Tother One and useful hurdler/top-class chaser (stayed 3¼m) Carlingford
Lough: no form in bumpers. *Harriet Graham*

DOTHRAKI PRINCE 5 b.g. Sulamani (IRE) – Crystal Princess (IRE) (Definite Article) **b84**
[2018/19 b16.4g³ b15.6m³ Feb 28] fourth foal: half-brother to 3 winners, including bumper
winner/useful hurdler Harambe (2m/19f winner, by Malinas) and fair hurdler/chaser
Diamond Rock (17f-19f winner, by Kayf Tara): dam unraced half-sister to useful hurdler/
smart chaser up to 3m Bags Groove: modest form in bumpers: better effort when third at
Newcastle in November. *Chris Grant*

DOTHRAKI RAIDER 8 b.g. Kayf Tara – French Spice (Cadeaux Genereux) [2018/19 **h90**
h87: h22.1g⁴ h19.7s Nov 28] workmanlike gelding: modest handicap hurdler: stays 2¾m:
acts on good to firm going: tried in hood: wears tongue tie: has awkward head carriage.
Sophie Leech

DOTTIES DILEMA (IRE) 11 b.g. Pierre – Tellarue (IRE) (Rhoman Rule (USA)) **c112**
[2018/19 c103, h98: h26d⁶ h23g² h23.9g⁴ c25.5d* c24g* c24g³ c25gᵖᵘ Oct 26] **h102**
fair handicap hurdler: fair handicap chaser: won at Cartmel in August and Southwell in
September: stays 3¼m: acts on heavy going: wears headgear/tongue tie: can finish weakly.
Peter Bowen

DOUBLE COURT (IRE) 8 b.g. Court Cave (IRE) – Miss Top (IRE) (Tremblant) **h82**
[2018/19 h77: h20g⁴ h20g³ h18.6g* h18.5m Nov 6] poor handicap hurdler: won at Market
Rasen in September: stays 23f: acts on good to firm and heavy going: often wears headgear.
Nigel Twiston-Davies

DOUBLE MISS 8 b.m. Double Trigger (IRE) – Ladyalder (Alderbrook) [2018/19 h20g **h82**
h23g⁶ Jul 4] poor form over hurdles: placed in points later in season: tried in headgear.
Robert Stephens

DOUBLE ROSS (IRE) 13 ch.g. Double Eclipse (IRE) – Kinross (Nearly A Hand) **c116**
[2018/19 c141, h–: c23.8g⁵ c23.6dᶠ c25gᵖᵘ c24s c15.7g² c23.6d* Mar 21] strong gelding: **h–**
winning hurdler: fairly useful chaser nowadays: won hunter at Chepstow in March: stays
3¼m: acts on heavy going: has worn cheekpieces: tried in tongue tie: usually races close
up. *Nigel Twiston-Davies*

DOUBLE SHUFFLE (IRE) 9 b.g. Milan – Fiddlers Bar (IRE) (Un Desperado (FR)) **c155**
[2018/19 c162?, h–: c24.2gᶠ c25s² c24g⁵ c24g² c26.3dᵖᵘ c21.1d Apr 5] lengthy, useful- **h–**
looking gelding: winning hurdler: very smart chaser: second in Many Clouds Chase at
Aintree (4½ lengths behind Definitly Red) in December and Grade 3 handicap at Kempton
(length behind Walt) in February: stays 25f: acts on soft going: usually wears hood.
Tom George

DOUBLE TREASURE 8 b.g. King's Theatre (IRE) – Double Red (IRE) (Thatching) **c–**
[2018/19 c142, h–: h21.7g* h21.6m* h19.5d² h21gᵖᵘ h21.7g² h21.7g* Apr 24] sturdy **h128**
gelding: has had breathing operation: fairly useful hurdler: won novices at Fontwell and
Newton Abbot in June and again at Fontwell in April: second in Persian War Novices'
Hurdle at Chepstow (2 lengths behind Secret Investor) in October: useful chaser: stays
2¾m: acts on good to firm and good to soft going: tried in hood: wears tongue tie: front
runner. *Jamie Snowden*

DOUBLE WHAMMY 13 b.g. Systematic – Honor Rouge (IRE) (Highest Honor (FR)) **c126**
[2018/19 c126, h–: c23.8g² c26.2g² c26.3dᵖᵘ c23.8g² Apr 25] leggy gelding: maiden **h–**
hurdler: fairly useful hunter chaser: runner-up 3 times in 2018/19: stays 31f: acts on good
to firm and heavy going: wears headgear: has joined Linda Jewell. *Iain Jardine*

DOUBLE W'S (IRE) 9 ch.g. Fruits of Love (USA) – Zaffre (IRE) (Mtoto) [2018/19 **c135**
c125, h–: c17.1g⁶ c16g* Apr 25] tall gelding: winning hurdler: useful handicap chaser: won **h–**
at Perth (by 1¾ lengths from Eyes of A Tiger) in April: best around 2m: acts on soft going:
usually races off pace. *Ruth Jefferson*

DOUBLY CLEVER (IRE) 7 ch.g. Iffraaj – Smartest (IRE) (Exceed And Excel (AUS)) **c102**
[2018/19 h125: h18.5v³ h21.4g⁶ h19.8s⁶ c16.5g⁴ Apr 11] workmanlike gelding: fair **h114**
handicap hurdler: 8/1, fourth in novice handicap at Huntingdon (15 lengths behind Paddy's
Poem) on chasing debut: stays 2½m: acts on soft and good to firm going: has worn
headgear: tried in tongue tie: often races lazily. *Michael Blake*

DOUG THE WELDER 7 ch.g. Schiaparelli (GER) – Mewstone (Supreme Leader) **b–**
[2018/19 b16d⁶ Aug 29] tailed off in bumper: placed once from 3 starts in points later in
season. *Nigel Hawke*

DOUNIKOS (FR) 8 b.g. Smadoun (FR) – Baby Sitter (FR) (Nikos) [2018/19 c153, h–: **c152**
c24d c24.5g c25sᶠ c28.7d* c34.3gᵖᵘ c29dᵖᵘ Apr 22] rangy gelding: winning hurdler: smart **h–**
handicap chaser: won at Punchestown (by 4¼ lengths from Wishmoor) in February: stays
29f: acts on heavy going. *Gordon Elliott, Ireland*

DOUX PRETENDER (FR) 6 b.g. Great Pretender (IRE) – Lynnka (FR) (Passing Sale **h124** (FR)) [2018/19 h122: h19.2g* h21.6g* h24s⁵ h21g^pu Jan 12] tall gelding: fairly useful form over hurdles: won novices at Towcester in May and Ascot in November: stays 2¾m: acts on good to soft going. *Nicky Henderson*

DOVE MOUNTAIN (IRE) 8 b.g. Danehill Dancer (IRE) – Virginia Waters (USA) **h–** (Kingmambo (USA)) [2018/19 h101: h16.3m^ur h15.7d Nov 20] has had breathing operation: fair hurdler, well below form in 2018/19: raced around 2m: acts on soft going: wears headgear/tongue tie. *Olly Murphy*

DOVILS DATE 10 gr.g. Clodovil (IRE) – Lucky Date (IRE) (Halling (USA)) [2018/19 **h98** h103: h19.9g⁴ h21.4f⁴ h24g³ h23.3d⁶ Mar 30] sturdy gelding: modest handicap hurdler: stays 3m: acts on soft going: in tongue tie last 2 starts. *Tim Vaughan*

DOWHATUDODOBEST (IRE) 6 b.m. City Honours (USA) – Crowning Virtue (IRE) **h78** (Jimble (FR)) [2018/19 h15.7g⁶ h20.3g⁶ h17.7g⁴ h20.5m⁴ h23.4d³ h19d h20.5d⁵ h20.5g³ Feb 25] £22,000 5-y-o: first foal: dam, lightly raced over hurdles, half-sister to useful hurdler/smart chaser (stayed 25f) Magnanimity out of half-sister to Grand National winner Amberleigh House: placed both starts in Irish points: poor maiden hurdler: stays 21f: acts on good to firm going: in headgear last 3 starts. *Phil Middleton*

DOWNBYTHESTRAND (IRE) 10 b.g. Vertical Speed (FR) – Fancyfacia (IRE) **c90** (Luso) [2018/19 c22.7m⁴ c20.9s⁴ Mar 11] point winner: modest form in novice hunter chases. *F. A. Hutsby*

DOWNE MILKING LANE 5 b.g. Fair Mix (IRE) – Downe Payment (IRE) (Saddlers' **b–** Hall (IRE)) [2018/19 b17.7s b17.7d Feb 24] tailed off in bumpers. *Diana Grissell*

DOWNLOADTHEAPP (IRE) 6 b.g. Definite Article – Chase A Dream (IRE) (Lord of **h87** Appeal) [2018/19 h91: h19.9g³ h25.8g² h25g^pu h19.2v⁵ Dec 26] modest maiden hurdler: stays 3¼m: tried in cheekpieces: usually races freely. *David Bridgwater*

DOWN THE HIGHWAY (IRE) 6 b.g. Duke of Marmalade (IRE) – Petit Moselle (IRE) **h124** (Sadler's Wells (USA)) [2018/19 h19.5s* h19.8v^pu h19.5d⁴ h24.3g Feb 16] £80,000 5-y-o: strong gelding: second foal: dam unraced: won on debut in Irish point: fairly useful form over hurdles: won novice at Lingfield in November: should stay beyond 2½m. *Emma Lavelle*

DOWNTOWN GETAWAY (IRE) 6 b.g. Getaway (GER) – Shang A Lang (IRE) **h121** (Commander Collins (IRE)) [2018/19 b114: h20.5s² h21.6d* h24.7d Apr 5] sturdy gelding: useful bumper performer: fairly useful form over hurdles: won novice at Ascot in January. *Nicky Henderson*

DOWNTOWN REBEL (USA) 5 b.g. Arch (USA) – Downtown Drifter (USA) (Devil **h94** His Due (USA)) [2018/19 h16g h16m⁴ h17.6g⁵ h20g Aug 15] dam half-sister to useful 2m hurdle winner Arch Rebel (by Arch): modest maiden hurdler: left A. Slattery after third start: unproven beyond 2m: acts on heavy going: wears headgear: front runner/races prominently. *Denis Quinn*

DOYEN MCKAY (IRE) 5 b.m. Doyen (IRE) – Mawly Day (IRE) (Fourstars Allstar **b–** (USA)) [2018/19 b16.8g⁶ Oct 21] closely related to fair hurdler/useful chaser Kilmurry (2m/17f winner, by King's Theatre): dam, unraced, out of sister to high-class hurdler/smart chaser (stayed 3¼m) Cab On Target: in tongue strap, 25/1, well held in bumper at Sedgefield. *Mrs Sarah Dawson, Ireland*

DOYOUMIND 7 b.g. Grape Tree Road – Lady Devondale (IRE) (Broken Hearted) **h–** [2018/19 h16.3m Jun 19] failed to complete all 3 starts in points: in tongue tie, tailed off in novice on hurdling debut. *Jack R. Barber*

D'PINESFLYER (IRE) 7 b.m. Westerner – Diskretion (GER) (Acatenango (GER)) **h–** [2018/19 h94: h20.3s h20.5g^pu Feb 25] modest hurdler, no impact both starts in 2018/19: stays 2½m: acts on good to soft going. *Johnny Farrelly*

DRACARYS 4 b.g. Sepoy (AUS) – Fen Guest (Woodborough (USA)) [2018/19 h17.7d^pu **h–** Nov 18] behind all starts on Flat: downed tools when pulled up in juvenile on hurdling debut. *Ken Cunningham-Brown*

DRAFT PICK (IRE) 8 b.g. Court Cave (IRE) – Kilmington Breeze (IRE) (Roselier (FR)) **c–** [2018/19 b–: c24.2s⁵ Apr 16] point winner: in cheekpieces, well held in novice hunter at Exeter on chasing debut. *J. M. Ridley*

DRAGON D'ESTRUVAL (FR) 6 b.g. Enrique – Rose d'Estruval (FR) (Lavirco (GER)) **c–**
[2018/19 h21.9d* h24.2s h20.5d³ h23.1d Feb 22] tall gelding: third foal: half-brother to **h126**
fairly useful hurdler/useful chaser Beguin d'Estruval (17f-21f winner, by Martaline): dam
French 17f-19f hurdle/chase winner: fairly useful hurdler: won novice at Ffos Las in May:
third in handicap at Newbury in December: winning chaser: left Guillaume Macaire after
final start in 2017/18: stays 2¾m: acts on soft going: tried in cheekpieces. *Nicky Henderson*

DRAGONHOV (FR) 6 b.g. Dragon Dancer – Kalistina (FR) (Sillery (USA)) [2018/19 **h–**
h15.7v Dec 22] half-brother to several winners, including fair hurdlers Comber Mill
(2m/17f winner, by Le Fou) and Ouest Eclair (ungenuine 2m winner, by Sagacity): dam ran
once on Flat: fair 17f hurdle winner in France for Francois Nicolle: last in handicap on
British debut. *Lucinda Russell*

DRAGON KHAN (IRE) 10 b.g. Dr Fong (USA) – Desert Magic (IRE) (Green Desert **h79**
(USA)) [2018/19 h83: h15.8s h15.8d⁴ h16d⁵ Mar 21] poor handicap hurdler: unproven
beyond 2m: acts on heavy going: has worn headgear: wears tongue tie: usually races off
pace. *Rosemary Gasson*

DRAGON TATTOO (IRE) 4 b.f. Zoffany (IRE) – Geisha Lily (FR) (Gone West (USA)) **h–**
[2018/19 h15.9s h17.7vᵖᵘ Feb 14] poor maiden on Flat, stays 1m: little impact over hurdles:
in cheekpieces final start. *Linda Jewell*

DRAMA KING (IRE) 8 b.g. King's Theatre (IRE) – Miss Arteea (IRE) (Flemensfirth **h96**
(USA)) [2018/19 h–: h21.6s⁵ h18.5s h23.9d Feb 28] sturdy gelding: modest form over
hurdles: best effort at 2¾m: often in headgear: tried in tongue tie: temperament under
suspicion. *David Pipe*

DRAMATIC APPROACH (IRE) 5 b.m. Flemensfirth (USA) – Sea Breeze Lady (IRE) **b86 p**
(Oscar (IRE)) [2018/19 b16d³ Feb 23] €30,000 3-y-o: first foal: dam unraced sister to
Grand National runner-up Oscar Time: clear when left alone last on debut in Irish point:
16/1, third in conditionals/amateurs maiden bumper at Chepstow (4¾ lengths behind Some
Detail): sure to progress. *Neil Mulholland*

DRAMATIC PAUSE (IRE) 6 b.g. Oscar (IRE) – Night Heron (IRE) (St Jovite (USA)) **h75**
[2018/19 b101: b16.7v⁶ h19.5s h20s⁵ Apr 7] has had breathing operation: failed to complete **b84**
sole start in points: modest form in bumpers: well held both starts over hurdles.
Tom Symonds

DR DES (IRE) 8 b.g. Double Eclipse (IRE) – Dans Belle (IRE) (Rising) [2018/19 h135: **c125**
c17.2g³ c19.2s⁵ c20s⁵ c24.5s⁴ c24v⁵ c19.2dᵖᵘ Apr 9] sturdy gelding: useful hurdler: fairly **h–**
useful form over fences: stays 3m: acts on heavy going: tried in blinkers. *Henry Oliver*

DR DUNRAVEN 8 b.g. Dr Massini (IRE) – Bajan Girl (FR) (Emperor Jones (USA)) **c116**
[2018/19 c–, h97: h19.6g³ c16.5g* c15.7g* h20g² c16.5g⁵ h16g⁵ c16.5g³ c17g³ c19.7g* **h102**
c16.4s⁴ Nov 27] fair maiden hurdler: fairly useful handicap chaser: won at Worcester
(novice) and Southwell in June, and Plumpton in November: left Martin Keighley after
eighth start: stayed 2½m: acted on soft going: tried in headgear: wore tongue tie: dead.
Peter Bowen

DREAM BAIE (FR) 6 b.g. Crillon (FR) – Montaraza (FR) (Anabaa Blue) [2018/19 **h83**
h102, b74: h15.8g⁶ h17.7g⁵ h15.9s h15.9d³ Jan 6] lengthy gelding: disapointing maiden
hurdler: unproven beyond 2m: acts on soft going: tried in hood: wears tongue tie. *Michael
Roberts*

DREAM BERRY (FR) 8 gr.g. Dream Well (FR) – Kalberry (FR) (Kaldounevees (FR)) **c–**
[2018/19 c–, h142: c20.9dᶠ h24.7g Nov 10] rather leggy gelding: useful hurdler, well held **h–**
final start in 2018/19: twice-raced over fences: stays 21f: acts on heavy going: wears
tongue tie. *Jonjo O'Neill*

DREAM BOLT (IRE) 11 ch.g. Urban Ocean (FR) – Riviera Dream (IRE) (Over The **c120**
River (FR)) [2018/19 c127, h–: c21g c19.4g² c17.8s⁴ c19.4g³ c19.9d³ c21g⁶ c20d c23.8g⁵ **h–**
Feb 28] rather leggy gelding: has had breathing operation: winning hurdler: fairly useful
handicap chaser: third at Newbury in November: stays 21f: acts on any going: tried in
tongue tie. *David Rees*

DREAM BROTHER (IRE) 7 b.g. Oscar (IRE) – Warmley's Gem (IRE) (Phardante **h–**
(FR)) [2018/19 b79: h23sᵖᵘ May 25] well-made gelding: has had breathing operation: won
Irish point on debut: modest form in bumper: pulled up in novice on hurdling debut.
Warren Greatrex

DREAMCATCHING (FR) 6 b.g. Al Namix (FR) – New Zealand (FR) (Smadoun (FR)) **c94**
[2018/19 c–, h88: c16.3g⁵ c21.4m⁵ Jul 21] good-topped gelding: winning hurdler: modest **h–**
form over fences: stays 2½m: acts on firm and soft going. *Paul Nicholls*

DREAM CHOPE (FR) 10 ch.g. Muhaymin (USA) – Snow In Summer (FR) (Limnos (JPN)) [2018/19 c–, h–: c21.6g^{pu} May 17] maiden pointer: winning hurdler: fair form over fences in France, pulled up both starts in hunters: unproven beyond 2m: acts on soft and good to firm going: tried in headgear. *Miss L. Luxton*   **c–** **h–**

DREAM DU GRAND VAL (FR) 6 b.g. Puit d'Or (IRE) – Apple Mille (FR) (Apple Tree (FR)) [2018/19 h16.4g^6 h17.7s* h16.2g* h16s h16g Apr 27] well-made gelding: half-brother to French hurdler/chaser Reveur du Grandval (17f-2¾m winner, by Maresca Sorrento): runner-up only start on Flat: useful hurdler: won handicap at Fontwell (by 10 lengths from Arthington) in January and novice at Kelso (by 7 lengths from Skiddaw Valleys) in February: left D. Sourdeau de Beauregard after final start in 2017/18: stays 2¼m: acts on soft going: in hood last 4 starts: temperament under suspicion. *Nicky Henderson*   **h132**

DREAM FREE 6 b.g. Oasis Dream – Freedonia (Selkirk (USA)) [2018/19 h–: h16.7g h16.8g^5 h18.5d^5 h18.5g^6 h16.8m^5 h19.8g^4 h18.5d^4 Apr 9] modest maiden hurdler: stays 2¼m: acts on good to firm going: wears headgear: tried in tongue tie. *David Pipe*   **h86**

DREAM OF CAMELOT (IRE) 4 b.f. Camelot – Definite Opinion (IRE) (Kheleyf (USA)) [2018/19 h16p^{pu} Oct 31] fair maiden on Flat, stays 1m: pulled up in fillies juvenile on hurdling debut. *Gary Moore*   **h–**

DREAM ON DREAMER (IRE) 5 b.m. Dream Ahead (USA) – Marula (IRE) (Sadler's Wells (USA)) [2018/19 h15.7g h15.7g c19.2m^4 c16.5g^4 c21.4g^{pu} Mar 20] fair maiden on Flat, stays 1m: unplaced in Irish point: little form over hurdles/fences: wears tongue tie: front runner/races prominently. *Lucinda Egerton*   **c59** **h–**

DREAM RUN 5 b.m. Phoenix Reach (IRE) – Function Dreamer (Overbury (IRE)) [2018/19 b16g^6 Sep 2] half-sister to 3 winners, including fairly useful hurdler Ellens Way (21f-3m winner, by Black Sam Bellamy) and bumper winner/fairly useful hurdler McGowan's Pass (2m winner, by Central Park): dam unraced half-sister to useful hurdler/top-class chaser (stayed 3m) Captain Chris: tailed off in mares bumper. *Henry Daly*   **b–**

DREAMSOFTHEATRE (IRE) 11 gr.g. King's Theatre (IRE) – Caroline Fontenail (IRE) (Kaldounevees (FR)) [2018/19 c103§, h106§: h25g^5 h25.8g^6 h25.4m* h25.4g^{pu} h26.4g^2 h26g* h25.5g^3 c25.6g^{pu} h24.4g h21.2d Feb 20] workmanlike gelding: fair handicap hurdler: won at Cartmel in July and Warwick in September: fairly useful chaser at best: stays 27f: acts on soft and good to firm going: usually wears cheekpieces: has worn tongue tie: unreliable. *Jonjo O'Neill*   **c– §** **h113 §**

DREAMSUNDERMYFEET (IRE) 4 b.g. Yeats (IRE) – Change of Plan (IRE) (Alderbrook) [2018/19 b16.3d Mar 23] tailed off in Goffs UK Spring Sales Bumper. *Martin Keighley*   **b–**

DRENEK (FR) 6 gr.g. Turgeon (USA) – Sireva (FR) (Simon du Desert (FR)) [2018/19 b–: b16g May 7] well held in 2 bumpers: in hood first start. *James Ewart*   **b–**

DREWMAIN LEGEND 7 b.m. Midnight Legend – Ryders Hill (Zaffaran (USA)) [2018/19 h97: h21d^4 h24.1d^5 h23.9g c19.7s^4 c19.4d* Apr 6] modest handicap hurdler: similar form over fences: won handicap at Chepstow in April: stays 19f: acts on heavy going: has worn headgear, including final start. *Ali Stronge*   **c95** **h90**

DREYFUS (IRE) 8 ch.g. Notnowcato – Trauquebise (FR) (Kaldounevees (FR)) [2018/19 h15.5g^5 h21d h15.8d^6 c17g^4 Apr 21] angular gelding: has had breathing operation: modest form over hurdles: tailed off in novice handicap on chasing debut. *Paul Webber*   **c–** **h94**

DR HOOVES (IRE) 6 b.g. Yeats (IRE) – Sejour (IRE) (Bob Back (USA)) [2018/19 b91: h19.8m^2 Mar 22] has had breathing operations: fair bumper performer: 20/1, second in novice at Musselburgh (3 lengths behind Grey Mist) on hurdling debut: in tongue tie last 4 starts. *Lucinda Russell*   **h107**

DRIFT 6 b.m. With The Flow (USA) – Lady Exe (Karinga Bay) [2018/19 b–: b16.3m^6 ab16g Nov 13] has had breathing operation: poor form in bumpers: in hood last 2 starts. *Noel Williams*   **b74**

DRIFTING STAR (IRE) 4 b.g. Sea The Stars (IRE) – Drifting (IRE) (Sadler's Wells (USA)) [2018/19 h16s^{pu} Feb 2] sturdy gelding: poor maiden on Flat: in tongue tie, pulled up in novice on hurdling debut. *Gary Moore*   **h–**

DRIFTWOOD HAZE 11 b.g. Nomadic Way (USA) – Kristal Haze (Krisinsky (USA)) [2018/19 c–, h109: c20.9v^3 h23.8g^2 h26s^4 h23.9s Apr 7] angular gelding: winning pointer: fairly useful handicap hurdler: won at Bangor in March: similar form over fences: third in novice handicap at Ffos Las in December: stays 3m: acts on heavy going: tried in blinkers. *Phillip Dando*   **c117** **h120**

DRIFTWOOD PRIDE (IRE) 11 b.g. Balmont (USA) – Olivia's Pride (IRE) (Digamist (USA)) [2018/19 c94: c21.6g May 17] point winner: modest maiden hunter chaser: stays 23f: wears headgear: tried in tongue tie. *Miss Jane Western*   **c–**

DRILL BABY DRILL 8 b.m. Black Sam Bellamy (IRE) – Tulipa (POL) (Jape (USA)) [2018/19 h92p: h24g³ h23.3d h27d c25.1spu Mar 7] fair form over hurdles: pulled up in novice handicap on chasing debut: stays 3m: in tongue tie last 2 starts: often let down by jumping. *Tom George*   **c– h100 x**

DRINKS INTERVAL 7 b.m. King's Theatre (IRE) – Dame Fonteyn (Suave Dancer (USA)) [2018/19 h120, b63: h23.3d h24.7g² c21m* c21m² c24g* c23.6d* c23.9gF c23.4s² c20.5g³ c24.4spu c24.1mF c23.8dpu Apr 26] sturdy mare: fairly useful handicap hurdler: second in mares event at Aintree in June: useful chaser: won novices at Newton Abbot in July, Uttoxeter in September and Chepstow (by 11 lengths from Debece) in October: stays 25f: acts on good to firm and heavy going: wears tongue tie. *Colin Tizzard*   **c138 h121**

DRIVE THE BUS (IRE) 10 b.g. Helissio (FR) – Curraghs Annie (IRE) (Darazari (IRE)) [2018/19 c–, h–: c17dF c23.8gpu Feb 28] little impact in points: winning hurdler/chaser, retains little ability: usually wears cheekpieces/tongue tie. *Mrs B. Thomas*   **c– h–**

DR MIKEY (IRE) 10 b.g. Dr Massini (IRE) – Nicola Marie (IRE) (Cardinal Flower) [2018/19 h140: h16g h16s⁴ h24d⁶ h16g⁶ c20d* c17dF c16d⁴ h16v² h16d⁴ Apr 21] useful hurdler: fourth in handicap at Galway (2½ lengths behind Top Othe Ra) in August and second in minor event at Cork (2 lengths behind Landofhopeandglory) in March: similar form over fences: won maiden at Gowran (by neck from A Plus Tard) in November: stays 2½m: acts on heavy going: tried in hood: usually leads: often let down by jumping over fences. *Ms M. Flynn, Ireland*   **c136 x h141**

DR MOLONEY (IRE) 12 b.g. Dr Massini (IRE) – Solal Queen (Homo Sapien) [2018/19 c107§, h–: c19.2g⁴ c16g⁴ c21.4g Aug 18] winning hurdler: modest maiden chaser: barely stays 3m: acts on good to firm and heavy going: usually wears headgear: has worn tongue tie, including in 2018/19: irresolute. *Olly Murphy*   **c93 § h–**

DR OAKLEY (IRE) 5 ch.g. Le Fou (IRE) – Two Choices (IRE) (Persian Mews) [2018/19 h16.2g⁴ h16.2g h15.8s h15.5g h16gro h19.7g h19.6g Apr 13] sturdy gelding: third on completed start in Irish points: poor maiden hurdler: temperamental. *Henry Oliver*   **h79 §**

DROMINEER (IRE) 6 b.g. Oscar (IRE) – Aileen Supreme (IRE) (Presenting) [2018/19 b16.5d* Apr 24] second foal: dam, ran twice, out of half-sister to smart hurdler/very smart chaser up to 3m Colonel Braxton: in hood/tongue tie, 6/5, won maiden bumper at Taunton by 11 lengths from We Move On, travelling powerfully. *David Pipe*   **b104**

DROMORE LAD (IRE) 7 ch.g. Flemensfirth (USA) – Mini Karinga (Karinga Bay) [2018/19 h20d³ h20s h19d Mar 10] useful handicap hurdler: back to best when 3¾ lengths fifth of 23 to My Sister Sarah at Punchestown shortly after end of British season: stays 3m: acts on heavy going. *Dermot Anthony McLoughlin, Ireland*   **h131**

DROPS OF JUPITOR (IRE) 7 gr.m. Dylan Thomas (IRE) – Fancy Intense (Peintre Celebre (USA)) [2018/19 h108: c20gF c17.4v⁵ c18.2s⁵ c18.2s³ Mar 19] tall, good-topped mare: fair hurdler: similar form over fences: stays 19f: acts on heavy going: has worn hood, including final start. *Anthony Honeyball*   **c101 h–**

DROPZONE (USA) 10 b.g. Smart Strike (CAN) – Dalisay (IRE) (Sadler's Wells (USA)) [2018/19 c–, h72§: h21.7g h25.8g⁴ h23g⁴ h25.8g³ Aug 30] sturdy gelding: poor handicap hurdler: maiden chaser: stays 3¼m: acts on soft and good to firm going: usually wears headgear: tried in tongue tie: hard to win with. *Brian Forsey*   **c– h65 §**

DROVERS LANE (IRE) 7 b.g. Oscar (IRE) – Minnie Turbo (IRE) (General View) [2018/19 h–99, b–: h23s⁴ h19.9m* h16g* h18.5m² c25.2g* c25g c21.4d* c20.6d* c24.4s⁶ Mar 13] well-made gelding: has had breathing operation: fairly useful form over hurdles: won maiden at Uttoxeter and novice at Worcester in July: smart form over fences: won novice handicaps at Hereford in October and Market Rasen (by 11 lengths from Soupy Soups) in November, and novice at Cheltenham (by 1½ lengths from Le Breuil) in December: stays 25f: acts on good to firm and good to soft going: usually travels strongly. *Rebecca Curtis*   **c147 h116**

DR RHYTHM (IRE) 6 b.g. Kalanisi (IRE) – Muscova Rose (IRE) (Sevres Rose (IRE)) [2018/19 b–p: h20.7g⁵ May 10] rather unfurnished gelding: point winner: well held in bumper: 10/1, fifth in maiden at Huntingdon (25¼ lengths behind Potterman) on hurdling debut. *Paul Nicholls*   **h91**

DR RICHARD KIMBLE (IRE) 4 b.g. Lawman (FR) – Aoife Alainn (IRE) (Dr Fong   **h103**
(USA)) [2018/19 h16.4g³ h16.7d h16.6d³ h15.8g⁴ Apr 11] fairly useful on Flat, stays 1½m:
fair form over hurdles. *Mark Johnston*

DR ROBIN (IRE) 9 b.g. Robin des Pres (FR) – Inter Alia (IRE) (Dr Massini (IRE))   **c116 §**
[2018/19 c119§, h–: c24m h23.9m⁴ h23.3g⁶ h20m c22.6gʳᵒ c21.2s³ c21.1m⁶ h23.3g²   **h111 §**
c20.9d* c22.6g h23.3v⁴ h23.3v⁵ Mar 16] lengthy gelding: fair handicap hurdler: fairly
useful handicap chaser: won at Ffos Las in October: stays 3m: acts on good to firm and
heavy going: wears headgear: has worn tongue tie: usually front runner/races prominently:
moody. *Peter Bowen*

DR SANDERSON (IRE) 5 b.g. Jeremy (USA) – Guydus (IRE) (Old Vic) [2018/19 b99:   **h126**
h20m* h19.7s⁴ h15.8s* h21.2m* h20.3g⁵ Apr 17] bumper winner: fairly useful form over
hurdles: won maiden at Worcester in October, and novices at Ffos Las in February and
Ludlow in April: stays 21f: acts on soft and good to firm going. *Paul Nicholls*

DR TIME (IRE) 7 b.g. Dubai Destination (USA) – Long Long Time (IRE) (Dr Massini   **h105**
(IRE)) [2018/19 b15.8d h21.3s³ h20.7d Feb 17] second foal: dam winning pointer: mid-   **b84**
field in bumper: fair form over hurdles: better effort when third in novice at Wetherby in
December: will be suited by 3m. *Tom Symonds*

DRUIDE PREMIER (FR) 6 gr.g. Martaline – Bellissima de Mai (FR) (Pistolet Bleu   **h93**
(IRE)) [2018/19 h16.8g³ b15.8g³ h16.5d³ h16.5d h16d h23.1d Feb 22] sixth foal: brother to   **b87**
very smart hurdler/top-class chaser Dynaste (19f-25f winner) and half-brother to fairly
useful chaser Dauphine Ereine (2¼m-2½m winner in France, by Saint des Saints), stays
3m: dam French maiden (second in 17f chase): fair form in bumpers: better effort when
third in conditionals/amateurs event at Newton Abbot in June: modest form over hurdles:
bred to prove best at 2½m+: tried in hood/tongue tie. *David Pipe*

DRUID'S DIAMOND 6 b.g. Piccolo – Faithful Beauty (IRE) (Last Tycoon) [2018/19   **h82**
h98: h17.2m⁶ Jun 29] smallish gelding: modest maiden on Flat, stays 12.5f: modest maiden
hurdler: raced around 2m: acts on heavy going: sometimes in headgear: tried in tongue tie:
sold £5,000 to join Laura Grizzetti, Italy. *Mark Walford*

DRUID'S FOLLY (IRE) 9 b.g. Beneficial – Sweet Vale (IRE) (Supreme Leader)   **c–**
[2018/19 c–, h98: h19m² h19.2g⁵ h16.8g³ h21d h19.2v⁶ h20.7g h20.5gᵖᵘ h20.3d⁵ Apr 24]   **h102 §**
tall gelding: has had breathing operation: fair handicap hurdler: pulled up both starts over
fences: left Robert Walford after fifth start: stays 2¾m: acts on good to firm and heavy
going: has worn hood/tongue tie: unreliable. *Caroline Fryer*

DRUMCLIFF (IRE) 8 b.g. Presenting – Dusty Too (Terimon) [2018/19 c143, h114:   **c142**
c20g* c22.5dᶠ Aug 1] well-made gelding: maiden hurdler: useful form over fences: won   **h–**
handicap at Uttoxeter (by length from Viconte du Noyer) in May: stays 2½m: acts on heavy
going: wears tongue tie: has joined Aidan Anthony Howard. *Harry Fry*

DRUMCONNOR LAD (IRE) 9 b.g. Winged Love (IRE) – Drumconnor Lady (IRE)   **c128**
(Shahrastani (USA)) [2018/19 c131, h–: c16m* c19.9s⁴ c21g⁴ c20g⁶ c18.2g c20gᵖᵘ c16.5g³   **h117**
c22.6g⁴ c20d⁴ c20d c24.5gᵖᵘ c16d⁶ h24d⁵ c26dᶠ h20.2s c20.5m Apr 12] fairly useful form
over hurdles: fairly useful chaser: won handicap at Down Royal in May and minor event at
Gowran in November: stays 2½m: acts on good to firm and heavy going: has worn
headgear: usually wears tongue tie. *A. P. Keatley, Ireland*

DRUMHART (IRE) 10 ch.g. Beneficial – Nancylu (IRE) (Luso) [2018/19 c100, h–:   **c98 x**
c22.6m³ c19.4m⁶ c23g⁴ Aug 22] multiple point winner: maiden hurdler: modest handicap   **h–**
chaser: stays 23f: acts on good to firm and good to soft going: tried in hood: usually wears
tongue tie: usually races in rear: not a fluent jumper. *Alastair Ralph*

DRUMLEE SUNSET (IRE) 9 br.g. Royal Anthem (USA) – Be My Sunset (IRE) (Bob   **c135**
Back (USA)) [2018/19 c131, h–: c25.8g* c26.1m c20d* Feb 22] compact gelding: winning   **h–**
hurdler: useful handicap chaser: won at Newton Abbot in May and Warwick (by short head
from Diable de Sivola) in February: stays easy 3¼m, effective at much shorter: acts on soft
going: in tongue tie last 4 starts. *Tom George*

DRUMLEE WATAR (IRE) 6 ch.g. Watar (IRE) – Dolly of Dublin (IRE) (Be My Native   **h102**
(USA)) [2018/19 h19.5s⁴ h20.8g³ Nov 30] £65,000 5-y-o: third foal: dam well held in
bumpers/over hurdles: won Irish point on debut: fair form over hurdles: better effort when
third in novice at Doncaster in November: will be suited by 2¾m+. *Warren Greatrex*

DRUMLYNN (IRE) 8 b.g. Definite Article – Miss Florida (IRE) (Florida Son) [2018/19   **c108**
b91: c20.2f² c24.2s² Apr 16] has had breathing operation: point/bumper winner: fair form
in hunter chases: better effort when second in novice at Exeter in April. *Luke Harvey*

DRUMNAGREAGH (IRE) 6 b.m. September Storm (GER) – Saffron Pride (IRE) (Be **h–**
My Native (USA)) [2018/19 h72, b77: h21.4g^{pu} h16.2g May 16] won completed start in
Irish points: poor maiden hurdler: tried in cheekpieces/tongue tie. *Sam Crawford, Ireland*

DRUMOCHTER 5 br.m. Bated Breath – Dixey (Diktat) [2018/19 h16.7g^5 h16d^4 h16.2s^3 **h99 p**
Dec 12] fairly useful on Flat, stays 1¼m: modest form over hurdles: best effort when third
in mares novice at Hexham: remains with potential. *Sam England*

DRUMS OF WAR (IRE) 7 b.g. Youmzain (IRE) – Min Asl Wafi (IRE) (Octagonal (NZ)) **h81**
[2018/19 h106, b87: h16.8s^5 Dec 7] fair hurdler, well below form sole start in 2018/19:
stays 19f: acts on heavy going: in cheekpieces last 3 starts. *Chris Grant*

DRUNKEN PIRATE 6 b.g. Black Sam Bellamy (IRE) – Peel Me A Grape (Gunner B) **h101 p**
[2018/19 b94p: b16.3d* h20.5s h18.5d^5 Jan 1] big, strong gelding: fairly useful form in **b100**
bumpers: won at Newbury in November: fair form over hurdles: tried in tongue tie: should
do better. *Noel Williams*

DR WALUIGI (IRE) 9 b.g. Shirocco (GER) – Daruliyya (IRE) (Highest Honor (FR)) **c–**
[2018/19 c16.5g Jun 2] has had breathing operation: winning pointer: modest maiden **h–**
hurdler: similar form over fences: trained prior to only outing in 2018/19 by Eoin Doyle:
stays 21f: acts on heavy going: has worn headgear/tongue tie. *Jamie Snowden*

DR WELLS 7 b.g. Dr Massini (IRE) – Aristi (IRE) (Dr Fong (USA)) [2018/19 h–, b–: **h–**
h19.9g h19.5g Oct 30] well held in bumper: no form over hurdles: tried in cheekpieces.
Peter Bowen

DRY LIGHTENING (IRE) 5 b.g. Arcadio (GER) – Waydale Hill (Minster Son) [2018/19 **h–**
h21.2g h21.2d^{pu} Feb 6] maiden Irish pointer: no form over hurdles. *Donald McCain*

DRY OL'PARTY 9 ch.m. Tobougg (IRE) – Emergence (FR) (Poliglote) [2018/19 h16.8g **c56**
h19.6g h23m³ c25.8g³ c25.8g³ c25.8g Sep 10] fair handicap hurdler at best for Philip **h73**
Hobbs: missed 2017/18: poor form over fences: best form up to 2¼m: acts on soft and good
to firm going: has worn headgear, including final start: usually races towards rear: won
twice in points later in season. *Stuart Kittow*

DUARIGLE (IRE) 7 ch.g. Dubai Destination (USA) – Silver Valley (IRE) (Henbit **h122**
(USA)) [2018/19 h16v h20.5s^5 h23s^5 h19.8s* h16.3d^3 h19.9v h20.3g^6 Apr 17] sturdy
gelding: seventh foal: brother to fair 2m hurdle winner/winning pointer Port Rashid and
half-brother to smart hurdler/high-class chaser Tranquil Sea (2m-3m winner, by Sea
Raven) and a winning pointer by Blueprint: dam placed in points: Irish point winner: fairly
useful handicap hurdler: won novice event at Sandown in February: stays 2½m: acts on
soft going: usually races towards rear. *Paul Henderson*

DUBAI ANGEL (IRE) 8 b.g. Dubai Destination (USA) – Just Another Penny (IRE) **c–**
(Terimon) [2018/19 c132, h128: h20g h20s h21.3s^{pu} h20.5s^3 h19.7g^4 Mar 29] fairly useful **h117**
handicap hurdler: third at Ayr in March: useful form over fences: stays 2¾m: acts on heavy
going. *Ruth Jefferson*

DUBAI DIRHAM 6 ch.m. Dubai Destination (USA) – Rolline (IRE) (Revoque (IRE)) **h–**
[2018/19 h–, b79: h16.8m May 8] rather unfurnished mare: modest form in bumpers: poor
form over hurdles. *Suzy Smith*

DUBA PLAINS 4 b.g. Sixties Icon – Selinda (Piccolo) [2018/19 h16.4g h15.6g h16.8s^{pu} **h–**
h16.8v^{pu} Mar 12] modest maiden on Flat, stays 1m: no form over hurdles. *Victor Thompson*

DUBH DES CHAMPS (IRE) 7 br.g. Robin des Champs (FR) – Aneda Dubh (IRE) **h93**
(Presenting) [2018/19 h71: h22.1s^{pu} h16.2s h19.3g^5 h23.3g^4 h24.4g* Nov 30] modest
handicap hurdler: won at Doncaster in November: thorough stayer: best form on good
going: in cheekpieces last 2 starts. *Philip Kirby*

DUBLIN FOUR (IRE) 5 ch.g. Arakan (USA) – Eluna (Unfuwain (USA)) [2018/19 **b82**
b16v² b16d Jan 4] €10,000 3-y-o: half brother to fairly useful hurdler/useful chaser Viva
Steve (2m-3m winner, by Flemensfirth) and fair 2m hurdle winner/winning pointer
Shaluna (by Shantou): dam (c83/h118) 2m hurdle winner: unplaced in points: modest form
in bumpers. *John Joseph Hanlon, Ireland*

DUCA DE THAIX (FR) 6 b.g. Voix du Nord (FR) – Nouca de Thaix (FR) (Subotica **c149 §**
(FR)) [2018/19 h133: c16.2g² c16d³ c17d² c17d² c16.5g* c17d* c17g⁴ c17s³ c18g³ Mar 23] **h–**
lengthy gelding: useful hurdler: smart chaser: won handicap at Fairyhouse (by 5 lengths
from Arvico Bleu) in December and Dan Moore Memorial Handicap Chase there (by ½
length from Cubomania) in January: stays 2¼m: acts on heavy going: wears cheekpieces/
tongue tie: unreliable. *Gordon Elliott, Ireland*

DUC DE BEAUCHENE (FR) 6 b.g. Saddler Maker (IRE) – Quatia d'Angron (FR) **h118** (Verglas (IRE)) [2018/19 h16d⁵ h16.2g h15.9s⁴ h20.5s* h19.8s² Mar 8] fairly useful form over hurdles: won handicap at Plumpton in February: second in novice handicap at Sandown 3 weeks later: stays 21f: acts on soft going. *David Pipe*

DUC DES GENIEVRES (FR) 6 gr.g. Buck's Boum (FR) – Lobelie (FR) (Round **c162 +** Sovereign (FR)) [2018/19 h145: c19d² c16s³ c20d* c15.9s* Mar 12] **h–**

After such a prolonged dry winter, it came as something of a surprise when the weather took a sudden turn and the Cheltenham Festival got under way on soft going. Less of a surprise, perhaps, was another memorable opening day for trainer Willie Mullins who is making a habit of creating headlines on Cheltenham's Tuesday card. It had been four years since the bookmakers escaped what would have been their 'worst day in Festival history' when odds-on Annie Power came down at the last flight with the David Nicholson Mares' Hurdle at her mercy, after three Mullins-trained short-priced favourites had obliged in the Supreme Novices' Hurdle, the Arkle and the Champion Hurdle. Mullins still won the David Nicholson Mares' Hurdle with 6/1-shot Glens Melody but Annie Power's fall saved the bookies tens of millions because of the linked accumulators on the four Mullins favourites. Annie Power (in the Champion Hurdle) was one of three winners for Mullins when he had the favourites for the same opening day events the following year, though the accumulator went down in the first when Min was foiled by Altior in his bid to become the fourth successive winner of the Supreme Novices' for Closutton (and for Min's owners the Riccis). Mullins drew an opening day 'blank' in 2017, when his great rival Gordon Elliott enjoyed a three-timer (two of the winners at the chief expense of Mullins-trained runners), but 'normal' service was resumed in 2018 when Footpad, Benie des Dieux and Rathvinden gave Mullins another first-day hat-trick, though the pre-race publicity that year was about a potential four-horse accumulator on favourites Getabird (Mullins-trained), Footpad, Buveur d'Air (the Champion Hurdle winner) and Apple's Jade (in the David Nicholson Mares' Hurdle which Benie des Dieux won). The latest Cheltenham Festival opened with a double for the Mullins team when 6/1-shot Klassical Dream won the Supreme and 5/1-shot Duc des Genievres took the Arkle, before odds-on Benie des Dieux was beaten in almost identical circumstances to Annie Power, though the Closutton second string Stormy Ireland couldn't compensate for her stablemate's fall, finding one too good for her in Roksana who was only the third non-Mullins-trained winner in the twelve runnings of the David Nicholson Mares' Hurdle. Klassical Dream was the fourth winner for Mullins in the last seven editions of the Supreme and Duc des Genievres the fourth in five years in the Arkle.

'I didn't dream of making a start like this,' said Mullins. 'I thought Klassical Dream would go close but I believed Duc des Genievres might need a little further and I gave him only an each-way chance.' Duc des Genievres was one of the runners who relished the soft ground on the day, with Mullins himself claiming the going 'changed the horse completely'. Duc des Genievres had been a smart novice hurdler the previous year, running several creditable races in Grade 1 company that season without ever looking like winning (his performances included a second in the Deloitte Novices' Hurdle at Leopardstown and a fifth in the Baring Bingham at Cheltenham, both won by Samcro, jumping's most exciting young prospect at the time). Duc des Genievres showed that he stayed twenty-one furlongs in the Baring Bingham, running as well as in any race all that season, but his campaign rather tailed off with below-par performances at Fairyhouse's premier spring meeting and at Punchestown.

In common with many of his stable's young chasing prospects and some of its seasoned performers over fences, Duc des Genievres was held up by the dry autumn and it was the week before Christmas when he made his debut over fences. He was beaten in a maiden chase at Naas by A Plus Tard, who had already had a run over fences and probably enjoyed a fitness edge, though there was plenty of encouragement to be taken from the sound jumping of Duc des Genievres. Down in trip to two miles in a similar event at Gowran in January, Duc des Genievres ran below his Naas form, finishing third behind stablemate Cilaos Emery (who started

Racing Post Arkle Challenge Trophy Novices' Chase, Cheltenham—
Duc des Genievres and Paul Townend are in complete control at the last

favourite) and Impact Factor. Finally off the mark over fences with a fifteen-length win in another Gowran maiden in February, over two and a half miles this time, Duc des Genievres became his stable's only representative in the Racing Post Arkle Trophy (his sole Cheltenham entry) after an injury to Cilaos Emery, who had been generally regarded as the stable's clear number-one for the race. The value of wide margin victories in conditions races isn't always straightforward to pinpoint by form-study alone, but the time for Duc des Genievres was very good, his timerating of 155 providing independent confirmation of the value of the form, as well as confirming the strong visual impression created by the performance (he travelled well all the way, was in command from three out and won with plenty in hand). The form of the Gowran win would have been good enough to see Duc des Genievres make the places in the three previous runnings of the Arkle.

Duc des Genievres started third favourite in the twelve-runner Arkle (just the second double figure field in eight runnings) behind the Elliott-trained Hardline and the shortest-priced home-trained contender Glen Forsa who had won the rearranged Kingmaker Novices' Chase at Sandown from 4/1-on shot Kalashnikov (runner-up in the Supreme at the previous year's Festival). Kalashnikov and Lalor, who had won the trial at Cheltenham's November meeting, were the only others in the line-up to start at single-figure odds. There were some notable absentees through injury, in addition to one-time ante-post favourite Cilaos Emery, and they included Dynamite Dollars, who had won the Henry VIII Novices' Chase at Sandown (from the Arkle 14/1-shot Ornua and Lalor), and the winner of the Arkle at Leopardstown Le Richebourg, for whom stablemate Us And Them (runner-up to him) was the deputy. There have been some vintage winners of the Arkle in recent years but too many good novices were missing from the latest edition for it to be regarded as anything but a substandard renewal beforehand. In the event, though, it produced a clear-cut winner, Duc des Genievres putting up another outstanding time performance in recording a timerating of 168 and routing his field by thirteen lengths after putting in a flawless round of jumping and leaving his rivals for dead in the

Sullivan Bloodstock Limited's "Duc des Genievres"

final straight. The competition, however, had been greatly reduced long before that, with Glen Forsa unseating his rider at the fourth and Ornua falling and hampering Kalashnikov (who parted company with his jockey) at the sixth. Lalor was out too, pulled up some way from home after receiving reminders on the final circuit. Us And Them and 25/1-shot Articulum were the closest pursuers of Duc des Genievres, giving Irish-trained horses a one, two, three. Hardline never threatened.

The Arkle, incidentally, was the first race to be run on Cheltenham's Old Course after another change had been made to the second last, which was moved a further ten yards beyond the home bend to give jockeys another two or three strides on the short run from the turn to balance their mounts (leaving just 110 yards— it is 169 yards on the New Course—between the penultimate fence and the last). Al Boum Photo had fallen at the fence twelve months earlier in the RSA Chase, leaving Ruby Walsh with a broken leg, and the course executive acted in response to advice from riders. Until the 2011 Festival, there was just one fence in the home straight with the sometimes controversial second last situated before the turn, where the ground drops away (the cause of the problems, rather than the fence itself). After moving the second last into the straight on safety grounds, a further adjustment was made in the 2016/17 season when it was moved ten yards or so closer to the final fence, after seven horses at the 2016 Festival had departed at the fence in the four steeplechases on the opening day.

Cheltenham's run-in also looked slightly different to previous Festivals in that the system of using a tape across the bend to prevent runners in steeplechases from going out on another circuit had been replaced by a temporary running rail. A tape had been used for as long as anyone could remember to guide the runners past the junction with the round course and up the finishing hill. It was replaced in the latest season by sections of plastic rail moved into place once all the runners had gone out on the final circuit. The move was prompted by two incidents at Cheltenham's first meeting of the season, both on the first day, when One For Billy and Oighear Dubh both jinked and ran out through the tape when holding winning chances. Oighear Dubh's exit handed the long distance handicap chase to Sam Red who provided trainer Dan Skelton with his hundredth winner of the season, the earliest such a feat had ever been achieved. Skelton was also the trainer of One For Billy, who was about a length down on Diakali after the last in the earlier two-mile novice chase when running out. The incidents brought back memories of the 2013 Festival when Salsify was a fortunate winner of the Foxhunter Chase after Oscar Delta swerved left and unseated his rider as he ran out through the temporary tape on the run-in when looking all over the winner. Replacing the tape across the bend with a rail had been considered after the Oscar Delta incident but had been ruled out because of the short time between the final runners leaving the home straight and returning on the final circuit. Using a wider, more visible tape was considered but discounted because of problems in high winds. Putting up a plastic rail needs a team of nine because the uprights supporting the rail have to be secured. There is still concern about loose horses on the course being a danger to the staff erecting the temporary rail (the tape was also safer for loose horses coming back the other way, as it could be lowered quickly to allow them through).

Duc des Genievres (FR) (gr.g. 2013)	Buck's Boum (FR) (b 2005)	Cadoudal (br 1979)	Green Dancer / Come To Sea
		Buck's (b 1993)	Le Glorieux / Buckleby
	Lobelie (FR) (gr 1999)	Round Sovereign (gr 1986)	Kaldoun / Anadyr
		Forlane V (b 1993)	Quart de Vin / Grande Tirelire

After a runaway victory in the Arkle, it seemed hard to think that his stable might have a better two-mile novice chaser than Duc des Genievres. However, shortly after the end of the British season, Duc des Genievres and the Golden Miller Novices' Chase winner Defi du Seuil were comprehensively defeated by the former's unexposed stablemate Chacun Pour Soi in the Ryanair Novices' Chase at the Punchestown Festival. Duc des Genievres managed only third behind Chacun Pour Soi and Defi du Seuil, beaten over twenty lengths by the winner who coped easily with a very big step up in class. Duc des Genievres wasn't in the same form as he had been at Cheltenham and he was headed on the home turn after travelling well and going on before the third last before fading in the straight. The going was good to soft at Punchestown, nowhere near as testing as it had been at Cheltenham which might have contributed to Duc des Genievres' below-par performance. Judged on his Arkle form, he is clearly capable of winning more good races on his return from a summer break, particularly if there is a wet winter.

The sturdy Duc des Genievres is by French-based Buck's Boum who is also the sire of Cheltenham Gold Cup winner Al Boum Photo, in whose essay more can be found about him. On the distaff side, Duc des Genievres is the only winner out of Lobelie, a French AQPS (other than thoroughbred) who was a prolific winner in non-thoroughbred bumpers at around a mile and a half (her last three wins came in Corsica). Lobelie is a half-sister to the fairly useful hurdler/chaser Pacha d'Oudairies who stayed three and a quarter miles. The grandam of Duc des Genievres, Forlane V, was a bumper-winning daughter of the Grande Course de Haies winner Quart de Vin who was one of the leading sires of jumpers in France during the 'nineties. Duc des Genievres stays twenty-one furlongs and goes very well in the mud (acts on heavy going). *W. P. Mullins, Ireland*

DUC DU MEE (FR) 6 b.g. Corri Piano (FR) – British Nellerie (FR) (Le Pontet (FR)) **h–** [2018/19 h16.5d^pu Dec 13] little impact in points: pulled up in novice on hurdling debut. *Richenda Ford*

DU CHATELIER (FR) 6 ch.g. Network (GER) – Elza III (FR) (Lazer (FR)) [2018/19 **h–** h20.5g^ur h19.3d^pu h16.5d Mar 11] smallish gelding: little show in Irish points: no form over hurdles: tried in cheekpieces. *David Flood*

DUCHESS OF BRONTE 4 b.f. Mount Nelson – Reaf (In The Wings) [2018/19 b13.7m **b–** b12.6s Dec 19] sister to useful 1m-1½m winner Duke of Bronte and half-sister to 3 winners, including fair 2m hurdle winner Taws (by Hernando): dam unraced: little show in bumpers. *Rod Millman*

DUCHESS RAVENWAVES 5 br.m. Harbour Watch (IRE) – Neila (GER) (Diktat) **h105** [2018/19 h16d⁴ h16.3g h18.9m Apr 20] fair on Flat, stays 11.5f: fair form over hurdles: left Andrew Oliver after first start. *Gavin Patrick Cromwell, Ireland*

DUC KAUTO (FR) 6 b.g. Ballingarry (IRE) – Kauto Lorette (FR) (Useful (FR)) [2018/19 **h86** h–, b–: h15.8g⁰ʳ h16.8g⁶ h15.7g⁵ h15.8m h20.5d* h19.6dᵖᵘ h15.3g h16g Apr 26] lengthy gelding: modest handicap hurdler: won at Plumpton in January: stays 21f: acts on good to soft going: sometimes in tongue tie. *Colin Tizzard*

DU DESTIN (FR) 6 gr.g. Fuisse (FR) – Parenthese (FR) (Fragrant Mix (IRE)) [2018/19 **h101** h73p, b–: h20.6s² Dec 26] has had breathing operation: fair form over hurdles: will be suited by 2¾m+: acts on soft going: usually races close up. *Nicky Henderson*

DUDETTE 7 ch.m. Apple Tree (FR) – Whatagale (Strong Gale) [2018/19 h74: h24gᵖᵘ **h–** h21.2mᵘʳ h23.3g h19.3g h23.8gᵖᵘ Nov 26] of little account: in headgear last 2 starts. *Andrew Crook*

DUEL AT DAWN (IRE) 9 b.g. Presenting – Phillis Hill (Karinga Bay) [2018/19 c142, **c125** h–: c22.9v c29.2g c24.2dᵖᵘ c24.2d³ c25.6mᵖᵘ Apr 20] sturdy gelding: winning hurdler: **h–** fairly useful handicap chaser nowadays: third at Exeter in March: stays 25f: acts on heavy going: usually wears headgear. *Alex Hales*

DUE REWARD (IRE) 6 b.g. Westerner – Long Acre (Mark of Esteem (IRE)) [2018/19 **h132** h16g⁴ h16g* h16g* h16dᶠ h16.6g² h16g⁶ h16g h16.8d Mar 15] €42,000 3-y-o: fifth foal: half-brother to bumper winner/useful hurdler Katie T (2m winner, by Beneficial) and fair hurdler/chaser Pied du Roi (2m-21f winner, by Robin des Pres): dam, ran twice on Flat, half-sister to smart hurdler/chaser (2m-19f winner) Briareus: well held completed start in maiden points: useful hurdler: won maiden at Gowran in June, handicap at Kilbeggan in July and novice at Punchestown in December: will stay beyond 2m: acts on good to soft going. *Henry de Bromhead, Ireland*

DUE SOUTH (IRE) 8 b.g. City Honours (USA) – Lady Shackleton (IRE) (Zaffaran **c–** (USA)) [2018/19 h16d h23s h25dᵖᵘ Mar 3] no form: tried in cheekpieces: dead. **h–** *Linda Jewell*

DUFFY ALLEN (FR) 6 b.g. Lucarno (USA) – Parade (FR) (Robin des Champs (FR)) **h92** [2018/19 h96p, b72: h24g³ h23.4g⁵ h23.1g⁵ Mar 14] modest maiden hurdler: should be suited by 2¾m+: acts on good to soft going. *Nick Kent*

DUHALLOWCOUNTRY (IRE) 13 b.g. Beneficial – Milltown Lass (IRE) (Mister **c74 §** Lord (USA)) [2018/19 c–§, h–§: c16.4gᵘʳ c15.6g⁴ c17.2g⁶ c19.3g⁴ c19.2g² c19.2sᵖᵘ **h– §** c15.6s³ c16.4sᵘʳ c20.1g⁴ c16.4d⁴ c20.3g³ c16.4s c15.8m⁶ c16.4v* c20.1m c16.3d* c15.6g⁴ Apr 15] sturdy gelding: maiden hurdler: poor handicap chaser: won at Sedgefield in March and Newcastle in April: unproven beyond 17f: acts on heavy going: wears headgear: temperamental. *Victor Thompson*

DUHALLOW GESTURE (IRE) 7 b.m. King's Theatre (IRE) – Rare Gesture (IRE) **h125** (Shalford (IRE)) [2018/19 b103: h16.3d³ h19.5d² h16.5s* h19.8s⁴ h17.7v* h18.9m⁵ Apr 20] good-topped mare: point/bumper winner: fairly useful form over hurdles: won mares novice at Taunton in February and mares handicap at Fontwell in March: stays 19f: acts on heavy going. *Anthony Honeyball*

DUHALLOW LAD (IRE) 7 b.g. Papal Bull – Macca Luna (IRE) (Kahyasi) [2018/19 **c103** c114p, h100, b–: c19.2v⁵ c16.4g⁴ Mar 23] fair form over hurdles/fences: stays easy 2½m: **h–** acts on heavy going: usually races towards rear. *Alan Jones*

DUHALLOW TORNADO (IRE) 7 b.g. Golden Tornado (IRE) – Cappard Ridge (IRE) **c94** (Executive Perk) [2018/19 c125p: c26g⁴ May 4] multiple point winner: fairly useful form in hunter chases, winning both starts in 2017/18. *C. C. Pimlott*

DUHR (IRE) 5 b.g. Mawatheeq (USA) – Diljah (Linamix (FR)) [2018/19 h15.9g⁵ Apr 21] **h–** has had breathing operation: fair maiden on Flat, stays 10.5f: tailed off in maiden on hurdling debut. *Ralph Smith*

DUKE DEBARRY (IRE) 8 b.g. Presenting – Blue Dante (IRE) (Phardante (FR)) **c125** [2018/19 h115: h23.1g c25.2g* c24d⁵ c30.7dᵖᵘ c25.3gᵖᵘ Apr 17] well-made gelding: has **h–** had breathing operation: fairly useful form over hurdles: similar form over fences: won novice at Catterick in January: stays 25f: acts on heavy going. *Nicky Henderson*

DUKE DES CHAMPS (IRE) 9 b.g. Robin des Champs (FR) – Ballycowan Lady (IRE) **c135**
(Accordion) [2018/19 c135, h–: c23.6v c24.2d⁴ c20s* Mar 9] lengthy gelding: winning **h–**
hurdler: useful form over fences: won handicap at Sandown (by ½ length from The Kings
Writ) in March: stays 2¾m: acts on heavy going. *Philip Hobbs*

DUKE OF KILCORRAL (IRE) 6 gr.g. Duke of Marmalade (IRE) – Miss Shaan (FR) **c–**
(Darshaan) [2018/19 h116, b73: h19.5s* h19.9s⁵ h24.2d c20d^F Apr 21] fair hurdler: won **h112**
maiden at Chepstow in November: struggling when fell 4 out in maiden won by Beyond
The Law at Cork on chasing debut: left Neil Mulholland after third start: should stay
beyond 2½m: acts on heavy going: tried in cheekpieces. *David Harry Kelly, Ireland*

DUKE OF NAVAN (IRE) 11 b.g. Presenting – Greenfieldflyer (IRE) (Alphabatim **c144**
(USA)) [2018/19 c145, h–: c15.9d² c16.8gᵖᵘ c15.2d⁵ c17g³ c16.5m^F Apr 13] well-made **h–**
gelding: winning hurdler: useful handicap chaser: second at Cheltenham (head behind
Modus) in October: stays 2¼m: acts on good to firm and heavy going. *Nicky Richards*

DUKE'S AFFAIR 11 b.g. Fair Mix (IRE) – Dunsfold Duchess (IRE) (Bustino) [2018/19 **h87**
h23s⁴ May 25] useful-looking gelding: modest handicap hurdler: stays 2¾m: acts on heavy
going: wears hood. *Jeremy Scott*

DUKE'S GIRL 5 b.m. Poet's Voice – Juniper Girl (IRE) (Revoque (IRE)) [2018/19 h16d² **h94**
h16s⁴ h21gᵇᵈ h17.3g h20g h20.5g^F h19.8g² h16d⁴ h21vᵖᵘ h20.2g h20g⁴ h24g⁶ h20d Apr 7]
half-sister to useful 2m hurdle winner Forced Family Fun (by Refuse To Bend) and
Italian Group 1 2½m hurdle winner Kifaaya (by Intikhab): modest maiden hurdler: left
James A. Nash after twelfth start: stays 3m: acts on good to soft going: has worn hood: in
tongue tie last 3 starts. *Gordon Elliott, Ireland*

DUKE STREET (IRE) 7 b.g. Duke of Marmalade (IRE) – Act of The Pace (IRE) (King's **c134 p**
Theatre (IRE)) [2018/19 c130, h–: c20g* Jun 2] compact gelding: winning hurdler: useful **h–**
form over fences: won novice at Worcester (by 5 lengths from Gustave Mahler) in June:
stays 21f: acts on soft and good to firm going: usually wears cheekpieces: looked open to
further improvement but not seen out again. *Dr Richard Newland*

DULCE PANEM (FR) 7 ch.g. Panis (USA) – Danissima (FR) (Fabulous Dancer (USA)) **c80**
[2018/19 c–, h100: h20d h19.5v c19.4s^F c15.6s⁴ h19.9s³ h20.6d³ h24.1d³ Mar 19] modest **h98**
maiden hurdler: poor form over fences: stays 3m: acts on heavy going: wears headgear.
Rebecca Menzies

DULWICH HILL (IRE) 7 b.m. Milan – Madam Leader (IRE) (Supreme Leader) **h–**
[2018/19 h20.6g⁴ Jul 8] £12,000 4-y-o: fourth foal: sister to fairly useful hurdler/useful
chaser Mighty Leader (2½m-3¼m winner): dam (h91) bumper/2m-2½m hurdle winner:
point winner: well beaten in novice on hurdling debut. *Caroline Bailey*

DUN BAY CREEK 8 b.g. Dubai Destination (USA) – Over It (Overbury (IRE)) [2018/19 **h–**
h–: h21.7dᵖᵘ h16.7s⁶ Mar 23] lengthy gelding: winning hurdler in 2016/17: no form since:
should stay 3m: acts on good to soft going. *Roy Brotherton*

DUNDRUM WOOD (IRE) 5 b.g. Flemensfirth (USA) – Ruby Isabel (IRE) (Great Palm **b92**
(USA)) [2018/19 b16g³ Apr 25] £28,000 3-y-o, £270,000 4-y-o: third foal: dam (c99/h89),
2m chase winner, half-sister to useful hurdler/fairly useful chaser (stayed 3½m) Valley
Ride: off mark in Irish points at second attempt: 5/6, third in bumper at Warwick (3¼
lengths behind Stoner's Choice). *Olly Murphy*

DUN FAW GOOD 12 br.g. Grape Tree Road – Dun Rose (Roscoe Blake) [2018/19 c89: **c96**
c20.1d² c24.2g³ c25.5g* c23.8g⁵ c24.2g² Sep 17] modest handicap chaser: won at Cartmel
in July: stays 25f: acts on good to soft going. *James Walton*

DUNLY (FR) 6 b.g. Gris de Gris (IRE) – Octavine du Meix (FR) (Le Tajer (FR)) [2018/19 **h65**
h–p: h16v h16.4g⁶ h20.5s h16.4m⁶ Mar 28] has had breathing operation: poor form over
hurdles. *James Ewart*

DUNN'S RIVER (FR) 8 gr.g. Mastercraftsman (IRE) – Prairie Moon (Halling (USA)) **h–**
[2018/19 h91: h18.5gᵖᵘ h18.7m Jun 19] multiple point winner: modest maiden hurdler, no
form in 2018/19: stays 2¾m: acts on good to soft going: in blinkers last 4 starts: tried in
tongue tie: front runner/races prominently. *Jack R. Barber*

DUN SCAITH (IRE) 11 b.g. Vinnie Roe (IRE) – Scathach (IRE) (Nestor) [2018/19 c–, **c–**
h101§: h20g^F Oct 11] fair hurdler, tailed off when fell on sole start in 2018/19: fell both **h–**
starts over fences: stays 3m: acts on good to firm and heavy going: often hooded: wears
tongue tie: temperamental. *Sophie Leech*

DUNSTALL DOLLY 6 b.m. Midnight Legend – Toungara (FR) (Smadoun (FR)) [2018/19 **b–**
b–: b15.8g Jun 14] has had breathing operation: no form in bumpers: tried in tongue tie.
Tom George

DUNVEGAN (FR) 6 gr.g. Le Havre (IRE) – Or des Joncs (FR) (Turgeon (USA)) **h133**
[2018/19 h122p, b112: h20d* h22g h21s^pu Mar 13] compact gelding: useful bumper
performer: similar form over hurdles: won maiden at Fairyhouse in December: front
runner/races prominently. *P. A. Fahy, Ireland*

DURATION (IRE) 4 b.g. Champs Elysees – Fringe (In The Wings) [2018/19 h16.3d^6 **h88**
h15.8d Mar 13] sturdy gelding: modest on Flat, stays 16.5f: modest form over hurdles:
wears cheekpieces. *J. R. Jenkins*

DURBANVILLE 7 b.g. Black Sam Bellamy (IRE) – Kealshore Lass (Alflora (IRE)) **c–**
[2018/19 h105: c24.2g c24.2s^pu Dec 26] fair hurdler: little show over fences: stays 3m: acts **h–**
on heavy going: tried in cheekpieces. *Stef Keniry*

DUSKY HERCULES (IRE) 5 b.g. Shantou (USA) – Annalecky (IRE) (Bob's Return **h93**
(IRE)) [2018/19 b–: b15.8d^5 h20.5s^4 h23.3s Dec 31] fair form in bumpers: modest form **b89**
over hurdles: tried in cheekpieces. *David Pipe*

DUSKY LARK 9 b.g. Nayef (USA) – Snow Goose (Polar Falcon (USA)) [2018/19 c117x, **c129**
h114: c20.9g^6 c19.2s^2 c19.4s^2 c24.2d Mar 24] good-topped gelding: fair hurdler: fairly **h–**
useful handicap chaser: second at Exeter and Chepstow in December: stays 2½m: acts on
heavy going: has worn cheekpieces, including last 2 starts: has worn tongue tie: usually
leads. *Robert Walford*

DUSKY RAIDER (IRE) 6 gr.g. Clodovil (IRE) – Rahila (IRE) (Kalanisi (IRE)) **h86**
[2018/19 h102: h15.8g h20g^4 h19.2g^pu Aug 23] fair hurdler at best, disappointing in
2018/19: stays 19f: acts on good to soft going. *Tim Vaughan*

DU SOLEIL (FR) 7 ch.g. Zambezi Sun – Cykapri (FR) (Cyborg (FR)) [2018/19 h118: **c117**
c15.9d^3 c20d^f Mar 24] fairly useful form over hurdles: similar form when third in novice **h–**
handicap at Carlisle on completed start over fences: should stay 2½m: acts on heavy going:
in hood last 3 starts. *Venetia Williams*

DUSTIN DES MOTTES (FR) 6 b.g. Kapgarde (FR) – Puszta des Mottes (FR) (Useful **c132**
(FR)) [2018/19 h18.9d* h17.9s* c16.4d^3 c16.8s^2 c20.6d^6 c19.9d^6 Mar 2] sturdy gelding: **h119**
fourth foal: half-brother to fairly useful hurdler/chaser Boss des Mottes (2m/17f winner, by
Califet): dam French 10.5f-13f bumper winner: fairly useful form over hurdles: won minor
event at Dax in June: useful form over fences: won minor event at Clairefontaine later in
June: second in novice handicap at Ascot (½ length behind Azzerti) in December: left
Francois Nicolle after second start: stays 19f: acts on soft going. *Dr Richard Newland*

DUTCH CANYON (IRE) 9 b.g. Craigsteel – Chitabe (IRE) (Lord of Appeal) [2018/19 **c– §**
c60§, h81§: h23.9g^4 h23.9g^4 h23.9g Aug 18] poor maiden hurdler: maiden chaser: stays **h77 §**
3m: acts on soft and good to firm going: has worn headgear/tongue tie: has joined Stuart
Coltherd: ungenuine. *N. W. Alexander*

DUTCH MELODY 5 b.m. Dutch Art – Mystic Melody (IRE) (Montjeu (IRE)) [2018/19 **h–**
h22d^pu Mar 5] has had breathing operation: poor maiden on Flat: pulled up on hurdling
debut. *Lucinda Egerton*

D'WATERSIDE 5 b.g. Sir Percy – Santorini Sunset (Haafhd) [2018/19 h93: h16.7g^3 **h97**
h16.3m^6 h16.7g Aug 3] neat gelding: modest maiden hurdler: raced around 2m: has worn
headgear, including final start:. *David Loughnane*

DWIGHT D 6 b.g. Duke of Marmalade (IRE) – Almatinka (IRE) (Indian Ridge) [2018/19 **h–**
h17d h15.7g Nov 23] fair on Flat, stays 1¼m: well held in 2 novice hurdles. *Stuart Coltherd*

DYLANSEOGHAN (IRE) 10 b.g. Pierre – Sabbatical (IRE) (Jurado (USA)) [2018/19 **c103**
c104, h–: c24.5g* c26.1d^4 c25.7s^4 c25.7s^4 c25.7s Jan 16] maiden hurdler: fair handicap chaser: **h–**
won novice event at Towcester in May: stays 3½m: acts on heavy going: wears cheekpieces:
usually races towards rear. *Zoe Davison*

DYLAN'S SEA SONG 5 b.m. Dylan Thomas (IRE) – Mary Sea (FR) (Selkirk (USA)) **b89**
[2018/19 b16.3s b16.3d^2 b15.7d Apr 9] close-coupled mare: sixth foal: half-sister to 2
winners on Flat, including 1m-1½m winner Jamaica Grande (by Doyen): dam maiden on
Flat: fair form in bumpers: best effort when second in mares event at Newbury in March.
Mark Usher

DYLIEV (FR) 6 ch.m. Dylan Thomas (IRE) – Coreliev (IRE) (Fasliyev (USA)) [2018/19 **h116**
h98: h15.8g h20.7g^4 h15.5g h15.5d^2 h16g* h16s^2 h15.8g* h15.8d* h15.8g^2 Mar 19] sturdy
mare: fairly useful handicap hurdler: won at Warwick (novice) in January, and Huntingdon
in February and March: likely to prove best at 2m: acts on soft going: usually wears hood:
usually travels strongly. *Caroline Bailey*

DYNA MIGHT 5 b.m. Foxwedge (AUS) – Dyna Bowl (USA) (Dynaformer (USA)) **h63**
[2018/19 h16.7g^5 h16.2g h15.7g^4 h22m Aug 2] modest on Flat, stays 1¾m: well held over
hurdles: in cheekpieces last 2 starts. *Ollie Pears*

DYNAMITE DOLLARS (FR) 6 b.g. Buck's Boum (FR) – Macadoun (FR)   **c153 +**
(Cardoun (FR)) [2018/19 h127: c17.2g* c15.9g^2 c15.5s* c16g* c16.4g* Jan 26]   **h–**

    Elite sport is littered with high profile roles that are 'too good to turn down',
even though they come with low job security. The average reign of managers among
the current twenty Premier League clubs stood at just two years and twenty-nine
days at the end of the latest football season, statistics which were affected by no
fewer than three of those managers leaving their roles during the close season.
Ironically, this trigger-happy trend has even extended to clubs with a reputation
for remaining loyal to their managers. Manchester United, for example, are on
to their fifth manager in six years since Sir Alex Ferguson retired his
remarkable reign at the club of nearly twenty-seven years. Ferguson's immediate
successor David Moyes was himself recruited after a lengthy tenure (eleven years)
at Everton, a club which has now had six managers since he left. The problems of
replacing a highly successful long-term incumbent have also been felt at Manor
Farm Stables where eleven-times champion trainer Paul Nicholls has rung the
changes with his stable jockeys since Ruby Walsh ended his most successful eleven-
year association with the yard in 2013 (when he opted to ride full time in Ireland).
Daryl Jacob became stable jockey (Walsh's initial understudy Sam Thomas had been
dispensed with several years earlier) but he lasted just twelve months, losing the
post to Sam Twiston-Davies in the spring of 2014 when sidelined with a broken leg
(Twiston-Davies had been given the ride on stable star Big Buck's earlier that year).
Twiston-Davies lasted longer in the hot seat, though regularly having to endure the
disappointment and/or embarrassment of losing the ride on some of the yard's high
profile horses—which included Clan des Obeaux (part-owned by Sir Alex Ferguson)
during his novice chasing campaign. Twiston-Davies turned freelance at the end of
the 2017/18 season with Nicholls understandably prickly on the subject, explaining
that there were outside pressures involved in replacing Twiston-Davies with his
number-two Harry Cobden (then aged nineteen) for 2018/19: 'Harry has been with
us since the age of sixteen. A lot of my owners have wanted to use him—we've lots
of good jockeys here and it's hard to keep everybody happy.'

    The decision to promote from within has so far reaped benefits, with both
Cobden and champion conditional Bryony Frost enjoying their best-ever campaigns,
reaching their first century and half-century respectively, all of which helped Nicholls
to regain the trainers' championship for the first time since 2015/16. Cobden, who
was champion conditional himself in 2016/17, had reportedly been offered the job as
stable jockey to Colin Tizzard just three days before Nicholls offered him the same
post, but he has never had much reason to regret his decision to stay at Manor Farm

randoxhealth.com Henry VIII Novices' Chase, Sandown—
a first Grade 1 win for Harry Cobden since being promoted to stable jockey for Paul Nicholls
as Dynamite Dollars (right) overhauls Irish raider Ornua

Napoleons Casino & Restaurant Owlerton Sheffield Lightning Novices' Chase,
Doncaster—a hat-trick of graded wins for Dynamite Dollars as he lands the odds from Ballywood

Stables, ending the season with one hundred and nine wins, which included eighty-four for Nicholls (compared to Twiston-Davies' forty-seven for the yard in 2017/18) and twenty-three for Tizzard. If the jockeys' championship had been decided on prize-money, rather than the number of wins, Cobden would have been celebrating his first title, his mounts winning £2,207,952 in first-three prize money in the latest season, putting him ahead of Richard Johnson and Harry Skelton.

Cobden's first big-race win as Nicholls stable jockey came on Dynamite Dollars in the randoxhealth.com Henry VIII Novices' Chase at Sandown in December, which was one of four Grade 1 wins for the jockey in 2018/19, all of them coming over fences. The latter point isn't a coincidence either, as an ability to get horses jumping fluently over fences is presumably one of the qualities that most attracted the yard's owners to Cobden (and Frost for that matter). Dynamite Dollars didn't look anything out of the ordinary in bumpers or over hurdles, winning twice from six starts in the latter sphere, showing just fairly useful form. His strike rate and level of form both improved considerably, however, once switched to the larger obstacles. It was clear from the outset that Dynamite Dollars was going to be a different proposition as a chaser. He ran out an impressive winner of a four-runner novice event at Market Rasen on his chasing debut in October, jumping most fluently under Cobden when easily defeating Highway One O One (who was conceding him 6 lb) by nine lengths.

Dynamite Dollars was immediately stepped up in class, his next start coming in the Grade 2 November Novices' Chase at Cheltenham, where a seven-length second to the impressive Lalor represented significant improvement on his debut effort. However, an uneven gallop did not really play to Dynamite Dollars' strength that day, as subsequent events more than proved. He took his revenge on Lalor in the Henry VIII three weeks later, the latter sent off 11/8-on favourite in a field of six and managing only a laboured third in a race run at a much more searching gallop, and on softer ground. It was the experienced Irish raider Ornua who pushed Dynamite Dollars the closest, going down by a length and three quarters after Dynamite Dollars overhauled him on the run-in, the pair pulling ten lengths clear of Lalor, with a further two and a half lengths back to Highway One O One in fourth. It was a record-breaking seventh win in the race for Nicholls, one more than his tally now in the 32Red.com Wayward Lad Novices' Chase at Kempton, which was the scene of Dynamite Dollars' next (and arguably best) win of the campaign later in December. Unfortunately, thick mist prevented a proper assessment of the race—the useful mare Maria's Benefit, for example, departed out of sight in the back straight having reportedly just taken up the running—but the fact that Dynamite Dollars lowered the colours of odds-on Kalashnikov, beating that rival by a length and a quarter, conceding him 5 lb, made for very good reading regardless of the visibility, particularly as there was a further twenty-eight lengths back to old rival Highway One O One in third. Dynamite Dollars was clearly the leading home-trained two-mile novice chaser at this stage of the season, a position he cemented with a routine win over the smart handicapper Ballywood in a four-runner renewal of the Napoleons Casino & Restaurant Owlerton Sheffield Lightning Novices' Chase at Doncaster in late-January (a sixth win in the race for Nicholls). Alas, injury ruled out Dynamite Dollars for the remainder of the campaign but his reputation was, if anything, enhanced even further by the performances of Ornua and Kalashnikov in winning Grade 1 novices at the Aintree Festival.

		Cadoudal	Green Dancer
	Buck's Boum (FR)	(br 1979)	Come To Sea
	(b 2005)	Buck's	Le Glorieux
Dynamite Dollars (FR)		(b 1993)	Buckley
(b.g. 2013)		Cardoun	Kaldoun
	Macadoun (FR)	(b 1989)	Cable Car
	(b 1999)	Marowa	Rex Magna
		(b 1983)	La Romantique

A good-topped gelding, Dynamite Dollars is from the second crop of smart French juvenile hurdler Buck's Boum, who finished runner-up to Long Run in the 2008 Prix Cambaceres before switching to stallion duties, his best representative to date being Cheltenham Gold Cup winner Al Boum Photo, in whose essay more can be found. Dynamite Dollars is the fifth foal out of Macadoun, runner-up over hurdles on her only start in France, and her only winner. Her only two other offspring to reach the racecourse included the ill-fated Tete A Queue (by Robin des Champs), who was snapped up by Gigginstown after finishing fourth in a four-year-old hurdle in the French Provinces but died the following year after just one start on Irish soil. There is more to recommend the family in this pedigree, though, with Macadoun being a half-sister to the dam of Nicholls' 2008 Henry VIII winner Al Ferof, who also won the Supreme Novices' Hurdle earlier that year before going on to become a top-class chaser at up to three miles later in his career (trained latterly by Dan Skelton).

Dynamite Dollars' injury may give some cause for concern with regards to his immediate future, but his trainer wasn't unduly worried when announcing the setback in his Betfair blog in February. 'You have to try to look on the bright side in these situations. I remember the nightmare when Kauto Star was forced to miss the Arkle after sustaining a hairline fracture,' the trainer explained. 'I told Kauto Star's owner Clive Smith he might actually benefit from the time off to mature, and that certainly proved to be the case.' It is most unlikely that Dynamite Dollars will ever scale the heights of Kauto Star, but he remains a good prospect and it is certainly not out of the question that he will go on to even better things in the next season provided he returns none the worse, particularly as his sound jumping is likely to continue to stand him in good stead. Although he was tried several times at around two and a half miles over hurdles, it seems likely that he will be kept at the minimum trip for now over fences given his free-going style of racing. Although he has winning form on soft and heavy going, the style of his wins at Market Rasen, Kempton and Doncaster suggests he may prove ideally suited by top-of-the-ground conditions which put the emphasis more firmly on speed and fluent jumping. *Paul Nicholls*

DYSTONIA'S REVENGE (IRE) 14 b.g. Woods of Windsor (USA) – Lady Isaac (IRE) **c– §**
(Le Bavard (FR)) [2018/19 c21.6g May 17] good-topped gelding: multiple point winner: **h–**
once-raced hurdler: fairly useful chaser at best, retains little ability: stays 25f: acts on soft
and good to firm going: in cheekpieces last 4 starts: unreliable. *Mrs Libby Lawson*

E

EAGER TO KNOW (IRE) 9 b.g. Sayarshan (FR) – Drew (IRE) (Double Schwartz) **c82**
[2018/19 c–, h80: c24.2g c20.1g³ c20.1g² c21.2m³ c25.5g c26.3mᵖᵘ c20.1g³ c24.2sᵖᵘ **h–**
c20.9m⁴ Apr 20] lengthy gelding: has had breathing operation: point winner: maiden
hurdler: poor maiden chaser: stays 3m: acts on good to firm going: tried in cheekpieces.
Micky Hammond

EAGLE CRAG (IRE) 7 b.g. Azamour (IRE) – Irish Style (IRE) (Mujadil (USA)) **h–**
[2018/19 b16.5g h22.7g Dec 29] fair maiden on Flat, stayed 1¾m: poor form in bumpers: **b71**
tailed off on hurdling debut: left Joseph G. Murphy after first start: tongue tied both starts
in 2018/19: dead. *Iain Jardine*

EAGLE RIDGE (IRE) 8 b.g. Oscar (IRE) – Azaban (IRE) (Be My Native (USA)) **h–**
[2018/19 h97, b–: h22.7g h16.4g h20.5d h20.2d Apr 26] runner-up in Irish point on debut:
poor maiden hurdler on balance: in tongue tie last 4 starts. *N. W. Alexander*

EAMON AN CNOIC (IRE) 8 b.g. Westerner – Nutmeg Tune (IRE) (Accordion) **c139**
[2018/19 c134, h–: h20g c20.2g⁵ c19.2s⁶ c16d* c20.6d⁴ c15.8d Apr 4] tall gelding: has had **h–**
breathing operation: fairly useful hurdler at best: useful handicap chaser: won at Chepstow
in February: fourth in Brown Advisory & Merriebelle Stable Plate at Cheltenham (3½
lengths behind Siruh du Lac) in March: stays 21f: acts on heavy going: wears cheekpieces:
tongue tied all starts in 2018/19. *David Pipe*

EARCOMESALI 6 b.m. Passing Glance – Earcomesannie (IRE) (Anshan) [2018/19 **h–**
b16.2s b16d b16d h19gᵖᵘ h22gᵖᵘ Apr 14] third foal: dam (c104/h72) fair chaser (3m/3¼m **b–**
winner): no form in bumpers/over hurdles: tried in tongue tie. *Peter Pritchard*

EARCOMESTOM 7 b.g. Passing Glance – Earcomesannie (IRE) (Anshan) [2018/19 **h90**
h77, b–: h23.3d² h24g⁵ h22g³ h24gᵖᵘ Jun 25] workmanlike gelding: maiden pointer:
modest maiden hurdler: stayed 3m: acted on good to soft going: wore hood: tried in tongue
tie: usually raced nearer last than first: dead. *Peter Pritchard*

EARL OF BUNNACURRY (IRE) 5 b.g. Approve (IRE) – Bonkers (Efisio) [2018/19 **h87**
h16g h16g h16s h16s h16d⁶ h16.7g Mar 14] fair on Flat, stays 1½m: modest form over
hurdles: left E. G. Barry after second start: raced around 2m: sometimes in tongue tie.
Gavin Patrick Cromwell, Ireland

*Martin Pipe Conditional Jockeys' Handicap Hurdle, Cheltenham—Jonjo O'Neill Jr produces
2018 third Early Doors (hoops) with a well-timed run to defeat the Gigginstown pair
Dallas des Pictons (white blaze) and Defi Bleu (left)*

Mr John P. McManus' "Early Doors"

EARLOFTHECOTSWOLDS (FR) 5 bl.g. Axxos (GER) – Sissi Land (FR) (Grey Risk (FR)) [2018/19 b89: b16.7g* b16.4d⁶ h18.6g² h17s* h21.4g⁵ h20.6d* h21.2g² h20.6g* Apr 3] useful-looking gelding: fairly useful form in bumpers: won at Market Rasen in September: useful form over hurdles: won novice at Carlisle in December, and handicaps at former course in February and April (by 1¼ lengths from The Sweeney): stays 21f: acts on soft going: usually front runner/races prominently. *Nigel Twiston-Davies*   **h130 b100**

EARL OF WISDOM 4 ch.g. Flemensfirth (USA) – Golden Sunbird (IRE) (Bob Back (USA)) [2018/19 b13.7g Apr 12] 4/1, well beaten in bumper. *Colin Tizzard*   **b–**

EARLSHILL (IRE) 8 b.g. Milan – Mrs Marples (IRE) (Sexton Blake) [2018/19 h116: h20.3g* c19.9gᵖᵘ c21.4d⁶ h24.4g⁴ c21.4g⁶ Mar 27] sturdy gelding: has had breathing operation: Irish point winner: fairly useful hurdler: won novice at Southwell in May: similar form over fences: stays 21f: acts on heavy going: tried in cheekpieces: has worn tongue tie: usually front runner/races prominently. *Stuart Edmunds*   **c122 h118**

EARLY BOY (FR) 8 b.g. Early March – Eclat de Rose (FR) (Scribe (IRE)) [2018/19 h–: h16.7g h16.7g⁶ c17.2g⁴ c19.3g² c16.4s⁴ c19.4sᵖᵘ c15.2g⁶ c15.6gᵖᵘ Apr 15] little form over hurdles or fences: usually wears eyeshields. *Andrew Crook*   **c61 h56**

EARLY DOORS (FR) 6 b.g. Soldier of Fortune (IRE) – Ymlaen (IRE) (Desert Prince (IRE)) [2018/19 h140: h20g⁵ h24g² h20.3d* Mar 15] smart hurdler: won Martin Pipe Conditional Jockeys' Handicap Hurdle at Cheltenham (by 1¼ lengths from Dallas des Pictons) in March: stays 3m: acts on heavy going: usually races towards rear. *Joseph Patrick O'Brien, Ireland*   **h152**

EARLY DU LEMO (FR) 6 gr.g. Early March – Kiswa (FR) (Top Waltz (FR)) [2018/19 h122: c16s c20sᵘʳ c16.4d² c15.9mᵘʳ c16d* Jan 15] good-topped gelding: fairly useful hurdler: useful form over fences: won handicap at Lingfield (by 2 lengths from Air de Rock) in January: unproven beyond 17f: acts on soft going: usually races close up: should improve further as a chaser. *Gary Moore*   **c136 p h–**

307

EARLY LEARNER 7 b.m. Sulamani (IRE) – Slow Starter (IRE) (Dr Massini (IRE)) **h104**
[2018/19 b–: h15.5g² h20.5g⁵ h20.8g⁶ h26gᵖᵘ Apr 10] point winner: fair form over hurdles only on first start: should be suited by 2½m: tried in cheekpieces. *Kim Bailey*

EARLY MORNING RAIN (FR) 5 gr.m. Martaline – Rosewater (GER) (Winged Love **b92**
(IRE)) [2018/19 b15.8s b16.5d² b17.7g* b16.8g⁵ Apr 18] €12,000 3-y-o: seventh foal: half-sister to 1¼m winners Rosa Damascena (by Kalanisi) and Matavia Bay (by Bahamian Bounty): dam ran 3 times on Flat in France (third at 1½m): fair form in bumpers: won mares event at Plumpton in February. *Jamie Snowden*

EARLY RETIREMENT (IRE) 7 b.g. Daylami (IRE) – Deep Lilly (Glacial Storm **c119**
(USA)) [2018/19 h116: h19.6g³ c24g² c24s⁵ c24dᵖᵘ h20.7d Jan 25] fair handicap hurdler: **h114**
fairly useful form over fences: best effort when second in novice handicap at Southwell in October: stays 3m: acts on heavy going: usually in headgear. *Caroline Bailey*

EARTH LADY 7 b.m. Presenting – Simply Divine (IRE) (Be My Native (USA)) [2018/19 **h–**
h–: h22.1gᵖᵘ May 30] has had breathing operation: modest maiden hurdler for Philip Hobbs, has lost way: should be suited by 2½m+: tried in hood. *Martin Todhunter*

EARTH LEADER (IRE) 6 br.g. Presenting – Full of Spirit (IRE) (Exit To Nowhere **h80**
(USA)) [2018/19 b–: h21.6gʳᵒ h20g⁶ Jun 2] poor form over hurdles: completed hat-trick in points later in season. *Paul Nicholls*

EARTH MOOR (IRE) 5 ch.g. Ask – Merrylas (IRE) (Mister Lord (USA)) [2018/19 b78: **h107 p**
b16.8m² b16g² b17.7s* h18.5m* Oct 23] fairly useful form in bumpers: won at Fontwell in **b97**
October: 1/4, also won maiden at Exeter (by neck from Zoffany Bay) on hurdling debut: usually races close up: should progress. *Philip Hobbs*

EARTHMOVES (FR) 9 b.g. Antarctique (IRE) – Red Rym (FR) (Denham Red (FR)) **c116 §**
[2018/19 c127, h–: c25.8m³ c25.5g⁶ c22.6m c21.4gᵖᵘ c19.4d³ Oct 20] lengthy gelding: **h–**
winning hurdler: fairly useful handicap chaser: third at Newton Abbot in July: stays 21f: acts on heavy going: usually wears headgear/tongue tie: front runner/races prominently: placed in points later in season: temperamental. *Peter Bowen*

EARTH PRINCE (FR) 5 gr.g. Al Namix (FR) – Quarline de L'Ecu (FR) (Lavirco **b85**
(GER)) [2018/19 b16.8g² May 16] 7/2, second in bumper at Newton Abbot (5 lengths behind Colonel Custard): dead. *Paul Nicholls*

EARTH SPIRIT 6 b.g. Black Sam Bellamy (IRE) – Samandara (FR) (Kris) [2018/19 **h–**
b16.8m h21.4gᵖᵘ Jan 5] tailed off in bumper: in hood, pulled up in novice on hurdling **b–**
debut. *Jack R. Barber*

EARTH STORM (IRE) 7 b.g. Getaway (GER) – Aguida (FR) (Kahyasi) [2018/19 h85: **h–**
h21.4mᵖᵘ May 10] point winner: little show over hurdles: should stay at least 3m. *Jack R. Barber*

EASKEY LAD (IRE) 4 b.g. Most Improved (IRE) – Lilakiya (IRE) (Dr Fong (USA)) **h87**
[2018/19 h16.5s h16g h16d h19d⁴ Apr 24] half-brother to fairly useful hurdler Minstrels Gallery (17f-2½m winner, by Refuse To Bend), stayed 3m: modest maiden on Flat, stays 1½m: modest form over hurdles: left F. Birrane after third start. *Noel Williams*

EASON (FR) 5 b.g. Coastal Path – Maitresse de Maison (FR) (Video Rock (FR)) [2018/19 **b99**
b16g* b15.7s⁶ b16.3d⁶ Mar 22] €115,000 3-y-o: good-topped gelding: fourth foal: half-brother to smart French hurdler/chaser Tir Au But (17f-25f winner, by Trempolino): dam French 2¼m-2½m hurdle/chase winner: fairly useful form in bumpers: won conditionals/amateurs event at Chepstow in October. *Paul Nicholls*

EASTER ERIC 5 b.g. Martaline – Easter Comet (Gunner B) [2018/19 b15.7g³ h20g⁵ **h97**
h19.3g⁴ h21d h20v Jan 14] rangy gelding: seventh foal: half-brother to smart chaser Easter **b91**
Meteor (17f-19f winner) and useful hurdler/chaser Easter Legend (19f-2¾m winner) (both by Midnight Legend): dam unraced: fair form when third in bumper at Southwell (4¼ lengths behind Genius) in May: modest form over hurdles. *David Pipe*

EASTER GOLD (FR) 5 b.m. Kapgarde (FR) – Une Dame d'Or (FR) (Astarabad (USA)) **b87**
[2018/19 b89: b15.7d⁵ b16s Mar 9] close-coupled mare: fair form in bumpers. *Lucy Wadham*

EASTER IN PARIS (IRE) 10 b.m. Bienamado (USA) – Easter Saturday (IRE) (Grand **c–**
Plaisir (IRE)) [2018/19 c71, h–: c21.2gᵖᵘ May 8] modest maiden hurdler at best: winning **h–**
chaser: stayed 2¾m: acted on heavy going: tried in hood: usually raced close up: dead. *Paul Henderson*

EASTERN HARBOUR 5 ch.g. Harbour Watch (IRE) – Eastern Lily (USA) (Eastern **h84**
Echo (USA)) [2018/19 h16g⁶ h16.2gᶠ Aug 18] poor form completed start (tongue tied) over hurdles for Henry de Bromhead: dead. *Leonard Kerr*

EASTERN LADY (IND) 6 ch.m. Dancing Forever (USA) – Oriental Lady (IRE) (King's **c82** Best (USA)) [2018/19 h84: c20g⁶ c20.9d⁵ c21.6g⁴ c20gᶠ c21g c21g c20.9g* c20.3d* Apr **h–** 26] workmanlike mare: maiden hurdler: poor chaser: won handicaps at Hereford (mares event) in March and Bangor (mares novice) in April: stays 2¾m: acts on soft going: has worn hood/tongue tie. *Richard Price*

EASTERN PROMISES 6 gr.m. Eastern Anthem (IRE) – Chilli Rose (Classic Cliche **h–** (IRE)) [2018/19 b16g h21dᵖᵘ Dec 31] first foal: dam (c107/h116, bumper winner (placed **b–** up to 3m over jumps), half-sister to useful hurdler/chaser (stayed 25f) Ross River: behind in mares bumper: pulled up in mares novice on hurdling debut. *Robert Walford*

EASTER ROCKET 5 b.g. Shirocco (GER) – Easter Legend (Midnight Legend) [2018/19 **b–** b16g Jun 2] second foal: dam (c140/h137), 19f-2¼m hurdle/chase winner, sister to smart chaser (stayed 21f) Easter Meteor: 4/1, well beaten in bumper. *Tom Lacey*

EAST INDIES 6 b.g. Authorized (IRE) – Elan (Dansili) [2018/19 h116: h17.7g⁴ h15.9g **c104** c18mᶠ Oct 21] rather leggy gelding: fairly useful hurdler, below form in 2018/19: tiring **h86** when fell heavily 2 out in novice handicap won by A Place Apart at Kempton on chasing debut: stays 2¼m: acts on good to firm and good to soft going: has worn headgear: sold £2,000 in March. *Gary Moore*

EASTLAKE (IRE) 13 b.g. Beneficial – Guigone (FR) (Esprit du Nord (USA)) [2018/19 **c104 §** c–§, h–§: c18g⁴ c19.4g c15.9gᵖᵘ Mar 8] winning hurdler: smart chaser at best: stayed 21f: **h– §** acted on good to firm and heavy going: sometimes in cheekpieces: wore tongue tie: unreliable. *Jonjo O'Neill*

EAST WING (IRE) 7 b.g. Winged Love (IRE) – Eastender (Opening Verse (USA)) **h78** [2018/19 h–, b89: h23.3d h25g⁵ h25.4m Jul 1] good-topped gelding: poor maiden hurdler: left Anthony Honeyball after second start: little impact in points in 2019: tried in blinkers: wears tongue tie. *Mike Sowersby*

EASY GAME (FR) 5 b.g. Barastraight – Rule of The Game (FR) (Lavirco (GER)) **h138** [2018/19 h20.5g* h16.6g* h20s² h16g³ h20d* h20d* h21s h20d³ Apr 7] third foal: dam, French 1½m/13f bumper winner, half-sister to useful French hurdler/smart chaser (15f-2¼m winner) Echiquier Royal: useful hurdler: won maiden at Killarney and novice at Galway in July, Monksfield Novices' Hurdle at Navan (by neck from Magnium) in November and Navan Novices' Hurdle (by 2 lengths from Getareason) in December: third in Grade 2 novice at Fairyhouse (length behind Dommage Pour Toi) in April: stays 2½m: acts on good to soft going: usually races off pace. *W. P. Mullins, Ireland*

EASYONTHEEYE (IRE) 8 br.m. Kalanisi (IRE) – Lady Bernie (IRE) (Supreme **h–** Leader) [2018/19 h20.7g⁶ h20.7g h15.9s h25gᵖᵘ Mar 19] no form in bumpers/over hurdles: tried in headgear. *Linda Jewell*

EASYRUN DE VASSY (FR) 5 b.g. Muhtathir – Royale The Best (FR) (Cadoudal (FR)) **h91** [2018/19 h19.5s⁵ h23.6v⁵ Dec 8] €52,000 3-y-o, £105,000 4-y-o: half-brother to French hurdlers/chasers My Fair Lady (15f-17f winner, by Poliglote) and Royale Majesty (2¼m winner, by Nikos), latter dam of smart French chaser up to 3¾m Roi Mage: dam French maiden (ran 3 times on Flat): won 2 Irish points (awarded first one): modest form over hurdles: better effort when fifth in maiden at Chepstow in November. *Paul Nicholls*

Navan Novices' Hurdle, Navan—a seventh win in this race in eleven years for Willie Mullins as Easy Game (right) holds off stable-companion Getareason

EASY STREET (IRE) 9 b.g. High Chaparral (IRE) – Victorine (IRE) (Un Desperado (FR)) [2018/19 c–x, h–: c20m* c24.2g^{pu} c26.1m c25.5g^2 c22.6m^2 c29.2g^{ur} c32.4g c23s^{pu} c23.6m^{pu} Apr 22] maiden hurdler: fairly useful handicap chaser: won at Warwick early in season: stayed 25f: acted on soft and good to firm going: raced off pace: often let down by jumping: dead. *Jonjo O'Neill*   **c128 x** **h–**

EASY WOOD (FR) 5 gr.g. Martaline – Ball of Wood (FR) (Cadoudal (FR)) [2018/19 b16.8s Dec 7] 5/1, down field in bumper at Exeter. *Tom George*   **b–**

EATON HILL (IRE) 7 b.g. Yeats (IRE) – Guilt Less (FR) (Useful (FR)) [2018/19 h125: h20g^6 h20g^5 Oct 28] good-topped gelding: fairly useful handicap hurdler: stays 2¾m: acts on soft going: in tongue tie last 3 starts: usually races towards rear. *Kerry Lee*   **h115**

EATON MILLER (IRE) 7 b.g. Milan – Four Fields (IRE) (Fourstars Allstar (USA)) [2018/19 h76, b–: h23s^2 h23g^3 h23.9d^3 h24d^5 c23.6d^2 c25.2d h26g c26.1d^3 c26.2d c23.6g* c24g^3 Apr 25] poor maiden hurdler: similar form over fences: won handicap at Huntingdon in April: stays 3m: acts on soft going: sometimes in headgear: one to treat with caution. *Tom Symonds*   **c78 §** **h78**

EAU DE NILE (IRE) 6 b.g. Robin des Champs (FR) – Rivervail (IRE) (River Falls) [2018/19 h90, b79: h21.2g^{pu} h21.2m May 13] tall gelding: poor maiden hurdler on balance: little impact in points. *Henry Daly*   **h–**

EAU TOP (FR) 5 b.g. Barastraight – Monepopee (FR) (Panoramic) [2018/19 b17.7d^5 b17d^6 Mar 24] modest form in bumpers. *Ben Pauling*   **b80**

EBNAL EXPLORER 4 ch.g. Universal (IRE) – Vedora (Alflora (IRE)) [2018/19 b15.7d^6 Apr 24] in hood, 40/1, sixth of 7 in bumper at Southwell. *Gary Hanmer*   **b–**

EBONY GALE 5 br.g. Shirocco (GER) – Glenora Gale (IRE) (Milan) [2018/19 b97: h16s^F h16s^F h15.5d* h18.5d^2 h16.3d h18.5d^6 h21.4g^6 Apr 14] lengthy gelding: bumper winner: fairly useful hurdler: won maiden at Leicester in December: second in handicap at Exeter in January: probably stays 2¼m: acts on good to soft going. *Philip Hobbs*   **h118**

EBONY JEWEL (IRE) 5 b.g. Westerner – Lady Roania (IRE) (Saddlers' Hall (IRE)) [2018/19 b15.7v^2 b16s* b17d^6 Apr 5] €30,000 3-y-o: well-made gelding: third foal: half-brother to bumper winner Princess Roania (by Dubai Destination): dam (c83/h99), unreliable bumper/3m hurdle winner, half-sister to useful hurdler (stayed 2¾m) Some Article: fairly useful form in bumpers: won at Ayr in March: left Ronald O'Leary after first start: will stay beyond 2m. *N. W. Alexander*   **b101**

EBONY ROSE 7 br.m. Kalanisi (IRE) – Cogolie (FR) (Cyborg (FR)) [2018/19 h112: h20.6s^5 h24.3d Feb 25] fair hurdler at best, well below form both starts in 2018/19: stays 25f: acts on soft going: wears hood/tongue tie: races well off pace. *Susan Corbett*   **h–**

EBONYS ENCORE (IRE) 7 b.m. Oscar (IRE) – Ebony Queen (Classic Cliche (IRE)) [2018/19 h96p: h16g^{pu} Sep 2] has had breathing operation: won Irish point on debut: modest form over hurdles, pulled up sole start in 2018/19. *Christian Williams*   **h–**

EBONY'S MANOR 8 b.m. Beat All (USA) – Winnetka Gal (IRE) (Phardante (FR)) [2018/19 h16g h15.8m^6 Apr 23] half-sister to fairly useful chaser Perfect Timing (2½m/21f winner, by Shantou), stays 3m, and fair chaser Chicago Alley (17f-2½m winner, by Bob Back): dam, lightly raced, out of half-sister to Cheltenham Gold Cup winner Garrison Savannah: pulled up all 5 starts in points: well held in 2 novice hurdles. *Robin Dickin*   **h–**

ECCO 4 b.g. Maxios – Enjoy The Life (Medicean) [2018/19 h16m^6 h16.8d^6 Mar 15] sturdy gelding: useful on Flat, stays 11f: fairly useful form over hurdles: sixth in Triumph Hurdle at Cheltenham in March: open to further improvement. *Paul Nicholls*   **h129 p**

ECEPARTI (FR) 5 b.g. Enrique – La Pommeraie (FR) (Apple Tree (FR)) [2018/19 h15.8v h15.8d h19.5d^4 h16.3s^2 h18.9d^3 Mar 20] fourth foal: brother to French 9f/11f bumper winner Cyr Nea and half-brother to French 9f/11½m bumper winner Dulcezza (by Redback): dam, French 2¼m hurdle winner (also prolific bumper winner), half-sister to fairly useful 2m hurdle winner Miss Academy: fair maiden hurdler: similar form when winning on sole start over fences for Guillaume Macaire in 2017/18: stays 19f: acts on soft and good to firm going. *Venetia Williams*   **c–** **h112**

ECHO EXPRESS (IRE) 7 b.g. Echo of Light – If Dubai (USA) (Stephen Got Even (USA)) [2018/19 h95: h20.7g^{pu} c15.6s^2 c15.6s* c16.5s^4 c16.3d^{pu} Apr 6] modest form over hurdles: fair form over fences: won handicap at Hexham in December: unproven beyond 2m: acts on soft going: in cheekpieces last 3 starts. *Nicky Richards*   **c100** **h–**

ECHO (IRE) 4 b.g. Zoffany (IRE) – Aweebounce (IRE) (Dubawi (IRE)) [2018/19 h15.7s **h–** h16d^ur Jan 4] fairly useful on Flat, stays 2m: well held completed start over hurdles. *Jedd O'Keeffe*

ECHO WATT (FR) 5 gr.g. Fragrant Mix (IRE) – Roxane du Bois (FR) (Passing Sale **h–** (FR)) [2018/19 h97, b89: h23.6d h23.1s^pu h21.6v Dec 20] useful-looking gelding: bumper winner: maiden hurdler, little show in handicaps in 2018/19: usually wears hood. *Richard Hobson*

ECLAIR D'AINAY (FR) 5 b.g. Network (GER) – Etoile d'Ainay (FR) (Dom Alco (FR)) **h102** [2018/19 h20.5s^4 h15.7s Dec 21] well-made gelding: fifth foal: dam, useful French hurdler/ fairly useful chaser (17f-3¼m winner), closely related to high-class hurdler/useful chaser (stayed 29f) Crystal d'Ainay: fair form over hurdles: left Gabriel Leenders, better effort in 2018/19 when fourth in novice at Newbury in November. *Dan Skelton*

ECLAIR DE BEAUFEU (FR) 5 b.g. Monitor Closely (IRE) – Tenebreuse Gemm (FR) **h133** (Visionary (FR)) [2018/19 h16d^3 h16s^2 h16g^3 h16d^3 h16s* h16g* h16g^4 h16.8d^ur h16d^6 Apr 7] first foal: dam, placed in French bumpers around 1½m/ran once over hurdles, half-sister to smart hurdler (2m/17f winner) Ronaldo des Mottes and fairly useful hurdler/useful chaser (stays 3m) A Sizing Network: won both starts in bumpers for A. Lefeuvre: useful hurdler: won maiden at Limerick in December and minor event at Fairyhouse in January: fourth in Ladbrokes Hurdle (Handicap) at Leopardstown (3 lengths behind Off You Go) in February: likely to stay beyond 2m: acts on soft going. *Gordon Elliott, Ireland*

ECLAIR DE GUYE (FR) 5 gr.g. Lord du Sud (FR) – Jouvence de Guye (FR) (Hawker's **h112** News (IRE)) [2018/19 b–: h20.8g^6 h20.5s^4 h20.5d^6 h19.8s^4 h21s^2 Mar 10] angular gelding: fair form over hurdles: stays 21f: acts on soft going. *Lucy Wadham*

ECLAIR DES SABLONS (FR) 5 b.g. Noroit (GER) – Jolie Fabi (FR) (Villez (USA)) **h114** [2018/19 h23.1s^6 h19.8g^2 h19.6g^2 Apr 11] €42,000 3-y-o, £64,000 5-y-o: sixth foal: half-brother to 3 winners, including fairly useful 2½m chase winner Taratata Sivola (by Assessor): dam, unraced, half-sister to fairly useful French hurdler/fair chaser (17f-19f winner) King of Landhor: off mark in Irish points at fifth attempt: fair form over hurdles: best effort when second in novice at Huntingdon in April. *Katy Price*

ECLAT DES BIEFFES (FR) 5 b.g. Enrique – Poliada (IRE) (Poliglote) [2018/19 b16g^pu **b–** Oct 11] little impact in 2 points: fatally injured in bumper. *Harry Whittington*

ECLAT DE STAR (FR) 5 b.g. Special Kaldoun (IRE) – Rose Star (FR) (Passing Sale **h100** (FR)) [2018/19 h16.8s^2 h16d Dec 27] useful-looking gelding: third foal: half-brother to French 11f/1½m bumper winner Beau Star (by Khalkevi): dam, French 1½m/12.5f bumper winner, half-sister to useful hurdler/chaser (stayed 3m) Tony Star: won only start in bumpers for J-F. Doucet: fair form over hurdles: better effort when second in maiden at Sedgefield. *Jonjo O'Neill*

ECO WARRIOR 9 b.g. Echo of Light – Kryssa (Kris) [2018/19 c–, h–: c21.6g^3 May 9] **c89** good-topped gelding: multiple point winner: maiden hurdler: modest form over fences: **h–** unproven beyond 17f: acts on heavy going: tried in headgear. *N. Orpwood*

ECTOR (FR) 5 b.g. Coastal Path – Evane (FR) (Lute Antique (FR)) [2018/19 h16.3d h21d **h–** h23.1v h24.6g^ur h19.5v h25g^pu Mar 19] well beaten in bumper: no form over hurdles: tried **b–** in cheekpieces. *Warren Greatrex*

ECU DE LA NOVERIE (FR) 5 b.g. Linda's Lad – Quat'sous d'Or (FR) (Lost World **c125** (IRE)) [2018/19 h16.3d* h19.5d^2 c20.6s^3 c18.8d^2 Jan 19] rangy gelding: fifth foal: half- **h130** brother to French chasers Cinq Sou d'Or (17f-19f winner, by Al Namix) and Aventure d'Or (2¼m winner, by Tomorrows Cat): dam, won both starts in French 12.5f bumpers (pulled up only start over hurdles), half-sister to fairly useful/unreliable hurdler/chaser (stayed 3¼m) River d'Or: useful form over hurdles: won novice at Newbury in November: second in handicap at Lingfield (7 lengths behind Rough Night) next time: fairly useful chaser: in cheekpieces, won 4-y-o event at Pau on final start in 2017/18 for Patrice Quinton: stays 21f: acts on heavy going. *Philip Hobbs*

EDABEAN (IRE) 5 b.m. Arcadio (GER) – Victorian Lady (Old Vic) [2018/19 b16.3m^pu **h89 §** b15.8g^ro b16.7m^pu b19.6g^6 b19.7s^6 b15.8d^5 b15.8g^pu h20.7g^4 Apr 22] angular mare: fifth **b86 §** foal: half-sister to fairly useful hurdler/chaser Malapie (2½m-3m winner, by Westerner): dam (c98/h92) 2½m-3m hurdle/chase winner: failed to complete in bumpers, second when running out near finish at Huntingdon in May: modest form over hurdles: usually wears headgear: ungenuine. *Giles Smyly*

EDDIEMAURICE (IRE) 8 ch.g. Captain Rio – Annals (Lujain (USA)) [2018/19 c109, **c122** h118: h16v⁴ h16g* h16g⁴ c16d³ c16.4d² c16sᵘʳ c16.8m* Mar 31] compact gelding: fairly **h122** useful handicap hurdler: won at Kempton in March: similar form over fences: won novice handicap at Ascot in March: unproven beyond 17f: acts on good to firm and heavy going: tried in headgear: races towards rear. *John Flint*

EDDIES MIRACLE (IRE) 11 b.g. Beat of Drums – Ballinamona Gold (IRE) (Pierre) **c112** [2018/19 c114x: c23m² c23.5g⁵ c27.5dᵖᵘ Jun 8] multiple point winner: fair hunter chaser: stays 23f: acts on good to firm and heavy going. *David Christie, Ireland*

EDDIES PEARL (IRE) 9 b.m. Craigsteel – Florida Bay (IRE) (Florida Son) [2018/19 **c55** h–: h21.6gᵖᵘ h23m h21.7v⁶ c23.6dᵖᵘ c19.2s⁶ Apr 16] point winner: little show over hurdles/ **h55** fences. *Brian Forsey*

EDDY 10 b.g. Exit To Nowhere (USA) – Sharway Lady (Shareef Dancer (USA)) [2018/19 **c–** h100: h23.1m h25.8m⁴ h23.6d c19.2s c24vᵖᵘ h21.7s⁴ h23.9s⁵ h23.1d h21.7g⁶ Apr 12] **h96** strong gelding: modest handicap hurdler: well held completed start over fences: stays 23f: acts on heavy going: tried in hood: usually wears tongue tie: races towards rear. *Susan Gardner*

EDEN DU HOUX (FR) 5 b.g. Irish Wells (FR) – Maralypha (FR) (Louveteau (USA)) **b112** [2018/19 b17.7s* Dec 21] €20,000 3-y-o: rather unfurnished gelding: first foal: dam unraced half-sister to fairly useful French hurdler up to 21f Lord Lyphard: won on debut in Irish point: useful form in bumpers: won at Plumpton (by 2 lengths from On The Slopes) and Ascot (listed event, by 1¼ lengths from Imperial Alcazar, finding plenty) in December. *David Pipe*

EDENE D'ARC (FR) 5 b.m. Maresca Sorrento (FR) – Pretty Moon (FR) (Moon **h117** Madness) [2018/19 h20s⁴ h16.5d² h19.4d³ h16s* h22v h16.2d² Apr 26] French mare: half-sister to useful hurdler/very smart chaser Ball d'Arc (2m-2½m winner, by Network): dam unraced: bumper winner: fairly useful form over hurdles: won maiden at Gowran in March: stays 2½m: acts on soft going: usually races prominently. *Gordon Elliott, Ireland*

EDEN FLYER 6 b.g. With The Flow (USA) – Cool Shuil (IRE) (Glacial Storm (USA)) **b–** [2018/19 b16d b16.5d⁵ Apr 24] well held in 2 bumpers: tried in tongue tie. *Colin Tizzard*

EDGAR (GER) 9 b.g. Big Shuffle (USA) – Estella (GER) (Acatenango (GER)) [2018/19 **c92** c17s² c15.9m* c17.8v³ c19.5m⁵ Mar 29] maiden hurdler: modest handicap chaser: won at **h–** Leicester in February: stays 21f: acts on good to firm and heavy going: wears headgear: has worn tongue tie. *David Bridgwater*

EDWARD ELGAR 8 ch.g. Avonbridge – Scooby Dooby Do (Atraf) [2018/19 c95§, **c– §** h91§: h19.2g⁴ h15.8g⁶ h15.8m⁴ h18.6m Aug 5] sturdy gelding: modest handicap hurdler: **h85 §** modest maiden chaser: stays 2¾m: acts on good to firm and heavy going: usually wears headgear: front runner/races prominently: temperamental. *Caroline Bailey*

EDWARDSTONE 5 b.g. Kayf Tara – Nothingtoloose (IRE) (Luso) [2018/19 b16.3d² **b99** b16d² b16s² Mar 10] strong, lengthy gelding: second foal: dam, winning pointer, half-sister to useful hurdler/fair chaser (stayed 3½m) The Parishioner: fairly useful form when runner-up all 3 starts in bumpers. *Alan King*

EDWULF 10 b.g. Kayf Tara – Valentines Lady (IRE) (Zaffaran (USA)) [2018/19 c161, h–: **c154** c20.2d⁵ c24g c20d³ Feb 16] tall gelding: has stringhalt: won only completed start over **h–** hurdles: high-class chaser, below best in 2018/19: stays 25f: best form on soft/heavy going: wears tongue tie. *Joseph Patrick O'Brien, Ireland*

EEZE A SAINT (FR) 5 b.g. Saint des Saints (FR) – Reflexion (FR) (Discover d'Auteuil **b78** (FR)) [2018/19 b16d⁵ b16v⁶ Dec 8] point winner: modest form in bumpers. *Warren Greatrex*

EFFET SPECIAL (FR) 5 b.g. Network (GER) – Tisane (FR) (Dear Doctor (FR)) **c111** [2018/19 c19.9s⁶ c18.9s* c16.5d³ Feb 6] first foal: dam (c135/h121) French 2¼m-21f **h–** hurdle/chase winner: fair form over hurdles: similar form over fences: won 4-y-o event at Nantes in June: left G. Cherel after second start: stays 19f: acts on heavy going: tried in cheekpieces. *Lucinda Russell*

EFFRETAIS (FR) 5 b.g. Blue Bresil (FR) – Teriniere (FR) (Robin des Pres (FR)) **b–** [2018/19 b16.3g Mar 30] tailed off in bumper. *Peter Bowen*

EGGESFORD 5 b.g. Foxwedge (AUS) – Elegant Pride (Beat Hollow) [2018/19 h–: **h–** h16.8s Jan 20] no form over hurdles: tried in hood. *Laura Young*

EGLANTIER (FR) 5 b.g. Bonbon Rose (FR) – Kyalami (FR) (Kahyasi) [2018/19 **b85** b17.7v* Mar 6] fourth foal: half-brother to French hurdler/chaser Intouchable (2m-2½m winner, by Kap Rock): dam unraced: 7/2, won bumper at Fontwell (by ¾ length from Lily The Pink, rallying well) on debut. *Mark Bradstock*

National Hunt Breeders Supported By Tattersalls Mares' Novices' Hurdle (Dawn Run),
Cheltenham—a final Festival win for Noel Fehily as 50/1-shot Eglantine du Seuil (far left) swoops
late to pip stable-companion Concertista (white blaze)

EGLANTINE DU SEUIL (FR) 5 b.m. Saddler Maker (IRE) – Rixia du Seuil (FR) **h141**
(Ultimately Lucky (IRE)) [2018/19 h16g* h16s³ h16.8d* h20g³ Apr 21] close-coupled
mare: second foal: dam French 1½m bumper winner: won bumper for M. Seror in 2017/18:
useful form over hurdles: won mares maiden at Sligo in August and Dawn Run Mares'
Novices' Hurdle at Cheltenham (by short head from Concertista, finding plenty to lead on
line) in March: third in Champion Novices' Hurdle at Punchestown (2¼ lengths behind
Reserve Tank) shortly after end of British season: stays 2½m: acts on soft going.
W. P. Mullins, Ireland

EGYPT MILL DUKE 4 b.g. Intikhab (USA) – Questama (Rainbow Quest (USA)) **b–**
[2018/19 b13m b15.8d Mar 21] well held in 2 bumpers: has joined Tom George.
Ian Williams

EHMAJ (JPN) 4 b.g. Empire Maker (USA) – Upward Spiral (Teofilo (IRE)) [2018/19 **b72**
b13.7d⁴ ab16g b15.8d⁵ Mar 13] poor form in bumpers: tried in tongue tie. *Jane Chapple-*
Hyam

EIGHT TILL LATE (IRE) 11 ch.g. Desert King (IRE) – Princess Lek (IRE) (Bob Back **c138**
(USA)) [2018/19 c16m⁶ c17g² h18.8d³ c17.4g² h20g² h16g* c16.7g³ c16.5g* c22m³ c24d **h132**
c20d h16g⁵ Dec 22] useful hurdler: won minor event at Punchestown (by 4 lengths from
Stooshie) in October: useful handicap chaser: won at Down Royal in November: last of 3
in listed event at Thurles (1¼ lengths behind Alpha des Obeaux) next start: stays 2¾m: acts
on good to firm and heavy going: usually wears headgear. *Francis Casey, Ireland*

EKAYBURG (FR) 5 b.g. Sageburg (IRE) – Kayseri (FR) (Dress Parade) [2018/19 h16s⁴ **h107**
h15.5g³ h16.3sᵖᵘ Mar 11] has had breathing operation: third foal: half-brother to 2 French
bumper winners, including 11.5f/15f winner Daisery (by Apsis): dam French 2¼m/21f
chase winner: won 2 bumpers in France for Alain Couetil in 2017/18: fair form over
hurdles: best effort when third in novice at Leicester in December: tried in cheekpieces:
temperament under suspicion. *David Pipe*

EL BANDIT (IRE) 8 b.g. Milan – Bonnie Parker (IRE) (Un Desperado (FR)) [2018/19 **c–**
c141p, h–: c25.1gᵖᵘ c26gᵖᵘ h23.6d Feb 23] tall, useful-looking gelding: useful hurdler: **h–**
similar form when winning on chasing debut, out of sorts in 2018/19 after long absence:
tried in hood. *Paul Nicholls*

EL DEGUELLO 6 b.m. Shirocco (GER) – Competa (Hernando (FR)) [2018/19 b–: **b–**
b15.7g May 6] unfurnished mare: no form in bumpers. *Tony Carroll*

ELDORADO ALLEN (FR) 5 gr.g. Khalkevi (IRE) – Hesmeralda (FR) (Royal Charter **h115 p**
(FR)) [2018/19 h16v* h17sᵘʳ Dec 8] half-brother to several winners, including fairly useful
hurdler/smart chaser Auvergnat (2¼m-33f winner, by Della Francesca) and to dam of
Champion Bumper winner Envoi Allen: dam, French 2½m-25f cross-country chase
winner, half-sister to grandam of Champion Hurdle winner Espoir d'Allen: placed in
bumper in France: fairly useful form over hurdles: left P. Peltier after final start in 2017/18:
won maiden at Sandown in November: remains with potential. *Colin Tizzard*

313

ELEANOR BOB 4 b.f. Midnight Legend – Red And White (IRE) (Red Ransom (USA)) **b69**
[2018/19 b12.4g⁴ b15.7d² b16d⁴ b16.7d Apr 26] fourth foal: sister to fairly useful 2m
hurdle winner Pink Legend and half-sister to modest 2½m hurdle winner Pink Tara (by
Kayf Tara): dam (h96), maiden hurdler, 6f winner on Flat: poor form in bumpers.
Venetia Williams

ELEANOROFAQUITAINE (IRE) 6 b.m. Flemensfirth (USA) – Misty Heather (IRE) **b88**
(Oscar (IRE)) [2018/19 b16.8g² b16.8g² b16g² b15.8d⁶ b16s⁶ Mar 9] €75,000 3-y-o:
useful-looking mare: second foal: half-sister to bumper winner/useful hurdler Simon
Squirrel (2¼m winner, by Robin des Champs): dam once-raced sister to Champion Hurdle
winner Rock On Ruby: fair bumper performer: wears tongue tie. *Harry Fry*

ELECTRON BLEU (FR) 5 b.g. Saddex – Odyssee du Cellier (FR) (Dear Doctor (FR)) **c106**
[2018/19 b14.9sʳᵒ b14.4d⁵ c19.4vᶠ c22.9v³ h16d³ c23.8m⁵ Apr 23] fifth foal: closely related **h79**
to fairly useful French 2¾m chase winner Duo d'Enfer (by Linda's Lad) and half-brother **b76**
to useful hurdler/top-class chaser Aso (2m-21f winner, by Goldneyev) and French bumper
winner/smart chaser Unmix (2½m-2¾m winner, by Al Namix): dam lightly raced in France
(third at 17f over hurdles): in frame in bumpers: twice-raced over hurdles: fairly useful
chaser at best: won handicap at Compiegne in 2017/18: left Mme I. Pacault after fourth
start: stays 23f: acts on heavy going: has worn hood. *Tim Vaughan*

ELEGANT ESCAPE (IRE) 7 b.g. Dubai Destination (USA) – Graineuaile (IRE) **c161**
(Orchestra) [2018/19 c151, h–: c24.2v* c26s² c29.5s* c25.3d² c26.3d⁶ c25d⁶ Apr 4] **h–**
    Thirteen-year-olds defied Old Father Time to fill the first two places in the
Welsh Grand National in the 2017/18 season, but it was the turn of youth to come to
the fore in the latest edition. Running in only his second handicap (and from a BHA
mark of 151), the consistent six-year-old Elegant Escape followed in the footsteps
of his illustrious stablemate Native River who won the race at the same age two
years earlier. Like Native River, Elegant Escape had ended his novice campaign
over fences with good efforts in Grade 1 events at Cheltenham and Aintree. Native
River had finished second in the National Hunt Chase before winning the Mildmay,
while Elegant Escape was placed in the RSA Chase and the Mildmay, looking—
particularly in the RSA—like a horse who would be suited by long distances.
Elegant Escape really came into his own in the autumn but he couldn't quite match
Native River's achievement of winning two of the great handicap steeplechases, the
Hennessy (now the Ladbrokes Trophy) and the Welsh Grand National, on his first
two starts over fences outside novice company.
    Native River had been warmed up for his Hennessy with a preparatory
outing in the West Yorkshire Hurdle at Wetherby, but Elegant Escape reappeared in
an intermediate chase in November at Sandown, where he beat the most progressive
Thomas Patrick, another second-season chaser, by half a length, leading near the
finish. The weights had already been published for the Ladbrokes Trophy and
Elegant Escape picked up a 4-lb penalty. Thomas Patrick, 5 lb better off, started 3/1
favourite at Newbury, ahead of Elegant Escape at 4/1, but it was the latter's own
stable companion 12/1-shot Sizing Tennessee who forged clear in the prevailing
testing conditions to beat Elegant Escape by ten lengths. Elegant Escape stayed on
without making any impression on Sizing Tennessee and looked as if he was going
to be worth trying over further still. Both first and second held an entry in the Coral
Welsh Grand National but it was Elegant Escape who represented his stable, starting
3/1 favourite in a field of twenty, his trainer Colin Tizzard praising him as 'not too
far behind Native River at the equivalent stage of his career.'
    Top weight Native River avoided a penalty in his year for winning the
Hennessy because the Welsh National weights cannot go above 11-12. The Welsh
National weights come out before the Ladbrokes Trophy (Hennessy), but they are
after the intermediate chase at Sandown which Elegant Escape had won. Elegant
Escape was actually 4 lb lower in the Welsh National than he had been at Newbury
which made him look favourably treated, particularly as he seemed likely to relish
his first crack at a marathon distance. Irish-trained Folsom Blue started second
favourite ahead of Vintage Clouds who had finished third behind Raz de Maree (in
the line-up again) and Alfie Spinner in the previous renewal. Ballyoptic and Yala
Enki, the two top weights, had plenty of big-race handicap form, while another six-
year-old Ramses de Teillee had won the Chepstow trial three weeks earlier and still

Coral Welsh Grand National Handicap Chase, Chepstow—a second win in the race in 3 years for the Tizzard stable as Elegant Escape beats Ramses de Teillee

looked well in under a 4-lb penalty. The going was soft but, as in Native River's year, conditions were nowhere near so extreme as they can be at Chepstow's Welsh National meeting. Yala Enki, Elegant Escape and Ramses de Teillee drew clear of the rest from five out and Elegant Escape saw the trip out thoroughly to get the better of the three-way battle in the home straight, winning by a length and a quarter and four lengths from Ramses de Teillee and Yala Enki, who was eleven lengths clear of fourth-placed Rons Dream (Raz de Maree and Ballyoptic filled fifth and sixth). Elegant Escape idled on the run-in and could have pulled out more had it been required, his performance still the best of his career at up to that time.

Native River ended his second season over fences contesting his first Cheltenham Gold Cup, in which he finished third, and Elegant Escape followed the same route, finishing a respectable sixth, starting at 20/1, behind Al Boum Photo, again giving the impression that ideally he needs more of a test of stamina (the Grand National should be right up his street with another year on his back). Elegant Escape was also beaten in his races either side of the Gold Cup, running up to his best when a rallying three quarters of a length second to Frodon in the Cotswold Chase on Cheltenham's Trials day but giving a lacklustre performance in the Aintree Bowl on his final start when he was probably over the top (made mistakes and was never travelling well).

Elegant Escape (IRE) (b.g. 2012)	Dubai Destination (USA) (b 1999)	Kingmambo (b 1990)	Mr Prospector
			Miesque
		Mysterial (b or br 1994)	Alleged
			Mysteries
	Graineuaile (IRE) (ch 1996)	Orchestra (ch 1974)	Tudor Music
			Golden Moss
		Hennywood (ch 1990)	Henbit
			Galawood

The well-made Elegant Escape, who had a breathing operation before the latest season, began his racing career chasing home Samcro in an Irish maiden point before he joined the Tizzard stable as a four-year-old after making €150,000 at the select Punchestown Sale, held in conjunction with that course's spring festival.

Elegant Escape's sire Dubai Destination wasn't a success as a Flat sire and was transferred to Glenview Stud in Ireland in 2010, but jumping breeders didn't support him well enough either and he is now in Saudi Arabia. Since his export, some of his daughters have started to enjoy success as broodmares, producing the likes of Golden Horn, Postponed and Thunder Snow on the Flat. Dubai Destination himself sired a number of significant purpose-bred jumpers in his time in Ireland, Next Destination, Kildisart and the mare Roksana also among them. Elegant Escape is the most distinguished member of his immediate family on the distaff side, though his dam the Orchestra mare Graineuaile, a winning chaser over two and a half miles, has bred three other winners, the winning two-mile hurdler Dubai Shen (a brother to Elegant Escape), the fairly useful handicap chaser Fear Glic (by Dr Massini) and the fair staying hurdler/chaser Cailleach Annie (by Blueprint). Elegant Escape, who has been tried in cheekpieces, is a thorough stayer who acts on heavy going. Still only seven, he may progress again, though he will have his work cut out to follow Native River on to the Cheltenham Gold Cup's winning roll. *Colin Tizzard*

ELEGANT (IRE) 8 b.m. Oscar (IRE) – Good Thought (IRE) (Mukaddamah (USA)) [2018/19 h–: h17.7m⁵ h19.2g³ h19.2g Aug 30] lengthy mare: has had breathing operation: modest form over hurdles: in tongue tie last 2 starts. *Michael Roberts* **h86**

ELENA SUE 6 b.m. Zamindar (USA) – Elasouna (IRE) (Rainbow Quest (USA)) [2018/19 b15.8g⁴ Jan 3] sixth foal: half-sister to 2 winners, including bumper winner/useful hurdler Babbling Stream (2m-2½m winner, by Authorized): dam, useful performer up to 1½m on Flat, half-sister to useful/temperamental hurdler Erzen: 6/1, fourth in mares bumper at Ludlow (10 lengths behind Subway Surf): entitled to progress. *Olly Murphy* **b79 p**

ELF DE RE (FR) 5 ch.g. Anabaa Blue – Ninon de Re (FR) (Denham Red (FR)) [2018/19 b16.2g⁶ b16.4v⁵ Mar 16] £20,000 3-y-o: seventh foal: half-brother to fairly useful hurdler/ fair chaser Brook (2m-3m winner, by Kandidate): dam, French 1½m/13f bumper winner, half-sister to Grand National winner Pineau de Re: fair form in bumpers: better effort when sixth at Kelso in February. *Sandy Thomson* **b88**

ELFILE (FR) 5 b.m. Saint des Saints (FR) – Rapide (FR) (Assessor (IRE)) [2018/19 h20g* h16.8d⁶ h20g² Apr 21] compact mare: second foal: half-sister to fairly useful French 17f chase winner Diligent (by Kapgarde), stays 2¾m: dam (c107/h123), French 19f hurdle/ chase winner, half-sister to smart French hurdler/fairly useful chaser (17f-21f winner) Vladimir (by Saint des Saints): won 2 bumpers in France for T. Fourcy in 2017/18: useful form over hurdles: won mares maiden at Punchestown in January and listed mares novice at same course (by 10 lengths from Rhythm Divine) shortly after end of British season: second in Irish Stallion Farms EBF Mares Novices' Hurdle Championship Final at Fairyhouse (5½ lengths behind Honeysuckle) in April: will be suited by 3m: open to further improvement. *W. P. Mullins, Ireland* **h135 p**

EL HAGEB ROSE (FR) 5 b.g. Coastal Path – Ile Rose (FR) (Le Riverain (FR)) [2018/19 b17.7g⁶ h19.3g h21.6s⁶ h23s⁶ h19.8s h19.5d² h21.7g² Apr 24] £85,000 3-y-o: sturdy gelding: half-brother to several winners, including bumper winner/useful hurdler Dame Rose (2m winner, by Network), stayed 2½m, and fairly useful French hurdler/fair chaser Prime Rose (2¼m/19f winner, by Video Rock): dam French 11f/1½m bumper winner: modest form sole start in bumper: fair form over hurdles: should be suited by 2½m+: acts on good to soft going: usually races off pace. *Gary Moore* **h102 b78**

ELIMAY (FR) 5 gr.m. Montmartre (FR) – Hyde (FR) (Poliglote) [2018/19 h20g² h19.9s⁶ Mar 12] angular mare: dam half-sister to fair French hurdler/fairly useful chaser (19f winner) Innovate: lightly raced on Flat: useful hurdler: left C. & Y. Lerner, second in EBF Mares' Hurdle at Leopardstown (½ length behind Good Thyne Tara) in December: resumed progress when winning minor event at Punchestown (by 17 lengths from Days Without End, in control when left clear last) shortly after end of British season: stays 2½m: acts on soft going. *W. P. Mullins, Ireland* **h137**

ELIOS D'OR (FR) 5 b.g. Puit d'Or (IRE) – Naker Mome (FR) (Nashamaa) [2018/19 ab16.3s⁵ Jan 15] €25,000 3-y-o: fourth foal: dam unraced half-sister to fairly useful hurdler/useful chaser (17f winner) Pesoto out of half-sister to dam of Grand National winner Mon Mome: 9/2, finished lame when fifth in maiden bumper at Newcastle (4¾ lengths behind Basildon): capable of better. *Nicky Richards* **b85 p**

ELISEZMOI (FR) 5 gr.g. Lord du Sud (FR) – Diva de La Borie (FR) (Bonnet Rouge (FR)) [2018/19 h17.4g² h17.6s⁵ h17.6s* h16.3d h17.7gᵘʳ Apr 24] third foal: dam French 17f chase winner: fairly useful form over hurdles: won 4-y-o event at Fontainebleau in November for A. Adeline de Boisbrunet: stays 2¼m: acts on soft going. *Gary Moore* **h117**

ELITE GARDE (FR) 5 b.g. Kapgarde (FR) – Queyrann (FR) (Sheyrann) [2018/19 b85: **h87**
h16v h15.8g h15.5g h21d⁴ Jan 28] modest form over hurdles. *Paul Webber*

ELIXER (IRE) 6 b.g. Oscar (IRE) – Sunny Native (IRE) (Be My Native (USA)) [2018/19 **h–**
h19.9s h18.1d h17m⁶ Apr 20] placed in Irish points: well held in 3 novice hurdles: in hood
last 2 starts. *Barry Murtagh*

ELIXIR DE NUTZ (FR) 5 gr.g. Al Namix (FR) – Nutz (FR) (Turgeon (USA)) **h141**
[2018/19 h–: h15.8dᶠ h16.4g² h16.4g* h16.8g* h16s* Jan 5]

    What a pity that lameness on the eve of the race prevented Elixir de Nutz from
taking his chance in the Supreme Novices' Hurdle, as he deserved his place in the
field, having completed a hat-trick with victory in the Tolworth Hurdle at Sandown
in January. Elixir de Nutz would have needed to improve to reach the frame at
Cheltenham, but he had beaten the third Itchy Feet when landing the Grade 2 Sharp
Novices' Hurdle and been collared only late when second to the Supreme runner-up
Thomas Darby on his return in the autumn. That was his first start for Colin Tizzard
and provided the first sign of what was to come through the winter. Until he changed
stables, Elixir de Nutz had been in danger of not fulfilling his obvious potential. He
had overcome inexperience to lead close home in a bunched finish to a bumper at
Argentan the previous October on his only start for Guy Cherel. He joined Philip
Hobbs after that, and made his hurdling debut in the Finesse, the juvenile hurdle
on Cheltenham Trials day in January, against the then-Triumph favourite Apple's
Shakira. He looked the part beforehand, but, having jumped sketchily, he dropped
right out before the straight. Elixir de Nutz wasn't seen again until April, when he
was withdrawn at Kempton after misbehaving in the preliminaries. His second and
final run for the Hobbs yard came at Uttoxeter the following month when, fitted
with a hood, he would have finished second to Not That Fuisse had he not fallen
at the last.

    It was soon clear when he returned in the autumn that Elixir de Nutz was
going to be a different proposition. Tactics were changed to making the running,
which made an asset of some of the exuberance he had shown for his previous
stable, and his jumping became much more polished. He showed useful form in
winning the Sharp at the Cheltenham November meeting—run as the Sky Bet
Supreme Trial Novices' Hurdle—under a well-judged ride by Harry Cobden; for
the second year in a row only five hurdles were jumped in the race due to the low
sun, an unsatisfactory state of affairs, which is seemingly unresolvable because of

*Unibet Tolworth Novices' Hurdle, Sandown—a second Tolworth win in three years for Colin Tizzard
as Elixir de Nutz (centre) shows a very willing attitude to hold off the Paul Nicholls-trained pair
Grand Sancy (right) and Southfield Stone*

Mr Terry Warner's "Elixir de Nutz"

the needs of television and sponsors. Elixir de Nutz followed up at short odds in an EBF qualifier at Cheltenham again in December, not needing to improve. The task of Elixir de Nutz in that race might have been stiffer had not the well-touted newcomer Angels Breath been withdrawn due to the ground. Another Nicky Henderson-trained novice Rathhill, an exciting prospect after a win at Newbury on his hurdling debut, looked the chief opponent in the Unibet-sponsored Tolworth in which Paul Nicholls fielded two, Grand Sancy and Southfield Stone, with outsider Mercy Mercy Me completing the field of five. With Cobden required to ride Southfield Stone, Tom O'Brien took over on Elixir de Nutz, employing the now-expected front-running tactics. The well-backed Rathhill failed to run his race, in trouble before the straight, but the Nicholls pair looked serious threats between the last two flights, Grand Sancy in particular challenging strongly, but Elixir de Nutz found extra under pressure to score by half a length, with Southfield Stone beaten a further three and a quarter lengths in third. Grand Sancy won the Kingwell Hurdle at Wincanton on his next start while Southfield Stone went on to win the Dovecote Novices' at Kempton.

		Linamix	Mendez
Elixir de Nutz (FR) (gr.g. 2014)	Al Namix (FR) (gr 1997)	(gr 1987)	Lunadix
		Dirigeante	Lead On Time
		(b 1991)	Daytona
	Nutz (FR) (gr 2001)	Turgeon	Caro
		(gr 1986)	Reiko
		Friandise II	Mistigri
		(ch 1993)	Kaidora

Elixir de Nutz is a tall gelding in appearance, the sort to make a chaser on looks, and it would be no surprise were he to develop into a leading novice over fences in 2019/20. He wasn't the only notable novice hurdler to represent his sire

Al Namix during the latest season, Al Dancer landing the Betfair Hurdle at Ascot for him. Nutz, the dam of Elixir de Nutz, didn't show much on the track—she ran five times with a modest third over fences at Montlucon-Neris the high point—but she has more than made up for that at stud, all five of her foals to race having won. Elixir de Nutz is her seventh and best, the pick of the others being the fairly useful chaser Calnutz (by Balko), a listed winner at around two and a half miles at Nantes in October, and Friandise Girl (by Hurricane Cat), a bumper winner who was runner-up in a Group 3 at Saint-Cloud in March. Nutz is the only one of the grandam Friandise II's nine foals not to win a race; the others include a couple of useful jumpers at up to two and a half miles in the British Isles in Upepito and Bonbon Au Miel. Kaidora, the third dam, won nine times in cross-country events, her other offspring, apart from Friandise, including the dam of the smart French chaser Objectif Special, who won the 2009 Prix du President de La Republique. Elixir de Nutz has raced only at around two miles, his free-going nature perhaps a factor in that, though he is bred to stay further. He has raced only on good going or softer, his win in the Tolworth coming on soft. *Colin Tizzard*

ELIXIR DU GOUET (FR) 5 ch.g. Vision d'Etat (FR) – My Asadore (FR) (Kadounor (FR)) [2018/19 h17.4s h17.9s* h17.9s⁴ c18.9d² c17.9s* c15.7vᵖᵘ c16d c20d² Mar 24] half-brother to 3 winners in France, including fairly useful hurdler/winning chaser My Alco (15f/17f winner, by Dom Alco) and chaser Tete A Tete (2¼m winner, by Epalo): dam (h110), French 15f hurdle winner, sister to winning hurdler/useful chaser (stayed 19f) Asador: fairly useful form over hurdles: won 4-y-o event at Clairefontaine in August: similar form over fences: won 4-y-o event at Fontainebleau in October: left T. Fourcy after fifth start: stays 2¼m: acts on soft going. *Venetia Williams* **c123 h123**

EL KALDOUN (FR) 5 b.g. Special Kaldoun (IRE) – Kermesse d'Estruval (FR) (Cadoudal (FR)) [2018/19 ab16g* b16.7d⁴ h16s h16.3d⁶ Mar 23] €85,000 3-y-o: well-made gelding: half-brother to several winners, including fairly useful hurdler/smart chaser Rival d'Estruval (2½m-3m winner, by Khalkevi): dam unraced: fair form in bumpers: won at Lingfield in November: modest form over hurdles: will prove suited by further than 2m: likely to progress further. *Nicky Henderson* **h99 p b93**

ELKSTONE 8 b.g. Midnight Legend – Samandara (FR) (Kris) [2018/19 c92§, h–: c21.4g² c19.2d² c22.5gᵖᵘ c19.2g* c19.2m² c20.9g* c19.2g⁶ c24m* c23.9g⁵ Nov 8] workmanlike gelding: maiden hurdler: fairly useful handicap chaser: won at Market Rasen in July, Stratford (novice) in August and Kempton in October: stays 3m: acts on soft and good to firm going: wears headgear: has worn tongue tie: has found little. *Caroline Bailey* **c115 h–**

ELLARNA (FR) 5 b.m. Lucarno (USA) – Oeuvre d'Art (FR) (Robin des Champs (FR)) [2018/19 b15.8s³ b16.5d³ b16.8g Apr 18] fourth foal: half-sister to fairly useful French cross-country chaser Art And Co (2½m-3¼m winner, by Dom Alco) and French chaser Dragee Haute (2½m/21f winner, by Buck's Boum): dam (c120/h113), French 17f-21f hurdle/chase winner, half-sister to useful hurdler/chaser (stayed 21f) Une Artiste and fairly useful hurdler/useful chaser (stays 3m) Coup de Pinceau: fair form in bumpers: best effort when third in mares event at Ludlow in December: in tongue tie last 2 starts. *Paul Nicholls* **b90**

ELLA'S DENE 8 ch.m. Millkom – Oh So Perky (IRE) (Executive Perk) [2018/19 h–, b–: h20.9g⁴ h23.9g⁶ h20.2gᵖᵘ Jun 23] no form in bumper/over hurdles. *Tim Reed* **h–**

ELMONO (FR) 8 ch.g. Epalo (GER) – Monareva (FR) (Montjeu (IRE)) [2018/19 h101: h20.2g² h20.1g² h20.1m³ c20.3g² c23.8g² c23.8g* c23.8m* c20.3s⁴ c20.3m⁴ Mar 22] fair handicap hurdler: fairly useful form over fences: won handicaps at Musselburgh in January and February (novice): stays 3m: acts on soft and good to firm going. *Lucinda Russell* **c118 h110**

EL MONO VERDE (IRE) 6 b.g. Dubai Destination (USA) – Bonny Hall (IRE) (Saddlers' Hall (IRE)) [2018/19 h16gᵖᵘ May 7] no form in maiden hurdles. *Mark McNiff, Ireland* **h–**

EL PRESENTE 6 b.g. Presenting – Raitera (FR) (Astarabad (USA)) [2018/19 h115, b84: h23.1g⁴ May 11] fairly useful form over hurdles: stays 23f: best form on good going: front runner/races prominently. *Kim Bailey* **h119**

EL SCORPIO (IRE) 7 b.g. Scorpion (IRE) – El Monica (IRE) (Kahyasi) [2018/19 h79, b75: h19.6g⁵ h23.1g³ h24d⁶ h21d⁶ Dec 13] workmanlike gelding: modest maiden hurdler: stays 23f. *John Groucott* **h87**

ELSKA 7 b.m. Norse Dancer (IRE) – Alska (FR) (Leading Counsel (USA)) [2018/19 **h74** b15.7d h19.2v⁴ h17.7vᵖᵘ h20.7g h23.9gᵖᵘ h25g Apr 22] fourth foal: half-sister to fairly **b71** useful 3m chase winner Alskamatic (by Systematic), stayed 33f: dam (c94) 3m chase winner (stayed 33f): failed to complete all 4 starts in points: poor form in bumper/over hurdles: in cheekpieces last 2 starts. *Richard Bandey*

EL TERREMOTO (FR) 7 b.g. Spirit One (FR) – By Decree (USA) (With Approval **c134** (CAN)) [2018/19 c–, h134: c15.7g* c22.6g² c20.1gᶠ c19.4mᶠ c17.1d² c20.5s c20g Apr 27] **h–** lengthy gelding: useful hurdler: useful chaser: won novice at Southwell in July: stays 23f: acts on good to firm and heavy going: usually races prominently: has joined David Pipe. *Nigel Twiston-Davies*

ELTON DES MOTTES (FR) 5 b.g. Maresca Sorrento (FR) – Ouhetu des Mottes (FR) **h–** (Ungaro (GER)) [2018/19 b91p: b15.8d h16s h16d⁵ Apr 6] sturdy gelding: has had **b–** breathing operation: fair form on first of 2 outings in bumpers: well held in 2 novice hurdles: tried in hood. *Dan Skelton*

ELTON JACK 4 ch.g. Malinas (GER) – Santoria (FR) (Limnos (JPN)) [2018/19 b16.7g⁴ **b89** Apr 13] fifth foal: half-brother to 2 winners, including smart hurdler/fairly useful chaser Up And Go (19f/2½m winner, by Martaline): dam unraced: 16/1, fourth in conditionals/ amateurs bumper at Bangor (5½ lengths behind L'Air du Vent). *Sophie Leech*

ELUSIVE BELLE (IRE) 5 b.m. Elusive Pimpernel (USA) – Soviet Belle (IRE) (Soviet **h129** Star (USA)) [2018/19 h17m⁵ b16.4g³ b16g² h15.3g* h16s² h16.8d h16g* Apr 10] useful- **b98** looking mare: seventh foal: half-sister to 2 winners on Flat, including 1m winner Bellini Bliss (by Big Bad Bob): dam 6f winner: fairly useful form in bumpers for Peter Fahey: best effort when second in listed mares event at Gowran (½ length behind Yukon Lil, closing all way to line) in October: similar form over hurdles: won novices at Wincanton in January and Warwick in April: in hood last 2 starts. *Nicky Henderson*

ELUSIVE COWBOY (USA) 6 ch.g. Elusive Quality (USA) – Sarmad (USA) **h62** (Dynaformer (USA)) [2018/19 h94: h15.9g h15.8gᵖᵘ h15.9g h20.5m h19.5vᵖᵘ Dec 10] close-coupled gelding: poor maiden hurdler on balance: has worn cheekpieces, including in 2018/19: tried in tongue strap. *Michelle Bryant*

ELUSIVE INTRUSIVE (IRE) 4 br.f. Elusive Pimpernel (USA) – Kleinova (IRE) **h76** (Trans Island) [2018/19 h16v h16s h16g Feb 13] little impact on Flat: poor form over hurdles. *Liam Lennon, Ireland*

ELUSIVE THEATRE (IRE) 8 b.m. King's Theatre (IRE) – Miss Best (FR) (Grand **c113 §** Tresor (FR)) [2018/19 c121, h126: h24.3d⁴ h18.1g⁵ h20dʳʳ h21.4s c19.5g⁵ Apr 11] neat **h115 §** mare: fairly useful handicap hurdler: fourth at Ayr in November: fair form over fences: left Stuart Crawford after fourth start: stays 3m: acts on heavy going: has worn headgear: temperamental. *Patrick Griffin, Ireland*

ELUSIVEVISION (IRE) 4 b.f. Elusive Pimpernel (USA) – Alyska (IRE) (Owington) **h–** [2018/19 b13.7m h15.8g h16dᵖᵘ Dec 4] half-sister to 3 winners on Flat, including useful **b–** 6f-1m winner Brilliant Vanguard (by Fast Company): dam, 1m winner, half-sister to fairly useful hurdler (stayed 2¾m) Athlumney Lad: tailed off in junior bumper: no form over hurdles: tried in headgear. *Denis Quinn*

ELVIS MAIL (FR) 5 gr.g. Great Pretender (IRE) – Queenly Mail (FR) (Medaaly) **h131** [2018/19 b71: h20.5v⁴ h16.2g* h16d² h18.1d³ h18.1d* Apr 8] useful form over hurdles: won novices at Kelso in December and April: third in Premier Kelso Novices' Hurdle (4 lengths behind Rouge Vif): stays 2¼m: acts on good to soft going: wears hood. *N. W. Alexander*

ELVIZ 5 b.g. Medicean – Estrela (Authorized (IRE)) [2018/19 b–: b16.7g b16g³ h16.3mᵘʳ **h–** Jul 15] has had breathing operation: poor form in bumpers: tailed off when unseated third **b68** in novice on hurdling debut. *Tony Carroll*

ELYSEES (IRE) 4 ch.g. Champs Elysees – Queen of Tara (IRE) (Sadler's Wells (USA)) **h125** [2018/19 h16d³ h16g* h15.8g* h16.6g² h18.8d⁴ Mar 23] fairly useful on Flat, stays 16.5f: fairly useful form over hurdles: won juveniles at Warwick and Ludlow in November: second in Summit Juvenile Hurdle at Doncaster (neck behind Quel Destin) in December: will be suited by 2½m: acts on good to soft going: usually responds generously to pressure. *Alan King*

ELYSIAN PRINCE 8 b.g. Champs Elysees – Trinkila (USA) (Cat Thief (USA)) [2018/19 **c85** h95: h19m⁶ h15.8g³ h18.7m³ h15.8g⁶ h18.7m⁴ h16.8m² h18.7g⁴ h20.5gᵖᵘ h19.3s h15.6g⁵ **h94** c16.4d c15.8m³ c16.9s⁴ h16.4m Mar 20] compact gelding: modest handicap hurdler: similar form over fences: best effort when third in handicap at Musselburgh in February: left Neil King after eighth start: stays 19f: acts on good to firm going: usually wears headgear: has worn tongue tie. *Andrew Hamilton*

EMBITTERED (IRE) 5 b.g. Fame And Glory – Kilbarry Classic (IRE) (Classic Cliche **b116** (IRE)) [2018/19 b16d⁴ b16g³ Feb 2] €46,000 3-y-o: second foal: half-brother to bumper winner/useful 2m hurdle winner Precious Cargo (by Yeats): dam (b101) bumper winner: third on completed start in maiden points: smart form in bumpers: won maiden at Punchestown (by 2½ lengths from Santana Plessis) in December: progressed again when 2 lengths fourth of 10 to Colreevy in Champion INH Flat Race at same course shortly after end of British season: likely to be suited by further than 2m: wears hood/tongue tie. *Joseph Patrick O'Brien, Ireland*

EMBOLE (FR) 5 b.g. Buck's Boum (FR) – Urielle Collonges (FR) (Dom Alco (FR)) **c118** [2018/19 h122, b–: h15.8g⁴ c16g² c19.9g⁵ h19d⁶ h16d c17.2gᵖᵘ Apr 3] close-coupled **h109** gelding: has had breathing operation: fair handicap hurdler: fairly useful form over fences: best effort when second in maiden at Hereford in November: unproven beyond 2m: acts on heavy going: has worn headgear, including in 2018/19: wears tongue tie: usually front runner/races prominently. *Dan Skelton*

EMERALD CHIEFTAN (IRE) 9 b.g. Oscar (IRE) – Its Only Gossip (IRE) (Lear Fan **c102** (USA)) [2018/19 h107: c20.5gᶠ h22.8v⁵ c20.1v⁴ h25.3g h21.2d* c20.3g³ c21.4g⁶ Mar 20] **h106** Irish point winner: fair form over hurdles: won novice handicap at Sedgefield in January: similar form over fences: stays 23f: acts on heavy going: sometimes in headgear: in tongue tie last 4 starts. *Rebecca Menzies*

EMERALD ROCKET (IRE) 4 b.g. Society Rock (IRE) – Lady From Limerick (IRE) **h115 p** (Rainbows For Life (CAN)) [2018/19 h16d² Mar 15] half-brother to French 19f hurdle winner Porte Dauphine (by Hurricane Run): fair on Flat, stays 11f: 8/1, second in conditionals maiden at Fakenham (½ length behind Swaffham Bulbeck) on hurdling debut: sure to do better. *Olly Murphy*

EMERALD ROSE 12 b.m. Sir Harry Lewis (USA) – Swiss Rose (Michelozzo (USA)) **c118** [2018/19 c117, h–: c29.1g* c24v³ c27.6s c24s Mar 23] angular mare: winning hurdler: **h–** fairly useful handicap chaser: won at Fakenham early in season: stays 29f: acts on good to firm and heavy going: usually wears cheekpieces. *Julian Smith*

EMILY MOON (IRE) 5 b.m. Beneficial – Wood Lily (IRE) (Definite Article) [2018/19 **h123** b16s* b16d h16s⁵ h20d⁶ h16g* h16.8dᵖᵘ h16d* h20g Apr 21] lengthy, rather unfurnished **b89** mare: second foal: half-sister to fair 23f hurdle winner Scented Lily (by Presenting): dam (h114) 2m hurdle winner out of half-sister to triple Cheltenham Gold Cup winner Best Mate: fair form in bumpers: won mares maiden at Cork early in season: fairly useful form over hurdles: won maiden at Naas in February and minor event at Limerick in March: stays 2½m: acts on good to soft going: usually leads. *Mrs J. Harrington, Ireland*

EMILYOGUE (IRE) 6 b.m. Scorpion (IRE) – Presenting Tara (IRE) (Presenting) **c–** [2018/19 h–: h16.2g⁵ h16m h20d h20.2s⁶ c17.4g h20.1s³ h16.4d Dec 13] poor maiden **h76** hurdler: well beaten in mares maiden on chasing debut: stays 2½m: acts on soft going: has worn tongue tie, including last 5 starts. *John Patrick Ryan, Ireland*

EMILY WEBB 4 b.f. Franklins Gardens – Lofaire (IRE) (Deploy) [2018/19 h15.8d³ **h80** h15.8g⁶ h15.8m⁶ h16.8g⁴ Apr 18] well held in seller on Flat: poor form over hurdles. *Alex Hales*

EMINENT POET 8 b.g. Montjeu (IRE) – Contare (Shirley Heights) [2018/19 h130: **h136** h23.4v* h23.4s h24d Mar 14] compact gelding: useful handicap hurdler: won at Sandown (by 6 lengths from Another Emotion) in December: stays 3¼m: acts on heavy going. *Venetia Williams*

EMIRAT DE CATANA (FR) 5 b.g. Linda's Lad – Kolada (FR) (Cyborg (FR)) [2018/19 **h77** b16d h16.2v⁴ h16.4m⁴ h20.2g⁴ Apr 24] pulled up both starts in Irish points: well beaten in **b–** bumper: poor form over hurdles. *Lucinda Russell*

EMISSAIRE (FR) 5 b.g. Kap Rock (FR) – Jacee (FR) (Royal Charter (FR)) [2018/19 **h97** b92: h16.2g⁵ h16v³ h19.3s⁴ h16.4g h17s⁶ Mar 7] bumper winner: modest form over hurdles: will stay 2½m+: acts on heavy going: often in hood. *Lucinda Russell*

The Spero Partnership Ltd's "Emitom"

EMITOM (IRE) 5 b.g. Gold Well – Avenging Angel (IRE) (Heron Island (IRE)) [2018/19 **h146 p** b95: b15.7m* h20s* h16d* h20.5d* h24.7d² Apr 5] good-topped gelding: fairly useful **b96** form in bumpers: won at Ascot in November: smart form over hurdles: won maiden at Ffos Las in November, and novices at Lingfield in January and Newbury in March: second in Sefton Novices' Hurdle at Aintree (3 lengths behind Champ) in April: stays 25f: open to further improvement. *Warren Greatrex*

EMKAE (IRE) 11 b.g. Milan – Hindi (FR) (Cadoudal (FR)) [2018/19 c24.2gᵖᵘ Jun 16] **c–** has had breathing operation: winning pointer: lightly-raced hurdler: poor maiden chaser: **h–** wears tongue tie. *Alison Hamilton*

EMMA BEAG (IRE) 8 b.m. Westerner – Emma Jane (IRE) (Lord Americo) [2018/19 **h86** h89: h24.3d* h24.3sᵖᵘ Mar 9] modest handicap hurdler: won at Ayr in January: stays 3m: acts on heavy going: has worn hood: usually races in rear. *Julia Brooke*

EMMA LAMB 5 b.m. Passing Glance – Lucinda Lamb (Kayf Tara) [2018/19 b16.2g⁵ **h105** b16.2g⁵ b16.8m² b16.8gᵘʳ h16.6gᵖᵘ h16.7g² h15.7d⁴ h16.4m⁴ Mar 28] lengthy, rather **b94** unfurnished mare: has had breathing operation: fourth foal: half-sister to bumper winner Tom Lamb (by Central Park): dam (h69), placed 3 times in bumpers, half-sister to useful hurdler/fairly useful chaser (stayed 25f) Lord Lamb and useful 2m hurdler Mr Lamb: fair form in bumpers/over hurdles. *Jedd O'Keeffe*

EMMAS DILEMMA (IRE) 7 b.m. Gold Well – Emmas Island (IRE) (Heron Island **h99** (IRE)) [2018/19 h16.7g³ h23.4g³ h24g⁶ Jun 25] first foal: dam, point winner (also runner-up in bumper/3m hurdle), sister to fairly useful hurdler/fair chaser (stayed 3m) Misala: fair form in bumpers: modest maiden hurdler: left Miss Elizabeth Doyle after final (2017/18) start: stays 23f: acts on heavy going: tried in cheekpieces. *Olly Murphy*

EMMAS JOY (IRE) 6 b.m. Gold Well – Emma Jane (IRE) (Lord Americo) [2018/19 **b102** b15.7d* b15.8d² b16g⁵ b17d Apr 4] neat mare: third foal: half-sister to modest 3m hurdle winner Emma Beag (by Westerner) and a winning pointer by Stowaway: dam (c134/h118) 19f-25f hurdle/chase winner: won on debut in Irish point: fairly useful form in bumpers: won mares event at Southwell in November: second in listed mares event at Huntingdon (½ length behind Timetochill) in December: will be suited by further than 2m. *Dan Skelton*

EMMPARA 5 ch.g. Black Sam Bellamy (IRE) – Maria Antonia (IRE) (King's Best (USA)) **h82** [2018/19 b–: h20.5d h16.5d³ h16s Feb 15] rather leggy gelding: poor form over hurdles: wears hood. *Dominic Ffrench Davis*

EMMPRESSIVE LADY (IRE) 4 b.f. Jeremy (USA) – Court Lexi (IRE) (Court Cave **b82** (IRE)) [2018/19 b15.7d⁶ Apr 9] second foal: dam (h117), bumper/19f hurdle winner, sister to fairly useful hurdler (stays 2½m) Clondaw Banker: third on debut in point bumper: in cheekpieces/tongue tie, sixth in conditionals/amateurs maiden bumper at Southwell. *Steve Flook*

EMOJIE 5 b.g. Captain Gerrard (IRE) – Striking Pose (IRE) (Darshaan) [2018/19 b13.7m **b–** Mar 29] last in bumper. *Jane Chapple-Hyam*

EMPEROR COMMODOS 12 b.g. Midnight Legend – Theme Arena (Tragic Role **c– §** (USA)) [2018/19 c–§, h–§: h19m h15.3m May 15] sturdy gelding: has had breathing **h– §** operation: fair maiden hurdler/chaser at best, no form since 2016/17: usually wears headgear: wears tongue tie: prone to mistakes over fences: untrustworthy. *Robin Mathew*

EMPHATIC QUALM (IRE) 4 b.g. Califet (FR) – Supreme Touch (IRE) (Supreme **b–** Leader) [2018/19 b16.7m⁵ Apr 21] 9/1, last of 5 in bumper at Market Rasen. *Nigel Twiston-Davies*

EMPIRE DE MAULDE (FR) 5 b.g. Spanish Moon (USA) – Ondine de Brejoux (FR) **h119** (Murmure (FR)) [2018/19 h77: h16.4g³ h16.2g h16.4g* h16.6g* Mar 2] bumper winner: fairly useful form over hurdles: won handicaps at Newcastle (novice) in January and Doncaster in March: raced around 2m: best form on good going: tried in hood. *James Ewart*

EMPORTEPARLAFOULE (FR) 5 gr.g. Smadoun (FR) – Sempiternelle (FR) (Lavirco **b–** (GER)) [2018/19 b16d b16d Feb 25] tailed off in 2 bumpers. *Andrew Crook*

EMPREINTE RECONCE (FR) 5 b.m. Voix du Nord (FR) – Petite Fille (FR) (Robin **h107** des Champs (FR)) [2018/19 b66: h16.8g* h19.5d⁶ h15.9s⁵ h16d² h16d⁵ Jan 28] bumper winner: fair form over hurdles: won mares novice at Newton Abbot in June: unproven beyond 17f: acts on good to soft going: tried in tongue tie. *Colin Tizzard*

ENA BAIE (FR) 5 b.m. Crillon (FR) – Trema Baie (FR) (Snow Cap (FR)) [2018/19 **h102 p** h15.7d⁴ Nov 20] good-topped mare: has had breathing operation: bumper winner in France for Y. Fertillet in 2017/18: 3/1, fourth in mares novice at Southwell (7¾ lengths behind Kimberley Point) on hurdling debut: should improve. *Harry Fry*

ENCHANTING ENYA (IRE) 4 ch.f. Champs Elysees – Miss Honorine (IRE) (Highest **h–** Honor (FR)) [2018/19 h15.8dᵖᵘ Feb 6] dam half-sister to smart hurdler (17f-2½m winner) Blue Canyon: fair on Flat, stays 2m: pulled up in fillies juvenile on hurdling debut. *Steph Hollinshead*

EN COEUR (FR) 5 b.g. Kap Rock (FR) – Fairyleap (FR) (Leeds (IRE)) [2018/19 b15.3s **b75** b17.7g⁶ Apr 7] modest form in bumpers: in hood final start. *Seamus Mullins*

ENCORE CHAMPS (IRE) 5 b.g. Robin des Champs (FR) – Dani California (Beat All **h126** (USA)) [2018/19 b16.7g² b15.8d⁸ h16d⁶ h15.7s h16.2g² h16.5g h19.8g Apr 27] €45,000 **b96** 3-y-o: compact gelding: third foal: half-brother to fair 2m hurdle winner Borderlinedecision and bumper winner Dani Theatre (both by King's Theatre): dam (h132), 2m hurdle winner, also 1½m-2m winner on Flat: fairly useful form in bumpers: won maiden at Ffos Las in October: similar form over hurdles: won novices at Wetherby in November and Kelso in January: unproven beyond 2m: acts on good to soft going. *Warren Greatrex*

ENDEAVOR 14 ch.g. Selkirk (USA) – Midnight Mambo (USA) (Kingmambo (USA)) **c– §** [2018/19 c91§, h72§: c17.3m Jul 1] winning hurdler: modest chaser: stayed 2½m: acted on **h– §** any going: sometimes wore cheekpieces: dead. *Dianne Sayer*

ENDLESS CREDIT (IRE) 9 b.g. High Chaparral (IRE) – Pay The Bank (High Top) **c123** [2018/19 c108, h–: c15.6g* c17.3g⁶ c16gᵖᵘ h15.8g h15.8d³ h15.7s h17m⁴ Apr 20] compact **h99** gelding: modest handicap hurdler: fairly useful form over fences: won handicap at Hexham early in season: left Micky Hammond after third start: raced around 2m: acts on soft going: tried in cheekpieces/tongue tie: usually races close up: temperament under suspicion. *Lucinda Egerton*

ENDLESS FLIGHT (IRE) 5 b.g. Winged Love (IRE) – Lady Oakwell (IRE) (King's **h–** Ride) [2018/19 b84: b16v³ b16.8d⁴ b18.5s Mar 18] fair form in bumpers: tailed off in **b85** maiden on hurdling debut. *Susan Gardner*

ENEMY COAST AHEAD 5 b.g. Malinas (GER) – Penang Princess (Act One) [2018/19 **b108** b16.3g* Mar 30] €10,000 3-y-o: second foal: dam 1¾m-2m winner: 7/2, won bumper at Stratford (by 10 lengths from In Rem, impressively) on debut. *Tom George*

ENFIN PHIL (FR) 5 ch.g. No Risk At All (FR) – Nheyranne (FR) (Sheyrann) [2018/19 **h116** h18.9s³ h17.4s⁴ h18.4s* h20.1s⁶ h16d³ h15.7m⁴ h19.9s² h20.6d⁴ Apr 6] fifth foal: dam French 21f chase winner: unplaced in bumpers: fairly useful hurdler: won claimer at Vichy in September for Emmanuel Clayeux: placed in novices at Wetherby in December and Sedgefield in March: stays 2½m: acts on soft going: sometimes in cheekpieces: usually leads. *Micky Hammond*

ENFORCEMENT (IRE) 4 b.g. Lawman (FR) – Elodie (Dansili) [2018/19 h16.2g³ **h92** h16.5g⁵ h16.3m⁶ h16d⁵ h15.9d* h16.8g⁴ Apr 5] modest form over hurdles: won handicap at Plumpton in March: raced around 2m: acts on good to soft going: usually wears hood: sometimes in tongue tie. *Martin Keighley*

ENGLISH PALE (IRE) 6 b.g. Elusive Pimpernel (USA) – Terme Cay (USA) (Langfuhr **h–** (CAN)) [2018/19 h103: h16.8g h16.3m h16v h16d Mar 31] fair maiden hurdler at best, has lost his way: left John Flint after second start: has worn headgear/tongue tie, including in 2018/19. *S. J. Mahon, Ireland*

ENJOY RESPONSIBLY (IRE) 10 b.g. Flemensfirth (USA) – Spice Patrol (IRE) **c128** (Mandalus) [2018/19 c128, h–: c19.9g⁵ c20.9g³ c21.2d³ c24g³ c25.7d⁴ c21.6g⁴ Apr 12] **h–** workmanlike gelding: maiden hurdler: fairly useful handicap chaser: third at Hereford in November: stays 3m: acts on good to firm and heavy going: has worn headgear/tongue tie. *Oliver Sherwood*

ENLIGHTEN 5 b.g. Kayf Tara – Rapturous (Zafonic (USA)) [2018/19 b88: b16d⁴ **h– p** b16.2g* h15.8d Mar 13] big gelding: fair form in bumpers: won at Kelso in February: raced **b93** too freely on hurdling debut: sure to do better. *Michael Easterby*

EN MEME TEMPS (FR) 5 b.g. Saddler Maker (IRE) – Lady Reine (FR) (Ragmar (FR)) **h114** [2018/19 b66: h21.6g⁶ h17.1d⁴ h17d² h16s² h16.3d h16d² h19.3m* Mar 31] has had breathing operation: fair hurdler: won maiden at Ascot in March: stays 19f: acts on soft and good to firm going: has worn headgear, including last 2 starts: wears tongue tie: front runner/races prominently: has joined Philip Kirby. *Tom Lacey*

ENNISCOFFEY OSCAR (IRE) 7 b.g. Oscar (IRE) – Enniscoffey (IRE) (Old Vic) **c124** [2018/19 h134: h22.8g⁵ c23.6d⁵ c24g² h24.4g Dec 29] tall gelding: useful handicap **h130** hurdler: fifth at Haydock (6 lengths behind Monbeg Theatre) in May: fairly useful form over fences: better effort when second in maiden at Kempton: stays 3m: acts on soft going: tried in cheekpieces. *Emma Lavelle*

ENNISTOWN 9 b.g. Authorized (IRE) – Saoirse Abu (USA) (Mr Greeley (USA)) **c101** [2018/19 h–§: h23g² h23.3s⁵ h25.4s³ h25g* c21.6m² Oct 5] good-topped gelding: useful **h138 §** handicap hurdler: won at Plumpton in September: 9/5, second in maiden at Fontwell (12 lengths behind Graasten) on chasing debut: stays 25f: acts on soft going: has worn headgear, including in 2018/19: wears tongue tie: temperamental. *Anthony Honeyball*

ENOLA GAY (FR) 6 br.g. Fuisse (FR) – Enolaland (FR) (Daliapour (IRE)) [2018/19 **c121** c112, h112: c16s³ c15.5s² c20.2g² c20.6d⁵ c20s⁴ c20.2g* c19.9m⁵ Apr 20] useful-looking **h–** gelding: fair hurdler: fairly useful handicap chaser: won at Wincanton in April: stays 2½m: acts on soft going: tried in cheekpieces: usually races prominently. *Venetia Williams*

ENRICHISSANT (FR) 5 b.g. Speedmaster (GER) – Quibble (FR) (Jimble (FR)) **h113** [2018/19 b88: h16.7g⁵ h19.5g³ h19.6g* h23.5s Dec 22] good-topped gelding: fair form in bumpers: similar form over hurdles: won novice at Huntingdon in November. *David Bridgwater*

ENRILO (FR) 5 bl.g. Buck's Boum (FR) – Rock Treasure (FR) (Video Rock (FR)) **b109** [2018/19 b16g* b15.7s⁴ b16m* Feb 23] €100,000 3-y-o: tall, rather unfurnished gelding: second foal: half-brother to French 17f/2¼m hurdle/chase winner Colere Noire (by Network): dam, French 17f/2¼m chase winner, out of smart French chaser up to 29f Harmonie Tresor: useful form in bumpers: won at Worcester (by 1½ lengths from Glen Vine) in October and Kempton (by 3 lengths from House Island) in February. *Paul Nicholls*

ENVIRONMENT ALLY 4 b.g. Bated Breath – Wemyss Bay (Sadler's Wells (USA)) **h–**
[2018/19 h16m[6] h15.6g[5] h16.7s[pu] Dec 6] little show over hurdles: tried in tongue tie.
Stuart Colthred

ENVOI ALLEN (FR) 5 b.g. Muhtathir – Reaction (FR) (Saint des Saints (FR)) **b125**
[2018/19 b16g* b16d* b16g* b16.4s* Mar 13]

    The giant chaser Party Politics—whose career features in the essay on
Topofthegame—must have cut quite a figure in his later years among the foals and
yearlings galloping round their paddocks at Cheveley Park Stud near Newmarket.
The 1992 Grand National winner lived out a lengthy retirement until his death in
2009 at the age of twenty-five at the stud belonging to his owner Patricia Thompson
and her husband David. Party Politics was also runner-up in the 1995 Grand National,
and over the last decade other Grand National entries have changed hands late in the
day to give Mrs Thompson further shots at winning the race again. The most recent
to carry her colours of pink, purple cross belts, hooped sleeves and cap at Aintree
was the well-fancied Seeyouatmidnight in 2018. Much better known, though, are the
Cheveley Park silks of red, white sash, blue cap, which have been carried to success
in a One Thousand Guineas, and at Royal Ascot and at the Breeders' Cup. Whilst
synonymous with the Flat, the Cheveley Park colours were doubly represented in the
Grand National during the 'eighties when both Classified and Northern Bay carried
them in two consecutive editions; Classified finished third to West Tip in 1986 on
his first start for Cheveley Park (he had finished fifth in different ownership the year
before) but unseated on the flat when his saddle slipped a year later. Since purchasing
the run-down Cheveley Park Stud in 1975, the Thompsons have developed the most
successful British-owned stud in the country, which now stands nine stallions and
owns one hundred and fifty broodmares, with almost as many horses in training
on the Flat. More recently, the Thompsons have expanded their National Hunt
interests from having a runner or two in the Grand National to investing heavily
in younger jumping stock with top-class potential. Cheveley Park was rewarded
almost immediately with two Cheltenham Festival winners. A day after A Plus Tard
had run away with the Close Brothers Novices' Handicap Chase, another five-year-
old, Envoi Allen, kept his unbeaten record when winning the Weatherbys Champion
Bumper in the manner of one with a big future over jumps.

    A field of fourteen was the smallest yet for the Champion Bumper, with
the British challenge looking weak despite several major stables being represented
(including Paul Nicholls who, unusually, had two runners) while Willie Mullins,
who had saddled the first three the year before, relied on a single entry, four-year-old
Blue Sari. Envoi Allen and Blue Sari headed the betting at 2/1 and 7/2 respectively

Weatherbys Champion Bumper, Cheltenham—
the smallest field in the race's history but it was business as usual with Irish yards dominating.
Envoi Allen just getting the better of Blue Sari (hoops)

Cheveley Park Stud's "Envoi Allen"

and the well-touted pair duly fought out the finish. Waited with under Mr Jamie Codd, Envoi Allen made ground smoothly on the outside down the hill to lead over three furlongs out and initially looked like quickening clear of the rest once in line for home. But Blue Sari joined him a furlong out, forcing Envoi Allen to knuckle down for a three quarter length win, though the runner-up might have got closer still but for going lame and losing his action in the final strides. Thyme Hill fared best of the British contingent, finishing a length and three quarters back in third for Philip Hobbs, with Envoi Allen's stable-companion Abacadabras completing the frame. The Nicholls pair finished down the field, but their stable-companion McFabulous, a half-brother to Waiting Patiently, looked one of the best British bumper horses when winning three of his four starts, including the Grade 2 contest at Aintree.

Blue Sari had been bought by J. P. McManus after an impressive winning debut at Gowran, while Envoi Allen had more experience as the odds-on winner of all three of his bumpers before Cheltenham. Envoi Allen had been heavily backed on his Rules debut at Fairyhouse at the beginning of December, by which time Cheveley Park and Gordon Elliott had already introduced another exciting prospect in Malone Road who was ante-post favourite for the Champion Bumper after winning both his starts the previous month. A setback meant Malone Road wasn't seen out again, whereas Envoi Allen soon followed up in a listed event at Navan a fortnight later which Elliott had won with Samcro two years earlier and future Gold Cup winner Don Cossack further back. Elliott all but ruled out running Envoi Allen at the Festival after that win, but his owners were keen to have runners at Cheltenham and he booked his ticket by completing his hat-trick in the Grade 2 bumper at the Dublin Racing Festival at Leopardstown in which all bar one of the field of ten were already winners. Kept wide as others met trouble in running,

Envoi Allen found plenty to hold off the Joseph O'Brien-trained pair Meticulous and Embittered, though Abacadabras would have been placed but for running out through the rail in the final furlong.

Envoi Allen (FR) (b.g. 2014)	Muhtathir (ch 1995)	Elmaamul (ch 1987)	Diesis / Modena
		Majmu (b 1988)	Al Nasr / Affirmative Fable
	Reaction (FR) (b 2005)	Saint des Saints (b 1998)	Cadoudal / Chamisene
		Hesmeralda (ro 1995)	Royal Charter / Violeta

Cheveley Park bought their 2003 One Thousand Guineas winner Russian Rhythm for 440,000 guineas as a yearling. Winning Irish pointers can readily fetch similar sums these days, and Envoi Allen and Malone Road were bought for £400,000 and £325,000 respectively after winning their only starts in that sphere early in 2018. Envoi Allen did so for renowned trainer of pointers Colin Bowe, winning by ten lengths over two and a half miles at Ballinaboola. His point win came in the colours of Wexford vet Walter Connors for whom Don Cossack also made his debut (in a bumper, before selling privately to Gigginstown), as did the latest Champion Hurdle winner, the ill-fated Espoir d'Allen, in a French bumper. Connors, along with agent Seamus Murphy, sources foals from France to sell on later as store horses, though the more precocious among them are given the opportunity to advertise themselves to would-be purchasers, either in bumpers or points. As might be surmised, Envoi Allen and Espoir d'Allen are related, albeit fairly distantly, the pair sharing the same great grandam Violeta. The fortunes of this AQPS family were therefore transformed by two Festival winners in as many days after being developed over generations by the Vagne family in central France, members of whom made the trip to Cheltenham. Violeta failed to win in AQPS races on the Flat but she produced ten winners at stud. Besides the grandams of both Espoir d'Allen and Envoi Allen, another of Violeta's winners was Imposant, notable for winning the first two editions of the valuable Prix Anjou-Loire Challenge at Le Lion d'Angers which is Europe's longest race, featuring fifty cross-country obstacles over more than four and a half miles. In the inaugural running in 2005 Imposant beat his elder half-brother Galapagos into second. Envoi Allen's grandam Hesmeralda was also a highly successful cross-country chaser, winning nine such races at distances up to three miles and a furlong. Hesmeralda is doing well at stud, too. As well as Envoi Allen's dam Reaction, winner of two cross-country chases at Cluny over twenty-three furlongs, Hesmeralda is the dam of Une Epoque, winner of the Prix Sytaj, a Group 3 chase for fillies and mares at Auteuil, and Auvergnat who kept up the family tradition in cross-country events by winning Ireland's most prestigious banks race, the La Touche Cup at Punchestown, for J. P. McManus and Enda Bolger in 2018. Twice fourth in the Cheltenham Festival's cross-country chase, Auvergnat was another big winner for the family in the latest season when landing the valuable Christmas feature the Paddy Power Chase at Leopardstown over regular fences. Hesmeralda is also the dam of Eldorado Allen who made a winning British debut in a novice hurdle at Sandown for Colin Tizzard in November. Envoi Allen is Reaction's first foal and only runner to date. Envoi Allen's sire Muhtathir, winner of the Prix Jacques le Marois for Godolphin, is probably best known in Britain for siring Pacha du Polder who was bidding to win the Foxhunter for the third time in March. Muhtathir's best Flat performer, Doctor Dino, a dual winner of the Hong Kong Vase, is also making a name for himself as a sire of jumpers, with Sceau Royal, Master Dino, Sharjah and La Bague Au Roi all winners of note in the latest season.

The good-topped Envoi Allen, who stands 17 hands, was a second Champion Bumper winner for Gordon Elliott in three years after the ill-fated mare Fayonagh, who was also ridden by Mr Jamie Codd. She followed up her Cheltenham victory in the Grade 1 bumper at Punchestown and made a perfect start to her hurdling career the following autumn only to break a leg on the gallops shortly afterwards. Envoi Allen is a first-rate prospect for novice hurdles in the shorter term and 'a three-mile chaser one day' according to his trainer. Describing him as 'a big baby', Codd added that he felt Envoi Allen's bumper campaign was all about educating him for his future career over jumps. Not many Irish-trained horses meet softer ground at Cheltenham than they've ever encountered back home, but that was the case with Envoi Allen and he had no problems handling the more testing conditions. *Gordon Elliott, Ireland*

ENVOL DE LA COUR (FR) 5 b.g. Maresca Sorrento (FR) – Reveuse de La Cour (FR) (Saint Cyrien (FR)) [2018/19 c20.4d⁴ c17.4g* h18.9v h18.5d⁴ h26s⁶ Mar 10] good-topped gelding: first foal: dam French maiden half-sister to useful hurdler/chaser (stayed 2¼m) Astre de La Cour: fair form over hurdles: similar form over fences: won 4-y-o event at Toulouse in June for Francois Nicolle: stays 2½m: acts on soft going: has joined Claire Dyson. *Henry Oliver*   **c112 h105**

ENVOLE TOI (FR) 5 b.g. Enrique – Orphee de Vonnas (FR) (Jimble (FR)) [2018/19 c17.4s* h15.7m⁵ c17.5s h16.5d* h15.3g³ h16.5g⁴ c16d⁶ c19.4g Mar 30] sixth foal: brother to 2 winners, including useful hurdler/smart chaser Ballotin (2m-2¾m winner), and half-brother to fairly useful hurdler/chaser Contre Tous (2m/17f winner, by Forestier); dam, French 2m-19f hurdle/chase winner, half-sister to dam of top-class French hurdler (stays 21f) Blue Dragon: fair hurdler: won novice at Taunton in December: fair chaser: won claimer at Auteuil early in season for Guillaume Macaire: stays 2¼m: acts on soft and good to firm going: usually front runner/races prominently. *Alexandra Dunn*   **c111 h113**

ENVOYE SPECIAL (FR) 5 b.g. Coastal Path – Santa Bamba (FR) (Saint des Saints (FR)) [2018/19 c17s² c20.5g⁶ c16s² Mar 16] good-topped gelding: has had breathing operation: third foal: brother to French 19f-21f hurdle/chase winner Saint Path and half-brother to high-class French hurdler De Bon Coeur (17f-25f winner, by Vision d'Etat): dam (c136/h115) French 15f-2½m hurdle/chase winner: winning hurdler in France for Francois Nicolle: useful form over fences: second in novice handicap at Kempton (7 lengths behind Timoteo) in March: unproven beyond 17f: acts on heavy going: in hood/tongue tie last 3 starts. *Paul Nicholls*   **c130 h–**

ENZILLERYA (FR) 5 b.g. Anzillero (GER) – Trieste (FR) (Valanour (IRE)) [2018/19 b16.8s⁴ Dec 7] 12/1, fourth of 5 in bumper at Sedgefield (22¾ lengths behind Champagne Well). *Rose Dobbin*   **b63**

ENZO BARBIERI (IRE) 6 b.g. Milan – Cappamore Girl (IRE) (Commanche Run) [2018/19 b16.2g² b16.2g⁴ Jun 3] placed both starts in Irish points: fair form in bumpers: dead. *Pauline Robson*   **b90**

EOLIAN 5 b.g. Poet's Voice – Charlecote (IRE) (Caerleon (USA)) [2018/19 h84: h16.7g h15.7s h16.7s h19.3m⁴ h15.8d² h18.6g² Apr 3] fair maiden hurdler: stays 19f: acts on good to soft going: sometimes in headgear. *Olly Murphy*   **h101**

EOS (FR) 5 gr.m. Martaline – Oreli (FR) (Robin des Pres (FR)) [2018/19 b16g h19.5d h19.2v⁵ h19.2d Feb 24] rather leggy mare: fourth foal: dam, maiden hurdler/chaser, half-sister to fairly useful hurdler/chaser (stayed 21f) Utopian: tailed off in bumper for John W. Nicholson: well held all 3 starts over hurdles. *Diana Grissell*   **h– b–**

EPALO DE LA THINTE (FR) 5 b.g. Anzillero (GER) – Spy de La Thinte (FR) (Dounba (FR)) [2018/19 b16.7g Oct 30] made frame on first of 2 starts in Irish points: tailed off in bumper. *P. M. J. Doyle, Ireland*   **b–**

EPATANTE (FR) 5 b.m. No Risk At All (FR) – Kadjara (FR) (Silver Rainbow) [2018/19 h16g* h16.8d* h16.8d Mar 14] compact mare: half-sister to 3 winners, including bumper winner/fairly useful hurdler Tante Sissi (19f-21f winner, by Lesotho): dam French 13f bumper winner: won last 2 of 3 starts in French bumpers for A. Lefeuvre, including Grade 1 event: fairly useful form over hurdles: won novice at Kempton in November and mares novice at Exeter in February: tried in hood: remains with potential. *Nicky Henderson*   **h123 p**

EPISODE (FR) 5 ch.m. Kotky Bleu (FR) – Morvandelle (FR) (Video Rock (FR)) [2018/19 h16s⁴ h16d³ Mar 21] half-sister to several winners, including fairly useful hurdler/useful chaser Demi Sang (2m-19f winner, by Gris de Gris) and fairly useful chaser Commodore (21f-3m winner, by Fragrant Mix): dam maiden sister to high-class hurdler/smart chaser (stayed 2¾m) Osana and to dam of high-class staying chaser Notre Pere: placed in bumper in France for Mlle M.-L. Mortier: modest form over hurdles: open to further improvement. *Gary Moore*   **h95 p**

EPSOM DAY (IRE) 6 b.g. Teofilo (IRE) – Dubai Flower (Manduro (GER)) [2018/19 h16g Apr 10] fairly useful at best on Flat, stays 1½m: hooded when tailed off in novice on hurdling debut. *Rob Summers*   **h–**

EPSOM DES MOTTES (FR) 5 b.g. Maresca Sorrento (FR) – Nellyssa Bleu (FR) (Epervier Bleu) [2018/19 h20.1vᵖᵘ h16.4m Mar 28] little impact both starts over hurdles. *Philip Kirby*   **h–**

EPSOM SECRET 5 ch.m. Sakhee's Secret – My Amalie (IRE) (Galileo (IRE)) [2018/19 h–
h17.7g^F Sep 23] modest on Flat, stays 1½m: tailed off when fell 2 out in novice at Plumpton
on hurdling debut. *Pat Phelan*

EQULEUS 7 b.g. Equiano (FR) – Merle (Selkirk (USA)) [2018/19 h–: h19s^{pu} h16.8s^{pu} Mar h–
18] maiden hurdler, no form since 2016/17: sometimes in cheekpieces: wears tongue tie.
Katie Stephens

EQUUS AMADEUS (IRE) 6 b.g. Beat Hollow – Charade (IRE) (Danehill (USA)) c– p
[2018/19 h125, b93: h20.6g^5 h21.6g^4 c16.5g^6 h15.3m* h16.4g h16.6g* h16.8d h15.7d^6 h132
h16.3d^4 h16m^3 h15.9g^4 Apr 21] lengthy gelding: has had breathing operation: useful
handicap hurdler: won at Wincanton in October and Doncaster in December: 5/2, last of 6
in novice at Worcester on chasing debut (should do better): stays 2¾m: acts on soft and
good to firm going: in tongue tie last 2 starts. *Tom Lacey*

EQUUS DANCER (IRE) 5 b.g. Jeremy (USA) – Celtic Cailin (IRE) (Beneficial) b100
[2018/19 b15.8s^5 b15.7m^4 b17d* b16.2d* Apr 26] first foal: dam (h122), maiden hurdler
(best at 2m), out of half-sister to smart chaser (winner up to 3m) Can't Buy Time: every
chance when fell in point on debut: fairly useful form in bumpers: won at Carlisle in March
and Perth in April. *Peter Bowen*

EQUUS FLIGHT (IRE) 6 b.g. Vinnie Roe (IRE) – Maiden Flight (IRE) (Jurado (USA)) h107
[2018/19 h–, b80: h21.6g^2 h21.9d^2 h24g^2 h22.2g^3 h23g^5 Apr 13] placed in Irish points: fair
form over hurdles: should stay 3m: acts on good to soft going: tried in cheekpieces/tongue
tie. *Peter Bowen*

EQUUS MILLAR (IRE) 6 b.g. Masterofthehorse (IRE) – Lets Get Busy (IRE) h124
(Presenting) [2018/19 h104: h15.8g* h16.7g^4 h20m^2 h19.9g* h16.2g* h19.5d^6 h21g
h16m Apr 12] rather unfurnished gelding: fairly useful handicap hurdler: won at Ludlow
(amateurs) early in season, and Uttoxeter and Perth in September: stays 21f: best form on
good going: has worn hood. *Nigel Twiston-Davies*

EQUUS PANDORA (IRE) 5 ch.g. Shantou (USA) – Pandorama Lady (IRE) (Cloudings h87
(IRE)) [2018/19 b17g h16g^{ur} h16.3m h20m^6 h19.9g^5 h22.1s^5 h20.2g^3 h23.3g^3 Oct 5] b85
second foal: dam unraced half-sister to smart hurdler/high-class chaser (stayed 3m)
Pandorama: won point bumper on debut: mid-field in bumper: modest maiden hurdler:
stays 23f: best form on good going: in tongue tie last 2 starts. *Peter Bowen*

EQUUS SECRETUS (IRE) 7 b.g. Brian Boru – Bodega Bay (IRE) (Presenting) c130
[2018/19 h130: c20d^2 c24.2s^5 c23.6d^2 c21.1d Apr 5] strong gelding: point winner: useful h–
form over hurdles: similar form over fences: second in maiden at Ludlow (2½ lengths
behind Psychedelic Rock) in December and novice at Huntingdon (½ length behind Station
Master) in March: likely to stay beyond 3m: acts on good to soft going: front runner/races
prominently. *Ben Pauling*

ERAGON DE CHANAY (FR) 5 b.g. Racinger (FR) – Rose Celebre (FR) (Authorized h132
(IRE)) [2018/19 h124: h16.4g^{pu} h19.8v* h19.8g^3 h16v h16s^3 h21.4g* h21s^{pu} h19.8g
Apr 27] close-coupled gelding: useful handicap hurdler: won at Sandown (conditionals, by
8 lengths from The Bottom Bar) in November and Wincanton (by 2½ lengths from
Townshend) in February: stays 21f: acts on heavy going: wears visor: usually races
prominently. *Gary Moore*

ERICAS LAD 8 b.g. Mutazayid (IRE) – Kingsmill Quay (Noble Imp) [2018/19 h–: c81
h18.5m^5 h21.6g^{pu} c23.6d^5 c16d^{ur} c17.5v* c19.2d^2 c21g^3 Apr 20] little show over hurdles: h–
poor form over fences: won handicap at Exeter in March: stays 21f: acts on heavy going:
has worn cheekpieces, including last 3 starts: usually races towards rear. *Jackie du Plessis*

ERICK LE ROUGE (FR) 5 ch.g. Gentlewave (IRE) – Imperia II (FR) (Beyssac (FR)) h134
[2018/19 h100: h19.6g* h19g* h21g* h21m* h21s^{pu} Mar 13] lengthy gelding: useful
handicap hurdler: completed 4-timer when winning at Bangor in October, Warwick
(conditionals) in November, and Kempton in December and February (by neck from
Burrows Edge): stays 21f: acts on good to firm and heavy going: front runner/races
prominently. *Mrs Jane Williams*

ERIC THE THIRD (IRE) 10 b.g. Mountain High (IRE) – Commanche Princess (IRE) c112
(Commanche Run) [2018/19 c–, h78: h15.8m^5 c16.3g* h15.8m^2 h15.8g* c17.3g^2 c21g* h95
c21.6g^2 c19.7g* c20.2f* h23.8g^5 Nov 26] modest handicap hurdler: won at Uttoxeter
(conditionals) in July: fair handicap chaser: won at Newton Abbot in June and August, and
novice events at Plumpton in September and Wincanton in October: stays 3m: acts on firm
and good to soft going: has worn hood: tried in tongue tie: front runner/races prominently.
Tim Vaughan

ERIK THE RED (FR) 7 b.g. Kendargent (FR) – Norwegian Princess (IRE) (Fairy King **h105 P**
(USA)) [2018/19 h16.2g* Jan 22] useful on Flat, stays 1½m: 4/6, won novice at Kelso (by
3 lengths from Northern Soul, easily) on hurdling debut: should make considerable
progress. *Kevin Ryan*

ERITAGE (FR) 5 b.g. Martaline – Sauves La Reine (FR) (Passing Sale (FR)) [2018/19 **b104**
ab11.9g* b16.8d³ b15.3g* Apr 14] lengthy, useful-looking gelding: has scope: first foal:
dam, French 19f hurdle winner, sister to useful hurdler/chaser (winner up to 3m) Terminal:
fairly useful form in bumpers: won at Pornichet (maiden, for F. Foucher) in July and
Wincanton in April. *Paul Nicholls*

ERMYN'S EMERALD 7 b.g. Alflora (IRE) – Emerald Project (IRE) (Project Manager) **h87**
[2018/19 h85: h15.9g h17.7gᶠ h17.7gᶠ h17.7d² h19.6d² h20.7g⁴ h15.9d Mar 18]
modest maiden hurdler: stays 2½m: acts on good to soft going: usually races prominently.
Pat Phelan

EROS (FR) 5 b.g. Diamond Boy (FR) – Madame Lys (FR) (Sheyrann) [2018/19 b16d⁶ **b80**
Apr 6] sixth foal: half-brother to 3 winners, including useful hurdler/smart chaser Bouvreuil
(15f-19f winner) and smart hurdler around 2½m Messire des Obeaux (both by Saddler
Maker): dam French 17f hurdle/chase winner: 6/1, sixth in bumper at Chepstow.
Olly Murphy

ESCORT'NAMIX (FR) 6 b.m. Al Namix (FR) – Escortee (FR) (Cadoudal (FR)) **h90**
[2018/19 b17.7s⁴ b16g⁶ h19.9vᶠ h22.8dᵘʳ h21.9g³ Apr 21] £30,000 5-y-o: half-sister to 3 **b80**
winners, including useful 2m hurdle winner Escort'men (stayed 2½m) and fairly useful
French 2m-2¼m hurdle/chase winner Escort'beauty (both by Robin des Champs): dam ran
once over hurdles: won completed start in Irish points: modest form in bumpers/over
hurdles. *Warren Greatrex*

ESHTIAAL (USA) 9 b.g. Dynaformer (USA) – Enfiraaj (USA) (Kingmambo (USA)) **c86**
[2018/19 c19.9sᵘʳ c19.9g⁶ c24.1g⁴ c24.6g⁵ c21.2s⁴ Jan 1] winning hurdler: modest form **h–**
over fences: stays 25f: acts on firm and good to soft going: has worn cheekpieces, including
in 2018/19: wears tongue tie. *Gordon Elliott, Ireland*

ESKENDASH (USA) 6 ch.g. Eskendereya (USA) – Daffaash (USA) (Mr Greeley **h123**
(USA)) [2018/19 h122: h16g* h16gᶠ h16m³ h15.8d³ h16.7g² h16.3s⁵ Mar 11] workmanlike
gelding: fairly useful hurdler: won novice at Kempton early in season: placed in handicaps
at Huntingdon in December and Market Rasen in February: raced around 2m: acts on good
to firm and good to soft going. *Pam Sly*

ESPALION (FR) 5 b.g. Khalkevi (IRE) – Somosierra (FR) (Blushing Flame (USA)) **h112**
[2018/19 b66: b15.7g⁵ b16.3m⁵ h15.8g⁴ h16.5d⁶ h18.5d h21.7sᵖᵘ h19.5d* h19.5g* Apr 26] **b75**
has had breathing operation: modest form in bumpers: fair form over hurdles: won
2 handicaps at Chepstow in April: left Tim Vaughan after second start: stays 19f: acts on
good to soft going. *Jeremy Scott*

ESPECIALLY SO 4 b.f. So You Think (NZ) – Behra (IRE) (Grand Lodge (USA)) **b71**
[2018/19 b15.7g⁴ b14g⁴ b16.2v⁵ Dec 15] workmanlike filly: half-sister to several winners,
including smart hurdler Baradari (2m-23f winner, by Manduro) and useful hurdler/chaser
Barizan (2m-2¼m winner, by Kalanisi): dam, useful 1¼m winner, half-sister to very smart
hurdler/top-class chaser (winner up to 25f) Behrajan: poor form in bumpers. *Steve Gollings*

ESPION DE SAFLO (FR) 5 b.g. Princeton – Neacoddes (FR) (Kadalko (FR)) **h117 p**
[2018/19 h17.4g⁶ h17.1g⁵ h17.6s⁴ h19.4s* h20.5s⁴ h19.6g⁴ Apr 11] sixth foal: half-brother
to French 19f chase winner Tosca de Coddes (by Dear Doctor): dam lightly-raced half-
sister to dam of smart staying chaser Saint Are/grandam of very smart hurdler/smart
chaser up to 3m Vroum Vroum Mag: fairly useful form over hurdles: won 4-y-o event at
Nantes in November for J. Delaunay: stays 19f: acts on soft going: remains with potential.
Gary Moore

ESPION (FR) 5 ch.g. Coastal Path – Toutamie (FR) (Epalo (GER)) [2018/19 b15.3g⁵ Nov **b72**
10] 5/1, green when fifth in bumper at Wincanton (15¾ lengths behind Flic Ou Voyou).
Philip Hobbs

ESPOIR D'ALLEN (FR) 5 b.g. Voix du Nord (FR) – Quadanse (FR) (Maille Pistol **h170**
(FR)) [2018/19 h142: h16d* h16s* h16d* h16.4s* Mar 12]

Ten races, nine wins—including the Champion Hurdle by a record winning
margin for the race. The freak accident at home that led to the ultimate demise of
Espoir d'Allen, after a two-week fight to save him, robbed National Hunt racing not
only of one of its reigning champions, but of an outstanding hurdler with more to

give to the sport, still only five. Espoir d'Allen had the world at his feet and it is hard to think of too many parallels for his loss. For the death of a top-notch performer who truly could have been anything, it might be necessary to go back forty years when Irish racing suffered the loss of another tremendous young hurdler Golden Cygnet. An outstanding winner of the Supreme Novices' Hurdle (he won running away by fifteen lengths), Golden Cygnet died as a result of a bad fall at the last flight on his next outing in the Scottish Champion Hurdle in which he would have beaten a field including Sea Pigeon, Night Nurse and Beacon Light, second, third and fourth in that year's Champion Hurdle (Golden Cygnet received only 1 lb from Sea Pigeon and was giving 5 lb to Night Nurse and 7 lb to Beacon Light). Unlike Espoir d'Allen, six-year-old Golden Cygnet never got the opportunity to run in a Champion Hurdle but all the superlatives heaped on him were fully justified by the performance he was in the process of putting up at Ayr. Golden Cygnet was unarguably one of the best hurdlers never to win the Champion Hurdle, and might arguably have been the best two-mile hurdler never to run in it (*Chasers & Hurdlers 1977/78* rated him at 176). There can be no greater tribute to Espoir d'Allen, in terms of his loss to the sport, than the fact that he deserves to be mentioned in the same breath as Golden Cygnet. Espoir d'Allen had just returned from a summer break at his owner's Martinstown Stud when he reared over one day after a routine canter and suffered an injury to a shoulder that, eventually, could not be remedied despite the best efforts of Fethard Equine Hospital. Espoir d'Allen's death was keenly felt by jumping's followers, but the feelings of those closest to him, particularly those who handled him at Gavin Cromwell's County Meath stables, were unimaginable.

A farrier by trade, Gavin Cromwell proudly claims on his website that he has shod Gold Cup and Grand National winners, as well as Olympic competitors. But now the small matter of training a Champion Hurdle winner must rival the achievements in his other occupation which he describes as 'a passion'. Cromwell trains not far from Gordon Elliott who is one of his clients, and Cromwell believed he had a better chance of shoeing a Champion Hurdle winner in the latest season than actually training one. 'I shod Apple's Jade last week and she's an absolutely amazing mare,' said Cromwell, speaking after 16/1-shot Espoir d'Allen had provided him with his first Festival winner. 'I thought Apple's Jade would win.' Cromwell wasn't alone in that belief, with Apple's Jade sent off the 7/4 favourite in a race in which she dominated the betting to the exclusion of the seven other runners with fellow mare Laurina at 5/2, and the reigning champion Buveur d'Air (seeking his third win) at 11/4.

It was conceivable beforehand, perhaps, that not all the fancied horses would be involved in the finish, but for none of them to be sighted at all was a major shock, particularly in a championship event such as the Champion Hurdle in which the placed horses Melon and Silver Streak were returned at 20/1 and 80/1, the latter the rank outsider of the whole field. For a similar result in the Champion Hurdle, you had to go back to 1985 when the five-year-old See You Then, also a 16/1-chance, was followed home by Robin Wonder and Stans Pride at 66/1 and 100/1. The first of what were to be See You Then's three Champion Hurdles was widely regarded as a two-horse race beforehand, involving 6/4-on shot Browne's Gazette, who had put up a top-class effort to beat Desert Orchid and See You Then (who was beaten twenty-five lengths) in the Christmas Hurdle, and former champion Gaye Brief, who had been beaten by Browne's Gazette in the Bula Hurdle and started at 4/1 for the Champion. Browne's Gazette lost his race in unsatisfactory circumstances when diving away from the tapes at the start, leaving him a detached last going to the first, while Gaye Brief was found wanting at the finish, finding nothing up the hill after leading See You Then over the final flight. Clearly, See You Then had not needed to improve the twenty-five lengths he was beaten at Kempton to win the 1985 Champion Hurdle but, by the same token, he did run his best race up until then and ran out a most decisive winner by seven lengths.

So what happened to the market leaders in the latest Champion Hurdle and how should Espoir d'Allen's win be assessed as a result of their failure to perform? Buveur d'Air fell at the third, bringing down Sharjah who appealed as much as

Unibet Champion Hurdle Challenge Trophy, Cheltenham—the game is up for the 'big three' come the home turn, with Buveur d'Air (riderless) and Apple's Jade (last) already out of things, whilst Laurina (second left) begins to send out distress signals ...

any on form among those at longer odds. Apple's Jade's involvement in the race barely lasted much longer, though even before losing her prominent pitch at the next she had never been going like a winner. That left only Laurina to prevent an upset, but a mistake when holding every chance three out soon made that unlikely. Meanwhile, Mark Walsh was carrying out the instructions discussed beforehand to ride Espoir d'Allen for a place. 'We got a place—it was first place!' commented a surprised Walsh after he had brought Espoir d'Allen to take over from Melon on the bridle two out before quickening clear to win impressively. 'I was in front soon enough,' said Walsh, 'and I heard a horse coming but only realised after the last that it was a loose horse.' Chased by the riderless Buveur d'Air, Espoir d'Allen put fifteen lengths between himself and Melon (who had run Buveur d'Air to a neck twelve months earlier) to establish a record winning margin for a Champion Hurdle winner. Rooster Booster had won by eleven lengths in 2003, with the previous record of twelve lengths shared by Istabraq in 1998 and Insurance who beat his only two rivals by twelve lengths and a distance in 1932. A neck separated Melon and Silver Streak, winner of the Swinton at Haydock and the Welsh Champion Hurdle at Ffos Las earlier in the campaign, with Laurina fourth and Apple's Jade (who returned an unsatisfactory scope afterwards) only sixth. Laurina and Apple's Jade were separated by another mare Verdana Blue who was given a sympathetic ride on unsuitably soft ground for her. The other finisher Global Citizen was out of his depth and tailed off, while Brain Power, who had beaten Silver Streak in a substandard International Hurdle, was pulled up, running one of his lesser races. Much like See You Then, Espoir d'Allen's task was made considerably easier by the poor showing of the favourites but, regardless of the race falling apart around him, he looked well worth crediting with a top-class performance that would have made him very much the one to beat in any future meeting with those who didn't give their running at Cheltenham.

It was not the first time that owner J. P. McManus had won the Champion Hurdle with a runner in the distinguishing green cap with a white star, rather than the white cap of his first colours which Barry Geraghty wore on Buveur d'Air. Jezki had been the McManus second string when beating the shorter-priced My Tent Or Yours in 2014, and McManus has now won eight Champion Hurdles in a Festival total that now stands at fifty-nine, both of which are records. McManus was leading owner at the latest Festival with five winners. Mark Walsh had his first Festival winner twelve months earlier when Bleu Berry won the Coral Cup in the emerald green, yellow hoops, and Walsh added to his Champion Hurdle victory at the latest Festival when City Island won the Baring Bingham. McManus spreads his patronage of Irish trainers far and wide, and Espoir d'Allen was one of three horses he had in training with Cromwell who handled another good horse of his, Jer's Girl. As a juvenile, Jer's Girl won Grade 1 novice events against older rivals at Fairyhouse and Punchestown and contested two editions of the David Nicholson Mares' Hurdle at Cheltenham, and was going well when falling three out in the 2017 renewal won by Apple's Jade. Cromwell, whose training career began with a few pointers, has no plans to give up farriery, not least, he says, because it helps to make training his string of forty-five pay—'You'd need to train one hundred and forty-five horses to make a decent living.' Besides Jer's Girl and Espoir d'Allen, Cromwell has enjoyed other big days with Raz de Maree winning the 2018 Welsh Grand National at the age of thirteen and, on the Flat, the mare Princess Yaiza winning the Prix de Royallieu at the Arc meeting before running at the Breeders' Cup. Cromwell worked for Raz de Maree's original trainer, the late Dessie Hughes, who won two Champion Hurdles with Hardy Eustace.

'A trainer with a difference'—a reference to his farriery work—is how Cromwell is described on his own website. Because of his age, Espoir d'Allen was just as much a Champion Hurdle winner with a difference, as five-year-old winners of the race are rare. The only one between See You Then and Espoir d'Allen was Katchit in 2008 who had been placed in the 'Fighting Fifth' and International Hurdle before winning the Kingwell at Wincanton on his way to the Champion Hurdle. Rarer still, Espoir d'Allen had run only once in open company prior to the Champion, when facing opposition that was, for the most part, well below Champion Hurdle standard when winning the Limestone Lad Hurdle at Naas in January. Conceding 7 lb to his four rivals, Espoir d'Allen landed the odds by two and a half lengths from

... Espoir d'Allen and Mark Walsh are already clear at the last; Melon (checks) is runner-up for the second year running, with outsider Silver Streak taking third

an out-of-sorts Wicklow Brave who had finished only seventh in the last couple of Champion Hurdles but returned to form at the latest Festival to be narrowly beaten under top weight in the Coral Cup.

The Limestone Lad was Espoir d'Allen's seventh win from eight starts over hurdles. He had looked the best juvenile in Ireland in the first half of the previous season when winning his first four starts, culminating in a Grade 2 win in the Knight Frank Juvenile Hurdle at Leopardstown from the Gordon Elliott-trained newcomer Farclas. Odds on again for the Spring Juvenile Hurdle at the same track, Espoir d'Allen clearly wasn't himself when finishing only fourth of the five runners and he missed the remaining big juvenile contests of the season in which the other top juveniles took turns beating each other. Farclas turned the tables on the Spring Juvenile winner Mr Adjudicator in the Triumph Hurdle while, at Punchestown, the Triumph fifth Saldier beat the pair of them in a race where Willie Mullins trained the first four home. In short, the 2018 crop of juveniles looked most unlikely to throw up a Champion Hurdle contender, though the Irish programme gives four-year-old hurdlers opportunities to continue competing against their own age group in their second season, and Espoir d'Allen restored his reputation at the start of the latest season by winning two such contests before the turn of the year. On his reappearance in the Fishery Lane Hurdle at Naas in November, he beat Mr Adjudicator by eleven lengths, though it might have been a different story if Saldier had not fallen when looking to be going better than Espoir d'Allen at the last. Espoir d'Allen came up against Farclas again in another Grade 3 contest, the Irish Independent Hurdle at Limerick in December, but Farclas was an early faller, hampering Espoir d'Allen in the process. Even so, Espoir d'Allen ran his best race before the Champion Hurdle when giving an eight-length beating to odds-on Stormy Ireland who went on to fill the same position in the David Nicholson Mares' Hurdle at the Festival. With the Limestone Lad giving him his third Grade 3 win of the season, Espoir d'Allen went into the Champion Hurdle with his limits arguably still unknown, though realistically—judged on his bare form—the best either his trainer or jockey could have hoped for was that he would not disgrace himself.

A posed portrait appeared in *Chasers & Hurdlers 2017/18* of the sturdy Espoir d'Allen, an AQPS gelding like Buveur d'Air, who was sourced from France by Charlie Swan, according to his trainer, after he won a maiden bumper over a mile and a half at Lignieres for Anne-Sophie Pacault. Espoir d'Allen comes from the final crop of the smart French middle-distance colt Voix du Nord whose death at the age of only twelve looks still more of a loss after the latest season in which his son Kemboy emerged as another top-class jumper. Golden Miller winner Defi du Seuil gave Voix du Nord a second winner at the latest Festival, that horse having himself been a top juvenile hurdler for McManus two years earlier. It goes almost without saying that a Champion Hurdle winner is the best thing to have happened to this family, but lightning struck twice at the Festival when Envoi Allen, a great grandson of the mare Violeta, who is also Espoir d'Allen's great grandam, won the Champion Bumper. Further details of Violeta's other descendants, who include some notable cross-country performers, can be found in Envoi Allen's essay.

		Valanour (b 1992)	Lomond
	Voix du Nord (FR) (b 2001)		Vearia
		Dame Edith (b 1995)	Top Ville
Espoir d'Allen (FR) (b.g. 2014)			Girl of France
		Maille Pistol (ch 1998)	Pistolet Bleu
	Quadanse (FR) (b 2004)		Bric Mamaille
		Etoile d'Or II (b 1992)	Lute Antique
			Violeta

Espoir d'Allen is the fourth foal of his unraced dam Quadanse whose first two foals were fillies who were also unraced. Next came Caviar d'Allen (by Laveron) who was a fair maiden hurdler for Christian Williams and has more recently been seeking a first career success in points. Quadanse is out of Etoile d'Or II who raced only in what would now be classed as French bumpers, winning six times at around a mile and a half. She has produced six winners in France, the best of them the smart chaser Mikador who ran in some of the top chases at Auteuil including the

Grand Steeple-Chase de Paris. Etoile d'Or II is also the dam of Toreador, a winning pointer in Britain, and she is the grandam of Arbre de Vie, a smart hurdler and chaser who ran at three Festivals for Willie Mullins, finishing fourth in the Spa. There is evidently no shortage of stamina in the family, though that was likely to be academic for the time being—Espoir d'Allen had done all his racing at two miles and a defence of his Champion Hurdle crown would no doubt have been his main objective. He had been raced only on soft or good to soft ground over hurdles so it remained to be seen how he handled conditions that put the emphasis more on speed (the last couple of Champion Hurdles have been run in more testing conditions than usual), but, in that respect, it was encouraging that he travelled well through his races. Unusually for a Champion Hurdle winner, Espoir d'Allen was still something of an unknown quantity. That's partly because of the way the latest renewal unfolded, but also because of Espoir d'Allen's age and his unexposed profile. He was ante-post favourite (as short as 3/1) at the time of his injury to retain the Champion Hurdle and there seemed every chance he would have confirmed himself a top-class hurdler in the next season. His demise is a reminder that serious injury can strike at home as well as on the racecourse. *Gavin Patrick Cromwell, Ireland*

ESPOIR DE GUYE (FR) 5 b.g. Khalkevi (IRE) – Penelope de Guye (FR) (Dom Alco (FR)) [2018/19 h17.9s⁵ h18.9g* h19.7s h16s² Mar 10] compact gelding: has had breathing operation: third foal: half-brother to French 19f chase winner Camille de Guye (by Buck's Boum): dam French maiden: fairly useful form over hurdles: won 4-y-o event at Les Sables-d'Olonne in June for G. Taupin: second in novice at Warwick in March. *Venetia Williams* **h116**

ESPOIR DE LOIRE (FR) 5 b.g. Anabaa Blue – Grischa (FR) (Septieme Ciel (USA)) [2018/19 h19.6g² h19.6g³ h19.4g⁵ h21s⁴ h21.7m⁶ h21g⁴ Apr 10] €20,000 3-y-o, €60,000 4-y-o: good-topped gelding: has had breathing operation: fifth foal: half-brother to French chasers Vertige de Loire (17f winner, by Trempolino) and All In de Loire (19f winner, by Loup Solitaire): dam French 11f-12.5f winner: won sole start in Irish points: fair form over hurdles: won handicap at Warwick in March: stays 21f: acts on soft going. *Ben Pauling* **h113**

ESPOIR DE ROMAY (FR) 5 b.g. Kap Rock (FR) – Miss du Seuil (FR) (Lavirco (GER)) [2018/19 h21.2d³ Mar 21] £22,000 3-y-o: third foal: dam French maiden jumper (placed up to 19f): 20/1, held back by inexperience when third in novice hurdle at Ludlow (20 lengths behind Jatiluwih) on debut: sure to progress. *Kim Bailey* **h95 p**

ESPOIR DE TEILLEE (FR) 7 b.g. Martaline – Belle de Lyphard (FR) (Lyphard's Wish (FR)) [2018/19 h124p: h18.5d³ h20.3g Apr 17] bumper winner: useful form over hurdles: third in handicap at Exeter (length behind Trans Express) in March. *Tom George* **h134**

ESPOIR MORIVIERE (FR) 5 ch.g. Saddex – Sagesse Moriviere (FR) (Vaguely Pleasant (FR)) [2018/19 h73: h16.2d h20.2g⁶ h20.9g h23.3g h23.3s³ h24.1d h25g Feb 18] poor maiden hurdler: stays 23f: acts on soft going. *Rose Dobbin* **h72**

ESPRIT DE BAILEYS (FR) 7 b.g. Le Havre (IRE) – Lit (IRE) (Danehill (USA)) [2018/19 h15.8g² h16.6g* Dec 15] half-brother to modest 2m hurdle winner Lit Et Mixe (by Linamix): fairly useful on Flat, stays 1½m: fairly useful form over hurdles: won novice at Doncaster in December. *Amy Murphy* **h117**

ESPRIT DE SOMOZA (FR) 5 b.g. Irish Wells (FR) – Topaze de Somoza (FR) (Discover d'Auteuil (FR)) [2018/19 h125: h17.9s⁶ h16.4g⁵ h19.5d⁴ h19d* h18.5d Mar 24] tall gelding: fairly useful handicap hurdler: won at Taunton in February: stays 19f: acts on soft going. *Nick Williams* **h128**

ESPRIT DU LARGE (FR) 5 b.g. No Risk At All (FR) – Tuffslolyloly (FR) (Double Bed (FR)) [2018/19 b16s h15.8s* h15.7d⁴ h19.7d* h20d Apr 5] €50,000 3-y-o: tall gelding: chasing type: half-brother to several winners in France, including fairly useful hurdler/chaser Thyflori (17f-21f winner, by Apsis): dam French 2m hurdle winner: shaped as if needing run in bumper: fairly useful form over hurdles: won maiden at Uttoxeter in December and novice at Hereford in March: remains with potential. *Evan Williams* **h120 p** **b72**

ESSGEE NICS (IRE) 6 b.g. Fairly Ransom (USA) – Vannuccis Daughter (IRE) (Perugino (USA)) [2018/19 b16.8mᵘʳ b16.3g³ Aug 23] fourth foal: dam, lightly raced on Flat, closely related to fairly useful 2m hurdle winner Aquila Oculus and fairly useful hurdler/chaser (stayed 2½m) Piercing Sun: modest form in bumpers: leading when swerved and unseated rider 1f out on debut at Newton Abbot: little show on Flat. *Paul George* **b83**

ESSTEEPEE 10 b.g. Double Trigger (IRE) – Lamper's Light (Idiot's Delight) [2018/19 **c–** c74, h–: c22.6d^{pu} Jun 8] point winner: maiden hurdler: little show in hunter chases: in **h–** headgear last 2 starts: tried in tongue tie. *Mrs Sherree Lean*

EST ILLIC (IRE) 5 b.g. Court Cave (IRE) – Ten Friends (IRE) (Shantou (USA)) **h112** [2018/19 h19.7s^6 h21.3d^2 h21.2d h21s Mar 10] €28,000 3-y-o: rather unfurnished gelding: second foal: dam, ran twice in bumpers/once in point, sister to fairly useful hurdler/chaser (stayed 21f) Clondaw Draft: Irish point winner: fair form over hurdles. *Tom Symonds*

ETAMINE DU COCHET (FR) 5 gr.m. Martaline – Nuance du Cochet (FR) (Siam **h113** (USA)) [2018/19 h103p: h15.8d^2 h16.2g^2 h21.2d^{pu} h20.7g^4 h19.9d^3 h20.5d^{ur} h20.1g^3 Apr 15] has had breathing operations: fair hurdler: won mares maiden at Huntingdon in January: stays 21f: acts on good to soft going: in tongue tie last 2 starts. *Dan Skelton*

ET APRES THOU (FR) 5 b.g. Network (GER) – Lady Thou (FR) (Kadalko (FR)) **b81** [2018/19 b16s^5 b15.3g Apr 14] half-brother to French bumper/fairly useful 19f chase winner Thouva (by Ragmar) and French 2½m chase winner Utathou (by Secret Singer): dam unraced: modest form in bumpers. *Philip Hobbs*

ETERNALLY YOURS 6 b.m. Sulamani (IRE) – Well Disguised (IRE) (Beneficial) **h126** [2018/19 h93p, b91: h20.5v^2 h20.6s* h20.5s^2 Mar 9] bumper winner: fairly useful form over hurdles: won mares handicap at Newcastle in December: held up. *Donald Whillans*

ETHANDEXTER 4 ch.g. Alkaased (USA) – Miss Venice (IRE) (Fasliyev (USA)) **b–** [2018/19 b16.3s ab16g Feb 18] well held in 2 bumpers: in hood first start. *Michael Madgwick*

ET MOI ALORS (FR) 5 b.g. Kap Rock (FR) – Qui L'Eut Cru (FR) (Lavirco (GER)) **h111** [2018/19 h117: h19.5s^5 h16d h21g h20.5s^5 h16.7g^2 h17.7g^3 Apr 12] useful-looking gelding: fair maiden hurdler: stays 2¼m: acts on heavy going. *Gary Moore*

ETTILA DE SIVOLA (FR) 5 gr.g. Noroit (GER) – Wild Rose Bloom (FR) **h116** (Kaldounevees (FR)) [2018/19 b85: h16.8s* h16.8s^3 h18.9d^2 Mar 20] lengthy, good-topped gelding: impresses in appearance: bumper winner: fairly useful form over hurdles: won maiden at Sedgefield in December: tried in tongue tie. *James Ewart*

EURATO (FR) 9 ch.g. Medicean – Double Green (IRE) (Green Tune (USA)) [2018/19 **h–** h98: h16.7g Mar 20] modest form over hurdles, well held only outing in sphere in 2018/19: wears cheekpieces. *Derek Shaw*

EUREU DU BOULAY (FR) 5 b.g. Della Francesca (USA) – Idole du Boulay (FR) **c123** (Useful (FR)) [2018/19 h120: h15.7g^6 h19.9g^6 h19.9m^2 h23g^{pu} c16g^4 c15.7s^5 c19.2s* **h115** c19.3s* c19.2g^2 c21.6g^4 c15.9m^2 c24v^{pu} Mar 16] good-topped gelding: has had breathing operation: fairly useful handicap hurdler: second at Uttoxeter in July: fairly useful handicap chaser: won at Catterick (novice) and Sedgefield in December: stays easy 2½m: acts on soft and good to firm going: tried in cheekpieces: wears tongue tie: front runner/races prominently. *Richard Hobson*

EUR GONE WEST (IRE) 6 b.g. Westerner – Floating Euro (IRE) (Beneficial) [2018/19 **h124** b74: h15.8g^4 h15.8s^2 h19.9s^4 h23.1d h19d^4 h23.1d* h23.9d* h23.9g^6 Apr 24] has had breathing operation: third in Irish point: fairly useful handicap hurdler: won at Exeter (novice) in March and Taunton in April: stays 3m: acts on soft going: usually wears hood/tongue tie: usually leads. *David Pipe*

EURKASH (FR) 5 b.g. Irish Wells (FR) – Meralda (FR) (Baby Turk) [2018/19 b86: **b78** b15.7g^4 b15.8g Nov 17] useful-looking gelding: modest form in bumpers. *Paul Webber*

EUXTON LANE (IRE) 7 b.g. Getaway (GER) – Local Hall (IRE) (Saddlers' Hall (IRE)) **c136** [2018/19 h134, b96: c20s^3 c20.3v^F Dec 1] useful form over hurdles: similar form over **h–** fences: every chance when fell last in maiden won by Jerrysback at Bangor: stayed 21f: acted on heavy going: dead. *Oliver Sherwood*

EVA'S OSKAR (IRE) 5 gr.g. Shirocco (GER) – Sardagna (FR) (Medaaly) [2018/19 b–: **h104** h16s h15.8v^3 h15.8v h20.5d^2 h24.2d^4 Mar 22] rather unfurnished gelding: fair form over hurdles: stays 3m: acts on good to soft going. *Tim Vaughan*

EVENT OF SIVOLA (FR) 5 ch.g. Noroit (GER) – Surprise de Sivola (FR) (Discover **c96** d'Auteuil (FR)) [2018/19 h17.9s^6 c16.9m* h18.6d c20s^{pu} Feb 18] third foal: dam, placed **h91** up to 2¾m over fences in France, half-sister to fair hurdler/fairly useful chaser (winner up to 21f) Take Over Sivola: modest form over hurdles: similar form over fences: won maiden at Wissembourg in June for A. Adeline de Boisbrunet: unproven beyond 17f: acts on good to firm going. *Mark Walford*

EVEQUE (FR) 5 ch.g. Kotky Bleu (FR) – Gloria IV (FR) (Video Rock (FR)) [2018/19 **b–**
b16s b16.2d Mar 26] little impact in 2 Irish points: last in 2 bumpers. *Jane Walton*

EVERLANES 6 br.m. Shirocco (GER) – Good Thinking (Kayf Tara) [2018/19 b89: h20g⁴ **h104**
h18.5g² h16.2s² h15.3d⁶ h16d⁴ Jan 28] has had breathing operation: fair form in bumpers:
similar form over hurdles: left Anthony Honeyball after first start: stays 19f: acts on soft
going: wears tongue tie: front runner/races prominently. *Keiran Burke*

EVER SO MUCH (IRE) 10 b.g. Westerner – Beautiful World (IRE) (Saddlers' Hall **c106**
(IRE)) [2018/19 c86, h93: h24g⁴ c20.1g* c20.1m* c20g c21.1m² c21.6m⁵ c19.3m⁴ **h85**
c21.3d^pu c23.4g^pu h19.9s^pu Mar 3] modest handicap hurdler: fair handicap chaser: won at
Hexham (twice) in June: should stay 3m: acts on good to firm and good to soft going: wears
headgear. *Ben Haslam*

EVERYBODY'S TALKIN (IRE) 6 ch.g. Robin des Champs (FR) – Miss Otis Regrets **c–**
(IRE) (Bob Back (USA)) [2018/19 h104: c19.4m⁶ May 20] won twice in points, including **h–**
in 2019: fair form over hurdles: 9/2, well held in novice handicap at Stratford on chasing
debut: wears tongue tie. *Nigel Twiston-Davies*

EVERY CHANCE (IRE) 6 b.g. Frozen Power (IRE) – Runway Dancer (Dansili) **h92**
[2018/19 h88: h20.5g⁵ h17.2g h18.5m⁶ h16g³ h16.8g^F h16.8g^pu Sep 28] modest maiden
hurdler: best effort at 2m: tried in cheekpieces: in tongue tie last 3 starts. *Noel C. Kelly,
Ireland*

EVERYDAY EVERYHOUR 8 b.g. Presenting – Candello (Supreme Leader) [2018/19 **c–**
c114, h–: c16.2m c20g⁵ c20.9g c16g Nov 19] won 2-runner Irish point: winning hurdler: **h–**
fair form at best in chases: tried in cheekpieces: dead. *Kerry Lee*

EVIDENCE DE THAIX (FR) 5 b.m. Network (GER) – Nacre de Thaix (FR) (Roi de **h109 p**
Rome (USA)) [2018/19 h19.5d² h18.5v* h19.5d^pu h21.4s Mar 7] lengthy mare: has scope:
sixth foal: half-sister to 2 winners in France by Dom Alco, including useful 17f/2¼m chase
winner Brin de Thaix: dam, ran twice in bumpers, sister to smart French hurdler/useful
chaser (15f-2½m winner) Havre de Thaix and half-sister to smart hurdler/chaser (stayed
25f) Quartz de Thaix: won 2 bumpers in France for G. Cherel in 2017/18: fair form over
hurdles: won mares novice at Exeter in December: tried in hood: remains with potential.
Philip Hobbs

EVRON (FR) 5 b.g. Secret Singer (FR) – Rive Droite (FR) (Ragmar (FR)) [2018/19 h17g⁵ **c–**
h19.5s⁶ h19.6g Jan 11] has had breathing operation: little form over hurdles: fairly useful **h–**
form over fences in France for Francois-Marie Cottin in 2017/18: tried in hood.
Warren Greatrex

EXCALIBUR (POL) 6 gr.g. Youmzain (IRE) – Electra Deelites (With Approval (CAN)) **h–**
[2018/19 h–: h16.2d h16.8s⁶ h22.7g h19.9v^pu Mar 12] no form over hurdles: tried in
cheekpieces. *Micky Hammond*

EXCELLENT RESULT (IRE) 9 b.g. Shamardal (USA) – Line Ahead (IRE) (Sadler's **h–**
Wells (USA)) [2018/19 h91: h16.2g⁵ h16m^su Oct 19] sturdy gelding: fairly useful hurdler
at best, no form in 2018/19: best efforts around 2m: acts on good to firm going: tried in
headgear. *Richard Spencer*

EXCELLENT TEAM 7 b.g. Teofilo (IRE) – Seradim (Elnadim (USA)) [2018/19 h106: **h106**
h15.8g⁵ h15.8g* h16m⁴ h16g⁴ h16.8m⁵ h16.7g⁴ h16g² h15.8m³ h16.3g² h15.8g² h15.5g²
h15.8g Apr 11] rather leggy gelding: has had breathing operation: fair handicap hurdler:
won at Uttoxeter in June: left Dan Skelton after ninth start: stays 2½m: acts on good to firm
and good to soft going: tried in blinkers: wears tongue tie: usually leads. *Michael Blake*

EXCITABLE ISLAND (IRE) 12 b.g. Heron Island (IRE) – Miss Excitable (IRE) **c113**
(Montelimar (USA)) [2018/19 c107: c32.5g* c27.5d⁴ c20v⁴ Feb 18] multiple point winner:
fair hunter chaser: awarded race at Cheltenham early in season: stays 33f: acts on good to
soft going. *N. W. Padfield*

EXCLUSIVE RIGHTS 11 b.m. Fair Mix (IRE) – Rosie Ring (IRE) (Phardante (FR)) **c98**
[2018/19 c91, h–: c17.8g² c17d^pu c17.2g³ c19.4m³ c19.3g^pu Apr 23] has had breathing **h–**
operation: point winner: twice-raced chaser: modest maiden chaser: trained by Richard
Phillips third/fourth starts: stays 23f: acts on good to firm and good to soft going: usually
front runner/races prominently. *Mrs Claire Hardwick*

EXCUSE ME (FR) 5 b.g. Saddler Maker (IRE) – Mexcala (FR) (Astarabad (USA)) **b–**
[2018/19 b15.8s⁶ Apr 7] 8/1, badly in need of experience when sixth in bumper at Ffos Las.
Venetia Williams

EXECUTIVE CAPILANO (IRE) 6 b.m. Milan – Capilano (IRE) (Executive Perk) **h110**
[2018/19 h18.5g⁴ h24s² h21sᵖᵘ Jan 21] off mark in Irish points at second attempt: fair form
over hurdles: best effort when second in mares maiden at Southwell: dead. *Dan Skelton*

EXECUTIVE PRINCE (IRE) 9 bl.g. Presenting – Callanagh Pride (IRE) (Executive **h–**
Perk) [2018/19 h16g Jun 24] placed in Irish points: modest maiden hurdler, well held sole
start in 2018/19: best effort at 2m: acts on good to firm going: tried in hood. *Jeremy Scott*

EXELERATOR EXPRESS (FR) 5 b.g. Poliglote – Reine de Lestrade (FR) (Sabrehill **b94**
(USA)) [2018/19 b15.8s² Apr 7] third foal: half-brother to fairly useful French 17f hurdle
winner Discours d'Un Roi (by Vision d'Etat): dam French 10.5f winner: in tongue tie,
25/1, showed plenty when second in bumper at Ffos Las (5 lengths behind Prudhomme).
Neil Mulholland

EXITAS (IRE) 11 b.g. Exit To Nowhere (USA) – Suntas (IRE) (Riberetto) [2018/19 c132, **c142**
h–: h16m⁵ h15.7g h19.9g³ h22.1g⁵ h20g⁴ h18.7g² h20.3g³ c22.6m⁴ c21.4g* c23.6d² h25m² **h116**
c25g* c24g² c28.8v³ c24gᵖᵘ c24.2d⁶ h23.5d c23.8mᵖᵘ c24.2m³ Apr 22] lengthy gelding:
fairly useful handicap hurdler: second at Plumpton in October: useful handicap chaser:
won at Market Rasen in September and Aintree (veterans event, by 11 lengths from Beat
That) in October: stays 25f: acts on good to firm and heavy going: has worn tongue tie.
Phil Middleton

EXIT TO FREEDOM 13 ch.g. Exit To Nowhere (USA) – Bobanvi (Timeless Times **c–**
(USA)) [2018/19 c–, h69§: h20.6g h22.1g h23gᵖᵘ h16.7g Aug 18] poor hurdler: fell sole **h– §**
start over fences: wore headgear: tried in tongue tie: front runner/raced prominently: dead.
John Wainwright

EXIT TO WHERE (FR) 5 b.r. Kapgarde (FR) – Rapsodie Sea (FR) (April Night (FR)) **c101**
[2018/19 h20.5d h16d h19.8s⁵ c24.2g² Apr 15] fourth foal: half-brother to 3 winners, **h80**
including fair chaser Cap Horner (23f-3½m winner, by Apsis): dam ran twice in French
bumpers (third at 1½m): poor maiden hurdler: fair form over fences: second in handicap at
Hexham in April: stays 3m: acts on soft going: has worn headgear, including in 2018/19: in
tongue tie last 4 starts. *Lucinda Russell*

EXMOOR MIST 11 gr.g. Kayf Tara – Chita's Flora (Alflora (IRE)) [2018/19 c106§, h–: **c98 §**
c20gᵖᵘ c16.5g⁴ c17.4s⁵ c16d⁵ c20.5d⁴ c16d c17.5vᵖᵘ Mar 18] rangy gelding: winning **h–**
hurdler: modest handicap chaser nowadays: stays 2¼m: acts on heavy going: wears
headgear/tongue tie: untrustworthy. *Victor Dartnall*

EXOTIC FRIEND (IRE) 11 ch.g. Croco Rouge (IRE) – Prima Nox (Sabrehill (USA)) **h88**
[2018/19 h–: h19.9g h21dᵖᵘ h22g⁴ h19.6g Apr 13] workmanlike gelding: has had breathing
operation: modest handicap hurdler: stays 2¾m: acts on good to soft going: tried in
cheekpieces: in tongue tie last 2 starts. *Adrian Wintle*

EXPANDING UNIVERSE (IRE) 12 b.g. Galileo (IRE) – Uliana (USA) (Darshaan) **c82**
[2018/19 c23.6d⁴ Mar 21] sturdy gelding: point winner: maiden hurdler: poor chaser **h–**
nowadays: stays 25f: acts on heavy going: tried in headgear. *Mrs S. Bowen*

EX PATRIOT (IRE) 6 b.g. Elusive Pimpernel (USA) – Carolobrian (IRE) (Mark of **c143**
Esteem (IRE)) [2018/19 h140: c19d⁵ c16s⁴ c16.3g* c18s* Mar 9] sparely-made gelding: **h–**
useful hurdler: similar form over fences: won maiden at Thurles in February and handicap
at Gowran (by 2¾ lengths from Goulane Chosen) in March: stays 2½m: acts on heavy
going: usually front runner/races prominently. *Ellmarie Holden, Ireland*

EXPRESS DES MOTTES (FR) 5 b.g. Network (GER) – Uzelle des Mottes (FR) **h–**
(Robin des Champs (FR)) [2018/19 b15.6g⁵ h16.2gᵖᵘ Dec 9] third on debut in Irish point: **b–**
tailed off in bumper: pulled up in maiden hurdle. *Alison Hamilton*

EXPRESS DU BERLAIS (FR) 10 b.g. Saint des Saints (FR) – Euil Eagle (FR) (Saint **c86**
Preuil (FR)) [2018/19 c26.2g⁶ May 27] point winner: winning hurdler: fairly useful at **h–**
best over fences, well held in hunter in 2018/19: stays 3m: acts on soft going: has worn
headgear: usually wears tongue tie. *Miss L. V. Horner*

EXPRESSTIME (IRE) 6 b.m. Scorpion (IRE) – Glenair Dante (IRE) (Phardante (FR)) **c90**
[2018/19 c90, h–: h20.5g³ c23.4g² c21.6d⁴ c17.1g⁴ c16.3d³ c19.3g Apr 23] has had **h79**
breathing operation: runner-up both starts in Irish points: well held completed start over
hurdles: modest maiden chaser: stays 23f: has worn tongue tie, including last 3 starts:
usually races close up. *Chris Grant*

338

EX S'ELANCE (FR) 5 b.g. Saddex – Pampa Brune (FR) (Robin des Champs (FR)) **h114**
[2018/19 h17.9d⁴ h17.4d* h16.2s h17g⁶ h20.9d⁶ h16.2g h16.8s h16s⁶ h17g h20.6d* Apr 6]
fourth foal: dam, French 1½m bumper winner, half-sister to fairly useful hurdler (stayed
21f) Tabac Brun: bumper winner in 2017/18: fair hurdler: won claimer at Vichy in May
(for G. Cherel) and handicap at Newcastle in April: stays 21f: acts on good to soft going:
has worn headgear, including in 2018/19: tried in tongue tie. *Micky Hammond*

EXTRA BALD (FR) 5 b.g. Linda's Lad – Palatyne (FR) (Passing Sale (FR)) [2018/19 **c–**
b68: b15.7g h16.4d⁵ h17s⁴ h16.7d⁴ h16s c19.3v⁵ Mar 12] tall gelding: poor form in **h102**
bumpers: fair form over hurdles: well beaten in novice handicap on chasing debut: likely **b–**
to stay 2½m: acts on soft going: tried in cheekpieces: front runner/races prominently: has
joined Mark Walford. *Richard Hobson*

EXTRA MAG (FR) 5 b.g. Kapgarde (FR) – Qrystale Mag (FR) (Vertical Speed (FR)) **h127**
[2018/19 h16dᵘʳ h16.8d* h16d² Jan 28] brother to fairly useful 19f hurdle winner Crystal
Lad (stays 3¼m): dam, French 17f hurdle winner, half-sister to smart French hurdler/fair
chaser (winner up to 2½m) Crylza Royal and smart hurdler/useful chaser (stayed 4m)
Royal Rosa: won sole Flat start in France for Alain Couetil: fairly useful form over hurdles:
won novice at Exeter in January: second in similar event at Kempton later in month: will
stay 2½m. *David Pipe*

EXTREME APPEAL (IRE) 7 b.g. Excellent Art – Silk Mascara (IRE) (Barathea (IRE)) **c100**
[2018/19 c16.3g h20.3s c21.2g³ Mar 4] lengthy, angular gelding: multiple point winner: **h–**
modest form over hurdles: fair form over fences: better effort when third in handicap at
Fakenham: stays 21f: acts on heavy going: wears headgear. *Kelly Morgan*

EXTRODINAIR 4 b.g. Captain Gerrard (IRE) – Mindfulness (Primo Dominie) [2018/19 **b–**
b16.3s b13.7v⁵ Feb 14] last in 2 bumpers. *Jane Chapple-Hyam*

EXXARO (IRE) 9 b.g. Presenting – Mandys Gold (IRE) (Mandalus) [2018/19 c128§, h–: **c121 §**
c20.6g⁴ c20.2m⁴ c26.1g* c23g³ c25.8g² c21.6g³ c25.8d⁶ c25.1m⁵ Oct 19] sturdy gelding: **h–**
winning hurdler: fairly useful handicap chaser: won at Uttoxeter in June: stays 3¼m: acts
on good to firm and good to soft going: wears headgear: usually wears tongue tie:
temperamental. *Colin Tizzard*

EYEHAVEAGOODIDEA 6 b.g. Black Sam Bellamy (IRE) – Aphrodisia (Sakhee **b91**
(USA)) [2018/19 b15.8m² b16g³ Jun 11] second foal: dam 1m-1¼m winner: fair form in
bumpers: better effort when second at Uttoxeter: wears tongue tie. *Peter Bowen*

EYE IN THE SKY (IRE) 8 gr.h. Sinndar (IRE) – Saudade (GER) (Linamix (FR)) **h95**
[2018/19 h15.9s* h19.5v Feb 18] useful on Flat, stays 2m: modest form over hurdles: won
minor event at Ovrevoll in October for Niels Petersen. *John E. Long*

EYE OF AN EAGLE (FR) 6 b.g. Linda's Lad – Vie des Aigles (FR) (Alamo Bay **b83**
(USA)) [2018/19 ab16g b16.3g⁴ Mar 30] second foal: half-brother to French 1¼m-1½m
winner Vision des Aigles (by Vision d'Etat): dam French maiden half-sister to top-class
middle-distance performer Cirrus des Aigles: modest form in bumpers. *David Arbuthnot*

EYES OF A TIGER (IRE) 8 ch.g. Golan (IRE) – Backtothekingsnest (IRE) (King's **c132**
Theatre (IRE)) [2018/19 c127, h–: c16g² Apr 25] winning hurdler: useful form over fences: **h–**
second in handicap at Perth (1¾ lengths behind Double W's) on sole outing in 2018/19:
stays 19f: acts on heavy going: usually wears hood: front runner/races prominently.
Brian Ellison

EYESOPENWIDEAWAKE (IRE) 8 b.g. Stowaway – Namesake (Nashwan (USA)) **c–**
[2018/19 c124, h107: c20.3gᵖᵘ c20.5g⁶ Nov 26] fair form over hurdles: fairly useful form **h–**
over fences, little show in 2018/19: stays 2¼m: acts on good to soft going: tried in hood/
tongue tie: front runner. *Richard Bandey*

EYES RIGHT 4 b.f. Passing Glance – Call Me A Star (Midnight Legend) [2018/19 b14g **b95**
b12.6s² b15.7d⁴ b15.7s* b17d Apr 4] good-topped filly: first foal: dam (h137), bumper/2m-
19f hurdle winner, sister to fairly useful hurdler/useful chaser (stayed 21f) Call Me A
Legend: fairly useful bumper performer: won conditionals/amateurs maiden at Southwell
in March. *Alan King*

EYREN (IRE) 4 b.f. Rip Van Winkle (IRE) – Ella Ransom (GER) (Ransom O'War **b94**
(USA)) [2018/19 b16.6g* b17d Apr 4] strong filly: third foal: half-sister to German 15f
winner Eyla (by Shirocco): dam German 1¼m winner: fair form in bumpers: easily won
5-runner conditionals/amateurs event at Doncaster in March. *Dan Skelton*

EYRESHILL (IRE) 6 ch.g. Beneficial – Eyres And Graces (IRE) (Saddlers' Hall (IRE)) **h97**
[2018/19 h22g³ h15.5g⁴ h19.9vᵖᵘ Dec 21] strong gelding: third foal: brother to fairly useful
hurdler/fair chaser Gracemount (2m-2¾m winner) and half-brother to a winning pointer by

Trans Island: dam, winning pointer, closely related to fairly useful hurdler/smart chaser (stayed 3m) Mount Oscar: well held in Irish point: modest form over hurdles only on first outing: has joined Andrew Hamilton. *Nigel Twiston-Davies*

EY UP ROCKY 6 b.g. Dylan Thomas (IRE) – Polo (Warning) [2018/19 h94, b101: h16g² h16.6g² h20.7dᵖᵘ h20.5d* Mar 1] good-bodied gelding: bumper winner: fairly useful handicap hurdler: won at Newbury (conditionals) in March: stays 21f: acts on good to soft going. *Jonjo O'Neill* **h119**

EZANAK (IRE) 6 b.g. Sea The Stars (IRE) – Ebaza (IRE) (Sinndar (IRE)) [2018/19 h15.7g² h16g² h16g² h16.7m⁴ h16g⁵ Oct 31] has had breathing operation: half-brother to fair hurdler Ebazan (2m-2½m winner, by Lemon Drop Kid): fair on Flat, stays 1½m: fair form over hurdles: raced around 2m: tried in cheekpieces: wears tongue tie: has joined Michael Appleby. *Dan Skelton* **h107**

F

FABIANSKI (IRE) 4 ch.f. Raven's Pass (USA) – Fabia (IRE) (Sadler's Wells (USA)) [2018/19 h16d* h15.7s* h16.6g³ Jan 25] fair on Flat, stays 1m: fair form over hurdles: easy winner of juveniles at Wetherby (maiden) in November and Catterick in December. *Rebecca Menzies* **h112**

FACT FLOW (IRE) 10 br.g. Whitmore's Conn (USA) – Beaver Run (IRE) (Be My Native (USA)) [2018/19 c–, h–: c22.5d* c20.9dᵖᵘ h16s c20d* c25.2s h20v c24d³ c19.4g³ Apr 21] sturdy gelding: little form over hurdles: modest handicap chaser: won at Uttoxeter in May (novices) and November: stays 3m: acts on good to soft going: tried in cheekpieces: usually front runner/races prominently. *Dai Burchell* **c97**
h–

FACTION 6 b.g. Champs Elysees – Belladora (Alzao (USA)) [2018/19 h92: h21.4m h19.9m⁴ May 19] modest maiden hurdler at best: should stay further than 2½m: acts on good to firm going: in cheekpieces last 4 starts. *Nigel Hawke* **h70**

FACT OF THE MATTER (IRE) 9 b.g. Brian Boru – Womanofthemountain (IRE) (Presenting) [2018/19 c128, h–: c25g⁴ h22.1g⁴ c25.5s² h26g² c29.2gᶠ c30.2g² c30.2g* c30.2s c21.1d Apr 5] good-topped gelding: has had breathing operations: fairly useful form over hurdles: second in handicap at Warwick in September: useful handicap chaser: won cross-country event at Cheltenham in December: stays 3¾m: acts on soft and good to firm going: wears headgear/tongue tie. *Jamie Snowden* **c136**
h117

FADING ICON 4 b.f. Sixties Icon – Fading Away (Fraam) [2018/19 h15.8g⁴ h16g⁶ h17.7d⁶ h17.7v³ h19d h20.5dᵖᵘ h19.2v² Feb 14] sister to modest hurdler Sixties Idol (2½m/2¾m winner) and half-sister to fair hurdler Brilliant Barca (2m winner, by Imperial Dancer), stayed 21f: modest form on Flat: modest maiden hurdler: stays 19f: acts on heavy going: has joined Philip Kirby. *Sheena West* **h90**

FAINT HOPE 7 ch.g. Midnight Legend – Rhinestone Ruby (Kayf Tara) [2018/19 h108, b67: h21g* h20dᵖᵘ May 26] has had breathing operation: fair form over hurdles: won handicap at Kempton in May: stays 21f: acts on heavy going: tried in tongue tie: usually races nearer last than first. *Grace Harris* **h110**

FAIR ALICE 10 gr.m. Fair Mix (IRE) – Mrs White (IRE) (Alflora (IRE)) [2018/19 h20gᵖᵘ May 10] first foal: dam winning pointer out of fairly useful hurdler up to 3m Annicombe Run: failed to complete in maiden hurdle/points. *Martin Wilesmith* **h–**

FAIR AND DANDY 6 gr.m. Fair Mix (IRE) – Ashnaya (FR) (Ashkalani (IRE)) [2018/19 b15.7s⁶ Mar 18] fifth foal: dam (c108/h93), 17f-23f hurdle/chase winner, also 2m winner on Flat: well beaten in bumper. *Henry Daly* **b–**

FAIRE PART SIVOLA (FR) 4 b.g. Noroit (GER) – Lettre d'Estruval (FR) (Vertical Speed (FR)) [2018/19 b15.3g* b16m⁶ Feb 23] rather unfurnished gelding: closely related to French 2¼m chase winner Bulle de Sivola (by Network): dam, prolific French 1½m bumper winner, half-sister to fairly useful hurdler/chaser (stayed 21f) Plaisir d'Estruval: fairly useful form in bumpers: won maiden at Wincanton in January. *Nick Williams* **b95**

FAIR EXCHANGE (IRE) 9 ch.g. Beneficial – Kazan Lady (IRE) (Petardia) [2018/19 c24.2dᵖᵘ c21.2g² c27.5dᴿ c20s³ c21.2d² c21.2sᵖᵘ c25.8dᵖᵘ c20m⁴ c26.1gᵖᵘ Nov 17] third foal: half-brother to fairly useful chaser Forever My Friend (19f-3m winner, by King's Theatre): dam (h96), 17f hurdle winner, half-sister to useful hurdler (stayed 2½m) Brogella, herself dam of smart hurdler up to 2½m Swamp Fox: multiple point winner: **c119**

fairly useful maiden chaser: placed in novices at Uttoxeter in July and Cartmel in August: left J. J. O'Shea after third start: stays 21f: acts on soft going: has worn headgear: has rejoined former yard: temperament under suspicion. *Peter Bowen*

FAIR FRANK 8 gr.g. Fair Mix (IRE) – Firstflor (Alflora (IRE)) [2018/19 c97, h72, b–: c16.3g^pu c22.6m^6 c22.6m^pu c17.8g^pu Aug 23] lightly raced over hurdles: modest form when successful on chasing debut, none since: tried in headgear/tongue tie: usually leads. *David Bridgwater* **c–**
h–

FAIR HOUXTY 7 bl.m. Fair Mix (IRE) – Border Mist (IRE) (Mull of Kintyre (USA)) [2018/19 h19.8g^pu Jan 7] second foal: half-sister to bumper winner Banks O' Houxty (by Generous): dam ran twice in bumpers: little show in points: in hood, pulled up in maiden on hurdling debut. *Tim Reed* **h–**

FAIR KATE 5 b.m. Fair Mix (IRE) – Silver Kate (IRE) (Insan (USA)) [2018/19 b15.8s^5 h16d^3 h19g h16d^2 Mar 21] second foal: half-sister to bumper winner/useful hurdler Kateson (19f/2½m winner, by Black Sam Bellamy): dam (c136/h136) 2½m-3¼m hurdle/chase winner: poor form sole start in bumpers: fair form over hurdles: best effort when third in maiden at Chepstow in January: will be suited by 2½m. *Tom Lacey* **h101**
b73

FAIR LADY 5 b.m. Fair Mix (IRE) – Lady Sambury (Overbury (IRE)) [2018/19 b16.2g Apr 15] third foal: dam (h86) 2½m-3m hurdle winner: tongue tied when well beaten in bumper. *Maurice Barnes* **b–**

FAIRLEE GRACE 8 b.m. Fair Mix (IRE) – Halo Flora (Alflora (IRE)) [2018/19 h21.4d^4 h21.4d h19.8m^4 Mar 22] poor form over hurdles: stays 21f: acts on good to soft going. *Stuart Coltherd* **h71**

FAIR LOCH 11 gr.g. Fair Mix (IRE) – Ardentinny (Ardross) [2018/19 c124§, h–§: c15.2d c15.2s^5 c17.2s^pu c15.2g^6 c17.1g^3 c15.2g^3 c16.4g* Apr 23] good-topped gelding: winning hurdler: fairly useful handicap chaser: won at Sedgefield in April: unproven beyond 17f: acts on heavy going: tried in headgear: has worn tongue tie: inconsistent: weak finisher. *Brian Ellison* **c116 §**
h– §

FAIR MINX 5 gr.m. Fair Mix (IRE) – Blazing Diva (IRE) (Blueprint (IRE)) [2018/19 b17g b16.2d^2 Mar 26] has had breathing operation: first foal: dam (c105/h98) 3m-3¼m chase winner: modest form in bumpers. *Sandy Thomson* **b75**

FAIR MOUNTAIN (GER) 7 b.g. Tiger Hill (IRE) – Fair Breeze (GER) (Silvano (GER)) [2018/19 h15.8m^2 h16.7g* h15.8m* h16.7m^2 Jul 21] leggy gelding: smart on Flat in Germany for Andreas Wohler, stays 1½m: useful form over hurdles: won maiden at Bangor in June and novice at Uttoxeter in July: second in Summer Hurdle (Handicap) at Market Rasen (2¼ lengths behind L'Inganno Felice) final outing. *Dan Skelton* **h134**

FAIR SHERIFF 5 gr.m. Fair Mix (IRE) – Sheriff's Falcon (IRE) (Presenting) [2018/19 b15.7d^4 b16.8d^6 Apr 23] third foal: sister to a winning pointer: dam, no form in bumpers/novice hurdles, out of sister to useful chaser up to 3m Force Seven: poor form in bumpers. *Rebecca Menzies* **b67**

FAIR TO DREAM 6 b.g. Fair Mix (IRE) – Sahara's Dream (Alphabatim (USA)) [2018/19 b16.3s Mar 11] little show in maiden bumper at Stratford. *Sarah-Jayne Davies* **b–**

FAIR TO MIDDLING 9 gr.g. Fair Mix (IRE) – Mtilly (Mtoto) [2018/19 c100, h–: h23g May 10] fair hurdler, well held sole start in 2018/19: similar form over fences: stays 2½m: acts on good going: wears headgear/tongue tie. *Peter Bowen* **c–**
h–

FAIRWAY FREDDY (IRE) 6 b.g. Elusive Pimpernel (USA) – Silent Supreme (IRE) (Supreme Leader) [2018/19 h–, b90: h15.9g^5 h15.3g* h16g* h16.7g h16m^3 Apr 12] lengthy gelding: chasing type: fair handicap hurdler: won at Wincanton (conditionals/amateurs novice) and Kempton (conditionals) in November: raced around 2m: acts on good to firm going: usually races close up. *Nick Gifford* **h113**

FAITHFUL MOUNT 10 b.g. Shirocco (GER) – Lady Lindsay (IRE) (Danehill Dancer (IRE)) [2018/19 h20s^5 h17.7v h23.5d^f h24.4g^2 h23.1g^2 h24.3m^pu Apr 20] sturdy gelding: fairly useful on Flat, stays 16.5f: fair handicap hurdler: stays 3m: best form on good going: wears cheekpieces. *Ian Williams* **h114**

FAITHFULNESS (IRE) 6 b.m. Robin des Champs (FR) – Ballycowan Lady (IRE) (Accordion) [2018/19 h20s^pu Nov 23] £80,000 5-y-o: fifth foal: sister to useful hurdler/chaser Duke des Champs (19f-2¾m winner): dam unraced half-sister to top-class chaser Harbour Pilot: won Irish point on debut: pulled up in maiden on hurdling debut. *Charlie Longsdon* **h–**

JCB Triumph Trial Juvenile Hurdle (Finesse), Cheltenham—heavily-backed Irish raider Fakir d'Oudairies runs out a wide-margin winner

FAKIR D'OUDAIRIES (FR) 4 b.g. Kapgarde (FR) – Niagaria du Bois (FR) (Grand **c96 P** Tresor (FR)) [2018/19 h15.9s² h17.4s⁶ c18.4d⁴ c18.4s^bd h16s* h16.8d* h16.4s⁴ h17d² **h143** Apr 4] medium-sized gelding: fourth foal: half-brother to French 19f chase winner Val d'Oudairies (by Robin des Pres): dam placed in French cross-country chases up to 2¾m: ran once in bumpers: useful hurdler: won maiden at Cork and Triumph Hurdle Trial (Finesse) at Cheltenham (by 13 lengths from Fine Brunello) in January: in frame in Grade 1 events after, including when second in Anniversary Hurdle at Aintree (neck behind Pentland Hills) then Champion Four Year Old Hurdle at Punchestown (2¾ lengths behind Fusil Raffles) shortly after end of British season: fourth on completed start over fences in France: left G. Cherel after fourth start: will prove suited by further than 2m: acts on soft going: front runner/races prominently, often travels strongly: should do much better over fences. *Joseph Patrick O'Brien, Ireland*

FALAK (IRE) 6 b.g. Teofilo (IRE) – Family (USA) (Danzig (USA)) [2018/19 h16g h16g* **h127** h20.9m³ Sep 19] fairly useful on Flat, stays 1¾m: fairly useful hurdler: won maiden at Kilbeggan in August: best effort when fourth in conditionals handicap at Punchestown shortly after end of British season: stays 21f: acts on heavy going: tried in blinkers. *Gordon Elliott, Ireland*

FALCO BLITZ (IRE) 5 b.g. Falco (USA) – Ignited (Red Ransom (USA)) [2018/19 **h115** h16.7s^pu h19g² h21.2d² h18.5g² Apr 20] €16,000 3-y-o, £40,000 4-y-o: first foal: dam ran once on Flat in France: runner-up in Irish point: fairly useful form over hurdles, runner-up last 3 starts. *Nicky Henderson*

FALCON CLIFFS (IRE) 5 b.m. Canford Cliffs (IRE) – Circle (IRE) (Galileo (IRE)) **h94 p** [2018/19 h19.4m² Dec 1] fair on Flat, stays 16.5f: 7/4, beaten 4½ lengths by Rubenesque in 2-runner mares novice at Doncaster on hurdling debut: should do better. *Tony Carroll*

FALCONS FALL (IRE) 8 ch.g. Vertical Speed (FR) – Ellie Park (IRE) (Presenting) **c–** [2018/19 c–, h–: h23.6v^pu h26d Dec 31] has had breathing operation: fair hurdler at best, **h–** has lost way: pulled up on chasing debut: stays 3m: acts on heavy going: in headgear last 3 starts: has joined Jamie Snowden. *Tom Symonds*

FALCON SUN (FR) 5 b.g. Falco (USA) – Pray For Sun (IRE) (Fantastic Light (USA)) **h114** [2018/19 h105: h16.4g h16.2g⁵ h15.5d* h15.5d* h16.3d^F h16g⁶ Mar 29] good-topped gelding: has had breathing operation: fair handicap hurdler: won at Leicester in December and January: likely to stay 2½m: acts on soft going: in blinkers last 5 starts: wears tongue tie: usually leads. *Dan Skelton*

FALCOS (FR) 7 ch.g. Falco (USA) – Olvera (IRE) (Sadler's Wells (USA)) [2018/19 h–: **c91** h20.6g c15.6m³ c17.3g⁵ c17.2g⁵ c15.6g⁴ c21.6m⁶ Oct 7] maiden hurdler: modest form over **h–** fences: stays 2¼m: in headgear last 3 starts: wears tongue tie. *Rebecca Menzies*

FALDO (IRE) 4 gr.g. Jukebox Jury (IRE) – Fusca (GER) (Lando (GER)) [2018/19 h16s² **h120** h16.3d³ Mar 1] fair on Flat, stayed 9f: fairly useful form over hurdles: dead. *Ian Williams*

FALMOUTH LIGHT (FR) 4 b.g. Cape Cross (IRE) – Wonderous Light (IRE) (Montjeu **h–** (IRE)) [2018/19 h16.2g Apr 25] fairly useful on Flat, stays 1¼m: 16/1, little impression in novice at Perth on hurdling debut. *Iain Jardine*

FAMILY MAN (IRE) 6 b.g. Gold Well – Greenacre Mandalay (IRE) (Mandalus) **h92** [2018/19 h16g⁵ h21.2g⁶ h23.8d h23.1g Mar 27] has scope: half-brother to fairly useful chaser Kandinski (2½m winner, by Bienamado): dam, well beaten in bumper, half-sister to useful hurdler (stayed 3m) Special Rate: placed twice in Irish points: modest form over hurdles: tried in visor/tongue tie. *Nigel Twiston-Davies*

FANFAN DU SEUIL (FR) 4 b.g. Racinger (FR) – Nina du Seuil (FR) (Blushing Flame **h129** (USA)) [2018/19 h16dᶠ h16.8s* h16.8d² h16.4s⁵ h17d Apr 4] good-topped gelding: fourth foal: half-brother to fair French hurdler/fairly useful chaser Casimir du Seuil (17f/2¼m winner, by Voix du Nord): dam French 1½m bumper winner (placed up to 21f over fences): won on sole start over hurdles in France for M. Seror in late-2017/18: fairly useful form in Britain: won juvenile at Exeter in November: raced around 2m: acts on soft going. *Tom George*

FANFAN LA COLMINE (FR) 4 b.g. No Risk At All (FR) – Union Leto (FR) (Laveron) **b–** [2018/19 b16.2v³ Dec 15] 5/1, well beaten in junior bumper. *Stuart Kittow*

FANZIO (FR) 4 b.g. Day Flight – Tu L'As Eu (FR) (Dark Moondancer) [2018/19 b11.4g³ **h109** b12.2g² b11.9g⁴ b11.4d⁵ h15.7s³ h16.4g* h15.7g³ h18.8d h16.2g³ Apr 25] first foal: dam **b?** French maiden (second in 2¾m cross-country chase): placed in French bumpers for B. Lefevre: fair form over hurdles: won juvenile maiden at Newcastle in January: will stay 2½m: best form on good going: in hood last 3 starts. *Richard Hobson*

FAR BIHOUE (FR) 4 b.g. Konig Turf (GER) – Vann Rouhanne (FR) (Robin des Champs **h95** (FR)) [2018/19 b16g³ b16.8s⁴ h16.3d h16g⁶ Apr 10] €4,500 3-y-o: first foal: dam unraced **b81** half-sister to fairly useful hurdler/useful chaser (stays 21f) Bagad Bihoue: modest form in bumpers/over hurdles. *Stuart Edmunds*

FARCLAS (FR) 5 gr.g. Jukebox Jury (IRE) – Floriana (GER) (Seattle Dancer (USA)) **h136** [2018/19 h149: h20g⁶ h16sᶠ h16g⁵ h16d⁵ h21spu Mar 13] good-topped gelding: smart hurdler, largely disappointing in 2018/19: unproven beyond 17f: acts on heavy going: in headgear last 3 starts: wears tongue tie. *Gordon Elliott, Ireland*

FAR CRY 6 b.m. Sakhee's Secret – Yonder (And Beyond (IRE)) [2018/19 b83: b15.7g⁵ **h59** h16g Jul 17] modest form in bumpers: well beaten in mares maiden on hurdling debut: **b82** modest maiden on Flat. *Hughie Morrison*

FARLAM KING 6 br.g. Crosspeace (IRE) – Second Bite (Gildoran) [2018/19 h16.2d **h86** h16.2g h16.2g⁶ h17.1d h16.2g h16.4g⁶ h16g⁴ h16.4m h24d² Apr 6] eighth foal: dam winning pointer: modest maiden hurdler: may prove best at short of 3m: best form on good going: wears tongue tie: usually races close up. *Maurice Barnes*

FARMER BOY (IRE) 6 b.g. Scorpion (IRE) – Absent Beauty (IRE) (Dancing Dissident **h105** (USA)) [2018/19 h88, b–: h21m⁵ h20.3gpu h20.6gur h20.6m* Apr 21] fair handicap hurdler: won at Market Rasen in April: stays 21f: acts on good to firm going: tried in blinkers/tongue tie. *Nigel Hawke*

FARMER MATT (IRE) 13 b.g. Zagreb (USA) – Ashville Native (IRE) (Be My Native **c–** (USA)) [2018/19 c100, h–: c32.5gpu May 4] lengthy, useful-looking gelding: point winner, **h–** pulled up both starts in 2019: winning hurdler/chaser: in cheekpieces last 2 starts: wears tongue tie. *Thomas Murray*

FARM THE ROCK (IRE) 8 b.g. Yeats (IRE) – Shades of Lavender (IRE) (Peintre **c109** Celebre (USA)) [2018/19 c108, h–: c22.5d h23.1g* h23 1m* h23.9d³ c23.6d⁴ c19.4g² Apr **h109** 21] lengthy gelding: has had breathing operation: Irish point winner: fair handicap hurdler: won at Bangor (novice) in October and Exeter in November: fair maiden chaser: stays 23f: acts on good to firm and good to soft going: has worn tongue tie, including last 2 starts: usually front runner/races prominently. *Katy Price*

FARNE (IRE) 5 b.m. Stowaway – Bonnies Island (IRE) (Turtle Island (IRE)) [2018/19 **b103** b16d² b15.8s² b16s³ b17d⁴ Apr 4] €12,000 3-y-o: well-made mare: first foal: dam unraced half-sister to fairly useful hurdler/useful chaser (19f-3¼m winner) Ruben Cotter: fairly useful form in bumpers: third in listed mares event at Sandown (1½ lengths behind Misty Whisky) in March and fourth in Nickel Coin Mares' National Hunt Flat Race at Aintree (5 lengths behind The Glancing Queen) in April. *Neil King*

FAROCCO (GER) 6 b.g. Shirocco (GER) – Fantasmatic (GER) (Lomitas) [2018/19 h–, **h100** b–: h16.2m³ h20.2g² h20.2gᵖᵘ h20.9m⁴ h23.3gᵖᵘ h20.1s h21.2g⁶ h19.7g h16.2d⁵ h20.2g Apr 25] has had breathing operation: fair maiden hurdler: stays 21f: acts on good to firm going: tried in cheekpieces: wears tongue tie. *Maurice Barnes*

FARRAN DANCER (IRE) 6 b.g. Winged Love (IRE) – Fairylodge Scarlet (IRE) **h–** (Mister Lord (USA)) [2018/19 h20.2g Apr 24] off mark in points at sixth attempt: tailed off in maiden on hurdling debut. *R. Mike Smith*

FARRANTS WAY (IRE) 5 b.g. Shantou (USA) – Shuil A Hocht (IRE) (Mohaajir **b96** (USA)) [2018/19 b15.8v³ b15.8s⁴ b15.7d³ Mar 20] €85,000 3-y-o: fifth foal: closely related to bumper winner/useful 2m chase winner Space Cadet (by Flemensfirth), stays 25f, and half-brother to 2 winners, including useful hurdler Gallant John Joe (2m-2¾m winner, by Presenting): dam (h96), bumper/19f hurdle winner, half-sister to useful chaser (winner up to 3m) The Outlier: fairly useful form in bumpers: best effort when fourth at Ffos Las in February. *Venetia Williams*

FAST AND FRIENDLY (IRE) 5 b.g. September Storm (GER) – Merewood Lodge **h–** (IRE) (Grand Lodge (USA)) [2018/19 h16.8g h16.4g⁶ h16.2d h16.2gᵘʳ Apr 25] poor form **b74** in bumpers: unseated first on hurdling debut: wears hood. *Barry Murtagh*

FATEH (IRE) 6 b.g. Big Bad Bob (IRE) – Passarelle (USA) (In The Wings) [2018/19 **c86** c23.6g³ Apr 26] lightly raced on Flat: point winner: in tongue tie, 14/1, third in novice hunter at Chepstow (27 lengths behind Pink Eyed Pedro) on chasing debut. *Mickey Bowen*

FATIMA BLUSH 6 b.m. Black Sam Bellamy (IRE) – Samar Qand (Selkirk (USA)) **h–** [2018/19 ab16g⁴ b17.7g⁵ h15.8gᵖᵘ Apr 11] has had breathing operation: third foal: half- **b79** sister to 2 winners on Flat, including 1½m winner The Lampo Genie (by Champs Elysees): dam ran once over hurdles/maiden on Flat: modest form in bumpers: pulled up in mares maiden on hurdling debut: in tongue tie last 2 starts. *Jamie Snowden*

FAT SAM 5 ch.g. Denham Red (FR) – Emergence (FR) (Poliglote) [2018/19 b16v h16.3s **h–** Nov 30] sturdy gelding: well beaten in bumper/maiden hurdle. *Gary Moore* **b–**

FAUGHEEN (IRE) 11 b.g. Germany (USA) – Miss Pickering (IRE) (Accordion) **h154** [2018/19 h165: h16.2g² h24gᶠ h24d³ h20dᵖᵘ Apr 4] good-topped gelding: top-class hurdler in his prime: showed plenty of ability remains in 2018/19, second in Morgiana Hurdle at Punchestown (7½ lengths behind Sharjah) in November and third in Stayers' Hurdle at Cheltenham (6¾ lengths behind Paisley Park) in March: reported to have fibrillating heart when pulled up at Aintree final start: possibly better at 3m than shorter nowadays: acts on good to firm and heavy going: tried in cheekpieces: front runner/races prominently. *W. P. Mullins, Ireland*

FAUSTINOVICK 5 b.g. Black Sam Bellamy (IRE) – Cormorant Cove (Fair Mix (IRE)) **b93 p** [2018/19 b16.3d² Mar 2] €26,000 3-y-o, £170,000 4-y-o: good-topped gelding: first foal: dam, unraced, out of half-sister to dam of top-class staying hurdler Inglis Drever: runner- up on debut in Irish point: 4/1, second in bumper at Newbury (6 lengths behind McFabulous): useful prospect. *Colin Tizzard*

FAVORI DE SIVOLA (FR) 4 b.g. Noroit (GER) – Suave de Sivola (FR) (Assessor **h95 p** (IRE)) [2018/19 h18.7s⁴ Mar 11] first foal: dam (c117/h117), French 17f-21f hurdle/chase winner, out of half-sister to dam of high-class staying hurdler Reve de Sivola: 7/1, fourth in juvenile hurdle at Stratford (19½ lengths behind Phoenician Star) on debut: will be suited by 2½m+: should improve. *Nick Williams*

FAVORITO BUCK'S (FR) 7 b.g. Buck's Boum (FR) – Sangrilla (FR) (Sanglamore **c131** (USA)) [2018/19 c132, h–: c24g⁴ c24.2m⁴ c23.8g* c23.8s⁶ c24.2sᵖᵘ c21m² Mar 31] tall **h–** gelding: winning hurdler: useful handicap chaser: won at Ascot (by 2½ lengths from Vice Et Vertu) in November: stays easy 3¼m: acts on soft and good to firm going: has worn cheekpieces, including last 4 starts: tried in tongue tie. *Paul Nicholls*

FAWSLEY SPIRIT (IRE) 6 b.g. Stowaway – Apple Trix (IRE) (Flemensfirth (USA)) **c110** [2018/19 h108: c20.9sᵘʳ c24.2s³ c26gᵖᵘ h25.5d⁴ h21.7m³ Mar 29] has had breathing **h111** operation: fair form over hurdles: similar form over fences: stays 3m: acts on soft and good to firm going: usually wears blinkers. *Ben Pauling*

FAZAMOUR (FR) 4 b.f. Legolas (JPN) – Salina d'Airy (FR) (Ungaro (GER)) [2018/19 **b–** b13m Dec 1] £7,000 3-y-o: second foal: dam, French 2m hurdle winner, half-sister to useful French 17f hurdle winner Vadero d'Airy: hooded when tailed off in junior bumper. *Ronald Thompson*

FEAR GLIC (IRE) 13 b.g. Dr Massini (IRE) – Graineuaile (IRE) (Orchestra) [2018/19 **c108** c103, h–: c20g⁴ c23g² c22.6m² c21g⁶ c24sᵖᵘ c22.6g* Aug 23] winning hurdler: fair **h–** handicap chaser: won at Stratford in August: stays 23f: acts on good to firm and heavy going: in headgear last 5 starts: front runner/races prominently. *Jackie du Plessis*

FEARLESS (IRE) 4 b.g. Arakan (USA) – La Spezia (IRE) (Danehill Dancer (IRE)) **b89** [2018/19 b15.3g* b14d⁵ Jan 1] lengthy gelding: sixth foal: half-brother to 2 winners, including smart hurdler Thomas Hobson (2m-21f winner, by Halling): dam, 8.6f winner, half-sister to useful hurdler/smart chaser (stayed 21f) Torphichen: fair form in bumpers: won junior event at Wincanton in December for Oliver Sherwood. *Rebecca Menzies*

FEARNIE LOU (IRE) 5 b.m. Mahler – Wet And Dry (IRE) (Catcher In The Rye (IRE)) **h–** [2018/19 b–: b15.8d h16g h16g h16.7m Aug 5] compact mare: no form in bumpers/over **b–** hurdles. *Christian Williams*

FEARSOME 5 b.g. Makfi – Lixian (Linamix (FR)) [2018/19 h16g⁵ h16m* h15.7m³ Nov **h113** 3] dam half-sister to fairly useful hurdler (stayed 3m) Harristown: useful on Flat, stays 2m: fair form over hurdles: won novice at Fakenham in October. *Nick Littmoden*

FEARSOME FRED 10 b.g. Emperor Fountain – Ryewater Dream (Touching Wood **c86** (USA)) [2018/19 h91: h23.3d h25d⁴ c23.6dᶠ h25d² c23.6d⁶ c24.2s⁶ c25.1gᶠ c25.1s⁵ **h85** c25.1g⁵ Apr 3] modest maiden hurdler: similar form over fences: stays 25f: acts on soft going. *Dr Jeremy Naylor*

FEDERICI 10 b.g. Overbury (IRE) – Vado Via (Ardross) [2018/19 c129, h–: c25.9s⁵ c24g **c128** c25gᵖᵘ Apr 6] sturdy gelding: winning hurdler: fairly useful handicap chaser: fifth in **h–** Becher Chase at Aintree in December: stays 3¼m: acts on heavy going: wears headgear. *Donald McCain*

FEEL THE PINCH 5 b.g. Librettist (USA) – Liqueur Rose (Alflora (IRE)) [2018/19 b–: **b82** b15.8g⁶ Apr 11] good-topped gelding: modest form in bumpers. *Fergal O'Brien*

FEETRONIE DE KERVI (FR) 4 b.f. No Risk At All (FR) – Malandra (Mtoto) **b–** [2018/19 b12.4s Dec 8] half-sister to several winners, including fairly useful French hurdler/chaser Bretaye (17f-2½m winner, by Astarabad) and useful hurdler/winning chaser Chablais (2m/21f winner, by Saint des Saints): dam ran once in bumper: in hood, well beaten in junior bumper. *James Ewart*

FELICIDAD (FR) 4 b.f. Racinger (FR) – Sacade (FR) (Robin des Champs (FR)) **b85** [2018/19 b11.9d⁴ b13.1g² b14g² b13.7m³ Mar 29] lengthy, rather unfurnished filly: half-sister to several winners, including French bumper winner/useful hurdler Bloody Mary (2m-2¼m winner, by Fragrant Mix) and French hurdler/chaser Daimiel (19f/2½m winner, by Gris de Gris): dam ran once in French bumper: fair form in bumpers. *Nick Williams*

FELIX DESJY (FR) 6 ch.g. Maresca Sorrento (FR) – Lamadoun (FR) (Smadoun **h146** (FR)) [2018/19 b112: h16.3d* h16d h20d⁵ h20s² h16d* h16.4s⁵ h16.5d* Apr 5]
   There were decidedly mixed fortunes for the latest crop of Gigginstown novice hurdlers at the major spring festivals. None of them carried expectations as high as those that had accompanied Samcro the year before, but the Gordon Elliott-trained pair Battleoverdoyen and Commander of Fleet were leading fancies for their respective races among the team Gigginstown sent to Cheltenham. Battleoverdoyen is a big, rangy chasing type who really fills the eye but he lost his unbeaten record when favourite for the Baring Bingham in which he was eventually pulled up. Commander of Fleet, another future chaser, fared better in his race, the Spa, when two lengths second to Minella Indo, but he too ended his campaign amiss, losing his action when pulled up in the War of Attrition Novices' Hurdle won by the same horse at Punchestown. Two more Gigginstown novices trained by Gordon Elliott, Dallas des Pictons (sent off favourite) and Defi Bleu, were placed in the Martin Pipe Conditional Jockeys' Handicap at Cheltenham, but they also finished their campaigns on low notes, Dallas des Pictons trailing home in the Sefton at Aintree, also reportedly losing his action, and Defi Bleu going wrong in the War of Attrition, said to have struck into himself. Felix Desjy, on the other hand, who had proved himself useful but not particularly progressive beforehand, managed to avoid any such mishaps and represented Elliott and Gigginstown at all three big meetings, winning at Aintree and running well in defeat at Punchestown.
   First, though, was the Supreme Novices' Hurdle at Cheltenham in which Felix Desjy, backed at long odds, was simply beaten on merit, after holding every chance two out, eventually finishing eleven lengths behind the winner Klassical

Betway Top Novices' Hurdle, Aintree—
Felix Desjy makes all under an enterprising ride from Jack Kennedy

Dream in fifth. Felix Desjy was held up on that occasion by Sean Flanagan, though the rider had been able to adopt much more positive tactics to really good effect in a smaller field for the Grade 2 Sky Bet Moscow Flyer Novices' Hurdle at Punchestown in January in which Felix Desjy was soon in a clear lead and ended up winning by five lengths from the useful Jetez. Jack Kennedy rode the stable's other Gigginstown runner in the Supreme, Vision d'Honneur, who finished ninth, but he was reunited with Felix Desjy for the Betway Top Novices' Hurdle at Aintree. Kennedy had been on board when Felix Desjy was an impressive ten-length winner of a maiden at Galway in October on his hurdling debut. Felix Desjy wore a hood on his first three starts over hurdles and the headgear was back on at Aintree where the smaller field—he had six to beat in an open-looking race—proved ideal for forcing tactics to be successfully employed again. Soon building a clear lead and going with zest, Felix Desjy misjudged the fourth where he stood off too far and dragged his hind legs through the flight, but he maintained his advantage and was still going well turning for home. Still in front but with a reduced lead jumping the last, Felix Desjy found extra on the run-in to hold off the favourite Aramon, who had finished just a head behind him in sixth in the Supreme, by a length and a half. Beaten another seven lengths was the Kelso Grade 2 winner Rouge Vif who chased the winner for a long way and just held on to take third by a head from Itchy Feet, who had finished in front of both the first two when third in the Supreme but never looked like threatening on this occasion. The same tactics didn't pay off to quite the same effect in the Champion Novices' Hurdle at Punchestown, but Felix Desjy confirmed the improvement he had shown at Aintree with another smart performance, finishing closer to Klassical Dream than he had done at Cheltenham. Even so, the result was in little doubt once Klassical Dream loomed up to him two out, though Felix Desjy kept on to finish clear of the rest, five and a half lengths behind the winner.

Felix Desjy had won his only start in points (already in Gigginstown ownership) as a four-year-old and was successful on his first two starts in bumpers later that year, at Punchestown and Down Royal, though he proved too headstrong when contesting the Grade 1 bumpers at Cheltenham and Punchestown the following spring. Cheltenham was the first time he was tried in a hood and he probably did well to finish sixth behind Relegate given how hard he pulled under restraint. The hood was left off when he was allowed to make the running at Punchestown, but he refused to settle and weakened into fifth. Felix Desjy didn't initially build on the promise of his winning debut over hurdles when he returned in the autumn and was beaten on his next three starts. The first two of those were Grade 3 novice contests at Navan (he was last of seven behind Aramon in the first of them), before he finished second to the Willie Mullins-trained mare Salsaretta at Limerick on Boxing Day in a minor event for horses that had not won more than once over hurdles. He was collared at the last after establishing a large lead; that race was over two and a half miles, and for his remaining starts he was kept to two miles.

Felix Desjy (FR) (ch.g. 2013)	Maresca Sorrento (FR) (b 1995)	Cadoudal (br 1979)	Green Dancer / Come To Sea
		French Free Star (b 1981)	Carmarthen / Vaga
	Lamadoun (FR) (gr 2003)	Smadoun (gr 1990)	Kaldoun / Mossma
		Lamakara (b 1990)	Akarad / Lady Jeff

Felix Desjy was one of Gigginstown's less expensive acquisitions, picked up for just €29,000 as an unbroken three-year-old at the Goffs Land Rover Sale in 2016. His French sire Maresca Sorrento, who died from colic in 2017, is best known in Britain as the sire of the 2014 Grand National winner Pineau de Re. Felix Desjy's dam Lamadoun ran only four times over jumps in France, winning a chase over nearly two and a half miles at Gemozac. Felix Desjy is her third foal and second winner after Carladoun (by Roli Abi) who raced only on the Flat, winning five times at up to an extended thirteen furlongs. Felix Desjy's grandam Lamakara was also a Flat performer, winning three times at up to a mile and a half, though all four of her winners were successful over jumps, two of them, Eaux Les Coeurs and L'Eau du Nil successful in Britain, the latter being a fairly useful hurdler. The great grandam

Gigginstown House Stud's "Felix Desjy"

Lady Jeff was a five-time winner in Austria who bred the Prix Penelope winner La Monalisa, and she was also a half-sister to the high-class French middle-distance colt Bon Sang whose wins included the Criterium de Saint-Cloud and Prix Niel. The tall and still rather unfurnished Felix Desjy is best making the running around two miles and he should make into an exciting novice over fences. He acts on soft ground. He wore a hood in the parade ring, and ear plugs in the race itself, at Cheltenham. *Gordon Elliott, Ireland*

FELIX MENDELSSOHN (IRE) 8 b.g. Galileo (IRE) – Ice Queen (IRE) (Danehill Dancer (IRE)) [2018/19 h110: h16.2g h16.2s⁵ h17.1v h16.4s⁵ h15.6g h16g⁶ h16d⁶ h16.2d h16.8d² Apr 23] modest maiden hurdler: unproven beyond 17f: acts on soft going: in blinkers last 2 starts: usually wears tongue tie: usually front runner/races prominently. *Stuart Coltherd* **h91**

FENJACK (IRE) 7 b.g. Jimble (FR) – Katie Baby (IRE) (Bustomi) [2018/19 h24d⁶ h24sᵖᵘ h15.7sᵖᵘ c23.6d⁴ c26.3g⁴ c23.6g⁴ c23.6gᶠ Apr 22] runner-up on second start in maiden points: no form over hurdles: poor form over fences: stayed 3m: usually wore headgear: dead. *Laura Morgan* **c73 h—**

FENLONS COURT (IRE) 7 b.g. Court Cave (IRE) – Classic Note (IRE) (Classic Secret (USA)) [2018/19 h97, b82: h22g² h21.7m⁷ h23.1s⁵ h19.8s³ h19.8s⁶ h26.5g⁵ Apr 20] lengthy, rather sparely-made gelding: placed in 2 Irish maiden points: fair handicap hurdler: won at Fontwell in October: stays 2¾m: acts on soft and good to firm going: usually front runner/races prominently. *Seamus Mullins* **h106**

FENLON'S HILL (IRE) 8 b.g. Court Cave (IRE) – Eva's Lass (IRE) (Flemensfirth (USA)) [2018/19 c118, h94: c17d⁵ c19.7g* c23.5g² c22.5d h20.8g³ c20.1g⁴ c20g³ c18.2d h18.8g c19.5g Apr 11] modest maiden hurdler: fairly useful handicap chaser: won at Down Royal in May: stays 23f: acts on soft going: tried in cheekpieces: has worn tongue tie. *Paul Stafford, Ireland* **c122 h98**

FENRIR BINDING 4 b.g. Norse Dancer (IRE) – Bethany Lewis (Sir Harry Lewis (USA)) [2018/19 b16d⁶ Mar 28] 50/1, sixth in maiden bumper at Warwick. *Giles Smyly* **b76**

FERGALL (IRE) 12 br.g. Norwich – Gaybrook Girl (IRE) (Alderbrook) [2018/19 c—, h135: h15.9g h16.5dᶠ Dec 30] useful handicap hurdler at best: well held only start over fences: stayed 2½m: acted on soft and good to firm going: often in cheekpieces: dead. *Seamus Mullins* **c— h120**

FERGIETHELEGEND (IRE) 13 b.g. Flying Legend (USA) – Hardy Cracker (IRE) (Lord Americo) [2018/19 c25v* c24g² c25.3g⁴ c25.3g c23s c25g c24.6g³ c24d³ c25s³ c24.1d Feb 6] maiden hurdler: modest handicap chaser: won at Wexford early in season: stays 25f: acts on heavy going: wears headgear: tried in tongue tie: front runner/races prominently. *John G. Carr, Ireland* **c88 h—**

FERLOCH 4 b.g. Rail Link – Modesta (IRE) (Sadler's Wells (USA)) [2018/19 b16.2g Feb 14] in rear in bumper. *Alistair Whillans* **b—**

FERROBIN (IRE) 5 br.g. Robin des Champs (FR) – Fedaia (IRE) (Anabaa (USA)) [2018/19 b87p: b16g³ h15.8g² h15.8d* h16s² h22gᶠ Apr 14] sturdy gelding: has had breathing operation: fairly useful form in bumpers: similar form over hurdles: won novice at Huntingdon in March. *Dan Skelton* **h122 b95**

FERRY ALL (FR) 4 ch.g. No Risk At All (FR) – Ohe Les Aulmes (FR) (Lute Antique (FR)) [2018/19 b16.2g Feb 14] 9/1, ninth in bumper at Kelso (8½ lengths behind Enlighten). *Brian Ellison* **b77**

FESTIVAL DAWN 7 b.m. Kayf Tara – Keel Road (IRE) (Luso) [2018/19 h112p: h19.5d² h20.6g h20.7g⁴ Feb 21] maiden pointer: fair maiden hurdler: bred to stay 3m. *Philip Hobbs* **h105**

FESTIVAL D'EX (FR) 4 b.g. Saddler Maker (IRE) – Une d'Ex (FR) (Brier Creek (USA)) €30,000 3-y-o: second foal: dam, French bumper maiden, half-sister to fairly useful French chaser up to 3¼m Azrou d'Ex: 9/1, created very good impression when winning 19-runner Goffs Land Rover Bumper at Punchestown shortly after end of British season by 10 lengths from Whatsnotoknow, still plenty to do 4f out but staying on strongly to lead around 1f out: exciting prospect. *Gordon Elliott, Ireland* **b115 p**

FESTIVE AFFAIR (IRE) 11 b.g. Presenting – Merry Batim (IRE) (Alphabatim (USA)) [2018/19 c135: c16m* c16m³ c17m⁴ Jul 22] tall gelding: useful handicap chaser: won at Ludlow (by 2¼ lengths from Noche de Reyes) in May: unproven beyond 17f: acts on soft and good to firm going: usually wears cheekpieces: wears tongue tie: front runner/races prominently. *Jonjo O'Neill* **c137**

FEU ARDENT (FR) 4 ch.g. Secret Singer (FR) – Vierge Sainte (FR) (Robin des Champs (FR)) [2018/19 b13.2m⁴ Oct 23] has had breathing operation: in tongue tie, 7/2, fourth in junior bumper at Exeter (13¼ lengths behind Ripplet). *Christian Williams* **b68**

FIBONACCI 5 ch.g. Galileo (IRE) – Tereschenko (USA) (Giant's Causeway (USA)) [2018/19 h16.3d h15.7v⁴ h16.6g⁶ Jan 9] fairly useful on Flat, stays 2m: modest form over hurdles. *Alan King* **h85**

FIDDLERS BOW (IRE) 10 b.g. Whitmore's Conn (USA) – Soraleda (IRE) (Toulon) [2018/19 c25.5d³ c20.1g² c16.5s* c21.5d* Jan 20] has had breathing operation: winning hurdler: fair handicap chaser: won twice at Ayr in January: stays 23f: acts on heavy going: has worn blinkers/tongue tie. *Julia Brooke* **c110 h–**

FIDUX (FR) 6 b.g. Fine Grain (JPN) – Folle Tempete (FR) (Fabulous Dancer (USA)) [2018/19 h128: h19g³ h18.5g⁴ h15.7g* h15.7m* h15.7s h16.5g h20.3g³ Apr 17] compact gelding: useful handicap hurdler: won at Southwell in October and listed event at Ascot (by 8 lengths from Global Citizen) in November: stays 2½m: acts on soft and good to firm going. *Alan King* **h138**

FIELD EXHIBITION (IRE) 9 b.m. Great Exhibition (USA) – Leefield Rose (IRE) (Parthian Springs) [2018/19 h16v c16m⁶ c20gᶠ c16m⁵ c20g* c20.9mᶠ c16.3s³ h20.3g³ h20gᵘʳ c20gᶠ h16.8m⁶ h19.5g⁵ h21d* h15.8d² h19.9v* h19d⁶ h16d³ h21.2d² h23.8g* h16.8s⁶ h21.2m⁵ h21.9g⁶ Apr 21] fourth foal: sister to modest hurdler/fair chaser Omega Springs (2m winner) and half-sister to a winning pointer by Bach: dam unraced: fair handicap hurdler: won at Warwick (mares) in November, Uttoxeter (conditionals) in December and Musselburgh (mares) in February: fair handicap chaser: won at Worcester in July: left Liam Casey after third start, Christian Williams after fourteenth: stays 3m, at least when emphasis is on speed: acts on heavy going: wears hood. *Grace Harris* **c103 h111**

FIELDS OF FIRE 5 b.g. Aqlaam – Blazing Field (Halling (USA)) [2018/19 b16.2g b16.2m b16.8g Oct 21] has had breathing operation: well held in bumpers: poor maiden on Flat. *Alistair Whillans* **b–**

FIELDS OF FORTUNE 5 b.g. Champs Elysees – Widescreen (USA) (Distant View (USA)) [2018/19 h107: h16.7m* h16.7g⁴ h16.4g h23.5s Dec 22] compact gelding: fair hurdler: won maiden at Market Rasen in August: best effort at 17f: acts on good to firm going. *Alan King* **h107**

FIELDS OF GLORY (FR) 9 b.g. King's Best (USA) – Lavandou (Sadler's Wells (USA)) [2018/19 c102, h–: c20.5mᶠ h21.6g h23.8gᵖᵘ Nov 26] fair hurdler/chaser at best, no form in 2018/19: tried in visor: wears tongue tie. *Tim Vaughan* **c– h–**

FIERCLY FORGIE (IRE) 6 b.g. Court Cave (IRE) – Bosanova Girl (IRE) (Exit To Nowhere (USA)) [2018/19 h22.1s⁴ h20.1s⁶ h21.2g h15.8g Nov 17] first foal: dam, no impact in points, half-sister to useful hurdler/high-class chaser (stayed 2¾m) Sound Investment: Irish point winner: poor form over hurdles: has joined Donald McCain. *James Moffatt* **h81**

FIESOLE 7 b.g. Montjeu (IRE) – Forgotten Dreams (IRE) (Olden Times) [2018/19 h16.2d h16g* h15.7s h16.5g⁶ h16.3sᶠ h15.9g* Apr 21] small, close-coupled gelding: fairly useful on Flat, stays 1¾m: useful handicap hurdler: won at Tipperary in October and Plumpton (by 9 lengths from Legal History) in April: left Eoin Doyle after second start: raced only at 2m: acts on good to firm and heavy going: has worn hood. *Olly Murphy* **h131**

FIFTH SYMPHONY (IRE) 5 b.g. Mahler – Nicolemma (IRE) (Heron Island (IRE)) [2018/19 b16.3d h21.3s⁵ h21.6d⁶ h21gᵖᵘ Apr 10] €24,000 3-y-o: tall, rather unfurnished gelding: third foal: dam runner-up in point: modest form in bumper: fair form over hurdles: best effort when fifth in novice at Wetherby in December. *Ben Pauling* **h103 b79**

FIFTY BALES OF HAY 6 ch.m. Indian Haven – Leading Role (Cadeaux Genereux) [2018/19 b15.3m May 15] sixth foal: half-sister to 2 winners, including bumper winner/fair 2m hurdle winner Seefin Dancer (by Groom Dancer): dam, 7f winner, half-sister to fairly useful hurdler (stayed 19f) Lindop: tailed off in mares bumper/minor event on Flat. *Brendan Powell* **b–**

FIFTY PEACH WAY 7 b.m. Black Sam Bellamy (IRE) – Aphrodisia (Sakhee (USA)) [2018/19 h72: h15.7g⁴ h18.7m⁴ h15.8gᶠ Jul 27] poor form in bumpers/over hurdles. *Alex Swinswood* **h82**

FIFTY SHADES (IRE) 6 gr.g. Tajraasi (USA) – Baylough Mist (IRE) (Cloudings (IRE)) [2018/19 c77p, h–: c20g* h25g² h23.4g* c25.8g* c23.8m³ c23.9mᵖᵘ c25g² c24.2s⁵ c26g⁴ c23.9s⁵ c25.2m² c24.2g* c24gⁱ c29.2g* Apr 10] good-topped gelding: modest form over **c109 h88 p**

hurdles: won novice handicap at Fakenham in June: fair handicap chaser: won at Worcester in May, Newton Abbot in July, Fakenham in March and Warwick in April: stays 29f: acts on good to firm going: should do better as a hurdler. *Christian Williams*

FIGARELLA BORGET (FR) 4 b.f. Network (GER) – Kashima (FR) (Kadalko (FR)) **b–** [2018/19 b15.7d b16m⁶ Apr 22] first foal: dam, French 2½m-3m cross-country chase winner, half-sister to outstanding 2m-2½m chaser Sprinter Sacre (by Network): well held in 2 bumpers. *Stuart Edmunds*

FIGEAC (FR) 5 gr.g. Kendargent (FR) – Faviva (USA) (Storm Cat (USA)) [2018/19 h91: **h86** h15.8g⁴ h20.3g Sep 5] modest maiden hurdler: unproven beyond 2m: in blinkers last 2 starts: wears tongue tie. *Nick Littmoden*

FIGHT COMMANDER (IRE) 10 b.g. Oscar (IRE) – Creidim (IRE) (Erins Isle) **c108 §** [2018/19 c105§, h–: c24s⁵ c21.6d² c21.4d³ c23.6gᵖᵘ h23.9d⁵ Apr 24] lengthy gelding: has **h–** had breathing operation: maiden hurdler: fair handicap chaser: stays 29f: acts on good to firm and heavy going: wears headgear: tried in tongue tie: moody. *Olly Murphy*

FIGHT FOR LOVE (FR) 6 b.g. Fuisse (FR) – Love Affair (FR) (Arctic Tern (USA)) **h–** [2018/19 h–, b82: h20.5s h20.5s Dec 17] modest form in bumpers: no form over hurdles. *Laura Mongan*

FIGHTING BACK 8 b.g. Galileo (IRE) – Maroochydore (IRE) (Danehill (USA)) **h72** [2018/19 h68: h16.2d h16.8g³ May 15] robust, workmanlike gelding: poor maiden hurdler: raced around 2m. *Henry Hogarth*

FIG'S PRIDE (IRE) 6 br.m. Stowaway – Roseboreen (IRE) (Roselier (FR)) [2018/19 b–: **h–** h16.2g h16.4g h16.2d⁴ Apr 26] sturdy mare: poor form in bumpers: no form over hurdles: usually in hood. *N. W. Alexander*

FILATORE (IRE) 10 ch.g. Teofilo (IRE) – Dragnet (IRE) (Rainbow Quest (USA)) **h57 §** [2018/19 h74§: h23.9d⁶ h20v³ h21.9vᵖᵘ Jan 14] sturdy gelding: poor handicap hurdler: stays 2¾m: acts on heavy going: wears headgear: has worn tongue tie: moody. *Bernard Llewellyn*

FILEMON 7 gr.g. Kayf Tara – L'Ultima (FR) (Verglas (IRE)) [2018/19 h–, b83: c16.3sᵘʳ **c99** c22.6g³ c20g⁵ h16.7g³ h15.9sᵖᵘ Dec 17] lengthy gelding: has had breathing operation: **h98** modest form over hurdles: similar form over fences: best effort when third in novice handicap at Stratford in September: stays 23f: best form on good going: tried in hood: wears tongue tie. *Jamie Snowden*

FILIPINE (FR) 4 gr.f. Network (GER) – Promo d'Alienor (FR) (April Night (FR)) **h69** [2018/19 b15.7g⁶ b14gᶠ b14d h16.6g⁶ h16.6g⁶ h16.8d Feb 22] angular filly: fifth foal: sister **b60** to 2 winners, including fairly useful 19f hurdle winner Denwork, and half-sister to French bumper/19f hurdle winner Elzillera (by Buck's Boum): dam French 11.5f-12.5f bumper winner: poor form in bumpers/over hurdles: tried in headgear/tongue tie. *Richard Hobson*

FILLE DES CHAMPS (IRE) 8 b.m. Robin des Champs (FR) – South Queen Lady **c95** (IRE) (King's Ride) [2018/19 h101: h21.2m³ h23.9d* c20.9v c19.4vᵖᵘ c25.2d⁴ Mar 9] **h105** sturdy mare: fair handicap hurdler: won at Ffos Las in May: modest form over fences: stays 3m: acts on heavy going: tried in cheekpieces: wears tongue tie. *Evan Williams*

FILLYDELPHIA (IRE) 8 b.m. Strategic Prince – Lady Fonic (Zafonic (USA)) [2018/19 **h–** h75: h16.4mᵘʳ Mar 22] poor maiden hurdler: raced mainly around 2m: tried in hood: modest/temperamental on Flat. *Liam Bailey*

FINAGHY AYR (IRE) 11 ch.g. Lahib (USA) – Ali Ankah (IRE) (Insan (USA)) [2018/19 **c92 x** c102x, h–: c26.9d c24.1dᵖᵘ c31.9v³ c26.2dᵖᵘ Mar 24] winning hurdler: modest handicap **h–** chaser: stays 4m: acts on heavy going: wears cheekpieces: tried in tongue tie: usually races towards rear: makes mistakes over fences. *Ian Duncan*

FINAL CHOICE 6 b.g. Makfi – Anasazi (IRE) (Sadler's Wells (USA)) [2018/19 h117: **h117** h20g h16s* h17.7vᵘʳ h16s* h15.8g³ Mar 19] good-topped gelding: fairly useful handicap hurdler: won at Lingfield in November: left Warren Greatrex after first start: should stay beyond 2m: acts on heavy going: wears headgear: tried in tongue tie. *Adam West*

FINAL NUDGE (IRE) 10 b.g. Kayf Tara – Another Shot (IRE) (Master Willie) [2018/19 **c110** c139, h–: c24d c29.5sᵖᵘ c25.1g Feb 16] strong gelding: has had breathing operation: **h–** winning hurdler: useful handicap chaser: well below form in 2018/19: probably best up to 29f: acts on heavy going: has worn cheekpieces, including in 2018/19: tried in tongue tie. *David Dennis*

FINAL REMINDER (IRE) 7 b.m. Gold Well – Olde Kilcormac (IRE) (Supreme **h108** Leader) [2018/19 h84: h21.4g* h25.4g* h24.7g* h24.3m Apr 12] won Irish maiden point on debut: fair handicap hurdler: won at Ayr and Cartmel (mares) in May, and Aintree (mares) in June: stays 25f: best form on good going. *N. W. Alexander*

FINALSHOT 6 b.g. Phoenix Reach (IRE) – Ryoshi (Rakaposhi King) [2018/19 b96: **h112** h15.8g² h19.6d h19.4gᵘʳ Feb 20] useful-looking gelding: fairly useful form in bumpers: fair form over hurdles. *Henry Daly*

FINANCIAL CLIMATE (IRE) 12 b.g. Exit To Nowhere (USA) – Claudia's Pearl **c97** (Deploy) [2018/19 c–, h–: c23g⁴ c24.5v³ c24.2d Apr 9] lengthy gelding: point winner: **h–** winning hurdler: modest hunter chaser nowadays: stays 3¼m: acts on heavy going: wears headgear. *Major Harry Wallace*

FINANCIAL CONDUCT (IRE) 5 b.g. Harbour Watch (IRE) – Popolo (IRE) (Fasliyev **h114 p** (USA)) [2018/19 h21.2g² Jan 3] dam half-sister to fairly useful hurdler (stayed 2½m) Ivan Vasilevich: useful on Flat, stays 1½m: 13/2, plenty of encouragement when second in maiden at Ludlow (4 lengths behind Smackwater Jack) on hurdling debut: entitled to progress. *Charlie Mann*

FINANCIAL OUTCOME (IRE) 6 b.g. Financial Reward (IRE) – Catriona's Mare **h122** (IRE) (Taipan (IRE)) [2018/19 h25.5s³ h20v³ h24.2d⁴ h21d² h23g² Apr 13] £50,000 5-y-o: fourth foal: half-brother to a winning pointer by Rock Hopper: dam placed in point: Irish point winner: fairly useful form over hurdles: fourth in handicap at Newbury in March: stays 3m: acts on heavy going: wears tongue tie. *Rebecca Curtis*

FINANCIER 6 ch.g. Dubawi (IRE) – Desired (Rainbow Quest (USA)) [2018/19 b16s³ **b83** b15.8s b16d⁵ Apr 6] £16,000 3-y-o, £115,000 5-y-o: half-brother to numerous winners on Flat, including smart French performers up to around 1½m Poet Laureate (by Highest Honor) and Desideratum (by Darshaan): dam unraced: won point on debut: modest form in bumpers: best effort when third at Chepstow in December. *Kerry Lee*

FIN AND GAME (IRE) 7 b.g. Oscar (IRE) – Miss Cilla (IRE) (Shernazar) [2018/19 **c116** h125: c15.9d⁶ c16.4s⁵ h15.7v² h16.5gᵖᵘ Apr 6] fairly useful form over hurdles: second in **h123** handicap at Haydock in December: similar form over fences: raced around 2m: acts on heavy going. *Donald McCain*

FINAWN BAWN (IRE) 6 b.g. Robin des Champs (FR) – Kayanti (IRE) (Old Vic) **h130** [2018/19 b16g* h16v³ h19.6v* h21g³ h20.7d* Mar 13] third foal: dam unraced sister to **b98** useful hurdler/fairly useful chaser (stayed 3¼m) Bellflower Boy: won bumper at Ayr (by 8 lengths from Leather Belly) on debut in May: useful form over hurdles: won novices at Bangor in December and Huntingdon (by ¾ length from Kingofthecotswolds) in March: third in Leamington Novices' Hurdle at Warwick (5¼ lengths behind Beakstown) in between: will be suited by 3m: usually responds generously to pressure. *Olly Murphy*

FINCH FANCY 7 b.m. Arvico (FR) – Ewar Finch (FR) (Kayf Tara) [2018/19 b16.8g⁶ **b67** b17.7g b16.8g⁵ Jul 6] second foal: dam winning pointer: well held in point: poor form in bumpers. *Richard Mitchell*

FINDLAY'S FIND (IRE) 13 ch.g. Medicean – Lady Pahia (IRE) (Pivotal) [2018/19 **c100 x** c25.3g² May 4] good-topped gelding: prolific point winner: fair hunter chaser: stays 3½m: acts on good to soft going: has worn headgear: tried in tongue tie: often let down by jumping. *Mrs Julie Mansell*

FINDUSATGORCOMBE 7 b.g. Tobougg (IRE) – Seemma (Romany Rye) [2018/19 **c91** h79: c25.8gᵖᵘ c26g* c25.8m² c25.8mᵖᵘ c25.8gᵖᵘ c24g c26g² c26v² c24.2s⁴ c25.1g² c25.1s* **h–** c26.7g² Mar 25] winning hurdler: modest handicap chaser: won novice events at Fontwell in June and Wincanton in March: stays 27f: acts on good to firm and heavy going: wears tongue tie: races prominently. *Jimmy Frost*

FINE ARK 6 b.m. Multiplex – Do It On Dani (Weld) [2018/19 h–, b–: h20.3gᵖᵘ Jul 15] **h–** well held in bumper: pulled up both starts over hurdles. *Henry Daly*

FINE BRUNELLO (FR) 4 b.g. Al Namix (FR) – Sweet Brune (FR) (Laveron) [2018/19 **h125** b11.9g b11.9g* h17.9s⁴ h16s⁴ h16.8d² h16.4s Mar 13] compact gelding: second foal: **b?** brother to French 1½m bumper winner Dark And Sweet: dam French 11f-13.5f bumper winner and 2¼m hurdle winner: won maiden bumper at Vittel in August: fairly useful form over hurdles: second in Triumph Hurdle Trial (Finesse) at Cheltenham (13 lengths behind Fakir d'Oudairies) in January: left G. Cherel after third start: should be suited by further than 2m. *Joseph Patrick O'Brien, Ireland*

FINE RIGHTLY (IRE) 11 b.g. Alflora (IRE) – Bealtaine (IRE) (Zaffaran (USA)) **c–** [2018/19 c139, h134: h21.4s³ Jan 2] useful handicap hurdler: third at Ayr sole start in **h129** 2018/19: useful chaser: stays 3¼m: acts on heavy going: usually wears hood: has worn tongue tie: usually races nearer last than first. *Stuart Crawford, Ireland*

FINE THEATRE (IRE) 9 b.g. King's Theatre (IRE) – Finemar Lady (IRE) (Montelimar **c–** (USA)) [2018/19 h21.9s c25.9s^F h20s h20s c23.5g^{pu} h20.3s* Mar 17] fairly useful handicap **h123** hurdler: won at Wexford in March: fairly useful chaser, failed to complete both starts over fences in 2018/19: stays 3m: acts on heavy going: usually wears headgear: has worn tongue tie. *Paul Nolan, Ireland*

FINGAL GIRL (IRE) 7 ch.m. Thewayyouare (USA) – She's Our Girl (IRE) (Royal **h–** Abjar (USA)) [2018/19 h15.3g^F Feb 27] dam half-sister to high-class hurdler up to 3m Golden Cross: tailed off only start on Flat, for S. J. Treacy in 2014: fell first on hurdling debut. *Steven Dixon*

FINGERONTHESWITCH (IRE) 9 b.g. Beneficial – Houseoftherisinsun (IRE) **c122** (Fourstars Allstar (USA)) [2018/19 c–, h120: h25g* h26.4m³ h23.1g h23g⁵ h24g⁴ c24.2g* **h117** c25.1g³ c24.2g³ Apr 11] lengthy gelding: has had breathing operation: fairly useful handicap hurdler: won at Huntingdon early in season: fairly useful handicap chaser: won at Wetherby in November: stays 25f: acts on heavy going: wears cheekpieces/tongue tie: usually races towards rear. *Neil Mulholland*

FINISH THE STORY (IRE) 13 b.g. Court Cave (IRE) – Lady of Grange (IRE) **c75** (Phardante (FR)) [2018/19 c90, h–: c24d⁶ May 5] compact gelding: winning hurdler: **h–** modest handicap chaser, below form sole start in 2018/19: out-and-out stayer: acts on heavy going: wears headgear/tongue tie. *Johnny Farrelly*

FINLEY'S EYES (IRE) 6 b.g. Beneficial – Badia Dream (IRE) (Old Vic) [2018/19 **h98** b87p: h16g¹ h16d² h16.3g² h16g Nov 9] rangy gelding: modest form only start in bumpers: similar form over hurdles: in hood last 3 starts: pulls hard. *Dan Skelton*

FINNEGAN'S GARDEN (IRE) 10 b.g. Definite Article – Tri Folene (FR) (Nebos **c100** (GER)) [2018/19 c95, h–: c20s² c20d c19.7s³ c19.7d² c19.2v⁶ c17.8v* c19.7g* c17.8g* **h–** Apr 12] sturdy gelding: lightly-raced hurdler: fair handicap chaser: completed hat-trick at Fontwell (twice) and Plumpton (conditionals) in March/April: stays 2½m: acts on heavy going: has worn hood. *Zoe Davison*

FINNICK GLORY (IRE) 5 gr.m. Fame And Glory – Jeu de Dame (Perugino (USA)) **b81** [2018/19 b15.7d⁴ b14d² Dec 19] £10,000 3-y-o: sixth foal: half-sister to bumper winner Stigh Collain (by Until Sundown): dam, French 1m winner, sister to top-class/ungenuine 2m hurdler Harchibald: modest form in bumpers. *Martin Keighley*

FIOSRACH (IRE) 9 b.g. Bachelor Duke – Saana (IRE) (Erins Isle) [2018/19 **h84** h106: h17.2g⁶ h17.2g^{ur} h15.8g h16.4s³ h16d Feb 25] compact gelding: poor handicap hurdler nowadays: unproven beyond 2m: acts on soft going³: has worn cheekpieces, including in 2018/19: has worn tongue tie. *James Moffatt*

FIRE AHEAD (IRE) 6 b.g. Yeats (IRE) – Ring of Fire (USA) (Nureyev (USA)) [2018/19 **c–** h58: h18.6g h20.6s^F h15.3g h19d c24g^{pu} Apr 25] pulled up only start in Irish points: no **h–** form over hurdles: pulled up in novice handicap on chasing debut. *Ian Williams*

FIREBIRD FLYER (IRE) 12 b.g. Winged Love (IRE) – Kiora Lady (IRE) (King's **c114 x** Ride) [2018/19 c–, h104: c25.2s² c30.7s^{pu} h23.1s² Mar 5] small, sturdy gelding: fair **h114** handicap hurdler/chaser nowadays: stays 33f: acts on heavy going: has worn headgear: tried in tongue tie: usually races towards rear: often let down by jumping over fences. *Evan Williams*

FIRMAGE BURG (FR) 5 b.m. Sageburg (IRE) – Firmini (FR) (Mansonnien (FR)) **h99 §** [2018/19 h16.8g⁶ h16m³ h15.8d^{rr} h17.7g* Nov 9] fourth foal: sister to 2 winners in France, including 21f hurdle winner Ferruccio, and half-sister to fairly useful French hurdler/chaser Niquos (17f-2½m winner, by Poliglote): dam (c114/h114), French 15f/17f hurdle/chase winner, half-sister to smart hurdler/chaser (stayed 21f) Far West: fair maiden on Flat, stays 12.5f: modest form over hurdles: won conditionals novice at Fontwell in November: wears hood: one to treat with caution (has refused to race). *Mrs B. Ewart*

FIRMOUNT GENT (IRE) 13 b.g. Beneficial – Tinkers Lady (Sheer Grit) [2018/19 c97, **c95** h–: c25.5g⁴ May 30] lengthy, plain gelding: point winner: twice-raced hurdler: modest **h–** chaser: stays 3m: acts on good to soft going: has worn cheekpieces/tongue tie. *Mrs B. Ewart*

FIRST ACCOUNT 5 b.g. Malinas (GER) – Kind Nell (Generous (IRE)) [2018/19 **h121 ▶** h17.1d³ h19.3s² Dec 16] €22,000 3-y-o: second foal: dam, ran twice in bumpers, sister to useful hurdler/fairly useful chaser (stayed 3m) Close House: won Irish point on debut: fairly useful form over hurdles: better effort when second in novice at Carlisle: remains with potential. *Donald McCain*

FIRST APPROACH (IRE) 6 b.g. Robin des Champs (FR) – Manhattan Babe (IRE) **h136** (Definite Article) [2018/19 b20g* b19g² h22g* h20d⁴ h20d⁶ h22.3g* h22g⁴ h24d Mar 15] **b105** €40,000 3-y-o: third foal: half-brother to fair hurdler/fairly useful chaser Hidden Charmer (19f/2½m winner, by Stowaway): dam, modest maiden hurdler, half-sister to smart hurdler/useful chaser Emotional Moment: point winner: useful bumper performer: won maiden at Tipperary in October: similar form over hurdles: won maiden at Down Royal in November and novice at Thurles (fortunate, finished alone) in January: best effort when 5 lengths fourth to Minella Indo in Irish Daily Mirror Novices' Hurdle at Punchestown shortly after end of British season: stays 3m: acts on good to soft going: in cheekpieces last 3 starts. *Noel Meade, Ireland*

FIRST ASSEMBLY (IRE) 5 b.g. Arcadio (GER) – Presenting Katie (IRE) (Presenting) **h–** [2018/19 b17.7s⁶ b16d h16.7g b21.7g⁵ Apr 12] €15,000 3-y-o, £6,000 4-y-o: third foal: **b82** half-brother to fair hurdler/chaser Achill Road Boy (2½m-3¼m winner, by Morozov): dam (b72), ran once each in point/bumper, half-sister to useful hurdler (winner up to 2¼m) Steviemac: maiden pointer: modest form in bumpers: well held in 2 novice hurdles. *Richard Bandey*

FIRST ASSIGNMENT (IRE) 6 b.g. Vinnie Roe (IRE) – Rebel Dream (IRE) (Dushyantor **h138** (USA)) [2018/19 h121: h21g* h23.9g* h24.3g³ h25g³ h24g⁴ Apr 17] workmanlike gelding: won Irish maiden point on debut: useful handicap hurdler: won at Cheltenham in October and November (listed event, by 9 lengths from Boyhood): fourth at same course (9¼ lengths behind Tobefair) in April: stays 3m: acts on heavy going. *Ian Williams*

FIRST DESTINATION 7 b.m. Rail Link – Hollow Quaill (IRE) (Entrepreneur) [2018/19 **h73 p** b80: h16.8s⁶ Apr 16] won sole start in bumpers in 2017/18: off 21 months, 33/1, probably in need of run when sixth in maiden at Exeter on hurdling debut: entitled to progress. *Robert Stephens*

FIRST DRIFT 8 ch.g. Generous (IRE) – Supreme Cove (Supreme Leader) [2018/19 h118: **c127** c21.4dᵖᵘ c16v* c16d² c20.6d h20.5d* h24.7g Apr 6] sturdy gelding: useful handicap **h130** hurdler: won at Newbury (by 2½ lengths from Betameche) in March: fairly useful form over fences: won novice at Hereford in December: stays 21f: acts on heavy going: usually races close up. *Ben Case*

FIRST DU CHARMIL (FR) 7 ch.g. Ballingarry (IRE) – Famous Member (FR) (Peintre **h–** Celebre (USA)) [2018/19 h111: h19.5dᵖᵘ Nov 27] workmanlike gelding: fair form over hurdles, pulled up sole start in 2018/19: best effort at 2m: acts on heavy going. *Samuel Drinkwater*

FIRST FIGARO (GER) 9 ch.g. Silvano (GER) – Felina (GER) (Acatenango (GER)) **h114** [2018/19 h110, b115: h16.2g* h15.7s h17.7s⁵ h16.7g h16.8d⁴ Apr 9] angular gelding: smart bumper performer: fair hurdler: won novice at Hereford in November: raced around 2m: acts on heavy going: tried in blinkers. *Venetia Williams*

FIRST FLOW (IRE) 7 b.g. Primary (USA) – Clonroche Wells (IRE) (Pierre) [2018/19 **h129** h133, b91: h16s⁵ Mar 9] well-made gelding: useful form over hurdles, fifth in Imperial Cup at Sandown sole start in 2018/19: will stay at least 2½m: acts on heavy going: usually front runner/races prominently. *Kim Bailey*

FIRST LORD DE CUET (FR) 5 gr.g. Lord du Sud (FR) – Alyce (FR) (Villez (USA)) **b100 p** [2018/19 b16.5d² b17.7d* Mar 18] £85,000 4-y-o: second foal: dam, lightly raced over hurdles in France, out of half-sister to dam of top-class chaser (winner up to 3¼m) Madison du Berlais: won Irish point on debut: fairly useful form in bumpers: won at Plumpton in March by 13 lengths from Mr Harp: promising. *David Pipe*

FIRST OF NEVER (IRE) 13 b.g. Systematic – Never Promise (FR) (Cadeaux **h87 §** Genereux) [2018/19 h66§: h16.8v³ h16g* h16.6dꟳ h16.4m h16.8g² h16.8d* Apr 23] modest handicap hurdler: won at Wetherby (conditionals) in February and Sedgefield in April: unproven beyond 17f: acts on soft going. *Lynn Siddall*

FIRST QUEST (USA) 5 b.g. First Defence (USA) – Dixie Quest (USA) (Coronado's **h112** Quest (USA)) [2018/19 h94: h15.8s* h16.7s⁴ h15.9d* h15.8g Feb 21] good-bodied gelding: has had breathing operation: fair handicap hurdler: won at Uttoxeter in July and Plumpton in January: raced around 2m: acts on soft going. *Jim Boyle*

FIRST UP (IRE) 5 b.g. Rip Van Winkle (IRE) – Doregan (IRE) (Bahhare (USA)) **h–** [2018/19 h99: h15.8g May 10] fairly useful on Flat, stays 1¼m: modest form over hurdles: tried in cheekpieces: in tongue tie last 3 starts: usually races towards rear. *Oliver Greenall*

FIRTH OF THE CLYDE 14 b.g. Flemensfirth (USA) – Miss Nel (Denel (FR)) [2018/19 **c–** c130, h–: h19.9s⁶ Dec 26] tall gelding: maiden hurdler: useful chaser: stays 3m: acts on **h–** heavy going: wears headgear. *Keith Dalgleish*

FISHER GREEN (IRE) 6 b.g. Rip Van Winkle (IRE) – Prealpina (IRE) (Indian Ridge) **h108**
[2018/19 h16.8s⁴ h16.8s³ h16.4g h15.6g* h15.6m* h16g⁴ h20.1gᵖᵘ Apr 15] fair on Flat,
stays 1½m: fair hurdler: won maiden and novice at Musselburgh in February: unproven
beyond 17f: acts on soft and good to firm going: wears tongue tie. *Maurice Barnes*

FISHERMAN'S TALE (IRE) 5 b.m. Jeremy (USA) – So You Said (IRE) (Definite **b–**
Article) [2018/19 b–: b15.8s Nov 23] well held in 2 bumpers. *Giles Smyly*

FIT FOR FIFTY 7 ch.g. Lucarno (USA) – Just For Jean (IRE) (Presenting) [2018/19 c–p, **c94**
h82: c16g⁵ c21.2m² c20g* c21.2d³ Aug 25] sturdy gelding: poor maiden hurdler: modest **h–**
form over fences: won handicap chase at Worcester in July: stays 21f: acts on good to firm and
good to soft going. *Donald McCain*

FITZHENRY (IRE) 7 b.g. Flemensfirth (USA) – She Took A Tree (FR) (Sri Pekan **c134**
(USA)) [2018/19 c131p, h121: h20d⁶ c29g³ c24.5g³ c28.7d⁴ Feb 10] maiden hurdler: **h110**
useful handicap chaser: third in Paddy Power Chase at Leopardstown (9 lengths behind
Auvergnat) in December: stays 29f: acts on heavy going: usually in headgear nowadays.
Paul Nolan, Ireland

FITZROY (IRE) 5 b.g. Fame And Glory – Forces of Destiny (IRE) (Luso) [2018/19 **b95**
b16d⁵ b16.3s² Mar 11] €110,000 3-y-o: second foal: dam unraced half-sister to smart
hurdler/useful chaser (stayed 3m) Emotional Moment: fairly useful form in bumpers:
better effort when second in maiden at Stratford in March. *Olly Murphy*

FIXED ASSET 7 b.g. Dr Massini (IRE) – Sharayna (Generous (IRE)) [2018/19 b–: **h–**
b16.2m⁶ h18.1dᵖᵘ Apr 8] poor form in bumpers: pulled up in novice on hurdling debut: **b69**
tried in tongue tie. *Lucinda Egerton*

FIXED RATE 6 b.g. Oasis Dream – Pretty Face (Rainbow Quest (USA)) [2018/19 h119: **c134**
h21g³ h20.6g c19.9g* c21.6d* Nov 10] close-coupled gelding: fair handicap hurdler: **h114**
useful form over fences: won novice handicap chase at Huntingdon (by head from Heydour)
in October and handicap at Kelso (by 14 lengths from Some Reign) in November: stays
2¾m: acts on good to firm and good to soft going: wears headgear/tongue tie: often leads.
Charlie Mann

FLABELLO (IRE) 9 br.g. Publisher (USA) – Uptodate (IRE) (Gothland (FR)) [2018/19 **c–**
h15.6g c26.3sᵖᵘ Feb 21] point winner: poor maiden hurdler: well held completed start over **h–**
fences: often wears headgear. *Sean Conway*

FLAKA 7 ch.m. Lucarno (USA) – A Fistful of Euros (East Wood) [2018/19 b15.8gᵖᵘ b16g⁶ **b–**
Jun 27] first foal: dam (h89), maiden hurdler (stayed 3¼m), half-sister to useful hurdler/
chaser (stayed 3m) Mon Villez: no form in bumpers. *Tim Pinfield*

FLAMING CHARMER (IRE) 11 ch.g. Flemensfirth (USA) – Kates Charm (IRE) **c120 §**
(Glacial Storm (USA)) [2018/19 c122§, h–§: c24.2v⁵ c19.4s* c25.1g c20.3dᵖᵘ Apr 9] tall **h– §**
gelding: winning hurdler: fairly useful handicap chaser: won at Chepstow in November:
left Colin Tizzard after third start: stays 3m: acts on heavy going: tried in cheekpieces:
wears tongue tie: untrustworthy. *G. Slade-Jones*

FLAMINGER (FR) 4 gr.g. Racinger (FR) – Landalouse (FR) (Iris Noir (FR)) [2018/19 **h106**
b11.9f² h16g⁵ h17.7v² h17.7v² h15.9g³ Apr 22] good-topped gelding: fifth foal: half-brother **b?**
to French 1½m winner Suffit de Le Dire (by Le Malemortois): dam ran twice in
French bumpers: second at Paray-Le-Monial on sole start in bumpers for A. Adeline de
Boisbrunet: fair form over hurdles. *Gary Moore*

FLAMING GLORY (IRE) 5 b.g. Gold Well – Pearlsforthegirls (Cloudings (IRE)) **h–**
[2018/19 h19.5d h16.2v⁶ h16.4m Mar 28] placed on 2 of 3 starts in Irish points: little
impact in novice hurdles. *Katie Scott*

FLAMINGO LANE (IRE) 6 ch.g. Arakan (USA) – Eluna (Unfuwain (USA)) [2018/19 **c–**
c20g h23g Jul 26] has had breathing operation: unplaced in points: poor form over hurdles: **h–**
well held completed start over fences: tried in cheekpieces: sometimes in tongue tie.
Donald McCain

FLANAGANS FIELD (IRE) 11 b.g. Araafa (IRE) – Zvezda (USA) (Nureyev (USA)) **h80 §**
[2018/19 h92: h15.5g⁵ h20v⁶ h15.8s³ h17.7d h19s³ h19g h15.7g⁴ h16d* h16.8g⁴ Apr 20]
poor handicap hurdler: won at Chepstow in March: stays 21f: acts on good to firm and
heavy going: wears headgear: has worn tongue tie: one to treat with caution. *Bernard
Llewellyn*

FLASHDANZA 4 ch.g. Sepoy (AUS) – Photo Flash (IRE) (Bahamian Bounty) [2018/19 **h90**
h17.7v³ h16s⁴ h19.2vᵖᵘ h21.7g Apr 12] compact gelding: modest maiden on Flat: modest
form over hurdles. *Richard Rowe*

FLASHING GLANCE 6 b.g. Passing Glance – Don And Gerry (IRE) (Vestris Abu) **c125**
[2018/19 h127: h15.8m c15.7g³ c20m³ c15.7g² h16v^{ur} h19.7v⁶ h15.5g² h16.8d³ h15.8d* **h129**
h16.5g⁵ Apr 6] smallish gelding: has had breathing operation: fairly useful handicap hurdler:
won at Ludlow in February: similar form over fences: best effort when second in novice
handicap at Southwell: unproven beyond 17f: acts on good to soft going: has worn hood:
usually races prominently. *Tom Lacey*

FLASHJACK (IRE) 9 br.g. Soapy Danger – Open Miss (Dracula (AUS)) [2018/19 c–, **c–**
h123: h21.9s² h25s³ h24.3d⁵ h25.8v* h23s Mar 23] well-made gelding: useful handicap **h130**
hurdler: won at Fontwell (by 1½ lengths from Vive Le Roi) in March: maiden chaser: stays
3¼m: acts on heavy going: has worn cheekpieces: races towards rear. *Henry Daly*

FLASHMAN 10 ch.g. Doyen (IRE) – Si Si Si (Lomitas) [2018/19 c104§, h–§: c20.5m^{pu} **c74 §**
c16.5g⁵ c19.7g⁵ c26g⁴ Apr 24] workmanlike gelding: winning hurdler: fair chaser, well **h– §**
below form in 2018/19: stays 2¼m: acts on soft going: wears headgear: temperamental.
Gary Moore

FLASH THE STEEL (IRE) 7 b.g. Craigsteel – Anna's Melody (IRE) (Luso) [2018/19 **h127**
b99: b16.3g³ h16.7d² h15.8d⁴ h16.6g* h16.8d² h16s* h16g⁵ Apr 27] workmanlike gelding: **b91**
off mark in Irish points at second attempt: fairly useful form in bumpers: similar form over
hurdles: won handicap at Doncaster in December and novice at Warwick in March: raced
around 2m: acts on soft going: often wears tongue tie. *Dan Skelton*

FLAXEN FLARE (IRE) 10 ch.g. Windsor Knot (IRE) – Golden Angel (USA) (Slew O' **c131**
Gold (USA)) [2018/19 c127, h138: h20m² h20m⁵ c23.8g² h24d² c22g⁴ Aug 17] sturdy **h132**
gelding: useful hurdler: second in minor event at Down Royal (½ length behind The Game
Changer) in June: useful chaser: second in handicap at Perth (11 lengths behind Swingbridge)
in July: stays 3m: acts on good to firm and heavy going: wears headgear: front runner/races
prominently. *Gordon Elliott, Ireland*

FLED OR PLED (IRE) 7 b.g. Shantou (USA) – Desert Gail (IRE) (Desert Style (IRE)) **c– §**
[2018/19 c76§, h60§: h23.9d^{pu} h24g^{pu} Jul 15] has had breathing operation: poor handicap **h– §**
hurdler: similar form over fences: stays 3m: acts on good to firm going: usually wears
headgear: often wears tongue tie: temperamental. *Tim Vaughan*

FLEETING VISIT 6 b.g. Manduro (GER) – Short Affair (Singspiel (IRE)) [2018/19 **h115**
h16.7g⁵ h20g³ h16.3m³ h18.7m^f h18.6g² h19.9g* h20.3g² Oct 2] dam half-sister to useful
hurdler (stayed 3¼m) Bourne: fairly useful on Flat, stays 2m: fairly useful hurdler: won
maiden at Uttoxeter in September: stays 2½m: acts on good to firm going: sometimes in
cheekpieces. *Graeme McPherson*

FLEGMATIK (FR) 4 ch.g. Fuisse (FR) – Crack d'Emble (FR) (Poliglote) [2018/19 **h113**
h17.9d⁵ h16d* h16g² Feb 22] second foal: dam French 17f-21f hurdle/chase winner: fair
form over hurdles: won juvenile at Wetherby (by 14 lengths from Travel Lightly,
impressively) in December: left G. Cherel after first start. *Dan Skelton*

FLEMCARA (IRE) 7 b.g. Flemensfirth (USA) – Cara Mara (IRE) (Saddlers' Hall (IRE)) **c102**
[2018/19 h127: c23.8v c23.6v^{ur} h23.4s³ h23.1d* h24d h24.7g Apr 6] sturdy gelding: **h131**
runner-up in Irish point: useful handicap hurdler: won at Exeter (by 3½ lengths from Poker
Play) in February: well held completed start over fences: stays 3m: acts on heavy going:
wears tongue tie. *Emma Lavelle*

FLEMENCO TEMPO (IRE) 5 ch.g. Flemensfirth (USA) – Tap The Beat (IRE) (Oscar **b77**
(IRE)) [2018/19 b16.3g⁵ Oct 8] €41,000 3-y-o: workmanlike gelding: first foal: dam,
unraced, closely related to useful hurdlers/smart chasers Finger Onthe Pulse (winner up to
2¾m) and Buddy Bolero (winner up to 3m): 9/2, fifth in bumper at Stratford (10¼ lengths
behind Tight Call). *Colin Tizzard*

FLEMEN MAJIC (IRE) 7 b.m. Flemensfirth (USA) – Majic Times Ahead (Weld) **h91**
[2018/19 h18.8g^{ur} h20g h19.9g^{ur} h20g⁴ h20d⁶ h16v Dec 13] €3,000 4-y-o: fourth foal:
sister to a winning pointer: dam unraced half-sister to smart hurdler/useful chaser (stayed
3¾m) Better Times Ahead: modest maiden hurdler: stays 2½m: tried in hood. *Gavin
Patrick Cromwell, Ireland*

FLEMENS STORY (IRE) 8 b.g. Flemensfirth (USA) – Amelia Earhart (IRE) (Be My **h108**
Native (USA)) [2018/19 h100: h19.9s² h22.7g⁵ h22.8d³ Mar 20] strong, workmanlike
gelding: off mark in Irish points at fourth attempt: fair form over hurdles: stays 23f: acts on
soft going: tried in tongue tie: usually leads. *Donald McCain*

FLEMENSTRIX (IRE) 6 b.g. Flemensfirth (USA) – Laurens Trix (IRE) (Presenting) **h–**
[2018/19 b–: h19.2g⁴¹ May 21] well held in bumper/maiden hurdle: tried in cheekpieces/
tongue tie: little impact in 2 points later in season. *Charlie Longsdon*

355

FLEMINPORT (IRE) 6 b.g. Flemensfirth (USA) – Geek Chic (IRE) (Saffron Walden (FR)) [2018/19 h124p: c20s⁶ c24v² c23.6s⁴ Dec 27] fairly useful form over hurdles: similar form over fences: best effort when second in handicap at Bangor in December: stays 3m: acts on heavy going. *Jonjo O'Neill* **c121 h–**

FLEMISH MAID (IRE) 7 b.m. Flemensfirth (USA) – Lucy May (IRE) (Supreme Leader) [2018/19 h22.1g³ May 28] fifth foal: dam (c79), 17f chase winner, half-sister to fairly useful hurdler/useful chaser (stays 3¼m) Herdsman (by Flemensfirth): poor maiden hurdler: stays 2¾m: has worn cheekpieces: front runner/races prominently. *Joanne Foster* **h78**

FLERE IMSAHO (IRE) 4 b.g. Kodiac – Florida City (IRE) (Pennekamp (USA)) [2018/19 h15.8g⁵ h15.8g h18.7sᵖᵘ Mar 11] fair maiden on Flat, stayed 1¼m: no form in juvenile hurdles: in hood last 2 starts: dead. *Rebecca Curtis* **h–**

FLEUR DU POMMIER 6 br.m. Apple Tree (FR) – Jersey Countess (IRE) (Supreme Leader) [2018/19 h70, b82: h15.3m May 10] modest form in bumpers: poor form over hurdles: likely to stay 2½m: placed in points later in season. *G. C. Maundrell* **h–**

FLIC OU VOYOU (FR) 5 b.g. Kapgarde (FR) – Hillflower (FR) (Sabrehill (USA)) [2018/19 b69: h15.3g* h15.3d* b16.4s Mar 13] well-made gelding: has had breathing operation: useful form in bumpers: won at Wincanton in November and December (by 3¼ lengths from Now Look At Me). *Paul Nicholls* **b109**

FLIGHT DECK (IRE) 5 b.g. Getaway (GER) – Rate of Knots (IRE) (Saddlers' Hall (IRE)) [2018/19 h16.7g⁶ h16.3s h16.8s Jan 20] second foal: dam (c124/h113) 19f-2¾m hurdle/chase winner (stayed 31f): modest form over hurdles: will stay at least 2½m: remains with potential. *Jonjo O'Neill* **h96 p**

FLIGHTS 8 b.m. King's Theatre (IRE) – Motcombe (IRE) (Carroll House) [2018/19 c26g³ May 17] multiple point winner: well held in 2 bumpers for Robert Walford in 2016: 15/8 and in blinkers, third in mares hunter at Fontwell (1½ lengths behind Kimora) on chasing debut. *Mrs S. Alner* **c91**

FLIGHT TO MILAN (IRE) 6 b.g. Milan – Kigali (IRE) (Torus) [2018/19 h107: h16.8g h19.5v⁶ h18.5d⁶ c17s³ c18.2s¹⁷ c16s² c17.4g Apr 13] fair maiden hurdler, below form first 3 starts in 2018/19: similar form over fences: unproven beyond 2m: acts on heavy going. *Evan Williams* **c111 h80**

FLIGHT TO NOWHERE 7 ch.m. Aeroplane – River Beauty (Exit To Nowhere (USA)) [2018/19 h94: h19.6gᵖᵘ h16d² h16g Apr 26] modest handicap hurdler: raced mainly around 2m: acts on soft going: has worn hood: usually wears tongue tie. *Richard Price* **h93**

FLIGHTY FILIA (IRE) 7 gr.m. Raven's Pass (USA) – Coventina (IRE) (Daylami (IRE)) [2018/19 h88: h21.6v h18.5m Nov 6] workmanlike mare: poor hurdler on balance: stays 2¾m: acts on good going: in blinkers last 2 starts. *Jimmy Frost* **h–**

FLINCK (IRE) 5 b.g. Fame And Glory – Princess Supreme (IRE) (Supreme Leader) [2018/19 h23.1v⁵ h19s³ Mar 19] closely related to fairly useful hurdler Casper King (2m-2¼m winner, by Scorpion) and half-brother to a winning pointer by Milan: dam unraced sister to useful hurdler/smart chaser (stayed 3m) Supreme Prince and useful hurdler/fairly useful chaser (17f-2¾m winner) Supreme Serenade: unplaced on debut in Irish point: fair form over hurdles: better effort when third in maiden at Taunton: open to further improvement. *Philip Hobbs* **h106 p**

FLINTS LEGACY 7 gr.m. Sagamix (FR) – Luneray (FR) (Poplar Bluff) [2018/19 h19.5d h19.5g⁵ Apr 26] poor maiden hurdler: stays 19f: acts on good to soft going. *Nigel Hawke* **h82**

FLOATING ROCK (GER) 4 b.g. It's Gino (GER) – Fly Osoria (GER) (Osorio (GER)) [2018/19 b15.7m* Feb 22] second foal: dam German 9f/1¼m winner: 15/8, won bumper at Catterick by ¾ length from Picks Flight. *Tom Lacey* **b99**

FLOKI 5 b.g. Kalanisi (IRE) – La Dame Brune (FR) (Mansonnien (FR)) [2018/19 b86p: b15.7m⁵ h19g³ Apr 25] rangy gelding: modest form in bumpers: 6/1, third in maiden at Warwick on hurdling debut: open to improvement. *Dan Skelton* **h87 p b83**

FLORAL BOUQUET 6 bl.m. Fair Mix (IRE) – Florarossa (Alflora (IRE)) [2018/19 h112: h15.8gᶠ h20m³ h15.8dᶠ c20.2d⁴ h20.6g⁴ h20.5s⁶ h24.3m⁵ Apr 12] lengthy mare: has had breathing operations: fairly useful handicap hurdler: let down by jumping only start over fences: probably stays 21f: acts on soft going: tried in cheekpieces: wears tongue tie. *Jamie Snowden* **c106 h116**

FLORAL QUEEN 6 b.m. Emperor Fountain – Florentino (Efisio) [2018/19 b–: h15.8d May 26] poor form in bumpers: well beaten in novice on hurdling debut: has joined Colin Tizzard. *Neil Mulholland* **h–**

FLORELLA (IRE) 9 b.m. Presenting – Shiminnie (IRE) (Bob Back (USA)) [2018/19 **c78** c26g⁴ May 17] third foal: half-sister to bumper winner/fairly useful hurdler Minnie Milan (23f-3¼m winner, by Milan): dam (h107) 2¼m hurdle winner: multiple point winner: 9/2, last of 4 finishers in mares hunter at Fontwell on chasing debut. *Mrs Cynthia Woods*

FLORESCO (GER) 9 ch.g. Santiago (GER) – Fiori (GER) (Chief Singer) [2018/19 **c105** c98p, h109: c19.4m⁴ c16sᵘʳ h21d h19d³ h18.5s⁵ h21.4g⁵ c18.2dᶠ h19.5gᵖᵘ Apr 26] compact **h107** gelding: has had breathing operation: fair handicap hurdler: similar form over fences: best at shorter than 2½m: acts on heavy going: wears headgear: has worn tongue tie, including last 2 starts: front runner/races prominently. *Kayley Woollacott*

FLORESSA (FR) 4 b.f. Poliglote – Dona Rez (FR) (Trempolino (USA)) [2018/19 **b97 p** b15.8d* b16.8g² Apr 18] sixth foal: sister to useful French hurdler/chaser Polygona (17f-19f winner) and half-sister to 2 winners in France, including fairly useful chaser Saint Lino (17f-2¾m winner, by Saint des Saints): dam, French 2m/17f hurdle/chase winner, sister to smart French hurdler up to 19f Don Lino: fairly useful form in bumpers: won at Ludlow in March: open to further improvement. *Nicky Henderson*

FLORRIE BOY (IRE) 8 b.g. Milan – Second Best (IRE) (Supreme Leader) [2018/19 **c123 p** h22.8g⁶ c21.4m⁶ c23d³ Aug 29] sturdy gelding: fairly useful handicap hurdler: similar form **h117** over fences: better effort when third in handicap at Worcester: stays 23f: acts on soft going: open to further improvement as a chaser. *Nigel Twiston-Davies*

FLORRIE KNOX (IRE) 6 gr.g. Gold Well – Miss Orphan (FR) (Round Sovereign (FR)) **h123** [2018/19 h126: h23.1g⁴ h22.8v⁵ Dec 22] runner-up on second of 2 starts in Irish points: fairly useful handicap hurdler: fourth at Market Rasen in November: stays 23f: acts on heavy going: front runner/races prominently. *Alex Hales*

FLO'SBOY SAM 6 b.g. Tobougg (IRE) – Madam Flora (Alflora (IRE)) [2018/19 h92§: **c–** h21.4m* h19.9g⁵ c21g⁴ h19.2d⁶ h21.4gʳʳ Feb 16] has had breathing operation: fair handicap **h103 §** hurdler: won at Wincanton early in season: well held in novice handicap on chasing debut: stays 21f: acts on good to firm going: wears blinkers: one to treat with caution (has twice refused to race, including final start). *Colin Tizzard*

FLOW AWAY (IRE) 5 br.m. Stowaway – Water Rock (El Conquistador) [2018/19 **b85** b15.7d⁶ b15.8s³ b15.7d⁶ Feb 16] rather unfurnished mare: seventh foal: half-sister to 2 winners by Presenting, including fairly useful 2½m hurdle winner Aliandy, and winning pointers by Luso and Karinga Bay: dam unraced: fair form in bumpers. *Alex Hales*

FLOWERY (IRE) 7 b.g. Millenary – Dato Vic (IRE) (Old Vic) [2018/19 h16v h16g h24g **c127** h16gʳᵒ h19.9s* h15.7g* h16.8v² c19.3v* c21.3g* Mar 29] third foal: half-brother to useful **h106 §** hurdler/smart chaser Knocknanuss (2m-2¼m winner) and fair 2m hurdle winner Summerhill Lewis (both by Beneficial): dam, unraced, closely related to top-class 2m hurdler Dato Star: fair handicap hurdler: won at Sedgefield in December and Catterick in January: fairly useful form over fences: won novice handicap at Sedgefield and handicap at Wetherby in March: left G. Webb after third start, M. Hourigan after fourth: stays 21f: acts on heavy going: usually wears hood: tried in tongue tie: hard ride (often hangs badly left and has run out). *Iain Jardine*

FLOW FROM DEVON 6 b.m. With The Flow (USA) – Sally Army (Silver Patriarch **h70** (IRE)) [2018/19 h16.3m⁴ h18.5g⁵ h18.7m h21.6mᵖᵘ Jul 14] pulled up in bumper for Ron Hodges in 2016/17: no form over hurdles. *Jamie Snowden*

FLOWING CADENZA 5 b.m. Yeats (IRE) – Over The Flow (Overbury (IRE)) [2018/19 **h91** b16.5d b16.5d³ b16d h21.6s⁵ Apr 16] second foal: dam (c98/h95), 21f chase winner, half- **b–** sister to fair hurdler/useful chaser (stays 4¼m) Regal Flow: well held in bumpers: 250/1, fifth in novice at Exeter on hurdling debut. *Bob Buckler*

FLOW WITH EVE 10 b.m. With The Flow (USA) – Vercheny (Petoski) [2018/19 h94: **h89** h20.6g⁴ h22.1g³ h21.6g h23.9dᶠ Apr 24] sturdy mare: modest maiden hurdler: left Olly Murphy after third start: stays 2¾m: acts on heavy going: wears headgear: has worn tongue tie. *Kevin Bishop*

FLUGZEUG 11 gr.g. Silver Patriarch (IRE) – Telmar Flyer (Neltino) [2018/19 c79, h–: **c69 §** c26g³ c25.7g³ c25.8g h25.8sᵖᵘ c26m⁴ c26gᵖᵘ Feb 20] maiden pointer: winning hurdler: **h–** poor handicap chaser: left Seamus Mullins after fifth start: stays 3¼m: acts on good to firm and heavy going: wears cheekpieces: temperamental. *L. Humphrey*

FLUTTER DOWN (FR) 4 b.g. Rob Roy (USA) – Florifere (FR) (Robin des Pres (FR)) **b–** [2018/19 b16.2d Apr 26] well held in bumper. *Lucinda Russell*

FLY HOME HARRY 10 b.g. Sir Harry Lewis (USA) – Fly Home (Skyliner) [2018/19 c112, h–: c24.2g⁴ c22.6g c24mᵖᵘ c28.5d⁴ c23.8g⁵ c23.6gᵖᵘ c25.7g⁵ Feb 25] compact gelding: maiden hurdler: fair handicap chaser: stays 3½m: acts on soft going: usually wears cheekpieces: wears tongue tie: temperament under suspicion. *Charlie Longsdon*   **c106 h–**

FLYING ANGEL (IRE) 8 gr.g. Arcadio (GER) – Gypsy Kelly (IRE) (Roselier (FR)) [2018/19 c152, h–: c19.9g⁶ c21g² c26s c23.8s c21.6d⁵ c25s⁵ c21.1d⁶ Apr 5] good-topped gelding: has had breathing operation: winning hurdler: useful handicap chaser when in the mood, second at Ascot (3 lengths behind Mr Medic) in November: stays 25f: acts on heavy going: wears visor nowadays: has worn tongue tie: hard to catch right. *Nigel Twiston-Davies*   **c143 § h–**

FLYING DISMOUNT (IRE) 6 b.g. St Jovite (USA) – Posh Posy (IRE) (Kadeed (IRE)) [2018/19 h16.2g h16.2g⁵ h19.3dᵖᵘ Mar 24] pulled up in Irish point: little show over hurdles. *Sandy Forster*   **h67**

FLYING EAGLE (IRE) 11 b.g. Oscar (IRE) – Fille d'Argent (IRE) (Desert Style (IRE)) [2018/19 c121§, h–: c20sᵖᵘ c23.8dᵖᵘ c23.8m³ Feb 27] lengthy, good sort: multiple point winner: winning hurdler: fairly useful chaser, below form in 2018/19: stays 3m: acts on good to firm and heavy going: wears headgear: has worn tongue tie, including in 2018/19: temperamental. *Mickey Bowen*   **c102 § h–**

FLYING FEATHERS (IRE) 6 b.m. Westerner – Miss Molly Malone (IRE) (Accordion) [2018/19 b–: b15.7g May 6] little show in 2 bumpers. *Louise Allan*   **b–**

FLYING JACK 9 b.g. Rob Roy (USA) – Milladella (FR) (Nureyev (USA)) [2018/19 c105, h98: c19.3gᶠ c24.1s⁶ c23.4g³ c21.1s³ c23.8sᵖᵘ c21.6d⁵ c24.2g⁶ Apr 15] long-backed gelding: modest hurdler: fair maiden chaser: stays 3m: acts on soft going: tried in cheekpieces: wears tongue tie. *Maurice Barnes*   **c105 h–**

FLYING TIGER (IRE) 6 bl.g. Soldier of Fortune (IRE) – Ma Preference (FR) (American Post) [2018/19 h137: c16.3d² c16.3v³ h15.7gᵇᵈ h15.7s h16.5gᵘʳ h16.3d⁵ Mar 2] good-topped gelding: has had breathing operation: fairly useful handicap hurdler: similar form over fences: better effort when second in novice at Newton Abbot in September: raced around 2m: acts on heavy going: usually races off pace/freely. *Nick Williams*   **c129 h127**

FLYING VERSE 7 b.g. Yeats (IRE) – Flight Sequence (Polar Falcon (USA)) [2018/19 h83, b79: h24gᵘʳ h24g* h23g h24g* h26.5g⁵ h26.5d³ h23.1g² h23.1g* h23.1m⁴ h21.6d⁵ h24d² Apr 24] compact gelding: fair handicap hurdler: won at Southwell in May (novice) and July, and Bangor in October: stays 3¼m: acts on good to soft going: wears headgear/tongue tie. *David Dennis*   **h110**

FLYNNVINCIBLE 8 b.g. Tobougg (IRE) – Shiny Thing (USA) (Lear Fan (USA)) [2018/19 h99: h22m³ h23.3sᵖᵘ h23sᵖᵘ Jan 4] sturdy gelding: fair maiden hurdler: stays 2¾m: acts on good to firm and heavy going: tried in cheekpieces: has joined Martin Todhunter. *Olly Murphy*   **h102**

FLY RORY FLY (IRE) 7 b.g. Milan – Thousand Wings (GER) (Winged Love (IRE)) [2018/19 c121, h104: c23.8g² c24.2g⁶ c23.4d⁴ c23.4g⁴ c21.6d* c26.3s³ c23.8g² Apr 24] fair form over hurdles: fair handicap chaser: won at Kelso in March: stays 25f: acts on good to soft going: usually wears headgear: has worn tongue tie, including last 4 starts: usually races towards rear. *N. W. Alexander*   **c110 h–**

FLY TO MARS 5 b.g. Schiaparelli (GER) – Patsie Magern (Alderbrook) [2018/19 b16.8m⁶ h20.5s² h16g⁶ h15.9s² h18.5d⁴ h18.5sᶠ Mar 18] €40,000 3-y-o: well-made gelding: first foal: dam once-raced sister to fairly useful hurdler/high-class chaser (stayed 27f) Ollie Magern: shaped as if needed experience when sixth in bumper at Exeter: fairly useful form over hurdles: stays 21f: acts on soft going. *Colin Tizzard*   **h119 b80**

FLY VINNIE (IRE) 10 b.g. Vinnie Roe (IRE) – Great Days (IRE) (Magical Strike (USA)) [2018/19 h120: h25.8d⁵ h23.8g⁶ h23.8g³ Jan 7] has had breathing operation: placed in Irish points: fairly useful handicap hurdler: third at Musselburgh in January: stays 3m: acts on soft and good to firm going: usually leads. *Alistair Whillans*   **h115**

FOLAU 4 br.g. Aussie Rules (USA) – Sky High Diver (IRE) (Celtic Swing) [2018/19 b15.8g Mar 19] in tongue tie, well beaten in conditionals/amateurs bumper. *Ian Williams*   **b–**

FOLIES BERGERES 4 ch.f. Champs Elysees – May Fox (Zilzal (USA)) [2018/19 h16sᵖᵘ Jan 21] fair on Flat, stays 2m: bled on hurdling debut: has joined Grace Harris. *Dai Burchell*   **h–**

FOLLOWING MAMA (IRE) 8 b.m. Beneficial – Follow Mama (IRE) (Saddlers' Hall (IRE)) [2018/19 c26g May 4] multiple point winner: well held all starts under Rules. *Mrs D. J. Ralph*   **c– h–**

FOLLOW THE BEAR (IRE) 7 b.g. King's Theatre (IRE) – Mrs Dempsey (IRE) **h120**
(Presenting) [2018/19 h124: h24.7g h21g^F h24.3m^3 Apr 12] good-topped gelding: off mark
in points at second attempt: fairly useful handicap hurdler: third at Ayr in April: stays 3m:
acts on soft and good to firm going: usually front runner/races prominently. *Nicky Henderson*

FOLLOW THE SWALLOW (IRE) 11 b.g. Dr Massini (IRE) – Old Chapel (IRE) **c108 x**
(Royal Fountain) [2018/19 c–, h–: c20g^5 c21.4g^2 c24.2g^{pu} c23m^{pu} c22.5g^4 c21.4g^2 c21.7d^F **h–**
c23.8g^2 c23.9s^4 c21.4g^5 c24g* Apr 25] strong, close-coupled gelding: once-raced hurdler:
fair handicap chaser: won at Warwick in April: stays 3m: acts on soft going: wears
headgear/tongue tie: races off pace: often let down by jumping. *Graeme McPherson*

FOLLY BERGERE (IRE) 6 ch.m. Champs Elysees – Rainbow Queen (FR) (Spectrum **h–**
(IRE)) [2018/19 h102: h20.6g^{pu} May 20] fair form over hurdles: dead. *James Eustace*

FOLSOM BLUE (IRE) 12 b.g. Old Vic – Spirit Leader (IRE) (Supreme Leader) **c135**
[2018/19 c148, h129: h24.3g^4 c29.5s h23.4s^4 c34v^6 c34.3g Apr 6] sturdy gelding: fairly **h123**
useful handicap hurdler: fourth at Sandown in February: useful handicap chaser: sixth in
Midlands Grand National at Uttoxeter (21 lengths behind Potters Corner) in March: stays
4¼m: acts on heavy going: wears headgear/tongue tie. *Gordon Elliott, Ireland*

FONTLEY HOUSE (IRE) 7 ch.g. Getaway (GER) – Down Town Cork (IRE) (Saddlers' **h108**
Hall (IRE)) [2018/19 b16d h23d^{pu} h21.2m^3 Apr 1] has had breathing operation: second **b–**
foal: dam unraced half-sister to Champion Bumper winner/fairly useful hurdler (stayed
3m) Liberman and fairly useful hurdler (stayed 2¼m) Jimmy Ber: fairly useful form when
third at Punchestown for Peter Fahey on first of 2 starts in bumpers: fair form over hurdles:
better effort when third in novice at Ludlow: tried in tongue tie. *Tom George*

FONTSANTA (IRE) 6 b.g. Flemensfirth (USA) – Day's Over (Overbury (IRE)) [2018/19 **h124 p**
b94: h20.5s^5 h23.6d^5 h25.5d* Mar 9] fair form in bumpers: fairly useful form over
hurdles: won novice at Hereford in March: tried in hood: open to further improvement.
Emma Lavelle

FOOTLOOSE 5 b.g. Sulamani (IRE) – Altesse de Sou (FR) (Saint Preuil (FR)) [2018/19 **b79**
b16.7g^4 Oct 30] has had breathing operation: in tongue tie, 16/1, fourth in bumper at
Bangor (17½ lengths behind Tel'art). *Jamie Snowden*

FOOTPAD (FR) 7 b.g. Creachadoir (IRE) – Willamina (IRE) (Sadler's Wells (USA)) **c161**
[2018/19 c174p, h–: c16d^F c17g^2 c20.6d Mar 14] good-topped gelding: winning hurdler: **h–**
top-class chaser as a novice: beaten 6l on reappearance, again suffered overreach when second
in Paddy's Rewards Club Chase at Leopardstown (½ length behind Simply Ned) in
December: bled final outing: stays 19f: acts on heavy going: tried in hood: usually travels
strongly. *W. P. Mullins, Ireland*

FORBIDDING (USA) 6 ch.g. Kitten's Joy (USA) – La Coruna (USA) (Thunder Gulch **h–**
(USA)) [2018/19 h–: h17m Apr 20] modest on Flat, stays 17f: made frame in bumpers:
well held in 2 novice hurdles. *Barry Murtagh*

FOR CARMEL (IRE) 9 b.g. Mr Dinos (IRE) – Bobalena (IRE) (Bob Back (USA)) **c90**
[2018/19 c104, h95: h23.6d^6 c23.5v^{pu} c25.7s^4 Mar 11] modest maiden hurdler/fair **h79**
handicap chaser, below best in 2018/19: stays 3¼m: acts on heavy going: wears tongue tie:
front runner/races prominently. *Paul Henderson*

FORECAST 7 ch.g. Observatory (USA) – New Orchid (USA) (Quest For Fame) [2018/19 **h124**
h23.3g h20g h15.7g^2 h20g^3 h19.5s* h15.7s h24d^4 h19.9v Mar 16] sturdy gelding: has had
breathing operation: fairly useful handicap hurdler: won at Lingfield in November: stays
3m: acts on soft and good to firm going: usually wears hood: wears tongue tie: usually
races off pace. *Martin Keighley*

FOREIGN SECRETARY 4 ch.g. Galileo (IRE) – Finsceal Beo (IRE) (Mr Greeley **h120 p**
(USA)) [2018/19 h16g h16d h16v* h16d^3 Mar 31] fairly useful form on Flat: likewise over
hurdles: won minor event at Limerick in March: third in novice there later in month: likely
to progress further. *John Halley, Ireland*

FORESEE (GER) 6 b.g. Sea The Stars (IRE) – Four Roses (IRE) (Darshaan) [2018/19 **h99**
h16g^5 h15.8g^5 Nov 26] neat gelding: has had breathing operation: modest on Flat, stays
15f: modest form over hurdles. *Tony Carroll*

FOREST BIHAN (FR) 8 ch.g. Forestier (FR) – Katell Bihan (FR) (Funny Baby (FR)) **c153**
[2018/19 c154, h–: c15.9g^3 c16.4s^F c15.2d^3 c16.4g^2 c16.3d^4 c16.5m Apr 13] good-topped **h–**
gelding: has had breathing operation: winning hurdler: smart handicap chaser: made frame
at Wetherby in December, Doncaster in January, and in Grand Annual at Cheltenham in
March: stays 19f: acts on heavy going: wears headgear: tends to find little. *Brian Ellison*

FOREST DES AIGLES (FR) 8 b.g. Balko (FR) – Rose des Aigles (FR) (Le Nain Jaune **c138** (FR)) [2018/19 c132, h–: c21.5d* c21.1s⁵ c20.6d c16.5s² c21.1dᵖᵘ Apr 5] useful-looking **h–** gelding: winning hurdler: useful handicap chaser: won at Ayr in November: fatally injured in Topham Chase at Aintree: stayed 3m: acted on heavy going: wore tongue tie. *Lucinda Russell*

FOREST FUSION (IRE) 5 b.g. Flemensfirth (USA) – Qui Plus Est (FR) (Dark Moon- **h–** dancer) [2018/19 b–: b15.7g⁶ h20.1vᵖᵘ h16g Mar 29] poor form in bumpers: no form over **b67** hurdles. *Tim Easterby*

FOREST LORD 5 b.g. Native Ruler – La Belle Au Bois (IRE) (Val Royal (FR)) [2018/19 **b–** b16.3s Jan 16] behind in bumpers, first one a point version. *Nick Lampard*

FOREVER DYLAN (IRE) 8 b.g. Stowaway – Long Long Time (IRE) (Dr Massini **c78** (IRE)) [2018/19 c26.3s⁵ c23.4d⁶ c26.3gᵖᵘ Apr 5] maiden pointer: fair maiden hurdler at **h–** best for Henry de Bromhead: poor maiden chaser: stays 23f: acts on good to soft going: wears headgear: tried in tongue tie. *Micky Hammond*

FOREVER FIELD (IRE) 9 b.g. Beneficial – Sarahs Reprive (IRE) (Yashgan) [2018/19 **c134** c131, h–: c21.4m⁶ h20g³ h20.9m² c23.8m² c25.1gᵖᵘ Nov 10] fairly useful handicap hurdler: **h129** second at Kelso in September: useful handicap chaser: second at Ludlow (¾ length behind Belmount) in October: stays easy 3m: acts on good to firm going: in cheekpieces last 2 starts. *Nicky Henderson*

FOREVER MY FRIEND (IRE) 12 b.g. King's Theatre (IRE) – Kazan Lady (IRE) **c116 §** (Petardia) [2018/19 c123§, h65§: c20.8g c21.6g* c20.9d² c19.4m⁴ Jul 3] smallish gelding: **h– §** maiden hurdler: fairly useful chaser: won lady riders' hunter at Fontwell in May: stays 3m: acts on soft and good to firm going: wears headgear: tried in tongue tie: usually races close up: unreliable. *Peter Bowen*

FOREWARNING 5 b.g. Cacique (IRE) – Buffering (Beat Hollow) [2018/19 b91: **b83** b16.7m² Aug 5] fair form in bumpers: wears tongue tie: fair maiden on Flat, stays 1¼m: has joined Julia Brooke. *Susan Corbett*

FORGE MEADOW (IRE) 7 b.m. Beneficial – Ballys Baby (IRE) (Bob Back (USA)) **c123** [2018/19 h143: c18.2d³ c16.1d² c16.7v⁴ h20g⁴ h16d⁴ h16d² h16d Apr 23] useful hurdler: **h135** second in Red Mills Trial Hurdle at Gowran (11 lengths behind Darasso) in February: fairly useful form over fences: best effort when second in maiden at Punchestown in November: stays 2½m: acts on heavy going: tried in hood: front runner/races prominently. *Mrs J. Harrington, Ireland*

FORGET ME KNOT (IRE) 6 b.m. Presenting – J'y Reste (FR) (Freedom Cry) **h100** [2018/19 b–p: b16.3g* h19.6g³ h20.6gᵖᵘ h19.5m* Apr 22] has had breathing operation: **b84** modest form in bumpers: won maiden at Stratford in June: fair form over hurdles: won mares novice at Chepstow in April. *Emma Lavelle*

FORGE VALLEY 15 b.g. Bollin William – Scalby Clipper (Sir Mago) [2018/19 c94: **c–** c25.5g⁶ May 30] lengthy gelding: multiple point winner: modest maiden hunter chaser: well held sole start under Rules in 2018/19: stays 3¼m: acts on soft going: wears cheekpieces. *Miss G. Walton*

FOR GOOD MEASURE (IRE) 8 b.g. King's Theatre (IRE) – Afdala (IRE) (Hernando **c119** (FR)) [2018/19 c132p, h–: c25g⁵ c25g⁶ h23.1d⁶ c24.2dᶠ c24m² Apr 25] sturdy gelding: **h122** fairly useful handicap hurdler: similar form over fences: stays 25f: acts on heavy going. *Philip Hobbs*

FORGOTTEN GOLD (IRE) 13 b.g. Dr Massini (IRE) – Ardnataggle (IRE) (Aristocracy) **c105** [2018/19 c138, h–: c26g³ c23.4d³ c23.8gᵖᵘ Apr 25] stocky gelding: winning hurdler: useful **h–** chaser, well below form in hunters in 2018/19: stays 27f: acts on any going: wears headgear. *Tom George*

FORGOT TO ASK (IRE) 7 b.g. Ask – Lady Transcend (IRE) (Aristocracy) [2018/19 **c–** h109p, b–: h15.8d³ h20.6g⁴ c23.9gᶠ c23dᶠ h21.4g³ h19g³ Apr 25] has had breathing **h114** operation: fair hurdler: won maiden at Market Rasen in May: fell both starts over fences: stays 21f: acts on soft going: in tongue tie last 2 starts. *Tom George*

FOR JIM (IRE) 7 gr.g. Milan – Dromhale Lady (IRE) (Roselier (FR)) [2018/19 h96p: **c–** h16.8g h15.8g h22.1s c16.4m h18.6g c24.2g Apr 15] unplaced in Irish points: poor maiden **h70** hurdler: well held both starts over fences: stays 2½m: acts on good to soft going: tried in cheekpieces. *Jennie Candlish*

FOR LUCK (FR) 4 ch.g. Coastal Path – Isis de Sormain (FR) (Useful (FR)) [2018/19 **b–** b16g⁵ Apr 25] well beaten in bumper. *Ben Pauling*

FORMIDABLEOPPONENT (IRE) 12 b.g. Arakan (USA) – Sliding (Formidable (USA)) [2018/19 c89, h–: c20.5d^{pu} Nov 3] point winner: winning hurdler: fairly useful chaser at best, pulled up sole start under Rules in 2018/19: stays 3m: acts on soft and good to firm going: wears blinkers: has worn tongue tie. *William Young Jnr* **c–** **h–**

FOR PLEASURE (IRE) 4 ch.g. Excelebration (IRE) – Darsan (IRE) (Iffraaj) [2018/19 h15.8g^f h15.7g³ h16d⁵ Dec 4] fairly useful on Flat for James M. Barrett, stays 1½m: fair form over hurdles: best effort when third in juvenile at Catterick in November: wears hood. *Alex Hales* **h102**

FORRARDON XMOOR 10 gr.g. Fair Mix (IRE) – The Nuns Song (Sir Harry Lewis (USA)) [2018/19 c84, h–: c23.8g^{pu} c23.5s^{pu} Oct 12] multiple point winner: no form over hurdles: poor form only completed start in chases: tried in tongue tie: dead. *Gordon Elliott, Ireland* **c–** **h–**

FORRESTERS PARK (IRE) 5 b.g. Scorpion (IRE) – Creanna Lady (IRE) (Flemensfirth (USA)) [2018/19 b16m Apr 13] pulled up both starts in Irish points: well beaten in bumper. *Alistair Whillans* **b**

FORTESCUE 5 b.g. Shirocco (GER) – Last of Her Line (Silver Patriarch (IRE)) [2018/19 b15.8d b15.8g³ b15.8s h18.5d^{pu} h20.5d h19.7d³ h21g⁴ Apr 10] well-made gelding: fifth foal: half-brother to fairly useful hurdler Lord Grantham (2½m-2¾m winner, by Definite Article) and fairly useful/temperamental hurdler/chaser Go West Young Man (2m-21f winner, by Westerner), stays 3m: dam unraced half-sister to fairly useful hurdler/useful chaser (19f-3¼m winner) Sail By The Stars: modest form in bumpers: fair form over hurdles: ungenuine. *Henry Daly* **h101 §** **b76**

FORT GABRIEL (FR) 8 ch.g. Ange Gabriel (FR) – Forge Neuve (FR) (Tel Quel (FR)) [2018/19 c112, h–: c20s² c26.1g* c23g³ c24.1g Aug 3] maiden hurdler: fairly useful handicap chaser: won at Uttoxeter in June: stays 3¼m: acts on soft and good to firm going: has worn headgear. *David Bridgwater* **c120** **h–**

FORTH BRIDGE 6 b.g. Bernardini (USA) – Sally Forth (Dubai Destination (USA)) [2018/19 c113, h134: h15.7g c16.2d² c23g² c23.8g² c22.5g⁴ c20.2g³ c21.2d² c20.3g² c22.7m² c20.5s* c20.5m⁴ Apr 12] lengthy, useful-looking gelding: useful hurdler: useful handicap chaser: won at Kempton (by 6 lengths from Onefortheroadtom) in March: stays 23f: acts on soft and good to firm going: usually wears cheekpieces: tried in tongue tie. *Charlie Longsdon* **c133** **h–**

FORTH CAVE (IRE) 7 b.g. Court Cave (IRE) – Supreme Departure (IRE) (Supreme Leader) [2018/19 h–: h23.9g h22.1g^{pu} May 28] placed in points: no form over hurdles: in cheekpieces last 2 starts: tried in tongue tie. *Dianne Sayer* **h–**

FORTHEFUNOFIT (IRE) 10 b.g. Flemensfirth (USA) – Sommer Sonnet (IRE) (Taipan (IRE)) [2018/19 c–, h118: h25.4g⁵ c23g² h26.4m* c26.2g^F Oct 25] sturdy gelding: fairly useful handicap hurdler: won at Stratford in July: similar form over fences: second in handicap at Worcester in June: stays 3¼m: acts on good to firm and heavy going: usually wears cheekpieces. *Jonjo O'Neill* **c118** **h124**

FOR THREE (IRE) 5 b.g. Pour Moi (IRE) – Asmaa (USA) (Canadian Frontier (USA)) [2018/19 h16.4g² h17g² h16.4s⁵ h16g³ Apr 11] modest maiden on Flat, stays 10.5f: fair form over hurdles: wears hood. *James Ewart* **h108**

FORTIA 5 b.m. Nathaniel (IRE) – Veenwouden (Desert Prince (IRE)) [2018/19 h19.6g⁴ h16g² h16.8g³ h19.5s h20.3d h20.5g Apr 22] has had breathing operation: half-sister to bumper winner/useful hurdler Hurricane Hollow (2m/17f winner, by Beat Hollow), stayed 2½m: modest maiden on Flat, stays 11.5f: modest form over hurdles. *Emma Lavelle* **h99**

FORT JEFFERSON 6 br.g. Passing Glance – Florida Heart (First Trump) [2018/19 h102: h16.7g* h16.7g³ h17.2d⁴ Aug 25] fairly useful on Flat, stays 1¾m: fair hurdler: won maiden at Bangor early in season: unproven beyond 17f: acts on good to soft going: wears headgear. *Oliver Greenall* **h105**

FORT SMITH (IRE) 10 b.g. Presenting – Land of Honour (Supreme Leader) [2018/19 c–§, h–§: c26g⁴ May 9] maiden hurdler: useful chaser at best, lightly raced nowadays and retains little ability: usually wears headgear/tongue tie: one to leave alone. *Oliver Sherwood* **c– §** **h– §**

FORTUNATE GEORGE (IRE) 9 b.g. Oscar (IRE) – Fine Fortune (IRE) (Bob Back (USA)) [2018/19 c129, h133: h21g h23.4v h21.4d h20.5d³ c24.2d^{pu} Mar 24] good-topped gelding: fairly useful handicap hurdler: third at Newbury in March: fairly useful chaser, pulled up final start: stays 3m: acts on heavy going: wears headgear. *Emma Lavelle* **c–** **h117**

FORTUNE BOUND (IRE) 10 ch.g. Primary (USA) – Special Artist (IRE) (Rock Hopper) [2018/19 c26g* May 4] multiple point winner: fair form when won at Cheltenham on completed start in hunter chases. *Richard Bandey* **c107**

FORTUNES HIDING (IRE) 6 b.g. Beat Hollow – Sambre (FR) (Turgeon (USA)) [2018/19 b–: b16g* b16.7m³ h20.1s³ h20g⁶ h19.5s c20.3g⁵ Jan 7] fairly useful form in bumpers: won at Worcester in June: fair form over hurdles: best effort when third in maiden at Hexham: tailed off in novice handicap on chasing debut: wears tongue tie: should do better. *Peter Bowen*
c– p
h100 p
b99

FOR YES (IRE) 10 b.g. Kutub (IRE) – Oscartan (IRE) (Oscar (IRE)) [2018/19 c100, h–: c24.2d³ c26.2g c27.5dᵖᵘ c24.2gᵖᵘ Jun 16] multiple point winner: pulled up sole start over hurdles: modest maiden chaser: stays 3m: acts on good to soft going: wears headgear/tongue tie. *Stuart Coltherd*
c93
h–

FORZA MILAN (IRE) 7 b.g. Milan – Nonnetia (FR) (Trempolino (USA)) [2018/19 h135: c20s c23.6dᵖᵘ h19.8s* h24.7gᵖᵘ Apr 6] useful-looking gelding: has had breathing operation: useful handicap hurdler: won at Sandown (by 2 lengths from Magoo) in March: not given hard time both starts over fences: stays 25f: acts on heavy going: tried in tongue tie: usually races off pace: should do better as a chaser. *Jonjo O'Neill*
c– p
h134

FOSTERED PHIL (IRE) 5 b.g. Arcadio (GER) – Knock Na Shee (IRE) (Classic Cliche (IRE)) [2018/19 b16.9g² b16.2g³ b16.2g² Feb 14] first foal: dam twice-raced half-sister to useful hurdler/chaser (stayed 21f) Chasing Cars: fair form when placed all 3 starts in bumpers: left Paul Nolan after first one: tried in hood. *James Ewart*
b92

FOUNDATION MAN (IRE) 12 b.g. Presenting – Function Dream (IRE) (Strong Gale) [2018/19 c117§, h–: c20.3g³ c20.3g⁵ c21g c20.3g c21g⁴ c23.6g c20g c19.2s³ Dec 6] very big gelding: has reportedly suffered breathing problems: lightly-raced hurdler: fair handicap chaser: stays 3m: acts on firm and soft going: has worn headgear/tongue tie: unreliable. *Jonjo O'Neill*
c112 §
h–

FOUNTAINS CIDER 11 b.g. Pasternak – Fountain Crumble (Dr Massini (IRE)) [2018/19 c21.6g⁵ May 17] point winner: little impact under Rules: usually wears tongue tie. *Steve Spice*
c–
h–

FOUR KINGDOMS (IRE) 5 b.g. Lord Shanakill (USA) – Four Poorer (IRE) (Oasis Dream) [2018/19 h16.2g⁴ Sep 17] fair on Flat, stays 2m: 8/1, fourth in maiden at Hexham (11 lengths behind Globetrotter) on hurdling debut. *R. Mike Smith*
h93

FOUR MILE BEACH 6 gr.g. Dalakhani (IRE) – Rappel (Royal Applause) [2018/19 h85§: h20.3g⁴ h20.6g h18.6g⁶ Apr 3] poor maiden hurdler: left Ruth Jefferson after second start: unproven beyond 17f: acts on good to firm going: usually wears headgear: one to treat with caution. *Michael Chapman*
h76 §

FOUROVAKIND 14 b.g. Sir Harry Lewis (USA) – Four M's (Majestic Maharaj) [2018/19 c117, h–: c26.3g⁵ May 4] winning hurdler: fairly useful chaser, well held in hunter sole start in 2018/19: stays 31f: acts on heavy going: wears blinkers. *Matt Hazell*
c79
h–

FOURSHOES 4 b.f. Passing Glance – Peel Me A Grape (Gunner B) [2018/19 b12.4g² b16g⁶ b16.5d Apr 4] half-sister to 3 winners, including bumper winner/useful hurdler Letsby Avenue (2¾m winner, by Tikkanen): dam unraced sister to useful chaser (2m-21f winner) Air Shot and useful staying hurdler Flying Gunner, and half-sister to useful chaser (stayed 25f) Windross: modest form in bumpers. *Alan King*
b78

FOURTH ACT (IRE) 10 b.g. King's Theatre (IRE) – Erintante (IRE) (Denel (FR)) [2018/19 c125, h119: c25.8gᵖᵘ May 9] angular gelding: has had breathing operation: fairly useful hurdler: fairly useful chaser, pulled up sole start in 2018/19: stays 3½m: acts on good to firm and heavy going: has worn headgear, including last 3 starts: wears tongue tie: front runner/races prominently. *Colin Tizzard*
c–
h–

FOURTH OF JULY (IRE) 4 b.g. Salutino (GER) – Akasha (IRE) (Stowaway) [2018/19 b14.6s h15.6m³ h16g h16.2g⁶ Apr 25] €8,000 3-y-o: fourth foal: dam unraced: well held in bumper: modest form over hurdles: tried in hood. *R. Mike Smith*
h87
b–

FOX APPEAL (IRE) 12 b.g. Brian Boru – Lady Appeal (IRE) (Phardante (FR)) [2018/19 c140x, h–: c23.8d³ c23g² c20.5g⁶ c23.8m² c21g⁴ Apr 20] smallish gelding: winning hurdler: useful handicap chaser: second at Taunton in November and January (2 lengths behind Romain de Senam): stays 3m: acts on good to firm and heavy going: wears headgear/tongue tie: often let down by jumping over fences. *Emma Lavelle*
c130 x
h–

FOXCUB (IRE) 11 b.g. Bahri (USA) – Foxglove (Hernando (FR)) [2018/19 c100, h–: c25.3g* May 4] sturdy gelding: point winner: winning hurdler: fair form in hunter chases: won at Cheltenham early in season: stays 25f: acts on heavy going: has worn cheekpieces, including last 3 starts. *R. D. Potter*
c105
h–

FOXEY 4 b.g. Foxwedge (AUS) – Blue Lyric (Refuse To Bend (IRE)) [2018/19 b13.1g **b90** b14.6s[3] b16.2g b15.7d[2] Mar 20] fourth foal: half-brother to 3 winners on Flat, including 8.6f winner Ode To Glory (by Poet's Voice), stayed 1½m: dam 7f winner: fair form in bumpers: wears hood. *James Ewart*

FOX NORTON (FR) 9 b.g. Lando (GER) – Natt Musik (FR) (Kendor (FR)) [2018/19 **c164** c167, h–: c16.8d[2] c21d[3] Feb 16] well-made gelding: winning hurdler: high-class chaser: **h–** second in Clarence House Chase at Ascot (7 lengths behind Altior) in January and third in Betfair Ascot Chase (18¼ lengths behind Cyrname) in February: stays 2½m: acts on soft going: usually wears hood, left off both starts in 2018/19. *Colin Tizzard*

FOX PRO (FR) 4 b.g. Coastal Path – Devise II (FR) (Djarvis (FR)) [2018/19 h16.9s[3] **h125** h16.9s* h17.4v[6] h16.4s h17.9s* Apr 9] half-brother to 3 winning chasers in France by Video Rock, including cross-country chase winners Qonqerant (21f) and Osko d'Aron (23f): dam French 25f/3¼m cross-country chase winner: fairly useful form over hurdles: won juveniles at Compiegne in November and April: well held in Fred Winter Juvenile Handicap at Cheltenham only outing in Britain: stays 2¼m: raced only on soft/heavy going: usually front runner/races prominently. *Mrs Jane Williams*

FOXTAIL HILL (IRE) 10 b.g. Dr Massini (IRE) – Flynn's Girl (IRE) (Mandalus) **c129** [2018/19 c141, h–: c15.9d[3] c20.6d c20.6d[5] c20d[4] c19.9g[4] c16g[6] Apr 25] workmanlike **h–** gelding: winning hurdler: fairly useful handicap chaser nowadays: fourth at Warwick in February: stays 21f: acts on soft going: usually front runner/races prominently. *Nigel Twiston-Davies*

FOXTROT JULIET 6 b.m. Shirocco (GER) – Miami Explorer (Pennekamp (USA)) **h108** [2018/19 b78: h16.7g h15.8g[2] h15.3f* h16g[F] h15.7g[2] h15.7g[3] h16d h16.5d[5] Apr 24] has had breathing operation: fair hurdler: won novice at Wincanton in October: raced around 2m: acts on firm going: usually front runner/races prominently. *Olly Murphy*

FOXWORTHY 7 b.g. Yeats (IRE) – Candy Creek (IRE) (Definite Article) [2018/19 **h– p** h23.6d Jan 18] second foal: closely related to fairly useful hurdler Asum (2m winner, by Kayf Tara), stayed 2½m: dam (h122), bumper/2m-2½m hurdle winner, half-sister to useful hurdler/smart chaser (2m/17f winner) Crossbow Creek: off mark in points at second attempt: reportedly struck into when tailed off in maiden on hurdling debut: should do better. *Nicky Henderson*

FOXY ACT 8 ch.m. Act One – Brown Fox (FR) (Polar Falcon (USA)) [2018/19 h115: **h–** h21g[pu] h20s May 25] fair hurdler, no form in 2018/19: stays 2¾m: acts on good to firm and good to soft going: tried in cheekpieces: usually leads. *Chris Down*

FOXY LASS 5 b.m. Foxwedge (AUS) – Domitia (Pivotal) [2018/19 h102: h16d[3] h16.5g[6] **c79 §** h20m[3] h16.9g h19.5s c20d[6] c23.5v[pu] h23.1s[pu] Mar 18] modest hurdler: poor form over **h85 §** fences: left Denis Hogan after fourth start: unproven beyond 2m: acts on heavy going: usually wears headgear: one to treat with caution. *Alexandra Dunn*

FOXY SINGER (FR) 4 b.f. Secret Singer (FR) – Newport (FR) (Hawker's News (IRE)) **b–** [2018/19 b16.2v[4] Dec 15] seventh foal: dam unraced half-sister to useful chaser (stayed 29f) Kamillo: well beaten in junior bumper: won point in March: has joined Clare Hobson. *Dan Skelton*

FOXY'S SPIRIT 4 b.f. Foxwedge (AUS) – Jessie's Spirit (IRE) (Clodovil (IRE)) **h–** [2018/19 h16.6g h16s h16.7d[6] h15.8d h16.6d[6] h15.9d Mar 18] poor maiden on Flat: little form over hurdles: tried in tongue tie. *Joanne Thomason-Murphy*

FRAME RATE 4 b.g. Arcano (IRE) – Miss Quality (USA) (Elusive Quality (USA)) **h100** [2018/19 h16.2g[6] h15.6g[2] h15.7g[F] h19.3s[pu] h15.6g h19.8s* h19.8m[5] Mar 22] modest maiden on Flat, best effort at 1m: fair handicap hurdler: won at Musselburgh in March: stays 2½m: acts on soft going. *Iain Jardine*

FRANCE DU LUKKA (FR) 5 bl.m. Kap Rock (FR) – Orlamonde Queen (FR) (Royal **h–** Charter (FR)) [2018/19 h–, b–: h16.8s Dec 7] little form in bumpers/novice hurdles: tried in hood. *Jackie du Plessis*

FRANCKY DU BERLAIS (FR) 6 b.g. Saint des Saints (FR) – Legende du Luy (FR) **h118** (Bonnet Rouge (FR)) [2018/19 h110, b77: h16.8g[3] h15.8d* h18.7g[2] h20.3g[2] h20g[5] h20.5g[4] Apr 21] good-bodied gelding: fairly useful hurdler: won novices at Ffos Las in May and Worcester in September: will stay 3m: acts on soft going: often wears hood/tongue tie: front runner/races prominently. *Peter Bowen*

FRANKIE BALLOU (IRE) 10 br.g. Norwich – One Up (IRE) (Bob Back (USA)) **c–** [2018/19 c103, h–: c17.3g[ur] c20d[pu] c17.4s[6] c16.4s[pu] c16.3d[4] Apr 6] quite good-topped **h–** gelding: maiden hurdler: fair chaser, out of form in 2018/19: wears headgear: tried in tongue tie. *Joanne Foster*

FRANKIE RAPPER (IRE) 7 b.g. Milan – Parkdota (IRE) (Good Thyne (USA)) **h114**
[2018/19 h89: h23g* h25g⁶ h25m² h19.9d² h25.5d⁶ Jan 2] fair handicap hurdler: won at
Worcester in May: stays 25f: acts on good to firm and good to soft going: in cheekpieces
last 2 starts: in tongue tie last 3: carries head awkwardly. *Dan Skelton*

FRANKIES FIRE 6 b.m. Flying Legend (USA) – Watch The Wind (High Kicker (USA)) **b–**
[2018/19 b16.2g⁶ b16.2g Aug 18] first foal: dam (c80/h76) maiden jumper (raced mainly at
2m): well held in 2 bumpers: multiple point winner. *James Walton*

FRANKIE'S PROMISE (IRE) 11 ch.g. Fruits of Love (USA) – According To Molly **c–**
(IRE) (Accordion) [2018/19 h23.3g⁶ h20.2g Jun 23] placed in points: fair hurdler at best, **h70**
well below form both starts in 2018/19: lightly-raced chaser: stays 2½m: acts on heavy
going: has worn headgear, including last 4 starts. *N. W. Alexander*

FRANKLY ALL TALK (IRE) 6 b.g. Fracas (IRE) – Take My Word (IRE) (Alhaarth **c114**
(IRE)) [2018/19 b17.3g h16d h20d h24.3v³ c20d⁶ c22.5d³ c24d² c16.2d⁵ c23.4d* Feb 28] **h94**
€11,000 3-y-o: third foal: dam unraced: tailed off in bumper: modest form over hurdles: fair **b–**
form over fences: won novice at Clonmel in February: stays 3m: acts on heavy going. *R. K.
Watson, Ireland*

FRANKLY SPEAKING 9 ch.g. Flemensfirth (USA) – No More Money (Alflora (IRE)) **c102**
[2018/19 h112: h23.6s c24.2s⁴ c26d c28.8v^pu Feb 18] lengthy gelding: fair maiden hurdler: **h86**
similar form over fences: best effort when fourth in novice handicap at Wetherby in
December: stays 25f: acts on heavy going: races towards rear. *Tom Symonds*

FRANK N FAIR 11 br.m. Trade Fair – Frankfurt (GER) (Celtic Swing) [2018/19 c104, **c–**
h–: c29.1g^pu May 8] winning hurdler: fair chaser, pulled up sole start in 2018/19: stays **h–**
3½m: acts on heavy going: tried in cheekpieces. *Zoe Davison*

FRANK THE SLINK 13 b.g. Central Park (IRE) – Kadari (Commanche Run) [2018/19 **c83**
c78, h–: c24.2g^pu c24.2s² c24.2g² c24.5v^pu c26.7d⁵ Jan 4] strong gelding: maiden hurdler: **h–**
poor handicap chaser nowadays: stays 3¼m: acts on heavy going: has worn cheekpieces,
including last 5 starts: wears tongue tie: front runner/races prominently. *Micky Hammond*

FRANSHAM 5 b.g. Sulamani (IRE) – Circus Rose (Most Welcome) [2018/19 b15.7g **h120**
b16g² b16v h15.8g⁴ h15.8g⁴ h15.8g^co h16g² h16g* h16m* Apr 25] fifth foal: half-brother **b86**
to fairly useful chaser Popelys Gull (19f winner, by Recharge), stays 3m, and fairly useful
hurdler Acertain Circus (2m-23f winner, by Definite Article): dam (h128), 2m-2½m hurdle
winner, half-sister to fairly useful hurdler/chaser (stayed 3¼m) Harrycone Lewis: fair form
in bumpers: fairly useful form over hurdles: won maiden at Wetherby and novice at
Kempton in April: raced only at 2m: acts on good to firm going. *Pam Sly*

FRANZ KLAMMER 7 b.g. Midnight Legend – Ski (Petoski) [2018/19 h94: h16.8g^pu **h54**
h20.3g h23g^pu h20g⁵ h19.5g Oct 30] poor maiden hurdler: left Charlie Longsdon after
second start: best efforts at 2m: in hood last 2 starts: tried in tongue tie. *Peter Pritchard*

FRASER CANYON 7 b.g. Halling (USA) – Valley of Gold (FR) (Shirley Heights) **h–**
[2018/19 h96: h25.8s Oct 6] modest hurdler, lame sole start in 2018/19: stays 3m: acts on
soft going: in headgear last 3 starts: wears tongue tie. *Tim Vaughan*

FRAU GEORGIA (IRE) 5 b.m. Germany (USA) – Sumability (IRE) (Oscar (IRE)) **b85**
[2018/19 b16g² b16g Feb 19] €10,000 3-y-o, resold £115,000 3-y-o: fourth foal: half-sister
to a winning pointer by Kalanisi: dam, unraced, out of sister to useful hurdler/smart chaser
(stayed 3m) Supreme Prince: fair form in bumpers: better effort when second in maiden at
Warwick in January. *Neil Mulholland*

FREDDY FANATAPAN 4 b.g. Nathaniel (IRE) – Pan Galactic (USA) (Lear Fan (USA)) **b79**
[2018/19 b13.2m³ b16d Feb 23] modest form in bumpers. *Stuart Kittow*

FRED'S FILLY 6 ch.m. Avonbridge – Regal Quest (IRE) (Marju (IRE)) [2018/19 h–: **h87**
h15.3m⁶ h15.8g⁴ h15.8m h15.3g h15.3d^pu Dec 26] modest form over hurdles: wears
headgear. *Nick Mitchell*

FREE BOUNTY 6 b.g. Dick Turpin (IRE) – Native Ring (FR) (Bering) [2018/19 h99: **h95**
h15.8g⁴ h20.6g h23.3g^pu h21.6m* h21.6m^ur h20.3g^ur h19.6m Oct 4] neat gelding: modest
handicap hurdler: won at Newton Abbot in July: stays 2¾m: acts on good to firm going:
wears tongue tie: usually forces pace: has joined Clare Ellam. *Neil Mulholland*

FREEDOM CHIMES 5 b.g. Champs Elysees – Ombre (Galileo (IRE)) [2018/19 h16s³ **h99**
h15.7g h16d^ur h16m⁶ h15.8s⁶ h19.7g^pu Feb 19] has had breathing operation: modest
maiden hurdler: left Ms Margaret Mullins after first start: raced mainly around 2m: acts on
heavy going. *Rosemary Gasson*

FREEDOM RUN 6 ch.m. Presenting – Mathine (FR) (Malinas (GER)) [2018/19 b74: b16g[2] b16g[4] h21.2d[5] Dec 19] modest form in bumpers: second in mares event at Worcester in September: 20/1, fifth in mares novice at Ludlow (19 lengths behind Liberty Bella) on hurdling debut: should improve. *Emma Lavelle* **h84 p b82**

FREE (FR) 5 b.m. Mr Sidney (USA) – Funny Feerie (FR) (Sillery (USA)) [2018/19 h16d[6] Mar 21] sister to fairly useful 21f hurdle winner Full and half-sister to 3 winning jumpers, including French hurdler/chaser Flagstaff (17f-3¼m winner, by Numerous): dam French 2¼m winner: useful on Flat in France for Mme C. Head-Maarek, stays 13f: sold €125,000 and off 17 months, 9/2, sixth in mares novice at Chepstow (13¼ lengths behind Deadringerforlove) on hurdling debut: should do better. *Anthony Honeyball* **h– p**

FREE RANGE (IRE) 9 b.g. Subtle Power (IRE) – Tullyspark Rose (IRE) (Beneficial) [2018/19 c111, h112: c21.6g[2] c22.5g[4] c24.1g[pu] c20.1s h19.6g[pu] c16.3g* Nov 16] fair form over hurdles: fairly useful handicap chaser: won novice events at Kelso early in season and Newcastle in November: left Micky Hammond after first start: stays 2¾m: acts on soft going: wears headgear. *Stella Barclay* **c115 h–**

FREE RETURN (IRE) 8 b.g. Mr Combustible (IRE) – Marisha (IRE) (Gulland) [2018/19 c–, h–: c20.9m[pu] c23m c24g[6] Jul 18] runner-up on second of 2 starts in Irish points: little form under Rules: wears headgear: tried in tongue tie. *Tom Weston* **c56 h–**

FREE STONE HILL (IRE) 9 b.g. Beneficial – Claramanda (IRE) (Mandalus) [2018/19 c115, h114: c16.2m[2] c16.3g[2] c15.7g[2] Jun 25] workmanlike gelding: fair hurdler: fairly useful maiden chaser: runner-up all 3 starts in 2018/19: stays 19f: acts on good to firm going: wears tongue tie: usually races nearer last than first: has joined Milton Bradley: no battler. *Dan Skelton* **c115 § h–**

FREE TRAVEL (IRE) 8 b.g. Stowaway – Janet Lindup (Sabrehill (USA)) [2018/19 h63: h15.8v h19.2d Feb 24] third in Irish point on debut: little show over hurdles. *Ben Case* **h–**

FRELIA (IRE) 8 b.m. Oscar (IRE) – Hannabelle (IRE) (Rudimentary (USA)) [2018/19 c109: c25.3g[pu] May 4] multiple point winner: tailed off in mares hunter chases, pulled up sole start in sphere in 2018/19: tried in tongue tie. *D. C. Gibbs* **c–**

FRENCH CRUSADER (FR) 6 b.g. Kapgarde (FR) – Largesse (FR) (Saumarez) [2018/19 h122p, b95: h15.7g* h20.3g[2] h16.3d* Nov 8] bumper winner: useful form over hurdles: won maiden at Towcester early in season and handicap at Newbury (conditionals, by 8 lengths from Majestic Touch) in November: stays 2½m: acts on soft going: usually travels strongly. *Nicky Henderson* **h133**

FRENCH KISS (IRE) 4 b.g. French Fifteen (FR) – Ms Cordelia (USA) (Anabaa (USA)) [2018/19 h16.7d[3] Nov 14] modest maiden at best on Flat: 33/1, well-beaten third in juvenile maiden at Bangor on hurdling debut. *Tony Carroll* **h60**

FRENCH MADE (FR) 4 b.f. Dream Well (FR) – Sempiternelle (FR) (Lavirco (GER)) [2018/19 b11.9g[2] h16.5d* h16.8d h16d* Apr 22] useful-looking filly: third foal: closely related to French bumper winner/fair 2½m hurdle winner Diocese (by Linda's Lad): dam once-raced half-sister to fairly useful hurdler/chaser (stayed 3m) Ocean du Moulin: second in maiden bumper at Le Lion d'Angers for J-F. Doucet very early in season: useful form over hurdles: won mares maiden at Clonmel in January and Rathbarry & Glenview Studs Juvenile Hurdle at Fairyhouse (by ½ length from Gardens of Babylon) in April: best effort when 6¾ lengths third to Feu Follet in Prix Alain du Breil at Auteuil soon after end of British season: will stay beyond 19f. *W. P. Mullins, Ireland* **h142 b?**

FRENCH PIECE 5 ch.g. Alkaased (USA) – Aster (IRE) (Danehill (USA)) [2018/19 b17.7g[6] h19.7s[pu] h15.5d h15.5g h15.8d Jan 25] big, workmanlike gelding: tailed off in bumper: no form over hurdles. *David Bridgwater* **h– b–**

FRENCH SEVENTYFIVE 12 b.g. Pursuit of Love – Miss Tun (Komaite (USA)) [2018/19 c72, h66: h24g[4] c24g[ur] Jul 15] multiple point winner: poor handicap hurdler/chaser: stays 3m: acts on soft going: usually wears headgear, left off both starts under Rules in 2018/19. *Gillian Boanas* **c– h59**

FRENCHY DU LARGE (FR) 4 gr.g. Al Namix (FR) – Quadence de Sivola (FR) (Mansonnien (FR)) [2018/19 b14d[2] b16.7d[2] Jan 8] fourth foal: half-brother to French 17f hurdle/chase winner Danse du Large (by Astarabad): dam, French maiden (second at 10.5f), half-sister to fairly useful hurdlers/useful chasers up to 2½m/21f Turn Over Sivola and Bel Ami de Sivola: fairly useful form in bumpers: better effort when second at Warwick in November. *Venetia Williams* **b96**

FRESH NEW DAWN (IRE) 7 ch.g. Flemensfirth (USA) – Star Shuil (IRE) (Soviet Star **h97** (USA)) [2018/19 h109, b94: h24.3g⁵ May 7] runner-up on sole start in Irish points: fair maiden hurdler: stays 3¼m: acts on heavy going: has worn hood: usually races towards rear. *Olly Murphy*

FRESNO EMERY (FR) 4 b.g. Vision d'Etat (FR) – Urfie Star (FR) (Visionary (FR)) **h107** [2018/19 h17.7v* h15.7d⁶ h16.3d Mar 1] well-made gelding: first foal: dam French 12.5f-13.5f bumper winner: third in maiden bumper in France for F. Grizon: fair form over hurdles: won juvenile at Fontwell in December. *Robert Walford*

FRET D'ESTRUVAL (FR) 4 br.g. No Risk At All (FR) – Udine d'Estruval (FR) (Le **c117** Fou (IRE)) [2018/19 b13.4gᶠ h16.4g* h16.9d* h16.8d⁵ h15.8g³ c17.4s⁵ c16.9g* Apr 22] **h117** compact gelding: third foal: half-brother to fairly useful French 17f-19f hurdle/chase **b–** winner Defit d'Estruval (by Balko): dam ran twice over hurdles in France: fell shortly after start only outing in bumper: fairly useful form over hurdles: won juveniles at Vittel in August and Lyon Parilly in September: similar form over fences: won 4-y-o event at Strasbourg in April: left Guillaume Macaire after third start, Alan King after fifth: raced only around 2m: acts on good to soft going. *Patrice Quinton, France*

FRIARY GOLD (IRE) 7 b.g. Mountain High (IRE) – Platinium Ambition (IRE) (Good **c101** Thyne (USA)) [2018/19 h89, b97: h15.8g⁶ h15.8g⁵ h18.5m² h19.6g h18.5d c15.9m³ Apr **h95** 20] maiden Irish pointer: modest maiden hurdler: 11/1, last of 3 in novice handicap at Carlisle (13½ lengths behind Wishfull Dreaming) on chasing debut: stays 2¼m: acts on good to firm going: tried in tongue tie: usually races off pace. *Katy Price*

FRICKA 6 b.m. Sulamani (IRE) – Distant Florin (Medicean) [2018/19 b16g⁶ b15.8d² **b88** b15.7d³ b15.8m² Apr 23] second foal: dam (b81) bumper winner: fair form in bumpers. *Anthony Carson*

FRIDAY FEELING 5 b.m. Schiaparelli (GER) – Lac Marmot (FR) (Marju (IRE)) **b–** [2018/19 b–: b16gᵖᵘ Feb 22] rather unfurnished mare: no form in bumpers, lame sole start in 2018/19: tried in cheekpieces. *John O'Shea*

FRIDAY NIGHT LIGHT (FR) 6 b.g. Air Chief Marshal (IRE) – Peninsula (FR) **h113** (Dansili) [2018/19 h122: h23.1m⁶ h16v⁵ h15.7s h18.6d² h20.5dᶠ Mar 1] fair handicap hurdler: stayed 19f: acted on heavy going: wore headgear/tongue tie: dead. *David Pipe*

FRIEND OR FOE (FR) 4 b.g. Walk In The Park (IRE) – Mandchou (FR) (Mansonien **h103** (FR)) [2018/19 h16.9s⁴ h17.4g⁴ h16.5d* h18.8d h16m* Apr 22] fourth foal: dam, ran once over hurdles (pulled up) in France, out of half-sister to very smart cross-country chaser (stayed 4¼m) Garde Champetre: fair form over hurdles: won juvenile at Taunton in December and novice at Chepstow (2-runner race) in April: left Emmanuel Clayeux after second start: should stay beyond 2m: acts on good to firm and good to soft going: tried in tongue tie. *Paul Nicholls*

FRIENDS IN HEAVEN (IRE) 7 br.g. Asian Heights – Native Bev (IRE) (Be My **h82** Native (USA)) [2018/19 h–: h16.2d h20.1g h16.4gᵖᵘ Jan 15] runner-up on completed start in Irish points: poor form over hurdles. *Andrew Wilson*

FRIGHTENED RABBIT (USA) 7 b.g. Hard Spun (USA) – Champagne Ending (USA) **h81** (Precise End (USA)) [2018/19 h89: h20.2g³ May 17] sparely-made gelding: modest handicap hurdler: stays 2½m: acts on heavy going: has worn headgear/tongue tie: front runner/races prominently. *Dianne Sayer*

FRIPPON DE VAIGE 4 b.g. Apsis – Ratina de Vaige (FR) (April Night (FR)) **b–** [2018/19 b16.3d Mar 23] 50/1, well held in Goffs UK Spring Sales Bumper at Newbury. *Paul Webber*

FRIZZLE 6 b.m. Rocamadour – Dizzy Frizzy (Loup Sauvage (USA)) [2018/19 b68: **h–** h21.6gᵖᵘ May 9] poor form in bumpers: pulled up in mares novice on hurdling debut. *Emma Lavelle*

FRODON (FR) 7 b.g. Nickname (FR) – Miss Country (FR) (Country Reel (USA)) **c167** [2018/19 c160, h–: c19.9g* c20.2g² c20.6d* c25.3d* c20.6d* Mar 14] **h–**

A sound-jumping, front-running chaser in full flight is a thrilling sight and Cheltenham has certainly enjoyed its share of them over the years, from probably the greatest of them all, Dunkirk, whose breathtaking all-the-way twenty-length triumph in the Two-Mile Champion Chase of 1965 was one of the iconic performances, to the likes of Anaglogs Daughter, Dublin Flyer, Edredon Bleu, Fair Along, and others whom readers will recall for themselves. Frodon is a chaser whose career, like those of Dublin Flyer and Edredon Bleu, has included victories in big handicaps as well as top weight-for-age events and his three wins in the latest season on Cheltenham's

Caspian Caviar Gold Cup Handicap Chase, Cheltenham—a fine weight-carrying performance as Frodon makes most to beat fellow pacesetter Cepage (left)

New Course (where he has won five times in all) each featured a textbook, forcing ride by his regular partner, the champion conditional Bryony Frost, coupled with a nigh-on perfect round of jumping from an enthusiastic and ultra-game Frodon. The partnership turned into something of a 'dream team' for the sport's marketing people who got plenty of mileage—both before and afterwards—out of their tilt at the Grade 1 Ryanair Chase (registered as the Festival Trophy) at the sport's greatest four-day festival. Occasions like Frodon's victory in the Ryanair—followed forty minutes later by Paisley Park's Stayers' Hurdle win for owner Andrew Gemmell who has been blind since birth—cannot be produced to order. That they combined to form a 'golden hour' for jumping, which put the sport on the front pages as well as the sports pages of the next day's newspapers, was the best possible outcome. It provided the Cheltenham Festival, and the whole season, with one of the most satisfying days the sport has known in recent times. It was gold dust, with the two victories—overshadowing other newsworthy stories including three winners on the day for owner J. P. McManus—touching the hearts of millions who do not usually follow the sport and ostensibly presenting racing in the best possible light (though the BHA itself had done its best to put a damper on the Festival with its well-publicised intervention on the first day into a brutal National Hunt Chase, something examined in the essay on Le Breuil).

The high-class Frodon returned as good as ever in the Monet's Garden Old Roan Chase, a limited handicap at Aintree at the end of October (having had a breathing operation during his six-month break). Carrying top weight of 11-10, Frodon raced with typical zest and was always prominent before pressing on from the second last to win by a length and a quarter and half a length from Javert and Cloudy Dream. A career best, at up to that stage, followed in the BetVictor Gold Cup, the big handicap at Cheltenham's November meeting (staged on the Old Course). Starting at 16/1 and up against another heart-on-sleeve, front-running handicapper in Baron Alco, Frodon didn't have things all his own way but he kept on well to go down by two lengths, conceding 15 lb to the winner. The pair dominated the race throughout, providing a good example of how the Cheltenham course can reward enterprising riding tactics, particularly on horses who jump well (the fine jumping of Baron Alco and Frodon drew plenty of mistakes from their rivals and there were just six finishers at the end of a strongly-run race in which nothing that was held up was able to get into the race).

Frodon and Baron Alco faced each other again the following month at Cheltenham in the Caspian Caviar Gold Cup, which Frodon had won as a four-year-old. Off a mark 15 lb higher than for his first win in the event, and carrying top weight of 11-12, Frodon took the race by the scruff of the neck from the start, denying Baron Alco the advantage he had enjoyed in the BetVictor. As in that race, front-running tactics paid dividends, with most of those ridden to come from behind failing to get involved and in trouble from some way out. Similar tactics to those employed on Frodon have paid off with other recent winners of Cheltenham's December Gold Cup, most notably Village Vic and Niceonefrankie, with good

BetBright Trial Cotswold Chase, Cheltenham—Frodon's stamina just lasts out over this longer trip as he holds off Elegant Escape (noseband) and Terrefort (grey)

jumpers increasingly seeming to benefit from turning such races into a helter-skelter test. Frodon again kept on very gamely, winning by a length and a quarter from Cepage, who was also handily placed all the way, with the previous year's winner Guitar Pete fifteen lengths back in third, matching his placing in the BetVictor (Baron Alco came fourth). Frodon and Poquelin (also trained by Paul Nicholls) are the only dual winners of the December Gold Cup.

Another all-the-way success was achieved by Frodon in the BetBright Cotswold Chase on Cheltenham's Trials day at the end of January, which answered questions about his stamina over the longest trip he has so far tackled. He didn't have to improve on his handicap form to win ridden out from the Welsh Grand National winner Elegant Escape who rallied well to run Frodon to three quarters of a length, after the latter had looked in control at the last with his rider having made a decisive move by kicking for home turning into the straight. Frodon, Elegant Escape and third-placed Terrefort all looked possible Cheltenham Gold Cup contenders, but, in the end, the connections of Frodon and Terrefort preferred the option of the Ryanair Chase. Frodon started at 9/2 joint second favourite, behind the previous year's Arkle winner Footpad, with the JNwine.com Champion Chase winner Road To Respect (another defector from the Gold Cup, in which he had come fourth the previous year). One of the strongest fields assembled for the Ryanair also included two previous winners Un de Sceaux (making his fifth Festival appearance) and Balko des Flos, as well as Monalee who had been runner-up at the last two Festivals over longer distances in the Spa Hurdle and the 'novices' Gold Cup', the RSA Chase. Ryanair has been the sponsor of the Festival Trophy since its second running and the race has gradually assumed greater importance, fulfilling the course executive's wish to establish an open championship event for chasers over an intermediate distance. The Ryanair, however, can be a distraction for traditional Gold Cup and Queen Mother Champion Chase contenders and looks set to become even more of one now that its value has been boosted to make it the feature event, ahead of the Stayers' Hurdle, on the third day (which is now promoted as Ryanair Chase day, rather than Stayers' Hurdle day). The twelve-strong line-up provided a welcome return to double-figures after fields of eight and six for the two previous editions.

Eight of the latest Ryanair field were trained in Ireland, which had won the last three runnings, but the first two places went to home-trained French imports Frodon and 33/1-shot Aso, the last-named having finished third when Un de Sceaux won the race. Frodon had to find plenty in the closing stages to beat Aso, who headed him two out before he rallied to challenge again early on the run-in and forged ahead up the steep climb to the finish to win by a length and a quarter. Road To Respect and Monalee completed the frame, ahead of Un de Sceaux who wasn't at his best, as well as being disadvantaged by being held up in mid-field in another Cheltenham chase in which it paid to be handy. Aso had won a valuable handicap at the track on New Year's Day, making most, and Siruh du Lac won the Plate, the race after the Stayers' Hurdle, in similar style (the first four in the following day's Grand Annual all raced prominently). Perhaps more jockeys and trainers need to be aware of the advantage of racing prominently in big fields on Cheltenham's steeplechase courses which are on the turn for a good part of the circuit. The courses are also dolled out at certain times of the year (to save fresh ground for the Festival) which narrows the track, though it seems odd that ground is still preserved on the Thursday of the Festival for the following day's Gold Cup. The Ryanair Gold Cup is itself a championship race and should be run over its proper course, not one that adds over fifty yards to its correct distance because of rail movements.

Frodon's Ryanair was one of six Grade 1s won by Manor Farm Stables in the latest season when Paul Nicholls regained the trainers' championship from Nicky Henderson. Bryony Frost, who rode out her claim in November, is an important part of the operation (eighteen of her fifty winners were for Nicholls), backing up the stable's number-one Harry Cobden (who won four of the six Grade 1s on Dynamite Dollars, Clan des Obeaux, Cyrname and Topofthegame) and freelance Sam Twiston-Davies (who partnered Quel Destin in the Finale Junior Hurdle). Frost's strengths are not confined to her prowess in the saddle and she has become one of the most recognised names in jumps racing through some memorable post-race interviews. Her success on Frodon was the first by a female jockey in a Grade 1 over obstacles at the Cheltenham Festival (the amateur Katie Walsh won the Champion Bumper on Relegate in 2018), and two of Frost's contemporaries among the professionals, Lizzie Kelly and Irish-based Rachael Blackmore, also won races at the latest Festival (female riders had won four races at the previous year's Festival). Frost's post-race interview was typical of her: 'He's Pegasus, he's got wings and is the most incredible battler. He travelled, my God he jumped. The moment he got overtaken two out, most horses would quit. But no, he grabbed me and said "No, don't you dare give up. Don't you dare not send me into the last. I want this more than you, so come on, where are you?"' Her remarks certainly conveyed the bond she enjoys with a horse like Frodon, as well as the thrill of riding him. Another noted equine ally Black Corton gave Frost her fiftieth winner of the campaign in the Oaksey Chase

Ryanair Chase (Festival Trophy), Cheltenham—prominent racers dominate again as Frodon (right) and Bryony Frost hold off outsider Aso (white sleeves); Irish raiders Road To Respect (left) and Monalee (stars) complete the frame

at Sandown's Finale meeting on the day she returned from an injury that had ruled her out of the Grand National meeting; the pair were given a rousing reception on returning to the winner's enclosure.

The good-topped Frodon is another fine advertisement for purpose-bred French jumpers who tend to begin their racing careers earlier than their Irish and British counterparts. Frodon and his imported stablemates Clan des Obeaux (King George VI Chase) and Cyrname (Ascot Chase) raced as three-year-olds in France, as, incidentally, did the Cheltenham Gold Cup winner Al Boum Photo and the Champion Hurdle winner Espoir d'Allen. There is no recognised programme in Britain and Ireland to encourage horses bred specifically for jumping to gain experience over hurdles and fences as three-year-olds, something that could certainly do with some thought in the light of the continued success of imported French jumpers (Clan des Obeaux and Frodon both put their early experience to good use and ran in the Triumph Hurdle after joining Paul Nicholls, their juvenile campaigns arguably helping, rather than hindering, their development into top-class chasers). Frodon is by the top French juvenile hurdler Nickname who went on to become a high-class two-miler chaser (there is more about him in the essay on Cyrname). French breeders have greater access to stallions who have done well over jumps, some other examples given in the essay on Al Boum Photo, and they seem to strongly favour winning mares over well-bred ones who might have shown little ability, or who didn't race at all. Frodon's dam Miss Country won over hurdles in France at two and a quarter miles and his grandam Miss d'Hermite was a winner too, albeit being successful just once—in a nine-furlong maiden in the Provinces—in thirty-four outings, all on the Flat. Miss d'Hermite has had seven winners from ten foals and is the dam of the top-class chaser Medermit who won the Scilly Isles Novices' Chase and the Haldon Gold Cup, among other races (he went down by a neck in the 2009 Supreme Novices' Hurdle at Cheltenham and was placed over fences in the Ryanair Chase and other good races). Another of Miss d'Hermite's winners Miss Pistol is the dam of the smart French chaser Saint Pistol who finished third in a Grand Steeple-Chase de Paris. Frodon's dam has now had three winners from three runners, the others being Tidjy (a filly by Slickly), a winner over fifteen furlongs over hurdles in France, and Sao (by Great Pretender) who has shown fairly useful form over hurdles at around two miles since joining Frodon at Manor Farm Stables. Frodon's pedigree contains more speed than stamina (his dam's sire Country Reel won the Gimcrack) but he stays twenty-five furlongs, which gives his connections plenty of options for his next campaign. A strong-travelling front runner, he acts on good to firm and heavy going. He wears a tongue tie. *Paul Nicholls*

FROM EDEN (USA) 6 gr.g. Paddy O'Prado (USA) – Mizzcan'tbewrong (USA) (Mizzen Mast (USA)) [2018/19 h20.2g h16.6g h24.4g h18.6d h20d h20s h20s* h20s² h18.8g² h24.3m* h26.6g⁴ Apr 25] fairly useful handicap hurdler: won at Navan in March and Ayr in April: left V. T. O'Brien after sixth start: stays 3m: acts on soft and good to firm going: usually wears headgear. *Gordon Elliott, Ireland*   **h119**

FROM THE HEART (IRE) 5 b.g. Jeremy (USA) – Zephyr Lilly (IRE) (Alhaarth (IRE)) [2018/19 b–: h16.7g³ h16.7d h15.8s³ h20.5d h19.9d Mar 30] useful-looking gelding: fair form over hurdles: should stay 2½m. *Philip Hobbs*   **h103**

FRONTLINE (IRE) 11 b.g. King's Theatre (IRE) – Thunder Road (IRE) (Mtoto) [2018/19 c–, h–: c16.5g Jun 2] robust gelding: winning hurdler: fair maiden chaser in 2015/16, lightly raced and little form since: stays 2¼m: acts on heavy going: tried in headgear/ tongue tie. *Paul Cowley*   **c–** **h–**

FROSTY DAWN 11 b.m. Desideratum – Frosty Petal (Silver Patriarch (IRE)) [2018/19 h71: h23.1spu Dec 6] placed in points: poor maiden handicap hurdler: tried in blinkers: dead. *Mike Sowersby*   **h–**

FROZEN FLAME (IRE) 6 b.g. Frozen Fire (GER) – Flame Supreme (IRE) (Saddlers' Hall (IRE)) [2018/19 h109: h24g³ h23.1g* h23.3g^pu c23d^pu Dec 13] runner-up in Irish point on debut: fair handicap hurdler: won at Bangor in June: pulled up in novice handicap on chasing debut: stayed 25f: acted on good to soft going: tried in cheekpieces/tongue tie: dead. *Jonjo O'Neill* **c– h112**

FROZON 6 b.g. Kheleyf (USA) – Crozon (Peintre Celebre (USA)) [2018/19 h–: h16.7g⁴ h18.6g⁵ h20g⁴ h20d⁶ h15.7g^F Jan 1] modest maiden hurdler: stays 2½m: best form on good going: tried in hood. *Harriet Bethell* **h98**

FS LOLA 5 ch.m. Arvico (FR) – Semi Colon (FR) (Robin des Champs (FR)) [2018/19 b–: b16.8s^ro b16.8g⁴ Aug 15] has had breathing operation: modest form in bumpers: ran out circuit out on reappearance: in tongue tie last 2 starts. *Martin Hill* **b82**

FUBAR (IRE) 5 ch.g. Le Fou (IRE) – Petite Mielle (IRE) (Pasternak) [2018/19 b16.7g² b15.7m⁴ b16d³ b16.6g³ Feb 20] €15,000 3-y-o: third foal: dam (b77), lightly raced in bumpers, half-sister to fairly useful hurdler/winning chaser (stayed 27f) Little Shilling: fairly useful form in bumpers: second at Market Rasen in September. *Kim Bailey* **b99**

FU FU 6 b.m. Eastern Anthem (IRE) – Kasamba (Salse (USA)) [2018/19 b16.5d b16.5d⁴ Apr 4] sixth foal: half-sister to fairly useful hurdler Spellbound (19f winner, by Doyen) and fair hurdler Welcometothejungle (2½m winner, by Lucky Story): dam, 7f winner, half-sister to useful hurdlers/winning chasers (stayed 3m) Dancing Bay and Mister Dillon: poor form in bumpers. *Robert Walford* **b73**

FUGITIVES DRIFT (IRE) 4 b.g. Yeats (IRE) – Shebeganit (IRE) (Alflora (IRE)) [2018/19 b16.3d³ Mar 23] £24,000 3-y-o: third foal: dam unraced half-sister to useful hurdler (stayed 2¾m) Couleur France: 10/1, third in Goffs UK Spring Sales Bumper at Newbury (5¾ lengths behind Get In The Queue). *Nicky Henderson* **b96**

FUKUTO (FR) 4 b.g. Cokoriko (FR) – Hargaux de Saisy (FR) (Bad Conduct (USA)) [2018/19 h16.9s⁴ h17.9g* h16s² h16.8d Jan 26] sturdy gelding: half-brother to several winners in France, including 17f/2¼m chase winner Peppito (by Subotica): dam French 1¼m winner: fair form over hurdles: won juvenile at Argentan in October for Gabriel Leenders. *David Bridgwater* **h110**

FULL BATTEN (IRE) 8 ch.g. Shantou (USA) – Spanker (Suave Dancer (USA)) [2018/19 c21.6g May 17] point winner: modest maiden hurdler: well beaten in maiden hunter on chasing debut: stayed 21f: acted on soft going: usually wore headgear: tried in tongue tie: dead. *J. P. Owen* **c– h–**

FULL BORE (IRE) 6 b.g. Milan – Senora Snoopy (IRE) (Un Desperado (FR)) [2018/19 b15.8g² b16.8g* b15.8g² h16.7g* h16g² h19.6g* Nov 4] €50,000 3-y-o: third foal: half-brother to fairly useful hurdler/chaser Ten Sixty (2½m-2¾m winner) and a winning pointer (both by Presenting): dam (h100), bumper winner/maiden hurdler (stayed 21f), half-sister to useful hurdler/high-class chaser (stayed 3¼m) Snoopy Loopy: fairly useful form in bumpers: won at Newton Abbot in July: similar form over hurdles: won maiden at Bangor in August and novice at Huntingdon in November. *Nicky Henderson* **h126 b98**

FULL CRY (IRE) 9 b.g. Milan – Gaye Melody (IRE) (Un Desperado (FR)) [2018/19 c132, h–: h24.7d² h24.5g⁶ c25g² c20.1g^pu c25g* c24g⁴ c24g^ur c30.2g Dec 14] medium-sized gelding: fair form over hurdles: useful handicap chaser: won at Kilbeggan (by neck from Freewheelin Dylan) in September: stays 25f: acts on soft and good to firm going: wears cheekpieces/tongue tie. *Henry de Bromhead, Ireland* **c131 h108**

FULL (FR) 7 b.g. Mr Sidney (USA) – Funny Feerie (FR) (Sillery (USA)) [2018/19 c118, h109: c16.5g³ c16.5d⁴ c20g h18.7g h21.4m* h21.4f* c20.2g⁴ c16.1m^ur h19d Dec 13] strong gelding: fair hurdler: won handicap and novice at Wincanton in October: fair maiden chaser: stays 21f: acts on firm and soft going: wears headgear: has worn tongue tie. *Neil Mulholland* **c108 h109**

FULL GLASS (FR) 6 b.g. Diamond Green (FR) – Full Tune (FR) (Green Tune (USA)) [2018/19 c141p, h124: c21.6g^ur c23.8s^pu h24.3g^pu Feb 16] compact gelding: fairly useful hurdler/useful chaser, no form in 2018/19. *Alan King* **c– h–**

FULL IRISH (IRE) 8 b.g. Flemensfirth (USA) – Miss Kettlewell (IRE) (Saddlers' Hall (IRE)) [2018/19 c134, h–: c24d^pu c22.4s^R c19.4s^pu h19.8s c17.4g³ c16m³ Apr 22] well-made gelding: has had breathing operation: fairly useful hurdler/useful chaser at best, disappointing in 2018/19: stays 23f: acts on heavy going: often wears headgear: tried in tongue tie. *Emma Lavelle* **c111 h–**

FULLMOON LUNA LADY (FR) 4 b.f. Spanish Moon (USA) – Question de Temps (FR) (Epistolaire (IRE)) [2018/19 b16.8d^ur Apr 23] in tongue tie, 20/1, fatally injured in mares bumper at Sedgefield on debut. *Micky Hammond* **b–**

FULL OF ROQUE (FR) 4 b.g. Blue Bresil (FR) – Pearl de La Roque (FR) (Villez (USA)) **b86**
[2018/19 b16.8s² Apr 16] third foal: half-brother to fairly useful French 2¼m hurdle/chase
winner Dream Roque (by Youmzain): dam, French 2m-19f hurdle/chase winner, half-sister
to smart French hurdler/useful chaser (stayed 3¼m) Salder Roque: runner-up in point on
debut: 12/1, second in maiden bumper at Exeter (3 lengths behind Merchant House).
Tim Vaughan

FULL SHIFT (FR) 10 b.g. Ballingarry (IRE) – Dansia (GER) (Lavirco (GER)) [2018/19 **c104 §**
c–, h–: h20.1g⁵ h20.1g c24s⁴ c21g⁵ c21g⁵ c21.6d² c20d⁵ c15.9g⁵ c18.2d⁴ c19.2s Apr 16] **h97 §**
well-made gelding: useful hurdler at best: fair handicap chaser nowadays: left Ben Haslam
after third start, Sophie Leech after seventh: stays 2¾m: acts on soft going: has worn
headgear/tongue tie: temperamental. *Roy Brotherton*

FULL TILT 6 b.g. Flying Legend (USA) – Proper Posh (Rakaposhi King) [2018/19 **h99**
h23.6v³ h23.3s h23.6dᵖᵘ Jan 18] off mark in Irish points at third attempt: modest form over
hurdles: dead. *Kim Bailey*

FULL TIME PARTY (IRE) 6 b.g. Milan – Native Singer (IRE) (Be My Native (USA)) **b94**
[2018/19 b16.7m² b16.3s Mar 11] closely related to 2 winners, including fairly useful
hurdler/chaser Knockavilla (2m-2½m winner, by Saddlers' Hall), and half-brother to
bumper winner/fair hurdler Golden Child (21f winner, by Supreme Leader), stayed 3m:
dam unraced sister to high-class hurdler/smart chaser up to 2½m Ned Kelly and half-sister
to very smart staying chaser Nick Dundee: pulled up both starts in Irish points: fair form in
bumpers: better effort when second at Market Rasen in June for Tom George. *Rebecca Curtis*

FULL TROTTLE (IRE) 10 ch.g. Vertical Speed (FR) – Keerou Lady (IRE) (Be My **c123**
Native (USA)) [2018/19 c127: c20.8g² c20v* Feb 18] has had breathing operation:
multiple point winner: fairly useful hunter chaser: won at Lingfield in February: stays
2¾m: acts on heavy going: tried in hood: wears tongue tie. *Miss L. Thomas*

FULLY BOOKED 6 b.g. Beat Hollow – Friendly Craic (IRE) (Mister Lord (USA)) **h94**
[2018/19 b16d⁶ h20.5v h22.7g⁴ h16.2g⁵ h20.9g h20.2dᵖᵘ Apr 26] seventh foal: closely **b–**
related to 2 winners by King's Theatre, including useful hurdler/very smart chaser Royal
Regatta (2m-21f winner), and half-brother to useful hurdler/smart chaser Three Musketeers
(2½m-2¾m winner, by Flemensfirth): dam unraced: well beaten in bumper: modest form
over hurdles. *Sandy Thomson*

FUMAROLE 4 b.g. Maxios – Solar Midnight (USA) (Lemon Drop Kid (USA)) [2018/19 **b75**
b13.7m⁴ b14g Nov 4] modest form in bumpers: wears tongue tie. *Michael Wigham*

FUNKI (FR) 4 ch.g. Sinndar (IRE) – Medine (FR) (Mansonnien (FR)) [2018/19 b15.3g **b–**
Apr 14] lengthy gelding: tailed off in bumper. *Robert Walford*

FURIA D'OUDAIRIES (FR) 4 b.f. Hurricane Cat (USA) – Sonate d'Oudairies (FR) **h94**
(Until Sundown (USA)) [2018/19 b11.9g³ b15.3g⁵ h17.7v⁴ h15.8g² Mar 19] first foal: dam, **b72**
French 2¼m-2¾m chase winner, half-sister to useful hurdler/smart chaser (stayed 3m)
Toner d'Oudairies: poor form in bumpers: modest form over hurdles: better effort when
second in fillies juvenile at Huntingdon in March: left L. Viel after first start. *Gary Moore*

FURIOUSLY FAST (IRE) 7 b.g. Fast Company (IRE) – Agouti (Pennekamp (USA)) **h113**
[2018/19 h16.2g⁵ h15.8d⁵ Dec 9] sturdy gelding: fair handicap hurdler: raced around 2m:
acts on good to soft going. *Dai Burchell*

FURTHER NORTH (FR) 5 ch.g. Muhtathir – Shamah (Unfuwain (USA)) [2018/19 **h–**
h15.9gᵖᵘ h20.5sᵖᵘ h20.5dᵖᵘ h17.7vᵖᵘ Mar 16] lengthy, rather unfurnished gelding: pulled up
in maiden/novice hurdles. *Seamus Mullins*

FURY ROAD (IRE) 5 b.g. Stowaway – Molly Duffy (IRE) (Oscar (IRE)) [2018/19 b16g⁵ **b107**
b16d* Feb 23] €205,000 3-y-o: third foal: half-brother to bumper winner/fairly useful
hurdler Monbeg Worldwide (2½m winner, by Lucarno) and fairly useful hurdler Rebel
Royal (2m winner, by Getaway), stays 2½m: dam, unraced, closely related to smart hurdler
City Island Again: off mark in points at second attempt: won maiden in bumpers: won maiden
at Fairyhouse (tongue tied, by 7 lengths from The Rubinator) in February: improved again
when length third of 4 to Sixshooter at Punchestown shortly after end of British season,
short of room 2f out: will be suited by further than 2m. *Gordon Elliott, Ireland*

FUSEAU (FR) 4 b.g. Barastraight – Monepopee (FR) (Panoramic) [2018/19 b13m² b14d⁴ **b90**
b15.8d⁵ Mar 3] lengthy, rather unfurnished gelding: half-brother to several winners in
France, including 2¼m hurdle winner Beaugency (by Tunduru) and 17f chase winner
Deaupamine (by Smadoun): dam unraced half-sister to useful chaser (2m/17f winner)
L'Ange Au Ciel: fair form in bumpers: second in junior event at Doncaster in December.
Alan King

FUSIL RAFFLES (FR) 4 b.g. Saint des Saints (FR) – Tali des Obeaux (FR) **h147 p**
(Panoramic) [2018/19 h16.9s* h17.1m² h16m* Feb 23]

For the fourth time in twenty years, a Nicky Henderson-trained juvenile
landed the Champion Four Year Old Hurdle at the Punchestown Festival. Fusil
Raffles followed Katarino (1999), Punjabi (2007) and Grandouet (2011), Grandouet
having been the last British-trained winner of the race. Like Katarino and Punjabi,
Fusil Raffles had also landed the Adonis Hurdle at Kempton in late-February; but,
unlike Katarino, Punjabi and Grandouet, Fusil Raffles did not contest the Triumph
Hurdle—a race Katarino won—having picked up an injury when winning at
Kempton. The Henderson-trained trio, incidentally, are not the only horses to
complete that particular Kempton-Punchestown double. Thirty years ago, the
Neville Callaghan-trained Royal Derbi won both the Tote Placepot Hurdle—as the
Adonis was then known—and the Champion Four Year Old Hurdle. His was very
much a rags to riches story, as he had been bought off the Flat out of a Windsor
seller and he was having his fifteenth start of a hurdling campaign, which had begun
on firm ground at Plumpton in August, when he won the Champion Four Year Old
Hurdle. He was also running in his second race at the meeting, having been a beaten
favourite running against the best older novices two days previously, on the first of
the three days over which the Festival was then run—the addition of a fourth day and
championship races for two-mile hurdlers and staying chasers still a decade away. At
Punchestown, Royal Derbi produced the best performance by a juvenile that season
in defeating the filly Lunulae by ten lengths. He had finished fourth in the Triumph,
but turned the tables on the first and second from Cheltenham, the 66/1 winner
Ikdam and Highland Bud, with those further behind at Punchestown including the
favourite Vayrua, who had beaten Highland Bud in style in the Anniversary Hurdle
at Aintree. The field was one of the most representative assembled in the history of
the race and Royal Derbi beat his rivals fairly and squarely.

It is fair to say that there wasn't the same strength in depth to the opposition
that faced Fusil Raffles in the latest AES-sponsored renewal of the Champion Four
Year Old Hurdle. He faced just four opponents, all of them Irish-trained and two
of them looking to have something to find. The two others did, however, look
worthy opponents: Fakir d'Oudairies had finished fourth in the Supreme Novices'
Hurdle and gone down narrowly, back against four-year-olds, to Fusil Raffles' stable
companion the Triumph winner Pentland Hills in the Anniversary at Aintree; and
French Made had beaten the Triumph third Gardens of Babylon in a Grade 2 juvenile

*888Sport Take 'Em On Adonis Juvenile Hurdle, Kempton—the mistake two out which arguably
cost Fusil Raffles (left) a Triumph win, the French import running out an impressive winner but
returning with a nasty cut which ruled him out of Cheltenham; also pictured are eventual third
Praeceps (right) and fifth Petit Palais (centre)*

AES Champion Four Year Old Hurdle, Punchestown—Fusil Raffles establishes his position as the season's leading juvenile with a ready victory over Fakir d'Oudairies (left)

at Fairyhouse earlier in April. French Made, her stable's sole representative, was bidding to give Willie Mullins a seventh straight success in the race, but it was Fusil Raffles who shaded favouritism, despite his absence that had been caused by a cut to a hind leg at Kempton. Fusil Raffles won the Adonis most impressively, as he showed himself to be simply a class apart from some fairly useful rivals, and the form had largely been upheld subsequently. Kempton actually marked his British debut and the way in which he drew clear in the straight suggested there was a fair bit more to come. The race at Punchestown went in similarly straightforward fashion to the Adonis. Fakir d'Oudairies established a lead by the second flight, with Fusil Raffles travelling smoothly in third; the pace was sound and when Fakir d'Oudairies was sent for home in earnest on the climb to the straight, Fusil Raffles was able to cover his move easily enough and he asserted himself almost immediately after the last to score by two and three quarter lengths, with the time and the distance back to the rest after Fakir d'Oudairies leaving no reason to think that horse was much, if anything, below his best on the day. As such, the winning performance earned Fusil Raffles the title of leading juvenile, of those raced in Britain and Ireland at least, in this Annual, narrowly ahead of his stable-companion Pentland Hills.

		Cadoudal	Green Dancer
	Saint des Saints (FR)	(br 1979)	Come To Sea
	(b 1998)	Chamisene	Pharly
Fusil Raffles (FR)		(b 1980)	Tuneria
(b.g. 2015)		Panoramic	Rainbow Quest
	Tali des Obeaux (FR)	(b 1987)	Immense
	(gr 2007)	Alpaga	Le Pontet
		(gr 1988)	Danaee II

Fusil Raffles arguably ought to be unbeaten over hurdles. In his two starts for Guillaume Macaire back in July, he hacked up in a newcomers race at Senonnes-Pouance but then was beaten a neck at Les Sables d'Olonne by Ch'ti Diamond, who had been no match for him on his debut. Ridden with a lot of confidence both times, Fusil Raffles came to challenge at the last in the latter, but went down narrowly in a sprint finish. If there was a concern about Fusil Raffles, it was that his jumping had not been without blemish in the two races and needed to be a bit slicker. The sturdy Fusil Raffles is by the excellent French sire Saint des Saints and, bred by his owners Simon Munir and Isaac Souede, he is the second foal out of Tali des Obeaux, a useful hurdler/chaser in France at up to two and three quarter miles. The first Eddy's Raya (a sister to Fusil Raffles) won twice from five starts over hurdles for Macaire in 2018 and was due to be offered for sale at the Munir-Souede breeding stock dispersal in December but was withdrawn after being injured close to the sale; Tali des Obeaux herself was sold for €20,000. The most notable name in the family in recent generations is the high-class chaser and smart hurdler Alpha des Obeaux, who was runner-up in the Thyestes Chase in the latest season. He is out of a half-sister to Tali des Obeaux. As for the future, there is a fair bit of encouragement for Fusil Raffles from the subsequent exploits of those horses who have won both the Adonis and the Champion Four Year Old Hurdle at Punchestown. Katarino never won again over hurdles after his Punchestown triumph, though he twice won the Fox Hunters' at Aintree; Grandouet won an International Hurdle; and Punjabi went on to win three Grade 1 hurdles in open company, notably the 2009 Champion Hurdle. Royal Derbi overcame his lack of scope and the effects of a tough first season to have a long and successful career over hurdles, sporting, after his first season, Michael Tabor's royal blue, orange disc, striped sleeves which have since been famously carried by so many of the Coolmore stars on the Flat. Royal Derbi finished second in Granville Again's Champion Hurdle and his wins included a 'Fighting Fifth' and a Bula, as well as a couple of races of yesteryear, the City Trial at Nottingham and the New Year's Day Hurdle at Windsor. Fusil Raffles' pedigree offers plenty of encouragement too, suggesting he should have a long-term future as he is bred to stay further and looks likely to make an impact over fences. He is unlikely ever to have fifteen runs in a season, but hopefully will have an uninterrupted campaign and enhance his record further in 2019/20. *Nicky Henderson*

FUTURE BOY (IRE) 7 b.g. Beneficial – Money Clip (IRE) (Oscar (IRE)) [2018/19 h–: h15.8d h25g h19.7s c26v^{pu} Dec 11] workmanlike gelding: placed once in Irish maiden points: well held over hurdles: pulled up in novice handicap on chasing debut. *Robin Dickin* c–
h–

FUTURE SECURITY (IRE) 10 ch.g. Dalakhani (IRE) – Schust Madame (IRE) (Second Set (IRE)) [2018/19 h108: h16d^6 Jan 15] fair hurdler, below form only outing in 2018/19: stays 21f: acts on soft and good to firm going: tried in headgear: usually wears tongue tie. *Milton Harris* h–

G

GAELIC FLOW 8 ch.g. With The Flow (USA) – Gaelic Lime (Lomitas) [2018/19 h55: h22m^3 h22g^4 h21.6m h22m^4 h23g^5 h20g^2 h18.7g* h19.5g* Oct 30] modest handicap hurdler: won at Stratford (novice event) and Chepstow in October: stays 2¾m: acts on good to firm going: front runner/races prominently: signs of temperament. *Chris Down* h88

GAELIC POET (IRE) 5 b.g. Yeats (IRE) – Hasainm (IRE) (Grand Lodge (USA)) [2018/19 b–: b16.8g h19.5g h16.5d^4 h21.2g^5 h20.5d h19.5g Apr 26] rather unfurnished gelding: has had breathing operation: well held in bumpers: modest form over hurdles: in tongue tie last 4 starts. *Tim Vaughan* h94
b–

GAELIC PRINCE (FR) 7 b.g. Martaline – Gaelic Jane (FR) (Hero's Honor (USA)) [2018/19 h–p: h16g Nov 12] strong gelding: off a year and 6/1, well beaten on completed start in novice hurdles. *Philip Hobbs* h–

GAELIC SURPRISE 7 b.m. Arvico (FR) – Gaelic Lime (Lomitas) [2018/19 h–, b73: h19d^6 Apr 4] angular mare: some promise in bumpers, but no form over hurdles (off 20 months before reappearance). *Chris Down* h–

GAELIK COAST (FR) 5 b.g. Coastal Path – Gaelika (IRE) (Pistolet Bleu (IRE)) [2018/19 b16.7v^2 b15.7s^5 Dec 30] €40,000 3-y-o, £110,000 4-y-o: half-brother to several winners in France, including 17f hurdle winner Kilala (by Irish Wells) and 19f/2¾m chase winner Gaelick Kap (by Kapgarde): dam French maiden (placed around 2m over jumps): won Irish point on debut: fair form when second at Bangor on first of 2 outings in bumpers. *Donald McCain* b86

GALA BALL (IRE) 9 b.g. Flemensfirth (USA) – Nuit des Chartreux (FR) (Villez (USA)) [2018/19 c19.9d^2 c19.9g* Mar 23] rangy gelding: winning hurdler: smart handicap chaser, off 2 years before return: won at Newbury (by length from Valdez) in March: stays 2½m: acts on heavy going: tried in blinkers. *Philip Hobbs* c147
h–

GALA CELEBRATION (IRE) 5 b.g. Excelebration (IRE) – Elusive Galaxy (IRE) **h–**
(Elusive City (USA)) [2018/19 h16.3g Jun 9] fair on Flat, stays 8.5f: hooded/tongue tied,
well beaten in novice at Stratford on hurdling debut. *Ian Williams*

GALACTIC POWER (IRE) 9 ch.g. Gamut (IRE) – Celtic Peace (IRE) (Deploy) **c–**
[2018/19 c–, h101: h25g h20.3g h21.2g h18.5s² h21.2d⁴ h18.5s⁶ h20.7g⁵ h21.7d^bd **h96**
Mar 9] compact gelding: modest handicap hurdler: let down by jumping sole start over
fences: stays 21f: acts on soft and good to firm going: has worn headgear: races off pace.
Robin Dickin

GALAHILL 6 gr.m. Ferrule (IRE) – Gala Queen (Accondy (IRE)) [2018/19 b16s b16.2g **b–**
Jan 22] first foal: dam, no form over hurdles, placed in points: no sign of ability in points/
bumpers. *William Young Jnr*

GALLAHERS CROSS (IRE) 7 b.g. Getaway (GER) – Raheen Lady (IRE) (Oscar **h107**
(IRE)) [2018/19 b107: h21.6s⁴ h20.5d Mar 1] sturdy gelding: has had breathing operation:
winning pointer: useful bumper winner: better effort over hurdles (only fair form) when
fourth in maiden at Ascot: should prove suited by further than 2m. *Nicky Henderson*

GALLANT JOHN JOE (IRE) 6 b.g. Presenting – Shuil A Hocht (IRE) (Mohaajir **h134**
(USA)) [2018/19 h16g⁴ h20g* h22g* h20g² h22g³ h16d* h20d Apr 7] €61,000 3-y-o:
fourth foal: half-brother to bumper winner/useful 2m chase winner Space Cadet (by
Flemensfirth), stays 25f, and bumper winner Jot'em Down (by Kalanisi): dam (h96),
bumper winner/19f hurdle winner, half-sister to useful chaser (winner up to 3m) The
Outlier: regressed in bumpers: useful hurdler: won maiden at Punchestown in November
(subsequently awarded similar event at Ballinrobe 6 months earlier) and listed novice at
Naas (by ½ length from Mister Blue Sky) in March: third in Nathaniel Lacy & Partners
Solicitors Novices' Hurdle at Leopardstown (6½ lengths behind Commander of Fleet) in
February: effective at 2m to 2¾m: acts on good to soft going: has worn headgear, including
last 2 starts. *Oliver McKiernan, Ireland*

GALLERY EXHIBITION (IRE) 12 b.g. Portrait Gallery (IRE) – Good Hearted (IRE) **c83**
(Broken Hearted) [2018/19 c103, h–: c21.4g^ur c24.2m⁴ c23.6g^pu c21.1d^pu Apr 4] **h–**
rangy gelding: has had breathing operation: point/hurdle winner: formerly useful handicap
chaser: regressed further in 2018/19, leaving Kim Bailey after third outing: wears tongue
tie. *P. W. Mason*

GALLIC DESTINY (IRE) 8 b.g. Champs Elysees – Cross Your Fingers (USA) **h–**
(Woodman (USA)) [2018/19 h21.2g⁵ h21.4g h25s⁶ Jan 16] fairly useful novice hurdle
winner in 2015/16: no comparable form: often in cheekpieces: usually in tongue tie.
Jo Davis

GALLIC GEORDIE 6 b.g. Geordieland (FR) – Je Ne Sais Plus (FR) (Spadoun (FR)) **b– p**
[2018/19 b15.8v⁶ Dec 17] first foal: dam (h112), 2m-19f hurdle winner, also 10.5f-1½m
winner on Flat in France: 3/1, well held in maiden bumper at Fontwell: presumably felt
capable of better. *Samuel Drinkwater*

GALLOWS POINT 6 b.g. Black Sam Bellamy (IRE) – Jolika (FR) (Grand Tresor (FR)) **h92**
[2018/19 b16g⁶ h19.9g h19.7s h19.7s h19.7g h24.1d² h23.1d Apr 9] rangy gelding: fourth **b83**
foal: half-brother to bumper winner/fairly useful hurdler Bonne Fee (19f-2¾m winner, by
Karinga Bay): dam (c96/h102) 2m-2½m hurdle/chase winner (stayed 25f): green in
bumper: form (modest) over hurdles only when second in 3m novice handicap at Wetherby,
and even then looked hard work: in headgear last 3 starts: probably ungenuine. *Kim Bailey*

GALLOX BRIDGE 14 b.g. Kayf Tara – Explorer (Krisinsky (USA)) [2018/19 c17d^pu **c–**
Jun 8] tall, lengthy gelding: point winner: winning hurdler/chaser: no form outside points **h–**
since autumn 2013: wears tongue tie. *Mrs Annabel Wheatley*

GALTEE MOUNTAIN (IRE) 4 br.g. Mountain High (IRE) – Kings Queen (IRE) **h80**
(Wizard King) [2018/19 b16.8d b16d h16g Apr 10] little show in bumpers (left Jose Santos **b–**
after debut) or over hurdles. *Pat Murphy*

GALVIN (IRE) 5 b.g. Gold Well – Burren Moonshine (IRE) (Moonax (IRE)) [2018/19 **h138**
b16.2g* b16d* h16.2g* h16d* h16d* h21s⁶ h16m² Apr 12] €34,000 3-y-o: third foal: dam **b105**
(c102/h117) 2½m-3½m hurdle/chase winner: useful form when winning bumpers at
Roscommon (maiden event) and Limerick (by 16 lengths) in July: useful novice hurdler:
won at Perth (maiden) in August, Navan in January and Ayr in April: should prove well
suited by at least 2½m: acts on soft going. *Gordon Elliott, Ireland*

GALWAY JACK (IRE) 14 b.g. Witness Box (USA) – Cooldalus (IRE) (Mandalus) **c119**
[2018/19 c130: c20.3g² c24s⁴ Mar 23] rangy gelding: fairly useful hunter chaser: stays 3m:
acts on heavy going: tried in tongue tie: front runner. *G. T. H. Bailey*

GAMAIN (IRE) 10 b.g. Gamut (IRE) – Glass Curtain (IRE) (Old Vic) [2018/19 c109, **c104** h107: h26.4g⁴ h26.5dᵖᵘ h26d⁵ c23.6d c21.6d⁵ c26.7g* c25.1g* Apr 14] good-topped **h92** gelding: fair handicap hurdler/chaser: won over fences at Wincanton in March and April: stays 27f: acts on heavy going: normally in headgear. *Mrs Jane Williams*

GAMBLING GAMUT (IRE) 7 ch.g. Gamut (IRE) – Red Promise (IRE) (Old Vic) **h102** [2018/19 h–: h23g⁴ h22g⁴ h23.1s³ h21.7sᵖᵘ h21.6d² Apr 9] unplaced completed start in Irish points: fair form over hurdles: stays 23f: acts on soft going. *Keiran Burke*

GAMBOLING GIGI 7 ch.m. Black Sam Bellamy (IRE) – Gundreda (Gunner B) **h–** [2018/19 b–: h18.7mᵘʳ h15.8g Jul 18] no form in bumper/novice hurdles: wears tongue tie. *Gary Hanmer*

GAMEFACE (IRE) 5 b.g. Oscar (IRE) – Queensland Bay (Primitive Rising (USA)) **h65 p** [2018/19 h16.3s Dec 19] £70,000 3-y-o, £145,000 4-y-o: fifth foal: dam, lightly raced in bumpers, half-sister to fairly useful hurdler/useful chaser (2½m-25f winner) Silver Knight: placed both starts in Irish points: 14/1, needed experience when well held in maiden at Newbury on hurdling debut: will improve. *Harry Fry*

GAME IN THE PARK (IRE) 6 b.g. Walk In The Park (IRE) – Learning Game (USA) **h92** (Carnegie (IRE)) [2018/19 b16.3g h16.7m⁵ h19m⁶ h19.5v h15.8s h21.2g Jan 17] **b–** half-brother to 3 winners in France, including 2m-2¼m hurdle winner Dark Strength (by Miesque's Son): dam, unraced, closely related to fairly useful/ungenuine hurdler/chaser (stayed 27f) Montevideo: seemingly modest form when sixth in 19f maiden hurdle at Taunton in November: no show in varied company otherwise, leaving Conrad Allen after second start: tried in blinkers: usually in tongue tie: usually races freely/leads. *Tracey Barfoot-Saunt*

GAMEKEEPER BILL 5 b.g. Beat All (USA) – Granny McPhee (Bahri (USA)) [2018/19 **h87** h–, b74: h16g h18.7gᵘʳ h19.6m² h21.7m⁶ h20d⁴ h19.5dᵖᵘ h20.7g⁶ Feb 21] rather unfurnished gelding: modest maiden hurdler: stays easy 2½m: acts on good to firm and good to soft going: in cheekpieces last 2 starts. *Alan Bailey*

GANACHE (IRE) 6 b.g. Scorpion (IRE) – Spring Baloo (IRE) (Definite Article) [2018/19 **h–** b93: h19.5dᵖᵘ Jan 18] good-topped gelding: fair form in bumpers: off 9 months, pulled up in novice won by Lisnagar Oscar at Chepstow on hurdling debut. *Nicky Henderson*

GANBEI 13 ch.g. Lomitas – Native Ring (FR) (Bering) [2018/19 c115, h102: c24m c23.8g **c117** c24.1g³ c23.8g⁵ c23.8g⁴ c25.5g² Nov 9] sturdy gelding: fair hurdler: fairly useful handicap **h–** chaser: stays 3¼m: acts on soft and good to firm going: has worn cheekpieces/tongue tie. *Michael Easterby*

GANG WARFARE 8 b.g. Medicean – Light Impact (IRE) (Fantastic Light (USA)) **h88** [2018/19 h104: h16m³ Jul 9] maiden hurdler, fair form at best: fairly useful stayer on Flat, won in August: unproven beyond 2m: acts on good to soft going: in cheekpieces last 3 starts: tried in tongue tie. *Alexandra Dunn*

GANNICUS 8 b.g. Phoenix Reach (IRE) – Rasmani (Medicean) [2018/19 h99: h15.7g⁴ **h98** h19.2g⁶ h15.9g² h15.7g⁵ h17.7gᵇᵈ h15.9d Jan 6] rather leggy gelding: modest handicap hurdler: best around 2m: best form on good going: wears cheekpieces/tongue tie: front runner/races prominently. *Brendan Powell*

GARBANZO (IRE) 5 gr.g. Mastercraftsman (IRE) – Noble Fantasy (GER) (Big Shuffle **h102 p** (USA)) [2018/19 h15.7s⁶ h16g⁴ Jan 12] good-topped gelding: developed into fairly useful performer on Flat (stays 1¾m) for Ed Walker: highly tried on hurdling debut: still in need of experience (test also insufficient) when fourth in maiden at Wetherby next time: remains with potential. *Dr Richard Newland*

GARDE FORESTIER (FR) 7 b.g. Forestier (FR) – Nette Rousse (FR) (Robin des Pres **c79** (FR)) [2018/19 h108: h21.4mᵖᵘ c20s c20.3gᶠ c24.2sᵖᵘ h19.9s Dec 26] fair hurdle winner in **h–** 2017/18: little show since, including over fences (left Seamus Mullins before chasing debut): should stay beyond 2m: acts on soft going: wears tongue tie. *Rebecca Menzies*

GARDEFORT (FR) 10 b.g. Agent Bleu (FR) – La Fresnaie (FR) (Exit To Nowhere **c133** (USA)) [2018/19 c137, h–: c16.8g c18.8sᵖᵘ c20dᵘʳ c20.6dᵖᵘ c20.1g² Apr 25] rangy gelding: **h–** winning hurdler: smart handicap chaser at best: largely disappointing in 2018/19: stays 21f: acts on good to firm and heavy going: tried in cheekpieces. *Venetia Williams*

GARDE LA VICTOIRE (FR) 10 b.g. Kapgarde (FR) – Next Victory (FR) (Akarad **c140** (FR)) [2018/19 c129, h135: c19.4d⁴ Oct 14] tall gelding: smart hurdler/high-class chaser at **h–** best: just useful form since 2016/17: stays 2½m: acts on good to firm and heavy going. *Philip Hobbs*

GARDENS OF BABYLON (IRE) 4 b.g. Camelot – Condition (Deploy) [2018/19 **h142 p**
h16g* h16d² h16g² h16.8d³ h16d² Apr 22] compact gelding: twice-raced in Flat maidens:
useful juvenile hurdler: won maiden event on hurdling debut and novice shortly after end
of British season, both at Punchestown: placed in good company all 4 outings in between,
notably when ½-length second to French Made in Rathbarry & Glenview Studs Juvenile
Hurdle at Fairyhouse: will be suited by 2½m+: acts on good to soft going: has worn
cheekpieces: wears tongue tie: remains capable of better granted a stamina test. *Joseph
Patrick O'Brien, Ireland*

GARDE VILLE (FR) 9 ch.g. Kapgarde (FR) – Ville Eagle (FR) (Villez (USA)) [2018/19 **c122**
c25.5d* c27.5d* c23.8g⁴ c24s³ Mar 23] smallish gelding: prolific point winner: disappointing **h–**
maiden hurdler: developed into fairly useful hunter chaser in 2018/19, winning at Warwick
in May and Stratford (novice event) in June: stays 3½m: acts on heavy going: has worn
headgear: tried in tongue tie: ridden by Mr Stephen Paul Davies (7) nowadays. *Patricia
Rigby*

GARDINERS HILL (IRE) 9 br.g. Stowaway – Mysterious Lass (IRE) (Satco (FR)) **c111**
[2018/19 c98, h–: h23.9d² c25.5g* c25.6g* h21.9s³ c25.6s⁵ h25.5d* h23d⁵ c25.5s⁵ h26.4g² **h108**
Mar 30] sturdy gelding: has had breathing operation: fair handicap hurdler/chaser: won
over fences at Warwick and Ludlow in November and over hurdles at Hereford in January:
likely to stay extreme distances: acts on heavy going: wears tongue tie: waited with.
David Rees

GARO DE JUILLEY (FR) 7 b.g. Ungaro (GER) – Lucy de Juilley (FR) (Goldneyev **h134**
(USA)) [2018/19 h120: h19.8m² h16.8g² h15.9g⁴ h19.5d* h18.9g⁴ h24.4s⁶ h16.5g⁵ h20.3d
Mar 15] tall gelding: useful handicap hurdler: improved in 2018/19 (left Paul Nicholls after
first start), winning Silver Trophy at Chepstow in October: stays 3m, effective at shorter:
acts on soft and good to firm going: tried in hood: wears tongue tie: held up: signs of
temperament for former yard: has bled. *Sophie Leech*

GARRANE (IRE) 7 b.g. Tikkanen (USA) – Ballooley (IRE) (Winged Love (IRE)) **c122**
[2018/19 h105: c26.2g² c23.6s² c30.7s² c26.7gᵖᵘ c24.2v³ c24.2d² Mar 24] fair hurdler: **h–**
fairly useful novice chaser: placed in handicaps all 5 completed starts in 2018/19: stays 31f:
acts on heavy going. *Jeremy Scott*

GARRETTSTOWN (IRE) 6 b.g. Doyen (IRE) – Azur (IRE) (Brief Truce (USA)) **h121**
[2018/19 b104: h16.3d⁶ h20v² h18.6d* h20.6d² h19.8sᵖᵘ h18.6g² Apr 3] tall gelding:
bumper winner: fairly useful form over hurdles: won novice at Market Rasen in January:
stays 21f: acts on heavy going. *Olly Murphy*

GARS BAR DINE (FR) 8 b.g. Martaline – Treekle Toffee (FR) (Cadoudal (FR)) **c102**
[2018/19 h19.7d h24.3s⁵ c24.1d⁴ c23.4d⁵ Mar 5] fair maiden hurdler nowadays: left **h107**
Francois Nicolle before return: similar form in handicap chases at Ayr and Newcastle:
probably stays 3m: acts on heavy going: has joined Dan Skelton. *Lucinda Russell*

GAS LINE BOY (IRE) 13 b.g. Blueprint (IRE) – Jervia (Affirmed (USA)) [2018/19 c148, **c–**
h–: c26.1mᵖᵘ Jul 1] tall, useful-looking gelding: winning hurdler: smart handicap chaser: **h–**
pulled up only outing in 2018/19: probaly stays 4¼m: acts on heavy going: wears headgear.
Ian Williams

GASOLINE (IRE) 7 b.g. Mahler – Judelle de Thou (FR) (Trebrook (FR)) [2018/19 h–: **h–**
h20.6gᵖᵘ h24gᵖᵘ Jun 25] of little account: tried in headgear: has worn tongue tie.
Mike Sowersby

GASSIN GOLF 10 b.g. Montjeu (IRE) – Miss Riviera Golf (Hernando (FR)) [2018/19 **h– §**
h119§: h16.2s Nov 21] useful-looking gelding: fairly useful handicap hurdler: stayed 2½m:
acted on heavy going: wore headgear/tongue tie: temperamental: dead. *Kelly Morgan*

GASTARA 4 b.g. Kayf Tara – Gaspaisie (FR) (Beyssac (FR)) [2018/19 b16d² Apr 6] **b98**
half-brother to numerous winners, including smart 2m-2½m hurdle winners Mr Thriller
(by Kapgarde) and Gaspara (by Astarabad), and fairly useful hurdler/chaser Larry
(19f/2½m winner, by Midnight Legend): dam French 17f-2½m hurdle/chase winner: 20/1,
2¾ lengths second of 16 to One Touch in bumper at Chepstow. *Johnny Farrelly*

GATACRE STREET 7 b.g. Lucarno (USA) – Sherry Darling (IRE) (Alflora (IRE)) **h64**
[2018/19 h24s⁵ h19.3s h20.6dᵖᵘ Apr 6] placed in Irish points: poor form over hurdles.
Sam England

GAUCHO 6 b.g. Shirocco (GER) – Gulshan (Batshoof) [2018/19 b–: h16g⁵ h16d⁶ h16g⁵ **h85**
h16.8g⁵ Aug 15] tall gelding: has had breathing operation: modest form over hurdles: tried
in hood (free-going sort). *Nigel Twiston-Davies*

GAUCHO GIL (IRE) 6 b.g. Getaway (GER) – Ballys Baby (IRE) (Bob Back (USA)) **h–**
[2018/19 b–: h16m h16d May 30] tall gelding: well held in bumpers/over hurdles: tried in
hood. *Philip Hobbs*

GAYTON 5 ch.m. Haafhd – Wistow (Sir Harry Lewis (USA)) [2018/19 b73: b16.7g May **b60**
19] poor form in bumpers. *Pam Sly*

G'DAY AUSSIE 6 b.g. Aussie Rules (USA) – Moi Aussi (USA) (Mt Livermore (USA)) **c105**
[2018/19 h94: h16g⁶ h16m⁵ h18.7m* c16.3s* h16.3g⁵ c20g⁶ Sep 11] fair handicap hurdler: **h105**
won at Stratford in July: similar form when winning at Newton Abbot later that month on
first of 2 outings in novice handicap chases: best short of 2½m: acts on soft and good to
firm going: usually in cheekpieces: wears tongue tie: held up. *Dave Roberts*

GEE SIXTY SIX 5 b.g. Mount Nelson – Azure Mist (Bahamian Bounty) [2018/19 h16.7gᵖᵘ **h–**
May 11] modest maiden on Flat, stays 1¾m: pulled up in maiden on hurdling debut. *Mark
H. Tompkins*

GEMOLOGIST (IRE) 4 b.f. Sir Percy – Tiffany Diamond (IRE) (Sadler's Wells (USA)) **h101**
[2018/19 h15.7s⁵ h16.6g² h15.7g⁴ h16.4s³ h16.4m³ h20.2g⁴ Apr 24] has had breathing
operation: half-sister to Grey Gem (2m hurdle winner in Jersey, by Danehill Dancer):
modest maiden on Flat, stays 13.5f: fair form over hurdles: left Mark Johnston after third
start: stays 2½m: acts on soft and good to firm going: in tongue tie last 3 starts.
Lucinda Russell

GENERAL ALLENBY 5 b.g. Medicean – Cat Hunter (One Cool Cat (USA)) [2018/19 **h104**
h72p: h17.7g⁵ h21.9d³ h21gᵖᵘ h20.5gᵖᵘ h25.3d⁴ h20.9g³ h26.5g³ Apr 20] has had breathing
operation: fair maiden hurdler: left Henry Tett after fourth start: stays 3¼m: acts on good
to soft going: in headgear 3 of last 4 outings: usually makes running/races prominently.
Peter Bowen

GENERAL BUX 8 b.g. Lucarno (USA) – Cadoutene (FR) (Cadoudal (FR)) [2018/19 c–, **c116**
h94p: c20sᶠ h23.4d² c19.9d* c19.9gᵖᵘ c23.6m* Apr 22] big gelding: fair form over hurdles: **h102**
better over fences: left Olly Murphy, won handicaps at Huntingdon in December and
Chepstow (novice event) in April: stays 3m: acts on soft and good to firm going: tried in
hood/tongue tie: usually makes running/races prominently. *Sophie Leech*

GENERAL CONSENSUS 7 br.g. Black Sam Bellamy (IRE) – Charlottes Webb (IRE) **h–**
(Luso) [2018/19 h114: h23.9dᵖᵘ Oct 27] rangy gelding: maiden pointer: fairly useful hurdle
winner in 2017/18: pulled up in handicap only outing in 2018/19. *Samuel Drinkwater*

GENERAL CUSTARD 6 b.g. Shirocco (GER) – Diamant Noir (Sir Harry Lewis (USA)) **h118**
[2018/19 h–, b67: h16g* h20m² h24d³ h18.6s* Dec 6] has had breathing operation: fairly
useful novice hurdler: won at Warwick in October and Market Rasen in December: stays
2½m: acts on soft and good to firm going: in tongue tie last 4 starts. *Olly Murphy*

GENERAL GIRLING 12 b.g. General Gambul – Gold Charm (Imperial Fling (USA)) **c–**
[2018/19 c90, h–: c25.1m⁶ May 10] tall, angular gelding: winning hurdler: modest handicap **h–**
chaser: stays 3¼m: acts on heavy going: wears headgear: usually leads. *Ron Hodges*

GENERAL MAHLER (IRE) 9 b.g. Mahler – High Dough (IRE) (High Roller (IRE)) **c109**
[2018/19 c112, h95: c20.1d² c19.3g³ May 15] has had breathing operation: winning **h–**
hurdler: fair maiden chaser: barely stays 3¼m: acts on heavy and good to firm going: tried
in cheekpieces: wears tongue tie: has looked half-hearted. *Brian Ellison*

GENERAL MALARKEY (IRE) 7 b.g. Scorpion (IRE) – Andreas Benefit (IRE) **h–**
(Beneficial) [2018/19 h–: h21d h19.6g Apr 13] little form in bumpers/over hurdles.
Peter Bowen

GENERAL PICTON (IRE) 7 b.g. Beneficial – Back To Cloghoge (IRE) (Bob Back **c97**
(USA)) [2018/19 h–: h19m h16.7g h21d⁴ c22.5g² h23.9sᵖᵘ Feb 26] workmanlike gelding: **h87**
little show over hurdles: fared better when 13 lengths second to Blagapar in novice handicap
at Uttoxeter (tongue tied, left Kim Bailey after) on chasing debut: stays 2¾m: signs of
temperament. *Rebecca Curtis*

GENERAL PRINCIPLE (IRE) 10 b.g. Gold Well – How Provincial (IRE) (Be My **c143**
Native (USA)) [2018/19 c142, h134: c24d c24.5g c25s⁵ c28.7d³ c25sᵖᵘ c34.3gᶠ c29dᵖᵘ Apr **h–**
22] well-made gelding: winning hurdler: useful handicap chaser: stays 29f: acts on heavy
going: wears tongue tie: usually races prominently. *Gordon Elliott, Ireland*

GENERATION GAP (IRE) 5 b.g. Olden Times – Kerso (IRE) (Luso) [2018/19 h19.9g⁶ **h100 p**
h16gᵘʳ h21d Nov 29] €8,000 3-y-o, £45,000 4-y-o: good-topped gelding: first foal: dam ran
twice in bumpers/pulled up in points: off mark in points at second attempt: promise in
maidens both completed outings over hurdles: remains capable of better. *Jonjo O'Neill*

GENERATOR CITY (IRE) 6 b.g. Primary (USA) – Sabbatical (IRE) (Jurado (USA)) **h–**
[2018/19 b16g⁴ h17.6g Apr 12] off mark in Irish points at fifth attempt: some encouragement **b80**
when fourth in bumper at Wetherby: down field in maiden on hurdling debut. *Denis Hogan,*
Ireland

GENEROUS CHIEF (IRE) 11 br.g. Generous (IRE) – Yosna (FR) (Sicyos (USA)) **c98 §**
[2018/19 c98§, h102§: h26.4m* h25.8g c24g³ c25.8mᵖᵘ h22g⁶ Sep 4] good-topped gelding: **h103 §**
fair handicap hurdler: won at Stratford in May: modest handicap chaser: stays 27f: acts on
soft and good to firm going: wears headgear: lazy sort. *Graeme McPherson*

GENEROUS DAY (IRE) 7 b.g. Daylami (IRE) – Our Pride (Generous (IRE)) [2018/19 **c122**
h111: c20.9g⁴ c20.3s² c16.2g* c15.2g c16.2g* Mar 28] fair handicap hurdler: fairly useful form over **h–**
fences: won handicaps at Warwick in January and March (further progress): stays 2½m:
acts on soft going. *Henry Oliver*

GENEROUS HELPINGS (IRE) 10 ch.g. Generous (IRE) – Saffron Pride (IRE) (Be **c– x**
My Native (USA)) [2018/19 c–x, h–x: h25g h20.5d h25dᵖᵘ h23.1d Apr 9] good-topped **h69 x**
gelding: poor and error-prone handicap hurdler: let down by jumping in novice handicap
chases: stays 25f: acts on good to firm and good to soft going: usually in headgear.
Gary Moore

GENEROUS JACK (IRE) 10 ch.g. Generous (IRE) – Yosna (FR) (Sicyos (USA)) **h103**
[2018/19 h15.9s³ h15.9s⁶ h15.9s* h16g³ h16d³ h16m⁵ Apr 22] fair handicap hurdler: won
at Plumpton in January and Fakenham (selling event, then left Suzi Best) in February: best
efforts at 2m: acts on soft and good to firm going: usually in headgear. *John Ryan*

GENI JOHNSON (IRE) 7 b.m. Mountain High (IRE) – Garrymorris (IRE) (Old Vic) **c–**
[2018/19 h83, b–: h20g h16.3m² c15.7gᵖᵘ Dec 28] poor maiden hurdler: pulled up in **h59**
novice handicap on chasing debut: should stay 2½m: acts on soft going: has worn
cheekpieces. *Alexandra Dunn*

GENIUS 5 b.g. Beat Hollow – Natsuke (FR) (Chichicastenango (FR)) [2018/19 b15.7g* **h96**
b16.3d h16.5d³ h15.8d⁴ h16.7gᶠ Mar 14] has had breathing operation: first foal: dam, **b96**
unraced, out of half-sister to useful French hurdler/fairly useful chaser up to 21f N’Oublie
Jamais: fairly useful form when winning at Southwell in May on first of 2 outings in
bumpers: modest form over hurdles: bled final outing. *Harry Whittington*

GENNADY (IRE) 5 b.g. Arakan (USA) – Topathistle (IRE) (Broadway Flyer (USA)) **b84**
[2018/19 b16g⁴ Oct 29] €15,000 3-y-o: has had breathing operation: first foal: dam
unraced half-sister to fairly useful chaser (stayed 3¼m) Thistlecraft: some encouragement
when fourth in maiden bumper at Ayr: joined Keith Dalgleish. *Stuart Crawford, Ireland*

GENRES 7 b.g. Champs Elysees – Musical Horizon (USA) (Distant View (USA)) **h–**
[2018/19 h–: h16.2dᵘʳ h16.8g May 15] narrow gelding: formerly fair handicapper on Flat
(stays 12.5f): no promise over hurdles: in tongue tie last 2 starts. *Rebecca Menzies*

GENTLEMAN FARMER 7 ch.g. Tobougg (IRE) – Sweet Shooter (Double Trigger **h91**
(IRE)) [2018/19 h–: h19.2g* h23.3g h23.9d* Oct 20] tall, lengthy gelding: winning
pointer: modest handicap hurdler: won at Towcester (amateurs) in May and Ffos Las
(further improvement) in October: stays 3m: acts on good to soft going: in cheekpieces last
3 starts. *Richard Hawker*

GENTLEMAN JAMES 7 b.g. Sixties Icon – Cashback Rose (IRE) (Alflora (IRE)) **c–**
[2018/19 h61: h20.2g² h20.2g⁶ h20.2g c19.4mᵖᵘ h24.3g h22g⁶ h24g⁶ Nov 16] has had **h64**
breathing operation: poor maiden hurdler: pulled up in novice on chasing debut: stays
2½m: best form on good going: wears cheekpieces/tongue tie. *Dianne Sayer*

GENTLEMAN JON 11 b.g. Beat All (USA) – Sudden Spirit (FR) (Esprit du Nord (USA)) **c129 §**
[2018/19 c125§, h–: c25.1m* h21.4g Apr 14] tall, well-made, attractive gelding: winning **h–**
hurdler: fairly useful handicap chaser nowadays: won at Wincanton in May: stays 27f: acts
on good to firm and heavy going: wears blinkers/tongue tie: unreliable. *Colin Tizzard*

GENTLEMAN MOORE (IRE) 9 b.g. Royal Anthem (USA) – Near Dunleer (IRE) **c91 §**
(Soviet Lad (USA)) [2018/19 h20.5dᵖᵘ h21d⁶ c20.2g² c19.2dᵖᵘ c20.3d³ c23.6g² Apr 22] **h–**
good-bodied gelding: winning hurdler: modest handicap chaser nowadays: barely stays
3m: best form on good going: wears headgear: tried in tongue tie: races prominently: one
to treat with caution. *Natalie Lloyd-Beavis*

GEORDIE B 6 gr.g. Geordieland (FR) – Sari Rose (FR) (Vertical Speed (FR)) [2018/19 **h124 p**
b94: h19.3g⁶ h19.7s² h23s* h23.1s* Mar 18] rather unfurnished gelding: bumper winner:
fairly useful novice hurdler: won at Lingfield in January and Exeter in March: will be
suited by 3m+: type to do better still. *Venetia Williams*

GEORDIEBEST 5 b.g. Geordieland (FR) – Lady Blade (IRE) (Daggers Drawn (USA)) **b81**
[2018/19 b18.8d³ b16.2m⁴ b16.4d Oct 27] €7,000 3-y-o: seventh foal: half-brother to fair
2m hurdle winner Thegaygardener (by Sulamani), stayed 2½m, and modest hurdler Billy
Blade (2¾m/23f winner, by Generous); dam, maiden on Flat/ran twice over hurdles, half-
sister to fairly useful hurdler (stayed 2½m) Lucaindubai: modest form first 2 outings in
bumpers: tried in blinkers. *Graham McKeever, Ireland*

GEORDIE DES CHAMPS (IRE) 8 br.g. Robin des Champs (FR) – Kilcoleman Lady **c131**
(IRE) (Presenting) [2018/19 c135p, h–: c26.1m⁵ c23.8m Nov 3] useful-looking gelding: **h–**
winning hurdler: useful handicap chaser: stays 3¼m: acts on soft and good to firm going:
tried in tongue tie. *Rebecca Curtis*

GEORDIE GEORGE (IRE) 7 b.g. Kodiac – Trika (First Trump) [2018/19 h16.8g **h–**
h17.2gᶠ May 28] smallish gelding: fair on Flat (races mostly around 1m nowadays): never
threatened on completed outing over hurdles: wears tongue tie. *Rebecca Menzies*

GEORDIELAD 5 ch.g. Geordieland (FR) – Adees Dancer (Danehill Dancer (IRE)) **h85**
[2018/19 h–: h16g⁵ h20g Jun 11] modest stayer on Flat: similar form over hurdles when
sixth in maiden at Worcester. *Oliver Sherwood*

GEORDIELANDGANGSTA 6 br.g. Geordieland (FR) – Dunsfold Duchess (IRE) **h–**
(Bustino) [2018/19 h74, b–: h17s h16.2g Jan 22] second on completed start in points: poor
form in bumper/novice hurdles: will prove suited by further than 17f. *Rose Dobbin*

GEORGES CONN (IRE) 11 b.g. Whitmore's Conn (USA) – Georges Girl (IRE) **c110 x**
(Montelimar (USA)) [2018/19 h23.7g⁵ c24s² c21g* c25mᵖᵘ c22.5s³ c28s c31.9sᵖᵘ Nov 21] **h82**
winning hurdler: fair chaser: won maiden at Sligo in September: stays 3¾m: acts on good
to firm and heavy going: tried in cheekpieces/tongue tie: front runner/races prominently:
prone to mistakes. *John Patrick Ryan, Ireland*

GEORGIAN FIREBIRD 9 b.m. Firebreak – Skovshoved (IRE) (Danetime (IRE)) **h90**
[2018/19 h93: h19.9gᵖᵘ h17sᶠ h15.8s² h15.8s² h15.7dᵖᵘ h20.6gᵖᵘ Mar 20] modest handicap
hurdler: stays 21f: acts on heavy going: in tongue tie last 5 starts: often races lazily
(temperament under suspicion). *Barry Leavy*

GEORGIATOR (FR) 6 b.g. Simplex (FR) – Princess Demut (GER) (Tannenkonig (IRE)) **b91 p**
[2018/19 b15.8m* Jul 13] second foal: dam, ran once on Flat in Germany, half-sister to
Italian Group 1 2½m hurdle winner Prince Nico: won conditionals/amateurs maiden
bumper at Ffos Las by 1¼ lengths from Ring The Moon: open to improvement. *Olly Murphy*

GEORGIE BEAR 5 gr.m. Proclamation (IRE) – Glen Clova (Elmaamul (USA)) [2018/19 **h–**
b16.2m h20.1gᵖᵘ Apr 15] fifth foal: dam unraced half-sister to fairly useful hurdler/chaser **b–**
(stayed 3m) Thedrinkymeister: no promise in bumper/novice hurdle. *Chris Grant*

GEORGINA JOY 6 b.m. Midnight Legend – First Katoune (FR) (Poliglote) [2018/19 **c75**
h74: h20.6g³ c25.8m⁵ c24g² c25.8m³ c25.8g h25.5g* h23.9m² h23.9d⁴ c25.2dᵖᵘ Jan 2] poor **h77**
handicap hurdler: won at Hereford (conditionals) in November: similar form over fences:
stayed 3¼m: acted on soft and good to firm going: wore headgear/tongue tie: usually led:
dead. *Nigel Hawke*

GERONIMO 8 ch.g. Kadastrof (FR) – Triggers Ginger (Double Trigger (IRE)) [2018/19 **c125**
h109: c24.2g³ c24.1s* c26.2g² c26.9d* c31.8mᵖᵘ Apr 13] runner-up all 4 outings over **h–**
hurdles: fairly useful form over fences: won handicaps at Ayr in November and January
(improved again): excuses in Scottish Grand National there final outing: should stay
extreme distances: acts on heavy going. *Sandy Thomson*

GETABIRD (IRE) 7 b.g. Getaway (GER) – Fern Bird (IRE) (Revoque (IRE)) [2018/19 **c150**
h144: c16d* c19.7s² Dec 26] strong, compact gelding: useful novice hurdler in 2017/18: **h–**
smart form over fences, winning maiden at Punchestown (by 7½ lengths from Articulum)
before close second to Hardline in Grade 1 novice at Limerick 17 days later: stays 2½m
(pulled too hard over 3m at Punchestown shortly after end of British season): acts on heavy
going: usually leads. *W. P. Mullins, Ireland*

GETABUCK (IRE) 6 ch.g. Getaway (GER) – Buck's Blue (FR) (Epervier Bleu) [2018/19 **b–**
b16.8s Apr 16] off mark in points at fourth attempt: tailed off in bumper. *P. W. Mason*

GETADOLLAR (IRE) 6 b.m. Getaway (GER) – Pure Beautiful (IRE) (Un Desperado **h86**
(FR)) [2018/19 b16g³ h21.6d h16.8g⁵ h16.8v h18.5m³ h18.5m h23.9m³ h23.9d⁶ Dec 13] **b56**
rather leggy mare: fourth foal: half-sister to useful 19f hurdle winner Mentor and fair
chaser Only Gorgeous (19f-31f winner) (both by Vertical Speed): dam winning pointer:
pulled up all 3 starts in Irish points: well-held third in mares bumper: modest maiden
hurdler: stays 3m: acts on good to firm going: tried in cheekpieces. *Alexandra Dunn*

GET AN OSCAR (IRE) 5 ch.m. Getaway (GER) – Lady Perspex (IRE) (Oscar (IRE)) **h95**
[2018/19 b16.3g² b16.2m* b16.7g⁶ b16.2s⁴ h19.5s h16d h21.4g⁵ h25s⁵ h21.9g³ Apr 21] **b89**
second foal: dam (h102), winning pointer/placed up to 3m over hurdles, sister to fairly
useful hurdler (stayed 3m) Moonlight Drive: point winner: fair form in bumpers: won at
Hexham in June: modest form over hurdles: should stay beyond 21f. *Peter Bowen*

GETAREASON (IRE) 6 ch.g. Getaway (GER) – Simple Reason (IRE) (Snurge) **h129**
[2018/19 b105: b20g³ h21s* h21g* h20s³ h21g⁴ h24d⁴ h20d² h20d³ h22g h20.3d Mar 15] **b101**
bumper winner: fairly useful hurdler: won maiden at Tramore in August, and later awarded
similar event at Galway earlier in month: second in Navan Novices' Hurdle (2 lengths
behind Easy Game) and third in Lawlor's of Naas Novices' Hurdle (4¾ lengths behind
Battleoverdoyen): stays 21f: acts on soft going: tried in hood. *W. P. Mullins, Ireland*

GETARIVER (IRE) 6 br.m. Getaway (GER) – Watson River (IRE) (Presenting) [2018/19 **b98**
b14g* b16.3d* Mar 1] £30,000 5-y-o: rather unfurnished mare: fifth foal: half-sister to
fairly useful 2m hurdle winner Capital Force (by Kayf Tara) and fair hurdler/modest chaser
Dallas Cowboy (17f-2½m winner, by Beneficial): dam unraced sister to fairly useful
hurdler (stayed 2¾m) Trimbellina and half-sister to useful hurdler/smart chaser (stayed
2½m) Watson Lake: off mark on debut in Irish point: looked promising when also winning
bumpers at Ludlow in January and Newbury (mares race) in March, leading from halfway
when beating Dylan's Sea Song 1¼ lengths at latter: wears tongue tie. *Dan Skelton*

GETAWAY FLYER (IRE) 6 b.m. Getaway (GER) – No Moore Bills (Nicholas Bill) **h–**
[2018/19 b16.3m h16g Sep 11] €8,000 3-y-o: half-sister to several winners, including fairly **b–**
useful hurdler Fionn Mac Cul (19f winner, by Oscar) and fair hurdler Mtpockets (27f
winner, by Deploy): dam (h75) maiden hurdler (stayed 2½m): maiden Irish pointer: no
threat in mares bumper/maiden hurdle. *Christian Williams*

GETAWAY GERRY 5 b.g. Getaway (GER) – Loch Dhu (IRE) (Oscar (IRE)) [2018/19 **h–**
b69: b16.2s⁶ b16d h16.4d Dec 1] poor form in bumpers: never-dangerous seventh in **b–**
maiden at Newcastle on hurdling debut. *Katie Scott*

GETAWAY HONEY (IRE) 7 ch.m. Getaway (GER) – Knappogue Honey (IRE) (Anshan) **h92**
[2018/19 b16g² b16.3m* h16d⁶ h21.7dᵖᵘ h16.7g⁵ Feb 17] £16,000 6-y-o: medium-sized **b86**
mare: third foal: half-sister to bumper winner/fairly useful chaser Man of Steel (2½m-27f
winner) and bumper winner/winning pointer Who You For (both by Craigsteel): dam
unraced: Irish point winner: fair form in bumpers: won mares event at Stratford in July:
best effort over hurdles (modest form) when fifth in novice at Market Rasen. *David Dennis*

GETAWAY JOHN (IRE) 6 ch.g. Getaway (GER) – Present Your Own (IRE) (Presenting) **h132**
[2018/19 b115: h16s³ h16v³ h23g* h20d³ h22.5g³ h22d Apr 22] smart bumper performer:
useful novice hurdler: won at Fairyhouse (maiden) in January: stays 23f: acts on good to
soft going: tried in cheekpieces. *Gordon Elliott, Ireland*

GETAWAY MISSION (IRE) 5 b.g. Getaway (GER) – Emeranna (IRE) (Dr Massini **h92 ?**
(IRE)) [2018/19 b15.7v⁶ h19.4g⁴ h19gᶠ h20.5d h19g⁵ Apr 25] €38,000 3-y-o: tall **b–**
gelding: chasing type: sixth foal: half-brother to fairly useful hurdler/chaser You Can't
Catch Me (19f-2¾m winner, by Catcher In The Rye) and fair chaser Warwickshire (19f
winner, by Westerner): dam (h102), ungenuine 2m-19f hurdle winner, also 13f winner on
Flat: well beaten in bumper: seemingly modest form when last in maiden on hurdling
debut: none after. *Ian Williams*

GETAWAY MIXIE (IRE) 6 b.m. Getaway (GER) – Mixie The Pixie (IRE) (Court Cave **b–**
(IRE)) [2018/19 b15.8d Dec 9] first foal: dam unraced sister to fairly useful hurdler/chaser
(stayed 3m) Hold Court: runner-up on last of 3 starts in Irish points: tailed off in listed
mares bumper at Huntingdon. *Stuart Edmunds*

GETAWAY TRUMP (IRE) 6 b.g. Getaway (GER) – Acinorev (IRE) (Cape Cross **h153 p**
(IRE)) [2018/19 b89: h19.5g⁴ h20.5g* h16.8s* h20.5d² h15.7d⁴ h18.1d⁴ h16m*
h16g* Apr 27]
    Following enhancements earlier in the decade to the late-season programme
for juvenile hurdlers and novice chasers with the addition of several valuable
handicaps in late-March and April, some of them more successful than others, the
British Horseracing Authority in 2018 introduced a very valuable handicap for
novice hurdlers to the card at Sandown on the final day of the season, mirrored by a
similar race for novice chasers at Ayr on Scottish National day. As additions filling
a gap in the programme, both already look to be unqualified successes, particularly
the Sandown event. Run as the bet365 Novices' Championship Final, the inaugural
running attracted a field of twenty, running off BHA marks of between 137 and

bet365 Novices' Championship Final Handicap Hurdle, Sandown—Getaway Trump confirms himself a very exciting prospect as he defies top weight in a cracking second running of this valuable race; Harambe (stars) fills the runner-up spot

118 and was won by Ballymoy. Ballymoy scored that day off 132 and went on to win three further handicaps in the latest season, notably the Holloway's Handicap Hurdle at Ascot off a mark 15 lb higher than in the Championship Final. Five fewer runners went to post for the second running of the Sandown race, in part due to the presence of Getaway Trump under top weight off a BHA mark of 147, conceding 11 lb and upwards to his rivals. Getaway Trump defied the mark in good style, showing himself to be in the front rank of novice hurdlers in 2018/19—the form was good enough to have seen him finish second in the Supreme Novices' Hurdle—and if he proves as good over fences, then he could develop into a serious Festival contender by the spring.

Getaway Trump's progression into such a good prospect was yet another testament to the skill of his trainer, for whom he was one of two winners on the card as he celebrated regaining the trainers' championship. Getaway Trump won the third of three starts in points in Ireland in 2017, and was bought for £90,000 at the Cheltenham November Sales that year. He had two considerately-handled runs in bumpers in the first part of the following year, shaping with promise though held each time, with the bare form nothing to write home about. The same was true of his hurdling debut at Chepstow in October, when he was easy to back and not given a hard time once held. From that point, however, Getaway Trump's career began on a sharp upward curve. He won his next two starts, both by five lengths, his first victory coming in a novice lacking depth at Plumpton in which the third was fifty-four lengths back, and his second in a much stronger one under a penalty at Exeter, in which he was followed home by the useful Tedham. Getaway Trump was clearly now ready for a higher grade and was sent next to Newbury for the Grade 1 Challow Hurdle in which he was no match for the even-money favourite Champ, though the manner in which he cruised into contention off a steady pace, before finishing two and a half lengths second, was impressive. Getaway Trump has won at two and a half miles and ran well over the trip in the Challow, but his subsequent efforts suggest he might be even better at around two miles.

Getaway Trump should have been back at Newbury for his next outing, but the equine flu outbreak meant that the Betfair Hurdle was delayed a week and staged at Ascot. Sent off 4/1 second favourite behind another novice Al Dancer, Getaway Trump ran well in the rearranged showpiece, though he was probably further back than ideal, the way the race was run, and could manage no better than fourth behind Al Dancer, still shaping as if there was better to come. The one blip in his season came next, when he was beaten at odds on in the Grade 2 Premier Novices' Hurdle at Kelso. Whatever the reason for that reverse, it was soon put behind him, Getaway Trump easily outpointing the Baring Bingham sixth Galvin in a novice event at Ayr's

Owners Group 023's "Getaway Trump"

Scottish National meeting, the sharp two miles much more in his favour than it was for the runner-up. Getaway Trump had won an EBF qualifier at Exeter, so could have run in that novice hurdle Final against fellow 'National Hunt' novices. As it was, though, he turned up for the open novice Final (the Ayr race was a qualifier) six weeks later, a race in which plenty of his rivals, by contrast, had had experience on the Flat. Getaway Trump was sent off the 9/2 favourite in an open betting market, five others starting at odds of between 6/1 and 17/2. Off a mark 5 lb higher than in the Betfair Hurdle, Getaway Trump was ridden more prominently than at Ascot, travelling smoothly as usual. Most of the field still had a chance early in the straight, but Getaway Trump went to the front at the second-last and soon had the race in the bag before being ridden out on the run-in to beat Harambe by two and three quarter lengths. The trio that chased home Getaway Trump were all handicap debutants and the form is likely to prove strong for a race of its kind.

Getaway Trump (IRE) (b.g. 2013)	Getaway (GER) (b 2003)	Monsun (br 1990)	Konigsstuhl Mosella
		Guernica (b 1994)	Unfuwain Greenvera
	Acinorev (IRE) (br 2003)	Cape Cross (b 1994)	Green Desert Park Appeal
		Tocade (b 1995)	Kenmare Trojan River

Getaway Trump might have looked fairly expensive when he went through the sale-ring at Cheltenham, having changed hands three times before for a combined sum that added up to less than a third of what he made that day, though subsequent events provided satisfaction for both parties to the sale. Getaway Trump had been sold twice as a yearling, for €5,000 and €10,000, and then made €11,500 as a three-year-old store. He has an ordinary pedigree on the dam's side, being Acinorev's third foal and first runner. Her 2015 foal Lively Citizen (by Frammassone) was placed in a point before being sold for £48,000 in May. Acinorev herself ran just twice, easily her better effort in bumpers when fourth at Limerick on her debut. She is a half-sister to four winners, probably the best of them Paco Jack, who won a Galway Blazers Handicap over fences and a Grade 3 juvenile event over hurdles. Getaway Trump wasn't the only winner for his up-and-coming sire on the Sandown card, as Talkischeap, another son of Getaway, landed the feature bet365 Gold Cup over three miles five furlongs, the high-class two-mile hurdler Verdana Blue also representing him in 2018/19. Getaway Trump is much more likely to take after Verdana Blue than Talkischeap, so far as stamina goes. He is a well-made gelding, very much a chaser on looks, and is an exciting novice prospect with fences the plan for him from now on in preference to going down the Champion Hurdle route. Getaway Trump has shown his best form at two miles and has won on soft and good to firm going. *Paul Nicholls*

GET HELP (IRE) 6 b.g. Gold Well – Present Abbey (IRE) (Presenting) [2018/19 h16.2d⁴   **h113** h16.8s⁴ h18.1d² Apr 8] sixth foal: dam (c94/h94), 2m/17f hurdle/chase winner, half-sister to fairly useful 2½m hurdle winner Lodge Hill: maiden pointer: fair form in novice hurdles: improved again when second to Elvis Mail at Kelso in April. *Stuart Colthern*

GET HOME NOW 11 b.g. Diktat – Swiftly (Cadeaux Genereux) [2018/19 h122:   **h–** h20.6gᵖᵘ h16.3g⁶ h20gᶠ h21.7g⁶ h20.3gᵖᵘ Sep 5] sturdy gelding: fairly useful handicap hurdler at best: out of sorts in 2018/19: usually in headgear: wears tongue tie. *Peter Bowen*

GET IN THE QUEUE 5 b.g. Mount Nelson – Amarullah (FR) (Daylami (IRE)) [2018/19   **b119** b15.8s* b16.8d* b16.3d* Mar 23] £40,000 3-y-o: fourth foal: half-brother to 3 winners, including a winning hurdler in Italy by Mawatheeq: dam unraced half-sister to fairly useful hurdler (stayed 21f) Trevisani: smart form in bumpers: won at Uttoxeter in December and Exeter (by 16 lengths from Sheshoon Sonny) in February: 1/3, completed hat-trick in 13-runner Goffs UK Spring Sales Bumper at Newbury by 4½ lengths from Prince Llywelyn, never far away and in command final 1f: most exciting prospect for novice hurdles. *Harry Fry*

Goffs UK Spring Sale Bumper, Newbury—a third successive win in this valuable bumper for trainer Harry Fry, though the main story concerns Noel Fehily, who rides off into retirement by steering home 3/1-on shot Get In The Queue

GETONSAM 7 ch.g. Black Sam Bellamy (IRE) – Pennepoint (Pennekamp (USA)) **c–** [2018/19 h–: h16.8m c15.7gᵖᵘ Oct 25] little sign of ability: has worn hood/tongue tie: **h–** headstrong. *Sue Smith*

GET ON THE YAGER 9 b.g. Tamure (IRE) – Florentino (Efisio) [2018/19 c138, h–: **c128** c19.4s⁶ c21d c34v³ Mar 16] good-topped gelding: has had breathing operation: winning **h–** hurdler: useful handicap chaser: easily best effort in 2018/19 when 15 lengths third to Potters Corner in Midlands Grand National at Uttoxeter in March: stays 4¼m: acts on heavy going. *Dan Skelton*

GET OUT THE GATE (IRE) 6 b.g. Mahler – Chartani (IRE) (King's Theatre (IRE)) **h125** [2018/19 h116: h15.6g* h15.6g³ h18.1g² h18.1d⁶ h16.2g⁴ h16m h23.9g³ Apr 24] tall gelding: will make a chaser: Irish point winner: fairly useful hurdler: won maiden at Musselburgh in December: stays 3m, at least when emphasis is on speed: acts on soft going. *Jim Goldie*

GET READY FREDDY 9 b.g. Sixties Icon – Summer Shades (Green Desert (USA)) **c96** [2018/19 c102, h77: h15.8m* h15.7g⁴ c16.5g⁶ h16.7g Aug 3] sparely-made gelding: **h90** modest handicap hurdler: won at Uttoxeter in May: fair handicap chaser: best around 2m: acts on good to firm and good to soft going: tried in cheekpieces: usually in tongue tie: held up. *Dan Skelton*

GET RHYTHM (IRE) 9 b.g. Kayf Tara – Ninna Nanna (FR) (Garde Royale) [2018/19 **c95** c120, h117: c15.7g c16.5g⁶ c16.4g⁴ h16.3d⁵ Jan 16] good-topped gelding: fairly useful **h–** hurdler: similar form over fences as a novice in 2017/18: disappointing since, including over hurdles: unproven beyond 17f: acts on heavy going: front runner/races prominently. *Tom George*

GETTYSBURG ADDRESS (IRE) 8 b.g. Milan – Cat Burglar (IRE) (Robellino (USA)) **c122** [2018/19 h120: c19.2s⁴ c24d² Jan 8] fairly useful hurdler: similar form when runner-up at **h–** Bangor on second of 2 starts in handicap chases: stays 3m: acts on heavy going: wears headgear: tried in tongue tie: front runner/races prominently. *Dr Richard Newland*

GET UP THEM STEPS 5 b.g. Excelebration (IRE) – Flag Day (Pivotal) [2018/19 **b86** b16.3d b14d⁴ b17.7d⁵ Mar 18] second foal: dam unraced: fair form in bumpers: tried in hood. *John O'Shea*

GET WISHING (IRE) 7 b.g. Getaway (GER) – Third Wish (IRE) (Second Empire **h95** (IRE)) [2018/19 h86: h16s* h16.8s³ h18.5s³ h21.9vᵖᵘ h16.8s⁴ Mar 18] has had breathing operations: modest handicap hurdler: won at Chepstow (conditionals) in November: unproven beyond 17f: acts on heavy going: often in headgear: wears tongue tie. *Victor Dartnall*

G FOR GINGER 9 ch.m. Lucarno (USA) – Kaream (Karinga Bay) [2018/19 h108: **h117** h19.9g* h16g* h16g³ h20g⁶ h21.4g Nov 10] has had breathing operation: fairly useful handicap hurdler: ridden by 10-lb claimer, won at Uttoxeter (mares) and Worcester in July: stays 2½m: best form on good going: tried in hood: wears tongue tie: front runner/races prominently. *Anthony Honeyball*

GHOSTLY ARC (IRE) 7 b.g. Arcano (IRE) – Cheyenne's Spirit (IRE) (Sadler's Wells **h–** (USA)) [2018/19 h16.8g May 15] fair handicapper on Flat (stays 1¾m): little promise in novice/maiden hurdles, tongue tied in latter. *Noel Wilson*

GHOST SERGE (IRE) 4 gr.g. Zebedee – Cornakill (USA) (Stormin Fever (USA)) **h124** [2018/19 h17.2s² h16.2g* h16m² h16.9s² h16.8d⁴ h18.8d h17.9s² Apr 9] sturdy gelding: fair on Flat, stays 1¼m: fairly useful juvenile hurdler: won maiden event at Perth in September: best effort when close second at Compiegne final outing: acts on soft and good to firm going. *Sophie Leech*

GIBBES BAY (FR) 7 gr.g. Al Namix (FR) – Nouvelle Donne (FR) (Sleeping Car (FR)) **c– x** [2018/19 c–, h115: h25g⁴ May 10] tall gelding: maiden pointer: fair maiden hurdler: failed **h111 x** to complete in handicap chases: stays 25f: acts on soft and good to firm going: prone to mistakes. *Paul Nicholls*

GIBB HILL 5 ch.g. Frozen Fire (GER) – River Reine (IRE) (Lahib (USA)) [2018/19 b–: **h–** b16.8g b16g b16.8d h19.5dᵘʳ h18.5d h19.3m⁶ Mar 31] workmanlike gelding: no form in **b–** bumpers/over hurdles. *Bob Buckler*

GIBBSTOWN (IRE) 13 b.m. Bob Back (USA) – Kitty Maher (IRE) (Posen (USA)) **c84 §** [2018/19 c89§, h–: c23.8g³ c24.2g⁶ Jun 16] maiden hurdler: modest handicap chaser: stays **h–** 25f: acts on heavy going: normally in headgear: has worn tongue tie: temperamental. *Paul Stafford, Ireland*

GIFT FROM PARIS 4 b.f. Champs Elysees – Blush's Gift (Cadeaux Genereux) [2018/19 **b–** b13.7m b14d Nov 29] first foal: dam unraced: well held in bumpers. *Philip McBride*

GI JAYNE (IRE) 8 b.m. Millenary – Lady of Appeal (IRE) (Lord of Appeal) [2018/19 c78, h61: h20.3g* h19.9g h21.6g^pu Jul 6] has had breathing operation: maiden pointer: modest handicap hurdler: won mares event at Southwell in May: well held only outing over fences: stays 2½m: acts on good to soft going: in hood last 3 starts: has worn tongue tie: waited with: not one to rely on. *Dan Skelton*   **c–** **h88 §**

GILLS PET (IRE) 8 b.m. Flemensfirth (USA) – Gleaming Spire (Overbury (IRE)) [2018/19 h20d^pu Apr 27] third foal: sister to fairly useful hurdler/smart chaser Knockgraffon (2m-2½m winner): dam unraced: won point in January 2018: pulled up otherwise, including in mares maiden hurdle (tongue tied). *David Harry Kelly, Ireland*   **h–**

GILLY GRACE 9 b.m. Morpeth – Miss Grace (Atticus (USA)) [2018/19 c–, h63: h21.6g^5 h16g h19.2d c16s^5 c16.1d^pu c19.2d^5 c19.2s^4 Apr 16] angular mare: poor maiden hurdler: similar form over fences: stays 2¾m: acts on soft going: has worn cheekpieces, including last 3 starts. *Jimmy Frost*   **c57** **h68**

GILWEN GRACELYN 5 b.m. Dick Turpin (IRE) – Gilwen Glory (IRE) (Saddlers' Hall (IRE)) [2018/19 b15.8s h21.9g^F h15.8m^4 Apr 23] second foal: dam (c84/h111) unreliable bumper/19f-3m hurdle winner: tailed off in bumper/completed start over hurdles. *Evan Williams*   **h–** **b–**

GILWEN GRACIE 6 b.m. Multiplex – Gilwen Glory (IRE) (Saddlers' Hall (IRE)) [2018/19 b16g^6 b15.7g Jul 15] first foal: dam (c84/h111) unreliable bumper/19f-3m hurdle winner: well beaten in bumpers. *Evan Williams*   **b–**

GIN AND TONIC 9 ch.g. Phoenix Reach (IRE) – Arctic Queen (Linamix (FR)) [2018/19 c93, h79: h15.9g* h15.8g^2 c16.3g^2 c16.3g^pu h15.8d^2 h15.8d^3 h16.4m h16m Apr 22] modest handicap hurdler: won at Plumpton in May: poor maiden chaser: best around 2m: acts on heavy going: wears headgear. *Michael Wigham*   **c81** **h88**

GIN COBBLER 13 b.g. Beneficial – Cassia (Be My Native (USA)) [2018/19 c70§, h–: c19.3g^6 c19.2g^4 c19.2s^pu c16.4s^2 c16.4s c15.8m^4 c20.1v^pu Mar 14] maiden hurdler: poor handicap chaser: stayed 2½m: acted on good to firm and heavy going: unreliable: dead. *Victor Thompson*   **c64 §** **h–**

GINGE DE SOPHIA (IRE) 6 b.m. Presenting – Me Grannys Endoors (IRE) (Tremblant) [2018/19 h98: h20g h20g h18.7g^5 Oct 20] compact mare: modest maiden hurdler: should stay 2½m: acts on good to soft going: wears tongue tie. *Nigel Twiston-Davies*   **h94**

GINGER FIZZ 12 ch.m. Haafhd – Valagalore (Generous (IRE)) [2018/19 h104: h16d^5 h15.7g h16g^4 h16g^6 Sep 2] lengthy, angular mare: has had breathing operation: modest handicap hurdler nowadays: stays easy 2¼m: acts on good to firm and good to soft going: wears headgear/tongue tie: free-going front runner. *Ben Case*   **h88**

GINGILI 9 b.g. Beat All (USA) – Gentian (Generous (IRE)) [2018/19 c127§, h116§: c24d^pu c27.7d^4 c25.6s Dec 5] has had breathing operation: fairly useful hurdler/chaser: probably stays 3½m: acts on soft and good to firm going: wears headgear/tongue tie: moody. *Johnny Farrelly*   **c122 §** **h– §**

GINJO 9 b.m. Sakhee (USA) – Gulshan (Batshoof) [2018/19 h16.8g^3 Apr 20] poor handicap hurdler: stays 19f: acts on good to firm and probably heavy going: wears cheekpieces: has worn tongue tie. *Bernard Llewellyn*   **h80**

GINO TRAIL (IRE) 12 br.g. Perugino (USA) – Borough Trail (IRE) (Woodborough (USA)) [2018/19 c153, h–: c15.5s^2 c15.7g^2 c16.3d^pu Mar 15] good-topped gelding: has had breathing operation: winning hurdler: smart handicap chaser: best around 2m: acts on heavy going: wears headgear: front runner. *Kerry Lee*   **c151** **h–**

GIRL POWRE 4 br.f. Great Pretender (IRE) – Annieegan (Zaha (CAN)) [2018/19 b16.3s^5 b16.7g^6 Apr 13] first foal: dam winning pointer: behind in bumpers: wears hood. *Steve Flook*   **b–**

GIVEAWAY GLANCE 6 br.m. Passing Glance – Giving (Generous (IRE)) [2018/19 h125: h19.2m^6 h19.2g* h15.8d* h20.3s^ur h18.5d Feb 22] fairly useful handicap hurdler: won mares events at Fontwell in November and Ludlow in December: stays 19f: acts on soft going: normally hooded: patiently ridden. *Alan King*   **h121**

GIVE HIM TIME 8 b.g. Kalanisi (IRE) – Delayed (FR) (Fijar Tango (FR)) [2018/19 c97, h–: h20.5d^6 h15.8d Feb 17] big, workmanlike gelding: has had breathing operation: maiden hurdler, fair form at best: placed all 3 starts in handicap chases: stays 2¼m: acts on soft going: has worn headgear: in tongue tie last 5 starts. *Nick Gifford*   **c–** **h76**

GIVE ME A COPPER (IRE) 9 ch.g. Presenting – Copper Supreme (IRE) (Supreme Leader) [2018/19 c140p, h–: c24.2s⁴ c25sᶠ c28.8g⁴ Apr 27] strong gelding: winning hurdler: useful chaser: fourth in valuable handicaps at Sandown in February and April (laboured effort) on completed starts in 2018/19: probably stays 29f: acts on heavy going: wears tongue tie. *Paul Nicholls* **c135 h–**

GIVEN NAME 4 b.g. Nathaniel (IRE) – Poly Pomona (Green Desert (USA)) [2018/19 h15.9s⁶ h16v h15.9d Mar 18] poor form on Flat: little show over hurdles. *Seamus Mullins* **h–**

GIVING BACK 5 br.m. Midnight Legend – Giving (Generous (IRE)) [2018/19 b90: ab16g* b15.8d b17d Apr 4] compact mare: fair bumper performer: won mares event at Lingfield in November. *Alan King* **b92**

GIVING GLANCES 4 b.f. Passing Glance – Giving (Generous (IRE)) [2018/19 h16.2g* h17spu h16.6g* h16m Feb 23] good-topped filly: sister to fairly useful hurdlers Giveaway Glance (2m/19f winner) and Forgiving Glance (2m winner): fairly useful on Flat, stays 1½m: fair form in juvenile hurdles: won at Hereford (fillies race) in November and Doncaster (weak listed event) in January. *Alan King* **h114**

GLAMOROUS GOLD (IRE) 6 b.m. Gold Well – Glamorous Leader (IRE) (Supreme Leader) [2018/19 h16m h16d h21g⁵ h20d³ h22g h22.4d⁵ h20.6dpu Dec 13] modest maiden hurdler: left N. Stokes after sixth start: stayed 2¾m: acted on good to soft going: tried in cheekpieces/tongue tie: dead. *Lucy Normile* **h88**

GLANCE BACK 8 b.g. Passing Glance – Roberta Back (IRE) (Bob Back (USA)) [2018/19 c97, h–: c17.4g² c17.4s* c16.1d⁵ c17.8s² c15.9g³ c17.8m³ c16.2g³ Apr 25] lengthy gelding: has had breathing operation: maiden hurdler: fair handicap chaser: won at Bangor in December: stays 2¼m: acts on heavy going: has worn headgear: wears tongue tie: front runner/races prominently. *Emma-Jane Bishop* **c104 h–**

GLANVILLES GUEST 7 ch.m. Sulamani (IRE) – Doubly Guest (Barathea Guest) [2018/19 h84: h19m⁵ h21.6g* h22mᶠ h23.3g² h21.6g⁴ h23g² h21.4m Oct 19] fair handicap hurdler: won mares event at Newton Abbot in June: stays 23f: acts on soft and good to firm going. *Nick Mitchell* **h105**

GLASHA'S PEAK 5 b.m. Flemensfirth (USA) – Peggies Run (Kayf Tara) [2018/19 b16.5d⁴ b16.3d⁵ Mar 1] useful-looking mare: fifth foal: half-sister to bumper winner/fair hurdler Peggies Venture (2½m/21f winner, by Presenting): dam unraced half-sister to fair hurdler/useful chaser (stayed 3¼m) Latimer's Place and useful hurdler/fairly useful chaser (19f-2¾m winner) Penneyrose Bay: modest form in mares bumpers. *Alan King* **b84**

GLENDUFF (IRE) 5 b.g. Gold Well – Last of The Bunch (Silver Patriarch (IRE)) [2018/19 b16.2g² h16.4m⁴ Mar 28] €90,000 3-y-o: second foal: half-brother to Champion Bumper winner/fairly useful 2m hurdle winner Relegate (by Flemensfirth): dam (h113) bumper and 2½m/21f hurdle winner (stayed 3m): fair form when second at Kelso on first of 2 outings in bumpers. *Nicky Richards* **b91**

GLENDUN (USA) 5 b.g. First Defence (USA) – La Mina (USA) (Mineshaft (USA)) [2018/19 h16g h15.8g³ Apr 22] compact gelding: fair on Flat, stays 1¼m: better effort in novice hurdles when seventh at Warwick. *James Eustace* **h96**

GLENFINN HALL 4 b.g. Mawatheeq (USA) – Hallingdal (UAE) (Halling (USA)) [2018/19 b13.7g Nov 13] always behind in junior bumper. *Kevin Bishop* **b–**

GLEN FORSA (IRE) 7 b.g. Mahler – Outback Ivy (IRE) (Bob Back (USA)) [2018/19 h16.8v² h20g² c23.6s* c20.5g⁴ c15.5d* c15.9sur c19.9dpu Apr 4] medium-sized gelding: fairly useful form over hurdles (remains capable of better): much better form over fences: won novice handicaps at Chepstow in November and Kempton (by 2¾ lengths from Glen Rocco) in December, and Kingmaker Novices' Chase at Sandown (by 19 lengths from Kalashnikov, jumping superbly) in February: effective from 2m to 3m: acts on heavy going. *Mick Channon* **c150 h119 p**

GLENGAR (IRE) 5 b.g. Stowaway – Accordeon Royale (IRE) (Accordion) [2018/19 b15.8v ab16g⁶ h19s h15.3g Apr 3] runner-up on sole completed start in Irish points: little form in bumpers/maiden hurdles. *Neil Mulholland* **h– b63**

GLENGRA (IRE) 10 gr.g. Beneficial – Zaraza (IRE) (Darshaan) [2018/19 c68, h–: c20.5m⁶ c19.2gpu Jul 8] rather leggy gelding: lightly-raced maiden hurdler: no form over fences since runner-up in novice handicap on chasing debut in 2016/17: stays 21f: acts on good to soft going: tried in tongue tie. *Ian Williams* **c78 h–**

GLENLOE (IRE) 8 br.g. Kayf Tara – Mandys Native (IRE) (Be My Native (USA)) [2018/19 h144: c19.7d⁵ c21.5s⁴ Jan 26] tall gelding: useful hurdler: better effort over fences when 11 lengths fourth to Real Steel in maiden at Fairyhouse in January: stays 3m: acts on heavy going: open to further improvement as a chaser. *Gordon Elliott, Ireland* **c130 p h–**

GLENLORA 6 ch.m. Supreme Sound – Rainha (Alflora (IRE)) [2018/19 b–: h16.2g⁵ h23.8g⁴ h16.2g h17d Mar 24] well held in bumper: in tongue tie, modest form over hurdles. *Sandy Thomson* **h87**

GLEN MOOAR (IRE) 5 br.g. Presenting – Supreme Serenade (IRE) (Supreme Leader) [2018/19 b16.4d Mar 5] green when well held in maiden bumper at Newcastle. *Tim Easterby* **b–**

GLENO (IRE) 7 ch.g. Ask – Lwitikila (Denel (FR)) [2018/19 b91: h16v h20.5s h20.5d h15.8d h21.4g* h19.8s* h20.6g⁶ h21.7g* Apr 24] angular gelding: fairly useful hurdler: much improved when winning handicaps at Wincanton in February, Sandown (novice event) in March and Fontwell in April: stays 2¾m: acts on soft going (won bumper on heavy): usually races close up. *Gary Moore* **h122**

GLENPARK (FR) 4 b.g. Enrique – Sweet Jaune (FR) (Le Nain Jaune (FR)) [2018/19 h16.2g⁴ h16.7d h16s⁴ h16s³ h18.8d Mar 23] useful-looking gelding: half-brother to numerous winners, including useful hurdler/chaser Viking Blond (23f/3m winner, by Varese), stayed 29f, and useful but ungenuine hurdler Rosemauve (2¾m-3m winner, by Cyborg): dam unraced: modest form over hurdles: bred to prove best at 2½m+: acts on soft going. *Lucinda Russell* **h96**

GLEN ROCCO 8 ch.g. Shirocco (GER) – Adees Dancer (Danehill Dancer (IRE)) [2018/19 h97p: c16sᵘʳ c21.6d* c20s³ c20.5g² c24g* c24g⁶ Feb 23] strong, workmanlike gelding: maiden hurdler: useful form over fences: won handicaps at Fontwell (novice) in November and Kempton (by 23 lengths, finding plenty) in January: stays well beyond 3m: acts on soft going: races off pace: remains open to improvement. *Nick Gifford* **c135 p h–**

GLEN ROE (IRE) 11 b.g. Vinnie Roe (IRE) – Belgrove Girl (IRE) (Supreme Leader) [2018/19 h20.1s* c24.2d⁴ Apr 9] point winner: 25/1-winner of maiden at Hexham (by ¾ length from Sheriff Garrett) in October on hurdling debut: left Andrew Martin, fourth in hunter chase at Exeter 6 months later: should stay beyond 2½m: wears tongue tie. *M. J. Linehan* **c82 h103**

GLENRUA (IRE) 6 b.g. Stowaway – Ceol Rua (IRE) (Bob Back (USA)) [2018/19 h19d c26.7dᵖᵘ h18.5g Mar 26] failed to complete in points: little form over hurdles/in chases: tried in cheekpieces. *John Joseph Hanlon, Ireland* **c– h–**

GLENS COUNTY (IRE) 6 b.m. Court Cave (IRE) – Glendante (IRE) (Phardante (FR)) [2018/19 h19.2vᵖᵘ h20.5dᵖᵘ Jan 6] sturdy mare: fifth foal: closely related to useful hurdler/chaser Dursey Sound (2½m-25f winner, by Milan): dam 2½m chase winner: pulled up in novice hurdles. *Neil Mulholland* **h–**

GLENTROOL 6 b.g. Passing Glance – Killala Bay (IRE) (Executive Perk) [2018/19 b92: h20vᵖᵘ Nov 11] bumper winner: pulled up in maiden on hurdling debut: should be suited by 2½m+. *Sam Thomas* **h–**

GLEN VINE 5 ch.g. Robin des Champs (FR) – Gaspara (FR) (Astarabad (USA)) [2018/19 b16g² h18.5d⁴ h19.5d⁵ Mar 20] €95,000 3-y-o: has had breathing operation: first foal: dam (h149), 2m-2½m winner (stayed 3m), half-sister to very smart 2m-2½m hurdle winner Mr Thriller: strong-finishing second in bumper at Worcester: fair form in maiden hurdles: will stay 2½m. *David Pipe* **h105 b96**

GLIMPSE OF GOLD 8 b.g. Passing Glance – Tizzy Blue (IRE) (Oscar (IRE)) [2018/19 c–, h89: h16.8g h15.8g³ h16.8s³ h17.7d⁵ h15.7g* h15.8d³ h16m⁴ Apr 22] workmanlike gelding: fair handicap hurdler: won selling event at Southwell in March: little aptitude for chasing: best around 2m: acts on heavy going: wears tongue tie. *Tim Vaughan* **c– h100**

GLINGER FLAME (IRE) 7 ro.g. Daylami (IRE) – Titian Flame (IRE) (Titus Livius (FR)) [2018/19 b87p: b16g³ h20.5s² h20.5d³ h20.1d* h16.2g* Apr 15] third in bumpers: fairly useful form over hurdles: in cheekpieces, won handicap in March and novice in April, both at Hexham: stays 2½m: acts on soft going: has looked tricky ride. *Nicky Richards* **h124 b87**

GLINGERSIDE (IRE) 8 b.g. Milan – Kettle 'N Cran (IRE) (Zaffaran (USA)) [2018/19 c–, h99: h20.2g³ h19.3g⁴ h19.5vᵖᵘ Nov 14] modest handicap hurdler: little promise in novice handicap chases: should stay beyond 2½m: acts on heavy going: in cheekpieces last 3 starts: often races prominently. *R. Mike Smith* **c– h90**

The New One Unibet Hurdle (Champion Hurdle Trial), Haydock—Global Citizen takes full advantage of a good opportunity, getting first run on Silver Streak

GLITTERING LOVE (IRE) 7 b.g. Winged Love (IRE) – Glittering Image (IRE) (Sadler's Wells (USA)) [2018/19 h89: c20.1v* c24.1s* c24.1d* c24.1s* Mar 9] good-topped gelding: lightly-raced maiden hurdler: vastly better in handicap chases, winning at Hexham (novice event) in December and Ayr in January, February (novice race) and March (further marked progress when beating Capard King 5 lengths, pair clear): stays 3m well: acts on heavy going: tried in tongue tie: will go on improving. *Nicky Richards* — **c125 p**
h–

GLOBAL ANCHOR (IRE) 5 b.g. Stowaway – Loreley (IRE) (Oscar (IRE)) [2018/19 b15.8m³ h16g⁶ h16.7v h15.8d h19s⁶ Feb 4] placed in bumper: poor form in novice hurdles. *Jonjo O'Neill* — **h68**
b80

GLOBAL CITIZEN (IRE) 7 b.g. Alkaadhem – Lady Willmurt (IRE) (Mandalus) [2018/19 h142, b104: h15.7m² h16.3s* h16g⁴ h15.7d* h16.4s Mar 12] sturdy gelding: point/bumper winner: smart hurdler: won listed handicap at Newbury in December and Champion Hurdle Trial at Haydock (by 3 lengths from Silver Streak) in January: will prove best around 2m: acts on heavy going: strong-travelling front runner: fluent jumper. *Ben Pauling* — **h153**

GLOBAL DOMINATION 11 b.g. Alflora (IRE) – Lucia Forte (Neltino) [2018/19 c85, h–: c20.3g² c20d³ c20.9sᵖᵘ c23.6g² c23.6d⁶ c21.4g* Apr 3] has had breathing operation: maiden hurdler: modest handicap chaser: won at Market Rasen in April: stays 3m: acts on heavy going: wears cheekpieces/tongue tie. *Caroline Bailey* — **c95**
h–

GLOBAL DREAM 9 ch.g. Lucarno (USA) – Global Girl (Shambo) [2018/19 c27.6sᵖᵘ c25.5s⁴ c25.5d² c29.2d³ c24dᵖᵘ Apr 9] good-topped gelding: winning hurdler: fairly useful handicap chaser: stays 29f: acts on good to firm and heavy going: tried in cheekpieces: consistent. *Caroline Bailey* — **c122**
h–

GLOBAL HARMONY (IRE) 4 b.f. Flemensfirth (USA) – Violin Davis (FR) (Turgeon (USA)) [2018/19 b12.6s Dec 19] first foal: dam (c131/h131), 2½m-3m hurdle/chase winner, out of sister to top-class 2m chaser Klairon Davis: 7/2, only ninth in fillies junior bumper at Newbury. *Dan Skelton* — **b–**

GLOBAL JACKPOT 6 b.g. Flying Legend (USA) – A Fistful of Euros (East Wood) [2018/19 b17.3g² b18.8g² b16.7m² h17.6g⁴ h19.8g² h16g* h16.2g* h16.2g* h19.6g² c16.7d³ Apr 23] €23,000 3-y-o, £90,000 4-y-o: second foal: dam (h89), maiden hurdler (stayed 3¼m), half-sister to useful hurdler/chaser (stayed 3m) Mon Villez: winning pointer: fair in bumpers: useful novice hurdler: won at Tramore (maiden) in August and twice at Perth in September (by 12 lengths from Kapgarry second occasion): length third to Or Jaune de Somoza in maiden at Fairyhouse on chasing debut: probably stays 2½m: acts on good to soft going: wears tongue tie: usually front runner/races prominently. *Gordon Elliott, Ireland* **c129 h130 b94**

GLOBAL RHAPSODY (IRE) 5 b.g. Presenting – Rhapsody In Blue (GER) (Winged Love (IRE)) [2018/19 b15.7g h15.8v h15.9s h18.5s Mar 18] €110,000 3-y-o: fifth foal: half-brother to a winner on Flat abroad by Samum: dam German 11f winner: well beaten in bumper: some promise over hurdles: remains capable of better. *Neil Mulholland* **h80 p b–**

GLOBAL RULER 7 b.g. Kalanisi (IRE) – Queen's Leader (Supreme Leader) [2018/19 h19.7g⁵ h19.7d⁵ h16s⁴ Dec 26] fair maiden hurdler: stays 2½m: acts on good to soft going: in tongue tie last 2 starts. *Dan Skelton* **h100**

GLOBAL THRILL 10 b.g. Big Shuffle (USA) – Goonda (Darshaan) [2018/19 h104: h16.8g* h16.5g⁴ h16.5d⁵ h15.5d h15.8s² h16d h16m³ Apr 25] good-topped gelding: modest handicap hurdler: won at Newton Abbot in May: unproven beyond 17f: acts on heavy going: has worn headgear, including last 5 starts: usually tongue tied. *Bernard Llewellyn* **h99**

GLOBAL TOUR (IRE) 6 b.g. Arakan (USA) – Galant Tour (IRE) (Riberetto) [2018/19 h–, b–: h16g h16.7d h19.8g h18.8g h16g⁶ h16d⁵ h16g h19.2d⁶ Nov 18] poor form over hurdles: should stay beyond 17f: acts on good to soft going: tried in hood: wears tongue tie: waited with: signs of temperament: has joined Fergal O'Brien. *Paul W. Flynn, Ireland* **h81**

GLOBETROTTER (IRE) 5 ch.g. Helmet (AUS) – Shimna (Mr Prospector (USA)) [2018/19 h16.2g³ h16.2g* Sep 17] has had breathing operation: half-brother to 3 winning jumpers, including fairly useful hurdler Hazeymm (2m winner, by Marju), stayed 2½m, and fairly useful hurdler/chaser Colebrooke (2m-2¾m winner, by Shamardal): fairly useful on Flat, stays 1½m: fair form over hurdles: won maiden at Hexham in September: open to further improvement. *Julia Brooke* **h106 p**

GLOI 8 b.m. Overbury (IRE) – Go Gwenni Go (Bold Fox) [2018/19 h64, b60: h16.8g⁵ h20g Jul 26] little form over hurdles: tried in hood. *Debra Hamer* **h87 ?**

GLORIOUS BORU (IRE) 8 b.g. Brian Boru – Sea Off The Gales (IRE) (Luso) [2018/19 h21g⁶ h16d h15.9s h20.7g h16.8s h21.7g³ Apr 12] workmanlike gelding: Irish point winner: modest hurdler over hurdles: stays 2¾m: usually held up. *Zoe Davison* **h93**

GLORIOUS LADY (IRE) 5 b.m. Fame And Glory – Lady Secret (FR) (Lord of Men) [2018/19 b16.2d⁶ b15.6g* Nov 26] €16,000 3-y-o: fifth foal: half-sister to a winning pointer by Court Cave: dam, placed at 17f over hurdles/fences in France, half-sister to useful hurdler/very smart chaser (stayed 2½m) Mansony: won on debut in Irish point: modest form in bumpers: won at Musselburgh in November. *Keith Dalgleish* **b80**

GLORVINA (IRE) 5 b.m. Dragon Pulse (IRE) – Hawk Dance (IRE) (Hawk Wing (USA)) [2018/19 h97: h20.6g⁶ h16d⁵ Dec 18] compact mare: modest hurdler: stays 21f: acts on soft going. *Charlie Mann* **h–**

GLORY AND FORTUNE (IRE) 4 b.g. Fame And Glory – Night Heron (IRE) (St Jovite (USA)) [2018/19 b14d* Jan 1] €75,000 3-y-o: sturdy gelding: fourth foal: half-brother to bumper winner Dramatic Pause (by Oscar) and modest 2½m hurdle winner Way of The World (by Flemensfirth): dam unraced half-sister to useful hurdler (2½m-2¾m winner) Flemenson: 7/2, won listed bumper at Cheltenham on debut by 4½ lengths from Cascova: sure to improve. *Tom Lacey* **b99 p**

GNARLY 7 b.m. Midnight Legend – Diamant Noir (Sir Harry Lewis (USA)) [2018/19 h67: h20.3g⁵ h20g³ c23g⁴ c23m Sep 17] poor form over hurdles/fences: dead. *Jonjo O'Neill* **c81 h77**

GOAL (IRE) 11 b.g. Mujadil (USA) – Classic Lin (FR) (Linamix (FR)) [2018/19 c–, h96: h15.8g h15.8m⁶ h15.8g⁴ Jun 6] modest handicap hurdler: fell only start over fences: stays 2¼m: acts on good to firm and good to soft going: wears headgear/tongue tie. *Tracey Watkins* **c– h93**

BetVictor Michael Purcell Memorial Novices' Hurdle, Thurles—the fourth of five wins in a very productive campaign for Go Another One

GO ANOTHER ONE (IRE) 7 b.g. Stowaway – Missusan (IRE) (King's Ride) [2018/19 **h135** h24m² h20.2g* h18.8d² h22g* h20.9m* h21g² h20g² h20g* h23.9g* Apr 24] workmanlike gelding: runner-up in point: useful hurdler: won maiden at Perth in July, novice at Stratford in August, handicap at Kelso in September, Michael Purcell Memorial Novices' Hurdle at Thurles (by 2¼ lengths from Notebook) in February and listed novice at Perth in April: stays 3m: acts on good to firm and good to soft going: wears tongue tie: often travels strongly: tough and likeable. *John McConnell, Ireland*

Sky Bet Handicap Chase, Doncaster—a second win in the race for Tom Bellamy as he brings home the fluent-jumping Go Conquer in front of the pace-setting Monbeg River (right)

GO AS YOU PLEASE (IRE) 6 b.g. Jeremy (USA) – Aweebounce (IRE) (Dubawi (IRE)) [2018/19 b92p: h15.7s h15.5d h15.5g h15.8d h16.7g Mar 20] compact gelding: runner-up in bumper: little form over hurdles. *Paul Webber* **h–**

GO CONQUER (IRE) 10 b.g. Arcadio (GER) – Ballinamona Wish (IRE) (Kotashaan (FR)) [2018/19 c150, h–: c23.8m³ c24g² c24g* c34.3g^pu c22.7g^pu Apr 27] strong gelding: winning hurdler: smart handicap chaser: won Sky Bet Chase at Doncaster (by 6 lengths from Monbeg River) in January: best up to 3m: acts on soft and good to firm going: has worn tongue tie, including last 3 starts: front runner/races prominently. *Nigel Twiston-Davies* **c154** **h–**

GOD'S OWN (IRE) 11 b.g. Oscar (IRE) – Dantes Term (IRE) (Phardante (FR)) [2018/19 c154+, h–: c17.5m* c19.9d² c15.9s^pu c19.9d⁵ c15.5g³ Apr 27] sturdy gelding: winning hurdler: very smart chaser: won Haldon Gold Cup at Exeter (by ½ length from Ozzie The Oscar) on reappearance in November: placed after in Peterborough Chase at Huntingdon (8 lengths second to Charbel) and Celebration Chase at Sandown (beaten 5½ lengths into third by Altior): stays 21f: acts on soft and good to firm going: tried in tongue tie. *Tom George* **c159** **h–**

GOFFSBRIDGE GIRL (IRE) 6 b.m. Touch of Land (FR) – The Bosses Mare (IRE) (Beneficial) [2018/19 b16.2g b15.8g h15.6g⁵ h15.7g⁶ h21s Jan 21] £20,000 5-y-o: has had breathing operation: fourth foal: dam winning pointer: won Irish point on debut: well held in bumpers/mares novice hurdles. *Donald McCain* **h–** **b–**

GO FORRIT (IRE) 5 b.g. Jeremy (USA) – Ben Roseler (IRE) (Beneficial) [2018/19 b–: b17.7g⁴ b15.8g³ h19.2m³ h20.5g⁴ Nov 19] fair form in bumpers: improved again when third at Huntingdon: much better effort over hurdles when third in maiden at Fontwell: tried in hood. *David Arbuthnot* **h107** **b92**

Crossed Fingers Partnership's "God's Own"

GO GEORGE GO (IRE) 6 gr.g. Zebedee – La Bella Grande (IRE) (Giant's Causeway (USA)) [2018/19 h17.7g^{ur} h15.9s^{pu} h20d^4 h23s^{pu} h19.2d Jan 14] compact gelding: fairly useful on Flat, stays 12.5f: no form over hurdles: tried in hood. *Anna Newton-Smith* **h–**

GOGO BALOO 7 b.m. Schiaparelli (GER) – Tarabaloo (Kayf Tara) [2018/19 h94: h24g c15.6s^{pu} c19.3s^2 c26.7d^4 c23.9d^R Jan 17] has had breathing operation: modest maiden hurdler: poor form over fences: stays 2½m: acts on heavy going: in blinkers/tongue tie last 3 starts: best treated with caution. *Tim Easterby* **c76 §** **h–**

GO GUARANTOR 5 b.g. Medicean – Furbelow (Pivotal) [2018/19 h17.3g^2 h18.8g^2 h16d h20.5s^{pu} h16.4m^{pu} h20.2d^{pu} Apr 26] regressive maiden on Flat: likewise over hurdles, leaving Andrew Oliver after second outing: in cheekpieces/tongue tie last 2 starts: usually front runner/races prominently. *R. Mike Smith* **h98**

GOING GOLD (IRE) 7 b.g. Gold Well – Wednesday Girl (IRE) (Rudimentary (USA)) [2018/19 h119, b96: c16g^6 c16g^4 Jan 3] lengthy gelding: point winner: fairly useful hurdler: last both starts in novice handicap chases: stayed 19f: acted on soft going: dead. *Ian Williams* **c99** **h–**

GOLAN CLOUD (IRE) 6 b.g. Golan (IRE) – Mite Be Cloudy (IRE) (Cloudings (IRE)) [2018/19 h16.9s h20v h16.2g Apr 25] fair form on hurdling debut in 2017/18: none since, leaving Michael Winters after second start. *Jennie Candlish* **h–**

GOLANDER (IRE) 9 b.g. Golan (IRE) – Bonnie And Bright (IRE) (Topanoora) [2018/19 c–, h68: c24.2m^5 May 8] Irish point winner: poor maiden hurdler: no form in chases: stays 3m: acts on good to firm going: has worn cheekpieces/tongue tie. *G. Chambers* **c–** **h–**

GOLANS CHOICE (IRE) 10 b.g. Golan (IRE) – Sea Voyager (IRE) (High Roller (IRE)) [2018/19 c24.2g^2 c23.9m^{ro} c23.9g^{pu} h23.3g^4 h27g^{pu} Nov 8] winning pointer: fair maiden hurdler at best: modest form over fences: stays 3m: acts on soft and good to firm going: in cheekpieces last 2 starts. *Olly Williams* **c89** **h83**

GOLAN WARRIOR (IRE) 6 br.g. Golan (IRE) – Taisilk (IRE) (Taipan (IRE)) [2018/19 h16.6d h20.5s h20.5d Jan 20] has had breathing operation: maiden pointer: no sign of ability over hurdles: tried in tongue tie. *Stuart Crawford, Ireland* **h–**

GOLDANBLEU (IRE) 6 b.g. Gold Well – Lisa Bleu (IRE) (Pistolet Bleu (IRE)) [2018/19 b16g^5 Aug 15] well held in bumpers 16 months apart: tried in hood. *Deborah Faulkner* **b–**

GOLD BONNE RAINE (IRE) 8 b.m. Gold Well – Be My Bonne (Be My Native (USA)) [2018/19 h20.3g^3 h23.1g^6 h23.3g^3 h23.9d^2 h25.8g^5 c20d^{pu} Dec 5] modest maiden hurdler: bled on chasing debut: stays 3m: acts on good to soft going: often in cheekpieces. *Evan Williams* **c–** **h83**

GOLD CHAIN (IRE) 9 b.m. Authorized (IRE) – Mountain Chain (USA) (Royal Academy (USA)) [2018/19 h107§: h20.2g h23.1g^5 h22.1d^{pu} h23.3g^{pu} h23.4g^4 h20.6d* h18.6s^3 h23.8g* h24.4g^3 h23.8g^2 Feb 28] neat mare: has had breathing operation: fair handicap hurdler: won at Newcastle in December and Ludlow (mares) in January: left Clare Ellam after fourth start: stays 3m: acts on soft and good to firm going: has worn headgear/tongue tie: not straightforward. *Dan Skelton* **h110**

GOLD CLASS 8 ch.g. Firebreak – Silken Dalliance (Rambo Dancer (CAN)) [2018/19 h101: h15.8g^2 h18.6g Sep 29] modest handicap hurdler: stays 21f: acts on good to soft going: has worn headgear/tongue tie. *Clare Hobson* **h96**

GOLDEN BIRTHDAY (FR) 8 b.g. Poliglote – Gold Or Silver (FR) (Glint of Gold) [2018/19 h139: c20s^2 c22.6g* c19.4m* c20g^{pu} h19.5d h21g h20.5s h20.3g^f Apr 17] rather leggy gelding: useful handicap hurdler: similar form in small fields over fences, winning novices at Stratford in August and September: stayed 23f: acted on good to firm and heavy going: wore tongue tie: dead. *Harry Fry* **c133** **h135**

GOLDEN CANNON 8 b.m. Winker Watson – Kalmina (USA) (Rahy (USA)) [2018/19 h69: h16g^6 h15.9g^5 h15.8g^{pu} h15.9m^4 h17.7g* h15.9s^4 h15.9s^f h17.7d h15.9s^6 h15.9d^5 h17.7g^5 Apr 22] poor handicap hurdler: won at Plumpton in November: stays 2¼m: tried in tongue tie. *Sheena West* **h83**

GOLDENCARD (IRE) 6 b.g. Golden Lariat (USA) – Flemensfirth Lady (IRE) (Flemensfirth (USA)) [2018/19 b16.2m^3 b16.8m^3 h16.2g* h15.7g^5 h16.2g^4 h17g^4 h16.4s^3 Mar 10] €12,000 3-y-o: sixth foal: dam unraced: runner-up twice in points: placed in bumpers: fair form over hurdles: won maiden at Kelso on hurdling debut in October: raced around 2m: best form on good going. *Keith Dalgleish* **h110** **b92**

GOLDEN DRUMLEE (IRE) 7 ch.g. Golden Lariat (USA) – Geraldine's Pet (IRE) (Old Vic) [2018/19 h16v^F h20d h20.5s^6 h16g h16d Apr 7] fourth foal: dam unraced: won maiden point in 2016: form under Rules only when mid-field in 2½m maiden hurdle at Ayr third outing. *Sean McParlan, Ireland* **h89**

GOLDEN EMBLEM (IRE) 5 ch.m. Presenting – Merry Excuse (IRE) (Flemensfirth **b88 p**
(USA)) [2018/19 b16d³ Mar 21] second foal: half-sister to useful 19f hurdle winner/
winning pointer Dickie Diver (by Gold Well), stays 3m: dam, ran out only start in points,
half-sister to useful chaser around 2m Festive Affair (by Presenting) out of half-sister to
top-class chaser (winner up to 25f) Merry Gale: 20/1, promise when third behind Subway
Surf in mares bumper at Chepstow: better to come. *Neil Mulholland*

GOLDEN ESTHER (IRE) 6 b.m. Scorpion (IRE) – Mascareigne (FR) (Subotica (FR)) **h–**
[2018/19 b–: h20gᵖᵘ Aug 22] little show in bumpers: tried to refuse and pulled up third in
mares maiden on hurdling debut. *Alan Phillips*

GOLDEN ETOILE (FR) 5 b.m. Muhtathir – Golden Firebird (IRE) (Old Vic) [2018/19 **h–**
h15.7s Dec 4] dam sister to useful hurdler/chaser (stayed 21f) Cavite Beta: no sign of
ability, including on Flat (left J-P. Gallorini before return). *Colin Tizzard*

GOLDEN FOOTSTEPS (IRE) 4 b.f. Footstepsinthesand – Contemplate (Compton **h– §**
Place) [2018/19 h16.4gᵘʳ h16.8sᵖᵘ h16.5d h15.3g h15.8d Feb 6] regressive maiden on Flat:
no form over hurdles: left Mrs J. Harrington after debut: tried in cheekpieces: temperamental.
Mark Gillard

GOLDEN FRIDAY (IRE) 6 b.g. Gold Well – Azulada (FR) (Pistolet Bleu (IRE)) **h94**
[2018/19 b84: h16.7gꜰ h16g h16m⁵ h16.3m³ h22.1s² h23.3g⁶ Sep 23] fair form both
outings in bumpers: modest form over hurdles: stays 2¾m: acts on soft going. *Donald
McCain*

GOLDEN GIFT (IRE) 5 b.g. Gold Well – Five Star Present (IRE) (Presenting) [2018/19 **b96**
b15.3g² b16d² Feb 23] €100,000 3-y-o: first foal: dam unraced sister to smart hurdler/top-
class staying chaser First Lieutenant: fairly useful form when second in bumpers at
Wincanton and Chepstow (conditionals/amateurs maiden event). *Paul Nicholls*

GOLDEN HOOF (IRE) 11 b.g. Oscar (IRE) – Nuovo Style (IRE) (Be My Native **c68**
(USA)) [2018/19 c22.6d⁵ c23g Jul 4] lengthy, useful-looking gelding: multiple point **h–**
winner: winning hurdler: useful novice chaser in 2014/15: well beaten in hunter/handicap
only outings under Rules since: should stay 2¾m: acts on good to firm and heavy going.
Jack R. Barber

GOLDEN HOUR (USA) 5 b.g. Medaglia d'Oro (USA) – Morrow (Pivotal) [2018/19 **h–**
b16d ab16s ab16s⁵ h16.3dᵖᵘ h16mᵖᵘ Apr 25] stocky, workmanlike gelding: well held in **b67**
bumpers: pulled up in novice hurdles: tried in tongue tie. *Simon Earle*

GOLDEN IMAGE 4 b.f. Havana Gold (IRE) – Photographie (USA) (Trempolino (USA)) **h79**
[2018/19 h16.6g⁴ h15.8d h16g h16.2g⁶ h16g Apr 10] has had breathing operation: half-
sister to fairly useful hurdler Downing Street (2½m-3m winner, by Sadler's Wells) and fair
hurdler Little Dutch Girl (17f winner, by Dutch Art): fairly useful on Flat, stays 1½m: poor
form over hurdles: tried in tongue tie. *Tom Symonds*

GOLDEN INVESTMENT (IRE) 10 b.g. Gold Well – Mangan Pet (IRE) (Over The **c96 §**
River (FR)) [2018/19 c109, h–: c26.2gᵇᵈ c24.1g c23.6g³ c24.1g c26m³ c23.4g² Jan 13] **h–**
angular gelding: winning hurdler: fair handicap chaser at best: stayed 25f: acted on soft and
good to firm going: wore headgear/tongue tie: temperamental: dead. *Donald McCain*

GOLDEN JEFFREY (SWI) 6 b.g. Soldier Hollow – Ange Doree (FR) (Sinyar (IRE)) **h120**
[2018/19 h124, b95: h16.2g² h17.2mᵘʳ h17.2d h16.2g⁶ h15.6g² h16g² h19.8g* h19.4g*
h19.7g h20.5m h16.2g⁵ Apr 24] sturdy gelding: bumper winner: fairly useful handicap
hurdler: won at Musselburgh (conditionals) and Doncaster in December: stays 2½m: acts
on good to firm and heavy going: wears headgear: usually leads. *Iain Jardine*

GOLDEN PROMISE (IRE) 5 b.g. Flemensfirth (USA) – Loadsapromise (IRE) (Brian **h109**
Boru) [2018/19 b16m² h16.2g² h16.2g⁵ h16.8s³ Jan 20] runner-up in bumper: fair form **b92**
over hurdles: would have been suited by 2½m: dead. *Jonjo O'Neill*

GOLDEN SANDSTORM (IRE) 10 ch.g. Golden Tornado (IRE) – Killoughey Fairy **h91**
(IRE) (Torus) [2018/19 h–: h20.3g⁴ h20.3g⁴ h20.3g h18.7g h23.3g h19.9g Oct 18] maiden
hurdler, modest form when fourth at Southwell in June, standout effort: tried in hood/
tongue tie: usually makes running/races prominently: headstrong. *Mark Loughnane*

GOLDEN SOVEREIGN (IRE) 5 b.g. Gold Well – Fugal Maid (IRE) (Winged Love **h109**
(IRE)) [2018/19 b89: b15.8s h19.9v³ h21.2d⁵ h19.8s⁴ Mar 7] fair form on first of 2 starts in **b–**
bumpers: fair form over hurdles: further progress when fourth in maiden at Wincanton in
March. *Philip Hobbs*

GOLDEN SPEAR 8 ch.g. Kyllachy – Penmayne (Inchinor) [2018/19 h130: h16.5g* Nov **h136**
3] angular gelding: useful handicap hurdler: won at Down Royal (by 5 lengths from
Shanning) in November: unproven beyond 2m: acts on soft going: has worn cheekpieces:
wears tongue tie: waited with. *A. J. Martin, Ireland*

GOLDEN SPREAD 6 b.g. Duke of Marmalade (IRE) – Purely By Chance (Galileo (IRE)) [2018/19 h18.3d³ b16d² b16g* b16d* Apr 22] second foal: dam (h113), 2m-21f hurdle winner, also 2m winner on Flat: useful form in bumpers: won at Thurles (maiden event) in March and Fairyhouse (by 1¼ lengths from Mt Leinster) in April: likely to stay 2½m. *W. P. Mullins, Ireland* **b107**

GOLDEN SUNRISE (IRE) 6 ch.g. Stowaway – Fairy Dawn (IRE) (Old Vic) [2018/19 h120: c20spu c22.4d⁴ c24.2s³ Jan 20] big, workmanlike gelding: has had breathing operation: fairly useful hurdler: similar form over fences: easily best effort when staying-on third in novice at Exeter in January: stays 3m: acts on heavy going: in tongue tie 3 of last 4 outings, also in cheekpieces last 2. *Colin Tizzard* **c126 h–**

GOLDEN TAIPAN (IRE) 5 b.g. Golden Lariat (USA) – Rose of Taipan (IRE) (Taipan (IRE)) [2018/19 b16v⁴ b15.7s b16.3s⁴ Mar 11] €12,000 3-y-o, £25,000 4-y-o: workmanlike gelding: has had breathing operation: fourth foal: dam unraced half-sister to fairly useful hurdler/chaser (2m/17f winner) Dominican Monk out of sister to top-class staying chaser The Grey Monk: placed on second start in Irish points: fair form in bumpers: tried in tongue tie. *Fergal O'Brien* **b90**

GOLDEN TOWN (IRE) 8 b.g. Invincible Spirit (IRE) – Princesse Dansante (IRE) (King's Best (USA)) [2018/19 h104: h16.2d h17.2g⁴ h17.2g³ h17.2m* h22.1m⁵ h17.2g h17.2d h16.2g h16.8spu Nov 27] lengthy gelding: has had breathing operation: fair handicap hurdler: won novice event at Cartmel in June: should stay 2½m: acts on soft and good to firm going: has worn headgear/tongue tie. *James Moffatt* **h99**

GOLDEN VISION (FR) 7 bl.m. Vision d'Etat (FR) – My Gold du Fanil (FR) (Goldneyev (USA)) [2018/19 c–, h–: c15.7g⁴ c16.5g³ c16.4m⁵ c16.5mF Oct 4] tall mare: has had breathing operations: winning hurdler: fairly useful form over fences: stays 2¼m: acts on soft going: has worn headgear: wears tongue tie: takes strong hold/finishes weakly. *Dan Skelton* **c119 h–**

GOLDEN WHISKY (IRE) 6 ch.g. Flemensfirth (USA) – Derry Vale (IRE) (Mister Lord (USA)) [2018/19 h109, b79: h16s⁵ h20.3s² h20v* h19.8s Mar 9] lengthy, unfurnished gelding: fair form over hurdles: won handicap at Ffos Las in January: stays 2½m: acts on heavy going. *Evan Williams* **h114**

GOLDEN WOLF (IRE) 5 b.g. Big Bad Bob (IRE) – Jeunesse Doree (IRE) (Rock of Gibraltar (IRE)) [2018/19 h15.6m² h16.4s h16g Apr 11] fairly useful at best on Flat (stays 16.5f): modest form over hurdles: tried in hood: tricky ride (pulls hard). *Iain Jardine* **h93**

GOLD FIELDS 5 b.g. Sakhee (USA) – Realms of Gold (USA) (Gulch (USA)) [2018/19 b–: b16g⁵ b15.7g⁴ b15.6g³ h18.6d⁶ h15.8d h16g h15.8g Apr 22] lengthy gelding: modest form in bumpers: no show over hurdles. *Laura Morgan* **h– b83**

GOLD MOUNTAIN (IRE) 9 b.g. Gold Well – La Belle de Serk (IRE) (Shernazar) [2018/19 c116, h113: h21.2vpu Jan 27] lightly-raced maiden hurdler: pulled up only outing in 2018/19: fairly useful form over fences: stays 3m: acts on good to firm going: wears tongue tie. *Martin Keighley* **c– h–**

GOLD OPERA (IRE) 10 b.g. Gold Well – Flute Opera (IRE) (Sharifabad (IRE)) [2018/19 c121§, h–: c20.1s² c20.6s² c26.2g⁵ c25g⁴ c30.6d⁴ Apr 26] rangy gelding: maiden hurdler: fairly useful handicap chaser: stays 25f: acts on heavy going: usually in headgear: often travels strongly: has looked temperamental. *Keith Dalgleish* **c128 h–**

GOLD PATROL (IRE) 11 b.g. Gold Well – One Love (IRE) (Bravefoot) [2018/19 c23.6g³ c24d⁴ c22.7m⁴ c24spu Mar 18] winning hurdler: fair handicap chaser nowadays: left Colin Bowe before return: stays 3¼m: acts on heavy going: usually in cheekpieces/tongue tie for former yard. *Jake Thomas Coulson* **c111 h–**

GOLD PRESENT (IRE) 9 br.g. Presenting – Ouro Preto (Definite Article) [2018/19 c155, h–: c21g³ c23.8s c20.5mF c22.7g² Apr 27] strong, lengthy gelding: has had breathing operation: winning hurdler: very smart chaser: placed 2 of 3 completed outings in 2018/19, second in Oaksey Chase at Sandown (11 lengths behind Black Corton) final one: stays 3m: acts on good to soft going: tends to jump right. *Nicky Henderson* **c155 h–**

GOLDRAPPER (IRE) 6 b.g. Gold Well – Mrs Bukay (IRE) (Bishop of Cashel) [2018/19 b16.8m⁵ h16.7g h16m h19.7s⁵ h19.5d h20.7g² Apr 22] €10,000 3-y-o, £11,000 5-y-o: sturdy gelding: first foal: dam bumper winner: placed in Irish points: well beaten in bumper: modest form over hurdles: stays 21f: acts on soft going. *Katy Price* **h96 b–**

GOLD RUNNER (IRE) 7 b.m. Gold Well – Copper Coast (IRE) (Old Vic) [2018/19 **h102** h16g⁶ h15.8d h15.7s⁶ h16s h19.5d² h16.2d h20.3d² Apr 9] £5,000 6-y-o: third foal: dam, ran once in bumper, out of sister to useful hurdler/chaser (stayed 29f) Feathered Leader: placed twice in Irish points: fair maiden hurdler: stays 2½m: acts on good to soft going. *Sam England*

GOLDSLINGER (FR) 7 b.g. Gold Away (IRE) – Singaporette (FR) (Sagacity (FR)) **h94** [2018/19 h100: h21m² h15.9dᵖᵘ h19.2v h15.9d⁴ Mar 18] neat gelding: modest handicap hurdler: stays 21f: acts on soft and good to firm going: tried in hood/tongue tie: races freely. *Gary Moore*

GOLIATH (IRE) 7 br.g. Golan (IRE) – Lady Shanakill (IRE) (Witness Box (USA)) **h–** [2018/19 h–: h20.2gᵖᵘ May 16] lightly raced and no sign of ability for various stables: tried in cheekpieces/tongue tie. *Maurice Barnes*

GO LONG (IRE) 9 b.g. Hurricane Run (IRE) – Monumental Gesture (Head For Heights) **c132** [2018/19 h125: c15.7v³ c16d* c16d³ Mar 9] rangy gelding: useful hurdler: similar form **h–** over fences: won novice at Hereford in January: unproven beyond 17f: acts on heavy going. *Evan Williams*

GONALSTON CLOUD (IRE) 12 gr.g. Cloudings (IRE) – Roseoengus (IRE) (Roselier **c–** (FR)) [2018/19 c130, h–: c23.9g⁵ c29.4g⁶ h24s⁴ Dec 4] poor maiden hurdler: useful chaser **h78** at best: well below form first 2 outings in 2018/19: stays 33f: acts on heavy going: usually in cheekpieces: front runner/races prominently. *Nick Kent*

GONE PLATINUM (IRE) 10 b.g. Mountain High (IRE) – Miss Platinum (IRE) (Oscar **c122** (IRE)) [2018/19 c107, h–: c19.4d⁴ c20.9g⁴ c19.4m² c20.9m⁶ c20g c20.9d² c20.9gᵖᵘ **h116** c20.9s⁵ c20.9v⁵ c20.3d* h20v² c19.4s⁴ c19.4g⁴ h20s* c20.3g* c20g² Apr 27] workmanlike gelding: has had breathing operation: fairly useful handicap hurdler: won at Ffos Las in April: fairly useful handicap chaser: won novice events at same track in May and Bangor in January and April: stays 21f: acts on soft and good to firm going: tried in cheekpieces: wears tongue tie: patiently ridden. *David Rees*

GONNABEGOOD (IRE) 8 b.g. Kutub (IRE) – Angels Flame (IRE) (Un Desperado **c–** (FR)) [2018/19 c–p, h87: h23.9d* h21.6s² h23.1s* c24sᵖᵘ h23.9sᵖᵘ Mar 19] modest **h99** handicap hurdler: won at Ffos Las in October and Exeter in December: pulled up both starts in handicap chases: stays 3m: acts on heavy going: wears headgear: usually races close up. *Jeremy Scott*

GONN AWAY (IRE) 7 b.m. Mahler – Supreme Call (IRE) (Supreme Leader) [2018/19 **b96** b16.2g² b16.2g* b16.2m² Jun 24] €2,200 3-y-o, £10,000 5-y-o: half-sister to fairly useful 2m hurdle winner Prairie Call (by Oscar), stayed 3m, and fair hurdler Lights of Broadway (19f/2½m winner, by Broadway Flyer): dam unraced half-sister to smart hurdler (stayed 3m) Whatever Jacksays: runner-up on completed start in points: fairly useful form in bumpers, winning at Perth in June. *Philip Kirby*

GO NOW GO NOW (IRE) 4 b.g. Kodiac – Ms Mary C (IRE) (Dolphin Street (FR)) **h91** [2018/19 h16.3m³ h15.8s⁵ Jul 29] fair on Flat, stays 1m: better effort in juvenile hurdles (modest form) when third at Stratford: wears cheekpieces: in tongue tie final start. *Jennie Candlish*

GOOD AND HARDY (IRE) 6 b.g. Westerner – Kilganey Maid (IRE) (Rudimentary **h111** (USA)) [2018/19 b80: h23.6v⁴ h23.3s² h23.1d⁵ h25.5d² Mar 9] off mark in Irish points at third attempt: fair form over hurdles: improved when second in handicap at Hereford final outing. *Fergal O'Brien*

GOOD AULD TIMES (IRE) 8 b.m. Olden Times – Hazelhall Princess (IRE) (Hubbly **h–** Bubbly (USA)) [2018/19 h20.6gᵖᵘ Oct 20] £10,000 7-y-o: third foal: dam (c105), 3m chase winner, half-sister to fairly useful hurdler/chaser (2½m-25f winner) Netminder: point winner: pulled up in mares novice on hurdling debut. *Fiona Kehoe*

GOOD BOY ALFIE 4 b.g. Showcasing – Costa Brava (IRE) (Sadler's Wells (USA)) **h97** [2018/19 h17.2s³ h16.2g³ h15.6g⁶ Nov 7] half-brother to fair 2m/17f hurdle winner Costa Percy (by Sir Percy): fairly useful on Flat, stays 9f: modest form first 2 outings in juvenile hurdles. *Keith Dalgleish*

GOOD BOY BOBBY (IRE) 6 b.g. Flemensfirth (USA) – Princess Gaia (IRE) (King's **h132** Theatre (IRE)) [2018/19 b113: h17.1d* h15.8v³ h15.7g* h20s* Apr 7] good-topped gelding: chasing type: useful bumper performer: similar form in novice hurdles, landing odds at Carlisle in October, Southwell (by 44 lengths) in March and Ffos Las (by 7 lengths from Quoi de Neuf) in April: stays 2½m: usually hooded. *Nigel Twiston-Davies*

GOODBYE DANCER (FR) 8 b.g. Dragon Dancer – Maribia Bella (FR) (Urban Ocean c–
(FR)) [2018/19 h23.9d h23.9g³ h24g⁶ h24.3d h26s³ h24g Apr 17] rather leggy gelding: **h128**
fairly useful handicap hurdler: pulled up both outings this season: stays 25f: acts on good
to firm and heavy going: tried in hood: races off pace. *Nigel Twiston-Davies*

GOODEYEFORDEER 6 b.m. Arvico (FR) – Liberty Rose (Relief Pitcher) [2018/19 b–
b16.5d⁶ Apr 24] first foal: dam, unraced, out of half-sister to fairly useful hurdler/chaser up
to 21f Lets Be Frank: last in maiden bumper. *Kevin Bishop*

GOODGIRLTERESA (IRE) 9 b.m. Stowaway – Decheekymonkey (IRE) (Presenting) c110
[2018/19 h100: h24g h21.6g⁴ h20g h20g c20g³ c24.2v c19.4v* c19.4d* h19.2v Feb 14] **h94**
modest maiden hurdler: better form over fences: won handicaps at Ffos Las (mares) and
Chepstow in January: left Neil Mulholland after fourth start: stays 21f: acts on heavy
going: has worn tongue tie: travels strongly waited with. *Kayley Woollacott*

GOOD IMPRESSION 4 b.g. Showcasing – Daintily Done (Cacique (IRE)) [2018/19 **h71**
h16.7d⁴ h16.5d h16.2d⁵ h16g³ h15.9d Mar 18] modest maiden on Flat, stays 1½m: poor
form over hurdles: raced around 2m: acts on good to soft going: tried in blinkers.
Ali Stronge

GOOD LITTLE WIFE 6 b.m. Sulamani (IRE) – Emergence (FR) (Poliglote) [2018/19 **b75**
b16.8g⁴ b16.8s⁴ b16.8g⁶ Aug 15] third foal: half-sister to bumper winner/fair hurdler Dry
Ol'party (2¼m winner, by Tobougg): dam French maiden hurdler: modest form when
fourth first 2 outings in bumpers. *Philip Hobbs*

GOOD MAN HUGHIE (IRE) 10 ch.g. Flemensfirth (USA) – Good Dawn (IRE) (Good c–
Thyne (USA)) [2018/19 c92, h–: h23s h19g c24g Mar 28] winning Irish pointer: winning h–
hurdler/maiden chaser: left Gary Moore, no form in 2018/19 (left Barry Brennan after first
start): stays 2½m: acts on heavy going: often in headgear: tried tongue tied. *Sean Curran*

GOOD MAN JIM (FR) 6 gr.g. Martaline – Precious Lucy (FR) (Kadrou (FR)) [2018/19 **h110**
b–: h15.8g h15.8d* h15.8d² Mar 21] good-topped gelding: has had breathing operation: off
mark in Irish points at second attempt: fair form over hurdles: won maiden at Ludlow (by
2 lengths from Ashutor) in January: likely to stay beyond 2m: in tongue tie last 3 starts:
makes running. *Tom George*

GOOD MAN PAT (IRE) 6 b.g. Gold Well – Basically Supreme (IRE) (Supreme Leader) c138
[2018/19 h128: c19.7d³ c19.7s* c20.5g³ c20.2sᵖᵘ c20g⁵ Apr 27] good-topped gelding: h–
fairly useful handicap hurdler: useful novice chaser: won handicap event at Plumpton in February:
third of 4 in Pendil Novices' Chase at Kempton (5¼ lengths behind Bags Groove) next
outing: stays 3m: acts on heavy going: held up. *Alan King*

GOOD MAN VINNIE (IRE) 8 ch.g. Vinnie Roe (IRE) – Pellerossa (IRE) (Good Thyne c116
(USA)) [2018/19 c107, h96: c25.8g* c26.1g* c26.1m h26.5g Aug 21] workmanlike h–
gelding: modest maiden hurdler: fairly useful form over fences: won handicaps at Newton
Abbot (novice event) and Uttoxeter in May: will stay long distances: acts on soft going:
temperament under suspicion. *Paul Henderson*

GOOD NEWS 7 b.g. Midnight Legend – Venetian Lass (First Trump) [2018/19 h91: **h85**
h25gᵘʳ h25.8m⁵ May 27] modest maiden hurdler: stays 25f: acts on good to soft going.
Lydia Richards

GOODNIGHT CHARLIE 9 gr.m. Midnight Legend – Over To Charlie (Overbury c119
(IRE)) [2018/19 c96, h96: c24d³ c24g* c26.1gᵖᵘ c24d² c25.5s h26g² c29.2d* h26gᵖᵘ c26g* **h100**
Apr 18] workmanlike mare: fair handicap hurdler: fairly useful handicap chaser: won at
Warwick (conditionals) in May and March and Cheltenham (mares event) in April: stays
29f: acts on soft going: wears headgear: strong-travelling front runner. *Caroline Fryer*

GOODNIGHT VIENNA (IRE) 13 b.g. High Roller (IRE) – Curragh Bridge (Pitpan) c86
[2018/19 c–: c21.6g³ May 17] multiple winning pointer: modest maiden hunter chaser:
stays 2¾m: acts on good to soft going: in cheekpieces last 2 starts. *Mrs L. Redman*

GOODNITESWEETHEART 8 b.m. Midnight Legend – Over To Charlie (Overbury **h108**
(IRE)) [2018/19 h21.7s⁶ h23.9g* h24.2dᵖᵘ Mar 22] sturdy mare: point winner: fair handicap
hurdler: won mares event at Taunton in February: stays 3m: best form on good going.
Harry Fry

GOOD SHOT SIR (IRE) 4 b.g. Casamento (IRE) – Miss Inferno (IRE) (Tagula (IRE)) h–
[2018/19 h16.2g⁵ h16v⁴ h16dᵖᵘ Apr 21] no promise over hurdles: tried in tongue tie.
Madeleine Tylicki, Ireland

GOODTHYNEAWAY (IRE) 6 b.g. Stowaway – Calling Classy (IRE) (Good Thyne (USA)) [2018/19 h16g⁴ h19.9g h16g h16.7v c19.2mᵘʳ c20.3g* c20.3d* Apr 9] well-made gelding: has had breathing operation: seventh foal: half-brother to 3 winners, including fair hurdler/fairly useful chaser Goodthynemilan (2½m-3m winner, by Milan) and fair chaser The Rockies (3m winner, by Oscar): dam (h101) 2m-2½m hurdle winner: maiden Irish pointer: well held over hurdles: fair form over fences: won handicaps at Southwell in March (mares event) and April (landed odds in ease): stays 2½m: acts on good to soft going: in tongue tie last 3 starts. *Dan Skelton* — c112 h–

GOOD THYNE TARA 9 b.m. Kayf Tara – Good Thyne Mary (IRE) (Good Thyne (USA)) [2018/19 h17d² h16.3g* h20m* h16s⁶ h18g* h22.5g³ h18.1g² h20g* h20.2d⁶ h19.9s³ Mar 12] sturdy mare: useful hurdler: won minor events at Ballinrobe in May and Cork in July, listed mares race at Gowran in October and EBF Mares' Hurdle at Leopardstown (by ½ length from Elimay) in December: also good third in David Nicholson Mares' Hurdle at Cheltenham (4¼ lengths behind Roksana) in March: stays 2½m: acts on good to firm and heavy going. *W. P. Mullins, Ireland* — h139

GOODTOKNOW 11 b.g. Presenting – Atlantic Jane (Tamure (IRE)) [2018/19 c125, h–: c29.4g⁴ May 28] useful-looking gelding: winning hurdler: formerly smart handicap chaser, found little only start in 2018/19: stays 29f: acts on heavy going: wears headgear. *Kerry Lee* — c110 h–

GOOD TRADITION (IRE) 8 b.g. Pivotal – Token Gesture (IRE) (Alzao (USA)) [2018/19 h110: h17.2g² h19.9g² h22m* h23g⁴ h20.2g* h20.9m h21g Oct 26] compact gelding: fairly useful handicap hurdler: won at Stratford in July and Perth in August: stays 2¾m: acts on soft and good to firm going: has worn cheekpieces, including last 3 starts. *Donald McCain* — h123

GOOHAR (IRE) 10 b.g. Street Cry (IRE) – Reem Three (Mark of Esteem (IRE)) [2018/19 c120, h–: c24m⁶ c25gᵘʳ Oct 26] rangy gelding: winning hurdler: fairly useful handicap chaser: let down by jumping in 2018/19: stays 3¼m: acts on heavy going: wears cheekpieces: signs of temperament. *Henry Daly* — c108 h–

GOONJIM (IRE) 8 ch.g. Beneficial – Clogga Native (IRE) (Good Thyne (USA)) [2018/19 c77, h–: c22.5mᵖᵘ c17gᵖᵘ c17g³ Apr 22] maiden hurdler: poor handicap chaser: stays 2½m: acts on soft going: used to regularly wear hood: wears tongue tie. *Alexandra Dunn* — c– h–

GO ON MAYSON 5 br.g. Mayson – Red Tiara (USA) (Mr Prospector (USA)) [2018/19 h20m³ h18.5g⁶ h16.7g⁴ h18.5g Oct 1] regressive maiden on Flat: modest form over hurdles: wore tongue tie: dead. *Sam Thomas* — h93

GOOSE MAN (IRE) 7 b.g. Gold Well – Young Amelie (FR) (Garde Royale) [2018/19 c132p, h104: c20d c24.5g^f h20d* h21.6v² c24.7d² Apr 22] fairly useful form over hurdles: won handicap at Navan in January: useful form over fences: best effort when second in handicap at Fairyhouse (length behind Sizing Rome) in April: stays 25f: acts on heavy going: even better to come. *Tom J. Taaffe, Ireland* — c140 p h122 p

GOOSEN MAVERICK (IRE) 8 b.g. Morozov (USA) – Bonny River (IRE) (Exit To Nowhere (USA)) [2018/19 c81x, h–: c24dᵖᵘ Nov 29] compact gelding: maiden hurdler: poor and error-prone handicap chaser: stays 25f: acts on heavy going. *Grant Cann* — c– x h–

GORHAM'S CAVE 5 b.g. Rock of Gibraltar (IRE) – Moiava (FR) (Bering) [2018/19 h16.3g h16m^f Apr 25] modest maiden on Flat, stays 1½m: poor form in novice hurdles, racing freely: wears hood. *Ali Stronge* — h81

GORING ONE (IRE) 14 b.g. Broadway Flyer (USA) – Brigette's Secret (Good Thyne (USA)) [2018/19 c94, h–: c20s⁶ c26.7g⁴ c20s* c21.6s⁶ c23.5v c25.7sᵖᵘ c26v² Mar 16] compact gelding: maiden hurdler: poor handicap chaser nowadays: won at Lingfield (conditionals event) in January: stays 27f: acts on good to firm and heavy going: wears headgear: not one to trust. *Anna Newton-Smith* — c80 § h–

GORSKY ISLAND 11 b.g. Turtle Island (IRE) – Belle Magello (FR) (Exit To Nowhere (USA)) [2018/19 c120, h–: c23.8g² c27.5g⁴ c25.8g⁴ c24.2g³ Nov 14] good-topped gelding: lightly-raced maiden hurdler: fair handicap chaser nowadays: stays 3½m: acts on soft going: tried in cheekpieces: usually travels strongly held up. *Tom George* — c110 h–

GORTNAGIRL (IRE) 7 b.m. Mahler – Rebel Flyer (IRE) (Presenting) [2018/19 h86: h21m^f May 14] off mark in Irish points at fifth attempt: tongue tied, poor form over hurdles. *Paul Cowley* — h78

GORTROE JOE (IRE) 7 b.g. Beneficial – Rowlands Star (IRE) (Old Vic) [2018/19 **c134** h114: h19m* h19.9g² h15.8g² c16.8s³ c20mᶠ c20d* c20dᵖᵘ c21.4m* Apr 21] tall, useful- **h114** looking gelding: has had breathing operation: fair hurdler: won novice at Warwick in May: much better form over fences: won handicaps at Ludlow in February and Market Rasen (novice event, by 12 lengths from Rio Quinto) in April: stays 21f: acts on good to firm and heavy going: front runner/races prominently: has found less than seemed likely. *Dan Skelton*

GOSHEVEN (IRE) 6 b.g. Presenting – Fair Choice (IRE) (Zaffaran (USA)) [2018/19 **h104** h125p, b72: h19.5d³ Oct 14] well-made gelding: mid-field in bumper: fairly useful form in novice hurdles in 2017/18: well-held third in Persian War Novices' Hurdle at Chepstow sole outing since: will be suited by 2¾m+. *Philip Hobbs*

GOT AWAY (FR) 6 b.m. American Post – Hideaway Girl (Fasliyev (USA)) [2018/19 **c140** c137, h137: c20vᵖᵘ c19.9d⁵ c20.2m* c20.2g² c19.9g³ c20.6g² c23.8d³ Apr 26] strong mare: **h–** useful hurdler: useful handicap chaser: won mares event at Leicester in February: stays 23f: acts on good to firm and heavy going: wears headgear: in tongue tie last 5 starts. *Oliver Sherwood*

GOTHIC EMPIRE (IRE) 7 b.g. Dark Angel (IRE) – Box of Frogs (IRE) (One Cool Cat **h89** (USA)) [2018/19 h102p: h15.9g² h15.8gᵖᵘ May 28] leggy gelding: formerly useful on Flat (unproven beyond 7f): modest form over hurdles. *Richard Rowe*

GO TO COURT (IRE) 6 b.m. Court Cave (IRE) – Go Franky (IRE) (Hollow Hand) **h82** [2018/19 h24.1g³ h19.9d⁶ Apr 23] £18,000 6-y-o: half-sister to 3 winners, including fairly useful hurdler/useful chaser Imjoeking (2m-2½m winner, by Amilynx) and fairly useful hurdler Go Odee Go (19f/2½m winner, by Alkaadhem): dam unraced half-sister to useful chaser up to 3m Super Franky: off mark in Irish points at fourth attempt: poor form when third in novice at Wetherby on first of 2 outings over hurdles. *Micky Hammond*

GOTTA GETAWAY (IRE) 5 b.m. Getaway (GER) – Dark Mist (IRE) (Mister Lord **h–** (USA)) [2018/19 b16g b16s b16d h17.6g h16g Apr 21] €14,000 3-y-o: half-sister to fair **b–** hurdler/useful chaser Bennys Mist (21f-3m winner, by Beneficial) and winning pointers by Beneficial and Flemensfirth (2): dam unraced: well beaten in bumpers/over hurdles: wears tongue tie. *Shane Nolan, Ireland*

GOT TRUMPED 4 ch.g. Thewayyouare (USA) – Madam President (Royal Applause) **h127** [2018/19 h16g² h16.6g* h16g³ h16d⁴ h16g⁶ h16.4s h16d⁵ Apr 22] fairly useful form on Flat (stays 1½m): fairly useful juvenile hurdler: won at Punchestown in November: raced around 2m: probably acts on soft going. *Mrs J. Harrington, Ireland*

GOULANE CHOSEN (IRE) 10 b.g. Well Chosen – Vixen's Cry (IRE) (Miner's Lamp) **c144** [2018/19 c136, h–: c20.6m c20dᵘʳ c19.7s⁴ c18s² c20s² c17.7g* Mar 31] winning hurdler: **h–** useful handicap chaser: career-best when winning at Limerick (by nose from Tycoon Prince) in March: stays 2¾m, effective at shorter: acts on heavy going: has worn cheekpieces: races prominently. *Seamus Spillane, Ireland*

GOUTEZ MOI (FR) 6 b.g. Dragon Dancer – Titi Jolie (FR) (Blushing Flame (USA)) **h–** [2018/19 h87: h17.7g⁴ h15.8g Mar 19] rather unfurnished gelding: fair form on second of **b65** 4 outings in bumpers: well beaten in maiden on hurdling debut. *Laura Mongan*

GOWANAUTHAT (IRE) 11 ch.g. Golan (IRE) – Coolrua (IRE) (Commanche Run) **c65** [2018/19 c85, h–: c17d⁶ Jun 8] winning pointer: maiden hurdler: developed into useful **h–** handicap chaser in 2016/17: little form since: stays 3m: acts on good to firm and heavy going: usually in cheekpieces: wears tongue tie. *Francesca Nimmo*

GOWELL (IRE) 8 b.m. Gold Well – Glen Supreme (IRE) (Supreme Leader) [2018/19 **c– §** c82§, h–§: c23.6gᵖᵘ Apr 26] point winner: modest maiden hurdler/chaser: pulled up in **h– §** novice hunter sole outing under Rules in 2018/19: stays 2½m: acts on soft going: in tongue tie last 4 outings, also in headgear last 3: ungenuine. *T. Faulkner*

GO WEST YOUNG MAN (IRE) 11 b.g. Westerner – Last of Her Line (Silver Patriarch **c118 §** (IRE)) [2018/19 c113§, h–§: c23.6gᵘʳ c24.1g⁴ h16.7g⁶ c16g* c17.2mʳᵒ c16gᵘʳ Aug 1] rangy **h–** gelding: winning hurdler: fairly useful handicap chaser: won at Perth in July: left Henry Daly after second start: stays 3m, effective at much shorter: acts on good to firm and heavy going: in headgear last 4 starts: ungenuine. *Laura Morgan*

GOWITHTHEFLOW (IRE) 6 b.g. Westerner – Maryiver (IRE) (Runyon (IRE)) [2018/19 **c122** h130: c19.1g² c22.7m³ h20.3gᵖᵘ Apr 17] sturdy gelding: has had breathing operation: Irish **h–** point winner: useful hurdler: better effort over fences (just fairly useful form) when 23 lengths third of 5 to Another Stowaway in novice handicap at Leicester: likely to stay 3m: acts on soft and good to firm going: front runner/races prominently. *Ben Pauling*

GRAASTEN (GER) 7 ch.g. Sholokhov (IRE) – Golden Time (GER) (Surumu (GER)) **c127 ?**
[2018/19 h125: c21.6m* c19.8d³ c20.2gᵘʳ c19.7g² c25.7dᶠ h26.4g Mar 30] good-topped **h–**
gelding: winning hurdler: fairly useful form over fences: won maiden at Fontwell in
October: seemingly easily best effort when 4¼ lengths last of 3 finishers behind Cubomania
in novice at Cheltenham next start: stays 2¾m: acts on good to firm and heavy going.
Gary Moore

GRACEFUL JAMES (IRE) 6 ch.g. Rock of Gibraltar (IRE) – Little Miss Gracie **h94**
(Efisio) [2018/19 h16.3d Mar 23] fairly useful on all-weather Flat, stays 1¼m: never a
threat in novice at Newbury on hurdling debut. *Jimmy Fox*

GRACEFUL LEGEND 8 b.m. Midnight Legend – Clover Green (IRE) (Presenting) **c130**
[2018/19 h132: c21.6g³ c19.9g³ c20d⁴ h24.4g⁵ c22.5v² c21.3g³ c22.4d* c20.6g⁶ Apr 18] **h116**
compact mare: fairly useful handicap hurdler: useful form over fences: won handicap at
Newbury (by 4 lengths from Master Burbidge) in March: stays 2¾m: acts on heavy going:
wears headgear. *Ben Case*

GRACELAND (FR) 7 gr.m. Mastercraftsman (IRE) – Jeunesse Lulu (IRE) (Montjeu **h106**
(IRE)) [2018/19 h15.7g³ h15.7d³ h16.8g* h15.8g⁵ Apr 22] good-topped mare: useful on
Flat, stays 16.5f: fair form over hurdles: won mares novice at Sedgefield in April: tried in
hood. *Donald McCain*

GRACEMEADOW (IRE) 5 b.g. Arcano (IRE) – Puttore (IRE) (High Chaparral (IRE)) **b84**
[2018/19 b16s³ Jan 8] first foal: dam 9f winner: tongue tied, 8/1, third in bumper at Ayr.
John McConnell, Ireland

GRACE TARA 10 b.m. Kayf Tara – Fenney Spring (Polish Precedent (USA)) [2018/19 **c–**
c106, h105: h23g⁶ Jun 2] has had breathing operation: Irish point winner: fair handicap **h95**
hurdler/maiden chaser: stays 25f: acts on heavy going: tried in cheekpieces: in tongue tie
last 5 starts. *Michael Scudamore*

GRAGEELAGH GIRL (IRE) 8 b.m. Craigsteel – Smiths Lady (IRE) (Anshan) **h113**
[2018/19 b101: h18.5g* h18.7m* h16.2g³ h21g⁶ h21.4g⁶ h20.2g⁵ Apr 24] useful-looking
mare: point/bumper winner: fairly useful form over hurdles: won mares maiden at Newton
Abbot and mares novice at Stratford, both in June: should stay beyond 19f: acts on good to
firm going (runner-up in bumper on soft). *Fergal O'Brien*

GRAINEYHILL (IRE) 8 b.g. Craigsteel – Inca Hill (IRE) (Insan (USA)) [2018/19 **c107**
h20g⁵ c16g³ h20.8g* h20.2gᵖᵘ h20s c17.5d* c17d⁴ c20.1gᵖᵘ Apr 25] fairly useful handicap **h127**
hurdler: won at Sligo in August: not so good over fences, though won maiden at Fairyhouse
in February: stays 21f: acts on heavy going: usually in headgear nowadays. *Gordon Elliott,
Ireland*

GRAMS AND OUNCES 12 b.g. Royal Applause – Ashdown Princess (IRE) (King's **c–**
Theatre (IRE)) [2018/19 c–, h96: h20m* h15.8m⁵ h21.6m⁴ h19.6g h19.5g Oct 30] sturdy **h95**
gelding: modest handicap hurdler: won at Ffos Las in June: maiden chaser: stays easy
2¾m: acts on good to firm and heavy going: has worn cheekpieces: wears tongue tie.
Grace Harris

GRANARD (IRE) 7 br.g. Getaway (GER) – Yes Darling (IRE) (Oscar (IRE)) [2018/19 **c–**
h118, h85: c20.1s h23.9vᵖᵘ h24.5g⁶ Nov 26] fairly useful form when making successful **h–**
hurdling debut in 2¾m novice in late-2017/18: disappointing since (tailed off in novice
handicap on chasing debut): tried in cheekpieces. *Nigel Twiston-Davies*

GRANDADS HORSE 13 br.g. Bollin Eric – Solid Land (FR) (Solid Illusion (USA)) **c100**
[2018/19 c121, h–: c25.5g³ c26.1gᵖᵘ Jun 20] strong gelding: winning hurdler: fairly useful **h–**
handicap chaser: stays 25f: acts on good to firm and heavy going: usually in headgear: has
worn tongue tie, including last 2 starts. *Jennie Candlish*

GRAND CANYON (IRE) 7 b.g. High Chaparral (IRE) – Cleide da Silva (USA) **h104**
(Monarchos (USA)) [2018/19 h16.5s* h16g⁴ h16.4g h20.2g Dec 28] fair on Flat, stays 2m:
fair handicap hurdler: won at Ballinrobe in September: should stay beyond 2m: acts on soft
going. *Miss Amanda Mooney, Ireland*

GRAND COUREUR (FR) 7 b.g. Grand Couturier – Iris du Berlais (FR) (Bonnet Rouge **c–**
(FR)) [2018/19 c94, h89: c22.5dᵖᵘ h19.9m⁶ h15.8d c15.2g⁴ Apr 11] maiden hurdler/chaser: **h–**
no form since autumn 2017: has worn cheekpieces. *Barry Leavy*

GRAND ENTERPRISE 9 b.g. Fair Mix (IRE) – Miss Chinchilla (Perpendicular) **c–**
[2018/19 c–, h104: h24.4gᵖᵘ h25.3sᵖᵘ h24.4gᵖᵘ Jan 9] fair hurdler at best: pulled up all 3 **h–**
outings in 2018/19: fell only chase start: stays 27f: acts on good to firm and good to soft
going: in cheekpieces last 2 starts: tried in tongue tie: held up. *Henry Hogarth*

GRANDE WALTZ (GER) 6 b.g. Wiener Walzer (GER) – Giralda (IRE) (Tenby) **h75**
[2018/19 h16s⁶ h21.5g h16g h17.3g⁶ h18.8g h16.8gᵖᵘ Apr 20] has had breathing operation:
poor maiden hurdler: left Andrew McNamara after fifth start: unproven beyond 2m: acts on
soft going: tried in cheekpieces: wears tongue tie. *Dan Skelton*

GRAND GIGOLO (FR) 10 b.g. Enrique – Belle d'Ecajeul (FR) (Le Nain Jaune (FR)) **c–**
[2018/19 h25g h24gᵖᵘ Jun 25] modest hurdler: no form in 2018/19: maiden chaser: stayed **h–**
25f: acted on soft and good to firm going: tried in cheekpieces: dead. *Mike Sowersby*

GRAND INQUISITOR 7 b.g. Dansili – Dusty Answer (Zafonic (USA)) [2018/19 h92: **h116**
h15.3g² h15.8d³ h15.8g⁵ h16d³ Mar 15] good-topped gelding: useful on Flat (stays 1½m):
fairly useful form over hurdles: likely to stay beyond 2m: acts on good to soft going: in
headgear last 3 starts: usually races freely. *Ian Williams*

GRAND INTRODUCTION (IRE) 9 b.g. Robin des Pres (FR) – What A Breeze (IRE) **c–**
(Naheez (USA)) [2018/19 c101, h–: c24.5gᶠ May 14] maiden hurdler: fair form when **h–**
winning handicap chase at Towcester in 2017/18: failed to complete in similar events
otherwise: stays 3m: acts on heavy going: has worn tongue tie. *Fergal O'Brien*

GRAND MORNING 7 b.g. Midnight Legend – Valentines Lady (IRE) (Zaffaran (USA)) **c110**
[2018/19 h123p: c20gᵖᵘ c24.2dᵖᵘ c23.4d⁴ Mar 2] well-made gelding: has had breathing **h–**
operation: won 3 of 4 outings over hurdles: let down by jumping/attitude over fences: stays
2¾m: acts on heavy going: tried in visor: in tongue tie last 5 starts. *Lucinda Russell*

GRAND SANCY (FR) 5 b.g. Diamond Boy (FR) – La Courtille (FR) (Risk Seeker) **h144**
[2018/19 h112, b89: h16d³ h16m² h15.3g* h15.7g* h15.7s⁴ h16s² h15.3g* h16.4s Mar 12]
good-topped gelding: has had breathing operation: useful hurdler: won handicap at
Chepstow in October, novices at Wincanton and Haydock (listed event) in November and
Kingwell Hurdle at Wincanton (by ¾ length from Sceau Royal) in February: raced around
2m: acts on soft and good to firm going: wears hood. *Paul Nicholls*

GRAND TURINA 8 b.m. Kayf Tara – Cesana (IRE) (Desert Prince (IRE)) [2018/19 h110: **c–**
c20g⁵ Jun 2] sturdy mare: fair hurdler: last of 5 in novice at Worcester on chasing debut: **h–**
stays 21f: acts on heavy going: has worn hood. *Venetia Williams*

GRAND VISION (IRE) 13 gr.g. Old Vic – West Hill Rose (IRE) (Roselier (FR)) **c125**
[2018/19 c133, h–: c19.4s c25.1g⁵ c26g⁵ Mar 23] tall gelding: has had breathing operation: **h–**
winning hurdler: fairly useful handicap chaser nowadays: stays 3¼m: acts on heavy going:
tried in cheekpieces. *Colin Tizzard*

GRANGE RANGER (IRE) 7 b.g. Kalanisi (IRE) – Grangeclare Flight (IRE) (Old Vic) **h104**
[2018/19 h19.2s⁴ h19.2d h20.3s⁵ Mar 18] £48,000 5-y-o: second foal: half-brother to fairly
useful chaser Present Flight (23f-27f winner, by Presenting): dam (b94), bumper winner,
sister to useful hurdler (stayed 2½m) Grangeclare Lark: in front when fell last in Irish
point: best effort over hurdles (fair form) when fourth in maiden at Fontwell: in tongue tie
last 2 starts. *Jamie Snowden*

GRANGEROSIE (IRE) 6 b.m. Court Cave (IRE) – Comings (IRE) (Grand Lodge **b–**
(USA)) [2018/19 b16dᵖᵘ Aug 29] €800 3-y-o: sixth foal: sister to a winning pointer and
closely related to a winning pointer by Gold Well: dam unraced: runner-up in Irish mares
maiden point: hooded and 5/1, lame when pulled up in bumper. *Suzi Best*

GRANGE WALK (IRE) 4 ch.g. Thewayyouare (USA) – A Woman In Love (Muhtarram **b74**
(USA)) [2018/19 b15.3g⁶ ab16s⁶ Jan 4] rather unfurnished gelding: mid-field in bumpers:
fair form on Flat (stays 1¼m). *Pat Phelan*

GRANIA O'MALLEY (IRE) 6 ch.m. Beat Hollow – Oh Susannah (FR) (Turgeon **h119**
(USA)) [2018/19 h101, b93: h16g³ h15.7g* h16g³ h15.8s* h15.7g³ h16.4m² h20.3g Apr
18] rather unfurnished mare: fairly useful hurdler: won mares novices at Southwell in May
and Uttoxeter in July: best around 2m: acts on good to firm and heavy going: usually in
cheekpieces: usually races close up. *Evan Williams*

GRANITIC (IRE) 6 b.g. Court Cave (IRE) – Like A Miller (IRE) (Luso) [2018/19 **h96**
b15.7g* h16.8s h16.8d h16s³ h16.8s⁴ Apr 16] €18,000 3-y-o: second foal: dam unraced **b86**
half-sister to useful staying chasers Maljimar and Kymandjen: won maiden bumper at
Towcester (by nose from Jen's Boy) in debut on May: only modest form over hurdles:
should be well suited by further than 17f. *Seamus Mullins*

GRAN MAESTRO (USA) 10 ch.g. Medicean – Red Slippers (USA) (Nureyev (USA)) **c–**
[2018/19 c–, h109: h16.7g³ h20.7g⁴ h22.1g h16.3m⁵ h18.6gᵘʳ Aug 18] plain gelding: fair **h109**
handicap hurdler: little aptitude for chasing: stayed 2½m: acted on soft and good to firm
going: wore headgear: tried in tongue tie: dead. *Peter Winks*

GRAN PARADISO (IRE) 7 ch.g. Galileo (IRE) – Looking Lovely (IRE) (Storm Cat (USA)) [2018/19 h96: c23.8mᶠ c24.2g³ Apr 15] multiple winning pointer: fair hurdle winner for Micky Hammond: similar form when third at Hexham on completed start in hunter chases: stays 3m: acts on good to soft going: wore cheekpieces for former yard: tried in tongue tie. *Norman Sanderson* **c103 h–**

GRANVILLE ISLAND (IRE) 12 b.g. Flemensfirth (USA) – Fox Glen (Furry Glen) [2018/19 c128, h–: c19.9s c15.7v⁶ c16.5s⁶ Mar 9] workmanlike gelding: winning chaser: fairly useful handicap chaser: lightly raced and below form in 2018/19: stays 2½m: acts on heavy going: tried in cheekpieces: usually leads. *Jennie Candlish* **c105 h–**

GRAY DAY (IRE) 8 gr.g. Daylami (IRE) – Carrigeen Diamond (IRE) (Old Vic) [2018/19 c122p, h–: h21g h23.3vᵖᵘ Dec 21] rather sparely-made gelding: fairly useful hurdle winner in 2016/17: off 14 months, well below form both starts in 2018/19: shaped quite well in well-contested maiden at Uttoxeter only outing over fences: stays 23f: acts on soft going. *Donald McCain* **c– h–**

GRAYHAWK (IRE) 9 gr.g. Kalanisi (IRE) – Saddler Regal (IRE) (Saddlers' Hall (IRE)) [2018/19 c59x, h–: c21.6g c19.7g⁵ c21.6dᶠ h25g c19.5m⁶ c26g² Apr 24] sturdy gelding: winning pointer: little form over hurdles: poor and error-prone maiden chaser: stays 3¼m: best form on good going: usually in cheekpieces/tongue tie. *Diana Grissell* **c63 x h–**

GRAYSTOWN (IRE) 7 b.g. Well Chosen – Temple Girl (IRE) (Luso) [2018/19 h106: h22.7g⁵ c26.3g⁶ c24.2s⁶ c24.1d⁶ c20.5dᴿ c20.1d³ c20m² Apr 20] modest maiden hurdler: fair form over fences: won handicap at Ayr in February: best short of 3m: acts on good to firm and heavy going: tried in cheekpieces: prone to mistakes. *Stuart Coltherd* **c102 x h93**

GREANETEEN (FR) 5 b.g. Great Pretender (IRE) – Manson Teene (FR) (Mansonnien (FR)) [2018/19 h16v⁶ h18.5d* h17.7s* Jan 27] rangy gelding: fifth foal: half-brother to 3 winners, including useful French hurdlers Turteene (17f/2¼m winner, by Turgeon) and Poly Teen (2¼m winner, by Poliglote): dam French 2¼m-2½m winner/chase winner: fairly useful form over hurdles: won maiden at Exeter and novice at Fontwell, both in January: should go on improving. *Paul Nicholls* **h127 p**

GREAT COLACI 6 b.g. Sulamani (IRE) – Fairlie (Halling (USA)) [2018/19 h78: h16.7g* h15.8g h16.2g² h16.2g² h16.4m h15.8d⁴ h16.4m Mar 22] modest handicap hurdler: won conditionals/amateurs event at Market Rasen in May: raced around 2m: best form on good going: usually leads. *Gillian Boanas* **h93**

GREAT FAIRY (FR) 6 b.g. Great Pretender (IRE) – Salsa Fairy (FR) (Kingsalsa (USA)) [2018/19 b16m⁵ h16g⁶ h20g h16.8d⁴ c15.7gᵖᵘ h19.5s⁴ h21.6vᵖᵘ h21.7dᶠ h19.5d h19.5d Apr 6] €27,000 3-y-o: third foal: half-brother to French 17f-19f hurdle winner Line Fairy (by Martaline): dam French maiden: placed in Irish points: last in bumper: modest maiden hurdler: pulled up in novice handicap on chasing debut: stays 19f: acts on soft going: tried in tongue tie. *Neil Mulholland* **c– h93 b–**

GREAT FIELD (FR) 8 b.g. Great Pretender (IRE) – Eaton Lass (IRE) (Definite Article) [2018/19 c170p, h–: c16.7vᶠ c17gᶠ Dec 27] winning hurdler: high-class chaser: won first 5 starts: fell both outings in winter of 2018/19, tiring in share of second when coming down last in Paddy's Rewards Club Chase won by Simply Ned at Leopardstown on second occasion: well beaten at Punchestown shortly after end of British season: free-going sort, best around 2m: acts on heavy going. *W. P. Mullins, Ireland* **c156 h–**

GREAT HALL 9 b.g. Halling (USA) – L'Affaire Monique (Machiavellian (USA)) [2018/19 h15.8d² h16g Dec 27] fairly useful handicap hurdler: should be suited by 2½m: acts on good to soft going: tried in cheekpieces. *Mick Quinn* **h120**

GREAT LOVER (FR) 7 gr.g. Smadoun (FR) – Dominelle (FR) (Pinmix (FR)) [2018/19 h97: h19.9gᵖᵘ c20.9m h21.6mᵖᵘ Jul 14] form over hurdles only when fourth in novice at Taunton in 2017/18: tailed off in novice handicap on chasing debut: in headgear last 3 starts. *Philip Hobbs* **c– h–**

GREAT TEMPO (FR) 6 b.g. Great Pretender (IRE) – Prima Note (FR) (Nononito (FR)) [2018/19 h103: c20g³ c20.9g² c24g⁶ h21.2g⁵ h20.3s⁴ c23.8g³ h21.9vᵖᵘ Jan 14] rather leggy gelding: modest handicap hurdler: fair form over fences: stays 3m: acts on heavy going: wears headgear: temperament under suspicion. *David Pipe* **c106 h90**

GREAT TRANGO (IRE) 6 b.g. Canford Cliffs (IRE) – Tarascon (IRE) (Tirol) [2018/19 h24s* h24g h20s Jan 5] angular gelding: fairly useful handicap hurdler: fit from Flat win, awarded race at Listowel in September after first past post Vent de La Cote disqualified: stays 3m: acts on heavy going: wears blinkers. *David Harry Kelly, Ireland* **h125**

GREAT VIZIER 4 b.g. Sir Percy – Special Green (FR) (Sadler's Wells (USA)) [2018/19 **h114** h16s h16d h16g h16g h20.2g³ Apr 25] half-brother to a winning jumper in Italy by Halling: fair form on Flat: much improved form over hurdles when third in novice handicap at Perth in April: stays 2½m: in tongue tie last 4 starts, also in blinkers last 2. *Gordon Elliott, Ireland*

GREEBA 5 ch.g. Getaway (GER) – Ladyday Lady (Old Vic) [2018/19 b16s Jan 8] well **b—** beaten in bumper. *Chris Grant*

GREEN DOLPHIN (IRE) 5 b.g. Oscar (IRE) – Shamrock Miss (IRE) (Bob's Return **b101** (IRE)) [2018/19 b16d³ b15.3s* b16.3d⁵ Mar 22] €52,000 3-y-o: lengthy gelding: third foal: dam unraced sister to useful chaser (stayed 2½m) Sizing Africa: fairly useful form in bumpers: won maiden at Wincanton in March: will prove suited by 2½m. *Harry Fry*

GREEN LIGHT 8 b.g. Authorized (IRE) – May Light (Midyan (USA)) [2018/19 h–: **h—** h17.2g^pu May 28] formerly useful handicapper on Flat (stays 1½m): no solid form over hurdles: tried in cheekpieces. *Brian Ellison*

GREEN OR BLACK (IRE) 7 gr.m. Zebedee – Boucheron (Galileo (IRE)) [2018/19 **h107** h104: h16d⁶ h16.8m² h16g² h16g² h16.8m³ h16.8g* h15.3g⁴ h15.8g³ Apr 22] workmanlike mare: has had breathing operations: fair hurdler: won races novice at Newton Abbot in October: raced around 2m: acts on good to firm and heavy going: in cheekpieces last 3 starts: wears tongue tie: travels well. *Neil Mulholland*

GREENSALT (IRE) 11 b.g. Milan – Garden City (IRE) (Shernazar) [2018/19 c122, h–: **c100** c24.2d^ur c21.1d Apr 4] good-bodied gelding: multiple point winner: maiden hurdler: fair **h—** maiden hunter chaser on balance: stays easy 25f: acts on heavy going: tried in cheekpieces: wears tongue tie. *W. H. Easterby*

GREEN TIKKANA 6 gr.m. Tikkanen (USA) – Think Green (Montjeu (IRE)) [2018/19 **h89** h91: h21.4g⁴ May 7] leggy mare: modest maiden hurdler: stays 3m: acts on heavy going: usually held up. *James Ewart*

GREENVIEW PARADISE (IRE) 5 gr.m. Exchange Rate (USA) – Senza Rete (IRE) **h—** (Barathea (IRE)) [2018/19 h16g Nov 12] modest on Flat (stays 1¾m), won twice in April: tailed off in novice on hurdling debut. *Brian Barr*

GREENWORLDSOLUTION 7 b.g. Lucarno (USA) – Basford Lady (IRE) (Accordion) **h91** [2018/19 h91: h15.8m³ h19.9g h15.8g Jul 10] modest maiden hurdler: stays 2½m: acts on good to firm going: tried in visor: often in tongue tie. *Jennie Candlish*

GREEN ZONE (IRE) 8 b.g. Bushranger (IRE) – Incense (Unfuwain (USA)) [2018/19 **h99** h105: h16.2d h16.2g⁶ h16.2g⁶ h16.2g h20.2g⁵ h20.2g⁴ h23.9g⁶ h20.2g³ h18.1m² h20.2g* h20.9g⁴ h17.1d⁴ h20.9g³ h17.1g² h19.5v h17.1v⁵ h19.8g⁴ h16.4s* h16.6g^F h19.8g⁵ h18.1g⁴ h19.3g⁴ h19.8s⁴ h16.4m³ h17m⁵ Apr 20] compact gelding: modest handicap hurdler: won at Perth (fifth course success) in September and Newcastle in December: should stay beyond 21f: acts on good and good to firm going: usually waited with. *Lisa Harrison*

GREGARIOUS (IRE) 6 gr.g. Big Bad Bob (IRE) – Sense of Greeting (IRE) (Key of **c—** Luck (USA)) [2018/19 c106, h114: h20d h16v h16v h17g* h19.2v³ h16d Apr 6] well-made **h120** gelding: fairly useful handicap hurdler: won at Carlisle (by 16 lengths) in February: little aptitude for chasing: stays easy 19f: acts on heavy going: formerly hooded/tongue tied: usually leads. *Lucy Wadham*

GREY ATLANTIC WAY (IRE) 6 gr.g. Dahjee (USA) – Altregan Touch (IRE) **h100** (Roselier (FR)) [2018/19 h16g⁴ h20g h17m³ h16g h16d³ h19.8s³ h16.8s h16d³ Apr 22] second foal: dam pulled up in points: fair maiden hurdler: stays 2½m: acts on soft and good to firm going: has worn headgear/tongue tie. *E. D. Linehan, Ireland*

GREYBOUGG 10 gr.g. Tobougg (IRE) – Kildee Lass (Morpeth) [2018/19 c115, h–: **c117** c19.9d c19.1g³ c15.7d^ur Mar 6] lengthy gelding: winning hurdler: fairly useful handicap **h—** chaser: effective at 2m to 3m: acts on good to firm and heavy going: has worn hood: front runner. *Nigel Hawke*

GREY DIAMOND (FR) 5 b.g. Gris de Gris (IRE) – Diamond of Diana (FR) (Kapgarde **h117** (FR)) [2018/19 b15.8d* h16.7g⁴ h16.2g⁵ h16.7s⁵ h15.9g⁴ h16g^F h16g* Apr 26] second **b87** foal: half-brother to fair 2m/17f hurdle winner Christmas In USA (by Shaanmer): dam unraced sister to useful French hurdler/fairly useful chaser (2¼m/19f winner) Boston Paris: won bumper at Ffos Las on debut in May: fairly useful form over hurdles: ridden more positively when winning maiden at Chepstow in April: raced around 2m: best form on good going: has worn hood/tongue tie: free-going sort. *Alan King*

GREYED A (IRE) 8 gr.g. Daylami (IRE) – Broadcast (Broadsword (USA)) [2018/19 **c111** c114, h–: c25.2s² c30g⁴ c28.8vᵖᵘ c19.4s⁵ Feb 26] winning hurdler: fair handicap chaser: **h–** stays 3¼m: acts on heavy going: has worn headgear: front runner/races prominently. *Dr Richard Newland*

GREY GETAWAY (IRE) 5 gr.g. Getaway (GER) – Miss Greylands (Alflora (IRE)) **b65 p** [2018/19 b16s⁶ Mar 16] €44,000 3-y-o, £190,000 4-y-o: second foal: dam, unraced, out of half-sister to Cheltenham Gold Cup winner See More Business: runner-up on debut in Irish point: 3/1, better than result when sixth in maiden bumper at Kempton, paying for taking on impressive winner Shishkin: sure to improve. *Paul Nicholls*

GREY GOLD (IRE) 14 gr.g. Strategic Choice (USA) – Grouse-N-Heather (Grey Desire) **c–** [2018/19 c121, h–: c15.5d⁶ Feb 15] rather leggy gelding: winning hurdler: smart chaser at **h–** best: only fairly useful form since 2016/17: stays 2½m: acts on heavy going. *Kerry Lee*

GREY MESSENGER (IRE) 10 gr.g. Heron Island (IRE) – Turlututu (FR) (Turgeon **c– x** (USA)) [2018/19 c67, h–: c20gᵘʳ May 10] sturdy gelding: poor maiden hurdler: completed only once in handicap chases (sketchy jumper): stays 23f: acts on good to firm going: in cheekpieces last 2 starts: wears tongue tie. *Emma-Jane Bishop*

GREY MIST 5 gr.g. Mastercraftsman (IRE) – Kekova (Montjeu (IRE)) [2018/19 h19.8m* **h110 p** Mar 22] half-brother to a winning jumper in Italy by Aussie Rules: fair stayer on Flat, unbeaten since leaving Tim Easterby, including making successful hurdling debut in novice at Musselburgh (hooded) by 3 lengths from Dr Hooves: entitled to progress. *Karen McLintock*

GREY MONK (IRE) 11 gr.g. Alderbrook – Thats The Bother (IRE) (Roselier (FR)) **c–** [2018/19 c–, h94§: h24gᵖᵘ h23.1m Aug 5] point winner: modest handicap hurdler **h–** nowadays: let down by jumping only chase start: stays 23f: acts on good to firm and heavy going: wears headgear/tongue tie: front runner/races prominently. *Sara Ender*

GRIMTHORPE 8 ch.g. Alflora (IRE) – Sally Scally (Scallywag) [2018/19 h–, b–: h20.1g **c–** h20.3s c20.1v⁵ c23.4gᶠ c21.6d Apr 8] tall, lengthy gelding: of no account: in hood last 2 **h–** starts. *Tina Jackson*

GRIPPER 4 b.g. Thewayyouare (USA) – Hold On Tight (IRE) (Hernando (FR)) [2018/19 **h–** h16.2g Apr 25] fair on Flat, stays 1¾m: well beaten in novice at Perth on hurdling debut. *Lucinda Russell*

GRIS DE PRON (FR) 6 b.g. Gris de Gris (IRE) – Say Say (FR) (Garde Royale) [2018/19 **c100** c112p, h79: c16.4g³ c15.8g⁵ c15.7g⁴ c17.2m⁴ c16.4m³ c19.3mᵖᵘ h17.1g h16.8sᵖᵘ c15.9g **h–** c16.3dᵖᵘ Apr 6] strong gelding: winning hurdler: fair maiden chaser: unproven beyond 17f: acts on good to soft going: usually wears headgear: has worn tongue tie. *Henry Hogarth*

GRITT 4 b.g. Pour Moi (IRE) – Elasouna (IRE) (Rainbow Quest (USA)) [2018/19 b13.7d **b–** Jan 25] tailed off in bumper. *Derek Shaw*

GROOVY CHICK 5 ch.m. Shirocco (GER) – Alina Rheinberg (GER) (Waky Nao) **h–** [2018/19 h16gᴿ Oct 24] tailed off when refused fourth in mares novice hurdle: dead. *Evan Williams*

GROUNDUNDERREPAIR (IRE) 8 b.g. Milan – Discerning Air (Ezzoud (IRE)) **c116** [2018/19 h120: c20s⁵ c23.4g³ c24.5s c24.2gᵖᵘ Apr 11] has had breathing operation: fairly **h–** useful hurdler: similar form first 2 outings over fences: stays 3¼m: acts on heavy going: usually in headgear nowadays. *Warren Greatrex*

GROVEMAN 4 b.g. Holy Roman Emperor (IRE) – Raving Monsun (Monsun (GER)) **h115** [2018/19 h15.7g* h16.6g² h16.8s² h18.8d⁵ h15.7m³ Mar 31] fairly useful on Flat, stays 16.5f: similar level as juvenile hurdler: won at Catterick in January: mostly shaped well after: should be well suited by at least 19f: best form on good going. *Jedd O'Keeffe*

GROVE SILVER (IRE) 10 gr.g. Gamut (IRE) – Cobbler's Well (IRE) (Wood Chanter) **c92** [2018/19 c118, h–: c29.1g⁵ c24dᵖᵘ Apr 9] rather leggy gelding: winning hurdler: fairly **h–** useful handicap chaser at best: well below form both outings in 2018/19, off 11 months in between: stays 29f, effective at much shorter when conditions are testing: acts on heavy going: wears headgear: tried in tongue tie. *Jennie Candlish*

GROW NASA GROW (IRE) 8 ch.g. Mahler – Dereenavurrig (IRE) (Lancastrian) **c92** [2018/19 c77, h57: c20.3g c19.2d* c22.5g³ c25.5g c19.4m⁵ c21.4g* c20.3g c19.3g* **h–** c19.2g* Nov 23] tall gelding: maiden hurdler: modest handicap chaser: won at Market Rasen in May and August (novice event), and at Sedgefield and Catterick in November: stays 2¾m: acts on heavy going: usually leads: tends to idle. *Peter Winks*

GRUMPY CHARLEY 4 b.g. Shirocco (GER) – Whisky Rose (IRE) (Old Vic) [2018/19   **b82**
b16.8s³ Apr 16] £52,000 3-y-o: fourth foal: closely related to bumper winner/useful hurdler
One For Rosie (winner up to 2½m, by Getaway), and half-brother to 2 winners, including
useful bumper winner/useful hurdler Air Horse One (17f-19f winner, by Mountain High):
dam unraced: won point bumper on debut: some promise when third to Merchant House in
amateurs maiden bumper at Exeter. *Chris Honour*

GUARD OF HONOUR (IRE) 8 b.g. Galileo (IRE) – Queen of France (USA) (Danehill   **h114 §**
(USA)) [2018/19 h20.3g* Oct 25] fair handicap hurdler: won at Southwell in October:
likely to stay 2¾m: acts on good to firm and heavy going: usually blinkered (wasn't at
Southwell): temperamental. *George Baker*

GUERRILLA TACTICS (IRE) 9 b.g. Presenting – Karens Flight (IRE) (Broadway   **c109**
Flyer (USA)) [2018/19 c102, h96: c24g² c26g³ c25.8g² h26.4g* h26.5d c25.1g⁴ Nov 22]   **h104**
fair handicap hurdler/chaser: won over hurdles at Stratford in August: thorough stayer: acts
on soft going: tried in cheekpieces: front runner/races prominently. *Jeremy Scott*

GUIDING STARS (FR) 6 b.g. Bonbon Rose (FR) – Furika (FR) (Kadalko (FR))   **h–**
[2018/19 b89: h16g Jun 3] fair form in bumpers: mistakes when well beaten in maiden on
hurdling debut: sold only £800, placed just once from 4 starts in points subsequently.
Harry Whittington

GUIDO RENI (IRE) 5 b.g. Excelebration (IRE) – Out of Thanks (IRE) (Sadler's Wells   **h110**
(USA)) [2018/19 h16g* h16.5g h16.7m h16g² h16.2d⁴ h16.2g⁴ h16.4g⁴ h16d² h16g
h15.8d⁵ h16d Apr 22] angular, plain gelding: fair handicap hurdler: won at Tipperary in
May: raced around 2m: acts on good to firm and good to soft going: has worn hood: wears
tongue tie. *Karl Thornton, Ireland*

GUITAR PETE (IRE) 9 gr.g. Dark Angel (IRE) – Innishmore (IRE) (Lear Fan (USA))   **c137**
[2018/19 c138, h130: c19.4m² c20.2g³ c20.6d³ Dec 15] rather leggy gelding: useful   **h–**
hurdler: useful handicap chaser: placed in good company all 3 starts in 2018/19, including
third to Frodon in Caspian Caviar Gold Cup at Cheltenham (had won race previous year):
stays 21f: acts on good to firm and heavy going:used to wear headgear/tongue tie.
Nicky Richards

GUITING POWER 8 b.g. Lucarno (USA) – Sparkling Jewel (Bijou d'Inde) [2018/19   **c–**
c16.3g May 4] maiden in points: poor maiden hurdler (for Nigel Twiston-Davies): tailed   **h–**
off in hunter on chasing debut: stays 3¼m: acts on soft going: has worn visor.
Mrs Alice Campbell

GULSHANIGANS 7 b.g. Sakhee (USA) – Gulshan (Batshoof) [2018/19 h21.4g² h21.4g⁶   **h109**
Jan 5] big gelding: fair maiden hurdler: stays 3m: acts on soft and good to firm going: wears
tongue tie. *Jack R. Barber*

GUMBALL (FR) 5 gr.g. No Risk At All (FR) – Good Time Girl (FR) (Slickly (FR))   **h122**
[2018/19 h140: h16.4g⁴ h16.3s Dec 1] sturdy gelding: useful juvenile hurdler in 2017/18:
below former best when starts in 2018/19, but won 3 times on Flat subsequently (useful form): will
stay beyond 17f: acts on soft going: tried in tongue tie. *Philip Hobbs*

GUN DIGGER (IRE) 7 ch.g. Stowaway – Booley Bay (IRE) (Gulland) [2018/19 c20d³   **c139**
c20d² c21g* c20d⁴ c31.7sF c29dpu Apr 22] €78,000 3-y-o: good-topped gelding: first foal: **h–**
dam (c88/h111), bumper/19f hurdle winner, half-sister to useful hurdler/chaser (stayed
2½m) De Dollar Man: bumper/novice hurdle winner: much better over fences, placed
twice prior to winning maiden at Leopardstown in December by 18 lengths from
Whisperinthebreeze: failed to complete when tongue tied last 2 outings: unproven beyond
21f: acts on heavy going: wears headgear: usually races prominently. *Gordon Elliott, Ireland*

GUNFLEET (IRE) 7 b.g. Oscar (IRE) – Lady Lincon (IRE) (Great Palm (USA))   **c137**
[2018/19 h130p: c24.2g² c25.3g³ c26.7gpu h24.7g Apr 6] lengthy gelding: fairly useful   **h–**
hurdle winner: better form when close second to Just A Sting in novice handicap at Exeter
on chasing debut: disappointing after, including over hurdles: will stay long distances: acts
on soft going: tried in hood. *Emma Lavelle*

GUNNER ROAD 10 ch.g. Grape Tree Road – Glory Be (Gunner B) [2018/19 c23d⁵   **c–**
Apr 4] winning pointer: well-held fifth in maiden hunter at Taunton on chasing debut.
M. Ainsworth

GUN SHY (IRE) 11 b.g. Norwich – Debbies Scud (IRE) (Roselier (FR)) [2018/19 c–, h–:   **c93**
c20m³ c23gpu c21gpu Aug 15] winning hurdler: fairly useful handicap chaser at best: **h–**
regressed further in 2018/19: stays 21f: acts on heavy going: front runner/races prominently.
Deborah Faulkner

GUSTAVE MAHLER (IRE) 9 ch.g. Mahler – Kloetta (IRE) (Grand Lodge (USA)) **c129**
[2018/19 h126: c20g² c20g³ c15.7g² c15.7g² c16.5g⁴ c20m² Oct 10] sturdy gelding: point **h–**
winner: fairly useful hurdler: similar form over fences: in frame all 6 starts: likely to stay
beyond 2½m: acts on good to firm and good to soft going: usually leads. *Alastair Ralph*

GUSTAV (IRE) 9 b.g. Mahler – Pakaradyssa (FR) (Roakarad) [2018/19 c99, h–: c20m **c–**
May 7] compact gelding: maiden hurdler: modest handicap chaser: stays 21f: acts on soft **h–**
going: wears cheekpieces. *Zoe Davison*

GUY (IRE) 4 ch.g. Getaway (GER) – Sept Verites (FR) (Turgeon (USA)) [2018/19 b16.2d² **b93 p**
Apr 26] second foal: dam (c113/h117), French 15f hurdle winner, out of half-sister to smart
French chaser (stayed 27f) Turgot: 10/3, promising 2½ lengths second to Big Bad Bear in
bumper at Perth: sure to progress. *Nigel Twiston-Davies*

GWALIA (IRE) 6 b.g. Beat Hollow – Payphone (Anabaa (USA)) [2018/19 b92: h16.2g³ **h115**
h16.2g⁴ h16.5d* h16.5d² h19g⁴ Jan 9] fairly useful form over hurdles: won handicap at
Taunton in December: unproven beyond 2m: acts on good to soft going: front runner/races
prominently. *Evan Williams*

GYPSY CHARM 5 b.m. Yorgunnabelucky (USA) – Lady Santana (IRE) (Doyoun) **b–**
[2018/19 b17g May 18] third in maiden point: hooded, tailed off in amateurs bumper at
Aintree: dead. *I. Chanin*

GYPSY ISLAND (IRE) 5 b.m. Jeremy (USA) – Thieving Gypsy (IRE) (Presenting) **h105 P**
[2018/19 b16.2d* h16d² b16d* b16d* Apr 7] €6,000 3-y-o: second foal: dam, lightly raced **b117**
in bumpers/over hurdles, half-sister to fairly useful hurdler/smart chaser (stays 25f) Master
Dee out of 2m hurdle winner Miss Lauren Dee: smart form in bumpers: won mares races
at Ballinrobe (maiden) in August, Naas in March and Fairyhouse (listed event) in April:
also won 15-runner EBF (Mares) INH Flat Race at Punchestown shortly after end of
British season by 5 lengths from Daylight Katie, quickening clear approaching final 1f: fair
form when length second to Put The Kettle On in mares maiden at Navan on hurdling debut
(sure to progress significantly). *Peter Fahey, Ireland*

H

HAAFAPIECE 6 ch.g. Haafhd – Bonnet's Pieces (Alderbrook) [2018/19 h110: h16mᵖᵘ **h115**
h16g³ h16g* h15.7g³ h16vᶠ h16.6m⁴ h15.5g⁴ Dec 28] fairly useful handicap hurdler: won
at Worcester in July: stays 19f: acts on soft going. *Pam Sly*

HAAFAPRINCESS 6 b.m. Haafhd – Mystic Glen (Vettori (IRE)) [2018/19 b–: h15.7g **h–**
h16.8m⁵ h16.7g h16.8g Nov 1] little form, including on Flat: in cheekpieces last 3 starts.
Peter Niven

HAASAB (IRE) 6 b.g. Sakhee (USA) – Badweia (USA) (Kingmambo (USA)) [2018/19 **h104**
h96, b88: h24gᵖᵘ h16.7g² h15.5g² h19.3s³ h18.6g* h16.2g⁶ Apr 25] has had breathing
operation: fair handicap hurdler: won at Market Rasen in April: stays 19f: best form on
good going: wears headgear: sometimes in tongue tie: usually front runner/races
prominently. *Laura Morgan*

HAB SAB (IRE) 7 b.g. Papal Bull – Tamburello (IRE) (Roi Danzig (USA)) [2018/19 c–, **c–**
h79: c23.6gᵖᵘ h15.9s³ Jan 16] good-topped gelding: poor form over hurdles: little show **h83**
over fences: stays 2¾m: acts on soft going: in headgear last 2 starts. *Linda Jewell*

HAHADI (IRE) 7 ch.g. Getaway (GER) – Derrygowna Lord (IRE) (Mister Lord (USA)) **h89**
[2018/19 h20vᵖᵘ h24s⁶ h20.5gᵖᵘ h20.7d⁶ h24g⁵ h22g³ h21.2m³ Apr 23] first foal: dam
winning pointer: Irish point winner: modest maiden hurdler: stays 3m: acts on good to firm
going: tried in cheekpieces. *David Dennis*

HALCYON DAYS 10 b.g. Generous (IRE) – Indian Empress (Emperor Jones (USA)) **c114**
[2018/19 c110, h–: c15.6g⁶ c15.9d* c20.1d⁶ c15.7s² c16.3g² c15.7d* c17.1d⁴ Apr 8] **h–**
maiden hurdler: fair handicap chaser: won at Carlisle in October and Catterick in March:
stays 19f: acts on heavy going: wears headgear. *Rebecca Menzies*

HALDON HILL (IRE) 6 b.g. Mahler – Qui Plus Est (FR) (Dark Moondancer) [2018/19 **h113 p**
b84: b16.8s* h16.8s² h18.5d⁵ h18.5s³ Mar 18] fairly useful form in bumpers: won at Exeter **b98**
in December: fair form over hurdles: best effort when second in maiden at same course in
January: will stay 2½m: tried in hood: remains with potential. *Victor Dartnall*

HALF NELSON 4 ch.g. Mount Nelson – Maria Antonia (IRE) (King's Best (USA)) **b–**
[2018/19 b15.8s Feb 26] tailed off in bumper. *Grace Harris*

HALLINGHAM 9 b.g. Halling (USA) – In Luck (In The Wings) [2018/19 h81: c15.7m⁴ **c–**
h15.8g⁴ Nov 2] stocky, compact gelding: poor handicap hurdler: well beaten in novice **h72**
handicap on chasing debut: stays 19f: acts on firm going: has worn headgear. *Ken Cunningham-Brown*

HALLINGS COMET 10 ch.g. Halling (USA) – Landinium (ITY) (Lando (GER)) **c–**
[2018/19 c–, h120: h20.5d h19.9d h19g⁴ Apr 25] sturdy gelding: fair handicap hurdler: **h107**
winning chaser: stays 2½m: acts on good to firm and good to soft going: front runner.
Shaun Lycett

HALLOWEEN HARRY (IRE) 6 b.g. Wareed (IRE) – Leteminletemout (IRE) (Be My **h105**
Native (USA)) [2018/19 h22.8v³ h23.3s⁶ h23.8d⁶ h23.1dᵘʳ h21.6dᵖᵘ Apr 9] closely related
to fairly useful hurdler Letemgo (2½m-3¼m winner, by Brian Boru) and half-brother to
bumper winner Canaradzo (by Flemensfirth): dam unraced: point winner: fair form over
hurdles: should be suited by 3m+: acts on good to soft going. *Philip Hobbs*

HALO MOON 11 br.g. Kayf Tara – Fragrant Rose (Alflora (IRE)) [2018/19 c122, h–: **c104**
c23.8g c24.2d c21.2g⁴ c22.9d⁴ Mar 20] well-made gelding: maiden hurdler: fairly useful **h–**
handicap chaser, below form in 2018/19: stays 3m: acts on heavy going: wears cheekpieces:
in tongue tie last 2 starts: held up. *Neil Mulholland*

HAMELIN POOL 5 b.g. High Chaparral (IRE) – Presbyterian Nun (IRE) (Daylami **h–**
(IRE)) [2018/19 h–: h16g Jun 3] has had breathing operation: little form, including on Flat:
tried in tongue tie. *Michael Chapman*

HAMILTON ISLAND (IRE) 4 b.f. So You Think (NZ) – Chatham Islands (USA) **b–**
(Elusive Quality (USA)) [2018/19 b13.7m b13.7g Nov 13] sixth foal: half-sister to 3
winners on Flat, including smart 6f-9f winner Balty Boys (by Cape Cross): dam 6f winner:
down the field in bumpers/Flat maiden. *Gary Moore*

HAMMER AND ANVIL (IRE) 8 b.g. Tikkanen (USA) – Fall O' The Hammer (IRE) **c–**
(Broken Hearted) [2018/19 c21.6gᵖᵘ May 17] placed in points: in cheekpieces, pulled up in
lady riders' hunter on chasing debut. *Miss L. Horsfall*

HAMMERSLY LAKE (FR) 11 b.g. Kapgarde (FR) – Loin de Moi (FR) (Loup Solitaire **c157**
(USA)) [2018/19 c154, h–: c24d c20g³ c21.2m* c20s² c20.1g* h21d c21g⁶ c19.9d⁵ c20.5g⁴ **h–**
c24g³ c24.2m* Apr 22] good-topped gelding: winning hurdler: very smart handicap chaser:
won at Cartmel (by 3¾ lengths from Princeton Royale) in July, Perth (by 3¾ lengths from
Imperial Presence) in September and Fakenham (veterans, by 8 lengths from Vaxalco) in
April: stays 3m: acts on good to firm and heavy going. *Charlie Longsdon*

HANDS OF STONE (IRE) 7 b.g. Shantou (USA) – Hayabusa (Sir Harry Lewis (USA)) **c79**
[2018/19 h85: c17.4g⁶ c16g³ c16g⁴ c20.3sᵖᵘ c20.3dᵖᵘ c16d² c17.5v⁶ Mar 18] lengthy **h–**
gelding: maiden hurdler: poor maiden chaser: unproven beyond 2m: acts on soft going: has
worn headgear, including last 2 starts: has worn tongue tie. *Evan Williams*

HANDSOME DAN (IRE) 13 b.g. Busy Flight – Beautiful City (IRE) (Jurado (USA)) **c–**
[2018/19 c–, h118: h19.6g h18.6g h18.6g⁶ h18.6gᵖᵘ Nov 8] fair handicap hurdler: winning **h98**
chaser: stays 3m, effective at much shorter: acts on good to firm and good to soft going:
has worn headgear, including last 3 starts: tried in tongue tie: usually races in rear.
Sarah Hollinshead

HANDSOME SAMSON 4 b.g. Nathaniel (IRE) – Factice (USA) (Known Fact (USA)) **b–**
[2018/19 b15.3g b14d Jan 1] compact gelding: in tongue strap, well held in 2 bumpers: in
hood second one. *Richard Spencer*

HANDY HOLLOW (IRE) 6 ch.g. Beat Hollow – Hesperia (Slip Anchor) [2018/19 h91, **h100**
b88: h16.8g h19.9g⁴ h22.1m³ h22.1g⁴ h23.1g⁴ h19.6g* h27m² h23.3g* h23.1gᵘʳ h25.8g³
h27g⁶ h20.7gᵘʳ Apr 22] smallish, angular gelding: fair handicap hurdler: won at Bangor in
August and Uttoxeter in September: stays 27f: acts on soft and good to firm going: has
worn hood, including in 2018/19. *Donald McCain*

HANG TOUGH 5 b.g. Geordieland (FR) – Allerford Lily (Pasternak) [2018/19 h21gᵖᵘ **h–**
h23gᵖᵘ Apr 13] made frame both starts in Irish points: no form over hurdles: in blinkers
second start. *Jonjo O'Neill*

HANNA HVAR 5 b.m. Pour Moi (IRE) – Visanilla (FR) (Danehill (USA)) [2018/19 **b85** b15.8m⁴ Oct 10] seventh foal: half-sister to 2 winners abroad on Flat: dam, useful French 1¼m/10.5f winner, half-sister to fairly useful/ungenuine hurdler/chaser Visibility (2m-19f winner): in hood, 14/1, fourth in mares bumper at Ludlow (8 lengths behind Mrs Hyde). *Donald McCain*

HANNON (IRE) 4 b.g. Canford Cliffs (IRE) – Lady Rua Dargent (IRE) (Redback) **h126** [2018/19 h16m² h15.6g* h16g² h16.8d h16d⁶ Apr 22] strong gelding: third foal: half-brother to 1¼m winner Steelyeyed (by Duke of Marmalade): dam unraced: fairly useful form over hurdles: won juvenile at Musselburgh in January: second in Grade 2 novice at Naas (nose behind Chosen Mate) in February: left Mrs Jessica Magnier after first start: raced around 2m: best form on good going: wears tongue tie. *John McConnell, Ireland*

HANSUPFORDETROIT (IRE) 14 b.g. Zagreb (USA) – Golden Needle (IRE) (Prince **c80** of Birds (USA)) [2018/19 c100, h90: c25.3v⁵ c24s⁶ c24.2vᵖᵘ Mar 5] strong gelding: **h–** winning hurdler: fair handicap chaser, below form in 2018/19: stays 3¼m: acts on heavy going: has worn cheekpieces, including in 2018/19: wears tongue tie. *Bernard Llewellyn*

HAPPY DIVA (IRE) 8 b.m. King's Theatre (IRE) – Megans Joy (IRE) (Supreme Leader) **c145** [2018/19 c140, h–: c20g² c20.2gᵇᵈ c20.6d² c21d³ c19.9d* c19.9dᵘʳ c16.3g² Apr 18] good- **h–** bodied mare: winning hurdler: smart chaser: won listed mares event at Huntingdon (by length from Magic of Light) in January: has won at 3m, but at least as effective at shorter: acts on heavy going: wears tongue tie: strong traveller: sound jumper. *Kerry Lee*

HAPPY NEWS 6 gr.m. Fair Mix (IRE) – Welcome News (Bob Back (USA)) [2018/19 **b–** b16.3g b15.8g Apr 11] fourth foal: half-sister to fairly useful chaser Big News (3m winner, by Karinga Bay): dam winning pointer: no form in bumpers. *John Groucott*

HARAMBE 6 br.g. Malinas (GER) – Crystal Princess (IRE) (Definite Article) [2018/19 **h136** b108: h16sᵇᵈ h16g² h20.5s⁴ h16.3d⁴ h16s* h18.6g* h16g² Apr 27] tall, rather unfurnished gelding: bumper winner: useful hurdler: won novices at Kempton in March and Market Rasen in April: second in novice handicap at Sandown (2¾ lengths behind Getaway Trump) final start: stays 19f: acts on soft going: often races freely. *Alan King*

HARBOUR FORCE (FR) 5 b.g. Harbour Watch (IRE) – Dam Beautiful (Sleeping **h–** Indian) [2018/19 h93: h17.7g⁶ Apr 22] modest maiden hurdler, well held sole outing in 2018/19 (retried in headgear): usually races towards rear. *Neil Mulholland*

HARDBACK (IRE) 8 b.g. Morozov (USA) – Alphablend (IRE) (Alphabatim (USA)) **c130** [2018/19 h131: c17d² c19.9g* Jun 5] useful hurdler: similar form over fences: won maiden **h–** at Kilbeggan in June: stays 2½m: acts on heavy going: in tongue tie last 4 starts: often travels strongly. *Joseph Patrick O'Brien, Ireland*

HARDESSA 6 b.m. Kayf Tara – Phardessa (Pharly (FR)) [2018/19 b16.3mᵖᵘ May 20] **b–** runner-up in point bumper: pulled up in bumper at Stratford: dead. *Laura Hurley*

HARD KNOCKS (IRE) 9 b.g. Turtle Island (IRE) – Celtic Tigress (IRE) (Over The **c87** River (FR)) [2018/19 c24.2gᵖᵘ c20.1g c21.2mᶠ h22.2g⁴ c25.5g² c23.9m⁶ h27m c24.2g Sep **h71** 17] runner-up on first of 2 starts in points: poor form over hurdles: modest form in chases: stays 25f: best form on good going: often in cheekpieces: tried in tongue tie. *Kenny Johnson*

HARDLINE (IRE) 7 b.g. Arcadio (GER) – Hidden Reserve (IRE) (Heron Island (IRE)) **c153** [2018/19 h139: c16g* c16.2g² c17d* c19.7s* c21g³ c15.9s Mar 12] sturdy gelding: useful **h–** hurdler: smart form over fences: won maiden at Fairyhouse in October, and Klairon Davis Novices' Chase at Navan (by 10 lengths from Us And Them) and Grade 1 novice at Limerick (by ½ length from Getabird) in December: also placed in Craddockstown Novices' Chase at Punchestown in November, Flogas Novices' Chase at Leopardstown in February and valuable novice handicap at Punchestown (6½ lengths second to Real Steel) shortly after end of British season: stays 21f: acts on heavy going: wears hood. *Gordon Elliott, Ireland*

HARDNESS (IRE) 6 b.g. Makfi – Hideaway (FR) (Cape Cross (IRE)) [2018/19 h75: **h–** h21.4mᵖᵘ h21.6gᵖᵘ Jun 4] maiden hurdler, no form in 2018/19: tried in blinkers. *Philip Hobbs*

HARDROCK DAVIS (FR) 8 b.g. Saint des Saints (FR) – Trumpet Davis (FR) (Rose **c93 p** Laurel) [2018/19 h85: c26.2dᵇᵈ Apr 8] useful-looking gelding: won 2 of 4 starts in points **h–** in 2018/19 (runner-up other 2): maiden hurdler: yet to be asked for effort when brought down 3 out in maiden hunter won by Longtymegone at Kelso on chasing debut: tried in hood. *Mrs K. Lynn*

HARD STATION (IRE) 10 b.g. Bandari (IRE) – Vinecroft (IRE) (Executive Perk) **c111**
[2018/19 c–, h–: c32.5g^F c25.8g² c23.9d* c20d² Dec 13] maiden hurdler: fair chaser: won **h–**
handicap at Market Rasen in November: stays 3m: acts on good to firm and good to soft
going: has worn hood, including in 2018/19: in tongue tie last 4 starts: front runner.
Richard Bandey

HARD TO FORGET (IRE) 6 b.g. Gold Well – Raheen Na Hoon (IRE) (Boyne Valley) **h108**
[2018/19 h15.8g h16.2g h16.7v⁵ h20.6s³ h19.9s* h21.6d Apr 9] €17,500 3-y-o, £15,000
5-y-o: fifth foal: half-brother to winning pointers by Heron Island and Trans Island: dam,
winning pointer, half-sister to fair hurdler/fairly useful chaser (stayed 25f) Night Safe:
Irish point winner: fair form over hurdles: won handicap at Sedgefield in March: stays 21f:
acts on soft going. *Henry Oliver*

HARDTOROCK (IRE) 10 b.g. Mountain High (IRE) – Permissal (IRE) (Dr Massini **c79 §**
(IRE)) [2018/19 c72§, h–: c26m³ c26g c25.8m⁴ c25.8g³ c21.6g* c26m^{pu} c26g^{pu} Nov 9] **h–**
sturdy gelding: maiden hurdler: poor handicap chaser: won at Fontwell in September: stays
3¼m: acts on good to firm going: wears cheekpieces: has worn tongue tie, including final
start: often races lazily: unreliable. *Seamus Mullins*

HAREFIELD (IRE) 6 b.g. Doyen (IRE) – Bobbi's Venture (IRE) (Bob Back (USA)) **h–**
[2018/19 h122: h16v^{pu} h16.6m^F Dec 1] rangy, rather unfurnished gelding: fairly useful
hurdler: seemed amiss on reappearance: fell (for third time in 5 starts) only other start of
season: should stay 2½m+: acts on heavy going: has joined Chris Gordon. *Alan King*

HARGAM (FR) 8 gr.g. Sinndar (IRE) – Horasana (FR) (Galileo (IRE)) [2018/19 c119, **c123**
h–: c16.2m* c20.3g⁴ Aug 19] rather leggy gelding: winning hurdler: fairly useful handicap **h–**
chaser: won novice event at Warwick in May: unproven beyond 17f: acts on soft and good
to firm going: has worn cheekpieces: races towards rear, often lazily. *John Quinn*

HARLEYS MAX 10 b.g. Winged Love (IRE) – Researcher (Cosmonaut) [2018/19 c–, h–: **c–**
c20.1m c19.3g⁶ Apr 23] maiden hurdler: modest chaser at best, lightly raced and no form **h–**
since 2016/17: stays 2¾m: acts on soft and good to firm going. *Susan Corbett*

HARMONISE 5 b.m. Sakhee's Secret – Composing (IRE) (Noverre (USA)) [2018/19 **h–**
h108: h16v^{pu} Nov 11] fair on Flat, stays 1½m: fair form on first 2 starts over hurdles, little
show since: has worn hood/tongue tie: front runner/races prominently. *Sheena West*

HARRIER 6 b.g. Flying Legend (USA) – Kullu Valley (Turgeon (USA)) [2018/19 b17.7g² **b86**
May 13] 12/1, second in bumper at Plumpton (4½ lengths behind Andapa): dead.
Seamus Mullins

HARRISONS PROMISE 7 b.m. Westerner – Hello My Lovely (Presenting) [2018/19 **h–**
b94: h20.2g h20.9g Dec 9] close-coupled mare: fairly useful bumper winner: in hood, no
form over hurdles: should stay further than 2m: tongue tied since debut. *Susan Corbett*

HARRY HAZARD 5 b.g. Schiaparelli (GER) – Eveon (IRE) (Synefos (USA)) [2018/19 **h86**
b16d h15.9d⁵ h15.9g h16s⁶ h20.5g⁵ Apr 7] good-topped gelding: fourth foal: half-brother **b–**
to fair hurdler Midtech Valentine (2m-19f winner, by Act One): dam (c76) 23f chase
winner: little impact in Irish bumper: modest form over hurdles: should be suited by at least 2½m: wears hood. *Zoe Davison*

HARRY HAZE 7 b.g. Dr Massini (IRE) – Gypsy Haze (Romany Rye) [2018/19 h16d **h84**
h16.8s h16d⁵ h19.5g⁶ Apr 26] brother to a winning pointer, and half-brother to bumper
winner/useful chaser Midnight Haze (2½m-25f winner, by Midnight Legend) and modest
hurdler Sahara Haze (3¼m winner, by Rainbow High): dam winning pointer: last of 4 in
point: poor form over hurdles. *Phillip Dando*

HARRY HUNT 12 b.g. Bertolini (USA) – Qasirah (IRE) (Machiavellian (USA)) [2018/19 **c– §**
c110§, h–§: c23.8g May 8] lengthy gelding: winning hurdler: fair chaser at best, behind **h– §**
sole outing in 2018/19: stays 3m: acts on heavy going: has worn headgear: unreliable.
Graeme McPherson

HARRY SENIOR (IRE) 5 b.g. Oscar (IRE) – Surf Like A Lady (IRE) (Presenting) **b91**
[2018/19 b16.7g³ Apr 13] first foal: dam once-raced half-sister to fairly useful hurdler/
high-class chaser (stayed 25f) Foxrock: placed in Irish point: 7/2, third in conditionals/
amateurs bumper at Bangor (2 lengths behind Orrisdale). *Colin Tizzard*

HARRY THE POTTER 6 b.g. Sulamani (IRE) – Glen Clova (Elmaamul (USA)) **b77**
[2018/19 b17s⁵ b17d⁵ Mar 24] modest form in bumpers. *Chris Grant*

HARRY THE VIKING 14 ch.g. Sir Harry Lewis (USA) – Viking Flame (Viking (USA)) **c122 §**
[2018/19 c122§, h–: c26.2g c32.4g* c32.6g c30.6d^{pu} Apr 26] useful-looking gelding: **h–**
winning hurdler: fairly useful handicap chaser: won at Kelso in December: stays 33f: acts
on heavy going: wears headgear: usually races prominently: temperamental. *Sandy Thomson*

HARTSHORNE ABBIE (IRE) 6 ch.m. Getaway (GER) – Lala Nova (IRE) (Zaffaran (USA)) [2018/19 b–: b15.7g6 b16.3g b16.3g6 h16g h23g5 Sep 28] poor form in bumpers: no form over hurdles: in hood last 3 starts: usually races nearer last than first. *Martin Keighley* **h– b67**

HARTSIDE (GER) 10 b.g. Montjeu (IRE) – Helvellyn (USA) (Gone West (USA)) [2018/19 h90: h16g h17g4 h16d h15.8d6 h15.7d Apr 9] sturdy gelding: modest handicap hurdler, below form in 2018/19: unproven beyond 17f: acts on heavy going: often wears headgear/tongue tie. *Peter Winks* **h64**

HASSLE (IRE) 10 b.g. Montjeu (IRE) – Canterbury Lace (USA) (Danehill (USA)) [2018/19 h15.7g h18.6g4 h16.7m h20g5 Aug 22] sturdy gelding: fairly useful handicap hurdler: won at Market Rasen in June: stays 19f: acts on soft going: wears headgear. *Dr Richard Newland* **h123**

HASTRUBAL (FR) 9 br.g. Discover d'Auteuil (FR) – Miss Montrose (Tina's Pet) [2018/19 h19.6g2 h21d2 h22.8s2 c24v6 h26g4 Apr 10] useful-looking gelding: fair maiden hurdler: well beaten in novice handicap on chasing debut: should be suited by 3m: acts on soft going. *Henry Daly* **c73 h114**

HATCHER (IRE) 6 b.g. Doyen (IRE) – African Keys (IRE) (Quws) [2018/19 h114, b97: h15.8gF h16.3m2 h16.3m* h16.3m* h18.7m* h18.7g* h16.7g c15.9g* c15.7d* Apr 9] lengthy gelding: has had breathing operation: useful hurdler: won maiden and novice (by 30 lengths from Cybalko) in July, and 2 more novices in August, all at Stratford: useful form over fences: won maiden at Leicester (by 16 lengths from Boite) in March and novice at Southwell in April: stays 19f: acts on good to firm and good to soft going: wears headgear: usually leads. *Dan Skelton* **c139 h132**

HATCHET JACK (IRE) 7 b.g. Black Sam Bellamy (IRE) – Identity Parade (IRE) (Witness Box (USA)) [2018/19 h118: h20g2 h8g] workmanlike gelding: maiden pointer: fairly useful maiden hurdler, below form sole outing in 2018/19: stays 3m: acts on heavy going. *Paul Henderson* **h96**

HATEM (FR) 6 gr.g. Kendargent (FR) – Escolhida (IRE) (Montjeu (IRE)) [2018/19 h–: h16g2 h15.7g3 h15.8g6 h15.8g h15.7g6 h16gpu Jun 24] modest maiden hurdler: left Nick Littmoden after first start: raced mainly around 2m: best form on good going: wore headgear: tried in tongue tie: dead. *Conor Dore* **h99**

HATS OFF TO LARRY 5 b.g. Sixties Icon – Highland Jig (Norse Dancer (IRE)) [2018/19 h15.7m6 h15.8g6 Nov 24] fairly useful on Flat, stays 10.5f: fair form over hurdles: will stay beyond 2m: open to further improvement. *Mick Channon* **h106 p**

HATTAAB 6 b.g. Intikhab (USA) – Sundus (USA) (Sadler's Wells (USA)) [2018/19 h101, b89: h15.8g h15.8g h15.7d2 h18.5s3 Apr 16] fair maiden hurdler: left Tom George after second start: probably stays 19f: acts on soft going: tried in cheekpieces. *Henry Oliver* **h109**

HATTONS HILL (IRE) 10 b.g. Pierre – Cluain Chaoin (IRE) (Phardante (FR)) [2018/19 c106, h–: c24.2g4 c20.1s4 c24.2vpu c26.7dF c23.9sur c26.2gpu c24.2dpu Mar 26] maiden hurdler: fair handicap chaser, below form in 2018/19: stays 3m: acts on heavy going: wears headgear: temperament under suspicion. *Henry Hogarth* **c92 h–**

HAUL AWAY (IRE) 6 b.g. Stowaway – Lisacul Queen (IRE) (Old Vic) [2018/19 h116, b95: h20.7g6 h20.3g* h21.6s* h21.7g* h19.2s* h20g4 h21g Nov 12] useful hurdler: won maiden at Southwell in June, novices at Newton Abbot and Fontwell in August, and handicap at Fontwell (by length from High Secret) in October: stays 2¾m: acts on soft going: usually wears headgear. *Nicky Henderson* **h130**

HAVANA BEAT (IRE) 9 b.g. Teofilo (IRE) – Sweet Home Alabama (IRE) (Desert Prince (IRE)) [2018/19 h130: h15.7gF h21gF Oct 26] useful hurdler at best: stayed 2½m: acted on soft going: dead. *Tony Carroll* **h–**

HAVANA HERMANO (IRE) 5 b.g. Flemensfirth (USA) – Senorita Rumbalita (Alflora (IRE)) [2018/19 b16.7g b16g4 h16g4 h15.8d6 h16d* h15.8d3 h16.5g5 Apr 6] fourth foal: brother to fair hurdler/chaser Havana Dancer (2m-21f winner): dam (c115/h124) 2m-21f hurdle/chase winner: placed in Irish point: modest form in bumpers: fairly useful form over hurdles: won maiden at Fakenham in January: third in novice at Huntingdon next time: will stay 2½m: acts on good to soft going. *Stuart Edmunds* **h118 b81**

HAVANA JACK (IRE) 9 b.g. Westerner – Hackler Poitin (IRE) (Little Bighorn) [2018/19 c91: c23.8g* c21.2g5 May 26] modest handicap chaser: won at Perth in May: stays 3¼m: acts on good to firm and heavy going: has worn headgear, including last 2 starts. *Leonard Kerr* **c97**

HAVANA RIVER (IRE) 6 b.m. Mahler – Dancingonthemoon (IRE) (Milan) [2018/19 **h90** h18.5s⁶ h16d h22g³ Apr 14] first foal: dam, unraced, closely related to useful hurdler/top-class chaser (stays 25f) Sub Lieutenant and half-sister to Cheltenham Gold Cup winner Lord Windermere: awarded Irish point: modest form over hurdles: best effort when third in novice at Stratford in April: will stay at least 3m. *Johnny Farrelly*

HAVE A GO HERO (IRE) 11 b.g. Flemensfirth (USA) – Blue Bank (IRE) (Burslem) **c–** [2018/19 c109: c27.6s^pu c23.6d^pu c25.7s^pu c26.7g⁶ Mar 25] fair chaser at best, no form in 2018/19: wears visor. *Dai Williams*

HAVENTTHEFROGGIEST 7 b.m. Bollin Terry – Froglet (Shaamit (IRE)) [2018/19 **h–** h16g h16g h16v^pu h15.8d^pu Nov 25] has had breathing operation: fifth foal: half-sister to fairly useful 17f hurdle winner The Tiddly Tadpole (by Tipsy Creek): dam 2m/17f winner on Flat: virtually pulled up in point bumper: no form over hurdles. *Dai Williams*

HAVINGAGOODTIME 4 ch.f. Mount Nelson – Don't Stop Me Now (FR) (Zamindar **h130** (USA)) [2018/19 h16m⁶ h16v⁶ h16d* h16g⁴ h16.8g* Apr 18] modest maiden on Flat up to 1½m: useful form over hurdles: won juvenile maiden at Fairyhouse in December and Grade 3 fillies juvenile handicap at Cheltenham (by 18 lengths from Via Delle Volte) in April: enthusiastic sort, likely to prove best around 2m: acts on heavy going: races close up. *Henry de Bromhead, Ireland*

HAVISHAM 7 b.g. Mount Nelson – Ile Deserte (Green Desert (USA)) [2018/19 h76: **h98** h20g* h20.3g^pu h16.3m² h16.8g⁴ h25.8m^pu Oct 5] has had breathing operation: modest handicap hurdler: won lady riders event at Fakenham in June: stays 2½m: acts on good to firm going: has worn headgear, including last 3 starts: wears tongue tie: usually leads. *Jamie Snowden*

HAWKERLAND (IRE) 6 b.g. Sea The Stars (IRE) – Zarara (USA) (Manila (USA)) **h100** [2018/19 h16.3d h16.3d h15.9s h19.5d⁴ h21.7g^ur Apr 12] good-topped gelding: half-brother to fairly useful hurdler Guardian of Truth (2¼m winner, by Barathea): fairly useful on Flat, stays 2m: fair form over hurdles: stays 2¾m: acts on good to soft going. *Nick Gifford*

HAWK HIGH (IRE) 9 b.g. High Chaparral (IRE) – Septembers Hawk (IRE) **c134** (Machiavellian (USA)) [2018/19 c15.9g³ c15.2g* c16.3d⁴ c16.3g* Jan 5] close-coupled **h–** gelding: useful hurdler: similar form over fences: won novices at Wetherby in November and Newcastle (by ½ length from Cool Mix) in January: unproven beyond 17f: acts on good to firm and heavy going: wears headgear. *Tim Easterby*

HAWK'S WELL (IRE) 5 b.g. Yeats (IRE) – Our Song (Classic Cliche (IRE)) [2018/19 **b90** b16d⁴ b15.3s³ Mar 7] €45,000 3-y-o: fourth foal: closely related to fairly useful hurdler/ chaser Rooster Byron (2m-3m winner, by Oscar): dam unraced half-sister to smart hurdler/ useful chaser (stays 2½m) Value At Risk and useful hurdler/chaser (stayed 3½m) Battlecry: fair form in bumpers: better effort when fourth at Warwick. *Emma Lavelle*

HAWRIDGE GLORY (IRE) 5 b.g. Royal Applause – Saint Lucia (IRE) (Whipper **h–** (USA)) [2018/19 h17.7g⁵ Sep 9] fair on Flat, stays 11.5f: 16/1, never involved in novice at Fontwell on hurdling debut. *Rod Millman*

HAWTHORN COTTAGE (IRE) 6 b.m. Gold Well – Miss Kilkeel (IRE) (Religiously **b87** (USA)) [2018/19 b98: b17d Apr 4] useful-looking mare: point winner: fairly useful form at best in bumpers: in cheekpieces last 2 starts. *Amy Murphy*

HAWTHORNE BUSH (IRE) 6 ch.g. Bushranger (IRE) – Jinx Johnson (IRE) (Desert **b–** King (IRE)) [2018/19 b16.8g May 15] tailed off in bumper. *David Thompson*

HAYMOUNT (IRE) 10 ch.g. Presenting – Ali's Dipper (IRE) (Orchestra) [2018/19 **c138** c22.5d^pu c22.5g³ c24s c26.3d^pu Mar 15] workmanlike gelding: unbeaten in 3 points: **h–** winning chaser: useful chaser nowadays: third in minor event at Galway (8 lengths behind Sub Lieutenant) in August, standout effort under Rules in 2018/19: left W. P. Mullins after third start: stays 4m: acts on heavy going: tried in cheekpieces: in tongue tie last 4 starts. *T. Ellis*

HAYWARD FIELD (IRE) 6 b.g. Cape Blanco (IRE) – Keepers Hill (IRE) (Danehill **h–** (USA)) [2018/19 h16.7m Aug 5] modest on Flat, stays 12.5f: well beaten in maiden on hurdling debut. *Noel Wilson*

HAZAMAR (IRE) 6 gr.g. Manduro (GER) – Hazarafa (IRE) (Daylami (IRE)) [2018/19 **c–** c88, h90: h21.2g^F h22.1g h16.2g h16.5d⁶ h16.5d⁵ Dec 13] good-topped gelding: modest **h91** handicap hurdler: fell only start over fences: will prove best at 2m: acts on good to firm and good to soft going: has worn cheekpieces: wears tongue tie: usually races towards rear. *Sophie Leech*

St James's Place Foxhunter Challenge Cup, Cheltenham—well-backed favourite Hazel Hill is in command at the last; 2018 runner-up Top Wood (left) has to settle for third this time

HAZEL HILL (IRE) 11 b.g. Milan – Resenting (IRE) (Presenting) [2018/19 c116p: c24s* c26.3d* Mar 15] prolific point winner: useful form in hunter chases: unbeaten in 4 starts, including at Warwick in January and Cheltenham (Foxhunter Chase, beating Shantou Flyer 4 lengths) in March: stays 3¼m. *Philip Rowley* **c137**

HAZM (IRE) 4 br.g. Shamardal (USA) – Hikari (IRE) (Galileo (IRE)) [2018/19 b16.3s* b17dpu Apr 5] 2,000 3-y-o: good-topped gelding: first foal: dam, useful 11.7f winner, sister to fairly useful hurdler (stayed 2½m) Deor: fairly useful form when won maiden bumper at Stratford on debut in March: pulled up in Grade 2 event next time. *Tim Vaughan* **b95**

HAZY MANOR (IRE) 5 b.m. Tagula (IRE) – Hazarama (IRE) (Kahyasi) [2018/19 h98: h18.7m³ h16.8m⁶ h16.8m³ Oct 2] modest maiden hurdler: stays 2½m: acts on heavy going: has worn hood, including in 2018/19. *Julia Brooke* **h90**

HAZY TOM (IRE) 13 b.g. Heron Island (IRE) – The Wounded Cook (IRE) (Muroto) [2018/19 h–: h21.6g⁴ May 17] tall, lengthy gelding: point winner: winning hurdler: fair chaser at best, little impact since 2016/17: stays 3m: acts on soft going: tried in headgear: in tongue tie last 3 starts. *Miss K. Phillips-Hill* **c72 h–**

HAZZAAR (IRE) 5 b.g. Flemensfirth (USA) – Una Sorpresa (GER) (Banyumanik (IRE)) [2018/19 b15.7d* b15.7s Dec 21] second foal: dam unraced half-sister to smart hurdler (2m-3m winner) United: fairly useful form in bumpers: won at Ascot (by 2 lengths from Prince Llywelyn) on debut in November: shaped better than result in listed event there next time: remains capable of better. *Tom Lacey* **b102 p**

HEAD LAD (FR) 6 b.g. Linda's Lad – Orabelle (FR) (Freedom Cry) [2018/19 h–: h18.7g² h16s² h19d⁶ h21.7d⁶ h26.4g Apr 14] useful-looking gelding: modest maiden hurdler: stays 19f: acts on soft going. *Jonjo O'Neill* **h93**

HEADS UP CLEMMIE 6 b.m. Sulamani (IRE) – M'lady Rousseur (IRE) (Selkirk (USA)) [2018/19 b16.8s⁴ Dec 26] first foal: dam (h85), maiden hurdler, 2m winner on Flat: 16/1, fourth in mares bumper at Sedgefield (18¼ lengths behind Dares To Dream). *Laura Morgan* **b68**

HEAD TO THE STARS 8 br.g. Kayf Tara – Sail By The Stars (Celtic Cone) [2018/19 h132: c24.2gF c23.8spu c22.4d⁵ Dec 29] rangy gelding: useful hurdler: fairly useful form over fences: stays 23f: acts on heavy going: held up. *Henry Daly* **c120 h–**

HEANEY (IRE) 12 b.g. Flemensfirth (USA) – The Red Wench (IRE) (Aahsaylad) [2018/19 c24.2d* Apr 9] sturdy gelding: multiple point winner: winning hurdler: fair chaser nowadays: won hunter at Exeter in April: stays 29f: acts on good to firm and heavy going: tried in blinkers. *Mrs C. L. Wonnacott* **c105 h–**

HEARTASIA (IRE) 6 b.m. Danehill Dancer (IRE) – Big Heart (Mr Greeley (USA)) [2018/19 h101, b102: h16.8g⁴ Nov 8] has had breathing operation: bumper winner: fair form over hurdles: has worn hood: wears tongue tie: held up. *Susan Corbett* **h75**

413

HEAR THE CHIMES 10 b.g. Midnight Legend – Severn Air (Alderbrook) [2018/19 **h103**
h97: h16.8g⁴ h15.8g h19.9g h19.9g* h19.9d⁴ h20.7g* h22.8d² h23.4m⁶ Apr 22] sturdy
gelding: has had breathing operation: fair handicap hurdler: won at Sedgefield in November
and Huntingdon in February: stays 23f: acts on heavy going: held up. *Shaun Harris*

HEART OF KERNOW (IRE) 7 b.g. Fruits of Love (USA) – Rathturtin Brief (IRE) **c–**
(Saddlers' Hall (IRE)) [2018/19 h104: c20.1sᶠ c18g Nov 12] fair form over hurdles, **h–**
winning 2 of 3 starts: well held completed start over fences: stays 23f: best form on soft/
heavy going. *Nigel Hawke*

HEARTS ARE TRUMPS (IRE) 6 b.g. Oscar (IRE) – Polly's Present (IRE) (Presenting) **h139**
[2018/19 h16.5g* h16.7g⁴ h16.2d² h16.6d* h16.3d² h16.2g* h16g⁴ h16g h16d³ h16d³
Apr 23] second foal: dam unraced sister to Cheltenham Gold Cup winner Denman: useful
handicap hurdler: won at Clonmel in May, Galway in October and Punchestown in
November: raced around 2m: acts on good to soft going: usually races prominently.
Desmond McDonogh, Ireland

HEATHER BURNING (IRE) 8 b.g. Mountain High (IRE) – Go To Blazes (IRE) **h73**
(Aahsaylad) [2018/19 h–: h19.5v⁶ h22.7g⁴ h21.4d Feb 6] poor maiden hurdler. *Rose Dobbin*

HEATHER SONG 5 b.m. Kayf Tara – Bella Macrae (Bustino) [2018/19 b17.1d Oct 18] **b73**
half-sister to bumper winner/useful hurdler Jack Frost (2m-19f winner, by Midnight
Legend) and fairly useful hurdler Pipe Banner (2½m winner, by Silver Patriarch): dam
(h120) bumper/2m hurdle winner: 11/1, ninth in mares bumper at Carlisle (17½ lengths
behind Mega Yeats). *Charlie Longsdon*

HEATSTROKE (IRE) 7 b.g. Galileo (IRE) – Walklikeanegyptian (IRE) (Danehill **h123**
(USA)) [2018/19 h15.8d* h16s⁴ h15.3g² h16g Apr 27] well-made gelding: has had
breathing operation: fairly useful on Flat, winning 3 races over hurdles: won maiden
at Huntingdon in February: in tongue tie 3 of 4 starts. *Nicky Henderson*

HEAVEN HALL (FR) 6 b.g. Born King (JPN) – Sola Luna (FR) (Loup Solitaire (USA)) **h–**
[2018/19 b15.8g b16g⁶ h20.3gᵖᵘ Sep 5] behind in bumpers: pulled up in novice on hurdling **b–**
debut (hooded). *Nick Littmoden*

HEAVENLY PROMISE (IRE) 8 ch.m. Presenting – Ambrosia's Promise (IRE) **c83**
(Minster Son) [2018/19 c80, h–: c24d⁴ c24.1g* c21.4g⁴ h24g c23.6gᵖᵘ Apr 11] maiden **h–**
hurdler: poor handicap chaser: won at Bangor in May: stays 3m: acts on heavy going: has
worn hood, including in 2018/19. *John Groucott*

HEAVENLY SECRET (IRE) 4 b.g. Sea The Stars (IRE) – Prime Run (Dansili) **b–**
[2018/19 b16.6g⁴ Mar 2] tailed off in bumper: little impact in minor events on Flat.
Tony Coyle

HEAVENLY SHADES 4 ch.f. Haafhd – Kaloni (IRE) (Kalanisi (IRE)) [2018/19 b13.7g **b–**
Nov 13] second foal: dam 1¼m winner: well beaten in junior bumper. *Pam Sly*

HEAVEY 5 b.g. Trans Island – Clohamon Gossip (IRE) (Lord Americo) [2018/19 b17.7d⁴ **b86**
Feb 24] £45,000 4-y-o: half-brother to a winning pointer by Dapper: dam unraced: made
frame both starts in Irish points: in tongue strap, 33/1, fourth in maiden bumper at Fontwell
(5 lengths behind Hugos Other Horse). *Neil Mulholland*

HEDGEINATOR (IRE) 9 ch.g. Beneficial – Annalecky (IRE) (Bob's Return (IRE)) **c111**
[2018/19 c111, h–: c29.1g⁴ c24.2g³ c24g² Oct 7] workmanlike gelding: twice-raced **h–**
hurdler: fair handicap chaser: left Christian Williams after second start: stays 3¼m: acts
on heavy going: wears cheekpieces: tried in tongue tie: front runner/races prominently.
Robert Stephens

HE IS ROSY (IRE) 7 b.g. Helissio (FR) – Sister Rose (IRE) (Roselier (FR)) [2018/19 h–: **h–**
h23.9sᵖᵘ h16d h21.7gᵖᵘ Apr 12] point winner: maiden hurdler, no form in 2018/19.
Susan Gardner

HEIST (IRE) 9 b.g. Galileo (IRE) – Matikanehanafubuki (IRE) (Caerleon (USA)) **c118 §**
[2018/19 c131, h118: h24.5g c23g⁵ c25g c22.5sᵘʳ c24g c22.6gᵖᵘ Nov 18] compact gelding: **h–**
winning hurdler: useful handicap chaser, below form in 2018/19: stays 3¼m: acts on good
to firm and good to soft going: wears headgear/tongue tie: temperamental. *Patrick Griffin,*
Ireland

HELAMIS 9 b.m. Shirocco (GER) – Alnoor (USA) (Danzig (USA)) [2018/19 h–: h19.9g **h69**
h19.9gᵖᵘ h19.9v h23.3s³ h25g⁴ Feb 18] poor handicap hurdler: stays 25f, effective at much
shorter: acts on heavy going: has worn headgear, including in 2018/19. *Barry Leavy*

HELF (IRE) 5 b.g. Helmet (AUS) – Causeway Song (USA) (Giant's Causeway (USA)) **h74**
[2018/19 h–: h15.8g h16.8g h18.6m* h19.8g⁵ h15.5g⁶ Dec 2] poor handicap hurdler: won
at Market Rasen in August: stays 19f: acts on good to firm going: in headgear last 5 starts:
wears tongue tie. *Oliver Greenall*

HELFORD RIVER 5 b.g. Presenting – Lovely Origny (FR) (Robin des Champs (FR)) **h98**
[2018/19 b15.8g⁵ h18.5d h20.5s⁵ h19.2d h19.5d⁵ h19.6gᵖᵘ Apr 13] £45,000 3-y-o: fifth **b88**
foal: brother to fair hurdler/chaser Is Love Alive (2½m-3m winner, by Presenting) and
half-brother to fairly useful 2m hurdle winner What's Occurring (by Rail Link) and a
winning pointer by Black Sam Bellamy: dam unraced half-sister to fair hurdler/useful
chaser (stayed 3m) Forzy Origny out of half-sister to top-class chaser (stayed 25f) Cyfor
Malta: fifth in bumper at Uttoxeter on debut: modest form over hurdles: will stay 2¾m+:
acts on good to soft going: tried in tongue tie. out *Colin Tizzard*

HELIUM (FR) 14 b.g. Dream Well (FR) – Sure Harbour (SWI) (Surumu (GER)) [2018/19 **c88 §**
c107§, h–: c19.4m c17.2g³ c19.2s* Dec 6] strong gelding: winning hurdler: modest **h–**
handicap chaser nowadays: retired in headgear, won at Market Rasen in December: stays
2½m: acts on any going: has worn tongue tie: unreliable. *Alexandra Dunn*

HELLAVASHOCK 6 gr.g. Hellvelyn – Surprise Statement (Proclamation (IRE)) **h73**
[2018/19 h16.2g³ h16.2g h16.2gᵖᵘ h15.6g⁴ h16.4s Dec 22] angular gelding: poor form over
hurdles: raced only at 2m: usually in headgear: tried in tongue tie. *Alistair Whillans*

HELLO BERTIE 7 b.g. Kayf Tara – I'm Delilah (Overbury (IRE)) [2018/19 h92, b87: **h90**
h16.7g h19.7s h19.9d h20.2d Apr 26] has had breathing operations: modest maiden
hurdler: unproven beyond 17f: acts on heavy going. *Ruth Jefferson*

HELLO BOB 4 ch.f. Cityscape – Maid of Perth (Mark of Esteem (IRE)) [2018/19 **b103**
b16.4m* Mar 22] sixth foal: half-sister to modest hurdler/fair chaser Thankyou Very Much
(2m/17f winner, by Lucky Story): dam unraced: in hood, 5/1, won mares bumper at
Musselburgh (by 11 lengths from Methodtothemadness) on debut. *James Bethell*

HELLO BUDDY (IRE) 5 ch.g. Salutino (GER) – Cotton Candy (IRE) (Exit To Nowhere **b–**
(USA)) [2018/19 b16g⁶ Apr 25] well beaten in bumper. *Graeme McPherson*

HELLO FELLAS 7 b.g. Gold Well – Archdale Ambush (IRE) (Heron Island **c– p**
(IRE)) [2018/19 h96: h20.2g² h23.1g³ h23.9g² c25.8gᵘʳ Sep 1] has had breathing operation: **h103**
fair form over hurdles: well backed when unseated first on chasing debut: left Nicky
Richards at third start: stays 3m: best form on good going: has worn hood, including in
2018/19. *Dan Skelton*

HELL'S KITCHEN 8 b.g. Robin des Champs (FR) – Mille Et Une (FR) (Trempolino **c158**
(USA)) [2018/19 c146, h–: c19.9g c18.8s* c15.9s⁴ c19.9d⁴ Apr 5] big, well-made gelding: **h–**
winning hurdler: high-class chaser: won handicap at Ascot (by 2¼ lengths from Janika) in
December: fourth in Queen Mother Champion Chase at Cheltenham (9½ lengths behind
Altior) next time: stays 21f: acts on heavy going: wears hood/tongue tie. *Harry Fry*

HELMSLEY LAD 8 gr.g. Fair Mix (IRE) – Wuchowsen (IRE) (King's Ride) [2018/19 **h92 §**
h96§: h20.3g³ May 23] tall gelding: has had breathing operation: modest maiden hurdler:
should stay beyond 2m: acts on heavy going: finds little. *Ruth Jefferson*

HELUVAGOOD 7 b.g. Helissio (FR) – Cape Siren (Warning) [2018/19 h100: c22.5d **c102**
h18.5d h19.5g³ c24.2g* c23d³ c23.6d⁵ c21.6dᵖᵘ c24.2v⁵ c24.2dᵖᵘ Apr 9] lengthy gelding: **h100**
has had breathing operation: fair handicap hurdler: fair handicap chaser: won at Exeter in
November: stays 3m: acts on heavy going: wears tongue tie. *Victor Dartnall*

HENCHARD 8 b.g. Deltic (USA) – Kittenkat (Riverwise (USA)) [2018/19 h23.6vᵖᵘ **h–**
h21.6vᵖᵘ h21.9vᵖᵘ h23.1sᵖᵘ Mar 18] maiden hurdler, no form in 2018/19: tried in
cheekpieces. *Richard Mitchell*

HENLLAN HARRI (IRE) 11 br.g. King's Theatre (IRE) – Told You So (IRE) (Glacial **c131**
Storm (USA)) [2018/19 c124, h124: c24dᵘʳ h24.7g c23.8g* c26.1m² c24.2dᵖᵘ c23.8m³ **h111**
c27.9g⁵ Apr 21] lengthy gelding: fairly useful handicap hurdler: useful handicap chaser:
won at Perth in June: second in Summer Cup at Uttoxeter (3¾ lengths behind Virgilio) next
time: stays 29f: acts on good to firm and heavy going: wears headgear/tongue tie: usually
front runner/races prominently. *Peter Bowen*

HENRIETTA BELL (IRE) 6 b.m. Shantou (USA) – Close To Shore (IRE) (Bob Back **b87**
(USA)) [2018/19 b17g⁴ b16.3d b15.7d⁴ Apr 9] €1,500 3-y-o: sturdy mare: fourth foal:
sister to useful hurdler/fairly useful chaser Mr Shantu (19f-3¼m winner) and fair hurdler/
fairly useful chaser Lake Takapuna (2m/17f winner): dam unraced: runner-up in Irish
point: fair form in bumpers. *Harry Whittington*

HENRI LE BON (IRE) 4 b.g. Sea The Stars (IRE) – Speed Song (Fasliyev (USA)) **b77**
[2018/19 b15.8s⁵ Apr 7] 20/1, fifth in bumper at Ffos Las (14½ lengths behind Prudhomme).
Kerry Lee

HENRI PARRY MORGAN 11 b.g. Brian Boru – Queen of Thedaises (Over The River **c116**
(FR)) [2018/19 c137x, h–: c23d⁶ c25.5g c23.6d c29.2gᵖᵘ Oct 21] sturdy gelding: winning **h–**
hurdler: useful handicap chaser, well below form in 2018/19: stays 3½m: acts on good to
firm and heavy going: wears headgear: usually tongue tied. *Peter Bowen*

HENRY'S JOY (IRE) 6 b.g. Craigsteel – Shocona (IRE) (Oscar Schindler (IRE)) **c117**
[2018/19 h114, b87: h22m² h20.5v⁵ c20.3g² c19.3s³ c20.3g* c23.8m³ c21.3g³ Mar 29] fair **h109**
hurdler: fairly useful form over fences: won novice handicap at Musselburgh in January:
stays 3m: acts on good to firm and heavy going: usually wears headgear. *Donald McCain*

HENRY SMITH 7 b.g. Firebreak – So Discreet (Tragic Role (USA)) [2018/19 h16.7g² **h114**
h16.3m⁴ h16.7g* h18.7g* Sep 4] fairly useful on Flat, stayed 12.5f: fair form over hurdles:
won maiden at Bangor in August and novice at Stratford in September: in hood last 2 starts:
tried in tongue tie: dead. *Dr Richard Newland*

HENRY'S REGIME 4 b.g. Bollin Eric – Regime Change (Morpeth) [2018/19 b16.5d³ **b88**
Apr 24] first foal: dam winning pointer: runner-up on second of 2 starts in points: 3/1, third
in maiden bumper at Taunton (13 lengths behind Dromineer). *Stuart Kittow*

HENRYVILLE 11 b.g. Generous (IRE) – Aquavita (Kalaglow) [2018/19 c147, h–: c21gᶠ **c139**
c20g c21g⁶ h23.6s c20dᵖᵘ c20.2gᵘʳ c24.2d² c21.1d c26g⁶ Apr 17] sturdy gelding: winning **h–**
hurdler: useful handicap chaser nowadays: left Harry Fry after third start: stays 25f: acts on
soft and good to firm going: has worn hood/tongue tie, including in 2018/19: usually races
in rear. *Peter Bowen*

HEPBURN 6 b.m. Sixties Icon – Mighty Splash (Cape Cross (IRE)) [2018/19 c91, h97: **c99**
h23.3d⁴ h20v c23.5v³ c26v³ c23.8s³ Apr 7] modest maiden hurdler: similar form over **h93**
fences: seems to stay 3¼m: acts on heavy going: wears cheekpieces/tongue tie. *Ali Stronge*

HEPIJEU (FR) 8 b.g. Palace Episode (USA) – Helenjeu (Montjeu (IRE)) [2018/19 c104, **c115**
h–: h15.8g c20.3gᵖᵘ h23.3g* h25m* h25g* c21.2g² c25.6g² c24d² h23.8m³ Apr 23] good- **h111**
topped gelding: fair handicap hurdler: won at Uttoxeter in September and Huntingdon
(twice) in October: fairly useful handicap chaser: second at Southwell in April: left
Geoffrey Deacon after second start: stays 3¼m: acts on soft and good to firm going: wears
headgear/tongue tie. *Stuart Edmunds*

HERBERT PARK (IRE) 9 b.g. Shantou (USA) – Traluide (FR) (Tropular) [2018/19 **c107 §**
c110§, h–: c26g⁵ c24.2d² Apr 9] tall gelding: winning hurdler: fair chaser: stays 3m: acts **h–**
on heavy going: has worn headgear: temperamental. *R. J. Alford*

HER DREAM (IRE) 7 b.m. Yeats (IRE) – High Benefit (IRE) (Beneficial) [2018/19 h–, **h–**
b–: h24g h19.9gᵖᵘ Nov 17] no form: wears tongue tie. *Claire Dyson*

HERECOMESNELSON (IRE) 10 b.g. Morozov (USA) – Undesperado View (IRE) **h73**
(Un Desperado (FR)) [2018/19 h–: h16.2d h20.2g⁴ h16.2g³ h19.5v⁴ h20.6d³ h22g⁵ Jan 5]
poor maiden hurdler: stayed 2½m: acted on heavy going: tried in hood: dead. *Katie Scott*

HERECOMESTHEBOOM (IRE) 7 b.g. Darsi (FR) – Dympnajane (Dushyantor **h–**
(USA)) [2018/19 b106: h15.8dᵖᵘ Feb 6] lengthy gelding: useful bumper winner: pulled up
in novice on hurdling debut: dead. *Fergal O'Brien*

HEREFORDSHIRE 11 b.g. Beneficial – Handmemy Moneydown (IRE) (Saddlers' Hall **c–**
(IRE)) [2018/19 c16v⁶ c23.6dᵖᵘ Jan 18] point winner: no impact in maiden/novice chases:
tried in tongue tie. *Sarah-Jayne Davies*

HERE I AM (IRE) 12 br.g. Presenting – The Last Bank (IRE) (Phardante (FR)) [2018/19 **c94**
c103, h–: c19.9g⁴ c21.6v⁶ c19.7dᵖᵘ c17.8g³ Apr 12] tall, workmanlike gelding: maiden **h–**
hurdler: modest handicap chaser nowadays: stays 2½m: acts on soft and good to firm
going: tried in cheekpieces: front runner. *Diana Grissell*

HERE'S BINGO 6 b.g. With The Flow (USA) – Winter Scene (IRE) (Oscar (IRE)) **h–**
[2018/19 b85: h18.5m h21.6g⁶ h16.8s Apr 16] placed in bumper: no form over hurdles.
Susan Gardner

HERE'S HERBIE 11 b.g. Classic Cliche (IRE) – Tyre Hill Lilly (Jupiter Island) [2018/19 **c–**
c–, h117: h19.8m³ h20d⁶ h19.8gᵘʳ h16.5d h19d* h20.7d⁴ h19d³ h19d³ h21.4g⁴ h18.5s* **h121**
h21.7g³ Apr 24] workmanlike gelding: fairly useful handicap hurdler: won at Taunton in
December and Exeter in April: fell both starts over fences: stays 21f: acts on heavy going:
tried in cheekpieces: wears tongue tie. *Susan Gardner*

HERESMYNUMBER (IRE) 9 b.g. Kalanisi (IRE) – Broken Rein (IRE) (Orchestra) **c–**
[2018/19 c99, h87: h19.5v⁵ h23s⁵ h23.4g⁴ c26.2dᵖᵘ Mar 20] sturdy gelding: modest maiden **h89**
hurdler: winning chaser: stays 3¼m: acts on heavy going: wears cheekpieces/tongue tie.
Ali Stronge

HERESTHETHING (IRE) 6 b.g. Milan – The Mighty Matron (IRE) (Montelimar **h91**
(USA)) [2018/19 b16.7g h20.5g³ h21.2d Feb 6] €37,000 3-y-o: brother to useful bumper **b–**
winner The Mighty Milan, and half-brother to unreliable but fair hurdler The Flaming
Matron (2½m-2¾m winner, by Flemensfirth), stayed 3m: dam unraced: well held in
bumper: better effort in maiden hurdles (modest form) when 20 lengths third of 7 to Chez
Hans at Leicester. *Ian Williams*

HERITAGE WAY 10 b.g. Tamayaz (CAN) – Morning Caller (IRE) (Zaffaran (USA)) **c63**
[2018/19 c–, h–: c21.4g⁵ May 11] maiden hurdler: poor form over fences. *Henry Hogarth* **h–**

HERMANUS (IRE) 7 ch.m. Golan (IRE) – Almost Trumps (Nearly A Hand) [2018/19 **h94**
h93: h20g⁶ h16.2g³ h19.9g³ h22.1m h17.2g* h16.7g* h18.7g³ h17.2d h15.8g⁵ h16g⁵
h21.3m Nov 2] angular mare: modest handicap hurdler: won at Cartmel (mares) in July and
Bangor in August: left James Ewart after first start: stays 21f: acts on soft going: usually
wears headgear: signs of temperament. *Stef Keniry*

HERMOSA VAQUERA (IRE) 9 b.m. High Chaparral (IRE) – Sundown (Polish **h98**
Precedent (USA)) [2018/19 h98: h16.3g³ h21.7g² h15.9g* h19.7gᶠ Oct 16] modest
handicap hurdler: won at Plumpton in September: stays 2¾m: acts on good to firm and
good to soft going: usually wears cheekpieces: has worn tongue tie: usually races
prominently. *Gary Moore*

HERON HEIGHTS (IRE) 10 b.g. Heron Island (IRE) – Inter Alia (IRE) (Dr Massini **c148**
(IRE)) [2018/19 c141, h–: c23g May 29] tall, close-coupled gelding: maiden hurdler: smart **h–**
chaser: won Pat Taaffe Handicap Chase at Punchestown (for second successive year, by 6½
lengths from Onefortheroadtom) shortly after end of British season: stays 25f: acts on
heavy going: in cheekpieces last 4 starts: wears tongue tie. *Henry de Bromhead, Ireland*

HERO'S CREEK (IRE) 6 br.g. Kalanisi (IRE) – Iktitafs Sister (IRE) (Val Royal (FR)) **b–**
[2018/19 b–: b15.7g b16g b13.7g⁶ Nov 24] no form in bumpers: dead. *Ben Pauling*

HERO'S STORY 9 b.g. Mount Nelson – Red Roses Story (FR) (Pink (FR)) [2018/19 **h82**
h16.2s h17.1d h20g⁵ h19.5v h23.8g² Feb 13] has had breathing operation: modest on Flat,
stays 16.5f: poor form over hurdles. *Barry Murtagh*

HE'S A GOER (IRE) 5 b.g. Yeats (IRE) – Tessas Girl (IRE) (Catcher In The Rye (IRE)) **h122**
[2018/19 b79: h19.6g⁴ h16g* h19.7m² h19.7sᵖᵘ h16v h15.7m³ h19.9d⁶ h21g² h20.5g³ Apr
21] fairly useful hurdler: won novice at Warwick in September: second in handicap there
in April: stays 21f: acts on good to firm and good to soft going: in headgear last 4 starts.
Tom Lacey

HE'S A TOFF (IRE) 5 br.g. Dandy Man (IRE) – Prevarication (IRE) (In The Wings) **h–**
[2018/19 h–: h15.8m h15.8g h16.8gᵖᵘ Aug 15] close-coupled gelding: has had breathing
operation: little form over hurdles: in headgear last 3 starts: tried in tongue tie. *Jo Davis*

Palmerstown House Pat Taaffe Handicap Chase, Punchestown—Heron Heights (stars) jumps the
last more cleanly than British raider Onefortheroadtom on his way to claiming this valuable race
for the second successive year

HES NO TROUBLE (IRE) 6 b.g. Scorpion (IRE) – She's No Trouble (IRE) (Zaffaran (USA)) [2018/19 h21d h15.8g* h15.8d⁴ Mar 22] €11,000 3-y-o, £45,000 5-y-o: seventh foal: dam unraced sister to Cheltenham Gold Cup winner Looks Like Trouble: Irish point winner: fairly useful form over hurdles: won novice at Huntingdon in February. *Kim Bailey* **h120**

HES OUR ROBIN (IRE) 9 b.g. Robin des Pres (FR) – Poly Sandstorm (IRE) (Presenting) [2018/19 c–, h86: h15.8m h15.8g h16g³ h16.7g⁶ h16.7g⁴ Aug 31] poor maiden hurdler: lightly-raced chaser: stays 21f, races over shorter nowadays: acts on good to firm going: usually wears hood: has worn tongue tie, including last 3 starts. *Michael Mullineaux* **c–** **h80**

HESSLE ROAD (IRE) 5 b.m. September Storm (GER) – Antinomy (IRE) (Anshan) [2018/19 b15.7g h16.7g h19.9dᵖᵘ h20.6g⁵ Mar 14] rather unfurnished mare: third foal: dam, winning pointer, half-sister to fairly useful hurdler/chaser (2m/17f winner) Fair Loch: no form in bumper/over hurdles. *Mike Sowersby* **h–** **b–**

HEURTEVENT (FR) 10 b.g. Hold That Tiger (USA) – Sybilia (GER) (Spectrum (IRE)) [2018/19 c69, h–: c16.5g² c16.1g⁴ c20g³ c16.5g* c23g⁵ c16.5g* c20g³ c17.8m⁵ c20d Nov 25] angular gelding: winning hurdler: poor handicap chaser: won at Worcester in July and September: stays 2½m: acts on heavy going: wears headgear: has worn tongue tie. *Tony Carroll* **c82** **h–**

HEY BILL (IRE) 9 b.g. Indian Danehill (IRE) – Grange More (IRE) (Ridgewood Ben) [2018/19 c124, h–: c25.6g⁶ c24.2sᵘʳ c26d⁶ c25.6d⁴ c25.5d⁵ c26m⁴ c23.8m³ Apr 23] sturdy gelding: winning hurdler: fairly useful handicap chaser: stays 3m: acts on soft and good to firm going: in cheekpieces last 3 starts. *Graeme McPherson* **c117** **h–**

HEY BOB (IRE) 7 br.g. Big Bad Bob (IRE) – Bounty Star (IRE) (Fasliyev (USA)) [2018/19 h75§: h16.8g h15.8g⁵ h15.7g h15.8mᵇᵈ h15.8s³ h16.8m h16.8m² h16.8g h15.6g⁴ h15.6g⁶ h16.8v h16d⁵ h15.7g* h16.8d⁴ Apr 23] close-coupled gelding: poor handicap hurdler: won selling event at Catterick in March: raced around 2m: acts on good to firm and heavy going: wears tongue tie: temperamental. *Chris Grant* **h78 §**

HEY BUD 6 b.g. Fair Mix (IRE) – Azione (Exit To Nowhere (USA)) [2018/19 b85: h16.8s h18.5d³ h15.3g³ h19.9g* Mar 25] fairly useful form over hurdles: won novice at Wincanton in March: open to further improvement. *Jeremy Scott* **h119 p**

HEYDOUR (IRE) 6 br.g. Presenting – Our Lucky Venture (IRE) (Golan (IRE)) [2018/19 h–, b–: h21.6s³ h20g³ h21.6d³ c19.9g² Oct 16] fair form over hurdles: 9/2, second in novice handicap at Huntingdon (head behind Fixed Rate) on chasing debut: stays 2¾m: acts on good to soft going: front runner/races prominently: open to improvement as a chaser. *Mick Channon* **c126 p** **h107**

HEY LISTEN (IRE) 7 b.g. Kutub (IRE) – Crescendor (FR) (Lavirco (GER)) [2018/19 c–, h96: h16.2g⁴ h16.2gᵖᵘ h16.2g⁶ h20.2gᵖᵘ Sep 10] point winner: poor maiden hurdler: twice-raced chaser: unproven beyond 2m: acts on soft going: usually wears cheekpieces. *Lucinda Russell* **c–** **h80**

HIDDEN CARGO (IRE) 7 b.g. Stowaway – All Heart (Alhaarth (IRE)) [2018/19 h102: c20.5mᵘʳ c20.3g⁵ h20m Jul 13] useful-looking gelding: won in point debut in December: fair maiden hurdler: held completed start in chases: stays 19f: acts on good to soft going: tried in cheekpieces. *Alan King* **c66** **h–**

HIDDEN CHARMER (IRE) 7 b.g. Stowaway – Manhattan Babe (IRE) (Definite Article) [2018/19 c20g² c21g³ c19.2gᵖᵘ c20.9dᵘʳ c22.6g⁶ c20m* Apr 1] good-topped gelding: winning hurdler: fair chaser: won hunter at Ludlow in April: left P. M. J. Doyle after first start, Christian Williams after fifth: stays 25f: acts on good to firm and good to soft going: wears tongue tie: often let down by jumping. *N. R. P. Williams* **c113 x** **h–**

HIDDEN DILEMMA (IRE) 6 b.m. Winged Love (IRE) – Kiss Jolie (FR) (Cadoudal (FR)) [2018/19 h84: h16.2g⁶ h16.5g h17s* h20.5v⁴ h20v* h20.6g² h18g h21.6v h24.3mᵖᵘ Apr 12] third on completed start in points: fairly useful handicap hurdler: won at Carlisle in November (mares) and December: second in mares novice at Newcastle in January: stays 21f: acts on heavy going: tried in tongue tie. *Stuart Crawford, Ireland* **h115**

HIDDEN GLEN (IRE) 8 ch.g. Stowaway – Gleanntan (IRE) (Lil's Boy (USA)) [2018/19 b95: h19m h21m* Oct 21] well-made gelding: fairly useful bumper winner: fair form over hurdles: won novice at Kempton in October: front runner/races prominently. *Ben Pauling* **h100**

HIDDEN IMPACT (IRE) 8 br.g. Oscar (IRE) – Maiden Flight (IRE) (Jurado (USA)) [2018/19 h–, b–: h20s⁶ May 25] runner-up in Irish maiden point: fair form on first of 2 starts in bumpers: lightly raced over hurdles: usually in tongue tie. *Rebecca Curtis* **h83**

HIDEAWAY VIC (IRE) 6 b.g. Stowaway – Cailin Vic Mo Cri (IRE) (Old Vic) [2018/19 b99: h20s³ h19.9v² Mar 16] has had breathing operation: bumper winner: fair form over hurdles: in tongue tie last 4 starts: remains open to improvement. *Anthony Honeyball* **h111 p**

HIDE THE BISCUIT (IRE) 9 br.m. Whitmore's Conn (USA) – Animo (IRE) (Idris (IRE)) [2018/19 h16m⁶ h19.5g³ h18.8g³ h16.5m⁵ h25.5g Nov 5] third foal: dam unraced: modest maiden hurdler: twice-raced chaser: left Mervyn Torrens after fourth start: stays 25f: acts on soft and good to firm going: tried in cheekpieces. *Tim Vaughan* **c– h90**

HIER ENCORE (FR) 7 ch.g. Kentucky Dynamite (USA) – Hierarchie (FR) (Sillery (USA)) [2018/19 h61: h23.4g h21.7g⁵ h21.7m² h21.7d² h21.7vᶠ h19.2v* h23d h19.2v⁴ h19.2v* Mar 16] fair handicap hurdler: won conditionals events at Fontwell in December and March: stays 23f: acts on good to firm and heavy going: tried in hood: usually races towards rear. *Nigel Dunger* **h102**

HIGGS (IRE) 6 b.g. Scorpion (IRE) – Captain Supreme (IRE) (Captain Rio) [2018/19 h110, b79: h16.8g* h16m⁴ h19.4m² h19.7v h15.3g⁶ h16d⁵ h21s Mar 16] strong gelding: fairly useful hurdler: won novice at Newton Abbot in May: stays 19f: acts on soft and good to firm going. *Sarah-Jayne Davies* **h118**

HIGH ACCLAIM (USA) 5 b.g. Elusive Quality (USA) – La Reine Lionne (USA) (Leroidesanimaux (BRZ)) [2018/19 h15.7s⁵ Dec 16] fairly useful on Flat, stays 9.5f: 20/1, fifth in maiden at Southwell (27½ lengths behind Umbrigado) on hurdling debut. *Roger Teal* **h84**

HIGHATE HILL (IRE) 5 b.g. Presenting – Lisrenny Lady (Oscar (IRE)) [2018/19 b15.6m⁴ Feb 28] Irish point winner: tailed off in bumper. *Olly Murphy* **b–**

HIGHBURY HIGH (IRE) 12 gr.g. Salford Express (IRE) – Betseale (IRE) (Step Together (USA)) [2018/19 c112x, h–: c21.6g⁵ c21m³ c21g⁴ h20g⁵ c21gᵖᵘ Sep 10] angular gelding: fair handicap hurdler/chaser: stays 2¾m: acts on good to firm and heavy going: wears headgear/tongue tie: often let down by jumping over fences. *Neil Mulholland* **c103 x h93**

HIGH COMMAND (IRE) 6 b.g. High Chaparral (IRE) – Plaza (USA) (Chester House (USA)) [2018/19 h17.7g³ h19.2m² h16.5d Nov 29] has had breathing operation: fairly useful on Flat, stays 16.5f: fair form over hurdles: best effort when third in novice at Plumpton in September: should stay beyond 2¼m. *Gary Moore* **h107**

HIGH COUNSEL (IRE) 10 br.g. Presenting – The Bench (IRE) (Leading Counsel (USA)) [2018/19 c93, h–: c26.1gᵖᵘ h23g Jul 26] winning hurdler/chaser, little show in 2018/19: stays 25f: acts on good to firm and good to soft going: has worn headgear, including in 2018/19: signs of temperament (has been reluctant at start). *Gary Hanmer* **c– h–**

HIGHDAWN (IRE) 6 b.m. Alflora (IRE) – Wychnor Dawn (IRE) (Broken Hearted) [2018/19 b16.3d b16d Mar 21] €19,000 3-y-o: lengthy mare: sister to bumper winner/useful hurdler Aegean Dawn (2m-21f winner) and half-sister to 3 winners, including smart hurdler Glingerburn (2m-2¼m winner, by King's Theatre): dam unraced half-sister to Cheltenham Gold Cup winner Cool Dawn: no form in bumpers. *Fiona Shaw* **b–**

HIGHEST SUN (FR) 5 b.g. Sunday Break (JPN) – Highest Price (FR) (Highest Honor (FR)) [2018/19 h15.7g³ h16.8g⁴ h15.3g² h16d* h21s Mar 13] well-made gelding: 15f winner on Flat: useful form over hurdles: won juvenile at Chateaubriant in 2017/18 for J-L. Guillochon: also won handicap at Chepstow (by 3½ lengths from Casa Tall) in February: should stay 2¼m+: acts on soft going: often travels strongly. *Colin Tizzard* **h132**

HIGH EXPECTATIONS (FR) 8 b.g. High Rock (IRE) – Tashifiya (FR) (Sendawar (IRE)) [2018/19 h117: h20g⁴ h18.8g⁵ h16.2g² h16.8m* h21g h16g³ h16.8d h16d⁵ Apr 23] compact gelding: fairly useful handicap hurdler: won at Sedgefield in September: third at Leopardstown in December: unproven beyond 17f: acts on soft and good to firm going: races off pace. *Gordon Elliott, Ireland* **h127**

HIGH HATTON 10 b.g. Silver Patriarch (IRE) – Leroy's Sister (FR) (Phantom Breeze) [2018/19 c73: c27.5d⁵ Jun 8] has had breathing operation: multiple point winner: fair maiden chaser at best, little impact under Rules since 2016/17: stays 27f: acts on soft and good to firm going: in hood last 2 starts: tried in tongue tie. *J. W. Tudor* **c–**

HIGH JINX (IRE) 11 b.g. High Chaparral (IRE) – Leonara (GER) (Surumu (GER)) [2018/19 h20.9g* h20g* h20.6g² h20.9m² Sep 19] smart on Flat, stays 2½m: fairly useful form over hurdles: won novices at Kelso in May and Aintree in June: runner-up other 2 starts. *Tim Easterby* **h129**

HIGH KITE (IRE) 13 b.g. High-Rise (IRE) – Sister Rose (IRE) (Roselier (FR)) [2018/19 c24.5g⁴ May 14] sturdy gelding: point winner, including in June: maiden hurdler: fair chaser at best, below form only 2 starts under Rules since 2015/16: stays 3m: acts on good to firm and heavy going: has worn headgear: sketchy jumper of fences. *Mrs Phillippa Taylor* **c86 x h–**

HIGHLAND BOBBY 4 b.g. Big Bad Bob (IRE) – Eolith (Pastoral Pursuits) [2018/19 **h107**
h15.7g⁶ h16d⁶ h15.7s⁴ h15.6g⁴ h15.7m³ h16.8s⁵ Mar 21] fair on Flat (unproven beyond
1m): fair form over hurdles: raced around 2m: acts on soft and good to firm going: in hood
last 5 starts: often races freely. *David O'Meara*

HIGHLAND HUNTER (IRE) 6 gr.g. Subtle Power (IRE) – Loughine Sparkle (IRE) **h126 p**
(Beneficial) [2018/19 b99: h20.5v* h20.1v* h21.3d³ h24.3g⁵ Feb 16] Irish
point winner: fairly useful bumper winner: similar form over hurdles: won maiden at Ayr
in November and novice at Hexham in December: third in handicap at Haydock in January:
remains capable of better. *Lucinda Russell*

HIGHLAND LIFE 9 b.m. Trans Island – High Life (Kayf Tara) [2018/19 c23.8s^pu Feb **c–**
26] has had breathing operation: placed once from 3 starts in points: modest hurdler: pulled **h–**
up in novice handicap on chasing debut after long absence: stays 2½m: acts on soft going:
tried in cheekpieces: usually wears tongue tie. *Steve Flook*

HIGHLAND LODGE (IRE) 13 b.g. Flemensfirth (USA) – Supreme Von Pres (IRE) **c93**
(Presenting) [2018/19 c134§, h–: c25.9s^F c21.1d Apr 5] strong gelding: winning hurdler: **h–**
useful handicap chaser, well below best in 2018/19: stays 27f: acts on heavy going: wears
headgear. *James Moffatt*

HIGHLAND PEAK 7 b.g. Distant Peak (IRE) – Flower Appeal (Diktat) [2018/19 h83: **c73**
h23.9g h23.9g^bd h23.9g h23.9g c15.7g⁴ c19.3s⁵ c21.6d⁵ Apr 8] has had breathing operation: **h87**
modest maiden hurdler: poor form over fences: stays 3m: acts on soft going: tried in
cheekpieces/tongue tie. *Jackie Stephen*

HIGHLAND WAY 5 b.m. Getaway (GER) – High Life (Kayf Tara) [2018/19 b16.2s **h– §**
b15.8s b16.7d h23.8d^ro Feb 20] fourth foal: half-sister to modest 19f hurdle winner **b– §**
Highland Life (by Trans Island): dam (c95/h105), ungenuine 17f hurdle winner, half-sister
to smart bumper winner/useful but ungenuine hurdler (stayed 3m) Secret Ploy: behind in
bumpers: ran out approaching first on hurdling debut: often in hood: in tongue tie last 2
starts: one to leave alone. *Steve Flook*

HIGHLY LIKELY (IRE) 10 b.g. Elnadim (USA) – Height of Fantasy (IRE) (Shirley **h–**
Heights) [2018/19 h19.2g h16m h18.7m⁵ h17.7g h17.7g^pu Nov 19] modest on Flat, stays
13f: no form over hurdles: in tongue tie last 2 starts. *Rebecca Woodman*

HIGHLY PRIZED 6 b.g. Manduro (GER) – Razzle (USA) (Danzig (USA)) [2018/19 **h110 p**
h17d⁵ h15.3g* Apr 14] good-topped gelding: fairly useful on Flat in USA, stays 1½m: fair
form over hurdles: in hood, won novice at Wincanton in April: left Jack O. Fisher after first
start: likely to prove best at sharp 2m: open to improvement. *Emma Lavelle*

HIGH NOON (IRE) 7 b.g. Westerner – Seymourswift (Seymour Hicks (FR)) [2018/19 **h96**
h100: h23.1g⁴ h19.5d⁵ h19.5g Apr 26] modest maiden hurdler: should stay beyond 19f:
acts on good to soft going. *Emma Lavelle*

HIGH PRIEST 4 b.g. High Chaparral (IRE) – Princess Aurora (USA) (Mr Greeley **b–**
(USA)) [2018/19 b16.7g^pu Mar 1] pulled up in bumper. *Jason Ward*

HIGH SECRET (IRE) 8 b.g. High Chaparral (IRE) – Secret Question (USA) (Rahy **h137**
(USA)) [2018/19 h111: h16.3g⁵ h20g³ h20.6m* h21.6g h20g h19.2s² h16m⁴ h24.1g⁴
Nov 3] good-topped gelding: useful handicap hurdler: won at Market Rasen (by 9 lengths
from North Hill) in July: stayed 21f: acted on soft and good to firm going: tried in headgear:
dead. *Dan Skelton*

HIGH UP IN THE AIR (FR) 5 ch.g. Famous Name – You Got The Love (Hawk Wing **h77 p**
(USA)) [2018/19 h20.5s⁶ h21.6s h19.2s⁵ Jan 27] €6,000 3-y-o: sturdy gelding: first foal:
dam, maiden on Flat (stayed 1¼m), half-sister to useful 2m hurdler Wingman: well-beaten
last of 2 finishers in Irish point: poor form over hurdles: type to do better in handicaps.
Gary Moore

HIGHWAY COMPANION (IRE) 5 b.g. Milan – Niffyrann (FR) (Sheyrann) [2018/19 **b96**
b15.7s² b16d⁵ Feb 25] €38,000 3-y-o: third foal: dam, French 17f hurdle winner, half-sister
to Triumph Hurdle winner Snow Drop: runner-up on second of 2 starts in Irish points:
fairly useful form in bumpers: better effort when second at Haydock in December.
Keith Dalgleish

HIGHWAY GIRL 6 b.m. Kayf Tara – Whichway Girl (Jupiter Island) [2018/19 b87: **h100 p**
h19.7g⁴ Nov 17] placed in bumpers: 7/2, shaped well when fourth in novice at Wetherby
(7½ lengths behind Captain Zebo) on hurdling debut: should improve. *Charlie Longsdon*

HIGHWAY ONE O ONE (IRE) 7 br.g. Stowaway – High Accord (IRE) (Accordion) **c144**
[2018/19 h137, b101: c16.3d* c17.2g² c15.9s* c15.5s⁴ c16g³ c20.6d² c20.2s c20.6g³ Apr **h–**
17] medium-sized gelding: bumper winner: useful hurdler: useful chaser: won novice at
Newton Abbot in September and graduation event at Carlisle (by ¾ length from Dolos) in

November: placed in Wayward Lad Novices' Chase at Kempton in December, Timeform Novices' Handicap at Cheltenham (2 lengths behind Kildisart) in January and Silver Trophy Chase (Limited Handicap) at Cheltenham (4¼ lengths behind Mister Whitaker) in April: stays 21f: acts on heavy going: usually front runner/races prominently. *Chris Gordon*

HIGHWAY ONE O TWO (IRE) 4 b.g. Shirocco (GER) – Supreme Dreamer (IRE) (Supreme Leader) [2018/19 b16.3s⁵ b16.3d Mar 2] rather unfurnished gelding: poor form in bumpers. *Chris Gordon* **b71**

HIGHWAY STAR (FR) 7 b.g. Vision d'Etat (FR) – Lyli Rose (FR) (Lyphard's Wish (FR)) [2018/19 b82: h18.7m² h20.6gᵖᵘ h16.3g³ h16g h16g² h15.9s Dec 3] good-topped gelding: has had breathing operation: modest form over hurdles: unproven beyond 2m: best form on good going. *Sarah Humphrey* **h96**

HIGH WELLS 5 b.g. High Chaparral (IRE) – Valencha (Domedriver (IRE)) [2018/19 h87: h17.7g² Aug 30] has had breathing operation: fair on Flat, stays 2m: similar form over hurdles: wears blinkers. *Seamus Durack* **h100**

HIGH WHEELER (IRE) 8 b.g. Kalanisi (IRE) – Penny Farthing (Mind Games) [2018/19 h–: h24gᵖᵘ h22gᵖᵘ Jun 9] no form over hurdles: tried in cheekpieces: dead. *Caroline Fryer* **h–**

HIJRAN (IRE) 6 ch.m. Mastercraftsman (IRE) – Sunny Slope (Mujtahid (USA)) [2018/19 h107: h16.3g⁴ h16.2s* h15.5g h16d* h15.8g* h15.7m⁶ Apr 20] fairly useful handicap hurdler: won mares events at Hereford in November and Kempton in January, and conditionals race at Ludlow in February: raced around 2m: acts on heavy going. *Henry Oliver* **h124**

HILLARY C 7 b.m. Kayf Tara – Dd's Glenalla (IRE) (Be My Native (USA)) [2018/19 b15.8d² b15.8m⁶ Jul 13] modest form in bumpers. *Nigel Twiston-Davies* **b79**

HILLARY JOHN (IRE) 8 ch.g. Gamut (IRE) – Dar Dar Supreme (Overbury (IRE)) [2018/19 h18.8g* h21.6g h17.7vᵖᵘ Dec 26] first foal: dam, winning pointer, half-sister to smart staying hurdler Tobefair and fairly useful hurdler/useful chaser (stayed 29f) Sweeney Tunes: point winner: fair form over hurdles: won maiden at Downpatrick in June, only start for B. R. Hamilton. *Warren Greatrex* **h108**

HILLARY VIEW (IRE) 7 b.g. Court Cave (IRE) – Tearaway Lady (IRE) (Tidaro (USA)) [2018/19 h98: c23g* c20g² c24.2g⁴ c25.8vᵖᵘ c20.9d c24dᶠ Mar 30] strong gelding: winning hurdler: fairly useful form over fences: won novice handicap at Worcester in August: stayed 23f: acted on heavy going: wore cheekpieces: dead. *Peter Bowen* **c118**
h–

HILLCREST FIRE (IRE) 5 b.m. Fast Company (IRE) – Firecrest (IRE) (Darshaan) [2018/19 h104: h20.6g² h20.5d² h15.3g⁴ Apr 3] fair handicap hurdler: stays 21f: acts on good to soft going: tried in hood: usually races off pace. *Stuart Edmunds* **h113**

HILL FORT 9 ch.g. Pivotal – Cairns (UAE) (Cadeaux Genereux) [2018/19 c89, h96: c25.7gᵖᵘ h21.6sᵖᵘ Nov 25] fairly useful hurdler at best, no form in 2018/19: twice-raced chaser: stays 21f: acts on good to firm and heavy going: usually in headgear: wears tongue tie. *Alexandra Dunn* **c–**
h–

HILL OF KEASH (IRE) 7 b.g. Craigsteel – Derrytown Girl (IRE) (Anshan) [2018/19 c21gᶠ h22g⁵ h19.7sᵖᵘ Dec 15] no form, including in points: has worn hood. *David Peter Dunne, Ireland* **c–**
h–

HILL SIXTEEN 6 b.g. Court Cave (IRE) – Chasers Chic (Karinga Bay) [2018/19 h20g³ h20.1s² h19.5s² h19.9d² h19.3g* h19.9v⁴ Mar 16] £20,000 4-y-o, £100,000 5-y-o: second foal: dam unraced half-sister to fairly useful hurdler (stayed 2½m) China Gold: Irish point winner: fairly useful form over hurdles: won novice at Carlisle in February: will stay 3m: acts on good going. *Sue Smith* **h119**

HILLS OF CONNEMARA (IRE) 7 gr.m. Tikkanen (USA) – Desirable Rhythm (IRE) (Hernando (FR)) [2018/19 h109, b72: h20.9g² May 9] Irish point winner: fair maiden hurdler: second in novice at Kelso on sole outing in 2018/19: in tongue tie last 2 starts. *Susan Corbett* **h106**

HILLS OF DUBAI (IRE) 10 ch.g. Dubai Destination (USA) – Mowazana (IRE) (Galileo (IRE)) [2018/19 c117, h–: c22.9v² c20.6s⁵ c21.5dᵖᵘ c22.9d⁶ Mar 20] maiden hurdler: fairly useful handicap chaser: stays 23f, effective at shorter: acts on heavy going: usually races close up. *Donald McCain* **c114**
h–

HILLVIEW LAD (IRE) 11 b.g. Vinnie Roe (IRE) – Kabale (IRE) (Ikdam) [2018/19 h21.2m⁶ Apr 23] point winner: poor maiden hurdler: stays 2½m: acts on good to soft going: tried in hood. *Sheila Lewis* **h56**

HINT OF GREY (IRE) 6 gr.m. Mastercraftsman (IRE) – Anamarka (Mark of Esteem (IRE)) [2018/19 h108: c18g⁵ c20d² c16s² Jan 4] workmanlike mare: fair hurdler: similar form over fences: best effort when second in novice handicap at Lingfield: stays 2½m: acts on soft going: has worn hood: often races freely. *Gary Moore*   **c106 h–**

HINXWORTH (IRE) 10 b.g. Milan – Open Cry (IRE) (Montelimar (USA)) [2018/19 c21.6g² c25.5d⁴ c20.2f⁶ Feb 26] good-topped gelding: multiple point winner: maiden hurdler: modest form over fences: best effort when second in maiden hunter at Fontwell in May: should stay beyond 2¾m: acts on good to firm going: wears headgear/tongue tie. *B. Clarke*   **c87 h–**

HIS DREAM (IRE) 6 b.g. Yeats (IRE) – Rosa Muscosa (USA) (Dixie Union (USA)) [2018/19 h72, b104: h21g h23.3g h22m* h23g³ h23.3g h25mᵖᵘ h23.1gᵖᵘ h26d* h24.4g³ h24.2d h24.2dᵘʳ h26gᵖᵘ Apr 10] sturdy gelding: fair handicap hurdler: won at Stratford (novice) in August and Warwick (conditionals) in December: stays 3¼m: acts on good to firm and good to soft going: in cheekpieces last 2 starts: tried in tongue tie: usually races towards rear. *Jonjo O'Neill*   **h101**

HIT AND RUN (IRE) 7 b.g. Getaway (GER) – Arrive In Style (IRE) (King's Theatre (IRE)) [2018/19 h106: h15.8g⁶ h15.8gᵖᵘ Jun 6] fair handicap hurdler: stayed 2½m: acted on soft going: wore headgear: dead. *Donald McCain*   **h88**

HITCHCOCK 5 b.g. Equiano (FR) – George's Gift (Haafhd) [2018/19 h16g⁶ h16g⁵ h16d⁶ h16g⁵ h16d⁴ h16.2gᵖᵘ h16g h20v h16d⁶ Apr 27] fair on Flat, stays 8.5f: modest maiden hurdler: left Barry John Murphy after sixth start: unproven beyond 2m: acts on good to soft going: usually in headgear: tried in tongue tie. *R. Donohoe, Ireland*   **h97**

HI THERE SILVER (IRE) 5 gr.g. Clodovil (IRE) – Elaborate (Sadler's Wells (USA)) [2018/19 h–: h19.2gᶠ Aug 23] modest on Flat, stays 1½m: no form over hurdles. *Michael Madgwick*   **h–**

HITHERJACQUES LADY (IRE) 7 br.m. Robin des Champs (FR) – Crackin' Liss (IRE) (Bob Back (USA)) [2018/19 h125: c20vᵖᵘ Nov 11] sturdy mare: has had breathing operation: fairly useful hurdler: pulled up in novice handicap on chasing debut: stays 2¾m: acts on heavy going: front runner/races prominently. *Oliver Sherwood*   **c– h–**

HITMAN FRED (IRE) 6 b.g. Getaway (GER) – Garravagh Lass (IRE) (Oscar (IRE)) [2018/19 b99: h17.1d h16.2g³ h20.8g⁵ h20.2g Apr 25] Irish point winner: fair form over hurdles: should be suited by further than 2m: tried in cheekpieces. *Rose Dobbin*   **h101**

HIT THE HIGHWAY (IRE) 10 b.g. Pierre – Highway Belle (Germany (USA)) [2018/19 c–, h121: h24.2s h21.6s h20.5dᶠ c24s⁵ c19.7g³ Apr 7] useful-looking gelding: point winner: useful hurdler at best, no form in 2018/19: modest maiden chaser nowadays: stays 3m: acts on heavy going: has worn cheekpieces, including last 4 starts: wears tongue tie: races prominently. *Chris Gordon*   **c99 h–**

HIT THE TOP (IRE) 12 b.g. Gold Well – Smooth Leader (IRE) (Supreme Leader) [2018/19 h20.3g⁵ h21.2m Aug 30] fairly useful hurdler at best, no form in 2018/19 after long absence: maiden chaser: stays 21f: acts on good to firm and heavy going. *Sue Smith*   **c– h–**

HIUPINTHESKY (IRE) 6 gr.m. Cloudings (IRE) – Cockpit Rose (IRE) (Be My Native (USA)) [2018/19 h21.4gᶠ Mar 25] point winner: modest form over hurdles: dead. *Oliver Sherwood*   **h92**

HOGAN'S HEIGHT (IRE) 8 b.g. Indian River (FR) – Electre du Berlais (FR) (Royal Charter (FR)) [2018/19 c138, h114: c24.2m³ c20.9gᵖᵘ h19.3g* h25.3m* Feb 26] sturdy gelding: has had breathing operation: fairly useful form over hurdles: won novices at Catterick in January and February: useful handicap chaser: stays 25f: acts on good to firm and heavy going: tried in hood: wears tongue tie. *Jamie Snowden*   **c127 h118**

HOKE COLBURN (IRE) 7 b.g. Beneficial – Ravaleen (IRE) (Executive Perk) [2018/19 h106: h24g c20.3g c23g² c24g⁵ h23g³ c23.6g* c20g* c20dᵖᵘ c19.9s³ Apr 26] compact gelding: fair hurdler: fair handicap chaser: won at Huntingdon and Ludlow (amateurs) in October: left Harry Whittington after second start, Brian Barr after eighth: stays 3m: acts on soft going: often wore cheekpieces/tongue tie in 2018/19: usually races off pace. *B. A. McMahon*   **c111 h104**

HOLBROOK PARK 9 b.g. Midnight Legend – Viciana (Sir Harry Lewis (USA)) [2018/19 c127, h–: c23.5d² c21.2d⁴ c24.2dᵖᵘ c30.7dᴿ c19.4gᵖᵘ Apr 14] compact gelding: has had breathing operation: winning hurdler: fairly useful handicap chaser: stays 3¼m: acts on heavy going: tried in cheekpieces: wears tongue tie: usually races close up. *Neil King*   **c125 h–**

HOLDBACKTHERIVER (IRE) 7 b.g. Presenting – Fairy Lane (IRE) (Old Vic) **c123**
[2018/19 h116: h23.6d⁵ c23.6v⁵ c24d* h23.3v⁴ c23.8s Apr 7] good-topped gelding: fair **h106**
handicap hurdler: fairly useful form over fences: won handicap at Bangor in January: stays
3m: acts on heavy going: usually races off pace. *Evan Williams*

HOLD ME TIGHT (IRE) 5 b.g. Zoffany (IRE) – All Embracing (IRE) (Night Shift **h85**
(USA)) [2018/19 h94: h21.4gᵖᵘ h19.8s⁴ h16d h19.5d⁵ Apr 6] workmanlike gelding: has had
breathing operation: modest maiden hurdler: stays 19f: acts on heavy going: wears tongue
tie. *Polly Gundry*

HOLD THE NOTE (IRE) 5 b.g. Jeremy (USA) – Keys Hope (IRE) (Luso) [2018/19 **h126 p**
b16.8v* b16.4g⁴ h16v³ h19.4g* h20.7d² Feb 17] €24,000 3-y-o: tall, unfurnished gelding: **b105**
second foal: half-brother to fair hurdler Supakalanistic (2½m-23f winner, by Kalanisi):
dam maiden out of sister to smart hurdler (stayed 21f) In Contrast: useful form in bumpers:
won at Newton Abbot (by 6 lengths from Poison Arrow) in October: fourth in listed event
at Cheltenham (2¾ lengths behind Master Debonair) month later: fairly useful form over
hurdles: won novice at Doncaster in December: remains with potential. *Mick Channon*

HOLEINTHEWALL BAR (IRE) 11 b.g. Westerner – Cockpit Lady (IRE) **c87**
(Commanche Run) [2018/19 c99, h–: c16.5g⁶ c15.7g² c17g⁵ c15.6g c21s⁵ c19.4d c20.2g **h–**
c16.5g⁶ Mar 19] workmanlike gelding: winning hurdler: modest handicap chaser
nowadays: stays 21f: acts on good to firm and heavy going: wears headgear: tried in tongue
tie. *Tracey Barfoot-Saunt*

HOLLINS HILL 9 b.g. Lucarno (USA) – Bonnie Buttons (Lord Bud) [2018/19 c21.2d³ **c–**
Aug 25] maiden hurdler: tailed off in novice on chasing debut. *Sam England* **h–**

HOLLOW PARK (IRE) 8 b.m. Flemensfirth (USA) – Love And Beauty (IRE) **c80**
(Presenting) [2018/19 h77: h25m² h23.3gᵖᵘ c25.8mᵖᵘ h25.8s³ c23g² Oct 24] runner-up in **h79**
Irish point: poor handicap hurdler: similar form in chases: stays 3¼m: acts on soft and good
to firm going: tried in cheekpieces: wears tongue tie: front runner/races prominently.
Katy Price

HOLLY BUSH HENRY (IRE) 8 b.g. Yeats (IRE) – Maslam (IRE) (Robellino (USA)) **c130**
[2018/19 c131, h132: h21g h23.4v⁶ c23.8d² c29.5sᵖᵘ h25g h26s c24.2d⁶ c27.7d³ Mar 18] **h96**
lengthy gelding: has had breathing operation: useful handicap hurdler, below form in
2018/19: useful handicap chaser: second at Ludlow (2 lengths behind Beau du Brizais) in
December: stays 25f: acts on good to firm and heavy going: wears headgear: has worn
tongue tie, including last 2 starts. *Phil Middleton*

HOLLY FLIGHT (FR) 7 b.m. Walk In The Park (IRE) – Lover Flight (FR) (Saint Cyrien **c110**
(FR)) [2018/19 h116: h16g⁵ c20g⁶ c18m c17gᵖᵘ c21g³ c22g³ c23sᵘʳ c23s⁴ c23g⁴ c22.5s⁴ **h110**
c20d³ Apr 22] won point in January: fair handicap chaser: fair maiden chaser: left Dan
Skelton after second start: stays 2¾m: acts on soft going: has worn hood: wears tongue tie:
usually races in rear. *Paul O'Flynn, Ireland*

HOLLYWOOD ALL STAR (IRE) 10 b.g. Kheleyf (USA) – Camassina (IRE) (Taufan **h–**
(USA)) [2018/19 h95: h16.7s⁵ h15.8vᵖᵘ h15.8sᵖᵘ Feb 26] compact gelding: fair hurdler at
best, no form in 2018/19: wears headgear. *Graeme McPherson*

HOLLYWOOD KEN (IRE) 6 b.g. Arcano (IRE) – Third Dimension (FR) (Suave **h–**
Dancer (USA)) [2018/19 h114: h16vᵖᵘ h16dᵖᵘ Feb 23] workmanlike gelding: has had
breathing operation: fair hurdler at best, no form in 2018/19: stays 2¼m: acts on soft going:
has worn headgear: wears tongue tie: often races freely. *Fiona Shaw*

HOLME ABBEY 6 b.g. Fair Mix (IRE) – Brockwell Abbey (Central Park (IRE)) **b83**
[2018/19 b16v⁶ b16s⁴ h16.2g⁴ Apr 15] first foal: dam, ran once in bumper, out of sister to
high-class staying chaser Grey Abbey: modest form in bumpers: will prove suited by
2½m+. *Nicky Richards*

HOLRYALE (IRE) 7 b.g. Trans Island – Lady Ramona (IRE) (Lord Americo) [2018/19 **c124**
h109, b90: h17.7g² h20.6g² h19.9g* h20m³ c16.5g* h17.7g² c16.5gᵖᵘ c16s³ c16.4gᵖᵘ **h113**
c20.3g⁶ c17.2mᵘʳ Apr 21] has had breathing operation: fair hurdler: won maiden at
Uttoxeter in June: fairly useful form over fences: won novice handicap at Worcester in
August: barely stays 21f: acts on good to firm going: sometimes in cheekpieces: wears
tongue tie. *Dan Skelton*

HOLY STREET (IRE) 7 b.g. Presenting – Vigna Maggio (FR) (Starborough) [2018/19 **c90**
h91: c25.2g² h26g c21.2gᵘʳ Mar 4] maiden hurdler: modest form over fences: stays 25f: **h–**
acts on good to soft going: in headgear last 3 starts. *Laura Morgan*

HOMING STAR 4 b.f. Harbour Watch (IRE) – Nightunderthestars (Observatory (USA)) **h69**
[2018/19 h16g h18.7s h16.2g Mar 26] modest on Flat, stays 1½m: poor form over hurdles.
Graeme McPherson

HONDA FIFTY (IRE) 5 b.g. Arakan (USA) – Shuil Le Vic (IRE) (Old Vic) [2018/19 **b78**
b16.4d² Mar 5] 50/1, second in maiden bumper at Newcastle (16 lengths behind Crypto).
Donald Whillans

HONEST VIC (IRE) 6 b.g. Kalanisi (IRE) – Miss Vic Lovin (IRE) (Old Vic) [2018/19 **h125**
h122p, b90: h20.6g⁶ h14d⁴ h21.2d² h21.4g⁵ h19.3d² h21sᵘʳ h20.3g⁵ Apr 17] medium-sized
gelding: bumper winner: fairly useful handicap hurdler: second at Ascot in February: stays
21f: acts on good to soft going: in headgear last 3 starts. *Henry Daly*

HONEY B 5 b.m. Shirocco (GER) – Bathwick Babe (IRE) (Sri Pekan (USA)) [2018/19 **b–**
b16.8g b16d Aug 29] half-sister to fairly useful hurdler/useful chaser Weather Babe (2m-
3m winner, by Storming Home) and modest 2m hurdle winner Bathwick Junior (by Reset):
dam, 13f winner, half-sister to fairly useful hurdler (stayed 3m) Tritonville Lodge: in
tongue tie, well held in bumpers. *Michael Blake*

HONEY BOO 6 ch.m. Tobougg (IRE) – Queen of The Bees (IRE) (Bob Back (USA)) **b–**
[2018/19 b16g third foal: half-sister to fair hurdler Easy Beesy (2½m-3m winner,
by Kalanisi): dam ran twice in bumpers: tailed off in mares bumper. *Geoffrey Deacon*

HONEYCHILE RYDER 8 ch.m. Black Sam Bellamy (IRE) – Dusky Dante (IRE) **c–**
(Phardante (FR)) [2018/19 c–, h65: h23.9g h17.2g⁵ h22.1g* h20.2g⁵ Jun 23] poor handicap **h70**
hurdler: won mares selling event at Cartmel in May: tailed off when refused last sole outing
over fences: stays 2¾m: acts on soft going: has worn headgear, including last 4 starts.
Dianne Sayer

HONEY P (IRE) 8 b.m. Winged Love (IRE) – Luck's A Lady (IRE) (Insan (USA)) **h–**
[2018/19 b–: h17.7g May 9] well beaten in bumper/maiden hurdle. *Rebecca Woodman*

HONEYSUCKLE 5 b.m. Sulamani (IRE) – First Royal (GER) (Lando (GER)) [2018/19 **h140 p**
h20g* h16g* h18s* h20g* Apr 21] €9,500 3-y-o, €110,000 4-y-o: fourth foal: half-sister to
winning pointers by Dr Massini and Black Sam Bellamy: dam German 1m winner: point
winner: useful form over hurdles: unbeaten in 4 starts, winning mares maiden at Fairyhouse
in November, listed mares novice at Thurles (by 3¼ lengths from Sassy Diva) in December,
and Solerina Mares Novices' Hurdle (by 6 lengths from Western Victory) in January and
Irish Stallion Farms EBF Mares Novices' Hurdle Championship Final (by 5½ lengths from
Elfile) in April, both also at Fairyhouse: stays 2½m: acts on soft going: will go on
improving. *Henry de Bromhead, Ireland*

HONORABLE (FR) 4 b.g. Lawman (FR) – Petite Noblesse (FR) (Galileo (IRE)) **h105**
[2018/19 h16sᵘʳ h15.7d⁵ h16.7d² h16g h18.7s⁵ h15.7m Mar 31] neat gelding: fairly useful
on Flat, stays 15f: fair form over hurdles: unproven beyond 17f: acts on good to soft going.
Gary Moore

HONOURABLE EXIT (IRE) 12 b.g. Exit To Nowhere (USA) – Honor Love (FR) **c–**
(Pursuit of Love) [2018/19 c78, h–: c16.1d⁴ Feb 28] multiple point winner: maiden hurdler: **h–**
little impact in chases: has worn hood. *J. Tickle*

Irish Stallions Farm EBF Mares' Novices' Hurdle Championship Final, Fairyhouse—
Honeysuckle maintains her unbeaten record with a very impressive display

HONOURABLE GENT 11 b.g. Gentleman's Deal (IRE) – Gudasmum (Primitive Rising (USA)) [2018/19 c16g* c16g³ c16g² c17.1m³ Sep 19] winning hurdler: fair handicap chaser: won at Perth in June: stays 2¼m: acts on soft and good to firm going: wears hood. *Rose Dobbin* **c112 h–**

HONOURARY GIFT (IRE) 6 b.g. City Honours (USA) – Zaffalong (IRE) (Zaffaran (USA)) [2018/19 b16.8g* b16s h19.5d h16.8s* h16.2g⁴ Apr 15] third foal: half-brother to fair 3m chase winner Mollies Gent (by Court Cave): dam ran once in bumper: fairly useful form in bumpers: won at Sedgefield in October, only start for Peter Fahey: fair form over hurdles: won novice at same course in March: should stay beyond 2m: in hood last 3 starts. *James Ewart* **h110 b96**

HONOURMISSION (FR) 5 b.g. Linda's Lad – Orabelle (FR) (Freedom Cry) [2018/19 b14g⁴ h19.7d h16.3d h16g Apr 10] fourth foal: brother to French 1¼m winner Larabelle (fairly useful maiden over jumps): dam, French 17f chase winner, also 11f/1½m winner on Flat: well held in bumper: modest form over hurdles: remains capable of better. *Harry Whittington* **h85 p b62**

HOO BALLY DIVA (IRE) 8 b.m. Scorpion (IRE) – Dr Sandra (IRE) (Dr Massini (IRE)) [2018/19 h96: h25m* c24.2m² c24.2s² c24s⁴ Dec 4] sturdy mare: fair form over hurdles: won handicap at Warwick in May: similar form over fences: stays 3¼m: acts on soft and good to firm going. *Bob Buckler* **c106 h102**

HOOK LANE ROOBEE 6 b.g. Spendent – Sharp Action (Overbury (IRE)) [2018/19 b94: h20.5spu h17.7v h20.7dpu Feb 17] good-topped gelding: bumper winner: poor form over hurdles: should stay at least 2½m. *Suzy Smith* **h54**

HOOLIGAN JACK 6 ch.g. Daylami (IRE) – Stravaigin (Primitive Rising (USA)) [2018/19 h–: h20.5g⁴ h23.3g³ May 12] poor form over hurdles: in cheekpieces last 2 starts. *Iain Jardine* **h83**

HOOT AT MIDNIGHT 4 b.f. Midnight Legend – Kahooting (Kahyasi) [2018/19 b12.6s⁴ b16.8g Apr 18] third foal: dam unraced out of useful 2m-2¼m hurdle winner Perle de Puce: modest form in bumpers: better effort when fourth in fillies junior event at Newbury: in tongue tie second start. *Charlie Longsdon* **b81**

HOOVER FEVER 5 b.m. Compton Place – Aswaaq (IRE) (Peintre Celebre (USA)) [2018/19 h18.7m h21.6g² h21.6g³ h16.8g h16.8g h26.5dpu h18.5g h19m⁴ h15.3g⁶ h19dpu Nov 29] half-sister to fair hurdler Stonecoldsoba (2m-2½m winner, by Aqlaam): poor maiden on Flat: poor maiden hurdler: stays 2¾m: acts on good to firm going: tried in blinkers/tongue tie. *Colin Tizzard* **h83**

HOPE AND GLORIA 4 b.f. Schiaparelli (GER) – Frangipani Lady (Milan) [2018/19 b16m⁵ Apr 22] first foal: dam twice-raced half-sister to fairly useful hurdlers Smart Mover (stayed 25f) and Malindi Bay (stayed 2¾m): mid-field in mares maiden bumper. *Fergal O'Brien* **b55**

HOPE FOR GLORY 10 b.g. Proclamation (IRE) – Aissa (Dr Devious (IRE)) [2018/19 c83, h–: c16.4sF c19.2s⁶ Dec 6] maiden hurdler: poor handicap chaser: unproven beyond 2m: often wore headgear: wore tongue tie: dead. *Maurice Barnes* **c78 h–**

HOPE'S WISHES 9 b.m. Kayf Tara – Otarie (FR) (Lute Antique (FR)) [2018/19 c92, h102: c16.3g⁴ c20.9g⁴ h16.2g² h16.7g⁶ h15.5g⁶ c17.5v³ c16g⁴ c15.9m² h15.9s* h19.8m h15.8v⁶ Mar 16] tall mare: modest maiden hurdler: won at Plumpton (conditionals) in February: fair form over fences: stays 21f: acts on good to firm and heavy going: tried in cheekpieces. *Barry Brennan* **c101 h94**

HOPONANDSEE 8 b.m. Nomadic Way (USA) – Jago's Girl (Bob's Return (IRE)) [2018/19 h15.8g h16.8g* h18.7g² h16g³ h18.7g h19.9g h15.5g⁴ Dec 6] modest handicap hurdler: won mares event at Newton Abbot in August: stays 19f: acts on good to firm going. *Nigel Twiston-Davies* **h87**

HORATIO HORNBLOWER (IRE) 11 b.g. Presenting – Countess Camilla (Bob's Return (IRE)) [2018/19 c121, h–: c24d⁵ c23.4d³ c25.5dur c24.2s³ c23.8mpu c23.8s⁵ Apr 7] rangy gelding: winning hurdler: fairly useful handicap chaser: third at Newbury in January: stays 3m: acts on good to firm and heavy going: wears cheekpieces. *Nick Williams* **c117 h–**

HORST (FR) 5 b.g. Soldier Hollow – Sternenkonigin (IRE) (Samum (GER)) [2018/19 h16.9g* c16.9g* c18.9s* c18.4d³ h16.9g* c17.1d³ c15.2dF h15.7m⁵ h16gF Mar 29] has had breathing operation: fair on Flat in Germany (winner at 1m): fairly useful hurdler: won 4-y-o event at Nancy in May and claimer at Cholet in September: similar form over fences: won 4-y-o events at Nancy in May and June: left Guillaume Macaire after fifth start: little show in Britain: stays 19f: acts on heavy going: usually leads. *Micky Hammond* **c118 h116**

HOSTILE 5 ch.g. Malinas (GER) – Skew (Niniski (USA)) [2018/19 b16d² Mar 28] **b103**
€40,000 3-y-o: half-brother to several winners, including useful hurdler/high-class chaser
Valdez (2m/17f winner), stays 2½m, and fair hurdler/fairly useful chaser Skewiff (2m-23f
winner), both by Doyen: dam unraced: 16/1, green when second in maiden bumper at
Warwick (1½ lengths behind Welsh Saint). *Alan King*

HOT GOSSIP (IRE) 5 b.m. Fast Company (IRE) – On The Make (IRE) (Entrepreneur) **h82**
[2018/19 h78: h16.2g h17.1d⁶ h17.1g⁵ h19.5v² Nov 29] poor maiden hurdler: likely to stay
further than 2½m: acts on heavy going. *Dianne Sayer*

HOT RYAN 6 b.m. Midnight Legend – Darn Hot (Sir Harry Lewis (USA)) [2018/19 b–: **h88**
b16d⁶ h21g h21.4g⁶ h21.4g⁴ h23.1s³ h23.1d Apr 9] rather unfurnished mare: has had **b69**
breathing operation: point winner: poor form in bumpers: modest form over hurdles: stays
23f: acts on soft going. *David Pipe*

HOT SMOKED 6 br.m. Eastern Anthem (IRE) – Waheeba (Pivotal) [2018/19 b–: b15.3m⁵ **h86**
h21d h21dᵖᵘ h17.7d⁶ h15.3g h16.8s² Mar 18] modest form in bumpers/over hurdles: should **b78**
prove suited by 2¼m+: acts on soft going: in cheekpieces last 2 starts. *Robert Walford*

HOTTER THAN HELL (FR) 5 ch.m. No Risk At All (FR) – Ombrelle (FR) (Octagonal **b91**
(NZ)) [2018/19 b95: b15.8d b16.6g² b16.3d⁶ Mar 23] fair form in bumpers. *Alan King*

HOTT LIPS 7 b.m. Midnight Legend – Major Hoolihan (Soldier Rose) [2018/19 b16d **b–**
Nov 28] seventh foal: half-sister to 3 winners by Kayf Tara, including useful hurdler/smart
chaser Ad Idem (2¾m winner) and fairly useful hurdler/useful chaser Gone Too Far
(2m-2½m winner): dam winning pointer: tailed off in mares bumper: won 3 times in points
in 2019. *James Evans*

HOUBLON DES OBEAUX (FR) 12 b.g. Panoramic – Harkosa (FR) (Nikos) [2018/19 **c142 §**
c142, h–: c23.6v⁶ c22.9v⁶ c24.2d* c24.2s c26d³ c24.5vᵖᵘ Mar 17] good-topped gelding: **h–**
winning hurdler: useful handicap chaser: won Veterans' Handicap Chase Final at Sandown
(by 15 lengths from Theatre Guide) in January: stays 3¼m: acts on heavy going: usually
wears headgear: temperamental. *Venetia Williams*

HOUNDSCOURT (IRE) 12 b.g. Court Cave (IRE) – Broken Rein (IRE) (Orchestra) **c86 §**
[2018/19 c–§, h88§: h24g⁶ h23.3g c24.2gᵇᵈ c23.9s* c26.7d³ c23.9d* c26.3s³ c21.4d⁴ **h57 §**
c26.3g⁶ Apr 5] poor handicap hurdler: modest handicap chaser: won at Market Rasen in
December and January: stays 27f: acts on heavy going: usually in headgear: wears tongue
tie: usually races prominently: unreliable. *Joanne Foster*

*Unibet Veterans' Handicap Chase (Series Final), Sandown—2018 winner Buywise departs at the
last to leave the gambled-on Houblon des Obeaux well clear*

HOUSE ISLAND (IRE) 5 ch.g. Casamento (IRE) – Fuaigh Mor (IRE) (Dubai **b102**
Destination (USA)) [2018/19 b17.7g² b16m² b16.3d* Mar 22] €11,500 3-y-o: strong,
compact gelding: half-brother to useful/untrustworthy winner up to 7f
Lexington Times (by Paco Boy): dam 5f winner: fairly useful hurdler in bumpers: won listed
event at Newbury (by neck from Nobby) in March: left Anthony Honeyball after first start.
Paul Webber

HOUSESOFPARLIAMENT (IRE) 6 ch.g. Galileo (IRE) – Sharp Lisa (USA) **h139**
(Dixieland Band (USA)) [2018/19 h17d h16.3g² h24g* Jun 23] useful handicap hurdler:
won at Gowran (by 1¾ lengths from High Nellie) in June: stays 3m: acts on heavy going:
has worn hood, including in 2018/19: usually wears tongue tie. *Joseph Patrick O'Brien,
Ireland*

HOWABOUTNEVER (IRE) 11 b.g. Shantou (USA) – Sarah's Cottage (IRE) **h– §**
(Topanoora) [2018/19 h92§: h23g Jun 11] smallish gelding: fairly useful hurdler at best,
behind sole outing in 2018/19: stays 3¼m: acts on heavy going: wears headgear: ungenuine.
Roger Teal

HOWLING MILAN 5 b.g. Milan – Fantasia Filly (FR) (Dadarissime (FR)) **h130**
[2018/19 h16.3s h16.3d⁶ h16.3d* Jan 16] €42,000 3-y-o: tall gelding: fifth foal: dam,
French 2m/17f hurdle/chase winner, half-sister to smart chaser (stayed 3m) Tresor de Mai:
first past post second start in Irish points: useful form over hurdles: much improved when
won novice at Newbury (by 26 lengths from Born To Please) in January. *Samuel Drinkwater*

HOWLONGISAFOOT (IRE) 10 b.g. Beneficial – Miss Vic (IRE) (Old Vic) [2018/19 **c100**
c–, h–: h21.7g² h21.7g² h23m* h23g h23g c23m² c21.6m⁴ c17g⁵ Apr 7] strong gelding: **h92**
modest handicap hurdler: won at Worcester in July: fair handicap chaser: stays 3m: acts on
good to firm and heavy going: wears headgear. *Chris Gordon*

HOW MUCH IS ENOUGH (IRE) 8 b.m. Moon Ballet (IRE) – Silankka (Slip Anchor) **c–**
[2018/19 h16.7g h20.1sᵖᵘ h23.1gᵖᵘ h23vᵖᵘ h24.1dᵖᵘ Mar 19] fourth on completed start in **h–**
points: no form under Rules. *Stella Barclay*

HOWS JOHNNY 6 b.g. Multiplex – Compton Chick (IRE) (Dolphin Street (FR)) **h93**
[2018/19 b–: h16.7m h19.9g Sep 12] fell all 3 starts in points: well held in bumper: modest
form over hurdles. *John Wainwright*

HOW'S MY FRIEND 14 b.g. Karinga Bay – Friendly Lady (New Member) [2018/19 **c87**
c97, h–: c23.5v c25.1s⁴ c26.7g⁴ c24.2dᵖᵘ Apr 9] workmanlike gelding: maiden hurdler: **h–**
modest handicap chaser: stays 27f: acts on good to firm and heavy going: has worn tongue
tie: usually races towards rear. *Grant Cann*

HOW'S VIENNA (IRE) 9 b.g. Westerner – Plant A Smacker (IRE) (Goldmark (USA)) **c–**
[2018/19 c23.8sᵖᵘ c26.7gᵖᵘ c26v³ Dec 26] sturdy gelding: maiden hurdler: modest chaser **h–**
at best, no form in 2018/19: tried in cheekpieces. *Mark Shears*

HOWTH SUMMIT 6 b.g. Stowaway – Rapid Heartbeat (IRE) (Old Vic) [2018/19 **h103**
h20g h16m* h16d⁵ h20d⁴ h24.1s⁵ Dec 8] fair form over hurdles: won maiden at Cork in
July: left Joseph Patrick O'Brien after third start: probably stayed 3m: acted on good to
firm and good to soft going: tongue tied first 3 starts: dead. *Pauline Robson*

HOWWOULDUNO (IRE) 11 b.g. Desert King (IRE) – Whadouno (IRE) (Abednego) **c– §**
[2018/19 h20.1gᵖᵘ May 12] lengthy gelding: maiden pointer: fairly useful hurdler at best, **h– §**
lightly raced and no form under Rules since 2016/17: winning chaser: stays 2½m: acts on
soft and good to firm going: tried in hood: has worn tongue tie: one to treat with caution
(has refused to race). *Liam Lennon, Ireland*

HUDSON YARD (IRE) 5 b.m. Yeats (IRE) – That's Moyne (IRE) (Flemensfirth (USA)) **b68**
[2018/19 b15.8d Mar 30] second foal: half-sister to a winning pointer by Scorpion: dam 3m
hurdle winner/winning pointer: winning pointer: 8/1, eighth in mares bumper at Uttoxeter
(19¼ lengths behind Wynn House): will be suited by further than 2m. *Emma Lavelle*

HUFF AND PUFF 12 b.g. Azamour (IRE) – Coyote (Indian Ridge) [2018/19 c123, h–: **c123**
c23.8g c25.6d* c24.2d² Feb 15] tall, workmanlike gelding: winning hurdler: fairly useful **h–**
handicap chaser: won at Ludlow in January: second in Royal Artillery Gold Cup (Amateur
Riders) at Sandown: stays 3¼m: acts on good to firm and heavy going: front runner/races
prominently. *Venetia Williams*

HUGOS HORSE (FR) 6 gr.g. Turgeon (USA) – Bella Eria (FR) (Nikos) [2018/19 h–: **c94**
h21m⁴ h21.6m³ c23.8g⁵ c23d Dec 13] good-topped gelding: point winner: modest form **h90**
over hurdles/fences: tried in cheekpieces: in tongue tie last 4 starts: dead. *Paul Nicholls*

HUGOS OTHER HORSE 5 b.g. Gold Well – Wicked Crack (IRE) (King's Ride) **b92**
[2018/19 b15.3d⁴ b17.7d* Feb 24] £80,000 3-y-o: seventh foal: closely related to very
smart hurdler/top-class chaser Cue Card (2m-25f winner, by King's Theatre) and
half-brother to fair hurdler/fairly useful chaser Hidden Crack (2m-2½m winner, by Lahib)
and fairly useful 21f chase winner Sidetracked (by Beneficial): dam (c137/h137) 21f-3m
hurdle/chase winner: fair form in bumpers: won maiden at Fontwell in February.
Paul Nicholls

HUGO'S REFLECTION (IRE) 7 b.g. Robin des Champs (FR) – Dawn Court **c108**
(Rakaposhi King) [2018/19 h–, b–: h19.7s h23sᶠ h21d⁶ c21.4g* c19.4d² Apr 6] rangy **h78**
gelding: has had breathing operation: poor form over hurdles: fair form over fences: won
novice handicap at Market Rasen in March: stays 21f: acts on soft going: in tongue tie last
2 starts. *Ben Case*

HUMBLE HERO (IRE) 5 b.g. High Chaparral (IRE) – Alamouna (IRE) (Indian Ridge) **h129 p**
[2018/19 h15.5g² h15.8g² h16.3d* h16g³ Apr 27] sturdy gelding: useful on Flat, stays
16.5f: fairly useful form over hurdles: won novice at Newbury in March: third in novice
handicap at Sandown: will stay beyond 2m: in tongue tie last 2 starts: open to further
improvement. *Dan Skelton*

HUMPHREY BOGART (IRE) 6 b.g. Tagula (IRE) – Hazarama (IRE) (Kahyasi) **h116 p**
[2018/19 h–p: h15.8g* May 28] smart on Flat, stays 1½m: fairly useful form over hurdles:
won maiden at Huntingdon on sole outing in 2018/19: tried in hood: open to further
improvement. *Nicky Henderson*

HUMPS AND BUMPS (IRE) 6 b.m. Court Cave (IRE) – Cat Burglar (IRE) (Robellino **h88**
(USA)) [2018/19 b16s⁶ b20g h21m⁵ h20.5g h24g b20g h18.8dᶠ h16g h18.8d⁶ h22.7g h20v **b–**
h24.6s² Apr 26] fourth foal: closely related to bumper winner/fairly useful hurdler
Gettysburg Address (2½m/21f winner, by Milan), stays 3m, and half-sister to fairly useful
hurdler/chaser Skylander (17f-23f winner, by Flemensfirth): dam maiden on Flat: point
winner: tailed off in maiden bumper: modest maiden hurdler: stays 25f: acts on soft and
good to firm going: tried in cheekpieces. *Peter Croke, Ireland*

HUNTRESS (IRE) 7 b.m. Flemensfirth (USA) – Madgehil (IRE) (Anshan) [2018/19 h60: **h–**
h16g h17.7m May 27] compact mare: bumper winner: little show over hurdles. *Suzy Smith*

HUNTSMANS JOG (IRE) 5 b.g. Milan – Faucon (Polar Falcon (USA)) [2018/19 b16g² **h113**
b17s⁴ h20v³ h23.6dᵖᵘ Jan 18] closely related to 2 winners, including bumper winner/useful **b86**
hurdler As I Am (2m-2½m winner, by Old Vic), and half-brother to 2 winners, including
bumper winner/fairly useful hurdler Western Way (19f-3m winner, by Westerner): dam
French 11f winner: fair form in bumpers: similar form over hurdles: better effort when third
in novice at Carlisle. *Don Cantillon*

HUNTSMAN SON (IRE) 9 b.g. Millenary – Daly Lady (IRE) (Lord of Appeal) **c134**
[2018/19 h129: c16.2g² c20s⁶ c16.4g² c19.9d* c20.2s Mar 12] well-made gelding: has had **h–**
breathing operation: fairly useful hurdler: useful form over fences: won novice at Newbury
(by 5 lengths from Slate House) in March: stays 21f: acts on heavy going: in tongue tie last
3 starts: usually races towards rear. *Alex Hales*

HURLSTONE POINT 6 br.m. Scorpion (IRE) – Dudeen (IRE) (Anshan) [2018/19 h–, **h92**
b–: h20g² h19.5d h23.1g h19dᵖᵘ Dec 30] has had breathing operation: modest form over
hurdles: stays 2½m: tried in cheekpieces/tongue tie. *Philip Hobbs*

HURRICANE ARCADIO (IRE) 5 b.g. Arcadio (GER) – Back To Favour (IRE) (Bob **h69**
Back (USA)) [2018/19 h19.5dᵖᵘ h15.3g⁶ Feb 16] placed both starts in Irish points: poor
form over hurdles: in hood first start. *Michael Blake*

HURRICANE DYLAN (IRE) 8 b.g. Brian Boru – Definetly Sarah (IRE) (Definite **c128**
Article) [2018/19 h116: h19.9m* h21g c25.2g² c24v³ c22.7m* c23d³ c23.4dᵖᵘ Mar 2] **h110**
good-topped gelding: fair hurdler: won novice at Uttoxeter in May: fairly useful form over
fences: won handicap at Leicester in February: stays 25f: acts on good to firm and heavy
going: front runner/races prominently. *Kevin Frost*

HURRICANE HARVEY 5 b.g. Doyen (IRE) – Camp Fire (IRE) (Lahib (USA)) **b94**
[2018/19 b16.8s² b15.7g² b16.3g³ Mar 30] £50,000 4-y-o: brother to useful hurdler/smart
chaser Kumbeshwar (2m/17f winner) and half-brother to several winners on Flat: dam 6f
winner: placed on second of 2 starts in Irish points: fair form in bumpers: placed all 3 starts.
Fergal O'Brien

HURRICANE HUGO 6 b.g. Iktibas – Nativus (IRE) (Be My Native (USA)) [2018/19 **b81**
ab16.3s⁶ ab16.3sᵖᵘ Feb 23] modest form in bumpers. *Philip Kirby*

HURRICANE MINNIE 6 b.m. Authorized (IRE) – Hurricane Milly (IRE) (Milan) **h85**
[2018/19 b77: h16d h15.5d h17.7d⁵ h16g⁴ h16.5d Apr 24] modest form over hurdles: wears
hood: usually leads/races freely. *Michael Scudamore*

HURRICANE RITA (FR) 9 gr.m. Sagamix (FR) – Madonna da Rossi (Mtoto) [2018/19 **c95**
h95: h20.3g⁶ c16.5gᶠ c16.5g³ c15.6g⁵ c17.2gᵖᵘ c16.5g² c17m⁵ c19.9m⁴ h15.7d c20.9s⁵ **h86**
c16.2d⁶ h16gᵘʳ h15.8d⁵ c16.4vᵖᵘ Mar 12] modest handicap hurdler: modest maiden chaser:
stays 2¾m: acts on heavy going: has worn headgear/tongue strap, including in 2018/19.
Conor Dore

HURRICANE VIC 9 b.g. Mount Nelson – Fountains Abbey (USA) (Giant's Causeway **c91**
(USA)) [2018/19 c20.9s³ c19.3g² Apr 23] tall, strong gelding: point winner: maiden **h–**
hurdler: modest form in chases: stays 21f: acts on soft going. *S. Robinson*

HURRY HENRY (IRE) 10 b.g. Blueprint (IRE) – Tower Princess (IRE) (King's Ride) **c–**
[2018/19 c–, h–: h15.9s c20s⁶ c19.4dᵖᵘ Jan 18] sturdy gelding: winning hurdler/maiden **h–**
chaser, no form since 2016/17: has worn cheekpieces, including last 2 starts: has worn
tongue tie, including in 2018/19. *Richenda Ford*

HUSSAR BALLAD (USA) 10 b.g. Hard Spun (USA) – Country Melody (USA) (Gone **h–**
West (USA)) [2018/19 h16.7mᵖᵘ Aug 5] fair on Flat, stays 1¾m: pulled up in maiden on
hurdling debut. *Antony Brittain*

HYMN AND A PRAYER 6 br.g. Eastern Anthem (IRE) – Kryssa (Kris) [2018/19 b81: **h77 p**
b16.8g³ b17.7g h15.3g h17.7sᵇᵈ h15.3g⁵ Feb 27] modest form in bumpers: poor form over **b81**
hurdles: in hood last 3 starts: remains capable of better. *Fiona Shaw*

I

IAMNOLADY 6 b.m. Millkom – Turbo Linn (Turbo Speed) [2018/19 b16.2g May 27] **b–**
second foal: dam (b118), unbeaten in 5 bumpers (also smart 1½m winner on Flat), sister to
fair hurdler/fairly useful chaser Bishops Heir (stayed 27f): in tongue tie, 17/2, well held in
bumper. *Susan Corbett*

I AM PLASTERED 4 b.g. Midnight Legend – One For Joules (IRE) (Choisir (AUS)) **b60**
[2018/19 b14d⁴ Nov 29] 4/1, well-held fourth in bumper at Warwick. *John Flint*

I AM SAM 8 b.g. Black Sam Bellamy (IRE) – Flinders (Henbit (USA)) [2018/19 c78, h82: **c75**
c25.7g⁵ c21.6g Jun 16] tall gelding: maiden pointer: poor form over hurdles/fences: often **h–**
in hood. *Emma Lavelle*

IAN'S GIFT (IRE) 6 b.g. Brian Boru – Cindy's Fancy (IRE) (Shernazar) [2018/19 b17s⁶ **b–**
Mar 7] 66/1, little impression in bumper at Carlisle. *George Bewley*

IBIS DU RHEU (FR) 8 b.g. Blue Bresil (FR) – Dona du Rheu (FR) (Dom Pasquini (FR)) **c142**
[2018/19 c134, h–: c24.4g⁴ c25.3g² c29.2g c24.1mᵖᵘ Apr 13] well-made gelding: winning **h–**
hurdler: useful chaser: won novice at Cheltenham (by length from Theatre Territory) in
November: stays 3m: acts on heavy going: has worn headgear, including final start: wears
tongue tie. *Paul Nicholls*

IBSEN (IRE) 10 b.g. Dubawi (IRE) – Really (IRE) (Entrepreneur) [2018/19 h–: h20g **h93**
h22.4m h23.9gᵖᵘ Sep 26] small, close-coupled gelding: fairly useful hurdler at best, well
below form since 2016/17: stays 2¾m: acts on heavy going: usually wears headgear: wears
tongue tie. *Gordon Elliott, Ireland*

I CAN'T EXPLAIN (IRE) 6 b.g. Getaway (GER) – Dr Sandra (IRE) (Dr Massini (IRE)) **h126**
[2018/19 h16v* h20.3d² h19.3dᵖᵘ Feb 16] €15,000 3-y-o: deep-girthed gelding: fifth foal:
brother to a winning pointer and half-brother to fair hurdler Hoo Bally Diva (3m/25f
winner, by Scorpion): dam unraced half-sister to Hennessy Gold Cup winner Strong Flow:
easy winner of Irish point on debut: fairly useful form over hurdles: won novice at
Sandown in December. *Nicky Henderson*

ICE COOL CHAMPS (IRE) 8 ch.g. Robin des Champs (FR) – Last of Many (IRE) **c–**
(Lahib (USA)) [2018/19 c122, h128: h23.4v⁴ h22.8s⁴ c24.2d⁶ Feb 22] well-made gelding: **h130**
useful form over hurdles: fourth in handicap at Haydock (3½ lengths behind Tomkevi) in
December: fairly useful form at best over fences: stays 3m: acts on heavy going: has joined
Kerry Lee. *Philip Hobbs*

ICEFALL (IRE) 6 b.g. Frozen Power (IRE) – Silvertine (IRE) (Alzao (USA)) [2018/19 **h102**
h15.8g² h16.7m² h17.2d³ h16.2g² h19.9m³ h16.2s⁴ h16.2g h15.6g⁶ h18.6s Dec 26] fair
maiden hurdler: stays 2½m: acts on good to firm and good to soft going: in headgear last 4
starts. *Tim Easterby*

ICE GALLEY (IRE) 6 br.g. Galileo (IRE) – Ice Queen (IRE) (Danehill Dancer (IRE)) **h106**
[2018/19 h21.3s^{pu} h19.3s h16d^6 h16.4g^5 h18.6g* h20.6g^5 Apr 3] sturdy gelding: fair but
temperamental on Flat, stays 2m: fair form over hurdles: won conditionals handicap at
Market Rasen in March after breathing operation: should be suited by at least 2½m.
Philip Kirby

ICE KONIG (FR) 10 gr.g. Epalo (GER) – Isarwelle (GER) (Sternkoenig (IRE)) [2018/19 **h82**
h85: h16.8g^3 h21.7m^4 h21.6g^4 h18.5s^{pu} h19g h16.5d Apr 4] rather leggy gelding: poor
handicap hurdler: stays 2¾m: acts on soft and good to firm going: tried in blinkers: has
worn tongue tie, including in 2018/19. *Jimmy Frost*

ICE TRES 10 br.m. Iceman – Tup Tim (Emperor Jones (USA)) [2018/19 h85: h16.8g^5 **h92**
h15.3m* May 15] modest handicap hurdler: won at Wincanton in May: unproven beyond
17f: acts on good to firm and good to soft going: usually wears headgear: has worn tongue
tie: front runner/races prominently. *Chris Down*

ICONIC BELLE 5 ch.m. Sixties Icon – Five Bells (IRE) (Rock of Gibraltar (IRE)) **h112**
[2018/19 h15.6g* h16.2s^4 h19.8g^F h16.4s^4 h16.6d^4 h19.8m^2 Mar 22] half-sister to fair
hurdlers Ding Ding (2m-2½m winner) and Marmont (2m winner), both by Winker Watson:
fairly useful on Flat, stays 1½m: fair form over hurdles: won mares novice at Musselburgh
in November: stays 2½m: acts on good to firm going. *Philip Kirby*

ICONIC MUDDLE 6 gr.g. Sixties Icon – Spatham Rose (Environment Friend) [2018/19 **h68**
h16.3s h16.3s Dec 19] rather leggy gelding: well held in 2 maiden hurdles. *Gary Moore*

I'D BETTER GO NOW (IRE) 6 b.g. Alkaadhem – Pohutakawa (FR) (Affirmed **h84 p**
(USA)) [2018/19 b96: h19.2d^5 h17.7s^5 h15.8d Feb 20] showed ability in bumper for
Charlie Longsdon in 2017/18: poor form over hurdles: in tongue tie last 3 starts: remains
with potential. *Dan Skelton*

IDDER (IRE) 8 br.g. Authorized (IRE) – Epiphany (Zafonic (USA)) [2018/19 h109: **h107**
h15.7g^4 h16g Jun 24] fair handicap hurdler: unproven beyond 17f: acts on good to firm and
heavy going: usually wears cheekpieces, not in 2018/19 when tongue tied instead. *Jack R.
Barber*

IDEE DE GARDE (FR) 6 b.g. Kapgarde (FR) – Idee Recue (FR) (Sicyos (USA)) **h106**
[2018/19 b93p: h16.4d^2 h15.7d^6 Jan 19] has had breathing operation: bumper winner: fair
form over hurdles: second in maiden at Newcastle in December: stiff task next time: in
tongue tie last 2 starts. *Dan Skelton*

IDENTITY THIEF (IRE) 9 b.g. Kayf Tara – Miss Arteea (IRE) (Flemensfirth (USA)) **c–**
[2018/19 c–, h161: h20d^{pu} Nov 11] rather leggy gelding: high-class hurdler: won Stayers **h–**
Hurdle (Liverpool) at Aintree in 2017/18: fatally injured at Navan on return: smart form
over fences: stayed 25f: acted on heavy going. *Henry de Bromhead, Ireland*

IDILICO (FR) 4 b.g. Lawman (FR) – Ydillique (IRE) (Sadler's Wells (USA)) [2018/19 **h114**
h15.8g* h16.7g^2 h18.9v^4 h15.8g^5 h16g^2 h18.8d^{ur} h15.7m Mar 31] fairly useful on Flat
in France for Christophe Ferland, stays 13.5f: fair hurdler: won juvenile at Uttoxeter in
October: unproven beyond 17f: best form on good going: in headgear last 2 starts.
Ian Williams

I'DLIKETHEOPTION (IRE) 8 b.g. Presenting – Supreme Dreamer (IRE) (Supreme **c129**
Leader) [2018/19 c126, h–: c20s^6 c20m^4 c16.5g* c16.3g* c16.3g^2 c16.5g^3 c15.8g^5 c16d^4 **h–**
Mar 21] winning hurdler: fairly useful handicap chaser: won at Worcester in July and
Newton Abbot in September: best around 2m: acts on good to firm and good to soft going:
usually wears tongue tie. *Jonjo O'Neill*

IDOLS'S EYE (FR) 4 b.g. Diamond Boy (FR) – Rose Caline (FR) (Astarabad (USA)) **b–**
[2018/19 b15.8g Apr 11] 14/1, seventh in maiden bumper at Huntingdon. *Mark Bradstock*

IFANDABUT (IRE) 7 b.g. Scorpion (IRE) – Native Wonder (IRE) (Good Thyne (USA)) **h88**
[2018/19 h–, b81: h21d h19.7d h16.8s* h15.3g Feb 27] modest handicap hurdler: won at
Exeter in January: should stay 2½m: acts on soft going. *Phillip Dando*

IFANDBUTWHYNOT (IRE) 13 b.g. Raise A Grand (IRE) – Cockney Ground (IRE) **c124**
(Common Grounds) [2018/19 c127, h–: c17.1g^2 c17.3g^5 c15.8g^3 c16g* c17.3s^2 c17.1m^5 **h–**
c15.2m^3 Oct 17] workmanlike gelding: winning hurdler: fairly useful handicap chaser:
won at Uttoxeter in July: raced mainly around 2m: acts on good to firm and heavy going:
has worn hood: wears tongue tie: can find little. *Tim Easterby*

IF THE CAP FITS (IRE) 7 b.g. Milan – Derravaragh Sayra (IRE) (Sayarshan (FR))   h159 +
[2018/19 h149p: h15.3g^2 h19.3g* h16g^3 h19.2d^2 h24.7g* Apr 6]

What was the largest string of any British-based jumping owners, that of Paul and Clare Rooney, is being halved in the next season to around thirty as the couple concentrate on 'quality rather than quantity', although other factors have undoubtedly played a part. One of the Rooneys' best horses, for example, has yet to run at Cheltenham. If The Cap Fits would have been worth his place at the Festival in any of the three seasons he has been racing, notably as a novice hurdler. Unbeaten in three starts in that campaign when looking most promising, he was second favourite for the Supreme Novices' Hurdle in ante-post lists when a muscle tear in his hindquarters caused him to miss the Festival and, it turned out, the rest of the season. If The Cap Fits had earlier looked Grade 1 material in bumpers after winning his first two starts, though, rather than Cheltenham, his spring target that season had been Aintree where he finished fourth. Aintree, rather than Cheltenham, was again the focus of his latest campaign which resulted in a career highlight to date with victory in a thrilling Liverpool Hurdle (run as the Ryanair Stayers' Hurdle), a first Grade 1 success and his seventh win from eleven starts.

If The Cap Fits was not alone among his owners' best horses in being absent from the latest Cheltenham Festival where the Rooneys were successful in the Baring Bingham in 2017 with Willoughby Court (whom they lost in the latest season, as recorded in the essay on Le Breuil). Earlier in the season, the Rooneys had instructed their various trainers not to make entries at the track for any of their string. They did so discreetly, with no public announcement of a boycott as such, though, when news did break, that was how the decision was widely interpreted, with a number of other high profile owners and trainers leaping to Cheltenham's defence. The Rooneys' concerns were over injury rates at the track and they were said to have their own data supporting their decision. As well as the high profile loss of Starchitect, who was well on his way to winning the Caspian Caviar Gold Cup at Cheltenham in 2017 when breaking a hind leg on the flat, they also had the misfortune to lose Melrose Boy who became the 2018 Festival's seventh fatality when having to be put down following an operation days after being struck into in the Martin Pipe. After a meeting took place in February between the Rooneys' racing manager Jason Maguire and representatives including Cheltenham's clerk of the course Simon Claisse, a statement issued on the owners' behalf confirmed that their trainers had been told that they could resume making entries for races at Cheltenham. Although some were made in the Festival's handicaps, in the event the Rooneys had no runners there in March, though a couple of runners at the April meeting were their first at Cheltenham since the previous November. Cheltenham's managing director Ian Renton's reaction to the lifting of the so-called boycott seemed to reveal that the state of the ground, rather than the obstacles, had been the Rooneys' main area of concern when he stressed that 'the team here takes immense care to provide a safe, world-class racing surface.' On the same subject, the Rooneys

Ryanair Stayers' Hurdle (Liverpool), Aintree—
all to play for after Apple's Jade (right) and If The Cap Fits (centre) both flatten the last ...

have apparently had few qualms about their horses running over the Grand National fences. The Last Samuri, who was retired in the latest season, ran in three Grand Nationals, finishing second on his first attempt, and was also placed on both his starts in the Becher Chase, while the familiar dark blue and yellow quartered colours were carried in the latest Grand National by Go Conquer who showed prominently for a long way before a lack of stamina told.

Earlier on the Grand National card, If The Cap Fits, stepping up markedly in trip for the Liverpool Hurdle and fitted with cheekpieces for the first time, came out on top in a stirring finish with the mares Roksana and Apple's Jade. The odds-on Apple's Jade set a strong pace and was still in front when making a mistake at the last. Held up and travelling well, If The Cap Fits had moved into third by the home turn and was switched around Apple's Jade and was only about a length down when making an even worse blunder than Apple's Jade at the final flight. Those mistakes briefly allowed the staying-on Roksana to emerge as a major threat wider out, but If The Cap Fits recovered to mount a determined challenge in between Apple's Jade and Roksana, as the gap between that pair narrowed. It was tight but If The Cap Fits rallied gamely to force his head in front of Roksana on the line, with only a neck back to Apple's Jade in third. The first three pulled eleven lengths clear of the Coral Cup winner William Henry in fourth. If The Cap Fits had a new jockey at Aintree and provided Sean Bowen with the first Grade 1 success of his career. If The Cap Fits' former regular partner Noel Fehily had retired a fortnight earlier after going out on a winner for the same connections' Get In The Queue in a valuable bumper at Newbury. Aged forty-three, Fehily, a former champion conditional, retired with 1,352 winners, putting him ninth on the all-time list of jump jockeys in Britain

... which results in a thrilling finish, as If The Cap Fits squeezes between Roksana (left) and Apple's Jade (right) to provide jockey Sean Bowen with a first Grade 1 success

and Ireland. Fehily's wins included two Champion Hurdles on Rock On Ruby and Buveur d'Air, the former trained at a satellite yard of Paul Nicholls run by his then assistant Harry Fry before he took out his own licence. Fehily also won two King Georges on Silviniaco Conti for Nicholls, and had the last of his seven Cheltenham Festival winners in the latest season when Eglantine du Seuil pulled off a 50/1 shock in the Dawn Run Mares' Novices' Hurdle.

Fehily's final success on If The Cap Fits had come in the Coral Hurdle at Ascot in November. In the absence of the Irish-trained pair Samcro and Laurina, who had been among the entries, If The Cap Fits started odds on in a field of six and won by a length and a half from Old Guard, in receipt of 6 lb from the runner-up, despite still being only fourth jumping the last after taking a keen hold in a muddling race. A fortnight earlier he had run well against a race-fit rival on his first start for the best part of eleven months when runner-up to Verdana Blue in the Elite Hurdle at Wincanton, meeting that mare on worse terms than when she inflicted a surprise defeat on her stable-companion Buveur d'Air in the Christmas Hurdle at Kempton, where If The Cap Fits was beaten six lengths into third behind the Nicky Henderson pair. On his only start between Kempton and Aintree, If The Cap Fits was stepped back up in trip for the National Spirit Hurdle at Fontwell in February but went down by a length and a half to Vision des Flos, to whom he was conceding 4 lb. Fehily had to bustle If The Cap Fits along at various stages at Fontwell, but the application of cheekpieces had the desired effect at Aintree where he travelled much more sweetly.

If The Cap Fits (IRE) (b.g. 2012)	Milan (b 1998)	Sadler's Wells (b 1981)	Northern Dancer
			Fairy Bridge
		Kithanga (b 1990)	Darshaan
			Kalata
	Derravaragh Sayra (IRE) (br 2004)	Sayarshan (b 1995)	Darshaan
			Sayyara
		Derravaragh Native (b 1995)	Be My Native
			Fairly Deep

If The Cap Fits looked a staying type right from his bumper days and it is no surprise on breeding that he has turned out to be suited by three miles over hurdles. He is by Milan who is also the sire of the useful staying chaser Duke of Lucca, a half-brother to his unraced dam, whose wins included two successive editions of the listed handicap on the Grand National card and who stayed nearly four miles, albeit over Cheltenham's cross-country course. A £30,000 three-year-old purchase at Doncaster's May Sales, If The Cap Fits is the third foal and only runner to date out of Derravaragh Sayra. His grandam Derravaragh Native showed only a little ability in Irish bumpers, but she had her second winner under Rules in the latest season when Duke of Lucca's brother Boot Camp won twice over hurdles and once over fences for Gigginstown and Gordon Elliott, though he has yet to prove himself over three miles. The great grandam Fairly Deep won a bumper and a couple of hurdles at around two miles in Ireland before breeding half a dozen winners, the pick of them being White Star Line who was still a maiden over fences when placed at two consecutive Cheltenham Festivals (in the novices' handicap and what is now the Ultima) before breaking his duck as a chaser in the Kerry National.

If The Cap Fits, who acts on soft ground but has raced mainly under less testing conditions, is therefore bred to be a staying chaser and has the right build for fences, being a good-topped gelding. But there must be a temptation to keep him over hurdles as he is still virtually unexposed over three miles and has the potential to be Paisley Park's biggest threat in the staying division. Harry Fry took full advantage of Paisley Park's absence from the Grade 1 staying hurdles at Aintree and Punchestown, as Unowhatimeanharry, beaten a long way behind If The Cap Fits in the Liverpool Hurdle, returned to form out of the blue to win the Champion Stayers' Hurdle at Punchestown for the second time in three years. *Harry Fry*

IFTIRAAQ (IRE) 8 b.g. Muhtathir – Alzaroof (USA) (Kingmambo (USA)) [2018/19 **c–** h20g Sep 2] has had breathing operation: well held in point: fair nowadays on Flat, stays **h–** 1½m, pulled up lame in January: fairly useful hurdler at best: placed only chase start: best at sharp 2m: wears headgear: tried in tongue tie: front runner/races prominently. *David Loughnane*

IFYOUCANSEEMENOW (IRE) 5 br.g. Stowaway – Sandrinechoix (FR) (Daliapour (IRE)) [2018/19 b16.7d b15.8d h19.2m⁵ Mar 29] good-topped gelding: little promise in bumpers: 6/1, fifth in maiden at Fontwell on hurdling debut. *Ben Pauling* **h72 b–**

IF YOU SAY RUN (IRE) 7 b.m. Mahler – De Lissa (IRE) (Zaffaran (USA)) [2018/19 h128: h21.4g⁴ h24.5g² h23.5d³ h18.9g² h20.3dᵖᵘ Mar 15] good-topped mare: won Irish maiden point on debut: useful hurdler: won mares handicap at Wincanton in November: placed after in listed mares event at Kempton, olbg.com Mares' Hurdle (Warfield) at Ascot and another listed mares event at Haydock: stays 3m: acts on heavy going: in cheekpieces last 2 starts: wears tongue tie: usually front runner/races prominently. *Paul Nicholls* **h133**

IGOR 6 b.g. Presenting – Stravinsky Dance (Stravinsky (USA)) [2018/19 h19.3g² h21.6s Dec 21] good sort: second foal: half-brother to 11f/1½m winner Storm Force Ten (by Shirocco): dam (h137) French 2m-2¼m hurdle winner: fairly useful form over hurdles: better effort when second in maiden at Ascot. *Nicky Henderson* **h118**

IGOUGO (IRE) 6 ch.g. Where Or When (IRE) – Giolldante (IRE) (Phardante (FR)) [2018/19 h–, b–: h21.6g⁴ h20gᵖᵘ Jul 26] well held in bumper: poor form over hurdles: tried in hood: in tongue tie last 3 starts. *Jeremy Scott* **h72**

I JUST KNOW (IRE) 9 b.g. Robin des Pres (FR) – Desperado Queen (IRE) (Un Desperado (FR)) [2018/19 c136, h112: h19.7m² c26.2gᶠ Oct 27] good-topped gelding: fair maiden hurdler: smart handicap chaser: still just in front when fell 2 out at Kelso in October: thorough stayer: acts on heavy and good to firm going: bold-jumping front runner. *Sue Smith* **c146 h109**

I K BRUNEL 5 b.g. Midnight Legend – Somethinaboutmolly (IRE) (Choisir (AUS)) [2018/19 b17s* h16.8g³ h16m⁶ Feb 23] €62,000 3-y-o: tall, good sort: third foal: half-brother to fairly useful/temperamental chaser Somewhere To Be (19f/2½m winner, by Golan): dam unraced: won bumper at Carlisle (by 1½ lengths from Tarada) in November on debut: fairly useful form over hurdles: better effort when third in novice at Cheltenham. *Olly Murphy* **h115 b96**

IKEJA (IRE) 5 b.g. Dahjee (USA) – Silly Mille (IRE) (Luso) [2018/19 b15.8v Dec 21] tailed off in bumper. *Graeme McPherson* **b–**

ILAYA (FR) 5 gr.m. Kapgarde (FR) – Tour Magic (FR) (Martaline) [2018/19 h16.8s⁵ h15.7g⁴ h15.7d⁶ h16d³ Mar 19] first foal: dam, French maiden hurdler (second at 17f), half-sister to useful French hurdler (2m-2¼m winner) Tornada: fair form over hurdles: placed on debut in France for A. Chaille-Chaille in 2017/18: raced around 2m: acts on heavy going: wears hood: often races freely. *Micky Hammond* **h103**

ILEWINDELILAH 11 b.m. Grape Tree Road – Bridepark Rose (IRE) (Kemal (FR)) [2018/19 h84: h25g⁴ h24g⁶ Jun 25] poor handicap hurdler: stays 3¼m: best form on good going: usually wears headgear. *Charlie Mann* **h79**

ILEWIN GEEZ 9 ch.g. Generous (IRE) – Ilewin Janine (IRE) (Soughaan (USA)) [2018/19 h112: h16.7g⁴ h15.8g* h16g³ h17.7g² h19.7g* h20g h21.2g⁶ Nov 8] fairly useful hurdler: won maiden at Uttoxeter in June and novice at Hereford in October: stays 2½m: acts on soft going. *Charlie Mann* **h115**

I'LL BE YOUR CLOWN (IRE) 8 b.g. Aqlaam – Lady Avenger (IRE) (Namid) [2018/19 h109: h21.4m h19.2d h15.3g h19.8s⁶ Mar 7] fair hurdler, well below form in 2018/19: unproven beyond 17f: acts on heavy going: tried in cheekpieces/tongue tie. *Steven Dixon* **h71**

ILLTELLMEMA (IRE) 7 gr.m. Milan – Cullenstown Lady (IRE) (Wood Chanter) [2018/19 h94: h19.5sᵖᵘ h19.5v h21.7v⁴ h21dᵘʳ h20.5g Feb 25] point winner: modest maiden hurdler: best effort at 2¾m: acts on heavy going: usually in hood: front runner/races prominently, tends to find little: has joined Gary Moore. *Suzy Smith* **h90**

ILLUMINATED BEAUTY (IRE) 6 b.m. Flemensfirth (USA) – Native Beauty (IRE) (King's Theatre (IRE)) [2018/19 h20.7g h15.3s⁵ h16.3g² Mar 30] €18,000 3-y-o, £55,000 5-y-o: has had breathing operation: first foal: dam (h113), 2m hurdle winner, out of fairly useful hurdler/useful chaser (stayed 3m) Woodville Star: off mark in Irish points at third attempt: fair form over hurdles: best effort when second in novice at Stratford in March, closing all way to line: will prove suited by 2½m: wears tongue tie: will go on improving. *Kim Bailey* **h104 p**

ILOVEMINTS 7 b.m. Kayf Tara – La Harde (FR) (Valanour (IRE)) [2018/19 h91: h20.3g⁵ h16.7m³ h21.6m² Jul 14] has had breathing operation: modest form over hurdles: stays 2¾m: acts on good to firm and heavy going: tried in hood/tongue tie. *David Pipe* **h99**

IL RE DI NESSUNO (FR) 4 b.g. Sinndar (IRE) – Lady Elgar (IRE) (Sadler's Wells (USA)) [2018/19 h16v³ Dec 7] rather leggy gelding: useful on Flat in Italy, stays 11f: 13/2, some encouragement when third in juvenile at Sandown (23 lengths behind Torpillo) on hurdling debut: should improve. *Gary Moore* **h92 p**

IL SICARIO (IRE) 5 b.g. Zebedee – Starring (FR) (Ashkalani (IRE)) [2018/19 h92: h16.8g h16.8g⁶ h16.8s Nov 25] fair on Flat, stays 11.5f: poor maiden hurdler: often in headgear. *Bill Turner* **h84**

I'M A BELIEVER 5 b.m. Sixties Icon – Fascinatin Rhythm (Fantastic Light (USA)) [2018/19 h20.7g⁴ h15.8d h15.3s Mar 7] fair maiden on Flat, stayed 2m: poor form over hurdles: tried in hood/tongue tie: dead. *Alan King* **h78**

IMADA (IRE) 9 br.g. Arcadio (GER) – Anck Su Namun (IRE) (Supreme Leader) [2018/19 h113: h20.6s³ c16.5s² c19.3v³ c20.1d* Apr 26] fair form over hurdles: fairly useful form over fences: won novice handicap at Perth in April: stays 21f: acts on heavy going. *Nicky Richards* **c119** **h112**

I'M A GAME CHANGER (IRE) 7 b.g. Arcadio (GER) – Drinadaly (IRE) (Oscar (IRE)) [2018/19 h136: h19g² h16d² c19.2g² h16v⁶ h20.5d* h20.3g² Apr 17] useful-looking gelding: useful handicap hurdler: won at Newbury in December: second at Warwick (short head behind Cultivator) early in season: 6/4, second in maiden at Exeter (5 lengths behind The Russian Doyen) on chasing debut: stays on soft going: keen-going sort, usually held up: should do better over fences. *Philip Hobbs* **c127 p** **h137**

IM ALL SET (IRE) 10 b.g. Darsi (FR) – Gathabawn Lass (IRE) (Norwich) [2018/19 c23d* c24.2s⁴ Apr 16] multiple point winner: fair form in hunter chases: won maiden at Taunton in April: stays 3m: acts on good to soft going: often in cheekpieces. *Mrs C. Hitch* **c106**

I'M ALWAYS TRYING (IRE) 6 b.g. Westerner – Pepsi Starlet (IRE) (Heavenly Manna) [2018/19 h94, b73: h25.8g* h23.3g⁵ h21.7g⁴ c24.1g⁴ Oct 3] fairly useful form over hurdles: won handicap at Fontwell in June: 11/2, fourth in novice handicap at Bangor (26 lengths behind Wandrin Star) on chasing debut: stays 3¼m: best form on good going: usually wears cheekpieces: often wears tongue tie: well held in 2 points later in season. *Dan Skelton* **c106** **h115**

I'M AN IZZ WIZZ (IRE) 11 ch.g. Desert King (IRE) – Lovely Native (IRE) (Be My Native (USA)) [2018/19 c119, h–: c20.1g⁴ c20g c19.9g² h24.4m c20g⁴ c18.2d c16.5g⁵ c22.6d c20d⁵ c20d⁴ c25s⁶ c23.5g⁶ c21.3s⁵ c19.2g⁶ Mar 24] maiden hurdler: fairly useful handicap chaser: second at Kilbeggan in August: stays 25f: acts on heavy going: has worn blinkers. *Liam Lennon, Ireland* **c115** **h–**

I'M A STARMAN 6 ch.g. Schiaparelli (GER) – Strathtay (Pivotal) [2018/19 h19.5d h19.5d³ h21g³ Apr 10] third foal: half-brother to 2m winner Sail With Sultana (by Black Sam Bellamy): dam (h88), ungenuine 17f hurdle winner, also 7f winner on Flat: fair form over hurdles: best effort when third in maiden at Chepstow in March. *Mark Rimell* **h107**

I'M BRITISH 6 b.g. Aqlaam – Libritish (Librettist (USA)) [2018/19 b68: b13.7d Jan 25] poor form in bumpers: tried in hood: modest form on Flat. *Don Cantillon* **b–**

I'M IMPROVING (IRE) 4 b.g. Most Improved (IRE) – Shebelia (GER) (Black Sam Bellamy (IRE)) [2018/19 h16.4g⁶ Jan 15] fairly useful on Flat, stays 1¼m: 2/1, tailed off in juvenile maiden on hurdling debut. *Keith Dalgleish* **h–**

IMPACT FACTOR (IRE) 7 b.g. Flemensfirth (USA) – Hello Kitty (IRE) (Houmayoun (FR)) [2018/19 h132: c19d c18g|² c19d c17g³ c17d² c16s² c16d² c20g⁵ c16.7g* Apr 21] sturdy gelding: useful form over hurdles: smart chaser: won novice handicap at Fairyhouse (by 5½ lengths from Quamino) in April: good 11 lengths second to Snugsborough Hall in handicap at Punchestown shortly after end of British season: best form around 2m: acts on heavy going: has worn hood: tried in tongue tie: usually races prominently. *Mrs J. Harrington, Ireland* **c146** **h–**

IMPERIAL ACOLYTE 5 b.g. Kalanisi (IRE) – Isabello (IRE) (Presenting) [2018/19 b64p: h16d* h16d⁵ h20.5d h16d Apr 6] has had breathing operation: fair form over hurdles: won novice at Wetherby in November: should stay 2½m. *Nigel Twiston-Davies* **h111**

IMPERIAL ALCAZAR (IRE) 5 b.g. Vinnie Roe (IRE) – Maddy's Supreme (IRE) (Supreme Leader) [2018/19 b16.3d⁴ b15.7s² b16.3d³ Mar 22] €42,000 3-y-o: good-topped gelding: seventh foal: half-brother to useful hurdler/winning pointer Jessber's Dream (2¼m-2½m winner, by Milan) and a winning pointer by Westerner: dam (h85) maiden hurdler (stayed 23f): useful form in bumpers: best effort when second in listed event at Ascot (1¼ lengths behind Eden du Houx) in December: will be suited by further than 2m. *Fergal O'Brien* **b110**

IMPERIAL AURA (IRE) 6 b.g. Kalanisi (IRE) – Missindependence (IRE) (Executive Perk) [2018/19 b94: h19.3g* h20.6g* Feb 23] bumper winner: fairly useful form over hurdles: won novices at Carlisle in October and Newcastle in February: sure to stay 3m: likely to progress further. *Kim Bailey* **h123 p**

IMPERIAL BAY (IRE) 7 br.g. Flemensfirth (USA) – Nun Better (IRE) (Presenting) [2018/19 c23.6s Nov 21] winning hurdler: off 21 months, well beaten in novice handicap on chasing debut: will stay beyond 3m. *Ben Pauling* **c–** **h–**

IMPERIAL ELIXIR (IRE) 6 b.g. Doyen (IRE) – Blond's Addition (IRE) (Lord Americo) [2018/19 b83: b16.8g⁵ h18.6g⁴ h19.3g h20.6g³ h20.2g Apr 24] lengthy gelding: has had breathing operation: modest form in bumpers: fair form over hurdles: tongue tied all starts in 2018/19. *Fergal O'Brien* **h107** **b74**

IMPERIAL ELOQUENCE (IRE) 7 b.g. Kalanisi (IRE) – Babble On (IRE) (Anita's Prince) [2018/19 h109: h20.3g⁴ May 13] rangy gelding: has had breathing operation: fair form over hurdles: stays 2½m: acts on soft going. *Fergal O'Brien* **h98**

IMPERIAL ELYSIAN (IRE) 5 br.g. Kalanisi (IRE) – Diva Antonia (IRE) (King's Theatre (IRE)) [2018/19 b16.2m⁵ b14d⁵ h20.8g⁵ h19.7d⁵ h21.7g³ h20.2d⁴ Apr 26] €28,000 3-y-o: has had breathing operation: sixth foal: half-brother to fairly useful 2½m-3m hurdle winner On The Record and fair 2m hurdle winner Have A Few (both by Presenting): dam unraced half-sister to smart staying chaser Goonyella: modest form in bumpers: similar form over hurdles: should stay beyond 21f: sometimes in tongue tie. *Fergal O'Brien* **h98** **b83**

IMPERIAL ESPRIT (IRE) 5 b.g. Scorpion (IRE) – Shesourpresent (IRE) (Presenting) [2018/19 b16s² b16d⁵ Feb 23] €32,000 3-y-o: fourth foal: half-brother to a winning pointer by Oscar: dam unraced sister to fairly useful hurdler/chaser (stayed 25f) Coin Man: shaped like a stayer in bumpers. *Harry Fry* **b84**

IMPERIAL FOCUS (IRE) 6 b.g. Intense Focus (USA) – Mrs Cee (IRE) (Orpen (USA)) [2018/19 h16.2m⁴ h16.2g² h16.2g³ h19.9s h15.6g⁴ h16.4g⁵ h15.7m⁶ h16.2g Apr 25] fair maiden on Flat, stays 2m: fair maiden hurdler: unproven beyond 2m: best form on good going: often wears cheekpieces. *Simon Waugh* **h101**

IMPERIAL KNIGHT (IRE) 7 b.g. Mahler – And Whatever Else (IRE) (Bob Back (USA)) [2018/19 b92: h16.7spu h19.3d³ h20.3s² Mar 18] rather leggy gelding: fair form in bumpers: similar form over hurdles: best effort when second in maiden at Southwell in March: left Olly Murphy after first start. *Ben Pauling* **h112**

IMPERIAL NEMESIS (IRE) 6 b.g. Stowaway – Liss Alainn (IRE) (Flemensfirth (USA)) [2018/19 h104p, b86: h21d⁴ h23.3v h15.5d⁶ h21spu Mar 10] close-coupled gelding: fair form in bumpers/over hurdles. *Nigel Twiston-Davies* **h103**

IMPERIAL PRESENCE (IRE) 8 ch.g. Presenting – Pennyrose Bay (Karinga Bay) [2018/19 c123, h–: c18g* c19.4g* c20s* c20.1g² c20.6g⁴ Apr 17] strong gelding: winning hurdler: smart handicap chaser: completed hat-trick when winning at Kempton in May, Stratford (by 5 lengths from Newton Geronimo) in June and Uttoxeter (by 8 lengths from Hammersly Lake) in July: fourth in Silver Trophy Chase (Limited Handicap) at Cheltenham (6¼ lengths behind Mister Whitaker) in April: stays 2½m: acts on soft going: tried in hood: front runner. *Philip Hobbs* **c149** **h–**

IMPERIAL PRINCE (IRE) 10 b.g. Subtle Power (IRE) – Satco Rose (IRE) (Satco (FR)) [2018/19 c94, h–: c24.1g³ c24.2g⁴ c24.2m³ c24.1g c20.5vᶠ c24.1s⁵ c24.1s³ c26.9d⁶ c24.1d² c24.2v⁴ Mar 14] winning hurdler: fair maiden chaser: stays 27f: acts on good to firm and heavy going. *Ian Duncan* **c100** **h–**

IMPROVED (IRE) 9 ch.g. Rainwatch – Show Potential (IRE) (Glacial Storm (USA)) [2018/19 h24gpu May 13] modest hurdler: off 15 months, pulled up sole start in 2018/19: stays 23f: acts on soft going: in cheekpieces last 3 starts. *Philip Kirby* **h–**

IMPULSIVE AMERICAN 7 b.g. American Post – Impulsive Decision (IRE) (Nomination) [2018/19 h18.6g h23.9g² h23gpu Sep 28] rather leggy gelding: fairly useful handicap hurdler, missed 2017/18: second at Perth in June: winning chaser: stays 3m: acts on soft going: wears headgear: tried in tongue tie. *David Pipe* **c–** **h117**

IMPULSIVE LEADER (IRE) 6 b.m. Westerner – Impulsive Ita (IRE) (Supreme Leader) [2018/19 h16g h19.5s⁶ h19.5d⁵ h16v⁵ h20.5dpu h16.8s Mar 18] €8,000 3-y-o: tall mare: third foal: half-sister to useful hurdler/chaser Impulsive Star (2½m-29f winner, by Busy Flight): dam failed to complete in 3 points: maiden pointer: too free in bumper: poor form over hurdles: left John Joseph Hanlon after first start: bred to stay beyond 2½m: acts on heavy going: in hood last 5 starts: usually races off pace. *Zoe Davison* **h82**

*McCoy Contractors Civil Engineering Classic Handicap Chase, Warwick—
second-season novice Impulsive Star (right) opens his account over fences with a victory over
Calett Mad (centre) and Crosspark*

IMPULSIVE STAR (IRE) 9 b.g. Busy Flight – Impulsive Ita (IRE) (Supreme Leader) **c138**
[2018/19 c134, h–: c25.7s² c29.2g* c31.7sᵖᵘ c31.8mᵖᵘ Apr 13] well-made gelding: winning **h–**
hurdler: useful chaser: won Classic Chase at Warwick (by 3¼ lengths from Calett Mad) in
January: probably stays 4m: acts on heavy going: usually in cheekpieces nowadays.
Neil Mulholland

I'M RUNNING LATE 5 ch.g. Sepoy (AUS) – Clinet (IRE) (Docksider (USA)) [2018/19 **h–**
h15.8g Nov 17] fair on Flat, stays 1½m: in cheekpieces/tongue tie, well held in novice on
hurdling debut. *Alex Hales*

I'M TO BLAME (IRE) 6 b.g. Winged Love (IRE) – Swap Shop (IRE) (Lord Americo) **h132**
[2018/19 b101: h16.8g* h20.6s³ h19.9d* h19.9s* h19.9s² Mar 21] won both starts in
bumpers: useful form over hurdles: won maiden in November, novice in January (by 26
lengths from Mance Rayder) and handicap in February (by 8 lengths from Quest For Life),
all at Sedgefield: will prove best up to 2½m: acts on soft going: in hood last 5 starts.
Keith Dalgleish

IM TOO GENEROUS 9 ch.g. Generous (IRE) – Something Major (IRE) (Zaffaran **h100**
(USA)) [2018/19 h16.4gᵖᵘ h19.7gᵖᵘ h19.8m* Mar 22] runner-up in point: fair form over
hurdles, off 47 months before return: tongue tied, won novice handicap at Musselburgh in
March: stays 2½m: acts on good to firm and good to soft going. *Rebecca Menzies*

I'M WISER NOW (IRE) 5 b.g. Presenting – Reine Angevine (FR) (Poliglote) [2018/19 **b98**
b15.7s³ b16d³ b15.7m³ Feb 22] €75,000 3-y-o: first foal: dam (h118), bumper/2m hurdle
winner, half-sister to smart hurdler/chaser (stays 3m) La Bague Au Roi: fairly useful form
in bumpers: best effort when third at Catterick in February. *Fergal O'Brien*

IN A BLUE DUST 10 gr.g. Portrait Gallery (IRE) – Two Hart Road (IRE) (Broken **c94**
Hearted) [2018/19 c26g⁴ May 17] multiple point winner: 3/1, fourth in novice hunter at
Fontwell (9 lengths behind Bally River Boy) on chasing debut. *N. R. W. Wright*

INAJIFFY (IRE) 6 b.m. Mahler – Spirit of Clanagh (IRE) (Zagreb (USA)) [2018/19 b–: **h–**
b17g h20.6g⁵ Nov 16] sturdy mare: no form in bumpers/maiden hurdle: tried in tongue tie. **b–**
Dianne Sayer

437

INAMINNA (IRE) 8 b.g. Oscar (IRE) – Amber Trix (IRE) (Scribano) [2018/19 h116p, **c119** b68: h20d⁴ c18.8mᵖᵘ c20sᵖᵘ c23d⁵ c23g³ c19.4d* c20.3g⁵ Apr 13] smallish, angular **h105** gelding: has had breathing operation: fair form over hurdles: fairly useful form over fences: won handicap at Chepstow in March: stays 23f: acts on soft going: in cheekpieces last 5 starts: in tongue tie last 3. *Neil Mulholland*

IN ARREARS (IRE) 7 b.m. Beneficial – Gullet Dawn (IRE) (Flemensfirth (USA)) **c99** [2018/19 c24.2v* c23.8m³ Mar 31] £5,000 6-y-o: second foal: dam winning pointer: multiple point winner: modest form in hunter chases: won novice at Exeter in March, easily. *Gordon Edwards*

INCERTAINE 6 b.m. Milan – La Dame Brune (FR) (Mansonnien (FR)) [2018/19 h15.8g⁶ **h67** h16d h16.7s h20d⁶ h22g Mar 30] £20,000 3-y-o: fourth foal: closely related to fair hurdler/ fairly useful chaser Cabaret Queen (21f-3m winner, by King's Theatre) and fair hurdler/ useful chaser Internal Transfer (19f-2¾m winner, by Kayf Tara): dam (h113), unreliable 2½m/21f hurdle winner, half-sister to fairly useful hurdler/useful chaser (2m-21f winner) Nikos Extra: poor form over hurdles. *Tom Gretton*

INCHCOLM (IRE) 9 br.g. Presenting – Rose of Inchiquin (IRE) (Roselier (FR)) **c113** [2018/19 c82§, h–: c24.2g* c24.2g³ c25.5m² c24.1g⁴ c24.2g* c26mᵘ c24.2s* c24.2sᵘʳ **h106** h25.3g* c26.3s³ c23.4d* Apr 6] tall gelding: fair form over hurdles: won handicap at Catterick in January: fair handicap chaser: won at Hexham in May (novice) and November (conditionals), Doncaster (conditionals) and Hexham again in December, and Newcastle in April: left Micky Hammond after third start: stays 3¼m: acts on soft and good to firm going: has worn headgear: tried in tongue tie. *Tristan Davidson*

INCH LALA (IRE) 7 ch.m. Mahler – Aboo Lala (IRE) (Aboo Hom) [2018/19 h100: **c112** c16g³ c19.3s* c20.6g³ c19.3d⁴ c20.2m³ c21.1g² Apr 5] sturdy mare: fair form over hurdles: **h–** similar form over fences: won handicap at Sedgefield in December: will stay 3m: acts on heavy going. *Evan Williams*

INCH RISE (IRE) 10 br.g. Heron Island (IRE) – Rosetown Girl (IRE) (Roselier (FR)) **c–** [2018/19 h20sᵖᵘ c24gᵖᵘ Jun 25] fairly useful hurdler/fair form over fences at best: pulled up **h–** all starts in 2018/19, including in point: left W. J. Burke after first start: stays 3m: acts on heavy going: has worn cheekpieces, including in 2018/19. *Dan Skelton*

INCLUDED 7 b.m. Champs Elysees – Cordoba (Oasis Dream) [2018/19 h97: h16.2g **h110** h16.7m⁴ h16.7g* h16g² Sep 2] fair handicap hurdler: won at Bangor in August: raced around 2m: acts on good to firm going: wears tongue tie. *Alastair Ralph*

INCUS 6 b.g. Bertolini (USA) – Cloudchaser (IRE) (Red Ransom (USA)) [2018/19 h71: **h87** h15.7s h16g h15.8dᵖᵘ Feb 17] modest form over hurdles: raced around 2m. *Ed de Giles*

INDEFATIGABLE (IRE) 6 b.m. Schiaparelli (GER) – Spin The Wheel (IRE) (Kalanisi **h132** (IRE)) [2018/19 b89: h16.3d h15.8d* h16.5d² h16.6g² h16.8d⁵ h20.3g* Apr 18] useful- looking mare: bumper winner: useful form over hurdles: won mares novices at Uttoxeter in November and Cheltenham (listed event, by 10 lengths from The Cull Bank) in April: second in Yorkshire Rose Mares' Hurdle at Doncaster (neck behind Lady Buttons) in January: stays 2½m: acts on good to soft going: races prominently. *Paul Webber*

INDIAN BRAVE (IRE) 8 b.g. Definite Article – Fridays Folly (IRE) (Flemensfirth **c–** (USA)) [2018/19 c24.2vᵖᵘ Mar 5] winning hurdler: off 23 months, pulled up in novice **h–** handicap on chasing debut: stays 2½m: acts on soft going. *Anthony Honeyball*

INDIAN CHIEF (IRE) 9 b.g. Montjeu (IRE) – Buck Aspen (Seeking The Gold **h–** (USA)) [2018/19 h16.8dᵖᵘ Jan 21] fairly useful on Flat, stays 1½m: lost shoe when pulled up in maiden on hurdling debut. *Rebecca Bastiman*

INDIAN HARBOUR 6 b.g. Indian Haven – Hawait Al Barr (Green Desert (USA)) **h97** [2018/19 h109, b62: h16.2d⁵ h16.8d h19.8sᵖᵘ h19s h17.7gᵇᵈ Apr 12] strong gelding: modest maiden hurdler: left Sally Haynes after first start: unproven beyond 2m: acts on good to soft going: tried in tongue tie. *Susan Gardner*

INDIAN HAWK (IRE) 7 b.g. Westerner – Yorkshire Girl (IRE) (Anshan) [2018/19 **c130** c116p, h123: c20.2m* h18d h20d h20d Nov 3] useful-looking gelding: fairly useful hurdler **h–** at best, no form in 2018/19: useful form over fences: won novice at Wincanton (by 10 lengths from Overland Flyer) in May: left Nicky Henderson after: stays 2¾m: acts on good to firm and heavy going: in headgear first 3 starts. *Leslie F. Young, USA*

INDIAN HERCULES (IRE) 7 b.g. Whitmore's Conn (USA) – Carrawaystick (IRE) **c100** (Old Vic) [2018/19 h119: c24.2g c19.9d⁴ Mar 2] good-topped gelding: Irish point winner: **h–** fairly useful form over hurdles: some promise on first of 2 starts in chases: should stay 3m: acts on heavy going. *Warren Greatrex*

INDIAN NATIVE (IRE) 9 b.m. Oscar (IRE) – Roman Native (IRE) (Be My Native (USA)) [2018/19 c109, h–: c25.5g⁶ h21.2d h20.3d⁶ Apr 24] point winner: modest handicap hurdler: fair form over fences, mistakes well held on return: stays 3m: acts on heavy going: tried in cheekpieces: wears tongue tie. *Alex Hales*   **c–** **h92**

INDIAN OPERA 7 b.m. Indian Danehill (IRE) – Minouchka (FR) (Bulington (FR)) [2018/19 b89: h24sᵖᵘ h19.8g* h16.6g⁵ h15.7m* h19.8sᶠ Mar 10] refused on sole point outing: fairly useful form over hurdles: won maiden at Musselburgh in January and handicap at Catterick in February: should stay beyond 2½m: acts on good to firm going, probably on soft: front runner/races prominently. *Iain Jardine*   **h125**

INDIAN REEL (IRE) 9 br.g. Indian River (FR) – Ceilidh Dancer (Scottish Reel) [2018/19 h95: h25m³ h23g⁵ c25.8m³ c24g c25.8m⁵ c21.6g⁶ h27m⁴ h19.6m h25g⁶ h20.7gᶠ h25g⁶ h23.1s h23.3s h20.7g² h20.6g³ Mar 14] modest handicap hurdler: similar form over fences: left Fergal O'Brien after seventh start: stays 3¼m: acts on good to firm and heavy going: usually wears headgear: has worn tongue tie. *Conor Dore*   **c95** **h90**

INDIAN STREAM 10 ch.m. Generous (IRE) – Zaffarimbi (IRE) (Zaffaran (USA)) [2018/19 c–, h133: c20g May 27] lengthy, workmanlike mare: has had breathing operation: useful hurdler: useful chaser, well held sole start in 2018/19: stays 3m: acts on soft going: wears tongue tie. *Neil Mulholland*   **c–** **h–**

INDIAN TEMPLE (IRE) 10 b.g. Indian River (FR) – Ballycraggan (IRE) (Beneficial) [2018/19 c132, h–: c19.9g² c20.1g* c15.8g⁶ c23.8g³ c20.1g⁵ c20.3s² c21.1dᶠ Apr 5] workmanlike gelding: maiden hurdler: useful handicap chaser: won at Perth (by 13 lengths from Ramonex) in June: stays 3m: acts on good to firm and heavy going: usually in cheekpieces in 2018/19: usually races close up. *Tim Reed*   **c136** **h–**

INDIAN VOYAGE (IRE) 11 b.g. Indian Haven – Voyage of Dreams (USA) (Riverman (USA)) [2018/19 c111§, h–: c15.6g⁴ c15.6g³ c15.6g Jun 16] strong gelding: maiden hurdler: modest handicap chaser nowadays: stays 21f: acts on good to firm and heavy going: wears tongue tie: unreliable. *Maurice Barnes*   **c97 §** **h–**

INDIEBURG (FR) 5 b.g. Sageburg (IRE) – Indietra (USA) (Vindication (USA)) [2018/19 b15.3g Nov 10] has had breathing operation: well beaten in bumper. *Harry Whittington*   **b–**

INDIGO STAMP 8 b.g. Rainbow High – Philatelic Lady (IRE) (Pips Pride) [2018/19 h75, b–: h16.8gᵖᵘ h21.6gᵖᵘ h15.3f⁴ Oct 28] has had breathing operation: little form in bumpers/over hurdles (has hinted at temperament). *Mark Gillard*   **h–**

INDIROCCO (GER) 6 ch.g. Shirocco (GER) – Indigo Girl (GER) (Sternkoenig (IRE)) [2018/19 h108: h21g c23.9g⁴ c26.1d³ Nov 25] good-topped gelding: has had breathing operation: fair form over hurdles: similar form over fences: will prove best up to 3¼m: acts on soft going: won on point debut in March. *Dan Skelton*   **c113** **h88**

INDUNO (IRE) 5 b.g. Flemensfirth (USA) – Vast Consumption (IRE) (Rudimentary (USA)) [2018/19 b16g² Apr 25] second foal: dam (h135) 2m-3m hurdle winner: 3/1, showed plenty when second in bumper at Warwick (2½ lengths behind Overthetop). *David Pipe*   **b94**

INDY FIVE (IRE) 9 b.g. Vertical Speed (FR) – Beesplease (IRE) (Snurge) [2018/19 c137, h–: c24d May 5] winning hurdler: useful form over fences, well held sole start in 2018/19: will stay long distances: acts on heavy going: usually races close up. *David Dennis*   **c–** **h–**

INESSA (FR) 6 b.m. Samum (GER) – Isantha (GER) (Dai Jin) [2018/19 h18.5g² h16g* h20.3g* h16.8g² h20.3g³ Apr 18] useful on Flat, stays 1¾m: fairly useful form over hurdles: won maiden at Worcester in June and mares novice at Southwell in July: third in listed mares handicap at Cheltenham in April: stays 2½m: raced only on good going. *Dr Richard Newland*   **h117**

INFINITI (IRE) 6 b.m. Arcano (IRE) – Seraphina (IRE) (Pips Pride) [2018/19 h15.8g h16.7s h15.5g h17sᵖᵘ h16g² Apr 10] compact mare: poor form over hurdles: tried in cheekpieces: in tongue tie last 2 starts. *Barry Leavy*   **h74**

INFLEXIBALL 7 b.m. Refuse To Bend (IRE) – Sphere (IRE) (Daylami (IRE)) [2018/19 h15.8v Jan 26] dam half-sister to fairly useful hurdler (stayed 2½m) Isle of Ewe: modest form on Flat, stays 1½m: tailed off in maiden on hurdling debut. *John Mackie*   **h–**

INFLUENTIAL LADY (IRE) 5 b.m. Doyen (IRE) – Lady Zephyr (IRE) (Toulon) [2018/19 b16.2g b15.8g³ b16g⁴ h19.5m⁵ Apr 22] €11,000 3-y-o: fifth foal: half-sister to fairly useful hurdler/useful chaser Owen Na View (15f-17f winner, by Presenting) and bumper winner Gowithdflo (by Flemensfirth): dam (h125) bumper/2m-21f hurdle winner: modest form in bumpers: best effort when third in mares event at Uttoxeter: mistakes when tailed off in mares novice on hurdling debut: tried in eyeshields. *Warren Greatrex*   **h–** **b81**

INFORMATEUR (FR) 6 b.g. Maresca Sorrento (FR) – Isarella (GER) (Second Set (IRE)) [2018/19 h100p, b87: h16.2s² h21.2g* h22d⁵ h20.6s² h19.3g⁴ h17v³ Mar 17] placed in bumpers: fairly useful hurdler: won novice at Sedgefield in November: second in similar event at Newcastle in December: stays 21f: acts on soft going. *Sue Smith* **h116**

INGLEBY HOLLOW 7 ch.g. Beat Hollow – Mistress Twister (Pivotal) [2018/19 h93p: h16g³ h16.8d* h16.8s* h16.2g Mar 23] fairly useful form over hurdles: won maiden at Sedgefield in January and novice there in February: raced around 2m: acts on soft going: wears tongue tie. *David O'Meara* **h123**

INHERITANCE THIEF 7 b.g. Black Sam Bellamy (IRE) – Red And White (IRE) (Red Ransom (USA)) [2018/19 b93: h16.7g Oct 30] has had breathing operation: placed in bumpers: tailed off in novice on hurdling debut. *Venetia Williams* **h–**

INICIAR (GER) 9 b.g. Galileo (IRE) – Iota (GER) (Tiger Hill (IRE)) [2018/19 h19.2g⁵ h21.9g⁵ h23.9m Jun 21] has had breathing operation: fairly useful handicap hurdler, below best in 2018/19: should stay beyond 2m: acts on soft going: in headgear last 5 starts. *David Pipe* **h112**

INIESTA (IRE) 8 b.g. Galileo (IRE) – Red Evie (IRE) (Intikhab (USA)) [2018/19 h103: h18.5g³ h18.7m⁴ h18.7m⁶ h19d⁶ h19d^pu h19.5d² h19g² h20.3s⁶ c21g* Apr 20] sturdy gelding: modest handicap hurdler: won at Stratford (conditionals) in June: 7/1, also won novice handicap at Newton Abbot (by head from Old Harry Rocks, well positioned) on chasing debut: stays 21f: acts on good to firm and heavy going: usually wears headgear: usually front runner/races prominently. *Michael Blake* **c101 h97**

INK MASTER (IRE) 9 b.g. Whitmore's Conn (USA) – Welsh Connection (IRE) (Welsh Term) [2018/19 c128, h112: c16.5g⁵ c16g⁵ h18.7m* c16g* c16.4m* c17m² c17.1m² c15.2m^F c16.8m⁴ c16m⁴ Apr 22] workmanlike gelding: fairly useful hurdler: won seller at Stratford in July: fairly useful handicap chaser: won at Perth and Sedgefield in August: second at Kelso in September: stays 19f: acts on good to firm and good to soft going: has worn hood: wears tongue tie: front runner/races prominently. *Donald McCain* **c126 h122**

INNISCASTLE LAD 7 b.g. Kyllachy – Glencal (Compton Place) [2018/19 h102: h17.2g h15.8s⁵ h18.7g⁶ h20.2g h19.6m Oct 4] modest maiden hurdler at best, has deteriorated: unproven beyond 17f: best form on good going: has worn blinkers, including last 4 starts. *Donald McCain* **h81**

INNOCENT GIRL (IRE) 10 b.m. King's Theatre (IRE) – Belle Innocence (FR) (Turgeon (USA)) [2018/19 c117, h96: c19.2m⁴ c21.6g⁴ Jun 5] sturdy mare: winning hurdler: fair handicap chaser: stays 21f: acts on good to firm and good to soft going: wears hood/tongue tie. *Harry Fry* **c99 h–**

INNOCENT TOUCH (IRE) 8 bl.g. Intense Focus (USA) – Guajira (FR) (Mtoto) [2018/19 h–: h16m² h16.7g* h16.3g h17.2g² h16.3m* h16.3m* h16.7g⁵ h16m* h16.8g^F Apr 17] useful hurdler: won at Bangor in May, Stratford in August and September, and Wetherby (by neck from Midnight Shadow) in October: raced around 2m: acts on good to firm going. *Henry Daly* **h132**

INNOKO (FR) 9 gr.g. Carlotamix (FR) – Chalana (Ashkalani (IRE)) [2018/19 h20g² h23d⁴ Aug 29] good-topped gelding: fair on Flat, stays 16.5f: fair handicap hurdler: stays 2½m: acts on good to soft going: wears headgear: tried in tongue tie. *Robert Stephens* **h102**

IN REM (FR) 4 b.g. Kapgarde (FR) – Etoile des Iles (FR) (Starborough) [2018/19 b16.3g² Mar 30] seventh foal: half-brother to French 17f chase winner South Pacific (by Martaline) and French 17f hurdle winner Turtle Bay (by Turtle Bowl): dam, French 17f hurdle winner, also 7f winner on Flat: 7/1, second in bumper at Stratford (10 lengths behind Enemy Coast Ahead). *Nick Williams* **b93**

INSPIREUS (IRE) 6 b.g. Scorpion (IRE) – Miniconjou (IRE) (Be My Native (USA)) [2018/19 h90: h21m h20g⁴ h21.6g⁴ h20.5m⁵ h21.6s h20.5d⁴ h23.1d⁵ Apr 9] workmanlike gelding: modest maiden hurdler: should stay 3m: acts on good to soft going. *Seamus Mullins* **h89**

INSTANT ATTRACTION (IRE) 8 b.g. Tagula (IRE) – Coup de Coeur (IRE) (Kahyasi) [2018/19 h94: h16.2g⁵ Oct 7] has had breathing operation: fairly useful on Flat, stays 10.5f: modest form both starts over hurdles. *Jedd O'Keeffe* **h94**

INSTANT KARMA (IRE) 8 b.g. Peintre Celebre (USA) – Kotdiji (Mtoto) [2018/19 h–: h15.8m h18.6g⁶ h19.2g⁶ h23.3g h18.5s^rr Jul 30] rather leggy gelding: has had breathing operation: fair handicap hurdler: stays 19f: acts on soft and good to firm going: tried in cheekpieces: wears tongue tie: one to treat with caution (refused to race final start). *Jamie Snowden* **h102 §**

INSTANT REPLAY (IRE) 7 ch.g. Fruits of Love (USA) – Ding Dong Belle (Minster **c121**
Son) [2018/19 c122, h93: h20d c20s c16.4g² c17.1g² c19.3d* c19.3d* h20.2g Apr 25] **h–**
lengthy gelding: maiden hurdler: fairly useful handicap chaser: won at Sedgefield in
January: stays 21f: acts on heavy going: in cheekpieces last 4 starts: usually leads.
Brian Ellison

INSTINGTIVE (IRE) 8 b.g. Scorpion (IRE) – Fully Focused (IRE) (Rudimentary **c94**
(USA)) [2018/19 c–, h87: h20.2g h16.2g h20.2g c20.1g³ c15.9d² c20.5d² c20s c16.5v² **h62**
c20v² c15.6s³ c16.5s³ c15.9g⁵ c20v² h17v⁴ c20m* Apr 20] tall gelding: modest handicap
hurdler, below form in 2018/19: modest handicap chaser: won at Carlisle in April: stays
2½m: acts on good to firm and heavy going: tried in blinkers: has worn tongue tie.
Lisa Harrison

INSUFFICIENT FUNDS (IRE) 9 b.g. Bach (IRE) – Peace Time Beauty (IRE) (Saddlers' **c–**
Hall (IRE)) [2018/19 h15.8g Jun 20] point winner: behind in hunter chase/maiden hurdle: **h–**
tried in cheekpieces. *Henry Oliver*

INSULT (IRE) 6 b.g. Scorpion (IRE) – Zenaide (IRE) (Zaffaran (USA)) [2018/19 h21s² **h130 p**
h20.2d* h24d⁴ Apr 23] €50,000 3-y-o: half-brother to 3 winners, including bumper winner/
useful hurdler Myska (2m-2¾m winner, by Presenting) and fair 2m hurdle winner/winning
pointer Six Gun Serenade (by Kalanisi): dam, bumper winner, half-sister to fair hurdler/
fairly useful chaser (stayed 3m) Very Stylish: useful form over hurdles: won maiden at
Punchestown (by 2¾ lengths from Opposites Attract) in February: 3½ lengths fourth of 23
to My Sister Sarah in handicap at same course shortly after end of British season, rallying
well near finish: open to further progress. *Henry de Bromhead, Ireland*

INTERCONNECTED 5 br.g. Network (GER) – R de Rien Sivola (FR) (Robin des **h122 p**
Champs (FR)) [2018/19 h20.5d² Mar 1] £220,000 4-y-o: well-made gelding: second foal:
half-brother to fairly useful hurdler/useful chaser Little Miss Poet (17f-2½m winner, by
Yeats): dam (c122/h112), 2m-2½m hurdle/chase winner, sister to fair hurdler/useful chaser
(stayed 21f) Pur de Sivola: easy winner on completed start in points: 8/1, plenty of promise
when second in novice at Newbury (¾ length behind Emitom) on hurdling debut: sure to
progress. *Nicky Henderson*

INTERCOOLER TURBO (IRE) 10 gr.g. Dr Massini (IRE) – Moigh Endeavour (IRE) **c–**
(Ala Hounak) [2018/19 c16.3g⁵ c15.7g⁵ h21.7m c25.7gᵖᵘ Nov 5] point winner: no form **h–**
over hurdles/fences: tried in headgear. *Phil York*

INTERNAL TRANSFER 8 b.g. Kayf Tara – La Dame Brune (FR) (Mansonnien (FR)) **c131 p**
[2018/19 h22.2m h20d³ h20s² h21g c22.5d* c19.5g* Apr 11] second foal: brother to a **h110**
winning pointer: dam (c99/h113), unreliable 2½m/21f hurdle winner, half-sister to fairly
useful hurdler/useful chaser (2m-21f winner) Nikos Extra: point winner: fair handicap
hurdler: useful form over fences: won novice in December and handicap in April (by 6
lengths from Damut), both at Limerick: stays 23f: acts on heavy going: front runner/races
prominently: likely to progress further as a chaser. *Eric McNamara, Ireland*

IN THE HOLD (IRE) 9 b.g. Stowaway – Carrigeen Kerria (IRE) (Kemal (FR)) [2018/19 **c–**
c104, h83: c26gᵖᵘ May 9] point winner: maiden hurdler: fair chaser: stayed 25f: acted on **h–**
good to soft going: dead. *Evan Williams*

IN THE PIPELINE (IRE) 6 b.g. Oscar (IRE) – Kerriemuir Lass (IRE) (Celtic Swing) **h101**
[2018/19 b–: h19.2g³ h19.2g² h16g Nov 9] fair form over hurdles: best effort when third
in novice at Towcester in May: will be suited by 2½m+: has joined Jonjo O'Neill.
Brendan Powell

INTIFADAH (IRE) 7 b.g. Intikhab (USA) – Cuilaphuca (IRE) (Danetime (IRE)) **c–**
[2018/19 c–, h80: h19.9g⁶ h15.8m³ h20g⁴ h16.7m³ h16.8m Aug 30] compact gelding: **h95**
modest handicap hurdler: didn't take to chasing: unproven beyond 17f: acts on good to firm
going: has worn headgear, including in 2018/19: wears tongue tie: usually races towards
rear. *Dan Skelton*

INTO THE BREACH (FR) 6 b.g. Al Namix (FR) – Arvicaya (Kahyasi) [2018/19 b–: **h94**
h16v⁵ h16.2g⁶ h20.1vᵖᵘ Mar 14] no form in bumpers: modest form over hurdles. *James Ewart*

INTO THE MIST 4 b.f. Black Sam Bellamy (IRE) – Kullu Valley (Turgeon (USA)) **b68**
[2018/19 b12.6s b17.7v⁵ Mar 6] £1,500 3-y-o: fourth foal: half-sister to bumper winner/fair
hurdler Horsted Valley (23f-27f winner, by Fair Mix): dam unraced sister to useful French
hurdler (2¼m/19f winner) Brighter Later: poor form in bumpers. *Jo Davis*

INVESTIGATION 5 gr.g. Rip Van Winkle (IRE) – Syann (IRE) (Daylami (IRE)) **h– §**
[2018/19 h–§: h16.2d h16.7g⁶ May 20] fair on Flat, stays 11.5f: no form over hurdles: in
hood last 2 starts: temperamental. *Shaun Harris*

INVICTA LAKE (IRE) 12 b.g. Dr Massini (IRE) – Classic Material (Classic Cliche **c91**
(IRE)) [2018/19 c108, h105: h20.5g⁵ h25g h23.1g c25.7s⁵ c21.6v⁴ c17.8v³ c26d⁴ c21.6v* **h–**
c21.6d⁶ c21.4g⁵ Mar 20] sturdy gelding: winning hurdler: modest handicap chaser: won at
Fontwell in February: stays 3¼m: acts on heavy going: wears headgear: usually races
towards rear. *Suzy Smith*

INVINCIBLE WISH (IRE) 7 b.g. Vale of York (IRE) – Moonlight Wish (IRE) (Peintre **h–**
Celebre (USA)) [2018/19 h16.7g Aug 3] fair on Flat, stays 1½m: modest form over
hurdles for Trevor Wall in 2016/17: well held only outing in sphere since: wears hood.
Matt Sheppard

INVISIBLE CLOUDS (IRE) 6 gr.g. Cloudings (IRE) – Go My Dream (Tirol) [2018/19 **h75**
b–: b17.7g h20g⁵ h20.3s⁵ h21.4g⁶ h16d h27sᵖᵘ Feb 21] behind in bumpers/over hurdles: **b–**
tried in cheekpieces. *Warren Greatrex*

INVISIBLE SHADOW 4 b.g. Oasis Dream – Tavy (Pivotal) [2018/19 b13.7m⁵ h16.3g **h–**
Mar 30] fifth in junior bumper on debut for Olly Murphy: little show on Flat or in novice **b70**
hurdle (in cheekpieces/tongue strap). *Alex Hales*

INVITATION ONLY (IRE) 8 b.g. Flemensfirth (USA) – Norabelle (FR) (Alamo Bay **c159**
(USA)) [2018/19 c154, h–: c21.5s³ c25s* c26.3dᶠ Mar 15] sturdy gelding: winning hurdler: **h–**
very smart chaser: won Thyestes Handicap Chase at Gowran (by 1¼ lengths from Alpha
des Obeaux) in January: fell fatally tenth in Cheltenham Gold Cup: stayed 25f: acted on
heavy going: usually raced close up. *W. P. Mullins, Ireland*

INVOLVE 5 b.g. Dansili – Popular (Oasis Dream) [2018/19 h–, b67: h16m h16d h16gᵖᵘ **h–**
Jun 24] rather leggy gelding: poor form in bumpers: none over hurdles. *Kim Bailey*

IOLANI (GER) 7 b.g. Sholokhov (IRE) – Imogen (GER) (Tiger Hill (IRE)) [2018/19 **h104**
h110, h103: h17.2g h16.8m⁴ h16.8m* h19.9g* h16.2g* h15.6g⁴ h17.1v h19.9sᵖᵘ h16g⁴
h16.8v Jan 27] has had breathing operation: fair handicap hurdler: won at Sedgefield
(twice) and Kelso in October: stays 2½m: acts on good to firm and good to soft going:
usually wears headgear/tongue tie: usually races towards rear. *Dianne Sayer*

Goffs Thyestes Handicap Chase, Gowran Park—a very smart performance by the ill-fated
Invitation Only as he proves too strong for top weight Alpha des Obeaux (blinkers)

IONA DAYS (IRE) 14 br.g. Epistolaire (IRE) – Miss Best (FR) (Grand Tresor (FR)) **c82**
[2018/19 c95, h–: c20.5m⁵ c21.4g⁴ Jun 1] tall gelding: maiden hurdler: modest handicap **h–**
chaser, below form in 2018/19: stays 3m: acts on good to firm and heavy going: usually
wears headgear. *Julian Smith*

IONA ISLAND 6 b.m. Dutch Art – Still Small Voice (Polish Precedent (USA)) [2018/19 **h–**
h18.5g h18.7g⁵ Aug 28] dam half-sister to smart hurdler (stayed 21f) Cotton Mill: modest
on Flat, stays 2m: well held in maiden/novice over hurdles. *Jean-Rene Auvray*

IONA LAD (IRE) 4 b.g. Scorpion (IRE) – April Thistle (IRE) (Alphabatim (USA)) **h–**
[2018/19 b16.6g³ h21.9gᵖᵘ Apr 21] well beaten in bumper: pulled up in maiden on hurdling **b61**
debut. *Tim Vaughan*

IRISH HAWKE (IRE) 7 b.g. Montjeu (IRE) – Ahdaab (USA) (Rahy (USA)) [2018/19 **h–**
h89: h21.2m Aug 30] modest hurdler, below form sole start in 2018/19: stays 21f: acts on
good to soft going: tried in blinkers: wears tongue tie: usually races towards rear.
Donald McCain

IRISH OCTAVE (IRE) 9 b.g. Gamut (IRE) – Fairytaleofnewyork (IRE) (Zaffaran **c108**
(USA)) [2018/19 c93, h–: c24d² c24g* c24.1g* c24.1g⁴ c25.5gᶠ c24d⁵ c24.2g c23.6d⁴ **h–**
c23.6d* c24g³ Apr 25] has had breathing operation: maiden hurdler: fair handicap chaser:
won at Warwick in May, Bangor in June and Chepstow in April: stays 3m: acts on soft
going: wears headgear: usually races off pace. *Rosemary Gasson*

IRISH PRINCE (IRE) 6 b.g. Presenting – Court Leader (IRE) (Supreme Leader) **h97 §**
[2018/19 h–p, b75: h23g² h21d h23.5dᵖᵘ Feb 16] compact gelding: has had breathing
operation: modest form over hurdles: stays 23f: in blinkers last 3 starts: one to avoid.
David Pipe

IRISH PROPHECY (IRE) 6 b.g. Azamour (IRE) – Prophets Honor (FR) (Highest **c–**
Honor (FR)) [2018/19 h121: c16gᵖᵘ h19.8gᵖᵘ Apr 27] tall, good sort: has had breathing **h–**
operation: fairly useful hurdler: bled on chasing debut. *Emma Lavelle*

IRISH ROE (IRE) 8 b.m. Vinnie Roe – Betty's The Best (IRE) (Oscar (IRE)) **h131**
[2018/19 h136: h16g³ h16.4g⁴ h16.6g² h15.6g h16.6g³ h16.2g h16m⁴ Apr 13] small,
sparely-made mare: has had breathing operation: useful handicap hurdler: second at
Doncaster (4½ lengths behind Equus Amadeus) in December and third in Yorkshire Rose
Mares' Hurdle at same course (3¼ lengths behind Lady Buttons) in January: raced around
2m: acts on soft and good to firm going: tried in cheekpieces. *Peter Atkinson*

IRISH THISTLE (IRE) 12 b.g. Luso – Which Thistle (IRE) (Saddlers' Hall (IRE)) **c71 x**
[2018/19 c93, h–: c20d³ c19.4m⁴ c23m⁵ c20g³ c21g⁶ h26.4g⁶ c20.2m⁴ c20g⁴ c22.7f⁴ **h–**
c23.6d⁵ c23.8mᵖᵘ Mar 31] workmanlike gelding: winning hurdler: poor handicap chaser:
stays 23f: acts on good to firm and heavy going: has worn headgear/tongue tie: often let
down by jumping. *Dai Williams*

IRON CHANCELLOR (IRE) 14 b.g. Alderbrook – Masriyna (IRE) (Shahrastani (USA)) **c–**
[2018/19 c–§, h–: c24.2gᶠ Mar 29] lengthy gelding: multiple point winner: handicap chaser, **h–**
fair hunter chaser: stays 3¼m: acts on heavy going: has worn headgear. *Miss J. I. Bedi*

IRON HORSE 8 b.g. Kayf Tara – What A Vintage (IRE) (Un Desperado (FR)) [2018/19 **h109**
h105: h21d⁵ h19.7s h21.2d h19sᵘʳ h19.5g² Apr 26] big, strong gelding: fair form over
hurdles: stays 2½m: acts on heavy going: in cheekpieces last 3 starts. *Richard Phillips*

IRONWIL (IRE) 8 b.g. Indian River (FR) – My Delight (IRE) (Un Desperado (FR)) **h–**
[2018/19 h21.6m⁴ Jun 26] Irish maiden pointer: in cheekpieces, tailed off in novice on
hurdling debut. *Ryan Chapman*

ISAACSTOWN LAD (IRE) 12 b.g. Milan – Friends of Friends (IRE) (Phardante (FR)) **c–**
[2018/19 c–, h127: h24.7g h24g h25s* h24.1d⁴ h26.6g⁶ Apr 25] sturdy gelding: Irish point **h123**
winner: fairly useful handicap hurdler: won at Carlisle in December: placed sole outing
over fences: stays 27f: acts on heavy going: tried in cheekpieces: usually races off pace.
Nicky Richards

ISAAC WONDER (IRE) 4 b.g. Born To Sea (IRE) – Najaaba (USA) (Bahhare (USA)) **h109**
[2018/19 h16g² h16.3s⁵ h16g⁵ h15.8g² h16g² Apr 11] fair on Flat, stays 1m: fair form over
hurdles: usually races prominently. *Michael Scudamore*

IS A REAL CHAMP (IRE) 5 ch.g. Getaway (GER) – Siobhans Charm (IRE) **b98**
(Flemensfirth (USA)) [2018/19 b16d³ Apr 6] €43,000 3-y-o: first foal: dam unraced half-
sister to useful hurdler (stayed 25f) Paperprophet: runner-up on sole start in Irish points:
9/4, third in bumper at Chepstow (4 lengths behind One Touch). *Paul Nicholls*

I SEE YOU WELL (FR) 6 b.g. Air Chief Marshal (IRE) – Bonne Mere (FR) (Stepneyev (IRE)) [2018/19 c113, h118: c16.2m⁵ c21.6g* c22.6m⁴ h20m⁵ c19.4s⁵ c25.7s* c28.5dᶠ c30.7dᵘʳ h25s⁴ c28.4m⁴ Apr 20] compact gelding: fair handicap hurdler: fairly useful handicap chaser: won at Fontwell in June and Plumpton in December: stays 3¼m: acts on soft and good to firm going: races off pace. *Seamus Mullins* **c122 h112**

ISHARAH (USA) 6 b.g. Kitten's Joy (USA) – Menekineko (USA) (Kingmambo (USA)) [2018/19 h72: h16g h22.1g h20d⁴ h19.5v Mar 16] modest nowadays on Flat, stays 16.5f: poor maiden hurdler: stays 2½m: acts on good to soft going: in cheekpieces last 2 starts. *Noel C. Kelly, Ireland* **h83**

ISHKHARA LADY 5 b.m. Scorpion (IRE) – Loxhill Lady (Supreme Leader) [2018/19 b17.7s* Dec 17] £27,000 3-y-o: fifth foal: half-sister to bumper winner/useful hurdler Zulu Oscar (2m-21f winner, by Oscar) and fair hurdler/fairly useful chaser Royal Salute (2¼m-3¼m winner, by Flemensfirth): dam unraced: 4/1, won bumper at Plumpton (by 15 lengths from Moroder, impressively) on debut: useful prospect. *Harry Fry* **b104 p**

ISIS BLUE 9 b.g. Cockney Rebel (IRE) – Bramaputra (IRE) (Choisir (AUS)) [2018/19 h96: c15.7mᵖᵘ h16m May 14] modest form on hurdling debut in 2017/18, standout effort in sphere: pulled up in novice handicap on chasing debut: in tongue tie last 3 starts: usually raced nearer last than first: dead. *Keiran Burke* **c– h–**

ISKABEG LANE (IRE) 8 b.g. Westerner – Nosey Oscar (IRE) (Oscar (IRE)) [2018/19 c107, h100: c24.2g⁶ c21.1g³ c20.3s⁴ c25.2g³ c23.4d² c21.4d² c21.4g* c23.4d Apr 6] workmanlike gelding: maiden hurdler: fair handicap chaser: won at Market Rasen in March: stays 25f: acts on heavy going: usually front runner/races prominently: carries head awkwardly. *Sue Smith* **c104 h–**

ISKRABOB 9 ch.g. Tobougg (IRE) – Honour Bolton (Past Glories) [2018/19 c–, h–: c23.5dᵖᵘ c19.7s Dec 17] workmanlike gelding: point winner: little impact under Rules. *Diana Grissell* **c– h–**

ISLAND HEIGHTS (IRE) 10 b.g. Heron Island (IRE) – La Reina (IRE) (Executive Perk) [2018/19 c–, h80: h23.9g² h25.4s⁴ h23.8g* h23.8g³ Dec 10] compact gelding: fairly useful handicap hurdler: won at Musselburgh in November: third at same course in December: winning chaser: stays 25f: acts on heavy going: tried in visor: front runner/races prominently. *Lucinda Russell* **c– h119**

ISLE OF DESTINY (IRE) 6 b.m. Gold Well – Young Amelie (FR) (Garde Royale) [2018/19 h19.4s⁵ h18.8g³ h18.8g³ h24d³ h20.1g* h24g h20.5v⁵ Nov 14] €30,000 3-y-o, €78,000 4-y-o: fourth foal: sister to fairly useful hurdler/useful chaser Goose Man (2m-2½m winner), stays 3m, and half-sister to bumper winners by Heron Island and Great Palm: dam once-raced half-sister to useful 2m chaser Best Lover: runner-up on sole start in points: fair hurdler: won mares handicap at Hexham in October: best effort at 2½m on good going: in cheekpieces last 4 starts. *Gordon Elliott, Ireland* **h110**

ISLEOFHOPENDREAMS 12 b.g. Flemensfirth (USA) – Cool Island (IRE) (Turtle Island (IRE)) [2018/19 c143, h–: c25sᵖᵘ c28.7dᵖᵘ c24d² c29d² Apr 22] winning hurdler: smart handicap chaser: runner-up in Irish Grand National at Fairyhouse for second successive season, beaten 1¾ lengths by Burrows Saint: fatally injured at Auteuil when next seen: stayed 3¾m: acted on heavy going: usually raced off pace. *W. P. Mullins, Ireland* **c152 h–**

ISLE ROAD (IRE) 10 b.g. Heron Island (IRE) – Corries Rein (IRE) (Anshan) [2018/19 c87, h–: h19.9m* c20.9m* c21.2m⁴ c17.4gᵖᵘ Aug 20] sturdy gelding: modest form over hurdles: won conditionals handicap at Uttoxeter early in season: similar form over fences: won novice handicap at Stratford in June: likely to prove best up to 21f: acts on good to firm going. *John David Riches* **c93 h93**

IS LOVE ALIVE 10 ch.g. Presenting – Lovely Origny (FR) (Robin des Champs (FR)) [2018/19 c66, h–: c21.7dᵖᵘ c23.6d* c20.3d⁶ c23.6dᵘʳ Jan 25] winning hurdler: poor handicap chaser nowadays: won at Huntingdon in December: stays 3m: acts on soft going: has worn headgear, including last 3 starts: wears tongue tie. *Adrian Wintle* **c76 h–**

ISOBEL BLEU 4 b.f. Arvico (FR) – Applepie Lady (IRE) (Lord Americo) [2018/19 b15.7d b16d Mar 21] angular filly: fifth foal: dam, placed in bumpers, winning pointer: last in 2 bumpers: in tongue tie second start. *James Grassick* **b–**

ISTIMRAAR (IRE) 8 b.g. Dansili – Manayer (IRE) (Sadler's Wells (USA)) [2018/19 c–, h56: c17g* Apr 21] winning hurdler: lightly raced over fences: off 21 months and retried in tongue tie, won novice handicap at Plumpton on sole outing in 2018/19: stays 2½m: acts on good to firm and heavy going: usually wears headgear. *Dan Skelton* **c79 h–**

ITALIAN RIVER 7 b.g. Milan – Over The Flow (Overbury (IRE)) [2018/19 h19.5s^{pu} h23.1s^{pu} c25.2g^{pu} Mar 26] pulled up all starts over hurdles/fences. *Bob Buckler*

c–
h–

ITALIAN SUMMER 4 br.f. Milan – Midsummer Magic (Muhtarram (USA)) [2018/19 b16m^4 Apr 22] fourth foal: half-sister to bumper winner/fair hurdler Summer Storm (2m/17f winner, by Lucarno): dam (h108), 2m hurdle winner (stayed 21f), half-sister to useful hurdlers/chasers Close Touch (stayed 2½m) and Open Hearted (stayed 3m): 5/4, seemed unsuited by track when fourth in mares maiden bumper at Fakenham (11¼ lengths behind Sopat): should do better. *Nicky Henderson*

b77 p

ITCHY FEET (FR) 5 b.g. Cima de Triomphe (IRE) – Maeva Candas (FR) (Brier Creek (USA)) [2018/19 b91: b16.3m* h15.7g* h16m* h16.4g^2 h16.4s^3 h16.5d^4 Apr 5] good-topped gelding: fairly useful form in bumpers: impressive when winning at Stratford in September: useful form over hurdles: won novice at Southwell and listed novice at Kempton (by 2¼ lengths from Grand Sancy) in October: third in Supreme Novices' Hurdle at Cheltenham (5 lengths behind Klassical Dream, bled) in March: likely to stay beyond 2m: acts on soft and good to firm going. *Olly Murphy*

h144
b100

ITOLDYOU (IRE) 13 ch.g. Salford Express (IRE) – Adisadel (IRE) (Petardia) [2018/19 c99§, h–§: c28.5d Nov 19] sturdy gelding: maiden hurdler: modest chaser: stays 29f: acts on good to firm and heavy going: wears headgear: has worn tongue tie: usually races prominently: temperamental. *Linda Jewell*

c– §
h– §

ITSABOUTIME (IRE) 9 gr.g. Whitmore's Conn (USA) – Blazing Love (IRE) (Fruits of Love (USA)) [2018/19 h56: h19d h23.9d^6 h23.9s^6 h21.7g* Apr 12] angular gelding: poor handicap hurdler: won at Fontwell in April: stays 2¾m: acts on heavy going: tried in cheekpieces: sometimes in tongue tie. *Helen Nelmes*

h77

Kate & Andrew Brooks's "Itchy Feet"

ITS'AFREEBEE (IRE) 9 br.g. Danroad (AUS) – Aphra Benn (IRE) (In The Wings) c–
[2018/19 c–, h96: h19.4g² Jan 26] workmanlike gelding: fairly useful handicap hurdler: h120
second at Doncaster sole start in sphere in 2018/19: winning chaser: stays 21f: acts on
heavy going: has worn headgear/tongue tie: has raced lazily. *Richard Spencer*

ITS A LITTLE RISKY 6 b.m. Windsor Castle – Risky Witness (IRE) (Witness Box b–
(USA)) [2018/19 b–: b15.8d^pu Oct 20] no form in bumpers. *Christian Williams*

IT'S ALL ABOUT ME (IRE) 7 b.m. King's Theatre (IRE) – Annie Spectrim (IRE) h89
(Spectrum (IRE)) [2018/19 h–, b73: h16.2g h17.2g h16.2g h22.1m h23.3g⁶ h25.3g²
h24.1g⁵ Apr 11] rather leggy mare: modest maiden hurdler: stays 25f: best form on good
going. *Micky Hammond*

ITS ALL A LARK (IRE) 6 b.m. Oscar (IRE) – Itsalark (IRE) (Definite Article) [2018/19 h117
h20.4m⁵ h16g³ h16m² h16d⁵ h18.1g* h16.4s² h16.6d* h16.3g⁴ Apr 14] €15,000 3-y-o: first
foal: dam (b102), bumper winner on only start, out of sister to fairly useful hurdler/useful
chaser (stayed 2¾m) Washington Lad: winning pointer: fairly useful hurdler: won
handicaps at Kelso (amateurs) in January and Doncaster (mares) in March: left Colin Bowe
after fourth start: stays 2¼m: acts on soft and good to firm going: wears tongue tie: front
runner. *Donald McCain*

ITS ALL GUESSWORK (IRE) 7 b.g. Mahler – La Lambertine (FR) (Glaieul (USA)) c125 p
[2018/19 h123, b91: c22.5d³ c19.9g² c22s² c20g* c24g^F h24d³ c26d Mar 14] tall gelding: h121
fairly useful hurdler: similar form over fences: won maiden at Navan in September: stays
3m: acts on soft going: wears tongue tie: remains with potential as a chaser. *Gordon Elliott,
Ireland*

ITS ALL OR NOTHING 10 gr.g. Terimon – Little Vera (Carlingford Castle) [2018/19 c–
c104: c23d⁶ Apr 4] multiple point winner: fair form in hunter chases, well held in maiden
in 2018/19: stays 3m: acts on good to firm and good to soft going. *Miss C. Rowe*

ITSAMANSLIFE (IRE) 6 b.g. Mahler – Medieval Banquet (IRE) (Mister Lord (USA)) c101
[2018/19 h94, b–: h21.4m^pu h19.5s⁶ h25.5v⁴ c23.6d* c24.2g⁵ c23.6g^pu Mar 19] poor h76
maiden hurdler on balance: fair form over fences: won novice handicap at Huntingdon in
January: stays 3m: acts on soft going: in tongue tie last 3 starts. *Katy Price*

ITS A STING (IRE) 10 b.g. Scorpion (IRE) – Wyndham Sweetmare (IRE) (Mister Lord c–
(USA)) [2018/19 c97, h–: c20d⁵ May 30] good-bodied gelding: has had breathing operation: h–
maiden hurdler: modest form on reappearance in 2017/18, standout effort over fences: stays
19f: acts on soft going: has worn hood: usually races nearer last than first. *Oliver Sherwood*

IT'S BUSTER (IRE) 8 b.g. Stowaway – Late Guest (IRE) (Gothland (FR)) [2018/19 h–, c–
b89: h16.8g⁴ h22.1g^F h22.1m h17.2g³ h20.3g⁴ c20.3g c20.3d^pu Nov 20] sturdy gelding: h83
poor maiden hurdler: didn't take to chasing: stays 2½m: best form on good going: front
runner/races prominently. *Sue Smith*

IT'S FINE WINE 6 b.g. Multiplex – Reem Two (Mtoto) [2018/19 h–, b80: h22g⁴ h19d h100
Dec 30] fair form over hurdles. *Graeme McPherson*

IT'S FOR ALAN 6 b.g. Multiplex – Miss Keck (Inchinor) [2018/19 h20g³ h20.5s⁶ h20.5s h91
h21.4g h21s Mar 10] close-coupled gelding: first foal: dam (b84), placed in bumpers/
winner around 2m on Flat, half-sister to fairly useful hurdler/useful chaser (stayed 2½m)
Psychomodo: off mark in Irish points at fifth attempt: modest form over hurdles: wears
hood: usually races towards rear. *Jo Davis*

IT'S GOT LEGS (IRE) 6 b.g. Getaway (GER) – Lady Cadia (FR) (Cadoudal (FR)) h123
[2018/19 h107, b92: h17.7g³ h16.8v³ h19.3m² h24.5g³ h23.5g⁶ h20.5d⁵ h19.8s² h19.8s⁵
h20.5g* h20.5g* Apr 21] sturdy gelding: fairly useful hurdler: won handicap and novice at
Plumpton in April: should prove as effective at 3m: acts on good to firm and heavy going:
wears visor. *Gary Moore*

IT'S GRAND (IRE) 6 b.g. Westerner – Calomeria (Groom Dancer (USA)) [2018/19 b–: h–
h15.7g⁶ h19.9m^pu Jul 1] no sign of ability. *Donald McCain*

IT'S HOW WE ROLL (IRE) 5 b.g. Fastnet Rock (AUS) – Clodora (FR) (Linamix h–
(FR)) [2018/19 h15.8d h16.5d Mar 11] poor maiden on Flat, stays 1¼m: well held in 2
maiden hurdles: wears cheekpieces. *John Spearing*

IT'S NEVER ENOUGH 5 b.g. Equiano (FR) – Swynford Pleasure (Reprimand) h60
[2018/19 b69: h16.4m⁶ Mar 28] fair maiden on Flat, barely stays 11f: in tongue tie, 25/1,
sixth in novice at Newcastle on hurdling debut. *James Ewart*

IT'S OBVIOUS 7 gr.g. Tobougg (IRE) – Hiho Silver Lining (Silver Patriarch (IRE)) c–
[2018/19 c110, h108: c25.8g^pu c25.8g^pu c19.4v c24s^ur Dec 31] workmanlike gelding: has h–
had breathing operation: fair form over hurdles: similar form over fences, no show in
2018/19: wears headgear: usually wears tongue tie. *David Pipe*

IT'S O KAY 6 b.m. Shirocco (GER) – Presenting Copper (IRE) (Presenting) [2018/19 b91: **h118**
h16.3d h15.5g* h16d⁴ h19.6g² h21.2d⁴ h23.8g⁴ h21.2m⁴ Apr 1] bumper winner: fairly
useful hurdler: won mares maiden at Leicester in December: likely to prove best up to
2¾m: acts on good to soft going: often in headgear. *Olly Murphy*

ITSONLYROCKNROLL (IRE) 7 ch.g. Shantou (USA) – Compelled (IRE) (Anshan) **h108**
[2018/19 h24g⁶ h20.5g h17.7d⁴ h17.7v⁶ h19.2d h19.8s h19.2v⁶ h17.7g⁴ h17.7g² Apr 22]
sturdy gelding: first foal: dam (c95/h110) 2m hurdle winner: bumper winner: fair maiden
hurdler: left W. P. Mullins after second start: stays 2¼m: acts on soft going: tried in hood:
wears tongue tie. *Chris Gordon*

ITS PANDORAMA (IRE) 9 b.g. Misternando – Gretchen's Castle (IRE) (Carlingford **c114**
Castle) [2018/19 h110: h20.1g² h20.1g⁶ c21.2m² c20.1g⁴ Sep 17] fair handicap hurdler: **h112**
similar form over fences: better effort when second in maiden at Cartmel: stayed 2¾m:
acted on good to firm and heavy going: wore headgear: front runner/raced prominently:
dead. *Brian Ellison*

IT'S PROBABLY ME 4 b.f. Great Pretender (IRE) – Sting In The Gale (Scorpion (IRE)) **b91**
[2018/19 b15.7d* Apr 9] second foal: dam unraced half-sister to useful 2m/17f hurdle
winner Kayf Grace out of useful hurdler/fairly useful chaser (stayed 2½m) Potter's Gale,
herself half-sister to Cheltenham Gold Cup winner Denman: 16/1, won conditionals/
amateurs maiden bumper at Southwell (by 3½ lengths from Konigin Ara) on debut.
Henry Daly

IUSETALUVHERONCE (IRE) 7 b.g. Golan (IRE) – Mollys Present (IRE) (Presenting) **c–**
[2018/19 h20m h21m⁶ h20m h16d c22.7g⁵ h21.7g Apr 12] €17,000 3-y-o: fifth foal: dam **h–**
failed to complete in points: fair maiden hurdler at best, little impact in 2018/19: well held
both starts over fences: left Patrick Neville after fifth start: stays 21f: acts on heavy going:
usually wears headgear: tried in tongue tie. *Tim Vaughan*

IVANHOE 9 b.g. Haafhd – Marysienka (Primo Dominie) [2018/19 h80: h19.5g Oct 30] **h–**
angular gelding: fair hurdler at best, little form since 2015/16: stays 19f: acts on heavy
going: tried in visor. *Michael Blanshard*

IVANOVICH GORBATOV (IRE) 7 b.g. Montjeu (IRE) – Northern Gulch (USA) **h145**
(Gulch (USA)) [2018/19 h–: h16g h16s h17d² h16s h16.5g h16g h16g h16g³ h16d* Apr 23]
round-barrelled gelding: smart handicap hurdler: won valuable event at Fairyhouse (by 2½
lengths from Tudor City) in April: unproven beyond 17f: acts on heavy going: has worn
headgear, including most starts in 2018/19: usually wears tongue tie. *Joseph Patrick
O'Brien, Ireland*

IVILNOBLE (IRE) 6 b.g. Alfred Nobel (IRE) – Almutamore (IRE) (Almutawakel) **h112**
[2018/19 h19.4g² h23.6d³ h20.7d³ Feb 17] €18,000 3-y-o, £26,000 5-y-o: fourth foal: dam
(h75), lightly raced over hurdles, 7.5f winner on Flat: third in Irish point on debut: fair form
when placed all 3 starts over hurdles. *Charlie Mann*

IVOR THE FOX 7 b.g. Sakhee (USA) – Florie (Alflora (IRE)) [2018/19 b–: h19.4g^pu Dec **h–**
29] no show in bumper/novice hurdle: tried in tongue tie. *Sara Ender*

IVY'S SHADOW (IRE) 4 b.f. Jammaal – Red Chili (IRE) (Scribano) [2018/19 b15.8d **b–**
Mar 30] €2,000 3-y-o: third foal: dam runner-up in point on only start: tailed off in mares
bumper. *Sam Thomas*

IWASTHEFUTUREONCE (IRE) 6 b.g. Fruits of Love (USA) – Ruthy Lukey (IRE) **c–**
(Oscar (IRE)) [2018/19 h19.7g h21.3s⁴ h19.9s⁴ c23.4g^pu h19.3s³ h19.9s³ Mar 21] €8,000 **h104**
3-y-o, £14,500 5-y-o: second foal: dam unraced half-sister to top-class staying chaser Suny
Bay: off mark in points at third attempt: fair form over hurdles: pulled up in novice on
chasing debut: likely to stay 3m: acts on soft going. *Tim Easterby*

IWILLDOIT 6 b.g. Flying Legend (USA) – Lyricist's Dream (Dreams End) [2018/19 b90: **h121**
h16m³ h19.9g h19.5v⁶ h23d* h23.1d⁶ h25.3d* h23.9s² Apr 7] fairly useful handicap
hurdler: won at Bangor in January and Catterick in March: stays 25f: acts on soft going.
Sam Thomas

IZZY'S CHAMPION (IRE) 5 b.g. Gold Well – Native Crystal (IRE) (Be My Native **h93**
(USA)) [2018/19 b16v h16.2g⁵ h16.2g³ h16.4m⁵ h17m Apr 20] €8,000 3-y-o: closely **b–**
related to 3 winners, including fairly useful hurdler Carrolls Milan (23f-3¼m winner, by
Milan): dam unraced half-sister to fairly useful hurdler/useful chaser (19f-3m winner)
Saxophone: tailed off in bumper: modest form over hurdles: tried in tongue tie. *Lucinda
Russell*

JABOTICABA (FR) 5 ch.g. Muhtathir – Janiceinwonderland (FR) (Ekraar (USA)) **h115**
[2018/19 h121: h16m³ h16.3m⁵ h16.2g² h15.3g h17.7v⁵ h16d⁴ Apr 6] has had breathing
operation: fairly useful handicap hurdler: first past post at Hereford in November, but
demoted after impeding rivals: unproven beyond 2m: acts on soft going: usually held up.
Alan King

JABULANI (FR) 6 gr.g. Martaline – Incorrigible (FR) (Septieme Ciel (USA)) [2018/19 **c98**
h119: c18m⁵ c20.3d⁵ h18.9s² h24.2d* h23.9s³ Apr 7] good-bodied gelding: fairly useful **h122**
handicap hurdler: won at Newbury in March: let down by jumping both outings in handicap
chases: stays 3m: acts on soft going. *Nigel Twiston-Davies*

JACAMAR (GER) 4 b.g. Maxios – Juvena (GER) (Platini (GER)) [2018/19 b14d **h115**
b13.7d⁶ b15.7m⁶ h15.3g* h16.8g³ Apr 20] good-topped gelding: closely related/half- **b70**
brother to 3 winners on Flat, including useful German 7.5f/1m winner Jardina (by
Shirocco): dam useful German 7.5f/1m winner: poor form in bumpers: fairly useful form
over hurdles: 33/1-winner of maiden at Wincanton in April. *Milton Harris*

JACBEQUICK 8 b.g. Calcutta – Toking N' Joken (IRE) (Mukaddamah (USA)) [2018/19 **h113**
h86: h16.7g⁴ h16g* h16.4g h16.5d² h16g¹ h16m² Apr 25] good-topped gelding:
fair handicap hurdler: won at Fakenham in October: raced around 2m: acts on good to firm
and good to soft going: wears visor: usually front runner/races prominently. *David Pipe*

JAC BROWN 5 b.g. Multiplex – Do It On Dani (Weld) [2018/19 b16.3d b16d⁴ Feb 23] **b91**
£10,000 3-y-o: half-brother to modest chaser Dingo Bay (2½m-25f winner, by Karinga
Bay): dam (h111) 3m-27f hurdle winner: much better effort in bumpers when fourth in
conditionals/amateurs maiden event at Chepstow, ending up too far back. *Debra Hamer*

JACKBLACK 7 b.g. Crosspeace (IRE) – Saharan Royal (Val Royal (FR)) [2018/19 h115: **h–**
h16.3m^pu h17.7g⁵ h20.3g^pu Oct 2] fair hurdler: out of sorts in 2018/19: stays easy 2¼m:
acts on good to soft going: usually wears hood: front runner. *Brett Johnson*

JACK DEVINE (IRE) 7 b.g. Kalanisi (IRE) – Sybil Says (IRE) (Flemensfirth (USA)) **c115**
[2018/19 h105: h23.9g* h23.9g* h23.1g⁶ h23.9g⁶ h25.8d* c23.4d⁴ c25.2g⁴ Jan 1] has had **h125**
breathing operations: multiple Irish point winner: fairly useful handicap hurdler: won at
Perth (2) in June and Kelso in November: fair form when fourth in novice handicap at
Newcastle on first of 2 outings over fences: let down by jumping next time: stays 3¼m: acts
on good to soft going: wears visor: tried in tongue tie. *Rose Dobbin*

JACKHAMMER (IRE) 5 b.g. Thewayyouare (USA) – Ask Annie (IRE) (Danehill **h75**
(USA)) [2018/19 h–: h16g h17.2g h15.6g⁵ h15.6g³ Dec 3] formerly useful performer on
Flat: only poor form over hurdles, making mistakes: will prove best around 2m: hooded 3
of last 4 outings, also in tongue tie last 2: held up. *Dianne Sayer*

JACK LAMB 7 gr.g. Sulamani (IRE) – Charlotte Lamb (Pharly (FR)) [2018/19 h97: **h104**
h20.3g h21.2m* h20.1g⁴ h20.9g* h21.3g² h21.2d^ur Apr 23] fair handicap hurdler: won at
Sedgefield in August and Kelso in October: stays 21f: acts on good to firm and good to soft
going: in visor last 5 starts. *Jedd O'Keeffe*

JACKOFHEARTS 11 b.g. Beat Hollow – Boutique (Selkirk (USA)) [2018/19 c68, h–: **c70**
c23.8g² c22.5g^pu c20.1g^pu c23.8g^pu c21.6d Apr 8] maiden hurdler: poor maiden chaser: **h–**
stays 3m: acts on soft and good to firm going: tried in cheekpieces. *Jean McGregor*

JACK REGAN 4 b.g. Rock of Gibraltar (IRE) – Chelsey Jayne (IRE) (Galileo (IRE)) **h122**
[2018/19 h16.7g* Sep 29] closely related to useful 2m hurdle winner Brandon Castle (by
Dylan Thomas) and half-brother to 2m hurdle winner The Statesman (by Zoffany): useful
on Flat, stays 1½m: 2/1, won juvenile at Market Rasen on hurdling debut by 2¼ lengths
from Cracker Factory: seemed sure to progress but not seen after running on Flat following
month, and sold 180,000 gns. *Ian Williams*

JACK RIDDELL 11 br.g. Grape Tree Road – Little Blackie (Royal Fountain) [2018/19 **h– §**
h20.5v^pu h21.3s^R h19.3s^pu Dec 16] shown more temperament than ability over hurdles: in
headgear last 2 starts. *George Bewley*

JACKS LAST HOPE 10 b.g. King's Theatre (IRE) – Ninna Nanna (FR) (Garde Royale) **c130**
[2018/19 c115p, h139: c23.8g* c20.1g² c23g³ c24g² c24g⁴ h24.1m³ h24.7g³ Nov 10] fairly **h129**
useful handicap hurdler: useful form over fences: won novice at Perth in May: stays 3m:
acts on heavy going: wears visor: usually tracks pace. *Chris Grant*

JACK SNIPE 10 b.g. Kirkwall – Sea Snipe (King Luthier) [2018/19 c106, h–: c25.8g* **c100**
c25.8g^pu Jul 6] maiden hurdler: fair handicap chaser: won at Newton Abbot in June: will **h–**
stay long distances: acts on heavy and good to firm going: wears headgear: races
prominently. *Jeremy Scott*

JACKSON HILL (IRE) 5 b.g. Jeremy (USA) – Definite Leader (IRE) (Definite Article) **b85**
[2018/19 b16v³ b17.7s⁴ b15.8v⁴ Mar 16] €36,000 3-y-o: has had breathing operation:
fourth foal: dam unraced half-sister to fair hurdler/useful staying chaser Kinburn: fair form
in bumpers, leaving Ellmarie Holden before reappearance. *Warren Greatrex*

JACK THE HAT (IRE) 14 b.g. Dr Massini (IRE) – Aunt Rose (IRE) (Caribo) [2018/19 **c–**
c108, h93: c20.2g^pu Feb 27] winning hurdler: fairly useful chaser at best: little form since **h–**
summer 2017, including in points: probably stays 25f: acts on heavy and good to firm
going: wears headgear/tongue tie. *Mark George Robinson*

JACKTHEJOURNEYMAN (IRE) 10 b.g. Beneficial – Maslam (IRE) (Robellino **c88 §**
(USA)) [2018/19 c92, h88: c16g³ c15.7g^ur c17.3g c16.5g³ Nov 4] has had breathing **h–**
operation: maiden hurdler: modest handicap chaser: unproven beyond 2m: acts on good to
firm and good to soft going: wears headgear/tongue tie: usually let down by jumping/
attitude. *Tom Gretton*

JACOBITE RISING (FR) 6 b.g. Rob Roy (USA) – Petillante Royale (FR) (Vertical **h–**
Speed (FR)) [2018/19 h110, b70: h15.8d h15.8d h15.7s Mar 18] sturdy gelding: maiden
pointer: fair 2m hurdle winner in 2017/18: lightly raced and no form since: tried in tongue
tie. *Charlie Longsdon*

J'AI FROID (IRE) 6 b.g. Flemensfirth (USA) – Park Wave (IRE) (Supreme Leader) **h110**
[2018/19 b90: h16s h19.5v⁵ h23.3s⁴ h24s h23.1s* Mar 5] fair form over hurdles: much
improved when winning handicap at Exeter in March, galloping on to lead near finish:
thorough stayer: raced on soft/heavy going. *Ben Case*

JAISALMER (IRE) 7 b.g. Jeremy (USA) – Shara (IRE) (Kahyasi) [2018/19 h127: **c112**
c16.3g² c19.2v c20g² Feb 28] stocky gelding: fairly useful hurdler: fair form when 21 **h–**
lengths second of 5 to Knocknanuss in novice at Fakenham on chasing debut: well beaten
in handicaps after: stays 21f: acts on heavy going. *Mark Bradstock*

JAKAMANI 5 b.g. Sulamani (IRE) – Kentford Grebe (Teenoso (USA)) [2018/19 b13.7d **b–**
Jan 25] hooded, well beaten in bumper. *Mark Bradstock*

JALEO (GER) 7 ch.g. New Approach (IRE) – Jambalaya (GER) (Samum (GER)) **c138**
[2018/19 h135: c23s² c20g* c20.3g c21.6g² h21d⁵ h20s³ Apr 20] tall gelding: fairly useful **h119**
hurdler: third in Grade 3 Temple Gwathmey Handicap at Middleburg in April: useful form
over fences: won novice at Worcester (by 7 lengths from Monbeg Legend) in June: left Ben
Pauling after fifth start: stays 23f: acts on heavy going: has worn headgear: usually races
close up. *Jack O. Fisher, USA*

JALINGO (IRE) 8 b.g. Cape Cross (IRE) – Just Special (Cadeaux Genereux) [2018/19 **h106**
h18.5s⁵ h21.7g³ h23.3g⁵ h21g^F h19.9d Nov 25] fair handicap hurdler nowadays: stays 23f,
effective at shorter: acts on heavy going: wears headgear: usually in tongue tie nowadays.
Ali Stronge

JALORS (IRE) 11 b.g. Invincible Spirit (IRE) – Julie Jalouse (USA) (Kris S (USA)) **h–**
[2018/19 h21.9d⁵ May 26] fair maiden on Flat, stays 1¾m: tongue tied, well beaten in
novice on hurdling debut. *Evan Williams*

JAMACHO 5 ch.g. Camacho – Obsessive Secret (IRE) (Grand Lodge (USA)) [2018/19 **h107**
h106: h16.8g* h16.3g² h16m² h16g⁵ h16.3g⁶ h15.8g⁶ h15.8g Oct 16] close-coupled
gelding: has had breathing operation: fair hurdler: won maiden at Sedgefield (left Brian
Ellison after) in May: raced around 2m: acts on good to firm and good to soft going: in
headgear last 2 starts: front runner/races prominently. *Charlie Longsdon*

JAMES BORU (IRE) 6 b.g. Brian Boru – Sparrow's Trap (IRE) (Magical Wonder **h97**
(USA)) [2018/19 b18.8g⁵ b18.3d h20m h18.5g⁴ h20d h16g h19.9s⁴ h23.9g⁵ Apr 24] €6,700 **b–**
4-y-o: third foal: closely related to useful hurdler Massini's Trap (2m-2½m winner, by
Dr Massini), stays 3m: dam poor maiden hurdler: point winner: no form in bumpers:
modest form over hurdles: stays 3m: acts on good to soft going: wears tongue tie: held up.
Noel C. Kelly, Ireland

JAMESON 7 br.g. Midnight Legend – Shatabdi (IRE) (Mtoto) [2018/19 c138, h–: c25g^F **c137**
Nov 16] good-topped gelding: winning hurdler: useful handicap chaser: stayed 21f: acted **h–**
on soft going: tried in hood: dead. *Nigel Twiston-Davies*

JAMESSAINTPATRICK (IRE) 6 b.g. Stowaway – Cadia's Lady (IRE) (Luso) **h77**
[2018/19 b16v h15.8s⁴ h19.7g h21g⁶ Apr 10] €5,500 3-y-o, £35,000 5-y-o: second foal: **b87**
dam unraced half-sister to fairly useful 2½m hurdle winner It's Got Legs: off mark in Irish
points at second attempt: fair form on second of 2 starts in bumpers: poor form both outings
over hurdles. *Amy Murphy*

JAMMIN MASTERS (IRE) 8 b.g. Sinndar (IRE) – Zara Million (ITY) (Zafonic **c134 §** (USA)) [2018/19 c–, h127: c20g² c23.8s² c23.4g² c26.2d² c34vᵖᵘ Mar 16] sturdy gelding: **h–** winning pointer: fairly useful hurdler: useful maiden chaser: second in Silver Cup at Ascot (8 lengths behind Valtor) in December: also runner-up 3 other times, but took little interest final outing: stays 3m: acts on heavy going: ungenuine. *Warren Greatrex*

JAMMY GEORGE (IRE) 6 b.g. Multiplex – Dantes Mile (Phardante (FR)) **h118** [2018/19 h16s² h16v⁴ h19.5s⁴ h22d* Mar 5] good-bodied gelding: half-brother to useful hurdler/smart chaser Lucky William (2m-2¼m winner, by All My Dreams): dam unraced half-sister to useful staying hurdler/chaser Mumbles Head: fairly useful form over hurdles: won novice at Newcastle in March: stays 2¾m: acts on soft going (won bumper on heavy): front runner/races prominently: travels strongly. *Harry Whittington*

JAMRHAM (IRE) 6 b.g. Great Palm (USA) – Appleway (IRE) (Lord Americo) **c65** [2018/19 c82, h–: c17.8g⁵ c17dᵖᵘ Jun 8] pulled up in novice hurdle: poor chaser: left Sam **h–** Thomas, little show in hunters in 2018/19: stays 21f: acts on good to firm and heavy going: in cheekpieces last 4 starts: wears tongue tie. *Miss S. McQueen*

JAM SESSION (IRE) 7 ch.g. Duke of Marmalade (IRE) – Night Dhu (Montjeu (IRE)) **h117** [2018/19 h–: h20.6s* h19.7v Dec 15] fairly useful stayer on Flat: similar form over hurdles: won handicap at Market Rasen in December: stays 21f: acts on soft going: in cheekpieces last 3 starts: has worn tongue tie. *Ian Williams*

J AND M GREENGAIRS 11 b.g. Flemensfirth (USA) – Smooth Technology (IRE) **h82** (Astronef) [2018/19 h73: h20.2g⁵ May 16] poor form over hurdles. *R. Mike Smith*

JANE LAMB 6 b.m. Haafhd – Lucinda Lamb (Kayf Tara) [2018/19 h88: h15.8g³ Apr 11] **h98 p** placed 3 times in bumpers: encouraging 1¾ lengths third to Saumur in mares maiden at Huntingdon on hurdling debut: in tongue tie last 2 starts: entitled to progress. *Dan Skelton*

JANIKA (FR) 6 b.g. Saddler Maker (IRE) – Majaka (FR) (Kapgarde (FR)) [2018/19 **c161** c18.8s² c20.6d² c20.6d² c21.1d⁴ Apr 5] good-topped gelding: first foal: dam, useful French **h–** 2½m chase winner, half-sister to useful hurdler/high-class chaser (17f-2¾m winner in France) Doumaya: high-class handicap chaser: left G. Cherel, in frame in good handicaps all 4 starts in 2018/19, including second in Brown Advisory & Merriebelle Stable Plate at Cheltenham (¾ length behind Siruh du Lac) in March: stays 2¾m: acts on heavy going. *Nicky Henderson*

JANUARY DON 8 br.g. Overbury (IRE) – Little Bud (Lord Bud) [2018/19 h20g Jun 27] **h–** dual point winner: poor form over hurdles, leaving Gary Moore before return (wore tongue tie). *Evan Williams*

JANUS (IRE) 4 br.g. Rock of Gibraltar (IRE) – Jardina (GER) (Shirocco (GER)) [2018/19 **h–** h16dᵖᵘ h16.2g Mar 26] second foal: half-brother to 9f-10.5f winner Jokohama (by Excelebration): dam 7f/1m winner: won twice on Flat in Belgium at 2 yrs, unplaced in Germany in 2018: little show in 2 juvenile hurdles (left Seamus Mullins in between). *Milton Harris*

JARLATH 8 b.g. Norse Dancer (IRE) – Blue Lullaby (IRE) (Fasliyev (USA)) [2018/19 **c118 x** c111, h75: c20m⁵ c23g c21.6m² c20g* c24dᵖᵘ c20.2m⁵ c22.7m³ c24s³ c19.4g* c19.9m³ **h–** Apr 20] good-topped gelding: winning hurdler: fairly useful handicap chaser: won at Warwick in November and Stratford in March: barely stays 2¾m: acts on good to firm and heavy going: tried in headgear: usually front runner/races prominently: prone to mistakes over fences. *Seamus Mullins*

JAROB 12 br.g. Beat All (USA) – Wishy (IRE) (Leading Counsel (USA)) [2018/19 c136, **c136** h124: h24g h24g³ c22.5g⁴ c22gᵖᵘ h20.2g⁴ c30.2g³ h16d⁵ c30.2s⁵ Mar 13] useful handicap **h132** hurdler: useful chaser: left Andrew Lynch after reappearance: stays 3¾m: acts on soft and good to firm going: has worn cheekpieces. *Gearoid O'Loughlin, Ireland*

JARVEYS PLATE (IRE) 6 ch.g. Getaway (GER) – She's Got To Go (IRE) (Glacial **h132** Storm (USA)) [2018/19 b104p: h16.2g³ h16.8g² h20.3d* h20.3d³ h21s³ Mar 13] well-made gelding: placed both starts in Irish points: bumper winner: useful form over hurdles: won listed novice at Cheltenham (by 13 lengths from I Can't Explain) in January: will be suited by 3m: acts on good to soft going. *Fergal O'Brien*

JASANI 11 b.g. Gentleman's Deal (IRE) – Bred For Pleasure (Niniski (USA)) [2018/19 h–: **h–** h17.7mᵖᵘ May 27] form only when 40/1-winner of 2½m novice handicap hurdle at Wetherby in March 2016: tried in cheekpieces/tongue tie. *Roger Teal*

JASMIN DES BORDES (FR) 5 b.g. Great Pretender (IRE) – Queen des Bordes (FR) **h114 p**
(Sleeping Car (FR)) [2018/19 b16.8s² h19.5s³ h19d⁴ Jan 19] €68,000 3-y-o, £145,000 **b94**
4-y-o: had breathing operation prior to debut under Rules: fifth foal: half-brother to French
1m/8.5f winner Kenne des Bordes (by Kendargent): dam lightly raced in France: runner-up
in Irish point: promising second in bumper at Exeter: much better effort over hurdles when
third in maiden at Chepstow: tongue tied next time: should still do better. *David Pipe*

JASSAS (FR) 7 ch.g. Fuisse (FR) – Sylverina (FR) (Numerous (USA)) [2018/19 h103: **c117**
c17.1g² c20g⁴ c23.8g² Jul 15] has had breathing operation: winning hurdler: fairly useful **h–**
form over fences: won novice handicap at Uttoxeter in June: stays 3m, effective at shorter:
best form on good going: tried in hood. *James Ewart*

JATILUWIH (FR) 5 ch.g. Linda's Lad – Jaune de Beaufai (FR) (Ultimately Lucky **c119**
(IRE)) [2018/19 h17.4sᶠ c18.9s⁶ c19.4s² c19.4s² h21.2d* h19.5g* Apr 26] fourth foal: half- **h118**
brother to useful French hurdler/fairly useful chaser Jubilatoire (17f/2¼m winner, by
Konig Turf) and fairly useful chaser Jaune Et Bleue (17f-2½m winner, by Al Namix): dam
unraced half-sister to smart French hurdler (19f winner) Diamant de Beaufai: ran once on
Flat: fairly useful form over hurdles: left Mme I. Pacault, won novices at Ludlow in March
and Chepstow in April: fairly useful chaser: left G. Cherel before second outing: stays 21f:
acts on heavy going: usually hooded in France. *Philip Hobbs*

JAUNTY FLYER 7 b.g. Sulamani (IRE) – Jaunty June (Primitive Rising (USA)) **c106**
[2018/19 h115: c23.6d⁴ c23.8g⁴ c23.8mᵖᵘ Apr 23] fairly useful hurdler: only fair form over **h–**
fences: stays 3m: acts on heavy going: in tongue tie last 4 starts. *Tim Vaughan*

JAUNTY SORIA 6 ch.m. Malinas (GER) – Jaunty Spirit (Loup Sauvage (USA)) [2018/19 **h104**
b74: b15.8s⁴ h19.7d⁴ h15.8m² h16.5d³ Apr 24] in frame twice in bumpers: fair form over **b89**
hurdles: should stay at least 2½m: tried in tongue tie. *Brian Eckley*

JAUNTY THOR 9 b.g. Norse Dancer (IRE) – Jaunty Walk (Overbury (IRE)) [2018/19 **c115**
c95x, h100: h20.2g² c20.1g² h23.9g* c20.1g* h19.6g⁵ c21g* c18m* c16.7s Nov 18] fair **h109**
handicap hurdler: won at Perth in September: fairly useful handicap chaser: won at
Hexham in October, and Fairyhouse (ladies event) and Thurles in November: stays 3m,
effective at much shorter: acts on good to firm and heavy going: has worn headgear: wears
tongue tie. *Gordon Elliott, Ireland*

JAUNTY VELOCITY 6 b.m. Sulamani (IRE) – Jaunty Walk (Overbury (IRE)) [2018/19 **h–**
b81: b15.8g⁶ b15.8v⁶ h19g h25.5d⁶ h21.2m⁵ Apr 1] poor form in bumpers: little show over **b61**
hurdles: in tongue tie last 4 starts. *Brian Eckley*

JAUNTY VIKING 4 b.g. Norse Dancer (IRE) – Jaunty Spirit (Loup Sauvage (USA)) **b–**
[2018/19 b15.8m⁴ Apr 23] well-held last of 4 in bumper at Ludlow. *Brian Eckley*

JAVERT (IRE) 10 b.g. Kayf Tara – Royalrova (FR) (Garde Royale) [2018/19 c20g* **c149**
c19.9g² c20.2g⁶ c19.9d⁴ Mar 2] strong gelding: maiden hurdler: smart handicap chaser: off **h–**
29 months, won at Uttoxeter (by 2 lengths from Crievehill) in September: good second in
Old Roan Chase at Aintree (1¼ lengths behind Frodon) next time: stays 2¾m, effective at
much shorter: acts on soft and good to firm going: has worn hood. *Emma Lavelle*

JAXLIGHT 7 b.m. Lucarno (USA) – Jaxelle (FR) (Lights Out (FR)) [2018/19 b83: **h–**
h15.7dᵖᵘ h16.8g Apr 5] sturdy mare: in front when fell in point on debut: bumper winner:
no show in mares novice hurdles. *Stef Keniry*

JAYCOLS STAR 4 ch.g. Medicean – A Lulu Ofa Menifee (USA) (Menifee (USA)) **h91**
[2018/19 h16.2g⁴ h16.5g³ h16.7mᵖᵘ h16.7m⁶ h21.3m h20.6s⁶ h24.4g⁴ Jan 9] half-brother to
fairly useful/unreliable hurdler Sakhee's City (2m-19f winner, by Sakhee): modest maiden
on Flat, stays 12.5f: modest maiden hurdler: should stay 2½m: best form on good going:
tried in blinkers. *Philip Kirby*

JAYTEE 4 ch.g. Schiaparelli (GER) – Archway Copse (Anshan) [2018/19 b16s b16.7g⁵ **b79**
Apr 13] lengthy, rather unfurnished gelding: modest form in bumpers. *Ian Williams*

JAYTRACK PARKHOMES 5 b.g. Multiplex – Sudden Beat (Beat All (USA)) **h80 p**
[2018/19 b86: b16.4d⁵ h16.3s h16s⁶ h18.5s⁵ Mar 18] good-topped gelding: fairly useful **b98**
bumper winner: only poor form in maiden/novice hurdles, but remains with potential.
Colin Tizzard

JAZRI 8 b.g. Myboycharlie (IRE) – Read Federica (Fusaichi Pegasus (USA)) [2018/19 **h–**
h16.3m Jul 3] modest and temperamental on Flat, stays 11f: in cheekpieces, tailed off in
maiden on hurdling debut. *Milton Bradley*

JAZZ THYME (IRE) 10 b.m. Helissio (FR) – Thyne Square (IRE) (Good Thyne (USA)) **h–**
[2018/19 h93: h16.8gᵖᵘ Aug 21] modest maiden hurdler: stays 19f: acts on good to firm
going: has worn tongue tie. *Robert Stephens*

JEANNOT DE NONANT (FR) 7 ch.g. Full of Gold (FR) – Jolie Puce (FR) (General **c126 §**
Assembly (USA)) [2018/19 c106, h133: c25.5g⁴ c23g³ h24.7g⁵ h24s h23.6s h20.5g³ **h117 §**
h23.5d Feb 16] angular gelding: fairly useful handicap hurdler: similar form over fences:
landed odds in weak maiden at Cartmel in May: stays 25f: acts on heavy going: usually in
headgear: regularly tongue tied: temperamental. *Peter Bowen*

JEANS GENIE 4 b.f. Kayf Tara – Aberdeen Park (Environment Friend) [2018/19 b13.7g⁴ **b71**
Apr 24] third foal: dam (h106) 2m-2¾m hurdle winner: 20/1, fourth in bumper at Fontwell.
Martin Keighley

JEFFERSON DAVIS (IRE) 6 b.g. Duke of Marmalade (IRE) – Samorra (IRE) (In The **c102**
Wings) [2018/19 c16v⁵ c17d⁵ c21.7g⁴ c23.5g⁵ h24m² h25d⁶ h21.2d h19g Apr 25] has had **h110**
breathing operation: fair handicap hurdler: similar form over fences: left Eoin Doyle after
fifth start: stays 3m: acts on soft and good to firm going: has worn headgear/tongue tie.
Tim Vaughan

JEFFREY 6 ch.g. Apple Tree (FR) – Jambles (Muhtarram (USA)) [2018/19 b–: h21.4m⁵ **h–**
h20g Jun 27] well held in bumpers/over hurdles. *Robert Walford*

JELLY MONGER (IRE) 7 b.m. Strategic Prince – Royal Jelly (King's Best (USA)) **h–**
[2018/19 h15.7g Jun 25] lengthy mare: fairly useful handicapper on Flat (stays 1¾m): fair
hurdler: stays 2¼m: acts on good to firm going: held up. *Dominic Ffrench Davis*

JELSKI (GER) 5 b.g. Kallisto (GER) – Just Zoud (Ezzoud (IRE)) [2018/19 h15.7d⁵ **b89**
b15.8v* b16.4s b16d Apr 6] €44,000 3-y-o: good-topped gelding: fourth foal: half-brother
to 2 winners, including French 17f hurdle winner Jaromier (by Saddex): dam German 7f
winner: fair form in bumpers: won at Ffos Las in January. *Nigel Twiston-Davies*

JEMBUG DRUMMER (IRE) 5 b.g. Jeremy (USA) – Drumbug (IRE) (Germany **h87**
(USA)) [2018/19 b16.4d⁵ b16.2d³ h15.8g³ Apr 21] €85,000 3-y-o: third foal: half-brother **b73**
to fairly useful 2m hurdle winner Grange (by Vinnie Roe): dam (h95), placed up to 19f over
hurdles, sister to high-class 2m hurdler/chaser Captain Cee Bee: poor form in bumpers:
some encouragement when third in novice at Ffos Las on hurdling debut. *Tim Vaughan*

JEMIMA P (IRE) 5 b.m. Jeremy (USA) – Peig Alainn (IRE) (Milan) [2018/19 b16g Nov **b79**
9] first foal: dam, maiden pointer, out of half-sister to useful hurdler/smart chaser (2m-2½m
winner) Watson Lake: 7/2, mid-field in 13-runner mares bumper at Warwick. *Emma Lavelle*

JENKINS (IRE) 7 b.g. Azamour (IRE) – Aladiyna (IRE) (Indian Danehill (IRE)) **c142**
[2018/19 h144: c19.4g* c20.2g⁴ c20.6d³ c20.2g² h20.3g Apr 17] good-topped gelding: **h127**
smart handicap hurdler at best: useful novice chaser: 25/1-on winner of 2-runner maiden at
Stratford in October on chasing debut: in frame next 3 outings: stays 21f: acts on heavy
going: regularly in headgear nowadays: usually races close up. *Nicky Henderson*

JENNIFER JUNIPER (IRE) 6 b.m. Kalanisi (IRE) – Assidua (IRE) (Anshan) [2018/19 **c–**
h70, b70: h20g³ h23g⁴ h23.3gᵖᵘ c23gᵖᵘ Aug 15] has had breathing operation: placed in Irish **h85**
points: modest form over hurdles: pulled up in novice handicap on chasing debut: stays
23f: best form on good going: tried in cheekpieces: front runner/races prominently. *Fergal
O'Brien*

JENNYS DAY (IRE) 8 b.g. Daylami (IRE) – Jennys Oscar (IRE) (Oscar (IRE)) [2018/19 **h107**
h104: h26.5g h21.4m² h21.2g² Nov 15] runner-up on second start in maiden points: fair
handicap hurdler: stays 21f: acts on heavy going: tried in hood: front runner/races
prominently. *Katy Price*

JENNYS SURPRISE (IRE) 11 b.m. Hawk Wing (USA) – Winning Jenny (IRE) **c129**
(Leading Counsel (USA)) [2018/19 c133, h–: c20v* c29.5sᵖᵘ Dec 27] workmanlike mare: **h–**
winning hurdler: fairly useful handicap chaser: won veterans race at Lingfield on return in
December: stays 3½m: acts on heavy going: tried in cheekpieces. *Fergal O'Brien*

JEN'S BOY 5 b.g. Malinas (GER) – Friendly Craic (IRE) (Mister Lord (USA)) [2018/19 **h89 p**
b–p: b15.7g² h20.5d h19.7dᵖᵘ h19.8g⁶ h16g⁴ Apr 26] rather unfurnished gelding: fair form **b85**
on second of 2 outings in bumpers: modest form over hurdles: will stay beyond 2½m:
should still do better as a hurdler. *Nicky Henderson*

JEPECK (IRE) 10 b.g. Westerner – Jenny's Jewel (IRE) (Be My Native (USA)) [2018/19 **c127**
c117: c23.8v* c30.7d⁶ c24.5v² Mar 17] fairly useful handicap chaser: won at Ffos Las on
return in November: stays 33f: acts on heavy going: consistent. *Anthony Honeyball*

JEREMIAH JAMES (IRE) 5 b.g. Jeremy (USA) – Lougholly Native (IRE) (Be My **b90**
Native (USA)) [2018/19 b15.3g b15.3d⁵ b17.7d Feb 24] €16,000 3-y-o: fifth foal: half-
brother to fairly useful hurdler/chaser House Rules (2m-2½m winner, by Overbury): dam
of little account over hurdles: easily best effort in bumpers when fifth at Wincanton.
Harry Fry

JEREMY'S JET (IRE) 8 b.g. Jeremy (USA) – Double Vie (IRE) (Tagula (IRE)) **h75**
[2018/19 h81: h15.8m⁵ h15.8s h16.3g⁴ Aug 23] poor maiden hurdler: raced around 2m:
acts on good to soft and good to firm going: wears tongue tie. *Tony Carroll*

JERRYSBACK (IRE) 7 b.g. Jeremy (USA) – Get A Few Bob Back (IRE) (Bob Back **c146**
(USA)) [2018/19 c20.2g⁵ c20.3v* c21s² c19.9d² c31.7s³ Mar 12] well-made gelding: **h–**
winning hurdler: smart form over fences: won maiden at Bangor (by length from Mulcahys
Hill) in December: endured hard race with remote third to Le Breuil in National Hunt
Chase at Cheltenham final outing: should stay at least 3m: acts on heavy going.
Philip Hobbs

JERSEY BEAN (IRE) 6 b.g. Court Cave (IRE) – Jennifers Diary (IRE) (Supreme **h134**
Leader) [2018/19 h127, b96: h20.6g* h24.2d* h23.1g² h24dᵖᵘ h25d⁵ h24.4gᵖᵘ Mar 2] **b96**
good-topped gelding: bumper winner: useful handicap hurdler: won at Market Rasen in
October and Newbury in November: stays 25f: acts on soft going. *Oliver Sherwood*

JESSE JUDE (IRE) 6 ch.g. Doyen (IRE) – La Belle Bleu (IRE) (Lahib (USA)) [2018/19 **h96**
h105, b71: h20.3g³ h23.1m⁶ h16.2g Sep 17] fair form over hurdles: stays 2½m: tried in
cheekpieces. *Simon West*

JESSICA RABBIT 5 b.m. Mawatheeq (USA) – Intersky High (USA) (Royal Anthem **h–**
(USA)) [2018/19 b16g⁶ b15.7g⁶ h15.7g h15.5d h19.6d Mar 3] rather sparely-made mare: **b70**
fourth foal: half-sister to fairly useful hurdler Cool Sky (2m-2½m winner, by Millkom):
dam (b84), third only start in bumper, ran twice on Flat: poor form in bumpers: never
dangerous in mares hurdles. *Graeme McPherson*

JESSIE LIGHTFOOT (IRE) 5 b.m. Yeats (IRE) – Needle Doll (IRE) (Needle Gun **b81**
(IRE)) [2018/19 b16.3s⁶ b16.7g Apr 13] seventh foal: closely related to useful hurdler/
chaser Mad Brian (2m-2¾m winner, by Brian Boru) and bumper winner Myblueeyedgirl
(by Milan): dam unraced: modest form on first of 2 outings in bumpers. *John Groucott*

JESSIEMAC (IRE) 5 br.m. Sholokhov (IRE) – All Our Blessings (IRE) (Statoblest) **h93**
[2018/19 b16g⁵ b16.2g h16d⁴ h16v⁴ h20.5s² h21.4d³ h19.5d⁶ h21.4s⁵ h17d⁴ Mar 24] **b71**
£8,000 3-y-o: closely related to bumper winner Black Ace (by Yeats), fair hurdler Boy In A
Bentley (2½m-2¾m winner) and a winning pointer (latter pair by Kayf Tara): dam (h64)
lightly raced over hurdles: little show in bumpers: modest maiden hurdler: stays 2½m: acts
on heavy going: wears tongue tie. *Ian Duncan*

JESTER JET (IRE) 9 br.m. Overbury (IRE) – Hendre Hotshot (Exit To Nowhere (USA)) **c136**
[2018/19 h135: h22.8g² c20.9d² c17.4d² c20d² h23.5d² h18.9g* h19.9s Mar 12] leggy **h137**
mare: useful hurdler: won listed mares event at Haydock (by neck from If You Say Run) in
February: similar form over fences: runner-up all 3 starts, notably when beaten 1¼ lengths
by Maria's Benefit (pair clear) in listed mares novice at Bangor second occasion: stays 25f:
acts on good to firm and heavy going. *Tom Lacey*

JE SUIS CHARLIE 5 b.g. High Chaparral (IRE) – Fin (Groom Dancer (USA)) [2018/19 **h118 §**
h117: h15.7g* h16.7m h16g³ h15.7g* Nov 23] has had breathing operation: fairly useful
novice hurdler: won at Southwell (maiden) in June and Catterick in November: raced
around 2m: acts on good to soft going: tried in cheekpieces: irresolute. *John Quinn*

JETEZ (IRE) 6 b.g. Getaway (GER) – Miss Squiff (IRE) (Saddlers' Hall (IRE)) [2018/19 **h134**
h16g* h20g⁵ h16.2g⁴ h20g² h16g* h16d² h16g h16gᶠ Feb 24] second foal: half-brother
to useful hurdler/chaser Jetz (17f-2½m winner, by Flemensfirth): dam twice-raced
close relative to Champion Hurdle winner Jezki: useful hurdler: won maiden at Limerick
in May and handicap at Leopardstown in December: stays 2½m: acts on soft going.
Mrs J. Harrington, Ireland

JET MASTER (IRE) 13 b.g. Brian Boru – Whats The Reason (IRE) (Strong Gale) **c124 x**
[2018/19 c121x, h110: h23.9g⁵ h16.2g c20g³ c20.1g* c22.3g² h23.8g* h22.7d³ c23.4mᶠ **h114**
Mar 28] neat gelding: fair handicap hurdler: won at Musselburgh in January: fairly useful
handicap chaser: won veterans race at Newcastle earlier in season: stays 3m: acts on good
to firm and heavy going: wears hood/tongue tie: held up: prone to mistakes. *N. W.
Alexander*

JET SET (IRE) 7 b.m. Getaway (GER) – Lavender Track (IRE) (Pistolet Bleu (IRE)) **c–**
[2018/19 h122, b91: c19.9gᵘʳ h20s⁴ h19.7g⁵ c22.5vᵘʳ h23.1g⁵ Apr 3] won Irish point on **h117**
debut: fairly useful handicap hurdler: unseated first in mares races both starts in chases:
stays 21f: acts on soft going: tried in cheekpieces/tongue tie. *Charlie Longsdon*

JETSET LAD 5 b.g. Sulamani (IRE) – Returning (Bob's Return (IRE)) [2018/19 b15.8g **b–**
Apr 11] no show in maiden bumper. *Nick Littmoden*

JETSTREAM (IRE) 4 b.g. Galileo (IRE) – Bewitched (IRE) (Dansili) [2018/19 **h–**
h15.8m^{ur} h15.8g Oct 18] fair on Flat, stays 1¼m: in hood, well beaten on completed start
in juvenile hurdles: wears tongue tie: headstrong. *Kerry Lee*

JETSTREAM JACK (IRE) 9 b.g. Beneficial – Westgrove Berry (IRE) (Presenting) **c127**
[2018/19 c119, h–: h20s^{pu} h16.7s^4 h23.6d^6 c34v^{pu} c23.6d^2 Apr 6] rangy gelding: winning **h104**
hurdler: fairly useful handicap chaser nowadays: left Olly Murphy after second start: stays
3m: acts on heavy going: usually in headgear: regularly tongue tied (not for current yard).
Sophie Leech

JETT (IRE) 8 b.g. Flemensfirth (USA) – La Noire (IRE) (Phardante (FR)) [2018/19 c144, **c151**
h–: c20.6m^4 c20d^3 c20d c24.5g^{ur} h20s^6 c20.5g^4 c18g^3 c21.3s^3 c20d* Apr 22] fairly useful **h120 +**
hurdler: smart chaser: won Devenish Chase at Fairyhouse (by 4¾ lengths from The
Storyteller) in April: stays 23f, effective at shorter: acts on heavy going: in cheekpieces 3
of last 4 outings. *Mrs J. Harrington, Ireland*

JETZ (IRE) 7 b.g. Flemensfirth (USA) – Miss Squiff (IRE) (Saddlers' Hall (IRE)) **c146**
[2018/19 h142: c17d^{ur} c17d* c20g^3 c19.7s^4 c20d^3 c21g^4 c17s* c20d^{ur} c18g^2 Mar 23] useful **h–**
hurdler: smart chaser: won maiden in November and Grade 3 novice in March, both at
Navan: best effort when third in Drinmore Novices' Chase at Fairyhouse (8½ lengths
behind Delta Work): stays 2¾m, effective at shorter: acts on heavy going: has worn
headgear: front runner/races prominently. *Mrs J. Harrington, Ireland*

JEU DE MOTS (FR) 6 b.g. Saint des Saints (FR) – Nanouska (GER) (Dashing Blade) **c100**
[2018/19 c92, h66p: c20.9d* c23.8m^6 c19.4g^{pu} Apr 21] maiden hurdler: fair form over **h–**
fences: won handicap at Ffos Las in May: stays 2½m: acts on good to soft going. *Mrs
Jane Williams*

JEZKI (IRE) 11 b.g. Milan – La Noire (IRE) (Phardante (FR)) [2018/19 h148d: h20d^2 **h152**
h16g h24g^4 h16g^2 h16d Apr 23] smallish, strong gelding: top-class hurdler in his prime,
won Champion Hurdle at Cheltenham in 2013/14: best effort in 2018/19 when length
second of 19 to Off You Go in Ladbrokes Hurdle (Handicap) at Leopardstown: stayed 3m,
at least as effective at shorter: acted on good to firm and heavy going: regularly in headgear:
retired. *Mrs J. Harrington, Ireland*

JIGSAW FINANCIAL (IRE) 13 b.g. Brian Boru – Ardcolm Cailin (IRE) (Beneficial) **h–**
[2018/19 h93: h21.6s^{ur} h18.5s h21.6v^{pu} Dec 20] leggy gelding: fair handicap hurdler at
best: off 17 months, no form in 2018/19: stays 23f: acts on good to firm and heavy going:
tried in cheekpieces. *Laura Young*

JILLYTHEJET (IRE) 5 bl.m. Jeremy (USA) – Listen Up (Good Thyne (USA)) [2018/19 **h108**
h15.8g h20.7g^F Jan 11] won Irish point on debut: running better race in mares maiden
hurdles when fallng last at Huntingdon: dead. *Nicky Henderson*

JIMAL MAGIC (FR) 5 b.g. Irish Wells (FR) – Night Cire (FR) (Lute Antique (FR)) **b92**
[2018/19 b15.3g^5 Jan 17] £22,000 3-y-o: third foal: dam, French maiden (placed at 13f),
half-sister to fairly useful 2m chaser Gentle John: fifth in maiden bumper at Wincanton.
Jack R. Barber

JIMMI CHEW (IRE) 6 br.g. Jimble (FR) – Katie Baby (IRE) (Bustomi) [2018/19 **h77**
b15.8g^5 ab16s^5 h16.7d h20.7d h20d^3 h15.8g Mar 19] rather leggy gelding: runner-up in **b74**
point on debut: poor form in bumpers/over hurdles. *Alex Hales*

JIMMY 6 ch.g. Norse Dancer (IRE) – Isintshelovely (IRE) (Broken Hearted) [2018/19 **h82**
h91: h21.7m^6 h21.7m h21.7d h21.7v h19.2v^4 h25g* h21.7g Apr 12] poor handicap hurdler:
won at Plumpton in February: will be suited by long distances: acts on heavy going: tried
in cheekpieces: often races lazily. *Chris Gordon*

JIMMY BELL 8 b.g. Tiger Hill (IRE) – Armada Grove (Fleetwood (IRE)) [2018/19 h98, **h93**
b–: h23.1g^5 h19.7d^4 h23d^4 h23.6d^6 h19.5d Apr 6] modest maiden hurdler: stays 3m: acts on
soft going: often in headgear nowadays: held up. *John O'Shea*

JIMMY BREEKIE (IRE) 9 b.g. Alkaadhem – Highland Breeze (IRE) (Kotashaan (FR)) **h130**
[2018/19 h126: h16d h22.5d^4 h20d^3 h24g^3 h19d^F Mar 10] failed to complete both starts in
points: useful handicap hurdler: stays 3m: acts on good to firm and heavy going: has worn
hood: in tongue tie last 4 starts. *Stuart Crawford, Ireland*

JIMMY RABBITTE (IRE) 6 b.g. Dubai Destination (USA) – Time To Act (Rakaposhi **h109**
King) [2018/19 h20d^{bd} h16g^5 h16g* h19.3g* h16.7g^4 Feb 17] €1,000 3-y-o: leggy,
close-coupled gelding: second foal: dam, no form, out of useful hurdler/chaser (winner up
to 25f) Bayrouge: fair hurdler: won maiden at Thurles in November and, having left
D. Broad, handicaps at Taunton (conditionals) in December and Catterick in January: stays
19f: acts on good to soft going: normally in hood. *Dr Richard Newland*

JIMMY'S SISTER 6 b.m. Denounce – Sementina (USA) (Silver Charm (USA)) **b–**
[2018/19 b15.7g Jun 5] second foal: half-sister to fair chaser Little Jimmy (2m-2½m winner, by Passing Glance): dam unraced: last in mares bumper. *Tom Gretton*

JIMMY THE DIGGER 6 b.g. Black Sam Bellamy (IRE) – The Lyme Volunteer (IRE) **h–**
(Zaffaran (USA)) [2018/19 b16.7g² b14d* h16sF h16dpu Apr 6] fourth foal: half-brother to **b99**
useful hurdler/smart chaser Crucial Role (19f-3m winner, by Westerner): dam (c105/h108) 3m/3¼m hurdle/chase winner: fairly useful form in bumpers: won at Ludlow in December: fell third on hurdling debut: bled next time: bred to be suited by 2½m+. *Henry Daly*

JINSHA LAKE (IRE) 7 b.g. Galileo (IRE) – Al Ihsas (IRE) (Danehill (USA)) [2018/19 **h–**
h–: h15.8m Jun 21] sturdy gelding: modest hurdler at best: lightly raced and little form since May 2016: tried in cheekpieces: wears tongue tie. *Evan Williams*

JO CASHFLOW 5 b.m. Getaway (GER) – Mary Kate O'Brien (Tiger Hill (IRE)) **h–**
[2018/19 b15.6g⁴ b16.8s h16.8dpu h16.8g h19.9d Apr 23] second foal: dam **b–**
unraced sister to useful hurdler/high-class chaser (stayed 21f) Ghizao: no form in bumpers/over hurdles. *Chris Grant*

JOE FARRELL (IRE) 10 b.g. Presenting – Luck of The Deise (IRE) (Old Vic) [2018/19 **c142**
c140, h–: c26d⁶ c26g² c34.3gpu c28.8gpu Apr 27] good-topped gelding: winning hurdler: **h–**
useful handicap chaser: second at Newbury (1½ lengths behind Chic Name) in March, easily best effort in 2018/19: stays 4m: acts on soft going. *Rebecca Curtis*

JOEY SASA (IRE) 10 b.g. Winged Love (IRE) – Brescia (FR) (Monsun (GER)) [2018/19 **h140**
h143: h16g* h20d⁶ Apr 22] useful hurdler: won Grimes Hurdle at Tipperary (by 1½ lengths from Wicklow Brave) in July: stays 2½m: acts on heavy going. *Noel Meade, Ireland*

JOEY STEEL (IRE) 6 b.g. Craigsteel – Tower Project (IRE) (Project Manager) [2018/19 **h–**
h15.8d h16d h19s h16d⁶ h16.8g Apr 20] unplaced in point: no form over hurdles. *Christian Williams*

JOG ON (IRE) 6 b.g. Definite Article – Azabu Juban (IRE) (Catcher In The Rye (IRE)) **h104**
[2018/19 b–: h19.5d h19.5v⁴ h18.5s⁴ Mar 18] well held in bumper (for Colin Tizzard): form over hurdles only when fourth in novice at Lingfield in February: will be suited by further than 2½m. *Nicky Martin*

JOHANOS (FR) 8 ch.g. Limnos (JPN) – Madame Johann (FR) (Johann Quatz (FR)) **c122**
[2018/19 c23.4s⁴ c31.7sF Mar 12] lengthy gelding: fairly useful novice hurdler in 2016/17: **h–**
similar form when fourth in novice handicap at Newbury on completed start over fences: out of depth in National Hunt Chase at Cheltenham next time (behind when falling seventeenth): probably stays 23f: acts on heavy going. *Nigel Hawke*

JOHNBB (IRE) 5 b.g. Stowaway – Flemins Evening (IRE) (Flemensfirth (USA)) **h120**
[2018/19 b16.7g² b21d³ h21d³ h20.5s* h19.8s³ Feb 2] €57,000 3-y-o: workmanlike gelding: **b95**
fourth foal: dam unraced half-sister to useful hurdler (stays 3m) Tommy Rapper and fairly useful hurdler/useful chaser (stayed 3½m) Operation Houdini: shaped well when second in bumper at Market Rasen: fairly useful form over hurdles: won maiden at Ayr in January. *Tom Lacey*

JOHN BISCUIT (IRE) 11 ch.g. Hawk Wing (USA) – Princess Magdalena (Pennekamp **c–**
(USA)) [2018/19 c–, h70: h21.7g⁵ h15.8g h20.7g⁵ h19.7g Mar 26] poor handicap hurdler: **h58**
fell only start over fences: stays 21f: acts on good to firm and good to sott going: tried in hood/tongue tie: waited with. *Jo Davis*

JOHN CONSTABLE (IRE) 8 b.g. Montjeu (IRE) – Dance Parade (USA) (Gone West **c112**
(USA)) [2018/19 h150: h15.7g c15.7g⁵ c16.5g³ h16.7g h15.3g⁶ h18.9gF h19.7v h20.5d **h138**
h16g⁶ h16.8d Jan 26] lengthy gelding: useful handicap hurdler: out of sorts for much of 2018/19, including in novice chases: unproven beyond 17f: acts on soft and good to firm going: wears tongue tie: held up. *Evan Williams*

JOHN DANIELL 14 b.g. Overbury (IRE) – Hottentot (Sula Bula) [2018/19 c24.2v³ **c75**
c24.2v⁶ c29.2g⁶ c26g³ Apr 24] multiple point winner: pulled up only hurdle start: poor **h–**
maiden chaser: stays 3¼m: acts on heavy going: patiently ridden. *Grant Cann*

JOHNI BOXIT 4 ch.g. Sakhee's Secret – Pink Supreme (Night Shift (USA)) [2018/19 **h72**
h16.8s h16d⁶ h15.3g Apr 14] smallish, close-coupled gelding: fair on Flat, stays 1¼m: well held over hurdles. *Brian Barr*

JOHNNY OCEAN (IRE) 7 b.g. Whitmore's Conn (USA) – Soda Bread (IRE) **c96**
(Beneficial) [2018/19 h–: h24d⁴ h15.8s c20.3dF Jan 8] well-made gelding: won Irish point **h85**
on debut: modest form over hurdles: showing more (though held in third) when falling heavily last in novice handicap at Bangor on chasing debut. *Kim Bailey*

JOHNNY OG 10 b.g. Flemensfirth (USA) – Mrs Roberts (Bob Back (USA)) [2018/19 c–, h–: c20.3g[6] c22.6d[6] c22.6m h26.4g Apr 14] workmanlike gelding: maiden hurdler: formerly useful chaser: left Martin Keighley, no better than mid-field in hunters/handicap in 2018/19: stays 2½m: acts on heavy going: has worn headgear. *Claire Dyson* **c96 h–**

JOHNNY PEDLAR 8 b.g. Revoque (IRE) – Festival Fancy (Le Coq d'Or) [2018/19 h86: h21.4g h16.2g[2] h20.2g h20.9g[5] Oct 7] modest maiden hurdler: stays 21f: tried in hood: temperamental (carries head awkwardly). *Sandy Thomson* **h98 §**

JOHNNY ROCCO 5 ch.g. Shirocco (GER) – Pickworth (IRE) (Milan) [2018/19 b17.7g[5] b15.7g[6] h15.9s[3] h16.7s[6] h15.8g[pu] Jan 11] modest form in bumpers/over hurdles: dead. *Harry Whittington* **h90 b82**

JOHNNY YUMA (IRE) 6 b.g. Alfred Nobel (IRE) – Rossbridge Lass (IRE) (Clerkenwell (USA)) [2018/19 c82p, h83, b–: c23.6g[5] c23.9s[pu] h19.9d[3] c17.5v[4] c15.6g* c15.7d* Apr 24] has had breathing operation: winning pointer: modest handicap chaser: won at Hexham and Southwell in April: best form around 2m: acts on good to soft going: in tongue tie last 5 starts, also in cheekpieces last 3: travels strongly, but sometimes finds less than promised. *Katy Price* **c99 h–**

JOHN WILLIAMS (IRE) 10 b.g. Presenting – Duhallow Park (IRE) (Flemensfirth (USA)) [2018/19 c102, h–: c15.6g c15.6s[3] c16.5v[5] c20.3g* c16.5s[2] c15.8m* c15.8m[5] c17.1d[5] Apr 8] maiden hurdler: fair handicap chaser: won at Musselburgh in December and February (fourth course success): stays 2¾m, effective at shorter: acts on good to firm and heavy going: wears cheekpieces: usually front runner/races prominently. *Sandy Thomson* **c103 h–**

JOIN THE CLAN (IRE) 10 b.g. Milan – Millicent Bridge (IRE) (Over The River (FR)) [2018/19 c123, h113: h26.4m[2] h26.5g Jul 6] workmanlike gelding: fairly useful handicap hurdler/chaser: stayed 3¼m: acted on good to firm and heavy going: often wore headgear: dead. *Jonjo O'Neill* **c– h116**

JOKE DANCER 6 ch.g. Authorized (IRE) – Missy Dancer (Shareef Dancer (USA)) [2018/19 h124: h16.4g* h16.2g h20d Apr 5] workmanlike gelding: has had breathing operation: fairly useful handicap hurdler: won at Newcastle on belated reappearance in February: disappointing after: unproven beyond 2m: acts on heavy going: usually held up. *Sue Smith* **h126**

JOKERS AND ROGUES (IRE) 11 b.g. Beneficial – Ashfield Girl (IRE) (Beau Sher) [2018/19 c76, h70: h16.2g[3] c16.4d* c16.4s[5] c16.4v[3] c16.4g[3] Apr 5] poor handicap hurdler: fair handicap chaser: won at Sedgefield in January: best around 2m: acts on heavy going: has worn tongue tie: usually forces pace. *Dianne Sayer* **c101 h63**

JOLIE CRICKETTE (FR) 7 b.m. Laverock (IRE) – Crickette River (FR) (Cricket Ball (USA)) [2018/19 c–, h88: h16.2g May 16] modest handicap hurdler: winning chaser in France: stays 2½m: acts on soft going: usually in blinkers: tried in tongue tie. *N. W. Alexander* **c– h–**

JOLLY JET (IRE) 7 b.m. Arcadio (GER) – Boarding Pass (IRE) (Accordion) [2018/19 h–: c23.6g[pu] May 10] no sign of ability: tried in cheekpieces. *Linda Jewell* **c– h–**

JOLLY'S CRACKED IT (FR) 10 b.g. Astarabad (USA) – Jolly Harbour (Rudimentary (USA)) [2018/19 h15.7g* h15.7s h15.3g[5] h19.9v[pu] Mar 16] well-made gelding: useful handicap hurdler: won at Ascot (by 6 lengths from Chatez) on belated return in November: disappointing after: best at 2m: acts on heavy going: travels notably strongly. *Harry Fry* **h141**

JONAGOLD 8 b.g. Apple Tree (FR) – Single Handed (Cloudings (IRE)) [2018/19 c102§, h–: h15.7g[3] h22m h24g[6] c21g[2] c20g* h21.7g[5] c21.7d[5] c23.8g[4] c20.1m[5] c19.4g[6] Apr 21] poor maiden hurdler: modest handicap chaser: won at Warwick in September: stays 21f: acts on soft going: usually wears headgear/tongue tie: unreliable. *Evan Williams* **c94 § h73**

JONES WELL (IRE) 6 b.g. Gold Well – Mrs Jones (FR) (Saint Preuil (FR)) [2018/19 h–: h23.3d[6] h20.7d[6] h16.7s h15.7d Apr 9] runner-up in Irish point on debut: well held over hurdles. *Olly Murphy* **h–**

JONJOELA (IRE) 8 b.m. Great Exhibition (USA) – Yorkshire Blade (IRE) (Sadler's Wells (USA)) [2018/19 h71: c23.9m[ur] h23.3g h23g[5] h25g[3] h25d[6] h25g[5] h26g c25.2g[4] c26g[4] Apr 12] winning pointer: poor maiden hurdler: no show over fences: stays 25f: best form on good going: tried in hood. *Tracey Leeson* **c– h65**

JONNIGRAIG (IRE) 6 b.g. Masterofthehorse (IRE) – Vanudski (IRE) (Pilsudski (IRE)) [2018/19 b16m[5] b17m[3] h16g[6] h18.8d[3] h19.9g h19.2m[4] h19.5g Apr 26] first foal: dam unraced: fair form in bumpers: best effort over hurdles when third in maiden at Downpatrick in August (left W. P. Mullins after): stays 19f: acts on good to soft going: in hood last 2 starts. *Roger Teal* **h96 b93**

JOSIES ORDERS (IRE) 11 b.g. Milan – Silent Orders (IRE) (Bob Back (USA))   **c147**
[2018/19 c143, h119: h21.9s c30.2g* c30.2g³ c25d* c30.2s² Mar 13] good-topped gelding: **h–**
winning hurdler: smart cross-country chaser: won at Cheltenham in November and
Punchestown in February: stays 33f: acts on heavy going: normally in headgear: usually
finds plenty. *Enda Bolger, Ireland*

JOSSES HILL (IRE) 11 b.g. Winged Love (IRE) – Credora Storm (IRE) (Glacial Storm   **c143 x**
(USA)) [2018/19 c149, h–: h22.8g c19.9d⁴ c24gᶠ c23.8mᵘʳ c22.7g⁵ Apr 27] strong, useful-   **h–**
looking gelding: has had breathing operation: winning hurdler: high-class but error-prone
chaser at best: stayed 2½m: acted on good to firm and heavy going: wore headgear:
collapsed and died after Oaksey Chase at Sandown on final day of season. *Nicky Henderson*

JOT'EM DOWN (IRE) 8 b.g. Kalanisi (IRE) – Shuil A Hocht (IRE) (Mohaajir (USA))   **c95**
[2018/19 h25.5s h19.9v h20.5s h20.7d c25.7g* Apr 21] good-topped gelding: has had   **h–**
breathing operation: well held over hurdles: vastly better when winning novice handicap at
Plumpton (easily) on chasing debut: stays 3¼m: tried in cheekpieces. *David Bridgwater*

JOUEUR BRESILIEN (FR) 7 b.g. Fuisse (FR) – Fille du Bresil (FR) (Smadoun (FR))   **c113 §**
[2018/19 c120, h–: c16.2m c16m⁴ h20m* h19.4gˢᵘ c23d⁴ c20.2gᵖᵘ Jan 17] lengthy, useful-   **h110**
looking gelding: fair hurdler: won maiden at Ffos Las in July: fair maiden chaser: best short
of 23f: acts on good to firm and heavy going: has worn headgear/tongue tie: temperamental.
Rebecca Curtis

JOVIAL JOEY (IRE) 8 b.g. St Jovite (USA) – Like A Bird (IRE) (Topanoora) [2018/19   **c126**
c–, h–: c20.5g⁵ c23.8g³ c23.8g³ c25.5g³ c20.1g* c20g³ c21.4g² c21.6d⁴ c25.2gᶠ Nov 23]   **h–**
maiden hurdler: fairly useful handicap chaser: won at Perth in August: stayed 25f: acted on
good to soft going: wore tongue tie: dead. *Maurice Barnes*

JOYCETICK (FR) 5 b.g. Myboycharlie (IRE) – Joyce (GER) (Chato (USA)) [2018/19   **h85**
h118: h16m h15.7gᵘʳ h16.3mᶠ h20g Aug 15] has had breathing operation: fair hurdle
winner in France: only modest form when completing in handicaps in 2018/19: unproven
beyond 17f: acts on heavy and good to firm going: wears tongue tie. *Nick Littmoden*

JOYRIDER (IRE) 7 b.g. Stowaway – Aileen Supreme (IRE) (Presenting) [2018/19 b98:   **h–**
h21d h23.1sᵖᵘ Mar 5] in frame in bumpers: off another 15 months, little promise in novice
hurdles: tried in hood. *Emma Lavelle*

JUBILYMPICS 7 b.m. Kapgarde (FR) – Pepite de Soleil (FR) (Fly To The Stars) [2018/19   **h116**
h119, b88: h21.6g h19.8v² h24.6g⁵ h19.5d h20.5s Mar 11] lengthy mare: bumper winner:
fairly useful handicap hurdler: should stay beyond 21f: acts on heavy going. *Seamus Mullins*

JUDGE EARLE (IRE) 7 b.g. Court Cave (IRE) – Louis's Teffia (IRE) (Presenting)   **c116**
[2018/19 h105, b86: h20.2g* h20.2g³ h20g³ h20.1g² c23.4m² h23.6s h21.4s h19.9d h20g   **h112**
Apr 21] has had breathing operation: bumper winner: fair hurdler: won maiden at Perth in
July: beaten 15 lengths by sole rival Rocky's Treasure in novice at Kelso on chasing debut
(left Richard Fahey after): should stay beyond 2½m: acts on good to firm and heavy going:
tried in blinkers: usually makes running/races prominently. *Peter Bowen*

JUDGE JUDY (IRE) 6 b.m. Oscar (IRE) – The Bar Maid (Alderbrook) [2018/19 h74:   **h–**
h25.8gᶠ May 9] more signs of temperament than ability in novice hurdles. *Lawney Hill*

JUDGEMENT DAY (IRE) 7 b.g. Martaline – Gaye Moscow (IRE) (Moscow Society   **c135**
(USA)) [2018/19 h16m⁴ h20g³ c20g² c19.9g* c25m* c20g* c20d* c24g⁵ Dec 29] £145,000   **h110**
4-y-o: fourth foal: dam unraced: fair maiden hurdler: much better over fences: won maiden
at Kilbeggan in August, and novices at Gowran and Cork in October and Punchestown in
November: stays 25f: acts on good to firm and heavy going: in cheekpieces last 5 starts:
tried in tongue tie: front runner/races prominently. *Henry de Bromhead, Ireland*

JUGE ET PARTI (FR) 6 gr.g. Martaline – Nakota Rag (FR) (Nikos) [2018/19 h116:   **h117**
h23.6d² h24.2s h24d⁶ h21.2d² h22d⁴ h21d³ h20.2g³ Apr 24] rather unfurnished gelding:
fairly useful maiden hurdler: placed 4 times in 2018/19: should stay beyond 3m: acts on
heavy going. *Nigel Twiston-Davies*

JULLY LES BUXY 9 b.m. Black Sam Bellamy (IRE) – Jadidh (Touching Wood (USA))   **c–**
[2018/19 h107: h23.1mᵖᵘ h25s² h25.5v² h23.5d c24.2vᵘʳ Mar 5] small mare: fair handicap   **h103**
hurdler: unseated on chasing debut: stays 3¼m: acts on heavy going: wears headgear/
tongue tie. *Keiran Burke*

JUMBO DAVIS (IRE) 6 b.m. Doyen (IRE) – Banjo Davis (IRE) (Definite Article)   **b75**
[2018/19 b63p: b15.7d⁵ Nov 20] has had breathing operation: runner-up on second start in
Irish points: fifth in bumpers 7 months apart. *Harry Whittington*

JUMBO'S BOY 5 b.g. Multiplex – Silver Gyre (IRE) (Silver Hawk (USA)) [2018/19   **h–**
h16.8gᵖᵘ h16.3m⁴ Aug 2] little form on Flat/over hurdles. *Peter Bowen*

JUMP FOR DOUGH (IRE) 8 b.g. Milan – Collopy's Girl (IRE) (Be My Native (USA))   **c–**
[2018/19 c92, h115: h20.1g⁵ h24.7g^ur Oct 28] good-topped gelding: fair handicap hurdler: **h107**
never a threat in novice handicap chases: stayed 3¼m: acted on soft going: tried in tongue
tie: dead. *Lucinda Russell*

JUMPING JACK (IRE) 5 b.g. Sir Prancealot (IRE) – She's A Character (Invincible   **h115**
Spirit (IRE)) [2018/19 h108: h15.9g^ur h15.8g² h15.9g² h15.9m* h15.7m h15.7g⁴ Nov 23]
good-quartered gelding: fairly useful hurdler: won maiden at Plumpton in October: raced
only at 2m: acts on good to firm and heavy going. *Chris Gordon*

JUMPSUIT 6 b.g. Tobougg (IRE) – Charmaine Wood (Double Trigger (IRE)) [2018/19   **h69**
b16g⁶ h19.5d⁶ Mar 20] well held in bumper/maiden hurdle. *Ian Williams*   **b–**

JUNCTION FOURTEEN (IRE) 10 b.g. King's Theatre (IRE) – Chevet Girl (IRE)   **c128 §**
(Roselier (FR)) [2018/19 c137§, h–: c30.2g c24g² c23.8m⁶ c19.9g⁴ Apr 22] sturdy gelding: **h–**
has had breathing operation: winning hurdler: fairly useful handicap chaser nowadays:
stays 3m: acts on soft and good to firm going: usually visored: wears tongue tie: front
runner/races prominently: temperamental. *Emma Lavelle*

JUPITERS WAY 7 b.m. Josr Algarhoud (IRE) – Jupiter's Fancy (Jupiter Island) [2018/19   **h94**
h19.9g³ h20.1g⁴ Apr 15] second foal: dam (c89) 2½m-25f chase winner: placed in points:
modest form in mares event on second of 2 starts in novice hurdles. *Philip Kirby*

JURBY 9 b.g. Motivator – Darariyna (IRE) (Shirley Heights) [2018/19 h127: c16g³ c16v⁴   **c116**
c19.9g⁴ c21.2g^pu h21.4g Apr 14] well-made gelding: modest handicap hurdler: fairly useful   **h97**
form over fences: stays 2½m: acts on heavy going. *Oliver Sherwood*

JURISTE (FR) 5 b.g. Lawman (FR) – Green Lassy (FR) (Green Tune (USA)) [2018/19   **b70**
b16.7m³ b16.2s^pu Oct 13] poor form on debut in bumpers: went wrong 2 months later.
Philip Kirby

JURY DUTY (IRE) 8 b.g. Well Chosen – Swan Heart (IRE) (Broken Hearted) [2018/19   **c156**
c150+, h–: c22.5d³ c24s c20m² h21d* c26.2v* c34.3g^ur c29d^pu Apr 22] well-made gelding: **h133**
useful hurdler: won Grand National Hurdle at Far Hills in October: very smart chaser: won
minor event at Down Royal in March: stays 3¼m: acts on heavy going: usually in tongue
tie. *Gordon Elliott, Ireland*

JURYS OUT (IRE) 6 b.g. Witness Box (USA) – No Complaints But (IRE) (Supreme   **h99**
Leader) [2018/19 h–: h20v h19.7s^pu h19.7d⁵ h19.3s* h23.1g² Mar 14] modest handicap
hurdler: won conditionals/amateurs event at Carlisle in March: likely to prove suited by
3m: acts on soft going. *Venetia Williams*

JUSTADREAMYEKEN 7 b.g. Scorpion (IRE) – Loxhill Lady (Supreme Leader)   **h97**
[2018/19 b84: h16.2g⁶ h22.7d³ Nov 10] in frame in bumper: modest form when third at
Kelso on second of 2 outings in novice hurdles. *Harriet Graham*

JUST A FEELING 9 ch.m. Flemensfirth (USA) – Precious Lady (Exit To Nowhere   **c82**
(USA)) [2018/19 c–, h68: h21.2m* c22.5m* c20.9m^pu Jun 19] angular mare: has had   **h87**
breathing operation: modest handicap hurdler: won at Ludlow on return in May: form over
fences only when winning handicap at Uttoxeter 6 days later: stays 2¾m: acts on good to
firm going: tried in visor/tongue tie. *Dan Skelton*

JUST A PAR (IRE) 12 b.g. Island House (IRE) – Thebrownhen (IRE) (Henbit (USA))   **c117**
[2018/19 c25.9s c34.3g^pu Apr 6] tall, lengthy, angular gelding: winning hurdler: smart   **h–**
handicap chaser: left Paul Nicholls/off 20 months, well below form both outings in 2018/19:
stays 29f: acts on heavy going, probably on good to firm: wears headgear. *James Moffatt*

JUST A SIP (IRE) 4 b.f. Great Pretender (IRE) – One Gulp (Hernando (FR)) [2018/19 b16.8g   **b– p**
Apr 18] £60,000 3-y-o: sixth foal: half-sister to 3 winners, including fair hurdlers/fairly
useful chasers Two Swallows (2½m-3m winner, by Kayf Tara) and One of Us (23f-31f
winner, by Presenting): dam (h143), bumper/2½m-3m hurdle winner, closely related to
Grand National winner Rule The World: 9/2: excuses when well held in mares bumper at
Cheltenham: clearly thought capable of better. *Warren Greatrex*

JUST A STING (IRE) 7 b.g. Scorpion (IRE) – Shanann Lady (IRE) (Anshan) [2018/19   **c134**
h121: c22.5g* c24.2g* c24g² c26d c28.8g^pu Apr 27] lengthy gelding: placed in novices 3 of   **h–**
4 starts over hurdles: useful form over fences: won novice handicaps at Uttoxeter in October
and Exeter in November: should stay further than 3m: acts on heavy going. *Harry Fry*

JUSTATENNER 8 b.g. Northern Legend – Shelayly (IRE) (Zaffaran (USA)) [2018/19 c–,   **c–**
h85: h23.3g^F h22.1m* h22.1g² h22.1s* h23.9g* h23.9g³ h24.3d² h24.6v⁴ h15.7v⁵ h25.8g²   **h116**
h19.3g Feb 18] workmanlike gelding: fairly useful handicap hurdler: left Barry Murtagh,
much improved when winning at Cartmel in June/August and Perth in September: let down
by jumping only outing over fences: stays 3¼m: acts on soft and good to firm going: wears
headgear: has worn tongue tie: dropped out. *Tristan Davidson*

JUST BOBBY (IRE) 6 b.g. Black Sam Bellamy (IRE) – Blackwater Bay (IRE) (Supreme **h109**
Leader) [2018/19 h112, b86: h19.5v h22.8v³ h19.9sᶠ Dec 26] fair hurdler: may have
proved best at shorter than 23f: acted on heavy going: dead. *Micky Hammond*

JUST BROOKE 9 ch.m. Black Sam Bellamy (IRE) – Sports Express (Then Again) **h71**
[2018/19 h67: h22.7g⁶ h21.4d h24.3sᵖᵘ Mar 9] poor maiden hurdler: in tongue tie last 4
starts. *N. W. Alexander*

JUST CALL ME AL (IRE) 6 br.g. Presenting – Tonaphuca Girl (IRE) (Saddlers' Hall **h101**
(IRE)) [2018/19 b90p: b16.4g² b16.4d h16.4s h17g⁴ h16.7g⁵ h20.3dᵘʳ h20.3d² Apr 24] fair **b89**
form in bumpers: similar form over hurdles: improved again when second in conditionals
handicap at Southwell final outing: stays 2½m: acts on good to soft going: tried in tongue
tie. *Gillian Boanas*

JUSTCALL'M JOHN (IRE) 5 b.g. Witness Box (USA) – Black N Amber (IRE) **h–**
(Alderbrook) [2018/19 b16.8d h16g h20.2s h21vᵖᵘ Apr 14] little sign of ability in varied **b–**
company: tried in hood: in tongue tie last 3 starts. *Seamus Spillane, Ireland*

JUST CAMERON 12 b.g. Kayf Tara – Miss Fencote (Phardante (FR)) [2018/19 c147, **c141**
h–: c19.4m⁶ c15.2s³ c15.2d Dec 27] tall gelding: winning hurdler: useful handicap chaser: **h–**
stays 2½m but usually races at shorter: acts on heavy going: wears headgear/tongue tie.
Micky Hammond

JUST CAUSE (IRE) 9 b.g. Court Cave (IRE) – Secret Can't Say (IRE) (Jurado (USA)) **c101**
[2018/19 c120§, h–: c26g² c22.7m² c26.3dᵖᵘ c21.1d Apr 4] lengthy gelding: multiple **h–**
winning pointer: winning hurdler: fair maiden hunter chaser nowadays: stays 3¼m: acts on
heavy going: has worn cheekpieces/tongue tie. *J. P. Owen*

JUST DON'T ASK (IRE) 7 ch.g. Ask – Lucys Mate (IRE) (Supreme Leader) [2018/19 **c121**
h124: c20s c19.4g* c20.1g Feb 23] rangy gelding: has had breathing operation: fairly **h–**
useful hurdler: similar form over fences only when winning novice at Wetherby in January:
stays 2½m: acts on heavy going: usually races close up: quirky sort. *Charlie Longsdon*

Sideways Syndicate's "Jury Duty"

JUSTFORJAMES (IRE) 10 b.g. Dr Massini (IRE) – Over The Road (IRE) (Executive **c119** Perk) [2018/19 c117, h–: c21.6d⁵ c24sᵖᵘ c19.2g c25.2m* Feb 26] winning hurdler: fairly **h–** useful handicap chaser: won at Catterick in February: stays 25f: acts on good to firm and heavy going: tried in hood, in cheekpieces 6 of last 7 outings. *Micky Hammond*

JUST FOR TARA 6 b.m. Malinas (GER) – Just For Jean (IRE) (Presenting) [2018/19 **h79** h16g⁵ h20g⁵ h16g³ h19g h21.6v h16g Oct 30] £11,000 5-y-o: second foal: half-sister to modest 2½m chase winner Fit For Fifty (by Lucarno): dam (h86), maiden hurdler, half-sister to fairly useful hurdler/chaser (stayed 3m) World Wide Web: runner-up in Irish point on debut: poor form over hurdles: should stay beyond 2½m: best form on good going. *Christian Williams*

JUST GEORGIE 9 b.g. Kayf Tara – Just Kate (Bob's Return (IRE)) [2018/19 c117, h92: **c104** c20.1d⁵ c27.6s Dec 26] maiden hurdler: fairly useful handicap chaser: below form in **h–** 2018/19: stays 3m: acts on heavy going: normally races prominently. *Sue Smith*

JUST GO FOR IT 6 b.m. Passing Glance – Just Jasmine (Nicholas Bill) [2018/19 h15.3g **h–** Feb 27] seventh foal: half-sister to fairly useful hurdler Queens Grove (17f-2½m winner) and modest hurdler/chaser Just Spot (15f-19f winner) (both by Baryshnikov): dam (c140/ h91) 2m-21f winner: tailed off in novice hurdle. *Kevin Bishop*

JUST GONE MIDNIGHT 5 ch.m. Midnight Legend – Precious Lady (Exit To Nowhere **b–** (USA)) [2018/19 b16d Mar 21] fourth foal: half-sister to modest hurdler/chaser Just A Feeling (21f/2¾m winner, by Flemensfirth): dam, unraced, out of sister to Best Mate: 8/1, well beaten in mares bumper at Chepstow. *Emma Lavelle*

JUST GOT TO GET ON 5 ch.g. Malinas (GER) – Just Cliquot (Gunner B) [2018/19 **h–** b15.8v³ b15.8s h19.3m⁵ Mar 31] half-brother to a winning pointer by Sir Harry Lewis: dam **b87** (c107) 3m chase winner: better effort in bumpers when third at Ffos Las on debut: tailed off in maiden hurdle at Ascot. *Sam Thomas*

JUST HEATHER (IRE) 5 gr.m. Zebedee – Miss Sundance (IRE) (Desert Sun) [2018/19 **h–** h20.6gᵖᵘ h16.6gᵖᵘ Oct 3] half-sister to modest 2m hurdle winner Mr Moondance (by Windsor Knot): of little account, including on Flat. *John Wainwright*

JUSTICE KNIGHT 7 b.g. Raven's Pass (USA) – New Story (USA) (Dynaformer **h96** (USA)) [2018/19 h91: h18.6g² h19.7s⁶ h15.3d h15.8d* Feb 17] modest handicap hurdler: won at Huntingdon in February: stays 19f: acts on heavy going: has worn headgear: tried in tongue tie: usually races freely in lead. *Michael Scudamore*

JUSTIFICATION 11 b.g. Montjeu (IRE) – Colorspin (FR) (High Top) [2018/19 h101: **h95** h19.2g⁶ h25.8g⁵ Jun 16] rather leggy gelding: fair handicap hurdler: stays 2½m: acts on heavy going. *Gary Moore*

JUST JANICE (IRE) 7 b.m. King's Theatre (IRE) – Liss Na Tintri (IRE) (Presenting) **h129** [2018/19 h130: h22.8g³ May 12] useful hurdler: stays 23f: acts on heavy going: has worn tongue tie: dropped out. *John E. Kiely, Ireland*

JUST LIKE BETH 11 b.m. Proclamation (IRE) – Just Beth (Carlingford Castle) [2018/19 **h–** h20.3sᵖᵘ Mar 18] no sign of ability. *Giuseppe Fierro*

JUST MARVIN (IRE) 6 b.g. Atraf – Gailybay Ellen (IRE) (Supreme Leader) [2018/19 **h71** b16.7g h15.7d³ Apr 24] sixth foal: half-brother to fair hurdler/fairly useful chaser Topper **b–** Thornton (2½m-3m winner, by Double Eclipse): dam (h76), maiden hurdler, half-sister to useful chaser (19f/2½m winner) Bible Lord: last in bumper/novice hurdle. *Alex Hales*

JUST MIDAS (IRE) 6 b.g. Shantou (USA) – Desert Gail (IRE) (Desert Style (IRE)) **h–** [2018/19 b84: h18.5m⁶ h20g h16.5dᵖᵘ h23.3sᵖᵘ Dec 31] promise on first of 2 outings in bumpers: no form over hurdles: tried in headgear. *David Pipe*

JUST MILLY (IRE) 8 b.m. Milan – Out Performer (IRE) (Persian Bold) [2018/19 h125: **h118** h23.1g³ h19.9g⁵ h21g⁵ h20.6gᵖᵘ Oct 20] fairly useful handicap hurdler: stays 3m: acts on good to soft going: wears hood. *John Mackie*

JUST MINDED (IRE) 8 b.g. Kayf Tara – Georgia On My Mind (FR) (Belmez (USA)) **c115** [2018/19 c116, h–: c20.3d⁴ c23.8g² c23.8m⁴ c24gᵖᵘ Apr 10] has had breathing operation: **h–** winning hurdler: fairly useful maiden chaser: stays 25f: acts on soft going: in cheekpieces last 5 starts, also in tongue tie last 4: temperament under suspicion. *Olly Murphy*

JUST PERFECT 4 ch.g. Mastercraftsman (IRE) – Downhill Dancer (IRE) (Montjeu **h–** (IRE)) [2018/19 b13.2m² h17.7v h17.7v⁵ h16d Jan 15] first foal: dam, maiden on Flat **b84** (stayed 1½m), half-sister to fairly useful/unreliable hurdler (2m-2½m winner) Heron Bay: second in junior bumper at Exeter: well held over hurdles. *George Baker*

JUST ROCKY 6 b.g. Yeats (IRE) – High Benefit (IRE) (Beneficial) [2018/19 b16g[4] b15.8s[3] h16.7d[F] Jan 8] compact gelding: fairly useful form in frame in bumpers: fell first on hurdling debut: dead. *Dan Skelton* — **h– b96**

JUST SKITTLES 11 b.g. Storming Home – Miss Roberto (IRE) (Don Roberto (USA)) [2018/19 c26g[pu] c23m Jul 9] no form outside points. *Richard Harper* — **c– h–**

JUST SPOT 12 ch.m. Baryshnikov (AUS) – Just Jasmine (Nicholas Bill) [2018/19 c–, h84: c20d[R] c20.2g[pu] h19s Feb 4] workmanlike mare: modest handicap hurdler/chaser: no form in 2018/19: stays 19f: acts on heavy going: has worn tongue tie. *Kevin Bishop* — **c– h–**

JUSTTHEGREY (IRE) 7 gr.g. Getaway (GER) – Line White (FR) (Pitchounet (FR)) [2018/19 b–73: h19.9g[2] h19.9g[pu] h15.8g[pu] h15.8s[pu] Dec 11] sturdy gelding: second of 3 in novice on hurdling debut: pulled up all 3 starts after. *Rosemary Gasson* — **h95**

JUST YOUR TYPE (IRE) 7 br.g. Morozov (USA) – Enistar (IRE) (Synefos (USA)) [2018/19 h123: c23.8v[4] c23.4s[5] c24.2s[F] c32.6g[6] c31.7s[F] Mar 12] tall, good-topped gelding: point winner: fairly useful hurdles winner: better form in defeat over fences: should be suited by long distances: acts on heavy going: tried in cheekpieces: usually races close up: room for improvement in jumping. *Charlie Longsdon* — **c139 h–**

K

KADASA 7 ch.m. Black Sam Bellamy (IRE) – Kadassa (IRE) (Shardari) [2018/19 h15.8d h19.5m[6] Apr 22] half-sister to several winners, including fairly useful hurdler/very smart chaser Kadarann (2m-2½m winner, by Bigstone) and useful hurdler Kadara (2m winner, by Slip Anchor), stayed 3m: dam, placed at 1¼m, half-sister to Derby winner Kahyasi: well beaten in novice hurdles. *Henry Oliver* — **h–**

KADDYS DREAM 8 b.m. Kadastrof (FR) – Symbiosis (Bien Bien (USA)) [2018/19 h94: h23.33d[F] h21m[6] h16g Oct 30] has had breathing operation: maiden hurdler, no form in 2018/19: left Robin Dickin after second start: has worn tongue tie, including in 2018/19: usually races towards rear. *Ali Stronge* — **h–**

KAHALEESI 7 b.m. Shirocco (GER) – Maiden Voyage (Slip Anchor) [2018/19 h–: h20.6g[2] Mar 14] useful-looking mare: poor form over hurdles: stays 21f. *Olly Murphy* — **h84**

KAHDIAN (IRE) 9 br.g. Rock of Gibraltar (IRE) – Katiykha (IRE) (Darshaan) [2018/19 c75, h–: c20.9d[pu] c19.5g[ur] h20g[5] h15.8v[4] h16.8s[3] c15.9m[2] h19g[6] h15.3g[3] c17.8v[ur] c16.5g[ur] c15.7g* h18.5d[2] Apr 9] compact gelding: modest maiden hurdler: poor handicap chaser: won at Wincanton in April: left Helen Rees after first start: stays 19f: acts on soft and good to firm going: wears headgear/tongue tie: usually races off pace. *Brian Barr* — **c78 h89**

KAISER BLACK (IRE) 8 b.g. Germany (USA) – Strong Red (Strong Gale) [2018/19 c23d[2] c23g* c24.5g* c21g[2] c20d* Mar 10] half-brother to fair hurdler/chaser Get Involved (23f/3m winner, by Milan): dam unraced: winning hurdler: smart chaser: won handicap at Ballinrobe (by 15 lengths from Spider Web) in May, Connacht National at Roscommon (by 4 lengths from Master Appeal) in June and Grade 3 novice at Naas (by 11 lengths from Camelia de Cotte) in March: second in Flogas Novices' Chase at Leopardstown (1¼ lengths behind La Bague Au Roi): stays 25f: acts on heavy going: wears tongue tie: open to even more improvement as a chaser. *P. M. J. Doyle, Ireland* — **c153 p h–**

KAIZER 4 ch.g. Nathaniel (IRE) – Perse (Rock of Gibraltar (IRE)) [2018/19 b13m[5] b15.6g[3] b16.2g[6] Jan 22] modest form in bumpers: down the field in minor event on Flat. *Alistair Whillans* — **b80**

KAJAKI (IRE) 6 gr.g. Mastercraftsman (IRE) – No Quest (IRE) (Rainbow Quest (USA)) [2018/19 h16.8g* h16g* h19.8g[2] Jan 1] has had breathing operation: fairly useful on Flat, stays 2m: fairly useful form over hurdles: won maiden at Sedgefield in October and introductory event at Wetherby in November: wears cheekpieces. *Kevin Ryan* — **h121**

KAKI DE LA PREE (FR) 12 b.g. Kapgarde (FR) – Kica (FR) (Noir Et Or) [2018/19 c–, h130: h23.3g[3] h23.9v[pu] h23s[6] Dec 14] good-bodied gelding: fairly useful handicap hurdler nowadays: useful chaser at best: stays 25f: acts on heavy going: tried in cheekpieces: usually races nearer last than first: temperament under suspicion. *Tom Symonds* — **c– h125**

KALABALOO (IRE) 7 b.m. Kalanisi (IRE) – Wild Spell (IRE) (Oscar (IRE)) [2018/19 c26g[2] May 4] sixth foal: half-sister to bumper winner/fair 2½m hurdle winner Kala Brandy: dam unraced half-sister to dam of top-class hurdler/very smart chaser (winner up to 21f) Oscar Whisky: multiple point winner: 33/1, third in hunter at Cheltenham (6¼ lengths behind Fortune Bound) on chasing debut. *T. Ellis* — **c95**

KALABEE (IRE) 4 b.g. Kalanisi (IRE) – American Honey (IRE) (Lord Americo) **b–**
[2018/19 b15.8v b16d Feb 23] no form in bumpers. *Keiran Burke*

KALAHARI QUEEN 6 br.m. Kalanisi (IRE) – Queen's Leader (Supreme Leader) **c129**
[2018/19 h125p: c20g² c21.5s³ c17.5v² c21.3g* c21.6g⁴ Mar 23] lengthy mare: has had **h–**
breathing operation: fairly useful hurdler: similar form over fences: won 3-runner mares
novice at Wetherby in February: will stay 3m: acts on heavy going: in cheekpieces last 3
starts. *Jamie Snowden*

KALAHARRY (IRE) 7 b.g. Kalanisi (IRE) – Full Imperatrice (FR) (Dernier Empereur **h108**
(USA)) [2018/19 h98: h19.5v h23.3s* h22.8s h24s* Jan 29] fair handicap hurdler: won at
Hexham in December and Newcastle in January: stays 3m: acts on soft going: often travels
strongly. *Alistair Whillans*

KALANGADOO 8 b.g. Grape Tree Road – Garota de Ipanema (FR) (Al Nasr (FR)) **h–**
[2018/19 h22.2g Jul 10] has had breathing operation: no form: tried in tongue tie. *Ben Case*

KALANITI (IRE) 8 b.m. Kalanisi (IRE) – Miss Twinkletoes (IRE) (Zafonic (USA)) **c–**
[2018/19 c–, h109: h16.4m h20.2gᶠ Apr 24] workmanlike mare: fair hurdler at best, well **h–**
held completed start in 2018/19: once-raced chaser: unproven beyond 17f: acts on soft
going: tried in cheekpieces. *Chris Grant*

KALARIKA (IRE) 6 br.m. Kalanisi (IRE) – Katariya (IRE) (Barathea (IRE)) [2018/19 **h97**
h86: h16g⁵ h19.2dᵖᵘ h18.5s⁴ Dec 7] sturdy mare: modest handicap hurdler: won
conditionals/amateurs event at Exeter in December: stays 19f: acts on heavy going: wears
headgear/tongue tie: races prominently. *Colin Tizzard*

KALASHNIKOV (IRE) 6 br.g. Kalanisi (IRE) – Fairy Lane (IRE) (Old Vic) **c154 p**
[2018/19 h152p: c16.2g* c17s* c16g² c15.5d² c15.9sᵘʳ c19.9d* Apr 4] **h–**

A third Grade 1 conditions event for novice chasers, over the intermediate
distance of two and a half miles, is now firmly embedded at the big spring festivals
at Cheltenham and Aintree. The Manifesto—named after one of the greatest of
all Grand National performers (two wins and three thirds in eight appearances)—
preceded Cheltenham's Golden Miller Novices' Chase (commemorating the most
famous chaser of the pre-war era) by two years and has been a Grade 1 since 2012,
two years before the Golden Miller was similarly upgraded. Both races quickly
developed into rivals for the longer-established Arkle (2m) and RSA Chase (3m)
at Cheltenham and the Maghull (2m) and the Mildmay Novices' (3m 1f, itself
only upgraded to Grade 1 as late as 2014). Since the Manifesto and Golden Miller
became Grade 1 events, they have taken runners from the other major novice
events at the two festivals and, in all honesty, should have remained as Grade 2s,
but with penalties (both started life with no penalties). Although there were double
figure fields in the latest season for both the Arkle and the RSA Chase, there are
really not enough good novice chasers around in an average year to justify having
three Grade 1s for them at each of the spring festivals (Punchestown doesn't have an
intermediate Grade 1). The proliferation of Grade 1s increases the opportunities for
the best horses to avoid one another, when, if Cheltenham is to live up to the hype of
being jumping's 'Olympics', the aim must surely be for the best horses to be racing
against each other.

One set of connections grateful for the intermediate Grade 1 at Aintree were
those associated with Kalashnikov, whose switch to two and a half miles paid off
when he gained consolation in the Devenish-sponsored Manifesto for an unfortunate
exit from the Arkle at Cheltenham. Five of the Arkle runners stuck to the two-mile
route by contesting the Maghull on Grand National day (Ornua and Us And Them
filled the first two places), but Kalashnikov was joined by another Arkle runner Glen
Forsa in the Manifesto. It was remarkable that it took until his twelfth start and
the final outing of his second full season before the smart hurdler/novice chaser
Kalashnikov was tried over a distance much beyond two miles. He had won one
notable prize in his runs at around the minimum trip—the very valuable Betfair
Hurdle at Newbury in 2017/8—and he had run some fine races in defeat against
other smart novices in graded company, including when finishing runner-up in the
Supreme Novices' at the Cheltenham Festival; however, it was really his win in
the Grade 1 Manifesto Novices' Chase at Aintree in April, run over nearly two and a
half miles, that saw him finally show just how good he might turn out to be.

Just six went to post for the Manifesto, the same number as contested the Mildmay and one fewer than for the Maghull, with the mare La Bague Au Roi, who was already a dual Grade 1 winner, sent off favourite at 7/4. Kalashnikov was next at 4/1, with Glen Forsa and the Pendil Novices' Chase winner Bags Groove at 11/2, the Golden Miller third Mengli Khan at 7/1 and Spiritofthegames, who had some strong handicap form, the outsider of the field at 8/1. There was no dead wood in a line-up in which La Bague Au Roi, unbeaten in four chases including the Kauto Star at Kempton and the Flogas at Leopardstown, stood out on form. Kalashnikov had already run against Glen Forsa twice. The previous month, in the Arkle at Cheltenham, Glen Forsa had already parted company with his rider by the time Kalashnikov was left with nowhere to go and unseated his rider when the leader Ornua fell in front of him at the sixth. Before that, Kalashnikov had started at 4/1-on to beat Glen Forsa in a three-runner affair for the Kingmaker Novices' Chase, transferred to Sandown from Warwick's fixture which had been lost because of the equine flu outbreak; Kalashnikov's attempt to try to keep pace with the bold-jumping Glen Forsa saw him crack before the straight that day and he finished nineteen lengths behind his rival. For Kalashnikov, the Kingmaker was a second consecutive reverse at odds-on. At Christmas, he had been decidedly flat in the Wayward Lad Novices' Chase, a race that became a virtual match with Dynamite Dollars after Maria's Benefit departed somewhere in the mist. Kalashnikov went down by a length and a quarter to Dynamite Dollars, the pair a long way clear of the two other finishers. He had fared better on his first two starts over fences, landing odds of 4/1-on and 7/1-on in novice events at Warwick and Plumpton, winning by eleven lengths and eighteen lengths respectively.

So, although he started second favourite at Aintree, Kalashnikov had a bit to prove on form going into the Manifesto, although he seemed sure to be suited by the step up in trip, judged on his pedigree. La Bague Au Roi was in front by the second, settling any issue about the battle for the lead, Kalashnikov more patiently ridden now stepped up in trip. Kalashnikov was within three lengths of the leader early on the final circuit and was asked for his effort as the race developed into a three-way tussle approaching the straight. After Mengli Khan made a bad mistake at the third last, Kalashnikov laid down his challenge to La Bague Au Roi in earnest and moved into a decisive lead despite blundering two from home. Maintaining a clear advantage with a better jump at the last, but only doing enough in front as La Bague Au Roi stuck to her task, Kalashnikov won by a length and a quarter, with Mengli Khan a further length and three quarters away in third. Bags Groove who was never travelling well, came a remote fourth, while Glen Forsa was pulled up in the straight after making significant mistakes. It seems probable that La Bague Au Roi wasn't quite at her best on the day, but Kalashnikov nonetheless appeared to show improvement to win.

Devenish Manifesto Novices' Chase, Aintree—Kalashnikov relishes the step up in trip as he lowers the colours of La Bague Au Roi (right); Irish raider Mengli Khan (star on cap) takes third

		Doyoun (b 1985)	Mill Reef
			Dumka
Kalanisi (IRE) (b 1996)		Kalamba (b 1991)	Green Dancer
			Kareena
Kalashnikov (IRE) (br.g. 2013)		Old Vic (b 1986)	Sadler's Wells
			Cockade
Fairy Lane (IRE) (b 2004)		Fairy Blaze (b 1991)	Good Thyne
			Fairy Tree

The good-topped Kalashnikov is certainly bred to stay two and a half miles and more, being out of an unraced daughter of strong stamina influence Old Vic. Furthermore, Fairy Lane is a sister to the top-class Kicking King, winner of the Cheltenham Gold Cup and two editions of the King George VI Chase, after he had been campaigned in his earlier days at two miles, finishing second (like Kalashnikov) in a Supreme and, the following year, in an Arkle. Kalashnikov's sister Kalane ran to form on her only try at three miles and won at up to two miles five furlongs; she ran only once at a bare two miles and that was on her debut. Kalashnikov's fairly useful half-brother Holdbacktheriver (by Presenting) won at three miles over fences in the latest season for Evan Williams. A brother to Holdbacktheriver, Classic Event, didn't win a race but stayed two and three quarter miles, while a half-sister Pixie Lane (by Gamut) was a fair winning hurdler at two and a half miles. Kalashnikov has been raced on good going or softer and acts on heavy. He has been ridden on all his starts to date by Jack Quinlan. Kalashnikov has more to offer as a chaser over two and a half miles and further and may well develop into a serious contender in his second season over fences for races like the Ryanair at the Cheltenham Festival and the Melling Chase back at Aintree. *Amy Murphy*

KALASKADESEMILLEY 8 b.g. Myboycharlie (IRE) – Congressional (IRE) (Grand Lodge (USA)) [2018/19 c86, h101: h15.9g h18.7m h16.8g h15.8g³ c20.9s² c20d c16d⁴ h19s⁶ h21.7g⁴ h19.6d² Apr 26] has had breathing operation: modest handicap hurdler: modest maiden chaser: stays 2¾m: acts on good to firm going: has worn headgear, including final start: wears tongue tie. *Johnny Farrelly* — c83 h85

KALASTAR (IRE) 10 b.g. Kalanisi (IRE) – Katsura (Alflora (IRE)) [2018/19 c71§: c24.2vᵖᵘ Mar 18] lengthy gelding: multiple point winner: maiden chaser, pulled up sole outing in 2018/19: stays 3m: acts on soft going: has worn blinkers: temperamental. *Mrs E. Scott* — c– § h–

KALIFORNIA (IRE) 5 br.m. Kalanisi (IRE) – Carrigeen Kalmia (IRE) (Norwich) [2018/19 b77: b16.7g* b17.1d⁵ b16.4g Nov 17] fair form in bumpers: won mares event at Bangor in May: will stay at least 2¼m. *Henry Daly* — b92

KALIFOURCHON (FR) 8 gr.g. Martaline – Kaly Flight (FR) (Great Palm (USA)) [2018/19 c–p, h115: c23g⁵ c23g⁵ c21gᵘʳ h26.5g⁶ h23.3g⁴ h21.6g h23.1m⁴ h23.1m⁶ Nov 6] rather leggy gelding: fair handicap hurdler: similar form over fences: stays 3m: best form on good going: wears headgear: usually tongue tied. *David Pipe* — c105 h99

KALMBEFORETHESTORM 11 ch.g. Storming Home – Miss Honeypenny (IRE) (Old Vic) [2018/19 h106: h26.5g Aug 21] close-coupled gelding: fair handicap hurdler, behind sole outing in 2018/19: stays 3¼m: acts on soft and good to firm going: tried in tongue tie. *Helen Nelmes* — h–

KALONDRA (IRE) 8 b.g. Spadoun (FR) – Mystic Vic (IRE) (Old Vic) [2018/19 c147p, h–: c22.5gᶠ c20.2gᵘʳ c21.6g⁴ c20.6dᵖᵘ Mar 14] workmanlike gelding: winning hurdler: smart chaser: looking sure to play hand in finish when falling heavily 2 out in minor event at Galway in August: went amiss final outing: stays 2¾m: acts on good to firm and heavy going: wears tongue tie: races off pace. *Neil Mulholland* — c149 h–

KALOOKI (GER) 5 b.g. Martaline – Karuma (Surumu (GER)) [2018/19 b16d b15.7d³ b16.8d² b16.8d⁵ Feb 22] half-brother to several winners, including useful hurdler/chaser Kruzhlinin (2m-3m winner, by Sholokhov): dam German 1¼m-1½m winner: fairly useful form in bumpers: second in maiden at Exeter in January. *Philip Hobbs* — b95

KAMIL (GER) 6 ch.g. Sholokhov (IRE) – Kastoria (GER) (Dulcero (USA)) [2018/19 h20g* c23d* c25g⁴ c20g⁵ Nov 4] £65,000 3-y-o: fourth foal: half-brother to a Flat winner abroad by Kahyasi: dam useful German 9.5f/1¼m winner: fair form over hurdles: won maiden at Limerick in July: fairly useful form over fences: won maiden at Ballinrobe in August: left Noel Meade after third start: stays 23f: acts on good to soft going: usually in headgear: usually races prominently. *Henry Hogarth* — c120 h109

KANDULA 6 b.m. Eastern Anthem (IRE) – Duchcov (Caerleon (USA)) [2018/19 b16.5d b16d b16g Apr 25] half-sister to several winners, including useful hurdler/smart chaser Brick Red (2m/17f winner, by Dubawi): dam useful 1¼m winner: poor form in bumpers. *Roger Teal* **b65**

KANSAS CITY CHIEF (IRE) 10 b.g. Westerner – Badawi Street (Thowra (FR)) [2018/19 c133, h131: h23s⁵ c29.5sᵖᵘ c24.2d⁵ c20.5sᵖᵘ c26gⁿ Mar 23] sturdy gelding: useful hurdler/chaser, below form in 2018/19: stays 3¼m: acts on heavy going: wears cheekpieces: tried in tongue tie. *Neil Mulholland* **c112 h–**

KAP AUTEUIL (FR) 4 b.g. Kapgarde (FR) – Turboka (FR) (Kahyasi) [2018/19 b15.8g² Apr 22] rather unfurnished gelding: fourth foal: brother to useful hurdler/very smart chaser A Plus Tard (2¼m-2½m winner): dam French 17f-2½m hurdle/chase winner: 13/2, second in bumper at Huntingdon (8 lengths behind Mister Coffey). *David Arbuthnot* **b81**

KAPCORSE (FR) 6 br.g. Kapgarde (FR) – Angesse (FR) (Indian River (FR)) [2018/19 c125p, h103: c19.9d c22.4s* h21.4g⁴ h23.6d Feb 23] well-made gelding: fair form over hurdles: won novice at Wincanton in January: useful form over fences: won handicap at Newbury (by 10 lengths from Brelan d'As) in December: stays 2¾m: acts on soft going: open to further improvement as a chaser. *Paul Nicholls* **c143 p h103**

KAPDAD (FR) 5 ch.g. Kapgarde (FR) – Reveries (FR) (Montjeu (IRE)) [2018/19 h118, b71: h15.9m² h16.4g h20.5s Dec 3] compact gelding: fair maiden hurdler: unproven beyond 2m: acts on good to firm and heavy going. *Gary Moore* **h113**

KAPGA DE LILY (FR) 6 ch.m. Kapgarde (FR) – Louvisy (FR) (Loup Solitaire (USA)) [2018/19 h106, b–: h16s⁴ h20.5d⁴ Dec 12] modest form over hurdles. *Venetia Williams* **h93**

KAPGARRY (FR) 6 b.g. Ballingarry (IRE) – Kaprissima (FR) (Epervier Bleu) [2018/19 b96: h16.2g² h19.7m* h21g⁵ h21.6s h19.7g⁶ h20.3d h26.6gᵖᵘ Apr 25] sturdy gelding: Irish point winner: fairly useful hurdler: won novice at Wetherby in October: stays 2½m: acts on good to firm going. *Nigel Twiston-Davies* **h117**

KAPSTADT (FR) 9 b.g. Country Reel (USA) – King's Parody (IRE) (King's Best (USA)) [2018/19 c127, h126: c16.2g² c20g⁶ May 27] rather leggy gelding: fairly useful hurdler: useful form over fences: second in handicap at Warwick (2¾ lengths behind Ozzie The Oscar) in May: unproven beyond 17f: acts on soft and good to firm going: has worn tongue tie. *Ian Williams* **c133 h–**

KARABUNGA DUDE 5 b.g. Black Sam Bellamy (IRE) – Danarama (Rock City) [2018/19 h19.5dᵖᵘ Mar 20] pulled up in maiden hurdle. *Ben Pauling* **h–**

KARAKORAM 4 b.g. Excelebration (IRE) – Portrait (Peintre Celebre (USA)) [2018/19 h16d⁵ h16.5d h15.8v³ h16v³ h16.8s⁵ h16d⁶ Apr 6] modest maiden on Flat, stays 1½m: fair form over hurdles: raced around 2m: acts on heavy going. *Grace Harris* **h104**

KARAMOKO (IRE) 7 b.g. Manduro (GER) – Virevolle (FR) (Kahyasi) [2018/19 h62, b68: h16g³ h20.2g⁴ h19.6g³ h21.4s³ Jan 8] modest form over hurdles: stays 21f: acts on soft going. *Nicky Richards* **h98**

KARAPIRO BOY 5 b.g. Arabian Gleam – Littlemiss (Cosmonaut) [2018/19 h16g Apr 11] well beaten in Flat maiden/maiden hurdle. *Ruth Jefferson* **h–**

KARAT OF GOLD 8 ch.m. Lucarno (USA) – Coole Presence (IRE) (Presenting) [2018/19 h20.9mᵖᵘ Sep 19] third foal: dam winning pointer: pulled up in novice hurdle. *Simon Waugh* **h–**

KARENS LAD (IRE) 9 b.g. Kalanisi (IRE) – Aremebooksready (IRE) (Good Thyne (USA)) [2018/19 c21.6gᵖᵘ May 17] placed in points: modest form over hurdles: pulled up in maiden hunter on chasing debut: should be suited by 2½m+. *J. D. Sole* **c– h–**

KAREZAK (IRE) 8 b.g. Azamour (IRE) – Karawana (IRE) (King's Best (USA)) [2018/19 h24.2s h24dᵖᵘ c24.2dᵖᵘ Mar 19] good-topped gelding: useful hurdler at best, no form in 2018/19 following long lay-off: twice-raced chaser: wears headgear. *Alan King* **c– h–**

KARINGA DANCER 13 b.g. Karinga Bay – Miss Flora (Alflora (IRE)) [2018/19 c20m⁴ Apr 1] lengthy gelding: multiple point winner: winning hurdler: smart chaser at best, behind in hunter only start under Rules in 2018/19: stays 21f: acts on soft going: wears tongue tie. *Miss L. Thomas* **c72 h–**

KARINGO 12 ch.g. Karinga Bay – Wild Happening (GER) (Mondrian (GER)) [2018/19 c–x, h81§: h21.4g h20.2g³ h23.9g* h23.9g⁵ h23.9g⁵ h23.9gᵖᵘ Apr 24] has had breathing operation: poor handicap hurdler: won at Perth in August: twice-raced chaser (let down by jumping): stays 3m: acts on soft and good to firm going: wears cheekpieces: unreliable. *Lucy Normile* **c– x h82 §**

KARL MARX (IRE) 9 b.g. Red Clubs (IRE) – Brillano (FR) (Desert King (IRE))   c– §
[2018/19 c–§, h84§: h15.3m⁵ h21.6mᵖᵘ h16s h19.8gᵖᵘ h16.5d Apr 4] leggy gelding: poor   **h63** §
handicap hurdler: no form in chases: stays 3¼m: acts on any going: wears headgear: tried
in tongue tie: temperamental. *Mark Gillard*

KASAKH NOIR (FR) 7 ch.g. Redback – Vale of Honor (FR) (Singspiel (IRE)) [2018/19   **c132**
c20g⁵ c16.4g³ Dec 29] tall, useful-looking gelding: useful hurdler: similar form over   **h–**
fences: jumped right when last of 3 in novice handicap at Doncaster (2¼ lengths behind
Ballywood) in December: unproven beyond 17f: acts on heavy going. *Dan Skelton*

KASPERENKO 5 b.g. Archipenko (USA) – Jardin (Sinndar (IRE)) [2018/19 h–: h15.8g⁶   **h–**
May 22] useful on Flat, stays 13.5f: no form over hurdles: wears tongue tie. *Brendan Powell*

KASTANI BEACH (IRE) 13 br.g. Alderbrook – Atomic View (IRE) (Old Vic) [2018/19   c–
c–, h85: h19.2g⁶ h15.9s⁶ h19.5d* h16s⁶ c17g⁴ Apr 22] angular gelding: modest handicap   **h87**
hurdler: won at Lingfield (amateurs) in January: fair chaser at best: effective at 2m when
conditions are testing, and stays 3m: acts on heavy going: has worn headgear, including last
2 starts. *Seamus Mullins*

KATABATIKA 5 b.m. Shirocco (GER) – Landinium (ITY) (Lando (GER)) [2018/19   **h81**
h15.7g⁵ h15.8d Jan 25] half-sister to fairly useful hurdler/useful chaser Hallings Comet
(2m-2½m winner, by Halling): fair on Flat, stays 1½m: poor form over hurdles. *Hughie
Morrison*

KATACHENKO (IRE) 10 b.g. Kutub (IRE) – Karalee (IRE) (Arokar (FR)) [2018/19   **c124** §
c133§, h–: c19.9g⁴ c19.4m⁴ c21.5d⁶ c19.9s Dec 8] lengthy gelding: winning hurdler: fairly   **h–**
useful handicap chaser nowadays: stays 25f: acts on heavy going: has worn headgear,
including last 2 starts: usually races close up: tends to hang/carry head awkwardly under
pressure. *Donald McCain*

KATALYSTIC (IRE) 8 br.g. Kalanisi (IRE) – Beltane Queen (IRE) (Strong Gale)   **c88**
[2018/19 h91: h22.7g h21.4s⁴ c24.1dᶠ c24.2v³ c20.1d Mar 26] modest maiden hurdler: **h93**
similar form over fences: best effort when third in novice handicap at Hexham in March:
stays 3m: acts on heavy going. *Lucinda Russell*

KATEBIRD (IRE) 5 gr.m. Dark Angel (IRE) – She Basic (IRE) (Desert Prince (IRE))   **h92**
[2018/19 h–: h20g⁵ h16.7g h16.7g h19.9g³ h20g³ h19.9s h19.4g⁴ h20.6⁶ Mar 20]
modest maiden hurdler: stays 2½m: acts on soft going: tried in cheekpieces. *Oliver Greenall*

KATESON 6 gr.g. Black Sam Bellamy (IRE) – Silver Kate (IRE) (Insan (USA)) [2018/19   **h132**
b108: h19.5s* h20.5s* h20.5d³ h24.3g h20g Apr 6] lengthy gelding: useful bumper
performer: similar form over hurdles: won maiden at Chepstow and novice at Newbury in
November: third in Challow Novices' Hurdle at latter course (3¼ lengths behind Champ)
in December: should be suited by at least 3m: acts on soft going. *Tom Lacey*

KATGARY (FR) 9 b.g. Ballingarry (IRE) – Kotkira (FR) (Subotica (FR)) [2018/19 c134,   **c118**
h130: c17.1g⁴ h16.4g⁶ h16.4v³ h20.5m⁴ Apr 13] good-topped gelding: fairly useful   **h125**
handicap hurdler/chaser: stays 21f: acts on any going: wears headgear: tried in tongue tie.
Pauline Robson

KATIE CONNELL (IRE) 6 b.m. Doyen (IRE) – Sylvertune (FR) (Green Tune (USA))   **h81**
[2018/19 h16g⁶ h16g⁶ h16.8g⁴ h16.8v⁵ h15.8v⁵ h15.8s h24.4gᵖᵘ Jan 9] bumper winner: poor form
over hurdles: left W. P. Mullins after second start: tried in blinkers: dead. *Philip Hobbs*

KATPOLI (FR) 4 b.g. Poliglote – Katkogarie (FR) (Ballingarry (IRE)) [2018/19 h16.9s⁴   **h119**
h16.9sᵖᵘ h15.8g* h16.4g⁴ h16.8d³ h15.3g⁵ h16sᵖᵘ Mar 9] good-topped gelding: first foal:
dam unraced half-sister to useful French hurdler/chaser (stayed 25f) Katkovana out of
sister/half-sister to Grand Steeple-Chase de Paris winners Kotkijet and Katko: fairly
useful hurdler: won juvenile at Huntingdon in November: left G. Cherel after second start:
raced around 2m: acts on good to soft going: tried in hood: in tongue tie last 5 starts.
Dr Richard Newland

KATY P 7 b.m. Ask – Kingara (Karinga Bay) [2018/19 h121: h23.1m³ h23g h24g⁴ Aug 19]   **h118**
leggy mare: fairly useful handicap hurdler: stays 23f: acts on soft and good to firm going.
Philip Hobbs

KATY ROYAL 7 b.m. King's Theatre (IRE) – Water Stratford (IRE) (Jurado (USA))   **h112**
[2018/19 h104: h23.3g* h22.1g² h24.7g³ h20.1gᶠ h25.3g⁶ h22.7g³ h27d* h24.4gᵖᵘ Feb 20]
quite good-topped mare: fair hurdler: won maiden at Hexham in May and handicap at
Sedgefield in January: stays 27f: acts on heavy going. *Chris Fairhurst*

KAUTO RIKO (FR) 8 b.g. Ballingarry (IRE) – Kauto Relstar (FR) (Art Bleu) [2018/19   **c143**
c136, h–: c19.9gᵖᵘ c15.7v* c15.2g³ c20.6d Mar 14] leggy gelding: winning hurdler: useful   **h–**
handicap chaser: won at Haydock (by 4½ lengths from Zalvados) in December: stays 21f:
acts on good to firm and heavy going. *Tom Gretton*

KAUTO THE KING (FR) 5 b.g. Ballingarry (IRE) – Kauto Luisa (FR) (Jeune Homme (USA)) [2018/19 b90: b16.8m⁴ h15.3g⁵ h16s⁴ h20.5d⁶ h19s² Mar 19] good-topped gelding: has had breathing operation: modest form in bumpers: fair form over hurdles: wears tongue tie: front runner/races prominently, often freely. *Colin Tizzard* **h108 b84**

KAVANAGHS CORNER (IRE) 10 b.g. Coroner (IRE) – Annacarney (IRE) (Moscow Society (USA)) [2018/19 c83, h–: c20d² c15.6s² c19.9d³ c19.2v* c17.5v⁵ Mar 18] maiden hurdler: modest handicap chaser: won at Exeter in March: stays 2½m: acts on heavy going: tried in hood: has worn tongue tie: usually races in rear. *Simon Earle* **c96 h–**

KAYF ADVENTURE 8 b.g. Kayf Tara – My Adventure (IRE) (Strong Gale) [2018/19 c137, h–: c22.4s⁵ c24.2s^F Feb 2] tall gelding: winning hurdler: useful handicap chaser: stays 2¾m: acts on heavy going. *Philip Hobbs* **c128 h–**

KAYF BLANCO 10 b.g. Kayf Tara – Land of Glory (Supreme Leader) [2018/19 c130, h129: c21.4d³ c23.6v³ c20.6s⁴ c21.2g* c20g* c20.5s⁴ Mar 16] tall gelding: fairly useful hurdler: fairly useful handicap chaser: won at Fakenham and Ludlow (novice) in February: stays 21f: acts on heavy going: tried in hood/tongue tie. *Graeme McPherson* **c129 h–**

KAYF CHARMER 9 b.m. Kayf Tara – Silver Charmer (Charmer) [2018/19 h81: h21.4m⁶ h20g² h21.6g⁶ h21.6s* h21.6v³ Dec 20] has had breathing operation: modest handicap hurdler: won at Exeter in November: stays 2¾m: acts on heavy going: tried in blinkers. *Linda Blackford* **h85**

KAYF MOSS 11 b.g. Kayf Tara – Madam Mosso (Le Moss) [2018/19 c–, h110: h24.2d h25.8v⁴ h23.9s⁴ Apr 7] sturdy gelding: fair handicap hurdler: maiden chaser: stays 3m: acts on heavy going: wears headgear/tongue tie: front runner/races prominently. *John Flint* **c– h102**

KAYF SERA SERA 4 b.f. Kayf Tara – Fernello (Presenting) [2018/19 b16.5d Mar 11] second foal: dam unraced half-sister to fairly useful hurdler/useful chaser (stays 4m) Cogry: well beaten in mares bumper. *Anthony Honeyball* **b–**

KAYF STORM 6 gr.m. Kayf Tara – Royal Keel (Long Leave) [2018/19 b79: h20g⁶ May 10] modest form in bumpers: well held in mares maiden on hurdling debut. *Kim Bailey* **h–**

KAYF SUPREME 10 b.g. Kayf Tara – Sonnet Supreme (IRE) (Supreme Leader) [2018/19 c25.1m³ May 15] point winner: fairly useful chaser at best, no form since 2015/16: wears tongue tie. *Miss Samantha Newby-Vincent* **c–**

KAYF TIGER 10 b.g. Kayf Tara – La Marette (Karinga Bay) [2018/19 h65: h23.9d h19.5d h15.8d⁶ h20.3s^pu h19.7g⁶ Mar 26] sturdy gelding: poor maiden hurdler: should prove best at 2½m+: acts on heavy going: wears headgear/tongue tie. *Matt Sheppard* **h59**

KAYLA 9 b.m. Kayf Tara – Palila (Petoski) [2018/19 c106, h112: h24.7g⁶ h23g⁴ Jul 31] fair handicap hurdler: maiden chaser: stayed 3m: acted on good to firm going: tried in cheekpieces: wore tongue tie: dead. *Stuart Edmunds* **c– h100**

KAZAWI 5 ch.g. Dubawi (IRE) – Kazeem (Darshaan) [2018/19 h21.6g⁵ Oct 1] fairly useful maiden on Flat, stays 12.5f: 9/1, well held in novice on hurdling debut. *Robert Stephens* **h–**

KEADY LADY (IRE) 8 bl.m. Definite Article – Balwaney (FR) (Exit To Nowhere (USA)) [2018/19 h21g h24.8g^pu h19.9g^pu Nov 8] first foal: dam unraced half-sister to useful hurdler/fair chaser (stayed 2½m) Balapour: maiden hurdler, no form in 2018/19: left Dermot Anthony McLoughlin after second start: tried in cheekpieces. *Hugh Burns* **h–**

KEEL OVER 8 b.g. Gamut (IRE) – Kayf Keel (Kayf Tara) [2018/19 h15.8g⁴ h22g² h19.5s³ h16.7s⁶ Dec 6] €10,000 3-y-o, €7,000 4-y-o: second foal: dam (h105), 2m hurdle winner, sister to fair hurdler/useful chaser (stays 2¾m) Mystifiable and half-sister to useful hurdler/chaser (stayed 21f) Hidden Keel: multiple point winner: fair form over hurdles: left Fiona Kehoe after first start: tried in cheekpieces. *David Bridgwater* **h102**

KEEPER HILL (IRE) 8 b.g. Westerner – You Take Care (IRE) (Definite Article) [2018/19 c136, h–: h24.1g⁵ h24g² h25g* h23.4s h24d h24.7g⁵ Apr 6] tall gelding: useful handicap hurdler: won at Warwick (by 3 lengths from Oh Land Abloom) in January: third at Aintree (6 lengths behind Aux Ptits Soins) in April: useful chaser: stays 25f: acts on soft going. *Warren Greatrex* **c– h143**

KEEPING FAITH (IRE) 5 br.m. Sholokhov (IRE) – Elphis (IRE) (Supreme Leader) [2018/19 b16g h18.5v h16d⁵ Mar 21] £26,000 3-y-o: closely related to a winning pointer by Milan and half-sister to 3 winners by Presenting, including fairly useful hurdler/useful chaser Themoonandsixpence (2½m-25f winner) and bumper/fair 2m hurdle winner Miss Accurate (stayed 2½m): dam, unraced, out of sister to smart staying chaser Buck Rogers: down the field in bumper: modest form over hurdles: should do better. *Evan Williams* **h92 p b–**

KEEPINUPWITDJONES 7 b.g. Multiplex – Ceoperk (IRE) (Executive Perk) [2018/19 **h–** h–, b82: h16.2g May 27] modest form in bumpers: no form over hurdles: usually wears tongue tie. *Sharon Watt*

KEEP MOVING (FR) 7 b.g. Linda's Lad – Keeping Gold (FR) (Goldneyev (USA)) **c116** [2018/19 c108, h–: c16g⁵ c20d* c20v⁴ c19.4d² c19.4g⁵ c19.4g* Apr 26] good-topped **h–** gelding: lightly-raced hurdler: fairly useful handicap chaser: won at Warwick in December and Chepstow in April: stays 2½m: acts on heavy going. *Philip Hobbs*

KEEP ROLLING (IRE) 6 ch.g. Mahler – Kayles Castle (IRE) (Good Thyne (USA)) **b102** [2018/19 b16.3d⁵ b16.3d* Mar 2] €16,500 3-y-o: rangy, workmanlike gelding: fourth foal: dam unraced: fairly useful form in bumpers: won at Warwick in December: wears hood. *Philip Hobbs*

KEEP THE RIVER 5 b.m. Scorpion (IRE) – River Alder (Alderbrook) [2018/19 b16.2g² **h108** b15.8g* b16.2g⁴ h20.2g³ h20.5g* h20.6g⁵ h19.4g² h20.6g³ h20.6g⁶ h16.4m⁶ Mar 28] **b88** second foal: half-sister to fairly useful hurdler River Icon (2¾m winner, by Sixties Icon): dam (h118) 2m-2¾m winner (stayed 25f): fair form in bumpers: won mares event at Uttoxeter in June: fair hurdler: won mares maiden at Ayr in October: will stay 3m: raced mainly on good going: usually races close up. *Iain Jardine*

KEEP TO THE BEAT 8 b.m. Beat Hollow – Cadeau Speciale (Cadeaux Genereux) **h80** [2018/19 h85: h25g² h25.8g³ h25.8g⁴ h25.8s⁵ h21.7m Oct 24] poor handicap hurdler nowadays: stays 3¼m: acts on good to firm and good to soft going: has worn cheekpieces. *Pat Phelan*

KEEPYOURHEADUP 8 b.g. Sir Percy – Sweet Lemon (IRE) (Oratorio (IRE)) [2018/19 **h–** h–: h18.5gᵖᵘ h21.6gᵖᵘ Jun 15] no form: in cheekpieces last 2 starts: has worn tongue tie, including final start. *Helen Nelmes*

KEITHS BROTHER 5 ch.g. Native Ruler – Judy The Drinker (Snurge) [2018/19 b16m⁴ **b–** Apr 22] tailed off in bumper. *Henry Oliver*

KELKA 7 b.m. Exit To Nowhere (USA) – Scarvagh Diamond (IRE) (Zaffaran (USA)) **c83** [2018/19 c120, h–: c15.6v⁴ h16m Apr 12] has had breathing operation: fairly useful hurdler **h–** at best: similar form on first of 3 outings over fences: stays 21f: acts on heavy going. *Donald McCain*

KELPIES MYTH 6 b.g. Dutch Art – Miss Respect (Mark of Esteem (IRE)) [2018/19 **h125** h119: h16.2gᵖᵘ h16.7g h15.6g³ h17.1v² h15.6g⁴ h19.3d h16.4m² h16.4s* Mar 10] well-made gelding: fairly useful handicap hurdler: won at Musselburgh in March: should stay 2¼m: acts on good to firm and heavy going: wears tongue tie. *Lucinda Russell*

KELSEY (IRE) 9 ch.g. Robin des Champs (FR) – Lady Mariah (IRE) (Moonax (IRE)) **c75 §** [2018/19 c26.3gᵖᵘ c23.8m⁵ Jun 21] multiple point winner: fair hurdler: poor form in **h– §** chases: stays 3m: acts on heavy going: has worn headgear, including in 2018/19: has worn tongue tie: temperamental. *Peter Bowen*

KELTUS (FR) 9 gr.g. Keltos (FR) – Regina d'Orthe (FR) (R B Chesne) [2018/19 c131, **c112** h–: c24.2d³ c24.2d c25.1g² Apr 14] rather leggy gelding: winning hurdler: fair chaser **h–** nowadays: stays 25f: acts on good to firm and heavy going: wears tongue tie. *Jeremy Scott*

KELVINGROVE (IRE) 9 b.g. Hurricane Run (IRE) – Silversword (FR) (Highest Honor **c116 §** (FR)) [2018/19 c121§, h123: c23.6d³ Mar 21] twice-raced pointer: winning hurdler: fairly **h–** useful chaser: stays 3m: acts on soft going: usually wears cheekpieces: temperamental. *A. B. Leyshon*

KEMBLE'S CASCADE (IRE) 4 b.g. Kalanisi (IRE) – Beauty Star (IRE) (Shalford **b93** (IRE)) [2018/19 b16g² Apr 25] seventh foal: half-brother to 3 winners, including fairly useful hurdler/chaser Pumped Up Kicks (2½m-3m winner, by Flemensfirth) and fair hurdler Wee Tiger (2¾m-3m winner, by Craigsteel): dam lightly-raced half-sister to fairly useful hurdler/useful chaser (best around 2m) Tiger Cry: 7/2, second in bumper at Warwick (1¼ lengths behind Stoner's Choice). *Warren Greatrex*

KEMBOY (FR) 7 b.g. Voix du Nord (FR) – Vitora (FR) (Victory Note (USA)) **c176** [2018/19 c157p, h–: c20g* c24g* c26.3dᵘʳ c25d* Apr 4] **h–**

    'Go out on a winner'. That's the ideal for a top jockey heading into retirement (Noel Fehily managed it in the latest season) but few have bowed out on such a 'high' as twelve-times Irish champion Ruby Walsh. He called it a day straight after winning the Punchestown Gold Cup on the campaign's top staying chaser Kemboy who got the better of his stablemate Al Boum Photo, the Cheltenham Gold Cup winner, in a thrilling climax to the showpiece event on the opening day of the Punchestown Festival which took place shortly after the end of the British season.

Savills Chase, Leopardstown—Kemboy thumps a competitive field after getting an enterprising ride from David Mullins; Monalee (striped cap) fares best of the rest

Walsh's decision came out of the blue for Kemboy's trainer Willie Mullins—'He got off and asked if I could find someone for Livelovelaugh later, I just looked at him and he said "I'm out of here" and that's when the penny dropped.' Walsh, who had turned to wave at the crowd in the grandstand after passing the post on Kemboy, went on to announce his retirement 'with immediate effect' over the course tannoy, which led to racegoers packing around the paddock to cheer and applaud him.

Jump jockeys go on longer these days than they used to, thanks largely to medical advances in the treatment of injuries and to modern professional management and care. Walsh himself was a few days short of his fortieth birthday, while Noel Fehily was forty-three, Tony McCoy was forty when he hung up his saddle and Richard Johnson was forty-one when he won his latest championship. Walsh said he had been thinking about retirement since breaking his right leg (for the fifth time—'they can't operate on it again') at the 2018 Cheltenham Festival in a fall on Al Boum Photo in the RSA Chase. 'People have been asking me about retirement since I was thirty, and it's been happening more since I passed thirty-five. What did they want me to say? I love competing but it doesn't get any easier recovering from injuries, though you tend to just get on with it, do the rehab and get back, and when you ride a winner and give a few horses rides you think "You know what, I haven't lost it yet" and away you go. There was never going to be a good time to retire but there was always going to be a time when I wasn't going to be riding. I was determined injury wouldn't beat me and I would go out the way I wanted to go out.'

Ruby Walsh went into retirement firmly established as one of the great jump jockeys after a career spanning nearly a quarter of a century. He rode 2,756 winners over jumps in Britain and Ireland, putting him third in the all-time list behind Tony McCoy and Richard Johnson. The resilient McCoy, never sidelined long enough to prejudice his run of twenty successive championships in Britain, was, in Walsh's words, 'obsessed with numbers and creating records.' For Walsh, on the other hand, it was 'all about riding the big winners on the big days and I was lucky enough to ride some of the best horses there have ever been.' Partnerships with two powerhouse trainers, Paul Nicholls in Britain and Willie Mullins in Ireland, overlapped for a time with Walsh balancing the two jobs and enjoying a career that for sheer quality of winners has never been matched. Think of any of the best jumpers in the twenty-first century and, perhaps with the most notable exceptions of Best Mate, Moscow Flyer, Sprinter Sacre, Don Cossack and Altior, there is a good chance that Walsh rode it. He won the Cheltenham Gold Cup twice and the King George VI Chase five times on Kauto Star (and partnered that horse's rival and stablemate Denman to wins in the RSA and the Hennessy Gold Cup), his three Queen Mother Champion Chase wins included two on Master Minded, his four wins in the Champion Hurdle included two on Hurricane Fly (on whom he won sixteen Grade 1 races) and he won four of his

469

five World [Stayers'] Hurdles on Big Buck's (whom he partnered to sixteen of his record-breaking eighteen consecutive victories). Walsh was leading jockey a record eleven times at the Cheltenham Festival where his fifty-nine wins is also a record.

During the first decade of the century Walsh commuted across the Irish Sea and was consistently in the top ten in the table in Britain (highest placing joint-fourth) and would have been champion in 2007/8 and 2008/9 if the title had been determined by first-three earnings. Another frequent traveller from Ireland, Barry Geraghty, has also enjoyed seasons in which he has ridden with notable success in both Ireland and Britain, but no jockey has yet matched the achievement of six-times Irish champion Martin Molony who was both champion in Ireland and runner-up in Britain (to his older brother Tim) in 1949/50. Martin Molony was light enough to ride on the Flat too and finished third in the 1951 Derby, having won that year's Cheltenham Gold Cup on Silver Fame (he fractured his skull in a fall at Thurles later that year which forced his retirement at the age of only twenty-six).

The essay on Walsh's third Irish Grand National winner, Burrows Saint, gives some insight into his wider involvement with the stables he rode for. 'He was always thinking, he'd get off one and had already formulated a plan—"We could do this or that"—and he had a big input with us as he did with Willie Mullins,' says Paul Nicholls. A shrewd tactician with a big-race temperament, as well as being hard to beat in a finish, the distinctive hunched figure of Walsh sometimes made it look easy, the mark of so many of the great sportsmen, but he made sure he knew his horses and always did his homework on the opposition. 'He knew the tracks and the way everybody rode, other riders were intimidated by him,' said his father Ted, for whom he rode Papillon to win the Grand National in 2000. Ruby Walsh also won the Grand National on Hedgehunter and he was successful in all four of the major Nationals in the British Isles, as well as in some of the biggest races in France, Japan, the United States and Australia.

The ride with which Ruby Walsh signed off on Kemboy in the Coral Punchestown Gold Cup could not have been bettered. He gave Kemboy a trademark front-running ride, doing just enough to shrug off the attentions of British challenger Definitly Red, who harried him for a long way at the head of affairs in a truly-run race, and then pressing on in earnest from three out when challenged by Al Boum Photo. Both horses made mistakes at the second last but Kemboy battled on just the better as the pair went toe-to-toe and he won by two lengths. The form was solid—considerably more solid than some of the other Grade 1 staying events over the campaign—and established the stablemates as the two best staying chasers in training. There was a twenty-two-length gap back to third-placed The Storyteller,

Betway Bowl Chase, Aintree—
Kemboy gains consolation for his early Gold Cup exit with an authoritative victory over
Clan des Obeaux (noseband) and Balko des Flos (partly hidden behind winner)

Coral Punchestown Gold Cup, Punchestown—Ruby Walsh goes out on a high as Kemboy holds off Al Boum Photo in one of the best races of the campaign

with the third Mullins-trained contender, the previous year's winner Bellshill, whom Walsh had chosen ahead of Kemboy and Al Boum Photo in the Cheltenham Gold Cup, completing the frame (Definitly Red paid the price for mixing it with Kemboy and weakened into fifth). With all the attention afterwards on Ruby Walsh, it was easy to overlook the fact that Kemboy was his trainer's fifth winner of the Punchestown Gold Cup. The master of Closutton had long since secured his thirteenth (twelfth in succession) domestic trainers' championship, the stable's first three earnings in the Irish season of €5,826,079 beating Mullins' own prize-money record which he had set the season before. Four more winners at the Cheltenham Festival, including a first Gold Cup with Al Boum Photo, took the Mullins total at the meeting to sixty-five, further extending his lead over Nicky Henderson at the top of the all-time list.

Kemboy had already made significant contributions—on both sides of the Irish Sea—to his stable's prize-money haul, even before his stellar victory at Punchestown. He had ended his first season over fences with wins in a Grade 3 novice at Limerick and in the valuable and typically competitive EMS Copiers Novices' Handicap at the Punchestown Festival, and he picked up where he left off by winning the Clonmel Oil Chase on his reappearance (only entered when the race was reopened) from four rivals headed by Alpha des Obeaux who had won the race the previous year. Kemboy incurred a 4-lb penalty for his next intended outing, in the Ladbrokes Trophy (formerly the Hennessy) at Newbury for which he was ante-post co-favourite. However, strong winds led to his ferry crossing being cancelled and Kemboy waited for the Savills Chase, the mid-season championship chase in Ireland for stayers which had been run the previous year as the Leopardstown Christmas Chase after long-term sponsors Lexus ended their involvement. The new sponsors were rewarded with a cracking renewal, with ten of the eleven runners having won at least once in a Grade 1 company. The line-up included the last two winners, Outlander (also third in 2017) and Road To Respect, the last-named sent off 9/4 favourite, ahead of the second-season chasers Monalee and Shattered Love, with Kemboy one of three who started at 8/1, the others being the previous season's Ryanair Chase winner Balko des Flos, who had been runner-up to Road To Respect twelve months earlier, and Bellshill, whom Ruby Walsh chose to ride ahead of Kemboy.

Kemboy trounced his rivals in the Savills Chase, stretching his winning sequence to four with a seven and a half length victory over close-finishers Monalee and Road To Respect, with Bellshill fourth and Outlander fifth. Sent on by David Mullins with a circuit to go, after the pace slowed, the keen-going Kemboy was

Supreme Horse Racing Club, Brett Graham & Ken Sharp's "Kemboy"

still on the bridle turning for home and stormed clear in the straight, putting himself firmly in the Cheltenham Gold Cup picture, slashed to 6/1 third favourite behind Presenting Percy after not even being quoted for the race beforehand by some bookmakers (50/1 had been available). There was a sad postscript to the Savills Chase with the news that Road To Respect's stable companion Disko had suffered fatal injuries when falling at the last. Kemboy wasn't seen out again until Cheltenham where he was the shortest-priced of the four Gold Cup runners from his stable at 8/1. Kemboy's race was over almost before it began, as he unseated his rider after landing awkwardly over the first.

Kemboy's jumping had a habit of letting him down on big occasions—he had fallen at the first in the previous season's Irish National—but he put his Gold Cup reverse behind him three weeks later in the Betway Bowl at Aintree where he put up a performance that was right up there—in terms of form—with Al Boum Photo's decisive display at Cheltenham. Kemboy was ridden by Ruby Walsh for the first time since the 2016/17 season when Kemboy won a maiden hurdle at Limerick on his first start for Closutton after being bought by Harold Kirk out of Francis Matzinger's stable in France (runner-up only start on the Flat). Walsh dictated a modest pace at Aintree and Kemboy was best placed when the race finally developed in earnest in the home straight where Kemboy was always in control and sprinted away on the flat in a style rarely seen from a staying chaser. The King George winner and Gold Cup fifth Clan des Obeaux pipped Balko des Flos for second, nine lengths behind the impressive winner, with the Gold Cup third Bristol de Mai completing the frame.

With Kemboy and Al Boum Photo both still only seven, the Mullins stable looks to have a very strong hand in the next season's top staying chases, though the yard may not be able to call on the considerable services in the saddle of Ruby Walsh who also won the Melling Chase, the big race on the Friday of Aintree, on Mullins-trained Min before finishing third in the Grand National on the same stable's Rathvinden (Walsh later said that, had he won the National, he had intended to retire there and then). The Grand National meeting was also a good one for the Supreme Horse Racing Club, an ownership group which has around thirty horses at Closutton and whose royal blue, light blue star was also carried to success by Cadmium in the Topham Chase over the National fences. Sixteen of the club's members are involved in Kemboy, with twenty having an interest in Cadmium. There is more about the club, which also saw Aramon come second in the Top Novices' Hurdle, in the essay on Kemboy in last year's Annual.

Kemboy (FR) (b.g. 2012)	Voix du Nord (FR) (b 2001)	Valanour (b 1992)	Lomond Vearia
		Dame Edith (b 1995)	Top Ville Girl of France
	Vitora (FR) (b 2004)	Victory Note (b 1995)	Fairy King Three Piece
		Mosstraye (b 1993)	Tip Moss Chevestraye

The sturdy Kemboy is by the now-deceased French stallion Voix du Nord, also sire of the Champion Hurdle winner Espoir d'Allen and the Golden Miller winner Defi du Seuil, among others. Kemboy is the only winner bred by his dam Vitora, who won at a mile and a half in France and is a half-sister to the very smart Karabak, winner of the Relkeel Hurdle, and to Mossville, a fairly useful staying hurdler. Kemboy's grandam Mosstraye won over seventeen furlongs on the Flat in France and was placed over hurdles, while his great grandam Chevestraye, also a winner on the Flat, had a very creditable record over hurdles, winning twice at Auteuil and finishing second in the Grand Prix d'Automne. Kemboy, who again wore ear plugs at the Cheltenham Festival, stays twenty-five furlongs and acts on heavy going (though he doesn't need the mud). *W. P. Mullins, Ireland*

KENMARE RIVER 4 gr.g. Kendargent (FR) – Isabella Glyn (IRE) (Sadler's Wells (USA)) [2018/19 h15.8v^{pu} Jan 26] has had breathing operation: modest maiden on Flat, stays 1¼m: pulled up in maiden on hurdling debut. *Tim Vaughan* — h–

KENNEDYS FIELD 6 b.g. Multiplex – Supreme Lady (IRE) (Supreme Leader) [2018/19 h80, b72: h16g⁴ h16.2g⁴ h20.6d h15.7g Jan 1] little show in Irish points: modest maiden hurdler: left Gemma Anderson after second start: unproven beyond 2m: best form on good going: has worn hood: usually leads. *George Bewley* — h92

KENNY GEORGE 4 b.g. Mawatheeq (USA) – One For Philip (Blushing Flame (USA)) [2018/19 h15.7d h17.7v⁴ h17.7v³ Mar 16] angular gelding: fair maiden on Flat, stays 1½m: little form over hurdles. *Sheena West* — h56

KENSUKES KINGDOM (IRE) 6 b.g. Stowaway – Hamalata (IRE) (Mujadil (USA)) [2018/19 b15.8g⁶ h15.6g* Dec 3] point winner: sixth in bumper at Uttoxeter: 6/5, won novice at Musselburgh (by 1¼ lengths from Constancio) on hurdling debut: dead. *Philip Hobbs* — h111 / b87

KEN'S WELL (IRE) 8 b.g. Trans Island – Tiergarten (IRE) (Brief Truce (USA)) [2018/19 c100p, h108p, b95: c17g c20.9d c20.20m⁵ Jan 10] rangy gelding: has had breathing operation: fair form over hurdles: maiden chaser, no form in 2018/19: tried in hood/tongue tie: usually races prominently. *Jo Davis* — c– / h–

KENTFORD HEIRESS 9 b.m. Midnight Legend – Kentford Duchess (Jupiter Island) [2018/19 h112: h23.1m⁵ h23.3m* h20.3g* h26.5g⁴ h26.4m h21.6g⁵ h21g⁴ h19.2g³ h21.6g c23d h19.2d h18.9m* Apr 20] fairly useful handicap hurdler: won mares events at Uttoxeter in May, Southwell in June and Haydock in April: well beaten in novice handicap on chasing debut (should do better): stays 3¼m: acts on soft and good to firm going. *Seamus Mullins* — c– p / h121

KENTFORD MALLARD 6 b.m. Sulamani (IRE) – Kentford Grebe (Teenoso (USA)) [2018/19 b–: h16.8m^{pu} h16.8g h19.5d h20.5g* h23.3d h20.5s⁶ h20.5g^F h20.5d⁴ Mar 18] modest hurdler: won mares novice at Plumpton in November: stays 21f: best form on good going: tried in blinkers: usually races off pace. *Seamus Mullins* — h97

KEPPEL ISLE (IRE) 10 b.g. Heron Island (IRE) – Wadi Khaled (FR) (Bering) [2018/19 **c71** c–, h–: h18.7m⁶ c17.2g c20g c19.7m⁴ c16g⁵ c16g Nov 19] good-topped gelding: maiden **h–** hurdler: poor handicap chaser: acts on good to firm and good to soft going: has worn headgear, including last 5 starts: often leads. *Tom Gretton*

KEREMAN (IRE) 5 b.g. Azamour (IRE) – Kerania (IRE) (Daylami (IRE)) [2018/19 **h107** h94p: h15.8d* h20.5g* h19.6d* Apr 26] has had breathing operation: fair handicap hurdler: unbeaten in 2018/19, winning at Uttoxeter (conditionals) in March, and Plumpton (conditionals) and Bangor in April: stays 21f: acts on good to soft going: often travels strongly. *Dan Skelton*

KERISPER (FR) 10 b.g. Robin des Champs (FR) – Tina Rederie (FR) (Cadoudal (FR)) **c–** [2018/19 c–, h–: c20.1g c19.4vᵇᵈ c25.2sᵘʳ h23s⁴ h20.9g⁵ Mar 23] strong, compact gelding: **h108** Irish point winner: fair handicap hurdler: maiden chaser, no form over fences in 2018/19: stays 3m: acts on heavy going. *Nigel Twiston-Davies*

KERROW (IRE) 9 b.g. Mahler – Olives Hall (IRE) (Saddlers' Hall (IRE)) [2018/19 **c130** c24dᶠ c26gᵖᵘ c25.1g⁶ Feb 16] smallish gelding: winning hurdler: useful handicap chaser: **h–** led when fell last at Bangor on return: stays 25f: acts on good to soft going. *Alan King*

KERRY'S BOY (IRE) 6 b.g. Oscar (IRE) – Kerry's Girl (IRE) (Flemensfirth (USA)) **h–** [2018/19 h93, b–: h21.2g h21.7m May 27] good sort: has had breathing operation: maiden hurdler, no form in 2018/19: in tongue tie last 5 starts. *Ben Pauling*

KERRY'S LORD (IRE) 10 br.g. Lend A Hand – Tesses Express (IRE) (Flemensfirth **c–** (USA)) [2018/19 h24gᵖᵘ h21.6vᵖᵘ h23d c19.7g⁵ c25.7s Mar 11] sturdy gelding: maiden **h–** pointer: maiden hurdler, no form in 2018/19 including in chases: has worn tongue tie, including last 3 starts. *Joanne Thomason-Murphy*

KESTREL VALLEY 5 b.m. Dr Massini (IRE) – Lady Karinga (Karinga Bay) [2018/19 **h100** h100, b74: h16v³ h16d⁶ h21sᶠ h19.5d h20sᵖᵘ Apr 7] sturdy mare: fair maiden hurdler: unproven beyond 17f: best form on soft/heavy going: usually wears hood: tried in tongue tie: usually leads. *Matt Sheppard*

KEYBOARD GANGSTER (IRE) 8 b.g. Gamut (IRE) – Vic O'Tully (IRE) (Old Vic) **h123** [2018/19 h130: h15.7v h19.9v⁶ h16.4d⁴ Apr 6] fairly useful handicap hurdler: unproven beyond 2m: acts on heavy going: has worn hood, including in 2018/19: wears tongue tie: usually races off pace: quirky sort, races freely. *Donald Whillans*

KEYNOTE (IRE) 4 b.g. Dragon Pulse (IRE) – Taalluf (USA) (Hansel (USA)) [2018/19 **h69** h15.8g h16gᵇᵈ h16d⁴ h16.7s⁵ h15.8g⁴ h20.7g h24.1g Apr 11] poor maiden on Flat/over hurdles. *Richard Armson*

KEY TO THE WEST (IRE) 12 b.g. Westerner – Monte Solaro (IRE) (Key of Luck **c99 §** (USA)) [2018/19 c92§, h–§: c16.5g⁴ c17.8m⁴ c17.2g* c16.3gᵖᵘ c16.5g² Jun 27] good sort: **h– §** has had breathing operation: winning hurdler: modest handicap chaser: won at Market Rasen in June: stays 2½m: acts on heavy going: usually wears headgear: has worn tongue tie: usually races towards rear: unreliable. *John Spearing*

KHAGE (IRE) 6 b.g. Stowaway – Made Easy (IRE) (Rudimentary (USA)) [2018/19 h92: **h124** h16.7gᶠ h15.7s² h16.5g* h20g h15.8s² h16d* h16d* Apr 6] well-made gelding: has had breathing operation: fairly useful hurdler: won maiden at Taunton in January, and novices at Chepstow in March and April: unproven beyond 2m: acts on good to soft going: has worn hood, including in 2018/19: front runner. *Harry Whittington*

KHAIRAGASH (FR) 4 b.g. Sinndar (IRE) – Khazina (FR) (Alhaarth (IRE)) [2018/19 **h63** h19.6vᵘʳ h19.7sᵖᵘ h16.8d h15.8v h19.3s⁶ h23.9sᵖᵘ Mar 19] has had breathing operation: fair form on Flat: little impact over hurdles: tried in hood: front runner/races prominently. *Venetia Williams*

KHANISARI (IRE) 5 gr.g. Dark Angel (IRE) – Kadayna (IRE) (Dalakhani (IRE)) **h101** [2018/19 b16m² b15.8d h19m⁴ h15.8g³ h19d Dec 13] €38,000 3-y-o: fourth foal: half- **b93** brother to useful 7f/1m winner Kadra (by Holy Roman Emperor): dam unraced sister to smart French 2¼m hurdle winner Kadabi: fair form in bumpers: similar form over hurdles: best effort when third in maiden at Ludlow in November: left Ellmarie Holden after first start. *Evan Williams*

KHELEYF'S GIRL 4 br.f. Kheleyf (USA) – Handsome Molly (Halling (USA)) [2018/19 **h–** h16dᵖᵘ h16.6gᵖᵘ Dec 29] modest maiden on Flat, stays 6f: no form over hurdles. *Clare Ellam*

KICK ON DOTTIE (IRE) 6 ch.m. Getaway (GER) – Oddly Presented (IRE) (Presenting) **h107** [2018/19 h–, b69: h16.2d* h20.1g* h23.3g⁵ Jun 16] fair form over hurdles: won novices at Hexham (twice) in May: stays 2½m: acts on good to soft going. *Ruth Jefferson*

KILBREE CHIEF (IRE) 11 b.g. Dr Massini (IRE) – Lame Excuse (IRE) (Presenting) [2018/19 c24.1v^{pu} c24.1s c26.2s^{pu} Dec 16] good-topped gelding: winning hurdler: fairly useful chaser at best, no form in 2018/19: in cheekpieces last 4 starts. *Lucinda Russell*
   c–
   h–

KILBREE KID (IRE) 12 b.g. Cloudings (IRE) – Bustingoutallover (USA) (Trempolino (USA)) [2018/19 c126, h–: c23.8g^3 c26.2g* c27.5d^6 c23.8g^2 c23.8g^{pu} c23.6g^{pu} Nov 13] sturdy gelding: winning hurdler: fairly useful chaser: won hunter at Kelso in May: stays 3¼m: acts on soft and good to firm going: wears headgear/tongue tie. *Tom George*
   c126
   h–

KILBREW BOY (IRE) 6 b.g. Stowaway – Bean Ki Moon (IRE) (King's Theatre (IRE)) [2018/19 b85: h15.3g^4 h21d^6 h20d^4 h20d^4 h24.4g^5 h23.4d^3 h26g^6 Apr 10] rather unfurnished gelding: second in Irish point: fair hurdler: won maiden at Fakenham in December: stays 3m: acts on good to soft going: often wears hood: usually leads. *Ben Case*
   h112

KILBRICKEN STORM (IRE) 8 b.g. Oscar (IRE) – Kilbricken Leader (IRE) (Supreme Leader) [2018/19 h151: c23.8v* c23.4s^6 h24d h24.7g Apr 6] strong gelding: smart hurdler at best, well held in Grade 1 events last 2 starts: useful form over fences: won novice at Ffos Las in November: stays 3m: best form on soft/heavy going: tried in blinkers: wears tongue tie. *Colin Tizzard*
   c132
   h–

KILCARAGH BOY (IRE) 10 b.g. King's Theatre (IRE) – Histologie (FR) (Quart de Vin (FR)) [2018/19 h18.7m h18.7m h23g^F h23.1g h16.3g^6 h23g^4 h23.3g^5 h18.5g h15.8g^5 h21.7g^F h16.8m h18.5m h15.5g^4 h19.3s^{pu} h20.5g^6 h16g^5 h15.7g^2 h18.7g Mar 30] angular gelding: poor handicap hurdler: lightly-raced chaser: left Matt Sheppard after thirteenth start: unproven beyond 17f: acts on good to soft going: often in headgear/tongue tie: races off pace. *Richard Armson*
   c–
   h65

KILCARA (IRE) 6 b.m. Court Cave (IRE) – Easter Day (IRE) (Simply Great (FR)) [2018/19 h16.8g^4 h19.5d h15.8g^4 h19m^3 c20g^4 c20.5m^{ur} Apr 25] €8,000 3-y-o, £3,000 5-y-o: good-topped mare: has had breathing operation: half-sister to fairly useful hurdler Dreambrook Lady (2m winner, by Alderbrook) and fair chaser Easter Hunt (25f winner, by Kalanisi): dam unraced: slight impact in Irish points: fair form over hurdles/in chases: stays 2½m: acts on good to firm going: tried in hood. *Jeremy Scott*
   c99
   h104

KILCASCAN 15 b.g. Alflora (IRE) – Peasedown Tofana (Teenoso (USA)) [2018/19 c73: c24g^{pu} Jun 25] modest chaser at best, pulled up sole outing in 2018/19: stays 3¼m: acts on good to firm and heavy going: wears cheekpieces: front runner/races prominently. *Rosemary Gasson*
   c–

KILCHREEST MOON (IRE) 8 ch.g. Moon Ballad (IRE) – Kilchreest Queen (IRE) (Teamster) [2018/19 h19d h16.3d^3 h22.5m^3 h20s^4 h23.2g h16d h19g Apr 25] fair maiden hurdler: left Barry T. Murphy after fifth start: stays 23f: acts on good to firm and good to soft going. *Christian Williams*
   h102

KILCOOLEY (IRE) 10 b.g. Stowaway – Bealaha Essie (IRE) (Denel (FR)) [2018/19 h24.3g^3 Feb 16] workmanlike gelding: high-class hurdler at best for Charlie Longsdon: third in Rendlesham Hurdle at Haydock (8¼ lengths behind Shades of Midnight) sole outing in 2018/19 after very long absence: stays 3m: acts on heavy going: has worn tongue tie. *Nicky Richards*
   h139

KILCREA BRIDGE 8 b.g. Kayf Tara – Ballyhoo (IRE) (Supreme Leader) [2018/19 c102, h–: c23.8v^3 c24.2v* c25.1g^5 c24.2v^4 c26.2d^2 c29.2g^5 Apr 26] maiden hurdler: fair handicap chaser: won at Exeter in December: stays 3¼m: acts on heavy going: often in cheekpieces: wears tongue tie: usually races off pace. *Richard Hawker*
   c100
   h–

KILCREA VALE (IRE) 9 b.g. Beneficial – Inflation (FR) (Port Etienne (FR)) [2018/19 c138, h–: c21.1s^3 c24g^5 c24.2s c23.8g^3 c21.1d Apr 5] well-made gelding: winning hurdler: useful handicap chaser: third in Grand Sefton Chase at Aintree (2¼ lengths behind Warriors Tale) in December: should stay beyond 21f: acts on heavy going: in cheekpieces last 2 starts: usually races prominently. *Nicky Henderson*
   c136
   h–

KILCULLEN BELLAMY 7 b.m. Black Sam Bellamy (IRE) – Fenney Spring (Polish Precedent (USA)) [2018/19 h86, b62: h21.6g^4 h19.7g Nov 13] Irish point winner: modest form over hurdles: dead. *Evan Williams*
   h91

KILCULLEN FLEM (IRE) 9 ch.g. Flemensfirth (USA) – Cansalrun (IRE) (Anshan) [2018/19 c114, h–: c31.9s^{pu} c26.2s^4 c28.8v^{pu} c31.9v^4 c30.7s^{pu} Apr 16] winning hurdler: fair handicap chaser: stays 4m: acts on heavy going: wears headgear: tried in tongue tie. *Philip Kirby*
   c103
   h–

KILCULLEN LADY (IRE) 9 b.m. Scorpion (IRE) – Glittering Star (IRE) (Good Thyne (USA)) [2018/19 c–, h–: h23.3g c21.1g^{ur} c19.2s^3 c16.4s^6 c20.1d Mar 26] Irish point winner: maiden hurdler: poor form in chases: wears headgear. *Henry Hogarth*
   c58
   h–

Timeform Novices' Handicap Chase, Cheltenham—
Kildisart (left) comes with a well-timed run to beat Highway One O One

KILDISART (IRE) 7 b.g. Dubai Destination (USA) – Princess Mairead (IRE) (Blueprint **c155**
(IRE)) [2018/19 h140: c18.8g² c21s* c20.6d* c19.8d⁴ c25g* Apr 6] strong, compact **h–**
gelding: useful hurdler: very smart form over fences: won graduation event at Ascot (by
short head from Activial) in December, Timeform Novices' Handicap at Cheltenham (by 2
lengths from Highway One O One) in January and Grade 3 handicap at Aintree (by 5
lengths from Mister Malarky) in April: will stay beyond 25f: acts on soft going: often
travels strongly. *Ben Pauling*

KILDOON LUCILLE (IRE) 5 br.m. Arcadio (GER) – Oscar Rebel (IRE) (Oscar **b75**
(IRE)) [2018/19 b15.7g² Sep 5] €8,000 3-y-o: third foal: half-sister to fair hurdler Birch
Vale (2m/17f winner) and 19f bumper winner Rebel Og (both by Presenting): dam (h140)
2¼m/2½m hurdle winner/winning pointer: 8/1, second in maiden bumper at Southwell (1¾
lengths behind The Rocket Park). *Harriet Bethell*

KILDORRERY (IRE) 6 b.g. Arakan (USA) – Killeen Castle (IRE) (Indian Danehill **c133**
(IRE)) [2018/19 h16g h19.5g* h16g⁵ c16.2g* c16.2g⁴ c20d² c17d⁴ c17g⁶ c20g⁴ c16.7g³ **h118**
Apr 21] fourth foal: half-brother to fair hurdler/fairly useful chaser Old Castletown
(2m-2¾m winner, by Fruits of Love): dam (c92/h108) 2m hurdle winner (stayed 2½m):
bumper winner: fairly useful form over hurdles: won maiden at Kilbeggan in September:
useful chaser: won maiden at Punchestown in October: sixth in Goffs Handicap at
Leopardstown (4¼ lengths behind Quamino) in February: stays 2½m: acts on good to soft
going: wears hood: usually races in rear. *T. M. Walsh, Ireland*

KILFENORA (IRE) 7 b.g. Yeats (IRE) – Blazing Liss (IRE) (Supreme Leader) [2018/19 **c120**
c120, h131: c20d⁵ c20s⁵ Jan 5] useful hurdler: best effort when 3 lengths third of 23 to My **h137**
Sister Sarah in handicap at Punchestown shortly after end of British season: fairly useful
maiden chaser: stays 3m: acts on heavy going. *Edward P. Harty, Ireland*

KILFILUM CROSS (IRE) 8 gr.g. Beneficial – Singh Street (IRE) (Dolphin Street (FR)) **c141**
[2018/19 h123: c20s⁴ c24.2d³ c23.8d* c26d² c24.1m⁴ Apr 13] workmanlike gelding: fairly **h–**
useful hurdler: useful form over fences: won handicap at Ludlow (amateurs) in February:
second in Fulke Walwyn Kim Muir Chase at Cheltenham (3¾ lengths behind Any Second
Now) in March: left Christopher Kellett after second start: stays 3¼m: acts on soft going:
front runner/races prominently. *Henry Oliver*

KILFINAN BAY (IRE) 4 b.g. Mahler – Midnight Special (IRE) (Danetime (IRE)) **b80**
[2018/19 b16.2d⁵ Apr 26] 66/1, fifth in bumper at Perth (9¼ lengths behind Equus Dancer).
Jackie Stephen

KILFINICHEN BAY (IRE) 11 b.g. Westerner – Cailin Deas (IRE) (Pistolet Bleu (IRE)) **c114 §**
[2018/19 c129, h–: c20.8g c23gᵖᵘ c25.5m* c25.8g⁴ c25.5s³ c26m² c24.2g³ c26.3s* c25.1d⁴ **h–**
c25.7s³ Jan 16] sturdy gelding: winning hurdler: fair handicap chaser: won at Cartmel in

476

July and Sedgefield in November: left F. A. Hutsby after first start to rejoin former yard: stays 3¼m: acts on good to firm and heavy going: wears cheekpieces/tongue tie: usually front runner/races prominently: unreliable. *Charlie Longsdon*

KILINAKIN (IRE) 9 ch.g. Definite Article – Topanberry (IRE) (Topanoora) [2018/19 c96, h–: c16s³ c16.4s³ c16d³ c20.5d⁶ c19.2s Apr 16] maiden hurdler: modest handicap chaser: stays 21f: acts on good to firm and heavy going: tried in cheekpieces: often races lazily. *Zoe Davison* **c94** **h–**

KILKISHEN (IRE) 9 b.g. Oscar (IRE) – Coming Home (FR) (Exit To Nowhere (USA)) [2018/19 h24.3g⁵ h22g⁶ h27m³ c24.4g⁴ c29gᵖᵘ c23.5d² c25s* c28.7d c32.6g⁴ c34vᵖᵘ Mar 16] fairly useful handicap hurdler: useful handicap chaser: won at Fairyhouse in January: stays 33f: acts on soft and good to firm going: has worn headgear, including last 5 starts. *John Joseph Hanlon, Ireland* **c132** **h122**

KILLER CROW (IRE) 10 ch.g. Presenting – Rivervail (IRE) (River Falls) [2018/19 c107, h–: c25g h19.5vᵖᵘ c23.8m² Feb 27] workmanlike gelding: won point in March: winning hurdler: fair chaser: stays 29f, most effective at shorter: best form on soft/heavy going: usually wears headgear/tongue tie: usually races towards rear. *N. W. Alexander* **c100** **h–**

KILLONE (IRE) 10 gr.g. Flemensfirth (USA) – Ceol Tire (IRE) (Roselier (FR)) [2018/19 c–, h68: h19.3g c23.8mᵖᵘ Mar 22] maiden pointer: modest form when second in novice in 2016/17, standout effort over hurdles: no form in chases: in tongue tie last 5 starts. *Alistair Whillans* **c–** **h–**

KILLULTAGH VIC (IRE) 10 b.g. Old Vic – Killultagh Dawn (IRE) (Phardante (FR)) [2018/19 c163x, h138: h25.4sᵖᵘ h20g⁵ h24s³ c20d⁴ h21s c24d² Apr 21] sturdy gelding: smart hurdler: third in John Mulhern Galmoy Hurdle at Gowran (1¼ lengths behind Presenting Percy) in January and fourth in Champion Stayers' Hurdle at Punchestown (in cheekpieces, 3½ lengths behind Unowhatimeanharry) shortly after end of British season: high-class form over fences, below best in 2018/19: stays 3m: acts on heavy going: prone to mistakes over fences. *W. P. Mullins, Ireland* **c137 x** **h147**

Betway Handicap Chase, Aintree—
a fine weight-carrying performance from Kildisart, who copes well with the longer trip and draws
clear of fellow novice Mister Malarky (left) and 2018 fourth Oldgrangewood

KILMACALLOGUE BAY 13 b.g. Karinga Bay – Wahiba Reason (IRE) (Robellino (USA)) [2018/19 c32.5g^{pu} c26.7d^{pu} h27s^{pu} Feb 21] multiple point winner: little show under Rules for various trainers: in headgear last 3 starts. *Sam England* c–
h–

KILMOGANNY (IRE) 7 b.g. Stowaway – Gowayourdat (IRE) (Saddlers' Hall (IRE)) [2018/19 h–: h19.7s h21d h21.9v⁶ c23.6d c26.1d c26.2d c23.6g³ c23.6g³ Apr 22] workmanlike gelding: has had breathing operation: poor maiden hurdler: similar form over fences: stays 3m: acts on heavy going: in cheekpieces last 5 starts: tried in tongue tie. *Katy Price* c71
h54

KILMURVY (IRE) 11 b.g. Shantou (USA) – Spagna (IRE) (Definite Article) [2018/19 c94, h–: c26m⁴ c25.8s* c25.5g^{pu} Nov 9] workmanlike gelding: winning hurdler: modest handicap chaser: won at Newton Abbot in July: stays 3½m: acts on good to firm and heavy going: wears headgear/tongue tie: temperamental. *Jeremy Scott* c99 §
h–

KILRONAN CASTLE 8 ch.g. Indian River (FR) – Greatest Friend (IRE) (Mandalus) [2018/19 c106, h–: h22m^{pu} May 20] fairly useful hurdler at best, pulled up sole outing in 2018/19: fair chaser: stays 2¾m: acts on good to firm and heavy going: in headgear last 4 starts: usually leads. *Donald McCain* c–
h–

KIMBERLEY POINT 6 b.m. Sixties Icon – Kingara (Karinga Bay) [2018/19 b88: h15.7g² h15.8g* h15.7d* h15.7s² h15.3g³ Mar 25] sturdy mare: fairly useful form over hurdles: won mares maiden at Uttoxeter and mares novice at Southwell in November: second in handicap at Southwell in December: raced around 2m: acts on soft going: wears hood: often races freely. *Alan King* h122

KIMBERLITE CANDY (IRE) 7 b.g. Flemensfirth (USA) – Mandys Native (IRE) (Be My Native (USA)) [2018/19 c136, h–: c24.1v* c22.9v c24.2s³ c32.6g⁵ c29d^{pu} Apr 22] winning hurdler: useful handicap chaser: won at Ayr (by 2¾ lengths from Silver Tassie) in November: third in Masters Handicap Chase at Sandown (2¼ lengths behind Classic Ben) in February: stays 3m: acts on heavy going. *Tom Lacey* c137
h–

KIMORA (IRE) 13 b.m. Bach (IRE) – Blue Gale (IRE) (Be My Native (USA)) [2018/19 c26g* May 17] multiple point winner: maiden hurdler: modest chaser: won mares hunter at Fontwell in May: stays 3¼m: acts on good to firm and heavy going: tried in cheekpieces: wears tongue tie: untrustworthy. *C. W. Loggin* c91 §
h– §

KIMS DIAMOND (IRE) 5 b.m. Mountain High (IRE) – Accordion To Pat (IRE) (Accordion) [2018/19 b16g b16g^{rr} Sep 2] second foal: dam unraced: no form in bumpers, refusing to race second outing. *Katy Price* b– §

KINARI (IRE) 9 b.g. Captain Rio – Baraza (IRE) (Kalanisi (IRE)) [2018/19 c115, h–: c23.8m Jul 13] placed in points: maiden hurdler: fairly useful chaser, well held sole outing under Rules in 2018/19: stays 3¼m: acts on soft and good to firm going: wears headgear/tongue tie. *Peter Bowen* c–
h–

KING ALFONSO 10 br.g. Desert King (IRE) – Satire (Terimon) [2018/19 c107, h92: h18.7m³ h16.7g* c20.3g* c16.5g* c16.5g⁶ c19.4d⁴ Oct 20] compact gelding: modest hurdler: won conditionals/amateurs seller at Market Rasen in August: fairly useful handicap chaser: won at Bangor in August and Worcester in September: stays 2½m: acts on firm and soft going: tried in tongue tie. *Dai Burchell* c118
h85

KING CALVIN (IRE) 7 b.g. King's Theatre (IRE) – Lerichi (IRE) (Shardari) [2018/19 h123: h21.6g* h23.9d^{su} c23.4s c23d^{pu} c20.2g^{pu} Mar 25] strong, compact gelding: has had breathing operation: point winner: fairly useful hurdler: won novice at Newton Abbot in May: no form in chases: stays 2¾m: acts on heavy going: wears tongue tie. *Jack R. Barber* c–
h113

KING CHARLIE (IRE) 9 b.g. Chevalier (IRE) – Desert Treat (IRE) (Desert Prince (IRE)) [2018/19 c–, h–: c25.7g^{pu} May 13] maiden hurdler/chaser, pulled up both starts since 2016/17: wears cheekpieces/tongue tie. *Suzy Smith* c–
h–

KING CNUT (FR) 5 ch.g. Kentucky Dynamite (USA) – Makadane (Danehill Dancer (IRE)) [2018/19 h96, b–: c19.7g² c19.7m* c20.5d^{ur} h19.2v c17s c19.2d³ Apr 9] sturdy gelding: maiden hurdler: fair form over fences: won handicap at Plumpton in October: stays 2½m: acts on soft and good to firm going. *Chris Gordon* c105
h–

KING COOL 8 b.g. King's Theatre (IRE) – Cool Spice (Karinga Bay) [2018/19 c90, h97: c25.7g* h25g⁵ h24d h21d* h24.2d h23.1g^{pu} Mar 14] fair handicap hurdler: won at Kempton in January: modest handicap chaser: won at Plumpton in May: stays 3¼m: acts on heavy going: has worn cheekpieces/tongue tie, including in 2018/19: races off pace. *Gary Moore* c99
h104

KING D'ARGENT (FR) 4 ch.g. Kendargent (FR) – Ephigenie (IRE) (Groom Dancer (USA)) [2018/19 h16m* h16m3 h16.7s2 h16.4s4 Mar 13] has had breathing operation: dam half-sister to fairly useful 3m hurdle winner Ephraim: fairly useful maiden on Flat, stays 13.5f: similar form over hurdles: won juvenile at Wetherby in October: third in Wensleydale Juvenile Hurdle at same course (8 lengths behind Cracker Factory) in November: wears tongue tie. *Dan Skelton*   **h123**

KING GOLAN (IRE) 8 b.g. Golan (IRE) – Crimson Bow (GER) (Night Shift (USA)) [2018/19 c69, h–: c20.3g4 c20.3g5 c20g c20g3 c22.6m5 c24g4 c20.1g4 c21.6m* c23.4g* c23.8m2 c20.3m2 c23.4dF Apr 8] maiden hurdler: fair handicap chaser: won 2 novice events at Kelso in October: stays 3m: acts on good to firm going: wears headgear: often tongue tied: usually leads. *Kenny Johnson*   **c106 h–**

KING LEON (IRE) 10 b.g. Mountain High (IRE) – None The Wiser (IRE) (Dr Massini (IRE)) [2018/19 h22.4m h24.3g h20.9dbd Nov 10] fairly useful hurdler/useful chaser at best, no form since 2016/17: left Joseph Patrick O'Brien after second start: has worn headgear, including in 2018/19: tried in tongue tie. *Iain Jardine*   **c– h–**

KING MURO 9 b.g. Halling (USA) – Ushindi (IRE) (Montjeu (IRE)) [2018/19 c111, h102: h16.3m h16.7g4 c16.5g6 c17.4g4 c16.5g3 c20.1g3 c16g4 c17.8m4 h15.9s2 h15.9s* h17.7m6 Mar 29] rather leggy gelding: has had breathing operation: fair handicap hurdler: won at Plumpton in March: fair handicap chaser: won novice event at Bangor in August: left Fergal O'Brien after seventh start: unproven beyond 17f: acts on good to firm and heavy going: usually wears hood: has worn tongue tie, including last 3 starts. *Michael Roberts*   **c105 h107**

KING OF FASHION (IRE) 9 ch.g. Desert King (IRE) – French Fashion (IRE) (Jamesmead) [2018/19 h120: h24.7g May 18] rather leggy gelding: fairly useful hurdler, excuses sole outing in 2018/19: stays 3m: acts on heavy going: wears tongue tie. *Kerry Lee*   **h–**

KING OF REALMS (IRE) 7 b.g. King's Theatre (IRE) – Sunny South East (IRE) (Gothland (FR)) [2018/19 h126p: c23.8g8* c24g4 c24.2s2 c24g* Mar 28] tall, good-topped gelding: has had breathing operation: fairly useful form over hurdles: useful form over fences: won handicaps at Ascot (novice) in November and Warwick in March: stays 3m: acts on soft going: tried in visor: usually front runner/races prominently. *Ian Williams*   **c140 h–**

KINGOFTHECOTSWOLDS (IRE) 5 b.g. Arcadio (GER) – Damoiselle (Sir Harry Lewis (USA)) [2018/19 b62: b16g2 h21.3d4 h15.8d2 h15.8d* h20.7d2 h23.9g4 Apr 24] lengthy gelding: fairly useful form in bumpers: fairly useful form over hurdles: won maiden at Ludlow in February: stays 21f: acts on good to soft going. *Nigel Twiston-Davies*   **h129 b97**

KING OF THE SAND (IRE) 4 ch.g. Footstepsinthesand – Lough Mewin (IRE) (Woodman (USA)) [2018/19 h16g Feb 22] fairly useful on Flat, stays 1¼m: 40/1, well held in juvenile on hurdling debut. *Gary Moore*   **h–**

KING OF THE SHARKS (IRE) 6 b.g. Flemensfirth (USA) – Kings Rose (IRE) (King's Ride) [2018/19 h23s h23.1s6 h23.1s3 Mar 18] €54,000 3-y-o: big, good-bodied gelding: half-brother to 3 winners, including fairly useful hurdlers/useful chasers Go All The Way (2½m winner, by Milan) and Dont Tell No One (2½m-23f winner, by Westerner): dam unraced: won 2 of 3 starts in points: modest form over hurdles: best effort when third in novice at Exeter in March. *Zoe Davison*   **h98**

KING ROLAND (IRE) 5 br.g. Stowaway – Kiltiernan Robin (IRE) (Robin des Champs (FR)) [2018/19 b15.8v* b15.8s* Feb 26] €40,000 3-y-o: first foal: dam unraced: Irish point winner: smart form in bumpers: won both starts, at Uttoxeter (by 22 lengths from Stung For Cash) in December and Ffos Las (by length from Stick With Bill) in February: wears hood: exciting prospect. *Harry Fry*   **b116 p**

KING'S COINAGE (IRE) 5 b.g. Holy Roman Emperor (IRE) – Seducing (IRE) (Galileo (IRE)) [2018/19 h16.4g h16.8d5 h16.8g3 h16.8gF Apr 5] had breathing operation: dam closely related to fairly useful hurdler/chaser (stayed 3¼m) Chesapeake: fair on Flat, stays 1½m: modest form over hurdles: in tongue tie last 2 starts: should do better. *Sam England*   **h96 p**

KINGS ECLIPSE (IRE) 9 c.g. Double Eclipse (IRE) – Good Times Ahead (IRE) (King's Ride) [2018/19 c99, h85: c24.1g5 c24.5v* c26.9d Jan 20] maiden hurdler: fair handicap chaser: won at Carlisle in December: stays 3¼m: acts on heavy going: tried in hood. *Andrew Wilson*   **c108 h–**

KINGS INN (IRE) 5 b.g. Mawatheeq (USA) – Afnoon (USA) (Street Cry (IRE)) [2018/19 h76: h15.8m4 h16s6 h16.6g2 h16d5 h15.8gF Feb 28] good-topped gelding: fair maiden on Flat (seems to stay 1½m): fair form over hurdles: raced around 2m: best form on good going: tried in cheekpieces: usually races freely. *Paul Nicholls*   **h106**

KINGS LAD (IRE) 12 b.g. King's Theatre (IRE) – Festival Leader (IRE) (Supreme Leader) [2018/19 c–, h117: c19.2m* c26m* h26.5g^2 c23.6d* c23.8m^5 c25.1g^{pu} c24.2d^{pu} h19d Jan 19] sturdy gelding: has had breathing operation: fairly useful handicap hurdler: useful handicap chaser: won at Exeter and Fontwell in May, and Chepstow (veterans, by ½ length from Exitas) in October: stays 3¼m: acts on good to firm and heavy going: tried in cheekpieces: wears tongue tie. *Colin Tizzard* **c133 h120**

KINGS MONARCH 6 b.g. Schiaparelli (GER) – Monarch's View (King's Ride) [2018/19 h100: c16g^5 c23.6d c21.6d* c20.9d* c20.6g^5 Apr 17] maiden hurdler: fairly useful form over fences: won handicaps at Fontwell in February and Hereford (novice) in March: stays 2¾m: acts on soft going. *Kerry Lee* **c127 h–**

KING'S ODYSSEY (IRE) 10 b.g. King's Theatre (IRE) – Ma Furie (FR) (Balleroy (USA)) [2018/19 c137, h–: c19.9g^2 c19.9d^F c19.4s^6 c20.6d^F Mar 14] well-made gelding: winning hurdler: useful handicap chaser: second at Aintree (6 lengths behind War Sound) in November: stays 21f: acts on heavy going: usually races prominently: temperamental. *Evan Williams* **c138 § h–**

KING SPIRIT (IRE) 11 b.g. Fruits of Love (USA) – Tariana (IRE) (Revoque (IRE)) [2018/19 c–, h–: c16g^{pu} c19.9g^4 c22.6m^2 c23g Jul 26] useful-looking gelding: maiden hurdler: fair handicap chaser: stayed 23f: acted on good to firm and heavy going: tried in cheekpieces: dead. *Tom Lacey* **c101 h–**

KINGSPLACE (IRE) 7 b.g. Ask – Winsome Breeze (IRE) (Glacial Storm (USA)) [2018/19 b95: h21d^4 h19.5s^5 h19.5d^2 h23.6d^2 h24.7d Apr 5] lengthy, angular gelding: runner-up in Irish point: bumper winner: fairly useful form over hurdles: will stay beyond 3m: acts on good to soft going: races prominently. *Nigel Twiston-Davies* **h119**

KING'S RESTE (IRE) 7 b.m. King's Theatre (IRE) – J'y Reste (FR) (Freedom Cry) [2018/19 h103, b–: c20g^4 c16.3m* c16g* h15.7g^2 c16.3g^2 h16.7g^2 c20.9g^4 c17.4d^{pu} Nov 14] lengthy mare: has had breathing operation: modest maiden hurdler: fair form over fences: won handicaps at Newton Abbot and Uttoxeter in July: left Amy Murphy after first start: probably stays 2½m: acts on soft and good to firm going: has worn headgear: wears tongue tie. *Dan Skelton* **c113 h99**

KINGS RYDE 7 b.g. King's Theatre (IRE) – Ryde Back (Bob Back (USA)) [2018/19 h123, b85: h21.4s* h23.5m^5 h21m^3 Apr 25] fairly useful form over hurdles: won handicap at Wincanton in March: should stay 3m: acts on soft going: usually races close up, often freely. *Nicky Henderson* **h128**

KING'S SOCKS (FR) 7 b.g. King's Best (USA) – Alexandrina (GER) (Monsun (GER)) [2018/19 c140, h–: c20.2g^{pu} Nov 17] good-topped gelding: has had breathing operation: winning hurdler: useful chaser, shaping encouragingly when unseating rider sole outing in 2018/19: stays 2½m: acts on heavy going: tried in tongue tie. *David Pipe* **c– h–**

KING'S SONG (FR) 9 b.g. King's Theatre (IRE) – Chanson Indienne (FR) (Indian River (FR)) [2018/19 c123, h70: h24g^{pu} h21.8d^4 h23.9g* h21.7d^3 h27m* c23.8g^4 c25m^6 h24g^6 c22.6g h20.5g^6 h16g h16d c25d^4 c24g^4 c28.5g^4 c21.2v* Apr 14] fairly useful handicap hurdler: won at Perth in August and Sedgefield in September: fairly useful handicap chaser: won at Tramore in April: left Gordon Elliott after tenth start: stays 29f: acts on good to firm and heavy going: has worn headgear, including last 2 starts: usually wears tongue tie. *D. Broad, Ireland* **c123 h115**

KINGS TEMPTATION 7 b.g. King's Theatre (IRE) – Temptation (FR) (Lando (GER)) [2018/19 c103p, h104: c23.6g* c23.6g^F c24g^3 c26g^2 c25.8d c23.9m^4 Apr 21] well-made gelding: maiden hurdler: fair handicap chaser: won novice event at Huntingdon in May: stays 3¼m: best form on good going: wears tongue tie. *Ben Case* **c109 h–**

KINGSTON (GER) 10 br.g. Dylan Thomas (IRE) – Katy Carr (Machiavellian (USA)) [2018/19 c–, h–: h15.8g h19.9g^3 h18.7m^4 h23.1g h19.6g^2 h19.6g* h19.9g^3 h19.9g* h20.7g* h19.7s^4 h20.7d^{ur} h20.5g^4 h19.4g^6 h21.4g^5 h23.3d^{pu} Mar 30] sturdy gelding: modest handicap hurdler: won at Bangor in August, Uttoxeter in October and Huntingdon in November: winning chaser: stays 23f: acts on heavy going: has worn headgear. *Tony Carroll* **c– h98**

KINGSTON MIMOSA 7 b.g. Kheleyf (USA) – Derartu (AUS) (Last Tycoon) [2018/19 h71: h17.7v h19.5d c18.2s^3 c19.2s^2 Apr 16] angular gelding: modest hurdler at best, no form in 2018/19: poor form over fences: stays 19f: acts on soft going: usually wears headgear: tried in tongue tie. *Mark Gillard* **c78 h–**

KINGS WALK (IRE) 8 b.g. King's Theatre (IRE) – Shuil Sionnach (IRE) (Mandalus) [2018/19 c106p, h120: h19.8v^3 c20s^{pu} c16.1d^3 c22.4d^2 c23.4d Mar 22] well-made gelding: fairly useful handicap hurdler: similar form over fences: second in novice handicap at Newbury in March: stays 2¾m: acts on heavy going. *Colin Tizzard* **c119 h112**

KINGS WATCH (IRE) 8 b.g. Rainwatch – Leavemealoneawhile (IRE) (Be My Native (USA)) [2018/19 h96: h26.5vᵖᵘ h19.5sᵖᵘ Nov 21] point winner: maiden hurdler, no form in 2018/19: often in headgear/tongue tie: front runner/races prominently. *Richard Price* — h–

KINGSWELL THEATRE 10 b.g. King's Theatre (IRE) – Cresswell Native (IRE) (Be My Native (USA)) [2018/19 c136, h–: c30.2s⁶ c27.9g² Apr 21] lengthy gelding: has had breathing operation: winning hurdler: useful chaser: second in handicap at Ffos Las (1½ lengths behind Pobbles Bay) in April: stays 31f: acts on heavy going: wears cheekpieces. *Michael Scudamore* — c139 h–

KING'S WHARF (IRE) 10 gr.g. Clodovil (IRE) – Global Tour (USA) (Tour d'Or (USA)) [2018/19 c131, h104: h20.2g⁴ c16g⁴ c20.1g⁴ Aug 1] fair handicap hurdler/chaser: stays 3m: acts on soft and good to firm going: has worn hood: has worn tongue tie, including final start. *Sandy Thomson* — c108 h98

KING UTHER 9 b.g. Master Blade – Cadbury Castle (Midyan (USA)) [2018/19 h119§: c24.2gᶠ Nov 14] good-topped gelding: fairly useful hurdler: fell ninth in novice handicap at Exeter on chasing debut: stays 3¼m: best form on soft/heavy going: has worn visor: front runner/races prominently: temperamental. *Venetia Williams* — c– p h– §

KING VINCE 6 gr.g. Mawatheeq (USA) – Tussah (Daylami (IRE)) [2018/19 h103, b93: h15.3m h20g² h23.1m³ c18g c19.7d⁴ c19.3d⁵ c21.4gᶠ c23.6gᵖᵘ Apr 22] lengthy gelding, has had breathing operation: bumper winner: fair form over hurdles/fences: stays 2½m: acts on good to soft going: in headgear last 4 starts: wears tongue tie: often let down by jumping over fences. *Jamie Snowden* — c100 x h96

KIRUNA PEAK (IRE) 5 ch.m. Arcano (IRE) – Kirunavaara (IRE) (Galileo (IRE)) [2018/19 h92: h17.7g² h15.8mᶠ h15.8g h16.8g³ h16g⁵ h18.6g h16.5d⁶ Apr 24] modest maiden hurdler: likely to prove best around 2m: acts on good to soft going: usually wears hood: has worn tongue tie. *Fergal O'Brien* — h93

KISSESFORKATIE (IRE) 5 b.m. Jeremy (USA) – Now Were Broke (IRE) (Beneficial) [2018/19 b13.7m* b16.4g³ b15.8d⁴ b17d⁶ Apr 4] close-coupled mare: first foal: dam (h81), maiden hurdler, half-sister to useful chaser (stayed 25f) Russian Regent: fairly useful bumper performer: won mares event at Fontwell in October: third in listed race at Cheltenham (1¾ lengths behind Master Debonair) in November. *Jeremy Scott* — b99

KISUMU 7 b.g. High Chaparral (IRE) – Arum Lily (USA) (Woodman (USA)) [2018/19 h83§: h16.2g h16.2g h16.2g³ h17.2g⁴ h16.8m c16.4m³ h17m Apr 20] poor maiden hurdler: tailed off in novice on chasing debut: raced mainly around 2m: acts on soft going: wears cheekpieces/tongue tie: temperamental. *Micky Hammond* — c– h76 §

KIT BARRY (IRE) 11 ch.g. Albano (IRE) – Traceyspecial (IRE) (Roselier (FR)) [2018/19 c25.3g³ c23s³ c22.6dᵖᵘ c24.2v² c23d⁴ c24.2s³ Apr 16] multiple point winner: fair form in hunter chases: stays 25f: acts on soft going: tried in cheekpieces. *David Dando* — c100

KITIKAT (IRE) 5 b.g. Fame And Glory – Felinious (Kayf Tara) [2018/19 b15.7g* h16m² h15.8g h15.8s⁶ Dec 11] won bumper at Southwell (by 1¾ lengths from Balleticon) in May on debut: modest form over hurdles: dead. *Jonjo O'Neill* — h98 b101

KITSUNE 5 b.m. Foxwedge (AUS) – Dance A Daydream (Daylami (IRE)) [2018/19 h–: h15.8g h15.5g⁴ h15.8gᵖᵘ Apr 22] sturdy mare: dam half-sister to smart hurdler (17f-21f winner) Elusive Dream: little show on Flat/over hurdles. *Denis Quinn* — h–

KITTY FISHER (IRE) 9 b.m. Scorpion (IRE) – Luck of The Deise (IRE) (Old Vic) [2018/19 h–: h23.3g⁶ h23.3g h20.2g h21.4d h19.8m⁶ h24d⁴ Apr 6] poor maiden hurdler: stays 3m: acts on good to firm and good to soft going: usually races prominently. *Sandy Forster* — h67

KIWAYU 10 b.g. Medicean – Kibara (Sadler's Wells (USA)) [2018/19 h–: h19.6g h19.9g h19.9g h24g* h23.3g² h23.3g* Jul 18] has had breathing operation: fair handicap hurdler: won at Southwell in June and Uttoxeter in July: stays 3m: best form on good going: tried in cheekpieces: wears tongue tie. *Mike Sowersby* — h108

KIWI MYTH 7 b.m. Midnight Legend – Kiwi Katie (Kayf Tara) [2018/19 h89, b–: h21.6g⁵ h21.7d h23.9dᵖᵘ c23.6dᵖᵘ c21.6s⁴ c24.2v* c24.2d⁴ Apr 9] has had breathing operation: poor maiden hurdler: similar form over fences: won handicap at Exeter in March: stays 3m: acts on heavy going: wears cheekpieces/tongue tie. *Fiona Shaw* — c79 h78

KK LEXION (IRE) 8 b.g. Flemensfirth (USA) – Kiloradante (IRE) (Phardante (FR)) [2018/19 h127: c20g⁴ c19.4g⁵ h19.4g³ h21.4g h24.2g² Jan 25] small gelding: fairly useful handicap hurdler: fair form over fences: stays 3m: acts on soft going: temperament under suspicion. *Tom George* — c112 h119

KLARE CASTLE 7 b.g. Black Sam Bellamy (IRE) – Always Forgiving (Commanche **h124** Run) [2018/19 h99p, b100: h16d⁴ h19.6d³ h23.6d h21m h19.5dᶠ Mar 20] lengthy gelding: fairly useful form over hurdles: should stay beyond 2½m: acts on good to soft going. *Stuart Edmunds*

KLASSICAL DREAM (FR) 5 b.g. Dream Well (FR) – Klassical Way (FR) **h157 p** (Septieme Ciel (USA)) [2018/19 h16g* h16g* h16.4s* Mar 12]

It is surprising, if not extraordinary, that no horse has managed to win the Supreme Novices' Hurdle and then the Champion Hurdle in consecutive years since the Fred Winter-trained Bula right back at the beginning of the 'seventies. The Supreme was still the Gloucestershire Hurdle when Bula won the second division of that contest in 1970 before winning not just the following year's Champion Hurdle but also the one after that. Also surprising is that only two Supreme winners since Bula have managed to win a Champion Hurdle subsequently. Hors La Loi III had to wait three years between his Festival successes, winning the Supreme as a four-year-old in 1999 before coming up against Istabraq in the following year's Champion Hurdle and then winning it in 2002, the year after the foot and mouth outbreak which led to the cancellation of the Festival. The 2004 winner Brave Inca was the last Supreme winner to add a Champion Hurdle, doing so two years later after being beaten two necks by Hardy Eustace and Harchibald in the edition in the interim. Since Brave Inca, future Champion Hurdle winners Sublimity, Binocular, Jezki and Buveur d'Air were all beaten in the Supreme, the last-named finishing third behind Altior and Min in 2016.

Perhaps Klassical Dream will be the one to add a Champion Hurdle to the Supreme that he won in clear-cut fashion at the latest Festival. He is a general 7/2 ante-post favourite following the demise of reigning Champion Hurdle winner Espoir d'Allen. In truth, Klassical Dream impressed more as a future chaser than a Champion Hurdle horse when he became Willie Mullins' sixth winner of the Supreme and the fourth since 2013. If he does take that route instead, Klassical Dream will have big shoes to fill following Mullins' most recent Supreme winners Champagne Fever, Vautour and Douvan who were all sent over fences the following season, the last two going on to have top-class chasing careers. However, a chasing career seems unlikely for Klassical Dream at the moment. After he followed up his Cheltenham success at Punchestown, to maintain his unbeaten record since joining Mullins, his trainer announced that he was going to 'try to make a Champion Hurdle horse out of him.'

Klassical Dream didn't arrive at Cheltenham with quite the same lofty reputation that has often accompanied his stable's runners in the Supreme in the past and he only took his chance in the race, instead of in the following day's Baring Bingham, when conditions softened. He was a leading contender on form but so too was his stable-companion Aramon with whom he was very closely matched judged on their last start when there had been just a head between them, in Klassical Dream's favour, in the Grade 1 Chanelle Pharma Novices' Hurdle (the sponsors taking over from Deloitte) at Leopardstown at the beginning of February. In an

Chanelle Pharma Novices' Hurdle (Brave Inca), Leopardstown—
a sixth win in the race in the last seven years for trainer Willie Mullins as Klassical Dream (hoops)
holds off stable-companion Aramon (stars)

Sky Bet Supreme Novices' Hurdle, Cheltenham—
nothing like so close this time as Klassical Dream already has the race in the bag at the last

unusually open renewal of the Supreme, the Betfair Hurdle winner Al Dancer, unbeaten over hurdles, shared 9/2 joint favouritism with the Joseph O'Brien-trained juvenile Fakir d'Oudairies, an impressive winner on Cheltenham's Trials day and bidding to become the first four-year-old winner since Hors La Loi. Ruby Walsh's mount Klassical Dream was next in the betting on 6/1, along with Angels Breath who had made a winning debut under Rules in the Kennel Gate at Ascot before finishing second in the Dovecote at Kempton on his other start. Paul Townend took the ride on Aramon, an 8/1 chance who had won the Future Champions Novices' Hurdle at Leopardstown in December before running Klassical Dream so close there next time. Always prominent and jumping well, though taking quite a keen hold and racing with a low head carriage, Klassical Dream went on after the fifth flight in the Supreme and was still travelling strongly in front turning for home. Another good jump at the last sealed matters, and Klassical Dream kept on well to win by four and a half lengths. The Olly Murphy-trained pair of outsiders Thomas Darby and Itchy Feet stayed on from much further back to be placed, separated by half a length, with Fakir d'Oudairies, Felix Desjy, faring the better of Gordon Elliott's two runners, Aramon and Angels Breath completing the first seven. Al Dancer was the biggest disappointment, finishing only tenth.

For what it's worth, the Supreme was officially run around half a second slower than the Champion Hurdle won by Espoir d'Allen a couple of hours later. The Supreme was the first jumps race to have an official time recorded electronically, using an invisible beam a metre from the starting tape, a welcome if belated step forward in recording accurate times and one that is due to be extended to other jumping tracks. The new timing procedure had to cope with a false start, however, one of three on the Festival's opening day, a reminder that vigilance will be required in checking the new technology against other methods and not simply assuming that it has worked correctly (the hand times taken by Timeform's reporters frequently highlight errors in official times). There is more on timing in the essay on Min.

Klassical Dream's win extended Ruby Walsh's record of having ridden at least one winner at every Cheltenham Festival since 2002. It gained further significance later on when the jockey announced his retirement twenty-four hours after partnering the same horse to his success at Punchestown. Walsh was leading rider at the Cheltenham Festival eleven times and his fifty-nine wins there (twenty-one more than Barry Geraghty in second) makes him the most successful jockey in Festival history. Like his final winner there, and many in between, the first of Walsh's Festival winners came for Willie Mullins in the 1998 Champion Bumper aboard Alexander Banquet. Described in that horse's essay in *Chasers & Hurdlers* as 'a highly promising Irish amateur', Walsh's subsequent Festival successes as a professional—his career is assessed in more detail in the essay on Kemboy—included two Gold Cups, four Champion Hurdles, two Queen Mother Champion Chases and five Stayers' Hurdles, while Klassical Dream became his sixth winner of the Supreme. That final Festival win provided a poignant success as it came in the colours of Mrs Joanne Coleman whose husband John, a long-time Festival goer, didn't live to see the fulfilment of his dream of having a runner at the meeting; he had died the previous summer, though Mrs Coleman brought some of his ashes with her.

When he followed up in the Herald Champion Novices' Hurdle at Punchestown, Klassical Dream was every bit as emphatic as he had been at Cheltenham. He started odds on with only five rivals to beat, three from his own stable, including Aramon again, plus Felix Desjy, who had won the Top Novices' Hurdle at Aintree since the Supreme, and Nicky Henderson's runner Champagne Platinum. Felix Desjy made the running, but the result was in little doubt once Klassical Dream loomed up on the bridle two out. He didn't do much in front on the run-in but still beat Felix Desjy by five and a half lengths with the rest well beaten. It was Mullins' seventh win in a contest which has gone to two of his subsequent Champion Hurdle winners, Hurricane Fly and Faugheen, and has also been won by another future Champion Hurdle winner, Jezki, in recent seasons.

Klassical Dream had made his debut for Mullins in a maiden hurdle at Leopardstown on Boxing Day which he won cosily on his first start for over a year. He had a Flat win to his name in France, successful in a maiden for future jumpers at Sable-sur-Sarthe and, while he hadn't won over hurdles for Isabelle Gallorini (also the former trainer of the same stable's Benie des Dieux), he had kept good company at Auteuil, running his best race when beaten around four lengths into fourth in the top French hurdle for three-year-olds, the Prix Cambaceres, won by Master Dino. The Guillaume Macaire-trained winner of that race, incidentally, also had Cheltenham in his sights in the latest season but sustained an injury when making a big impression in a novice chase at Plumpton in January.

Klassical Dream (FR) (b.g. 2014)	Dream Well (FR) (b 1995)	Sadler's Wells (b 1981)	Northern Dancer
			Fairy Bridge
		Soul Dream (br 1990)	Alleged
			Normia
	Klassical Way (FR) (b 2003)	Septieme Ciel (b 1987)	Seattle Slew
			Maximova
		Negligente (b 1996)	Quest For Fame
			Nobile Decretum

Mrs Joanne Coleman's "Klassical Dream"

By the Prix du Jockey Club and Irish Derby winner Dream Well, Klassical Dream is his dam's fifth foal and much the best of them to date, though she has had three other winners in France. Klassical Dance (by Nickname) won a hurdle over seventeen furlongs, while both Klassical Summer (by Polish Summer) and Klassical Risk (by My Risk) were winners at up to nineteen furlongs and successful over both hurdles and fences. Their dam Klassical Way's first win came in a claiming hurdle for three-year-olds at Auteuil but she went on to better things, winning two of her three starts over fences when still just three (she was third on her chasing debut in the Group 2 Prix Congress), showing fairly useful form, and ending her career with another win over hurdles over two and a quarter miles, the furthest she raced. The grandam Negligente was a middle-distance maiden on the Flat and great grandam Nobile Decretum also failed to win, in the States, though the family had its share of 'black type' winners on the Flat, including Negligente's smart half-brother Triarius, a winner of the Select Stakes at Goodwood in the early days of Godolphin. Layal, a sister to Triarius, was useful on the Flat but she had a successful jumping career too, including over fences at Auteuil. The good-topped Klassical Dream has raced only at around two miles and there will be little incentive to try him over further for the time being as he goes down the Champion Hurdle route. He acts on soft ground but his two wins at Leopardstown show that he is fully effective under firmer conditions and is not short of speed, travelling strongly close up for all his wins. Klassical Dream would have to progress further to improve the record of Supreme winners in the Champion Hurdle, but there is surely more to come from him. He wore ear plugs before the Supreme which were removed at the start. *W. P. Mullins, Ireland*

KLEPHT (IRE) 14 b.g. Great Palm (USA) – What A Mewsment (IRE) (Persian Mews) **c76** [2018/19 c106, h–: c19.9g⁵ c20.1m⁶ Mar 28] strong gelding: point winner: winning **h–** hurdler: useful chaser at best, little impact in handicaps in 2018/19: stays 2¾m: acts on good to firm and heavy going: wears tongue tie. *Jacqueline Coward*

KLOUD GATE (FR) 7 ch.g. Astronomer Royal (USA) – Talkata (IRE) (Suave Dancer **h118** (USA)) [2018/19 h99: h19m⁵ h20.5g* h19.4g* h21g⁶ Jan 12] rather leggy gelding: fairly useful handicap hurdler: won at Leicester and Doncaster (novice) in December: stays 2½m: acts on good to firm going. *Gary Moore*

KNAB ROCK 5 b.g. Mastercraftsman (IRE) – Hollow Quaill (IRE) (Entrepreneur) **b74** [2018/19 b16.8m³ Aug 6] 14/1, third in bumper at Newton Abbot (8 lengths behind Dorette): modest form on Flat. *Evan Williams*

KNIGHT COMMANDER 6 br.g. Sir Percy – Jardin (Sinndar (IRE)) [2018/19 h109: **h104** h15.7gᶠ h18.7m³ h18.6g⁴ h22g⁵ h15.8m h15.8g² h19.5s h16.5d h21.2d⁶ h21.7d Mar 9] rather sparely-made gelding: has had breathing operation: fair handicap hurdler: left Olly Murphy after third start: stays 21f: acts on good to soft going: tried in blinkers/tongue tie. *Steve Flook*

KNIGHT CRUSADER 7 b.g. Sir Percy – Lac Marmot (FR) (Marju (IRE)) [2018/19 **b80** b15.8d b15.8g* b16.7v Dec 1] rather sparely-made gelding: modest form in bumpers: won maiden event at Uttoxeter in November: tried in cheekpieces: fairly useful 2m winner on Flat. *John O'Shea*

KNIGHT DESTROYER (IRE) 5 b.g. Dark Angel (IRE) – Do The Deal (IRE) (Halling **h107** (USA)) [2018/19 h120: h16d⁶ h16.3d⁵ h15.8g h20gᵖᵘ Apr 21] strong gelding: fair handicap hurdler: unproven beyond 17f. *Jonjo O'Neill*

KNIGHTHOOD 5 b.g. Delegator – Love Roi (ITY) (Roi Danzig (USA)) [2018/19 b83: **h–** b15.8g⁴ h20m⁵ Jul 9] modest form in bumpers: well beaten in novice on hurdling debut. **b83** *Nicky Henderson*

KNIGHT IN DUBAI (IRE) 6 b.g. Dubai Destination (USA) – Bobbies Storm (IRE) **c– p** (Bob Back (USA)) [2018/19 h131, b76: c19.8dᶠ h20.5d² h21s h20d⁵ Apr 5] lengthy **h133** gelding: has had breathing operation: useful handicap hurdler: second at Newbury (nose behind I'm A Game Changer) in December: going well when fell twelfth in novice won by Cubomania at Cheltenham on chasing debut: will stay 3m: acts on soft going: wears tongue tie. *Dan Skelton*

KNIGHT OF NOIR (IRE) 10 b.g. Winged Love (IRE) – At Dawn (IRE) (Lashkari) [2018/19 c136, h142: h23g h23g⁵ h23.1g³ h23.3s⁴ h26.5g⁶ Sep 10] workmanlike gelding: useful handicap hurdler: third at Market Rasen (1½ lengths behind Wynford) in July: useful chaser: stays 25f: acts on heavy going: has worn headgear/tongue tie: usually leads. *Michael Blake* **c–** **h130**

KNIGHT OFTHE REALM 10 b.g. Kayf Tara – Flow (Over The River (FR)) [2018/19 c25.2d c24.2s^pu c21.7g^pu c23.8s^pu Apr 7] workmanlike gelding: winning hurdler: fair chaser at best, no form in 2018/19: has worn cheekpieces, including in 2018/19. *Bob Buckler* **c–** **h–**

KNOCKADERRY FLYER (IRE) 10 b.g. Aolus (GER) – Tastao (IRE) (Camden Town) [2018/19 c116: c25g^pu c23.8m^pu c24s⁶ Jan 21] point winner: fairly useful form when winning on chasing debut in 2017/18, little show since: left Fergal O'Brien after second start. *Max Comley* **c103**

KNOCKANRAWLEY (IRE) 11 gr.g. Portrait Gallery (IRE) – Hot Lips (IRE) (Good Thyne (USA)) [2018/19 c131, h–: c24.2s^pu c28.8v^pu c22.9d* Mar 20] workmanlike gelding: winning hurdler: fairly useful handicap chaser: won veterans event at Haydock in March: stays 33f: acts on heavy going: wears headgear: temperamental. *Kim Bailey* **c122 §** **h–**

KNOCKGRAFFON (IRE) 9 b.g. Flemensfirth (USA) – Gleaming Spire (Overbury (IRE)) [2018/19 c142, h–: c25g⁵ c20.3g* c20.3s³ Mar 10] tall gelding: winning hurdler: useful handicap chaser: won at Musselburgh (by 1¾ lengths from Forth Bridge) in January: stays 2½m: acts on soft going: wears cheekpieces/tongue tie. *Olly Murphy* **c142** **h–**

KNOCK HOUSE (IRE) 10 ch.g. Old Vic – Lady's Gesture (IRE) (Anshan) [2018/19 c–, h126: h24.7g c23.8g⁵ c24.5d h23s* h23.8g² h24.7g Apr 6] sturdy gelding: has had breathing operation: useful handicap hurdler: won at Bangor (by 10 lengths from Salmanazar) in December: useful chaser at best, no form over fences in 2018/19: stays 3¼m: acts on heavy going: wears headgear: tried in tongue tie. *Donald McCain* **c–** **h131**

KNOCKLAYDE (IRE) 7 b.g. Mountain High (IRE) – Foret Noire (IRE) (Barathea (IRE)) [2018/19 h62: h23.3g h23.3g c21.6m⁵ c21.6d⁵ c20.1s^pu Dec 12] poor maiden hurdler: no form over fences: has worn headgear, including in 2018/19. *Katie Scott* **c–** **h58**

KNOCKLONG (IRE) 11 b.g. Milan – Banningham Blaze (Averti (IRE)) [2018/19 c22.6d⁴ Jun 8] prolific point winner: winning hurdler: fairly useful chaser, well below best sole outing under Rules in 2018/19: stays 25f: acts on heavy going: has worn headgear: often let down by jumping over fences. *Justin Landy* **c79 x** **h–**

KNOCKMAOLE BOY (IRE) 7 b.g. Echo of Light – Kashmir Lady (FR) (Rock of Gibraltar (IRE)) [2018/19 h126: c16.4d³ c15.9m³ c15.9f⁴ c16s^F Mar 16] fairly useful hurdler: similar form over fences: raced around 2m: acts on firm and soft going: wears hood/tongue tie. *Jean-Rene Auvray* **c121** **h–**

KNOCKNAGOSHEL (IRE) 6 b.g. Kalanisi (IRE) – Granny Clark (IRE) (Welsh Term) [2018/19 b16.7d Jan 8] little show in points: tailed off in bumper. *Gary Hanmer* **b–**

KNOCKNAMONA (IRE) 8 b.g. Trans Island – Faraday Lady (IRE) (Lord Americo) [2018/19 c98, h89: c24.2s⁴ c24.2g⁶ c24.5v² c20.3s² c19.3s⁴ c20s* h20.5d⁵ c23.4d^F h23d⁶ Apr 26] modest handicap hurdler: fair handicap chaser: won at Carlisle in February: stays 3m: acts on heavy going: tried in cheekpieces. *Micky Hammond* **c107** **h85**

KNOCKNANUSS (IRE) 9 b.g. Beneficial – Dato Vic (IRE) (Old Vic) [2018/19 h128: c19.7m^F c16.3g* c16.4d* c19.7d² c17g^F c15.9s⁵ c15.8g⁵ Apr 6] sturdy gelding: winning hurdler: smart chaser: won novice at Fakenham (by 21 lengths from Jaisalmer) in October and novice handicap at Newbury (by 17 lengths from Kupatana) in November: stays 2½m: acts on heavy going: free-going front runner. *Gary Moore* **c147** **h–**

KNOCKOURA (IRE) 7 b.g. Westerner – Lisselton Thatch (IRE) (Generous (IRE)) [2018/19 h20.6d⁶ h20.2g Apr 24] £42,000 5-y-o: third foal: dam unraced half-sister to useful hurdler/very smart chaser (winner up to 3m) Scotsirish: Irish point winner: modest form over hurdles: in tongue tie second start. *Maurice Barnes* **h87**

KNOCKROBIN (IRE) 8 b.g. Robin des Pres (FR) – Tudor Style (IRE) (Montelimar (USA)) [2018/19 h128: c20g³ c20.6v³ c23.4s⁵ c23.4d² c20.6d³ c23.8g^pu Apr 24] lengthy gelding: has had breathing operations: Irish point winner: fairly useful hurdler: similar form in chases: stays 23f: acts on heavy going: in blinkers last 2 starts: wears tongue tie. *Donald McCain* **c125** **h–**

KNOW THE SCORE (IRE) 6 b.g. Flemensfirth (USA) – Prairie Bell (IRE) (Sadler's Wells (USA)) [2018/19 b105: h19.5s³ h20.1s* h23d³ h24.1d³ Mar 19] sturdy gelding: Irish point winner: useful bumper winner: fairly useful form over hurdles: won maiden at Hexham in December: third in handicap at Wetherby in March: may prove best up to 3m: tried in cheekpieces/tongue tie: usually races prominently. *David Pipe* **h119**

KOALA KEEL (IRE) 7 gr.m. Kirkwall – Kayf Keel (Kayf Tara) [2018/19 h99: h16.2g³ **h88** h16.2g Jun 3] placed in points: modest form over hurdles: unproven beyond 2m: acts on soft going: in tongue tie last 5 starts. *N. W. Alexander*

KOBROUK (FR) 8 b.g. Saint des Saints (FR) – Kotkira (FR) (Subotica (FR)) [2018/19 **c–** h20d^{pu} Apr 5] lengthy gelding: useful hurdler at best in France, pulled up sole outing in **h–** 2018/19 after long absence: smart chaser: stays 2¾m: acts on soft going. *Nicky Henderson*

KOHUMA 9 ch.m. Halling (USA) – Kohiba (IRE) (Rock of Gibraltar (IRE)) [2018/19 **h101** h101: h16.8m* h16.8s h16.3g Aug 28] fair handicap hurdler: won lady amateurs event at Newton Abbot in May: raced around 2m: acts on soft and good to firm going. *Robert Walford*

K O KENNY 8 b.g. Apple Tree (FR) – Cool Island (IRE) (Turtle Island (IRE)) [2018/19 **h61** h83: h22.7g⁶ h23.3s Dec 31] poor maiden hurdler: stays 3m: acts on heavy going: in cheekpieces last 4 starts. *Andrew Crook*

KONIGIN ARA (GER) 4 br.f. Kamsin (GER) – Konigin Arte (GER) (Artan (IRE)) **b87** [2018/19 b15.7d² Apr 9] fifth foal: closely related to a winning jumper in Czech Republic by Samum and half-sister to a winner abroad on Flat by Big Shuffle: dam, 7f/1m winner in Germany/Czech Republic, placed up to 25f over jumps: 25/1, second in conditionals/ amateurs maiden bumper at Southwell (3½ lengths behind It's Probably Me). *Dan Skelton*

KOOTENAY RIVER (IRE) 5 ch.g. Dubai Destination (USA) – Siwaara (IRE) (Peintre **h93** Celebre (USA)) [2018/19 b98: b17g² h21g h22.8v h21.4g³ h23.9d³ Apr 4] has had **b95** breathing operation: point winner: fairly useful form in bumpers: modest form over hurdles. *Alan King*

KOSHARI (FR) 7 br.g. Walk In The Park (IRE) – Honor May (FR) (Balleroy (USA)) **c–** [2018/19 c143, h–: c22.5d h19.8g² Aug 11] useful hurdler: second in minor event at **h133** Kilbeggan (4 lengths behind Woodland Opera) in August: useful chaser at best, well beaten in Galway Plate on return: stays 2½m: acts on heavy going. *W. P. Mullins, Ireland*

KOST A COAT (FR) 4 b.g. Diamond Boy (FR) – Charming Princesse (FR) (Charming **b86** Groom (FR)) [2018/19 b16s³ b13.7m Mar 29] €12,000 3-y-o: first foal: dam French maiden (no form over jumps): fair form in bumpers: better effort when third in maiden at Kempton on debut. *Gary Moore*

KOSTAQUARTA (IRE) 12 ch.g. Beneficial – Aclare Thyne (IRE) (Good Thyne (USA)) **c– x** [2018/19 c–x, h–: c23g⁵ c25.8m^{pu} Aug 6] strong gelding: multiple point winner: once- **h–** raced hurdler: little form in chases: wears headgear: has worn tongue tie: poor jumper. *Mark Gillard*

KOVERA (FR) 7 b.g. Antarctique (IRE) – Kesakao (FR) (Saint Estephe (FR)) [2018/19 **c82** h73: h24g⁵ c21.6g⁵ c24g² c26.3g* h24g* c26.7g^{pu} c26.3s⁵ c23.8m³ c26.2g⁶ Apr 26] poor **h81** handicap hurdler: won at Newcastle in November: poor handicap chaser: won novice event at Sedgefield in November: stays 3¼m: acts on good to firm going: wears visor: usually front runner/races prominently. *Tim Vaughan*

KRACQUER 5 ch.g. Schiaparelli (GER) – Norma Hill (Polar Prince (IRE)) [2018/19 **b–** b16g Jun 2] tailed off in bumper. *David Dennis*

KREB'S CYCLE (IRE) 5 ch.g. Helmet (AUS) – La Noe (Nayef (USA)) [2018/19 **h–** h16m^{pu} h15.8g^{pu} Oct 25] fairly useful on Flat, stays 1m: no form over hurdles: in tongue tie first start. *Ian Williams*

KRIS SPIN (IRE) 11 br.g. Kris Kin (USA) – Auditing Empress (IRE) (Accordion) **c–** [2018/19 c–, h142: h25s Dec 16] workmanlike gelding: useful hurdler, behind sole outing **h–** in 2018/19: maiden chaser: stays 3¼m: acts on heavy going. *Kerry Lee*

KRISTAL HART 10 b.m. Lucky Story (USA) – Moly (FR) (Anabaa (USA)) [2018/19 **h88** h90: h15.3m h15.8g⁶ h16.8g⁴ h18.7g* h19g* h15.9m² h17.7g³ Nov 19] modest handicap hurdler: won mares events at Stratford and Warwick in September: stays 19f: acts on soft and good to firm going: wears cheekpieces/tongue tie: front runner/races prominently. *Neil Mulholland*

KRISTJANO (GER) 7 b.g. Nayef (USA) – Kalahari Dancer (Dalakhani (IRE)) [2018/19 **h84** h–: h19d h16.8s h15.3g* h19.7g Mar 26] poor handicap hurdler: won at Wincanton in February: probably best around 2m: tried in cheekpieces: in tongue tie last 2 starts: dead. *Jimmy Frost*

KRUGERMAC (IRE) 8 b.g. Kalanisi (IRE) – Vindonissa (IRE) (Definite Article) **c85** [2018/19 h108: c24.5g⁵ c23.6g⁴ May 28] tall, useful-looking gelding: fair hurdler: modest **h–** form over fences: stays 21f: acts on heavy going: tried in visor. *Gary Moore*

KRUZHLININ (GER) 12 ch.g. Sholokhov (IRE) – Karuma (GER) (Surumu (GER)) **c118**
[2018/19 c22d³ c21.1d Apr 4] lengthy, useful-looking gelding: prolific point winner: **h–**
winning hurdler: useful chaser at best: third in hunter at Down Royal in December: stays
3¼m: acts on heavy going: has worn blinkers. *Gordon Elliott, Ireland*

KUBLAI (FR) 9 b.g. Laveron – Java Dawn (IRE) (Fleetwood (IRE)) [2018/19 c–, h91: **c–**
h16.8gᵖᵘ h16.8m h18.5m h16.8s h16.8g⁶ h18.6g² h20g* h19.9g² Oct 18] well-made **h89**
gelding: modest handicap hurdler: won at Worcester in October: pulled up both starts over
fences: stays 2¾m: acts on soft and good to firm going: has worn headgear: has worn
tongue tie, including in 2018/19. *Alexandra Dunn*

KUIPER BELT (USA) 5 b.g. Elusive Quality (USA) – Youre So Sweet (USA) (Storm **h126**
Cat (USA)) [2018/19 h24.6s h20.2g² h20.2g* h16.8m* h16d² h20g* h20g⁶ h16s h18.8g⁵
h16d² Apr 22] dam half-sister to smart hurdler/chaser (stayed 4¼m) Cause of Causes: fair
on Flat, stays 2m: fairly useful hurdler: won conditionals handicap at Perth and novice at
Sedgefield in August, and novice handicap at Clonmel in October: also first past post in
handicap at Listowel during that sequence, but demoted after causing interference: best
effort when second in novice handicap at Fairyhouse in April: left W. Ross after second
start: stays 2½m: acts on good to firm and good to soft going: tried in blinkers: wears
tongue tie. *Gordon Elliott, Ireland*

KUPATANA (IRE) 6 b.m. Westerner – Kildea Cailin (IRE) (Anshan) [2018/19 h108: **c144**
h20g* c18g* c16.4d⁷ c20.2dᵘʳ c20.2gᶠ c20m⁷ c20g² c21.6g* c20.6g* Apr 18] good-topped **h112**
mare: fair form over hurdles: won mares handicap at Aintree in May: useful chaser: won
novice handicap at Kempton in November, mares novice at Kelso in March and listed
mares novice handicap at Cheltenham (by 1¼ lengths from Little Miss Poet) in April: left
Nicky Henderson after sixth start: stays 2¾m: acts on heavy going: has worn hood,
including in 2018/19: front runner, often travels strongly. *Paul Nicholls*

KYLEMORE LOUGH 10 b.g. Revoque (IRE) – One of The Last (Supreme Leader) **c–**
[2018/19 c159, h–: c19.4mᵘʳ Nov 2] tall gelding: winning hurdler: very smart chaser at **h–**
best, unseated rider first only start in 2018/19: stayed 2¾m: acted on heavy going: tried in
tongue tie: dead. *Harry Fry*

KYLLACHY GALA 6 b.g. Kyllachy – Tenuta di Gala (IRE) (Nashwan (USA)) [2018/19 **h88**
h15.8d h16.5g⁵ Jan 9] useful on Flat, stays 1¼m: modest form over hurdles. *Warren Greatrex*

KYLLACHYS TALE (IRE) 5 b.m. Kyllachy – Betray (King's Best (USA)) [2018/19 **h–**
h16.3dᵖᵘ Jan 16] fairly useful on Flat, stays 1m: pulled up in novice on hurdling debut.
Roger Teal

KYMATA 5 b.m. Sulamani (IRE) – Miss Annabell (IRE) (Old Vic) [2018/19 ab16.3g⁶ Jan **b–**
5] first foal: dam, unraced, closely related to useful bumper winner Rapid Escape and half-
sister to fairly useful hurdler/chaser around 2m Nicolas Chauvin: placed in point: in
cheekpieces, 50/1, sixth of 7 in conditionals/amateurs bumper at Newcastle. *Sean Conway*

L

LA BAGUE AU ROI (FR) 8 b.m. Doctor Dino (FR) – Alliance Royale (FR) **c151 p**
(Turgeon (USA)) [2018/19 h145: c22.4d* c19.9d* c24g* c21g* c19.9d² Apr 4] **h–**
The opening line of the essay on Apple's Jade asks how long it will be before
another mare wins the Champion Hurdle. Not too long seems the likely answer,
given that it was short odds beforehand about a mare winning the latest edition
(Apple's Jade and Laurina started favourite and second favourite in a renewal which
was also contested by another of the season's best mares Verdana Blue). Pose the
same question about the Cheltenham Gold Cup and it is difficult to be so sanguine.
The previous year's Golden Miller Novices' Chase winner, Irish-trained Shattered
Love, ran in the latest edition of steeplechasing's blue riband event (well held,
reportedly suffered post-race ataxia) but she was the first mare to contest the race
since Dubacilla came second to Master Oats nearly a quarter of a century before.
Four mares, three of them trained in Ireland, have won the Cheltenham Gold Cup.
The 1925 winner Ballinode was Ireland's first winner of the Gold Cup and she was
followed in 1972 by Glencaraig Lady and in 1986 by the finest mare of them all, the
Champion Hurdle and Cheltenham Gold Cup winner Dawn Run (the 1958 winner

Kerstin was trained in Northumberland by Verly Bewicke and won her Gold Cup when the favourite Mandarin and Linwell, who had beaten Kerstin into second in the race the year before, both fell.

The planned, gradual enhancement of the British programme for jumping mares in recent years has led to a small increase in the number of mares in training and in the prices they make at auction. Mares are still very much second class citizens in the jumping world but they provided a record twenty-three per cent of the jumpers in training in Britain in the latest season when mares races accounted for nearly ten per cent of the jumps programme. Not exactly a breakthrough, but a good start nonetheless for the combined efforts of the British Horseracing Board and the Thoroughbred Breeders' Association. Encouraging more owners to have mares in training over jumps should lead to more mares coming to the fore in the big races and the BHA has also increased the number of 'black type' races. The David Nicholson Mares' Hurdle, held at the Cheltenham Festival (together with the Grade 2 Dawn Run Mares' Novices' Hurdle), remains the only Grade 1 event in Britain restricted to mares and includes Apple's Jade among its past winners. The 'black type' programme consisted of thirty-five races in the latest season, also including six Grade 2s, one Grade 3 and twenty-seven listed events. Most of the programme revolves, for the moment, around bumpers and races over hurdles, but good-class chasing mares are no longer quite the phenomenon they used to be and it cannot be many more years before there is a Grade 1 chase in Britain and Ireland for mares. Plans were announced after the end of the latest season for the introduction of a new Grade 2 mares chase at the Cheltenham Festival in 2021 which will replace an existing race (still to be decided) to maintain the Festival at twenty-eight races. Neither of the mares hurdles is under consideration for the axe and it remains to be seen whether there will be enough good quality mares around by 2021 to fill the three races. Two other recent winners of the David Nicholson Mares' Hurdle, Vroum Vroum Mag and Benie des Dieux, began their Irish careers over fences, showing smart form, before reverting to hurdling and establishing fine records in

32Red Kauto Star Novices' Chase, Kempton—
La Bague Au Roi rallies splendidly to beat Topofthegame (right)

Flogas Novices' Chase (Scalp), Leopardstown—
the only British challenger on the second day of the Dublin Racing Festival, La Bague Au Roi,
lands the odds in workmanlike fashion dropped back in trip

graded hurdles, kept largely, but not exclusively, to lucrative mares races. Shattered Love didn't reach the same heights as a novice hurdler and nor did La Bague Au Roi (seventh in Benie des Dieux's David Nicholson), but they proved to be in their element when sent over fences and won Grade 1 novices on both sides of the Irish Sea against their male counterparts, their successes doing plenty to promote the cause of running mares over fences (Shattered Love was the first mare to win a novice chase at the Cheltenham Festival for twenty-three years).

Unlike Vroum Vroum Mag and Benie des Dieux, who both started their careers in France, Shattered Love and La Bague Au Roi came through the domestic ranks, Shattered Love starting out in a point and then running in bumpers in Ireland, while La Bague Au Roi's wins, in a career which has seen her brought on steadily, include three in bumpers and seven over hurdles (including the Grade 2 Warfield Hurdle against her own sex) before she embarked on her career over fences in the latest season. Sent to Henrietta Knight at the beginning of the campaign for schooling, La Bague Au Roi's trainer reported that 'Hen said once she started jumping fences she was a different horse.' Sound-jumping La Bague Au Roi made an instant impression when winning a red-hot maiden chase at Newbury on her reappearance, her 7-lb weight-for-sex allowance just giving her the edge against Lostintranslation (Talkischeap and Thomas Campbell were third and fourth). La Bague Au Roi looked every bit as promising when following up in the Berkshire Chase over the same course at the Ladbrokes Trophy meeting (with Talkischeap second and Lostintranslation third) and she looked an obvious contender for the 32Red Kauto Star Novices' Chase at Kempton on Boxing Day. The Kauto Star (formerly the Feltham) is the first Grade 1 test of the season for staying novice chasers and La Bague Au Roi passed with flying colours, jumping well and rallying strongly, after being headed three out, to maintain her unbeaten start over fences, beating Topofthegame and Santini by a length and a half and two lengths, the trio clear of the rest (La Bague Au Roi was the first of her sex to win the race for over twenty years, since Fiddling The Facts who went on to start favourite, and departed when still going well at second Becher's, in the following year's Grand National).

Despite the healthy prize money on offer at the new Dublin Racing Festival in February, British challengers have been in short supply so far and La Bague Au Roi was the sole raider on the second day at Leopardstown when she contested the Flogas Novices' Chase (a Grade 1 that used to be known as the Dr P.J. Moriarty and is registered as the Scalp). The weather caused some problems for the meeting's organisers—as discussed in the essay on Bellshill—and the late defection of Delta Work, also unbeaten over fences at up to that time, made the task easier for odds-on La Bague Au Roi who didn't have to reach the level of her Kempton form to hold off 33/1-shot Kaiser Black and second favourite Hardline. La Bague Au Roi was the first mare to win the race since J'Y Vole eleven years earlier, that mare having benefited from an over-generous age allowance in Ireland for four- and five-year-old chasers, in addition to a mares allowance which was 5 lb at the time in Ireland.

La Bague Au Roi bypassed the Cheltenham Festival to wait for Aintree. She was an 8/1-shot straight after Leopardstown to emulate Shattered Love in the Golden Miller but connections always said she was unlikely to run. The Manifesto Novices' Chase provided La Bague Au Roi with a good opportunity to make it five out of five over fences but she wasn't quite at the top of her game on the day and couldn't quicken after being headed two out, rallying on the run-in in typical style but going down by a length and a quarter to Kalashnikov, with the Golden Miller third Mengli Khan filling the same position he had at Cheltenham.

La Bague Au Roi may well benefit from being stepped back up to three miles, her performance in the Kauto Star making a return to Kempton on Boxing Day for the King George VI Chase a possibility. She would be the first mare to run in the race since the 200/1-shot Sandymac in 2009 and only the fourth to do so this century. Lady Cricket, who finished down the field in 2000, and La Landiere, who was sixth in 2003, had both been among the leading novice chasers the previous season, just as La Bague Au Roi was. La Landiere, who caught the imagination of the racing public in a similar way to La Bague Au Roi, was also ridden by Richard Johnson who has partnered La Bague Au Roi to seven of her last eight victories, including all her wins over fences. Johnson, who received an OBE in the New Year's Honours, went on to become champion jumps jockey in Britain for the fourth time, after sixteen second places behind Tony McCoy (the only rider to have had more winners over jumps than Johnson). A hard-working, consummate professional, Johnson reached the landmark of two hundred wins for the season with a double on the penultimate day at Perth. It was the second time in his career that Johnson has ridden two hundred winners in a season (he rode 235 in 2015/16) and he has passed one hundred and fifty on nine occasions in the last ten years. He finished twenty-two ahead of runner-up Harry Skelton and fifty-four clear of third-placed, northern-based Brian Hughes, Johnson's only other serious rival for the title nowadays whose chances were ended in the latest season when he was sidelined for the rest of the campaign by a nasty facial injury received in a fall at Newcastle on Grand National day.

La Bague Au Roi (FR) (b.m. 2011)	Doctor Dino (FR) (ch 2002)	Muhtathir (ch 1995)	Elmaamul
			Majmu
		Logica (b 1994)	Priolo
			Salagangai
	Alliance Royale (FR) (gr 2002)	Turgeon (gr 1986)	Caro
			Reiko
		Allee Sarthoise (b 1993)	Pampabird
			Allee du Roy

The tall, useful-looking La Bague Au Roi always had the physical scope to jump fences. She was acquired as a yearling from France by her connections, her sire being the much travelled Doctor Dino, winner of two Hong Kong Vases and a Man o'War Stakes in America. Doctor Dino is also the sire, among others, of the high-class Sceau Royal, placed behind Altior in the Queen Mother Champion Chase and the Celebration Chase in the latest season, and the very smart Irish hurdler Sharjah, who won the Galway Hurdle, the Morgiana Hurdle and the Ryanair Hurdle (at Leopardstown), all before the turn of the year. La Bague Au Roi's dam, the unraced Alliance Royale, is a daughter of Turgeon who won the Irish St Leger and the Prix Royal-Oak and was twice placed in the Gold Cup at Royal Ascot. Turgeon was still active as a stallion at the age of thirty-two in 2018, when he covered twenty-six

Mrs Julien Turner & Andrew Merriam's "La Bague Au Roi"

mares, but he died in April, just after Siruh du Lac (whose essay makes further reference to Turgeon) had given him his second Cheltenham Festival winner (he was also the sire of Exotic Dancer, twice placed in the Gold Cup). La Bague Au Roi is the fourth winner out of Alliance Royale following: the useful staying handicap hurdler Kaysersberg (by Khalkevi) who went on to win over fences for La Bague Au Roi's trainer; Reine Angevine (by Poliglote) who won twice over hurdles at two miles for Willie Mullins and earned herself some dubious 'black type' when third in the Grade 1 Navan Novices' Hurdle, though she was last of three finishers, beaten seventy-two lengths; and the useful French hurdler/winning chaser Franche Alliance (also by Poliglote). La Bague Au Roi's grandam Allee Sarthoise is a half-sister to the smart staying chaser Clan Royal who was twice placed in the Grand National and was carried out by a loose horse when clear in the race in between those efforts. The tough and game La Bague Au Roi, who has had a breathing operation, stays three miles and acts on heavy going, though she doesn't need the mud. She makes the running or races prominently and is a slick jumper of fences who remains with potential as a chaser. She is a credit to herself and her stable. *Warren Greatrex*

LABEL DES OBEAUX (FR) 8 b.g. Saddler Maker (IRE) – La Bessiere (FR) (Loup Solitaire (USA)) [2018/19 c149, h–: h24.2d⁶ Nov 8] compact gelding: useful hurdler: not disgraced in handicap at Newbury, only outing in 2018/19: smart chaser: probably stays 4m: acts on heavy going: has worn cheekpieces. *Alan King* **c–**
h126

LA CAVSA NOSTRA (IRE) 7 b.g. Flemensfirth (USA) – Pharenna (IRE) (Phardante (FR)) [2018/19 h21d h18.5d c17.8d³ Feb 24] sturdy gelding: point winner: well held in maiden hurdles/novice chase. *Neil Mulholland* **c–**
h–

LACE BONNET (IRE) 5 gr.m. Mastercraftsman (IRE) – Lace (IRE) (Sadler's Wells **h96**
(USA)) [2018/19 h16g h20s h16s^F h16v^5 h20d^5 h15.8v^3 h16g* Apr 10] fair maiden on Flat,
stays 1¾m: modest hurdler: in cheekpieces, won mares handicap at Warwick in April: left
Eugene M. O'Sullivan after third start: stays 2½m: acts on heavy going. *Christian Williams*

LACKANEEN LEADER (IRE) 7 b.m. Oscar (IRE) – Shandora (IRE) (Supreme **c–**
Leader) [2018/19 h131, b86: h18.1g^4 c16.7v c19.7d^pu h20.2d^5 h19.9s^pu Mar 12] compact **h130**
mare: point/bumper winner: useful hurdler: lame final start: no promise in 2 chases: stays
2¾m: acts on heavy going: usually races off pace. *Gordon Elliott, Ireland*

LAC KIVU (FR) 6 b.g. Sakhee (USA) – Poliaurea (ARG) (Poliglote) [2018/19 h16d* Apr **h142**
21] fairly useful 15f winner on Flat in France: useful form over hurdles: off 21 months/
tongue tied, won minor event at Cork (by length from Whiskey Sour) in April, having
benefit of enterprising ride: likely to prove best up to 2½m. *W. P. Mullins, Ireland*

LAC SACRE (FR) 10 b.g. Bering – Lady Glorieuse (FR) (Le Glorieux) [2018/19 c108, **c104**
h–: c26.3s^4 c28.5d^4 c28.8v^pu c23.6d^pu c23.8s* c27.5g^F Apr 14] neat gelding: winning **h–**
hurdler: fair handicap chaser: won at Ffos Las in April: stays 31f: acts on heavy going:
wears headgear/tongue tie. *John Flint*

LADIES DANCING 13 b.g. Royal Applause – Queen of Dance (IRE) (Sadler's Wells **c–**
(USA)) [2018/19 c–, h89: h18.5g^4 h18.7m h21.6g h20g^3 h16.3g* h18.5d^pu h16.8m^3 **h81**
h18.5m^4 Nov 6] angular gelding: poor handicap hurdler: won at Stratford (amateurs) in
August: maiden chaser: stays 2½m: acts on soft and good to firm going: has worn headgear:
tried in tongue tie: front runner/races prominently. *Chris Down*

LADOFASH 5 b.g. Canford Cliffs (IRE) – Curras Spirit (Invincible Spirit (IRE)) [2018/19 **h–**
h99: h15.9g May 13] compact gelding: maiden hurdler, has gone wrong way: usually in
cheekpieces. *Chris Gordon*

LAD OF LUCK (FR) 6 b.g. Soldier of Fortune (IRE) – Baraka du Berlais (FR) (Bonnet **h–**
Rouge (FR)) [2018/19 h107: h20d^pu May 26] bumper winner: fair form over hurdles,
pulled up in handicap only outing in 2018/19. *Jonjo O'Neill*

LADRONNE (FR) 5 b.g. Linda's Lad – Wordeta (FR) (Lost World (IRE)) [2018/19 **b92**
b17g^6 b16.7g^3 Apr 3] £3,000 3-y-o: first foal: dam French 2¼m chase winner: fair form in
bumpers: better effort when third in maiden at Market Rasen, very much having run of
race. *Sue Smith*

LADURELLI (IRE) 7 b.g. Mastercraftsman (IRE) – Chanter (Lomitas) [2018/19 h16.3m **h–**
Jun 19] useful at best on Flat (stayed 11f), deteriorated markedly: pulled up both starts in
points: tailed off only outing (tongue tied) over hurdles: dead. *Alexandra Dunn*

LADY AVERY (IRE) 7 b.m. Westerner – Bobs Article (IRE) (Definite Article) [2018/19 **h–**
h63: h15.8g h15.8d Nov 25] point winner: well held over hurdles. *Alan Jones*

LADY BABS 5 br.m. Malinas (GER) – Jontys'lass (Tamure (IRE)) [2018/19 b16.2g^4 **b86**
b16.2g^3 May 27] third foal: half-sister to bumper winner/fairly useful hurdler Ryedale
Racer (2½m winner), by Indian Danehill), stays 23f: dam (h111) bumper/2½m hurdle
winner (stayed 23f): fair form in bumpers: better effort when third in mares event at Kelso.
Andrew Crook

LADY BUTTONS 9 b.m. Beneficial – Lady Chapp (IRE) (High Chaparral (IRE)) **c150**
[2018/19 c140, h131: h16g* c16.4s* c20.5g* h16.6g* h19.9s^4 c15.8d^2 Apr 4] **h138**
    The driest summer for many years was followed by an unusually dry autumn
and early-winter which caused some headaches for course executives trying to
provide uniform, safe ground. Exeter, Taunton and Leicester had to abandon fixtures
during the autumn because of hard going—Leicester staged others without any
steeplechases—and some courses were still watering extensively for meetings in
December (Kempton watered before a fixture in mid-January). More than half the
meetings in the first half of the season were run on good going or firmer (a figure
that would normally be less than a third) and average field sizes were inevitably
affected, with complaints made about some late withdrawals which were put down
to the inaccuracy of the advance going descriptions supplied by clerks of the courses
(as we have said before in these pages, given the frustration felt by owners, trainers
and racegoers who sometimes travel long distances, it might be time to consider
whether the BHA's course inspectorate should have some role as a neutral voice in
the issuing of advance going descriptions, and certainly in decisions about whether
a meeting goes ahead or not). Yorkshire's two top jumps courses, Wetherby and
Doncaster, suffered more than most during the dry spell. Doncaster had to abandon

Ladbrokes In Memory of Tara Von Ihering Handicap Chase,
Newbury—a lucrative trip down south for the prolific mare Lady Buttons

the last two races on the first day of a two-day meeting at the end of November because of a slippery bend, resulting in twenty non-runners on the following day's card; two weeks later, Doncaster staged a seven-race card with a mere thirty declared runners (the field sizes were four, three, three, five, three, five and seven, and odds-on favourites went down in the first three races!). Wetherby's biggest day of the year, Charlie Hall Chase day in October, was another left denuded, with seventeen non-runners, all taken out on account of the drying ground. The advance going for the two-day meeting had been given as 'good' but, after jockeys and trainers had walked the course before racing the previous day, there seemed to be a feeling that conditions were 'good to firm', certainly in the home straight, and the course changed the description to 'good, good to firm in places' after the second race on the first day. Star attractions Bristol de Mai and Thistlecrack had been withdrawn from the Charlie Hall Chase earlier in the week and there were only four runners on the day, the smallest field since 2000 when See More Business won at 3/1-on.

Definitly Red's victory in the bet365 Charlie Hall Chase was the first by a Yorkshire-trained runner in the race for over thirty years, since the Cheltenham Gold Cup runner-up Cybrandian made all in 1987. In fact, Charlie Hall Chase day was a good one all round for local horses, with Philip Kirby, whose stables are just off the A1 near Catterick, completing a treble on the card to supplement the success of Malton-trained Definitly Red in the feature event. The smart handicapper Nautical Nitwit stepped up in class to beat just four opponents in the West Yorkshire Hurdle (likely favourite Wholestone was one of two withdrawn on the day because of 'unsuitable ground'), Wemyss Point won the handicap hurdle (from two opponents after four more 'unsuitable ground' withdrawals) and the versatile Lady Buttons went one better than twelve months earlier (when she was two lengths behind La Bague Au Roi) in the listed OLBG.com Mares' Hurdle in which she led on the bridle after the second last and asserted to win by a length and three quarters and three quarters of a length from 20/1-shot Mystic Sky and Irish Roe.

Connections had successfully mixed chasing with hurdling in Lady Buttons' campaign the previous year and she was back over fences for her next two races, justifying favouritism under 11-3 in a fairly valuable two-mile handicap on Ladbrokes Trophy day at Newbury (leading two out and winning with plenty in hand from Shear Rock) and then landing the valuable Mansionbet Yorkshire Silver Vase Mares' Chase just after Christmas at Doncaster, beating the previous year's winner Rene's Girl. The Silver Vase is a very good prize for a listed mares event and Lady Buttons was rerouted after initially being lined up for the Castleford Chase at Wetherby two days earlier (her trainer cited not only the bigger prize on offer at Doncaster but also the fact that the Wetherby course had been raced on the day before on Boxing Day and 'with the leg troubles she's had in the past, we didn't really want to take any risks'). The Silver Vase saw Lady Buttons tried again at two and a half miles and, after sauntering into the lead at the third last, she appeared to be nearing the end of her tether on the run-in as Rene's Girl rallied to push her to three and three quarter lengths. Back at Doncaster—over two miles—a month later for the Grade 2 OLBG.com Yorkshire Rose Mares' Hurdle, Lady Buttons went two lengths up on the run-in but then idled as Indefatigable, whom she had initially readily brushed aside, reduced the winning margin to a neck, with Irish Roe three lengths further back in third.

Lady Buttons held Cheltenham Festival entries in both the Queen Mother Champion Chase—a tall order—and the David Nicholson Mares' Hurdle, and her winning run came to an end behind Roksana, Stormy Ireland and Good Thyne Tara in the last-named, in which Benie des Dieux fell at the last with the race at her mercy. Two and a half miles stretches Lady Buttons' stamina and, patiently ridden over the trip at Cheltenham, she found herself still with plenty to do turning for home and could make no further impression after moving into fourth in the straight. Lady Buttons ended her latest campaign in the Red Rum Handicap Chase at Aintree's Grand National meeting and, back over two miles, she typically travelled well in

OLBG.com Yorkshire Rose Mares' Hurdle, Doncaster—Tommy Dowson takes over from the sidelined Adam Nicol as Lady Buttons (noseband) holds off Indefatigable and Irish Roe

touch and did nothing wrong in finishing second to the well-backed 'handicap blot' Moon Over Germany who went clear between the last two to beat Lady Buttons by ten lengths.

Lady Buttons (b.m. 2010)	Beneficial (b 1990)	Top Ville (b 1976)	High Top
			Sega Ville
		Youthful (b 1980)	Green Dancer
			First Bloom
	Lady Chapp (IRE) (b 2006)	High Chaparral (b 1999)	Sadler's Wells
			Kasora
		A-To-Z (b 1989)	Ahonoora
			Zenga

The lengthy Lady Buttons is by the now deceased Beneficial, a good sire of jumpers who tended to shine more with his chasers than his hurdlers. Lady Chapp, the dam of Lady Buttons, never ran but is a close relative of the useful two-mile hurdler and winning chaser Royal Alphabet (by another son of Sadler's Wells, King's Theatre), out of A-To-Z. Lady Chapp was bought privately by the owners of Lady Buttons at the Doncaster Sales; she was in foal, carrying Lady Buttons, her first offspring, who has been with the Kirbys since her early days. She started out in junior bumpers and was beaten a head in the graded mares bumper at Aintree on her final start in that first season. It hasn't all been plain sailing since, though, and, after showing fair form kept over hurdles in her second season, Lady Buttons suffered a leg injury which led to her being off the course for twenty months. She has gone on to make a name for herself and has become a popular mare with the northern racing public, with purple and white scarves (based on her purple, white triple diamond colours) sometimes evident among the crowd when she races. The grandam of Lady Buttons, A-To-Z, won the Nell Gwyn Stakes at Newmarket and two of her other winners, Queen Alphabet, who was fairly useful, and Appy Days (both sisters to Royal Alphabet), did their winning over jumps at two miles. There isn't a lot of stamina in the family and, although she stays two and a half miles, Lady Buttons is possibly at her very best at two miles (she is a strong traveller in her races). She acts on soft going but doesn't need the mud. Although she mixes chasing with hurdling, she is better over fences and should continue to more than pay her way, provided connections continue to enjoy a clear run with her. Never out of the frame over the last two seasons, she is most consistent and a credit to those who handle her at Green Oaks stables where she is understandably a great favourite. *Philip Kirby*

LADY CAMELOT (IRE) 4 b.f. Camelot – Queen Jock (USA) (Repent (USA)) [2018/19 h16.6g h16d⁶ h17s³ h16sᵘʳ h19.3m² h15.7d² h20.6g* h16.8g⁵ Apr 18] leggy filly: fairly useful on Flat, stays 1½m: fair hurdler: won 3-runner maiden at Market Rasen in March: left Gavin Patrick Cromwell after fourth start: stays easy 21f: acts on soft going. *Philip Kirby* **h105**

LADY CARDUROS (IRE) 5 b.m. Byron – Saranjo (IRE) (Carrowkeel (IRE)) [2018/19 h16dᵖᵘ Mar 21] no form on Flat: pulled up in mares novice on hurdling debut. *Neil Mulholland* **h—**

LADY CHARTREUSE (IRE) 6 ch.m. Flemensfirth (USA) – Verde Goodwood (Lomitas) [2018/19 b59: h16.7dᵖᵘ h16d h16v² h16d Jan 7] modest form over hurdles. *Venetia Williams* **h87**

LADY CHUFFNELL (IRE) 5 b.m. Jeremy (USA) – Taraval (IRE) (Milan) [2018/19 b15.8d Mar 30] €30,000 3-y-o: first foal: dam (h114), 2½m hurdle winner, closely related to top-class hurdler/very smart chaser (2m-21f winner) Oscar Whisky: tailed off in mares bumper. *Ben Pauling* **b—**

LADY CYLLA 4 b.f. Malinas (GER) – Lady Samantha (Fraam) [2018/19 b14g⁵ h16.6g³ h16.6g h15.8d² h19.9v³ h21.9gᵖᵘ Apr 21] sturdy filly: fourth foal: half-sister to bumper winner/fairly useful hurdler Before Midnight (19f winner, by Midnight Legend), stays 3m: dam (h76), 3m hurdle winner, half-sister to useful hurdler (stayed 25f) Lord Generous out of top-class 2½m-3m hurdle winner Lady Rebecca: some promise in fillies junior bumper: fair form over hurdles: should stay at least 2½m: acts on good to soft going. *Tom Lacey* **h111 b69**

LADY INGLEBY 9 b.m. Multiplex – Lady Jay Jay (Commanche Run) [2018/19 h16m h15.7g⁴ h16.3g h18.7g⁴ Aug 28] has had breathing operation: second foal: dam ran once in bumper: no form over hurdles. *Charlie Longsdon* **h—**

LADY IN HIDING (IRE) 5 br.m. Stowaway – Crackin' Liss (IRE) (Bob Back (USA)) **b84**
[2018/19 b16.3d⁴ Mar 1] €28,000 4-y-o: compact mare: seventh foal: half-sister to bumper winner/fairly useful hurdler Hitherjacques Lady (19f-21f winner, by Robin des Champs): dam (b99), bumper winner, half-sister to fairly useful hurdler (2m-2¼m winner) Blazing Liss out of half-sister to very smart hurdler up to 2½m Liss A Paoraigh: 9/2, fourth in mares bumper at Newbury (4¾ lengths behind Getariver). *Oliver Sherwood*

LADY KINGSMILL 8 b.m. Bandmaster (USA) – Kingsmill Lake (Broadsword (USA)) **h–**
[2018/19 h23.1sᵘʳ Mar 5] first foal: dam winning pointer: placed twice from 3 starts in points: 200/1, unseated third on hurdling debut. *Jackie du Plessis*

LADY KYRIA (FR) 5 b.m. Holy Roman Emperor (IRE) – Segesta (IRE) (Vettori (IRE)) **h102**
[2018/19 h15.7gᶠ h20.5s³ h16.4g³ h16.8v³ h16.4m* h17m⁶ Apr 20] fair on Flat, stays 1½m: fair form over hurdles: won mares handicap at Newcastle in March: unproven beyond 2m: acts on good to firm going: often in hood. *Philip Kirby*

LADY LONDON (IRE) 8 b.m. Beneficial – Torduff Storm (IRE) (Glacial Storm (USA)) **c87 §**
[2018/19 h89: h23.3g c23.9m⁵ h23.9g⁵ h23.9g⁵ h23.0g³ c23.8g² c23.4g⁴ c23.8g² c23.6dᵖᵘ **h77 §**
Dec 26] quite good-topped mare: winning pointer: poor handicap hurdler: modest form in chases: stays 3m: acts on good to firm going: wears headgear: usually tongue tied: temperamental. *Rose Dobbin*

LADY LONGSHOT 8 b.m. Needle Gun (IRE) – So Long (Nomadic Way (USA)) **h102**
[2018/19 h81: h17.7g* h18.5m* h21.4g* Mar 25] fair handicap hurdler: won all 3 starts in 2018/19, conditionals mares event at Fontwell and novice contest at Newton Abbot, both in June, and mares event at Wincanton in March: stays 21f: acts on good to firm going: usually wears hood/tongue tie: usually races towards rear. *Jeremy Scott*

LADY MAKFI (IRE) 7 b.m. Makfi – Dulcet Tones (IRE) (Singspiel (IRE)) [2018/19 **h–**
h21d May 30] rather leggy mare: dam half-sister to useful hurdler/chaser (stayed 3m) Made In Japan: modest on Flat, stays 16.5f: tailed off in novice on hurdling debut. *Johnny Farrelly*

LADY MALEFICENT 5 b.m. Malinas (GER) – Lush Lady (IRE) (Kris Kin (USA)) **h94**
[2018/19 b87: h20g² h15.7g² h15.8g h18.6g h21d⁶ h20.5g⁴ Apr 22] modest form over hurdles: stays 21f: in cheekpieces last 2 starts. *Dan Skelton*

LADY MARKBY (IRE) 8 b.m. Oscar (IRE) – Leitrim Bridge (IRE) (Earl of Barking **h107 §**
(IRE)) [2018/19 h23.3m³ h23.9m h23.1m² h21.7gʳʳ h26g h23.9s⁶ h23.1sᵖᵘ Mar 5] fair handicap hurdler: stays 23f: acts on good to firm and heavy going: has worn headgear: one to treat with caution (has refused to race). *Emma Lavelle*

LADY MARWAH (IRE) 6 b.m. Iffraaj – Eyrecourt (IRE) (Efisio) [2018/19 b90: b15.7g³ **h89**
h15.3d⁴ h16g⁴ h19.5m³ Apr 22] fair form in bumpers: modest form over hurdles: tried in **b90**
hood. *Michael Scudamore*

LADY MASTER 6 b.m. Native Ruler – Elmside Katie (Lord David S (USA)) [2018/19 **c97**
h73: h19.9g c19.4s* c20dᵖᵘ c23.6d⁴ c20.2m² c20.2f³ c23.6g² Mar 19] maiden hurdler: **h–**
modest form over fences: won novice handicap at Wetherby in December: stays 3m: acts on soft and good to firm going. *Caroline Bailey*

LADY MIX 6 gr.m. Fair Mix (IRE) – Et Voila (Alflora (IRE)) [2018/19 h106: h23g² **h112**
h23.3m⁴ h20.1g² Oct 5] fair maiden hurdler: stays 3m: acts on good to soft going: has worn cheekpieces: usually leads. *Nigel Hawke*

LADY NATASHA (IRE) 6 b.m. Alfred Nobel (IRE) – Hot To Rock (IRE) (Kalanisi **h–**
(IRE)) [2018/19 h15.8s h16.3d h16d⁶ h16.8s Mar 18] lengthy mare: has had breathing operation: modest maiden on Flat, stays 14.5f: no form over hurdles. *James Grassick*

LADY OF DERRYGALLY (IRE) 7 gr.m. September Storm (GER) – Lady of **h–**
Gortmerron (IRE) (Orchestra) [2018/19 h15.8gᵖᵘ h16.8sᵖᵘ Dec 7] half-sister to 3 winners, including fair hurdler Pure Genius (21f winner, by Exit To Nowhere) and bumper winner/ fair hurdler Pure Anticipation (2¾m winner, by Old Vic): dam (c119/h106) 3m-3½m hurdle/chase winner: placed in Irish points: no form over hurdles: in hood first start. *Sam England*

LADY OF LONGSTONE (IRE) 9 ch.m. Beneficial – Christdalo (IRE) (Glacial Storm **c–**
(USA)) [2018/19 c–, h104: h21.4m May 10] workmanlike mare: fairly useful hurdler at **h–**
best, on downgrade: maiden chaser: stays 3¼m: acts on soft and good to firm going: usually wears headgear: has worn tongue tie. *David Pipe*

LADY OF THE REA (IRE) 8 b.m. Scorpion (IRE) – Sonnys Girl (IRE) (Broken **h–**
Hearted) [2018/19 h62: h20.6g May 11] maiden pointer: little show over hurdles: in tongue tie last 2 starts. *Micky Hammond*

Racing Post Arkle Trophy Trial Novices' Chase (November), Cheltenham—the high point of an anti-climactic campaign for Lalor as he lowers the colours of Dynamite Dollars (left), Claimantakinforgan (hooped cap) and Defi du Seuil (second right)

LADY ROBYN (IRE) 9 b.m. Robin des Champs (FR) – Iseefaith (IRE) (Perugino (USA)) [2018/19 c–, h–: h23.3d May 5] runner-up all 4 completed starts in Irish points: maiden hurdler/chaser: has worn cheekpieces: in tongue tie last 5 starts: signs of temperament. *Peter Bowen* **c– h–**

LADY SALLY (IRE) 5 b.m. Scorpion (IRE) – Broken Gale (IRE) (Broken Hearted) [2018/19 b15.8m⁶ Oct 10] fourth foal: half-sister to modest 3m hurdle winner Our Morris (by Milan): dam (c81/h88), winning pointer, half-sister to fairly useful hurdler/useful chaser Takagi (19f-25f winner): 33/1, sixth of 7 in mares bumper at Ludlow. *Dominic Ffrench Davis* **b–**

LADY SAMBACK 7 ch.m. Black Sam Bellamy (IRE) – Bob Back's Lady (IRE) (Bob Back (USA)) [2018/19 b61: h16g h16.7g⁴ h20.2g⁵ h20.2g⁶ h19.6gᵖᵘ h16.8m⁴ h16.4s⁴ h16.2g² h15.7dᵖᵘ h17d² h17m* Apr 20] has had breathing operation: modest hurdler: won handicap at Carlisle (conditionals) in April: unproven beyond 17f: acts on good to firm and good to soft going: tried in hood: wears tongue tie: usually races prominently. *Maurice Barnes* **h87**

LADYVIE (FR) 12 b.m. Vic Toto (FR) – Ladykish (FR) (Comte du Bourg (FR)) [2018/19 c25.5g Jul 21] multiple point winner, including in 2019: maiden hurdler: fair chaser at best, never on terms in handicap only outing under Rules since 2013/14: wears headgear: usually tongue tied: signs of temperament. *Jackie Stephen* **c– h–**

LADY VITESSE 6 b.m. Rail Link – Sainte Gig (FR) (Saint Cyrien (FR)) [2018/19 h80, b–: h15.3m⁵ h20.3g³ h19.9g⁵ h15.8g h23gᵖᵘ Aug 22] has had breathing operation: poor maiden hurdler: stays 2½m: acts on heavy going: usually wears hood: often in tongue tie: temperamental. *Martin Keighley* **h83 §**

LADY VIVONA 11 gr.m. Overbury (IRE) – Ladylliat (FR) (Simon du Desert (FR)) [2018/19 h76: h22.1g⁶ h19.9g Jun 20] maiden hurdler, no form in 2018/19: stays 23f: acts on good to soft going: tried in cheekpieces: has worn tongue tie. *Lisa Harrison* **h–**

LADY WETHERED (IRE) 7 br.m. Westerner – Vics Miller (IRE) (Old Vic) [2018/19 h88: h15.3mᵖᵘ h18.5g h19s h21.4gᵖᵘ Apr 26] poor maiden hurdler: stays 2½m: acts on heavy going: in tongue tie last 2 starts. *Linda Blackford* **h85**

LA FILLE FRANCAISE (FR) 6 b.m. Kapgarde (FR) – Pondimari (FR) (Marignan (USA)) [2018/19 h108: h24g* h24g⁴ h21d⁵ h19.5d h24.2d Mar 1] close-coupled mare: fair handicap hurdler: won novice event at Southwell in May: stays 3m: acts on soft going: often travels strongly. *Robin Dickin* **h108**

LAHLOO 5 b.m. Native Ruler – Clipper Line (USA) (Mizzen Mast (USA)) [2018/19 b–: **b–** b16.7g b15.7s Dec 4] no form in bumpers. *Nick Kent*

LA HULPE (FR) 5 ch.m. No Risk At All (FR) – Belle Yepa (FR) (Mansonnien (FR)) **b78** [2018/19 b15.7d Apr 9] half-sister to several winners, including very smart hurdler/top-class chaser Whisper (2½m-3m winner) and smart French hurdler/fairly useful chaser Chuchoteuse (15f-19f winner) (both by Astarabad): dam French 17f-19f hurdle winner: 20/1, seventh in conditionals/amateurs maiden bumper at Southwell. *Sam Thomas*

L'AIR DU VENT (FR) 5 b.g. Coastal Path – Bleu Perle (FR) (Pistolet Bleu (IRE)) **b101 P** [2018/19 b16.7g* Apr 13] €70,000 3-y-o: half-brother to several winners, including useful hurdler/chaser Si C'etait Vrai (2m-21f winner, by Robin des Champs) and fairly useful French hurdler/chaser Perle Sainte (17f-21f winner, by Saint des Saints): dam unraced: fell when in contention sole start in Irish points: 10/11, won conditionals/amateurs bumper at Bangor in good style by 4½ lengths from Poniente: useful prospect. *Colin Tizzard*

LAKE SHORE DRIVE (IRE) 7 b.g. Thewayyouare (USA) – Labrusca (Grand Lodge **h101** (USA)) [2018/19 h103: h26.5m⁴ h26.5g⁵ Jul 22] fair handicap hurdler: stays 3¼m: acts on good to firm and good to soft going. *Johnny Farrelly*

LAKESIDE PEARL (IRE) 7 b.m. Presenting – Asigh Pearl (IRE) (Lord of Appeal) **h82** [2018/19 h16g h24g h19.9s⁵ h23.9d² Apr 24] first foal: dam (h128) bumper and 2m/17f hurdle winner: poor maiden hurdler: left Patrick G. Kelly after second start: stays 3m: acts on good to soft going: tried in tongue tie. *Jamie Snowden*

LAKETOUR LEADER (IRE) 7 b.g. Publisher (USA) – Gay da Cheen (IRE) (Tenby) **h74** [2018/19 h70, b–: h15.9g⁶ h17.7vᵖᵘ h20.5dᵖᵘ Jan 6] Irish point winner: poor maiden hurdler. *Richard Rowe*

LAKE VIEW LAD (IRE) 9 gr.g. Oscar (IRE) – Missy O'Brien (IRE) (Supreme Leader) **c157** [2018/19 c137, h–: c23.4d* c24.2s* c25s³ c34.3gᵖᵘ Apr 6] sturdy gelding: winning hurdler: **h–** very smart handicap chaser: won Rehearsal Chase at Newcastle (by 2¾ lengths from Captain Chaos) and Rowland Meyrick Chase at Wetherby (by 4 lengths from Captain Chaos) in December: good third in Ultima Handicap Chase at Cheltenham (3¼ lengths behind Beware The Bear) in March: missed break and never figured in Grand National at Aintree: stays 3¼m: acts on heavy going: sound jumper. *N. W. Alexander*

LAKE WASHINGTON (FR) 6 ch.g. Muhtathir – La Curamalal (IRE) (Rainbow Quest **h–** (USA)) [2018/19 h–, b–: h20.2gᵖᵘ May 17] little sign of ability: races freely. *Venetia Williams*

LALOR (GER) 7 b.g. It's Gino (GER) – Laviola (GER) (Waky Nao) [2018/19 h147: **c146** c15.9g* c15.5s³ c15.9sᵖᵘ c15.8g⁶ Apr 6] good-topped gelding: has had breathing operation: **h–** smart hurdler: similar form when won Grade 2 novice at Cheltenham (by 7 lengths from Dynamite Dollars) on chasing debut in November: went wrong way after: raced around 2m: acts on soft going. *Kayley Woollacott*

LA MADRINA (IRE) 7 b.m. Milan – Edermine Blossom (IRE) (Bach (IRE)) [2018/19 **h–** h–: h25.8gᵖᵘ h21.6g Jul 6] has had breathing operation: little sign of ability: usually in headgear: tried in tongue tie. *Katie Stephens*

LAMANVER BEL AMI 5 b.g. Black Sam Bellamy (IRE) – Lamanver Homerun (Relief **b82** Pitcher) [2018/19 b16.8s⁴ b15.8v⁵ Jan 14] fifth foal: half-brother to several winners, including bumper winner/fairly useful hurdler Lamanver Odyssey (2¼m-21f winner) and fairly useful 19f hurdle winner Lady of Lamanver (both by Lucarno): dam (c136/h123) 19f-3m hurdle/chase winner: modest form in bumpers: better effort when fourth at Exeter in December. *Jack R. Barber*

LAMANVER ODYSSEY 7 b.m. Lucarno (USA) – Lamanver Homerun (Relief Pitcher) **h114** [2018/19 h126: h21.9s⁴ h19.7v⁵ h24.3g h17.7v⁴ h23.9sᵖᵘ Apr 7] good-topped mare: fairly useful handicap hurdler, largely disappointing in 2018/19: stays 2¾m: acts on heavy going: wears tongue tie: usually front runner/races prominently. *Jack R. Barber*

LAMANVER PIPPIN 6 b.g. Apple Tree (FR) – Lamanver Homerun (Relief Pitcher) **h117** [2018/19 b94: h21.6d h20v* h19.5d h23.1s⁴ h19.9v Mar 16] fairly useful form over hurdles: won novice at Ffos Las in December: should stay beyond 2½m: acts on heavy going: usually races prominently. *Colin Tizzard*

LAMB OR COD (IRE) 12 ch.g. Old Vic – Princess Lizzie (IRE) (Homo Sapien) **c122 §** [2018/19 c114, h–: c25.8g² c29.4g c23.8mᵖᵘ c20d c24s⁴ Mar 2] lengthy gelding: has **h–** reportedly had breathing operation: winning hurdler: fairly useful handicap chaser: ran poorly after second at Newton Abbot in May: left Philip Hobbs after third start: stays 3¼m: acts on good to firm and heavy going: has worn headgear, including final start: wears tongue tie: unreliable. *Gordon Elliott, Ireland*

LAMH AR LAMH (IRE) 5 ch.m. Teofilo (IRE) – Tintreach (CAN) (Vindication (USA)) **h91**
[2018/19 h18.5g h16.8g h16g h18.7g³ h20g⁴ h23.3g⁵ h23.9d^{ro} h25g² h25d² h23d^{pu} h23.9g²
h23.9s* h19.7g⁵ h23.9d* Apr 24] modest maiden on Flat, stays 12.5f: modest handicap
hurdler: won at Taunton in March (conditionals) and April (mares): stays 25f: acts on soft
going: wears headgear/tongue tie. *Nigel Hawke*

LAMMTURNER (IRE) 7 b.m. Brian Boru – Deploy Or Die (IRE) (Deploy) [2018/19 **h81**
h–: h20.3g⁶ h23.3g^{pu} h23.1s⁴ h24.1d⁶ h25g⁶ h27s* h27g⁶ Apr 5] poor handicap hurdler:
won at Sedgefield in March: stays 27f: acts on soft going: in cheekpieces last 2 starts.
Joanne Foster

LANCASTER ROSE (IRE) 5 ch.m. Windsor Knot (IRE) – Tara Tara (IRE) (Fayruz) **b74**
[2018/19 b73: b15.7g b15.8m⁴ Jul 13] poor form in bumpers: tried in hood. *Sam Thomas*

LANDECKER (IRE) 11 br.g. Craigsteel – Winsome Breeze (IRE) (Glacial Storm **c–**
(USA)) [2018/19 c–, h116§: h23.9g h25.8d⁶ h21.4v⁶ h22.7g² h25.8g* h24.3d h22.7d^{pu} Apr **h106**
8] rather leggy gelding: has had breathing operation: fair handicap hurdler: won at Kelso in
January: no show only chase start: stays 3¼m: acts on heavy going: has worn headgear,
including most starts in 2018/19: tried in tongue tie: usually races off pace. *N. W. Alexander*

LANDIN (GER) 6 b.g. Sir Percy – Lupita (GER) (Niniski (USA)) [2018/19 h128: **h106**
h23.9d^{bd} h21g h23.3d⁶ h23.5d⁶ Feb 16] smallish gelding: fairly useful handicap hurdler at
best, has become disappointing: stays 2½m: acts on heavy going: has worn cheekpieces.
Seamus Mullins

LAND LEAGUE (IRE) 8 b.g. Touch of Land (FR) – Be My Sunset (IRE) (Bob Back **c–**
(USA)) [2018/19 c102, h114: h19.9d h16g⁴ Apr 26] tall gelding: Irish point winner: fair **h97**
handicap hurdler: maiden chaser: stays 2¼m: acts on heavy going: in tongue tie last 3
starts. *Stuart Edmunds*

LANDOFHOPEANDGLORY (IRE) 6 b.g. High Chaparral (IRE) – Wurfklinge **c128**
(GER) (Acatenango (GER)) [2018/19 c20d c19.7s⁵ c21g⁶ c18g² h16v* Mar 21] strong **h134**
gelding: useful hurdler: won minor event at Cork (by 2 lengths from Dr Mikey) in March:
fairly useful handicap chaser: stays 21f: acts on heavy going: usually wears headgear/
tongue tie: often races towards rear. *Joseph Patrick O'Brien, Ireland*

LANDOFSMILES (IRE) 6 b.g. Beneficial – Sadie Supreme (IRE) (Supreme Leader) **h111**
[2018/19 b92: h20g⁴ h20v⁶ h20s⁴ h19.5s h19.5d⁶ h23.3d² h24.3m³ Apr 12] placed on
second of 2 starts in Irish points: fair maiden hurdler: stays 3m: acts on good to firm and
good to soft going. *Peter Bowen*

LANDSCAPE (FR) 11 b.g. Lando (GER) – Universelle (USA) (Miswaki (USA)) **h63 §**
[2018/19 h86§: h19.9g⁶ h15.9s h21.4g⁶ h25s Mar 11] rather leggy gelding: poor handicap
hurdler nowadays: left Michael Appleby after second start: stays 25f: acts on heavy going:
often wears headgear/tongue strap: unreliable. *Dai Williams*

LANDSMAN (IRE) 6 b.g. Canford Cliffs (IRE) – Mowaadah (IRE) (Alzao (USA)) **h121**
[2018/19 h15.8d³ h19.8m* h15.8d² h20d h19d³ Apr 24] compact gelding: fairly useful on
Flat, stays 13f: fairly useful hurdler: left A. J. Martin after final start in 2017/18: won
maiden at Musselburgh in February: stays 2½m: acts on good to firm and good to soft
going: wears tongue tie: usually leads. *Tim Vaughan*

L'ANE FOU (IRE) 9 b.m. Robin des Pres (FR) – Katcharto Lady (IRE) (Victory Note **h–**
(USA)) [2018/19 h20.7d^{pu} Feb 17] point winner: pulled up in novice on hurdling debut.
Alex Hales

LANGNESS (IRE) 6 b.g. Milan – Bally Robin (IRE) (Fourstars Allstar (USA)) [2018/19 **h–**
h99: h23.3d^{pu} h24.1g^{pu} Apr 11] has had breathing operation: lightly-raced hurdler, no form
in 2018/19: tried in tongue tie. *Mike Sowersby*

LANTA'S LEGACY 9 ch.m. Central Park (IRE) – Purple Patch (Afzal) [2018/19 c56, h–: **c–**
h22g⁵ c25.8m^{pu} Jun 26] point winner: little form under Rules: wears tongue tie. *Jeremy Scott* **h–**

LANTIERN (IRE) 5 ch.g. Salutino (GER) – Luas Luso (IRE) (Luso) [2018/19 b15.7m⁵ **b99**
b15.7s⁵ ab16g* b15.8g³ Mar 19] €8,000 3-y-o, resold £35,000 3-y-o: has had breathing
operation: sixth foal: half-brother to bumper winner/useful chaser Call It Magic (2½m-23f
winner, by Indian River) and fairly useful 2m hurdle winner/winning pointer Wes Hardin
(by Beneficial): dam (b92) won bumper on only start: fairly useful form in bumpers: won
at Lingfield in February: wears hood. *Harry Whittington*

LAOCH BEAG (IRE) 8 gr.g. King's Theatre (IRE) – Innocentines (FR) (Linamix (FR)) **h82**
[2018/19 h21.7g⁴ Apr 12] poor maiden hurdler: stays 2¾m: acts on good to firm going.
Helen Nelmes

LA PAIMPOLAISE (FR) 7 b.m. Linda's Lad – Medievale (FR) (Lost World (IRE)) **c–**
[2018/19 h21.7g⁴ Sep 9] good-topped mare: fairly useful hurdler at best: disappointing in **h–**
Britain, including on sole start over fences: dead. *Dr Richard Newland*

LAPALALA (IRE) 8 b.m. Oscar (IRE) – Lala Nova (IRE) (Zaffaran (USA)) [2018/19 h–: **h79**
h22.1g⁶ h17.2m⁴ h22.1g⁵ h22.1s h19.7g Oct 16] sturdy mare: poor maiden hurdler
nowadays: should stay further than 2½m: acts on soft going: in cheekpieces last 3 starts.
James Moffatt

LAPFORD LAD 7 ch.g. Arvico (FR) – State of Grace (Generous (IRE)) [2018/19 h64, **h66**
b82: h24gʳᵒ h23.9dᵖᵘ h23.1d h19.5g⁴ Apr 26] poor maiden hurdler: in hood last 3 starts:
tried in tongue tie: often races freely. *Susan Gardner*

LARA TROT (IRE) 7 b.m. Scorpion (IRE) – Honour Own (IRE) (City Honours (USA)) **c–**
[2018/19 h93: h16mᵖᵘ h20.3g c20.3g⁶ h20.5d* Jan 22] modest handicap hurdler: won at **h85 §**
Leicester (conditionals) in January: well beaten in novice handicap on chasing debut: stays
21f: tried in blinkers: temperamental. *Robin Dickin*

LARCH HILL (IRE) 6 ch.g. Presenting – Misty Move (IRE) (Saddlers' Hall (IRE)) **c111**
[2018/19 h–, b–: h16g³ h16.3g⁶ h21.7gᵖᵘ h20.5g⁴ h25.5v h16s* h17g c17.2g* c17.2m³ Apr **h107**
21] rather unfurnished gelding: fair handicap hurdler: won at Warwick in January: similar
form over fences: won novice handicap at Market Rasen in April: stays 2½m: acts on soft
and good to firm going: usually wears hood. *Nigel Twiston-Davies*

LARGY MOUNTAIN (IRE) 5 b.g. Yeats (IRE) – Leith Walk (IRE) (Posidonas) **b82**
[2018/19 b16.2s³ Oct 13] first foal: dam (h107) 2½m/21f hurdle winner: maiden pointer,
placed in 2019: 10/1, third in conditionals/amateurs bumper at Hexham (13½ lengths
behind Mr Scrumpy): will be suited by further than 2m. *Stuart Crawford, Ireland*

LARGY PERK (IRE) 5 b.g. Scorpion (IRE) – Ellens Perk (IRE) (Executive Perk) **b80**
[2018/19 b16s⁵ b17d³ Mar 24] modest form in bumpers: tried in tongue tie. *Stuart
Crawford, Ireland*

LARGY PROSPECT (IRE) 7 b.g. Stowaway – Thrilling Prospect (IRE) (King's Ride) **h111**
[2018/19 h19.5d⁶ h20.5s* h23.3d⁵ Mar 26] £20,000 5-y-o, £1,800 6-y-o: fifth foal: dam
(h102), 2m-23f hurdle winner, out of half-sister to useful staying chaser Gola Cher: Irish
point winner: fair form over hurdles: won novice at Ayr in March: should stay 3m. *Ian
Duncan*

LARKBARROW LAD 6 b.g. Kayf Tara – Follow My Leader (IRE) (Supreme Leader) **h121 §**
[2018/19 b97: b15.7g⁴ h19.6g² h21.6s² h24.6g² h20.3s* Mar 18] well-made gelding: fair **b86**
form in bumpers: fairly useful form over hurdles: won maiden at Southwell in March after
breathing operation: wears tongue tie: temperamental. *Philip Hobbs*

LARKHALL 12 b.g. Saddlers' Hall (IRE) – Larkbarrow (Kahyasi) [2018/19 c77§, h–§: **c65 §**
c19.2d³ c21.4g⁶ c24gᵖᵘ c24g⁴ Jul 15] good-topped gelding: maiden hurdler: poor handicap **h– §**
chaser: stays 3m: acts on firm and good to soft going: tried in headgear/tongue tie: often
races in rear: weak finisher. *Mike Sowersby*

LARRY 6 b.g. Midnight Legend – Gaspaisie (FR) (Beyssac (FR)) [2018/19 h126: c18.8m⁴ **c142**
c19.7gᶠ c20d* c22.7m⁴ c23.4d² c20g⁴ Apr 27] sturdy gelding: fairly useful hurdler: useful **h–**
form over fences: won handicaps at Sandown in January and April (novice, by neck from
Gone Platinum): stays 23f: acts on heavy going: usually tongue tied. *Gary Moore*

LASKADINE (FR) 4 b.f. Martaline – Laskadoun (FR) (Smadoun (FR)) [2018/19 h17.9s* **h123**
h16s* h18.9g⁵ Feb 16] third foal: dam, French 2¼m chase winner, half-sister to useful
French hurdler/chaser up to 21f Laskaline (by Martaline): once-raced on Flat: fairly useful
form over hurdles: won listed newcomers race at Auteuil (by 6 lengths from Statuaire) in
September and juvenile at Warwick in January: disappointed final outing: left G. Cherel
after first start. *Nicky Henderson*

LA SORELITA (FR) 4 gr.f. Martaline – Sary Flight (FR) (Turtle Bowl (IRE)) [2018/19 **h121**
h16.9d* h16.9d³ h16g⁴ h16d³ h16d⁴ h16.4s h17.6g³ Apr 12] first foal: dam, French 2m
hurdle winner, half-sister to fairly useful French hurdler/fair chaser (17f/2¼m winner) Star
Flight: fairly useful hurdler: won newcomers race at Clairefontaine in July: third in
handicap at Ballinrobe in April: left Guillaume Macaire after second start: stays 2¼m: in
tongue tie last 2 starts. *W. P. Mullins, Ireland*

LASSANA ANGEL 5 b.m. High Chaparral (IRE) – Diara Angel (IRE) (Hawk Wing **h103**
(USA)) [2018/19 h15.6g⁶ h15.8d³ h15.7g* h16d⁶ h16.3g⁵ Apr 14] fair maiden on Flat,
stays 1½m: fair form over hurdles: won mares novice at Catterick in January: raced only at
2m: tried in headgear: wears tongue tie. *Tom Gretton*

LAST CHANCE PADDY (USA) 5 gr.g. Paddy O'Prado (USA) – Mizzcan'tbewrong (USA) (Mizzen Mast (USA)) [2018/19 h15.8m Apr 23] modest maiden on Flat, stays 1½m: well beaten in novice on hurdling debut. *Sarah-Jayne Davies* **h–**

LAST ENCHANTMENT (IRE) 4 b.f. Camelot – Illandrane (IRE) (Cape Cross (IRE)) [2018/19 h16.4d⁴ h16d⁵ h16sᶠ Jan 5] leggy filly: has had breathing operation: fairly useful on Flat, stays 1½m: modest form over hurdles. *Neil Mulholland* **h90**

LASTIN' MEMORIES 7 b.g. Overbury (IRE) – Dusky Dante (IRE) (Phardante (FR)) [2018/19 h88: h19.5v⁴ h19.5v h20.6d* h16.4sᶠ h21.4d⁴ h19.3g³ h20.6v² h20.6d⁶ Apr 6] modest handicap hurdler: won at Newcastle in December: stays 21f: acts on heavy going: wears cheekpieces: usually races prominently. *Sandy Forster* **h88**

LASTOFTHECOSMICS 4 b.g. Shirocco (GER) – Cosmic Case (Casteddu) [2018/19 b14g b16.2g⁵ b16.4m⁶ h20.2g⁵ Apr 24] modest form in bumpers: well beaten in maiden on hurdling debut: tried in tongue tie. *Iain Jardine* **h77** **b78**

LAS TUNAS (FR) 7 b.g. Country Reel (USA) – Grey Winner (FR) (Take Risks (FR)) [2018/19 c86, h–: c20.1g² h16.2g⁴ c16.5v³ h16.2g² c16.5sᶠ c16.5s* c16.3s² c15.7d³ c15.2g* c15.2g* h16.2g Apr 25] poor handicap hurdler nowadays: fair handicap chaser: won at Ayr in January, and Wetherby in March and April: stays 2½m: acts on heavy going: wears tongue tie nowadays: usually front runner/races prominently, often travels strongly. *R. Mike Smith* **c111** **h73**

LAST WATCH 6 br.m. Sagamix (FR) – Watcha (USA) (Blushing Stage (USA)) [2018/19 b80: h15.7g⁴ h19.6gᶠ Aug 3] showed a bit on first of 2 starts in bumpers/completed outing over hurdles: should be suited by 2½m. *David Bridgwater* **h81**

LATE AGAIN (IRE) 5 b.m. Presenting – Hannigan's Lodger (IRE) (Be My Native (USA)) [2018/19 b16.5mᵖᵘ b16s⁶ b16.6d h16d h16g h19.1d⁴ h21vᶠ h16g⁵ h19g³ h19.9dᶠ Apr 23] sister to fairly useful hurdler Leave At Dawn (2m-2¾m winner) and fairly useful chaser Present Lodger (2½m winner), stays 3m, and half-sister to 3 winners: dam (c129/h107) 17f-2½m hurdle/chase winner: poor bumper performer: fair maiden hurdler: should stay further than 19f: acts on heavy going. *Charles Byrnes, Ireland* **h104** **b72**

LATE DATE (IRE) 8 b.g. Oscar (IRE) – Regents Ballerina (IRE) (Commanche Run) [2018/19 h98: c24.2gᵖᵘ c26.3s* c24.2vᵖᵘ c26.3s⁴ c26.3s* c30.6dᵖᵘ Apr 26] winning hurdler: fair form over fences: won handicaps at Sedgefield in December and March (3 ran): should stay further than 3¼m: acts on soft going: front runner/races prominently. *Micky Hammond* **c102** **h–**

LATE NIGHT LILY 8 b.m. Midnight Legend – Ready To Crown (USA) (More Than Ready (USA)) [2018/19 h124: h16.3d h16.3d⁶ h20.3g Apr 10] fairly useful handicap hurdler, below form in 2018/19 after long lay-off: stays 2½m: acts on good to firm and heavy going. *Dan Skelton* **h107**

LATE ROMANTIC (IRE) 9 b.g. Mahler – Mere Gaye (IRE) (Gildoran) [2018/19 h113: c23.4d² c27.6s³ c24.2d⁵ c24v² Mar 16] sturdy gelding: multiple point winner: maiden hurdler: fairly useful form in chases: second in novice handicap at Newcastle in December: probably stays 3½m: acts on heavy going: wears tongue tie: usually front runner/races prominently. *Oliver Greenall* **c123** **h–**

LATE SHIPMENT 8 b.g. Authorized (IRE) – Time Over (Mark of Esteem (IRE)) [2018/19 h111: h23.6s⁶ h25.5v⁶ h25.5d h23.6d* h26.4g⁵ Apr 14] sturdy gelding: fair handicap hurdler: won at Chepstow in March: stays 3¼m: acts on heavy going: wears cheekpieces: temperamental. *Nikki Evans* **h104 §**

L'ATTENDUE (IRE) 5 br.m. Oscar (IRE) – Triptoshan (IRE) (Anshan) [2018/19 h62: h19m h16g h19.5ᵖᵘ h19.9s* h20.6d Apr 6] poor maiden hurdler: won mares event at Sedgefield in March: will stay further than 2½m: acts on soft going. *Philip Kirby* **h78**

L'ATTESA (IRE) 10 b.g. Kalanisi (IRE) – Tara Brooch (IRE) (Supreme Leader) [2018/19 c16.3m h23gᵖᵘ h16.8m h17.7vᵖᵘ h19gᵖᵘ Feb 19] winning hurdler/maiden chaser, no form in 2018/19: wears headgear: tried in tongue tie. *Mark Gillard* **c–** **h–**

L'AUBERGE DU BOIS (IRE) 7 br.g. Olden Times – Midway (IRE) (Warcraft (USA)) [2018/19 h98, b75: h22g⁶ Oct 20] modest form on first of 3 starts over hurdles: dead. *Jeremy Scott* **h–**

LAUGHARNE 8 b.g. Authorized (IRE) – Corsican Sunset (USA) (Thunder Gulch (USA)) [2018/19 h113: h24g* h23.6s³ c26gᵖᵘ Jan 9] rather leggy gelding: fairly useful handicap hurdler: won at Southwell in May: pulled up in novice handicap on chasing debut: stays 3m: acts on good to firm and heavy going. *Tim Vaughan* **c–** **h116**

LAUGHING LUIS 5 b.g. Authorized (IRE) – Leitzu (IRE) (Barathea (IRE)) [2018/19 **h118** b82: b16g* b16.3g* h16g⁴ h16g h15.5g* h20.5d⁵ h16.3d* h16.8g Apr 17] sturdy gelding: **b101** fairly useful form in bumpers: won at Worcester and Stratford in August: fairly useful form over hurdles: won novice at Leicester in December and novice handicap at Newbury in March: should stay beyond 2m: acts on good to soft going. *Nicky Henderson*

LAUGHING MUSKETEER (IRE) 8 b.g. Azamour (IRE) – Sweet Clover (Rainbow **c–** Quest (USA)) [2018/19 h–: h16g c15.7gᵖᵘ Jul 15] little sign of ability in various events: **h–** dead. *Tracey Barfoot-Saunt*

LAURINA (FR) 6 b.m. Spanish Moon (USA) – Lamboghina (GER) (Alkalde (GER)) **h154** [2018/19 h150p: h19.8s* h20.2d* h16.4s⁴ Mar 12] tall, lengthy mare: smart hurdler: extended winning run in listed mares events at Sandown (2 ran) in January and Punchestown (beating Stormy Ireland by 6 lengths) in February: well-backed 5/2, below expectations when 16¾ lengths fourth of 10 to Espoir d'Allen in Champion Hurdle at Cheltenham, every chance when mistake 3 out: stays 2½m: acts on heavy going. *W. P. Mullins, Ireland*

LAURIUM 9 ch.g. Gold Away (IRE) – Silver Peak (FR) (Sillery (USA)) [2018/19 c–, h–: **c141 §** h22.8gᵖᵘ c25.5g* c25gᵖᵘ h21gᵖᵘ Nov 12] sturdy gelding: has had breathing operation: useful **h– §** hurdler at best: useful handicap chaser: won at Warwick (by 1¾ lengths from Pickamix) in September, only completed start under Rules in 2018/19: won all 3 outings in points later in season: stays 25f: acts on soft and good to firm going: unreliable. *Nicky Henderson*

LAWMAKING 6 b.g. Zamindar (USA) – Canada Water (Dansili) [2018/19 h15.8dᵖᵘ May **h–** 26] fairly useful on Flat, stays 1¼m: pulled up in novice on hurdling debut. *Michael Scudamore*

LAWTOP LEGEND (IRE) 7 b.g. Milan – Nolagh Supreme (IRE) (Supreme Leader) **h84** [2018/19 h–, b–: h23.3g² h20.2g h23.3g⁴ h23.3g² h23.3g* h25.3g⁴ h23.3s⁵ Dec 12] sturdy gelding: poor handicap hurdler: won at Hexham in November: stays 23f: best form on good going: tried in cheekpieces. *George Bewley*

LAWYERSGUNSN'MONEY 4 gr.g. Indian Haven – Non Disclosure (IRE) (Clodovil **b–** (IRE)) [2018/19 b13.7d Jan 25] well beaten in bumper: modest form on Flat. *Roger Teal*

LAXEY (IRE) 5 b.g. Yeats (IRE) – Nerissa (IRE) (Great Palm (USA)) [2018/19 b16.2s⁵ **h111 p** b15.7s⁴ h15.8d⁵ h16s⁴ h16g² Apr 10] £42,000 3-y-o: tall gelding: will make a chaser: sixth **b78** foal: half-brother to bumper winner Pectora (by Kalanisi): dam unraced half-sister to smart 2m hurdler Spirit Leader, herself dam of high-class staying hurdler Prince of Scars and smart staying chaser Folsom Blue: modest form in bumpers: fair form over hurdles: best effort when second in novice at Warwick: will be suited by 2½m+: open to further improvement. *Henry Daly*

LAYERTHORPE (IRE) 7 b.g. Vale of York (IRE) – Strobinia (IRE) (Soviet Star (USA)) **h80** [2018/19 h20m² Jun 21] poor maiden hurdler nowadays, off 21 months before only outing in 2018/19: stays 2½m: acts on good to firm going: tried in headgear/tongue tie. *Debra Hamer*

LAZARUS (IRE) 5 b.g. Zoffany (IRE) – Knysna (IRE) (Rock of Gibraltar (IRE)) **h113** [2018/19 h94: h15.7gᵘʳ h15.7g⁴ h15.8g* h20g² h15.5d⁶ h16.6g² h16d⁵ h16m⁶ Apr 22] has had breathing operation: fair hurdler: won claimer at Huntingdon in November: stays 2½m: best form on good going: wears tongue tie. *Amy Murphy*

L'CHAMISE 6 b.m. Apple Tree (FR) – Colline de Fleurs (Alflora (IRE)) [2018/19 b88: **h114** h20.6g* h19g³ h19.9d* Feb 25] won point on debut: fair form over hurdles: won mares novices at Market Rasen in October and Uttoxeter in February: stayed 21f: dead. *Jack R. Barber*

LEADER OF THE LAND (IRE) 12 ch.g. Halling (USA) – Cheerleader (Singspiel **h75** (IRE)) [2018/19 h20g h16.3g⁴ Aug 23] fair 17f hurdle winner: shaped as if retaining some ability on second of 2 starts (tongue tied) after 5-year absence. *Robert Stephens*

LEADER WRITER (FR) 8 b.h. Pivotal – Miss Emma May (FR) (Hawk Wing (USA)) **h89** [2018/19 h15.8s⁵ h16gᵖᵘ h16dᵖᵘ Jan 28] useful at one time on Flat, stays 1m: modest form on completed start over hurdles: has joined David Elsworth. *Henry Spiller*

LEAGUE OF HIS OWN (IRE) 10 ch.g. Beneficial – Miss Eastwood (IRE) (Commanche **c–** Run) [2018/19 c16.5gᵖᵘ c17.2gᵖᵘ Jul 8] lengthy gelding: of little account outside points: has **h–** worn hood: wears tongue tie. *Tim Vaughan*

LEANNES LADY (IRE) 7 b.m. Ask – Wizzy (IRE) (Presenting) [2018/19 h17.2g **h–** h19.7gᵖᵘ Apr 11] second foal: half-sister to fairly useful hurdler/fair chaser Mr Mafia (19f-3¼m winner, by Zerpour): dam unraced: of no account. *Alan Berry*

LEAPAWAY (IRE) 7 b.g. Stowaway – Gisela (IRE) (King Charlemagne (USA)) [2018/19 **h127** h98: h16m³ h15.8g³ h16g* h17.2m* h16.3m* h16.8g* h18.5g* h16m³ h15.9g³ Apr 21] lengthy gelding: fairly useful hurdler: completed 5-timer in first half of season in handicaps at Worcester and Cartmel, and novices at Stratford and Newton Abbot (2): stays 2¼m: acts on good to firm going. *Philip Hobbs*

LEAPT 5 b.g. Nathaniel (IRE) – Liel (Pivotal) [2018/19 h16.7g³ h15.7g* h16.7g³ h18.7g⁵ **h100** Aug 23] fair maiden on Flat, stays 1¾m: fair form over hurdles: won novice at Southwell in June. *Graeme McPherson*

LEATHER BELLY 6 ch.g. Phoenix Reach (IRE) – Gertrude Webb (Central Park (IRE)) **b87** [2018/19 b16g² b15.6gˢᵘ Dec 31] fair form when second at Ayr on completed start in bumpers: dead. *Rebecca Menzies*

LEAVE MY ALONE (IRE) 6 br.m. Getaway (GER) – Glenda King (IRE) (King's Theatre **h95** (IRE)) [2018/19 h15.3s⁶ h16d⁴ Mar 21] £20,000 6-y-o: second foal: dam, winning pointer, out of half-sister to high-class 2m hurdler Colonel Yeager: winning Irish pointer: modest form over hurdles: better effort when fourth in mares novice at Chepstow. *Richenda Ford*

LEAVING HOME (IRE) 6 b.g. Getaway (GER) – Snuff (FR) (Al Nasr (FR)) [2018/19 **h–** b15.8d b16.3m* b16.2s h15.8v h19.8sᵖᵘ Mar 7] half-brother to French hurdler/chaser **b90** Thury (2m-21f winner, by Turgeon): dam, maiden on Flat, half-sister to useful French chaser (stayed 27f) Turgot: fair form in bumpers: won conditionals/amateurs event at Stratford in July: no show over hurdles: tried in hood. *Peter Bowen*

LE BACARDY (FR) 13 b.g. Bahhare (USA) – La Balagna (Kris) [2018/19 c–§, h–§: **c– §** c17.8gᵘʳ May 17] rangy gelding: point winner: winning hurdler: useful chaser at best, no **h– §** form in hunters: stays 2½m: acts on heavy going: usually wears headgear nowadays: tried in tongue tie: usually races nearer last than first: temperamental. *A. Gardner*

LE BOIZELO (FR) 8 b.g. Irish Wells (FR) – Bois Tendre (FR) (Murmure (FR)) [2018/19 **c128** c125, h–: c23.8g^F c19.2v³ c24.2d² c23sᵖᵘ c30.7d c22.4d⁶ Mar 22] strong gelding: winning **h–** hurdler: fairly useful handicap chaser: second at Exeter in January: stays 3m: acts on heavy going: temperament under suspicion. *Robert Walford*

LE BRAYE (IRE) 7 b.g. Court Cave (IRE) – Salsaparilla (FR) (Lost World (IRE)) **c–** [2018/19 c–, h104: h24gᵖᵘ h24m³ h24.8g⁶ h22m c25.2d^F h23.9g⁶ Apr 24] workmanlike **h101** gelding: point winner: fair handicap hurdler: lightly-raced chaser: stays 3m: acts on soft and good to firm going: wears tongue tie. *Gavin Patrick Cromwell, Ireland*

LE BREUIL (FR) 7 ch.g. Anzillero (GER) – Slew Dancer (Fabulous Dancer (USA)) **c147** [2018/19 h140: c19.9g* c20.2g² c23.4s³ c20.6d² c19.9d⁴ c31.7s* Mar 12] **h–**

The climate of opinion in racing's corridors of power seems currently to be influenced as much by the perceived views of a wider public, as by the opinions held by the majority of racing's own followers. As a result, when it comes to horse welfare issues, in particular, the sport's regulator the British Horseracing Authority cannot see a nut these days without reaching for the sledgehammer. The storm in a teacup over the wholesale shutdown of racing in February, following the emergence of a handful of cases of equine influenza, was very much of the BHA's own making (more on the subject appears in the essay on Al Dancer). The initial action was driven by welfare issues—'The welfare of our horses is paramount, above all economics,' was the BHA's justification—and the precipitate halting of racing came amid something of a general crisis of confidence within the sport in those responsible for regulating it. The spectre of outside interference in racing, which came to a head when a debate on the sport in Parliament the previous autumn considered setting up an independent body for horse welfare, seemed to alarm the BHA, as did remarks from the floor of the House about elements of racing being 'undoubtedly incredibly cruel' and the use of the whip being 'barbaric'. The BHA responded by creating its own Welfare Board, with an independent chairman, to steer racing on a course aimed at making it more acceptable 'in the modern world'. The fining of trainer Henry Oliver for waving his arms behind the moody Burrenbridge Hotel to encourage him to take part in a race at Uttoxeter in February was a minor incident in itself, but the BHA was ridiculed by the sport's professionals when it defended the actions of the race stewards (in applying a dubious rule) in a statement which referred to horses racing of their own 'free will' ('We do not force horses to race'), suggesting that even the act of cajoling a horse into action was a welfare issue. The BHA quickly backtracked on its laughable assertion but its original statement illustrated that 'welfare' was right at the top of the agenda.

The approach of the Cheltenham Festival coincided with a warning that, if a spate of whip offences occurred over the four days, racing's ruling body would be toughening the penalties for jockeys ('Jockeys will be reminded of their responsibilities'). A raft of measures had already been announced as a result of a drawn-out BHA review into the 2018 Festival, which had taken the best part of eight months to report. The review went beyond the examination of the seven equine deaths (that of Melrose Boy a sad subsequent addition as a result of complications from surgery following an injury sustained at the Festival). The review concluded— as Cheltenham's management had already done—that no single factor was 'definitely responsible' for the seven deaths, but it examined all races run at the Festival since 2007 and decided that all runners should in future be trotted up and examined by Cheltenham's vets on raceday, with their medical records, covering the weeks up to the Festival, being submitted ten days before the meeting (this resulted in a number of horses reportedly being pulled out before the final declaration stage and two horses trained by Gary Moore being ruled out after veterinary concerns on the day).

The BHA, indicating a move towards more direct data-driven management of the sport, announced it would be undertaking analysis of faller rates at Cheltenham by each trainer and jockey with a view to 'engaging' with those whose average is significantly higher than the norm. There was to be a major research project to 'develop a predictive model for identifying risk factors for all jump racing, including horse history and performance, rider and training factors.' As for the Festival itself, the safety limit for all two-mile chases was reduced from twenty-four to twenty (three of the fatalities had been in the Grand Annual) and riding allowances were dropped from the conditions of the conditional jockeys handicap hurdle to encourage the use of more experienced riders. The BHA report had a warning for amateur riders at the Festival to be 'aware that they are subject to particular public scrutiny', with the four-mile National Hunt Chase (for novices ridden by amateurs), in which Mossback had been one of the previous Festival's fatalities, singled out as one of the races with the highest rate of fallers (one in eight of the runners having fallen or been brought down in the period under review).

High-class jumps racing in testing conditions had been something of a rarity in the dry conditions that prevailed for most of the latest season and the soft ground on the opening day of the Cheltenham Festival meant that the National Hunt Chase turned into a particularly gruelling contest. The BHA's remarks beforehand, putting amateur riders on notice about their Festival participation, led some commentators to ponder whether the furore that broke out after the National Hunt Chase had been part of a planned agenda to make an example of some of the riders if the race turned into a fiasco. As part of a rejig of the order of some of the races at the meeting, the National Hunt Chase was moved from the second last race on the first day to the final race (the Grand Annual changed places with the conditional jockeys handicap on the final day so it was not the last race, which some thought had been a factor in the fatalities). Moving the National Hunt Chase meant that it was no longer on free-to-air TV and therefore less likely to attract so much attention if there was carnage. However, after the stewards had handed suspensions to three of the riders for 'continuing to ride when it appeared to be contrary to the horse's welfare', one of the trio being punished for excessive use of the whip as well, the BHA saw fit to issue its own statement saying it was 'extremely disappointed by the conduct of a small number of riders in the National Hunt Chase…amateur participation in its current form at future Festivals will be under material threat.'

The BHA's statement, open to being interpreted as an apology on behalf of the whole sport, ensured that plenty of attention was given in the media to the National Hunt Chase (in which the favourite Ballyward was a fatality and the race finished with screens up at three fences where horses were still on the ground). The ammunition that the race itself, and the BHA's statement, gave to racing's enemies was priceless for them and must put the future of the National Hunt Chase in doubt. Often referred to as 'the four-miler', the race will have its distance tinkered with—

reduced by two furlongs—in 2020, following a review of the latest running, with other changes meaning that runners must have a BHA mark of at least 120 (as for the Grade 1 novice chases), have run in two novice chases and finished in the first four over fences in a race of two miles seven and a half furlongs or further. Runners must have had at least one outing over fences in the current season and riders must have taken part in a minimum of twenty races under Rules and ridden five winners. Reducing the distance of the National Hunt Chase will mean a shorter run to what will be the first fence, which will be followed quickly by a left-handed downhill turn which worries some of the leading amateurs (Mr Patrick Mullins, Mr Jamie Codd and Mr Derek O'Connor asked to be involved in the 'review and consultation' process but say they were not invited by the BHA to make a submission). The National Hunt Chase survived more or less intact from a similar review after the runnings in 2006 (three fatalities) and 2007 (another fatality), but some changes—even if largely cosmetic—were surely needed if it was to continue after the latest running, with the BHA clearly wrong to lay the blame solely at the feet of the amateur riders. It should be said that, despite raising question marks over the race in its own earlier review, the BHA still sanctioned an event which is an extreme test for novices even in normal conditions. Two of the runners, Impulsive Star and rank outsider Clondaw Cian (whose rider eventually became a fourth to be interviewed by the Cheltenham stewards), had run in the previous year's National Hunt Chase, in which there had been six finishers on soft ground in addition to the fatal accident to Mossback and a six-day ban for the winning rider for overuse of the whip. A third runner in the latest edition, Just Your Type, had finished sixth in the Eider Chase at Newcastle last time, but four miles was unknown territory for the rest in the National Hunt Chase field (a number of the runners in the latest edition had not finished in the first four in a chase of two miles seven and a half furlongs or further).

The quality of the runners in the National Hunt Chase has improved significantly since the race was opened to winning hurdlers seventeen years ago (it was formerly for horses who had not won a race of any description before the current season, except for certain types of hunter chases). An increase in prize money also helped and the National Hunt Chase has been largely on an upward curve since, being upgraded to listed status in 2014 and then promoted to Grade 2 in 2017 (unique for a race for amateur jockeys). Defenders of the race—one of five at the Festival for novice chasers—will point to the number of subsequent high profile winners of big staying handicaps that have come from those who have won it or featured prominently. They include winners of the Irish, Scottish and Welsh Nationals, as well as of the Grand National itself (Tiger Roll the most recent example), while the first two in 2016, the six-year-olds Minella Rocco and Native River, finished second and third in the 2017 Gold Cup, with Native River going on to win the blue riband event in 2018. In terms of the quality of runners alone, it can no longer be said—as it used to be—that the National Hunt Chase is not really worth its place at the Festival, but it could be argued that reducing the number of chases restricted to novices from five to four would be no bad thing, given that the RSA Chase, the traditional 'novices' Gold Cup', could only benefit from the scrapping of the National Hunt Chase in its present form. One of the existing twenty-eight races at the Festival is due to be axed to make way for a new Grade 2 mares chase in 2021 and, although any one of half a dozen of the races at the Festival could be removed without too much concern, the National Hunt Chase would appear to be a prime candidate given the bloated novice programme at the meeting and the race's high rate of fallers (a further review is pencilled in for after the 2022 running but could be brought forward). The novices handicap chase, sponsored by Close Brothers, seems the favourite to go at the time of writing.

Whatever the long-term future for the Festival's most historic race (first run in 1860), there is no doubt that the latest renewal of the National Hunt Chase will go down as one of the most controversial. Only four completed, and there were twice as many fallers as finishers, but the BHA's intervention and the Cheltenham stewards' suspensions provoked an angry reaction. Sir Anthony McCoy was furious on the following day's ITV broadcast from Cheltenham, saying the publicity was an embarrassment. 'Talk about bringing racing into disrepute, I have never seen as bad a decision in twenty-five years in racing.' The suspensions meted out to the riders of Just Your Type and Mulcahy's Hill, both of whom fell late on, were less contentious than the ten days given to Mr Declan Lavery on third-placed Jerrysback. Mr Robert James was suspended for twenty days for persevering 'contrary to the horse's welfare' and seven days for hitting Just Your Type when the horse was showing no response, Mr Noel McParlan receiving eight days for continuing on Mulcahy's Hill 'contrary to the horse's welfare', although, in both cases, the veterinary officer told the stewards that an examination of their mounts had not revealed any abnormalities. The fourth rider interviewed by the stewards, Mr Damien Skehan, who finished fourth on Clondaw Cian, a length behind Jerrysback, was absolved at a hearing two days after the race. The stewards accepted his explanation that his mount's welfare had not been compromised and that the reason he had got so far behind was as a result of significant ground and momentum lost when Clondaw Cian was hampered by fallers at the seventeenth fence; his mount had also been inconvenienced by fallers at the second last and at the final fence, and it was claimed that the horse's concentration had been affected because he had lost one of his cheekpieces.

The first intimation that Mr Lavery intended to lodge an appeal against his suspension came when the BHA's chief executive Nick Rust told the Racing TV programme *Luck On Sunday* that he could not comment on the ride because it was the subject of an appeal. That said, when the programme showed the closing stages and the host pointed out to viewers that Jerrysback was 'tired', Rust interjected to say the horse was '*very* tired'. Whether it was 'tired' or '*very* tired', of course, should have occasioned no surprise given that it was at the end of a four-mile steeplechase in the mud. What was apparent from the video was that Mr Lavery had used his whip considerably less than the riders of the three other finishers (including Mr Skehan who had been found not in breach of the rules) and, in fact, Mr Lavery had merely pushed out his horse with hands and heels after he had jumped the last better than the second last. Jerrysback's trainer Philip Hobbs, who was also on the TV programme,

National Hunt Challenge Cup Amateur Riders' Novices' Chase, Cheltenham—
Le Breuil and Discorama (left) fight it out at the end of a gruelling race;
Jerrysback (hoops/partly hidden) is a controversial remote third

reported that no veterinary officer had asked to see Jerrysback after the race and added that the horse had been fine the next day. The obvious justification for the rider of Jerrysback was that he was doing his very best, within the rules, to comply with the requirement to 'obtain the best possible placing'. What would the reaction have been if he had pulled up Jerrysback after jumping badly right two out and the first two had then fallen at the last? The BHA is drawing a very fine line between the integrity of competition and the interests of horse welfare, a line that put Mr Lavery in an almost impossible position in the circumstances in which he found himself. Jerrysback finished forty-seven lengths behind the runner-up Discorama, securing just over £13,000 in prize money for the horse's connections and ensuring that each-way backers of the 16/1-shot got paid out. Justice prevailed when Mr Lavery won his appeal.

The damage was already done, however, to the BHA which continued to face a barrage of criticism from within the sport for days afterwards, one letter to the *Racing Post* from Henrietta Knight, Mick Channon and Charles Egerton labelling Nick Rust as 'clearly not qualified for his role…unable to grasp the relevant welfare issues facing racing…including a horse population which is staffed inadequately, racecourses over-racing and racing on false watered ground, and trainers with unsustainable businesses being granted licences.' There had been an earlier fallout with trainers over a regulation introduced without consultation on February 1st (quickly returned to the pending tray) that all runners in jumps races must be fully shod; a few runners currently do not wear hind shoes in case they overreach and cause tendon and foreleg injuries. Some trainers were not happy with the extra regulations introduced for the Cheltenham Festival either, arguing that trainers had already passed suitability tests when they were licenced by the BHA whose policies and actions were themselves contributing to the misguided impression that racing has a welfare problem. It was undermining trainers to give veterinary surgeons the final say on whether a horse is fit to run or not, especially when such veterinary opinion—and it can only be 'opinion'—is based on a cursory trot-up before racing and a brief examination of a horse's medical records (the trainer is more likely to be the better judge as he is with the horse every day). Nick Rust stood his ground on *Luck On Sunday*, saying 'I'm looking at the lessons of history—hunting, coursing, circuses—it's all changing and they didn't move with public opinion. I don't want us to appease the so-called antis, but just look at the draft manifestos of the political parties [Labour is committed to an independent review of whip use in the sport]. I want us to stay ahead of it by robustly arguing that we're doing all we can as a sport to manage avoidable risk…the sport needs to wake up a little bit to this.' The 'Twitter storm' is a phenomenon of modern life, influential to such a degree that authority ignores the power of social media at its peril. To that extent, Nick Rust deserves credit for trying to make sure that racing stays ahead of the curve. The racing professional may be much better informed than the average keyboard warrior but the world is more conditioned to treating all opinions as equal these days, something recognised by Nick Rust.

Nick Rust's critics might point out, on the other hand, that a record 266,779 paid to go to the latest Cheltenham Festival (where there wasn't a protester in sight) and such an attendance reflects the strength of public support for jump racing more accurately than the simmering discontent of an unrepresentative anti-racing faction, whose campaign eventually made its way to Parliament through a petition with over 100,000 signatures. If Parliament pursues the idea that there can be some utopian solution for racing that eliminates risks, it will only find, like racing itself has found, that it cannot legislate for everything! Jump racing is a challenging sport but it is a multi-million-pound operation which brings with it so many economic benefits, especially in terms of employment, as well as providing entertainment for millions.

To return to the National Hunt Chase, the winner Le Breuil had already shown form in graded company over fences, quickly progressing from a useful handicap hurdler into an even better chaser, beating his sole opponent in a novice event at Huntingdon on his reappearance in November before being placed in the Steel Plate & Sections Novices' Chase at Cheltenham later the same month and the Grade 2 John Francome Novices' at Newbury's Ladbrokes Trophy meeting. Another solid performance followed in the Ryman Novices' Chase back at Cheltenham, where Le Breuil looked a stout stayer when second to Drovers Lane. On his final run before the National Hunt Chase, Le Breuil managed only a below-form fourth of five (with Jerrysback second) in the Grade 2 Altcar Novices' Chase at Haydock, again performing as if he needed the emphasis more on stamina, staying on again after being headed four out when trying to make all.

Le Breuil relished the markedly increased emphasis on stamina at Cheltenham, starting at 14/1 under top Irish amateur Mr Jamie Codd and showing improved form when rallying for a half-length win over Discorama, who headed Le Breuil at the last and kept on well. Apart from the two other finishers, whose performances have already been covered, second favourite Ok Corral was never in the hunt, while his well fancied stablemate Chef des Obeaux had his chance ruined by some shoddy jumping and trouble in running. Le Breuil was a second Cheltenham Festival winner for his trainer who won the 2017 Baring Bingham with Willoughby Court who sadly had to be put down in January following surgery on a sesamoid bone. Willoughby Court had been a first Cheltenham Festival winner for Paul and Clare Rooney who also became embroiled in the Cheltenham controversy in the latest season when instructing their trainers not to enter horses at the course because of safety concerns (a decision later rescinded after talks with the track's management). The Rooneys owned the ill-fated Melrose Boy and had also lost Starchitect who sustained a fatal injury on the flat when about to win the 2017 Caspian Caviar Gold Cup. Le Breuil wasn't seen out again after Cheltenham but the runner-up Discorama did his bit to uphold the form when finishing runner-up to the impressive Delta Work in the three-mile Champion Novices' Chase at the Punchestown Festival.

Le Breuil (FR) (ch.g. 2012)	Anzillero (GER) (b 1997)	Law Society (br 1982)	Alleged / Bold Bikini
		Anzille (b 1986)	Plugged Nickle / Allegretta
	Slew Dancer (ch 1992)	Fabulous Dancer (b 1976)	Northern Dancer / Last of The Line
		Slew of Fortune (b 1984)	Seattle Slew / Whydidju

Mrs Emma Palmer's "Le Breuil"

The good-topped Le Breuil is by the German mile and a half Group 1 winner Anzillero, whose dam is a half-sister to Urban Sea, the dam of Galileo and Sea The Stars. Unlike his illustrious relatives, Anzillero has spent his career covering mostly non-thoroughbred mares in France. Le Breuil's dam Slew Dancer, a maiden on the Flat, is a half-sister to Slew Man who was claimed off the Flat in France and became a fairly useful two-mile hurdler for Martin Pipe, and later a prolific winner in points. Le Breuil is a brother to Belenien, a French hurdler/chaser who won at up to two and a half miles. Slew Dancer has also bred three winners on the Flat, the best of them Belfortain (by Riche Mare), a mile and a half listed winner at Longchamp. The sound-jumping Le Breuil usually makes the running or races prominently. He stays four miles, acts on heavy going and should have a future in good long-distance handicap chases. He has been tried in cheekpieces. *Ben Pauling*

LE CAMELEON 4 b.g. Great Pretender (IRE) – Countess Camilla (Bob's Return (IRE)) **b87**
[2018/19 b16.3d⁶ Mar 2] good-topped gelding: half-brother to several winners, including useful hurdler/chaser Horatio Hornblower (2m-3m winner, by Presenting) and bumper winner/fairly useful hurdler Moonlighter (19f winner, by Midnight Legend): dam (h116), bumper/2m-2¾m hurdle winner, half-sister to very smart chaser (stayed 3m) Our Ben: 6/1, sixth in bumper at Newbury (8¼ lengths behind McFabulous). *Nick Williams*

LE CAPRICIEUX (FR) 8 b.g. Alberto Giacometti (IRE) – Eria Flore (FR) (Hero's **c108**
Honor (USA)) [2018/19 h104: c16s⁴ c19.9d³ c19.7d³ c17.8v* c17s⁴ c19.7dᵖᵘ Mar 18] **h–**
close-coupled gelding: fair hurdler: similar form over fences: won handicap at Fontwell in February: stays 2½m: acts on heavy going. *Gary Moore*

LECHLADE MAGICIAN (IRE) 6 b.g. Getaway (GER) – Run Supreme (IRE) **h–**
(Supreme Leader) [2018/19 b101: h15.8v Nov 11] good-topped gelding: poor mover in slower paces: won bumper on debut: well beaten since, including in novice hurdle when tongue tied. *Anthony Honeyball*

LE COEUR NET (FR) 7 ch.g. Network (GER) – Silverwood (FR) (Garde Royale) **c112**
[2018/19 c105, h91: c16v* c17.8v⁵ c17.8v³ Mar 16] maiden hurdler: fair handicap chaser: **h–**
won at Ffos Las in November: best form up to 2¼m: acts on heavy going: tried in hood: usually wears tongue tie: usually races off pace. *Anthony Honeyball*

LE CURIEUX (FR) 7 br.g. Lauro (GER) – La Curieuse (FR) (Robin des Champs (FR)) **c98**
[2018/19 c109, h–: c20g⁴ c20.9g⁵ c16.5g⁶ Jun 11] compact gelding: winning hurdler: **h–**
modest maiden chaser: stays 2½m: acts on soft going: in cheekpieces last 2 starts: tried in tongue tie. *Brendan Powell*

LE DAUPHIN (IRE) 8 b.g. Robin des Champs (FR) – Miss Denman (IRE) (Presenting) **c–**
[2018/19 h104: h25gᵘʳ c20.1gᶠ Aug 18] good-topped gelding: fairly useful hurdler at best: **h–**
struggling when fell fatally on chasing debut: left Nicky Henderson after first start: stayed 21f: acted on good to firm going. *Andrew Hamilton*

LE DRAPEAU (FR) 7 ch.g. Satri (IRE) – La Bandera (Bahhare (USA)) [2018/19 h105: **c98**
h20d c24.2g c21.3d³ c24.2s² c26.2g⁶ Feb 24] fair maiden hurdler: modest form over **h86**
fences: stays 3m: best form on soft/heavy going. *Sue Smith*

LEE SIDE LADY (IRE) 9 ch.m. Mountain High (IRE) – Vicante (IRE) (Old Vic) **c91**
[2018/19 c65, h106: c21.6g⁵ c26g³ c24g⁴ h21.6v⁴ h21.6s h21.7v³ h20.5d³ h21.7s³ h20.5g **h93**
h21.4g² Mar 25] smallish, close-coupled mare: winning pointer: modest handicap hurdler: similar form in chases: stays 3¼m: acts on good to firm and heavy going: wears cheekpieces nowadays: signs of temperament. *Neil Mulholland*

LE FOU ROYAL (FR) 8 b.g. Le Fou (IRE) – Kalon Ced'a (FR) (Grand Tresor (FR)) **c–**
[2018/19 c21.6g May 17] winning pointer: well held in maiden hunter on chasing debut (tongue tied). *Mrs B. Ansell*

LE FRANK (IRE) 7 b.g. King's Theatre (IRE) – Dream Lass (IRE) (Bob Back (USA)) **c108**
[2018/19 h91: c20.1s⁴ c15.6s* c16.3sᶠ c16.9s⁵ c17.1dᵘʳ Apr 8] has had breathing operation: **h–**
maiden hurdler: fair form over fences: won novice handicap at Hexham in November: best effort at 2m: acts on soft going: wears tongue tie: usually front runner/races prominently. *Lucinda Russell*

LEFT BACK (IRE) 7 b.g. Oscar (IRE) – Baldrica (FR) (Lost World (IRE)) [2018/19 h–: **c67 x**
c21.6d⁶ c23.8g⁶ c24.1s⁵ c24.1dᶠ c21.6d³ c21.6d Apr 8] little show over hurdles: poor form **h–**
over fences: has worn hood: wears tongue tie: sketchy jumper. *N. W. Alexander*

LEGAL EYES (IRE) 6 br.g. Court Cave (IRE) – Grass Tips (IRE) (Bob Back (USA))   **h120**
[2018/19 b98: h19.9g³ h19.6d h20.5d⁵ h23d² Apr 26] tall gelding: has had breathing
operation: fairly useful form over hurdles: improved when second in handicap at Bangor:
will stay 3m. *Ben Pauling*

LEGAL HISTORY (IRE) 4 b.g. Lawman (FR) – Nina Celebre (IRE) (Peintre Celebre   **h122**
(USA)) [2018/19 h3.3d³ h16.5g⁴ h16.6d² h18.8d² h15.7m* h16.8d* h15.9g² Apr 21]
compact gelding: fairly useful maiden on Flat, stays 1½m: fairly useful handicap hurdler:
won at Ascot (juvenile) in March and Exeter in April: stays 19f: acts on good to firm and
good to soft going: in headgear last 5 starts: usually travels strongly. *David Pipe*

LEGALIZED 5 br.m. Authorized (IRE) – Laurena (GER) (Acatenango (GER)) [2018/19   **h120**
h16.4g⁵ h15.7g⁴ h19.3g² h19.9v* h19.9s² h19.9v* h20.5mᵇᵈ Apr 13] modest maiden on
Flat, stays 2m: fairly useful hurdler: won maiden novices at Sedgefield in January and March:
stays 2½m: acts on heavy going: has worn hood: often travels strongly. *Dianne Sayer*

LE GAVROCHE (IRE) 6 b.g. Flemensfirth (USA) – Knockieran (IRE) (Oscar (IRE))   **h76**
[2018/19 h–, b–: h16.4d h20.6d⁶ Dec 13] poor form over hurdles: usually races towards
rear. *Rose Dobbin*

LEGEND LADY 8 b.m. Midnight Legend – Aoninch (Inchinor) [2018/19 h–: h19.5sᵖᵘ   **c–**
c17.5dᵘʳ h18.5d⁴ h16.5d⁵ Mar 11] fair handicap hurdler: unseated fourth on chasing debut: **h95**
should stay further than 2m: acts on soft going: in hood last 2 starts: usually races off pace.
Jackie du Plessis

LEGEND OF FRANCE 6 ch.m. Flying Legend (USA) – Bonne Anniversaire (Alflora   **h94**
(IRE)) [2018/19 h84, b77: h16gᵖᵘ h16m h15.9s* h15.9s³ h16d⁴ h16s⁵ Feb 15] rather
unfurnished mare: modest handicap hurdler: won at Plumpton in December: will stay
further than 2m: acts on soft going: often wears hood. *Pat Phelan*

LEGEND OF ZORRO (IRE) 6 ch.g. Touch of Land (FR) – Wotaglen (IRE) (Heavenly   **c–**
Manna) [2018/19 h16sᵖᵘ h21.4g² h19d c16.1d⁵ Jan 19] €7,200 3-y-o, £10,000 5-y-o: first   **h102**
foal: dam placed in point: off mark in Irish points at fifth attempt: fair form over hurdles:
standout effort when second in novice at Wincanton: tailed off in novice handicap on
chasing debut: tried in tongue tie. *Jimmy Frost*

LEGENDS GOLD (IRE) 5 b.m. Gold Well – Fu's Legend (IRE) (Pistolet Bleu (IRE))   **h124**
[2018/19 b17g² h16.4g h21.2d² h20.5s³ h23.8g³ h16.3g* Apr 14] €2,500 3-y-o: sixth foal: **b92**
half-sister to fairly useful 19f winner Mount Pelier (by Milan) and bumper winner/fair
hurdler Fu's Island (19f/2½m winner, by Turtle Island): dam unraced daughter of smart
chaser up to 2½m Fu's Lady: won Irish point on debut: fair form in bumpers: better effort
when second in mares event at Aintree: fairly useful form over hurdles: quickly resumed
progress when won mares handicap at Stratford in April. *Rebecca Curtis*

LEGENDS RYDE 4 ch.f. Midnight Legend – Ryde Back (Bob Back (USA)) [2018/19   **b83**
b16g³ b16.3d⁵ Mar 23] £55,000 3-y-o: second foal: half-sister to fairly useful hurdler Kings
Ryde (2½m/21f winner, by King's Theatre): dam (h131) bumper and 2½m/21f hurdle
winner: modest form in bumpers: fifth in Goffs UK Spring Sales Bumper at Newbury,
possibly doing too much too soon. *Jamie Snowden*

LEG LOCK LUKE (IRE) 9 b.g. Indian River (FR) – Delirious Tantrum (IRE) (Taufan   **c100 §**
(USA)) [2018/19 c105§, h–§: c24gᵘʳ c23.8g* c26gᵖᵘ c25.7g³ c20.2g⁶ c19.7g⁵ c22.7mᵖᵘ   **h– §**
c21.7gᵖᵘ Feb 19] lengthy gelding: maiden hurdler: fair handicap chaser: won at Ffos Las in
May: left Colin Tizzard after sixth start: stays 3¼m: acts on soft and good to firm going:
usually wears headgear/tongue tie: usually races close up: temperamental. *Tom George*

LE GRAND ROCHER (FR) 3 b.g. Saint des Saints (FR) – Belle du Roi (FR) (Adieu   **h110 p**
Au Roi (IRE)) [2018/19 h14.9s Apr 27] brother to 2 winners, including smart hurdler/
useful chaser Le Rocher (2m-21f winner), and half-brother to several winners, including
fairly useful/unreliable hurdler/chaser Poli Roi (21f/2¾m winner, by Poliglote): dam
(h118), placed over hurdles in France, 6f-10.5f winner on Flat: 29/1, seventh of 9 in listed
3-y-o hurdle at Auteuil on debut, never dangerous: should do better. *Nick Williams*

LE HACHETTE (IRE) 6 b.m. Yeats (IRE) – Tafseer (IRE) (Grand Lodge (USA))   **h85**
[2018/19 h24.6s⁴ h21.4v⁵ h23.9g⁶ h24.8g⁶ h24.8m h24g h21v³ h21s⁴ Jan 1] €3,800 3-y-o:
fifth foal: half-sister to modest 2m hurdle winner Saint Helena (by Holy Roman Emperor):
dam, unraced, closely related to fairly useful 2m hurdle winner Aather: point winner:
modest maiden hurdler: stays 25f: acts on heavy going: tried in cheekpieces/tongue tie.
John Patrick Ryan, Ireland

LEITH HILL LAD 9 b.g. Kayf Tara – Leith Hill Star (Comme L'Etoile) [2018/19 c123x, **c119 x** h–: c26.1g³ c25.2g⁵ c24.2m⁵ c23.5dᵖᵘ Nov 27] good-topped gelding: winning hurdler: **h–** fairly useful handicap chaser: third at Uttoxeter in May: stays 3¼m: acts on soft and good to firm going: in cheekpieces last 2 starts: usually races close up: often let down by jumping. *Charlie Longsdon*

LEITH HILL LEGASI 10 b.m. Kahyasi – Leith Hill Star (Comme L'Etoile) [2018/19 **c72** c83, h–: c23.8s⁶ c24.2v c25.7s⁵ c26.2d³ Mar 20] has had breathing operation: maiden **h–** hurdler: poor handicap chaser: stays 3¼m: acts on good to firm and heavy going: wears headgear/tongue tie: front runner/races prominently. *Charlie Longsdon*

LE LIGERIEN (FR) 6 b.g. Turgeon (USA) – Etoile de Loir (FR) (Lost World (IRE)) **h118** [2018/19 b15.8d b13.7g⁴ h16.5d³ h15.3g⁴ h16.5g² h15.8d² h15.8g² h19.2m* h16.8g Apr **b83** 17] £32,000 3-y-o: fourth foal: half-brother to French 19f chase winner Chambord du Loir (by Ange Gabriel): dam unraced half-sister to fairly useful French hurdler/useful chaser (17f/2¼m winner) Symphonie d'Anjou (by Turgeon): pulled up in point: some promise in bumpers: fairly useful hurdler: won maiden at Fontwell in March: stays 19f: acts on good to firm and good to soft going: wears hood: usually races close up. *Philip Hobbs*

LE MARTALIN (FR) 8 ch.g. Martaline – Hembra (FR) (Croco Rouge (IRE)) [2018/19 **c138** c140, h–: c17d* c16g² c16m* c22.7g² c18.2d⁰ Aug 2] winning hurdler: useful chaser: won **h–** maiden at Killarney (by 6 lengths from Hardback) in May and novice at Wexford in July: stayed 23f: acted on heavy and good to firm going: wore headgear: usually tongue tied: front runner/raced prominently: dead. *Noel Meade, Ireland*

LE MILOS 4 b.g. Shirocco (GER) – Banjaxed Girl (King's Theatre (IRE)) [2018/19 **h119** h16.9s h15.9g⁶ h17.4sᵖᵘ h17.4g⁵ h17.9s⁵ h16.8s⁴ h16.8s* h15.7m Mar 31] angular gelding: second foal: dam (c135/h144), 2m-21f hurdle/chase winner (stayed 3m), half-sister to useful hurdler/chaser (stayed 2½m) Mountain King and useful chaser (25f winner) Gorsky Island: fairly useful hurdler: won juvenile handicap at Sandown (wore hood) in March: left P. Raussin after fifth start: stays 2¼m: acts on soft going: tried in cheekpieces. *Tim Vaughan*

LEMONADE DRINKER 6 gr.g. Fair Mix (IRE) – Sheknowsyouknow (Petrizzo) **b–** [2018/19 b–: b16g Oct 30] last in bumpers. *Mike Hawker*

LEMON T 6 gr.g. Sulamani (IRE) – Altogether Now (IRE) (Step Together (USA)) **b94** [2018/19 b16.7g⁵ b16.4m* Mar 28] brother to fair 2m hurdle winner Temple Man (stays 21f) and half-brother to several winners, including fairly useful hurdler/chaser Mac Aeda (2½m-25f winner, by Kayf Tara): dam, unraced, out of half-sister to top-class staying chaser Marlborough: fair form in bumpers: won at Newcastle in March, very much having run of race: will be suited by further than 2m. *Ruth Jefferson*

LE MUSEE (FR) 6 b.g. Galileo (IRE) – Delicieuse Lady (Trempolino (USA)) [2018/19 **h126** h118: h21g h20.5s² h21.6s⁵ h24.3d h23.9s* h20.3d Mar 15] close-coupled gelding: has had breathing operation: fairly useful handicap hurdler: won at Taunton in February: stays 3m: acts on heavy going: has worn headgear: usually tongue tied (not last 2 starts): has raced lazily. *Nigel Hawke*

LEN BRENNAN (IRE) 6 b.g. Westerner – Letthedancebegin (IRE) (Flemensfirth **c120** (USA)) [2018/19 b17.7g h22g³ c24.2g² c25.7s³ c26.7g² c24.5s² c25.1sᵖᵘ c30.7s Apr 16] **h102** €800 3-y-o: second foal: dam, winning pointer, out of sister to useful staying chaser Merry **b–** Master: third on completed start in Irish points: tailed off in bumper: some encouragement when third in maiden hurdle (4¼ lengths behind Dandolo du Gite) at Stratford: fairly useful form over fences: second in handicap at Carlisle in February: should stay beyond 27f: acts on soft going. *Tim Vaughan*

LEODIS (IRE) 7 ch.g. Shirocco (GER) – Leonica (Lion Cavern (USA)) [2018/19 b86: **h86** h19.7m³ h19.7mᶠ h19.7g h19.3s⁵ Dec 18] fair in bumpers/on Flat: modest form over hurdles. *Micky Hammond*

LEOFRIC (IRE) 5 b.g. Galileo (IRE) – Ice Mint (USA) (Awesome Again (CAN)) **b–** [2018/19 b16.7g Sep 29] well beaten in bumper. *David O'Meara*

LEONASISLAND (IRE) 7 b.g. Trans Island – Ashanti Dancer (IRE) (Dancing Dissident **c–** (USA)) [2018/19 h–: c16gᵖᵘ c20.1gᵖᵘ h16.2m h16v h16.4s h15.6gᵖᵘ c16.4sᵖᵘ c15.8m⁵ **h–** c16.9s⁶ c15.2gᵖᵘ Mar 29] no form: usually wears hood: tried in tongue tie. *Stuart Coltherd*

LEONCAVALLO (IRE) 7 br.g. Cape Cross (IRE) – Nafura (Dubawi (IRE)) [2018/19 **c134** h121: h15.8m* h16s³ c20m² h16.8d h16m⁵ Apr 13] neat gelding: useful handicap hurdler: **h139** won at Ludlow (by 5 lengths from Peruvien Bleu) in May: third in Galway Hurdle (3½ lengths behind Sharjah) in August: 1/2, mistakes when second in maiden at Worcester

(1¼ lengths behind Cultivator) on chasing debut: stays 2½m: acts on good to firm and good to soft going: usually wears headgear nowadays: front runner/races prominently. *Dr Richard Newland*

LEOPARD (IRE) 5 b.g. Iffraaj – Appletreemagic (IRE) (Indian Danehill (IRE)) [2018/19 h17.2g⁵ h16.8gᶠ h22.8v⁶ h19.7s h25.3g³ h25gᵖᵘ h24.1d⁴ Mar 19] modest maiden on Flat, stays 1¾m: modest maiden hurdler: stays 3m: acts on good to soft going: usually wears hood: in tongue tie last 5 starts: often races towards rear. *Joanne Foster* **h87**

LEORO (IRE) 5 ch.g. Campanologist (USA) – Ledicea (Medicean) [2018/19 h–: h21.4m⁶ h19.2g⁵ h18.5m⁴ h20g Jul 31] workmanlike gelding: fairly useful on Flat, stays 2m: modest form over hurdles: sometimes in headgear: in tongue tie last 5 starts: often races towards rear. *Charlie Mann* **h90**

LEOSTAR 5 ch.g. Nathaniel (IRE) – Gaditana (Rainbow Quest (USA)) [2018/19 b89: h16g² h16.2g⁴ Dec 9] placed in bumpers: modest form in maiden hurdles: will stay 2½m. *Alistair Whillans* **h98**

LE PATRIOTE (FR) 7 b.g. Poliglote – Sentosa (FR) (Kaldounevees (FR)) [2018/19 h127: h19.5d h16d* h20.3g* Apr 17] well-made gelding: useful/progressive handicap hurdler: won at Ayr in November and Cheltenham (by 3½ lengths from No Hassle Hoff) in April: stays 2½m: acts on heavy going: in cheekpieces last 5 starts: strong traveller. *Dr Richard Newland* **h143**

LE PRECIEUX (FR) 6 b.g. Diamond Boy (FR) – Bab Khaldoun (FR) (Kaldoun (FR)) [2018/19 c–, h109: c16.2m⁶ c16.3gᵘʳ c17.8g³ c17.8g³ c17.8m² c15.9m* c16g* c16.4dᵖᵘ Jan 16] good-topped gelding: fair hurdler: fairly useful handicap chaser: won small-field events at Leicester in December and Ludlow (novice) in January: stayed 2¼m: acted on good to firm and heavy going: dead. *Gary Moore* **c118 h–**

LE PREZIEN (FR) 8 br.g. Blue Bresil (FR) – Abu Dhabi (FR) (Saint Cyrien (FR)) [2018/19 c156x, h–: h15.8d² h15.9g⁵ h15.5s c16.3d Mar 15] useful-looking gelding: smart handicap hurdler: second in Welsh Champion Hurdle (Limited Handicap) at Ffos Las (3 lengths behind Silver Streak) on return: very smart chaser at best, disappointing in 2018/19: stays 2½m: acts on heavy going: wears tongue tie: often let down by jumping. *Paul Nicholls* **c– x h147**

L'EQUINOXE (FR) 5 b.g. Enrique – Nebuleuse (IRE) (Definite Article) [2018/19 h–: h18.5dᵖᵘ Apr 9] pulled up in novice selling hurdle. *Gary Moore* **h–**

LE REVE (IRE) 11 br.g. Milan – Open Cry (IRE) (Montelimar (USA)) [2018/19 c24g³ c24.2d c24.2sᵖᵘ c28.8v* c24.2d* c26.2g⁴ c28.8g Apr 27] tall, good sort: winning hurdler: useful chaser: won handicap at Lingfield in February and Grand Military Gold Cup (Amateur Riders) at Sandown (by 13 lengths from Spanish Arch) in March: stays 29f: acts on heavy going: wears headgear. *Lucy Wadham* **c131 h–**

LE RICHEBOURG (FR) 6 br.g. Network (GER) – Fee Magic (FR) (Phantom Breeze) [2018/19 h137: h16s⁵ c17d* c20g* c20g² c17g* c17g* Feb 2] **c158 p h130**

　　Michael Dickinson's feat of saddling the first five home in the 1983 Cheltenham Gold Cup is no closer to being equalled (let alone surpassed) some thirty-six years later, despite the super-sized, powerhouse yards now operating on both sides of the Irish Sea. Paul Nicholls (who had one hundred and sixty-one individual runners in 2018/19) has come closest, saddling the first three in the 2008 Cheltenham Gold Cup and then four of the first five twelve months later. Willie Mullins (who had two hundred and sixty-seven individual runners in 2018/19) only ended his Gold Cup drought in the latest season, though he did saddle the first three in the 2015 Champion Hurdle, and four of the first five (including the first three) in the latest edition of the Irish Grand National. All of which shows Dickinson's feat

Racing Post Novices' Chase, Leopardstown—Mark Walsh and Le Richebourg have matters well under control at the last; stable-companion Us And Them (near side) fills the runner-up spot

Frank Ward Solicitors Arkle Novices' Chase, Leopardstown—Voix du Reve (centre) comes to grief at the last as Le Richebourg (hoops) again pulls well clear of Us And Them

in an even better light, particularly as his string at Harewood in Yorkshire never exceeded fifty-five. Aged just thirty-three when the 1983 Gold Cup took place, Dickinson remarked that just getting any horse fit and ready to run well on the day in a showpiece event like the Gold Cup was 'a hell of an achievement' in its own right, never mind getting five to post. Willie Mullins would have vouched for that after the latest renewal of the Arkle Challenge Trophy at Cheltenham in March. Although the perennial Irish champion trainer had just saddled the runaway winner Duc des Genievres (his fourth winner of the race in five years), the chances are that he was only the third best two-mile novice chaser housed at Closutton in the latest season, with those missing from the line-up including both Cilaos Emery (who had comprehensively beaten Duc des Genievres earlier in the season before suffering an injury) and the lightly-raced Chacun Pour Soi (who didn't make his debut for current connections until March 10th after a three-year absence). In fact, the 2019 Arkle was very much a story of who wasn't there, rather than the twelve who did show up. No fewer than four of the first six in the ante-post Arkle betting less than five weeks earlier were missing come the Tuesday of the Cheltenham Festival, a quartet which included the Nicholls-trained Dynamite Dollars, the leading hope in the home defence, who joined Cilaos Emery on the easy list in the build-up to the race. Arguably the most significant absentee, however, was Irish-trained Le Richebourg, who had headed the betting for much of the winter and would surely have gone close had he been fit and well enough to make the line-up.

In truth, when Le Richebourg finished fifteenth off a BHA mark of 145 in the County Hurdle at the 2018 Cheltenham Festival, it seemed unlikely he would have gone into many notebooks as a candidate to become one of the leading novice chasers in 2018/19. His three hurdle wins had come in the summer of 2017 and, although impressive on each of those occasions, he rather had his hurdling limitations exposed in Grade 1 company subsequently, which presumably influenced the decision to plump for the handicap at the Cheltenham Festival. A switch to the larger obstacles proved to be the making of Le Richebourg. After finishing a respectable fifth in the Galway Hurdle on his reappearance, Le Richebourg created a very good impression when landing the odds in a nine-runner maiden chase over seventeen furlongs at Listowel. A step up to Grade 3 company yielded a similarly impressive display, with Le Richebourg making light work of the Mullins-trained Robin des Foret in the two and a half mile Like A Butterfly Novices' Chase at Tipperary in October. Although he coped with the longer trip that day, Le Richebourg was edged out by a stronger stayer on his next start, going down by half a length to Delta Work in the

Drinmore Novices' Chase at Fairyhouse having traded as low as 1.05 in running on the exchanges, although an uncharacteristic mistake at the last by the winner was as much responsible for that as the strong-travelling display from Le Richebourg.

Despite losing his unbeaten record over fences, Le Richebourg still enhanced his reputation in what was a competitive renewal of the Drinmore. Fourth-placed Cadmium went on to win the Topham Chase, while fifth-placed Discorama was a good second at both the Cheltenham and Punchestown Festivals. Le Richebourg himself hammered home the point when convincingly winning Grade 1 events at Leopardstown back over seventeen furlongs on his next two starts, taking the Racing Post Novices' Chase in December and the Frank Ward Solicitors Arkle Novices' Chase in February, posting a strong timefigure both times. Both were six-runner events featuring many of the same rivals, with stable-companion Us And Them chasing home Le Richebourg on each occasion, although Voix du Reve (third in the Racing Post) would have pushed him closest in the latter but for falling at the last (the penultimate fence on each circuit in the Arkle was omitted because of low sun). It was clear that Le Richebourg was a cut above the opposition, though, and he became a warm favourite in the ante-post market for the Arkle at Cheltenham before he had to be ruled out in late-February with a season-ending injury. The Leopardstown form was franked in his absence, with Us And Them finishing runner-up again in Grade 1 company at both Cheltenham (in the Arkle) and at Aintree, whilst Voix du Reve won the Grade 1 Ryanair Gold Cup at Fairyhouse in late-April.

The angular Le Richebourg is by French-based Network, who is best known as the sire of outstanding two-mile chaser Sprinter Sacre but is also responsible for several high-profile performers over longer trips, including Grand National regular Saint Are (placed in 2015 and 2017) and the aforementioned Delta Work, in whose essay Network's death is reported and his career summarised. There is also plenty of stamina to be found in the bottom half of Le Richebourg's pedigree, with his half-brother Grands Crus (by Dom Alco) being a top-class staying hurdler/high-class staying chaser for David Pipe. Unfortunately, weak finishes became the norm for the strong-travelling Grands Crus late in his career when he often shaped like one with problems. Grands Crus' brother Gevrey Chambertin also had problems, though his seemed to be mainly temperamental in nature, which led to a very in-and-out career for Pipe, although he showed useful winning form at up to twenty-five furlongs over both hurdles and fences. Happily, Le Richebourg seems a more straightforward type than either Grands Crus or Gevrey Chambertin. He is the sixth foal of the unraced Fee Magic, whose only other runner to date is the fairly useful French two and a half mile hurdler/chaser Nuits Premier Cru (by Buck's Boum). Fee Magic's unraced daughter La Romanee (by Robin des Champs) has already tasted success as a broodmare, her first runner Le Bearn winning a four-year-old chase in the French Provinces in the spring. Notable jumping winners in the family don't end there either, as Fee Magic is a half-sister to the 2014 Scottish Grand National winner Al Co (also by Dom Alco), whose latest success came in a long-distance veterans event shortly after the end of the season at Cartmel at the age of fourteen. Fee Magic is also a half-sister to the grandam of the Cheltenham Gold Cup winner Al Boum Photo. Fee Magic has produced one foal since Le Richebourg, the unraced five-year-old Le Musigny (by Anzillero), who is in training with Henry de Bromhead having changed hands for €45,000 as a three-year-old.

Given the speed he's shown to date (very best form on good ground), it seems likely that the sound-jumping Le Richebourg will be kept at two to two and a half miles for the time being, particularly as the Irish programme offers a liberal helping of graded events over these trips. It is to be hoped he forms part of another strong Cheltenham raiding party from Joseph O'Brien come the next Festival. Although he had to endure the disappointments of Le Richebourg's absence and Sir Erec's fatal injury when odds-on in the Triumph Hurdle, their ambitious young trainer still enjoyed a most productive Festival in 2019, saddling two winners and having a further four runners finish in the frame. It would be no surprise to see him build on those achievements in the years to come. After all, at twenty-six, Joseph O'Brien is still seven years younger than Michael Dickinson was at the time of his Cheltenham Gold Cup heroics in 1983. *Joseph Patrick O'Brien, Ireland*

LERICHI BELLE (IRE) 8 b.m. King's Theatre (IRE) – Lerichi (IRE) (Shardari) **c96** [2018/19 h106: c24.5g^2 c20g^6 c16v^{pu} h19.5s c20.9g^{pu} c19.4g^4 Apr 14] maiden hurdler: **h–** modest form over fences: left Martin Keighley after fourth start: stays 3m: acts on heavy going: usually wears headgear: headstrong. *Ian Williams*

LE ROCHER (FR) 9 b.g. Saint des Saints (FR) – Belle du Roi (FR) (Adieu Au Roi **c134** (IRE)) [2018/19 c146, h123: c21v^3 h23.9s^5 h21.4v^2 c19.4s^4 h20.4v^2 Feb 3] tall gelding: **h136** useful hurdler: second in Prix Leon Olry-Roederer at Auteuil (12 lengths behind Galop Marin) in November and listed event at Pau (in cheekpieces, 6 lengths behind Forthing) in February: useful chaser: fourth in handicap at Chepstow (14¾ lengths behind Doitforthevillage) in December: stays 21f: acts on heavy going. *Nick Williams*

LESANTI 5 b.g. Royal Applause – Kammaan (Diktat) [2018/19 h15.9g^{ur} Apr 21] poor **h–** maiden on Flat, stays 8.5f: unseated first on hurdling debut. *Ed de Giles*

L'ES FREMANTLE (FR) 8 b.g. Orpen (USA) – Grand Design (Danzero (AUS)) **c75 §** [2018/19 c–, h–: c19.2d^4 c17.2g^{ur} c23.9m^3 c25.5m c24g^{pu} c23.9g^{pu} c15.7g^4 c24g c21.4g* **h–** c23.9d^4 c19.2s^2 c21.4s^5 Dec 26] plain gelding: maiden hurdler: poor handicap chaser: 80/1, won at Market Rasen in November: stays 3m: acts on soft and good to firm going: has worn cheekpieces: held up: not one to trust. *Michael Chapman*

LESKINFERE (IRE) 6 b.g. Darsi (FR) – Taipans Girl (IRE) (Taipan (IRE)) [2018/19 **c–** h106: h20d^5 c20.9s c21.5d^{pu} h22.8d Mar 20] has had breathing operation: fair maiden **h97** hurdler: no show over fences: should stay beyond 2½m: acts on soft going: in cheekpieces last 3 starts: temperament under suspicion. *Oliver Greenall*

LESTER KRIS (IRE) 5 b.g. Fame And Glory – Wood Sprite (Mister Baileys) [2018/19 **h106** h16.7g^3 h16.7g^6 h15.7g^3 h16s^3 h19.3g^3 h19.9d Mar 30] fairly useful maiden on Flat, stays 1¾m: fair form over hurdles: left Dan Skelton after second start, Micky Hammond after fifth: stays 19f: acts on soft going: wears tongue tie. *Kayley Woollacott*

LETBESO (IRE) 11 ch.g. Vinnie Roe (IRE) – Go Hunting (IRE) (Abednego) [2018/19 **c88 §** c90§, h–§: c24.5g^3 May 14] winning hurdler: fairly useful chaser at best, has deteriorated **h– §** markedly (achieved little in points in 2019): stays 3¼m: acts on good to firm and heavy going: wears headgear: has worn tongue tie: temperamental. *Mrs K. Lawther*

LETEMGO (IRE) 11 b.g. Brian Boru – Leteminletemout (IRE) (Be My Native (USA)) **c93** [2018/19 c–, h112: h20d h23.8g^3 h24.6v^3 h24.3s h24.3d c31.9v^6 h25d c26.3g^3 Apr 5] **h105** compact gelding: fair handicap hurdler: maiden chaser, only modest form in 2018/19: stays 27f: acts on good to firm and heavy going: has worn headgear: tried in tongue tie: usually races off pace. *Andrew Hamilton*

LETHAL STEPS 4 gr.g. Lethal Force (IRE) – Tanda Tula (IRE) (Alhaarth (IRE)) [2018/19 **h123** h16d^5 h16d^2 h20d^3 h16.4s h20.2s^3 h17.6g^2 h20d^3 Apr 23] useful on Flat, stays 1¼m: fairly useful maiden hurdler: stays 2½m: acts on good to soft going: tried in cheekpieces/tongue tie: usually races prominently. *Gordon Elliott, Ireland*

L'ETOILE (IRE) 6 ch.g. Champs Elysees – Cross Your Fingers (USA) (Woodman **h–** (USA)) [2018/19 h–, b76: h16.8g^{pu} May 15] strong gelding: has had breathing operation: mid-field in bumper: no form over hurdles. *Micky Hammond*

LET'S BE HAPPY (IRE) 5 gr.m. Mastercraftsman (IRE) – Corrozal (GER) (Cape Cross **h68** (IRE)) [2018/19 h78: h15.3m^3 h17.7g h15.8g Oct 7] poor maiden hurdler: in cheekpieces last 3 starts: tried in tongue tie. *Ali Stronge*

LET'S GET AT IT (IRE) 6 b.g. Mustameet (USA) – Last Hope (IRE) (Jurado (USA)) **h120** [2018/19 h80: h15.8g h16m^6 h16.3g^5 h16v h20.6s* h23.1d h25.3m* h23.1g* h24.1g^4 Apr 11] fairly useful hurdler: won handicaps at Market Rasen (novice) in December, Catterick in February and Market Rasen again in March: stays 25f: acts on soft and good to firm going: in cheekpieces last 3 starts: in tongue tie back? *Olly Murphy*

LETS GO DUTCHESS 9 b.m. Helissio (FR) – Lets Go Dutch (Nicholas Bill) [2018/19 **c110** h107: h18.5g^F h19.9g^4 c20g^3 c21m^2 Jun 26] sturdy mare: fair handicap hurdler: similar **h95** form over fences: stays 2¾m: acts on good to firm and good to soft going: often races in rear. *Kevin Bishop*

LETSKEEPIT SIMPLE (IRE) 9 b.g. Saffron Walden (FR) – Diaconate (IRE) (Cape **c91**
Cross (IRE)) [2018/19 c–: c26g⁶ May 17] multiple point winner: last of 6 finishers in
novice hunter at Fontwell on completed start in chases. *Ian Cobb*

LET'S SWAY 5 b.m. Authorized (IRE) – Let's Dance (IRE) (Danehill Dancer (IRE)) **h113**
[2018/19 h105: h15.3m* h15.8d² h16.3m³ h16.3m² h16.8g² h19.7g³ h15.8d* h16.7s² Dec
26] has had breathing operation: fair hurdler: won novice at Wincanton in May and novice
claimer at Ludlow in December: left Tracey Barfoot-Saunt after fourth start, Olly Murphy
after seventh: unproven beyond 17f: acts on soft and good to firm going: wears hood: in
tongue tie last 4 starts: usually races. *Katy Price*

LETTHERIVERRUNDRY (IRE) 9 br.g. Diamond Green (FR) – Dissitation (IRE) **c–**
(Spectrum (IRE)) [2018/19 c112, h111: h16g Jun 24] big, strong, workmanlike gelding: **h–**
fairly useful hurdler at best, well beaten only start in 2018/19: maiden chaser: stays 21f:
acts on good to soft going: wears headgear: in tongue tie last 5 starts. *Brendan Powell*

LEVASSEUR 5 b.g. Black Sam Bellamy (IRE) – Tiger Line (Kayf Tara) [2018/19 h20.5d **h–**
Mar 1] rather unfurnished gelding: runner-up both starts in points: well beaten in novice on
hurdling debut. *Ben Case*

LEVEL OF INTENSITY (IRE) 5 b.g. Intense Focus (USA) – Teofolina (IRE) (Teofilo **h118**
(IRE)) [2018/19 h106: h16m* h16g⁵ h18.5g h16.3m⁴ Jul 15] sturdy gelding: has had
breathing operation: fairly useful handicap hurdler: won at Kempton in May: went wrong
way after: unproven beyond 17f: acts on good to firm going: in headgear last 5 starts: wears
tongue tie. *Nigel Hawke*

LEVER DU SOLEIL (FR) 4 b.g. Le Havre (IRE) – Morning Dust (IRE) (Invincible **h123**
Spirit (IRE)) [2018/19 h16m³ h16g³ h16.5s² h16.6g⁶ h16d* h16g³ h16d⁵ h16d⁴ h18.7s²
h16d² h16d Apr 22] modest on Flat, stays 1¾m: fairly useful hurdler: won juvenile maiden
at Gowran in November: third in Bar One Racing Juvenile 3-Y-O Hurdle at Fairyhouse (9½
lengths behind Chief Justice) in December and second in novice at Limerick in March:
stays 19f: acts on good going. *Gavin Patrick Cromwell, Ireland*

LEVEROCK LASS (IRE) 6 b.m. Olden Times – Hazelhall Princess (IRE) (Hubbly **h95**
Bubbly (USA)) [2018/19 h22.8v h20.5s* h19.5d h24.1d⁵ Mar 19] £20,000 5-y-o: fourth
foal: sister to a winning pointer: dam (c105), 3m chase winner, half-sister to fairly useful
hurdler/chaser (2½m-25f winner) Netminder: won Irish point on debut: modest form over
hurdles: won mares novice at Ayr in January. *Tim Reed*

LEXINGTON LAW (IRE) 6 b.g. Lawman (FR) – Tus Nua (IRE) (Galileo (IRE)) **h–**
[2018/19 h103: h16gᵖᵘ Nov 12] fairly useful hurdler, fair form
at best: raced only at 2m: in cheekpieces last 2 starts. *Alan King*

LEX TALIONIS (IRE) 6 b.g. Thewayyouare (USA) – Dawn Air (USA) (Diesis) **c113 §**
[2018/19 h116: h23.1g⁶ h19.8v⁶ c23d² c20.9v c25.1g⁶ c25.6d² c22.7m² c22.4d c24d⁴ **h91 §**
c25.8g⁴ Apr 20] fair handicap hurdler/maiden chaser: stays 3¼m: acts on good to firm and
heavy going: wears cheekpieces/tongue tie: usually races towards rear: temperamental.
Charlie Mann

LIBBRETTA 4 ch.f. Libranno – Dispol Katie (Komaite (USA)) [2018/19 b13.7m⁶ b13.7g **b–**
ab16g Feb 18] seventh foal: half-sister to 3 winners, including modest 2m hurdle winner
Bahrikate (by Bahri): dam 5f-7f winner: no form in bumpers. *John E. Long*

LIBBY T VALANCE (IRE) 8 b.m. Scorpion (IRE) – Dipp In The Dark (IRE) (Presenting) **h–**
[2018/19 h98: h20s h20m Jun 21] bumper winner: maiden hurdler, no form in 2018/19:
tried in cheekpieces. *Rebecca Curtis*

LIBERTY BELLA 5 b.m. Librettist (USA) – Classy Crewella (Lahib (USA)) [2018/19 **h116**
b75: h21g⁶ h21.2d* h21.7d* h19.8s⁵ h20.3g⁴ Apr 18] workmanlike mare: fairly useful
form over hurdles: won mares novices at Ludlow in December and Hereford in January:
stays 2¾m: acts on good going: usually leads. *Brian Eckley*

LICKPENNY LARRY 8 gr.g. Sagamix (FR) – Myriah (IRE) (Strong Gale) [2018/19 **c94**
c94, h72: c17.4s² c16d⁵ c16d⁶ c15.5d² c20.2g⁵ c20.3d⁵ Apr 26] lengthy, angular gelding: **h–**
maiden hurdler: modest handicap chaser: won at Chepstow in February: best form around
2m: acts on heavy going: tried in hood: wears tongue tie. *Tom Gretton*

LIEUTENANT COLONEL 10 b.g. Kayf Tara – Agnese (Abou Zouz (USA)) [2018/19 **c113 §**
c109§, h137§: h20m h20m⁶ h23.4vᵖᵘ c29.5sᵖᵘ c20m³ c23sᵖᵘ c16.2g³ Mar 28] tall gelding: **h– §**
smart hurdler/fairly useful chaser at best, has lost his way: left Gordon Elliott after second
start: stays 3m, effective at shorter: acts on good to firm and heavy going: has worn
headgear, including in 2018/19: wears tongue tie: usually races in rear: one to leave alone.
Sophie Leech

LIFEBOAT (IRE) 4 b.g. Born To Sea (IRE) – Mrs Seek (Unfuwain (USA)) [2018/19 **h–**
h16.7s⁶ h15.7s Dec 18] disappointing maiden on Flat: no form over hurdles. *Dan Skelton*

LIFE KNOWLEDGE (IRE) 7 ch.g. Thewayyouare (USA) – Rosa Bellini (IRE) (Rossini **h86**
(USA)) [2018/19 h83: h16.8m h15.6g² h15.7g³ h15.6g² Jan 7] modest maiden hurdler:
trained by Lawrence Mullaney only on reappearance: raced around 2m: best form on good
going: in headgear last 4 starts. *Andrew Crook*

LIFFEYDALE DREAMER (IRE) 4 b.f. Azamour (IRE) – Owega Dale (IRE) (Refuse **h107**
To Bend (IRE)) [2018/19 h16.6g⁶ h17s² h16g⁵ h16.6d⁵ h20d² h21.4s⁴ Mar 9] fair on Flat,
stays 12.5f: fair form over hurdles: stays 2½m: acts on soft going: wears hood: in tongue
tie last 5 starts. *Madeleine Tylicki, Ireland*

LIGHTENTERTAINMENT (IRE) 11 b.g. King's Theatre (IRE) – Dochas Supreme **c96**
(IRE) (Supreme Leader) [2018/19 c91, h92: c16.2d* c16dᵖᵘ c17g⁴ Apr 7] workmanlike **h–**
gelding: winning hurdler: modest handicap chaser: won at Warwick in December: stays
21f: acts on heavy going: wears cheekpieces: front runner/races prominently. *Barry Brennan*

LIGHT FLICKER (IRE) 7 b.g. Royal Anthem (USA) – Five Cents More (IRE) **c–**
(Flemensfirth (USA)) [2018/19 c25.3gᶠ May 4] off mark in points at sixth attempt in
November: 66/1, joined when fell 4 out in hunter won by Foxcub at Cheltenham on chasing
debut. *A. Campbell*

LIGHT GUNNER (IRE) 5 b.g. Lawman (FR) – Neve Lieve (IRE) (Dubai Destination **h98**
(USA)) [2018/19 h19.6gᵖᵘ h16.3d h16.3d⁵ h16m² Apr 25] sturdy gelding: modest maiden
on Flat, stays 1½m: modest form over hurdles: left Henry Tett after third start: tried in
tongue tie. *Richard Bandey*

LIGHTLY SQUEEZE 5 b.g. Poet's Voice – Zuleika Dobson (Cadeaux Genereux) **h103**
[2018/19 h84: h16.8s⁴ h15.3d³ Dec 26] sturdy gelding: fair form over hurdles: best effort
when third in novice handicap at Wincanton: sometimes in headgear: often races in rear.
Harry Fry

LIGHT OF AIR (FR) 6 b.g. Youmzain (IRE) – Height of Vanity (IRE) (Erhaab (USA)) **h–**
[2018/19 h–: h18.7g h15.9m h15.9s Jan 16] good-topped gelding: fair on Flat, stays 13f:
little impact over hurdles: often in headgear. *Gary Moore*

LIGHT OF ATHENA (IRE) 5 b.m. Doyen (IRE) – Reflecting (IRE) (Daylami (IRE)) **b–**
[2018/19 b16.2s b15.8g b16s Mar 10] €8,000 3-y-o: fourth foal: dam, maiden on Flat
(stayed 1¼m), half-sister to very smart hurdler/high-class chaser (2m-3m winner) Shooting
Light: no form in bumpers: tried in hood/tongue tie. *Ronald Harris*

LIGHT THAT (IRE) 7 b.g. Echo of Light – Tucum (IRE) (Diktat) [2018/19 c115, h130: **c134**
c16g* May 16] useful hurdler: similar form over fences: won novice at Punchestown **h–**
(by ½ length from Robin des Foret) only start in 2018/19: raced around 2m: acts on heavy
going: in tongue tie last 2 starts: front runner/races prominently. *Mrs J. Harrington, Ireland*

LIGNY (FR) 6 ch.g. Fuisse (FR) – Light Wave (FR) (Marignan (USA)) [2018/19 b–: **h–**
h16.7gᵖᵘ Aug 20] good-topped gelding: no show in bumpers/maiden hurdle. *Sarah-
Jayne Davies*

LIKEABATOUTOFHELL (IRE) 4 b.g. Virtual – Bond Holder (IRE) (Hawkeye **b–**
(IRE)) [2018/19 b16s Mar 16] tailed off in maiden bumper. *Chris Gordon*

LIKEAMONKEY 7 b.g. Phoenix Reach (IRE) – Naturally Inspired (FR) (Ungaro **h97**
(GER)) [2018/19 h16.2gʳᵒ Apr 15] second foal: dam (c91/h85) placed over hurdles/fences
up to 2½m: 66/1, keeping on into share of third when ran out last in novice hurdle won by
Glinger Flame at Hexham on debut. *Laura Morgan*

LIKE SULLY (IRE) 11 b.g. Presenting – Swing Into Action (IRE) (Be My Native **c–**
(USA)) [2018/19 c91, h–: c20.5m May 14] good-topped gelding: winning hurdler: fair **h–**
chaser at best, well held only start in 2018/19: stays 3¼m: acts on heavy going: tried in
cheekpieces. *Richard Rowe*

LIKETHEMUDDA (IRE) 6 b.m. Court Cave (IRE) – Quivvy Bridge (IRE) (Alflora **h–**
(IRE)) [2018/19 h16m h16.2gʳᵒ Sep 17] first foal: dam (h120), 2m-3m hurdle winner,
half-sister to useful hurdler (stays 21f) Serosevsky: no form over hurdles: tried in hood.
P. E. Collins, Ireland

LIKE THE SOUND (FR) 8 b.g. Soldier of Fortune (IRE) – Zalida (IRE) (Machiavellian **c136**
(USA)) [2018/19 c26.3g² c23.8g⁶ c26v² c26.7g* c25.1gᵖᵘ c28.4dᵘʳ c28.4s* Mar 19] **h–**
winning hurdler: useful handicap chaser: won at Wincanton in January and Taunton in
March: stays 3½m: acts on heavy going: in tongue tie last 4 starts: usually races close up.
Charlie Mann

LIL LAZARUS (FR) 6 ch.g. Anabaa Blue – Santoria (FR) (Limnos (JPN)) [2018/19 b15.8d h15.8d h15.8g Feb 28] tailed off in bumper/over hurdles: in hood/tongue tie last 2 starts. *Sophie Leech* **h– b–**

LILLIAN (IRE) 8 b.m. Milan – Kay Tully (Kahyasi) [2018/19 h119: h24g h26.5g⁵ h26.4m⁴ h26.5g⁵ h26g⁴ c21.6g⁴ c24.2g³ Nov 20] small mare: fair handicap hurdler: behind both starts over fences, all but fell second occasion: stays 3¼m: acts on good to firm and good to soft going: front runner/races prominently: remains open to improvement as a chaser. *Seamus Mullins* **c107 p h114**

LILLINGTON (IRE) 7 br.g. Westerner – Kind Word (IRE) (Yashgan) [2018/19 c102, h–: c16.3g* c17g* c15.9d⁴ c16s* c18.2d c20d² c16.4d* c16.4g* c16.5mᵖᵘ Apr 13] tall gelding: maiden hurdler: useful handicap chaser: won at Newton Abbot in June, Stratford in October, Lingfield in November and Newbury (twice, by 2¾ lengths from Master Work second occasion) in March: stays 2¼m: acts on soft and good to firm going: wears headgear/tongue tie: often races prominently. *Colin Tizzard* **c133 h–**

LILLIPUT LANE (IRE) 7 b.m. Yeats (IRE) – Charade (IRE) (Danehill (USA)) [2018/19 b87: b15.3m* May 15] fair form in bumpers: won mares event at Wincanton in May. *Johnny Farrelly* **b87**

LILLY PEDLAR 4 b.f. Yeats (IRE) – Mathine (FR) (Malinas (GER)) [2018/19 b16.7d Apr 26] third foal: dam, pulled up only start over hurdles in France, half-sister to Cheltenham Gold Cup winner Long Run: 11/1, seventh in mares bumper at Bangor (18 lengths behind The Milan Girl). *Nicky Henderson* **b71**

LILLY'S ARC (IRE) 5 b.m. Arcadio (GER) – Eye And Ear (IRE) (Old Vic) [2018/19 b15.7g b16d⁶ h20.6g³ Mar 1] poor form in bumpers: showed bit more when third in mares novice at Market Rasen (8¼ lengths behind Mega Yeats) on hurdling debut: dead. *Stuart Edmunds* **h91 b73**

LIL ROCKERFELLER (USA) 8 ch.g. Hard Spun (USA) – Layounne (USA) (Mt Livermore (USA)) [2018/19 h152: c20g* c24.4g* c24.2s* c25.3gᵘʳ c21s³ h24d⁵ h19.2d³ h21s Mar 13] well-made gelding: has had breathing operation: smart hurdler: third in National Spirit Hurdle at Fontwell (3¾ lengths behind Vision des Flos) in February: useful form over fences: won maiden at Uttoxeter in October, and novices at Cheltenham (by 4 lengths from Treackle Tart) later in October and Exeter in November: let down by jumping other 2 chase starts: stays 3m: acts on heavy going: wears headgear: usually leads: can take plenty of driving but normally responds. *Neil King* **c144 h147**

LILY OF LEYSBOURNE 6 b.m. Shirocco (GER) – Alegralil (King's Theatre (IRE)) [2018/19 h15.8g² h20.6g² h20.6g² h16.7s² Dec 6] £47,000 3-y-o: first foal: dam (h128), bumper/2m-19f hurdle winner, sister to useful staying chaser Theatrical Star: unplaced in bumpers: fair form over hurdles: left James Joseph Mangan after final (2017/18) start: will prove suited by further than 2m: acts on soft going: in hood last 4 starts: usually races towards rear. *Fergal O'Brien* **h108**

LILY'S GEM (IRE) 6 b.m. Scorpion (IRE) – Kegster (IRE) (Bach (IRE)) [2018/19 b96: b16s⁶ h19.3g⁴ h16sᵛ Mar 18] bumper winner: fair form over hurdles: better effort when third in maiden at Navan (tongue tied). *Stuart Crawford, Ireland* **h100 b80**

LILY THE PINK 5 b.m. Malinas (GER) – Carrigeen Queen (IRE) (Darnay) [2018/19 b17g⁶ b16.3d* b17.7v² Mar 6] £1,800 3-y-o: first foal: dam, ran twice over hurdles, half-sister to useful hurdler/smart chaser (stays 3m) Benatar and smart 3m hurdle winner Minella Indo: won point bumper on debut: fair form in bumpers under Rules: won at Stratford in June: left J. Tickle after second start. *Anthony Honeyball* **b86**

LIME STREET (IRE) 8 b.g. Presenting – Specifiedrisk (IRE) (Turtle Island (IRE)) [2018/19 c83, h111: h20dᵖᵘ May 26] sturdy gelding: fair handicap hurdler: lightly-raced maiden chaser: stays 3m: acts on heavy going: usually wears headgear/tongue tie. *Peter Bowen* **c– h–**

LIMINI (IRE) 8 ch.m. Peintre Celebre (USA) – Her Grace (IRE) (Spectrum (IRE)) [2018/19 h20g³ h20g³ h24s⁴ h19.9sᵖᵘ Mar 12] angular mare: smart on Flat, stays 17f: similar at one time over hurdles, only useful in 2018/19 but not beaten far when fourth in Galmoy Hurdle at Gowran: bled final outing: stayed 3m: acted on heavy going: retired (reportedly in foal to Australia). *W. P. Mullins, Ireland* **h137**

LINCOLN COUNTY 8 b.g. Authorized (IRE) – Lane County (USA) (Rahy (USA)) [2018/19 h78: h21.2g⁶ c23.9mᵖᵘ h20.6g³ h26.5g⁴ h23.9g² h23.9g⁴ h27m h23.3gᵖᵘ Sep 17] poor maiden hurdler: pulled up in novice handicap on chasing debut: stays 3m: acts on good to firm going: wears headgear/tongue tie: temperamental. *Oliver Greenall* **c– h78 §**

L'INCORRIGIBLE (FR) 4 b.g. No Risk At All (FR) – Incorrigible (FR) (Septieme Ciel **b102 p**
(USA)) [2018/19 b14d* Nov 29] €75,000 3-y-o: brother to bumper winner Nickolson
and half-brother to several winners by Martaline, including fair hurdler/useful chaser
Hollywoodien (2m-19f winner) and bumper winner/fairly useful hurdler Jabulani (19f-3m
winner): dam unraced: 2/1, won junior bumper at Warwick on debut impressively by 3½
lengths from Frenchy du Large: looked sure to go on to better things but not seen out again.
Tom Lacey

LINED WITH SILVER (IRE) 10 gr.g. Cloudings (IRE) – Tinkers Lady (Sheer Grit) **c99**
[2018/19 c97, h–: c20.8g May 4] maiden hurdler: modest chaser: probably stays 23f, **h–**
though effective at much shorter: acts on good to firm going. *Miss Hannah Taylor*

LINEMASON (IRE) 7 b.g. Sandmason – Superline (IRE) (Darnay) [2018/19 h19.9gᵖᵘ **h–**
h16g Sep 25] Irish maiden pointer: no form over hurdles. *Derek Shaw*

LINENHALL (IRE) 7 ch.g. Stowaway – Option (IRE) (Red Ransom (USA)) [2018/19 **c111**
h124: c24.5g⁴ May 6] fairly useful hurdle winner: 4/1, jumped left when fourth in novice **h–**
handicap at Towcester (13¼ lengths behind Dylanseoghan) on chasing debut: should be
suited by 3m: tried in cheekpieces: front runner/races prominently. *Ben Pauling*

LINE OUT (IRE) 7 b.g. Shantou (USA) – Bluebell Line (IRE) (Charnwood Forest (IRE)) **h132**
[2018/19 h20g⁶ h17m² Jul 19] fifth foal: brother to bumper/fairly useful 2m hurdle winner
Toe The Line: dam, placed at 2m over hurdles, 1½m winner on Flat: useful handicap
hurdler: second at Killarney (½ length behind Play The Game) in July: stays 2½m: acts on
good to firm and heavy going. *John E. Kiely, Ireland*

L'INGANNO FELICE (FR) 9 br.g. Librettist (USA) – Final Overture (FR) (Rossini **h138**
(USA)) [2018/19 h109p: h16.7g⁴ h15.8g* h16.7m* h16.7gᵖᵘ Sep 29] useful form over
hurdles: won novices at Market Rasen in May and Uttoxeter in June, and Summer Hurdle
(Handicap) at Market Rasen (by 2¼ lengths from Fair Mountain) in July: raced around 2m:
acts on good to firm going: wears hood: usually leads. *Iain Jardine*

LINGUINE (FR) 9 ch.g. Linngari (IRE) – Amerissage (USA) (Rahy (USA)) [2018/19 **h99**
h109: h16g h18.5g h26.5m⁶ h26.5m² h26.5gᵖᵘ h23.4m⁵ Apr 22] small gelding: fair
handicap hurdler: stays 25f: acts on soft and good to firm going: has worn headgear (only
once in 2018/19). *Dai Williams*

LION OF LACKABANE (IRE) 8 b.g. Welsh Lion (IRE) – Lackabane Julie (IRE) **h–**
(Broken Hearted) [2018/19 h65: h17.7d h21.4g Feb 27] maiden pointer: little form over
hurdles: tried in visor. *Jimmy Frost*

LION ROUGE (FR) 5 b.g. Rajsaman (FR) – Serpenta (GER) (Protektor (GER)) [2018/19 **h109**
h15.8g² h19.9g² h19.9gᶠ Jul 18] fair form over hurdles: left L. Maceli after final start in
2017/18: stayed 2½m: dead. *Stuart Edmunds*

LIOSDUIN BHEARNA (IRE) 6 b.g. Beneficial – Cloth Fair (IRE) (Old Vic) [2018/19 **h129**
b15.7g² b15.8g³ h19.9v² h23.6d² h20.5d* h19.5d* Mar 20] €7,000 3-y-o: second foal: **b89**
brother to fairly useful hurdler/useful chaser Cloth Cap (21f-25f winner), stays 4m: dam,
2m hurdle winner (stayed 3m), half-sister to fair hurdler/fairly useful chaser (stayed 25f)
Askmeroe: placed both starts in bumpers: fairly useful form over hurdles: won handicaps
at Ayr in February and Chepstow in March: will prove suited by 3m. *Fergal O'Brien*

LIP SERVICE (IRE) 10 ch.g. Presenting – Top Her Up (IRE) (Beneficial) [2018/19 c–, **c117**
h110: c19.2m³ c22.6m* Jun 19] well-made gelding: has had breathing operation: maiden **h–**
hurdler: fairly useful form over fences: won handicap at Stratford in June: stays 23f: acts
on good to firm and heavy going: usually wears hood: has worn tongue tie. *Fergal O'Brien*

LISA DE VASSY (FR) 4 b.f. Cokoriko (FR) – Mona Vassy (FR) (Sleeping Car (FR)) **h–**
[2018/19 h16gᵖᵘ Oct 31] half-sister to fairly useful hurdler Or de Vassy (17f-2½m winner,
by Assessor) and French 19f chase winner Grassland Sulpice (by Epalo): dam, placed up to
19f over hurdles/fences in France, half-sister to smart hurdler (2m-21f winner) James de
Vassy: fairly useful winner around 1¼m on Flat in France: 5/4, reportedly bled when pulled
up in fillies juvenile at Fakenham on hurdling debut. *Paul Nicholls*

LISDOONVARNA LAD (IRE) 7 br.g. Westerner – Socialite Girl (Glacial Storm **c119**
(USA)) [2018/19 h118, b95: c16.2g⁴ c21.4d⁴ c20.5g c19.2Dᶠ h21m Feb 23] tall gelding: **h–**
fairly useful hurdle winner: similar form over fences (has been let down by jumping): stays ,
21f: acts on soft going: tried in cheekpieces. *Charlie Longsdon*

LISHEEN CASTLE (IRE) 4 b.g. Most Improved (IRE) – Mafaaza (USA) (Jazil (USA)) **h108 p**
[2018/19 h16d* h16.7d⁴ Feb 5] fairly useful on Flat, should stay at least 1¼m: fair form
over hurdles: won juvenile maiden at Wetherby in January: should still improve. *Nicky
Henderson*

Albert Bartlett Prestige Novices' Hurdle, Haydock—Lisnagar Oscar storms clear

LISHEEN PRINCE (IRE) 8 b.g. Oscar (IRE) – Dino's Monkey (IRE) (Mr Dinos (IRE)) **h–** [2018/19 h–: h20g May 18] lengthy gelding: won Irish point on debut: fairly useful 2½m hurdle winner, well beaten in handicap only start in 2018/19. *Olly Murphy*

LISNAGAR OSCAR (IRE) 6 b.g. Oscar (IRE) – Asta Belle (FR) (Astarabad (USA)) **h135** [2018/19 b16d³ h20s² h24s² h19.5d* h24.3g* h24d⁵ h24.7d³ Apr 5] £105,000 5-y-o: rather **b95** unfurnished gelding: fourth foal: dam unraced sister to high-class hurdler/top-class chaser (stays 3¼m) Whisper: won Irish point on debut: shaped well when third in bumper at Chepstow (6¾ lengths behind McFabulous): useful form over hurdles: won novice at Chepstow in January and Prestige Novices' Hurdle at Haydock (by 10 lengths from Ask Ben) in February: third in Sefton Novices' Hurdle at Aintree (10 lengths behind Champ) final start: stays 25f: acts on soft going: good chasing prospect. *Rebecca Curtis*

LISP (IRE) 5 ch.g. Poet's Voice – Hora (Hernando (FR)) [2018/19 h122: h17.7d* h16.3s² **h139** h15.7s² h15.7d h16.8d⁵ Mar 15] sturdy gelding: useful handicap hurdler: won at Fontwell in November: second in Betfair Exchange Trophy at Ascot (2¼ lengths behind Mohaayed) and fifth in County Hurdle at Cheltenham (8½ lengths behind Ch'tibello): likely to prove best at 2m: acts on heavy going. *Alan King*

LISRONAGH STONE (IRE) 6 b.g. Arcadio (GER) – From Above (IRE) (Anshan) **h91** [2018/19 h20.5s⁵ Mar 11] second foal: dam unraced sister to fairly useful hurdler/chaser (2½m-25f winner) Baily Storm: off mark in Irish points at sixth attempt: 40/1, fifth of 6 in novice at Plumpton (17¼ lengths behind Myplaceatmidnight) on hurdling debut. *Paul Henderson*

LISSEN TO THE LADY (IRE) 5 b.m. Fame And Glory – Liss Rua (IRE) (Bob Back **b60** (USA)) [2018/19 b16.2g⁶ b16.2g⁶ Apr 15] €8,000 3-y-o: half-sister to several winners, including fairly useful hurdler/useful chaser Minella Aris (2½m-3m winner, by King's Theatre) and bumper winner/fairly useful hurdler Pym (2m-21f winner, by Stowaway): dam (h97), bumper winner (placed up to 3m over hurdles), half-sister to very smart hurdler (winner up to 2½m) Liss A Paoraigh: poor form in bumpers. *Sandy Forster*

LISSYCASEY (IRE) 6 b.g. Rule of Law (USA) – Forever Mates (IRE) (Un Desperado **h101**
(FR)) [2018/19 h115, b–: h19.9m³ h16g³ h19.6g h21.2g h21.2d h21.2m² Apr 23] rather
unfurnished gelding: runner-up on completed start in Irish points: fair maiden hurdler: left
Sheila Lewis after fifth start: stays 21f: acts on soft and good to firm going: tried in tongue
tie. *Kim Bailey*

LISTEN DEAR (IRE) 9 b.m. Robin des Champs (FR) – Crescendor (FR) (Lavirco **c141**
(GER)) [2018/19 c141, h–: c18.2g² c17d² c20s² c16d³ Nov 11] winning hurdler: useful **h–**
chaser: runner-up first 3 starts in 2018/19, including in handicap at Galway (3½ lengths
behind Show And Go) and minor event at Listowel (head behind Don't Touch It): stays
2½m: acts on soft going: usually races close up/travels strongly. *W. P. Mullins, Ireland*

LISTENTOTHEWOMEN (IRE) 6 b.m. Millenary – Dipper's Double (IRE) (Taipan **c–**
(IRE)) [2018/19 h22.1mᵖᵘ c21g Aug 7] sturdy mare: fourth foal: dam unraced half-sister to **h–**
Midlands Grand National winner G V A Ireland: runner-up both completed starts in points:
no show in maiden hurdle/chase. *Mrs Caroline McCaldin, Ireland*

LIST ONE 7 b.m. Tobougg (IRE) – Minibelle (Macmillion) [2018/19 b15.8d⁶ b15.8s² **b91**
Dec 5] fifth foal: half-sister to fairly useful hurdler/winning pointer Queens Bay (2m
winner, by Karinga Bay), stayed 25f: dam (c69/h74) 27f chase winner: fair form in
bumpers: better effort when second in mares event at Ludlow: left Neil Mulholland after
first start. *Colin Tizzard*

LITHIC (IRE) 8 b.g. Westerner – Acoola (IRE) (Flemensfirth (USA)) [2018/19 c124, **c128 §**
h117: c20g⁴ c21.4m⁴ c25.1m⁴ c20v² c20sᶠ c20d⁵ c24v² c24.2v² c25.3g³ Apr 17] good- **h–**
topped gelding: fairly useful hurdler: fairly useful maiden chaser: placed 7 times, including
in novice handicap at Cheltenham in April: stays 25f: acts on good to firm and heavy going:
has worn headgear, including last 4 starts: no battler. *Jonjo O'Neill*

LITTERALE CI (FR) 6 b.m. Soldier of Fortune (IRE) – Cigalia (Red Ransom (USA)) **h132**
[2018/19 h122: h20d* h20g⁴ h21.6g* h21.4g² Nov 10] useful handicap hurdler: won at
Ffos Las in May and Newton Abbot in September: stays 2¾m: acts on soft going: usually
travels strongly. *Harry Fry*

LITTLE ALLSTAR (IRE) 6 b.g. Morozov (USA) – Little Twinkle (IRE) (Fourstars **c84**
Allstar (USA)) [2018/19 h94, b68: c20.9m⁶ h20.3gᵖᵘ Oct 10] placed in Irish point on debut: **h–**
modest form at best over hurdles, lame final start: sixth in novice handicap at Stratford
(25½ lengths behind Isle Road) on chasing debut: wears tongue tie. *Sam Thomas*

LITTLE BAVINGTON 6 b.g. Strategic Prince – Vanilla Delight (Orpen (USA)) **h–**
[2018/19 b–: b16.4g h16.4d h16.2g Jan 13] little show in bumpers/over hurdles: tried in **b–**
tongue tie. *Ann Hamilton*

LITTLE BOY BORU (IRE) 11 b.g. Brian Boru – How Is Things (IRE) (Norwich) **c–**
[2018/19 h23.4vᵖᵘ h21.6s h23s h25s⁵ h25s⁵ c24sᵘʳ Mar 23] lengthy gelding: fair handicap **h105**
hurdler: won at Plumpton in February: twice-raced chaser, unseated fourth final start in
2018/19: stays 25f: acts on heavy going: tried in headgear. *Suzy Smith*

LITTLE BRUCE (IRE) 7 b.g. Yeats (IRE) – Lady Rolfe (IRE) (Alzao (USA)) [2018/19 **c130**
h108§: c20.1d⁴ c24.2g* c28.4gᶠ c24.2sᵖᵘ c23.4s² c30g² c25.2m³ c30.7d* c25.3g² Apr 17] **h–**
sturdy gelding: fair hurdler: useful handicap chaser: won at Hexham in November
and Huntingdon in March: second in another novice event at Cheltenham (7 lengths behind
Bob Mahler) in April: stays 31f: acts on good to firm and heavy going: wears headgear:
tried in tongue tie: front runner/races prominently. *Philip Kirby*

LITTLE CHARLOTTE (FR) 4 b.f. Diogenes (IRE) – Neicha (FR) (Neverneyev **b–**
(USA)) [2018/19 b14g b16g Feb 22] close-coupled filly: half-sister to several winners,
including smart 2m/17f hurdle winner Ch'tibello (stays 2½m) and French 2¼m chase
winner J'ai Oublie Nico (both by Sageburg): dam French maiden (placed at 11f): well
beaten in bumpers. *Christian Williams*

LITTLE CHIP (IRE) 12 b.g. Dushyantor (USA) – Aunt Chris (IRE) (Moscow Society **c– §**
(USA)) [2018/19 c27.7gᵖᵘ May 17] multiple point winner: maiden hurdler: fairly useful **h–**
chaser at best, pulled up in hunter in early-2018/19: stays 27f: acts on soft and good to firm
going: has worn headgear/tongue tie: temperamental. *Richard Bandey*

LITTLE CHUNK (IRE) 7 ch.g. Mr Dinos (IRE) – Daly Lady (IRE) (Lord of Appeal) **c–**
[2018/19 c–, h120: c16mᶠ Jun 21] sturdy gelding: fairly useful hurdler: no aptitude for **h–**
chasing: acted on good to soft going: in tongue tie last 4 starts: usually raced
close up: dead. *Kim Bailey*

LITTLE DOTTY 10 br.m. Erhaab (USA) – Marsh Marigold (Tina's Pet) [2018/19 h76: **h–**
h16.2sᶠ h21.2dᵖᵘ Apr 23] bumper winner: lightly-raced maiden hurdler, little show since
debut in 2016/17. *Giuseppe Fierro*

522

LITTLE FOLKE 8 gr.m. Sagamix (FR) – Little Choice (IRE) (King's Theatre (IRE)) [2018/19 h16g⁶ h16.5g h16d h16.3gᶠ Apr 14] has had breathing operation: first foal, dam, third in point, half-sister to dam of Queen Mother Champion Chase winner Special Tiara: fair hurdler: once-raced chaser: left Henry de Bromhead after second start: raced around 2m: often in tongue tie. *Nikki Evans*   **c– h99**

LITTLE GINGE (FR) 6 ch.g. Kapgarde (FR) – Aconit (FR) (Shining Steel) [2018/19 b16.8s b16s Mar 10] sturdy gelding: little promise in bumpers. *Venetia Williams*   **b–**

LITTLE IMBER 6 b.m. Sulamani (IRE) – Clover Dove (Overbury (IRE)) [2018/19 b15.3m May 15] £2,000 3-y-o: fourth foal: half-sister to fairly useful hurdler/chaser Top Smart (19f-3m winner, by Karinga Bay): dam, ran twice in bumpers, out of half-sister to Champion Hurdle winner Flakey Dove: well beaten in mares bumper. *Seamus Mullins*   **b–**

LITTLE JACK 5 b.g. Malinas (GER) – Persian Forest (Presenting) [2018/19 b17.7g* b16.7g³ h21.2gʳʳ h19.2d h23.1s⁵ Mar 18] €38,000 3-y-o: has had breathing operation: third foal: dam lightly-raced sister to useful hurdler/very smart chaser (stayed 3m) Our Ben: fairly useful form in bumpers: won at Fontwell in June: poor form over hurdles: should stay at least 2½m: temperamental (has refused to race). *Warren Greatrex*   **h73 § b97**

LITTLE JIMMY 12 br.g. Passing Glance – Sementina (USA) (Silver Charm (USA)) [2018/19 c92, h–: c20.3g³ c24.1gᵖᵘ c16.3d⁵ c20d⁴ c19.4d³ c21.2g⁵ c15.7dᵖᵘ Apr 24] close-coupled gelding: maiden hurdler: poor handicap chaser nowadays: stays 21f: acts on heavy going: wears headgear/tongue tie. *Tom Gretton*   **c84 h–**

LITTLE JIMMY BROWN (IRE) 11 b.g. Perugino (USA) – Kings Glory (IRE) (King's Ride) [2018/19 h20gᵖᵘ Jul 4] point winner: maiden hurdler, modest at best: unseated only run in chase: in hood last 4 starts: dead. *Kevin Bishop*   **c– h–**

LITTLE JON 11 b.g. Pasternak – Jowoody (Gunner B) [2018/19 c124x, h–: c19gᵖᵘ c23.8m⁵ c20.9v⁵ Mar 7] tall gelding: maiden hurdler: useful chaser at best, no form in 2018/19: wears cheekpieces. *Nigel Twiston-Davies*   **c– h–**

LITTLE LADY LU (IRE) 4 ch.f. Mahler – Sparrow's Trap (IRE) (Magical Wonder (USA)) [2018/19 b14.6g⁴ b16gˢᵘ b16s⁵ Mar 3] fourth foal: half-sister to useful hurdler Massini's Trap (2m-2½m winner, by Dr Massini), stays 3m, and a winning pointer by Brian Boru: dam poor maiden hurdler: no form in bumpers. *James A. Nash, Ireland*   **b–**

LITTLE MILLIE (IRE) 7 b.m. Milan – Sweetbitter (FR) (Turgeon (USA)) [2018/19 h106: h24g² h23.3m² h23g³ h23.3d⁴ h23.4d⁴ h24.1d⁶ h20.7g³ h19.6d⁴ h25.5g² h23.3d* h26g* Apr 10] compact mare: has had breathing operation: Irish point winner: fairly useful handicap hurdler: won at Uttoxeter in March and Warwick in April: stays 3¼m: acts on soft and good to firm going: usually wears headgear: has worn tongue tie. *Neil King*   **h116**

LITTLE MISS DARSI (IRE) 6 b.m. Darsi (FR) – Shaylejon (IRE) (Old Vic) [2018/19 h21g⁶ h21.2g² h21g Nov 12] off mark in Irish points at second attempt: fair form over hurdles: best effort when second of 4 in mares novice at Ludlow: dead. *Charlie Mann*   **h101**

LITTLE MISS POET 7 b.m. Yeats (IRE) – R de Rien Sivola (FR) (Robin des Champs (FR)) [2018/19 h116: h23.3d³ h19.8m* h21.4g⁴ h21.6g⁵ c20.2d² c20m* c21.3g² c20.6g² Apr 18] lengthy mare: fairly useful handicap hurdler: won at Wincanton in May: useful form over fences: won 3-runner mares novice at Ludlow in January: second in listed mares novice handicap at Cheltenham in April: stays 23f: acts on good to firm and heavy going: has worn hood: often travels strongly. *Philip Hobbs*   **c137 h121**

LITTLE PIPPIN 6 b.m. Sir Percy – Lady Le Quesne (IRE) (Alhaarth (IRE)) [2018/19 h87: h16.2g⁵ h16.2g* h15.5d³ h16s Dec 26] modest handicap hurdler: won at Hexham in November: unproven beyond 2m: acts on good to soft going: in cheekpieces last 4 starts. *Tony Coyle*   **h95**

LITTLE RED LION (IRE) 5 b.g. Sans Frontieres (IRE) – Rever Up (IRE) (Revoque (IRE)) [2018/19 b15.8v² h16.5d h19.5d h16.5d h19s Mar 19] dam winning pointer: second in maiden bumper at Ffos Las: poor form over hurdles. *David Pipe*   **h81 b84**

LITTLE RICH (IRE) 4 b.g. Arakan (USA) – Brioney (IRE) (Barathea (IRE)) [2018/19 h15.8g h17.7v⁴ h16.2d³ h21.7v² h22g Mar 30] brother to 2 winners on Flat, including 1½m-2m winner Conkering Hero, and half-brother to several winners on Flat: dam, ran once over hurdles, 1¼m-1½m winner on Flat: modest form over hurdles: in cheekpieces last 3 starts. *David Bridgwater*   **h89**

LITTLE ROBIN (IRE) 7 b.m. Robin des Pres (FR) – Soi (IRE) (Bob Back (USA)) [2018/19 h16g⁴ h16.8v⁶ h18.5dᵘʳ h16.5g Jan 9] €2,000 3-y-o: first foal: dam lightly-raced sister to useful hurdler/high-class staying chaser Burton Port: no sign of ability. *Laura Hurley*   **h– b–**

LITTLE RORY MAC (IRE) 5 b.g. Yeats (IRE) – Solar Quest (IRE) (King's Ride) **h116 p**
[2018/19 b91p: b16.2s⁵ h15.8s⁴ h15.8v³ Jan 26] runner-up on first of 2 starts in bumpers: **b–**
fairly useful form over hurdles: better effort when third in maiden at Uttoxeter: left Philip
Hobbs after first start: open to further improvement. *Henry Oliver*

LITTLE STEVIE 7 b.g. Overbury (IRE) – Candy's Room (IRE) (Alderbrook) [2018/19 **c103**
c17.1g³ c16g⁴ c16.5g⁵ h20.1g h20.9g h16.2g² h15.8d h19.6g⁵ h19.6d⁵ Apr 26] modest **h94**
handicap hurdler: fair maiden chaser: left Donald McCain after third start, Russell Ross
after sixth: stays 19f: acts on soft going: tried in cheekpieces: has worn tongue tie, including
final start: usually races off pace: has finished weakly. *Stella Barclay*

LITTLE VERN (IRE) 5 b.g. Oscar (IRE) – Silver Valley (IRE) (Henbit (USA)) [2018/19 **h–**
b–: b17.7s³ h17.7v^pu h16s h21.4g Feb 27] unfurnished gelding: has had breathing **b88**
operation: fair form when third in bumper at Plumpton: little show in novice hurdles.
Colin Tizzard

LITTLE VIC 8 br.g. Overbury (IRE) – Vicky Bee (Alflora (IRE)) [2018/19 h20g⁵ h23s³ **h98**
h24g³ Jun 12] modest form when third in novice hurdle at Worcester, standout effort: tried
in hood. *Amy Murphy*

LITTLE WELSHCAKE 6 ch.m. Generous (IRE) – Retro's Lady (IRE) (Zaffaran (USA)) **h–**
[2018/19 h16.3g h16g h16g Jul 26] no sign of ability: in hood last 2 starts: tried in tongue
tie. *Kevin Bishop*

LITTLE WINDMILL (IRE) 9 ch.g. Mahler – Ennismore Queen (IRE) (Glacial Storm **c114 §**
(USA)) [2018/19 c100§, h65: c22.5m⁶ h20.3g⁴ c25.5m³ h23g* c25.8m* h24g³ c25.7g* **h95 §**
c24g² c21.2g^pu c25.6g^pu h23.9d^pu c25.7s^pu c25.7g² c24d² Apr 24] small gelding: has had
breathing operation: modest handicap hurdler: won at Worcester (amateurs) in July: fair
handicap chaser: won at Newton Abbot in August and Plumpton in September: stays 3¼m:
acts on good to firm and heavy going: wears headgear/tongue tie: usually races close up:
unreliable. *Neil King*

LIVA (IRE) 4 ch.g. Champs Elysees – Resistance Heroine (Dr Fong (USA)) [2018/19 **h122**
h15.7g² h15.6g* h15.6g² h19.8s* h15.7m h17m⁴ Apr 20] has had breathing operation: dam
half-sister to fairly useful 2m hurdle winner Szabo's Destiny: fair on Flat, stays 1½m: fairly
useful form over hurdles: won juvenile at Musselburgh in December and handicap at same
course in March: stays 2½m: acts on soft going: often in cheekpieces: usually front runner/
races prominently. *Donald McCain*

LIVE FOR TODAY (IRE) 8 b.g. Alflora (IRE) – Uppermost (Montjeu (IRE)) [2018/19 **c–**
c–, h–: h23g^pu h20g² h23.3g h15.8v³ h20v⁵ c16.1d⁶ Mar 11] winning pointer: poor maiden **h72**
hurdler: little show in 2 chases: left Kevin Bishop after fourth start: stays 2½m: in headgear
last 5 starts: wears tongue tie. *Tim Vaughan*

LIVELOVELAUGH (IRE) 9 b.g. Beneficial – Another Evening (IRE) (Saddlers' Hall **c146**
(IRE)) [2018/19 c134, h–: c24.5g^pu c21g² c26d c34.3g Apr 6] good-topped gelding: **h–**
winning hurdler: smart chaser: second to Whisperinthebreeze in Leopardstown Handicap
Chase in February and O O Seven in Guinness Handicap Chase at Punchestown shortly
after end of British season: best around 2½m (shaped well long way in Grand National):
acts on heavy going. *W. P. Mullins, Ireland*

LIVELY ARTICLE (IRE) 8 b.g. Definite Article – Mountain Time (IRE) (Bishop of **h119**
Cashel) [2018/19 h23.3g* h24g² Oct 12] €5,200 3-y-o: first foal: dam (b82) ran twice in
bumpers (second on debut): point winner: fairly useful form over hurdles: won novice at
Uttoxeter in June: improved when second in similar event at Southwell 4 months later.
Fiona Kehoe

LIZ'S DREAM 6 b.m. Dick Turpin (IRE) – Whatcameoverme (USA) (Aldebaran (USA)) **h89**
[2018/19 b81: b16.3g² b17.1d^rr h20.7g³ Jan 11] modest form in bumpers: 50/1, third in **b81 §**
mares maiden at Huntingdon (18½ lengths behind Etamine du Cochet) on hurdling debut:
has worn hood: one to treat with caution (has refused to race). *Robyn Brisland*

LIZZIE LANGTON 8 b.m. Kayf Tara – Madam Flora (Alflora (IRE)) [2018/19 h85: **c88**
h15.3m h15.3m^pu c20s³ c26.7g* c26v^pu c25.1g⁵ c25.1g³ c25.1s³ c26.7g³ Mar 25] has had **h–**
breathing operation: maiden hurdler: modest handicap chaser: won at Wincanton in
December: stays 27f: acts on heavy going: wears tongue tie. *Colin Tizzard*

LLANCILLO LORD (IRE) 9 b.g. Beneficial – Llancillo Lady (IRE) (Be My Native **c111**
(USA)) [2018/19 c–, h–: c16s c19.4v c21.2m* Apr 22] winning hurdler: fair chaser: won **h–**
on point debut then 3-runner novice hunter at Fakenham in April: left Robert Walford after
second start: stays 21f: acts on soft and good to firm going: often wears hood/tongue tie. *R.
D. Potter*

LLANDINABO LAD 4 ch.g. Malinas (GER) – Hot Rhythm (Haafhd) [2018/19 b16s⁴ **b93 p** Mar 10] sturdy gelding: first foal: dam (b76) ran twice in bumpers (third on debut): 50/1, shaped well when fourth in bumper at Warwick (5½ lengths behind Chantry House): should improve. *Tom Symonds*

LLANTARA 8 b.m. Kayf Tara – Lady Llancillo (IRE) (Alflora (IRE)) [2018/19 h109: **h112** h15.8d³ h15.8v³ h16.2v* Mar 14] fair handicap hurdler: won at Hexham (conditionals) in March following breathing operation: unproven beyond 17f: acts on heavy going: wears tongue tie: often races towards rear. *Tom Symonds*

LOAD UP TIME (IRE) 5 br.g. Stowaway – Orinocco Blue (IRE) (Pistolet Bleu (IRE)) **h110** [2018/19 h16g h20d h21v h19s h16.5d⁴ h20d³ h24d h21v⁵ h21v³ h23.9g² h20.2d* Apr 26] fourth foal: dam (b78), ran once in bumper, half-sister to fair hurdlers/fairly useful chasers Avoca Promise (stayed 2½m) and Point Blank (stayed 3m): fair handicap hurdler: in first-time cheekpieces/tongue strap, won at Perth in April: stays 3m: acts on heavy going. *Gordon Elliott, Ireland*

LOCAL SHOW (IRE) 11 br.g. Oscar (IRE) – Loughaderra Rose (IRE) (Roselier (FR)) **c–** [2018/19 c126, h–: h25gᵖᵘ May 10] lengthy gelding: multiple point winner, mostly in 2019: **h–** fairly useful hurdler/useful chaser at best: stays 3m: acts on heavy going: in headgear last 3 starts: tried in tongue tie: usually races close up. *Sarah Humphrey*

LOCH GARMAN ARIS (IRE) 9 b.g. Jammaal – See Em Aime (IRE) (Little Bighorn) **c86** [2018/19 h–: h23.1g⁶ c20.3g³ c20d⁴ c20.3s³ c21.4g³ Mar 20] bumper winner: no form over **h–** hurdles: modest form over fences: should stay 3m: acts on soft going: usually races nearer last than first. *Gary Hanmer*

LOCHINVER (FR) 5 b.g. American Post – Golden Gleam (IRE) (Acclamation) [2018/19 **h–** b16.8m⁴ h16s h15.8d h16.3s Dec 19] has had breathing operation: won point bumper on **b–** debut: well held under Rules, mainly over hurdles: left David Pipe after first outing: in hood last 3 starts. *Charlie Longsdon*

LOCH LINNHE 7 b.g. Tobougg (IRE) – Quistaquay (El Conquistador) [2018/19 h109: **c110** c20.1d* c24.1gᵖᵘ c20.1g³ c24gᵖᵘ c24s³ c21.6m⁶ h23.1d³ h24s² h23.1d⁴ h25.3m³ c23.4d **h108** c24d* Apr 24] has had breathing operation: fair handicap hurdler: similar standard as chaser: won novice at Hexham in May and handicap at Southwell in April: left Mark Walford after fifth start: stays 3m: acts on soft going: wears headgear: tried in tongue tie: usually front runner/races prominently. *Gillian Boanas*

LOCKER ROOM TALK (IRE) 6 b.g. Beneficial – Whistling Gypse (IRE) (Good **h119** Thyne (USA)) [2018/19 b–p: h15.8g h16.2g⁶ h15.8g⁴ h15.8g* h16.5g Apr 6] runner-up in Irish point on debut: fairly useful form over hurdles: won maiden at Huntingdon in March: raced only at 2m: in hood last 5 starts: usually races freely. *Nigel Twiston-Davies*

LOCK'S CORNER (IRE) 5 b.g. Gold Well – Last Century (IRE) (Glacial Storm **h121** (USA)) [2018/19 h15.8d² h16s⁵ Mar 10] €39,000 3-y-o, £215,000 4-y-o: useful-looking gelding: has had breathing operation: closely related to fairly useful hurdler/chaser Steele's Rock (2½m winner, by King's Theatre) and a winning pointer by Oscar, and half-brother to a winning pointer by Ashkalani: dam unraced sister to useful hurdler (stayed 3¼m) Glacial Sunset: easy winner of Irish point on debut: fairly useful form over hurdles: much better effort when second in maiden at Huntingdon: will be suited by 2½m+. *Jonjo O'Neill*

LOFGREN 8 b.g. Multiplex – Sherry Darling (IRE) (Alflora (IRE)) [2018/19 c127, h–: **c131** c20.6g² c25g³ c24.1g² c25.5s* c25.5g c20.3g* c26.2gᵖᵘ c19.4g³ c24g⁴ Dec 15] sturdy **h–** gelding: winning hurdler: useful handicap chaser: won at Cartmel in August and Bangor (by 6 lengths from Mill Quest) in October: stays 25f: acts on soft and good to firm going: wears headgear/tongue tie. *Donald McCain*

LOGAN ROCKS (IRE) 4 b.g. Yeats (IRE) – Countess Comet (IRE) (Medicean) **b94** [2018/19 b13.7m² b13.7g³ b16.2v² b15.8d⁴ b16.3d⁴ Mar 22] angular gelding: first foal: dam (c107/h108), 2m hurdle winner (stayed 2½m), also 1½m winner on Flat: fair bumper performer, in frame all 5 starts including in listed event. *Amy Murphy*

LOMACHENKO (IRE) 5 ch.g. Sans Frontieres (IRE) – Midnight Orchid (IRE) **h114** (Petardia) [2018/19 b15.8d h20m⁴ h20.5g* h24.6g⁴ h19.6s² Mar 23] €18,500 3-y-o: big, **b–** lengthy gelding: has had breathing operation: half-brother to fair hurdler/chaser Castletown Bridge (2m-27f winner, by Bienamado): dam, 6f winner, half-sister to useful hurdler/fairly useful chaser Buddy Marvel (stayed 21f): shaped as if needed experience in bumper: fair form over hurdles: won maiden at Leicester in December: has joined Stuart Crawford, Ireland. *Nicky Henderson*

LON

LONDON GRAMMAR (IRE) 5 b.m. Sir Prancealot (IRE) – Emmas Princess (IRE) **h–**
(Bahhare (USA)) [2018/19 h15.9g⁶ h19.5g h19.5d Nov 27] half-sister to a winning jumper
in Slovakia by Frozen Power: poor/temperamental on Flat, stays 1½m: no form over
hurdles. *Ralph Smith*

LONDONIA 7 gr.g. Paco Boy (IRE) – Snowdrops (Gulch (USA)) [2018/19 h104: h16.7g⁶ **c–**
h20.3g³ c20g⁴ Jun 27] fair handicap hurdler: well beaten in novice on chasing debut: stays **h103**
2½m: acts on good to firm and good to soft going: wears hood/tongue tie. *Graeme McPherson*

LONG CALL 6 b.g. Authorized (IRE) – Gacequita (URU) (Ride The Rails (USA)) **c100 p**
[2018/19 h16.4g c16g³ Nov 19] lengthy gelding: fairly useful hurdler: fit from Flat when **h–**
well held on return: 12/1, last of 3 in maiden at Hereford on chasing debut: raced only at
2m: acts on heavy going: wears tongue tie: should do better over fences. *Tony Carroll*

LONGHOUSE POET (IRE) 5 b.g. Yeats (IRE) – Moscow Madame (IRE) (Moscow **b110 p**
Society (USA)) sixth foal: closely related to fair hurdler/winning pointer Longhousesignora
(21f winner, by Milan), and half-brother to fairly useful hurdler Moscow Presents (2m-3m
winner, by Presenting): dam, of little account, half-sister to fairly useful hurdler/useful
chaser (2½m-2¾m winner) Well Presented: won maiden point on debut: 6/1, also won
17-runner maiden bumper at Punchestown shortly after end of British season by 2½ lengths
from Monkfish, travelling well and in command final 1f: good prospect. *Martin Brassil,
Ireland*

LONGHOUSE SALE (IRE) 5 b.g. September Storm (GER) – Sweetbriar Rose (IRE) **b111**
(Dushyantor (USA)) [2018/19 b16.7m* b15.8g* b16.7m* b17.7g* Aug 23] €8,000 3-y-o:
fifth foal: half-brother to fair 2m hurdle winner Long House Island (by Turtle Island) and a
winning pointer by Tikkanen: dam unraced half-sister to useful hurdler/fairly useful chaser
(winner up to 21f) Line Ball: won Irish point on debut: useful form in bumpers: unbeaten
in 4 starts, winning at Market Rasen in June, Uttoxeter (by 17 lengths from De Young
Warrior) in July, and Market Rasen again (by 14 lengths from Forewarning) and Fontwell
in August: wears tongue tie. *Dan Skelton*

LONGHOUSESIGNORA (IRE) 7 b.m. Milan – Moscow Madame (IRE) (Moscow **c101 p**
Society (USA)) [2018/19 h106: c20.3g⁴ c20d³ c24.2d⁶ h21.2d* h20.6g² h25s h25d⁶ Mar **h110**
24] angular mare: winning Irish pointer: fair handicap hurdler: won mares event at Ludlow
in January: fair form in chases: stays 21f: acts on heavy going: remains with potential over
fences. *Venetia Williams*

LONG RIVER DANCER 6 b.g. Bollin Eric – Artist's Muse (USA) (Royal Academy **h–**
(USA)) [2018/19 b14d h19g⁵ h19.2d⁻ h16d Mar 20] no form in bumper/novice hurdles: **b–**
tried in tongue tie. *Neil Mulholland*

LONGTYMEGONE (IRE) 9 b.g. Portrait Gallery (IRE) – Katie O'Toole (IRE) **c80**
(Commanche Run) [2018/19 c26.2d* Apr 8] winning pointer: in cheekpieces, 16/1, very
fortunate when successful in maiden hunter at Kelso on chasing debut, all bar one rival
failing to complete. *Stuart Coltherd*

LOOKFORARAINBOW 6 b.g. Rainbow High – Look Here's May (Revoque (IRE)) **h105**
[2018/19 h95p, b83: h15.8d⁴ h16.7v h15.8d⁶ h15.8d⁵ h18.9d⁵ Mar 20] has had breathing
operation: fair form over hurdles: stays 19f: acts on good to soft going: wears hood: in
tongue tie last 5 starts: often races in rear. *Sarah Hollinshead*

LOOKING WELL (IRE) 10 b.g. Gold Well – Different Level (IRE) (Topanoora) **c141**
[2018/19 c137, h–: c23.8g² c27.3g c32.4g⁻ c24g* c26g⁻ Mar 2] winning hurdler: useful **h–**
handicap chaser: won veterans event at Doncaster in February: running well when falling
last in Grimthorpe Chase there 10 days later: stays 4m: acts on soft and good to firm going:
in cheekpieces last 3 starts. *Nicky Richards*

LOOK NOW 6 b.g. Observatory (USA) – One For Philip (Blushing Flame (USA)) **h–**
[2018/19 b16.4g⁵ b15.6g³ h19.8g⁴ Jan 7] £2,500 5-y-o: sixth foal: half-brother to fairly **b74**
useful hurdler/chaser One Lucky Lady (2m-21f winner, by Lucky Story) and fair hurdler
Onemix (2m winner, by Fair Mix): dam (b83) placed in bumpers: poor form in bumpers:
bled on hurdling debut. *James Ewart*

LOOKS FROZEN (IRE) 5 ch.g. Frozen Fire (GER) – Miss Beverley (Beveled (USA)) **h75**
[2018/19 b86: h15.9g⁶ h15.8s⁶ h16d h15.8d⁶ h15.8g Feb 21] lengthy gelding: placed in
bumpers: poor form over hurdles: raced around 2m: sometimes in hood: tried in tongue tie:
dead. *Neil Mulholland*

LOOKS LIKE MURT (IRE) 6 b.g. Well Chosen – Ninetypenceapound (IRE) (Treasure Hunter) [2018/19 b16s² h19.5d³ h20.6d² Apr 6] £20,000 4-y-o: fourth foal: dam lightly raced in points/bumpers: runner-up in Irish point and Ayr bumper 20 months apart: fair form when placed in novice hurdles at Ayr and Newcastle: should still improve. *Lucinda Russell*   **h108 p** **b84**

LOOKS LIKE POWER (IRE) 9 ch.g. Spadoun (FR) – Martovic (IRE) (Old Vic) [2018/19 c123, h104: c24.2s⁴ h23.6s³ h23.5d⁵ h23s³ c23.8s³ Apr 7] angular gelding: fairly useful handicap hurdler/chaser: stays 3m: acts on heavy going: wears headgear: usually tongue tied: races off pace. *Debra Hamer*   **c125** **h116**

LOOKSNOWTLIKEBRIAN (IRE) 8 b.g. Brian Boru – Sheebadiva (IRE) (Norwich) [2018/19 c125, h–: c24.5d* c26.2g* c29.5sᵖᵘ h23.6d Feb 23] fair hurdler: useful handicap chaser: won at Carlisle in October and November (by 10 lengths from Bako de La Saulaie): should stay long distances: acts on heavy going: tried in tongue tie: often races towards rear: sketchy jumper. *Tim Vaughan*   **c135 x** **h–**

LOOSE CHIPS 13 b.g. Sir Harry Lewis (USA) – Worlaby Rose (Afif) [2018/19 c136, h–: c24.5d⁵ c24.2v* h23.4v³ c24.2d⁵ c24.2sᵖᵘ c24.2s⁵ c23.8mᵖᵘ c25.6m⁵ Apr 20] close-coupled gelding: fairly useful handicap hurdler/chaser nowadays: won veterans event over fences at Sandown in November: stays 3½m: acts on good to firm and heavy going: wears headgear: usually leads. *Charlie Longsdon*   **c129** **h125**

LOPE DE LOOP (IRE) 4 b.f. Lope de Vega (IRE) – Patroller (USA) (Grand Slam (USA)) [2018/19 h16.8gᵖᵘ h15.8gᵖᵘ Apr 22] workmanlike filly: modest maiden at best on Flat: no form over hurdles: wears hood: tried in tongue tie. *Aytach Sadik*   **h–**

LOPES DANCER (IRE) 7 b.g. Lope de Vega (IRE) – Ballet Dancer (IRE) (Refuse To Bend (IRE)) [2018/19 h16d⁶ Nov 28] dam half-sister to fairly useful hurdler/useful chaser (stayed 2½m) Castafiore: fairly useful on Flat, stays 1¾m: 2/1, sixth in novice at Wetherby (19½ lengths behind Imperial Acolyte) on hurdling debut, tiring when bad mistake last: likely to improve. *Harriet Bethell*   **h90 p**

LOQUACIOUS LADY (IRE) 5 b.m. Milan – Jennifers Diary (IRE) (Supreme Leader) [2018/19 h15.3s h23.6d h21gᵖᵘ Apr 10] sixth foal: closely related to useful hurdler Mischievous Milly (2m/17f winner, by Old Vic), stayed 21f, and bumper winner/useful hurdler Jersey Bean (19f-3m winner, by Court Cave) and half-sister to bumper winner Robinesse (by Robin des Champs): dam (h88) placed in bumpers/over hurdles (stayed 3m): no form over hurdles. *Harry Fry*   **h–**

LORD ALDERVALE (IRE) 12 br.g. Alderbrook – Monavale (IRE) (Strong Gale) [2018/19 c77, h–: c26m⁵ c21.6g c23m⁴ Jul 9] well-made gelding: point winner: maiden hurdler: poor maiden chaser: stays 3¼m: acts on soft and good to firm going: has worn headgear/tongue tie: front runner/races prominently. *Steve Woodman*   **c67** **h–**

LORD BALLIM (FR) 9 ch.g. Balko (FR) – Lady Pauline (FR) (Hamas (IRE)) [2018/19 c106, h117: c20s* c23.8g h20m h23g² h27m⁵ c26.2g⁴ h23.6s c23.8d c19.4dᵘʳ c17.4g Apr 13] fairly useful handicap hurdler/chaser: won over fences at Worcester in May: lost way later in season: stays 27f: acts on good to firm and heavy going: wears headgear: usually tongue tied: races well off pace. *Nigel Hawke*   **c122** **h122**

LORD BEN (IRE) 14 b.g. Beneficial – Lady Bluebell (IRE) (Mister Lord (USA)) [2018/19 c114, h–: h16.8m⁴ c16g⁴ c17m³ c16.5g² c16.4m⁶ Aug 30] well-made gelding: fairly useful hurdler at one time: fair handicap chaser nowadays: stays 3m: acts on good to firm and heavy going: has worn headgear: front runner. *Dai Williams*   **c108** **h92**

LORD BRYAN (IRE) 8 b.g. Brian Boru – Run Cat (IRE) (Lord Americo) [2018/19 c123, h84: c19.2d³ c19.9s c23.4d⁴ c20s³ c19.4d³ c23.8s c21g* Apr 20] maiden hurdler: fairly useful handicap chaser: won at Newton Abbot in April: stays 3¼m: acts on heavy going: wears tongue tie: usually leads. *Peter Bowen*   **c124** **h–**

LORD CAPRIO (IRE) 4 b.g. Lord Shanakill (USA) – Azzurra du Caprio (IRE) (Captain Rio) [2018/19 h16.2g* h15.8s³ h16.8g² Oct 21] fair on Flat, stays 1¼m: fair form over hurdles: won juvenile at Hexham in June: best effort when second in similar event at Sedgefield: wears tongue tie. *Ben Haslam*   **h113**

LORD CONDI (IRE) 6 ch.g. Papal Bull – Wings To Soar (USA) (Woodman (USA)) [2018/19 b77: b17.7g* b16m³ h17.7g³ h17.7g* h21.2m* h16.4g h17.7g² Apr 24] sturdy gelding: fair form in bumpers: won at Fontwell in May: fairly useful form over hurdles: won novices at Plumpton in September and Ludlow in October: stays 21f: acts on good to firm going: usually races prominently. *Martin Keighley*   **h120** **b88**

888Sport Heroes Handicap Hurdle, Sandown—a strong staying performance from Lord Napier, who pulls clear of outsider Coole Cody (striped sleeves)

LORD COUNTY (FR) 5 gr.g. Lord du Sud (FR) – County County (FR) (Medaaly) [2018/19 c–, h117: c20.5v^{pu} c19.1g* c19.2g^5 c19.4g^2 c24g^4 c25.2m^4 c19.4g^3 Apr 26] good-topped gelding: fairly useful hurdler: fairly useful handicap chaser: won 3-runner event at Doncaster in December: stays 2½m: acts on heavy going: wears headgear. *Oliver Greenall* **c117 h–**

LORD DE LA MINE (FR) 4 gr.g. Lord du Sud (FR) – Brezole (FR) (Panoramic) [2018/19 h16.9g h16.9s c16.9d^4 h16g Apr 11] no form over hurdles/fences: left Emmanuel Clayeux after third start: tried in hood/tongue tie. *Oliver Greenall* **c– h–**

LORD DU MESNIL (FR) 6 b.g. Saint des Saints (FR) – Ladies Choice (FR) (Turgeon (USA)) [2018/19 c22.5g^F c25g^{ur} h19.9g^5 h22d^3 h25s^2 h24d h22s^3 h23.4g^6 c25.2g^F h22v^3 Mar 16] good-topped gelding: has had breathing operation: fourth foal: half-brother to fairly useful chaser Kings Cross (17f-2½m winner, by King's Theatre), stayed 3m: dam (c121/h121), French 2¼m-2½m hurdle/chase winner, sister to useful French hurdler up to 19f Ladytown: fairly useful maiden hurdler/chaser: left D. Bressou after final start in 2017/18: stays 25f: acts on heavy going: wears headgear/tongue tie: often let down by jumping over fences. *Richard Hobson* **c124 x h116**

LORD DUVEEN (IRE) 6 br.g. Doyen (IRE) – Afdala (IRE) (Hernando (FR)) [2018/19 h116p: h16d^6 h15.3g^4 h19.8s^3 Mar 7] tall gelding: fairly useful form first 2 starts over hurdles, well below best in 2018/19: bred to be suited by 2½m+: acts on soft going. *Philip Hobbs* **h99**

LORD FENDALE (IRE) 10 ch.g. Erewhon (USA) – Upton Lady (IRE) (Lord Upton (IRE)) [2018/19 h94: h15.8m^5 h18.7m^2 h17.2g^2 h18.5g^3 h15.7g^2 h15.6g^2 c16s^{ur} c17.8v^F Dec 26] modest handicap hurdler: departed early both starts over fences: stayed easy 19f: acted on soft and good to firm going: often wore headgear: tried in tongue tie: dead. *Tim Vaughan* **c– h96**

LORD GETAWAY (IRE) 7 b.g. Getaway (GER) – Terre d'Orient (FR) (Kabool) [2018/19 h108, b80: h20d^6 h21g c23.6d* h23.3v* c24.5g^F c23.9d^2 c25.3g^4 Apr 17] good-topped gelding: fair handicap hurdler: won at Uttoxeter in December: fairly useful form over fences: won novice handicap at Huntingdon earlier in December: should stay beyond 3m: acts on heavy going: tried in cheekpieces. *James Evans* **c121 h108**

LORD IN RED (GER) 7 ch.g. Noroit (GER) – Lady In Red (GER) (General Assembly (USA)) [2018/19 h24.5g^4 h24g h16g^3 h20g* h22d^5 c21g^3 h20g^4 c20d h19.5d^3 c21.2d^5 c23.6d^{pu} c25.8g^5 Apr 20] fourth foal: half-brother to German 10.5f-12.5f winner Lord Of The Dark (by Lavirco): dam German 7.5f-9.5f winner: fair hurdler: won maiden at Roscommon in October: similar form over fences: left Noel Meade after ninth start: stays 3m: acts on heavy going: tried in blinkers: often tongue tied. *Christian Williams* **c112 h114**

LORD MARMADUKE 6 ch.g. Duke of Marmalade (IRE) – Maid To Treasure (IRE) **c– §**
(Rainbow Quest (USA)) [2018/19 h107§: h16.2g h20.5g² h20.7d c15.9m^pu h15.8d³ h19.9s⁶ **h104 §**
h20.3d^ur Apr 9] sturdy gelding: has had breathing operation: fair maiden hurdler: pulled up
in novice handicap on chasing debut: left Paul Webber after fourth start: stays 2½m: acts
on soft going: in cheekpieces last 3 starts: temperamental. *Stuart Edmunds*

LORD NAPIER (IRE) 6 b.g. Galileo (IRE) – Jacqueline (IND) (King Charlemagne **h139**
(USA)) [2018/19 h126: h15.7g⁶ h15.3g⁴ h15.7s⁶ h21g³ h23.4s* h19.9v⁶ h24.7g⁵ Apr 6]
compact gelding: useful handicap hurdler: won Grade 3 event at Sandown (by 9 lengths
from Coole Cody) in February: stays 25f: acts on heavy going: tried in cheekpieces: wears
tongue tie. *Peter Bowen*

LORD OF THE ISLAND (IRE) 11 b.g. Heron Island (IRE) – Miss Morose (IRE) **h125**
(Arctic Lord) [2018/19 h21g h23.1d⁴ h24v Mar 21] sturdy gelding: fairly useful handicap
hurdler: missed 2017/18: fourth at Exeter in February: stays 23f: acts on heavy going.
Fergal O'Brien

LORD OF THE ROCK (IRE) 7 b.g. Rock of Gibraltar (IRE) – La Sylphide **h114**
(Rudimentary (USA)) [2018/19 h16.8s* h16.4g⁴ h15.8d⁴ Mar 3] fairly useful form over hurdles, stays
10.5f: fair form over hurdles: won novice at Sedgefield in November. *Lawrence Mullaney*

LORD ROCCOCO (FR) 4 b.g. Shirocco (GER) – Lady Chloe (Noverre (USA)) **b80**
[2018/19 b13.7m⁴ b13.1g b16.7g b15.7d⁴ Apr 24] modest form in bumpers. *Philip Kirby*

LORD SCOUNDREL (IRE) 10 b.g. Presenting – Noble Choice (Dahar (USA)) **c131**
[2018/19 c141, h–: h20m⁴ c22.5d Aug 1] fairly useful hurdler: smart chaser at one time, not **h125**
as good nowadays: stays 25f: acts on good to firm and heavy going: has worn headgear,
including last 4 starts: wears tongue tie. *Gordon Elliott, Ireland*

LORDS PARK STAR (IRE) 10 b.g. Presenting – Mary's View (IRE) (Phardante (FR)) **c82 §**
[2018/19 c22.6d c20.2f⁴ Feb 26] multiple point winner: maiden hurdler: poor form in **h– §**
hunter chases: in cheekpieces last 4 starts: has worn tongue tie: unreliable. *Mrs L. Pomfret*

LORD SPARKY 5 ch.g. Sulamani (IRE) – Braybrooke Lady (IRE) (Presenting) [2018/19 **h104 p**
h15.8d⁴ h18.6g⁴ h20.7g* Apr 22] workmanlike gelding: second foal: dam (h73) maiden
hurdler: fair form over hurdles: won handicap at Huntingdon (conditionals) in April: will
be suited by further than 2½m: open to further improvement. *Caroline Bailey*

LORD SPRINGFIELD (IRE) 6 ch.g. Well Chosen – Super Thyne (IRE) (Good Thyne **h103 p**
(USA)) [2018/19 h20.5v⁶ h17s³ h20.5d⁵ Jan 20] €42,000 5-y-o: has had breathing
operation: half-brother to a winning pointer by Indian River: dam unraced: won Irish point
on debut: fair form over hurdles: best effort when fifth in maiden at Ayr: open to further
improvement. *Donald McCain*

LORD TOPPER 6 b.g. Sir Percy – Fugnia (Hurricane Run (IRE)) [2018/19 c–p, h114: **c93**
h19.8m⁶ h25.8g³ h26.5m* h26.5g* h26.5g c24.1g³ Oct 11] fairly useful handicap hurdler: **h120**
won at Newton Abbot in July (lady riders event) and August: modest form in chases: won
point in February: stays 3¼m: acts on good to firm going: wears headgear. *Jamie Snowden*

LORD WALSINGHAM 5 b.g. Shirocco (GER) – Glorious Twelfth (IRE) (Old Vic) **h–**
[2018/19 b–p: b16.3d h16.6d⁶ h19g⁴ Apr 25] has had breathing operation: well held in **b–**
bumpers/over hurdles: tried in tongue tie. *Alan King*

LORD WESSEX 8 b.g. Deltic (USA) – Society Night (IRE) (Moscow Society (USA)) **h–**
[2018/19 b–: h15.3m Oct 19] has had breathing operation: no form, including in points.
Richard Mitchell

LORD WISHES (IRE) 12 b.g. Milan – Strong Wishes (IRE) (Strong Gale) [2018/19 c–, **c113**
h102: h22.7g⁴ h20.9g⁴ c20.1d³ Apr 6] tall, good-bodied gelding: fair handicap hurdler/ **h108**
chaser nowadays: stays 3m: acts on good to firm and heavy going: wears headgear: tried in
tongue tie. *James Ewart*

LORD YEATS 6 b.g. Yeats (IRE) – Bogside Theatre (IRE) (Fruits of Love (USA)) **h128**
[2018/19 h16d² h16.8s* h16.2g² h16.2v* h16.5g⁴ h16g Apr 27] useful-looking gelding:
dam (h122), 2m hurdle winner, half-sister to useful 2m/17f hurdle winner Lindenhurst:
smart on Flat, stays 15f: fairly useful form over hurdles: won maiden at Sedgefield in
December and novice at Hexham (6/1-on) in March: fourth in conditionals/amateurs
handicap at Aintree: will stay beyond 2m: acts on heavy going. *Jedd O'Keeffe*

LOS CERRITOS (SWI) 7 ch.g. Dr Fong (USA) – La Coruna (SWI) (Arazi (USA)) **h63**
[2018/19 h–: h15.3g h15.7m⁴ h15.8d h16.8g Apr 20] angular gelding: poor maiden hurdler:
in cheekpieces/tongue tie last 3 starts. *Milton Harris*

LOSSIEMOUTH 4 b.g. Makfi – First Bloom (USA) (Fusaichi Pegasus (USA)) [2018/19 **b101**
b13.7gro b14.6s* b17g* Feb 18] sixth foal: half-brother to 6f winner At A Clip (by Green
Desert): dam lightly raced on Flat: fairly useful form in bumpers: ran out on debut but then
won at Newcastle (junior) in December and Carlisle in February. *Tom Lacey*

LOST FREQUENCY 7 b.g. Yeats (IRE) – Lauderdale (GER) (Nebos (GER)) [2018/19 **c–**
h16.2v³ c16.5s c20.5d c20.1vpu Mar 14] off mark in Irish points at third attempt: modest **h90**
form over hurdles: no show in chases: tried in tongue tie: temperament under suspicion.
Lucinda Russell

LOST HISTORY (IRE) 6 b.g. Strategic Prince – Prelude (Danzero (AUS)) [2018/19 **h–**
h97: h15.8s Feb 26] workmanlike gelding: fair on Flat, stays 1½m: maiden hurdler, modest
form at best: will prove best at sharp 2m. *John Spearing*

LOSTIN A FOG (IRE) 7 ch.m. Mahler – Spirit Rock (IRE) (Rock Hopper) [2018/19 **h–**
b15.8d h19.5dpu Nov 27] €7,500 3-y-o: compact mare: fourth foal: dam unraced half-sister **b–**
to useful hurdler/smart chaser (2m-3m winner) Southern Vic: multiple point winner: no
show in bumper/maiden hurdle. *Thomas Gallagher*

LOST IN NEWYORK (IRE) 12 b.g. Arakan (USA) – Lace Flower (Old Vic) [2018/19 **c59**
c55, h–: c20.3g c17.2g⁵ h20.6gur h15.8g Jul 18] workmanlike gelding: poor hurdler/maiden **h–**
chaser: stays 2¾m: acts on soft and good to firm going: has worn headgear/tongue tie,
including last 3 starts: usually races towards rear. *Nick Kent*

LOSTINTRANSLATION (IRE) 7 b.g. Flemensfirth (USA) – Falika (FR) (Hero's **c160 p**
Honor (USA)) [2018/19 h147: c22.4d² c19.9d³ c20.6d* c20s² c19.8d² c25d* Apr 5] **h–**
There wasn't much to choose between the pick of a good crop of novice
chasers competing at two and a half miles or more in the latest season, and it is hard to
say with confidence, at this stage, which of them will break through into the top open
races, though it will be disappointing if at least one or two of them don't make the
grade. Although he wasn't quite the best of the bunch as a novice, Lostintranslation
has good claims to bridge the divide: he is consistent, straightforward, and a bold
jumper who is, as yet, largely unexposed at three miles or more. Lostintranslation
won just two of his six starts over fences, and was beaten twice by La Bague Au Roi
and twice also by Defi du Seuil. He also had a verdict over the latter in the Dipper
Novices' Chase at Cheltenham and ended his campaign with a victory over the RSA
Insurance Chase winner Topofthegame in the Grade 1 Betway Mildmay Novices'
Chase at Aintree.

*BetBright Dipper Novices' Chase, Cheltenham—Lostintranslation rallies splendidly
after Defi du Seuil (left) had been produced with what looked a race-winning challenge;
Black Op (right) takes third*

Betway Mildmay Novices' Chase, Aintree—the step up in trip suits Lostinstranslation down to the ground as he impressively sees off Topofthegame (left) and the front-running Top Ville Ben (stripes)

Lostintranslation's victory in the Mildmay meant that for the second successive season he saved his best till last, when stepped up in trip at Aintree. As a novice hurdler in 2017/18, he had taken a significant step forward when chasing home the Baring Bingham runner-up Black Op in the Mersey Novices' Hurdle on his first start at two and a half miles. In the latest season, Lostintranslation was one of six that went to post in the Mildmay, with Topofthegame the pick on form after his Cheltenham win and starting a shade of odds on. Lostintranslation was second in the betting at 3/1, with the others potential improvers who had something to find on form. Having made the running on most of his starts over fences, Lostintranslation was ridden more patiently in the Mildmay, with an extra half mile to travel. Top Ville Ben went off in front as Lostintranslation was waited with travelling strongly and once again jumping fluently. All six runners were still in with a chance approaching three out, where Crucial Role fell fatally before Lostintranslation moved to the front going best at the next, as Topofthegame began to struggle. Shaken up after the last, Lostintranslation forged ahead to score by six lengths, as Topofthegame—clearly not at his best on the day—passed Top Ville Ben for second late on. In truth, the Mildmay wasn't a very strong Grade 1 and the bare form can't be rated particularly highly, though Lostintranslation is a horse to view positively, value for more than his winning margin. His efforts against Defi du Seuil also suggest that he is not far behind the RSA principals. All three encounters between Lostintranslation and Defi du Seuil swung one way and then the other. In defeat in the Scilly Isles Novices' Chase at Sandown and the Golden Miller at Cheltenham, Lostintranslation traded at 1.12 and 1.20 in running on the exchanges before going down by three quarters of a length and two and a quarter lengths respectively. There was an even more extreme switch in fortune in the Dipper (one of the last major sponsorships for BetBright bookmakers, which ceased trading in controversial circumstances just before the

Cheltenham Festival, about which there is more in the essay on Min). Defi du Seuil looked all but past the post at Cheltenham and traded at the basement price, 1.01, before Lostintranslation rallied on the run-in, turning a two-length deficit at the last fence into victory by a length and a quarter. Before the Dipper, Lostintranslation had been beaten twice by La Bague Au Roi at Newbury, a bad mistake three from home when still cruising in the Berkshire Novices' Chase in November his only significant jumping error in his six starts over fences.

Lostintranslation (IRE) (b.g. 2012)	Flemensfirth (USA) (b 1992)	Alleged (b 1974)	Hoist The Flag	Princess Pout
			Diesis	Royal Bund
		Etheldreda (ch 1985)		
	Falika (FR) (ch 1996)	Hero's Honor (b 1980)	Northern Dancer	Glowing Tribute
		Karifale (ch 1990)	Lashkari	La Rafale

Lostintranslation is a strong gelding, a typical son of his sire Flemensfirth in appearance. Flemensfirth was champion sire over jumps for the second successive year in Britain and Ireland combined in the latest season with total prize money of £2,298,726 in sires' tables published by the *Racing Post*. While Flemensfirth is still going strongly at Coolmore (fee €15,000), his now-retired compatriot Oscar finished second (£2,132,209) and Milan (£2,044,382) made it a one, two, three for Coolmore's jumps roster, ahead of Presenting, Beneficial and King's Theatre who completed the top six. Lostintranslation's pedigree on the dam's side is ordinary, to put it politely. He is the seventh foal out of his dam Falika and her first winner outside points, the six others having drawn a blank from thirty-six starts under Rules. I No Understand (by Overbury) won a point, but the only other to show better than modest form is Master Todd (by Dream Well), a fairly useful maiden hurdler at up to three miles. Falika was a winner up to a mile and a half on the Flat in France and was placed over hurdles, including in the Prix Wild Monarch, a listed race for newcomers. Neither Lostintranslation's grandam Karifale nor his great grandam La Rafale raced. Lostintranslation went through the sale-ring twice, making €8,500 as a foal and €38,000 as a three-year-old. He was fourth in a point in Ireland before joining his current yard, his British and hurdling debut coming in a novice hurdle at Chepstow in which he finished second to another Grade 1-winning novice chaser in the latest season, Dynamite Dollars. Lostintranslation has raced only on going softer than good and he acts on soft going (the only poor run of his career came on his only start on heavy). He will stay beyond twenty-five furlongs and, given his sound-jumping, strong-travelling nature, he might well be an ideal type for the Ladbrokes Trophy at Newbury (though there is talk of a prep run followed by the Betfair Chase). That will only be a starting point for his second campaign as a chaser. His trainer has called him 'a dream horse, poetry in motion, we've loved him for a long time and see him as our future. He's got everything and we hope he'll be our next good one.' The King George VI Chase is said to be a target for Lostintranslation in the next season, with Colin Tizzard saying 'Hopefully he'll run in the Gold Cup, he's ready for the big time.' *Colin Tizzard*

LOSTNFOUND 6 b.m. Midnight Legend – La Cerisaie (Old Vic) [2018/19 h107: h23.3d⁶ c17.4d⁵ h21.7v² c22.5vᵖᵘ h16v² h17.7v⁵ h24.3mᵘʳ h21.9g² Apr 21] sturdy mare: has had breathing operation: fair handicap hurdler: little show over fences: stays 2¾m: acts on heavy going: tried in tongue tie. *Jamie Snowden* **c–** **h110**

LOSTOCK HALL (IRE) 7 b.g. Lord Shanakill (USA) – Cannikin (IRE) (Lahib (USA)) [2018/19 h16.2s h20.1s h15.7d⁵ h16g² h16.4m* Mar 28] fair handicap hurdler, off over 2 years before return: won at Newcastle in March: stays 19f: acts on good to firm going. *Tristan Davidson* **h106**

LOTS OF LUCK (IRE) 5 b.g. Millenary – Lovely Hand (IRE) (Phardante (FR)) [2018/19 h19g h19.7dᵖᵘ Mar 9] no promise over hurdles. *Kim Bailey* **h–**

LOTTOLOVE (IRE) 11 b.m. Court Cave (IRE) – Lady Lotto (IRE) (Lord Americo) [2018/19 c25.5m Jun 29] fourth foal: closely related to a winning pointer by Dushyantor: dam (h80), maiden hurdler (stayed 2½m), half-sister to useful chaser (stayed 29f) Winning Dream: winning pointer: little form under Rules: tried in cheekpieces: wears tongue tie. *Ms Claire O'Connell, Ireland* **c–** **h–**

LOTUS POND (IRE) 11 b.g. Beneficial – Capard Lady (IRE) (Supreme Leader) **c112**
[2018/19 c90, h–: c23.8m* c24g* c23.8m* c23.8g⁴ Jul 31] maiden hurdler: fair handicap **h–**
chaser: completed hat-trick at Ffos Las (twice) and Southwell in June/July: stays 3m: acts
on good to firm and heavy going: has worn hood, including last 4 starts: wears tongue tie:
often races towards rear/travels strongly. *Peter Bowen*

LOUD AND CLEAR 8 b.g. Dalakhani (IRE) – Whispering Blues (IRE) (Sadler's Wells **h113**
(USA)) [2018/19 h111: h23.9g³ h20.2g³ h23.9g⁵ Jul 31] dual bumper winner: fairly useful
on Flat, stays 16.5f: fair form over hurdles: stays 3m: tried in hood/tongue tie. *Iain Jardine*

LOUD AS LIONS (IRE) 6 b.g. Flemensfirth (USA) – Misspublican (IRE) (Overbury **h95**
(IRE)) [2018/19 b62: h16.2g³ h21d⁹ h19.7s⁵ h20v h20.7g h19.5d⁶ Apr 6] useful-looking
gelding: modest form over hurdles: should stay beyond 2m. *Tom Symonds*

LOUGHADERRA PRINCE (IRE) 10 b.g. Oscar (IRE) – Loughaderra Rose (IRE) **c102**
(Roselier (FR)) [2018/19 c100, h–: c16.3g² May 4] bumper winner: fair form over hurdles/ **h–**
fences: second in hunter at Cheltenham in May: stays 2¾m: acts on soft going. *Tom George*

LOUGH DERG DIAMOND (IRE) 6 b.g. Flemensfirth (USA) – Ballerina Laura (IRE) **h98**
(Riot Helmet) [2018/19 h15.7g⁵ h16.4d⁴ h24s h16.8s Jan 20] sturdy gelding: well beaten in
Irish points: modest form over hurdles: dead. *Colin Tizzard*

LOUGH DERG FARMER (IRE) 7 b.g. Presenting – Maryiver (IRE) (Runyon (IRE)) **c122 §**
[2018/19 c–, h119: h24.7g h24.1m⁵ c26.3g³ c26.1d² c26.2s² c26.2g³ c24.5g* c24v⁶ **h– §**
c28.4m² Apr 20] sturdy gelding: fairly useful hurdler at best, disappointing in 2018: fairly
useful handicap chaser: won novice event at Carlisle in February: left Nicky Henderson
after first start: stays 3½m: acts on soft and good to firm going: has worn headgear: usually
front runner/races prominently: temperamental. *Sue Smith*

LOUGH DERG JEWEL (IRE) 8 b.g. Oscar (IRE) – River Valley Lady (IRE) (Salt **c128**
Dome (USA)) [2018/19 c126, h–: c23.4g³ c23.8g⁶ c26.2g⁹ᵘ c26g* c23.4g² Jan 13] winning **h–**
hurdler: fairly useful handicap chaser: won 3-runner event at Doncaster in December: stays
3¼m: acts on heavy going: often races prominently. *Donald McCain*

LOUGH DERG MYSTERY (IRE) 8 b.g. Oscar (IRE) – Have To Go (IRE) (Le Moss) **c–**
[2018/19 c20s c26.7g⁹ᵘ Dec 6] sturdy gelding: maiden pointer/hurdler: no show in 2 chases **h–**
after long absence: tried in visor. *Nick Mitchell*

LOUGH DERG SPIRIT (IRE) 7 b.g. Westerner – Sno-Cat Lady (IRE) (Executive **c139**
Perk) [2018/19 h134: c19.4m* c20.5g⁵ c20d* c20.2s⁹ᵘ c20.5m⁶ Apr 13] well-made **h–**
gelding: has had breathing operation: useful hurdler: similar form over fences: won novice
at Wetherby in October and novice handicap at Ludlow (by 12 lengths from Lillington) in
January: stays 2½m: acts on soft and good to firm going: in cheekpieces last 3 starts.
Nicky Henderson

LOUGH KENT 10 b.g. Barathea (IRE) – King's Doll (IRE) (King's Best (USA)) [2018/19 **c–**
c–, h115: h17.2g h17.2m⁵ h17.2g h17.2d² c17.3s⁴ c16g⁵ h15.7g⁴ h17g³ Feb 24] good-topped **h103**
gelding: fair handicap hurdler: winning chaser, behind both starts over fences in 2018/19:
stays 19f: acts on soft going: has worn headgear, including last 5 starts. *James Moffatt*

LOUGH LEGEND (IRE) 5 b.g. Watar (IRE) – Gibboghstown (IRE) (Second Empire **h101**
(IRE)) [2018/19 b79: h17.1d h16g³ h15.7g Nov 23] placed in bumpers: fair form over
hurdles: disqualified after rider weighed in light after fourth past post in novice at Carlisle
on first outing: will stay beyond 2m. *Sue Smith*

LOUGH RYN (IRE) 7 br.g. Court Cave (IRE) – Media View (IRE) (Presenting) [2018/19 **h77**
h105, b–: h15.8d⁶ h23.5s h23.1s Mar 5] compact gelding: fair form when fourth in maiden
in 2017/18, standout effort over hurdles: tried in tongue tie: usually races towards rear.
Neil Mulholland

LOUGH SALT (IRE) 8 b.g. Brian Boru – Castlehill Lady (IRE) (Supreme Leader) **c114**
[2018/19 h115: h24g⁴ h20g⁶ h23.1g h23.1m h23.3g² h26g⁶ h24.1m⁴ c24.2m⁴ c24.2g⁴ **h109**
c24.2s⁵ c24.2d² c24g³ c24.2g² c21.3d² c21.3g⁴ c24.2g⁴ Apr 11] close-coupled gelding: has
had breathing operation: fair handicap hurdler/maiden chaser: stays 3m: acts on soft going:
has worn headgear, including last 6 starts. *Richard Guest*

LOUIS' VAC POUCH (IRE) 7 b.g. Oscar (IRE) – Coming Home (FR) (Exit To **c141**
Nowhere (USA)) [2018/19 h138: h19.5d c16d* c19.2m* c24.2d⁶ c20.5m² Apr 13] useful- **h–**
looking gelding: useful hurdler: similar form over fences: won 4-runner novices at Ludlow
and Catterick in February: second in Future Champions Novices' Chase at Ayr (3¾ lengths
behind Secret Investor) in April: left Philip Hobbs after first start: stays 25f: acts on soft and
good to firm going: wears hood. *Henry Oliver*

LOULOUMILLS 9 b.m. Rob Roy (USA) – Etching (USA) (Groom Dancer (USA)) [2018/19 h87: h16.2g⁶ h23.3g⁴ h17.2g⁵ h17.2g⁵ h23.9g² h21.2m⁶ c23.8g⁵ c24.2gᶠ c19.3g² c20.9m⁵ Apr 20] poor handicap hurdler: poor form over fences: stays 3m: acts on heavy going: tried in cheekpieces: has worn tongue tie. *Maurice Barnes* **c72 h80**

LOUSE TALK (IRE) 7 b.g. Mahler – Foxy-Lady (IRE) (Yashgan) [2018/19 h120: h21g c23.6vᵖᵘ c24dᵘʳ c24v⁵ c23.9dᶠ Mar 14] tall gelding: has had breathing operation: Irish point winner: fairly useful hurdle winner: in cheekpieces, running easily best race in chases when falling 2 out in handicap at Market Rasen, though tiring at time: should be suited by 3m: acts on heavy going: front runner/races prominently. *Charlie Longsdon* **c114 h–**

LOVATO (GER) 7 br.g. Lauro (GER) – Larella (GER) (Anabaa (USA)) [2018/19 h120: h16.3g² h16.7g* h15.3m h20.5g² h19.7g Nov 17] fairly useful handicap hurdler: won at Bangor in October: stays 21f: acts on good to firm going: wears headgear. *Dr Richard Newland* **h117**

LOVE AT DAWN (IRE) 6 br.m. Winged Love (IRE) – Presentingatdawn (IRE) (Presenting) [2018/19 h90, b69: h21.3m h20.1sᵖᵘ h20.6d h25.3g⁵ h27s⁶ Mar 21] angular mare: has had breathing operation: poor maiden hurdler: should be suited by 3m: acts on heavy going: tried in headgear. *Peter Niven* **h59**

LOVEHERANDLEAVEHER (IRE) 7 b.m. Winged Love (IRE) – Rowdy Exit (IRE) (Exit To Nowhere (USA)) [2018/19 h–p: h20.5gᶠ h21.7d² h20.7g* Feb 21] winning pointer: fair form over hurdles: won mares maiden at Huntingdon in February: will stay 3m: likely to progress further. *Nicky Henderson* **h108 p**

LOVE LANE (IRE) 6 b.m. Stowaway – Inquisitive Look (Montjeu (IRE)) [2018/19 h106: h16.2g⁶ h16.7s* h16d* h18.5d³ h17.7v² Mar 16] placed in Irish points: fairly useful handicap hurdler: won at Market Rasen (conditionals) in December and Chepstow (mares) in January: stays 19f: acts on heavy going: usually races prominently. *Henry Oliver* **h121**

LOVELY JOB (IRE) 9 ch.g. Touch of Land (FR) – Wyckoff Queen (IRE) (Carefree Dancer (USA)) [2018/19 c136, h–: c23.6d⁴ c25g⁵ c25.2m⁴ c28.4dᵖᵘ c23.6m* Apr 22] workmanlike gelding: winning hurdler: useful handicap chaser: won 4-runner event at Chepstow in April: stays 3¼m: acts on good to firm and heavy going: in headgear last 3 starts. *Fergal O'Brien* **c136 h–**

LOVELY JUBBLY 4 ch.f. Harbour Watch (IRE) – Ruthie (Pursuit of Love) [2018/19 b16.3d Mar 1] leggy filly: seventh foal: closely related to a winner on Flat and half-sister to 2 winners, including 1¾m bumper winner Rodneythetrotter (by Royal Applause): dam, 7.5f winner, half-sister to fairly useful hurdler/useful chaser (stayed 2½m) Lease Lend: tailed off in mares bumper/Flat maiden. *Pat Phelan* **b–**

LOVELY SCHTUFF (IRE) 7 b.g. Court Cave (IRE) – The Long Bill (IRE) (Phardante (FR)) [2018/19 h106, b84: h20.2g h20.1m⁴ c23.4g⁵ c16.5s⁵ c20.9v⁶ c20.1vᵘʳ c21.6d Apr 8] winning pointer: fair form at best over hurdles, has regressed: modest form in chases: should stay further than 19f: acts on good to soft going. *Jackie Stephen* **c91 h71**

LOVENORMONEY (IRE) 8 br.g. Winged Love (IRE) – Dixies Gem (IRE) (Anzillero (GER)) [2018/19 h136: c20s c23.5s² Jan 4] good-topped gelding: won completed start in Irish points: useful hurdler: laboured efforts in chases: stays 3m: acts on heavy going: wears headgear: temperament under suspicion. *Warren Greatrex* **c121 h–**

LOVE OF MIDNIGHT 5 b.m. Midnight Legend – Love of Tara (Kayf Tara) [2018/19 b16d⁵ b16.5d⁴ Apr 24] first foal: dam (h125) 2½m-23f hurdle winner: poor form in bumpers: will be suited by 2½m. *Jennifer Mason* **b70**

LOVE THE LEADER (IRE) 11 b.g. Fruits of Love (USA) – Suelena (IRE) (Supreme Leader) [2018/19 c–, h95: h20.3g h25.8s h25.8g* h23.9m* c25.2g* c23.9d³ c25.2s⁵ h26.5g⁶ Apr 20] fair handicap hurdler/chaser: completed hat-trick at Fontwell, Taunton and Hereford in November: stays 3¼m: acts on good to firm and heavy going: has worn headgear. *Johnny Farrelly* **c104 h104**

LOWANBEHOLD (IRE) 12 gr.g. Cloudings (IRE) – Marble Quest (IRE) (Roselier (FR)) [2018/19 c104, h–: c24.1v³ c26.2s⁶ c26.9d c23.8m² c23.4d³ c29.6d³ Apr 26] lightly raced over hurdles: fair handicap chaser: stays 4m: acts on good to firm and heavy going: tried in cheekpieces. *Sandy Forster* **c101 h–**

LOW SUN 6 b.g. Champs Elysees – Winter Solstice (Unfuwain (USA)) [2018/19 h135: h22.8d* Aug 4] useful handicap hurdler: improved when won at Galway (by 2½ lengths from Minella Awards) in August: also landed Cesarewitch Handicap on Flat later in year: stays 23f: acts on soft going: wears cheekpieces: races prominently. *W. P. Mullins, Ireland* **h140**

LUCA BRAZI (IRE) 7 b.g. Mahler – Carriacou (Mark of Esteem (IRE)) [2018/19 c–§, h–§: h20g^{pu} c21.2g^5 c21.2m^{pu} h15.7g^F c21.2g^6 Jul 23] leggy gelding: of no account: has worn headgear: temperamental. *Aytach Sadik*   **c– §** **h– §**

LUCARNO DANCER 9 b.m. Lucarno (USA) – Sing And Dance (Rambo Dancer (CAN)) [2018/19 h79: h16.2g^F h16.2m h16.4d^2 c15.7g* c16.4v^{ur} Mar 12] poor handicap hurdler: better form when won novice handicap at Catterick on chasing debut in December: left Raymond Shiels after second start: unproven beyond 2m: acted on soft going: often in hood: wore tongue tie: dead. *Donald Whillans*   **c85** **h80**

LUCCA LADY (IRE) 8 b.m. Milan – Trail Storm (IRE) (Supreme Leader) [2018/19 h116, b95: h20g^3 h17.2g^6 h20g^3 h16.8m^2 h15.8g^2 h21.6v^5 c20d* c23.8d^4 Apr 26] lengthy mare: has had breathing operation: fair maiden hurdler: fairly useful form over fences: easily won mares novice at Warwick in March: stays 3m: acts on good to soft going. *Katy Price*   **c122** **h109**

LUCKOFTHEDRAW (FR) 6 gr.g. Martaline – La Perspective (FR) (Beyssac (FR)) [2018/19 h118p, b95: c15.9d* c15.8g c20.9s^2 c19.9g^{pu} c26g^{pu} c20.1d^{pu} Apr 26] bumper/ hurdle winner: useful form over fences: won novice handicap at Carlisle (by 2¼ lengths from Mister Kit) in October: lost form later in season: stays 21f: acts on heavy going: has worn hood, including in 2018/19. *Nigel Twiston-Davies*   **c131** **h–**

LUCKY FINNEGAN 7 b.g. Dr Massini (IRE) – Himitas (FR) (Lomitas) [2018/19 b16g h18.5g^{pu} Apr 20] no show in bumper/maiden hurdle: left Ivan Furtado after first start. *Ali Stronge*   **h–** **b–**

LUCKY JIM 8 b.g. Lucky Story (USA) – Lateralle (IRE) (Unfuwain (USA)) [2018/19 c20m^4 c23.6g^2 c21m^{pu} Jun 26] compact gelding: winning hurdler: fair maiden chaser: stays 2¾m: acts on good to firm and heavy going: has worn cheekpieces, including in 2018/19: wears tongue tie. *David Dennis*   **c103** **h–**

LUCKY LOVER BOY (IRE) 4 b.g. Teofilo (IRE) – Mayonga (IRE) (Dr Fong (USA)) [2018/19 h15.8d^2 h15.8d^2 h16.4m* h15.8g* h16.7d^8 Apr 26] dam half-sister to fairly useful hurdler/useful chaser (2m winner) Massena: fair maiden on Flat, stays 1¾m: fairly useful form over hurdles: completed hat-trick in novice at Newcastle, handicap at Huntingdon and novice at Bangor in March/April: raced around 2m: acts on good to firm and good to soft going: in tongue tie last 4 starts: open to further improvement. *Oliver Greenall*   **h129 p**

LUCKY LUCARNO 7 b.g. Lucarno (USA) – Sari Rose (FR) (Vertical Speed (FR)) [2018/19 h–, b63: h17.2g^4 h22.1m^4 h16.4d^4 h16.2d^6 Mar 26] lengthy gelding: fair form over hurdles: should be suited by 2½m+: acts on good to soft going. *Sue Smith*   **h104**

LUCKY ROBIN (IRE) 7 ch.g. Mister Fotis (USA) – Bewilderment (IRE) (Loup Sauvage (USA)) [2018/19 h15.7g^2 h18.6m* h18.6g* h16.8m^2 h20g h19.9s^6 c21.1s^4 c17.2g^4 c19.3g^4 Apr 23] first foal: dam unraced half-sister to useful hurdler/smart chaser (stayed 21f) Claret Cloak: no form on Flat: fair handicap hurdler: won at Market Rasen (twice) in August: modest form over fences: stays 19f: acts on good to firm going: hs worn cheekpieces: tried in tongue tie: front runner/races prominently. *Brian Ellison*   **c98** **h109**

LUCKY'S DREAM 4 ch.g. Yorgunnabelucky (USA) – Dream Esteem (Mark of Esteem (IRE)) [2018/19 h15.8d^5 h16g h18.7s Mar 11] fair on Flat, stays 1¼m: poor form over hurdles: may do better in handicaps. *Ian Williams*   **h80**

LUCKY WIND (IRE) 5 ch.g. Grandera (IRE) – Florida Onyx (IRE) (Florida Son) [2018/19 ab16.3s Jan 15] reluctant when tailed off in bumper: dead. *Susan Corbett*   **b– §**

LUCY CROSS 8 b.m. Alflora (IRE) – My Beautiful Loser (IRE) (Silver Patriarch (IRE)) [2018/19 h23.3g^{pu} May 12] £1,500 5-y-o: second foal: dam, little sign of ability, half-sister to useful/ungenuine staying chaser Double Dizzy: failed to complete all starts, most in points. *David Thompson*   **h–**

LUCYHILUCYLOW 7 b.m. Josr Algarhoud (IRE) – Shardda (Barathea (IRE)) [2018/19 b16.4g Nov 16] fourth foal: dam maiden on Flat (stayed 1m): tailed off in bumper. *Fred Watson*   **b–**

LUGG RIVER 5 b.m. Kayf Tara – Supreme Gem (IRE) (Supreme Leader) [2018/19 b15.8s^5 b15.8s^4 b16s^5 Mar 9] lengthy, unfurnished mare: has had breathing operation: fifth foal: sister to 2 winners, including fairly useful hurdler River Arrow, and closely related to fairly useful hurdler/chaser Perfect Pirate (2½m/21f winner, by Black Sam Bellamy): dam (h81), lightly raced in bumpers/over hurdles, half-sister to winning hurdler/fairly useful chaser (stayed 27f) He's The Gaffer: fair form in bumpers: best effort when fifth in listed mares event at Sandown. *Tom Symonds*   **b93**

LUNA JUNE (IRE) 6 gr.m. Mahler – Halfway Home (Presenting) [2018/19 b66: b16.7g **b–** May 19] poor form on first of 2 starts in bumpers. *Fergal O'Brien*

LUNAR BABY (IRE) 4 b.f. Fame And Glory – Fiddlededee (IRE) (Beneficial) [2018/19 **b92** b14g* b15.7d b15.7d⁵ Apr 9] sturdy filly: first foal: dam (h117), bumper/3m hurdle winner, also winning pointer: fair form in bumpers: won fillies junior event at Warwick in November. *Jonjo O'Neill*

LUNAR FLOW 8 b.g. With The Flow (USA) – Misty Move (IRE) (Saddlers' Hall (IRE)) **c–** [2018/19 c114, h–: c24g⁶ c23.8vᵖᵘ Dec 17] has had breathing operations: winning **h–** hurdler: fair chaser at best, no form in 2018/19: wears headgear: in tongue tie last 5 starts: temperament under suspicion. *Jamie Snowden*

LUNAR JET 5 ch.g. Ask – Lightning Jet (Dutch Art) [2018/19 h16.4gᵘʳ h15.8g⁵ h15.7s⁵ **h117** h16.6g² h16.6g² Jan 9] sturdy gelding: useful on Flat, stays 10.5f: fairly useful form over hurdles: second in novices at Doncaster in December and January: will prove best with emphasis on speed around 2m. *John Mackie*

LUNGARNO PALACE (USA) 8 b.g. Henrythenavigator (USA) – Good Time Sally **h122** (USA) (Forestry (USA)) [2018/19 h121: h19m² h16.3g* h21g⁴ h21g³ h25g⁵ h23.4s h20.3g⁴ Apr 17] sturdy gelding: fairly useful hurdler: won novice at Stratford in October: third in intermediate handicap at Cheltenham in November: stays 21f: acts on soft and good to firm going: tried in cheekpieces/tongue tie: usually races towards rear. *Fergal O'Brien*

LUST FOR GLORY (IRE) 6 b.m. Getaway (GER) – Maisie Presenting (IRE) **h128** (Presenting) [2018/19 b86p: b15.8g* h16.3d* h16.3s² h16.4g* h16.8d h16m⁵ Apr 12] **b92** good-topped mare: won Irish point on debut: fair form in bumpers: won mares event at Ludlow in May: fairly useful form over hurdles: won mares novices at Newbury in November and Newcastle (8/1-on) in February: second in listed mares novice at Newbury (3¼ lengths behind Posh Trish) in between: will stay beyond 2m: acts on soft going: often travels strongly. *Nicky Henderson*

LUVLY BOY BLUE 8 b.g. Blueprint (IRE) – Mellouise (Handsome Sailor) [2018/19 **c–** h96p: h16.2g h20g h22.7g c20dᵘʳ h24d Apr 6] maiden hurdler, no form in 2018/19: **h–** unseated rider second on chasing debut: tried in hood: wears tongue tie. *Susan Corbett*

LYFORD (IRE) 4 ch.g. Intense Focus (USA) – Nurture (IRE) (Bachelor Duke (USA)) **h–** [2018/19 h15.7s h16.8gᵖᵘ Apr 20] modest on Flat, stays 1¾m: no form over hurdles. *Dan Skelton*

LYGON ROCK (IRE) 6 b.g. Robin des Champs (FR) – Cute Lass (IRE) (Flemensfirth **h123** (USA)) [2018/19 h115, b85: h21.2m* h20g² h21g h24g⁵ h23.5d³ h25.5d⁵ h24.3mᵖᵘ Apr 20] workmanlike gelding: has had breathing operation: fairly useful hurdler: won novice at Ludlow in May: third in handicap at Ascot in February: stays 3m: acts on soft and good to firm going: in cheekpieces last 3 starts. *Henry Daly*

LYNDSAYS LAD 6 b.g. Kayf Tara – Ceilidh Royal (Erhaab (USA)) [2018/19 b76: **h97** h15.8g⁵ h15.8d⁵ h20d⁴ h18.6g⁵ Apr 3] modest form over hurdles. *Nicky Henderson*

LYN'S SECRET (IRE) 4 ch.f. Sakhee's Secret – Blase Chevalier (IRE) (Chevalier **h–** (IRE)) [2018/19 h16.8g⁴ Jul 22] dam (h97), bumper/2m hurdle winner, half-sister to fairly useful hurdler (stayed 2¾m) Front of House: fair form on Flat: tailed off in juvenile on hurdling debut. *Seamus Mullins*

LYRICAL KING 5 b.g. Librettist (USA) – Priscilla (Teenoso (USA)) [2018/19 b17.7d **b–** Feb 24] tailed off in maiden bumper. *Jamie Snowden*

LYRIC VERSE 5 b.m. Librettist (USA) – Delayed (FR) (Fijar Tango (FR)) [2018/19 **b–** b17.7sᵖᵘ Oct 6] half-sister to 13f bumper winner Comte d'Anjou (by Desert King) and fair 2½m chase winner Pack Your Bags (by Black Sam Bellamy): dam (c119/h121), 2m hurdle/ chase winner, also 10.5f winner on Flat: pulled up in bumper. *Polly Gundry*

M

MAB DAB (IRE) 8 b.g. Papal Bull – Pret A Porter (UAE) (Jade Robbery (USA)) [2018/19 **h104** h106: h25g³ May 10] good-topped gelding: fair handicap hurdler: stays 25f: acts on good to firm and good to soft going. *Linda Jewell*

MABELA 5 b.m. Oscar (IRE) – Histoire de Moeurs (FR) (Kaldounevees (FR)) [2018/19 **h106** b82: h15.7g⁴ h16d⁵ h15.3g h20.7d* h21.2m² h20.6m² Apr 21] has had breathing operations: bumper winner: fair form over hurdles: won mares handicap at Huntingdon in March: stays 21f: acts on good to firm and good to soft going: wears tongue tie: waited with. *Dan Skelton*

MACA CAILIN (IRE) 9 ch.m. Rainwatch – Melodic Accord (IRE) (Accordion) **h–**
[2018/19 h23.3g^{pu} h23.9g^{pu} Sep 27] first foal: dam, no form over hurdles, half-sister to
fairly useful 2m hurdle winner Maca Rince (by Rainwatch): Irish point winner: little form
over hurdles: tried in visor. *Sheena Walton*

MAC AMARA 5 b.m. Dick Turpin (IRE) – Macnance (IRE) (Mandalus) [2018/19 b15.8s **h94 p**
h15.8m h22g^2 Apr 14] half-sister to several winners, including fair hurdlers Mac Beattie **b60**
(19f winner) and Mac Bertie (2½m winner), both by Beat All: dam (c108/h105), 2m-2½m
hurdle/chase winner (stayed 3m), sister to fair hurdler/very smart chaser (stayed 3¼m)
Macgeorge and half-sister to smart hurdler/chaser (stayed 4m) Chief Dan George: well
beaten in bumper: modest form over hurdles: open to further progress. *Evan Williams*

MACARDLE (IRE) 6 b.g. Beneficial – Monavale (IRE) (Strong Gale) [2018/19 h98, **h102**
b87: h20.1g^3 h16.2g^2 h20.2g^{pu} Sep 26] fair form in bumpers: similar form over hurdles:
usually leads: has joined Susan Corbett. *Philip Kirby*

MAC BELLA 7 ch.m. Black Sam Bellamy (IRE) – Macnance (IRE) (Mandalus) [2018/19 **h95**
h95: h20g^F h23g^5 h20.3g^3 h20g h20d^6 h25g^6 h23.9s^5 h25.5g^5 h21.9g* Apr 21] modest
handicap hurdler: won mares event at Ffos Las in April: stays 2¾m: best form on good
going: usually leads. *Evan Williams*

MACCA'S STOWAWAY (IRE) 6 b.m. Stowaway – Julies Vic (IRE) (Old Vic) [2018/19 **c55**
c19.2g^6 h18.5m h19.8g h23.9d^3 h21.6v c24.2s h23.9g h23.9d c26.2d^{pu} h21.4g^5 h23.9d^{pu} **h78**
Apr 24] angular mare: poor maiden hurdler: well held both completed starts over fences:
left Gordon Elliott after first start: stays 3m: acts on good to soft going: has worn headgear,
including last 3 starts: in tongue tie last 2: has joined Christian Williams. *Kevin Bishop*

MAC CENNETIG (IRE) 7 b.g. Brian Boru – Buslane (IRE) (Tidaro (USA)) [2018/19 **h75 §**
h99: h16.7g h16.2g h16.2g h17.1d h21.3m^5 h20.1s^{pu} h16.8s^6 h19.3s h15.7g^4 h15.7g^5 h16g^5
h16.8g^3 h16.8d^6 Apr 23] lengthy gelding: has had breathing operations: poor maiden
hurdler: stays 21f: acts on good to firm and good to soft going: wears headgear/tongue tie:
temperamental. *Micky Hammond*

MACHIATO (IRE) 8 b.g. Milan – Wychnor Dawn (IRE) (Broken Hearted) [2018/19 **h–**
h21d h23.6d^{pu} h19d^{pu} Feb 28] won sole start in bumpers for Colin Tizzard in 2016/17: off
29 months, no show over hurdles: left Ian Williams after second start: tried in tongue tie.
Brian Barr

MACH ONE 5 b.g. Makfi – Perfect Spirit (IRE) (Invincible Spirit (IRE)) [2018/19 h15.9g^3 **h103**
h16.6g^{pu} h15.9s^3 h15.8d^5 h15.9g^3 Apr 21] compact gelding: dam half-sister to fairly useful
hurdler/fair chaser (stayed 3m) First Row: fairly useful at best on Flat for Archie Watson,
stays 1¼m: fair form over hurdles. *Charlie Longsdon*

MAC KAYLA 4 b.f. Kayf Tara – Macnance (IRE) (Mandalus) [2018/19 b15.8d^6 Mar 30] **b74**
half-sister to several winners, including fair hurdlers Mac Beattie (19f winner) and Mac
Bertie (2½m winner), both by Beat All: dam (c108/h105), 2m-2½m hurdle/chase winner
(stayed 3m), sister to fair hurdler/very smart chaser (stayed 3¼m) Macgeorge and half-
sister to smart hurdler/chaser (stayed 4m) Chief Dan George: 40/1, sixth in mares bumper
at Uttoxeter (13½ lengths behind Wynn House). *Evan Williams*

MACKSVILLE (IRE) 6 gr.g. Mastercraftsman (IRE) – Fairest of All (IRE) (Sadler's **h102**
Wells (USA)) [2018/19 h94: h20g^5 h18.7g^2 h22g^3 h19.6m* h17.7m Mar 29] has had
breathing operation: fair handicap hurdler: won at Huntingdon in October: left James
Eustace after fourth start: stays 2½m: acts on soft and good to firm going: in headgear last
2 starts: tried in tongue tie. *Emma-Jane Bishop*

MACK THE MAN (IRE) 5 b.g. Flemensfirth (USA) – Nifty Nuala (IRE) (Saddlers' **h118**
Hall (IRE)) [2018/19 b80: h19.5s h15.7s^3 h15.8v^2 h19.8s^{pu} Mar 8] modest form sole start
in bumpers: fairly useful form over hurdles: second in maiden at Uttoxeter in January: bred
to stay 2½m+. *Evan Williams*

MAC N CHEESE (IRE) 9 b.g. Milan – Fox Burrow (IRE) (Supreme Leader) [2018/19 **c87**
c118, h118: c24.1s h25s^3 c24.7d^6 Apr 22] fairly useful handicap hurdler: similar form at **h116**
best over fences: left Keith Dalgleish after second start: stays 25f: acts on heavy going:
tried in hood. *Gavin Patrick Cromwell, Ireland*

MAC TOTTIE 6 b.g. Midnight Legend – Tot of The Knar (Kayf Tara) [2018/19 b88: **h124**
h15.8d^5 h16.7g^2 h20g* h20.2g^3 h22.1g* h22.1s* h23.3g* h20.3g Apr 17] fair form in
bumpers: fairly useful hurdler: won maiden at Worcester in June, and novices at Cartmel
in July/August and Hexham in October: stays 23f: acts on soft going: usually in hood:
wears tongue tie. *Peter Bowen*

MADAM ANNA (IRE) 6 b.m. Papal Bull – Melaaya (USA) (Aljabr (USA)) [2018/19 b81: b15.7d h19.2v⁶ h15.9d h15.8g Feb 21] rather leggy mare: modest form in bumpers: well held in novice hurdles: tried in hood. *Linda Jewell* **h–ь–**

MADAM CLOUD (IRE) 6 gr.m. Cloudings (IRE) – Model Girl (Classic Cliche (IRE)) [2018/19 b17g h20.1s⁴ h16.2s⁵ h19.7s⁴ h24sᵖᵘ Jan 29] fourth foal: sister to modest 2¾m chase winner Model Cloud and a winning pointer, and half-sister to bumper winner/fairly useful hurdler Spider's Bite (3m winner, by Scorpion): dam (b75), ran once in bumper, half-sister to smart hurdler/useful chaser (winner up to 25f) Silver Wedge: Irish point winner: well beaten in mares bumper: modest form over hurdles: should stay beyond 2½m. *Tim Easterby* **h86 ь–**

MADAME VOGUE 6 b.m. Multiplex – Roslin (Roscoe Blake) [2018/19 b16.8g⁵ Aug 15] half-sister to fairly useful hurdler/fair chaser Georgian King (2¾m-3¼m winner, by Overbury) and bumper winner/fair hurdler Madame Jasmine (25f winner, by Karinga Bay): dam unraced: 8/1, fifth in mares bumper at Newton Abbot (18½ lengths behind Nanny Pat's). *Suzy Smith* **b63**

MADAM MALINA 5 b.m. Malinas (GER) – Madam Jolie (IRE) (King's Theatre (IRE)) [2018/19 b15.8s b15.8g² b16.7g⁴ Mar 20] £8,000 3-y-o: third foal: half-sister to fairly useful hurdler Chateauneuf du Pap (2m-19f winner, by Definite Article): dam unraced sister to fairly useful hurdler/chaser (stayed 2½m) I'm All You Need: fair form in bumpers: best effort when second in mares event at Ludlow in January: possibly amiss final start. *Warren Greatrex* **b88**

MADAM SCULLY 6 ch.m. Flying Legend (USA) – Sally Scally (Scallywag) [2018/19 b–: b15.7s b16d h19.9v⁶ h16.8s⁶ h15.7d h20.6d Apr 6] no form in bumpers/over hurdles: tried in tongue tie. *Tina Jackson* **h–ь–**

MADIBA PASSION (FR) 5 b.g. Al Namix (FR) – Birsheba (FR) (Always Fair (USA)) [2018/19 b16m³ b16.3d Mar 22] €50,000 3-y-o, £100,000 4-y-o: sturdy gelding: half-brother to 3 winners abroad on Flat: dam French 1m winner: won 2 of 3 starts in Irish points: fairly useful form in bumpers. *Alan King* **b97**

MAD JACK MYTTON (IRE) 9 b.g. Arcadio (GER) – Gilt Ridden (IRE) (Heron Island (IRE)) [2018/19 c131, h133: c16m⁵ c16.5g⁴ h16.3m³ h16.4g⁴ h16.4g c20.2mᵖᵘ h15.5g⁴ h15.8d Feb 20] lengthy gelding: has had breathing operation: fairly useful handicap hurdler/chaser, below form over fences in 2018/19: stays 2½m: acts on soft and good to firm going: tried in blinkers: has worn tongue tie: has joined Sean Thomas Doyle, Ireland: irresolute. *Jonjo O'Neill* **c109 § h121 §**

MAEBH (IRE) 5 b.m. Doyen (IRE) – South Queen Lady (IRE) (King's Ride) [2018/19 b86: h15.8g³ h21g* h19.8v⁶ h19.9d² h24.4g⁴ h18.9m⁶ Apr 20] bumper winner: fair form over hurdles: won mares novice at Warwick in November: should stay 3m: acts on good to soft going: in cheekpieces last 2 starts. *Seamus Mullins* **h114**

MAESTRO ROYAL 10 b.g. Doyen (IRE) – Close Harmony (Bustino) [2018/19 c131, h131: c24gᵖᵘ May 23] tall gelding: useful hurdler: similar form over fences, pulled up sole start in 2018/19: stays 21f: acts on heavy going: tried in cheekpieces: often let down by jumping. *Nicky Henderson* **c– x h–**

MAFATE FORTIN (FR) 9 b.g. Enrique – Shining of Crystal (FR) (Shining Steel) [2018/19 h16.2g Jun 16] maiden pointer: fair form in bumpers for Keith Reveley in 2016/17: no form over hurdles: wears tongue tie. *Katie Scott* **h–**

MAGELLAN 5 b.g. Sea The Stars (IRE) – Hector's Girl (Hector Protector (USA)) [2018/19 h16.6g⁴ h16.6g⁶ h16g⁴ Apr 11] has had breathing operation: useful on Flat, stays 12.5f: fair form over hurdles: remains open to improvement. *Philip Kirby* **h101 p**

MAGGIEOFTHEVALLEY 8 b.m. Sleeping Indian – Fabulously Red (Red Ransom (USA)) [2018/19 h15.8gᵖᵘ May 31] first foal: dam unraced: pulled up in mares novice hurdle. *Debra Hamer* **h–**

MAGGIES LEGEND 6 b.m. Midnight Legend – Very Special One (IRE) (Supreme Leader) [2018/19 h101, b–: h20g⁴ h15.8gh20.6g h20.3s⁵ h23.4d⁶ h26g Feb 22] workmanlike mare: poor maiden hurdler: wears tongue tie. *Alex Hales* **h84**

MAGGIO (FR) 14 b.g. Trempolino (USA) – La Musardiere (FR) (Cadoudal (FR)) [2018/19 c132, h126: c23.8g⁶ Jun 3] rather leggy gelding: fairly useful hurdler: useful chaser: stays 25f: acts on good to firm and heavy going: has worn headgear: wears tongue tie. *Patrick Griffin, Ireland* **c120 h–**

MAGICAL MAN 12 b.g. Lahib (USA) – Majestic Di (IRE) (Zaffaran (USA)) [2018/19 **c75 §**
c90§, h–: c23.8s^{ur} c26.2d c23.8s^6 Apr 7] maiden hurdler: modest handicap chaser, below **h–**
form in 2018/19: stays 25f: acts on heavy going: has worn headgear, including in 2018/19:
temperamental (has run out). *Debra Hamer*

MAGICAL MISS (IRE) 6 ch.m. Beat Hollow – Sorivera (Irish River (FR)) [2018/19 **b87**
b16.3m^2 May 20] closely related to smart hurdler/useful chaser Mossley (2m-3m winner,
by Old Vic) and fairly useful hurdler/chaser Rebel Yeats (2m-2½m, by Yeats) and half-
sister to several winners: dam, useful German 6f-1m winner, half-sister to Irish Grand
National winner Commanche Court: fair form in bumpers: left W. P. Mullins, second at
Stratford only start in 2018/19. *Ian Williams*

MAGICAL THOMAS 7 ch.g. Dylan Thomas (IRE) – Magical Cliche (USA) (Affirmed **h111**
(USA)) [2018/19 h91: h15.8m h15.8m^4 h15.8g^2 h16.3g* h17.7g* h17.7m^3 h16.5m^4
h17.7g* Apr 12] fair handicap hurdler: won at Stratford (amateurs) and Fontwell in August,
and at Fontwell again in April: stays 2¼m: acts on good to firm and heavy going: wears
cheekpieces/tongue tie: usually leads. *Neil Mulholland*

MAGIC DANCER 7 b.g. Norse Dancer (IRE) – King's Siren (IRE) (King's Best (USA)) **h127**
[2018/19 h128: h16.4g^2 h15.7m^6 h18.9g^5 h16.8g h16g^2 h15.7d^2 h16.8g^3 Apr 17] sturdy
gelding: has had breathing operation: fairly useful handicap hurdler: second at Kempton in
January and third in conditionals/amateurs event at Cheltenham in April: stays 21f: acts on
soft going: wears cheekpieces/tongue tie. *Kerry Lee*

MAGIC DRAGON (IRE) 5 b.g. Dragon Pulse (IRE) – Milenka (USA) (Cape Cross **h94**
(IRE)) [2018/19 b15.7g^6 b16.8m h20.1s^{pu} h16.8s^6 h19.3s h19.9d* h19.7g^{pu} Feb 19] behind **b–**
in bumpers: modest form over hurdles: won handicap at Sedgefield in January: stayed
2½m: acted on good to soft going: in cheekpieces last 2 starts: dead. *Philip Kirby*

MAGIC MUSIC MAN 8 b.g. Authorized (IRE) – Magic Music (IRE) (Magic Ring **c104**
(IRE)) [2018/19 c17d^3 Jun 8] off mark in points at third attempt: winning hurdler: 9/2, third **h–**
in hunter at Stratford (2¾ lengths behind Robin des People) on chasing debut: unproven
beyond 17f: acts on soft and good to firm going: in headgear last 5 starts. *Philip Rowley*

MAGIC MUSTARD (IRE) 8 ch.g. Stowaway – Honey Mustard (IRE) (Roselier (FR)) **c–**
[2018/19 c24v^{pu} c24.2v^{pu} Mar 5] stocky gelding: has had breathing operation: winning **h–**
hurdler in 2016/17, missed following season: pulled up both starts over fences: should stay
3m: acts on soft going: has worn headgear: in tongue tie last 4 starts. *Kerry Lee*

MAGIC OF LIGHT (IRE) 8 b.m. Flemensfirth (USA) – Quest of Passion (FR) **c155**
(Saumarez) [2018/19 c134, h105: c24d^3 c23.4s* h23.5d* c19.9d^2 c25d^{ur} c25s **h132 +**
c34.3g^2 Apr 6]
As the watching millions collectively held their breath as Tiger Roll loomed
up at the last in his bid to become the first back-to-back Grand National winner since
Red Rum, not many spared a thought for the 66/1 outsider upsides him battling for
her own piece of Aintree history. Magic of Light would have been the first mare to
win the Grand National in sixty-eight years and, although she eventually gave best to
Tiger Roll, her second place was still the highest finishing position for one of her sex
since 1958. Only two mares have won the Aintree marathon in the past one hundred
and sixteen years and both did so in the period after World War II, Sheila's Cottage
in 1948 and Nickel Coin in 1951.

'Vicious', 'an absolute swine' and 'a real old brute' were just some of the
descriptions used by trainer Neville Crump and jockey Arthur Thompson about the
headstrong Sheila's Cottage, whose obstinate nature was perhaps best exemplified
after the 1947 Scottish Grand National, then staged at Bogside. Having fallen at
the third last when still holding every chance, Sheila's Cottage proceeded to gallop
into the sea and swim across the inlet before finally being retrieved by Crump from the
local police station at midnight. She put it all together at Aintree on March 20th
1948, however, and even benefited from the waywardness of others on that occasion.
Another mare, the 100/1-shot Zahia ran out between the last two fences, leaving the
way for the staying-on Sheila's Cottage to overhaul long-time leader First of The
Dandies to win by a length—third-placed Cromwell was the other hard-luck story
of the race, his jockey, the popular amateur Lord Mildmay, being incapacitated for
the final mile by severe cramp following the recurrence of a neck injury. It was a
significant win for Crump as he battled to re-establish himself after the war, his
string growing from just six to thirty in the immediate aftermath. Crump became

OLBG.com Mares' Hurdle (Warfield), Ascot—a valuable win back over hurdles for the versatile Magic of Light, who is chased home by Jester Jet (second right)

one of the most respected trainers of staying chasers, winning the National again in 1952 with Teal (also ridden by Thompson) and in 1960 with Merryman II (the first televised edition). Sheila's Cottage never ran after her National success and the intervention of Crump saved her when her owner (who had run into financial difficulties) planned to have her put down following an unsuccessful stud career, Sheila's Cottage spending her final days on Thompson's farm in Wexford, obviously forgiven for biting the top off one of the jockey's fingers when the pair posed for a photo at Crump's Middleham stables after the National!

By contrast, Nickel Coin was a far more straightforward mare all round, even enjoying a successful stint as a show-jumper before having her attentions turned to steeplechasing by Surrey trainer Jack O'Donoghue. Nickel Coin's National win also owed something to its share of luck, albeit at a very different stage of the race. The 1951 renewal was marred by an extremely ragged getaway after the starter released the tape with nearly half the field unawares and/or facing the wrong way, resulting in no fewer than twelve runners crashing out at the first as some of the runners rushed to recover ground lost at the start. Further casualties followed and only two managed to complete the course without incident (third-placed Derrinstown was remounted after being brought down at second Becher's). The sure-footed Nickel Coin came home six lengths clear of Royal Tan (the winner three years later), providing the biggest win in the career of jockey John Bullock—who, like Thompson, had been a prisoner of war.

Only eight mares reached the frame in the National between Nickel Coin and Magic of Light, with nearly a quarter of century elapsing before the first of that octet. Gentle Moya finished runner-up in 1956, as did the redoubtable Tiberetta two years later, though that barely scratches the surface of Tiberetta's association with Aintree as she finished third in 1957 and fourth in 1959, having also won the Becher Chase and Grand Sefton Chase there during this period, whilst her offspring included the top-class staying chaser Spanish Steps, who also made the frame in three successive Nationals in the 'seventies (fourth in 1973 and 1974, third in 1975). Third place finishes were achieved by Miss Hunter in 1970, Eyecatcher in 1976 and 1977 and Auntie Dot in 1991, and there were honourable fourths for Rainbow Battle in 1965, Ebony Jane in 1994 (just five days after finishing third in the Irish Grand National!) and Dubacilla in 1995. The closest a mare came to winning again before Magic of Light didn't involve any of these eight, however (Gentle Moya would have finished a distant third in 1956 but for Devon Loch's infamous bellyflop on the

540

run-in and Tiberetta finished thirty lengths adrift of the winner Mr What in 1958). Instead, that honour goes to Sandy Sprite, at least in terms of distance beaten. Sandy Sprite led over the last seemingly going best in 1971, only to break down on the run-in and fade into fifth, beaten just over four lengths—she was trained by John Edwards whose National luck didn't get any better, with his former inmate Little Polveir (in front when unseating five out in 1988) winning the 1989 edition just six weeks after being sold to join Toby Balding. Dubacilla, runner-up in the same season's Cheltenham Gold Cup, is the only one of the featured mares to have started at single-figure odds in the National and she was very much the exception to the rule. In common with Sheila's Cottage (50/1) and Nickel Coin (40/1), the other mares were largely ignored by Grand National punters, returning an average SP of 34/1.

Magic of Light's odds of 66/1 were longer than those of any of her predecessors in this group, perhaps a reflection of the poor recent record of mares in the National (of the ten mares to contest the race between Dubacilla and Magic of Light, the 2007 fifth Liberthine was the only one who even came close to troubling the judge). Magic of Light, who has carried the colours of Ann and Alan Potts since changing hands for £75,000 as a six-year-old, had, in fact, enjoyed an excellent campaign prior to Aintree and certainly shouldn't have been a 66/1-shot. Always in the front rank (tactics which often work well over the National fences), Magic of Light took extremely well to the National course and raced with plenty of zest, surviving a blunder at the Chair which would surely have proved far more costly in years gone by. Having taken the lead at second Valentine's when fellow pacesetter Rathvinden made a mistake, Magic of Light was notably fluent thereafter until making another error at the last when challenging the strong-travelling Tiger Roll under pressure. Tiger Roll shot clear at the elbow and Magic of Light gamely held off the rallying Rathvinden for second, even reducing the distance to the winner to just two and three quarter lengths by the line (Magic of Light was taken straight to the cooling down area after the race instead of to the winner's enclosure). Magic of Light was a first National runner for trainer Jessica Harrington and a first ride in the race for Paddy Kennedy, who came in for the mount after regular rider Robbie Power was released for the better-fancied Jury Duty (unseated eighteenth) for another yard. Thirty-year-old Kennedy, who had finished third in a mares handicap hurdle at Limerick in late-2016/17 on his only previous ride on Magic of Light, had also teamed up with the same connections for his biggest win to date on Whisperinthebreeze in the valuable Leopardstown Handicap Chase just two months earlier, though his career has been plagued by injuries (he also had surgery to remove a tumour from his bladder in 2017). Kennedy is probably best known for being the older brother of teenage jockey Jack Kennedy (who rode the pulled-up Dounikos in the 2019 National). Magic of Light was, in fact, her jockey's first ride in Britain for five years and just his sixth in total.

In contrast to her jockey, Magic of Light's Aintree run was her fifth British start of 2018/19, though she began her campaign on home soil with a creditable third to Tout Est Permis in the Troytown Handicap Chase at Navan in November. That performance underlined that large-field handicaps held no fears for her (she'd rounded off 2017/18 with a lucrative win at the Punchestown Festival). Back in smaller fields in conditions events for her next three starts, all against her own sex, Magic of Light ran out a wide-margin winner from Drinks Interval and Molly The Dolly (a good winner at Ayr later in the season) in a listed mares chase at Newbury in December, before making a successful switch to the smaller obstacles in the OLBG.com Mares' Hurdle (registered as the Warfield) at Ascot the following month, overcoming a much steadier gallop to beat Jester Jet easily by three and a quarter lengths in the latter. Although she couldn't complete the hat-trick in a listed event back over fences at Huntingdon, she still emerged with plenty of credit when going down by just a length, conceding 4 lb, to the smart Happy Diva. Magic of Light wasn't disgraced either when seventh (beaten just over eleven lengths) to Beware The Bear in the Ultima Handicap Chase at Cheltenham on her final run before Aintree, though the slightly more patient tactics than usual employed at Cheltenham arguably didn't play to her strengths.

The distaff side of Magic of Light's pedigree was awash with 'black type' long before Magic of Light came along. Her lightly-raced dam Quest of Passion, who was runner-up twice at up to fifteen furlongs on the Flat in France, was a sister to the useful listed performer Supreme Commander who enjoyed success in both Germany and France at around ten furlongs. Quest of Passion was also related to several above-average Flat performers, including her Group 2-winning half-sister Fair of The Furze, who went on to even greater things at stud, being the dam of 1993 Arc de Triomphe runner-up White Muzzle. Fair of The Furze also produced the 2001 German St Leger winner Fair Question, who went on to show useful winning form over both hurdles and fences. The National Hunt arena has been the scene for most of the success achieved by Quest of Passion's offspring, which no doubt influenced the decision to send her to jumps-oriented sires during the latter part of her stud career. Her first foal Mughas (by Sadler's Wells) had rather set the tone, developing into a smart staying hurdler after failing to meet expectations when carrying Hamdan Al Maktoum's colours on the Flat. Quest of Passion's other notable jumpers before Magic of Light were the smart pair Sizing Platinum and Pingshou (both by Definite Article), who also run under the Potts' banner but are now trained by Colin Tizzard after beginning their careers in Ireland with Henry de Bromhead. Pingshou won the Grade 1 Top Novices' Hurdle at Aintree in 2017 but has been lightly raced since, winning a three-mile novice chase at Ffos Las in May after a mixed 2018/19 campaign. Sizing Platinum has stood far more racing and, although an in-and-out performer nowadays, he showed that he is still capable of smart form when defying a BHA mark of 145 to land a two-mile handicap chase at Chepstow in April. Magic of Light's maiden half-sister Prairie Bell (by Sadler's Wells) was the dam of the Harrington-trained prolific winning hurdler/chaser Cailin Annamh (also by Definite Article), who showed useful form at up to two and three quarter miles. Quest of Passion's final foal, the seven-year-old mare Carrowmore (by Yeats), never reached the racecourse but recently launched her broodmare career with a 2018 Shirocco filly.

			⎧ Alleged	⎧ Hoist The Flag
	⎧ Flemensfirth (USA)	⎧	⎨ (b 1974)	⎩ Princess Pout
		(b 1992)	⎨ Etheldreda	⎧ Diesis
Magic of Light (IRE)	⎨	⎩ (ch 1985)	⎩ Royal Bund
(b.m. 2011)			⎧ Saumarez	⎧ Rainbow Quest
	⎩ Quest of Passion (FR)	⎧	⎨ (b or br 1987)	⎩ Fiesta Fun
	(b 1994)	⎨ Autocratic	⎧ Tyrant
		⎩ (b 1974)	⎩ Flight Table

A useful-looking mare, Magic of Light has yet to race on ground firmer than good but she has proved effective on all types of underfoot conditions she has encountered to date (acts on heavy). She is certainly versatile with regards to trip, showing her form at two and a half miles up to four and a quarter miles in the latest campaign. Ideally suited by being ridden up with the pace, Magic of Light is essentially a sound jumper but, as her Aintree performance showed, she can still throw in the odd jumping error—she unseated Power at the eleventh when favourite for the Bobbyjo Chase at Fairyhouse (won by Rathvinden) in February. Magic of Light is likely to be kept in training and seems sure to have another campaign geared around a tilt at the Aintree showpiece. If she makes the line-up, she will be attempting to overcome another daunting historical statistic: by the time of the 2020 renewal it will be forty-three years since the last runner-up went on to win the National twelve months later. That horse was none other than Aintree legend Red Rum whose achievement of being the only horse to win three Grand Nationals will also feature strongly in previews of the race if Tiger Roll takes the field again. *Mrs J. Harrington, Ireland*

MAGIC OF MILAN (IRE) 6 b.m. Milan – Laughing Lesa (IRE) (Bob Back (USA)) **c86** [2018/19 h74: h20.2g⁶ h19.9g h16.8s² h19.9s⁴ h21.4s* h22g² h21.4d c20.9v² c26.2d⁶ **h83** Mar 24] medium-sized mare: poor handicap hurdler: won at Ayr (conditionals) in January: modest form over fences: stays 2¾m: acts on heavy going: in cheekpieces last 5 starts: wears tongue tie: usually races prominently. *Sam England*

MAGIC RIVER (IRE) 8 ch.g. Indian River (FR) – All Magic (IRE) (Ashkalani (IRE)) [2018/19 h101: h19d h21.4g c24g c19.4g^2 c25.7g^F Apr 21] off mark in Irish points at fourth attempt: fair form over hurdles: modest form over fences: stays 19f: best form on good going: in headgear last 3 starts: in tongue tie last 2. *Milton Harris* **c98 h–**

MAGIC SAINT (FR) 5 b.g. Saint des Saints (FR) – Magic Poline (Trempolino (USA)) [2018/19 c21.6g^2 c18.8s^5 c15.7g* c16.3d c16.5m^F c16m^2 Apr 22] sturdy gelding: half-brother to fairly useful French hurdler/chaser Liberatore (15f-19f winner, by Poliglote): dam fairly useful French 17f hurdle winner (stayed 2½m): won both starts over hurdles (in France for Guillaume Macaire): smart handicap chaser: won at Wincanton (by 4½ lengths from Gino Trail) in February: second at Chepstow (5 lengths behind Sizing Platinum) in April: best form up to 2¼m: acts on soft and good to firm going: tried in hood. *Paul Nicholls* **c147 h–**

MAGNA CARTOR 9 b.g. Motivator – Hora (Hernando (FR)) [2018/19 h122: h16v c16g^3 c16g^6 c17g h16.8m^6 h16.6d^4 h18.5s Apr 16] lengthy gelding: fair handicap hurdler: similar form over fences: best effort when third in maiden at Clonmel in June: left John Joseph Hanlon after sixth start: should stay beyond 17f: acts on good to soft going: has worn hood. *Dr Richard Newland* **c109 h108**

MAGNA SAM 5 b.g. Black Sam Bellamy (IRE) – Angie Marinie (Sabrehill (USA)) [2018/19 b–: b16.3d Mar 23] off mark in points at fourth attempt: no form in bumpers. *Steve Flook* **b–**

MAGNETIZE (IRE) 6 b.m. Gold Well – Ersa (IRE) (Alhaarth (IRE)) [2018/19 b16g^4 b15.8d h21.7d Jan 2] third foal: half-sister to a winning pointer by Arcadio: dam, maiden in Greece, half-sister to very smart hurdler/useful chaser (winner up to 3m) Muirhead and smart 2m hurdle winner Thomas Darby: fair form in bumpers: tailed off in mares novice on hurdling debut. *Tom Symonds* **h– b86**

MAGNOLIA RIDGE (IRE) 9 b.g. Galileo (IRE) – Treasure The Lady (IRE) (Indian Ridge) [2018/19 h82: c16g^{pu} May 16] winning hurdler: pulled up in novice handicap on chasing debut: stays 2½m: best form on good going: usually wears headgear. *Andrew Hamilton* **c– h–**

MAGNUM (IRE) 6 gr.g. Lawman (FR) – Coventina (IRE) (Daylami (IRE)) [2018/19 h87: h15.8m May 19] fairly useful on Flat (stays 1¼m), well below best in 2018: maiden hurdler: tried in cheekpieces: wears tongue tie. *Susan Corbett* **h–**

MAGOO (IRE) 7 gr.g. Martaline – Noche (IRE) (Night Shift (USA)) [2018/19 h121p: c20s^F h21.4g^4 h19.8s^2 h19.9v^5 Mar 16] strong, compact gelding: has had breathing operation: fairly useful form over hurdles: second in handicap at Sandown in March: fell eleventh in novice handicap at same course on chasing debut: will probably stay 3m: acts on heavy going: in tongue tie last 5 starts: usually races prominently. *Paul Nicholls* **c– p h123**

MAGUIRE'S GLEN (IRE) 11 b.g. Craigsteel – Next Venture (IRE) (Zaffaran (USA)) [2018/19 c113, h115: h21g h19.4v^6 c20v^4 h20v^5 c19.4s^{bd} h20s Apr 7] fairly useful hurdler/fair chaser, below best in 2018/19: stays 23f: acts on heavy going: tried in cheekpieces. *Grace Harris* **c100 h97**

MAHLER BAY (IRE) 9 b.g. Mahler – Belalzao (IRE) (Alzao (USA)) [2018/19 c80§, h–: h22.1m^{pu} c24g^{ur} Jul 15] good-topped gelding: maiden hurdler/chaser: has worn headgear/tongue tie: temperamental. *Rebecca Menzies* **c– § h– §**

MAHLERDRAMATIC (IRE) 9 br.g. Mahler – Image of Vermont (IRE) (Accordion) [2018/19 c96, h79: c21.4g c21.4g c19.2g^3 c23.9s^5 Dec 6] winning hurdler: modest maiden chaser, below form in 2018/19: left Brian Ellison after first start: should be suited by further than 2½m: acts on soft going: has worn headgear/tongue tie, including in 2018/19: front runner/races prominently: one to leave alone. *Jacqueline Coward* **c80 § h–**

MAHLER LAD (IRE) 9 b.g. Mahler – Sister Merenda (IRE) (Dr Massini (IRE)) [2018/19 c112, h–: c24.5g* c24.2g^{pu} c26.2g^2 c24.5v c29.6d^{pu} Apr 26] lightly-raced hurdler: fair handicap chaser: won at Towcester early in season: stays 3¼m: acts on heavy going: wears headgear: usually races prominently. *Donald McCain* **c111 h–**

MAHLERMADE (IRE) 6 ch.g. Mahler – Double Concerto (IRE) (Brahms (USA)) [2018/19 h108, b81: h19m^3 h19.9g^3 h23.3g^4 h23.1g^4 c23d^2 c23d^2 c24g^2 c25.5d^3 c24d^{ur} c25.6m* Apr 20] has had breathing operation: fair form over hurdles: fairly useful form over fences: won handicap at Haydock in April: stays 3¼m: acts on soft and good to firm going: has worn headgear: wears tongue tie: usually races prominently. *Alan King* **c125 h113**

MAHLER'S FIRST (IRE) 7 b.g. Mahler – Fridays Folly (IRE) (Flemensfirth (USA)) **c94**
[2018/19 h84: c21.6d^{pu} c24.2v^{ur} c24.2s^3 Jan 20] modest form over hurdles/fences: stays **h–**
3m: acts on soft going: has worn cheekpieces, including last 2 starts. *Victor Dartnall*

MAHLERS SPIRIT (IRE) 9 ch.g. Mahler – Belle Dame (IRE) (Executive Perk) **c–**
[2018/19 c26g^{pu} May 4] multiple point winner: no form under Rules. *A. Pennock* **h–**

MAHLER SUPREME (IRE) 5 b.g. Mahler – Site Alite (IRE) (Supreme Leader) **h101**
[2018/19 b18g^6 h19.9s^3 h18.1d^5 h19.9d^4 Apr 23] third foal: dam (b89) in frame in bumpers: **b–**
tailed off in bumpers for T. S. Costello: fair form over hurdles: best effort when third in
novice at Sedgefield. *George Bewley*

MAHLERVOUS (IRE) 6 b.g. Mahler – Brook Style (IRE) (Alderbrook) [2018/19 h117, **h128**
b–: h21g^2 h20s^6 h20.9g* h21s^5 h21.4m* Apr 13] good-topped gelding: has had breathing
operation: fairly useful handicap hurdler: won at Kelso in January and Ayr in April: stays
21f: acts on good to firm and good to soft going: in cheekpieces last 2 starts. *Warren Greatrex*

MAH MATE BOB (IRE) 7 b.g. Mahler – Bobset Leader (IRE) (Bob Back (USA)) **h97**
[2018/19 h–: h21.2g^5 h25.3g h20.1s^4 h22g^4 h20.6d^2 h19.9v* h20.6d^4 Apr 6] workmanlike
gelding: modest handicap hurdler: won at Sedgefield in March: stays 2¾m: acts on heavy
going: in hood last 3 starts: usually leads. *George Bewley*

MAID OF MILAN (IRE) 8 br.m. Milan – Joes Lady (IRE) (Win Quick (IRE)) [2018/19 **c114**
c116, h–: c23.8g^4 c26.1g^{pu} c25.8g^{pu} Jul 6] winning hurdler: fair form over fences: stays **h–**
3¼m: acts on soft and good to firm going: in cheekpieces last 3 starts. *Charlie Mann*

MAIFALKI (FR) 6 b.g. Falco (USA) – Makila (IRE) (Entrepreneur) [2018/19 h15.8g^3 **h91 p**
May 28] useful on Flat, stays 1½m: 16/1, third in maiden at Huntingdon (19 lengths behind
Humphrey Bogart) on hurdling debut: should improve. *Jason Ward*

MAIGH DARA (IRE) 10 br.g. Cacique (IRE) – Dara Diva (IRE) (Barathea (IRE)) **h–**
[2018/19 h21.7d^{pu} Nov 18] little show over hurdles: dead. *Lydia Richards*

MAIRE BANRIGH 7 b.m. King's Theatre (IRE) – La Marianne (Supreme Leader) **h115**
[2018/19 h67: h16.7g* h17g* Oct 25] type to make a chaser: has had breathing operation:
won Irish point on debut: fairly useful form over hurdles: won maiden at Market Rasen
early in season and intermediate handicap at Carlisle in October: in tongue tie last 3 starts.
Dan Skelton

MAISIEBELLA 6 b.m. Black Sam Bellamy (IRE) – Lucylou (IRE) (Bob Back (USA)) **b79**
[2018/19 b16.7d^4 Apr 26] half-sister to fairly useful hurdler/chaser Cool Mix (2m-2½m
winner) and a winning pointer (both by Fair Mix): dam unraced out of half-sister to useful
hurdler up to 2½m Mayasta, herself dam of Cheltenham Gold Cup winner Synchronised:
66/1, fourth in mares bumper at Bangor (11¾ lengths behind The Milan Girl). *John Groucott*

MAISY BELLE (IRE) 8 b.m. Westerner – Sabbiosa (IRE) (Desert Prince (IRE)) **h88**
[2018/19 h20.5g^5 h15.9s h15.9d h20.5d^{pu} h20.5g^6 h20.5g^{pu} h25g^{pu} Apr 22] close-coupled
mare: third foal: dam (h92), maiden hurdler (stayed 19f), 1m-1½m winner on Flat: modest
maiden hurdler: left Stuart Crawford after first start: stays 2½m: often in hood. *Zoe Davison*

MAITREE EXPRESS 5 br.g. Malinas (GER) – Shatabdi (IRE) (Mtoto) [2018/19 b16d **b–**
Mar 28] 4/1, well beaten in maiden bumper. *Warren Greatrex*

MAJDOOL (IRE) 6 b.g. Acclamation – Maany (Mr Greeley (USA)) [2018/19 **h–**
h16.2g h16.2m Jun 24] fair on Flat, stays 1m: well held in 2 maiden hurdles: tried in hood.
Noel Wilson

MAJESTIC LORD 5 b.g. Youmzain (IRE) – Majestic Roi (USA) (Street Cry (IRE)) **b–**
[2018/19 b15.8g Nov 2] angular gelding: 3/1, tailed off in maiden bumper. *Harry Whittington*

MAJESTIC MAN (IRE) 6 b.g. Majestic Missile (IRE) – Windomen (IRE) (Forest Wind **h–**
(USA)) [2018/19 b–: h16.6m^6 h15.7g^4 Mar 4] no show in bumper/novice hurdles. *Ronald
Thompson*

MAJESTIC MOLL (IRE) 7 b.m. King's Theatre (IRE) – Artist's Muse (IRE) (Cape **c126**
Cross (IRE)) [2018/19 h112p: h23.3d h20g* h19.9g^4 c20g* c20.2g^{pu} c19.9g* c20.6g^{pu} **h122**
Apr 18] has had breathing operation: fairly useful handicap hurdler: won at Worcester in
August: similar form over fences: won mares novices at same course in October and
Huntingdon in November: stays 21f: acts on good to soft going. *Emma Lavelle*

MAJESTIC TOUCH (IRE) 8 br.g. Kalanisi (IRE) – Alexander Divine (Halling (USA)) **h119**
[2018/19 h115: h16.8g* h19.2s^4 h16.4g^6 h16.3d^2 h19d^3 Dec 13] well-made gelding: fairly
useful handicap hurdler: won at Newton Abbot in September: placed at Newbury
(conditionals) and Taunton last 2 starts: should stay 2½m: acts on soft going: wore hood in
2018/19: races towards rear. *Philip Hobbs*

MAJOR DAVIS (FR) 7 b.g. Vision d'Etat (FR) – Majorica Sancta (FR) (Saint des Saints (FR)) [2018/19 h101: h15.7g³ May 14] angular gelding: fair form over hurdles: won first 2 starts in Irish points in October. *Warren Greatrex* — h105

MAJOR HINDRANCE (IRE) 9 ch.g. Kris Kin (USA) – Ten Dollar Bill (IRE) (Accordion) [2018/19 c121§, h–: c19.9dᵖᵘ c24.2d⁶ c23.9dᵖᵘ h20s Apr 7] fair hurdler/fairly useful chaser, well below form in 2018/19: should be suited by 3m+: acts on heavy going: temperamental. *Henry Oliver* — c105 § h– §

MAJOR MINUS 5 b.g. Sir Percy – Eminencia (Sadler's Wells (USA)) [2018/19 h19.9m Oct 2] no form on Flat: well beaten in novice on hurdling debut: placed first 3 starts in points. *Tim Easterby* — h–

MAJURCA (FR) 5 b.g. Maresca Sorrento (FR) – Majature (FR) (Turgeon (USA)) [2018/19 c17.9s⁴ c18.4s* c21.9s⁴ c19.7sᶠ c24d⁵ Jan 27] fourth foal: half-brother to French 19f chase winner Majacalie (by Califet): dam unraced half-sister to useful hurdler/smart chaser (2m-2½m winner) Majala: winning hurdler in France: useful form over fences: won 4-y-o event at Auteuil in June: left G. Cherel after third start: stays 2¾m: acts on soft going. *Joseph Patrick O'Brien, Ireland* — c131 h–

MAKE IT HAPPEN (IRE) 10 b.g. Saffron Walden (FR) – Kelpie (IRE) (Kahyasi) [2018/19 c–, h98: h20.2gʳᵒ h20.2g h16.2g³ h22.1sᵖᵘ h18.1m h17vᵖᵘ h18.1d* h16.2g Apr 25] modest handicap hurdler: won at Kelso (conditionals) in April: twice-raced chaser: stays 2½m: acts on heavy going: wears cheekpieces: usually wears tongue tie. *Lucinda Russell* — c– h97

MAKE ME A FORTUNE (IRE) 11 b.g. Heron Island (IRE) – Biora Queen (IRE) (Old Vic) [2018/19 c–, h–: h19.6g h24gᵖᵘ May 23] medium-sized gelding: useful hurdler at best, no form last 2 seasons: maiden chaser: wears cheekpieces: tried in tongue tie. *Steve Gollings* — c– h–

MAKE MY HEART FLY (IRE) 7 b.m. Stowaway – Poppy Maroon (Supreme Leader) [2018/19 h18.8g* h16g h16.2g* h23.9g* h16.8m* h20.2g* h18g² c21g⁴ h21g³ h16d⁵ Nov 11] sturdy mare: fairly useful hurdler: completed 4-timer in handicaps at Perth in July (amateurs) and August, and mares novices at Sedgefield and Perth again in September: third in Irish EBF Mares Novices' Hurdle at Down Royal (5 lengths behind Sancta Simona) in November: 3/1, fourth in mares maiden at Fairyhouse (8¾ lengths behind Bargy Lady) on chasing debut: stays 3m: acts on good to firm going: tried in hood: wears tongue tie: should do better over fences. *Gordon Elliott, Ireland* — c112 p h124

MAKETHEDIFFERENCE (IRE) 11 b.g. Shantou (USA) – La Panthere (USA) (Pine Bluff (USA)) [2018/19 h15.9g⁴ h20.1gᵖᵘ h15.8mᶠ h18.6mᵖᵘ Aug 5] well-made gelding: modest handicap chaser: maiden chaser: effective from 2m to 21f: acts on good to firm and heavy going: has worn headgear, including last 3 starts. *Kevin Bishop* — c– h89

MAKETY 5 ch.m. Black Sam Bellamy (IRE) – Mi Money (Alflora (IRE)) [2018/19 h21.7d⁶ h16.8d² h16.3d⁴ Mar 23] has had breathing operation: second foal: dam, well held in bumpers/over hurdles, out of half-sister to Grand National winner Red Marauder: won point bumper on debut: fair form over hurdles. *Oliver Sherwood* — h108

MAKEYAMINDUPMAIZ 5 gr.m. Geordieland (FR) – Pems Gift (Environment Friend) [2018/19 b15.8s Dec 31] half-sister to fair hurdler/fairly useful chaser Mick The Jiver (2¾m-3m winner, by Apple Tree) and bumper winner Maggie Aron (by Generous): dam unraced: tailed off in maiden bumper. *Jake Thomas Coulson* — b–

MAKIN IT 4 b.f. North Light (IRE) – Saltpetre (IRE) (Selkirk (USA)) [2018/19 h19.2m Mar 29] modest maiden on Flat, stays 1½m: no show in point/maiden hurdle. *Phil York* — h–

MAKITORIX (FR) 6 gr.g. Makfi – Goldamix (IRE) (Linamix (FR)) [2018/19 h130: h16s h16.2g² Nov 18] useful handicap hurdler: second at Punchestown (2½ lengths behind Hearts Are Trumps) in November: raced only at 2m: acts on heavy going: tried in hood: in tongue tie last 4 starts. *W. P. Mullins, Ireland* — h133

MALA BEACH (IRE) 11 b.g. Beneficial – Peppardstown (IRE) (Old Vic) [2018/19 c155, h–: h24s c26.2v² c34.3gᵖᵘ Apr 6] strong gelding: winning hurdler: very smart chaser, below best in 2018/19: second in minor event at Down Royal (6½ lengths behind Jury Duty) in March: stays 3¼m: acts on heavy going. *Gordon Elliott, Ireland* — c140 h–

MALACHITE 6 gr.g. Malinas (GER) – Kali (Linamix (FR)) [2018/19 h111, b93: h16.4g h19g³ h20.5d³ h18.5s Apr 16] tall, good-topped gelding: fair form over hurdles: stays 21f: acts on soft going. *Nicky Henderson* — h112

Matchbook Imperial Cup Handicap Hurdle, Sandown—a belated first win in this race for Paul Nicholls as Malaya (noseband) wears down the leader Monsieur Lecoq; 2018 runner-up Call Me Lord (third left) takes third this time

MALACHYS GIRL (IRE) 6 b.m. Darsi (FR) – Borleagh Princess (IRE) (Presenting) **h91** [2018/19 b92: h21.2d⁴ h21.7d⁴ Jan 2] Irish point winner: fair form in bumper: modest form over hurdles: will be suited by 3m: tried in hood. *Ben Pauling*

MALANGEN (IRE) 4 b.g. Born To Sea (IRE) – Lady's Locket (IRE) (Fasliyev (USA)) **h111 §** [2018/19 h16d⁴ h15.9g² h18.7g² h19.3g⁵ h18.6g³ h15.3gᶠ h16v⁴ h15.8v h16.8d* h19.6g* h16.8g* Apr 20] rather leggy gelding: fair hurdler: completed hat-trick in novice seller at Exeter in March, and handicaps at Bangor and Newton Abbot in April: stays 2½m: acts on good to soft going: usually wears headgear: has worn tongue tie, including in 2018/19: usually front runner/races prominently: temperamental (carries head awkwardly). *David Pipe*

MALAPIE (IRE) 11 b.g. Westerner – Victorian Lady (Old Vic) [2018/19 c122, h122: **c–** h23.3d⁵ c30.7sᵖᵘ h25g h19.9v⁵ Jan 26] workmanlike gelding: fairly useful handicap hurdler/ **h115 ?** winning chaser, below best in 2018/19: stays 3¼m: acts on heavy going. *Caroline Bailey*

MALASPINA (ITY) 7 b.m. Pounced (USA) – Modern Goddess (USA) (Gulch (USA)) **h–** [2018/19 h15.5d Dec 12] fairly useful on Flat, stays 1¼m: in hood/tongue tie, well beaten in maiden on hurdling debut. *Dan Skelton*

MALAYA (FR) 5 b.m. Martaline – Clarte d'Or (FR) (Kendor (FR)) [2018/19 h133: **h138** h19.4sᶠ h16gᶠ h19.3d⁴ h16s* h16m Apr 13] leggy mare: useful handicap hurdler: won Imperial Cup at Sandown (by 1¼ lengths from Monsieur Lecoq) in March: stays 19f: acts on soft going. *Paul Nicholls*

MALINDI BAY (FR) 6 b.m. Malinas (GER) – La Grande Villez (FR) (Villez (USA)) **h87** [2018/19 h91p, b92: h19.9g⁵ h17.1d⁵ h21.6g⁶ Nov 24] won Irish point on debut: bumper winner: modest form over hurdles: held up, races freely. *James Evans*

MALL DINI (IRE) 9 b.g. Milan – Winsome Breeze (IRE) (Glacial Storm (USA)) **c134** [2018/19 c148, h–: c20g³ c25s⁶ c17.7v² Mar 17] good-topped gelding: winning hurdler: **h–** useful maiden chaser: should stay long distances: acts on heavy going: tried in blinkers: usually wears tongue tie. *Patrick G. Kelly, Ireland*

MALLY COLLIER 6 ch.g. Flying Legend (USA) – Isaflo (Alflora (IRE)) [2018/19 **b68** b16.8d⁵ b15.7g Mar 4] poor form in bumpers: tried in hood. *Ronald Thompson*

MALONE ROAD (IRE) 5 b.g. Kalanisi – Zaffarella (IRE) (Zaffaran (USA)) **b117 p** [2018/19 b16.5g* b16.2g* Nov 18] £325,000 4-y-o: fourth foal: half-brother to bumper winner/fairly useful 17f hurdle winner Ravenhill Road (by Exit To Nowhere) and bumper winner/useful 2½m hurdle winner Windsor Avenue (by Winged Love): dam (h112) 2m-3m hurdle winner: won maiden point on debut: smart form in bumpers: won at Down Royal (maiden, by 7½ lengths from Valdieu) and Punchestown (by 8½ lengths from Mt Leinster, storming clear) in November: met set-back but remains very exciting prospect. *Gordon Elliott, Ireland*

MALTON ROSE (IRE) 8 b.g. Milan – Pharney Fox (IRE) (Phardante (FR)) [2018/19 **h122**
h118, b98: h25g⁵ h20g⁴ h20g³ h21dᵖᵘ Nov 29] bumper winner: fairly useful form over
hurdles: third in handicap at Worcester: should stay 2¾m. *Nicky Henderson*

MALYSTIC 5 b.g. Malinas (GER) – Mystic Glen (Vettori (IRE)) [2018/19 b16.4g* **b98**
b15.6g² ab16.3s* b17d Apr 5] tall, rather unfurnished gelding: second foal: dam (c81/h75),
ungenuine 2m hurdle/chase winner (stayed 21f), half-sister to useful hurdler (2m-2¼m
winner) Clever Cookie: fairly useful form in bumpers: won at Newcastle in November and
February. *Peter Niven*

MAMNOON (IRE) 6 b.g. Cape Cross (IRE) – Masaafat (Act One) [2018/19 h16g **h–**
h15.7g⁵ Oct 2] modest on Flat, stays 11f: well held in 2 novice hurdles. *Roy Brotherton*

MAMOO 6 ch.g. Sir Percy – Meredith (Medicean) [2018/19 h99: h22m h21.7g⁴ h26.5g* **h94**
h26.5g⁴ h25m³ h25g h23.4g⁶ h25g⁴ Nov 24] modest handicap hurdler: won at Newton
Abbot in July: stays 3¼m: acts on soft and good to firm going: wears headgear: front
runner/races prominently: has joined Mike Sowersby. *Neil King*

MAM TRASNA (IRE) 5 b.g. Morozov (USA) – Eimear Supreme (IRE) (Supreme **b95**
Leader) [2018/19 b16.2g³ b16.2g* b16.2d⁵ Apr 26] €12,000 3-y-o, resold £30,000 3-y-o:
fifth foal: closely related to a winning pointer by Oscar: dam unraced half-sister to smart
hurdler/very smart chaser up to 3m Colonel Braxton: fairly useful form in bumpers: won
at Kelso in January for D. Broad. *Gordon Elliott, Ireland*

MANAMITE (FR) 6 b.g. Kentucky Dynamite (USA) – Masaya (SWI) (In The Wings) **h121**
[2018/19 h16.7dᵖᵘ h16.8s h16.2v* h19.9d⁴ h16.4m* h16.4dᵖᵘ Apr 6] closely related to
French 17f/2¼m hurdle winner Ma Cagnotte (by King's Best): fairly useful hurdler: won
maiden at Hexham in December and handicap at Musselburgh in February: left Gordon
Elliott after first start: mainly raced around 2m: acts on good to firm and heavy going:
usually races off pace. *Ben Haslam*

MANCE RAYDER (IRE) 6 b.g. Flemensfirth (USA) – J'y Viens (FR) (Smadoun (FR)) **h107**
[2018/19 h111: h23sᵖᵘ h21.2g² h19.9s³ h19.7s h19.9d² h21.2v³ h19.3g* Feb 24] sturdy
gelding: fair hurdler: won handicap at Carlisle (conditionals) in February: left Philip Hobbs
after first start: stays 23f: acts on heavy going: in cheekpieces last 5 starts. *Henry Hogarth*

MANDY'S QUINE (IRE) 5 b.m. Tikkanen (USA) – Mandy Mac (IRE) (Amilynx (FR)) **h72**
[2018/19 b16d⁵ b16.1d h16v h16d h20d Apr 27] first foal: dam unraced: poor form in **b65**
bumpers/over hurdles: in hood late 4 starts. *Stuart Crawford, Ireland*

MANETTI (IRE) 7 b.g. Westerner – Mrs Wallensky (IRE) (Roselier (FR)) [2018/19 **h101**
h20.5v³ h22d⁴ h20.5s⁵ h19.5d⁴ Feb 25] multiple point winner: fair form over hurdles.
N. W. Alexander

MANHATTAN SPRING 8 b.g. Central Park (IRE) – Risky May (Petoski) [2018/19 h94: **h104**
h21.4m h23.3g² Jun 6] lengthy gelding: fair form over hurdles: tried in blinkers.
Seamus Mullins

MANICMAN (IRE) 5 ch.g. Getaway (GER) – Quinsborohall (IRE) (Saddlers' Hall **h–**
(IRE)) [2018/19 h15.7gᵖᵘ h20.6dᵖᵘ Apr 6] placed in Irish points: pulled up both starts in
novice hurdles. *Sam England*

MAN LOOK 7 b.g. Nayef (USA) – Charlecote (IRE) (Caerleon (USA)) [2018/19 h118: **h117**
h19.9g⁶ h19.9m² h16.2gᵖᵘ Oct 7] useful-looking gelding: fairly useful handicap hurdler:
stayed 21f: acted on good to firm going: sometimes in hood: dead. *Donald McCain*

MANNING ESTATE (IRE) 5 b.g. Stowaway – Specifiedrisk (IRE) (Turtle Island **h119**
(IRE)) [2018/19 b17.7g² b15.7m⁶ h15.9s² h17.7v⁴ h20.5s² h19.4g* h21.7m⁴ h23.8m² Apr **b87**
23] €57,000 3-y-o: half-brother to several winners, including smart hurdler/very smart
chaser Glencove Marina (2m-2¾m winner, by Spectrum) and fairly useful hurdler/useful
chaser Theatre Territory (2m-3m winner, by King's Theatre): dam unraced half-sister to
Ascot Gold Cup winner Mr Dinos: fair form in bumpers: fairly useful form over hurdles:
won novice at Doncaster in March: stays 3m: acts on soft and good to firm going.
Oliver Sherwood

MANNOCHMORE 4 b.g. Dylan Thomas (IRE) – Loch Dhu (IRE) (Oscar (IRE)) **b–**
[2018/19 b16.2d⁶ Apr 26] 33/1, sixth of 7 in bumper at Perth. *Lucinda Russell*

MAN OF PLENTY 10 ch.g. Manduro (GER) – Credit-A-Plenty (Generous (IRE)) **h127**
[2018/19 h125: h16.7g⁶ h16.4g⁵ h16.4g h20.5s⁴ h16v* h15.7s h19.3d⁵ h23.4s⁶ h24.3g⁶
h24d Mar 14] good-topped gelding: fairly useful handicap hurdler: won listed event at
Sandown in December: stays 3m: acts on heavy going: usually wears headgear: wears
tongue tie: races off pace. *Sophie Leech*

MAN OF STEEL (IRE) 10 b.g. Craigsteel – Knappogue Honey (IRE) (Anshan) [2018/19 c117, h–: c25.5g* May 30] multiple point winner: maiden hurdler: fairly useful hunter chaser: won at Cartmel early in season: stays 27f: acts on good to firm and heavy going: has worn headgear, including last 5 starts: wears tongue tie: temperamental. *Alan Hill*

c108 h– §

MANOFTHEMOMENT (IRE) 5 b.g. Jeremy (USA) – Endless Ambition (IRE) (Luso) [2018/19 b15.7d h15.3g h16d⁵ h16.3d h16.8s* Apr 24] €15,000 3-y-o, £58,000 4-y-o: sturdy gelding: first foal: dam unraced half-sister to useful staying hurdler No Hassle Hoff: won Irish point on debut: modest form on sole start in bumper: fair form over hurdles: won handicaps at Exeter (novice) in March and Southwell (conditionals) in April: stays 2½m: acts on soft going. *Tom George*

h105 b82

MANOFTHEMOUNTAIN (IRE) 6 b.g. Mahler – Womanofthemountain (IRE) (Presenting) [2018/19 b15.8s h19d⁴ h19.4g² Jan 25] has had breathing operation: third foal: half-brother to bumper winner/useful chaser Fact of The Matter (2½m-3¾m winner, by Brian Boru): dam ran once in bumper: last of 3 finishers in Irish point: well beaten in bumper: fair form over hurdles: better effort when second in maiden at Doncaster: will be suited by 2½m+: has joined Emma Lavelle. *Jamie Snowden*

h107 b–

MAN OF THE NORTH 6 b.g. And Beyond (IRE) – Latin Beauty (IRE) (Sadler's Wells (USA)) [2018/19 b–: h16m⁴ h16d h16.7g h19.6g⁰⁰ h19d⁰⁰ h20.5g h16.6g* h15.8d h18.9d⁴ Mar 20] workmanlike gelding: modest handicap hurdler: won novice event at Doncaster in January: stays 19f: acts on good to soft going: in headgear last 4 starts. *Tony Carroll*

h89 x

MANON 5 b.m. Malinas (GER) – La Creole (FR) (Astarabad (USA)) [2018/19 b87: b16d h19.9d⁶ Jan 21] modest form in bumpers: well beaten in novice on hurdling debut. *Michael Easterby*

h– b–

MANSION (IRE) 7 b.g. Invincible Spirit (IRE) – Manoeuvre (IRE) (Galileo (IRE)) [2018/19 h18.5d h15.9s⁵ h23.9s⁴ h19.5d Apr 6] strong gelding: modest maiden hurdler: missed 2017/18: may prove best at short of 3m: acts on soft going. *Venetia Williams*

h88

MANTOU (IRE) 8 ch.g. Teofilo (IRE) – Shadow Roll (IRE) (Mark of Esteem (IRE)) [2018/19 c100, h–: c16.3g c20.9d³ c23.8m⁰⁰ c22.7f⁰⁰ Feb 26] has had breathing operation: winning hurdler: fair form in hunter chases: stays 21f: acts on heavy going: wears cheekpieces/tongue tie. *Sam Allwood*

c102 h–

MANTOVANI (FR) 4 b.g. High Chaparral (IRE) – Ripley (GER) (Platini (GER)) [2018/19 h16.8s³ h16.5d⁵ Dec 30] half-brother to useful 2m hurdle winner Soldier In Action (by Soldier of Fortune): fairly useful maiden on Flat, stays 1½m: fair form over hurdles: better effort when third in juvenile at Exeter in November. *Harry Fry*

h114

MANVERS HOUSE 6 b.g. Schiaparelli – Freydis (IRE) (Supreme Leader) [2018/19 b97: h19.5s h16.3d⁴ h21d⁴ h19.8s⁶ Mar 7] lengthy gelding: fairly useful form in bumpers: fair form over hurdles: should be suited by 21f+. *Robert Walford*

h108

MANWELL (IRE) 9 b.g. Gold Well – Roborette (FR) (Robore (FR)) [2018/19 c105, h–: c20.3d² c19.2s² c19.2g* c19.4g* c16.4s² c19.9g⁴ c21.1s⁴ Mar 3] lengthy, workmanlike gelding: has had breathing operation: winning hurdler: fairly useful handicap chaser: won at Catterick and Wetherby in January: stays 2½m: acts on heavy going: tried in hood: wears tongue tie: races off pace. *Sam England*

c124 h–

MAN WITH VAN (IRE) 13 b.g. Milan – Delibonne (IRE) (Erdelistan (FR)) [2018/19 c–, c89, h114: h23.9g c22.5d Dec 28] useful hurdler/chaser at best, on downgrade: stays 3½m: acts on heavy going: has worn headgear, including in 2018/19: has worn tongue tie: usually races towards rear. *Patrick Griffin, Ireland*

c– h–

MAQUISARD (FR) 7 ch.g. Creachadoir (IRE) – Gioiosa Marea (IRE) (Highest Honor (FR)) [2018/19 h122: h19.2g⁰⁰ h19.2m h16g³ h16.8d⁶ h16s² h16.3d⁰⁰ h16.3d⁴ Mar 22] sturdy gelding: fairly useful handicap hurdler: second at Sandown (conditionals) in February: left Gary Moore after second start: unproven beyond 17f: acts on heavy going: tried in cheekpieces: has joined Michael Madgwick. *Chris Gordon*

h123

MARAAKIB (IRE) 9 b.g. Dark Angel (IRE) – Mrs Cee (IRE) (Orpen (USA)) [2018/19 h18.7m⁴ h18.5g h16.8d⁵ h16.5d h16.5d Dec 13] modest on Flat, stays 10.5f: poor form over hurdles. *Alexandra Dunn*

h82

MARADA 4 ch.f. Martaline – Kerada (FR) (Astarabad (USA)) [2018/19 b16.7g⁴ Apr 3] third foal: half-sister to fairly useful 19f hurdle winner Tarada (by Kayf Tara) and fair 25f hurdle winner Royal Claret (by Yeats): dam (c137/h127) 2m-3m hurdle/chase winner: 2/1, fourth in maiden bumper at Market Rasen (2 lengths behind Stormin Norman): should do better. *Dan Skelton*

b81 p

MARATT (FR) 6 gr.g. Martaline – Lavi (FR) (Evening World (FR)) [2018/19 h68, b–: **c98** h17.7g h16.8g h23g^pu h15.9g^4 h15.9m^3 h16s h15.3g^4 c17.5d^4 c17s^pu Jan 16] poor maiden **h78** hurdler: modest form over fences: raced mainly around 2m: acts on good to firm going: tried in hood. *Seamus Mullins*

MARAWEH (IRE) 9 b.g. Muhtathir – Itqaan (USA) (Danzig (USA)) [2018/19 h94§: **h– §** h23.9g h23.9g h23.9g^pu Aug 1] maiden pointer: modest hurdler, well below form in 2018/19: wears headgear: temperamental. *Lucinda Russell*

MARBETH (IRE) 6 b.m. Frozen Power (IRE) – Suddenly (Puissance) [2018/19 h–: **h–** h20.6g^pu May 11] maiden hurdler. *Hugh Burns*

MARBLE BAR 4 b.g. Makfi – Presbyterian Nun (IRE) (Daylami (IRE)) [2018/19 h15.7g **h–** h15.6g^6 h15.6g^6 Jan 1] fairly useful on Flat, best at 6f: well held over hurdles: tried in hood/ tongue tie. *Iain Jardine*

MARBLE MOON (IRE) 7 b.g. Millenary – Royal Marble (IRE) (Anshan) [2018/19 h66, **c105** b85: h20g* h23.9m* h21.6g* h25.5g* h23.6s c23d c23g^4 c23g Feb 19] fair handicap **h114** hurdler: completed 4-timer at Ffos Las in May and June, and Newton Abbot and Hereford in October: similar form over fences: stays 3¼m: acts on good to firm going. *Evan Williams*

MARCEL DEBRUXELLES (FR) 7 b.g. Librettist (USA) – Forcaster (FR) (Cadoudal **h– p** (FR)) [2018/19 h19.8s Mar 7] fair on Flat in France for P. Van de Poele, stays 15f: well beaten in maiden on hurdling debut: should do better. *Nicky Henderson*

MARCH IS ON (IRE) 6 b.g. Gold Well – Shannon Tiara (IRE) (Erins Isle) [2018/19 h83: **h97** h19m h19g^3 h22m^3 h21d^2 h23.1s Mar 5] off mark in Irish points at second attempt: modest form over hurdles: should stay 2¾m+: acts on good to soft going. *Jonjo O'Neill*

MARCILHAC (FR) 10 b.g. Smadoun (FR) – One Way (FR) (Exit To Nowhere (USA)) **c–** [2018/19 c139, h–: c26d^pu c26g^pu Mar 23] well-made gelding: winning hurdler: useful **h–** chaser, pulled up both starts in 2018/19: stays 3m: acts on heavy going. *Venetia Williams*

MARETTIMO (IRE) 5 b.g. Harbour Watch (IRE) – Renowned (IRE) (Darshaan) **h111** [2018/19 h93: h15.3m^5 h15.3m^2 h18.5g^5 h16.8g h16g^3 h15.3m^2 h15.9g^2 Nov 5] tall gelding: fair maiden hurdler: unproven beyond 2m: acts on soft and good to firm going. *Bill Turner*

MARGARET'S ROSE (IRE) 9 b.m. Millenary – Alannah Rose (IRE) (Roselier (FR)) **c–** [2018/19 h20.5s c16.5d^5 c24.1d^pu Feb 6] winning pointer: maiden hurdler, no show on **h–** return after leaving Nigel Twiston-Davies/22 months off: no promise either in chases: tried in visor. *Andrew Hamilton*

MARIA FRANCESCA (IRE) 4 b.f. Califet (FR) – Miss Kettlewell (IRE) (Saddlers' **b84** Hall (IRE)) [2018/19 b15.7d b16.7g^3 Apr 13] useful-looking filly: fifth foal: half-sister to fairly useful hurdler/useful chaser Full Irish (2½m-23f winner, by Flemensfirth): dam unraced daughter of fairly useful hurdler/chaser up to 2½m Native Endurance: modest form in bumpers: better effort when third in conditionals/amateurs event at Bangor. *Nigel Twiston-Davies*

MARIAH'S LEGEND 7 b.m. Flying Legend (USA) – Mariah Rollins (IRE) (Over The **c–** River (FR)) [2018/19 c107, h118: h20g^5 h20.3g^2 Jun 5] fair handicap hurdler: similar form **h110** over fences: stays 21f: acts on soft going: has worn headgear: usually races close up. *Amy Murphy*

MARIA'S BENEFIT (IRE) 7 b.m. Beneficial – Youngborogal (IRE) (Anshan) [2018/19 **c138 p** h137: c16.3v* c17.4d* c16g^ur Dec 27] useful hurdler: similar form over fences: won **h–** 3-runner novice at Newton Abbot (by 9 lengths from Mont des Avaloirs, easily) in October and listed mares novice at Bangor (by 1¼ lengths from Jester Jet) in November: raced around 2m: acts on heavy going: usually leads: remains with potential as a chaser. *Stuart Edmunds*

MARIENSTAR (IRE) 8 b.m. Marienbard (IRE) – Starofdonickmore (IRE) (Fourstars **c128** Allstar (USA)) [2018/19 c110, h110: c23g* c20.5g* c20g* c19.9d^F Jan 25] sturdy mare: **h–** has had breathing operation: fair hurdler: fairly useful handicap chaser: completed hat-trick in mares events at Worcester in October, and Kempton and Warwick (novice) in November: stays 3m: acts on heavy going: wears tongue tie: usually leads. *Neil King*

MARILYN MONROE (IRE) 6 b.m. Scorpion (IRE) – Go On Eileen (IRE) (Bob Back **b89 p** (USA)) [2018/19 b17.7g^3 Feb 25] £50,000 5-y-o: fifth foal: half-sister to useful hurdler/ smart chaser Regal Encore (2m-3m winner, by King's Theatre) and bumper winner/useful hurdler The Organist (19f-3m winner, by Alkaadhem): dam (c98/h87) 3m hurdle winner: won completed start in Irish points: 5/4, third in mares bumper at Plumpton (1¼ lengths behind Early Morning Rain): should improve. *Anthony Honeyball*

MARINERO (IRE) 10 b.g. Presenting – Peggy Maddock (IRE) (Oscar (IRE)) [2018/19 **c108** c131, h117: c23.8m³ c23.8d⁴ c20gᵖᵘ Mar 28] rangy gelding: fairly useful hurdler: useful **h–** chaser, below best in hunters in 2018/19: stays 3m: acts on heavy going: has worn headgear/tongue tie. *David Christie, Ireland*

MARINERS MOON (IRE) 8 ch.g. Mount Nelson – Dusty Moon (Dr Fong (USA)) **c79** [2018/19 h82: h15.8g⁴ h15.8s c17.4g⁶ h20.3g⁴ c20g² c24g⁵ c21.4gᵖᵘ Nov 8] compact **h83** gelding: poor maiden hurdler: similar form over fences: stays 2½m: acts on good to soft going: wears headgear: has worn tongue tie, including last 4 starts. *Caroline Bailey*

MARIO DE PAIL (FR) 4 gr.g. Blue Bresil (FR) – Sauveterre (FR) (Turgeon (USA)) **b87** [2018/19 b17.7d³ Mar 18] second foal: dam French 2¼m-21f chase winner: 2/1, third in bumper at Plumpton (13½ lengths behind First Lord de Cuet). *Sam Thomas*

MARJU'S QUEST (IRE) 9 b.g. Marju (IRE) – Queen's Quest (Rainbow Quest (USA)) **c96 §** [2018/19 c–, h100§: h15.8m⁴ c17.2g² h20g c17.2g² h16.7g⁵ h15.8g h18.6g³ Sep 29] **h92 §** compact gelding: modest handicap hurdler: similar form over fences: stays 2½m: acts on firm and good to soft going: usually hooded in 2018/19: tried in tongue tie: temperamental. *Adrian Wintle*

MARKET ROAD (IRE) 9 gr.g. Tikkanen (USA) – Clydeside (IRE) (General Ironside) **c101** [2018/19 c109, h104: h23g⁴ c20.9dᵘʳ c23.8vᵖᵘ h23.8g⁴ c21.6v² c20.2m* c25.6dᵖᵘ c19.4sᶠ **h101** c19.4d⁶ c19.4d⁴ Apr 6] sturdy gelding: fair handicap hurdler: fair handicap chaser: won at Leicester in January: stays 23f: acts on good to firm and heavy going: has worn headgear, including in 2018/19: wears tongue tie. *Evan Williams*

MARKHAN (USA) 6 b.g. Birdstone – Royal Flush (USA) (Smart Strike (CAN)) **h115 p** [2018/19 h16g h16.9g³ h16.7g² h19.8g² Nov 1] fairly useful on Flat, stays 16.5f: fairly useful form over hurdles: second in maiden at Clonmel in November: wears tongue tie: open to further improvement. *Gordon Elliott, Ireland*

MARKMYWORD 6 b.m. Resplendent Glory (IRE) – Spring Creek (Tipsy Creek (USA)) **b72** [2018/19 b16d⁵ b16d b15.7g⁵ Nov 23] fourth foal: dam lightly raced on Flat: poor form in bumpers: wears hood: placed in points. *Stuart Crawford, Ireland*

MARKOV (IRE) 9 b.g. Morozov (USA) – Willoughby Sue (IRE) (Dabali (IRE)) **c–** [2018/19 c133, h–: c19.4g c23.8gᵖᵘ h19.4d² h23.1g⁵ h24.3m⁴ Apr 12] close-coupled **h116** gelding: has had breathing operation: fairly useful maiden hurdler: second in handicap at Doncaster in March: useful chaser, well below form in 2018/19: stays 3m: acts on soft and good to firm going: tried in tongue tie. *Ben Pauling*

MARLAIS 7 b.g. Dylan Thomas (IRE) – Super Motiva (Motivator) [2018/19 h–: h20sᵖᵘ **h–** Apr 7] maiden hurdler: tried in cheekpieces/tongue tie. *Arthur Whitehead*

MARLEE MASSIE (IRE) 10 b.g. Dr Massini (IRE) – Meadstown Miss (IRE) **c–** (Flemensfirth (USA)) [2018/19 h24.1s h24.3s h24.3d h24.3s Mar 9] sturdy gelding: fair **h–** hurdler at best, no form in 2018/19: winning chaser: has worn cheekpieces, including final start. *N. W. Alexander*

MARLEY FIRTH (IRE) 7 b.g. Flemensfirth (USA) – Merrill Gaye (IRE) (Roselier **c102** (FR)) [2018/19 h117: c16s c20.1dᶠ c19.2sᵖᵘ h26d Dec 31] has had breathing operation: **h–** won Irish point on debut: fairly useful hurdler, well below form final start: fair form over fences: stays 2½m: acts on heavy going: in headgear last 2 starts: tried in tongue tie: temperament under suspicion. *Dan Skelton*

MARLOW MOSS (IRE) 5 b.m. Fame And Glory – Moss Artiste (IRE) (Beneficial) **h–** [2018/19 b15.8s h17.7dᵖᵘ h21.7v⁴ h15.8g Apr 11] €10,000 3-y-o: seventh foal: half-sister **b76** to a winning pointer by Subtle Power: dam, maiden pointer, sister to smart hurdler/very smart chaser (stayed 3¼m) Cooldine and useful hurdler/chaser (stayed 25f) Fists of Fury: modest form sole start in bumpers: no form over hurdles. *Jamie Snowden*

MARMALADE MIST (IRE) 6 ch.m. Stowaway – Shean Rose (IRE) (Roselier (FR)) **h–** [2018/19 b15.8d b15.8g h20g Aug 22] has had breathing operation: sister to 2¾m **b–** chase winner Sonowyouknow and half-sister to 3 winners, including smart hurdler/useful chaser Blow By Blow (2½m-23f winner, by Robin des Champs): dam unraced half-sister to smart hurdler/very smart chaser (stayed 3¼m) Cooldine and useful hurdler/chaser (stayed 25f) Fists of Fury: behind in bumpers: well held in mares maiden on hurdling debut. *Jonjo O'Neill*

MARMONT 6 ch.g. Winker Watson – Five Bells (IRE) (Rock of Gibraltar (IRE)) [2018/19 **c–** h108: c15.7g⁵ h17.7d⁵ h19.2v² h16.5s* Mar 19] rather leggy gelding: has had breathing **h108** operation: fair handicap hurdler: won at Taunton in March: well beaten in novice handicap on chasing debut: should stay 19f+: acts on soft going: wears hood: has worn tongue tie, including last 2 starts. *Jo Davis*

MAROC 6 b.g. Rock of Gibraltar (IRE) – Zietory (Zieten (USA)) [2018/19 h–: h16g[6] **h91**
h16.7s[3] h16.6g[ro] h15.8d[2] Feb 17] modest maiden hurdler: unproven beyond 17f: acts on
soft going: wears cheekpieces: has worn tongue tie: usually front runner/races prominently:
has run out. *Nikki Evans*

MAROCCHINO 6 gr.g. Tikkanen (USA) – Mocha (FR) (Mansonnien (FR)) [2018/19 b–: **h63**
b16.8g[6] h19.5s h20.5s h15.3g h20.5s[ur] h19.2s h20.5g h25g[4] Apr 22] has had breathing **b–**
operation: no form in bumpers: poor maiden hurdler: left James Ewart after first start: has
worn headgear, including last 2 starts. *Chris Gordon*

MARONETTE 6 b.m. Milan – Wyldello (Supreme Leader) [2018/19 h66: h18.7g h23.4g[3] **h75**
h19.9s h24.1g[pu] Apr 11] rather unfurnished mare: poor maiden hurdler: bred to stay at least
3m: best form on good going. *Tim Vaughan*

MAROWN (IRE) 5 b.g. Milan – Rosie Suspect (IRE) (Presenting) [2018/19 b16.4v* Mar **b92**
16] €80,000 3-y-o: first foal: dam unraced half-sister to useful hurdler/smart chaser (stayed
3½m) Cannington Brook: 3/1, overcame inexperience when winning bumper at Newcastle
(by length from Show Promise) on debut: will be suited by further than 2m. *Nicky Richards*

MARQUIS OF CARABAS (IRE) 9 b.g. Hurricane Run (IRE) – Miss Otis Regrets **c131**
(IRE) (Bob Back (USA)) [2018/19 c126, h–: c19.2m[f] c20s[4] c21.4m c23.8m[2] c24.1g[4] c23d **h–**
c25.5g[6] c26g[3] Apr 17] winning hurdler: useful handicap chaser: second at Ffos Las (short
head behind Lotus Pond) in July: stays 3m: acts on good to firm and heavy going: tried in
cheekpieces. *David Dennis*

MARRACUDJA (FR) 8 b.g. Martaline – Memorial (FR) (Homme de Loi (IRE)) **c141**
[2018/19 c142, h–: c16m[4] c20.1g[6] c20g c19.4d[6] c16.8g[3] c15.2d[2] c16.3d c16g[3] Apr 25] **h–**
useful-looking gelding: has had breathing operation: winning hurdler: useful handicap
chaser: second at Wetherby (nose behind Cracking Find) in December: left Paul Nicholls
after first start: unproven beyond 17f: acts on soft going: has worn hood, including final
start: wears tongue tie: usually races off pace: temperament under suspicion. *Dan Skelton*

MARTABOT (FR) 8 gr.g. Martaline – Reine de Sabot (FR) (Homme de Loi (IRE)) **h103**
[2018/19 h94: h21.6v[2] h19d[3] h20v[pu] h21d[2] Jan 28] has had breathing operation: fair
maiden hurdler: stays 2¾m: acts on heavy going: wears headgear: has worn tongue tie:
usually races towards rear. *David Pipe*

MARTEN (FR) 7 b.g. Martaline – Commande Blue (FR) (Commands (AUS)) [2018/19 **c–**
h114: c23.9g[pu] h21.4g h21s[pu] Mar 10] sturdy gelding: has had breathing operation: fair **h91**
form when winning on hurdling debut in 2017/18: disappointing since, including on
chasing debut: stays 2½m: acts on good to soft going: in blinkers last 2 starts: usually front
runner/races prominently. *Ben Pauling*

MARTHA BRAE 4 b.f. Shirocco (GER) – Harringay (Sir Harry Lewis (USA)) [2018/19 **b–**
b16.8d Apr 23] fifth foal: half-sister to bumper winner/fair hurdler Danielle's Journey (2m
winner, by Presenting), stayed 2¾m, and fair hurdler Playhara (2m-2½m winner, by King's
Theatre): dam (c109/h120) 19f-21f hurdle/chase winner: tailed off in mares bumper.
Warren Greatrex

MARTHA'S BENEFIT (IRE) 10 b.m. Beneficial – Trajectus (Homo Sapien) [2018/19 **c104**
c96, h–: c25.3g[6] c20.3g[4] c25.5g[3] h19.9g* c21.2m* h22.1d[4] Aug 25] stocky mare: multiple **h99**
point winner: modest form over hurdles: won mares handicap at Uttoxeter in June: fair
chaser: won handicap at Cartmel later in June: stays 21f: acts on good to firm and good to
soft going. *Mark Walford*

MARTHA'S DREAM 5 ch.m. Captain Gerrard (IRE) – Rose Bounty (Polar Falcon **h–**
(USA)) [2018/19 h–: h15.8d[pu] May 5] no show over hurdles. *Sarah Robinson*

MARTILA (FR) 7 b.m. Martaline – Paola Pierji (FR) (Cadoudal (FR)) [2018/19 h117: **h120**
h16.2g[2] h17.2m[4] h16d[4] h20.6g[4] h16.2g* h16.2g[5] h18.9m Apr 20] rather leggy mare: fairly
useful handicap hurdler: won at Kelso in January: unproven beyond 17f: acts on heavy
going: wears hood. *Pauline Robson*

MARTILOO (FR) 9 b.m. Martaline – Paola Pierji (FR) (Cadoudal (FR)) [2018/19 c109, **c122**
h–: c20.5g* c19.9g* c23.8g[4] c19.9g[5] Nov 10] maiden hurdler: fairly useful handicap **h–**
chaser: won at Ayr and Aintree early in season: stays 2½m: acts on soft going: has worn
hood: usually wears tongue tie. *Pauline Robson*

MARVELLOUS JOE (IRE) 4 b.g. Mahler – Marvellous Dream (FR) (Muhtathir) **b–**
[2018/19 b16.4d Mar 5] tailed off in maiden bumper. *Micky Hammond*

MARVELLOUS MONTY (IRE) 9 br.m. Oscar (IRE) – Montys Miss (IRE) **h96** (Presenting) [2018/19 h105: h20s[3] h20m[6] h23g h19.9g[4] h21.6v[6] Dec 20] has had breathing operation: modest maiden hurdler nowadays: barely stays 25f: acts on heavy going: tried in blinkers: has worn tongue tie, including last 2 starts. *Johnny Farrelly*

MARYAM JAAN 10 b.m. Tiger Hill (IRE) – Persian Ruby (IRE) (Grand Lodge (USA)) **c–** [2018/19 c105] third foal: dam unraced: point winner: in tongue tie, tailed off in hunter chase on Rules debut. *K. Jacka*

MASH POTATO (IRE) 9 b.g. Whipper (USA) – Salva (Grand Lodge (USA)) [2018/19 **c91** h84: h16g h18.5g[3] h18.5g[4] h22.5s[3] h24g[3] c21.2g[pu] c24.1s[4] h24.3d Jan 20] modest handicap **h88** hurdler: similar form over fences: stays 3m: acts on soft going: wears cheekpieces/tongue tie. *Noel C. Kelly, Ireland*

MASON DIXON (IRE) 8 b.g. Presenting – Bronx Girl (IRE) (Quws) [2018/19 c26g[2] **c85** c20g[4] Jun 24] maiden hurdler: modest maiden handicap chaser: stayed easy 3¼m: wore **h–** blinkers: dead. *Tim Vaughan*

MASSINI MAN 6 b.g. Dr Massini (IRE) – Alleged To Rhyme (IRE) (Leading Counsel **h109** (USA)) [2018/19 b80: h16.2g* h15.8d[4] h19.9d[pu] h18.5d h21g[5] h20.2g Apr 25] fair form over hurdles: won novice at Hereford in November: stays 21f: acts on good to soft going. *Tom George*

MASSINIS ADVENTURE (IRE) 11 b.g. Dr Massini (IRE) – Deirdre Eile (IRE) **c74 §** (Supreme Leader) [2018/19 c25.7g[4] c24.1g[F] c23m c23g[pu] c20g[pu] Sep 25] winning hurdler: **h– §** poor handicap chaser: stays 25f: acts on soft and good to firm going: usually wears headgear: temperamental. *Arthur Whiting*

MASSINI'S DREAM 8 b.m. Dr Massini (IRE) – Cathy's Dream (IRE) (Husyan (USA)) **h102 §** [2018/19 h21m[2] h18.5g[ro] h20g[3] h20m[2] h20g[2] h23g[2] h19g h23g[3] Oct 11] point winner: fair maiden hurdler: stays 21f: acts on good to firm going: temperamental. *Christian Williams*

MASSINI'S LADY 8 b.m. Dr Massini (IRE) – Lady du Bost (FR) (Royal Charter (FR)) **c91 §** [2018/19 c80§, h77§: c22.6m* c25.8m[pu] Aug 6] has had breathing operation: maiden **h– §** hurdler: modest form over fences: won handicap at Stratford in August: stays 3¼m: acts on good to firm and heavy going: tried in headgear: front runner/races prominently: unreliable. *Dan Skelton*

MASSINI'S TRAP (IRE) 10 b.g. Dr Massini (IRE) – Sparrow's Trap (IRE) (Magical **h127** Wonder (USA)) [2018/19 h133: h20g h18.8g[pu] h19.8g[3] h20.9m[3] h20g h24g[6] Nov 15] smallish gelding: fairly useful handicap hurdler: third at Kelso in September: stays 3m: acts on good to firm and heavy going: usually wears headgear: tried in tongue tie. *James A. Nash, Ireland*

MASTER BAKER 10 b.g. Kayf Tara – Fashion House (Homo Sapien) [2018/19 c114: **c121** c27.5d[F] c16.1d* c23.4d* c22.6g[2] Apr 14] has had breathing operation: prolific point winner: fairly useful form in hunter chases: won at Taunton in February and Newbury in March: stays 3m: acts on heavy going. *Mrs L. J. Jefford*

MASTER BURBIDGE 8 b.g. Pasternak – Silver Sequel (Silver Patriarch (IRE)) **c120** [2018/19 c124, h–: c20m[3] c17m[5] h20g[2] h19d[6] c20.5g[5] c22.4d[2] c23.8m[4] Apr 23] strong **h115** gelding: fairly useful handicap hurdler: second at Les Landes in August: fairly useful handicap chaser: stays 21f: acts on soft going: wears cheekpieces. *Neil Mulholland*

MASTER CARD 6 ch.g. Presenting – Subtilty (With Approval (CAN)) [2018/19 h65: **h108** h21.6m[4] h25.5s[2] h23.6d h25.5d[3] h23g[pu] Apr 13] strong gelding: chasing type: fair form over hurdles. *Warren Greatrex*

MASTER DANCER 8 gr.g. Mastercraftsman (IRE) – Isabella Glyn (IRE) (Sadler's **h121** Wells (USA)) [2018/19 h125: h19.5d h23.9g[F] h23.8m[5] Apr 23] good-topped gelding: fairly useful handicap hurdler: may prove best at shorter than 3m: acts on good to firm and good to soft going: wears cheekpieces: tried in tongue tie. *Tim Vaughan*

MASTER DEBONAIR 5 br.g. Yeats (IRE) – Swincombe Flame (Exit To Nowhere **b109** (USA)) [2018/19 b16.8g* b16.4d[2] b16.4g* b16.4s b17d[5] Apr 5] rather unfurnished gelding: first foal: dam (c103/h133) bumper/2m-2½f hurdle winner (stayed 3m): useful bumper performer: won conditionals/amateurs maiden at Sedgefield early in season and listed event at Cheltenham (by neck from Thyme Hill) in November. *Colin Tizzard*

MASTER DEE (IRE) 10 b.g. King's Theatre (IRE) – Miss Lauren Dee (IRE) (Montelimar **c–** (USA)) [2018/19 c151, h–: c21.4g[pu] c19.9d[pu] Mar 2] compact, workmanlike gelding: has **h–** had breathing operation: winning hurdler: smart chaser, pulled up both starts in 2018/19: stays 3m: acts on soft and good to firm going: has worn cheekpieces: wears tongue tie. *Fergal O'Brien*

Follow At The Races on Twitter Novices' Chase, Plumpton—
a winning debut on British soil for exciting French jumper Master Dino

MASTER DINO (FR) 5 gr.g. Doctor Dino (FR) – Mind Master (USA) (Mizzen Mast (USA)) [2018/19 h19.4s³ h19.4s* h17.9s* h19.4s* h19.4s* c17.9v* c19.7d* Jan 6] good-topped gelding: third foal: half-brother to French 11f winner Mind Story (by Diamond Green): dam French maiden on Flat: very smart hurdler: successful at Auteuil in Prix Questarabad in June, Prix de Maisons-Laffitte in September, Prix Pierre de Lassus in October (all Group 3s) and Prix Renaud du Vivier (by 8 lengths from Tunis) in November: smart form over fences: won 4-y-o event at Auteuil (by 30 lengths) in November and novice at Plumpton (impressively by 7 lengths from Knocknanuss) in January: stays 2½m: acts on heavy going: has worn tongue tie: sustained hairline fracture of a leg at Plumpton and underwent operation: still open to improvement over fences if recovering. *Guillaume Macaire, France*
c150 p
h158

MASTER MAJIC (IRE) 8 b.g. Flemensfirth (USA) – Majic Times Ahead (Weld) [2018/19 h19.2dᵖᵘ h16.8s⁵ h23.1d Apr 9] workmanlike gelding: modest form over hurdles. *Colin Tizzard*
h91

MASTER NEWTON (IRE) 4 gr.g. Mastercraftsman (IRE) – French Friend (IRE) (Teofilo (IRE)) [2018/19 b14.6s b16.6g⁶ Feb 20] tailed off in 2 bumpers. *Philip Kirby*
b–

MASTEROFDECEPTION (IRE) 11 b.g. Darsi (FR) – Sherberry (IRE) (Shernazar) [2018/19 c124, h–: h23d³ c24.1g⁵ Oct 3] good-topped gelding: fairly useful handicap hurdler: similar form over fences: stays 3m: acts on soft and good to firm going: wears headgear: in tongue tie last 5 starts. *Dr Richard Newland*
c–
h119

MASTER OF FINANCE (IRE) 8 ch.g. Mastercraftsman (IRE) – Cheal Rose (IRE) (Dr Devious (IRE)) [2018/19 c106§, h114§: h19.6g⁶ c16.3g* c15.7g³ h20m³ h16g⁶ c16.3g³ h23.4d⁶ Dec 18] sturdy gelding: has had breathing operation: fair handicap hurdler: similar form over fences: won novice handicap at Fakenham in June: stays 2½m: acts on soft and good to firm going: wears headgear: temperamental. *Lucy Wadham*
c103 §
h104 §

MASTER OF SPEED (IRE) 7 ch.g. Mastercraftsman (IRE) – Mango Groove (IRE) **h81**
(Unfuwain (USA)) [2018/19 h16g h19.2d h19d^{pu} h17.7m^F h16m^4 Apr 25] rather leggy
gelding: fair hurdler: off 32 months, little show in 2018/19: stays 19f: acts on good to firm
going: in blinkers last 3 starts. *Gary Moore*

MASTERPLAN (IRE) 9 b.g. Spadoun (FR) – Eurolucy (IRE) (Shardari) [2018/19 c117, **c–**
h–: c20m^{pu} c19.9m^{pu} h20d^{pu} h23.1m c22.9v^{pu} Dec 5] useful-looking gelding: fairly useful **h–**
hurdler/chaser at best, no form in 2018/19: has worn headgear, including in 2018/19: has
worn tongue tie: usually races close up. *Charlie Longsdon*

MASTER RING (IRE) 6 b.g. Dalakhani (IRE) – Luce (IRE) (Sadler's Wells (USA)) [2018/19 **h89**
h16.3g^5 h20g^6 h19.9g^3 h19.2g^3 Aug 23] fairly useful on Flat, stayed 1¼m: modest form
over hurdles: wore tongue tie: dead. *Dan Skelton*

MASTER SAM BELLAMY (IRE) 6 b.g. Black Sam Bellamy (IRE) – Mistress Nell **b87**
(Thethingaboutitis (USA)) [2018/19 b17.7d^4 Mar 18] second foal: dam (c118) 3m chase
winner: unplaced in point: 66/1, fourth in bumper at Plumpton (14¼ lengths behind First
Lord de Cuet). *Dominic Ffrench Davis*

MASTERSON (IRE) 6 gr.g. Lawman (FR) – Indian Dumaani (Indian Ridge) [2018/19 **h–**
h23.3g^{pu} Jul 18] leggy gelding: fair hurdler, pulled up sole start in sphere in 2018/19: stays
2¾m: acts on soft going: in blinkers last 2 starts: wears tongue tie: usually travels strongly.
Gordon Elliott, Ireland

MASTER SUNRISE (IRE) 10 ch.g. Blueprint (IRE) – Aunty Dawn (IRE) (Strong **c104 §**
Gale) [2018/19 c93: c25.3g^4 c27.5d^2 c23m^6 c24g* c23g^3 c24g^6 c20g^3 c24.2s^6 Apr 16] fair
chaser: won handicap at Southwell in July: stays 3½m: acts on good to soft going: wears
cheekpieces: temperamental. *Alastair Ralph*

MASTER TOMMYTUCKER (IRE) 8 b.g. Kayf Tara – No Need For Alarm (Romany Rye) **c– p**
[2018/19 h129p: c19.4d^F Oct 13] useful form over hurdles, successful both starts in **h–**
2017/18: closing when fell 4 out in listed novice won by Spiritofthegames at Chepstow on
chasing debut, looking sure to play hand in finish. *Paul Nicholls*

MASTER TRADESMAN (IRE) 8 ch.g. Marienbard (IRE) – Tobeornotobe (IRE) **c–**
(Mister Lord (USA)) [2018/19 c–, h113: h23.6s h25.5s^5 c23d^{pu} h23.3d^6 h23.3d^{pu} h23.9d^3 **h92**
Apr 24] point winner: fair maiden hurdler, below best in 2018/19: pulled up both starts in
chases: should stay 3m+: acts on soft going: tried in cheekpieces: usually front runner/
races prominently. *Richard Mitford-Slade*

MASTER VINTAGE 11 b.g. Kayf Tara – What A Vintage (IRE) (Un Desperado (FR)) **c107**
[2018/19 h107: h20.7d c16.5d^2 c17s^5 c19.4d c24d^{pu} Apr 24] fair hurdler: similar form over **h–**
fences: stays 19f: acts on heavy going: wears hood. *Richard Phillips*

MASTER WORK (FR) 6 b.g. Network (GER) – Mascarpone (FR) (Mansonnien (FR)) **c127**
[2018/19 h112: h19.6g h16g* h15.5g* h16.8g^5 h15.5g^3 c15.9f^3 c16.4g^2 h18.5s^5 Apr 16] **h120**
sturdy gelding: fairly useful handicap hurdler: won at Warwick in November and Leicester
in December: similar form over fences: better effort when second in handicap at Newbury
in March: stays 2¼m: acts on firm and good to soft going: temperament under suspicion.
Philip Hobbs

MASTER WORKMAN (IRE) 13 b.g. Posidonas – Bobbie Magee (IRE) (Buckskin **c–**
(FR)) [2018/19 c120: c24.2g^{pu} May 8] multiple point winner: fairly useful hunter chaser,
pulled up sole start in 2018/19: stays 3m: acts on good to firm and heavy going: wears
cheekpieces: tail flasher. *David Kemp*

MATRAVERS 8 b.g. Oasis Dream – Maakrah (Dubai Destination (USA)) [2018/19 **h81**
h15.3m h16.3g h15.7g^5 h16.3g^{pu} h15.8m h18.7g^{pu} Nov 1] modest on Flat, stays 1¼m: poor
form over hurdles: tried in headgear: often in tongue tie. *Martin Keighley*

MATTS COMMISSION (IRE) 6 b.g. Beneficial – Sonus Beo (IRE) (Sonus (IRE)) **b93**
[2018/19 b17g^3 May 18] €9,000 3-y-o: third foal: dam, ran twice in points, out of half-
sister to dam of Cheltenham Gold Cup winner See More Business: multiple point winner:
14/1, third in bumper at Aintree (3½ lengths behind Rob The Getaway). *J. Teal*

MAUNA KEA (IRE) 7 b.g. Mountain High (IRE) – The Bench (IRE) (Leading Counsel **c–**
(USA)) [2018/19 c–, h87: h25m^3 h21.6g^4 h25g^{pu} h23.9d h25.8g^6 h25d^5 h23.9d* h21.6v* **h96**
h25s^{pu} h21.4g^6 h23.9d^4 h23.9d h23.6d h23.1d h26.4g^3 Apr 14] modest handicap hurdler:
won at Taunton and Exeter (amateurs) in December: well held on chasing debut: stays 25f:
acts on good to firm and heavy going: wears headgear. *Polly Gundry*

MAUREEN'S STAR (IRE) 6 b.m. Gold Well – Serpentine Mine (IRE) (Rashar (USA)) **c78**
[2018/19 h89, b–: h23.3g h19.5g h21.3g³ h23.9g* h22.1g³ h21.8dᶠ h22g c17g c23.5s⁴ **h86**
h24.3g h20.5v h22g c19.2g c20.9m⁶ Apr 20] modest handicap hurdler: won novice event
at Perth in July: poor form over fences: stays 3m: acts on soft going: tried in blinkers. *Liam Lennon, Ireland*

MAURICIO (IRE) 5 ch.g. Helmet (AUS) – Essexford (IRE) (Spinning World (USA)) **h108**
[2018/19 h59: h16g⁶ h15.8g* h15.8g³ h16g⁵ h15.7g* h16g² Oct 31] fair handicap hurdler:
won at Uttoxeter in September and Southwell (conditionals) in October: raced only at 2m:
best form on good going. *Dr Richard Newland*

MAX DO BRAZIL (FR) 7 b.g. Blue Bresil (FR) – Lili Valley (FR) (Cadoudal (FR)) **h103**
[2018/19 h108: h19.5v² h15.8s⁴ h21s⁶ Mar 10] sturdy gelding: fair handicap hurdler: stays
2½m: acts on heavy going: wears headgear/tongue tie. *David Pipe*

MAX FORTE (IRE) 9 br.g. Indian River (FR) – Brook Forte (Alderbrook) [2018/19 c–, **c–**
h113: h23.1m* h23.9d⁵ h21g c25.1d c25.1g h23.1d⁶ h26s h25g² Apr 25] rather leggy **h111**
gelding: has had breathing operation: fair handicap hurdler: won at Exeter early in season:
little show over fences: stays 25f: acts on soft and good to firm going: wears cheekpieces.
Chris Down

MAXI JAZZ (FR) 4 gr.g. Enrique – Andria (FR) (Martaline) [2018/19 b15.8d Mar 3] **b–**
rather unfurnished gelding: tailed off in bumper. *Paul Webber*

MAX LIEBERMANN (IRE) 5 b.g. Galileo (IRE) – Anna Karenina (IRE) (Green **h92**
Desert (USA)) [2018/19 h106: h20g⁴ h20m⁶ h23.4g⁵ h16s⁶ h15.6g h19.8g⁶ h23.8g⁶
h19.8m⁵ h19.8s Mar 10] has had breathing operation: modest maiden hurdler: left John
Ryan after fourth start: best effort at 2m: acts on good to soft going: usually in headgear:
has worn tongue tie, including final start: usually races in rear: temperament under
suspicion. *Lucinda Russell*

MAX WARD (IRE) 10 b.g. Milan – Made Easy (IRE) (Rudimentary (USA)) [2018/19 **c100**
c145, h–: c18g⁵ May 7] good-topped gelding: winning hurdler: smart chaser at best, well **h–**
held sole start in 2018/19: stays 2½m: acts on soft going. *Tom George*

MAYBE MICKEY 6 b.g. Multiplex – Mays Delight (IRE) (Glacial Storm (USA)) **h90**
[2018/19 h20.1g h16.2g⁶ h17.1d⁵ h21.3m Nov 2] fifth foal: half-brother to fair hurdler/
chaser Maybe Plenty (21f-3m winner, by Overbury): dam winning pointer: modest form
over hurdles. *Simon Waugh*

MAYBE PLENTY 10 b.m. Overbury (IRE) – Mays Delight (IRE) (Glacial Storm (USA)) **c94**
[2018/19 c25.3g^pu c24d³ c25.2s³ c25.5s⁶ c25.2d⁵ c26.2d⁶ Mar 20] sturdy mare: winning **h–**
hurdler: modest handicap chaser: stays 25f: acts on heavy going: has worn cheekpieces,
including last 5 starts: usually races close up. *Giles Smyly*

MAYLLAN 5 ch.m. Malinas (GER) – Mystery Lot (IRE) (Revoque (IRE)) [2018/19 **b85**
b15.8g² b16.3m² Jul 22] fair form in bumpers: dead. *Alan King*

MAY MIST 7 b.m. Nayef (USA) – Midnight Mist (IRE) (Green Desert (USA)) [2018/19 **h–**
h–: h16.7g h16g h15.8d⁵ Dec 5] no form over hurdles. *Trevor Wall*

MAYOHILL (IRE) 6 b.g. Beneficial – Daras Mayo (IRE) (Kasmayo) [2018/19 h19.7m⁵ **c–**
h19.9v h21.2g^pu c20.3g^pu c24g^pu Mar 28] £20,000 5-y-o: second foal: half-brother to fair **h93**
chaser Sideways (21f-3¼m winner, by Gamut): dam, ran 3 times in points, half-sister to
useful hurdlers/chasers Shoreacres (stayed 3½m) and Call Me Vic (stays 3¼m): off mark
in Irish points at seventh attempt: modest maiden form over hurdles: pulled up both starts in chases
when in cheekpieces. *Nigel Twiston-Davies*

MAYPOLE CLASS (IRE) 5 b.g. Gold Well – Maypole Queen (IRE) (Bob Back (USA)) **h72**
[2018/19 h19.5s h15.8d Feb 6] runner-up second start in Irish points: poor form over
hurdles. *Jonjo O'Neill*

MAYTHEORSEBEWITHU (IRE) 4 b.f. Shirocco (GER) – Amoya (GER) (Royal **h–**
Dragon (USA)) [2018/19 h15.9g h15.9d⁶ Mar 18] poor maiden on Flat: well held both
starts over hurdles. *Pat Phelan*

MAYZE BELL 10 br.m. And Beyond (IRE) – Eleanor May (Crofthall) [2018/19 h76: **h–**
h23.9g^pu Aug 18] little form over hurdles. *Alistair Whillans*

MAZALTO (IRE) 6 b.m. Teofilo (IRE) – Mazaaya (USA) (Cozzene (USA)) [2018/19 **h105**
h90: h19.2d h17.7v* h19.9v² h19.8s³ Mar 8] lengthy mare: fair handicap hurdler: won at
Fontwell in December: stays 2½m: acts on heavy going. *Pat Phelan*

Weatherbys Racing Bank Standard Open National Hunt Flat, Aintree—
McFabulous (left) holds on grimly from Thebannerkingrebel (right) and Santa Rossa (centre)

MAZE RUNNER (IRE) 4 b.g. Authorized (IRE) – Alice Rose (IRE) (Manduro (GER)) **h123**
[2018/19 h16v* h16g h16g² h16d⁵ Mar 31] dam half-sister to useful hurdler/chaser (stays
2¾m) Altruism (by Authorized): fairly useful on Flat, stays 1½m: fairly useful form over
hurdles: won juvenile maiden at Cork in December: second in novice at Naas in February:
in cheekpieces last 2 starts. *W. P. Mullins, Ireland*

MAZURATI (IRE) 10 b.g. Definite Article – Mazuma (IRE) (Mazaad) [2018/19 c73§, **c– §**
h–§: c24gᵖᵘ May 12] compact gelding: point winner: maiden hurdler: little form over **h– §**
fences: stays 3¼m: acts on good to soft going: has worn headgear: tried in tongue tie:
ungenuine. *Ben Case*

MCCABE CREEK (IRE) 9 b.g. Robin des Pres (FR) – Kick And Run (IRE) (Presenting) **c119**
[2018/19 c122, h–: c15.7g² c17g⁴ c20g⁶ c17m⁴ c16.5g⁴ c16.5gᵘʳ Nov 4] sturdy gelding: **h–**
winning hurdler: fairly useful handicap chaser: second at Southwell early in season: stays
21f: acts on heavy going: usually wears headgear: front runner/races prominently. *Caroline
Bailey*

MCFABULOUS (IRE) 5 b.g. Milan – Rossavon (IRE) (Beneficial) [2018/19 b16d* **b116**
b16.4g b16.3d* b17d* Apr 5] €88,000 3-y-o: sturdy gelding: fourth foal: half-brother to
useful hurdler/top-class chaser Waiting Patiently (2m-21f winner) and bumper winner/
useful hurdler Walking In The Air (21f winner), both by Flemensfirth: dam unraced: smart
form in bumpers: won at Chepstow in October, Newbury in March and Grade 2 at Aintree
(by length from Thebannerkingrebel) in April. *Paul Nicholls*

MCGINTY'S DREAM (IRE) 8 b.g. Flemensfirth (USA) – Laboc (Rymer) [2018/19 **c98**
c81, h–: h23.3g⁴ c24.2g⁴ c24.2g h19.5v c24.2s² c24.2v* c24.1d* c24.2vᶠ Mar 14] poor **h71**
handicap hurdler: modest handicap chaser: won at Hexham in December and Ayr in
February: stays 3m: acts on heavy going: has worn headgear/tongue tie: usually travels
strongly. *N. W. Alexander*

MCGOWAN'S PASS 8 b.g. Central Park (IRE) – Function Dreamer (Overbury (IRE)) **h112**
[2018/19 h117: h16sᵘʳ h15.7v⁴ h19.3g Feb 18] fair handicap hurdler: unproven beyond 2m:
acts on heavy going: usually races freely. *Sandy Thomson*

MCGROARTY (IRE) 8 b.g. Brian Boru – Uffizi (IRE) (Royal Academy (USA)) **c135**
[2018/19 h118, b98: h19.2g⁵ c16.5m* c15.7g* c16gᶠ c15.8g³ c16.5m³ Apr 13] good- **h–**
topped gelding: has had breathing operation: fairly useful hurdler: useful form over fences:
won novice handicaps at Huntingdon and Southwell in October: likely to prove best up to
2½m: acts on good to firm going: tried in cheekpieces: wears tongue tie: front runner/races
prominently. *Dr Richard Newland*

MCNAMARAS BAND (IRE) 6 b.g. Getaway (GER) – Katies Pet (IRE) (Glacial Storm **h120 p**
(USA)) [2018/19 b89: h19.5sˢᵘ h19.5d³ h19.5d* Mar 20] bumper winner: fairly useful
form over hurdles: won maiden at Chepstow in March, easily: open to further improvement.
Philip Hobbs

MEAD VALE 6 ch.g. Schiaparelli (GER) – Devon Peasant (Deploy) [2018/19 h81: **h111**
h23.3g² h23.1g⁵ h16.5m* h16.5d⁴ h19.5d³ h23.8d² Jan 28] fair handicap hurdler: won at
Taunton in November: stays 3m: acts on good to firm and good to soft going: usually races
prominently. *Nigel Hawke*

MEASUREOFMYDREAMS (IRE) 11 b.g. Shantou (USA) – Le Bavellen (Le Bavard (FR)) [2018/19 c23.5g³ c26d c29dᶠ Apr 22] sturdy gelding: winning hurdler: useful chaser: off 22 months, third in minor event at Fairyhouse (6½ lengths behind Snugsborough Benny) in February: stays 4m: acts on heavy going: tried in cheekpieces. *Gordon Elliott, Ireland* — **c136 h–**

MEDIEVAL BISHOP (IRE) 10 b.g. Bachelor Duke (USA) – On The Backfoot (IRE) (Bob Back (USA)) [2018/19 h–: h15.8g h23.3g Jun 20] poor maiden hurdler on balance: sometimes in cheekpieces. *Tony Forbes* — **h61**

MEEP MEEP (IRE) 6 ch.m. Flemensfirth (USA) – Charming Leader (IRE) (Supreme Leader) [2018/19 b102: h19.5d⁴ h16s⁵ h18.9vᵖᵘ h20.5dᵖᵘ Mar 23] lengthy mare: fairly useful form in bumpers: fair form over hurdles: should stay beyond 19f. *Tom Lacey* — **h100**

MEGABOOST (IRE) 6 b.m. Court Cave (IRE) – Sweetasanu (IRE) (Sri Pekan (USA)) [2018/19 h96, b66: h24g c25.7gᵖᵘ c20d⁶ c24s² c26v² c26dᵖᵘ Jan 14] angular mare: runner-up in Irish point: modest form over hurdles: poor form over fences: stays 3¼m: acts on heavy going: usually wears headgear: temperamental. *Ben Case* — **c82 § h–**

MEGA DOUBLE (IRE) 5 b.m. Westerner – Distant Dreams (IRE) (Saddlers' Hall (IRE)) [2018/19 h15.7g⁶ h15.7g² h16.4g² Feb 23] £9,000 4-y-o: half-sister to modest 19f hurdle winner/winning pointer Distant Sound (by Luso), stayed 3m: dam unraced half-sister to smart staying chaser Can't Buy Time and Galway Plate winner Stroll Home: runner-up on second start in Irish points: poor form in bumpers: fair form over hurdles: better effort when second in mares novice at Newcastle in February: will be suited by further than 2m. *James Moffatt* — **h102 b71**

MEGALODON (IRE) 6 b.g. Getaway (GER) – Fitzgrey (IRE) (Great Palm (USA)) [2018/19 b16s h16.3s h16.3d h16d² h20.6d h16.3d⁶ h16.8d³ Apr 9] workmanlike gelding: second foal: half-brother to a winning pointer by Scorpion: dam, unraced, out of half-sister to Grand National winner Rough Quest: placed in Irish points: tailed off in bumper: fair form over hurdles: should stay 2½m: acts on good to soft going: in tongue tie last 2 starts: usually races towards rear. *Paul Henderson* — **h103 b–**

MEGA MIND (IRE) 6 ch.g. Captain Rio – Final Leave (IRE) (Glacial Storm (USA)) [2018/19 h–: h16.7gᵖᵘ h18.6gᵖᵘ Sep 29] no show over hurdles. *Sam Thomas* — **h–**

MEGAN'S CHOICE (IRE) 5 b.g. Doyen (IRE) – Megan's Bay (Muhtarram (USA)) [2018/19 b15.7g² Oct 10] 5/2, second in maiden bumper at Southwell (6 lengths behind Adjourned) on debut: dead. *Tom Lacey* — **b89**

MEGAUDAIS SPEED (FR) 7 b.g. Puit d'Or (IRE) – La Rouadiere (FR) (Murmure (FR)) [2018/19 h23.1v h18.5s⁵ Mar 18] fourth foal: dam unraced: Irish point winner: fair form over hurdles: better effort when fifth in maiden at Exeter in March. *Laura Young* — **h108**

MEGA YEATS (IRE) 5 br.m. Yeats (IRE) – Mega Mum (IRE) (Presenting) [2018/19 b17.1d* b16.4g² h19.7s* h18.9g³ h20.6g* Mar 14] €22,000 3-y-o, £60,000 4-y-o: first foal: dam unraced sister to useful hurdler/fairly useful chaser (stayed 3m) Sam Adams and half-sister to useful hurdler/high-class chaser (stayed 3¼m) Snoopy Loopy: won Irish point on debut: fairly useful form in bumpers: won mares race at Carlisle in October: second in listed mares event at Cheltenham (1¼ lengths behind The Glancing Queen) month later: similar form over hurdles: won mares novices at Wetherby in December and Market Rasen in March: remains open to improvement. *Ruth Jefferson* — **h125 p b104**

MELCHIOR KING (IRE) 5 br.g. Stowaway – Miss Ira Zarad (IRE) (Darazari (IRE)) [2018/19 b–: b16g h15.3g h16.3s⁶ h16d* h16dᵖᵘ h16s⁵ Mar 8] good-bodied gelding: modest form in bumpers: fair form over hurdles: won maiden at Chepstow in January: temperamental. *Philip Hobbs* — **h112 § b77 §**

MELDRUM WAY (IRE) 6 b.g. Getaway (GER) – Meldrum Hall (IRE) (Saddlers' Hall (IRE)) [2018/19 h19.3s h19.9g Oct 18] pulled up in point: poor form over hurdles: left David Harry Kelly after first start. *Mark Campion* — **h–**

MELEKHOV (IRE) 5 b.g. Sholokhov (IRE) – Yorkshire Girl (IRE) (Anshan) [2018/19 b97: h16.7g⁴ h16.5d² h16.8s* Apr 16] fairly useful form in bumpers: similar form over hurdles: won maiden at Exeter in April: should be suited by 2¼m+. *Philip Hobbs* — **h115**

MELLOW BEN (IRE) 6 b.g. Beneficial – Mellowthemoonlight (IRE) (Un Desperado (FR)) [2018/19 h110, b–: h20.5g² h19.6g⁵ h19.2g* h17.7mᶠ h21g h21g⁴ h21g² h21g h20.5g² Apr 7] useful-looking gelding: runner-up sole start in Irish points: fairly useful handicap hurdler: won at Fontwell in September: second at Plumpton in April: stays 21f: acts on soft going: tried in hood. *Chris Gordon* — **h126**

Mrs J. Donnelly's "Melon"

MELLO YELLO 5 b.m. Milan – Fernello (Presenting) [2018/19 b15.7d b16d Mar 28] **b–**
first foal: dam unraced half-sister to fairly useful hurdler/useful chaser (stays 4m) Cogry:
tailed off in 2 bumpers: wears hood. *Martin Keighley*

MELODY OF SCOTLAND (FR) 5 b.m. Youmzain (IRE) – This Melody (FR) (Saint **h123**
Preuil (FR)) [2018/19 h16.5g³ h16.3m³ h20g² h15.9g⁶ h21g h16g h16s h19.9v h23.8g³
h16.4vᵖᵘ Mar 16] third foal: half-sister to fairly useful hurdler Pas Trop Tard (2m-2½m
winner) and French 19f chase winner Jacobite Honor (both by Caballo Raptor): dam placed
over hurdles at 15f/2m in France: fairly useful handicap hurdler: won juvenile in France for
Guillaume Macaire in 2017/18: third at Aintree on British debut: left Alan King after fifth
start: stays 2½m: acts on soft going: usually races off pace. *Ben Haslam*

MELON 7 ch.g. Medicean – Night Teeny (Platini (GER)) [2018/19 h166: h16g⁴ h16g⁴ **h155 x**
h16.4s² h20dᶠ Apr 4] well-made gelding: high-class hurdler: below best in 2018/19,
including when second in Champion Hurdle at Cheltenham for second successive season,
beaten 15 lengths by Espoir d'Allen: unproven beyond 2m: acts on soft going: has worn
headgear: prone to a bad mistake nowadays: to be sent chasing. *W. P. Mullins, Ireland*

MENAPIAN (IRE) 8 b.g. Touch of Land (FR) – Mannequin (IRE) (In The Wings) **h83**
[2018/19 h63: h16.5d⁵ h19d⁴ h21.4g h19s² Mar 19] poor form over hurdles: stays 19f: acts
on soft going: usually races towards rear. *Helen Nelmes*

MENDIP EXPRESS (IRE) 13 br.g. King's Theatre (IRE) – Mulberry (IRE) (Denel **c127**
(FR)) [2018/19 c129, h–: c23.8g⁵ c24.2v⁶ c24.2s* c24.2d Feb 15] tall, good-topped **h–**
gelding: prolific point winner: winning hurdler: fairly useful handicap chaser: won at
Sandown (amateurs) in December: stays 3¼m: acts on heavy going: wears tongue tie.
Philip Hobbs

MENGLI KHAN (IRE) 6 b.g. Lope de Vega (IRE) – Danielli (IRE) (Danehill (USA)) **c151**
[2018/19 h149: c16.1d* c17g⁴ c17g³ c19.8d³ c19.9d³ c20g⁴ Apr 21] strong gelding: smart **h–**
hurdler: similar form over fences: won maiden at Punchestown (by 10 lengths from Forge
Meadow) in November: third in JLT Novices' Chase (Golden Miller) at Cheltenham (9¼
lengths behind Defi du Seuil) in March and Manifesto Novices' Chase at Aintree (3 lengths
behind Kalashnikov) in April: stays 2½m: acts on heavy going: wears tongue tie. *Gordon
Elliott, Ireland*

MERCENAIRE (FR) 5 gr.g. Soldier of Fortune (IRE) – Southwold (FR) (Take Risks **c–**
(FR)) [2018/19 h126: h16d c19.2g⁵ h23.6v⁴ h21.4gᵖᵘ Jan 17] fairly useful handicap **h117**
hurdler: fourth at Chepstow in December: well beaten in maiden on chasing debut:
unproven beyond 17f: acted on heavy going: tried in cheekpieces: dead. *Nick Williams*

MERCERS COURT (IRE) 11 b.g. Court Cave (IRE) – Vikki's Dream (IRE) (Kahyasi) **c121**
[2018/19 c116, h–: c29.1g⁶ c24.5g² c24.2g⁴ c26.1g³ c25.5m⁴ c23g⁵ c23g* c26g* c26m* **h–**
c29.2g² c23.6g² c25.1g⁴ c24.2g⁵ Apr 11] angular gelding: winning hurdler: fairly useful
handicap chaser: completed hat-trick at Worcester and Fontwell in August, and Fontwell
again (conditionals) in October: second at Huntingdon in November: stays 29f: acts on soft
and good to firm going: has worn headgear: tried in tongue tie. *Neil King*

MERCER'S TROOP (IRE) 4 b.g. Canford Cliffs (IRE) – Meek Appeal (USA) **h96**
(Woodman (USA)) [2018/19 h17.7g h16.7g h15.8g h15.9s² h16g h15.8d* h20.3d⁶ Apr 9]
has had breathing operation: half-brother to fairly useful 2m hurdle winner Triumphant (by
Danehill Dancer), stayed 2¾m, and fair 2m hurdle winner In Bloom (by Montjeu): fairly
useful on Flat, stays 1½m: modest handicap hurdler: won at Uttoxeter in February:
unproven beyond 2m: acts on soft going. *Dan Skelton*

MERCHANT HOUSE (IRE) 5 b.g. Fairly Ransom (USA) – Skyra (IRE) (Scorpion **b91**
(IRE)) [2018/19 b16.8s* Apr 16] €8,000 3-y-o: first foal: dam unraced half-sister to useful
2m chaser Bambi De L'Orme: won point bumper on debut: 20/1, also won maiden bumper
at Exeter (by 3 lengths from Full of Roque) on Rules bow. *L. Jefford*

MERCIAN KING (IRE) 8 b.g. Robin des Pres (FR) – Mariah Rollins (IRE) (Over The **c121**
River (FR)) [2018/19 c116, h–: c17m² c17.8g² c17m³ h16g² h16.3m⁶ c16.5g* c16.5g² **h93**
c15.8g c16.4g³ Nov 30] lengthy gelding: has had breathing operation: modest maiden
hurdler: fairly useful handicap chaser: won at Worcester in October: stays 2½m: acts on
firm and soft going: has worn headgear: front runner/races prominently. *Amy Murphy*

MERCIAN KNIGHT (IRE) 5 b.g. Saint des Saints (FR) – Carole's Legacy (Sir Harry **b83 p**
Lewis (USA)) [2018/19 b16.3d Mar 2] well-made gelding: third foal: dam (c154/h145),
19f-3m hurdle/chase winner, half-sister to useful hurdler/smart chaser (stayed 2½m) Mad
Max: 25/1, badly in need of experience when ninth in bumper at Newbury: will improve.
Amy Murphy

MERCIAN PRINCE (IRE) 8 b.g. Midnight Legend – Bongo Fury (FR) (Sillery (USA)) **c146**
[2018/19 c142, h–: c19.9g⁶ c16d c20.5g* c19.9d c21.1d c19.7g* Apr 22] sturdy gelding: **h–**
has had breathing operation: maiden hurdler: smart handicap chaser: won small-field
events at Kempton (by 17 lengths from Poker School) in January and Plumpton (by 3
lengths from Romain de Senam) in April: stays 21f: acts on good to soft going: tried in
cheekpieces/tongue tie: front runner/races prominently. *Amy Murphy*

MERCY MERCY ME 7 b.g. Shirocco (GER) – Monsignorita (IRE) (Classic Cliche **h115**
(IRE)) [2018/19 h109: h19.5s² h19.8v³ h16s⁵ h19.5d² Mar 20] tall gelding: has had
breathing operation: useful bumper performer: fairly useful form over hurdles: third in
Winter Novices' Hurdle at Sandown (13½ lengths behind Alsa Mix) in December: tried in
cheekpieces. *Fergal O'Brien*

MERE ANARCHY (IRE) 8 b.g. Yeats (IRE) – Maracana (IRE) (Glacial Storm (USA)) **h103 §**
[2018/19 h96: h20g³ h16s³ h19.5s³ h19d h16.8s³ h20s⁵ h16g³ Apr 26] fair handicap
hurdler: stays 2½m: acts on soft going: has worn cheekpieces, including in 2018/19: tried
in tongue tie: temperamental (has awkward head carriage). *Robert Stephens*

MERE IRONMONGER 7 ch.g. Galileo (IRE) – Kindling (Dr Fong (USA)) [2018/19 **h83**
b15.7m h16.3s h17.7v h20.5d h21s Mar 10] workmanlike gelding: useful form when **b–**
winning bumper on debut in 2015/16: disappointing since, off 2½ years before return: left
Brendan Powell after fourth start: tried in visor/tongue tie. *Richard Bandey*

MERGEELA (IRE) 4 b.f. September Storm (GER) – Sweetbriar Rose (IRE) (Dushyantor **b–**
(USA)) [2018/19 b12.4s b16m Apr 22] sixth foal: sister to useful bumper winner/winning
pointer Longhouse Sale and half-sister to fair 2m hurdle winner Long House Island (by
Turtle Island) and a winning pointer by Tikkanen: dam unraced half-sister to useful hurdler/
fairly useful chaser (winner up to 21f) Line Ball: well held in 2 bumpers. *Kim Bailey*

MERRYDOWN VINTAGE (IRE) 12 ch.g. Ballingarry (IRE) – Cure The Blues (IRE) **c– x** (Phardante (FR)) [2018/19 c26g Jun 5] multiple point winner: maiden hurdler/chaser, well **h–** held sole start under Rules in 2018/19: stays 3m: acts on soft going: wears headgear: tried in tongue tie: often let down by jumping. *Patrick Chamings*

MERRY MILAN (IRE) 7 b.g. Milan – Timerry (IRE) (Alphabatim (USA)) [2018/19 **c116** h113: h21d² c23.8g^F c23.6v⁴ c24d h21.4g³ h25s Mar 11] good-topped gelding: off mark in **h120** Irish points at third attempt: fairly useful form over hurdles: third in handicap at Wincanton in January: similar form over fences: will prove best at 3m+: acts on good to soft going. *Nicky Martin*

METATRONS CUBE (IRE) 4 b.g. Artie Schiller (USA) – Quiet Down (USA) (Quiet **h103** American (USA)) [2018/19 h15.8g⁴ h16.8s⁶ h16d² h15.8g² h16s Jan 21] fairly useful on Flat, stays 1½m: fair form over hurdles: raced around 2m: in tongue tie last 3 starts. *Matt Sheppard*

METEORITE 5 b.g. Bollin Eric – Running Hotter (Wace (USA)) [2018/19 b16.2s⁴ h20.3s **h105** h20s³ Apr 7] £10,000 4-y-o: fourth foal: dam well held in bumpers: in frame in point/ **b72** bumper: fair form over hurdles: better effort when third in novice at Ffos Las. *Tom Symonds*

METHAG (FR) 6 b.m. Pour Moi (IRE) – Kyria (Grand Lodge (USA)) [2018/19 h76: **h90** h16.7m² h19.9g⁶ Nov 17] close-coupled mare: fair on Flat, stays 2m: modest maiden hurdler: unproven beyond 17f: acts on good to firm going. *Alex Hales*

METHODTOTHEMADNESS (IRE) 5 b.m. Gold Well – Odeeka (IRE) (Posen **b90** (USA)) [2018/19 b16.6g³ b16.4m² Mar 22] €25,000 3-y-o: fifth foal: half-sister to fair hurdler/fairly useful chaser Grange Hall (2½m winner, by Flemensfirth): dam, winning pointer, half-sister to very smart hurdler (stayed 3m) Celestial Wave: every chance when falling late all 3 starts in Irish points: fair form when placed both starts in bumpers. *Lucinda Russell*

METICULOUS (IRE) 5 b.g. Fame And Glory – Refinement (IRE) (Oscar (IRE)) [2018/19 **b110** b17m* b16g⁴ b16g² b16.4s Mar 13] lengthy gelding: fifth foal: half-brother to bumper winner/fairly useful 2m hurdle winner West Coast Time (by Westerner), stays 2¾m: dam (h152) bumper winner/2m-3m hurdle winner: useful form in bumpers: won maiden at Killarney in July: second in Grade 2 at Leopardstown (1¼ lengths behind Envoi Allen) in February: bred to stay at least 2½m: wears tongue tie. *Joseph Patrick O'Brien, Ireland*

METRO BOULOT DODO (IRE) 6 br.g. Robin des Champs (FR) – Lizzy Langtry **h96** (IRE) (King's Theatre (IRE)) [2018/19 b16.4d⁵ b16s³ h15.6g⁵ h20.6d³ Apr 6] €46,000 **b84** 3-y-o, £6,000 5-y-o: fifth foal: brother to fairly useful 2m/17f hurdle winner Mardale and half-brother to fair hurdler Onlyfoolsownhorses (19f-3m winner, by Presenting): dam unraced half-sister to smart 2m hurdler Farmer Brown: unplaced in 2 Irish points: modest form in bumpers/over hurdles. *Daragh Bourke*

MIAH GRACE 4 b.f. Malinas (GER) – Silver Gypsy (IRE) (Luso) [2018/19 b16g² **b84** b16.2g³ Apr 15] £18,000 3-y-o: second foal: half-sister to a winning pointer by Sulamani: dam (c101/h128), bumper/2m-19f hurdle winner (stayed 3m), half-sister to useful hurdler/ fairly useful chaser (stayed 3m) Quickbeam: modest form in bumpers: better effort when second in mares event at Wetherby in February. *Jedd O'Keeffe*

MIA'S STORM (IRE) 9 b.m. September Storm (GER) – Letitia's Gain (IRE) (Zaffaran **c–** (USA)) [2018/19 c145, h132: h23.3g* h24.5g* h24.7g h21.5g⁶ Apr 27] lengthy mare: **h140** useful hurdler: won handicap at Uttoxeter (by 4 lengths from Boreham Bill) in October and listed mares event at Kempton (by 2 lengths from If You Say Run) in November: smart form over fences: stays 3m: acts on good to firm and good to soft going: in cheekpieces last 2 starts. *Alan King*

MICHAEL JAMES (IRE) 8 b.g. Baltic King – Flying Cockatoo (IRE) (Flying Spur **h96** (AUS)) [2018/19 h97: h24m h21g h20.2g⁵ Sep 10] compact gelding: modest maiden hurdler: stays 2½m: acts on soft going: sometimes in tongue tie. *Paul Stafford, Ireland*

MICKIEBLUEEYES (IRE) 7 b.g. Dilshaan – Killerig Park (I'm Supposin (IRE)) **c–** [2018/19 h99: h24g c24g^{pu} Mar 28] modest form over hurdles: pulled up in novice **h–** handicap on chasing debut: stays 25f: acts on good to soft going: in tongue tie last 4 starts. *Diana Grissell*

MICK MAESTRO (FR) 6 b.g. Air Chief Marshal (IRE) – Mick Maya (FR) (Siam **h116** (USA)) [2018/19 b90: h15.8d* h16d³ h16.3m⁴ h15.8g² h16g⁴ h15.3g³ Jan 17] strong gelding: fair form in bumpers: fairly useful form over hurdles: won maiden at Uttoxeter in May: left Tom George after third start: raced around 2m: acts on good to soft going: tried in hood. *Alan King*

MICK MANHATTAN (FR) 5 b.g. Blue Bresil (FR) – Normanville (IRE) (Anabaa Blue) [2018/19 b93: h15.8v⁵ h20s Nov 23] won sole start in bumpers: modest form over hurdles. *Evan Williams* **h86**

MICK MONA (FR) 5 ro.m. Blue Bresil (FR) – Mick Toscane (FR) (Ultimately Lucky (IRE)) [2018/19 b15.8s b15.7d h15.8g³ Apr 11] rather unfurnished mare: first foal: dam unraced half-sister to fairly useful chaser/useful chaser (stays 2½m) Mick Thonic: little show in bumpers: in hood, 33/1, third in mares maiden at Huntingdon (4¼ lengths behind So Lonely) on hurdling debut: tried in tongue tie. *Alastair Ralph* **h101 b–**

MICK'S WISH (IRE) 7 b.g. Westerner – Bells Chance (IRE) (Needle Gun (IRE)) [2018/19 h–, b69: h20.5gᶠ May 7] smallish gelding: poor form in bumpers/over hurdles: dead. *Jackie Stephen* **h85**

MICK THE POSER (IRE) 5 b.g. Art Connoisseur (IRE) – Naked Poser (IRE) (Night Shift (USA)) [2018/19 h101: h15.8g h15.7g h22.1mᵖᵘ Jun 29] compact gelding: modest maiden hurdler, below form in 2018/19: raced mainly around 2m: acts on good to soft going: usually wears cheekpieces: in tongue tie last 3 starts. *Jennie Candlish* **h83**

MICK THONIC (FR) 9 gr.g. Maresca Sorrento (FR) – Mick Madona (FR) (Dadarissime (FR)) [2018/19 c121, h110: c21g² c19.2gᵘʳ h16.5g⁵ h15.8m⁴ h15.3m² h15.3f³ h16g⁶ h19.8g⁶ h19dᶠ Jan 19] lengthy gelding: has had breathing operation: fair handicap hurdler/chaser: stays 21f: acts on any going: has worn blinkers, including final start: wears tongue tie: front runner/races prominently: temperamental. *Colin Tizzard* **c111 § h110 §**

MICQUUS (IRE) 10 b.g. High Chaparral (IRE) – My Potters (USA) (Irish River (FR)) [2018/19 c59, h–: c23.8gᵖᵘ h21.7g h17.7g³ h15.9s⁵ h21.7v⁴ h23dᵖᵘ c17s* c19.7s* c17g² Apr 7] poor maiden hurdler: modest handicap chaser: won novice events at Plumpton in February and March: left Emma Lavelle after second start: stays 2½m: acts on good going: has worn headgear, including last 3 starts: often let down by jumping. *Seamus Mullins* **c87 x h73**

MICRAS 8 b.m. Medicean – Purple Heather (USA) (Rahy (USA)) [2018/19 c20g⁵ c23.6dᶠ h19.5g h21.6s h15.5g² h15.8s h16.8s² h15.3g² h16.5d³ h16.7g³ h16.5d h16.5d² Apr 24] modest handicap hurdler: poor maiden chaser: stays 21f: acts on heavy going: wears headgear/tongue tie. *Matt Sheppard* **c80 h92**

MID DAY GUN (IRE) 6 ch.g. Robin des Champs (FR) – Crackin' Liss (IRE) (Bob Back (USA)) [2018/19 b16g⁵ b16g³ b17.3g⁵ h15.8gᵘʳ h16.2g h16.7v h20.3sᵖᵘ h25g² h23.9s⁶ h24.1d c24g⁴ Apr 25] €60,000 3-y-o: sixth foal: brother to bumper winner/fairly useful hurdler Hitherjacques Lady (19f-21f winner): dam (b99), bumper winner, half-sister to fairly useful hurdler (2m-2¼m winner) Blazing Liss out of half-sister to very smart hurdler up to 2½m Lisa A Paoraigh: modest form in bumpers for W. P. Mullins: modest maiden hurdler: 28/1, fourth in novice handicap at Warwick (20¼ lengths behind Danseur du Large) on chasing debut: stays 25f: best form on good going: in cheekpieces last 3 starts: usually in tongue tie. *Oliver Greenall* **c80 p h90 b77**

MIDDLEBROW (IRE) 8 b.g. Oscar (IRE) – O What A Girl (IRE) (Anshan) [2018/19 c116, h68: h16.2g⁴ c17.4g⁴ c15.9d³ c17.1g* c15.7s⁵ c16.4g⁴ Apr 23] maiden hurdler: fair handicap chaser: won at Kelso in October: stays 2½m: acts on soft going: in cheekpieces last 3 starts: usually wears tongue tie. *Donald McCain* **c113 h75**

MIDDLESCENCE (IRE) 5 ch.g. Lope de Vega (IRE) – Silesian (IRE) (Singspiel (IRE)) [2018/19 h15.8d Mar 3] angular gelding: modest maiden on Flat, stays 1m: in tongue tie, tailed off in novice on hurdling debut. *Lucinda Egerton* **h–**

MIDNIGHT ANTICS (IRE) 5 b.m. Midnight Legend – Toungara (FR) (Smadoun (FR)) [2018/19 b15.7s² b16.8d⁵ Apr 23] £3,000 3-y-o: second foal: dam lightly-raced sister to fairly useful hurdler/top-class chaser (stayed 25f) Nacarat: fair form in bumpers: better effort when second in conditionals/amateurs maiden at Southwell in March: in tongue tie next start. *Sue Smith* **b89**

MIDNIGHT AURORA 6 ch.m. Midnight Legend – Bekkaria (FR) (Clafouti (FR)) [2018/19 h16.7gᵖᵘ h16d⁵ h16.3g h18.7m⁵ h15.8g⁵ h23g* h23.3g² h25g² h20.3d³ Apr 24] compact mare: half-sister to several winners, including useful chaser Bekkensfirth (2½m winner, by Flemensfirth): dam, French 10.5f-1½m winner, half-sister to dam of outstanding 2m chaser Azertyuiop: modest handicap hurdler: won at Worcester in August: stays 25f: best form on good going: has worn hood. *Dan Skelton* **h94**

MIDNIGHT BLISS 9 b.m. Midnight Legend – Violet Elizabeth (Overbury (IRE)) [2018/19 c24.2g* c26g* c25.6s² c23.6dᵖᵘ c26d* c25.7g³ c24.2g⁴ c24sᶠ h27gᵖᵘ Apr 5] no form over hurdles: fair handicap chaser: won at Fakenham (novice) and Fontwell in June, and again at Fontwell in January: stays 3¼m: acts on soft going: tried in cheekpieces: wears tongue tie: usually leads. *Caroline Fryer* **c101 h–**

MIDNIGHT CHILL 7 b.g. Midnight Legend – Chilla Cilla (Glacial Storm (USA)) **c121**
[2018/19 h114: h19.6g c16.4s* c15.7s* c15.9m² c18.2s² c20d* c21.4m³ Apr 21] good- **h–**
topped gelding: has had breathing operation: fair form over hurdles: fairly useful handicap
chaser: won at Sedgefield (novice) in November, Catterick in December and Ludlow
(novice) in March: stays 2½m: acts on soft and good to firm going: wears tongue tie.
Jamie Snowden

MIDNIGHT GEM 9 b.m. Midnight Legend – Barton Flower (Danzero (AUS)) [2018/19 **c96 §**
c103, h–: c23.6g⁵ c21.4g³ c21.6g⁵ c23m³ c20g⁵ c21.4g c21.6g⁵ c23.6g⁴ c23.8g⁴ c23.6g⁵ **h–**
h23.9d Apr 24] smallish mare: winning hurdler: modest maiden chaser: left Charlie
Longsdon after seventh start: stays 3m: acts on good to firm and good to soft going: has
worn cheekpieces: races prominently: unreliable. *Sophie Leech*

MIDNIGHT GLANCE 4 b.g. Passing Glance – Magical Legend (Midnight Legend) **b80**
[2018/19 b16.3s⁴ b15.3s Mar 7] modest form in bumpers. *Alan King*

MIDNIGHT GLEN 7 b.m. Midnight Legend – Kali (Linamix (FR)) [2018/19 b15.8d **b–**
b16.8s Dec 26] sister to fairly useful hurdler/useful chaser Midnight Cowboy (19f/2½m
winner), stays 3m, and half-sister to several winners, including fairly useful hurdler
Danceintothelight (2m-21f winner, by Dansili): dam 7f winner: well held in bumpers: tried
in hood. *Seamus Mullins*

MIDNIGHT GLORY 7 b.m. Midnight Legend – Land of Glory (Supreme Leader) **h114**
[2018/19 h104: h21.6v h21.2g* h20.7d⁴ h24.1d* h23.8g⁴ h24.3m³ Apr 12] compact mare:
fair handicap hurdler: won at Ludlow (amateurs) in November and Wetherby (mares) in
January: stays 3m: acts on soft and good to firm going. *Philip Hobbs*

MIDNIGHT JITTERBUG 7 b.g. Midnight Legend – Heebie Jeebie (Overbury (IRE)) **h82**
[2018/19 h96: h15.3d h15.8vᵖᵘ h16.5d³ h17.7g³ Apr 22] lengthy gelding: modest maiden
hurdler, below best in 2018/19 after 19-month absence: stays 2¼m: acts on good to soft
going. *Martin Bosley*

MIDNIGHT KATE (IRE) 5 gr.m. Midnight Legend – Primrose Time (Alflora (IRE)) **h–**
[2018/19 h82, b–: h16.2g May 17] well held in bumpers: poor form over hurdles.
Jackie Stephen

MIDNIGHT MAESTRO 7 b.g. Midnight Legend – Calamintha (Mtoto) [2018/19 h124: **c– p**
h20.6g* c20s c20.2gᶠ Jan 5] useful-looking gelding: fairly useful handicap hurdler: won at **h127**
Market Rasen in May: well held completed start over fences: stays 21f: acts on heavy
going: should do better as a chaser. *Alan King*

MIDNIGHT MAGIC 7 b.g. Midnight Legend – Arctic Magic (IRE) (Saddlers' Hall **c93 §**
(IRE)) [2018/19 h92: h24g h23g h21.6g⁵ c23.8s⁴ c26.2dᵖᵘ c24.2d c26.2g² Apr 26] has had **h76 §**
breathing operation: poor maiden hurdler: modest form over fences: stays 3¼m: acts on
soft going: wears headgear/tongue tie: temperamental. *David Pipe*

MIDNIGHT MIDGE 5 b.g. Midnight Legend – Posh Emily (Rakaposhi King) [2018/19 **h104**
h77, b70: h21.4f³ h23.1g⁴ h21.4g h15.3d⁴ h15.3g⁶ h16.8s² h16.5s² Mar 19] neat gelding:
fair handicap hurdler: won at Wincanton (novice) in December: likely to prove best at short
of 23f: acts on firm and soft going: wears hood: usually races close up. *Ron Hodges*

MIDNIGHT MONTY 9 ch.g. Midnight Legend – Marello (Supreme Leader) [2018/19 **c– §**
c117, h111: c24mᵖᵘ h23.1sᵖᵘ Dec 7] workmanlike gelding: has had breathing operation: **h– §**
fair hurdler/fairly useful chaser: pulled up all starts in 2018/19, including in points: has
worn blinkers, including final start: usually wears tongue tie: temperamental. *Jamie
Snowden*

MIDNIGHT MUSTANG 12 b.g. Midnight Legend – Mustang Molly (Soldier Rose) **c79**
[2018/19 c73, h–: c21.2g⁵ c21.4g* c24.1g⁴ c21.6g h23.3g c21.7d⁴ c25.6s⁴ c23.6d⁵ c22.7f⁵ **h–**
c25.7s⁶ c27.5g² c26.2g⁵ Apr 26] stocky gelding: maiden hurdler: poor handicap chaser:
won at Market Rasen early in season and Southwell in December: stays 3½m: acts on
heavy going: wears cheekpieces. *Andrew Martin*

MIDNIGHT OWLE 9 ch.g. Midnight Legend – Owlesbury Dream (IRE) (Luso) **c82**
[2018/19 c–, h–: h23.3gᵖᵘ c21.6d³ c22.8gᵖᵘ c20.9sᵖᵘ c19.9d⁴ c16.2d² c19.4d **h–**
c19.9d² c18.2s* c15.7gᶠ c19.4g Apr 14] workmanlike gelding: maiden hurdler: poor
handicap chaser: won novice event at Taunton in March: stays 2½m: acts on soft going:
wears tongue tie. *Claire Dyson*

MIDNIGHT POPSTAR 5 b.m. Midnight Legend – It's Missy Imp (Fearless Action **b–**
(USA)) [2018/19 b16.3g Mar 30] second foal: dam, winning pointer, half-sister to fairly
useful hurdler/chaser (2m-3m winner) Sunny Ledgend (by Midnight Legend): last in
bumper. *Andrew Martin*

Dornen Engineering Relkeel Hurdle, Cheltenham—northern raider Midnight Shadow battles well to defeat 2018 winner Wholestone (right) as third-placed Old Guard challenges in between them

MIDNIGHT QUEEN 9 b.m. Rainbow High – Questionit (Sovereign Water (FR)) [2018/19 c–, h71: c24g^F c25.8g* h27m^F h25.8s^4 h23.4d* h25.3g^3 h23.8g^F Feb 13] modest handicap hurdler: won at Fakenham in December: poor form over fences: won handicap at Newton Abbot (conditionals) in August: stays 3¼m: acts on soft going: wears headgear: usually races close up: temperament under suspicion. *Tim Vaughan* **c77 h89**

MIDNIGHTREFERENDUM 6 b.m. Midnight Legend – Forget The Ref (IRE) (Dr Massini (IRE)) [2018/19 b106: h19.5d h19.2v* h20.5s^4 h19g^4 h19g* Apr 25] rather unfurnished mare: has had breathing operation: useful bumper performer: fairly useful form over hurdles: won mares novice at Fontwell in December and handicap at Warwick in April: bred to stay further than 2½m: acts on heavy going. *Alan King* **h121**

MIDNIGHTREFLECTION 4 b.f. Midnight Legend – Hymn To Love (FR) (Turgeon (USA)) [2018/19 b15.8d Mar 30] second foal: dam French 2¼m hurdle winner: in hood, 33/1, ninth in mares bumper at Uttoxeter. *Ben Case* **b–**

MIDNIGHT RUN (IRE) 5 b.g. Well Chosen – Knockamullen Girl (IRE) (Alderbrook) [2018/19 b16.6d* b16d^2 b16g* Feb 24] €15,000 3-y-o: third foal: brother to smart bumper winner/fairly useful 2¾m hurdle winner Carefully Selected: dam unraced half-sister to dam of smart hurdler/chaser (stayed 3m) Lord Sam: useful form in bumpers: won at Galway (maiden, by 5½ lengths from Poker d'Ainay) in October and Naas (by 3½ lengths from Column of Fire, impressively) in February: will be suited by further than 2m. *Joseph Patrick O'Brien, Ireland* **b109**

MIDNIGHT SAPPHIRE 9 ch.m. Midnight Legend – Norton Sapphire (Karinga Bay) [2018/19 h26.5g^2 h23m^4 Sep 17] angular mare: has had breathing operation: fair handicap hurdler: stays 3¼m: acts on heavy going: wears tongue tie: has joined Gail Haywood. *David Pipe* **h113**

MIDNIGHT SHADOW 6 b.g. Midnight Legend – Holy Smoke (Statoblest) [2018/19 h137: h16m^2 h16.4g h20s* h20.3d* h24d Jan 26] workmanlike gelding: smart hurdler: won handicap at Aintree (by ½ length from Ch'tibello) in December and Relkeel Hurdle at Cheltenham (by 2¼ lengths from Wholestone) in January: stays 2½m: acts on good to firm and heavy going. *Sue Smith* **h154**

MIDNIGHT SHOT 9 b.g. Midnight Legend – Suave Shot (Suave Dancer (USA)) [2018/19 c135, h–: c20.6g^6 c23g^{pu} h23g^6 c21.2s* c20g^5 c24.2m* c30.2g^6 c24g^5 c24.2d^3 c23.4d^{pu} Apr 8] sturdy gelding: winning hurdler: useful handicap chaser: won at Cartmel in August and Fakenham (by 13 lengths from Ballykan) in October: stays 3m: acts on soft and good to firm going: wears cheekpieces. *Charlie Longsdon* **c132 h–**

MIDNIGHT SONATA (IRE) 5 b.g. Big Bad Bob (IRE) – Symphonique (FR) (Epervier Bleu) [2018/19 b90p: b16g^5 h15.8g Nov 13] fair form on first of 2 outings in bumpers: well beaten in novice on hurdling debut: tried in hood: has joined Venetia Williams. *Charlie Longsdon* **h– b66**

MIDNIGHT STROLL 7 b.g. Midnight Legend – Late For Class (IRE) (Bob's Return **c124 p** (IRE)) [2018/19 h132: c19d⁴ h20s*ᵈ Jan 5] good-topped gelding: useful handicap hurdler: **h134** retried in hood, first past post at Cork in January, ½ length ahead of Chatham Street Lad, but later disqualified due to banned substance: 25/1, fourth in maiden at Naas (19 lengths behind A Plus Tard) on chasing debut: stays 2½m: acts on soft going: should do better over fences. *Robert Tyner, Ireland*

MIDNIGHT TARGET 9 b.m. Midnight Legend – Right On Target (IRE) (Presenting) **c112** [2018/19 c117, h–: c20.5g² c20.6g⁵ h23.8g² c23.8d⁴ h21.2m⁶ Apr 1] lengthy mare: fair **h113** handicap hurdler: fairly useful handicap chaser, below best in 2018/19: stays 3m: acts on heavy going: wears hood/tongue tie: usually races close up. *John Groucott*

MIDNIGHT TIPPLE 5 b.m. Fair Mix (IRE) – Farewellatmidnight (Midnight Legend) **h–** [2018/19 h16.8s Dec 7] first foal: dam (c100/h82), 2½m/21f hurdle/chase winner, half-sister to fairly useful hurdler/smart chaser (stayed 21f) Cocktails At Dawn (by Fair Mix): pulled up in 2 points: tailed off in novice on hurdling debut. *Neil Mulholland*

MIDNIGHT TROUBLE 7 b.g. Midnight Legend – Friendly Request (Environment **h–** Friend) [2018/19 h92, b79: h19m h23.9g Sep 27] sturdy gelding: modest form in bumpers: similar form over hurdles, well held both starts in 2018/19: should be suited by 3m. *Nigel Twiston-Davies*

MIDNIGHT TUNE 8 b.m. Midnight Legend – Harmonic Motion (IRE) (Bob Back **c130** (USA)) [2018/19 h131: c24g² c19.7sᶠ Feb 13] compact mare: useful hurdler: similar form **h–** over fences: second in mares novice at Uttoxeter (2½ lengths behind Molly The Dolly) on completed start: will stay 3½m+: acts on heavy going: wears tongue tie: front runner. *Anthony Honeyball*

MIDNIGHT WALK (IRE) 9 b.m. Oscar (IRE) – Lady Belvedere (IRE) (Lord Americo) **c55** [2018/19 c108, h102: c20.3g⁶ h18.1g³ h19.3g⁶ c21.1g⁴ Apr 5] fair handicap hurdler: **h100** similar form at best over fences: left Donald McCain after first start: stays 2½m: acts on soft going: has worn headgear, including last 2 starts: usually wears tongue tie. *Julia Brooke*

MIDTECH VALENTINE 8 b.m. Act One – Eveon (IRE) (Synefos (USA)) [2018/19 **c–** c104, h108: h19.6g⁴ Aug 3] lengthy mare: fair handicap hurdler, below form sole start in **h94** 2018/19: maiden chaser: stays 2½m: acts on heavy going: sometimes in cheekpieces: tried in tongue tie: has joined Ken Wingrove. *Ian Williams*

MIGHT BITE (IRE) 10 b.g. Scorpion (IRE) – Knotted Midge (IRE) (Presenting) **c–** [2018/19 c171, h–: c25.6g⁵ c24g c26.3dᵖᵘ Mar 1] tall gelding: has had breathing operation: **h–** winning hurdler: top-class chaser at best, most disappointing in 2018/19 (folded tamely all 3 starts): stays 3¼m: front runner/races prominently: usually strong traveller/superb jumper. *Nicky Henderson*

MIGHTY LEADER (IRE) 11 b.g. Milan – Madam Leader (IRE) (Supreme Leader) **c131** [2018/19 c–, h123: c25.8g* c24.2g² c23.8g* c25.8m⁴ h24g³ c23.8g* c26.7f⁴ c27.7dᵖᵘ Nov **h119** 18] angular gelding: fairly useful handicap hurdler: useful chaser: won maiden at Newton Abbot early in season, and novice in June (by 2½ lengths from Tanarpino) and handicap in September (by 3½ lengths from Forth Bridge), both at Perth: little impact in points later in season: stays 3¼m: acts on soft and good to firm going: usually wears headgear: wears tongue tie: usually races close up. *Fergal O'Brien*

MIGHTY MEG 5 b.m. Malinas (GER) – Harry's Bride (Sir Harry Lewis (USA)) [2018/19 **b82** ab16.3s³ Jan 15] half-sister to bumper winner/useful hurdler Carlton Jack (2½m winner, by Erhaab) and fairly useful hurdler U B Carefull (2m-21f winner, by Roi de Rome): dam unraced half-sister to useful 2m chaser Shamana: 11/4, third in maiden bumper at Newcastle (1¾ lengths behind Basildon). *Olly Murphy*

MIGHTY MISSILE (IRE) 8 ch.g. Majestic Missile (IRE) – Magdalene (FR) (College **h77** Chapel) [2018/19 h91: h18.5g⁶ h16.8g⁵ Apr 20] sturdy gelding: has had breathing operation: poor handicap hurdler nowadays: stays 2½m: acts on firm and soft going: usually wears headgear: has worn tongue tie, including last 5 starts: temperament under suspicion. *Brian Barr*

MIGHTY MUSTANG 9 b.g. Passing Glance – Mustang Molly (Soldier Rose) [2018/19 **h–** h16.2g h16g Feb 19] sturdy gelding: has had breathing operation: of no account: tried in tongue tie. *Andrew Martin*

MIGHTY THUNDER 6 b.g. Malinas (GER) – Cool Island (IRE) (Turtle Island (IRE)) **h111**
[2018/19 h107, b91: h20.2g² h20.9d² h21.4v⁵ h22.7g* h25.8g³ h26.6g³ Apr 25] lengthy
gelding: has had breathing operation: bumper winner: fair hurdler: won maiden at Kelso in
December: stays 27f: acts on heavy going: in cheekpieces last 2 starts: wears tongue tie.
Lucinda Russell

MIGHTY VIC (IRE) 11 b.g. Old Vic – Mighty Marble (IRE) (Satco (FR)) [2018/19 h95: **h82**
h23.1spu h26d h21.7s⁵ h25s⁵ Feb 13] compact gelding: Irish point winner: maiden hurdler,
only poor form in 2018/19: wears tongue tie. *Suzy Smith*

MIGHTY WHITEY (IRE) 13 b.g. Sesaro (USA) – Deeco Valley (IRE) (Satco (FR)) **c–**
[2018/19 c–, h95: h21.4g h15.8mF Jul 1] fairly useful hurdler at best, on downgrade: **h–**
winning chaser: stays 21f: acts on good to firm and heavy going: has worn headgear: wears
tongue tie: front runner. *Noel C. Kelly, Ireland*

MILAN DANCER (IRE) 8 b.m. Milan – Pawnee Trail (IRE) (Taipan (IRE)) [2018/19 **c–**
h21.4d⁵ Jan 20] multiple point winner: modest maiden hurdler: twice-raced chaser: stays **h91**
2½m: acts on heavy going: usually races nearer last than first. *Noel C. Kelly, Ireland*

MILAN NATIVE (IRE) 6 br.g. Milan – That's The Goose (IRE) (Be My Native (USA)) **h131**
[2018/19 b20g³ h16d* h16g³ h22.5v² h20d⁵ Apr 7] seventh foal: brother to bumper winner **b89**
Alice Pink, closely related to smart hurdler/chaser Colour Squadron (2m-2½m winner, by
Old Vic) and half-brother to modest hurdler/chaser Western Goose (2½m/21f winner, by
Westerner): dam (c92/h104) bumper/2½m hurdle winner: third in maiden bumper at
Leopardstown (15½ lengths behind Neptune) on debut: useful form over hurdles: won
maiden at Navan in February: third in Grade 2 novice at Naas (3½ lengths behind Chosen
Mate) week later: will probably stay further than 2¾m. *Gordon Elliott, Ireland*

MILAN OF CRYSTAL (IRE) 10 b.m. Milan – Native Crystal (IRE) (Be My Native **c–**
(USA)) [2018/19 c–, h96: h15.7g⁶ h19.9g h16g* h20d h16g³ h16g³ h19g⁶ h16g⁴ h19.7g³ **h96**
Oct 16] angular mare: point winner: modest handicap hurdler: won mares event at
Worcester in July: twice-raced chaser: stays 21f: acts on good to firm going: wears tongue
tie: usually races nearer last than first. *Dave Roberts*

MILANO MAGIC (IRE) 13 b.r.g. Milan – Magical Mist (IRE) (Be My Native (USA)) **c– §**
[2018/19 c24.2dpu May 5] multiple point winner: fair maiden hurdler at best: maiden **h– §**
chaser: stays 3m: acts on heavy going: wears cheekpieces: temperamental. *Daragh Bourke*

MILANO'S MELODY (IRE) 5 br.m. Milan – Tizzy Frizzy (Alflora (IRE)) [2018/19 **b73**
b13.7m⁶ Oct 24] 5/1, sixth in mares bumper at Fontwell: dead. *Colin Tizzard*

MILANSBAR (IRE) 12 b.g. Milan – Ardenbar (Ardross) [2018/19 c143§, h–: c28.8v⁵ **c133 §**
c29.2g c26d⁴ c34vpu c23.8spu Apr 7] big gelding: winning hurdler: useful handicap chaser: **h–**
fourth in veterans event at Newbury (9 lengths behind Carole's Destrier) in March: stays
4¼m: acts on heavy going: has worn headgear, including in 2018/19: unreliable (often
sulks if unable to lead). *Neil King*

MILANSTORM (IRE) 6 b.g. Milan – Deise Rose (IRE) (Glacial Storm (USA)) **h92 p**
[2018/19 b93: h20s⁶ h20.5g³ h15.8v⁶ Jan 14] bumper winner: modest form over hurdles:
best effort when third in maiden at Leicester in December: will be suited by 2¾m+:
remains capable of better. *Nigel Twiston-Davies*

MILANS WELL (IRE) 13 b.g. Milan – Panoora Queen (IRE) (Topanoora) [2018/19 **c83**
c23.8gpu c20.1g⁴ c15.6g c20.1m³ c20.1gpu c20.1g c25.5g Jul 21] winning hurdler: poor **h–**
handicap chaser nowadays: stays 25f: acts on good to firm and heavy going: wears
headgear. *William Young Jnr*

MILESHA (IRE) 4 b.f. Milan – Shameena (IRE) (Indian Danehill (IRE)) [2018/19 **b–**
b16.7d Apr 26] £16,000 3-y-o: third foal: half-sister to 5f-10.7f winner Shelbe (by Big Bad
Bob): dam (h82) maiden hurdler: well beaten in mares bumper. *Henry Daly*

MILES TO MILAN (IRE) 9 b.g. Milan – Princesse Rooney (FR) (Baby Turk) [2018/19 **c117**
h106: c24.1g* h20m⁴ c26.2g³ c24.2g* c21.4s³ Dec 26] fair handicap hurdler: fairly useful **h113**
form over fences: won maiden at Ayr early in season and handicap at Wetherby in
November: stays 3¼m: acts on heavy going: in cheekpieces last 4 starts. *Olly Murphy*

MILITARIAN 9 b.g. Kayf Tara – Mille Et Une (FR) (Trempolino (USA)) [2018/19 c118, **c139**
h–: c16d³ c20g⁴ c20g² c23d* c21.2d* c24g⁴ c15.9m* c20.2spu h15.8m⁶ c19.7g³ c20g⁴ **h–**
Apr 27] strong gelding: lightly-raced hurdler: useful handicap chaser: won at Taunton
(novice) in November, Fakenham in December and Leicester (3-runner novice) in
February: fourth at Sandown (novice, 3½ lengths behind Larry) in April: stays 3m: acts on
soft and good to firm going: tried in tongue tie. *Andrew Martin*

MILK KING (IRE) 6 gr.g. Cloudings (IRE) – Snow Keeper (Rocamadour) [2018/19 b–: **h–**
h16g^{pu} Aug 22] has had breathing operation: no form in bumpers/novice hurdle: tried in
tongue tie. *Claire Dyson*

MILKWOOD (IRE) 5 b.g. Dylan Thomas (IRE) – Tropical Lake (IRE) (Lomond (USA)) **b96**
[2018/19 b86p: b17.7g^5 b13.7m^2 b13.7g* Apr 24] has had breathing operation: fairly
useful form in bumpers: won at Fontwell in April. *Neil Mulholland*

MILLANISI BOY 10 b.g. Kalanisi (IRE) – Millennium Rose (IRE) (Roselier (FR)) **c–**
[2018/19 c125, h–: c25.7s^{pu} c19.4s^{pu} Feb 26] workmanlike gelding: winning hurdler: fairly **h–**
useful chaser, pulled up both starts in 2018/19: stays 3m: acts on heavy going: has worn
cheekpieces, including in 2018/19: tried in tongue tie: usually races prominently.
Kayley Woollacott

MILLARVILLE (IRE) 6 b.m. Court Cave (IRE) – Portavoe (IRE) (Pilsudski (IRE)) **h112**
[2018/19 h21g h17.7d^4 h17.7v^3 h20.5d h20.3d* Apr 24] €5,000 3-y-o, £52,000 5-y-o:
compact mare: has had breathing operation: first foal: dam, ran twice in points, half-sister
to useful hurdler/smart chaser (stays 3¼m) Mendip Express: won Minip point on debut: fair
form over hurdles: won maiden at Fontwell in January and 3-runner mares novice at
Southwell in April: likely to stay beyond 2½m: acts on heavy going. *Oliver Sherwood*

MILLDEAN SILVA (IRE) 6 ch.m. Presenting – Impudent (IRE) (In The Wings) **h91**
[2018/19 b17.7g^5 b16.3g b15.7g* h15.3m^3 h15.3f^3 h19.7g^2 h16.5g^3 Jan 9] €38,000 3-y-o: **b77**
third foal: half-sister to smart hurdler/chaser Rock The Kasbah (19f-27f winner, by
Shirocco): dam (h114), 17f hurdle winner, also 1¾m-17f winner on Flat, closely related to
smart hurdler/useful chaser (2m-19f winner) Royal Shakespeare: modest form in bumpers:
won mares event at Southwell in July: similar form over hurdles: should be suited by
2½m+: tried in hood: in tongue tie last 5 starts. *Suzi Best*

MILLE NAUTIQUE (FR) 8 b.g. Panis (USA) – Anoush (USA) (Giant's Causeway **c–**
(USA)) [2018/19 c112, h–: h20.6g^{pu} c21g^6 c17.8g^6 c19.2g^{pu} Sep 29] lengthy gelding: **h–**
maiden hurdler: fair chaser at best, no form in 2018/19: tried in blinkers: usually leads.
Fergal O'Brien

MILLEN DOLLAR MAN (IRE) 10 b.g. Millenary – Rare Dollar (IRE) (Bob's Return **c76**
(IRE)) [2018/19 c73, h83: c21.2g* c24.2g^{ur} h21.6g h20g c21.6g^{pu} h18.5g^{pu} Oct 1] winning **h–**
hurdler: poor handicap chaser: won at Fakenham early in season: stayed 21f: acted on soft
going: wore headgear: tried in tongue tie: dead. *Alexandra Dunn*

MILLERS BANK 5 b.g. Passing Glance – It Doesn't Matter (Karinga Bay) [2018/19 **b86**
ab16g^2 ab16s^2 b16.3g^5 Mar 30] tall, angular gelding: first foal: dam unraced sister to fairly
useful hurdler (stayed 23f) Lady Karabaya out of fairly useful hurdler/chaser (winner up to
2¾m) Supreme Lady: fair form in bumpers: runner-up first 2 starts. *Alex Hales*

MILL FORGE 12 b.g. Grape Tree Road – Agara (Young Ern) [2018/19 c–, h100: h23.9g^2 **c–**
h20.2g^6 h20.2g h20s^2 h24.3m^F Apr 12] fair handicap hurdler: lightly-raced chaser: stayed **h102**
3m: acted on heavy going: wore headgear: tried in tongue tie: dead. *Stuart Crawford,
Ireland*

MILL GREEN 7 b.g. Black Sam Bellamy (IRE) – Ceilidh Royal (Erhaab (USA)) **h132**
[2018/19 b88: b15.7g^3 h19.2g* h21.6m* h20g^3 h19.8s^4 h20.3g^3 Apr 17] fair form in **b94**
bumpers: useful form over hurdles: won novices at Fontwell in June and Newton Abbot
in July: stays 2¾m: acts on soft and good to firm going: usually races prominently.
Nicky Henderson

MILLIE KHEE 7 b.m. Sakhee (USA) – Cugina (Distant Relative) [2018/19 b15.7g **h–**
h15.8g h15.8g^{pu} Apr 11] sister to bumper winner/fairly useful hurdler Cousin Khee **b–**
(2m-19f winner) and half-sister to bumper/fair 2m hurdle winner There And Then (by
Where Or When): dam useful 1¼m winner: no show in bumper/over hurdles: wears hood.
Lydia Pearce

MILLIE THE MINX (IRE) 5 b.m. Medicean – Popocatepetl (FR) (Nashwan (USA)) **h94**
[2018/19 h–, b–: h16.8g h17.2m^3 h16.8g^2 h16.9g^3 h16.8s* h16.8^6 h19.9s^F h16.8g^6
h16.8d^3 Apr 23] modest handicap hurdler: won at Sedgefield in November and December
(novice): stays 2½m: acts on soft going. *Dianne Sayer*

MILLIONDOLLARBILL (IRE) 7 b.g. Dubai Destination (USA) – Rapid Dawn (IRE) **b–**
(Un Desperado (FR)) [2018/19 b16.3d Jun 8] maiden pointer: in tongue tie, tailed off in
bumper. *J. Slatter*

MILL QUEST (IRE) 9 br.m. Milan – Solar Quest (IRE) (King's Ride) [2018/19 h20m^4 **c131**
h24m^4 h20m* h22g^4 h21s^2 h21.8d* c22g* c25g^3 c20g^{pu} c21g^2 c20.3g^2 c20g^4 c19.6v^3 **h123**
c20s^4 c21.5g* Apr 21] fairly useful handicap hurdler: won at Limerick and Cork (mares)

in July, and Downpatrick (mares) in August: useful chaser: won handicap at Tramore in August and novice at Fairyhouse (by 3¾ lengths from Uisce Beatha) in April: stays 25f: acts on good to firm and heavy going: wears tongue tie. *Gordon Elliott, Ireland*

MILL RACE KING (IRE) 6 b.g. Scorpion (IRE) – Oso Special (Teenoso (USA)) [2018/19 h19.9d⁵ h19.3v² Mar 17] £26,000 5-y-o: half-brother to several winners, including fairly useful 2m hurdle winner Specialagent Alfie and fairly useful hurdler/ chaser Special Wells (2m-2½m winner), both by Alflora: dam unraced: off mark in Irish points at second attempt: fair form over hurdles: better effort when second in novice at Carlisle. *Tim Easterby* — **h104**

MILLROSE BELL (IRE) 7 b.m. Flemensfirth (USA) – Laboc (Rymer) [2018/19 h77: h20.1sᵖᵘ h19.9s⁴ h20.6dᵖᵘ h23.3v h22g⁶ h22g⁶ h21.2d³ h23.8g⁴ h27s³ h23.8m⁶ h23.3v² h27g⁵ Apr 5] sturdy mare: poor maiden hurdler: stays 23f: acts on heavy going: wears cheekpieces: usually races close up. *Victor Thompson* — **h79**

MILLSTONE 5 b.g. Alkaased (USA) – Stoney Path (Petoski) [2018/19 b16g⁵ b15.8g³ Apr 11] half-brother to several winners, including fair hurdler/useful chaser Stoney's Treasure (19f-3m winner, by Silver Patriarch) and fair hurdler/chaser Shady Lane (2m winner, by Alflora): dam (h94), 19f/2½m hurdle winner, half-sister to fairly useful hurdler/very smart chaser (2m winner) Martin's Lamp: fair form in bumpers: better effort when third in maiden at Huntingdon. *Alan King* — **b90**

MILLY BALOO 8 b.m. Desideratum – Tarabaloo (Kayf Tara) [2018/19 c110, h105: c24.2d* May 5] fair hurdler: fair handicap chaser: won at Hexham in May: stays 25f: acts on heavy going: tried in tongue tie. *Tim Easterby* — **c113** **h–**

MILORD (GER) 10 br.g. Monsun (GER) – Montserrat (GER) (Zilzal (USA)) [2018/19 c110, h107: h20gᵖᵘ Jun 11] compact gelding: fair hurdler at best, pulled up sole start in 2018/19: fair form over fences: stays 3m: acts on good to firm and heavy going: wears headgear: front runner/races prominently: temperament under suspicion. *Kim Bailey* — **c–** **h–**

MILROW (IRE) 6 b.g. Tamayuz – Cannikin (IRE) (Lahib (USA)) [2018/19 h123: h19.2sᶠ h23.9d h24.3g⁶ h21.6s² h21g h23.9s Feb 4] neat gelding: fairly useful handicap hurdler: standout effort in 2018/19 when second at Ascot (conditionals) in December: stays 3m: acts on soft going: has worn cheekpieces, including last 3 starts: wears tongue tie: usually races nearer last than first. *Sophie Leech* — **h115**

MILTON 7 br.g. Nomadic Way (USA) – Jesmund (Bishop of Cashel) [2018/19 b–: h20.5s⁶ h15.9g Feb 25] well held in bumpers/over hurdles. *Diana Grissell* — **h–**

MILVALE (IRE) 5 b.g. Ask – House-Of-Hearts (IRE) (Broken Hearted) [2018/19 b16s² b16s² b16.2d⁶ Apr 26] €12,500 3-y-o, £40,000 4-y-o: half-brother to 3 winners by Flemensfirth, including fairly useful hurdler/useful chaser Emperor's Choice (23f-29f winner): dam (b86), placed in bumper, half-sister to smart hurdler/top-class chaser (stayed 3½m) Our Vic: runner-up in Irish point: fair form in bumpers: best effort when second at Ayr in January: will stay at least 2½m. *Sandy Thomson* — **b86**

MIND'S EYE (IRE) 7 b.g. Stowaway – Joleen (IRE) (Bob's Return (IRE)) [2018/19 h133: c18.2d² c16d* c20g⁶ c17g⁵ c17g⁵ c16.3dᵖᵘ c16.7gʳᵒ Mar 21] well-made gelding: useful hurdler: useful chaser: won maiden at Wexford in October: joined when ran out 2 out in novice handicap at Fairyhouse in April: stays 2½m: acts on soft going: tried in tongue tie: best treated with caution. *Henry de Bromhead, Ireland* — **c143 §** **h–**

MIND YOUR BACK (IRE) 6 b.g. Getaway (GER) – Local Hall (IRE) (Saddlers' Hall (IRE)) [2018/19 b84p: b15.8d⁴ h20.7d⁴ h20s⁶ Apr 7] modest form in bumpers/over hurdles. *Neil Mulholland* — **h95** **b84**

MINELLA AWARDS (IRE) 8 b.g. Oscar (IRE) – Montys Miss (IRE) (Presenting) [2018/19 h144: h22.8d² c23.6d³ c25g* c24.4g⁴ Nov 17] good sort: smart handicap hurdler: second at Galway (2½ lengths behind Low Sun) in August: useful form over fences: easy winner of 2-runner novice at Aintree in November: stays 25f: acts on heavy going: wears tongue tie. *Harry Fry* — **c144** **h148**

MINELLA BOBO (IRE) 6 gr.g. Oscar (IRE) – Line Kendie (FR) (Bonnet Rouge (FR)) [2018/19 b16.3d⁶ h20.8g² h23.6d⁴ h22g* Apr 14] £100,000 5-y-o: second foal: closely related to useful 19f hurdle winner Minellatillmorning (by King's Theatre): dam once-raced half-sister to useful hurdler/chaser around 2½m Granit Jack: won sole start in Irish points: much better than result when sixth in bumper at Newbury: fairly useful form over hurdles: won novice at Stratford in April, hard held: remains open to improvement. *Rebecca Curtis* — **h118 p** **b89**

MINELLACELEBRATION (IRE) 9 b.g. King's Theatre (IRE) – Knocktartan (IRE) **c136** (King's Ride) [2018/19 c136, h–: c24d* May 5] sturdy gelding: has had breathing **h–** operation: winning hurdler: useful handicap chaser: won at Uttoxeter (by ½ length from Sizing Codelco) on sole start in 2018/19: stays 25f: acts on good to firm and heavy going. *Katy Price*

MINELLA CHARMER (IRE) 8 b.g. King's Theatre (IRE) – Kim Hong (IRE) **c–** (Charnwood Forest (IRE)) [2018/19 c–, h118x: c25.5gF h25.4spu h18.9v³ h16.4v* Mar 16] **h131 x** useful-looking gelding: has had breathing operation: useful handicap hurdler: won at Newcastle (by 1¾ lengths from Dali Mail) in March: lightly-raced chaser: stays 21f: acts on heavy going: has worn tongue tie: often let down by jumping. *James Moffatt*

MINELLA DADDY (IRE) 9 b.g. Flemensfirth (USA) – Old Moon (IRE) (Old Vic) **c134** [2018/19 c138, h–: c24g² c23.8g c23.8s c24g⁶ c24.5spu c28.4m* Apr 20] strong gelding: **h–** winning hurdler: useful handicap chaser: won at Haydock (by 4 lengths from Lough Derg Farmer) in April: stays 3½m: acts on good to firm and heavy going: usually wears headgear: tried in tongue tie. *Peter Bowen*

MINELLA EXAMINER 6 b.g. Beat Hollow – Bold Fire (Bold Edge) [2018/19 h20v⁵ **h–** h19.2s Jan 27] runner-up in Irish point on debut: weakened tamely both starts over hurdles. *Warren Greatrex*

MINELLA FIVEO (IRE) 11 b.g. Westerner – Autumn Sky (IRE) (Roselier (FR)) **c–** [2018/19 c–, h98: h16.2g⁶ h20.3g⁶ h17.2g⁶ h17.2dF h17.1d² h15.7g⁶ h16.2g² h16.2s h16.7s* **h110** h18.6d* h20.6d⁶ h16.7g³ Mar 29] well-made gelding: has had breathing operation: maiden pointer: fair handicap hurdler: won at Market Rasen in December (seller) and January (conditionals): fell only chase start: stays 3m: acts on heavy going: has worn cheekpieces. *Sue Smith*

MINELLAFORLEISURE (IRE) 11 br.g. King's Theatre (IRE) – Dame Foraine (FR) **c–** (Raintrap) [2018/19 c–, h113: h16.4g h21g h15.8g³ h15.3g h16.6g⁴ h16g h16.8gbd Apr 17] **h117** lengthy gelding: fairly useful handicap hurdler: third in lady riders event at Huntingdon in November: well held completed start over fences: unproven beyond 17f: acts on good to soft going. *Alex Hales*

MINELLA FOR ME (IRE) 9 b.g. King's Theatre (IRE) – Irish Mystics (IRE) (Ali- **c121** Royal (IRE)) [2018/19 c107, h–: c20.3g* c18g³ c19.1g² c24.2g* c24s* c25.3g⁶ Apr 17] **h–** good-topped gelding: has had breathing operation: lightly-raced hurdler: fairly useful handicap chaser: won at Southwell (novice) early in season, Wetherby in February and Kempton in March: stays 3m: acts on soft going: tried in hood: wears tongue tie. *Tom George*

MINELLA FRIEND (IRE) 10 b.g. King's Theatre (IRE) – Don't Waste It (IRE) (Mister **c–** Lord (USA)) [2018/19 c25.3g⁵ May 4] smallish, leggy gelding: multiple point winner: **h–** fairly useful form over hurdles for Evan Williams in 2013/14: 5/1, well held in hunter at Cheltenham on chasing debut: stays 21f: acts on good to soft going. *Mrs Kim Smyly*

MINELLA GATHERING (IRE) 10 b.g. Old Vic – A Plus Ma Puce (FR) (Turgeon **c–** (USA)) [2018/19 h91x: h19.5v⁴ h23.4d⁵ h23d h23.1d c19.7spu Mar 11] compact gelding: **h72 x** maiden pointer: poor handicap hurdler nowadays: pulled up in novice handicap on chasing debut: stays 25f: acts on heavy going: often let down by jumping. *Paul Henderson*

MINELLA INDO (IRE) 6 b.g. Beat Hollow – Carrigeen Lily (IRE) (Supreme **h147** Leader) [2018/19 h20s³ h24d² h24d* Mar 15]

'It's Cheltenham we're going to, not Lourdes.' Irish trainer Philip Dempsey was apparently not expecting miracles from his runner Derrinross in the Spa Novices' Hurdle, though Derrinross had a better chance than many in an open-looking twenty-runner field for the Spa which is gaining a reputation at the Festival for producing surprises, if not exactly 'miraculous' results. Berties Dream, Very Wood and, in 2018, Kilbricken Storm, all won the race at 33/1, while the latest winner Minella Indo was a 50/1-shot, only two in the field starting at longer odds. The nature of the Spa, or Albert Bartlett to give it its branded title, makes it susceptible to upsets. A well-run race over a stiff three miles (conditions on the soft side were also a factor in the latest renewal) makes it a test which many of the novices will not have faced before, and it turned out that a thorough test of stamina suited Minella Indo better than all his rivals. He was among many in the field who still looked open to improvement beforehand, having run only twice over hurdles after one start in a bumper, and he had already improved a good deal from his first to his second start over hurdles. The main factor in his being virtually overlooked in the betting was doubtless his

Albert Bartlett Novices' Hurdle (Spa), Cheltenham—50/1-maiden Minella Indo becomes the longest-priced winner in the race's 15-year history as he holds off the favourite Commander of Fleet (right)

maiden status under Rules—he was the only one in the line-up without a previous win over hurdles—while he also needed to turn around form with one of the leading contenders Allaho who had been an impressive four-length winner from Minella Indo in a Grade 3 contest, the Surehaul Mercedes-Benz Novices' Hurdle, at Clonmel the previous month. Minella Indo made the running on that occasion, stepped up to three miles after he had finished a promising third when given a considerate introduction to hurdling over two and a half miles in a maiden at Limerick at the end of December.

The 4/1 favourite for the Spa was Commander of Fleet, representing Gigginstown and Gordon Elliott, who had beaten another of the leading Irish contenders Rhinestone in the Grade 1 Nathaniel Lacy & Partners Solicitors Novices' Hurdle at Leopardstown, while the main home-trained hopes were Birchdale and Lisnagar Oscar, winners of Grade 2 contests at Cheltenham and Haydock respectively on their latest starts. With Derrinross making the running, Minella Indo showed prominently, travelling notably well throughout, and jumped into the lead three out at the top of the hill. Shaken up and brought to the stands rail turning into the straight, Minella Indo briefly looked under threat of losing the lead to Allaho before Commander of Fleet emerged as his main challenger at the final flight. Minella Indo stayed on strongly to maintain his advantage to the line, finishing two lengths clear of the favourite who in turn pulled seven clear of Allaho in an Irish-trained one, two, three. Dickie Diver, a stable companion of the disappointing Birchdale, fared best of the home team ahead of Lisnagar Oscar in fifth. The first three all met again in the War of Attrition Novices' Hurdle (branded as the Irish Daily Mirror) at Punchestown where Minella Indo was a 5/1-shot this time, though still at longer odds than Allaho (sent off favourite) and Commander of Fleet. Minella Indo confirmed his superiority over those rivals and became the first Spa winner to win the Punchestown race. He again looked better the further he went, going on approaching the last after Allaho had made the running and beating his old rival by two lengths with Carefully Selected a length and a half back in third, Willie Mullins saddling both the placed horses. Commander of Fleet was pulled up soon after the fifth, reportedly having lost his action.

Minella Indo was a second winner of the week at Cheltenham for his trainer Henry de Bromhead and jockey Rachael Blackmore who had been successful with the impressive A Plus Tard in the Close Brothers Novices' Handicap Chase. They were Blackmore's first Cheltenham Festival winners, her victory on Minella Indo

Irish Daily Mirror Novices' Hurdle (War of Attrition), Punchestown—Minella Indo shows his Cheltenham win to be no fluke with another fine staying display to beat Allaho (No.1)

coming just a day after Bryony Frost had become the first female jockey to ride a Grade 1 winner over jumps at the meeting when successful on Frodon in the Ryanair Chase, in which Blackmore finished fourth on Monalee for Minella Indo's owner Barry Maloney. De Bromhead, who himself enjoyed his best season, finishing third in the Irish trainers' championship, supplied the majority of Blackmore's ninety winners in Ireland where she led the jockeys' championship for a good part of the season before finishing runner-up to Paul Townend. Initially with ambitions to become a vet, Blackmore's first winner under Rules had come as an amateur in 2011 but her riding career gained momentum once she turned professional in March 2015, when she became only the second female jump jockey in Ireland to do so. A first big success came in the Leinster National on Abolitionist in March 2017 and she ended that season as the first female winner of Ireland's conditional jockeys title before riding out her claim in June 2017. Blackmore had three winners at the 2018 Punchestown Festival which was also where Minella Indo had made his Rules debut, finishing third in a newcomers bumper (the future Baring Bingham winner City Island was runner-up) having won his only start in points earlier that spring.

Minella Indo (IRE) (b.g. 2013)	Beat Hollow (b 1997)	Sadler's Wells (b 1981)	Northern Dancer Fairy Bridge
		Wemyss Bight (b 1990)	Dancing Brave Bahamian
	Carrigeen Lily (IRE) (b 1991)	Supreme Leader (b 1982)	Bustino Princess Zena
		Carrigeensharragh (gr 1976)	Walshford Rock Forest

The latest Spa winner shares the familiar 'Minella' prefix with plenty of other good jumpers that have passed through the John Nallen academy (see the essay on Minella Foru in *Chasers & Hurdlers 2015/16*), National Hunt Chase winner Minella Rocco another to be successful at the Festival in recent years. However, it's the 'Carrigeen' name which predominates in Minella Indo's pedigree as he was bred by the Lalor family who stamp most of their home breds with that prefix (Minella Indo was bought by Nallen, for whom he won his point, as a foal for €24,000). Minella Indo's dam Carrigeen Lily was a fairly useful chaser whose four wins all came at between nineteen and twenty-one furlongs. Like Minella Indo, most of her other winning offspring graduated from success in points to winning under Rules, chief among them the smart Gary Moore-trained chaser Benatar (by Beneficial) from the latest season Benatar (by Beneficial). Also by Beneficial are the modest two-mile hurdle winner Carrigeen Lantana and the fairly useful Irish chaser Carrigeen Lechuga who stayed twenty-nine furlongs, while Minella Indo is a close relative of the bumper winner Carrigeen Lonicera (by Old Vic, a son of Sadler's Wells like Minella Indo's sire

Beat Hollow), she too a winning pointer who would have stayed further than three miles over fences. Minella Indo's grandam Carrigeensharragh won a total of ten races over hurdles and fences and was a fairly useful chaser who stayed twenty-five furlongs. Besides Minella Indo's dam, her other winner Carrigeen Kerria, also a winning hurdler and fairly useful chaser at up to twenty-five furlongs, has become a broodmare of note. Among several at least fairly useful jumpers, she produced the Grade 1 Dr P. J. Moriarty Novices' Chase winner Carrigeen Victor, and has more recently become grandam of the 2016 Irish Grand National winner Rogue Angel on whom Rachael Blackmore finished third in the Kerry National in the latest season. Carrigeensharragh, who ran in two Irish Grand Nationals herself (sixth to Bentom Boy in 1984) is also the grandam of Chicago Grey who provided Gordon Elliott with his first Cheltenham Festival winner when successful in the 2011 National Hunt Chase. The Irish Grand National and the National Hunt Chase are just the sort of races that could feature in the sturdy Minella Indo's own programme in seasons to come as he seems sure to be suited by further than three miles when he goes over fences. Raced only on soft or good to soft ground, he has already achieved a lot from just five starts under Rules and looks sure to give his trainer Henry de Bromhead and jockey Rachael Blackmore plenty more chances of success in top races when stamina is at a premium. *Henry de Bromhead, Ireland*

MINELLA MELODY (IRE) 5 b.m. Flemensfirth (USA) – Cottage Theatre (IRE) **b107** (King's Theatre (IRE)) [2018/19 b18s* b17d² Apr 4] €65,000 3-y-o: lengthy, rather unfurnished mare: second foal: half-sister to bumper winner Forty One Winks (by Getaway): dam unraced sister to smart hurdler (stayed 2¾m) Glens Melody: easy winner of mares maiden point on debut: useful form in bumpers: won maiden at Gowran (by 12 lengths from Miss Pernickety) in March: placed after in Nickel Coin Mares' National Hunt Flat Race at Aintree 2¼ lengths by The Glancing Queen) and EBF (Mares) INH Flat Race at Punchestown (9¾ lengths behind Gypsy Island), latter shortly after end of British season. *Henry de Bromhead, Ireland*

MINELLA MOJO (IRE) 7 b.g. King's Theatre (IRE) – On The Horizon (IRE) (Definite **h99** Article) [2018/19 h20g⁴ h21.6m³ Jul 14] sixth foal: closely related/half-brother to 3 winners, including fairly useful 3m hurdle winner/winning pointer M M D Sizer (by Shirocco): dam, 1¼m winner, half-sister to Triumph Hurdle winner Rare Holiday: point winner: modest form over hurdles: better effort when fourth in maiden at Worcester. *Chris Down*

MINELLA ON LINE (IRE) 10 b.g. King's Theatre (IRE) – Bally Bolshoi (IRE) (Bob **c130 x** Back (USA)) [2018/19 c133x, h116: c22.4s^pu c24g² Dec 29] well-made gelding: fairly **h–** useful hurdler: useful handicap chaser: second at Doncaster (1½ lengths behind Treackle Tart) in December: stays 3¼m: acts on heavy going: has worn headgear, including in 2018/19: tried in tongue tie: often let down by jumping. *Oliver Sherwood*

MINELLA ROCCO (IRE) 9 b.g. Shirocco (GER) – Petralona (USA) (Alleged (USA)) **c– x** [2018/19 c159x, h–: c25.3d⁵ h23.1d c25s^pu c34.3g^pu c29d^pu Apr 22] big gelding: has had **h–** breathing operation: winning hurdler: top-class chaser at best, looked one with major problems in 2018/19: has worn cheekpieces, including in 2018/19: usually wears tongue tie: often let down by jumping. *Jonjo O'Neill*

MINELLA SCAMP (IRE) 10 b.g. King's Theatre (IRE) – Forgotten Star (IRE) (Don't **c124** Forget Me) [2018/19 c114, h–: c21.7g* c23.8g^F Jun 23] maiden hurdler: fairly useful **h–** handicap chaser: won at Towcester early in season: stays 2¾m: acts on heavy going: usually tongue tied (not for both starts in 2018/19). *Fergal O'Brien*

MINELLA STYLE (IRE) 9 b.g. King's Theatre (IRE) – Rose of The Erne (IRE) **c–** (Presenting) [2018/19 c–, h94: h21.7g h25.8g Jun 5] off mark in Irish points at fourth **h–** attempt: modest maiden hurdler, well held both starts in 2018/19: well held completed start over fences: stays 19f: tried in cheekpieces: has joined Claire Dyson. *Dai Williams*

MINELLA SUITE (IRE) 8 br.g. Oscar (IRE) – Ballymaguirelass (IRE) (Phardante **c–** (FR)) [2018/19 c–, h–: c21.2m Jun 29] big, lengthy gelding: point winner: maiden hurdler: **h–** modest form over fences, in cheekpieces when well held sole start in 2018/19: should stay beyond 2m: acts on soft going. *Rose Dobbin*

MINELLATILLMORNING (IRE) 7 gr.g. King's Theatre (IRE) – Line Kendie (FR) **c108** (Bonnet Rouge (FR)) [2018/19 h109: c23.6s c18.2s^F Feb 4] placed on completed starts in **h–** Irish points: fair form over hurdles: running to similar level when falling fatally 3 out in novice handicap chase at Taunton: stayed 19f: acted on heavy going. *Neil Mulholland*

MINELLA VOUCHER 8 b.g. King's Theatre (IRE) – All Rise (GER) (Goofalik (USA)) c78
[2018/19 c89, h81: h16s h18.5s c16.1d⁴ c17.2d³ Feb 17] lengthy gelding: poor hurdler: h–
modest form at best over fences: stays 19f: acts on heavy going: has worn tongue tie,
including in 2018/19. *Alexandra Dunn*

MINELLA WARRIOR (IRE) 7 b.g. King's Theatre (IRE) – Bobbi's Venture (IRE) h134
(Bob Back (USA)) [2018/19 h19g* h19.9g* h19.5d⁴ h25d² h24.1d* Mar 19] good sort: has
had breathing operation: runner-up in Irish point: useful form over hurdles: won novices at
Warwick in May and Uttoxeter in September, and handicap at Wetherby (by 3¼ lengths
from Skipthescales) in March: stays 25f: acts on good to soft going: in tongue tie last 3
starts. *Kim Bailey*

MINELLA WHISPER 8 b.g. Kayf Tara – Celtic Native (IRE) (Be My Native (USA)) h–
[2018/19 h102: h25g May 22] Irish point winner: fair hurdler, well held sole start in
2018/19: stays 3¼m: acts on soft going: usually races prominently. *Richard Phillips*

MINER DISTRACTION 11 b.m. Desert King (IRE) – Miner Yours (Miner's Lamp) c–
[2018/19 h–: h21.2m c20.9gᵖᵘ May 31] sturdy mare: maiden hurdler: pulled up in novice h–
handicap on chasing debut: tried in tongue tie. *Debra Hamer*

MINERFORTYNINER (IRE) 10 br.g. Catcher In The Rye (IRE) – Hungry Eyes (IRE) c98
(Old Vic) [2018/19 h21.6d⁶ h19.7s² h23.5s h19.2d⁴ c25.2g³ c24g⁴ Apr 10] strong gelding: h106
multiple point winner: fair form over hurdles: well held both starts in chases, though
shaped better than result on first: should be suited by 3m: acts on soft going: wears tongue
tie. *Giles Smyly*

MINE'S A PINT 7 b.g. Network (GER) – Ryme Bere (FR) (Until Sundown (USA)) c112
[2018/19 h23.9d⁶ h16.5dᶠ h16.8d⁵ h20v h19.2v⁵ c19.7g* c20.2g³ c20.2g² Apr 14] £6,200 h94
5-y-o, £6,000 6-y-o: sturdy gelding: first foal: dam, placed up to 21f over hurdles/fences in
France, half-sister to smart French hurdler/high-class chaser (stayed 27f) Matinee Lover:
off mark in points at fourth attempt: modest form over hurdles: fair form over fences: won
novice at Plumpton in February: stays 2½m: acts on heavy going: wears hood/tongue tie.
Keiran Burke

MIN (FR) 8 b.g. Walk In The Park (IRE) – Phemyka (FR) (Saint Estephe (FR)) c174
[2018/19 c169, h–: c20.2d* c17g* c15.9s⁵ c19.9d* Apr 5] h–
'It's an awful lot easier when Altior isn't around.' Ruby Walsh's initial
summing up of Min's performance in the Melling Chase (branded as the JLT Chase)
at Aintree in April scarcely did justice to a magnificent performance by a chaser
who has been consistently underrated by some. Min really showed British racegoers
what he is capable of when finally winning his first Grade 1 in Britain, handing out
a twenty-length beating to Politologue who had just edged him out in the same
race twelve months earlier. Min's three other defeats on earlier visits to Britain had
come in Grade 1s at the Cheltenham Festival, all won with top drawer displays by
Altior, one in the Supreme Novices' Hurdle and two in the Queen Mother Champion
Chase. Min came second to Altior in a very strong edition of the Supreme and
second to him in their first meeting over fences in the Queen Mother Champion
Chase, coincidentally beaten seven lengths each time but putting up performances
that would have been good enough to have won several recent editions of those two
races. Min had always looked capable of the tip-top performance he recorded in the
latest Melling Chase, in which he put behind him a subdued showing three weeks
earlier in his second Queen Mother Champion Chase in which he failed to give his
running (fifth behind Altior) after racing keenly for a long way under restraint. The
patient tactics were a change from those usually adopted as connections had 'wanted
to try something new' but Min's trainer Willie Mullins concluded that the horse had
'sulked when we didn't let him do what he wanted to do.'
      Min started 2/1 favourite for the Melling Chase, narrowly preferred to
Waiting Patiently and Politologue, the three of them dominating the betting in a
six-runner line-up which, unusually, had no representative from the Ryanair Chase,
the equivalent event at the Cheltenham Festival (Politologue and Waiting Patiently
had both bypassed Cheltenham to wait for Aintree). Min was allowed free rein in
the Melling and the return to front-running made him look like a new horse as he
jumped boldly out in front under a motionless Ruby Walsh before easily stretching
clear after a good jump at the third last and thereafter always being in complete
control. Measuring the last fence superbly, Min sauntered home from Politologue

John Durkan Memorial Punchestown Chase, Punchestown—a fourth win in six years for Ruby Walsh and Willie Mullins as Min proves far too strong for the Gigginstown-owned pair Shattered Love (noseband) and Balko des Flos (centre)

who had been left behind from two out but still finished nine lengths ahead of third-placed Waiting Patiently who could make no impression. Hell's Kitchen, fourth in the Queen Mother Champion Chase, filled the same position—though beaten much further—in the Melling, with the 2016 Melling winner God's Own, who had been struck into and pulled up in the Queen Mother Champion Chase, the only other finisher. Min's performance was the best seen all season in a steeplechase over two and a half miles, just surpassing, at least the way Timeform reads the form-book, Cyrname's demolition of a very good Ascot Chase field (he won by seventeen lengths from Waiting Patiently, with Politologue fourth).

Min may well have been feeling the effects of his exertions at Cheltenham and Aintree when beaten four lengths by his rejuvenated stablemate Un de Sceaux in the Champion Chase at the Punchestown Festival (which took place shortly after the end of the British season). Odds-on Min travelled smoothly enough but wasn't in quite the same brilliant form as Aintree (he had been a below-form fourth behind Un de Sceaux in the same Punchestown race twelve months earlier, running as if races at the Cheltenham and Aintree Festivals might have taken the edge off him). Min won on both his other appearances in Ireland during his latest campaign, adding two more Grade 1s to his Racing Post Novices' Chase, the Boxing Day highlight he had won at Leopardstown in his curtailed first season over fences (he missed the Arkle—and another meeting with Altior—after suffering a 'little stress fracture' while being prepared for that race). Min reappeared in the latest season in the two-and-a-half-mile John Durkan Memorial Punchestown Chase in December when, travelling strongly as usual and jumping soundly, he was always handy until quickening clear before the last to win by a length and a half and two and a half lengths from Shattered Love and front-running Balko des Flos, both of whom had won at the Cheltenham Festival the previous season.

Min bypassed the Grade 1 Paddy's Rewards Club Chase at Leopardstown's Christmas meeting (a race he had lost in the stewards' room the previous year) but he dropped back to around two miles for the newly-upgraded Ladbrokes Dublin Chase at the Dublin Racing Festival in February and made the most of a straightforward opportunity to see off Ordinary World and British-trained challenger Saint Calvados by six lengths and the same (the final fence on both circuits was omitted because of low sun). The occasion was marred by an incident before the field had even reached the first when the veteran Special Tiara broke down so badly that he had to be destroyed (Ruby Walsh felt that Min's disappointing effort in the Queen Mother Champion Chase might have been partly accounted for by his being jarred up as a result of the unseasonably resilient underfoot conditions that prevailed at the Dublin Racing Festival, about which there is more in the essay on Bellshill). Min's Cheltenham Festival target came down to a late choice between the Queen Mother Champion Chase and the Ryanair Chase (under a new rule, connections are no longer able to declare a horse, at the final stage, for more than one race at the Festival).

573

Min's performance was one of a number of disappointments at the meeting for his multi-millionaire owners the Riccis who drew a blank at the Festival for the first time since 2011 (odds-on Benie des Dieux fell at the last with the David Nicholson Mares' Hurdle at her mercy). As BetBright's executive chairman, Rich Ricci also found himself in the firing line at the Cheltenham Festival after the company had ceased trading the previous week, a move that led initially to the voiding of ante-post bets with the company (outstanding multiple bets with winning legs were settled as winning bets). The Gambling Commission received a number of complaints about the decision on the grounds that BetBright (which had not 'gone bust') had 'shirked their obligations'. There was a feeling that the 'consumer rights' of punters ought to be protected in such situations. In response, 888Sport, who had bought part of BetBright, said they would honour existing Cheltenham ante-post bets, while Ricci, who took the brunt of the criticism on social media at the time, was behind a scheme in which BetVictor were subsequently involved in reviving the rest of the unsettled ante-post wagers (with Rich Ricci reportedly putting in considerable funds of his own to secure the favoured outcome for BetBright's punters).

The latest Cheltenham Festival also marked the beginning of electronically-generated official times for races over jumps, a big step in the right direction for the sport which has lagged behind for far too long. The break-beam technology will eventually be rolled out to all jumps courses in Britain. More accurate race distances have been available since 2015 (the distances of jumps races were formerly advertised to the nearest half furlong) but there are still instances of rail movements not always being reported (Southwell one of the main culprits), or being reported incorrectly. Rail movements can also add significantly to the race distance published in the *Racing Calendar*, Market Rasen and Fontwell among the main perpetrators in this respect, with extra yardage sometimes extending the distances of races by up to three hundred yards from their advertised distance (something connections perhaps ought to be more aware of). Timeform reporters have taken hand times over the years for every race over jumps, including sectional times, but the frequent repositioning of rails, not to mention imprecise or inaccurate distance measurements, held up plans for Timeform to publish its computer timefigures for jumps. The rule changes about more accurate measurement made by the British Horseracing Authority, and the wholesale remeasuring of courses (following an investigation by Timeform in the 2014/15 season which revealed alarming inaccuracies), enabled Timeform to publish timefigures for the first time in the 2017/18 season (along with figures for some Irish tracks where historical data provides confidence to do so). The strength of 'time', as a guide to true merit, is that a very fast time performance establishes a horse without question as a good horse, sometimes before it can be recognised by other means. Min's timefigures firmly established him as a top performer from

Ladbrokes Dublin Chase, Leopardstown—a disappointing turnout for this newly-installed Grade 1 contest, with Min proving far too good on the extended run-in for Ordinary World (stripes) and Saint Calvados (noseband)

JLT Chase (Melling), Aintree—
a scintillating performance from Min with prominent tactics back in use

an early stage in his chasing career and, in the two seasons for which timefigures have been published, no other horse has recorded four timeratings over 165 on the Timeform scale. Three of those were recorded by Min in the 2017/18 season, when winning a three-runner minor event at Gowran on his reappearance and the inaugural Dublin Chase at Leopardstown (which was Grade 2 at the time), and when he was second to Altior in the Queen Mother Champion Chase. Min recorded timeratings of 167, 167 and 170 respectively, but those performances on the clock were bettered in the latest season by Min's timerating of 174, the best recorded by any horse over any distance all season, when he annihilated his field in the Melling Chase at Aintree.

		Walk In The Park (IRE) (b 2002)	Montjeu (b 1996)	Sadler's Wells Floripedes
Min (FR) (b.g. 2011)			Classic Park (b 1994)	Robellino Wanton
		Phemyka (FR) (b 1996)	Saint Estephe (b 1982)	Top Ville Une Tornade
			Stormyka (b 1990)	Akarad Stormy Scene

Min is a well-made individual who always had the looks to suggest he would make up into a chaser. His sire Walk In The Park, also the sire of Douvan, has been covering more than two hundred mares a season since being transferred from France to join Coolmore's jumping roster in early-2016. Walk In The Park was second in the Derby and Min's pedigree on the distaff side is principally a Flat one as well, the best jumper to come from the family before Min being the smart if temperamental staying chaser Stormez who was a half-brother to Min's grandam Stormyka who won three races in the French Provinces at up to eleven furlongs.

Mrs S. Ricci's "Min"

Min's dam Phemyka won a handicap at Vittel in the Provinces over an extended ten furlongs and Min is the fourth winner she has bred, following the Flat winners Satwa Princess and Belamage (both by Daliapour) and Gaone (by Sagacity), the last-named also successful at nineteen furlongs over hurdles. Min's tendency to race freely has tended to lead to the conclusion—borne out by his pedigree—that he is likely to find two and a half miles the limit of his stamina. Interestingly, though, connections have mooted the possibility that he might go for the King George VI Chase at Kempton in the next season. Min has so far raced only on good going or softer (he acts on heavy) but he should not be inconvenienced if he encounters top-of-the-ground conditions on Boxing Day at well-drained Kempton (such conditions might even favour him). Interestingly, if Min is trained for the King George he could well be set for another meeting with Altior, with that horse also being stepped up in trip in the next season when a tilt at the Kempton highlight is said to be very much on the agenda. Whether or not he runs in the King George, the sound-jumping Min should have another good season for Closutton which starts the campaign awash with high-class chasers at all distances. The exuberant Min has worn ear plugs on his three visits to the Cheltenham Festival, but they were left out for the Melling Chase. *W. P. Mullins, Ireland*

MING DYNASTY (FR) 7 b.g. King's Best (USA) – Memoire (FR) (Sadler's Wells (USA)) [2018/19 h16g h16.7d h19d h20d h16d² h16s³ h16d⁵ h16g* h16s h16.3s⁶ h15.7m Apr 20] very smart at best on Flat, stays 1½m: fairly useful handicap hurdler: won at Naas in February: may prove best around 2m: acts on good to soft going: wears tongue tie. *Gavin Patrick Cromwell, Ireland* **h117**

MINIATURE DAFFODIL (IRE) 4 b.g. Thewayyouare (USA) – Queen of Stars (USA) (Green Desert (USA)) [2018/19 h16d Dec 13] modest on Flat, stays 1¼m: tailed off in juvenile maiden on hurdling/stable debut. *Jo Davis* **h–**

MINI DREAMS 7 b.m. Josr Algarhoud (IRE) – Mini Minster (Minster Son) [2018/19 h–, b–: h16.2g⁶ h15.7g³ h16.2m h16.2v⁶ h24dᵖᵘ Apr 6] has had breathing operation: poor form over hurdles: sometimes in tongue tie. *Peter Atkinson* **h70**

MINISTERFORSPORT (IRE) 8 b.g. Dubai Destination (USA) – Lady Alacoque (IRE) (Anshan) [2018/19 h137: c16dᶠ c19d³ c16s⁵ Jan 24] multiple point winner: useful form over hurdles: similar form over fences: best effort when third in maiden at Naas (4 lengths behind A Plus Tard) in December: will be suited by 2½m+: acts on heavy going: tried in tongue tie: remains with potential as a chaser. *Noel O'Neill, Ireland* **c139 p h–**

MINMORE GREY (IRE) 10 gr.g. Primary (USA) – Hopeful Memory (IRE) (Roselier (FR)) [2018/19 c–§, h–: c28.5d Nov 19] maiden pointer: little form under Rules: has worn headgear: temperamental. *Nick Lampard* **c– § h–**

MINMORE PRESENT (IRE) 8 ch.g. Presenting – Ballagh Dawn (IRE) (Buckskin (FR)) [2018/19 c107: c21.2d³ c23.6dᵖᵘ c23.6d⁴ Mar 13] point winner: maiden chaser, no form in 2018/19. *Gary Moore* **c84**

MINNIE ESCAPE 7 b.m. Getaway (GER) – Minnie Hill (Oscar (IRE)) [2018/19 b–: b15.7s⁴ b15.8s h17.7sᶠ h16.5s⁶ h15.3g h17.7v⁴ Mar 16] poor form in bumpers: none over hurdles. *Victor Dartnall* **h– b74**

MINNIE MILAN (IRE) 10 b.m. Milan – Shiminnie (IRE) (Bob Back (USA)) [2018/19 h97: h22.1m² Jun 29] sturdy mare: modest handicap hurdler: stays 3¼m: acts on good to firm and good to soft going: usually in cheekpieces: often in tongue tie: front runner/races prominently. *Barbara Butterworth* **h92**

MINNIE MUSTANG 11 b.m. Midnight Legend – Mustang Molly (Soldier Rose) [2018/19 h20.6m⁵ Apr 21] well held in bumpers/maiden hurdles, off nearly 5 years prior to sole start in 2018/19. *Andrew Martin* **h–**

MINNIES SECRET (IRE) 7 b.m. Beneficial – Caltra Royale (IRE) (Moscow Society (USA)) [2018/19 h20.2s c17.4g⁵ c18.2d⁴ c18.2d² c19d c20d c20g⁵ c19.7d⁴ c19.4g² Jan 12] second foal: sister to fair hurdler/chaser (2m-2½m winner) Rosie Alice: dam (h97), 2¾m hurdle winner/winning pointer, sister to fairly useful 2½m hurdle winner Mask of Darkness and half-sister to fairly useful hurdler (stayed 3m) Alpha Royale: bumper winner: fair hurdler: fairly useful maiden chaser: stays 2½m: acts on soft going: often wears cheekpieces. *Charles Byrnes, Ireland* **c117 h–**

MINSTREL ROYAL 9 b.g. Kayf Tara – Close Harmony (Bustino) [2018/19 h109: h22.7gᵖᵘ h20.3gᵖᵘ h19.5v h24.4gᵖᵘ Nov 30] strong gelding: will make a chaser: fair hurdler, no form in 2018/19: tried in cheekpieces: wears tongue tie. *Philip Kirby* **h–**

MINSTREL SONG 6 br.g. Dark Angel (IRE) – Sing Acapella (IRE) (Cape Cross (IRE)) [2018/19 b16g b20g b16.6g h16gᴳ h19.9m⁴ Sep 6] first foal: dam unraced half-sister to fairly useful hurdler (2m/17f winner) Dynamic Drive: well held in 2 bumpers: modest form over hurdles: best effort when fourth in maiden at Tramore. *John Joseph Hanlon, Ireland* **h89 b–**

MINT GOLD (IRE) 5 b.g. Gold Well – Lady Flyer (IRE) (Eagle Eyed (USA)) [2018/19 b16.2g³ b16.7g⁶ h16.2g⁶ h16.2g h17g* h16.2d³ Mar 26] €30,000 3-y-o: fifth foal: half-brother to a winner on Flat in Italy by Le Vie dei Colori: dam of little account on Flat/ran once over hurdles: modest form in bumpers: fair form over hurdles: won novice at Carlisle in February: in tongue tie last 3 starts. *Lucinda Russell* **h109 b83**

MIN TIKY (IRE) 7 b.m. King's Theatre (IRE) – Kon Tiky (FR) (Perrault) [2018/19 h–: h20.3gᵖᵘ h19g h15.9m⁵ h19.2d⁵ h19.7d Jan 22] has had breathing operation: poor maiden hurdler: usually in headgear: tried in tongue tie. *Mark Bradstock* **h70**

MIRANDA (IRE) 4 b.f. Camelot – Great Artist (FR) (Desert Prince (IRE)) [2018/19 h15.8d* h15.3s* h15.3gᵖᵘ Mar 25] half-sister to fairly useful/unreliable hurdler Vercingetorix (2m-2½m winner, by Dylan Thomas) and French hurdler Hear My Voice (17f/2¼m winner, by Shirocco): fairly useful on Flat, stays 1½m: fairly useful form over hurdles: won fillies juvenile at Ludlow in February and mares novice at Wincanton in March. *Paul Nicholls* **h115**

MIRO (IRE) 7 b.g. Rock of Gibraltar (IRE) – Mission Secrete (IRE) (Galileo (IRE)) [2018/19 h16g⁴ h23.9g³ h20.2g h23.1s⁴ h20.5g³ Dec 6] has had breathing operation: fair handicap hurdler: left Gordon Elliott after third start: stays 23f: acts on soft going: has worn headgear: sometimes in tongue tie. *David Pipe* **h104**

MIRSAALE 9 ch.g. Sir Percy – String Quartet (IRE) (Sadler's Wells (USA)) [2018/19 **h118 §** h136: h16.2g⁴ h16.2g⁶ Aug 18] smallish, angular gelding: useful on Flat, stays 2¼m: useful handicap hurdler, below form both starts in sphere in 2018/19: stays 19f: acts on soft going: has worn cheekpieces: temperamental. *Keith Dalgleish*

MIRS CHOICE (IRE) 9 br.m. Coroner (IRE) – Dummy Run (IRE) (Glacial Storm **c95** (USA)) [2018/19 c74, h–: c23s² c22.6d c25.8m c24g³ c20g⁶ c23g Aug 15] point winner: **h–** once-raced hurdler: modest maiden chaser: stays 3m: acts on soft going: wears headgear. *Tony Carroll*

MIRZAM (IRE) 5 gr.m. Mastercraftsman (IRE) – Luxie (IRE) (Acclamation) [2018/19 **h92** h74: h16g¹ h20s² May 25] fairly useful on Flat, stays 1½m: modest form over hurdles: likely to prove best short of 2½m when conditions are testing: acts on soft going. *Tom Symonds*

MISCHIEVIOUS MAX (IRE) 6 ch.g. Dubai Destination (USA) – Saabga (USA) **h–** (Woodman (USA)) [2018/19 h132, b95: h20g h19.7g h15.7v Dec 22] neat gelding: useful hurdler at best for Joseph Patrick O'Brien, below form all 3 starts in 2018/19. *Harriet Bethell*

MISDFLIGHT (IRE) 9 ch.g. Indian River (FR) – Jody's Girl (IRE) (Oscar (IRE)) **c96** [2018/19 h24s⁶ h23g h25g⁶ c25.3g c20.5d⁴ c23.6d² c27.5g³ Apr 14] modest handicap **h88** hurdler: modest maiden chaser: left John F. Gleeson after fourth start: stays 3½m: acts on good to soft going: usually wears headgear: has worn tongue tie. *Olly Murphy*

MISFITS (IRE) 8 b.g. Beneficial – Park Rose (IRE) (Roselier (FR)) [2018/19 c100, h–: **c109** c24.2g⁽ᵖᵘ⁾ h23.3g⁶ c24.2s* c24.5v⁴ h23.3s² h23.3v³ h24s h25g c31.9v² c30.6d² Apr 26] **h99** sturdy gelding: modest maiden hurdler: fair handicap chaser: won at Hexham in October: stays 4m: acts on heavy going: tried in hood: wears tongue tie: usually races towards rear. *Lucinda Russell*

MISKIN 10 b.g. Motivator – Castellina (USA) (Danzig Connection (USA)) [2018/19 **h83** h18.5g² h19d⁽ᵖᵘ⁾ Feb 28] modest on Flat, stays 16.5f: poor form over hurdles: better effort when second in seller at Newton Abbot: wears hood. *Robert Stephens*

MISS ADVENTURE (IRE) 7 b.m. Brian Boru – Blue Fire Lady (IRE) (Blueprint **h102 §** (IRE)) [2018/19 h105: h21m⁽ᵖᵘ⁾ h16.3m* h20.3g⁵ h15.8g³ Jun 20] lengthy, angular mare: placed both starts in Irish points: fair hurdler: won novice seller at Stratford early in season: stays 19f: acts on good to firm and heavy going: usually wears headgear: tried in tongue tie: front runner/races prominently: temperamental. *Phil Middleton*

MISS ALOUD (IRE) 5 br.m. Azamour (IRE) – Key Stage (IRE) (King's Best (USA)) **b87** [2018/19 b16g⁶ b16.2m² b17.3g² b16.9g³ b16g³ b16s⁽ʳᵒ⁾ b16d⁶ Dec 18] third foal: half-sister to winner Oak Bluffs (by Royal Applause): dam unraced: fair bumper performer: wears hood. *Gordon Elliott, Ireland*

MISS AMELIA 6 b.m. Midnight Legend – Miss Pross (Bob's Return (IRE)) [2018/19 c–, **c84** h88, b–: c20.1d⁽ᵖᵘ⁾ h20.1s⁽ᵖᵘ⁾ c17.4s⁴ h16.6g² c17.2d* c16.4s⁴ c15.6g² Apr 15] rather leggy **h83** mare: has had breathing operation: poor maiden hurdler: poor handicap chaser: won at Market Rasen in February: unproven beyond 17f: acts on soft going. *Mark Walford*

MISS ANTIPOVA 7 b.m. Pasternak – Herballistic (Rolfe (USA)) [2018/19 b17.7g⁵ **h–** b15.7m b15.8d h16.8g Apr 5] has had breathing operation: half-sister to winning hurdler/ **b–** fairly useful chaser Quel Ballistic (15f-3¼m winner, by Kayf Tara) and modest hurdler Miniballist (2¾m winner, by Tragic Role): dam, (b72) ran twice in bumpers, half-sister to top-class staying chaser Go Ballistic: behind in bumpers/mares novice hurdle: usually in hood: temperament under suspicion. *Martin Keighley*

MISS AUSTEN (IRE) 4 b.f. Fame And Glory – Swap Shop (IRE) (Lord Americo) **b85** [2018/19 b16.5d³ Mar 11] half-sister to bumper winner/useful hurdler I'm To Blame (17f-2½m winner) and 2½m bumper winner/fairly useful 2¾m hurdle winner Showem Silver (both by Winged Love): dam unraced half-sister to useful hurdler/smart chaser (2m-2½m winner) Aran Concerto: well-backed 3/1, promise when third in mares bumper at Taunton (1½ lengths behind Miss Honey Ryder). *Hughie Morrison*

MISS BATTEN (IRE) 5 b.m. Vinnie Roe (IRE) – Awesome Miracle (IRE) (Supreme **h– p** Leader) [2018/19 h20.1s Nov 21] €18,000 3-y-o, £115,000 4-y-o: has had breathing operation: seventh foal: half-sister to 3 winners, including useful hurdler/smart chaser Shotgun Paddy (2½m-29f winner, by Brian Boru) and fairly useful hurdler/chaser Buster Thomas (19f/2½m winner, by Westerner): dam unraced: easy winner on debut in Irish point: in tongue tie, well beaten in novice hurdle: should do better. *Lucinda Russell*

MISS BENEFITZ (IRE) 8 ch.m. Beneficial – African Keys (IRE) (Quws) [2018/19 **h57 §**
h69§: h16.8g⁶ h16.7m Jun 22] sparely-made mare: has had breathing operation: poor
maiden hurdler: left Dan Skelton after first start: wears headgear: temperamental.
Laura Morgan

MISS BISCOTTI 11 ch.m. Emperor Fountain – Bellaccacia (IRE) (Beau Sher) [2018/19 **c90**
c90, h–: c23.8g c21.2g² c25.5gᵖᵘ c20.1g Jul 31] winning hurdler: modest handicap chaser: **h–**
stays 3¼m: acts on soft going: has worn cheekpieces. *Gemma Anderson*

MISS BROOKLYN 5 ch.m. Notnowcato – Serraval (FR) (Sanglamore (USA)) [2018/19 **b–**
b16g⁵ Oct 29] sixth foal: half-sister to bumper winner/fairly useful 2m hurdle winner Steel
City (by Act One) and bumper winner/fair 2m hurdle winner Miss Sassypants (by
Hernando), stayed 2½m: dam (h82), placed at 2m/17f over hurdles, 1m-1¼m winner on
Flat: 9/1, shaped as if needed experience when fifth of 6 in maiden bumper at Ayr.
Michael Easterby

MISS CLICK (IRE) 6 b.m. Getaway (GER) – Catu (IRE) (Snurge) [2018/19 b16g Jul 4] **b–**
€1,000 3-y-o: first foal: dam (h71), maiden hurdler, half-sister to fair hurdler/fairly useful
chaser (stayed 27f) Intac: pulled up all 3 starts in points: tongue tied when tailed off in
mares bumper. *Kevin Bishop*

MISS CONWAY 8 br.m. Midnight Legend – Miss Pross (Bob's Return (IRE)) [2018/19 **c91**
c103, h–: c15.6g c15.6g³ c19.2g⁶ Jul 8] neat mare: maiden hurdler: modest handicap **h–**
chaser: stays 2½m: acts on good to soft going: front runner/races prominently. *Mark Walford*

MISS CRICK 8 b.m. Midnight Legend – Kwaheri (Efisio) [2018/19 c117, h129: c20g³ **c120**
c21.2g² h19.2s³ h21.4g⁵ Nov 10] lengthy mare: fairly useful on Flat, stays 1½m: fairly **h121**
useful handicap hurdler: third at Fontwell in October: similar form over fences: stays 2¾m:
acts on soft going. *Alan King*

MISS DELIGHTED (IRE) 6 b.m. Getaway (GER) – Abhainn Ri (IRE) (Saddlers' Hall **h115**
(IRE)) [2018/19 b15.8s h20.7g⁵ h19.6d² h22.8d* h20.1g* Apr 15] €1,000 3-y-o: leggy **b–**
mare: second foal: dam (b77), lightly raced in bumpers, half-sister to fairly useful hurdler/
chaser (stayed 3m) Baily Rock: placed in points: fair form on first of 2 outings in bumpers
when trained by James Kieran King: fairly useful form over hurdles: won mares novices at
Haydock in March and Hexham in April: will stay 3m. *Oliver Greenall*

MISSED APPROACH (IRE) 9 b.g. Golan (IRE) – Polly's Dream (IRE) (Beau Sher) **c129**
[2018/19 c143, h–: c25.9s⁶ Dec 8] lengthy gelding: has had breathing operation: winning **h–**
hurdler: useful handicap chaser: very slowly away when sixth in Becher Chase at Aintree
on sole start in 2018/19: stays 33f: acts on heavy going: wears headgear: front runner/races
prominently. *Warren Greatrex*

MISSESGEEJAY 9 br.m. Beat All (USA) – Riverbank Rainbow (Overbury (IRE)) **h82**
[2018/19 h15.5d h16.4gʳᵒ h16.4v⁵ h16g Apr 10] little show over hurdles, off 31 months
prior to 2018/19 return: ran out second start. *Stella Barclay*

MISS GEMSTONE 5 ch.m. Midnight Legend – Real Treasure (Rainbow High) [2018/19 **b–**
b15.8g b16g Feb 19] first foal: dam (c112/h118) 2m-2¾m hurdle/chase winner: little show
in bumpers: tried in cheekpieces. *Kim Bailey*

MISS GOTAWAY 10 b.m. Midnight Legend – Strollaway (IRE) (Jurado (USA)) [2018/19 **c–**
c–, h–: h23.9s Feb 26] multiple point winner: modest form over hurdles: pulled up both **h–**
starts over fences: in tongue tie last 3 starts. *Polly Gundry*

MISS HAMDA (IRE) 5 gr.m. Mastercraftsman (IRE) – Erstwhile (FR) (Desert Prince **b–**
(IRE)) [2018/19 b72: b16.2g May 27] poor form in bumpers. *Brian Ellison*

MISS HERITAGE (IRE) 5 b.m. Pour Moi (IRE) – Haretha (IRE) (Alhaarth (IRE)) **b104**
[2018/19 b95p: b15.8m² b15.7d* b17d Apr 4] close-coupled mare: fairly useful bumper
performer: won conditionals/amateurs mares event at Catterick in March. *David Elsworth*

MISS HONEY RYDER (IRE) 6 b.m. Stowaway – Seesea (IRE) (Dr Massini (IRE)) **h97**
[2018/19 b–p: ab16g² b16.5d* b16.5d* Mar 11] fairly useful form in bumpers: won mares
events at Taunton in January and March: 13¼ lengths fourth of 15 to Gypsy Island in EBF
(Mares) INH Flat Race at Punchestown shortly after end of British season. *Warren Greatrex*

MISSION TRIO (IRE) 7 b.g. Presenting – Miss Brandywell (IRE) (Sadler's Wells **c–**
(USA)) [2018/19 h–: h20.6g h23.3g³ h23.9g² h23.3g h23.9g c23.8g Dec 3] has had **h76**
breathing operation: poor maiden hurdler: well beaten in novice handicap on chasing
debut: stays 3m: best form on good going: has worn headgear, including last 5 starts: tried
in tongue tie. *Stef Keniry*

MISS KATNISS 5 br.m. Kayf Tara – Kate Hill Dancer (IRE) (Presenting) [2018/19 b16.8d⁶ **b70**
b15.3g Apr 14] second foal: dam of little account: poor form in bumpers. *Jeremy Scott*

MISS MACKIE (IRE) 8 b.m. Mr Combustible (IRE) – Grannys Kitchen (IRE) **c76** (Flemensfirth (USA)) [2018/19 c83, h–: c20.1d May 5] maiden hurdler: poor form over **h–** fences: unproven beyond 17f: acts on soft going: tried in cheekpieces. *R. Mike Smith*

MISS MALARKY (IRE) 6 b.m. Presenting – The Shan Gang (IRE) (Anshan) [2018/19 **h–** h–, b–: h21m⁵ h21.7g⁶ h21.7g h20.5g Apr 22] rather unfurnished mare: no form in bumpers/over hurdles: in tongue tie last 2 starts. *Linda Jewell*

MISS MASH 8 b.m. Multiplex – Shanxi Girl (Overbury (IRE)) [2018/19 c–, h103x: h20d³ **c–** h23m² h21.6v* h21.7g² h21.6g h20.3s⁶ h19.5d⁶ h23.8g⁵ h18.9m³ Apr 20] compact mare: **h116 x** fairly useful handicap hurdler: won at Newton Abbot (mares) in October: second at Hereford in November: pulled up only chase start: stays 23f: acts on heavy going: races off pace: often let down by jumping. *Henry Daly*

MISS MAYFAIR (IRE) 12 b.m. Indian Danehill (IRE) – Cocktail Party (USA) (Arctic **h–** Tern (USA)) [2018/19 h96: h25d⁶ h23.8d h27sᵖᵘ Feb 21] modest hurdler, below form in 2018/19: wears headgear: in tongue tie last 2 starts: usually leads. *Lawney Hill*

MISS MCILROY (IRE) 7 ch.m. Fracas (IRE) – Monthly Sessions (IRE) (Pistolet Bleu **h81** (IRE)) [2018/19 h16g h16.6s h20.1g h16m⁶ h20s h16sᵖᵘ h16.1d⁶ h16v⁵ h18.5g³ h21gᵇᵈ h24.6s Apr 26] fourth foal: sister to modest 19f hurdle winner Rock On Barney: dam unraced half-sister to fair hurdler/fairly useful chaser (stayed 25f) No Half Session: poor maiden hurdler: stays 2¾m: acts on heavy going: wears cheekpieces: has worn tongue tie, including last 3 starts. *G. T. Lynch, Ireland*

MISS MOLINARI 5 b.m. Malinas (GER) – Maiden Voyage (Slip Anchor) [2018/19 **h–** h20.7g⁵ h20.7gᵖᵘ Feb 21] €30,000 3-y-o: sixth foal: half-sister to fairly useful hurdler/ chaser Crest (2½m-23f winner) and a winning pointer (both by Kayf Tara): dam (h105), 2m-2½m hurdle winner, half-sister to Grand National winner Rule The World: well held completed start over hurdles. *Charlie Longsdon*

MISS MOLLY MAE (IRE) 7 b.m. Getaway (GER) – Miss Mary Mac (IRE) (Dushyantor **h79** (USA)) [2018/19 h–, b–: h20.7gᵖᵘ h21.7vᵖᵘ Mar 16] poor form over hurdles. *Neil Mulholland*

MISS MUMTAZ (IRE) 4 ch.f. Lope de Vega (IRE) – Ispanka (Invincible Spirit (IRE)) **h105** [2018/19 h17sꟳ h15.8g* h16.3g⁵ h16.8g Apr 18] fairly useful on Flat, stays 1¼m: fair form over hurdles: won fillies juvenile at Huntingdon in March. *Ian Williams*

MISS NIGHT OWL 9 ch.m. Midnight Legend – Moyliscar (Terimon) [2018/19 h124: **c104** c16.5g³ c16.3g² c17.4d³ c20.6gꟳ Dec 14] compact mare: placed 3 times in Irish mares **h–** maiden points: fairly useful hurdler: fair form over fences: unproven beyond 2m: acts on heavy going: usually races close up. *Tom George*

MISS ROCHER (IRE) 5 b.m. Arcadio (GER) – Madam Rocher (IRE) (Roselier (FR)) **h–** [2018/19 b–: h18.5g h16.5d⁶ Nov 29] pulled up in bumper: well held in 2 novice hurdles: in hood last 2 starts. *Nigel Hawke*

MISS SPENT (IRE) 9 b.m. Presenting – Cash And New (IRE) (Supreme Leader) **c–** [2018/19 c–, h119: h16g⁵ h16.3mᵖᵘ h20g⁶ h18.7g h19g⁵ h24d* h24.4g* h21.3s⁵ Dec 26] **h112** good-topped mare: fair handicap hurdler: won at Southwell in November and Doncaster (mares) in December: let down by jumping only chase outing: stays 3m: acts on soft going: tried in cheekpieces: wears tongue tie: waited with. *Dan Skelton*

MISS TONGABEZI 10 b.m. Overbury (IRE) – Shiwa (Bustino) [2018/19 c119, h108: **c92** c20.5g³ h19.8v⁵ c24.2d⁵ Dec 27] compact mare: modest handicap hurdler/chaser **h86** nowadays: stays 3m: acts on soft going: wears hood/tongue tie. *Paul Webber*

MISS TYNTE (IRE) 7 b.m. Mahler – Top Quality (Simply Great (FR)) [2018/19 h111, **h– §** b78: h17.7v⁶ h18.9m Apr 20] fair hurdler, no form in 2018/19: stays 21f: acts on heavy going: in headgear last 5 starts: has worn tongue tie: weak finisher. *David Pipe*

MISS YEATS (IRE) 8 b.m. Yeats (IRE) – Mrs Wallensky (IRE) (Roselier (FR)) [2018/19 **c100** h97: c23.6g⁴ c20d⁴ c25.2v c20.5d⁵ c24s⁴ Mar 16] good-topped mare: modest maiden **h–** hurdler: fair form over fences: won mares handicap at Lingfield in November: probably stays 3m: acts on soft going: usually front runner/races prominently. *Laura Mongan*

MISSY TATA (FR) 7 b.m. Astarabad (USA) – Queen Running (FR) (Cadoudal (FR)) **c134** [2018/19 c21g* c22.5vᵖᵘ Mar 17] good-topped mare: useful hurdler, unbeaten in 5 starts in **h–** 2016/17: useful form over fences: off over 2 years, won mares maiden at Fairyhouse in February, upsides when left clear 2 out: lame next time: stays 21f: acts on soft and good to firm going. *Gordon Elliott, Ireland*

MISTER BLUE SKY (IRE) 5 gr.g. Royal Applause – Mujdeya (Linamix (FR)) **h139**
[2018/19 h16.5d* h16d² h16d* Apr 7] fairly useful on Flat, stays 1¼m: useful form over
hurdles: won maiden at Wexford in October and novice at Fairyhouse (by ¾ length from
Cash Back) in April: 16½ lengths third of 6 to Klassical Dream in Champion Novices'
Hurdle at Punchestown shortly after end of British season. *W. P. Mullins, Ireland*

MISTERCOBAR (FR) 7 b.g. Nicobar – Miss Decca (FR) (Smadoun (FR)) [2018/19 **c107**
c20s h19.6dᵖᵘ c19.4g³ c24v c21.1s² c20.9d⁶ Mar 9] point winner: pulled up in novice on **h–**
hurdling debut: fair form over fences: stays 21f: acts on soft going: in hood last 3 starts:
tried in tongue tie. *Tony Carroll*

MISTER COFFEY (FR) 4 b.g. Authorized (IRE) – Mamitador (Anabaa (USA)) **b98 p**
[2018/19 b15.8g* Apr 22] tall, good sort: sixth foal: half-brother to 2 winners in France,
including fairly useful 2m/17f hurdle winner Myboy (by American Post): dam French
7.5f-10.5f winner: 8/11, won bumper at Huntingdon (by 8 lengths from Kap Auteuil,
impressively) on debut: useful prospect. *Harry Whittington*

MISTER FISHER (IRE) 5 b.g. Jeremy (USA) – That's Amazing (IRE) (Marignan **h143 p**
(USA)) [2018/19 b98: h16.3d² h16g* h15.7d* h16.4s Mar 12] sturdy gelding: bumper
winner: useful form over hurdles: won novice at Kempton (by 2¾ lengths from Rouge Vif)
in December and Rossington Main Novices' Hurdle at Haydock (by 2½ lengths from
Bright Forecast) in January. *Nicky Henderson*

MISTER FIZZ 11 b.g. Sulamani (IRE) – Court Champagne (Batshoof) [2018/19 h119: **h139**
h19.8m h20.3g* h18.5s* h21.6g* h19.6d⁶ h16.8d h20d h16.8g Apr 17] leggy gelding:
useful handicap hurdler: completed hat-trick for Alex Hales when winning at Southwell
and Newton Abbot in July, and Newton Abbot again (by 2¾ lengths from Qualando) in
August: trained next start only by Alastair Ralph: stays 2¾m: acts on soft and good to firm
going: wears cheekpieces: usually races close up. *Miss Imogen Pickard*

MISTER KALANISI (IRE) 10 b.g. Kalanisi (IRE) – Maxis Girl (IRE) (Mister Mat **h95**
(FR)) [2018/19 h20.3g⁶ h20.3g h24g² Jun 25] maiden hurdler, fair form at best, off 27
months/left Dan Skelton prior to return: stays 3m: acts on heavy going. *Sara Ender*

Sky Bet Supreme Trial Rossington Main Novices' Hurdle, Haydock—Mister Fisher justifies
favouritism by holding off his main market rival Bright Forecast

*Sodexo Reynoldstown Novices' Chase, Ascot—a race of changing complexions,
with Mister Malarky (stars) staying on best to beat Now McGinty (partly hidden),
Yalltari (grey) and Top Ville Ben (right)*

MISTER KIT 11 gr.g. Tikkanen (USA) – Rosie Mist (Missed Flight) [2018/19 c15.9d² **c126**
c15.9s⁵ Nov 12] winning hurdler: fairly useful form over fences: second in novice handicap **h–**
at Carlisle in October: stayed 2½m: acted on good to soft going: dead. *Chris Grant*

MISTER MALARKY 6 ch.g. Malinas (GER) – Priscilla (Teenoso (USA)) [2018/19 **c149**
h115: c19.7g* c23.4s³ c23.4d* c23.8d* c24.4s⁴ c25g² Apr 6] lengthy gelding: fairly useful **h–**
hurdler: smart form over fences: won novice handicap at Plumpton in November, handicap
at Newbury (by 13 lengths from Carlos du Fruitier) in January and Reynoldstown Novices'
Chase at Ascot (by 1½ lengths from Now McGinty) in February: second in Grade 3
handicap at Aintree (5 lengths behind Kildisart) in April: will stay long distances: acts on
heavy going: reliable, and a sound jumper. *Colin Tizzard*

MISTER MISTER (IRE) 8 b.g. September Storm (GER) – The Long Bill (IRE) **c84**
(Phardante (FR)) [2018/19 h102: c20g⁵ c21m⁴ c23g⁴ c23.9g⁶ c26.3mF c21g⁴ c23m c23.6g⁶ **h–**
c23.8g³ c19.7g³ c21.7d* c19.7g*] useful-looking gelding: fair hurdler: poor
handicap chaser: won at Taunton in November and Plumpton in April: stays 23f: acts on
good to soft going: tried in headgear: has worn tongue tie. *Dai Williams*

MISTER MIYAGI (IRE) 10 b.g. Zagreb (USA) – Muckle Flugga (IRE) (Karinga Bay) **c126**
[2018/19 h–: c20g* c19.2m² c20s⁴ Jul 29] lengthy gelding: winning hurdler: fairly useful **h–**
form over fences: won maiden at Uttoxeter in May and novice at Market Rasen (sole rival
unseated first) in June: finished lame final start: stays 2½m: acts on good to firm and good
to soft going: has joined W. P. Mullins. *Stuart Edmunds*

MISTERMOONBOY (IRE) 5 ch.g. Mister Fotis (USA) – Sister Moon (IRE) **h109**
(Flemensfirth (USA)) [2018/19 b16v h16v² h20.5s³ h22.7g⁶ Feb 14] £10,000 4-y-o: close- **b–**
coupled gelding: second foal: dam (c65/h79), maiden jumper, half-sister to useful hurdler/
chaser (2m-2¾m winner) Santa's Son: made frame all 4 starts in Irish points: well held in
bumper: fair form over hurdles: best effort when second in maiden at Ayr in November.
Leonard Kerr

MISTER MURCHAN (IRE) 6 b.g. Westerner – So Supreme (IRE) (Supreme Leader) **b87**
[2018/19 b17.7g⁵ Apr 7] half-brother to 3 winners, including fairly useful hurdler/chaser
Emcon (2m-2½m winner, by Vinnie Roe) and fair 2m hurdle winner Juan de Gracia (by
Milan): dam (h103), bumper/2m hurdle winner, half-sister to useful hurdler/chaser (stayed
25f) Native Estates: off mark in Irish points at third attempt: fair form in bumpers.
Richard Rowe

MISTER ROBBO (IRE) 8 ch.g. Indian River (FR) – Bu Hagab (IRE) (Royal Academy **c–**
(USA)) [2018/19 b18d c23.6g^{pu} Apr 26] multiple point winner: tailed off in maiden bumper **b–**
for Diarmuid P. Ryan: pulled up in novice hunter on chasing debut. *T. Faulkner*

MISTER SERIOUS (IRE) 10 b.g. Kalanisi (IRE) – Mack Tack (IRE) (Shardari) **h100**
[2018/19 h–: h21.4m^4 h25.8m^3 h25.8g^6 Jun 5] multiple point winner: fair form over
hurdles: stays 3¼m: acts on good to firm going: tried in cheekpieces. *Robert Walford*

MISTER TICKLE (IRE) 5 b.g. Morozov (USA) – Tatiana (IRE) (Erins Isle) [2018/19 **h101**
h24.6g^{ur} h23.8d^5 h23.3d^2 Mar 30] €22,000 3-y-o, £35,000 4-y-o: short-backed gelding:
eighth foal: dam (h71) lightly-raced sister to useful hurdler/chaser (2m-2½m winner) Cuan
Na Grai: Irish point winner: fair form over hurdles: best effort when second in novice at
Uttoxeter: will prove best at 3m+. *Martin Smith*

MISTER TIMMYTUCKS 6 b.g. Kayf Tara – No Need For Alarm (Romany Rye) **b73**
[2018/19 b16.8d^6 b15.3g^5 Apr 14] rangy gelding: poor form in bumpers. *Paul Nicholls*

MISTERTON 8 gr.g. Sagamix (FR) – Mighty Splash (Cape Cross (IRE)) [2018/19 h140: **h134**
h16.5g^F Feb 19] useful handicap hurdler: stayed 2½m: acted on soft going: usually raced
close up: dead. *Harry Fry*

MISTER UNIVERSUM (GER) 7 b.g. Cape Cross (IRE) – Miss Europa (IRE) (Monsun **h122**
(GER)) [2018/19 h123: h16g* h16.7m^5 h16.3m^2 h20g^6 h16.4g h15.8g^4 h16.6m^2 h15.8d^6
h15.9g^6 Apr 21] rather leggy gelding: has had breathing operation: fairly useful handicap
hurdler: won at Warwick in May: second at Stratford in September: stays 2½m: acts on
good to firm and good to soft going: tried in cheekpieces: wears tongue tie. *Dan Skelton*

MISTER VALENTINE 6 b.g. Alflora (IRE) – Aberdeen Park (Environment Friend) **h88 p**
[2018/19 b–: h23g^4 Sep 11] well held in bumpers: 33/1, some encouragement when fourth
in novice at Worcester (31 lengths behind Present In Court) on hurdling debut: should
improve. *Martin Keighley*

MISTER WHITAKER (IRE) 7 b.g. Court Cave (IRE) – Benbradagh Vard (IRE) (Le **c153**
Bavard (FR)) [2018/19 c146p, h–: c20g* c20.2g^4 c21d^4 c25s^{pu} c20.6g* Apr 17] lengthy **h–**
gelding: lightly-raced hurdler: smart chaser: won intermediate event at Carlisle (by 2¼
lengths from Happy Diva) in November and Silver Trophy Chase (Limited Handicap) at
Cheltenham (in cheekpieces, by neck from Got Away) in April: should stay further than
21f: acts on good to firm and heavy going. *Mick Channon*

MISTIROC 8 br.g. Rocamadour – Mistinguett (IRE) (Doyoun) [2018/19 h16.2g^4 h16d^4 **h102 p**
h16.7s^5 Dec 26] half-brother to several winning jumpers, including smart hurdler
Mistanoora (2m-25f winner, by Topanoora) and useful hurdler/fairly useful chaser Rimsky
(2m-2¾m winner, by Silver Patriarch), stayed 33f: dam (h156) 2m-21f hurdle winner:
fairly useful on Flat, stays 12.5f: fair form over hurdles: best effort when fifth in novice at
Market Rasen: remains with potential. *John Quinn*

MISTRAL SONG (FR) 5 b.m. Hurricane Cat (USA) – Song of India (Dalakhani (IRE)) **b67**
[2018/19 b13.7m b13.7g^6 Apr 12] second foal: dam ran once on Flat: poor form in bumpers.
Michael Blanshard

*Cure Parkinson's and Hambo Foundation Silver Trophy Chase (Limited Handicap), Cheltenham—
Mister Whitaker (centre) gets back on track in first-time cheekpieces to beat Got Away (noseband)
and Highway One O One (right)*

MISTRESS MASSINI 8 b.m. Dr Massini (IRE) – Mistress Willie (Master Willie) **c93** [2018/19 h78, b86: c24.2m⁴ c23.8g⁴ c25.2g* c25.6d³ Jan 28] sturdy mare: once-raced **h—** hurdler: modest form over fences: won conditionals/amateurs handicap at Ludlow and novice handicap at Catterick in January: trained on reappearance only by Mrs Teresa Clark: stays 25f: best form on good going: usually races off pace. *Anthony Honeyball*

MISTY BLOOM (IRE) 6 b.m. Yeats (IRE) – Misty Mountain (IRE) (Namaqualand **h108** (USA)) [2018/19 b79: h15.7g² h15.8g³ h20gᵖᵘ h18.5m* h19m* h20.7d³ h19d² h23.1d⁴ h18.9m² Apr 20] fair handicap hurdler: won at Exeter and Taunton (mares) in November: stays 23f: acts on good to firm and good to soft going. *Emma Lavelle*

MISTY MAI (IRE) 9 b.m. Westerner – Arcanum (IRE) (Presenting) [2018/19 c113, h80: **c90** c20.9d⁶ c23.8v⁴ c25.2v⁶ c19.4v⁵ h23.9g⁴ c24sᵖᵘ Mar 23] modest hurdler/chaser nowadays: **h90** stays 25f: acts on heavy going. *David Rees*

MISTY WHISKY 5 gr.m. Stowaway – Whisky Rose (IRE) (Old Vic) [2018/19 b17g² **b105** b15.8s* b16s* b17d Apr 4] good-topped mare: third foal: half-sister to bumper winners/ useful hurdlers Air Horse One (17f-19f winner, by Mountain High) and One For Rosie (19f/2½m winner, by Getaway): dam unraced: useful form in bumpers: won mares race at Ludlow in December and listed mares event at Sandown (by length from Silver Forever) in March. *Harry Fry*

MISU BULA 4 b.f. Misu Bond (IRE) – Bula Rose (IRE) (Alphabatim (USA)) [2018/19 **b72** b15.7d b16.8d³ Apr 23] half-sister to fairly useful 2m hurdle winner Bulas Belle (by Rob Roy): dam (h104), 2m/17f hurdle winner (also 7f winner on Flat), out of Anniversary Hurdle winner Titled Dancer: poor form in bumpers. *Philip Kirby*

MITCD (IRE) 8 gr.m. Mastercraftsman (IRE) – Halicardia (Halling (USA)) [2018/19 h88: **h96** h16.7m* h16.2g⁴ h18.1m h16.8mᶠ Oct 2] modest handicap hurdler: won mares event at Market Rasen in June: stays 2½m: acts on soft and good to firm going. *George Bewley*

MITCHOUKA (FR) 5 b.g. Creachadoir (IRE) – Minnaloushe (FR) (Black Minnaloushe **c120** (USA)) [2018/19 h138: c18mᶠ c18.8g⁵ c16d⁴ c17g⁴ c17d⁵ h16g h16.8dᵖᵘ h16d Apr 23] **h129** useful hurdler: in blinkers/tongue strap, best effort for a while when 5 lengths third to Pearl of The West in handicap at Punchestown shortly after end of British season: fairly useful form over fences: fourth in maidens at Punchestown and Leopardstown: unproven beyond 17f: acts on soft going: tried in cheekpieces. *Gordon Elliott, Ireland*

MITEBEALL FORLUCK 11 b.g. Westerner – Iborga (FR) (Cyborg (FR)) [2018/19 **c—** c20.8g c23.9mᵖᵘ c21gᵖᵘ c16.5gᵖᵘ Sep 28] placed in points: maiden hurdler: fairly useful **h—** chaser at best, no form in 2018/19 (left A. L. T. Moore before return): wears headgear: has worn tongue tie, including final start. *David Brace*

MIXBOY (FR) 9 gr.g. Fragrant Mix (IRE) – Leston Girl (FR) (Lesotho (USA)) [2018/19 **c143** c142, h—: c17.3g³ h16.8m* c20.3g³ c15.2g² c20.3s* Mar 10] angular gelding: fairly useful **h127** on Flat, stays 2¼m: fairly useful form over hurdles: won handicap at Sedgefield in October: useful handicap chaser: won at Musselburgh in March: has won over 21f, effective over shorter: acts on good to firm and heavy going: has worn hood: front runner/races prominently. *Keith Dalgleish*

MIXCHIEVOUS 8 gr.g. Fair Mix (IRE) – Cheeky Mare (Derrylin) [2018/19 h106: h20.7d⁶ **c115** c20.9v* c19.2dʳᵒ c23.9dᵖᵘ Mar 14] good-topped gelding: fair handicap hurdler: fairly **h108** useful form over fences: won novice handicap at Ffos Las in December: stays 21f: acts on heavy going: tried in blinkers: usually races off pace: signs of temperament. *Venetia Williams*

MIX OF CLOVER 5 b.g. Fair Mix (IRE) – Allforclover (IRE) (Alflora (IRE)) [2018/19 **h98** b16dᵖᵘ b16.3g⁴ b16.2s⁶ h15.8dᵘʳ h21.2g⁶ Jan 3] sturdy gelding: first foal: dam, winning **b77** pointer, half-sister to useful 2m chaser Wilde Pastures: modest form in bumpers: similar form over hurdles: tried in hood: usually races nearer last than first. *Alastair Ralph*

MIZEN MASTER (IRE) 6 b.g. Captain Rio – Nilassiba (Daylami (IRE)) [2018/19 **h121** h121: h20g* h18.7m⁵ h20g* Nov 20] angular gelding: has had breathing operation: modest on Flat, stays 16.5f: fairly useful hurdler: won claimer at Worcester in August and selling handicap at Fakenham in November: stays 2¾m: acts on good to soft going: in headgear last 4 starts: wears tongue tie. *Olly Murphy*

MIZZ MOONDANCE 4 b.f. Yeats (IRE) – Mizzurka (Alflora (IRE)) [2018/19 b16.5d **b—** Apr 4] second foal: dam (h127), bumper/2½m hurdle winner, half-sister to useful/ ungenuine staying chaser Double Dizzy: tailed off in maiden bumper. *Bob Buckler*

MOABIT (GER) 7 b.g. Azamour (IRE) – Moonlight Danceuse (IRE) (Bering) [2018/19 **c–** c99, h132: h17.7d^F Nov 18] good-topped gelding: useful hurdler: stumbled and fell first on **h–** sole start in 2018/19: modest form in 2 novice chases: strong-travelling sort, will prove best at 2m: acts on good to firm and heavy going: wears tongue tie: usually races close up. *Paul Nicholls*

MOAYADD (USA) 7 b.g. Street Cry (IRE) – Aryaamm (IRE) (Galileo (IRE)) [2018/19 **h92** h15.7s^pu h15.9s h19.3m^3 h16.5d^4 h15.8d h16.5d Apr 24] fairly useful on Flat, stays 1½m: modest form over hurdles: raced mainly around 2m: acts on good to soft going: tried in tongue tie. *Neil Mulholland*

MODELIGO (IRE) 10 b.g. Indian Danehill (IRE) – Glens Lady (IRE) (Mister Lord **c107** (USA)) [2018/19 c105, h–: c20m^6 c17m* c20g^pu c17.4g^6 h18.7g c17m^3 c16g^2 c17g^5 **h–** c16.5g^5 c20g^6 c19.4s c20d c16d^pu Feb 23] angular gelding: winning hurdler: fair handicap chaser: won at Stratford in May: stays 2½m: acts on good to firm and heavy going: wears headgear/tongue tie: usually races off pace. *Matt Sheppard*

MODERN WARFARE (IRE) 5 b.g. Well Chosen – Brooklyn Brook (IRE) (Alderbrook) **h112** [2018/19 h21.6d^4 h22.8v^2 h24.4g* h23.5d Feb 16] €15,000 3-y-o, £80,000 4-y-o: first foal: dam unraced half-sister to fairly useful hurdler/useful chaser (stayed 3½m) Brooklyn Brownie and useful hurdler (stayed 27f) Barnhill Brownie: runner-up in Irish point on debut: fair form over hurdles: won handicap at Doncaster in January. *Tim Vaughan*

MODULUS 10 b.g. Motivator – Wild Academy (IRE) (Royal Academy (USA)) [2018/19 **c–** c–, h98: h16.6g^6 h16s h19.3g h19.9v^6 h15.8d^pu Mar 30] point winner: modest hurdler, no **h–** form in 2018/19: pulled up only chase outing: usually wears headgear. *Peter Winks*

MODUS 9 ch.g. Motivator – Alessandra (Generous (IRE)) [2018/19 c147, h–: c15.9d* **c147 x** c16.8g c16.4g^3 c24g c20.6d Mar 14] lengthy gelding: winning hurdler: smart handicap **h–** chaser: won at Cheltenham (by head from Duke of Navan) in October: stays 21f: acts on good to firm and heavy going: has worn hood: usually races off pace: often let down by jumping. *Paul Nicholls*

MOGESTIC (IRE) 10 b.g. Morozov (USA) – Crosschild (IRE) (Buckskin (FR)) **h95** [2018/19 h96: h25g* h25.8g* h26.5m^5 h23.1g^5 h26d^pu h25s h23.1s h23.6d h19.8g^6 Apr 14] close-coupled gelding: modest handicap hurdler: won at Plumpton in May and Fontwell in June: stays 3¼m: acts on heavy going: tried in cheekpieces. *Seamus Mullins*

MOHAAYED 7 b.g. Intikhab (USA) – Reyaada (Daylami (IRE)) [2018/19 h146: **h147** h15.8d^4 h16.4g h15.7s* h15.7d^4 h16.8d h20d Apr 5]

'Hopefully I'll train plenty of good horses in my career, but I'll never forget Willow's Saviour, that's for sure!' That was the reaction of rookie trainer Dan Skelton, just four months into his new career, after Willow's Saviour had landed the first big-race win for his fledgling yard. Over seven hundred wins later, Skelton might be forgiven if his memory was hazy on the finer details of many of the other former inmates of his yard, considering the number of horses he has handled during his rapid rise up the training ranks—two hundred and forty-four horses ran for the stable in 2018/19, in contrast to a string of just twelve when Skelton started out in August 2013! That said, Mohaayed is one who seems certain to join Willow's Saviour in the 'unforgettable' folder having provided the ambitious Skelton team with two of its biggest wins of the last two seasons. Mohaayed was the stable second string when the 33/1 winner of the 2018 County Hurdle at Cheltenham, with fifth-placed Spiritofthegames the choice of Skelton's stable jockey brother Harry that day, though the latter still celebrated wildly as Mohaayed was steered home by his fiancée Bridget Andrews. Harry Skelton was back on board when Mohaayed lined up for the Betfair Exchange Trophy at Ascot in December—the same race Willow's Saviour had won (as the Ladbroke) five years earlier—and went on to become the first horse to win that prestigious handicap hurdle as well as the County at the Festival.

With Newbury's Betfair Hurdle run with a reduced prize after being transferred to Ascot, the Betfair Exchange Trophy was the most valuable handicap hurdle staged on British soil in 2018/19 and it attracted a competitive field. Paul Nicholls, to whom Mohaayed's trainer was once assistant, saddled two runners, the well-backed favourite Mont des Avaloirs and the prolific-winning novice Grand Sancy, in his bid to land one of the few big prizes still missing from his record. Mohaayed wasn't the only big-race winner in the field, Jolly's Cracked It, who had

Betfair Exchange Trophy (Handicap Hurdle), Ascot—another lucrative pot for the likeable Mohaayed (cheekpieces); Lisp (partly hidden) and Western Ryder (noseband) fill the places

dead-heated in 2015, being fresh from a comeback win after a lengthy spell on the sidelines, while outsiders Fidux and Man of Plenty had both won valuable listed handicaps on their most recent starts. The Imperial Cup winner Mr Antolini was also in the line-up, as was northern raider Nietzsche who had won the Greatwood Hurdle at Cheltenham. Mohaayed had managed only seventh in the last-named race, though things didn't really go his way that day when he was shuffled back when outpaced at the top of hill, before being hampered by a faller at the last (usual two out), then keeping on when it was all too late on the extended run-in. Mohaayed's reappearance fourth (beaten under four lengths) to Silver Streak in the Welsh Champion Hurdle at Ffos Las in October had been far more encouraging, though, particularly as he shaped as if the outing was just needed. Nevertheless, 16/1-shot Mohaayed was ninth choice in the betting at Ascot, having been dropped just 1 lb after those two defeats since his County win. He proceeded to produce a career-best effort, arguably deserving extra credit too given that he was in the teeth of the race throughout, being the only one of the first six home to race prominently in what was a well-run affair. Jumping into the lead at the third last, Mohaayed kicked for home turning in and was always holding the well-fancied runner-up Lisp, who was two and a quarter lengths adrift at the line, with a further length back to Western Ryder in third and another two and three quarter lengths to Grand Sancy in fourth (Mont des Avaloirs faded into fourteenth).

The demands of truly-run handicaps with big fields clearly suit Mohaayed down to the ground, but his lucrative win left him difficult to place. He falls below Champion Hurdle class (he was a remote fourth in Haydock's Champion Hurdle Trial in January), and a new BHA mark of 153 (8 lb higher than at Ascot) left him vulnerable judging by his seventh place when bidding to repeat his County Hurdle win in March, when the roles were reversed this time as Bridget Andrews (back on board Mohaayed) rushed to embrace Harry Skelton as the runners were pulling up, with Ch'tibello providing the Skelton yard with its third win in the County Hurdle in four years.

Royal Ascot, rather than Ascot in December, was almost certainly the plan when Moyaahed's dam Reyaada was sent to Intikhab in 2011. Reyaada's family descends from a successful strand of Hamdan Al Maktoum's Irish operation.

Mohaayed's grandam Walayef was a Group 3 winner over seven furlongs but finished lame when last in the 2003 Irish One Thousand Guineas (her final outing). Her brother Haatef was a smart sprinter who won the 2007 Diadem Stakes (then a Group 2 event) to earn himself a stud career. Their sister Ulfah and half-sister Shimah were both listed winning sprinters for Sheikh Hamdan and Kevin Prendergast (who also trained Walayef and Haatef). Reyaada might not have reached those heights on the racecourse (when also trained by Prendergast) but she did display more stamina than most of her relatives, winning over seven furlongs at two before showing fairly useful form when placed over a mile and a half at three. Mohaayed is her third foal and the only winner from just two runners to date, the lightly-raced maiden Nabat Sultan (by Invincible Spirit), now a broodmare herself, being the other one. Durability certainly hasn't proved a concern for Mohaayed so far. Having shown useful form at up to nine and a half furlongs on the Flat for Prendergast, winning twice and finishing sixth in the 2015 Irish Two Thousand Guineas, Mohaayed was bought by current connections for 32,000 guineas at the end of a disappointing four-year-old campaign. That outlay was quickly recouped, with Mohaayed winning twice (and recording lucrative placed efforts in the Scottish Champion Hurdle and Christmas Hurdle) before his County Hurdle win in 2018. He has now won nearly £200,000 in three seasons for Skelton.

	Intikhab (USA) (b 1994)	Red Ransom (b 1987)	Roberto
Mohaayed (b.g. 2012)			Arabia
		Crafty Example (ch 1987)	Crafty Prospector
			Zienelle
	Reyaada (b 2005)	Daylami (gr 1994)	Doyoun
			Daltawa
		Walayef (b 2000)	Danzig
			Sayedat Alhadh

Effective held up or ridden prominently (the more favoured tactics of late), the sturdy Mohaayed handles the mud surprisingly well for one so speedily-bred, his two biggest wins having come on soft and heavy, but clearly he isn't inconvenienced

Mrs June Watts's "Mohaayed"

by top-of-the-ground conditions either. He has been raced mainly at around two miles and, although he didn't shape noticeably like a non-stayer when finishing in mid-division in a two and a half mile handicap at Aintree on his final start, there must be doubts about his stamina over that sort of trip. Mohaayed might prove difficult to place in the short term, with connections presumably not considering him a chasing type given that he is now rising eight and has yet to tackle the larger obstacles. Willow's Saviour was, however, switched to chasing at the same age, winning two novice events from small fields (beating the subsequent top-class performer Aso on the first occasion). Tongue tied throughout his hurdling career, Mohaayed was tried in headgear latterly on the Flat and has worn cheekpieces on his last four starts, though it is hard to crab his attitude given his largely consistent record over jumps. *Dan Skelton*

MOIDORE 10 b.g. Galileo (IRE) – Flash of Gold (Darshaan) [2018/19 h104: h23.3v h26s[5] h25d[5] Mar 24] good-topped gelding: fair handicap hurdler, lightly raced in 2018/19: probably stays 25f: acts on heavy going: has worn headgear: tried in tongue tie. *Charles Pogson* **h91**

MOLINEAUX (IRE) 8 b.g. King's Theatre (IRE) – Steel Grey Lady (IRE) (Roselier (FR)) [2018/19 h123: c20v[5] c19.2sur c20.2g* c24.2d[2] c19.9d[3] c15.8d[6] c20g Apr 27] workmanlike gelding: fairly useful hurdler: fairly useful handicap chaser: won novice event at Wincanton in January: stays 3m: acts on heavy going: in tongue tie last 4 starts: usually races close up. *Colin Tizzard* **c129 h–**

MOLLIANA 4 b.f. Olden Times – The Screamer (IRE) (Insan (USA)) [2018/19 h16.8g[5] h15.9g h16d[5] h15.9s[4] h20d* h19.9s[3] h20.5g[2] Apr 7] half-sister to fair hurdler Chilworth Screamer (2½m/21f winner, by Imperial Dancer): dam (c110/h109) 2m hurdle/chase winner: lightly raced on Flat: modest handicap hurdler: won mares event at Fakenham in March: stays 2½m: acts on good to soft going. *Neil Mulholland* **h93**

MOLLY CAREW 7 b.m. Midnight Legend – Moyliscar (Terimon) [2018/19 h108: c20s[2] c22.5vur c19.4s* c20v[3] c21.6m[4] Apr 20] sturdy mare: fair hurdler: fairly useful form over fences: won handicap at Ffos Las in February: stays 2½m: acts on heavy going: usually races off pace. *Neil Mulholland* **c120 h–**

MOLLY CHILDERS (IRE) 7 b.m. Stowaway – Hushaby (IRE) (Eurobus) [2018/19 h121: h23.3d[2] c24.1g[2] c21.6g[2] c24g[3] h24.6g[2] c25.1g* c25.1g[2] c24g[4] c26g[3] Apr 18] sturdy mare: has had breathing operation: fairly useful handicap hurdler: second in mares events at Uttoxeter early in season and Kempton in December: fairly useful chaser: won 3-runner mares handicap at Wincanton in January: likely to stay long distances: acts on soft going: wears cheekpieces: tried in tongue tie. *Stuart Edmunds* **c129 h125**

MOLLY OLLYS WISHES 5 b.m. Black Sam Bellamy (IRE) – September Moon (Bustino) [2018/19 b16.3s[3] b15.8d[4] Mar 30] second foal: dam (c105/h96) ungenuine 2¾m-3¼m hurdle/chase winner: modest form in bumpers. *Dan Skelton* **b81**

MOLLYOW (IRE) 11 ch.m. Iceman – Corryvreckan (IRE) (Night Shift (USA)) [2018/19 h18.5g[5] h15.8v h19.9v[4] h21.9v[4] h23.9d[5] Mar 11] small, plain mare: poor handicap hurdler: stays 2½m: acts on heavy going: has joined Adrian Wintle. *Dai Burchell* **h73**

MOLLY THE DOLLY (IRE) 8 b.m. Flemensfirth (USA) – Pistol Flash (IRE) (Pistolet Bleu (IRE)) [2018/19 h119: c25g* c24g* c23.4s[3] c24.1m* Apr 13] fairly useful hurdler: useful form over fences: won novice handicap at Aintree in October, mares novice at Uttoxeter in November and novice handicap at Ayr (by 3¾ lengths from Dandy Dan) in April: stays 25f: acts on good to firm and heavy going: open to further improvement as a chaser. *Dan Skelton* **c144 p h–**

MOLLY WHUPPIE 6 br.m. Beat Hollow – Daisies Adventure (IRE) (Flemensfirth (USA)) [2018/19 b16g[6] h16.8d[3] h15.7d[3] h19.9s[6] h18.6g[6] h16g h19.9d[2] Apr 23] £800 4-y-o: second foal: dam unraced out of half-sister to dam of very smart hurdler/top-class chaser (stayed 25f) Menorah: poor form in bumpers: modest form over hurdles: left John Wainwright after first start: usually in hood: temperament under suspicion. *Tim Fitzgerald* **h89 b68**

MOLTEN BROWN 14 b.g. Needle Gun (IRE) – Molten (Ore) [2018/19 c90: c26.2gpu May 27] multiple point winner: modest hunter chaser at best, pulled up sole start under Rules in 2018/19: stays 3m: acts on soft and good to firm going: wears cheekpieces. *Tony Hogarth* **c–**

MOLTOIR (IRE) 4 b.g. Vocalised (USA) – Gleigeal (USA) (Mr Greeley (USA)) [2018/19 h16.2g Sep 26] fair on Flat, stays 8.5f: well held in juvenile maiden on hurdling debut. *Brian Ellison* **h–**

J & D Pierce Novices' Champion Handicap Chase, Ayr—a smaller field than expected for this valuable prize due to some trainers being caught out by new race conditions, with the mare Molly The Dolly in command

MOMELLA (IRE) 7 ch.m. Sholokhov (IRE) – Missing Link (IRE) (Elusive Quality (USA)) [2018/19 h137: h24.2sF h24.6gpu h19.9s Mar 12] sturdy mare: has had breathing operation: Irish point winner: useful hurdler: stays 2¾m: acts on soft going: in tongue tie last 3 starts. *Harry Fry*   **h131**

MOM SAID (IRE) 4 b.g. Lawman (FR) – Istishaara (USA) (Kingmambo (USA)) [2018/19 h17d⁵ h16m h16m⁵ Oct 21] sturdy gelding: modest maiden on Flat: easily best effort over hurdles when fifth in juvenile at Kempton, possibly flattered: tried in cheekpieces/tongue tie. *Gavin Patrick Cromwell, Ireland*   **h103 ?**

MONALEE (IRE) 8 b.g. Milan – Tempest Belle (IRE) (Glacial Storm (USA)) [2018/19 c157p, h–: c19.5g³ c24g² c20d* c20.6d⁴ Mar 14] tall gelding: winning hurdler: top-class chaser: won Red Mills Chase at Gowran (by 2 lengths from Anibale Fly) in February: second in Savills Chase at Leopardstown (7½ lengths behind Kemboy) in December and fourth in Ryanair Chase at Cheltenham (5¼ lengths behind Frodon) in March: shaped as if amiss at Punchestown shortly after end of British season: effective from 2½m to 25f: acts on heavy going: front runner/races prominently. *Henry de Bromhead, Ireland*   **c165 h–**

Red Mills Chase, Gowran Park—a win under new jockey Rachael Blackmore for Monalee despite having to give weight to Anibale Fly

MON AMI BOB 6 ch.g. Schiaparelli (GER) – Maid of Perth (Mark of Esteem (IRE)) **h88 p**
[2018/19 b79: h16.2g⁴ h15.6m⁴ Feb 28] modest form in bumpers for James Bethell: similar
form over hurdles: in tongue tie last 5 starts: better to come. *Lucinda Russell*

MONARCH (IRE) 6 b.g. Galileo (IRE) – Secret Garden (IRE) (Danehill (USA)) **c129 p**
[2018/19 h16g⁶ h16.5m* h16.7m* h16s c17g⁴ c16.5g^F Oct 1] useful handicap hurdler: **h138**
won at Down Royal in June and Bellewstown (by ½ length from Stormey) in July: fairly
useful form over fences: won maiden at Killarney in August: raced around 2m: acts on soft
and good to firm going: wears tongue tie: remains with potential as a chaser. *Joseph
Patrick O'Brien, Ireland*

MONAR LAD (IRE) 7 b.g. Mountain High (IRE) – Cottage Lady (IRE) (Moscow Society **c–**
(USA)) [2018/19 h78: c16.3g⁴ c17.2g^pu Jul 8] good-topped gelding: poor form over hurdles: **h–**
no show over fences: raced around 2m: often in tongue tie. *Dai Burchell*

MONAR ROSE 7 b.m. Yeats (IRE) – Rhapsody Rose (Unfuwain (USA)) [2018/19 c–p, **c106 §**
h110: c20.5m² c19.2g³ c19.2m⁵ Aug 5] lengthy mare: has had breathing operation: fair **h–**
hurdler: similar form over fences: stays 2½m: acts on soft and good to firm going: has worn
hood, including in 2018/19: wears tongue tie: irresolute. *Ben Case*

MONATOMIC (IRE) 6 b.g. Arcadio (GER) – Star Island (IRE) (Heron Island (IRE)) **c134**
[2018/19 c16g^F c16g² c16.3s² c16.2g³ c20d⁵ c16.2d* c16d^F c20g² c21.3s^F c21.2v^pu Apr 14] **h–**
€26,000 3-y-o: first foal: dam unraced half-sister to useful hurdler (stays 19f) Fairly Legal:
fair form over hurdles: useful chaser: won novice at Down Royal in January: second in
novice handicap at Naas (2 lengths behind Poker Party) in February: stays 21f: acts on
heavy going. *Gordon Elliott, Ireland*

MONBEG AQUADUDE (IRE) 8 b.g. Flemensfirth (USA) – Mite Dash (IRE) (Anshan) **c– p**
[2018/19 c20.9s Nov 23] won Irish maiden point on debut: winning hurdler: well beaten in **h–**
novice handicap on chasing debut: should stay further than 2½m: acts on heavy going:
should be better over fences. *Michael Scudamore*

MONBEG CAVE (IRE) 7 b.g. Court Cave (IRE) – Reynella Cross (IRE) (Torus) **c58**
[2018/19 c66, h–: c16.4g⁵ c20.1g^pu Jun 2] maiden hurdler: little form over fences: in **h–**
cheekpieces last 3 starts. *Martin Todhunter*

MONBEG CHARMER (IRE) 8 br.g. Daylami (IRE) – Charming Present (IRE) **c128**
(Presenting) [2018/19 c130, h–: c19.2d² May 20] lengthy, angular gelding: winning **h–**
hurdler: useful form over fences: stays 3m: acts on good to soft going: wears hood: in
tongue tie last 5 starts: front runner/races prominently. *Charlie Longsdon*

MONBEG GOLD (IRE) 9 b.g. Gold Well – Little Hand (IRE) (Carroll House) [2018/19 **c129**
c–, h–: h23.3g⁴ c24.2s* c24d* Apr 9] rangy gelding: has had breathing operation: fair **h106**
handicap hurdler: fairly useful handicap chaser: won at Exeter in November and Southwell
in April: stays 3m: acts on heavy going: has worn headgear, including in 2018/19. *Jonjo
O'Neill*

MONBEG LEGEND 9 b.g. Midnight Legend – Reverse Swing (Charmer) [2018/19 **c140**
h126: c20g* c20g² c20s* c22.6m* c19.4d² c19.8d² c20.5m³ Apr 13] strong gelding: fairly **h–**
useful form over hurdles: useful chaser: won novice handicap at Ludlow early in season,
novice at Uttoxeter in July and handicap at Stratford (by 2¼ lengths from Easy Street) in
September: stays 23f: acts on soft and good to firm going: front runner. *Nicky Henderson*

MONBEG NOTORIOUS (IRE) 8 b.g. Milan – Borleagh Princess (IRE) (Presenting) **c143 §**
[2018/19 c149, h–: c25s c28.7d c24d⁶ c34.3g^pu c29d^pu Apr 22] rangy gelding: winning **h–**
hurdler: useful handicap chaser: sixth in Leinster National Handicap Chase at Naas (16¾
lengths behind Pairofbrowneyes) in March: stays 25f: acts on heavy going: wears headgear:
temperamental. *Gordon Elliott, Ireland*

MONBEG RIVER (IRE) 10 br.g. Indian River (FR) – So Pretty (IRE) (Presenting) **c132**
[2018/19 c134, h–: c25g³ c21.5d² c24g² c20.5m⁵ Apr 12] workmanlike gelding: maiden **h–**
hurdler: useful handicap chaser: third at Aintree (8 lengths behind Virgilio) early in season:
stays 25f: acts on good to firm and heavy going: tried in tongue tie. *Martin Todhunter*

MONBEG THEATRE (IRE) 10 b.g. King's Theatre (IRE) – Amberina (IRE) (Bob **c–**
Back (USA)) [2018/19 c–, h128: h22.8g* h24.1m* h24.1g³ h24.2s⁴ h21.4d² h21s^pu Mar **h142**
13] sturdy gelding: has had breathing operations: useful handicap hurdler: won at Haydock
early in season and Wetherby in October: second at Wincanton (2 lengths behind
Padleyourowncanoe) in December: completed only once from 3 starts in chases: stays 3m:
acts on good to firm and heavy going: wears cheekpieces/tongue tie: front runner.
Jamie Snowden

MONBEG ZENA (IRE) 7 ch.m. Flemensfirth (USA) – Mandys Gold (IRE) (Mandalus) **h113 p**
[2018/19 h24s* Dec 16] €31,000 3-y-o, £110,000 5-y-o: fourth foal: sister to useful
hurdler/chaser Sizing Gold (2½m winner, stayed 3m) and half-sister to fairly useful
hurdler/chaser Exxaro (2½m-3¼m winner, by Presenting): dam 2½m bumper/3m chase
winner: won Irish point on debut in Feb 2017: 11/10, also won mares maiden at Southwell
(by 3½ lengths from Executive Capilano) on hurdling debut: should improve. *Olly Murphy*

MONDA'S LEGACY 6 b.m. Tamure (IRE) – Monda (Danzig Connection (USA)) **h–**
[2018/19 h15.3g^pu Apr 3] no form in bumpers: pulled up in maiden on hurdling **b–**
debut: in hood last 2 starts. *Chris Down*

MONDAY CLUB 6 ch.g. Strategic Prince – Support Fund (IRE) (Intikhab (USA)) **h110**
[2018/19 h105: h19.2g⁴ h19.2g³ h16g h16.8s² h17.7g³ h15.8g* h15.8g³ h16g³ h15.8g²
h16g² h17.7v² h16s Feb 15] neat gelding: fair handicap hurdler: won novice event at
Uttoxeter in September: stayed 19f: acted on good to firm and heavy going: effective with
or without headgear: usually raced in rear: dead. *Dominic Ffrench Davis*

MONDO CANE (IRE) 12 b.g. Beneficial – La Vita E Bella (FR) (Le Nain Jaune (FR)) **c–**
[2018/19 c99, h–: c20.3g May 15] winning hurdler: modest chaser: stays 27f: acts on heavy **h–**
going: wears headgear. *Charles Pogson*

MON ELDORADO (FR) 7 b.g. Gentlewave (IRE) – Miryea (FR) (Shining Steel) **h–**
[2018/19 h119, b86: h16.2g h21.4g Apr 3] fairly useful form over hurdles, behind both
starts in handicaps in 2018/19: has worn hood: tried in tongue tie. *Peter Bowen*

MONETAIRE (FR) 13 b.g. Anabaa (USA) – Monitrice (FR) (Groom Dancer (USA)) **c90**
[2018/19 c–, h–: c23s⁵ May 25] compact gelding: multiple point winner: winning hurdler: **h–**
useful chaser at best, has deteriorated markedly: best up to 21f: acts on good to firm and
heavy going: has worn headgear, including last 2 starts: has worn tongue tie. *W. M. Wanless*

MONET MOOR 10 b.m. Morpeth – Miracle Monarch (Elegant Monarch) [2018/19 c56, **c56**
h–: c21.6d^pu c24.2v^pu c20s³ h23.1s⁶ h20.9g⁴ Mar 26] sturdy mare: little form over hurdles/ **h54**
fences: has looked hard ride. *Jimmy Frost*

MONFASS (IRE) 8 b.g. Trans Island – Ajo Green (IRE) (Moscow Society (USA)) **h–**
[2018/19 h115: h17.1v h16s h17g h16.2g Apr 24] fair hurdler, well below form in 2018/19:
wears hood: races off pace. *Rose Dobbin*

MON GARCON FRANKIE 7 ch.g. Sulamani (IRE) – Rhetorique (FR) (Smadoun (FR)) **c–**
[2018/19 h23d⁵ c15.9g^ur c25.2g Mar 26] of no account: tried in cheekpieces. *Steve Flook* **h–**

MONJENI 6 b.g. Montjeu (IRE) – Polly's Mark (IRE) (Mark of Esteem (IRE)) [2018/19 **h81 p**
h15.5g⁶ h15.8d h19s Mar 19] good-topped gelding: dam half-sister to fairly useful
2m-2¼m hurdle winner Instant Karma: fairly useful on Flat, stays 2m: poor form over
hurdles: tried in cheekpieces: remains with potential. *Ian Williams*

MONKEY HARRIS (IRE) 7 b.g. Oscar (IRE) – Benefit Ball (IRE) (Beneficial) **h85**
[2018/19 h16s h16s Nov 21] fourth foal: closely related to fairly useful 19f hurdle winner
My Charity (by King's Theatre) and half-brother to fair hurdler/winning pointer Uimhir A
Seacht (2¼m-2½m winner, by Millenary): dam, unraced, closely related to fairly useful
hurdler/useful chaser (stayed 3m) Seven Is My Number: placed once from 4 starts in Irish
points: modest form over hurdles. *Richenda Ford*

MONKFISH (IRE) 5 ch.g. Stowaway – Martovic (IRE) (Old Vic) €36,000 3-y-o, **b107**
£235,000 4-y-o: fifth foal: half-brother to fairly useful hurdler/useful chaser Looks Like
Power (2m-3m winner, by Spadoun): dam (h95) maiden hurdler out of smart chaser
(stayed 25f) Martomick: off mark in points at second attempt: 5/2, shaped well when 2½
lengths second of 17 to Longhouse Poet in maiden bumper at Punchestown shortly after
end of British season. *W. P. Mullins, Ireland*

MONK'S VIEW 6 bl.g. Multiplex – Evelith Abbey (IRE) (Presenting) [2018/19 b69: **h93 x**
h15.8g⁶ h21.4g⁴ h21.2g h20.7g^pu Feb 21] has had breathing operation: modest form over
hurdles: clumsy jumper. *Ben Pauling*

MON PALOIS (FR) 7 b.g. Muhaymin (USA) – Gastinaise (FR) (Cadoudal (FR)) **c121**
[2018/19 h119: h24g⁵ c23.9g³ c24.2s^F h24g^pu Mar 4] good-topped gelding: Irish point **h116**
winner: fairly useful handicap hurdler: similar form over fences: stays 3m: acts on firm and
good to soft going. *Kim Bailey*

MON PARRAIN (FR) 13 b.g. Trempolino (USA) – Kadaina (FR) (Kadalko (FR)) **c107**
[2018/19 c108§, h–: c32.5g² c27.5dᵖᵘ c25.8gᵖᵘ Jul 6] maiden hurdler: one-time very smart **h–**
chaser: barely stayed 33f: acted on heavy going: wore headgear/tongue tie: dead.
Giles Smyly

MON PORT (IRE) 7 b.g. Scorpion (IRE) – Sounds Charming (IRE) (Presenting) **h116**
[2018/19 b92: h15.8g* h16m² h17.7g² h20.5d³ h21.2g⁵ h16.7g* h16.7m* Apr 21] has had
breathing operation: bumper winner: fairly useful hurdler: won maiden at Huntingdon
early in season, and novices at Market Rasen in March and April: stays 2½m: acts on good
to firm and good to soft going: tried in hood: often leads. *Olly Murphy*

MONSART (IRE) 7 gr.g. Echo of Light – Monet's Lady (IRE) (Daylami (IRE)) [2018/19 **h–**
h20.7g Nov 13] modest form at best over hurdles, well held sole start in 2018/19 after
2-year absence. *Shaun Lycett*

MONSIEUR ARKADIN (FR) 8 b.g. Dream Well (FR) – Quenta des Bordes (FR) **c97**
(Bateau Rouge) [2018/19 c–, h108: c20.9g³ c21.6d³ c23.8gᵖᵘ Nov 26] angular, rather **h–**
lightly-made gelding: winning pointer: fair hurdler: modest form over fences: stays 3¼m:
acts on soft and good to firm going: in tongue tie last 4 starts. *Tim Vaughan*

MONSIEUR BAGOT (IRE) 7 b.g. Robin des Pres (FR) – Hardabout (IRE) (Alderbrook) **c92**
[2018/19 b–: h18.8g h20.9g h20m⁶ h21.5g h17d⁶ c24.2sᵖᵘ c20.1g² h27s⁶ c23.8m² c24.2gᵖᵘ **h88**
Apr 15] modest form over hurdles/fences: left Christian Delcros after fourth start and
returned to former yard: stays 3m: acts on good to firm going: tried in cheekpieces.
Rebecca Menzies

MONSIEUR CO (FR) 6 b.g. Turgeon (USA) – Cayras Style (FR) (Trempolino (USA)) **c128**
[2018/19 c121, h–: c17.1d⁵ c15.8g³ c15.8g* h16.6g⁵ c17.1g* c15.8m* c16.5m⁶ Apr 13] **h98**
winning hurdler: fairly useful handicap chaser: won at Musselburgh in December, Kelso in
January and again at Musselburgh in February: should stay 2½m: acts on good to firm and
heavy going: wears headgear/tongue tie. *Keith Dalgleish*

MONSIEUR D'ARQUE (IRE) 5 b.g. Muhtathir – Nervous Breakdown (FR) **h111**
(Miesque's Son (USA)) [2018/19 h16.8g⁴ h15.8d⁴ h15.8d* h16.8g⁴ Apr 20] €50,000 3-y-o,
£32,000 4-y-o: compact gelding: second foal: dam French maiden on Flat (placed at 1m):
off mark in Irish points at second attempt: fair form over hurdles: won maiden at Ludlow
in February. *Dan Skelton*

MONSIEUR GIBRALTAR (FR) 8 ch.g. Spirit One (FR) – Palabras de Amor (FR) **c131**
(Rock of Gibraltar (IRE)) [2018/19 c–, h–: c16.3g* c21.6g* c22.6d c21.4m c20.2g* **h–**
c20.3d* c20.5m* Apr 25] good-topped gelding: prolific point winner: winning hurdler:
useful hunter chaser: won at Cheltenham and Fontwell early in season, and completed hat-
trick at Wincanton in February, and Southwell and Kempton in April: stays 2¾m: acts on
good to firm and heavy going: has worn blinkers: wears tongue tie. *Mrs Rose Loxton*

MONSIEUR LECOQ (FR) 5 b.g. Diamond Boy (FR) – Draga (FR) (Smadoun (FR)) **h135**
[2018/19 h114: h15.8g³ h17.9vᵘʳ h15.8v* h16s* h16s² h16.8d Mar 15] lengthy gelding:
useful hurdler: won maiden at Ffos Las in December and handicap at Sandown in January:
second in Imperial Cup at latter course (1¼ lengths behind Malaya) in March: likely to stay
beyond 2m: acts on heavy going. *Mrs Jane Williams*

MONTALBANO 7 ch.g. Monsieur Bond (IRE) – Alpen Glen (Halling (USA)) [2018/19 **c142 x**
c139, h–: c16g³ c19gᴾᶠ c19.5s* c19.5g² h21gᵖᵘ c15.2g² Feb 19] winning hurdler: useful **h–**
chaser: won minor event at Ballinrobe in September: left W. P. Mullins after fourth start:
stayed 2½m: acted on heavy going: wore hood: dead. *Jonjo O'Neill*

MONTANA GREY (IRE) 6 gr.g. Watar (IRE) – Wapiti Creek (IRE) (Great Palm (USA)) **b75**
[2018/19 ab16s⁴ Dec 10] 12/1, fourth in bumper at Lingfield (13½ lengths behind Nimby).
Emma Lavelle

MONTANNA 5 ch.g. Notnowcato – Asi (USA) (El Prado (IRE)) [2018/19 h20m* h20.2g* **h116**
h15.8s⁵ h23.8g Dec 10] fairly useful on Flat for Jedd O'Keeffe, stays 16.5f: fairly useful
form over hurdles: won novices at Ffos Las in June and Perth in July. *Peter Bowen*

MONT DES AVALOIRS (FR) 6 b.g. Blue Bresil (FR) – Abu Dhabi (FR) (Saint Cyrien **c133**
(FR)) [2018/19 h136, b98: c16.3v² h16.3s³ h15.7s h15.7d h20dᵖᵘ Apr 5] tall gelding: **h133**
bumper winner: useful handicap hurdler: third in listed event at Newbury (½ length behind
Global Citizen) in December: 15/8, similar form when second of 3 in novice at Newton
Abbot (9 lengths behind Maria's Benefit) on chasing debut: unproven beyond 17f: acts on
heavy ground: has worn hood. *Paul Nicholls*

MONTEGO GREY (FR) 5 gr.g. Montmartre (FR) – Anna Kalinka (GER) (Lion Cavern **b108**
(USA)) [2018/19 b17g⁴ b15.7s⁵ b16.7m* Apr 21] €42,000 3-y-o: good-topped gelding:
half-brother to several winners on Flat, including 1m/9f winner Another For Joe (by
Lomitas): dam German 7f/8.5f winner: useful form in bumpers: won at Market Rasen (by
8 lengths from Akarita Lights) in April. *Dan Skelton*

MONTELIMAR 4 b.f. Raven's Pass (USA) – Mascarene (USA) (Empire Maker (USA)) **b66**
[2018/19 b14g b12.4s^pu b16.2d Mar 26] 7,500 3-y-o: leggy filly: third foal: half-sister to
8.6f winner Vice Versa (by Oasis Dream): dam maiden on Flat (stayed 11f): poor form in
bumpers. *Andrew Crook*

MONTESTREL 4 b.g. Montmartre (FR) – La Estrella (GER) (Desert King (IRE)) **h125**
[2018/19 h16d* h16.4g⁶ h16.5g⁵ Feb 19] good-topped gelding: half-brother to several
winners, including useful hurdler Los Nadis (2m-3m winner, by Hernando) and French
17f-19f hurdle/chase winner Estraline (by Martaline): dam, German 1m winner, half-sister
to Grande Course de Haies d'Auteuil winner Laveron: fairly useful form over hurdles: won
juvenile at Chepstow in October: tried in hood. *Mrs Jane Williams*

MONTHYNE 8 ch.g. Nomadic Way (USA) – Captivating Tyna (IRE) (Presenting) **h76**
[2018/19 h–: h20.6g* May 11] poor form over hurdles: won handicap at Market Rasen only
start in 2018/19. *Warren Greatrex*

MONT ROYALE 11 b.g. Hurricane Run (IRE) – Wild Academy (IRE) (Royal Academy **c118**
(USA)) [2018/19 c128, h–: c20s h20g c20g* c21.2s⁴ c21.4g^pu c20.9g⁵ c25.6d^pu c22.7m^ur **h–**
c19.1d⁴ c24d⁶ c24d^pu Apr 24] good-topped gelding: winning hurdler: fairly useful handicap
chaser: won at Uttoxeter in July: stays 23f: has won on soft, but probably ideally suited to
less testing ground nowadays: usually wears headgear/tongue tie. *Jonjo O'Neill*

MONT ROYAL (FR) 5 gr.g. Naaqoos – Take Blood (FR) (Take Risks (FR)) [2018/19 **h91**
h15.7g³ h15.7g⁵ Jun 12] fair on Flat, stays 1½m: modest form over hurdles: better effort
when third in novice at Southwell. *Ollie Pears*

MONTYCRISTO 6 br.g. Motivator – Water Gipsy (Piccolo) [2018/19 h85: h18.5g h22m **h–**
Aug 2] modest maiden on Flat, stays 1¾m: poor form over hurdles. *Paul Henderson*

MONTYDARKDESTROYER 8 b.g. Lucarno (USA) – Markila (FR) (Mark of Esteem **h86**
(IRE)) [2018/19 h–: h16.2d May 5] modest form in bumpers/over hurdles: has joined
Philip Kirby. *John Davies*

MONTY MASSINI 8 b.g. Dr Massini (IRE) – Miss Montgomery (IRE) (Montekin) **c–**
[2018/19 h–, b–: h24g c20.9g^pu h16.8s c26.2g^pu Apr 26] little form over hurdles: pulled up **h–**
both starts over fences: left Evan Williams after second start. *Sarah Robinson*

MONTYS ANGEL (IRE) 9 b.m. Definite Article – Montys Bank (IRE) (Montelimar **h99**
(USA)) [2018/19 h21.5g^ur h16.5d² h18.8s³ h16.6g³ h16g⁴ h20.3d³ Apr 9] dam half-sister to
fairly useful staying chaser Ask Frank: poor maiden on Flat: modest maiden hurdler: stays
2½m: acts on soft going: tried in tongue tie: has joined Dan Skelton. *John McConnell,
Ireland*

MONTY'S AWARD (IRE) 7 b.g. Oscar (IRE) – Montys Miss (IRE) (Presenting) **h116**
[2018/19 h104: h16g² h20g* h22d⁶ h20.6g⁴ Apr 3] sturdy gelding: has had breathing
operation: fairly useful hurdler: won novice handicap at Worcester in October: stays 21f:
acts on soft going: wears hood. *Charlie Longsdon*

MONZINO (USA) 11 b.g. More Than Ready (USA) – Tasso's Magic Roo (USA) (Tasso **c– x**
(USA)) [2018/19 c–x, h–§: h16.7g⁴ h24g^pu h15.7g c17.2d^R Feb 17] workmanlike gelding: **h– §**
little form over hurdles/fences (sketchy jumper): ungenuine. *Michael Chapman*

MOODY MAGGIE (IRE) 6 b.m. Milan – Golden Bay (Karinga Bay) [2018/19 b95: **h–**
h19.6g⁶ Oct 16] fairly useful bumper performer: tailed off in maiden on hurdling debut.
Suzy Smith

MOONLIGHT CAMP (GER) 5 br.g. Kamsin (GER) – Moonlight Symphony (GER) **h–**
(Pentire) [2018/19 b15.8v³ h15.8v h19.8s^pu Mar 7] modest form in bumpers: pulled up in **b76**
maiden on hurdling debut. *Neil Mulholland*

MOONLIGHT DANCER 6 gr.m. Kayf Tara – Dissolve (Sharrood (USA)) [2018/19 **h99**
h79, b75: h20.6g⁵ h19.5d⁴ h23.3v^pu h21.4g h23.3d Mar 30] sturdy mare: has had breathing
operation: modest form over hurdles: in cheekpieces last 2 starts. *Dan Skelton*

MOONLIGHTER 6 b.g. Midnight Legend – Countess Camilla (Bob's Return (IRE)) **h120**
[2018/19 b106: h16.7g³ h19.3g* h20.5s^F h21.6d Jan 19] tall, unfurnished gelding: useful
bumper performer: fairly useful form over hurdles: won maiden at Ascot in November.
Mrs Jane Williams

Red Rum Handicap Chase, Aintree—the gambled-on novice Moon Over Germany routs the opposition; the consistent Lady Buttons takes second

MOON OVER GERMANY (IRE) 8 ch.g. Germany (USA) – Elea Moon (IRE) (Moonax (IRE)) [2018/19 c16d³ c17g² c17g c18g⁴ c15.8d* Apr 4] angular gelding: winning hurdler: smart form over fences: won Red Rum Handicap Chase at Aintree (by 10 lengths from Lady Buttons) in April: raced mainly around 2m: acts on heavy going. *Henry de Bromhead, Ireland*
     c147
     h–

MOON RACER (IRE) 10 b.g. Saffron Walden (FR) – Angel's Folly (Wesaam (USA)) [2018/19 h141: h24.2d³ c18.8g⁴ Nov 23] good-topped gelding: has had breathing operation: useful handicap hurdler: third at Newbury (8½ lengths behind Jersey Bean) in November: 5/1, fourth in novice at Ascot (13¾ lengths behind Wenyerreadyfreddie) on chasing debut: stays 3m, effective at shorter: acts on soft going: in tongue tie last 5 starts: should do better over fences. *David Pipe*
     c124 p
     h133

MOON RUA (IRE) 6 b.g. Sandmason – Dusky Palm (IRE) (Great Palm (USA)) [2018/19 h22s⁶ h19.7g h22dᵖᵘ h19.3dᵖᵘ Mar 24] made frame all 3 starts in Irish points: no form over hurdles. *Sharon Watt*
     h–

MOONSHINE BAY (IRE) 6 b.g. Milan – Chantoue Royale (FR) (Cadoudal (FR)) [2018/19 h24m* c21.2g⁴ c24.6g* c24g⁴ c24dᵖᵘ c24d⁴ c24.5g⁴ Mar 31] £120,000 4-y-o: sixth foal: closely related to modest/unreliable 2½m hurdle winner Cinematique (by King's Theatre) and half-brother to fairly useful 23f hurdle winner Preseli Rock (by Flemensfirth), later successful in USA, and bumper winner Westhorpe (by Westerner): dam 15f-2¼m hurdle/chase winner: fairly useful form over hurdles: won minor event at Down Royal early in season: useful form over fences: won maiden at Thurles in December: stays 25f: acts on good to firm and heavy going: tried in cheekpieces: usually races prominently. *Mrs J. Harrington, Ireland*
     c140
     h127

MOONTRIPPER 10 b.m. Doyen (IRE) – Moon Spinner (Elmaamul (USA)) [2018/19 c60, h76: c20.9d³ h21.6g c16.5gᵘʳ h23.9d Oct 20] point winner: poor maiden hurdler: similar form over fences: stays 21f: acts on soft going: usually races towards rear. *Phillip Dando*
     c71
     h–

MOORES NOVELTY (IRE) 7 b.g. Sholokhov (IRE) – Moricana (GER) (Konigsstuhl (GER)) [2018/19 h–: h20.2g⁴ h23.8gᵖᵘ h20.6dᵖᵘ Dec 13] has had breathing operation: in frame completed starts in Irish points: poor maiden hurdler: best effort at 2½m: tried in tongue tie. *N. W. Alexander* — **h83**

MOORES ROAD (IRE) 10 ch.g. Vertical Speed (FR) – Lady Quesada (IRE) (Alflora (IRE)) [2018/19 h–: h19.2g Jul 8] point winner: little form in chases: stays 2¾m: acts on heavy going: tried in blinkers: front runner/races prominently. *Richard Spencer* — **c– h–**

MOOR FREEDOM 6 b.m. Beat Hollow – Line Freedom (FR) (Freedom Cry) [2018/19 b86: b16.4g b16.8s h19g h18.5s⁶ Mar 18] smallish mare: fair form in bumpers only on debut in 2017/18: well held both starts over hurdles. *Polly Gundry* — **h– b–**

MOORLANDS GEORGE 11 b.g. Grape Tree Road – Sandford Springs (USA) (Robellino (USA)) [2018/19 c108, h–: c25.8d c25.2s³ c24dᵖᵘ Dec 31] has had breathing operation: maiden hurdler: fair handicap chaser, below form in 2018/19: stays 3¼m: acts on soft and good to firm going: wears tongue tie. *Jeremy Scott* — **c95 h–**

MOORLANDS JACK 14 b.g. Cloudings (IRE) – Sandford Springs (USA) (Robellino (USA)) [2018/19 c107§, h–§: c21g* c21g³ c20.9g⁴ c20g Nov 9] strong gelding: winning hurdler: fair handicap chaser: won at Newton Abbot in May: stays 23f: acts on soft and good to firm going: usually wears headgear: tried in tongue tie: usually races nearer last than first: unreliable. *Jeremy Scott* — **c107 § h– §**

MOORLANDS MIST 12 gr.g. Fair Mix (IRE) – Sandford Springs (USA) (Robellino (USA)) [2018/19 c97§, h100: h23.3g* h27g* h24.6vᵖᵘ h23.1gᵖᵘ h20.1g⁶ Apr 15] good-topped gelding: fair handicap hurdler: won at Hexham in October and Sedgefield in November: maiden chaser: stays 27f: acts on heavy going: has worn headgear: tried in tongue tie: front runner: not one to trust. *Sara Ender* — **c– § h101 §**

MOORSTOWN (IRE) 9 b.g. Oscar (IRE) – Glacial Princess (IRE) (Glacial Storm (USA)) [2018/19 c81§, h–: c24.2vᵖᵘ Dec 20] lightly-raced hurdler: modest chaser at best, pulled up sole start in 2018/19: stays 3m: acts heavy going: tried in headgear: has worn tongue tie: temperamental. *Lucinda Russell* — **c– § h–**

MORAL HAZARD (IRE) 10 br.g. Milan – Maria Thai (FR) (Siam (USA)) [2018/19 c–, h–: c27.5dᵖᵘ Jun 8] multiple point winner: once-raced hurdler: fair form on debut in hunter chases, none since: in tongue tie last 2 starts. *Miss Beverley Thomas* — **c– h–**

MORE BUCK'S (IRE) 9 ch.g. Presenting – Buck's Blue (FR) (Epervier Bleu) [2018/19 c110, h–: c26.7m² c23.8g* c21.4m* h23.9vᵖᵘ c21g c21.1sᵖᵘ c20m* c23.8gᵖᵘ c20.2g⁴ c21.1dᵘʳ c23.8g⁵ Apr 24] well-made gelding: winning hurdler: useful handicap chaser: won at Perth in June, Summer Plate at Market Rasen (by ½ length from Too Many Diamonds) in July and Ludlow in January: left Paul Nicholls after first start: stays 3m: acts on good to firm and heavy going: has worn headgear: wears tongue tie: front runner. *Peter Bowen* — **c136 h–**

MOREECE (IRE) 10 b.g. Chevalier (IRE) – Jumbo Romance (IRE) (Tagula (IRE)) [2018/19 c–, h–: c23.6g⁵ Apr 26] multiple point winner: maiden hurdler: fair form at best in hunter chases: stays 3m: acts on soft and good to firm going: in headgear last 5 starts: has joined John Flint. *Alexander Gibbons* — **c– h–**

MOREHURRYLESSHASTE (IRE) 6 b.m. Court Cave (IRE) – Hasty Quest (IRE) (Sesaro (USA)) [2018/19 h16m h16g h16g h21.6sᵖᵘ Nov 25] €800 3-y-o, £2,500 5-y-o: fifth foal: dam well held in bumpers: maiden Irish pointer: no form over hurdles. *Christian Williams* — **h–**

MORE THAN LUCK (IRE) 8 br.g. Gothland (FR) – Pretty Impressive (IRE) (Presenting) [2018/19 c109, h102: h16.7g h19.6gᵖᵘ h20.3g⁶ h25.8g* c25.7g² h27g⁴ Nov 1] has had breathing operation: fair handicap hurdler: won at Fontwell in August: fair handicap chaser: stays 3¼m: acts on heavy going: usually wears headgear: has worn tongue tie, including last 4 starts. *Olly Murphy* — **c105 h103**

MORGA (IRE) 9 b.m. Whipper (USA) – Langfuhrina (USA) (Langfuhr (CAN)) [2018/19 h16.3d³ h18.1g h16g h18g h17.6g⁵ h16d Apr 27] useful handicap hurdler: third at Galway (4 lengths behind Off You Go) in October: unproven beyond 2m: acts on soft and good to firm going: has worn hood. *Desmond McDonogh, Ireland* — **h130**

MORIANOUR (FR) 8 b.g. Valanour (IRE) – Moriane (FR) (Manninamix) [2018/19 h112: c19.4m³ c23.6s² c25.6sᵖᵘ Dec 5] fair form over hurdles: similar form over fences: best effort when second in handicap at Chepstow: stayed 3m: acted on heavy going: dead. *Evan Williams* — **c114 h–**

MORNEY WING (IRE) 10 b.g. Antonius Pius (USA) – Tillan Fuwain (FR) (Unfuwain (USA)) [2018/19 c111§, h–: c26m* c25.5g³ c25.7d² c28.8v* c32.6g³ c25.7d² c31.8m^pu Apr 13] workmanlike gelding: maiden hurdler: fairly useful handicap chaser: won at Fontwell in October and Betfair London National at Sandown (by length from Red Infantry) in December: third in Eider (Handicap Chase) at Newcastle: stays 33f: acts on good to firm and heavy going: wears headgear/tongue tie: usually races prominently. *Charlie Mann* **c129 h–**

MORNING HERALD 8 br.m. Lucky Story (USA) – Wakeful (Kayf Tara) [2018/19 h–: h23.3d c22.5g³ h19.9g Jul 10] angular mare: fairly useful hurdler, below form since 2016/17: 6/1, third of 4 in novice handicap at Uttoxeter (13¾ lengths behind Blagapar) on chasing debut: stays 2¾m: acts on good to firm going: tried in cheekpieces. *Martin Keighley* **c110 h–**

MORNING ROYALTY (IRE) 12 b.g. King's Theatre (IRE) – Portryan Native (IRE) (Be My Native (USA)) [2018/19 c135, h125: h25.4g⁴ c25.5g⁵ c25.5s⁵ c24.1v c20.1s^pu c24.5s^ur h24.3d⁶ h22.8d⁴ Mar 20] small, sturdy gelding: fair handicap hurdler nowadays: useful chaser, below form in 2018/19: stays 25f, at least as effective at shorter: acts on good to firm and heavy going: tried in tongue tie: waited with. *James Moffatt* **c– h108**

MORNING SEQUEL 6 b.m. Revoque (IRE) – Silver Sequel (Silver Patriarch (IRE)) [2018/19 h–: h18.5g h23m h17.7d⁶ h20.5g^bd h20.5g⁵ Apr 21] poor maiden hurdler: in cheekpieces last 4 starts: stays 2½m: acts on soft going: tried in tongue tie last 3. *Neil Mulholland* **h67**

MORNING VICAR (IRE) 6 b.g. Beneficial – Mary's Little Vic (IRE) (Old Vic) [2018/19 h105: h20.5s³ h21.2d* h20.5d Mar 22] well-made gelding: useful bumper performer: fairly useful form over hurdles: won maiden at Ludlow in February: likely to stay 3m. *Nicky Henderson* **h118**

MORNING WITH IVAN (IRE) 9 b.m. Ivan Denisovich (IRE) – Grinneas (IRE) (Barathea (IRE)) [2018/19 c–, h110: h16.2g* h16.2g⁴ h15.6g h17.1v^pu Dec 2] fair handicap hurdler: won at Perth early in season: maiden chaser: stays 2½m: acts on soft going: has worn headgear: wears tongue tie: usually races nearer last than first. *Susan Corbett* **c– h108**

MORODER (IRE) 5 b.g. Morozov (USA) – Another Tonto (IRE) (Definite Article) [2018/19 b17.7s² b15.8v* Mar 16] €11,000 3-y-o: first foal: dam, unraced, out of half-sister to smart chaser (winner up to 21f) Go Roger Go: fair form in bumpers: won at Uttoxeter in March. *Seamus Mullins* **b94**

MOROSINI (FR) 4 b.g. Martaline – Iris du Berlais (FR) (Bonnet Rouge (FR)) [2018/19 h16d² Feb 23] half-brother to fair hurdler/fairly useful chaser Ivresse du Berlais (15f-19f winner, by Poliglote) and fairly useful hurdler La Croix Sonnet (17f winner, by Kapgarde), both in France: dam, French 2¼m hurdle winner, half-sister to useful/unreliable hurdler/ chaser (stayed 29f) Ipsos du Berlais: runner-up only start on Flat for Mlle A-S. Pacault: 20/1, promising second in Winning Fair Juvenile Hurdle at Fairyhouse (3½ lengths behind Way Back Home) on hurdling debut: open to improvement. *Mrs J. Harrington, Ireland* **h127 p**

MORRAMAN (IRE) 6 b.g. Gold Well – Casa Queen (IRE) (Great Palm (USA)) [2018/19 h16.8g⁶ h21.2g³ h23d³ h23.8g* h19.3s³ h19.8m⁴ h21.3g* Apr 11] £10,000 5-y-o: has had breathing operation: second foal: dam, ran once over hurdles, out of sister to useful chaser up to 25f All The Aces: Irish point winner: fairly useful hurdler: won maiden at Musselburgh in December and handicap at Wetherby in April: stays 3m: acts on good to firm going. *Donald McCain* **h122**

MORTAL (IRE) 7 b.g. King's Theatre (IRE) – Pomme Tiepy (FR) (Apple Trec (FR)) [2018/19 c21.2g* c24g² c21g⁶ c24.4s⁵ Mar 13] €100,000 3-y-o: good-topped gelding: first foal: dam (c134/h124), 17f-3m hurdle/chase winner (stayed 3¾m), also 1½m winner on Flat in France: fairly useful form over hurdles: useful form over fences: won maiden at Fairyhouse in December: second in Neville Hotels Novices' Chase at Leopardstown (8 lengths behind Delta Work) later in month: stays 3m: acts on heavy going: wears tongue tie. *Joseph Patrick O'Brien, Ireland* **c143 h–**

MORTENS LEAM 7 b.g. Sulamani (IRE) – Bonnet's Pieces (Alderbrook) [2018/19 c122, h97: h23g⁶ h20.3g h15.8s^pu h19.2g c26g^ur c21.6d* c20d⁵ c21.6v* c27.6s⁶ c19.5d⁵ c19.5v² Mar 6] maiden hurdler: fairly useful handicap chaser: won at Fontwell in November and December: stays 2¾m: acts on heavy going: held up. *Mike Hawker* **c117 h–**

MOSCANISI (IRE) 8 b.m. Kalanisi (IRE) – Renvyle Society (IRE) (Moscow Society (USA)) [2018/19 h20.1g May 12] Irish point winner: fair form over hurdles, well held on sole start in 2018/19 after 17 months off: will stay 2¾m+. *Rebecca Menzies* **h–**

MOSSING 7 b.m. Passing Glance – Missy Moscow (IRE) (Moscow Society (USA)) [2018/19 b15.8m h15.8s h21s⁵ h19.6d⁵ h24.2d⁶ Mar 22] lengthy mare: first foal: dam (c86) 2¾m-3m chase winner: offered little in bumper: modest form over hurdles. *James Evans* **h85 b–**

MOSS ON THE MILL 11 br.g. Overbury (IRE) – Mimis Bonnet (FR) (Bonnet Rouge (FR)) [2018/19 c105, h–: c26.1g³ c25.8gᵖᵘ c23.6s⁶ c25.2sᶠ h23dᵖᵘ Jan 8] winning hurdler: fair handicap chaser: stays 3¼m: acts on good to firm and heavy going: wears headgear: often let down by jumping. *Tom George* **c108 x** **h–**

MOTION TO STRIKE (IRE) 9 b.g. Beneficial – Comeragh Girl (IRE) (Imperial Ballet (IRE)) [2018/19 c–, h87§: c16g² c17.3g³ c16g² c17.3gᵖᵘ Jul 21] Irish point winner: modest maiden hurdler: similar form over fences: stayed 2½m: acted on soft going: often wore headgear/tongue tie earlier in career: dead. *Jackie Stephen* **c91** **h– §**

MO TOTTIE 5 b.m. Midnight Legend – Tot of The Knar (Kayf Tara) [2018/19 b17.7v⁴ Mar 6] second foal: sister to fairly useful hurdler Mac Tottie (2½m-23f winner): dam (c120/h132) 2m-23f hurdle/chase winner: tailed off in bumper. *Peter Bowen* **b–**

MOTTS CROSS (IRE) 8 b.g. Scorpion (IRE) – Rainy Season (IRE) (Sulamani (IRE)) [2018/19 h21.6v c23.6d c24.2sᵖᵘ h26g⁶ h23.9d* Mar 11] lengthy gelding: maiden chaser: modest handicap hurdler: won at Taunton in March: no show in chases: stays 3m: acts on good to firm and good to soft going: usually wears cheekpieces: usually races prominently. *Chris Down* **c–** **h91**

MOTUEKA (IRE) 7 b.g. King's Theatre (IRE) – Tchouina (FR) (Broadway Flyer (USA)) [2018/19 h111§: h22.2g* h23.9g² h24g² h21.6g* h23g* Oct 11] fairly useful hurdler: won maiden at Uttoxeter in July, and novices at Newton Abbot and Worcester in October: stays 3m: best form on good going: in headgear/tongue tie last 5 starts: usually leads: has joined Hannah James: temperamental. *Olly Murphy* **h120 §**

MOUCHEE (IRE) 4 b.g. Zebedee – Nashaat (Redoute's Choice (AUS)) [2018/19 h16.8g⁵ h16d Aug 29] fair on Flat, stays 1½m: well held in 2 juvenile hurdles: in visor first start. *Michael Blake* **h–**

MOUNTAIN CHIMES 7 b.g. Winged Love (IRE) – Threerockmountain (IRE) (Lahib (USA)) [2018/19 h15.8d h15.7g h16g h15.8g c17.4g³ c17g⁴ c16s³ c16.2dʳᵒ c20.3d Jan 8] has had breathing operation: modest form over hurdles/fences: left Evan Williams after first start: raced mainly around 2m. *Henry Oliver* **c89** **h90**

MOUNTAIN CLICHE (IRE) 12 b.g. Classic Cliche (IRE) – Quarry Girl (IRE) (Lord Americo) [2018/19 c98, h–: c24.2d⁶ Apr 9] multiple point winner: once-raced over hurdles: modest form in hunter chases. *N. J. Dawe* **c–** **h–**

MOUNTAIN HAWK (IRE) 7 b.g. Mountain High (IRE) – Septembers Hawk (IRE) (Machiavellian (USA)) [2018/19 h16g⁴ h21.3s⁶ h16.2v² h16.4g* h19.9s³ h17v⁴ Mar 17] fair form over hurdles: won novice at Newcastle in January: should stay at least 2½m: acts on heavy going. *Tim Easterby* **h109**

MOUNTAIN OF ANGELS 10 b.m. Midnight Legend – Landsker Missile (Cruise Missile) [2018/19 c–, h–: c19.4m² c17gᵖᵘ Aug 28] point winner: maiden hurdler: poor form over fences: stays 19f: acts on good to firm going: in headgear last 4 starts: in tongue tie last 2. *Evan Williams* **c66** **h–**

MOUNTAIN OF MOURNE (IRE) 10 ch.g. Mountain High (IRE) – Katies Native (IRE) (Be My Native (USA)) [2018/19 c–§, h95§: h21.6s h19.5d⁴ c19.4d⁵ c30.7dᵖᵘ h23.6d Mar 20] compact gelding: poor handicap hurdler: poor maiden chaser: stays 3m: acts on heavy going: usually wears headgear: temperamental. *Linda Blackford* **c64 §** **h78 §**

MOUNTAIN PATH 6 b.m. Mount Nelson – Vino (Efisio) [2018/19 h101: h16.7gᵖᵘ May 20] leggy mare: bumper winner: fair form over hurdles: dead. *Jonjo O'Neill* **h–**

MOUNTAIN RANGER (IRE) 7 b.g. Mountain High (IRE) – Oscareen (IRE) (Oscar (IRE)) [2018/19 h21sᵖᵘ h16g⁶ h19.5g⁵ h16g⁵ h20g h19.4g³ h19.9sᵖᵘ Dec 31] fifth foal: brother to fair 2m hurdle winner/winning pointer Highandmighty, closely related to fairly useful 2m hurdle winner Billbushay (by Westerner) and half-brother to bumper winner/fair hurdler Catimini (2½m winner, by Golan): dam unraced sister to smart hurdler/useful chaser (winner up to 3m) Oscar Park: unplaced in point: fair form in bumpers: fair maiden hurdler: left Sean Byrne after fifth start: stays 19f: has worn tongue tie. *Alex Hales* **h102**

MOUNTAIN ROCK (IRE) 7 b.g. Mountain High (IRE) – Ajo Green (IRE) (Moscow Society (USA)) [2018/19 h19.9g⁴ h19.9g² Apr 7] bumper winner: fair form over hurdles: stays 2¾m: acts on good to firm going: tried in cheekpieces: has joined Johnny Farrelly. *Ian Williams* **h113**

MOUNTAIN SO HIGH (IRE) 6 b.g. Mountain High (IRE) – Marigier (IRE) (Presenting) [2018/19 b15.7g b16.3d Nov 8] well held in bumpers. *Thomas Gallagher* **b–**

MOUNT BECKHAM (IRE) 10 b.g. Desert King (IRE) – Nowhere Like Home (IRE) **c107**
(Exit To Nowhere (USA)) [2018/19 c123, h–: h16.5m c20.1g³ c20.1g⁴ Aug 25] winning **h–**
hurdler: fairly useful form at best over fences: stays 2½m: acts on heavy going: tried in
cheekpieces/tongue tie. *Miss Clare Louise Cannon, Ireland*

MOUNT CLESHAR 5 b.g. Mount Nelson – Resal (IRE) (Montjeu (IRE)) [2018/19 **h77**
h15.8v h16d⁶ Mar 4] modest maiden on Flat, stays 2m: poor form over hurdles. *Paul
D'Arcy*

MOUNT MEWS (IRE) 8 b.g. Presenting – Kneeland Lass (IRE) (Bob Back (USA)) **c129**
[2018/19 c138p, h138: c21.6g² h20.3dʳ h20d Apr 5] well-made gelding: useful handicap **h– §**
hurdler, let down by jumping final start: similar form over fences: second in handicap at
Kelso in January: stays 3m: acts on heavy going: temperamental (refused to race second
outing). *Donald McCain*

MOUNT NELLY 5 b.m. Mount Nelson – Candle (Dansili) [2018/19 b16.8s⁴ Apr 16] **b74**
£12,500 5-y-o: third foal: dam (h107), 2m-2¾m hurdle winner, also useful 1¼m-1½m
winner on Flat: placed in point on debut: 10/1, fourth in maiden bumper at Exeter (8¼
lengths behind Merchant House). *David Pipe*

MOUNT RUSHMOORE (IRE) 7 b.g. Shantou (USA) – Knock On The Door (IRE) **c–**
(Saddlers' Hall (IRE)) [2018/19 h116, h84: h19.9g c23.6vᵖᵘ c22.4dᵖᵘ Dec 29] workmanlike **h82**
gelding: won Irish point on debut: fairly useful form over hurdles: disappointing in
2018/19, including in chases: stays 19f: acts on heavy going: tried in cheekpieces.
Colin Tizzard

MOUNT RUSSELL (IRE) 9 b.g. Indian River (FR) – Norwich Breeze (IRE) (Norwich) **c–**
[2018/19 c16.5g⁶ c20.3g Oct 3] maiden pointer/hurdler: well held in chases. *Henry Oliver* **h–**

MOUNT VESUVIUS (IRE) 11 b.g. Spartacus (IRE) – Parker's Cove (USA) (Woodman **c–**
(USA)) [2018/19 c68, h82§: h18.5g⁶ h25.8s h20.5m* h18.5m h19.8g Nov 22] compact **h78 §**
gelding: poor handicap hurdler: won at Plumpton in October: maiden chaser: barely stays
3¼m: acts on good to firm and heavy going: has worn cheekpieces: wears tongue tie: no
battler. *Paul Henderson*

MOUNT WINDSOR (IRE) 4 br.g. Mountain High (IRE) – Mrs Bukay (IRE) (Bishop **b93**
of Cashel) [2018/19 b13.7v² b13.7g* Apr 12] second foal: dam bumper winner: fair form
in bumpers: won at Fontwell in April. *Chris Gordon*

MOUSEINTHEHOUSE (IRE) 5 b.g. Milan – Mandysue (IRE) (Mandalus) [2018/19 **h90 p**
h19.7sᵘʳ h15.8v⁴ h19s⁶ Mar 19] €22,000 3-y-o: fourth foal: half-brother to a winning
pointer by Great Palm: dam unraced sister to top-class chaser (stayed 29f) Sir Rembrandt:
modest form over hurdles: remains with potential. *Evan Williams*

MOVE ABOVE (IRE) 5 br.g. Dubai Destination (USA) – From Above (IRE) (Anshan) **h104**
[2018/19 b16g³ b16.7v* b16s⁵ h15.8d⁴ h15.8d³ h21.6d Apr 9] €20,000 3-y-o: third foal: **b88**
half-brother to a winning pointer by Arcadio: dam unraced sister to fairly useful hurdler/
chaser (2½m-25f winner) Baily Storm: fair form in bumpers: won at Bangor in December:
similar form over hurdles: best effort when third in novice at Ludlow in March: should be
suited by further than 2m: tried in cheekpieces. *Alastair Ralph*

MOVE TO THE GROOVE (IRE) 9 b.g. Catcher In The Rye (IRE) – Valley of Love **c– x**
(IRE) (Lure (USA)) [2018/19 c22.5gᶠ Oct 18] winning pointer/hurdler: no form in chases, **h–**
fell heavily first only outing in 2018/19 after 24 months off: stays 2½m: acts on good to
firm and good to soft going: often let down by jumping. *Donald McCain*

MOVEWITHTHETIMES (IRE) 8 ch.g. Presenting – Dare To Venture (IRE) (Darazari **c136**
(IRE)) [2018/19 c140, h–: c16.3gᵘʳ c20.2gᶠ c20.2s Mar 12] well-made gelding: winning **h–**
hurdler: useful maiden chaser: stays 2½m: acts on good to soft going: has joined Enda
Bolger. *Paul Nicholls*

MOVIE LEGEND 9 b.g. Midnight Legend – Cyd Charisse (Kayf Tara) [2018/19 c125, **c130**
h–: h20m* c15.9g² c15.2s² c18.8s³ c16.2g² c15.2g* c16.4g* c15.8d Apr 4] workmanlike **h115**
gelding: has had breathing operations: fairly useful hurdler: won novice at Fakenham in
October: useful handicap chaser: won at Wetherby in February and Doncaster in March:
stays 21f: acts on good to firm and heavy going: wears cheekpieces: has worn tongue tie.
Lucy Wadham

MOVIE SET (USA) 7 b.g. Dubawi (IRE) – Short Skirt (Diktat) [2018/19 h115p: h16g³ **h117**
h15.8g² h15.8g³ Jul 10] good-topped gelding: fairly useful form over hurdles: third in
novice at Kempton early in season: raced only at 2m: tried in cheekpieces: front runner/
races prominently. *Richard Spencer*

MOVIE THEATRE 7 b.g. Multiplex – Tintera (IRE) (King's Theatre (IRE)) [2018/19 **h—**
h20s^{pu} h19.7s^{pu} h19d^5 h19d^5 Feb 28] off mark in Irish points at third attempt: no form over
hurdles: in hood last 2 starts. *Jack R. Barber*

MOVING IN STYLE (IRE) 8 ch.g. Mountain High (IRE) – Good To Travel (IRE) **c119**
(Night Shift (USA)) [2018/19 h104: c25.8v^{pu} c24.2s* c23.6d^4 c26.3s* c24.2v^3 Mar 18] **h—**
compact gelding: has had breathing operation: fair form over hurdles: fairly useful form
over fences: won handicaps at Wetherby (novice) in December and Sedgefield in March:
stays 3¼m: acts on soft going: has joined Robert Walford. *Neil Mulholland*

MOYASZOV (IRE) 5 b.g. Morozov (USA) – Moyas Charm (IRE) (Carroll House) **h—**
[2018/19 h17.1d h16.2g Nov 9] no show in 2 novice hurdles. *Nicky Richards*

MOYHENNA (IRE) 7 b.m. Westerner – Moskova (IRE) (Montjeu (IRE)) [2018/19 **c140**
c16.7v^2 c19.7d^2 c21g^F c18g^{ur} c22.5v* Mar 17] first foal: dam (c139/h140), ungenuine 2m- **h—**
3m hurdle/chase winner, also 1½m winner on Flat: bumper winner: fairly useful form over
hurdles: useful form over fences: won Grade 2 mares novice at Limerick (by 25 lengths
from Oh Me Oh My) in March: improved again when following up in 15-runner mares
handicap at Punchestown shortly after end of British season by 4½ lengths from
Timeforwest, going with enthusiasm again and drawing clear run-in: stays 3m: acts on
heavy going: front runner/races prominently. *Denis Hogan, Ireland*

MOYNIHANS GIRL (IRE) 5 ch.m. Frammassone (IRE) – Catch Ball (Prince Sabo) **h—**
[2018/19 h—: h15.3m May 10] no form over hurdles. *Laura Young*

MR ADJUDICATOR 5 b.g. Camacho – Attlongglast (Groom Dancer (USA)) **h156**
[2018/19 h147: h16d^2 h16.8d h16d^{pu} Apr 23]
It is notoriously difficult for the leading juvenile hurdlers to make the
transition to top open company against older rivals. Recent Triumph Hurdle winners
have certainly struggled in their second seasons over hurdles. The most recent
to be successful in the following season was Tiger Roll, though even his win, at
Cheltenham in the autumn of 2014, came in a four-runner minor event against fellow
four-year-olds, not older horses. The five-year-old Espoir d'Allen's Champion
Hurdle victory in the latest season was therefore a rare achievement as he became
the first of his age since Katchit in 2008 to win hurdling's top prize. Strictly speaking,
another of the top juvenile hurdlers from the previous season, Mr Adjudicator, drew a
blank, just like Farclas, the horse who beat him into second in the Triumph
Hurdle. He may not have won in the latest season, but important victories in Ireland
and France shortly after the end of the British season (performances not included in
the form figures above) mean that Mr Adjudicator can, after all, go down as another
success story from the 2017/18 crop of Irish juveniles.
Three of the top Irish four-year-old hurdlers made their return in a Grade 3
contest restricted to their age group, the Fishery Lane Hurdle at Naas in November.
The ill-fated Espoir d'Allen was having his first start since suffering what was the
only defeat of his career in the Spring Juvenile Hurdle at Leopardstown the previous
February, a race Mr Adjudicator had won from Farclas with the odds-on Espoir
d'Allen a well-beaten fourth. Also in the Fishery Lane line-up was Mr Adjudicator's
stablemate Saldier, who had beaten him into second in the Champion Four Year Old
Hurdle at Punchestown. Saldier looked all set to make a winning return at Naas when
falling at the last, leaving Espoir d'Allen clear to beat Mr Adjudicator by eleven
lengths. While Espoir d'Allen won twice more before the Cheltenham Festival,
Mr Adjudicator went straight there without another run to contest the County Hurdle.
Whiskey Sour, who started favourite, fared best of the Mullins runners in fourth
while Mr Adjudicator caught the eye back in eighth, staying on under a patient ride
without coming under firm pressure once it was clear he wasn't going to be involved
in the finish, impressing as one to note for another big handicap. Runner-up behind
the winner Ch'tibello, incidentally, under a big weight, was another of the previous
season's leading juvenile hurdlers We Have A Dream, winner of the Anniversary
Hurdle at Aintree.
The promise of Mr Adjudicator's run in the County Hurdle was duly fulfilled
at rewarding odds of 20/1 at Punchestown, though that was surely one race too late
for many. By then, his name had doubtless been scrubbed from many notebooks
after he had run no sort of race following his County Hurdle effort when strongly
supported for another valuable handicap at Fairyhouse. Sent off the 4/1 favourite for

the Rybo Handicap Hurdle (which went to Ivanovich Gorbatov—his first victory since winning the Triumph Hurdle more than three years earlier), Mr Adjudicator was pulled up by Ruby Walsh before jumping the fifth flight, his rider reporting, when asked to account for Mr Adjudicator's poor showing, that he had been 'reluctant to race'. Veterinary checks had found nothing wrong physically.

Mr Adjudicator's contrasting display when winning the twenty-five-runner Ballymore Handicap Hurdle on the final day of the Punchestown Festival attracted the stewards' attention again, and they noted the explanations that Mr Adjudicator was running without the ear plugs he had worn at Fairyhouse, and that he was tried in a new bit. Willie Mullins fielded ten runners in the Ballymore, including the very lightly-raced Lake Kivu who started one of the 7/1 joint favourites, but it was four of the longer-priced stablemates who dominated the finish as Mr Adjudicator, carrying top weight and ridden by Mr Patrick Mullins, stayed on to lead close home after an untidy jump at the last to win by three quarters of a length and half a length from Contingency and Dorrells Pierji, with Stratum completing the frame (Mullins also had the sixth Cut The Mustard). Under his big weight, Mr Adjudicator produced one of the handicap performances of the season, a very smart effort which suggested he was well worth his place back in graded company.

The Ballymore, over two and a half miles, was Mr Adjudicator's first race at much beyond two miles and the longer trip clearly suited him, though the three miles plus of the Grande Course de Haies d'Auteuil later in May proved too far for him. Mr Adjudicator was not entirely discredited in finishing seventh behind stable-companion Benie des Dieux, though his jumping was not foot perfect on his first experience of French hurdles. He was due to have had his first taste of the brush obstacles at the same meeting the year before but was prevented from running in the Prix Alain du Breil as his vaccinations were not in order. A return to shorter promised to suit Mr Adjudicator and he got the chance when sent back to Auteuil in June for the Prix La Barka over just short of two and a half miles.

Having swapped dates with the Grande Course de Haies for the first time in 2018, the La Barka now provides an opportunity for some sort of consolation three weeks after France's top hurdling prize, rather than serving as its main trial beforehand (it was run over a couple of furlongs further in its former guise). The alteration to the calendar has made no difference to Mullins' excellent record in a race he won for the first time with Thousand Stars in 2012, the year that horse also won his second Grande Course de Haies. Thousand Stars won the La Barka again

Ballymore Handicap Hurdle, Punchestown—a remarkable 1, 2, 3, 4 for Willie Mullins as top-weight Mr Adjudicator (No.1) beats Contingency (left), Dorrells Pierji (centre/mostly hidden) and Stratum (out of shot)

Prix La Barka Hurdle, Auteuil—the Mullins yard dominates again as Mr Adjudicator (dark colours/right) keeps on too well for 2018 winner Bapaume (left)

in 2014, while Mullins had also won the last three renewals with Un de Sceaux, Shaneshill and Bapaume. The last-named finished runner-up in the Grande Course de Haies in 2018 and joined Mr Adjudicator in a five-strong Mullins team in a field of ten for the latest running of the Prix La Barka, Bapaume having finished fourth in his most recent Grande Course de Haies attempt. Bapaume and Mr Adjudicator, in fact, were the only two in the La Barka field who had contested the Grande Course de Haies three weeks earlier, and it was they who fought out the finish, albeit some apart on Auteuil's broad run-in. Bapaume came up the stand rail but Mr Adjudicator, having put in a better round of jumping than on his last visit, stayed towards the far side and kept on best after joining issue at the final hurdle for a three-length win. Seven lengths behind Bapaume in third was the favourite Blue Dragon who made most of the running, though he had already shown that he is no longer the top-class hurdler he once was. For the record, the three other Mullins runners Quick Grabim, Stormy Ireland and Pravalaguna finished fifth, sixth and seventh. Bapaume had been the stable's first string and was the mount (as he had been when successful the year before) of Paul Townend who had also partnered Benie des Dieux to her win in the Grande Course de Haies. Indeed, all Mullins' earlier La Barka victories and all five of his successes in the Grande Course de Haies had been gained with Irish jockeys, making Mr Adjudicator's victory notable for having a local jockey in the saddle, Bertrand Lestrade, French champion for a third time in four years in 2018 and clear again in the 2019 standings.

	Camacho (b 2002)	Danehill (b 1986)	Danzig
Mr Adjudicator			Razyana
(b.g. 2014)		Arabesque (b 1997)	Zafonic
			Prophecy
	Attlongglast (b 2001)	Groom Dancer (b 1984)	Blushing Groom
			Featherhill
		My Way (b 1995)	Marju
			Ausherra

The rather leggy Mr Adjudicator, who won over seven furlongs as a two-year-old, has an unlikely sire for a good hurdler in the smart six- to seven-furlong performer Camacho, himself a half-brother to the fine sire of sprinters Showcasing. But there is stamina in Mr Adjudicator's distaff family—his great grandam Ausherra, winner of the Lingfield Oaks Trial, was a sister to the Epsom, Irish and Yorkshire Oaks winner and St Leger runner-up Ramruma—and others in the family have successfully taken to jumping despite this being an essentially Flat pedigree. Among Ausherra's foals, the ex-Godolphin gelding Red Admiral won a Rising Stars' Novices Chase at Wincanton for Charlie Mann, while Yorkshire, a close fifth in the Melbourne Cup when trained by Paul Cole on the Flat, won his first five races as a novice over hurdles. Devil To Pay, a half-brother to Mr Adjudicator's unraced dam Attlongglast, was a fairly useful hurdler for Alan King, while Attlongglast herself now numbers three winning hurdlers among her foals. Vlannon (by Captain Gerrard) won a juvenile hurdle at Kempton in January, while her modest six-year-old daughter Multigifted (by Multiplex, a son of Danehill like Camacho) got off the mark in a handicap at Fontwell in May 2019. As for Mr Adjudicator, he was returned to the Flat after the Prix La Barka to exploit a potentially lenient handicap mark, something he achieved in a valuable handicap over a mile and a half at the Galway Festival. Mr Adjudicator stays two and a half miles and has been raced only on ground softer than good over hurdles (acts on heavy), though his Galway win came on good to firm. He wore a hood on his successful debut over hurdles and has also worn headgear on the Flat. *W. P. Mullins, Ireland*

MR ANTOLINI (IRE) 9 b.g. Catcher In The Rye (IRE) – Victory Run (IRE) (Old Vic) **h134**
[2018/19 h136: h21g⁵ h18.9g² h15.7s⁵ h23.4sᵖᵘ h20.3d Mar 15] rather leggy gelding:
maiden pointer: useful handicap hurdler: fifth in Betfair Exchange Trophy at Ascot in
December: stays 21f: acts on heavy going: has worn hood. *Nigel Twiston-Davies*

MR BACHSTER (IRE) 14 b.g. Bach (IRE) – Warrior Princess (IRE) (Mister Lord **c–**
(USA)) [2018/19 c74, h74: c20.9dᶠ h21.2g h20.3s⁶ h23.8dᵖᵘ Jan 28] compact gelding: **h–**
modest hurdler/chaser at best: stayed 2½m: acted on heavy going: usually wore
cheekpieces: dead. *Kerry Lee*

MR BIG SHOT (IRE) 8 br.g. Flemensfirth (USA) – Une Etoile (IRE) (Un Desperado **c132**
(FR)) [2018/19 h142p: c23.4s⁵ Dec 1] big gelding: useful form over hurdles: 9/2, fifth in **h–**
John Francome Novices' Chase at Newbury (17½ lengths behind Santini) on chasing
debut: stays 25f: acts on soft going. *David Pipe*

MR CAFFREY 7 b.g. Duke of Marmalade (IRE) – Quest For Eternity (IRE) (Sadler's **h118**
Wells (USA)) [2018/19 h100§: h19.9g² h19.6g² h20g² h22g* h23.3g* Sep 12] fairly useful
handicap hurdler: won at Stratford and Uttoxeter in September: stays 23f: acts on good to
firm and good to soft going: wears headgear. *Dr Richard Newland*

MR CLARKSON (IRE) 7 b.g. Jeremy (USA) – Wynsleydale (USA) (Theatrical) **h95**
[2018/19 h21.4dᵖᵘ h23.4sᵖᵘ h21.4s⁶ Mar 7] compact gelding: runner-up in point: fairly
useful handicap hurdler, out of form in 2018/19 after 20 months off: stays 2½m: acts on
heavy going: in headgear last 2 starts: tried in tongue tie. *David Pipe*

MR DEALER (IRE) 7 b.g. Mr Dinos (IRE) – Vera Glynn (IRE) (Alderbrook) [2018/19 **b–**
b15.7s Dec 30] fair form when placed in bumpers, for J. G. Cosgrove in 2017/18.
Ashley Dodgson

MR DIABLO (IRE) 10 br.g. Presenting – Aremebooksready (IRE) (Good Thyne (USA)) **c136**
[2018/19 h20d c24d² c20d⁵ c25s c24s² Mar 2] workmanlike gelding: winning hurdler: **h–**
useful handicap chaser: second in Troytown Handicap Chase at Navan (4½ lengths behind
Tout Est Permis) in November: stays 25f: acts on good to firm and heavy going: has worn
headgear, including final start: has worn tongue tie, including in 2018/19: usually races
close up. *J. P. Dempsey, Ireland*

MR DORRELL SAGE (FR) 6 b.g. Sageburg (IRE) – Miss Breezy (FR) (Sicyos (USA)) **h113**
[2018/19 b–: h17.7g* h16dᶠ h16.3g h16.5d⁶ h16.3d h21.4g⁵ Apr 3] strong, lengthy gelding:
has had breathing operations: fair form over hurdles: won maiden at Fontwell early in
season: stays 2¼m: acts on good to soft going. *Oliver Sherwood*

MR FENTON (IRE) 8 b.g. Trans Island – Carnagh Girl (IRE) (Saddlers' Hall (IRE)) **h74 §**
[2018/19 h109§: h24.2dᵖᵘ h19.5g Apr 26] chunky gelding: fair maiden hurdler, below form
in 2018/19 after 18 months off: stays 23f: acts on good to firm going: has worn headgear:
temperamental. *Emma Lavelle*

MR FICKLE (IRE) 10 b.g. Jeremy (USA) – Mamara Reef (Salse (USA)) [2018/19 h–§: **h101 §**
h17.7m h21.7g³ h19.2g* h20.5g⁵ Nov 19] smallish gelding: fair handicap hurdler: won at
Fontwell in August: stays 2¾m: acts on good to firm and heavy going: has worn headgear,
including last 3 starts: temperamental. *Gary Moore*

MR FIFTYONE (IRE) 10 b.g. Jeremy (USA) – Maka (USA) (Diesis) [2018/19 c138, **c133**
h–: c16g c19g⁴ Jun 4] sturdy gelding: winning hurdler: useful handicap chaser: stays 21f: **h–**
acts on good to firm and heavy going: has worn cheekpieces, including last 4 starts: tried
in tongue tie. *Mrs J. Harrington, Ireland*

MR FITZROY (IRE) 9 ch.g. Kyllachy – Reputable (Medicean) [2018/19 c–, h95: **c–**
h15.8s⁵ h19.5d Mar 20] small gelding: has had breathing operation: fairly useful handicap **h82**
hurdler at best, regressed further in 2018/19: maiden chaser: stays 2½m: acts on heavy
going: has worn headgear, including final start: wears tongue tie. *Jo Davis*

MR GREY SKY (IRE) 5 gr.g. Fame And Glory – Lakil Princess (IRE) (Bering) [2018/19 **b105**
b15.7v* b15.7s* Dec 30] €92,000 3-y-o: fourth foal: half-brother to 3 winners, including
fairly useful hurdler/useful chaser Lastbutnotleast (2m-3m winner, by Flemensfirth) and
useful hurdler/winning pointer Danny Whizzbang (23f/25f winner, by Getaway): dam
(c120/h115), 2m-2¼m hurdle/chase winner, half-sister to useful/ungenuine hurdler/chaser
(2m-3m winner) Moskova: useful form in bumpers: won at Haydock (twice, by length
from Highway Companion second occasion) in December: will be suited by 2½m+.
Kim Bailey

MR GRUMPY 6 b.g. Sir Percy – Panna (Polish Precedent (USA)) [2018/19 h105: h16.2g³ **h99**
Sep 27] fair form over hurdles: raced around 2m: tried in hood. *Lucinda Russell*

MR HARP (IRE) 6 b.g. Court Cave (IRE) – Chapel Wood Lady (IRE) (Zaffaran (USA)) **b88**
[2018/19 b17.7d² b17.7g³ Apr 7] third foal: closely related to fair chaser Mr Raj (19f-23f winner, by Oscar): dam (h86), lightly raced over hurdles, out of half-sister to smart staying chaser Seven Towers: fair form when placed in 2 bumpers at Plumpton. *Thomas Gallagher*

MR JACK (IRE) 7 ch.g. Papal Bull – Miss Barbados (IRE) (Hawk Wing (USA)) **h105**
[2018/19 h101: h16s⁴ h20.7d h15.9d² h19.6d⁴ h20.5s² h19.8s⁴ Mar 8] angular gelding: fair maiden hurdler: stays 21f: acts on heavy going. *Linda Jewell*

MR JIM 10 b.g. Fraam – Coddington Susie (Green Adventure (USA)) [2018/19 c92: c21.4g⁴ **c86**
May 11] modest handicap chaser: stays 2¾m: acts on good to firm going. *Tony Carroll*

MR K (IRE) 8 b.g. Kheleyf (USA) – Undertone (IRE) (Noverre (USA)) [2018/19 h19.5dᵖᵘ **h–**
Apr 6] workmanlike gelding: pulled up in point: modest form over hurdles, pulled up sole start under Rules since 2016/17: tried in cheekpieces. *Adrian Wintle*

MR KIT CAT 9 ch.g. Lucarno (USA) – Makeabreak (IRE) (Anshan) [2018/19 c102, h116: **c–**
c16.3s³ c20.1gᵖᵘ Jan 5] good-topped gelding: winning hurdler: fair form over fences, no **h–**
show in 2018/19: should stay 2½m: acts on good to firm and good to soft going: has worn hood. *Russell Ross*

MR KITE 8 b.g. Sixties Icon – Mar Blue (FR) (Marju (IRE)) [2018/19 h105: h16.7g May **h89**
20] well-made gelding: fair handicap hurdler at best, lightly raced nowadays: raced mainly around 2m: acts on soft going: wears tongue tie. *Susan Corbett*

MR LANDO 10 b.g. Shirocco (GER) – Capitana (GER) (Lando (GER)) [2018/19 c–, **c77**
h102: h19.6g h15.8m h16.8s h16.8m h16.5m h18.5s h17.7d h19d⁶ h23.9d⁶ h23.9s⁴ c21g⁵ **h80**
Apr 20] close-coupled gelding: fair handicap hurdler, below form in 2018/19: poor form over fences: stays 3m: acts on good to firm and heavy going: has worn headgear: wears tongue tie: front runner. *Johnny Farrelly*

MR LOVE (IRE) 7 b.g. Winged Love (IRE) – Bonny Rathlin (IRE) (Beauchamp King) **c95 §**
[2018/19 c105§, h–: c20.3g⁶ c21.2dᵘʳ c23.6g⁴ c23.8s c24g⁶ Apr 25] sturdy gelding: has **h–**
had breathing operation: maiden hurdler: fair maiden chaser, below form in 2018/19: stays 3m: acts on heavy going: wears headgear: temperamental. *Lucy Wadham*

MR MACHO (IRE) 7 b.g. Flemensfirth (USA) – Accordian Rules (IRE) (Accordion) **h116 p**
[2018/19 b–p: h20.3g² h19.5g² Oct 30] fairly useful form over hurdles: better effort when second in maiden at Chepstow: should go on improving. *Kim Bailey*

MR MACLENNANE (IRE) 8 b.g. Witness Box (USA) – Sally Maclennane (IRE) (Anshan) **c87**
[2018/19 c26g May 4] multiple point winner: in cheekpieces, 16/1, seventh in hunter at Cheltenham (26½ lengths behind Fortune Bound) on chasing debut. *N. R. W. Wright*

MR MAFIA (IRE) 10 b.g. Zerpour (IRE) – Wizzy (IRE) (Presenting) [2018/19 c73, h92: **c105**
h22m* h23g* h20.3g* h26.5g* h26.4m³ c24g² h25.8m² h23.3g³ h21g Nov 18] compact **h115**
gelding: fairly useful handicap hurdler: completed 4-timer at Stratford (conditionals) in May, Worcester and Southwell (conditionals) in June, and Newton Abbot in July: fair handicap chaser: stays 3¼m: acts on soft and good to firm going: tried in cheekpieces: has worn tongue tie. *Martin Keighley*

MR MAGILL (FR) 7 b.g. Hamairi (IRE) – Marie Cuddy (IRE) (Galileo (IRE)) [2018/19 **h85**
h–: h19.8g h19dᵖᵘ h15.3g h16.8s⁵ h21d⁵ h21.4g* h21.4g h23.9s² h23.1d Apr 9] modest handicap hurdler: won at Wincanton in February: stays 3m: acts on soft going: has worn hood: wears tongue tie: usually races off pace. *Keiran Burke*

MR MCGO (IRE) 8 b.g. Touch of Land (FR) – La Principal (IRE) (Saddlers' Hall (IRE)) **c120**
[2018/19 c20.3vᵖᵘ c19sᶠ c20s⁵ c23.6d⁴ Apr 6] sturdy gelding: won completed start in **h–**
points: winning hurdler: missed 2017/18: fairly useful form over fences: stays 19f: acts on soft going. *Donald McCain*

MR MCGUINESS (IRE) 9 b.g. Kalanisi (IRE) – Maig Mandy (IRE) (Mandalus) **c95**
[2018/19 c–, h120: h23g⁵ h23g⁵ h23.3s² h20g⁴ h23m⁶ c24.2mᵘʳ c23.6s Nov 21] lengthy **h118**
gelding: fairly useful handicap hurdler: second at Uttoxeter in July: modest form over fences: stays 23f: acts on soft and good to firm going: held up. *Rosemary Gasson*

MR MEDIC 8 b.g. Dr Massini (IRE) – Danse Slave (FR) (Broadway Flyer (USA)) **c138**
[2018/19 c132, h–: c21g* c20.6d⁶ c21d⁶ c16.3dᵖᵘ Mar 15] sturdy gelding: maiden hurdler: **h–**
useful handicap chaser: won at Ascot (by 3 lengths from Flying Angel) in November: stays 21f: acts on good to firm and good to soft going. *Robert Walford*

MR MERCURIAL (IRE) 11 b.g. Westerner – Arcanum (IRE) (Presenting) [2018/19 **c130**
c123: c20.8g* c23.4g² c24.2d³ c21.1d c23.8g* Apr 25] good-topped gelding: multiple point winner: useful hunter chaser: won at Cheltenham early in season (for Mrs Sheila Crow) and Perth (by 2½ lengths from Double Whammy) in April: stays 3½m: acts on soft and good to firm going: tried in headgear: usually wears tongue tie. *Will Ramsay*

MRM

MR MICHANDA (IRE) 13 b.g. Heron Island (IRE) – Clown Around (True Song) [2018/19 c32.5g^{pu} May 4] point winner: pulled up in hunter on chasing debut. *Mrs Sarah Tickle* — c—

MR MIX (FR) 8 gr.g. Al Namix (FR) – Royale Surabaya (FR) (Turgeon (USA)) [2018/19 c141, h–: c24s^2 c21.1d^{ur} Apr 4] angular gelding: winning pointer/hurdler: useful chaser at best: second in hunter at Warwick in January: stays 27f: acts on heavy going: has worn cheekpieces. *S. C. Robinson* — c121 h—

MR MONOCHROME 8 br.g. Indian Danehill (IRE) – Our Ethel (Be My Chief (USA)) [2018/19 c110, h–: c20g c17.4v^{pu} Dec 1] leggy, useful-looking gelding: winning hurdler: lightly raced over fences, no show in 2018/19: stays 19f: acts on soft going. *Donald McCain* — c— h—

MR MUDDLE 12 gr.g. Imperial Dancer – Spatham Rose (Environment Friend) [2018/19 c108, h–: c16.5g c17.8m May 27] compact gelding: winning hurdler: fair chaser, well held both starts in 2018/19: stays 2¾m: acts on heavy going: wears headgear. *Gary Moore* — c— h—

MR MULLINER (IRE) 10 b.g. Millenary – Mrs Battle (IRE) (Be My Native (USA)) [2018/19 c–, h–: c20d^{pu} h21.7g^{pu} h23g c25.8m^{ur} h23g^4 h25.8g^2 h25.8s c19.7m^6 h25.8g^3 h19.8g^3 c21.2d^5 h15.8d Mar 30] poor handicap hurdler: maiden chaser, no form in 2018/19: stays 3¼m: acts on good to soft going: wears headgear: has worn tongue tie: usually front runner/races prominently: temperamental. *Paul Henderson* — c— § h69 §

MR PALMTREE (IRE) 6 gr.g. Robin des Pres (FR) – Mattys Joy (IRE) (Beneficial) [2018/19 b16s b16d h21.2g h20.5d^6 c20d^2 c24g^F c24g^{pu} Apr 25] £17,000 5-y-o: third foal: half-brother to fair hurdler/fairly useful chaser Padraig's Joy (2½m/21f winner, by Vinnie Roe), stayed 3m: dam (c106/h85) 2m chase winner: placed both starts in Irish points: little impact under Rules: in cheekpieces/tongue tie last 3 starts. *Robin Dickin* — c83 h74 b—

MR PEPPERPOT 10 b.g. Sir Harry Lewis (USA) – Parslin (The Parson) [2018/19 c24.5v^F Mar 17] point winner: 9/1, second when fell heavily eleventh in hunter at Carlisle on chasing debut. *R. Tate* — c—

MR PERFECT (IRE) 4 b.g. Mustameet (USA) – Crescendor (FR) (Lavirco (GER)) [2018/19 b15.8g^2 Apr 11] €15,000 3-y-o: half-brother to useful hurdler/chaser Listen Dear (2m-19f winner, by Robin des Champs) and a winning pointer by Kutub: dam unraced half-sister to prolific French hurdler/chaser up to 25f Tempo d'Or: 8/1, second in maiden bumper at Huntingdon (1¾ lengths behind Willie Butler): likely to stay 2½m. *Ian Williams* — b89

MR PIPPIN 8 gr.g. Daylami (IRE) – Fionnula's Rainbow (IRE) (Rainbows For Life (CAN)) [2018/19 h20g^{pu} c25.8g^6 c16.3d^4 Sep 21] failed to complete in points: little show under Rules: often in headgear: in tongue tie last 2 starts. *Tracey Barfoot-Saunt* — c— h—

MR PUMBLECHOOK 5 b.g. Midnight Legend – Definitely Pip (IRE) (Definite Article) [2018/19 b76: h16.7d^3 h20.5s^2 h20.5s* h20.3d^6 h20.7d^4 h21.6s^6 Apr 16] sturdy gelding: fairly useful form over hurdles: won maiden at Plumpton in December: second in novice at Newbury previous month: stays 21f: acts on soft going. *Alan King* — h122

MR RAJ (IRE) 11 b.g. Oscar (IRE) – Chapel Wood Lady (IRE) (Zaffaran (USA)) [2018/19 c109: c19.7g^4 c21.2d^6 Dec 4] multiple point winner: fair form in chases: stays 23f: acts on good going: in tongue tie last 4 starts. *Thomas Gallagher* — c103

MR ROBINSON (FR) 12 b.g. Robin des Pres (FR) – Alberade (FR) (Un Desperado (FR)) [2018/19 c–, h–: h18.6m^5 Aug 5] maiden pointer: poor maiden handicap hurdler: winning chaser: stays 2¾m: acts on soft going: has worn headgear: not straightforward. *Lucinda Egerton* — c— h64

MR SANDGATE (IRE) 6 b.g. Sandmason – Ballybeg Princess (IRE) (The Bart (USA)) [2018/19 h–, b–: h16.2g May 17] no form in bumpers/over hurdles: tried in cheekpieces/tongue tie. *R. Mike Smith* — h—

MR SATCO (IRE) 11 b.g. Mr Combustible (IRE) – Satlin (IRE) (Satco (FR)) [2018/19 c119§, h–: c21g^3 h20g c21m^4 c23g^3 c25.8m^{pu} c23g^3 c25.8g^{pu} c20.2m^2 c20g^4 c25.1g^5 Nov 22] workmanlike gelding: winning hurdler: fair handicap chaser: stays 23f: acts on good to firm and good to soft going: wears headgear: usually leads: unreliable. *Chris Down* — c102 § h— §

MR SAWYER 10 b.g. Striking Ambition – Willows World (Agnes World (USA)) [2018/19 c85: c16.3g^{pu} May 4] multiple point winner: modest chaser at best, pulled up in hunter in 2018/19. *K. Jacka* — c—

MRS BELLAMY 6 b.m. Black Sam Bellamy (IRE) – Jaxelle (FR) (Lights Out (FR)) [2018/19 b73: b15.8s Dec 11] poor form in bumpers. *Michael Appleby* — b—

MRS BURBIDGE 9 b.m. Pasternak – Twin Time (Syrtos) [2018/19 c91, h97: h20s⁴ h19.9g h20g h19m² h19d c19.4v⁴ c19.7g² Apr 7] modest handicap hurdler: modest maiden chaser: stays 2½m: acts on heavy going: wears cheekpieces/tongue tie: races towards rear. *Neil Mulholland* **c87 h90**

MR SCRUMPY 5 b.g. Passing Glance – Apple Days (Sovereign Water (FR)) [2018/19 b94p: b16.2s* b17s³ h16.7g³ Apr 15] fairly useful form in bumpers: won conditionals/amateurs event at Hexham in October: fair form over hurdles: better effort when second in novice at same course: will be suited by 2½m: open to further improvement. *Jedd O'Keeffe* **h107 p b100**

MRS DAVIES (IRE) 5 b.m. Court Cave (IRE) – Bandelaro (IRE) (Beneficial) [2018/19 b17g b16.4m⁴ h16.8g⁵ h20.1g h19.9d⁵ Apr 23] €8,000 3-y-o, £30,000 4-y-o: second foal: dam unraced sister/half-sister to hurdler/chaser Marlbrook and hurdler I'm A Game Changer, both useful up to 2½m: second on completed start in Irish points: modest form in bumpers: poor form over hurdles: tried in hood. *Keith Dalgleish* **h72 b76**

MRS GREY (IRE) 5 gr.m. Court Cave (IRE) – Caroline Fontenail (IRE) (Kaldounevees (FR)) [2018/19 h16.7s h15.8d⁵ h15.8d⁶ h21.2m³ Apr 1] €7,000 3-y-o: fifth foal: closely related to fairly useful/unreliable hurdler/chaser Dreamsoftheatre (2¾m-27f winner, by King's Theatre) and half-sister to fair hurdler/chaser Definitly Grey (2½m-3m winner, by Daylami): dam unraced half-sister to fairly useful hurdler/chaser (stayed 25f) Dom Fontenail: runner-up in Irish mares maiden point on debut: fair form over hurdles: likely to stay further than 21f. *Henry Oliver* **h101**

MR SHANTU (IRE) 10 b.g. Shantou (USA) – Close To Shore (IRE) (Bob Back (USA)) [2018/19 c114, h118x: c24sᵖᵘ c22.6gᵖᵘ Aug 23] good-topped gelding: fairly useful hurdler: similar form over fences, pulled up both starts in 2018/19: stays 3¼m: acts on good to soft going: usually wears headgear: has worn tongue tie, including in 2018/19. *Jonjo O'Neill* **c– h–**

MRS HYDE (IRE) 6 b.m. Flemensfirth (USA) – Funny Times (Silver Patriarch (IRE)) [2018/19 b78p: b15.8m* b16.4g⁴ b16.7d² b17d Apr 4] rather unfurnished mare: fairly useful bumper performer: won mares event at Ludlow in October: fourth in listed mares event at Cheltenham (3¼ lengths behind The Glancing Queen) month later. *Fergal O'Brien* **b101**

MRS JACK (IRE) 5 ch.m. Papal Bull – Miss Barbados (IRE) (Hawk Wing (USA)) [2018/19 b17.7g h15.9gᵖᵘ Apr 21] fourth foal: dam unraced: no show in bumper/maiden hurdle. *Linda Jewell* **h– b–**

MRS LOVETT (IRE) 6 ch.m. Sir Percy – Madame Boulangere (Royal Applause) [2018/19 h16.5m³ c17g² c18.2d⁴ c18m* c20g* c20d⁶ c16d⁴ c22g* c17s⁴ c23.8d⁵ Apr 26] fairly useful form over hurdles, won twice in France for D. Windrif: fairly useful chaser: won mares maiden at Thurles in November, mares handicap at Fairyhouse in December and mares novice at Thurles again in February: stays 2¾m: acts on soft and good to firm going. *Gordon Elliott, Ireland* **c120 h115**

MRS MIGGINS (IRE) 6 b.m. Presenting – Carrigeen Lunaria (IRE) (Saddlers' Hall (IRE)) [2018/19 b72: h16.8m³ h18.5g³ h23.9d⁴ h21.2d³ h20.5g⁴ h23.9s³ h23.1d⁶ Apr 9] has had breathing operation: fair maiden hurdler: stays 3m: acts on soft and good to firm going: in cheekpieces last 4 starts: wears tongue tie: usually races close up. *David Pipe* **h100**

MR SNOOZY 10 b.g. Pursuit of Love – Hard To Follow (Dilum (USA)) [2018/19 c–, h114: h16.2d³ h16.2g* h20g³ h19.9m³ h20.3g³ Jul 15] sturdy gelding: fair handicap hurdler: won at Hexham in May: pulled up only chase outing: no impact in points later in season: stays 21f: acts on soft and good to firm going: wears headgear: usually races close up. *Mark Walford* **c– h107**

MRS ROBIN (IRE) 9 b.m. Robin des Pres (FR) – Regents Dancer (IRE) (Flemensfirth (USA)) [2018/19 c85§, h87§: c24d* c21.6g* c23.9mᵖᵘ c24.2gᵖᵘ c25.3v Dec 17] lengthy mare: winning hurdler: fair handicap chaser: won at Uttoxeter and Fontwell early in season for Dan Skelton: trained by Kevin Bishop fourth start: stays 3¼m: acts on good to firm and heavy going: has worn headgear: has joined Dai Williams: ungenuine. *Tim Vaughan* **c104 § h– §**

MR STAN 4 b.g. Scorpion (IRE) – Dametori (FR) (Vettori (FR)) [2018/19 b16g Feb 15] 7/2, last in maiden bumper at Fakenham. *Nigel Twiston-Davies* **b–**

MR STUBBS (IRE) 8 b.g. Robin des Pres (FR) – Crystal Stream (IRE) (Dr Massini (IRE)) [2018/19 b17m⁶ b16g h15.9d h15.3g c19.7g³ c26v⁴ Mar 16] lengthy gelding: in frame numerous times in points: well held in bumpers for David Kenneth Budds: well held in 2 novice hurdles: modest form in chases: tried in cheekpieces. *Paul Henderson* **c93 h– b–**

MRS VONN (IRE) 7 b.m. Scorpion (IRE) – Mrs Ritchie (Teenoso (USA)) [2018/19 h20.2g⁵ h20.5g⁶ h20.9g h20.6s c16.4d c19.3d² c19.2s⁴ c23.8sᵖᵘ c21.6d* Apr 8] fifth foal: half-sister to modest hurdler Goochypoochyprader (2m-2¼m winner, by Karinga Bay) and **c87 h81**

winning pointers by Milan and Brian Boru: dam (h95), maiden hurdler (stayed 3m), half-sister to smart hurdler (winner up to 3m) Material World: poor form over hurdles: modest form over fences: won handicap at Kelso in April: stays 2¾m: acts on good to soft going: tried in hood. *Stuart Coltherd*

MR WASHINGTON (IRE) 6 b.g. Vinnie Roe (IRE) – Anna Bird (IRE) (Be My Native (USA)) [2018/19 h90, b82: h18.7g Oct 8] good-topped gelding: won point on debut: modest form in bumpers/over hurdles: in tongue tie last 3 starts. *David Dennis* **h–**

MR WHIPPED (IRE) 6 br.g. Beneficial – Dyrick Daybreak (IRE) (Ali-Royal (IRE)) [2018/19 h140: c20.2g³ c20.6v* c25d⁴ Apr 5] well-made gelding: useful form over hurdles: similar form over fences: won novice at Haydock in December: fourth in Mildmay Novices' Chase at Aintree (13½ lengths behind Lostintranslation) in April: stays 25f: acts on heavy going: tried in cheekpieces: has joined Brian Ellison. *Nicky Henderson* **c141 h–**

MR WOODY (IRE) 5 b.g. Shantou (USA) – She's On The Case (IRE) (Witness Box (USA)) [2018/19 b16d² b15.3g Apr 14] €54,000 3-y-o: angular gelding: second foal: dam (c98/h105) bumper/2½m winner (stayed 3m): fair form in bumpers: best effort when second at Warwick in December. *Nicky Henderson* **b91**

MR WOOLLEY 5 b.g. Shirocco (GER) – Evella (IRE) (Beneficial) [2018/19 b15.3g b17.7d⁶ b15.8g⁶ b15.8g³ Apr 22] workmanlike gelding: has had breathing operation: modest form in bumpers. *Neil King* **b79**

MR YOUNG (FR) 5 ch.g. Mr Sidney (USA) – Young Majesty (USA) (Maria's Mon (USA)) [2018/19 h15.8gᵖᵘ Jun 14] fairly useful on Flat in France for F. Head, stays 9.5f: pulled up in novice on hurdling debut. *Oliver Greenall* **h–**

MSASSA (FR) 5 b.g. Sholokhov (IRE) – Ramina (GER) (Shirocco (GER)) [2018/19 h136: h16d* h19.4s⁶ May 19] useful hurdler: won minor event at Sligo in May: sixth to Wildriver in Prix Alain du Breil at Auteuil later in month: probably stays 19f: raced only on ground softer than good (acts on heavy). *W. P. Mullins, Ireland* **h131**

MS PARFOIS (IRE) 8 ch.m. Mahler – Dolly Lewis (Sir Harry Lewis (USA)) [2018/19 c146, h–: c26s⁶ c34v² Mar 16] lengthy mare: had breathing operation: winning hurdler: smart handicap chaser: second in Midlands Grand National at Uttoxeter (3 lengths behind Potters Corner) in March: stayed 4¼m: acted on heavy going: tried in hood: wore tongue tie: usually front runner/raced prominently: retired, and visits Getaway. *Anthony Honeyball* **c149 h–**

MT LEINSTER (IRE) 5 b.g. Beat Hollow – Sixhills (FR) (Sabrehill (USA)) [2018/19 b16.5s* b16.2g² b16g³ b16g⁵ b16d² Apr 22] brother to bumper/1½m winner Diamond Hill, closely related to 2 winners by Imperial Ballet, including smart hurdler/chaser Blackstairmountain (2m-21f winner), and half-brother to 3 winners, including bumper winner/useful 2½m hurdle winner Allure of Illusion (by Captain Rio): dam 14.4f mare who stayed 17.5f: useful bumper performer: won maiden at Ballinrobe (by 22 lengths from Dona Katharina) in September: placed 3 times after: in hood last 3 starts. *W. P. Mullins, Ireland* **b106**

MUCH TOO MUCH 6 b.m. Stimulation (IRE) – Complication (Compton Place) [2018/19 b74: b15.3m May 15] poor form in bumpers. *Paul Nicholls* **b–**

MUCKLE ROE (IRE) 10 b.g. Westerner – Island Crest (Jupiter Island) [2018/19 c123x, h–: c25g⁵ c25.6g⁵ c24d² c24d³ c25.5s³ c23.8d Feb 20] tall gelding: maiden hurdler: fairly useful handicap chaser: third at Warwick in December: stays 25f: acts on heavy going: often let down by jumping. *Nigel Twiston-Davies* **c121 x h–**

MUDDLE THINKING (IRE) 5 b.g. Haafhd – Just Josie (Josr Algarhoud (IRE)) [2018/19 h17.7g h15.9s h15.9d⁶ h16s h20.5d Mar 22] compact gelding: tailed off in bumper: no form over hurdles. *Gary Moore* **h– b–**

MUFTAKKER 5 gr.g. Tamayuz – Qertaas (IRE) (Linamix (FR)) [2018/19 b77: b16.7g⁴ b15.7g⁶ May 23] fair form in bumpers/on Flat. *John Norton* **b88**

MUHTAMAR (FR) 4 ch.g. Muhtathir – Martalina (FR) (Martaline) [2018/19 b16.4d Mar 5] in hood, tailed off in maiden bumper. *James Ewart* **b–**

MUHTARIS (IRE) 9 b.g. Teofilo (IRE) – Fann (USA) (Diesis) [2018/19 h72: h19.9g* May 27] sturdy gelding: fair handicap hurdler: won at Uttoxeter on sole start in 2018/19: stays 21f: acts on heavy going: has worn cheekpieces, including last 2 starts. *Ian Williams* **h112**

MUILEAN NA MADOG (IRE) 8 b.g. Papal Bull – Truly Precious (USA) [2018/19 h16dᵇᵈ h16g⁴ h16.3g h20.7g c20d² c19.7s c17s⁵ c20.2m⁵ c20.2gᵖᵘ Mar 8] has had breathing operation: no form over hurdles: poor form over fences: stays 2½m: acts on good to soft going: has worn headgear, including final start: tried in tongue tie: has joined Dan Skelton. *David Bridgwater* **c80 h–**

MULCAHYS HILL (IRE) 7 b.g. Brian Boru – Belsalsa (FR) (Kingsalsa (USA)) **c138**
[2018/19 h138, b103: c23.8v⁶ c20.3v² c20s⁴ c31.7s^F Mar 12] rather leggy gelding: has had **h–**
breathing operation: useful form over hurdles: similar form over fences: second in maiden
at Bangor (length behind Jerrysback) in December: stays 21f: raced mainly on heavy
going: in cheekpieces last 3 starts: front runner/races prominently: has flashed tail.
Warren Greatrex

MULLAGHBOY (IRE) 8 b.g. Beneficial – Mellowthemoonlight (IRE) (Un Desperado **c100 x**
(FR)) [2018/19 c103, h99: c20.3g⁴ c19.2g h23.1g² h23.1g⁶ h26g h23.1g⁶ h19.9g h20g **h96**
h16.7s⁶ h15.8s Dec 31] modest handicap hurdler: fair form over fences: left Olly Murphy
after fourth start: stays 23f: acts on heavy going: wears headgear: usually wears tongue tie:
often let down by jumping. *Sean Conway*

MULSANNE CHASE 5 b.g. Sixties Icon – Hot Pursuits (Pastoral Pursuits) [2018/19 **h–**
h15.8m h15.8g^{pu} Oct 16] modest on Flat, stays 1½m: no show in novice hurdles: wears
tongue tie. *Conor Dore*

MULTIFACTORIAL (IRE) 5 br.g. Stowaway – Zuzka (IRE) (Flemensfirth (USA)) **b105**
[2018/19 b16g² b16s⁴ b16d² b16s² h17.3g* Mar 24] €82,000 3-y-o: first foal: dam (h142),
bumper winner/2¼m-21f hurdle winner, half-sister to useful hurdler/smart chaser (stayed
25f) Puffin Billy and useful hurdler/chaser (stays 2½m) Tycoon Prince: useful bumper
performer: won maiden at Downpatrick in March: runner-up 3 times earlier in season.
Gordon Elliott, Ireland

MULTIGIFTED 6 b.m. Multiplex – Attlongglast (Groom Dancer (USA)) [2018/19 h97: **h87**
h21.7d h15.9s h20.5g⁵ h21.4g⁴ h21.7g² Apr 12] has had breathing operation: modest on
Flat, stays 2m: modest maiden hurdler: stays 2¾m: acts on heavy going: has worn tongue
tie, including in 2018/19. *Michael Madgwick*

MUMGOS DEBUT (IRE) 11 b.g. Royal Anthem (USA) – Black Queen (IRE) (Bob **c106**
Back (USA)) [2018/19 c105, h–: c16g² c16.5v⁴ c16.5s* c16.3g* c16.3s³ c15.9g³ c20.1v^{pu} **h–**
Mar 16] has had breathing operation: maiden hurdler: fair handicap chaser: won at Ayr and
Newcastle in January: stays 2½m: acts on heavy going: wears tongue tie: usually races
prominently. *Lucinda Russell*

MUNSAAB (IRE) 13 b.g. Alhaarth (IRE) – Claustra (FR) (Green Desert (USA)) [2018/19 **c85**
c119, h–: c25.5g⁶ h25.4m^{pu} Jul 1] neat gelding: fairly useful hurdler/chaser at best, little **h–**
show in 2018/19: stays 25f: acts on good to firm and heavy going: wears headgear: has
worn tongue tie, including final start. *James Moffatt*

MURATELLO (FR) 5 b.g. Blue Bresil (FR) – Nesle de La Roque (FR) (Villez (USA)) **h120**
[2018/19 h17.4g* h17.4s² h15.7d³ h20.6d³ h19.8s Mar 9] fifth foal: half-brother to French
15f hurdle winner Callista Nera (by Balko): dam lightly-raced half-sister to fairly useful
French cross-country chaser (stayed 31f) Pasquini Rouge: fairly useful form over hurdles:
won 4-y-o event at Rochefort-sur-Loire in July for Guillaume Macaire: third in Rossington
Main Novices' Hurdle at Haydock (5½ lengths behind Mister Fisher) in January and novice
at Market Rasen in February: stays 21f: acts on good to soft going. *Nigel Twiston-Davies*

MURCHISON RIVER 5 b.g. Medicean – Free Offer (Generous (IRE)) [2018/19 h16.7g **h89 §**
h15.7g⁶ h15.7g⁴ h20.3g h20.3g h15.8g h15.5g* h20.6d² h16.4g⁴ h18.6g³ h21.2d⁴ Apr 23]
half-brother to fair 2½m hurdle winner Tunnel Creek (by Tobougg): fair on Flat for Henry
Candy, stays 1½m: modest handicap hurdler: won at Leicester in December: stays 21f: acts
on good to soft going: in headgear last 5 starts: usually wears tongue tie: usually races close
up: temperamental. *Sam England*

MURPHY'S LAW (IRE) 5 b.g. Gold Well – Balleen Rose (IRE) (Old Vic) [2018/19 **h109**
h19.3g⁵ h19.8m⁴ h16.4s⁴ h16.2d Mar 26] €29,000 3-y-o: third foal: closely related to fairly
useful 21f hurdle winner Old Rascals (by Ask): dam (b75), placed in bumpers, half-sister
to fair hurdler/fairly useful chaser (stayed 2¾m) Fireball Macnamara: placed in Irish point:
fair form over hurdles. *Keith Dalgleish*

MURPHY'S NAILS 7 b.g. Milan – Definite Artist (IRE) (Definite Article) [2018/19 h83: **c–**
c26v^{pu} c23.6d^{pu} c26.1d^{pu} Feb 25] modest form over hurdles: pulled up all 3 starts over **h–**
fences: has worn headgear, including last 2 starts. *Kerry Lee*

MURRAY MOUNT (IRE) 9 b.g. Trans Island – Ash (Salse (USA)) [2018/19 c109, h–: **c93**
h16g c20.3g⁵ h20g* c24g³ Oct 2] good-topped gelding: little impact in points: modest **h96**
handicap hurdler: won conditionals/amateurs event at Worcester in September: fair
handicap chaser, below form over fences in 2018/19: stays 2½m: best form on good going:
tried in blinkers: held up: has joined Sarah-Jayne Davies. *Henry Oliver*

MUSICAL SLAVE (IRE) 6 b.g. Getaway (GER) – Inghwung (Kayf Tara) [2018/19 h–: h128 p h16.8s⁶ h15.8v⁵ h16.7g* h15.8d* Mar 21] fairly useful form over hurdles: won handicaps at Market Rasen and Ludlow in March: completed hat-trick in 24-runner conditionals handicap at Punchestown shortly after end of British season by 1¼ lengths from Conron, jumping better and staying on to lead close home: stays 21f: acts on good to soft going: will go on improving. *Philip Hobbs* **h128 p**

MUSICAL STARDUST 6 b.m. Passing Glance – Royal Musical (Royal Abjar (USA)) [2018/19 b56: b17.7g b16.3m⁴ h20.3g⁶ h16.3m⁴ h18.7m³ h18.7g h18.6g⁵ h20g Oct 11] poor form in bumpers/over hurdles: left Sam Thomas after first start. *Alex Hales* **h77 b71**

MUSKETEER 7 ch.g. Schiaparelli (GER) – Suave Shot (Suave Dancer (USA)) [2018/19 h–: h20m⁶ Jun 21] well held in bumpers/over hurdles: tried in hood. *Robert Stephens* **h–**

MUSTAAQEEM (USA) 7 b.g. Dynaformer (USA) – Wasseema (USA) (Danzig (USA)) [2018/19 h16.2g⁶ h15.8v h19.7g⁴ Nov 19] fair on Flat, stays 12.5f: well held over hurdles: wears headgear. *Bernard Llewellyn* **h58**

MUSTMEETALADY (IRE) 9 b.g. Mustameet (USA) – Ladymcgrath (IRE) (Jamesmead) [2018/19 c129, h–: c24d c25.9sᵖᵘ c24.2d c24.2s c28.4m³ Apr 20] good-topped gelding: winning hurdler: fairly useful handicap chaser: third at Haydock in April: stays 3½m: acts on good to firm and heavy going: usually wears cheekpieces: usually races off pace. *Jonjo O'Neill* **c120 h–**

MUTAMAYEL (IRE) 5 b.g. Mawatheeq (USA) – Musharakaat (IRE) (Iffraaj) [2018/19 b–: b16.8d⁶ Jan 11] poor form in bumpers. *John Norton* **b63**

MUTANAQEL 4 b.g. Havana Gold (IRE) – Audaz (Oasis Dream) [2018/19 h17.7g⁵ h15.9g⁴ h16.7g⁵ h16.8sᵖᵘ Nov 25] has had breathing operation: half-brother to fairly useful hurdler/chaser Authorized Too (2m winner, by Authorized): fair maiden on Flat, stays 1m: modest form over hurdles: tried in hood: wears tongue tie: has joined Ray Peacock. *David Pipe* **h97**

MUTASHABEK (USA) 9 b.g. Arch (USA) – Siyadah (USA) (Mr Prospector (USA)) [2018/19 h21.4g⁵ h23.9sᵖᵘ Mar 19] point winner: poor form over hurdles. *Tracey Barfoot-Saunt* **h77**

MUTAWAASEL 7 b.g. Teofilo (IRE) – Muwakleh (Machiavellian (USA)) [2018/19 h86, b80: h16.2g⁴ h15.7gᵖᵘ h16.8g⁵ h16.8gᶠ h16.8dᵖᵘ Jan 21] sturdy gelding: poor maiden hurdler: raced around 2m. *Sue Smith* **h80**

MUTHABIR (IRE) 9 b.g. Nayef (USA) – Northern Melody (IRE) (Singspiel (IRE)) [2018/19 h116: h24g h24.5g⁴ h23.8g* h24.4g⁴ h24.4g⁵ h23.9d⁶ Apr 4] sturdy gelding: fair handicap hurdler: won at Ludlow in January: stays 3m: acts on heavy going: tried in cheekpieces. *Richard Phillips* **h113**

MUTOONDRESDASHORSE 5 ch.g. Harbour Watch (IRE) – Mutoon (IRE) (Erhaab (USA)) [2018/19 h–: h15.3m h15.8g⁵ h15.8m⁵ h18.6m⁶ h16.8g⁶ h18.5gᶠ h20gᵖᵘ c16.4sᵘʳ c15.7d⁴ Apr 24] has had breathing operation: little impact in 2 points: poor maiden hurdler: similar form over fences: unproven beyond 2m: acts on soft going: sometimes in headgear/tongue tie. *Nigel Hawke* **c72 h77**

MY ANCHOR 8 b.g. Mount Nelson – War Shanty (Warrshan (USA)) [2018/19 c–, h–: h20.6g⁵ h20.3g⁵ May 23] sturdy gelding: poor maiden hurdler: pulled up sole start over fences: stays 21f: acts on good to soft going: has worn tongue tie. *Anthony Day* **c– h61**

MY BOY COLIN 8 ch.g. Midnight Legend – Killala Bay (IRE) (Executive Perk) [2018/19 h25.5dᵖᵘ h22g⁴ Apr 14] placed in points: modest form over hurdles: in tongue tie final start. *Alex Hales* **h86**

MYBOYSAM 5 b.g. Delegator – Fantastisch (IRE) (Fantastic Light (USA)) [2018/19 b87: b15.3g⁶ h16.5d Dec 13] smallish gelding: fair form in bumpers only on debut: well beaten in novice on hurdling debut. *Alan King* **h– b71**

MY BROTHER (IRE) 6 b.g. Roderic O'Connor (IRE) – Victory Peak (Shirley Heights) [2018/19 h20.2g² h16.7g⁴ h16g³ h16.4g² h16v⁶ h19.2d⁴ Jan 14] good-topped gelding: fairly useful on Flat for L. Smyth, stays 11f: fair form over hurdles: stays 19f: acts on good to soft going: wears hood: usually races nearer last than first. *Neil Mulholland* **h109**

MY BROWN EYED GIRL 6 b.m. Ferrule (IRE) – Chalosse (Doyoun) [2018/19 h68: h19.3g Feb 24] small, leggy mare: poor maiden handicap hurdler: has worn headgear, including last 2 starts: wears tongue tie. *Susan Corbett* **h–**

MY CHARITY (IRE) 8 b.g. King's Theatre (IRE) – Benefit Ball (IRE) (Beneficial) [2018/19 h116, b86: c23dF c22gF h20.6d h24.2d h21.3g² h19g* Apr 25] tall gelding: fairly useful hurdler: won maiden at Warwick in April: second in handicap at Wetherby earlier in month: fell both starts over fences: stays 2¾m: acts on good to soft going: in tongue tie last 2 starts. *Graeme McPherson* **c–**
h116

MY DESTINY (IRE) 6 ch.g. Flemensfirth (USA) – Gaye Melody (IRE) (Un Desperado (FR)) [2018/19 h19.2d* Jan 14] sixth foal: half-brother to fair hurdler/useful chaser Full Cry (2½m-25f winner, by Milan): dam unraced half-sister to high-class chaser (stayed 3¼m) Kingsmark: 66/1, won maiden hurdle at Fontwell (by nose from Carrick Roads) on hurdle debut: bred to be suited by further than 2½m: entitled to progress. *Brendan Powell* **h107 p**

MY DIAMOND (IRE) 8 b.g. Brian Boru – Our Idol (IRE) (Mandalus) [2018/19 c–, h66: c15.7m⁶ May 10] maiden hurdler/chaser: bred to stay at least 3m: wears headgear. *Laura Young* **c–**
h–

MY DIXIE 5 br.m. High Chaparral (IRE) – My Petra (Midnight Legend) [2018/19 h21g⁴ h21.4gᵖᵘ Dec 6] third foal: closely related to fairly useful hurdler/winning pointer My Dance (2¼m-2½m winner, by Kayf Tara): dam (c142/h134), 2m-19f hurdle/chase winner (also 11.6f winner on Flat), sister to fairly useful hurdler/useful chaser (stayed 25f) Midnight Appeal: last of 4 finishers in point: fair form over hurdles. *Alan King* **h101**

MY ESCAPADE (IRE) 8 ch.m. Tamayuz – Highly Respected (IRE) (High Estate) [2018/19 c–, h85: h20.2g* h25.2g* c24.2g⁵ h23.9g h21.3h⁶ Nov 2] modest handicap hurdler: won at Perth and Cartmel early in season: poor form over fences: stays 3m: acts on soft and good to firm going: should do better as a chaser. *Simon Waugh* **c83 p**
h92

MY FANTASEA (IRE) 6 b.g. Sea The Stars (IRE) – Speed Song (Fasliyev (USA)) [2018/19 h16.7g Oct 3] fair on Flat, stays 1½m: 14/1, seventh of 8 in novice at Bangor on hurdling debut: has joined Philip Kirby. *Ian Williams* **h–**

MY FOXY LADY 7 br.m. Sagamix (FR) – Marlbrook Fox (Bob Back (USA)) [2018/19 b15.8g⁶ h16.8v⁶ h21.9gᵖᵘ Apr 21] has had breathing operation: first foal: dam well held in bumper: poor form in bumpers: pulled up in maiden on hurdling debut: in tongue tie last 2 starts. *John Needham* **h–**
b71

MY HOMETOWN (IRE) 9 b.g. Presenting – Amathea (FR) (Exit To Nowhere (USA)) [2018/19 c120, h–: c19.2d c21g c21g⁶ c16.7s⁵ c24g* c30.2g² Dec 14] rangy gelding: won sole start over hurdles: fairly useful chaser: won cross-country event at Punchestown in November: stays 3¾m: acts on heavy going: tried in tongue tie. *Enda Bolger, Ireland* **c127**
h–

MY LADY GREY 5 gr.m. Presenting – Wassailing Queen (Generous (IRE)) [2018/19 b85: b15.8g⁴ h19d h20.5sᵖᵘ h17.7v h23.9d h21.7g Apr 12] modest form in bumpers/over hurdles. *Colin Tizzard* **h87**
b83

MY LIEGE (IRE) 8 b.g. Marienbard (IRE) – Smashing Leader (IRE) (Supreme Leader) [2018/19 h99: h20.1s⁶ h18.9s Dec 30] bumper winner: maiden hurdler, fair form at best for Evan Williams: raced only on soft/heavy going. *Sam England* **h64**

MYLITTLEOULBUDDY (IRE) 6 br.m. Darsi (FR) – She Will Return (IRE) (Bob's Return (IRE)) [2018/19 b16.2g Feb 14] first foal: dam placed in bumper/lightly raced over hurdles: tailed off in bumper. *Hugh Burns* **b–**

MYLITTLERUNAWAY (IRE) 4 ch.f. Getaway (GER) – Running Wild (IRE) (Anshan) [2018/19 b13.7v⁴ h17.7vᵘʳ h16dᶠ Mar 21] well held in bumper: failed to complete over hurdles: dead. *Susan Gardner* **h–**
b–

MY MANEKINEKO 10 b.g. Authorized (IRE) – Echo River (USA) (Irish River (FR)) [2018/19 h19.8gᵖᵘ h20.2g h16g² c16.2g³ h16.5g c16gᶠ c18g⁵ h15.5g⁶ c18gᵘʳ c16.2gᶠ c16g² c16.2d⁶ c16d³ h16s⁵ c16.7d⁴ Apr 23] good-topped gelding: useful hurdler at best, below that in 2018/19: fair maiden chaser: unproven beyond 2m: acts on good to firm and heavy going: has worn hood: usually races in rear. *James A. Nash, Ireland* **c112**
h102

MY MATE MARK 6 b.g. Sakhee (USA) – Florie (Alflora (IRE)) [2018/19 h16.7g² h16g* Nov 21] good-topped gelding: bumper winner: fairly useful form over hurdles: won novice at Warwick in November: dead. *Ben Pauling* **h119**

MYMILAN (IRE) 6 b.g. Milan – Jill's Girl (IRE) (Be My Native (USA)) [2018/19 h16.4s h16.2dᶠ h20.1v⁶ Mar 14] £7,500 5-y-o: closely related to fairly useful chaser Auldthunder (2½m-3¼m winner) and fair hurdler/chaser Terfel's Toscar (3m-27f winner), both unreliable/ by Oscar: dam unraced: placed in Irish points: modest form over hurdles. *Sandy Thomson* **h87**

MY MUMS POSH 5 b.m. Malinas (GER) – Posh Bird (IRE) (Winged Love (IRE)) [2018/19 b15.7d Apr 9] first foal: dam (c122/h106) temperamental 2½m-3¾m hurdle/ chase winner: down the field in bumper. *Peter Niven* **b–**

MY OLD GOLD (IRE) 9 b.m. Gold Well – Tenbo (IRE) (Sexton Blake) [2018/19 h118: **c136** h24.7g⁵ c24.2d* c23.4g² c21.6g² c23.8d* Apr 26] fairly useful form over hurdles: useful **h118** form over fences: won novice handicap at Wetherby in January and listed mares event at Perth (by 4 lengths from Treackle Tart) in April: stays 27f: acts on heavy going. *Nicky Richards*

MY PEGGY (IRE) 7 b.m. Yeats (IRE) – Last Century (IRE) (Glacial Storm (USA)) **h87** [2018/19 b17.3g⁰ᵘ b16.2g² b16g⁶ h20g⁵ h18g h16g h18.8g⁵ h16g Apr 21] seventh foal: **b85** closely related to fairly useful hurdler/chaser Steele's Rock (2½m winner, by King's Theatre) and a winning pointer by Oscar, and half-sister to a winning pointer by Ashkalani: dam unraced sister to useful hurdler (stayed 3¼m) Glacial Sunset: fair bumper performer: modest form over hurdles: has worn cheekpieces: tried in tongue tie: usually races off pace. *N. Hynds, Ireland*

MYPLACEATMIDNIGHT 7 b.g. Midnight Legend – Zahra's Place (Zaha (CAN)) **h131** [2018/19 b96: h20.7g² h21d³ h21.4g⁴ h21.4g* h21.4g³ h21.4s² h20.5s* h24.3mᶠ Apr 12] close-coupled gelding: useful hurdler: won handicap at Wincanton in January and novice at Plumpton in March: stays 21f: acts on soft going: usually leads. *Neil King*

MY RENAISSANCE 9 b.g. Medicean – Lebenstanz (Singspiel (IRE)) [2018/19 c82, **c100** h76: c16.4g* c15.7g⁴ c17.3m c17.3g* c17.4g³ c16.4m⁴ c21.1m³ c19.2g⁰ᵘ c17.4gᵘʳ h16.8g⁴ **h82** Nov 1] has had breathing operation: poor handicap hurdler: fair handicap chaser: won at Sedgefield early in season and Cartmel in July: stays 21f: acts on good to firm and good to soft going: has worn headgear, including in 2018/19: has worn tongue tie, including last 2 starts: usually races nearer last than first. *Sam England*

MYROUNDORURS (IRE) 9 b.g. Arakan (USA) – Six Bob (IRE) (Anshan) [2018/19 **c95** c103, h–: c16gᵘʳ c17mᵖᵘ c15.7gᵖᵘ c24g⁵ c20g⁰ᵘ c16.5gᵖᵘ Jul 31] has had breathing **h–** operation: maiden hurdler: fair chaser at best, lost his way in 2018/19: unproven beyond 2m: acts on good to firm and heavy going: usually wears headgear: tried in tongue tie: temperament under suspicion. *Robin Dickin*

MY SHIROCCO 4 ch.f. Shirocco (GER) – Auberge (IRE) (Blueprint (IRE)) [2018/19 **h–** h20.6gᴿ h16.2gᵖᵘ Apr 15] first foal: dam (h98) 2¾m/3m hurdle winner: more signs of temperament than ability in novice hurdles: in hood first start. *Dianne Sayer*

MY SISTER SARAH (IRE) 5 ch.m. Martaline – Reste Ren Or (IRE) (Goldneyev **h136** (USA)) [2018/19 b16.4g* h20g* h20g² h18s* h16.8d h24d⁶ Apr 23] rather sparely-made **b99** mare: first foal: dam lightly-raced half-sister to fairly useful hurdler/very smart chaser (stayed 21f) J'y Vole and useful French hurdler/chaser (winner up to 23f) Si Tu Viens (by Martaline): won maiden bumper at Roscommon on debut in August, impressively: useful form over hurdles: won maiden at Punchestown in October and mares novice at Fairyhouse in January: progressed again when also winning 23-runner handicap at Punchestown shortly after end of British season by 2 lengths from Young Ted: stays 3m: acts on soft going: usually races off pace. *W. P. Mullins, Ireland*

MY SON JOHN 5 b.g. Bahri (USA) – Cogolie (FR) (Cyborg (FR)) [2018/19 b16.4d **b–** b16.2g Jan 22] well held in 2 bumpers. *N. W. Alexander*

MYSTEREE (IRE) 11 b.g. Gold Well – Hillside Native (IRE) (Be My Native (USA)) **c132** [2018/19 c–, h–: c27.3gᵖᵘ c32.4g c29.5s c32.6g² Feb 23] angular gelding: winning hurdler: **h–** useful handicap chaser: second in Eider (Handicap Chase) at Newcastle (neck behind Crosspark) in February: stays 33f: acts on heavy going: wore headgear in 2018/19. *Michael Scudamore*

MYSTICAL CLOUDS (IRE) 6 gr.g. Cloudings (IRE) – Silent Valley (Forzando) **h114** [2018/19 h119, b88: h19.6g* h19.9gᶠ h21.2g² h21d³ Jan 28] useful-looking gelding: fair form in bumpers: similar form over hurdles: won novice at Bangor in October: likely to stay 3m: acts on soft going. *Alan King*

MYSTICAL KNIGHT 10 b.g. Kayf Tara – Dark Diva (Royal Fountain) [2018/19 c123, **c–** h–: c25.1sᵖᵘ Mar 7] well-made gelding: winning hurdler: fairly useful chaser, pulled up **h–** sole start in 2018/19: stays 25f: acts on heavy going: wears tongue tie. *Anthony Honeyball*

MYSTIC COURT (IRE) 6 b.g. Court Cave (IRE) – My Mystic Rose (IRE) (Arctic **b85** Lord) [2018/19 b15.7g⁵ b16.7g⁶ b15.3g Apr 14] £32,000 5-y-o: compact gelding: fourth foal: dam unraced sister to fair hurdler/useful chaser (winner up to 21f) Lord Ryeford: won completed start in Irish points: fair form in bumpers: tried in hood. *Ben Pauling*

MYSTIC DREAMER (IRE) 5 b.m. Sans Frontieres (IRE) – Free Dreamer (IRE) **b99**
(Turtle Island (IRE)) [2018/19 b15.7d² b16s b16.8g* Apr 18] rather unfurnished mare: fifth
foal: half-sister to a winning pointer by Scorpion: dam unraced half-sister to smart hurdler/
useful chaser (stayed 3m) Deputy Dan and useful hurdler/chaser (stayed 21f) Minella
Class: fairly useful form in bumpers: won mares event at Cheltenham in April. *Nick Gifford*

MYSTIC SKY 8 b.m. Midnight Legend – Kentucky Sky (Cloudings (IRE)) [2018/19 **h126**
h121: h16g² h16.3g² h16.7m h16.3m h19.2m³ h16g² h15.8g* h15.8d² h16g h15.9g
Apr 21] lengthy mare: has had breathing operation: fairly useful handicap hurdler: won at
Huntingdon in November: second in Mares' Hurdle at Wetherby (1¾ lengths behind
Lady Buttons) earlier in month: stays 2½m: acts on good to firm and good to soft going:
wears headgear. *Lucy Wadham*

MYSTIFIABLE 11 gr.g. Kayf Tara – Royal Keel (Long Leave) [2018/19 c121, h–: **c–**
c20.1g⁶ Jun 3] sturdy gelding: winning hurdler: fairly useful chaser, well held sole start in **h–**
2018/19: stays 2¾m: acts on soft going: tried in hood: wears tongue tie: tends to find little.
Fergal O'Brien

MY STORY (IRE) 7 b.g. Court Cave (IRE) – Holloden (IRE) (Shantou (USA)) [2018/19 **h109**
b80: h19.4g³ h19.5d h21g⁴ Apr 10] won Irish maiden point on debut: fair form over
hurdles: best effort when third in novice at Doncaster in December: tried in hood: bled last
2 starts. *Tom George*

MYTHICAL LEGEND 8 ch.m. Midnight Legend – Materiality (Karinga Bay) [2018/19 **h97**
h97: h23.3m h23.1m* h23.3gᵘʳ h26.5gᵘʳ Jul 22] workmanlike mare: modest hurdler: won
maiden at Market Rasen in June: stays 23f: acts on good to firm going: in visor last 3 starts.
Emma Lavelle

MYTHICAL PRINCE (IRE) 7 b.g. Beneficial – Conker Nails (IRE) (Carroll House) **h106**
[2018/19 b95: b16.3m³ h16.7g⁶ h19.3g³ h20.7dᵖᵘ h16.7g² h20.6m⁵ Apr 21] failed to **b74**
complete in 2 Irish maiden points: fair form on first 2 outings in bumpers: similar form over
hurdles: best effort at 2m: best form on good going: in hood last 4 starts: usually races
towards rear. *Warren Greatrex*

MY TURGEON (FR) 6 gr.g. Turgeon (USA) – My Belle (FR) (Smadoun (FR)) [2018/19 **h84**
b66p: h21.2g⁵ h21.3s h19.9v h26g h25d³ h25gᵖᵘ Mar 19] poor form over hurdles: in
cheekpieces last 3 starts: tried in tongue tie. *Ben Pauling*

MY VALENTINO (IRE) 6 ch.g. Duke of Marmalade – Nadwah (USA) (Shadeed **h–**
(USA)) [2018/19 h–: h16.4m⁶ h16.2g Apr 25] modest on Flat, stays 7f: no form over
hurdles: often in cheekpieces: in tongue tie last 2 starts. *Dianne Sayer*

MY WAY (FR) 5 ch.g. Martaline – Royale Majesty (FR) (Nikos) [2018/19 h19.8v⁶ h15.3g **c–**
h19s² h19g³ h21s² h24.3m Apr 12] good-topped gelding: has had breathing operation: third **h121**
foal: brother to French 17f hurdle/chase winner Ribambelle and half-brother to fairly
useful French hurdler/smart chaser Roi Mage (2¼m-2¾m winner, by Poliglote): dam
French 2¼m hurdle/chase winner: fairly useful maiden hurdler: second in novice at
Taunton in February and handicap at Kempton in March: useful form over fences in France
for Francois Nicolle: stays 21f: acts on soft going: usually in tongue tie. *Paul Nicholls*

MY WIGWAM OR YOURS (IRE) 10 b.g. Beneficial – Midnight Pond (IRE) (Long **c105**
Pond) [2018/19 h20mᵖᵘ c24.2g⁶ c24.2g⁴ c21.1gᶠ Oct 21] useful hurdler at best: fair maiden **h–**
chaser: left Stephen Francis Magee after first start: best up to 21f: acted on soft and good
to firm going: tried in headgear: dead. *Simon West*

N

NAASIK 6 b.g. Poet's Voice – Shemriyna (IRE) (King of Kings (IRE)) [2018/19 h70, b81: **h69**
h19.6g h20.3s h16.6g⁵ h16g Feb 19] poor maiden hurdler. *John Norton*

NABHAN 7 b.g. Youmzain (IRE) – Danidh Dubai (IRE) (Noverre (USA)) [2018/19 h111: **h103**
h16.8g h16.8g² h16.8mᵘʳ h18.5g³ h16.5s² h16.8g³ h16.9g h16.2g h16d³ h16g⁶ Apr 26]
angular gelding: fair handicap hurdler: unproven beyond 2m: acts on heavy going: wears
headgear/tongue tie. *Bernard Llewellyn*

NACHI FALLS 6 ch.g. New Approach (IRE) – Lakuta (IRE) (Pivotal) [2018/19 c119, h–: **c–**
h24g h16m h23gᵖᵘ h19.2gᵖᵘ h21.4m⁵ h16g h21.4gᵖᵘ h16.5d² h15.7d Apr 9] compact **h105**
gelding: has had breathing operation: fair handicap hurdler nowadays: winning chaser:
stays 3m: acts on good to firm and good to soft going: tried in blinkers: has worn tongue
tie, including in 2018/19. *Nigel Hawke*

NADAITAK 5 b.g. Teofilo (IRE) – Tanfidh (Marju (IRE)) [2018/19 h15.7m⁴ h20.8g* **h134** h24.4g² h24.4g* h24d h24.7g Apr 6] good-topped gelding: fairly useful on Flat, stays 2m: useful form over hurdles: won novice at Doncaster in November and River Don Novices' Hurdle there (by 22 lengths from Truckers Lodge) in January: stays 3m: best form on good going: in cheekpieces last 3 starts: races prominently. *Ben Pauling*

NAKADAM (FR) 9 b.g. Nickname (FR) – Cadoudame (FR) (Cadoudal (FR)) [2018/19 **c108** c108, h–: c20.5d⁴ c24.1v⁶ c26.2s* c26.9d c30.7dᵖᵘ c30.6d³ Apr 26] sturdy gelding: maiden **h–** hurdler: fair handicap chaser: won at Carlisle in December: stays 27f: acts on heavy going: wears cheekpieces/tongue tie. *R. Mike Smith*

NAMAZEE (USA) 4 b.g. Gio Ponti (USA) – Eagle Sound (USA) (Fusaichi Pegasus **h90** (USA)) [2018/19 h16d h18.1d⁵ h17m⁵ Apr 20] fair on Flat, stays 10.5f: modest form over hurdles: left A. Slattery after first start. *Chris Grant*

NAMIB DANCER (IRE) 5 b.g. Westerner – Derriana (IRE) (Snurge) [2018/19 b16.3s⁶ **b90** b15.8d³ Mar 3] €44,000 3-y-o: lengthy gelding: fifth foal: half-brother to 2 winning pointers by Scorpion: dam, ran twice in points, half-sister to smart hurdler/useful chaser (stayed 3m) Kicks For Free: fair form in bumpers. *Emma Lavelle*

NANCY MAHER (IRE) 6 gr.m. Well Chosen – Loughaderra Rose (IRE) (Roselier (FR)) **h77** [2018/19 h16g h19.8gᵘʳ h24g h20sᵖᵘ h21s h20g h16gᶠ h19.3m h15.8v⁵ h17d⁵ h16g Apr 10] closely related to fairly useful hurdler/useful chaser Local Show (23f/3m winner) and 19f bumper winner Loughaderra Prince (both by Oscar): dam unraced: poor maiden hurdler: left Miss Elizabeth Doyle after sixth start: tried in cheekpieces: usually races off pace. *Christian Williams*

NANNY PAT'S 6 b.m. Kayf Tara – Megalex (Karinga Bay) [2018/19 b15.8g⁴ b16.8g* **b90** Aug 15] sister to several winners, including smart hurdler/useful chaser Ballyandy (2m-2½m winner) and smart bumper winner/useful but ungenuine hurdler Megastar (2m winner), stayed 21f, and half-sister to a winner on Flat by Proclamation: dam (h92) 2½m hurdle winner: fair form in bumpers: won mares event at Newton Abbot in August. *Gary Moore*

NAPOLEON BLUE (IRE) 6 ch.g. Beat Hollow – Myown (IRE) (Le Bavard (FR)) **h107** [2018/19 h19.4s⁴ h18.6d h20g h21d h20d h23.3g* h23.9g² Apr 24] €18,000 3-y-o: closely related to 2 winners, including smart hurdler/useful chaser Ninetieth Minute (2m-2¾m winner, by Old Vic), stayed 3¼m, and half-brother to bumper winner/fair 2½m hurdle winner Gortnahulla (by Bravefoot): dam unraced: point winner: fair handicap hurdler: won at Thurles in March: stays 3m: acts on soft going: in cheekpieces last 2 starts. *Adrian Murray, Ireland*

NATHANS PRIDE (IRE) 11 ch.g. Definite Article – Tricias Pride (IRE) (Broken **c–** Hearted) [2018/19 c123, h119: c20.2mᵖᵘ h20.5d Mar 1] workmanlike gelding: fairly useful **h–** hurdler/chaser, little show in 2018/19: stays 2½m: acts on good to firm going: wears tongue tie. *Tim Vaughan*

NATIVE FIGHTER (IRE) 5 b.g. Lawman (FR) – Night of Magic (IRE) (Peintre **h86 p** Celebre (USA)) [2018/19 h16.4s⁶ h19.3d³ h20.6d Apr 6] dam half-sister to high-class 2m hurdler Melon: fairly useful on Flat, stays 1½m: modest form over hurdles: will prove best at short of 2½m: remains open to improvement. *Jedd O'Keeffe*

NATIVE GAMUT (IRE) 9 b.g. Gamut (IRE) – Gonearethedays (IRE) (Be My Native **c94** (USA)) [2018/19 c88: c16d⁶ c20.9dᶠ c20g Jun 24] point winner: modest form in chases: stays 21f: acts on good to soft going. *Alastair Ralph*

NATIVEGETAWAY (IRE) 6 b.g. Getaway (GER) – Clonsingle Native (IRE) (Be My **h112** Native (USA)) [2018/19 h23.9d³ h19.5s² h19.5s Dec 27] £24,000 3-y-o, €34,000 4-y-o, £20,000 5-y-o: tall gelding: half-brother to useful hurdler/smart chaser Ackertac (2½m-25f winner, by Anshan), a winning jumper in Sweden by Presenting and a winning pointer by Blueprint: dam unraced: placed twice in Irish points: fair form over hurdles: best effort when second in maiden at Chepstow. *Colin Tizzard*

NATIVE OPTIMIST (IRE) 12 b.g. Broadway Flyer (USA) – Native Orchid (IRE) (Be **h105 §** My Native (USA)) [2018/19 h108§: h24.3g³ h23.9g⁶ h23.3g³ h23.9g³ Jul 15] angular gelding: fair handicap hurdler: stays 25f: acts on heavy going: tried in tongue tie: temperamental. *Sheena Walton*

NATIVE RIVER (IRE) 9 ch.g. Indian River (FR) – Native Mo (IRE) (Be My Native **c165 +** (USA)) [2018/19 c172, h–: c25.6g² c24g³ c26.3d⁴ Mar 15] well-made gelding: winning **h–** hurdler: top-class chaser: second in Betfair Chase at Haydock (4 lengths behind Bristol de Mai) in November, third in King George VI Chase at Kempton (13½ lengths behind

Clan des Obeaux, jumping left and never travelling well) in December and fourth in Cheltenham Gold Cup (9¼ lengths behind Al Boum Photo) in March: stays 4m: goes very well on soft/heavy going: wears cheekpieces: front runner/races prominently. *Colin Tizzard*

NATIVE ROBIN (IRE) 9 br.g. Robin des Pres (FR) – Homebird (IRE) (Be My Native (USA)) [2018/19 c114, h–: c20.2g⁴ c21.2d* c19.2v² c19.5d³ c20s² Feb 18] maiden hurdler: fairly useful handicap chaser: won at Fakenham in December: stays 21f: acts on heavy going. *Jeremy Scott*   **c119 h–**

NATIVE SOLDIER (IRE) 5 b.g. Sepoy (AUS) – Electra Star (Shamardal (USA)) [2018/19 h–: h23gᵖᵘ h20v h21d Nov 29] fairly useful at best on Flat (stays 1m): no form over hurdles: tried in headgear. *John Flint*   **h–**

NATTER JACK CROAK (IRE) 7 b.g. Gold Well – Native Euro (IRE) (Be My Native (USA)) [2018/19 h105: h20.2g⁶ Sep 26] workmanlike gelding: Irish point winner: modest maiden hurdler: stays 23f: acts on soft going. *Nigel Twiston-Davies*   **h97**

NATURELLE (FR) 4 gr.f. Martaline – Adamantina (FR) (Muhtathir) [2018/19 h16.9s⁴ h17.4s* h17.4s² h17.4v* h16.4s Mar 13] fair on Flat, stays 13f: fairly useful form over hurdles: won fillies juvenile at Auteuil in October and listed event at Pau in February: seventh in Fred Winter at Cheltenham: raced around 2m on soft/heavy going. *Alain Couetil, France*   **h128**

NAUGHTY NANCIE 4 b.f. Bahri (USA) – Oh So Perky (IRE) (Executive Perk) [2018/19 b16.8v⁵ Mar 12] second foal: dam winning pointer: tailed off in mares bumper. *Tim Reed*   **b–**

NAUTICAL NITWIT (IRE) 10 b.g. Let The Lion Roar – Mrs Pugwash (IRE) (Un Desperado (FR)) [2018/19 h130: h23g⁶ h22.1g⁴ h25.4s* h23.9g h24.1m² h24.1g* h24d⁵ h24d h24.7gᵖᵘ Apr 6] compact gelding: smart hurdler: won handicap at Cartmel (by 17 lengths from Court King) in August and West Yorkshire Hurdle at Wetherby (by 1½ lengths from Old Guard) in November: stays 25f: acts on soft and good to firm going: wears cheekpieces: usually races close up. *Philip Kirby*   **h146**

NAUTICAL TWILIGHT 9 gr.m. Proclamation (IRE) – Anabranch (Kind of Hush) [2018/19 c–§, h99§: c20.9v³ c22.6g⁴ Apr 14] lengthy mare: placed in points: winning hurdler: modest chaser nowadays: stays 21f: acts on heavy going: wears headgear: untrustworthy. *A. Fielding*   **c99 § h– §**

NAVAJO WAR DANCE 6 br.g. Makfi – Navajo Rainbow (Rainbow Quest (USA)) [2018/19 h106: h16g² h17.7m h16g⁴ h20.5g² h18.6s⁵ h16.3dᶠ h16.6d³ h16d Apr 6] has had breathing operation: fair maiden hurdler: stays 2½m: acts on heavy going: tried in tongue tie. *Ali Stronge*   **h102**

NAVY WINGS (IRE) 5 b.m. Shirocco (GER) – Mew Gull (Generous (IRE)) [2018/19 b16d Apr 6] second foal: dam, lightly raced in bumpers/over hurdles, half-sister to fair hurdler/useful chaser (stayed 3m) Duncliffe: in hood, tailed off in bumper. *Jack R. Barber*   **b–**

bet365 Hurdle (West Yorkshire), Wetherby—the biggest win on a red-letter day for trainer Phil Kirby as Nautical Nitwit beats Old Guard (mostly hidden) and Monbeg Theatre (right)

NAYATI (FR) 5 b.g. Spirit One (FR) – Smadouce (FR) (Smadoun (FR)) [2018/19 h119: **h121**
h16d³ h16.8g⁶ h18.9v h16.3s h15.7m⁵ Apr 20] compact gelding: fairly useful handicap
hurdler: left Alan King after third start: should stay 2¼m: acts on heavy going: tried in
cheekpieces. *Donald McCain*

NEACHELLS BRIDGE (IRE) 7 ch.g. Getaway (GER) – Strawberry Lane (IRE) **h124**
(Moscow Society (USA)) [2018/19 h108p, b97: h15.8g⁵ h19.7g* h21.3s² Dec 26] fairly
useful form over hurdles: won novice handicap at Hereford in November: imsproved again
when second in handicap at Wetherby following month: stays 21f: acts on soft going.
Neil Mulholland

NEAR KETTERING 5 ch.g. Medicean – Where's Broughton (Cadeaux Genereux) **h77**
[2018/19 h17s h16.2g h16.6g h16.2g⁴ Feb 14] fairly useful on Flat, stays 1½m: poor form
over hurdles. *Sam England*

NEARLY FAMOUS 6 b.m. Rip Van Winkle (IRE) – Ermena (Dalakhani (IRE)) [2018/19 **h105**
h16g h16g⁴ h17.6g* h16s⁶ Jan 21] dam half-sister to fairly useful hurdler/chaser (stayed
3¼m) Fin Vin de Leu: fairly useful on Flat, stays 13f: fair handicap hurdler: won at
Ballinrobe in July: left Mrs J. Harrington after third start: will be suited by 2½m+: acts on
soft going. *Grace Harris*

NEARLY MAN (FR) 5 b.g. Turgeon (USA) – La Loute (FR) (Saint des Saints (FR)) **h–**
[2018/19 b20g⁴ h19.5d h20.6d Apr 6] €70,000 3-y-o: has had breathing operation: fourth **b85**
foal: half-brother to fairly useful French hurdler/chaser La Symphonie (2¼m-21f winner,
by Martaline) and fairly useful French chaser Au Combat (17f winner, by Ballingarry),
stayed 2¾m: dam, placed in French hurdles/chases up to 2¼m, half-sister to useful French
hurdler/chaser (stayed 23f) Mirmillon: fair form in bumpers: little impact over hurdles: left
Gordon Elliott after first start: tried in hood: in tongue tie last 3 starts. *Alistair Whillans*

NEARLY PERFECT 5 b.g. Malinas (GER) – The Lyme Volunteer (IRE) (Zaffaran (USA)) **h117**
[2018/19 b85: b16.3d h24s² h23.1v h21.6d h23.1d³ h23.3v² Mar 16] lengthy gelding: **b–**
runner-up in Irish point: down the field in bumpers: fairly useful form over hurdles: will be
suited by further than 3m: acts on heavy going: usually races close up. *Neil King*

NEARLY THERE 6 b.g. Virtual – Nicoise (IRE) (Lear Spear (USA)) [2018/19 b16.2g³ **b78**
b16.2g² b16.2g⁵ Aug 1] placed in bumpers: modest maiden on Flat, stays 1½m. *Wilf Storey*

NEBUCHADNEZZAR (FR) 4 b.g. Planteur (IRE) – Trexana (Kaldoun (FR)) [2018/19 **h106**
h16.7d² h16g⁴ h16g⁴ Feb 22] useful-looking gelding: half-brother to fairly useful French
hurdler Biens Nanti (2¼m/19f winner, by Montjeu): fairly useful maiden on Flat, stays
1½m: fair form over hurdles: best effort when second in juvenile maiden at Bangor: will be
suited by further than 2m. *Alan King*

NEEDS TO BE SEEN (FR) 4 b.g. Motivator – Morning Line (FR) (Anabaa (USA)) **h104**
[2018/19 h15.8g³ h15.5g⁴ h15.6g* h15.6g⁴ h16mᵖᵘ h16.4sꟳ Mar 10] leggy gelding: fairly
useful maiden on Flat, stays 10.5f: fair form over hurdles: won juvenile at Musselburgh in
November: raced only at 2m: best form on good going: sometimes in blinkers: temperament
under suspicion. *John Ryan*

NEETSIDE (IRE) 7 b.m. Getaway (GER) – Lady Wagtail (IRE) (Milan) [2018/19 h98, **h91**
b83: h18.7g⁶ h21.7d⁵ h19.9s⁶ Dec 11] modest maiden hurdler: stays 21f: acts on soft going:
tried in cheekpieces: wears tongue tie. *David Dennis*

NEFYN BAY 10 b.g. Overbury (IRE) – So Cloudy (Cloudings (IRE)) [2018/19 c115, **c119**
h108: c23.8g⁵ c20.1g* c20.1g⁴ c20.1gᵖᵘ Aug 1] smallish gelding: winning hurdler: fairly **h–**
useful handicap chaser: won at Perth in July: stays 3m: acts on soft and good to firm going:
wears cheekpieces/tongue tie. *Donald McCain*

NEFYN POINT 5 gr.g. Overbury (IRE) – So Cloudy (Cloudings (IRE)) [2018/19 b97: **h98**
h15.6g³ h19.9s⁵ h19.8g³ h18.9d Mar 20] placed in bumper: modest form over hurdles.
Donald McCain

NELLEMANI 7 ch.m. Sulamani (IRE) – Send Me An Angel (IRE) (Lycius (USA)) **h–**
[2018/19 b–: h15.8gꟳ h16g⁶ h15.8g h16.7vᵖᵘ Dec 1] little impact in bumpers/over hurdles.
John Groucott

NELSON RIVER 4 b.g. Mount Nelson – I Say (IRE) (Oratorio (IRE)) [2018/19 h16.7d* **h132**
h16.8d* h16.8d⁶ h16.8d⁴ Mar 15] compact gelding: fair on Flat, stays 1½m: useful form
over hurdles: won juveniles at Bangor (maiden) in November and Cheltenham in
December: best effort when fourth in Triumph Hurdle (9¾ lengths behind Pentland Hills)
at Cheltenham: will be suited by further than 17f. *Tony Carroll*

NELSON ROAD (IRE) 6 b.g. Mount Nelson – Merciful (IRE) (Cape Cross (IRE)) **h113 p**
[2018/19 h19.7g⁴ h20.6d* Apr 6] dam sister to useful hurdler (stayed 19f) Maputo: fair on

Flat, stays 2¼m: fair form over hurdles: won novice at Newcastle in April with plenty in hand: will stay beyond 2½m: will go on improving. *Tristan Davidson*

NELSON'S TOUCH 6 gr.g. Mount Nelson – Lady Friend (Environment Friend) [2018/19 **h120** h108: h15.8g* h16v² h16v² h16.8d⁶ h15.7d h18.5s² Apr 16] angular gelding: fairly useful handicap hurdler: won at Uttoxeter in May: stays 19f: acts on heavy going. *Seamus Mullins*

NEMEAN LION (IRE) 7 b.g. Mahler – Sandy Desert (Selkirk (USA)) [2018/19 h107, **c99** b92: h20.1g⁶ h20.3g^pu h20.3g³ c20g^pu h23.1g⁵ c26.3m^F c24.2g⁵ h24g⁵ h27g* h24d⁴ **h102** h23.3s h25.3g* h25.3g⁶ h23.1g⁶ h24d^pu Apr 24] tall gelding: fair handicap hurdler: won at Sedgefield in November and Catterick in December: modest form over fences: still in front when fell heavily last in novice handicap at Sedgefield in August, likely to have won: stays 27f: acts on good to firm and good to soft going: wears cheekpieces/tongue tie: front runner. *Philip Kirby*

NENDRUM (IRE) 10 br.g. Westerner – Westgrove Berry (IRE) (Presenting) [2018/19 **h111** h104: h16.2g² h16.2g² h16.2g³ h17g⁴ h19.8g^F h19.8g⁴ Jan 1] fair handicap hurdler: stays 2½m: acts on heavy going: has worn hood: usually wears tongue tie: front runner. *Sandy Thomson*

NENERGY'S QUEST 8 b.m. Pasternak – Coolers Quest (Saddlers' Hall (IRE)) [2018/19 **h–** h–: h16.8g^pu h16.8m h23.9m^pu Nov 15] no form: has worn hood, including in 2018/19: in tongue tie last 3 starts. *Richenda Ford*

NERUAL (IRE) 8 b.m. Craigsteel – Central Arch (Dilum (USA)) [2018/19 h24s h24.2v⁶ **h98** h24g³ h22d h24d h24s^pu h19.9s h20.3s^pu h23.9d^pu Apr 24] €2,200 3-y-o: fourth foal: half-sister to fairly useful hurdler/smart chaser Spring Heeled (2m-25f winner, by Old Vic) and fair hurdler Derrylea Girl (21f winner, by Presenting): dam (h101), bumper/19f hurdle winner, half-sister to very smart chaser (best around 2m) Central House: modest maiden hurdler: left Miss Elizabeth Doyle after sixth start: stays 3m: acts on heavy going: has worn headgear, including in 2018/19: often races lazily. *Jake Thomas Coulson*

NESSFIELD BLUE 5 b.g. Kayf Tara – Bella Medici (Medicean) [2018/19 b17.7s b16d **h–** h21d⁶ Mar 28] no form in bumpers for Jose Santos: well beaten in maiden on hurdling **b–** debut. *Pat Murphy*

NESTERENKO (GER) 10 b.g. Doyen (IRE) – Nordwahl (GER) (Waajib) [2018/19 c–, **c113** h118: h20.5d⁶ c22.6s² c19.2d⁵ Apr 9] sturdy gelding: fairly useful handicap hurdler: fair **h102** form over fences: stays 3m: acts on heavy going: has worn hood: usually front runner/races prominently. *Venetia Williams*

NESTOR PARK (FR) 6 b.g. Walk In The Park (IRE) – Cila (FR) (Saint Preuil (FR)) **h124** [2018/19 b101: h21g⁶ h21d* h20.5d h22s* h24.7g^pu h25g^pu Apr 25] tall, useful-looking gelding: bumper winner: fairly useful form over hurdles: won maiden at Warwick in November and novice at Catterick in January: stays 2¾m: acts on soft going. *Ben Pauling*

NET D'ECOSSE (FR) 9 ch.g. Network (GER) – Ecossette (FR) (Ecossais (FR)) **c133** [2018/19 c19.9s* c23g^pu c24.5g⁵ c22.2m⁴ c24s c20v^pu Feb 18] rangy gelding: has had **h–** breathing operation: winning hurdler: useful chaser: won handicap at Kilbeggan (by 11 lengths from Thirsty Work) in May: left Noel Meade after fourth start: won point shortly after end of season: stays 25f: acts on good to firm and heavy going: has worn headgear, including last 4 starts: wears tongue tie: usually races prominently. *J. P. Owen*

NET DE TREVE (FR) 6 b.g. Network (GER) – Dame de Treve (FR) (Cadoudal (FR)) **h113** [2018/19 b87: b16.8m⁵ h19.9g* h21g h24d⁵ Nov 20] well-made gelding: runner-up in Irish **b84** point: modest form in bumpers: fair form over hurdles: won maiden at Uttoxeter in October. *Tom George*

NETWORK ROUGE (FR) 10 b.g. Network (GER) – Lychee de La Roque (FR) (Officiel **c120 §** (FR)) [2018/19 c24g^pu c23g^pu c24.1g² c23.8g c22.6g⁵ Nov 1] useful-looking gelding: has **h–** had breathing operation: winning hurdler: fairly useful handicap chaser: will stay long distances: acts on heavy going: has worn headgear/tongue tie, including in 2018/19: temperamental. *Kim Bailey*

NEVER ADAPT (FR) 4 ch.f. Anabaa Blue – She Hates Me (IRE) (Hawk Wing (USA)) **h118 p** [2018/19 h16.4g³ Nov 17] strong filly: fifth foal: sister to French 15f winner Pti Paul and half-sister to fairly useful French hurdler/winning chaser He Loves Me (17f-21f winner, by Enrique) and fairly useful French 2m hurdle winner Mercenario (by Soldier of Fortune): dam, placed at 2m-2¼m over hurdles in France and 1¼m winner on Flat, half-sister to high-class hurdler/top-class chaser (stays 3m) Top Notch: fairly useful form when winning fillies newcomers race at Compiegne for Guillaume Macaire: in hood, third in Prestbury Juvenile Hurdle at Cheltenham on sole outing since: remains with potential. *Nicky Henderson*

NEVER A WORD (USA) 5 br.g. Lonhro (AUS) – Janetstickettocats (USA) (Storm Cat **h95**
(USA)) [2018/19 h92: h15.8g⁵ h19.6g h16.7g² h15.8g³ h15.8g³ h18.7g³ h15.8g Nov 2]
lengthy, angular gelding: modest maiden hurdler: stays 19f: best form on good going: in
headgear last 5 starts: wears tongue tie: front runner/races prominently. *Oliver Greenall*

NEVERBEEN TO PARIS (IRE) 4 b.g. Champs Elysees – Island Paradise (IRE) (Trans **h116 p**
Island) [2018/19 h16s⁵ h15.9g⁶ h15.8d⁵ h21.2m* Apr 23] compact gelding: fairly useful on
Flat, stays 13.5f: similar form over hurdles: won novice handicap at Ludlow in April: stays
21f: open to further improvement. *David Arbuthnot*

NEVER COMPLAIN (IRE) 11 ch.g. Beneficial – Polly Native (IRE) (Be My Native **c97**
(USA)) [2018/19 c118, h–: c21.6g³ c21.1d Apr 4] workmanlike gelding: has had breathing **h–**
operation: multiple point winner: maiden hurdler: fairly useful hunter chaser, below form
in 2018/19: stays 3m: acts on good to firm and heavy going: wears cheekpieces: tried in
tongue tie: usually races towards rear. *Mrs F. Marshall*

NEVER EQUALLED (IRE) 10 br.g. Brian Boru – Broken Thought (IRE) (Broken **c–**
Hearted) [2018/19 c–, h126: h21.9s h20.5g⁵ h19.9s⁵ h19d⁴ h23s⁵ c23.6dᵖᵘ h20g² Apr 21] **h105**
lengthy gelding: fair handicap hurdler nowadays: maiden chaser: stays 23f: best form on
soft/heavy going: wears headgear. *Bernard Llewellyn*

NEVER GO SHORT 7 ch.m. Midnight Legend – Tulipa (POL) (Jape (USA)) [2018/19 **h–**
b–: h16.8m h19.9g⁶ h18.5g Jun 4] down the field in bumper: no form over hurdles.
Tom George

NEVER LEARN (IRE) 8 b.g. King's Theatre – Hamari Gold (IRE) (Priolo **c108**
(USA)) [2018/19 c98, h88: c26m* c21.6m* Oct 24] workmanlike gelding: maiden hurdler: **h–**
fair form over fences: won handicaps at Fontwell in May and October: stays 3¼m: acts on
soft and good to firm going: wears tongue tie. *Colin Tizzard*

NEVER UP (GER) 8 b.g. Danehill Dancer (IRE) – Never Green (IRE) (Halling (USA)) **c115**
[2018/19 c115, h–: c20s⁵ c20v* c24.2g⁶ Apr 11] sturdy gelding: winning hurdler: fairly **h–**
useful handicap chaser: won at Carlisle in March: stays 2½m: acts on good to firm and
heavy going: usually leads. *Sue Smith*

NEVERUSHACON (IRE) 8 b.g. Echo of Light – Lily Beth (IRE) (Desert King (IRE)) **c143**
[2018/19 c143, h125: h17d² c19.5m* c22.5d h17d⁴ h24m⁶ Oct 6] fairly useful handicap **h127**
hurdler: won at Killarney in May: useful chaser: won minor event at Limerick (by 12
lengths from The Game Changer) in July: stays 3m, effective at much shorter: acts on soft
and good to firm going: wears cheekpieces/tongue tie. *Mrs J. Harrington, Ireland*

NEW AGE DAWNING (IRE) 5 ch.g. Stowaway – Captain Supreme (IRE) (Captain **h119 p**
Rio) [2018/19 b16.8d* h19.5v² h23.6d* Mar 21] second foal: half-brother to fairly useful **b96**
hurdler Higgs (17f winner, by Scorpion): dam, unraced, sister to useful hurdler (2½m
winner) Allure of Illusion and half-sister to smart hurdler/chaser (stayed 21f)
Blackstairmountain: runner-up in Irish point: won maiden bumper at Exeter (by length
from Kalooki) in January: fairly useful form over hurdles: tongue tied, won novice at
Chepstow in March: open to further improvement. *David Pipe*

NEW AGENDA 7 b.g. New Approach (IRE) – Prove (Danehill (USA)) [2018/19 c–, h115: **c–**
c16.5gᵖᵘ h16.7g h15.8g* Oct 25] good-topped gelding: fairly useful handicap hurdler: won **h123**
at Ludlow in October: no show over fences: raced around 2m: acts on good to firm going:
has worn hood, including in 2018/19: front runner/races prominently. *Paul Webber*

NEWBERRY NEW (IRE) 7 b.g. Kodiac – Sunblush (UAE) (Timber Country (USA)) **c111**
[2018/19 c114, h–: c26.1d⁶ c20.1s⁵ c23.9s⁶ c23.4d⁴ c23.4v* Mar 16] good-topped gelding: **h–**
winning hurdler: fair handicap chaser: won at Newcastle in March: stays 3m: acts on heavy
going: has worn cheekpieces, including in 2018/19. *Harriet Bethell*

NEW GUARD 5 b.m. Kayf Tara – Easibrook Jane (Alderbrook) [2018/19 b16.5dᵖᵘ Feb **b–**
28] in tongue tie, 3/1, fatally injured in bumper at Taunton. *Paul Nicholls*

NEWHALL GRANGE 4 ch.g. Equiano (FR) – Wotatomboy (Captain Rio) [2018/19 **b–**
b15.7m Feb 22] well beaten in bumper. *Richard Whitaker*

NEW KID IN TOWN (IRE) 10 b.g. Gamut (IRE) – Echo Queen (IRE) (Luso) [2018/19 **c– §**
c–§, h–§: h16m h16.7gᵖᵘ c17.3g⁶ c15.7g⁶ h23g h20g c17.3g⁶ h19.6gᵖᵘ Aug 20] fair hurdler/ **h– §**
fairly useful chaser at best, no form in 2018/19: has worn headgear, including in 2018/19:
usually races close up: temperamental. *Peter Winks*

NEWLANDS CROSS (IRE) 7 b.g. Stowaway – Honey Mustard (IRE) (Roselier (FR)) **c86**
[2018/19 h16.3d h18.6g h21d h20.3s⁴ c23.8s⁵ Feb 26] €38,000 3-y-o: brother to fairly **h84**
useful 3m chase winner Viking Splash and fair 2¾m/23f hurdle winner Magic Mustard,
and half-brother to 2½m bumper winner Ballytobin (by Shahanndeh) and to dam of high-
class staying hurdler Kilcooley (by Stowaway): dam unraced: point winner: poor form

over hurdles: 12/1, fifth in novice handicap at Ffos Las (17½ lengths behind dead-heaters Alminar and Top And Drop) on chasing debut: stays 3m: acts on soft going: tried in cheekpieces. *Olly Murphy*

NEW LIST 6 ch.g. Pivotal – Angel's Tears (Seeking The Gold (USA)) [2018/19 h79: h16.2g⁵ h23.1g h19.3g h16.2g⁵ h16.8sᶠ h15.7g⁶ Jan 10] has had breathing operation: won point bumper: modest maiden hurdler: has worn cheekpieces, including last 4 starts. *Brian Ellison*   **h90**

NEW MILLENNIUM (IRE) 6 b.g. Galileo (IRE) – Banquise (IRE) (Last Tycoon) [2018/19 h105: h16m⁴ c16.5g³ c16.3g³ c16.3m² c17.8m* c17.5s⁴ c16.4s⁴ c15.9m* c15.5d c17.8m² Mar 29] lengthy gelding: maiden hurdler: fairly useful handicap chaser: won at Fontwell in October and Leicester (novice) in January: stays 2¼m: acts on soft and good to firm going: tried in hood: usually leads: not straightforward (often carries head awkwardly). *Philip Hobbs*   **c116 h88**

NEWQUAY CARDS (IRE) 7 gr.g. Tikkanen (USA) – Sanadja (IRE) (Slip Anchor) [2018/19 h70: h15.8m² h16s⁶ h15.7d c16.4d⁴ c16.4s⁴ c16.5gᶠ Mar 19] big, workmanlike gelding: poor maiden hurdler: similar form over fences: raced around 2m: acts on good to firm going: tried in cheekpieces: wears tongue tie: usually front runner/races prominently. *Evan Williams*   **c73 h82**

NEW QUAY (IRE) 6 b.g. Mahler – Beg La Eile (IRE) (Lahib (USA)) [2018/19 h112p: h19.3m* h16.3d⁶ h19.3d h19g h18.6g³ Apr 3] sturdy gelding: has had breathing operation: Irish point winner: fairly useful handicap hurdler: won novice event at Ascot in November: stays 19f: acts on good to firm and heavy going: wears tongue tie. *Dan Skelton*   **h123**

NEWS FOR PASCAL (IRE) 11 b.g. Kutub (IRE) – Direction (Lahib (USA)) [2018/19 h83: h24g² c25.5g² h22.1g h27m c24.2g c19.2m³ c25.2g² c20.9m Apr 20] point winner: poor maiden hurdler: similar form in chases: stays 25f: acts on good to firm and heavy going: has worn headgear/tongue tie: usually races towards rear. *Simon West*   **c73 h77**

NEWSTART (IRE) 8 br.g. Stowaway – Joes Annie (IRE) (Norwich) [2018/19 h108: h16.2d* h16.2g⁴ h17.1g h16.2s h16.2g⁴ h22.7g⁶ h19.9d h16.4d h16.4m h16.8g Apr 5] has had breathing operation: modest hurdler: won seller at Hexham in May for Brian Ellison: stays 21f: acts on good to firm and heavy going: has worn headgear, including last 4 starts: tried in tongue tie. *Katie Scott*   **h90**

NEWSWORTHY (IRE) 9 br.g. Presenting – Cousin Jen (IRE) (Oscar (IRE)) [2018/19 c125, h115: c19.5v* c19.9s⁵ c23g c25g⁴ h21s⁶ h16.7g c24s c23g² c20v⁵ Feb 18] lengthy, angular gelding: placed in points: fair handicap hurdler: fairly useful chaser: won handicap at Ballinrobe in May: left Mrs D. A. Love after seventh start: stays 3m: acts on heavy going: has worn headgear, including in 2018/19: tried in tongue tie: unreliable. *J. H. Henderson*   **c124 § h105**

NEWT 5 b.m. Sixties Icon – Froglet (Shaamit (IRE)) [2018/19 h88: h15.8g h15.8g* Jul 27] modest form over hurdles: won mares handicap at Uttoxeter in July: raced around 2m: in cheekpieces last 2 starts: none too resolute. *Alastair Ralph*   **h98 §**

NEW TARABELA 8 ch.g. New Approach (IRE) – Tarabela (CHI) (Hussonet (USA)) [2018/19 h15.8sᵖᵘ Jul 29] compact gelding: maiden hurdler, pulled up sole outing in 2018/19: tried in blinkers: ungenuine. *Tony Carroll*   **h– §**

NEWTIDE (IRE) 6 br.g. Getaway (GER) – C'est Fantastique (IRE) (Hernando (FR)) [2018/19 h19.5s⁴ h22.8v* h23.5s³ h26s⁴ h23.9s* Apr 7] £21,000 3-y-o, €100,000 4-y-o: tall gelding: chasing type: seventh foal: dam (c99/h112), 2m-2½m hurdle winner, also 9.5f/1¼m winner on Flat in Germany: runner-up in Irish point: useful form over hurdles: won maiden at Haydock in December and handicap at Ffos Las (by 9 lengths from Iwilldoit) in April: stays 3m: raced only on soft/heavy going: usually front runner/races prominently. *Kim Bailey*   **h132**

NEWTON GERONIMO (IRE) 10 b.g. Brian Boru – Newton Commanche (IRE) (Commanche Run) [2018/19 c130§, h–§: c19.4g² c20g* c20.3g h19.9gʳʳ Sep 12] fairly useful hurdler, refused to race final outing: useful handicap chaser: won at Worcester (by 1¼ lengths from Call To Order) in June: stays 21f: acts on good to firm and good to soft going: has worn hood: not one to trust. *Ben Pauling*   **c135 § h– §**

NEW TO THIS TOWN (IRE) 8 b.g. Milan – Jade River (FR) (Indian River (FR)) [2018/19 h134: c20s⁴ c16.3d Jan 19] well-made gelding: useful hurdler: fairly useful form over fences: stays 21f: acts on soft going: tried in cheekpieces: wears tongue tie. *Colin Tizzard*   **c123 h–**

Unibet Greatwood Handicap Hurdle, Cheltenham—7-lb conditional Danny McMenamin has 20/1-shot Nietzsche (checks/centre) well positioned with the run-in extended due to low sun

NEWTOWN BELLE 6 b.m. And Beyond (IRE) – Coldwells (IRE) (Presenting) **h–** [2018/19 b–: h19.9gpu May 15] no show in bumpers/mares novice hurdle: tried in hood. *George Bewley*

NEWTOWN BOY (IRE) 6 b.g. Beneficial – Tanit Lady (IRE) (Presenting) [2018/19 **h124** b99: b15.7g² h16.2g* h16.6g³ h19.7d² h16g⁴ Apr 10] has had breathing operation: fairly **b95** useful form in bumpers: similar form over hurdles: won novice at Hereford in November: should be suited by 2½m: tried in tongue tie. *Alan King*

NEWTOWN LAD (IRE) 9 b.g. Craigsteel – Rocher Lady (IRE) (Phardante (FR)) **c120 §** [2018/19 c124§, h–: c26.1gpu c23.4d³ c25.5sur c24.5spu c23.6d* c26m² c24.2gpu Apr 11] **h–** winning hurdler: fairly useful handicap chaser: won at Chepstow in March: stays 3¼m: acts on good to firm and heavy going: wears headgear: has worn tongue tie, including in 2018/19: usually races close up: temperamental. *Michael Scudamore*

NEXT EXIT (IRE) 14 b.g. Exit To Nowhere (USA) – Pilgrim Star (IRE) (Marju (IRE)) **c59 x** [2018/19 c61x, h–: h16g⁵ c20.3g c17.2g⁴ Jun 1] winning hurdler: poor handicap chaser: **h–** stays 3m: acts on any going: wears tongue tie: often let down by jumping over fences. *John Cornwall*

NEXT LEVEL (IRE) 8 b.g. Mahler – Molly Be (First Trump) [2018/19 h87: c20.1g **c–** c22.6mpu h20g c22.5gpu Oct 7] sturdy gelding: has had breathing operation: point winner: **h–** maiden hurdler: no form in chases: tried in cheekpieces: usually wears tongue tie. *Jamie Snowden*

NIBLAWI (IRE) 7 b.g. Vale of York (IRE) – Finnmark (Halling (USA)) [2018/19 h123p: **h119** h20d* Mar 4] fairly useful hurdler: won novice at Fakenham sole outing in 2018/19. *Neil Mulholland*

NICEANDEASY (IRE) 6 b.g. Kalanisi (IRE) – High Priestess (IRE) (Priolo (USA)) **h118** [2018/19 h115: h21.4v⁴ h19.9s³ h18.9s⁴ h27d³ h20.1d⁶ h26.6g² Apr 25] lengthy, angular gelding: fairly useful handicap hurdler: left Keith Dalgleish after fourth start: stays 27f: acts on heavy going: tried in headgear. *N. W. Alexander*

NICELY INDEED (IRE) 9 b.g. Marienbard (IRE) – Rare Dollar (IRE) (Bob's Return **h110** (IRE)) [2018/19 h108: h18.6g h20.3g h20.3g³ h20.3s² h19.9s* h21.2v* Jan 27] good-topped gelding: unseated in Irish point: fair handicap hurdler: won at Sedgefield in December and January: stays 21f: acts on heavy going: has worn headgear, including last 2 starts: races off pace. *Philip Kirby*

NICE THOUGHTS (IRE) 7 b.g. Shamardal (USA) – Zacheta (Polish Precedent (USA)) **h–** [2018/19 h88: h15.8gF h19.7spu Nov 28] angular gelding: maiden hurdler, failed to complete in 2018/19: stays 2½m: acts on heavy going: usually wears headgear: has worn tongue tie, including last 2 starts: temperament under suspicion. *Mark Shears*

NICHEINTHEMARKET (IRE) 7 b.m. Oscar (IRE) – Supreme Kellycarra (IRE) **h–** (Supreme Leader) [2018/19 h84: h23.3d h15.7gpu May 21] unplaced in Irish points: maiden hurdler, no form in 2018/19. *Caroline Fryer*

NICKELSONTHEDIME (IRE) 5 b.g. Shantou (USA) – Penny Fiction (IRE) (Welsh **b91**
Term) [2018/19 b16d² b15.7g² Nov 23] €26,000 3-y-o: brother to 3 winners, including
useful hurdler/chaser Carriganog (2m-2¾m winner) and bumper winner/fairly useful
hurdler Eyesontheprize (2m winner), stayed 2½m: dam (h95) bumper winner/second in 2m
hurdle: fair form in bumpers: better effort when second in maiden at Ayr on debut.
Keith Dalgleish

NICK LOST (FR) 7 ch.g. Nickname (FR) – Loumie (FR) (Loup Solitaire (USA)) **c135**
[2018/19 h24g* c21g* c24g² c20.1g² c22.6g³ c24g⁶ c24.5g⁶ Mar 31] €48,000 3-y-o: sixth **h121**
foal: half-brother to fairly useful French hurdler/chaser Policy Jumper (17f-21f winner, by
Poliglote) and fair French hurdler/chaser Baltic Speed (17f-2½m winner, by Ballingarry):
dam (c131/h132), French 15f-2½m hurdle/chase winner, also 15f winner on Flat: fairly
useful form over hurdles: won handicap at Limerick in May: useful form over fences: won
maiden at Punchestown in June and minor event at Limerick (by 7 lengths from Childrens
List) in July: third in Florida Pearl Novices' Chase at Punchestown (8¾ lengths behind
Some Neck) in November: stays 3m: best form on good going: front runner. *Henry de
Bromhead, Ireland*

NICKNAME EXIT (FR) 9 b.g. Nickname (FR) – Exit To Fire (FR) (Exit To Nowhere **c98 §**
(USA)) [2018/19 c106§, h–: c19.2v⁴ Mar 5] winning hurdler: fair handicap chaser: stays **h–**
3m: acts on heavy going: usually wears headgear: temperamental. *Henry Oliver*

NICKOLSON (FR) 5 b.g. No Risk At All (FR) – Incorrigible (FR) (Septieme Ciel **b92 p**
(USA)) [2018/19 b16d* Feb 25] half-brother to several winners by Martaline, including
fair hurdler/useful chaser Hollywoodien (2m-19f winner) and bumper winner/fairly
useful hurdler Jabulani (19f-3m winner): dam unraced: 10/11, won conditionals/amateurs
bumper at Ayr (by 2¼ lengths from Sirwilliamwallace) on debut: open to improvement.
Olly Murphy

NICOLAS CHAUVIN (IRE) 11 b.g. Saffron Walden (FR) – Kenzie (IRE) (Presenting) **c93**
[2018/19 c124, h118: c17.3g h17.2m c17.3g⁴ c19.3m³ c15.8g⁵ c15.7s³ h15.7g Jan 1] sturdy **h–**
gelding: fairly useful hurdler/chaser, well below best in 2018/19: unproven beyond 17f:
acts on soft and good to firm going: has worn headgear, including last 5 starts. *James Moffatt*

NIETZSCHE 6 ch.g. Poet's Voice – Ganga (IRE) (Generous (IRE)) [2018/19 h119: h16g⁶ **h130**
h16.4g* h15.7s h16.5g³ Apr 6] angular gelding: useful handicap hurdler: won Greatwood
Hurdle at Cheltenham (by neck from Silver Streak) in November: raced mainly around 2m:
acts on soft going: has worn hood: in tongue tie last 3 starts. *Brian Ellison*

NIFTY AT FIFTY (IRE) 6 b.g. Gold Well – Tropical Sunset (IRE) (Overbury (IRE)) **h105**
[2018/19 b76: b15.7g⁶ h15.3g⁵ h19.7gᵇᵈ h16.5d⁴ h18.5s h21.4g⁴ h23.3d⁴ Mar 30] modest **b76**
form in bumpers: fair form over hurdles: may prove best at shorter than 23f: acts on good
to soft going: sometimes in hood: usually races towards rear. *Jeremy Scott*

NIGH OR NEVER (IRE) 5 b.g. Excelebration (IRE) – Nigh (IRE) (Galileo (IRE)) **h113**
[2018/19 h110: h19.7g² h18.6s h18.5s h19.9d³ h19g² Apr 25] compact gelding: has had
breathing operation: fair maiden hurdler: left Rebecca Curtis after first start: stays 2½m:
acts on heavy going: has worn headgear, including in 2018/19: has worn tongue tie.
Ian Williams

NIGHTBOATTOCLYRO 5 ch.g. Sulamani (IRE) – Wychwoods Legend (Midnight **b81**
Legend) [2018/19 b15.8m³ Apr 23] second foal: dam (c122/h120), 21f-25f hurdle/chase
winner (stayed 3½m), sister to fairly useful hurdler/useful chaser (stayed 25f) Wychwoods
Brook: 5/2, third in bumper at Ludlow (10 lengths behind Bergamot). *David Dennis*

NIGHT COMES IN (IRE) 7 b.g. Definite Article – Couture Daisy (IRE) (Desse Zenny **h63**
(USA)) [2018/19 h–: h20.2g⁵ May 17] has had breathing operation: poor maiden hurdler.
Donald Whillans

NIGHTFLY 8 br.m. Midnight Legend – Whichway Girl (Jupiter Island) [2018/19 c112, **c132**
h105: c16g* c16.5g² c19.4g* c19.1g² c19.9d⁴ c19.3d⁵ c20.2g⁵ Mar 25] good-topped mare: **h–**
maiden hurdler: useful handicap chaser: won at Ludlow in May and Wetherby in
November: bred to stay 3m: acts on heavy going: wears tongue tie. *Charlie Longsdon*

NIGHT GENERATION (GER) 7 ch.g. Sholokhov (IRE) – Night Woman (GER) **h105 §**
(Monsun (GER)) [2018/19 h105§: h25g² h26.5m² h26.5g h26.5d⁶ h23.9d⁵ h26.5g Apr 20]
has had breathing operation: fair handicap hurdler: left Chris Gordon after first start: stays
3¼m: acts on good to firm and heavy going: usually wears headgear/tongue tie: usually
front runner/races prominently: temperamental. *Jackie du Plessis*

NIGHTHAWKER 6 b.g. Bollin Eric – Bird Without Wings (IRE) (Flemensfirth (USA)) [2018/19 b15.3g b17.7d h16d⁶ h21.4g⁶ Apr 3] no form in bumpers/over hurdles. *Fiona Shaw* **h– b–**

NIGHTLINE 9 b.g. Midnight Legend – Whichway Girl (Jupiter Island) [2018/19 c119, h–: c24.1g* May 19] tall gelding: winning hurdler: fairly useful handicap chaser: won novice event at Bangor sole outing in 2018/19: stays 3m: acts on heavy going: tried in hood: has worn tongue tie: usually leads. *Charlie Longsdon* **c124 h–**

NIGHT MANAGER (FR) 5 b.g. Sageburg (IRE) – Pretty Soon (FR) (Zafonic (USA)) [2018/19 b77: b16.2g³ h16.2g⁴ h19.9g³ h17.1d Oct 18] modest form in bumpers/over hurdles. *Micky Hammond* **h96 b83**

NIGHT OF GLORY 5 b.g. Sea The Stars (IRE) – Kesara (Sadler's Wells (USA)) [2018/19 h118: h15.7d² Jan 19] lengthy gelding: useful on Flat, stays 14.5f: fairly useful form over hurdles: in cheekpieces, second in handicap at Haydock sole outing in sphere in 2018/19. *Iain Jardine* **h119**

NIGHT OF SIN (FR) 6 gr.g. Sinndar (IRE) – Natt Musik (FR) (Kendor (FR)) [2018/19 h125: h19.8m⁵ c20.9g c16.1m* c17.5s³ c19.2v⁶ c23d c19.5d* c20.2f* c20d⁴ Mar 21] lengthy gelding: fairly useful handicap hurdler, below form first outing in 2018/19: fairly useful chaser: won novice at Taunton in November, handicap at Fontwell in January and novice handicap at Leicester in February: stays 2½m: acts on any going: has worn headgear, including in 2018/19: usually races close up. *Nick Williams* **c120 h105**

NIKAP (FR) 5 b.m. Kapgarde (FR) – Nika Glitters (FR) (Nikos) [2018/19 b85: b16.7g^ro Apr 13] fair form when second in bumper on debut in 2017/18: ran out sole outing since. *Nigel Hawke* **b– §**

NIKGARDE (FR) 4 b.g. Kapgarde (FR) – Nikoline (FR) (Martaline) [2018/19 ab16.3s² ab16.3s³ Feb 23] £40,000 3-y-o: second foal: half-brother to useful French 17f chase winner Confuceen (by Konig Turf): dam French 15f-2¼m hurdle/chase winner (useful over hurdles): fair form in bumpers, placed both starts. *James Ewart* **b86**

NIKKI STEEL (IRE) 9 b.g. Craigsteel – Nikikita (IRE) (Nikos) [2018/19 h–: h15.8g² h15.7g² c16m³ c17.2g* c19.2d⁴ Apr 9] lengthy, sparely-made gelding: fair handicap hurdler: similar form over fences: won handicap at Market Rasen in March: stays 2¾m: acts on soft going: in cheekpieces last 3 starts. *Dr Richard Newland* **c110 h111**

NIMBY (IRE) 5 ch.g. Doyen (IRE) – Ain't Misbehavin (IRE) (Trempolino (USA)) [2018/19 ab16s* b13.7g Apr 12] £42,000 3-y-o: sixth foal: closely related to bumper winner/useful hurdler Caius Marcius (2m/17f winner, by King's Theatre) and half-brother to modest 2¾m hurdle winner Petite Ganache (by Presenting): dam unraced half-sister to dam of very smart hurdler/useful chaser (winner up to 21f) Diamond King: fair form in bumpers: won at Lingfield in December. *Dan Skelton* **b92**

NINEOHTWOONEOH (IRE) 5 b.g. Fame And Glory – Oscar's Beauty (IRE) (Oscar (IRE)) [2018/19 h15.3g h19.5d h16.7s⁵ h16.8s Apr 16] poor form over hurdles. *Paul Nicholls* **h71**

NINE O THREE (IRE) 7 gr.g. Central Park (IRE) – That's My Sister (IRE) (Aboo Hom) [2018/19 h20.1s^pu c20s c24.2s^ur h20.8g h20.1v⁶ c24s c25.2g^pu Jan 10] Irish point winner: no form under Rules: usually in headgear/tongue tie. *Micky Hammond* **c– h–**

NINEPOINTSIXTHREE 9 b.g. Bertolini (USA) – Armada Grove (Fleetwood (IRE)) [2018/19 c102§, h110§: h15.7g h18.6g^pu h16.8s² h16.8s* h16.8g h19.9s⁴ h16.8v* h15.7m^pu h16.4d^rr Apr 6] lengthy gelding: has had breathing operation: fairly useful handicap hurdler: won at Sedgefield in December and January: maiden chaser: stays 21f, though races mainly around 2m nowadays: acts on good to firm and heavy going: wears headgear: in tongue tie last 3 starts: ungenuine. *Sam England* **c– § h120 §**

NINTH WAVE (IRE) 5 b.g. September Storm (GER) – Royale Pearl (Cloudings (IRE)) [2018/19 b15.8d⁴ h19.9g h19.7s⁴ h19.4g³ h15.7s⁶ c20.3g Apr 13] €10,000 3-y-o, £40,000 4-y-o: fourth foal: dam, 13f winner, out of half-sister to high-class 2m hurdler Royal Derbi: point winner: fourth in maiden bumper at Ffos Las: modest form over hurdles: 22/1, seventh in novice handicap at Bangor (26 lengths behind Gone Platinum) on chasing debut: stays 2½m: acts on soft going: open to improvement as a chaser. *Philip Hobbs* **c87 p h99 b89**

NI SIN E MO AINM (IRE) 11 b.g. Balakheri (IRE) – Bramslam (IRE) (Glacial Storm (USA)) [2018/19 c75, h–: c20.8g May 4] multiple point winner: winning hurdler: lightly raced in hunter chases, well beaten in last 2: has worn cheekpieces. *Miss Alexandra Bell* **c– h–**

NIVEN (IRE) 6 b.g. Elusive Pimpernel (USA) – Ginger Lily (IRE) (Lucky Guest) **c134**
[2018/19 h16s⁶ h16.5g* h16.5m³ h16.7m⁵ h17.5g³ c18.2d³ c19.9g² c19.9g⁴ c19.5g² **h122**
c16.7s⁵ c15.6v* c19.9g³ c16.3g² c16.5m² Apr 12] half-brother to fair 2m hurdle winner
Captain Sully (by Pairumani Star), stayed 2½m: fairly useful hurdler: won maiden at
Ballinrobe in May: useful chaser: won novice at Hexham in December: left Noel Meade
after tenth start: stays 2½m: acts on good to firm and heavy going: wears cheekpieces/
tongue tie. *Philip Kirby*

NOAH AND THE ARK (IRE) 5 ch.g. Vinnie Roe (IRE) – Well Water (IRE) (Old Vic) **h117**
[2018/19 h16.3m⁶ h17.2g⁵ h16.7g⁵ h16.3m* h16.2g* h16.4g h15.6g³ Nov 7] €9,000 3-y-o, **b–**
£20,000 4-y-o: good-topped gelding: fourth foal: half-brother to bumper winner/fairly
useful hurdler Collen Beag (2m winner, by Mountain High): dam, unraced, out of half-
sister to Scottish Grand National winner Moorcroft Boy: point winner: found little only
bumper start: fairly useful form over hurdles: won novices at Stratford in September and
Kelso in October: will stay 2½m: acts on good to firm going: usually races in rear.
Donald McCain

NO ALARM (IRE) 7 b.g. Getaway (GER) – Chapanga (IRE) (Un Desperado (FR)) **h95**
[2018/19 h93: h16.7g h20.3gᵖᵘ h16.7gᵖᵘ h19.6g h20.6g* h19.6g⁶ Apr 13] pulled up both
starts in points: modest handicap hurdler: won at Market Rasen (conditionals) in March:
stays 21f: acts on heavy going: has worn tongue tie, including last 2 starts. *Olly Murphy*

NOBBY 5 b.g. Authorized (IRE) – Magic Music (IRE) (Magic Ring (IRE)) [2018/19 b89p: **b109**
b16g* b16d* b16.3d² Mar 22] good-topped gelding: point winner: useful form in bumpers:
won at Warwick in May and December by 8 lengths from Mr Woody): second in listed
event at Newbury (neck behind House Island) in March. *Alan King*

NOBEL LEADER (IRE) 9 b.g. Alflora (IRE) – Ben Roseler (IRE) (Beneficial) [2018/19 **c114**
c20d c20.3s* c19.9d* c21.2d² Mar 15] has had breathing operation: maiden hurdler: fair **h–**
handicap chaser: won at Bangor in December and Huntingdon in February: stays 21f: acts
on soft going: has worn headgear. *James Evans*

NOBLE ATTITUDE (FR) 5 b.g. Dunkerque (FR) – Silent Flight (FR) (Sicyos (USA)) **h–**
[2018/19 h17.7gᵖᵘ Sep 23] little impact on Flat: pulled up in novice on hurdling debut.
Linda Jewell

NOBLE CALL (IRE) 11 b.g. King's Best (USA) – Really (IRE) (Entrepreneur) [2018/19 **c66**
c89, h–: c19.4gᵖᵘ h22g⁴ c17.2d⁴ Feb 17] compact gelding: poor handicap hurdler: poor **h63**
maiden chaser: stays 21f: acts on soft going: has worn headgear: wears tongue tie.
Joanne Foster

NOBLE ENDEAVOR (IRE) 10 b.g. Flemensfirth (USA) – Old Moon (IRE) (Old Vic) **c139**
[2018/19 c25.9s c25s c34.3gᵖᵘ Apr 6] strong gelding: winning hurdler: very smart chaser, **h–**
below best 2018/19 after long absence (pulled up in Grand National): probably stays 29f:
acts on heavy going: has worn cheekpieces, including last 2 starts. *Gordon Elliott, Ireland*

NOBLE FRIEND (IRE) 11 b.g. Presenting – Laragh (IRE) (Oscar (IRE)) [2018/19 c–, **c–**
h–: c17.8gᵘʳ c17dᶠ Jun 8] workmanlike gelding: maiden pointer/hurdler: fairly useful **h–**
chaser at best, failed to complete all 3 starts under Rules since 2016/17: wears headgear:
has worn tongue tie, including last 3 starts. *Miss Beth Childs*

NOBLE QUEST 7 b.g. Kalanisi (IRE) – Katalina (Hernando (FR)) [2018/19 h21g Nov **h–**
12] well beaten in bumper/novice hurdle. *Warren Greatrex*

NOBLE ROBIN (IRE) 8 b.g. Robin des Champs (FR) – Which Thistle (IRE) (Saddlers' **c–**
Hall (IRE)) [2018/19 h122: c23.6vᵖᵘ Dec 8] Irish point winner: fairly useful hurdler: pulled **h–**
up in novice handicap on chasing debut: should stay further than 2½m: raced only on soft/
heavy going. *Jonjo O'Neill*

NOBLE SAFFRON 4 br.g. Trans Island – Renada (Sinndar (IRE)) [2018/19 b13.7g **h–**
b15.3g h16.2dᵖᵘ h15.9s⁵ h17.7vᵖᵘ h18.7s Mar 11] poor form in bumpers: none over hurdles. **b71**
David Bridgwater

NOBLE WARRIOR (IRE) 6 b.g. Vertical Speed (FR) – Everdane (IRE) (Danetime **h106**
(IRE)) [2018/19 h19.9g* h15.7v⁵ h19.3sᵘʳ h19.3g⁴ Jan 1] £18,000 5-y-o: rather unfurnished
gelding: second foal: dam unraced half-sister to fairly useful 2m hurdler Noble Choice,
herself dam of fairly useful hurdler/smart chaser (stays 25f) Lord Scoundrel: runner-up on
completed start in Irish points: fair form over hurdles: won novice at Uttoxeter in
November. *James Moffatt*

NO BOUNDARIES (IRE) 7 ch.g. Spadoun (FR) – Dawn Princess (IRE) (Old Vic) **h56**
[2018/19 h99, b–: h20.2g h17.1g h16.2g⁶ h24.1d Dec 27] poor maiden hurdler on balance:
unproven beyond 2m: acts on heavy going: sometimes in hood: usually races in rear.
Simon Waugh

NO BUTS 11 b.g. Kayf Tara – Wontcostalotbut (Nicholas Bill) [2018/19 c105, h110: **c94 §**
c29.1g c24.5g³ c21.6g⁶ c22.6mᵖᵘ Jun 19] leggy, lengthy gelding: maiden hurdler: modest **h–**
handicap chaser nowadays: stays 3½m: acts on good to firm and heavy going: has worn
headgear, including in 2018/19: tried in tongue tie: hard to catch right. *David Bridgwater*

NOBUTTABOY 8 b.g. Darsi (FR) – Buckalong (IRE) (Buckskin (FR)) [2018/19 **c– §**
c109§, h–§: c24.2sᵖᵘ h25.3m⁵ h23.1g Mar 27] good-topped gelding: point winner: fairly **h– §**
useful hurdler at best, no form in 2018/19: little show in chases: has worn cheekpieces,
including in 2018/19: unreliable. *Tim Fitzgerald*

NO CEILING (IRE) 9 b.g. Turtle Island (IRE) – Pyrexie (FR) (Pistolet Bleu (IRE)) **c100**
[2018/19 c114, h–: c17m⁴ c15.7g⁴ c19.4m³ c19.2g Jan 1] rather leggy gelding: winning **h–**
hurdler: fair handicap chaser: left Ian Williams after third start: stays 2½m: acts on good to
soft going: has worn hood, including in 2018/19: tried in tongue tie. *Mike Sowersby*

NOCHE DE REYES (FR) 10 b.g. Early March – Cochinchine (IRE) (Namaqualand **c132**
(USA)) [2018/19 c134, h–: c16m² c17g³ c16m⁶ Jul 1] lengthy gelding: winning hurdler: **h–**
useful handicap chaser: second at Ludlow in May: best around 2m: acts on good to firm
and heavy going: has worn tongue tie, including last 3 starts. *Tom George*

NO COMMENT 8 br.g. Kayf Tara – Dizzy Frizzy (Loup Sauvage (USA)) [2018/19 **c131 p**
c122P, h–: c20.9d⁵ c26d⁵ Mar 14] well-made gelding: winning hurdler: useful form over **h–**
fences: fifth in Fulke Walwyn Kim Muir Chase at Cheltenham (14½ lengths behind Any
Second Now) in March: stays 3¼m: acts on heavy going: wears hood: likely to progress
further as a chaser. *Philip Hobbs*

NO CRUISE YET 4 b.g. Passing Glance – Claradotnet (Sri Pekan (USA)) [2018/19 **h81**
h15.8d h18.7s⁶ h16.2g Mar 26] seventh foal: dam, 11.6f winner who stayed 2m on the Flat,
half-sister to fairly useful hurdler (stayed 2½m) Tokala: poor form over hurdles: tried in
hood/tongue tie. *Oliver Greenall*

NOCTURNAL MYTH 6 b.g. Midnight Legend – Gan On (Missed Flight) [2018/19 b85: **h71**
h19.5s h19s⁴ h16.5g Feb 19] has had breathing operation: poor form over hurdles: tried in
tongue tie. *Anthony Honeyball*

NO DICE (IRE) 10 ch.g. Presenting – Roxbury (Overbury (IRE)) [2018/19 c–, h–: **c–**
c19.4d⁶ c19.4m⁵ c22.6m⁵ Jul 15] sturdy gelding: maiden hurdler: maiden chaser, little **h–**
impact last 2 seasons: in cheekpieces last 2 starts: has worn tongue tie. *Fergal O'Brien*

NO DUFFER 12 ch.g. Karinga Bay – Dolly Duff (Afflora (IRE)) [2018/19 c137, h–: c24d⁵ **c129**
c25gᵖᵘ c23.8m⁴ Jan 17] deep-girthed gelding: maiden hurdler: useful handicap chaser: left **h–**
Tom George after second start: stays 3¼m: acts on heavy going: has worn cheekpieces/
tongue tie, including in 2018/19: usually races prominently. *A. Lake*

NO GETAWAY (IRE) 6 ch.g. Getaway (GER) – Nonnetia (FR) (Trempolino (USA)) **h114 p**
[2018/19 b85: h15.8g⁴ h16.7g h16v h19.7s⁴ h21s² Mar 10] useful-looking gelding: will
make a chaser: fair form over hurdles: will be suited by 3m: acts on soft going: still
unexposed. *Dan Skelton*

NO HASSLE HOFF (IRE) 7 b.g. Craigsteel – Endless Patience (IRE) (Miner's Lamp) **c133**
[2018/19 h136: c20v⁴ c21.5s² c24gᵘʳ c24.2s h20.3g² Apr 17] good-topped gelding: useful **h129**
handicap hurdler: similar form over fences: stays 3¼m: acts on heavy going: races towards
rear. *Dan Skelton*

NO HIDDEN CHARGES (IRE) 6 b.g. Scorpion (IRE) – Soniadoir (IRE) (Presenting) **h102**
[2018/19 h23.1s⁴ h15.3g⁴ Apr 14] lengthy gelding: has scope: has had breathing operation:
third foal: half-brother to bumper winner/fair hurdler The Wicket Chicken (2¼m-2½m
winner, by Milan), stays 3¼m: dam (h86) 2¼m hurdle winner: Irish point winner: fair form
over hurdles: better effort when fourth in novice at Wincanton in April: should be suited by
further than 2m. *Neil Mulholland*

NO HIDING PLACE (IRE) 6 b.g. Stowaway – Subtle Gem (IRE) (Subtle Power (IRE)) **c–**
[2018/19 h113, b89: h15.7g* h19.9g⁴ c19.4m⁶ c24.1g h21.6d² h24g³ h23.3g² h24.5g* **h127**
h21.6s⁴ h24.4g⁶ h24.3m³ Apr 20] compact gelding: fairly useful handicap hurdler: won at
Towcester in May and Kempton in November: third at Haydock in April: little impact in 2
starts over fences: stays 3m: acts on soft and good to firm going: in cheekpieces last 4 starts.
Nicky Henderson

NOISY NEIGHBOUR 5 b.m. Malinas (GER) – Mooreheigh (Sir Harry Lewis (USA)) **h–** [2018/19 b–: b15.7d h23s Jan 4] smallish mare: behind in bumpers/novice hurdle: in visor **b–** 2 of 3 starts. *Louise Allan*

NOLANS HOTSPUR (IRE) 7 b.g. Bushranger (IRE) – Cayambe (IRE) (Selkirk **b–** (USA)) [2018/19 b15.7g b16.7g b15.7g Oct 25] no form in bumpers. *Michael Chapman*

NO LIKEY (IRE) 12 b.g. Helissio (FR) – Money Galore (IRE) (Monksfield) [2018/19 **c–** c104, h–: c23spu May 25] winning hurdler: fairly useful chaser at best, pulled up in hunter **h–** sole outing in 2018/19: stays 21f: acts on good to firm and heavy going: wears headgear: has worn tongue tie. *Mrs Julie Mansell*

NOMINATION GAME (IRE) 8 b.g. Oscar (IRE) – Tiarella (IRE) (Supreme Leader) **c88** [2018/19 h79: h16gpu h16.7g6 h16.2g4 h19.7g3 c20d5 c20.2m2 c22.7mpu c22.7f4 c17.2g6 **h61** Mar 27] lengthy gelding: has had breathing operation: poor maiden hurdler: modest form in chases: stays 2½m: acts on good to firm going: wears hood: usually races in rear. *Robin Dickin*

NONESUCH (IRE) 5 b.m. Shirocco (GER) – N'Avoue Jamais (FR) (Marignan (USA)) **b80** [2018/19 h14d3 h16.6g5 b16.3d6 Mar 1] €155,000 3-y-o: rather unfurnished mare: half-sister to several winners in France, including useful hurdler/fairly useful chaser N'Oublie Jamais (15f-21f winner, by Loup Solitaire) and fair hurdler/chaser Nickelle (15f/17f winner, by Sagamix): dam, French 15f-19f (Prix Alain du Breil) hurdle winner, half-sister to high-class chaser up to 21f Nickname: modest form in bumpers. *Nicky Henderson*

NO NO CARDINAL (IRE) 10 ch.g. Touch of Land (FR) – Four Moons (IRE) (Cardinal **c80 §** Flower) [2018/19 c85§, h–§: c16.4g6 c16.3g2 c16.3m3 c16.3m2 c16.5gf c16.3gf h18.5mpu **h– §** c16.3d c15.7g4 c17.8g2 c17g* Apr 22] leggy, angular gelding: maiden hurdler: poor handicap chaser: won at Plumpton in April: stays 2¼m: acts on good to firm going: usually wears headgear: has worn tongue tie: temperamental. *Mark Gillard*

NO NO JOLIE (FR) 7 gr.m. Martaline – Virgata (FR) (Turgeon (USA)) [2018/19 h–: **h89** h17.7g4 h16g h15.5g2 h19.7d Jan 2] modest form over hurdles: stayed 2¼m: best form on good going: dead. *Oliver Sherwood*

NO NO JULIET (IRE) 6 br.m. Scorpion (IRE) – Full Imperatrice (FR) (Dernier **h105** Empereur (USA)) [2018/19 h98, b77: h15.7g3 h21.7g4 h21.7d4 h21.7v* h21.6s3 h23.8g3 h20.5s4 Mar 11] sturdy mare: fair handicap hurdler: won at Fontwell in December: stays 3m: acts on heavy going. *Oliver Sherwood*

NO NO LEGEND 6 b.m. Midnight Legend – Karinga Madame (Karinga Bay) [2018/19 **h–** h100, b74: h16.8g h18.5m h21.6m h19.8gf Nov 22] sturdy mare: poor maiden hurdler on balance: dead. *Mark Gillard*

NO NO MAC (IRE) 10 b.g. Oscar (IRE) – Whatdoyouthinkmac (IRE) (Supreme Leader) **c101** [2018/19 c111, h–: h23.1g4 h20g h21.6m h24.3s h24.2d c20.5d3 c21.6s6 c23.8m* c23.4d5 **h96** Apr 6] sturdy gelding: modest handicap hurdler nowadays: fair handicap chaser: won at Musselburgh (conditionals) in March: left Tim Vaughan after third start, R. Mike Smith after fifth: stays 25f: acts on good to firm and heavy going: has worn headgear, including last 2 starts: wears tongue tie. *Ian Duncan*

NO NO TONIC 5 b.m. Sulamani (IRE) – Karinga Madame (Karinga Bay) [2018/19 **b–** b16.8g Apr 18] second foal: dam, ran once in bumper, half-sister to fairly useful hurdler/ smart chaser (stayed 19f) Overtown Express: tailed off in mares bumper. *Mark Gillard*

NO QUARTER ASKED (IRE) 4 b.g. Jeremy (USA) – Louis's Teffia (IRE) (Presenting) **b89** [2018/19 b16.2d2 Apr 26] €30,000 3-y-o: third foal: half-brother to fairly useful hurdler Court Dreaming (2½m/21f winner) and bumper winner/fair 2½m hurdle winner Judge Earle (both by Court Cave): dam, winning pointer, half-sister to fairly useful hurdler/useful chaser (stayed 3¾m) Night In Milan: 6/1, promise when second in bumper at Perth (2¼ lengths behind Equus Dancer). *Stuart Crawford, Ireland*

NORDENFELT (IRE) 6 b.g. Lilbourne Lad (IRE) – There With Me (USA) (Distant **h–** View (USA)) [2018/19 h16d h16d h15.3g Apr 14] sturdy gelding: modest maiden on Flat, stays 2¼m: no form over hurdles. *Susan Gardner*

NORDICAN BLEUE (FR) 4 b.f. Anabaa Blue – Nordican Queen (FR) (Chineur (FR)) **h104** [2018/19 h16d2 h17.7g2 h15.8m3 Oct 4] has had breathing operation: fair on Flat, stays 11f: fair form over hurdles: best effort when second in juvenile at Worcester: tried in hood. *Dr Richard Newland*

NORDIC COMBINED (IRE) 5 b.g. Haafhd – Chilly Filly (IRE) (Montjeu (IRE)) **h118** [2018/19 h16.3d5 h16d2 h16.3s2 h15.8v2 h15.7d h19.8sf h16.3d Mar 22] smallish gelding: fairly useful on Flat, stays 1¼m: fairly useful maiden hurdler: unproven beyond 2m: acts on heavy going: tried in visor. *David Pipe*

NO REGRETS (IRE) 5 b.g. Presenting – E Mac (IRE) (Old Vic) [2018/19 b16m⁴ Apr **b94 p** 13] €42,000 3-y-o: first foal: dam (h112), 19f hurdle winner, closely related to useful hurdler (stayed 2¾m) Blue Buttons: 11/4, shaped well when fourth in bumper at Ayr (8 lengths behind December Second), caught further back than ideal: open to improvement. *Nicky Richards*

NO REMATCH (IRE) 5 b.g. Westerner – Loadsofability (IRE) (Supreme Leader) **h112 p** [2018/19 b15.8s² h15.8v⁴ h18.5s² Mar 18] £20,000 3-y-o: fourth foal: half-brother to fairly **b84** useful hurdler/winning pointer Plan of Attack (21f/23f winner, by Court Cave) and fair hurdler/fairly useful chaser Definite Soldier (2½m-3m winner, by Definite Article): dam, ran twice over hurdles, half-sister to fairly useful hurdler/useful chaser (winner up to 23f) See U Bob and useful hurdler (2m-2¼m winner) Gold Ability: second in conditionals/ amateurs bumper at Ffos Las (9 lengths behind Thor de Cerisy): fair form over hurdles: better effort when second in maiden at Exeter: will stay 2½m+: will go on improving. *Evan Williams*

NORMAL NORMAN 5 ch.g. Shamardal (USA) – Ambria (GER) (Monsun (GER)) **h123** [2018/19 b96: h15.8m² h16.7g* h15.6g² h16.4g h15.6g* h16m³ h16.4sᵖᵘ Mar 12] sturdy gelding: bumper winner: fairly useful hurdler: won maiden at Market Rasen in October and handicap at Musselburgh in January: raced around 2m: best form on good going. *John Ryan*

NORMAN THE RED 9 ch.g. Tobougg (IRE) – Linden Lime (Double Trigger (IRE)) **h109** [2018/19 h110: h23.3gᵘʳ May 27] angular gelding: fair handicap hurdler: challenging when unseated rider 2 out sole outing in 2018/19 stays 2¾m: acts on heavy going: tried in hood. *John E. Long*

NORM THE STORM 6 b.g. Multiplex – Macnance (IRE) (Mandalus) [2018/19 b–: **h–** h15.8m⁶ h20gᵖᵘ h15.8m⁵ h19.9g⁵ h25.8gᵖᵘ h19.6m Oct 4] compact gelding: no form in bumpers/over hurdles. *Evan Williams*

NORSE DA 9 b.g. Norse Dancer (IRE) – End of An Error (Charmer) [2018/19 h–: h21.6gᵖᵘ **c–** h21.6gᵖᵘ c24.2sᵖᵘ Nov 25] no form over hurdles: pulled up in novice on chasing debut: **h–** tried in cheekpieces/tongue tie. *Helen Nelmes*

NORSE LEGEND 8 b.g. Norse Dancer (IRE) – Methodical (Lujain (USA)) [2018/19 **c101** h108: h23.1g* h23.1s h23s c23gᵖᵘ c19.2v³ c23.6dᵘʳ Mar 21] angular gelding: fair handicap **h108** hurdler: won at Exeter in November: similar form over fences: standout effort when third in handicap at same course in March: stays 23f: acts on heavy going: wears headgear. *Colin Tizzard*

NORSE LIGHT 8 ch.g. Norse Dancer (IRE) – Dimelight (Fantastic Light (USA)) **c–** [2018/19 c97, h99: h20.6g² h20.7g h18.5d c20.2m⁵ h18.5m h19d h20.7d h19d Jan 19] **h84** strong gelding: modest handicap hurdler: winning chaser: stays 21f: acts on good to firm and heavy going: wears headgear/tongue tie. *David Dennis*

NORTHANDSOUTH (IRE) 9 ch.g. Spadoun (FR) – Ennel Lady (IRE) (Erin's Hope) **c109** [2018/19 c–, h94: c16.5g* h15.8m c16.5g² c25.5dᵖᵘ c16g h19.7g h16.4d Mar 5] poor **h83** handicap hurdler nowadays: fair handicap chaser: won at Worcester in May: left Samuel Drinkwater after third start, Aytach Sadik after fifth: stays 21f: acts on heavy going: has worn hood. *Sara Ender*

NORTHERN BEAU (IRE) 6 b.m. Canford Cliffs (IRE) – View (IRE) (Galileo (IRE)) **c118** [2018/19 h105: h20g³ h15.7g³ h20.3g² h19.6g³ h23g³ c23.8g⁴ c20g² c20.2m² c20.2f* **h104** c25.2d² c16.3g* Apr 18] has had breathing operation: fair maiden hurdler: fairly useful form over fences: won mares handicaps at Leicester in February and Cheltenham in April: stays 25f: acts on any going: has worn cheekpieces, including last 3 starts: in tongue tie last 4 starts: front runner/races prominently. *Michael Scudamore*

NORTHERN BOUND (IRE) 5 b.g. Fruits of Love (USA) – Noble Choice (Dahar **h106** (USA)) [2018/19 b16.4d h15.8g* h21d⁵ Jan 28] £55,000 4-y-o: compact gelding: half- **b–** brother to several winners, including fairly useful hurdler/smart chaser Lord Scoundrel (2¼m-2¾m winner), stays 25f, and useful hurdler/useful chaser Balnaslow (2m-3m winner), both by Presenting: dam (h127), 2m hurdle winner, also 1m-11f winner on Flat: runner-up sole start in Irish points: down the field in bumper: fair form over hurdles: won maiden at Ludlow in November: should stay 21f. *Ben Pauling*

NORTHERN GIRL (IRE) 6 b.m. Westerner – Janebailey (Silver Patriarch (IRE)) **h96** [2018/19 h94: h21.3m² h19.9g h19.7s⁶ h21.4d* h20.6v⁴ Mar 16] leggy mare: modest handicap hurdler: won mares event at Ayr in January: stays 21f: acts on heavy going. *Philip Kirby*

NORTHERN PRINCESS 5 b.m. Authorized (IRE) – Julatten (IRE) (Alhaarth (IRE)) **b90**
[2018/19 b15.7d² b15.8s b15.8s⁶ Dec 31] fourth foal: dam, ran twice over hurdles/maiden
on Flat (stayed 1¼m), sister to high-class hurdler (2m-19f winner) Iktitaf: fair form in
bumpers: best effort when second in mares event at Southwell on debut. *Lucy Wadham*

NORTHERN SKY (IRE) 6 b.g. Danehill Dancer (IRE) – Moon Flower (IRE) (Sadler's **h69**
Wells (USA)) [2018/19 h17.6g h18.8d h16.8s⁶ Dec 7] close-coupled gelding: fair on Flat,
stayed 13f: poor form over hurdles: tried in tongue tie: dead. *A. P. Keatley, Ireland*

NORTHERN SOUL 6 ch.g. Presenting – Our Ethel (Be My Chief (USA)) [2018/19 h98: **h113**
h20g^pu h16d* h16.2g² h19.5d Feb 25] bumper winner: fair form over hurdles: won novice
at Wetherby in December: should be suited by 2½m. *Ruth Jefferson*

NORTH HILL (IRE) 8 b.g. Westerner – Hill Fairy (Monsun (GER)) [2018/19 h107: **h111**
h21g h20.6m² h23.9g⁴ h20.6g³ Oct 20] sturdy gelding: fair handicap hurdler: stays 2¾m:
acts on good to firm going: usually wears hood: usually races nearer last than first.
Ian Williams

NORTHOFTHEWALL (IRE) 5 b.g. Mahler – Sherchanceit (IRE) (Norwich) [2018/19 **h103 p**
b16d h16.3d h15.7s⁴ h19g⁵ Feb 22] €38,000 3-y-o: has had breathing operation: second **b76**
foal: dam (h100), 2m/17f hurdle winner, half-sister to fair hurdler/fairly useful chaser
(stayed 4m) Canada Street: unplaced in bumper: fair form over hurdles: will stay beyond
19f: should do better. *Dan Skelton*

NORTH STAR OSCAR (IRE) 5 b.g. Oscar (IRE) – North Star Poly (IRE) (Presenting) **h78**
[2018/19 b15.8g⁴ b15.8s² h19.5d h23.1s h21g⁵ Apr 10] €38,000 3-y-o: has had breathing **b97**
operation: fourth foal: closely related to fairly useful hurdler/useful chaser Audacious Plan
(3m-29f winner, by Old Vic) and half-brother to bumper winner/fairly useful hurdler Savoy
Court (21f winner, by Robin des Champs): dam unraced half-sister to smart hurdler
(2m-2¼m winner) She's Our Mare: fairly useful form in bumpers: poor form over hurdles:
tried in cheekpieces. *Warren Greatrex*

NORTH WEST WIND 6 b.g. Shirocco (GER) – Crystal Ballerina (IRE) (Sadler's Wells **c108**
(USA)) [2018/19 h88: h23.1g⁴ c24g³ c16g³ c17.4g^ur Oct 30] fair form over hurdles/fences: **h101**
stayed 23f: best form on good going: tried in cheekpieces: dead. *Evan Williams*

NORTONTHORPELEGEND (IRE) 9 b.g. Midnight Legend – Tanit (Xaar) [2018/19 **c97**
c114, h–: c24.2d^pu c25.5g^pu c24.1g^pu c24.5v⁶ c25.2g* c26.7d* c26.3d⁴ Jan 11] lightly- **h–**
raced hurdler: modest handicap chaser: won at Catterick in December and Wetherby
(amateurs) in January: stays 27f: acts on soft and good to firm going: tried in cheekpieces.
Rebecca Menzies

NORUKI (IRE) 9 b.g. Flemensfirth (USA) – Classic Material (Classic Cliche (IRE)) **c107**
[2018/19 c24d^pu c26.2d⁴ c24.2d^f c25.2g⁶ Mar 26] €43,000 3-y-o: brother to bumper winner
Colonel Mortimer and half-brother to 2 winners, including fairly useful hurdler/winning
chaser Invicta Lake (2¼m-25f winner, by Dr Massini): dam unraced half-sister to smart
hurdler (winner up to 3m) Material World: Irish point winner: fair form in novice chases.
Dai Williams

NORWEGIAN WOODS (IRE) 6 b.g. Arcadio (GER) – Water Ore (IRE) (Ore) [2018/19 **h–**
b16g⁶ h16.6g Jan 9] Irish point winner: well beaten in bumper/novice hurdle. *Tim Vaughan* **b65**

NOSPER (FR) 7 b.g. Whipper (USA) – Nostaltir (FR) (Muhtathir) [2018/19 h62: h21.4m **h–**
May 10] maiden hurdler: tried in tongue tie. *Bob Buckler*

NO SUCH NUMBER 11 b.g. King's Best (USA) – Return (USA) (Sadler's Wells **c106**
(USA)) [2018/19 c110, h–: h22.7g^pu c23.9d² c24.2g⁵ c20.1m^pu c20.1g⁶ c23.9m^pu c21.6m **h–**
Sep 19] winning hurdler: fair handicap chaser: stays 3m: acts on good to soft going: has
worn cheekpieces, including in 2018/19: wears tongue tie. *Maurice Barnes*

NOTACHANCE (IRE) 5 b.g. Mahler – Ballybrowney Hall (IRE) (Saddlers' Hall (IRE)) **h117**
[2018/19 h23d² h24s³ h23.1d³ h24.2d⁵ h24.2d* Mar 22] £18,000 3-y-o, £80,000 4-y-o:
useful-looking gelding: fourth foal: dam, (h89) winning pointer, out of half-sister to Over
The Deel and Smarty, both placed in Grand National: runner-up in Irish point: fairly useful
form over hurdles: won handicap at Newbury in March: stays 3m: acts on good to soft
going. *Alan King*

NOT A NAIL (IRE) 5 b.g. Flemensfirth (USA) – Mandys Gold (IRE) (Mandalus) **b92**
[2018/19 b16.8s³ b15.8s Feb 26] £100,000 3-y-o: sixth foal: brother to 3 winners, including
useful hurdler/chaser Sizing Gold (2½m winner) and fairly useful 2m hurdle winner Ten

Ten, and half-brother to fairly useful hurdler/chaser Exxaro (2½m-3¼m winner, by Presenting): dam 2½m bumper/3m chase winner: fair form in bumpers: better effort when third at Exeter on debut. *Paul Nicholls*

NOT ANOTHER MUDDLE 8 b.g. Kayf Tara – Spatham Rose (Environment Friend) [2018/19 c131p, h–: c15.5s³ c15.5d* c16.3d⁵ c21.6g² Apr 12] good-topped gelding: winning hurdler: useful form over fences: won handicap at Sandown in February: second in similar event at Fontwell (length behind Romain de Senam) in April: barely stays 2¾m: acts on heavy going: usually races off pace, often freely. *Gary Moore*   **c141** **h–**

NOTARFBAD (IRE) 13 b.g. Alderbrook – Angels Flame (IRE) (Un Desperado (FR)) [2018/19 c129§, h–: c20.3g⁶ c21g⁴ Jun 15] lengthy gelding: winning hurdler: fairly useful handicap chaser, below form in 2018/19: stays 2¾m: acts on good to firm and heavy going: wears hood: usually leads: temperamental. *Jeremy Scott*   **c113 §** **h–**

NOT A ROLE MODEL (IRE) 7 b.g. Helissio (FR) – Mille Et Une Nuits (FR) (Ecologist) [2018/19 c106, h103: c20.5m* c21.6g² c21m* c21.4m⁴ c21.4g⁴ Sep 29] lightly-raced hurdler: fairly useful form over fences: won handicaps at Kempton in May and Newton Abbot in June: fourth in Summer Plate at Market Rasen in July: stays 2¾m: acts on good to firm going: usually leads. *Sam Thomas*   **c122** **h–**

NOT AT ALL (FR) 6 b.g. Martaline – Not Lost (FR) (Lost World (IRE)) [2018/19 h66: c22.5g Jun 6] has had breathing operation: poor maiden hurdler on balance: well beaten in novice handicap on chasing debut: placed in points in 2019: tried in tongue tie. *Jonjo O'Neill*   **c–** **h–**

NOTAWORDOFALIE (IRE) 4 br.f. Presenting – Saddleeruppat (IRE) (Saddlers' Hall (IRE)) [2018/19 b16g⁴ Feb 22] €60,000 3-y-o: fifth foal: half-sister to useful hurdler/smart chaser Winter Escape (2m-2½m winner, by Robin des Pres) and bumper winner/fairly useful hurdler Lughnasa (2m-2¼m winner, by Westerner): dam (b102), bumper winner, closely related to high-class hurdler (stayed 25f) Black Jack Ketchum: 10/1, fourth in mares bumper at Warwick (23 lengths behind Yeavering Belle): should improve. *Jonjo O'Neill*   **b63 p**

NOTEBOOK (GER) 6 b.g. Samum (GER) – Nova (GER) (Winged Love (IRE)) [2018/19 h16d² h19.6g² h16s* h20g² h21s Mar 13] £70,000 5-y-o: lengthy gelding: will make a chaser: half-brother to bumper winner Neck Or Nothing (by Intikhab) and 2 winners on Flat in Italy: dam German 9f-1½m winner: point winner: useful form over hurdles: won maiden at Tramore in January: second in Michael Purcell Memorial Novices' Hurdle at Thurles in February and novice at Punchestown (6½ lengths behind Gardens of Babylon) shortly after end of British season: stays 2½m: acts on soft going: in tongue tie last 4 starts. *Henry de Bromhead, Ireland*   **h134**

NOT FOR YOU (IRE) 11 b.g. Beneficial – Bonnie Thynes (IRE) (Good Thyne (USA)) [2018/19 c20.6dᶠ c20g c20.7m* c20s⁵ c24gᵖᵘ Sep 5] winning hurdler: fair handicap chaser: won at Killarney in July: stayed 25f: acted on good to firm and heavy going: often wore headgear: tried in tongue tie: often let down by jumping over fences: dead. *Charles Byrnes, Ireland*   **c100 x** **h–**

NOT GOING OUT (IRE) 5 ch.g. Doyen (IRE) – Alannico (Overbury (IRE)) [2018/19 b16.8d h23.1s h15.3g³ h18.5g⁴ Apr 20] €28,000 3-y-o: closely related to fairly useful hurdler/chaser Kashline (2¾m/23f winner, by Oscar) and half-brother to fair hurdler War On (2½m winner, by Presenting): dam, placed in bumper, half-sister to useful hurdler/fair chaser (stayed 3m) Rudi Knight: maiden Irish pointer: tailed off in bumper: fair form over hurdles: best effort when third in maiden at Wincanton: in tongue tie last 2 starts. *Mark Gillard*   **h108** **b–**

NOTHING MAN (IRE) 5 b.g. Ask – Holly Gaga (IRE) (Golan (IRE)) [2018/19 b16v⁴ b16.3g Mar 30] €16,000 3-y-o: first foal: dam, unraced, out of half-sister to top-class 2m-2½m hurdle winner Mister Morose: fair form in bumpers: better effort when fourth at Ayr on debut (for Stuart Crawford). *David Dennis*   **b85**

NOT MANY LEFT (IRE) 6 b.g. Oscar (IRE) – Lasado (IRE) (Jurado (USA)) [2018/19 h131, b83: h20s⁴ h25d* h24d³ h20d² Apr 22] compact gelding: point winner: smart hurdler: won handicap at Huntingdon in January: placed after in Pertemps Final at Cheltenham (1½ lengths behind Sire du Berlais) and Keelings Irish Strawberry Hurdle at Fairyhouse (1½ lengths behind Rashaan): again running well when falling last in Champion Stayers' Hurdle won by Unowhatimeanharry at Punchestown shortly after end of British season: stays 25f: acts on heavy going: in cheekpieces last 4 starts. *Mrs J. Harrington, Ireland*   **h147**

NOT NEVER 7 ch.g. Notnowcato – Watchoverme (Haafhd) [2018/19 h120: h15.7s h19.2d* Jan 14] neat gelding: fairly useful handicap hurdler: won at Fontwell in January: stays 19f: acts on heavy going: usually races prominently. *Gary Moore*   **h129**

NOT NORMAL (IRE) 6 b.g. Robin des Champs (FR) – Mardi Roberta (IRE) (Bob Back (USA)) [2018/19 b99: h19.5s^ur h16.7v^2 Dec 1] placed both starts in bumpers: fair form when second in novice at Bangor on completed latest start over hurdles: dead. *Emma Lavelle* — **h109**

NOTNOWSAM 8 ch.g. Notnowcato – First Fantasy (Be My Chief (USA)) [2018/19 c–, h77: h22.1g h22.1m Jun 29] workmanlike gelding: poor handicap hurdler: winning chaser: stays 23f: acts on soft going: wears headgear: tried in tongue tie. *Micky Hammond* — **c–**, **h56**

NOTNOW SEAMUS 8 b.g. Notnowcato – Special Beat (Bustino) [2018/19 h102: h24g^6 h23.1g^pu h20.3g* h19.9m* h19.9g* h20g^2 h19.9g* h24.1m Oct 17] has had breathing operation: useful handicap hurdler: won at Southwell in June, and Uttoxeter in July (twice) and September (by 18 lengths from Venue): stays 3m: acts on good to firm and heavy going: has worn headgear: wears tongue tie: usually races close up. *Dan Skelton* — **h136**

NOTONEBUTTWO (IRE) 12 b.g. Dushyantor (USA) – Daiquiri (IRE) (Houmayoun (FR)) [2018/19 c78§, h–§: c19.3g^f c20.1g^2 c17.4g^4 c19.3g^pu c20.1s^3 c25.2g c26.3s^6 Feb 21] compact gelding: winning hurdler: poor handicap chaser: stays 3¼m: acts on heavy going: has worn headgear/tongue tie: temperamental. *Sue Smith* — **c83 §**, **h– §**

NOTRE AMI (IRE) 8 br.g. Kalanisi (IRE) – Shuilan (IRE) (Good Thyne (USA)) [2018/19 h120: c16.5m^F h19.5s^2 c18g^3 c16v^3 c17.5d^3 h20.7d h21.7d Feb 24] good-topped gelding: fairly useful handicap hurdler, below best in 2018/19: fair form over fences: stays 19f: acts on heavy going: has worn hood, including in 2018/19: tried in tongue tie. *Nick Gifford* — **c101**, **h112**

NOTRE PARI (IRE) 5 b.g. Jeremy (USA) – Glynn Approach (IRE) (Zagreb (USA)) [2018/19 h16g^3 Apr 10] €22,000 3-y-o, £47,500 4-y-o: second foal: dam, unraced, out of sister to smart hurdler/useful chaser up to 3m Adamant Approach: runner-up in Irish point: 16/1, considerably handled when third in novice at Warwick (4½ lengths behind Elusive Belle) on hurdling debut: sure to improve. *Olly Murphy* — **h110 p**

NO TRUMPS 5 b.m. Black Sam Bellamy (IRE) – Magic Score (Shambo) [2018/19 h19.5d h21.7d^5 h21s^4 h25g^4 h24.1d^6 Mar 19] fourth foal: half-sister to bumper winner Side Step (by Norse Dancer): dam (b91) runner-up sole start in bumper: modest form over hurdles: stays 25f: acts on soft going: usually races prominently. *Charlie Longsdon* — **h93**

NOT SO SLEEPY 7 ch.g. Beat Hollow – Papillon de Bronze (IRE) (Marju (IRE)) [2018/19 h16d^4 h15.3g* h15.3g^5 Mar 25] closely related to modest hurdler/winning pointer Fine Resolve (2½m winner, by Refuse To Bend): useful on Flat, stays 1½m: fairly useful form over hurdles: won novice at Wincanton in February: tried in tongue tie. *Hughie Morrison* — **h122**

NOT THAT FUISSE (FR) 6 b.g. Fuisse (FR) – Edelmira (FR) (Kahyasi) [2018/19 h107p: h15.8d* h17g* h16d^5 h16.3g^2 h16.4g^6 h16.8g^2 h19g* h21m^4 h20.3d^f Mar 15] rangy gelding: fairly useful hurdler: won maiden at Uttoxeter and novice at Aintree in May, and handicap at Taunton in January: stays 21f: acts on soft and good to firm going. *Dan Skelton* — **h129**

NOT THE CHABLIS (IRE) 5 b.g. Scorpion (IRE) – De Street (IRE) (Sunshine Street (USA)) [2018/19 b17d^3 b16.5m* h16v^4 h16s^6 h16.2d^3 h16.2d^4 h20.2g Apr 25] €10,000 3-y-o: second foal: half-brother to fair 2m hurdle winner Penneys Hun (by Arakan): dam unraced half-sister to fairly useful hurdler/smart chaser (2m-2½m winner) Hold Fast: fair form in bumpers: won at Down Royal in June: modest form over hurdles: left Edward P. Harty after second start: unproven beyond 2m: acts on heavy going. *N. W. Alexander* — **h99**, **b87**

NOTWHATIAM (IRE) 9 b.g. Morozov (USA) – Riverfort (IRE) (Over The River (FR)) [2018/19 c–, h118: h22.2m h23.3g* h23.9d^f h23.3d* h20s^3 h25g^4 h24d^pu h26.4g^4 Mar 30] strong gelding: has had breathing operation: fairly useful handicap hurdler: won at Uttoxeter in October and November: behind when unseated only chase outing: left A. P. Keatley after first start: stays 3¼m: acts on heavy going: has worn hood, including in 2018/19: wears tongue tie: races off pace. *Dan Skelton* — **c–**, **h129**

NOVIS ADVENTUS (IRE) 7 b.g. New Approach (IRE) – Tiffed (USA) (Seattle Slew (USA)) [2018/19 h118: h16.3m h20m h20g* h20g^5 Sep 28] fairly useful handicap hurdler: won at Worcester in September: stays 2½m: acts on good to firm going: in cheekpieces last 2 starts: in tongue tie last 3: usually travels strongly. *Neil Mulholland* — **h127**

NOW BEN (IRE) 11 ch.g. Beneficial – Bannow Beach (IRE) (Saddlers' Hall (IRE)) [2018/19 c121, h–: c27.5d^pu c23.8g^2 c23.8m^2 Apr 23] prolific point winner, including in 2018/19: once-raced hurdler: fairly useful hunter chaser at best, below that level in 2018/19: stays 3½m: acts on good to firm and good to soft going. *Philip Rowley* — **c107**, **h–**

NOWHERETOEXIT 5 b.m. Exit To Nowhere (USA) – Lady of Scarvagh (IRE) **h62** (Zaffaran (USA)) [2018/19 b–: h20m b20m⁴ h16g⁵ h15.8d h15.8v Dec 21] poor form over hurdles: left David Rees after third start: often in hood. *Dai Burchell*

NOW IS THE WINTER (IRE) 5 b.g. Fame And Glory – Supreme Melody (IRE) **b96** (Supreme Leader) [2018/19 b16.3s* Mar 11] €55,000 3-y-o, £30,000 4-y-o: fifth foal: dam (b78), placed in bumpers, sister to useful hurdler/smart chaser (stayed 3m) Supreme Prince: runner-up in point bumper: 6/1, won maiden bumper at Stratford by ½ length from Fitzroy, digging deep. *Ben Pauling*

NOW LISTEN HERE (IRE) 7 b.g. Captain Marvelous (IRE) – Thanks Eileen (Emperor **h93** Fountain) [2018/19 h94: h25g³ h21.7m² Mar 27] modest maiden hurdler: barely stays 25f: acts on good to firm going: in cheekpieces last 3 starts. *Gary Moore*

NOW LOOK AT ME (IRE) 5 ch.g. Shantou (USA) – Similan (IRE) (Milan) [2018/19 **b106** b15.3g* b15.3d² b16.6g* Feb 20] €40,000 3-y-o: second foal: dam, unraced, half-sister to useful hurdler/smart chaser (stayed 25f) My Murphy: useful form in bumpers: won at Wincanton in November and Doncaster (by 1½ lengths from Welsh Saint) in February. *Tom George*

NOW MCGINTY (IRE) 8 b.g. Stowaway – Western Whisper (IRE) (Supreme Leader) **c142** [2018/19 h141: c23.6g² c23.6dᵘʳ c20s² c23.6d* c23.8d² c24.4s Mar 13] angular gelding: **h–** useful hurdler: similar form over fences: won novice at Chepstow in January: second in Reynoldstown Novices' Chase at Ascot (1½ lengths behind Mister Malarky) in February: will stay long distances: acts on heavy going: wears cheekpieces: front runner/races prominently. *Stuart Edmunds*

NUBE NEGRA (SPA) 5 br.g. Dink (FR) – Manly Dream (FR) (Highest Honor (FR)) **h134** [2018/19 h131: h16.4g h16.5gᵇᵈ h16.3d³ h16m⁶ Apr 13] good-topped gelding: has had breathing operation: useful handicap hurdler: third at Newbury (1¾ lengths behind Zanza) in March: raced around 2m: acts on soft going: tried in tongue tie: strong traveller. *Dan Skelton*

NUMBERCRUNCHER (IRE) 13 b.g. Beneficial – Josie's Turn (IRE) (Kambalda) **c114** [2018/19 c106, h–: c20.8g c17.8g* c17dᵖᵘ c15.9g³ c20d⁴ c21.1dᵖᵘ Apr 4] good-topped **h–** gelding: multiple point winner: maiden hurdler: fair hunter chaser: won at Fontwell in May: stays 3m: acts on good to firm and heavy going. *David O'Brien*

NUMITOR 5 gr.g. Schiaparelli (GER) – Just Popsy (Turgeon (USA)) [2018/19 b16d⁵ Mar **b85** 28] first foal: dam (b74) ran twice in bumpers: 14/1, fifth in maiden bumper at Warwick (15¼ lengths behind Welsh Saint). *Heather Main*

NUTS WELL 8 b.g. Dylan Thomas (IRE) – Renada (Sinndar (IRE)) [2018/19 c132p, h–: **c143** c17.1m* c15.9sᵖᵘ h16s⁴ h15.6g⁶ c15.2g² c16.4gᶠ c16.4g⁴ c16.5m⁴ c20.1g⁶ Apr 25] fairly **h122** useful handicap hurdler: useful handicap chaser: won at Kelso in October: stays 2½m: acts on good to firm and heavy going: in cheekpieces last 3 starts. *Ann Hamilton*

NYE BEVAN (IRE) 4 b.g. Arcadio (GER) – Emma Jane (IRE) (Lord Americo) [2018/19 **b–** b16.3d Mar 23] tailed off in Goffs UK Spring Sales Bumper at Newbury. *Nigel Twiston-Davies*

NYLON SPEED (IRE) 5 b.g. Campanologist (USA) – Neuquen (IRE) (Rock of **h112** Gibraltar (IRE)) [2018/19 h16g* h15.8g² h16g⁶ Nov 26] has had breathing operation: fairly useful on Flat, stays 1½m: fair form over hurdles: won novice at Warwick in September. *Alan King*

O

OAKIDOAKI 7 b.g. Sulamani (IRE) – Sweet Robinia (IRE) (Bob Back (USA)) [2018/19 **c94** c94, h61: c19.9g² c23.9m Jun 22] sturdy gelding: maiden hurdler: modest maiden chaser: **h–** won point in April: stays 21f: acts on heavy going: wears cheekpieces/tongue tie. *Brendan Powell*

OAKLEY HALL (IRE) 7 b.g. Milan – Rockwell College (IRE) (Supreme Leader) **c–** [2018/19 h121: h24.5g² c25gᵖᵘ h21dᵖᵘ Nov 29] good-topped gelding: fairly useful maiden **h120** hurdler: pulled up in novice handicap on chasing debut: stays 25f: acts on soft going: tried in cheekpieces. *Jonjo O'Neill*

OAKLEY (IRE) 6 b.g. Oscar (IRE) – Tirolean Dance (IRE) (Tirol) [2018/19 b94: h16v⁵ h15.7s² h15.8d* h16g*] Jan 12] lengthy gelding: useful form over hurdles: won novice at Ludlow in December and handicap at Kempton (much improved when beating Magic Dancer 1¾ lengths) in January: open to further progress. *Philip Hobbs* **h131 p**

OAKMONT (FR) 6 ch.g. Turtle Bowl (IRE) – Onega Lake (IRE) (Peintre Celebre (USA)) [2018/19 h16g² h16.7m⁵ h16.7g³ h16.7g h16.7g h16g⁶ Apr 26] fairly useful on Flat, stays 10.5f: fair maiden hurdler: unproven beyond 17f: acts on good to firm and good to soft going: has worn hood: wears tongue tie. *John McConnell, Ireland* **h101**

OAK VINTAGE (IRE) 9 b.g. Fruits of Love (USA) – Brandam Supreme (IRE) (Supreme Leader) [2018/19 c105, h–: c17.1g* h16.2g⁶ c19.3m* c15.2m⁴ c15.2d⁴ c19.4s² c19.3d⁵ c20.1g c21.3d⁴ c17.1d⁶ Apr 8] sturdy gelding: winning hurdler: fairly useful handicap chaser: won at Kelso in May and Sedgefield in October: left Ann Hamilton after fifth start: stays 21f: acts on good to firm and heavy going: usually front runner/races prominently: sometimes let down by jumping. *Philip Kirby* **c121 x h–**

OBORNE LADY (IRE) 6 b.m. Watar (IRE) – Lady Shackleton (IRE) (Zaffaran (USA)) [2018/19 h–, h16.8m⁶ h22.1gm⁶ h22.1gᵖᵘ h21.6g h18.5mᵖᵘ Jun 26] poor form over hurdles: will stay beyond 2¾m: acts on good to firm going. *Seamus Mullins* **h83**

OCCASIONALLY YOURS (IRE) 15 b.g. Moscow Society (USA) – Kristina's Lady (IRE) (Lafontaine (USA)) [2018/19 c–, h103: h20.7g h20g³ Jun 3] tall gelding: modest handicap hurdler: fell only chase start: stays 23f: acts on good to firm and heavy going: has worn headgear. *Alan Blackmore* **c– h98**

OCEAN COVE (IRE) 7 ch.g. Ask – Sand Eel (IRE) (Sandalay) [2018/19 h123, b84: h24.2d h23.3d³ h26s³ h26s* Mar 10] has had breathing operation: third in Irish point: fairly useful handicap hurdler: won at Warwick in March: stays 3¼m: acts on heavy going: tried in cheekpieces/tongue tie. *Fergal O'Brien* **h129**

OCEAN GALE 6 b.m. Shirocco (GER) – Ocean Transit (IRE) (Trans Island) [2018/19 h16mᵘʳ Sep 17] dam (h128) 2m-21f hurdle winner: modest on Flat, stays 2m: unseated first on hurdling debut. *Richard Price* **h–**

OCEAN JIVE 6 b.g. Norse Dancer (IRE) – Kaylianni (Kalanisi (IRE)) [2018/19 h105p: h18.5g³ h15.8m² h16.7m⁶ h20gᵖᵘ Aug 22] fairly useful form over hurdles: stayed 2¼m: acted on good to firm going: dead. *Charlie Mann* **h120**

OCEANUS (IRE) 5 b.g. Born To Sea (IRE) – Alkhawarah (USA) (Intidab (USA)) [2018/19 h99: h15.8m⁵ Oct 4] modest on Flat, stays 11f: similar form on first of 2 outings over hurdles. *Julia Feilden* **h63**

OCH AYE 4 b.g. Declaration of War (USA) – Di Moi Oui (Warning) [2018/19 b16.4d Mar 5] behind in bumper/minor event on Flat. *Mark Johnston* **b–**

O CONNELL STREET (IRE) 5 b.g. Fame And Glory – Victorine (IRE) (Un Desperado (FR)) [2018/19 b16.7g² b16g⁴ Apr 25] €125,000 3-y-o: half-brother to several winners, including bumper winner/smart hurdler City Island (2m-21f winner, by Court Cave) and fairly useful hurdler/useful chaser Fort Worth (2½m-3m winner, by Presenting): dam unraced half-sister to Champion Hurdle winners Morley Street and Granville Again: fair form in bumpers. *Nicky Henderson* **b92**

ODDS ON DAN (IRE) 13 b.g. Oscar (IRE) – Grange Classic (IRE) (Jurado (USA)) [2018/19 c–: h16.2d⁶ h16.7g c21.2m c20g Jul 26] strong gelding: poor form over hurdles: poor handicap chaser: stays 2½m: acts on soft going: wears headgear/tongue tie: often races lazily off pace. *Lucinda Egerton* **c– h68**

ODEN 5 ch.g. Lope de Vega (IRE) – Dashing (IRE) (Sadler's Wells (USA)) [2018/19 h–: h16.3d h16.7d h16v² h15.9d⁴ Jan 6] good-quartered gelding: fair form over hurdles: likely to stay beyond 2m: acts on heavy going: tried in cheekpieces. *Nick Gifford* **h102**

OENOPHILE (GER) 4 b.f. Mamool (IRE) – Ormita (GER) (Acatenango (GER)) [2018/19 h16gᵖᵘ h16.2g⁴ h16.6g h15.8g³ Jan 3] modest maiden on Flat, stays 1½m: poor form over hurdles: wears headgear. *Tom Gretton* **h68**

OFCOURSEIWILL (IRE) 7 b.g. Publisher (USA) – Camden Princess (IRE) (Alderbrook) [2018/19 h97, b88: h19.6g* h15.8m² h22.1g² c16.5g⁴ h22.1s⁵ c24.1g² c20.5gᶠ Oct 29] won Irish point on debut: fair hurdler: won novice handicap at Bangor in May: fairly useful form in novice handicap chases, set to finish in frame again when falling 4 out at Ayr final outing: stays 3m: acts on soft and good to firm going: usually leads. *Donald McCain* **c118 h108**

OFFICER HOOLIHAN 9 b.g. Kayf Tara – Major Hoolihan (Soldier Rose) [2018/19 c121, h–: c20.5g Nov 26] winning hurdler: fairly useful novice chaser in 2017/18: well beaten only outing since: stays 2½m: acts on soft and good to firm going: wears hood/tongue tie. *Tim Vaughan*

OFFICERNISI (IRE) 6 b.g. Kalanisi (IRE) – Some Say (IRE) (King's Theatre (IRE)) [2018/19 b–: b15.8g b17.7s⁶ b18.5d h21.6sᵖᵘ Apr 16] rangy gelding: little promise in bumpers/over hurdles: tried in hood: temperament under suspicion. *Seamus Mullins*

OFFSHORE OSCAR (IRE) 8 gr.g. Oscar (IRE) – La Fiamma (FR) (General Assembly (USA)) [2018/19 h16.5g h20d* h24g² h21g³ h20sᵖᵘ Dec 29] angular gelding: fair handicap hurdler: won at Killarney in August: stays 3m: acts on good to soft going. *Eric McNamara, Ireland*

OFF THE BEAT 5 ch.g. Black Sam Bellamy (IRE) – Off By Heart (Royal Applause) [2018/19 b–: b15.8m May 19] well held in bumpers. *John Mackie*

OFF THE HOOK (IRE) 7 b.m. Getaway (GER) – Call Her Again (IRE) (Old Vic) [2018/19 h104p: h20.5v³ h20.9g² h18.9v³ h20.5d* h20.5d⁴ Mar 23] fairly useful hurdler: won maiden at Ayr in January: in frame all 4 starts otherwise: will stay beyond 2½m: acts on heavy going. *N. W. Alexander*

c–
h–

h–
b–

h109

b–

h118

OFF YOU GO (IRE) 6 b.g. Presenting – Ozzy Oscar (IRE) (Oscar (IRE)) [2018/19 h131p: h16.3d* h16g h16g* h21d² h20d³ Apr 22]

h151

The big handicap hurdle that now features on the first day of the Dublin Racing Festival at Leopardstown in February (moved from its familiar January spot when the new festival was framed two years ago) has had a colourful history. Its origins are to be found in the Irish Sweeps Hurdle, which used to be run just before Christmas, initially at Fairyhouse before being transferred to Leopardstown in 1971, and included the likes of Persian War, Comedy of Errors (twice) and Night Nurse among its winners. The Sweeps Hurdle was turned into a handicap in 1976 and has had a number of sponsors over the years, including lengthy spells supported by Ladbrokes and then by Pierse who took over from Ladbrokes in 2001. The race, one of the strongest handicap hurdles of the year in Ireland, proved a very successful promotional vehicle, known in its days under Ladbrokes sponsorship simply by the sponsor's name (The Ladbroke), which was the most valuable handicap hurdle run in Britain and Ireland until it was overtaken by the Tote Gold Trophy, now the Betfair Hurdle, at Newbury. Ladbrokes ended their sponsorship when only fourteen runners were declared for the race in 2000, the smallest field in fourteen runnings under the bookmaker whose spokesman accused Irish racing of 'disregarding' the race (the presence of Theatreworld, runner-up in three Champion Hurdles, compressed the weights that year, with the rest of the runners receiving between 12 lb and 28 lb from him). The latest running saw the return of the Ladbrokes name to the race title, with the Ladbrokes Hurdle (Extended Handicap) the second most valuable handicap hurdle of the year in Ireland behind the feature event at the summer Galway Festival, the Galway Hurdle.

The last horse to win the Ladbrokes Hurdle twice was Redundant Pal, back in the days when it was The Ladbroke, his successive victories came at 16/1 and 20/1 (he was the longest-priced of his stable's three runners on the first occasion—the only novice in the field—and had been beaten at 5/1-on in a two-runner minor event on his previous outing when winning for the second time). By contrast, the victories of Off You Go in the last two runnings were anything but unexpected, judging by his single-figure starting prices. In a subject also touched on in the essay on Irish Grand National winner Burrows Saint, the 'unknown quantity', the horse that for one reason or another the handicapper has seriously underestimated, can be a thorn in the side for the hard-working, consistent types who make up the bulk of the field in big handicaps. Off You Go's first win in the race, carrying bottom weight of 9-10, was a masterpiece of quite legitimate preparation. Three runs in maiden hurdles, never really involved, got his handicap career under way off a handy mark and he won at Limerick on his second start in handicap company, showing much improved form and earning a 15 lb rise in the weights which just got him into Leopardstown's feature handicap. One of the least exposed (only his sixth start)

Ladbrokes Hurdle (Extended Handicap), Leopardstown—Off You Go does very well to recover from an unpromising position on the extended run-in and repeat his 2018 win; fellow McManus-owned runners Jezki and Ivanovich Gorbatov fill the places

in a highly competitive twenty-seven-runner line-up, 6/1-shot Off You Go won in the manner of one well ahead of the handicapper, scoring from another relatively unexposed runner Deal d'Estruval (well-backed 9/1-chance), the pair pulling clear.

Off You Go didn't run again that season but he picked up where he left off when winning his third handicap in a row, a fairly valuable event at Galway, on his reappearance in October. After being a touch disappointing when claimer ridden in a valuable handicap at Fairyhouse in early-December, Off You Go next made his second appearance in Leopardstown's traditional big handicap, now in its new guise as the Ladbrokes Handicap. Off You Go carried 11-5 this time, racing off a mark 21 lb higher than the previous year, and, again coming in for plenty of support (sent off at 8/1 in a field of nineteen), he progressed once more to run out a ready winner from two others also carrying the McManus emerald green, yellow hoops, the veteran Jezki (who was retired at the end of the season) and another former Cheltenham Festival winner Ivanovich Gorbatov. Redundant Pal finished fifth in the Supreme Novices' and then down the field in the Champion Hurdle in the years when he won The Ladbroke, but Off You Go has yet to pay a visit to the Cheltenham Festival and was taken out of the Coral Cup ('at the wrong end of the handicap') after being beaten by Tiger Roll in the Boyne Hurdle at Navan later in February on his first outing in graded company. Off You Go met interference just as the race was starting in earnest but he kept on, after Tiger Roll got first run, to go down by four lengths. Off You Go had no excuses, however, on his only subsequent outing, when third to Rashaan and the Pertemps Final third Not Many Left in the Grade 2 Keelings Irish Strawberry Hurdle at Fairyhouse at Easter.

Off You Go, purchased for €40,000 as a foal, is from the same family as the J.P. McManus-owned Irish Grand National winner Shutthefrontdoor, a close relative (also by a son of Sadler's Wells out of Hurricane Girl) of Off You Go's unraced dam Ozzy Oscar. Off You Go's grandam Hurricane Girl ran only twice over hurdles but did well at stud, producing four winners who also included the fairly useful hurdler and useful chaser Strong Project who was effective at up to three miles. Off You Go's two biggest wins have come at two miles but he stays twenty-one furlongs and acts on heavy going (though he doesn't need the mud). No horse has won the Ladbrokes Hurdle or its equivalent three times and, if he attempts it, it will represent a stiff task for Off You Go, who may well have reached his ceiling over hurdles. A novice chasing career might be the more likely option in the next season. *Charles Byrnes, Ireland*

OH DEAR OH DEAR 11 b.m. Pasternak – Post It (Thowra (FR)) [2018/19 c–, h68: h15.3m⁴ h17.7g Jun 5] poor maiden hurdler: fell only start over fences: stays 19f: acts on good to soft going: tried in blinkers/tongue tie. *Ron Hodges*   c–
h–

OH LAND ABLOOM (IRE) 9 b.g. King's Theatre (IRE) – Talinas Rose (IRE) (Definite Article) [2018/19 h129: c23g⁴ h23.3d² c23.6dᵖᵘ c27.6sᵖᵘ h25g² h26s² h23.3d* h24d Mar 14] close-coupled gelding: has had breathing operation: useful handicap hurdler: won at Uttoxeter in February: nothing like so good over fences: stays 3¼m: acts on good to firm and heavy going: has worn headgear/tongue tie, including last 4 starts: usually leads. *Neil King*   c112
h132

OH MICHELLE 8 br.m. Kayf Tara – Grenfell (IRE) (Presenting) [2018/19 h110: h23.8g⁶ h21g Apr 10] fair form over hurdles in 2017/18: tailed off both starts since: stays 21f: acts on soft going: tried in tongue tie. *Nigel Twiston-Davies*   h–

OH NO 7 b.g. Indian Danehill (IRE) – See My Girl (Terimon) [2018/19 h23.3gᵖᵘ h16.2g h19.9m⁶ h16g³ h20.5s h20.5d Jan 20] fifth foal: half-brother to fair 2m hurdle winner My Farmer Girl (by Karinga Bay): dam lightly raced in bumpers/over hurdles: well held in point: modest form over hurdles: left Iain Jardine after first start: should stay beyond 2m: in tongue tie last 5 starts. *Maurice Barnes*   h89

OIGHEAR DUBH (IRE) 8 gr.g. Verglas (IRE) – Silly Goose (IRE) (Sadler's Wells (USA)) [2018/19 h22g⁵ h20.5g³ c20g* c16g³ c20.1g³ c21.6m² h24g³ c21g³ c19.5g³ c25gʳᵒ c28s Nov 4] angular gelding: modest maiden on Flat, stays 2m: fair handicap hurdler: fairly useful handicap chaser: won at Tipperary in July: stays 3m: acts on soft and good to firm going: in cheekpieces last 3 starts: wears tongue tie. *Eugene M. O'Sullivan, Ireland*   c123
h101

OI OI (IRE) 6 b.m. Oscar (IRE) – Mandys Native (IRE) (Be My Native (USA)) [2018/19 h70: h24g May 6] poor form over hurdles: temperament under suspicion. *Jonjo O'Neill*   h–

OISHIN 7 b.g. Paco Boy (IRE) – Roshina (IRE) (Chevalier (IRE)) [2018/19 h93: h16.2d h16.2g⁵ May 22] poor handicap hurdler: effective at 2m to easy 3m: acts on soft going: wears tongue tie. *Maurice Barnes*   h77

OI THE CLUBB OI'S 4 gr.g. Champs Elysees – Red Boots (IRE) (Verglas (IRE)) [2018/19 h15.8g² h16.4d² h16.6g³ h16.4sᵖᵘ Mar 13] fair on Flat, stays 1½m: fairly useful juvenile hurdler: placed first 3 outings: out of depth final one. *Ian Williams*   h120

OK CORRAL (IRE) 9 b.g. Mahler – Acoola (IRE) (Flemensfirth (USA)) [2018/19 h148: c25.7s* c24g* c31.7sᵖᵘ Mar 12] lengthy gelding: smart form over hurdles: similar form over fences: won novice at Plumpton in December and listed novice at Warwick (by 6 lengths from Secret Investor) in January: mistakes and hampered more than once when pulled up in National Hunt Chase won by Le Breuil at Cheltenham: stays 25f: acts on heavy going: often travels strongly: remains open to improvement as a chaser. *Nicky Henderson*   c148 p
h–

OK JK (IRE) 5 b.m. Yeats (IRE) – Shebeganit (IRE) (Alflora (IRE)) [2018/19 b17s b16d h16s Mar 2] second foal: dam unraced half-sister to useful hurdler (stayed 2¾m) Couleur France: down field in bumpers/mares maiden hurdle: in tongue tie last 2 starts. *Stephen Francis Magee, Ireland*   h–
b–

OKMYWAY 6 br.m. Passing Glance – Highlight Girl (Forzando) [2018/19 b16g h19.9gᵖᵘ h16.3g⁴ h15.8d h16.7s⁵ h19d h20.5dᵖᵘ Jan 22] sturdy mare: no form in bumpers/over hurdles: often in headgear. *James Evans*   h–
b–

OKOTOKS (IRE) 9 b.g. Gamut (IRE) – Whats Another One (IRE) (King's Theatre (IRE)) [2018/19 h113: c20gᵘʳ c15.6m* c16g⁵ c17.1dᵘʳ Mar 2] angular gelding: fairly useful hurdler: similar form over fences: won novice at Hexham in June: stays 2½m: acts on soft and good to firm going: waited with. *Fergal O'Brien*   c122
h–

OKSANA 6 b.m. Midnight Legend – La Harde (FR) (Valanour (IRE)) [2018/19 h102, b85: h20.3g³ h19.9g⁶ h20g h20d h18.7m Sep 8] modest maiden hurdler: stays 21f: acts on soft going: usually in headgear: tongue tied first 4 starts in 2018/19: usually waited with. *Ben Case*   h94

OLDABBEY BRIDGE (IRE) 5 b.g. Morozov (USA) – Jacks Joy (IRE) (Persian Bold) [2018/19 b17.7v³ h20.3sᵖᵘ h16g h15.8g⁴ Apr 22] €7,000 3-y-o: angular gelding: fourth foal: dam, no form over hurdles, half-sister to modest hurdler/useful chaser (2½m winner) Sir Ian: pulled up in Irish point on debut: well beaten in bumper: poor form over hurdles. *Clare Hobson*   h83
b–

OLDGRANGEWOOD 8 b.g. Central Park (IRE) – Top of The Class (IRE) (Rudimentary (USA)) [2018/19 c145, h133: c20.6d c20d⁶ c25s c25g³ Apr 6] rangy gelding: useful hurdler: useful handicap chaser: third in Grade 3 at Aintree (9 lengths behind Kildisart) in April: barely stays 25f: acts on heavy going: wears tongue tie: usually held up. *Dan Skelton* **c136 h—**

OLD GUARD 8 b.g. Notnowcato – Dolma (FR) (Marchand de Sable (USA)) [2018/19 c–, h151: h16m² h24.1g² h16.4g³ h19.3g² h16.8s⁶ h20.3d³ h19.2d⁴ Feb 24] useful-looking gelding: smart hurdler: largely creditable efforts in 2018/19, placed 5 times in good company: winner on sole completed start over fences: stays 3m: acts on good to firm and heavy going: has worn cheekpieces, including last 5 starts: tracks pace. *Paul Nicholls* **c— h150**

OLD HARRY ROCKS (IRE) 7 b.g. Milan – Miss Baden (IRE) (Supreme Leader) [2018/19 h118: h25.4g h16g h15.8d h23.3d c21g² Apr 20] smallish gelding: fair hurdler, below form in 2018/19: back on track when close second in novice handicap at Newton Abbot on chasing debut: should stay beyond 2¾m: acts on soft going: has worn cheekpieces, including last 2 starts. *Sophie Leech* **c105 h—**

OLD JEROBOAM (IRE) 5 b.g. Jeremy (USA) – Old Line (IRE) (Old Vic) [2018/19 b16g⁶ b15.7d⁴ Apr 24] €50,000 3-y-o: sixth foal: half-brother to fair hurdler/chaser Whiskey And Red (2¾m-3m winner) and bumper winner/modest 2½m hurdle winner Line d'Aois (both by Craigsteel): dam unraced: fairly useful form when winning bumpers at Wetherby and Southwell in spring, finding plenty both times. *Charlie Longsdon* **b101**

OLD PRIDE (IRE) 11 ch.g. Old Vic – Feel The Pride (IRE) (Persian Bold) [2018/19 c16.3g⁴ c23sᵖᵘ c22.6m² c20.3g² c20g³ Sep 11] winning hurdler: fair maiden chaser: stays 23f: acts on soft and good to firm going: has worn hood. *Alastair Ralph* **c105 h—**

OLD RASCALS (IRE) 6 b.g. Ask – Balleen Rose (IRE) (Old Vic) [2018/19 h21g³ h20.5sᵖᵘ h21.4g⁸ Feb 27] €31,000 3-y-o, £25,000 5-y-o: second foal: dam (b75), placed in bumpers, half-sister to fair hurdler/fairly useful chaser (stayed 2¾m) Fireball Macnamara: placed all 3 completed starts in Irish points: had breathing operation, much improved form (fairly useful) over hurdles when winning novice at Wincanton with something in hand. *Emma Lavelle* **h119**

OLD SALT (IRE) 7 b.g. Craigsteel – Andrea Gale (IRE) (Presenting) [2018/19 c107, h—: c22.5dᵖᵘ h15.8g⁸ h15.8g⁸ c16g² c17.2m⁸ c16.4m c16.4m⁵ c19.2g⁵ h15.7g⁵ h18.6g h19.7g h16.6g⁵ h16.6gᵖᵘ c20.3g⁴ c20.3m⁸ Feb 28] sturdy gelding: fair hurdler: won sellers at Ffos Las (left Evan Williams after) in May and Uttoxeter (only outing for John Flint) in June: fair handicap chaser: won at Market Rasen in July and twice at Musselburgh (novice event second occasion) in February: stays 2½m: acts on good to firm and heavy going: normally in headgear/tongue tie. *Stef Keniry* **c105 h113**

OLDTIMER (IRE) 8 br.g. Olden Times – Supreme Surprise (IRE) (Presenting) [2018/19 h16.2g h15.7g h16.8s⁵ h16.8s⁶ Mar 21] unplaced in Irish point: modest form over hurdles. *Martin Todhunter* **h89**

OLDTOWN POLLY (IRE) 7 b.m. Publisher (USA) – Oldtown Gill (Robertico) [2018/19 b—: h19.2g⁶ h21.6g⁶ h23sᵖᵘ h20.5sᵖᵘ Jan 16] lengthy mare: winning Irish pointer: no form in bumper/novice hurdles: tried in tongue tie. *Brendan Powell* **h—**

OLEG (GER) 4 gr.g. Kamsin (GER) – Dramraire Mist (Darshaan) [2018/19 h17.4s² h16.2d* h16d² Apr 6] fair form on Flat (stays 1½m) in Germany for H. Grewe: similar form over hurdles: left David Cottin, won novice at Kelso in March. *Paul Nicholls* **h110**

OLIVER'S GOLD 11 b.g. Danehill Dancer (IRE) – Gemini Gold (IRE) (King's Best (USA)) [2018/19 c125, h103: h16.2d³ c15.7g* c17.3g² h15.7gᵘʳ c16m⁴ c17.3g³ c16.5g⁵ c15.2s⁶ c17.1g⁶ c16.3d c15.2g c15.7g² c15.2g² c15.2g² Apr 11] sturdy gelding: fair handicap hurdler: fairly useful handicap chaser: won at Southwell in May: unproven beyond 17f: acts on soft and good to firm going: has worn cheekpieces: often races lazily. *Mark Walford* **c125 h106**

OLIVER'S HILL (IRE) 10 b.g. Shantou (USA) – River Rouge (IRE) (Croco Rouge (IRE)) [2018/19 c119, h—: c17m⁴ c17m⁶ c17.8g* h19.2g⁵ c17.8s* c18m⁵ Oct 21] lengthy gelding: winning hurdler: fairly useful handicap chaser: won at Fontwell in August and October: has form at 3¼m, effective at much shorter: acts on any going: wears headgear/tongue tie: sometimes let down by jumping. *Lawney Hill* **c124 h—**

OLIVER'S ISLAND (IRE) 7 b.g. Milan – Leading Rank (IRE) (Supreme Leader) [2018/19 h—: h15.8gᵖᵘ h23.1s⁵ h20.6s⁵ h23.3s* h23.8g³ h20.3s⁵ Mar 18] good-topped gelding: poor handicap hurdler: won at Uttoxeter in December: should stay beyond 23f: acts on soft going: in blinkers last 5 starts. *Sean Conway* **h80**

OLLIE VAAR 7 b.g. Sulamani (IRE) – It's A Discovery (IRE) (Grand Plaisir (IRE)) [2018/19 h97: c16vᶜᵒ c16.4d⁴ c19.4gᶠ Apr 21] fair form over hurdles: running best race in chases when falling 2 out in handicap at Ffos Las: probably stays 2½m: tried in hood. *Richard Price* — c111 h–

OLLISU LAD (IRE) 10 b.g. Westerner – Nick's Jule (IRE) (Perugino (USA)) [2018/19 h80: h20.2g Jun 23] poor maiden hurdler: should be suited by further than 23f. *Ian Duncan* — h–

OLLY THE BRAVE 6 b.g. Black Sam Bellamy (IRE) – September Moon (Bustino) [2018/19 b15.7d² Apr 24] first foal: dam (c105/h96) ungenuine 2¾m-3¼m hurdle/chase winner: showed plenty when second in bumper at Southwell, beaten length by Old Jeroboam (pair clear). *Dan Skelton* — b93

OLYMNIA 8 b.m. Teofilo (IRE) – Diotima (High Estate) [2018/19 h15.9g⁵ h17.7g⁴ Jun 5] poor maiden hurdler: off over 2½ years before reappearance: stays 2¼m: best form on good going: in headgear last 4 starts. *Gary Moore* — h72

OLYMPIC ODYSSEY 4 b.g. Camelot – Field of Hope (IRE) (Selkirk (USA)) [2018/19 h16g h15.8s⁴ h15.3g Apr 14] sturdy gelding: fair on Flat, stays 1½m: modest form over hurdles. *Harry Fry* — h99

O MAONLAN (IRE) 11 b.g. Oscar (IRE) – Another Gaye (IRE) (Classic Cliche (IRE)) [2018/19 c129, h–: c23.8dᶠ Feb 6] workmanlike gelding: winning hurdler: useful chaser at best: lightly raced and mostly disappointing since 2016/17: placed in points in 2019: best short of 3¼m: acts on heavy going: tried in cheekpieces: waited with. *Miss H. Welch* — c– h–

OMEGA SPRINGS (IRE) 11 b.g. Great Exhibition (USA) – Leefield Rose (IRE) (Parthian Springs) [2018/19 c16v c16g⁵ c16g² c17.4g³ c20.3g⁶ c16g* c15.2m⁵ c16s⁵ c17.2sᶠ Dec 26] winning hurdler: fair handicap chaser: won at Uttoxeter in September: left Liam Casey after second start: stays beyond 17f: acts on soft going. *Dai Williams* — c102 h–

ON ALBERTS HEAD (IRE) 9 b.g. Mountain High (IRE) – Dear Money (IRE) (Buckskin (FR)) [2018/19 c–, h88: c20.9g c20g⁶ h20g Jul 26] modest hurdler at best: lightly-raced maiden chaser, well held in handicaps in 2018/19: stays easy 3m: acts on good to firm and soft going: wears headgear: usually in tongue tie. *Neil Mulholland* — c64 h–

ONBOARD 4 gr.g. Dalakhani (IRE) – Emplane (USA) (Irish River (FR)) [2018/19 b16.7m⁴ Apr 21] £12,000 3-y-o: has had breathing operation: half-brother to several winners, including fair hurdler/fairly useful chaser Coach Lane (2m-19f winner, by Barathea) and fair hurdler Painted Sky (2m-3¼m winner, by Rainbow Quest), both temperamental: dam useful 1m winner: tongue tied, fourth in bumper at Market Rasen. *Nigel Hawke* — b83

ONCE AN ANGEL (IRE) 7 br.m. Robin des Pres (FR) – Easter Day (IRE) (Simply Great (FR)) [2018/19 h79, b–: h22.1gᵖᵘ May 28] has had breathing operation: runner-up in point: poor form over hurdles: tongue tied 4 of last 5 outings: signs of temperament. *Martin Todhunter* — h–

ON DEMAND 8 ch.m. Teofilo (IRE) – Mimisel (Selkirk (USA)) [2018/19 c116, h121: c21g² c20g⁵ c21g* c20.9g² c25.1g Nov 10] rather leggy mare: fairly useful hurdler: similar form over fences: won novice at Newton Abbot in October: unproven beyond 2¾m: acts on good to firm and heavy going: has worn headgear, including last 3 starts (replacing usual tongue strap): front runner/races prominently. *Colin Tizzard* — c123 h–

ONDERUN (IRE) 10 b.g. Flemensfirth (USA) – Warts And All (IRE) (Commanche Run) [2018/19 c103, h–: c23.8gᵖᵘ c24.1s c24.2s³ c26.2g c23.4v³ c26.2dᵖᵘ Mar 24] well-made gelding: maiden handicap chaser nowadays: stays 31f: acts on heavy going: has worn headgear: usually leads. *George Bewley* — c92 h–

ONE BIG LOVE 11 b.m. Tamure (IRE) – Sound Appeal (Robellino (USA)) [2018/19 c26g² May 17] workmanlike mare: multiple point winner: fair maiden hurdler: close second in mares hunter at Fontwell on chasing debut: stays easy 3¼m: acts on good to soft going. *Mrs S. Alner* — c91 h–

ONECALLAWAY (IRE) 5 b.m. Getaway (GER) – Pocket Call (IRE) (Milan) [2018/19 b16d b16.8d Apr 23] €2,000 3-y-o: first foal: dam, unraced, out of sister to smart hurdler/very smart chaser (stayed 3¼m) Cooldine: last in bumpers. *Donald Whillans* — b–

ONE CONEMARA (IRE) 11 b.g. Milan – Rose of Kerry (IRE) (Roselier (FR)) [2018/19 c–, h–: c26.3dᵖᵘ Mar 15] useful-looking gelding: multiple point winner, but little promise in chases: winning hurdler: should stay beyond 3m: acts on heavy going: in headgear 3 of last 4 outings. *Mrs C. A. Coward* — c– h–

ONE COOL BOY (IRE) 10 b.g. One Cool Cat (USA) – Pipewell (IRE) (Lake Coniston (IRE)) [2018/19 h93: h15.8g h15.8g⁶ Jun 6] lengthy gelding: modest handicap hurdler: stays easy 19f: acts on soft going: has worn headgear: in tongue tie last 4 starts. *Tracey Watkins* — **h77**

ONE COOL POET (IRE) 7 b.g. Urban Poet (USA) – Oasis Star (IRE) (Desert King (IRE)) [2018/19 h16g h17.2m³ h16g³ h16g³ h20g⁵ h20g⁵ Nov 6] close-coupled gelding: fair on Flat, stays 1½m: fair maiden hurdler: stays 2½m: acts on good to firm going: in headgear last 4 starts: wears tongue tie. *Matthew J. Smith, Ireland* — **h104**

ONE FINE MORNING 13 ch.g. Generous (IRE) – Flagship Princess (IRE) (Topanoora) [2018/19 c24.2gᵖᵘ May 8] winning pointer/hurdler: modest chaser: stays 23f: acts on firm and good to soft going: regularly wears headgear. *Tom Clover* — **c–** **h–**

ONEFITZALL (IRE) 9 b.g. Indian Danehill (IRE) – Company Credit (IRE) (Anshan) [2018/19 h–: c22.4dᵖᵘ Dec 29] well-made gelding: winning hurdler: failed to complete since 2016/17, including in novice handicap on chasing debut: stays 21f: acts on soft going. *Nicky Henderson* — **c–** **h–**

ONE FOR ARTHUR (IRE) 10 b.g. Milan – Nonnetia (FR) (Trempolino (USA)) [2018/19 c25sᵘʳ c25.6dᵘʳ c34.3g⁶ Apr 6] tall gelding: winning hurdler: smart handicap chaser: won Grand National at Aintree in 2016/17: missed following season due to leg injury: looked as good as ever when 25½ lengths sixth of 40 to Tiger Roll in latest renewal of race on completed start in 2018/19, unable to sustain huge effort from rear: suited by extreme distances: acts on heavy going: in tongue tie last 5 starts. *Lucinda Russell* — **c142 +** **h–**

ONE FOR BILLY 7 b.g. Midnight Legend – Saxona (IRE) (Jade Robbery (USA)) [2018/19 h113: c16m² c17m* c16g* c16.5g² c16.5g² c15.9gʳᵒ c16.8g Nov 24] strong gelding: fair hurdler: useful novice chaser: won at Stratford (handicap) and Perth in July: raced mainly around 2m: acts on good to firm and good to soft going: wears tongue tie. *Dan Skelton* — **c144** **h–**

ONE FOR HARRY (IRE) 11 b.g. Generous (IRE) – Strawberry Fool (FR) (Tel Quel (FR)) [2018/19 h135: h20g h21.4s⁵ h18.1g⁴ h20.5s⁴ h20.2dᵖᵘ Apr 26] sturdy gelding: useful handicap hurdler: stays 3m, effective at much shorter when conditions are testing: acts on heavy going: tried in cheekpieces: front runner: has been let down by jumping. *Nicky Richards* — **h129**

ONE FOR ROSIE 6 gr.g. Getaway (GER) – Whisky Rose (IRE) (Old Vic) [2018/19 b100p: h20g* h19.3s³ h19g* h19.8s² h20g³ Apr 6] sturdy gelding: bumper winner: useful novice hurdler: won at Carlisle in November and Warwick in February: placed both starts after, in EBF 'National Hunt' Novices' Handicap Hurdle Final at Sandown (short-headed by Third Wind) and Mersey Novices' Hurdle at Aintree (5½ lengths third to Reserve Tank): will stay 3m: acts on soft going: travels strongly. *Nigel Twiston-Davies* — **h139**

ONE FOR THE GUV'NR (IRE) 10 b.g. Oscar (IRE) – Wintry Day (IRE) (Presenting) [2018/19 h16.5g h17.2mᶠ Jul 1] lengthy gelding: useful hurdler at best: left Nicky Henderson, well beaten completed start in 2018/19: twice-raced over fences: best around 2m: acted on soft going: dead. *Nicky Martin* — **c–** **h–**

ONEFORTHEROADTOM 6 gr.g. Fair Mix (IRE) – Ifni du Luc (FR) (Chamberlin (FR)) [2018/19 h125: c18.8g⁶ c16v⁵ c19.7d⁶ c20.6d⁶ c20.5s² c24.1mᶠ Apr 13] good-topped gelding: lightly-raced winning hurdler: fairly useful maiden chaser: runner-up twice, including when beaten 6½ lengths by Heron Heights in Pat Taaffe Handicap Chase at Punchestown shortly after end of British season, upsides when pecking last: stays 3m: acts on soft going: in cheekpieces last 2 starts. *Harry Fry* — **c121** **h–**

ONE FOR THE TEAM 5 b.g. Shirocco (GER) – One Gulp (Hernando (FR)) [2018/19 b89p: h20g⁴ h19g⁴ Feb 22] bumper winner: fair form when fourth in novice hurdles at Aintree and Warwick: remains open to improvement. *Nick Williams* — **h109 p**

ONE FORTY SEVEN (IRE) 7 b.g. Beneficial – Still Bubbly (IRE) (Hubbly Bubbly (USA)) [2018/19 h114: c24.1g⁵ c19.2g² c20.9g* c22.6g⁴ c24vᵖᵘ c19.2dᵖᵘ c23g⁵ c24d* c23.8g⁵ Apr 24] workmanlike gelding: maiden hurdler: fairly useful handicap chaser: won at Stratford in October and Uttoxeter in March: stays 3m: acts on good to soft going: has worn visor, including last 3 starts: often let down by jumping. *Nigel Twiston-Davies* — **c120 x** **h–**

ONE HANDSOME DUDE (IRE) 4 b.g. Canford Cliffs (IRE) – Allegrina (IRE) (Barathea) [2018/19 b15.3g³ ab16s⁴ b16d Apr 6] smallish gelding: modest form in bumpers, best effort on debut: wears tongue tie. *Adam West* — **b80**

ONEHELLUVATOUCH 6 gr.m. Hellvelyn – Soft Touch (IRE) (Petorius) [2018/19 h80: h23.3g⁴ h23.3gᵖᵘ Jul 27] poor maiden hurdler: stays 21f: acts on good to firm and good to soft going: wears cheekpieces. *Suzy Smith* — **h58**

ONEIDA TRIBE (IRE) 10 b.g. Turtle Island (IRE) – Glory Queen (IRE) (Taipan (IRE))   **c102**
[2018/19 c108, h–: c24d⁶ c25.5s² c22.9d⁵ c24s⁵ c29.2gᵖᵘ Apr 10] winning pointer: maiden   **h–**
hurdler: fair handicap chaser: stays 25f: acts on heavy going: wears headgear. *Robin Dickin*

ONELASTHAND 6 b.m. Haafhd – Miss Molly Be Rude (IRE) (Perugino (USA))   **h–**
[2018/19 b–: b16.2g³ b15.8g² b16.2m h15.7g h15.7d h16.8sᵖᵘ Nov 27] has had breathing   **b78**
operation: modest form in bumpers for Ruth Jefferson: no promise over hurdles: in tongue
tie last 2 starts. *Sam England*

ONE LEADER (IRE) 8 b.g. Oscar (IRE) – Be My Leader (IRE) (Supreme Leader)   **c–**
[2018/19 h62, b–: c20g c24.2sᵖᵘ c24.2vᵖᵘ Mar 5] has had breathing operation: little show   **h–**
over hurdles/in handicap chases: tried in tongue tie. *Tim Vaughan*

ONE MORE BID (IRE) 7 b.g. Grandera (IRE) – Martin's Oscar (IRE) (Oscar (IRE))   **c105**
[2018/19 b–: c20gᶠ h23gᵖᵘ c20mᵖᵘ Sep 17] has had breathing operation: little sign of ability.   **h–**
Jo Hughes

ONE MORE FLEURIE (IRE) 5 b.g. Mustameet (USA) – Auburn Cherry (IRE)   **h104**
(Treasure Hunter) [2018/19 b16.6g⁴ h21.2d⁵ h19g² Apr 25] €18,500 3-y-o, £40,000 4-y-o: **b86**
fifth foal: brother to a winning pointer: dam placed in point: runner-up in Irish point on
debut: fourth in bumper at Doncaster: fair form over hurdles: clear second in maiden at
Warwick on second of 2 outings over hurdles. *Ian Williams*

ONE MORE TUNE (IRE) 11 b.g. Luso – Strong Gale Pigeon (IRE) (Strong Gale)   **c–**
[2018/19 c26gᵖᵘ May 17] strong gelding: multiple winning pointer: winning hurdler: easily   **h–**
best effort in hunter chases when runner-up at Doncaster in 2015/16: stays 3¼m: acts on
good to firm going: tried in cheekpieces/tongue tie. *Miss Laura Bradley*

ONE NIGHT IN MILAN (IRE) 6 b.g. Milan – Native Mo (IRE) (Be My Native   **h121 p**
(USA)) [2018/19 h82p, b76: h23.9g³ h19.9m⁴ h19.3g* h20.9g* h20.9dᶠ h25.3g* Nov 23]
fairly useful handicap hurdler: won at Carlisle and Kelso in October, and Catterick in
November: stays 25f: acts on good to firm going: tried in cheekpieces: usually races
prominently: will go on improving. *Keith Dalgleish*

ONE OF US 7 b.g. Presenting – One Gulp (Hernando (FR)) [2018/19 h105: c22.5d⁵ c24m²   **c115**
c26.1g⁵ c25.1d² c25.1s² c30.7s* Apr 16] well-made gelding: fair hurdler: better over   **h–**
fences: won handicap at Exeter in April: stays 31f: acts on soft and good to firm going: tried
in cheekpieces. *Nick Williams*

ONE TOUCH (IRE) 5 b.g. Court Cave (IRE) – Star Bui (IRE) (Fourstars Allstar (USA))   **b104**
[2018/19 b16d⁴ b16.4g b16d* Apr 6] €21,000 3-y-o: rangy gelding: sixth foal: half-brother
to a winning pointer by Alderbrook: dam once-raced half-sister to smart hurdler/useful
chaser (stayed 3m) Emotional Moment: point winner: left Michael Scudamore, much
improved form (fairly useful) in bumpers when winning at Chepstow in April. *Ben Pauling*

ONLY GORGEOUS (IRE) 10 b.g. Vertical Speed (FR) – Pure Beautiful (IRE) (Un   **c100**
Desperado (FR)) [2018/19 c109, h90: c25.8g⁶ c23.8g⁵ c24.2g² c24.2s³ c25.2sᵖᵘ c19.2d⁶ Jan   **h–**
1] lengthy gelding: maiden hurdler: fair handicap chaser: stays 31f: acts on good to firm
and heavy going. *Susan Gardner*

ONLY MONEY (IRE) 5 ch.g. Getaway (GER) – Kings Diva (IRE) (King's Theatre   **b97**
(IRE)) [2018/19 b15.7d⁴ b15.3d⁶ b13.7m* Mar 29] first foal: dam unraced sister to bumper
winner/useful chaser Kings Grey (stayed 2½m) and fairly useful hurdler/useful chaser
Wings of Smoke (stayed 2¾m): fairly useful form in bumpers: won at Fontwell in March:
keen-going sort. *Chris Gordon*

ONLY ORSENFOOLSIES (IRE) 10 b.g. Trade Fair – Desert Gold (IRE) (Desert Prince   **c–**
(IRE)) [2018/19 c–, h126: h16s³ h22.8v⁴ h16.4v⁴ Mar 16] fairly useful handicap hurdler: **h120**
lightly-raced maiden chaser: stays 21f: acts on heavy going. *Micky Hammond*

ONLY ORVIETO (IRE) 8 b.m. Kayf Tara – Vigna Maggio (FR) (Starborough) [2018/19   **h97**
h96: h19.9g⁶ h20.1g⁴ h23.3g² Nov 9] modest maiden hurdler: stays 23f: acts on heavy
going: tried in headgear. *Mark Walford*

ON PAROLE (IRE) 6 b.g. Kayf Tara – Ain't Misbehavin (IRE) (Trempolino (USA))   **h–**
[2018/19 b–: h16gᵘʳ h16.7vᵖᵘ Dec 1] good-topped gelding: pulled hard when well beaten
in bumper: failed to complete in novice hurdles. *Olly Murphy*

ON RAGLAN ROAD (FR) 7 b.g. Walk In The Park (IRE) – Millessima (FR) (Bering)   **c73**
[2018/19 h16m⁴ h16g² c15.7g c20dᵖᵘ h19d² h19.6dᵖᵘ h21sᵖᵘ Mar 10] €80,000 3-y-o: strong   **h96**
gelding: has had breathing operation: fourth foal: half-brother to French 13.5f winner
Mapenzi (by Sagamix): dam French 2m-19f hurdle/chase winner: modest form over
hurdles: little show in handicap chases: stays 19f: acts on good to soft and good to firm
going: wears hood/tongue tie. *Charlie Longsdon*

ON THE BLIND SIDE (IRE) 7 b.g. Stowaway – Such A Set Up (IRE) (Supreme Leader) [2018/19 h146: c20.6d⁴ c24d* c24.4sᵖᵘ h21.5g² Apr 27] good-topped gelding: has had breathing operation: smart form over hurdles: 9 lengths second to Younevercall in Select Hurdle at Sandown final outing: form over fences only when winning novice at Kempton (by 3¼ lengths from Talkischeap) in January: stays 3m: acts on soft going: in cheekpieces last 2 starts: has a lazy streak. *Nicky Henderson* **c142 h147**

ONTHEFRONTFOOT (IRE) 5 b.g. Shantou (USA) – On The Backfoot (IRE) (Bob Back (USA)) [2018/19 b16.8s* b17d Apr 5] €23,000 3-y-o, £30,000 4-y-o: sturdy gelding: fifth foal: half-brother to 2 winners, including fairly useful hurdler/chaser Star Foot (2m-19f winner, by Soviet Star): dam lightly raced on Flat: winning pointer: fair form when winning at Sedgefield in March on first of 2 outings in bumpers. *Donald McCain* **b92**

ON THE GO AGAIN (IRE) 6 b.g. Arakan (USA) – Lady Bolino (IRE) (King's Theatre (IRE)) [2018/19 h16s³ h16s Sep 13] smart on Flat, stays 1½m: useful handicap hurdler: best effort when third at Galway (length behind Top Othe Ra) in August: raced only at 2m: acts on heavy going: wears tongue tie. *Michael Mulvany, Ireland* **h137**

ON THE METER (IRE) 5 b.g. Eastern Anthem – Party Belle (Silver Patriarch (IRE)) [2018/19 b16d² b15.8g⁴ Nov 2] €15,000 3-y-o: leggy gelding: first foal: dam, maiden on Flat (stayed 9.5f), half-sister to high-class 2m hurdler Countrywide Flame: fair form in bumpers: better effort when second at Worcester on debut: wears tongue tie. *Alan Jones* **b86**

ON THE QUIET (FR) 4 b.f. Ballingarry (IRE) – Royale Sulawesie (FR) (Jimble (FR)) [2018/19 b16d⁶ Mar 21] £6,000 3-y-o: half-sister to bumper winner Strike The Pose (by Saint des Saints): dam, French maiden (placed up to 19f over hurdles), half-sister to fairly useful French hurdler (2¼m/19f winner) Question de Chance: 20/1, sixth in mares bumper at Chepstow. *Evan Williams* **b60**

ON THE ROAD (IRE) 9 b.g. Stowaway – B Greenhill (Gunner B) [2018/19 c–, h119: h23.6v⁵ h23.3vᵖᵘ c22.6s⁵ c23.8s⁶ c27.9g³ Apr 21] sturdy gelding: fairly useful handicap hurdler/chaser at best: below that level in 2018/19: stays 3¼m: acts on heavy going: has worn cheekpieces/tongue tie. *Evan Williams* **c108 h106**

ONTHEROPES (IRE) 5 b.g. Presenting – Dushion (IRE) (Dushyantor (USA)) [2018/19 b16s⁶ b20s⁴ h21v* Apr 14] €38,000 3-y-o, £240,000 4-y-o: first foal: dam, ran 3 times in points, out of half-sister to useful hurdler/winning chaser (stayed 3m) Gentle Buck: runner-up sole start in points: fair form in bumpers: 6/4, won maiden at Tramore (by 10 lengths from Spyglass Hill, comfortably) on hurdling debut: open to improvement. *W. P. Mullins, Ireland* **h130 p b92**

ON THE ROX (IRE) 6 b.g. Fastnet Rock (AUS) – Dance Parade (USA) (Gone West (USA)) [2018/19 h102: h15.8s⁴ h15.8v⁶ h16.7d h16.5s h16.8dᶠ Mar 24] bumper winner (for Sally Haynes): regressive maiden hurdler: tried in cheekpieces/tongue tie. *Evan Williams* **h86**

ON THE SLOPES 5 b.g. Librettist (USA) – Dalriath (Fraam) [2018/19 b17.3g³ b17.7s² h17.7v* h17.7s² h20g⁴ h19.8s h19d³ Apr 4] €50,000 3-y-o, £17,000 4-y-o: workmanlike gelding: third foal: half-brother to fair hurdler Sauvignon (23f winner, by Yeats): dam (c97/h93), 2m-21f hurdle/chase winner, also 1m winner on Flat: in frame twice in Irish points: fairly useful form in bumpers: similar form in novice hurdles: won at Fontwell in December: placed twice after: should stay further than 19f: acts on heavy going. *Chris Gordon* **h127 b96**

ONTOPOFTHEWORLD (IRE) 10 ch.g. Desert King (IRE) – Zaffre (IRE) (Mtoto) [2018/19 c19.9s⁵ c17g³ c22.6g⁴ c17m* c16g⁴ c16.3g* c16.5g³ c16.5d² c16.3g* c15.8g² c15.7v c15.7d² c15.8g* c19.2dᵖᵘ Jan 17] maiden hurdler: fairly useful handicap chaser: won at Stratford and Perth in September, Newton Abbot in November, Fakenham in November and Musselburgh (match) in January: left A. L. T. Moore after second start: unproven beyond 17f: acts on good to firm and heavy going: wears cheekpieces: tried in tongue tie: usually front runner/races prominently. *Peter Bowen* **c125 h–**

ON TOUR (IRE) 11 b.g. Croco Rouge (IRE) – Galant Tour (IRE) (Riberetto) [2018/19 c140, h–: c24d⁶ c23.6d⁵ c22.4s⁶ c24.2d³ c24gᵖᵘ c25g⁵ Apr 6] workmanlike gelding: winning hurdler: fairly useful handicap chaser nowadays: stays 25f: acts on heavy going: races well off pace. *Evan Williams* **c128 h–**

ONURBIKE 11 b.g. Exit To Nowhere (USA) – Lay It Off (IRE) (Strong Gale) [2018/19 c75, h–: c23.6gᵖᵘ c23.6dᵖᵘ c23.5v⁵ c26.2d* Mar 20] maiden hurdler: poor handicap chaser: won at Chepstow in March: will stay extreme distances: acts on heavy going: tried in headgear/tongue tie. *John O'Neill* **c78 h–**

ONWITHTHEPARTY 10 b.g. Sir Harry Lewis (USA) – Kentford Fern (El Conquistador) [2018/19 h27g⁵ h23.3s⁶ h27s⁴ h27g⁴ Apr 5] modest handicap hurdler: well held in novice handicap only start over fences: stays 27f: acts on heavy going: usually in headgear: ungenuine. *Dianne Sayer* **c– h82 §**

OOLOGIST 8 gr.g. Proclamation (IRE) – Orchid's Silver (Silver Patriarch (IRE)) [2018/19 h79: h20.6g³ h20.7g² h20.3s⁵ h19d Jan 19] modest maiden hurdler: stays 21f: probably acts on heavy going: tried in hood. *John Gallagher* **h89**

O O SEVEN (IRE) 9 b.g. Flemensfirth (USA) – Kestral Heights (IRE) (Eagle Eyed (USA)) [2018/19 c150, h–: c24g* c24g c25s c21.1d Apr 5] good sort: has had breathing operation: winning handicap chaser: smart handicap chaser: won at Doncaster (by ½ length from Go Conquer) in December and Guinness Handicap Chase at Punchestown (by 2½ lengths from Livelovelaugh, jumping well and making all) shortly after end of British season: stays 3m: acts on heavy going: in blinkers last 3 starts: has bled. *Nicky Henderson* **c154 h–**

OPECHEE (IRE) 8 b.g. Robin des Champs (FR) – Falcons Gift (IRE) (Zaffaran (USA)) [2018/19 c91, h–: c19.4m* c21.4gᵘʳ c19.7g⁴ c20.9g² c23.6g⁴ c21.6vᵖᵘ c21.6dᵖᵘ c20m³ c17.2m² Apr 21] maiden hurdler: modest handicap chaser: won at Stratford in August: left David Bridgwater after sixth start: probably stays 23f: acts on firm going: tried in hood: usually held up. *Lucinda Egerton* **c99 h–**

OPENING BATSMAN (IRE) 13 b.g. Morozov (USA) – Jolly Signal (IRE) (Torus) [2018/19 h112: c20.9g⁴ c23.8d c20.2g³ c20.2g⁴ c20.2g² c20.2gᵖᵘ Apr 14] workmanlike gelding: winning hurdler: fairly useful handicap chaser: stays 3m: acts on heavy going: used to wear headgear: wears tongue tie: temperamental. *Harry Fry* **c127 § h–**

OPERA BUFFA (IRE) 6 b.m. Exceed And Excel (AUS) – Dubai Opera (USA) (Dubai Millennium) [2018/19 c–, h–: h16.3m⁵ c16.5gᶠ h20g c18.2sᵖᵘ h18.5d h16.5d Apr 24] has had breathing operation: of little account: left Steve Flook after third start: tried in cheekpieces: usually tongue tied. *Laura Hurley* **c– h–**

OPTIMA PETAMUS 7 gr.g. Mastercraftsman (IRE) – In A Silent Way (IRE) (Desert Prince (IRE)) [2018/19 h–: h15.8g Oct 7] poor maiden hurdler: tried in cheekpieces. *Lawrence Mullaney* **h–**

OPTIMISED (IRE) 7 br.g. Stowaway – Apterous (IRE) (King's Theatre (IRE)) [2018/19 c26g⁶ c24s* Mar 23] €55,000 3-y-o: second foal: dam unraced: multiple point winner: modest maiden hurdler: much improved form in chases when winning hunter at Bangor in March: stays 25f: acts on heavy going: tried in cheekpieces: has looked temperamental. *Philip Rowley* **c115 h–**

OPTIMISTIC BIAS (IRE) 10 b.g. Sayarshan (FR) – Dashers Folly (IRE) (Dr Massini (IRE)) [2018/19 c124, h–: h26d c25.5s c29.2d² Mar 10] strong, compact gelding: winning hurdler: fairly useful handicap chaser: barely stays 29f: acts on soft going: tried in tongue tie. *James Evans* **c120 h–**

OPTIMUS PRIME (FR) 7 b.g. Deportivo – Diluvienne (FR) (Kaldoun (FR)) [2018/19 c146, h125: h15.7g⁴ h19f* h20d³ h17s* Oct 27] well-made gelding: useful hurdler: left Dan Skelton after first start: won New York Turf Writers Cup Handicap at Saratoga (by 1¼ lengths from New Member) in August and Grade 2 David L. (Zeke) Ferguson Memorial Handicap at Great Meadow (by 18 lengths from Sempre Medici) in October: third in Lonesome Glory Handicap at Belmont (2 lengths behind Zanjabeel) in between: winning chaser: stays 2½m: acts on firm and soft going: tried in cheekpieces: has worn tongue tie, including in 2018/19: strong traveller. *Richard J. Hendriks, USA* **c– h136**

O'RAHILLY (IRE) 7 b.g. Aristotle (IRE) – Linoora (IRE) (Lil's Boy (USA)) [2018/19 h17.7vᵖᵘ h15.9g⁴ Apr 7] fifth foal: dam, lightly raced on Flat, half-sister to dam of useful hurdler/chaser Emmpat: pulled up in Irish point: in hood, little impact in maiden hurdles. *Zoe Davison* **h85**

ORBASA (FR) 8 b.g. Full of Gold (FR) – Ierbasa de Kerpaul (FR) (Cadoubel (FR)) [2018/19 c128§, h–: c25.1m³ May 10] good-topped gelding: winning hurdler: fairly useful handicap chaser: stayed 25f: acted on soft and good to firm going: wore headgear: often wore tongue tie: ungenuine: dead. *Paul Nicholls* **c123 § h–**

ORBURSTOCK (IRE) 4 b.g. Millenary – Auction Girl (IRE) (Saddlers' Hall (IRE)) [2018/19 b16g Mar 29] well beaten in bumper. *Jedd O'Keeffe* **b–**

ORCHARD LANE (IRE) 7 b.g. Gamut (IRE) – Me No Puppet (Mtoto) [2018/19 b73: h20g³ h23gᵇᵈ h19.9g⁶ h20g⁶ h23.9d⁶ Oct 20] maiden pointer: modest form over hurdles. *Katy Price* **h89**

Guinness Handicap Chase, Punchestown—
a third British win in four years as O O Seven makes all from Livelovelaugh (second left)

ORCHARD MOON 6 b.m. Apple Tree (FR) – Flaviola (IRE) (Moscow Society (USA)) **b–**
[2018/19 b70: b16.7g May 19] well held in bumpers: tried in tongue tie. *Nigel Twiston-Davies*

ORCHARDSTOWN CROSS (IRE) 8 b.g. Westerner – Shang A Lang (IRE) **c122 p**
(Commander Collins (IRE)) [2018/19 c–, h102: c20d² c23g* c22.4d* Mar 1] maiden **h–**
hurdler: fairly useful form over fences: won novice handicaps at Taunton in February and
Newbury (further marked improvement) in March: stays 23f: acts on good to soft going:
travels strongly: useful chaser in making. *Jeremy Scott*

ORCHARD THIEVES (IRE) 7 b.g. Ask – Ballycleary (IRE) (Phardante (FR)) **h115**
[2018/19 h23s* h21.6d Nov 14] €22,000 3-y-o, £115,000 4-y-o: closely related to fair
hurdler Cheiliuradh (2½m winner, by Oscar) and half-brother to useful hurdler
Getoutwhenyoucan (2m-2½m winner, by Beneficial): dam unraced half-sister to useful
hurdler/smart chaser (stayed 25f) Sparky Gayle: runner-up in Irish maiden point: much
better effort in novice hurdles (fairly useful form) when winning at Worcester in May: in
cheekpieces, went in snatches 6 months later. *David Pipe*

ORCHESTRATED (IRE) 8 b.g. Mahler – Rose Island (Jupiter Island) [2018/19 c93, **c101**
h–: c23m* c25.8g² c25.7g⁴ c22.6g c20.3d c21.6v⁵ Dec 11] compact gelding: maiden **h–**
hurdler: fair handicap chaser: won at Worcester in July: stays 3¼m: acts on good to firm
going: has worn headgear. *David Bridgwater*

ORDER OF THISTLE (IRE) 4 b.g. High Chaparral (IRE) – Law of The Jungle (IRE) **b85**
(Catcher In The Rye (IRE)) [2018/19 b16.2g⁴ Feb 14] third foal: brother to German
9.5f-11f winner Chalcot: dam maiden on Flat (stayed 1½m): 25/1, nearest finish when
fourth in bumper at Kelso (2¾ lengths behind Enlighten). *Lucinda Russell*

OR DE VASSY (FR) 7 b.g. Assessor (IRE) – Mona Vassy (FR) (Sleeping Car (FR)) **h113**
[2018/19 h117: h16.2d⁴ h20.6g⁵ May 20] compact gelding: fairly useful handicap hurdler:
stayed 2½m: acted on soft going: made running/raced prominently: dead. *Dan Skelton*

ORDINARY WORLD (IRE) 9 br.g. Milan – Saucy Present (IRE) (Presenting) [2018/19 **c155**
c155, h–: c20m⁴ c16d² c17g³ c17g² c15.9s c20d³ Apr 22] good-topped gelding: winning **h–**
hurdler: very smart chaser: best efforts in 2018/19 when third in Paddy's Rewards Club
Chase (5¼ lengths behind Simply Ned) in December and second in Dublin Chase (beaten
6 lengths by Min) in February, both at Leopardstown: unproven beyond 17f: acts on good
to firm and heavy going: has worn hood/tongue tie. *Henry de Bromhead, Ireland*

Doom Bar Maghull Novices' Chase, Aintree—Henry de Bromhead saddles his third winner in this race in a decade as Ornua holds off Us And Them (right) and Destrier

ORDO AB CHAO (IRE) 10 b.g. Heron Island (IRE) – Houldyurwhist (IRE) (Supreme Leader) [2018/19 h125: c16.1g² h18.7m⁵ Jul 22] useful-looking gelding: failed to complete in points: smart hurdler at best: tailed off in seller in July: fairly useful form when 6 lengths second to Our Three Sons in maiden at Towcester on chasing debut: stays 21f: acts on soft going. *Olly Murphy* — **c116 h–**

OREGON GOLD (FR) 6 b.g. Confuchias (IRE) – Gold Wine (FR) (Holst (USA)) [2018/19 h102: h24g h23.1g h15.7d³ h20.3s* h18.6s* h18.6d⁶ h25.3dᵖᵘ Mar 6] fair handicap hurdler: won at Southwell and Market Rasen in December: stays 2½m: acts on soft going: in cheekpieces last 5 starts: usually leads (didn't when pulled up final outing). *Nick Kent* — **h106**

ORGANDI (FR) 7 br.m. Early March – Creme Pralinee (FR) (Kashtan (FR)) [2018/19 b15.3m² b15.7d h21.2g⁴ h19g* Feb 19] half-sister to fair hurdler/chaser Jupiter Rex (3m-27f winner, by Dano-Mast) and French chaser Dans Tes Reves (19f-2¾m winner, by Evening World): dam, French 17f-3m chase winner, half-sister to Grand National runner-up Encore Un Peu): better effort in mares bumpers when second at Wincanton on debut: fair form over hurdles: won novice at Taunton in February, despite barely adequate test: will be suited by 3m: should do better still. *Richard Phillips* — **h104 p b83**

ORIENTAL CROSS (IRE) 6 b.m. Cape Cross (IRE) – Orion Girl (GER) (Law Society (USA)) [2018/19 b86: h16.7d h24s³ h17.7d⁴ h20.6d* h21.9g⁴ Apr 21] has had breathing operation: bumper winner: fair form over hurdles: won novice handicap at Newcastle in March: stays 21f: acts on good to soft going: in tongue tie last 2 starts. *Tim Vaughan* — **h102**

ORIENTAL FIXER (IRE) 10 b.g. Vertical Speed (FR) – Hannah Rose (IRE) (Un Desperado (FR)) [2018/19 c100, h92: c25.5gʳʳ c25.8sᵖᵘ c25.8g⁵ c25.8g c24.2g c24gᵖᵘ Oct 18] tall, lengthy gelding: has had breathing operation: maiden hurdler: modest handicap chaser: stays 3¼m: acts on heavy going: has worn headgear, including last 2 starts: one to treat with caution (edgy sort who often gives trouble at start). *Michael Scudamore* — **c87 § h–**

ORIENTAL FLAME 6 b.m. Norse Dancer (IRE) – Eastern Paramour (IRE) (Kris Kin (USA)) [2018/19 b91: h16.5d⁵ h16.5d⁶ h17.7d³ h15.8g⁴ h16.5d h15.3g Apr 3] fair form over hurdles: stays 2¼m: acts on good to soft going: usually hooded. *Charlie Mann* — **h109**

ORIENTAL TIGER 8 b.g. Tiger Hill (GER) – Cal Norma's Lady (IRE) (Lyphard's Special (USA)) [2018/19 h16.2g Dec 29] regressive on Flat in 2018 after long absence: in cheekpieces/hood, and tailed off in novice on hurdling debut. *R. Mike Smith* — **h–**

ORIONINVERNESS (IRE) 8 b.g. Brian Boru – Woodville Leader (IRE) (Supreme Leader) [2018/19 c96, h–: c23.8gᶠ c20.1g* c20.5d³ c20.1d² c23.4d² c21.5d⁴ c21.6dᵖᵘ Mar 2] maiden hurdler: fair handicap chaser: won at Perth in September: stays 23f: acts on heavy going: wears cheekpieces/tongue tie: usually makes running/races prominently. *Lucinda Russell* — **c109 h–**

OR JAUNE DE SOMOZA (FR) 7 ch.g. Bernebeau (FR) – Planete d'O (FR) (Son of **c132** Silver) [2018/19 c17d³ c17d³ h16g⁶ c16.7d* Apr 23] €70,000 3-y-o: half-brother to 2 **h106** winners in France by Discover d'Auteuil, including smart hurdler/chaser Or Noir de Somoza (15f-2¾m winner): dam French 15f hurdle winner: fair form over hurdles: useful form over fences: won maiden at Fairyhouse in April: raced around 2m: acts on heavy going. *Henry de Bromhead, Ireland*

ORKAN 5 b.g. Shirocco (GER) – Zefooha (FR) (Lomitas) [2018/19 h88: h17g² h16.6d⁴ **h96** h19.9dᵖᵘ h20.3d Apr 24] modest form over hurdles. *Mark Walford*

ORMESHER 4 b.g. Sir Percy – Marakabei (Hernando) [2018/19 h15.8s* h17.2s* **h114** h16m⁵ h16.7m⁴ Apr 21] dam half-sister to fairly useful hurdler (stayed 27f) Kattegat: fair maiden on Flat, stays 1½m: fair juvenile hurdler: won at Uttoxeter in July and Cartmel in August. *Donald McCain*

ORMSKIRK 6 gr.g. Hellvelyn – River Song (USA) (Siphon (BRZ)) [2018/19 h99: **h113** h15.8g⁴ h17.2m² h16.8s⁵ h20g* h21.2g h16gᶠ h15.3d h19.5d h19s h25g h20.6g⁴ Mar 20] rather leggy gelding: fair handicap hurdler: won at Les Landes in August: stays 2½m: acts on good to firm and heavy going: has worn headgear. *Johnny Farrelly*

ORNUA (IRE) 8 ch.g. Mahler – Merry Heart (IRE) (Broken Hearted) [2018/19 h131: **c151** c17d³ c16g² c16.3g* c18.2d² c16.5g* c18.6g² c15.5s² c15.9sᶠ c15.8g* Apr 6] angular **h–** gelding: has had breathing operation: useful hurdler: smart chaser: won maiden at Wexford in June, novice at Newton Abbot in July, Grade 3 novice at Roscommon (by 3¾ lengths from Cadmium) in October and Maghull Novices' Chase at Aintree (by 1¾ lengths from Us And Them) in April: placed all 4 other completed outings: stays 19f: acts on soft and good to firm going: usually goes with enthusiasm in lead: generally a sound jumper. *Henry de Bromhead, Ireland*

OROMO (IRE) 6 b.g. High Chaparral (IRE) – Miss Beatrix (IRE) (Danehill Dancer (IRE)) **h101** [2018/19 h19.7g h19.5g² h16g h20m h18g h16m⁶ h20g h16g4 h16m h16.4m² h16.2g* Apr 25] modest maiden on Flat, stays 2m: fair handicap hurdler: won at Perth in April: stays 19f: acts on good to firm going: tried in blinkers: wears tongue tie. *Karl Thornton, Ireland*

ORO REBELDE 6 b.g. Cockney Rebel (IRE) – Corsa All Oro (USA) (Medaglia d'Oro **b–** (USA)) [2018/19 b14g⁵ b15.7d⁵ Apr 27] little show in bumpers: in tongue tie last 2 starts. *Gary Hanmer*

ORRISDALE (IRE) 5 b.g. Oscar (IRE) – Back To Loughadera (IRE) (Bob Back (USA)) **b94** [2018/19 b16d⁶ b16.7g* Apr 13] €125,000 3-y-o: second foal: closely related to a winning pointer by Well Chosen: dam unraced half-sister to useful hurdler/chaser (2½m-2¾m winner) Strong Pursuit and to dam of useful hurdler/smart chaser (stays 3½m) Robinsfirth: fair form in bumpers: won conditionals/amateurs event at Bangor with bit in hand. *Jonjo O'Neill*

ORTENZIA (IRE) 5 b.m. Lawman (FR) – Ondoyante (IRE) (Slickly (FR)) [2018/19 **c97** h102: h15.7g² h15.7g⁵ h18.7m h20g⁴ h16g c17.4g* c17.8m³ c19.7gᵘʳ c20d c17.8g⁴ Apr 24] **h101** has had breathing operation: fair maiden hurdler: modest form over fences: won novice handicap at Bangor on chasing debut in October: regressive after: barely stays 2½m: probably acts on good to firm going: has worn blinkers/tongue tie, in latter last 5 starts. *Charlie Longsdon*

OSCAR BLUE (IRE) 9 gr.g. Oscar (IRE) – Blossom Rose (IRE) (Roselier (FR)) [2018/19 **c72** c21.4mᵖᵘ c23.9mᵖᵘ c26.3m² h22.7dᵖᵘ Apr 8] fairly useful hurdler at best: some promise on **h–** chasing debut, but then off nearly 2 years and offered little in 2018/19: left Brian Ellison after third start: stays 23f: acts on heavy going: tried in headgear. *Jean McGregor*

OSCAR CEREMONY (IRE) 8 b.g. Oscar (IRE) – Native Singer (IRE) (Be My Native **h101** (USA)) [2018/19 h19.5s⁴ h21d h23.3s³ h23.1d⁵ h23.9d⁵ Feb 28] €46,000 3-y-o: brother to fair 2m chase winner Martin Cash, closely related to fairly useful hurdler/chaser Knockavilla (2m-2½m winner, by Saddlers' Hall), and half-brother to bumper winner/fair hurdler Golden Child (21f winner, by Supreme Leader), stayed 3m: dam unraced sister to high-class hurdler/smart chaser up to 2½m Ned Kelly and half-sister to very smart staying chaser Nick Dundee: fair form over hurdles: probably stays 3m: acts on good to soft going. *Charlie Mann*

OSCAR HOOF (IRE) 11 b.g. Oscar (IRE) – New Legislation (IRE) (Dominion Royale) **h108** [2018/19 h20g² h20.5g⁴ h20.5g² h16s⁶ h19.7g³ Apr 11] good-topped gelding: lightly raced: formerly fairly useful hurdler: deteriorated in 2018/19 (beaten 3 times in selling company): stays 21f: acts on good to firm and good to soft going: in cheekpieces last 5 starts, also in tongue tie last 3. *Ian Williams*

OSCAR KNIGHT (IRE) 10 b.g. Oscar (IRE) – Cool Supreme (IRE) (Supreme Leader) c–
[2018/19 c136, h131: h22.8d c24s^{pu} h24g^6 h24d h21s Mar 13] sturdy gelding: useful **h130**
handicap hurdler/chaser: stays 3m: acts on heavy going. *Thomas Mullins, Ireland*

OSCAR LIGHT (IRE) 6 b.m. Oscar (IRE) – Sound of Light (IRE) (General Monash h–
(USA)) [2018/19 b73: b16.2d h20d h16d h20g Jan 14] point winner: some promise on first **b–**
of 2 outings in bumpers: no show over hurdles: tongue tied 4 of 5 starts. *Noel C. Kelly,
Ireland*

OSCAR MAGUIRE (IRE) 6 b.g. Oscar (IRE) – Ballymaguirelass (IRE) (Phardante **h63**
(FR)) [2018/19 b15.8g h16.3d h16d h16.5g h15.9d h15.7d Apr 9] €42,000 3-y-o: closely **b82**
related to a winning pointer by Saddlers' Hall: dam, ran once in bumper/point, sister to
fairly useful hurdler/chaser (stayed 21f) Dante's Battle: eighth in bumper at Uttoxeter:
poor form over hurdles: will be suited by 2½m+: acts on good to soft going. *Olly Murphy*

OSCAR NOMINATION (IRE) 7 b.g. Getaway (GER) – Nightofthe Oscars (IRE) c–
(Oscar (IRE)) [2018/19 h18.6s^4 h16.7d^5 h20.6g* h20.3d* Apr 9] €2,800 3-y-o: first foal: **h103**
dam, unraced, closely related to useful hurdler/chaser (best up to 2½m) Ceasar Milan:
placed in Irish points: fair form over hurdles: won handicap at Market Rasen in March and
novice handicap at Southwell in April: pulled up in maiden hunter only chase start: stays
21f: acts on good to soft going: held up. *Gary Hanmer*

OSCAR O'SCAR (IRE) 11 b.g. Oscar (IRE) – Shining Lights (IRE) (Moscow Society **c98 §**
(USA)) [2018/19 c107§, h–§: c19.3g^2 c21.2g^4 c20.3g^2 c20.1m^{pu} Jun 24] maiden hurdler: **h– §**
modest handicap chaser nowadays: stays 3m: acts on good to firm and heavy going: wears
headgear: untrustworthy. *Micky Hammond*

OSCAR ROSE (IRE) 7 b.m. Oscar (IRE) – Ben Roseler (IRE) (Beneficial) [2018/19 **h121**
h121: h16g* h16g^5 h21.6g^4 h20.3s^2 h16.5d^3 h21.2d^5 h19.4d^2 h20.5d^5 h20.3g Apr 18]
lengthy mare: fairly useful hurdler: won mares novice at Worcester in October: stays 2¾m:
acts on soft going. *Fergal O'Brien*

OSCARS LEADER (IRE) 6 b.g. Oscar (IRE) – Lead'er Inn (IRE) (Supreme Leader) **h100**
[2018/19 h118, b84: h19.6v^6 h16s^4 Feb 15] unfurnished gelding: fourth in Irish maiden
point on debut: fair maiden hurdler: should stay beyond 2m: acts on soft going: tried in
cheekpieces: front runner/races prominently. *Jo Davis*

OSCAR STAR (IRE) 6 b.m. Oscar (IRE) – Tucacas (FR) (Highest Honor (FR)) [2018/19 h–
h114, b–: h21.2m^{pu} h25s^4 Dec 3] smallish mare: has had breathing operation: fair hurdler:
shaped much better than bare result on second of 2 outings in mares handicaps in 2018/19:
stays 3m: acts on soft going: tried in cheekpieces: usually waited with. *Jamie Snowden*

OSCAR SUNSET (IRE) 12 b.g. Oscar (IRE) – Derravarra Sunset (IRE) (Supreme c–
Leader) [2018/19 c–, h107: h21.9g^{pu} h21.7g^{pu} Nov 13] lengthy gelding: useful hurdler at **h–**
best: lightly raced and little form since 2016/17: winning chaser: stays 2¾m: acts on heavy
going. *Evan Williams*

OSCAR VESPASIAN (IRE) 11 b.g. Oscar (IRE) – Quinnsboro Native (IRE) (Be My h–
Native (USA)) [2018/19 h15.8g^F h15.8d h16s Mar 10] workmanlike gelding: maiden
pointer: fair handicap hurdler at best: lightly raced and little form since 2014/15: has worn
cheekpieces. *Jake Thomas Coulson*

OSCAR WILDE (IRE) 5 b.g. Oscar (IRE) – Deep Supreme (IRE) (Supreme Leader) **h110**
[2018/19 h16.4d^3 h16g h16.4s^3 h20.6g^3 h16.4m^3 Mar 28] €13,000 3-y-o, £16,000 4-y-o:
half-brother to bumper winner/useful hurdler Heath Hunter (2m-2½m winner, by Shantou)
and fair chaser Pretty Reckless (19f/2½m winner, by Scorpion): dam unraced sister to very
smart staying chaser Nick Dundee and half-sister to high-class hurdler/smart chaser up to
2½m Ned Kelly: maiden Irish pointer: fair form over hurdles: likely to stay 3m: acts on soft
going. *Sue Smith*

OSCAR WORLD (IRE) 7 b.m. Oscar (IRE) – Maresin (I'm Supposin (IRE)) [2018/19 **c89**
h88, b85: h19.9g^6 h20.3g^6 c23.6d c20.2f^2 c25.2d^3 Mar 9] lengthy mare: has had breathing **h88**
operation: modest form over hurdles: similar form over fences: stays 2½m: acts on firm
going, probably on heavy: in cheekpieces last 2 starts. *Martin Keighley*

OSKAR DENARIUS (IRE) 8 b.g. Authorized (IRE) – Elizabethan Age (FR) (King's **h106**
Best (USA)) [2018/19 h100: h16g* h18.5g* h19.9g h16.5g h18g^3 h19f Mar 30] fair
handicap hurdler: won at Worcester (conditionals) and Newton Abbot in May: left Ben
Pauling after fourth start: stays 19f: acts on heavy going: regularly in headgear/tongue tie:
often leads. *Richard L. Valentine, USA*

OSKAR HIGH (IRE) 7 b.g. Mountain High (IRE) – Kiwi Lass (IRE) (Oscar (IRE)) **h97**
[2018/19 h19g h16.5g⁴ h17.6gᵖᵘ h16g h20d h20d² h20.2s h20g h19.3g³ Oct 25] modest
handicap hurdler: stays 2½m: acts on soft going: usually races close up. *Norman Lee, Ireland*

OSKAR'S EVA (IRE) 9 gr.m. Black Sam Bellamy (IRE) – Sardagna (FR) (Medaaly) **h–**
[2018/19 h20vᵖᵘ Jan 14] workmanlike mare: fair handicap hurdler in 2016/17: pulled up
only outing since: stays 21f: acts on good to soft going. *Tim Vaughan*

OSKEMEN 4 gr.g. Mastercraftsman (IRE) – Ollie Olga (USA) (Stormy Atlantic (USA)) **h103**
[2018/19 h16g h16.7m² Apr 21] fair maiden on Flat, stays 8.5f: similar form when runner-
up at Market Rasen on second of 2 starts in novice hurdles. *Olly Murphy*

OSSIE'S DANCER 10 ch.g. Osorio (GER) – Nina Ballerina (Kahyasi) [2018/19 h109: **h–**
h24.2d h21.4g h20.7g⁵ Apr 22] sturdy gelding: fairly useful handicap hurdler at best: off 22
months, well held in 2018/19: stays 21f: acts on heavy going: tried in hood/tongue tie:
races off pace. *Neil King*

OSTUNI (FR) 6 b.g. Great Pretender (IRE) – Mamassita (FR) (Loup Solitaire (USA)) **h109**
[2018/19 b–: h16g h15.8d h16.5g h19s⁴ h21.7d* h21.4g² Feb 27] strong gelding: fair form
over hurdles: won handicap at Fontwell in February: stays 2¾m: acts on soft going: in
tongue tie last 2 starts. *Paul Nicholls*

OTAGO TRAIL (IRE) 11 b.g. Heron Island (IRE) – Cool Chic (IRE) (Roselier (FR)) **c152**
[2018/19 c23.4d³ c23.8s c25.6d Jan 19] medium-sized gelding: winning hurdler: smart **h–**
handicap chaser: shaped well under forcing ride when third in Rehearsal Chase at
Newcastle (3½ lengths behind Lake View Lad) on belated return: well held both subsequent
starts: stays 3m well: acts on heavy going. *Venetia Williams*

OTTER MOON 7 b.g. Midnight Legend – Highland Dawn (Primitive Rising (USA)) **c120**
[2018/19 h126: h20.6g c15.7g³ c16s⁶ c18.2dᵖᵘ c15.9m⁴ c20dᵖᵘ Mar 21] well-made gelding: **h114**
fair hurdler/fairly useful form over fences: stayed 2½m: acted on soft and good
to firm going: dead. *Tom George*

OUR BOY (IRE) 5 ch.g. Raven's Pass (USA) – Burren Rose (USA) (Storm Cat (USA)) **h–**
[2018/19 h19m h16d Jan 7] fair on Flat, stays 1½m: hooded, well held both outings in
maiden hurdles. *Sam Thomas*

OUR BUBBA (IRE) 5 b.g. Scorpion (IRE) – Lady Marnay (IRE) (Darnay) [2018/19 b16s **h101**
h15.8v⁴ h15.8d⁶ Feb 17] £25,000 4-y-o: has had breathing operation: third foal: half- **b–**
brother to fairly useful hurdler/winning pointer Big Penny (19f winner, by Oscar) and
bumper winner/fair hurdler Lockeen Girl (2m winner, by Beneficial), both stay 3m: dam
twice-raced half-sister to smart hurdler (winner up to 21f) Coolnagorna: off mark in Irish
points at third attempt: well beaten in bumper: promise both outings in maiden hurdles:
will be suited by 2½m. *Stuart Edmunds*

OUR CILLA 5 gr.m. Sixties Icon – Kinetix (Linamix (FR)) [2018/19 h16.4g⁴ h15.7d **h87**
h19.9s⁵ h24d³ Apr 6] modest on Flat, stays 1¾m: similar form over hurdles. *Andrew Crook*

OUR DELBOY 7 gr.g. Multiplex – Dawn's Della (Scottish Reel) [2018/19 h19.9v **h–**
h21.2dᵖᵘ Jan 21] fair form over hurdles in 2016/17 (off 20 months after): no promise since:
should stay 2½m: acts on heavy going. *Donald McCain*

OUR DOT'S BABY (IRE) 7 b.m. Helissio (FR) – Our Dot (IRE) (Supreme Leader) **h123**
[2018/19 h15.8d* h16.3dᵘʳ h15.8dᶠ h18.5v² h20.5s* h20.5d³ h20.3g³ Apr 18] £12,000
5-y-o: third foal: half-sister to poor hurdler Dolly's Dot (2½m winner, by Vertical Speed)
and a winning pointer by Craigsteel: dam, unraced, out of half-sister to dual Whitbread
Gold Cup winner Topsham Bay: point winner: fairly useful hurdler: won mares maiden at
Ffos Las in October and novice at Newbury in January: placed all 3 other completed starts:
stays 21f: acts on heavy going: usually leads. *Jeremy Scott*

OUR FOLLY 11 b.g. Sakhee (USA) – Regent's Folly (IRE) (Touching Wood (USA)) **h84**
[2018/19 h104: h23.3g h26.5d⁴ Sep 21] rather leggy gelding: has had breathing operation:
fair handicap hurdler, below form in 2018/19: stays 3¼m: acts on good to firm and heavy
going: tried in headgear: usually tongue tied. *Stuart Kittow*

OUR GIRL ACORN 5 b.m. Bushranger (IRE) – Dominatrix (Whipper (USA)) [2018/19 **h–**
b17.7g b13.7m h15.9s Dec 17] first foal: dam French maiden (third at 7f): no promise in **b–**
bumpers/novice hurdle. *Linda Jewell*

OUR HENRIETTA (IRE) 9 b.m. Winged Love (IRE) – Nut Eile (IRE) (Torus) [2018/19 **c–**
c20g⁴ Oct 11] half-sister to fairly useful hurdler/useful chaser Jazz Dance (2m-2½m
winner, by Arctic Lord): dam ran once over hurdles: multiple Irish point winner: well
beaten in mares novice on chasing debut. *Nick Mitchell*

OUR IDIC BOY (IRE) 5 b.g. Royal Anthem (USA) – Next Best Thing (IRE) (Taipan **h–**
(IRE)) [2018/19 b15.8g h19.5d^pu Jan 18] tailed off in bumper: also no show in novice on **b–**
hurdling debut. *Ian Williams*

OUR JERRY (IRE) 8 b.g. Jeremy (USA) – Sonic Night (IRE) (Night Shift (USA)) **h94**
[2018/19 h16d² h16v* h17.6g h16d³ Apr 27] pulled up in point: modest handicap hurdler:
won at Cork in March: stays 2¼m: acts on heavy going: wears tongue tie. *Miss Evanna
McCutcheon, Ireland*

OUR KAEMPFER (IRE) 10 b.g. Oscar (IRE) – Gra-Bri (IRE) (Rashar (USA)) **c131**
[2018/19 c–, h124: h23.1g⁵ c24g⁴ c23.6d⁵ c21.5d³ Nov 3] tall gelding: has had breathing **h119**
operation: fairly useful handicap hurdler: useful handicap chaser: respectable efforts in
2018/19: stays 25f: acts on soft going: tried in cheekpieces: has worn tongue tie: travels
strongly held up: temperament under suspicion (often finds little). *Charlie Longsdon*

OUR KYLIE (IRE) 7 b.m. Jeremy (USA) – Prakara (IRE) (Indian Ridge) [2018/19 h121: **h111**
h16.2d h15.7g² h17.2d⁶ h16.2g Apr 24] sturdy mare: fairly useful handicap hurdler: left
Brian Ellison after third start: unproven beyond 17f: acts on good to soft going: tried in
cheekpieces. *Donald McCain*

OUR LEGEND (IRE) 4 b.g. Finsceal Fior (IRE) – Thrift (IRE) (Green Desert (USA)) **h122**
[2018/19 h16m⁴ h16g² h16.5g² h16g⁴ h16s* Mar 2] has had breathing operation:
half-brother to fair 2m/17f hurdle winner Darwins Theory (by Montjeu): fair maiden on
Flat, stays 1½m: fairly useful juvenile hurdler: won maiden event at Navan in March: raced
only at 2m: acts on soft going: tried in hood: usually races close up: joined Jack O. Fisher
in USA. *Thomas Mullins, Ireland*

OUR LUCAS (IRE) 7 b.g. Jeremy (USA) – Alassio (USA) (Gulch (USA)) [2018/19 **h115**
h107: h16.2g* h16m Apr 12] fairly useful handicap hurdler: won at Perth in August, then
left Iain Jardine: unproven beyond 17f: acts on heavy going. *Ian Duncan*

OURMANMASSINI (IRE) 11 b.g. Dr Massini (IRE) – Aunty Dawn (IRE) (Strong **c105 §**
Gale) [2018/19 c27.5d⁵ h24.8g² h24.4g³ c22g² h22m⁶ Aug 31] sturdy gelding: prolific **h103 §**
winner in points: fair maiden hurdler: similar form in chases: stays 25f: acts on heavy
going, probably on good to firm: has worn headgear: wears tongue tie: usually races
prominently: has shown temperament. *Gordon Elliott, Ireland*

OUR MERLIN 7 b.g. Pasternak – Lorgnette (Emperor Fountain) [2018/19 h124: h16.4g **h127**
h16.3d³ h15.3g* h16s² h16.8d^F h16s h16.3d² Mar 22] sturdy gelding: fairly useful
handicap hurdler: won at Wincanton in December: stays 2¼m: acts on heavy going:
usually leads. *Robert Walford*

OUR MORRIS (IRE) 8 b.g. Milan – Broken Gale (IRE) (Broken Hearted) [2018/19 h80: **h87**
h23.9g* h23.3g² h23.9g^pu h27m³ Sep 6] modest handicap hurdler: won novice event at
Perth in May: barely stays 27f: acts on good to firm going. *George Bewley*

OURMULLION 5 b.g. Mullionmileanhour (IRE) – Queen Ranavola (USA) (Medaglia **h91**
d'Oro (USA)) [2018/19 h16.5d⁵ h19s h16.5g h15.8g^pu h16.5d⁵ h16.5d⁴ Apr 24] fair on Flat,
stays 11f: modest form over hurdles: will prove best around 2m: acts on good to soft going:
tried in cheekpieces: wears tongue tie. *David Pipe*

OUR PERCY (IRE) 5 b.g. Stowaway – Another Present (IRE) (Presenting) [2018/19 **b90**
b16.7g⁵ Apr 13] €45,000 3-y-o; fourth foal: dam, winning pointer, half-sister to top-class
hurdler/very smart chaser (stayed 3¼m) Time For Rupert: 11/2, 8¼ lengths fifth to L'Air
du Vent in conditionals/amateurs bumper at Bangor. *Charlie Longsdon*

OUR PHILLIE LILY 7 b.m. Sulamani (IRE) – Tyre Hill Lilly (Jupiter Island) [2018/19 **h–**
h76: h15.3m h15.7g⁶ May 21] lengthy mare: poor maiden hurdler. *Susan Gardner*

OUR POWER (IRE) 4 b.g. Power – Scripture (IRE) (Sadler's Wells (USA)) [2018/19 **h124**
h16.7g* h16.8s² h16.3s* h16.8d⁴ h16.4s h16m⁴ Apr 12] sturdy gelding: dam sister to
useful hurdler/fairly useful chaser (winner up to 21f) Fontanesi: fairly useful on Flat, stays
1½m: fairly useful juvenile hurdler: won at Market Rasen in November and Newbury in
December: will be suited by 2½m: acts on soft going. *Alan King*

OUR PROMISE 5 ch.m. Malinas (GER) – Hello My Lovely (Presenting) [2018/19 b17d⁴ **b73**
Mar 24] third foal: half-sister to bumper winner Harrisons Promise (by Westerner): dam
(c85/h71), ungenuine 3m chase winner, sister to useful chaser (stayed 25f) Another
Promise: fourth in bumper at Carlisle. *Susan Corbett*

OUR REWARD (IRE) 9 b.g. Morozov (USA) – Paddyeoin (IRE) (Insan (USA)) **c107 §**
[2018/19 c110, h–: c24.5g^pu c24.1g² c23.5m² c25.8g⁵ h27m h25m⁴ h23.4g* c23.6s³ **h116**
h25.3g² h25.3s⁵ Dec 18] lengthy, angular gelding: winning Irish pointer: fairly useful
handicap hurdler: won at Fakenham in October: fair but temperamental maiden chaser:
stays 25f: acts on soft and good to firm going: wears headgear: front runner. *Jamie Snowden*

OUR ROCKSTAR (IRE) 5 b.m. Gold Well – Hazel Mist (IRE) (Flemensfirth (USA)) **h106**
[2018/19 b16.7g b15.8s h21.2d h15.8d³ h15.8g h22g* h20.5g* Apr 22] first foal: dam **b–**
unraced sister to useful hurdler (stayed 3m) Abbey Lane: well held in bumpers for Mark
Loughnane: fair form over hurdles: won handicaps at Stratford in March and Plumpton
(mares event, improved still further) in April: stays 2¾m: acts on good to soft going.
Alastair Ralph

OUR THREE SONS (IRE) 8 b.g. Shantou (USA) – Ballyquinn (IRE) (Anshan) [2018/19 **c125**
h118: c16.1g* c17.8g² c19.4m² c21.4m³ c16.5g⁴ c22.6m⁵ c19.5s⁵ Oct 6] fairly useful **h–**
hurdler: fairly useful novice chaser: beat sole rival Ordo Ab Chao 6 lengths in maiden at
Towcester in May on chasing debut: stays 21f: acts on good to firm and good to soft going:
usually in cheekpieces: usually races close up. *Jamie Snowden*

OUR UNCLE PAT (IRE) 8 b.g. Daylami (IRE) – Springmount (IRE) (Beneficial) **c–**
[2018/19 h85: h20.3g c21.2g⁶ h16.2g h20g³ c17.2g⁴ c19.4m h19.9m⁵ Aug 30] little sign **h–**
of ability: usually in hood/tongue tie. *Kenny Johnson*

OUTBACK BLUE 6 gr.g. Aussie Rules (USA) – Beautiful Lady (IRE) (Peintre Celebre **h95**
(USA)) [2018/19 h85: h15.8g³ h20.2g³ h20.2g h19.9g h17.1g h16.8s⁵ h16.4d h19.3s⁴
h19.9s h16.8v⁴ Mar 12] has had breathing operation: modest maiden hurdler: stays 2½m:
best form on good going: tried in cheekpieces: has worn tongue tie (not so regularly
nowadays). *George Bewley*

OUTCROP (IRE) 5 b.g. Rock of Gibraltar (IRE) – Desert Sage (Selkirk (USA)) [2018/19 **h103**
h101: h17.2g h17.2m h16.7g³ h16.8g* h15.6g³ h19.8g⁵ Dec 10] sturdy gelding: fair
handicap hurdler: won at Sedgefield in November: probably stays 2½m: acts on good to
soft going: has worn headgear. *Jennie Candlish*

OUT FOR JUSTICE (IRE) 6 b.g. Beneficial – Dustys Delight (IRE) (Oscar (IRE)) **c89 p**
[2018/19 b–: h15.8d h15.3m⁶ h15.8g³ h15.8g⁶ h22.1g h19.6g⁶ h20g² h19.5g² c24g² h20.2d **h85**
Apr 26] has had breathing operation: runner-up in Irish point on debut: modest maiden
hurdler: similar form when second in novice handicap at Bangor on chasing debut (should
improve): stays 3m: tried in tongue tie. *Katy Price*

OUTLANDER (IRE) 11 b.g. Stowaway – Western Whisper (IRE) (Supreme Leader) **c160 §**
[2018/19 c164§, h–: c25g² c24g³ c24g⁵ c24g⁴ c25d⁴ c34.3g Apr 6] lengthy gelding: **h–**
winning hurdler: high-class chaser, but on lengthy losing run: left Gordon Elliott after
fifth start: probably stays 4¼m: acts on heavy going: normally in headgear nowadays: not
one to trust. *Richard Spencer*

OUTLAW JACK (IRE) 7 b.g. Mr Dinos (IRE) – Bonus Issue (IRE) (Treasure Hunter) **h–**
[2018/19 h–: h19.5dᵖᵘ h18.5s h19d⁵ Apr 4] winning pointer: little show over hurdles.
Johnny Farrelly

OUTNUMBERED (IRE) 6 b.g. Stowaway – Back Market Lass (IRE) (Bob Back **c95**
(USA)) [2018/19 h100: c24.2mᶠ c21.3dᵖᵘ c20.1v³ c20.1g⁶ c20.5d⁶ c20.1vᵖᵘ c20.1m² Mar **h–**
28] maiden hurdler: modest maiden chaser: stays 23f: acts on good to firm and heavy
going: tried in cheekpieces. *Chris Grant*

OUT OF STYLE 8 b.g. Court Cave (IRE) – Portanob (IRE) (Be My Native **h62**
(USA)) [2018/19 h84: h16m⁵ Jul 9] won Irish maiden point on debut: poor form in maiden
hurdles. *Alastair Ralph*

OUTOFTHEQUESTION 5 b.g. Delegator – Why Dubai (USA) (Kris S (USA)) [2018/19 **h71**
h16g h16.6m⁴ h16.3s h16.6g⁵ Jan 9] fair on Flat, stays 13.5f: disappointing over hurdles.
Alan King

OUTOFTHISWORLD (IRE) 6 b.m. Shantou (USA) – Mystic Masie (IRE) (Turgeon **h117**
(USA)) [2018/19 b–: h20.6gᵘʳ h20.6g* h19.2v³ h21.2dᵖᵘ h20.5d Mar 23] bumper winner:
fairly useful form over hurdles: won mares maiden at Market Rasen in November:
disappointing last 2 outings: stays 21f: acts on heavy going: tried in cheekpieces. *Harry Fry*

OUTONPATROL (IRE) 5 gr.m. Stowaway – Burnt Oil Babe (IRE) (Beneficial) [2018/19 **b71**
b15.8d Mar 30] €6,800 3-y-o: second foal: dam (c115/h74), 2¼m-21f chase winner, stayed
3m: winning Irish pointer: raced too freely in mares bumper at Uttoxeter. *Alan King*

OUTRAGEOUS ROMANA (IRE) 8 b.m. Mahler – South West Nine (IRE) (Oscar **c–**
(IRE)) [2018/19 h74: h22.1g⁵ h23.3g* h23g³ h23.1g* h23g* h23m⁵ h23.1g⁵ c20.3d³ **h91**
Apr 26] modest handicap hurdler: won at Uttoxeter (mares event) in June, and at Bangor
(conditionals) and Worcester in August: well held in mares novice handicap on chasing
debut: stays 23f: acts on good to soft going: usually in cheekpieces. *John O'Shea*

OUT SAM 10 b.g. Multiplex – Tintera (IRE) (King's Theatre (IRE)) [2018/19 c134§, h–§: **c139 §**
c28s* c24d5 c29g c25s4 c28.5gpu c29d Apr 22] lengthy gelding: winning hurdler: useful **h– §**
handicap chaser: won Cork National (by 1¼ lengths from Rogue Angel) in November:
stays 29f: acts on heavy going: usually in headgear: wears tongue tie: unreliable. *Gordon
Elliott, Ireland*

OUTSMARTIN (IRE) 7 b.g. Marienbard (IRE) – Fair Gina (IRE) (Long Pond) [2018/19 **h–**
h18.5gpu Aug 15] some promise on first of 2 outings in bumpers: off 22 months, pulled up
in maiden on hurdling debut. *Deborah Faulkner*

OUT THE GLEN (IRE) 6 b.g. Millenary – Dicera (IRE) (Flemensfirth (USA)) [2018/19 **h–**
h23.6d h20s h15.8g5 Apr 21] placed in points: no show in novice hurdles. *Debra Hamer*

OVERAWED 8 b.m. Overbury (IRE) – Alleged To Rhyme (IRE) (Leading Counsel **c98**
(USA)) [2018/19 c76, h–: c15.7m5 c16s2 c19.4s4 c19.4d2 c20.3g5 c20.9g3 c24g4 Apr 13] **h–**
winning hurdler: modest maiden chaser: left Tom George after reappearance: stays 21f:
acts on heavy going. *John Groucott*

OVERFLOW (FR) 4 b.g. Bonbon Rose (FR) – Furika (FR) (Kadalko (FR)) [2018/19 **b83**
b15.8g5 Apr 11] €15,000 3-y-o: half-brother to 3 winners in France, including Deception
Island (17f-19f hurdle/chase winner, by Antarctique) and Worldly Wise (2m-19f hurdle/
chase winner, by Lost World): dam, failed to complete over hurdles in France, out of half-
sister to top-class chaser (stayed 25f) Cyfor Malta: 11/4, only fifth in maiden bumper at
Huntingdon. *Dan Skelton*

OVERLAND FLYER (IRE) 8 b.g. Westerner – Love Train (IRE) (Sadler's Wells **c124**
(USA)) [2018/19 h–: c25.8g2 c20.2m2 c23gpu c25.1g c20.2g* Feb 27] has had breathing **h–**
operation: winning hurdler: fairly useful form over fences: won handicap at Wincanton in
February: stays 3m: acts on good to firm going: wears tongue tie. *Paul Nicholls*

OVERRIDER 9 b.g. Cockney Rebel (IRE) – Fustaan (IRE) (Royal Applause) [2018/19 **h–**
h–: h15.8g h16.8g h16g h16.3g Aug 23] has had breathing operation: poor maiden hurdler:
in headgear last 3 starts: usually in tongue tie. *Shaun Lycett*

OVERSHOT 7 b.m. Overbury (IRE) – Aya (Double Trigger (IRE)) [2018/19 b16.8g b16g **h–**
h20.3gpu Jul 15] second foal: dam (h89) bumper winner/maiden hurdler (stayed 25f): no **b–**
sign of ability, including in points. *Phil York*

OVER THE ARCH (IRE) 7 br.g. Presenting – On The Outside (IRE) (Anshan) [2018/19 **c92 ?**
h93: h24.5gF h19.5g c19.2g4 c23.6dpu c22.7fpu c24s6 c25.1g4 Apr 14] workmanlike **h–**
gelding: maiden hurdler: seemingly modest form in maiden on chasing debut, no show
subsequently: tried in cheekpieces. *Richard Rowe*

OVERTHEEDGE (IRE) 10 b.g. Morozov (USA) – Ballyroe Hill (IRE) (Over The River **c–**
(FR)) [2018/19 c–, h103: h19.7d h23.3spu c20.3dpu c26.3dpu Jan 11] point winner: fair **h–**
hurdler: ran badly in 2018/19: failed to complete in chases: stays 23f: unraced on heavy
going, acts on any other: tried in headgear/tongue tie. *Simon West*

OVERTHETOP (IRE) 5 br.g. Flemensfirth (USA) – Dawn Bid (IRE) (Mazaad) **b99**
[2018/19 b16g* Apr 25] €115,000 3-y-o, £150,000 4-y-o: brother to bumper winner/useful
3m hurdle winner On Raglan Road and half-brother to bumper winners by King's Theatre
and High Chaparral: dam unraced half-sister to useful hurdler/very smart chaser (stayed
27f) Therealbandit and useful hurdler/chaser (stayed 3¼m) The Bajan Bandit: won Irish
point on debut: 3/1, also looked good prospect when winning bumper at Warwick by 2½
lengths from Induno, asserting final 1f. *Olly Murphy*

OVER TO BREE 7 b.m. Overbury (IRE) – Nouf (Efisio) [2018/19 b16gpu b16.3mpu Sep **b–**
8] £800 5-y-o: seventh foal: dam (h110), 2m hurdle winner, also 7f/1m winner on Flat:
pulled up in bumpers. *Tracey Leeson*

OVERTOUJAY 9 b.g. Overbury (IRE) – Ouh Jay (Karinga Bay) [2018/19 h89: c20.3g2 **c98**
c17.2g3 c20g2 c17.2g5 c20.3g3 c24g6 c24g4 c21.1gur c21.4g3 c20.3d5 Nov 20] winning **h–**
hurdler: modest handicap chaser: won novice event at Stratford in September: stays easy
23f, effective at much shorter: acts on good to soft going: has worn cheekpieces, including
last 5 starts. *Charles Pogson*

OVERTOWN EXPRESS (IRE) 11 br.g. Overbury (IRE) – Black Secret (Gildoran) **c128**
[2018/19 c149, h129: c18.8spu c15.5s4 c16dpu Feb 23] workmanlike gelding: winning **h–**
hurdler: smart handicap chaser at best: stayed 19f: acted on heavy going: usually raced
towards rear: dead. *Harry Fry*

OVERWORKDUNDERPAID (IRE) 6 b.g. Getaway (GER) – Another Whiparound (IRE) (Saddlers' Hall (IRE)) [2018/19 h109, b95: c20.9s⁴ c23.4dᶠ c21.4dᵘʳ c24.2g⁴ c20.9d³ c20.3g Apr 13] useful-looking gelding: has had breathing operation: finished alone in Irish point: fair maiden hurdler: similar form in handicap chases: should stay 3m: acts on soft going: tried in cheekpieces: in tongue tie last 4 starts. *Charlie Longsdon*   c113 h−

OWEN GLENDOWER (IRE) 14 br.g. Anshan – Native Success (IRE) (Be My Native (USA)) [2018/19 c26.3g⁴ c22.6d⁷ Jun 8] winning hurdler: fair chaser: won lady riders' hunter at Stratford in June: stayed 23f: acted on good to firm and heavy going: sometimes wore cheekpieces: wore tongue tie: sketchy jumper: dead. *Miss Hannah Gregory*   c113 x h−

OWNERS DAY 9 gr.m. Fair Mix (IRE) – Charmeille (FR) (Exit To Nowhere (USA)) [2018/19 h−: h20s⁶ h20g h16.3g⁵ h16s h17.7v Dec 11] rather leggy mare: has had breathing operation: modest handicap hurdler: left Neil Mulholland after second start: unproven beyond 2m: acts on good to soft going: tried in tongue tie. *Jimmy Frost*   h85

OXFORD BLU 5 b.g. Aqlaam – Blue Zealot (IRE) (Galileo (IRE)) [2018/19 h120: h19.2g h19.5d⁶ h26d h23.4d⁵ h18.6gᶠ Mar 27] close-coupled gelding: has had breathing operation: fair handicap hurdler nowadays: should stay beyond 2¼m: acts on heavy going: usually in headgear: tried in tongue tie: temperament under suspicion. *Olly Murphy*   h103

OXWICH BAY (IRE) 7 b.g. Westerner – Rose de Beaufai (FR) (Solon (GER)) [2018/19 h119: c16s⁴ c19.4sᵘʳ c19.4vᶠ c16g³ c20dᶠ h15.8d⁴ h16.5s⁵ h20g⁵ Apr 21] fair handicap hurdler: fairly useful maiden chaser: stays 2½m: acts on heavy going: tried in cheekpieces: not a fluent jumper of fences. *Evan Williams*   c118 x h104

OYSTER PERCH 5 b.m. Yeats (IRE) – Dudeen (IRE) (Anshan) [2018/19 b16.5d b16.3d h21.7g⁵ h21.6s h19d⁵ Apr 24] unfurnished mare: fifth foal: closely related to 2 winners, including fairly useful hurdler Catherines Well (19f winner, by Kayf Tara), and half-sister to bumper winner/winning pointer Neville (by Revoque): dam (h89) 2½m hurdle winner: poor form in mares bumpers: little show in novice hurdles. *Bob Buckler*   h− b60

OZZIE THE OSCAR (IRE) 8 b.g. Oscar (IRE) – Private Official (IRE) (Beneficial) [2018/19 c150+, h−: c16.2g* h15.8d³ c17.5m² c16.8g⁵ c16.3d* c16.4g⁴ c16.5m⁵ Apr 13] useful-looking gelding: useful handicap hurdler: very smart handicap chaser: won at Warwick in May and Cheltenham (by 3½ lengths from Bun Doran) in December: raced around 2m: acts on soft and good to firm going: enthusiastic sort, makes running/races prominently. *Philip Hobbs*   c155 h141

OZZY THOMAS (IRE) 9 b.g. Gold Well – Bramble Leader (IRE) (Supreme Leader) [2018/19 c139, h−: h24g² h24g⁶ c24.1g⁵ c23d⁵ Aug 29] rather leggy gelding: has had breathing operation: fairly useful handicap hurdler/chaser: stays 3m: acts on soft and good to firm going: usually in cheekpieces: tried in tongue tie. *Henry Oliver*   c127 h120

P

PACHA DU POLDER (FR) 12 b.g. Muhtathir – Ambri Piotta (FR) (Caerwent) [2018/19 c134, h−: c22.2g⁵ c26.3dᵖᵘ Mar 15] well-made gelding: winning hurdler: useful hunter chaser, winning Foxhunter Chase at Cheltenham in 2017 and 2018: pulled up attempting hat-trick in race: stayed 3½m: acted on good to firm and heavy going: tried in cheekpieces: retired. *Paul Nicholls*   c92 h−

PACIFIC DE BAUNE (FR) 6 gr.g. Al Namix (FR) – Perle de Baune (FR) (En Calcat (FR)) [2018/19 h133: c16.2g* c19.1gᵘʳ h16g⁶ Dec 27] rather unfurnished gelding: has had breathing operation: useful form at best over hurdles: similar form over fences: won novice at Warwick in November: should stay 2½m: acts on soft going: often travels strongly: remains open to improvement as a chaser. *Nicky Henderson*   c131 p h122

PAC IT IN 5 b.m. Paco Boy (IRE) – Bisaat (USA) (Bahri (USA)) [2018/19 b−: b16.3g b16.3m³ b16.3m³ h19.6g⁵ h18.5gᵖᵘ h23g⁴ h23gᵖᵘ h15.3m Oct 19] modest form in bumpers: poor form over hurdles. *David Weston*   h83 b80

PACKETTOTHERAFTERS (IRE) 10 b.g. Craigsteel – Darazari River (IRE) (Darazari (IRE)) [2018/19 c91: c26.1gᵖᵘ c24g³ c24gᵖᵘ c25.6s⁵ c27.5g⁴ c29.6d* Apr 26] lengthy gelding: modest handicap chaser: won at Bangor in April: stays 3¾m: acts on soft going: wears cheekpieces: tried in tongue tie. *Gary Hanmer*   c90

PACK IT IN (IRE) 6 br.g. Big Bad Bob (IRE) – Evening Dress (Medicean) [2018/19 h−: h16g⁵ h18.7gᵖᵘ h15.3m⁶ Oct 19] form over hurdles only when fifth in novice at Worcester: tried in blinkers. *Alexandra Dunn*   h90

PACOFILHA 5 b.m. Paco Boy (IRE) – Seradim (Elnadim (USA)) [2018/19 h–: h17.7g⁴ **h–** Nov 19] fair on Flat, stays 1½m: no form over hurdles. *John Flint*

PADDLING (FR) 8 b.g. Walk In The Park (IRE) – Sea Mamaille (FR) (Sea Full (FR)) **c84** [2018/19 c96, h–: c17.1d³ c16g⁵ c20.1s c19.2g³ c15.2g⁴ c19.3g⁵ Apr 23] close-coupled **h–** gelding: maiden hurdler: modest handicap chaser: stays 19f: acts on heavy going: tried in cheekpieces. *Micky Hammond*

PADDOCKS LOUNGE (IRE) 12 b.g. Oscar (IRE) – Sister Rosza (IRE) (Roselier **c86** (FR)) [2018/19 c102, h–: h23.1gᵖᵘ c19.3g³ c20.9s⁴ c15.6v⁵ c16.5s⁵ c17.2d⁵ Feb 17] lengthy **h–** gelding: has had breathing operation: winning hurdler: modest maiden chaser: stays 21f: acts on good to firm and heavy going: has worn hood/tongue tie: front runner/races prominently. *Clare Ellam*

PADDY A (IRE) 5 b.g. Holy Roman Emperor (IRE) – Lilting (IRE) (Montjeu (IRE)) **h78** [2018/19 h15.5gʳᵒ h16s h15.8d h15.8g Feb 28] smallish gelding: fairly useful on Flat, stays 2m: poor form over hurdles: will be suited by further than 2m: tried in cheekpieces. *Ian Williams*

PADDY'S POEM 8 b.g. Proclamation (IRE) – Ashleys Petale (IRE) (Ashley Park (IRE)) **c117** [2018/19 h113: h15.8d³ c17s³ c16d³ c16.5d* c17s² c16.5g* Apr 11] fair maiden hurdler: **h108** fairly useful form over fences: won novice handicaps at Huntingdon in February and April: raced around 2m: acts on heavy going: in tongue tie last 4 starts: usually front runner/races prominently. *Nick Gifford*

PADDYS RUNNER 7 gr.g. Sir Percy – Frosty Welcome (USA) (With Approval (CAN)) **h98** [2018/19 h117: h21g⁵ h21.7gᵖᵘ h22.8v⁶ h23d³ h23.1gᵖᵘ Mar 20] close-coupled gelding: fairly useful handicap hurdler, below form in 2018/19: stays 23f: acts on soft going: wears headgear: usually races close up. *Graeme McPherson*

PADDY THE CHEF (IRE) 4 b.g. Dandy Man (IRE) – The Reek (Tiger Hill (IRE)) **h106 p** [2018/19 h15.6g³ h16s³ h16s⁵ Jan 21] useful-looking gelding: fairly useful on Flat, stays 11f: fair form over hurdles: likely to prove best around 2m with emphasis on speed: remains with potential. *Ian Williams*

PADDY THE OSCAR (IRE) 16 b.g. Oscar (IRE) – Parsonage (The Parson) [2018/19 **c–** c115, h–: c24dᵖᵘ c23.6dᵖᵘ Mar 21] maiden hurdler: fairly useful chaser at best, no form in **h–** 2018/19: stays 3¼m: acts on heavy going: tried in cheekpieces/tongue tie: front runner. *Grace Harris*

PADDY THE STOUT (IRE) 14 b.g. Oscar Schindler (IRE) – Misty Silks (Scottish **c–** Reel) [2018/19 c–§, h–: c24.2gᵖᵘ May 8] strong gelding: maiden pointer/hurdler: fair **h–** chaser at best, lightly raced and no form under Rules since 2016/17: stays 21f: acts on heavy going: wears tongue tie. *L. Humphrey*

PADGE (IRE) 10 b.g. Flemensfirth (USA) – Mona Vic (IRE) (Old Vic) [2018/19 c–, h103: **c–** h21.9s⁶ Nov 23] sturdy gelding: useful handicap hurdler at best: in cheekpieces, well **h–** beaten sole outing in 2018/19: winning chaser: stays 23f: acts on heavy going. *Evan Williams*

PADLEYOUROWNCANOE 5 b.g. Nayef (USA) – Pooka's Daughter (IRE) (Eagle **h137** Eyed (USA)) [2018/19 h124: h16d² h16.4g³ h20.5s⁶ h21.4d* h24d Mar 14] compact gelding: useful handicap hurdler: won at Wincanton (by 2 lengths from Monbeg Theatre) in December: probably stays 3m: acts on heavy going. *Colin Tizzard*

PADS (IRE) 9 b.g. Luso – Augusta Victoria (Callernish) [2018/19 c74, h98: h20.6d h21.4s **c–** h19.3g⁵ h17s⁵ Mar 7] placed in points: modest maiden hurdler, below form in 2018/19: **h79** once-raced chaser: stays 2¾m: acts on soft going: has worn headgear, including in 2018/19. *Daragh Bourke*

PAGERO (FR) 4 b.g. Nathaniel (IRE) – Pagera (FR) (Gentlewave (IRE)) [2018/19 h16.8d **h112 p** h16m h17m³ Apr 20] lengthy, useful-looking gelding: dam sister to fairly useful 2m hurdle winner Pakora: useful on Flat in France, stays 10.5f: fair form over hurdles: best effort when third in novice at Carlisle: open to further improvement. *Jonjo O'Neill*

PAHASKA (GER) 6 b.m. Saddex – Pacific Sun (GER) (Dashing Blade) [2018/19 h19.7g **c–** h23.1g² h23.1s h21.2d h21.4g h26.5g⁴ Apr 20] has had breathing operation: fourth foal: **h100** sister to French 1¼m winner Pai Mei and half-sister to a winner on Flat abroad by Paolini: dam German 6.5f winner: fair handicap hurdler: lightly-raced chaser: stays 3¼m: acts on soft going: wears headgear: usually leads. *Chris Down*

PAIN AU CHOCOLAT (FR) 8 b.g. Enrique – Clair Chene (FR) (Solido (FR)) [2018/19 **c139** c139, h–: c23.8g c19.4g⁶ c19.4s³ h19.3g c20.1d* Apr 6] good-topped gelding: has had **h–** breathing operation: winning hurdler: useful handicap chaser: won at Newcastle (by 10 lengths from The Paddy Pie) in April: stays 2½m: acts on heavy going: has worn headgear/ tongue tie, including final start: usually races prominently. *Rebecca Menzies*

PAINTERS LAD (IRE) 8 b.g. Fruits of Love (USA) – Great Cullen (IRE) (Simply Great **h68** (FR)) [2018/19 h–: h20.9gᵖᵘ h19.3gᵖᵘ h15.6g⁵ h15.6g h16.8d Apr 23] has had breathing operation: poor maiden hurdler: tried in tongue tie. *Alison Hamilton*

PAINT THE DREAM 5 b.g. Brian Boru – Vineuil (FR) (Muhtathir) [2018/19 b16.2s **h122** h19.6d⁴ h19s³ h20.5d⁵ h21.4g² h20.2g* Apr 25] good-topped gelding: second foal: dam, **b–** French 2m hurdle winner, half-sister to useful French hurdler/fairly useful chaser (stayed 25f) Drole de Drame: tailed off in bumper: fairly useful form over hurdles: won novice handicap at Perth in April: stays 21f: in tongue tie last 5 starts: often travels strongly. *Fergal O'Brien*

PAIROFBROWNEYES (IRE) 10 b.g. Luso – Frankly Native (IRE) (Be My Native **c155** (USA)) [2018/19 c148, h103: c24.5g c25s c24d* c29dꟳ Apr 22] workmanlike gelding: **h–** winning hurdler: smart handicap chaser: won Leinster National Handicap Chase at Naas (by 5 lengths from Isleofhopendreams) in March: stays 3m: acts on heavy going: has worn cheekpieces. *W. P. Mullins, Ireland*

PAISLEY PARK (IRE) 7 b.g. Oscar (IRE) – Presenting Shares (IRE) (Presenting) **h166 p** [2018/19 h137: h20g* h24.3g* h24.4s* h24d* h24d* Mar 14]

What a difference a year makes! As well as being one of the stars of the latest season, Paisley Park was also one of the most unheralded newcomers to jump racing's top table. There was certainly nothing in his performance at the 2018 Cheltenham Festival to hint at the feats he would go on to accomplish on his return there twelve months later, or indeed during the whole of a season in which he went undefeated. Wearing a visor and sent off at 33/1 in the Spa Novices' Hurdle at Cheltenham in 2018, Paisley Park was beaten more than fifty lengths when trailing home last of the thirteen finishers, a performance which even led to his resolution being called into question. A year later, starting 11/8 favourite against seventeen rivals in the Stayers' Hurdle, he stormed up the Cheltenham hill to cap an unbeaten campaign with a stirring success.

No horse has managed to dominate the staying hurdling scene for any length of time since Big Buck's, winner of a record four Stayers' [World] Hurdles between 2009 and 2012. Those wins formed part of his unbeaten sequence of eighteen races in the top staying hurdles, a record over jumps surpassed in the latest season by Altior. Whilst not achieving the same longevity, other hurdlers have come along since Big Buck's who have managed to dominate the staying division for a season. Thistlecrack did so in a superb campaign in 2015/16 during which he ran up a sequence of clear-cut wins in the Long Distance Hurdle at Newbury, the Long Walk at Ascot, the Cleeve and World Hurdles at Cheltenham and the Liverpool Hurdle at Aintree. It was only a switch to chasing, culminating in a win in the King George as a novice, which curtailed Thistlecrack's reign as the top staying hurdler. His successor was Unowhatimeanharry who enjoyed an unbeaten campaign of his own in novice and handicap company that same season before emulating Thistlecrack by winning the Long Distance, the Long Walk and the Cleeve in 2016/17. He came unstuck when beaten into third at odds on in the Stayers' Hurdle but reasserted his dominance when beating the Stayers' Hurdle winner Nichols Canyon at Punchestown. Age prevented Unowhatimeanharry lasting longer as the top staying hurdler—he was already nine when reaching his peak—though he did win in Grade 1 company at Punchestown again as an eleven-year-old, shortly after the end of the latest British season. Honours were spread much more widely among the top staying hurdles in 2017/18 when the Stayers' Hurdle was won by the fragile Penhill who hadn't run at all previously that season and missed the whole of the latest campaign. Therefore, the way was clear for a new young contender to emerge as the top staying hurdler and it was Paisley Park who unexpectedly took the division by storm.

He made his breakthrough in the big staying hurdles in the Long Walk at Ascot in December, having returned in top form in handicaps in the autumn. To be fair to Paisley Park, his effort in the Spa the previous March, on his first attempt at

JLT Hurdle (Long Walk), Ascot—a first Grade 1 win for Paisley Park (spotted cap), who has the measure of eventual third Top Notch at the last

three miles, was much his worst run of a light novice campaign during which he had looked a potentially smart recruit to hurdling, winning on his debut at Hereford (upsetting the long odds-on Vision des Flos, a smart performer himself in due course) and then finishing second at Warwick (in the Leamington Novices') and Doncaster. Under top weight, from a BHA mark of 140 for his handicap debut, Paisley Park made an impressive return to action at Aintree in October, showing no lack of speed in a race where the flights in the home straight were omitted due to the low sun. Off a mark 7 lb higher, he carried top weight again for the Betfair Exchange Stayers' Handicap Hurdle at Haydock the following month. The £100,000 added Grade 3 contest, just the second renewal over conventional hurdles (after beginning life over the 'fixed brush' obstacles), attracted an unusually small field of seven, the good ground doubtless a factor, contrasting with the very heavy conditions in which Sam Spinner had been successful twelve months earlier. Paisley Park not only proved himself effective at three miles, but showed himself well suited by the trip as he did well to wear down Shades of Midnight and the favourite First Assignment, both of whom got first run on him. Still having plenty to do at the last, he kept on very gamely to lead close home and win by half a length and a length and a quarter.

Sam Spinner had successfully taken the step up in grade in his stride when following up in the Long Walk the year before, and Paisley Park started at 8/1 to follow suit in an open and competitive field of eleven for a race branded as the JLT Hurdle. With the staying division still in search of a leader, both the last two winners were in the line-up again and prominent in the betting, Unowhatimeanharry having won the Long Distance Hurdle at Newbury for a second time in a renewal in which Sam Spinner was beaten when unseating two out. The 7/2 favourite at Ascot, though, was Call Me Lord who had signed off the previous season with a win in Sandown's Select Hurdle, while another proven on the prevailing soft ground, and ahead of Paisley Park in the betting, was the previous season's Cleeve Hurdle winner Agrapart. Little went right for the favourite, who wasn't a proven stayer in any case, and both former winners failed to complete, Sam Spinner unseating his jockey again as early as the second flight when seemingly trying to refuse, with Unowhatimeanharry falling at the same hurdle a circuit later, badly hampering Call Me Lord. There was still little between the remainder jumping two out before Paisley Park, who had travelled more smoothly than at Haydock, and Thistlecrack's half-brother West Approach moved ahead at the final flight. Keeping on well on the run-in, Paisley Park was ridden out by Aidan Coleman for a two-length win over the 40/1 runner-up, with Call Me Lord's stable-companion the high-class chaser Top Notch beaten another three and three quarter lengths in third. Call Me Lord was only seventh, while Agrapart, left in the lead early on, faded to finish last of the nine who completed.

Paisley Park's rise to the top of the staying hurdle division, which was now well under way, was as much one of the human stories of the season as it was about the horse himself. After the Long Walk, it was Coleman and Paisley Park's trainer Emma Lavelle who were the main focus of attention as each, surprisingly, had a first Grade 1 victory to celebrate, despite both being well established in successful careers. Coleman, a former champion conditional, had ridden his first winner more than twelve years earlier and ended the latest season with just short of a thousand career wins to his name, a milestone he went on to reach in June 2019. Lavelle, now based near Marlborough, had been training for twenty years since taking out a licence in her mid-twenties after serving as pupil assistant to Toby Balding, though she gave much of the credit for Paisley Park's training to her husband, former jockey Barry Fenton.

The Grade 2 galliardhomes.com Cleeve Hurdle at Cheltenham, Paisley Park's next race, may not have quite the same status as the Long Walk, but it brought together several of the field Paisley Park had already faced at Ascot, including the two who had failed to complete. The new challengers included the former Coral Cup winner Aux Ptits Soins who had been a ready winner of a handicap over the same course and distance earlier in the month. Sent off favourite, Paisley Park had little in hand on form but, showing further considerable improvement, he put up a top-class performance that suddenly seemed to bring some clarity to the ante-post Stayers' Hurdle picture, establishing him as the one to beat in March. West Approach chased him home again, but the two-length gap between them at Ascot was widened to twelve this time as Paisley Park made good progress early in the straight to lead before the last and stayed on strongly up the hill (he was conceding 6 lb to the runner-up after meeting him at level weights in the Long Walk). Third place was filled by one of the top novices of the previous season, Black Op, beaten another two lengths on his return to hurdles after being let down by his jumping in a couple of starts over fences. There was a better showing from Sam Spinner, although he was beaten another ten lengths into fourth. A best-priced 12/1 for the Stayers' Hurdle beforehand, Paisley Park was no bigger than 7/2 after demolishing all the main British opposition in the Cleeve, and his odds shortened still further when Willie Mullins announced that Penhill would be unable to defend his Cheltenham crown.

galliardhomes.com Cleeve Hurdle, Cheltenham—
Ascot runner-up West Approach again fares best of the rest but is beaten much further this time as
Paisley Park cements his Stayers' Hurdle credentials in fine style

By now, Paisley Park's owner Andrew Gemmell had become an integral part of the horse's story and accounted for much of the media interest in the build-up to the Festival. Gemmell has been a life-long and very active sports fan, his interests including football, cricket and tennis (he had to forego an intended trip to the Australian Open to be present for the Cleeve) as well as racing. He grew up with the radio as the main means of following his passion, having been blind since birth. Gemmell nominated racing as the easiest sport for him to attend 'because you have the public address and the commentators all day. The halcyon days of Sir Peter O'Sullevan are long since gone, I'm afraid, but some of the current commentators like Richard Hoiles, and Jim McGrath not so long ago, are very good and can make a big difference to everybody's pleasure, not just mine.'

Gemmell insists that his love of sport is no less strong for not being able to see it. For those who perhaps take being able to see too much for granted, Paisley Park's surge up the Cheltenham straight to win the Stayers' Hurdle belongs with the most stirring conclusions to any race in recent Festival history. The field of eighteen for the Sun Racing-sponsored contest was the second largest this century. Paisley Park was hot favourite, with only the senior runner Faugheen, bidding to become the first former Champion Hurdle winner to win the race, and Supasundae, runner-up the year before, also starting at single-figure odds. Among those at longer prices were Wholestone and Sam Spinner, third and fifth in 2018, the last-named a 33/1 chance this time, having been sent off favourite twelve months earlier. Ridden much more aggressively, Sam Spinner, pressed by Faugheen, led the field over the second last when Paisley Park was still only ninth. But improving from the home turn, Paisley Park made relentless progress up the stand rail to overhaul the two leaders on the run to the last, coming to it with his ears pricked, only to make a bad mistake which gave Sam Spinner half a chance of capitalising. However, with half a furlong to go, Paisley Park began to pull away again and ran out the winner by two and three quarter lengths, with Faugheen another four lengths back in third and another Mullins-trained runner Bapaume completing the frame well clear of the rest in a race which, unlike the year before, was a true test of stamina. Supasundae came only seventh and back in eleventh was Kilbricken Storm, winner of the Spa all that way ahead of Paisley Park twelve months earlier. Paisley Park's trainer had enjoyed success at the Festival before in a couple of handicaps, with Crack Away Jack in the 2008 Fred Winter and Pause And Clause in the 2010 Martin Pipe, while Aidan Coleman had gone ten years since his only other winner still in the record books when Kayf Aramis won the 2009 Pertemps Final. His win on Any Currency in the 2016 Cross Country Chase was expunged when his mount failed a drugs test. 'Although coming down the hill you'd like to be going that little bit better, you do know that when you meet the rising ground you're going to get there,' said Coleman who described Paisley Park's mistake at the last as 'just a bit of complacency'.

Sun Racing Stayers' Hurdle, Cheltenham—
a customary late surge has taken Paisley Park to the front at the last, where a blunder doesn't
prevent him beating Sam Spinner, Faugheen (left) and Bapaume

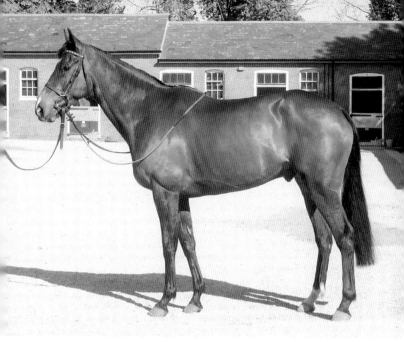

Andrew Gemmell's "Paisley Park"

		Oscar (IRE)	Sadler's Wells	Northern Dancer
Paisley Park (IRE)		(b 1994)	(b 1981)	Fairy Bridge
(b.g. 2012)			Snow Day	Reliance II
			(b 1978)	Vindaria
		Presenting Shares (IRE)	Presenting	Mtoto
		(b 1999)	(br 1992)	D'azy
			Royal Shares	Royal Fountain
			(b 1994)	Four Shares

The well-made Paisley Park was bought as an unbroken three-year-old for €60,000 at the Goffs Land Rover Sale in 2015. His career was apparently close to being ended almost before it had begun as he suffered a life-threatening bout of colic after his only start in a bumper in which he finished second. His Stayers' Hurdle win completed a full set of the Festival's big four championship races for his sire Oscar who has also been responsible for Champion Hurdle winner Rock On Ruby, Queen Mother Champion Chase winner Big Zeb and Gold Cup winner Lord Windermere (Oscar, now retired, finished second in the combined Anglo-Irish sires' table for 2018/19 behind Flemensfirth, with Milan ensuring that Coolmore stallions filled all three places on the podium). Paisley Park is much the best of six winners out of his unraced dam Presenting Shares. Of the rest, Va'vite (by Vinnie Roe), Henry King and Mr Grey (both by Great Palm) were all fairly useful hurdlers. The mare Va'vite stayed three miles, while the latter pair stayed two and a half miles. Henry King also showed fairly useful form over fences without winning, while Mr Grey was also a winning pointer. Presenting Shares is also dam of the fair two and a half mile hurdle winner Society Shares (by Moscow Society), while her latest winner is Present Value (by Gold Well) who looked a good prospect when winning a maiden hurdle at Chepstow in December for Evan Williams. Presenting Shares is a half-sister to the useful Irish staying chaser Priests Leap who was a dual winner of the Thyestes. Grandam Royal Shares was also unraced, and she was out of Four Shares who won four times over hurdles and twice over fences and was a sister to Book of Gold who showed useful form as a novice hurdler.

Paisley Park was put away after Cheltenham with the retention of his Stayers' crown his main aim in 2020. The path to Cheltenham for the top staying hurdlers is well defined, and he is scheduled to return in the Long Distance Hurdle at Newbury, which could be a big day for his owner as Andrew Gemmell is a member of the Makin' Bacon Partnership which owns De Rasher Counter whom Lavelle is aiming at the Ladbrokes Trophy on the same card after the progressive novice won at Uttoxeter on the Saturday after Cheltenham. Effective on soft ground, Paisley Park will be the one to beat in the top staying hurdles again, all the more so since there is probably still further improvement in him. Paisley Park's style of racing—he has shown an occasional tendency to idle—has already drawn comparisons with that of Big Buck's, and, while there's a long way to go before he can rival his record, there could be further reasons for mentioning the two in the same breath if Paisley Park can retain his position as the top staying hurdler for another season. *Emma Lavelle*

PALIXANDRE (FR) 5 b.g. Kapgarde (FR) – Palmeriade (FR) (Kouroun (FR)) [2018/19 b15.7g[5] h19.8s[4] Mar 7] €100,000 3-y-o: has had breathing operation: sixth foal: half-brother to 2 winners in France by Doctor Dino, including 19f hurdle winner Palmerino: dam, French maiden, ran once over hurdles/placed up to 11f on Flat, half-sister to fairly useful hurdler/useful chaser (stayed 27f) Pantxoa: fifth of 7 in bumper at Southwell (6¾ lengths behind Genius): 9/1, fourth in maiden at Wincanton (34 lengths behind Storm Arising) on hurdling debut 10 months later: should do better. *Nicky Henderson* — **h88 p** **b88**

PALMARIA 9 b.m. Kayf Tara – Ollejess (Scallywag) [2018/19 c99, h–: c25.3g[5] May 4] multiple point winner: maiden hurdler: modest form in chases: stays 3m: best form on soft/heavy going: in hood last 3 starts. *Caroline Keevil* — **c90** **h–**

PALMERS HILL (IRE) 6 b.g. Gold Well – Tosca Shine (IRE) (Topanoora) [2018/19 h116: h21g* Nov 18] lengthy gelding: Irish point winner: useful form over hurdles: won handicap at Cheltenham (conditionals, by 1¼ lengths from Unblinking) on sole outing in 2018/19: likely to stay 3m: open to further improvement. *Jonjo O'Neill* — **h131 p**

PALOMA BLUE (IRE) 7 br.g. Stowaway – Court Leader (IRE) (Supreme Leader) [2018/19 h148: c17d[4] c17g* c15.9s[6] Mar 12] lengthy gelding: smart hurdler: useful form over fences: won maiden at Leopardstown (by 6½ lengths from Moon Over Germany) in December: unproven beyond 17f: acts on soft going: usually front runner/races prominently. *Henry de Bromhead, Ireland* — **c142** **h–**

PALOMA ROSA 5 b.m. Native Ruler – Moonlight Babe (USA) (Thunder Gulch (USA)) [2018/19 b15.7g b15.7s Mar 18] first foal: dam no form on Flat: no form in bumpers, trained by Sarah Hollinshead on debut (wore hood). *Jennie Candlish* — **b–**

PANDINUS IMPERATOR (IRE) 6 b.g. Scorpion (IRE) – Casiana (GER) (Acatenango (GER)) [2018/19 h–, b–: h19.9m[5] h20g h25m[5] Oct 4] close-coupled gelding: poor form over hurdles. *Martin Smith* — **h78**

PANIA 5 b.m. Sakhee (USA) – Maori Legend (Midnight Legend) [2018/19 b15.3g[4] Nov 22] fourth foal: dam (c114/h81), 3m/25f chase winner, sister to fairly useful hurdler/chaser (stayed 25f) Winsley Hill: tailed off in bumper. *Neil Mulholland* — **b–**

PANIC AND RUN (IRE) 6 b.g. Roderic O'Connor (IRE) – Bolas (Unfuwain (USA)) [2018/19 b77: h15.8g[5] h16.2g h15.5d[6] h19.6g[4] h21.2d[5] h20.3d[5] Apr 9] fair form over hurdles: should stay 3m. *Henry Daly* — **h100**

PANIS ANGELICUS (FR) 10 b.g. Panis (USA) – Pyu (GER) (Surumu (GER)) [2018/19 h97: h20g[ur] Sep 11] workmanlike gelding: modest hurdler, unseated rider sole outing in 2018/19: stays 3m: acts on soft and good to firm going: has worn visor. *Tim Vaughan* — **h–**

PANKO (IRE) 6 b.g. Iffraaj – Engraving (Sadler's Wells (USA)) [2018/19 h16.3m[2] h15.7g[ur] h16g[6] Nov 12] fairly useful form over hurdles, stays 1¾m: fair form over hurdles: best effort when second in novice at Stratford in September. *Alex Hales* — **h102**

PANTOMIME (IRE) 7 gr.m. Mastercraftsman (IRE) – Dama'a (IRE) (Green Desert (USA)) [2018/19 h–: h16.2g[4] h23.1m[6] h19.9m[3] Sep 6] poor form over hurdles: tried in cheekpieces: in tongue tie last 2 starts. *Rebecca Menzies* — **h78**

PAPAGANA 6 b.m. Martaline – New Destiny (FR) (Highest Honor (FR)) [2018/19 b83:
h15.8g* h20.6g⁴ h19.8v* h18.9v⁴ h19.8s³ h24.4g* Mar 2] workmanlike mare: will make a
chaser: fairly useful form over hurdles: won mares novice at Ffos Las in May, mares
handicap at Sandown in December and listed mares novice at Doncaster (by 12 lengths
from Danse Idol) in March: third in Jane Seymour Mares' Novices' Hurdle at Sandown (3
lengths behind Queenohearts): stays 3m: acts on heavy going: usually races prominently.
Oliver Sherwood **h127**

PAPER PROMISE (IRE) 7 ch.m. Gamut (IRE) – Rose Vic (IRE) (Old Vic) [2018/19
b99: h20v⁵ h16d⁶ h16.4v* Mar 16] good-topped mare: dual bumper winner: modest form
over hurdles: won mares novice at Newcastle in March: should stay further than 2m.
Donald Whillans **h99**

PAPER ROSES (IRE) 8 b.m. Gamut (IRE) – Rose Vic (IRE) (Old Vic) [2018/19 h111:
h16.2s² h19.5d⁴ h16.2v² Mar 14] fair maiden hurdler: stays 2½m: best form on heavy
going. *Donald Whillans* **h107**

PARDON ME 6 ch.m. Tobougg (IRE) – Andromache (Hector Protector (USA)) [2018/19
b86: b15.3m b17g⁶ h15.8d² h19.2v³ h15.3d h17.7dF h16.8d⁶ h20.3d Apr 9] modest form in
bumpers: fair form over hurdles: should prove suited by 2½m: acts on good to soft going.
Seamus Mullins **h103
b80**

PARELLI GOLD 5 ch.m. Schiaparelli (GER) – All My Gold (GER) (Deploy) [2018/19
b17.7g⁶ h16.8gᵖᵘ Oct 1] fifth foal: dam German 10.5f winner: no show in mares bumper/
novice hurdle. *Nigel Hawke* **h–
b–**

PARIS DIXIE 4 b.f. Champs Elysees – Last of The Dixies (Halling (USA)) [2018/19
b13.7m b14g³ ab16.3g³ b17g* Feb 24] second foal: half-sister to a winner on Flat in Italy
by Kyllachy: dam unraced: modest form in bumpers: won mares event at Carlisle in
February. *Julie Camacho* **b81**

PARISIAN AFFAIR 4 b.f. Champs Elysees – Trinkila (USA) (Cat Thief (USA))
[2018/19 b14g b12.6s ab16g² b15.8g⁴ Mar 19] good-topped filly: fifth foal: sister to fair 2m
hurdle winner Elysian Prince and closely related to bumper winner Fforbidden Love (by
Fastnet Rock): dam 8.6f winner: modest form in bumpers. *Neil King* **b75**

PARIS PROTOCOL 6 b.g. Champs Elysees – Island Vista (Montjeu (IRE)) [2018/19
h96p: h16.8s⁵ Feb 21] useful at best on Flat, stays 2m: maiden hurdler, well held sole
outing in sphere in 2018/19. *Mark Walford* **h–**

PARKER (IRE) 5 b.g. Cape Cross (IRE) – Mount Elbrus (Barathea (IRE)) [2018/19 b–:
h16.2m Jun 24] has had breathing operation: little show in bumper/maiden hurdle (wore
tongue tie). *Lucinda Russell* **h–**

PARKIN 5 b.g. Passing Glance – Patacake (Pasternak) [2018/19 b14d⁶ b16g⁵ Feb 15] poor
form in bumpers. *Harry Whittington* **b65**

PARK PHILOSOPHER (IRE) 6 gr.g. Milan – Fantasia Filly (FR) (Dadarissime (FR))
[2018/19 h16.7dF Nov 14] placed in Irish point: behind when fell fatally 2 out in maiden
hurdle at Bangor. *Robin Dickin* **h–**

PARLOUR MAID 8 gr.m. Dr Massini (IRE) – Charliebob (Nomadic Way (USA))
[2018/19 c–, h100: h21d h21.6v⁵ c20d* c19.2s* c19.2v⁵ c19.4d Apr 6] has had breathing
operation: fair handicap hurdler, below form first 2 starts in 2018/19: fair form over fences:
won novice handicap at Lingfield in January and mares handicap at Market Rasen in
February: stays 21f: acts on soft going: wears cheekpieces/tongue tie. *Richard Hawker* **c107
h79**

PARMENTER 4 b.f. Dick Turpin (IRE) – Triple Cee (IRE) (Cape Cross (IRE)) [2018/19
h16.3m² h16.7m³ Aug 5] dam half-sister to fairly useful hurdler/fair chaser (stayed 2½m)
Giocomo: modest maiden on Flat, stays 1¾m: fair form over hurdles: better effort when
second in juvenile at Stratford: in cheekpieces next time: sent to Germany. *Alan King* **h102**

PARODY 5 br.m. Presenting – Arctic Actress (King's Theatre (IRE)) [2018/19 ab16g⁵
b16.6g⁶ Jan 26] £62,000 3-y-o: second foal: half-sister to fair hurdler/winning pointer
Arctic Road (21f/23f winner, by Flemensfirth): dam (h102), bumper/19f hurdle winner,
half-sister to fairly useful hurdlers/useful chasers up to 3m Wee Robbie and Isn't That
Lucky: little impact in bumpers. *Paul Nicholls* **b–**

PARSONAL (IRE) 6 b.g. Oscar (IRE) – Rith Ar Aghaidh (IRE) (Phardante (FR))
[2018/19 h97, b–: h23.3s h23.3s Dec 31] has had breathing operation: placed twice in Irish
points: modest form over hurdles. *Sarah Humphrey* **h87**

PARSONS AVENUE 7 b.g. Grape Tree Road – Kentford Duchess (Jupiter Island) [2018/19 h16.3d Jun 8] tailed off in bumper: finally off mark in points soon after end of
season. *A. Pennock* **b–**

PARTHENIUS (GER) 6 b.g. Soldier Hollow – Princess Li (GER) (Monsun (GER)) **h122**
[2018/19 h109: h16.5g² h16.3m² h16.2g⁵ h16.8m⁵ Sep 6] has had breathing operation:
fairly useful handicap hurdler: raced around 2m: acts on good to firm and good to soft
going: tried in blinkers: in tongue tie last 2 starts: temperament under suspicion.
Dan Skelton

PARWICH LEES 7 ch.g. Pasternak – Barton Dante (Phardante (FR)) [2018/19 h82: **h75**
h23.3d h20g⁵ h20.6gᵖᵘ Jul 8] poor maiden hurdler: should be suited by further than 2m:
tried in cheekpieces. *Neil Mulholland*

PASSAM 7 b.g. Black Sam Bellamy (IRE) – One Wild Night (Rakaposhi King) [2018/19 **h102**
h104, b95: h19.9dᵘʳ h18.9s h23.9s³ h23.9d² Feb 28] bumper winner: fair maiden hurdler:
stays 3m: acts on heavy going: wears tongue tie. *Claire Dyson*

PASSING CALL 6 b.m. Passing Glance – Call Me A Legend (Midnight Legend) [2018/19 **h123**
h116: h20g² h16.8g² h16g* h16.7g* h16.8g* h16.3s³ h16.5d⁴ Dec 30] lengthy mare: fairly
useful hurdler: won mares maiden at Worcester in July, and novice at Bangor and handicap
at Newton Abbot in August: third in listed mares novice at Newbury in December: stays
2½m: acts on soft going: wears cheekpieces: often travels strongly. *Alan King*

PASSING DREAM 6 br.m. Passing Glance – Violet's Walk (Dr Fong (USA)) [2018/19 **h106**
h94p: h15.7g* h16.8gᵘʳ h18.7mᶠ h16g⁴ h15.8g² h16.5d h15.3g h17.7g* Apr 22] fair
hurdler: won mares maiden at Towcester in May and novice handicap at Plumpton in May:
stays 2¼m: best form on good going: in hood last 3 starts: races well off pace.
Seamus Mullins

PASSING OCEANS 5 gr.g. Passing Glance – Sherwood Rose (IRE) (Mandalus) **h78**
[2018/19 h19.5s h16.7s⁴ h19d⁶ h19s h20.3d Apr 9] unplaced in Irish point: poor form over
hurdles. *Neil Mulholland*

PASSING SHADOW 5 b.g. Passing Glance – Peel Me A Grape (Gunner B) [2018/19 **b58**
b15.8d b15.7m Feb 22] poor form in bumpers. *Graeme McPherson*

PASS THE HAT 12 ch.g. Karinga Bay – Moor Spring (Primitive Rising (USA)) [2018/19 **c126**
c20.3g* c20.9v* c21.1dᵖᵘ Apr 4] sturdy gelding: placed in points: winning hurdler: fairly **h–**
useful chaser: won hunters at Southwell in May and Carlisle in March: left D. Holmes after
first start: stays 3m: acts on good to firm and heavy going: wears tongue tie.
Miss Sarah Rippon

PASTORAL MUSIC 6 b.g. Pastoral Pursuits – Jasmeno (Catcher In The Rye (IRE)) **h–**
[2018/19 h98: h15.8g Jul 18] maiden hurdler, no form since debut in 2017/18: sold £1,800.
Donald McCain

PATH TO FREEDOM (IRE) 7 b.g. Mr Dinos (IRE) – Old Kentucky (IRE) (Mandalus) **c114**
[2018/19 c103: c24.2dᵖᵘ c25.2d² Mar 6] multiple point winner, including in 2019: fair form
in chases: best effort when second in novice hunter at Catterick. *Mrs C. A. Coward*

PATIENCE TONY (IRE) 8 b.g. Windsor Knot (IRE) – Johar Jamal (IRE) (Chevalier **h79**
(IRE)) [2018/19 h85: h16.7m⁶ h18.6m³ h16.8s⁵ h19.8g² h20.6dᵖᵘ h19.4g h20.7g h25dᵖᵘ
Mar 3] workmanlike gelding: has had breathing operation: poor maiden hurdler: stays 19f:
acts on good to firm going: has worn cheekpieces, including in 2018/19: sometimes in
tongue tie: usually races close up. *Lucinda Egerton*

PATRICKS PARK (IRE) 8 b.g. Insatiable (IRE) – Rose Gallery (FR) (Gallery of Zurich **c141**
(IRE)) [2018/19 c141p, h90: c22.5d² Aug 1] maiden hurdler: useful handicap chaser: **h–**
second in Galway Plate (6 lengths behind Clarcam) sole outing in 2018/19: stays 23f: acts
on soft and good to firm going: has worn headgear: tried in tongue tie. *W. P. Mullins,
Ireland*

PATRICKTOM BORU (IRE) 12 b.g. Brian Boru – Brehon Law (IRE) (Alphabatim **c91**
(USA)) [2018/19 c114, h106: c22.6d³ Jun 8] prolific winning pointer: winning hurdler: fair **h–**
chaser: stays 3¼m: acts on soft and good to firm going: front runner/races prominently. *R.
W. J. Willcox*

PATSIO (IRE) 11 b.g. Moscow Society (USA) – Supreme Favour (IRE) (Supreme **c–**
Leader) [2018/19 h19d h21g⁶ c16gᶠ h20d h16.5d³ c23.6dᵖᵘ c16.1d Mar 11] fair handicap **h98**
hurdler: fair chaser at best, no form over fences in 2018/19: left J. R. Barry after fifth start:
stays 2½m: acts on heavy going: has worn headgear, including in 2018/19. *David Brace*

PAT'S OSCAR (IRE) 8 b.m. Oscar (IRE) – Coming Home (FR) (Exit To Nowhere **h119**
(USA)) [2018/19 h114: h16d h16s h27d⁴ h19.5dᶠ Feb 6] fairly useful handicap hurdler: in
control when fell last at Ayr in February: likely to prove best up to 3m: acts on heavy going:
in cheekpieces last 3 starts. *Gordon Elliott, Ireland*

PAULS HILL (IRE) 7 b.g. Marienbard (IRE) – Lunar Star (IRE) (King's Theatre (IRE)) c122
[2018/19 h115: c23.6d c26.3g* c20.2m³ c22.7m⁵ c29.2dᵘʳ Mar 10] strong gelding: fairly h–
useful form over hurdles: similar form over fences: won novice handicap at Sedgefield in
November: stays 3¼m: acts on soft going: in headgear last 4 starts: front runner/races
prominently. *Fergal O'Brien*

PAWN STAR (IRE) 9 b.g. Beneficial – Missindependence (IRE) (Executive Perk) c127
[2018/19 c128, h–: c22.6g* Aug 23] smallish gelding: winning hurdler: fairly useful h–
handicap chaser: won at Stratford sole outing in 2018/19: stays 3m: acts on soft and good
to firm going: usually travels strongly. *Emma Lavelle*

PAXMAN (IRE) 5 b.g. Jeremy (USA) – Dreamy Lagoon (IRE) (Bahri (USA)) [2018/19 h83
h19.5s⁶ h16.5dᶠ h15.8s⁶ Feb 26] £110,000 4-y-o: first foal: dam unraced half-sister to
useful hurdler Sivota (stayed 3m) and to dam of smart 2m hurdler Silver Streak: won Irish
point on debut: poor form over hurdles. *Evan Williams*

PC DIXON 6 ch.g. Sixties Icon – Lakaam (Danzero (AUS)) [2018/19 h97: h16.2d² h19.3s c85
h16.4g⁴ h18.1g⁶ h16.8v⁶ c20.9v³ c16.4sᵖᵘ c20.1d⁶ Mar 26] compact gelding: modest h93
handicap hurdler: similar form over fences: stays 21f: acts on heavy going. *Victor Thompson*

PEACEFUL VALLEY (FR) 5 b.m. No Risk At All (FR) – Si Parfaite (FR) (Solon b–
(GER)) [2018/19 b16d Nov 28] £19,000 3-y-o: seventh foal: half-sister to fairly useful
hurdler/useful chaser Sea Wall (2m winner, by Turgeon) and modest 2½m chase winner
Kings River (by Lost World): dam, French maiden, sister to fairly useful French hurdler/
winning chaser up to 21f Si Sol: tailed off in mares bumper. *Lucy Wadham*

PEACHEY (IRE) 5 b.g. Robin des Champs (FR) – Zita Hall (IRE) (Saddlers' Hall (IRE)) h113 p
[2018/19 b16.7g⁵ h15.8g⁴ Nov 24] €50,000 3-y-o: has had breathing operation: fourth foal: b86
dam (h92) 19f hurdle winner: fifth in bumper at Market Rasen (2¼ lengths behind Tokay
Dokey): 14/1, fourth in maiden at Huntingdon (tongue tied, 2½ lengths behind Cervaro
Mix) on hurdling debut: will stay further than 2m: open to improvement. *Olly Murphy*

PEACOCKS SECRET (IRE) 7 b.g. Court Cave (IRE) – Secret Can't Say (IRE) c120
(Jurado (USA)) [2018/19 h96, b105: c16v c21.7g⁵ c17g² h16.7g c24s⁴ c23.5g³ c18.2dᶠ h104
h19g⁶ c20d* c20d* c18.5sᶠ c20d* c16.2d² c20g c20.5s c20s⁵ c22.5dᵖᵘ Apr 23] fair form
over hurdles: fairly useful chaser: won maiden at Wexford in October, novice handicap at
Naas in November and handicap at Punchestown (conditionals) in January: stays 3m: acts
on soft going: wears headgear: usually leads. *John Joseph Hanlon, Ireland*

PEAK TIME 6 ch.g. Distant Peak (IRE) – Redwing (Luso) [2018/19 h20.1s h19.9d⁴ h102
h19.3g h21.2d* Apr 23] second foal: dam unraced: fair form over hurdles: tongue tied, won
handicap at Sedgefield in April. *Rebecca Menzies*

PEAK TO PEAK (IRE) 7 br.g. Authorized (IRE) – Bayourida (USA) (Slew O' Gold h121
(USA)) [2018/19 h123: h21.4gᵖᵘ h21.4s h23.5m³ h21.4gᵖᵘ Apr 14] well-made gelding:
fairly useful handicap hurdler: barely stays 3m: acts on soft and good to firm going.
Paul Nicholls

PEANUTSPONYPETITE (IRE) 6 b.m. Gold Well – Powerlove (FR) (Solon (GER)) h–
[2018/19 b16g b16g⁵ h16m h20g Aug 15] sturdy mare: fourth foal: dam (h94) bumper/3m b–
hurdle winner: no form in bumpers/over hurdles: tried in hood. *Mike Hammond*

PEARL OF THE WEST (IRE) 5 b.m. Teofilo (IRE) – Creese (Halling (USA)) h136
[2018/19 h115p: h16.7m* h16.2g² h16.7g* h16g⁴ h16.4g* h16m Apr 13] sturdy mare:
useful hurdler: won minor events at Bellewstown in July/August and Cheltenham (by 3¼
lengths from Redicean) in October, and handicap at Punchestown (by 1¼ lengths from
Cosmo's Moon) shortly after end of British season: raced around 2m: acts on soft and good
to firm going: wears tongue tie: usually leads. *John McConnell, Ireland*

PEARL ROYALE (IRE) 7 b.m. Robin des Champs (FR) – Dartmeet (IRE) (Presenting) c137
[2018/19 c136p, h–: c20v* c23.4sᵖᵘ c26dᵖᵘ Mar 14] workmanlike mare: winning hurdler: h–
useful form over fences: won listed mares event at Carlisle (by 6 lengths from Rons
Dream) in December: pulled up next 2 starts: stays 2½m: best form on heavy going:
usually front runner/races prominently. *Nigel Hawke*

PEARLS LEGEND 12 b.g. Midnight Legend – Pearl's Choice (IRE) (Deep Run) c127
[2018/19 c128, h–: c19g⁴ c16.5g* c16.5g² c15.8g² Jun 15] rather leggy gelding: winning h–
hurdler: fairly useful handicap chaser: won at Huntingdon in May: stays 2½m: acts on good
to firm and heavy going: has worn cheekpieces, including last 3 starts. *John Spearing*

PEARL SWAN (FR) 11 gr.g. Gentlewave (IRE) – Swanson (USA) (Diesis) [2018/19 c115
c128, h–: c28.5d³ c28.8vᵖᵘ Feb 18] good-topped gelding: winning hurdler: useful handicap h–
chaser at best, laboured effort final start in 2018/19: barely stays 4m: acts on soft going:
wears headgear/tongue tie. *Peter Bowen*

PECULIAR PLACES (IRE) 7 b.g. Presenting – Blu Louisiana (IRE) (Milan) [2018/19 **h112 x** h112, b86: h23.3g² h21.7g² h23.1m^pu Jun 22] has had breathing operation: bumper winner: fair form over hurdles: stays 23f: best form on good going: tried in cheekpieces: in tongue tie last 2 starts: usually let down by attitude/jumping. *Warren Greatrex*

PEDDLER (IRE) 5 b.g. Scorpion (IRE) – Don't Waste It (IRE) (Mister Lord (USA)) **h–** [2018/19 h19.7s Nov 28] tailed off in novice hurdle. *Mark Bradstock*

PEEPING TOM (IRE) 6 b.g. Morozov (USA) – Orcadian Dawn (Alflora (IRE)) **h107** [2018/19 h15.8g³ h19.5v Dec 8] €3,200 3-y-o, £13,000 5-y-o: first foal: dam unraced: Irish point winner: fair form over hurdles: easily better effort when third in novice at Uttoxeter in November: should stay 2½m. *Kim Bailey*

PEGASE AMOUR (IRE) 8 b.g. Winged Love (IRE) – Lovely Native (IRE) (Be My **h95** Native (USA)) [2018/19 h20.2g b18.8g⁶ h20d h23g⁶ h19.5v³ h25m⁴ Apr 20] point winner: **b–** tailed off in maiden bumper: modest form over hurdles: should be suited by further than 19f: acts on heavy going. *Liam Lennon, Ireland*

PEGASUS WALK (IRE) 10 b.g. Beneficial – Porter Tastes Nice (IRE) (Dry Dock) **h–** [2018/19 h20.1s h23.3g h24g Nov 16] point winner: maiden hurdler, no form in 2018/19: tried in blinkers. *Harriet Graham*

PEGGIES VENTURE 8 b.m. Presenting – Peggies Run (Kayf Tara) [2018/19 h114: **h113** h20g⁸ h20d⁴ h20g² h20g⁶ h21m* Apr 25] smallish, sturdy mare: has had breathing operation: fair hurdler: won mares maiden at Worcester in May and handicap at Kempton in April: stays 21f: acts on good and good to firm going: strong traveller. *Alan King*

PEGGY'S ACRE (IRE) 6 b.m. Yeats (IRE) – Lorraine's Secret (IRE) (Desert King **c–** (IRE)) [2018/19 h80, b–: h16s h16g h15.8g c19.5g Jul 14] poor maiden hurdler: tailed off **h58** in maiden on chasing debut: raced mainly around 2m: acted on soft going: retried in hood in 2018/19, wore tongue tie prior to that: dead. *Paul Stafford, Ireland*

PELORIC 4 ch.g. Intello (GER) – New Orchid (USA) (Quest For Fame) [2018/19 b13.7m³ **h100** h16g⁵ h17.7d h16d^F h16.5d³ Dec 30] £5,000 3-y-o: half-brother to several winners, **b82** including fairly useful hurdler Forecast (19f/2½m winner, by Observatory), stays 3m, and fair hurdler Sand Blast (2½m winner, by Oasis Dream): dam useful 1¼m winner: third in junior bumper at Huntingdon (4 lengths behind Carry On): fair form over hurdles: tried in hood/tongue tie: usually races towards rear. *Jeremy Scott*

PELTWELL (IRE) 6 b.m. Milan – Fast Finisher (IRE) (Wizard King) [2018/19 h16.5d **h–** h17.7g³ Apr 24] first foal: dam, unraced, out of half-sister to useful hurdler/smart chaser **b–** (stayed 3m) Risk Accessor: behind in mares bumper/novice hurdle. *Neil Mulholland*

PEMBERLEY (IRE) 6 b.g. Darsi (FR) – Eyebright (IRE) (Zaffaran (USA)) [2018/19 **h102** b76: h16.2g⁵ h15.8d h15.9d⁴ h19.8s² Mar 7] lengthy gelding: fair form over hurdles: will stay 3m. *Emma Lavelle*

PEMBROKE HOUSE 12 gr.g. Terimon – Bon Coeur (Gunner B) [2018/19 c95, h–: **c96** c23.8g* c23.8g² c25.2g² c25.6s⁶ c19.9d⁶ c20v³ c20v⁴ c19.9g³ Apr 11] sturdy gelding: **h–** winning hurdler: modest handicap chaser: won at Ludlow in May: stays 25f: acts on good to firm and heavy going: wears headgear. *Sarah-Jayne Davies*

PENA DORADA (IRE) 12 b.g. Key of Luck (USA) – Uluwatu (IRE) (Unfuwain (USA)) **c–** [2018/19 c89, h–: c25.5m^pu Jun 29] stocky gelding: winning hurdler: fairly useful chaser at **h–** best, pulled up sole outing in 2018/19: stays 3¼m: acts on soft and good to firm going: usually wears headgear. *Alistair Whillans*

PENDRA (IRE) 11 ch.g. Old Vic – Mariah Rollins (IRE) (Over The River (FR)) [2018/19 **c–** c–, h–: c25g⁴ Oct 28] rather plain gelding: has had breathing operation: winning hurdler: **h–** smart handicap chaser at best, lightly raced and little show since only start in 2016/17: stays 3¼m: acts on good to firm and heavy going: wears headgear: in tongue tie last 2 starts. *Charlie Longsdon*

PENGO'S BOY 10 gr.g. Proclamation (IRE) – Homeoftheclassics (Tate Gallery (USA)) **h–** [2018/19 h109: h21.6g Oct 1] rather leggy gelding: fair hurdler at best, well held sole outing in 2018/19: stays 19f: acts on good to soft going: wears hood: held up, often travels strongly. *Richard Hawker*

PENNANT LEGEND 6 b.m. Flying Legend (USA) – Pennant Princess (Alflora (IRE)) **h–** [2018/19 b70: b16g b16g⁵ h15.8d Oct 20] little impact in bumpers: tailed off in mares **b–** maiden on hurdling debut: tried in tongue tie. *Debra Hamer*

PENNEYS HUN (IRE) 6 b.g. Arakan (USA) – De Street (IRE) (Sunshine Street (USA)) **h–**
[2018/19 h109, b88: h16.8m h21.2g⁶ Nov 26] fair hurdler at best, no form in 2018/19: stays
2¼m. *Michael Blanshard*

PENNIES AND POUNDS 12 b.m. Sir Harry Lewis (USA) – Sense of Value (Trojan **c–**
Fen) [2018/19 c–, h–§: h21.6g h21d³ h21.4g Mar 25] poor handicap hurdler: unseated rider **h64 §**
sole outing over fences: stays 2¾m: acts on good to soft going: has worn cheekpieces:
temperamental. *Julian Smith*

PENN LANE (IRE) 8 b.g. Scorpion (IRE) – Belsalsa (FR) (Kingsalsa (USA)) [2018/19 **h128**
h122: h21.9s* h21g h21.4g Feb 16] rangy gelding: has had breathing operation: fairly
useful handicap hurdler: won at Ffos Las in November: stays 2¾m: acts on heavy going.
Warren Greatrex

PENNY JANE (IRE) 7 b.m. King's Theatre (IRE) – Shannon Rose (IRE) (Topanoora) **c132**
[2018/19 c111, h111, b85: c18.2d* c16.7g* c16.5g⁶ Nov 2] fair hurdler: useful handicap **h–**
chaser: won at Galway and Cork (by 2 lengths from Lakemilan) in October: stays 2½m:
acts on heavy going: wears hood. *Gordon Elliott, Ireland*

PENNY MALLOW (FR) 5 b.m. Kapgarde (FR) – Louvisy (FR) (Loup Solitaire (USA)) **b89**
[2018/19 b16g* b16.8g Apr 18] €15,000 3-y-o: second foal: sister to 2m hurdle winner
Kapga de Lily: dam, French 17f/2¼m hurdle/chase winner, half-sister to fairly useful
hurdler/smart chaser (stayed 2½m) Kapga de Cerisy (by Kapgarde): fair form in bumpers:
won maiden at Fakenham in February. *Venetia Williams*

PENNY POET (IRE) 6 b.m. Intikhab (USA) – Mnene (FR) (Ocean of Wisdom (USA)) **h101**
[2018/19 h15.3d² h16.8d h15.3s Mar 7] fair on Flat, stays 1¾m: similar form over hurdles:
best effort when second in mares novice at Wincanton. *Neil Mulholland*

PENSION MADNESS (IRE) 6 b.g. Vocalised (USA) – Grinneas (IRE) (Barathea **h64**
(IRE)) [2018/19 h82: h15.8g⁴ h16.8g⁴ h19.2g Aug 23] compact gelding: poor maiden
hurdler: left Johnny Farrelly after first start: stays 2¼m: acts on good to soft going: has
worn headgear, including in 2018/19. *Mark Shears*

PENTIFFIC (NZ) 16 br.g. Pentire – Sailing High (NZ) (Yachtie (AUS)) [2018/19 c–§: **c105 §**
c26.3g³ May 4] sturdy gelding: point winner: useful chaser at best, still retains some
ability: stays 33f: acts on soft going: has worn headgear, including only start in 2018/19:
unreliable. *P. P. C. Turner*

PENTLAND HILLS (IRE) 4 b.g. Motivator – Elle Galante (GER) (Galileo (IRE)) **h146 p**
[2018/19 h15.9g* h16.8d* h17d* Apr 4]

Nicky Henderson already held the record for the most number of wins in the
Triumph Hurdle and, when Pentland Hills became his seventh winner of the race
in the latest season, it equalled his record total of wins in the Champion Hurdle,
the two races being those in which he has had the most success at the Cheltenham
Festival. Henderson won both races for the first time in 1985, the Champion Hurdle
with See You Then (runner-up in the Triumph the year before) and the Triumph with
First Bout. Henderson's subsequent success in the championship event for juvenile
hurdlers contrasts with the record of another champion trainer Fred Winter, to whom
Henderson had been assistant. Winter never won the Triumph despite saddling the
favourite on more than one occasion and he came to dislike a race which he said
could be 'the ruination of good young horses.' Winter's main misgiving was that
thirty runners—a huge field was the norm in those days—was too many and he
proposed a qualifying system to limit the number of runners. There was a field of
fourteen for the latest Triumph, the much smaller number nowadays being mainly
due to the introduction to the Festival in 2005 of the race that carries Fred Winter's
name, albeit only in its registered title now. Run as the Boodles Juvenile Handicap
Hurdle in the latest season (Winter's name was dropped from the full title for the first
time), the Fred Winter provides an alternative at the Festival for four-year-olds who
previously would have been making up the numbers, or at least faced a stiff task, at
level weights in the Triumph. The Fred Winter is one of the races on the short list,
incidentally, to make way for the new Grade 2 mares chase being introduced at the
Festival in 2021; given that its existence has changed the Triumph Hurdle for the
better, and that it provides a second opportunity for the juvenile hurdlers, it would be
a pity to see the Fred Winter go.

JCB Triumph Hurdle, Cheltenham—a seventh Triumph for Nicky Henderson as 20/1-shot Pentland Hills (right) stays on well to beat fellow outsider Coeur Sublime

Henderson's first Triumph winner had something of a rushed preparation to make it to Cheltenham. First Bout had made his hurdling debut at Plumpton little more than two weeks beforehand and was turned out again at Newbury later the same week to avoid the risk of being balloted out of the Triumph. Winning both his starts ensured him of a place in the line-up and he started 5/1 second favourite in a field of twenty-six others, half starting at 50/1 or longer. Whilst one of the least experienced over hurdles in the line-up, First Bout boasted the best Flat form after enjoying an excellent three-year-old season for Ben Hanbury, winning the Coral Autumn Handicap at Newbury before being sold privately to go jumping. Henderson's second winner Alone Success came along just two years later and, like First Bout, he won both his starts beforehand, also not making his hurdling debut until February. First Bout and Alone Success were typical Triumph winners of the time in being recruited domestically from the Flat (Alone Success had been a maiden in Ireland). But by the time Henderson won the race for a third time in 1999, things had changed and France was starting to become popular as a source of top juveniles. Katarino, Zaynar, Soldatino and Peace And Co were Henderson's next four Triumph winners, all of them bred across the Channel. The Aga Khan-bred Zaynar was the exception among them in coming off the Flat, but the rest all had jumping experience of one sort or another in France. Soldatino in 2010 had been another late starter for Seven Barrows, not entering the Triumph Hurdle picture until winning the Adonis Juvenile at Kempton on his British debut less than three weeks beforehand. Henderson looked to have another leading contender for the latest Triumph when Fusil Raffles won the same race on his first start since coming from France, but he was forced to miss Cheltenham after sustaining a nasty cut at Kempton.

The two most recent Triumph winners, Defi du Seuil and Farclas, had also begun their careers in France but Pentland Hills was something of a throw-back to Henderson's first two winners of the race in the 'eighties. He had been a fairly useful handicapper for Chris Wall, winning a couple of times at around a mile and a half at Yarmouth and Windsor. Besides increased domestic opportunities, and bigger prizes on the all-weather over the winter nowadays, there is a thriving export market for middle-distance types, many destined for Australia or the Middle East. These factors have reduced the domestic pool of horses that traditionally supplied Triumph Hurdle candidates. But Pentland Hills' wins were gained off BHA marks of just 65 and 69 which perhaps explains why he wasn't snapped up to go abroad. Like some of his stable's other Triumph winners, his debut over hurdles was a belated one at the end of February, coincidentally at the corresponding Plumpton meeting at which First Bout had also won, all those years earlier. There is no longer a juvenile hurdle on that card, though, and Pentland Hills made his hurdling debut instead against mainly older rivals in a maiden contest which he won in fine style by fourteen lengths from odds-on The Flying Sofa, quickening clear after the second last. Unlike with First Bout, there was no time, or any need, for Pentland Hills to have another run before Cheltenham and he started at 20/1 for the JCB-sponsored Triumph in a market dominated by the 11/10 Irish-trained favourite Sir Erec. Third in the Long Distance Cup at Ascot on his final Flat start for Aidan O'Brien, Sir Erec had won both his starts over hurdles for Joseph O'Brien, including the Spring Juvenile Hurdle at Leopardstown in impressive fashion by six lengths from stable-companion Gardens of Babylon who joined him in the Triumph line-up. Among three representing Paul Nicholls, French recruit Quel Destin was well backed at 4/1 to keep the prize at home, having won his last five races. Besides Pentland Hills, Henderson also fielded the 16/1 chance Adjali, another who had begun his career in France, and had run Quel Destin to a neck in the Finale Juvenile Hurdle at Chepstow in December.

The complexion of the Triumph altered suddenly when the favourite met a sad end, going wrong soon after jumping the fourth flight where he was close up behind the pace being set by Quel Destin. The latter lasted in front until after two out where 20/1-shot Coeur Sublime, bidding to give Gordon Elliott a second consecutive win in the race after Farclas, took over in front going well. However, from further back after surviving a blunder at the first, Pentland Hills improved under Nico de Boinville to take the lead soon after the final flight and stayed on well for a three-length win over Coeur Sublime, with Gardens of Babylon keeping on well to take third, three and a quarter lengths behind the runner-up. Quel Destin faded into fifth, while Adjali, who had improved to challenge entering the straight, was another to weaken late on, finishing seventh. Despite his lack of experience jumping hurdles in public, both trainer and rider praised Pentland Hills' professionalism, his early schooling having been done under the expert eye of Henrietta Knight. 'He knows exactly what he is doing and settles well, which is nice,' said de Boinville afterwards. 'Usually, these Flat horses come and they are really revved up and used to running over a mile or a mile and a half. He is so settled and his jumping is his main asset.' Not for the first time, the Triumph was won by a large band of owners, the three thousand-plus members of 'Owners Group 031' being a spin-off of the hugely successful Elite Racing Club in whose colours Penzance won the 2005 renewal. Another high-profile horse to carry the mauve, black chevrons on sleeves, black cap of another of the Owners Group syndicates in the latest season was the novice Getaway Trump for Paul Nicholls.

Doom Bar Anniversary 4-Y-O Juvenile Hurdle, Aintree—Pentland Hills (left) reels in Fakir d'Oudairies to become just the sixth horse to complete this Cheltenham-Aintree double in 44 years

The ill-fated Sir Erec, whose demise rather overshadowed the aftermath of the Triumph, had headed a particularly strong team of juveniles from the O'Brien stable which won the Fred Winter with Band of Outlaws and was represented by another four-year-old, Fakir d'Oudairies, in the Supreme in which he had finished fourth, starting as joint favourite. Although Pentland Hills looked to have marginally the best form, the O'Brien pair were slightly shorter in the betting when the three met in the Doom Bar Anniversary 4-Y-O Juvenile Hurdle at Aintree, with Band of Outlaws 9/4, Fakir d'Oudairies 5/2 and Pentland Hills 11/4. The only beaten horse from the Triumph to take on Pentland Hills again in a field of nine was his stablemate Adjali. Doubtless due to Sir Erec's accident, Pentland Hills had perhaps not been given full credit for what he achieved at Cheltenham and he followed up in similar fashion to become the fifth Triumph winner this century (sixth in all), after Detroit City, Katchit, Zarkandar and Defi du Seuil, to follow up at Aintree. Fakir d'Oudairies set out to make it a good test of stamina but Pentland Hills, who took more of a hold than he had done at Cheltenham, made smooth headway before leading after the last, winning by a neck with a bit in hand. Christopher Wood, winner of both his previous starts for Paul Nicholls, was another six lengths back in third, ahead of Adjali and the disappointing Band of Outlaws. Henderson had won the Anniversary twelve months earlier with We Have A Dream, who had had to miss Cheltenham, with his other success in the race coming with Binocular in 2008 who had finished second in the Supreme beforehand. That was it for Pentland Hills' season, but Adonis winner Fusil Raffles was fit again for Punchestown where he represented the stable in the Champion Four Year Old Hurdle and gave a bigger beating to Fakir d'Oudairies than Pentland Hills had done at Aintree.

There cannot be many broodmares who can boast winning offspring at both Royal Ascot and the Cheltenham Festival. Elle Galante has now achieved that as she was already the dam of the 2015 King Edward VII Stakes winner Balios (by

Owners Group 031's "Pentland Hills"

Shamardal). Pentland Hills is Elle Galante's sixth winner on the Flat; the only one previously to have gone on to win over jumps is the versatile Camlann (by Cape Cross), a fairly useful hurdler who won twice over fences in Ireland early in the latest season, showing useful form, before finishing first past the post back on the Flat at the Galway Festival. By Galileo out of a champion filly/mare in Germany, Elle Galante didn't quite live up to her breeding but she was useful and won three times in Germany at up to fifteen furlongs. Her own dam Elle Danzig won twelve races, all bar one of them pattern races, among them both of Germany's fillies' classics and two editions of the Premio Roma, then still a Group 1. Elle Danzig went on to be equally prolific as a broodmare, with Elle Galante one of her eleven winners. The others included the smart filly Elle Shadow, second in the Preis der Diana (the German Oaks), and several useful performers, including Asyad, third in the Park Hill Stakes for Sir Michael Stoute, and El Vip, a mile to mile and a quarter winner for Luca Cumani. Another of her useful Flat winners, Lyric Street, went on to be a fairly useful hurdler at up to two and a half miles for Donald McCain in the colours of former Timeform handicapper Matthew Taylor.

Pentland Hills (IRE) (b.g. 2015)	Motivator (b 2002)	Montjeu (b 1996)	Sadler's Wells
			Floripedes
		Out West (br 1994)	Gone West
			Chellingoua
	Elle Galante (GER) (b 2003)	Galileo (b 1998)	Sadler's Wells
			Urban Sea
		Elle Danzig (b 1995)	Roi Danzig
			Elegie

The sturdy Pentland Hills, bought for 40,000 guineas as a yearling, is by Derby winner Motivator who will always be best known as the sire of dual Arc winner Treve. However, Motivator's own sire Montjeu has been particularly influential in the Triumph Hurdle in recent years. As well as siring the 2016 winner Ivanovich Gorbatov, two more of his sons, Authorized and Jukebox Jury, are responsible for other recent winners, Tiger Roll and Farclas respectively. Montjeu's best jumper was dual Champion Hurdle winner Hurricane Fly who was also the last Champion Hurdle winner to have begun his career on the Flat. Pentland Hills will need to improve a good deal further if he is to keep his unbeaten record in top open company. None of Henderson's previous Triumph winners won the Champion Hurdle (Zaynar went closest, third to stablemate Binocular a year later), though two of his Champion Hurdle winners had previously made the frame in the Triumph, See You Then, already mentioned, and Punjabi who was fourth in the Triumph two years before winning the Champion. *Nicky Henderson*

PEPPAY LE PUGH (IRE) 8 b.g. Arakan (USA) – Pinaflore (FR) (Formidable (USA)) [2018/19 c91§, h91§: c17g* c16.4m* c16.2g^f c17.8s² c16.5g* c18.8m³ c15.9g³ c15.7g² c16.4g* c16.5g² h16.6d* h16.7g² h16.3g⁴ c16.5m* c15.9m² Apr 20] workmanlike gelding: fair hurdler: won novice at Doncaster in March: useful handicap chaser: won at Stratford in August, Sedgefield (novice) in September, Worcester in October, Doncaster in November and Ayr (novice, by 6 lengths from Niven) in April: stays 19f: acts on good to firm and heavy going: has worn headgear: wears tongue tie: races freely held up (5 of 6 wins for Harry Skelton): has joined Jack O. Fisher in USA. *Dan Skelton*   **c130 h113**

PEPPERDEW (USA) 5 ch.g. Street Cry (IRE) – Spice Island (USA) (Tabasco Cat (USA)) [2018/19 b16.8g h18.6d⁴ h21.2d⁶ Mar 21] tailed off in bumper: poor form over hurdles. *Sarah-Jayne Davies*   **h75 b–**

PEPPER STREET (IRE) 4 b.f. Born To Sea (IRE) – Mindy (IRE) (Zamindar (USA)) [2018/19 h16d³ h16.3s⁶ Dec 19] fair on Flat, stays 1¾m: modest form over hurdles: better effort when third in juvenile maiden at Wetherby in November. *Amy Murphy*   **h88**

PERCY PROSECCO 4 b.g. Sir Percy – Grapes Hill (Kingsalsa (IRE)) [2018/19 h15.8m* h16g⁴ h16g⁴ h16s^{pu} h17.7m Mar 29] close-coupled gelding: fair on Flat, stays 2m: similar form over hurdles: won juvenile at Huntingdon in October: will stay 2½m: acts on good to firm going. *Noel Williams*   **h104**

PERCY STREET 6 br.g. Sir Percy – Star of Gibraltar (Rock of Gibraltar (IRE)) [2018/19 h111§: h16.7g³ h19d⁴ h15.5g² h16.5d⁴ h16.3d⁴ h21.4g⁴ Apr 3] compact gelding: fair   **h112 §**

handicap hurdler: left Nicky Henderson after first start: stays 21f: acts on good to firm and good to soft going: has worn headgear, including in 2018/19: ungenuine. *David Pipe*

PERCY'S WORD 5 b.g. Sir Percy – Laverre (IRE) (Noverre (USA)) [2018/19 h16.3d² Dec 29] compact gelding: useful on Flat, stays 2m: 16/1, showed plenty when second in introductory event at Newbury (4½ lengths behind Champagne Platinum) on hurdling debut: will improve. *Dan Skelton*   **h110 p**

PERCY THROWER (IRE) 5 ch.g. Sir Percy – Dayrose (Daylami (IRE)) [2018/19 h–: h16.7g⁶ h20g⁵ h18.5m Jul 14] modest form over hurdles. *Sarah-Jayne Davies*   **h85**

PERCY VEER 7 ch.g. Sir Percy – Fandangerina (Hernando (FR)) [2018/19 h19d³ h22g^ur h24g* h21g* h24d⁵ h21g³ Nov 16] neat gelding: fairly useful on Flat, stays 21f: useful hurdler: won maiden at Listowel in September and listed novice at Limerick (by 3 lengths from Calie du Mesnil) in October: third in Hyde Novices' Hurdle at Cheltenham (5¼ lengths behind Coolanly) final outing: stays 3m: acts on heavy going. *Eric McNamara, Ireland*   **h130**

PEREGRINE RUN (IRE) 9 b.g. King's Theatre (IRE) – Masriyna's Article (IRE) (Definite Article) [2018/19 c141, h–: c22.5d c20.1g* h24.4m² c20m³ c23d* c19.5g⁴ h23.3g² c21.1dᶠ Apr 5] good-topped gelding: useful chaser: smart chaser: won handicap at Killarney (by 5½ lengths from Kilcarry Bridge) in August and listed event at Wexford (by 8 lengths from Dinaria des Obeaux) in October: third in PWC Champion Chase at Gowran (15½ lengths behind Woodland Opera) earlier in October: barely stays 3m: acts on soft going: wears blinkers: often travels strongly. *Peter Fahey, Ireland*   **c151** **h125 +**

PERFECT CANDIDATE (IRE) 12 b.g. Winged Love (IRE) – Dansana (IRE) (Insan (USA)) [2018/19 c153, h–: c25g c27.3g^pu c22.3g⁶ c26.3d³ c26d^pu c26g⁵ Apr 17] strong gelding: winning hurdler: useful handicap chaser nowadays: third at Cheltenham (13 lengths behind Beware The Bear) in January: stays 27f: acts on heavy going: has worn headgear, including last 4 starts: has worn tongue tie. *Fergal O'Brien*   **c132 h–**

PERFECT LEADER (IRE) 9 b.g. Let The Lion Roar – Peace Leader (IRE) (Supreme Leader) [2018/19 c19.9g⁴ h16.2g h24g c18m⁵ c16d c21.5s c16.2d² c20dᶠ c16.3g⁴ c17d* c15.2g³ Mar 29] modest maiden hurdler, below form in 2018/19: modest handicap chaser: won at Leopardstown in March: stays 2½m: acts on good to soft going. *Ms Margaret Mullins, Ireland*   **c96 h64**

PERFECT LEGEND 8 b.g. Norse Dancer (IRE) – Flamjica (USA) (Real Quiet (USA)) [2018/19 h20g^pu Jun 27] little impact on Flat/in points: pulled up in maiden on hurdling debut. *Polly Gundry*   **h–**

PERFECT MAN (IRE) 8 b.g. Morozov (USA) – Garrisker (IRE) (King's Ride) [2018/19 h23.1g* h26.5g³ h23.9d h23.1g⁵ h25g⁶ h23.3d⁴ h23.3v³ Mar 16] rather leggy gelding: maiden pointer: fairly useful handicap hurdler: won at Market Rasen in August: out-and-out stayer: acts on heavy going: has worn headgear, including last 5 starts: wears tongue tie: usually races towards rear. *Olly Murphy*   **h121**

PERFECT MOMENT (IRE) 6 b.m. Milan – Faucon (Polar Falcon (USA)) [2018/19 b80: b17.7g² h16g h16d⁵ h15.9s⁶ h17.7vᶠ h20.5g Apr 22] leggy, lightly-built mare: poor form in bumpers: modest form over hurdles. *Michael Roberts*   **h90 b72**

PERFECT MYTH 5 b.m. Midnight Legend – Perfect Silence (Dansili) [2018/19 b81: b15.8g⁵ b15.7g h16d³ h15.8d⁴ h15.3s³ Mar 7] has had breathing operation: modest form in bumpers/on Flat: fair form over hurdles: best effort when third in mares novice at Fakenham in December: front runner/races prominently. *Harry Whittington*   **h102 b83**

PERFECT PIRATE 7 b.g. Black Sam Bellamy (IRE) – Supreme Gem (IRE) (Supreme Leader) [2018/19 c124§, h–: c25g c26.1d^pu h26d⁴ h27d⁵ h24.2d³ h26g⁵ Apr 10] compact gelding: fair handicap hurdler nowadays: fairly useful chaser at best, no form over fences in 2018/19: stays 3¼m: acts on heavy going: has worn headgear, including last 5 starts: temperamental. *Ben Pauling*   **c– §** **h112 §**

PERFECT POISON (IRE) 11 b.g. Vinnie Roe (IRE) – Noddys Confusion (IRE) (Supreme Leader) [2018/19 h23.3g h23.1g⁴ Oct 30] fair handicap hurdler: maiden chaser, often let down by jumping: stays 25f: acts on good to firm and good to soft going: has worn cheekpieces. *Donald McCain*   **c– x** **h99**

PERFECT PREDATOR 4 b.g. Passing Glance – Cosmea (Compton Place) [2018/19 b15.3g b14g² b16.5d* b15.3g² Apr 14] sturdy gelding: fourth foal: half-brother to 3 winners, including fairly useful hurdler Cosmeapolitan (2m winner, by Mawatheeq) and   **b101**

fair hurdler Sula Island (17f winner, by Sulamani): dam (h117), 2m hurdle winner, also 1¼m-11.6f winner on Flat: fairly useful form in bumpers: won at Taunton in February. *Alan King*

PERFECT SUMMER (IRE) 9 b.m. High Chaparral (IRE) – Power of Future (GER) (Definite Article) [2018/19 h95: h21.6g³ h23.3v⁶ h23.8g⁵ Jan 17] compact mare: fair handicap hurdler: stays 2¾m: acts on good to firm and heavy going: usually wears headgear: usually races prominently. *Ian Williams* **h102**

PERFECT TIMING 11 b.g. Shantou (USA) – Winnetka Gal (IRE) (Phardante (FR)) [2018/19 c121, h–: c19.2m⁵ c19.2g³ c20.1g² c24.1gᵘʳ c23.8g Sep 27] strong gelding: maiden hurdler: useful handicap chaser: stays 3m: acts on good to firm and heavy going: wears headgear: tried in tongue tie. *Neil Mulholland* **c119**
h–

PERFORM (IRE) 10 b.g. King's Theatre (IRE) – Famous Lady (IRE) (Presenting) [2018/19 c–, h–: c24.2g c24.2s⁴ c25.1d³ c26.7g³ c26dᵖᵘ Mar 2] strong gelding: winning hurdler: fairly useful maiden chaser: stays 25f: acts on heavy going: tried in cheekpieces. *Philip Hobbs* **c124**
h–

PERLE'S AN ICON 5 b.m. Sixties Icon – Kahooting (Kahyasi) [2018/19 h17.7dᵖᵘ h20.7g Feb 21] second foal: dam unraced out of useful 2m-2¼m hurdle winner Perle de Puce: no form over hurdles. *Charlie Longsdon* **h–**

PERMISSION GRANTED (IRE) 7 b.g. Oscar (IRE) – Ask The Misses (IRE) (Supreme Leader) [2018/19 h88: h20.2g⁶ h20.9g³ h19.3g h24g⁵ h20.2d Apr 26] has had breathing operation: poor maiden hurdler: should stay 3m: best form on good going. *Rose Dobbin* **h75**

PERSEID (IRE) 9 br.g. Robin des Pres (FR) – Cowanstown Miss (IRE) (Presenting) [2018/19 c101, h89: h22.1g h22.1g³ h25.4m⁴ h22.1g⁶ h21.2m h20.9g h23.8g h22g h19.9d⁶ Jan 11] medium-sized gelding: has had breathing operation: poor handicap hurdler: maiden chaser: stays 3m: acts on soft and good to firm going: tried in headgear/tongue tie: usually races close up. *Barbara Butterworth* **c–**
h71

PERSHING 8 gr.g. Mount Nelson – La Gandilie (FR) (Highest Honor (FR)) [2018/19 c–, h111: h16g⁶ h15.8g⁵ h20.3d Apr 24] fair hurdler at best, no form in 2018/19: once-raced chaser: has worn headgear, including in 2018/19: has worn tongue tie: usually races off pace. *Kevin Frost* **c–**
h–

PERSHING MISSILE (IRE) 7 b.g. Milan – Banbury Cross (IRE) (Supreme Leader) [2018/19 h102, b89: h19.9d h23.3sᵖᵘ h23.1dᵖᵘ Jan 17] has had breathing operation: maiden hurdler, no form in 2018/19: tried in cheekpieces/tongue tie. *Graeme McPherson* **h–**

PERSIAN SNOW (IRE) 13 b.g. Anshan – Alpine Message (Tirol) [2018/19 c–, h–: c20.9dᵖᵘ Jun 8] good-topped gelding: winning hurdler: useful chaser at best, little show since 2016/17: wears tongue tie: front runner/races prominently. *Philip Hobbs* **c–**
h–

PERSISTANTPRINCESS (IRE) 7 b.m. Scorpion (IRE) – Classy Conflict (IRE) (Close Conflict (USA)) [2018/19 h–: h20m⁴ h23m h23.1s c24g³ Apr 13] point winner: poor form over hurdles: 25/1, in cheekpieces when third in novice handicap at Bangor (26 lengths behind Change Ur Tune) on chasing debut: stays 3m: acts on good to firm going. *David Rees* **c65**
h75

PERSONAL COACH (FR) 6 b.g. Motivator – Castellina (USA) (Danzig Connection (USA)) [2018/19 b91: b16.8g⁴ h16.3m⁴ h20gᵖᵘ h16m Sep 17] fair form at best in bumpers: no form over hurdles: left Robert Stephens after first start: tried in hood. *David Dennis* **h–**
b75

PERUVIEN BLEU (FR) 7 b.g. Fuisse (FR) – Edelmira (FR) (Kahyasi) [2018/19 h122: h15.8m² h16.3m⁶ h16.7mᵖᵘ h15.8d⁶ h15.8m³ h15.7m³ Apr 20] fairly useful handicap hurdler: raced around 2m: acts on soft and good to firm going: has worn tongue tie, including in 2018/19: usually races off pace: temperament under suspicion. *Mrs Jane Williams* **h125**

PETAPENKO 8 b.g. Archipenko (USA) – Tricoteuse (Kris) [2018/19 c–, h91: h15.7g⁵ c17.1gᵖᵘ May 27] workmanlike gelding: maiden hurdler/chaser, no form in 2018/19: unproven beyond 17f: acts on good to soft going: has worn blinkers, including last 3 starts. *Pauline Robson* **c–**
h–

PETERBOROUGH (FR) 6 b.g. Fuisse (FR) – Peony Girl (FR) (Phantom Breeze) [2018/19 b–: h16.8g³ h15.7g² h16g h16.8s⁸ h15.3g h15.7m Apr 20] Irish point winner: fair form over hurdles: won handicap at Exeter (conditionals) in November: raced around 2m: acts on soft going: usually front runner/races prominently. *Evan Williams* **h107**

PETERS COUSIN (IRE) 6 b.m. Presenting – Sunwake (GER) (Tiger Hill (IRE)) **h109**
[2018/19 b90: h16d² h20.9g* h19.5d³ h16.6d² h23.1g⁴ h20.2g Apr 24] bumper winner: fair
form over hurdles: won novice at Kelso in December: should stay further than 21f: acts on
good to soft going: tried in hood. *Nicky Richards*

PETER'S PORTRAIT (IRE) 6 b.g. Portrait Gallery (IRE) – Fancyfacia (IRE) (Luso) **h108**
[2018/19 h19.7gᶠ h23.3d⁴ Mar 30] £37,000 5-y-o: fifth foal: half-brother to a winning
pointer by Vertical Speed: dam unraced: Irish point winner: fair form over hurdles.
Charlie Longsdon

PETER THE MAYO MAN (IRE) 9 ch.g. Dylan Thomas (IRE) – Mommkin (Royal **c143**
Academy (USA)) [2018/19 c145, h–: c18gᵖᵘ c16.5mᶠ Sep 17] strong gelding: winning **h–**
hurdler: useful chaser: looked set to go close when fell last in handicap at Worcester in
September: left Paul Nicholls after first start: stays 19f: acts on good to firm and good to
soft going. *Dan Skelton*

PETE'S CHOICE (IRE) 6 b.g. Arcadio (GER) – Definite Design (IRE) (Definite **c–**
Article) [2018/19 b16v h20.5gᵖ h20.5s h15.9s³ h19.5d³ h19.7gⁱ Feb 25] first foal: **h87**
dam (b71), showed little in bumpers, sister to fairly useful 19f chase winner Clouded **b–**
Thoughts: well beaten in 2 Irish points: tailed off in bumper: modest form over hurdles:
tailed off in novice on chasing debut: usually in cheekpieces. *Zoe Davison*

PETE THE FEAT (IRE) 15 b.g. King's Theatre (IRE) – Tourist Attraction (IRE) **c129**
(Pollerton) [2018/19 c133, h–: c24.2v c24.2s³ c24.2dᵖᵘ c24.2dᶠ Mar 8] angular gelding: **h–**
winning hurdler: useful handicap chaser: third at Sandown (amateurs) in December: stays
29f: acts on heavy going: wears tongue tie. *Charlie Longsdon*

PETITE GANACHE (IRE) 7 ch.g. Presenting – Ain't Misbehavin (IRE) (Trempolino **c99**
(USA)) [2018/19 h69: h21.4g³ h23.3gᵘʳ h23.9gᶠ h23.9g³ h22g* h25g⁵ c20.9m² Apr 20] **h95**
good-topped gelding: modest handicap hurdler: won at Newcastle in January: 6/5, second
in novice handicap at Carlisle (1¾ lengths behind Roll of Thunder) on chasing debut: stays
3m: acts on good to firm going: wears headgear. *Nicky Richards*

PETITE JACK 6 ch.g. Champs Elysees – Pilcomayo (IRE) (Rahy (USA)) [2018/19 **h97 p**
h16.6g⁴ h16d h16.3d³ Jan 16] useful form on Flat, stays 12.5f: modest form over hurdles:
remains capable of better. *Neil King*

PETITE POWER (IRE) 10 b.g. Subtle Power (IRE) – Little Serena (Primitive Rising **c–**
(USA)) [2018/19 c123, h–: c26.1g May 27] smallish gelding: winning hurdler: fairly useful **h–**
chaser, little show only outing in 2018/19: stays 29f: acts on heavy going: has worn
cheekpieces: wears tongue tie. *Fergal O'Brien*

PETITIONER (IRE) 5 b.g. Dansili – Reflective (USA) (Seeking The Gold (USA)) **h95**
[2018/19 h16.6g⁴ h19.9s⁴ Mar 3] fairly useful on Flat, stays 1½m: modest form over
hurdles. *John Davies*

PETIT MOUCHOIR (FR) 8 gr.g. Al Namix (FR) – Arnette (FR) (Denham Red (FR)) **c–**
[2018/19 c159+, h–: h16g⁶ h16g³ h24d h20d⁴ Apr 22] good-topped gelding: high-class **h155**
hurdler: in cheekpieces, back near best when 4¼ lengths fourth to Buveur d'Air in
Punchestown Champion Hurdle shortly after end of British season: very smart form over
fences: unproven beyond 17f: acts on heavy going: has worn hood. *Henry de Bromhead,
Ireland*

PETIT PALAIS 4 ch.g. Champs Elysees – Galicuix (Galileo (IRE)) [2018/19 h15.8d* **h117**
h16m⁵ h16.3g* h16.3g* Apr 27] compact gelding: fairly useful 1½m winner on Flat: fairly
useful form over hurdles: won juvenile at Ludlow in January and novice at Stratford in
March: likely to prove best at around 2m. *Tom George*

PETIVILLE (FR) 7 gr.g. Montmartre (FR) – Aegle (IRE) (Night Shift (USA)) [2018/19 **c112**
h117: h24.7gᵖᵘ c20dᵘʳ c23.4g³ c24.5g² c29.2d c23.8g³ Apr 24] compact gelding: fairly **h–**
useful hurdler: fair form over fences: stays 25f: acts on good to soft going: tried in tongue
tie: usually races off pace. *Richard Hobson*

PETRIFY 9 b.g. Rock of Gibraltar (IRE) – Frigid (Indian Ridge) [2018/19 h59: h15.3m⁶ **h76**
h18.5m³ h21.6g* h16.8g³ h22m³ h21.6g* h23.3g h18.5g Oct 1] poor handicap hurdler:
won at Newton Abbot in July (selling event) and September: stays 2¾m: acts on good to
firm going: wears cheekpieces/tongue tie. *Bernard Llewellyn*

PETRONELLA MANNERS 6 b.m. Shirocco (GER) – Last of Her Line (Silver **h101**
Patriarch (IRE)) [2018/19 h108, b76: h15.8d h21.6g h19.4g² h20.6g⁵ h20.7d Mar 13]
sturdy mare: fair maiden hurdler: stays 21f: acts on good to soft going: in cheekpieces last
3 starts. *Henry Daly*

PETROU (IRE) 9 b.g. Mountain High (IRE) – Evnelu (IRE) (Old Vic) [2018/19 c136, h118: c19.9g³ c25g² h26.5g⁶ c23.8g⁶ Jul 31] fairly useful handicap hurdler: useful handicap chaser: second at Aintree (1¼ lengths behind Ballyboker Breeze) in June: stays 25f: acts on heavy going: has worn headgear, including in 2018/19: usually races nearer last than first, often travels strongly. *Dan Skelton* — **c136 h116**

PETTICOAT TAILS 7 b.m. Presenting – Theatre Girl (King's Theatre (IRE)) [2018/19 h121: h20g⁴ h21.6g² h20.3s³ h23.5d⁴ h24.3g² Feb 16] lengthy mare: has had breathing operation: fairly useful hurdler: second in Rendlesham Hurdle at Haydock (8 lengths behind Shades of Midnight) in February: stays 3m: acts on heavy going: has worn cheekpieces, including last 3 starts. *Warren Greatrex* — **h127**

PEUR DE RIEN (FR) 6 b.g. Kapgarde (FR) – Tango Princess (FR) (Fabulous Dancer (USA)) [2018/19 h115, b–: h19m h19.7g h15.5d⁴ h18.5s⁴ h21s Mar 10] sturdy gelding: fair maiden hurdler: stays 19f: acts on soft going. *Oliver Sherwood* — **h100**

PHANGIO (USA) 10 ch.g. Invasor (ARG) – Muneera (USA) (Green Dancer (USA)) [2018/19 c99, h83: c26.1g⁴ c25.8g⁴ c23m h25.5g Nov 5] sturdy gelding: poor hurdler: modest handicap chaser: stays 29f: acts on good to firm and heavy going: wears headgear/tongue tie: usually races prominently. *Matt Sheppard* — **c91 h–**

PHANTOM ISLE 6 b.g. Teofilo (IRE) – Antillia (Red Ransom (USA)) [2018/19 h82, b77: h21.4g May 7] has had breathing operation: placed in bumper: poor form over hurdles: has joined Rebecca Menzies. *Chris Grant* — **h71**

PHARAWAY VIEW 5 br.m. Beat All (USA) – High Park Lady (IRE) (Phardante (FR)) [2018/19 b–: b16g⁵ h15.8g⁶ Jun 6] no form in bumpers: tailed off in maiden on hurdling debut. *David Bridgwater* — **h– b–**

PHOBIAPHILIAC (IRE) 8 b.g. Beneficial – Denys Eyre (IRE) (Eurobus) [2018/19 c109, h–: h16.7g May 19] sturdy gelding: fairly useful hurdler at best, well held sole outing in 2018/19: fair form over fences: stays 2½m: acts on good to firm going: usually wears hood: often races freely. *Nicky Martin* — **c– h–**

PHOEBUS LESCRIBAA (FR) 7 b.g. Policy Maker (IRE) – Mia Lescribaa (FR) (Saint des Saints (FR)) [2018/19 c98, h98: c20.3g⁵ h20g⁶ h24.1g^pu Apr 11] sturdy gelding: Irish point winner: modest maiden hurdler: similar form in chases: left Fergal O'Brien after second start, though rejoined that yard for 2019/20 season: stays 19f: acts on good to firm and good to soft going: tried in hood. *Olly Murphy* — **c90 h85**

PHOENICIAN STAR (IRE) 4 ch.g. Mastercraftsman (IRE) – Place de L'Etoile (IRE) (Sadler's Wells (USA)) [2018/19 h16d⁶ h16g⁶ h18.7s* Mar 11] has had breathing operation: fair maiden on Flat, stays 1½m: fairly useful form over hurdles: won juvenile at Stratford in March: will prove suited by 2½m+: will go on improving. *Fergal O'Brien* — **h118 p**

PHOENIX DAWN 5 b.g. Phoenix Reach (IRE) – Comtesse Noire (CAN) (Woodman (USA)) [2018/19 h119: h16.5g⁶ h15.9g* h16d⁵ Oct 13] lengthy gelding: fairly useful handicap hurdler: won at Plumpton in September: unproven beyond 2m: acts on soft and good to firm going: wears headgear: often in tongue tie: usually leads. *Brendan Powell* — **h119**

PHOENIX FIREBIRD 6 b.m. Flying Legend (USA) – Flamebird (IRE) (Mukaddamah (USA)) [2018/19 h81: h15.3d^pu Dec 26] little impact in bumper/over hurdles. *Nigel Hawke* — **h–**

PHOENIX PARK (GER) 7 b.g. Sholokhov (IRE) – Piercetown (IRE) (Germany (USA)) [2018/19 h–: h20g^pu Jul 17] has had breathing operation: maiden pointer: little form over hurdles: tried in cheekpieces: has worn tongue tie. *David Dennis* — **h–**

PHOENIX RIVER 5 b.g. Phoenix Reach (IRE) – Griselina (IRE) (Mandalus) [2018/19 b–: b16g ab16g⁵ Nov 27] lengthy gelding: no form in bumpers. *Paul Webber* — **b–**

PHOENIX ROCK (IRE) 7 br.m. Winged Love (IRE) – Guillaume Rock (IRE) (Definite Article) [2018/19 h74: h24g⁴ h23g⁴ h23g h23g⁶ c22.6g^su c27.5g⁶ Apr 14] poor maiden hurdler: similar form over fences: has worn headgear. *Jonjo O'Neill* — **c68 h70**

PHOENIX SONG 6 b.g. Phoenix Reach (IRE) – Temple Heather (Faustus (USA)) [2018/19 b16g⁵ b15.7s h20.5g^pu h19.5d h21g⁵ Apr 10] poor form in bumpers/over hurdles: in blinkers last 2 starts. *John O'Neill* — **h69 b71**

PHOENIX WAY (IRE) 6 b.g. Stowaway – Arcuate (Arch (USA)) [2018/19 h16.7d⁵ h16v² h20.5d* Jan 6] £15,000 3-y-o, £270,000 5-y-o: tall, rather unfurnished gelding: third foal: dam unraced half-sister to useful hurdler (stayed 2½m) Castlemorris King: easy winner of Irish point: fairly useful form over hurdles: won novice at Plumpton in January: remains open to improvement. *Harry Fry* — **h119 p**

PHYSICAL POWER (IRE) 4 b.f. Power – Street Shaana (FR) (Darshaan) [2018/19 h15.9g⁵ h17.7m⁴ h16g⁶ᵖᵘ Oct 31] half-sister to fairly useful French 2¼m hurdle winner Sourabad (by Halling): fair maiden on Flat, stays 1¼m: poor form over hurdles. *Neil Mulholland*   **h78**

PICCALILLI PIE 5 b.m. Weetman's Weigh (IRE) – Piece of Pie (Contract Law (USA)) [2018/19 b16.4g h15.7gᵖᵘ h16g h16.8sᵖᵘ Feb 21] third foal: dam unraced: behind in bumper: no form over hurdles. *Sam England*   **h– b–**

PICCOLO RAMOSCELLO 6 b.m. Malinas (GER) – Dusky Dancer (Ziggy's Dancer (USA)) [2018/19 b16.7v b14d Dec 19] first foal: dam unraced: no form in bumpers. *Lisa Williamson*   **b–**

PIC D'ORHY (FR) 4 b.g. Turgeon (USA) – Rose Candy (FR) (Roli Abi (FR)) [2018/19 h17.4s² h17.9s* c17.4sᶠ h17.9s² h17.9s² h16.8d Mar 15] close-coupled gelding: half-brother to fairly useful French hurdler/useful chaser Eclair Gris (15f-21f winner, by Fairly Ransom) and French 2¼m hurdle winner Forsus (by Great Pretender): dam unraced: smart hurdler: won juvenile at Auteuil in September: second in Prix Aguado in June, Prix Georges de Talhouet-Roy in October and Prix Cambaceres in November, all at same course: fell in juvenile there on chasing debut: left Francois Nicolle, disappointing when only tenth of 14 in Triumph Hurdle at Cheltenham: stays 2¼m: acts on heavy going: has worn tongue tie. *Paul Nicholls*   **c– p h145**

PICKAMIX 8 gr.g. Sagamix (FR) – Star of Wonder (FR) (The Wonder (FR)) [2018/19 c131, h120: c23.9g⁴ c23.8g² c25.8m* c25.5g² c24.4g⁴ c25.2gᵖᵘ Nov 23] rather leggy gelding: fairly useful hurdler: useful handicap chaser: won at Newton Abbot in July: second at Warwick in September: stays 3¼m: acts on good to firm and good to soft going: in visor last 4 starts: wears tongue tie: front runner/races prominently: temperament under suspicion. *Charlie Mann*   **c133 h–**

PICKNICK PARK 7 b.g. Sulamani (IRE) – Eva's Edge (IRE) (Good Thyne (USA)) [2018/19 h92: h20.6g⁶ h18.6g⁴ h20.6s c20.3d⁴ c17.2d² c19.2g⁵ Mar 20] close-coupled gelding: modest maiden hurdler: similar form over fences: stays 19f: acts on soft going: in cheekpieces last 3 starts: front runner/races prominently. *Nick Kent*   **c87 h80**

PICKS FLIGHT 4 br.g. Aeroplane – Picks Magic (Medicean) [2018/19 b15.7m² Feb 22] first foal: dam unraced: 20/1, second in bumper at Catterick (¾ length behind Floating Rock). *Micky Hammond*   **b97**

PICTURE PAINTER (IRE) 6 gr.g. Zoffany (IRE) – Sisceal (Dalakhani (IRE)) [2018/19 h104: h21.7g h16.5d h19.5dᵖᵘ h19.5m² Apr 22] fair handicap hurdler: stays 2½m: acts on good to firm and good to soft going: has worn headgear, including last 5 starts: tried in tongue tie. *David Pipe*   **h105**

PICTURE YOUR DREAM 4 ch.f. Kheleyf (USA) – Another Sunset (Doyen (IRE)) [2018/19 ab16.3g Jan 5] had breathing operation prior to debut: first foal: dam unraced: in tongue tie, 66/1, last of 7 in bumper: modest form on Flat in 7f minor events. *Lucinda Egerton*   **b–**

PIECEOFTHEACTION (IRE) 6 br.g. Oscar (IRE) – Homebird (IRE) (Be My Native (USA)) [2018/19 b84: h24.3d⁴ h20.6g⁵ h20.1v² h20.1d h24.1g⁵ Apr 11] multiple point winner: fair form over hurdles: stays 2½m: acts on heavy going. *Chris Grant*   **h104**

PIERLOW (IRE) 10 ch.g. Double Eclipse (IRE) – Dooleys Daughter (IRE) (Mister Lord (USA)) [2018/19 c20.3g⁴ c17.8m⁶ May 27] winning hurdler/chaser for Henry de Bromhead: fit from points (little show), modest form at best over fences in 2018/19: stays 2½m: acts on good to firm and good to soft going: has worn cheekpieces, including in 2018/19. *Diana Grissell*   **c85 h–**

PILANSBERG 7 b.g. Rail Link – Posteritas (USA) (Lear Fan (USA)) [2018/19 h24.2d h21.6s h21.4g⁶ h21.2d h19d³ Feb 28] compact gelding: has had breathing operation: fair handicap hurdler nowadays: stays 2¾m: best form on good going: wears headgear/tongue tie. *Paul Nicholls*   **h110**

PILEON (IRE) 5 b.g. Yeats (IRE) – Heath Heaven (Alflora (IRE)) [2018/19 b16.8d* Mar 24] £60,000 4-y-o: fourth foal: dam, lightly raced in points, half-sister to useful hurdler (stayed 2½m) That's A Wrap out of half-sister to dam of Cheltenham Gold Cup winner Long Run: runner-up on second of 2 starts in Irish points: well-backed 2/1, won bumper at Exeter by 4½ lengths from Story of Friends: open to improvement. *Philip Hobbs*   **b99 p**

PILGRIM SOUL 4 b.f. Yeats (IRE) – Sabah (Nashwan (USA)) [2018/19 h16d⁴ h16m h16.2g³ h15.8g⁴ h16.8g Apr 18] closely related to fairly useful 2m/17f hurdle winner Roserrow (by Beat Hollow): fairly useful maiden on Flat, stays 1½m: modest form over hurdles: will prove best around 2m (free-going sort): tried in hood/tongue tie. *Kerry Lee*   **h92**

PINCH OF GINGER (IRE) 8 ch.g. Golden Lariat (USA) – Espiritu Santo (IRE) (Trans Island) [2018/19 c100, h90: c23.8s² c27.5g^{pu} Apr 14] maiden hurdler: modest chaser: stays 3m: acts on heavy going: has worn headgear: front runner/races prominently. *Donald McCain* **c98 h—**

PINEAPPLE RUSH 6 b.m. Kayf Tara – Celtic Native (IRE) (Be My Native (USA)) [2018/19 h120, b100: h20g⁵ h20d h21.4g² h21.2d Feb 6] tall mare: has had breathing operation: fairly useful hurdler: will be suited by 3m: acts on heavy going. *Philip Hobbs* **h116**

PINE MOSS 6 b.rm. Shirocco (GER) – Pochard (Inchinor) [2018/19 b15.7g Jun 5] second foal: half-sister to bumper winner Emperor Sakhee (by Sakhee): dam (h105), 2½m-23f hurdle winner, half-sister to fairly useful hurdler (stayed 3m) Habitual Dancer: well beaten in mares bumper. *Lucy Wadham* **b—**

PINE WARBLER 10 b.g. Pilsudski (IRE) – Cetti's Warbler (Sir Harry Lewis (USA)) [2018/19 c99, h—: c24s² c24.2v c26.2d Mar 20] has had breathing operation: maiden hurdler: maiden chaser: stays 3m: best form on soft/heavy going: wears cheekpieces/tongue tie. *Stuart Edmunds* **c100 h—**

PINGLEY LAD 6 b.g. Jamaican Flight (USA) – Worlaby Rose (Afif) [2018/19 b15.7s³ b16.6g b16.7g⁵ Mar 14] poor form in bumpers: tried in hood. *Charles Pogson* **b64**

PINGSHOU (IRE) 9 b.g. Definite Article – Quest of Passion (FR) (Saumarez) [2018/19 c15.9g⁴ c15.5s⁵ h15.7d⁵ h16.8d Mar 15] rangy gelding: smart hurdler at best, behind last 2 outings in 2018/19: fairly useful form over fences: stays 2½m: acts on soft going: tried in blinkers/tongue tie: should do better as a chaser. *Colin Tizzard* **c120 p h—**

PINK EYED PEDRO 8 b.g. Dr Massini (IRE) – Poacher's Paddy (IRE) (Jurado (USA)) [2018/19 c96: c27.5d^{pu} c20.9g³ c20g⁴ c19.2g³ c21.6s² h19.5g⁶ c23.6g* Apr 26] prolific point hunter, including in 2018/19: poor form only start over hurdles: fair chaser: won novice hunter at Chepstow in April: stays 3m: acts on good to firm going: has worn hood/tongue tie, including in 2018/19: often travels strongly. *David Brace* **c111 h81**

PINK GIN 11 ch.g. Alflora (IRE) – Miss Mailmit (Rakaposhi King) [2018/19 c107, h—: c24.2g⁴ c23.5v⁶ c25.1g* c24.2v⁴ c25.1g⁴ Mar 3] workmanlike gelding: winning hurdler: fair handicap chaser: won novice event at Wincanton in January: stays 25f: acts on heavy going: wears tongue tie. *Nigel Twiston-Davies* **c107 h—**

PINK LEGEND 5 b.m. Midnight Legend – Red And White (IRE) (Red Ransom (USA)) [2018/19 b16.7g⁶ h19.9v⁶ h16.7d² h15.7d* h16.5g h16.7d³ Apr 26] third foal: half-sister to modest hurdler Pink Tara (2½m winner, by Kayf Tara): dam (h96), maiden hurdler, 6f winner on Flat: sixth in mares bumper at Bangor: fair form over hurdles: won mares novice at Catterick in March: should stay 2½m: acts on good to soft going: usually front runner/races prominently. *Venetia Williams* **h114 b68**

PINK ROCK (IRE) 5 b.m. Westerner – Eliane di Rupette (Cosmonaut) [2018/19 b16.4g Nov 17] strong mare: fourth foal: sister to useful hurdler/chaser Azorian (2½m winner): dam (b72) ran once in bumper: 20/1, tenth in listed mares bumper at Cheltenham (18¾ lengths behind The Glancing Queen). *Eoin Griffin, Ireland* **b—**

PINK SHEETS (IRE) 5 b.m. Gold Well – Soft Skin (IRE) (Rudimentary (USA)) [2018/19 b16d² Feb 6] €4,500 3-y-o: sixth foal: half-sister to fairly useful 21f hurdle winner Yellow Dockets (by Getaway) and a winning pointer by Gamut: dam unraced: fell in point: 11/2, second in mares bumper at Ayr (6 lengths behind Arion Sky): has joined Mick Channon. *Shane Nolan, Ireland* **b86**

PINNACLE PEAK 4 b.g. Passing Glance – Giovanna (Orpen (USA)) [2018/19 b16.3s Mar 11] 16/1, seventh in maiden bumper at Stratford (6¼ lengths behind Now Is The Winter). *Martin Keighley* **b85**

PINO BOY (IRE) 5 b.g. Scorpion (IRE) – Lisagore Lady (IRE) (Indian Danehill (IRE)) [2018/19 b18.1g b16g h16d h20.5g⁵ h20.2g h20.2d h23.3g^f h19.6g h24.6s Apr 26] no form in bumpers: poor maiden hurdler: in cheekpieces last 2 starts: usually races off pace. *Mrs Ann Mooney, Ireland* **h73 b—**

PINSPOT 5 ch.g. Presenting – Amber Cloud (Lomitas) [2018/19 h16.2g⁴ b16.2g⁵ h16.2g⁶ h16v h16.2g h22g³ h23.8m⁵ h27s^f Mar 21] £8,000 3-y-o: has had breathing operation: first foal: dam (h97) bumper/2m hurdle winner out of useful 2m-3m hurdle winner Diamant Noir: modest form in bumpers/over hurdles: stays 3m: acts on good to firm going: in cheekpieces last 2 starts: in tongue tie last 5. *Lucinda Russell* **h90 b82**

PIQUE ROCK 7 b.m. King's Theatre (IRE) – Flutter Bye (IRE) (Alflora (IRE)) [2018/19 h—: c22.6d⁴ h19.6g* h21.2g* h21.2g³ h24.4g⁴ c19.1g³ c20.2f² c19.9g* c16.3g⁴ Apr 18] close-coupled mare: fair form over hurdles: won mares novices at Bangor and Ludlow in **c121 h112**

October: fairly useful form over fences: won handicap at Huntingdon in April: left Philip Rowley after first start: stays 21f: acts on firm going: wears hood: usually front runner/races prominently. *Henry Daly*

PIRATE LOOK (IRE) 5 b.g. Canford Cliffs (IRE) – Gerika (FR) (Galileo (IRE)) [2018/19 h104: h19.2g h18.7g Oct 8] compact gelding: fairly useful on Flat, stays 1¼m: fair form over hurdles in 2017/18, little impact in handicaps since: tried in cheekpieces. *Martin Keighley* h–

PIRI MASSINI (IRE) 8 b.g. Pierre – Lady Doctor (IRE) (Dr Massini (IRE)) [2018/19 h117: c20s c25.2g^F Jan 1] Irish point winner: fairly useful form over hurdles: well held completed start in chases: stayed 3m: acted on heavy going: tried in cheekpieces: dead. *Olly Murphy* c–
h–

PIROLO (IRE) 7 ch.g. Teofilo (IRE) – Zavaleta (IRE) (Kahyasi) [2018/19 h–: h15.3m h17g^3 h15.7g h16.8g h23g^6 Sep 28] has had breathing operations: poor maiden hurdler: in headgear last 2 starts: wears tongue tie. *Nigel Hawke* h78

PISTOL (IRE) 10 b.g. High Chaparral (IRE) – Alinea (USA) (Kingmambo (USA)) [2018/19 c–, h107§: h17.1g h16.2s h17.1v^4 h24.3s^4 h17g^2 h25d^4 Mar 24] useful-looking gelding: fair handicap hurdler: maiden chaser: stays 3m: acts on heavy going: has worn headgear: in tongue tie last 3 starts: untrustworthy. *John Dixon* c–
h98 §

PISTOL PARK (FR) 8 b.g. Poliglote – Pistolera (GER) (Monsun (GER)) [2018/19 c133, h–: c16.5d^3 Nov 3] has had breathing operation: winning hurdler: useful handicap chaser, folded tamely sole outing in 2018/19 (retried in cheekpieces): stays 2½m: acts on heavy going: in tongue tie last 5 starts. *Brian Ellison* c94
h–

PISTOL WHIPPED (IRE) 5 b.g. Beneficial – Holiday Time (IRE) (Turtle Island (IRE)) [2018/19 h16.3s^3 h20g* h19.8s^{pu} Mar 8] €35,000 3-y-o, £110,000 4-y-o: first foal: dam unraced half-sister to useful chaser (stayed 3m) Ballinvarrig (by Beneficial): runner-up completed start in Irish points: fairly useful form over hurdles: won novice at Fakenham in February: remains with potential. *Nicky Henderson* h124 p

PITON PETE (IRE) 8 b.g. Westerner – Glenair Lucy (IRE) (Luso) [2018/19 h118: c18.8g^5 c20d^{ur} c23.6d^3 c20d* c20.1g^4 Apr 25] sturdy gelding: fairly useful hurdler: useful form over fences: won novice at Carlisle (by 23 lengths from Elixir du Gouet) in March: stays 3m: acts on heavy going. *Oliver Sherwood* c131
h–

PIVOTAL FLAME (IRE) 6 b.m. Pivotal – Saadiah (IRE) (Dubai Destination (USA)) [2018/19 h91: h16g Nov 12] sparely-made mare: fair on Flat, stays 13f: modest maiden hurdler: raced only at 2m: acts on good to soft going: usually races towards rear. *Pat Phelan* h79

PIXIEPOT 9 b.m. Alflora (IRE) – Folly Foster (Relkino) [2018/19 h99: h18.6g^3 Jun 1] modest handicap hurdler: stays 21f: acts on good to firm and heavy going: has worn cheekpieces: front runner/races prominently. *Peter Niven* h93

PLACEDELA CONCORDE 6 b.g. Champs Elysees – Kasakiya (IRE) (Zafonic (USA)) [2018/19 h–: h16.2g* h16.2g^3 h16.2g* h16.2g^2 h16.2g^4 h17.2d h19.9m^2 h20.1g^3 h17g^3 h19.7g^6 Nov 17] fair hurdler: won novices at Kelso in May and Perth in July: stays 2½m: acts on good to firm going: wears tongue tie. *Maurice Barnes* h107

PLAISIR D'AMOUR (FR) 7 b.m. Linngari – Analfabeta (FR) (Anabaa (USA)) [2018/19 h129, h–: c24g^6 May 23] good-topped mare: winning hurdler: useful chaser at best, behind sole outing in 2018/19: stays 3m: acts on heavy going. *Venetia Williams* c–
h–

PLAN AT THE MINUTE (IRE) 6 b.m. Getaway (GER) – Skipping Along (IRE) (Anshan) [2018/19 b15.7d^{pu} Apr 9] Irish point winner: pulled up in bumper: dead. *Phil Middleton* b–

PLANET NINE (IRE) 7 b.g. Flemensfirth (USA) – Old Moon (IRE) (Old Vic) [2018/19 h122p: h24.3d^5 Nov 3] fairly useful hurdler, below form sole outing in 2018/19: stays 25f: acts on soft going: tried in hood. *Rose Dobbin* h102

PLAN OF ESCAPE (IRE) 6 ch.g. Presenting – Pilgara (IRE) (Pilsudski (IRE)) [2018/19 h16g^6 h16.2g Apr 15] second foal: dam unraced half-sister to smart hurdler/high-class chaser (stayed 2¾m) Woolcombe Folly (by Presenting): placed in Irish points: modest form over hurdles: will be suited by at least 2½m. *Martin Todhunter* h85

PLANSINA 4 b.f. Planteur (IRE) – Sina (GER) (Trans Island) [2018/19 h16.2d^{pu} h15.8g^6 Apr 11] fair on Flat, stays 9f: poor form over hurdles: in hood second start. *Tom Symonds* h71

PLANTAGENET 7 b.g. Midnight Legend – Marsh Court (Overbury (IRE)) [2018/19 c107, h104: c23.6g^{pu} h25g^3 h23.1m^2 h24.5g^2 c23d* c26g^2 c25.7g* c31.7s^{pu} c30.7s^F Apr 16] angular gelding: fair handicap hurdler: fairly useful handicap chaser: won novice event c118
h102

at Taunton in December and amateurs race at Plumpton in February: stays 3¼m: acts on good to firm and heavy going: has worn headgear, including in 2018/19: usually front runner/races prominently. *Seamus Mullins*

PLATINUM BEN (IRE) 7 br.g. Beneficial – Justines Joy (IRE) (Taipan (IRE)) [2018/19 **b79** b17g May 18] point winner: in hood, 40/1, ninth in bumper at Aintree (15 lengths behind Rob The Getaway). *N. W. Padfield*

PLAYA BLANCA (IRE) 4 b.g. Zoffany (IRE) – Aiming Upwards (Blushing Flame **h107** (USA)) [2018/19 h17.7v h16g h16d³ h16v h15.8d* h15.7m Mar 31] lengthy gelding: half-brother to fairly useful 3m hurdle winner Easy Gold (by Mastercraftsman): fair maiden on Flat, stays 7f: similar form over hurdles: won maiden at Huntingdon in March: unproven beyond 2m: acts on good to soft going. *Seamus Mullins*

PLAYING GAMES 6 b.m. Pastoral Pursuits – Flirtatious (Generous (IRE)) [2018/19 **b—** ab16s Jan 4] rather unfurnished mare: fourth foal: half-sister to bumper winner/fairly useful hurdler Canoodle (2m winner, by Stimulation) and bumper winner Trigger Point (by Double Trigger): dam lightly-raced half-sister to very smart 2m hurdler Marble Arch: tailed off in bumper. *Hughie Morrison*

PLAYIT AGAIN HARRY 6 b.g. Tobougg (IRE) – Sunshine Rays (Alflora (IRE)) **b—** [2018/19 b16g Oct 24] tailed off in bumper. *Warren Greatrex*

PLAY PRACTICE 9 b.m. Josr Algarhoud (IRE) – More Flair (Alflora (IRE)) [2018/19 **h—** h78: h22.1g^{pu} May 30] point winner: maiden hurdler, pulled up sole outing in 2018/19. *James Walton*

PLAY THE ACE (IRE) 10 b.g. Scorpion (IRE) – Henris Blaze (IRE) (Be My Native **c131** (USA)) [2018/19 c136: c21g⁶ c19.9g^{pu} h21.6g⁴ h20m* h20g² h24g* c23.8g h21g⁶ c21.4g² **h120** c23.8m c23.8g⁴ Apr 25] fairly useful form over hurdles: won novices at Worcester in July and Southwell in September: useful handicap chaser: second at Market Rasen (3¼ lengths behind Royal Village) in October: stays 3m: acts on good to firm and heavy going: wears cheekpieces/tongue tie: usually front runner/races prominently. *Mickey Bowen*

PLAY THE GAME (IRE) 6 b.g. Lawman (FR) – Neutral (Beat Hollow) [2018/19 h118: **h131** h16v⁵ h16.7m⁴ h17m* h17d Aug 24] useful handicap hurdler: won at Killarney (by ½ length from Line Out) in July: raced around 2m: acts on good to firm and heavy going. *T. Gibney, Ireland*

PLEASANT COMPANY (IRE) 11 b.g. Presenting – Katie Flame (IRE) (Alderbrook) **c—** [2018/19 c152, h—: h24g c25s c34.3g^{ur} Apr 6] tall gelding: maiden hurdler: smart chaser at **h—** best, runner-up in Grand National at Aintree in 2017/18: prominent until unseated 4 out in latest renewal of race: stays 4¼m: acts on heavy going: has worn hood, including in 2018/19: tried in tongue tie. *W. P. Mullins, Ireland*

PLENEY 5 b.g. Martaline – Knock Down (IRE) (Oscar (IRE)) [2018/19 b15.7g⁴ b16.3g **h94** h19.7g h19.3g h23.6d h19.5g⁴ Apr 26] €60,000 3-y-o: half-brother to 3 winners, including **b83** fairly useful hurdler/chaser Hello Sweetie (2m-2¼m winner, by Westerner) and bumper winner/fairly useful hurdler Carries Darling (2½m winner, by Flemensfirth): dam (c121/ h131), 2m-2½m hurdle/chase winner, sister to smart/moody hurdler/chaser (stays 29f) Buachaill Alainn: modest form in bumpers/over hurdles. *Tim Vaughan*

PLENTY OF BUTTY (IRE) 6 b.g. Germany (USA) – Jump For Joy (IRE) (Liboi **h—** (USA)) [2018/19 h—, b—: h16.2g h21.7g^{pu} h21g^{pu} Apr 10] no form: tried in hood/tongue tie. *Michael Scudamore*

PLUS JAMAIS (FR) 12 b.g. Caballo Raptor (CAN) – Branceilles (FR) (Satin Wood) **c—** [2018/19 c125, h96: h21.4v^{pu} c20.1s⁶ h20.5d c22.9d Mar 20] sturdy gelding: fair hurdler/ **h—** fairly useful chaser at best, no form in 2018/19: usually wears headgear. *Iain Jardine*

PLUS ONE (IRE) 7 b.g. Winged Love (IRE) – Balwaney (FR) (Exit To Nowhere (USA)) **c109** [2018/19 h115: c21.6d³ c25.5s^{pu} h26g^{pu} Apr 10] Irish point winner: fairly useful form over **h—** hurdles, pulled up final outing (blinkered) in 2018/19: fair form over fences: easily better effort when third in novice handicap at Fontwell: should be suited by 3m: acts on good to soft going. *Ben Pauling*

PLYMOUTH SOUND 7 b.g. Fastnet Rock (AUS) – Shardette (IRE) (Darshaan) **h—** [2018/19 h16g^{pu} h16.8g Sep 1] fairly useful at one time on Flat, stays 1½m: no form over hurdles: wears headgear. *Bernard Llewellyn*

POBBLES BAY (IRE) 9 b.g. Oscar (IRE) – Rose de Beaufai (FR) (Solon (GER)) **c133** [2018/19 c119, h—: h23.9v³ c28.4g^{ur} c28.4d^F c28.4s² c27.9g* Apr 21] good-topped gelding: **h114** fairly useful handicap hurdler: useful handicap chaser: won at Ffos Las (by 1½ lengths from Kingswell Theatre) in April: stays 3½m: acts on heavy going: usually races off pace. *Evan Williams*

POETIC LADY (IRE) 8 b.m. Yeats (IRE) – Apollo Lady (Alflora (IRE)) [2018/19 h108: h— h19.9gᵖᵘ h21.6v Oct 12] fair hurdler at best, no form in 2018/19: stays 2¾m: acts on soft and good to firm going: wears headgear/tongue tie. *Neil Mulholland*

POETIC PRESENCE (IRE) 9 b.m. Presenting – Johnston's Crest (IRE) (Be My Native c– § (USA)) [2018/19 c71§, h71§: h22.1gᵖᵘ May 30] point winner: poor maiden under Rules: h— § has worn headgear: tried in tongue tie: front runner/races prominently: temperamental. *Stuart Coltherd*

POETIC RHYTHM (IRE) 8 ch.g. Flemensfirth (USA) – Sommer Sonnet (IRE) (Taipan c103 (IRE)) [2018/19 h138: c19.4dᵖᵘ c24.2m² Nov 2] strong gelding: point winner: useful h— hurdler: disappointing both starts in chases: should be suited by 3m: acts on heavy going: races prominently. *Fergal O'Brien*

POET'S CHARM (IRE) 5 b.g. Poet's Voice – Antillia (Red Ransom (USA)) [2018/19 h71 h78: h16.8g⁴ h16.8g⁵ h16g⁶ Jun 24] poor maiden hurdler: raced around 2m: wears hood: races well off pace. *Martin Hill*

POET'S REFLECTION (IRE) 4 b.f. Dylan Thomas (IRE) – Lola's Reflection h— (Presenting) [2018/19 b16.8d b16d h21.4g⁴ Apr 3] fifth foal: dam unraced: well beaten in b— bumpers/novice hurdle. *Linda Blackford*

POGO I AM 5 b.m. Passing Glance – Orbital Orchid (Mujahid (USA)) [2018/19 b15.8s⁶ b89 b17.7g² b15.8d³ Mar 30] second foal: sister to 2m Flat winner Sir Pass I Am: dam (h109) temperamental 2m hurdle winner: fair form in bumpers, placed 2 of 3 starts. *Harry Fry*

POGUE (IRE) 6 gr.g. Stowaway – Night Palm (IRE) (Great Palm (USA)) [2018/19 h109 h19.6v³ h16.2d² h19.3d² Mar 24] £100,000 5-y-o: fourth foal: dam, unraced, out of half-sister to Coral Cup winner Big Strand: Irish point winner: fair form over hurdles, placed all 3 starts. *Donald McCain*

POINT BREAK (IRE) 5 b.g. Westerner – Pertinent Point (IRE) (Barathea (IRE)) h112 [2018/19 b18d⁵ b16g³ b16.7m⁴ b16m⁶ b16d³ h16.4g⁶ h16.4g³ h16.4s² h16.2g³ Feb 14] b87 €55,000 3-y-o: fourth foal: dam winning pointer: fair bumper performer: similar form over hurdles: left E. U. Hales after first start, T. E. Hyde after fifth: tried in headgear: in tongue tie last 3 starts: often travels strongly. *Ann Hamilton*

POINTED AND SHARP (IRE) 7 b.g. Scorpion (IRE) – Leamybe (IRE) (Religiously c– (USA)) [2018/19 h113: h16.8g⁵ h19.2m⁴ h21.7g c20sᶠ h19d c20.2gᶠ Mar 25] lengthy h109 § gelding: fair handicap hurdler: fell both starts over fences: stays 19f: acts on soft and good to firm going: usually wears hood: ungenuine. *Philip Hobbs*

POINT N SHOOT (IRE) 8 b.g. Broadway Flyer (USA) – Ali's Dipper (IRE) (Orchestra) c– x [2018/19 c–x, h100: h23.1sᵖᵘ h23d⁵ h27s³ h27g⁴ h24dᵖᵘ Apr 24] fair handicap hurdler: won h106 at Sedgefield in April: let down by jumping over fences: stays 27f: acts on heavy going: wears headgear/tongue tie. *Nigel Hawke*

POINT OF DEPARTURE (IRE) 8 b.g. Mahler – Miranda's Lace (IRE) (Bach (IRE)) c86 [2018/19 h19.5s h21.2dᵖᵘ c21.2d² c23.8sᵖᵘ Apr 7] Irish point winner: modest form on h— hurdling debut, little show first 2 starts in 2018/19: modest form over fences: easily better effort when second in novice handicap at Fakenham: stays 23f: acts on good to soft going: in cheekpieces last 2 starts: temperament under suspicion. *Peter Bowen*

POINT OF PRINCIPLE (IRE) 6 b.g. Rip Van Winkle (IRE) – L'Ancresse (IRE) h139 (Darshaan) [2018/19 h133, b89: h19.5d² h21g⁵ h19.9v h20d² Apr 5] sturdy gelding: bumper winner: useful handicap hurdler: second in Grade 3 at Aintree (1¾ lengths behind Three Musketeers) in April: should stay 3m: acts on soft going: races prominently. *Tim Vaughan*

POINT TAKEN (IRE) 5 b.g. Papal Bull – Grand Isla (Selkirk (USA)) [2018/19 h16.3d h96 p h15.8d h15.3g⁴ Feb 27] has had breathing operation: won 10.5f Flat maiden on debut: modest form over hurdles: best effort when fourth in novice at Wincanton: better to come. *Dan Skelton*

POISON ARROW (IRE) 5 b.g. Scorpion (IRE) – Lobatica (GER) (Acatenango (GER)) b91 [2018/19 b16.8v² b16v⁴ b16.8dᵖᵘ Feb 22] fair form in bumpers: best effort when second at Newton Abbot on debut: dead. *Nicky Martin*

POKARI (FR) 7 ch.g. Bonbon Rose (FR) – Pokara (FR) (Kutub (IRE)) [2018/19 h85p: h90 h16.3g⁶ h18.5g² h16.5d Dec 13] angular gelding: bumper winner: modest form over hurdles. *Alan Jones*

POKER PARTY (FR) 7 ch.g. Gentlewave (IRE) – Becquarette (FR) (Nombre Premier) **c139**
[2018/19 c17d⁵ c16d⁶ c21sᵘʳ c16.3s⁵ c21g² c20d* c20g* Feb 24] half-brother to smart **h—**
French hurdler/useful chaser Storminator (17f-19f winner, by Stormy River) and fairly
useful French hurdler/useful chaser Pokerdor (17f winner, by Martaline): fair hurdler, won
twice in 2017/18: useful chaser: won novice handicaps at Naas in January and February (by
2 lengths from Monatomic): stays 21f: acts on heavy going: usually travels strongly. *Henry
de Bromhead, Ireland*

POKER PLAY (FR) 6 ch.g. Martaline – Becquarette (FR) (Nombre Premier) [2018/19 **c120**
h123: c23g³ h23.6vᵖᵘ h23.1d² h19.9v* h24.7g Apr 6] good-topped, attractive gelding: has **h132**
had breathing operation: useful handicap hurdler: won at Uttoxeter (by 9 lengths from Bold
Plan) in March: 5/1, third in novice handicap at Worcester (13 lengths behind Allelu
Alleluia) on chasing debut: barely stays 23f: acts on heavy going: wears cheekpieces: has
worn tongue tie, including in 2018/19. *David Pipe*

POKER SCHOOL (IRE) 9 b.g. Gold Well – Broken Pockets (IRE) (Broken Hearted) **c125**
[2018/19 c132, h—: c19g³ c17g⁵ h19.8v c16g² c15.5d³ c20.5g² c20d⁵ c16d³ c20.2g* Apr 14] **h—**
lengthy gelding: winning hurdler: fairly useful handicap chaser: won at Wincanton in
April: stays 21f: acts on soft going: wears headgear: has worn tongue tie, including in
2018/19: temperament under suspicion. *Ian Williams*

POKORA DU LYS (FR) 8 b.g. Saint des Saints (FR) – Shailann (FR) (Gaspard de La **c99**
Nuit (FR)) [2018/19 h102: c20.1d³ May 5] has had breathing operation: fair maiden **h—**
hurdler: 16/1, third in novice at Hexham (12 lengths behind Loch Linnhe) on chasing
debut: barely stays 25f: acts on soft going: in tongue tie last 2 starts: usually races
prominently, tends to find little. *Rebecca Menzies*

POLARBROOK (IRE) 12 br.g. Alderbrook – Frozen Cello (IRE) (Arctic Lord) **c—**
[2018/19 c—, h91: h19.9g⁴ h25g⁵ h20.7g³ h20.3s h20.3d Apr 24] angular gelding: poor **h81**
handicap hurdler nowadays: winning chaser: stays 3m: acts on good to firm and heavy
going: wears headgear: has worn tongue tie. *Derek Shaw*

POLAR LIGHT 4 b.f. Norse Dancer (IRE) – Dimelight (Fantastic Light (USA)) [2018/19 **h86**
h17.7d⁵ h17.7v h15.3g h20.5g² h15.9s Mar 11] sister to fairly useful 2m hurdle winner
Odin and fair hurdler/modest chaser Norse Light (2m-21f winner): fair maiden on Flat,
stays 11f: modest form over hurdles: stays 21f. *Paul Henderson*

POLIDAM (FR) 10 b.g. Trempolino (USA) – Eladame (FR) (Snurge) [2018/19 c148, h—: **c138**
c21.9s⁴ c24.5g c25s c20.6d c20g³ c21.1dᵖᵘ Apr 5] good-topped gelding: has had breathing **h—**
operation: winning hurdler: useful handicap chaser: third in minor event at Clonmel (22½
lengths behind Acapella Bourgeois) in March: stays 23f: acts on heavy going: has worn
headgear, including in 2018/19. *W. P. Mullins, Ireland*

POLISHED ROCK (IRE) 9 ch.g. Rock of Gibraltar (IRE) – Where We Left Off (Dr **c106**
Devious (IRE)) [2018/19 h—: h15.7g* c20.9g² h20.3g* c22.5g* h23.4g h25.5v Dec 15] fair **h104**
handicap hurdler: won at Southwell in August and October: similar form over fences: won
handicap at Uttoxeter later in October: stays 2¾m: acts on good to firm going: has worn
cheekpieces, including last 3 starts: wears tongue tie: temperament under suspicion.
Johnny Farrelly

POLITENESS (FR) 10 b.g. Poliglote – Martiniquaise (FR) (Anabaa (USA)) [2018/19 **h109**
h99: h16.2g⁵ h20.2g* h20.2g* h16.2g³ h16.2g³ Aug 18] fair handicap hurdler: won at Perth
in June and July (conditionals): stays 2½m: acts on good to firm and good to soft going:
usually wears hood. *Rose Dobbin*

POLITICAL POLICY (IRE) 8 b.g. Bushranger (IRE) – Alexander Express (IRE) (Sri **h131**
Pekan (USA)) [2018/19 h16.7m⁴ h17.5g* h18.8d⁴ h17d⁴ h16s h16.7g³ h16g² h16g⁴ Feb
24] fairly useful on Flat, stays 17f: useful hurdler: won maiden at Bellewstown and minor
event at Downpatrick in July: second in handicap at Thurles in December: unproven
beyond 17f: acts on good to firm going: wears tongue tie. *Gavin Patrick Cromwell, Ireland*

POLITOLOGUE (FR) 8 gr.g. Poliglote – Scarlet Row (FR) (Turgeon (USA)) [2018/19 **c166**
c166, h—: c21g* c24g⁴ c21d⁴ c15.9s² c19.9d² Apr 5] good-bodied gelding: winning hurdler: **h—**
top-class chaser: won 1965 Chase at Ascot (by ½ length from Charbel) in November:
second in Queen Mother Champion Chase at Cheltenham (1¾ lengths behind Altior) and
Melling Chase at Aintree (20 lengths behind Min, reportedly bled) last 2 starts: effective at
2m-21f: acts on heavy going: has worn hood, including most starts in 2018/19: wears
tongue tie. *Paul Nicholls*

POLLYKAN (IRE) 6 b.m. Arakan (USA) – Polly's Joy (IRE) (Oscar (IRE)) [2018/19 **h–**
h16.5m^F h20.2g^F Jul 31] fourth foal: half-sister to fairly useful hurdler/useful chaser Chitu
(2m-19f winner, by Desert King): dam (h105), 19f/2½m hurdle winner, closely related to
fairly useful 3m hurdle winner Oberon Moon: behind when fell both starts over hurdles.
Stuart Crawford, Ireland

POLO THE MUMM (FR) 9 b.g. Great Journey (JPN) – Maido (FR) (French Glory) **c87**
[2018/19 c84, h97: h21.6m^6 h23g^4 h19.6m c20.2m^6 c26g^4 c20.2g* c21.2d^4 c21.6s c22.7f^3 **h97**
c18.2d* c17.8g^2 Apr 24] workmanlike gelding: modest handicap hurdler, below form first **h79**
3 starts in 2018/19: modest handicap chaser: won at Wincanton (amateurs) in December
and Taunton in April: left Jackie du Plessis after second start: stays 2¾m: acts on soft and
good to firm going: wears headgear/tongue tie. *Alexandra Dunn*

POLYDORA (IRE) 7 b.g. Milan – Mandysway (IRE) (Mandalus) [2018/19 h118: **c138**
h24.7g^2 c25g^3 c23.4d* c22.4d^3 c24v^4 c25g Apr 6] useful-looking gelding: fairly useful **h125**
form over hurdles: useful form over fences: won novice handicap at Newcastle (by 1¼
lengths from Late Romantic) in December: stays 25f: acts on heavy going: tried in blinkers.
Tom Lacey

POLYMATH (IRE) 8 ch.g. Stowaway – Godlylady (IRE) (Old Vic) [2018/19 c107, **c87**
h100: c23.6s^6 c23d Dec 13] point winner: fair hurdler: similar form on chasing debut, little **h–**
impact since: stays 3m: best form on good going: has worn cheekpieces. *Deborah Faulkner*

POMME DE NUIT 6 b.m. Midnight Legend – Apple Days (Sovereign Water (FR)) **h–**
[2018/19 b–: b16.7g h19.5s^pu h20.5g^4 h20.5g^4 h17.7v h20.5g^pu Apr 21] no form: left **b–**
Martin Keighley after fourth start: tried in tongue tie. *Charlie Longsdon*

POND ROAD (FR) 5 ch.g. No Risk At All (FR) – Califea (FR) (Nikos) [2018/19 b15.8d^3 **h83 p**
b15.8v^4 h15.8s^5 h15.8g h16d^3 Apr 6] £40,000 3-y-o: fourth foal: half-brother to a winning **b85**
pointer by Bonbon Rose: dam unraced half-sister to winning French hurdler/fairly useful
chaser (2m-3m winner) Calideo: fair form in bumpers: poor form over hurdles: will be
suited by 2½m+: remains with potential. *Kim Bailey*

PONIENTE 5 br.m. Shirocco (GER) – Tazzarine (FR) (Astarabad (USA)) [2018/19 **b85**
b16.7g^2 Apr 13] third foal: half-sister to a point bumper winner by Beat Hollow: dam
(b90), bumper winner, sister to very smart hurdler/top-class chaser (stays 3¼m) Whisper:
14/1, second in conditionals/amateurs bumper at Bangor (4½ lengths behind L'Air du
Vent). *Venetia Williams*

PONTBLYDDYN 4 ch.g. Mount Nelson – Daring Damsel (IRE) (Van Nistelrooy (USA)) **b–**
[2018/19 b13.7g Nov 13] well held in junior bumper. *Mark Loughnane*

PONTRESINA (IRE) 6 b.g. Milan – Gilt Benefit (IRE) (Beneficial) [2018/19 h109: **h109**
h21.7g^3 h21g^2 h21.4f^2 Oct 28] point winner: fair form over hurdles: stays 2¾m: acts on
good to firm going: front runner/races prominently. *Oliver Sherwood*

POOKIE PEKAN (IRE) 6 b.g. Putra Pekan – Shii-Take's Girl (Deploy) [2018/19 h94: **c113**
c20s c21.3d* c23.9s^2 c21.4s^2 c21.5d^5 c20s c20v^4 c20d^9 Mar 24] winning hurdler: fair **h–**
handicap chaser: won at Wetherby in November and Carlisle in March: stays 21f: acts on
heavy going. *Stuart Coltherd*

POPAWAY 14 b.m. Nomadic Way (USA) – Sea Poppy (Baron Blakeney) [2018/19 c–: **c111**
c25.3g* May 4] prolific point winner: fair chaser: won mares hunter at Cheltenham on sole
outing in 2018/19: stays 25f: acts on soft and good to firm going: wears tongue tie. *Mrs
Pauline Harkin*

POPELYS GULL (IRE) 7 ch.g. Recharge (IRE) – Circus Rose (Most Welcome) **c64**
[2018/19 c127, h–: h25g c24.2g^3 Feb 15] maiden hurdler: fairly useful chaser at best: little **h–**
show in 2018/19, including in points: left Pam Sly after first start: stays 3m: acts on heavy
going. *L. Humphrey*

POPERINGHE GINGER (IRE) 6 ch.m. Beneficial – Masamor (IRE) (Saddlers' Hall **h110**
(IRE)) [2018/19 b84: b17g^3 b16.4g h18.9v^6 h20.7g^2 h19.8g^2 h24.2d^5 Mar 22] workmanlike **b85**
mare: fair form in bumpers/over hurdles. *Graeme McPherson*

POPPY KAY 9 b.m. Kayf Tara – Double Red (IRE) (Thatching) [2018/19 h134: c20g^5 **c99 x**
c16.4d* Mar 1] sturdy mare: has had breathing operation: useful hurdler: jumped with no **h–**
conviction on chasing debut: simple task in match at Doncaster (novice, in cheekpieces)
next time: left Philip Hobbs after first start: stays 2½m: acts on heavy going. *Olly Murphy*

POP ROCKSTAR (IRE) 7 b.g. Flemensfirth (USA) – Special Ballot (IRE) (Perugino **c127**
(USA)) [2018/19 h114: c22.5g^5 c19.4s c19.4v^2 c23d^F c23.6d* Apr 6] has had breathing **h–**
operation: fairly useful hurdler: similar form over fences: won novice handicap at Chepstow

in April: stays 3m: acts on heavy going: wears tongue tie: usually races nearer last than first/travels strongly. *Jonjo O'Neill*

POP THE CHAMPERS (IRE) 8 b.g. Scorpion (IRE) – Manesbil (IRE) (Fourstars Allstar (USA)) [2018/19 h54: c25.2d^{pu} h21g^{pu} Apr 10] Irish point winner: next to no form under Rules: tried in visor. *Nick Kent*   **c–** **h–**

PORTHLEDDEN FLIGHT 5 b.m. Kayf Tara – Molly Flight (FR) (Saint Cyrien (FR)) [2018/19 b15.7g b16.8g Aug 15] third foal: sister to fair hurdler/fairly useful chaser Return Flight (2m-21f winner): dam unraced sister to Prix La Haye Jousselin winners Sunny Flight and Golden Flight: no form in bumpers. *Jean-Rene Auvray*   **b–**

PORT LAIRGE 9 b.g. Pastoral Pursuits – Stylish Clare (IRE) (Desert Style (IRE)) [2018/19 h–: h16.7g^6 h16.7g h25.4g h18.6g^5 h16.7m^6 Apr 21] poor maiden hurdler: stays 21f: acts on good to firm going: tried in blinkers: usually races in rear. *Michael Chapman*   **h60**

PORT MELON (IRE) 11 br.g. Presenting – Omyn Supreme (IRE) (Supreme Leader) [2018/19 c113, h–: c24.5g^2 c25.5d^3 c22.6g^5 Apr 14] tall, good sort: has had breathing operation: prolific point winner: winning hurdler: fair hunter chaser: left Paul Nicholls after second start: stays 3½m: acts on soft and good to firm going: has worn headgear, including in 2018/19: tried in tongue tie. *J. T. Guerrieri*   **c113** **h–**

PORTO DU SUD (FR) 6 gr.g. Lord du Sud (FR) – Queen du Vallon (FR) (Jeune Homme (USA)) [2018/19 h101, b–: h16.2g h20.3g^F h20.2g^6 h19.5v h20.6d^6 h24d^5 Apr 6] has had breathing operation: modest maiden hurdler: may prove best at short of 3m: acts on soft going: usually wears hood: in tongue tie last 2 starts. *Rebecca Menzies*   **h86**

PORT ROYALE 7 b.m. King's Theatre (IRE) – Easibrook Jane (Alderbrook) [2018/19 b–: b15.3m h16.8g h16g^3 Jul 17] poor form in bumpers: fair form over hurdles: better effort when third in mares maiden at Worcester: in tongue tie last 2 starts: dead. *Anthony Honeyball*   **h100** **b69**

PORTRUSH TED (IRE) 7 b.g. Shantou (USA) – Village Queen (IRE) (King's Theatre (IRE)) [2018/19 b112: h23.9g* Aug 1] well-made gelding: Grade 2 bumper winner: 2/9, won novice at Perth (by 17 lengths from Motueka) on hurdling debut: in tongue tie last 2 starts: front runner/races prominently: looked sure to progress but not seen out again. *Warren Greatrex*   **h119 p**

PORTSTORM 4 b.g. Shirocco (GER) – Viva Victoria (Old Vic) [2018/19 b16d^3 b17d^2 b16m Apr 13] £15,000 3-y-o: second foal: dam unraced out of fairly useful chaser (winner up to 3½m) Rosie Redman: fair form in bumpers. *Ian Duncan*   **b86**

POSH TOTTY 12 ch.m. Midnight Legend – Well Bred (Rakaposhi King) [2018/19 c82p, h75: c25.8g^2 c22.5g* Jun 6] angular mare: prolific point winner: maiden hurdler: modest form in chases: won novice handicap at Uttoxeter in June: stays 3m: acts on good to soft going: races prominently, often travels strongly. *Jack R. Barber*   **c87** **h–**

POSH TRISH (IRE) 6 b.m. Stowaway – Moscow Demon (IRE) (Moscow Society (USA)) [2018/19 b107: h19.5d* h16.3d^2 h16.3s* h15.3d* h16.5d* h16.8d Mar 14] rangy mare: Irish point winner: useful bumper performer: similar form over hurdles: won mares novices at Chepstow in October, and Newbury (listed event, by 3¼ lengths from Lust For Glory), Wincanton and Taunton (another listed race, by 2 lengths from Indefatigable) in December: will be suited by 2½m+: acts on soft going: usually front runner/races prominently. *Paul Nicholls*   **h133**

POSITIVELY DYLAN 8 b.g. Multiplex – Wou Oodd (Barathea (IRE)) [2018/19 c137, h121: c15.8g^f Nov 10] fairly useful hurdler: useful handicap chaser: stayed 2¾m: acted on heavy going: dead. *Evan Williams*   **c132** **h–**

POSTBRIDGE (IRE) 8 br.m. Robin des Pres (FR) – Dartmeet (IRE) (Presenting) [2018/19 c–, h–: h19m^{pu} May 7] has had breathing operation: fair hurdler at best, no form since 2016/17 (including in chases): has worn headgear/tongue tie: front runner/races prominently. *Sarah Humphrey*   **c–** **h–**

POSTMAN (FR) 6 ch.g. American Post – Pepperjuice (GER) (Big Shuffle (USA)) [2018/19 h15.3g^6 Apr 14] tall gelding: fair on Flat in France, stays 12.5f: 50/1, sixth in novice at Wincanton (16½ lengths behind Highly Prized) on hurdling debut. *Seamus Mullins*   **h89**

POT DE FLEUR 7 b.m. Revoque (IRE) – Glen Clova (Elmaamul (USA)) [2018/19 h–: h15.8d^{pu} h15.8g h15.8d Dec 5] no form in bumper/over hurdles. *Christian Williams*   **h–**

POTTERMAN 6 b.g. Sulamani (IRE) – Polly Potter (Kayf Tara) [2018/19 h113p, b101: h20.7g* h19.6g* h21g^4 h19.4m^5 h21m^5 h20.5m^2 Apr 13] bumper winner: fairly useful hurdler: won maiden at Huntingdon in May and novice at Bangor (challenging when sole   **h126**

rival fell 2 out) in June: stays 21f: acts on soft and good to firm going: usually races prominently, often travels strongly. *Alan King*

POTTERS ANGELIQUE 7 b.m. Midnight Legend – Craughwell Suas (IRE) (Turtle Island (IRE)) [2018/19 b15.7d Nov 20] poor in bumpers. *Amy Murphy*   **b–**

POTTERS APPROACH (IRE) 8 b.g. Scorpion (IRE) – Moon Approach (IRE) (Shernazar) [2018/19 h–: c20g⁶ c26.2g* c27.7dᵖᵘ c24.2sᵖᵘ Mar 9] sturdy gelding: has had breathing operation: fair hurdler: fairly useful form over fences: won novice handicap at Chepstow in October: disappointing both starts after: stays 3¼m: acts on good to soft going: in cheekpieces last 3 starts. *Dan Skelton*   **c122 h–**

POTTERS AWAY (IRE) 5 ch.m. Getaway (GER) – Polly's Present (IRE) (Presenting) [2018/19 b16.8v⁴ h15.8g⁶ h16.7d⁶ Apr 26] third foal: half-sister to useful hurdler Hearts Are Trumps (2m/17f winner, by Oscar): dam unraced sister to Cheltenham Gold Cup winner Denman: tailed off in mares bumper: poor form over hurdles. *Oliver Greenall*   **h78 b–**

POTTERS CORNER (IRE) 9 b.g. Indian Danehill (IRE) – Woodford Beauty (IRE) (Phardante (FR)) [2018/19 c24.2g c24.2sᵖᵘ c25.1d* c26.7gᶠ c32.6gᶠ c34v* Mar 16] sturdy gelding: winning hurdler: useful handicap chaser: won at Wincanton in December and Midlands Grand National at Uttoxeter (by 3 lengths from Ms Parfois) in March: stays 4¼m: acts on good to firm and heavy going: in cheekpieces last 5 starts: often travels strongly. *Christian Williams*   **c140 h–**

POTTERS HEDGER 7 b.g. Midnight Legend – Loose Morals (IRE) (Luso) [2018/19 h110: h20g* h23.5s⁵ h25s* h25d h23.5d⁴ h25s³ h25g³ Apr 25] good-topped gelding: has had breathing operation: fairly useful hurdler: won maiden at Fakenham in May and handicap at Plumpton in January: stays 25f: acts on heavy going: wears cheekpieces. *Lucy Wadham*   **h121**

POTTERS MIDNIGHT 9 b.m. Midnight Legend – Craughwell Suas (IRE) (Turtle Island (IRE)) [2018/19 h116: h20g⁴ h16d³ h16d* h16.7g³ h16d⁴ Mar 15] sturdy mare: fairly useful handicap hurdler: won at Lingfield in January: stays 21f: acts on heavy going. *Lucy Wadham*   **h128**

POTTERS SAPPHIRE 6 gr.m. Aussie Rules (USA) – Arabescato (UAE) (Gone West (USA)) [2018/19 h104: h21mᵖᵘ h20.6g³ h20.7d h19.6d³ h20.5g h20.3d Apr 9] compact mare: fair maiden hurdler: left Lucy Wadham after first start: stays 21f: acts on soft going: wears headgear. *Amy Murphy*   **h99**

Marston's 61 Deep Midlands Grand National (Open Handicap Chase), Uttoxeter—
the biggest win in the fledgling training career of Christian Williams as 20/1-shot Potters Corner
slogs it out to win from Ms Parfois

POTTERS STORY 7 b.g. Kayf Tara – Lily Potter (Karinga Bay) [2018/19 h134: h20.5s c16v³ c19.2dᵖᵘ Apr 9] good-bodied gelding: useful hurdler at best, no form in 2018/19 (including over fences): unproven beyond 2m: acts on heavy going: tried in cheekpieces: has worn tongue tie, including in 2018/19. *Peter Bowen* **c–** **h–**

POTTERS TALE 6 b.g. Kayf Tara – Lily Potter (Karinga Bay) [2018/19 b91: b16.7gᵖᵘ May 11] fair at best in bumpers: tried in hood: in tongue tie last 2 starts: dead. *Peter Bowen* **b–**

POTTERS VISION (IRE) 6 b.m. Getaway (GER) – Peripheral Vision (IRE) (Saddlers' Hall (IRE)) [2018/19 b16.7g⁵ b15.8d⁶ Dec 26] sixth foal: half-sister to fairly useful chaser By The Boardwalk (19f-3m winner) and a winning pointer (both by Presenting): dam (h84), 2½m hurdle winner/winning pointer, out of half-sister to Cheltenham Gold Cup winner Denman: runner-up in Irish point: poor form in bumpers. *Alan King* **b69**

POTTLEREAGHEXPRESS (IRE) 6 b.m. Beneficial – Needle Doll (IRE) (Needle Gun (IRE)) [2018/19 h15.8s⁴ h15.7g⁵ h16g⁴ h19.7g⁴ h23d h15.8d h16g h23.9d⁴ Apr 24] £15,000 5-y-o: sixth foal: half-sister to useful hurdler/chaser Mad Brian (2m-2¾m winner, by Brian Boru) and bumper winner Myblueeyedgirl (by Milan): dam unraced: runner-up on completed start in Irish points: modest maiden hurdler: probably stays 3m: best form on good going. *Jonjo O'Neill* **h90**

POUCOR 4 b.g. Pour Moi (IRE) – Corinium (IRE) (Turtle Island (IRE)) [2018/19 h17.7v² h16.2d* h15.7d h16.5s⁴ Mar 19] sturdy gelding: half-brother to fair hurdler Decision (19f winner, by Royal Applause): modest maiden on Flat, stays 1½m: fair form over hurdles: won juvenile maiden at Hereford in January. *Mick Channon* **h111**

POUR JOIE 4 b.g. Pour Moi (IRE) – Lupa Montana (USA) (Giant's Causeway (USA)) [2018/19 b16g⁴ ab16g³ Feb 18] first foal: dam maiden on Flat (stayed 9f): fair form in bumpers: won maiden at Warwick in January. *Ian Williams* **b92**

POWERFUL SOCIETY (IRE) 4 b.f. Power – Society Gal (IRE) (Galileo (IRE)) [2018/19 h17.7g h17.7m⁵ h15.3fᵘʳ h16g² h16.8s⁵ h15.3g h15.8d⁵ h15.3g³ h16.5d² h15.3g³ h16.8g² h16.5d² Apr 24] modest on Flat, stays 1½m: fair maiden hurdler: unproven beyond 17f: acts on good to soft going: usually races prominently. *Mark Gillard* **h102**

POWERFUL SYMBOL (IRE) 9 b.g. Robin des Champs (FR) – Be My Rainbow (IRE) (Be My Native (USA)) [2018/19 c122, h–: c23.9d² c23g³ c24.1g⁵ c22.6g* c24.2mᶠ c23.4dᵖᵘ Jan 16] good-topped gelding: has had breathing operation: maiden hurdler: fairly useful handicap chaser: won at Stratford in October: stays 3m: acts on good to soft going: wears cheekpieces/tongue tie: usually leads: often let down by jumping. *Ben Pauling* **c124 x** **h–**

POWERSTOWN PARK (IRE) 6 b.g. Craigsteel – Smiths Lady (IRE) (Anshan) [2018/19 h81, b–: h24g³ h21.6g⁵ h16.8g² Jul 22] rather unfurnished gelding: has had breathing operation: point winner: modest form over hurdles: should stay beyond 2m: best form on good going: usually wears headgear: tried in tongue tie. *Sam Thomas* **h93**

POWER SURGE (IRE) 5 ch.g. Power – Silver Skates (IRE) (Slip Anchor) [2018/19 h15.3g h15.8d Mar 13] won 9.5f maiden in 2017 on first of 2 Flat starts: no form over hurdles. *Robert Stephens* **h–**

PRABENI 4 ch.g. Teofilo (IRE) – Nyarhini (Fantastic Light (USA)) [2018/19 h16g³ h15.8g* h16.6g* h16.4s h18.8d h20.5g² Apr 21] compact gelding: fairly useful on Flat, stays 1½m: similar form over hurdles: won juvenile at Huntingdon in January and novice at Doncaster in February: stays 21f: best form on good going: tried in cheekpieces: wears tongue tie. *Charlie Mann* **h126**

PRAECEPS (IRE) 4 b.g. Canford Cliffs (IRE) – Sliding Scale (Sadler's Wells (USA)) [2018/19 h16.3d² h16.7d* h16m³ h16.4s⁶ h15.7m⁶ h15.9g* Apr 22] good-topped gelding: fairly useful on Flat, stays 16.5f: similar form over hurdles: won juveniles at Market Rasen in February and Plumpton in April: will be suited by 2½m+: acts on soft and good to firm going: in blinkers last 3 starts. *Alan King* **h121**

PRAIRIE IMPULSE 6 b.m. Major Cadeaux – Prairie Sun (GER) (Law Society (USA)) [2018/19 h86: h15.8m h18.6m Aug 5] modest hurdler at best, no form in 2018/19: unproven beyond 17f: best form on good going: held up. *Rebecca Menzies* **h–**

PRAIRIE TOWN (IRE) 8 b.g. High Chaparral (IRE) – Lake Baino (Highest Honor (FR)) [2018/19 c119, h113: c20d⁶ h15.5d⁵ h16s⁴ h16.5g Apr 6] rather leggy gelding: fair handicap hurdler: fairly useful chaser at best, well held first outing in 2018/19: unproven beyond 2m: acts on heavy going: has worn headgear, including in 2018/19: usually races in rear. *Tony Carroll* **c–** **h106**

PRAVALAGUNA (FR) 7 b.m. Great Pretender (IRE) – Arnette (FR) (Denham Red (FR)) **c138**
[2018/19 h136: c17d⁴ c19.7d* c16d* c19.8d c20d² Apr 23] smallish mare: useful hurdler: **h–**
similar form over fences: won mares maiden at Limerick in December and listed mares
event at Naas (by 14 lengths from Baie des Iles) in February: second in Grade 3 mares
event at Fairyhouse (5½ lengths behind Camelia de Cotte) in April: stays 2½m: acts on
heavy going: has worn hood, including in 2018/19: usually races close up. *W. P. Mullins,
Ireland*

PRAY FOR A RAINBOW 8 b.g. Rainbow High – Blackchurch Lass (IRE) (Taum Go **c89**
Leor (IRE)) [2018/19 c–, h88: h24g³ c24.1g² h23.3g⁴ h25g² c23.5v⁵ h23.3s h26g c22.7g⁴ **h88**
h25g² h24.1g³ h25g³ Apr 22] point winner: modest handicap hurdler: similar form in
chases: stays 25f: acts on heavy going: has worn headgear, including in 2018/19.
Samuel Drinkwater

PRECIOUS BOUNTY (IRE) 5 b.g. Yeats (IRE) – Zaharath Al Bustan (Gulch (USA)) **h108**
[2018/19 h16.2g⁶ h16.5d² h16.8d² h15.8g⁵ h16.3d Mar 2] €25,000 3-y-o, £52,000 **b–**
4-y-o: neat gelding: third foal: dam, 1m winner, out of half-sister to high-class 2m hurdler
I'm Supposin: maiden Irish pointer: tailed off in bumper: fair form over hurdles: raced
around 2m: acts on good to soft going: front runner/races prominently. *Philip Hobbs*

PRECIOUS CARGO (IRE) 6 b.g. Yeats (IRE) – Kilbarry Classic (IRE) (Classic Cliche **h126 p**
(IRE)) [2018/19 b96: h16d* h16s* h16.5d⁶ Apr 5] useful-looking gelding: has had
breathing operation: bumper winner: fairly useful form over hurdles: won novices at
Kempton in January and Sandown in March: has worn tongue tie: remains with potential.
Nicky Henderson

PRECIOUS ELEANOR (FR) 4 gr.f. Maresca Sorrento (FR) – Precious Lucy (FR) **b61**
(Kadrou (FR)) [2018/19 b16.7d Apr 26] £15,000 3-y-o: fifth foal: half-sister to 2 winners,
including fair 2m hurdle winner/winning pointer Good Man Jim (by Martaline): dam (h88)
17f hurdle winner: well beaten in mares bumper. *Henry Daly*

PRECIOUS GROUND 9 b.g. Helissio (FR) – Wild Ground (IRE) (Simply Great (FR)) **c–**
[2018/19 c19.4s Nov 21] workmanlike gelding: winning hurdler: maiden chaser, little **h–**
impact sole outing in 2018/19 after long absence. *Kevin Bishop*

PRECIOUS MOMENTO (IRE) 4 ch.g. Casamento (IRE) – Precious Citizen (USA) **b–**
(Proud Citizen (USA)) [2018/19 b16s Mar 16] well beaten in maiden bumper.
Mark Loughnane

PREMIER KING (IRE) 11 b.g. Brian Boru – Miracle Run (IRE) (Commanche Run) **c129**
[2018/19 c20g* c24g* c24.1g* h23g² Sep 11] has had breathing operation: fair form over **h113**
hurdles: fairly useful form over fences: completed hat-trick in handicaps at Uttoxeter (both
novice events) in July and Bangor in August: stays 3m: best form on good going: wears
headgear: in tongue tie last 5 starts: often leads. *Dan Skelton*

PREMIER ROSE (IRE) 10 b.m. Westerner – Alltoplayfor (IRE) (Broken Hearted) **h97**
[2018/19 h92: h15.8gᵘʳ h18.6m⁵ h22.1s h25.8s⁶ h19.3g⁴ h19.9g* h20.5d* h21.7v Dec 26]
Irish point winner: modest handicap hurdler: won at Carlisle in October, and mares events
at Uttoxeter in November and Leicester in December: stays 3m, at least as effective over
shorter: acts on good to soft and good to firm going: has worn cheekpieces, including in
2018/19: wears tongue tie. *Dan Skelton*

PRESENCE FELT (IRE) 11 br.g. Heron Island (IRE) – Faeroe Isle (IRE) (Erins Isle) **c–**
[2018/19 c–§, h–: h23.9g* h20d h24.3d⁶ h24.1s³ h21.3s h25m³ Apr 20] good-topped **h117**
gelding: fairly useful handicap hurdler: won at Perth in May: winning chaser: stays 25f:
acts on good to firm and heavy going: has worn headgear: usually races close up.
John Dixon

PRESENT CHIEF (IRE) 5 b.g. Presenting – Daizinni (Dr Massini (IRE)) [2018/19 **b76**
b16.7g⁵ Oct 30] 11/2, fifth in bumper at Bangor: has joined Jonjo O'Neill. *Ronald O'Leary,
Ireland*

PRESENT DESTINY (IRE) 7 b.g. Dubai Destination (USA) – Anns Present (IRE) **h104**
(Presenting) [2018/19 h103: h19.2g³ h21.7g⁵ h18.5g⁵ h15.3gᵖᵘ h21.7sᵖᵘ Jan 27] lengthy
gelding: fair maiden hurdler: left Seamus Mullins after third start: stays 19f: acts on soft
going. *Paul Henderson*

PRESENTEDWITHWINGS (IRE) 5 br.g. Presenting – Rosa Rugosa (IRE) (In The **b85**
Wings) [2018/19 b77: b17.7g³ May 13] fair form in bumpers. *Tom Symonds*

PRESENT FLIGHT (IRE) 10 ch.g. Presenting – Grangeclare Flight (IRE) (Old Vic) **c102**
[2018/19 c114, h–: c20.1g⁵ c20.5d⁵ c20v³ c24.1s² c26.9d⁴ c26.2g c23.8m⁵ Mar 22] maiden **h–**
hurdler: fair handicap chaser nowadays: stays 27f: acts on good to firm and heavy going: in
cheekpieces last 4 starts: wears tongue tie: inconsistent. *Lucinda Russell*

PRESENT FROM DUBAI (IRE) 6 b.g. Dubai Destination (USA) – Inch Promise **h109**
(IRE) (Presenting) [2018/19 h99, b–: h15.8d² h19.4g⁴ Jan 26] placed both starts in Irish
points: fair form over hurdles: better effort in 2018/19 when second in maiden at Uttoxeter:
should stay 19f+. *Richard Phillips*

PRESENT IN COURT (IRE) 6 b.g. Court Cave (IRE) – Present Line (IRE) (Presenting) **h125**
[2018/19 b16m³ b18.8g* h21.8d² h21.7d* h23g* Sep 11] €15,000 3-y-o, £65,000 4-y-o: **b95**
second foal: dam unraced half-sister to useful hurdler/fairly useful chaser (stayed 3m) Line
Ball: point winner: fairly useful form in bumpers: won maiden at Downpatrick in July:
similar form over hurdles: won maiden at Downpatrick in August and novice at Worcester
(in cheekpieces) in September: stays 23f. *Gordon Elliott, Ireland*

PRESENTING BERKLEY (IRE) 9 br.g. Presenting – Tynelucy (IRE) (Good Thyne **c81 §**
(USA)) [2018/19 c–, h85: c20.3g c25.8m* c25.5g c25.8g⁵ c24g⁶ c25.7gᶠ Nov 5] maiden **h–**
hurdler: poor handicap chaser: won novice event at Newton Abbot in June: stayed 3¼m:
acted on good to firm going: sometimes wore headgear, including last 2 starts: in tongue tie
last 5 starts: temperamental: dead. *Tim Vaughan*

PRESENTING JULIO (IRE) 11 b.g. Presenting – Ouro Preto (Definite Article) **c112**
[2018/19 c114, h113: h24.5g c25g⁶ c25g³ c24g³ c25gᶠ c21gᵘʳ c22.5dᵖᵘ Apr 23] lengthy **h–**
gelding: winning hurdler: fair handicap chaser: stays 25f: acts on good to firm and good to
soft going: has worn headgear, including last 5 starts: wears tongue tie. *Gordon Elliott,
Ireland*

PRESENTING LUCINA (IRE) 7 b.m. Presenting – Lucina (GER) (Groom Dancer **h81**
(USA)) [2018/19 h–: h19.2vᵖᵘ h19s⁶ h23.9sᵖᵘ h23.1s⁴ Mar 18] poor maiden hurdler: stays
23f: best form on soft/heavy going: tried in tongue tie. *Neil Mulholland*

PRESENTING PERCY 8 b.g. Sir Percy – Hunca Munca (IRE) (Presenting) **c165 +**
[2018/19 c164p, h152: h24s* c26.3d Mar 15] **h160 +**
    You probably had to be living on the moon itself to have missed the fact that
2019 marked the fiftieth anniversary of the Apollo 11 landings. Surviving Apollo 11
astronauts Michael Collins and Buzz Aldrin were typically generous with their time
at public events and for TV and film projects to commemorate the occasion, though
whether the mission's commander Neil Armstrong would have been anything like
so co-operative had he still been alive (he died in 2012) must be open to debate. The
publicity-shy Armstrong became a case study on dealing with extreme celebrity,
his decision to shun the limelight reportedly heavily influenced by the experiences
of aviation pioneer Charles Lindbergh. The two men were friends, yet Lindbergh
still turned down an invitation from President Richard Nixon to personally greet
the three Apollo 11 astronauts on their triumphant return to the USS Hornet aircraft
carrier, explaining that he had spent a quarter of a century 're-achieving a position
in which I can live, work and travel under normal circumstances' and feared that the
resulting attention would force him back into a 'press relationship and way of life I
am most anxious not to re-enter.' Lindbergh was thrust into global superstardom in
1927 as a humble twenty-five-year-old US Air Mail pilot when becoming the first
to fly non-stop from New York to Paris, his mammoth stint at the controls of *The
Spirit of St Louis* (the flight lasted over thirty-three hours) not only landing him
the lucrative 25,000-dollar prize (over 360,000 dollars in modern day terms) but
also making him the most famous person on the planet for a while. Lindbergh's
subsequent marriage to author Anne Morrow only intensified this, the couple
attracting the kind of attention reserved for royalty and A-list celebrities nowadays.
Things soon turned sour, however, as the Lindberghs' baby son was murdered after
being kidnapped (despite Lindbergh paying the ransom fee), whilst the resulting
court case was dubbed the 'Trial of the Century' with saturation media coverage. The
couple moved to Europe soon afterwards in a bid to escape the unrelenting public
attention. That decision, combined with Lindbergh becoming a spokesman for the
America First pressure group urging his home country to keep out of the escalating
World War II, led to a fierce backlash and Lindbergh's retreat from the public eye
(then in his forties, he flew some fifty bombing missions in the Pacific as part of
the Allied effort). Armstrong regretted not immediately adhering to Lindbergh's
advice of 'Never sign an autograph' in the wake of his new-found celebrity, but he
made very few slip-ups once his NASA duties were over. A dislike of the limelight

prompted Armstrong to largely shun the lucrative speaking circuit and the world of celebrity endorsement in favour of a career as a college lecturer, refusing the vast majority of media interview requests for the remainder of his life. Close friends reported that Armstrong was anything but reclusive, however, and lived a perfectly happy life once out of the limelight.

The 2018 RSA Novices' Chase might not have attracted anything like the same audience as the 1969 moon landing (for which there was a reputed global TV audience of 500m), but it cemented Presenting Percy's position as one of the most popular Irish horses in training, while further elevating the reputation of Pat Kelly's small County Galway yard, which was triumphing at the Cheltenham Festival for the third year in a row, following successive wins in the Pertemps Final by Mall Dini in 2016 and by Presenting Percy himself in 2017. Presenting Percy and Kelly, however, proceeded to do their best impressions of Armstrong and Lindbergh for much of the 2018/19 campaign. Despite his prominent position in the Cheltenham Gold Cup ante-post market, Presenting Percy regularly shunned public appearances during the winter as his planned comeback kept being put back again and again. If anything, this series of 'no-shows' seemed only to swell his popularity among Irish racing fans, earning him the tag of the 'people's horse' as he attracted the strength of following reserved previously for the likes of former Irish jumping stars such as Danoli (also from a small yard) and Dawn Run. The column inches devoted to the elusive Presenting Percy during this period couldn't be blamed on Kelly either, as the publicity-shy trainer steadfastly refused to talk to anyone in the media. Admittedly, he had been involved in a controversial disciplinary case in September, which saw Kelly fined €1,000 (and ordered to pay €3,000 costs) when one of his point-to-point winners tested positive for cobalt, a situation that might have prompted some awkward questions for him. However, Kelly's career in recent years has featured far more good news stories than bad ones and he had been equally reluctant to talk about them too.

Trainers, of course, are under no obligation to talk to the media and Kelly certainly isn't the first to take such a stance—legendary northern trainer Arthur Stephenson, for example, shunned the racing press for much of his career (famously he was at Sedgefield when his horse The Thinker won the 1987 Cheltenham Gold Cup!), while the reticent Nigel Twiston-Davies never spoke on camera for the first decade or so of his career. That said, a blanket ban on media contact can be counterproductive as Kelly discovered in 2018/19, when his own reclusive behaviour became just as big a story as that of Presenting Percy himself. 'It would be better if Pat would speak and give people an insight into how much of a genius he is. I think he'd do a lot better off the back of that, to be honest, but he doesn't want to,' explained Presenting Percy's owner Philip Reynolds, who stepped into the breach to provide updates. Reynolds presumably learned a thing or two about the art of diplomacy from his father (former Taoiseach Albert Reynolds) and he has stated that he understands the media's frustrations with Kelly and has tried to persuade his trainer to soften his stance, although he added: 'We're all different and I think we should respect that.'

Given the background, there was plenty of interest (and a bumper mid-week crowd) when Presenting Percy finally made his reappearance on Thyestes Chase day at Gowran Park in late-January, unseasonably dry conditions having prevented several earlier planned appearances. True to form, Kelly broke with convention and, instead of the Thyestes Chase, opted for a spin over hurdles with his Cheltenham Gold Cup hopeful, saddling him for the Grade 2 John Mulhern Galmoy Hurdle (named after Ireland's only Cheltenham Festival winner in the late-'eighties). Presenting Percy had successfully reverted to hurdling when winning the same race twelve months earlier and he was sent off 9/4 favourite after his eleven-month lay-off, though a quick scan of the official racecard merely added to the David and Goliath narrative that so appealed to his followers. No fewer than ten of Presenting Percy's eleven rivals hailed from the stables of the training superpowers Willie Mullins and Gordon Elliott, while the other runner was owned by J.P. McManus and trained by Joseph O'Brien (responsible for the third highest number of wins on Irish

John Mulhern Galmoy Hurdle, Gowran Park—the elusive Presenting Percy makes light of an eleven-month absence as he repeats his 2018 win back over hurdles

soil in 2018/19). By contrast, in the latest season Kelly had just twenty-two horses (seven more than in the previous campaign), with Presenting Percy one of only three winners sent out by his yard. Presenting Percy's second successive Galmoy Hurdle win ended a five and a half month drought under Rules for the yard and proved to be Kelly's final win of the campaign. There was plenty to like about the comeback win, with Presenting Percy looking every bit as good as ever and, after being produced to lead two out, he typically left the impression that there was more in the tank if it had been required. Presenting Percy had a length and a quarter to spare over Mullins' Prix La Barka winner Bapaume, with the latter's stable-companions Killultagh Vic and Limini close up in third and fourth. A return visit to Gowran for the Red Mills Chase (in which Presenting Percy finished second twelve months earlier) in mid-February was mooted, but Presenting Percy was scratched at the overnight stage—predictably without prior warning or subsequent explanation from Kelly to the media and punters. Instead, Presenting Percy completed his Festival preparations with behind-closed-doors schooling sessions at Galway, where the racecourse executive reversed the fences so that Presenting Percy and Mall Dini (also owned by Reynolds) could work left-handed to replicate Cheltenham.

The Cheltenham Gold Cup attracted a competitive sixteen-strong field, featuring plenty of leading contenders who had followed far more orthodox campaigns for top stables. The trainers involved included Willie Mullins (who saddled four runners), Colin Tizzard (three runners), Paul Nicholls, Nicky Henderson and Gordon Elliott. Even so, punters sided with the horse who had not jumped a fence in public for twelve months and hailed from a yard with just one win in the past eight months. Presenting Percy was sent off 100/30 favourite but there was a hugely anti-climactic ending to the year-long story when Presenting Percy managed only eighth of nine finishers, never travelling nor jumping with quite his usual fluency and then unable to sustain his effort after briefly getting into contention on the home

681

turn. Plausible excuses soon emerged, however, as Presenting Percy was found to be lame afterwards (which ruled him out for the remainder of the campaign), while regular jockey Davy Russell reported that he had also had to contend with a slipping saddle. In addition, the fact that victory went to Al Boum Photo, whom Presenting Percy had comprehensively defeated in the 2018 RSA Novices' Chase, stoked the speculation about what might have been.

Presenting Percy (b.g. 2011)	Sir Percy (b 2003)	Mark of Esteem (b 1993)	Darshaan
			Homage
		Percy's Lass (b or br 1984)	Blakeney
			Laughing Girl
	Hunca Munca (IRE) (b 1999)	Presenting (br 1992)	Mtoto
			D'azy
		Tulladante (b 1990)	Phardante
			Tullow Performance

Presenting Percy's pedigree has been discussed in detail in previous editions of *Chasers & Hurdlers* and there isn't a great deal to add. The main update is that his dam Hunca Munca, a dual winning pointer, is now responsible for two winners under Rules, as Presenting Percy's year-younger half-brother Monkey Puzzle (by Sulamani) won a two and a half mile maiden hurdle for Oliver Sherwood in the early weeks of 2019/20. It should also be noted that Presenting Percy's exploits on the track haven't gone unnoticed at the sales in recent years either. His unraced half-brother Maxwell Swift (by Shirocco) sold for €46,000 as a three-year-old in 2017, whilst Hunca Munca's 2018 foal, a full brother to Presenting Percy, made €50,000 in November. Hunca Munca has also produced unnamed fillies by Malinas in 2016 and by Jack Hobbs in 2019.

A good-topped gelding, Presenting Percy stays long distances but certainly isn't short of speed and is usually a strong traveller in his races. He handles the mud well (three wins on heavy) but showed he doesn't need such conditions when winning the 2016 Pertemps Final on good ground, which remains the most resilient surface he has tackled to date. Neil Armstrong, of course, had different conditions to cope with when making his 'one giant leap for mankind' and, unlike Presenting Percy's connections, he knew there would be no second chances if something went wrong (Apollo 11 command module pilot Michael Collins was under the grim orders to return to Earth alone, leaving Armstrong and Aldrin stranded, should the lunar module break down). Happily, Presenting Percy (who is still only eight) should get at least one more chance in the Cheltenham Gold Cup, his ante-post odds of 16/1 for the 2020 renewal looking attractive, considering the odds at which he was trading for most of the latest winter. One final point before considering whether to take the plunge: don't expect regular updates from Mission Control in County Galway along the way, while it is also probably safe to rule out Pat Kelly ever attending any ticker tape parades or welcome parties should he manage to launch Presenting Percy on a successful Gold Cup mission. *Patrick G. Kelly, Ireland*

PRESENTING RIO (IRE) 6 b.m. Presenting – Oh My Rubie (GER) (Law Society (USA)) [2018/19 h15.8g⁶ h21.2dᵖᵘ h21d c23.6dᵖᵘ c19.2s⁵ c22.7g⁶ Mar 8] £14,000 5-y-o: first foal: dam ran once in bumper/over hurdles: maiden pointer: modest form over hurdles: little impact in chases: in cheekpieces last 3 starts: wears tongue tie. *Ben Case*   c– h87

PRESENTING STREAK (IRE) 10 b.g. Presenting – Kuwalla (IRE) (New Frontier (IRE)) [2018/19 h16.7gᵖᵘ h18.6g h15.8g h18.8mᶠ h18.7g c20g c16.4s³ h16.6g⁴ Dec 15] modest maiden hurdler/handicap chaser nowadays: stays 3m, effective at much shorter: acts on soft and good to firm going: tried in hood: has worn tongue tie, including in 2018/19. *Peter Winks*   c96 h87

PRESENTING SUN (IRE) 5 b.g. Presenting – Sunwake (GER) (Tiger Hill (IRE)) [2018/19 h19.9m⁵ h16g h20gᵖᵘ h20.2d⁵ Oct 28] €40,000 3-y-o: second foal: brother to bumper winner/fair 21f hurdle winner Peters Cousin: dam (h112) 2m hurdle winner (stayed 3m): modest form over hurdles. *John Joseph Hanlon, Ireland*   h92

PRESENT LODGER (IRE) 11 b.g. Presenting – Hannigan's Lodger (IRE) (Be My Native (USA)) [2018/19 c21.2g⁶ c21.6m⁴ Sep 19] useful-looking gelding: maiden hurdler: fairly useful handicap chaser, below form in 2018/19 after long absence: stays 3m: acts on heavy going: wears tongue tie. *Lucinda Russell*   c104 h–

PRESENT MAN (IRE) 9 b.g. Presenting – Glen's Gale (IRE) (Strong Gale) [2018/19 **c148** c143, h106: c25.1g* c25.9s c28.4d⁴ c28.8gᵖᵘ Apr 27] rangy gelding: has had breathing **h–** operation: winning hurdler: smart handicap chaser: won Badger Ales Trophy Handicap Chase at Wincanton (by 2½ lengths from Sumkindofking) in November: failed to see races out subsequently: barely stays 29f: acts on good to firm and heavy going: tried in headgear: wears tongue tie: front runner/races prominently. *Paul Nicholls*

PRESENT RANGER (IRE) 6 b.g. Presenting – Papoose (IRE) (Little Bighorn) **h113** [2018/19 h114p: h20g³ h19.6d h20.6m* Apr 21] sturdy gelding: runner-up in point: fair hurdler: won maiden at Market Rasen in April: stays 21f: acts on soft and good to firm going: tried in tongue tie. *Dan Skelton*

PRESENT TIMES (IRE) 8 b.g. Kalanisi (IRE) – Beguiling (IRE) (Dr Massini (IRE)) **h–** [2018/19 h117: h24s⁶ h25.5d h24.2d Mar 22] sturdy gelding: fairly useful hurdler at best, no form in 2018/19. *Evan Williams*

PRESENT VALUE (IRE) 5 b.g. Gold Well – Presenting Shares (IRE) (Presenting) **h123** [2018/19 h15.8s² h19.5s* h23.1s³ Mar 5] £35,000 3-y-o: closely related to top-class staying hurdler Paisley Park (by Oscar) and half-brother to several winners, including bumper winner/fairly useful hurdler Henry King (17f-19f winner, by Great Palm): dam unraced half-sister to fair hurdler/useful chaser (stayed 3m) Priests Leap: fairly useful form over hurdles: won maiden at Chepstow in December: should stay 2½m+. *Evan Williams*

PRESIDENTE LINE (FR) 5 ch.m. Martaline – Presidence (FR) (Nikos) [2018/19 **h128** h17.9s² h17.9s² h17.4s* h16.5s² h16.8d h17.9s Apr 27] rather leggy mare: half-sister to several winners, including useful French hurdler/fairly useful chaser Invicter (2m-2¼m winner, by Sholokhov): fairly useful on Flat, stays 14.5f: fairly useful form over hurdles: won handicap at Pau in December: seventh to Églantine du Seuil in Dawn Run Mares' Novices' Hurdle at Cheltenham on fifth start: stays 2¼m: acts on soft going. *Alain Couetil, France*

PRES (IRE) 5 ch.g. Sans Frontieres (IRE) – Present Company (IRE) (Presenting) [2018/19 **h93** h19.8s⁶ h20.5d⁶ Mar 22] good-topped gelding: fifth foal: dam winning pointer: placed twice from 3 starts in Irish points: modest form over hurdles. *Chris Gordon*

PRESS GANG 6 b.g. Mount Nelson – Rutba (Act One) [2018/19 h16.5d h16.8d h15.8v **h84** h15.9s Mar 11] dam half-sister to useful hurdler/fairly useful chaser (2m/17f winner) Alfie Flits: fair maiden on Flat, stays 1¾m: poor form over hurdles. *Harry Fry*

PRESSURIZE (IRE) 13 b.g. Witness Box (USA) – Cockpit Rose (IRE) (Be My Native **c119** (USA)) [2018/19 c131d, h–: c20s⁵ c22.9d² Mar 20] sturdy gelding: maiden hurdler: fairly **h–** useful handicap chaser nowadays: second in veterans event at Haydock in March: stays 23f: acts on heavy going: tried in headgear: often races lazily. *Venetia Williams*

PRETTY LITTLE LIAR (IRE) 6 br.m. Excellent Art – Pont Allaire (IRE) (Rahy **h80** (USA)) [2018/19 h16m h18.7g⁶ Sep 4] modest maiden hurdler: stays 2½m: acts on good to firm going: tried in tongue tie: tends to find little. *David Peter Dunne, Ireland*

PRETTY MISS MAHLER (IRE) 8 b.m. Mahler – So Pretty (IRE) (Presenting) **c100** [2018/19 c100, h98: c26.2gᶠ c25.5g⁵ h23.9g³ c24.2d* c26.9d⁵ c26.2g³ c26.2d⁴ Mar 24] **h85** modest handicap hurdler: fair handicap chaser: won mares event at Wetherby in December: stays 27f: acts on heavy going: has worn headgear, including in 2018/19. *Martin Todhunter*

PRETTY RECKLESS (IRE) 6 b.m. Scorpion (IRE) – Deep Supreme (IRE) (Supreme **c109 §** Leader) [2018/19 c106, h–: c20m² c19.2g² h15.8g² h19.6g Aug 20] modest maiden hurdler: **h95 §** fair handicap chaser: stays 21f: acts on good to firm and good to soft going: has worn headgear, including in 2018/19: weak finisher. *Dan Skelton*

PRIDE OF LECALE 8 b.g. Multiplex – Rock Gossip (IRE) (Inchinor) [2018/19 h20v⁵ **h106 p** h18.5d⁶ h20.5d Mar 1] well-made gelding: chasing type: Irish point winner: useful bumper performer in 2015/16: fair form over hurdles: usually wears tongue tie: remains with potential. *Fergal O'Brien*

PRIMAL FOCUS (IRE) 5 b.g. Intense Focus (USA) – Churn Dat Butter (USA) **c109** (Unbridled (USA)) [2018/19 b16.8s² b16g³ h16g⁴ h16d⁵ h16.4gᶠ h16.8g⁵ h16v h19d⁴ **h101** c20.2g³ c23.8d⁵ c21.2g² c21.2dᶠ c25.8g* Apr 20] good-topped gelding: half-brother to **b87** several winners on Flat: dam US maiden: fair form in bumpers/over hurdles: similar form over fences: won handicap at Newton Abbot in April: stays 3¼m: acts on good to soft going: tried in cheekpieces: sometimes in tongue tie. *Christian Williams*

PRIME VENTURE (IRE) 8 br.g. Primary (USA) – Next Venture (IRE) (Zaffaran **c138** (USA)) [2018/19 h135: h22.8g c20.9d⁶ c23.8v c20gᴿ c23.6v² c23.6s³ c34v⁴ c28.8g Apr 27] **h105** useful-looking gelding: useful handicap hurdler, below form first outing in 2018/19: useful maiden chaser: second in handicap at Chepstow (2½ lengths behind Ramses de Teillee) in December: stays 3m: acts on good to firm and heavy going: races towards rear. *Evan Williams*

PRIMOGENITURE (IRE) 8 b.g. Glory of Dancer – Jacqueline (IND) (King Charlemagne (USA)) [2018/19 h83: h19g³ h20g⁵ h18.7m⁵ h18.7gᵖᵘ h20g c15.7g h15.8g⁵ h15.5g³ h16d⁴ h19.7d h19.5d c17.8g³ Apr 24] sturdy gelding: has had breathing operation: modest maiden hurdler: poor form over fences: stays 19f: best form on good going: often wears headgear: tried in tongue tie: temperamental. *Martin Keighley*   c75 h97 §

PRINCE CHARMIN' (IRE) 6 b.g. High Chaparral (IRE) – Dream Club (Dansili) [2018/19 h16.2g² h16.3d Mar 22] rather leggy gelding: has had breathing operation: dam half-sister to smart hurdler (stayed 3m) Hora, herself dam of smart hurdler/useful chaser (stays 25f) Thomas Campbell: fair on Flat, stays 17f: fairly useful handicap hurdler: left A. J. Martin after final start in 2017/18: stays 2½m: acts on heavy going: tried in cheekpieces: wears tongue tie. *Tim Vaughan*   h123

PRINCE DUNDEE (IRE) 6 b.g. Stowaway – Miss Dundee (IRE) (Bob Back (USA)) [2018/19 h84: h16g⁶ h16.2g⁵ c16.5s⁶ c24.1d⁵ c20.9v⁵ c24.2d* c24.2g* Apr 15] good-topped gelding: poor maiden hurdler: modest form over fences: won handicaps at Hexham in March and April: stays 3m: acts on good to soft going: in cheekpieces last 2 starts: wears tongue tie. *Lucinda Russell*   c93 h58

PRINCE FLORBURY 6 b.g. Prince Flori (GER) – Lady Sambury (Overbury (IRE)) [2018/19 h–, b–: h16gᵖᵘ May 7] no form: tried in hood: in tongue tie last 3 starts. *Maurice Barnes*   h–

PRINCE GARYANTLE (IRE) 9 b.g. Exit To Nowhere (USA) – Last Sunrise (IRE) (Shahanndeh) [2018/19 c111p, h134: c21g³ c21.2m³ h22.5d⁶ h24s³ h24g Dec 28] tall gelding: fairly useful handicap hurdler: fair form in maiden chases: stays 25f: acts on soft going: wears headgear/tongue tie: front runner/races prominently. *Matthew J. Smith, Ireland*   c103 h125

PRINCE KHURRAM 9 b.g. Nayef (USA) – Saree (Barathea (IRE)) [2018/19 c–, h108: h19.6g h17.2m⁶ h16.2g* h20.2g Aug 1] good-topped gelding: fair handicap hurdler: won at Perth (conditionals) in July: winning chaser: stays 21f: acts on any going: has worn cheekpieces: wears tongue tie. *Donald McCain*   c– h108

PRINCE LLYWELYN 5 ch.g. Schiaparelli (GER) – La Marette (Karinga Bay) [2018/19 b15.7d² b16d* b16.3d² Mar 23] £30,000 3-y-o: third foal: dam (h90) 2m-2¾m hurdle winner (stayed 25f): fairly useful form in bumpers: won at Wetherby in January: best effort when second in Goffs UK Spring Sales Bumper at Newbury (4½ lengths behind Get In The Queue) in March. *Kim Bailey*   b104

PRINCE MAHLER (IRE) 9 b.g. Mahler – Strokestown Queen (IRE) (Presenting) [2018/19 c–, h98: h21.4m⁵ May 10] modest handicap hurdler: fifth at Wincanton sole outing under Rules in 2018/19: subsequently placed in points: well held completed start in chases: stays 25f: acts on soft and good to firm going: tried in headgear: has worn tongue tie, including last 4 starts. *Kayley Woollacott*   c– h91

PRINCE OF STEAL (IRE) 9 b.g. Craigsteel – Princess Gloria (IRE) (Prince Rupert (FR)) [2018/19 h15.8dᵖᵘ h23.8g h25d Jan 25] good-topped gelding: Irish point winner: useful hurdler at best, no form in 2018/19 after lengthy lay-off: failed to complete both starts in chases: has worn headgear, including last 2 outings in 2018/19. *James Evans*   c– h–

PRINCESS MIDNIGHT 5 ch.m. Midnight Legend – Setter's Princess (Generous (IRE)) [2018/19 b–: b15.3m h18.5g h18.5gᵖᵘ h16.3g⁴ h21.6s⁴ h23.9d⁵ h23.9g h23.9d³ h21.4g h23.9d⁵ Apr 24] rather unfurnished mare: no form in bumpers: poor maiden hurdler: left Ron Hodges after third start: stays 2¾m: acts on soft going: tried in tongue tie. *Colin Tizzard*   h77 b–

PRINCESS MONONOKE (IRE) 8 b.m. Oscar (IRE) – Grande Solitaire (FR) (Loup Solitaire (USA)) [2018/19 h104: h20v³ h16.2v⁵ Mar 14] Irish point winner: fair handicap hurdler, below form in 2018/19: stays 2½m: best form on soft/heavy going. *Donald McCain*   h89

PRINCESS ROXY 6 ch.m. Midnight Legend – Royal Roxy (IRE) (Exit To Nowhere (USA)) [2018/19 b94: h19.5d h16.3g³ h15.7d⁵ Nov 20] rather unfurnished mare: has had breathing operation: Irish point winner: bumper winner: modest form over hurdles: wears tongue tie. *Ben Case*   h95

PRINCETON ROYALE (IRE) 10 br.g. Royal Anthem (USA) – Shelikesitstraight (IRE) (Rising) [2018/19 c131, h–: c24.2g* c21.2m² c20s⁴ c21.6m⁴ c21m* c19.9m² Apr 20] lengthy gelding: winning hurdler: useful handicap chaser: won at Fakenham in June and Ascot in March: stays 25f: acts on soft and good to firm going: wears headgear: usually leads. *Neil King*   c142 h–

PRINTING DOLLARS (IRE) 6 br.m. Doyen (IRE) – Printing Polly (IRE) (Blueprint (IRE)) [2018/19 b16g* h21.4g² h21d² h23.1s* h23.1d* h26s h24.3m² Apr 12] £60,000 5-y-o: rather unfurnished mare: first foal: dam, winning pointer, half-sister to fairly useful hurdler/useful chaser (2m-19f winner) The Russian Doyen (by Doyen): Irish point winner: won mares bumper at Warwick (by length from Eleanorofaquitaine) in November: useful form over hurdles: won mares maiden at Exeter in January and handicap there in February: second in mares handicap at Ayr in April: stays 3m: acts on soft and good to firm going: usually races prominently. *Warren Greatrex* **h130 b89**

PRIVATE MALONE (IRE) 10 b.g. Darsi (FR) – Native Artist (IRE) (Be My Native (USA)) [2018/19 c125, h–: c20sᵘʳ h20.5dᵖᵘ Mar 2] rangy gelding: useful hurdler/fairly useful maiden chaser, failed to complete both starts in 2018/19: stays 23f: acts on heavy going: wears headgear. *Emma Lavelle* **c– h–**

PROGRESS DRIVE (IRE) 8 b.g. Stowaway – Dolphins View (IRE) (Dolphin Street (FR)) [2018/19 c132, h–: c24.1v⁴ c32.4g³ c32.6g c23.8gᵖᵘ Apr 24] has had breathing operation: winning hurdler: useful handicap chaser: third at Kelso (7½ lengths behind Harry The Viking) in December: stays 4m: acts on heavy going: has worn headgear, including last 3 starts. *Nicky Richards* **c131 h–**

PROJECT BLUEBOOK (FR) 6 bl.g. Sinndar (IRE) – Apperella (Rainbow Quest (USA)) [2018/19 h133: h16s h20d Apr 5] workmanlike gelding: useful hurdler at best, no form in 2018/19: barely stays 2½m: acts on soft going. *John Quinn* **h–**

PROJECT MARS (IRE) 7 b.g. Presenting – Molly Massini (IRE) (Dr Massini (IRE)) [2018/19 h97: h21.7g May 9] modest maiden hurdler, behind sole outing in 2018/19: stays 2¾m: acts on good to firm and heavy going: has worn headgear, including last 4 starts. *Nick Gifford* **h–**

PROMISE OF PEACE (JPN) 5 ch.g. King Kamehameha (JPN) – Peace of World (JPN) (Sunday Silence (USA)) [2018/19 h16.7g⁵ h16.2g³ h15.8g⁵ h16.8s² h16.4d Mar 5] has had breathing operation: useful on Flat in Germany, stays 1½m: modest form over hurdles: raced around 2m: acts on soft going: tried in cheekpieces: in tongue tie last 4 starts. *Donald McCain* **h97**

PRONTO TONTO (IRE) 6 b.g. Thousand Words – Island Sun (IRE) (Trans Island) [2018/19 h82: h16.7g² May 11] modest form over hurdles: tried in blinkers: usually races towards rear. *Tim Easterby* **h91**

PROPHETS PRAYER (IRE) 5 b.m. Azamour (IRE) – Prophets Honor (FR) (Highest Honor (FR)) [2018/19 b16.7g⁴ b15.7g* h16.6m⁵ h20.3d³ Apr 24] fourth foal: sister to bumper winner/fairly useful 2m hurdle winner Irish Prophecy: dam (b88), runner-up in bumper only start, half-sister to high-class hurdler/very smart chaser (2m-2½m winner) Wahiba Sands: fair form in bumpers: won maiden at Southwell in October: modest form over hurdles: better effort when third in mares novice at same course: wears hood. *Emma Lavelle* **h98 b85**

PROTEK DES FLOS (FR) 7 b.g. Protektor (GER) – Flore de Chantenay (FR) (Smadoun (FR)) [2018/19 c–, h133: h23g³ Jun 2] useful-looking gelding: useful handicap hurdler: third at Worcester sole outing in 2018/19: twice-raced chaser: should stay 3m: acts on heavy going: tried in cheekpieces. *Nicky Henderson* **c– h126**

PROTEKTORAT (FR) 4 b.g. Saint des Saints (FR) – Protektion (FR) (Protektor (GER)) [2018/19 h17.9s² h16.8dᵘʳ h16.8d⁵ h16m Feb 23] good-topped gelding: third foal: half-brother to French 2¼m chase winner Protektrice (by Turgeon): dam (c133/h135) French 15f-21f hurdle/chase winner: fairly useful form over hurdles: second in listed newcomers race at Auteuil in September, only start for G. Cherel: remains capable of better. *Dan Skelton* **h122 p**

PROUD GAMBLE (IRE) 10 b.g. Brian Boru – Sister Anna (Gildoran) [2018/19 c25.5gᵖᵘ c25.5m⁴ Jun 29] workmanlike gelding: maiden hurdler: modest handicap chaser: lame final outing: stays 3m: acts on soft going: wears tongue tie. *Rose Dobbin* **c90 h–**

PRUDHOMME (FR) 4 ch.g. Martaline – Panzella (FR) (Kahyasi) [2018/19 b15.3gᵘʳ b16.3s² b15.8s* Apr 7] sixth foal: half-brother to several winners, including smart hurdler/useful chaser Pont Alexandre (17f-2¾m winner, by Dai Jin) and fairly useful French hurdler Ponte Fortune (17f winner, by Soldier of Fortune): dam unraced: fairly useful form in bumpers: won at Ffos Las in April: open to further improvement. *Nick Williams* **b100 p**

PRUSSIA WITH LOVE 5 b.m. Presenting – Ruby Royale (King's Theatre (IRE)) [2018/19 b16.3s³ Mar 11] first foal: dam unraced sister to fairly useful hurdler/chaser (stayed 2¾m) Kings Lodge out of sister to high-class hurdler (stayed 25f) Marello: 11/1, third in maiden bumper at Stratford (¾ length behind Now Is The Winter). *Dan Skelton* **b88**

PSYCHEDELIC ROCK 8 b.g. Yeats (IRE) – Gemini Lucy (IRE) (Glacial Storm **c133 p** (USA)) [2018/19 h126, b–: h20g² h23.1g⁴ h20g* h25g⁴ c20g² c20d* c20gᵖᵘ Apr 27] tall **h129** gelding: fairly useful handicap hurdler: won at Worcester in August: useful form over fences: won maiden at Ludlow (by 2½ lengths from Equus Secretus) in December: stays 21f: acts on good to firm and good to soft going: wears cheekpieces: remains with potential as a chaser. *Ian Williams*

PSYCHOCANDY (IRE) 7 b.m. Oscar (IRE) – Derrigra Sublime (IRE) (Flemensfirth **c82 §** (USA)) [2018/19 c–, h83: c24g³ c24g³ c22.5g² c23.9m⁴ c25.8s³ c22.5g³ c24g⁶ c23g³ Oct **h–** 24] lengthy mare: maiden hurdler: poor maiden chaser: stays 25f: acts on good to firm and good to soft going: wears headgear: usually in tongue tie: irresolute. *Ian Williams*

PSYCHOLOGY 6 b.g. Shamardal (USA) – Emotion Parade (ARG) (Parade Marshal **c–** (USA)) [2018/19 h16.7mᵖᵘ h16.8m⁶ h16.2g c16.4m⁴ c19.3g⁴ c19.3gᵖᵘ c19.2gᶠ Nov 23] **h–** modest maiden on Flat, probably stays 2m: no form over hurdles/fences: wears headgear: usually in tongue tie. *Kenny Johnson*

PULLING POWER 9 br.m. Erhaab (USA) – Pulling Strings (IRE) (Accordion) [2018/19 **c111** h–: c23g⁵ c22.5g* c20g³ c23gᵖᵘ Feb 19] good-bodied mare: has had breathing operation: **h–** fair hurdler: similar form over fences: won mares handicap at Uttoxeter in November: should stay 3m: acts on heavy going: wears tongue tie: front runner/races prominently. *Jeremy Scott*

PULLMAN BROWN (USA) 7 b.g. Big Brown (USA) – Touch Too Much (USA) (Holy **h–** Bull (USA)) [2018/19 h19.3g⁵ h16.2g h20.8gᵖᵘ h16.8s h15.8vᵖᵘ h15.7g h16.6d⁵ Mar 1] modest on Flat, probably stays 1½m: no form over hurdles: tried in hood: usually races off pace. *Philip Kirby*

PULL TOGETHER (IRE) 7 b.g. Curtain Time (IRE) – Whos To Know (IRE) **c115** (Bravefoot) [2018/19 h112, b–: c21.6d⁶ c15.7dᶠ c19.4d Mar 20] fairly useful hurdler: **h–** similar form over fences: stays 21f: best form on soft/heavy going: usually leads. *Stuart Edmunds*

PUPPETONASTRING 4 b.f. Sixties Icon – Valbuena (IRE) (Bob Back (USA)) [2018/19 **b76** b12.4g³ b16g Feb 19] £5,500 3-y-o: third foal: dam (b94), bumper winner, out of half-sister to Cheltenham Gold Cup winner Imperial Call: modest form in bumpers. *Tim Easterby*

PUPPET WARRIOR 7 ch.g. Black Sam Bellamy (IRE) – Rakajack (Rakaposhi King) **c112** [2018/19 h113: c22.5d⁴ May 5] sturdy gelding: fair maiden hurdler: 18/1, fourth in novice **h–** handicap at Uttoxeter (4¾ lengths behind Fact Flow) on chasing debut: stays 2¾m: acts on soft going: tried in cheekpieces. *Nick Gifford*

PURCELL'S BRIDGE (FR) 12 b.g. Trempolino (USA) – Theatrical Lady (USA) **c113** (Theatrical) [2018/19 c93, h–: c23.4g⁴ c23.8g³ Apr 25] winning hurdler/pointer: fair **h–** chaser: stays 3¼m: acts on good to firm and heavy going: usually wears hood: usually races off pace. *Rose Dobbin*

PURDEY (IRE) 5 ch.m. Mastercraftsman (IRE) – Corryvreckan (IRE) (Night Shift **h–** (USA)) [2018/19 h15.7gᵖᵘ Oct 10] half-sister to modest 2½m hurdle winner Mollyow (by Iceman): poor maiden on Flat: little impact over hurdles. *Lawrence Mullaney*

PURE AFFECTION (IRE) 8 b.m. Beneficial – Regents Dancer (IRE) (Flemensfirth **h87** (USA)) [2018/19 b86: h15.5d⁶ h15.8d h16.7g⁶ h19.6g³ Apr 13] sturdy mare: Irish point winner: fair form in bumpers: modest form over hurdles: tried in cheekpieces. *Ian Williams*

PURE SCIENCE (IRE) 11 ch.g. Galileo (IRE) – Rebelline (IRE) (Robellino (USA)) **c–** [2018/19 h21.3s Dec 26] compact gelding: fairly useful handicap hurdler at best: won **h103** completed start over fences: stayed 23f: acted on heavy going: tried in cheekpieces: dead. *Sue Smith*

PURE VISION (IRE) 8 b.g. Milan – Distillery Lane (IRE) (Exit To Nowhere (USA)) **c–** [2018/19 c131, h–: h27.3g Nov 17] useful-looking gelding: winning hurdler: useful chaser **h–** at best, well held sole outing in 2018/19: will be suited by extreme distances: acts on heavy going: wears tongue tie: usually races towards rear. *Anthony Honeyball*

PURPLE HARRY 11 gr.g. Sir Harry Lewis (USA) – Ellfiedick (Alfie Dickins) [2018/19 **c95** c88, h–: c24.5v⁵ c24.1s h23.3vᵖᵘ c26.2dᵖ c23.4d² Apr 6] winning hurdler: modest handicap **h–** chaser: won at Carlisle in March: stays 3¼m: acts on heavy going: has worn headgear, including in 2018/19: in tongue tie last 2 starts: usually front runner/races prominently. *Tina Jackson*

PURPLE JAZZ (IRE) 4 b.g. Red Jazz (USA) – Breakmeheart (IRE) (Galileo (IRE)) **h62** [2018/19 h15.8d h16.5d h16.8g⁵ Apr 20] modest on Flat, stays 1½m: poor form over hurdles: in tongue tie last 2 starts. *Jeremy Scott*

PURPLE 'N GOLD (IRE) 10 b.g. Strategic Prince – Golden Dew (IRE) (Montjeu (IRE)) [2018/19 c122§, h104§: h16g³ h20.7g c16.3g⁴ c17.8g⁴ Jun 16] compact gelding: fair handicap hurdler nowadays: useful handicap chaser at best, little show last 2 starts: stays 2½m: acts on good to firm and good to soft going: wears headgear: has worn tongue tie: unreliable. *David Pipe* **c72 §** **h97 §**

PUSH THE TEMPO (IRE) 6 b.g. Gold Well – Fairpark (IRE) (Shardari) [2018/19 b16g* h21.6g* h21.6d* h19.5d⁵ h20.5s³ h20d h19.8g⁵ Apr 27] €18,000 3-y-o, £12,000 5-y-o: sturdy gelding: half-brother to bumper winner/useful chaser War of The World (2½m-23f winner, by Shernazar): dam unraced: Irish point winner: won conditionals/ amateurs bumper at Worcester (by 8 lengths from Rose Crown) in June: fairly useful form over hurdles: won maiden at Newton Abbot in July and novice there in September: stays 2¾m: acts on soft going: wears hood. *Robert Stephens* **h123** **b96**

PUTDECASHONTHEDASH (IRE) 6 b.g. Doyen (IRE) – Be My Adelina (IRE) (Be My Native (USA)) [2018/19 h23.1sᵖᵘ h23.6d c26g³ Apr 12] £7,500 5-y-o: sixth foal: half-brother to useful hurdler/winning pointer Arthurian Legend (2m-2½m winner, by Alflora), stayed 3m: dam (b92) bumper winner: made frame on first of 2 starts in Irish points: no form in novice hurdles/chase: in tongue tie last 2 starts. *Keiran Burke* **c–** **h–**

PUT THE LAW ON YOU (IRE) 4 b.g. Declaration of War (USA) – Spirit of Tara (IRE) (Sadler's Wells (USA)) [2018/19 ab16.3s⁴ Jan 15] half-brother to several winners, including fair 2m hurdle winner Akarem (by Kingmambo): dam useful 1½m winner: 16/1, fourth in maiden bumper at Newcastle (3 lengths behind Basildon): little show in 2 minor events on Flat. *Alistair Whillans* **b82**

PUTTING GREEN 7 ch.g. Selkirk (USA) – Ryella (USA) (Cozzene (USA)) [2018/19 h16v h19.7s² h19.8sᵖᵘ h19d² h20.2g⁵ Apr 25] strong, compact gelding: fair maiden hurdler: stays 2½m: acts on soft going: in cheekpieces last 3 starts. *Neil Mulholland* **h113**

PUZZLE CACHE 5 b.m. Phoenix Reach (IRE) – Secret Queen (Zafeen (FR)) [2018/19 b–: b16.8g May 16] no form in bumpers: in blinkers last 2 starts: modest form on Flat. *Martin Hill* **b–**

PYJAMA GAME (IRE) 13 b.g. Hernando (FR) – Princess Claudia (IRE) (Kahyasi) [2018/19 c24.2g⁵ Apr 15] multiple point winner: maiden hurdler: fair chaser at best: stays 27f: acts on good to firm and heavy going: has worn headgear: temperamental. *Miss Lucy Brown* **c– §** **h– §**

PYM (IRE) 6 b.g. Stowaway – Liss Rua (IRE) (Bob Back (USA)) [2018/19 h102: h16d* h15.7m² h21g² h21d* h20.3d Mar 15] compact gelding: bumper winner: fairly useful form over hurdles: won novices at Chepstow in October and Kempton in January: second in Hyde Novices' Hurdle at Cheltenham: will stay 3m: acts on good to firm and good to soft going: usually front runner/races prominently. *Nicky Henderson* **h127**

PYRIOS (FR) 6 b.g. Heliostatic (IRE) – Nuance Tartare (FR) (Nononito (FR)) [2018/19 h104, b83: h21.4m³ May 10] maiden pointer: fair maiden hurdler: will stay 3m: acts on soft and good to firm going. *Philip Hobbs* **h100**

PYROMANIAC (IRE) 9 b.g. Invincible Spirit (IRE) – Silly Goose (IRE) (Sadler's Wells (USA)) [2018/19 h17d h18.6m h16sᵖᵘ h16.8g Apr 17] sturdy gelding: useful handicap hurdler, went wrong way in 2018/19: maiden chaser: left A. J. Martin after second start: unproven beyond 17f: acts on good to firm and heavy going: has worn headgear, including in 2018/19: wears tongue tie. *Alastair Ralph* **c–** **h127**

Q

QAWAMEES (IRE) 4 b.g. Exceed And Excel (AUS) – Jabhaat (USA) (Hard Spun (USA)) [2018/19 h16d³ h16.4s⁵ h15.6g⁶ Feb 13] has had breathing operation: fairly useful on Flat (should stay beyond 1¼m): fair form in juvenile maiden on hurdling debut: excuses both outings after: tried in tongue tie. *Michael Easterby* **h104**

QUALANDO (FR) 8 b.g. Lando (GER) – Qualite Controlee (FR) (Poliglote) [2018/19 c133, h133: c20g³ c23g³ h21.6g² Aug 15] good-topped gelding: fairly useful handicap hurdler/maiden chaser nowadays: stays 2¾m, effective at shorter: acts on heavy going: wears headgear. *Alan Jones* **c124** **h128**

QUAMINO (GER) 6 ch.g. Lord of England (GER) – Quintana (GER) (Fantastic Light (USA)) [2018/19 h16s² h16g⁶ c21g* c20d³ c17gᵘʳ c16d² c17g* c20.2sᵖᵘ c16.7g² Apr 21] workmanlike gelding: fourth foal: half-brother to a winning pointer by Black Sam Bellamy and 2 winners abroad on Flat, including smart 1m-1¼m winner Quelindo (by Aussie **c138** **h108**

Rules): dam placed around 1¼m in Germany: winning hurdler: useful chaser: won maiden at Fairyhouse in November and Goffs Handicap at Leopardstown (by ½ length from Dakota Moirette) in February: stays 21f: acts on heavy going: wears tongue tie. *Paul Nolan, Ireland*

QUANTATMENTAL (IRE) 4 ch.g. New Approach (IRE) – Anayid (A P Indy (USA)) **h110**
[2018/19 h16d⁴ h16g h16d h16g* h15.7m⁵ h16d Apr 22] fairly useful on Flat, stays 1½m: fair form over hurdles: won novice at Fairyhouse in February: raced at 2m: acts on good to soft and good to firm going. *Gavin Patrick Cromwell, Ireland*

QUANTUM OF SOLACE 9 b.m. Kayf Tara – Fashion House (Homo Sapien) [2018/19 **c108**
c–, h–: h16.2g* h16.7m⁴ h15.8g⁴ c19.9d² c19.4v² c19.2s² c16d* c15.9g⁴ c17.2g³ Mar 27] **h96**
compact mare: modest handicap hurdler: won mares race at Perth early in season: fair handicap chaser: won novice event at Ludlow in February: stays 2½m: acts on good to firm and heavy going: usually wears hood: tried in tongue tie. *Fergal O'Brien*

QUARENTA (FR) 7 b.g. Voix du Nord (FR) – Negresse de Cuta (FR) (Baroud d'Honneur **c132**
(FR)) [2018/19 h115: h19.2m c23.6s⁴ c24d* c23.4d⁶ c25.5d* c25.6m² Apr 20] compact **h–**
gelding: fair hurdler: useful form over fences: won handicaps at Warwick in December and February: second in similar event at Haydock (¾ length behind Mahlermade) in April: stays 3¼m: acts on good to firm and good to soft going: tried in cheekpieces: has shown some quirks. *Jonjo O'Neill*

QUARRY WIZARD (IRE) 9 b.g. Trans Island – Hazel Green (IRE) (Teamster) **c62**
[2018/19 h71: h23.3d⁶ h23.9d c24g⁵ c26.2g Apr 26] strong gelding: Irish point winner: **h76**
poor maiden hurdler: similar form in chases: left Oliver Greenall after first start: should stay further than 19f: acts on heavy going: usually wears headgear: in tongue tie last 2 starts. *Milton Harris*

QUASHA 6 b.m. Black Sam Bellamy (IRE) – Gloriana (Formidable (USA)) [2018/19 b–: **h96**
b16.2m⁴ b15.7g⁴ h20.6gᵘʳ h15.8g⁶ h15.7dꟳ h15.7s h24.1d⁴ h25d⁵ h20.7d⁴ Mar 13] rather **b69**
leggy mare: poor form in bumpers: modest maiden hurdler: left John Wainwright after second start: stays 3m: acts on good to soft going. *Charles Pogson*

QUASI (IRE) 7 ch.g. Presenting – Pink Mist (IRE) (Montelimar (USA)) [2018/19 h–: **h–**
h22.8v h21.2mᵖᵘ Apr 1] no form over hurdles. *John Groucott*

QUEEN ADELAIDE 4 b.f. Helmet (AUS) – Spunger (Fraam) [2018/19 h16g³ h16.2g² **h98**
h16.6g h16d⁶ h16g² h16.5dᵖᵘ Mar 11] dam half-sister to fairly useful hurdler (stayed 2½m) Priors Gold: modest on Flat, stays 1¾m: modest form over hurdles: left John Ryan after fifth start: raced around 2m. *David Pipe*

QUEEN OF THE COURT (IRE) 6 b.m. Court Cave (IRE) – Waydale Hill (Minster **b69**
Son) [2018/19 b16.8s b16.8d⁵ Jan 1] €1,000 3-y-o, £15,000 5-y-o: seventh foal: closely related to fair hurdler/winning pointer Theatre Evening (2¾m winner, by King's Theatre) and bumper winner/useful hurdler Captain Zebo (19f/2½m winner, by Brian Boru): dam (h73), maiden hurdler (stayed 23f), half-sister to fairly useful hurdler/useful chaser (2½m/21f winner) Buckby Lane: off mark in Irish points at third attempt: poor form in bumpers. *Grant Cann*

QUEEN OF THE WIND 6 b.m. Shirocco (GER) – Kaydee Queen (IRE) (Bob's Return **h104**
(IRE)) [2018/19 h96, b–: h20.3g h15.8v* h20.6g* h19d Dec 30] fair handicap hurdler: won at Ffos Las (conditionals) and Market Rasen (mares) in November: stays 21f: acts on heavy going: usually races prominently. *Colin Tizzard*

QUEENOHEARTS (IRE) 6 ch.m. Flemensfirth (USA) – Chars (IRE) (Old Vic) **h130 p**
[2018/19 b107: h19.5s² h18.9v* h19.8s* h16.8d Mar 14] lengthy, rather unfurnished mare: useful bumper performer: similar form over hurdles: won listed mares novice at Haydock (by 1½ lengths from Danse Idol) in December and Jane Seymour Mares' Novices' Hurdle at Sandown (by 2¼ lengths from Danse Idol) in February: will be suited by 3m: remains with potential. *Stuart Edmunds*

QUEEN OLIVIA 11 b.m. King's Theatre (IRE) – Queen's Leader (Supreme Leader) **c114**
[2018/19 c113, h–: c25.3g³ c23.8d² c23.8g³ c23.8m² Mar 31] has had breathing operation: **h–**
point winner: winning hurdler: fair hunter chaser: stays 25f: acts on good to firm and heavy going: usually wears hood: tried in tongue tie. *Miss V. Collins*

QUEENS CAVE (IRE) 6 b.m. Court Cave (IRE) – Shuilan (IRE) (Good Thyne (USA)) **h– p**
[2018/19 b107: h20.5sᵖᵘ Jan 8] strong mare: won Irish point on debut: useful bumper performer: pulled up in mares novice on hurdling debut, found to be suffering from a fibrillating heart: should do better. *David Pipe*

QUEENS CLOAK (IRE) 6 b.m. Definite Article – Love Divided (IRE) (King's Ride) **h–**
[2018/19 h–: h20g Aug 22] shown little in bumper/2 starts over hurdles. *Jamie Snowden*

QUEEN'S MAGIC (IRE) 7 b.m. Kalanisi (IRE) – Black Queen (IRE) (Bob Back (USA)) [2018/19 b101: h19.9g[4] h16g[2] h15.8g[2] h20.3s[4] h16d[4] h16.7g[3] h20.5d[2] h20.2g[3] Apr 24] lengthy mare: placed in Irish point: bumper winner: fair maiden hurdler: should prove best up to 2½m: acts on soft going. *Neil Mulholland* **h112**

QUEENS PRESENT (IRE) 8 ch.m. Presenting – Fairy Dawn (IRE) (Old Vic) [2018/19 c23.4d[pu] c24g[pu] Apr 10] angular mare: point winner: fair hurdler: pulled up both starts in chases: stays 3¼m: acts on heavy going: tried in cheekpieces. *David Arbuthnot* **c–** **h–**

QUEL DESTIN (FR) 4 ch.g. Muhtathir – High Destiny (FR) (High Yield (USA)) [2018/19 h15.9m[F] h14.9s* h16d[2] h16m* h16.4g* h16.6g* h16s* h15.7g* h16.8d[5] Mar 15] **h135**

'Getting the maximum out of every horse we train' may be the aim of every racing stable, but not many fulfil that aspiration quite so well as Manor Farm Stables which provided no better example of the art in the latest season than the juvenile hurdler Quel Destin. Imported from France in the summer—having won at Auteuil in May on his final start for Guy Cherel—Quel Destin won five in a row after being beaten on his first start for Paul Nicholls at Chepstow in October. Quel Destin had to carry a penalty for his win at Auteuil on his first two starts but he made light of it when winning by twelve lengths at Kempton on his second appearance for Nicholls. His front-running, zestful style of racing, coupled with some fluent jumping, soon became the hallmark of Quel Destin's performances as he progressed into graded company, picking up the first such event of the winter for juveniles, the Grade 2 Prestbury at Cheltenham's November meeting (a race branded as the JCB Triumph Trial). The Prestbury provided a good early pointer to the state of play in the juvenile division as Quel Destin recorded a game victory over Cracker Factory, Never Adapt and Katpoli (with Montestrel, who had beaten Quel Destin at Chepstow, trailing home last).

More was needed, of course, if Quel Destin was to go on to make an impact in the Triumph Hurdle itself at the Cheltenham Festival, but two further victories in graded company saw him near the head of the Triumph ante-post betting at the turn of the year. Manor Farm Stables isn't known for holding back on its in-form horses, or for training its good horses just for Cheltenham, and Quel Destin completed his hat-trick for the yard with a battling display to land the odds by a neck from Elysees in the bet365 Summit Juvenile Hurdle at Doncaster in mid-December (Cracker

William Hill Victor Ludorum Juvenile Hurdle, Haydock—
Sean Bowen does the steering as Quel Destin completes his five-timer

Martin Broughton & Friends' "Quel Destin"

Factory ran poorly, coming last). Quel Destin was out again twelve days later in the Grade 1 Coral Finale Juvenile Hurdle at Chepstow where all the qualities that had made him tough to beat were on show again as he resolutely held off odds-on Adjali by a neck, the pair twenty-two lengths clear of the French-trained third Arverne. Quel Destin and Adjali each had one more run before meeting again in the Triumph Hurdle, Adjali finishing third (starting a short-priced favourite) to the Joseph O'Brien-trained pair Fakir d'Oudairies and Fine Brunello in the Finesse on Cheltenham's Trials day (another graded race confusingly also branded as the JCB Triumph Trial). Quel Destin waited for the William Hill Victor Ludorum at Haydock in mid-February, a long-standing race for juveniles which has fallen from grace since the days, back in the 'sixties, when it was won by the likes of Persian War and Coral Diver, both of whom went on to win the Triumph. Frodon and Top Notch have been among the best of the Victor Ludorum's most recent winners and Quel Destin didn't have to improve on his best form to land the odds by six lengths from Capone and two others (including the disappointing Torpillo who had been expected to give Quel Destin most to do). Quel Destin's winning run came to an end next time in the Triumph when, sent off 4/1 second favourite, he managed only fifth (two places ahead of Adjali) behind 20/1-shot Pentland Hills and Irish challengers Coeur Sublime and Gardens of Babylon, in a race marred by the fatal accident to the short-priced favourite Sir Erec. Quel Destin possibly did a little too much in front on this occasion and was headed before the last, fading to finish over ten lengths behind the winner. He wasn't seen out again, while Adjali was among the Triumph runners

690

who went on to Aintree for the Anniversary Hurdle, in which he came a good fourth behind his stablemate Pentland Hills, finishing one place behind Christopher Wood who was stepped up in grade to represent Quel Destin's stable.

Quel Destin (FR) (ch.g. 2015)	Muhtathir (ch 1995)	Elmaamul (ch 1987)	Diesis	
			Modena	
		Majmu (b 1988)	Al Nasr	
			Affirmative Fable	
	High Destiny (FR) (ch 2008)	High Yield (ch 1997)	Storm Cat	
			Scoop The Gold	
		Such Is Life (b 1990)	Akarad	
			Arosa	

Quel Destin is a strong gelding with the physique to make a chaser and it would come as no surprise to see him sent straight over fences in the next season, following in the footsteps of his stablemate Frodon, who finished eighth in the Triumph after winning the Victor Ludorum. French-bred youngsters are a major influence in jumping in Britain nowadays—Quel Destin was the sixth successive French-bred winner of the Finale Junior Hurdle—and they frequently go on to make their mark over fences after a short hurdling career (Defi du Seuil and Bristol De Mai are among those last half dozen Finale winners). Quel Destin's sire the Prix Jacques le Marois winner Muhtathir is also the sire of the Champion Bumper winner Envoi Allen, as well as of Doctor Dino who is making a name for himself as a sire of jumpers with such as La Bague Au Roi, Sharjah and Sceau Royal. Quel Destin's dam High Destiny was a fairly useful juvenile, winning twice at Clairefontaine, and Quel Destin is the only winner she has bred so far. Quel Destin's grandam Such Is Life won at a mile and a quarter as a two-year-old and is a sister to La Tirana, a useful performer at around a mile and a quarter who won in listed company, and to the very smart Arokar who ran in the Derby after winning the Prix Greffulhe and coming second in the Prix Lupin. This is basically a Flat family but La Tirana's numerous winners include a couple who did well over jumps, the useful French hurdler Fools Rush In, and the Finale Juvenile Hurdle and Anniversary Hurdle winner and Triumph Hurdle runner-up Walkon, who went on to show smart form over fences too, after returning from a tendon injury suffered at the end of his juvenile season. The genuine Quel Destin, a front runner who races with plenty of enthusiasm, has been seen only at around two miles to date but should stay further. He acts on soft and good to firm going. *Paul Nicholls*

QUERRY HORSE (FR) 7 b.g. Equerry (USA) – La Richelandiere (FR) (Garde Royale) [2018/19 c–, h115?: h21g⁵ h20g⁶ h23.3g⁴ h24.5g h25d² h23.1g⁴ Mar 27] good-topped gelding: has had breathing operation: fair handicap hurdler: winning chaser: stays 25f: acts on soft going: has worn headgear, including in 2018/19: has joined Leslie F. Young in USA. *Oliver Sherwood*   **c– h111**

QUEST FOR LIFE 7 b.g. Dapper – Lewesdon Duchess (Alhaatmi) [2018/19 h117, b94: h20.1g* h24.7g h19.7g⁵ h21.3s h19.4g³ h19.9s² c19.3v² c20d⁵ h20.5m⁵ Apr 13] fairly useful handicap hurdler: won at Hexham early in season: similar form over fences: better effort when second in novice handicap at Sedgefield: stays 21f: acts on good to firm and heavy going: usually in cheekpieces. *Mark Walford*   **c118 h120**

QUESTIONATION (IRE) 8 b.m. Dubai Destination (USA) – How Is Things (IRE) (Norwich) [2018/19 c25.8g⁵ h16s h15.9s⁵ h15.9d Jan 6] sturdy mare: placed in Irish points: modest bumper performer: well held in novice hurdles/chase: has worn headgear. *Paul Henderson*   **c– h69**

QUESTION OF FAITH 8 b.m. Yeats (IRE) – Anastasia Storm (Mozart (IRE)) [2018/19 h19.9g² h20.5v Nov 14] fairly useful on Flat, stays 17.5f: modest handicap hurdler: stays 2½m: acts on heavy going. *Martin Todhunter*   **h91**

QUICK BREW 11 b.g. Denounce – Darjeeling (IRE) (Presenting) [2018/19 c102, h–: c19.3g* c21.2g c24.2m⁶ c20.1g⁶ c23.8g² c24.2gᶠ c23.8g⁶ c21.1g² c21.3d⁵ c19.3dᵖᵘ Jan 21] winning hurdler: fair handicap chaser: won at Sedgefield early in season: stays 3m: acts on soft going: wears headgear/tongue tie. *Maurice Barnes*   **c101 h–**

QUICK GRABIM (IRE) 7 b.g. Oscar (IRE) – Top Her Up (IRE) (Beneficial) [2018/19 h16s* h16g* h16d⁴ h16g* Dec 2] smallish gelding: smart form over hurdles: won maiden at Listowel in September, Joe Mac Novices' Hurdle at Tipperary (by 5½ lengths) in October   **h145**

and Royal Bond Novices' Hurdle at Fairyhouse (by 3¾ lengths) in December, last 2 from Triplicate: raced around 2m: acts on soft going. *W. P. Mullins, Ireland*

QUICK N' EASY (IRE) 9 ch.g. Vertical Speed (FR) – Tarmons Duchess (IRE) (The c81
Parson) [2018/19 c91, h–: c26m^pu c25.8m⁴ c24g Jul 18] placed in points: lightly-raced h–
hurdler: modest form in chases: will stay beyond 3¼m: acts on good to firm and good to
soft going: wears hood: has joined David Brace. *Susan Gardner*

QUICK PICK (IRE) 8 b.g. Vinnie Roe (IRE) – Oscars Arrow (IRE) (Oscar (IRE)) c– p
[2018/19 h120: c20.5v^pu h23.3s⁴ h26d³ h27d² Jan 21] Irish point winner: fair handicap h113
hurdler: pulled up in novice handicap on chasing debut: stays 27f: acts on heavy going:
should do better over fences. *Jennie Candlish*

QUICK WAVE (FR) 6 b.m. Gentlewave (IRE) – Magicaldoun (FR) (Kaldoun (FR)) c–
[2018/19 c116, h102+: h16.8s² Apr 16] fair form over hurdles, second in maiden at Exeter h107
on sole start in 2018/19: fairly useful form over fences in France for Y. Fouin in 2017/18:
stays 2¼m: acts on soft going. *Venetia Williams*

QUIDS IN (IRE) 6 b.g. Pour Moi (IRE) – Quixotic (Pivotal) [2018/19 h114: h16.7g⁵ h113
h20d³ h24.1s² h22.8s h21.3g Apr 11] useful-looking gelding: has had breathing operation:
fair handicap hurdler: stays 3m: acts on heavy going: has worn headgear, including in
2018/19: wears tongue tie. *Donald McCain*

QUIET ACCOUNT (IRE) 11 b.g. Jimble (FR) – Celia's Pet (IRE) (Kemal (FR)) c94
[2018/19 c23.5g⁵ c23.8g⁵ c23g⁶ h24.4m h22g c23.5s³ c24.1g^ur c20d⁴ Dec 26] modest h87
maiden hurdler: modest handicap chaser: stays 3½m: acts on good to firm and heavy going:
tried in cheekpieces. *Colin A. McBratney, Ireland*

QUIET MOMENT (IRE) 5 b.m. Dandy Man (IRE) – Easee On (IRE) (Hawk Wing h–
(USA)) [2018/19 h15.7d^pu h16.4m Mar 28] has had breathing operation: modest on Flat,
stays 1m: hasn't taken to hurdling: wears tongue tie. *Maurice Barnes*

QUIETO SOL (FR) 8 ch.g. Loup Solitaire (USA) – First Wonder (FR) (Mansonnien c103
(FR)) [2018/19 h102: c20.9v⁴ c23.8s⁶ Feb 26] angular gelding: has had breathing operation: h–
fair hurdler: similar form over fences: better effort when fourth in novice handicap at Ffos
Las: possibly best at shorter than 3m: acts on heavy going: tried in cheekpieces. *Kerry Lee*

QUIET PENNY 5 b.m. Sholokhov (IRE) – Pennys Pride (IRE) (Pips Pride) [2018/19 h98
b16.2d⁵ b16d b15.8s h16.4s h16.4g⁵ h19.9v⁴ h16.4m⁵ h24d* Apr 6] closely related to fairly b80
useful hurdler/useful chaser Victor Hewgo (2½m-3m winner, by Old Vic) and half-sister to
several winners, including bumper winner/useful hurdler Crowning Jewel (2½m-2¾m
winner, by Sulamani): dam, (b104) bumper winner (also 1¼m winner on Flat), half-sister
to top-class chaser (stayed 2½m) Direct Route: modest form in bumpers: similar form over
hurdles: won novice handicap at Newcastle in April: stays 3m: acts on good to soft going:
has joined Dr Richard Newland. *Gillian Boanas*

QUIMBA (SPA) 5 b.m. Dink (FR) – Die Beste (SPA) (Spartacus (IRE)) [2018/19 h–, b–: h–
h16.3m³ May 20] sturdy mare: well held in bumper/over hurdles. *Nigel Twiston-Davies*

QUINTO 9 ch.g. Desideratum – Cruz Santa (Lord Bud) [2018/19 c–, h92: c23.8g³ c25.8m⁶ c89 §
c24g^pu h21.6g^pu c26m² h25.8g⁴ c24.2v^pu c25.2d² c21.6v³ Feb 14] medium-sized gelding: h77 §
point winner: modest handicap hurdler: modest maiden chaser: stays 25f: acts on heavy
going: wears headgear: usually wears tongue tie: temperamental. *Jimmy Frost*

QUITE BY CHANCE 10 b.g. Midnight Legend – Hop Fair (Gildoran) [2018/19 c144, c134
h–: c16m⁵ c25.8m² c20s⁵ c23d h21.6d⁴ c21d c25.1g³ c25.1s^pu c20.2g⁴ Mar 25] sturdy h87
gelding: has had breathing operations: maiden hurdler: useful handicap chaser: second at
Newton Abbot (½ length behind Pickamix) in July: stays 3¼m: acts on good to firm and
heavy going: tried in blinkers: wears tongue tie. *Colin Tizzard*

QUITE RIGHT 8 b.m. Lucarno (USA) – Thebelloftheball (Classic Cliche (IRE)) h–
[2018/19 h–: h16.8m h20s h20g Jun 11] well-made mare: unplaced in point: no form over
hurdles: in hood last 2 starts. *Polly Gundry*

QUIZ MASTER (IRE) 7 b.g. Ask – Good Bye Dolly (IRE) (Buckskin (FR)) [2018/19 c–
h115: h21g² h23.9v² h19.9d³ c23g^pu c20.3g Apr 13] lengthy gelding: fairly useful handicap h117
hurdler: placed first 3 starts in 2018/19: no form over fences: stays 3m: acts on heavy
going: wears tongue tie. *Colin Tizzard*

QUIZZACLE NOMAD 10 b.m. Nomadic Way (USA) – Quizzal (Afzal) [2018/19 c–
h15.8g^pu h15.7d h18.6s⁶ h15.7s c17.2g^pu c24.2g^pu Apr 15] first foal: dam, winning pointer, h–
half-sister to useful staying chaser Gypsy George: point winner: no form over hurdles/in
chases: tried in cheekpieces. *Laura Morgan*

QUOI DE NEUF (FR) 5 b.g. Anzillero (GER) – Qualite Controlee (FR) (Poliglote) **h119**
[2018/19 h20g* h19.8v⁴ h20s² Apr 7] €180,000 4-y-o: lengthy gelding: half-brother to
several winners, including useful hurdler Qualando (2m-19f winner, by Lando) and
bumper winner/useful hurdler Au Quart de Tour (2m winner, by Robin des Champs): dam,
French 17f-19f hurdle/chase winner, also 13f winner on Flat: easy winner of Irish point on
debut: fairly useful form over hurdles: won novice at Aintree in November. *Evan Williams*

QURI (IRE) 6 b.m. Gold Well – Wigwam Mam (IRE) (Commanche Run) [2018/19 h21g¹ **h118**
h20.5g² h23.3d* h22.8v² Dec 5] half-sister to bumper winner/top-class hurdler Brave Inca
(2m-2½m winner, including Champion Hurdle, by Good Thyne) and useful hurdler/fairly
useful chaser Yurok (2½m winner, by Alflora): dam unraced: fair form on first of 3 outings
in Irish bumpers: fairly useful form over hurdles: won mares handicap at Uttoxeter in
November: left Terence O'Brien after first start: often in hood: held up. *Tom Lacey*

R

RABUNDA (IRE) 9 b.g. Milan – Cush Ramani (IRE) (Pistolet Bleu (IRE)) [2018/19 h–: **c–**
c23.6d^pu Jan 25] useful-looking gelding: point winner: maiden hurdler: pulled up in novice **h–**
handicap on chasing debut: should stay 2¾m: tried in cheekpieces/tongue tie. *Tom George*

RACING SPIRIT 7 ch.g. Sir Percy – Suertuda (Domedriver (IRE)) [2018/19 h93: **h–**
h16.7s⁵ Mar 23] modest maiden hurdler, well held only start in 2018/19: stays 23f: acts on
good to soft going: tried in headgear/tongue tie. *Dave Roberts*

RADICAL ARCHIE 8 ch.g. Prince Arch (USA) – Radical Gunner (Gunner B) [2018/19 **h112**
h105: h19.5s* h15.8v² h23.9s^pu Apr 7] fair handicap hurdler: won at Chepstow in
November: stayed 19f: acted on heavy going: front runner/raced prominently: dead.
Evan Williams

RAECIUS FELIX (IRE) 5 ch.g. Stowaway – Dances With Waves (IRE) (Presenting) **h95 p**
[2018/19 h17.1d⁶ h16.4g⁴ h16.2g² Dec 29] €20,000 3-y-o: second foal: dam, no form, out
of sister to high-class chaser around 2½m Thisthatandtother: modest form over hurdles:
best effort when second in novice at Kelso: will be suited by 2½m: should progress further.
Ruth Jefferson

RAFFERTY (IRE) 5 b.g. Arcadio (GER) – Mighty Star (IRE) (Arctic Lord) [2018/19 **h88**
b15.7g³ h16.8m⁶ h16.2g^F h16.4d⁶ h15.5g⁶ h16.6g h17s Mar 7] €14,000 3-y-o: fourth foal: **b76**
dam (h109), 19f hurdle winner (stayed 3m), out of half-sister to triple King George VI
Chase winner Wayward Lad: modest form in bumpers/over hurdles: raced around 2m: tried
in hood: often races freely. *Stef Keniry*

RAFFLES SURPRISE (FR) 4 b.f. Sageburg (IRE) – Ruthenoise (FR) (Robin des **h84**
Champs (FR)) [2018/19 h16.9g⁵ h15.9g h18.7s Mar 11] second foal: half-sister to bumper
winner Raya Time (by Al Namix): dam (c134/h127) French 17f-19f hurdle/chase winner:
poor form over hurdles: left Francois Nicolle after first start, Ben Pauling after second.
Robert Bevis

RAHMAH (IRE) 7 b.g. Vale of York (IRE) – Sweet Home Alabama (IRE) (Desert Prince **h104**
(IRE)) [2018/19 h16.3s h16.3d h15.5g⁴ h15.8d⁶ h16d Apr 6] close-coupled gelding: half-
brother to useful hurdler Havana Beat (2m winner, by Teofilo), stayed 2½m, and fairly
useful hurdler King's Realm (2m-19f winner, by King's Best): dam half-sister to smart
hurdler/fairly useful chaser (stayed 25f) No Refuge: fair on Flat, stays 2m: fair form over
hurdles: standout effort when fourth in novice at Leicester. *Geoffrey Deacon*

RAID STANE (IRE) 13 b.g. Morozov (USA) – Rashhattan (IRE) (Rashar (USA)) **c–**
[2018/19 c–, h–: h25.4m⁵ Jul 1] sturdy gelding: multiple point winner: fair handicap **h84**
hurdler at best, very lightly raced nowadays: maiden chaser: stays 3¼m: acts on good to
firm and heavy going: wears headgear: has worn tongue tie. *Lucinda Egerton*

RAIFTEIRI (IRE) 12 b.g. Galileo (IRE) – Naziriya (FR) (Darshaan) [2018/19 c–x, h–: **c– x**
h16.2d May 5] rather leggy gelding: winning hurdler/maiden chaser, no longer of much **h–**
account: has worn headgear/tongue tie. *William Young Jnr*

RAILROAD JUNKIE (IRE) 6 b.g. Thousand Words – Eckbeag (USA) (Trempolino **c117**
(USA)) [2018/19 b86: b16.8g h15.8d³ h15.7g² h18.7m⁴ h15.7g⁶ c16.2g* c18g^ur c15.7g³ **h105**
c18.2d⁴ c16.1d* c16.1d² c16.5g³ c16m² Apr 1] sturdy gelding: placed in bumper: fair form **b72**
over hurdles: fairly useful handicap chaser: won at Warwick (novice event) in September
and Taunton in December: unproven beyond 2m: acts on good to soft going: wears tongue
tie. *Evan Williams*

RAILWAY STORM (IRE) 14 ch.g. Snurge – Stormy Bee (IRE) (Glacial Storm (USA)) **c86**
[2018/19 c94, h–: c21.6g⁴ c26g⁶ Jun 16] tall gelding: winning pointer: once-raced hurdler: **h–**
modest chaser: left C. White after first start: stays 31f: acts on good to firm and heavy
going: has worn cheekpieces, including in 2018/19: has worn tongue tie. *Bill Turner*

RAINBOW DREAMER 6 b.g. Aqlaam – Zamhrear (Singspiel (IRE)) [2018/19 h20s **h–**
h20.5d⁶ Dec 29] lengthy gelding: fairly useful hurdler in 2016/17: below best both starts
following long absence, but won on return to Flat in February: should be suited by 2½m:
acts on soft going: has worn headgear. *Alan King*

RAINBOW STRIPES 10 b.g. Rainbow High – Retorrick Rose (Lancastrian) [2018/19 **h–**
h26g^pu h24d^pu Nov 20] has had breathing operation: placed in points: pulled up both starts
in novice hurdles: tried in cheekpieces. *Nick Gifford*

RAIN IN THE FACE 6 b.g. Naaqoos – Makaaseb (USA) (Pulpit (USA)) [2018/19 c–, **c–**
h–: c16g⁶ May 16] has had breathing operation: no form over hurdles/fences: in tongue tie **h–**
last 2 starts. *Sam England*

RAINY CITY (IRE) 9 b.g. Kalanisi (IRE) – Erintante (IRE) (Denel (FR)) [2018/19 **c110 §**
c119§, h117§: c20.5g⁴ c23.8g c20s⁴ c24.1s⁴ h25.3s⁴ h23.8g² h25d h19.7g⁵ Apr 11] lengthy, **h114 §**
useful-looking gelding: fair handicap hurdler/chaser: left Iain Jardine after second start:
stays 25f: acts on firm and soft going: wears headgear/tongue tie: temperamental.
Donald McCain

RAINY DAY DYLAN (IRE) 8 br.g. Spadoun (FR) – Honeyed (IRE) (Persian Mews) **c106**
[2018/19 h118: c16.3d³ c16s^pu c19.2v^F c16d⁶ c16.1d⁴ c19.2d² c20.1v^F Mar 16] workmanlike **h–**
gelding: has had breathing operation: fairly useful hurdler: disappointing maiden chaser:
stays 2½m: acts on heavy going: wears hood/tongue tie. *Neil Mulholland*

RAISE A SPARK 9 b.g. Multiplex – Reem Two (Mtoto) [2018/19 h122: h16.2g⁴ c21.2g* **c136**
c17.3g* c21.2s² c20.1g³ c16.5d* c15.2s⁴ c15.7v^R c16.5d⁴ Feb 6] fairly useful handicap **h115**
hurdler: useful chaser: won maiden in May and handicap in July, both at Cartmel, and
3-runner handicap at Ayr (by 5 lengths from Ontopoftheworld) in November: stays 21f:
acts on heavy going: usually wears hood. *Donald McCain*

RAISE YOUR SHADES (IRE) 5 b.g. Morozov (USA) – Couleurs de Barra (IRE) **h84**
(Luso) [2018/19 h16g⁶ h17.7g^ur h15.8g h15.8g h15.5d h21.2d^pu h20.3s^pu Mar 18] €2,600 **b–**
3-y-o, £10,000 4-y-o: second foal: dam unraced half-sister to useful hurdler (stayed 3m)
Slim Pickens: third in point on debut: well beaten in bumper: poor form over hurdles.
Ben Pauling

RAISING THE BAR (IRE) 7 b.g. Kalanisi (IRE) – Cool Quest (IRE) (Turtle Island **h115**
(IRE)) [2018/19 b89: h16s⁴ h20d² h21g Apr 10] tall, useful-looking gelding: has had
breathing operation: placed in bumper: fairly useful form over hurdles: best effort when
second in novice at Fakenham: should be suited by further than 2½m. *Nicky Henderson*

RAJAPUR 6 gr.g. Dalakhani (IRE) – A Beautiful Mind (GER) (Winged Love (IRE)) **h–**
[2018/19 h105: h20.1g⁴ h16.8s^pu Dec 7] maiden hurdler, no form in 2018/19: won seller on
Flat in March: wears cheekpieces. *David Thompson*

RAKAIA ROSA (IRE) 10 b.m. Balakheri (IRE) – Ashanti's Dream (IRE) (Right Win **c–**
(IRE)) [2018/19 c91, h–: c16.5g c19.4m⁶ c22.6m^pu c17g^pu Aug 28] maiden hurdler: modest **h–**
chaser at best, no form in 2018/19: has worn headgear/tongue tie: usually leads.
Dai Williams

RAKHINE STATE (IRE) 6 b.g. Arakan (USA) – Oiselina (FR) (Linamix (FR)) **h112**
[2018/19 h20d⁶ h19.5d³ h20s h16.4d* h16d⁴ h16.2g* Apr 25] €7,000 3-y-o: half-brother to
several winners, including fair/ungenuine hurdler Diktalina (2m/17f winner, by Diktat),
stayed 2¾m: dam French 10.5f winner: fair hurdler: won maiden at Clonmel in February
and novice at Perth in April: stays 19f: acts on heavy going. *Gordon Elliott, Ireland*

RAKTIMAN (IRE) 12 ch.g. Rakti – Wish List (IRE) (Mujadil (USA)) [2018/19 c83, h–: **c–**
h24g^pu Jun 12] quite good-topped gelding: fairly useful hurdler/chaser at best, lightly raced **h–**
and no form since 2016/17: has worn cheekpieces: wears tongue tie. *Sam England*

RAMBLING RECTOR (FR) 7 ch.g. Bonbon Rose (FR) – Califea (FR) (Nikos) **h98**
[2018/19 h100: h22g² Nov 1] useful-looking gelding: has had breathing operation: won
Irish point on debut: modest form over hurdles. *Warren Greatrex*

RAMBLING RIVER 8 b.g. Revoque (IRE) – Just Beth (Carlingford Castle) [2018/19 **h–**
b–: h21d^pu h23.3s^pu h22g^pu Apr 14] no sign of ability. *Giuseppe Fierro*

RAMONEX (GER) 8 b.g. Saddex – Ramondia (GER) (Monsun (GER)) [2018/19 c130, **c115**
h115: c20.1g² Jun 3] workmanlike gelding: fairly useful hurdler/chaser: stays 19f: acts on **h–**
soft going: tried in cheekpieces/tongue tie: front runner/races prominently. *Richard Hobson*

RAMORE WILL (IRE) 8 gr.g. Tikkanen (USA) – Gill Hall Lady (Silver Patriarch (IRE)) [2018/19 c107, h106: h19.2g⁵ h19.8v⁵ Nov 11] tall, angular gelding: fair handicap hurdler/chaser: stays 3m: acts on good to firm and heavy going: wears headgear: often travels strongly. *Chris Gordon* **c–** **h101**

RAMSES DE TEILLEE (FR) 7 gr.g. Martaline – Princesse d'Orton (FR) (Saint Cyrien (FR)) [2018/19 c144, h119: c25.1g⁵ c23.6v* c29.5s² c28.4g² c34.3gᵖᵘ Apr 6] leggy gelding: has had breathing operation: maiden hurdler: smart handicap chaser: won at Chepstow (by 2½ lengths from Prime Venture) in December: second in Welsh Grand National (beaten 1¼ lengths by Elegant Escape) at same course and Grand National Trial (¾ length behind Robinsfirth) at Haydock: never better than mid-field in Grand National at Aintree: stays 29f: acts on heavy going: often travels strongly. *David Pipe* **c152** **h–**

RANCHER LASS (IRE) 8 gr.m. Tikkanen (USA) – Belledornie (IRE) (Buckskin (FR)) [2018/19 c93x, h–: c24.6g c20.1g⁵ Sep 26] maiden hurdler: modest chaser at best, no form in 2018/19: stays 3m: best form on good going: has worn hood, including in 2018/19: wears tongue tie: often races towards rear: often let down by jumping. *Karl Thornton, Ireland* **c– x** **h–**

RANDY PIKE (IRE) 9 b.g. Mahler – Niamh's Leader (IRE) (Supreme Leader) [2018/19 h117: h16.2d May 5] has had breathing operation: fairly useful handicap hurdler: stays 2¾m: acts on heavy going: in tongue tie last 4 starts. *Tim Easterby* **h106**

RANSKILL ROAD (IRE) 4 b.g. Jeremy (USA) – Tarziyma (IRE) (Kalanisi (IRE)) [2018/19 b16.8d Jan 11] tailed off in bumper. *Brian Ellison* **b–**

RAPAPORT 7 b.m. Dr Massini (IRE) – Seemarye (Romany Rye) [2018/19 b17g⁴ b16.3d² Jun 8] £1,500 3-y-o: second foal: dam, placed in point, half-sister to useful hurdler/chaser (stayed 25f) See You Sometime: won second of 2 starts in point bumpers: fair form in bumpers under Rules: better effort when second at Stratford: unseated in point in 2019: wears hood. *T. S. M. Bulgin* **b85**

RAPID FRITZ (IRE) 10 ch.g. Kutub (IRE) – Another Pet (IRE) (Un Desperado (FR)) [2018/19 c–, h90: h16.7g c16.4g⁴ c19.2d⁵ c17.3gᶠ h16.9gᶠ h15.6g h16.4d⁶ h16.4gᵖᵘ c16.4d c16.4sᵖᵘ c15.8mᵖᵘ h19.3s h19.9vᵖᵘ h16.8sᵖᵘ h16.8dᵘʳ Apr 23] maiden hurdler/chaser, no longer of any account: has worn blinkers: wears tongue tie. *Victor Thompson* **c–** **h–**

RAPPER 5 b.g. Scorpion (IRE) – Bling Noir (FR) (Moscow Society (USA)) [2018/19 b16.3m³ b16g⁴ h16.7d⁶ h16.7s³ h21.2g* h20g⁶ h21.2m² Apr 1] £8,500 3-y-o: third foal: dam, ran once over hurdles in France, half-sister to useful chaser up to 3m Katnap: fair form in bumpers: fairly useful form over hurdles: won maiden at Ludlow in January: stays 21f: acts on good to firm going. *Henry Daly* **h118** **b93**

RARE CLOUDS 5 b.g. Cloudings (IRE) – Rare Vintage (IRE) (Germany (USA)) [2018/19 b16d⁶ Jan 4] seventh foal: brother to useful hurdler/smart chaser Vintage Clouds (19f-25f winner), stays 4m, and half-brother to fairly useful hurdler/useful chaser Vintage Star (17f-3¼m winner, by Presenting): dam winning pointer: 18/1, sixth in bumper at Wetherby (11½ lengths behind Prince Llywelyn). *Sue Smith* **b84**

RARE LEGEND (IRE) 12 b.g. Stowaway – Shambala (IRE) (Imperial Ballet (IRE)) [2018/19 c82, h95: c23.5gᵖᵘ c20.1gᶠ Jun 2] winning hurdler: maiden chaser: left John Joseph Hanlon after first start: stayed 25f: acted on heavy going: wore cheekpieces: tried in tongue tie: dead. *Gemma Anderson* **c–** **h–**

RASASEE (IRE) 6 gr.g. Rip Van Winkle (IRE) – Gleaming Silver (IRE) (Dalakhani (IRE)) [2018/19 h107: h15.7g⁵ h20m h16g⁶ h16.3g h20.5m² h23.8g⁵ h19.9vᵖᵘ Dec 21] sturdy gelding: modest handicap hurdler: stays 21f: acts on good to firm going: has worn headgear, including in 2018/19. *Tim Vaughan* **h89**

RASHAAN (IRE) 7 ch.g. Manduro (GER) – Rayyana (IRE) (Rainbow Quest (USA)) [2018/19 h144: c19.5d² c19.5g² c18.2d* c22.5d² c20g⁴ c20gᵗʳ h16d³ h20d* Apr 22] smart hurdler: won Keelings Irish Strawberry Hurdle at Fairyhouse (by 1½ lengths from Not Many Left) in April: useful form over fences: won Grade 3 novice at Galway (by ½ length from Ornua) in August: stays easy 3m: acts on good to firm and heavy going: temperamental (refused to race when tried in cheekpieces). *Colin Thomas Kidd, Ireland* **c140 §** **h146 §**

RASHEE (IRE) 7 gr.m. Daylami (IRE) – Celtic Angel (IRE) (Bob Back (USA)) [2018/19 b85: b16.2g⁵ b17.1d h20.6g Jan 15] rather leggy mare: modest form in bumpers: well beaten in mares novice on hurdling debut: left Stuart Crawford after second start. *Simon Waugh* **h–** **b77**

RATFACEMCDOUGALL (IRE) 6 b.g. Robin des Champs (FR) – Milano Bay (IRE) (Milan) [2018/19 b16.4d h21g⁴ h24.4g* h26s h21.7g* Mar 26] €25,000 3-y-o, £50,000 5-y-o: sturdy gelding: first foal: dam (h94), placed over hurdles (stayed 2½m), half-sister **h112** **b–**

to Triumph Hurdle winner Spectroscope: off mark in Irish points at third attempt: well beaten in bumper: fair form over hurdles: won novices at Doncaster (3 ran) in December and Hereford in March: stays 3m. *Ben Case*

RATHER BE (IRE) 8 b.g. Oscar (IRE) – Irish Wedding (IRE) (Bob Back (USA)) [2018/19 c152p, h–: c20.2g^bd c20.6d^5 c24g h20.3g^pu Apr 17] good-topped gelding: useful hurdler/smart chaser at best, disappointing in handicaps in 2018/19: should stay 3m: acts on heavy going: tried in hood/tongue tie. *Nicky Henderson* — **c130 h–**

RATHHILL (IRE) 6 b.g. Getaway (GER) – Bella Venezia (IRE) (Milan) [2018/19 h16.3s* h16s^4 Jan 5] well-made gelding: first foal: dam, lightly raced, closely related to smart hurdler/top-class chaser (stays 29f) Bellshill: runner-up sole start in Irish points: fairly useful form over hurdles: won maiden at Newbury in December: 6/5, only fourth in Tolworth Novices' Hurdle at Sandown (11¾ lengths behind Elixir de Nutz) 17 days later: remains open to improvement. *Nicky Henderson* — **h125 p**

RATHLIN ROSE (IRE) 11 b.g. Bonbon Rose (FR) – A Plus Ma Puce (FR) (Turgeon (USA)) [2018/19 c131, h–: c24.2v^4 c24.2d c24.2d^ur c24.2d c23.8m* c31.8m c28.8g Apr 27] good-topped gelding: winning hurdler: fairly useful handicap chaser: won veterans event at Ascot in March: barely stays 3½m: acts on good to firm and heavy going: wears headgear: held up. *David Pipe* — **c129 h–**

RATHVINDEN (IRE) 11 b.g. Heron Island (IRE) – Peggy Cullen (IRE) (Presenting) [2018/19 c153, h–: c25d* c34.3g^3 Apr 6] sturdy gelding: winning hurdler: high-class chaser: off 10 months, better than ever when won Bobbyjo Chase at Fairyhouse (by 3½ lengths from Alpha des Obeaux) in February: couple of mistakes when 5 lengths third of 40 to Tiger Roll in Grand National at Aintree: stays 4¼m: acts on good to firm and heavy going. *W. P. Mullins, Ireland* — **c162 h–**

RATOUTE YUTTY 6 b.m. Midnight Legend – Easibrook Jane (Alderbrook) [2018/19 h15.7g^4 h20.3s^5 h19.5d^5 h16.6d^3 h16.3g^2 Apr 14] £11,000 3-y-o: good-topped mare: has had breathing operation: fifth foal: half-sister to useful hurdler Draco (2m/17f winner, by Hernando): dam (c98/h109) 19f-21f hurdle/chase winner: placed in bumpers: fairly useful form over hurdles: won maiden at Navan in 2017/18 for R. P. McNamara: second in mares handicap at Stratford in April: should stay beyond 2m: acts on heavy going: in tongue tie last 4 starts. *Dan Skelton* — **h115**

RAVEN COURT (IRE) 5 b.g. Court Cave (IRE) – Lady Kate Ellen (IRE) (Supreme Leader) [2018/19 b17g^3 b15.3s^6 b15.3g Apr 14] €80,000 3-y-o: strong gelding: fourth foal: dam (c97/h95), 2½m-3m hurdle/chase winner, half-sister to fairly useful hurdler/chaser (stayed 3m) Native Coral: fairly useful form in bumpers: easily best effort when third at Aintree on debut. *Philip Hobbs* — **b98**

BetVictor Bobbyjo Chase, Fairyhouse—Rathvinden goes on to many a Grand National short list following his smooth victory over Alpha des Obeaux

RAVENHILL (IRE) 9 b.g. Winged Love (IRE) – Rhythm Hill (IRE) (Orchestra) [2018/19 h18.8g² h21.3g* h24.8m* h24d² h19.9m* Aug 30] fifth foal: half-brother to useful chaser Ballycarney (23f/3m winner, by Classic Cliche): dam (h86) maiden in bumpers/over hurdles: point winner: useful form over hurdles: won maiden at Downpatrick in June, and novices at Kilbeggan later in June and Sedgefield in August: stays 25f: acts on good to firm and good to soft going: usually responds generously to pressure. *Gordon Elliott, Ireland* **h131**

RAVENHILL ROAD (IRE) 8 ch.g. Exit To Nowhere (USA) – Zaffarella (IRE) (Zaffaran (USA)) [2018/19 h123: c15.2g² c16.3d³ c16.4g³ c16.5m⁵ Apr 12] has had breathing operation: winning hurdler: fairly useful form over fences: unproven beyond 17f: acts on soft going: tried in cheekpieces/tongue tie. *Brian Ellison* **c128 h–**

RAVENOUS 8 b.g. Raven's Pass (USA) – Supereva (IRE) (Sadler's Wells (USA)) [2018/19 h16.3d h15.3g² h16m³ Apr 22] angular gelding: fairly useful on Flat, stays 14.5f: fair maiden hurdler: unproven beyond 2m: acts on soft and good to firm going: has worn cheekpieces. *Luke Dace* **h109**

RAVENSDALE (IRE) 7 ch.g. Flemensfirth (USA) – Thunder Belle (IRE) (Glacial Storm (USA)) [2018/19 h116, b93: h23.3g⁴ h19.9s c24v^pu h23.1d Feb 22] Irish point winner: fairly useful hurdle winner, but has become disappointing: pulled up in novice handicap on chasing debut: stays 19f: acts on heavy going: tried in visor. *Nigel Twiston-Davies* **c– h101**

RAVEN'S TOWER (USA) 9 b.g. Raven's Pass (USA) – Tizdubai (USA) (Cee's Tizzy (USA)) [2018/19 c–, h125: c19g^pu h16m³ h16g³ h15.8d h19d³ Jan 19] compact gelding: fairly useful handicap hurdler: useful chaser at best, pulled up in handicap on return: stays 2½m: acts on good to firm and heavy going: tried in blinkers/tongue tie. *Ben Pauling* **c– h125**

RAVING BONKERS 6 ch.g. Notnowcato – Harriet's Girl (Choisir (AUS)) [2018/19 b84: b15.7g h16g⁶ h16.5g h15.8g h16.8s⁵ Apr 16] bumper winner: poor form over hurdles. *Martin Keighley* **h81 b–**

RAVISHED (IRE) 11 b.g. Oscar (IRE) – Fair Present (IRE) (Presenting) [2018/19 c114, h–: c19.9g c22.6m³ c23.9m⁵ c24.2g* c24.2g² Mar 26] winning hurdler: fair chaser nowadays: won 3-runner hunter at Wetherby in March: left Charlie Longsdon after third start: stays 25f: acts on good to firm and heavy going: has worn headgear/tongue tie, including in 2018/19: usually races prominently. *G. C. Brewer* **c114 h–**

RAYA TIME (FR) 6 gr.g. Al Namix (FR) – Ruthenoise (FR) (Robin des Champs (FR)) [2018/19 b17m* h16.5g⁵ h16g³ h16s³ h16d² h16g² Mar 26] first foal: dam (c134/h127) French 15f-19f hurdle/chase winner: won ladies maiden bumper at Killarney (by 14 lengths from Jan Maat) on debut in May: fairly useful form over hurdles, placed 4 times in maidens: left S. Curling after first start: raced around 2m: tried in hood: front runner/races prominently, often freely. *Henry de Bromhead, Ireland* **h122 b105**

RAYMOND (IRE) 4 b.g. Tobougg (IRE) – Crack The Kicker (Anshan) [2018/19 b16.4d⁴ Mar 5] €11,500 3-y-o: seventh foal: half-brother to fairly useful hurdler/useful chaser Cracking Find (15f-2½m winner, by Robin des Pres): dam unraced half-sister to useful hurdler (2½m-3m winner) Master of The Sea and to dam of top-class staying chaser First Lieutenant: well beaten in maiden bumper: should do better. *Keith Dalgleish* **b60 p**

RAY'S THE MONEY (IRE) 5 b.g. Dragon Pulse (IRE) – Riymaisa (IRE) (Traditionally (USA)) [2018/19 h–: h15.8g² Jul 18] fair form over hurdles: second in novice at Uttoxeter on sole outing in 2018/19: tried in cheekpieces. *Amy Murphy* **h101**

RAYVIN BLACK 10 b.g. Halling (USA) – Optimistic (Reprimand) [2018/19 c132, h130: h19.3g² c21s⁴ h16s⁴ c20d⁴ h21.5g Apr 27] good-topped gelding: useful hurdler/chaser: enterprisingly ridden when third in Coral Hurdle at Ascot (5 lengths behind If The Cap Fits) in November: disappointing after: stays 2½m: acts on good to firm and heavy going: wears headgear: usually leads: temperament under suspicion. *Oliver Sherwood* **c111 h140**

RAZ DE MAREE (FR) 14 ch.g. Shaanmer (IRE) – Diyala III (FR) (Quart de Vin (FR)) [2018/19 c144x, h118: c24g c28s c24d c29.5s⁵ c32.6g c34v^pu Mar 16] sturdy gelding: fairly useful hurdler: useful handicap chaser: won Welsh Grand National at Chepstow in 2017/18: only fifth in latest renewal of race during season he started to show his age: stays 33f: acts on heavy going: has worn headgear: often let down by jumping. *Gavin Patrick Cromwell, Ireland* **c131 x h–**

READ'EM AND WEEP (IRE) 9 b.g. Kutub (IRE) – Amalita (IRE) (Brief Truce (USA)) [2018/19 h87: h21.4g h20.2g^pu May 17] in frame completed start in Irish points: maiden hurdler, no form in 2018/19: best effort at 2m: in cheekpieces last 3 starts. *R. Mike Smith* **h–**

READER'S CHOICE 5 b.g. Redoute's Choice (AUS) – Forever Times (So Factual (USA)) [2018/19 b15.8g³ b16.7g⁵ Sep 29] closely related/half-brother to several winners on Flat, including 6f winner Question Times (by Shamardal), herself dam of Irish Derby winner Latrobe: dam useful 5f-7f winner: fair form in bumpers. *Ian Williams* **b85**

READY AND ABLE (IRE) 6 b.g. Flemensfirth (USA) – Gypsy Mo Chara (IRE) (Oscar (IRE)) [2018/19 h95: h19.6g* h19.9g* h24.7g* h24.2dᶠ Nov 8] useful handicap hurdler: completed hat-trick when winning at Huntingdon in May, Uttoxeter in June and Aintree (conditionals), by 3 lengths from Settimo Milanese) in October: stays 25f: best form on good going. *Jonjo O'Neill* **h131**

READY TOKEN (IRE) 11 gr.g. Flemensfirth (USA) – Ceol Tire (IRE) (Roselier (FR)) [2018/19 c113, h–: c24.5g⁴ c25.8g⁴ c23gᵖᵘ Jul 26] workmanlike gelding: maiden hurdler: fairly useful chaser at one time, has lost his way: pulled up in point in April: stays 25f: acts on soft and good to firm going: has worn headgear: wears tongue tie: front runner/races prominently. *Charlie Longsdon* **c90**
h–

REAL ARMANI 7 ch.g. Sulamani (IRE) – Reel Charmer (Dancing High) [2018/19 b16g b16.4d h19.8g² h16.4s h24.1g⁶ Apr 11] second foal: dam (c120/h131) 2½m-25f hurdle/chase winner: well held in bumpers/over hurdles. *Jane Walton* **h90**
b–

REALLYRADICAL (IRE) 6 b.g. Insatiable (IRE) – Glenogra Cailin (IRE) (Alderbrook) [2018/19 h20.5s⁴ h15.9g³ h24.2d Mar 22] good-topped gelding: second foal: dam, placed in points, half-sister to dam of very smart chaser (stayed 25f) Joncol: placed in Irish points: fair form over hurdles. *Chris Gordon* **h106**

REALLY SUPER 5 b.m. Cacique (IRE) – Sensationally (Montjeu (IRE)) [2018/19 h90: h20g² h20d* h20g* h21g Oct 26] rather leggy mare: fairly useful handicap hurdler: won at Worcester in August (mares) and September: stays 2½m: acts on good to soft going: often races prominently. *Amy Murphy* **h115**

REALMS OF FIRE 6 ch.g. Malinas (GER) – Realms of Gold (USA) (Gulch (USA)) [2018/19 b87: h16.7g h16.7g h18.6d h20.7g Feb 21] rather unfurnished gelding: poor form over hurdles. *Dan Skelton* **h68**

REAL STEEL (FR) 6 b.g. Loup Breton (IRE) – Kalimina (FR) (Monsun (GER)) [2018/19 h136: c17gᶠ c21.5s* c18g* c19.8d⁶ c20g² Apr 21] rather unfurnished gelding: winning hurdler: very smart form over fences: won maiden at Fairyhouse in January and minor event at Thurles (by 10 lengths from Landofhopeandglory) in February: very strong 5/2, also won 12-runner valuable novice handicap at Punchestown shortly after end of British season by 6½ lengths from Hardline, suited by positive ride and greater emphasis on stamina: should stay 3m: acts on soft going: often travels strongly: open to further improvement as a chaser. *W. P. Mullins, Ireland* **c159 p**
h–

REALTA DAWN (IRE) 7 b.m. Craigsteel – Silver Grouse (IRE) (Zagreb (USA)) [2018/19 h16m h16m⁶ h17.3g³ h16.2g h16g h16g³ h16.7g⁴ h16Fᵈ h19.5g Apr 26] second foal: half-sister to bumper winner Outrath (by Captain Rio): dam, unraced, out of half-sister to dam of Grand National winner Silver Birch: modest maiden hurdler: left Peter Fahey after eighth start: should stay 2½m: acts on good to firm going: has worn hood. *Christian Williams* **h89**

REALT OR (IRE) 6 b.g. Gold Well – Starventure (IRE) (Insan (USA)) [2018/19 b15.8m⁶ h22gᵖᵘ h19m h21d h21.7v² h20.5d h23.9s Feb 26] €32,000 3-y-o: fifth foal: half-brother to fairly useful staying 23f hurdle winner/winning pointer Ocean Venture (by Urban Ocean): dam, little form, out of sister to useful staying chaser St Mellion Freeway: little impact in bumper: modest form over hurdles: left Jo Hughes after second start: stays 2¾m: acts on heavy going: in headgear last 3 starts: tried in tongue tie: usually races off pace. *Dominic Ffrench Davis* **h91**
b–

REAL WARRIOR (IRE) 8 b.g. Tikkanen (USA) – Muffin Top (IRE) (Synefos (USA)) [2018/19 c112, h–: c19.9g² c16.4gᵖᵘ c21.4sᵖᵘ Dec 26] off mark in Irish points at fourth attempt: pulled up only hurdle start: fair form in chases: front runner/races prominently. *Charles Pogson* **c107**
h–

REAPLEE 6 ch.g. Recharge (IRE) – Chant de L'Aube (FR) (Bon Sang (FR)) [2018/19 b–: h20.9gᵖᵘ h20.1gᵖᵘ h19.9mᵘʳ h16.2g⁵ Jul 31] has had breathing operation: no form in bumpers/over hurdles: in tongue tie last 2 starts. *Chris Grant* **h–**

REAR ADMIRAL (IRE) 13 b.g. Dushyantor (USA) – Ciaras Charm (IRE) (Phardante (FR)) [2018/19 c121§, h–: c19g⁵ c19.2g⁴ c20.1g* c20.1g³ c20g² c19.4mᵖᵘ Oct 17] big, lengthy gelding: winning hurdler: fairly useful handicap chaser: won at Perth in July: stays 21f: acts on soft going: wears tongue tie: often races towards rear: temperamental. *Michael Easterby* **c124 §**
h–

REASON TO BELIEVE (FR) 5 b.m. Rip Van Winkle (IRE) – Showcall (USA) **h78**
(Kingmambo (USA)) [2018/19 h16m⁴ h15.8s⁵ h17.7g⁴ h16.8g Sep 10] modest maiden on
Flat, stays 13.5f: poor form over hurdles: tried in hood. *David Bridgwater*

REBEL COMMANDER (IRE) 7 b.g. Flemensfirth (USA) – Pharney Fox (IRE) **h92**
(Phardante (FR)) [2018/19 h–, b98: h16g³ h16.7g⁵ h16.8spu h19dur Jan 19] useful-looking
gelding: has had breathing operation: modest form over hurdles: left Nicky Henderson
after first start. *Jack R. Barber*

REBEL ROCK (IRE) 4 b.g. Rock of Gibraltar (IRE) – Star Bonita (IRE) (Invincible **b–**
Spirit (IRE)) [2018/19 b13.7m b14g Nov 4] no form in bumpers. *Donald McCain*

REBEL ROYAL (IRE) 6 b.g. Getaway (GER) – Molly Duffy (IRE) (Oscar (IRE)) **h116**
[2018/19 h115p, b76: h20s² h19.2s² h20g h21.4sF h20.6g Apr 3] fairly useful hurdler: left
Dan Skelton after third start: stays 21f: acts on soft and good to firm going. *Alan King*

REBEL YEATS (IRE) 7 b.m. Yeats (IRE) – Sorivera (Irish River (FR)) [2018/19 h115: **c123**
h19g⁵ h19.2g* c16.3s² c16.5g³ c20.1g* c20.9g³ c19.9g² c20d Dec 13] workmanlike mare: **h119**
fairly useful handicap hurdler: won at Fontwell in June: similar form over fences: won
novice handicap at Hexham in September: stays 21f: acts on good to firm and good to soft
going: has worn cheekpieces. *Ian Williams*

RECIPROCITY 4 gr.f. Mastercraftsman (IRE) – Cleide da Silva (USA) (Monarchos **b–**
(USA)) [2018/19 b15.7s Mar 18] £2,500 3-y-o: sixth foal: half-sister to 2 winners,
including fair 2m hurdle winner Grand Canyon (by High Chaparral): dam 7f winner: tailed
off in bumper. *Sean Conway*

RECKLESS BEHAVIOR (IRE) 7 b.g. Gold Well – Wee Wallis (Windsor Castle) **c108 §**
[2018/19 h112: c21.7g² c20.3g h20.3g⁵ h24d c20dpu c20v² c21.4d⁴ c20vur c24spu Mar 18] **h105 §**
lengthy gelding: fair handicap hurdler/maiden chaser: stays 2¾m: acts on heavy going:
wears headgear: temperamental. *Caroline Bailey*

*EMS Copiers Novices' Handicap Chase (Punchestown), Punchestown—Real Steel emulates
stable-companion Kemboy from twelve months earlier with an impressive win under top weight*

RECOGNITION (IRE) 6 gr.g. Rip Van Winkle (IRE) – Bali Breeze (IRE) (Common Grounds) [2018/19 h–: h17.1g^{pu} h16.8s^{pu} Nov 27] fair hurdler at best, has lost his way: often in cheekpieces. *Barry Murtagh* h–

RED ADMIRABLE (IRE) 13 b.g. Shantou (USA) – Eimears Pet (IRE) (Lord Americo) [2018/19 c–x, h96: h21.2g^4 h23.8g^6 h25d^3 h23.8d h26g^5 h25g^3 h26.4g^2 Apr 14] modest handicap hurdler: winning chaser: stays 3¼m: acts on heavy going: wears headgear/tongue tie: often let down by jumping. *Graeme McPherson* c– x h86

REDBRIDGE GOLD (IRE) 6 b.m. Gold Well – Marikala (IRE) (Sri Pekan (USA)) [2018/19 b17.1d^2 b16.6g* b16s Mar 9] £30,000 5-y-o: sturdy mare: half-sister to 19f bumper winner/winning pointer Cheyenne Girl (by Indian Danehill): dam unraced half-sister to dam of fairly useful hurdler/useful chaser (2m winner) Maralan: off mark in Irish points at fourth attempt: fair form in bumpers: won mares event at Doncaster in January. *Jamie Snowden* b94

RED CHARMER (IRE) 9 b.g. Red Clubs (IRE) – Golden Charm (IRE) (Common Grounds) [2018/19 h16s h15.9s Feb 13] tall gelding: fairly useful on Flat, stays 1½m: well held in novice hurdles. *Suzi Best* h–

RED DANAHER (IRE) 12 ch.g. Shantou (USA) – Red Rover (Infantry) [2018/19 c89§, h104§: h20.1g^4 May 12] sturdy gelding: fair handicap hurdler: modest chaser: stays 25f: acts on heavy going: usually races close up: temperamental. *Sue Smith* c– § h89 §

RED DEVIL LADS (IRE) 10 b.g. Beneficial – Welsh Sitara (IRE) (Welsh Term) [2018/19 c86x, h132: c25.1m^{pu} c20.9d^{pu} h24g^{pu} Mar 4] useful hurdler/chaser at best, no form in 2018/19: left Mrs Sherree Lean after first start, Grace Harris after second: usually wears hood: has worn tongue tie, including in 2018/19: front runner/races prominently: often let down by jumping over fences. *Louise Davis* c– x h–

RED DEVIL STAR (IRE) 9 b.g. Beneficial – Gortbofearna (IRE) (Accordion) [2018/19 c123, h–: c19.9d c15.5s^{pu} c15.5d^5 c19.5v^3 c17.8m^{ur} c19.4d^5 Apr 6] lengthy gelding: winning hurdler: fairly useful handicap chaser, below form in 2018/19: stays 19f: acts on heavy going: tried in cheekpieces: wears tongue tie. *Suzi Smith* c110 h–

REDDINGTON (IRE) 7 b.g. Getaway (GER) – Nikkis Alstar (IRE) (Fourstars Allstar (USA)) [2018/19 h–: h19.9m^5 May 19] good-topped gelding: no form: tried in visor. *Tim Vaughan* h–

RED EMPEROR (IRE) 5 b.g. Holy Roman Emperor (IRE) – Rougette (Red Ransom (USA)) [2018/19 h15.3g h15.8v^{pu} Jan 14] poor maiden on Flat: no form over hurdles. *Sheila Lewis* h–

REDEMPTION SONG (IRE) 7 gr.m. Mastercraftsman (IRE) – Humilis (IRE) (Sadler's Wells (USA)) [2018/19 h110: h20g^3 c24g^3 c24.1g^3 Oct 3] workmanlike mare: has had breathing operation: point/bumper winner: fair hurdler: fairly useful form in chases: better effort when third in novice at Uttoxeter: stays 3m: tried in cheekpieces: in tongue tie last 3 starts. *Kevin Frost* c121 h111

RED FORCE ONE 4 ro.g. Lethal Force (IRE) – Dusty Red (Teofilo (IRE)) [2018/19 h16m^4 h18.7s^3 Mar 11] angular gelding: has had breathing operations: useful on Flat, stays 11f: fairly useful form over hurdles: better effort when fourth in Adonis Juvenile Hurdle at Kempton (13½ lengths behind Fusil Raffles) in February. *Paul Nicholls* h115

REDFORD ROAD 5 b.g. Trans Island – Maryscross (IRE) (Presenting) [2018/19 b15.8g^2 Mar 19] third foal: dam (h96), 23f hurdle winner/winning pointer, half-sister to dam of high-class hurdler/smart chaser (stayed 21f) Oscars Well: 11/2, second in conditionals/amateurs bumper at Huntingdon (length behind Roque It). *Nigel Twiston-Davies* b94

RED FOUR 9 ch.m. Singspiel (IRE) – Protectorate (Hector Protector (USA)) [2018/19 h94: h20g^6 May 8] fairly useful hurdler at best, lightly raced: well held only start in 2018/19: unproven beyond 17f: acts on good to firm and heavy going: often wears headgear. *Sarah-Jayne Davies* h–

RED GIANT (IRE) 8 ch.g. Beneficial – Barrack Star (IRE) (Overbury (IRE)) [2018/19 c105, h–: c19.3g^4 c26.1g^{ur} c24.2m^{ur} h23.3g c23.9m* c24.1g* c24.1g^2 c25.5g^5 c29.2g^{ro} c26.2g^2 c25.2g^2 c25g^{pu} c23.8g* Apr 24] good-topped gelding: winning hurdler: useful handicap chaser: won at Market Rasen and Bangor in August, and Perth (by 3 lengths from Swingbridge) in April: stays 25f: acts on good to firm going: wears headgear. *Jennie Candlish* c133 h–

RED HANRAHAN (IRE) 8 b.g. Yeats (IRE) – Monty's Sister (IRE) (Montelimar (USA)) [2018/19 c123§, h–§: c19.7g^{pu} c19.9m^F c20.2f^2 h19.5s h19d^{pu} Mar 11] sturdy gelding: has had breathing operation: fairly useful hurdler/maiden chaser at best, disappointing in 2018/19: left Suzi Best after fourth start: stays 3m: acts on soft going: tried in headgear: usually tongue tied: ungenuine. *Emma Owen* c106 § h– §

RED HOT CHILLY (IRE) 6 ch.g. Frozen Power (IRE) – She's Got The Look (Sulamani **h118**
(IRE)) [2018/19 h–: h15.8g⁴ h15.8m² h16m* h16.7m⁵ h16.3m³ h16g² h16.7g² h15.3m⁴
h16.4g* h16.8g⁴ Apr 17] rather leggy gelding: fairly useful handicap hurdler: won at
Worcester in July and Cheltenham (novice) in November: will be suited by further than
2m: acts on good to firm going: has worn hood. *Fergal O'Brien*

REDICEAN 5 b.g. Medicean – Red Halo (IRE) (Galileo (IRE)) [2018/19 h141: h16.4g² **h141**
h15.3g⁴ h16m Apr 13] compact gelding: useful on Flat, stays 1¾m, won twice in late-2018:
useful hurdler: second in minor event at Cheltenham (3¼ lengths behind Pearl of The West)
in October: raced around 2m: acts on heavy going: sent to USA. *Alan King*

RED INCA 11 ch.g. Pivotal – Magicalmysterykate (USA) (Woodman (USA)) [2018/19 c–, **c–**
h–: c20.8g May 4] close-coupled gelding: point winner: winning hurdler: stiff tasks in **h–**
hunter chases: unproven beyond 2m: acts on heavy going: has worn cheekpieces: in tongue
tie last 5 starts. *Con Rutledge*

RED INDIAN 7 b.g. Sulamani (IRE) – Rafiya (Halling (USA)) [2018/19 h136: c21.5s* **c145**
c24g⁴ c21.6gᵘʳ c20.2s h24.7g Apr 6] sturdy gelding: useful hurdler: smart form over fences: **h–**
won novice at Ayr (by 15 lengths from No Hassle Hoff) in November: stays 3m: acts on
heavy going: tried in cheekpieces: usually front runner/races prominently. *Kelly Morgan*

RED INFANTRY (IRE) 9 ch.g. Indian River (FR) – Red Rover (Infantry) [2018/19 **c138**
c126, h116: h23.9d c28.4g* c28.8v² c25.6d⁵ c28.4gᵘʳ c31.8m Apr 13] stocky gelding: fairly **h104**
useful handicap hurdler: useful handicap chaser: won at Haydock in November: second in
Betfair London National at Sandown (length behind Morney Wing) in December and fifth
in Peter Marsh Chase at Haydock (6 lengths behind Wakanda) in January: stays 29f: acts
on heavy going: wears headgear: usually races close up. *Ian Williams*

RED MIRACLE 4 b.f. Dylan Thomas (IRE) – Under Milk Wood (Montjeu (IRE)) **h77**
[2018/19 h16.3mᶠ h16.8g⁴ h17.7g h15.8m⁶ Oct 4] modest maiden on Flat, stays 1½m: little
form over hurdles: tried in hood. *Rod Millman*

RED MIX (FR) 6 b.g. Al Namix (FR) – Fidelety (FR) (Villez (USA)) [2018/19 c18.4s² **c116**
c18.9d³ c15.5sᵖᵘ h15.8d² h19d⁴ h15.8gᶠ h16.8d⁶ Apr 9] lengthy gelding: seventh foal: half- **h124**
brother to 3 winners, including useful French hurdler/fairly useful chaser Red Name
(17f-21f winner, by Nickname) and fairly useful chaser Rouge Et Blanc (2m-2½m winner,
by Mansonnien): dam (c107/h121), French 17f/2¼m hurdle/chase winner, also 11f winner
on Flat: fairly useful handicap hurdler: second at Ludlow in February: fairly useful chaser:
left D. Bressou after second start: stays 2½m: acts on soft going: in hood last 2 starts:
usually leads. *Dr Richard Newland*

REDMOND (IRE) 9 b.g. Tikkanen (USA) – Medal Quest (FR) (Medaaly) [2018/19 c98, **c91**
h–: c21.6m³ c24.2g c20dᵖᵘ c21.6s² c21.6d⁵ c19.4dᵖᵘ Apr 6] rangy gelding: maiden hurdler: **h–**
modest handicap chaser: stays 3¼m: acts on good to firm and heavy going: tried in
blinkers: wears tongue tie: usually races close up. *Jack R. Barber*

RED OCHRE 6 b.g. Virtual – Red Hibiscus (Manduro (GER)) [2018/19 h103: h16.2g² **c96**
h16.2g² h16.7m² h16.8m⁵ c16.4g² c20.3g⁴ Nov 26] fair maiden hurdler: modest form over **h103**
fences: better effort when second in novice handicap at Sedgefield: should stay at least
2½m: acts on good to firm and heavy going. *Chris Grant*

RED PENNY (IRE) 12 b.m. Definite Article – Hurricane Dawn (IRE) (Strong Gale) **c–**
[2018/19 c–, h–: c26mᵖᵘ May 27] winning pointer: maiden hurdler/chaser: stays 3¼m: acts **h–**
on good to firm and heavy going: has worn tongue tie. *Jimmy Frost*

RED REMINDER 5 b.m. Mount Nelson – Red Hibiscus (Manduro (GER)) [2018/19 **b74**
b16.2g b17g⁶ b16.8v³ b16.8d⁴ Apr 23] second foal: dam unraced half-sister to fairly useful
hurdler/useful chaser (stayed 27f) Samstown: poor form in bumpers: will be suited by
2½m. *Chris Grant*

RED RISING (IRE) 8 ch.g. Flemensfirth (USA) – Fugal Maid (IRE) (Winged Love **c126**
(IRE)) [2018/19 h134: c20s⁴ c23.6d³ c24.2d² c24.5g⁵ c23.4d Mar 22] well-made gelding: **h–**
winning Irish pointer: useful hurdler: fairly useful form in chases, went wrong way: stays
25f: acts on heavy going: in cheekpieces last 2 starts. *Dan Skelton*

RED RIVER (IRE) 6 ch.g. Beneficial – Socker Toppen (IRE) (Great Palm (USA)) **c– p**
[2018/19 h139p: c23.8sᵖᵘ Dec 5] rangy gelding: has had breathing operation: runner-up on **h–**
sole outing in Irish points: useful form over hurdles, won 2 of 3 starts: 6/5, upsides when
all but came down 4 out in novice at Ludlow on chasing debut: in tongue tie last 3 starts:
should do better over fences. *Kim Bailey*

RED ROYALIST 5 b.g. Royal Applause – Scarlet Royal (Red Ransom (USA)) [2018/19 **h119**
h15.8g³ h16.6m² h20m* Apr 22] fairly useful on Flat, stays 2m: fairly useful form over
hurdles: won 4-runner novice at Fakenham in April. *Stuart Edmunds*

701

RED SPINNER (IRE) 9 b.g. Redback – Massalia (IRE) (Montjeu (IRE)) [2018/19 c128, **c–** h–: c18g^{pu} May 7] sturdy gelding: winning hurdler: useful chaser: bad mistake when pulled **h–** up only outing under Rules in 2018/19: unplaced in points later in season: stays 2½m: acts on good to firm and heavy going: in cheekpieces last 3 starts. *Kim Bailey*

RED SQUARE REVIVAL (IRE) 8 b.g. Presenting – Alder Flower (IRE) (Alderbrook) **c113** [2018/19 c107, h–: c20g^{pu} c19.2g* Jun 1] maiden hurdler: fair handicap chaser: won at **h–** Market Rasen in June: stays 2½m: acts on good to soft going: wears headgear/tongue tie: front runner/races prominently. *David Pipe*

RED TORNADO (FR) 7 ch.g. Dr Fong (USA) – Encircle (USA) (Spinning World **h130** (USA)) [2018/19 h127: h19g h18.5g^2 h16.3m* h16.8g^4 h16.3s^3 h15.7m Apr 20] smallish, good-bodied gelding: useful handicap hurdler: won at Stratford (by 11 lengths from Regulation) in July: left Dan Skelton after fourth start: stays 2¼m: acts on soft and good to firm going. *Chris Fairhurst*

RED TORTUE (IRE) 10 b.g. Turtle Island (IRE) – Howrwedoin (IRE) (Flemensfirth **c83** (USA)) [2018/19 c64, h64: h19m^3 h15.8g^3 c17.3m^3 Jul 1] sturdy gelding: point winner: **h80** poor handicap hurdler/maiden chaser: stays 2½m: acts on good to firm and heavy going: wears headgear: tried in tongue tie: front runner/races prominently. *Jennie Candlish*

REDWOOD BOY (IRE) 10 b.g. Definite Article – Native Sunset (IRE) (Be My Native **c89** (USA)) [2018/19 h19.7g* h19.5g h21.3g^6 h16g h20.8g^4 c16.4m^4 c21g^2 h20g^{su} h19.8g^5 **h87** c21g^4 c23.5g^{pu} c18g h20s* Dec 6] sturdy gelding: modest handicap hurdler: won at Clonmel in May and December: similar form over fences: stays 21f: acts on good to firm and good to soft going: usually wears headgear: has worn tongue tie. *John Joseph Hanlon, Ireland*

REDZOR (IRE) 6 b.g. Shantou (USA) – Knockara One (IRE) (Snurge) [2018/19 h20g^2 **h120** h21d^3 h21.3d^5 h23.8d* h25.5d^2 h23.1g Mar 27] €55,000 3-y-o, £80,000 5-y-o: tall gelding: has had breathing operation: first foal: dam unraced half-sister to fairly useful hurdler/very smart chaser (stayed 29f) One Knight: Irish point winner: fairly useful form over hurdles: awarded maiden at Ludlow in February: stays 3¼m: acts on good to soft going: in tongue tie last 3 starts. *Dan Skelton*

REECELTIC 4 b.g. Champs Elysees – Sense of Pride (Sadler's Wells (USA)) [2018/19 **b79** b13.7g ab16g^4 b16.3d Mar 2] lengthy gelding: modest form on second of 3 starts in bumpers: has worn cheekpieces. *Pat Phelan*

REFLEX ACTION (IRE) 4 b.g. Sans Frontieres (IRE) – Monanig Lass (IRE) **b–** (Topanoora) [2018/19 b16.8s Apr 16] runner-up on first of 2 starts in point bumpers: 50/1, eighth in maiden bumper at Exeter. *J. Tickle*

REFUSAL 11 b.g. Teofilio (IRE) – Frankie Fair (IRE) (Red Sunset) [2018/19 c21.2g* **c103** c22.6d^3 Jun 8] has had breathing operation: multiple winning pointer: maiden hurdler: fair **h–** chaser: won maiden hunter at Cartmel in May: stays 23f: acts on soft and good to firm going: in hood last 2 starts: tried in tongue tie. *G. C. Brewer*

REGAL ENCORE (IRE) 11 b.g. King's Theatre (IRE) – Go On Eileen (IRE) (Bob Back **c146 §** (USA)) [2018/19 c152§, h–: h24.7g^6 c23.8d^3 c34.3g Apr 6] compact gelding: useful **h128** hurdler: smart handicap chaser: third in listed event at Ascot (9¼ lengths behind Calipto) in February and second to Cloudy Morning at Punchestown (beaten 18 lengths after late mistakes) shortly after end of British season: barely stays 4¼m: acts on good to soft going: has worn hood/tongue tie: temperamental. *Anthony Honeyball*

REGAL FLOW 12 b.g. Erhaab (USA) – Flow (Over The River (FR)) [2018/19 c139, h–: **c129** h23.9d c24d^6 c25.9s^{ur} c29.5s c28.4d^5 c28.4d^3 c34v^{pu} c23.8m^3 c27.9g^6 Apr 21] sturdy **h–** gelding: fair hurdler: fairly useful handicap chaser: third in veterans event at Ascot in March: stays 4¼m: acts on any going: tried in cheekpieces. *Bob Buckler*

REGAL FLUTE 7 b.m. Schiafilio (GER) – Regal Music (Bandmaster (USA)) [2018/19 **h–** h19d^{pu} Dec 30] first foal: dam (b88) in frame both starts in bumpers: soon detached in novice hurdle. *Richard Hawker*

REGARDE MOI 11 b.g. King's Best (USA) – Life At Night (IRE) (Night Shift (USA)) **h101** [2018/19 h19.9m^5 h16.8g h16d^3 Nov 28] smart on Flat at one time over 7f/1m, has deteriorated: fair form over hurdles: best effort when third in novice at Wetherby: wears tongue tie. *Maurice Barnes*

REGARDING RUTH (IRE) 5 b.m. Flemensfirth (USA) – May's June (IRE) (Oscar **h107** (IRE)) [2018/19 b88: b17.1d^4 b15.8d h16d^3 h17.7v^4 h19.6d^3 h20.6g Apr 3] neat mare: fair **b85** form in bumpers/over hurdles: stays 2½m: acts on good to soft going: tried in cheekpieces. *Lucy Wadham*

REGGIE B 6 ch.g. Midshipman – Dot Up (Weld) [2018/19 b–: h16.3m Jun 19] workmanlike **h–** gelding: tailed off in bumper/novice hurdle. *Henry Oliver*

REGULATION (IRE) 10 br.g. Danehill Dancer (IRE) – Source of Life (IRE) (Fasliyev **h114** (USA)) [2018/19 h119: h16m⁶ h16.3m² h17.2m h16.3m² h16.3m⁴ h16.3g⁴ h16.8g² h15.9g⁵ h20.5g³ h16.7s h20.5g* h21.2d h19d h18.7g⁵ h20.6mᶠ Apr 21] lengthy gelding: fair hurdler: won seller at Leicester in January: stays 2½m: acts on good to firm and good to soft going: often wears headgear: tried in tongue tie: front runner/races prominently. *Neil King*

REIGN BACK DANCER (IRE) 5 b.g. Jeremy (USA) – Back The Queen (IRE) (Bob **b–** Back (USA)) [2018/19 ab16.3s b16s Mar 9] towards rear in bumpers. *George Bewley*

REIGNING SUPREME (IRE) 8 b.g. Presenting – Gli Gli (IRE) (Supreme Leader) **c132** [2018/19 c132, h–: c25gᵖᵘ c24g* Nov 12] strong gelding: winning hurdler: useful form **h–** over fences: won 3-runner maiden at Kempton in November: stays 3m: acts on heavy going. *Nicky Henderson*

REIKERS ISLAND (IRE) 6 b.g. Yeats (IRE) – Moricana (GER) (Konigsstuhl (GER)) **c141** [2018/19 h114: c24.2g³ c25.1g* c26d⁴ c23.8d⁶ c25gᵖᵘ Apr 3] strong, lengthy gelding: **h–** winning hurdler: useful form over fences: won handicap at Wincanton in December: stays 3¼m: acts on soft going: usually front runner/races prominently. *Philip Hobbs*

REIVERS LAD 8 b.g. Alflora (IRE) – Reivers Moon (Midnight Legend) [2018/19 **c133 p** c16.3d* Dec 13] strong gelding: fairly useful hurdler: 11/2, even better form when won **h–** novice at Newcastle (by ¾ length from Cool Mix) on chasing debut after 20-month absence: should stay beyond 2m: acts on heavy going: capable of better still over fences. *Nicky Richards*

REIVERS LODGE 7 b.m. Black Sam Bellamy (IRE) – Crystal Princess (IRE) (Definite **h96** Article) [2018/19 h99: h23.9gˢᵘ h23.9g² h23.9g⁵ h23.9g⁶ h20.1g h19.9gᵘʳ h20vᵖᵘ h19.8s³ h20.9g⁶ Mar 23] modest handicap hurdler: stays 3m: acts on heavy going: usually in hood: has often worn tongue tie. *Susan Corbett*

REJAAH 7 b.m. Authorized (IRE) – Dhan Dhana (IRE) (Dubawi (IRE)) [2018/19 c–, **c126** h126: h23g⁶ c21.4g² h23.9dᵖᵘ Oct 27] fairly useful handicap hurdler: similar form over **h115** fences: second in handicap at Market Rasen in July: stays 21f: acts on good to firm and good to soft going: wears tongue tie. *Nigel Hawke*

RELAX (FR) 14 b.g. Fragrant Mix (USA) – Magik (FR) (Kadalko (FR)) [2018/19 c23.8gᵖᵘ **c–** Apr 25] good-topped gelding: maiden pointer: once-raced hurdler: useful chaser at best, **h–** pulled up on hunter debut: stays 3¼m: acts on heavy going: tried in cheekpieces. *Will Ramsay*

RELEGATE (IRE) 6 b.m. Flemensfirth (USA) – Last of The Bunch (Silver Patriarch **h125 p** (IRE)) [2018/19 b116: h22g² h16d⁴ h22g⁵ Feb 2] compact mare: smart bumper performer: fairly useful form over hurdles: won mares maiden at Naas in December: laboured when fifth in Nathaniel Lacy & Partners Solicitors Novices' Hurdle at Leopardstown: likely to stay 3m: often races in rear: remains with potential. *W. P. Mullins, Ireland*

RELENTLESS DREAMER (IRE) 10 br.g. Kayf Tara – Full of Elegance (FR) **c140** (Cadoudal (FR)) [2018/19 c137, h–: c26.1m³ c25g* Oct 27] tall gelding: winning hurdler: **h–** useful handicap chaser: won at Cheltenham (by neck from Cogry) in October: stays 3¼m: acts on good to firm and heavy going: wears headgear/tongue tie. *Rebecca Curtis*

RELIGHT THE FIRE 8 ch.g. Firebreak – Alula (In The Wings) [2018/19 h–: h20.6s **h–** h15.9sᵖᵘ Jan 16] placed in bumpers: no form over hurdles: tried in cheekpieces/tongue tie. *Denis Quinn*

RELKADAM (FR) 5 ch.g. Muhtathir – Gloirez (FR) (Saumarez) [2018/19 h17d³ **c–** h16.8sᵖᵘ Dec 7] fourth foal: half-brother to fairly useful French hurdler/chaser Fiestine **h99** (17f-19f winner, by Martaline): dam useful French 1½m winner: maiden hurdler, modest form on completed start in Britain: well held both starts over fences: tried in cheekpieces. *Tim Easterby*

REMASTERED 6 ch.g. Network (GER) – Cathodine Cayras (FR) (Martaline) [2018/19 **h124** b102: h15.8v* h16.8s⁵ h20.5d² Mar 22] big, strong gelding: bumper winner: fairly useful form over hurdles: won novice at Ffos Las in November: stays 2½m. *David Pipe*

REMEMBER FOREVER (IRE) 9 b.g. Indian River (FR) – Running Wild (IRE) **c83** (Anshan) [2018/19 c76, h–: c25.7g⁶ c19.7m³ c20s* c24dᵖᵘ c21.6v³ Dec 11] lengthy **h–** gelding: maiden hurdler: poor handicap chaser: won at Lingfield in November: stays 2½m: acts on good to firm and heavy going. *Richard Rowe*

REMEMBER ME WELL (IRE) 6 b.m. Doyen (IRE) – Creidim (IRE) (Erins Isle) **h57** [2018/19 h–, b–: h17.7g h17.7m h16g h15.9s h21.7v⁵ h23d h21d h23.6dᵖᵘ Mar 20] sturdy mare: little form over hurdles. *Richard Rowe*

REMEMBER NERJA (IRE) 5 ch.m. Lord Shanakill (USA) – Tequise (IRE) (Victory Note (USA)) [2018/19 h15.8g⁶ h16.3g⁶ h15.8g h15.5g⁵ h16.5g⁶ h15.8d h15.8v⁴ Mar 16] lengthy, rather unfurnished mare: poor maiden on Flat/over hurdles. *Barry Leavy*   **h76**

REMEMBER THE DAYS (IRE) 5 b.g. Kyllachy – Pointed Arch (IRE) (Rock of Gibraltar (IRE)) [2018/19 h16.8g⁴ h16.4g² h16.6g* h16.6g⁶ Dec 29] fairly useful on Flat, stays 10.5f: fair form over hurdles: won handicap at Doncaster in December. *Jedd O'Keeffe*   **h109**

REMIND ME LATER (IRE) 10 b.g. Zerpour (IRE) – Two T'three Weeks (Silver Patriarch (IRE)) [2018/19 c126, h–: c26.1g² May 27] sturdy gelding: winning hurdler: fairly useful handicap chaser: stayed 3¼m: acted on any going: dead. *Gary Moore*   **c128 h–**

REMMY D (IRE) 4 b.g. Lawman (FR) – Evening Time (IRE) (Keltos (FR)) [2018/19 h16.8g³ Oct 21] fair on Flat, stays 1½m: 25/1, none too fluent when well-held third in juvenile at Sedgefield on hurdling debut. *Roger Fell*   **h75**

RENDEZVOUS PEAK 10 b.g. High-Rise (IRE) – Jurado Park (IRE) (Jurado (USA)) [2018/19 c105, h–: c17.8mᶠ c19.5g² Apr 24] winning pointer/hurdler: maiden chaser: has often worn hood. *Phil York*   **c– h–**

RENE'S GIRL (IRE) 9 b.m. Presenting – Brogella (IRE) (King's Theatre (IRE)) [2018/19 c144, h128: c20g⁴ c19.9d c20.5g² c20.6g⁶ Apr 17] tall mare: fairly useful hurdler: useful chaser: second in listed mares event at Doncaster (3¾ lengths behind Lady Buttons) in December: stays 25f: acts on firm and soft going: in tongue tie last 3 starts: usually front runner/races prominently. *Dan Skelton*   **c144 h–**

RENWICK (IRE) 6 b.g. Milan – Come In Moscow (IRE) (Over The River (FR)) [2018/19 b80p: h19.2g² h19.7g* h20.6s⁵ h19.9d* h18.5s⁶ Apr 16] has had breathing operation: fairly useful form over hurdles: won maiden at Hereford in November and handicap at Uttoxeter in March: likely to stay beyond 2½m: acts on good to soft going: in cheekpieces/tongue tie last 2 starts. *Dan Skelton*   **h115**

REPRESENTED (IRE) 6 b.g. Presenting – Lunar Path (IRE) (Night Shift (USA)) [2018/19 b92p: b17.7g⁴ b17.7g² b16m⁶ h19m³ h16.5dᵖᵘ Nov 29] fairly useful form in bumpers: fair form over hurdles: better effort when third in maiden at Taunton: in tongue tie last 4 starts. *Anthony Honeyball*   **h100 b97**

REPUBLICAN 4 b.g. Kayf Tara – Noun de La Thinte (FR) (Oblat (FR)) [2018/19 b13.7m⁴ Mar 29] €72,000 3-y-o: third foal: dam (c123/h96), 2¼m/2½m hurdle/chase winner (stayed 3¼m), half-sister to useful chaser (stayed 3m) Royal de La Thinte: 4/1, fourth in bumper at Fontwell (7¾ lengths behind Only Money). *Oliver Sherwood*   **b82**

REPUTATIONAL RISK (IRE) 5 b.g. Watar (IRE) – She's All There (IRE) (Tragic Role (USA)) [2018/19 h–, b–: h16m⁶ May 7] well held in bumper/maiden hurdles: tried in cheekpieces. *Matt Sheppard*   **h69**

RESCUED GLORY (IRE) 10 b.g. Milan – Stand Girl (IRE) (Standiford (USA)) [2018/19 c25.1s⁴ c23.8s⁵ Apr 7] winning pointer: maiden hurdler: modest form in chases after 2-year absence: stays 23f: acts on soft going. *Jeremy Scott*   **c88 h–**

RESERVE TANK (IRE) 5 b.g. Jeremy (USA) – Lady Bellamy (IRE) (Black Sam Bellamy (IRE)) [2018/19 h16d³ h16.3d h16s* h21s* h20g* Apr 6]   **h150 p**

The death of the stallion Jeremy after an injury sustained while at exercise in September 2014, aged only eleven, potentially robbed racing of a major source of quality jumpers. Jeremy, a son of Danehill Dancer, had already had success on the Flat with several smart performers, and judged on his racing record—he won the Jersey Stakes and finished runner-up in the Queen Anne Stakes—he seemed an unlikely one to transfer to covering National Hunt mares. However, Jeremy has more stamina in his pedigree than his career on the track might suggest, his dam being a half-sister to Deep Impact and from the family of Nashwan and Unfuwain. The fifteen-length victory of his son Our Conor in the 2013 Triumph Hurdle was the catalyst for a change of focus with Jeremy's last two crops—each numbering around one hundred and fifty—which were purely jumps-oriented. His penultimate crop, who are now five-year-olds, contained three graded hurdles winners in the latest season. Two of those, Mister Fisher and Birchdale, still have untapped potential, but it is Reserve Tank, successful in Grade 1 novices at both Aintree and Punchestown in the spring, who looks the best of the bunch at this stage.

Reserve Tank went straight into novice hurdles in the autumn, running twice, finishing a promising third at Chepstow before running slightly less encouragingly at Newbury less than four weeks later. He then had a three-month break before

Betway Mersey Novices' Hurdle, Aintree—
Robbie Power and Colin Tizzard team up to win the race for the second time in three years as
Reserve Tank lowers the colours of favourite Brewin'upastorm (star on cap)

returning to win a novice event at Sandown in mid-February, and then following up in another at Kempton the day after the Cheltenham Festival. Both wins came in races that became tactical affairs, both looking as if they might have been lost by the favourite rather than won by Reserve Tank, who traded at long odds in running on each occasion. Nevertheless, Reserve Tank was clearly promising and showed fairly useful form at Kempton in his first race beyond two miles. A step up to Grade 1 company for the Betway Mersey Novices' Hurdle at Aintree nonetheless looked to set him quite a demanding task. Only two of the nine runners started at longer odds than 20/1-shot Reserve Tank, with the Supreme Novices' disappointment Angels Breath and the Baring Bingham fourth Brewinupastorm at the head of the market. That pair were clearly smart novices, but Reserve Tank proved more than up to

Alanna Homes Champion Novices' Hurdle, Punchestown—Reserve Tank holds off Sams Profile to
complete an Aintree-Punchestown double

the challenge and, on ground less testing than he had previously encountered, he travelled smoothly at the head of affairs and found plenty once sent for home in the straight. Reserve Tank had three and a quarter lengths to spare over Brewinupastorm at the line, with Angels Breath dead-heating for third with One For Rosie, who had been touched off in the EBF Final at Sandown on his previous start in a race which earned notoriety after One For Rosie was initially named the winner in error in a mix-up over Sandown's two winning posts (about which there is more in the essay on Talkischeap).

Reserve Tank was evidently much improved, even if Brewinupastorm and Angels Breath weren't quite at their best at Aintree, and he got the chance to confirm his progress in the Alanna Homes Champion Novices' Hurdle, the two and a half mile Grade 1 novice event at Punchestown, in which the Baring Bingham winner City Island was the short-priced favourite. Colin Tizzard's previous winner of the Mersey, Finian's Oscar, had failed by a short head when attempting the same double two years previously but Reserve Tank went one better. The only British-trained runner in a representative field of twelve, 13/2-shot Reserve Tank was more patiently ridden than at Aintree, travelling strongly before being sent on before three out. He was firmly in control when the pursuing Sams Profile made an error at the last. Reserve Tank had to be driven out to score by half a length as Sams Profile rallied. City Island managed only sixth, and clearly wasn't at his best, though the form has a very solid look to it overall. Sams Profile had come fifth in the Baring Bingham and third-placed Eglantine du Seuil had won the Dawn Run at the Festival, suggesting that Reserve Tank wasn't far behind the pick of the season's novice hurdlers.

The Reserve Tankers' "Reserve Tank"

Reserve Tank (IRE) (b.g. 2014)	Jeremy (USA) (b 2003)	Danehill Dancer (b 1993)	Danehill Mira Adonde
		Glint In Her Eye (b 1996)	Arazi Wind In Her Hair
	Lady Bellamy (IRE) (b 2005)	Black Sam Bellamy (b 1999)	Sadler's Wells Urban Sea
		Miss Nowhere (bl 1995)	Exit To Nowhere Miss Carina

Reserve Tank is a strong gelding in appearance and has the physique to make an even better chaser than hurdler. The ill-fated Finian's Oscar didn't quite make up into the exciting novice chaser that was anticipated after his novice hurdling campaign, but he did win a Grade 1 novice event over fences. So too did the Tizzard-trained 2018 Mersey runner-up Lostintranslation who also has an essay in this edition and proved far more convincing over the larger obstacles. The dam's side of Reserve Tank's pedigree isn't particularly notable. His dam Lady Bellamy (by Galileo's brother Black Sam Bellamy, the sire of the likes of The Giant Bolster and Sam Spinner) was a winning pointer out of Miss Nowhere, herself a mile winner at two in France. Miss Nowhere has produced two Flat winners in India and another in Germany. She is a half-sister to Mendez, a high-class miler whose biggest success came in the Prix du Moulin but who is best known for siring leading French stallion Linamix. Reserve Tank was bought for €35,000 at the Goffs Land Rover Sale as an unraced three-year-old. He will stay beyond twenty-one furlongs and has so far raced only on good going or softer (acts on soft). He is open to further improvement. *Colin Tizzard*

RESIDENCE AND SPA (IRE) 11 b.g. Dubai Destination (USA) – Toffee Nosed (Selkirk (USA)) [2018/19 c–, h–: h23.9d May 26] sturdy gelding: modest hurdler at best, lightly raced and no form since 2013/14: maiden chaser: has worn headgear: has worn tongue tie, including last 3 starts. *Helen Rees* — **c–** **h–**

RETRACE (FR) 5 b.m. Red Roy (USA) – Puerta Grande (FR) (Lesotho (USA)) [2018/19 b–: b16.2d h16d⁶ h16.6d⁶ h20.6g⁵ h19.3g⁶ Feb 18] fell in point: well held in bumpers: poor form over hurdles: in tongue tie last 3 starts: remains open to improvement. *Stuart Crawford, Ireland* — **h83 p** **b–**

RETRIEVE (AUS) 12 b.g. Rahy (USA) – Hold To Ransom (USA) (Red Ransom (USA)) [2018/19 h–: h15.7gᵇᵈ Jun 5] sturdy gelding: fairly useful 2m hurdler at best, very lightly raced and no form in sphere since 2014/15: in headgear/tongue tie last 2 starts. *Johnny Farrelly* — **h–**

RETURN FLIGHT 8 b.g. Kayf Tara – Molly Flight (FR) (Saint Cyrien (FR)) [2018/19 c118, h–: c23.9g² c23.8g⁴ c20.1g³ c20.1g⁶ c20.1g⁶ c20.9gᵘʳ c20s Nov 12] lengthy gelding: winning hurdler: fairly useful handicap chaser: lost form after third start: stays 3m: acts on heavy going: has worn headgear, including last 5 starts: tried in tongue tie: front runner/races prominently: irresolute. *Rebecca Menzies* — **c115 §** **h–**

RETURN TICKET (IRE) 6 b.g. Getaway (GER) – Capelvenere (IRE) (Barathea (IRE)) [2018/19 b100: h16g* h17.1d⁶ h15.6g* h16.4m² Mar 28] bumper winner: fairly useful form over hurdles: won maiden at Ayr in May and novice at Musselburgh in November: likely to prove best at 2m. *Ruth Jefferson* — **h123**

REVE 5 b.g. Nathaniel (IRE) – Rouge (FR) (Red Ransom (USA)) [2018/19 h19.9g h24d² h20.5gᶠ h21.6s h21.2g² h19.3m* h24gᵖᵘ Apr 17] rather unfurnished gelding: fair on Flat in France, stays 13.5f: fairly useful hurdler: won maiden at Catterick in February: stays 3m: acts on good to firm and good to soft going: in hood/tongue tie last 3 starts: usually front runner/races prominently. *Martin Keighley* — **h117**

R'EVELYN PLEASURE (IRE) 7 b.g. Getaway (GER) – Alwayshavnpleasure (IRE) (Oscar (IRE)) [2018/19 h16.5g² h16g c21sᶠ c16.3s* c17.7d² c20d* c17g⁴ c18s³ c15.8dᵖᵘ c21.5g³ Apr 21] lengthy gelding: first foal: dam unraced sister to useful hurdler/fairly useful chaser (stayed 2½m) Wilde Wit Pleasure: fair form over hurdles: fairly useful chaser: won maiden at Clonmel in December and novice at Fairyhouse in January: stays 21f: acts on heavy going: tried in hood: room for improvement in jumping. *Sean O. O'Brien, Ireland* — **c128** **h107**

REVERANT CUST (IRE) 8 gr.g. Dalyami (IRE) – Flame Supreme (IRE) (Saddlers' **c113** Hall (IRE)) [2018/19 h120: c19.2g* c20.9s^{pu} c16.3g³ c16.3g³ c19.3v⁴ c17.1g⁵ Mar 23] **h–** fairly useful hurdler: fair form over fences: won maiden at Catterick in November: stays 2½m: acts on heavy going: tried in cheekpieces: wears tongue tie: races off pace. *Peter Atkinson*

REVEREND JACOBS 5 b.g. Nathaniel (IRE) – Light Impact (IRE) (Fantastic Light **h– p** (USA)) [2018/19 h16.3d Dec 29] sturdy gelding: dam half-sister to useful hurdler (stays 19f) Nietzsche: useful on Flat, stays 1½m: 4/1, well held in introductory event at Newbury on hurdling debut: should do better. *Alan King*

REVERSE THE CHARGE (IRE) 12 b.g. Bishop of Cashel – Academy Jane (IRE) **c84** (Satco (FR)) [2018/19 c70§, h–: c16.4g³ c15.6g² c15.6g* c17.3m⁶ c17.3g³ c20.1g³ c17.2g⁴ **h–** c15.6g* c21.1g* c15.7g c15.2g⁵ Apr 11] has had breathing operation: no form over hurdles: modest handicap chaser: won at Hexham in June and September, and at Sedgefield in October: stays 21f: acts on good to soft going: wears cheekpieces: tried in tongue tie: usually races close up. *Jane Walton*

REVOCATION 11 b.g. Revoque (IRE) – Fenella (Phardante (FR)) [2018/19 c20.1g^{pu} **c116** c20.1g^{ur} Sep 27] winning hurdler: fairly useful handicap chaser: shaped as if retaining his **h–** ability before unseating 2 out in race won by Creadan Grae at Perth: stays 3¼m: acts on soft going: in tongue tie last 2 starts. *Lucinda Russell*

RHAEGAR (IRE) 8 b.g. Milan – Green Star (FR) (Green Tune (USA)) [2018/19 h115, **c119** b95: c24g* c23.5d⁵ c24d^{pu} c24d^{pu} Apr 9] tall, good-topped gelding: fairly useful hurdler: **h–** similar form over fences: won novice handicap at Southwell in October: left Kim Bailey after third start: stayed 3m: acted on heavy going: tried in cheekpieces/tongue tie: dead. *Olly Murphy*

RHINESTONE (IRE) 6 b.g. Montjeu (IRE) – Apticanti (USA) (Aptitude (USA)) **h141** [2018/19 b119: h16d* h20d⁴ h22g² h24d^{pu} Mar 15] smallish gelding: smart bumper performer: useful form over hurdles: won maiden at Naas in November: progressed again when second in Nathaniel Lacy & Partners Solicitors Novices' Hurdle at Leopardstown (½ length behind Commander of Fleet) in February: lost action final start: stays 2¾m: wears tongue tie. *Joseph Patrick O'Brien, Ireland*

RHYMERS STONE 11 b.g. Desideratum – Salu (Ardross) [2018/19 h115: c16.3d **c101** c17.1g³ c20s⁶ Feb 18] fairly useful hurdler: below that level over fences: stays 21f: acts on **h–** heavy going: wears cheekpieces. *Harriet Graham*

RHYTHM DIVINE (IRE) 5 b.m. Milan – Diandrina (Mondrian (GER)) [2018/19 b17.3g⁴ **h118** b16s⁵ b16v⁵ h20d³ h20g³ h21v³ h16d² Apr 7] €6,500 3-y-o: half-sister to several winners **b78** abroad, including fair French hurdler/chaser Daisy Fay (17f winner, by Dubawi): dam German winner around 1m: unplaced completed start in points: modest form in bumpers: fairly useful form over hurdles: improved again when 10 lengths second to Elfile in listed novice at Punchestown shortly after end of British season: left J. G. Cosgrave after fifth start: stays 21f: acts on heavy going: usually front runner/races prominently. *T. Gibney, Ireland*

RHYTHM IS A DANCER 6 b.g. Norse Dancer (IRE) – Fascinatin Rhythm (Fantastic **h128** Light (USA)) [2018/19 b91: b16.8m* h15.3f² h21.4g* h21.4g* h21.4d⁵ h21m^{pu} h21.2g* **b100** h24.3m⁴ Apr 12] useful-looking gelding: fairly useful form in bumpers: won at Exeter in May: fairly useful hurdler: won novice at Wincanton in November, and novice handicaps at Wincanton in December and Ludlow in February: stays 21f: best form on good going: wears tongue tie: front runner/races prominently. *Paul Nicholls*

RHYTHM OF SOUND (IRE) 9 ch.g. Mahler – Oscarvail (IRE) (Oscar (IRE)) [2018/19 **c79 §** c80§, h–§: c15.6g c15.6g c19.2g² c20.1g^{pu} c20.3g^{pu} c20.3g^{pu} Aug 31] maiden hurdler: poor **h– §** handicap chaser: stays 19f: acts on soft and good to firm going: wears headgear/tongue tie: often races towards rear: unreliable. *Micky Hammond*

RI AN RIAN (IRE) 6 b.g. Arcadio (GER) – Live A Lot (IRE) (Saddlers' Hall (IRE)) **c109** [2018/19 c19.2g² c21.7g c20g* c19.9g⁶ c19.7g^{pu} h17.7g⁵ Apr 12] second foal: half-brother **h71** to fair hurdler/chaser Cillian's Well (2m-19f winner, by Trans Island): dam (h89) maiden hurdler (stayed 2¾m)/winning pointer: fair maiden hurdler: similar form over fences: won maiden at Tipperary in July: left Miss Elizabeth Doyle after third start: stays 2½m: acts on soft going: has worn headgear, including in 2018/19. *Laura Mongan*

RIBBLE VALLEY (IRE) 6 b.g. Westerner – Miss Greinton (GER) (Greinton) [2018/19 **b101** b16d⁴ b16.4g⁶ b16s* Jan 8] strong gelding: half-brother to 3 winners, including fairly useful hurdler Alla Svelta (17f-21f winner) and fairly useful hurdler/chaser Gran Torino

(2¼m-2½m winner), both by Milan: dam, placed in 2m hurdles in Germany, 6.5f-8.5f winner on Flat: fairly useful form in bumpers: won at Ayr in November and January: will stay further than 2m. *Nicky Richards*

RICHARDOFDOCCOMBE (IRE) 13 b.g. Heron Island (IRE) – Strike Again (IRE) **c–**
(Phardante (FR)) [2018/19 c–, h83: h15.8s⁵ h19.8s Mar 7] poor handicap hurdler: maiden **h77**
chaser: stays 2½m: acts on heavy going: wears tongue tie. *Gail Haywood*

RICHARDSON 4 ch.g. Kirkwall – Makeover (Priolo (USA)) [2018/19 b16.5d Apr 4] **b–**
well beaten in maiden bumper. *John Groucott*

RICHARD STRAUSS (IRE) 5 b.g. Kheleyf (USA) – Symfony (IRE) (Monsun (GER)) **h93**
[2018/19 h99: h16.7g h16.7g h15.6g* h19.4g⁶ h18.9s³ Dec 30] modest handicap hurdler:
won novice event at Musselburgh in November: unproven beyond 2m: acts on good to soft
going: in cheekpieces last 4 starts: has worn tongue tie. *Philip Kirby*

RICH COAST 11 b.g. King's Best (USA) – Costa Rica (IRE) (Sadler's Wells (USA)) **c– §**
[2018/19 h24.3dᵖᵘ Nov 3] useful hurdler at best: maiden chaser: left Noel Meade/off over **h– §**
2 years before only start in 2018/19: unproven beyond 17f: acted on good to firm and heavy
going: often hooded early in career: tried in tongue tie: untrustworthy: dead. *Lucinda Russell*

RICHIDISH (FR) 4 b.g. Spanish Moon (USA) – Briere (FR) (Kahyasi) [2018/19 b13.7g³ **b84**
Apr 24] £36,000 3-y-o: sixth foal: half-brother to fairly useful 2m hurdle winner Lareena
(by Full of Gold): dam, ran twice on Flat in France, half-sister to useful French 2¼m hurdle
winner Bilboquet: 7/1, third in bumper at Fontwell (7 lengths behind Milkwood).
Gary Moore

RICHIE VALENTINE 5 b.g. Native Ruler – Karmest (Best of The Bests (IRE)) **h91**
[2018/19 b–: ab16g h19.2m² Mar 29] little show in bumpers: 28/1, did better when second **b–**
in maiden at Fontwell (15 lengths behind Le Ligerien) on hurdling debut: in tongue tie last
2 starts. *Jamie Snowden*

RICHMOND (FR) 14 b.g. Assessor (IRE) – Hirondel de Serley (FR) (Royal Charter **c85**
(FR)) [2018/19 c107, h–: c32.5g⁴ May 4] sturdy gelding: point winner: maiden hurdler: fair **h–**
hunter chaser: stays 3m: acts on good to firm and heavy going: wears cheekpieces
nowadays. *P. P. C. Turner*

RIDDLESTOWN (IRE) 12 b.g. Cloudings (IRE) – Gandi's Dream (IRE) (Commanche **c109 §**
Run) [2018/19 c115, h114: c24.5g² c24.5g* c20.3g⁴ c26.1g c20.3s c22.7m c24.2gᵖᵘ c24s⁴ **h– §**
c26.3g² c29.2g⁴ h24dᵖᵘ Apr 24] strong gelding: winning hurdler: fair handicap chaser: won
at Towcester in May: stays 3¼m: acts on good to firm and heavy going: wears headgear:
usually front runner/races prominently: unreliable. *Caroline Fryer*

RIDERS ONTHE STORM (IRE) 6 br.g. Scorpion (IRE) – Endless Moments (IRE) **c144**
(Saddlers' Hall (IRE)) [2018/19 h133: c16.1d⁴ c19.7s³ c16d⁴ c20.2sᶠ c16.7gᵖᵘ Apr 21] tall **h–**
gelding: useful hurdler: even better form when won novice at Punchestown in February,
standout effort over fences: unproven beyond 2m: acts on heavy going. *Tom J. Taaffe,*
Ireland

RIDE THE LIGHTNING 6 b.g. Dalakhani (IRE) – Bright Halo (IRE) (Bigstone (IRE)) **h– p**
[2018/19 h16v h16.2g h16d Feb 6] fairly useful on Flat, stays 1¾m: well held in maiden/
novice hurdles: should do better now qualified for handicaps. *N. W. Alexander*

RIDGEWAY FLYER 8 b.g. Tobougg (IRE) – Running For Annie (Gunner B) [2018/19 **c136**
c134, h–: c26.7f² c21gᵖᵘ c23.8g⁵ Feb 28] good-topped gelding: has had breathing **h–**
operation: winning hurdler: useful form over fences: second in handicap at Wincanton (1¾
lengths behind Bigbadjohn) in October: reportedly bled next time: stays 27f: acts on firm
and soft going: wears hood/tongue tie: has hinted at temperament. *Paul Nicholls*

RIDGEWAY PEARL 6 b.m. Malinas (GER) – Sparkling Jewel (Bijou d'Inde) [2018/19 **h67**
b80: b15.7g h19.9v h16.7gᵘʳ h19.9v h15.8d Mar 30] mid-field at best in bumpers: little **b–**
show over hurdles. *Mike Sowersby*

RIGHTDOWNTHEMIDDLE (IRE) 11 b.g. Oscar (IRE) – Alternative Route (IRE) **c126 §**
(Needle Gun (IRE)) [2018/19 c–, h106: h23.9g* c20.1g c23.8g² h24m c25g h20.5g* **h110 §**
c23.8d c28.5d h24.2d h24.2d h21g h19.5m⁶ Apr 22] compact gelding: fair hurdler: won
handicap at Perth in July and conditionals seller at Leicester in December: fairly useful
handicap chaser: left Gordon Elliott after sixth start: stays 25f: acts on good to firm and
heavy going: has worn cheekpieces: in tongue tie last 4 starts: unreliable (behind all starts
for current yard). *Sean Curran*

RIGHT OF REPLY (IRE) 8 b.g. Presenting – Baliya (IRE) (Robellino (USA)) [2018/19 **c–**
c105, h103: c24.5g⁵ c17dᵖᵘ Jun 8] strong gelding: fair 23f hurdle winner: maiden chaser: **h–**
no form in 2018/19: tried in cheekpieces. *J. P. Owen*

RIGHT OLD TOUCH (IRE) 6 b.g. Stowaway – No Easy Way (IRE) (Mandalus) **b–**
[2018/19 b16v Nov 11] useful-looking gelding: no form in bumpers 20 months apart.
Gary Moore

RIGHT ROYALS DAY 10 b.m. Beneficial – Just For A Laugh (Idiot's Delight) [2018/19 **h79**
h16g h21.2m³ h15.8g⁴ h15.5g h15.8v⁵ h15.8s Dec 31] poor maiden hurdler: has worn
tongue tie, including last 2 starts: often races towards rear. *John Needham*

RINGA DING DING 6 b.g. Shirocco (GER) – Blue Dante (IRE) (Phardante (FR)) **c–**
[2018/19 h117, b90: h21.4m² h17.7m² h21.6g³ h21.6g⁵ c16.3s⁵ Jul 30] fair maiden hurdler: **h103**
well held in novice handicap on chasing debut: tried in tongue tie: usually races close up.
Paul Nicholls

RINGARINGAROSIE (IRE) 6 ch.m. Stowaway – Megan's Magic (Blue Ocean **c79**
(USA)) [2018/19 h16.2s h17.1d h16g⁴ h16d³ c15.6s⁵ c19.3sᵘʳ c16.4s³ c16.4d c16.4d **h73**
c16.4s³ c20.1vᵖᵘ c16.4s² c15.6g⁶ Apr 15] €7,200 4-y-o: fourth foal: half-sister to bumper
winner/fairly useful hurdler Come On Laurie (2½m/21f winner, by Oscar): dam (h71),
maiden hurdler, 1m-1¼m winner on Flat: pulled up both starts in Irish points: poor form
over hurdles: unproven beyond 2m: acts on soft going: tried in tongue
tie: usually front runner/races prominently. *Martin Todhunter*

RING EYE (IRE) 11 b.g. Definite Article – Erins Lass (IRE) (Erins Isle) [2018/19 c–, **c–**
h75: h21.2gᵇᵈ h23g⁴ h24g² h24g⁵ h20.3g h19.6m h21.7gᵖᵘ Oct 16] poor maiden hurdler: **h72**
well beaten only outing over fences: stays 3m: best form on good going: has worn tongue
tie: often races in rear. *Sarah-Jayne Davies*

RING MINELLA (IRE) 8 b.g. King's Theatre (IRE) – Ring of Water (USA) (Northern **c–**
Baby (CAN)) [2018/19 h80: h25m* h21.7d⁶ h23.4d⁴ c20dᶠ c21.6sᵖᵘ Jan 27] poor handicap **h74**
hurdler: won at Warwick in May: no aptitude for chasing: stays 25f: acts on soft and good
to firm going: wears tongue tie. *Paul Henderson*

RINGMOYLAN (IRE) 7 b.g. Mahler – La Speziana (IRE) (Perugino (USA)) [2018/19 **c–**
c–, h108: c24.1gᵖᵘ h21g h23.4dᵖᵘ Dec 18] workmanlike gelding: fair form when second in **h–**
maiden on hurdling debut in 2017/18: most disappointing since, including over fences: left
Jonjo O'Neill after first start. *Tracey Leeson*

RING THE MOON 6 b.g. Spanish Moon (USA) – Get The Ring (FR) (Linamix (FR)) **b89**
[2018/19 b17m³ b15.8m² Jul 13] €15,000 3-y-o: fifth foal: half-brother to 2 winners on Flat
by Layman, including French 7f/1m winner Eternal Gift: dam unraced: fair form in
bumpers: best effort when second in conditionals/amateurs maiden at Ffos Las in July: left
M. P. Collins after first start. *Evan Williams*

RINTULLA (IRE) 5 ch.g. Tobougg (IRE) – The Millers Tale (IRE) (Rashar (USA)) **b93**
[2018/19 b16.7v³ b15.8d b17s* Mar 7] fifth foal: half-brother to fair hurdler/fairly useful
chaser Tales of Milan (2¾m-29f winner, by Milan) and modest 2½m chase winner Go On
Henry (by Golan): dam unraced half-sister to useful staying chaser Dunbrody Millar: fair
form in bumpers: won at Carlisle in March. *Ben Pauling*

RIOJA DAY (IRE) 9 b.g. Red Clubs (IRE) – Dai E Dai (USA) (Seattle Dancer (USA)) **h73**
[2018/19 h16.2g h15.6g* h15.6g h16d³ h19.8s⁶ h16.4m⁴ h20.2d Apr 26] poor handicap
hurdler: won at Musselburgh in November: stays 19f: acts on heavy going: wears headgear.
Jim Goldie

RIO QUINTO (FR) 6 b.g. Loup Breton (IRE) – Seal of Cause (IRE) (Royal Academy **c132**
(USA)) [2018/19 h123, b–: h24.2d c23.5s* c24.1d⁴ c21.4m² Apr 21] good-topped gelding: **h–**
has had breathing operation: fairly useful hurdler: useful form over fences: won novice at
Lingfield (by 12 lengths from Lovenormoney) in January: stays 23f: acts on good to firm
and heavy going: tried in cheekpieces: in tongue tie last 4 starts: front runner/races
prominently. *Olly Murphy*

RIPPLET 4 b.f. Rip Van Winkle (IRE) – Seradim (Elnadim (USA)) [2018/19 b13.2m* **b82**
b14d⁶ Jan 1] rather unfurnished filly: fourth foal: closely related to fairly useful hurdler
Excellent Team (2m-2¼m winner, by Teofilo) and half-sister to a winner on Flat by
Raven's Pass: dam 7f/7.5f winner: modest form in bumpers: won 4-runner junior event at
Exeter in October: similar form on Flat. *Hughie Morrison*

RIPSTICK 8 b.g. Lucarno (USA) – Posh Stick (Rakaposhi King) [2018/19 c–, h85: **c84**
c21.2g⁴ c21.2g h23.9g Aug 1] winning pointer: poor form over hurdles/fences. *James Walton* **h–**

RISE AND DINE (FR) 4 gr.g. Authorized (IRE) – Here She Comes (FR) (Take Risks **b–**
(FR)) [2018/19 b16m Feb 23] useful-looking gelding: 7/1, badly needed experience when
last in bumper at Kempton: won on Flat at Angouleme following month. *N. Clement, France*

RISE OF AN EMPIRE (IRE) 9 br.g. Stowaway – Kymin (IRE) (Kahyasi) [2018/19 c104
c114, h–: c26.7m³ h26.5mᵖᵘ Jul 14] fairly useful hurdler at best: fair maiden chaser: stays h–
3m: acts on soft going: tried in cheekpieces: wears tongue tie: often races prominently.
Harry Fry

RISING BLUSH 6 b.m. Phoenix Reach (IRE) – Rosie All Over (Overbury (IRE)) b–
[2018/19 b17s⁴ Dec 16] first foal: dam (c113/h99) 2m-3½m hurdle/chase winner: tailed off
in mares bumper. *Donald McCain*

RISING MARIENBARD (IRE) 7 b.g. Marienbard (IRE) – Dromkeen Wood (Primitive c101
Rising (USA)) [2018/19 h99: h23.3g² c24.2g³ c24.2g³ Sep 17] won Irish maiden point on h98
debut: modest maiden hurdler: fair form in chases: stays 3m: usually tongue tied.
Lucinda Russell

RISING TIDE (IRE) 8 b.g. Dubai Destination (USA) – Erins Love (IRE) (Double Bed c–
(FR)) [2018/19 c–, h–: h15.7gᵖᵘ May 13] maiden hurdler, no form since 2016/17 including h–
over fences: tried in headgear: has worn tongue tie. *Laura Morgan*

RISK A FINE (IRE) 10 ch.g. Saffron Walden (FR) – Portanob (IRE) (Be My Native c133
(USA)) [2018/19 c24.2g* c20.2g² c20g* c22.6g* Apr 14] sturdy gelding: winning hurdler: h–
useful chaser: won hunters at Fakenham in February, Warwick in March and Stratford (by
15 lengths from Master Baker) in April: stays 3m: acts on soft and good to firm going:
wears hood: in tongue tie last 4 starts. *Gareth Moore*

RISK AND CO (FR) 5 b.g. No Risk At All (FR) – Chin'ba (FR) (Take Risks (FR)) h98 p
[2018/19 b74: b16.7g³ b16.8g² h19.7g³ Nov 5] fairly useful form in bumpers: 5/2, last of 3 b95
in maiden at Hereford on hurdling debut: should do better. *Jamie Snowden*

RISK AND ROLL (FR) 5 b.g. No Risk At All (FR) – Rolie de Vindecy (FR) (Roli Abi c126
(FR)) [2018/19 h125: c21g² c20gᶠ c19.7g² c19.2s³ c16.8s⁴ c18.8d⁵ c20s³ h21.7g² Apr 24] h126
good-topped gelding: has had breathing operation: fairly useful handicap hurdler/maiden
chaser: stays 2¾m: acts on heavy going: often in headgear: has worn tongue tie, including
last 2 starts: temperament under suspicion. *Paul Nicholls*

RISKS EMERY (FR) 4 ch.g. Vision d'Etat (FR) – Take Emery (FR) (Take Risks (FR)) b–
[2018/19 b13.7g Apr 24] has had breathing operation: last in bumper. *Michael Roberts*

RISKY GOLD (IRE) 6 b.g. Gold Well – Ask Me Sister (IRE) (Safety Catch (USA)) h78
[2018/19 b17g h21d h19.5v⁵ h19.9v⁴ Mar 16] has had breathing operation: winning b–
pointer: well held in bumper/over hurdles: in tongue tie last 2 starts. *Fergal O'Brien*

RITUAL OF SENSES (IRE) 9 b.g. Milan – Nonnetia (FR) (Trempolino (USA)) h114
[2018/19 h25g h20.5d Mar 2] good-topped gelding: fairly useful hurdler at best, off over 2
years before return: stays 19f: tried in blinkers. *Warren Greatrex*

RIVABODIVA (IRE) 9 ch.m. Flemensfirth (USA) – Sheebadiva (IRE) (Norwich) c–
[2018/19 c–, h110: h23.9g⁴ h23.3s* h24.6v h20.6s⁴ h21.4s² h25d h22.7d⁵ Apr 8] compact h114
mare: Irish point winner: fair handicap hurdler: won at Hexham in October: lightly-raced
maiden chaser: stays 27f: acts on heavy going: tried in cheekpieces: wears tongue tie:
usually front runner/races prominently. *Lucinda Russell*

RIVER ARROW 8 b.m. Kayf Tara – Supreme Gem (IRE) (Supreme Leader) [2018/19 h118
h124: h19.9v h20.3g⁵ Apr 18] sturdy mare: fairly useful handicap hurdler, lightly raced:
fifth in listed mares event at Cheltenham in April: will stay 3m: acts on heavy going.
Tom Symonds

RIVER BEND 5 b.m. Winged Love (IRE) – Retro's Lady (IRE) (Zaffaran (USA)) h–
[2018/19 b16d h20sᵖᵘ Apr 7] half-sister to fairly useful hurdler/useful chaser And The Man b–
(2½m-25f winner, by Generous): dam (c115/h115) bumper/2½m-3m hurdle winner:
showed nothing in bumper/novice hurdle. *Neil Mulholland*

RIVER BRAY (IRE) 6 ch.g. Arakan (USA) – Cill Fhearga (IRE) (Lahib (USA)) [2018/19 h124
h117, b93: h19.9g³ h16.8g³ h19.5d h15.3g* h15.7g³ h16.8g* Apr 20] lengthy, rather
sparely-made gelding: has had breathing operations: fairly useful hurdler: won novices at
Wincanton in February and Newton Abbot in April: stays 19f: acts on soft going: has worn
hood: in tongue tie last 3 starts. *Victor Dartnall*

RIVER DART (IRE) 7 ch.g. Dutch Art – Sky Galaxy (USA) (Sky Classic (CAN)) h–
[2018/19 h16gᵖᵘ Nov 12] has had breathing operation: fair on Flat, stays 16.5f: pulled up
in novice hurdle. *Tony Carroll*

RIVER FROST 7 b.g. Silver Frost (IRE) – River Test (Beat Hollow) [2018/19 h139: c– p
h19.5d c20sᶠ h19.8g Apr 27] good-topped gelding: useful handicap hurdler, shaped as if h129
retaining ability on return: fell tenth in maiden at Uttoxeter on chasing debut: stays 21f:
acts on good to soft going: has joined Ben Haslam. *Alan King*

JNwine.com Champion Chase, Down Royal—
Road To Respect and Sean Flanagan go one better than in 2017

RIVER GLADES 4 b.g. Cape Cross (IRE) – Everglades (Teofilo (IRE)) [2018/19 h16.4s⁴ **h99 p**
h17g^ur Feb 24] dam half-sister to fairly useful hurdler (2m/17f winner) Vancouverite: fairly
useful on Flat, stays 16.5f: modest form when fourth in novice at Newcastle on completed
start over hurdles, racing freely: remains with potential. *Tom Tate*

RIVER ICON 7 b.m. Sixties Icon – River Alder (Alderbrook) [2018/19 h119: h25.4g⁴ **c119**
h22.1d³ c20.1g² c24.2g⁴ c20.6g⁴ h16.4m⁵ h20.5m^ur h20.2g⁶ Apr 24] rather leggy mare: **h117**
fairly useful handicap hurdler: similar form over fences: best effort when second in novice
handicap at Hexham: stays 25f: acts on good to soft going: races off pace. *Iain Jardine*

RIVER OF INTRIGUE (IRE) 9 b.g. Indian River (FR) – Molly Hussey (IRE) **c113**
(Flemensfirth (USA)) [2018/19 c112, h–: c20.9m³ c21g³ c25.7m* c23.9g^pu c22.7m⁵ **h–**
c25.1s² c25.1g* Apr 3] winning hurdler: fair handicap chaser: won at Plumpton (novice) in
October and Wincanton in April: left Fergal O'Brien after fourth start: stays 3¼m: acts on
soft and good to firm going: has worn headgear, including last 3 starts: tried in tongue tie:
usually front runner/races prominently. *John O'Shea*

RIVER PURPLE 12 b.g. Bollin Eric – Cerise Bleue (FR) (Port Lyautey (FR)) [2018/19 **c– §**
c–§, h–: c16g^pu c20d⁶ c17g⁶ c16.5g c16d^pu c16.2d c20d^pu Mar 21] lengthy gelding: maiden **h–**
hurdler: fairly useful chaser at best, no form since 2016/17: wears tongue tie: temperamental.
Lady Susan Brooke

RIVERSIDE CITY (IRE) 10 ch.g. Presenting – Blazing Sky (IRE) (Beneficial) **c– §**
[2018/19 c107, h–: c24.1g^pu May 19] winning hurdler: fairly useful chaser at best, has lost **h–**
his way: stays 3½m: acts on good to firm and heavy going: has worn blinkers/tongue tie:
usually races nearer last than first: temperamental. *Jonjo O'Neill*

RIVER WYLDE (IRE) 8 b.g. Oscar (IRE) – Clarin River (IRE) (Mandalus) [2018/19 **c151**
c140p, h–: c21.6g^F c20.6d^pu c20.5m⁶ Apr 12] strong, compact gelding: has had breathing **h–**
operation: winning hurdler: smart form over fences: in front and running best race when
fell last in graduation event at Haydock on return: stays 2¾m: acts on soft going.
Nicky Henderson

RIVIERE ARGENTEE (FR) 5 gr.m. Hurricane Cat (USA) – River Trebor (USA) **h89**
(Myrakalu (FR)) [2018/19 h15.7g h18.7m³ h15.7g³ h20.3s h16d² h15.9s² h16v⁵ h16.5d⁶
h16g³ h16.3g³ Apr 14] has had breathing operation: sister to French 17f hurdle winner Grey
Owl: fair on Flat, stays 1½m: modest maiden hurdler: left Robin Dickin after fourth start:
unproven beyond 2m: acts on soft going: wears headgear: usually in tongue tie: usually
races off pace, often travels strongly. *Milton Harris*

712

RIZZARDO 7 gr.g. Tikkanen (USA) – Last Spruce (USA) (Big Spruce (USA)) [2018/19 **h108** h–, b–: h21.2g⁵ h16s⁶ h23.1g² h20.2g Apr 25] strong, lengthy gelding: very much a chaser on looks: fifth in Irish point on debut: fair form over hurdles: will stay 3m: best form on good going. *Nigel Twiston-Davies*

ROACHDALE HOUSE (IRE) 8 b.g. Mastercraftsman (IRE) – Golden Legacy (IRE) **h108** (Rossini (USA)) [2018/19 h16gᶠ h16d h16d⁶ h16m⁶ Apr 12] fair on Flat, also 7f: fair handicap hurdler: raced around 2m: acts on soft and good to firm going: tried in cheekpieces/tongue tie: usually races off pace. *Paul W. Flynn, Ireland*

ROAD TO FREEDOM 10 b.g. Revoque (IRE) – Go Classic (Classic Cliche (IRE)) **c–** [2018/19 c21.4g Aug 18] lengthy gelding: maiden pointer: winning hurdler: maiden chaser, **h–** no show only start in 2018/19: stays 3m: acts on heavy going: tried in cheekpieces. *Sarah-Jayne Davies*

ROAD TO GOLD (IRE) 10 b.g. Gold Well – Haut de Gamme (IRE) (Carmelite House **c101** (USA)) [2018/19 c–, h118: h21.4v* h22.8vᵖᵘ h21.4s² c24.1d⁵ Feb 6] winning Irish pointer: **h119** fairly useful handicap hurdler: won at Ayr in November: fair form in chases: stays 23f: acts on heavy going: tried in visor: signs of temperament. *N. W. Alexander*

ROAD TO RESPECT (IRE) 8 ch.g. Gamut (IRE) – Lora Lady (IRE) (Lord Americo) **c165** [2018/19 c167, h–: c24g* c24g³ c24g² c24g² c20.8d⁵ Apr 4] strong gelding: winning **h–** hurdler: top-class chaser: won JNwine.com Champion Chase at Down Royal (by 16 lengths from Woodland Opera) in November: placed after in Savills Chase (7½ lengths behind Kemboy) and Irish Gold Cup (short head behind Bellshill), both at Leopardstown, and in Ryanair Chase (Festival Trophy) at Cheltenham (3 lengths behind Frodon): stays 25f: acts on heavy going: has worn hood, including in 2018/19: tried in tongue tie. *Noel Meade, Ireland*

ROAD TO RICHES (IRE) 12 b.g. Gamut (IRE) – Bellora (IRE) (Over The River (FR)) **c123 §** [2018/19 c133, h–: c22.5d⁶ h24.4m c20.9v² c24.5v* c21.1d³ c24.7dᵖᵘ Apr 23] rangy **h–** gelding: winning hurdler: fairly useful chaser nowadays: won 4-runner hunter at Carlisle in March: third to Top Wood in Foxhunters' Chase at Aintree next time: left Noel Meade after second start: stays 4¼m: acts on heavy going: has worn headgear, including last 4 starts: wears tongue tie: usually races close up: one to treat with caution. *David Christie, Ireland*

ROAD TO ROME (IRE) 9 b.g. Choisir (AUS) – Tibbie (Slip Anchor) [2018/19 c111, **c134** h93: c20.3g² c23g* c23.8m* c22.2g* c26.3d⁴ c21.1d⁵ Apr 4] good-topped gelding: **h–** has had breathing operation: unbeaten in points: maiden hurdler: useful hunter chaser: completed 4-timer when winning at Taunton, Ludlow (twice) and Haydock (by 34 lengths from Sybarite) in January/February: left Oliver Sherwood after first start: stays 3m: acts on good to firm and good to soft going: tried in hood: front runner. *J. J. O'Shea*

ROARING BULL (IRE) 6 b.g. Milan – Gift of Freedom (IRE) (Presenting) [2018/19 **c138** h16.5g* c17d⁶ c16d² c21.2s* c21.6g⁴ c20d* c20.2s⁶ c24.5g³ c29d⁶ Apr 22] €35,000 3-y-o: **h117** well-made gelding: second foal: dam, no form in bumpers, out of half-sister to top-class 2m chaser Buck House: fairly useful hurdler: won minor event at Clonmel in November: useful chaser: won maiden at Fairyhouse in January and handicap at Naas in February: third in Grade 3 novice at Limerick (4½ lengths behind Burrows Saint) in March: stays 25f: acts on heavy going: wears headgear. *Gordon Elliott, Ireland*

ROARING FURY (IRE) 5 br.m. Sholokhov (IRE) – Bongo Fury (FR) (Sillery (USA)) **b84** [2018/19 b13.7d⁵ b17.7g⁴ b16.7g² b15.7d Apr 9] has had breathing operation: sixth foal: half-sister to smart chaser Mercian Prince (19f-21f winner, by Midnight Legend): dam (c124/h132), 2m hurdle/chase winner (stayed 19f), also 9f winner on Flat in France: modest form in bumpers. *Amy Murphy*

ROBBINA (IRE) 9 b.m. Robin des Champs (FR) – Sorrentina (IRE) (Muroto) [2018/19 **c–** c21.1s h24gᵖᵘ h20gᵖᵘ h23.9d⁵ h23.4g⁵ Nov 20] first foal: dam (c96/h99) bumper winner/ **h76** maiden jumper (stayed 2½m): maiden hurdler: poor nowadays: no form over fences: left W. Harney after second start: stays 3m: acts on heavy going: has worn headgear: has worn tongue tie, including in 2018/19: held up. *Christian Williams*

ROBBING THE PREY (IRE) 8 b.g. Robin des Pres (FR) – Derravarra Lady (IRE) **c128** (Flemensfirth (USA)) [2018/19 c128, h–: c19g* c15.8g c15.2dᵘʳ c19.1g⁴ h16.8s² c19.9gᵖᵘ **h106** Apr 22] good-topped gelding: fair maiden hurdler: fairly useful handicap chaser: won at Haydock in May: left Ruth Jefferson/disappointing after first start: stays 19f: acts on soft going: tried in hood. *Donald McCain*

ROBBIN'HANNON (IRE) 8 ch.g. Robin des Champs (FR) – Culleen Lady (IRE) **c–** (Presenting) [2018/19 c–, h134: h24s² h24g h23.3g⁵ Mar 23] sturdy gelding: won Irish **h132** maiden point on debut: useful hurdler: well beaten only chase outing: stays 3m: acts on heavy going. *M. A. Gunn, Ireland*

ROBERT'S STAR (IRE) 9 b.g. Oscar (IRE) – Halona (Pollerton) [2018/19 c–p, h120: c23.6g* c23g⁴ c22.6g³ c27.7d⁶ h25.5d Jan 2] sturdy gelding: fairly useful hurdler: similar form over fences: won novice handicap at Huntingdon in May: should stay beyond 3m: acts on heavy going: wears headgear: often races towards rear. *Mark Bradstock* **c123 h–**

ROBERTTOWN ROSE (IRE) 6 b.m. Milan – Windfola (FR) (Bonbon Rose (FR)) [2018/19 b–: h16.2g h19.9m³ h20.9m⁵ h19.9g⁶ h24.1gᵘʳ Apr 11] poor form over hurdles. *Andrew Crook* **h61**

ROBIN DE BROOME (IRE) 7 b.g. Robin des Pres (FR) – Croghan Lass (IRE) (Vestris Abu) [2018/19 h85, b–: h21.7g h23g h20g² h24g⁴ h23g⁵ c19.7gᵘʳ h20g⁴ h23.1d⁴ Apr 9] placed twice in Irish points: poor maiden hurdler: unseated fifth in novice handicap at Plumpton on chasing debut: stays 2½m: usually wears cheekpieces: races off pace. *Brian Barr* **c– h76**

ROBIN DE CARLOW 6 br.m. Robin des Champs (FR) – La Reine de Riogh (IRE) (Presenting) [2018/19 b16.5g* h19.8g* h18.1g³ h22.5g* h24d* h24v⁵ h18s⁴ h22v* h20gᶠ Apr 21] €40,000 3-y-o: first foal: dam (b76), ran once in bumper, out of fairly useful hurdler/chaser (winner up to 23f) Nas Na Riogh: won mares maiden bumper at Ballinrobe in May: useful hurdler: won mares maiden at Kilbeggan in July, listed mares event at Limerick (by 2 lengths from Awayinthewest) in October, listed novice at Cork (by 11 lengths from Milliner) in November and Kerry Group EBF Shannon Spray Mares Novices' Hurdle at Limerick (by nose from Well Set Up) in March: stays 3m: acts on heavy going: usually races off pace. *W. P. Mullins, Ireland* **h131 b95**

ROBIN DE PLAN (IRE) 8 b.m. Robin des Pres (FR) – Nice Resemblance (IRE) (Shernazar) [2018/19 h16vᵖᵘ h16s h20.5dᵖᵘ Jan 20] €3,800 3-y-o, £5,000 6-y-o: fourth foal: half-sister to fairly useful hurdler/smart chaser Bishops Road (2m-3½m winner, by Heron Island): dam unraced: runner-up in Irish point on debut: no form over hurdles: in tongue tie last 2 starts. *Barry Murtagh* **h–**

ROBIN DES FORET (IRE) 9 br.g. Robin des Pres (FR) – Omyn Supreme (IRE) (Supreme Leader) [2018/19 h142: c17v* c16g² c19.9m* c22.7g³ c18.2d³ c20s* c20g² c20sᶠ c20d³ c24.5g² Mar 31] useful hurdler: useful chaser: won maiden at Ballinrobe in May, and novices at Kilbeggan in June and Listowel (by 14 lengths from Gusty Rocky) in September: second in Like A Butterfly Novices' Chase at Tipperary (7 lengths behind Le Richebourg) and Grade 3 novice at Limerick (4 lengths behind Burrows Saint): stays 25f, effective at shorter: acts on good to firm and heavy going: usually races off pace/travels strongly. *W. P. Mullins, Ireland* **c144 h–**

ROBIN DES MANA (IRE) 8 br.g. Robin des Pres (FR) – Kokopelli Mana (IRE) (Saddlers' Hall (IRE)) [2018/19 h16g* h15.7g* h17.7g³ h21.7g³ h19.2g⁴ Sep 9] fair hurdler: won novice at Worcester and novice seller at Southwell in July: remained chaser: left Gordon Elliott/well below form after second start: stays 2¼m: acts on heavy going: has worn hood: has worn tongue tie, including in 2018/19. *Phil York* **c– h112**

ROBIN DES PEOPLE (IRE) 9 b.g. Robin des Pres (FR) – Zelea (IRE) (Be My Guest (USA)) [2018/19 c102, h–: c17d⁴ c16.5d³ Aug 29] multiple point winner: maiden hurdler: fair chaser: won hunter at Stratford in June: stays 3m, effective at much shorter: acts on good to firm and heavy going: has worn headgear/tongue tie. *David Brace* **c107 h–**

ROBIN DEUZ POIS (IRE) 7 ch.m. Robin des Champs (FR) – Native Wood (IRE) (Be My Native (USA)) [2018/19 h80: h23.3g⁴ h23.3g⁴ h25g⁴ c23.6g² c26v³ c23.9d² c26.3s⁴ Feb 21] modest maiden hurdler: similar form over fences: stays 3m: acts on soft and good to firm going: tried in cheekpieces. *Paul Webber* **c89 h90**

ROBINESSE (IRE) 8 ch.m. Robin des Champs (FR) – Jennifers Diary (IRE) (Supreme Leader) [2018/19 h99: h23.3d² h21.7v h25s⁶ h20.1v³ Mar 14] good-topped mare: fair maiden hurdler: stays 23f: acts on good to soft going: in blinkers last 2 starts: front runner/ races prominently. *Oliver Sherwood* **h104**

ROBIN OF LOCKSLEY (IRE) 9 b.g. Robin des Pres (FR) – Duggary Dancer (IRE) (Saddlers' Hall (IRE)) [2018/19 c129§, h104§: h19.9g² Sep 23] good-topped gelding: fairly useful hurdler: maiden chaser: stayed 21f: acted on heavy going: usually wore headgear: tried tongue tied: unreliable: dead. *Sophie Leech* **c– § h114 §**

ROBINROYALE (IRE) 8 b.g. Robin des Champs (FR) – Rosafi (IRE) (Roselier (FR)) [2018/19 c–, h103: h26d⁵ c23g⁴ c22.6g c25gᵘʳ c23.6s c25.1d⁶ c26d³ c25.7gᵘʳ h23.1gᵖᵘ h26gᵖᵘ Apr 10] strong gelding: has had breathing operation: fair handicap hurdler/maiden chaser: left Seamus Mullins after fifth start: stays 3¼m: acts on good to soft going: wears headgear: in tongue tie last 4 starts: usually races prominently. *Johnny Farrelly* **c111 h111**

William Hill Grand National Trial Handicap Chase, Haydock—Robinsfirth (centre) comes through to get the better of the grey Ramses de Teillee and Chef d'Oeuvre

ROBINSFIRTH (IRE) 10 b.g. Flemensfirth (USA) – Phardester (IRE) (Phardante (FR)) [2018/19 c144, h–: c25.6d[2] c28.4g* Feb 16] rangy gelding: winning hurdler: smart handicap chaser, lightly raced: progressed again when won Grand National Trial at Haydock (by ¾ length from Ramses de Teillee) in February: stays 3½m: acts on heavy going: in tongue tie last 4 starts: often races towards rear/travels strongly. *Colin Tizzard*
c152
h–

ROBINSHILL (IRE) 8 ch.g. Robin des Champs (FR) – I Remember It Well (IRE) (Don't Forget Me) [2018/19 c137, h–: c18m c16g[3] c16d c16.2g[6] h16d[6] h16.3d h19g Apr 25] sturdy gelding: useful hurdler/chaser at best, largely out of form in 2018/19: stays 19f: acts on heavy going: often wears tongue tie: usually front runner/races prominently: often let down by jumping. *Nigel Twiston-Davies*
c127 x
h108

ROBINS LEGEND (IRE) 7 b.g. Robin des Pres (FR) – Lemons Legend (Midnight Legend) [2018/19 c79, h–: c24.2g[6] May 22] sturdy gelding: poor maiden hurdler/chaser: won point in 2019: stays 3m: acts on good to soft going: wears headgear: usually races close up. *Chris Grant*
c–
h–

ROBINSSON (IRE) 9 b.g. Robin des Champs (FR) – Silver Proverb (Silver Patriarch (IRE)) [2018/19 h107: h21.9g c20.9s[pu] Nov 23] sturdy gelding: maiden hurdler: pulled up in novice handicap on chasing debut: stayed 2¾m: acted on heavy going: in cheekpieces last 4 starts: dead. *Oliver Sherwood*
c–
h–

ROBINTHEAULAD (IRE) 8 b.g. Robin des Champs (FR) – Brotenstown (IRE) (Presenting) [2018/19 c96, h75: c21.6g[pu] h23.9g[6] Jul 5] has had breathing operations: maiden hurdler/chaser, little show in 2018/19: wears tongue tie. *Sandy Thomson*
c–
h78

ROBIN THE RAVEN (IRE) 7 b.g. Robin des Pres (FR) – Omyn Supreme (IRE) (Supreme Leader) [2018/19 h135: c23s[3] c23g[F] h25g* Apr 25] good-topped gelding: useful form over hurdles: won handicap at Warwick (by 7 lengths from Max Forte) in April: similar form when third in novice at Worcester (2½ lengths behind Deauville Crystal) on completed start over fences: stays 25f: acts on soft and good to firm going: wears cheekpieces: in tongue tie last 4 starts: usually races prominently: should still do better over fences. *Kim Bailey*
c134 p
h138

ROBIN WATERS (FR) 6 b.g. Irish Wells (FR) – Skandia (FR) (Robin des Champs (FR)) [2018/19 h140p: c25g[2] h23.1d[pu] Feb 22] tall, good-topped gelding: has had breathing operation: easy winner of point on debut: useful form over hurdles: beaten both starts in 2018/19, including on chasing debut: stays 3m: acts on heavy going: often travels strongly. *Dan Skelton*
c–
h–

ROBSAM (IRE) 4 b.g. Mahler – Silver Set (IRE) (Accordion) [2018/19 b17.7d[6] Mar 18] well beaten in bumper. *Martin Keighley*
b–

ROB'S LEGACY 6 ch.g. Phoenix Reach (IRE) – Clumber Pursuits (Pastoral Pursuits) **h–**
[2018/19 h–: h16.7gpu Jul 8] little form over hurdles. *Shaun Harris*

ROB THE GETAWAY (IRE) 6 b.g. Getaway (GER) – Kinard True (IRE) (Snurge) **b97**
[2018/19 b17g* May 18] €20,000 3-y-o: second foal: dam winning pointer: won twice in
points: 5/1, also won bumper at Aintree (by ½ length from Kootenay River) in May. *Mrs
Sheila Crow*

ROBYNDZONE (IRE) 5 b.g. Frammassone (IRE) – Rebecca Susan (Petoski) [2018/19 **h–**
b16.4d b15.7d h19.5d h21g6 h19g Apr 25] smallish gelding: has had breathing operation: **b–**
won sole start in Irish points: well held in bumpers/over hurdles: in tongue tie last 3 starts.
Fergal O'Brien

ROCCO (IRE) 6 b.g. Shantou (USA) – Navaro (IRE) (Be My Native (USA)) [2018/19 **h124**
h89, b77: h16d* h21g4 h21.9s5 h24s3 h20.3d5 h21m Feb 23] good-topped gelding: won
completed start in Irish points: fairly useful hurdler: won novice at Chepstow in October:
third in Albert Bartlett Novices' Hurdle (Bristol) at Cheltenham (5¾ lengths behind
Rockpoint): stays 3m: acts on soft going: front runner/races prominently.
Nigel Twiston-Davies

ROCCOWITHLOVE 5 b.g. Shirocco (GER) – Love Train (IRE) (Sadler's Wells (USA)) **h89**
[2018/19 b15.7d h20.5d h23.1s4 h23.3d3 Mar 30] €55,000 3-y-o: third foal: half-brother to **b–**
fairly useful hurdler/chaser Overland Flyer (2½m-3m winner, by Westerner): dam (b71),
ran twice in bumpers, sister to useful hurdler/fairly useful chaser (2½m/21f winner) Sizing
Symphony and closely related to useful hurdler (stays 3m) Monbeg Theatre: well beaten in
bumper: modest form over hurdles: in cheekpieces last 2 starts. *Warren Greatrex*

ROC D'APSIS (FR) 10 gr.g. Apsis – Rocapina (FR) (Solon (GER)) [2018/19 c130x, h–: **c113**
c20.5g c22.6g4 Mar 30] well-made gelding: maiden hurdler: useful handicap chaser: below **h–**
form both starts in 2018/19 after long absence: stays 3m: acts on soft and good to firm
going: wears cheekpieces. *Tom George*

ROCKALZARO (FR) 7 gr.g. Balko (FR) – Royale Wheeler (FR) (Rusticaro (FR)) **c86**
[2018/19 h108, b88: h16.2g4 h20.1g3 h16.7g h16.7g3 h20.3g5 c20.3g5 h23.8g2 h25d4 **h101**
h21.2v6 h23.8m3 h19.6g Apr 13] has had breathing operation: fair handicap hurdler: well
held in novice handicap on chasing debut: stays 3m: acts on good to firm and good to soft
going: wears headgear/tongue tie. *Donald McCain*

ROCKET MAN RODNEY 6 b.g. Black Sam Bellamy (IRE) – Miss Quickly (IRE) **c–**
(Anshan) [2018/19 b–: b16.2g6 b15.7g c23.4gpu h22.7gpu h22spu h18.1dpu Apr 8] has had **h–**
breathing operation: mid-field at best in bumpers: no form over hurdles/fences. **b71**
Harriet Graham

ROCKET RONNIE (IRE) 9 b.g. Antonius Pius (USA) – Ctesiphon (USA) (Arch **h93**
(USA)) [2018/19 h96: h22m4 h20.6g5 h18.7m5 h19.6g2 h16.8g2 h18.5d* h15.8m2 h16g2
h19d Nov 29] compact gelding: modest handicap hurdler: won at Newton Abbot
(conditionals) in September: stays 2½m: acts on good to firm and good to soft going: wears
headgear: has worn tongue tie. *Adrian Wintle*

ROCK GONE (IRE) 11 b.g. Winged Love (IRE) – Guillem (USA) (Nijinsky (CAN)) **c124**
[2018/19 c137, h–: c24.2v2 c24.2d4 Jan 5] tall gelding: winning hurdler: fairly useful **h–**
handicap chaser nowadays: second in veterans event at Sandown after year off then fourth
in Veterans' Handicap Chase Final there: stays 3m: acts on heavy going. *Dr Richard Newland*

ROCKINROLLDIXIE (IRE) 10 b.g. Garuda (IRE) – Witches Lane (IRE) (Petorius) **c–**
[2018/19 h20m2 Jul 9] multiple point winner: first form under Rules when second in novice **h101**
hurdle at Worcester (hooded): trained previously by Eugene M. O'Sullivan: tried in tongue
tie. *Alastair Ralph*

ROCKLANDER (IRE) 10 b.g. Oscar (IRE) – Rua Lass (IRE) (Beau Sher) [2018/19 **c133**
c147, h–: c20.6gpu c21v5 c22.4s4 c22.9vF c24gpu h25.8g Mar 23] sturdy gelding: useful **h–**
hurdler/chaser, largely out of form in 2018/19: stays 3m: acts on good to firm and heavy
going: tried in cheekpieces: usually races close up. *Tom George*

ROCKLIFFE 6 b.g. Notnowcato – Hope Island (IRE) (Titus Livius (FR)) [2018/19 h91: **h91**
h16.8gpu h17.2m3 h16.7g4 h16.8s6 h19.3s* h18.6d5 h19.3m3 h21.2d3 Apr 23] smallish
gelding: modest handicap hurdler: won at Catterick (amateurs) in December: stays 19f:
acts on soft and good to firm going: tried in cheekpieces. *Micky Hammond*

ROCK ME ZIPPO (IRE) 11 b.g. Millenary – Babylonia (IRE) (Be My Guest (USA)) **c–**
[2018/19 c–, h–: c26.2gpu May 27] maiden pointer: little form under Rules: tried in tongue **h–**
tie. *Miss L. V. Horner*

ROCK MY STYLE (IRE) 7 b.g. Marienbard (IRE) – Meara Trasna (IRE) (Rock Hopper) **c123**
[2018/19 h121: c23.4dur c22.5d2 c26gpu Mar 23] fairly useful hurdler: similar form when **h–**

second in novice handicap at Uttoxeter only completed start in chases: should stay beyond 3m: acts on heavy going: in cheekpieces last 4 starts: races lazily (has bled). *Warren Greatrex*

ROCK N ROLLA (IRE) 5 ch.g. Intikhab (USA) – Fantastic Opinion (IRE) (Fantastic Light (USA)) [2018/19 h16.2g² h16.2g h16.8g Oct 21] fairly useful on Flat, stays 1¼m: modest form over hurdles: easily best effort when second in novice at Perth: tried in visor. *Keith Dalgleish* **h98**

ROCKNROLLRAMBO (IRE) 12 b.g. Winged Love (IRE) – Lady Padivor (IRE) (Zaffaran (USA)) [2018/19 c109, h–: c24.1g Aug 31] winning hurdler: fair chaser at best, has lost his way: stays 3m: acts on heavy going: has worn cheekpieces/tongue tie. *Ian Williams* **c– h–**

ROCK N'STONES (IRE) 8 b.g. Stowaway – Rock Abbey (IRE) (College Chapel) [2018/19 h82x: h16.2d⁵ h16.2g² h16.2g⁶ h16.2m³ c20gᵖᵘ h23g h18.6m h20.3g⁵ h23.3g h16.2g h20.1sᵖᵘ h16.7s⁶ h19.3s h19.3m⁶ h15.7g⁵ Mar 4] has had breathing operation: modest on Flat, stays 2m: poor maiden hurdler: pulled up in novice handicap on chasing debut: stays 21f: acts on good to firm and good to soft going: wears headgear: tried in tongue tie: often let down by jumping. *Gillian Boanas* **c– h68 x**

ROCK OF LEON 8 b.g. Rock of Gibraltar (IRE) – Leonica (Lion Cavern (USA)) [2018/19 c–, h104§: h20g* h22.1g⁴ h20.3gᵘʳ Jul 15] sturdy gelding: modest hurdler: won seller at Worcester in May: winning chaser: stays 3m: acts on good to firm and heavy going: wears headgear/tongue tie: usually races close up: usually let down by jumping/attitude. *Philip Kirby* **c– x h95 §**

ROCK ON BARNEY (IRE) 8 b.g. Fracas (IRE) – Monthly Sessions (IRE) (Pistolet Bleu (IRE)) [2018/19 h21.4v³ c19.9s h19.7g⁶ c19.5g c21gᶠ c20gᵖᵘ c24.6g c20.1g c18.2s⁵ c23s³ c20.1g⁵ c22.5s h24.5v Mar 16] modest handicap hurdler/maiden chaser: stays 23f: acts on heavy going: wears headgear: has worn tongue tie. *G. T. Lynch, Ireland* **c94 h88**

ROCK ON FRUITY (IRE) 10 b.g. Fruits of Love (USA) – Sancta Miria (IRE) (Toulon) [2018/19 c19gᵖᵘ c25gᵘʳ c17s⁵ c25.2g c20.1s* c23.4s* c32.6g c24.5v⁵ c20.1d⁴ Apr 6] winning hurdler: useful handicap chaser: won at Newcastle in December and January: left Charles Byrnes after third start: stays 25f: acts on good to firm and heavy going: has worn headgear: usually races in rear: often let down by jumping. *Ben Haslam* **c135 x h–**

ROCK ON OSCAR (IRE) 9 b.g. Oscar (IRE) – Brogeen Lady (IRE) (Phardante (FR)) [2018/19 c116p, h–: c19.4dᵖᵘ h15.8g Nov 4] rangy gelding: won sole start in points: useful hurdler at best: maiden chaser: best form up to 21f: acted on good to soft going: wore hood/tongue tie: carried head awkwardly: dead. *Matt Sheppard* **c– h–**

ROCK ON ROCCO (IRE) 5 b.g. Shirocco (GER) – Katalina (Hernando (FR)) [2018/19 b16.4v³ Mar 16] €42,000 3-y-o, £55,000 4-y-o: third foal: dam (b86), second in bumper, sister to fairly useful hurdler/useful chaser (21f/2¾m winner) Carlitos out of useful hurdler/chaser (2m/17f winner) Queen of Spades: third on completed start in Irish points: 3/1, third in bumper at Newcastle (1½ lengths behind Marown). *Tom George* **b94**

ROCK ON ROCKY 11 b.g. Overbury (IRE) – Tachometer (IRE) (Jurado (USA)) [2018/19 c132, h–: h15.8d c16.8m³ c15.9g⁴ c16.4s⁶ c18.8s⁶ c16.2g⁴ c18.8dᶠ c19.4s³ c15.5d⁵ c16.4g⁵ c16sᵖᵘ Apr 7] lengthy gelding: useful hurdler at best: fairly useful handicap chaser nowadays: third in listed event at Ascot in November: stays 2½m: acts on heavy going: wears cheekpieces/tongue tie: inconsistent. *Matt Sheppard* **c120 h–**

ROCK ON TIGER (FR) 4 gr.g. Alberto Giacometti (IRE) – Kennaaly (FR) (Medaaly) [2018/19 b16.7g⁴ Apr 13] £10,000 3-y-o: fourth foal: half-brother to French 19f chase winner Summer Creek (by Brier Creek): dam French maiden (placed at 11.5f): 5/2, fourth in conditionals/amateurs bumper at Bangor (2¼ lengths behind Orrisdale). *Henry Daly* **b89**

ROCKPOINT 6 b.g. Shirocco (GER) – Tinagoodnight (FR) (Sleeping Car (FR)) [2018/19 h118: h18.5m² h16.4g h24.2s² h24s* h21g⁴ h24.3g⁶ h24d h24g Apr 17] stocky gelding: fairly useful hurdler: won Albert Bartlett Novices' Hurdle (Bristol) at Cheltenham (by 2¾ lengths from Lisnagar Oscar) in December: stays 3m: acts on heavy going: usually races close up. *Colin Tizzard* **h127**

ROCKPORTIAN (IRE) 9 b.g. Definite Article – Wilmott's Fancy (Buckley) [2018/19 h24g³ Sep 5] point/bumper winner: fair form over hurdles: dead. *Warren Greatrex* **h97**

ROCK STEADY (IRE) 6 ch.g. Intikhab (USA) – Mannsara (IRE) (Royal Academy (USA)) [2018/19 h15.7mᵘʳ h15.7g⁶ h16.8d⁶ h16.3d Mar 2] sturdy gelding: half-brother to fairly useful hurdler Russian George (2m/17f winner, by Sendawar): dam half-sister to useful hurdler (2m/17f winner) Marchand d'Argent: useful on Flat, stays 1¾m: fair form over hurdles. *Alan King* **h104**

Mrs Diana L. Whateley's "Rock The Kasbah"

ROCK THE KASBAH (IRE) 9 ch.g. Shirocco (GER) – Impudent (IRE) (In The Wings) [2018/19 c150, h–: c23.6d[6] c27.3g* c26g[6] c34.3g[f] c28.8g[pu] Apr 27] useful-looking gelding: winning hurdler: smart handicap chaser: won Grade 3 event at Cheltenham (by 1¼ lengths from Royal Vacation) in November, standout effort of season: stays 29f: acts on heavy going: wears cheekpieces: often races prominently. *Philip Hobbs*   **c150 h–**

ROCKU 9 b.g. Great Palm (USA) – Suetsu (IRE) (Toulon) [2018/19 h23.1s[3] h24.1d[4] h19.3g[bd] h19.9v[3] Mar 12] third in maiden point on debut: poor maiden hurdler: stays 23f: acts on soft going: wears headgear: in tongue tie last 4 starts. *Dan Skelton*   **h73**

Knight Frank Juvenile Hurdle, Leopardstown—
Coeur Sublime's fall at the last hands the race to Rocky Blue (striped cap)

ROCKWOOD 8 b.g. Rock of Gibraltar (IRE) – Hannah Frank (IRE) (High Chaparral (IRE)) [2018/19 h16.7g⁴ Mar 27] angular gelding: fair on Flat, stayed 1¼m: 33/1, fourth in novice at Market Rasen (13 lengths behind Benny's Bridge) on hurdling debut: dead. *Karen McLintock* **h91**

ROCKY BLUE (IRE) 4 ch.g. Society Rock (IRE) – Plumbago Blue (Manduro (GER)) [2018/19 h16.6g² h16g* Dec 26] fairly useful on Flat, stays 1¾m: useful form over hurdles: improved plenty from debut when won Knight Frank Juvenile Hurdle at Leopardstown (by 3¼ lengths from Chief Justice) in December, joined when left clear last. *Thomas Mullins, Ireland* **h132**

ROCKY COURT (IRE) 10 b.g. Court Cave (IRE) – Easter Bee (IRE) (Phardante (FR)) [2018/19 c17g*ᵈ h20m c17d* c18.2d⁵ Oct 9] winning hurdler: useful chaser: 50/1, won minor event at Ballinrobe (by 1¼ lengths from Listen Dear) in August: also first past post in handicap at same course on reappearance, but later disqualified due to banned substance: stays 2¼m: acts on soft and good to firm going: wears tongue tie: often travels strongly. *S. J. Mahon, Ireland* **c131 h–**

ROCKY'S TREASURE (IRE) 8 b.g. Westerner – Fiddlers Bar (IRE) (Un Desperado (FR)) [2018/19 h128: h25g⁴ c23.4m* c24.2m* c24.2m* c23.4s² c24g* c24g³ c26g⁵ c26g² Apr 17] sturdy gelding: fairly useful handicap hurdler: smart chaser: won novices at Kelso, Fakenham and Wetherby in October/November, and December Novices' Chase at Doncaster by 17 lengths from Theclockisticking, all small-field events: also second in John Francome Novices' Chase at Newbury (4 lengths behind Santini) before turn of year: stays 3¼m: acts on good to firm and heavy going: usually front runner/races prominently. *Kim Bailey* **c147 h121**

ROCOCO RIVER 5 b.g. Shirocco (GER) – Noun de La Thinte (FR) (Oblat (FR)) [2018/19 h–p: h16.8s⁶ h16.8s³ Apr 16] modest form over hurdles: third in maiden at Exeter in April: remains open to improvement. *Mrs Jane Williams* **h96 p**

Mr J. Perriss' "Rocky's Treasure"

ROCOCO STYLE 6 b.m. Shirocco (GER) – Akdara (IRE) (Sadler's Wells (USA)) **h92**
[2018/19 b85: h16.7g³ h20.6gᵘʳ h20.6g³ h19.9s h19.4g⁵ h16.8v⁵ Mar 12] sturdy mare:
bumper winner: modest form over hurdles: in cheekpieces last 4 starts. *Steve Gollings*

ROCONGA (IRE) 9 b.g. Rakti – Nafzira (IRE) (Darshaan) [2018/19 c132, h–: c16g³ **c130**
c16g³ c17m³ Jul 19] winning hurdler: useful maiden chaser: third in novice at Punchestown **h–**
(3¼ lengths behind Light That) in May: stays 19f: acts on soft and good to firm going: often
races prominently. *E. J. O'Grady, Ireland*

RODEO DODO (IRE) 9 b.g. Milan – Laney Mary (IRE) (Mister Lord (USA)) [2018/19 **h86**
h–: h19.7g* h24g⁶ Mar 4] winning pointer: modest form over hurdles: much improved
when won on handicap debut at Wetherby in February: should stay beyond 2½m: in tongue
tie last 2 starts. *Dan Skelton*

RODRIGO (IRE) 5 b.g. Roderic O'Connor (IRE) – Dixie Fine (USA) (L'Emigrant **b–**
(USA)) [2018/19 b16.2m Sep 19] tailed off in bumper. *Dianne Sayer*

ROE MILL (IRE) 6 ch.m. Papal Bull – Maria Milena (Stravinsky (USA)) [2018/19 **b–**
b17.7g May 13] first foal: dam ran twice on Flat: tailed off in bumper. *Linda Jewell*

ROEVIN STAR (IRE) 9 b.g. Vinnie Roe (IRE) – Morereason (IRE) (Indian Lodge **c89**
(IRE)) [2018/19 c25.3g c25.3g⁴ c24g⁴ c22g c25.2d⁴ c22.2gᵖᵘ Feb 16] winning pointer: **h–**
once-raced hurdler: modest handicap chaser: left Eoin Doyle after fifth start: stays 25f: acts
on good to soft going: usually wears headgear. *Tim Garton*

ROGUE ANGEL (IRE) 11 b.g. Presenting – Carrigeen Kohleria (IRE) (Luso) [2018/19 **c140**
c126§, h–: c25g* c24s³ c24g⁶ c28s² c24d c29g⁵ c24.5g c26d c24.7d Apr 22] workmanlike **h–**
gelding: winning hurdler: useful handicap chaser: awarded Midlands National Handicap
Chase at Kilbeggan in July after Timiyan was disqualified due to prohibited substance:
second in Cork National (1¼ lengths behind Out Sam) in November: stays 4m: acts on
good to firm and heavy going: wears headgear/tongue tie. *Gordon Elliott, Ireland*

ROGUE DANCER (FR) 14 b.g. Dark Moondancer – Esperanza IV (FR) (Quart de Vin **c77**
(FR)) [2018/19 c23.6g² c28.5d³ c23.6d⁴ Dec 26] tall gelding: maiden hurdler: poor **h–**
handicap chaser: stays 3½m: acts on good to firm and good to soft going: in cheekpieces
last 3 starts: has worn tongue tie, including in 2018/19. *Lawney Hill*

ROGUE DIAMOND (IRE) 6 b.m. Wareed (IRE) – La Brigantine (IRE) (Montelimar **b–**
(USA)) [2018/19 b17g May 18] £15,000 5-y-o: fifth foal: half-sister to bumper winner/
smart hurdler Quwetwo (2m-2¼m winner, by Karinga Bay): dam (c85/h93), 2m hurdle/
chase winner who became temperamental, half-sister to smart hurdler/chaser (stayed 25f)
Fundamentalist: won maiden point on debut: well beaten in bumper. *Graeme McPherson*

ROI DE DUBAI (IRE) 7 b.g. Dubai Destination (USA) – Miss Esther (GER) (Alkalde **h114**
(GER)) [2018/19 h20m* h24mᵘʳ h19.6g⁶ h21.7d* h20g⁴ h20g⁵ h21g Oct 26] £38,000
4-y-o: lengthy gelding: half-brother to several winners, including fairly useful hurdler/
smart chaser Moon Over Miami (2m-2½m winner, by Dashing Blade) and fair hurdler/
fairly useful chaser Presenting Lisa (2m-21f winner, by Presenting): dam German 8.5f
winner: off mark in points at fourth attempt: fair handicap hurdler: won at Down Royal in
June and Downpatrick in August: stays 2¾m: acts on good to firm and good to soft going:
usually races close up. *John McConnell, Ireland*

ROKSANA (IRE) 7 b.m. Dubai Destination (USA) – Talktothetail (IRE) **h149**
(Flemensfirth (USA)) [2018/19 h142: h16s³ h19.9s* h24.7g² Apr 6]
It is thirty years since Martin Pipe became the first trainer in Britain to saddle
two hundred winners or more in a season, a feat he went on to repeat seven more
times before his retirement at the end of the 2005/06 season (by which time the
feat had still not been achieved even once by any other trainer in Britain, Flat or
jumping). The year before he notched a double century for the first time, Pipe had
surpassed Michael Dickinson's supposedly unassailable record of one hundred and
twenty wins set in 1982/83, recording a total of one hundred and twenty-nine. The
1988/89 season began in late-July and ran until early-June, with Pipe passing the
hundred mark before the end of December, overtaking his previous season's total in
early-February and reaching the double century on May 19th before a final total of
two hundred and eight at the end of the season. It's worth pointing out that Pipe's
first double century was helped by what *Chasers & Hurdlers* called 'a freakishly-
mild winter in which there was hardly an interruption to the jumping programme', a
description which would apply just as well to the latest season when—in an era
when there is more racing—his feat was finally matched by another jumping trainer

in Britain. As was Pipe's way, he raised the bar still further, and in 1999/2000, despite the season ending earlier than previously, at Sandown in late-April, he set the current record of two hundred and forty-three wins in a season, clocking up new records for the fastest hundred and two hundred on the way. Pipe's final double century (235 winners) came in 2001/02, the only one he achieved during the current twelve-month format for the jumps season, and he set another record on the way for the fastest century, which came at Ascot on November 3rd.

Since Pipe's retirement, the highest seasonal total of winners by a jumps trainer in Britain had been one hundred and seventy-one, set by Paul Nicholls in 2016/17, ironically one of the few seasons in the post-Pipe era that Nicholls has ceded the trainers' championship, which is decided by prize money, to Nicky Henderson. There was an early indication that the two-hundred barrier might finally be broken again during the latest campaign when Dan Skelton clocked up a century of winners, eight days earlier than the Pipe record, when Sam Red won the amateur riders' handicap chase at Cheltenham on October 26th. Luck was on the Skelton runner's side on that occasion as he was handed the race when the clear leader ran out through the tapes on the run-in. It wasn't to be the only piece of good fortune that the stable enjoyed at Cheltenham during the season. Having banked plenty of prize money early on (becoming the first trainer to pass the £1m mark for the season), Skelton lost the lead in the trainers' championship to Paul Nicholls before the end of the year, but the winners kept flowing and a six-timer on Easter Sunday (four at Market Rasen ridden by brother Harry, and two at Plumpton), with a week of the season remaining, brought up the two hundred before the stable reached a final total of two hundred and five. Skelton finished in third place in the championship (on prize money) behind Nicholls and Henderson, sending out easily the largest number of individual horses of any stable during the season—two hundred and forty-four—who between them ran almost a thousand times, establishing a ratio of wins to runs of better than one in five.

Skelton completed only his sixth season with a licence and his seasonal totals of 27, 73, 104, 118, 156 and now 205 chart the progress of a rapidly-growing threat to the two trainers who have dominated the championship since Pipe won his record fifteen titles. Pipe also regularly increased his totals year on year, and that's not the only similarity between the two. Like Pipe, who took fifteen seasons to become champion for the first time, Skelton has founded his success to date on quantity of winners, rather than quality, and has quickly established a reputation for improving other stables' cast-offs whilst ruffling a few feathers along the way. Too Many Diamonds could have come straight from the Pipe textbook. A maiden who had been placed just twice (once in Jersey) from more than forty starts, most of those on the Flat in Ireland, Too Many Diamonds finished eighth at 40/1 in a selling handicap hurdle at Taunton in April 2017. The following month, having joined Skelton, Too Many Diamonds was sent off at even money on his debut for his new yard at Plumpton, off a BHA mark of 72, and won by thirteen lengths. He went on to add further wins at Sedgefield, Bangor and Market Rasen in a little over a week. Too Many Diamonds also ran up a hat-trick in handicap chases at Southwell when contributing to the stable's flying start to the latest season and reached a BHA mark in the mid-130s over fences.

Just as Pipe's success was shared by his stable's main jockeys, Peter Scudamore and then Tony McCoy, both also record-breakers, Dan Skelton's rapid ascent in the training ranks has come in tandem with his brother Harry who enjoyed his best season in the saddle, finishing runner-up to Richard Johnson in the championship with only six of his one hundred and seventy-eight winners coming for other yards. It is also true that both Pipe and Dan Skelton were set up as trainers with the help of their fathers, though that's where any similarities in their backgrounds end. Pipe, the son of a West Country bookmaker, started out as a permit holder from what had been a run-down farm in Somerset, while Skelton, who served as Paul Nicholls' assistant for six years, began training in 2013 from a modern purpose-built training establishment at Lodge Hill in Warwickshire, next door to the stables of his father Nick, winner of show-jumping gold medals at the last two Olympics.

OLBG Mares' Hurdle (David Nicholson), Cheltenham—
almost a replica of the fate that befell Annie Power in the same race as 2018 winner
Benie des Dieux comes down at the last, handing victory to Roksana

It is not hard to see, from the way Skelton's seasonal totals are growing, why Pipe believes his record number of wins in a season could be under threat before much longer. But he may be worrying unnecessarily about that. The first season that Pipe reached two hundred winners coincided with his becoming champion for the first time, thanks to a greater number of big-race winners than ever before, including Strands of Gold in the Hennessy Gold Cup and Bonanza Boy in the Welsh Grand National. As Skelton has acknowledged—and as Gordon Elliott has already found competing with Willie Mullins in Ireland—training a large quantity of winners will only take a trainer so far along the road towards becoming champion. Skelton intends changing his strategy in his bid to achieve that ambition. 'We have always bought quality but need to make an even more concerted effort to do that,' he said during the latest season. 'Next year we might not be beating records or be third, fourth, fifth in the trainers' championship table. We might be seventh or eighth but there is a growth stage we have to go through to get where we want to end up. Quite simply, if you want to be champion trainer, you can't do it simply on numbers and I am ambitious to get there.' It sounds, therefore, as though Nicholls and Henderson, rather than Pipe, may eventually have most to worry about from Dan Skelton!

Ch'tibello provided Skelton with a third win in four years in the County Hurdle and the essay on that horse highlights the impressive record which the trainer is compiling in valuable handicap hurdles. But the stable's other winner at the Cheltenham Festival provided an indication of the sort of races Skelton needs to be winning in future to be staking a claim for the championship. As alluded to earlier, and as connections readily admitted, Roksana's win in the David Nicholson Mares' Hurdle (run again as the OLBG Mares' Hurdle) was a hugely fortunate success, as well as being a first Grade 1 victory for both Skeltons. In a remarkable echo of Annie Power's last-flight fall when clear in the same race four years earlier, the previous year's winner Benie des Dieux looked all set to collect for the same connections only to depart in identical circumstances. Willie Mullins still won the 2015 David Nicholson with Glens Melody, but in the latest renewal a couple of his other runners, Stormy Ireland and Good Thyne Tara, had to settle for second and third. Roksana was held in second, but sticking to her task four lengths down on Benie des Dieux, when presented with the lead. She briefly looked like throwing away a golden opportunity, hanging right and giving a flash of her tail as she idled, before pulling away again to win by two and a quarter lengths and two. Roksana was the first mare to keep the prize at home since Whiteoak won the inaugural running in 2008 for Donald McCain, another trainer, incidentally, who has previously had the most winners in a season.

Roksana had been a useful and progressive novice the previous season, completing a hat-trick of wins in the Mares' 'National Hunt' Novices' Hurdle Finale at Newbury before going down fighting to Santini over three miles in the Sefton Novices' at Aintree. She had just the one start prior to Cheltenham in the latest season, shaping well under a sympathetic ride over an inadequate trip when third behind Buveur d'Air in the Contenders Hurdle at Sandown. But after Cheltenham, she again ended her season with an excellent effort back over three miles at Aintree, coming off narrowly second-best in a thrilling three-way finish with If The Cap Fits and Apple's Jade in the Liverpool Hurdle. Mistakes by her two closest rivals at the final flight almost gave Roksana another victory on a plate as she led briefly in the final hundred yards. However, she couldn't hold the late rally of If The Cap Fits who squeezed through to get up by a head, Roksana running a career best nonetheless.

Roksana (IRE) (b.m. 2012)	Dubai Destination (USA) (b 1999)	Kingmambo (b 1990)	Mr Prospector
			Miesque
		Mysterial (br 1994)	Alleged
			Mysteries
	Talktothetail (IRE) (b 2000)	Flemensfirth (b 1992)	Alleged
			Etheldreda
		Glenview Lady (b 1984)	Cheval
			Silent Lady

The good-topped Roksana is by Dubai Destination who was also responsible for the Welsh Grand National winner Elegant Escape and another potentially high-class staying chaser Kildisart in the latest season. Roksana comes from a family in Weatherbys' Non-Thoroughbred Register and is from a line of mares who were

Mrs Sarah Faulks's "Roksana"

all successful in the pointing field. Plenty of their offspring have been successful pointers themselves, the most prolific in that sphere being Real Value, a grandson of Roksana's third dam Silent Lady (winner of six such races herself), who finished second in the 2000 Foxhunter at the Cheltenham Festival after beating the previous year's winner of that race, Castle Mane, on his debut under Rules in a hunter chase at Newbury. Besides an Irish point, Roksana's dam Talktothetail won a Clonmel bumper and a mares maiden chase at Thurles over three miles on her only start over fences. Talktothetail's only other runner under Rules was Robin Roe (by Robin des Champs) who looked destined for a promising career with the Skeltons after winning a bumper and a maiden hurdle on his first two starts but sustained a knee injury in a fall when sent off favourite for the Challow Hurdle on his only other outing. Robin Roe was another Irish point winner, as was Talktothetail's daughter Talktotheblonde (by Royal Anthem). Talktothetail is the only winner under Rules out of Glenview Lady who won a bumper at Tipperary and a novice chase at Clonmel besides her point. Talktothetail's three-year-old by Yeats was bought for £105,000 by Olly Murphy at Doncaster in May. Roksana, who travels strongly and is patiently ridden, is due to have a similar campaign in the next season, with one run before going to Cheltenham and Aintree again. She stays three miles well and acts on heavy ground and wore a hood on her only start in bumpers. *Dan Skelton*

ROLL AGAIN (FR) 5 b.g. Walk In The Park (IRE) – Olina (FR) (Dounba (FR)) [2018/19   **h130** b18d² b19d⁴ h16.6v* h16d⁵ h24d⁵ Apr 23] €140,000 3-y-o: third foal: half-brother to useful   **b84** French hurdler/smart chaser Argentique (17f-21f winner, by Saint des Saints), stayed 27f: dam, French 17f-2½m chase winner, half-sister to smart French chaser (stayed 2¾m) Oculi: modest form in bumpers: useful form over hurdles: won maiden at Down Royal in March: upped markedly in trip, best effort when fifth in novice handicap at Fairyhouse (6½ lengths behind Ronald Pump) in April: in hood after first start. *W. P. Mullins, Ireland*

ROLLERBALL ROCCO (IRE) 7 b.g. Ask – Jamica Ginger (IRE) (Flemensfirth   **c92** (USA)) [2018/19 h–: h16dᵖᵘ c24v* c24s⁴ c24s² c24s⁴ Mar 23] no form over hurdles: **h–** modest form over fences: won novice handicap at Uttoxeter in December: stays 3m: acts on heavy going: usually front runner/races prominently. *Charles Pogson*

ROLLERCOSTER (IRE) 7 b.m. Helissio (FR) – Full Deck (IRE) (Roselier (FR))   **h79** [2018/19 h16.7s h15.5d⁵ h19.7d h16d Mar 21] £15,500 6-y-o: half-sister to 3 winners, including fair hurdler/fairly useful chaser Sparkling River (19f-2¾m winner, by Indian River): dam unraced sister to useful chaser (stayed 25f) All The Aces: off mark in Irish points at third attempt: poor form over hurdles. *Henry Oliver*

ROLLERRULER 5 b.g. Native Ruler – Roll Over Rose (IRE) (Beneficial) [2018/19   **h98** h16.8sᵖᵘ h16.2g³ h16.2g⁴ h19.5d⁵ h22d³ h20.1dᵖᵘ Mar 26] first foal: dam (h97), maiden hurdler (stayed 2½m), half-sister to fair hurdler/fairly useful chaser (stayed 2½m) Drumlee Lad: modest form over hurdles: wears tongue tie: usually races prominently. *Maurice Barnes*

ROLLING DYLAN (IRE) 8 ch.g. Indian River (FR) – Easter Saturday (IRE) (Grand   **c141 §** Plaisir (IRE)) [2018/19 c138, h–: c24d⁴ c26g³ c26.3d⁴ c24.2s⁵ c28.4d² c28.8g⁵ Apr 27]   **h–** sturdy gelding: winning hurdler: useful handicap chaser: second at Taunton (head behind Samuel Jackson) in March: stays 3½m: acts on heavy going: wears cheekpieces: temperamental. *Philip Hobbs*

ROLLING MAUL (IRE) 11 b.g. Oscar (IRE) – Water Sports (IRE) (Marju (IRE))   **c– §** [2018/19 c–§, h118§: h23g h23.9m³ h23g⁴ h27m⁴ h23m* h23.9g* h26.5v* h24.3d Nov 3]   **h132 §** good-topped gelding: useful handicap hurdler: completed hat-trick at Worcester, Perth and Newton Abbot in September/October: winning chaser: stays 3¼m: acts on good to firm and heavy going: wears headgear: has worn tongue tie: front runner/races prominently, though often lazily: temperamental. *Peter Bowen*

ROLL OF THE DICE (IRE) 7 b.g. Publisher (USA) – Dinah B (IRE) (Yashgan)   **h105** [2018/19 h103, b79: h17.7m* h19.2g⁶ Jun 16] useful-looking gelding: off mark in points at fourth attempt: fair hurdler: won maiden at Fontwell in May: stays 2¾m: acts on good to firm and good to soft going. *Gary Moore*

ROLL OF THUNDER 10 b.g. Antonius Pius (USA) – Ischia (Lion Cavern (USA))   **c75** [2018/19 c–, h–: c15.6g⁶ c20.1gᵘʳ c15.6g⁶ c17.3m⁵ c20.1d c20.9m* Apr 20] winning   **h–** hurdler: poor handicap chaser: won novice event at Carlisle in April: stays 21f: acts on good to firm and good to soft going: tried in tongue tie. *James Walton*

ROLL THE DOUGH (IRE) 10 b.g. Definite Article – High Dough (IRE) (High Roller (IRE)) [2018/19 c109, h–: c24g² c21g⁴ c21g* c22.6g⁴ c20.5g³ c23d⁵ Dec 13] sturdy gelding: has had breathing operation: winning hurdler: fairly useful handicap chaser: won at Newton Abbot (twice) in September and Hereford (novice event) in November: stays 23f: acts on soft going: wears tongue tie. *Philip Hobbs* **c118 h–**

ROMAIN DE SENAM (FR) 7 b.g. Saint des Saints (FR) – Salvatrixe (FR) (Housamix (FR)) [2018/19 c144, h–: c21.4g⁴ c19.9g³ c20.2g* c20.6dᵖᵘ c23g* c24g⁴ c21.6g* c19.7g² Apr 22] well-made gelding: has had breathing operation: winning hurdler: useful handicap chaser: won at Taunton in January and Fontwell (by length from Not Another Muddle) in April: stays 3m: acts on soft going: wears hood/tongue tie. *Paul Nicholls* **c141 h–**

ROMAN FLIGHT (IRE) 11 b.g. Antonius Pius (USA) – Flight Sequence (Polar Falcon (USA)) [2018/19 c21g³ c20g⁵ c19.4g c21.4g⁴ c20.3g c16.5m³ c23.8m⁵ Oct 10] smallish gelding: winning hurdler: useful handicap chaser: third at Newton Abbot (4¾ lengths behind Cut The Corner) in May: lost way after next start: stays 21f: acts on good to firm and heavy going: wears headgear: moody. *David Dennis* **c136 d h–**

ROMAN NUMERAL (IRE) 11 b.g. King's Best (USA) – Trespass (Entrepreneur) [2018/19 c82, h81: h16.2d c15.6g⁵ c15.7g* c15.6g Jun 16] poor hurdler: poor handicap chaser: won at Southwell in June: stays 2¾m: acts on good to firm and heavy going: has worn headgear/tongue tie: usually races towards rear. *David Thompson* **c81 h64**

ROMANOR 5 b.g. Holy Roman Emperor (IRE) – Salinia (IRE) (Rainbow Quest (USA)) [2018/19 h101: h15.9g⁴ h15.8g⁵ h16.3m³ h16.3m³ h17.7g* h16.3g* h16v h19.8g⁴ h15.8d⁴ h16g h16s³ h16g Apr 27] lengthy gelding: fairly useful handicap hurdler: won at Stratford in June, and Fontwell and Stratford again in August: stays 2¼m: acts on soft and good to firm going: has worn hood, including last 2 starts: usually races towards rear. *Seamus Mullins* **h120**

ROMEO BROWN 5 br.g. Yeats (IRE) – Santia (Kahyasi) [2018/19 b93p: b16.4d b16.5m² h16.2g* h19.9d³ h19.4g⁴ h17v* Mar 17] lengthy, rather unfurnished gelding: placed twice in bumpers: fairly useful form over hurdles: won maiden at Kelso in December and novice handicap at Carlisle in March: left Mrs Jane Williams after third start: should stay 2½m. *Philip Kirby* **h118 b95**

ROMEO IS BLEEDING (IRE) 13 b.g. Carroll House – Ean Eile (IRE) (Callernish) [2018/19 c100, h–: c20.3g h20g⁶ c21g Jul 22] maiden hurdler: fair chaser at best, no form over fences in 2018/19: stays 2¾m: acts on good to firm and good to soft going: has worn cheekpieces: wears tongue tie. *Kevin Bishop* **c– h71**

ROMULUS DU DONJON (IRE) 8 gr.g. Stormy River (FR) – Spring Stroll (USA) (Skywalker (USA)) [2018/19 c110, h103: c21.6g⁴ c23.4g⁵ c21.6m² c20.5d c20s c20v⁵ h19.3s Dec 18] lengthy gelding: winning hurdler: regressive maiden chaser: barely stays 3m: acts on soft going: has worn headgear, including last 3 starts. *Rose Dobbin* **c97 h–**

RONALD PUMP 6 ch.g. Schiaparelli (GER) – Fruit Yoghurt (Hernando (FR)) [2018/19 h24.2v⁴ h21.5g⁴ h22m h17.3g⁴ h16g h20v* h24s* h20d⁴ h24v* h24d* Apr 23] €1,000 3-y-o: first foal: dam, ran once in bumper, out of useful hurdler up to 3m Diamant Noir: useful handicap hurdler: progressed very well in second half of season, winning at Cork (novice event) in December, Fairyhouse in January, Cork again in March and Fairyhouse again (novice event, by 2 lengths from Ifyoucatchmenow) in April: stays 3m: acts on heavy going: wears hood/tongue tie: races off pace, responds generously to pressure. *Matthew J. Smith, Ireland* **h144**

RONNIE LAWSON (IRE) 10 b.g. King's Theatre (IRE) – Sarahs Quay (IRE) (Witness Box (USA)) [2018/19 c88, h76: c20.9dᵖᵘ c22.6mᵖᵘ Aug 2] rangy gelding: multiple point winner: maiden hurdler/chaser, no form in 2018/19: often in tongue tie nowadays: front runner/races prominently. *Tim Vaughan* **c– h–**

RONS DREAM 9 b.m. Kayf Tara – Empress of Light (Emperor Jones (USA)) [2018/19 c137, h133: c23.9g* c20v² c29.5s⁴ c25.1gᶠ c26.2g Mar 23] workmanlike mare: useful hurdler: useful chaser: won listed mares event at Market Rasen (by ½ length from Casablanca Mix) in November: fourth in Welsh Grand National (16¼ lengths behind Elegant Escape) at Chepstow following month: probably stays 29f: acts on heavy going: tried in tongue tie: tough and reliable. *Peter Bowen* **c137 h–**

ROOKIE TRAINER (IRE) 5 b.g. Gold Well – Crazy Falcon (IRE) (Polar Falcon (USA)) [2018/19 b15.8s Apr 7] off mark in Irish points at second attempt: tailed off in bumper. *Kayley Woollacott* **b–**

ROOM AT THE TOP (IRE) 4 b.g. New Approach (IRE) – Baila Me (GER) (Samum (GER)) [2018/19 ab16.3s⁵ Feb 23] 8/1, green when fifth in bumper at Newcastle (13¼ lengths behind Malystic). *Alistair Whillans* **b67**

ROO ROO (IRE) 5 b.g. Court Cave (IRE) – Shuil Sionnach (IRE) (Mandalus) [2018/19 **h103** b81: b16.2g⁴ h20.2g* h20.2g⁵ h19.7g h24.4gᵖᵘ Nov 30] modest form in bumpers: fair form **b76** over hurdles: won novice at Perth in June: should be suited by further than 2½m. *Iain Jardine*

ROOSTER COGBURN (IRE) 6 b.g. Westerner – Hollygrove (IRE) (Commander **h101 p** Collins (IRE)) [2018/19 h62p, h87: h15.8d⁴ h20gᵖᵘ h15.8v⁴ Nov 11] tall gelding: fair form over hurdles: left Emma Lavelle after first start: tried in hood: open to further improvement. *Peter Bowen*

ROOTLESS TREE (IRE) 4 b.g. Jeremy (USA) – Miss Compliance (IRE) (Broken **b83** Hearted) [2018/19 b13.7d* b13.7g⁵ Apr 12] €70,000 3-y-o: 3-y-o: half-brother to 3 winners, including fairly useful hurdler/useful chaser Bally Beaufort (2½m-25f winner, by Old Vic) and fairly useful hurdler/chaser Birch Hill (2m-2¾m winner, by Kalanisi): dam unraced half-sister to Grand National winner Comply Or Die: modest form in bumpers: won bumper at Huntingdon in January, just holding on. *Nigel Twiston-Davies*

ROPARTA AVENUE 12 b.g. Nomadic Way (USA) – Miss Fizz (Charmer) [2018/19 **c83 §** c72§, h77§: c25.7g² h25.8g² c26g⁵ c23g⁶ Jul 26] poor handicap hurdler/chaser: stayed **h74 §** 3¼m: acted on heavy going: wore headgear: unreliable: dead. *Chris Gordon*

ROQUE IT (IRE) 5 b.g. Presenting – Roque de Cyborg (IRE) (High Chaparral (IRE)) **b95** [2018/19 b16.7s³ b15.8g* Mar 19] second foal: brother to fair 23f hurdle winner Big Difference: dam unraced half-sister to useful hurdler/high-class chaser (2½m-25f winner) Quito de La Roque and high-class hurdler (2½m-3m winner) Kazal: fairly useful form in bumpers: won conditionals/amateurs event at Huntingdon in March. *Olly Murphy*

RORY'S VALENTINE (IRE) 8 br.m. Windsor Knot (IRE) – Housekeeping (Dansili) **c–** [2018/19 c–, h65: h20.2g* h23.9gᵖᵘ h20.9gᵖᵘ Oct 7] has had breathing operation: poor **h73** handicap hurdler: won at Perth in May: pulled up both starts over fences: stays 2½m: wears tongue tie: usually races nearer last than first. *Katie Scott*

ROSE CROWN 5 b.m. New Approach (IRE) – Silver Touch (IRE) (Dansili) [2018/19 **b77** b15.3m⁴ b16.8g⁴ b16g² b16g⁴ Jul 4] useful-looking mare: fifth foal: half-sister to 2 winners on Flat, including 1¼m-1½m winner Ya Jammeel (by Dubawi): dam smart 7f winner: modest form in bumpers/on Flat. *Mick Channon*

ROSEMARY RUSSET 7 b.m. Midnight Legend – Apple Days (Sovereign Water (FR)) **h110** [2018/19 h103: h21.6g² h21.6v h21.2g⁶ h23.9d² h25.5d⁴ h23.9s² h23.1s⁴ h21.6d³ Apr 9] fair maiden hurdler: stays 3m: acts on heavy going: wears tongue tie: usually races close up. *Harry Fry*

ROSEMAY (FR) 5 b.m. Mayson – Maine Rose (Red Ransom (USA)) [2018/19 h15.6g **h–** Nov 26] dam half-sister to fairly useful hurdler (2m-19f winner) Sunley Peace: modest maiden on Flat, stays 12.5f: well beaten in mares novice on hurdling debut (wore cheekpieces). *R. Mike Smith*

ROSE OF CIMARRON (IRE) 6 b.m. Westerner – Sharp Single (IRE) (Supreme **h101** Leader) [2018/19 h90, b94: h20g³ h19.5s² Nov 21] sturdy mare: bumper winner: fair form over hurdles: likely to stay 2¾m+: often races prominently. *Warren Greatrex*

ROSE OF DUBAI 6 b.m. Dubai Destination (USA) – Daraz Rose (IRE) (Darazari (IRE)) **b–** [2018/19 b13.7g⁵ Nov 24] first foal: dam (c108/h106), 2½m-2¾m hurdle winner/winning pointer, half-sister to fair hurdler/fairly useful chaser (stayed 25f) Arklow Ger: well held in bumper. *Barry Brennan*

ROSER MOTER (IRE) 4 b.f. Motivator – Rosia Bay (Rock of Gibraltar (IRE)) **h57** [2018/19 h17.7g h15.8m⁴ h16d h15.8d⁵ h15.7gᵖᵘ Mar 4] has had breathing operation: dam half-sister to fairly useful 17f hurdle winner Prompter (by Motivator): fair on Flat, stays 1½m: little form over hurdles. *Dan Skelton*

ROSE SEA HAS (FR) 4 gr.g. Kapgarde (FR) – Vaibuscar Has (FR) (Turgeon (USA)) **c123 p** [2018/19 h17.4s h17.4d* h18.4s³ c16.9s² h16m h16s² h18.8d Mar 23] well-made gelding: **h113** third foal: half-brother to fairly useful French hurdler Rose Amelie Has (15f/2m winner, by Martaline) and bumper winner Roseriver Has (by Astarabad): dam, lightly raced over jumps in France, sister to smart French hurdler/chaser (2¼m-25f winner) Formosa Joana Has: fair hurdler: won juvenile at Strasbourg in November: good start over fences when neck second to Bel Apsis in newcomers race at Pau: left Guillaume Macaire after: unproven beyond 17f: acts on soft going: open to improvement as a chaser. *Dr Richard Newland*

ROSE'S IN THE RAIN (IRE) 6 b.m. Yeats (IRE) – Midnight Flirt (IRE) (Flemensfirth (USA)) [2018/19 h16g h16g⁵ h16.2g h20.5dᵖᵘ Jan 22] €20,000 3-y-o: third foal: dam unraced half-sister to useful hurdler (stayed 21f) My Wigwam Or Yours: made frame both starts in Irish points: poor maiden hurdler: left Enda Bolger after second start: tried in cheekpieces: in tongue tie last 3 starts. *Donald McCain* — **h73**

ROSES POSES (IRE) 5 ch.m. Beat Hollow – Francesa (Silver Patriarch (IRE)) [2018/19 h21g³ h20.5g² h24.4g⁵ h23.4d Jan 1] first foal: dam (c107/h119), 21f hurdle winner, half-sister to smart hurdler/high-class staying chaser Blaklion: runner-up sole start in Irish points: modest form over hurdles. *Charlie Longsdon* — **h99**

ROSE TO FAME 5 b.m. Fame And Glory – Cinderella Rose (Midnight Legend) [2018/19 b–: b15.8g b13.7m² b15.7d³ h19.6d⁶ h15.8m* h16.5d* Apr 24] smallish, lengthy mare: has had breathing operation: placed in bumpers: fair form over hurdles: won novices at Ludlow (mares) and Taunton in April: in tongue tie last 3 starts. *Kim Bailey* — **h112 b85**

ROSE TREE (IRE) 6 b.m. Yeats (IRE) – Isabellareine (GER) (Goofalik (USA)) [2018/19 h81, b83: h23.3g h22.1g⁴ h22.1m⁴ h24g⁵ h23.3g Sep 17] close-coupled mare: has had breathing operation: poor maiden hurdler: left Susan Corbett after second start: stays 2¾m: acts on good to firm and heavy going: has worn headgear/tongue tie, including in 2018/19. *Seamus Mullins* — **h68**

ROSEY 5 b.m. Multiplex – Rose Street (IRE) (Noverre (USA)) [2018/19 b–: h19.7sᵖᵘ Dec 26] no show in bumper/novice hurdle. *Rose Dobbin* — **h–**

ROSEYROO (IRE) 12 b.m. Brian Boru – Rose Island (Jupiter Island) [2018/19 c25.3gᵘʳ May 4] has had breathing operation: multiple winning pointer: twice-raced hunter chaser, fair form when second on completed start (in 2015/16). *Louise Cabble* — **c–**

ROSIE AND MILLIE (IRE) 6 ch.m. Flemensfirth (USA) – Madgehil (IRE) (Anshan) [2018/19 b16g⁶ b16d³ b17s² h24.9gᵖᵘ Mar 2] £25,000 5-y-o: fourth foal: sister to useful hurdler Hunters Hoof (2m-2½m winner) and bumper winner Huntress: dam, lightly raced in bumpers, half-sister to smart 2m hurdler Kilcash and useful hurdler/fairly useful chaser (2m-2¼m winner) Snow Dragon: runner-up both completed starts in Irish points: fair in bumpers: best effort when third in mares event at Wetherby: pulled up in listed mares novice on hurdling debut: in hood last 3 starts. *Michael Scudamore* — **h– b89**

ROSIE HALL (IRE) 9 ch.m. Lion Heart (USA) – Baltic Dip (IRE) (Benny The Dip (USA)) [2018/19 h–: h16.7g May 20] no form over hurdles. *John Wainwright* — **h–**

ROSIE LEA (FR) 6 b.m. Manduro (GER) – Saralea (FR) (Sillery (USA)) [2018/19 b85: h15.8g⁵ h18.7m⁴ Jun 19] compact mare: bumper winner: poor form over hurdles: tried in tongue tie. *Stuart Kittow* — **h64**

ROSIE MCQUEEN (IRE) 7 b.m. Milan – Royal Rosy (IRE) (Dominion Royale) [2018/19 h105: h23g⁶ c20.9m⁵ c23.9m² c23.6d³ Oct 13] good-topped mare: Irish point winner: fair maiden hurdler: similar form over fences: will stay beyond 3m: acts on soft and good to firm going: in cheekpieces last 5 starts: tried in tongue tie. *Jonjo O'Neill* — **c110 h99**

ROSIERITA 5 b.m. Black Sam Bellamy (IRE) – Mtilly (Mtoto) [2018/19 b16s b16g b16g Apr 25] lengthy, angular mare: fifth foal: half-sister to fair hurdler Fair To Middling (19f winner, by Fair Mix): dam (h65), lightly raced over hurdles, half-sister to useful hurdler/chaser (stayed 3m) Robbie: no form in bumpers. *John Groucott* — **b–**

ROSIE ROYALE (IRE) 7 gr.m. Verglas (IRE) – Fearn Royal (IRE) (Ali-Royal (IRE)) [2018/19 h15.3d⁵ h23.1sᵖᵘ h19.6d Mar 3] compact mare: has had breathing operation: fair on Flat, stays 13f: little show over hurdles. *Roger Teal* — **h–**

ROSSAMILAN (IRE) 8 b.g. Milan – Beautiful Blue (IRE) (Xaar) [2018/19 c82, h80: c20.1d h20.2g² Jun 3] Irish point winner: fair form both starts in chases: well held both starts in chases: best effort at 2½m. *Lucinda Russell* — **c– h100**

ROSSETTI 11 gr.g. Dansili – Snowdrops (Gulch (USA)) [2018/19 h134: h16g h16.3g⁴ h20g⁵ c15.7g⁴ c16.3g² Jul 22] compact gelding: fairly useful handicap hurdler: similar form on completed start over fences: stays 2½m: acts on good to firm and good to soft going: wears hood: usually races close up. *Neil Mulholland* — **c120 h121**

ROSSMORE'S PRIDE (IRE) 11 br.g. Heron Island (IRE) – Parsons Supreme (IRE) (Supreme Leader) [2018/19 c17v⁵ c23.5g c16.5g c20.1s⁵ c16.4s* c16.3s⁴ c16.4s³ c16.4gᵖᵘ Apr 5] winning hurdler: fair handicap chaser: won at Sedgefield in December: left Christian Delcros after third start: stays 19f: acts on heavy going: in visor last 5 starts: usually races off pace. *Rebecca Menzies* — **c103 h–**

ROSY WORLD 6 b.m. Shirocco (GER) – Material World (Karinga Bay) [2018/19 b94: **h112 p** h15.9s⁶ h19.2s³ h19.8s⁶ h20.5s* Mar 11] angular mare: bumper winner: fair form over hurdles: won mares handicap at Plumpton in March: will stay beyond 2½m: front runner/ races prominently: open to further improvement. *Suzy Smith*

ROTHMAN (FR) 9 b.g. Michel Georges – Bravecentadj (FR) (True Brave (USA)) **c–** [2018/19 c109, h115: c21gⁱ h25.8mᵖᵘ May 27] rather leggy gelding: fair handicap hurdler/ **h107** chaser: went wrong final start: stays 21f: acts on heavy going: wears headgear/tongue tie. *Chris Gordon*

ROUDRAPOUR (FR) 4 gr.g. Redoute's Choice (AUS) – Rosanara (FR) (Sinndar (IRE)) **h–** [2018/19 h16v⁶ Dec 7] close-coupled gelding: fair maiden on Flat, stays 2m: tailed off in juvenile on hurdling debut. *Tony Carroll*

ROUE DE CHARRETTE 4 ch.f. Champs Elysees – Somersault (Pivotal) [2018/19 **b–** b13.7m b13.1g Oct 20] half-sister to several winners on Flat: dam 1m winner: no form in bumpers/on Flat. *Chris Dwyer*

ROUGE ET BLANC (FR) 14 ch.g. Mansonnien (FR) – Fidelety (FR) (Villez (USA)) **c–** [2018/19 c110, h–: c20.9vᴿ Mar 7] good-topped gelding: maiden hurdler: fairly useful **h–** chaser at best, bled only start in 2018/19: stays 21f: acts on heavy going: usually wears cheekpieces: tried in tongue tie. *Oliver Sherwood*

ROUGE VIF (FR) 5 b.g. Sageburg (IRE) – Rouge Amour (FR) (Cadoudal (FR)) [2018/19 **h142** b95: h16.8v⁵ h16.2g² h15.7s* h16g² h16.4s* h18.1d* h16.5d³ Apr 5] strong gelding: bumper winner: useful hurdler: won maiden at Southwell in December, novice at Newcastle in January and Premier Kelso Novices' Hurdle (by 4 lengths from Windsor Avenue) in March: third in Top Novices' Hurdle at Aintree (8½ lengths behind Felix Desjy) final start: stays 2¼m: acts on soft going: in hood last 5 starts: usually leads (unable to do so at Aintree). *Harry Whittington*

ROUGH JUSTICE (IRE) 11 b.g. Beneficial – Ringzar (IRE) (Shernazar) [2018/19 **c– §** c101§, h–: h24gᵖᵘ c23.9gᵖᵘ Aug 18] winning hurdler: useful chaser at best, has lost his form **h– §** completely: has worn headgear/tongue tie: unreliable. *John Wainwright*

ROUGH NIGHT (IRE) 6 b.g. Doyen (IRE) – Sunny Bob (IRE) (Bob Back (USA)) **h121** [2018/19 h16s h19.5d* h19.7vᵖᵘ h19.2d³ Jan 14] strong gelding: first foal: dam unraced sister to fairly useful staying chaser Dusky Bob and half-sister to fairly useful hurdler (stayed 3m) Hotterthanjuly: third in point on debut: fairly useful handicap hurdler: won at Lingfield in November: left E. U. Hales after first start: stays 19f: acts on heavy going: often races prominently. *Alex Hales*

ROUNDHEAD 4 ch.g. Helmet (AUS) – Blue Mistral (IRE) (Spinning World (USA)) **h–** [2018/19 h16d Dec 13] has had breathing operation: fairly useful on Flat, stays 1½m: well beaten in juvenile maiden on hurdling debut. *Richard Phillips*

ROWDY ROBIN 7 b.g. Revoque (IRE) – Youamazeme (Kayf Tara) [2018/19 h–: h20.1s⁶ **h–** h24.1dᵖᵘ Dec 27] has had breathing operation: maiden pointer: little impact over hurdles. *Ruth Jefferson*

ROWLEY PARK (IRE) 6 b.g. Golan (IRE) – Atomic Winner (IRE) (Poliglote) [2018/19 **h101** b–: b16.8m h16s h16.5d⁶ h15.3g⁵ h15.3g⁶ h15.3g⁶ Apr 3] well held in bumpers: fair form **b–** over hurdles: usually front runner/races prominently. *Linda Blackford*

ROXYFET (FR) 9 b.g. Califet (FR) – Roxalamour (FR) (Valanour (IRE)) [2018/19 c103, **c93 §** h85: c15.9d⁶ c17.4g⁵ c17.1d⁶ c16.4sᵖᵘ c17.4s³ c16.4sᵖᵘ c16.4d² c16.4s* c16.4v⁴ c20.1d⁶ **h–** c15.6g³ Apr 15] winning hurdler: modest handicap chaser: won at Sedgefield in February: best around 2m: acts on heavy going: has worn headgear/tongue tie: ungenuine. *Micky Hammond*

ROYAL ACT 7 br.g. Royal Anthem (USA) – Native's Return (IRE) (Presenting) [2018/19 **c92** c91, h58: c17.4gᵖᵘ c19.2s⁴ c16.4s⁵ c16.2d⁵ c16.1d* c17.2g Mar 27] tall gelding: maiden **h–** hurdler: modest handicap chaser: won at Taunton in March: stays 2¼m: acts on heavy going: normally wears headgear: usually front runner/races prominently. *Sarah-Jayne Davies*

ROYAL BEEKEEPER 6 ch.g. Champs Elysees – Lasso (Indian Ridge) [2018/19 h106: **h–** h15.8m h20.6g Jul 17] won both completed starts in points: fair hurdler at best, no form in 2018/19: wears cheekpieces. *Conor Dore*

ROYAL CHIEFTAIN (IRE) 9 b.g. Beneficial – Jensharandsue (IRE) (Lord Americo) **c62** [2018/19 h19.9g⁶ h21.6g³ h21.6g⁶ h23g⁶ c22.6g⁶ Sep 4] point winner: poor form over **h75** hurdles: never a danger in novice handicap on chasing debut. *Linda Blackford*

ROYAL CLARET 7 b.m. Yeats (IRE) – Kerada (FR) (Astarabad (USA)) [2018/19 h101: h23.6s² h25s* h23.9s⁵ Apr 7] fair handicap hurdler: won mares event at Plumpton in December: stays 3¼m: acts on heavy going: has worn tongue tie: usually races off pace. *Tom Symonds* **h108**

ROYAL CONCORDE (IRE) 8 br.g. Kalanisi (IRE) – Talinas Rose (IRE) (Definite Article) [2018/19 h15.9s⁶ h15.9d h19.2d h19.9d³ Mar 18] workmanlike gelding: poor form over hurdles: tried in tongue tie. *Linda Jewell* **h77**

ROYAL DEBUTANTE (IRE) 8 b.m. Presenting – Chinatownqueen (IRE) (Westerner) [2018/19 c102, h112: h16g⁶ May 7] fair handicap hurdler: beaten when falling only start over fences: stays 21f: acts on good to soft going: wears tongue tie: temperamental. *Paul Webber* **c–** **h97 §**

ROYALE DJANGO (IRE) 10 b.g. Kayf Tara – Royale Boja (FR) (Kadalko (FR)) [2018/19 c115§, h102§: c23.8g⁵ c25.8g⁵ c23g⁴ Jul 26] has had breathing operation: fairly useful hurdler/chaser at best, little show over fences in 2018/19: stays 3m: acts on good to firm and heavy going: wears headgear: in tongue tie last 5 starts: temperamental. *Tim Vaughan* **c84 §** **h– §**

ROYALE JONQUILLE (FR) 5 b.m. Indian Daffodil (IRE) – Royale Trophy (FR) (Vertical Speed (FR)) [2018/19 h16g⁵ h15.8g⁶ h16d h19d Dec 31] €1,200 3-y-o: fifth foal: closely related to French hurdler Royal Haven (15f/2m winner, by Sulamani) and half-sister to French hurdler Royal Piper (17f/2¼m winner, by Nickname): dam, lightly raced over hurdles in France, half-sister to fairly useful hurdler/useful chaser (stayed 3½m) King Barry: unplaced in 2 points: modest form over hurdles. *Henry Daly* **h96**

ROYAL ESCAPE (IRE) 7 b.g. Getaway (GER) – Echo Queen (IRE) (Luso) [2018/19 h90: h21.2mᵖᵘ h20g⁵ h20gᵖᵘ Jul 26] compact gelding: poor maiden hurdler: tried in headgear/tongue tie: front runner/races prominently. *Jonjo O'Neill* **h72**

ROYAL ETIQUETTE (IRE) 12 b.g. Royal Applause – Alpine Gold (IRE) (Montjeu (IRE)) [2018/19 h84: h25.8g Jun 5] angular gelding: poor maiden hurdler: stays 2½m: acts on good to firm and heavy going: wears headgear/tongue tie: usually races towards rear. *Lawney Hill* **h–**

ROYAL FLAG 9 b.g. New Approach (IRE) – Gonbarda (GER) (Lando (GER)) [2018/19 h86: h16.7g May 11] fair on Flat, stays 2¼m: modest form on first of 2 starts over hurdles. *Brian Ellison* **h–**

ROYAL FLUSH 8 b.g. Multiplex – Mystical Feelings (BEL) (Feelings (FR)) [2018/19 c22.6dᵘʳ Jun 8] winning pointer: no form in various events under Rules. *Simon Waugh* **c–** **h–**

ROYAL GOLDIE (IRE) 4 b.f. Havana Gold (IRE) – Dream Maker (IRE) (Bahamian Bounty) [2018/19 h15.9g⁶ h15.9g⁵ Apr 22] has had breathing operation: fair maiden on Flat, stays 1¼m: well held both starts over hurdles: wears visor/tongue tie. *Lydia Richards* **h–**

ROYAL HALL (FR) 7 b.g. Halling (USA) – Royal Fantasy (IRE) (King's Best (USA)) [2018/19 h15.9g² h17.7m* h19.2g* h25m* h20.5gᵘʳ h15.9g³ Feb 25] sturdy gelding: fair handicap hurdler: completed hat-trick at Fontwell in May/August and Plumpton in October: stays 25f: acts on good to firm going: usually in visor. *Gary Moore* **h110**

ROYAL HOUSEHOLD 4 b.g. Camacho – Dusting (IRE) (Acclamation) [2018/19 h16d⁶ h15.9g³ Sep 23] fair on Flat, stays 1¼m: modest form over hurdles: better effort when third in juvenile at Plumpton: sold £6,000 in October. *Alan King* **h88**

ROYAL ILLUSION (IRE) 7 b.m. King's Theatre (IRE) – Spirit Run (IRE) (Luso) [2018/19 b16g* b16d* b16.4g³ Nov 17] sturdy mare: third foal: dam (h112), 2¼m hurdle winner, half-sister to fairly useful hurdler (stayed 27f) General Duroc: fairly useful form in bumpers: won mares maiden at Punchestown in October and mares event at Cork in November: third in listed mares event at Cheltenham (1¼ lengths behind The Glancing Queen) final start. *W. P. Mullins, Ireland* **b104**

ROYAL IRISH HUSSAR (IRE) 9 b.g. Galileo (IRE) – Adjalisa (IRE) (Darshaan) [2018/19 h120: h18.5g⁵ h16.3m⁵ h21.7g Aug 23] close-coupled gelding: has had breathing operation: useful hurdler at best, has lost his way: left Nicky Henderson after first start: has worn cheekpieces: in tongue tie last 2 starts: often races freely. *Lawney Hill* **h–**

ROYAL MACNAB (IRE) 11 b.g. Beneficial – Tina McBride (IRE) (Oscar (IRE)) [2018/19 c20.3g Aug 19] lightly raced over hurdles: fairly useful chaser at best, pulled up only start in 2018/19 after long absence: stays 2½m: acts on heavy going: tried in hood: wears tongue tie. *Rebecca Menzies* **c–** **h–**

ROYAL MAGIC (IRE) 7 b.g. Whitmore's Conn (USA) – Room To Room Magic (IRE) **c109** (Casteddu) [2018/19 h120, b75: c21.6d^{pu} c20.5d³ c22.4d⁶ c21.4g⁴ Apr 3] fairly useful **h–** hurdle winner: fair form over fences: should stay 3m: acts on good to soft going: tried in cheekpieces: usually wears tongue tie: usually leads. *Sam Thomas*

ROYAL MANDATE (IRE) 7 ch.g. Manduro (GER) – Hesperia (Slip Anchor) [2018/19 **c85** h95: c21.6g³ c20.1g⁴ May 22] maiden hurdler: modest form over fences: barely stays 3m: **h–** acts on soft going: wears headgear: usually races close up. *Rebecca Menzies*

ROYAL PALLADIUM (FR) 11 gr.g. King's Theatre (IRE) – Dent Sucree (FR) **c101 §** (Turgeon (USA)) [2018/19 c125§, h–: c24.2s^F c25.1g c24.2d⁴ c23.6d^{pu} Apr 6] useful- **h–** looking gelding: maiden hurdler: fairly useful handicap chaser, well below best in 2018/19: stays 3¼m: acts on heavy going: has worn headgear: usually leads: unreliable. *Venetia Williams*

ROYAL PLAZA 8 b.g. King's Theatre (IRE) – Friendly Craic (IRE) (Mister Lord (USA)) **c122** [2018/19 c118, h–: c21.7g³ c17.8g* c17m² h16.3m* c16.3g⁴ c16.5g⁵ c19.5s² h19.2m **h102** c20.2g⁶ Apr 3] fairly useful hurdler at best: won seller at Stratford in August: fairly useful handicap chaser: won at Fontwell in June: left Olly Murphy after fourth start: stays 2½m: acts on soft and good to firm going: has worn headgear: usually wears tongue tie: front runner/races prominently. *Katie Stephens*

ROYALRAISE (IRE) 10 b.g. Royal Anthem (USA) – Raise The Issue (IRE) (Galileo **c109** (IRE)) [2018/19 c119, h–: c24.5g* c25.5d² c20.9d^{pu} Jun 8] lengthy gelding: winning **h–** hurdler: fair chaser nowadays: won hunter at Towcester in May: little impact in points later in season: stays 3m: acts on soft and good to firm going: wears blinkers. *Oliver Sherwood*

ROYAL REEF (IRE) 7 b.g. Duke of Marmalade (IRE) – Bintalreef (USA) (Diesis) **h–** [2018/19 h24s^{pu} h20.5d^{pu} h15.8g Feb 21] fairly useful at one time on Flat, stays 16.5f: no form over hurdles after long lay-off: wears headgear/tongue tie. *Claire Dyson*

ROYAL REEL 6 ch.g. Shirocco (GER) – Close Harmony (Bustino) [2018/19 b16.7g⁶ Apr **b82** 3] half-brother to several winners, including useful hurdler/very smart chaser Barbers Shop (17f-3¼m winner, by Saddlers' Hall) and useful hurdler/chaser Maestro Royal (2m-2½m winner, by Doyen): dam (h89) maiden hurdler (stayed 2½m): 9/4, sixth in maiden bumper at Market Rasen (6¼ lengths behind Stormin Norman). *Nicky Henderson*

ROYAL REGATTA (IRE) 11 b.g. King's Theatre (IRE) – Friendly Craic (Mister **c–** Lord (USA)) [2018/19 c–, h–: c21g c18.8s Dec 22] useful-looking gelding: has had **h–** breathing operation: winning hurdler: very smart chaser at best, no form in 2018/19: stays 21f: acts on soft going: wears headgear/tongue tie. *Philip Hobbs*

ROYAL RENDEZVOUS (IRE) 7 b.g. King's Theatre (IRE) – Novacella (FR) (Beyssac **h129 p** (FR)) [2018/19 b16.6g⁵ b18.8d* b16g* h16.3d* Oct 27] £130,000 5-y-o: fourth foal: dam **b113** (c85/h102), 2m-21f hurdle winner, half-sister to useful hurdler/chaser (stayed 2½m) Marcel: off mark in points at third attempt: useful form in bumpers: won Downpatrick (maiden, by 23 lengths) in August and Tipperary (by 4¼ lengths from Kalum River) in October: 4/6, also won maiden at Galway (by 16 lengths from Tara Dylan) on hurdling debut: ridden too aggressively when pulled up in Champion Novices' Hurdle at Punchestown when next seen shortly after end of British season: in hood after second start: remains with potential. *W. P. Mullins, Ireland*

ROYAL RESERVE 6 b.g. Duke of Marmalade (IRE) – Lady Hawkfield (IRE) (Hawk **h116** Wing (USA)) [2018/19 h16.4g* h16.4m³ h16.2g h18.1d³ Apr 8] lengthy gelding: useful on Flat, stays 2m: fairly useful handicap hurdler: won at Newcastle in January: should stay beyond 2m: acts on good to firm going. *Lucinda Russell*

ROYAL RUBY 7 b.g. Yeats (IRE) – Close Harmony (Bustino) [2018/19 h110: h19.6g **h110 §** h20g³ h19.9m³ h23.1g⁵ h19.6g* h20.3g³ Oct 25] has had breathing operation: fair handicap hurdler: won at Bangor in October: stays 2½m: acts on good to soft going: wore hood until last 2 starts: usually races close up: temperamental. *Nicky Henderson*

ROYAL SALUTE 9 br.g. Flemensfirth (USA) – Loxhill Lady (Supreme Leader) [2018/19 **c98 d** c–, h109: c20s⁵ c26.3s^F c20.1s² c24.2v⁵ c26.9d c23.4d h23.3v h27g^{pu} Apr 5] well-made **h–** gelding: has had breathing operation: fair hurdler/chaser at best, has lost his way: stays 3¼m: acts on heavy going: has worn headgear/tongue tie, including in 2018/19. *George Bewley*

ROYALS AND REBELS (IRE) 9 b.g. Robin des Pres (FR) – Native Deal (IRE) (Be **c102 §** My Native (USA)) [2018/19 c106§, h–§: c26g* c25.5g^F c25.8g^{pu} h26.5m^{pu} h25.8g⁵ **h85 §** c25.7g⁵ c28.5d⁶ c25.2d³ c23.9s c26v^{pu} Mar 16] maiden hurdler: fair handicap chaser: won at Fontwell in May: stays 3½m: acts on heavy going: wears headgear/tongue tie: ungenuine. *Charlie Mann*

ROYAL SEA (IRE) 10 b.g. Refuse To Bend (IRE) – Janayen (USA) (Zafonic (USA)) h– §
[2018/19 h23.3g^{pu} Sep 12] fair 2½m winner on hurdling debut in 2015/16, no subsequent
form (off 2½ years before comeback): tried in hood: temperamental. *Michael Mullineaux*

ROYAL SUMMIT 8 b.g. Kayf Tara – Nas Na Riogh (IRE) (King's Theatre (IRE)) h–
[2018/19 h–, b–: h23.8g^{pu} Nov 26] has had breathing operation: no form: in tongue tie last
2 starts. *Alison Hamilton*

ROYAL SUNDAY (FR) 5 gr.g. Never On Sunday (FR) – Royale Malaisie (FR) (Villez h108
(USA)) [2018/19 h108p: h16v^{pu} h16v^5 h15.5g h16s h21s Mar 10] workmanlike gelding:
fair hurdler: largely disappointing in handicaps in 2018/19: unproven beyond 2m: acts on
heavy going: front runner/races prominently. *Alex Hales*

ROYAL SUPREMO (IRE) 8 b.g. Beneficial – Slaney Athlete (IRE) (Warcraft (USA)) c122
[2018/19 h102: c20.5m^{pu} h26.5m c24g^2 c20.3g* c20.2g^{pu} Apr 14] sturdy gelding: fair h–
hurdler: fairly useful form over fences: won handicap at Southwell in August: stays 25f:
best form on good going. *Kim Bailey*

ROYAL TARA (IRE) 10 b.g. Kayf Tara – The Irish Whip (Presenting) [2018/19 c119, c113
h65: c23.8g^2 c25.6g^3 c23.6d^2 c28.8v^{pu} Feb 18] has had breathing operation: twice-raced h–
over hurdles: fair handicap chaser: stays 3m: acts on good to soft going: usually races close
up. *Venetia Williams*

ROYAL VACATION (IRE) 9 b.g. King's Theatre (IRE) – Summer Break (IRE) c149
(Foxhound (USA)) [2018/19 c131, h136: c27.3g^2 c28.8v^6 c28.4d* c28.4g^4 c25s^{pu} Mar 12] h–
useful-looking gelding: has had breathing operation: useful hurdler: smart chaser: won
minor event at Taunton (by 6 lengths from The Last Samuri) in January: stays 3½m: acts
on heavy going: usually wears headgear: has worn tongue tie. *Colin Tizzard*

ROYAL VILLAGE (IRE) 7 b.g. Scorpion (IRE) – Etoile Margot (FR) (Garde Royale) c131
[2018/19 h122: h20.6g^4 h24g^4 c21.4m* c22.6g^3 c22.6m^3 c23.8g^4 c21.4g* c21g^3 c20g^6 Apr h122
27] good-topped gelding: has had breathing operation: fairly useful handicap hurdler:
useful handicap chaser: won at Market Rasen in July (novice event, dead-heated) and
October: stays 3m: acts on good to firm and heavy going: in cheekpieces last 3 starts.
Ian Williams

ROYBUOY 12 b.g. Royal Applause – Wavy Up (IRE) (Brustolon) [2018/19 c–§, h–: c21g^F c– §
Apr 20] no longer of any account: has worn headgear/tongue tie: temperamental. h–
Derrick Scott

ROYCANO 9 ch.g. Lucarno (USA) – Royal Distant (USA) (Distant View (USA)) h112
[2018/19 h116: h24.3d^6 Jan 19] workmanlike gelding: multiple point winner: fairly useful
handicap hurdler at best, very lightly raced nowadays: stays 3m: acts on heavy going.
Michael Easterby

ROYSTORY (IRE) 5 b.g. Thousand Words – Chase A Dream (IRE) (Lord of Appeal) h–
[2018/19 b17.7g^{pu} h19.2s^{pu} Oct 6] showed nothing in bumper/novice hurdle. b–
Seamus Mullins

RUACANA 10 b.g. Cape Cross (IRE) – Farrfesheena (USA) (Rahy (USA)) [2018/19 c–, c–
h–: h19.5d^5 h18.9s^6 h23.8m^4 Apr 23] smallish, sturdy gelding: useful hurdler at best, has h108
deteriorated: jumped sketchily only chase outing: stays 21f: acts on heavy going: has worn
headgear, including in 2018/19. *Tim Vaughan*

RUARAIDH HUGH (IRE) 10 b.g. Craigsteel – Decent Shower (Decent Fellow) h102
[2018/19 h–: h25g^5 h20g* h20g* h20.2g^F h23d^5 h16m^2 h23.1g^{pu} h16.5d h19d^{pu} Dec 30]
fair handicap hurdler: won at Worcester (twice, selling event on first occasion) in July: left
Julia Brooke after sixth start: stays 23f: acts on good to firm and good to soft going: wears
headgear: usually races prominently. *Ryan Chapman*

RUBENESQUE (IRE) 7 b.m. Getaway (GER) – Shouette (IRE) (Sadler's Wells (USA)) h111
[2018/19 h16.2g^3 h22.1m* h22.1d^2 h20.5v h19.4m* h24.4g^2 h24.4g^F h23.1g^{pu} h20.2g^2 Apr
24] sturdy mare: dam (h123) 2m hurdle winner (stayed 3m): fair on Flat, stays 21.5f: fair
hurdler: won maiden at Cartmel in June and 2-runner mares novice at Doncaster in
December: left Gemma Anderson after first start: stays 3m: acts on good to firm and good
to soft going: tried in cheekpieces: wears tongue tie. *Tristan Davidson*

RUBHEIRA 7 ch.m. Arkadian Hero (USA) – Devon Ruby (Zilzal (USA)) [2018/19 h–
h18.5m^4 h18.5g h16d h16.8g h18.5g h21.7m Oct 24] of little account: wears hood/tongue
tie. *Brian Barr*

RUBY BEAR (IRE) 5 b.g. Gold Well – Noble Nell (IRE) (Luso) [2018/19 b16d h20s^4 h77
Apr 7] has had breathing operation: limited encouragement in bumper/novice hurdle: b–
wears tongue tie. *Harry Fry*

RUBY DU BERLAIS 5 b.m. Beat All (USA) – Marina du Berlais (FR) (Mister Sicy **h–** (FR)) [2018/19 h15.5g⁵ Dec 2] half-sister to 3 winners, including useful hurdler/chaser Report To Base (2m winner, by Westerner), stayed 2½m, and useful hurdler Surtee du Berlais (2m-3m winner, by High Chaparral): dam, French 1¾m winner, half-sister to useful hurdler/smart chaser (stayed 3¼m) Michel Le Bon: in cheekpieces, well held in mares maiden hurdle. *David Bridgwater*

RUBY FOOL 9 b.m. Apple Tree (FR) – Westbourne (IRE) (King's Ride) [2018/19 h–: **h69** h20g⁶ h23.9d h23.9m⁴ h23.1d h23.9dᵖᵘ Apr 24] has had breathing operation: winning pointer: poor maiden hurdler: wears headgear. *Richard Mitford-Slade*

RUBY RING 6 b.m. Sulamani (IRE) – Royal Bride (Kayf Tara) [2018/19 b15.8g b16.3d **b–** Mar 1] unfurnished mare: second foal: dam unraced sister to useful hurdler/smart chaser (stayed 3¼m) The Package: no form in bumpers. *Ben Pauling*

RUBY RUSSET 7 b.m. Apple Tree (FR) – Fair Coppelia (Saddlers' Hall (IRE)) [2018/19 **c76** h79: h15.3m² h15.3m³ h17.7g h21.6g h18.5m c25.8g⁴ c19.5g² c21g⁵ c20dᵖᵘ h17.7d h19s⁵ **h83** h19g h16.5dᶠ Mar 11] poor maiden hurdler/chaser: stayed 19f: acted on good to firm going: often in headgear in 2018/19: wore tongue tie: dead. *Colin Tizzard*

RUBYS CUBE 6 b.m. Multiplex – Cresswell Ruby (IRE) (Rashar (USA)) [2018/19 h58: **h85** h21.6g h16gᵖᵘ h23g² h23g* Sep 2] modest handicap hurdler: won at Worcester in September: stays 23f: raced only on good going: tried in cheekpieces: held up. *Debra Hamer*

RUBY TAYLOR 7 b.m. Passing Glance – Bold Rose (Bold Edge) [2018/19 h15.9sᵖᵘ **h–** h15.3g h15.3g h15.9d h16g Apr 10] of no account. *Nick Lampard*

RUBY TIGER (IRE) 5 b.m. Sulamani (IRE) – Fenney Spring (Polish Precedent (USA)) **h–** [2018/19 b73: b15.8g³ b15.8m⁵ h21.7dᵖᵘ Jan 2] modest form in bumpers: pulled up in **b84** mares novice on hurdling debut: should be suited by 2½m. *Henry Daly*

RUBYTWO 7 b.m. Sulamani (IRE) – Miss Nellie (Presenting) [2018/19 b85: **h101** b16.2g* h20.2g⁴ h20.6g⁴ h20.6s² h19.8m² h16.4m³ h18.9m⁴ Apr 20] fair form in bumpers: **b89** won mares event at Kelso in May: fair form over hurdles: stays 2½m: acts on soft and good to firm going. *Nicky Richards*

RUBY WHO (IRE) 7 gr.g. Daylami (IRE) – Lelepa (IRE) (Inchinor) [2018/19 c–, h–: **c–** c19.4sᵖᵘ Dec 8] little sign of ability. *Rose Dobbin* **h–**

RUBY YEATS 8 b.m. Yeats (IRE) – Newbay Lady (Terimon) [2018/19 c117, h93: c18g **c–** h21.7v³ h25s³ h21.4g⁴ h25g² h20.5s³ h25.5g³ h20.5g Apr 22] workmanlike mare: fair **h104** handicap hurdler: lightly raced in chases: stays 3¼m: acts on heavy going: usually wears headgear. *Gary Moore*

RUFFLING FEATHERS (IRE) 5 b.g. Presenting – Oilily (IRE) (Dr Massini (IRE)) **h–** [2018/19 b85: b16.8g b20.5g⁵ h19.5v h19d⁶ Jan 19] modest form on second of 3 starts in **b69** bumpers: well held in novice hurdles. *Colin Tizzard*

RUFIO 5 b.g. Schiaparelli (GER) – Mole End (Slip Anchor) [2018/19 b15.8s³ b16.8d³ Jan **b82** 1] £25,000 3-y-o: first foal: dam unraced half-sister to fairly useful hurdler/useful chaser (stayed 25f) Dover's Hill: modest form in bumpers. *Harry Fry*

RUGGIERO (IRE) 6 ch.g. Robin des Champs (FR) – Kayf Vera (IRE) (Kayf Tara) **h88** [2018/19 h–, b70: h19m⁶ h16d h19.9m Jul 1] lengthy gelding: mid-field at best in bumper/ over hurdles: won 2-runner point in April. *Emma Lavelle*

RULE THE OCEAN (IRE) 9 gr.m. Stowaway – Page Ten (IRE) (Great Palm (USA)) **c73** [2018/19 c20g⁵ c16.5g⁶ c20.9mᵖᵘ h23gᵖᵘ c20.3g⁶ h16g h21d² h19.9s² h19.7d h23.1s⁵ **h69** c20.9g² c19.2s³ Apr 16] third foal: dam unraced half-sister to useful hurdler/fairly useful chaser (stayed 23f) River Maigue: poor maiden hurdler/chaser: stays 21f: acts on soft going: tried in cheekpieces: wears tongue tie. *Matt Sheppard*

RUMOR 6 ch.g. Windsor Castle – Whispering Wind (IRE) (Sunshine Street (USA)) **c–** [2018/19 h–, b69: h23.1g c23g⁴ Sep 28] smallish gelding: little sign of ability: tried in **h–** cheekpieces. *John Flint*

RUM RATION 4 b.g. Mount Nelson – Myriades d'Etoiles (IRE) (Green Tune (USA)) **h–** [2018/19 h16d Aug 29] little form on Flat: tailed off in juvenile on hurdling debut. *Mark H. Tompkins*

RUN DON'T HIDE (IRE) 8 b.g. High Chaparral (IRE) – Right Key (IRE) (Key of Luck **c–** (USA)) [2018/19 c81, h78: c16v⁶ c20dᵖᵘ Nov 29] has had breathing operation: maiden **h–** hurdler: maiden chaser, no form in 2018/19: tried in cheekpieces: wears tongue tie. *Paul Henderson*

RUN FOR EVA 6 b.m. Westerner – Glorybe (GER) (Monsun (GER)) [2018/19 h69, b68: **h61** h20.3g h23.3g⁶ Jun 20] leggy mare: little form: wears hood. *Laura Morgan*

RUNNING CLOUD (IRE) 4 b.g. Cacique (IRE) – Nimbus Star (Nayef (USA)) **h96**
[2018/19 h16.3d⁴ h16g⁴ Jan 12] sturdy gelding: fairly useful on Flat, stays 1½m: modest
form over hurdles: better effort when fourth in juvenile at Kempton. *Alan King*

RUNNING IN HEELS (IRE) 10 br.m. September Storm (GER) – Ceo Draiochta (IRE) **c105**
(Erins Isle) [2018/19 c93, h90: h24.6s* h23g⁴ h24.6g² c25.3g h24m* c24g* h24d⁴ h24.4g **h106**
c26.3m* c23.8g⁶ Sep 10] fair handicap hurdler: won at Kilbeggan very early in season and
Bellewstown in July: fair handicap chaser: won at Limerick later in July and Sedgefield
(novice event) in August: stays 3¼m: acts on soft and good to firm going: has worn
headgear: wears tongue tie: often races towards rear. *Gavin Patrick Cromwell, Ireland*

RUNNING WOLF (IRE) 8 b.g. Amadeus Wolf – Monet's Lady (IRE) (Daylami (IRE)) **c106 §**
[2018/19 c108§, h–§: c24.2g² c25.5m³ c25.5gᵖᵘ Nov 9] lengthy, workmanlike gelding: **h– §**
winning hurdler: fair handicap chaser: stays 3m: acts on soft and good to firm going:
usually wears tongue tie: unreliable. *Alex Hales*

RUNRIZED (FR) 4 b.g. Authorized (IRE) – Courseulles (FR) (Monsun (GER)) [2018/19 **h110**
h16d⁴ h16.8d Mar 15] compact gelding: dam half-sister to fairly useful French hurdler/
chaser (stays 2½m) Attalco: fairly useful 1¼m winner on Flat in France: fair form over
hurdles: never a threat in Triumph Hurdle at Cheltenham. *W. P. Mullins, Ireland*

RUN TO MILAN (IRE) 7 b.g. Milan – Run Supreme (IRE) (Supreme Leader) [2018/19 **c127**
h125: c22.5gᵘʳ c24.2g⁴ c24.2d³ Jan 1] fairly useful hurdler: similar form over fences: best **h–**
effort when fourth in novice handicap at Exeter: stays 3m: acts on heavy going: has worn
hood. *Victor Dartnall*

RUPERRA TOM 11 b.g. Kayf Tara – Cathy's Dream (IRE) (Husyan (USA)) [2018/19 **c99**
c109p, h–: c21.6s³ c25.1g² c25.1g⁶ c25.7sᵖᵘ Jan 16] multiple point winner: maiden hurdler: **h–**
fair maiden chaser: stays 25f: acts on good to soft going: has worn hood, including in
2018/19: wears tongue tie nowadays. *Peter Bowen*

RUPERT VALENTINO 6 b.g. Schiaparelli (GER) – Magic Valentine (Magic Ring **h–**
(IRE)) [2018/19 b–: b16.8s b16.8d h16.8s h23.1sᵖᵘ Mar 5] mid-field at best in bumpers: no **b74**
show over hurdles: tried in hood/tongue tie. *Jackie du Plessis*

RUSSBOROUGH (FR) 10 b.g. Turgeon (USA) – Heritage River (FR) (Kaldounevees **c104 §**
(FR)) [2018/19 c114§, h–: c24.1g⁵ Jun 5] strong gelding: maiden hurdler: fair handicap **h–**
chaser: probably stays 3m: acts on heavy going: has worn headgear, including last 3 starts:
unreliable. *Venetia Williams*

RUSSIAN HAWK 5 b.g. Malinas (GER) – Sparron Hawk (FR) (Hawker's News (IRE)) **h127**
[2018/19 b94: h21.6d⁴ h21.6d³ h19.3d² h19.8s Mar 9] well-made gelding: will make a
chaser: fairly useful form over hurdles: won novice at Exeter in November: stays 2¾m.
Colin Tizzard

RUSSIAN RASCAL 6 b.g. Kyllachy – Russian Ruby (FR) (Vettori (IRE)) [2018/19 h89: **h91**
h16.8g* h16.7g² h16.2g⁵ h16.8g⁴ Nov 1] modest handicap hurdler: won at Sedgefield in
May: may prove best around 2m: best form on good going: wears tongue tie: front runner/
races prominently. *Maurice Barnes*

RUSSIAN ROYALE 9 b.m. Royal Applause – Russian Ruby (FR) (Vettori (IRE)) **h91**
[2018/19 h89: h22.1g² h16.2m* h21.2m⁵ h19.9g⁴ h17s⁶ h18.6g⁵ Mar 27] smallish mare:
modest handicap hurdler: won at Hexham in June: stays 2¾m: acts on good to firm and
good to soft going: usually wears cheekpieces nowadays. *Micky Hammond*

RUSSIAN SPY (IRE) 6 b.g. Sholokhov (IRE) – Elle Desert (GER) (Next Desert (IRE)) **h73**
[2018/19 h–, b72: h16.8g⁶ h16g⁴ Jun 24] poor form over hurdles: best effort at 2m: tried in
cheekpieces/tongue tie. *Evan Williams*

RUSSIANTOM (IRE) 8 b.m. Dylan Thomas (IRE) – Russian Roubles (IRE) (Sadler's **h–**
Wells (USA)) [2018/19 h–, b–: h20.9g⁵ h16.2g h23.9gᵖᵘ Jul 5] no form: wears tongue tie.
Susan Corbett

RUSTY FOX (FR) 6 ch.g. Excellent Art – Damoiselle (USA) (Sky Classic (CAN)) **b90**
[2018/19 b15.7g⁴ b15.8g⁶ Jun 6] fourth foal: closely related to French 10.5f-15f winner
Shorn Grass (by Pivotal) and half-brother to 2 other winners on Flat abroad: dam useful
French 6f/7f winner: fair form in bumpers: easily better effort when fourth at Southwell.
Pam Sly

RUTHLESS ARTICLE (IRE) 6 b.g. Definite Article – Lady Kamando (Hernando **h– p**
(FR)) [2018/19 b15.3g² b16.7g⁴ h19g Apr 25] sixth foal: brother to a winning pointer and **b86**
half-brother to fairly useful hurdler/winning pointer Steel Bob (23f-25f winner, by
Craigsteel): dam (h68), maiden hurdler, closely related to useful hurdler (stayed 2½m)
Doctor Goddard: fair form in bumpers: tailed off in maiden on hurdling debut: in tongue tie
last 4 starts: should do better. *Rebecca Curtis*

RYALEX (IRE) 8 b.g. Arcadio (GER) – Lady Ramona (IRE) (Lord Americo) [2018/19 c97, h–: h20.2g c15.9d⁵ c20s* c23.9d² c20.9s³ c21.4dF c20s⁴ c20vF c20d² Mar 24] maiden hurdler: fair handicap chaser: won at Carlisle in November: stays 3m: acts on soft going: has worn hood: usually front runner/races prominently. *Lucinda Russell* **c113 h86**

RYEDALE RACER 8 b.g. Indian Danehill (IRE) – Jontys'lass (Tamure (IRE)) [2018/19 h119: h21.4v h20.1d² Mar 26] fairly useful handicap hurdler: not disgraced either start in 2018/19: stays 23f: acts on heavy going. *Ruth Jefferson* **h107**

S

SACKETT 8 b.g. Midnight Legend – Gloriana (Formidable (USA)) [2018/19 h109: h25g h23.3g* h20.5g² c23d h26d⁶ h25s⁴ c19.9g² c24.2g² h24.2d h24d³ Apr 24] strong gelding: winning pointer: fair handicap hurdler: won at Uttoxeter in November: better form when runner-up last 2 outings in handicap chases: stays 25f: acts on heavy going: tried in tongue tie. *Neil King* **c115 h109**

SACKFULLOFDREAMS (IRE) 6 b.g. Rock of Gibraltar (IRE) – Nymphaea Alba (IRE) (Monsun (GER)) [2018/19 h89: h18.7mᵖᵘ h20g h19.6gᵖᵘ Aug 31] maiden hurdler, no form in 2018/19: often in headgear: normally tongue tied. *Mike Hammond* **h–**

SAD EYED DYLAN 6 br.g. Multiplex – Congressional (IRE) (Grand Lodge (USA)) [2018/19 h23g³ h16.7g² c16.5m² c16.5g² Nov 4] €21,000 3-y-o, £30,000 5-y-o: sixth foal: half-brother to 2 winners, including fair hurdler Kalaskadesemilley (2m winner, by Myboycharlie): dam, 1m winner, half-sister to useful hurdler/fairly useful chaser (stayed 3m) Ainama: off mark in Irish points at seventh attempt: fair form over hurdles: tongue tied, similar form when runner-up in handicap chases at Huntingdon. *Tim Vaughan* **c113 h109**

SADLERMOR (IRE) 5 b.g. Morozov (USA) – Lucyjane (IRE) (Luso) [2018/19 b15.3g³ b15.8d* b15.8g⁵ Apr 22] £12,000 3-y-o: strong gelding: second foal: dam unraced: fair form in bumpers: won at Huntingdon in March. *Kim Bailey* **b93**

SADLER'S RISK (IRE) 11 b.g. Sadler's Wells (USA) – Riskaverse (USA) (Dynaformer (USA)) [2018/19 c129§, h–§: c23.8gᵖᵘ h24gᵖᵘ c23gᵖᵘ c23.8mᵖᵘ Jan 17] strong, sturdy gelding: formerly smart hurdler/chaser: pulled up all 4 starts in 2018/19 (left Tom George after second one): stays 25f: acts on heavy going: tried in headgear/tongue tie: moody. *T. M. Frost* **c– § h– §**

SADMA 10 gr.g. Street Cry (IRE) – Blue Dress (USA) (Danzig (USA)) [2018/19 c–, h–: c16.3g h16.3g³ c16gᵖᵘ c16gᵘʳ h15.9s h15.3g h15.3g⁴ h16.5d⁴ c17gᵖᵘ Apr 21] modest handicap hurdler: little form over fences: unproven beyond 2m: acts on soft and good to firm going. *Nick Lampard* **c82 h87**

SAFARHI 4 b.g. Farhh – Swarm (IRE) (Hurricane Run (IRE)) [2018/19 h16s Jan 21] fair maiden on Flat (stays 1½m) for Alan King: well beaten in juvenile on hurdling debut. *Alex Hales* **h–**

SAFFRON PRINCE 11 b.g. Kayf Tara – Jan's Dream (IRE) (Executive Perk) [2018/19 c101, h–: c15.7g³ c16.3mᵖᵘ c16.5g⁶ c17g⁴ c17g* h15.7d⁶ Nov 20] big, workmanlike gelding: winning hurdler: fair handicap chaser: won at Stratford in October: stays 2¼m: acts on heavy going: tried in cheekpieces. *David Bridgwater* **c103 h83**

SAGA SUCCES (FR) 5 b.m. Irish Wells (FR) – Frija Eria (FR) (Kadalko (FR)) [2018/19 b16g b15.8s h21.2d⁶ h19.7d⁶ Mar 9] fifth foal: half-sister to 3 winners, notably smart hurdler/top-class chaser Balder Succes (2m-21f winner, by Goldneyev): dam unraced: well held in bumpers: sixth both starts in novice hurdles, better effort (modest form) in cheekpieces at Hereford second one. *Henry Daly* **h90 b–**

SAGE MONKEY (IRE) 10 br.g. Craigsteel – Braw Lass (Alflora (IRE)) [2018/19 c94, h–: c17m⁴ Jul 15] maiden hurdler: modest handicap chaser: stays 19f: acts on soft and good to firm going: tried in cheekpieces/tongue tie. *Kerry Lee* **c– h–**

SAGLAWY (FR) 5 b.g. Youmzain (IRE) – Spasha (Shamardal (USA)) [2018/19 h138: h19.4s h19.4s⁵ h16g³ h16s³ Dec 28] smart hurdler: best effort in 2018/19 when 1¼ lengths third to Wonder Laish in handicap at Fairyhouse: unproven beyond 2m: acts on heavy going. *W. P. Mullins, Ireland* **h145**

SAHARA HAZE 10 b.m. Rainbow High – Gypsy Haze (Romany Rye) [2018/19 h99: h23.3dᵖᵘ May 5] placed twice from 3 starts in points: modest handicap hurdler: stays 3¼m: acts on heavy going. *Phillip Dando* **h–**

Poplar Square Chase, Naas—Saint Calvados and Gavin Sheehan are left clear by Footpad's exit

SAILING AWAY (IRE) 6 ch.m. Stowaway – Drama Chick (Riverwise (USA)) [2018/19 **h80 ?** b–: b16.2g h20.1vur h16.8gpu h16.2g6 Apr 15] behind in bumpers: seemingly first form over **b–** hurdles when sixth in novice at Hexham in April: tricky ride. *Sheena Walton*

SAINLOUIS DES PRES (FR) 6 b.g. Saint des Saints (FR) – Miss Courteillaise (FR) **h104** (Lavirco (GER)) [2018/19 h19.5d4 Mar 20] fourth in bumper and maiden hurdle 2 years apart. *Evan Williams*

SAINT ANTHONY 4 ch.g. Pastoral Pursuits – Mega (IRE) (Petardia) [2018/19 h16.7mpu **h–** Jun 22] no promise on Flat or in juvenile hurdle. *Mark H. Tompkins*

SAINT CALVADOS (FR) 6 b.g. Saint des Saints (FR) – Lamorrese (FR) (Pistolet Bleu **c156** (IRE)) [2018/19 c157+, h–: c16d* c15.5v3 c17g3 c15.9s Mar 13] lengthy gelding: winning **h–** hurdler: very smart chaser: won Poplar Square Chase at Naas (by 4½ lengths from Tycoon Prince) on return in November: failed to go on: best around 2m: acts on heavy going: tried in cheekpieces: front runner. *Harry Whittington*

SAINT CONTEST (FR) 6 b.g. Air Chief Marshal (IRE) – Sainte Adresse (Elusive City **c–** (USA)) [2018/19 c–p, h105: h16.2mpu Jun 24] good-topped gelding: fair form over **h–** hurdles: left Alan King, bled sole outing in 2018/19: failed to complete in handicap chases. *Keith Dalgleish*

SAINT DALINA (FR) 5 b.m. Saint des Saints (FR) – Dalina (FR) (Trempolino (USA)) **b81** [2018/19 b16g3 Jan 12] third foal: half-sister to useful hurdler/fairly useful chaser Mon Lino (21f-3m winner, by Martaline): dam (h122), French 2¼m/19f hurdle winner, also 10.5f-15f winner on Flat: 8/1, third in maiden bumper at Warwick (6¾ lengths behind Pour Joie): will be suited by 2½m. *Charlie Longsdon*

SAINT DE REVE (FR) 5 b.g. Saint des Saints (FR) – Ty Mat (FR) (Panoramic) [2018/19 **b85** b–: b16.8s4 b15.3s4 Mar 7] fair form in bumpers: temperament under suspicion (carries head awkwardly). *Paul Nicholls*

SAINT DE VASSY (FR) 6 br.g. Saint des Saints (FR) – Mona Vassy (FR) (Sleeping Car **h118** (FR)) [2018/19 h15.8s3 h16d2 h19.3g3 h18.5s2 Mar 18] fairly useful form over hurdles: placed all 4 outings, including in handicap: will stay 2½m+. *Tom Symonds*

SAINTE LADYLIME (FR) 8 b.m. Saint des Saints (FR) – Lady Pauline (FR) (Hamas **c–** (IRE)) [2018/19 c134, h132: h24s3 h24.6gpu Dec 27] workmanlike mare: useful handicap **h126** hurdler/chaser: stays 3m: acts on heavy going. *Kim Bailey*

735

SAINTEMILION (FR) 6 b.g. Diamond Green (FR) – Matakana (FR) (Green Tune (USA)) [2018/19 h16s^{pu} h16s c20.9d^2 c19.2d* c20.2g^3 Apr 3] good-topped gelding: fairly useful hurdler: similar form over fences: won novice handicap at Exeter in March: stays 21f: acts on soft going: often in tongue tie. *Paul Nicholls*   **c125 h–**

SAINT FREULE (FR) 6 br.g. Saint des Saints (FR) – Topsy Blue (FR) (Anabaa Blue) [2018/19 h108§: h16.2d^6 h17.1d h16.2s* h16.2d* h20.1g^3 Apr 15] winning Irish pointer: fairly useful handicap hurdler: won at Hexham in November and March (novice event): stays 2½m: acts on heavy going: wears hood: has worn tongue tie: usually races freely close up: one to treat with caution (has refused to race). *Lucinda Russell*   **h124 §**

SAINT JUDE (IRE) 6 ch.g. Presenting – Native Monk (IRE) (Be My Native (USA)) [2018/19 b17.7d Feb 24] well held in maiden bumper. *Oliver Sherwood*   **b–**

SAINT LEO (FR) 6 b.g. Maresca Sorrento (FR) – Sainte Lea (FR) (Sirk) [2018/19 c20g^5 c15.2d^4 c16.5s^F h16.2g^6 c20.1g^3 Apr 25] brother to 1¾m winner, including useful hurdler/chaser Easter Day (2¼m-2¾m winner, by Malinas) and useful chaser Mon Successeur (17f-19f winner, by Forestier): dam French 2½m/21f chase winner: fairly useful form over hurdles: useful handicap chaser: likely to prove best up to 2½m: acts on heavy going: in tongue tie last 4 starts. *Sandy Thomson*   **c131 h127**

SAKHEE'S CITY (FR) 8 b.g. Sakhee (USA) – A Lulu Ofa Menifee (USA) (Menifee (USA)) [2018/19 h130§: h16m^6 h18.9g h16s^6 h21.3s^3 h19.3g^2 h20.3d h21.4m Apr 13] rangy gelding: fairly useful handicap hurdler: stays 21f: acts on heavy going: wears cheekpieces: temperamental. *Philip Kirby*   **h127 §**

SALAZAR (IRE) 4 ch.g. Raven's Pass (USA) – Queen Padme (IRE) (Halling (USA)) [2018/19 h16.8s Apr 16] has had breathing operation: regressive on Flat: well beaten in maiden on hurdling debut. *Sarah-Jayne Davies*   **h–**

SALDIER (FR) 5 b.g. Soldier Hollow – Salve Evita (Monsun (GER)) [2018/19 h145: h16d^F Nov 10] angular gelding: smart form over hurdles: going well in lead when falling heavily last in Fishery Lane Hurdle won by Espoir d'Allen at Naas only start in 2018/19: raced around 2m: acts on heavy going: travels strongly close up. *W. P. Mullins, Ireland*   **h151 +**

SALIX (FR) 5 gr.g. Grey Risk (FR) – Yes Mate (FR) (Lord of Men) [2018/19 h90p: h15.7g^4 h20.7g* h19.9g* h19g^6 h21d Oct 20] sturdy gelding: fairly useful handicap hurdler: won at Huntingdon in May and Uttoxeter (novice event) in June: left Ben Pauling after third start: stays 21f: best form on good going. *Katherine Neilson, USA*   **h116**

SALLY CAN'T WAIT 6 b.m. Sulamani (IRE) – Kate Hill Dancer (IRE) (Presenting) [2018/19 b16.3m^4 h15.8g h15.7s h15.8g h16.5d^6 h19.5d Apr 6] £600 3-y-o, £9,000 5-y-o: first foal: dam no sign of ability: runner-up in point: fourth in bumper at Stratford for Roy Brotherton: modest form in mares maiden on hurdling debut: failed to reproduce it: should stay beyond 2m. *Henry Oliver*   **h91 b65**

SALMANAZAR 11 b.g. Classic Cliche (IRE) – Leroy's Sister (FR) (Phantom Breeze) [2018/19 c–, h120: h23s^2 c24.2d^4 c24.2s^4 c26g^3 c25.6m^{pu} Apr 20] good-topped gelding: fairly useful handicap hurdler/chaser: stays 25f: acts on heavy going: tried in hood: moody. *Alan King*   **c120 § h117**

SALMON RUN (IRE) 7 b.g. Getaway (GER) – Abhainn Ri (IRE) (Saddlers' Hall (IRE)) [2018/19 b15.3d Dec 26] well beaten in bumper. *Ben Pauling*   **b–**

SALSARETTA (FR) 6 b.m. Kingsalsa (USA) – Kendoretta (FR) (Kendor (FR)) [2018/19 h117: h16d* h20s* h22g^{ur} h24d h20g Apr 21] angular mare: fairly useful hurdler: won mares maiden at Sligo in May and minor event at Limerick in December: stays 2½m: acts on soft going. *W. P. Mullins, Ireland*   **h121**

SALTO CHISCO (IRE) 11 b.g. Presenting – Dato Fairy (IRE) (Accordion) [2018/19 c120, h108: c16.3g^3 c17m^2 c17.4g^2 h16.8m^3 h18.7g^3 c16.5g^2 h16g^4 h19.8g^2 h20.6m^3 Apr 21] sturdy gelding: fair handicap hurdler: fairly useful handicap chaser: stays 21f: acts on soft and good to firm going: tried in cheekpieces. *Harry Whittington*   **c118 h111**

SALTY BOY (IRE) 6 b.g. Stowaway – Ballons Oscar (IRE) (Oscar (IRE)) [2018/19 h20.9g^3 h24g^4 b17.3g^3 h19.6g* h22.5d^3 h20d* h24g h22.5g Mar 7] £3,000 3-y-o, resold €4,000 3-y-o: second foal: dam unraced: won maiden point on debut: inadequate test when third in maiden bumper at Downpatrick: useful hurdler: won maiden at Clonmel in November and handicap at Navan (by ½ length from Golden Jewel) in December: should stay 3m: acts on good to soft going: front runner/races prominently. *Ms Margaret Mullins, Ireland*   **h133 b90**

SALUBRIOUS (IRE) 12 b.g. Beneficial – Who Tells Jan (Royal Fountain) [2018/19 **c106** c121, h–: c20.8g May 4] useful-looking gelding: very smart hurdler/useful chaser at one **h–** time (for Paul Nicholls): found little in hunter at Cheltenham only outing in 2018/19: stays 25f: acts on heavy going: tried in headgear: has suspect attitude. *Miss Chloe Roddick*

SALVEN 6 b.g. Presenting – Montelfolene (IRE) (Montelimar (USA)) [2018/19 h20v **h–** h20.5d Jan 20] placed completed start in Irish points: well held both outings over hurdles. *Chris Grant*

SAMANNTOM (IRE) 11 ch.g. Portrait Gallery (IRE) – Native Ocean (IRE) (Be My **c114** Native (USA)) [2018/19 c23.7g² c26.3dpu Mar 15] multiple point winner: winning hurdler: **h–** fair chaser: stays 3m: acts on good to firm and heavy going: has worn headgear: wears tongue tie. *P. M. J. Doyle, Ireland*

SAMARQUAND 5 b.g. Malinas (GER) – Samandara (FR) (Kris) [2018/19 h103p: **h128** h21.2g* h16.8s³ h20.5sPu Dec 19] impressive winner on sole outing in bumpers: fairly useful form over hurdles: won introductory event at Ludlow in November: wears hood. *Harry Fry*

SAMBA TIME 7 gr.m. Black Sam Bellamy (IRE) – Tikk Tokk (IRE) (Tikkanen (USA)) **h–** [2018/19 b–: h20.1spu h19.9v⁴ h25.3m³ h20.1vpu Mar 14] has had breathing operation: no form in bumpers or over hurdles (tongue tied). *George Bewley*

SAMBURU SHUJAA (FR) 6 b.g. Poliglote – Girelle (FR) (Le Nain Jaune (FR)) **h130** [2018/19 h120: h19.5s h21d² h21d⁵ h23s² h23.6d* h23.6d* h24d Mar 14] lengthy gelding: useful hurdler: won maiden in January and handicap in February (by 2¼ lengths from Tobefair), both at Chepstow: stays 3m: acts on soft going: usually front runner/races prominently. *Philip Hobbs*

SAM CAVALLARO (IRE) 13 b.g. Oscar Schindler (IRE) – Gaelic Holly (IRE) (Scenic) **c105** [2018/19 c101: c16.3g³ c20.3g³ c20.9d⁴ c20d² c20m³ Apr 1] good-topped gelding: has had breathing operation: multiple winning pointer: fair hunter chaser: stays 21f: acts on good to soft going: usually wears headgear: tried tongue tied. *Miss H. Brookshaw*

SAM CHISOLM (IRE) 6 br.g. Getaway (GER) – Undecided Hall (IRE) (Saddlers' Hall **h101** (IRE)) [2018/19 b16s⁴ h21d h16.7s⁶ h16.7d³ h19.9vpu h18.9d⁶ Mar 20] €85,000 3-y-o: first **b55** foal: dam, runner-up in point/race once over hurdles, sister to fairly useful hurdler/chaser (stayed 2½m) Knockavilla: well held in bumpers (for Mrs J. Harrington): fair form over hurdles: should stay beyond 17f: acts on good to soft going. *Sarah-Jayne Davies*

SAMCRO (IRE) 7 ch.g. Germany (USA) – Dun Dun (IRE) (Saddlers' Hall (IRE)) **h159** [2018/19 h163p: h16g² h16.4d² h16g⁵ Dec 29] strong gelding: will make a chaser: point winner: high-class hurdler as a novice (won all completed starts): beaten at short odds in 2018/19, including when second in WKD Hurdle at Down Royal (beaten 1½ lengths by Bedrock) and 'Fighting Fifth' Hurdle at Newcastle (no match for 8-length winner Buveur d'Air): will stay beyond 21f: acts on heavy going: usually jumps/travels well: hobdayed over the summer: to be sent novice chasing. *Gordon Elliott, Ireland*

SAME CIRCUS (IRE) 8 b.m. Brian Boru – Curragh Orpen (IRE) (Orpen (USA)) **c129** [2018/19 c127, h–: h25.4g⁵ h27gF c25.2g⁴ c24s* c30g⁵ h25.3d² h25.5g⁶ c26g⁵ Apr 18] **h119** smallish mare: fairly useful handicap hurdler/chaser: won over fences at Bangor in December: should stay long distances: acts on soft going: wears cheekpieces: usually front runner/races prominently: signs of temperament. *Donald McCain*

SAMMAMISH (IRE) 6 b.m. Oscar (IRE) – Issaquah (IRE) (Supreme Leader) [2018/19 **h–** b–: h22.1g May 26] well held in mares bumpers/novice hurdle. *Ruth Jefferson*

SAMMY B 9 br.g. Overbury (IRE) – This Thyne (Good Thyne (USA)) [2018/19 c–, h–: **c–** h24.3d h24.3d³ h25d³ Mar 24] fair handicap hurdler: excuses when well held in novice **h114** handicap chase: stays 25f: acts on heavy going. *Lucinda Russell*

SAMMY BILL 6 b.g. Black Sam Bellamy (IRE) – Samrana (FR) (Tagula (IRE)) [2018/19 **h97 p** h16.8s⁵ h15.8d³ h16g⁵ Apr 10] €50,000 3-y-o, £90,000 5-y-o: tall gelding: sixth foal: brother to fair 2m hurdle winner Samarayia: dam unraced half-sister to useful hurdler/ winning chaser (stayed 2½m) Samapour and to dam of useful hurdler/smart chaser (stays 3m) Warriors Tale: runner-up in point: modest form over hurdles, catching eye in novice final outing: remains with potential. *Oliver Sherwood*

SAMMYLOU (IRE) 6 b.g. Beneficial – Carrigeen Diamond (IRE) (Old Vic) [2018/19 **h107** h91p, b90: h19g⁵ h16g h19d h16gbd h19.6d* h23.9d³ h21.7m⁵ h21.6d Apr 9] good-topped gelding: has had breathing operation: in frame on completed start in Irish points: fair handicap hurdler: won novice event at Huntingdon in January: stays 3m: acts on good to soft going: wears tongue tie. *Graeme McPherson*

SAM

SAM NOIR 7 ch.g. Black Sam Bellamy (IRE) – United (GER) (Desert King (IRE)) **c95 §** [2018/19 c–, h105: c25.5g^{ur} c22.6m^6 c25.5m^6 Jul 1] sturdy gelding: fair hurdler: below that **h–** level in handicap chases: stays 3¼m: acts on soft and good to firm going: wears cheekpieces/tongue tie: best treated with caution. *Peter Bowen*

SAM RED (FR) 8 b.g. Denham Red (FR) – Call Me Nana (FR) (Call Me Sam (FR)) **c117** [2018/19 c133, h125: c20g c22.6g^5 c25g* c25.1g^{pu} c28.4g^F h21.6s c23.8g^{pu} c23.4d4 c24.2d^5 **h–** Apr 9] lengthy gelding: winning hurdler: fairly useful handicap chaser: fortunate winner at Cheltenham (amateurs) in October: left Dan Skelton after sixth start: stays 25f: acts on good to firm and heavy going: wears headgear/tongue tie: none too reliable. *A. B. Leyshon*

SAM'S ADVENTURE 7 b.g. Black Sam Bellamy (IRE) – My Adventure (IRE) (Strong **h116** Gale) [2018/19 h20.5v^3 h22.7g^{ro} h20.5d^2 h22v* h24.3m^5 Apr 12] useful-looking gelding: has had breathing operation: 3-time bumper winner: fairly useful form over hurdles: won novice handicap at Newcastle in March: should stay 3m: acts on heavy going: in cheekpieces last 2 starts. *Brian Ellison*

SAMSARA (FR) 7 b.m. Early March – Quatz Melody (FR) (Johann Quatz (FR)) [2018/19 **c–** h20m h21.8d h25.4s^{pu} c22d Dec 26] maiden hurdler/winning chaser: little show since **h–** 2016/17 when trained by Alain Lyon, France, including in points: often in blinkers: tried in tongue tie. *Graham McKeever, Ireland*

SAM'S GUNNER 6 ch.g. Black Sam Bellamy (IRE) – Falcon's Gunner (Gunner B) **c91** [2018/19 h132: c16.5d^3 c24.2d^2 Mar 19] rangy gelding: progressive novice hurdler in **h–** 2017/18: in need of experience both outings in novice chases: should stay 3m: acts on heavy going. *Michael Easterby*

SAMSON 8 ch.g. Black Sam Bellamy (IRE) – Riverine (Risk Me (FR)) [2018/19 c101p, **c102** h102: c20.5m^F c23.6g^3 c20g^2 c16.5g c21.6g^4 c20.9g^2 c23d^5 Nov 29] angular gelding: fair **h–** hurdler: fair maiden chaser: stays 2¾m: acts on good to firm and heavy going: usually in headgear: tried in tongue tie: lazy sort: joined Dr Richard Newland. *Sophie Leech*

SAMSON'S REACH 6 b.g. Phoenix Reach (IRE) – Court Wing (IRE) (Hawk Wing **h109** (USA)) [2018/19 h103: h21.2g^3 h21.9g^6 h21.7g* h21d^6 h19.5d h21.2d^2 h20.5d^4 h23s^2 h21.4g^{pu} Apr 14] angular gelding: fair handicap hurdler: won at Hereford in November: stays 23f: acts on heavy going: in headgear last 4 starts: usually front runner/races prominently. *Richard Price*

SAMSON THE MAN 6 b.g. Black Sam Bellamy (IRE) – Princess Cara (Rakaposhi **h98** King) [2018/19 h98, b89: h20.7g^5 h21d^F h19.6d h21.4g^4 Feb 27] angular gelding: has had breathing operation: modest maiden hurdler: stays 21f: acts on soft going: wears hood. *Noel Williams*

SAM SPINNER 7 b.g. Black Sam Bellamy (IRE) – Dawn Spinner (Arctic Lord) [2018/19 **h158** h158: h24.2s^{ur} h24.4s^{ur} h24d^4 h24d^2 h24.7g Apr 6] angular gelding: high-class hurdler: easily best effort in 2018/19 when 2¾ lengths second of 18 to Paisley Park in Stayers' Hurdle at Cheltenham in March: stays 3m: acts on heavy going: in cheekpieces last 4 starts: front runner/races prominently: prone to mistakes. *Jedd O'Keeffe*

SAMS PROFILE 5 b.g. Black Sam Bellamy (IRE) – Lucylou (IRE) (Bob Back (USA)) **h150** [2018/19 h16s* h24v^2 h20d^2 h21s^5 Mar 13] £80,000 4-y-o: compact gelding: half-brother to fairly useful hurdler/chaser Cool Mix (2m-2½m winner) and a winning pointer (both by Fair Mix): dam, unraced, out of half-sister to dam of Cheltenham Gold Cup winner Synchronised: winning pointer: placed only start in bumper: smart form over hurdles: won maiden at Cork in November: better form in defeat subsequently, especially when unlucky close second to Reserve Tank in Champion Novices' Hurdle at Punchestown (rallied strongly after mistake last) shortly after end of British season: stays 3m: acts on heavy going: front runner/races prominently. *M. F. Morris, Ireland*

SAMSTOWN 12 b.g. Kingsalsa (USA) – Red Peony (Montjeu (IRE)) [2018/19 c–, h–: **c–** c26.2s^5 c24.5s^{pu} c22.9d^F Mar 20] has had breathing operation: winning hurdler: useful **h–** handicap chaser at best: missed 2 seasons after 2014/15 and no form since: has worn cheekpieces/visor: signs of temperament. *Alistair Whillans*

SAMTARA 5 b.g. Kayf Tara – Aunt Harriet (Overbury (IRE)) [2018/19 b16d Mar 28] well **b–** beaten in maiden bumper. *Martin Keighley*

SAMTU (IRE) 8 b.g. Teofilo (IRE) – Samdaniya (Machiavellian (USA)) [2018/19 h–: **c106** h22.1m^6 h16.7g^5 h16.7g^5 h16.2g h20.9g^2 h19.3g^F h23.8g^3 h20.6d^5 h25.3g^2 h25.3g c23.8g* **h99** c23.8m^F h23.8m^5 c20.9m^{pu} Apr 20] modest handicap hurdler: fair form over fences: won novice handicap at Musselburgh in February: stays 25f: acts on soft and good to firm going: wears cheekpieces: formerly tongue tied. *Barry Murtagh*

738

SAMUEL JACKSON 7 b.g. Alflora (IRE) – Primitive Quest (Commanche Run) **c133**
[2018/19 h132: c23.8v⁵ c24s³ c24.2s* c30.7d⁴ c28.4d* c27.9g⁴ Apr 21] good-topped **h–**
gelding: useful hurdler: similar form over fences: won novice at Exeter in January and
handicap at Taunton (by head from Rolling Dylan) in March: stays 3½m: acts on heavy
going: in cheekpieces last 4 starts: races prominently. *Richard Mitford-Slade*

SAN BENEDETO (FR) 8 ch.g. Layman (USA) – Cinco Baidy (FR) (Lure (USA)) **c153**
[2018/19 c158, h128: c16.2g³ h16m⁶ c17.5m³ c16.8g⁴ c19.9d⁶ c21d c19.9d* c21.1d **h–**
c22.7g³ Apr 27] tall gelding: winning hurdler: smart handicap chaser: won Greatwood
Gold Cup at Newbury (by 2¼ lengths from Gala Ball) in March: stays 21f: acts on good to
firm and heavy going: usually in headgear: wears tongue tie. *Paul Nicholls*

SANCTA SIMONA (FR) 6 b.m. Saddex – Desimona (GER) (Monsun (GER)) [2018/19 **h126**
b16s* b16s³ h19d* h16g* h16g² h16.8d^pu h20g Apr 21] sturdy mare: fifth foal: half-sister **b99**
to 2 winners on Flat in Germany, including smart performer up to 1½m Destor (by
Sternkoenig): dam German 7f/1m winner: fairly useful form in bumpers: won maiden at
Kilbeggan in May: similar form over hurdles: won maiden at Galway in October and Irish
EBF Mares Novices' Hurdle at Down Royal (by 1¼ lengths from Holding Pattern) in
November: will prove best around 2m: acts on good to soft going: in hood last 2 starts:
wears tongue tie: strong-travelling sort. *W. P. Mullins, Ireland*

SAND BLAST 8 b.g. Oasis Dream – New Orchid (USA) (Quest For Fame) [2018/19 c77, **c–**
h84: c24.2g^pu c22.6d^pu Jun 8] maiden pointer: winning hurdler: little form in chases: stays **h–**
2½m: acts on good to firm and good to soft going: normally in cheekpieces/tongue tie. *B.
Dowling*

SANDFORD CASTLE (IRE) 9 b.g. Norwich – Pegs Polly (IRE) (Phardante (FR)) **c– p**
[2018/19 h–: h19.5s h21.9v³ c25.1s^pu Mar 7] point winner: fair maiden hurdler: failed to **h87**
stay in novice handicap on chasing debut (entitled to do better): unproven beyond 19f: acts
on heavy going. *Johnny Farrelly*

Caron & Paul Chapman's "Sam Spinner"

SANDHURST LAD (IRE) 8 b.g. Presenting – Off She Goes (IRE) (Sadler's Wells (USA)) [2018/19 h109: c21.6d⁴ c19.4v⁴ c23.6d³ c25.1g* c23.6d³ c30.7s² Apr 16] strong gelding: fair hurdler: fairly useful form over fences: won handicap at Wincanton in February: stays 31f: acts on heavy going: usually in headgear: has worn tongue tie: usually races prominently. *Warren Greatrex* **c115 h–**

SANDRO BOTTICELLI (IRE) 7 b.g. Galileo (IRE) – Ask For The Moon (FR) (Dr Fong (USA)) [2018/19 h63: h21.6d Nov 14] regressive on Flat: poor form over hurdles: tried in cheekpieces. *Alexandra Dunn* **h84**

SANDS COVE (IRE) 12 b.g. Flemensfirth (USA) – Lillies Bordello (IRE) (Danehill Dancer (IRE)) [2018/19 c96, h–: c23.9d⁵ c25.2s⁶ c23.9d³ c23.6d² Feb 17] good-topped gelding: winning hurdler: formerly fairly useful handicap chaser: only modest form since 2015/16: stays 25f: acts on good to firm and heavy going: tried in headgear: has worn tongue tie. *James Evans* **c93 h–**

SANDY BEACH 9 b.g. Notnowcato – Picacho (IRE) (Sinndar (IRE)) [2018/19 c118, h–: c26.1d* c26d⁵ c24.2sᵖᵘ c30.7d³ c24.2d Mar 24] good-topped gelding: has had breathing operation: maiden hurdler: fairly useful handicap chaser: won at Uttoxeter on return in November: stays 31f: acts on heavy going: wears cheekpieces/tongue tie. *Colin Tizzard* **c125 h–**

SANDY BOY (IRE) 5 b.g. Tajraasi (USA) – Annienoora (IRE) (Topanoora) [2018/19 h15.8g h16.3g h16.2g h21dᶠ h23.9dᵘʳ h22g² Mar 30] sturdy gelding: fifth foal: half-brother to fairly useful hurdler/winning pointer Patsys Castle (23f-3¼m winner, by Windsor Castle): dam ran twice: modest form over hurdles: should stay 3m. *Philip Hobbs* **h94**

SANDYMOUNT DUKE (IRE) 10 b.g. Hernando (FR) – Joleah (IRE) (Ela-Mana-Mou) [2018/19 c155, h–: c26m c22.5g² c25g³ c24gᶠ h19d h23.3g³ Mar 23] strong, lengthy gelding: winning hurdler: useful chaser nowadays: stays 3m: acts on good to firm and good to soft going: wears cheekpieces nowadays: usually leads. *Mrs J. Harrington, Ireland* **c140 h120**

SANDYMOUNT (IRE) 8 b.g. Yeats (IRE) – Flaiha (FR) (Esprit du Nord (USA)) [2018/19 h123: h21.4g h23.6dᵖᵘ h26.6g⁵ Apr 25] fairly useful handicap hurdler: below form in 2018/19: should stay beyond 23f: acts on heavy going. *Tom George* **h109**

SANDYMOUNT ROSE (IRE) 5 b.m. Yeats (IRE) – Ma Furie (FR) (Balleroy (USA)) [2018/19 b15.7d Feb 16] lengthy, dipped-backed, unfurnished mare: sixth foal: bumper winner Irish Odyssey, and closely related to useful hurdler/smart chaser King's Odyssey (2½m/21f winner) and bumper winner Queen Odessa (both by King's Theatre): dam (c122/h110) 2m-2½m hurdle/chase winner: well beaten in mares bumper at Ascot. *Neil Mulholland* **b–**

SAN PEDRO DE SENAM (FR) 6 br.g. Saint des Saints (FR) – Tetiaroa (FR) (Poliglote) [2018/19 c122, h–: h20.5g⁶ h17.7d³ h20.7d* h20.7d² h20.7d h20.5g³ Apr 7] good-topped gelding: fair handicap hurdler: won at Huntington (conditionals event) in December: fairly useful chaser: stays 21f: acts on heavy going: wears blinkers: has worn tongue tie: often travels strongly. *Gary Moore* **c– h113**

SAN PIETRO (FR) 11 b.g. Poliglote – Sainte Berinne (FR) (Bering) [2018/19 c94, h–: c24.1g⁵ May 19] maiden hurdler: fair handicap chaser at best (for Richard Ford): below par since 2016/17: stays 3¼m: acts on heavy going: in blinkers last 2 starts. *Donald McCain* **c81 h–**

SAN RUMOLDO 4 ch.g. Malinas (GER) – Ancora (IRE) (Accordion) [2018/19 b15.7g* Mar 4] sixth foal: half-brother to bumper winner En Joule (by Shirocco): dam unraced sister to very smart chaser (stayed 3¼m) The Tother One, closely related to top-class chaser (stayed 3¼m) Carlingford Lough and half-sister to high-class chaser (stayed 21f) Thisthatandtother: won bumper at Southwell on debut by neck from Hurricane Harvey. *Alan King* **b91**

SAN SATIRO (IRE) 8 b.g. Milan – Longueville Quest (IRE) (Witness Box (USA)) [2018/19 h–: c20gᵘʳ h21g h19d c25.1g³ c23g⁶ h21.4g Apr 14] well-made gelding: won both completed starts in points: fairly useful hurdler at one time: best effort in novice handicap chases (fairly useful form) when third at Wincanton in January: stays 25f: acts on firm going: in headgear last 2 starts: temperament under suspicion. *Paul Nicholls* **c121 h99**

SAN SEB (GER) 4 br.g. Mamool (IRE) – Sunshine Story (IRE) (Desert Story (IRE)) [2018/19 h13.7m³ h13.7g h16d* h16g⁵ Dec 27] compact gelding: half-brother to several winners, including fairly useful hurdler/winning pointer Serious Ego (2m winner, by Sholokhov) and fairly useful hurdler/smart chaser Sammy Black (2m-2¾m winner, by Black Sam Bellamy): dam, German 15f-19f hurdle/chase winner, also 7f winner on Flat: poor form in 3-y-o bumpers: much better form when winning juvenile at Fakenham in December on hurdling debut: stiffer task next time. *Stuart Edmunds* **h119 b73**

SANTA ANNA (IRE) 4 b.f. Canford Cliffs (IRE) – Ardent Lady (Alhaarth (IRE)) [2018/19 **h83** h16m⁵ h16.5s h20.1g Apr 15] poor maiden on Flat: similar level over hurdles. *Mrs Caroline McCaldin, Ireland*

SANTANI (GER) 4 b.g. Jukebox Jury (IRE) – Sun Society (GER) (Law Society (USA)) **h120** [2018/19 h15.8m* Apr 23] fairly useful maiden on Flat, stays 1½m: 11/10, won novice at Ludlow on hurdling debut by 25 lengths from Cock A Doodle Doo. *Tom Symonds*

SANTA ROSSA (IRE) 5 b.m. Jeremy (USA) – Panther Moon (IRE) (Almutawakel) **b108** [2018/19 b16d* b16g* b17d³ Apr 5] sturdy mare: second foal: dam unraced: useful form in bumpers: won 4-y-o fillies race at Fairyhouse in December and Grade 2 mares event at Leopardstown (by 3¼ lengths from Bigbadandbeautiful) in February: also ran well when 3¼ lengths third to McFabulous in Grade 2 event at Aintree. *Dermot Anthony McLoughlin, Ireland*

SANTIAGO DE CUBA (IRE) 6 b.g. Pour Moi (IRE) – Marjalina (IRE) (Marju (IRE)) **h109** [2018/19 h99p, b110: h16g³ h16g² h20g⁵ h21s h16.6g h16.3d⁶ h21g Apr 10] useful bumper performer: disappointing maiden hurdler: left Joseph Patrick O'Brien after fourth start: should stay 2½m: tongue tied for former yard. *Jonjo O'Neill*

SANTINI 7 b.g. Milan – Tinagoodnight (FR) (Sleeping Car (FR)) [2018/19 h150: **c161 p** c23.4s* c24gj³ c24.4s² Mar 13] **h–**

A trio of top-notch novices dominated the 2011 renewal of the Feltham Novices' Chase, with a hitherto unbeaten chaser maintaining his one hundred per cent record over fences when defeating highly-regarded runners from the powerful yards of Paul Nicholls and Nicky Henderson. There was a similar scenario in the latest edition of the Grade 1 staying event at Kempton on Boxing Day, which had its name changed to the Kauto Star Novices' Chase in 2012 in honour of the five-times King George VI Chase winner. Three very promising sorts pulled clear at the end of what looked a strong renewal, with the runners saddled by Nicholls and Henderson again having to settle for minor honours. The 2011 winner Grands Crus never won another race, increasingly looking like a horse with physical problems as he developed into a chronic weak finisher during the remainder of his career. There seem to be no such issues for La Bague Au Roi and she has already bettered Grands Crus by following up her Kauto Star win with another Grade 1 success in the Flogas Novices' Chase at Leopardstown and, despite subsequently losing her unbeaten record over fences, she looks sure to continue to warrant respect in good company. That said, as in 2011, it would be no surprise if the placed horses at Kempton emerge as the most serious candidates for top staying honours over the coming years. The 2011 runner-up Silviniaco Conti went on to win seven Grade 1 events, including two Betfair Chases and two King George VI Chases, while third-placed Bobs Worth, although not quite so prolific as his rival, landed steeplechasing's blue riband, the following season's Cheltenham Gold Cup (Silviniaco Conti fell three out when close up), and also won the Lexus Chase at Leopardstown later in 2013. The Nicholls-trained Topofthegame and Henderson-trained Santini, second and third behind La Bague Au Roi, both appeal as worthy successors to their illustrious predecessors and ended 2018/19 ranked more highly (with the 7-lb mares allowance taken into account) than their Kempton conqueror.

Bobs Worth's match score with Silviniaco Conti ended up four-two against him and Santini begins 2019/20 with similar ground to make up against his Nicholls-trained rival as he is already two-nil down to Topofthegame following their novice chasing campaign. The pair fought out a thrilling finish to the RSA Chase at Cheltenham in March (a race won by Bobs Worth in 2012 when Silviniaco Conti was absent and Grands Crus came only fourth), with Topofthegame shading the verdict by half a length from Santini, with a further length and three quarters back to Irish-trained favourite Delta Work. Things had hardly gone smoothly for Santini during the run-up to Cheltenham, however. A planned preparatory run in the Reynoldstown Chase at Ascot in February (in which Bobs Worth and Silviniaco Conti finished second and fourth respectively in 2012) had to be scrapped because of the fallout from the short-lived equine flu shutdown, with protocol preventing Santini from running for seven days after having to be re-vaccinated that week. Much worse was to follow in the week before Cheltenham, when lameness prompted a seemingly endless cycle of 'shoes on, shoes off, poultices on and poultices off', according to

Ladbrokes John Francome Novices' Chase, Newbury—
chasing debutant Santini has Rocky's Treasure (noseband) and Le Breuil (No.2) in his sights

Henderson, before Santini was eventually declared fit to run. Despite that scare, Santini was still the shortest priced of the home-trained contingent on the day, sent off 3/1 second choice behind Delta Work at 15/8 and preferred in the betting to 4/1-shot Topofthegame, even though he had two lengths to find with that rival from Kempton. The big three in the betting dominated the race itself, deserving plenty of credit for pulling sixteen lengths clear of the remainder late on after a gallop that had been surprisingly steady for a race of its quality. Although Topofthegame was a good winner on the day, connections of both Santini and Delta Work have grounds for hoping the placings might be reversed another day. An uncharacteristic mistake at the second last put Delta Work on the back foot just as the race was taking shape, while Santani finished with just three shoes, with the plate on his problematic near-fore coming off during the race. Apart from that, Santini had every chance on the day, jumping soundly out wide (his only scare being a stumble shortly after four out) and he was just run out of things by the strong-finishing winner after leading briefly between the last two fences. Cheltenham certainly suited him better than Kempton, where he had seemed to be outpaced from the end of the back straight before keeping on strongly again at the end, finishing with plenty of running left in him. Santini started 11/10 favourite for the Kauto Star after an impressive chasing debut win in the Grade 2 John Francome Novices' Chase at Newbury earlier in December, when he had made light work of beating Rocky's Treasure and subsequent National Hunt Chase winner Le Breuil, winning by four lengths and three and three quarter lengths.

Santini (b.g. 2012)	Milan (b 1998)	Sadler's Wells (b 1981)	Northern Dancer
			Fairy Bridge
		Kithanga (b 1990)	Darshaan
			Kalata
	Tinagoodnight (FR) (b 2004)	Sleeping Car (b or br 1988)	Dunphy
			Lorelta
		Tinarctica (ch 1995)	Arctic Tern
			Tinopasa

Santini's pedigree was covered extensively in *Chasers & Hurdlers 2017/18* and there isn't a great deal to add. To recap, he is the third foal out of Tinagoodnight and one of just three runners for her to date, though all three have proved to be above-average performers. The main addition is that Santini's year-younger half-brother Rockpoint (by Shirocco) finally broke his duck over hurdles, in the Grade 2 Bristol Novices' Hurdle at Cheltenham no less. The step up to three miles prompted the upturn in fortunes for Rockpoint and it bears repeating that staying is very much

Santini's forte—he'll stay much further than twenty-five furlongs (the longest trip he's tackled to date) if required. His strength at the end of races has been the feature of his career so far, while the fact that he responds so generously to pressure is encouraging given that there is some temperament in his family. Indeed, Tinagoodnight herself was packed off to stud after refusing to race on her third start (she won the other two), whilst Rockpoint hasn't always looked the most straightforward either (has started slowly). Santini has proved a model of consistency, though, and is yet to finish out of the first three in eight starts, his record including a wide-margin win on his sole outing in points and three wins over hurdles, his battling qualities seen to particularly good effect for his wins in the Grade 2 Classic Novices' at Cheltenham and Grade 1 Sefton Novices' at Aintree in the latter sphere.

A strong gelding, Santini has raced only on good going or softer and clearly handles the mud well. He wore ear plugs at the Cheltenham Festival which were removed at the start. He will warrant plenty of respect should conditions be testing for day four of the 2020 Cheltenham Festival—the last Gold Cup run on heavy going went to a similar type in Native River (who had also finished third in the Kauto Star, being outpaced at one stage, during his novice campaign). The last Gold Cup run on soft ground was won by Bobs Worth. Both Bob's Worth and Native River won the Hennessy Gold Cup (now the Ladbrokes Trophy) in their second season over fences and the Newbury showpiece appeals as an ideal autumn target for Santini in the next season (if all the contenders that look likely 'Hennessy' types were to turn up at Newbury, the Ladbrokes Trophy could turn into the race of the season!). *Nicky Henderson*

SAO (FR) 5 b.g. Great Pretender (IRE) – Miss Country (FR) (Country Reel (USA)) [2018/19 **h124** h124: h16g h16.8d² Apr 9] useful-looking gelding: has had breathing operations: fairly useful handicap hurdler: raced around 2m: acts on soft going: in hood last 5 starts, also tongue tied last 3: tricky ride (races freely/looks awkward). *Paul Nicholls*

SAPPHIRE NOIRE (IRE) 6 b.m. Shantou (USA) – Cool Cool (FR) (Anabaa (USA)) **c–** [2018/19 h–: c25.8mᵖᵘ Jun 26] point winner: poor maiden hurdler: pulled up in novice **h–** handicap on chasing debut: should stay beyond 17f: acts on soft going: in headgear last 2 starts. *Nigel Hawke*

SAROQUE (IRE) 12 b.g. Revoque (IRE) – Sarakin (IRE) (Buckskin (FR)) [2018/19 **c–** c102, h–: c20v Feb 18] workmanlike gelding: lightly raced in points: winning hurdler: fair **h–** chaser: stayed 27f: acted on heavy going: tried blinkered: dead. *Alexandra Dunn*

SARPECH (IRE) 8 b.g. Sea The Stars (IRE) – Sadima (IRE) (Sadler's Wells (USA)) **c–** [2018/19 c102, h–: h16.7s Dec 14] sturdy gelding: fair hurdler: thrice-raced maiden chaser: **h–** raced around 2m: acts on soft and good to firm going: tried in cheekpieces. *Louise Davis*

SARTENE'S SON (FR) 8 ch.g. Linda's Lad – Sartene (FR) (Bakharoff (USA)) [2018/19 **c100** h110, b–: h25gᵖᵘ c19.4d h17g⁶ h23.3d c20.3d⁴ Apr 26] rather unfurnished gelding: modest **h95** maiden hurdler: fair form over fences (left Nigel Twiston-Davies after chasing debut): stays 3m: acts on heavy going: has worn tongue tie. *Robert Bevis*

SARTORIAL ELEGANCE 8 b.g. Kayf Tara – Blue Ride (IRE) (King's Ride) [2018/19 **c102 §** c–, h94: c20.9d⁵ c24.2g⁶ c25.7s³ c24s c21.6s* c21.6v² c20v⁵ c24.2d Apr 9] strong gelding: **h–** has had breathing operation: winning hurdler: fair handicap chaser: won at Fontwell in January: stays 3¼m: acts on heavy going: usually in blinkers/tongue tie: temperamental. *Colin Tizzard*

SARVI 4 br.f. Intello (GER) – Crystal Swan (IRE) (Dalakhani (IRE)) [2018/19 h15.6g⁴ **h100** h15.6g² h18.1g⁴ h15.6g³ h15.6g³ h23.8g² h20.5d³ h21.4s⁶ h20.2g Apr 24] fair on Flat, stays 1¼m: fair maiden hurdler: stays 2½m: acts on good to soft going: tried in cheekpieces. *Jim Goldie*

SARYSHAGANN (FR) 6 gr.g. Iffraaj – Serasana (Red Ransom (USA)) [2018/19 **h109** h16.6g³ h15.6g² h15.7m⁴ Feb 26] half-brother to fairly useful hurdler/chaser Souriyan (17f-23f winner, by Alhaarth): dam half-sister to smart hurdler (stayed 2½m) Serabad: fairly useful on Flat, stays 12.5f: fair form in frame over hurdles. *David O'Meara*

SASSY DIVA (IRE) 8 b.m. Kalanisi (IRE) – Regal Spirit (IRE) (Alflora (IRE)) [2018/19 **h124** h16d* h16g² h16g² h18g* h20g Apr 21] bumper winner: fairly useful hurdler: won mares events at Ayr (maiden) in November and Leopardstown (handicap) in February: stays 2½m: acts on heavy going: wears tongue tie. *Shane Crawley, Ireland*

SATELLITE (IRE) 8 b.g. Danehill Dancer (IRE) – Perihelion (IRE) (Galileo (IRE)) h–
[2018/19 h–: h19.9m^pu Jul 1] useful-looking gelding: fairly useful hurdle winner: little
form since reappearance in 2016/17: stays 2¼m: acts on soft going: in tongue tie last 3
starts, also in headgear last 2. *Tim Vaughan*

SATIS HOUSE 5 b.m. Bahri (USA) – Ex Mill Lady (Bishop of Cashel) [2018/19 h99: h–
h17.1g Nov 4] modest maiden hurdler: raced round 2m: wears tongue tie. *Susan Corbett*

SATOSHI (IRE) 5 b.g. Shirocco (GER) – Morar (Kalanisi (IRE)) [2018/19 h22g* h16d^3 **h121**
h20d h24g^4 h24d^3 h20g^5 h20g^6 Apr 21] first foal: dam, ran twice over hurdles, 14.5f-2m
winner on Flat: fairly useful hurdler: awarded maiden at Punchestown in November: left
Gordon Elliott after sixth start: stays 3m: acts on good to soft going. *Johnny Farrelly*

SATURDAYNIGHTFEVER 7 b.g. King's Theatre (IRE) – Get Me Home (IRE) **h105**
(Alderbrook) [2018/19 b93: h20.5g^3 h20.3s^F h19.5d h21.6d^6 Apr 9] compact gelding: fair
form in bumpers/over hurdles. *Fergal O'Brien*

SATURNAS (FR) 8 b.g. Davidoff (GER) – Sayuri (GER) (Acatenango (GER)) [2018/19 **c149**
c141, h–: c22.5d c22.5g^3 c24s^2 Sep 12] winning hurdler: smart handicap chaser: improved h–
when neck second of 18 to Snow Falcon in Kerry National Handicap Chase at Listowel
final outing: stays 3m: acts on heavy going: tried in tongue tie. *W. P. Mullins, Ireland*

SAUCYSIOUX 9 b.m. Tobougg (IRE) – Mohican Pass (Commanche Run) [2018/19 c–, c–
h107: c22.5g^F h20d h23.4d^pu h16.2g^6 h23.8m Feb 27] fair hurdler at best: no form in h–
2018/19: failed to complete both starts in handicap chases: stays 3m: acts on heavy going:
usually in headgear: has worn tongue tie. *Barry Brennan*

SAUMUR 7 b.m. Mawatheeq (USA) – Sparkling Montjeu (IRE) (Montjeu (IRE)) [2018/19 **h101**
h16d^4 h15.3s* h15.8g* h15.8g^2 Apr 22] sturdy mare: dam (h98) 2m-23f hurdle winner: fair
on Flat, stays 1½m: fair form over hurdles: won mares maiden at Huntingdon in April.
Denis Coakley

SAUSALITO SUNRISE (IRE) 11 b.g. Gold Well – Villaflor (IRE) (Religiously (USA)) **c115**
[2018/19 c23.6d^2 c24.2g* Apr 15] well-made gelding: has had breathing operation: h–
winning hurdler: fair hunter chaser nowadays: off 2 years before return: won at Hexham in
April: stays 29f: acts on heavy going: wears cheekpieces. *Olly Murphy*

SAUVIGNON 8 b.m. Yeats (IRE) – Dalriath (Fraam) [2018/19 h89: h23s* h23g^6 h23.1g^4 c–
c20.3g^pu h23.3s^4 h25g h23.1s^2 h23.9d^2 Apr 24] fair handicap hurdler: won at Worcester on **h105**
return in May: pulled up in novice handicap on chasing debut: left Dan Skelton after fourth
start, Henry Daly after seventh: stays 3m: acts on heavy going: wears hood: held up.
George Baker

SAVANNAH MOON (IRE) 5 b.m. Canford Cliffs (IRE) – Tennessee Moon (Darshaan) **h104**
[2018/19 h20.5s^4 h16.8d^3 h16.8g^3 h19.9d^F Apr 23] fair on Flat, stayed 1¼m: similar form
over hurdles: left Gordon Elliott after second start: in hood last 2 outings: dead. *Philip Kirby*

SAVANNA ROAR (IRE) 6 b.g. Let The Lion Roar – Addie's Choice (IRE) (Norwich) **h87**
[2018/19 b75: h17.7g^5 h16g^5 h16.3s h26d h21s^5 Mar 10] lengthy gelding: modest form
over hurdles: stays 21f: acts on soft going. *Ben Pauling*

SAVELLO (IRE) 13 ch.g. Anshan – Fontaine Frances (IRE) (Lafontaine (USA)) [2018/19 **c117**
c119, h–: c16.5g^5 c16s^2 c15.2d^3 c17.2s^4 c15.7g^4 c15.7s* Mar 18] lengthy gelding: winning h–
hurdler: fairly useful handicap chaser: won at Southwell in March: best around 2m: acts on
heavy going: wears headgear/tongue tie: waited with. *Dan Skelton*

SAVE THE PENNIES (IRE) 8 ch.m. Shantou (USA) – Penny Fiction (IRE) (Welsh **h92**
Term) [2018/19 b84: h19.5v h23d^4 h19s h25d* h25g^5 Mar 19] compact mare: runner-up on
completed start in Irish maiden points: modest form over hurdles: won handicap at
Huntingdon in March, easily best effort: stays 25f: acts on good to soft going. *Grant Cann*

SAVOY COURT (IRE) 8 b.g. Robin des Champs (FR) – North Star Poly (IRE) **c103**
(Presenting) [2018/19 h123: c24.5g^4 c20d^ur Mar 24] fairly useful hurdler: fair form when h–
fourth in novice event at Carlisle on completed start in handicap chases: stays 21f: acts on
heavy going: tried in cheekpieces: front runner/races prominently. *George Bewley*

SAXO JACK (FR) 9 b.g. King's Best (USA) – Gamma (FR) (Sadler's Wells (USA)) **h90**
[2018/19 h114: h15.8m^5 h16.8m^F Jun 26] workmanlike gelding: fair handicap hurdler:
raced around 2m: acts on good to soft going: has worn headgear: wears tongue tie: usually
held up. *Sophie Leech*

SCAFFOLD 6 ch.g. Apple Tree (FR) – Ocarina Davis (FR) (Ballingarry (IRE)) [2018/19 h–
b16g^2 b16g^4 h20m Jul 13] first foal: dam unraced half-sister to useful hurdler/chaser **b84**
(stayed 3m) Violin Davis out of sister to top-class 2m chaser Klairon Davis: modest form
on first of 2 outings in bumpers: laboured effort in maiden on hurdling debut. *Nigel Hawke*

SCALES (IRE) 13 b.g. Bob Back (USA) – Mrs Avery (IRE) (Supreme Leader) [2018/19 c–, h102: h18.5s h21.7d⁵ Mar 9] has had breathing operation: modest handicap hurdler: let down by jumping only start in chase: stays easy 2¾m: acts on heavy going: has worn headgear/tongue tie: usually held up. *Kerry Lee* **c– h91**

SCALES OF JUSTICE (IRE) 5 b.g. Galileo (IRE) – Half Queen (USA) (Deputy Minister (CAN)) [2018/19 h16.2g h20.2g⁶ h20.9g² h22.7g² h22.7gᶠ Dec 29] fair maiden on Flat, stayed 1¼m: fair form over hurdles: stayed 23f: raced only on good going: in cheekpieces last 2 starts: dead. *Lucinda Russell* **h109**

SCAPPATO 5 b.g. Librettist (USA) – Rhetorique (FR) (Smadoun (FR)) [2018/19 b–: b16.8g⁵ May 15] poor form in bumpers. *Oliver Greenall* **b60**

SCARAMANGA (IRE) 4 b.g. Mastercraftsman (IRE) – Herboriste (Hernando (FR)) [2018/19 h15.8d³ h16.5g² h16.5d* h15.7m² Mar 31] dam half-sister to fairly useful hurdler (2m/17f winner) Hartside: useful maiden on Flat, stays 1½m: fairly useful form over hurdles: won maiden at Taunton in March: open to further improvement. *Paul Nicholls* **h123 p**

SCARLET COUTURE 6 b.m. Schiaparelli (GER) – Little Red Spider (Bustino) [2018/19 b–: h19.5v⁶ h21.7v³ Mar 16] last in bumper: modest form on second of 2 starts in novice hurdles. *Gary Moore* **h88**

SCARLET DRAGON 6 b.g. Sir Percy – Welsh Angel (Dubai Destination (USA)) [2018/19 h132: h15.8d* h16m⁵ h16g⁴ Apr 27] sturdy gelding: has had breathing operation: fairly useful hurdler: won novice at Huntingdon in January: raced only at 2m: acts on good to soft going: has worn hood. *Alan King* **h129**

SCARPETA (FR) 6 b.g. Soldier of Fortune (IRE) – Sanada (IRE) (Priolo (USA)) [2018/19 h146: h24s* h20g³ h21s h23.3g* Mar 23] compact gelding: smart hurdler: won minor events at Clonmel in December and Thurles in March: stays 3m: acts on heavy going: in cheekpieces last 2 starts. *W. P. Mullins, Ireland* **h146**

SCARTARE (IRE) 8 br.g. Trans Island – La Speziana (IRE) (Perugino (USA)) [2018/19 h81: h24g⁴ h23.3g⁴ h20.3s³ c20.3d⁵ c20.3g² c20.3d² Apr 9] sturdy gelding: has had breathing operation: poor maiden hurdler: slightly better form in handicap chases, runner-up last 2 starts: stays 2½m: acts on heavy going: has worn hood. *Rosemary Gasson* **c85 h81**

SCEAU ROYAL (FR) 7 b.g. Doctor Dino (FR) – Sandside (FR) (Marchand de Sable (USA)) [2018/19 c157, h–: c15.9g* c15.5v⁴ h15.3g² c15.9s³ c15.5g² Apr 27] good-topped gelding: winning hurdler: high-class chaser: won Shloer Chase at Cheltenham (by 2¼ lengths from Simply Ned) on return in November: career-best third in Queen Mother Champion Chase at Cheltenham (3½ lengths behind Altior) in March: strong-travelling sort, best around 2m: acts on good to firm and heavy going. *Alan King* **c164 h141**

SCENEMAKER (IRE) 6 b.g. Stowaway – Kilmac Princess (IRE) (King's Ride) [2018/19 b16s Dec 27] well beaten in 2 points/bumper. *Peter Bowen* **b–**

Shloer Chase, Cheltenham—Sceau Royal (left) shows a good turn of foot to beat the veteran Simply Ned, who finishes runner-up in the race for the third time

SCENIC STAR (IRE) 9 b.g. Erewhon (USA) – African Scene (IRE) (Scenic) [2018/19   **c–**
c97, h81: c24g^{pu} h21.6g^{pu} Jul 6] lengthy gelding: winning hurdler: modest handicap chaser: **h–**
stays 3m: acts on good to firm and good to soft going: tried in hood: wears tongue tie:
usually held up. *Mark Shears*

SCENTED LILY (IRE) 6 b.m. Presenting – Wood Lily (IRE) (Definite Article) [2018/19   **h105**
h104, b80: h21.2g^{F} h20.7g^{6} h19g^{3} h23.1g^{8}* h25.3g^{5} h23.1g^{3} h23.4m^{3} Apr 22] fair handicap
hurdler: won novice event at Market Rasen in October: stays 23f: acts on soft going: has
worn headgear: tried in tongue tie. *Charlie Longsdon*

SCHAP 7 ch.m. Schiaparelli (GER) – Royal Keel (Long Leave) [2018/19 h95: h24g^{5} **h96**
h23.3m h16d^{6} h20d^{4} h20.7d^{5} h23.1g Mar 27] stocky mare: modest maiden hurdler: stays
3m: acts on soft going: has worn headgear, including last 3 starts. *Caroline Fryer*

SCHEU TIME (IRE) 6 b.g. Arakan (USA) – Time Limit (IRE) (Alzao (USA)) [2018/19   **h120**
h131, b100: h19.3s^{4} h20g^{3} h16g^{4} h16.5g^{4} h15.7g^{F} h16g h15.6g h16.5g^{6} h16d Apr 23]
sturdy gelding: fairly useful hurdler: won novice at Ayr in October: stays 2½m: acts on soft
going: has worn hood. *James A. Nash, Ireland*

SCHIAPARANNIE 7 b.m. Schiaparelli (GER) – Annie's Answer (IRE) (Flemensfirth   **h102**
(USA)) [2018/19 h111, b97: h20.5v^{6} h16.8s^{4} h18.1g^{6} Dec 29] bumper winner: fair hurdler:
stays 2½m: acts on soft going: regularly hooded. *Ruth Jefferson*

SCHIEHALLION MUNRO 6 ch.g. Schiaparelli (GER) – Mrs Fawlty (Kayf Tara)   **h121**
[2018/19 b85: h19.7g^{2} h19.9s* h19.9s^{2} h19.7g* h20.2d^{3} Apr 26] fairly useful form over
hurdles: won novices at Sedgefield (conditionals/amateurs) in December and Wetherby in
February: stays 2½m: acts on soft going: in hood last 4 starts. *Micky Hammond*

SCHIEHALLION RIDGE (IRE) 4 b.g. Mountain High (IRE) – Upton Lodge (IRE)   **b–**
(Clearly Bust) [2018/19 b16.2d Apr 26] last in bumper. *Jackie Stephen*

SCHINDLER'S PRINCE 14 ch.g. Oscar Schindler (IRE) – Coppeen Storm   **c–**
(IRE) (Glacial Storm (USA)) [2018/19 c103: c26.1g^{pu} c23.8m^{pu} Jun 21] workmanlike
gelding: fair handicap chaser: stays 3¼m: acts on good to firm and heavy going: wears
cheekpieces/tongue tie. *Katy Price*

SCHLIPF 6 b.g. Supreme Sound – Zahara Joy (Cayman Kai (IRE)) [2018/19 h88, b78:   **h76**
h22g^{pu} h19.9v^{4} h20.6d^{pu} Apr 6] modest maiden hurdler, below best in 2018/19: stays 2¾m:
best form on good going: usually races prominently. *Daragh Bourke*

SCHNABEL (IRE) 7 b.g. Ask – Velsatis (IRE) (Commanche Run) [2018/19 h106p: **c–**
h21.4m* h21.9g h20.7d c22.4d^{pu} Mar 1] fourth in Irish point: fair handicap hurdler: won at   **h113**
Wincanton on return in May: pulled up in novice handicap on chasing debut: stays 21f: acts
on good to firm and good to soft going. *David Dennis*

SCHOOL LANE (IRE) 6 b.g. Winged Love (IRE) – Mangan Monte (IRE) (Montelimar   **c111**
(USA)) [2018/19 c21.5s^{5} c20d^{6} c16d^{3} c25s^{4} c24d^{2} c23.5g^{4} c21.3s^{2} c28.5g^{2} c20m^{4} Apr 20]
sixth foal: dam unraced: point winner: fair maiden chaser: stays 29f: acts on soft going: in
blinkers last 2 starts: usually leads. *Liam Lennon, Ireland*

SCOIR MEAR (IRE) 9 gr.g. Exit To Nowhere (USA) – Princess Rosie (IRE) (Roselier   **c133**
(FR)) [2018/19 c20g c20d^{6} c24.5g c20d^{6} c24d c24s* Mar 18] lengthy gelding: winning   **h–**
hurdler: useful handicap chaser: won novice event at Navan (by 3½ lengths from Young
Paddymc) in March: stays 3m: acts on heavy going. *Thomas Mullins, Ireland*

SCOOBY (IRE) 8 b.g. Dubai Destination (USA) – Maggie Howard (IRE) (Good Thyne   **h107**
(USA)) [2018/19 h105: h23g^{5} h25.8m* h23.4g^{2} Oct 31] well-made gelding: fair handicap
hurdler: won at Fontwell in May: stays 3¼m: acts on soft and good to firm going: has worn
headgear, including last 2 starts. *Graeme McPherson*

SCOOP THE POT (IRE) 9 b.g. Mahler – Miss Brecknell (IRE) (Supreme Leader)   **c131**
[2018/19 c121p, h126: h23g^{3} c23g^{2} c24.1g^{pu} c23d^{4} c25.8d^{2} c25.2g^{3} c24.2m* c26v* Dec   **h121**
11] good-topped gelding: fairly useful handicap hurdler: useful handicap chaser: won at
Exeter in November and Fontwell (by 24 lengths from Like The Sound) in December: stays
3¼m: acts on good to firm and heavy going: in cheekpieces last 2 starts: wears tongue tie:
usually held up. *Philip Hobbs*

SCORCHIN 5 b.g. Multiplex – Lemon Queen (IRE) (Desert Sun) [2018/19 b15.7g^{3} Nov   **b86**
23] second foal: dam, lightly raced in bumpers/on Flat, half-sister to smart hurdler (stayed
25f) Son of Flicka: 7/1, third in bumper at Catterick. *Sue Smith*

SCORPION HAZE (IRE) 6 b.g. Scorpion (IRE) – Sea Maiden (IRE) (Presenting)   **h110**
[2018/19 h95: h19.3g^{3} h21.6d^{5} h19.5d^{5} h19.3m^{4} Mar 31] tall, useful-looking gelding: in

frame in bumpers: fair form over hurdles: should be suited by further than 2½m: tried in cheekpieces. *Ali Stronge*

SCORPION SEA (IRE) 8 b.m. Scorpion (IRE) – Peinture Rose (IRE) (Marathon (USA)) **h–**
[2018/19 h16g h19.9g Nov 17] first foal: dam, unraced, out of sister to fairly useful hurdler/ useful chaser (stayed 3m) Vodka Bleu: in frame in bumper: no form over hurdles: tried in tongue tie. *Robin Dickin*

SCORPION SID (IRE) 7 b.g. Scorpion (IRE) – Gaye Lady (IRE) (Pistolet Bleu (IRE)) **c134**
[2018/19 h130: c16.2g³ c19s* c19.9g*ur c20.6d* Mar 20] useful hurdler: useful form over **h–**
fences: won maiden in December and novice handicap in March (by length from Whoshotwho), both at Haydock: should stay beyond 2½m: acts on heavy going: usually leads. *Jamie Snowden*

SCORPION STAR (IRE) 10 b.g. Scorpion (IRE) – Chapanga (IRE) (Un Desperado **c85 §**
(FR)) [2018/19 c97, h84: h16.8g h21.6g⁵ h22m⁶ h16.8g³ h21.6g*pu h18.5d⁴ h18.5g* h19.9g **h77 §**
h18.5m³ c20.5m⁴ Apr 25] lengthy gelding: multiple point winner: poor handicap hurdler: won conditionals selling event at Newton Abbot in October: modest form in chases: left Martin Hill after seventh start, Jimmy Frost after ninth: stays 19f: acts on good to firm going: normally wore cheekpieces for former yards: tried in tongue tie: usually front runner/races prominently: temperamental. *J. D. Sole*

SCORPO (IRE) 8 b.g. Scorpion (IRE) – Maltesse (IRE) (Never So Bold) [2018/19 c–: **c76**
c20.1d c21.4g c20.1g⁶ c21.4g*pu c20.1v*pu c16.4d³ c19.3d⁴ c19.3s⁴ c23.8g³ c26.3s³ c20.3m⁵
c23.8s⁵ c20.1m³ c26.3g* c24.2g*pu Apr 15] poor handicap chaser: won at Sedgefield (5 lb out of weights) in April: stays 3¼m: acts on heavy going: wears blinkers. *Victor Thompson*

SCOTCHTOWN (IRE) 7 ch.g. Beneficial – Always Present (IRE) (Presenting) [2018/19 **c126**
c127x, h–: c20g⁶ c23.5d⁴ c26d³ c24.2d² c24v*pu Mar 16] tall gelding: winning hurdler: fairly **h–**
useful handicap chaser: stays 3¼m: acts on heavy going: in visor last 3 starts: tried in tongue tie: usually races close up: has been let down by jumping. *Nigel Twiston-Davies*

SCOTSBROOK NIGHT 6 b.m. Midnight Legend – Won More Night (Kayf Tara) **h91**
[2018/19 h81: h15.7g³ h15.7g² h16g³ h15.8g² h15.8g³ h18.7g* h18.7g*F Sep 4] angular mare: modest handicap hurdler: won novice event at Stratford in August: stays 19f: best form on good going: tried in hood: usually leads. *Shaun Lycett*

SCOTSWELL 13 b.g. Endoli (USA) – Tofino Swell (Primitive Rising (USA)) [2018/19 **c93 §**
c–§, h–§: c26.2g⁵ c26.2g c32.4g*ur c26.2g*F Dec 29] plain gelding: winning hurdler: one- **h– §**
time fairly useful handicap chaser: only modest form since 2016/17: stays 4m: acts on good to firm and heavy going: usually leads: unreliable. *Harriet Graham*

SCOTTSHILL (IRE) 7 ch.g. Flemensfirth (USA) – Loch Lomond (IRE) (Dry Dock) **c–**
[2018/19 h83p, b92: h19g⁶ h23.3g h20.3g⁵ h19.3g h24.2g*pu c24g*ur Apr 13] sturdy gelding: **h94**
placed in Irish points: modest maiden hurdler: hampered and unseated fifth in novice handicap at Bangor on chasing debut: should stay beyond 2½m: best form on good going: tried in headgear. *Jonjo O'Neill*

SCRAFTON 8 b.g. Leporello (IRE) – Some Diva (Dr Fong (USA)) [2018/19 h–: h16.3m **c66**
c15.7g Oct 25] fairly useful hurdle winner: lightly raced and little form in sphere since **h–**
2015/16 (including in novice handicap chase): won on Flat in 2018: stays 2¼m: acts on heavy going: tried in blinkers/tongue tie: none too genuine. *Tony Carroll*

SCRIPTURIENT (IRE) 7 ch.g. Arakan (USA) – Kelso Magic (USA) (Distant View **c– §**
(USA)) [2018/19 c105§, h81: h20.1m*pu h19.3g h15.6g*pu Dec 3] poor maiden hurdler: fair **h–**
form over fences in 2017/18 (left Gavin Patrick Cromwell after final start): stays 23f: acts on good to firm going: normally blinkered: wears tongue tie: temperamental. *John Hodge*

SCRUMPY BOY 7 b.g. Apple Tree (FR) – Presuming (Mtoto) [2018/19 h81: h25m⁵ **c76**
h22m⁵ c20.9m⁴ c20g⁴ c20g² Jul 26] poor maiden hurdler/chaser: stays 21f: acts on good to **h65**
firm going: usually in tongue tie nowadays. *Brian Barr*

SCRUPULEUX (FR) 8 b.g. Laveron – Rouge Folie (FR) (Agent Bleu (FR)) [2018/19 c–, **c91**
h–: h18.5m⁴ c16.5g⁵ c16.5g* c16.3m⁶ h19.5g c16s c16.2d*pu Dec 31] has had breathing **h86**
operation: modest maiden chaser: won novice event at Worcester in June: stays 19f: acts on good to firm going: wears hood: tried in tongue tie. *Chris Down*

SCRUTINISE 7 b.g. Intense Focus (USA) – Tetravella (IRE) (Groom Dancer (USA)) **h–**
[2018/19 h84: h15.9g h20d h19d Dec 31] useful-looking gelding: disappointing maiden hurdler: tried in headgear. *Tim Vaughan*

SEABOROUGH (IRE) 4 b.g. Born To Sea (IRE) – Nobilissima (IRE) (Orpen (USA)) **h112**
[2018/19 h16m² h16.7s⁴ Dec 6] fair on Flat, stays 1¼m: much better effort in juvenile hurdles (fair form) when clear second to King d'Argent at Wetherby. *Alan King*

SEAMUSJAY (IRE) 7 b.g. Craigsteel – Black Manipulator (IRE) (Glacial Storm (USA))   **c–**
[2018/19 c22.6d^pu Jun 8] dual point winner: in cheekpieces/tongue tie, pulled up in novice hunter on chasing debut. *O. Brissenden*

SEAN O'CASEY (IRE) 6 b.g. Galileo (IRE) – Lahinch (IRE) (Danehill Dancer (IRE))   **h–**
[2018/19 h–: h15.8g^6 Jun 14] fairly useful on Flat (stays 11.5f): raced freely when down field both starts over hurdles: sold 7,000 gns, sent to Italy. *Michael Appleby*

SEA OF MYSTERY (IRE) 6 b.g. Sea The Stars (IRE) – Sassenach (IRE) (Night Shift   **h89**
(USA)) [2018/19 h78: h20m^3 h21.6m^3 h19.5d Apr 6] has had breathing operation: modest maiden hurdler: stays 2½m: acts on good to firm going: in cheekpieces last 3 starts: tried in tongue tie. *Dan Skelton*

SEAPOINT (IRE) 5 b.m. Footstepsinthesand – Genuinely (IRE) (Entrepreneur) [2018/19   **h93**
h16.6g h16g^4 h19.7d^6 h16g h16d h19d h16g h20g h20.6d^4 h19.9s^6 h20.6d^2 h19.6d^6 Apr 26] regressive maiden on Flat, stays 1m: modest maiden hurdler: left John Joseph Hanlon after eighth start: stays 21f: acts on good to soft going: has worn cheekpieces. *Joanne Foster*

SEA PRESENT (IRE) 7 b.m. Presenting – Nautical Lady (IRE) (Strong Gale) [2018/19   **h–**
h16.8s h23.1s h19s^pu Feb 4] seventh foal: half-sister to a winning pointer by Dubai Destination: dam (h94), 2m hurdle winner, sister to useful hurdler/fairly useful chaser (2m/17f winner) Sea Gale: no form in points/over hurdles: in cheekpieces last 2 starts. *Jackie du Plessis*

SEARCHING (IRE) 7 ro.g. Mastercraftsman (IRE) – Miracolia (IRE) (Montjeu (IRE))   **h88**
[2018/19 h84: h20g^2 May 10] sturdy gelding: modest hurdler nowadays: stays 2¼m: acts on heavy going: wears headgear. *Gary Moore*

SEA'S ARIA (IRE) 8 b.g. Sea The Stars (IRE) – Speed Song (Fasliyev (USA)) [2018/19   **c101**
c16.2m c19.4m^3 c20.3g^6 h19.2g^4 h19.2g^2 h19.2g^3 h20g h20.5m^6 h20.5g^6 Apr 7] modest on   **h95**
Flat, stays 17f: modest handicap hurdler: fair maiden chaser: stays 2½m: acts on good to firm going: has worn headgear/tongue tie: front runner/races prominently. *Mark Hoad*

SEASTON SPIRIT 6 b.g. Kayf Tara – Aphrodisias (FR) (Double Bed (FR)) [2018/19   **c110**
h113, b94: h21g^bd h19.9g c24g^f c23d^4 c23d^4 c24v h21.7d^4 h19.5d^3 Mar 20] well-made   **h98**
gelding: modest handicap hurdler: fair form over fences: should be suited by 3m+: acts on heavy going: has worn headgear, including last 2 starts. *Oliver Sherwood*

SEA STORY 6 b.m. Black Sam Bellamy (IRE) – Charlottes Webb (IRE) (Luso) [2018/19   **h105**
b98: h15.7d^2 h20.9g^4 h16d h16v^6 Feb 18] sturdy mare: bumper winner: went wrong way over hurdles after second in mares novice on debut: should stay at least 2½m. *Kim Bailey*

SEATON CAREW (IRE) 5 b.m. Getaway (GER) – Millys Gesture (IRE) (Milan)   **b91 p**
[2018/19 b16g^5 b16g* Feb 19] fifth foal: half-sister to useful hurdler/very smart chaser Coney Island (2m-3m winner, by Flemensfirth): dam, unraced, closely related to smart hurdler/chaser (winner up to 3m) Wichita Lineman and half-sister to top-class hurdler (stayed 3m) Rhinestone Cowboy: fair form in mares bumpers, staying on well when winning at Wetherby in February: should do better still. *Jonjo O'Neill*

SEAWEED (IRE) 7 b.g. Winged Love (IRE) – Grangeclare Rhythm (IRE) (Lord   **c– p**
Americo) [2018/19 h19g h24g h19.2d^4 h15.9s^2 h15.9s* h19.2v^3 c17s^ur Feb 13] €18,000   **h97**
3-y-o: first foal: dam (h97), maiden hurdler (best at 2m), half-sister to smart hurdler/chaser (stayed 2½m) Real Steel: modest handicap hurdler: won at Plumpton in December: stumbled and unseated 5 out in novice handicap on chasing debut: left A. J. Martin after second start: best around 2m: acts on soft going: tried in tongue tie: usually travels strongly. *Chris Gordon*

SEBASTIAN'S WISH (IRE) 6 b.g. Aqlaam – Swish (GER) (Monsun (GER)) [2018/19   **h68**
h15.7m^5 h20.5s^pu h19.8m^6 h18.1d Apr 8] has had breathing operation: fair on Flat, stays 2m: poor form over hurdles. *Keith Dalgleish*

SEBASTOPOL (IRE) 5 b.g. Fame And Glory – Knockcroghery (IRE) (Pelder (IRE))   **h113 p**
[2018/19 b101p: h16.4g^4 h16s^3 Jan 2] lengthy, rather unfurnished gelding: point/bumper winner: fair form in frame both starts over hurdles: will stay beyond 2m: remains with potential. *Tom Lacey*

SEBS SENSEI (IRE) 8 ch.g. Art Connoisseur (IRE) – Capetown Girl (Danzero (AUS))   **h–**
[2018/19 h–: h17.7g^5 h15.9g Sep 23] regressive maiden hurdler: tried in cheekpieces/tongue tie. *Daniel Steele*

SECOND TIME AROUND 7 b.g. Midnight Legend – Silk Rope (IRE) (Presenting)   **c116**
[2018/19 h99, b91: h19.6g^4 h23.3g^2 h26.4m^5 c19.9d^2 c20.5d^F c21.4g^3 Mar 27] lengthy   **h112**
gelding: bumper winner: fair maiden hurdler: fairly useful form when placed both completed outings over fences: stays 3¼m: acts on good to firm and good to soft going. *Alan King*

SECRET BERI 5 ch.m. Schiaparelli (GER) – Secret Whisper (Infantry) [2018/19 b16.3g b16g Apr 25] fourth foal: half-sister to 3 winners, including poor hurdler/modest chaser Red Whisper (2m/17f winner, by Midnight Legend): dam winning pointer: hooded, well held in bumpers. *Rob Summers*

b–

SECRET DOOR (IRE) 8 b.m. Stowaway – Cellar Door (IRE) (Saddlers' Hall (IRE)) [2018/19 c–, h118: h19.8m⁴ h26.5vᵖᵘ h19.2g⁵ h19.8v³ h20.5s Mar 11] good-topped mare: fair handicap hurdler: little promise in handicap chases: probably stays 23f: acts on heavy going: sometimes in cheekpieces: temperament under suspicion. *Harry Fry*

c–
h108

SECRET ESCAPE (IRE) 7 ch.m. Getaway (GER) – Portorosa (USA) (Irish River (FR)) [2018/19 b100: h16.8m² h16.7g³ h17.2m* h17.2g³ h19.9g² h20v h18.1g³ Dec 29] smallish mare: fair novice hurdler: won mares event at Cartmel in July: should stay 2½m: acts on good to firm going (won bumper on soft): in cheekpieces last 2 starts. *Donald McCain*

h108

SECRETE STREAM (IRE) 10 ch.g. Fruits of Love (USA) – Bonny River (IRE) (Exit To Nowhere (USA)) [2018/19 c127, h123: h18.9v* h20.2d⁶ Apr 26] close-coupled gelding: useful handicap hurdler, lightly raced: won at Haydock (by neck from Becky The Thatcher) on return in December: ran badly another 5 months later: let down by jumping over fences: stays 2½m: acts on heavy going: tried in blinkers: usually races prominently. *Ruth Jefferson*

c–
h131

SECRET GETAWAY (IRE) 5 ch.g. Getaway (GER) – Good Tune (IRE) (Good Thyne (USA)) [2018/19 b16d Nov 28] second foal: dam, 2¼m bumper winner, half-sister to useful hurdler/chaser (19f-3m winner) Here's Johnny: well beaten in mares bumper. *Stuart Edmunds*

b–

SECRET INVESTOR 7 b.g. Kayf Tara – Silver Charmer (Charmer) [2018/19 h129: h24.5g* h19.5d* c20.2g² c24g² c20.5g⁴ c20.2g* c20.5m* Apr 13] good-bodied gelding: has had breathing operation: useful hurdler: won novice at Kempton in May and Persian

c147 p
h134 +

Hills of Ledbury (Aga)'s "Secret Investor"

War Novices' Hurdle at Chepstow in October: better form over fences: won novice at Wincanton (by 20 lengths) in March and Future Champions Novices' Chase at Ayr (by 3¾ lengths from Louis' Vac Pouch) in April: stays 3m: acts on good to firm going, probably also on heavy: wears tongue tie: often travels strongly: remains with potential as a chaser. *Paul Nicholls*

SECRET LEGACY (IRE) 8 b.g. Flemensfirth (USA) – Wingfield Lady (IRE) (Erdelistan (FR)) [2018/19 h117, b102: h19.6d⁵ c20sᵖᵘ Dec 31] bumper winner: fairly useful hurdle winner in 2017/18: pulled up in novice handicap on chasing debut (should do better): stays 2½m: acts on heavy going: usually travels strongly. *Ian Williams*   **c– p** **h96**

SECRET MELODY 6 b.g. Sakhee's Secret – Montjeu's Melody (IRE) (Montjeu (IRE)) [2018/19 h91: h16.7gᶠ h16.4g h15.8s h16.6g⁴ h15.8d⁴ h16.8g Apr 20] workmanlike gelding: has had breathing operation: modest maiden hurdler: left Tim Easterby after first start: unproven beyond 17f: acts on heavy going: in tongue tie last 3 starts. *Sarah-Jayne Davies*   **h92**

SECRET PALACE 7 ch.m. Pastoral Pursuits – Some Sunny Day (Where Or When (IRE)) [2018/19 h21.6g⁶ h21.6gᵖᵘ Jul 22] modest maiden on Flat, stays 7f: no show in maiden hurdles. *Gail Haywood*   **h–**

SECRET PASSENGER (IRE) 6 ch.g. Stowaway – Mtpockets (IRE) (Deploy) [2018/19 h95: h21.2m h23.3g³ Sep 17] has had breathing operation: poor maiden hurdler on balance: probably stays 2½m: acts on soft going: tried in cheekpieces. *Brian Ellison*   **h74**

SECRET REPRIEVE (IRE) 5 b.g. Flemensfirth (USA) – Oscar's Reprieve (IRE) (Oscar (IRE)) [2018/19 b17g⁵ h19.5v* h23.1s⁵ Mar 5] €45,000 3-y-o: third foal: dam unraced half-sister to fair hurdler/useful chaser (stayed 27f) Keepitsecret: shaped as if needing run in bumper: fairly useful form when winning novice at Chepstow on hurdling debut in December: excuses when well held in similar event at Exeter 3 months later. *Evan Williams*   **h116** **b–**

SEDDON (IRE) 6 b.g. Stowaway – Andreas Benefit (IRE) (Beneficial) [2018/19 b107p: h16.3g* h16.4g³ h15.7s³ h19.3d³ h21s h16m³ Apr 12] good-topped gelding: chasing type: useful bumper winner: useful novice hurdler: won at Stratford in November: best effort when third in Holloway's Handicap Hurdle at Ascot (4 lengths behind Ballymoy) in January: should stay 2½m: acts on soft going. *Tom George*   **h132**

SEDGEMOOR EXPRESS (IRE) 11 b.g. Presenting – Pretty Native (Be My Native (USA)) [2018/19 c22.6d² c21.4g h26.5mᵖᵘ Jul 14] winning hurdler: developed into useful chaser in early-2015/16 (for Nigel Hawke): missed following 2 seasons: fit from point win, went wrong way in 2018/19: stayed 25f: acted on good to firm and good to soft going: sometimes wore headgear: normally tongue tied: dead. *Lawney Hill*   **c102** **h–**

SEE DOUBLE YOU (IRE) 16 b.g. Saddlers' Hall (IRE) – Mandy's Treasure (IRE) (Mandalus) [2018/19 c79, h91: c24.2g⁸ h24.3g⁵ h23.3g c24.2v² c25s² c20d² c24.1d³ h24g⁵ c25d Apr 27] angular gelding: modest handicap hurdler/chaser: won over fences at Hexham on return in September: stays 25f: acts on heavy going: often in cheekpieces. *Ronan M. P. McNally, Ireland*   **c97** **h90**

SEEFOOD (IRE) 12 b.g. Kahyasi – Anne Theatre (Saddlers' Hall (IRE)) [2018/19 c21.4m c22.6g⁶ c22.7f* c21.1dᵘʳ Apr 4] lengthy, angular gelding: winning hurdler: fairly useful chaser: left Dr Richard Newland, won hunter at Leicester in February: stays 25f, effective at shorter: acts on any going: regularly wears headgear. *Justin Landy*   **c128** **h–**

SEE FOREVER (IRE) 5 gr.m. Stowaway – Flaming Poncho (IRE) (Accordion) [2018/19 h19.9g h16v³ h17.7dᵇᵈ h15.5d⁴ h20.7d⁶ h20.3d⁴ Apr 9] €16,000 3-y-o, £36,000 4-y-o: fourth foal: dam, no form, half-sister to useful hurdler/fairly useful chaser (stayed 3½m) Garruth: runner-up in Irish point on debut: modest form over hurdles: should prove suited by further 2½m: acts on heavy going. *Paul Webber*   **h94**

SEEMINGLY SO (IRE) 6 br.g. Dubai Destination (USA) – Jane Hall (IRE) (Saddlers' Hall (IRE)) [2018/19 h18.6g* h20.3s³ h20.6d⁴ h24.3d Feb 25] €32,000 3-y-o, £100,000 5-y-o: third foal: half-brother to fairly useful hurdler/useful chaser Shanroe Santos (21f-3½m winner, by Definite Article): dam unraced half-sister to smart French hurdler/high-class chaser (stayed 25f) Boca Boca: runner-up in Irish point on debut: fair form over hurdles: won novice at Market Rasen on debut in November: should be well suited by 3m. *Olly Murphy*   **h114**

SEEMORELIGHTS (IRE) 7 b.g. Echo of Light – Star Lodge (Grand Lodge (USA)) [2018/19 h18.9v⁴ h20.5s⁴ h25.8g⁶ Mar 23] maiden Irish pointer: fairly useful handicap hurdler: stays 3m: acts on heavy going: tried in hood. *Sandy Thomson*   **h129**

SEE MORES FINALE 11 b.g. Grand Finale (IRE) – See More Castles (Seymour Hicks (FR)) [2018/19 c21.6g⁴ c21.2g⁶ May 28] multiple point winner: modest form in novice event on first of 2 outings in hunter chases. *S. Clark* **c89**

SEERO 9 b.g. Arkadian Hero (USA) – Seem of Gold (Gold Dust) [2018/19 c20.2g⁴ Mar 25] placed in points: tailed off in novice on chasing debut. *Amaryllis Goschen* **c–**

SEE THE SEA (IRE) 5 b.m. Born To Sea (IRE) – Shahmina (IRE) (Danehill (USA)) [2018/19 h15.8g² Apr 11] fair on Flat, stays 1¼m: similar form when 3¾ lengths second to So Lonely in mares maiden at Huntingdon on hurdling debut. *Donald McCain* **h101**

SEE WHAT (IRE) 9 b.m. Craigsteel – See For Yourself (IRE) (Lord Americo) [2018/19 h21.7dᵖᵘ h19.7dᵖᵘ Mar 9] first foal: dam, winning pointer, out of half-sister to smart chaser up to 2½m Brockley Court: winning pointer: pulled up both starts in novice hurdles. *Hannah James* **h–**

SEHAYLI (IRE) 6 b.g. Iffraaj – Quaich (Danehill (USA)) [2018/19 h19.9m⁴ h21d⁶ h16.3m h16.3m h16g h16.5d⁶ Apr 4] dam closely related to useful hurdler/fairly useful chaser (2m/17f winner) Tempo Mac: one-time fairly useful maiden on Flat (stays 7.5f): little form over hurdles. *Johnny Farrelly* **h86**

SEI BELLA 5 b.m. Crosspeace (IRE) – Dizzy Whizz (Kayf Tara) [2018/19 b15.8d Mar 3] sturdy mare: second foal: dam (b88) bumper winner: needed experience in bumper. *Murty McGrath* **b–**

SELDOM INN 11 ch.g. Double Trigger (IRE) – Portland Row (IRE) (Zaffaran (USA)) [2018/19 c131§, h131§: c29.4gᵖᵘ May 28] workmanlike gelding: winning hurdler: formerly smart chaser: only fairly useful form after 2016/17: stayed 3¼m: acted on heavy going: regularly wore headgear: temperamental: dead. *Sandy Thomson* **c– §** **h– §**

SELFCONTROL (FR) 8 b.g. Al Namix (FR) – L'Ascension (FR) (River Sand (FR)) [2018/19 h–: h16v h16dᵖᵘ Feb 25] lightly raced and no form over hurdles: tried in hood/tongue tie. *Tristan Davidson* **h–**

SEMPO (IRE) 5 b.g. Oscar (IRE) – Miss Cozzene (FR) (Solid Illusion (USA)) [2018/19 b16d⁴ b16g³ b16d* b16.4s⁶ Mar 13] lengthy, rather unfurnished gelding: sixth foal: half-brother to useful hurdler/chaser Aqua Dude (2m-2½m winner, by Flemensfirth): dam, 2m-2¼m hurdle winner, half-sister to useful hurdler/very smart chaser (2m-2¼m winner) Andreas: useful form in bumpers: won maiden at Thurles (by 15 lengths from Casamari Abbey) in February: improved further when 7¾ lengths sixth of 14 to Envoi Allen in Champion Bumper at Cheltenham: wears tongue tie. *Joseph Patrick O'Brien, Ireland* **b113**

SENDIYM (FR) 12 b.g. Rainbow Quest (USA) – Seraya (FR) (Danehill (USA)) [2018/19 c89, h86: h22.1g h21.2m h23.3g h19.3g h19.5v h19.9sᵘʳ h22g Jan 15] poor handicap hurdler: winning chaser: stays 3m: acts on soft and good to firm going: has worn headgear/tongue tie. *Andrew Wilson* **c–** **h70**

SENIERGUES 7 ch.g. Midnight Legend – Lady Samantha (Fraam) [2018/19 h101: h23.3gᵖᵘ h20.3gᵖᵘ Jun 25] lightly-raced maiden hurdler: fair form at best: tried in cheekpieces. *Robert Stephens* **h–**

SENIOR CITIZEN 6 b.g. Tobougg (IRE) – Mothers Help (Relief Pitcher) [2018/19 b92: h19.5g* h21.6g³ h19.4g⁶ h20.6d⁴ h19.8s h24.3m⁶ Apr 12] runner-up in Irish point: fairly useful form over hurdles: won maiden at Chepstow on debut in October: should stay 3m: best form on good going. *Alan King* **h119**

SENOR LOMBARDY (IRE) 6 b.g. Milan – Killoughey Babe (IRE) (Alderbrook) [2018/19 h131p, h103: c24.2s⁴ c23.4gꟳ h21.4s Jan 2] rather unfurnished gelding: point/ bumper winner: useful novice hurdle winner in 2017/18: possibly amiss only outing since: running much better race in novice chases when falling 3 out in race won by Donna's Diamond at Kelso (remains open to improvement): should stay 3m: acts on heavy going. *Keith Dalgleish* **c118 p** **h–**

SENSE OF ADVENTURE (IRE) 5 ch.g. Getaway (GER) – Lady Jurado (IRE) (Jurado (USA)) [2018/19 b16.7g⁴ Mar 14] €25,000 3-y-o: half-brother to 3 winners by Beneficial, including fairly useful hurdler/very smart chaser Tanks For That (2m/17f winner) and fair chaser Truckers Benefit (17f-21f winner): dam unraced: in lead when fell last in point: considerably handled when fourth of 6 in bumper at Market Rasen: should improve. *Dan Skelton* **b85 p**

SENSE OF URGENCY (IRE) 7 ch.m. Captain Rio – Itsallaracket (IRE) (Rudimentary **h86** (USA)) [2018/19 h98, b82: h16.2g⁴ h16.2g* h16.2g³ h16.2g⁴ h19.6g h20.9g h16.2g⁶ h17.1g⁶ h16.2g Apr 25] modest handicap hurdler: won at Hexham in June: barely stays 21f: best form on good going: often hooded. *Lucy Normile*

SENSIBLE FRIEND (GR) 6 b.g. Reel Buddy (USA) – Senseansensibility (USA) **h103** (Capote (USA)) [2018/19 h98p: h19.2g⁴ h20g⁴ h21.7g² h19.2g² h17.7m⁵ h16g⁵ Jan 12] has had breathing operation: fair maiden hurdler: stays 2¾m: raced on good/good to firm going: tried in tongue tie. *Amanda Perrett*

SENSULANO (IRE) 6 b.m. Milan – Espresso Lady (IRE) (Shantou (USA)) [2018/19 **h130** h122, b88: h21.6g* h20.3s* h19.8s² h18.9g⁴ Feb 16] useful-looking mare: useful hurdler: won mares handicaps at Ascot in November and Cheltenham in December: stays 2¾m: acts on heavy going: tried in cheekpieces. *Noel Williams*

SENTIMENTALJOURNEY (IRE) 12 ch.g. Portrait Gallery (IRE) – Hazy Rose (IRE) **c101** (Roselier (FR)) [2018/19 c108, h–: c26.3gᵖᵘ c23.8d⁵ c24.2d⁵ Mar 8] winning pointer: **h–** winning hurdler: fair hunter chaser: stays 3½m: acts on soft and good to firm going: has worn headgear. *R. W. Varnham*

SEQUINSATDAWN 7 ch.m. Tobougg (IRE) – Two Aye Em (Double Trigger (IRE)) **h–** [2018/19 h–: h16.3m May 20] well held in novice hurdles, including selling event: tried tongue tied. *Sarah-Jayne Davies*

SERGEANT BRODY 8 ch.g. Black Sam Bellamy (IRE) – Ardent Bride (Ardross) **c99** [2018/19 h106: c24.1g⁶ c25gᵖᵘ c23.6g³ c20v⁶ c23.8s⁴ Apr 7] lengthy gelding: has had **h–** breathing operation: winning pointer: fair maiden hurdler: modest form in chases: stays 3m: acts on soft going: tried in cheekpieces: has worn tongue tie, including last 3 outings. *Samuel Drinkwater*

SERGIO (IRE) 7 b.g. Flemensfirth (USA) – Aventia (IRE) (Bob Back (USA)) [2018/19 **h81** h87: h22mᶠ h21.7gᵇᵈ h21.7dᵖᵘ h19d³ h23.8m³ Feb 27] sturdy gelding: poor maiden hurdler: stays 3m: acts on soft and good to firm going: in visor last 3 starts: wears tongue tie. *Tim Vaughan*

SERMANDO (FR) 5 ch.g. Fuisse (FR) – Josephjuliusjodie (IRE) (Galileo (IRE)) **h106 p** [2018/19 h15.8d h16.8d³ h15.8d⁶ Jan 25] fairly useful on Flat, stays 15f: fair form in novice hurdles: type to progress further. *Jonjo O'Neill*

SEROSEVSKY (IRE) 6 b.g. Morozov (USA) – Be My Rainbow (IRE) (Be My Native **h132** (USA)) [2018/19 h91, b86: h18.5m* h19g² h18.5g* h21.6g² h20g³ h21gᵖᵘ h21.4g* Apr 14] angular gelding: point winner: useful hurdler: won novices at Exeter in May and Newton Abbot in August, and handicap at Wincanton (by 1¾ lengths from Champagne Champ) in April: will stay 3m: acts on good to firm going: wears tongue tie. *Harry Fry*

SERPICO (IRE) 8 br.g. Scorpion (IRE) – Call Her Again (IRE) (Old Vic) [2018/19 h105: **h92 §** h25g⁴ h25.4m⁶ h25mᵖᵘ Oct 4] lengthy, raw-boned gelding: modest maiden hurdler: stays 3¼m: acts on soft going: has worn headgear, including last 3 starts: wears tongue tie: temperamental. *Graeme McPherson*

SERVEONTIME (IRE) 8 b.g. Echo of Light – Little Lovely (IRE) (Mizzen Mast **h88** (USA)) [2018/19 h96: h18.5m⁶ h16.8s h19.2g⁶ h19m h16.5d³ Nov 29] rather leggy gelding: modest maiden hurdler: unproven beyond 2m: acts on good to firm and good to soft going: wears cheekpieces/tongue tie. *Helen Nelmes*

SET LIST (IRE) 10 b.g. Heron Island (IRE) – Copper Magic (IRE) (Zaffaran (USA)) **c113 x** [2018/19 c113, h109: c29.1g² c24.2d⁴ c22.6g⁵ h16d⁶ h26.5g² Apr 20] sturdy gelding: has **h111** had breathing operation: fair maiden hurdler/handicap chaser: stays 3¼m: acts on good to firm and good to soft going: regularly in headgear: not straightforward: sketchy jumper of fences. *Dan Skelton*

SETTIE HILL (USA) 6 b.g. Cape Blanco (IRE) – Claire Soleil (USA) (Syncline (USA)) **h121** [2018/19 h128p: h20.3g* h20.6gᵘʳ h21.6g* Jun 15] rather leggy gelding: fairly useful hurdler: won maiden at Southwell in May and novice at Newton Abbot in June: stays 2¾m: acts on good to soft going. *Nicky Henderson*

SETTIMO MILANESE (IRE) 7 b.g. Milan – Ad Gloria (IRE) (Shernazar) [2018/19 **h128** h24gᵖᵘ h23g² h23g* h24g* h24.7g² h23.6s⁵ h21m* Apr 25] €46,000 3-y-o: sixth foal: brother to a winning pointer and closely related to another by King's Theatre: dam unraced half-sister to useful hurdler/very smart chaser (stayed 33f) Ad Hoc: fairly useful hurdler:

won conditionals maiden at Worcester in September, and novices at Southwell in October and Kempton in April: left M. F. Morris after reappearance: stays 25f: acts on soft and good to firm going: tried in tongue tie: usually front runner/races prominently. *Dr Richard Newland*

SETTLEDOUTOFCOURT (IRE) 13 b.g. Court Cave (IRE) – Ardagh Princess (Proverb) [2018/19 c24.5v² c24.2g⁶ Apr 15] lengthy gelding: placed in points: winning hurdler: fair hunter chaser: stays 4m: acts on good to firm and heavy going: normally forces pace: temperamental. *Miss A. E. Mcclung* **c102 §** **h–**

SEVARANO (IRE) 6 b.g. Shantou (USA) – Eva La Diva (IRE) (Azamour (IRE)) [2018/19 b101: h16v² h16.3s² h16d⁴ h16s³ Feb 15] good-topped gelding: fairly useful bumper winner: only fair form in frame over hurdles. *Oliver Sherwood* **h108**

SEVENBALLS OF FIRE (IRE) 10 b.g. Milan – Leadamurraydance (IRE) (Supreme Leader) [2018/19 c–, h95: h24.1s h25.3s⁶ h24.3d c24.2v⁵ c24.2dᵘʳ c26.3gᵖᵘ Apr 5] fairly useful hurdler/fair maiden chaser at best: out of sorts since 2016/17: stays 4m: acts on heavy going: sometimes in cheekpieces: usually front runner/races prominently: not straightforward. *George Bewley* **c–** **h–**

SEVEN DE BAUNE (FR) 6 ch.g. Tiger Groom – Venus de Baune (FR) (Le Coureur (FR)) [2018/19 b15.8m* h16.4g⁶ h21.2g* h19.4g Dec 29] £75,000 4-y-o: rather unfurnished gelding: third foal: brother to French 2¼m-2¾m hurdle/chase winner Tiger de Baune: dam French 2½m-2¾m cross-country chase winner: runner-up in Irish point: won bumper at Uttoxeter in May with plenty in hand by 6 lengths from Eyehaveagoodidea: fairly useful form over hurdles: landed odds in novice at Ludlow in November by wide margin: stays 21f. *Ian Williams* **h118** **b99**

SEVEN DEVILS (IRE) 9 b.g. Definite Article – Top Lot (IRE) (Topanoora) [2018/19 c97x, h–: c20.1g⁶ c15.6s² c17.4g³ c16.5vᵖᵘ Nov 14] maiden hurdler: modest handicap chaser: probably stays 2¾m: acts on soft and good to firm going: wears tongue tie: often let down by jumping. *Lucinda Russell* **c94 x** **h–**

SEVEN KINGDOMS (IRE) 7 b.g. Yeats (IRE) – Valrhona (IRE) (Spectrum (IRE)) [2018/19 c–x, h–: h23.9d h21.4m Oct 19] rather leggy gelding: has had breathing operation: disappointing hurdler/chaser: usually in headgear: wears tongue tie: sketchy jumper of fences. *David Dennis* **c– x** **h–**

SEVEN NATION ARMY (IRE) 10 gr.g. Rock of Gibraltar (IRE) – Crepe Ginger (IRE) (Sadler's Wells (USA)) [2018/19 c92, h70: h23m⁵ h22m c24g h16gᵖᵘ Nov 20] rather leggy gelding: disappointing maiden hurdler: no solid form over fences: wears headgear: formerly tongue tied. *Alexandra Dunn* **c–** **h81**

SEYMOUR SOX 5 b.g. Multiplex – Seymour Chance (Seymour Hicks (FR)) [2018/19 b15.7v b16.7d h23.8d h23.6d Mar 21] well held in bumpers/over hurdles. *Alastair Ralph* **h–** **b–**

SEYMOUR STAR 11 b.g. Alflora (IRE) – Seymour Chance (Seymour Hicks (FR)) [2018/19 c124, h123: h19.7v h23.8g Jan 3] good-topped gelding: fairly useful hurdler: well below form both outings in 2018/19: not always fluent when last of 3 finishers in novice in 2017/18, only chase outing: stays 23f: acts on heavy going. *Alastair Ralph* **c–** **h–**

SGROPPINO (IRE) 7 b.g. Getaway (GER) – Boadicea (Celtic Swing) [2018/19 h85: h16g² h20.3gᵖᵘ Jun 25] useful-looking gelding: modest form over hurdles: tried in cheekpieces. *Philip Hobbs* **h93**

SGT BULL BERRY 12 b.g. Alflora (IRE) – Cede Nullis (Primitive Rising (USA)) [2018/19 c–, h–: c24gᵖᵘ c26mᵖᵘ c25.2gᵖᵘ c23.6gᵖᵘ Apr 22] workmanlike gelding: of no account nowadays: tried in headgear/tongue tie. *Peter Maddison* **c–** **h–**

SHACKLES 5 b.g. Equiano (FR) – Silent Waters (Polish Precedent (USA)) [2018/19 h16.2g h16.7g⁶ h16.2g⁵ h16.7gᵖᵘ Aug 31] poor form on Flat: modest form over hurdles: dead. *Nicky Richards* **h87**

SHADARPOUR (IRE) 10 b.g. Dr Fong (USA) – Shamadara (IRE) (Kahyasi) [2018/19 h–: h23gᵖᵘ h23mᵖᵘ h23gᵖᵘ Sep 2] sturdy gelding: formerly fairly useful handicap hurdler: little form since 2015/16: stays 23f: acts on soft and good to firm going: regularly in headgear. *Katie Stephens* **h88**

SHADES OF MIDNIGHT 9 b.g. Midnight Legend – Hannah Park (IRE) (Lycius (USA)) [2018/19 c137, h–: h24.3d³ h24.3g² c22.3g* h24.3g* Feb 16] good-topped gelding: smart hurdler: won Rendlesham Hurdle at Haydock (by 8 lengths from Petticoat **c137 +** **h146**

*William Hill Rendlesham Hurdle, Haydock—a winning return to hurdles for Shades of Midnight;
Kilcooley (left) weakens into third*

Tails) in February: useful novice chaser: landed odds at Kelso in December: stays 3¼m:
acts on heavy going: in cheekpieces 4 of last 5 outings: normally tongue tied. *Sandy
Thomson*

SHADES OF SILVER 9 b.g. Dansili – Silver Pivotal (IRE) (Pivotal) [2018/19 h–: h18.5d **h—**
Apr 9] regressive on Flat: no show in novice hurdles: tried blinkered. *Alexandra Dunn*

SHADOW SADNESS (GER) 7 b.g. Soldier Hollow – Shadow Queen (GER) (Lando **h100**
(GER)) [2018/19 h16m⁴ h16dᶠ h16.2g³ h17.1d h19.6gᵖᵘ Oct 30] has had breathing
operation: useful on Flat, stays 2m: fair form over hurdles: should stay beyond 2m:
acts on good to firm and good to soft going: in cheekpieces 4 of 5 outings: tongue tied.
Oliver Greenall

SHADOW'S BOY 10 gr.g. Norse Dancer (IRE) – Inspired Role VII (Damsire **h109**
Unregistered) [2018/19 h112: h18.5g² h18.5g⁵ h20g h25g⁶ h21.7g h21.9s h20.5g² h20.5sᵖᵘ
h19d⁵ h18.7g³ h20.5g⁴ Apr 7] sturdy gelding: maiden pointer: fair handicap hurdler: stays
21f: acts on good to firm and heavy going: usually in cheekpieces nowadays. *Bernard
Llewellyn*

SHADOW'S GIRL 7 gr.m. Fair Mix (IRE) – Special Beat (Bustino) [2018/19 b69: **h80**
h18.5g⁶ h18.7m⁶ h16.3m h18.7g h15.9g³ h16.7g⁵ h16g* h15.3g⁵ h15.5g³ h16.5g² h15.9s⁵
h16.5d⁴ Mar 11] failed to complete in points: poor handicap hurdler: won mares event at
Chepstow in October: unproven beyond 2m: acts on soft going: wears cheekpieces.
Bernard Llewellyn

SHADY GLEN (IRE) 10 br.g. Dr Massini (IRE) – Poppins (IRE) (Invited (USA)) **c116**
[2018/19 c115, h74: c23.9g* c26m³ c21.4mᵖᵘ c23g⁶ c24.1g c24.1g⁶ c24.2g⁵ c21.2d⁵ **h—**
c27.6sᵖᵘ Dec 26] has had breathing operation: maiden hurdler: fairly useful handicap
chase: won at Market Rasen on return in May: stays 3m: acts on soft and good to firm
going: usually in headgear: wears tongue tie. *Graeme McPherson*

SHADY OAKS (IRE) 6 b.g. Getaway (GER) – Naked Poser (IRE) (Night Shift (USA)) **c120**
[2018/19 c15.7g³ c15.7g⁴ c20g c19.1m³ c16.4g⁴ c16.3g³ Feb 15] €32,000 3-y-o, £7,000
5-y-o: half-brother to several winners, including fairly useful 2m hurdler Artist's Muse (by
Cape Cross): dam 6f winner: unplaced in 2 Irish points: fairly useful form in chases: stays
19f: acts on good to firm going. *Charles Pogson*

SHADY OPERATOR (IRE) 6 b.g. Court Cave (IRE) – Native Artist (IRE) (Be My Native (USA)) [2018/19 h135p: c20d³ c25.2g* c24d⁴ c20.2s c29dpu Apr 22] tall, rather unfurnished gelding: useful hurdler: similar form over fences: won maiden at Punchestown (by short head from Ballyward) in December: stays 25f: acts on heavy going. *Joseph Patrick O'Brien, Ireland* **c137 h–**

SHAH AN SHAH 5 ch.g. Shirocco (GER) – Queen Soraya (Persian Bold) [2018/19 b16.7m³ Apr 21] fifth foal: half-brother to bumper winner/fairly useful hurdler Snow Leopardess (19f/2½m winner, by Martaline) and fairly useful chaser Shah of Persia (3m winner, by Fair Mix): dam (c96/h114) bumper/19f hurdle winner: some encouragement when 9¼ lengths third to Montego Grey in bumper at Market Rasen. *Charlie Longsdon* **b90**

SHAIYEM (IRE) 6 b.g. Starspangledbanner (AUS) – Shaanbar (IRE) (Darshaan) [2018/19 h15.7gpu Nov 23] useful on Flat, stayed 1m: pulled up in novice on hurdling debut: dead. *Tim Easterby* **h–**

SHAIYZAR (IRE) 10 b.g. Azamour (IRE) – Shaiyzima (IRE) (Polish Precedent (USA)) [2018/19 c85, h–: c20.1d c20.3g⁵ c24.2g c24g⁵ c25.5g³ c23.9g⁵ c25.5d² h27m⁶ c24.2g⁵ c24g³ c26.3g⁵ h25.3g c23.8g³ c25.2g⁴ c26.7d² c23.8g² c26.3s* c23.8s³ c26.3g⁵ c24.2g⁵ Apr 15] strong gelding: poor handicap hurdler: modest handicap chaser: won at Sedgefield in February: stays 27f: acts on soft and good to firm going: wears headgear: has worn tongue tie. *David Thompson* **c85 h77**

SHAJI 4 b.g. Exceed And Excel (AUS) – Eclaircie (IRE) (Thunder Gulch (USA)) [2018/19 h16d h15.8g⁶ h16s Jan 21] modest maiden on Flat (barely stays 13.5f): little show in juvenile hurdles. *David Bridgwater* **h84**

SHAKE IT UP (IRE) 10 br.g. Presenting – Miss Fresher (FR) (Pampabird) [2018/19 c117, h–: c26.2gF c25.5g² h25.4m³ c25.5g* c25.5spu Aug 27] compact gelding: fair maiden hurdler: fair handicap chaser: won at Cartmel in July: stayed 25f: acted on good to firm and heavy going: tried in headgear: dead. *Micky Hammond* **c114 h100**

SHAKEM UP'ARRY (IRE) 5 b.g. Flemensfirth (USA) – Nun Better (IRE) (Presenting) [2018/19 b15.8s³ Feb 26] fifth foal: brother to fairly useful 3m hurdle winner Imperial Bay and half-brother to fair 19f hurdle winner Feenakilmeedy (by Alflora): dam, lightly raced in bumpers, half-sister to fairly useful hurdler/chaser Dedigout (2½m winner, by Bob Back): Carmelite: showed plenty when 4¼ lengths third to exciting King Roland in bumper at Ffos Las. *Ben Pauling* **b100**

SHALAKAR (FR) 6 b.g. Cape Cross (IRE) – Shalanaya (IRE) (Lomitas) [2018/19 h121p: h19.6d³ h18.5v² h24d Jan 1] close-coupled gelding: fairly useful handicap hurdler: will prove best at short of 3m: acts on heavy going: front runner/races prominently. *Venetia Williams* **h123**

SHALAMZAR (FR) 10 ch.g. Selkirk (USA) – Shamalana (IRE) (Sinndar (IRE)) [2018/19 h76: h16m⁵ h15.8g⁶ h16s⁵ h15.9s Dec 3] close-coupled gelding: poor handicap hurdler: best around 2m: acts on soft going: wears headgear: has worn tongue tie. *Phil McEntee* **h77**

SHALLTOO (IRE) 6 b.m. Shantou (USA) – Dainty Daisy (IRE) (Buckskin (FR)) [2018/19 b16.3d³ Jun 8] €20,000 3-y-o: closely related to fair hurdler/chaser Winning Counsel (21f-3m winner, by Leading Counsel) and half-sister to 2 winners, including high-class hurdler/smart chaser Dedigout (2½m-3m winner, by Bob Back): dam bumper winner: won point bumper on debut: evens, looked unlucky when 2½ lengths third to Lily The Pink in amateurs bumper at Stratford, badly hampered entering back straight and finishing with running left. *Philip Rowley* **b84**

SHALUNA (IRE) 9 b.m. Shantou (USA) – Eluna (Unfuwain (USA)) [2018/19 c20dpu h24.1d Jan 4] won completed start in Irish points: fair hurdler: folded second outing in 2018/19: little form in chases: stays 19f: acts on soft and good to firm going. *John Joseph Hanlon, Ireland* **c– h–**

SHAMAN DU BERLAIS (FR) 6 b.g. Saint des Saints (FR) – Shinca (FR) (Port Lyautey (FR)) [2018/19 b64: b17.5s h19.5s³ h20v² h23.4g² h25.3mF h23.3d² h23g⁴ Apr 13] runner-up on completed start in points: poor form in bumpers: much better form when in frame all 5 completed outings over hurdles: stays 23f: acts on heavy going: wears hood: made running last 3 starts. *Tim Vaughan* **h119 b–**

SHAMBRA (IRE) 5 b.m. Clodovil (IRE) – Shambodia (IRE) (Petardia) [2018/19 h113: h16.3g² h19.2g² h16.2s³ h24.6g³ Dec 27] neat mare: fairly useful handicap hurdler: probably stays 3m, effective at much shorter: acts on heavy going: hooded 7 of 8 starts. *Lucy Wadham* **h118**

SHAMILAN (IRE) 6 b.g. Milan – Shatani (IRE) (Shahrastani (USA)) [2018/19 b90: h19.5s h19.7g² h23.1v² h23.6d⁶ Jan 18] fair form over hurdles when runner-up in maiden/ novice: stays 23f. *Tom George* **h109**

SHAMITSAR 5 b.g. Shami – Tsarina Louise (Red Ransom (USA)) [2018/19 b84: b16.8g⁴ b16.2d Mar 26] modest form when third on debut in 2017/18, easily best effort in bumpers. *Ray Craggs* **b64**

SHANAHAN'S TURN (IRE) 11 b.g. Indian Danehill (IRE) – Chanson Indienne (FR) (Indian River (FR)) [2018/19 c137§, h–: c19.4d³ c15.9g c21.1s c16d⁶ c19.9dᵘʳ c23.6m² Apr 22] well-made gelding: has had breathing operation: winning hurdler: useful handicap chaser: form in 2018/19 only when third to Charbel at Chepstow on return: stays 23f: acts on soft and good to firm going: tried in cheekpieces: wears tongue tie: unreliable. *Colin Tizzard* **c130 § h–**

SHANANN STAR (IRE) 13 br.m. Anshan – Baile An Droichid (IRE) (King's Ride) [2018/19 c82, h–: c26.7g³ c25.2v⁵ c25.2d⁴ c24.2vᵖᵘ Mar 5] workmanlike mare: twice-raced hurdler: poor handicap chaser: stays 27f: acts on heavy going: wears headgear. *Gordon Edwards* **c74 h–**

SHANAWAY (IRE) 8 b.g. Stowaway – Shannagh Run (IRE) (Denel (FR)) [2018/19 h90: h23.9g² h22.1g⁶ h23.9g⁴ h20.2g Sep 26] pulled up in point: modest maiden hurdler: left Stuart Coltherd after third start: stays 3m: acts on soft going: has worn headgear/tongue tie: front runner/races prominently. *R. Mike Smith* **h88**

SHAN BLUE (IRE) 5 b.g. Shantou (USA) – Lady Roberta (IRE) (Bob Back (USA)) [2018/19 b16s³ Mar 10] strong gelding: first foal: dam (h110) bumper/2½m hurdle winner (stayed 3m): Irish point winner: showed plenty when third in bumper at Warwick (4¼ lengths behind Chantry House): should improve. *Dan Skelton* **b98 p**

SHANDON (IRE) 4 b.g. Big Bad Bob (IRE) – Rum Raisin (Invincible Spirit (IRE)) [2018/19 h16d⁶ h15.7g⁶ Jan 10] well held on Flat/in juvenile hurdles. *Lucinda Egerton* **h–**

SHANESHILL (IRE) 10 b.g. King's Theatre (IRE) – Darabaka (IRE) (Doyoun) [2018/19 c152, h154: c20.6m³ h19.4s h20g h24g⁵ h24sᵖᵘ Jan 24] sturdy gelding: smart hurdler/ chaser: mostly well below form in 2018/19: stays easy 25f: acts on heavy going: prone to mistakes over fences. *W. P. Mullins, Ireland* **c131 x h150**

SHANG TANG (IRE) 5 b.g. Shantou (USA) – Ballyguider Bridge (IRE) (Accordion) [2018/19 b16s⁶ b16.8s³ b16.3s³ Mar 11] €80,000 3-y-o: fifth foal: dam (h101), bumper/2m hurdle winner, half-sister to fairly useful hurdler (2½m-2¾m winner) Mrs Wallensky and to dam of useful hurdler/chaser (stayed 3m) Minella Foru: fair form in bumpers. *Emma Lavelle* **b86**

SHANKILL CASTLE 6 b.g. Lord Shanakill (USA) – Sagina (Shernazar) [2018/19 b84: h16g* h20.2g⁴ h16.2g⁶ h19.8m⁶ Mar 22] has had breathing operation: modest form over hurdles: won maiden at Ayr on debut in May: regressed, leaving R. Mike Smith before final start: tried in tongue tie: has finished weakly. *Ian Duncan* **h99**

SHANKSFORAMILLION 10 b.g. Needle Gun (IRE) – Cool Connie (IRE) (Commanche Run) [2018/19 h99: c24gᵖᵘ c23mᵖᵘ h20g⁴ h19.5gᵖᵘ Oct 30] workmanlike gelding: has had breathing operation: modest handicap hurdler: pulled up both outings in handicap chases: stays 21f: best form on good going: tried in visor: patiently ridden. *Debra Hamer* **c– h83**

SHANNING (FR) 6 b.m. Spanish Moon (USA) – Idaho Falls (FR) (Turgeon (USA)) [2018/19 h22.8d³ h16s² h16.5g² Nov 3] third foal: half-sister to French 11f/1½m winner Shannoise (by Racinger): dam unraced sister to useful staying chaser Tarquinius: useful hurdler: placed in handicaps all 3 outings in 2018: probably stays 2¾m, effective at much shorter: acts on heavy going. *W. P. Mullins, Ireland* **h136 p**

SHANNON BRIDGE (IRE) 6 ch.g. Flemensfirth (USA) – Bridgequarter Lady (IRE) (King's Ride) [2018/19 h135: c24.4g³ c24.4g⁵ h23.6s h19.9v Mar 16] good-topped gelding: has had breathing operation: useful hurdler: disappointing in handicaps in 2018/19: better effort in novice chases when 10 lengths third to Lil Rockerfeller in novice at Cheltenham: stays 3m: acts on soft going: tried in cheekpieces: in tongue tie last 4 starts: has looked tricky ride. *Dan Skelton* **c131 h104**

SHANNON HILL 5 b.g. Kayf Tara – Shannon Native (IRE) (Be My Native (USA)) [2018/19 h22g* h21.2g⁴ h19.2d⁴ Feb 24] £85,000 4-y-o: good-topped gelding: closely related to fairly useful hurdler Abruzzi (19f winner, by Milan), stayed 25f, and half-brother to bumper winner/fairly useful hurdler Gaelic Myth (21f winner, by Midnight Legend): dam unraced half-sister to fairly useful hurdler/chaser (stayed 3¼m) Bunratty Castle: easy winner of 2-finisher maiden point: fair form over hurdles: won maiden at Stratford in November: tried in hood. *Alan King* **h103**

SHANNON LIGHT (IRE) 7 ch.g. Ask – Shannon Mist (IRE) (Perugino (USA)) **b–**
[2018/19 b75: b17.7g^{pu} May 9] runner-up both starts in Irish points: modest form on
completed start in bumpers (went wrong sole outing in 2018/19). *Brett Johnson*

SHANROE 5 b.g. Multiplex – Pugnacious Lady (Hernando (FR)) [2018/19 b15.8d^3 **b100**
b16.2g* Apr 15] €12,000 3-y-o: fourth foal: brother to fairly useful 21f hurdle winner
Boldmere: dam maiden on Flat (stayed 1½m): fairly useful form in bumpers: much
improved from debut when winning at Hexham in April with something in hand. *Karl
Thornton, Ireland*

SHANROE AL C (IRE) 6 br.g. Arcadio (GER) – Dromroe Dreamer (IRE) (Insan **c–**
(USA)) [2018/19 h16d h22g h20s c24d^5 c20.2d h20s h21g* h23.9g* Apr 24] £40,000 **h100**
5-y-o: fourth foal: half-brother to a winning pointer by Indian Danehill: dam pulled up both
starts in points: winning pointer: fair form over hurdles: won handicaps at Limerick and
Perth (amateurs event) in April: never dangerous in maiden chases: stays 3m: best form on
good going. *Karl Thornton, Ireland*

SHANROE IN MILAN (IRE) 7 b.g. Milan – Shanroe Scenario (IRE) (Presenting) **c114**
[2018/19 c123, h110: c21.6d^3 c21.4g^{ur} Mar 27] good-topped gelding: maiden hurdler: **h–**
fairly useful handicap chaser: stays 3m: acts on soft going: has made mistakes over fences.
Charlie Longsdon

SHANROE SANTOS (IRE) 10 b.g. Definite Article – Jane Hall (IRE) (Saddlers' Hall **c134 x**
(IRE)) [2018/19 c135x, h–: c24.5d^4 c27.7d^4 c28.8v^4 c26.3d^2 c24.2s c26d c23.8s^4 Apr 7] **h–**
lengthy gelding: winning hurdler: useful handicap chaser: won Southern National at
Fontwell (by 5 lengths from Morney Wing) in November: stays 3½m: acts on heavy going:
wears headgear: sketchy jumper. *Lucy Wadham*

SHANROE SMOOCH (IRE) 6 b.g. Ask – Lady Quesada (IRE) (Alflora (IRE)) **h–**
[2018/19 h16d h15.9m^3 h19.5s^{pu} h16.5d^4 h20.5d h19.8s^{pu} Mar 7] smallish gelding: off
mark in Irish points at fourth attempt: little form over hurdles. *Richenda Ford*

SHANROE STREET (IRE) 9 b.g. Mustameet (USA) – Zaffran Lady (IRE) (Zaffaran **c–**
(USA)) [2018/19 c110, h–: c23.8g^6 c23.8g^5 Sep 27] Irish point winner: winning hurdler: **h–**
fair handicap chaser: stays 31f: acts on heavy going: usually leads. *Lucinda Russell*

SHANROE TIC TEC (IRE) 7 b.g. Flemensfirth (USA) – Bonny Hall (IRE) (Saddlers' **h116**
Hall (IRE)) [2018/19 h107: h20.7g^4 h20.3g h16g h20g^f h19.3m h20.7d h16s* h15.8d*
h16.7g* h16.7s^4 Mar 23] maiden pointer: fairly useful handicap hurdler: completed hat-
trick at Sandown (amateurs event), Huntingdon (ladies race) and Market Rasen in March:
left Jennifer Mason after first outing: should stay beyond 17f: acts on soft going: wears
headgear. *Ben Pauling*

SHANTALUZE (IRE) 7 b.g. Shantou (USA) – Nut Touluze (IRE) (Toulon) [2018/19 **h121**
b100: h16.7g* h16.7v* h19.9s^5 h16.7s^{pu} Mar 23] winning Irish pointer: bumper winner:
fairly useful form over hurdles: won maiden in October and December, both at
Bangor: should prove suited by at least 2½m: tried in hood. *Donald McCain*

SHANTEWE (IRE) 5 b.m. Shantou (USA) – Step On My Soul (IRE) (Dr Massini (IRE)) **b102**
[2018/19 b16d* b16.7d^3 b17d^5 Apr 4] first foal: dam unraced half-sister to useful hurdler/
fairly useful chaser (2m-2¾m winner) Chief Yeoman: fairly useful form in bumpers: won
mares event at Wetherby on debut in November: best effort when fifth to The Glancing
Queen in Nickel Coin Mares' National Hunt Flat Race at Aintree. *Jamie Snowden*

SHANTOU EXPRESS (IRE) 4 ch.g. Shantou (USA) – Spanker (Suave Dancer (USA)) **b99**
[2018/19 b15.8d^2 Mar 21] €34,000 3-y-o: brother to a winning pointer and half-brother to
3 winners, including fairly useful hurdler First Trim (2m winner, by Acclamation): dam
irresolute maiden (stayed 1½m): favourite, 1¼ lengths second to Floressa in bumper at
Ludlow. *Kim Bailey*

SHANTOU FLYER (IRE) 9 b.g. Shantou (USA) – Carrigmorna Flyer (IRE) (Bob Back **c133**
(USA)) [2018/19 c155, h–: c24s^5 c23.4g^4 c26d* c26.3d^2 Mar 15] workmanlike gelding: **h–**
has had breathing operation: winning hurdler: useful hunter chaser nowadays: won at
Kelso and Fontwell in February: second in Foxhunter Chase at Cheltenham (4 lengths
behind Hazel Hill) in subsequently: stays 3¼m: acts on good to firm and heavy going: wears
headgear/tongue tie. *Richard Hobson*

SHANTOU MAGIC (IRE) 12 b.g. Shantou (USA) – Supreme Magical (Supreme **c95**
Leader) [2018/19 c70, h–: c26.2g^5 c21.1d^{pu} Apr 4] sturdy gelding: point winner: winning **h–**
hurdler: useful chaser at best: little form in hunters since 2016/17 (trained first start only by
Rose Dobbin): stays 3m: acts on heavy going: tried in cheekpieces/tongue tie. *Will Ramsay*

SHANTOU PRINCE (IRE) 10 b.g. Shantou (USA) – Princess Nina (IRE) (King's **c105** Theatre (IRE)) [2018/19 c106: c21.6g* May 9] multiple point winner: fair hunter chaser: won novice event at Kelso in May: stays 3¼m: acts on good to soft going: in tongue tie last 2 starts. *Mrs G. B. Walford*

SHANTOU ROCK (IRE) 7 b.g. Shantou (USA) – Cool Cool (FR) (Anabaa (USA)) **c–** [2018/19 c146, h–: c16.8m^{pu} Nov 3] angular gelding: winning hurdler: smart novice chaser **h–** in 2017/18: 11/8-on, fatally injured in listed handicap at Ascot: best around 2m: acted on soft going: wore tongue tie: usually led. *Dan Skelton*

SHANTOU TIGER (IRE) 10 b.g. Shantou (USA) – Opus One (Slip Anchor) [2018/19 **c61 §** c65§, h107§: c26.3g^6 May 4] close-coupled gelding: point winner (yet little aptitude for **h– §** chasing): fair hurdler (for Donald McCain): stays 25f: acts on soft and good to firm going: wore headgear for former yard: tried in tongue tie: front runner/races prominently: moody. *A. B. Leyshon*

SHANTOU VILLAGE (IRE) 9 b.g. Shantou (USA) – Village Queen (IRE) (King's **c142** Theatre (IRE)) [2018/19 c–, h–: c20g c21.2m^4 c21.4m^3 c23d* c25g^6 c20.2g^{ur} c25s^{pu} **h–** Mar 12] sturdy gelding: winning hurdler: useful handicap chaser: won at Worcester in August: stays 3m: acts on soft and good to firm going: in cheekpieces last 4 starts, also tongue tied last 2. *Neil Mulholland*

SHANTUNG (IRE) 6 ch.m. Shantou (USA) – Sarah's Cottage (IRE) (Topanoora) **h112** [2018/19 b90: h20.6g^6 h19.5d* h18.9v^5 h21s^3 h20.5s Mar 11] sturdy mare: fair form over hurdles: won mares maiden at Lingfield in November: stays 21f: acts on soft going (found less than promised sole start on heavy). *Lucy Wadham*

SHANTY ALLEY 5 b.g. Shantou (USA) – Alexander Road (IRE) (Kaldounevees (FR)) **h114** [2018/19 b78: h16.2g^4 h15.7s h15.8g* h16.3d h19.9d^5 Mar 30] good-topped gelding: fair form over hurdles: won maiden at Huntingdon in January: stays 2½m: acts on good to soft going. *Ben Case*

SHANTY TOWN (IRE) 10 b.g. Zagreb (USA) – Rapsan (IRE) (Insan (USA)) [2018/19 **c99** c109, h–: c23.8g^6 May 8] tall gelding: maiden handicap chaser: fair handicap chaser: acts **h–** on good to firm and heavy going: in cheekpieces last 5 starts: tried tongue tied. *David Dennis*

SHAPIRO 6 b.m. Schiaparelli (GER) – Lady Turk (FR) (Baby Turk) [2018/19 b84: **h108 p** h21.7v* Mar 16] placed twice in bumpers: 5/4, won novice at Fontwell (by 10 lengths from Smart Getaway) on hurdling debut: likely to improve. *Anthony Honeyball*

SHARJAH (FR) 6 b.g. Doctor Dino (FR) – Saaryeh (Royal Academy (USA)) **h157 +** [2018/19 h137: h16g^3 h16s* h16g^3 h16.2g* h16g* h16.4s^{bd} Mar 12]

Few would have picked out Sharjah at the start of the season as the horse who would earn the most prize money in Ireland for his owners Susannah and Rich Ricci. He had been a useful novice the previous season, winning his first two starts at Gowran, but his best chance of winning a Grade 1 contest looked to have passed him by when he fell, upsides and going best, at the final flight in the Future Champions Novices' Hurdle at Leopardstown on his next start. He never went so close in four more outings in good novice company that season and finished eighth in the Supreme Novices' at Cheltenham under Paul Townend, starting as the 20/1 stable second string, Ruby Walsh partnering 7/4 favourite Getabird in the same colours and finishing even further back as it turned out. But Sharjah was much improved in his second season over hurdles, unexpectedly so, it seemed, with Walsh again riding shorter-priced stable-companions in all three of the valuable contests which Sharjah won.

Sharjah netted the bulk of his season's earnings early on when winning the Guinness Galway Hurdle in August, far and away Ireland's richest handicap hurdle and worth much more than many of its Grade 1 races, including the two which Sharjah won later in the season. He carried top weight at Galway in what was his first start in a handicap and was one of six trained by Willie Mullins in a twenty-runner field. Walsh rode the other runner in the Ricci colours, Max Dynamite, runner-up in 2015 and contesting the race for a third time, but it was another of the Mullins entries Whiskey Sour (who had been the main beneficiary of Sharjah's fall at Leopardstown) who was sent off the 9/2 favourite. Sharjah was a 12/1 chance back under Mr Patrick Mullins who had ridden him on a couple of occasions as a novice, including when he fell. The pair had a much happier experience at Galway,

leading early, remaining prominent and looming up again as another of his stable-companions, Blazer, led entering the straight. The leader didn't meet the last on a good stride, though, and Sharjah overhauled him on the run-in to win by three lengths. There were three British-trained runners in the field and two of them, Leoncavallo and Bedrock, completed the frame, with Whiskey Sour seventh and Max Dynamite eleventh, both ridden further off the pace than ideal.

Sharjah had warmed up for the Galway Hurdle by finishing third in the Grimes Hurdle at Tipperary earlier in the summer and after Galway he was given a couple of starts on the Flat in the autumn, sent off favourite for a valuable contest at Leopardstown on Irish Champions' Weekend and then contesting the Irish Cesarewitch at Navan. He cut little ice in either contest, and initially failed to run up to his Galway form back over hurdles when only third of four behind Bedrock and odds-on Samcro in the WKD Hurdle at Down Royal, receiving weight from both. But it was a different story on his next start, his smart effort under a big weight at Galway entitling him to a return to Grade 1 company. Good ground resulted in a depleted field for the Unibet Morgiana Hurdle at Punchestown in November, with Samcro and Supasundae both withdrawn to leave the Mullins trio of Faugheen, Sharjah and Wicklow Brave and the Gordon Elliott-trained outsider Tombstone. Walsh's mount Faugheen was 5/2-on to win the Morgiana for the second year running, but he had been thwarted by a stable companion in a small field at even shorter odds in the race previously, when Nichols Canyon ended his unbeaten record in 2015. This time it was Sharjah who lowered his colours, Paul Townend content to sit some way off the pace as Faugheen, pressed by Tombstone, set the gallop. Moving closer, Sharjah quickened to lead early in the straight and was driven clear to beat Faugheen by seven and a half lengths.

Mullins has now won the Morgiana in each of the last eight years and, of his previous winners, both Nichols Canyon and Hurricane Fly had gone on to win the December Festival Hurdle (run as the Ryanair Hurdle again in the latest season) at Leopardstown. Nichols Canyon won the Morgiana twice, following up at Leopardstown the year he beat Faugheen at Punchestown, while Hurricane Fly won both races three years running. This time it was Melon, having his first start since falling at the Punchestown Festival, who was Walsh's selected ride, leaving Patrick

Ryanair Hurdle, Leopardstown—
a second successive Grade 1 win for Sharjah (centre) as he lowers the colours of Supasundae
(almost hidden), Tombstone (right), Melon (left) and the disappointing Samcro (second right)

Mullins to partner Sharjah again. Sharjah's task looked a stiffer one with both Samcro (6/4 favourite) and Supasundae standing their ground and the 2016 winner Petit Mouchoir also in the line-up. The last couple of renewals had seen hot favourites turned over, with Petit Mouchoir beating Nichols Canyon and then Faugheen being pulled up and coming back in the horse ambulance in 2017. With Melon, who looked rusty for his return, and, Samcro, who had no such excuses, failing to run anywhere near their best, it was 6/1 chance Sharjah who again exceeded expectations, winning a steadily-run race with much the best turn of foot. Samcro initially looked the winner after two out when looming up to leader Tombstone, the outsider again, but he was unable to open up any sort of gap on his stable companion, while Sharjah, creeping closer after being waited with, quickened to lead approaching the last and drew clear to beat Supasundae by three and three quarter lengths. Tombstone kept on for third, beaten another length and three quarters, with Melon and Samcro only fourth and fifth and Petit Mouchoir last throughout. Sharjah was missing from the Irish Champion Hurdle line-up, where he surely wouldn't have beaten Apple's Jade in any case, and purposely kept fresh for Cheltenham, making his only other appearance of the season in the Champion Hurdle. Sent off 20/1, he was ridden again by Mr Patrick Mullins, with Walsh taking the ride on the stable's well-backed Laurina, but his participation lasted only until the third hurdle where Buveur d'Air fell in his path and he was brought down.

		Doctor Dino (FR)	Muhtathir	Elmaamul
Sharjah (FR)		(ch 2002)	(ch 1995)	Majmu
(b.g. 2013)			Logica	Priolo
			(b 1994)	Salagangai
		Saaryeh	Royal Academy	Nijinsky
		(b 1998)	(b 1987)	Crimson Saint
			Belle Argentine	Fijar Tango
			(br 1991)	Jarlina

Sharjah's sire Doctor Dino didn't reach his peak for Richard Gibson in France until he was an older horse, winning consecutive editions of the Hong Kong Vase aged five and six. He didn't win at the top level in Europe, but his globe-trotting also won him the Man o' War Stakes at Belmont. His own sire Muhtathir is a successful sire of jumpers, and Doctor Dino had a good season with Sceau Royal, La Bague Au

Roi and the French-trained Master Dino also among his best horses. Sharjah started out on the Flat in France with Jonathan Pease and, following his retirement, Henri-Francois Devin for whom he won a minor event on the polytrack at Deauville over an extended mile and a half. Sharjah's dam Saaryeh won a mile maiden at Ascot for Marcus Tregoning in the colours of Sheikh Ahmed Al Maktoum and she has bred three other French Flat winners, the best of them the useful French performer at up to a mile and a half Sahawar (by Dark Angel). The others are Songeur (by Elusive City), a winner in France from a mile to a mile and a quarter, and Jaassey (by Josr Algarhoud) whose only win came in a claimer at Beverley over seven and a half furlongs (he ran over hurdles but showed nothing). Sharjah's grandam was the smart French filly Belle Argentine who won twice at a mile, including in listed company, and was third in the Poule d'Essai des Pouliches and fourth in the Prix de Diane. Other than Sharjah, her most notable descendants have been sprinters, her daughter Alzerra winning the Cornwallis Stakes and her grandson, the smart Gifted Master, counting the Stewards' Cup among his wins. Sharjah's unraced great grandam Jarlina was a half-sister to the high-class middle-distance colt Lovely Dancer. The well-made Sharjah has raced only at two miles over hurdles and acts on heavy ground. He had to make his own running in the small field at Down Royal but was ridden much more patiently for the most part to make best use of his good turn of foot. He wore a tongue tie on his final start as a novice and was fitted with cheekpieces for all his starts on the Flat as a three-year-old. Another campaign in the top two-mile hurdles will presumably be mapped out for him in the next season. Finally, a few words on Mr Patrick Mullins who is 'in a different league compared to me when I was riding many years ago', according to his father speaking after the Galway Hurdle. It was only a few weeks earlier at Sligo that Mr Mullins had ridden his 546th career victory to break Mr Ted Walsh's record and become Ireland's most successful amateur rider.

Mrs S. Ricci's "Sharjah"

Mr Mullins has announced his intention to reach a thousand winners. He claimed his eleventh amateur title in Ireland at the end of the latest season to equal the record number of championships achieved by Mr Walsh. *W. P. Mullins, Ireland*

SHARNEY SIKE 13 ch.g. And Beyond (IRE) – Squeeze Box (IRE) (Accordion) [2018/19 c102x, h–: c20.1d* c20.1g Jun 2] tall, lengthy, angular gelding: maiden hurdler: fair handicap chaser: won at Hexham in May: stays 3m: acts on heavy going: in headgear last 5 starts: front runner/races prominently: sketchy jumper of fences. *Stuart Colthred* **c97 x h–**

SHARPE'S RIFLES 5 b.g. Arabian Gleam – High Meadow Jo (Silver Patriarch (IRE)) [2018/19 b16v ab16s Jan 4] rather leggy gelding: well beaten in bumpers. *Fergal O'Brien* **b–**

SHARP GETAWAY (IRE) 7 b.g. Getaway (GER) – Thanks Noel (IRE) (Tel Quel (FR)) [2018/19 h–, b71: h19.5s h23.6v⁶ h24.1g⁴ Apr 11] tall gelding: poor form over hurdles: left Ben Case after second start: tried in cheekpieces. *Fergal O'Brien* **h82**

SHARP REPLY (IRE) 5 b.g. Holy Roman Emperor (IRE) – Sabindra (Magic Ring (IRE)) [2018/19 h24.4g³ h21.3dᵘʳ h18.6d⁵ h15.8d h20.6g⁶ Mar 14] fair maiden on Flat, stays 11.5f: only poor form over hurdles. *Charles Pogson* **h69**

SHARP RESPONSE (IRE) 8 b.g. Oscar (IRE) – Lambourne Lace (IRE) (Un Desperado (FR)) [2018/19 c120, h–: h23.3s⁴ c26.2g* c27.3g c23.4d⁴ c22.9v⁴ c30g* Jan 10] winning hurdler: useful handicap chaser: progressed well in 2018/19, winning at Carlisle in October and Catterick in January: stays 3¾m: acts on heavy going: sound jumper. *Sue Smith* **c141 h97**

SHARP ROCK 4 b.g. Kheleyf (USA) – Fair View (GER) (Dashing Blade) [2018/19 b16.5d⁵ b16.3s Mar 11] well beaten in bumpers. *Alastair Ralph* **b–**

SHATTERED LOVE (IRE) 8 b.m. Yeats (IRE) – Tracker (Bustino) [2018/19 c154, h–: c19.5g² c20.2d² c24g c26.3d c29dᵖᵘ Apr 22] tall mare: has had breathing operation: winning hurdler: very smart chaser: runner-up in Grade 2 events at Down Royal and John Durkan Memorial Punchestown Chase (1½ lengths behind Min) first 2 outings in 2018/19: disappointing subsequently: stays 3m, at least as effective at shorter: acts on heavy going: wears tongue tie. *Gordon Elliott, Ireland* **c156 h–**

SHAUGHNESSY 6 b.g. Shantou (USA) – Sudden Beat (Beat All (USA)) [2018/19 b102: b15.7g* h21.6d³ h23.1v⁴ h20s³ Apr 7] fairly useful form in bumpers: won at Towcester in May: fair form in frame all 3 starts over hurdles, including in handicap: may prove best short of 23f when conditions are testing: tried in cheekpieces. *Oliver Sherwood* **h114 b102**

SHAWS BRIDGE (IRE) 6 b.g. Kalanisi (IRE) – Zaffarella (IRE) (Zaffaran (USA)) [2018/19 b16.6d³ b16v⁶ b16.2d⁴ Apr 26] third foal: half-brother to bumper winner/fairly useful 17f hurdle winner Ravenhill Road (by Exit To Nowhere) and bumper winner/useful 2½m hurdle winner Windsor Avenue (by Winged Love): dam (h112) 2m-3m hurdle winner: fair form in bumpers. *Stuart Crawford, Ireland* **b91**

SHAW'S CROSS (IRE) 7 b.g. Mr Dinos (IRE) – Capparoe Cross (IRE) (Saddlers' Hall (IRE)) [2018/19 h16.5g h21m h16g h19.2d² h16v* h15.3d² h16d h19.8s⁵ Feb 15] sturdy gelding: second foal: dam (h92) maiden hurdler (stayed 2½m): fair handicap hurdler: won novice event at Sandown in December: left E. J. O'Grady after third start: stays 19f: acts on heavy going: usually hooded. *Paul Henderson* **h104**

SHAW'S DILEMMA 5 bl.m. Sakhee (USA) – Donastrela (IRE) (Tagula (IRE)) [2018/19 b16.3m⁵ h15.5d h20.5d³ Mar 18] third foal: dam, lightly raced over hurdles, 1¼m winner who stayed 2m on Flat, half-sister to useful hurdler/fairly useful chaser (stayed 23f) Kanpai: fifth in mares bumper at Stratford: well held in mares novice hurdles. *Tom Gretton* **h75 b74**

SHAZZAMATAZ (IRE) 7 br.m. Presenting – Dame O'Neill (IRE) (Dr Massini (IRE)) [2018/19 h104p, b–: h21m* h22.1m⁴ h20.3g⁴ h19.6g³ h21.2g⁴ Oct 25] smallish mare: placed once in points: fair hurdler: won mares maiden at Kempton in May: stays easy 21f: acts on good to firm going: waited with. *Alex Hales* **h105**

SHEAR ROCK (IRE) 9 b.g. Spadoun (FR) – Sleeping Diva (FR) (Sleeping Car (FR)) [2018/19 c121, h–: c16.4s² c15.7v³ Dec 22] useful-looking gelding: winning hurdler: useful maiden chaser: best around 2½m: acted on soft and good to firm going: hooded until 2017/18: tried tongue tied: dead. *Kerry Lee* **c134 h–**

SHEELBEWHATSHEELBE (IRE) 9 b.m. Oscar (IRE) – Cheerymount (IRE) (Oscar Schindler (IRE)) [2018/19 h87: h24g⁵ h25g³ h23.9g* h24g² Aug 19] modest handicap hurdler: left Richard Phillips, won at Perth in August: stays 25f: acts on heavy going: in tongue tie last 2 starts. *Dan Skelton* **h94**

SHEEZA LEGEND 5 b.m. Midnight Legend – Roberta Back (IRE) (Bob Back (USA)) [2018/19 b16.5d⁶ b16.7g³ b16g⁶ Apr 25] has had breathing operation: third foal: sister to fair hurdler/fairly useful chaser Back By Midnight (2m-2¼m winner) and half-sister to fair **b80**

chaser Glance Back (2m/17f winner, by Passing Glance): dam, winning pointer, half-sister to fairly useful/irresolute chaser (19f winner) Ballywatt: form in bumpers only when third in maiden at Market Rasen in March: wears tongue tie. *Emma-Jane Bishop*

SHEILA'S EMPIRE (IRE) 4 b.f. Holy Roman Emperor (IRE) – Silk Mascara (IRE)   **h–**
(Barathea (IRE)) (Hdg Dec 27] modest maiden on Flat, stays
1½m: tailed off in juvenile on hurdling debut. *J. S. Moore*

SHEILA'S FANCY (IRE) 5 ch.g. Casamento (IRE) – Fancy Vivid (IRE) (Galileo (IRE))   **h105**
[2018/19 h19.2m⁴ h20.5g h21d h21.7s* h21.7d⁵ h24.2d h20.7g⁶ Apr 22] tall gelding: fair
maiden on Flat, stays 16.5f: fair handicap hurdler: won at Fontwell in January: should stay
beyond 2¾m: acts on soft going: usually front runner/races prominently. *Michael Attwater*

SHEILA TANIST (IRE) 6 b.m. Court Cave (IRE) – Douglas Park (IRE) (Definite   **h104**
Article) [2018/19 b15.8g b15.7g h16g⁶ h15.8s³ h20g² h16g* h21.2m² Oct 10] £20,000   **b67**
5-y-o: third foal: dam unraced half-sister to Maryland Hunt Cup winner Guts For Garters
and fairly useful hurdler/chaser (stayed 25f) Nom de Guerre: winning pointer: poor form
in bumpers: fair form over hurdles: won mares maiden at Worcester in September: stays
21f: acts on soft and good to firm going: in hood last 5 starts: wears tongue tie. *Ben Case*

SHELCOMEONFORDRUN (IRE) 6 b.m. Flemensfirth (USA) – Hazel Sylph (IRE)   **h–**
(Executive Perk) [2018/19 b20g⁶ b20m b17g⁵ b16.7d b18.1g h21.2g h18.5d Feb 22]   **b83**
€8,000 3-y-o, £12,000 5-y-o: sister to useful hurdler/winning pointer Abbey Lane (2m-3m
winner) and half-sister to a winning pointer by Good Thyne: dam unraced: point winner:
modest bumper performer (for T. E. Hyde): well held both outings over hurdles: tried in
hood/tongue tie. *Kayley Woollacott*

SHELFIELD (IRE) 4 b.c. Kayf Tara – Isabello (IRE) (Presenting) [2018/19 b15.7g h16.7g⁶ Mar   **h–**
27] good-topped colt: well beaten in bumper/novice hurdle. *Dan Skelton*   **b–**

SHELFORD (IRE) 10 b.g. Galileo (IRE) – Lyrical (Shirley Heights) [2018/19 c129,   **c117**
h130: h18.9s⁵ c24m⁵ c23.8m⁴ c24s c24.2dᵘʳ c24s³ Mar 2] winning gelding: winning   **h122**
hurdler: fairly useful handicap chaser: left Dan Skelton after second start: stays 3¼m: acts
on good to firm and heavy going: regularly in headgear: held up. *Kevin Frost*

SHELL CRYSTAL 5 b.m. Schiaparelli (GER) – Solent Crystal (Generous (IRE)) [2018/19   **b–**
b–: b15.3mᵖᵘ May 15] tongue tied, folded tamely in bumpers 7 months apart (had breathing
operation in between). *David Pipe*

SHELTER BELT 5 b.m. Josr Algarhoud (IRE) – Watch The Wind (High Kicker (USA))   **b–**
[2018/19 b16.4m Mar 22] second foal: half-sister to a winning pointer by Flying Legend:
dam (c80/h76) maiden jumper (raced mainly at 2m): made frame in point: tailed off in
mares bumper. *James Walton*

SHE MITE BITE (IRE) 6 b.m. Scorpion (IRE) – That's Moyne (IRE) (Flemensfirth   **h118**
(USA)) [2018/19 h21g² h20.5dᶠ h21d³ h19.8s² h23.8gᵇᵈ h20.5dᵖᵘ Mar 23] £28,000 5-y-o:
well-made mare: first foal: dam (c70/h100) 3m hurdle winner/winning pointer: off mark in
Irish points at second attempt: fairly useful form over hurdles: bred to stay 3m: acts on soft
going: travels strongly: has shown temperament. *Nicky Henderson*

SHENEEDEDTHERUN (IRE) 9 b.m. Kayf Tara – Lady Moon (FR) (Monsun (GER))   **c103**
[2018/19 c107, h–: c24.2d c23.6d⁶ c23.4g³ c25.2v² c24.2d⁴ c24d² c29.2d⁵ c26gᵖᵘ Apr 18]   **h–**
sturdy mare: has had breathing operation: winning hurdler: fair handicap chaser: left
Michael Scudamore after fifth start: stays 25f: acts on heavy going: normally tongue tied:
increasingly lazy. *Ben Pauling*

SHEPHERD'S BIGHT (IRE) 7 b.g. Court Cave (IRE) – Orador Sur Glane (IRE)   **h102**
(Shernazar) [2018/19 h90: h22.7g* h20g⁴ Nov 4] fair form over hurdles: won handicap at
Kelso on return in May: will stay 3m: acts on soft going. *Ruth Jefferson*

SHEPHERD STORM (IRE) 9 b.g. September Storm (GER) – Clerhane Belle (IRE)   **c92 ?**
(Astarabad (USA)) [2018/19 c16.3d c16.3gᶠ c21.6g² Jan 22] well beaten in bumpers: no
solid form in novice chases. *Chris Grant*

SHERIFF 4 br.g. Lawman (FR) – Chatline (IRE) (One Cool Cat (USA)) [2018/19 h16.3m⁵   **h–**
h15.8sᵖᵘ Jul 29] fair on Flat, stays 1m: tongue tied, no show in juvenile hurdles. *Amy Murphy*

SHERIFF GARRETT (IRE) 5 b.g. Lawman (FR) – Few Are Chosen (IRE) (Sulamani   **h119**
(IRE)) [2018/19 h16.7m⁶ h20.6g³ h22.1s² h20.1s² h23.1g³ h21.2g⁴ h20.1g² h19.7d²
h20.1s* h19.9s² Dec 26] dam sister to useful 2m hurdle winner Much Acclaimed: fair on
Flat, stays 16.5f: fairly useful hurdler: won handicap at Hexham in December: best around
2½m: acts on soft going: in cheekpieces last 4 starts, also tongue tied last 2. *Tim Easterby*

SHE'S A LEGEND 4 b.f. Midnight Legend – Sylroy (Silver Patriarch (IRE)) [2018/19   **h–**
b16.5d h15.8dᵖᵘ Jan 28] second foal: sister to a winning pointer: dam (h89) 2½m hurdle   **b–**
winner: no promise in mares bumper or juvenile hurdle. *Bill Turner*

SHE'S A PRIMADIVA 7 b.m. Primitive Academy – Petrovka (IRE) (King's Theatre **b–**
(IRE)) [2018/19 b16.2m b16.8s Dec 26] first foal: dam (h99) unreliable 2m maiden
hurdler: down field in bumpers. *Sean Regan*

SHE'SASUPERMACK (IRE) 6 b.m. Arakan (USA) – Castleknock (IRE) (Executive **h89**
Perk) [2018/19 h16.8g⁶ h19.9d³ Apr 23] third foal: dam unraced half-sister to useful
hurdler (stayed 3m) Vast Consumption: maiden Irish pointer: modest form over hurdles:
stays 2½m: acts on good to soft going: waited with. *Iain Jardine*

SHE'S BLORENGE 4 ch.f. Arvico (FR) – Lefty's Dollbaby (USA) (Brocco (USA)) **b–**
[2018/19 b12.4s⁴ Dec 8] half-sister to 3 winners, including fair 2½m hurdle winner See Me
Here (by State City): dam US 1m winner: hooded, never on terms in junior bumper at
Wetherby. *Michael Scudamore*

SHE'S GINA (GER) 6 b.m. It's Gino (GER) – Song of Night (GER) (Tiger Hill (IRE)) **h107**
[2018/19 h105: h16d⁴ h19.2g h16.2s⁴ h16d h16v⁴ h19.2v⁶ h15.3g⁶ h23.9d^pu Apr 24] good-
topped mare: fair handicap hurdler: won mares event at Warwick in May: should stay
beyond 2m: acts on heavy going: in headgear last 3 starts. *Seamus Mullins*

SHESHOON SONNY (FR) 4 b.g. Youmzain (IRE) – Minnie's Mystery (FR) (Highest **b95**
Honor (FR)) [2018/19 b15.3g⁴ b16.8d² b16d* Mar 19] brother to 1¼m bumper winner
White Valiant and half-brother to several winners on Flat: dam 7f-1½m winner in Jersey:
fairly useful form in bumpers, improving further when winning at Wetherby in March.
Alan King

SHESTHEBUSINESS 8 b.m. Midnight Legend – Sabreflight (Sabrehill (USA)) **h–**
[2018/19 h–, b72: h23.3g h22.1g h23.9g^pu Aug 18] smallish, lengthy mare: little sign of
ability: has worn hood: wears tongue tie. *Susan Corbett*

SHILLINGSWORTH (IRE) 6 b.g. Presenting – Miss Bobs Worth (IRE) (Bob Back **h99**
(USA)) [2018/19 h104, b71: h17.7m³ h19.9m^F h15.3g^F h21.4g h21.4g⁵ h19s^ur h15.3g⁵ Apr
3] well-made gelding: fair maiden hurdler: stays 21f: acts on good to firm going. *Colin Tizzard*

SHIMBA HILLS 8 b.g. Sixties Icon – Search Party (Rainbow Quest (USA)) [2018/19 h–: **c62**
c17.8g⁴ h15.9s⁵ h20.5d^pu Jan 6] sturdy gelding: fair handicap hurdler at best: lightly raced **h57**
and little form since 2016/17, including novice chase: best around 2m: acts on heavy
going: wears cheekpieces/tongue tie. *Lawney Hill*

SHIMLA DAWN (IRE) 11 b.g. Indian Danehill (IRE) – Tina Thyne (IRE) (Good Thyne **c113**
(USA)) [2018/19 c109, h106: c26.2g³ c23.8m* c21.1d^pu Apr 4] lengthy gelding: winning **h–**
pointer: winning hurdler: fair hunter chaser nowadays: won at Musselburgh in February:
stays 3m: acts on good to firm and heavy going: tried in hood. *Mrs C. Drury*

SHIMMER'S ROCK (IRE) 7 b.m. Westerner – Thuringe (FR) (Turgeon (USA)) **c–**
[2018/19 h17d^pu h16g⁶ h16v h20g⁶ h23.5d^pu c21g^ur Feb 13] £35,000 3-y-o: sturdy mare: **h–**
fourth foal: half-sister to smart bumper winner/top-class hurdler The New One (2m-21f
winner, by King's Theatre): dam French maiden (third in 15f hurdle): runner-up both starts
in points: bumper winner: fairly useful hurdler: little impact in various events in 2018/19:
unseated early on chasing debut: stays 2½m: acts on heavy going. *P. E. Collins, Ireland*

SHINE AWAY (IRE) 9 b.m. Robin des Pres (FR) – Bramble Bree (IRE) (Rashar (USA)) **c77**
[2018/19 c100, h70: h19.9g² c25.5g⁴ c24.2g^pu c21.2m h20.1g^pu Oct 5] workmanlike mare: **h84**
maiden hurdler: fair handicap chaser at best: stayed 21f: acted on soft going: dead.
Sue Smith

SHINE BABY SHINE 5 b.m. Aqlaam – Rosewood Belle (USA) (Woodman (USA)) **h95**
[2018/19 h108: h19.7g^pu h16.6m⁵ h20.6s^pu h20.5d^pu h20.3d Apr 24] leggy mare: has had
breathing operation: modest handicap hurdler: should be suited by further than 2m: acts on
soft going. *Philip Kirby*

SHINING ROMEO 7 b.g. Royal Applause – Silver Pivotal (IRE) (Pivotal) [2018/19 **h122**
h120: h19.6g* h15.9g³ h15.7g^pu Oct 10] fairly useful handicap hurdler: won at Huntingdon
in May: stayed 2½m: acted on soft and good to firm going: raced towards rear: dead.
Denis Quinn

SHININSTAR (IRE) 10 b.g. Westerner – Shiny Button (Bob's Return (IRE)) [2018/19 **c86**
c80, h–: c16.5g³ c20.3g³ c17.4g⁵ c20.3g³ c20.3d³ c20d* c19.9d⁴ c20.3d c19.4g* Apr 14] **h–**
maiden hurdler: modest handicap chaser: won novice events at Ludlow in December and
Stratford in April: stays 2½m: acts on good to soft going: has worn hood: often travels
strongly. *John Groucott*

SHINOOKI (IRE) 12 br.g. Blueprint (IRE) – Rapid Response (IRE) (Be My Native **c–**
(USA)) [2018/19 c109, h105: c29.1g^pu h26d May 30] fair handicap hurdler/chaser: well **h–**
below form in 2018/19: stays 25f: acts on heavy going: has worn headgear: often leads.
Alex Hales

SHINTORI (FR) 7 b.g. Enrique – La Masai (FR) (Bernebeau (FR)) [2018/19 c–, h83: h21.7m³ h21.6s⁶ c19.7s* c19.4d⁴ c17s³ c16.1d⁵ c19.5m* Mar 29] lengthy, workmanlike gelding: maiden handicap chaser: won at Plumpton in December and Fontwell in March: stays easy 2¾m: acts on soft and good to firm going: has worn headgear/ tongue tie: irresolute. *Jack R. Barber*
c99 §
h80

SHIPWRECK (IRE) 8 b.m. Shantou (USA) – Skeleton Coast (IRE) (Bob Back (USA)) [2018/19 h21.5g⁶ h21.3g* h23.9g h21.8g h18.8d⁴ h24.8g⁴ c21g h22.5s h19d h24g Jan 14] fourth foal: dam unraced: modest handicap hurdler: won at Downpatrick in June: mistakes when well beaten in maiden on chasing debut: stays 25f: best form on good going. *Colin A. McBratney, Ireland*
c–
h90

SHIROCCAN ROLL 5 b.g. Shirocco (GER) – Folie Dancer (Exit To Nowhere (USA)) [2018/19 b77: b16.8m³ h16.8d* h16g² h15.3g² h15.8d h19d^pu h19.5g³ Apr 26] fair form in bumpers: fairly useful novice hurdler: won at Newton Abbot in September: unproven beyond 17f: acts on good to soft going. *Emma Lavelle*
h116
b88

SHIROCCODEE 6 b.m. Shirocco (GER) – La Marianne (Supreme Leader) [2018/19 h–, b–: h23.3d May 5] well held in bumpers: little form in novice hurdles. *Alex Hales*
h–
b–

SHISHKIN (IRE) 5 b.g. Sholokhov (IRE) – Labarynth (IRE) (Exit To Nowhere (USA)) [2018/19 b16s* Mar 16] €28,000 3-y-o, £170,000 4-y-o: third foal: half-brother to a winning pointer by Presenting: dam, winning pointer, half-sister to very smart hurdler (stayed 3m) Voler La Vedette and useful hurdler/staying chaser Hennessy: off mark in Irish points at second attempt: 4/6, won maiden bumper at Kempton impressively by 8 lengths from Certainly Red: exciting prospect. *Nicky Henderson*
b104 p

SHIVERMETIMBERS (IRE) 7 br.g. Black Sam Bellamy (IRE) – Kimouna (FR) (Round Sovereign (FR)) [2018/19 h111§: h16d h19.5s h25.5d⁵ Mar 9] good-bodied gelding: form over hurdles only when runner-up in maiden at Ludlow in 2017/18: tried in hood: temperamental. *Venetia Williams*
h– §

SHOAL BAY (IRE) 6 b.g. Gold Well – Ring Hill (Bering) [2018/19 h118, b90: h22g⁶ h16.4g h15.7g⁵ h24.3g⁶ h21s⁴ h24.3m⁵ Apr 12] well-made gelding: will make a chaser: bumper winner: fair handicap hurdler: should stay further than 19f: acts on soft going: tried in blinkers: wears tongue tie. *Colin Tizzard*
h114

SHOCONA'S JOY (IRE) 5 b.m. Primary (USA) – Shocona (IRE) (Oscar Schindler (IRE)) [2018/19 b17s³ Dec 16] £7,000 4-y-o: second foal: half-sister to fair hurdler/fairly useful chaser Henry's Joy (2½m winner, by Craigsteel): dam winning pointer: made frame both starts in Irish points: well beaten in mares bumper. *Donald McCain*
b58

SHORT FLIGHT (IRE) 7 b.g. Trans Island – Surricate (FR) (True Brave (USA)) [2018/19 h59: h22.1g* h23.9g⁵ Aug 18] third in Irish point: modest handicap hurdler: won at Cartmel on return in July: stays 2¾m: acts on soft going: in visor last 2 starts. *Julia Brooke*
h89

SHOTAVODKA (IRE) 13 ch.g. Alderbrook – Another Vodka (IRE) (Moscow Society (USA)) [2018/19 c129, h–: c20.8g⁵ May 4] stocky gelding: point winner: winning hurdler: fairly useful hunter chaser: stays 3¼m: acts on heavy going: wore headgear for former yard: tried in tongue tie: travels strongly held up. *Miss H. Brookshaw*
c115
h–

SHOTGUN SALLY (IRE) 6 b.m. Milan – Awesome Miracle (IRE) (Supreme Leader) [2018/19 h17.1d h19.9s⁵ h20.6g h15.8d h23.9g h23.1s c24g^pu Apr 13] €10,000 3-y-o: sixth foal: closely related to useful hurdler/smart chaser Shotgun Paddy (2½m-29f winner, by Brian Boru) and half-sister to 2 winners, including fairly useful hurdler/chaser Buster Thomas (19f/2½m winner, by Westerner), stays 3m: dam unraced: won Irish point on debut: little form in varied company under Rules: tried in cheekpieces: tongue tied bar on hurdling debut. *Oliver Greenall*
c–
h–
b–

SHOWEM SILVER (IRE) 8 b.g. Winged Love (IRE) – Swap Shop (IRE) (Lord Americo) [2018/19 c19.9s⁶ c19.7g c25g h24g^pu c25g^f h24s^pu c20.1s^pu c20g c23.9d^pu c19.2s⁵ c21.4g^pu Apr 3] fairly useful hurdle winner: little form since 2016/17 (including over fences), leaving Noel Meade after sixth start: has worn headgear. *Jennie Candlish*
c98
h–

SHOW OF FORCE 4 gr.f. Lethal Force (IRE) – Craighall (Dubawi (IRE)) [2018/19 h15.5g⁴ h17.7v Dec 11] fair on Flat, stays 1¼m: poor form over hurdles. *Nick Mitchell*
h72

SHOW ON THE ROAD 8 b.g. Flemensfirth (USA) – Roses of Picardy (IRE) (Roselier (FR)) [2018/19 h128: h20.6g⁴ c19.2g³ c19.2s^su h21.4g⁵ c22.6s⁶ h21.4g⁵ Apr 14] lengthy, useful-looking gelding: fairly useful handicap hurdler: easily better completed effort over fences when third in maiden at Exeter on chasing debut: stays 21f: acts on heavy going: usually hooded. *Philip Hobbs*
c123
h120

SHOW PROMISE 5 b.g. Josr Algarhoud (IRE) – Show Potential (IRE) (Glacial Storm **b91** (USA)) [2018/19 b15.7g ab16.3s² b16.4v² Mar 16] second foal: half-brother to bumper winner/fair hurdler Improved (23f winner, by Rainwatch): dam lightly-raced half-sister to useful staying chaser Well Refreshed: fair form when runner-up last 2 outings in bumpers. *Philip Kirby*

SHOW'S OVER (IRE) 8 b.g. Curtain Time (IRE) – Sailors Run (IRE) (Roselier (FR)) **c84 §** [2018/19 c78, h–: c20g c20.3g² c21.4g⁵ c16g² c16.4s* c16.3d⁴ c19.7s Dec 17] maiden **h–** hurdler: poor handicap chaser: won at Sedgefield in November: left Tim Vaughan after first start: stays 23f, effective at shorter: acts on heavy going: wears headgear/tongue tie: usually races prominently: unreliable. *Fergal O'Brien*

SHPADOINKLE DAY (IRE) 4 ch.g. Champs Elysees – Idle Chatter (IRE) (Galileo **b92** (IRE)) [2018/19 b13.7g² Nov 13] close second in junior bumper at Huntingdon: dead. *Keith Dalgleish*

SHREWD TACTICS (IRE) 8 ch.g. Broadway Flyer (USA) – Taking My Time (IRE) **c61** (High Roller (IRE)) [2018/19 c16v⁵ c16sᵘʳ c20v⁵ Dec 21] rangy gelding: winning Irish **h–** pointer: modest form over hurdles: no show in chases since close second in novice handicap on debut over fences in 2016/17 (missed following season): stays 2¼m: acts on heavy going: in tongue tie first 3 starts over fences. *Evan Williams*

SHROUGHMORE LASS (IRE) 8 b.m. Flemensfirth (USA) – Smokey Bandit (IRE) **c–** (Oscar (IRE)) [2018/19 h100: c20.3gᵖᵘ h16v³ h21.7d⁴ h16g Apr 10] sturdy mare: has had **h97** breathing operation: runner-up all 3 starts in Irish points: modest handicap hurdler: pulled up in novice handicap on chasing debut: stays 2½m: acts on heavy going: tried in cheekpieces. *Henry Oliver*

SHRUBLAND 6 b.g. High Chaparral (IRE) – Ratukidul (FR) (Danehill (USA)) [2018/19 **h101** h106: h16.8g² h19.9g⁶ h16g⁴ Jun 24] sturdy gelding: fair handicap hurdler: stays 21f: acts on good to soft going: wears headgear: held up. *Dan Skelton*

SHTAN ON (IRE) 8 b.g. Generous (IRE) – Lady Oakwell (IRE) (King's Ride) [2018/19 **h102** h101: h21.4v h24.3s³ h24.3d⁵ h20.6v⁵ Mar 16] runner-up in Irish point: fair maiden hurdler: stays 3m: acts on heavy going: in cheekpieces last 2 starts. *Alistair Whillans*

SHUFOOG 6 b.m. Mawatheeq (USA) – Hamloola (Red Ransom (USA)) [2018/19 h76: **h103** h15.3m* h16d⁴ h15.7g h15.8m² h16g³ h15.3m⁵ h15.3g⁵ h15.8g⁴ Apr 22] leggy mare: fair handicap hurdler: won at Wincanton (conditionals) in May and Warwick (mares) in October: raced around 2m: acts on good to firm and heavy going. *Mark Usher*

SHUHOOD (IRE) 4 b.g. Tamayuz – Walayef (USA) (Danzig (USA)) [2018/19 h15.8m³ **h97** Oct 10] useful on Flat, stays 11.5f: 1/3, keen and not fluent when close third in juvenile maiden at Ludlow on hurdling debut: sold 60,000 gns. *Ian Williams*

SHUTSCOMBE HILL 7 b.g. Arvico (FR) – Storm Kitten (IRE) (Catrail (USA)) **h–** [2018/19 b–: h17.7s⁶ h15.3gᵖᵘ Apr 3] has had breathing operations: no form in bumper/ over hurdles (in tongue tie). *Victor Dartnall*

SHUT THE BOX (IRE) 5 ch.g. Doyen (IRE) – Bond Holder (IRE) (Hawkeye (IRE)) **h106 p** [2018/19 b89: b17.7s³ b16.7v⁴ h15.9g⁵ h15.9d* Mar 18] fair form in bumpers: similar form **b86** in maiden hurdles at Plumpton, much better effort when landing odds in March: will prove suited by further than 2m: should do better again. *Chris Gordon*

SHUTTHEGATE (IRE) 5 b.g. Milan – Miss Conduct (Overbury (IRE)) [2018/19 **b–** b15.8s Feb 26] well beaten in bumper. *John Spearing*

SIANNES STAR (IRE) 6 b.g. Arakan (USA) – Musical Madam (IRE) (Musical Pursuit) **h126** [2018/19 b79: h16.8g⁵ h20.6gᵘʳ h23.1m² h22.1m⁶ h19.9g³ h15.7m⁵ h16.7g⁴ h18.6g⁶ h16.2g* Apr 24] rather unfurnished gelding: fairly useful hurdler: much improved when winning handicap at Perth in April: best efforts around 2m: acts on good to firm going: tried in hood (has pulled hard). *Brian Ellison*

SIDBURY HILL 11 ch.g. Midnight Legend – Flora Macdonald (Alflora (IRE)) [2018/19 **c–** c26gᵖᵘ May 17] workmanlike gelding: winning pointer/hurdler: fairly useful form in **h–** novice handicaps in 2015/16: pulled up in novice hunter sole outing in chases since: best around 2½m: acts on heavy going: in cheekpieces last 2 starts. *Mrs Sally Rawlins*

SIDE OF THE ROAD (IRE) 7 b.m. Beneficial – Roses And Wine (IRE) (Roselier (FR)) **h84** [2018/19 h85: h19.5v h19.9s⁵ h21.4d h16d⁴ h16.4m* Mar 22] poor handicap hurdler: won at Musselburgh in March: should stay 2½m: acts on good to firm and heavy going: tried in cheekpieces/tongue tie. *Donald Whillans*

SIDEWAYS (IRE) 8 b.g. Gamut (IRE) – Daras Mayo (IRE) (Kasmayo) [2018/19 c25.8v³ c20g c19.4s⁶ c25.3v³ c21.2d* c26.3d* c21.2g³ c26.3s² c24.2d* Mar 15] maiden hurdler: fair handicap chaser: progressed well in 2018/19, winning at Fakenham (amateurs event) and Sedgefield in January and Fakenham again in March: stays 3¼m: acts on heavy going: in cheekpieces last 5 starts. *Christian Williams* **c114** **h–**

SID HOODIE (IRE) 5 b.m. Rip Van Winkle (IRE) – Universe (Cape Cross (IRE)) [2018/19 b16.7g b15.8g⁴ b16.8g² b16.8s* h16g⁶ h19.6g⁴ h15.8g⁴ h15.3g² h16g⁴ h16m* Apr 22] second foal: half-sister to a winner on Flat abroad by Dream Ahead: dam unraced: modest form in bumpers: won maiden at Newton Abbot in July: similar form over hurdles: won handicap at Fakenham in April: unproven beyond 2m: acts on good to firm going (bumper win on soft): tried in cheekpieces: wears tongue tie. *Charlie Mann* **h104** **b83**

SIDI ISMAEL (FR) 5 b.g. Great Pretender (IRE) – Tetouane (FR) (Colonel Collins (USA)) [2018/19 b17g⁴ b16s³ b16.2d* Mar 26] €48,000 3-y-o: third foal: dam lightly-raced half-sister to dam of smart French chaser (stayed 3¾m) Sidi Bouknadel: runner-up in Irish point: fair form in bumpers: best effort when well-backed winner of maiden at Hexham in March: will be suited by 2½m. *Keith Dalgleish* **b93**

SIDSTEEL (IRE) 8 b.g. Craigsteel – Clare Hogan (IRE) (Moscow Society (USA)) [2018/19 h75: c24g Apr 25] poor maiden hurdler: off 17 months, tailed off in novice handicap on chasing debut: stays 23f: in tongue tie last 3 starts. *John Groucott* **c–** **h–**

SIENNA ROYALE (IRE) 5 b.m. Sholokhov (IRE) – Dartmeet (IRE) (Presenting) [2018/19 h77, b–: h18.5g⁵ h19.5d⁶ h19.9s h23.9g Feb 19] leggy mare: modest form over hurdles: should be suited by 2½m+. *Nigel Hawke* **h89**

SIERRA OSCAR (IRE) 7 b.g. Robin des Champs (FR) – John's Eliza (IRE) (Dr Massini (IRE)) [2018/19 h94: h20.2g³ h19.9g h20.2g⁶ h23.9g h20.2g h18.1m⁶ h19.8gᵖᵘ Dec 3] compact gelding: poor handicap hurdler: stayed 21f: best form on good going: dead. *Jean McGregor* **h79**

SIGNIFICANT OTHER (IRE) 5 b.m. Fame And Glory – Etoile Margot (FR) (Garde Royale) [2018/19 b15.7g⁶ Jun 5] closely related to 2 winners by Scorpion, including bumper winner/fairly useful hurdler Royal Village (2½m-23f winner), and half-sister to 2 winners, including useful hurdler/very smart chaser Village Vic (17f-21f winner, by Old Vic): dam, French 17f chase winner, also 11f winner on Flat: sixth in mares bumper at Southwell. *Dan Skelton* **b79**

SIGN OF WAR (IRE) 5 b.g. Oscar (IRE) – Irish Wedding (IRE) (Bob Back (USA)) [2018/19 b17.7g⁴ h15.5d⁵ h19g³ h16d⁴ h20s Apr 7] £40,000 3-y-o: fifth foal: brother to useful hurdler/smart chaser Rather Be (2m-2½m winner) and closely related to bumper winner/smart 2m hurdler Sign of A Victory (2m by Kayf Tara) and bumper winner/useful hurdler Art of Security (2m-2½m winner, by High Chaparral): dam (b94) bumper winner: well beaten in bumper: modest form first 2 starts over hurdles. *Evan Williams* **h95** **b71**

SIGURD (GER) 7 ch.g. Sholokhov (IRE) – Sky News (GER) (Highest Honor (FR)) [2018/19 h–: h20.1g c21.2g³ c20.1g⁵ c21.2gꟳ h20.1g⁶ h20.3g h19.7g² h23.1g³ h21.3g⁵ Apr 11] sturdy gelding: has had breathing operation: fair handicap hurdler: stiff tasks on completed outings over fences: stays 23f: acts on good to firm going: sometimes in cheekpieces: in tongue tie last 3 starts. *Joanne Foster* **c98** **h102**

SILENT ACCOUNT (IRE) 8 b.g. Jimble (FR) – Mary Money (Vettori (IRE)) [2018/19 c89, h88: c21g c16m⁴ c19.5g c16.5g⁵ c21.4g⁵ c22.5g⁵ c15.7gᴿ Oct 25] placed in points: modest maiden hurdler/chaser: left Des Donovan after fourth start: stayed 21f: best form on good going: tried in headgear: in tongue tie last 4 starts: dead. *Conor Dore* **c86** **h–**

SILENT ASSISTANT (IRE) 5 b.g. Sans Frontieres (IRE) – Monanig Lass (IRE) (Topanoora) [2018/19 h21d h19.4g⁴ Dec 29] €24,000 3-y-o, £50,000 4-y-o: fifth foal: dam, winning pointer, half-sister to useful hurdler/chaser (2¾m-25f winner) Wise Oscar: won Irish point on debut: much better effort over hurdles when fourth in novice at Doncaster: likely to progress further. *Emma Lavelle* **h109 p**

SILENT ENCORE (IRE) 7 ch.g. Curtain Time (IRE) – What Can I Say (IRE) (Mister Lord (USA)) [2018/19 h107: h19.9d h23.3s⁵ h23.4d c20d⁴ c24.2vᵖᵘ c24gᵖᵘ Mar 28] workmanlike gelding: has had breathing operation: maiden hurdler, fair form at best: modest form when fourth in novice event at Lingfield, sole completion in handicap chases: should stay 3m: acts on good to soft going: in cheekpieces last 3 starts: wears tongue tie. *Ben Case* **c94** **h82**

SILENT MAN (IRE) 9 br.g. Morozov (USA) – Outdoor Heather (IRE) (Presenting) **c93**
[2018/19 c97, h72: c22.5m⁵ c23.8g⁶ c20g⁵ Jul 4] good-topped gelding: winning hurdler: **h—**
modest handicap chaser: stays 3¼m: acts on soft going: wears tongue tie. *Tom Weston*

SILENT STEPS (IRE) 8 b.m. Milan – Taking Silk (IRE) (Mister Lord (USA)) [2018/19 **c109 §**
c111, h107: c23.8m³ c22.5g³ c20d⁵ c24s* c20.6gᵖᵘ c24.2d³ c22.5vᵖᵘ c25.2d⁶ h25.5g⁴ h26.4g⁴ **h102**
c24d⁴ Apr 24] good-topped mare: fair maiden hurdler: fair handicap chaser: won mares
event at Southwell in December: left Paul Nicholls after first start: stays 3¼m: acts on soft
and good to firm going: usually in headgear: wears tongue tie: temperamental. *Neil King*

SILK OR SCARLET (IRE) 7 ch.g. Mahler – Spirit of Clanagh (IRE) (Zagreb (USA)) **h98**
[2018/19 h100: h22.7g h21.4s² h24s⁵ Jan 29] compact gelding: modest maiden hurdler:
stays 21f: acts on heavy going. *N. W. Alexander*

SILK RUN (IRE) 6 b.m. Oscar (IRE) – Asian Alliance (IRE) (Soviet Star (USA)) [2018/19 **h115**
h86, b80: h16.2g² h18.5g³ h15.8mᶠ h17.2m⁵ h19.6g* h23.1g* h26g³ h21.2m h19.5m* Apr
22] angular mare: fairly useful hurdler: won mares maiden and handicap at Bangor in
August and, having had breathing operation, another handicap at Chepstow in April:
probably stays 3¼m: acts on good to firm going: in tongue tie last 3 starts: front runner/
races prominently. *Tom Lacey*

SILVA ECLIPSE 6 gr.g. Multiplex – Linen Line (Double Eclipse (IRE)) [2018/19 h120: **h125**
h19.6d⁴ h23.3d⁴ h22.8v² h24.3d² h24.3g² h20.5sᵖᵘ h23.1g⁶ Mar 27] fairly useful handicap
hurdler: stays 3m: acts on heavy going: usually races prominently. *Sue Smith*

SILVER CONCORDE 11 b.g. Dansili – Sacred Pearl (IRE) (Daylami (IRE)) [2018/19 **h97**
h137: h20.1g⁴ Jun 16] smallish gelding: useful hurdler at best: well below form in handicap
sole outing in 2018/19: stays 2½m: acts on soft going: front runner/races prominently,
often travels strongly. *Keith Dalgleish*

SILVER DRAGON 11 gr.g. Silver Patriarch (IRE) – Gotogeton (Le Moss) [2018/19 c–§, **c– §**
h74§: h25mᵖᵘ May 7] poor maiden hurdler/chaser: stays 4m: acts on heavy going: usually **h– §**
in headgear: tried in tongue tie: often leads: temperamental. *Mike Sowersby*

SILVER FOREVER (IRE) 5 gr.m. Jeremy (USA) – Silver Prayer (IRE) (Roselier (FR)) **b104**
[2018/19 b16s* b15.8d³ b15.7d* b16s² Mar 9] compact mare: seventh foal: half-sister to
fairly useful hurdler/chaser Crown Hill (2m-3¼m winner, by Definite Article) and fairly
useful chaser Ruapehu (25f/3¼m winner, by Presenting): dam unraced: won on debut in
Irish point: fairly useful form in bumpers: won at Chepstow in November and Ascot
(mares) in February: placed in listed mares events at Huntingdon and Sandown (length
behind Misty Whisky) otherwise. *Paul Nicholls*

SILVERGROVE 11 b.g. Old Vic – Classic Gale (USA) (Classic Cliche (IRE)) [2018/19 **c104**
c24.2d² c23.8m⁴ c24.2m* Apr 22] workmanlike gelding: won last 4 outings in points: **h—**
maiden hurdler: fair hunter chaser nowadays: beat below-par sole rival Jack Yeats by wide
margin at Fakenham in April: stays 27f: acts on good to firm and heavy going: wears
tongue tie. *J. P. Owen*

SILVER HALLMARK 5 br.g. Shirocco (GER) – Gaye Sophie (Environment Friend) **b92**
[2018/19 b16.3d³ Mar 2] £115,000 4-y-o: rather unfurnished gelding: sixth foal: half-
brother to 3 winners, including bumper winner/useful hurdler Gayebury (2½m-3m winner,
by Overbury) and fair hurdler/fairly useful chaser Monbeg Chit Chat (2m-2½m winner, by
Kayf Tara): dam once-raced half-sister to smart staying chaser Simon: won on debut in
Irish point: 11/2, promise when 7 lengths third to McFabulous in bumper at Newbury: will
stay at least 2½m. *Fergal O'Brien*

SILVERHOW (IRE) 8 br.g. Yeats (IRE) – Monte Solaro (IRE) (Key of Luck (USA)) **c109**
[2018/19 c129, h–: c23.6d c19.9d⁵ c23s⁵ c20.2g⁵ h18.5d h23.9s Apr 7] good-topped **h108**
gelding: fairly useful hurdler/chaser, below best in 2018/19: stayed 21f: acted on heavy
going: tried in tongue tie: dead. *Colin Tizzard*

SILVER KAYF 7 gr.g. Kayf Tara – Silver Spinner (Silver Patriarch (IRE)) [2018/19 h127: **c– p**
c23.6d⁵ h23.8g h21.4s³ Mar 7] well-made gelding: fairly useful handicap hurdler: not fluent **h129**
when remote fifth in novice at Huntingdon on chasing debut (should do better): should stay
3m: acts on soft going: tried in cheekpieces: front runner/races prominently. *Kim Bailey*

SILVER MAN 12 gr.g. Silver Patriarch (IRE) – Another Mans Cause (FR) (Highest Honor **c107**
(FR)) [2018/19 c130, h–: c24dᵖᵘ c29.4g⁵ c26.1mᵖᵘ c24.2g c24g⁴ Apr 25] lengthy **h—**
gelding: maiden hurdler: fair handicap chaser nowadays: left Jo Hughes after fourth start:
stays 29f: acts on good to firm and good to soft going: normally in headgear. *Steve Flook*

SILVER NICKEL (IRE) 5 g.g. Gold Well – Cooper's Rose (IRE) (Roselier (FR)) **b80 ?**
[2018/19 b17.7d b15.3g b16m³ Apr 22] workmanlike gelding: seemingly modest form in
bumpers, though probably flattered when third at Chepstow. *Seamus Mullins*

SILVER QUAY (IRE) 7 gr.g. Dark Angel (IRE) – She Runs (FR) (Sheyrann) [2018/19   **h104**
h91: h18.5g^{pu} h21.6g^6 h18.5m^5 h18.5m h16.5m^5 h19d^4 h16.5d^3 h19d* h19s* h19.2v h19d
Mar 11] sturdy gelding: fair handicap hurdler: won at Taunton in January and February
(conditionals): stays 19f: acts on soft and good to firm going: tried in hood. *Jimmy Frost*

SILVER ROQUE (FR) 13 b.g. Laveron – Bible Gun (FR) (Pistolet Bleu (FR)) [2018/19   **c117**
c–, h–: c20.8g^3 May 4] good-topped gelding: multiple point winner: maiden hurdler: **h–**
formerly useful chaser: third in hunter at Cheltenham sole outing in 2018/19: unproven
beyond 21f: acts on heavy going: has worn cheekpieces/tongue tie. *Mary Vestey*

SILVER SEA 6 b.g. Sholokhov (IRE) – Sword Roche (GER) (Laroche (GER)) [2018/19   **h104**
h18.5m^3 h17.7g^5 h16.8g^4 h21.6g^3 h21.4m^4 h21.7d^7 h20.7d^5 h19d Dec 30] fair handicap
hurdler: won novice event at Fontwell in November: stays 2¾m: acts on good to firm and
good to soft going: in tongue tie last 3 starts. *Seamus Mullins*

SILVER STAR (FR) 6 gr.g. Silver Frost (IRE) – Suerte (Halling (USA)) [2018/19   **h124**
h16.7d^6 h16g^3 h18.8d^2 h16g* h16g^3 h18.8s* h16g^3 h16.4g h16d^F h16s Mar 3] useful-
looking gelding: once-raced on Flat: fairly useful hurdler: won conditionals maiden at
Kilbeggan in September and minor event at Downpatrick in October: stays 19f: acts on soft
going: has worn hood: wears tongue tie. *Gordon Elliott, Ireland*

SILVER STREAK (IRE) 6 gr.g. Dark Angel (IRE) – Happy Talk (IRE) (Hamas   **h154**
(IRE)) [2018/19 h128: h15.7g* h15.8d* h16.4g^2 h16.8s^2 h15.7d^2 h16.4s^3 h20d^5
Apr 4]

    'There were fears that despite the sponsor's generosity there would be a
disappointing turn-out for an event due to be run so late in the season on ground that
would probably be on the firm side; the best hurdlers, those trained for the Champion
Hurdle in mid-March, normally complete their racing programme by mid-April at
the latest.' That was how *Chasers & Hurdlers 1977/78* prefaced its report on the
inaugural running of the Royal Doulton Handicap Hurdle, by far the most valuable
handicap hurdle ever staged on British soil at that time, and the fourth biggest
stake on offer that season behind only the Grand National, the Gold Cup and the
Champion Hurdle. Fears that the Royal Doulton would be a damp squib proved to
be unfounded, as the race, staged at Haydock on May 1st, attracted a field of twenty
which included the first four from that season's Champion Hurdle, Monksfield, Sea
Pigeon, Night Nurse and Beacon Light and another hurdling luminary from that era
Bird's Nest, the race run on going officially described as firm! Victory went to one
of the lighter weights, the Fred Rimell-trained Royal Gaye, who held on by three
quarters of a length from Monksfield (conceding the winner 28 lb) in a course record
time (over seven seconds inside the previous one), with the typically reliable Night
Nurse a further two and a half lengths away in third. Monksfield put up another
fine weight-carrying performance when runner-up again twelve months later, going
down by two lengths, conceding 13 lb to the winner Beacon Light, who had finished
third behind Monksfield when the latter gained his second Champion Hurdle less
than two months before.

    After initial fears for this long-standing valuable spring prize had proved
unfounded, the race eventually, and inevitably, lost some of its lustre. Renamed
the Swinton in 1985 after Royal Doulton ended its sponsorship, the race suffered
a severe dip in prize money for the 2011 renewal which saw winning connections
receive just £28,505—which was £2,000 less than the first prize thirty years earlier!
That 1981 renewal was won by Royal Gaye's half-brother Gaye Chance who
provided the final big-race win in the illustrious training career of Rimell, who died
a couple of months later aged sixty-eight. Gaye Chance rounded off a fine novice
campaign with victory under Sam Morshead, who died in September 2018 at the
age of just sixty-three after his own cancer battle. Haydock proved a happy hunting
ground for Morshead, his first big win coming there when an amateur on subsequent
Cheltenham Gold Cup winner Royal Frolic in the 1976 Greenall Whitley Gold Cup.
Perth is the track with which Morshead will be forever linked, though, having acted
as clerk of the course and then general manager there after retiring from the saddle,
his association with Perth stretching for nearly thirty years.

    Perth is a bit out of the way for Vale of Glamorgan-based trainer Evan
Williams, who has made the 922-mile round trip just five times during the past five
seasons (and not once in 2018/19). Merseyside isn't anything like so daunting a

Pertemps Network Swinton Handicap Hurdle, Haydock—
the grey Silver Streak pounces late to overhaul Chesterfield, providing trainer Evan Williams with a
record-equalling fourth win in the race

journey in the horsebox, however, and Haydock Park in May has been the subject of several lucrative journeys for Williams in recent years. The trainer took advantage of a significant prize money rise for the 2018 renewal of the Pertemps Network Swinton Handicap Hurdle, which saw its first prize raised to £57,000—from £34,170 twelve months earlier—to make it the joint third most valuable handicap hurdle run in Britain in 2018/19. There was nothing approaching the calibre of Monksfield, or even Bird's Nest (top weight in 1981 as an evergreen eleven-year-old), in the line-up for the 2018 Swinton, but the cash injection paid off by attracting a strong field in the context of the modern-day jumping landscape. The Swinton, of course, now takes place in the first few weeks of the National Hunt season (as opposed to the final few weeks) after the calendar was changed in 2000 to bring the curtain down on the season at Sandown in late-April, while the much enhanced Punchestown Festival is now the destination for Champion Hurdle-level performers at the time of year.

Top weight in the latest Swinton was Williams' 2017 winner John Constable, who had managed only ninth in the Champion Hurdle on his previous start. However, John Constable looked the stable second string behind Silver Streak, who was among the favourites in a market headed by the Paul Nicholls-trained Capitaine at 6/1, with the juvenile Act of Valour and 2017 runner-up Optimus Prime joint second favourites with Silver Streak on 13/2. The front-running Capitaine ensured a truly-run affair, but he had already cried enough when the race's pivotal moment occurred two out, where Act of Valour fell fatally while disputing the lead, hampering Silver Streak in the process as he was poised to challenge. This left 2017 Scottish Champion Hurdle winner Chesterfield with what looked like an unassailable lead (he was four lengths up clearing the last), only for him to be reeled in after a strong late rally from Silver Streak, who had three quarters of a length to spare at the line, with a further five lengths and a length and a quarter back to the Skelton-trained pair Ashkoul and Optimus Prime (John Constable came seventh, with Capitaine fading into thirteenth). It was a fourth Swinton win in six years for Evan Williams, who joined Martin Pipe as the most successful trainer in the race's forty-year history. Barizan in 2013 and Ballyglasheen in 2014 began that sequence, during which period Williams has saddled a trio of fourth-placed finishers as well.

Silver Streak had been among the lightly-weighted runners at Haydock (off a BHA mark of 132), which left him with ground to make up if he was to emulate previous Swinton winners Macs Joy (2004), Intersky Falcon (2002) and Past Glories

(1988), who all went on to be placed in the Champion Hurdle. Silver Streak was even 1 lb out of the handicap for the Welsh Champion Hurdle at Ffos Las on his next start five months later but, sent off 3/1 joint favourite, he ran out a convincing winner after a typically smooth-travelling display, beating Le Prezien by three lengths, with Ozzie The Oscar a further short head away in third. Both placed horses are better known as chasers, but the fact that the field also included Cheltenham Festival winners Mohaayed, Ch'tibello and The New One gave the form plenty of substance. Silver Streak became only the second horse to win both the Swinton and Welsh Champion Hurdle, though the latter race was staged at its original home of Chepstow, and in its traditional slot on Easter Monday, when Past Glories completed the double in 1988.

Silver Streak continued on an upward curve when runner-up in the Greatwood Hurdle at Cheltenham, failing by just a neck to peg back outsider Nietzsche on the extended run-in. Stepped up to graded company for the remainder of the campaign, Silver Streak continued to more than pay his way. Further second places in the International Hurdle at Cheltenham (beaten a length and three quarters by Brain Power) and the Champion Hurdle Trial at Haydock (beaten three lengths by Global Citizen) in January represented career-best efforts, with a mistake three out in the latter race proving costly. The Haydock race, incidentally, was branded as The New One Unibet Hurdle to mark the retirement of the gelding who had won the last four renewals. His trainer Nigel Twiston-Davies confirmed he had run his final race the previous month when pulled up in the International Hurdle, a race he had won three times in a career whose other highlights included victories in the Baring Bingham and the Aintree Hurdle, as well as twice making the frame in the Champion Hurdle.

Silver Streak was the 80/1 rank outsider of ten when he lined up in the Champion Hurdle back at Cheltenham in March. The early fall of twice champion Buveur d'Air reduced the race's competitiveness, as did the flop of hot favourite Apple's Jade who was beaten by the top of the hill. Well suited by the strong gallop, Silver Streak crept closer under a trademark patient ride from Adam Wedge and it was clear from some way out that he was going to figure in the prize money. Although no match for wide-margin winner Espoir d'Allen from the home turn, Silver Streak stuck to his task willingly and finished a fine third (picking up £47,745), only a neck behind 2018 runner-up Melon—Global Citizen was seventh, while Brain Power was pulled up. Silver Streak's odds were the longest for a placed runner in the Champion Hurdle since Past Glories finished third at 150/1 in 1990, whilst Yeniesi (third in 1974) and Stans Pride (third under Morshead in 1985) are the only other placed horses in the race's history to be sent off at bigger odds (both 100/1).

Silver Streak (IRE) (gr.g. 2013)	Dark Angel (IRE) (gr 2005)	Acclamation (b 1999)	Royal Applause
			Princess Athena
		Midnight Angel (gr 1994)	Machiavellian
			Night At Sea
	Happy Talk (IRE) (b 1999)	Hamas (b or br 1989)	Danzig
			Fall Aspen
		Mamara Reef (b 1990)	Salse
			Fanny's Cove

The rather leggy Silver Streak is the seventh foal out of the Hamas mare Happy Talk and one of seven winning offspring from her ten runners to date. Happy Talk was a lightly-raced ten-furlong winner in Ireland, the decision to send her to stud at the end of her three-year-old campaign presumably owing plenty to the fact that she is a half-sister to the 2000 Irish One Thousand Guineas third Storm Dream, who was later a Grade 3 winner in the States. The 'black type' in this family doesn't end there as Silver Streak's grandam Mamara Reef, who was a fair mile and three quarter winner on the Flat and later successful over hurdles over nearly two and a half miles, was a half-sister to Park Hill Stakes runner-up Nibbs Point, herself the dam of Two Thousand Guineas and Derby third Border Arrow. As that background would suggest, this is a Flat-oriented pedigree. Mica Mika (by Needwood Blade) is the only other one of Happy Talk's foals to have won over hurdles, though he is far better known as a useful middle-distance performer who won ten times on the Flat during a long career with Richard Fahey. Other siblings of Silver Streak include his half-sisters Nagham (by Camacho) and Foreign Rhythm (by Distant Music), who were both sprinters, with the former capable of useful form at her best. His brother Evoke, meanwhile, won over six furlongs at two before going on to win a further five races in Greece. Silver Streak drew a blank himself on the Flat, though he was placed three times at up to seven furlongs from seven starts in that sphere for Ann Duffield. Two further placed efforts followed once he was sent hurdling but, after being bought out of Duffield's yard for £25,000 in the autumn of 2016, Silver Streak rewarded his new connections immediately by winning three of his first four starts for them (his first off a BHA mark of just 96), winning a limited four-year-old handicap at Chepstow on the final occasion.

As his pedigree might suggest, Silver Streak is far from certain to stay further than two miles, though lack of stamina didn't seem the cause of an uncharacteristically lacklustre display when he was stepped up in trip on his final start in the Aintree Hurdle, a long campaign possibly just catching up with him by that stage. Even if there was an excuse for that rare below-par effort, he could still prove harder to place in the short term as he starts the new campaign off a BHA mark of 154 (9 lb higher than when runner-up in the Greatwood), while he will do well to earn better than minor honours in top graded company. Nevertheless, Silver Streak is an admirable sort who seems versatile with regards to ground and has a zest for racing that should continue to stand him in good stead, with strongly-run races at around two miles always likely to show him in a good light. *Evan Williams*

SILVER TASSIE (IRE) 11 b.g. Shantou (USA) – Silver Castor (IRE) (Indian Ridge) [2018/19 c130, h–: c23.9g³ c24.1v² c22.3g c24.5v³ Mar 17] winning hurdler: fairly useful handicap chaser: stays 3¼m: acts on good to firm and heavy going: tried in headgear/tongue tie: held up. *Micky Hammond* — **c124 h–**

SILVER TICKET (IRE) 8 gr.g. Tikkanen (USA) – Windmill View (IRE) (Glacial Storm (USA)) [2018/19 h67: h23d^pu Jan 15] sturdy gelding: poor maiden hurdler on balance. *Laura Mongan* — **h–**

SILVERTON 12 gr.m. Silver Patriarch (IRE) – Gretton (Terimon) [2018/19 c81, h–: c20.1s c20.1v^pu Mar 14] maiden hurdler: poor handicap chaser nowadays: stays 3m: acts on heavy going: tried in cheekpieces. *Lucy Normile* — **c– h–**

SIMAFAR (IRE) 5 b.g. Makfi – Simawa (IRE) (Anabaa (USA)) [2018/19 h97: h15.8g h16g Jun 24] has had breathing operation: formerly fair on Flat: well held over hurdles: tried in headgear/tongue tie. *Olly Murphy* — **h–**

SIMONE (IRE) 7 b.m. Presenting – Dusty Too (Terimon) [2018/19 h97, b94: h20.2g^bd h23.9g³ c21.6d⁴ c23.8g⁴ Dec 3] bumper winner: fair form over hurdles: showed aptitude in novice handicap chases: stays 3m: acts on heavy going. *Lucinda Russell* — **c94 h100**

SIMON THE GREAT 6 b.g. Great Palm (USA) – Miss Royello (Royal Fountain) [2018/19 b16g b16.8g⁵ b16.8s⁶ b16d* Aug 29] £1,800 4-y-o: tall gelding: fourth foal: dam (c98) 25f/27f chase winner: won at Worcester in August: in headgear after debut. *Paul George* — **b86**

SIMPLY A LEGEND 10 b.g. Midnight Legend – Disco Danehill (IRE) (Danehill Dancer (IRE)) [2018/19 h19.7g² h19.7g² Mar 29] workmanlike gelding: useful handicap hurdler: runner-up at Wetherby both outings in 2018/19: stays 21f: acts on good to firm and heavy going: usually hooded. *Alan King* — **h133**

SIMPLY BUSINESS (FR) 6 b.m. Maresca Sorrento (FR) – Fabulous Darling (FR) (Freedom Cry) [2018/19 c–, h76: h15.7g^pu May 13] has had breathing operation: poor maiden hurdler: pulled up in novice handicap only chase outing: raced around 2m: acts on heavy going: has worn hood: tongue tied 4 of last 5 outings: weak finisher. *Sam England* — **c– h–**

SIMPLY LOVELEH 6 b.m. Beneficial – Pippedatthepost (Exit To Nowhere (USA)) [2018/19 b89: b15.8g² b13.7g² b17.7s⁵ Dec 17] sturdy mare: fair form in bumpers. *Dan Skelton* — **b87**

SIMPLY LUCKY (IRE) 10 b.g. Flemensfirth (USA) – Derrygowna Court (IRE) (Rakaposhi King) [2018/19 h24g* h24g⁴ h23.3g* h24g³ h22m⁵ h27m⁵ h21.3m^F h25.3g³ h23.1s⁶ h25.3g⁶ h23.1g⁶ h23.3d^pu h24.1g⁶ Apr 11] has had breathing operation: point — **c– h88**

winner: modest handicap hurdler: won at Towcester in May and Uttoxeter (novice event) in June: let down by jumping over fences: left Dan Skelton after fifth start: stays 25f: best form on good going: has worn headgear: usually in tongue tie. *Mike Sowersby*

SIMPLY MANI 7 ch.g. Sulamani (IRE) – Simply Mystic (Simply Great (FR)) [2018/19 **h102** h–, b72: h20.3g² h20.3g⁵ h23.9g³ h24g⁵ h23.9g Sep 10] fair form over hurdles: stays 3m. *Peter Niven*

SIMPLY NED (IRE) 12 ch.g. Fruits of Love (USA) – Bishops Lass (IRE) (Marju **c162** (IRE)) [2018/19 c157, h–: c17.1m⁴ c15.9g² c17g* Dec 27] **h–**

    The Old Testament story of David and Goliath is a lesson in overcoming what might look impossible. In the same way that King Saul thought the Philistine giant was too powerful to fight, most of the top British-based jumps trainers seem to regard the powerhouse Irish stables of Willie Mullins and Gordon Elliott as presenting too formidable a barrier to be challenging for Ireland's top prizes. Until British trainers 'breached the dam' with four Grade 1 winners (including two for Nicky Henderson) at the Punchestown Festival, the only British-trained success in Grade 1s in Ireland in the last two campaigns had come with horses trained by Lambourn trainer Warren Greatrex (with La Bague Au Roi in the Flogas Novices' Chase at the Dublin Racing Festival) and Cumbrian-based Nicky Richards whose stable in the village of Greystoke is the home of Simply Ned, the first Grade 1 winner for the yard since the days of Monet's Garden. Nicky Richards didn't exactly 'slay' the Irish Goliath Willie Mullins with Simply Ned's successive victories in the Paddy's Rewards Club Chase, the two-mile Grade 1 chase at Leopardstown's Christmas meeting, but the 'five smooth stones' represented by Simply Ned's five successive appearances in that race have all been on target, Simply Ned's victories in 2017 and 2018 preceded by a second and two thirds.

    Simply Ned's first victory in the Paddy's Rewards Club Chase came at the expense of the Mullins-trained 7/2-on shot Min who was first past the post but impeded Simply Ned on the run-in. Simply Ned did not require the assistance of

Paddy's Rewards Club 'Sugar Paddy' Chase, Leopardstown—
no need for any help from the stewards this time as Simply Ned (striped sleeves) reels in hot
favourite Footpad to claim a second successive win in this Grade 1

the stewards when taking the scalp of another Mullins-trained hot pot, the previous season's top novice Footpad, in the latest Paddy's Rewards Club 'Sugar Paddy' Chase. Simply Ned's preparation for his annual Christmas visit to Leopardstown followed a familiar path, a seasonal reappearance in a handicap at Kelso in October (shaping as if he'd be better for the run when fourth under top weight to Nuts Well) and then a fifth crack at the Shloer Chase at Cheltenham in November. Simply Ned came second in the Shloer for the third time, beaten two and a quarter lengths by Sceau Royal who had met with a setback and been forced to miss the previous season's Arkle for which he had been ante-post second favourite behind Footpad. Simply Ned ran right up to his best to finish second in the Shloer, in which he conceded 3 lb to the winner, and he started at 16/1 (the same odds as the previous year) in the seven-runner Paddy's Rewards Club Chase, in which Footpad, who had reportedly suffered an overreach when falling on his reappearance at Naas, was sent off at evens, with the Fortria Chase winner Ballyoisin second favourite at 11/4 and Footpad's stablemate Great Field next at 5/1. Simply Ned lost his place briefly at the third last and came under a strong ride from two out. Footpad loomed up to his front-running stablemate Great Field entering the home straight and looked to have the race in the bag when sent for home before the last, where Great Field fell. Simply Ned was finding plenty under pressure, though, and came with a strong run to wear down Footpad close home. The winning margin was half a length, with Ordinary World adding to his collection of placed efforts in Grade 1s, a further four and three quarter lengths back. Ballyoisin managed only fifth, unable to dominate with Great Field in the line-up and not given a hard time after briefly losing his footing on the approach to the second last. Simply Ned bruised a knee in his stable at home and was a late withdrawal from the Dublin Chase at the Dublin Racing Festival in February. It was then hoped to have him ready for a third tilt at the Queen Mother Champion Chase (fifth to Dodging Bullets his better effort in that race) but he wasn't seen out again. Although now twelve, Simply Ned is set to remain in training 'if he stays in the same sort of form he showed at Leopardstown.'

			Hansel	Woodman
	Fruits of Love (USA)		(b 1988)	Count On Bonnie
	(b 1995)		Vallee Secrete	Secretariat
Simply Ned (IRE)			(b 1977)	Midou
(ch.g. 2007)			Marju	Last Tycoon
	Bishops Lass (IRE)		(br 1988)	Flame of Tara
	(b 1999)		Priorite	Kenmare
			(ch 1994)	Princess Dixieland

The tall, rather sparely-made Simply Ned is easily the best representative of his sire Fruits of Love, a tough performer who twice won the Hardwicke Stakes and also won the Dubai Sheema Classic. Simply Ned's dam Bishops Lass never raced and has bred one other winner, Apt Manor (by Craigsteel), a winner of a bumper and a two-mile mares maiden hurdle. Unproven beyond seventeen furlongs, Simply Ned acts on good to firm and heavy going. He is usually patiently ridden. *Nicky Richards*

SIMPLY THE BETTS (IRE) 6 b.g. Arcadio (GER) – Crimson Flower (IRE) (Soviet **h122** Lad (USA)) [2018/19 h129, b98: h16m* h16.2s* h15.7m h19.4m⁴ Dec 1] sturdy gelding: bumper winner: fairly useful hurdler: won maiden at Warwick in May and novice at Hexham in October: unproven beyond 2m: acts on soft and good to firm going. *Harry Whittington*

SINAKAR (IRE) 8 br.g. Manduro (GER) – Siniyya (IRE) (Grand Lodge (USA)) [2018/19 **h94** h21.7gᵖᵘ h23.8d h20.7g³ Apr 22] compact gelding: fair handicap hurdler: stays 23f: acts on soft going: tried in cheekpieces: in tongue tie last 5 starts. *Kerry Lee*

SINGAPORE SAGA 4 b.f. Midnight Legend – Kim Tian Road (IRE) (King's Theatre **b85** (IRE)) [2018/19 b16.8g⁶ Apr 18] first foal: dam (h120), 17f/19f hurdle winner, sister to fair hurdler/fairly useful chaser (winner up to 21f) Saunders Road: some encouragement when sixth in mares bumper at Cheltenham. *Philip Hobbs*

SINGER IN THE SAND (IRE) 4 b.f. Footstepsinthesand – Village Singer (USA) **h–** (Rahy (USA)) [2018/19 h15.9d⁵ h15.9g⁵ Apr 7] behind all starts on Flat/over hurdles. *Pat Phelan*

SINGLE ESTATE 5 b.g. Tamayuz – Duo de Choc (IRE) (Manduro (GER)) [2018/19 **h97**
h16.2g⁶ h20.2g⁵ h23.9g³ h19.8g⁴ Dec 3] dam half-sister to useful French hurdler (best up
to 19f) Rock The Race: modest maiden on Flat, should stay beyond 1¼m: similar form
over hurdles. *Simon Waugh*

SINGLEFARMPAYMENT 9 b.g. Milan – Crevamoy (IRE) (Shardari) [2018/19 c147, **c145**
h–: c27.3g⁴ c26g² c25s c34.3g Apr 6] good-topped gelding: winning hurdler: smart handicap **h–**
chaser: in frame in Grade 3 events at Cheltenham first 2 starts in 2018/19: stays 27f: acts
on heavy going: wears hood: held up: infrequent winner (has been outbattled). *Tom George*

SINORIA (IRE) 6 b.m. Oscar (IRE) – Petralona (USA) (Alleged (USA)) [2018/19 h16d⁴ **h131**
h20d⁴ h16d⁴ h16.8d Mar 14] £130,000 5-y-o: angular mare: closely related to 2 winners,
including fair 23f hurdle winner Petrovic (by Old Vic), and half-sister to 3 winners,
including useful hurdler/top-class chaser Minella Rocco (21f-4m winner, by Shirocco) and
smart hurdler/fairly useful chaser Big Moment (2m-2½m winner, by Be My Guest): dam
useful French 12.5f winner: winning pointer: useful form over hurdles: won maiden at
Down Royal in December and listed novice at Punchestown (by ¾ length from Chosen
Mate) in February: in season when down field in Dawn Run Mares' Novices' Hurdle at
Cheltenham. *Henry de Bromhead, Ireland*

SIN SIN (IRE) 5 b.m. Intense Focus (USA) – Saor Sinn (IRE) (Galileo (IRE)) [2018/19 **h73**
h83: h21.2m⁵ h16.8m h21.7dᵖᵘ h16.5d⁵ h23.9dᵖᵘ Apr 24] poor maiden hurdler: stays 21f:
acts on soft and good to firm going: in headgear last 4 starts: tried in tongue tie. *Nigel Hawke*

SIR DU BEARN (FR) 13 b.g. Passing Sale (FR) – Girl du Bearn (FR) (Sarpedon (FR)) **c–**
[2018/19 c23.8vᵖᵘ Nov 11] workmanlike gelding: winning hurdler: useful chaser at best: **h–**
lightly raced and no form outside points (prolific winner) since 2013/14: in cheekpieces
last 4 starts. *Peter Bowen*

SIR DYLAN 10 b.g. Dylan Thomas (IRE) – Monteleone (IRE) (Montjeu (IRE)) [2018/19 **c98 §**
h106§: c20.2gᵖᵘ c17.8g⁵ c17.8g⁴ Apr 24] fair hurdler: modest form over fences: won **h–**
handicap at Fontwell in April: stays 2½m: acts on good to firm going: usually hooded:
temperamental. *Polly Gundry*

SIRE DU BERLAIS (FR) 7 b.g. Poliglote – Royale Athenia (FR) (Garde Royale) **h151**
[2018/19 h141: h20d h24g⁶ h24d⁴ h24.7g Apr 6] good-topped gelding: smart handicap
hurdler: won Pertemps Final at Cheltenham (by neck from Tobefair) in March: let down by
jumping at Aintree subsequently: stays 3m: acts on soft going: in cheekpieces last 2 starts:
wears tongue tie. *Gordon Elliott, Ireland*

SIR EGBERT 6 b.g. Kayf Tara – Little Miss Flora (Alflora (IRE)) [2018/19 h117: c20.9s² **c128 p**
c16.4s⁴ c17.2s² c15.5d Feb 15] rangy gelding: fairly useful handicap hurdler: similar form **h–**
over fences: won handicap at Newbury (conditionals) in December: probably stays 21f, at
least as effective around 2m: acts on soft going: hooded in 2017/18: sound jumper who
remains capable of better as a chaser. *Tom Lacey*

Pertemps Network Final Handicap Hurdle, Cheltenham—
Barry Geraghty needs to be at his strongest as Sire du Berlais (hoops) beats Tobefair (second right),
Not Many Left (centre) and Cuneo (second left)

SIR EREC (IRE) 4 b.c. Camelot – Quiritis (Galileo (IRE)) [2018/19 h16g* h16g* **h143** h16.8d^{pu} Mar 15]

Not many horses switched to hurdling from the Flat are of the quality of Sir Erec who got to within two and a half lengths of star stayer Stradivarius in the Long Distance Cup on British Champions' Day on his final start. Fairly lightly raced and barely out of maiden company, Sir Erec looked the type to do better still as a four-year-old but, instead of recharging his batteries over the winter in preparation for another tilt at Stradivarius, he was transferred—still an entire—from Ballydoyle to Joseph O'Brien to run in the colours of J.P. McManus. He made his jumping debut in a maiden hurdle at Leopardstown's Christmas fixture, justifying short-priced favouritism and holding off second favourite Tiger Tap Tap by a neck, the pair eight lengths clear of the rest of a big field. There was room for improvement in Sir Erec's jumping but he was installed as Triumph Hurdle favourite straight afterwards and regained that position, after temporarily losing it to stablemate Fakir d'Oudairies, when successfully stepped up to Grade 1 company in the Tattersalls Ireland Spring Juvenile Hurdle at the Dublin Racing Festival at Leopardstown in early-February. Making his own running this time, Sir Erec travelled smoothly all the way and quickened clear impressively on the run-in, after a fluent jump at the last, to win by six lengths from another stablemate Gardens of Babylon, with Tiger Tap Tap (again second favourite behind Sir Erec) a respectable fourth in a race in which the field was weakened by ground-related withdrawals of four of the intended runners, including the useful Coeur Sublime.

After looking so promising and arriving at the Cheltenham Festival hailed as an Irish banker (sent off at 11/10 in the Triumph Hurdle), Sir Erec met a very sad end. Close up, he went wrong at the fourth flight in the Triumph, shattering his off-fore on the flat when landing awkwardly, the horrific accident taking place in full view of the TV cameras. Sir Erec was the best of a fine collection of juvenile hurdlers in the latest season for his young trainer. Stablemate Band of Outlaws had won the Fred Winter, Fakir d'Oudairies had finished in the frame in the Supreme and Gardens of Babylon filled third behind Pentland Hills and Coeur Sublime in the Triumph (Fakir d'Oudairies went on to finish runner-up to Pentland Hills in the Anniversary at Aintree and to Fusil Raffles in the Champion Four Year Old Hurdle at Punchestown). Sir Erec had been re-shod on his off-fore after shedding a plate on the way to the start.

Sir Erec was one of three fatalities at the latest Cheltenham Festival—Ballyward and Invitation Only could not be saved after being injured in falls in the National Hunt Chase and the Gold Cup—and the fact that his participation had been in some doubt, after he suffered a stone bruise in the run up to the race, had the animal rights activists in full voice afterwards. PETA, which campaigns to end horse racing, got plenty of publicity in the media for its claim that Sir Erec 'should not have run and cruelty charges should be brought.' Sir Erec was given the green light early in Cheltenham Festival week by his stable after his injury scare and, like all runners at the latest Festival, he was checked on the day of the race by Cheltenham's vets who found that he 'moved well and displayed no signs of lameness or injuries.'

Tattersalls Ireland Spring Juvenile Hurdle, Leopardstown—
the ill-fated Sir Erec cements his position at the head of the Triumph Hurdle betting with an
impressive victory from stable-companion Gardens of Babylon (No.4)

Risks are inherent in horse racing and around one hundred and twenty-five jumpers die on the track in Britain each season, an uncomfortable, but sadly unavoidable, consequence of the dangers inherent in the sport. The sport is honest about such consequences, openly publishing figures on fatalities (something it has done for many years) and holding numerous reviews into safety which have undoubtedly helped to improve equine welfare (the number of fatalities has fallen over the years and is now at 0.2 per cent of runners). Such transparency should be applauded as it enables the wider public to make up its own mind based on the facts, rather than just swallowing the propaganda of those who would ban the sport. Aintree's Grand National meeting, where three horses died, also featured another particularly grim sight for ITV viewers as Forest des Aigles suffered an untreatable fracture to his near-fore cannon bone approaching the final fence in the Topham Trophy when he was challenging the eventual winner Cadmium. Crucial Role suffered a fatal fall in the Mildmay Novices' Chase on the same day and, in the Grand National itself, Up For Review broke his neck when brought down at the first (ITV commentators told viewers that the fence was being bypassed on the second circuit but it would have helped if some explanation had also been provided of what might have been going on behind the green screens in the corner of the picture; when the National was reshown, the ITV coverage began, without explanation, at the second fence, presumably to 'sanitize' events for the audience, though surely viewers could have been told).

All equine fatalities are investigated by the turf authorities, like the four on the same day at Musselburgh in early-December, none of which were attributed to any problems with the track or the racing surface on the day (the ground was on the soft side of good, there was a full covering of grass and the weather was perfect). By no means all racecourse fatalities occur at the obstacles and, in a dry winter like the latest one, it was often difficult for racecourses to produce ideal ground conditions, a subject touched on in the essay on Lady Buttons. Sir Erec, for example, had had his most recent race at the Dublin Racing Festival in early-February from which there were a significant number of late, ground-related withdrawals, with a number of those horses that ran reportedly returning jarred up. Continually improving ground management is probably the paramount priority in making racing as safe as possible for its participants, equine and human.

Sir Erec's excellent pedigree raised speculation that he might eventually have had a stallion career. He was by Camelot, a son of the influential Montjeu (the first four in the Spring Juvenile were all by sons of Montjeu, as was the Triumph winner Pentland Hills), out of the unraced Galileo mare Quiritis who is a sister to the St Leger runner-up Mahler who is now on the roster of Coolmore's jumps stallions. Sir Erec's grandam Rainbow Goddess was a sister to Glatisant, the dam of another Coolmore stallion, the Two Thousand Guineas winner Footstepsinthesand. Coolmore supremo John Magnier has close ties with Sir Erec's owner and it would have been no surprise to see Sir Erec given his chance at stud. Magnier's father, incidentally, stood the 1947 Cheltenham Gold Cup winner Fortina, the only entire to win steeplechasing's blue riband, and Fortina went on to sire two Gold Cup winners, Fort Leney and Glencaraig Lady. *Joseph Patrick O'Brien, Ireland*

SIRIUS STAR 10 b.g. Beat All (USA) – Miss Sirius (Royal Vulcan) [2018/19 c81, h–: c21.4g c24g^{pu} c23.9g^{pu} Aug 18] workmanlike gelding: has had breathing operation: of little account nowadays: has worn hood. *Brian Rothwell*   **c–**
h–

SIR IVAN 9 b.g. Midnight Legend – Tisho (Sir Harry Lewis (USA)) [2018/19 c137, h–: c26d^{pu} h18.5d² h24g Apr 17] angular gelding: has had breathing operation: useful handicap hurdler/chaser: stays 3m: acts on heavy going: tried in hood: wears tongue tie. *Harry Fry*   **c–**
h133

SIR JACK YEATS (IRE) 8 b.g. Yeats (IRE) – Quadrennial (IRE) (Un Desperado (FR))   **c122**
[2018/19 c128, h109: c23.4g³ c24.2d* c21.1d⁶ c24.2m² Apr 22] workmanlike gelding: fair   **h–**
hurdler: fairly useful hunter chaser: won at Fakenham in March: stays 3m: acts on heavy
going: wears headgear. *Richard Spencer*

SIR LONICA (IRE) 8 b.g. Craigsteel – Flashey Thyne (IRE) (Good Thyne (USA))   **c87 p**
[2018/19 c26.2dᵘʳ Apr 8] half-brother to modest chaser Alright Benny (2½m/21f winner, by
Beneficial) and winning pointers by Satco and Mandalus: dam unraced: dual point winner:
odds on, upsides when unseated 2 out in maiden hunter won by Longtymegone at Kelso on
chasing debut. *Justin Landy*

SIR MANGAN (IRE) 11 b.g. Darsi (FR) – Lady Pep (IRE) (Cajetano (USA)) [2018/19   **c127**
c134, h132: h22.8gᶠ h22g h24.7g c24d² c26g² c26.3d c24g⁵ h23.4d⁴ Mar 4] sturdy gelding: **h116**
fairly useful handicap hurdler/chaser: stays 27f: acts on heavy going: has worn headgear.
Dan Skelton

SIR MIX 6 gr.g. Fair Mix (IRE) – Highland Cherry (Milan) [2018/19 h–: h19dᵖᵘ Apr 4] no   **h–**
form in points/over hurdles: tried in hood. *Kevin Bishop*

SIROBBIE (IRE) 5 br.g. Arakan (USA) – Presentbreeze (IRE) (Presenting) [2018/19   **h90**
b85: h16.7dᵘʳ h16d h15.8d⁵ h15.8g⁵ h20.5g⁴ Apr 7] close-coupled gelding: modest form
over hurdles: left Sam Thomas after second start: will be well suited by 3m: in hood last 3
starts. *Harry Whittington*

SIROP DE MENTHE (FR) 9 ch.g. Discover d'Auteuil (FR) – Jolie Menthe (FR)   **h–**
(Bateau Rouge) [2018/19 h–: h19.5dᵖᵘ Mar 20] angular gelding: fairly useful hurdler at
best: no show since early-2017: stays 2¾m: acts on good to firm and heavy going: tried in
headgear: has looked hard ride. *Susan Gardner*

SIR PASS I AM 6 b.g. Passing Glance – Orbital Orchid (Mujahid (USA)) [2018/19 h21.4g   **h–**
Feb 27] fair stayer on Flat: tailed off in novice on hurdling debut. *Alan King*

SIR RUNS A LOT 7 b.g. Sir Percy – Monjouet (IRE) (Montjeu (IRE)) [2018/19 h19.3s⁴   **h86**
h19.3g h18.6d³ Jan 17] half-brother to a winning hurdler in Italy by Hawk Wing: modest
on Flat, stays 12.5f: similar form over hurdles. *Micky Hammond*

SIR TOMMY 10 ch.g. Sir Harry Lewis (USA) – Rose of Overbury (Overbury (IRE))   **h59**
[2018/19 h100: h16.2g h16.2gᵖᵘ Jul 5] modest handicap hurdler: lame final outing: should
stay beyond 2m: acts on good to soft going: wears tongue tie. *Maurice Barnes*

SIRUH DU LAC (FR) 6 b.g. Turgeon (USA) – Margerie (FR) (Le Balafre (FR))   **c147 p**
[2018/19 c123, h–: c19.9d* c19.2s* c20.6d* c20.6d* Mar 14]   **h–**
There is a long history of rivalry between the British hosts and the Irish
visitors at the Cheltenham Festival. It's a good-natured and informal aspect of the
meeting, though since 2014 silverware has been at stake in the form of the Prestbury
Cup awarded to the nation having the most winners, decided by which side of the
Irish Sea those winners are trained. The result of the latest Prestbury Cup went right
down to the final race of the Festival, when Early Doors' win for Joseph O'Brien
in the Martin Pipe Conditional Jockeys' Handicap Hurdle was an 'equaliser' which
brought Ireland's total to fourteen and resulted in a draw between the two nations.
But the raw material for many of those winners, both British- and Irish-trained, was
supplied by the breeding industry of a third nation, France. In fact, the French-bred
Early Doors was also the fourteenth winner at the Festival bred across the Channel,
equalling the number of Irish-bred winners at the meeting at which British-bred jumpers
drew a blank.

You have to go back to 1997 to find the last Festival at which there was only
a single French-bred winner when Or Royal, trained by Martin Pipe, one of the
pioneers of importing French-bred jumpers in the modern era, won the Arkle. At the
2009 Festival, that total reached a record ten, including the Paul Nicholls-trained
trio of Kauto Star, Master Minded and Big Buck's, winners of the Gold Cup, Queen
Mother Champion Chase and Stayers' Hurdle. In 2018, the number of French-bred
winners hit a new high of eleven. With another record set at the latest Festival,
where half of the winners were bred in France, there must be a chance that they will
achieve a majority before much longer. Besides Early Doors, the other French-bred
winners were; Klassical Dream (Supreme Novices'), Duc des Genievres (Arkle),
Espoir d'Allen (Champion Hurdle), A Plus Tard (Close Brothers Novices' Handicap
Chase), Le Breuil (National Hunt Chase), Envoi Allen (Champion Bumper), Defi du
Seuil (Golden Miller), Sire du Berlais (Pertemps Final), Frodon (Ryanair Chase),

Siruh du Lac (Brown Advisory & Merriebelle Stable Plate), Eglantine du Seuil (Dawn Run Mares' Novices' Hurdle), Ch'tibello (County Hurdle) and, not least, Al Boum Photo who led home a French-bred one, two, three in the Gold Cup. While the number of French-bred winners matched the Irish-bred total, that doesn't reflect a level playing field as French-bred horses were outnumbered, accounting for not much more than a third of the total runners at the Festival.

One trainer who has founded much of his stable's success on French-bred jumpers, with the likes of Reve de Sivola, Fox Norton, Le Rocher and Agrapart, is Nick Williams. Coo Star Sivola won the Ultima Handicap Chase in 2018 and it was another French-bred six-year-old, Siruh du Lac, who provided the trainer and his stepdaughter Lizzie Kelly (who became the first professional female jockey to win at the meeting the year before) with another Festival handicap success in the latest season. It was also the third year running that Williams had been successful in a Festival handicap, his first winner at the meeting coming with Flying Tiger in the Fred Winter in 2017. Unraced in France, Siruh du Lac showed some promise in three starts in juvenile hurdles but he was quickly put over fences the following season and, while still only a four-year-old, won handicap chases against more seasoned rivals at Bangor and Exeter in another light campaign. His Bangor win was off a BHA handicap mark of 112 but in the Plate he was up to 141 after winning all three of his starts before the Festival, at Newbury, Exeter and Cheltenham.

Excellent jumping was a hallmark of Siruh du Lac's progress over fences, and he was a joy to watch in his win over the Plate course and distance at Cheltenham's Trials day in January. Willingness under pressure is another of his qualities as he showed when rallying for a head win over another unexposed French-bred six-year-old Janika, from whom he was receiving more than a stone, in the Spectra Cyber Security Solutions Trophy in which Siruh du Lac made most of the running. The same two horses fought out another close finish to the Brown Advisory & Merriebelle Stable Plate in March when they headed the betting in a twenty-two-runner field. Under top weight, Janika was only a pound better off from their meeting in January, having been put up 6 lb compared to Siruh du Lac's 7 lb, but Janika was sent off the heavily-backed 3/1 favourite to turn the tables on 9/2 chance Siruh du Lac. However, another superb round of jumping in front and a further demonstration of resolution under pressure when tackled by Janika two out, meant

Brown Advisory Merriebelle Stable Plate Handicap Chase, Cheltenham—
another notably fluent display from Siruh du Lac as he confirms his superiority over Janika (left)
from Trials day; Spiritofthegames (noseband) and Eamon An Cnoic (right) complete the frame

that Siruh du Lac kept his unbeaten record for the season, beating his rival by three quarters of a length. That smart effort ended Siruh du Lac's campaign as one of the most progressive chasers around and the Plate form looked particularly strong, with two more of those prominent in the betting, novice Spiritofthegames and Eamon An Cnoic, completing the frame.

A range of stallions contributed to the French-bred success at Cheltenham but none could match the extraordinary career of Siruh du Lac's sire Turgeon who died at the ripe old age of thirty-three less than a month after the Festival. What made Turgeon remarkable was that he was still an active stallion, said to be the world's oldest, at the time of his death. Trained by Jonathan Pease in his racing days, Turgeon's most notable victories came as a five-year-old in 1991 in the Irish St Leger and Prix Royal-Oak for his breeder George Strawbridge, while he subsequently finished third in two Gold Cups at Royal Ascot after being bought by Sheikh Mohammed. Turgeon's stallion career began late, at the age of eight, and for most of his career at the Haras du Mesnil he covered books of only fifty or sixty mares, though he was champion sire of jumpers in France in 2006 and 2011. Among his notable winners was Shannon Rock, who won a Prix La Haye Jousselin as well as finishing runner-up four times in the Grand Steeple-Chase de Paris, while much the best of his imports to Britain was the top-class chaser Exotic Dancer who was placed twice behind Kauto Star in Cheltenham Gold Cups and won several other big chases for Jonjo O'Neill. The New One, as well as important winners in the latest season Politologue, Aux Ptits Soins, La Bague Au Roi, Vision des Flos, Elixir de Nutz and Angels Breath are all out of Turgeon's daughters.

		Caro	Fortino Ii
	Turgeon (USA)	(gr 1967)	Chambord
	(gr 1986)	Reiko	Targowice
Siruh du Lac (FR)		(b 1979)	Beronaire
(b.g. 2013)		Le Balafre	Groom Dancer
	Margerie (FR)	(b 1990)	Tuneria
	(b 2000)	Matelica	R B Chesne
		(b 1987)	Minnehowhow

Whilst the leading British and Irish yards tend to import French jumpers who have already shown promise on the racecourse, Williams' policy is to buy young unraced horses in France and bring them on himself, sometimes starting them off in French races. Siruh du Lac was bought for €32,000 as a two-year-old at Deauville's Autumn Mixed Sale. Apart from being by Turgeon, his main selling point on pedigree was that his grandam Matelica is a half-sister to the Grande Course de Haies d'Auteuil winner Matchou. The winner of eight races over hurdles in all, Matchou had a short comment in *Chasers & Hurdlers 1995/96* in which he was rated 165. Among those he beat in the 1995 Grande Course de Haies, incidentally, was Apple's Girl, now the grandam of Apple's Jade. Raced only on the Flat, Matelica won twice at around a mile, while her three winners at stud included Siruh du Lac's dam Margerie. She was a fairly useful jumper whose four wins at up to two and a half miles, three over fences and one over hurdles, all came at Pau. Siruh du Lac is Margerie's fourth foal and second winner after the French two-mile hurdle winner Txamantxoia (by Sinndar). A full sister to Siruh du Lac, Acta Est Fabula, showed fair form in France in the latest season without winning. The tall Siruh du Lac stays twenty-one furlongs and acts on heavy ground. It bears repeating that he is a superb jumper of fences, a formidable weapon which goes hand in hand with his usual tactics of making the running. There is no telling how much more improvement there is to come and the BetVictor Gold Cup back at Cheltenham would be an obvious autumn target, though the way Siruh du Lac has been sparingly campaigned to date, his trainer has explained, is because he doesn't take too much racing. His name, incidentally, is apparently inspired by nothing more than his breeder's home address—6 rue du Lac! *Nick Williams*

SIRWILLIAMWALLACE (IRE) 6 b.g. Getaway (GER) – Mrs Milan (IRE) (Milan) **b89**
[2018/19 b16d² Feb 25] fourth foal: half-brother to a winning pointer by Westerner: dam unraced half-sister to dam of useful chaser (stays 21f) Templehills: 2¼ lengths second to Nickolson in conditionals/amateurs bumper at Ayr. *Sandy Thomson*

SIR WILL (IRE) 8 b.g. Yeats (IRE) – Tinopasa (FR) (No Pass No Sale) [2018/19 c–, h130: h26s h24.3g^{pu} h23.5m^4 Mar 31] good-topped gelding: has had breathing operation: fairly useful handicap hurdler: fell first on chasing debut: stays 3¼m: acts on heavy going: wears cheekpieces/tongue tie: usually races close up. *Kerry Lee*　**c–ₕ122**

SISANIA (IRE) 6 gr.m. Mastercraftsman (IRE) – Avril Rose (IRE) (Xaar) [2018/19 h84: h21d^3 h23.9g^5 h25g^4 h21.7g^{pu} Apr 12] poor handicap hurdler: stays 3m: acts on good to firm and good to soft going: has worn headgear: temperament under suspicion. *Suzy Smith*　**h75**

SISSINGHURST (IRE) 9 b.g. Kalanisi (IRE) – Sissinghurst Storm (IRE) (Good Thyne (USA)) [2018/19 c–, h105p: c23.8g^{pu} c23.9m^2 c23.9g^2 Aug 18] workmanlike gelding: fair hurdler: similar form over fences: stays 3m: acts on any going: tried in cheekpieces/tongue tie: held up. *Fergal O'Brien*　**c101 h–**

SISTER SIBYL (IRE) 8 br.m. King's Theatre (IRE) – Rose of The Erne (IRE) (Presenting) [2018/19 c122, h–: c20g* c15.9g^2 c20.5g^4 c20.5g^{pu} Dec 29] lengthy mare: winning hurdler: fairly useful chaser: won novice handicap at Warwick in May: stayed 2½m: acted on soft going: held up: dead. *Hughie Morrison*　**c129 h–**

SIX ONE NINE (IRE) 4 b.g. Cloudings (IRE) – Indian Athlete (IRE) (Indian River (FR)) [2018/19 b16.2g Apr 15] never involved in bumper at Hexham. *Chris Grant*　**b–**

SIXTIES GLENARK 6 b.g. Sixties Icon – Cashback Rose (IRE) (Alflora (IRE)) [2018/19 b16.2g h20.5d^{pu} h16d Feb 6] little promise in bumper/over hurdles. *Dianne Sayer*　**h– b–**

SIXTIES IDOL 6 b.m. Sixties Icon – Fading Away (Fraam) [2018/19 h85: h21.7m^5 h21.7g* h21.7m h25g^5 h21d h21.7v h20.5d^5 h20.5g^{pu} Apr 21] compact mare: modest handicap hurdler: won at Fontwell in June: stays 2¾m: acts on good to firm and heavy going: normally blinkered: wears tongue tie. *Sheena West*　**h88**

SIXTIES SECRET 4 b.f. Sixties Icon – Jollyhockeysticks (Fantastic Light (USA)) [2018/19 h16.8g^F h15.9g* h17.7m^{pu} h17.7m^4 h20.5g^6 Apr 22] modest maiden on Flat, stays 1½m: fair form over hurdles: won juvenile at Plumpton in September: stays 21f. *Sheena West*　**h102**

SIXTIES STAR 5 b.g. Sixties Icon – Songbook (Singspiel (IRE)) [2018/19 b84: b16.8g^2 h16d^{pu} h16.8d^{pu} h16.2g^5 Apr 15] close-coupled gelding: fair form in bumpers: modest form on last of 3 outings over hurdles: tried in tongue tie. *Chris Fairhurst*　**h92 b90**

SIXTY'S BELLE 5 b.m. Gold Well – Over Sixty (Overbury (IRE)) [2018/19 h76: h15.8g h21d^4 h20.7g^2 h20.5d^2 Mar 23] progressive form over hurdles: will be suited by 2¾m+: open to further improvement. *Alan King*　**h110 p**

SIZING AT MIDNIGHT (IRE) 7 br.g. Midnight Legend – Issaquah (IRE) (Supreme Leader) [2018/19 h15.8d h19.5d^{pu} h20s^2 Apr 7] fair form over hurdles: much improved when runner-up in handicap at Ffos Las final outing: stays 2½m: acts on soft going. *Colin Tizzard*　**h105**

SIZING BRISBANE 11 b.g. Nayef (USA) – Elaine Tully (IRE) (Persian Bold) [2018/19 c20v^4 c19.2d^5 c19.4d^{pu} c20.2g^5 Feb 27] fair form over hurdles/fences, little show in 2018/19 after long lay-off: has worn tongue tie. *Colin Tizzard*　**c90 h–**

SIZING CODELCO (IRE) 10 b.g. Flemensfirth (USA) – La Zingarella (IRE) (Phardante (FR)) [2018/19 c160?, h–: c24d^2 c29.2g c25s^{pu} c31.8m^{pu} Apr 13] useful-looking gelding: has had breathing operation: winning hurdler: very smart handicap chaser: close second to Minellacelebration at Uttoxeter in May: lost way after: stays 25f: acts on heavy going: has worn headgear/tongue tie. *Colin Tizzard*　**c155 d h–**

SIZING CUSIMANO 6 b.g. Midnight Legend – Combe Florey (Alflora (IRE)) [2018/19 h101, b77: h15.8d^2 h20.6g* h21g^5 h16.8g h23.3s* h19.9s^{pu} h26s^{pu} Mar 10] sturdy gelding: fairly useful hurdler: won novice at Market Rasen (joined when left alone 2 out) in June and handicap at Uttoxeter in December: stays 23f: acts on heavy going. *Colin Tizzard*　**h118**

SIZING GRANITE (IRE) 11 br.g. Milan – Hazel's Tisrara (IRE) (Mandalus) [2018/19 c157, h139: h15.7g h15.8d^6 c15.9g^6 c21g^5 h24g c20.5m^2 Apr 12] tall, angular gelding: has had breathing operation: formerly useful hurdler: smart chaser: refound some form in spring, placed behind Born Survivor in listed handicap at Ayr and O O Seven in Guinness Handicap Chase at Punchestown, latter shortly after end of British season: stays 25f: acts on soft and good to firm going: has worn cheekpieces: usually tongue tied: waited with. *Colin Tizzard*　**c144 h–**

SIZING PLATINUM (IRE) 11 b.g. Definite Article – Quest of Passion (FR) (Saumarez) [2018/19 c148, h–: c21g^2 c21.2m^5 c20.2g^{ur} c20.6d c16m* Apr 22] workmanlike gelding: winning hurdler: smart handicap chaser: won at Chepstow (by 5 lengths from Magic Saint) in April: stays 21f: acts on good to firm and heavy going: wears tongue tie: usually front runner/races prominently. *Colin Tizzard*　**c147 h–**

SIZING ROME (IRE) 7 b.g. Milan – Timber Toes (IRE) (Mandalus) [2018/19 c23m* **c132 p** c23.5g⁴ c20s c25gᵘʳ c23.5g⁴ c25g⁴ c28s⁴ c20.4g* c24.7d* Apr 22] €100,000 3-y-o: half-brother to useful hurdler/fairly useful chaser Brave Right (2m-2½m winner) and fair hurdler/chaser Dun Masc (2½m-3m winner), both by Right Win: dam lightly raced: won point on debut: useful chaser: won hunter at Down Royal in May and handicaps at Punchestown (amateurs) in October, Thurles in March and Fairyhouse (by length from Goose Man) in April: stays 3½m: acts on soft and good to firm going: tried in cheekpieces: open to further improvement. *J. T. R. Dreaper, Ireland*

SIZING SAHARA 11 gr.g. Shirocco (GER) – Aristocratique (Cadeaux Genereux) **c–** [2018/19 c–, h80: h24g h25dᵖᵘ h23.4d⁵ c21.2d⁵ h21d⁵ h25g Feb 25] angular gelding: poor **h70** handicap hurdler/maiden chaser: stays 3¼m: acts on heavy going: tried in blinkers. *Paul Henderson*

SIZING SCORPION (IRE) 10 b.g. Scorpion (IRE) – Fair Present (IRE) (Presenting) **c–** [2018/19 c15.7gᵖᵘ c20gᵖᵘ c26.2gᵖᵘ Apr 26] fell in point: winning hurdler: pulled up all 4 **h–** outings in chases: form only at 2m: tried in cheekpieces/tongue tie. *Colin Tizzard*

SIZING TENNESSEE (IRE) 11 ch.g. Robin des Champs (FR) – Jolivia (FR) **c157** (Dernier Empereur (USA)) [2018/19 c148, h–: c21.6m* c26s* Dec 1] **h–**

The emerald green, yellow chevron and sleeves of Ann & Alan Potts Limited will become a rarer sight on Britain's racecourses in future years. A trust was reportedly set up to continue the legacy of the Yorkshire couple by racing their existing string, though the horses won't be replaced as their careers come to an end. 'In the meantime, we've got to make sure we win enough money to finance it,' said Colin Tizzard, one of the trainers who has been involved with the Potts horses in recent years. Mining tycoon Alan Potts died at the age of eighty in November 2017, just months after his wife Ann, their best known horse being Sizing John (still in training, missed 2018/19) who landed the Irish Gold Cup, Cheltenham Gold Cup, Punchestown Gold Cup treble in 2016/17. Jessica Harrington, Sizing John's trainer, contributed significantly at the Grand National meeting to keeping the coffers of the Potts' trust topped up, Supasundae winning the Aintree Hurdle and Magic of Light landing the big second prize in the Grand National itself. As for Colin Tizzard, he saddled Sizing Tennessee to win the second most valuable handicap over jumps in Britain, the Ladbrokes Trophy (formerly the Hennessy) at Newbury in December.

The sum of €76,000 may not be everyone's idea of a bargain purchase but, in the world of big-spending Alan Potts, the figure that secured Sizing Tennessee as an unraced three-year-old was relatively small change. Very much a chasing type on looks, he was sent into training with Willie Mullins, for whom he ran in the Champion Bumper at Cheltenham and the Punchestown equivalent (fifth) as a five-year-old after winning twice. He then made a winning start over jumps in a novice hurdle at Navan before next being seen, after a two-year layoff with leg trouble, with Henry de Bromhead. Sizing Tennessee resumed winning ways when making all over hurdles at Navan in January 2016, by which time he was eight, and had his final run for de Bromhead when a 66/1-shot in the County Hurdle at the 2016 Cheltenham Festival. An eight-month absence followed, during which time Sizing Tennessee was transferred to Colin Tizzard who finally turned his attentions to steeplechasing. Let down by his jumping on occasions and even tried in blinkers, Sizing Tennessee took eight races to get off the mark over the bigger obstacles and was still a novice entering his second season as a chaser when he developed into a smart performer, winning at Cheltenham in December and reaching a place at the same track in the Dipper Novices' Chase and the National Hunt Chase at the Festival. That season ended with Sizing Tennessee being pulled up in the Scottish National.

Sizing Tennessee reappeared in the latest season under top weight in a handicap over two and three quarter miles at Fontwell in early-October when he produced a career best—over a trip and on firmish ground that, on the face of it, seemed unlikely to show him at his best. Travelling and jumping well in the main, Sizing Tennessee went on at the tenth and forged clear in the later stages to win by eleven lengths from Capeland. Still to be fully exposed over three miles plus, Sizing Tennessee lined up in the Ladbrokes Trophy alongside his four-years-younger stablemate Elegant Escape (whose own performances as a novice the previous season had included placed efforts in the RSA at the Cheltenham Festival and the Mildmay

Ladbrokes Trophy Chase (Handicap), Newbury—
stayers very much to the fore as Sizing Tennessee runs out a wide-margin winner from
stable-companion Elegant Escape (centre) and Dingo Dollar (right)

at Aintree). Elegant Escape started second favourite behind another six-year-old, Thomas Patrick, while Sizing Tennessee, the oldest in the field, was sent off at 12/1 after the leading ante-post fancy, the Mullins-trained Kemboy, was a late absentee when his ferry was cancelled because of bad weather. With exuberant jumper Go Conquer also a defector on the day, only twelve lined up, a significantly smaller field than usual for the race and the smallest since Coome Hill beat ten opponents in the 1996 renewal. It was necessary to go back even further—to Diamond Edge in 1981—to find a winner of the race as old as ten, but Sizing Tennessee progressed again and overcame a rather mixed round of jumping to triumph, staying on strongly, by ten lengths from Elegant Escape, with another six-year-old Dingo Dollar a further seven lengths back in third. Conditions were testing, with rain continuing through the first part of the afternoon, and many of the runners were struggling a long way from home, only eight completing the course. Like Elegant Escape, Sizing Tennessee held a Welsh Grand National entry but he didn't run at Chepstow and, in fact, wasn't seen out again after suffering a setback. At his age, and with his history of leg trouble, it could be that the Ladbrokes Trophy turns out to be Sizing Tennessee's swansong. If so, he did his connections proud, handsomely repaying the patience that they had shown with him over the years.

Sizing Tennessee (IRE) (ch.g. 2008)	Robin des Champs (FR) (b 1997)	Garde Royale (br 1980)	Mill Reef
			Royal Way
		Relayeuse (b 1987)	Iron Duke
			Reliorneuse
	Jolivia (FR) (ch 1999)	Dernier Empereur (ch 1990)	Trempolino
			Dear Colleen
		Via Sou (bl 1989)	Sicyos
			Vestal Queen

Sizing Tennessee, a strong gelding, is by Robin des Champs, a very successful French sire who spent the last half of his career in Ireland at Glenview Stud in County Cork where he died, at the age of twenty-one, shortly before Sizing Tennessee's triumph in the Ladbrokes Trophy. Robin des Champs sired the likes of Quevega, Sir des Champs and Vautour from his French-bred crops, and Sizing Tennessee has the same origin. His dam Jolivia was a fairly useful hurdler and winning chaser at around two miles in France and has done well at stud, producing a fairly useful hurdler and winning French chaser Lordolivia (by Lord of Men) and three winners by Yeats, the useful Bargy Lady (successful in Ireland over hurdles and fences), the fairly useful chaser Compadre (won twice at Market Rasen in the latest season), both of whom stay three miles, and Mount Ida (winner of a mares bumper at Wexford in April). Sizing Tennessee is a strong traveller in his races and stays three and a quarter miles well, and he acts on good to firm and heavy going. As already mentioned, he was tried in blinkers once. *Colin Tizzard*

SKANDIBURG (FR) 5 b.g. Sageburg (IRE) – Skandia (FR) (Robin des Champs (FR)) [2018/19 b89: b16g* h16g³ h20d⁴ h22.7g² h19.8s h19.6g* Apr 11] rather leggy gelding: fair form in bumpers: won conditionals/amateurs event at Fakenham in October: fairly useful novice hurdler: won at same course in December and Huntingdon in April: stays 23f: acts on soft going: tried in cheekpieces. *Olly Murphy* — **h122 b94**

SKA RIDGE 7 b.g. Distant Peak (IRE) – Tandawizi (Relief Pitcher) [2018/19 b–: h23.3gᵖᵘ h16.2g h15.7g h19.3s⁶ h19.9dᵖᵘ h24.3sᵖᵘ Mar 9] poor form over hurdles: left Rebecca Menzies after first start: hooded 4 of last 5 outings, also tongue tied 3 of last 4. *George Bewley* — **h83**

SKELLIG ROCKS (FR) 8 b.g. Poliglote – Skellig Mist (FR) (Sleeping Car (FR)) [2018/19 c20.2g⁵ c20.2gᵖᵘ c21.6dᵖᵘ Feb 24] modest maiden hurdler: fair maiden chaser: left A. L. T. Moore before return: stays 3m: acts on heavy going: regularly in headgear: tried in tongue tie: races prominently. *Robert Walford* — **c96 h–**

SKEWIFF 7 b.m. Doyen (IRE) × Skew (Niniski (USA)) [2018/19 h112: h23.3d⁴ h20d² h24.7g⁵ h21.2m³ c24.2g⁶ c20.6gᵘʳ c19.2d c22.5v* c20.9d⁵ c21.6mᶠ Apr 20] lengthy, angular mare: fair handicap hurdler: fairly useful form over fences: won handicap at Uttoxeter in January: stays 3m: acts on heavy going: not a fluent jumper. *Evan Williams* — **c117 x h113**

SKIDDAW TARA 5 b.g. Kayf Tara – Bob Back's Lady (IRE) (Bob Back (USA)) [2018/19 b16s Mar 9] 6/1, well held in bumper at Ayr. *Nicky Richards* — **b–**

SKIDDAW VALLEYS 7 ch.g. Three Valleys (USA) – Skiddaw Wolf (Wolfhound (USA)) [2018/19 h16.2g³ h16.2g² h15.7d² h20.2g² Apr 24] fair on Flat (stays 1¾m): fairly useful form over hurdles: placed all 4 outings: stays 2½m. *Nicky Richards* — **h116**

SKIDOOSH 6 b.g. Midnight Legend – Southern Exit (Poliglote) [2018/19 h97: h16g⁴ h19.7m* h19.7g³ h20.5d² h19.3g² h24.4g* h24.2d h24.3m² Apr 20] rangy gelding: bumper winner: fairly useful hurdler: won novice at Wetherby in November and handicap at Doncaster in February: stays 3m: acts on good to firm and good to soft going. *Ben Pauling* — **h128**

SKILLED 8 b.g. Mastercraftsman (IRE) – Treacle (USA) (Seeking The Gold (USA)) [2018/19 c115, h–: h19.9g⁵ Jul 27] winning hurdler: fairly useful chaser: stays 2½m: acts on soft going: usually in hood: held up. *Olly Murphy* — **c– h81**

SKIN DEEP (IRE) 6 ch.m. Presenting – Maryota (FR) (Martaline) [2018/19 b15.3m³ b15.7g² b16g* h19.6gᵖᵘ h20gᵖᵘ h19.6gᵖᵘ Oct 3] £56,000 3-y-o: second foal: dam twice-raced half-sister to high-class hurdler/smart chaser (stays 25f) Yanworth: fair form in bumpers: won mares event at Worcester in July: also fair form when winning mares maiden hurdle at Worcester in August: pulled up either side, lame final outing. *Alan King* — **h104 b94**

SKINFLINT (IRE) 7 b.g. Scorpion (IRE) – Gales Hill (IRE) (Beau Sher) [2018/19 h101: h23.3gᵖᵘ Jun 20] has had breathing operation: runner-up in Irish point: modest maiden hurdler: should stay beyond 2m: acts on heavy going: in headgear last 2 starts: tried in tongue tie. *David Pipe* — **h–**

SKINT 13 b.g. King's Theatre (IRE) – No More Money (Alflora (IRE)) [2018/19 c98§, h–§: c17.8g² c15.6gᵖᵘ Sep 17] well-made gelding: winning hurdler: modest handicap chaser: stays 2¾m: acts on good to firm and heavy going: regularly wears headgear/tongue tie: temperamental. *Michael Scudamore* — **c91 § h– §**

SKIPPING ON (IRE) 10 b.g. Westerner – Skipping Along (IRE) (Anshan) [2018/19 c117, h–: h19.9s* h19.3g Feb 18] fair hurdler: won novice at Sedgefield in December: fairly useful handicap chaser: stays 2½m: acts on heavy going: wears hood: often travels strongly. *Laura Morgan* — **c– h113**

SKIP SKOOL 6 b.g. Alkaased (USA) – Good Wee Girl (Tagula (IRE)) [2018/19 b16g Jun 2] well beaten in bumper. *Brendan Powell* — **b–**

SKIPTHECUDDLES (IRE) 8 b.g. Westerner – Autumn Sky (IRE) (Roselier (FR)) [2018/19 h132: c23.4s⁴ c23.6s⁵ c23.9d* c31.8mᵖᵘ h25g⁶ Apr 25] sturdy gelding: winning hurdler: useful form over fences: beat sole rival Chosen Path 6 lengths in novice at Market Rasen in February: stays 3m: acts on soft going: wears headgear: hard ride. *Graeme McPherson* — **c136 § h–**

SKIPTHESCALES (IRE) 7 b.g. Winged Love (IRE) – Waterland Gale (IRE) (Fourstars Allstar (USA)) [2018/19 h115: h24.7g c24.2s* c23.4s* c24.5g⁶ h24.1d² Mar 19] fairly useful handicap hurdler: similar form over fences: won novice handicaps at Wetherby and Newcastle in December: stays 25f: acts on heavy going: wears headgear. *Philip Kirby* — **c121 h118**

SKYE CHIEF 7 b.g. Sulamani (IRE) – Isle of Skye (Terimon) [2018/19 h103, b92: h19.3s h16.4s⁶ c20.3m⁴ Feb 28] fair form on first of 3 outings over hurdles: shaped well when fourth in novice handicap at Musselburgh on chasing debut: entitled to progress. *Simon Waugh* **c103 p** **h63**

SKY FULL OF STARS (IRE) 9 b.g. Mahler – Gold Flo (IRE) (Fourstars Allstar (USA)) [2018/19 c99, h90: h19.2d³ h17.7v⁶ c17.8v² h17.7d* c17.8s* h19s c17.8vᵖᵘ Mar 16] workmanlike gelding: modest handicap hurdler: won at Fontwell in January: fair handicap chaser: won at same track later that month: best around 2m: acts on heavy going: regularly wears headgear. *Chris Gordon* **c103** **h96**

SKYHILL ALLSTAR (IRE) 8 b.g. Shareb (USA) – Rachels Allstar (IRE) (Fourstars Allstar (USA)) [2018/19 c21.2g⁴ May 28] multiple point winner: well beaten in maiden hunter on chasing debut. *Simon Edwards* **c55**

SKYHILL (IRE) 6 b.g. Gold Well – Classic Mari (IRE) (Classic Cliche (IRE)) [2018/19 h20.5vᵖᵘ h23.8g³ h16.2v⁵ h24s h20.6dᵖᵘ h20.6d⁵ Apr 6] £26,000 5-y-o: has had breathing operation: first foal: dam lightly-raced half-sister to Stayers' Hurdle winner Princeful: maiden pointer: poor maiden hurdler on balance: stays 3m: tongue tied second to fifth outings. *Alison Hamilton* **h97 ?**

SKY KHAN 10 b.g. Cape Cross (IRE) – Starlit Sky (Galileo (IRE)) [2018/19 h129: h20.6g³ h20.1g⁵ h22.1gᵖᵘ h20.2g² h21.3s⁴ h20.9g² h23.8m³ h21.4m⁵ h20.2d⁵ Apr 26] good-topped gelding: fairly useful handicap hurdler: stays 3m: acts on good to firm and heavy going: wears headgear/tongue tie: usually waited with. *Lucinda Russell* **h125**

SKYLANDER (IRE) 10 b.g. Flemensfirth (USA) – Cat Burglar (IRE) (Robellino (USA)) [2018/19 c25.8gᵖᵘ May 16] lengthy gelding: dual point winner: formerly fairly useful hurdler/chaser (for David Pipe): pulled up in hunter only outing in 2018/19: stays 27f: acts on good to firm and heavy going: usually in headgear/tongue tie. *A. S. T. Holdsworth* **c–** **h–**

SKYLARK LADY (IRE) 6 ch.m. Tamayuz – Allegrissimo (IRE) (Redback) [2018/19 h16.8gᶠ h19g h16g h19d Nov 29] modest juvenile hurdler in 2016/17: well held in handicaps all 3 completed outings since: in headgear 6 of last 7 starts, also tongue tied final one. *Nikki Evans* **h–**

SKYLINE 5 b.g. Stimulation (IRE) – Yonder (And Beyond (IRE)) [2018/19 b85: b15.8g⁵ May 10] lengthy, unfurnished gelding: has had breathing operation: modest form in bumpers: tried in tongue tie. *Hughie Morrison* **b83**

SKY OF STARS (IRE) 6 b.g. Frozen Power (IRE) – So So Lucky (IRE) (Danehill (USA)) [2018/19 h97: h16.3m³ c17.4gᵖᵘ h25.8g⁶ h20g Sep 11] rather leggy gelding: modest handicap hurdler: pulled up in novice handicap on chasing debut: stays 2½m: acts on good to firm and good to soft going: wears headgear. *Barry Brennan* **c–** **h87**

SKY PIRATE 6 b.g. Midnight Legend – Dancingwithbubbles (IRE) (Supreme Leader) [2018/19 h118: h24.7g³ h23g* h23g³ c24g² c24.5d² c25gᵇᵈ c24.2d⁴ c26d Mar 14] good-topped gelding: point winner: useful handicap hurdler: won at Worcester in June: similar form over fences: in frame 3 of 4 completed outings, and also shaped well when seventh to Any Second Now in Fulke Walwyn Kim Muir Chase at Cheltenham final outing: stays 25f: acts on good to soft going. *Jonjo O'Neill* **c135** **h131**

SLADE STORM (IRE) 6 b.g. September Storm (GER) – Katie Kelly (IRE) (Deploy) [2018/19 b16.2g⁵ h20.1g⁶ May 22] €6,500 3-y-o: second foal: brother to bumper winner Storm Forecast: dam, ran once in bumper, out of half-sister to smart chaser (stayed 3m) Young Spartacus: placed in Irish point: showed a bit in bumper/novice hurdle. *Alistair Whillans* **h82** **b77**

SLAINE 5 b.m. Brian Boru – Flowing On (Alflora (IRE)) [2018/19 b74: b15.8v⁴ h15.8vᶠ h15.8m h19.6g³ Apr 11] poor form in bumpers: fair form over hurdles: much improved when third in novice at Huntingdon. *Neil King* **h106** **b–**

SLAINTE AND THANKS (IRE) 7 b.m. Arakan (USA) – Danza Nera (IRE) (Dansili) [2018/19 h21g³ h16.5g* h16g⁵ h16m h19d h16g⁶ h16g⁶ h23.4g² h23d Dec 15] modest maiden on Flat (stays 12.5f): point winner: modest handicap hurdler: won mares event at Clonmel in June: barely stays 23f: best form on good going: tried in hood/tongue tie. *G. Ahern, Ireland* **h97**

SLAINTE MHOR (IRE) 5 b.g. Milan – Founding Daughter (IRE) (Anshan) [2018/19 b16g⁶ b17s Mar 7] last in bumpers. *Lucinda Russell* **b–**

SLANELOUGH (IRE) 7 b.g. Westerner – Tango Lady (IRE) (King's Theatre (IRE)) [2018/19 h126: c15.9g⁴ c20.9s⁵ c19sᵘʳ c19.9gᶠ Feb 16] workmanlike gelding: runner-up in Irish point: fairly useful hurdler: similar form over fences: stays 21f: acts on heavy going: wears hood. *Rose Dobbin* **c129** **h–**

SLANEMORE HILL (IRE) 7 br.g. Court Cave (IRE) – Goodonyou-Polly (IRE) (Good **c103 ?**
Thyne (USA)) [2018/19 c24.2m³ c23.4g^pu c23.4g^pu h23.1d Feb 5] €9,000 4-y-o, £20,000 **h–**
6-y-o: fourth foal: half-brother to a winning pointer by Desert King: dam (c92/h94)
2¼m-2½m hurdle/chase winner: point winner: last in handicap on hurdling debut: form in
novice chases only when third of 4 finishers at Wetherby, probably flattered: in headgear
last 2 starts. *Chris Grant*

SLANEY CRAIGLEGACY (IRE) 7 b.m. Craigsteel – Slaney Legacy (IRE) (Mr **h78**
Combustible (IRE)) [2018/19 h16.7g h16.2g h20.2g h21.2m⁴ h18.1m* h20.9g h19.3g⁴ Oct
25] first foal: dam placed in point: poor handicap hurdler: won at Kelso in September: stays
21f: acts on good to firm and good to soft going: wears headgear. *Hugh Burns*

SLATE HOUSE (IRE) 7 b.g. Presenting – Bay Pearl (FR) (Broadway Flyer (USA)) **c129**
[2018/19 h138: c19.7d⁴ c19.9d⁵ c19.9d² c15.9s Mar 12] strong, good sort: has had breathing **h–**
operation: Irish point winner: useful novice hurdler in 2017/18: fairly useful form over
fences: best effort when second in novice at Newbury in March: highly tried either side:
may prove best at shorter than 2½m: acts on soft going: wears tongue tie. *Colin Tizzard*

SLAVE TO LOVE (IRE) 5 b.m. Arcadio (GER) – Grape Love (FR) (Grape Tree Road) **b–**
[2018/19 b15.7d⁵ Mar 6] seventh foal: sister to fair 2m hurdle winner/winning pointer
Minella Berry (by King's Theatre) and bumper winner Chapel Garden (by Heron Island):
dam unraced half-sister to smart French hurdler/useful chaser (stayed 3¼m) Great Love: in
hood, well beaten in bumper. *Julia Brooke*

SLAYING THE DRAGON (IRE) 6 ch.g. Notnowcato – Empress Charlotte (Holy **h83**
Roman Emperor (IRE)) [2018/19 h–: h18.5m² h21.6m^pu h21.6m⁶ h18.5d² h16s h21.6s^pu
Nov 25] stocky gelding: poor maiden hurdler: left Martin Hill after fourth start: stays 2¼m:
acts on good to firm and good to soft going: wears headgear/tongue tie. *Nigel Hawke*

SLEEP EASY 7 b.g. Rip Van Winkle (IRE) – Strictly Lambada (Red Ransom (USA)) **c119**
[2018/19 h131: h18.5s⁴ h21.6g³ h22g² h20.5s h21g h21.4g c20.2g³ c21.6g³ Apr 12] **h124**
compact gelding: has had breathing operation: fairly useful handicap hurdler: similar form
both both outings over fences: stays 2¾m: acts on soft going: wears headgear: tried in
tongue tie. *Neil Mulholland*

SLEEP IN FIRST (FR) 13 b.g. Sleeping Car (FR) – First Union (FR) (Shafoun (FR)) **c102**
[2018/19 c–, h95: c15.6g² c15.6g* c20.1m² c21.2g² h18.6m⁴ h17.2d⁵ c15.9d⁴ Oct 18] **h91**
modest handicap hurdler: fair handicap chaser: won at Hexham in May: stays 21f: acts on
soft and good to firm going: has worn headgear/tongue tie. *James Ewart*

SLEEPY HAVEN (IRE) 9 b.g. Indian Haven – High Society Girl (IRE) (Key of Luck **c– x**
(USA)) [2018/19 c–x, h119: h16m⁶ h16.2s² h19.7d⁴ h16.4v⁵ Mar 16] sturdy gelding: fairly **h122**
useful handicap hurdler: maiden chaser (often let down by jumping): best up to 2½m: acts
on heavy going: often in headgear/tongue tie. *Jennie Candlish*

SLEIGHT OF HAND (IRE) 5 b.g. Kalanisi (IRE) – Katariya (IRE) (Barathea (IRE)) **b97**
[2018/19 b15.3d³ b16m⁴ Feb 23] €40,000 3-y-o: well-made gelding: has had breathing
operation: brother to fair hurdler Kalarika (2m-2¼m winner) and half-brother to a winner
on Flat by Noverre: dam ran twice on Flat: fairly useful form in frame in bumpers at
Wincanton and Kempton. *Nicky Henderson*

SLEPTWITHMEBOOTSON (IRE) 4 b.f. Universal (IRE) – Temple Heather (Faustus (USA)) **b–**
[2018/19 b14g Nov 21] compact filly: half-sister to useful chaser Embracing Change
(3m-29f winner, by Anshan) and a winning pointer by Presenting: dam unraced: tailed off
in fillies junior bumper. *John O'Neill*

SLICE OF LEMON 7 b.m. Dr Massini (IRE) – Lady Maranzi (Teenoso (USA)) [2018/19 **h–**
h–: h15.8m h15.8g⁴ h18.5g Oct 1] lengthy mare: no show over hurdles. *Debra Hamer*

SLIDING DOORS (IRE) 6 b.g. Ask – Reseda (GER) (Lavirco (GER)) [2018/19 h103: **h112**
h24.7g³ h21g h23.8g² h19.8s⁶ h24.2d Mar 22] good-topped gelding: fair maiden hurdler:
likely to stay beyond 25f: acts on soft going: in cheekpieces last 2 starts: usually waited
with. *Ian Williams*

SLIPPER SATIN (IRE) 9 b.m. Excellent Art – In The Ribbons (In The Wings) [2018/19 **h–**
h19.9g⁵ h19.9g^pu Nov 8] fair hurdle winner: lightly raced and no form since 2015/16: has
worn headgear, including last 2 starts: wears tongue tie. *Simon West*

SLOWMOTION (FR) 7 b.m. Soldier of Fortune (IRE) – Second Emotion (FR) (Medaaly) **c134**
[2018/19 c139, h–: h16g⁴ c22.5d⁶ c24s^pu h20.2d³ h19.9s⁵ c20d⁴ Apr 23] good-topped mare: **h127**
fairly useful hurdler: useful handicap chaser: best short of 3m when conditions are testing:
acts on heavy going: wears headgear. *Joseph Patrick O'Brien, Ireland*

SLUMBER PARTY 6 gr.g. Hellvelyn – In Some Style (IRE) (Grand Lodge (USA)) **b–**
[2018/19 b–: b15.8g⁶ Jul 18] last in bumpers 7 months apart. *Matthew Salaman*

SMACKWATER JACK (IRE) 5 b.g. Flemensfirth (USA) – Malachy's Attic (IRE) **h125**
(Old Vic) [2018/19 b94: h20g^F h16d^3 h21.2g* h19d^2 h19.8s h21.2m^4 Apr 1] rather
unfurnished gelding: fairly useful form over hurdles: won maiden at Ludlow in January:
stays 21f: acts on good to soft going: tried in cheekpieces. *Olly Murphy*

SMADYNIUM (FR) 11 gr.g. Smadoun (FR) – Sea Music (FR) (Bering) [2018/19 c124§, **c80 §**
h–§: c21.6g^5 May 17] rather leggy gelding: winning hurdler: formerly fairly useful chaser **h– §**
(for John Joseph Hanlon): well beaten in hunter only outing outside points in 2018/19:
stays 3m: acts on heavy going: regularly in headgear: tongue tied: front runner/races
prominently: unreliable. *Alan Hill*

SMAOINEAMH ALAINN (IRE) 7 b.m. Shantou (USA) – Dathuil (IRE) (Royal **h124**
Academy (USA)) [2018/19 h130: h16m^3 h15.3g^5 h16.8g^6 h19.5d^3 h16.5g Feb 19] good-
topped mare: fairly useful handicap hurdler: unproven beyond 17f: acts on good to firm and
heavy going: normally hooded. *Robert Walford*

SMART BOY (IRE) 8 b.g. Mahler – Supreme Style (IRE) (Supreme Leader) [2018/19 **h108**
h112: h19.2m^5 h23.6d^{pu} h19d^{pu} h21.7d Feb 24] runner-up in point: fair handicap hurdler:
stays 21f: acts on good to firm and heavy going: tried in cheekpieces: usually leads. *Jack
R. Barber*

SMART GETAWAY (IRE) 7 b.m. Getaway (GER) – Legendsofthefall (IRE) (Arctic **h98 p**
Lord) [2018/19 b82: b17.7s^3 h21.7v^2 Mar 16] modest form in bumpers: encouraging 10 **b76**
lengths second to Shapiro in novice at Fontwell on hurdling debut: open to improvement.
Dominic Ffrench Davis

SMART PACO 5 ch.g. Paco Boy (IRE) – La Gifted (Fraam) [2018/19 b–: b16.8m h15.6g^5 **h–**
h20.6s^4 h16.4s^{pu} Mar 10] no form in bumpers/over hurdles: wears tongue tie. **b–**
Maurice Barnes

SMART RULER (IRE) 13 ch.g. Viking Ruler (AUS) – Celebrated Smile (IRE) **c–**
(Cadeaux Genereux) [2018/19 c103, h100: h16.2d^4 h17.2g^6 h22.1m^6 h17.2g^3 h16.8m^3 **h88**
h16.8m h15.6g^{pu} Dec 3] modest handicap hurdler: placed in maiden chases: stayed 21f:
acted on good to firm and good to soft going: tried in headgear: dead. *James Moffatt*

SMARTY WILD 5 b.g. Fair Mix (IRE) – Blaeberry (Kirkwall) [2018/19 b16v^6 b15.8s^6 **h129 p**
h15.8g^3 h15.8d* h16.8s* h19d* Mar 11] third foal: half-brother to 1½m winner Bowberry **b70**
(by Cockney Rebel): dam (c134/h130), 19f-3m hurdle/chase winner, also 7f winner on
Flat: mid-field in bumpers: fairly useful form over hurdles: won novice at Ludlow in
February and handicaps at Exeter (conditionals) and Taunton in March: will be suited by
2½m: remains open to improvement. *Philip Hobbs*

SMILING ELIZA (IRE) 4 b.f. Rock of Gibraltar (IRE) – Gift Dancer (Imperial Dancer) **h111**
[2018/19 h16.4g^2 h17d^2 h16m* h16.2g^2 h16g* h17s^4 h16g^4 h18g^5 h20d h20.2g
Apr 24] fair on Flat, stays 1½m: fair juvenile hurdler: won at Down Royal (maiden event)
in August and Punchestown in October: best around 2m: acts on good to firm going: in
cheekpieces last 4 starts. *Gordon Elliott, Ireland*

SMILING JESSICA (IRE) 9 ch.m. Golden Tornado (IRE) – Charlie's Mary (IRE) **c86**
(Daar Alzamaan (IRE)) [2018/19 c83, h64, b–: h21.8g^6 c23g^2 h21.8d^3 c25.5d^{pu} Aug 25] **h88**
modest form over hurdles: modest handicap chaser: stayed 3m: acted on good to soft
going: usually wore headgear: dead. *Gavin Patrick Cromwell, Ireland*

SMITH'S BAY 6 b.g. Midnight Legend – Takotna (IRE) (Bering) [2018/19 b91: h19g^6 **h106 p**
h20.5d^5 Mar 22] sturdy gelding: bumper winner: fair form in novice hurdles, better effort
when fifth at Newbury in March: capable of better still. *Alan King*

SMITHS CROSS (IRE) 7 b.g. Westerner – Blue Supreme (IRE) (Pistolet Bleu (IRE)) **h114**
[2018/19 b101: h15.8v^2 h19.5v^2 h16v^4 Feb 18] smallish, strong gelding: Irish point winner:
bumper winner: fair form over hurdles, runner-up in novices first 2 outings.
Michael Scudamore

SMOKING DIXIE (IRE) 8 ch.g. Beneficial – Jacksister (IRE) (Flemensfirth (USA)) **c54**
[2018/19 c93, h–: h20.2g^5 c22.6g c16g Sep 23] has had breathing operation: modest form **h79**
over hurdles/fences: left John Groucott, disappointing in 2018/19: stays 2½m: acts on soft
going: tried in hood: usually races close up. *Warren Greatrex*

SMOKING GUN (IRE) 6 b.g. Gold Well – The Wounded Cook (IRE) (Muroto) **h132**
[2018/19 h16.9s* h16s* h16d^4 h20d* h20.2g* Mar 7] €80,000 3-y-o: fourth foal: half-
brother to useful hurdler/chaser Hazy Tom (2m-2½m winner) and fairly useful hurdler/
chaser The Housekeeper (2½m-3m winner), both by Heron Island: dam pulled up in point:
useful form over hurdles: won 4 of 5 starts in 2018/19, maiden at Clonmel and novice at

Limerick in December, and handicaps at Gowran in February and Thurles (by ¾ length from Plan of Attack) in March: likely to stay 3m: acts on soft going. *Joseph Patrick O'Brien, Ireland*

SMOKING JACKET (IRE) 9 b.g. Beneficial – Unalaska (IRE) (High Estate) [2018/19 c–, h–: h19.5d h19.6d^{pu} Jan 25] sturdy gelding: maiden hurdler: fair form over fences in 2016/17: lightly raced and no form since, including over hurdles. *Tom George*   **c–**
h–

SMOOTH STEPPER 10 b.g. Alflora (IRE) – Jazzy Refrain (IRE) (Jareer (USA)) [2018/19 c142, h–: h24s c23.8d^5 c34v^{pu} c25g^{pu} Apr 6] workmanlike gelding: winning hurdler: useful handicap chaser: below form in 2018/19: probably stays 4m: acts on heavy going:. *Alex Hales*   **c124**
h–

SMUGGLER'S BLUES (IRE) 7 b.g. Yeats (IRE) – Rosy de Cyborg (FR) (Cyborg (FR)) [2018/19 h109, b89: h15.8g c20s^4 c25.6d^5 c22.4d c20.3d* Apr 26] sturdy gelding: fair form over hurdles: fairly useful form over fences: won handicap at Bangor (conditionals) in April: likely to prove best up to 3m: acts on good to soft going. *Tom George*   **c116**
h96

SNAPDRAGON FIRE (IRE) 6 b.g. Getaway (GER) – Global Diamond (IRE) (Classic Music (USA)) [2018/19 h113, b87: h15.8g* h16.4g^{pu} h15.8g* h15.3g^2 h15.3g^4 h15.8g* h15.8m^2 Apr 1] useful hurdler: won handicaps at Huntingdon in October and November (lady riders), and novice at Ludlow in February: has form at 21f, very best efforts around 2m: acts on soft and good to firm going. *Tom Lacey*   **h133**

SNAP SHOTS (IRE) 7 b.g. Kodiac – Refuse To Give Up (IRE) (Refuse To Bend (IRE)) [2018/19 h16m^6 h16.3m^6 Jul 22] useful sprinter at best on Flat: no form over hurdles: wears tongue tie. *Oliver Greenall*   **h–**

SNATCHITBACK 8 b.g. Overbury (IRE) – Talk The Talk (Terimon) [2018/19 h–: h16.8s Jan 20] fourth only start in points: little impact under Rules: tried in hood/tongue tie. *Michael Scudamore*   **h–**

SNAZZ MAN 9 b.g. Beat All (USA) – Ela d'Argent (IRE) (Ela-Mana-Mou) [2018/19 h59: h21.7g* h21.7v^{pu} h22g^{pu} Mar 30] poor handicap hurdler: won at Fontwell in May: stays 2¾m: usually races close up. *Susan Gardner*   **h79**

SNEAKY FEELING (IRE) 7 b.g. Oscar (IRE) – Shuil Aris (IRE) (Anshan) [2018/19 h–: h19.5d h21.9s h23.9s^6 Apr 7] lengthy gelding: has had breathing operation: made frame in Irish point: fairly useful hurdler at best, below that level since 2016/17: stays 2½m: acts on soft going. *Philip Hobbs*   **h109**

SNEAKY GETAWAY (IRE) 6 b.g. Getaway (GER) – Aguida (FR) (Kahyasi) [2018/19 b16g^{ur} b16g^2 b19d* Apr 21] €8,000 3-y-o: fifth foal: brother to a winning pointer: dam lightly-raced half-sister to very smart French hurdler/useful chaser (17f-25f winner) Astonville: useful form in bumpers: won maiden event at Cork (by ½ length from General Counsel) in April. *Emmet Mullins, Ireland*   **b105**

SNIPPETYDOODAH 11 b.m. King's Theatre (IRE) – Kimpour (FR) (Hawker's News (IRE)) [2018/19 h97: h19.5s^4 h25s^{pu} h17.7v^3 h20.5g^{pu} Apr 7] has had breathing operation: modest handicap hurdler: stays 2¾m: acts on heavy going: has worn hood, including in 2018/19: wears tongue tie: usually front runner/races prominently: temperament under suspicion. *Michael Roberts*   **h97**

SNOBBERY (IRE) 6 b.g. Duke of Marmalade (IRE) – Boast (Most Welcome) [2018/19 h83: h21.2m h22g Jun 9] strong gelding: poor maiden hurdler: has worn tongue tie, including in 2018/19. *Nigel Twiston-Davies*   **h67**

SNOOKERED (IRE) 5 b.g. Born To Sea (IRE) – Secret Quest (Pivotal) [2018/19 h62p: h16.8g^2 h16.4g h16.4d^6 h16d^4 h16.2d^2 h16.2g^4 Apr 25] rather leggy gelding: fair maiden hurdler: raced around 2m: acts on good to soft going: usually in cheekpieces. *Brian Ellison*   **h106**

SNOUGAR (IRE) 6 b.g. Arakan (USA) – Thorbella (Deploy) [2018/19 h109, b–: h16s^5 Dec 26] fair form at best over hurdles, below that level sole outing in 2018/19: raced around 2m: acts on heavy going: tracks pace. *Donald McCain*   **h93**

SNOWBALL (IRE) 12 gr.g. Alderbrook – Rosafi (IRE) (Roselier (FR)) [2018/19 c75, h–: c28.5d^5 c23.5v^3 c23.5v Feb 18] rather leggy gelding: winning hurdler: poor handicap chaser: stays 3½m: acts on heavy going. *David Arbuthnot*   **c75**
h–

SNOWED IN (IRE) 10 gr.g. Dark Angel (IRE) – Spinning Gold (Spinning World (USA)) [2018/19 c–, h89: h17.2g h18.1m^3 h17.1d h20.1s^6 h19.3g^2 h19.7g^3 h17v^6 Mar 17] modest handicap hurdler: twice-raced chaser: stays 21f: acts on good to firm and heavy going: wears cheekpieces. *Barbara Butterworth*   **c–**
h89

Guinness Kerry National Handicap Chase, Listowel—Snow Falcon gains consolation for his luckless Galway Plate defeat with a narrow win over Saturnas (seams)

SNOWELL (IRE) 12 b.g. Well Chosen – Snow Water (IRE) (Jolly Jake (NZ)) [2018/19 h16.8s h16s[6] h15.7d Apr 9] compact gelding: modest handicap hurdler, below form in 2018/19 after 3-year absence: winning chaser: stays 2¾m: acts on heavy going: wears cheekpieces. *Emma-Jane Bishop* **c–** **h65**

SNOW FALCON (IRE) 9 b.g. Presenting – Flocon de Neige (IRE) (Kahyasi) [2018/19 c149+, h–: c22.5d[4] c24s* c19.5g* c20d[4] Apr 22] sturdy gelding: winning hurdler: very smart chaser: won Kerry National Handicap Chase at Listowel (by neck from Saturnas) in September and Grade 2 event at Down Royal (by 1½ lengths from Shattered Love) in November: stays 25f: acts on heavy going: has worn headgear. *Noel Meade, Ireland* **c156** **h–**

SNOW RESCUE (IRE) 7 gr.g. Stowaway – Annilogs Palm (IRE) (Great Palm (USA)) [2018/19 c–, h–: c20.3d[pu] c15.9g[2] c17.2g[4] c15.7g[pu] Apr 3] sturdy gelding: maiden hurdler: poor form over fences: unproven beyond 17f: raced mainly on good going: in cheekpieces last 3 starts: wears tongue tie. *Tom Gretton* **c82** **h–**

SNOWY OSCAR (IRE) 6 b.g. Oscar (IRE) – Reedsbuck (FR) (Cyborg (FR)) [2018/19 h94, b63: h19.2d[pu] h17.7v[5] h23d Jan 15] smallish, plain gelding: poor maiden hurdler: has worn hood, including in 2018/19: often in tongue tie. *Nick Gifford* **h75**

SNUFF BOX (IRE) 8 b.g. Witness Box (USA) – Dara Supreme (IRE) (Darazari (IRE)) [2018/19 h108, b–: c23.6s c24.2v[2] c23.6d[6] c30.7s[6] Apr 16] point winner: fair form over hurdles: fairly useful form over fences: second in novice handicap at Exeter in March: stays 3m: best form on heavy going. *Venetia Williams* **c122** **h–**

SNUGSBOROUGH BENNY (IRE) 9 b.g. Beneficial – Saddlers Arc (IRE) (Saddlers' Hall (IRE)) [2018/19 c19.5v[6] c19.7g* c22.2m[3] c22.5d* h20g c24.5g[ur] c23.5g* c29d[4] Apr 22] winning hurdler: useful chaser: won novice at Down Royal in May, handicap at Galway in August and minor event at Fairyhouse (by 6 lengths from Call It Magic) in February: should stay 3m+: acts on soft and good to firm going: races off pace. *Liam P. Cusack, Ireland* **c141** **h–**

SNUGSBOROUGH HALL (IRE) 8 b.g. Beneficial – Saddlers Arc (IRE) (Saddlers' Hall (IRE)) [2018/19 c22g[5] c21s[6] c25.7d[2] c20d[3] c25.5d[3] c20.2d* c17d* c16.7g[co] Apr 21] third foal: brother to fairly useful hurdler/useful chaser Snugsborough Benny (2½m-23f winner): dam showed a little ability in bumpers: winning hurdler: smart chaser: won maiden at Clonmel in February, novice at Leopardstown in March and handicap at **c147** **h–**

Punchestown (easily by 11 lengths from Impact Factor) shortly after end of British season: stays 3¼m, at least as effective at much shorter: acts on soft going: wears hood: usually travels strongly. *Liam P. Cusack, Ireland*

SOARLIKEANEAGLE (IRE) 7 b.g. Scorpion (IRE) – Wayward Cove (Karinga Bay) **h91**
[2018/19 h19.5s⁴ h20.5s h20.5sᵖᵘ h15.9g h24.2d h19.8g Apr 14] €5,000 3-y-o, £17,000
6-y-o: lengthy gelding: will make a chaser: seventh foal: dam lightly-raced half-sister to smart chaser (19f-21f winner) Wayward King: Irish point winner: modest form over hurdles. *Richard Rowe*

SOCKSY (IRE) 8 ch.m. Flemensfirth (USA) – Bachello (IRE) (Bach (IRE)) [2018/19 **c119**
c121, h–: h23.6s c26.3s² c24.2d² c28.8v⁶ c24s⁴ c26gᵖᵘ c23.8d⁶ Apr 26] winning hurdler: **h–**
fairly useful handicap chaser: stays 3¼m: acts on heavy going: usually wears headgear/tongue tie. *Fergal O'Brien*

SO ENJOY (IRE) 4 b.f. So You Think (NZ) – Winter Song (IRE) (Pivotal) [2018/19 **h94**
h16.6g h16g⁶ h15.6g⁴ h16.6d⁴ h16g³ h16.8g³ Apr 18] fair maiden on Flat, stays 9f: modest form over hurdles: raced around 2m: acts on good to soft going: tried in blinkers. *James A. Nash, Ireland*

SOEUR DE STROP (IRE) 6 b.m. Robin des Pres (FR) – Miss Twinkletoes (IRE) **h–**
(Zafonic (USA)) [2018/19 b16.2d b16d h15.7gᵖᵘ Dec 28] €3,000 4-y-o: half-sister to **b–**
several winners, including bumper winner/fair 2m hurdle winner Kalaniti (by Kalanisi): dam French 1m winner: no form in bumpers/novice hurdle: tried in cheekpieces. *Chris Grant*

SOFIA'S ROCK (FR) 5 b.g. Rock of Gibraltar (IRE) – Princess Sofia (UAE) (Pennekamp **h137 p**
(USA)) [2018/19 h16m* h16.5g³ h15.8d* Mar 21] has had breathing operation: useful on Flat, stays 13f: similar form over hurdles: won maiden at Worcester in September and novice at Ludlow (tongue tied) in March: open to further improvement. *Dan Skelton*

SOIESAUVAGE (FR) 8 b.m. Lauro (GER) – Taffetas (FR) (Nikos) [2018/19 h91: h16g⁴ **h100**
h15.8g* h16g² h19.6g⁶ Oct 30] sturdy mare: fair handicap hurdler: won mares event at Uttoxeter in September: stays 2½m: acts on soft going: wears hood/tongue tie. *Sophie Leech*

SOJOURN (IRE) 6 b.g. Getaway (GER) – Toscar (IRE) (Oscar (IRE)) [2018/19 b85: **h110 p**
b17g* h19.8s³ h21g² Apr 10] fairly useful form in bumpers: won at Aintree in November: **b100**
fair form over hurdles: better effort when third in maiden at Wincanton in March: tried in tongue tie: should still improve. *Anthony Honeyball*

SOLAR GLORY (IRE) 5 b.g. Fame And Glory – Cashalass (IRE) (Moscow Society **h89**
(USA)) [2018/19 b17.7g⁵ b17.7s b17.7s h17.7v⁵ h19.2m³ h21.7g³ Apr 24] €20,000 3-y-o: **b–**
has had breathing operation: third foal: half-brother to bumper winner/fairly useful hurdler Osco Mosco (2¼m-2½m winner, by Oscar): dam unraced sister to useful hurdlers Kopeck (2m winner) and Rouble (2m-2½m winner): no form in bumpers: modest form over hurdles: best effort when third in maiden at Fontwell: tried in tongue tie. *Nick Gifford*

SOLAR IMPULSE (FR) 9 b.g. Westerner – Moon Glow (FR) (Solar One (FR)) **c128**
[2018/19 c121§, h–: c15.2g⁵ c20.2gᵘʳ c17.4g* Apr 13] good-topped gelding: has had **h–**
breathing operation: winning hurdler: fairly useful handicap chaser nowadays: won at Bangor in April: stays 19f: acts on good to firm and heavy going: wears headgear: has worn tongue tie: quirky sort (can race freely). *Ian Williams*

SOLATENTIF (FR) 9 b.g. Solon (GER) – Indian Mist (FR) (River Mist (USA)) [2018/19 **c120 §**
c124§, h126§: c20g³ h17.2m h20g² h21.6g h15.9gᵖᵘ Sep 23] sturdy gelding: fairly useful **h122 §**
handicap hurdler/maiden chaser: stayed easy 3¼m: acted on soft and good to firm going: often wore headgear/tongue tie: temperamental: dead. *Colin Tizzard*

SOLDIER OF LOVE 6 b.g. Yeats (IRE) – Monsignorita (IRE) (Classic Cliche (IRE)) **h108**
[2018/19 b95: h16.7g³ h18.6s³ h19g² h23.9d⁴ Feb 28] good-topped gelding: fair form over hurdles: in cheekpieces, won novice handicap at Taunton in February. *Fergal O'Brien*

SOLDIER OF WAR (USA) 4 b.g. War Front (USA) – Praise (USA) (Mr Prospector **b–**
(USA)) [2018/19 b16.6g⁵ Mar 2] tailed off in bumper. *Sarah-Jayne Davies*

SOLEGLAD (IRE) 7 b.g. Scorpion (IRE) – Tilaiya (IRE) (Fantastic Light (USA)) **c–**
[2018/19 h92, b104: h16.5g h20.2g⁵ h18.8g⁶ h20.1g h16.5d c18m c20.3dᵖᵘ Nov 20] **h95**
bumper winner: modest maiden hurdler: no form over fences: stays 2½m: acts on soft going: tried in blinkers: in tongue tie last 3 starts. *Gavin Patrick Cromwell, Ireland*

SOLE PRETENDER (IRE) 5 b.g. Gold Well – Cool Quest (IRE) (Turtle Island (IRE)) **h134**
[2018/19 b16.3g* h16g⁴ h20g* h19.3g² h17.6g* h16d* Apr 27] €20,000 3-y-o: third foal: **b92**
dam (c131/h116), 2m/17f hurdle/chase winner, half-sister to fairly useful hurdler/useful

chaser (stayed 3m) Mister Hyde: won maiden bumper at Ballinrobe (by 1½ lengths from Russian Dancer) on debut in May: useful form over hurdles: won maiden at Clonmel in October, and handicap at Ballinrobe and minor event at Wexford (by 7½ lengths from Kingston Girl) in April: stays 2½m: acts on good to soft going: in hood last 2 starts: usually races close up. *Norman Lee, Ireland*

SOLID STRIKE 11 b.g. Sir Harry Lewis (USA) – Solid Land (FR) (Solid Illusion (USA)) [2018/19 c107: c19.3s⁵ c26.3s c22.7g² c20.1v* c26.2d² Mar 24] fair handicap chaser: won at Hexham in March: stays 3¼m: acts on heavy going: in cheekpieces last 2 starts: usually races prominently. *Paul Collins* **c105**

SOLIGHOSTER (FR) 7 ch.g. Loup Solitaire (USA) – Miss Martine (FR) (Waki River (FR)) [2018/19 c135, h–: c23.8m c23.4dᶠ c23.8s⁴ c23.4sᶠ h24.3g h23.9sᵖᵘ Apr 7] well-made gelding: fairly useful hurdler/useful chaser at best, largely out of sorts in 2018/19: stays 3m: acts on heavy going: tried in cheekpieces: usually races off pace. *Neil Mulholland* **c123 h–**

SOLOMN GRUNDY (IRE) 9 b.g. Westerner – Marika's King (IRE) (King's Ride) [2018/19 c126, h134: c20d² c24.5g⁴ c28.7d⁵ c20.2sᵖᵘ Mar 12] lengthy gelding: has had breathing operation: useful hurdler: useful maiden chaser: second in handicap at Navan (½ length behind De Name Escapes Me) in December: stays 3m: acts on heavy going: often travels strongly. *Henry de Bromhead, Ireland* **c137 h–**

SOLOMON GREY (FR) 7 gr.g. Sulamani (IRE) – Sardagna (FR) (Medaaly) [2018/19 h133, b101: h16.6g h21g² h21.4m² Apr 13] good-topped gelding: useful handicap hurdler: second at Ayr (1¾ lengths behind Mahlervous) in April: stays 21f: acts on soft and good to firm going: in tongue tie last 2 starts. *Dan Skelton* **h135**

SO LONELY (IRE) 5 b.m. So You Think (NZ) – Via Aurelia (IRE) (Antonius Pius (USA)) [2018/19 h87: b16g² b16s² h16g² b16.2d³ h16.3s h17.7d² h20.6g³ h20.5dᵖᵘ h15.8g* h15.8g* Apr 22] smallish mare: fair bumper performer: fair hurdler: won mares maiden and novice handicap at Huntingdon in April: left Charles O'Brien after fourth start: stays 2¼m: acts on good to soft going: has worn hood, including last 2 starts: in tongue tie last 4 starts: usually races off pace: signs of temperament. *Dan Skelton* **h114 b88**

SOLO SAXOPHONE (IRE) 5 b.g. Frankel – Society Hostess (USA) (Seeking The Gold (USA)) [2018/19 h113: h20.6g⁶ h21g h21d h15.8s⁵ h21.3g* h20.1g* Apr 15] rather leggy gelding: has had breathing operation: fairly useful handicap hurdler: won at Wetherby and Hexham in April: stays 21f: acts on heavy going: has worn blinkers, including in 2018/19: wears tongue tie: usually races off pace: has looked temperamental. *Dan Skelton* **h120**

SOLSTALLA 7 b.m. Halling (USA) – Solstice (Dubawi (IRE)) [2018/19 h105: h20g⁵ h16g⁵ h16g⁴ h15.8g³ h15.7g⁴ h16.3g* h19.2g⁴ h15.8g Nov 24] fair handicap hurdler: won at Worcester in September and Stratford (mares) in October: stays 2¼m: acts on good to soft going: has worn cheekpieces, including in 2018/19: front runner/races prominently. *David Weston* **h104**

SOLSTICE SON 10 b.g. Haafhd – Karasta (IRE) (Lake Coniston (IRE)) [2018/19 c129, h–: c26.1g Nov 17] sturdy gelding: winning hurdler: fairly useful chaser, well held sole outing in 2018/19: stays 27f: acts on soft going: wears blinkers/tongue tie. *Anthony Honeyball* **c– h–**

SOLSTICE STAR 9 b.g. Kayf Tara – Clover Green (IRE) (Presenting) [2018/19 c126, h100: h19.8m h23.6g* h23.6d⁴ h21.6s c25.2m* h23.3v⁶ c25.3gᵖᵘ Apr 17] well-made gelding, has had breathing operation: fairly useful handicap hurdler: won at Chepstow in October and November: fairly useful handicap chaser: won at Catterick in February: stays 25f: acts on good to firm and heavy going: wears headgear/tongue tie: usually races close up. *Martin Keighley* **c124 h118**

SOLSTICE TWILIGHT 7 b.m. Milan – Twilight Eclipse (IRE) (Presenting) [2018/19 h89, b78: h21.7d h23v² h25s⁴ Feb 13] modest maiden hurdler: stays 25f: best form on soft/heavy going. *Anthony Honeyball* **h86**

SOLWAY AVA 6 b.m. Overbury (IRE) – Solway Sunset (Primitive Rising (USA)) [2018/19 b16d Nov 3] third foal: dam (c83/h106) 2½m-3¼m hurdle/chase winner: tailed off in maiden bumper. *Lisa Harrison* **b–**

SOLWAY BERRY 8 b.m. Overbury (IRE) – Solway Rose (Minster Son) [2018/19 b74: h20.2g h23.9g⁴ h16.2g⁴ h23.3g⁶ h24.3g Oct 29] poor form over hurdles. *Lisa Harrison* **h69**

SOLWAY LARK 8 b.g. Beat All (USA) – Solway Larkin (IRE) (Supreme Leader) [2018/19 b–: h15.8g⁵ h20.2g⁵ h16.2g⁶ h23.9g² h23.9g h23.3gˢᵘ h20d h25.8gᵘʳ h23.8g⁵ h22.8v h16.4s h21.4s h23.8m h19.8s Mar 10] modest maiden hurdler: stays 3m: best form on good going: usually races in rear. *Lisa Harrison* **h92**

SOLWAY LIZZIE 7 ch.m. Tobougg (IRE) – Solway Rose (Minster Son) [2018/19 b–: b16.2g b16.2g⁶ h16.2gᵘʳ Sep 10] no form in bumpers: unseated second on hurdling debut. *Lisa Harrison* **h–** **b–**

SOLWAY PALM 9 gr.g. Great Palm (USA) – Solway Donal (IRE) (Celio Rufo) [2018/19 h83: h23.9g h23.3gᵘʳ Jun 2] maiden hurdler, no form in 2018/19. *Lisa Harrison* **h–**

SOLWAY STORM (IRE) 9 gr.g. Indian River (FR) – The Grey Lady (IRE) (Roselier (FR)) [2018/19 h20.2gᵖᵘ h16.2g Jun 16] placed in bumper: no form over hurdles. *Lisa Harrison* **h–**

SOLWAY TRIGGER 10 b.g. Double Trigger (IRE) – Double Flight (Mtoto) [2018/19 c66, h–: c23.8g⁶ h23.3gᵖᵘ c24.2gᵖᵘ c23.8gᵘʳ Jun 23] maiden hurdler: poor maiden chaser: stays 3m: best form on good going: temperamental. *Lisa Harrison* **c62 §** **h–**

SOMCHINE 11 b.g. Volochine (IRE) – Seem of Gold (Gold Dust) [2018/19 c126, h–: c19g⁶ May 12] lengthy gelding: maiden hurdler: fairly useful handicap chaser, below form sole outing in 2018/19: stays 21f: acts on heavy going: has worn hood: tried in tongue tie. *Seamus Mullins* **c105** **h–**

SOME ARE LUCKY (IRE) 8 b.g. Gold Well – Foreign Estates (IRE) (Be My Native (USA)) [2018/19 c122, h–: c26.3dᵘʳ Mar 15] well-made gelding: multiple point winner: winning hurdler: useful chaser at best, unseated in Foxhunter at Cheltenham only outing under Rules in 2018/19: stays 23f: acts on heavy going: usually in cheekpieces: usually races close up. *S. Curling, Ireland* **c–** **h–**

SOME BOY MCCOY (FR) 5 b.g. Enrique – Khaylama (IRE) (Dr Devious (IRE)) [2018/19 b–: ab16s² h16d⁴ h15.8d Feb 6] useful-looking gelding: has had breathing operation: modest form in bumpers: fair form over hurdles: better effort when fourth in maiden at Fakenham in January. *Olly Murphy* **h106** **b78**

SOME BUCKLE (IRE) 10 b.g. Milan – Miss Moppit (IRE) (Torus) [2018/19 c142, h–: c20.6d c25g Apr 6] useful-looking gelding: winning hurdler: useful handicap chaser, very lightly raced nowadays: stays 2¾m, effective at shorter: acts on soft going: wears tongue tie. *Richard Bandey* **c126** **h–**

SOME CAN DANCE (IRE) 6 b.g. Gold Well – Rocella (GER) (Goofalik (USA)) [2018/19 h16d⁴ h15.8g⁵ h16d h15.8v² h19.5v³ h23d⁶ h25g* h23.1s³ h25d* Mar 24] €20,000 3-y-o: sturdy gelding: sixth foal: half-brother to French 13f winner Roccamena (by Bests of The Bests) and a winning pointer by Robin des Pres: dam, Italian 15f hurdle winner, half-sister to dual Velka Pardubicka winner Registana: unplaced in Irish points: fair handicap hurdler: won at Carlisle in February and March: stays 25f: acts on heavy going: tried in cheekpieces. *Samuel Drinkwater* **h113**

SOME CHAOS (IRE) 8 b.g. Brian Boru – Iruna Iris (IRE) (Golden Tornado (IRE)) [2018/19 c20.3g* c23.9g* c25.1g² c26.3d⁵ c25.1g* c26.2g* Mar 23] short-backed gelding: lightly-raced hurdler: useful form over fences: won novice handicaps at Bangor in October and Market Rasen in November, and handicaps at Wincanton in February and Kelso (by 2¼ lengths from Blue Flight) in March: likely to stay long distances: acts on good to soft going: has worn hood: open to further improvement as a chaser. *Michael Scudamore* **c140 p** **h–**

SOME DAY SOON (IRE) 6 b.g. Robin des Champs (FR) – Creative Approach (IRE) (Toulon) [2018/19 b96: h16.7g² h16.4g⁵ h16.8m² h16.5d² Nov 29] close-coupled gelding: fairly useful form over hurdles: second in novice at Exeter in November: will be suited by 2½m: front runner/races prominently. *Jamie Snowden* **h116**

SOME DETAIL (IRE) 5 b.g. Getaway (GER) – You Should Know Me (IRE) (Oscar (IRE)) [2018/19 b16.2s² b15.7s³ b16d* b16.4s Mar 13] €38,000 3-y-o: compact gelding: first foal: dam unraced half-sister to fairly useful hurdler/useful chaser (stayed 3m) You Must Know Me: maiden Irish pointer: fairly useful form in bumpers: won conditionals/amateurs maiden at Chepstow in February: will be suited by at least 2½m. *Nigel Hawke* **b99**

SOME FINISH (IRE) 10 b.g. Kayf Tara – Kylie Kaprice (GER) (Big Shuffle (USA)) [2018/19 c82§, h–§: h25g⁶ c23.6gᵖᵘ c24.2vᵖᵘ c25.2d* c24.2vᵖᵘ Mar 5] maiden hurdler: poor handicap chaser: won at Hereford in January: stays 25f: acts on good to firm and heavy going: has worn headgear, including last 4 starts: temperamental. *Robin Dickin* **c74 §** **h– §**

SOME INVITATION (IRE) 8 b.g. Presenting – Bolly (IRE) (Jolly Jake (NZ)) [2018/19 c134, h–: c19.9gᵖᵘ Nov 10] well-made gelding: has had breathing operation: winning hurdler: useful chaser at best, no form under Rules in 2018/19 (runner-up in point in March): stays 3¼m: acts on soft going: in cheekpieces last 3 starts: wears tongue tie. *Dan Skelton* **c–** **h–**

SOME KINDA LAMA (IRE) 8 gr.g. Daylami (IRE) – Last Sunrise (IRE) (Shahanndeh) **c94**
[2018/19 c–, h–: c29.1g^{pu} h25.5g^2 c26.3g^4 c24v^{pu} Dec 1] fairly useful handicap hurdler: **h123**
only modest form over fences: left Charlie Mann after first start: stays 3¼m: acts on heavy
going: wears headgear/tongue tie. *Olly Murphy*

SOMEKINDOFSTAR (IRE) 6 ch.g. Getaway (GER) – Katty Barry (IRE) (Alderbrook) **h91 p**
[2018/19 h19g^F Apr 25] €17,000 3-y-o: fifth foal: dam unraced half-sister to very smart
staying chaser Hey Big Spender: runner-up in Irish point: third when fell heavily 2 out in
maiden won by My Charity at Warwick on hurdling debut: open to improvement.
Lucy Wadham

SOME MAN (IRE) 6 b.g. Beat Hollow – Miss Denman (IRE) (Presenting) [2018/19 **h96**
h109p: h20g^5 Feb 15] good-topped gelding: has had breathing operation: Irish point
winner: fair form over hurdles: tried in hood. *Paul Nicholls*

SOME NECK (FR) 8 gr.g. Yeats (IRE) – Maternelle (FR) (Machiavellian (USA)) **c143**
[2018/19 c144, h–: c26m^6 c22.6g* c25s^F c28.7d^6 Feb 10] winning hurdler: useful chaser: **h–**
won Florida Pearl Novices' Chase at Punchestown (by neck from Blow By Blow) in
November: should stay 3m+: acts on heavy going. *W. P. Mullins, Ireland*

SOME OPERATOR (IRE) 5 b.g. September Storm (GER) – Emilies Pearl (IRE) **c95**
(Accordion) [2018/19 h19.5g^5 h25.5s^4 h19.7s h23.3s h25d^3 c18.9s^3 Apr 15] €15,000 3-y-o, **h95**
£68,000 4-y-o: third foal: dam, ran twice in bumpers, out of half-sister to Grand National
winner Corbiere: won Irish point on debut: modest form over hurdles: left Ian Williams,
similar form on chasing debut: stays 3¼m: acts on soft going. *Mlle Louisa Carberry,
France*

SOME REIGN (IRE) 8 b.g. Kayf Tara – Bridge Love (FR) (Astarabad (USA)) [2018/19 **c124 §**
h124: c15.9d^4 c21.6d^2 c15.2s^{rr} c20.1s^4 c17.1g^2 Jan 22] fairly useful hurdler: similar form **h–**
over fences: stays 2¾m: acts on good to soft going: tried in hood: one to treat with caution
(has twice refused to race). *Rose Dobbin*

SOMETHING BREWING (FR) 5 gr.g. Clodovil (IRE) – Talwin (IRE) (Alhaarth **c–**
(IRE)) [2018/19 h102: h16.2d^6 h20.1g^3 h20.1m^2 h20.9g^2 c20.3g^F h22.7g^4 h22.7g^3 h16.4s^4 **h111**
Mar 10] smallish gelding: fair handicap hurdler: fell fifth on chasing debut: stays 23f: acts
on good to firm and good to soft going: wears cheekpieces: races off pace. *Iain Jardine*

SOMEWHERE TO BE (IRE) 7 ch.g. Golan (IRE) – Somethinaboutmolly (IRE) **c127 §**
(Choisir (AUS)) [2018/19 c116, h67: c20g^2 c23.5d^{pu} c20.2m^F c26g^{pu} Apr 17] workmanlike **h–**
gelding: maiden hurdler: fairly useful handicap chaser: stays 2½m: acts on heavy going:
wears headgear: temperamental. *Martin Keighley*

SOMMERVIEU (FR) 5 gr.g. Rajsaman (FR) – Simple Solution (USA) (Dynaformer **c–**
(USA)) [2018/19 h113: h16d c20g c20.1g^6 Oct 5] maiden hurdler: little show in Britain, **h78**
including over fences: has worn blinkers, including final start: in tongue tie last 3 starts.
Charlie Longsdon

SONG FOR SOMEONE (GER) 4 ch.g. Medicean – Sweni Hill (IRE) (Danehill Dancer **h125**
(IRE)) [2018/19 h17.4d^3 h17.4g* h15.8g^2 h16d^2 h16.3d* h16g* h17d^6 Apr 4] medium-
sized gelding: 2m winner on Flat in France: fairly useful juvenile hurdler: won at Le Lion-
d'Angers in July, Newbury in December and Warwick in February: left J. Boisnard after
second start: raced around 2m: acts on good to soft going. *Tom Symonds*

SONG SAA 9 b.m. Midnight Legend – Mystere (IRE) (Montelimar (USA)) [2018/19 c123, **c124**
h–: c19.2d^4 c20.5g^4 c19.2g^4 c20.5d* c24d^3 c20.1d* Mar 5] sturdy mare: winning hurdler: **h–**
fairly useful handicap chaser: won at Kempton in January and Newcastle (mares) in
March: stays 3m: acts on heavy going: wears tongue tie: often travels strongly. *Tom George*

SONIC (IRE) 6 b.g. Vinnie Roe (IRE) – Bella's Bury (Overbury (IRE)) [2018/19 h112, **h119**
b92: h15.8d^4 h20.3g^3 h19.6g^F h22.1m^2 h19.9g* h19.6g^2 h19.9m* h19.9g^4 Oct 21] compact
gelding: runner-up on second of 2 starts in Irish points: fairly useful hurdler: won maiden
at Uttoxeter in July and novice at Sedgefield in October: stays 2¾m: acts on soft and good
to firm going: in cheekpieces last 2 starts: front runner. *Donald McCain*

SONNEOFPRESENTING (IRE) 9 b.g. Presenting – Sonne Cinq (IRE) (Old Vic) **c128**
[2018/19 c132, h–: c25.8g^3 c23g Jun 27] lengthy gelding: winning hurdler: useful handicap **h–**
chaser: third at Newton Abbot in May: won point in late-2018: stays 23f: acts on soft going:
tried in cheekpieces: front runner. *Kim Bailey*

SONNETIST 5 b.g. Poet's Voice – Society Rose (Saddlers' Hall (IRE)) [2018/19 c16g^3 **c63**
c16v^{pu} Dec 15] angular gelding: fair on Flat, stays 1¾m: poor form over fences: wears
cheekpieces. *David Evans*

SON OF FEYAN (IRE) 8 ch.g. Nayef (USA) – Miss Penton (Primo Dominie) [2018/19 **h67** h–: h23.9g⁴ h24.3g⁴ h22g² h23.8gᵖᵘ Nov 26] poor maiden hurdler: stays 3m: acts on good to soft going: tried in tongue tie. *Lucy Normile*

SONOFTHEKING (IRE) 11 b.g. King's Theatre (IRE) – Nikadora (FR) (Nikos) **c95** [2018/19 c106, h–: c25.2s⁴ c23.6g⁶ c24s⁵ Mar 18] useful-looking gelding: maiden hurdler: **h–** fair handicap chaser: laboured effort final start: stays 25f: acts on good to firm and heavy going: has worn cheekpieces, including in 2018/19: wears tongue tie. *Nicky Martin*

SOPAT (IRE) 6 b.m. Gold Well – Silver Prayer (IRE) (Roselier (FR)) [2018/19 b13.7m⁶ **b94** b16m* Apr 22] £62,000 6-y-o: sixth foal: half-sister to fairly useful hurdler/chaser Crown Hill (2m-3¼m winner, by Definite Article) and fairly useful chaser Ruapehu (25f/3¼m winner, by Presenting): dam unraced: Irish point winner: fair form in bumpers: won mares maiden at Fakenham in April. *Phil Middleton*

SOPHIE FATALE 7 b.m. Robin des Champs (FR) – Buffy (Classic Cliche (IRE)) **h102** [2018/19 h16.2v² Mar 14] little impact in bumpers in 2016/17: 66/1, second in novice at Hexham (5 lengths behind Lord Yeats) on hurdling debut. *Sandy Thomson*

SOPHIE OLIVIA (IRE) 7 gr.m. Ask – Gill's Honey (IRE) (Celio Rufo) [2018/19 h108: **c114** c20.1s* c20.5vᵖᵘ c20.1d² Mar 5] fair hurdler: similar form over fences: won novice **h–** handicap at Hexham in October: will stay beyond 2½m: acts on soft going. *Martin Todhunter*

SORAYA 5 b.m. Black Sam Bellamy (IRE) – Star Ar Aghaidh (IRE) (Soviet Star (USA)) **h74** [2018/19 h18.5g h16d Jan 7] third foal: sister to a winning pointer and a point bumper winner: dam (b81), lightly raced in bumpers, half-sister to fairly useful hurdler/fair chaser (stayed 3m) King Ar Aghaidh out of Stayers' Hurdle winner Shuil Ar Aghaidh: finished alone in point on debut: poor form over hurdles: in tongue tie first start. *Tom Lacey*

SORBET 4 b.f. Passing Glance – Fireburst (Spectrum (IRE)) [2018/19 b13.7g⁵ b12.4s³ **b75** b15.8g³ Jan 3] has had breathing operation: ninth foal: dam lightly-raced half-sister to fairly useful/unreliable staying chaser Cedar Green: modest form in bumpers: little impact on Flat. *Lucy Wadham*

SORY 12 b.g. Sakhee (USA) – Rule Britannia (Night Shift (USA)) [2018/19 h71: h16.8s⁵ **c74** h24.1d h21.2d⁴ c19.3s³ c20.9v⁴ c20.1v³ c20.1d² Mar 26] maiden hurdler, no form in **h–** 2018/19: poor form over fences: stays 2½m: acts on soft going: tried in headgear. *Tina Jackson*

SO SATISFIED 8 b.g. Aqlaam – Pirouetting (Pivotal) [2018/19 c103, h–: c24.1sᵖᵘ c25.2g⁵ **c99** h24.3d c24.1d² c26.3sᵘʳ c23.8m* c23.8m⁴ c24.2gᵖᵘ Apr 15] winning handicap hurdler: modest **h76** handicap chaser: won at Musselburgh in February: stays 25f: acts on good to firm and heavy going: wears headgear. *Iain Jardine*

SO SORRY SARAH (IRE) 10 br.m. Beneficial – Greenhall Rambler (IRE) (Anshan) **c–** [2018/19 h23gᵖᵘ h20g³ h16.3g² h23v⁵ c21.2d⁴ Dec 18] €9,000 4-y-o: second foal: dam **h85** (c108/h115), 2¼m-2½m hurdle/chase winner, also 1¾m winner on Flat: point winner: modest maiden hurdler: well beaten in novice handicap on chasing debut: stays 2½m: acts on heavy going: in cheekpieces/tongue tie last 3 starts. *Olly Murphy*

SOTOMAYOR 4 b.c. Havana Gold (IRE) – No Frills (IRE) (Darshaan) [2018/19 h16dᵖᵘ **h–** Jan 28] fair on Flat, stays 1½m: pulled up in novice on hurdling debut. *Oliver Sherwood*

SOUL EMOTION (FR) 6 b.g. Martaline – Second Emotion (FR) (Medaaly) [2018/19 **c–** c–, h146p: h24.4s⁵ Dec 22] strong gelding: has had breathing operation: useful hurdler, **h140** lightly raced: twice-raced chaser: stays 3m: acts on soft going. *Nicky Henderson*

SOULSAVER 7 ch.g. Recharge (IRE) – Lapina (IRE) (Fath (USA)) [2018/19 h101: c20g **c– p** h17.7m⁴ h19.7s² h21.4g³ h17.7m Mar 29] fair handicap hurdler: 4/1, well held in novice **h105** handicap on chasing debut: stays 2¾m: acts on soft going: tried in blinkers: wears tongue tie: should do better over fences. *Anthony Honeyball*

SOUNDS OF ITALY (IRE) 10 b.g. Milan – Sound Hill (FR) (Green Tune (USA)) **c87** [2018/19 c70, h70: h23.3g³ c24g* c26g³ c24d* c24.2s⁵ Dec 26] has had breathing **h60** operation: poor maiden hurdler: modest handicap chaser: won at Uttoxeter in October and Warwick in November: stays 3m: acts on heavy going: has worn headgear: in tongue tie last 5 starts. *Dan Skelton*

SOUPY SOUPS (IRE) 8 ch.g. Stowaway – Near Dunleer (IRE) (Soviet Lad (USA)) **c124** [2018/19 c119, h–: c21.7gᵖᵘ c21.4m⁴ c20g* c20.1g³ c22.6g² c21.4d² c23.8gᵖᵘ Apr 24] **h–** good-topped gelding: has had breathing operation: winning hurdler: fairly useful handicap chaser: won at Uttoxeter in September: stays 3m: acts on good to firm and good to soft going: in cheekpieces last 3 starts. *Neil Mulholland*

SOURIYAN (FR) 8 b.g. Alhaarth (IRE) – Serasana (Red Ransom (USA)) [2018/19 c123, **c131** h126: h23.1g* h25.4g³ h24g⁵ c21.2m* c23g* c25.5s^{pu} Aug 27] rather leggy gelding: fairly **h120** useful handicap hurdler: won at Market Rasen in May: useful chaser: won maiden at Cartmel in June and novice at Worcester (by 3 lengths from Scoop The Pot) in July: stays 25f: acts on good to firm and heavy going: wears headgear/tongue tie. *Peter Bowen*

SOUTHEAST ROSE (IRE) 6 b.m. Beat Hollow – Sunny South East (IRE) (Gothland **h92** (FR)) [2018/19 b17.1d h16s h16.2g⁶ h16d h19.8m⁴ Feb 27] €16,000 3-y-o: sixth foal: **b–** closely related to fairly useful hurdler/useful chaser King of Realms (19f-3m winner, by King's Theatre): dam (c86) 25f chase winner: placed in Irish points: well beaten in mares bumper: modest form over hurdles. *Martin Todhunter*

SOUTHERN SAM 5 b.g. Black Sam Bellamy (IRE) – Pougatcheva (FR) (Epervier Bleu) **h123** [2018/19 h19.9g² h21.6s³ h20g² h19.8s⁵ Mar 9] €105,000 4-y-o: good-topped gelding: half-brother to fair hurdler The Big Dipper (3m winner, by Alflora): dam (c86/h102), 2m-19f hurdle winner, half-sister to fair hurdler/useful chaser (stayed 2¾m) Noisetine: runner-up in Irish point: fairly useful form over hurdles: second in novice at Fakenham in February: will be suited by 2¾m+. *Oliver Sherwood*

SOUTHERN STATES 6 b.g. Medaglia d'Oro (USA) – Little Belle (USA) (A P Indy **h–** (USA)) [2018/19 h19.5s^{pu} h17.7v^{pu} Dec 26] fair maiden on Flat, stays 16.5f: no form over hurdles: in visor final start. *Lydia Richards*

SOUTHFIELD HARVEST 5 b.g. Kayf Tara – Chamoss Royale (FR) (Garde Royale) **b93** [2018/19 b16.8d³ b16m* Apr 22] sixth foal: closely related to smart hurdler/chaser Southfield Theatre (2½m-23f winner, by King's Theatre) and useful hurdler/chaser Southfield Vic (2½m-3¼m winner, by Old Vic), and half-brother to 2 winners, including useful hurdler/smart chaser Southfield Royale (2½m-3m winner, by Presenting): dam (c134/h134) 17f-25f hurdle/chase winner: fair form in bumpers: won at Chepstow in April. *Paul Nicholls*

SOUTHFIELD ROYALE 9 b.g. Presenting – Chamoss Royale (FR) (Garde Royale) **c–** [2018/19 c–, h122: h26s^{pu} h26.5g Apr 20] good sort: useful hurdler at best, no form in **h–** 2018/19: one-time smart chaser: stays 4m: acts on heavy going: has worn headgear, including final start: tried in tongue tie: races prominently. *Mark Bradstock*

SOUTHFIELD STONE 6 gr.g. Fair Mix (IRE) – Laureldean Belle (IRE) (Supreme **h136** Leader) [2018/19 b88: b16.5m* h16.5d* h16.5d* h16s³ h19s² h16m* h16.5d Apr 5] well- **b101** made gelding: fairly useful form in bumpers: won maiden at Taunton in November: useful form over hurdles: won novices at Taunton in November and December, and Dovecote Novices' Hurdle at Kempton (by ¾ length from Angels Breath) in February: also third in Tolworth Novices' Hurdle at Sandown (3¾ lengths behind Elixir de Nutz): stays 19f: acts on soft and good to firm going: usually races close up. *Paul Nicholls*

SOUTHFIELD THEATRE (IRE) 11 b.g. King's Theatre (IRE) – Chamoss Royale **c– §** (FR) (Garde Royale) [2018/19 c139§, h–: c25.8g^{pu} c26.3d Mar 15] good-topped gelding: **h–** won 3 of 4 starts in points: winning hurdler: very smart chaser at best, little impact in 2018/19 (made mistakes in Foxhunter at Cheltenham having left Paul Nicholls): stays 25f: acts on soft going: wears headgear: has worn tongue tie: unreliable. *Mrs Sara V. Bradstock*

SOUTHFIELD TORR 6 gr.g. Fair Mix (IRE) – Chamoss Royale (FR) (Garde Royale) **h104** [2018/19 b94: h15.3m⁴ h19m² h16.5d² h15.3d h21.4g h19.8g* Apr 14] sturdy gelding: fair form over hurdles: won handicap at Wincanton (amateurs) in April: stays 2½m: acts on good to firm and good to soft going: races prominently, often freely. *Paul Nicholls*

SOUTHFIELD VIC (IRE) 10 ch.g. Old Vic – Chamoss Royale (FR) (Garde Royale) **c120** [2018/19 c143, h–: c25.8m⁶ c26d² c23.4d² c25.1g* Apr 14] lengthy gelding: winning **h–** hurdler: fairly useful hunter chaser nowadays: won at Wincanton in April: stays 3¼m: acts on soft and good to firm going: wears headgear. *Paul Nicholls*

SOUTHPORT 7 b.g. Robin des Pres (FR) – First Katoune (FR) (Poliglote) [2018/19 c–, **c94 x** h–: c24g⁶ c20g⁴ c20g⁴ c25.8g^{ur} c25.8g Sep 10] winning hurdler: modest maiden chaser: **h–** likely to prove best at short of 3m: best form on good going: often let down by jumping over fences. *Nigel Twiston-Davies*

SOVIET CASTLE (IRE) 6 b.g. Soviet Star (USA) – Castle Hope (IRE) (Old Vic) **b92** [2018/19 b16g² b15.7g* Nov 23] fifth foal: half-brother to bumper winner Sandanski (by Definite Article), stayed 3m over hurdles: dam (h98), 2½m-3m hurdle winner, half-sister to useful hurdler (stayed 3m) Vast Consumption: fair form in bumpers: won at Catterick in November. *Rebecca Menzies*

SOVINNIE (IRE) 10 ch.g. Vinnie Roe (IRE) – Sohapara (Arapahos (FR)) [2018/19 h–: **h–**
h23.9d[pu] May 26] maiden hurdler, no form since 2016/17: wears cheekpieces/tongue tie.
Jane Mathias

SOYOUTHINKSOAGAIN (IRE) 4 b.g. So You Think (NZ) – Al Saqiya (USA) **b85**
(Woodman (USA)) [2018/19 ab16s[3] b15.8d[3] Mar 13] sturdy gelding: half-brother to
several winners, including fairly useful hurdler Cashel Blue (3m-27f winner, by Aljabr):
dam maiden (stayed 7.5f): fair form in bumpers: better effort when third at Huntingdon in
March. *Dan Skelton*

SPACE ODDITY (FR) 8 br.g. Al Namix (FR) – Schoune (FR) (Majorien) [2018/19 **c116**
c136, h–: c18m[4] c16s[F] c16.4s[ur] h16.5g h20.5d[4] h19d[F] Apr 4] compact gelding: fairly useful **h110**
handicap hurdler/useful handicap chaser, below form in 2018/19: stays 19f: acts on good to
firm and heavy going: wears hood: usually races close up. *Harry Fry*

SPACE SAFARI (FR) 6 b.g. Kapgarde (FR) – Prodiga (FR) (Poliglote) [2018/19 b16s **b–**
Mar 9] point winner: tailed off in bumper. *Lucy Normile*

SPADER (IRE) 6 b.g. Jeremy (USA) – Poulkovo (IRE) (Sadler's Wells (USA)) [2018/19 **h88**
h94: h15.7g* h15.8g[5] h16g h15.8g h15.8d[4] h16g[bd] h16.6g h16.6d[4] h15.7d h19.6d Apr 26]
compact gelding: modest handicap hurdler: won novice event at Southwell in May: left
Dan Skelton after third start: stays 19f: acts on good to soft going: tried in cheekpieces: has
worn tongue tie, including in 2018/19: usually races off pace. *Louise Davis*

SPADES ARE TRUMPS (IRE) 6 b.g. Yeats (IRE) – Sway (FR) (Califet (FR)) [2018/19 **h132**
h19d[6] h22d[2] Apr 22] second foal: dam (c121/h142) 15f-19f hurdle/chase winner: useful
handicap hurdler: second at Fairyhouse (¾ length behind Maeve's Choice) in April: stays
2¾m: acts on heavy going. *Gavin Patrick Cromwell, Ireland*

SPANISH ARCH (IRE) 12 b.g. Westerner – Piepowder (In The Wings) [2018/19 c109§, **c114 §**
h–: c24.2d[2] Mar 8] compact gelding: point winner: winning hurdler: fair chaser: stays 3m: **h–**
acts on heavy going: has worn headgear/tongue tie: temperamental. *Mrs V. Sollitt*

SPANISH OPTIMIST (IRE) 13 b.g. Indian Danehill (IRE) – La Traviata (Spectrum **c– §**
(IRE)) [2018/19 c–§, h–: c24d[pu] h21.6g h23g c22.5g[ur] Oct 7] fairly useful hurdler/fair **h–**
chaser at best, no form since 2016/17: wears headgear: has worn tongue tie: not one to rely
on. *Sarah Robinson*

SPANISH STARLING 7 b.g. Fantastic Spain (USA) – Clarice Starling (Saddlers' Hall **h–**
(IRE)) [2018/19 h21.2m[pu] h21.6s[pu] Apr 16] last in bumper: no form over hurdles. *Sarah-Jayne Davies*

SPARKLEANDSHINE (IRE) 6 b.g. Olden Times – Little Flower (IRE) (Talkin Man **h120**
(CAN)) [2018/19 h113p: h15.7m[4] h15.8d h15.8d[3] h19d[5] Mar 11] little impact in Irish
points: fairly useful form over hurdles: left Sam Thomas after second start: unproven
beyond 2m: acts on good to soft going: sometimes in hood. *Harry Whittington*

SPARKLING DAWN 7 gr.m. Sulamani (IRE) – Clotted Cream (USA) (Eagle Eyed **h–**
(USA)) [2018/19 b98: h21.4g[ur] h21.2d[ur] h15.8g Apr 11] sturdy mare: bumper winner: no
form over hurdles: tried in blinkers: looks reluctant. *Johnny Farrelly*

SPARKLING RIVER (IRE) 9 gr.m. Indian River (FR) – Full Deck (IRE) (Roselier **c–**
(FR)) [2018/19 c125, h–: c24d c24s[pu] c20.1d[F] c23.8s[pu] Apr 7] angular mare: winning **h–**
hurdler: fairly useful chaser at best, no form in 2018/19: tried in blinkers: usually front
runner/races prominently: signs of temperament. *Henry Oliver*

SPARKY STOWAWAY (IRE) 7 b.g. Stowaway – Torose (IRE) (Torus) [2018/19 **h106**
h15.8g h15.5g[3] h15.5d Jan 22] fourth foal: dam (h106) bumper/2½m hurdle winner: fair
handicap hurdler: stays 2¼m: acts on good to soft going: tried in hood. *Paul Webber*

SPARKY VALENTINE (FR) 4 b.f. Kapgarde (FR) – Qualite Controlee (FR) (Poliglote) **h–**
[2018/19 b12.6s[3] h16.6g Jan 25] closely related to bumper winner/useful hurdler Au Quart **b85**
de Tour (2m winner, by Robin des Champs), half-sister to several winners, including
useful hurdler Qualando (2m-19f winner, by Lando): dam, French 17f-19f hurdle/chase
winner, also 13f winner on Flat: third in fillies junior bumper at Newbury (4¼ lengths
behind Who What When): tailed off in listed juvenile on hurdling debut. *Mrs Jane Williams*

SPEAKER CONNOLLY (IRE) 6 b.g. Court Cave (IRE) – Kylebeg Dancer (IRE) **c136 p**
(General Monash (USA)) [2018/19 c16d c19d c16.1d[6] c21g* c21g[3] c26d[ur] h20.2s[F] Apr 5] **h–**
€42,000 3-y-o: rangy gelding: third foal: half-brother to 2 winners, including bumper
winner/fairly useful 2¼m hurdle winner Dancing Meadows (by Alhaarth): dam (c77/
h103), 2m hurdle winner, also 1½m-1¾m winner on Flat: winning hurdler: useful form

over fences: won handicap at Leopardstown (by 5 lengths from Poker Party) in December: stays 21f: acts on heavy going: usually races off pace: remains capable of better as a chaser. *Alan Fleming, Ireland*

SPEAK OF THE DEVIL (IRE) 6 ch.g. Mahler – A Fine Romance (IRE) (Air Display (USA)) [2018/19 h24.3d³ h20.1v⁵ Mar 14] €15,000 3-y-o, £65,000 5-y-o: fifth foal: half-brother to a winning pointer by Beneficial: dam ran once in point: Irish point winner: modest form over hurdles. *Lucinda Russell*   **h97**

SPECIAL ACCEPTANCE 6 b.g. Malinas (GER) – Doubly Guest (Barathea Guest) [2018/19 h95: h16g⁴ h15.8d h15.8g² h19.8sur h19.2v² Mar 16] rather unfurnished gelding: fair form over hurdles: will prove suited by 2½m: acts on heavy going: in hood last 3 starts: usually races prominently. *Paul Webber*   **h110**

SPECIAL CATCH (IRE) 12 b.g. Catcher In The Rye (IRE) – Top Quality (Simply Great (FR)) [2018/19 c131, h–: c15.2d² c19.4s⁵ᵖᵘ c20.1g⁶ Feb 23] winning hurdler: fairly useful handicap chaser nowadays: second at Wetherby in November: stays 2½m: acts on heavy going: usually races towards rear. *Ruth Jefferson*   **c116 h–**

SPECIAL PREP (IRE) 7 b.g. Brian Boru – Schindler's Dame (IRE) (Oscar Schindler (IRE)) [2018/19 h113, b88: c24g³ h21.4g c22g² c26g* c25.2m² c23.4m* c23.8g⁵ᵖᵘ Apr 24] winning hurdler: useful handicap chaser: won at Doncaster (novice) in January and Newcastle (by 14 lengths from Ascot de Bruyere) in March: stays 3¼m: acts on good to firm and good to soft going: in cheekpieces last 4 starts: wears tongue tie: usually travels strongly. *Pauline Robson*   **c131 h–**

SPECIAL TIARA 12 b.g. Kayf Tara – Special Choice (IRE) (Bob Back (USA)) [2018/19 c155d, h–: c16.7v³ c16g³ c17g⁵ᵖᵘ Feb 2] big gelding: winning hurdler: top-class chaser at best, winner of 3 Grade 1 events, including Queen Mother Champion Chase in 2017: best effort in 2018/19 when third in Desert Orchid Chase at Kempton (24 lengths behind Altior) in December: fatally injured in Dublin Chase at Leopardstown: stayed 2¼m: acted on heavy going: tried in hood: usually raced close up. *Henry de Bromhead, Ireland*   **c140 h–**

SPECIAL WELLS 10 ch.g. Alflora (IRE) – Oso Special (Teenoso (USA)) [2018/19 c–, h–: c23.8m⁴ Feb 27] big gelding: maiden pointer: winning hurdler: fairly useful chaser at best, well held in hunter sole outing under Rules in 2018/19: stays 2½m: acts on heavy going. *R. A. Owen*   **c71 h–**

SPECTACULAR RIVAL (IRE) 4 b.g. Sageburg (IRE) – Consuelita (Singspiel (IRE)) [2018/19 b16.8s Apr 16] placed in point bumper: tailed off in maiden bumper. *Miss H. Brookshaw*   **b–**

SPECTACULIS 4 b.g. Champs Elysees – Merry Diva (Bahamian Bounty) [2018/19 h15.8g⁴ h15.8d h19.6g Apr 11] poor form on Flat/over hurdles. *Denis Quinn*   **h64**

SPECTATOR 8 br.g. Passing Glance – Averami (Averti (IRE)) [2018/19 h110: h21g³ h16.2g⁵ h18.7g⁵ h19.9g² Oct 21] good-topped gelding: fair handicap hurdler: stays 21f: acts on good to firm and heavy going: has worn headgear, including last 5 starts when also tongue tied: usually races towards rear. *Tim Vaughan*   **h112**

SPEED COMPANY (IRE) 6 b.g. Fast Company (IRE) – Trentini (IRE) (Singspiel (IRE)) [2018/19 h95: h15.8g² h15.7v³ h16.6g³ h16g³ Jan 12] smallish gelding: fairly useful form over hurdles: raced around 2m: acts on heavy going: has worn hood, including in 2018/19: tried in tongue tie: usually travels strongly. *Ian Williams*   **h121**

SPEEDO BOY (FR) 5 ch.g. Vision d'Etat (FR) – Shamardanse (IRE) (Shamardal (USA)) [2018/19 h110: h21g* h20.5s³ Dec 1] sturdy gelding: useful on Flat, stays 2¼m: fairly useful form over hurdles: won intermediate handicap at Cheltenham in November: stays 21f: acts on soft going: in tongue tie last 2 starts: often travels strongly: remains capable of better. *Ian Williams*   **h121 p**

SPEEDY BUCK (IRE) 6 b.g. Beat Hollow – Attymon Lill (IRE) (Marju (IRE)) [2018/19 h23sᵖᵘ h19.5d⁶ h20.7d⁵ h21.3gᵖᵘ Apr 11] workmanlike gelding: closely related to 1½m winner Absolutely Me (by Barathea) and half-brother to 2 winners, including 2¼m hurdle winner Ninfea (by Le Vie dei Colori): dam lightly raced on Flat: Irish point winner: modest form over hurdles. *Michael Scudamore*   **h96**

SPEEDY CARGO (IRE) 6 b.g. Stowaway – Vics Miller (IRE) (Old Vic) [2018/19 b17.7s⁴ h21.2g⁵ h19.9s² h19.3g³ h24s⁶ Jan 29] €11,000 3-y-o: second foal: dam unraced half-sister to fair hurdler/useful chaser (2¼m-3¾m winner) Maljimar: placed in Irish points: fourth in bumper at Fontwell: fair form over hurdles: stays 3m: front runner/races prominently: temperament under suspicion. *Harry Whittington*   **h102 b80**

SPEEDY GONZALEZ 5 b.g. Josr Algarhoud (IRE) – Tellmethings (Distant Music (USA)) [2018/19 b84: b16.8s³ h20s Nov 23] modest form in bumpers: tailed off in maiden on hurdling debut. *William Muir* — h– b83

SPENCER LEA 11 b.g. Overbury (IRE) – Castanet (Pennekamp (USA)) [2018/19 c21.4s^pu Dec 26] angular gelding: fairly useful hurdler: similar form on chasing debut in 2016/17, little show only start since: stays 21f: best form on soft/heavy going. *David Dennis* — c– h–

SPENDABLE 7 ch.m. Spendent – Eastern Point (Buckskin (FR)) [2018/19 b17.7g⁵ b17.7g⁴ b13.7m h20.5g h20.5g h19.5d Nov 27] lengthy mare: first foal: dam (c94/h86) 2¾m/23f hurdle/chase winner: no form in bumpers/over hurdles. *Phil York* — h– b–

SPEREDEK (FR) 8 b.g. Kapgarde (FR) – Sendamagic (FR) (Sendawar (IRE)) [2018/19 c153, h136: c16.8g² c16g⁴ c20.5g^F h16s⁶ Mar 9] good-topped gelding: has had breathing operation: useful handicap hurdler: smart chaser: second in Hurst Park Handicap Chase at Ascot (1¼ lengths behind Caid du Lin) in November: stays 23f: acts on heavy going: wears headgear: has worn tongue tie, including in 2018/19: front runner/races prominently. *Nigel Hawke* — c151 h128 +

SPICE BOAT 7 ch.g. Shamardal (USA) – Frizzante (Efisio) [2018/19 h–: h15.9g May 13] no form over hurdles: raced only at 2m: tried in cheekpieces/tongue tie. *Paddy Butler* — h–

SPICY FRUITY (IRE) 9 b.g. Fruits of Love (USA) – Rocksham (IRE) (Bluebird (USA)) [2018/19 h18.5g² h20.3g^pu Oct 2] placed in points: fair form over hurdles: stays 2¾m: acts on soft and good to firm going. *Louise Cabble* — h106

SPIDER'S BITE (IRE) 7 b.g. Scorpion (IRE) – Model Girl (Classic Cliche (IRE)) [2018/19 h113: h24.7g⁵ c23.8g² c23.8d^ur Dec 19] rangy, useful-looking gelding: fairly useful form over hurdles: similar form over fences: second in novice handicap at Ascot on completed start: stays 25f: acts on heavy going: often travels strongly: has looked ungenuine. *Henry Daly* — c128 h123

SPIDER WEB (IRE) 8 b.g. Presenting – Poetics Girl (IRE) (Saddlers' Hall (IRE)) [2018/19 c23g² c22.5d^F c24g* c24d^pu h19d³ Mar 10] fair handicap hurdler: useful handicap chaser: won Munster National Handicap Chase at Limerick (by ¾ length from Na Trachtalai Abu) in October: stays 3m: acts on heavy going: often travels strongly: has bled. *Thomas Mullins, Ireland* — c134 h113

SPIN A YARN (IRE) 6 b.g. Flemensfirth (USA) – Keeps Sake (IRE) (Old Vic) [2018/19 h21g² h19.9g⁵ Sep 23] €38,000 3-y-o: has had breathing operation: unraced half-sister to useful hurdler/smart chaser Watson Lake (2m-2½m winner): fair form over hurdles: stays 21f: acts on good to soft going: often in tongue tie: front runner/races prominently. *Warren Greatrex* — h110

SPINNING SCOOTER 9 b.g. Sleeping Indian – Spinning Coin (Mujahid (USA)) [2018/19 h95: c20.1d⁵ c24.2g² c24.2g³ c23.8g³ c24.2g⁴ c24.2s^pu c24.1g c26.3g⁴ c24.1s c25.2g³ Jan 10] modest maiden chaser: modest maiden hurdler: stays 3m: acts on good to soft going: has worn headgear, including last 3 starts: wears tongue tie. *Maurice Barnes* — c99 h–

SPINOLO 4 b.g. Piccolo – Spinning Coin (Mujahid (USA)) [2018/19 b15.3g Apr 14] good-topped gelding: behind in bumper. *Nigel Hawke* — b–

SPIN THE COIN (IRE) 6 b.g. Witness Box (USA) – Kempinski (IRE) (Moscow Society (USA)) [2018/19 h105p: h17.1g h15.6g* Dec 3] has had breathing operation: runner-up in point: fair form over hurdles: won handicap at Musselburgh in December: should stay 2½m: acts on good to soft going: tried in tongue tie. *Donald McCain* — h109

SPINY NORMAN 6 ch.g. Malinas (GER) – Helen Wood (Lahib (USA)) [2018/19 b–: h16.5g h18.5s Mar 18] no form in bumper/over hurdles: tried in tongue tie. *Alexandra Dunn* — h–

SPIRITOFCHARTWELL 11 ch.g. Clerkenwell (USA) – Rollin Rock (Rock Hopper) [2018/19 c93, h–: c17.8m² c21.6g² c20g c19.5g⁴ c21.6g² Sep 9] maiden hurdler: modest handicap chaser: stays 2¾m: acts on soft and good to firm going. *Phil York* — c91 h–

SPIRIT OF HALE (IRE) 8 ch.g. Stowaway – Roseboreen (IRE) (Roselier (FR)) [2018/19 c95, h–: c24v⁴ c23.6d^pu c26.1d⁶ c24s^pu Mar 23] tall gelding: maiden hurdler: modest handicap chaser, below form in 2018/19: stays 25f: acts on heavy going: has worn cheekpieces, including in 2018/19: tried in tongue tie. *Jennie Candlish* — c82 h–

SPIRIT OF KAYF 8 b.g. Kayf Tara – Over Sixty (Overbury (IRE)) [2018/19 h18.9v⁵ h16s⁴ h20.5s⁶ h20.2d⁴ Apr 26] fairly useful handicap hurdler: stays 2¾m: acts on soft going: tried in hood. *N. W. Alexander* — h124

SPIRIT OF MENDIP (IRE) 6 b.m. Arakan (USA) – Afdale (IRE) (Old Vic) [2018/19 **h83** h–, b–: h16.8m[5] May 8] little impact in bumpers/over hurdles: in hood last 2 starts: dead. *Philip Hobbs*

SPIRIT OF ROME (IRE) 5 ch.m. Mastercraftsman (IRE) – Zagreb Flyer (Old Vic) **h94** [2018/19 h98: h17.7m[3] h16.2s[5] h21.6v[pu] h16.5g[5] h20d[pu] h21.4g[3] h23.9d[6] Apr 24] modest maiden hurdler: left Harry Whittington after first start: stays 21f: acts on good to firm going. *Nick Mitchell*

SPIRITOFTHEGAMES (IRE) 7 b.g. Darsi (FR) – Lucy Walters (IRE) (King's Ride) **c150** [2018/19 h139: c19.4d* c19.9d[4] c20.6d[3] c20.6d[3] c19.9d[5] Apr 4] strong gelding: useful **h–** hurdler: smart form over fences: won listed novice at Chepstow (by 6 lengths from Monbeg Legend) in October: third in Brown Advisory & Merriebelle Stable Plate at Cheltenham (3 lengths behind Siruh du Lac) in March: will stay 3m: acts on heavy going: has worn cheekpieces, including in 2018/19: usually races towards rear. *Dan Skelton*

SPLASH OF GINGE 11 b.g. Oscar (IRE) – Land of Honour (Supreme Leader) [2018/19 **c– §** c140§, h–§: h24.2d[5] c20.2g[pu] c22.9v c20.6d Mar 14] lengthy gelding: useful handicap **h123 §** hurdler, below form first outing in 2018/19: useful chaser at best, no form in 2018/19: stays 3m: acts on heavy going: has worn visor: usually leads: not one to trust. *Nigel Twiston-Davies*

SPLASH THE CASH (IRE) 6 b.m. Scorpion (IRE) – Goldfeather (IRE) (Goldmark **h99** (USA)) [2018/19 b17.1d[6] b17s h16d[6] h15.7g[4] h16g h19.8s[2] h23.8m[F] Mar 22] £17,000 **b84** 5-y-o: first foal: dam, (h100) bumper winner, half-sister to fairly useful hurdler/useful chaser Brackloon High (stayed 3¼m) and fairly useful hurdler/chaser Bon Chic (stays 25f): runner-up in Irish point: modest form in bumpers/over hurdles: will prove suited by further than 2½m: acts on soft going: usually races off pace. *Jennie Candlish*

SPOCK (FR) 14 b.g. Lost World (IRE) – Quark Top (FR) (Perrault) [2018/19 c91§, h–: **c86 §** c20.9d[2] c24.1g[4] c19.4m[ro] c23g[pu] c25.2s[pu] c20d[6] c19.5v[4] c26v[6] c16m[3] Apr 23] winning **h–** hurdler: modest handicap chaser: stays 3m: acts on good to firm and heavy going: has worn headgear: tried in tongue tie: usually races close up: unreliable. *Lady Susan Brooke*

SPOILT ROTTEN 10 b.g. Kayf Tara – Rosita Bay (Hernando (FR)) [2018/19 c108, h–: **c84** c16.5g c19.4m[F] c19.7g[3] Sep 23] lightly-raced hurdler: poor maiden chaser nowadays: has **h–** worn hood, including in 2018/19: in tongue tie last 2 starts. *Fergal O'Brien*

SPOOKYDOOKY (IRE) 11 b.g. Winged Love (IRE) – Kiora Lady (IRE) (King's Ride) **c80** [2018/19 c126, h–: c26m[4] May 27] workmanlike gelding, has had breathing operation: **h–** winning hurdler: fairly useful handicap chaser, behind sole outing in 2018/19: stays 31f: acts on heavy going: has worn cheekpieces, including last 2 starts: wears tongue tie: usually races towards rear. *Jonjo O'Neill*

SPORTING BOY (IRE) 11 b.g. Barathea (IRE) – Sportsticketing (IRE) (Spectrum **c123** (IRE)) [2018/19 c133, h124: h18.5g[6] c27.5g[ur] c26.1m c24.1g h23.1g[2] c22.6m c25.8d[4] **h120** c25g[5] h19d[4] h20g[3] Apr 21] quite good-topped gelding: fairly useful handicap hurdler/ chaser: stays 3¼m: acts on firm and good to soft going: usually in headgear: wears tongue tie. *Johnny Farrelly*

SPORTING MILAN (IRE) 8 b.g. Milan – Sports Leader (IRE) (Supreme Leader) **h90** [2018/19 h75: h23.3g* h23.3g Jun 2] runner-up in Irish point: modest handicap hurdler: won at Hexham (conditionals) in May: will be suited by 3m+: acts on good to soft going: tried in cheekpieces. *Stuart Coltherd*

SPORTING PRESS (IRE) 6 b.g. Flemensfirth (USA) – Rudy Renata (IRE) (Rudimentary **c117** (USA)) [2018/19 b91: h15.6g[4] h16v[2] h16.2v[4] h16.8s[6] c20.3m* c17.1d* c16.4g[3] Apr 23] **h104** has had breathing operation: bumper winner: fair form over hurdles: fairly useful form over fences: won novice handicap at Musselburgh in March and handicap at Kelso in April: stays 2½m: acts on good to firm and heavy going: has worn hood, including last 3 starts. *Keith Dalgleish*

SPORTY YANKEE (USA) 6 gr.g. Paddy O'Prado (USA) – I Insist (USA) (Green **h–** Dancer (USA)) [2018/19 h105: h21.4m h16g h19g[5] h20.5g[4] h16.7s h15.8d[6] Mar 13] tall gelding: fair handicap hurdler, out of form in 2018/19: left Martin Keighley after first start: stays 2½m: acts on heavy going: has worn headgear/tongue tie, including in 2018/19. *Aytach Sadik*

SPOSALIZIO (IRE) 12 ch.g. Dr Fong (USA) – Wedding Cake (IRE) (Groom Dancer **c–** (USA)) [2018/19 c–, h–: c25.5g[5] May 30] multiple point winner: maiden hurdler: fair **h–** chaser at best, little show under Rules since 2014/15: has worn headgear: wears tongue tie. *C. T. Dawson*

SPRINGBOK SEIA (FR) 6 b.g. Saddler Maker (IRE) – Amaseia (FR) (Bateau Rouge) **h84**
[2018/19 h20.3g⁵ h20s⁵ h19.9g⁵ Jun 14] £78,000 3-y-o: has had breathing operation: fourth
foal: dam French 15f-2¼m hurdle/chase winner: poor form over hurdles. *Jonjo O'Neill*

SPRINGCOMBE JOE 7 b.g. Kayf Tara – Dissolve (Sharrood (USA)) [2018/19 b83: **h–**
b16.8s h23.1v h19.5d h17.7v³ Mar 6] modest at best in bumpers: no form over hurdles. **b–**
Bill Turner

SPRING STORM 7 b.m. Morozov (USA) – Presenting Gayle (IRE) (Presenting) **h–**
[2018/19 b16.8g b16m h16g⁶ h20.5g⁵ Nov 5] fifth foal: half-sister to fair chaser Somerset **b–**
Lias (23f winner, by Golan) and fair hurdler Western Sunrise (17f-3¼m winner, by
Westerner): dam winning pointer: well held in bumpers/over hurdles. *Johnny Farrelly*

SPRINGTOWN LAKE (IRE) 7 b.g. Gamut (IRE) – Sprightly Gal (IRE) (Old Vic) **c140**
[2018/19 h132: c20v* c20.6v² c24g⁴ c20.2s⁵ c25g^pu Apr 6] good-topped gelding: useful **h–**
hurdler: similar form over fences: won novice handicap at Sandown (by 1¼ lengths from
Lithic) in November: should stay 3m: acts on good to firm and heavy going: front runner/
races prominently. *Philip Hobbs*

SPRING WOLF 11 br.g. Loup Sauvage (USA) – Spring Grass (Pardigras) [2018/19 **c118**
c19.2s⁶ c19.2d* c18.2s* c24.2v^pu Mar 5] twice-raced hurdler: fairly useful form over **h–**
fences: won handicap at Exeter in January and novice handicap at Taunton in February:
stays 19f: acts on soft going. *Robert Walford*

SPROGZILLA 10 gr.m. Fair Mix (IRE) – Gentle Approach (Rakaposhi King) [2018/19 **c66 §**
h90: h15.7g⁴ h16g⁴ h18.7m⁶ h15.8g³ h15.8g c16d^ur c20.2f^F c16.5g² c15.7g⁵ Apr 3] poor **h71 §**
maiden hurdler: similar form over fences: raced mainly around 2m: best form on good
going: has worn hood, including in 2018/19: usually races close up: temperamental.
Hannah James

SPY FI 5 b.m. Dick Turpin (IRE) – Sindarbella (Sinndar (IRE)) [2018/19 b16.8g⁵ ab16.3g⁴ **b74**
b16.8d Apr 23] third foal: dam unraced half-sister to useful hurdler/fairly useful chaser
(stayed 2¾m) Bold Fire: poor form in bumpers. *John Norton*

SQUARE VIVIANI (FR) 8 b.g. Satri (IRE) – Idria (GER) (Kings Lake (USA)) [2018/19 **c93**
c102, h94: c21.1g⁴ c20s^pu c23.9s³ c20.5d^pu c24.2d^F c24.2g^pu Apr 15] has had breathing **h–**
operation: winning hurdler: modest handicap chaser: stays 21f: acts on heavy going: has
worn headgear, including in 2018/19: usually races off pace. *Micky Hammond*

SQUOUATEUR (FR) 8 gr.g. Martaline – Samansonnienne (FR) (Mansonnien (FR)) **c–**
[2018/19 c136, h–: c24d^pu h20d c24.5g^F c26d^pu Mar 14] strong, lengthy gelding: has had **h124**
breathing operation: useful handicap hurdler at best, below form second outing in 2018/19:
maiden chaser, no form in 2018/19: left Gordon Elliott after third start: stays 3¼m: acts on
heavy going: tried in headgear: wears tongue tie. *Ben Haslam*

STACEY SUE (IRE) 6 b.m. Robin des Champs (FR) – Antonia Hall (IRE) (Saddlers' **b101**
Hall (IRE)) [2018/19 b19d* b16m² b16m* b16.4g Nov 17] lengthy mare: second foal: dam
unraced: point winner: fairly useful form in bumpers: won at Cork (maiden) in August and
Worcester in September: left T. E. Hyde after third start. *Alex Hales*

STAGED ENGAGEMENT (IRE) 6 b.g. Darsi (FR) – Katishna (IRE) (Heron Island **h113 p**
(IRE)) [2018/19 b71: b16.8g³ b15.8g* h19.9g² h16.7g⁴ h17m² Apr 20] fairly useful form **b95**
in bumpers: won at Uttoxeter in June: fair form over hurdles: best effort when second in
novice at Carlisle in April: should be suited by 2½m: open to further improvement. *P. E.
Collins, Ireland*

STAGE SUMMIT (IRE) 6 gr.g. Tikkanen (USA) – Summittotalkabout (IRE) (Lahib **c115**
(USA)) [2018/19 h112, b87: h25g c20.9g⁵ c19.4s³ c19.5d² c19.1g^F Jan 25] rangy gelding: **h–**
has had breathing operation: maiden hurdler: fairly useful form over fences: second on
handicap debut at Fontwell in January: stays 2¾m: acts on soft going: sometimes in cheekpieces:
usually races prominently. *Ben Pauling*

STAGS LEAP (IRE) 12 b.g. Refuse To Bend (IRE) – Swingsky (IRE) (Indian Ridge) **h96**
[2018/19 h62: h22.1g⁶ h17.2g* h19.9m³ h20m^pu Oct 19] modest handicap hurdler
nowadays: won at Cartmel in July: stays 2¾m: acts on good to firm and good to soft going:
wears headgear: has looked temperamental. *Julia Brooke*

STAINSBY GIRL 5 ch.m. Shirocco (GER) – Charmaine Wood (Double Trigger (IRE)) **b96**
[2018/19 b17s* b17g³ b17d Apr 4] rather unfurnished mare: second foal: dam (h113),
bumper/2m hurdle winner, half-sister to useful hurdler/very smart chaser (stayed 3m) Our
Ben: fairly useful form in bumpers: won 4-runner mares event at Carlisle on debut in
December. *Donald Whillans*

STAMP YOUR FEET (IRE) 7 b.g. Galileo (IRE) – Nausicaa (USA) (Diesis) [2018/19 **c124** h131: h20g h24.7g c19.9g² c20d^bd c24.2d c19.4g⁵ Apr 14] sturdy gelding: useful hurdler at **h–** best, well held first 2 starts in 2018/19: fairly useful form over fences: second in novice handicap at Huntingdon in January: stays 2½m: acts on soft going: wears tongue tie: usually races off pace. *Tom George*

STAND BY ME (FR) 9 b.g. Dream Well (FR) – In Love New (FR) (Perrault) [2018/19 **h–** h–: h16.8d⁶ h21.4g⁵ h23.9d^pu Mar 11] has had breathing operations: bumper winner: no form over hurdles. *Alan Jones*

STANDER (IRE) 5 b.g. Famous Name – Coill Cri (IRE) (Shinko Forest (IRE)) [2018/19 **h102** h16g h19.5g h16g* h16.6d⁵ h20d h16d h16s⁴ h16d h16.2v⁵ h16d Apr 22] half-brother to fairly useful hurdler Causey Arch (2m-2½m winner, by Jeremy): little impact on Flat: fair hurdler: won maiden at Roscommon in October: unproven beyond 17f: acts on soft going: tried in cheekpieces. *Paul Stafford, Ireland*

ST ANDREWS (IRE) 6 ch.g. Rip Van Winkle (IRE) – Stellavera (FR) (Anabaa (USA)) **h88** [2018/19 h96: h24g^pu h20.6g⁴ h23.1m⁴ h20.6g⁵ Jul 8] rather sparely-made gelding: modest maiden hurdler: stays 3m: acts on firm going: has worn headgear, including in 2018/19: tried in tongue tie. *Gillian Boanas*

STAND UP AND FIGHT (IRE) 7 b.g. Flemensfirth (USA) – Aylesbury Park (IRE) **c128** (Old Vic) [2018/19 c22d* c26.3d⁶ Mar 15] won first of 2 starts in points: winning hurdler: **h–** fairly useful form in chases: won hunter at Down Royal in December: failed to live up to expectations subsequently: stays 2¾m: acts on heavy going. *Enda Bolger, Ireland*

STARCROSSED 7 b.g. Cape Cross (IRE) – Gretna (Groom Dancer (USA)) [2018/19 **h115** h119p: h15.7g⁴ h19.2g² h20m⁴ h20g h15.8v⁵ h21.2d^pu Dec 19] fairly useful handicap hurdler: second at Fontwell in June: left Dan Skelton after fourth start: stays 2½m: acts on soft and good to firm going: tried in cheekpieces. *Lady Susan Brooke*

STAR FOOT (IRE) 8 b.g. Soviet Star (USA) – On The Backfoot (IRE) (Bob Back **c118** (USA)) [2018/19 h120: h20.6g^pu h21.6g⁴ h19.9g c18g⁶ h20.5g³ c19.2g* c21.4g² Mar 27] **h97** sturdy gelding: has had breathing operation: fairly useful hurdler at best, well below that level in 2018/19: fairly useful form over fences: won handicap at Market Rasen in March: stays 21f: acts on soft going: has worn headgear: wears tongue tie. *Jo Davis*

STARJAC (FR) 5 gr.g. Linda's Lad – Star's Mixa (FR) (Linamix (FR)) [2018/19 b71: **h118** h15.8g³ h16g² h15.8g³ h16d h19.9d² Mar 30] rather unfurnished gelding: fairly useful form over hurdles: second in handicap at Uttoxeter in March: stays 2½m: acts on good to soft going. *Paul Webber*

STARKIE 12 b.g. Putra Sandhurst (IRE) – Lysways (Gildoran) [2018/19 c108, h–: c21.1d^ur **c–** Apr 4] good-topped gelding: point winner: winning hurdler: fair chaser: beaten when **h–** unseated 5 out in Foxhunters' Chase at Aintree sole outing under Rules in 2018/19: stays 2¼m: acts on heavy going: has worn headgear: in tongue tie last 2 starts. *Anthony Ward-Thomas*

STARLIT NIGHT 7 b.m. Nayef (USA) – Perfect Night (Danzig Connection (USA)) **h60** [2018/19 h74: h21.6g h21.6g h23m⁶ h23g h21.6g h16.8g Apr 20] rather leggy mare: has had breathing operation: poor handicap hurdler: stays 2¾m: has worn hood: has worn tongue tie, including in 2018/19: usually races close up. *Chris Down*

STAR MAX (GER) 4 b.g. Maxios – Startissima (Green Tune (USA)) [2018/19 h16g **h126** h16d³ h16d* h16.4s h16d* h16d Apr 22] useful on Flat in Germany, stays 11f: fairly useful form over hurdles: won maiden at Gowran in February and novice at Limerick in March: should stay further than 2m: acts on good to soft going: usually races prominently. *Joseph Patrick O'Brien, Ireland*

STAR OF LANKA (IRE) 5 b.g. Zoffany (IRE) – Indian Bounty (Indian Ridge) [2018/19 **h124** b92: h16v⁴ h19.7s* h19.7s⁵ h21g⁴ h24.3g⁴ h21s Mar 16] rather leggy gelding: bumper winner: fairly useful form over hurdles: won novices at Hereford in November and December: fourth in Lanzarote Hurdle at Kempton: stays 3m: acts on soft going. *Warren Greatrex*

STAR OF RORY (IRE) 5 b.g. Born To Sea (IRE) – Dame Alicia (IRE) (Sadler's Wells **h104** (USA)) [2018/19 h15.8g h19.6v⁴ h15.8s h16g² h15.8d⁴ h16s* Mar 10] sturdy gelding: closely related to fair hurdler Invincible Don (2m winner, by Invincible Spirit), stays 21f: useful on Flat, stays 1¼m: fair form over hurdles: in tongue tie, won conditionals/amateurs handicap at Warwick in March: seems best at 2m: acts on heavy going: tried in cheekpieces. *John Groucott*

STAROZOV (IRE) 6 b.g. Morozov (USA) – Star of Arcady (IRE) (Jurado (USA)) **h107 p**
[2018/19 h16.2g³ h22.7d² Nov 10] €15,000 3-y-o, £10,000 5-y-o: sixth foal: half-brother
to a winning pointer by Beneficial: dam once-raced half-sister to Midlands Grand National
winner G V A Ireland and useful 2m chaser Dines: Irish point winner: fair form over hurdles:
better effort when second in novice at Kelso: open to further improvement. *Jackie Stephen*

STARPLEX 9 b.g. Multiplex – Turtle Bay (Dr Fong (USA)) [2018/19 h91: h16.2spu h16.8s **h—**
h15.7g h16.8vpu h17g⁶ Feb 24] fair hurdler at best, no form in 2018/19 (including on Flat):
tried in tongue tie. *Kenny Johnson*

STARSHELL (IRE) 5 b.g. Sea The Stars (IRE) – Aquarelle Bleue (Sadler's Wells **h—**
(USA)) [2018/19 h–: h16.8m⁵ h16.2g h21.3mpu h15.8gpu h16.8spu Nov 27] no form over
hurdles: in cheekpieces last 2 starts: tried in tongue tie. *Barry Murtagh*

STARSKY (IRE) 5 b.g. Shantou (USA) – Lunar Star (IRE) (King's Theatre (IRE)) **b93**
[2018/19 b15.3g² b16.5d³ Apr 4] €48,000 3-y-o: third foal: half-brother to fairly useful
hurdler/chaser Pauls Hill (21f-3¼m winner, by Marienbard): dam unraced half-sister to
smart hurdler (stayed 3m) Make Your Mark: fair form in bumpers: better effort when third
in maiden at Taunton: wears tongue tie. *Paul Nicholls*

STARS ROYALE (IRE) 10 b.g. King's Best (USA) – Open Your Heart (IRE) (Soviet **c—**
Star (USA)) [2018/19 c26gpu May 17] rather leggy gelding: point winner: maiden hurdler/ **h—**
chaser: tried in tongue tie. *Mrs Cynthia Woods*

START SEVEN 7 br.g. Dilum (USA) – Dancingintheclouds (IRE) (Rainbow Quest **h—**
(USA)) [2018/19 h17.2gpu h15.7g h20.6s⁵ h16g Jan 12] has had breathing operation: fairly
useful on Flat, stays 2m: no form over hurdles: wears cheekpieces: in tongue tie last 3
starts. *James Moffatt*

STATE THE OBVIOUS (IRE) 7 ch.g. Presenting – New Vega (FR) (Blushing Flame **c105**
(USA)) [2018/19 h101: c20.3g⁶ c20.9g³ c23.9m* Jun 22] fair hurdler: similar form over **h—**
fences: won novice handicap at Market Rasen in June: stays 3m: acts on good to firm
going: in cheekpieces last 2 starts. *Jonjo O'Neill*

STATE VISION (FR) 5 b.g. Vision d'Etat (FR) – Dona Rez (FR) (Trempolino (USA)) **b73 p**
[2018/19 b16.2g⁵ Apr 15] fifth foal: half-brother to 3 winners in France, including useful
hurdler/chaser Polygona (17f-19f winner, by Poliglote) and fairly useful chaser Saint Lino
(17f-2¾m winner, by Saint des Saints): dam, French 2m/17f hurdle/chase winner, sister to
smart French hurdler up to 19f Don Lino: 7/2, better than result when fifth in bumper at
Hexham (22½ lengths behind Shanroe): sure to do better. *Charlie Longsdon*

STATION MASTER (IRE) 8 b.g. Scorpion (IRE) – Gastounette (IRE) (Presenting) **c137**
[2018/19 h131, b95: c22.5g² c25g² c24gpu c23.6d* c25.2g² c26g² Apr 12] well-made **h—**
gelding: bumper winner: useful hurdler: similar form over fences: won novice at
Huntingdon in March: likely to stay long distances: acts on good to soft going: has worn
cheekpieces, including last 3 starts. *Kim Bailey*

STATISTICAL (IRE) 7 b.g. Robin des Champs (FR) – Lusty Beg (IRE) (Old Vic) **c109**
[2018/19 h21m⁵ h17.3g⁶ c20g² c22g* h21.4gpu c20.5m* Apr 25] €75,000 3-y-o: second **h103**
foal: dam unraced half-sister to fair hurdler/smart chaser (stayed 3¼m) Treacle: fair
maiden hurdler: fair form over fences: won maiden at Tramore in August and novice
handicap at Kempton (sole rival unseated first) in April: left Henry de Bromhead after
fourth start: stays 2¾m: acts on good to firm and heavy going: tried in cheekpieces: front
runner/races prominently. *Emma Lavelle*

STATUARIO 4 b.g. Helmet (AUS) – Cat Hunter (One Cool Cat (USA)) [2018/19 h15.8g³ **h125**
h16.7s² h17d h15.8g* Apr 21] good-topped gelding: dam half-sister to smart hurdler/very
smart chaser (stays 21f) Charbel: fairly useful on Flat, stays 1¼m: fairly useful form over
hurdles: tongue tied, won novice at Ffos Las in April. *Peter Bowen*

STAUNTON 8 b.m. Kayf Tara – Aranga (IRE) (Supreme Leader) [2018/19 c58, h71: **c—**
h23.9d⁵ May 26] lengthy mare: poor maiden hurdler: once-raced chaser. *Tim Vaughan* **h70**

STAY IN TOUCH (IRE) 8 b.g. Touch of Land (FR) – Supreme Dancer (IRE) (Supreme **h105**
Leader) [2018/19 h105: h22.1g³ h15.8g³ h20.2g⁴ h23.1g Aug 20] point winner: fair maiden
hurdler: stays 2¾m: acts on good to soft going: wears headgear: usually races prominently.
Donald McCain

ST BASIL 6 gr.g. Geordieland (FR) – Wibble Wobble (Alflora (IRE)) [2018/19 b16m Apr **b—**
13] tailed off in bumper. *Stuart Colthred*

STEADY AWAY (IRE) 5 b.g. Fame And Glory – Inch Pride (IRE) (Beneficial) [2018/19 **b–**
b15.3g ab16g Feb 18] little impact in bumpers. *Nicky Martin*

STEAK AND SPUDS (IRE) 7 b.m. Flemensfirth (USA) – Pip 'N Pop (IRE) (Oscar **h90**
(IRE)) [2018/19 h19.5d h24.3s⁵ h16.4m h23.9g Apr 24] third foal: dam (c115) 3m chase
winner: multiple point winner: modest maiden hurdler: stays 19f: acts on good to soft
going. *R. Mike Smith*

STEALING MIX 9 b.g. Fair Mix (IRE) – Minimum (Terimon) [2018/19 c106, h94: **c81**
c17m⁶ May 20] good-topped gelding: fair hurdler: similar form at best over fences: stays **h–**
2½m: acts on firm going: wears tongue tie. *Neil Mulholland*

STEAMBOAT BILL (IRE) 8 b.g. Kalanisi (IRE) – Freemantle Doctor (IRE) (Luso) **c–**
[2018/19 h24g h24.3g h22m h22d h21.4vᵖᵘ Nov 29] fairly useful hurdler at best, no form **h–**
in 2018/19: maiden chaser: has worn cheekpieces. *Harry Smyth, Ireland*

STECCANDO (IRE) 6 b.g. Lawman (FR) – Second Act (Sadler's Wells (USA)) [2018/19 **h–**
h16d Nov 28] fair maiden on Flat, stays 1½m: tailed off in novice on hurdling debut.
Rebecca Menzies

STEEL BOB (IRE) 7 b.g. Craigsteel – Lady Kamando (Hernando (FR)) [2018/19 h111: **h115**
h23.6dᵖᵘ h25.5v³ h25s* h26g Apr 10] point winner: fairly useful handicap hurdler: won at
Plumpton in March: left Harry Fry after second start: stays 25f: acts on good going: has
worn cheekpieces, including in 2018/19: usually races prominently. *George Baker*

STEEL CITY 11 gr.g. Act One – Serraval (FR) (Sanglamore (USA)) [2018/19 c–x, h101x: **c–**
h16.4d h15.7g³ c16.4dᵖᵘ h15.7g³ Mar 6] useful-looking gelding: fair handicap hurdler: no **h99**
form over fences: unproven beyond 17f: acts on heavy going: has worn headgear: in tongue
tie last 2 starts. *Michael Easterby*

STEELES TERRACE (IRE) 7 b.g. Craigsteel – She's So Beautiful (IRE) (Bluebird **c105**
(USA)) [2018/19 c21.6g* c22.6d² Jun 8] €3,000 3-y-o: fifth foal: half-brother to fair 2¾m
hurdle winner Shaciara (by Shantou) and modest 3m chase winner Benefit In Kind (by
Beneficial): dam (h70), maiden hurdler, 7f winner on Flat: multiple point winner: fair form
in chases: won maiden hunter at Fontwell in May: in tongue tie last 2 starts. *A. Pennock*

STEEL EXPRESS (IRE) 7 b.g. Craigsteel – Assidua (IRE) (Anshan) [2018/19 h97: **h101**
h21.4g h23.6d² h23.1d² Apr 9] fair maiden hurdler: stays 3m: acts on heavy going.
Linda Blackford

STEEL HELMET (IRE) 5 ch.g. Helmet (AUS) – Marine City (JPN) (Carnegie (IRE)) **h77**
[2018/19 h–: h15.7d² Apr 24] poor form over hurdles. *Harriet Bethell*

STEEL KING (IRE) 10 b.g. Kalanisi (IRE) – Prairie Bell (IRE) (Sadler's Wells (USA)) **h–**
[2018/19 h24.3g h20.8g Aug 21] fairly useful hurdler at best, no form in 2018/19: stays
3m: acts on soft going: has worn headgear, including final start: in tongue tie last 2 starts.
Mark McNiff, Ireland

STEEL NATIVE (IRE) 8 b.g. Craigsteel – Princess Gloria (IRE) (Prince Rupert (FR)) **c101 x**
[2018/19 c96x, h94x: c23.8v² c25.3v* h21.9vᵖᵘ c24s* c30.7s⁵ Apr 16] winning hurdler: **h– x**
fair handicap chaser: won at Ffos Las in December and Bangor in March: stays 25f: acts on
heavy going: usually wears hood: often let down by jumping. *David Rees*

STEEL'S COTTON 10 b.m. Tikkanen (USA) – Last Spruce (USA) (Big Spruce (USA)) **c–**
[2018/19 c94, h–: c24.2dᵖᵘ c26.2dᵖᵘ Apr 8] point winner: maiden hurdler/chaser: has worn **h–**
cheekpieces/tongue tie. *Jane Clark*

STEEL WAVE (IRE) 9 br.g. Craigsteel – Musical Waves (IRE) (Orchestra) [2018/19 **c116**
c19.9s* c20g⁴ c19.9mᵇᵈ c22.5d⁵ c20.1g⁴ c20g⁶ h24m³ h20g² h19.6d h20.6s⁴ c20.2m³ h23s⁴ **h117**
h21.3g⁴ h23d³ Apr 26] fairly useful handicap hurdler: useful handicap chaser: won maiden at
Kilbeggan in May: left W. P. Mullins after eighth start: stays 3m: acts on soft and good to
firm going: has worn hood. *Gary Hanmer*

STEELY ADDITION (IRE) 7 b.g. Craigsteel – Blond's Addition (IRE) (Lord Americo) **c144**
[2018/19 h128p: c23.8v³ c23.6v* c23.6d⁴ c25.2g* Mar 26] fairly useful hurdler: useful **h–**
form over fences: won novice handicap at Chepstow (by 2½ lengths from Yalltari) in
December and novice at Hereford in March: stays 25f: acts on heavy going: often travels
strongly. *Philip Hobbs*

STELLAR NOTION (IRE) 11 b.g. Presenting – Green Star (FR) (Green Tune (USA)) **c133**
[2018/19 c122, h–: c23.4g* c26.1mᵖᵘ c20.3d² Apr 9] well-made gelding: won twice in **h–**
points in 2019: winning hurdler: useful chaser: won handicap at Kelso (by 6 lengths from

Blue Kascade) in May: left Tom George after second start: stays 3m: acts on heavy going: tried in cheekpieces: has worn tongue tie: usually races close up. *T. M. Frost*

STEP BACK (IRE) 9 ch.g. Indian River (FR) – Stepitoutmary (IRE) (Roselier (FR)) [2018/19 c146p, h–: c23.6d c29.2g⁶ c34.3gᵖᵘ c28.8g³ Apr 27] sturdy gelding: winning hurdler: useful handicap chaser: third in bet365 Gold Cup at Sandown (19 lengths behind Talkischeap, won race as novice previous year) in April: stays 29f: acts on soft going: often in cheekpieces: tried in tongue tie: usually leads. *Mark Bradstock*   **c141 h–**

STEPHANIE SUNSHINE (IRE) 6 b.m. Dubai Destination (USA) – Shyanne (IRE) (Mandalus) [2018/19 h16g⁴ h16dᵘʳ h15.8d⁵ h16d³ h19.5d⁴ h19.5m² Apr 22] half-sister to useful hurdler/chaser Sizing Rio (2m-2½m winner, by Heron Island) and bumper winner/fairly useful 2¾m hurdle winner Sizing Mexico (by Snurge): dam (h70) second in bumper/maiden hurdler: modest maiden hurdler: left Mrs J. Harrington after second start: stays 19f: acts on good to firm and good to soft going: tried in tongue tie. *Sophie Leech*   **h99**

STEPOVER 8 b.m. Midnight Legend – Ring Back (IRE) (Bob Back (USA)) [2018/19 h106: h15.7g² h15.7g⁴ h16g⁴ h16.7gᵖᵘ h16.2g³ Nov 5] workmanlike mare: fair handicap hurdler: won mares event at Worcester in September: raced around 2m: acts on good to soft going: has worn hood: wears tongue tie. *Alex Hales*   **h112**

STEPS AND STAIRS (IRE) 9 b.g. Robin des Pres (FR) – Be Mine Tonight (IRE) (Carroll House) [2018/19 c111, h–: c20.3d² c22.9v³ c24d⁴ c25.5d⁴ c23.6dᶠ Mar 21] winning hurdler: fair handicap chaser: stayed 3m: acted on heavy going: retried in cheekpieces penultimate start: dead. *Henry Oliver*   **c113 h–**

STEP YOU GAILY 6 b.m. Crosspeace (IRE) – Khadija (Kadastrof (FR)) [2018/19 b–: b15.8g b17.7g Jun 5] no form in bumpers. *Ben Pauling*   **b–**

ST ERNEY 8 ch.g. Kadastrof (FR) – Ticket To The Moon (Pollerton) [2018/19 c24.2s³ c26.2d³ c24.2v* Mar 18] second foal: dam (c98) 21f chase winner (stayed 25f): runner-up in point: fairly useful form in chases: won novice handicap at Exeter in March: open to further improvement. *Jackie du Plessis*   **c125 p**

STERNRUBIN (GER) 8 b.g. Authorized (IRE) – Sworn Mum (GER) (Samum (GER)) [2018/19 c138, h131: h20g c17.5m* c18.8m⁶ c16g* c16d³ h16.5g² h16.8d⁶ h20d⁴ Apr 5] tall gelding: useful handicap hurdler: second at Taunton (1½ lengths behind Capitaine) in February: useful chaser: won maiden at Exeter in October and handicap at Ludlow in November: stays 2½m: acts on good to firm and heavy going: wears headgear: front runner/races prominently: tough and reliable. *Philip Hobbs*   **c136 h136**

STEVE MEQUINE 6 ch.g. Native Ruler – Rabbit (Muhtarram (USA)) [2018/19 b–: h20s h20gᵖᵘ Jun 11] no form in bumpers/over hurdles: tried in hood: in tongue tie last 3 starts. *Katy Price*   **h–**

ST GEORGE'S OVAL (IRE) 6 b.g. Milan – Lisselton Lady (IRE) (Anshan) [2018/19 h92, b81: h15.8g² h17.2m⁴ h16.7g h17.1g h15.7d⁵ h22.7g⁵ h19.4g⁴ h21.4dᶠ h19.7g h20.6d⁵ h19.8s h17m³ h16.2g⁵ Apr 25] lengthy gelding: modest maiden hurdler: left Mark Loughnane after third start: should stay beyond 17f: acts on soft and good to firm going: in cheekpieces last 4 starts: wears tongue tie. *Lucinda Egerton*   **h97**

STICK TO THE PLAN (IRE) 7 b.g. Gold Well – Chloes Choice (IRE) (Presenting) [2018/19 h121: c24.1gᵖᵘ May 19] well-made gelding: fairly useful hurdler: pulled up in novice handicap on chasing debut: stayed 3m: acted on good to soft going: in cheekpieces last 2 starts: wore tongue tie: dead. *Dan Skelton*   **c– h–**

STICK WITH BILL (IRE) 5 b.g. Oscar (IRE) – Made In Kk (IRE) (Kris Kin (USA)) [2018/19 b15.8v* b15.8s² Feb 26] third foal: dam unraced half-sister to smart hurdler/chaser (stayed 2½m) Made In Taipan: useful form in bumpers: won maiden at Ffos Las (by 2¼ lengths from Little Red Lion) in December. *Harry Whittington*   **b112**

STILL BELIEVING (IRE) 11 ch.m. Blueprint (IRE) – Im A Believer (IRE) (Erins Isle) [2018/19 c104, h127: c23.8g⁵ h23.3m⁶ c20g c23.8d* c24.2m* h21.2g c25.2v* c23g³ c24s⁶ c21.6m³ Apr 20] angular mare: fairly useful handicap hurdler, below form in 2018/19: fairly useful handicap chaser: won at Chepstow (mares) and Exeter in October, and Hereford (mares) in December: stays 3¼m: acts on good to firm and heavy going: has worn cheekpieces, including in 2018/19. *Evan Williams*   **c116 h92**

STIMULATING SONG 4 ch.g. Stimulation (IRE) – Choral Singer (Daylami (IRE)) [2018/19 b15.3g⁶ Jan 17] fifth foal: dam unraced: 40/1, sixth in maiden bumper at Wincanton (5 lengths behind Faire Part Sivola). *Milton Harris*   **b86**

STIPULATE 10 b.g. Dansili – Indication (Sadler's Wells (USA)) [2018/19 h17.2g⁶ h15.8g⁵ h17.2m h15.8g Jul 18] compact gelding: modest maiden hurdler: raced mainly at 2m: has worn headgear, including final start. *Sam England* **h85**

ST JOHN'S 6 b.g. Aqlaam – Diam Queen (GER) (Lando (GER)) [2018/19 h91, b93: h21.2g² h20m⁵ h15.8m³ h23.3g⁴ h16.8g⁴ h20.3g⁴ h15.8v⁴ h15.5g⁶ Dec 6] sturdy gelding: bumper winner: modest maiden hurdler: stays 21f: acts on good to soft going: tried in cheekpieces. *Evan Williams* **h98**

ST MERRYN (IRE) 8 b.g. Oscar (IRE) – Kigali (IRE) (Torus) [2018/19 c80, h–: c20.3g⁶ c20d⁴ c19.4mᵖᵘ c20d⁶ c16.2d c19.2sᵖᵘ Apr 16] good-topped gelding: maiden hurdler: poor maiden chaser: tried in hood: has worn tongue tie, including in 2018/19. *Rob Summers* **c70 h–**

STOCKBURN (IRE) 6 b.g. Scorpion (IRE) – Hayabusa (Sir Harry Lewis (USA)) [2018/19 h110, b80: h21.7g h21d h25d⁴ c23.6d³ Apr 6] workmanlike gelding: fair maiden hurdler: 13/2, third in novice handicap at Chepstow (5 lengths behind Pop Rockstar) on chasing debut: likely to stay extreme distances: acts on soft going: tried in headgear. *Alan King* **c108 h100**

STOLBERG (IRE) 11 br.g. Vinnie Roe (IRE) – Giveherthewhistle (IRE) (Supreme Leader) [2018/19 c73, h102: h16.7s³ h15.3g⁶ h20sᵖᵘ h16.8gᵖᵘ h16m Apr 22] workmanlike gelding: has had breathing operation: modest handicap hurdler: maiden chaser: stays 2¾m: acts on heavy going: has worn cheekpieces/tongue tie, including final start. *Dai Williams* **c– h86**

STOLEAWAY (IRE) 9 b.g. Stowaway – Karsulu (IRE) (Mukaddamah (USA)) [2018/19 c25.3gᵘʳ May 4] multiple point winner: fair form in chases: looked sure to play hand in finish when unseating 4 out in hunter at Cheltenham sole outing under Rules in 2018/19. *Philip Rowley* **c–**

STOLEN SILVER (FR) 4 gr.g. Lord du Sud (FR) – Change Partner (FR) (Turtle Island (IRE)) [2018/19 b15.3s⁵ b16m² Apr 22] has had breathing operation: closely related to useful hurdler Karalee (17f-19f winner, by Martaline) and half-brother to 2 winners in France, including useful hurdler/fairly useful chaser Jamal Malik (15f-2¼m winner, by Lavirco): dam (c119/h127) French 2m-19f hurdle/chase winner: fair form in bumpers: in hood, better effort when second at Chepstow: wears tongue tie. *Sam Thomas* **b86**

STOLE THE SHOW (IRE) 7 ch.g. Mahler – Brideview Hamshire (IRE) (Blueprint (IRE)) [2018/19 h19.2g* h21.4m⁴ h15.7g³ h16g² h18.6m* Jul 21] fairly useful hurdler: won handicap at Fontwell (conditionals) in May and novice at Market Rasen in July: stayed 19f: acted on good to firm and heavy going: dead. *Dr Richard Newland* **h116**

STONEBRIGG LEGEND 7 b.m. Midnight Legend – Forget The Ref (IRE) (Dr Massini (IRE)) [2018/19 h72: h24g³ h24g h25.8g⁵ c19.9g⁴ c23.6dᶠ c21.2d² h26g³ c21.2g* c21.2d* c23.6g⁵ Apr 11] poor maiden hurdler: similar form over fences: won 2 handicaps (novice on second occasion) at Fakenham in March: stays 3m: acts on good to soft going: tried in cheekpieces. *Sarah Humphrey* **c84 h70**

STONECOLDSOBA 6 b.g. Aqlaam – Aswaaq (IRE) (Peintre Celebre (USA)) [2018/19 h107: h15.7g⁶ h20.3g⁴ h16g h15.8g⁴ h15.7gᵘʳ h18.6g h20g⁶ h15.5g³ h15.9d⁶ h15.8d* h16sᶠ Mar 10] leggy gelding: fair handicap hurdler: won at Huntingdon in February: stayed 2½m: acted on good to soft going: retried in cheekpieces in 2018/19: dead. *Denis Quinn* **h102**

STONEMADFORSPEED (IRE) 11 b.g. Fruits of Love (USA) – Diamond Forever (Teenoso (USA)) [2018/19 h108§: h20g h20g⁴ h23.3g h20.3g⁵ h21.7g² h21.7m⁵ h25g³ h21.6s h24.4g h21d² h19g* h25dᵖᵘ h22g Mar 30] sturdy gelding: point winner: modest handicap hurdler: won selling event at Taunton in February: stays 2¾m: acts on firm and soft going: wears headgear: tried in tongue tie: usually races close up: temperamental. *Roger Teal* **h93 §**

STONER'S CHOICE 4 br.g. Great Pretender (IRE) – High Benefit (IRE) (Beneficial) [2018/19 b16.7g² b16g* Apr 25] £75,000 3-y-o: third foal: dam (h113), bumper/2m hurdle winner, half-sister to fairly useful hurdlers/chasers Larks Lad (stayed 3m) and Hersov (stayed 33f) out of half-sister to Champion Hurdle winners Granville Again and Morley Street: fairly useful form in bumpers: won at Warwick in April. *Ben Case* **b95**

STONEY CROSS 7 b.m. Sulamani (IRE) – Stoney Path (Petoski) [2018/19 b15.8gᵘʳ b15.3m h15.8dᶠ h21.2dᵖᵘ Feb 6] half-sister to several winners, including fair hurdler/useful chaser Stoney's Treasure (19f-3m winner, by Silver Patriarch) and fair hurdler/chaser Shady Lane (2m winner, by Alflora): dam (h94), 19f/2½m hurdle winner, half-sister to smart 2m chaser Martin's Lamp and useful chaser up to 3m Hurricane Lamp: no form in bumpers/over hurdles. *Richard Phillips* **h– b–**

STONEY MOUNTAIN (IRE) 6 ch.g. Mountain High (IRE) – Cherry Pie (FR) **h127**
(Dolpour) [2018/19 b100: h20g* h21.6g² h20.3s* h21g² h24.3g³ h24dᵖᵘ Mar 15] medium-
sized gelding: bumper winner: fairly useful form over hurdles: won maiden at Aintree in
October and novice at Southwell in December: second in Leamington Novices' Hurdle at
Warwick (3¾ lengths behind Beakstown): will stay beyond 3m: acts on soft going. *Henry
Daly*

STONEY ROVER (IRE) 6 b.g. Scorpion (IRE) – Consultation (IRE) (Camden Town) **h117**
[2018/19 h16.2gᵘʳ h16g² h20.1s* h20.1v² h22.7g³ h20.5s⁴ h20.1d⁴ Mar 26] £16,000 5-y-o:
seventh foal: half-brother to fair hurdler Mo Chailin (2m winner, by Milan), stayed 2½m:
dam (b80), fourth in bumper (little other form), out of half-sister to high-class staying
chaser Kingsmark: placed twice from 3 starts in Irish points: fairly useful hurdler: won
novice at Hexham in November: stays 2½m: best form on soft/heavy going. *Katie Scott*

STONY STREAM (IRE) 5 b.g. Watar (IRE) – Chiminee Lamp (IRE) (Pierre) [2018/19 **b89**
b16g² b16.8s² Mar 3] first foal: dam unraced: fair form in bumpers: better effort when
second at Sedgefield in March: left Eoin Griffin after first start. *Jonjo O'Neill*

STOP TALKING (IRE) 7 b.m. Gamut (IRE) – Miss Snapdragon (IRE) (Topanoora) **h112**
[2018/19 h17.2d h16.3m⁶ h16.2g h18.7g⁵ h16g² h15.7d⁴ h21.2s* h19.9s* h22v⁴ h20.2g*
Apr 24] €2,200 4-y-o: workmanlike mare: has had breathing operation: sixth foal: half-
sister to fair 3m hurdle winner/winning pointer High Ho Sheriff (by Presenting) and a
winning pointer by Milan: dam unraced half-sister to useful staying hurdler What A
Question: placed in Irish points: fair handicap hurdler: won at Southwell (conditionals) in
November, Ludlow (conditionals novice) and Uttoxeter (novice) in December, and Perth
(mares) in April: stays 21f: acts on soft going: strong traveller. *Jennie Candlish*

STOP THE WORLD (IRE) 6 b.g. Oscar (IRE) – Coolsilver (IRE) (Good Thyne (USA)) **h118**
[2018/19 b89: h19.2g³ h19.8s⁵ h23.1d² h24.3m² Apr 12] has had breathing
operation: runner-up in Irish maiden point: fairly useful maiden hurdler: further
improvement when second in handicap at Ayr final outing: stays 3m: acts on soft and good
to firm going: in tongue tie last 3 starts. *Tom George*

STORM ARISING (IRE) 5 b.g. Yeats (IRE) – Ceol Rua (IRE) (Bob Back (USA)) **h123**
[2018/19 h19.5s⁶ h19.5v⁴ h19.5d⁵ h19.8s* h19.8g³ Mar 25] €42,000 3-y-o, £80,000 4-y-o:
second foal: dam (h134), bumper/2m-2¼m hurdle winner, stayed 2¾m), also 1¾m winner
on Flat, half-sister to smart hurdler (stayed 2¾m) Glens Melody: placed in Irish point:
fairly useful form over hurdles: won maiden at Wincanton in March: will be suited by
2¾m+: acts on soft going. *Paul Nicholls*

STORMBAY BOMBER (IRE) 10 b.g. September Storm (GER) – Top Tottie (IRE) **c91 §**
(Alzao (USA)) [2018/19 c99§, h–: c16.4g² c15.7gᵖᵘ c15.6g c21.2g⁴ c20.3g⁴ c16g⁴ c15.7g² **h–**
c17g³ c19.3g⁵ Nov 8] strong, close-coupled gelding: winning hurdler: modest handicap
chaser: unproven beyond 17f: acts on heavy going: has worn cheekpieces, including last 2
starts: tried in tongue tie: irresolute. *Rebecca Menzies*

STORM CONTROL (IRE) 6 b.g. September Storm (GER) – Double Dream (IRE) **c– p**
(Double Eclipse (IRE)) [2018/19 h117: h20g h21dᵖᵘ c19.4g⁴ Jan 12] tall, unfurnished **h–**
gelding: easy winner of Irish point: fairly useful form in maiden hurdles in 2017/18:
disappointing since, including in novice on chasing debut (weakened quickly once
headed): should stay beyond 19f: acts on soft going: tried in cheekpieces/tongue tie: front
runner/races prominently: should do better over fences. *Kerry Lee*

STORM FIRE 6 b.g. Fair Mix (IRE) – Tara Gale (Kayf Tara) [2018/19 b–: b16g³ b16.8g⁶ **h–**
h16.8mᵘʳ h20.5gᵖᵘ h21.4g h15.3g Jan 17] workmanlike gelding: little show in bumpers/ **b59**
novice hurdles: tried in visor/tongue tie. *Brian Barr*

STORM FORCE BEN (IRE) 5 b.g. Fame And Glory – Torduff Storm (IRE) (Glacial **b75**
Storm (USA)) [2018/19 b16d b16d Apr 6] well held in bumpers. *Philip Hobbs*

STORM GODDESS (IRE) 5 br.m. Oscar (IRE) – Afasheen (IRE) (Presenting) [2018/19 **h119**
b15.8g⁵ b15.8g⁵ b13.7m⁴ b15.8g³ h19.7s² h19.4g⁴ h16.3d² h20.3gᵘʳ Apr 18] fourth foal: **b83**
closely related to fair hurdler Countess Cathleen (19f winner, by Yeats): dam (h112),
2m-19f hurdle winner, half-sister to smart hurdler (stays 3m) Younevercall: modest form in
bumpers: fairly useful form over hurdles: won maiden at Doncaster in January: stays 2½m:
acts on soft going. *Charlie Longsdon*

STORM HOME (IRE) 7 br.g. King's Theatre (IRE) – Miss Mayberry (IRE) (Bob Back **c118**
(USA)) [2018/19 h127: c16d⁵ c15.9g⁴ c18.8g c20.5gᵖᵘ h16.8d⁵ h16.5g Feb 19] fairly useful **h101**
novice hurdler in 2017/18: similar form first 2 starts over fences: disappointing

subsequently, including back over hurdles: unproven beyond 2m: acts on heavy going: tried in tongue tie. *Colin Tizzard*

STORMINGIN (IRE) 6 gr.g. Clodovil (IRE) – Magadar (USA) (Lujain (USA)) [2018/19 h–: h15.9g⁴ h16d h16d³ h15.3g h15.8d Feb 17] good-topped gelding: fairly useful on Flat (stays 11f): modest form over hurdles: will prove best around 2m: acts on good to soft going. *Gary Moore* **h98**

STORMIN NORMAN 4 b.g. Sir Percy – Roses (Muhtarram (USA)) [2018/19 b13.1g⁴ b14g b14.6s b16.7g* Apr 3] second foal: half-brother to 2m winner Rosette (by Archipenko): dam (b109) won all 4 starts in bumpers/ran once on Flat: fair form in bumpers: won maiden at Market Rasen in April. *Micky Hammond* **b90**

STORM LANTERN 10 b.g. King's Theatre (IRE) – Katoune (FR) (Snurge) [2018/19 c22.6dᵖᵘ Jun 8] multiple point winner: pulled up both outings in chases: tried in tongue tie. *Ms J. Johnston* **c–**

STORM NELSON (IRE) 6 b.g. Gold Well – Dabiyra (IRE) (Linamix (FR)) [2018/19 h83, b74: h20.2g³ h24.3g* Oct 29] modest form over hurdles: won conditionals handicap at Ayr in October: stays 3m: usually races close up. *Lucy Normile* **h96**

STORM OF INTRIGUE (IRE) 7 b.g. Oscar (IRE) – Storminoora (IRE) (Topanoora) [2018/19 h–p, b90: h20.5d³ Mar 1] rangy gelding: bumper winner: off 15 months (had breathing operation), much better effort over hurdles when third in novice at Newbury: capable of better still. *Nicky Henderson* **h114 p**

STORM PATROL 8 b.m. Shirocco (GER) – Material World (Karinga Bay) [2018/19 h–: h15.8d³ Oct 20] lengthy mare: runner-up twice in bumpers: first form (modest) over hurdles when third in mares maiden at Ffos Las: tongue tied previously. *Suzy Smith* **h88**

STORM RISING (IRE) 6 b.g. Canford Cliffs (IRE) – Before The Storm (Sadler's Wells (USA)) [2018/19 h16s⁴ h16g² h16g² h16g² h16m* h17m⁵ h16.6g* h16d⁵ h16.4g* h16m* h16.4g h16s⁴ h16.8d h16.8g⁶ Apr 17] plain gelding: half-brother to fairly useful hurdler Landau (17f/2¼m winner, by Aussie Rules): fairly useful hurdler: won maiden at Limerick and handicap at Galway in July and, having left Denis Hogan, handicaps at Cheltenham (conditionals race) in October and Wetherby in November: will prove best around 2m: acts on soft and good to firm going: wears headgear. *Dr Richard Newland* **h125**

STORM WARNING (IRE) 7 b.g. September Storm (GER) – Ceo Draiochta (IRE) (Erins Isle) [2018/19 h–: h23sᵖᵘ May 25] compact gelding: runner-up in point: no form over hurdles: tried in cheekpieces. *Tim Reed* **h–**

STORM WIZARD (IRE) 7 b.g. Milan – Tempest Belle (IRE) (Glacial Storm (USA)) [2018/19 h16vᶠ h19.5v h19.5d h25d⁶ c24gᵘʳ Apr 13] poor form over hurdles: unseated ninth on chasing debut: bred to stay 2½m+. *Venetia Williams* **c–** **h79**

STORMY BLUES 5 b.g. Sepoy (AUS) – Miss Brown To You (IRE) (Fasliyev (USA)) [2018/19 h16.7g⁵ h16.8gᵖᵘ h15.8g h16.5d h16.5d Apr 24] fair maiden on Flat, stays 1½m: modest form on hurdling debut: none after: tongue tied 3 of 5 outings. *Nigel Hawke* **h90**

STORMY FLIGHT (IRE) 5 gr.g. Cloudings (IRE) – Help Yourself (IRE) (Roselier (FR)) [2018/19 b15.3s² Mar 7] €10,000 3-y-o: seventh foal: half-brother to fair hurdler/ winning pointer Royal Chief (21f winner, by Royal Anthem) and a winning pointer by Beat All: dam (h71), bumper winner/maiden hurdler (stayed 3m), half-sister to fairly useful hurdler/chaser (stayed 2¾m) Bridge Run: 33/1, shaped well when 11 lengths second to Green Dolphin in maiden bumper at Wincanton. *Jeremy Scott* **b86**

STORMY IRELAND (FR) 5 b.m. Motivator – Like A Storm (IRE) (Ultimately Lucky (IRE)) [2018/19 h137: h17d* h19.4s³ h18.1g* h16s² h20.2d² h19.9s² Mar 12] neat mare: useful hurdler: won listed mares events at Killarney in May and Punchestown (again beating Good Thyne Tara in clear-cut fashion) in November: placed all other starts, including when 2¼ lengths second to Roksana in David Nicholson Mares' Hurdle at Cheltenham and 9½ lengths second to Benie des Dieux in Mares Champion Hurdle at Punchestown, latter shortly after end of British season: stays 2½m: acts on heavy going: front runner. *W. P. Mullins, Ireland* **h140**

STORMY MILAN (IRE) 6 b.g. Milan – Socialite Girl (Glacial Storm (USA)) [2018/19 h102p, b69: h23.3g⁴ c20.2f⁴ c23.6g* Mar 19] tall, useful-looking gelding: has had breathing operation: fair form over hurdles: similar form over fences, winning novice handicap at Huntingdon in March: stays 3m: acts on firm and good to soft going: in cheekpieces last 2 starts: open to further improvement as a chaser. *Charlie Longsdon* **c109 p** **h82**

STORMY RECEPTION (IRE) 5 b.m. September Storm (GER) – Mandalus Lady (IRE) (Mandalus) [2018/19 h20.5s^{pu} h22s^{pu} h16.4g Feb 23] €3,800 3-y-o: seventh foal: dam unraced half-sister to dam of high-class hurdler/smart chaser (stayed 25f) Crack Away Jack: no promise in novice hurdles. *Chris Grant* h–

STORMY SEPTEMBER (IRE) 5 b.g. September Storm (GER) – Nechtan (IRE) (Generous (IRE)) [2018/19 h16.2g h24g^5 Oct 2] little impact in 2 Irish points: last both outings over hurdles. *Sam England* h–

STORNAWAY (IRE) 7 b.g. Stowaway – Lucy Cooper (IRE) (Roselier (FR)) [2018/19 b15.7s^4 h16.4s h16.2g^5 h15.7m^6 h20.6d h16.4m Mar 28] placed in Irish points: little sign of ability in bumper/over hurdles: tried in cheekpieces. *Russell Ross* h– b–

STORY OF FRIENDS (FR) 5 b.g. Kingsalsa (USA) – Royale Malinelle (FR) (Malinas (GER)) [2018/19 b16s^5 b16.8d^2 Mar 24] €27,000 3-y-o, £72,000 4-y-o: rather unfurnished gelding: first foal: dam, French 2¼m hurdle winner, out of half-sister to smart French staying hurdler Millenium Royal: winning pointer: fair form in bumpers: better effort when second at Exeter in March. *David Pipe* b93

STOWAWAY MAGIC (IRE) 8 b.g. Stowaway – Irish Mystics (IRE) (Ali-Royal (IRE)) [2018/19 c132p, h135: c15.9g^2 c20.9g* c16.3d^5 h21g h16d h21.4s h19.9v h20.5m^6 h21.7g^4 Apr 24] good-topped gelding: has had breathing operation: formerly useful handicap hurdler: disappointing in 2018/19: useful form over fences: simple task when winning maiden at Stratford in November: stays 21f: acts on soft and good to firm going: usually in headgear: wears tongue tie: temperament under suspicion. *Dan Skelton* c134 h120

ST PATRICK'S DAY (IRE) 7 b.g. Fastnet Rock (AUS) – Race For The Stars (USA) (Fusaichi Pegasus (USA)) [2018/19 h99: h15.8g h15.8g^5 h16g^5 Jun 14] tall gelding: modest maiden hurdler at best: raced only at 2m: acts on soft going: wears headgear: temperamental. *J. R. Jenkins* h64 §

ST PETER'S SQUARE (IRE) 8 b.g. Danehill Dancer (IRE) – Glamour (IRE) (Sadler's Wells (USA)) [2018/19 c–, h93: h16.3g^{pu} h21.6g^{pu} Sep 1] winning hurdler/maiden chaser, of little account nowadays: has worn headgear/tongue tie. *Katie Stephens* c– h–

ST QUINTIN 9 b.g. Act One – Gloriana (Formidable (USA)) [2018/19 c23.4g^3 h23.8g^4 Nov 26] poor maiden hurdler: well-held third in novice handicap at Kelso on chasing debut: stays 3m: best form on good going: tried in headgear. *Mark Walford* c64 h73

STRADIVARIUS DAVIS (FR) 6 b.g. Turgeon (USA) – Trumpet Davis (FR) (Rose Laurel) [2018/19 h–: h21.4m* h23.3g^3 h21.4f^4 Oct 28] has had breathing operation: won maiden point on debut: fair form in novice hurdles: won at Wincanton in May: should stay beyond 21f: acts on good to firm going: wears tongue tie: has looked temperamental. *Paul Nicholls* h109

STRAIDNAHANNA (IRE) 10 gr.g. Medaaly – Sue's Song (Alflora (IRE)) [2018/19 c132§, h–: c25.2g^6 c24g^3 c23.4s^4 c25.2m^F c24.5v^4 c23.4m^3 c28.4m^{pu} Apr 20] big, strong, close-coupled gelding: maiden hurdler: fairly useful handicap chaser: stays 3¾m: acts on good to firm and heavy going: front runner/races prominently: temperamental. *Sue Smith* c128 § h–

STRAIT OF MAGELLAN (IRE) 7 b.g. Captain Rio – Golden (FR) (Sanglamore (USA)) [2018/19 h–: h20.2g^3 h23.9g^6 Aug 1] fairly useful on Flat (stays 16.5f): modest maiden hurdler: stays 2½m: acts on good to soft going: has worn tongue tie. *Nicky Richards* h95

STRAIT RUN (IRE) 8 ch.g. Rock of Gibraltar (IRE) – Gentlemen's Guest (USA) (Gentlemen (ARG)) [2018/19 h82: h16.8s^4 h19.3s^6 h15.7g^5 h16.8v^5 h15.7g^2 h17v* h17m Apr 20] good-bodied gelding: poor handicap hurdler: won at Carlisle in March: unproven beyond 17f: acts on heavy going: usually in headgear/tongue tie: unreliable. *Micky Hammond* h79 §

STRANGSMILL (IRE) 10 b.m. Beneficial – Sweet Vale (IRE) (Supreme Leader) [2018/19 h100: h21.4g^{pu} h20s^{pu} h21.2m Apr 23] point winner: maiden hurdler, no form in 2018/19: tried in blinkers. *Sheila Lewis* h–

STRATHY 6 b.g. Mount Nelson – Rose Street (IRE) (Noverre (USA)) [2018/19 b–: b16g h20.2g^{pu} h20.2g^{pu} h16s h22.7g^{pu} Jan 13] no sign of ability: tried in tongue tie. *Jim Goldie* h– b–

STRATUM 6 b.g. Dansili – Lunar Phase (IRE) (Galileo (IRE)) [2018/19 h131p: h16.3g^4 h16g Dec 2] useful staying handicapper on Flat: smart form over hurdles: best effort when 3½ lengths fourth of 25 to Mr Adjudicator in Ballymore Handicap Hurdle at Punchestown shortly after end of British season: likely to stay beyond 2½m: acts on heavy going: tried in hood. *W. P. Mullins, Ireland* h145

STRAWBERRY SPIRIT (IRE) 6 b.m. Saint des Saints (FR) – Strawberry (IRE) **h95**
(Beneficial) [2018/19 h87, b67: h25m² h24g May 13] modest maiden hurdler: stays 25f:
acts on good to firm and heavy going: tried in headgear/tongue tie. *Amy Murphy*

STREAM LADY (IRE) 6 b.m. Curtain Time (IRE) – Victory Queen (IRE) (Victory Note **h104**
(USA)) [2018/19 b16d⁵ h18.5v⁵ h16.8d⁵ h16.5d h20s h25g* Apr 22] €2,000 3-y-o: has had **b74**
breathing operation: fifth foal: dam (h81), lightly raced over hurdles, half-sister to smart
hurdler/chaser (2m-2½m winner) Slaney Native: easy winner of Irish point on debut: fifth
in mares bumper at Wetherby: fair form over hurdles: won handicap at Plumpton in April:
stays 25f: acts on good to soft going: tried in blinkers. *David Pipe*

STREET ART (IRE) 7 ch.g. Excellent Art – Via Aurelia (IRE) (Antonius Pius (USA)) **h–**
[2018/19 h15.8d^pu Dec 5] regressive on Flat: tongue tied, pulled up in novice claimer on
hurdling debut. *Tracey Barfoot-Saunt*

STREETS OF FIRE (IRE) 5 br.m. Milan – Flaming Brandy (IRE) (Be My Native **b55**
(USA)) [2018/19 b16d Mar 21] €12,000 3-y-o, £37,000 5-y-o: eighth foal: closely related/
half-sister to winning pointers by Oscar and Flemensfirth: dam unraced: Irish point winner:
well beaten in mares bumper. *Jean-Rene Auvray*

STREETS OF MILAN (IRE) 8 b.g. Milan – Madame Jean (FR) (Cricket Ball (USA)) **c96**
[2018/19 c24.2d* May 5] £21,000 6-y-o: half-brother to 3 winners, including fairly useful
hurdler/useful chaser That's Rhythm (2½m-3½m winner, by Pistolet Bleu) and French
hurdler Greydoun (17f/2¼m winner, by Smadoun): dam French 11f winner: point winner:
won maiden hunter at Hexham (by 3 lengths from Wizadora) on chasing debut. *C. C. Pimlott*

STRICTLYADANCER (IRE) 5 b.g. Yeats (IRE) – Feale Dancer (IRE) (Supreme **h92**
Leader) [2018/19 h16g h16.8v h18.5m⁴ h16g h23.4d* h23.8d⁶ Jan 28] €16,500 3-y-o:
second foal: dam unraced half-sister to fairly useful hurdler/chaser (stayed 3m) Gortinard:
failed to complete both starts in points: modest form over hurdles: won handicap at
Fakenham in January: left Sean Thomas Doyle after first start: stays 23f: acts on good to
firm and good to soft going: tried in hood: patiently ridden. *Christian Williams*

STRIKE FEAR (IRE) 7 b.g. Scorpion (IRE) – Skatey Kate (IRE) (Oscar (IRE)) **h–**
[2018/19 h–: h20.3g^pu h23.3g^pu Jul 27] little form over hurdles: tried in hood. *Shaun Harris*

STRIKE HOLLOW 6 ch.m. Beat Hollow – Tazzarine (FR) (Astarabad (USA)) [2018/19 **b81**
b17g⁵ b16.3d⁵ Jun 8] second foal: dam (b90), bumper winner, sister to very smart hurdler/
top-class chaser (stays 3¼m) Whisper: won point bumper on debut: modest form on first of
2 starts in bumpers under Rules. *Miss H. Lewis*

STRIKE IN MILAN (IRE) 7 b.g. Milan – Great Days (IRE) (Magical Strike (USA)) **b99**
[2018/19 b84p: b16.3m* May 20] runner-up in Irish point: fairly useful form in bumpers:
much improved when winning at Stratford sole start in 2018/19: will stay further than 2m:
wears tongue tie. *Tom George*

STRIKE THE FLINT 5 b.m. Shirocco (GER) – Material World (Karinga Bay) [2018/19 **b94**
b15.7d b17.7g* Apr 7] sturdy mare: fifth foal: sister to bumper winner/fair 2½m hurdle
winner Rosy World: dam (h146) bumper/2¾m-3m hurdle winner: fair form in bumpers:
much improved from debut when winning at Plumpton in April. *Suzy Smith*

STRIKE WEST (IRE) 7 b.g. Westerner – Fuel Queen (IRE) (Flemensfirth (USA)) **h100**
[2018/19 h96: h20.1s³ h19.9s h19.3s² h27s² Mar 21] fair handicap hurdler: stays 27f: acts
on heavy going: usually races off pace. *Micky Hammond*

STRIPE OF HONOUR (IRE) 6 b.g. Court Cave (IRE) – Miss Top (IRE) (Tremblant) **h–**
[2018/19 h16.7m h19.7g h24s^pu Dec 4] no promise in maiden/novice hurdles. *Anthony Day*

STROLLAWAYNOW (IRE) 12 b.g. Oscar (IRE) – Rose of Salome (IRE) (Roselier **c110 x**
(FR)) [2018/19 c102x, h–: c24.2g⁴ c27.7g⁵ May 17] rangy gelding: dual point winner: **h–**
winning hurdler: fair but error-prone chaser: won hunter at Fakenham in May: stays 3m:
acts on heavy going: has worn headgear/tongue tie. *David Arbuthnot*

STRONGARM CHASER (IRE) 4 b.g. Footstepsinthesand – Sarawati (IRE) (Haafhd) **h86**
[2018/19 h16.7m² Jun 22] dam half-sister to fairly useful hurdler/useful chaser (2m-2¼m
winner) Priors Dale: modest maiden on Flat, stays 1½m: similar form when well-held
second in juvenile at Market Rasen on hurdling debut. *Donald McCain*

STRONG ECONOMY (IRE) 7 ch.g. Sandmason – Odd Decision (IRE) (Little **c109**
Bighorn) [2018/19 c109, h112: c20.5g⁴ c20.5v³ Nov 14] maiden pointer: fair hurdler: **h–**
similar form over fences: should be suited by 3m: acts on heavy going. *Ian Duncan*

STRONG GLANCE 6 bl.g. Passing Glance – Strong Westerner (IRE) (Westerner) [2018/19   **h108** b105: b16.4d* h16.3s h19.4g⁵ h18.1d⁵ Mar 2] lengthy gelding: has had breathing operation: **b108** useful form in bumpers: won at Cheltenham (by ½ length from Master Debonair) on return in October: fair form over hurdles: tongue tied, improved again when fifth in Premier Kelso Novices' Hurdle in March, though jumped badly right: bred to stay at least 2½m. *Fergal O'Brien*

STRONGLY SUGGESTED 12 b.g. Kayf Tara – Branston Lily (Cadeaux Genereux)   **c115 §** [2018/19 c123§, h–: c19g² c23g c20.3g⁵ c20g c20g c22.9v⁵ Dec 5] compact gelding: **h–** winning hurdler: fairly useful handicap chaser: stays 25f: acts on good to firm and heavy going: has worn cheekpieces/tongue tie (in former last 2 starts): held up: untrustworthy. *Jonjo O'Neill*

STRONG PURSUIT (IRE) 9 ch.g. Flemensfirth (USA) – Loughaderra (IRE) (Strong   **c134** Gale) [2018/19 c139p, h–: c24.2d³ c26gᵖᵘ Mar 23] rangy gelding: winning hurdler: useful   **h–** form over fences: won maiden on chasing debut in 2017/18: off 15 months, better effort in handicaps since when 8¾ lengths third to Achille at Sandown: should be suited by 3m+: acts on soft going: tried in tongue tie. *Philip Hobbs*

STRONG RESEMBLANCE (IRE) 8 b.g. Tikkanen (USA) – Shenamar (IRE)   **c118** (Beneficial) [2018/19 c–, h103: c21.2g h22.1m⁵ c25.5g⁶ c25.5d⁴ h24.3g² h25g* c23.6g*   **h120** c23.8s² h25d* h24.3s* c24.2g³ c24.1s⁵ Mar 9] workmanlike gelding: has had breathing operation: fairly useful handicap hurdler/chaser: left James Moffatt and much improved after fourth start, winning at Huntingdon in November (twice, second one novice event over fences) and December (conditionals hurdle race) and Ayr (also over hurdles) in January: stays 25f: acts on soft going: wears cheekpieces: front runner/races prominently. *Oliver Greenall*

STRONG TEAM (IRE) 6 b.g. Exceed And Excel (AUS) – Star Blossom (USA) (Good   **h98** Reward (USA)) [2018/19 h–, b79: h16.8g² h15.7g h16.2g* h16.8m² h15.8g³ h16.2g* h16.2g² Oct 7] rather leggy gelding: modest handicap hurdler: won at Perth in July and Hexham in September: raced around 2m: acts on good to firm going: tried in hood. *Chris Grant*

STRUMBLE HEAD (IRE) 14 b.g. Anshan – Milan Moss (Le Moss) [2018/19 c119§,   **c119 §** h–: c25.8g* c27.5dᵖᵘ c25.8g³ c20g c26mᵖᵘ c24m⁵ Oct 21] plain gelding: winning hurdler: **h–** fairly useful chaser: won hunter at Newton Abbot in May: stays 3¼m: acts on any going: wears headgear: tried in tongue tie: front runner/races prominently: not one to trust. *Peter Bowen*

STUBBORN LOGIC (IRE) 5 b.g. Dylan Thomas (IRE) – Peripheral Vision (IRE)   **h98** (Saddlers' Hall (IRE)) [2018/19 b16.4g h16g⁵ h16d⁶ h20g² h21.5g⁴ h21.4g Apr 14] €11,000   **b68** 3-y-o: compact gelding: seventh foal: half-brother to fairly useful chaser By The Boardwalk (19f-3m winner) and a winning pointer (both by Presenting): dam (h84), 2½m hurdle winner/winning pointer, out of half-sister to Cheltenham Gold Cup winner Denman: unseated in point: well beaten in maiden bumper: modest form over hurdles: left John Halley after fifth start: stays 21f: best form on good going. *Dr Richard Newland*

STUCCODOR (IRE) 10 b.g. Modigliani (USA) – Armilina (FR) (Linamix (FR))   **h104** [2018/19 h98: h20.6g⁵ h15.8g* h15.8g* h16g h16.7gᵘʳ h15.8gᵖᵘ h15.8g Nov 4] angular gelding: fair handicap hurdler: won at Huntingdon (twice) in May: unproven beyond 2m: acts on heavy going: wears headgear: has worn tongue tie. *Conor Dore*

STUNG FOR CASH (IRE) 6 b.g. Scorpion (IRE) – Cash A Lawn (IRE) (Executive   **h106** Perk) [2018/19 h15.8v² h20.5d⁶ h23.8d⁴ h23.3d⁴ Mar 26] €6,500 3-y-o: half-brother to a   **b85** winning pointer by Marienbard: dam unraced half-sister to useful hurdler/very smart chaser (stayed 25f) Mister Top Notch: Irish point winner: shaped well behind very promising King Roland (beaten 22 lengths into second) in bumper at Uttoxeter: fair form over hurdles, improving when fourth in novice at Hexham final outing. *Alastair Ralph*

STUPID CUPID (IRE) 8 b.m. Beneficial – Supreme Arrow (IRE) (Supreme Leader)   **h–** [2018/19 h–: h15.8d h15.7gᵖᵘ h23g Jun 2] Irish point winner: little form over hurdles. *Sheila Lewis*

STYLE DE GARDE (FR) 5 b.g. Kapgarde (FR) – Anowe de Jelois (FR) (Red Guest   **c131 §** (IRE)) [2018/19 h134: c16g* c16vʳʳ h19g² c16d² h20.3d c15.7d³ Apr 9] good-topped   **h137 §** gelding: has had breathing operation: useful handicap hurdler: similar form over fences: made all in maiden at Hereford in November: stays 19f: acts on soft going: wears hood: headstrong sort who's best treated with caution (has refused to race). *Nicky Henderson*

STYLE DE VOLE (FR) 4 gr.g. Vol de Nuit – Anowe de Jelois (FR) (Red Guest (IRE)) **h120 p**
[2018/19 h16.4d* h16.3s² Dec 19] useful-looking gelding: half-brother to useful hurdler/
chaser Style de Garde (2m-17f winner, by Kapgarde): dam (c125/h125) 17f-2½m hurdle/
chase winner: won 10.4f newcomers race at Saint-Cloud only outing on Flat: looked good
prospect when winning juvenile at Newcastle (by head from Oi The Clubb Oi's) in
December on hurdling debut: outstayed when 6 lengths second to Our Power in similar
event at Newbury: wears hood: remains open to improvement. *Nicky Henderson*

STYLISH DANCER 5 b.m. Nathaniel (IRE) – Hazy Dancer (Oasis Dream) [2018/19 **h103**
h103: h19.9m² h18.7m² h20.6g³ h15.8d h15.8d h15.7s h21.2m Apr 1] rather leggy mare:
fair handicap hurdler: stays 2½m: acts on good to firm going. *Dan Skelton*

STYLISH MOMENT (IRE) 6 b.g. Milan – Up The Style (IRE) (Ashkalani (IRE)) **c108**
[2018/19 h106p, b96: h19.6g³ h21.7g⁵ h21.4g⁶ c19.1g⁵ c24d² Mar 30] fair maiden hurdler: **h98**
better effort in handicap chases (fair form) when second at Uttoxeter in March: stays 3m:
acts on good to soft going: tried in visor. *Alan King*

STYNES (IRE) 9 b.g. Aussie Rules (USA) – Magic Princess (Bahhare (USA)) [2018/19 **c126**
c126, h–: c17.3g* May 28] rather leggy gelding: winning hurdler: fairly useful form over **h–**
fences: won handicap at Cartmel in May: not seen after following up on Flat following
month: probably stays 2½m: acts on soft and good to firm going: tried in cheekpieces:
wears tongue tie: often travels strongly. *Graeme McPherson*

SUBCONTINENT (IRE) 7 b.g. Dubawi (IRE) – Saree (Barathea (IRE)) [2018/19 h114: **h116**
h16.2g* h21d³ h19.7v² h20.5d⁴ h19.8s h16.5g h20.2g⁶ Apr 25] compact gelding: fairly
useful hurdler: won maiden at Perth in May: stays 21f: acts on heavy going. *Venetia Williams*

SUB LIEUTENANT (IRE) 10 b.g. Brian Boru – Satellite Dancer (IRE) (Satco (FR)) **c156**
[2018/19 c159, h–: c22.5d⁵ c22.5g* c25g* c24g⁵ c21.5s c20.5g² c20.6dᵖᵘ c21.1d² Apr 5] **h–**
strong gelding: winning hurdler: very smart chaser nowadays: won minor event at Galway
in August and Grade 3 race at Punchestown (by 9 lengths from Outlander) in October:
second in Topham Handicap Chase at Aintree (8 lengths behind Cadmium): stays 25f: acts
on heavy going: has worn headgear: wears tongue tie: usually front runner/races
prominently: bold jumper. *Henry de Bromhead, Ireland*

SUBTLE SOVEREIGN (IRE) 12 gr.g. Subtle Power (IRE) – Katonka (Emperor Jones **c–**
(USA)) [2018/19 c26.3g May 4] useful-looking gelding: prolific point winner: fair form in **h–**
bumpers/on first of 2 starts over hurdles: tailed off in hunter on chasing debut: tried in
blinkers. *Mrs Teresa Clark*

SUBWAY SURF (IRE) 5 b.m. Milan – Dante Rouge (IRE) (Croco Rouge (IRE)) **b102**
[2018/19 b15.8g* b15.7d³ b16d* Mar 21] £35,000 4-y-o: sturdy mare: first foal: dam
unraced half-sister to useful hurdler/chaser (stayed 23f) Loosen My Load: won Irish point
on debut: fairly useful form in bumpers: won mares events at Ludlow in January and
Chepstow in March. *Kim Bailey*

SUCH A LEGEND 11 ch.g. Midnight Legend – Mrs Fizziwig (Petoski) [2018/19 c123, **c–**
h–: c17dᵖᵘ Jun 8] strong gelding: has had breathing operation: winning hurdler: fairly **h–**
useful chaser: lost way since reappearance in 2017/18 (including in points): stays 2½m:
acts on soft and good to firm going: tried in cheekpieces: has worn tongue tie: front runner/
races prominently. *Tracey L. Bailey*

SUDDEN DESTINATION (IRE) 7 ch.g. Dubai Destination (USA) – Sudden Approach **h116**
(IRE) (Topanoora) [2018/19 h19.9v⁴ h21.2g⁶ h20m² Apr 22] has had breathing operation:
first foal: dam (h91), maiden hurdler/pointer (stayed 3m), half-sister to fairly useful
hurdler/useful chaser (stayed 3m) Graphic Approach: placed in Irish point/bumper: fairly
useful form over hurdles: easily best effort when second in novice at Fakenham: tried in
tongue tie. *Dr Richard Newland*

SUDSKI STAR (IRE) 11 br.g. Pilsudski (IRE) – Mogen's Star (IRE) (Be My Native **c108 §**
(USA)) [2018/19 c120, h106: c17.1g³ c23.4g⁴ c17.1m⁴ c17.1g⁵ c20s² c20.1dᵖᵘ Dec 1] fair **h–**
hurdler: fairly useful handicap chaser: below par in 2018/19: stays 2¾m: acts on heavy
going: wears headgear/tongue tie: temperamental. *Harriet Graham*

SUE BE IT (IRE) 8 b.m. Presenting – Runaround Sue (IRE) (Among Men (USA)) **h102**
[2018/19 h98: h15.7g* h18.7m* Jun 19] fair hurdler: won handicap at Towcester in May
and mares novice at Stratford in June: stays 2½m: acts on good to firm and heavy going:
normally tongue tied. *Nikki Evans*

SUENO TOMS 6 b.m. Oscar (IRE) – Smooth Technology (IRE) (Astronef) [2018/19 b–: **h–**
h16.2d^{ur} Apr 26] last in bumpers: 200/1, unseated second on hurdling debut: tried in hood.
Andrew Hamilton

SUFFICE (IRE) 10 b.g. Iffraaj – Shallat (IRE) (Pennekamp (USA)) [2018/19 h–: h23s **h75**
h19.9g² h18.7m^F Jul 15] poor handicap hurdler: stays 2½m: acts on good to firm and heavy
going: has worn headgear: in tongue tie last 5 starts. *Laura Young*

SUGAR STORM 8 b.m. Kayf Tara – Golden Buck (Golden Snake (USA)) [2018/19 h–: **h61**
h20.3g h17.7g⁶ Jun 5] well-made mare: has had breathing operation: poor maiden hurdler:
usually in tongue tie. *Martin Keighley*

SUGGESTION 7 gr.g. Dansili – Jibboom (USA) (Mizzen Mast (USA)) [2018/19 h103: **h124**
h16.2d⁵ h15.8g⁵ h16.2g² h20.3g³ h17.1g h17.1v h16s* h16.4g³ h15.7d* h19.4d³ h16g*
h16m Apr 12] fairly useful handicap hurdler: won at Wetherby in December, Haydock in
January and Wetherby again in March: barely stays 2½m: acts on heavy going: wears
headgear. *Philip Kirby*

SUITOR 7 ch.g. Dutch Art – Entreat (Pivotal) [2018/19 h16.5m^F Jun 22] dam half-sister to **h131**
fairly useful hurdler/chaser (stayed 3¼m) Font: fair on Flat, stays 13f: useful form over
hurdles: just headed when falling heavily last in handicap won by Monarch at Down Royal
sole outing in 2018/19: raced around 2m: acts on heavy and good to firm going: tried in
cheekpieces/tongue tie. *Gordon Elliott, Ireland*

SULA ISLAND 5 ch.m. Sulamani (IRE) – Cosmea (Compton Place) [2018/19 h16.7g* **h113**
h16.3d⁴ h16.2s⁶ h16d² h16.6d⁵ Mar 1] half-sister to fairly useful 2m hurdle winner
Cosmeapolitan (by Mawatheeq): dam (h117) 2m hurdle winner: fair on Flat (stays 1¾m),
successful in June: fair form over hurdles: won bumpers novice at Market Rasen in September:
raced around 2m: acts on good to soft going. *Alan King*

SULAMANI THE LATE (FR) 7 b.g. Sulamani (IRE) – Delayed (FR) (Fijar Tango **c98 §**
(FR)) [2018/19 h98§: c23.8g^{ur} c24g^{ur} c26.3m^{bd} c24.2g^R Oct 5] modest maiden hurdler: **h– §**
failed to complete in novice handicap chases: should stay further than 2½m: acts on good
to firm and good to soft going: has worn cheekpieces: usually races towards rear: ungenuine.
Rebecca Menzies

SULLY D'OC AA (FR) 5 b.g. Konig Turf (GER) – Samarra d'Oc (FR) (Moon Madness) **h–**
[2018/19 h19.9v^{pu} Mar 16] third foal: half-brother to 2 winners on Flat, including
11.5f/1½m winner Dismoitout d'Oc AA (by Full of Gold): dam 17f-19f chase winner:
bumper winner: fairly useful juvenile hurdler in 2017/18, winning Anglo-Arabian events at
Toulouse and Pau (2): left G. Cherel/off 15 months, lost shoe when pulled up in handicap
at Uttoxeter: unproven beyond 17f: acts on soft and good to firm going. *Anthony Honeyball*

SULTANS HERO 5 b.g. Sulamani (IRE) – Fairlie (Halling (USA)) [2018/19 b15.7s⁶ **h–**
b16d h20.6d h16.7g⁶ h16.4m h20.6d h16.8d Apr 23] well held in bumpers/over hurdles: in **b–**
cheekpieces last 4 starts. *Gillian Boanas*

SULTANS PRIDE 7 b.g. Sulamani (IRE) – Pennys Pride (IRE) (Pips Pride) [2018/19 **h94**
h99, b84: h23.3g⁵ h23.3g Nov 2] lengthy gelding: modest maiden hurdler: likely to stay
beyond 23f: acts on heavy going: held up. *Gillian Boanas*

SUMELIA 4 ch.f. Sulamani (IRE) – Aimela (FR) (Sagamix (FR)) [2018/19 b16d Mar 21] **b–**
£6,000 3-y-o: fifth foal: half-sister to 3 winners, including useful French 15f/2m hurdle
winner The Saint James, stayed 2½m, and fairly useful French 17f chase winner Sanpaco
(both by Saint des Saints): dam French 15f hurdle winner: well beaten in mares bumper.
Michael Scudamore

SUM FUN NOW (IRE) 5 b.g. Jeremy (USA) – Blond's Addition (IRE) (Lord Americo) **h–**
[2018/19 b–: h19m h16.7s^{pu} h19.3m^{pu} Feb 22] rather unfurnished gelding: has had breathing
operation: no promise in bumper/over hurdles: tried in hood/tongue tie. *Ali Stronge*

SUMKINDOFKING (IRE) 8 br.g. King's Theatre (IRE) – Shannon Rose (IRE) **c134**
(Topanoora) [2018/19 h119: c20g² c20.1g³ c21.4m* c21.4m⁵ c20m* c26.7f³ c25.1g² **h–**
c25.6s² c23.8d⁴ c26d c25.6m³ Apr 20] well-made gelding: has had breathing operation:
winning hurdler: useful handicap chaser: won at Market Rasen in June and Ludlow (novice
event) in October: stays 27f: acts on firm and soft going: wears tongue tie: usually waited
with. *Tom George*

SUMMER GETAWAY (IRE) 7 b.g. Getaway (GER) – Summer Crush (USA) (Summer **c63**
Squall (USA)) [2018/19 h93: h21.7g^{pu} c25.8g⁴ c22.5g Jun 6] workmanlike gelding: modest **h–**
maiden hurdler: in cheekpieces, well beaten both starts in novice handicap chases: stays
2½m: acts on good to firm and good to soft going: tried in tongue tie. *Nick Mitchell*

SUMMER LIGHTENING 5 gr.m. Fair Mix (IRE) – Kristineau (Cadeaux Genereux) [2018/19 b79: b16.2d ab16.3g⁵ h16.4s h16.4g⁶ h16.4v³ h20.6d Apr 6] modest form in bumpers: some promise over hurdles. *Dianne Sayer* **h77 b–**

SUMMER SOUNDS (IRE) 10 b.g. Definite Article – Marble Sound (IRE) (Be My Native (USA)) [2018/19 c26g⁵ May 4] prolific point winner: modest maiden hurdler/chaser: stays 21f: acts on good to soft going: tried in cheekpieces. *Francesca Nimmo* **c87 h–**

SUMMERVILLE BOY (IRE) 7 b.g. Sandmason – Suny House (Carroll House) [2018/19 h156p, b98: h16.4d⁴ h16.8s h20d⁴ Apr 4] lengthy gelding: smart novice hurdler in 2017/18: won Tolworth Novices' Hurdle at Sandown and Supreme Novices' Hurdle at Cheltenham: suffered hairline fracture and off 4 months after second outing: back on track when 6¼ lengths sixth of 7 to Buveur d'Air in Punchestown Champion Hurdle shortly after end of British season: should stay 2½m: acts on soft going. *Tom George* **h152**

SUMMIT LIKE HERBIE 7 ch.g. Sulamani (IRE) – Colline de Fleurs (Alflora (IRE)) [2018/19 b91§: h16.8v⁶ h19.5v h21.4g² h23.1sᵖᵘ Mar 5] bumper winner: form over hurdles only when runner-up in novice at Wincanton: tried in hood: ungenuine. *Nigel Twiston-Davies* **h100 §**

SUMMONED (IRE) 8 b.g. Kris Kin (USA) – Technohead (IRE) (Distinctly North (USA)) [2018/19 c74: c21.6g⁵ c21.2g⁵ c24gᵖᵘ Jul 15] has had breathing operation: multiple point winner: some promise in chases, though folded tamely in handicap final outing: tried in cheekpieces/tongue tie. *Chris Grant* **c–**

SUMMONS TO COURT (IRE) 8 b.m. Court Cave (IRE) – Jacinta's Dream (IRE) (Over The River (FR)) [2018/19 c22.5s² c20.6d⁵ c24.2v³ c23dᵘʳ Apr 4] €3,000 3-y-o: closely related/half-sister to winning pointers by Old Vic and Gamut: dam, unraced, out of half-sister to Triumph Hurdle winner Baron Blakeney: point winner: no form in bumper/maiden hurdles: modest in hunter chases: left John Andrew Kinsella after second start: stays 23f: acts on soft going: tried in tongue tie. *Jimmy Frost* **c92 h–**

SUN CLOUD (IRE) 12 b.g. Cloudings (IRE) – Miss Melrose (Bob Back (USA)) [2018/19 c104, h127: h23.9g h25.8g h24.3d² h26.6g Apr 25] smallish, good-topped gelding: fairly useful handicap hurdler/chaser: stays 3¾m, effective at shorter: acts on heavy going: wears headgear: tried in tongue tie: usually front runner/races prominently. *Ruth Jefferson* **c– h121**

SUNDANCE BOY 10 gr.g. Proclamation (IRE) – Just Beth (Carlingford Castle) [2018/19 h–: h19.9d h23.3s h19d h24g* h20.3s* Mar 18] poor handicap hurdler: improved when winning twice at Southwell in March: stays 3m: acts on soft going: wears blinkers. *Giuseppe Fierro* **h80**

SUNDAY AT AUGUSTA (IRE) 6 b.g. Arakan (USA) – Alla Marcia (IRE) (Marju (IRE)) [2018/19 h15.7s h16.3dᵖᵘ h16d h16s h16d Apr 6] workmanlike gelding: second of 4 in Irish bumper: disappointing maiden hurdler. *Richard Rowe* **h–**

SUNDAY IN THE PARK 6 gr.m. Fair Mix (IRE) – Just Smokie (Cloudings (IRE)) [2018/19 h93: h16gᶠ Sep 11] modest maiden hurdler: should have stayed beyond 2m: acted on soft going: wore hood 4 of first 5 outings: dead. *David Bridgwater* **h–**

SUNDAY SESSION (IRE) 5 b.g. Scorpion (IRE) – Casiana (GER) (Acatenango (GER)) [2018/19 h21d⁴ h21.9g⁵ Apr 21] €21,000 3-y-o: seventh foal: half-brother to fair hurdler/fairly useful chaser Today Please (2m/17f winner, by Westerner): dam German maiden (placed up to 11f): off mark in points at second attempt: fair form when fourth at Warwick on first of 2 outings in maiden hurdles. *Michael Scudamore* **h100**

SUNNY DESTINATION (IRE) 7 b.g. Dubai Destination (USA) – Railway House (IRE) (Ashkalani (IRE)) [2018/19 h96, b74: h19.5v² h21.4v³ h24s h20.9g* h22.7d³ Apr 8] fair handicap hurdler: won at Kelso in March: should stay 2¾m: acts on heavy going: in cheekpieces last 2 starts: usually races prominently. *George Bewley* **h106**

SUNNY EXPRESS (IRE) 4 b.g. Jeremy (USA) – Golden Summer (IRE) (Flemensfirth (USA)) [2018/19 b16m³ Apr 13] €75,000 3-y-o: first foal: dam unraced half-sister to fairly useful hurdlers/useful chasers Steel Summit (stays 25f) and On The Road (stays 2¾m): 11/2, green yet showed plenty when 5¼ lengths third to December Second in bumper at Ayr. *Warren Greatrex* **b96**

SUNNY GIRL (IRE) 5 b.m. Arcadio (GER) – Vincenta (IRE) (Bob Back (USA)) [2018/19 b16.2s b15.8g Jan 3] €3,500 3-y-o: fourth foal: dam unraced half-sister to very smart staying chaser Beware The Bear: no show in bumpers: tried tongue tied. *Adrian Wintle* **b–**

SUNNY LEDGEND 14 b.g. Midnight Legend – Swordella (Broadsword (USA)) [2018/19   c– c106, h–: c24d^{pu} May 5] tall gelding: winning hurdler: fair handicap chaser nowadays: best   h– up to 3m: acts on good to firm and heavy going: has worn headgear, including 5 of last 6 outings: tried in tongue tie: front runner/races prominently. *Andrew Martin*

SUNNYTAHLIATEIGAN (IRE) 7 b.g. Robin des Pres (FR) – Wavering Bee (IRE)   **h104** (Oscar (IRE)) [2018/19 h111: h16.4g³ h19.4m³ h26d h24.3m⁶ Apr 20] useful-looking gelding: fair handicap hurdler: stays 2½m: acts on soft going. *Ian Williams*

SUNNY WEST (IRE) 10 b.g. Westerner – Lunar Beauty (IRE) (Milan) [2018/19 h17.2d⁶   h– Aug 25] winning pointer: very lightly-raced maiden hurdler: should have proved suited by further than 2½m: dead. *Sue Smith*

SUNRISE RUBY (IRE) 5 ch.m. Sholokhov (IRE) – Maryota (FR) (Martaline) [2018/19   **h116 p** b15.7g* h20.5s² h16.3d³ Mar 23] third foal: half-sister to bumper winner/fair hurdler Skin   **b97** Deep (2½m winner, by Presenting): dam twice-raced half-sister to high-class hurdler/smart chaser (stays 25f) Yanworth: won mares bumper at Southwell in June: fairly useful form when placed in novice hurdles at Newbury 2 months apart: may prove best at 2½m+: remains open to improvement. *Nicky Henderson*

SUNSET MARQUIS (IRE) 8 b.m. Kayf Tara – Miss Abrahnovic (IRE) (Deploy)   h– [2018/19 h69: h20.9g h16.2g h19.8m^{pu} Feb 27] maiden hurdler, lightly raced and little form since 2016/17: tried in cheekpieces. *Alison Hamilton*

SUNSET SHOWDOWN (IRE) 6 b.g. Flemensfirth (USA) – Sunset Queen (IRE)   c– (King's Theatre (IRE)) [2018/19 h119p, b93: c23.4s c19.9g^{pu} Feb 16] good-topped   h– gelding: won Irish point on debut: fairly useful form on first of 2 starts in maiden hurdles: little show in novice handicap chases: should be suited by 2½m+: signs of temperament. *Rebecca Curtis*

SUNSET SKYE 6 b.m. Sea Freedom – Money Central (Central Park (IRE)) [2018/19 h–,   **h64** b–: h24g⁴ h19.9g Oct 18] poor maiden hurdler: tried in visor/tongue tie. *Lawney Hill*

SUNSHADE 6 b.m. Sulamani (IRE) – Spring Flight (Groom Dancer (USA)) [2018/19   **h137 p** h121: h16.3d⁵ h20.3g* Apr 18] rather unfurnished mare: has had breathing operation: useful form over hurdles: won listed mares handicap at Cheltenham (by 3½ lengths from Agusta Gold) in April: stays 2½m: acts on good to soft going: hooded first 4 outings: likely to progress further. *Nicky Henderson*

SUPAKALANISTIC (IRE) 6 b.g. Kalanisi (IRE) – Keys Hope (IRE) (Luso) [2018/19   **h113** h115, b91: h19g h20d⁵ h19.7g² h19d h23.8g⁴ h23.8d* h25d^{pu} h21g Apr 10] rather leggy gelding: has had breathing operation: fair handicap hurdler: won at Ludlow (amateurs) in January: stays 3m: acts on heavy going. *Nigel Twiston-Davies*

SUPASUNDAE 9 b.g. Galileo (IRE) – Distinctive Look (IRE) (Danehill (USA))   **h157** [2018/19 h162: h20g² h16g² h16g² h24d h20d* Apr 4]

The colours of his late owners Ann and Alan Potts were carried with distinction for another season by the very smart hurdler Supasundae. For the second year running he ran at all three major spring festivals and for the third year running he was successful at one of them. In 2017 he had won the Coral Cup at Cheltenham, in 2018 the Punchestown Champion Hurdle and in the latest season he completed a full set of wins at those big meetings by winning at Aintree, successful in another Grade 1 the Betway Aintree Hurdle. Versatility is one of Supasundae's attributes, and once again he ran over three different trips at Cheltenham, Aintree and Punchestown. Three miles rather stretches his stamina, while two miles is probably on the sharp side for him nowadays, with the two and a half miles of the Aintree Hurdle proving just right. It was Supasundae's second attempt at the Aintree Hurdle after he had gone down to L'Ami Serge on soft ground when a short-priced favourite twelve months earlier. He had also finished second at Aintree in 2017 when his first race over three miles saw him beaten only a length by Yanworth in the Liverpool Hurdle.

On form, though, Supasundae's task in the latest Aintree Hurdle looked a stiffer one than the year before, as he was up against the 2017 winner Buveur d'Air who was sent off at 6/5-on to atone for his fall in the Champion Hurdle. Another former Champion Hurdle winner, Faugheen, third in the latest Stayers' Hurdle, was next in the betting at 4/1, ahead of Supasundae on 15/2 and Melon, runner-up in the last two Champion Hurdles and running beyond two miles for the first time, on 8/1. The three longer-priced runners in the field, County Hurdle winner Ch'tibello,

Betway Aintree Hurdle, Aintree—the ultra-tough Supasundae goes one better than in 2018 with a hard-fought win over Buveur d'Air (hoops) and Ch'tibello

Champion Hurdle third Silver Streak and the previous season's Supreme winner Summerville Boy, also had stamina to prove, the last-named pair also trying two and a half miles for the first time. Faugheen made the running until passing the post for the first time, before Ruby Walsh pulled him up turning into the back straight leaving stable-companion Melon as the new leader. However, Melon fell at the first in the straight when still in front, at which point Buveur d'Air (whom he hampered), Ch'tibello and Supasundae were the only ones still in contention. All three were in the air together two out, with Supasundae and Buveur d'Air still inseparable at the last after Ch'tibello had been the first to crack. In what proved something of a slog up the run-in in driving rain, Supasundae managed to assert under Robbie Power in the last fifty yards or so to beat a below-par Buveur d'Air by a length and a quarter, with Ch'tibello keeping on to finish only half a length behind the runner-up. They were a long way clear of the two other finishers, a post-race examination revealing Faugheen to be suffering from a fibrillating heart.

The Aintree Hurdle, a race Jessica Harrington had also won in 2015 with Jezki, was Supasundae's best effort of the season up to that point, and he matched that form when bidding to win the Punchestown Champion Hurdle again, just after the end of the season in Britain. Supasundae's victory the year before had been overshadowed by the falls of Samcro and Melon late in the race which had made his task easier, while this time Supasundae found Buveur d'Air in better heart than he had been at Aintree. Though he stayed on well from the last, Supasundae could only finish two and a half lengths behind in second. Since his Coral Cup win over two years earlier, Supasundae has only once finished out of the first three and that was in his latest bid to win the Stayers' Hurdle, a race in which he had been beaten two lengths by Penhill in 2018. In contrast to that renewal of the Stayers' Hurdle, which played very much to Supasundae's strengths, the latest one was much more truly run, which seemed to make it far too much of a test for him. In fact, so quickly did Supasundae capitulate, from being third early in the straight to passing the post more than twenty lengths behind the winner Paisley Park in seventh, that it was hard to see him bouncing back in time for Aintree. It was very much to his credit, then, that he was able to win three weeks later and run well again after that at Punchestown. Supasundae had finished runner-up in his first three starts of the season, when even his best form would have been unlikely to have been sufficient to cope with Apple's Jade in either the Hatton's Grace Hurdle at Fairyhouse in December or the Irish Champion Hurdle, which he had won the year before, at Leopardstown in February.

Ann & Alan Potts Limited's "Supasundae"

Supasundae finished a long way behind Apple's Jade in both but, in between, was closer to Sharjah in the Ryanair Hurdle at Leopardstown (the old December Festival Hurdle), meeting some interference in the latter stages but ultimately unable to match the winner's turn of foot.

Supasundae (b.g. 2010)	Galileo (IRE) (b 1998)	Sadler's Wells (b 1981)	Northern Dancer
			Fairy Bridge
		Urban Sea (ch 1989)	Miswaki
			Allegretta
	Distinctive Look (IRE) (b 2003)	Danehill (b 1986)	Danzig
			Razyana
		Magnificent Style (b 1993)	Silver Hawk
			Mia Karina

Supasundae is a big gelding whose distinguished Flat pedigree, as well as his early career which involved several changes of stables, was covered in last year's Annual. His fairly useful half-brother Distingo (by Smart Strike) lost his form in handicaps during the latest season after finishing second on his reappearance, but another younger sibling, four-year-old Twenty Twenty (by Henrythenavigator), who is also with Gary Moore, won a couple of times at Fontwell. Once again, Supasundae's campaign tested both his versatility and toughness and he scored highly on both counts. He has raced only on good ground or softer and acts on heavy. He wore a tongue tie for the first time at Cheltenham and again on his two remaining starts. *Mrs J. Harrington, Ireland*

SUPER CHARGE 7 ch.g. Recharge (IRE) – Arctic Ring (Karinga Bay) [2018/19 h87: c15.7g^{pu} c15.6g^{pu} h16.8m^5 h19.3g h16.8g^5 c19.2g^{pu} Nov 23] point winner: poor maiden hurdler: pulled up all 3 starts in chases: in visor last 3 outings. *Chris Fairhurst*

c–
h71

SUPEREFFICIENT (IRE) 7 b.m. Beneficial – Mellowthemoonlight (IRE) (Un Desperado (FR)) [2018/19 h20.4g⁴ h17.3g⁵ h16m⁴ h16g³ h19d⁶ h16g⁶ h18.1m Sep 19] sixth foal: sister to fair hurdler/chaser (2m-21f winner) Mellow Ben and half-sister to modest 2¼m hurdle winner Hello Louie (by Luso): dam (h85) 2m hurdle winner: poor maiden hurdler: stays 2½m: acts on soft and good to firm going: in cheekpieces last 4 starts: races prominently. *Ms Michelle Duggan, Ireland* **h84**

SUPER LUNAR (IRE) 10 b.g. Super Celebre (FR) – Kapricia Speed (FR) (Vertical Speed (FR)) [2018/19 c24.2g⁵ c20.1g⁵ c24.2gᵖᵘ c24g⁴ c20gᵖᵘ Jul 10] lengthy gelding: maiden hurdler: poor maiden chaser: stays 3m: acts on soft going: usually in headgear: wears tongue tie. *Henry Hogarth* **c63** **h–**

SUPER MAC (IRE) 7 b.g. Yeats (IRE) – Midnight Flirt (IRE) (Flemensfirth (USA)) [2018/19 h15.8v h20.5dᵖᵘ h16.2g h16g Apr 26] has had breathing operation: tailed off in bumper: also showed little in novice/maiden hurdles: in tongue tie last 2 starts. *Donald McCain* **h–** **b–**

SUPER MOON 7 b.g. Black Sam Bellamy (IRE) – Aussie Deal (IRE) (Flemensfirth (USA)) [2018/19 h22.2g⁵ h20g⁵ Jul 26] poor form over hurdles: may prove best around 2m: tried in hood (pulls hard). *Fergal O'Brien* **h68**

SUPER SCORPION (IRE) 9 b.g. Scorpion (IRE) – Nolagh Supreme (IRE) (Supreme Leader) [2018/19 c129, h–: c23.8g³ h20m² c23.8m⁵ h21.6g² h21.2m² h16.2g² Nov 5] fair maiden hurdler: fairly useful handicap chaser: stays 3m: acts on good to firm and good to soft going: usually in headgear: in tongue tie last 3 starts. *Debra Hamer* **c124** **h113**

SUPER SID (IRE) 7 b.g. Westerner – Super Sammy (Mesleh) [2018/19 h117: c15.7s⁶ c20vᵖᵘ Dec 21] fairly useful hurdle winner: disappointing since second outing in 2017/18, including in handicap chases: should stay beyond 2m: acts on heavy ground. *Tom George* **c–** **h–**

SUPER SNIPE 8 b.g. Kayf Tara – Sea Snipe (King Luthier) [2018/19 h19.5s⁶ h19.5s h16.5d² h23.8g⁶ h23.1d h19s⁵ Mar 19] £18,000 3-y-o: second foal: half-brother to fair chaser Jack Snipe (23f-3¼m winner, by Kirkwall): dam prolific winning pointer: fair form over hurdles: bred to stay well: acts on good to soft going: held up. *Jeremy Scott* **h107**

SUPERVISOR (IRE) 5 b.g. Flemensfirth (USA) – Coolamaine Star (IRE) (King's Theatre (IRE)) [2018/19 b15.7v⁵ b17s⁴ Mar 7] modest form when fourth at Carlisle on second of 2 outings in bumpers. *Venetia Williams* **b80**

SUPREME DANEHILL (IRE) 11 b.g. Indian Danehill (IRE) – Monte Rosa (IRE) (Supreme Leader) [2018/19 c117: c32.5gᵖᵘ May 4] multiple point winner: fairly useful hunter chaser: stays 25f: acts on soft and good to firm going: wears cheekpieces. *Alan Hill* **c–**

SUPREMELY LUCKY (IRE) 7 b.g. Milan – Lucky Supreme (IRE) (Supreme Leader) [2018/19 h99: h16d⁴ h24d* h24s⁴ h20.3d⁴ h19.9v⁴ h26s² h23.3d* Mar 30] runner-up on second of 2 starts in Irish points: bumper winner: useful novice hurdler: won at Southwell in November and Uttoxeter (9/2-on) in March: best effort when second to Ocean Cove in handicap at Warwick: stays 3¼m: acts on heavy going. *Dan Skelton* **h131**

SUPREME SOVIET (IRE) 5 b.g. Sholokhov (IRE) – Bay Pearl (FR) (Broadway Flyer (USA)) [2018/19 b15.3g b16.3d b16.3g Mar 30] tall gelding: well held in bumpers. *Ben Pauling* **b–**

SURF AND TURF (IRE) 13 ch.g. Beneficial – Clear Top Waltz (IRE) (Topanoora) [2018/19 c116x, h119: h20.1g⁴ h19.8g³ h19.8g⁶ Jan 1] workmanlike gelding: has had breathing operation: fair handicap hurdler nowadays: fairly useful handicap chaser: stays 2½m: acts on good to firm and good to soft going: has worn cheekpieces, including last 2 outings: tongue tied 4 of last 5 starts: prone to mistakes over fences. *Richard Hobson* **c– x** **h107**

SURF INSTRUCTOR (IRE) 7 b.g. Stowaway – Corrie Hall (IRE) (Saddlers' Hall (IRE)) [2018/19 c19g c18.2d⁴ c22.5s c21g³ c21.6g³ c22.5d* Apr 23] €27,000 4-y-o: fourth foal: dam, unraced, out of half-sister to top-class hurdler (stayed 2½m) Fortune And Fame: winning hurdler: useful handicap chaser: won at Fairyhouse (by length from The Church Gate) in April: stays 23f: acts on heavy going: in cheekpieces last 3 starts, also tongue tied last 2. *Henry de Bromhead, Ireland* **c131** **h–**

SURIN (FR) 4 b.f. Authorized (IRE) – Sinopsy (FR) (Sinndar (IRE)) [2018/19 b13.1g* h16g² h16d* h16g³ Feb 3] second foal: half-sister to French 1½m winner Soliera (by Whipper): dam lightly raced on Flat: narrow winner of junior bumper at Market Rasen (for M. Hofer) in October: fairly useful form over hurdles: won minor event at Fairyhouse in **h129** **b78**

January: much improved again when 6½ lengths third to Sir Erec in Spring Juvenile Hurdle at Leopardstown. *Gordon Elliott, Ireland*

SURRENDER 4 b.g. Sixties Icon – Mango Music (Distant Music (USA)) [2018/19 **h87** h17.2s⁴ h16.7g⁴ h16m⁴ h15.7g h16.8sᵇᵈ h19.3s⁵ h19.7s h16.8vᵖᵘ Jan 27] smallish gelding: modest maiden on Flat, stays 1¾m: of similar merit over hurdles: tried in headgear. *Tim Easterby*

SUSIE MAC 4 ch.f. Dawn Approach (IRE) – La Pomme d'Amour (Peintre Celebre **b79 p** (USA)) [2018/19 b16.8d² Apr 23] 5,500 3-y-o: first foal: dam smart French 9f-12.5f winner: favourite, 14 lengths second to Ahorsewithnoname in mares bumper at Sedgefield: should do better. *Kevin Ryan*

SUSSEX RANGER (USA) 5 b.g. Hat Trick (JPN) – Purple (USA) (Royal Academy **h131** (USA)) [2018/19 h131: h15.7m h20.5s h17.7v* h19.3d h19.8s⁵ Mar 8] tall gelding: useful handicap hurdler: won at Fontwell (by 4½ lengths from Monday Club) in December: stays 2¼m: acts on heavy going: in headgear last 4 starts: usually front runner/races prominently. *Gary Moore*

SUSSEX ROAD (IRE) 9 b.g. Mahler – Rose Island (Jupiter Island) [2018/19 c80§, h–: **c– §** c16.1gᵖᵘ c21.2g c21.2m⁴ c15.7g c21.2g⁵ c23g⁶ c19.4g² c19.3g³ c20.9g³ c16.2g² c16.4d² **h–** c19.9d⁵ c15.7d⁴ c23.6g⁴ Apr 22] angular gelding: of little account: normally in headgear: temperamental. *Aytach Sadik*

SUSTAINABLE STAR (IRE) 8 gr.g. Winged Love (IRE) – Fooling Around (IRE) **c–** (Medaille Militaire) [2018/19 h81, b–: h23.9d⁶ c24.2sᵖᵘ c16d Feb 23] lengthy gelding: little **h–** form in varied company. *Richenda Ford*

SUTTER'S MILL (IRE) 8 b.g. Gold Well – Shamriyna (IRE) (Darshaan) [2018/19 **c101** c102, h104: c25.8g³ c23.8m⁴ c23.8g⁶ c23.8s³ c23.8g* c25.3v² c23.6d c23.8s c26.2dᵖᵘ **h–** c23.8s² Apr 7] fair hurdler: fair handicap chaser: won novice event at Ludlow in November: stays 3¼m: acts on heavy going: often in headgear: tried in tongue tie. *Evan Williams*

SUTTONWOOD SALLY 5 b.m. Delegator – Hip Hip Hooray (Monsieur Bond (IRE)) **b–** [2018/19 b16.3m b16g Sep 2] first foal: dam 6f-1m winner: no form in bumpers/on Flat. *Geoffrey Deacon*

SUZIE STAPLES 5 ch.m. Black Sam Bellamy (IRE) – Dawn Breaker (Rakaposhi King) **b–** [2018/19 b–: b16g May 12] leggy mare: well beaten in bumpers 5 months apart. *Richard Price*

SWAFFHAM BULBECK (IRE) 5 b.g. Jeremy (USA) – Ballygologue (IRE) (Montjeu **h118** (IRE)) [2018/19 h115: h16g² h16d² h16d³ h16d* Mar 15] has had breathing operation: fairly useful form over hurdles: won conditionals maiden at Fakenham in March: raced at 2m: acts on soft going: in tongue tie last 3 starts, also in cheekpieces last 2. *Olly Murphy*

SWALEDALE LAD (IRE) 12 b.g. Arakan (USA) – Tadjnama (USA) (Exceller (USA)) **c– §** [2018/19 c82§, h82§: h15.8m May 1] tall, narrow gelding: modest handicap hurdler/ **h– §** chaser nowadays: barely stays 2½m: acts on good to firm and heavy going: has worn cheekpieces, including last 4 starts: has finished weakly. *Graeme McPherson*

SWALLOW DANCER 5 b.m. Danehill Dancer (IRE) – Bay Swallow (IRE) (Daylami **h–** (IRE)) [2018/19 h16.9gᵖᵘ Feb 19] has had breathing operation: modest maiden on Flat (stays 9.5f) for Harry Dunlop: hooded, pulled up in novice on hurdling debut. *Nick Mitchell*

SWALLOWSHIDE 10 b.g. Hernando (FR) – Kentford Grebe (Teenoso (USA)) [2018/19 **c86** c97, h–: c16.3g c21.6g⁶ c20.9d⁵ Jun 8] dual winning pointer: winning hurdler: modest **h–** maiden hunter chaser: stays 2¾m: acts on soft going: tried in headgear. *J. H. Young*

SWAREZ (IRE) 7 b.g. Echo of Light – Behlaya (IRE) (Kahyasi) [2018/19 b17.3g h15.8g⁴ **c–** h20d h16g h20g h23.3v⁶ c16d Apr 27] of little account. *Paul Stafford, Ireland* **h–**

SWASHBUCKLE 6 b.g. Dashing Blade – Inhibition (Nayef (USA)) [2018/19 h106p: **h100 §** h16.2d⁴ h16.7g⁴ h19.9m⁴ Jul 1] fair maiden hurdler: should be suited by 2½m+: acts on soft going: in blinkers last 2 starts: front runner/races prominently: ungenuine. *Donald McCain*

SWATOW 7 b.m. Shantou (USA) – Sudden Beat (Beat All (USA)) [2018/19 h102: h21.6gᵘʳ **h101 §** h19.9g³ May 27] good-topped mare: fair maiden hurdler: stays 2½m: probably acts on good to firm going: tried in hood: one to treat with caution (has given trouble at start). *Emma Lavelle*

SWEEPING ROCK (IRE) 9 b.g. Rock of Gibraltar (IRE) – Sweeping Story (USA) **h89** (End Sweep (USA)) [2018/19 h98: h16g⁴ h17.7m⁶ h18.5m Jul 14] has had breathing operation: modest handicap hurdler: stays 2½m: acts on good to soft going: has worn cheekpieces: tried in tongue tie: waited with. *John Spearing*

SWEEP OF DIAMONDS 6 br.g. Mawatheeq (USA) – Apple Blossom (IRE) (Danehill **h70**
Dancer (IRE)) [2018/19 h16d h16d h15.9s h15.9s h15.9d h16.5d^{pu} Apr 24] no show on
Flat: poor form over hurdles: in headgear last 3 starts: tried in tongue tie. *Rebecca Woodman*

SWEET ADARE (IRE) 6 b.m. Getaway (GER) – The Adare Woman (IRE) (Oscar **h103**
(IRE)) [2018/19 b89: b17g b18.5g b19g^{2} h15.3s^{2} h20.5d Mar 23] has had breathing **b79**
operation: fair bumper winner: similar form in novice hurdles: in tongue tie last 3 starts.
Victor Dartnall

SWEET DESTINATION (IRE) 7 b.m. Dubai Destination (USA) – Sweet Liss (IRE) **c107**
(Saddlers' Hall (IRE)) [2018/19 h20g^{6} h20m^{F} c21g c22g c25.2d^{2} c21g^{3} c25g^{4} c25.7g* **h86**
c24.2g^{2} c21g h22.5d c22g^{2} c22.5v^{4} Mar 17] fourth foal: dam lightly-raced half-sister to
fairly useful hurdler (2m-2¼m winner) Blazing Liss out of half-sister to very smart hurdler
up to 2½m Liss A Paoraigh: modest form over hurdles: fair handicap chaser: won novice
event at Plumpton in November: stays 3¼m: acts on good to soft going: wears cheekpieces:
often leads. *G. Ahern, Ireland*

SWEET HOLLY 8 b.m. Kayf Tara – Presuming (Mtoto) [2018/19 h108: h22.1g^{3} h20.1g^{2} **h113**
h20.6g^{ur} h25.8d^{pu} Nov 10] fair handicap hurdler: stayed 2¾m: acted on soft and good to
firm going: tried in tongue tie: dead. *Ruth Jefferson*

SWEET HOME CHICAGO (IRE) 10 b.g. Shantou (USA) – Finnuala Supreme (IRE) **h118**
(Supreme Leader) [2018/19 h21s^{F} h23.7g^{4} h20d^{5} h24g* h24s* h23.9g^{4} h24g h20s^{pu} Jan 24]
unplaced in points: fairly useful hurdler: won handicap at Clonmel and minor event at
Galway in October: stays 3m: acts on soft going: tried in cheekpieces. *Colin Bowe, Ireland*

SWEET MARMALADE (IRE) 4 b.f. Duke of Marmalade (IRE) – Lady Chaparral **h–**
(High Chaparral (IRE)) [2018/19 h16d^{5} h15.7g h16.4g^{5} h25d^{pu} Mar 3] close-coupled filly:
placed in Flat maiden: no form over hurdles: tried in headgear. *Lawrence Mullaney*

SWEET'N'CHIC (IRE) 9 b.m. Midnight Legend – Sweetbitter (FR) (Turgeon (USA)) **h81**
[2018/19 h80: h25g^{4} h25g* h25d^{pu} Mar 3] smallish mare: poor handicap hurdler: won at
Huntingdon (conditionals) in May: stays 25f: acts on soft going. *Richard Rowe*

SWEET OBSESSION (IRE) 7 b.m. Getaway (GER) – Dual Obsession (Saddlers' Hall **h–**
(IRE)) [2018/19 h16.8s^{pu} h15.3g^{pu} h20.7d^{pu} Mar 13] €6,000 3-y-o: third foal: dam once-
raced half-sister to Hennessy Cognac Gold Cup winner Trabolgan: no form over hurdles.
Alexandra Dunn

SWEET VINETTA 5 gr.m. Fair Mix (IRE) – Vinetta (Grape Tree Road) [2018/19 b75: **h107**
h16.7g^{6} h16.2s^{5} h16.2g^{2} h19.3s* h20.6g^{4} h16.2v^{4} h17d h20.1g^{6} Apr 15] fair hurdler: won
novice at Catterick in December: stays 19f: acts on heavy going: tried in cheekpieces.
Gillian Boanas

SWIFT CRUSADER 8 b.g. Kayf Tara – Goldenswift (IRE) (Meneval (USA)) [2018/19 **c123**
c124, h–: c15.5s* c16.4d^{3} c15.5d^{4} Mar 8] rangy gelding: successful sole start over hurdles: **h–**
fairly useful handicap chaser: won at Sandown in December: stays 2½m: acts on heavy
going. *Alexandra Dunn*

SWIFT NATIVE (IRE) 7 br.m. Mahler – Hasty Native (IRE) (Be My Native (USA)) **h–**
[2018/19 h–: h17.7g h17.7m^{6} h21.7g^{pu} h19.6m h21.7m Oct 24] has had breathing
operation: Irish point winner: no form over hurdles: tried in cheekpieces. *Nick Gifford*

SWILLY SUNSET 6 b.g. Kyllachy – Spanish Springs (IRE) (Xaar) [2018/19 h15.8g^{6} Apr **h–**
22] sturdy gelding: fairly useful on Flat, stays 1¼m: well beaten in novice on hurdling
debut. *Tracey Leeson*

SWINCOMBE SCORCHIO 9 b.g. Scorpion (IRE) – Lady Felix (Batshoof) [2018/19 **c–**
c–: c25.1m^{5} c25.8g^{pu} Jun 4] long-backed gelding: has had breathing operation: fairly useful
chaser at best, no form since 2016/17: tried in cheekpieces: wears tongue tie. *Polly Gundry*

SWINCOMBE WIZ 4 b.f. Westerner – Lady Everywhere (Exit To Nowhere (USA)) **b–**
[2018/19 b16.3d Mar 1] tall filly: second foal: dam (c118/h97), 19f chase winner, sister to
useful hurdler (stayed 3m) Swincombe Flame: well beaten in mares bumper. *Colin Tizzard*

SWINGBRIDGE (IRE) 11 b.g. Milan – Creative Approach (IRE) (Toulon) [2018/19 **c129**
c119, h111: h24g c23.8g* h23.7g^{3} c23.8g^{6} c23.8g* c25g c24.1v^{5} c24d h22d c23.8g^{2} **h103**
Apr 24] good-topped gelding: fair handicap hurdler: fairly useful handicap chaser: won at
Perth in July and September: stays 25f: acts on heavy going: wears headgear/tongue tie.
Gordon Elliott, Ireland

SWING HARD (IRE) 11 br.g. Zagreb (USA) – Hurricane Jane (IRE) (Strong Gale) **c104 §**
[2018/19 c108§, h–: c24.2d³ May 5] maiden hurdler: fair handicap chaser: stays 25f: acts **h–**
on heavy going: front runner/races prominently: temperamental. *Sue Smith*

SWINTON DIAMOND (IRE) 8 b.g. Dubai Destination (USA) – Absent Beauty (IRE) **c101**
(Dancing Dissident (USA)) [2018/19 h101: h20.1g⁵ h20.1m⁵ c24g⁴ c21.6mᵘʳ c20g* Oct **h76**
25] fair handicap hurdler, below form first 2 starts in 2018/19: fair form over fences: won
handicap at Carlisle in October: stays 2¾m: acts on soft going: has worn hood: front
runner/races prominently: tail flasher. *Micky Hammond*

SWISS PSALM 4 b.f. Swiss Spirit – Athwaab (Cadeaux Genereux) [2018/19 h17.7gᵖᵘ **h–**
Sep 9] no form on Flat: pulled up in juvenile on hurdling debut. *Mark Gillard*

SWORDBILL 4 ch.g. Champs Elysees – Dream Wild (Oasis Dream) [2018/19 h16.4d³ **h108**
h16.8d⁶ h16g⁶ Apr 11] close-coupled gelding: fairly useful on Flat, stays 2m: fair form over
hurdles: best effort when third in juvenile at Newcastle: will be suited by 2¼m+: in
cheekpieces first 2 starts. *Ian Williams*

SWORD OF FATE (IRE) 6 b.g. Beneficial – Beann Ard (IRE) (Mandalus) [2018/19 **c131**
h118: c15.7g* h15.7g⁵ c19.4m* c21g* c21m⁴ h23.8g h16.4m⁶ c17.1d³ c20dᶠ c16.5mᵖᵘ Apr **h101**
12] lengthy gelding: fairly useful handicap hurdler, below form in 2018/19: useful handicap
chaser: won at Southwell (novice) in May, and Stratford and Newton Abbot (novice) in
July: left Tom Lacey after fifth start: stays 21f: acts on firm and good to soft going: tried in
visor: usually leads. *Leonard Kerr*

SYBARITE (FR) 13 b.g. Dark Moondancer – Haida III (FR) (Video Rock (FR)) [2018/19 **c102 §**
h115§: c22.2g² c26.3dᵖᵘ Mar 15] rangy, well-made gelding: prolific point winner: winning **h– §**
hurdler: fair maiden chaser nowadays: stays 33f: acts on heavy going: has worn headgear/
tongue tie: most temperamental (usually gets well behind). *Miss V. Collins*

SYDNEY DE BAUNE (FR) 8 b.g. Califet (FR) – Perle de Baune (FR) (En Calcat (FR)) **c–**
[2018/19 c99, h96: h23.1s Nov 25] sturdy gelding: modest hurdler, behind sole outing in **h–**
2018/19: twice-raced chaser: stays 23f: acts on soft going. *Robert Walford*

SYKES (IRE) 10 b.g. Mountain High (IRE) – Our Trick (IRE) (Flemensfirth (USA)) **c–**
[2018/19 c–, h137: h23.9d² h24.3g* h24.7gᵖᵘ Apr 6] compact gelding: useful handicap **h142**
hurdler: won at Haydock (by neck from Silva Eclipse) in February: winning chaser: stays
25f: acts on heavy going: usually front runner/races prominently. *Nicky Martin*

SYMBOLIC STAR (IRE) 7 b.g. New Approach (IRE) – Epitome (IRE) (Nashwan **h–**
(USA)) [2018/19 h16.2g h16.4sᵖᵘ h15.7m h17mᵖᵘ Apr 20] modest on Flat, stays 12.5f: no
form over hurdles: tried in cheekpieces. *Barry Murtagh*

SYMPHONY HALL (IRE) 4 b.g. Mahler – Coumhall (IRE) (Saddlers' Hall (IRE)) **b83**
[2018/19 b15.7d³ Apr 24] €20,000 3-y-o: third foal: dam unraced half-sister to smart
staying chaser Benvolio: 4/1, third in bumper at Southwell (9 lengths behind Old
Jeroboam). *Warren Greatrex*

SYMPHONY OF ANGELS 7 b.g. Sulamani (IRE) – Flying Lion (Hunting Lion (IRE)) **h132**
[2018/19 h117, b88: h15.7g* h15.8m* Jul 1] useful form over hurdles: won handicaps at
Southwell in June and Uttoxeter (by 2¾ lengths from Ocean Jive) in July: may prove best
at 2m: acts on good to firm and good to soft going. *Dan Skelton*

SYNOPSIS 7 b.m. Azamour (IRE) – Censored (Pivotal) [2018/19 c20g⁶ h20s c20.6g* **c132**
c19.9dᵖᵘ c16d⁵ c20dᶠ Apr 23] workmanlike mare: fairly useful on Flat, stays 1½m: winning **h–**
hurdler: useful chaser: won mares handicap at Cheltenham (by 10 lengths from Black
Tulip) in December: stays 21f: acts on heavy going: usually wears tongue tie. *Gordon
Elliott, Ireland*

SYRACUSE'S DREAM (FR) 8 gr.g. Lord du Sud (FR) – Laura's Dream (FR) (Bonnet **c–**
Rouge (FR)) [2018/19 c–, h68: h23g⁵ Jul 4] point winner: poor form over hurdles: maiden **h69**
chaser: has worn cheekpieces. *Jackie du Plessis*

T

TAAFFES CASTLE (IRE) 6 b.g. Sandmason – Pet Magpie (IRE) (Desert Sun) [2018/19 **h60**
h19s h20s h21.9g⁴ Apr 21] Irish point winner: poor form over hurdles. *Christian Williams*

TAB HOGARTH (IRE) 6 b.g. Westerner – Vintage Vic (IRE) (Old Vic) [2018/19 h–§, **h§§**
b–: h23.8gᵘʳ h19.3gʳʳ Dec 28] small gelding: failed to complete all 4 starts over hurdles,
twice refusing to race: usually in headgear: one to avoid. *Dianne Sayer*

TACTICAL MANOEUVRE (IRE) 8 b.g. Marienbard (IRE) – Pride O'Fleet (IRE) (Bob's Return (IRE)) [2018/19 c89, h101: h25g h23.9m⁶ h21.6s⁵ c24.2vᵖᵘ c21.7g⁴ c18.2s⁴ c24.2dᵖᵘ Apr 9] modest hurdler/chaser, below form in 2018/19: stays 23f: acts on heavy going: wears tongue tie. *Alexandra Dunn* **c56 h66**

TAGUR (IRE) 5 ch.g. Tagula (IRE) – Westcote (USA) (Gone West (USA)) [2018/19 h16.8dᵖᵘ Jan 21] fair on Flat, stays 1m: pulled up in maiden on hurdling debut. *Kevin Ryan* **h–**

TAILOR TOM (IRE) 7 b.g. Fruits of Love (USA) – Anfield Lady (IRE) (Safety Catch (USA)) [2018/19 h103: h23.1g² Oct 30] maiden pointer: fair handicap hurdler: thorough stayer: acts on heavy going: tried in cheekpieces. *Donald McCain* **h102**

TAKBEER (IRE) 7 b.g. Aqlaam – Precious Secret (IRE) (Fusaichi Pegasus (USA)) [2018/19 h15.8m⁸ h16gᶠ h15.8g⁶ h15.8g² Apr 22] sturdy gelding: fairly useful on Flat, stays 1¾m: fair form over hurdles: won novice at Ludlow in May. *Nikki Evans* **h109**

TAKE A BREAK (FR) 8 b.g. Sunday Break (JPN) – Popee (FR) (Take Risks (FR)) [2018/19 c96§, h113§: c16.5g³ c16.5g⁴ c19.2m³ h18.7m³ h23g² c15.6s* h17.1g⁸ h16.2s⁴ h17.1v h18.1g⁵ Jan 22] compact gelding: fair handicap hurdler: won at Carlisle in November: fair handicap chaser: won at Hexham in October: left Nigel Hawke after fifth start: stayed 23f: acted on good to firm and heavy going: wore headgear/tongue tie: temperamental: dead. *Mark Walford* **c104 § h107 §**

TAKE EM OUT (IRE) 7 b.g. Amadeus Wolf – Toorah Laura La (USA) (Black Minnaloushe (USA)) [2018/19 h105, b65: h19.2g* h22g² h23g⁶ h23.1m² Oct 23] runner-up both starts in Irish points: fair hurdler: won maiden at Towcester in May: stays 23f: acts on good to firm and heavy going: wears tongue tie. *Tim Vaughan* **h100**

TAKEIT EASY 4 b.g. Malinas (GER) – Circus Rose (Most Welcome) [2018/19 b16.7g⁵ Apr 3] sixth foal: half-brother to 3 winners, including fairly useful chaser Popelys Gull (19f winner, by Recharge), stays 3m, and fairly useful hurdler Acertain Circus (2m-2½m winner, by Definite Article): dam (h128), 2m-2½m hurdle winner, half-sister to fairly useful hurdler/chaser (stayed 3¼m) Harrycone Lewis: 3/1, fifth in maiden bumper at Market Rasen (4¼ lengths behind Stormin Norman), left poorly placed: should improve. *Pam Sly* **b85 p**

TAKEITFROMALADY (IRE) 10 b.g. Intikhab (USA) – Pinheiros (IRE) (Rock of Gibraltar (IRE)) [2018/19 h–: h15.9g May 13] maiden hurdler, no form since 2016 (including on Flat): wears headgear. *Daniel Steele* **h–**

TAKEN BY FORCE (IRE) 6 b.g. Millenary – Along Came Polly (IRE) (Old Vic) [2018/19 h64: h23g h16.3g⁵ Aug 23] placed both starts in points: little form over hurdles: in tongue tie last 2 starts. *Tom Weston* **h–**

TAKE THE HIGH ROAD 5 b.g. Kyllachy – China Tea (USA) (High Chaparral (IRE)) [2018/19 h85p: h18.7m h16.8g h18.5d h15.8d⁶ Dec 5] maiden hurdler, no form in 2018/19: in blinkers/tongue tie last 3 starts. *David Pipe* **h–**

TAKE TO HEART 7 b.g. Sakhee (USA) – Romantic Dream (Bustino) [2018/19 h126: c21.7g* May 21] tall, useful-looking gelding: fairly useful hurdler: evens, won 3-runner novice at Towcester (by 13 lengths from Reckless Behavior) on chasing debut: stays 2¾m: acts on good to firm going: tried in cheekpieces: front runner/races prominently. *Nicky Henderson* **c124 h–**

TAKING A CHANCE (IRE) 6 b.m. Flemensfirth (USA) – Northern Mill (IRE) (Distinctly North (USA)) [2018/19 h91: h15.8v⁶ h23.8d³ h26g⁴ c24gᶠ Apr 13] runner-up in Irish point: modest maiden hurdler: fell heavily fifth on chasing debut: stays 3¼m: acts on soft going. *Ian Williams* **c– h88**

TAKING AIM (IRE) 7 b.g. Acambaro (GER) – Sharp Missile (IRE) (Son of Sharp Shot (IRE)) [2018/19 b–: h16.2g h21.2gᵖᵘ h20.6sᵖᵘ h19.9d⁶ Jan 11] no show in bumper/over hurdles. *Chris Grant* **h–**

TAKING FLIGHT (IRE) 5 b.g. Stowaway – Cailin Vic Mo Cri (IRE) (Old Vic) [2018/19 b17g³ b16.2d⁴ Apr 26] €36,000 3-y-o: fourth foal: brother to bumper winner Hideaway Vic and a winning pointer, and half-brother to fairly useful hurdler Bryden Boy (19f-3m winner, by Craigsteel): dam (h113), bumper/2½m hurdle winner, half-sister to useful hurdler (stayed 2½m) Prince of Steal: fair form in bumpers: better effort when third at Carlisle on debut: will be suited by 2½m. *Nicky Richards* **b87**

TAKINGITALLIN (IRE) 5 b.m. Fame And Glory – Gilt Benefit (IRE) (Beneficial) [2018/19 b16.8s² b16.8v* b16.7d³ Apr 26] £26,000 4-y-o: fifth foal: half-sister to a winning pointer by Milan: dam (c88/h105) 19f/2½m hurdle winner: Irish point winner: fair form in bumpers: won mares event at Sedgefield in March: best effort when third in another mares race at Bangor: will prove suited by further than 17f. *Donald McCain* **b88**

TAKINGRISKS (IRE) 10 b.g. Golden Tornado (IRE) – Downtown Rosie (IRE) **c137**
(Good Thyne (USA)) [2018/19 c127, h101: c23.8g⁵ h24.3d* c25.6g² c24.2s³ c23.4s⁶ **h119**
c24.5v* c31.8m* Apr 13]

'A triumph for the North' was how trainer Nicky Richards hailed the victory
of Takingrisks in the Coral Scottish Grand National. 'I don't have £250,000 to spend
on a horse, this one cost €35,000 as a six-year-old!' The state of jump racing in the
North has been a recurring topic in recent times, with northern yards sometimes
finding it hard to compete against southern raiders in valuable races in their own
back yard, let alone in the big races in the South. No northern-trained horse has won
at the Cheltenham Festival, for example, since the Tim Easterby-trained Hawk High
in 2014, a far cry from that golden era, thirty or forty years ago, when the powerful
yards of such as Peter Easterby (Tim's father), the Dickinsons, Arthur Stephenson,
Jimmy FitzGerald and Nicky Richards's father Gordon were among those which
really put the North on the map (five different northern-based trainers won the
sport's blue riband, the Cheltenham Gold Cup, in the fifteen years between 1979
and 1993, with Peter Easterby and Michael Dickinson—both champion trainer three
times in that era—each winning the race twice).

The victory of Takingrisks in the Scottish National, the third-most valuable
handicap chase in Britain after the Grand National and the Ladbrokes Trophy
(formerly the Hennessy), helped to propel Nicky Richards into the top twenty in
the British trainers' championship for the first time since the 2008/9 season. There
were five northern-based trainers in the top twenty that season. One of them Howard
Johnson has since given up while Ferdy Murphy relocated from Middleham after the
end of the 2012/13 season, forced out because of declining numbers and increasing
costs ('I've been funding the business for a while with the horses we sell'). Murphy
sent out ten Cheltenham Festival winners and won three Scottish Nationals and
was one of the leading powers in northern jumping from the mid-'nineties until his

Coral Scottish Grand National Handicap Chase, Ayr—
Sean Quinlan asks for an all-or-nothing jump at the last from Takingrisks, who keeps on well to beat
Crosspark and the novices Cloth Cap (left) and Blue Flight (star on cap)

departure to Normandy before moving to the Loire Valley where he died in September 2019, aged seventy. Nicky Richards was the only northern trainer to make the top twenty in the latest season, though the stables of Philip Kirby, Sue Smith, Brian Ellison and Sandy Thomson housed horses which won in graded company. Simply Ned, who also has an essay in this Annual, won the Grade 1 Paddy's Rewards Club Chase for the second time at Leopardstown's Christmas meeting for Nicky Richards, while Iain Jardine was another northern-based trainer who won graded events in Ireland. Perhaps the number of wins in 'black type' races overall—better than in any other recent season—signals the beginning of a revival in fortunes for northern jumping. The successful Challenger Series, aimed at middle-tier performers, and the new Racing Post Go North Weekend being introduced in March 2020 (replacing the Northern Lights Series), provide some welcome increased prize money in the North, which has to appeal to more of the country's top owners if its leading jumping trainers are to have the extra good horses they need to compete successfully with their better off southern-based counterparts.

Takingrisks was bought at the 2015 Punchestown Sale shortly after winning a maiden point at Castletown (he had been brought down on his only previous start). He has raced under Rules for Penrith owner Frank Bird, who lives not far from the Greystoke stables of Nicky Richards, and has won in each of his four seasons to race, showing fairly useful form over hurdles in his first season and then quickly developing into a chaser of similar merit. He began the latest season with a staying-on victory over Justatenner and Shades of Midnight in a handicap hurdle at Ayr in November before a couple of creditable placed efforts in fairly valuable handicap chases at Haydock (a close second to Vintage Clouds on Betfair Chase day) and Wetherby (third to Lake View Lad in the Rowland Meyrick on Boxing Day). In both those races, he showed that he would be suited by further and, after resuming winning ways (following a poor run at Newcastle) in a veterans handicap at Carlisle, he got his first chance over a marathon trip in the Scottish National which was run on ground described by some of the jockeys as the firmest they had encountered all season. There were five withdrawals on the day, including top weight Beware The Bear whose presence meant that over a third of the field ran from out of the handicap proper. Takingrisks carried 10-1 and was a 25/1-shot in a betting market headed by the previous year's third Vintage Clouds (5/1), Irish challenger Crosshue Boy (7/1), the Ultima Handicap fourth Big River (8/1), the progressive novice Cloth Cap (9/1) and the Eider Chase winner Crosspark (10/1). Takingrisks barely took off at the first but, given plenty of time to recover, he worked his way into contention on the final circuit and took over in front early in the home straight before rallying very gamely to wrest back the advantage after being headed by Crosspark three out. Takingrisks beat Crosspark by four lengths with the sound-jumping Cloth Cap and fellow novice Blue Flight completing the frame, ahead of Big River and Vintage Clouds (Crosshue Boy came down after clipping heels).

Nicky Richards took over the yard at Greystoke when his father died in 1998 and Takingrisks was the third winner of the race for the family, Gordon Richards having won it with Playlord and Four Trix (when the stable also had the second Tartan Takeover). Gordon Richards trained two Grand National winners, Lucius and Hallo Dandy, and Takingrisks looks a likely sort for Aintree, particularly after proving himself in the drying conditions at Ayr which were similar to those which sometimes obtain on National day. The emergence of the winning jockey, thirty-five-year-old Irishman Sean Quinlan, warrants a mention as well, his career turning a corner riding in the North in the latest season when he rode over fifty winners for the first time. He had already passed the post first in a 'National'—the Durham National at Sedgefield in October—only for his mount Red Giant to be disqualified after Quinlan, who received a twelve-day suspension, steered him round a fence that had been reinstated after being bypassed on the previous circuit (the fact that the rules in Ireland prohibit a fence from being reintroduced in the same race was mentioned in Quinlan's defence, but it is every rider's responsibility to know the appropriate rules and avoid ambiguity by following the course unless direction markers indicate otherwise).

Takingrisks (IRE) (b.g. 2009)	Golden Tornado (IRE) (b 1996)	Sadler's Wells (b 1981)	Northern Dancer
			Fairy Bridge
		Broadway Joan (ch 1979)	Bold Arian
			Courtneys Doll
	Downtown Rosie (IRE) (br 1994)	Good Thyne (br 1977)	Herbager
			Foreseer
		North Rose VII (b 1981)	Northern Guest
			Night Rose

Takingrisks is by the minor jumps stallion Golden Tornado, an unraced son of Sadler's Wells and sire of Spa Hurdle winner Berties Dream. The dam of Takingrisks is the poor maiden jumper Downtown Rosie who has not bred another winner. The grandam North Rose VII was of humble origins, also unraced and never represented by a winner under Rules. Takingrisks is suited by long distances and acts on good to firm and heavy going. He was fitted with cheekpieces on his last two starts. *Nicky Richards*

TALENT TO AMUSE (IRE) 6 b.m. Manduro (GER) – Burn Baby Burn (IRE) (King's   **h119** Theatre (IRE)) [2018/19 h124: h20g[5] h21.4g[3] h21.6g[pu] h20.3g[4] Apr 18] fairly useful handicap hurdler: barely stays 21f: acts on good to firm going: wears tongue tie. *Emma Lavelle*

TALKINGPICTURESTV 6 b.m. Flying Legend (USA) – Banoo (IRE) (Hernando   **h75** (FR)) [2018/19 h16.3m[4] h16.8g h16g h16g h16.3g[5] h15.7d[4] h19.9s[5] h19.9s h23.1d[4]   **b78** h23.9d[3] Apr 24] sturdy mare: third foal: dam (h103) maiden hurdler (stayed 2¾m): modest form in bumpers: poor maiden hurdler: stays 3m: acts on good to soft going. *Henry Oliver*

TALKISCHEAP (IRE) 7 b.g. Getaway (GER) – Carrigmoorna Oak (IRE) (Milan)   **c155** [2018/19 h131: c22.4d[3] c19.9d[2] c24g* c24d[2] c24g[5] c28.8g* Apr 27]   **h–**

    For the second year running, a novice making his way on the staying scene ran away with the bet365 Gold Cup at Sandown's Finale meeting. On just his second appearance over fences in handicap company, seven-year-old Talkischeap jumped superbly and, very confidently ridden (his jockey looking over his shoulder after jumping the third last), he brushed aside two previous winners of the race The Young Master and Step Back to sprint clear on the run-in for a wide margin win. The nine finishers trailed home at lengthy intervals in a truly-run race in which Talkischeap's very good timerating backed up the positive view that has been taken of the form. Talkischeap won by ten lengths and nine lengths from The Young Master and Step Back, whom he stalked as the trio dominated the race from five out, and he looks very much one to keep on the right side in good handicap company—perhaps even in open graded events—in the next season, with the Ladbrokes Trophy (formerly the Hennessy) looking a likely starting point in a campaign that could well end up at the Grand National. The turn of foot that Talkischeap produced at the end of the bet365 Gold Cup was exceptional for a horse who stays so well and is a potent weapon in his armoury.

    The big handicap that is the centre piece of Sandown's programme on the last day of the season has a tradition of producing dramatic finishes, like the one in 2017 when 40/1-shot Henllan Harri held on in a four-way photo (a head and two necks were the distances). That edition saw the jockey on the runner-up seemingly mistaking the finishing line and riding out to the second winning post which is used for races over hurdles (as a consequence, he was banned for hitting his mount after the finish). It wasn't the first time that a jockey had been caught out by Sandown's two winning posts, which are only twenty-five yards apart, and ITV's cameraman also got it wrong on that particular occasion. The chase and hurdles tracks do not run parallel at Sandown and the separate winning posts are used because, if the hurdles finishing line was used for all races, it would apparently create a stands-side bias amounting to about a length on the run-in in steeplechases. That said, the confusion caused by having two winning posts so close together has gone on for too long and it makes the sport look amateurish when one is mistaken for the other (the situation inevitably also causes confusion for ordinary racegoers and those watching on television).

bet365 Gold Cup Handicap Chase, Sandown—the novice Talkischeap has the measure of previous winners The Young Master (noseband) and Step Back (cheekpieces/mostly hidden)

Incompetence, rather than amateurism, is the description that covers the latest 'two winning posts' fiasco when, in March, the Sandown stewards had to revise the result of the EBF 'National Hunt' Novices' Handicap Hurdle Final, a Saturday race shown live on terrestrial television, after 12/1-shot One For Rosie was incorrectly announced as the winner with the photo-finish taken from the camera aligned with the first winning post. The race was eventually correctly awarded to 9/1-chance Third Wind but the incident was humiliating for the sport and cost bookmakers, on and off course, thousands of pounds for a goodwill gesture which saw them paying out on two different results. The Sandown incident followed a number of other embarrassing photo-finish decisions, including dead-heats awarded at Bangor and Market Rasen because neither course was equipped with a reverse mirror to check the image, and judges at Kempton and Sandown having to reverse decisions after originally declaring the wrong horse as the winner. Sandown has taken steps, introduced at its Finale meeting, which it hopes will prevent confusion in future over its two winning posts. The design of the winning posts has been improved to make it easier to distinguish between the two finishes, and the movable 'lollipop' on top, switched between courses to denote the finish being used, has also been enlarged. Further pre-race checks of camera alignment have been introduced between the judge and the photo-finish operator which should prevent a repeat of what happened with the EBF Final.

To return to Talkischeap, he arrived at Sandown's Finale meeting after taking well to fences (he had useful form over hurdles at up to three miles). He boasted strong form with some of the season's classiest novices over fences, having finished third behind La Bague Au Roi and Lostintranslation at Newbury in November on his reappearance before splitting that pair (Lostintranslation made a bad mistake) in the Berkshire Novices' Chase on the same course later in the month. Talkischeap then beat his only opponent in a novice chase at Doncaster in January before finishing second to On The Blind Side (received 6 lb) at Kempton in another novice event. He ran below form when joint favourite on his handicap debut at Kempton in February for the 888Sport Handicap Chase (a valuable event that has lost some of its identity with the merry-go-round of sponsors since it was known as the Racing Post Chase).

Talkischeap (IRE) (b.g. 2012)	Getaway (GER) (b 2003)	Monsun (br 1990)	Konigsstuhl
			Mosella
		Guernica (b 1994)	Unfuwain
			Greenvera
	Carrigmoorna Oak (IRE) (b 2007)	Milan (b 1998)	Sadler's Wells
			Kithanga
		Cockney Star (ch 1993)	Camden Town
			Big Bugs Bomb

Mr Charles Dingwall's "Talkischeap"

Talkischeap, a sturdy gelding, won three times in points in Ireland before joining his present stable after changing hands for £55,000 as a four-year-old at the Cheltenham November Sales in 2016. His sire Getaway is establishing himself as a jumping sire to note, even though his oldest progeny are just seven, and he will stand at a fee of €7,500 for 2019, making him one of the more expensive stallions on the jumping roster at Coolmore. Talkischeap's dam Carrigmoorna Oak, an unraced daughter of Milan, has produced one other winner so far, Carrigmoorna Wood (by Shantou) who won a mares bumper at Tipperary. Talkischeap's grandam Cockney Star was also unraced but she is a sister to the high-class hurdler/useful chaser Cockney Lad, a genuine and consistent performer whose victories included a far from vintage edition of the Irish Champion Hurdle. A sister to Cockney Star and Cockney Lad, Cockney Lass, won the Tattersalls Gold Cup and was placed in the Irish Champion Stakes and a half-brother called Big Ash won on the Flat and over jumps, showing quite useful form in two-mile chases. Talkischeap stays twenty-nine furlongs and acts on heavy going, though he doesn't need the mud. He is a strong traveller in his races and a good jumper who may be open to even more improvement. *Alan King*

TALKOFGOLD (IRE) 7 gr.m. Gold Well – Talk of Rain (FR) (Turgeon (USA)) c– [2018/19 h103: c24.2g h19.5d⁵ h21.4s* h20.1d³ Mar 26] Irish point winner: fair handicap **h106** hurdler: won mares event at Ayr in March: well held in novice handicap on chasing debut: stays 21f: acts on soft going: in headgear last 3 starts. *Martin Todhunter*

TALK OF MONTY 6 b.g. Fair Mix (IRE) – Talk The Talk (Terimon) [2018/19 h76, b–: **h70** h16.7g⁶ h16g⁴ h15.8g Nov 2] angular gelding: poor form over hurdles: often races freely. *Lucy Wadham*

826

TALK OF THE SOUTH (IRE) 10 b.g. Milan – Smalltowntalk (IRE) (Carroll House) c– §
[2018/19 c108§, h–: c29.1g^pu May 8] sturdy gelding: winning hurdler: fair chaser, let down h–
by jumping sole outing in 2018/19: stays 29f: acts on heavy going: temperamental.
Paul Henderson

TALKONTHESTREET (IRE) 12 b.g. Milan – Super Size (IRE) (Shernazar) [2018/19 c110
c–, h–: c24.2g^2 c24.2m^2 c20.1g^2 c23.9m^4 Aug 5] well-made gelding: winning hurdler: h–
fairly useful handicap chaser at best: stayed 3½m: acted on soft and good to firm going:
tried in cheekpieces: dead. *Richard Fahey*

TALKTOMENOW 5 b.g. Shirocco (GER) – Sweet Stormy (GER) (Bluebird (USA)) h115
[2018/19 h20.5g^2 h21d h19.8s^5 h21.7g^4 Mar 26] £14,000 3-y-o: fourth foal: dam, German
1¼m winner, half-sister to useful 2m hurdler Sweet Wake and fairly useful hurdler/chaser
(stayed 25f) Sweet Shock: won point on debut: fairly useful form over hurdles: second in
novice at Plumpton, standout effort: tried in cheekpieces. *Warren Greatrex*

TAMARILLO GROVE (IRE) 12 b.g. Cape Cross (IRE) – Tamarillo (Daylami (IRE)) h104
[2018/19 h95: h15.7g^3 h16.8g^* h18.5g^2 h16.8s^* h16.7g^6 h16d h19.5m^3 Apr 22]
smallish gelding: fair handicap hurdler: won at Newton Abbot in June (conditionals) and
July: best around 2m: acts on soft and good to firm going: tried in cheekpieces: wears
tongue tie: usually races off pace. *Sophie Leech*

TAMAYEF (IRE) 5 b.g. Sir Prancealot (IRE) – Miss Glitters (IRE) (Chevalier (IRE)) h–
[2018/19 h85: h16.4g Oct 26] compact gelding: fairly useful on Flat, stayed 1m: little
impact over hurdles: in tongue tie last 2 starts: dead. *Matt Sheppard*

TAMBOURINE SAM 6 b.g. Black Sam Bellamy (IRE) – Tambourine Ridge (IRE) b–
(Tamure (IRE)) [2018/19 b13.7d Jan 25] failed to complete in points: well held in bumper.
Nick Littmoden

TAMBOUR MAJOR (FR) 12 b.g. Myrakalu (FR) – Joaillere (FR) (Silver Rainbow) c–
[2018/19 c59, h–: c21.6g^pu c23.8m^pu Feb 27] multiple point winner: of little account under h–
Rules nowadays: wears headgear: has worn tongue tie. *J. Threadgall*

TANACANDO (FR) 7 b.g. Ballingarry (IRE) – Tamaziya (IRE) (Law Society (USA)) c75
[2018/19 h94: h23.3d h19.9g^5 c24v^4 c26.1d h19.5g Apr 26] has had breathing operation: h85
modest maiden hurdler: poor form over fences: left Tim Vaughan after fourth start: should
stay beyond 19f: acts on heavy going: tried in tongue tie. *Ronald Harris*

TANARPINO 8 ch.g. Tobougg (IRE) – Got Tune (FR) (Green Tune (USA)) [2018/19 c131
c126, h126: c24m^2 c24.2g^* c23.8g^2 c23.4g^4 c22.5d^4 c20d^* c25.3g^5 Apr 17] workmanlike h–
gelding: winning hurdler: useful chaser: won novice at Hexham in June and novice
handicap at Uttoxeter (by 10 lengths from Terry The Fish) in March: stays 25f: acts on
good to firm and heavy going: wears headgear: front runner/races prominently.
Jennie Candlish

TANGO BOY (IRE) 6 ch.g. Flemensfirth (USA) – Hello Kitty (IRE) (Houmayoun (FR)) b93
[2018/19 b16.7g^* Mar 14] €36,000 3-y-o: second foal: brother to useful hurdler/smart
chaser Impact Factor (2m/17f winner): dam (c116/h119) 2½m-23f hurdle/chase winner:
2/1, won bumper at Market Rasen (by 1¼ lengths from O Connell Street) on debut.
Neil Mulholland

TANGOED (IRE) 6 ch.m. Papal Bull – Dainty Steps (IRE) (Xaar) [2018/19 h–, b91: h–
h20.3g May 15] point winner: placed in bumpers: little impact over hurdles: tried in
cheekpieces. *Harry Whittington*

TANGOLAN (IRE) 11 ch.g. Golan (IRE) – Classic Note (IRE) (Classic Secret (USA)) c100 §
[2018/19 c126, h103: c19.2d^5 h23.9g^6 c20.1g^5 h23.1g h20.2g c20.1g^5 Sep 27] fair handicap h93 §
hurdler/fairly useful handicap chaser, below form in 2018/19: stays 3m: acts on good to
firm and good to soft going: has worn headgear/tongue tie, including in 2018/19: unreliable.
Fergal O'Brien

TANIT RIVER (IRE) 9 br.g. Indian River (FR) – Tanit Lady (IRE) (Presenting) [2018/19 c–
c125, h102: c25.5g c23.4d^pu c24.2g Apr 11] tall gelding: fair hurdler: useful chaser at best, h–
no form in 2018/19: has worn headgear: wears tongue tie: usually leads. *Tim Vaughan*

TANKERTON BOY (IRE) 6 br.g. Marienbard (IRE) – Smashing Leader (IRE) h–
(Supreme Leader) [2018/19 b82: h23.1m^pu Jun 22] placed in bumper on debut: little show
since, including on hurdling debut: tried in tongue tie. *Neil King*

TANNADICE PARK (IRE) 4 b.f. Shirocco (GER) – Catcherinscratcher (IRE) (Catcher b–
In The Rye (IRE)) [2018/19 b16.4m^6 b16m Apr 13] second foal: dam (c123/h121) 2½m-
3m hurdle/chase winner: no form in bumpers. *Jim Goldie*

TANRUDY (IRE) 5 b.g. Presenting – Come In Moscow (IRE) (Over The River (FR)) **h92 p**
[2018/19 h19.3g⁴ h15.8s h23.8d h23.1d⁶ Apr 9] €46,000 3-y-o: sixth foal: brother to fair
chaser Wood Pigeon (21f winner), stays 25f, and half-brother to fairly useful 2½m hurdle
winner Renwick (by Milan): dam (c112/h89) 2m-2½m hurdle/chase winner: placed in Irish
points: modest form over hurdles: tried in hood/tongue tie: should do better. *Nigel Hawke*

TANTAMOUNT 10 b.g. Observatory (USA) – Cantanta (Top Ville) [2018/19 h116: **h117**
h24.7g⁶ May 18] good-bodied gelding: fairly useful handicap hurdler, lightly raced in
recent seasons: stays 25f: acts on soft and good to firm going: tried in hood: wears tongue
tie. *Lucinda Russell*

TAPACULO 8 b.g. Kayf Tara – Aniston (IRE) (Eurodeal (IRE)) [2018/19 h20.5dᵘʳ Mar 2] **h98**
strong gelding: useful form over hurdles in 2015/16: keeping on from rear when unseated
rider last in handicap at Newbury on only start since. *Philip Hobbs*

TAPENADE (IRE) 5 br.g. Scorpion (IRE) – Corravilla (IRE) (Yashgan) [2018/19 b16d⁵ **h71**
b16.2g⁴ b16g⁵ h16s⁶ h19.4s Apr 26] €12,000 3-y-o: half-brother to fairly useful hurdler/ **b87**
chaser An Capall Mor (2m-2½m winner, by Flemensfirth) and poor 2¼m hurdle winner
Ping (by Mahler): dam winning pointer: fair form in bumpers: poor form over hurdles:
tried in cheekpieces. *Gordon Elliott, Ireland*

TARA BRIDGE 11 b.g. Kayf Tara – Annie Greenlaw (Petoski) [2018/19 c121, h117: **c115**
h16s⁵ c15.5d c20s⁴ c19.4d⁴ Mar 20] well-made gelding: maiden hurdler: fairly useful **h–**
handicap chaser: stays 2¾m, at least as effective at much shorter: acts on heavy going: in
cheekpieces last 2 starts. *Chris Gordon*

TARADA 6 br.g. Kayf Tara – Kerada (FR) (Astarabad (USA)) [2018/19 b17s² h19.5d² **h123 p**
h19.2d* Feb 24] second foal: closely related to fair hurdler Royal Claret (3m/25f winner, **b94**
by Yeats): dam (c137/h127) 2m-3m hurdle/chase winner: second in bumper at Carlisle (1½
lengths behind I K Brunel) on debut: fairly useful form over hurdles: won novice at
Fontwell in February: will stay beyond 19f: likely to progress further. *Oliver Sherwood*

TARA FLOW 9 b.m. Kayf Tara – Poppet (Terimon) [2018/19 h19.5d⁴ c16.3g⁴ c19.4s² **c118**
c24vᵖᵘ Mar 16] fairly useful handicap hurdler, too free on comeback: fairly useful form **h102**
over fences: second in handicap at Ffos Las in February: stays 19f: acts on heavy going.
Venetia Williams

TARA FORCE 5 b.m. Kayf Tara – Whizz Back (IRE) (Bob Back (USA)) [2018/19 b–: **h–**
b16g h20.1gᵖᵘ Apr 15] no form in bumpers/novice hurdle. *Tim Easterby* **b–**

TARA MAC 10 b.m. Kayf Tara – Macklette (IRE) (Buckskin (FR)) [2018/19 c91, h98: **c105**
c21.6g* h20s c22.6g⁵ c20g* h20.1g⁶ c21.2d⁴ c19.2g³ c19.4vᵖ Jan 14] angular mare: modest **h91**
handicap hurdler: fair handicap chaser: won mares events at Fontwell in May and
Worcester in September: stays 3m: acts on heavy going: wears headgear: usually races
prominently. *Tim Vaughan*

TARA NIECE 6 b.m. Kayf Tara – Pepite de Soleil (FR) (Fly To The Stars) [2018/19 **b78**
b17.7g⁶ b15.3g⁶ Apr 14] rather unfurnished mare: second foal: half-sister to bumper
winner/fairly useful hurdler Jubilympics (21f winner, by Kapgarde) and (h129) 2m-19f
hurdle winner: modest form in bumpers. *Seamus Mullins*

TARAS DAY 6 b.m. Kayf Tara – One of Those Days (Soviet Lad (USA)) [2018/19 h–, b–: **h76**
h15.7g⁶ h20d h27g h20.3d⁴ Apr 24] has had breathing operation: poor maiden hurdler:
stays 2½m: acts on good to soft going: in cheekpieces last 3 starts: tried in tongue tie.
Laura Morgan

TARA VIEW 8 b.m. Kayf Tara – Temptation (FR) (Lando (GER)) [2018/19 h125: c20g⁵ **c–**
c20.5gᵖᵘ h24.4g Dec 29] angular mare: fairly useful hurdler: no form over fences. **h–**
Alan King

TARA WELL (IRE) 9 b.m. Kayf Tara – Miss Baden (IRE) (Supreme Leader) [2018/19 **h80**
h86: h21d⁴ h19.9v⁵ h15.8s h20.5d² Jan 22] Irish point winner: poor handicap hurdler: stays
23f: best form on soft/heavy going: wears cheekpieces: usually in tongue tie. *Robin Dickin*

TARA WEST 5 b.m. Kayf Tara – West River (USA) (Gone West (USA)) [2018/19 b15.8s³ **b87**
Apr 7] £24,000 3-y-o, and £100,000 4-y-o: sister to bumper winner Up The Bees and half-sister
to several winners, including modest hurdler Nero West (2¾m winner, by Pelder): dam ran
once on Flat: won Irish point on debut: 6/1, third in bumper at Ffos Las (5 lengths behind
Prudhomme). *Anthony Honeyball*

TARKS HILL 5 b.m. Brian Boru – Risky May (Petoski) [2018/19 b17.7g b17.7g Apr 7] **b–**
third foal: closely related to fair chaser Foxes Bridge (23f-3¼m winner, by Tamure) and
half-sister to bumper winner Manhattan Spring (by Central Park): dam no form in bumpers/
points: no form in bumpers. *Seamus Mullins*

TARRONA 10 b.g. Kayf Tara – Lisrona (IRE) (Presenting) [2018/19 h–: h20.6g³ h23.1s^{pu} h20.3s² h20v⁴ h20.5s^{pu} h21.7g² h21.4g Apr 3] fair maiden hurdler: stays 2¾m: acts on heavy going: tried in cheekpieces. *Alan Phillips* **h105**

TARSINI 5 b.m. Dr Massini (IRE) – Tarmac Girl (Alflora (IRE)) [2018/19 b15.8g^{pu} May 8] first foal: dam (h70), placed in bumper/2m hurdle, half-sister to useful hurdler (stayed 3m) Fahamore and fairly useful staying hurdler/chaser Brownville: pulled up in mares bumper. *Kevin Bishop* **b–**

TASHUNKA (IRE) 6 b.m. Flemensfirth (USA) – Las Palmlas (IRE) (Brian Boru) [2018/19 b94: b17g b16.4g Nov 17] good-topped mare: little impact in Irish points: fair in bumpers, below best in 2018/19. *Fergal O'Brien* **b–**

TASTE THE WINE (IRE) 13 gr.g. Verglas (IRE) – Azia (IRE) (Desert Story (IRE)) [2018/19 h88: h18.5g h20g h18.7m⁴ h21.6g³ Jul 6] close-coupled gelding: poor handicap hurdler: stays 2¾m: acts on good to firm and good to soft going: has worn cheekpieces/tongue tie, including in 2018/19. *Bernard Llewellyn* **h78**

TAWSEEF (IRE) 11 b.g. Monsun (GER) – Sahool (Unfuwain (USA)) [2018/19 h133: h20s h22.8v⁶ h19.9v h23s⁶ h25m² Apr 20] smallish gelding: fairly useful handicap hurdler: stays 27f: acts on good to firm and heavy going: has worn headgear. *Donald McCain* **h122**

TAXMEIFYOUCAN (IRE) 5 b.g. Beat Hollow – Accounting (Sillery (USA)) [2018/19 h127: h16d h18.9v h25.8g⁴ h19.3g⁶ h25.8g Mar 23] good-topped gelding: fairly useful handicap hurdler: stays 3¼m: acts on good to firm and heavy going: has worn headgear, including in 2018/19: temperament under suspicion. *Keith Dalgleish* **h125**

TAYARAT (IRE) 14 b.g. Noverre (USA) – Sincere (IRE) (Bahhare (USA)) [2018/19 c–§, h–§: h16.7g^{pu} Nov 22] rather leggy gelding: fairly useful hurdler/fair chaser at best, no form since 2014/15: has worn headgear/tongue tie: temperamental. *Michael Chapman* **c– §** **h– §**

TAYZAR 8 b.g. Kayf Tara – Matilda Too (Definite Article) [2018/19 h112, b–: h16.7g³ c15.9d c19.4g^{pu} c17.1d* c16.4s² c17.1g^{ur} c19.3d² c20.1g³ Feb 23] has had breathing operation: fair maiden hurdler: fairly useful handicap chaser: won novice event at Kelso in November: stays 19f: acts on soft going. *Ruth Jefferson* **c121** **h91**

TAZKA (FR) 4 b.f. Network (GER) – Tazminya (Fantastic Light (USA)) [2018/19 h16m³ h17.7d* h17.7v² h16s⁴ h16.6g⁵ h18.8d³ h16.8g Apr 18] lengthy filly: fair maiden on Flat, stays 1½m: fair hurdler: won juvenile at Fontwell in November: stays 19f: acts on heavy going: races prominently. *Gary Moore* **h108**

TB BROKE HER (IRE) 9 br.m. Indian River (FR) – Catch Ball (Prince Sabo) [2018/19 c100, h77: c23.8g³ c26.1g⁶ c23g c23.8m^{pu} Jan 17] point winner: winning hurdler: fair handicap chaser: left Matt Sheppard after third start: stays 3¼m: acts on soft going: has worn cheekpieces, including in 2018/19: tried in tongue tie: usually races off pace. *Sam Jukes* **c107** **h–**

TEACHER'S PET (IRE) 8 b.m. Oscar (IRE) – Castlecrossings (IRE) (Broken Hearted) [2018/19 c19.5d² c19.9m^F h16.5s c19.9g^{pu} c18.2d^{bd} h16d c20g³ c17g⁶ c25.5d⁴ c21.6g² c16d³ c21.3s^{ur} c28.5g⁵ Mar 24] second foal: closely related to modest hurdler/fairly useful chaser Whatareudoingtome (23f-3¾m winner, by High Chaparral): dam (h120) 2m-2½m hurdle winner: fairly useful handicap hurdler: fairly useful handicap chaser: second at Thurles (neck behind Double Portrait) in January: stays 25f: acts on heavy going: has worn cheekpieces, including in 2018/19: wears tongue tie: often let down by jumping over fences. *J. P. Dempsey, Ireland* **c130 x** **h121**

TEA FOR TWO 10 b.g. Kayf Tara – One For Me (Tragic Role (USA)) [2018/19 c160, h–: h25.4s^{pu} c19.9d³ c24g⁶ c28.4d^{pu} c30.2s^{ur} c34.3g^{pu} Apr 6] strong gelding: has had breathing operation: winning hurdler: useful chaser nowadays: third in Peterborough Chase at Huntingdon (12 lengths behind Charbel) in December: regressed further after: stays 25f: has won on heavy ground, but very best form under less testing conditions: tried in hood: races towards rear. *Mrs Jane Williams* **c144** **h–**

TEALS LAD 10 b.g. Kayf Tara – Derry Ann (Derrylin) [2018/19 h19.9g^{pu} h16d^{pu} Dec 27] little impact in bumper/over hurdles. *Lee James* **h–**

TEASER 4 b.g. Dansili – Tottie (Fantastic Light (USA)) [2018/19 h15.3f² h16d* h16.6g h15.8g³ h16.5s³ h15.7m h15.7m Apr 20] has had breathing operation: dam half-sister to useful hurdler/fairly useful chaser (stayed 2½m) Harry Tricker: fair on Flat, stays 1½m: fair hurdler: won juvenile maiden at Warwick in December: raced around 2m: acts on soft going: wears headgear/tongue tie: usually leads. *David Pipe* **h108**

TEA TIME FRED 10 b.g. Kayf Tara – Darjeeling (IRE) (Presenting) [2018/19 c87x, h106: h21.4m h26.4m⁴ h25.8g² h26.5m³ h26.5g² h26.5g⁴ h26.5d² h23.6g h23.1m³ h23.1s² h23.1s² h26.4g⁵ h19.8g⁵ Apr 14] lengthy gelding: fair handicap hurdler: maiden chaser (often let down by jumping): stays 3¼m: acts on good to firm and heavy going: wears cheekpieces. *Susan Gardner* — **c– x h112**

TEA TIME ON MARS 7 ch.g. Schiaparelli (GER) – Darjeeling (IRE) (Presenting) [2018/19 b79: h19.5g h20spu h16.8s h19.6d h21.4g* Feb 27] rangy gelding: fair form over hurdles: won handicap at Wincanton in February: stays 21f. *Susan Gardner* — **h106**

TED BACH (IRE) 8 b.g. Bach (IRE) – Rose Tanner (IRE) (Roselier (FR)) [2018/19 h20g⁵ h16g h16.6g h19.2v* h15.3g h19s⁵ Mar 19] poor maiden on Flat: modest maiden hurdler: won at Fontwell in February: left David Kenneth Budds after third start: stays 2½m: acts on heavy going: has worn headgear, including in 2018/19: tried in tongue tie. *Paul Henderson* — **h96**

TEDDY TEE (IRE) 10 b.g. Mountain High (IRE) – Knocksouna Lady (IRE) (Oscar (IRE)) [2018/19 c122x, h–: c26.9d² c31.9vᶠ c30.6d⁵ Apr 26] tall, lengthy gelding: has had breathing operation: winning hurdler: fairly useful maiden chaser: stays 27f: acts on heavy going: often let down by jumping. *Nicky Richards* — **c119 x h–**

TEDHAM 5 b.g. Shirocco (GER) – Alegralil (King's Theatre (IRE)) [2018/19 b91: h17.1d⁴ h16s³ h16.8s² h21.4g* h20d Apr 5] good-topped gelding: useful form over hurdles: won handicap at Wincanton (by 1¾ lengths from Tight Call) in January: stays 21f: acts on soft going: tracks pace: remains with potential. *Jonjo O'Neill* — **h130 p**

TEDSPEED (IRE) 9 ch.g. Vertical Speed (FR) – Clare Hogan (IRE) (Moscow Society (USA)) [2018/19 h19.5d Jan 18] point winner: well beaten in Irish bumper (for L. J. Archdeacon) and novice hurdle. *Richard Mitford-Slade* — **h–**

TED VEALE (IRE) 12 b.g. Revoque (IRE) – Rose Tanner (IRE) (Roselier (FR)) [2018/19 c137x, h125: h16s h20.9g³ h16.4g³ h16.2g³ h16.2g³ Apr 24] medium-sized gelding: fairly useful handicap hurdler nowadays: winning chaser (often let down by jumping): left A. J. Martin after first start: stays 21f: acts on heavy going: has worn hood. *N. W. Alexander* — **c– x h126**

TEESCOMPONENTS BOY (IRE) 5 b.g. Midnight Legend – Northern Native (IRE) (Be My Native (USA)) [2018/19 b15.7g May 13] tailed off in bumper. *Gillian Boanas* — **b–**

TEESCOMPONENTS LAD 6 b.g. Midnight Legend – Northern Native (IRE) (Be My Native (USA)) [2018/19 h115, b95: h20d² h16.2s³ h21.3s* h24.3d⁴ h19.3g* Feb 18] fairly useful handicap hurdler: won at Wetherby in December and Carlisle in February: stays 3m: acts on heavy going. *Gillian Boanas* — **h127**

TEESCOMPONENTS MAX 10 b.g. Grape Tree Road – Our Tees Component (IRE) (Saddlers' Hall (IRE)) [2018/19 c–, h78: h15.8m⁴ c17.2gur c15.6gpu h15.8gpu Jul 10] poor maiden hurdler/maiden chaser: raced around 2m: dead. *Gillian Boanas* — **c– h74**

TEESCOMPONENTSTRIG 4 ch.g. Black Sam Bellamy (IRE) – La Calinda (Presenting) [2018/19 b16.4d⁶ b16.2g Apr 15] poor form in bumpers. *Gillian Boanas* — **b63**

TEETON POWER 8 ch.m. Black Sam Bellamy (IRE) – Teeton Priceless (Broadsword (USA)) [2018/19 c25.3g² c27.5dpu Jun 8] multiple point winner: fair form in chases: better effort when second in mares hunter at Cheltenham in May. *Miss Liz Harris* — **c101**

TEGEREK (FR) 5 b.g. Mount Nelson – Takaniya (IRE) (Rainbow Quest (USA)) [2018/19 h16d⁵ h15.5g³ h15.8v⁵ h16.3d⁴ h19.5d² Mar 20] sturdy gelding: fairly useful on Flat, stays 10.5f: fair form over hurdles: stays 19f: acts on good to soft going: usually races in rear. *Jonjo O'Neill* — **h114**

TEKIBLUE DE L'ORME (FR) 6 b.g. Blue Bresil (FR) – Tekila de L'Orme (FR) (Ultimately Lucky (IRE)) [2018/19 h–: h22.1s³ Aug 27] good-bodied gelding: poor maiden hurdler. *Philip Kirby* — **h66**

TEL'ART (FR) 5 gr.g. Montmartre (FR) – Textuelle (FR) (Roakarad) [2018/19 b16g⁵ b16.7g* h17.7v h15.8d h19d⁶ Apr 24] €44,000 3-y-o: compact gelding: sixth foal: dam unraced half-sister to smart hurdler/useful chaser (stayed 2½m) Tarla: fairly useful form in bumpers: won at Bangor in October: no form over hurdles: should stay further than 17f. *Ben Pauling* — **h– b100**

TELEGRAPH PLACE (IRE) 6 br.g. Yeats (IRE) – Sea Skate (USA) (Gilded Time (USA)) [2018/19 h99p, b–: h20.6g⁴ h16d* h16g h19.5v h15.9d h21.4g h15.9s⁵ h20.5g⁵ Apr 7] sturdy gelding: pulled up in Irish point: fair hurdler: won novice at Warwick in May: left Olly Murphy after second start: should stay further than 2m: acts on soft going: tried in cheekpieces. *Chris Gordon* — **h100**

TELEKINETIC 4 b.f. Champs Elysees – Kinetix (Linamix (FR)) [2018/19 b13.7m Oct 4] fourth foal: half-sister to 1¾m winner Our Cilla (by Sixties Icon): dam maiden on Flat (placed up to 1½m): tailed off in junior bumper: modest form on Flat. *Julia Feilden* **b–**

TELL THE TALE (IRE) 9 b.g. Craigsteel – Club Member (IRE) (Flemensfirth (USA)) [2018/19 h91§: h16.8g h20g^ro Sep 11] sturdy gelding: maiden pointer: modest maiden hurdler, below form in 2018/19: stayed 19f: acted on good to soft going: wore headgear: sometimes in tongue tie: temperamental: dead. *Neil Mulholland* **h65 §**

TELSON BARLEY (IRE) 6 b.g. Scorpion (IRE) – El Monica (IRE) (Kahyasi) [2018/19 h–86, b–: h19.5v h19d^5 h19d^5 h23.8g* h23.1d^6 h26g^3 Apr 10] fair handicap hurdler: won novice event at Musselburgh in February: stays 3¼m: acts on good to soft going: tried in cheekpieces: in tongue tie last 4 starts. *Graeme McPherson* **h102**

TEME SPIRIT (IRE) 5 b.m. Sans Frontieres (IRE) – Newtown Dancer (IRE) (Danehill Dancer (IRE)) [2018/19 h16.8g2 b17g b15.8s h21d^pu h23.8d Feb 20] £28,000 3-y-o: sixth foal: half-sister to very smart hurdler/useful chaser Different Gravey (2m-2½m winner, by High Chaparral): dam (c104/h104), 2m-2¼m hurdle winner (stayed 21f), also 1½m/13f winner on Flat: fair form in bumpers: best effort when second in mares event at Bangor on debut: no form over hurdles: tried in hood. *Henry Daly* **h–** **b89**

TEMIR KAZYK 5 b.g. Oasis Dream – Tingling (USA) (Storm Cat (USA)) [2018/19 h–: h16.8g^pu May 9] has had breathing operation: no form over hurdles. *Henry Oliver* **h–**

TEMPESTATEFLORESCO 11 b.g. Storming Home – Empress Dagmar (Selkirk (USA)) [2018/19 c142, h117: h23g^4 c25.8m^5 h23.3s^3 h20g h26.5g^4 h25.8m^3 c23.8m^6 Oct 10] has had breathing operation: fairly useful handicap hurdler: useful chaser: stays 3¼m: acts on good to firm and good to soft going: tried in blinkers: wears tongue tie. *Colin Tizzard* **c128** **h125**

TEMPLE GUIDE 5 b.g. Bahri (USA) – Posh Stick (Rakaposhi King) [2018/19 b17d Mar 24] tailed off in bumper. *James Walton* **b–**

TEMPLE HIGH 4 b.f. Sulamani (IRE) – Uppermost (Montjeu (IRE)) [2018/19 b16g^5 Apr 25] seventh foal: half-sister to bumper winner/useful hurdler Midnight Tour (2m-21f winner, by Midnight Legend), 1¾m bumper winner Miss Fleming (by Flemensfirth) and a winning pointer by Alfora: dam unraced half-sister to useful hurdler/chaser (stayed 3m) Locksmith: fair form in bumper (8¾ lengths behind Overthetop). *Nicky Henderson* **b77**

TEMPLEHILLS (IRE) 8 b.g. Kalanisi (IRE) – Sissinghurst Storm (IRE) (Good Thyne (USA)) [2018/19 c136x, h–: c24d^4 c20g* c19.9g^4 c24d^F c23.4d^pu c19.4s c20.6d c24g^5 Mar 28] tall gelding: winning hurdler: useful handicap chaser: won at Warwick (by 11 lengths from Rear Admiral) in October: stays 21f: acts on good to firm and heavy going: wears hood: has worn tongue tie: often let down by jumping: has joined Jonjo O'Neill. *Nigel Twiston-Davies* **c137 x** **h–**

TEMPLE MAN 7 b.g. Sulamani (IRE) – Altogether Now (IRE) (Step Together (USA)) [2018/19 h95p: c16.3s^pu h20.9g^3 h20.2d Apr 26] fair form over hurdles: pulled up in novice handicap on chasing debut: stays 21f: best form on good going: usually races off pace. *Ruth Jefferson* **c–** **h103**

TEMPLENABOE (IRE) 7 b.g. Milan – Pretty Impressive (IRE) (Presenting) [2018/19 h75: h20.2g h20.2g^6 Jun 3] won Irish point on debut: maiden hurdler, no form in 2018/19. *Lucinda Russell* **h–**

TEMPLEPARK 6 b.g. Phoenix Reach (IRE) – Kenny's Dream (Karinga Bay) [2018/19 b16m^2 b16g^2 b17.7g^3 h19.9g^2 h19.9g^2 h19.3m^5 c16.5g^3 Apr 22] £75,000 4-y-o: lengthy gelding: fourth foal: half-brother to modest 2m hurdle winner Lusis Naturea (by Multiplex) and a winning pointer by Central Park: dam, unraced, closely related to Scottish Grand National winner Young Kenny: Irish point winner: fair form in bumpers/over hurdles, placed several times: 6/4, third in novice handicap at Huntingdon (5 lengths behind Cosmic King) on chasing debut: will stay further than 2½m: tried in cheekpieces: will improve as a chaser. *Ben Case* **c110 p** **h111** **b91**

TEMPLIER (IRE) 6 b.g. Mastercraftsman (IRE) – Tigertail (FR) (Priolo (USA)) [2018/19 h110: c16.5d^4 c19.7s^5 c17g^3 Apr 21] well-made gelding: fair hurdler: modest form over fences: unproven beyond 2m: acts on good to soft going: has worn cheekpieces, including in 2018/19. *Gary Moore* **c93** **h–**

TEMPURAN 10 b.g. Unbridled's Song (USA) – Tenderly (IRE) (Danehill (USA)) [2018/19 c–, h114: h16.7g^3 h21g^pu h23d^pu Apr 26] sturdy gelding: fair handicap hurdler: winning chaser: stays 21f: acts on good to firm going: tried in cheekpieces: front runner. *Alastair Ralph* **c–** **h107**

TEN

TENNEWROW (IRE) 7 b.m. Stowaway – Silent Supreme (IRE) (Supreme Leader) **h88**
[2018/19 h90?: h19m^{pu} h16g h23v^6 h24.4g^{pu} h20.7d^3 h20.5g^2 Apr 22] Irish point winner:
modest maiden hurdler: left Ben Pauling after fourth start: stays 21f: acts on good to soft
going: in tongue tie last 2 starts: usually races prominently. *Alastair Ralph*

TENOR (IRE) 9 b.g. Oratorio (IRE) – Cedar Sea (IRE) (Persian Bold) [2018/19 h16g **h86**
h15.8m^3 h16m^4 Oct 19] smart at best on Flat, stays 1½m: modest form over hurdles: tried
in tongue tie. *John Ryan*

TENOR NIVERNAIS (FR) 12 b.g. Shaanmer (IRE) – Hosanna II (FR) (Marasali) **c117**
[2018/19 c–§, h–§: c24.2v c23.8d^5 c24.2d^{pu} Jan 5] rangy, useful-looking gelding: winning **h– §**
hurdler: one-time smart chaser, little impact in handicaps since 2016/17: stays 3m: acts on
heavy going: has worn cheekpieces, including last 2 starts: usually races close up: not one
to trust. *Venetia Williams*

TENSION TIME (IRE) 5 b.g. Dubai Destination (USA) – Leader's Hall (IRE) (Saddlers' **b–**
Hall (IRE)) [2018/19 b15.8d^6 Mar 13] 7/1, never a threat in bumper at Huntingdon. *Lucy
Wadham*

TEN TREES 9 b.m. Millkom – Island Path (IRE) (Jupiter Island) [2018/19 h93: h20.1g^3 **h103**
h22.1d Aug 25] fair handicap hurdler: left Sally Haynes after first start: stays 21f: acts on
soft going. *Stella Barclay*

TEQUILA BLAZE 5 b.m. Sakhee (USA) – Miss Sassi (Terimon) [2018/19 b15.7s^3 Mar **b72 p**
18] third foal: half-sister to fair hurdler Dakota Grey (17f winner, by Fair Mix), stays 3m:
dam lightly-raced half-sister to useful 2m hurdler Amaretto Rose: 20/1, third in
conditionals/amateurs maiden bumper at Southwell (20 lengths behind Eyes Right): should
improve. *Fergal O'Brien*

TEQUILA SECRET (IRE) 8 b.m. Kayf Tara – Jubilee Queen (IRE) (Exit To Nowhere **c–**
(USA)) [2018/19 c–, h95, b76: c22.5m^{pu} c21.4g^{pu} Jun 1] maiden hurdler: maiden chaser, **h–**
no form in 2018/19: tried in blinkers: in tongue tie last 3 starts. *Nigel Hawke*

TERMINAL ONE (IRE) 5 b.m. Stowaway – Kalyfa Royale (IRE) (Blueprint (IRE)) **h–**
[2018/19 b67: h20.6g^6 h20v h19.7s^5 h16.2g^6 h15.7g Mar 6] no form over hurdles: in hood
last 5 starts: usually races freely. *Tim Reed*

TERREFORT (FR) 6 gr.g. Martaline – Vie de Reine (FR) (Mansonnien (FR)) [2018/19 **c158**
c156p, h124: c24.2v^4 c25.3d^3 c23.8d^2 c20.6d^{pu} Mar 14] tall gelding: winning hurdler: very **h–**
smart chaser: third in Cotswold Chase at Cheltenham (3 lengths behind Frodon) in January
and second in Betfair Denman Chase at Ascot (11 lengths behind Clan des Obeaux) 3
weeks later: stays 25f: acts on heavy going. *Nicky Henderson*

TERRY THE FISH (IRE) 7 b.g. Milan – Have More (Haafhd) [2018/19 h131: c23.6g^3 **c126**
c24g^{pu} c19.2d^2 c20d^2 Mar 30] strong gelding: useful hurdler: fairly useful form over **h–**
fences: stays 3¼m: acts on soft going: in headgear last 3 starts. *Jonjo O'Neill*

TESTIFY (IRE) 8 b.g. Witness Box (USA) – Tanya Thyne (USA) (Good Thyne (USA)) **c110**
[2018/19 c142, h–: c23.4d^6 c22.9v c20.6d^{pu} Mar 14] strong gelding: has had breathing **h–**
operation: winning chaser, well below best in 2018/19: has won over 23f, at
least as effective at much shorter: best form on soft/heavy going: tried in blinkers/tongue
tie: races prominently. *Donald McCain*

TEST RIDE (IRE) 5 b.g. Rip Van Winkle (IRE) – Easter Fairy (USA) (Fusaichi Pegasus **h–**
(USA)) [2018/19 b–: b15.8g^6 h15.9s h15.9d h15.9s h16v Feb 18] tall, rather unfurnished **b74**
gelding: poor form in bumpers: none over hurdles: left John Butler after first start.
Neil Mulholland

TEST VALLEY (IRE) 4 b.g. Footstepsinthesand – Rockabout (IRE) (Rock of Gibraltar **h–**
(IRE)) [2018/19 h15.9d^{ur} h16.7m^{pu} Jun 22] failed to complete both starts over hurdles:
tried in hood: joined Tracey Barfoot-Saunt, well held in minor event on Flat. *Harry Fry*

TETRAITES STYLE (IRE) 7 b.g. Court Cave (IRE) – Kilmessan (IRE) (Flemensfirth **c101**
(USA)) [2018/19 h106: c19.2g^F c19.2s^3 c16.9s^2 c16.4s^5 c16.4g^5 Apr 5] has had breathing **h–**
operation: maiden hurdler: fair form over fences: left Gillian Boanas after second start:
should be suited by further than 17f: acts on heavy going: tried in tongue tie. *Keith Dalgleish*

TEVIOT PRINCE (IRE) 9 ch.g. Strategic Prince – Nashville Skyline (Nashwan (USA)) **c–**
[2018/19 c20.1g^{pu} May 17] point winner: maiden hurdler: little show in 2 chases. *Gemma* **h–**
Anderson

TEXAN NOMAD 7 ch.g. Nomadic Way (USA) – Texas Belle (IRE) (Glacial Storm **h102**
(USA)) [2018/19 b76: h15.8m^4 h16g^4 h16.3m^5 h19.6m^4 h19d h15.3g^3 h16g^F h15.8g^6 h16s^5
h15.7d h16.5d* Apr 24] leggy gelding: fair handicap hurdler: won at Wincanton in January
and Taunton in April: unproven beyond 2m: acts on good to firm and good to soft going:
wears hood: races off pace. *Ronald Harris*

THAHAB IFRAJ (IRE) 6 ch.g. Frozen Power (IRE) – Penny Rouge (IRE) (Pennekamp (USA)) [2018/19 h107: h18.5g⁴ h18.7m² h16.7g h16.3g h19.8g* h20.5d⁴ h16.5d³ c16.5g⁵ Apr 11] fair handicap hurdler: won at Wincanton in November: 16/1, last of 5 in novice handicap at Huntingdon on chasing debut: stays 2½m: acts on good to firm going: tried in blinkers: usually races close up: should do better as a chaser. *Alexandra Dunn* **c– p h109**

THAMES KNIGHT 7 b.g. Sir Percy – Bermondsey Girl (Bertolini (USA)) [2018/19 h–: h16g² h15.8m* Jul 1] small, close-coupled gelding: fair handicap hurdler: won at Uttoxeter in July: likely to prove best around 2m: acts on good to firm going: tried in cheekpieces. *Jim Boyle* **h100**

THANK YOU BEFORE (FR) 6 b.m. Saddler Maker (IRE) – Before Royale (FR) (Dauphin du Bourg (FR)) [2018/19 b75: h21m³ May 14] made frame in bumpers: 16/1, third in mares maiden at Kempton (5¾ lengths behind Shazzamataz) on hurdling debut. *Gary Moore* **h99**

THAT'S A GIVEN (FR) 5 b.g. Great Pretender (IRE) – Aulne River (FR) (River Mist (USA)) [2018/19 b96: h15.8g³ h15.8g⁴ h19d² h21.4g⁴ h19.8g⁶ Apr 27] bumper winner: fairly useful form over hurdles: won handicap at Wincanton in April: stays 21f: acts on good to soft going. *Philip Hobbs* **h117**

THATS DIGBY 9 ch.g. Cayman Kai (IRE) – Jupiter's Fancy (Jupiter Island) [2018/19 h15.7m h19.9s Mar 3] placed in points: no form over hurdles. *Philip Kirby* **h–**

THAT'S EXACTLY (IRE) 10 ch.m. Bach (IRE) – Maracana (IRE) (Glacial Storm (USA)) [2018/19 h19.2vᵖᵘ Dec 11] unplaced in bumpers: pulled up in mares novice on hurdling debut after very long absence. *Nigel Dunger* **h–**

THAT'S GONNA STING (IRE) 8 b.g. Scorpion (IRE) – Creme d'Arblay (IRE) (Singspiel (IRE)) [2018/19 c69, h–: c24gᵖᵘ h25.8g h23g h21.6m Jul 14] strong gelding: modest handicap hurdler, below form in 2018/19: maiden chaser (often let down by jumping): stays 3m: acts on good to soft going: tried in blinkers: wears tongue tie. *Jeremy Scott* **c– x h56**

THAT'S LIFE (IRE) 7 b.g. Presenting – Leader's Hall (IRE) (Saddlers' Hall (IRE)) [2018/19 h–, b–: h24.3g Oct 29] no form. *Nicky Richards* **h–**

THAT'S THE DEAL (IRE) 15 b.g. Turtle Island (IRE) – Sister Swing (Arctic Lord) [2018/19 c93, h–: c21.2g³ c19.9g⁵ c21.4g⁵ c24g c19.2g c23.6g⁵ c25.6s⁶ c23.6d³ c23.6g³ Jan 11] well-made gelding: lightly-raced hurdler: poor handicap chaser nowadays: stays 25f: acts on good to firm and heavy going: one to treat with caution. *John Cornwall* **c78 § h–**

THATSY (FR) 5 gr.g. Martaline – Rainallday (FR) (Cadoudal (FR)) [2018/19 b16d* Feb 17] €47,000 3-y-o, £130,000 4-y-o: fifth foal: half-brother to French 15f/2m hurdle winner Magway (by Sulamani): dam lightly raced over hurdles in France (second at 17f): point winner: 10/11, looked good prospect when also won maiden bumper at Navan by 1¼ lengths from Multifactorial: sure to progress. *Gordon Elliott, Ireland* **b111 p**

THE ACCOUNTANT 4 ch.g. Dylan Thomas (IRE) – Glorybe (GER) (Monsun (GER)) [2018/19 h16.7m⁴ h15.8s⁶ h17.7g h15.7d Apr 9] dam (h103), 2m hurdle winner, half-sister to useful hurdler/high-class chaser (stayed 21f) Ghizao: little show in 2 starts on Flat: poor form over hurdles: in headgear last 2 starts. *Amy Murphy* **h81**

THE ARTFUL COBBLER 8 gr.g. Saint des Saints (FR) – Serhaaphim (Erhaab (USA)) [2018/19 c118, h–: c26.1gᵖᵘ Nov 17] sturdy gelding: winning hurdler: fairly useful chaser, pulled up sole outing in 2018/19: stayed 29f: acted on heavy going: tried in cheekpieces: usually led: dead. *Henry Daly* **c– h–**

THEATRE ACT 8 ch.m. Act One – Theatre Belle (King's Theatre (IRE)) [2018/19 h84: h20.1g⁴ h16.2m⁴ h18.1m⁵ h20.1g⁵ h19.3g² h20v⁴ h19.9s h19.3mᵖᵘ h17v⁵ Mar 17] leggy, close-coupled mare: poor handicap hurdler: stays 21f: acts on heavy going: wears headgear. *Chris Grant* **h79**

THEATREBAR 11 b.g. King's Theatre (IRE) – Ardenbar (Ardross) [2018/19 c–, h117: h23.1g² h23g* h23g² h23.3s⁶ h20g⁶ h21g h25d h23.3d⁵ h19.7g* Mar 29] good-topped gelding: fairly useful handicap hurdler: won at Worcester in June and Wetherby in March: placed both starts over fences: stays 3m: acts on heavy going: wears tongue tie. *Dan Skelton* **c– h127**

THEATRE EVENING (IRE) 11 b.g. King's Theatre (IRE) – Waydale Hill (Minster Son) [2018/19 c20.2g⁴ Feb 27] point winner: winning hurdler: modest form at best in hunter chases: will stay 3m: acts on good to firm going: tried in tongue tie. *Miss Harriet Brown* **c63 h–**

THEATRE GUIDE (IRE) 12 b.g. King's Theatre (IRE) – Erintante (IRE) (Denel (FR)) **c143**
[2018/19 c147, h–: c23.6d c24.2v c24.2d² c26d² Mar 2] tall gelding: winning hurdler: useful **h–**
handicap chaser nowadays: second in veterans event at Newbury in March: stays 29f, at
least when conditions aren't testing: acts on soft going: wears headgear/tongue tie: usually
races towards rear. *Colin Tizzard*

THEATRE LEGEND 6 b.g. Midnight Legend – Theatre Belle (King's Theatre (IRE)) **h130 p**
[2018/19 b98: h16.8s³ h19.7g³ h16d* h16m* Apr 12] useful-looking gelding: bumper
winner: useful form over hurdles: won handicaps at Wetherby in March and Ayr (by 1½
lengths from Champagne Mystery) in April: open to further improvement. *Chris Grant*

THEATRE MILL (IRE) 11 b.g. King's Theatre (IRE) – River Mill (IRE) (Supreme **c–**
Leader) [2018/19 c115d, h–: c17m c21m^pu Jun 26] workmanlike gelding: winning hurdler: **h–**
fairly useful chaser at best, no form in 2018/19: stays 21f: acts on soft and good to firm
going: has worn hood: wears tongue tie: usually races nearer last than first. *Richenda Ford*

THEATRE MIX 6 gr.m. Fair Mix (IRE) – Theatre Diva (IRE) (King's Theatre (IRE)) **h85**
[2018/19 b–: b16.8m h18.5g⁶ h18.5v⁴ Dec 20] made frame in point: little impact in **b–**
bumpers: modest form over hurdles. *Jackie du Plessis*

THEATRE ROUGE (IRE) 7 b.m. King's Theatre (IRE) – Toulon Rouge (IRE) (Toulon) **h–**
[2018/19 h–: h24g^pu h17.7g Jun 5] fair hurdler at best, lightly raced and no form since
2016/17: usually wears headgear: in tongue tie last 2 starts. *Neil Mulholland*

THEATRE STAGE (IRE) 7 b.g. Gamut (IRE) – Castletown Girl (Bob Back (USA)) **h80**
[2018/19 h87: h23.3d h19.6g⁴ h21.6m^pu Jul 14] poor maiden hurdler: usually races towards
rear. *Evan Williams*

THEATRE TERRITORY (IRE) 9 b.m. King's Theatre (IRE) – Specifiedrisk (IRE) **c134**
(Turtle Island (IRE)) [2018/19 c136, h–: c24.4g² c26g⁴ c24g² c25.1g³ c25g c24.2s* Apr 16] **h–**
useful-looking mare: has had breathing operation: winning hurdler: useful chaser: 4/1-on,
won novice hunter at Exeter in April: much better form when second in novice at
Cheltenham (length behind Ibis du Rheu) on return: stays 3m: acts on heavy going: wears
headgear: usually front runner/races prominently. *Warren Greatrex*

THEATRICAL STAR 13 b.g. King's Theatre (IRE) – Lucy Glitters (Ardross) [2018/19 **c106 x**
c125x, h–: c25.1m⁴ c26.1g May 27] angular gelding: winning hurdler: fairly useful **h–**
handicap chaser, below form in 2018/19: stays 31f: acts on heavy going: has worn
headgear/tongue tie: often let down by jumping. *Colin Tizzard*

THE BANASTOIR (IRE) 10 b.g. Presenting – Kimouna (FR) (Round Sovereign (FR)) **c79**
[2018/19 c–, h58: h20.2g h16.2m⁵ h16.2g² c15.6g⁶ Sep 17] placed in points: modest **h85**
handicap hurdler: poor maiden chaser: stays 2½m: acts on soft and good to firm going.
Lucinda Russell

THE BANNERKINGREBEL (IRE) 6 b.g. Arakan (USA) – One Love (IRE) (Bravefoot) **b115**
[2018/19 b105: b17d² Apr 5] sturdy gelding: has had breathing operation: smart form in
bumpers: second in Grade 2 at Aintree (length behind McFabulous) only outing in 2018/19.
Jamie Snowden

THE BAY BIRCH (IRE) 8 b.m. Beneficial – Tournant Vic (IRE) (Old Vic) [2018/19 **c139**
c125, h77: h19.9g* h15.8g⁶ h24.7g c22.4s³ c20.6g^ur c24.2d^pu c24d* c24.2s c24s* c21.6m* **h108**
Apr 20] compact mare: fair hurdler: won mares novice at Uttoxeter in May: useful handicap
chaser: won mares events at Warwick in February, Bangor in March and Haydock (by 9
lengths from Troubled Soul) in April: stays 25f: acts on good to firm and heavy going: in
tongue tie last 4 starts: usually races off pace, often travels strongly. *Matt Sheppard*

THE BIG BITE (IRE) 6 b.g. Scorpion (IRE) – Thanks Noel (IRE) (Tel Quel (FR)) **h134**
[2018/19 b107: h16s* h15.7v* h16g⁴ h16.4s h20g Apr 6] well-made gelding: useful
bumper performer: similar form over hurdles: won maiden at Chepstow in November and
introductory event at Haydock (by 13 lengths from Demopolis) in December: unproven
beyond 2m: acts on heavy going: usually races close up. *Tom George*

THE BIG GALLOPER (IRE) 5 ch.g. Mahler – Cuiloge Lady (IRE) (Beneficial) **c102 p**
[2018/19 h16.5g^ur h19.9s³ h16g⁵ h19.3g c20s⁵ Mar 9] fifth foal: half-brother to bumper **h100**
winner/useful chaser What A Moment (25f winner) and fair 2m hurdle winner/winning
pointer Important Moment (both by Milan): dam, unraced, closely related to fairly useful
hurdler/useful chaser (stayed 3m) Seven Is My Number: fair form over hurdles: 50/1, fifth
in maiden at Gowran (20 lengths behind Burrows Saint) on chasing debut: bred to stay 3m:
acts on soft going: should do better as a chaser. *Charles Byrnes, Ireland*

THE BIG YIN 5 ch.g. Malinas (GER) – Bright Spangle (IRE) (General Monash (USA)) **b94**
[2018/19 b15.8v² Mar 16] sixth foal: half-brother to modest hurdler/chaser Festival Dreams
(2½m-3m winner, by Largesse), bumper winner Go Annie (by Proclamation) and a
winning pointer by Thowra: dam 6f winner who stayed 1½m: 25/1, second in bumper at
Uttoxeter (neck behind Moroder). *Jo Davis*

THE BLACK MCGUIGAN (IRE) 6 b.g. Mahler – Castle Island Lass (IRE) (Turtle **h70**
Island (IRE)) [2018/19 h21.6g⁴ Jul 22] placed in Irish point: 25/1, fourth in maiden at
Newton Abbot (29½ lengths behind Push The Tempo) on hurdling debut. *Evan Williams*

THE BLACK SQUIRREL (IRE) 6 br.g. Craigsteel – Terra Lucida (IRE) (Alderbrook) **h103**
[2018/19 h97, b96: h21.4m² h19.9g² h25.8gᵖᵘ h26.5g⁶ Jul 22] runner-up in point: bumper
winner: fair maiden hurdler: stays 21f: acts on good to firm going: often leads.
Warren Greatrex

THE BLAME GAME (IRE) 5 b.g. Getaway (GER) – Tribal Princess (IRE) **b85**
(Namaqualand (USA)) [2018/19 b16.2g² b16.5⁵ b16.4m² Mar 28] €4,500 3-y-o: sixth
foal: half-brother to bumper winner Top Man Marty (by Westerner) and a winning pointer
by Old Vic: dam (c96/h98), 2m/2¼m hurdle/chase winner, also 1½m winner on Flat: fair
form in bumpers: left M. A. Gunn after second start. *James Ewart*

THE BLUE BOMBER 7 b.g. Stimulation (IRE) – Mar Blue (FR) (Marju (IRE)) **h91**
[2018/19 h94: h16.7g⁴ h15.8g^F May 22] modest handicap hurdler: best form around 2m:
acted on soft going: tried in hood: usually raced prominently, often travelled strongly:
dead. *Caroline Fryer*

THE BOO BOX (IRE) 6 b.g. Scorpion (IRE) – High Court Action (IRE) (Witness Box **h60**
(USA)) [2018/19 b16.2g b16.4d h19.3g h20.5s⁶ h20.6d Apr 6] poor form in bumpers/ **b58**
novice hurdles. *Donald Whillans*

THE BOOGIEMAN 5 b.g. Delegator – Great Quest (IRE) (Montjeu (IRE)) [2018/19 **b—**
b16d Dec 13] well held in bumper. *Richard Bandey*

THE BOOLA BEE (IRE) 6 b.m. Arcadio (GER) – Hy Kate (IRE) (Over The River **c80**
(FR)) [2018/19 b16g⁶ h19.9g⁴ h18.5m⁵ h18.5g h27m c15.7m³ c20d³ c24vᵖᵘ c17sᵖᵘ h19s **h79**
c21g⁴ Apr 20] £2,000 5-y-o: sparely-made mare: has had breathing operation: sixth foal: **b—**
half-sister to winning pointers by Craigsteel and Double Eclipse: dam placed in point:
point winner: well beaten in mares chase: poor form over hurdles/in chases: stays 2½m:
acts on good to soft going: usually wears headgear: usually races in rear. *Nigel Hawke*

THE BOOM IS BACK (IRE) 7 b.g. Publisher (USA) – Wild Coast (IRE) (Gothland **c78**
(FR)) [2018/19 h—: h16d h19.5g c23.6s c15.5s c24.2vᵖᵘ c23.8s Apr 7] lengthy gelding: **h—**
Irish point winner: poor form over hurdles/in chases: tried in cheekpieces. *Christian Williams*

THE BOSS'S DREAM (IRE) 11 b.g. Luso – Mrs Kick (IRE) (Supreme Leader) **c109**
[2018/19 c114, h83: c22.5d⁶ c24g⁵ c25.2sᵘʳ c23.6d⁵ c24v³ c23.5v* c26.1d² c29.2d⁴ c24d⁵ **h—**
Mar 30] workmanlike gelding: has had breathing operation: winning hurdler: fair handicap
chaser: won at Lingfield in February: best up to 3¼m: acts on heavy going: has worn
headgear/tongue tie, including in 2018/19: usually races prominently. *Neil King*

THE BOTTOM BAR (IRE) 7 br.g. Stowaway – Serenade Leader (IRE) (Supreme **c120**
Leader) [2018/19 h122p, b91: h23s² h20m³ h19.8v² c20sᵘʳ c20s⁶ c20d³ c19.4g⁴ Apr 14] **h121**
medium-sized gelding: has had breathing operation: fairly useful hurdler: similar form
over fences: stays 23f: acts on heavy going. *Nicky Henderson*

THE BROTHERS (IRE) 6 b.g. Flemensfirth (USA) – Laboc (Rymer) [2018/19 h109, **h103**
b73: h21.6g h23.6g⁴ h21.4g³ h15.3d⁵ h19.8s⁵ h21.4g⁶ h21.6d Apr 9] lengthy gelding: fair
maiden hurdler: stays 21f: acts on heavy going. *Colin Tizzard*

THE BUNNYMAN 5 b.g. Authorized (IRE) – Linnet (GER) (Dr Fong (USA)) [2018/19 **h108**
b83: h19.9v^F h19.7dᵖᵘ Mar 9] unplaced in bumper: fair form over hurdles: held in third
when fell last in maiden won by Captain Drake at Uttoxeter. *Emma Lavelle*

THE BUTCHER SAID (IRE) 6 b.g. Robin des Champs (FR) – Georgina Valleya (IRE) **h108**
(King's Theatre (IRE)) [2018/19 h80p, b91: h16.7v⁶ h20.6m² Apr 21] rangy gelding: has
had breathing operation: fair form over hurdles: best effort when second in maiden at
Market Rasen (wore hood/tongue tie): left Warren Greatrex after first start. *Olly Murphy*

THE CANNISTER MAN (IRE) 7 b.g. Arakan (USA) – Ladyrosaro (IRE) (Roselier **h118**
(FR)) [2018/19 h114, b—: h15.5g⁶ h15.8g⁴ h19.2v⁵ Mar 16] runner-up in Irish point: fairly
useful handicap hurdler: stays 2¼m: acts on heavy going: wears hood. *Sam Thomas*

THE

THE CAPTAIN (IRE) 6 b.g. Millenary – Quilt (Terimon) [2018/19 h97p: h15.7g⁵ **c94** h15.8g³ h20.3g h20d c15.9m³ c15.9m³ c19.9g⁴ c20.2gᵖᵘ Mar 8] sturdy gelding: has had **h80** breathing operation: modest form over hurdles/fences: should be suited by 2½m+: acts on good to firm going: sometimes in headgear: races prominently. *Caroline Bailey*

THE CAPTAINS INN (IRE) 5 b.g. Flemensfirth (USA) – Killeen (IRE) (Bob Back **h125 p** (USA)) [2018/19 b16d⁶ h20.5d⁴ h19.9v* h24.7dᵖᵘ Apr 5] £220,000 4-y-o: tall gelding: **b85** fourth foal: dam (h88), placed at 2½m over hurdles, sister to fairly useful hurdler (stayed 21f) Bobbina and half-sister to useful hurdler (stayed 3¼m) Glacial Sunset: runner-up in Irish point: sixth in bumper at Warwick: fairly useful form over hurdles: won novices at Leicester in January and Uttoxeter in March: will prove suited to 3m: remains with potential. *Ben Pauling*

THE CASHEL MAN (IRE) 7 b.g. High Chaparral (IRE) – Hadarama (IRE) (Sinndar **h125** (IRE)) [2018/19 h21d² h23.3d² h21s² Mar 16] dam half-sister to fairly useful hurdler (stayed 3m) Handazan: useful on Flat, stays 2¼m: fairly useful form over hurdles: best effort when second in novice at Kempton in March. *Nicky Henderson*

THE CELTIC MACHINE 4 b.g. Rip Van Winkle (IRE) – Lyra's Daemon (Singspiel **b55** (IRE)) [2018/19 b14d⁶ Nov 29] well beaten in bumper: little impact on Flat. *Pat Phelan*

THE CHARACTER (IRE) 8 b.g. Bushranger (IRE) – Operissimo (Singspiel (IRE)) **h103** [2018/19 h16.2s⁶ h15.7d⁴ h16.4m h16g Apr 26] fair handicap hurdler: raced around 2m: acts on good to soft going. *Donald McCain*

THE CITY COBBLER 4 b.f. Mount Nelson – Galante (FR) (Librettist (USA)) [2018/19 **b–** b15.8dʳᵒ b16.7d Apr 26] first foal: dam French maiden (placed at 1m): no form in bumpers. *Paul Webber*

THECLOCKISTICKING (IRE) 7 br.g. Gamut (IRE) – Curragheen (IRE) (Sadler's **c132 p** Wells (USA)) [2018/19 h137, b94: h20g⁴ h16.7g² h19.5d⁵ h23.9d⁴ c24.2g* c24g² h24d⁶ **h133** h24.7g⁵ Apr 6] tall gelding: useful handicap hurdler: sixth in Pertemps Final at Cheltenham (9¼ lengths behind Sire du Berlais) in March: similar form over fences: won 2-runner maiden at Fakenham in November: second in December Novices' Chase at Doncaster (17 lengths behind Rocky's Treasure): likely to stay long distances: acts on good to soft going: usually front runner/races prominently: open to further improvement as a chaser. *Stuart Edmunds*

THE CLOCK LEARY (IRE) 11 b.g. Helissio (FR) – Kiwi Babe (Karinga Bay) **c113** [2018/19 c128, h–: c21.2g⁴ c23.8g⁴ c20g c24.1g Aug 3] sturdy gelding: winning hurdler: **h–** fairly useful handicap chaser, below form in 2018/19: stays 3m: acts on heavy going: has worn headgear: tried in tongue tie: often beaten. *Donald McCain*

THE COB (IRE) 5 b.g. Let The Lion Roar – Millenium Love (IRE) (Great Commotion **b88** (USA)) [2018/19 b15.8v² b15.8v³ b17d Apr 5] €13,000 3-y-o: good-topped gelding: sixth foal: closely related to fairly useful hurdler Seeyouallincoppers (2m-2½m winner, by Saffron Walden) and half-brother to a winner on Flat by Tendulkar: dam 5f winner: fair form in bumpers: best effort when second at Ffos Las on debut. *Ben Pauling*

THE COMPELLER (IRE) 7 b.g. Lawman (FR) – Mark Too (IRE) (Mark of Esteem **h91** (IRE)) [2018/19 h91: h16.2g* Jun 23] modest handicap hurdler: won at Perth sole outing in 2018/19: best form at 2m: acts on soft going: tried in cheekpieces: in tongue tie last 5 starts. *Lucinda Russell*

THE CONDITIONAL (IRE) 7 b.g. Kalanisi (IRE) – Gorrie Vale (IRE) (Saddlers' Hall **c130** (IRE)) [2018/19 h24m² c20d⁴ c24.6gᶠ c25.2g⁴ c24d⁶ c20d⁵ c24d⁴ Mar 10] €9,000 3-y-o: **h119** fourth foal: half-brother to a winning pointer by Beneficial: dam, unraced, out of half-sister to smart 2m hurdler Cardinal Hill: point winner: fairly useful form over hurdles: useful form in chases: stays 25f: acts on good to firm and heavy going: in tongue tie last 2 starts. *Martin Hassett, Ireland*

THE CON MAN (IRE) 6 b.g. Oscar (IRE) – Phillis Hill (Karinga Bay) [2018/19 h20v* **h119 p** Dec 2] €50,000 3-y-o, £70,000 5-y-o: closely related to 2 winners by Old Vic, including bumper winner/fairly useful hurdler Miles To Memphis (2m-2¼m winner), stays 3m, and half-brother to 3 winners, including useful hurdler/chaser Duel At Dawn (23f/3m winner, by Presenting): dam (b64) ran once in bumper: Irish point winner: 3/1, looked good prospect when won novice at Carlisle (by 5 lengths from Garrettstown) on hurdling debut: sure to progress. *Donald McCain*

THE CONN (IRE) 9 b.g. Milan – Grandy Invader (IRE) (Presenting) [2018/19 h76: **h55** h23.3v⁵ h24d Apr 6] poor maiden hurdler: will stay long distances: acts on soft going: tried in headgear/tongue tie: usually races off pace. *Sheena Walton*

836

THE CRAFTY TOUCH (IRE) 6 ch.m. Touch of Land (FR) – Dicharachera (Mark of **h90 p**
Esteem (IRE)) [2018/19 h15.8g⁴ Apr 11] fourth foal: dam 1m winner who stayed 1¼m:
Irish point winner: 7/1, fourth in mares maiden at Huntingdon (7¾ lengths behind Saumur)
on hurdling debut: open to improvement. *Jonjo O'Neill*

THE CRAZED MOON (IRE) 7 b.m. Yeats (IRE) – Rose Gallery (FR) (Gallery of **h111**
Zurich (IRE)) [2018/19 h101: h16g⁵ h19.7g⁵ h16.7s* h15.8v* h15.8v* h16.4d⁵ Mar 5]
Irish point winner: fair handicap hurdler: won at Bangor (conditionals) and Uttoxeter
(novice) in December, and again at Uttoxeter (conditionals) in January: unproven beyond
17f: acts on heavy going. *Henry Oliver*

THE CROONER (FR) 4 gr.g. Martaline – Viva Maria (FR) (Kendor (FR)) [2018/19 **h105**
h17.4s⁶ h17.4s h16s³ h18.5s³ h16g⁶ Apr 26] seventh foal: half-brother to 3 winners,
including French 17f-19f hurdle winner Art Militaire (by Victory Note): dam 6f winner:
fair maiden hurdler: left Francois Nicolle after second start: unproven beyond 17f: acts on
soft going. *Venetia Williams*

THE CRUIX (IRE) 4 ch.g. Galileo (IRE) – Walklikeanegyptian (IRE) (Danehill (USA)) **b78**
[2018/19 b16g⁴ Feb 15] 16/1, fourth in maiden bumper at Fakenham (12¼ lengths behind
Penny Mallow). *Dean Ivory*

THE CULL BANK (IRE) 5 b.m. Yeats (IRE) – Creme d'Arblay (IRE) (Singspiel (IRE)) **h125**
[2018/19 h17.7v* h20.3g² Apr 18] €5,000 3-y-o, £50,000 4-y-o: fourth foal: half-
sister to modest 3m hurdle winner That's Gonna Sting (by Scorpion): dam (h102) 2m-3m
hurdle winner: fairly useful form over hurdles: won mares novices at
Fontwell in February and Plumpton in March: second in listed race at Cheltenham (10
lengths behind Indefatigable) in April. *Alan King*

THE DARLEY LAMA (IRE) 5 b.g. Carlotamix (FR) – Last Sunrise (IRE) (Shahanndeh) **b77**
[2018/19 b15.7g ab15.3g³ ab16s³ b15.8g⁴ Apr 22] compact gelding: modest form in
bumpers: tried in hood. *Charlie Mann*

THE DAWN MAN (IRE) 8 b.g. Milan – Calling Classy (IRE) (Good Thyne (USA)) **c85**
[2018/19 c70, h107: h20gᵖᵘ c20gᵖᵘ c24d⁴ c19.2g⁴ h20.3s⁷ Mar 18] Irish point winner: **h93**
modest maiden hurdler: similar form in chases: stays 2½m: acts on soft going: tried in
hood. *Henry Oliver*

THE DELLERCHECKOUT (IRE) 6 b.g. Getaway (GER) – Loreley (IRE) (Oscar **c123**
(IRE)) [2018/19 h114: h21g h21.2d³ c20.2g⁵ c23d* c23.6mᵖᵘ Apr 22] useful-looking **h118**
gelding: has had breathing operation: fairly useful form over hurdles: similar form over
fences: won novice handicap at Taunton in February: stays 23f: acts on soft going: in
blinkers last 2 starts: usually in tongue tie. *Paul Nicholls*

THE DETAINEE 6 b.g. Aqlaam – Jakarta Jade (IRE) (Royal Abjar (USA)) [2018/19 **h113**
h109: h15.3m³ h20.2g² h19.9g h21.7g⁵ h21.6d Apr 9] fair maiden hurdler: stays 2½m: best
form on good going: wears cheekpieces: usually front runner/races prominently.
Neil Mulholland

THE DEVILS DROP (IRE) 6 b.g. Court Cave (IRE) – Concernforkillen (IRE) (Anshan) **h134**
[2018/19 h111: h24g* h23g* h24g* Aug 19] has had breathing operation: runner-up in
Irish point winner: useful hurdler: won all 3 starts in 2018/19, maiden at Southwell in June, novice
at Worcester in July and handicap at Southwell in August: stays 3m: acts on soft going:
seemed sure to go on improving, but wasn't seen out again. *Alan King*

THEDFACTOR (IRE) 10 b.g. Kalanisi (IRE) – Insan Magic (IRE) (Insan (USA)) **c–**
[2018/19 c84?: c20.1g⁵ c24.2gᵖᵘ Nov 9] maiden chaser, no form in 2018/19: in cheekpieces
last 5 starts: tried in tongue tie. *Jane Walton*

THE DOMINO EFFECT (IRE) 5 b.g. Oscar (IRE) – Lively Lass (IRE) (Definite **b85**
Article) [2018/19 b15.7g⁴ Mar 4] €95,000 3-y-o: third foal: dam, bumper winner/winning
pointer, sister to fairly useful hurdler/fair chaser (stayed 3m) Model County Lass: 7/1,
fourth in bumper at Southwell (7¼ lengths behind San Rumoldo). *Emma Lavelle*

THE DOORMAN (IRE) 10 b.g. King's Theatre (IRE) – Amber Light (IRE) (Anshan) **c– x**
[2018/19 c107x, h109§: c24.2gᵖᵘ h20.1mᶠ Jun 24] fair hurdler/chaser at best: barely stayed **h– §**
25f: acted on soft and good to firm going: wore cheekpieces/tongue tie: often let down by
jumping/attitude: dead. *Ben Haslam*

THEDRINKYMEISTER (IRE) 10 b.g. Heron Island (IRE) – Keel Row (Relkino) **c124 §**
[2018/19 c127§, h–: c23.4g² c24.2d⁶ c22.6sᵖᵘ Mar 11] rangy gelding: winning hurdler: **h–**
fairly useful handicap chaser: stays 3m: acts on heavy going: wears headgear: usually races
close up: ungenuine. *Henry Daly*

THE DRONE (IRE) 8 b.g. Mahler – Liberess (IRE) (Saddlers' Hall (IRE)) [2018/19 **c103** h22m* h26.4m² h2꜀.7g³ h24.5g⁵ c21.2d³ h24d* Apr 24] unplaced in 2 Irish points: fair **h114** form over hurdles: won novice at Stratford in May and handicap at Southwell in April: 11/4, third in novice handicap at Fakenham (12¼ lengths behind Craigmor) on chasing debut: stays 3¼m: acts on good to firm and good to soft going: usually races close up. *Alex Hales*

THE DRUIDS NEPHEW (IRE) 12 b.g. King's Theatre (IRE) – Gifted (Shareef Dancer **c–** (USA)) [2018/19 c26.3dᵖᵘ Jan 1] smallish gelding: winning hurdler: very smart chaser at **h–** best, pulled up sole outing in 2018/19 after long absence: stays 29f: acts on heavy going: wears headgear. *Neil Mulholland*

THE DUBAI WAY (IRE) 7 b.g. Dubai Destination (USA) – Britway Lady (IRE) **c120** (Norwich) [2018/19 h123, b97: c15.7g⁴ c16s⁵ c16.3s² h16d c19.7d* Mar 18] good-topped **h–** gelding: winning hurdler: fairly useful form over fences: won novice handicap at Plumpton in March: left Harry Whittington after fourth start: stays 2½m: acts on heavy going: tried in cheekpieces. *Charlie Mann*

THE EAGLEHASLANDED (IRE) 9 b.g. Milan – Vallee Doree (FR) (Neverneyev **h127** (USA)) [2018/19 h–: h23.9d h23.9g⁵ h24g h24d³ h21.4g⁴ Feb 16] useful-looking gelding: point winner: fairly useful handicap hurdler: stays 25f: acts on heavy going: wears headgear/tongue tie. *Paul Nicholls*

THE EAGLE'S NEST (IRE) 5 ch.g. Lope de Vega (IRE) – Follow My Lead (Night **h–** Shift (USA)) [2018/19 h16.6g⁵ Jan 25] fairly useful on Flat, stays 1¼m: in tongue strap, well beaten in novice on hurdling debut. *Rae Guest*

THE ENCHANTER (FR) 5 gr.g. Martaline – Fille Formidable (USA) (Trempolino **b–** (USA)) [2018/19 b16s Mar 16] well beaten in maiden bumper. *Sam Thomas*

THE FINAL WHISTLE (IRE) 6 ch.g. Approve (IRE) – Fairnilee (Selkirk (USA)) **h82** [2018/19 h–, b–: h15.8g h20sᵖᵘ h19g Apr 25] poor form over hurdles: tried in cheekpieces. *Sheila Lewis*

THE FLAME (IRE) 6 b.g. Flemensfirth (USA) – Molly Round (IRE) (Old Vic) [2018/19 **c120** h93: h24g* h22mᵖᵘ h23.9m⁶ h23.3g c19.4m² c25.8v⁴ Oct 12] fair handicap **h106** hurdler: won at Southwell in May: fairly useful form over fences: won novice handicap at Newton Abbot in September: stayed 3¼m: acted on heavy and good to firm going: tried in hood/tongue tie: front runner/raced prominently: dead. *Jonjo O'Neill*

THEFLICKERINGLIGHT (IRE) 5 b.m. Flemensfirth (USA) – Turtle Lamp (IRE) **b79** (Turtle Island (IRE)) [2018/19 b16.8v² b16.4m⁵ Mar 28] sixth foal: sister to bumper winner Acronym and half-sister to fairly useful chaser The Cobbler Swayne (2½m winner, by Milan): dam unraced half-sister to smart hurdler/very smart chaser (stayed 3m) Colonel Braxton: won both starts in Irish points: modest form in bumpers. *Philip Kirby*

THEFLYINGPORTRAIT (IRE) 10 gr.g. Portrait Gallery (IRE) – Skule Hill Lass **c138** (IRE) (Close Conflict (USA)) [2018/19 c136, h–: c16m c15.8g⁴ c17m² c17.3s⁵ c17.1m³ **h–** c15.2m* c15.8g² c15.2d* c16.3d c15.8d c16g⁴ Apr 25] workmanlike gelding: winning hurdler: useful handicap chaser: won at Wetherby in October and November (by 14 lengths from Special Catch): stays 2½m: acts on good to firm and heavy going: tried in cheekpieces: wears tongue tie. *Jennie Candlish*

THE FLYING SOFA (FR) 6 b.g. Sholokhov (IRE) – La Julie (IRE) (Peintre Celebre **h119** (USA)) [2018/19 b107: h17.7s³ h15.9s² h15.9g² h16.4s h15.3g² h15.9g* Apr 21] compact gelding: useful bumper performer: fairly useful form over hurdles: won maiden at Plumpton in April: unproven beyond 2m: acts on soft going. *Gary Moore*

THE FRENCH HORSE (FR) 5 b.g. Fuisse (FR) – Malandra (Mtoto) [2018/19 b16.8d⁶ **b–** Mar 24] well held in bumper. *Jonjo O'Neill*

THE FRESH PRINCE (IRE) 9 b.g. Robin des Pres (FR) – Hayley Cometh (IRE) **c123** (Supreme Leader) [2018/19 c113, h–: c19.7g* c22.6g⁴ Aug 23] rangy gelding: has had **h–** breathing operation: winning hurdler: fairly useful handicap chaser: won at Plumpton in May: stays easy 2¾m: acts on heavy going: front runner/races prominently. *Oliver Sherwood*

THEFRIENDLYGREMLIN 11 b.g. Vinnie Roe (IRE) – Queens Fantasy (Grand Lodge **c–** (USA)) [2018/19 c–, h–§: h19.2g h20gᵖᵘ Sep 11] of little account nowadays: has worn **h– §** headgear: ungenuine. *Tracey Leeson*

THEGALLANTWAY (IRE) 6 b.g. Stowaway – Imogens Fancy (IRE) (Taipan (IRE)) **b89**
[2018/19 b16.8s³ b16d Mar 28] €6,000 3-y-o, £22,000 5-y-o: second foal: brother to a
winning pointer: dam (h90) maiden hurdler (stayed 3m): won Irish point on debut: fair
form in bumpers: better effort when third at Sedgefield in March. *Fergal O'Brien*

THE GALLOPING BEAR 6 b.g. Shantou (USA) – Cheshire Kat (King's Theatre **b78**
(IRE)) [2018/19 b16.8s⁵ Apr 16] second in point bumper: 8/1, fifth in maiden bumper at
Exeter (10½ lengths behind Merchant House). *B. Clarke*

THE GAME CHANGER (IRE) 10 b.g. Arcadio (GER) – Gilt Ridden (IRE) (Heron **c137**
Island (IRE)) [2018/19 c140, h134: h20m* h16g c19.5m² h16spu c18.2gur h19f Aug 23] tall **h139**
gelding: useful hurdler: won minor event at Down Royal (by ½ length from Flaxen Flare)
in June: useful chaser nowadays: second in minor event at Limerick (12 lengths behind
Neverushacon) in July: stays 2½m: acts on good to firm and heavy going: has worn
headgear, including in 2018/19: usually wears tongue tie: often leads. *Gordon Elliott,
Ireland*

THE GAME IS A FOOT (IRE) 12 b.g. Oscar (IRE) – Cooksgrove Rosie (IRE)
(Mandalus) [2018/19 h110: h16s³ Jan 4] tall gelding: placed in points: fair handicap
hurdler: stays 21f: acts on heavy going: tried in blinkers: races towards rear. *Zoe Davison* **h96**

THE GATECHECKER (IRE) 9 b.g. Classic Cliche (IRE) – Criaire Princess (IRE) **c134 x**
(Tidaro (USA)) [2018/19 c23g c22.2mro h22.4m⁵ h24g² c24s* h24g* c28s³ h24g h24g **h121**
h24g* h22.5g h24v⁵ Mar 21] fairly useful handicap hurdler: won at Limerick in October
and Thurles in February: useful handicap chaser: won at Listowel in September: third in
Cork National (2 lengths behind Out Sam) in November: stays 3½m: acts on heavy going:
wears headgear: usually races towards rear: temperament under suspicion (ran out second
start), and usually let down by jumping over fences. *M. Hourigan, Ireland*

THE GEEGEEZ GEEGEE (IRE) 10 b.g. Beneficial – Shanann Lady (IRE) (Anshan) **c–**
[2018/19 c121, h–: c21.2d c21.2d⁵ h23.4d Jan 1] fair hurdler/fairly useful chaser at best, no **h–**
form in 2018/19: wears headgear/tongue tie. *Olly Murphy*

THE GIPPER (IRE) 9 b.g. King's Theatre (IRE) – Merrill Gaye (IRE) (Roselier (FR)) **c–**
[2018/19 c118, h–: h16g h16v* h15.8v* h16.4v⁶ h15.7m Apr 20] sturdy gelding: fairly **h124**
useful handicap hurdler: won at Lingfield and Ffos Las in December: maiden chaser:
unproven beyond 2m: acts on heavy going: usually races prominently. *Evan Williams*

THEGIRLFROMMILAN (IRE) 9 b.m. Milan – Legendsofthefall (IRE) (Arctic Lord) **c98**
[2018/19 c91, h–: c26g² c23.6g² Apr 26] good-topped mare: prolific point winner: maiden **h–**
hurdler: modest form in chases: will stay beyond 3¼m: acts on heavy going: tried in
cheekpieces. *D. C. Gibbs*

THE GLANCING QUEEN (IRE) 5 b.m. Jeremy (USA) – Glancing (IRE) (Kayf Tara) **b110**
[2018/19 b16.4g* b15.7s³ b16.4s⁵ b17d* Apr 4] €8,500 3-y-o, £80,000 4-y-o: sturdy mare:
second foal: dam (h75), placed in bumper, closely related to fairly useful hurdler/useful
chaser (stayed 21f) Operating: Irish point winner: useful form in bumpers: won listed
mares event at Cheltenham (by 1¼ lengths from Mega Yeats) in November and Nickel
Coin Mares' National Hunt Flat Race at Aintree (by 2¼ lengths from Minella Melody) in
April: will stay 2½m. *Alan King*

Goffs UK Nickel Coin Mares' Standard Open National Hunt Flat, Aintree—
The Glancing Queen looks a smart prospect as she proves too strong for the Irish-trained favourite
Minella Melody (No.9)

THE GO TOU MAN (IRE) 6 b.g. Shantou (USA) – Golan Lady (IRE) (Golan (IRE))   c–
[2018/19 h105, b87: h21.6g h20.3g^2 h19.7g h20.5g^6 c23d^{pu} Dec 30] fair maiden hurdler: **h107**
pulled up in novice handicap on chasing debut: stays 2½m: acts on soft going: tried in
cheekpieces: front runner/races prominently. *Harry Whittington*

THE GRAND VISIR 5 b.g. Frankel – Piping (IRE) (Montjeu (IRE)) [2018/19 h17s^{ur} **h99 p**
h16.6g^4 Jan 25] useful on Flat, stays 2m: modest form when fourth in maiden at Doncaster
(in tongue tie) on completed start over hurdles: capable of better. *Ian Williams*

THE GREEN OGRE 9 b.g. Dubai Destination (USA) – Takegawa (Giant's Causeway   c–
(USA)) [2018/19 c–, h109: h16.6g^3 h15.5g Jan 10] workmanlike gelding: fair handicap   **h89**
hurdler, below form in 2018/19: winning chaser: stayed 19f: acted on heavy going: wore
blinkers prior to final season: dead. *Alastair Ralph*

THE GREENVET (IRE) 9 b.g. Acrobat (IRE) – Glacial Air (IRE) (Glacial Storm   c–
(USA)) [2018/19 c–, h84: h23.1d Apr 9] has had breathing operation: winning pointer: h–
maiden hurdler: failed to complete only chase start: wears cheekpieces: tried in tongue tie.
Laura Young

THE GRINDER (IRE) 7 b.g. Arcadio (GER) – Bincas Beauty (IRE) (Kayf Tara)   **h91**
[2018/19 h102: h18.6g^4 h20g h16.7m h18.7g h18.6g^{pu} Nov 8] in frame completed start in
Irish points: modest maiden hurdler: stays 21f: best form on good going. *Nick Kent*

THE GROOVE 6 b.g. Azamour (IRE) – Dance East (Shamardal (USA)) [2018/19 h–:   h–
h15.8g Nov 2] smallish gelding: fair on Flat, stays 8.5f: little impact over hurdles: tried in
headgear/tongue tie: temperament under suspicion. *David Evans*

THE GROOVY HOOVY 7 b.g. Sulamani (IRE) – Kingennie (Dunbeath (USA))   **h100**
[2018/19 h96, b90: h20.7g^{pu} h20.3g* h21.7g^6 h23.9d^{pu} h20.7d h24d^4 Apr 24] has had
breathing operations: fair handicap hurdler: won novice event at Southwell in October:
should stay further than 2½m: acts on soft going: tried in cheekpieces. *Oliver Sherwood*

THE GUNNER MURPHY (IRE) 6 br.g. Oscar (IRE) – River Finn (IRE) (Luso)   **h132**
[2018/19 h–p, b106: h22g^2 h16s^3 h20d^3 h24d^3 Apr 23] useful bumper performer: similar
standard over hurdles: third in novice handicap at Fairyhouse (3¼ lengths behind Ronald
Pump) in April: stays 3m: acts on good to soft going: tried in cheekpieces: wears tongue tie.
Joseph Patrick O'Brien, Ireland

THE HAPPY CHAPPY (IRE) 8 b.g. Flemensfirth (USA) – Native Design (IRE) (Be   **c103**
My Native (USA)) [2018/19 c120, h108: c26.1g c24.2g^4 c25.6g c22.7m^6 c30.7d^2 c26m^3 h–
c30.7s^{pu} Apr 16] lengthy, angular gelding: has had breathing operation: winning hurdler:
fair handicap chaser nowadays: stays 31f: acts on soft and good to firm going: in headgear
last 4 starts: wears tongue tie: lazy. *Sarah Humphrey*

THE HARD SHOULDER (IRE) 8 gr.g. Cloudings (IRE) – Our Witness (IRE)   h–
(Witness Box (USA)) [2018/19 h–, b–: h16.2g^6 May 27] has had breathing operation: little
impact in bumpers/over hurdles: tried in tongue tie. *Chris Grant*

THE HERDS GARDEN 10 b.g. Multiplex – Eternal Legacy (IRE) (Monashee Mountain   c–
(USA)) [2018/19 c–, h92: c17.4g^F h16.8s^4 h16.7s^2 h15.7g* h16.2g^3 h16.6g^3 h18.1d^2 Apr 8]   **h110**
fair handicap hurdler nowadays: won at Catterick in January: maiden chaser: stays 2½m:
acts on soft and good to firm going: has worn headgear, including last 5 starts: has worn
tongue tie: front runner/races prominently. *Donald McCain*

THE HIKING VIKING 6 b.g. Beat Hollow – Swaythe (USA) (Swain (IRE)) [2018/19   c–
h–: c16d^F Jan 2] well held in bumper/novice hurdle: beaten when fell 4 out in novice at   h–
Hereford on chasing debut: in hood last 2 starts. *Paul Webber*

THE HOLLOW CHAP (IRE) 5 ch.g. Beat Hollow – An Banog (IRE) (Anshan)   **h78**
[2018/19 h20g^6 h17s Dec 16] Irish point winner: poor form over hurdles: wears hood.
Rose Dobbin

THE HOLLOW GINGE (IRE) 6 b.g. Oscar (IRE) – Some Gem (IRE) (Flemensfirth   **h124**
(USA)) [2018/19 h118: h23.3s^2 h24.7g^4 h22.8v* h23.4s Feb 2] leggy gelding: fairly useful
handicap hurdler: won at Haydock in December: stays 25f: acts on heavy going. *Nigel
Twiston-Davies*

THE HORSECHESNUT (IRE) 11 ch.g. Definite Article – Ballinahowliss (IRE)   **c95**
(Supreme Leader) [2018/19 c–, h–: c21.5v^2 c21.5s^6 h24.3s* c24.2v* Mar 14] modest   **h98**
hurdler nowadays: won handicap at Ayr in March: modest handicap chaser: won novice
event at Hexham later in March: left David M. O'Brien after second start: stays 3m: best
form on soft/heavy going: has worn cheekpieces, including in 2018/19: wears tongue tie.
Jennie Candlish

THE IBBSTER (IRE) 9 b.g. Shantou (USA) – Annalisa (IRE) (Rhoman Rule (USA)) **h–**
[2018/19 h–: h19s⁵ h18.5d h23.9dᵖᵘ h19.7gᵖᵘ Mar 26] point winner: no form over hurdles: in headgear last 2 starts. *Brian Forsey*

THEINVAL (FR) 9 b.g. Smadoun (FR) – Kinevees (FR) (Hard Leaf (FR)) [2018/19 c148, **c119** h–: c16.8g c16.3d³ c20.2g⁶ Jan 5] sturdy gelding: winning hurdler: smart handicap chaser, **h–** well below best in 2018/19: stays 21f: acts on soft going: wears cheekpieces. *Nicky Henderson*

THE JAM MAN (IRE) 6 br.g. Papal Bull – Kathy Jet (USA) (Singspiel (IRE)) [2018/19 **c–** h107: h23.3g* h21.7d² h20.3g* c17d⁶ c17d c16.3s h20s² c16.3gᶠ h20d c20sᵖᵘ Apr 5] **h120** unplaced completed start in points: fairly useful handicap hurdler: won at Hexham in June and Southwell in September: no form in chases: stays 25f: acts on heavy going: usually races off pace. *Ronan M. P. McNally, Ireland*

THE JUGOPOLIST (IRE) 12 b.g. Oscar (IRE) – Chance My Native (IRE) (Be My **c77 §** Native (USA)) [2018/19 c56§, h–: c24d c22.5m² c20.3g c16g c24g⁴ c21.4gᵘʳ c20.9sᵖᵘ **h–** c19.9d c24s c23.9d⁶ c22.7f⁶ c23.6d* c23.6g⁶ Apr 11] lengthy, angular gelding: winning hurdler: poor handicap chaser nowadays: won at Huntingdon in March: stays 3¼m: acts on good to firm and heavy going: wears headgear: temperamental. *John Cornwall*

THE JUNGLE VIP 4 b.g. Leroidesanimaux (BRZ) – Alakananda (Hernando (FR)) **h–** [2018/19 h16.5gᵖᵘ h16.7mᵖᵘ Jun 22] modest maiden on Flat, stays 1¼m: no form over hurdles: wears tongue tie. *Amy Murphy*

THE JUNIOR MAN (IRE) 8 b.g. Darsi (FR) – Pear Tart (IRE) (Rock Hopper) [2018/19 **h–** h–: h24sᵖᵘ h27sᵖᵘ Feb 21] has had breathing operation: third on completed start in Irish points: no form over hurdles: in cheekpieces last 3 starts, tongue tied last 2. *John Norton*

THE KID 8 b.g. High Chaparral (IRE) – Shine Like A Star (Fantastic Light (USA)) **h76** [2018/19 h87: h18.5g⁵ h21.6g Jul 6] sturdy gelding: poor handicap hurdler: unproven beyond 2m: acts on soft going: has worn headgear, including in 2018/19: wears tongue tie. *Kevin Bishop*

THE KING OF BREGA (IRE) 12 b.g. Court Cave (IRE) – Heather Darling (IRE) (Be **c–** My Native (USA)) [2018/19 h16g⁵ h18.8g⁴ h24g h20g* h24g⁴ h16g* h16g* h16s³ Mar 3] **h138** useful handicap hurdler: won at Gowran in October, and Thurles in December and January (by 6½ lengths from Ask Nile): winning chaser: stays 3m, as effective at much shorter: acts on soft and good to firm going: wears headgear. *Henry de Bromhead, Ireland*

THE KINGS BABY (IRE) 8 b.m. King's Theatre (IRE) – Assidua (IRE) (Anshan) **c110** [2018/19 c21.1s² c16mᵖᵘ h19.8gᵖᵘ c22.5vᶠ h18.5d h16.8s⁴ h17.7m⁵ h20.5g³ Apr 22] rather **h107** leggy mare: has had breathing operation: fifth foal: sister to modest hurdler The Kings Assassin (2¾m-3¼m winner): dam unraced half-sister to grandam of Stayers' Hurdle winner Paisley Park: point winner: fair handicap hurdler: similar form over fences: best effort when second in mares maiden at Roscommon: left Moses McCabe after second start: stays 21f: acts on soft going: tried in tongue tie. *Harry Whittington*

THE KINGS WRIT (IRE) 8 b.g. Brian Boru – Letterwoman (IRE) (Fourstars Allstar **c134** (USA)) [2018/19 c113, h–: c19.4sᶠ c19.2v* c20.6d⁴ c20s² Mar 9] workmanlike gelding: **h–** maiden hurdler: useful handicap chaser: won at Exeter in December: stays 3m: acts on heavy going: tried in tongue tie: often travels strongly. *Kayley Woollacott*

THE KNOT IS TIED (IRE) 4 b.g. Casamento (IRE) – Really Polish (USA) (Polish **h119** Numbers (USA)) [2018/19 h16.3s³ h16d² h15.8g² h16s³ h18.8d* Mar 23] tall gelding: fairly useful on Flat, stays 2m: similar standard over hurdles: won juvenile handicap at Newbury in March: stays 19f: acts on soft going: front runner/races prominently. *Neil King*

THE KVILLEKEN 11 b.g. Fair Mix (IRE) – Wannaplantatree (Niniski (USA)) [2018/19 **c– §** c–, h66§: c19.4m⁵ c22.6mᵖᵘ c23gᶠ c22.6gᵖᵘ h20g Sep 11] tall gelding: winning hurdler/ **h– §** maiden chaser, no form in 2018/19: left Hannah James after second start: usually wears headgear: has worn tongue tie: usually races towards rear: ungenuine. *Alan Phillips*

THE LADY RULES 5 ch.m. Native Ruler – Lady Author (Authorized (IRE)) [2018/19 **h78** h91: h20.3g h20g⁶ h20g⁴ h18.7g³ h23.4d⁵ h15.8v³ h16.2g⁵ h19g⁴ h19.3s⁴ Mar 7] lengthy mare: poor maiden hurdler: left Sarah Humphrey after third start: stays 21f: acts on heavy going: tried in tongue tie: usually races lazily. *Barry Brennan*

THE LAST BRIDGE 12 b.g. Milan – Celtic Bridge (Celtic Cone) [2018/19 c97§, h–§: **c80 §** c23.8sᵖᵘ c25.2s c23.6d c26.2d⁴ c29.2g² Apr 10] winning hurdler: poor handicap chaser: **h– §** stays 29f: acts on heavy going: wears headgear/tongue tie: often races lazily, and is unreliable. *Susan Johnson*

THE LAST BUT ONE (IRE) 7 b.g. Kutub (IRE) – Last Hope (IRE) (Jurado (USA)) **c128** [2018/19 c132p, h96: h21.6m³ c20m² h20g* h21.6s² c22.7f² Feb 26] rangy gelding: **h116** multiple point winner: fairly useful hurdler: won novice at Worcester in July: useful chaser: second in hunter at Leicester in February: left Paul Nicholls after fourth start: stays 3m: acts on any going: tried in tongue tie: usually races close up. *Tom Malone*

THE LAST DAY (IRE) 7 b.g. Oscar (IRE) – The Last Bank (IRE) (Phardante (FR)) **c132 p** [2018/19 h121: c16.4d^F c17.5d² c16v² c15.9v* Mar 17] lengthy, angular gelding: fairly **h–** useful hurdler: useful form over fences: simple task when winning novice at Carlisle in March: unproven beyond 2m: best form on soft/heavy going: front runner/races prominently: remains open to improvement as a chaser. *Evan Williams*

THE LAST MARJU (IRE) 7 b.g. Marju (IRE) – Celestial Dream (IRE) (Oasis Dream) **c136** [2018/19 c16g³ c17m* c18.2d⁴ c20.1g* c20g³ Oct 7] fair on Flat, stays 13f: winning **h–** hurdler: useful form over fences: won maiden at Killarney in July and novice there (by 6 lengths from Nick Lost) in August: third in Like A Butterfly Novices' Chase at Tipperary (11 lengths behind Le Richebourg) final outing: stays 2½m: acts on good to firm and good to soft going: wears hood. *Denis W. Cullen, Ireland*

THE LAST MELON 7 ch.g. Sir Percy – Step Fast (USA) (Giant's Causeway (USA)) **h85** [2018/19 h16.3m⁵ h16.3m h22m h19.2g⁵ h23g Sep 2] modest form over hurdles: stays 2¾m: acts on good to firm going: has worn hood. *James Bennett*

THE LAST SAMURI (IRE) 11 ch.g. Flemensfirth (USA) – Howaboutthis (IRE) (Oscar **c144** (IRE)) [2018/19 c159, h156: c23.8s⁵ c28.4d² c26d^pu Mar 2] sturdy gelding: winning **h–** hurdler: very smart chaser at best, runner-up in Grand National at Aintree in 2016, and also placed another twice over same fences: best effort in 2018/19 when second in minor event at Taunton (6 lengths behind Royal Vacation) in January: stayed 4¼m: acted on good to firm and heavy going: often wore hood in 2014/15: tried in tongue tie: retired. *Harry Fry*

THELIGNY (FR) 8 gr.g. Martaline – Romilly (FR) (Subotica (FR)) [2018/19 h131: **c130** c20.2g³ c23.4s⁶ c23.4s³ Jan 29] angular gelding: has had breathing operation: useful **h–** hurdler: similar form over fences: best effort when third in handicap at Newcastle (2¾ lengths behind Rock On Fruity) in January: stays 23f: acts on good to firm and heavy going: in tongue tie last 2 starts: front runner/races prominently. *Tim Vaughan*

THE LINCOLN LAWYER 4 b.g. Lawman (FR) – Adventure Seeker (FR) (Bering) **h100** [2018/19 h15.8m² h16.8g⁴ h17.7d³ h16d^pu h17.7g⁴ Apr 12] fairly useful maiden on Flat, stays 11.5f: fair form over hurdles: stays 2¼m: acts on good to firm and good to soft going: in hood last 3 starts: often races freely. *Charlie Mann*

THE LINKSMAN (IRE) 7 b.g. Westerner – Lost Link (IRE) (Shernazar) [2018/19 **c– p** h123: c16.3g^ur Oct 31] workmanlike gelding: fairly useful hurdler: unseated rider fifth on **h–** chasing debut: raced around 2m: best form on soft/heavy going: tried in hood. *Sam England*

THE LION DANCER (IRE) 7 b.g. Let The Lion Roar – Shesadoll (IRE) (Naheez **c110** (USA)) [2018/19 c116, h78: c23.6d³ Apr 6] lightly-raced hurdler: fair handicap chaser: **h–** stays 3¼m: acts on heavy going: wears headgear: front runner/races prominently. *Charlie Mann*

THE LION MAN (IRE) 9 b.g. Let The Lion Roar – Just Smart (IRE) (Anshan) [2018/19 **c–** c–, h65: h24g² h24g* h23.3g h24g^pu c24g^ur h23.1g^pu Oct 30] poor handicap hurdler: won **h72** at Southwell in May: lightly-raced chaser: stays 3m: acts on soft and good to firm going: usually wears headgear. *Robin Dickin*

THE LION QUEEN 4 b.f. Helmet (AUS) – Bisaat (USA) (Bahri (USA)) [2018/19 **b–** b13.7g Apr 12] half-sister to several winners, including bumper winner/fair hurdler At First Light (2m-2¾m winner, by Echo of Light) and fair hurdler Khismet (17f winner, by Kheleyf): dam once-raced sister to fairly useful hurdler/fair chaser (stayed 3m) Maraafeq: well beaten in bumper. *David Weston*

THE LION ROARS (IRE) 5 b.g. Let The Lion Roar – Definite Blue (IRE) (Definite **h–** Article) [2018/19 b15.8m³ h15.8v h20v^pu Dec 17] €25,000 3-y-o: first foal: dam unraced **b75** half-sister to fairly useful French 2¼m hurdle winner Mt Speculation: third in conditionals/ amateurs maiden bumper at Ffos Las (11¼ lengths behind Georgiator): no form over hurdles. *Peter Bowen*

THE LIZARD KING (IRE) 10 b.g. Indian River (FR) – Norwich Breeze (IRE) **c90** (Norwich) [2018/19 c92?, h–: c24.2m² May 8] point winner: twice-raced hurdler: modest **h–** maiden chaser: stayed 3m: acted on good to firm going: in cheekpieces last 3 starts: dead. *Nicky Martin*

THELONGWAYAROUND (IRE) 6 b.g. Fruits of Love (USA) – Brass Neck (IRE) **h109**
(Supreme Leader) [2018/19 h16.2g² h19.7g⁵ h21.3s² h22.7g h19.7g⁶ h19.9d* Apr 23]
£10,000 5-y-o: has had breathing operation: fourth foal: half-brother to fair hurdler Walser
(2m winner, by Milan), stayed 2½m, and a winning pointer by Snurge: dam unraced: Irish
point winner: fair form over hurdles: won maiden at Sedgefield in April: should stay
beyond 21f: acts on soft going: usually races prominently. *Sue Smith*

THELUNARSCHOONER (IRE) 6 b.m. Milan – Garden City (IRE) (Shernazar) **h94**
[2018/19 h95, b94: h15.8s² h16.7g h16g⁵ h19gᵖᵘ Sep 25] bumper winner: modest maiden
hurdler: should stay 2½m: acts on soft going. *Warren Greatrex*

THE MACON LUGNATIC 5 b.g. Shirocco (GER) – Didbrook (Alzao (USA)) **b97**
[2018/19 b15.8g² b16.6d⁶ b16.3s* b16.3d Mar 2] good-topped gelding: fourth foal: half-
brother to 2 winners, including 1¾m bumper winner Hazel Brook (by High Chaparral):
dam bumper winner: fairly useful form in bumpers: won at Newbury in January.
Ben Pauling

THE MAD WELL (IRE) 10 b.g. Milan – Silverfortprincess (IRE) (Mull of Kintyre **h99**
(USA)) [2018/19 h–: h22m² h23g Jun 11] modest handicap hurdler: stays 2¾m: acts on
good to firm and heavy going: has worn cheekpieces: wears tongue tie. *Kevin Bishop*

THE MAESTRO (IRE) 5 b.g. Doyen (IRE) – Myown (IRE) (Le Bavard (FR)) [2018/19 **h94 p**
b15.7s² b16d h16g⁵ Apr 11] €30,000 3-y-o, £60,000 4-y-o: closely related to 3 winners, **b84**
including smart hurdler/useful chaser Ninetieth Minute (2m-2¾m winner, by Old Vic),
stayed 3¼m, and half-brother to bumper winner/fair 2½m hurdle winner Gortnahulla (by
Bravefoot): dam unraced: point winner modest form in bumpers: 33/1, fifth in maiden at
Wetherby (19¾ lengths behind Fransham) on hurdling debut: will be suited by further than
2m: tried in hood/tongue tie: likely to improve. *James Ewart*

THE MAJOR 6 b.g. Major Cadeaux – Ballerina Suprema (IRE) (Sadler's Wells (USA)) **c93**
[2018/19 h79: h15.3m² h15.8g h18.5s⁴ h15.3g c21gᵘʳ Apr 20] modest maiden **h88**
hurdler: yet to be asked for effort when unseated 2 out in novice handicap won by Iniesta
at Newton Abbot on chasing debut: stays 21f: acts on good to firm going: has worn hood,
including in 2018/19: wears tongue tie. *Kayley Woollacott*

THE MAJOR GENERAL (IRE) 6 b.g. Galileo (IRE) – Scribonia (IRE) (Danehill **h108**
(USA)) [2018/19 h16.6g⁵ h22g⁵ h22m h24g⁶ h18.6s⁶ h16d⁵ Jan 15] smart on Flat, stays
1½m: fair maiden hurdler: left Joseph Patrick O'Brien after fourth start: probably stays
2¾m: acts on good to firm going: has worn headgear/tongue tie, including in 2018/19.
Jonjo O'Neill

THE MANUSCRIPT (IRE) 6 b.g. Mahler – Limavady (IRE) (Executive Perk) [2018/19 **h88**
h–: h23.3g⁶ h23.9d⁵ h23.1s* h24.4g³ h26g Feb 22] good-topped gelding: modest handicap
hurdler: won at Market Rasen in December: stays 3m: acts on soft going: in cheekpieces
last 3 starts. *Jonjo O'Neill*

THE MIGHTY ASH (IRE) 9 b.g. Arcadio (GER) – She's Got To Go (IRE) (Glacial **c94**
Storm (USA)) [2018/19 h104: h19.5s h21.4g⁵ h15.3d c20d⁵ c17.8v² Feb 14] maiden Irish **h98**
pointer: modest maiden hurdler: similar form in chases: stays 21f: acts on heavy going:
wears headgear. *Fiona Shaw*

THE MIGHTY DON (IRE) 7 ch.g. Shantou (USA) – Flying Answer (IRE) (Anshan) **c–**
[2018/19 h132: c21.6mᵘʳ h23.9d* h24.2s³ h24.4s⁴ h24d h24d Mar 14] useful-looking **h140**
gelding: useful hurdler: won handicap at Cheltenham in October: third in Long Distance
Hurdle at Newbury (4½ lengths behind Unowhatimeanharry) next outing: jumped badly
right and unseated sixth in maiden at Fontwell on chasing debut: stays 25f: acts on soft
going: has worn cheekpieces, including in 2018/19: usually races towards rear. *Nick Gifford*

THE MILAN GIRL (IRE) 5 b.m. Milan – En Vedette (FR) (Astarabad (USA)) [2018/19 **b94**
b15.8d² b16.7d* Apr 26] €50,000 3-y-o: first foal: dam, French 2¼m hurdle winner, half-
sister to useful hurdler/winning chaser (stayed 21f) Chablais: fair form in bumpers: won
mares event at Bangor in April: will be suited by 2½m: wears tongue tie. *Kim Bailey*

THE MISSUS 8 b.m. Presenting – Violet Express (FR) (Cadoudal (FR)) [2018/19 h–: **h–**
h21.6m Jul 14] leggy, angular mare: has had breathing operation: fair hurdler at best,
lightly raced and no form since 2016/17: has worn hood: tried in tongue tie. *Warren Greatrex*

THE MISTRESS (IRE) 8 b.m. Kalanisi (IRE) – Sonnerschien (IRE) (Be My Native **c–**
(USA)) [2018/19 h79, b77: h20sᵖᵘ h16.7mᵖᵘ h20.5dᵖᵘ c19.4gᵖᵘ Apr 14] maiden hurdler, no **h–**
form in 2018/19: pulled up in novice handicap on chasing debut: left Oliver Greenall after
second start: in headgear last 4 starts: wears tongue tie. *Milton Harris*

THE MODEL COUNTY (IRE) 9 b.m. Robin des Champs (FR) – Ware It Vic (IRE)   **h–**
(Old Vic) [2018/19 h86: h26gᵖᵘ Feb 22] sturdy mare: point winner: modest hurdler, pulled
up sole outing in 2018/19: stays 3¼m: acts on heavy going: tried in cheekpieces: usually
races prominently. *Alan Phillips*

THE NAUGHTY STEP (IRE) 4 b.g. Camacho – Echad (IRE) (Kris Kin (USA))   **h–**
[2018/19 h17.7gᵖᵘ Sep 9] no form on Flat: pulled up in juvenile on hurdling debut.
Jim Boyle

THE NAVIGATOR 4 gr.g. Mastercraftsman (IRE) – Blessing (USA) (Pulpit (USA))   **h56**
[2018/19 h15.7gᶠ h16.8d⁶ h16d h17g⁵ Feb 24] fair on Flat, stays 11f: poor form over
hurdles: tried in hood. *Dianne Sayer*

THE NEW ONE (IRE) 11 b.g. King's Theatre (IRE) – Thuringe (FR) (Turgeon (USA))   **h–**
[2018/19 h157: h15.8d h16.8sᵖᵘ Dec 15] sturdy gelding: top-class hurdler at best, won
2 Grade 1 events as well as International Hurdle (twice) at Cheltenham and Champion
Hurdle Trial (4 times) at Haydock: also in frame twice in Champion Hurdle: stayed 21f:
acted on heavy going: tried in visor: front runner/raced prominently: retired. *Nigel Twiston-
Davies*

THE NEW PHARAOH (IRE) 8 b.g. Montjeu (IRE) – Out West (USA) (Gone West   **h–**
(USA)) [2018/19 h116: h24gᵖᵘ May 15] compact gelding: fairly useful hurdler, shaped as
if amiss sole outing in 2018/19: should stay beyond 2m: acts on heavy going: tried in
headgear. *Laura Morgan*

THENIGHTISYOUNG (IRE) 5 b.g. Gold Well – Larnalee (IRE) (Presenting) [2018/19   **h–**
h22gᵇᵈ Apr 14] brought down second in novice hurdle on debut. *Tom Gretton*

THE OGLE GOGLE MAN (IRE) 7 b.g. Yeats (IRE) – Miss Otis Regrets (IRE) (Bob   **c107 x**
Back (USA)) [2018/19 c102, h102: c23.6g³ c26.3g² c23.8g² c26v* c24s* c23.6d⁶ c24.2vᶠ   **h–**
c26m⁶ Mar 29] rangy gelding: maiden hurdler: fair handicap chaser: won at Fontwell
(novice) and Uttoxeter in December: stays 3¼m: acts on heavy going: wears headgear/
tongue tie: sketchy jumper of fences. *Charlie Mann*

THEO (IRE) 9 b.g. Westerner – Jemima Jay (IRE) (Supreme Leader) [2018/19 c134,   **c138 x**
h115: c16.5g* c16.5m* c19.9g⁵ c17.5m⁴ c16.4g² c16.3d⁶ c20.5m Apr 12] sturdy gelding: **h–**
winning hurdler: useful handicap chaser: won at Worcester in August and September (by 6
lengths from Dinsdale): best form at up to 2½m: acts on good to firm and heavy going:
wears headgear: races towards rear: often let down by jumping. *Dr Richard Newland*

THE ORANGE ROGUE (IRE) 12 br.g. Alderbrook – Classic Enough (Classic Cliche   **c99**
(IRE)) [2018/19 c99, h–: c23.4dᵘʳ c16.5s² c20vᵖᵘ Mar 7] has had breathing operation: **h–**
maiden hurdler: modest handicap chaser nowadays: lame final start: stays 3m: mainly
raced on soft/heavy going: has worn headgear: wears tongue tie. *N. W. Alexander*

THE ORGANIST (IRE) 8 b.m. Alkaadhem – Go On Eileen (IRE) (Bob Back (USA))   **c–**
[2018/19 c–, h137: h24.7g² Nov 10] compact mare: useful handicap hurdler: second at   **h133**
Aintree (10 lengths behind Abolitionist) sole outing in 2018/19: lightly-raced chaser: stays
25f: acts on heavy going. *Oliver Sherwood*

THEO'S CHARM (IRE) 9 b.g. Presenting – Kates Charm (IRE) (Glacial Storm (USA))   **c–**
[2018/19 c129, h134: h24.3g⁵ h22.8v³ h19.9v³ Jan 26] medium-sized gelding: useful   **h128**
handicap hurdler: maiden chaser: stays 23f: acts on heavy going: has worn headgear,
including in 2018/19: tried in tongue tie. *Nick Gifford*

THE OTMOOR POET 6 b.g. Yeats (IRE) – Kristalette (IRE) (Leporello (IRE))   **h66**
[2018/19 h84: h15.8s⁶ Jul 29] lengthy, rather sparely-made gelding: poor maiden hurdler:
should stay further than 2m: acts on heavy going: tried in cheekpieces. *Alex Hales*

THE OVERFLOW 8 b.m. With The Flow (USA) – Cornish Fort (Shaab) [2018/19 h20g⁵   **c–**
h15.3m h21.6m⁵ c24.2s⁵ Nov 25] sturdy mare: fourth foal: dam placed in points: point   **h72**
winner: poor form over hurdles: well beaten in novice on chasing debut. *Susan Gardner*

THE PADDY PIE (IRE) 6 b.g. Beneficial – Salsita (FR) (Fijar Tango (FR)) [2018/19 h–,   **c125**
b–: h15.8d h20.1g² h20.1m* c20.1s² c24.2g² c25.2g³ c19.3d³ c16.4s* c19.9g* c21.1s²   **h111**
c20.1d² c25.6m⁴ Apr 20] fair form over hurdles: won handicap at Hexham in June: fairly
useful handicap chaser: won novice events at Sedgefield in January and Haydock in
February: stays 3m: acts on soft and good to firm going. *Sue Smith*

THEPENSIONFUND (IRE) 7 b.g. Big Bad Bob (IRE) – Whizz (Salse (USA)) [2018/19   **h93**
b91p: h16d⁴ h16.2g⁵ h16.2sᵖᵘ h16.2gᵖᵘ h16d Feb 25] modest form over hurdles: raced only
at 2m: acts on good to soft going. *Lucinda Russell*

THE PHANTOM (FR) 7 b.g. Apsis – Idee Recue (FR) (Sicyos (USA)) [2018/19 h16g⁵ **c104 p** h15.8g² h17.2mᵘʳ c15.9d⁵ Oct 18] sturdy gelding: fair form over hurdles: 80/1, fifth in **h101** novice handicap at Carlisle (11¾ lengths behind Luckofthedraw) on chasing debut: raced around 2m: acts on good to soft going: usually wears hood. *Dianne Sayer*

THE PREMIER CELTIC 6 b.g. Black Sam Bellamy (IRE) – Maria Antonia (IRE) **h104** (King's Best (USA)) [2018/19 h111, b81: h19.2m h15.3g h20.7d⁵ h19.2d⁵ h21s Mar 10] workmanlike gelding: fair handicap hurdler: stays 21f: acts on soft going: tried in cheekpieces. *Pat Phelan*

THE RAVEN MASTER (IRE) 5 b.g. Raven's Pass (USA) – Rainbow Desert (USA) **h–** (Dynaformer (USA)) [2018/19 h108: h16.3s h16d Apr 6] fair hurdler at best, no form in 2018/19: raced around 2m: acts on good to firm going: in tongue tie last 5 starts. *Dan Skelton*

THE RAVEN'S RETURN 6 b.g. Scorpion (IRE) – Mimis Bonnet (FR) (Bonnet Rouge **h–** (FR)) [2018/19 b91: b16v* h21.6g⁶ h16.8sᵖᵘ Feb 25] unfurnished gelding: fair form **b92** in bumpers: won at Sandown in November: no form over hurdles: should stay further than 2m. *Seamus Mullins*

THEREDBALLOON 13 ch.g. Sulamani (IRE) – Sovana (FR) (Kadounor (FR)) [2018/19 **h92** h15.7g h15.7d² h20.7dᵖᵘ Dec 9] modest handicap hurdler: stays 2½m: acts on soft going: has worn hood. *Louise Allan*

THE RESDEV WAY 6 b.g. Multiplex – Lady Duxyana (Most Welcome) [2018/19 h–: **h–** h18.7g h22g Nov 7] sturdy gelding: fair on Flat, stays 2m: no form over hurdles. *Philip Kirby*

THE RETRIEVER (IRE) 4 ch.g. Shamardal (USA) – Silent Secret (IRE) (Dubai **b–** Destination (USA)) [2018/19 b16.2g Apr 15] well beaten in bumper. *Micky Hammond*

THERMISTOCLES 7 b.g. Oscar (IRE) – Alpine View (IRE) (Witness Box **h132** (USA)) [2018/19 h20g³ h24g* h24g³ h24d h24d Apr 23] €25,000 3-y-o: sturdy gelding: first foal: dam, maiden pointer, half-sister to Champion Hurdle winner Rock On Ruby (by Oscar): bumper winner: useful handicap hurdler: won at Clonmel in November: stays 3m: acts on heavy going: has worn tongue tie, including final start (also wore cheekpieces). *Joseph Patrick O'Brien, Ireland*

THE ROAD HOME (IRE) 7 b.g. Oscar (IRE) – In Fact (IRE) (Classic Cliche (IRE)) **c102** [2018/19 h110, b90: c17.1g⁴ c20.5g⁵ c20.3gᵖᵘ c20.3m² c20.3m³ c21.6d² Apr 8] lengthy **h–** gelding: has had breathing operation: Irish point winner: fair hurdler: similar form in chases: stays 2¾m: acts on soft and good to firm going: tried in cheekpieces: wears tongue tie: races prominently. *Lucinda Russell*

THE ROCKET PARK (IRE) 6 b.g. Rock of Gibraltar (IRE) – Snowpalm (Halling **h–** (USA)) [2018/19 b15.7g* b16g⁵ h16.3s h15.8d h16.6d⁵ Mar 1] angular gelding: third foal: **b83** closely related to Italian 9f/1¼m winner Super Dukessa (by Duke of Marmalade): dam unraced half-sister to fairly useful hurdler (2m/17f winner) Manjakani: modest form in bumpers: won maiden event at Southwell on debut in May: no form over hurdles. *John Berry*

THE ROMFORD PELE (IRE) 12 b.g. Accordion – Back And Fore (IRE) (Bob Back **c–** (USA)) [2018/19 c148, h–: c26.1mᵖᵘ Jul 1] rather leggy gelding: winning hurdler: smart **h–** chaser at best, fatally injured sole outing in 2018/19: stayed 3¼m: acted on good to firm and heavy going: wore headgear at peak of his career. *Tom George*

THE RORY STORY (IRE) 8 b.g. Flemensfirth (USA) – Phardester (IRE) (Phardante **h–** (FR)) [2018/19 h19.9sᵖᵘ Dec 31] won sole bumper start: fairly useful form over hurdles for Noel Meade, winning maiden at Galway in 2017/18: pulled up sole outing following season: should stay 2½m+: acts on heavy going: has worn tongue tie. *Julian Smith*

THE RUSSIAN DOYEN (IRE) 6 b.g. Doyen (IRE) – Namloc (IRE) (Phardante (FR)) **c138** [2018/19 h123p, b96: c19.2g³ c20.6d⁵ c16.4d* c20.2s⁴ Mar 12] big, lengthy gelding: fairly **h–** useful form over hurdles: useful form over fences: won maiden at Exeter in November and novice handicap at Newbury (by 4½ lengths from Charming Zen) in January: should stay 2½m: acts on heavy going. *Colin Tizzard*

THESAURUS (IRE) 4 b.g. Sea The Stars (IRE) – Night Fairy (IRE) (Danehill (USA)) **b60 p** [2018/19 b16.5d⁶ Apr 4] brother to 1m winner Stars So Bright and half-brother to smart 6f-1m winner Majestic Queen (by Kheleyf): dam 1¼m winner: needed experience when well beaten in maiden bumper: should improve. *Martyn Meade*

THE SECOND COMING (IRE) 5 b.g. Yeats (IRE) – Decent Dime (IRE) (Insan **h111**
(USA)) [2018/19 b15.7s* h20d⁴ h24d Apr 22] fifth foal: closely related to a winning **b93**
pointer by Clerkenwell and half-brother to fair hurdler/chaser Superior Command (2m/17f
winner, by Lahib), stayed 2¾m: dam unraced: well held in Irish point: won bumper at
Catterick (by 6 lengths from The Maestro) in December, sole start for Simon West: fair
form over hurdles: wears tongue tie. *Denis Hogan, Ireland*

THE SOCIETY MAN (IRE) 12 ch.g. Moscow Society (USA) – Redruth (IRE) (Sri **c– §**
Pekan (USA)) [2018/19 c83§, h–: c19.2d⁶ c21.4g c23.9m c17.2gᵖᵘ c21.2g Jul 23] **h–**
workmanlike gelding: winning hurdler: maiden chaser, no form in 2018/19: temperamental.
Michael Chapman

THE SOME DANCE KID (IRE) 6 b.g. Shantou (USA) – River Rouge (IRE) (Croco **h122 p**
Rouge (IRE)) [2018/19 b97: h17.1d³ h16.7d⁴ h16.7s* h19.3g* Jan 10] runner-up in Irish
point: bumper winner: fairly useful form over hurdles: won maiden at Bangor in November,
and novices there in December and Catterick in January: will stay 2½m+: front runner/
races prominently: will go on improving. *Donald McCain*

THE STEWARD (USA) 8 b.g. Street Cry (IRE) – Candlelight (USA) (Kingmambo **h105**
(USA)) [2018/19 h103: h16.2d² h17.2g² h22.1m³ h17.2g² h17.2d² h23.8g² h19.3g² h19.3g⁴
Jan 10] lengthy gelding: fair maiden hurdler: stays easy 3m, at least as effective around 2m:
acts on good to soft going: wears headgear: often races prominently. *James Moffatt*

THE STING (IRE) 6 br.g. Scorpion (IRE) – Moon Approach (IRE) (Shernazar) [2018/19 **h86**
b17s⁵ h20v⁶ h16.8s⁴ h19.3g⁵ h19.3s³ h24.1d Mar 19] €10,000 3-y-o, £2,000 5-y-o: seventh **b84**
foal: brother to fair hurdler/fairly useful chaser Potters Approach (3¼m winner) and half-
brother to fairly useful hurdler/useful chaser Foundry Square (2½m-23f winner, by Oscar),
stayed 3½m: dam unraced: little impact in points: fifth in bumper at Carlisle: modest form
over hurdles: stays 19f: acts on soft going: wears hood. *Micky Hammond*

THE STORYTELLER (IRE) 8 ch.g. Shantou (USA) – Bally Bolshoi (IRE) (Bob Back **c160**
(USA)) [2018/19 c153, h136: c19.5g⁵ c20.2d⁴ c24g⁶ c24g³ c20.6dᵖᵘ c20d² Apr 22] sturdy **h–**
gelding: useful hurdler: high-class chaser: usually highly tried in 2018/19, and again ran
respectably when 24 lengths third to Kemboy in Punchestown Gold Cup shortly after end
of British season: stays 25f: acts on heavy going. *Gordon Elliott, Ireland*

THE SWAGMAN (USA) 5 ch.g. Galileo (IRE) – Ventura (IRE) (Spectrum (IRE)) **b92**
[2018/19 b16.3d⁴ b16d⁴ b16g⁴ Apr 25] lengthy, angular gelding: brother/half-brother to
several winners on Flat, notably high-class 6.5f-1m winner Moonlight Cloud (by Invincible
Spirit): dam, 1m winner, half-sister to fairly useful hurdler/fair chaser (winner up to 23f)
Irish Legend: fair form in bumpers. *Seamus Durack*

THE SWEENEY (IRE) 7 b.g. Oscar (IRE) – Banningham Blaze (Averti (IRE)) [2018/19 **h120**
h115: h19.2g⁴ h20g³ h21g³ h21g⁵ h20.6g² h21.4g³ Apr 14] neat gelding: has had breathing
operations: fairly useful handicap hurdler: stays 21f: acts on heavy going: in cheekpieces
last 3 starts: usually travels strongly. *Emma Lavelle*

THE TAILGATER (IRE) 8 b.g. Oscar (IRE) – Zaffaran Express (IRE) (Zaffaran **c–**
(USA)) [2018/19 c124, h119: c19.9gᵖᵘ May 18] good-topped gelding: fairly useful hurdler: **h–**
similar form over fences in 2017/18: pulled up sole outing since: stays 21f: acts on soft
going: waited with. *Jonjo O'Neill*

THE TANGLER BARRY (IRE) 6 b.g. Ask – Royale Pour Moi (FR) (Cadoudal (FR)) **h93**
[2018/19 h22.1g⁵ h20g⁴ h18.7g³ h21.3m⁴ h24.4gᵖᵘ Nov 30] €11,500 3-y-o, £40,000 5-y-o:
sixth foal: half-brother to bumper winner/fair chaser Catspan (21f winner, by Turgeon),
stayed 3m: dam twice-raced sister to useful chaser (stayed 25f) Royal Predica: off mark in
Irish points at fifth attempt: modest form over hurdles: stays 21f: acts on good to firm
going. *Phil Middleton*

THE TARTAN SPARTAN (IRE) 6 ch.h. The Carbon Unit (USA) – The Real Thing **h108 p**
(IRE) (Traditionally (USA)) [2018/19 h16.3d h16d³ h16.6d⁵ Jan 29] medium-sized horse:
brother to modest 19f hurdle winner Sarah Joyce, later successful in USA: useful at best on
Flat (stays 2m), well held in 2018: inadequate tests over hurdles: will be suited by further
than 2m: remains with potential. *Andrew Hughes, Ireland*

THE TIN MINER (IRE) 8 br.g. Presenting – Sidalcea (IRE) (Oscar (IRE)) [2018/19 **c104**
c109p, h–: c25.7s* c25.7s² c25.8d⁶ c24.2gᶠ c19.7d³ h25g² Apr 22] sturdy gelding: **h99**
modest form over hurdles: fair handicap chaser: won at Plumpton in December: left David
Bridgwater after sixth start: stays 3¼m: acts on soft going: wears headgear: usually races
close up. *Chris Gordon*

THE TOOJUMPA 6 b.m. Midnight Legend – Sunnyland (Sovereign Water (FR)) **h102**
[2018/19 h77, b–: h19.7g h23v* h23.6v^pu h19.8s^6 Feb 2] sturdy mare: fair handicap
hurdler: won conditionals event at Bangor in December: should stay at least 3m: acts on
heavy going: tried in hood. *John Groucott*

THE TOURARD MAN (IRE) 13 b.g. Shantou (USA) – Small Iron (General Ironside) **c–**
[2018/19 c–, h141: h22.8g h25.4g^2 h23.1g^5 Jul 8] compact gelding: useful handicap **h136**
hurdler: winning chaser: stays 3¼m: acts on good to firm and heavy going: ridden by Kevin
Dowling (7). *Alan King*

THE TRIGGER (IRE) 10 ch.g. Beneficial – Ardrom (Ardross) [2018/19 c101, h88: **c91**
h20.2g* h20.6g^2 h20.8g c18.2d h24d^2 c22.6d c20d^F Dec 16] fair handicap hurdler/chaser: **h103**
won over hurdles at Perth in June: stays 3m: acts on good to soft going: has worn
cheekpieces/tongue tie: held up. *Ronan M. P. McNally, Ireland*

THE TWISLER 7 b.g. Motivator – Panna (Polish Precedent (USA)) [2018/19 h106: **h118**
h15.3m^2 h15.8g^6 h16g^3 h16g* h19.3m^6 h16.4g h15.2g^7 h15.3g* h16.7g^6 h15.3g^6 Mar 25]
workmanlike gelding: fairly useful hurdler: won novice at Worcester in July and handicap
at Wincanton in January: stays 19f: acts on good to firm going: has worn cheekpieces,
including last 4 starts. *Neil Mulholland*

THE TWO AMIGOS 7 b.g. Midnight Legend – As Was (Epalo (GER)) [2018/19 h93: **c137 p**
c25.8v* c23.9g^2 c30.7s* c28.5d* c28.4g^F Feb 16] stocky gelding: fair form over hurdles **h–**
(for David Pipe): vastly better over fences: won handicaps at Newton Abbot (novice event)
in October, Exeter in December and Plumpton (useful form when beating Calin du Brizais
2¼ lengths) in January: stays 31f: acts on heavy going: has worn tongue tie: usually leads:
strong-travelling sort who normally jumps boldly (rare error when falling final outing):
remains open to improvement. *Nicky Martin*

THE UNIT (IRE) 8 b.g. Gold Well – Sovana (FR) (Kadounor (FR)) [2018/19 c143, h137: **c140**
h15.7g c20.1g* c21m^2 c21m* c21.4g^3 c19.1g^2 Dec 15] sturdy gelding: useful handicap **h112**
hurdler: similar form over fences, winning novices at Hexham in June and Newton Abbot
(by 3 lengths from Drinks Interval) in August: effective at 2m to 21f: acts on good to firm
and heavy going: usually travels strongly held up. *Alan King*

THE UNMENTIONABLE (IRE) 6 b.g. Mustameet (USA) – Auburn Cherry (IRE) **b71**
(Treasure Hunter) [2018/19 b16.3d^4 Jun 8] off mark in points at fifth attempt: well-held
fourth in amateurs bumper at Stratford. *D. Peters*

THE VERY MAN (IRE) 5 b.g. Jeremy (USA) – Mill Meadow (IRE) (Kalanisi (IRE)) **b106**
[2018/19 b16d* b16d Apr 22] €28,000 3-y-o, £210,000 4-y-o: first foal: dam unraced half-
sister to fairly useful hurdler/useful chaser (stays 3m) Howlongisafoot: winning pointer:
useful form when winning maiden at Navan (by 3¾ lengths from Neptune) in December on
first of 2 outings in bumpers: most disappointing at Fairyhouse 4 months later. *Gordon
Elliott, Ireland*

THE VERY THING (IRE) 5 b.g. Getaway (GER) – Katie Quinn (IRE) (Glacial Storm **h106**
(USA)) [2018/19 b84p: h16g^3 h16d^2 h16d^2 h20d^5 h19.8m^3 h18.6g Mar 27] lengthy gelding:
fair form over hurdles: first past post in handicap at Fakenham in December, but demoted
after bumping rival run-in: stays 2½m: acts on good to firm and good to soft going: tried in
cheekpieces. *Olly Murphy*

THE VOCALIST 7 b.m. Recharge (IRE) – Ivy Edith (Blakeney) [2018/19 h115p: c16.3d^6 **c94 p**
h19.9s^6 h20.1g^4 Apr 15] has had breathing operation: fair handicap hurdler, lightly raced: **h113**
off 10 months and left Nicky Henderson, probably needed run when well-held sixth in
novice at Newcastle on chasing debut (should do better): stays easy 21f: acts on soft going:
in tongue tie last 2 starts. *Keith Dalgleish*

THE VOLLAN (IRE) 5 b.g. Scorpion (IRE) – Print It On Lips (IRE) (Blueprint (IRE)) **h107**
[2018/19 b15.7g h16.7d h16d^6 h15.5g^5 h15.8g^5 h19.5g Apr 26] €30,000 3-y-o: good- **b–**
topped gelding: first foal: dam twice-raced half-sister to useful 2m hurdle winner The Big
Bite (by Scorpion) out of half-sister to smart hurdler/very smart chaser (stayed 3¼m)
Cooldine: green in maiden bumper: fair form over hurdles: should stay 2½m. *Charlie
Longsdon*

THE WAY YOU DANCE (IRE) 7 b.g. Thewayyouare (USA) – Beautiful Dancer (IRE) **c–**
(Danehill Dancer (IRE)) [2018/19 c75, h105: h23.5d Feb 16] sturdy gelding: fair hurdler at **h–**
best: last only outing in sphere in 2018/19 (still fair on Flat, winning in May and July): little
aptitude for chasing: stays 23f, effective at much shorter: acts on good to firm going: wears
headgear. *Neil Mulholland*

THE WEALERDEALER (IRE) 12 b.g. Vinnie Roe (IRE) – Lantern Liz (IRE) **c–** (Montelimar (USA)) [2018/19 c122, h–: c26.3g^{ur} May 4] lengthy gelding: multiple point **h–** winner: winning hurdler: fairly useful hunter chaser: set for third when unseating 2 out at Cheltenham sole outing in 2018/19: stays 3¼m: acts on good to firm and heavy going: has worn headgear. *I. Chanin*

THE WELSH PADDIES (IRE) 7 b.g. Court Cave (IRE) – Masiana (IRE) (Daylami **h129** (IRE)) [2018/19 h111: h23.6s^{pu} h23.3v⁵ h25d* h26.4g* h24g³ Apr 17] fairly useful handicap hurdler: improved in 2018/19, winning at Huntingdon in February and Stratford in March: stays 3¼m: acts on soft going: in cheekpieces last 4 starts. *Kerry Lee*

THE WEST'S AWAKE (IRE) 8 b.g. Yeats (IRE) – Bilboa (FR) (Phantom Breeze) **c141** [2018/19 c138, h119: c19g² c18.2g c20.1g^F Aug 25] winning hurdler: useful handicap **h–** chaser: stays 2½m: acts on soft going: has worn headgear, including last 3 starts. *E. J. O'Grady, Ireland*

THE WHITE MOUSE (IRE) 5 br.m. Stowaway – Maxwells Demon (IRE) (King's **h122** Theatre (IRE)) [2018/19 b–: h19.5d* h15.5d² h19.4d* h20.5d^F Mar 23] good-topped mare: fairly useful form over hurdles: won mares maiden at Lingfield in November and mares novice at Doncaster in March: will be suited by 3m. *Lucy Wadham*

THE WICKET CHICKEN (IRE) 7 b.m. Milan – Soniadoir (IRE) (Presenting) [2018/19 **c114** h112, b88: h23.3d⁵ c23.6g² c24g² c24g³ c26g⁴ c23.6d² c25.2v⁴ c25.7g³ c26g² Apr 18] **h96** bumper winner: fair hurdler/maiden chaser: stays 3¼m: acts on good to soft going: wears cheekpieces. *Neil Mulholland*

THE WINKLER (IRE) 10 gr.g. Medaaly – Osirixa (FR) (Linamix (FR)) [2018/19 **c123** c26m⁴ c19.2d³ c28.8v^{pu} c23.9d^{pu} Mar 14] lengthy gelding: winning hurdler: fairly useful **h–** handicap chaser: left Eoin Doyle, out of sorts last 3 outings: stayed 3¼m: acted on good to firm and heavy going: usually wore headgear/tongue tie: dead. *Kelly Morgan*

THE WINNINGTIPSTER 6 ch.g. Kheleyf (USA) – Freedom Song (Singspiel (IRE)) **c–** [2018/19 h–: h17.7g^f c16.1d³ c20g^{pu} Mar 28] of no account: left Paul Henderson after first **h–** start: tried in cheekpieces. *A. J. Burks*

THE WOLF (FR) 5 ch.g. Kapgarde (FR) – Ges (FR) (Hours After (USA)) [2018/19 **h116** b16.3m⁴ b16s³ h20.5s h16.3d³ h20.3d⁴ h20.5d³ Mar 22] tall, rather unfurnished gelding: **b97** half-brother to several winners in France, notably dual Grande Course de Haies d'Auteuil winner Gemix (by Carlotamix): dam, French 13.5f hurdle winner, also 4.5f winner on Flat: fairly useful form on second of 2 outings in bumpers: similar form over hurdles. *Warren Greatrex*

THE WORLDS END (IRE) 8 b.g. Stowaway – Bright Sprite (IRE) (Beneficial) [2018/19 **c145** h153: c23.6g* c24.4g³ c25.3g* c24g⁶ c24.4s^{pu} h24.7g Apr 6] good-topped gelding: smart **h–** hurdler at best: similar form over fences: won maiden at Chepstow in October and novice at Cheltenham (by 26 lengths from Ibis du Rheu) in December: ended season out of sorts: stays 25f: acts on soft going: tried in cheekpieces. *Tom George*

THE YANK 10 b.g. Trade Fair – Silver Gyre (IRE) (Silver Hawk (USA)) [2018/19 c106§, **c96 §** h–: c17m³ c16.5g Jul 31] compact gelding: maiden hurdler: fair handicap chaser: free- **h–** going front runner, best around 2m: acts on firm and good to soft going: regularly in headgear: has worn tongue tie: temperamental. *David Bridgwater*

THEYDON PARK 6 b.g. Royal Applause – Velvet Waters (Unfuwain (USA)) [2018/19 **h102** h109: h15.8g⁴ h20g² h20g Jul 31] fair maiden hurdler: stays 3m: acts on soft going: wears headgear: in tongue tie last 2 starts. *Michael Roberts*

THE YOUNG MASTER 10 b.g. Echo of Light – Fine Frenzy (IRE) (Great Commotion **c144** (USA)) [2018/19 c130x, h–: c23.6d* c25g* c26s^{pu} c26d³ c28.8g² Apr 27] workmanlike **h–** gelding: has had breathing operation: winning hurdler: useful handicap chaser: won at Chepstow in October and Cheltenham (amateurs race) in November: also ran well when placed in valuable handicaps at Cheltenham and Sandown last 2 outings, 10 lengths second of 15 to Talkischeap in bet365 Gold Cup at Sandown final one: stays 29f: acts on heavy going: wears cheekpieces: tried in tongue tie: front runner/races prominently. *Neil Mulholland*

THIBAULT 6 b.g. Kayf Tara – Seemarye (Romany Rye) [2018/19 b90: h16g³ h15.6g⁴ **h103** h15.5g Dec 28] has had breathing operation: fair form on first of 2 outings in bumpers: similar form over hurdles only when third in novice at Kempton on return. *Kim Bailey*

THINK AHEAD 8 b.g. Shamardal (USA) – Moonshadow (Diesis) [2018/19 h114: h17.2g⁴ **h–** h17.2m^d h17.2d^{pu} h17g^{pu} h16d^{pu} Mar 19] sturdy gelding: has had breathing operation: fair hurdler at best, out of sorts in 2018/19: wears headgear. *James Moffatt*

European Breeders' Fund Matchbook VIP 'National Hunt'
Novices' Handicap Hurdle Final, Sandown—Third Wind (star on cap/partly hidden) rallies to pip
One For Rosie (grey) and Champagne Well (No.8) in a race which caused more controversy over
Sandown's second winning post (touched on in the essay on Talkischeap)

THIRD ACT (IRE) 10 b.g. King's Theatre (IRE) – Starry Lady (IRE) (Marju (IRE)) [2018/19 c102§, h–§: c15.7m³ c17.8mᶠ c16.5g⁴ c16.3g⁶ h21.6mᵖᵘ Jul 14] lengthy, useful-looking gelding: has had breathing operation: fair handicap hurdler/maiden chaser: badly lost way since early-2017/18: stays 2¾m: acts on soft and good to firm going: regularly wears headgear: usually tongue tied: temperamental. *Colin Tizzard*   **c73 §** **h–**

THIRD ESTATE (IRE) 7 b.g. Suleiman (IRE) – Fizanni (IRE) (Arzanni) [2018/19 h103: h19.6g⁶ h23.3g h21.6m⁵ h18.5g² h15.8g* h15.8g² h21.2g⁴ h15.8g² c16.5g² Apr 22] angular gelding: has had breathing operation: fair handicap hurdler: won at Uttoxeter in October: second of 3 in novice handicap at Huntingdon on chasing debut (should improve): stays 21f: acts on good to soft going: tried in hood/tongue tie: usually races prominently/travels well. *Neil King*   **c115 p** **h112**

THIRD OF THE THIRD 12 b.g. Presenting – Gavotte du Cochet (FR) (Urbain Minotiere (FR)) [2018/19 c93, h–: c24gᵖᵘ Jun 25] winning pointer: maiden hurdler: modest form on completed starts in hunter chases: stays 3¼m: acts on soft going: in cheekpieces last 2 outings. *Gary Hanmer*   **c–** **h–**

THIRD WIND 5 b.g. Shirocco (GER) – Act Three (Beat Hollow) [2018/19 h93: h20.5s* h20.5d² h19s* h19.8s* Mar 9] well-made gelding: useful form over hurdles: won maiden at Plumpton in December, novice at Taunton in February and EBF 'National Hunt' Novices' Handicap Hurdle Final at Sandown (by short head from One For Rosie) in March: open to further improvement. *Hughie Morrison*   **h132 p**

THIS BREAC (IRE) 8 br.g. Carlo Bank (IRE) – De Breac (IRE) (Windsor Castle) [2018/19 c26g³ c27.5dᵖᵘ Jun 8] dual winning pointer: modest form in chases: stays 3¼m: wears hood. *A. Pennock*   **c96**

THIS IS IT (IRE) 7 b.g. Milan – Riviera Sands (IRE) (Mister Lord (USA)) [2018/19 h119: c23.4sᵘʳ c23.5s⁴ c24.2v⁶ Mar 5] workmanlike gelding: has had breathing operation: fairly useful hurdler: last both completed outings in chases: stays 3m: acts on heavy going: tried in cheekpieces: joined Harry Fry. *Nick Mitchell*   **c–** **h–**

THIS LOVELY LADY (IRE) 6 b.m. Getaway (GER) – Princesse Rooney (FR) (Baby Turk) [2018/19 b15.7g⁴ b16.3m² b15.8g⁴ h20g⁶ h20.3g⁵ h15.8d h18.5mᵖᵘ h21.4g h16.5dᵖᵘ Apr 24] lengthy, plain mare: has had breathing operation: seventh foal: half-sister to fairly   **h80** **b83**

useful hurdler/chaser Miles To Milan (19f-3m winner) and fair hurdler Msmilan (2m-2½m winner), both by Milan: dam, French maiden, out of half-sister to dam of Queen Mother Champion Chase winners Viking Flagship and Flagship Uberalles: modest form in bumpers (for Olly Murphy): disappointing maiden hurdler. *Tim Vaughan*

THIS MIGHT WORK (IRE) 5 b.g. Mountain High (IRE) – Finallyfree (IRE) (Flemensfirth (USA)) [2018/19 b17.7d Mar 18] pulled up in point: also folded quickly in bumper. *Emma Lavelle*   **b–**

THISONETIME (IRE) 8 br.g. Kalanisi (IRE) – Dizzy's Whisper (IRE) (Supreme Leader) [2018/19 c111, h107: h19.7g Feb 19] angular gelding: fair maiden hurdler: similar form first 2 outings in handicap chases: should stay beyond 2¼m: acts on heavy going: has worn headgear/tongue tie. *Andrew Martin*   **c– h–**

THIS THYNE JUDE 11 gr.m. Silver Patriarch (IRE) – This Thyne (Good Thyne (USA)) [2018/19 h93: h20.9d⁵ Nov 10] modest handicap hurdler: will stay beyond 3m: acts on heavy going: tried in hood. *Lucy Normile*   **h72**

THISTIMENEXTYEAR 5 gr.g. New Approach (IRE) – Scarlet Empire (IRE) (Red Ransom (USA)) [2018/19 h107p: h16v² h14h⁸ h16.5g² Apr 6] rather leggy gelding: useful on Flat (stays easy 1¾m): fairly useful handicap hurdler: won at Fakenham in March: good second in conditionals/amateurs event at Aintree after: raced around 2m: acts on heavy going: hooded prior to Fakenham: tried in tongue tie. *Richard Spencer*   **h123**

THISTLECRACK 11 b.g. Kayf Tara – Ardstown (Ardross) [2018/19 c158+, h–: c25.6g³ c24g² c26.3dᵖᵘ Mar 15] sturdy gelding: winning hurdler: formerly top-class chaser: showed plenty of ability remains when third in Betfair Chase at Haydock (5¾ lengths behind Bristol de Mai) in November and second in King George VI Chase at Kempton (beaten 1½ lengths by Clan des Obeaux, pair clear) in December: stays 3¼m: acts on heavy going: travels powerfully: doesn't always jump fences fluently (several mistakes when pulled up in Cheltenham Gold Cup final outing). *Colin Tizzard*   **c164 h–**

THISTLE DO NICELY (IRE) 5 b.g. Arcadio (GER) – April Thistle (IRE) (Alphabatim (USA)) [2018/19 b94: h15.3m* h16g* h15.7s⁴ h15.3g² h19d² h16.8d h20.3g² Apr 17] sturdy gelding: bumper winner: useful hurdler: won maiden at Wincanton in October and novice at Wetherby in November: runner-up 3 of 5 starts after, beaten 3½ lengths by Dashel Drasher in novice at Cheltenham final outing: stays 2½m: acts on good to firm and good to soft going. *Jamie Snowden*   **h132**

THOMAS BLOSSOM (IRE) 9 b.g. Dylan Thomas (IRE) – Woman Secret (IRE) (Sadler's Wells (USA)) [2018/19 c90, h98: c17.8m⁵ h16.8m* c16g* c15.9g⁶ c18.2dᵖᵘ Apr 4] close-coupled gelding: has had breathing operation: fair handicap hurdler: won amateurs event at Exeter in October: similar form over fences: won conditionals handicap at Hereford (left Ali Stronge after) in November: best around 2m: acts on good to firm going: usually tongue tied. *Richard Harper*   **c105 h101**

THOMAS CAMPBELL 7 b.g. Yeats (IRE) – Hora (Hernando (FR)) [2018/19 h149: c22.4d⁴ c20g* c23.6d² h20.3d⁴ h23.1d h21.5g³ Apr 27] good-topped gelding: formerly very smart hurdler: mostly disappointing since autumn 2017: just useful form over fences, landing odds in maiden at Ludlow in November: stays 25f: acts on soft going: often in headgear nowadays. *Nicky Henderson*   **c139 h143**

THOMAS CRAPPER 12 b.g. Tamure (IRE) – Mollycarrs Gambul (General Gambul) [2018/19 c–, h–: c21.7g⁶ c19.9d c25.6d⁷ c24.2s² c26.3d Jan 1] tall gelding: winning handicap chaser at best: won veterans event at Southwell in November: stayed 3¼m: acted on heavy going: wore headgear: often in tongue tie: retired. *Robin Dickin*   **c119 h–**

THOMAS CROMWELL 6 b.g. Sixties Icon – Salim Toto (Mtoto) [2018/19 ab16s⁶ ab16s Jan 1] good-topped gelding: little show in bumpers: tried in tongue strap. *Brendan Powell*   **b59**

THOMAS CROWN (IRE) 5 b.g. Helmet (AUS) – Picture of Lily (Medicean) [2018/19 h16mᵖᵘ h16g h16g⁴ h16g h18.5d h19.5g h21.2s⁴ h21.9v⁵ Jan 14] modest maiden on Flat, stays 11f: poor maiden hurdler: tried in cheekpieces. *Deborah Faulkner*   **h72**

THOMAS DARBY (IRE) 6 b.g. Beneficial – Silaoce (FR) (Nikos) [2018/19 b15.8g* h16.4g* h15.7g² h16g³ h16.5d* h16.4s² Mar 12] €160,000 3-y-o: good-topped gelding: half-brother to very smart hurdler/useful chaser Muirhead (2m-3m winner, by Flemensfirth) and bumper winner/fairly useful hurdler Letterbelucky (2m-2½m winner, by Luso): dam (h102), lightly raced over hurdles, sister to high-class French hurdler (17f-2½m winner) Nononito: won maiden bumper at Huntingdon: smart novice hurdler: won at Cheltenham (maiden, by 3¼ lengths from Elixir de Nutz) in October and Taunton (simple task) in   **h147 b92**

Mrs Diana L. Whateley's "Thomas Darby"

January: 28/1, much improved when second in Supreme Novices' Hurdle at Cheltenham (4½ lengths behind Klassical Dream) final outing: likely to stay beyond 2m: acts on soft going. *Olly Murphy*

THOMAS DO (IRE) 8 b.g. Flemensfirth (USA) – Loughaderra (IRE) (Strong Gale) [2018/19 h20.5d c20.9v Mar 7] Irish maiden point winner: well held over hurdles, off 23 months before return: little show in novice handicap on chasing debut: tongue tied 3 of 5 outings. *Donald McCain* **c–** **h–**

THOMAS MACDONAGH 6 b.g. Black Sam Bellamy (IRE) – Taqreem (IRE) (Nashwan (USA)) [2018/19 b18d⁴ b15.8d² b17g² Feb 18] €20,000 3-y-o: closely related to 2 winners on Flat and half-brother to several winners, including bumper winner Another Moment (by Sakhee) and modest 2m hurdle winner Jayed (by Marju): dam maiden (stayed 1½m): placed both starts in points: fairly useful form in frame in bumpers: left Denis Hogan after first start: tried in tongue tie. *Jamie Snowden* **b95**

THOMAS PATRICK (IRE) 7 b.g. Winged Love (IRE) – Huncheon Siss (IRE) (Phardante (FR)) [2018/19 c147p, h123: c24.2v² c26sᵖᵘ c23.8s c28.4dᵖᵘ c23.8d⁴ Feb 16] tall gelding: fairly useful hurdler: smart chaser: encouraging second in listed event at Sandown (½ length behind Elegant Escape) on return: most disappointing subsequently: stays 3¼m: acts on heavy going: forces pace. *Tom Lacey* **c149 d** **h–**

THOMAS TODD 9 b.g. Passing Glance – Miss Danbys (Charmer) [2018/19 h–: c23.8g* c21.2d² c26g³ c23.9sᵖᵘ Feb 5] point winner: maiden hurdler: fair form in handicap chases, winning novice event at Musselburgh in December: stays 3¼m: acts on good to soft going: wears headgear: in tongue tie last 3 starts: held up. *Laura Morgan* **c107** **h–**

THOMOND (IRE) 11 b.g. Definite Article – Hushaby (IRE) (Eurobus) [2018/19 c113, h–: c23.8g⁶ May 16] strong gelding: point winner: winning hurdler: fairly useful chaser, well below best since early-2017/18: stays 29f: acts on firm and soft going: has worn headgear: wears tongue tie. *N. W. Alexander* **c–** **h–**

THOONAVOLLA (IRE) 11 ch.g. Beneficial – Another Partner (Le Bavard (FR)) **c86**
[2018/19 c–, h–: c20g^{pu} c22.5m^3 c23.8g^2 c20g^{pu} c23m^{ur} Jul 9] winning hurdler: modest **h–**
handicap chaser nowadays: stays 3m: acts on soft and good to firm going: has worn
cheekpieces, including last 5 starts. *Tom Weston*

THOR DE CERISY (FR) 5 b.g. Enrique – Midalisy (FR) (Medaaly) [2018/19 b15.8s* **b98**
b15.7s b16.4s Mar 13] €40,000 3-y-o: beaten favourite: sixth foal: half-brother to useful
French hurdler/winning chaser Vangel de Cerisy (2¼m/19f winner, by Vangelis): dam
French maiden on Flat: fairly useful form in bumpers: easy winner of conditionals/
amateurs event at Ffos Las on debut in November: tried in hood. *Michael Scudamore*

THOSEDAYSAREGONE (IRE) 6 b.g. Getaway (GER) – Gonearethedays (IRE) (Be **c129 p**
My Native (USA)) [2018/19 b99: h19.4s h20s^2 h19.9m^{pu} h19d h16d h19.7g* h19.3d^4 **h121**
h19.3g^5 c17.7v* h19.7g Mar 29] lengthy, angular gelding: bumper winner: fairly useful
hurdler: won handicap at Wetherby in January: better form when also won maiden at
Limerick on chasing debut readily by 4¼ lengths from Mall Dini (should progress): stays
2½m: acts on heavy going. *Charles Byrnes, Ireland*

THOSE TIGER FEET (IRE) 5 b.g. Shantou (USA) – Luca Lite (IRE) (Warcraft **h70**
(USA)) [2018/19 b16.2s* b15.7s h15.8v h15.8d h15.7g^2 Mar 4] €47,000 3-y-o: well-made **b100**
gelding: fourth foal: dam, unraced, out of useful hurdler/chaser Lucky Baloo (stayed
2½m): fairly useful form in bumpers: won at Hereford in November: disappointing all 3
outings over hurdles. *Kim Bailey*

THOUNDER (FR) 5 ch.g. Hurricane Cat (USA) – Meldown (FR) (Until Sundown **h121**
(USA)) [2018/19 h117: h16v^{pu} h15.5g^{ur} h15.5d^2 h15.8g^3 h15.8d^2 h15.8m^5 Apr 1] compact
gelding: fairly useful handicap hurdler: best around 2m: acts on good to soft going.
Gary Moore

THREE BULLET GATE (IRE) 6 b.g. Touch of Land (FR) – Brave Hope (IRE) (City **h105**
Honours (USA)) [2018/19 b15.7g^3 h16s^6 h20d^2 h24s h16g^6 h21.2g^4 h19.9d^4 Mar 30] **b87**
second foal: dam unraced half-sister to fairly useful hurdler/chaser (stayed 3m) Lochan
Lacha: third in maiden bumper at Southwell: fair form over hurdles: stays 2½m: acts on
good to soft going. *Robin Dickin*

THREE COLOURS RED (IRE) 7 b.g. Camacho – Colour's Red (IRE) (Red Ransom **h107**
(USA)) [2018/19 h92: h23.3g^3 h23g* h23.2g* Jul 31] rather leggy gelding: fair handicap
hurdler: ridden by Tom O'Brien, won twice at Worcester in July: stays 23f: acts on good to
soft going: wears headgear: has worn tongue tie. *Robert Stephens*

THREE COUNTY'S (IRE) 8 b.g. Beneficial – Pattern Queen (IRE) (Alderbrook) **h104**
[2018/19 h26g^4 h15.7s^6 h16d h16.7s Mar 23] €52,000 3-y-o: third foal: brother to fair 2¾m
hurdle winner Do We Like Him: dam unraced sister to fair hurdler/useful chaser (stayed
25f) Flaming Gorge: ran out in Irish point: fair form when fourth in novice at Warwick on
hurdling debut: went wrong way: tried in hood. *Olly Murphy*

THREE FACES WEST (IRE) 11 b.g. Dr Massini (IRE) – Ardnataggle (IRE) **c–**
(Aristocracy) [2018/19 c133, h–: c26d^{pu} Feb 24] workmanlike gelding: winning hurdler: **h–**
smart chaser at best: failed to complete since reappearance in 2017/18: stays 3m: acts on
heavy going: wears cheekpieces: front runner/races prominently. *Miss Beth Childs*

THREE IN ONE (IRE) 7 b.g. Court Cave (IRE) – Star Bui (IRE) (Fourstars Allstar **c–**
(USA)) [2018/19 h21.6d h20.5s h19.2s^6 c20.3g^{pu} h23.9d^4 Mar 11] has had breathing **h74**
operation: maiden pointer: poor form over hurdles: pulled up in novice handicap on
chasing debut: tried in cheekpieces/tongue tie. *Jack R. Barber*

THREE KINGS (IRE) 7 b.g. King's Theatre (IRE) – M M Magnifica (IRE) (Beneficial) **c110**
[2018/19 h16g h24m c20g h16g h20.5d^2 c21.3d^F c19.5g^2 c16d Apr 27] £42,000 3-y-o: first **h105**
foal: dam unraced sister to fairly useful hurdler (stayed 2½m) Chiltern Hills: point winner:
fair maiden hurdler: similar form over fences: left T. E. Hyde after fourth start: stays 2½m:
acts on heavy going: wears headgear: has worn tongue tie. *Gordon Elliott, Ireland*

THREE MUSKETEERS (IRE) 9 b.g. Flemensfirth (USA) – Friendly Craic (IRE) **c124 §**
(Mister Lord (USA)) [2018/19 c144, h134: h20g c19.9d^3 c25.6d h20d* Apr 5] strong, **h137 §**
workmanlike gelding: useful handicap hurdler: left Dan Skelton, back on track when
winning Grade 3 event at Aintree (by 1¾ lengths from Point of Principle) in April: formerly
smart chaser: became disappointing for former yard: should stay 3m: acts on heavy going:
often wears cheekpieces: untrustworthy. *Gordon Elliott, Ireland*

THREE STAR GENERAL 6 b.g. Montjeu (IRE) – Honorlina (FR) (Linamix (FR)) **h115 §**
[2018/19 h115: h24.7g h21g h23.1s^3 h23.3s^3 h18.9s^5 h25s^2 h23.8d^4 h25s^2 h24.2d^2 h26g^2
Apr 10] rather leggy gelding: fairly useful handicap hurdler: stays 3¼m: acts on soft and
good to firm going: wears headgear: tried in tongue tie: ungenuine. *David Pipe*

THREE WAYS 8 b.g. Flemensfirth (USA) – Serenique (Good Thyne (USA)) [2018/19 c134, h–: h24.4g⁶ Mar 2] sturdy gelding: has had breathing operation: fairly useful hurdler: useful novice chase winner in 2017/18: stays 25f: acts on soft going: often in headgear: wears tongue tie: races prominently. *Jamie Snowden* **c–** **h–**

THROCKLEY 8 b.g. Passing Glance – Porcelain (IRE) (Peintre Celebre (USA)) [2018/19 h16g⁴ h16.8g² h15.8g⁴ h15.8m⁴ h19.3m^pu Nov 3] modest form over hurdles: unproven beyond 17f: acts on good to firm going: tried in hood: in tongue tie last 5 starts. *Sophie Leech* **h98**

THUMB STONE BLUES (IRE) 9 b.g. High Chaparral (IRE) – Jade River (FR) (Indian River (FR)) [2018/19 c130, h–: c23g² Jul 31] has had breathing operation: winning hurdler: useful maiden chaser: stays 25f: acts on good to firm and heavy going: in cheekpieces last 3 starts: wears tongue tie: front runner/races prominently: takes plenty of driving. *Kim Bailey* **c131** **h–**

THUNDER BOY (FR) 4 b.g. Haatef (USA) – Nice To Know (FR) (Machiavellian (USA)) [2018/19 h16.8s^pu h16g h16.7d^pu Apr 26] fair maiden on Flat (stayed 11f) in France for Mme J-F. Bernard: no form over hurdles: dead. *Micky Hammond* **h–**

THUNDERHOOVES 4 ro.g. Raven's Pass (USA) – Regrette Rien (USA) (Unbridled's Song (USA)) [2018/19 h15.8m^pu h15.8g Nov 24] little form on Flat/over hurdles. *John Ryan* **h–**

THUNDERING HOME 12 gr.g. Storming Home – Citrine Spirit (IRE) (Soviet Star (USA)) [2018/19 h91: h16.8g^F h16.8m h16.5m Nov 15] smallish gelding: winning hurdler, retains little ability: wears headgear/tongue tie. *Richard Mitchell* **h–**

THUNDERSTRUCK (IRE) 5 b.g. Fame And Glory – Go Sandy Go (IRE) (Flemensfirth (USA)) [2018/19 b16v² b17.7d² Feb 24] €10,000 3-y-o, £125,000 4-y-o: first foal: dam (c116/h116) 2¾m-3m hurdle/chase winner: won Irish point on debut: fair form when runner-up in bumpers at Sandown and Fontwell. *Emma Lavelle* **b92**

THYME HILL 5 b.g. Kayf Tara – Rosita Bay (Hernando (FR)) [2018/19 b16g* b16.4g² b16.4s³ Mar 13] well-made gelding: fourth foal: brother to fair hurdler/fairly useful chaser Storming Strumpet (2m-19f winner): dam (h106), bumper/19f-21f hurdle winner, out of smart hurdler/fairly useful chaser (stayed 3¼m) Lemon's Mill: smart form in bumpers: won at Worcester (by 6 lengths from Timcoda) on debut in October: much better form when placed at Cheltenham, notably so when 2½ lengths third of 14 to Envoi Allen in Champion Bumper. *Philip Hobbs* **b121**

THYNE FOR GOLD (IRE) 8 b.g. Robin des Pres (FR) – My Name's Not Bin (IRE) (Good Thyne (USA)) [2018/19 c107, h–: c20.3d* c23.8g⁴ c19.4g³ c19.1d³ c19.2g⁴ c20.3d Apr 26] useful-looking gelding: winning hurdler: fair handicap chaser: won at Bangor on return in November: stays 23f: acts on good to soft going: tried in hood: front runner/races prominently. *Donald McCain* **c107** **h–**

TIBBIE TAMSON 8 b.m. Josr Algarhoud (IRE) – Midlem Melody (Syrtos) [2018/19 h–, b–: h17.2g^pu h16.2g^pu Jul 31] no promise in bumper/over hurdles. *Stuart Coltherd* **h–**

TICKANRUN (IRE) 9 gr.g. Tikkanen (USA) – Dusty Lane (IRE) (Electric) [2018/19 h91: h23.3g h24g^pu Jun 25] modest maiden hurdler: stayed 3m: acted on heavy going: tried in headgear: dead. *Micky Hammond* **h–**

TICKENWOLF (IRE) 9 gr.g. Tikkanen (USA) – Emma's Choice (IRE) (Indian Danehill (IRE)) [2018/19 c122, h–: c23.8g c24.2g⁴ c23.8g⁶ c25.5s⁴ h27m⁶ h23.3s³ h27g² c31.9s^pu h25.3g⁵ Dec 28] big, lengthy gelding: fair handicap hurdler: fairly useful handicap chaser: won at Hexham in June: stays 27f: acts on heavy going: wears cheekpieces. *Micky Hammond* **c118** **h109**

TICKERTY BOO (IRE) 7 gr.m. Tikkanen (USA) – La Fille d'Or (IRE) (Goldmark (USA)) [2018/19 b78: h16.2d³ h19.9g⁴ h22.1d⁵ h16.2g⁵ h20.6g⁵ h17.1g c19.3s^F c16.4s⁴ Dec 26] modest form over hurdles: little aptitude for chasing: should stay beyond 2m: acts on good to soft going: tried in cheekpieces: in tongue tie last 2 starts. *Brian Ellison* **c83** **h97**

TICKET TO RIDE (FR) 6 b.g. Al Namix (FR) – Eightdaysaweek (Montjeu (IRE)) [2018/19 c91, h81: c24d c20d³ c21.5s³ c21g² Jan 15] workmanlike gelding: twice-raced hurdler: modest maiden chaser: left Polly Gundry after first start: stayed 21f: acted on soft going: wore hood: dead. *Gordon Elliott, Ireland* **c97** **h–**

TIDAL FLOW 6 b.g. Black Sam Bellamy (IRE) – Mrs Philip (Puissance) [2018/19 b105: h21g* h20.5s* h21g⁶ h20.5d⁴ h23.1s² Mar 18] compact gelding: useful bumper performer: fairly useful form over hurdles: won novices at Kempton in November and Newbury in December: will be suited by 3m: acts on soft going: tried in cheekpieces. *Philip Hobbs* **h123**

TIDAL WATCH (IRE) 5 b.g. Harbour Watch (IRE) – Najmati (Green Desert (USA))   **h113**
[2018/19 h98: h15.7g³ h18.7m* h15.8g* h16.8g* h20g⁴ h16g⁴ h16m* Apr 25] has had
breathing operation: fair handicap hurdler: completed hat-trick in conditionals events at
Stratford and Uttoxeter and novice race at Newton Abbot, all in July, and also won another
conditionals contest at Kempton in April: stays easy 19f: acts on good to firm and good to
soft going: usually travels strongly. *Jonjo O'Neill*

TIDESTREAM 9 b.g. Galileo (IRE) – Sweet Stream (ITY) (Shantou (USA)) [2018/19 c–,   **c–**
h90: h22m⁶ May 20] good-topped gelding: modest handicap hurdler: little encouragement   **h71**
in handicap chases: stays 3m: acts on soft going: visored 4 of last 6 outings: wears tongue
tie. *Tim Vaughan*

TIDE TIMES (IRE) 5 gr.g. Vinnie Roe (IRE) – Lady Wagtail (IRE) (Milan) [2018/19   **b78**
b16.3d Mar 2] rather leggy gelding: won point on debut: showed a bit in bumper at
Newbury. *Ian Williams*

TIERRA VERDE 8 b.m. Josr Algarhoud (IRE) – La Corujera (Case Law) [2018/19 h100,   **h106**
b74: h19.9g h16.5g* h16d³ h16.5d* Mar 11] fair handicap hurdler: won mares events at
Taunton in January and March: unproven beyond 2m: acts on heavy going. *Emma Lavelle*

TIFFIN TOP 4 gr.g. Oasis Dream – Mussoorie (FR) (Linamix (FR)) [2018/19 h16.5d⁴   **h112**
h16g³ h16.2g* h15.3g³ Apr 14] sturdy gelding: half-brother to useful hurdler Thunder Zone
(2m-2½m winner, by Shamardal): fairly useful maiden on Flat, stays 1½m: fair form in
juvenile hurdles, winning maiden at Hereford in March. *Alan King*

TIGERALLEY 10 b.m. Revoque (IRE) – Run Tiger (IRE) (Commanche Run) [2018/19   **c91 p**
h17.7g⁴ h15.8g h16d h16.4d⁵ h21.7s² h23.9g³ c25.1sᶠ h15.8v* h16.7s² c21.1g³ Apr 5] half-   **h105**
sister to 3 winners, including fairly useful chaser Alpancho (2½m winner, by Alflora) and
fair hurdler Tiger Line (27f winner, by Kayf Tara): dam unraced out of sister to high-class
2m chaser Young Snugfit and half-sister to Grand National runner-up Mr Snugfit: point
winner: fair handicap hurdler: won mares event at Uttoxeter in March: modest form when
third in mares event at Sedgefield on completed start in handicap chases (capable of better):
stays 3m: acts on heavy going: in cheekpieces last 3 starts. *Dan Skelton*

TIGER ROLL (IRE) 9 b.g. Authorized (IRE) – Swiss Roll (IRE) (Entrepreneur)   **c167**
[2018/19 c155, h–: c30.2g⁴ h21d* c30.2s* c34.3g* Apr 6]   **h154**
   'Tigermania' hit the world of sport in April. An amazing month for comebacks
featured the Masters victory of the greatest golfer of the modern era, Tiger Woods,
whose world ranking had slipped to 1,199th in 2018 after a series of injuries and
other problems (it was feared at one time that his career might be over after three
back operations). The scenes at Augusta as Woods closed in on his first victory in a
major for eleven years were probably unprecedented in the history of golf and were
great for his sport, and for sport in general. Here was a comeback as remarkable as
any, set to become as famous as those involving some other sporting greats. Formula
One driver Niki Lauda, who died in May aged seventy, was given the last rites after
a horrifying crash in the 1976 German Grand Prix, but he was back at the wheel
just seven weeks later, finishing fourth in the Italian Grand Prix despite his painful
injuries (Lauda went on to regain the World Championship in 1977 and then came
out of retirement in 1982 to win the title again in 1984); Muhammad Ali regained
the world title after an effective three-year ban from boxing when he refused to be
inducted into the US army; George Foreman became the oldest heavyweight world
champion when reclaiming the title twenty years after last holding it; and Monica
Seles won the Australian Open after a two-year absence from the game when she
was stabbed by a spectator while playing a match at Hamburg. Tennis also provided
a comeback of a different sort that made the headlines in April, when British player
Tara Moore recovered to win from 0-6, 0-5, 30-40 down in a World Tour event,
and there was attention on James Cracknell, the former Olympic rower—twice a
gold medallist—who, at the age of forty-six (thirteen years after retiring from the
sport and after almost dying in a cycling accident in America in 2010), became the
oldest winner in the long history of the Oxford and Cambridge boat race (England's
number-one spectator sport, football, had to wait until May to make its own 'famous
comeback' headlines, when Liverpool overturned a 3-0 deficit from the first leg
of a Champions' League semi-final with a 4-0 home win against Barcelona, and
Tottenham, trailing 3-0 on aggregate with thirty-five minutes left, scored three times
to win the other semi-final against Ajax on away goals to set up an all-English final,
which Liverpool won).

Ladbrokes Ireland Boyne Hurdle, Navan—
a remarkable winning return to hurdles by 25/1-shot Tiger Roll

Racing's most popular event, the Grand National at Aintree, has produced its own share of incredible comebacks, two of those moments brought to mind in the latest season with the retirement from the training ranks of Brendan Powell and the death at the age of eighty-one in November of owner Nick Embiricos. Powell's amazing victory on Rhyme 'N' Reason in 1988 took its place among the legendary feats in Grand National history when horse and rider recovered from a near-fall at first Becher's (Rhyme 'N' Reason slithering on his belly before scrambling to his feet and setting off again at a walk); any hopes of victory seemed to have gone as the pair went in pursuit of the thirty-two others still standing, but Rhyme 'N' Reason was in front four out and then rallied strongly after being headed by Durham Edition at the second last. An estimated British television audience of sixteen and a half million saw the triumph in 1981 of Aldaniti, carrying the colours of shipbroker Embiricos and ridden by Bob Champion, in one of the happiest tales in Grand National history. Aldaniti had been plagued by injury for most of his career and had run only once in the previous sixteen months, kept in training primarily to give Champion, his regular jockey, 'something to keep him going' as he fought a lengthy and painful struggle against cancer. Aldaniti and Champion, who had finished third in the 1979 Cheltenham Gold Cup, led the National field throughout the final circuit to achieve the ultimate fairytale, a story that was made into a film (Nick Embiricos, whose colours were carried in the latest season by the smart novice hurdler Bright Forecast who raced for the Aldaniti Partnership, was chairman of the Bob Champion Cancer Trust for more than twenty years, actively campaigning to raise millions for research into testicular and prostate cancer).

Aldaniti's triumph came towards the end of the seven-year tenure of bookmakers Ladbrokes who leased the course at short notice to run the troubled Grand National meeting in 1976 after the turf authorities shilly-shallied and eventually suggested staging a substitute National at another course (likely to have been Doncaster). The 1975 National had been watched by the smallest crowd in living memory after its new owners the Walton Group introduced much increased admission charges. With the Walton Group in difficulties, the future of Aintree racecourse was seriously threatened before Ladbrokes saved the day and earned some valuable breathing space (Mike Dillon, who eventually became director of public relations and left Ladbrokes after forty-six years in June 2018, was among those instrumental in sowing the seeds of a revival at Aintree which was developed with flair into an all-jumps meeting). It almost strains credulity, looking back, that an event capable of attracting sixteen and a half million television viewers, and an irresistible draw, in one way or another, for well over half the country's population, should have come under threat of extinction in its traditional form. The Grand National was—and still is—an institution, racing's greatest asset, and, with eleven Grade 1 events over its three days, the Aintree meeting itself can no longer be labelled Cheltenham's poor relation. The Grand National still dominates the week's headlines, however, just as it has always done. Aldaniti's triumph was the main item on the day's television news bulletins and was prominent on the news pages, as well as the sports pages, of all the newspapers in the days that followed. It provided a perfect illustration of what the National could produce by way of drama and entertainment.

In the same way, Red Rum contributed enormously to the revival of the National during the Ladbrokes years. In all, he finished first or second in the race five years running and is the only horse to win the race three times, his third win coming in 1977 after he had finished second in Ladbrokes' first year. Red Rum twice won the National under top weight, carrying 12-0 and beating dual Cheltenham Gold Cup winner L'Escargot in 1974, and then conceding between 4 lb and 22 lb to forty-one rivals (including the current Gold Cup winner Davy Lad) when successful at the age of twelve in 1977. Red Rum is the only Grand National winner with a statue at Aintree (he is buried near the winning post) and no top weight has won the race since he did. Red Rum was a sporting phenomenon and his third win in the National was one of the great events in steeplechasing, accompanied by an O'Sullevan commentary that can still be recited, word for word, more than forty years afterwards—'They are willing him home now, the twelve-year-old Red Rum being preceded only by loose horses … he's coming up to the line to win it like a fresh horse in great style. It's hats off and a tremendous reception, you've never heard the like of it at Liverpool.'

Comparisons between Red Rum and the latest 'people's horse' Tiger Roll, the cause of racing's own 'Tigermania' in April, are not particularly useful. Tiger Roll became just the eighth horse to appear on the Grand National's roll of honour more than once—and the first since Red Rum—but, forty-five years on, the National is a different race. Even in Red Rum's day, there were those who complained that the fences had been made 'too easy', but the obstacles on today's National course are a far cry from those of yesteryear which made the National an even more fearsome test. The race remains the longest in Britain and is still an extreme test of stamina, courage and resolution, but the fences themselves have been built differently since the modifications made to the course before the 2013 running. The levelling work, and the reduction in the drop, on the landing side of some of the most famous fences is illustrated by the photographs on pages 858 and 859 which provide a striking contrast between Becher's as it was in Red Rum's day and as it is now, with the drop and the slope on the landing side much reduced and the ditch virtually filled in. The Grand National fences are still constructed with loose furze and spruce on top of a firm foundation, outwardly making them look much the same, but the traditional rigid, thick timber frames have been replaced by closely-packed plastic birch in plastic containers fixed at ground level, in the style of a French-style brush hurdle. The old timber frames were vertically bigger than the current plastic base, and the spruce which used to fill the top six inches or so of the big fences now amounts to at least fourteen inches, the less tightly-packed spruce sprays being thinner and more easily dislodged, which makes the fences more forgiving. Runners who make mistakes nowadays have a much better chance of getting away with them, as illustrated by those of Magic of Light (who carved a huge chunk out of the final fence) in the photographs of the race displayed in these pages.

The incidence of falls, horses being brought down and jockeys being unseated has been noticeably lower in the last seven Nationals than nearly all the earlier runnings this century, though the remodelled fences are still big. The Grand

National field taking Becher's, for example, may have lost its allure as one of the great sights in racing (it causes considerably fewer problems than it used to), but there still isn't a tougher event anywhere for horse and rider than the race widely known as 'the people's race'. The size of the field—there were the maximum forty runners in the latest edition—undoubtedly plays its part, coupled with the sense of occasion, in the Grand National remaining the finest spectacle that steeplechasing has to offer, even though the course modifications and the higher overall quality of the runners results in the race bearing a closer likeness to a conventional staying steeplechase, in the way it is run, with the field taking longer to get whittled down and become thinned out. Good horses ran in the Grand National in Red Rum's era but all the runners nowadays are in the handicap proper and the field contains more above-average performers than it did in the 'sixties and 'eighties, for example.

The field for the latest Randox Health Grand National was a good one by present-day standards. The weights were headed by the previous year's fourth Anibale Fly, on whom Barry Geraghty had to be replaced by Mark Walsh after breaking his leg in the Topham. Anibale Fly had finished third and second in the last two Cheltenham Gold Cups and carried 11-10 (the top weight was lowered from 11-12 in 2009). Anibale Fly's weight equated to a BHA handicap mark of 164 and the forty runners all fitted in a weight range of 22 lb, the bottom weights, including late reserve Just A Par, carrying 10-2 and running off a BHA mark of 142. Around half the field had previous experience of the Grand National fences, among them the last two winners of the big race itself, Tiger Roll and One For Arthur (trying to regain his crown after a lengthy absence with a tendon injury). Also in the field were two winners of the Becher Chase, Vieux Lion Rouge (appearing for the seventh time over the fences) and its most recent winner Walk In The Mill, as well as Grand Sefton winner Warriors Tale and dual Topham Chase winner Ultragold (running his fifth race over the big fences). The 2018 Grand National runner-up Pleasant Company, who had run a faltering Tiger Roll close, and the third, veteran Bless The Wings, were back again, as was Valseur Lido, eighth behind Tiger Roll. Pleasant Company had also completed the course in One For Arthur's Grand National, as

Glenfarclas Chase (Cross Country), Cheltenham—a fourth Festival success for Tiger Roll as he pulls twenty-two lengths clear under Keith Donoghue

had Regal Encore and Vieux Lion Rouge (who had never come lower than ninth in three appearances in the race). Among the others proven over very long distances were the 2017 Cheltenham Gold Cup second Minella Rocco, a former winner of the National Hunt Chase, a race Tiger Roll had also won, as had Rathvinden who had shown improved form when winning the Bobbyjo Chase at Fairyhouse on his reappearance. The first two in the previous year's Scottish National, Joe Farrell and Ballyoptic, and the first two in the Sandown Gold Cup, Step Back and Rock The Kasbah (a record twenty-first National ride for Richard Johnson), were others who had form over very long distances, while the same could be said for Irish National winner General Principle, the close second in the Welsh National Ramses de Teillee, and Vintage Clouds who had finished in the frame in both a Scottish and a Welsh National. Irish-trained Jury Duty had also won a Grand National, though that was a two mile five furlong race over hurdles in the States in October, since when he had won his warm-up for Aintree in a minor event at Down Royal in March, beating his better-fancied stablemate Mala Beach (also in the National line-up) on that occasion.

The fields for many of jumping's most valuable handicaps nowadays feature multiple entries from the top Irish stables of Gordon Elliott and Willie Mullins, and Jury Duty, Mala Beach and the Punchestown Grand National Trial winner Dounikos were among a record eleven saddled in the latest Grand National by Elliott who also had the high-class pair Outlander and Don Poli before they were sold out of his stable for £165,000 and £170,000 respectively at the Aintree Sales at the Grand National meeting on the Thursday evening before the race (both ran in the National under different trainers for their new owners, the 2016 Cheltenham Gold Cup third Don Poli bought as a replacement for an earlier Darren Yates £300,000 purchase, the high-class Blaklion, a horse with good Aintree form who had recently gone wrong). There were four Mullins-trained contenders, Rathvinden (the choice of the stable's number-one Ruby Walsh), Pleasant Company, Livelovelaugh and Up For Review. Nigel Twiston-Davies, the only current British-based trainer to have won the National more than once (his second winner Bindaree led the traditional pre-race parade of former winners), was doubly represented with Ballyoptic and Go Conquer, as was David Pipe (Ramses de Teillee and Vieux Lion Rouge) whose father Martin had set the previous record for the number of runners in the race with ten in the mudbath of 2001 when remounted Blowing Wind finished third for Pipe, one minute forty-three seconds behind the winner Red Marauder in a race in which only two got round without mishap.

Tiger Roll was undoubtedly the star turn among the big Elliott contingent and the bookmakers claimed to be braced for the biggest public gamble in the Grand National for years. Already dubbed a 'modern-day Red Rum', Tiger Roll

Randox Health Grand National Handicap Chase, Aintree—Step Back leads the field over the modern-day version of Becher's on the first circuit …

... which provides a far less daunting jumping test than Red Rum (No.1) had to contend with at the same stage of the 1974 Grand National

had a big following after also winning four times at the Cheltenham Festival—a group sporting matching suits with tiger patterning was prominent at Aintree—and there was even talk that Tiger Roll might go off the shortest-priced Grand National favourite since Red Rum himself started at 7/2 in the 1975 edition in which, carrying 12-0 and conceding weight all round, he was beaten by L'Escargot. The dual Grand National runner-up in the 'sixties Freddie was sent off at 7/2 and 11/4 on those two appearances. Golden Miller is the shortest-priced Grand National favourite in history, sent off at 2/1 under 12-7 when he unseated his rider in 1935 (the year after he had won). It was a hundred years since Poethlyn had become the shortest-priced winning favourite in the history of the race when it returned to its natural home after the end of World War I. Carrying 12-7 at Aintree and starting at 11/4, he won his ninth race in succession which had included the previous year's War National Steeplechase run over approximately the same distance but a vastly different course at Gatwick. The Grand National weights launch in February was moved to Liverpool in the latest season in recognition of the hundredth anniversary of Poethlyn's weight-carrying feat (the maximum top weight came down from 12-7 to 12-0 in the 'sixties).

It was once a questionable investment to wager on Tiger Roll—he still carried the '§' symbol, the Timeform squiggle, against his rating in the 2018 Grand National—but his unreliability seems very much a thing of the past, even though he still wears headgear. Tiger Roll was better than ever in the latest season when, after a satisfactory fourth under top weight in a handicap over Cheltenham's cross country course in November, he won the Ladbrokes Ireland Boyne Hurdle, a Grade 2 contest, at Navan in February before taking the Cross Country Chase (sponsored by Glenfarclas) at the Cheltenham Festival for the second year in succession. The latest Boyne Hurdle wasn't a vintage renewal by any means but, friendless in the market at 25/1 in a six-runner race, and having his first outing over hurdles for almost three years, Tiger Roll led on the bridle before the second last and drew clear to win by four lengths from Off You Go. Tiger Roll's form was comparable to that which he showed to win the 2014 Triumph Hurdle, the first of his four Cheltenham

The Chair—Magic of Light (noseband) survives a blunder as the Willie Mullins-trained pair Pleasant Company (right) and Rathvinden (diamonds) lead the way, with Tiger Roll (blinkers) tracking the latter

Festival wins. Tiger Roll's Boyne Hurdle performance still came as something of a revelation (it seemed to be presumed that the purpose was merely to blow away any remaining cobwebs before his spring campaign), but there was even better to come at Cheltenham. The separate cross country course at Cheltenham, with its assorted obstacles and twisting course, was regarded as no more than a novelty when it was introduced in the mid-'nineties. When a cross country chase featured for the first time at the Cheltenham Festival in 2005, it was described in these pages as 'the crowning insult to those who have reservations about jumping's premier meeting becoming four days.' The race drew on a small pool of Irish-trained cross country specialists who were taken on by a mixed bag, including ageing handicap chasers using it as something of a halfway house between running in better races over orthodox fences and their eventual retirement.

The Cross Country Chase has come a long way since those early days and has featured a number who have gone on to run well in Grand Nationals, including, before Tiger Roll, his stable's other Grand National winner Silver Birch (a good second) and two winners who have gone on to finish second at Aintree, dual scorer Balthazar King and Cause of Causes (another stablemate of Tiger Roll). The victories of Cause of Causes and Tiger Roll in the Cross Country Chase have come since its change from a handicap to a conditions event and Tiger Roll dominated the fifteen-runner field for the latest edition. Sent off 5/4 favourite, Tiger Roll showed that he was in the form of his life, sauntering clear to win by twenty-two lengths from the smart cross country performer Josies Orders (winner, on technical grounds, of the first running of the race as a conditions event in 2016), with French challenger Urgent de Gregaine (second to Tiger Roll the previous year) third in a representative field (Bless The Wings, Ultragold and Tea For Two, who all went on to the National, failed to complete).

Tiger Roll had 11-5 (equivalent to a BHA mark of 159, 9 lb higher than the previous year) in the Grand National, for which there are no penalties after the publication of the weights in February. He was third top weight behind Anibale Fly and the Henderson-trained French import Valtor (who vied with Tiger Roll as the smallest horse in the field). Tiger Roll's owner Michael O'Leary, whose ownership vehicle Gigginstown House Stud still had seven in the National line-up after Outlander and Don Poli were sold (six of the seven trained by Elliott), had suggested after his Cross Country Chase victory that Tiger Roll might sidestep the National because of the stiffness of his task. However, the BHA handicappers raised Tiger Roll's mark 8 lb after his Cheltenham victory and he undoubtedly looked well-in at the weights at Aintree, as did others who had shown improved form since the handicap was framed and would have had more to carry if the weights could have been framed again, notably Rathvinden, Anibale Fly and Jury Duty. Tiger Roll was as short as 7/2 in the ante-post market in the run up to the race but, on the day, he was sent off the 4/1 favourite, ahead of Rathvinden at 8/1 and Anibale Fly and Jury Duty both at 10/1. Next came the 11/1-shot Vintage Clouds, 12/1-shot Pleasant Company and 14/1-shots Joe Farrell and Lake View Lad (the last-named and Vintage Clouds among a trio representing octogenarian owner Trevor Hemmings who was seeking a record fourth win in the race). Rock The Kasbah and Dounikos, both at 16/1, were the only others shorter than 20/1. Seventeen of the field, including the only mare Magic of Light, were sent off at odds ranging from 50/1 to 66/1.

In contrast to the unusually wet winter of the year before, when the conditions for the Grand National were very testing, the latest winter was unusually dry and the going on Grand National day was good (although racegoers endured heavy rain and strong, bitingly-cold winds on the opening day of the meeting). For Tiger Roll, the contrasting underfoot conditions demanded versatility as he sought to join the exclusive club of dual Grand National winners; since Red Rum won successive editions in 1973 and 1974, incidentally, twenty-four winners had tried and failed to follow up the next year before Tiger Roll, with only Red Rum himself (second in 1975), Corbiere (third in 1984), Hedgehunter (second in 2006), Comply Or Die (second in 2009) and Don't Push It (third in 2011) reaching a place (West Tip, Papillon and Monty's Pass managed fourth). Hedgehunter and Comply Or Die (joint) were the last winning favourites in the Grand National, since when six of the ten editions before the latest one had featured winners at 100/1, 66/1, 33/1 (twice) and 25/1 (twice). Since Red Rum's era, only Grittar (11-5), Don't Push It (11-5), Neptune Collonges (11-6) and Many Clouds (11-9) had won carrying the same or more weight than Tiger Roll.

The Grand National fences have undergone changes throughout Aintree's history but the radical remodelling of them and the levelling work on the course before the 2013 running have proved more influential than anything that preceded them. It soon became apparent in the first 'plastic Grand National' in 2013 that the race had been changed as the field streamed over the first seven fences without a single casualty (no horse actually came down until the twelfth that year and there was only one other faller). The latest National was similarly largely incident-free, although there was an anxious moment before the start for Tiger Roll's jockey Davy Russell (taking over from the horse's regular rider Keith Donoghue for the first time since the previous year's race). As the runners were about to be called in, Tiger Roll began to show signs of reluctance to assemble with his thirty-nine rivals and had to be given a lead by stablemate A Toi Phil to rejoin them. That was probably the most worried that Russell became at any point before or during the race. Tiger Roll gave him just about as near to an armchair ride as is possible in a forty-runner steeplechase.

The National went off a few minutes late after a false start, Lake View Lad dwelling badly at the subsequent starting start. The patiently-ridden Tiger Roll settled towards mid-field on the inner, where he remained for most of the first circuit. After Vintage Clouds fell at the first, bringing down Up For Review, who looked very badly injured, the fences claimed no further casualties until after an unprecedented thirty-seven survivors had set off into the country towards Becher's

Second Canal Turn—Tiger Roll (No.3) is well placed alongside eventual fourth Walk In The Mill as Rathvinden leads from Magic of Light (noseband), Pleasant Company (checks) and Livelovelaugh (almost hidden)

on the second circuit. Step Back (racing on the outside and jumping to the right), Rathvinden, Walk In The Mill, Pleasant Company, Magic of Light, Go Conquer, Livelovelaugh and the smooth-travelling Tiger Roll were the leaders passing the winning post for the first time. The field had to bypass the seventeenth (where the ill-fated Up For Review was still being attended to), and after filing past, almost in formation, the survivors all cleared the next. However, what would have been the nineteenth, an open ditch, claimed Jury Duty, General Principle and Rock The Kasbah, the first runners to depart at one of the fences since the first. Tiger Roll was moving smoothly, close behind the leaders, but the Willie Mullins team was particularly strongly represented in the leading group as the field cleared Becher's for the second time, with Rathvinden, Livelovelaugh, taking extremely well to the fences, Walk In The Mill and Pleasant Company the first four. Mullins had the first three over the second Canal Turn, with Rathvinden, Livelovelaugh and Pleasant Company now ahead of Magic of Light.

It is becoming more usual to see a bigger group staying in contention for longer in the National and, crossing the Melling Road onto the main racecourse with two fences left, there were a dozen still in with some hope. Magic of Light led the way from Rathvinden, Tiger Roll, Livelovelaugh, Walk In The Mill, Captain Redbeard, Anibale Fly, Regal Encore, the improving One For Arthur, Outlander, Singlefarmpayment and Valseur Lido. Tiger Roll had quickly shrugged aside mistakes when pecking on landing over the fifth last (after stumbling slightly) and then making a similar error four out, and, with Russell sitting motionless, looked the winner in the home straight even before he moved through to take the lead, still on the bridle, at the last. Magic of Light, who had gone with plenty of zest after recovering well from a blunder at the Chair (a mistake that left her jockey with a bloody lip), ruined any chance she still had when crashing through the final fence. Tiger Roll was soon clear and, ridden out firmly from the elbow ('I was just a bit afraid he might get a puncture like last year,' said Russell), he won by two and three quarter lengths from the rallying Magic of Light (the first of her sex to finish in the first two since runner-up Tiberetta in 1958), with Rathvinden, who like the runner-up took some chances at the fences along the way (including at the water and at second Valentine's), finishing a further two and a quarter lengths behind in third to complete an Irish-trained one, two, three, after Irish horses had filled the first four places the previous year.

There was an eleven-length gap back to fourth-placed Walk In The Mill, who emerged with more credit in the National than most Becher winners have in recent times, and he was followed home by a staying-on Anibale Fly, recovering

Four out—2018 runner-up Pleasant Company (left) is about to part company with Paul Townend as Tiger Roll (right) moves alongside his main market rival Rathvinden

The last—Davy Russell still has plenty of horse under him as Tiger Roll takes over from the blundering Magic of Light

from a bad mistake at the fourteenth, and One For Arthur, whose effort flattened out after he had made ground from well off the pace with only three to jump. Regal Encore bettered his 2017 finish by one place, with Singlefarmpayment, Outlander and Valseur Lido (ridden by Rachael Blackmore, one of two female riders with a mount in the race) completing the first ten. Livelovelaugh ran out of stamina, shaping much better than his final placing of eleventh, and nineteen completed the course in all, with just six of those who failed to do so either falling or unseating their rider (including Pleasant Company who was still right there when departing at the fourth last). Although the early pace wasn't so strong as it can be sometimes in the National, Tiger Roll's time of 9m 1.5sec was the fastest by a National winner since the course modifications in 2013 (when the National distance was also shortened, with the start moved closer to the first fence). Tiger Roll's time was nearly thirty-nine seconds faster than the soft-ground National of twelve months earlier and, for the time being, he has the distinction of holding both the slowest and fastest winning times for the 'new' National. Red Rum's best performance on the clock came in the 1973 renewal when Crisp's front-running display resulted in a time of 9m 1.9sec, remarkable considering the longer trip and stiffer fences.

The form of the latest National looks strong and, among National winners of the last forty years or so, only Many Clouds (rated 168) has earned a higher Timeform rating in the race than Tiger Roll, with only Crisp (rated 173 when runner-up to Red Rum in 1973) and Suny Bay (171 in 1998 when also runner-up under 12-0) having achieved more in handicapping terms. The highest Timeform rating achieved by Red Rum, incidentally, was 166 after the 1973/4 season in which his second National was one of six wins from ten starts (he was also disqualified after finishing first under 12-4 at Perth on his reappearance and went down by just a short head under 11-4 in the Hennessy). Red Rum followed up his Grand National win that season with another top-class performance to win the Scottish National under 11-13 (including a 6-lb penalty for his Aintree win), after which his connections even considered tilts at the Whitbread [now the Sandown Gold Cup] and the Grand Steeple-Chase de Paris! Ratings, though, have only a minor role in the Red Rum

The run-in—history is made as Tiger Roll becomes the first to win successive Nationals since Red Rum in 1974; Magic of Light (noseband) and Rathvinden fill the places, whilst 2018 fourth Anibale Fly (hoops) takes fifth this time around

story who owes his immortality to his historic achievements at Aintree which have made him one of the legendary names, perhaps matched only by those of Arkle and Desert Orchid, in the now extensive post-war history of steeplechasing.

Tiger Roll's trainer announced in September that the horse would have a light programme in 2019/20 with a view to having a third crack at the National, which contradicted the stated view of his owner, who retired his previous National winner Rule The World almost straight afterwards. 'It's very unlikely Tiger Roll will come back and run in it for a third time, he will be carrying top weight and every time he runs now I get nervous, I'd hate for anything unfortunate to happen to him while he's racing. Tiger Roll isn't Red Rum—he's Tiger Roll—and I feel no pressure to go back and try to win a third time.' Michael O'Leary's stated concern, both for his horse and for the good of the Grand National itself, is perhaps understandable, given the huge public affection for Tiger Roll who has been voted the *Racing Post*'s Jumps Horse of the Year in each of the last two years, collecting over half the votes cast by readers in the latest season. Anyone labouring under the illusion that the radical modifications in 2013 would magically render the Grand National course and its fences 'safe' for its equine participants had a reminder with the death—from a broken neck—of the brought-down Up For Review (following that of Forest des Aigles over the National course in the Topham the previous day) that steeplechasing is inherently dangerous and no amount of course reconstruction can remove all the hazards. The Grand National has been a major target down the years for animal rights campaigners (who have plenty of supporters in the media) and Up For Review's demise—the first fatality in the race since the course was remodelled—would have received considerably more prominence if the headlines hadn't been made by Tiger Roll's second victory. Red Rum's own record-breaking feats largely overshadowed the far greater toll that the fences were taking at that time when no fewer than five horses—Grey Sombrero in 1973, Land Lark and Beau Bob in 1975, and Winter Rain and Zeta's Son in 1977—lost their lives in the five Grand Nationals contested by Red Rum.

The increased TV viewing figures on all three days of the Grand National meeting were in line with a general increase over the year for jump racing, when average figures across ITV and ITV4 rose by fourteen per cent year-on-year to 664,000 for each live show. Figures for the Grand National itself rose by more than a million, registering 9.6m (a figure calculated nowadays using a five-minute peak, which would always be higher compared to the previously long-established fifteen-minute peak). The National's television audience dwarfs that for any other race and the fact that the National has been the stage for Tiger Roll's most notable performances counts for more than the quality of those performances in having turned him into a household name. As usual, the Grand National was the major story in the sports pages of all the Sunday papers and the 'quality' Sundays all carried a picture of Tiger Roll on their front pages. Bookmakers quote Tiger Roll at around 8/1 for the 2020 Grand National at the time of writing, with the owner's brother having issued a challenge to the handicapper over the summer—'We've seen horses condensed 7 lb or more before in the National weights and, if they want him, it's up to them. If he has to run off anything above 165 he'll be retiring after Cheltenham!' If Tiger Roll's owner, who has the perfect right to make his own choice, changes his mind and sends him to Aintree he will line up at considerably shorter odds than 8/1 as millions of once-a-year punters watching in their living rooms make him the subject of their annual flutter (as a footnote on that subject, backers should always 'take a price' in the morning—and shop around for extra places on each-way bets—when it comes to the National, on which the SP overround in the latest edition was historically high at 162%, just below that in Many Clouds' year). The others, incidentally, who have won the Grand National twice, in addition to Tiger Roll (and Red Rum, of course), are Abd-el-Kader, Peter Simple, The Colonel, The Lamb and Manifesto (who ran in the race eight times, reaching the frame on four other occasions), all their successes in the nineteenth century before Reynoldstown added his name in 1935 and 1936.

Tiger Roll's big-spending owner said after the horse's latest win (the third time in four years that the winner had carried his famous maroon, white star and armlets) that 'Whatever amount of money I spend on horses, days like this justify it all, it's incredible.' Within a month, though, O'Leary was announcing his intention to wind up his huge string over the next five years, a decision with potentially seismic consequences for Irish racing and a topic that is discussed elsewhere in this edition, including in the essay on Battleoverdoyen. Tiger Roll's trainer Gordon Elliott, who trains around a hundred horses for O'Leary's Gigginstown House Stud operation, was born a racing outsider (like his good friend Martin Pipe for whom he worked and rode as an amateur in his early days in the sport). Elliott's Cullentra House stable has been built into one of the juggernauts of jumping in Britain and Ireland—three hundred and twenty individual horses ran for the yard in Ireland alone in the latest season—and Elliott is now right at the centre of the sport and just one Grand National winner away from joining Fred Rimell and Red Rum's trainer Ginger McCain as the joint holder of the record for training four winners of the race. Still only forty-one, and with no first-hand memories of Red Rum, Elliott may well end up holding the Grand National training record on his own eventually. Elliott describes Tiger Roll as 'a bit of a boyo, he's no child's pony, but he's a horse of a lifetime', an assessment broadly shared by the horse's Grand National jockey, thirty-nine-year-old Davy Russell, who has been champion in Ireland three times in a rather up-and-down career (he lost his job as first jockey to Tiger Roll's owner, resulting in a couple of tough years, but now rides regularly for him again). Russell reported that Tiger Roll 'got very wound up' before the start of the latest National and, commenting on his only two jumping errors late in the race, called him 'a little devil, he doesn't get very high at his fences, but he gets away with it and he's one hell of a horse.'

Like Red Rum, whose first racecourse appearance came when dead-heating in a two-year-old seller at the 1967 Grand National meeting, Tiger Roll was bred for the Flat. A cast-off from Sheikh Mohammed's racing operation, he fetched just £10,000 at Doncaster Sales as an unraced three-year-old and won at Market Rasen on his debut for jumping trainer Nigel Hawke before being bought on behalf of Michael O'Leary for £80,000 at the Cheltenham Sales that December. Gigginstown's purchases have tended to be slower-maturing chasing types with plenty of size and substance, and, although Tiger Roll had scope to fill into his frame (something he has never really done), he was not bred on lines that suggested he might develop into a chaser, let alone a Grand National winner. Memorably labelled 'a little rat of a thing' by his owner, the lengthy, leggy Tiger Roll is relatively small for a jumper, at 15.3 hands one of the smallest horses to win a National (physical comparisons have been made with the compact Red Rum but Red Rum was a stronger-looking individual than the more slight Tiger Roll, as well as being a little bigger). 'We bought him for the Fred Winter [the handicap for juveniles at the Cheltenham Festival],' said Eddie O'Leary, his brother's racing manager. If that was so, Tiger Roll evidently did better than expected to win the Triumph (under Russell), the juvenile hurdling championship, at the end of that first season, and he has continued

Gigginstown House Stud's "Tiger Roll"

to defy expectations on a fairly regular basis. He was a 50/1-shot when down the field in the World [Stayers'] Hurdle as a five-year-old, didn't run at the Cheltenham Festival as a six-year-old and then won the National Hunt Chase there at 16/1 as a seven-year-old before his successive victories in the Cross Country Chase which have made him one of only twelve horses who have won at least four times at the meeting (a full list appears in the essay on Altior).

Tiger Roll (IRE) (b.g. 2010)	Authorized (IRE) (b 2004)	Montjeu (b 1996)	Sadler's Wells Floripedes
		Funsie (b 1999)	Saumarez Vallee Dansante
	Swiss Roll (IRE) (b 2000)	Entrepreneur (b 1994)	Sadler's Wells Exclusive Order
		On Air (b 1988)	Chief Singer Green Light

Tiger Roll's pedigree has been covered fully in previous editions of *Chasers & Hurdlers* but, in summary, he is the first Grand National winner to be sired by an Epsom Derby winner since the 1884 winner Voluptuary and is a tribute to the influence that sons of Montjeu are having on jumping. Montjeu himself sired the record-breaking dual Champion Hurdle winner Hurricane Fly, and Authorized, one of his four Epsom Derby-winning sons, has certainly hit the heights with Tiger Roll. The late Fame And Glory, Walk In The Park, Montmartre, Scorpion, Camelot, Motivator and Jukebox Jury are among other sons of Montjeu advertising the line with big winners over jumps. Tiger Roll's pedigree features the phenomenal Sadler's Wells twice, as the grandsire of both Authorized and of Tiger Roll's dam, the fairly useful Flat mare Swiss Roll who was trained by Tommy Stack, Red Rum's jockey when he won his third Grand National. Swiss Roll has bred four winners so far, the best of them the Lonsdale Cup winner and Irish St Leger and Goodwood Cup runner-up Ahzeemah (by Dubawi) and the very smart staying handicapper Austrian

School (by Teofilo). Tiger Roll stays four and a quarter miles and acts on good to firm and heavy going. He is usually in headgear and a tongue tie (wore cheekpieces in the 2018 National and was blinkered in the latest edition). He has a low jumping technique but has never fallen (once unseated his rider). His owner reportedly has statues at his home of his Cheltenham Gold Cup winners War of Attrition and Don Cossack and he will doubtless be providing more work for the sculptor when Tiger Roll's racing career is over.

Food for thought: If Tiger Roll's owner sticks to his decision not to send Tiger Roll back to Aintree, perhaps he might consider a more ambitious Cheltenham Festival target for his versatile performer. Tiger Roll has already won two editions of the Cross Country Chase—he is far too good a horse for that company—and a tilt at the Stayers' Hurdle would be a more interesting challenge. Achieving a fifth Festival win would be much more straightforward in the Cross Country Chase, but Tiger Roll showed form in winning the Boyne Hurdle that is not far short of the standard required to win a Stayers' Hurdle. He travelled well throughout at Navan and was impressive, leading on the bridle before drawing clear in a manner that suggested he had more in the locker. Winning the Stayers' Hurdle is within his compass on that form and would make Tiger Roll the first horse to triumph in four different races at the Cheltenham Festival, which would be some legacy to go alongside his Grand National victories. *Gordon Elliott, Ireland*

TIGER SAM (IRE) 9 ch.g. Beneficial – Colleen Donn (Le Moss) [2018/19 c23.5g⁴ c24g **c92 x** c25.8gᵖᵘ h23.1m⁵ h21.6s Nov 25] maiden hurdler: modest handicap chaser: left Noel **h–** Meade after second start: stays 25f: acts on soft going: usually in blinkers: tried in tongue tie: front runner/races prominently: often let down by jumping. *Laura Hurley*

TIGER'S LEGACY 5 b.g. So You Think (NZ) – Tiger Moss (Classic Cliche (IRE)) **h–** [2018/19 b16.3d h15.8sᵖᵘ h15.8g⁴ Apr 21] little show in bumper/novice hurdles. **b–** *Michael Scudamore*

TIGER TAPTAP (GER) 4 ch.g. Jukebox Jury (IRE) – Tomato Finish (GER) (Starborough) **h134** [2018/19 h16g² h16g⁴ h16.8d Mar 15] angular gelding: twice-raced 1¼m winner on Flat in France: useful form in juvenile hurdles: best effort when fourth in Spring Juvenile Hurdle at Leopardstown (8¼ lengths behind Sir Erec) in February. *W. P. Mullins, Ireland*

TIGER TIME (IRE) 5 b.g. Scorpion (IRE) – Summertime Girl (IRE) (Glacial Storm **b–** (USA)) [2018/19 b–: b16.8gᵖᵘ May 15] little impact in bumpers: dead. *Philip Kirby*

TIGER TREK (IRE) 10 b.g. Tiger Hill (IRE) – Zayana (IRE) (Darshaan) [2018/19 **c– x** c114x, h–: h16g³ h16.7g² h19.9m⁵ Aug 30] winning hurdler: only poor form in 2018/19: **h80** fairly useful maiden chaser at best: left Dr Richard Newland after first start: stays 2½m: acts on good to soft going: has worn headgear: often leads: often let down by jumping over fences. *Rebecca Menzies*

TIGER TWENTY TWO 8 b.g. Authorized (IRE) – Collette's Choice (Royal Applause) **h79** [2018/19 h85: h20.6g⁶ h25g³ h23.3gᵖᵘ h18.6m³ Jul 21] poor maiden hurdler: probably stays 25f: acts on good to firm going. *Brian Rothwell*

TIGGER TWO (IRE) 7 b.g. Getaway (GER) – Anne Hathaway (IRE) (Definite Article) **h–** [2018/19 h–, b68: h20gᵖᵘ Jun 2] has had breathing operation: mid-field in bumpers: no show in novice/maiden hurdles: tried in cheekpieces. *David Pipe*

TIGHT CALL (IRE) 5 ch.g. Mahler – Victory Anthem (IRE) (Royal Anthem (USA)) **h121** [2018/19 b16g³ b16.3g* h19.7g* h16g² h21.4g² h19.3dᶠ h19.8m³ h17.7g* Apr 24] **b91** unfurnished gelding: second foal: brother to a winning pointer: dam, pulled up in point, half-sister to fairly useful 2m hurdle winner Yes Sir Brian: pulled up in point: fair form in bumpers: left Roger McGrath, won at Stratford in October: fairly useful form over hurdles: won maiden at Hereford in November and novice at Fontwell in April: stays 21f: best form on good going. *Tim Vaughan*

TIGRIS RIVER (IRE) 8 b.g. Montjeu (IRE) – Hula Angel (USA) (Woodman (USA)) **h137** [2018/19 h144: h16g⁵ h16s h22.5d h24g h24g h16d³ Apr 21] compact gelding: useful handicap hurdler: stays 2½m: acts on heavy going: has worn headgear, including last 2 starts: wears tongue tie. *Joseph Patrick O'Brien, Ireland*

TIKKANDEMICKEY (IRE) 13 gr.g. Tikkanen (USA) – Miss Vikki (IRE) (Needle **c–** Gun (IRE)) [2018/19 c100, h–: c20.1d May 5] winning hurdler: fair handicap chaser: stays **h–** 3m: acts on heavy going: regularly in headgear. *Raymond Shiels*

TIKKAPICK (IRE) 9 b.g. Tikkanen (USA) – Takeanotherpick (IRE) (Winged Love (IRE)) [2018/19 c26.7g² c23.6d c24.2s c21.7g* c20.2g⁶ Feb 27] workmanlike gelding: maiden hurdler: modest handicap chaser: won at Taunton in February: stays 3¼m: acts on soft going: wears headgear: often let down by jumping. *Colin Tizzard* **c86 x** **h–**

TIKKEN AWAY (IRE) 8 gr.g. Tikkanen (USA) – Lady Goldilocks (IRE) (Mister Lord (USA)) [2018/19 c–, h102: c21gᵘʳ c16.5g c16.3g⁵ h19.5g h16.8sᵖᵘ Nov 25] fair maiden hurdler at best: well below par in 2018/19: no form in handicap chases, mostly let down by jumping: unproven beyond 2m: acts on soft going: tried in blinkers/tongue tie. *Robert Walford* **c71 x** **h–**

TIKKINTHEBOX (IRE) 7 b.g. Tikkanen (USA) – Surfing France (FR) (Art Francais (USA)) [2018/19 c102, h–: c15.7m* c16.3g c16.3s* c16.3g³ c16.5m³ c18mᵖᵘ c20.2g⁴ Apr 3] workmanlike gelding: maiden hurdler: fairly useful handicap chaser: won novice events at Wincanton in May and Newton Abbot in July: stays 2¼m: acts on soft and good to firm going: has worn hood: wears tongue tie: free-going front runner. *Jeremy Scott* **c119** **h–**

TIKK TOCK BOOM (IRE) 7 gr.m. Tikkanen (USA) – Henrietta (IRE) (Hushang (IRE)) [2018/19 h96p, b–: h15.8d⁵ h23g² h23.1d⁶ h21s³ h25.5g* c24g² c25.3g Apr 17] lengthy mare: Irish point winner: fair handicap hurdler: won mares event at Hereford in March: fairly useful form when second at Warwick on first of 2 outings in novice handicap chases: stays 3¼m: best form on good going: in cheekpieces last 3 starts. *Ian Williams* **c115** **h108**

TILDAS ICON (IRE) 5 b.m. Sixties Icon – I Tilda (IRE) (Kris Kin (USA)) [2018/19 h89: h16g⁶ h16g⁶ h16g Jun 23] modest maiden hurdler: best around 2m: acts on heavy going: hooded 4 of last 5 outings, also tongue tied last 3. *Patrick Griffin, Ireland* **h92**

TILLYTHETANK (IRE) 6 b.m. Stowaway – All Heart (Alhaarth (IRE)) [2018/19 h80p: h16.8m* h18.7m² Jun 19] placed both starts in Irish points: fair form over hurdles: won mares maiden at Exeter in May: will stay at least 2½m. *Alan King* **h108**

TILSON (IRE) 7 b.g. Milan – Chaparral Lady (IRE) (Broken Hearted) [2018/19 h18.5d h16m² Apr 22] €50,000 3-y-o, £7,000 5-y-o: brother to 2 winners, including bumper winner/ fairly useful hurdler Benny In Milan (19f/2½m winner): dam, bumper winner, also 1½m-1¼m winner on Flat: placed in points: no solid form in novice hurdles, first a seller: wears headgear. *Bernard Llewellyn* **h85 ?**

TIMASSINI (IRE) 4 b.f. Dr Massini (IRE) – Timoca (IRE) (Marju (IRE)) [2018/19 h19g⁵ h15.8gᶠ h16.8s Apr 16] second foal: dam (c92/h94), temperamental 2m hurdle winner (stayed 2½m), also 10.7f winner on Flat: modest form when mid-field in novice hurdle at Taunton on debut: failed to progress. *Evan Williams* **h95**

TIMCODA (IRE) 6 b.g. Milan – Sorelia (FR) (Sillery (USA)) [2018/19 b16g² h16.7d h25.5s⁶ h19.2d⁶ h20.3s³ c24gᵘʳ c26.2gᵖᵘ Apr 26] €8,000 3-y-o: has had breathing operation: sixth foal: brother to a winning pointer and closely related to fair hurdler/chaser Who Let de Dogsout (2m-21f winner, by Oscar): dam lightly-raced half-sister to triple Grand Steeple-Chase de Paris winner Mid Dancer: placed on last 2 of 3 starts in Irish points: second in bumper at Worcester: modest form over hurdles: failed to complete in handicap chases: in tongue tie last 3 starts. *Jamie Snowden* **c–** **h89** **b90**

TIME AND AGAIN (FR) 9 b.g. Sassanian (USA) – Petillante Royale (FR) (Vertical Speed (FR)) [2018/19 c–, h80: h21.6m Jul 14] sturdy gelding: disappointing maiden hurdler/chaser: has worn headgear/tongue tie. *Tim Vaughan* **c–** **h–**

TIMEFORADANCE 4 b.g. Norse Dancer (IRE) – Timeforagin (Pasternak) [2018/19 b16d Apr 6] well beaten in bumper. *Brian Eckley* **b–**

TIME FOR ANOTHER (IRE) 6 ch.g. Shantou (USA) – Borleagh Blonde (IRE) (Zaffaran (USA)) [2018/19 b95: h19.3g⁴ Dec 28] fairly useful form when third in bumper: better than result when well-held fourth in maiden at Catterick on hurdling debut: should improve. *Olly Murphy* **h79 p**

TIMEFORASPIN 5 b.g. Librettist (USA) – Timeforagin (Pasternak) [2018/19 b75: b15.8s b16.7s² b16.7d³ Jan 8] fair form when placed last 2 starts in bumpers. *Brian Eckley* **b92**

TIMEFORBEN (IRE) 7 ch.m. Beneficial – Shokalocka Baby (IRE) (Accordion) [2018/19 h106, b82: h24g⁴ h23g* h23.3g² h23d² h26.5g* h26.5v² h23.9d h20.3g Apr 18] sturdy mare: has had breathing operation: winning Irish pointer: fairly useful handicap hurdler: won at Worcester (mares event) in June and Newton Abbot in September: stays 3¼m: acts on soft going: wears headgear: tried in tongue tie: often travels strongly. *David Pipe* **h120**

TIME FOR CHAMPERS (IRE) 9 b.m. Robin des Champs (FR) – Someone Told Me (IRE) (Saddlers' Hall (IRE)) [2018/19 h76: h19.9gʳʳ h15.8d⁶ h16.8s h19s h15.8d³ Feb 25] poor maiden hurdler: unproven beyond 2m: acts on good to soft going: wears hood: has worn tongue tie: temperamental. *Nikki Evans* **h79 §**

TIMEFORWEST (IRE) 7 b.m. Westerner – Shang A Lang (IRE) (Commander Collins (IRE)) [2018/19 c120, h–: c23.8g⁵ c24g* c20g² c20g² c24.5g h20.3s⁴ c24d* Apr 21] sturdy mare: fairly useful handicap hurdler: useful chaser: won novice handicap at Southwell in June and Imperial Call Chase at Cork (by ½ length from Killultagh Vic) in April: improved again when second in mares handicap at Punchestown (4½ lengths behind Moyhenna) shortly after end of British season: left Jonjo O'Neill after second start: stays 3m: acts on good to firm and heavy going: tried in cheekpieces. *Peter Fahey, Ireland*   **c138 h126**

TIME IS HONEY (IRE) 6 ch.m. Rajj (IRE) – Bob's Sarah (IRE) (Bob Back (USA)) [2018/19 h16.7s³ Dec 26] £11,500 5-y-o: fourth foal: sister to modest 23f hurdle winner Lady Quill: dam (h66), maiden hurdler, half-sister to fairly useful hurdler/useful chaser (stayed 2¾m) Schindler's Gold: won completed start in Irish points: 40/1, third in novice at Market Rasen (3¼ lengths behind War Brigade, having run of race) on hurdling debut. *Nick Kent*   **h106**

TIMELY GIFT (IRE) 6 b.g. Presenting – Give It Time (Kayf Tara) [2018/19 h84: h15.8d⁵ h20.3d Apr 24] poor handicap hurdler: unproved beyond 2m: acts on heavy going. *Tim Vaughan*   **h70**

TIMESAWAITING (IRE) 6 b.g. Arakan (USA) – Princess Nicole (IRE) (Alhaarth (IRE)) [2018/19 b83: h20.1g⁴ h16s h20.5d Jan 20] runner-up in Irish point: modest form over hurdles: should prove suited by further than 2½m: wears tongue tie. *Lucinda Russell*   **h98**

TIMES OF TROUBLE 9 b.g. Tobougg (IRE) – Let It Be (Entrepreneur) [2018/19 h20sᵖᵘ May 25] no show in bumper and novice hurdle (tongue tied) 30 months apart. *Fiona Shaw*   **h–**

TIMETOBENEFIT (IRE) 8 b.m. Beneficial – Shokalocka Baby (IRE) (Accordion) [2018/19 h86: h20.3g h25g⁴ Nov 4] has had breathing operation: point winner: poor maiden hurdler: tried in tongue tie: races towards rear. *Richard Phillips*   **h78**

TIMETOCHILL (IRE) 6 br.m. Scorpion (IRE) – Kilcoleman Lady (IRE) (Presenting) [2018/19 b16.2d* b15.8d* b17d Apr 4] €3,200 3-y-o: useful-looking mare: seventh foal: half-sister to hurdler/chaser Geordie des Champs (19f-25f winner, by Robin des Champs): dam unraced half-sister to useful hurdler/chaser (stayed 25f) Ashwell Boy: placed on second of 3 starts in Irish points: fairly useful form in bumpers: won mares events at Kelso in November and Huntingdon (listed, by ½ length from Emmas Joy) in December. *Kelly Morgan*   **b103**

TIME TO MOVE ON (IRE) 6 ch.g. Flemensfirth (USA) – Kapricia Speed (FR) (Vertical Speed (FR)) [2018/19 b107p: h21.3s Dec 8] useful bumper performer: 6/4, well held in novice at Wetherby on hurdling debut, found to be suffering from post-race heat stress: should do better. *Fergal O'Brien*   **h– p**

TIMEWAITSFORNOONE (IRE) 7 b.g. Oscar (IRE) – Trendy Attire (IRE) (Luso) [2018/19 c26.3dᵘʳ Mar 15] €34,000 3-y-o, £225,000 4-y-o: fourth foal: closely related to a winning pointer by Milan and half-brother to poor 2½m hurdle winner Present Trend (by Presenting): dam unraced half-sister to fairly useful staying hurdlers Phar From Frosty and Glacial Evening out of sister to high-class staying hurdler/very smart chaser Cab On Target: point winner: fairly useful form in chases: won maiden hunter at Downpatrick in 2017/18: unseated rider first in Foxhunters at Cheltenham on return: should stay beyond 3m. *Alan Fleming, Ireland*   **c–**

TIMI ROLI (FR) 7 b.g. Roli Abi (FR) – Tiana (FR) (Saint Cyrien (FR)) [2018/19 h24g* h22.8d c16d² Oct 29] brother to fairly useful French hurdler/chaser Tom Roli (17f-19f winner) and half-brother to 2 winners in France by Denham Red, including fairly useful hurdler/chaser Team Red (2¼m-3¼m winner): fairly useful hurdler: won minor event at Wexford in June: 7/1, second in maiden at same course (1¾ lengths behind Mind's Eye) on chasing debut: stays 3m: acts on good to firm and heavy going: should progress over fences. *W. P. Mullins, Ireland*   **c133 p h123**

TIMIYAN (USA) 8 b.g. Ghostzapper (USA) – Timarwa (IRE) (Daylami (IRE)) [2018/19 c94, h136: c19.9m⁶ c25g*ᵈ c24s c24g c28s c24dᵖᵘ Nov 25] winning hurdler: useful chaser: first past post in Midlands National Handicap Chase at Kilbeggan in July, but subsequently disqualified having tested positive for prohibited substance: went wrong way after: stays 25f: acts on heavy going: wears tongue tie: races off pace. *Gordon Elliott, Ireland*   **c133 d h–**

TIMOTEO (FR) 6 b.g. Diamond Green (FR) – Goldnella (FR) (Goldneyev (USA)) [2018/19 h16v h21.4g h20.6d⁵ c17s* c16s* Mar 16] sturdy gelding: fair maiden hurdler: useful form over fences: won novice handicaps at Stratford (by 13 lengths from Paddy's Poem) and Kempton in March: best around 2m: acts on soft going: tried in hood: open to further improvement as a chaser. *Alan King*   **c134 p h106**

TIM ROCCO (GER) 7 ch.g. Doyen (IRE) – Timbalada (GER) (Big Shuffle (USA)) h111
[2018/19 h16.7g h16.2g h16.7s h16.4g³ h15.8d⁴ h16.6d* h16.4d* h15.8m⁴ h15.7m Apr 20]
useful on Flat in Germany for Frau C. Barsig, trained in France for Frau C. Barsig: won at
Doncaster (novice event) and Newcastle in March: raced around 2m: acts on good to soft
going: wears hood/tongue tie: races off pace. *Oliver Greenall*

TINELYRA (IRE) 13 b.g. Mr Combustible (IRE) – Ladyogan (IRE) (Torus) [2018/19 c– §
c20.8g May 4] workmanlike gelding: point winner: maiden hurdler: one-time modest h– §
chaser, well held in hunter in 2018/19: has worn hood/tongue tie: unreliable. *A. Campbell*

TINGO IN THE TALE (IRE) 10 b.g. Oratorio (IRE) – Sunlit Skies (Selkirk (USA)) h72
[2018/19 h15.8m h18.7m⁶ h15.8g³ h20.3g⁶ h23.3g h15.8g⁶ Nov 2] compact gelding: poor
maiden hurdler: stays 2½m: acts on soft and good to firm going: in cheekpieces last 5 starts:
tried in tongue tie. *Tony Forbes*

TINKER TIME (IRE) 11 b.g. Turtle Island (IRE) – Gypsys Girl (IRE) (Husyan (USA)) c–
[2018/19 c118§, h–: h25d c24.2gᵘʳ Mar 4] workmanlike gelding: winning hurdler/useful h–
chaser at best, no form in 2018/19 after 20 months off: stays 3½m: acts on heavy going:
tried in headgear. *Alex Hales*

TINTANGLE (IRE) 6 b.m. Yeats (IRE) – Connaught Hall (IRE) (Un Desperado (FR)) h137
[2018/19 h16s¹ h16g* h16g³ h18s³ h16d¹ h16.8d³ h20g⁴ Apr 21] €52,000 3-y-o: well-made
mare: third foal: half-sister to smart hurdler/chaser Tombstone (2m-19f winner, by Robin
des Champs): dam (h108), bumper/2m hurdle winner (stayed 2½m), half-sister to useful
chaser (winner up to 3m) Storm Damage: bumper winner: useful hurdler: won minor event
at Thurles in November: 40/1, third in Dawn Run Mares' Novices' Hurdle at Cheltenham
(1¾ lengths behind Eglantine du Seuil) in March: probably stays 2½m: acts on soft going:
in cheekpieces after fourth start: usually races prominently. *Gordon Elliott, Ireland*

TINTERN THEATRE (IRE) 8 b.g. King's Theatre (IRE) – Rith Ar Aghaidh (IRE) c119
(Phardante (FR)) [2018/19 c139, h–: c24.5d c23.8g⁴ Nov 23] sturdy gelding: winning h–
hurdler: useful handicap chaser, below form both starts in 2018/19: stays 25f: acts on heavy
going. *Nigel Twiston-Davies*

TIQUER (FR) 11 b.g. Equerry (USA) – Tirenna (FR) (Sleeping Car (FR)) [2018/19 c128, c123
h–: c21.1s⁴ Dec 8] has had breathing operation: lightly-raced hurdler: fairly useful h–
handicap chaser: fourth in Grand Sefton Chase at Aintree, only outing in 2018/19: stays
21f: acts on heavy going: tried in cheekpieces. *Alan Jones*

TIR DUBH (IRE) 10 br.m. Sandmason – Turbine Hill (IRE) (Hubbly Bubbly (USA)) h80
[2018/19 h82: h23s⁶ h23.3g h23g³ h23.1g³ h24gᵖᵘ h23g⁶ h20.9g h25g² h25g Nov 24] poor
handicap hurdler: left Robert Stephens after third start: stays 25f: acts on good to firm
going: wears headgear. *Mike Sowersby*

TIS FANTASTIC (FR) 4 gr.g. Montmartre (FR) – Anadara (FR) (Xaar) [2018/19 h16s⁵ h–
h16s Mar 8] well-made gelding: well held in juvenile/novice hurdles: wears tongue tie.
Michael Blake

TIS WONDERFUL (IRE) 5 b.g. Casamento (IRE) – Cosenza (Bahri (USA)) [2018/19 h–
h15.3m h16.2g Nov 5] fair maiden on Flat, stays 1½m: little show both starts over hurdles.
Carroll Gray

TITIAN BOY (IRE) 10 ch.g. Spadoun (FR) – Leodotcom (IRE) (Safety Catch (USA)) c–
[2018/19 c93, h–: c20.1g⁵ c20.5d⁶ c26mᵖᵘ c20.1g⁵ c16.5sᵘʳ Jan 8] maiden hurdler: poor h–
chaser nowadays: usually wears tongue tie: front runner/races prominently. *N. W. Alexander*

TITUS BOLT (IRE) 10 b.g. Titus Livius (FR) – Megan's Bay (Muhtarram (USA)) h97
[2018/19 h94: h20.2g⁴ h16.2g* Jun 3] modest handicap hurdler: won at Perth in June: stays
2½m: acts on heavy going: has worn headgear, including at Perth. *Jim Goldie*

TOBACCO ROAD (IRE) 9 b.g. Westerner – Virginias Best (King's Best (USA)) h–
[2018/19 h100: h16gᵖᵘ Nov 12] modest on Flat, stays 11.5f: modest hurdler, pulled up sole
start in sphere in 2018/19: mainly raced around 2m: best form on good going: usually
wears headgear: in tongue tie last 5 starts. *Mark Pattinson*

TOBEFAIR 9 b.g. Central Park (IRE) – Nan (Buckley) [2018/19 c110, h134: h24.2d c105 +
c24.2s⁴ c23.4s c23.6dᵖᵘ h23.6d² h24d² h24g* Apr 17] big gelding: smart handicap hurdler: h147
won at Cheltenham (by 5 lengths from Broughtons Admiral) in April: second in Pertemps
Final three months earlier: fair form over fences: stays 3¼m: acts on soft and good to firm
going: has worn cheekpieces: tried in tongue tie: usually races off pace. *Debra Hamer*

TOBOGGAN'S FIRE 6 b.m. Firebreak – Toboggan Lady (Tobougg (IRE)) [2018/19 h100
h106: h15.8g⁴ h16.3g³ h17s³ h16.7sᵖᵘ h16.7g⁶ h16g h16.8dᵖᵘ Apr 23] fair handicap hurdler:
raced around 2m: acts on soft going: tried in blinkers: usually front runner/races
prominently. *Donald McCain*

TODD 9 b.g. Gentlewave (IRE) – Voice (Zamindar (USA)) [2018/19 h20g* h20.3g⁶ h20m² h105
h20g³ h23.4d* h23.4d² h23.8d⁵ Jan 28] compact gelding: fair handicap hurdler: won at
Worcester (conditionals/amateurs) in September and Fakenham in December: stays 23f:
acts on good to firm and heavy going: wears headgear: has worn tongue tie. *Olly Murphy*

TOE TO TOE (IRE) 11 br.g. Presenting – Tavildara (IRE) (Kahyasi) [2018/19 c75§, c– §
h72§: c20g⁰ h20g⁵ Sep 11] winning hurdler/maiden chaser, no form in 2018/19: stays 23f: h– §
best form on good going: has worn headgear/tongue tie: usually races towards rear:
irresolute. *Debra Hamer*

TOGETHERNESS (IRE) 6 b.g. Pour Moi (IRE) – Madeira Mist (IRE) (Grand Lodge h–
(USA)) [2018/19 h77: h21.2mᵖᵘ May 13] sturdy gelding: has had breathing operation: little
show over hurdles. *Patrick Chamings*

TOI STOREY (IRE) 6 b.g. Winged Love (IRE) – Where's Herself (IRE) (Shernazar) h108
[2018/19 b16.8g⁴ h21.2g⁴ h20.1s³ h20.1v³ h20.1v* Mar 14] first foal: dam unraced half- b83
sister to useful/unreliable hurdler/staying chaser Universal Soldier (by Winged Love):
modest form sole start in bumpers: fair form over hurdles: won maiden at Hexham in
March: will prove suited by 2¾m+: tried in hood: usually races in rear. *Rebecca Menzies*

TOKARAMORE 7 b.m. Sulamani (IRE) – More Likely (Shambo) [2018/19 h98: h16.2g c96 p
h23.8g² h15.6g⁴ h18.1g² h19.8m* c21.6g³ Mar 23] small mare: fair handicap hurdler: won h105
mares event at Musselburgh in February: stiff task when well held on chasing debut (should
do better): stays 3m: acts on soft and good to firm going: wears hood. *Iain Jardine*

TOKAY DOKEY (IRE) 5 b.g. Gold Well – Charming Present (IRE) (Presenting) h125
[2018/19 b16.7g* h15.8g* h15.8g* h16mᶠ Feb 23] £70,000 3-y-o: tall gelding: chasing b89
type: closely related to 2 winners by Dr Massini, including bumper winner/fairly useful 17f
hurdle winner Magic Spear (stayed 2½m), and half-brother to 2 winners, including useful
hurdler/chaser Monbeg Charmer (2½m-3m winner, by Daylami): dam unraced: won
bumper at Market Rasen (by ½ length from Encore Champs) early in season: fairly useful
form over hurdles: won both completed starts, novices at Uttoxeter in October and
November: will stay 2½m. *Dan Skelton*

TOMAHAWK WOOD 10 ch.g. Courteous – Meda's Song (Master Willie) [2018/19 c–, c–
h87: h21.4gᵖᵘ May 7] modest hurdler, bled sole start in 2018/19: mistakes only outing over h–
fences: stays 21f: acts on heavy going: tried in tongue tie. *Donald Whillans*

TOM AND TONY H (IRE) 4 b.g. Masterofthehorse (IRE) – Then Came Bronson (IRE) b–
(Up And At 'Em) [2018/19 b16s b16.2d Apr 26] last in 2 bumpers: in tongue tie second
start. *R. Mike Smith*

TOMBSTONE (IRE) 9 ch.g. Robin des Champs (FR) – Connaught Hall (IRE) (Un c141
Desperado (FR)) [2018/19 c147, h–: h16g⁵ c19.5g* h16.2g³ h16g h16g³ h16d³ h16g⁶ h147
h18s* h20d⁵ Apr 22] strong gelding: smart hurdler: won minor event at Leopardstown (by
2¼ lengths from Three Stars) in March: third in Ryanair Hurdle at same course (5½ lengths
behind Sharjah) in December: smart chaser: won minor event at Limerick (by 2 lengths
from Montalbano) in October: stays 3m: acts on heavy going: tried in hood: wears tongue
tie. *Gordon Elliott, Ireland*

TOMKEVI (FR) 8 b.g. Khalkevi (IRE) – Tamsna (FR) (Smadoun (FR)) [2018/19 c122x, c97 x
h115: c20s⁶ h24.1s* h22.8s* h24gᵘʳ h25.8g⁵ Mar 23] useful handicap hurdler: won at h130
Wetherby and Haydock in December: fairly useful handicap chaser at best: stays 3m: acts
on heavy going: usually wears headgear/tongue tie: races off pace: often let down by
jumping out of fences. *Rebecca Menzies*

TOMMYCOLE 4 b.g. Native Ruler – Tancred Miss (Presidium) [2018/19 b14g b14.6s b–
Dec 22] little impact in bumpers/on Flat: has joined Olly Williams. *Susan Corbett*

TOMMY HALLINAN (IRE) 5 b.g. Intense Focus (USA) – Bowstring (IRE) (Sadler's h96
Wells (USA)) [2018/19 h–: h16.3g³ h16m⁶ Jul 9] sturdy gelding: has had breathing
operation: fairly useful at best on Flat, stays 1¼m: modest form over hurdles: wears tongue
tie: has joined Marjorie Fife: has bled. *Paul Nicholls*

TOMMY O'DWYER (IRE) 10 b.g. Milan – Always Present (IRE) (Presenting) c62 §
[2018/19 c79§, h–: c24.2gᵖᵘ c24g⁶ c25.5g h23.1gᵖᵘ Aug 3] multiple point winner: maiden h– §
hurdler: poor maiden chaser: stays 3m: acts on good to soft going: usually wears headgear:
front runner/races prominently: ungenuine. *Neil Mechie*

TOMMY RAPPER (IRE) 8 b.g. Milan – Supreme Evening (IRE) (Supreme Leader) c131
[2018/19 h132: c20.9d³ c20.3v⁴ h23.6d⁴ h24.7g² Apr 6] useful-looking gelding: useful h136
handicap hurdler: second at Aintree (4½ lengths behind Aux Ptits Soins) in April: similar

form over fences: better effort when third in novice at Ffos Las (14 lengths behind Bags Groove) in October: stays 25f: acts on heavy going: wears tongue tie. *Dan Skelton*

TOMMYS GEAL 7 b.m. Halling (USA) – Steel Free (IRE) (Danehill Dancer (IRE)) **h78** [2018/19 h15.9s h17.7v⁵ Dec 26] modest on Flat, stays 2m: poor form over hurdles. *Michael Madgwick*

TOMMY SHELBY (FR) 4 b.g. Dabirsim (FR) – Interior (USA) (Fusaichi Pegasus **h–** (USA)) [2018/19 h16.4pu Dec 1] fair maiden on Flat for Richard Fahey, stays 1½m: pulled up in juvenile on hurdling debut. *Barry Murtagh*

TOMMY SILVER (FR) 7 b.g. Silver Cross (FR) – Sainte Mante (FR) (Saint des Saints **c139** (FR)) [2018/19 c141, h–: c20g c15.9d⁵ c15.8g⁴ c20.5g² c20dco c23.8g* c20.5mpu c24m* **h–** Apr 25] tall, good-topped gelding: winning hurdler: useful handicap chaser: won at Ludlow in February and Kempton (match, by 15 lengths from For Good Measure) in April: stays 3m: acts on soft and good to firm going: has worn cheekpieces/tongue tie, including final start. *Paul Nicholls*

TOMMY THE RASCAL 9 b.g. Multiplex – Tina Gee (Orchestra) [2018/19 c71§, h–: **c– §** h24.3g⁶ c24spu Mar 23] sturdy gelding: winning hurdler/maiden chaser, has lost his way: **h– §** wears headgear: races prominently: temperamental. *Jennie Candlish*

TOM NEARY (IRE) 12 b.g. Atraf – La Fandango (IRE) (Taufan (USA)) [2018/19 c61, **c–** h–: h19.2g Aug 23] lightly-raced hurdler, well held sole start in 2018/19: winning chaser: **h–** usually wears tongue tie. *Robert Walford*

TOMNGERRY (IRE) 9 b.g. Craigsteel – Lady Vic (IRE) (Old Vic) [2018/19 c108p, **c–** h132: h19.3g⁵ h24s⁵ Dec 4] useful hurdler at best: last on completed start over fences: **h117** stayed 2¾m: acted on heavy going: tried in cheekpieces: dead. *Brian Ellison*

TOMORROW MYSTERY 5 b.m. Nathaniel (IRE) – Retake (Reset (AUS)) [2018/19 **h116** h16g² h19d³ h15.3g² h17.7g² Apr 12] has had breathing operation: fairly useful on Flat, stays 1½m: fairly useful form over hurdles: placed all 4 starts: wears tongue tie. *Paul Nicholls*

TOMORROW'S ANGEL 4 ch.f. Teofilo (IRE) – Funday (Daylami (IRE)) [2018/19 **h100 p** h16.6g⁵ h16.4g² Jan 15] dam sister to useful hurdler/chaser (winner up to 3m) Pigeon Island: fair maiden on Flat, stays 15f: fair form over hurdles: better effort when second in juvenile maiden at Newcastle (visored): remains with potential. *Iain Jardine*

TONICNGIN (FR) 5 b.g. Irish Wells (FR) – Kahipiroska (FR) (Mansonnien (FR)) **b88** [2018/19 b17m² Apr 20] €17,000 3-y-o: has had breathing operation: fifth foal: brother to fairly useful hurdler/chaser Vodka Wells (2m/17f winner): dam twice-raced half-sister to fairly useful chaser (stayed 25f) Master Neo: 7/4, second of 3 in bumper at Carlisle (2 lengths behind Connective). *Keith Dalgleish*

TONTO'S SPIRIT 7 b.g. Authorized (IRE) – Desert Royalty (IRE) (Alhaarth (IRE)) **c131** [2018/19 h119: h17.2g* h16d³ c16.5d² c16.5s⁵ Mar 9] has had breathing operation: fairly **h126** useful handicap hurdler: won at Cartmel (conditionals) early in season: useful form over fences: better effort when second in novice at Ayr (4½ lengths behind Destrier) in January: stays 19f: acts on good to firm and heavy going: wears hood: front runner/races prominently. *Dianne Sayer*

TOODLEPIP (IRE) 5 b.m. Robin des Champs (FR) – Shannon Theatre (IRE) (King's **h83** Theatre (IRE)) [2018/19 b15.8d b16.6g⁴ b16.5d⁶ h15.8g⁵ Apr 11] has had breathing **b83** operation: second foal: half-sister to fair hurdler Colt Lightning (2¾m winner, by Flemensfirth): dam unraced half-sister to useful hurdler/fairly useful chaser (stays 2½m) Blacklough: modest form in bumpers: 7/2, fifth in mares maiden at Huntingdon (17¾ lengths behind So Lonely) on hurdling debut: tried in hood: wears tongue tie. *Harry Fry*

TOO MANY CHIEFS (IRE) 8 br.g. Indian River (FR) – Wahiba Hall (IRE) (Saddlers' **c–** Hall (IRE)) [2018/19 c–, h119: h25.8d⁴ h24.6v⁵ h25.3s* h20.5spu h23.3vpu Mar 16] fairly **h123** useful handicap hurdler: won at Catterick in December: twice-raced chaser: stays 25f: acts on heavy going: tried in cheekpieces: usually front runner/races prominently. *Sharon Watt*

TOO MANY DIAMONDS (IRE) 8 br.g. Diamond Green (FR) – Too Much Color **c131** (USA) (Spectrum (IRE)) [2018/19 c102, h97: c20.3g* c20.3g* c20.3g* c21.4m² c20.3g² **h–** c23.8m⁶ c20.9g c19.1g⁴ Nov 30] winning hurdler: useful handicap chaser: completed hat-trick at Southwell in May/June: second in Summer Plate at Market Rasen (½ length behind More Buck's) in July: stays 21f: acts on soft and good to firm going: has worn cheekpieces/tongue tie. *Dan Skelton*

TOO MUCH TOO SOON (IRE) 10 b.g. Craigsteel – Zara Rose (IRE) (Zaffaran (USA)) [2018/19 c21.4g³ c20d* c22.5g⁴ c20g² c20g³ h20g⁵ Nov 20] sturdy gelding: point winner: modest maiden hurdler: fair handicap chaser: won at Warwick early in season: stays 2½m: acts on soft going: wears cheekpieces/tongue tie. *Dan Skelton* **c105 h94**

TOOSEY 8 b.g. Lucarno (USA) – Quiz Night (Kayf Tara) [2018/19 h96: c22.5d c24.1g³ c24.2g³ c21.2d* h22.1s h24.8g c24g² c24.1g* h22.7g² h24d c25.1g³ c25dᵖᵘ Apr 27] fair maiden hurdler: fair handicap chaser: won at Cartmel in August and Ayr in October: left Tom Symonds after third start: stays 3m: acts on good to soft going: left in cheekpieces: wears tongue tie: usually front runner/races prominently. *Gavin Patrick Cromwell, Ireland* **c105 h102**

TOPALOVA 6 ch.m. Champs Elysees – Topatori (IRE) (Topanoora) [2018/19 h16g⁶ Jun 3] half-sister to fair 2m hurdle winner Toparudi (by Rudimentary): modest maiden on Flat, stays 2m: well beaten in maiden on hurdling debut. *Mark H. Tompkins* **h–**

TOP AND DROP 8 b.m. Kayf Tara – Ismene (FR) (Bad Conduct (USA)) [2018/19 c20d⁴ c19.4v³ c25.2vᵖᵘ c23.6d⁴ c23.8s* c25.2d* Mar 9] maiden hurdler: fairly useful handicap chaser: completed hat-trick at Chepstow in January and Ffos Las (dead-heated) in February, both novice events, and Hereford (mares race) in March: stays 25f: acts on heavy going: usually races prominently. *Venetia Williams* **c119 h–**

TOP BILLING 10 br.g. Monsun (GER) – La Gandilie (FR) (Highest Honor (FR)) [2018/19 c–§, h91§: h23.9g³ c23.8g⁴ h23.3g h24.6v* h22.7g h24s h22.8d⁵ h23.9g Apr 24] leggy gelding: fair handicap hurdler: won at Carlisle in December: lightly-raced chaser: stays 3¼m: acts on heavy going: has worn headgear, including in 2018/19: temperamental. *Nicky Richards* **c87 § h103 §**

TOP CAT DJ (IRE) 11 ch.g. St Jovite (USA) – Lady Coldunell (Deploy) [2018/19 c63§, h–: c23.8g c25.5gᵘʳ c20.1g⁴ c23.4g⁶ c24.2sᵖᵘ c23.8g³ c23.8g⁵ Dec 10] maiden hurdler: poor maiden chaser: stays 3m: acts on heavy going: has worn headgear: wears tongue tie: temperamental. *Maurice Barnes* **c69 § h–**

TOP CHIEF 11 b.g. Doyen (IRE) – For More (FR) (Sanglamore (USA)) [2018/19 c16.3m⁴ c21g* c21g⁴ c25.8g² c25.8g² c25.8d* Sep 21] multiple point winner: winning hurdler: fair handicap chaser: won at Newton Abbot in July and September: stays 3¼m: acts on good to firm and good to soft going: has worn headgear, including last 5 starts: wears tongue tie. *Colin Tizzard* **c103 h–**

TOP DECISION (IRE) 6 ch.g. Beneficial – Great Decision (IRE) (Simply Great (FR)) [2018/19 h93, b–: h16gᵖᵘ h18.5s⁵ h19d* h21.7d³ Mar 9] rather unfurnished gelding: has had breathing operation: third on sole outing in Irish points: modest handicap hurdler: won novice event at Warwick in December: stays 2¾m: acts on soft going: has worn hood: in tongue tie last 3 starts. *Samuel Drinkwater* **h97**

TOP GAMBLE (IRE) 11 ch.g. Presenting – Zeferina (IRE) (Sadler's Wells (USA)) [2018/19 c152, h–: c16.4s⁴ c16.3dᶠ c19.4sᶠ c16.3d Mar 15] rangy gelding: winning hurdler: useful handicap chaser: fourth at Newbury (19¼ lengths behind Lady Buttons) in December: stays 21f, effective over shorter: acts on good to firm and heavy going: tried in cheekpieces: usually wears tongue tie. *Kerry Lee* **c131 h–**

TOP MAN TIM (IRE) 12 b.g. Flemensfirth (USA) – Wont Change (IRE) (Luso) [2018/19 h24.4g⁵ h27s* h27s⁵ Mar 21] point winner: modest handicap hurdler: won at Sedgefield in February: stayed 27f: acted on soft going: tried in headgear: dead. *Thomas Gallagher* **h89**

TOP NOTCH (FR) 8 b.g. Poliglote – Topira (FR) (Pistolet Bleu (IRE)) [2018/19 c166, h139: h24.4s³ c20.5g* h24d c19.9dᵖᵘ Apr 5] compact gelding: useful hurdler: third in Long Walk Hurdle at Ascot (5¾ lengths behind Paisley Park) in December: top-class chaser: won listed event at Kempton (by 5 lengths from Black Corton) in January: stays 3m: acts on heavy going. *Nicky Henderson* **c162 h142 +**

TOP OF THE CHARTS (FR) 5 b.g. Great Pretender (IRE) – Precious Lucy (FR) (Kadrou (FR)) [2018/19 b16.8g b16g³ h16s h19.6vᵖᵘ h22.7g⁴ h16.5d c21.3d⁴ h16s⁶ Mar 17] €80,000 3-y-o: fourth foal: half-brother to 2m hurdle winners Good Man Jim (fair, by Martaline) and The Absent Mare (modest, by Fair Mix): dam (h88) 17f hurdle winner: fair form in bumpers: better effort when third at Worcester: modest form over hurdles: 20/1, fourth in maiden at Leopardstown (23½ lengths behind Roxboro Road) on chasing debut: left Warren Greatrex after fifth start: tried in cheekpieces. *Gavin Patrick Cromwell, Ireland* **c74 h96 b94**

TOPOFTHECOTSWOLDS (IRE) 5 b.g. Arcadio (GER) – Bambootcha (IRE) (Saddlers' Hall (IRE)) [2018/19 b86: b16.3m² h16g² h16v⁶ h16g² Mar 29] modest form in bumpers: similar form over hurdles: will be suited by 2½m: in hood last 3 starts. *Nigel Twiston-Davies* **h98 b81**

TOPOFTHEGAME (IRE) 7 ch.g. Flemensfirth (USA) – Derry Vale (IRE) (Mister Lord (USA)) [2018/19 c–p, h154: c19.2s² c24g² c24.4s* c25d² Apr 5]   c162 p
h–

Property experts warn about the perils of 'buying big', citing examples of 'dream homes' turning into money-guzzling white elephants. Similar issues can apply at equine auctions too, with bigger horses often more difficult to keep sound than the norm—though, in both instances, sometimes all the effort can prove worthwhile. Stable staff at Fred Winter's Uplands yard were distinctly underwhelmed when champion Australian chaser Crisp first arrived in Lambourn following a round-the-world trip which had included a hard race on American soil. The giant gelding, who stood at seventeen hands plus, stood out like a sore thumb against his new stable-companions, while an immobilising drug was required whenever his coat needed clipping, a regular occurrence as he encountered a British winter for the first time. Winter could see beyond Crisp's freakish appearance, though, and said: 'Just look at the depth of his chest. He must have a big heart in there.' Crisp, of course, soon went on to impress British racegoers, breaking course records left, right and centre. He ran out a wide-margin winner of the 1971 Two-Mile Champion Chase at Cheltenham, though his finest hour arguably came in defeat when just pipped by Red Rum in the 1973 Grand National after an epic display of front-running under 12-0. Crisp's giant frame proved an asset over Aintree's daunting fences as he made light work of them with a notably bold round of jumping, but it counted against him when tiring on the long run-in, where he lost vital ground and momentum by wandering on the run to the elbow as jockey Richard Pitman (who admitted to being equally exhausted!) struggled to keep his oversized partner on an even keel.

Nineteen years later, a horse measuring eighteen-plus hands went one better in the Aintree showpiece when Party Politics became one of the biggest and tallest winners in the race's long history. In many ways Party Politics wasn't typical for one of his size, with trainer Nick Gaselee highlighting an incident early in the race: 'For a big horse he was incredibly nimble. When Brown Windsor came down at first Becher's, he just sidestepped him which is remarkable considering how big he was—a lot of horses would have gone straight over him.' Party Politics still had his share of problems, though. He was actually sent back to Gaselee and his owner-breeder David Stoddart after failing the vet—said to be unsound in his wind—when sold as a six-year-old, while the long list of ailments from which he suffered during his career included broken blood vessels, a damaged hock and fragile feet which bruised easily (Stoddart eventually sold him for a reputed £80,000 to Cheveley Park Stud owner David Thompson forty-eight hours before he won the Grand National). By far the main issue with Party Politics, however, were the recurring problems with his breathing, which resulted in him being tubed for the final four seasons after his Grand National win.

Both Party Politics (pulled up in 1991) and Crisp (fifth when favourite in 1972) were out of luck when tackling the Cheltenham Gold Cup, but Cheltenham's blue riband proved the natural race for another giant in Denman. Nicknamed 'The Tank' on account of his size, the Paul Nicholls-trained Denman was another to stand at seventeen hands plus and had a terrific Cheltenham record, never finishing out of the first two in six successive Festivals, a run which included winning the Gold Cup in 2008 and finishing runner-up in the next three renewals. This relentless galloper wasn't quite so robust as his nickname or that record might suggest, however, as he also endured his fair share of training issues, notably a heart problem detected in the autumn following his Gold Cup win (he won just one more race from ten starts after the 2008 Gold Cup). His mammoth frame also contributed to his relatively short retirement, as he was put down at the age of eighteen due to a rapidly-deteriorating stifle injury, his devoted owner Paul Barber explaining: 'If you've got great big horses like him, there's a lot of strain and unfortunately they don't live forever'.

Nicholls and Barber have another giant on their hands in Topofthegame, who is described by the former as 'the tallest horse I've ever trained' (measured at 17.3 hands) and falls very much into the same mould as Denman. He looked a top-notch staying chaser in the making when emulating his illustrious predecessor with victory in the RSA Insurance Novices' Chase at Cheltenham in March (a race Denman won in 2007). 'He is very similar to Denman and he probably has more

boot than him. Denman was an out-and-out slogger. This fella has a touch of class and is very exciting,' remarked the trainer afterwards. The form-book doesn't fully endorse that verdict so far, as Denman was unbeaten in four starts over fences before his Festival novice win, while Topofthegame became the first maiden chaser to win the race since its sponsors (then known as just Sun Alliance) began their association way back in 1974. That 'maiden' tag is misleading, however, as Topofthegame had shown himself to be one of the leading novice chasers around prior to Cheltenham and he lined up for the RSA as 4/1 third favourite in a field of twelve, the market headed by Irish raider Delta Work at 15/8 and the Nicky Henderson-trained Santini at 3/1. Topofthegame and Santini had met on their previous start, when filling the minor placings behind the mare La Bague Au Roi (who missed Cheltenham by design) in a good renewal of the Kauto Star Novices' Chase at Kempton on Boxing Day. That doesn't tell the whole story, though, as Topofthegame might have been unlucky to come up against an ultra-tough winner after being produced to lead three out, which was arguably too soon for one still on the raw side—Topofthegame looked to be going best at one stage and traded as low as 1.20 in-running on Betfair, compared to a high of 17.00 for La Bague Au Roi. Similar rawness had been on display at the other end of the race on Topofthegame's reappearance in a hot novice chase at Exeter earlier in December, when he shied away as the tapes went up and found himself seventeen lengths adrift of eventual winner Defi du Seuil at the first. That deficit had been reduced to just three and a half lengths by the finishing line and, although Defi du Seuil won with plenty to spare, it was still a very promising performance by Topofthegame to finish second in the circumstances. Throw in the fact that he had fallen on his chasing debut in 2017/18 (when he was put back over hurdles for the remainder of the campaign), and Topofthegame clearly made a rather frustrating start to his chasing career.

Happily, there was no repeat of any of these traits as Topofthegame put it all together in the so-called 'novices' Gold Cup' at Cheltenham to reward his connections' patience. Travelling smoothly in mid-division, Topofthegame was produced with a much better-timed challenge to lead soon after the last and knuckled down really well to hold off the renewed effort of Santini (better suited by the track than Kempton) by half a length, with a further length and three quarters back to Delta Work in third. The fact that this trio pulled sixteen lengths clear of the remainder, in a race that wasn't run at an end-to-end gallop, reflects very well on each of them. Connections of both placed horses will be hopeful of reversing the form on another day, particularly those involved with Delta Work, who ran out an imperious winner at the Punchestown Festival on his only subsequent outing. Unfortunately, Topofthegame couldn't do his own bit for the RSA form when managing only second, beaten six lengths, to Lostintranslation in the Mildmay Novices' Chase at Aintree in April, though the manner in which he went through that race (uncharacteristically off the bridle a fair way out) suggests he may have been feeling the effects of his Cheltenham exertions, particularly as he is a horse who has been sparingly raced to date (the Mildmay was just his eleventh race from three full seasons under Rules). It seems far better to judge Topofthegame on his Cheltenham win and, with further improvement a distinct possibility, he looks very much one for the short list for the 2020 Cheltenham Gold Cup, for which he is third choice in the ante-post betting at 10/1 (behind the Willie Mullins-trained pair Kemboy and Al Boum Photo), with Santini a best priced 12/1 and Delta Work 14/1.

	Flemensfirth (USA) (b 1992)	Alleged (b 1974)	Hoist The Flag
			Princess Pout
		Etheldreda (ch 1985)	Diesis
Topofthegame (IRE) (ch.g. 2012)			Royal Bund
	Derry Vale (IRE) (ch 1997)	Mister Lord (b 1979)	Sir Ivor
			Forest Friend
		Nun Merrier (ch 1987)	The Parson
			Merry Memories

A raw-boned gelding, Topofthegame is a son of veteran stallion Flemensfirth, who is still going strongly at the age of twenty-seven (standing at a fee of €15,000 in 2019) and claimed his second successive champion jumps sire title in Britain and Ireland in 2018/19—Magic of Light, dual Irish Grand National runner-up Isleofhopendreams and the aforementioned Lostintranslation were among his other leading performers/earners. The bottom line of this pedigree also has plenty to recommend it, even if all three of the dams in question failed to see a racecourse themselves. Topofthegame's year-younger brother Golden Whisky is Derry Vale's only other winner, having shown fairly useful form when landing a two and a half mile handicap hurdle at Ffos Las for Evan Williams in the latest campaign. Derry

Chris Giles and Mr & Mrs P. K. Barber's "Topofthegame"

Vale was a half-sister to the useful hurdler Artadoin Lad, runner-up in the 1999 Royal & SunAlliance Novices' Hurdle at Cheltenham (now registered as the Baring Bingham). Over The Bar, out of a half-sister to Topofthegame's grandam Nun Merrier, was runner-up in the same race three years later and a brother to the very smart staying hurdler Merry Masquerade. Their half-brother Merry People was a useful chaser on his day and still had a chance of causing a 200/1 shock in the 1999 Grand National when falling two out. Third dam Merry Memories is also the third dam of useful two and a half mile chaser Arteea and the fourth dam of the high-class two-mile to three-mile hurdler Identity Thief (out of a Flemensfirth mare) whose career ended sadly when he sustained a fatal injury.

Notwithstanding those relatives, it was almost certainly the ease of Topofthegame's victory in a four-year-old maiden on his sole outing in points which prompted current connections (he is owned in partnership by Barber and Chris Giles) to pay £120,000 for him at the Aintree Sales shortly afterwards. The owners have had little reason to regret that decision, with Topofthegame's two wins over hurdles including one worth £56,000 at Sandown, while he failed by just a neck to win the Coral Cup (pipped in the dying strides by Bleu Berry) at the 2018 Cheltenham Festival. Tongue tied nowadays, Topofthegame underwent a breathing operation prior to his 2018/19 reappearance, though it is possibly best not to read too much into that for now, given that the Nicholls stable has long favoured such procedures. Effective on all types of ground that he has encountered to date (yet to race on firmer than good), Topofthegame will stay beyond twenty-five furlongs and, despite his chasing debut fall, is essentially a good jumper. It is easy to see why his trainer has 'big' plans for him in the next season. *Paul Nicholls*

TOP OF THE ROCKS (FR) 6 b.g. Rock of Gibraltar (IRE) – Runaway Top (Rainbow Quest (USA)) [2018/19 h74: h16.8s h15.3g⁵ h16d² h16.8g⁶ Apr 20] sturdy gelding: poor maiden hurdler: stays 2¼m: acts on good to firm and good to soft going: usually wears headgear: wears tongue tie. *Katie Stephens* — **h75**

TOP OF THE TOWN (IRE) 11 b.g. Craigsteel – Hil Rhapsody (Anshan) [2018/19 h24.5g⁵ h24g⁴ h22.4m³ c22.5d c19.9gᵖᵘ h23.9g Sep 26] fairly useful handicap hurdler: third at Killarney in July: useful chaser at best, well below form both starts over fences in 2018/19: stays 25f: acts on good to firm and good to soft going: has worn hood: usually races towards rear. *Gordon Elliott, Ireland* — **c–, h124**

TOPOTHE RA (IRE) 11 ch.g. Whitmore's Conn (USA) – The Top Road (IRE) (Toulon) [2018/19 h133: h16s* h16s c18.2d⁵ Oct 9] workmanlike gelding: fairly useful on Flat, stays 15f: useful handicap hurdler: won at Galway (by neck from Stormey) in August: tailed off in maiden on chasing debut: stays 2¼m: acts on heavy going: tried in hood. *Thomas Mullins, Ireland* — **c–, h137**

TOPPER THORNTON (IRE) 10 ch.g. Double Eclipse (IRE) – Gailybay Ellen (IRE) (Supreme Leader) [2018/19 c129§, h–: h23.6d⁴ h25.5v⁵ c25.7spᵘ Jan 16] sturdy gelding: fair handicap hurdler: fairly useful but unreliable chaser: stays 3¼m: acts on good to firm and heavy going: has worn headgear: races off pace. *Alex Hales* — **c– §, h103**

TOP ROCK TALULA (IRE) 4 b.f. Lord Shanakill (USA) – Spirit Watch (IRE) (Invincible Spirit (IRE)) [2018/19 h16.7m² h16g⁴ h17.7gᵘʳ h15.5g Dec 6] fair on Flat, stays 1¾m: modest form over hurdles: left Kenny Johnson after first start. *Warren Greatrex* — **h94**

TOPS NO 4 b.f. Mount Nelson – China Beads (Medicean) [2018/19 b14g⁶ b12.6s⁶ Dec 19] leggy filly: third foal: half-sister to 5f winner Little China (by Kyllachy): dam unraced: poor form in bumpers. *William Muir* — **b68**

TOP UP THE FASHION (IRE) 5 b.g. Court Cave (IRE) – Aqua Breezer (IRE) (Namaqualand (USA)) [2018/19 h21s³ h21g² Apr 10] €22,000 3-y-o, £48,000 4-y-o: sixth foal: brother to a winning pointer: dam (h104) bumper/2¼m hurdle winner: runner-up in Irish point: fair form over hurdles: better effort when second in maiden at Warwick: will stay beyond 21f: open to further improvement. *Charlie Mann* — **h105 p**

TOP VILLE BEN (IRE) 7 b.g. Beneficial – Great Decision (IRE) (Simply Great (FR)) [2018/19 h136: c24.2s* c24.2d* c23.8d⁵ c24.4sᶠ c24.2d* c25d³ Apr 5] useful-looking gelding: useful hurdler: smart form over fences: comfortably won small-field novices at Hexham in November, and Wetherby in December and March: third in Mildmay Novices' Chase at Aintree (6½ lengths behind Lostintranslation) in April: likely to stay long distances: acts on heavy going: wears hood: forces pace. *Philip Kirby* — **c150, h–**

Randox Health Foxhunters' Chase, Aintree—Top Wood and Tabitha Worsley withstand the challenge of the strong-travelling Burning Ambition (diamonds)

TOP WOOD (FR) 12 ch.g. Kotky Bleu (FR) – Heure Bleu (FR) (Grand Tresor (FR)) [2018/19 c133§, h–: c26.3d³ c21.1d* Apr 4] lengthy gelding: winning hurdler: useful chaser: won Foxhunters' Chase at Aintree (by 2 lengths from Burning Ambition) in April: third in Foxhunter at Cheltenham (11 lengths behind Hazel Hill) on return 3 weeks earlier: stays 3¼m: acts on good to firm and heavy going: wears headgear/tongue tie: formerly moody. *Kelly Morgan* — **c134 h–**

TOR 5 ch.g. Orientor – Dance In The Sun (Halling (USA)) [2018/19 h86p: h15.6g³ Dec 3] useful on Flat, stays 15f: fair form over hurdles: third in novice at Musselburgh on sole outing in 2018/19: remains with potential. *Iain Jardine* — **h104 p**

TORCELLO (IRE) 5 ch.g. Born To Sea (IRE) – Islandagore (IRE) (Indian Ridge) [2018/19 h16s³ h20.2gᵘʳ h16g* h19.2g² h16d⁵ h19d h16d Mar 31] half-brother to fair 2m hurdle winner Fool To Cry (by Fast Company): useful on Flat, stays 1½m: fairly useful hurdler: won maiden at Tramore in June: stays 19f: acts on heavy going: wears headgear. *Andrew McNamara, Ireland* — **h118**

TORHOUSEMUIR 8 b.g. Sagamix (FR) – Royal Musical (Royal Abjar (USA)) [2018/19 c81, h–: c21g² c17g³ c22.6g² c23mᵖᵘ c24g⁴ c26.3g³ Nov 8] maiden hurdler: modest maiden chaser: stays 23f: acts on soft going: has worn hood. *Sam Thomas* — **c94 h–**

TORNADO FLYER (IRE) 6 b.g. Flemensfirth (USA) – Mucho Macabi (IRE) (Exceed And Excel (AUS)) [2018/19 b125: h20d* h20dᵖᵘ Jan 6] sturdy gelding: smart bumper performer: useful form over hurdles: won maiden at Punchestown in December: flopped next time, but very much back on track when 8¾ lengths fourth to Reserve Tank in Champion Novices' Hurdle at same course shortly after end of British season, left lot to do and forced to switch early in straight: open to further improvement. *W. P. Mullins, Ireland* — **h141 p**

TORNADO IN MILAN (IRE) 13 b.g. Milan – Julika (GER) (Nebos (GER)) [2018/19 c137, h112: c19.4d² c16gᶠ Nov 26] winning hurdler: useful chaser: second in claimer at Ffos Las (2½ lengths behind Candy Burg) in October: stayed 2½m: acted on heavy going: tried in hood: dead. *Evan Williams* — **c132 h–**

TORNADO WATCH (IRE) 10 ch.g. Selkirk (USA) – Pattimech (USA) (Nureyev (USA)) [2018/19 h114: h16s* h21d² h16g⁵ h15.7s Dec 22] sturdy gelding: useful handicap hurdler: won at Kilbeggan in May: second in Grand National Hurdle at Far Hills (3¼ lengths behind Jury Duty) in October: stays 21f: acts on heavy going. *Emmet Mullins, Ireland* — **h130**

TORN AND FRAYED (FR) 5 b.g. Califet (FR) – Chic Et Zen (FR) (Chichicastenango (FR)) [2018/19 b15.7g⁵ Mar 4] third foal: half-brother to French 11.5f winner Scala Emery (by Spanish Moon): dam, French 14.5f winner, half-sister to smart French chaser (stayed 27f) Top of The Sky: 11/2, fifth in bumper at Southwell (8¼ lengths behind San Rumoldo). *Nigel Twiston-Davies* — **b84**

TORONTO SOUND 5 b.g. Aussie Rules (USA) – Caribana (Hernando (FR)) [2018/19 h–: h22.8v Dec 5] modest maiden on Flat, stays 1¼m: well held in maiden on hurdling debut. *Kevin Frost* — **h–**

TORPILLO (FR) 4 ch.g. Alanadi (FR) – Astherate (FR) (Balko (FR)) [2018/19 h16v* **h127**
h16s* h15.7g⁴ h16.4s Mar 13] tall gelding: first foal: dam ran once over hurdles in France:
fairly useful form over hurdles: won 3-y-o event at Nancy on debut for A. Adeline de
Boisbrunet: also successful in juveniles at Sandown in December and January: disappointing
last 2 starts: raced around 2m: acts on heavy going: in hood last 4 starts: usually leads.
Nigel Twiston-Davies

TORRAN NA DTONN (IRE) 11 b.g. Fruits of Love (USA) – Celtic Tigress (IRE) **c–**
(Over The River (FR)) [2018/19 c20.9sᵖᵘ Mar 11] multiple point winner: pulled up in
novice hunter on chasing debut. *A. Pennock*

TORRENT DES MOTTES (FR) 8 gr.g. Montmartre (FR) – Wavy (FR) (Lavirco **c93**
(GER)) [2018/19 h–, b94: h20gᵖᵘ h15.8m³ h15.7g² h24g⁶ h20.3g⁶ h15.8g h20.3g h20.7g⁶ **h91**
h16.7g⁵ h15.5g⁴ c20.3g c16.5g* c19.4g⁵ c15.7d² Apr 24] modest maiden hurdler: similar
form over fences: won handicap at Huntingdon in March: left Alexandra Dunn after third
start: unproven beyond 17f: acts on good to firm and good to soft going: wears cheekpieces/
tongue tie. *John Cornwall*

TORRID 8 ch.g. Three Valleys (USA) – Western Appeal (USA) (Gone West (USA)) **h113**
[2018/19 h16.2s³ h16.8s² h16.8d² h16.4s² Mar 10] fair on Flat, stays 8.5f: fair form over
hurdles: will prove best at sharp 2m. *Michael Easterby*

TORTUGA BAY 5 b.m. Sulamani (IRE) – Empress of Light (Emperor Jones (USA)) **b77**
[2018/19 b17g⁴ Feb 24] £60,000 4-y-o: half-sister to several winners, including bumper
winner/useful chaser Fistral Beach (2½m/21f winner, by Definite Article), stayed 3m, and
useful hurdler/chaser Rons Dream (2m-25f winner, by Kayf Tara): dam, lightly raced on
Flat, half-sister to high-class hurdler/very smart chaser Wahiba Sands (won point on debut: tongue tied, fourth in mares bumper at Carlisle. *James Ewart*

TOSHIMA (IRE) 4 b.g. Sea The Stars (IRE) – Sabreon (Caerleon (USA)) [2018/19 **h–**
h16dᵖᵘ h16.3d Mar 1] useful-looking gelding: fairly useful on Flat, stays 12.5f: no promise
in juvenile hurdles (had breathing operation between races): tried in cheekpieces/tongue
tie. *Robert Stephens*

TOSSAPENNY (IRE) 6 b.g. Presenting – Blueanna (IRE) (Blueprint (IRE)) [2018/19 **h91**
h122, b100: h19.5s⁵ Nov 7] fairly useful maiden hurdler: shaped as if needing run sole
outing under Rules in 2018/19: won both starts in points, second in 2019. *Evan Williams*

TOTAL ASSETS 11 b.m. Alflora (IRE) – Maid Equal (Pragmatic) [2018/19 c111, h120: **c112**
c24.2d c29.4g³ h23.9g c26.2gᵖᵘ c31.9s* c32.4g⁴ c26.3s⁵ c31.9v⁵ Mar 14] rather leggy mare: **h–**
fairly useful hurdler: fair handicap chaser: won at Hexham in November: stays 4m: acts on
good to firm and heavy going: has worn cheekpieces: held up. *Simon Waugh*

TOTAL RECALL (IRE) 10 b.g. Westerner – Augest Weekend (IRE) (Dr Massini (IRE)) **c153**
[2018/19 c163+, h143pᵘ c21.5s² c20.5g³ c29dᵖᵘ Apr 22] lengthy gelding: useful form over **h–**
hurdles: developed into high-class chaser in winter 2017/18, winning Ladbrokes Trophy at
Newbury by neck from Whisper: largely let down by jumping since, having tendency to go
left: stays 3¼m: acts on heavy going. *W. P. Mullins, Ireland*

TO THE CORE 6 b.m. Apple Tree (FR) – Pull The Wool (IRE) (Commander Collins **b–**
(IRE)) [2018/19 b16g b15.7dˢᵘ Nov 20] tailed off completed start in bumpers: tried in
hood: dead. *Keiran Burke*

TOTTERDOWN 8 b.g. Pasternak – Yeldham Lady (Mujahid (USA)) [2018/19 h112, b87: **h132**
h15.8m* h15.8g³ h16v* h16v³ h19g⁵ h16d⁴ h16sᵖᵘ h15.8m Apr 1] smallish gelding: useful
hurdler: won novice at Huntingdon (by 12 lengths) in October and handicap at Sandown in
November: best at 2m: acts on good to firm and heavy going: usually hooded: enthusiastic
front runner. *Richard Phillips*

TOUCHEDBYANANGEL (IRE) 7 gr.g. Beneficial – Gray's Anatomy (IRE) (Gothland **h109**
(FR)) [2018/19 h19.3s h21.5g h17.3g* h18.8g* h16g³ h16gᵖ h20.9gᵖᵘ h20.2g Apr 25]
second foal: dam, winning pointer, half-sister to fairly useful hurdler/useful chaser (2m-19f
winner) The Russian Doyen: fair handicap hurdler: won at Downpatrick in June and July
and Kilbeggan (left Andrew Oliver after) in August: stays 19f: best form on good going:
usually makes running/races prominently. *Lucinda Russell*

TOUCH KICK (IRE) 8 b.g. Presenting – Bay Pearl (FR) (Broadway Flyer (USA)) **c133**
[2018/19 c125, h–: c20.9g* c19.9d² c19.4s³ c23s* c26d c25gᵖᵘ Apr 6] good-topped **h–**
gelding: winning hurdler: useful handicap chaser: won at Hereford in November and
Taunton in February: best short of 3¼m: acts on soft going: hooded over jumps prior to last
4 outings: wears tongue tie. *Paul Nicholls*

TOUCH SCREEN (IRE) 9 b.g. Touch of Land (FR) – Capard Lady (IRE) (Supreme **c73 x**
Leader) [2018/19 c81x, h–: h19s c21.7g⁵ c24.2v³ c24.2d Apr 9] poor maiden hurdler: poor **h61**
handicap chaser: stays 3m: acts on heavy going: has been let down by jumping. *Mark
Gillard*

TOUCHY SUBJECT (IRE) 6 br.g. Tikkanen (USA) – Legal Lodge (IRE) (Carroll **h95**
House) [2018/19 h111, b–: h20g³ h19.9gᵖᵘ h22g³ Aug 23] has had breathing operation:
runner-up in Irish point on debut: maiden hurdler, fair form at best: stays 21f: acts on good
to soft going: tried in tongue tie. *Jo Davis*

TOUR DE PARIS (IRE) 4 b.g. Champs Elysees – Disco Lights (Spectrum (IRE)) **h96**
[2018/19 h16.7g⁴ h17.7d⁴ h16.5d Dec 13] fair on Flat, stays 1¾m: modest form over
hurdles: may prove best at 2m. *Alan King*

TOUR DE PUB (IRE) 5 ch.g. Aizavoski (IRE) – Gallant Express (IRE) (Flemensfirth **h95**
(USA)) [2018/19 h16.8s h19.9s⁶ h16.8s³ Mar 21] £14,000 3-y-o, £18,000 5-y-o: first foal:
dam, maiden pointer, half-sister to useful hurdler/chaser (stays 25f) On Tour: off mark in
points at second attempt: easily best effort in novice hurdles when third at Sedgefield:
should be suited by at least 2½m. *Mark Walford*

TOUT EST PERMIS (FR) 6 gr.g. Linda's Lad – Kadalbleue (FR) (Kadalko (FR)) **c154 p**
[2018/19 c16m c22.5s* c24d² c20.5g* c29d Apr 22] second foal: dam French maiden **h–**
jumper: winning hurdler: smart chaser: left M. F. Morris, won handicap at Galway in
October, Troytown Handicap Chase at Navan (by 4½ lengths from Mr Diablo) in November
and Kinloch Brae Chase at Thurles (by short head from Sub Lieutenant) in January: stays
3m well: acts on heavy going: has worn cheekpieces/tongue tie: remains open to
improvement over fences. *Noel Meade, Ireland*

TOVIERE (IRE) 8 ch.g. Presenting – Aventia (IRE) (Bob Back (USA)) [2018/19 c130p, **c117**
h118: c24g⁵ c26.1m⁶ c23dᵘʳ Aug 29] fairly useful hurdler: useful handicap chaser: below **h–**
par in 2018/19 (lame final outing): stays 3¼m: acts on good to firm and good to soft going.
Oliver Sherwood

TOWARDS THE DAWN 5 b.g. Midnight Legend – Wakeful (Kayf Tara) [2018/19 **h111 p**
h21.2g³ Jan 3] fourth foal: brother to fairly useful hurdler/chaser Awake At Midnight (2m
winner) and half-brother to fairly useful hurdler Morning Herald (2¼m-21f winner, by
Lucky Story): dam unraced sister to useful hurdler/very smart chaser (stayed 3¼m) Planet
of Sound: shaped well when third in maiden hurdle at Ludlow (6¼ lengths behind
Smackwater Jack) on debut: will improve. *Ben Pauling*

TOWER BRIDGE (IRE) 6 b.g. High Chaparral (IRE) – Walkamia (FR) (Linamix (FR)) **c140**
[2018/19 h143, b109: c20g⁵ c21g³ c20d² c20.2s² Mar 12] compact gelding: dual bumper **h–**
winner: useful novice hurdler in 2017/18: similar form over fences, second in Close Brothers
Novices' Handicap Chase at Cheltenham (16 lengths behind A Plus Tard) in March: stays
3m: acts on heavy going: tried in cheekpieces: wears tongue tie. *Joseph Patrick O'Brien,
Ireland*

TOWERBURN (IRE) 10 b.g. Cloudings (IRE) – Lady Newmill (IRE) (Taipan (IRE)) **c–**
[2018/19 c85, h74: c20.1gᵖᵘ h23.3g h17.2g h16.2g⁴ h20.1s* h20.1s² h23.3v Dec 20] has had **h77**
breathing operation: winning pointer: poor handicap hurdler: won at Hexham in November:
modest form on completed start in maiden hunter chases: stays 3m: acts on soft going: has
worn headgear: wears tongue tie: front runner/races prominently. *Alison Hamilton*

TOWERING (IRE) 10 b.g. Catcher In The Rye (IRE) – Bobs Article (IRE) (Definite **c– §**
Article) [2018/19 c–§, h104§: h21.2mᵖᵘ h20.7g h20.3gᵖᵘ Jun 12] good-topped gelding: fair **h74 §**
handicap hurdler: runner-up on completed start in novice handicap chases: stayed 3m:
acted on good to firm and heavy going: wore headgear: tried in tongue tie: temperamental:
dead. *Conor Dore*

TOWER OF ALLEN (IRE) 8 b.g. Beneficial – Baile An Droichid (IRE) (King's Ride) **c–**
[2018/19 c72, h88: h15.8g h20.3s⁴ Dec 14] has had breathing operation: modest maiden **h82**
hurdler/chaser: stays 21f: usually tongue tied. *Alex Hales*

TOWER VIEW (IRE) 5 b.g. Oscar (IRE) – Atomic Betty (IRE) (Anshan) [2018/19 **h–**
b15.7v h19.5d Feb 23] tailed off in bumper/maiden hurdle. *Nigel Twiston-Davies* **b–**

TOWN PARKS (IRE) 8 b.g. Morozov (USA) – Outdoor Heather (IRE) (Presenting) **c127**
[2018/19 c133, h–: c20.9gᵖᵘ c19.2sᵇᵈ c20d² c16d² c19.4g³ Apr 14] angular gelding: **h–**
winning hurdler: useful handicap chaser: best effort in 2018/19 when second at Hereford in
March: stays 21f: acts on heavy going. *Kerry Lee*

TOWNSHEND (GER) 8 b.g. Lord of England (GER) – Trikolore (GER) (Konigsstuhl **c139**
(GER)) [2018/19 h146, h–: c16g⁵ c19g³ c24s⁶ h23.1g⁶ h19.7v⁴ h21.4g² h21s⁶ c21m⁴ **h123**
c19.9g* Apr 22] compact gelding: has had breathing operation: fairly useful handicap

hurdler: useful handicap chaser nowadays: won at Huntingdon in April: left W. P. Mullins after third start: stays easy 21f: acts on heavy going: tried in hood: usually tongue tied. *Nigel Twiston-Davies*

TOWTON (IRE) 4 b.g. Zebedee – Amber Tide (IRE) (Pursuit of Love) [2018/19 h15.8spu Jul 29] poor maiden on Flat: pulled up in juvenile on hurdling debut: dead. *James Bethell* — **h–**

TRACTOR FRED (IRE) 5 br.g. Curtain Time (IRE) – Bonny Blackdoe (IRE) (Close Conflict (USA)) [2018/19 h22gpu h21g h20.5s³ h23.6dpu h25s³ Feb 13] €16,000 3-y-o, £12,000 4-y-o: first foal: dam, no form, half-sister to fairly useful chaser (2¾m-3m winner) Coljon: fell both starts in Irish points: fair form over hurdles: seemingly stays 25f: acts on soft going: tried in tongue tie. *Kate Buckett* — **h106**

TRADE FLOW (FR) 7 b.g. Danehill Dancer (IRE) – Dubai Rose (Dubai Destination (USA)) [2018/19 h22.1m Jun 29] sturdy gelding: fairly useful on Flat (stays 1½m) in France for H-A. Pantall: off 3 years, tailed off in maiden on hurdling debut. *Lucinda Egerton* — **h–**

TRADITIONAL DANCER (IRE) 7 b.g. Danehill Dancer (IRE) – Cote Quest (USA) (Green Desert (USA)) [2018/19 h119§: h24.3g² h20.2g* h23.1g² h20.2g⁴ c25g² h23.8g⁴ c24.5gur h20.5s c23.8g* Apr 24] tall gelding: fairly useful handicap hurdler: won conditionals race at Perth in May: useful form over fences: won novice handicap at same track in April: stays 25f: acts on good to firm and heavy going: wears headgear: tried in tongue tie: tactically versatile: temperamental. *Iain Jardine* — **c131 §**
h120 §

TRAFALGAR BOY 4 b.g. Mount Nelson – Aiaam Al Wafa (IRE) (Authorized (IRE)) [2018/19 b16s⁴ Mar 16] £8,000 3-y-o, resold €29,000 3-y-o: second foal: dam 1¼m winner who stayed 1½m: 25/1, needed experience when fourth to promising Shishkin in maiden bumper at Kempton. *Gary Moore* — **b84**

TRAFALGAR GIRL 4 ch.f. Champs Elysees – Lasting View (IRE) (Pivotal) [2018/19 h16.2gpu Nov 19] modest maiden on Flat, stays 1¼m: pulled up in fillies juvenile on hurdling debut. *Dominic Ffrench Davis* — **h–**

TRAFALGAR ROCK 8 b.g. Mount Nelson – Helter Helter (USA) (Seeking The Gold (USA)) [2018/19 c120x, h120: h15.8g² c20.9m⁴ c21.2g³ c19.4m⁵ h23.9spu c23.6m² Apr 22] fair hurdler/maiden chaser: left Alexandra Dunn after first start: stays 21f: acts on good to firm and good to soft going: often in headgear: lazy, and not one to trust. *Peter Bowen* — **c112 §**
h111 §

TRAFFIC FLUIDE (FR) 9 b.g. Astarabad (USA) – Petale Rouge (FR) (Bonnet Rouge (FR)) [2018/19 c145, h110: c23.6d² c23.8m* Nov 3] lengthy gelding: fair hurdler: smart handicap chaser: won Sodexo Gold Cup (Handicap Chase) at Ascot (by ½ length from — **c150**
h–

Sodexo Gold Cup Handicap Chase, Ascot—Traffic Fluide (second right) rallies to beat outsider Art Mauresque (right) and the leader Go Conquer

Art Mauresque) in November: stays 3m: acts on good to firm and heavy going: usually in headgear nowadays. *Gary Moore*

TRAILBOSS (IRE) 4 b.g. High Chaparral (IRE) – Seeking Solace (Exceed And Excel (AUS)) [2018/19 b16g² Feb 15] third foal: brother to Spanish 1m winner Learza: dam useful French 1¼m winner: 11/8, close second in maiden bumper at Fakenham. *Ed Vaughan* **b93**

TRAINWRECK (IRE) 7 b.g. Stowaway – Trail Storm (IRE) (Supreme Leader) [2018/19 h138: c16.2gᵘʳ c17d³ c16.1dᶠ Nov 28] winning pointer: useful hurdler: similar form when third in maiden at Navan (8 lengths behind Us And Them) on completed outing in maiden chases: unproven beyond 17f: acts on heavy going: usually races prominently. *Henry de Bromhead, Ireland* **c135 h–**

TRANS DES OBEAUX 5 br.g. Trans Island – Quechua des Obeaux (FR) (Ungaro (GER)) [2018/19 b16s b15.7m h25.3m² h20.1vᵖᵘ Mar 14] little promise in bumpers (trained second outing only by Philip Kirby) or over hurdles. *Russell Ross* **h– b–**

TRANS EXPRESS (IRE) 9 br.g. Trans Island – Hazel Fastrack (Shambo) [2018/19 h112: h19.2g³ h21g h16.8g² h20.5g⁴ h18.5v* h18.5d³ h18.5s³ h23.1d⁴ h18.5d* h19.8g⁴ Apr 27] close-coupled gelding: fairly useful handicap hurdler: won at Leicester and Exeter in December, and Exeter again (fifth course success) in March: stays 23f: acts on heavy going: wears cheekpieces: front runner/races prominently: tough and reliable. *Susan Gardner* **h119**

TRANSPENNINE STAR 6 ch.g. Mount Nelson – Brave Mave (Daylami (IRE)) [2018/19 h108: h19.9g h23.6g³ h23d⁴ h20.6d³ h19.9s³ h23.3d³ Mar 30] fair maiden handicap hurdler: stays 3m: acts on soft going: in headgear last 4 starts. *Jonjo O'Neill* **h109**

TRAPPER PEAK (IRE) 10 b.g. Westerner – Banningham Blaze (Averti (IRE)) [2018/19 c–§, h84§: h15.8g⁴ h16.8v* h19.3m* Feb 26] sturdy gelding: fair handicap hurdler: left Conor Dore, won at Sedgefield in January and Catterick (lady amateurs event) in February: winning chaser: has form at 23f, races mainly at much shorter nowadays: acts on good to firm and heavy going: usually wore headgear for former yards: regularly in tongue tie. *Stef Keniry* **c– h107**

TRAVEL LIGHTLY 4 b.f. Showcasing – Upton Seas (Josr Algarhoud (IRE)) [2018/19 h16m⁴ h15.7g* h17s⁵ h16d² h15.7g³ h16.8v⁵ Jan 27] modest on Flat, stays 7f: fair juvenile hurdler: won at Catterick in November: will prove best around 2m: best form on good going: tried in blinkers. *Tim Easterby* **h105**

TRAVERTINE (IRE) 9 b.g. Danehill Dancer (IRE) – Mer de Corail (IRE) (Sadler's Wells (USA)) [2018/19 h114: h19.2g⁶ h21.9g³ h23.3g³ h19.6g⁵ h26.5g³ c25.2g⁴ c25.5g⁴ c26.3s³ h24.2d² Mar 22] good-topped gelding: fairly useful handicap hurdler: never dangerous in handicap chases: stays 3¼m: acts on heavy going: often in headgear: held up. *Jonjo O'Neill* **c115 h117**

TREACKLE TART (IRE) 7 b.m. Winged Love (IRE) – Battle Over (FR) (Sillery (USA)) [2018/19 h124: c20g² c20g³ c23g* c24.4g² c24g⁵ c24g* c26d c23.8d² Apr 26] workmanlike mare: fairly useful hurdler: useful chaser: won novice at Worcester in September and handicap at Doncaster in December: should stay beyond 3m: acts on soft going. *Charlie Longsdon* **c134 h–**

TREASURE DILLON (IRE) 5 b.g. Sans Frontieres (IRE) – Treasure Trix (IRE) (Flemensfirth (USA)) [2018/19 h20v h21.2g⁴ h20.5g² h23d² h23.1d h19.9v² h19.5d* Mar 21] €10,000 3-y-o, £70,000 4-y-o: sixth foal: dam unraced half-sister to fairly useful hurdler/useful chaser (stayed 3m) Splendour: winning pointer: fair handicap hurdler: won novice event at Chepstow in March: stays 23f: acts on heavy going: in cheekpieces last 2 starts. *Evan Williams* **h112**

TREASURE THE RIDGE (IRE) 10 b.g. Galileo (IRE) – Treasure The Lady (IRE) (Indian Ridge) [2018/19 h108: h16.8g⁶ h18.5g⁶ h18.5m⁵ h16.8s³ h16.8g h21.6g⁵ Oct 1] has had breathing operation: fair handicap hurdler: stays 2¼m: acts on soft going: wears headgear: has worn tongue tie. *Martin Hill* **h101**

TREATY GIRL (IRE) 8 b.m. Milan – Back To Cloghoge (IRE) (Bob Back (USA)) [2018/19 h110, h–: c24mᵖᵘ c26.2gᵖᵘ Oct 30] sturdy mare: has had breathing operation: winning pointer/hurdler: fairly useful maiden chaser at best: pulled up both outings in 2018/19: stays 3¼m: acts on soft going. *Ben Pauling* **c– h–**

TREAT YOURSELF (IRE) 12 b.g. Beat Hollow – Cartesian (Shirley Heights) [2018/19 c116§, h–: c24.2g⁵ c17dᵖᵘ c23.8gᵖᵘ c20.5m³ Apr 25] winning hurdler: modest chaser on balance: probably stays 3¼m: acts on good to firm and heavy going: often in headgear/tongue tie: temperamental. *Miss Michelle Bentham* **c86 § h–**

TREE OF LIBERTY (IRE) 7 ch.g. Stowaway – The Wrens Nest (IRE) (Shernazar) c148
[2018/19 c141, h–: c16d² c15.2g⁴ c16.3d c20.6g^{ur} Apr 17] well-made gelding: winning h–
hurdler: smart handicap chaser: best effort when second at Ludlow (½ length behind
Capeland) on return: stays 21f: acts on heavy going. *Kerry Lee*

TRELIVER MANOR (IRE) 11 b.g. Flemensfirth (USA) – Loch Lomond (IRE) (Dry c–
Dock) [2018/19 c24.2d^{pu} May 5] point winner: poor maiden hurdler/chaser: stays 25f: acts h–
on heavy going: in cheekpieces last 3 starts: wears tongue tie. *A. G. Dobbin*

TRENCH BOX (IRE) 5 b.g. Scorpion (IRE) – Sonne Cinq (IRE) (Old Vic) [2018/19 b–
b16.5d⁴ Feb 28] well beaten in bumper. *Jeremy Scott*

TRESHNISH (FR) 6 ch.g. Gold Away (IRE) – Didn't I Tell You (IRE) (Docksider c122
(USA)) [2018/19 h123: c15.9g⁵ c15.9s⁴ c20.6v⁴ c16.3s* c17.1g⁵ c16.5s⁴ c20d⁶ Mar 30] h–
fairly useful hurdler: fairly useful handicap chaser: won novice event at Newcastle in
December: should stay beyond 17f: acts on heavy going. *Sue Smith*

TREVELYN'S CORN (IRE) 6 b.g. Oscar (IRE) – Present Venture (IRE) (Presenting) h121
[2018/19 h21.6g⁴ h19.8s* h24.7d Apr 5] €45,000 3-y-o, £400,000 4-y-o: well-made
gelding: will make a chaser: second foal: dam bumper winner/winning pointer: easy
winner of Irish point on debut: fairly useful form over hurdles: won maiden at Wincanton
in March, forging clear: wears tongue tie. *Paul Nicholls*

TRIANGLE ROCK (IRE) 6 b.g. Stowaway – Lucy Cooper (IRE) (Roselier (FR)) h103
[2018/19 h24g^{pu} h20.5g h24g⁵ h24g h21g⁴ h20m⁵ h23.8g² h22.7g h21.2v² h23.8m² Feb 27]
€62,000 3-y-o: sixth foal: half-brother to fairly useful hurdler/chaser Palm Grey (2½m-3m
winner, by Great Palm): dam, placed in points, half-sister to useful hurdler/fairly useful
chaser (stayed 3½m) Valley Ride out of half-sister to Cheltenham Gold Cup winner
Jodami: fair maiden hurdler: left M. F. Morris after sixth start: stays 3m: acts on good to
firm and heavy going: often in cheekpieces: wears tongue tie: front runner/races
prominently. *Keith Dalgleish*

TRIBESMANS GLORY (IRE) 5 b.g. Jeremy (USA) – Benecash (IRE) (Beneficial) b–
[2018/19 ab16s Dec 10] won Irish maiden point on debut: 11/4, pulled hard/weakened
quickly once headed in bumper at Lingfield. *Tom George*

TRICKS AND TRAILS (IRE) 6 b.g. Flemensfirth (USA) – Loughaneala (IRE) (Be My h–
Native (USA)) [2018/19 h21g h16.8g⁵ h15.7d⁵ Jan 19] good-topped gelding: placed twice
in Irish points: highly tried in novice hurdles. *Alan Jones*

TRIGGER NICHOL (IRE) 7 b.g. Dubai Destination (USA) – Run For Cover (IRE) c121
(Lafontaine (USA)) [2018/19 h91, b–: h15.8g^F h20.7d² h20.3s³ c15.9m⁵ c22.7m* c23.8d⁶ h108
Feb 20] sturdy gelding: fair form over hurdles: fairly useful form over fences: won
handicap at Leicester in January: should be suited by 3m+: acts on good to firm and good
to soft going, probably on heavy: in cheekpieces last 4 starts. *Dr Richard Newland*

TRIGGITAS 9 b.g. Double Trigger (IRE) – Suntas (IRE) (Riberetto) [2018/19 h105: c81
h19.5s⁵ c20s⁶ c23d Dec 30] rangy gelding: fair maiden hurdler, lightly raced: badly let h87
down by jumping in novice handicap chases: should have been suited by 2½m+: acted on
soft going: tried in hood: raced in rear: dead. *Paul Webber*

TRIGGYWINKLE (FR) 10 b.m. Le Triton (USA) – Periwinkle (FR) (Perrault) [2018/19 c– §
c77§, h73§: c16d^{pu} h23.1d h16.5d⁶ Apr 24] has had breathing operation: maiden hurdler/ h– §
winning chaser, no form in 2018/19: wears headgear/tongue tie: ungenuine. *Laura Hurley*

TRILLERIN MINELLA (IRE) 11 b.g. King's Theatre (IRE) – Eva Fay (IRE) (Fayruz) c– §
[2018/19 c–§, h–: c20.1g^{pu} Jun 2] lengthy gelding: maiden hurdler/winning chaser, of no h–
account nowadays: wears headgear: temperamental. *Kevin Hunter*

TRINCOMALEE 6 b.m. Malinas (GER) – Royal Tango (Petoski) [2018/19 b16g³ Oct 31] b84 p
sixth foal: half-brother to fair hurdler/chaser Midnight Macarena (2½m-3m winner, by
Midnight Legend): dam unraced: 11/4, encouraging third in conditionals/amateurs bumper
at Fakenham: open to improvement. *Lucy Wadham*

TRIO FOR RIO (IRE) 6 b.g. Getaway (GER) – Rio Trio (IRE) (Oscar (IRE)) [2018/19 h120
h19.3g³ h23d* h19.8v⁵ h23d² h23.3d⁴ h24.1g* Apr 11] £40,000 5-y-o: sturdy gelding:
second foal: brother to a winning pointer: dam, winning pointer, half-sister to useful
hurdler/smart chaser (stayed 21f) Rio's King: won twice in Irish points: fairly useful
novice hurdler: won at Bangor in November and Wetherby in April: stays 3m: acts on good
to soft going: in cheekpieces last 3 starts: usually leads. *Warren Greatrex*

TRIOLET (IRE) 9 b.g. Westerner – Trinity Belle (FR) (Tel Quel (FR)) [2018/19 h111: c– h16.2g⁵ c20g⁶ c19.2d h20d⁰ᵖᵘ Jan 19] fair hurdler in 2017/18: no form since, including over h– fences: stays 2½m: acts on soft and good to firm going: tried in cheekpieces/tongue tie. *Colin A. McBratney, Ireland*

TRIOPAS (IRE) 7 b.g. Stowaway – Aine Dubh (IRE) (Bob Back (USA)) [2018/19 c110p, c– h104: c22.5dᵖᵘ h25.8g⁴ h23.1g⁶ c24.2sꟳ c25.1sᵖᵘ h23.1d Apr 9] fair handicap hurdler at h86 best: well held in 2018/19: similar form in novice handicap on chasing debut: failed to complete in similar events since: stays 25f: acts on heavy going: tried in cheekpieces: usually races close up. *Tom Lacey*

TRIPARTITE (IRE) 6 b.g. Zebedee – Baltic Belle (IRE) (Redback) [2018/19 h15.8g h99 h16.3m⁵ h16.3m⁴ h15.9g⁵ h15.8m⁵ Oct 10] has had breathing operation: half-brother to fairly useful hurdler Rathealy (2m-2½m winner, by Baltic King): fair on Flat, stays 1¼m: modest form over hurdles: raced only at 2m: acts on good to firm going: in cheekpieces last 3 starts: tried in tongue tie. *Phil Middleton*

TRIPLE CHIEF (IRE) 8 b.g. High Chaparral (IRE) – Trebles (IRE) (Kenmare (FR)) c109 [2018/19 c113, h101: c19.2m² c18m⁶ c20.2gᵖᵘ c19.2vᵖᵘ c19.2d³ c19.5d⁶ c17.8v³ c17.5v² h– c18.2d² c19.4g² Apr 26] workmanlike gelding: winning hurdler: fair handicap chaser: stays 21f: acts on good to firm and heavy going: usually in headgear: has worn tongue tie. *Jimmy Frost*

TRIPLICATE (IRE) 6 b.g. Galileo (IRE) – Devoted To You (IRE) (Danehill Dancer h141 (IRE)) [2018/19 h16.7d* h16s* h16g² h16g² h16g⁴ h16g⁵ Feb 3] dam half-sister to fairly useful/ungenuine hurdler (stayed 2¾m) Rio de Janeiro: useful on Flat, stays 1½m: useful hurdler: won maiden at Galway in August and novice at Listowel in September: good efforts when runner-up behind Quick Grabim in Joe Mac Novices' Hurdle at Tipperary and Royal Bond Novices' Hurdle at Fairyhouse (beaten 3¾ lengths): unproven beyond 17f: acts on soft going: wears tongue tie. *Joseph Patrick O'Brien, Ireland*

TRIXIE MC (IRE) 6 b.m. Yeats (IRE) – Miss Cozzene (FR) (Solid Illusion (USA)) b85 [2018/19 b16.7g⁴ b16.5d³ b15.8m Oct 10] fifth foal: half-sister to useful hurdler/chaser Aqua Dude (2m-2½m winner, by Flemensfirth): dam, French 2m-2¼m hurdle winner, half-sister to useful hurdler/very smart chaser (2m-2¼m winner) Andreas: in frame first 2 outings in bumpers. *Gavin Patrick Cromwell, Ireland*

TRIXSTER (IRE) 6 b.g. Beneficial – Our Trick (IRE) (Flemensfirth (USA)) [2018/19 h128 h113: h21g* h24g² h23.6v* h22.7g* h23.5d² h19.8s h24.3m⁴ Apr 20] compact gelding: fairly useful novice hurdler: won at Warwick (maiden) in October, Chepstow (conditionals) in December and Kelso in January: stays 3m: acts on good to firm and heavy going: usually front runner/races prominently. *Tim Vaughan*

TROED Y MELIN (IRE) 7 b.g. Craigsteel – Kissangel (IRE) (Namaqualand (USA)) h85 [2018/19 h21.6g⁴ h19.7g⁶ h19.5sᵖᵘ Nov 7] point winner: well held in maiden bumper: form over hurdles only when fourth in novice at Newton Abbot. *Jimmy Frost*

TROIKA STEPPES 11 b.g. Pasternak – Killerton Clover (High Season) [2018/19 c83 c26.1gᵖᵘ c24.1g h23g c23.6gᵖᵘ c25.2gᵖᵘ c22.7m⁴ c22.7g³ c24.2dᵖᵘ Apr 9] big, strong h– gelding: maiden hurdler: fairly useful handicap chaser at best: deteriorated considerably in 2018/19: stays 25f: acts on heavy going: often in headgear: has worn tongue tie: front runner/races prominently. *Fergal O'Brien*

TROJAN STAR (IRE) 9 b.g. Tikkanen (USA) – Mystical Queen (IRE) (Dr Devious c85 § (IRE)) [2018/19 c89§, h–: c16.1g² May 21] maiden hurdler: modest handicap chaser h– nowadays: stays 3m: acts on good to firm and good to soft going: wears headgear: usually tongue tied: front runner/races prominently: one to treat with caution (tends to find little). *Kim Bailey*

TRONGATE (IRE) 7 b.g. Dansant – Val Eile (IRE) (Aahsaylad) [2018/19 h104: h24.3g⁴ c122 h20.2g³ c20.1g² c21.6m* c20.5g² c20.5v* c20.9s⁴ c24.1d³ c15.9v² c24.1m⁵ Apr 13] h97 modest handicap hurdler: fairly useful handicap chaser: won at Kelso in September and Ayr (novice) in November: left R. Mike Smith after reappearance: barely stays testing 3m: acts on good to firm and heavy going. *Iain Jardine*

TROOBLUE 7 gr.m. Great Palm (USA) – Touch of Ivory (IRE) (Rossini (USA)) [2018/19 c89 § h104, b81: h16.2g h17sᵇᵈ c15.6s⁴ c19.3s³ c15.9s³ c15.7g⁵ c16.4d* c16.4d⁶ c16.4sꟳ c15.2gᵖᵘ h– Mar 29] maiden hurdler, fair form at best: modest handicap chaser: won novice event at Sedgefield in January: unproven beyond 17f: acts on heavy going: irresolute. *Sue Smith*

TROOPER TURNBULL (IRE) 5 b.g. Arcadio (GER) – Clover Pearl (IRE) (Luso) **b85**
[2018/19 b16.4d⁴ Dec 13] £18,000 3-y-o: fourth foal: dam (h112), 2m-2½m hurdle winner,
half-sister to useful/unreliable chaser (stayed 2½m) Swift Arrow: some encouragement
when fourth in bumper at Newcastle. *Rose Dobbin*

TROTTINETTE (FR) 4 ch.f. No Risk At All (FR) – Princesse Irena (FR) (Apple Tree **b–**
(FR)) [2018/19 b16.7d Apr 26] seventh foal: half-sister to 3 winners, including useful 2m
hurdle winner Royal Mix (by Sagamix) and fairly useful French hurdler/chaser Prince
Sumitas (15f-21f winner, by Sumitas): dam French maiden (second at 1½m): tailed off in
mares bumper. *Tom Gretton*

TROUBLED SOUL (IRE) 10 ch.m. Definite Article – Dorrha Lass (IRE) (Fourstars **c109**
Allstar (USA)) [2018/19 h19.9m h20d h20g³ c23.6d⁴ c21.6d* c20.6gᶠ h20.5d⁴ c21.4g² **h93**
c21.6m² c20.3d² Apr 26] sturdy mare: modest handicap hurdler: fair handicap chaser: won
novice race at Kelso in November: best short of 3m: acts on soft and good to firm going:
has worn headgear/tongue tie (in former last 2 starts). *Fergal O'Brien*

TROUFION (FR) 10 gr.g. Smadoun (FR) – La Troussardiere (FR) (Maresca Sorrento **c–**
(FR)) [2018/19 c20.3dᵖᵘ Nov 20] winning pointer: maiden hurdler: modest handicap chaser: **h–**
stayed 3m: acted on soft and good to firm going: tried in tongue tie: dead. *Caroline Bailey*

TROY DEE KNEE 7 b.g. Rainbow High – Matthew's Bridey (El Conquistador) [2018/19 **h78**
b–: b15.8m⁶ b16g h16g⁴ h16d h18.5g³ h18.6gᵖᵘ h19.8g⁶ Nov 22] down field in bumpers: **b–**
poor form over hurdles. *Shaun Lycett*

TRUCKERS CAILIN (IRE) 6 b.m. Curtain Time (IRE) – Truckers Lady (IRE) **c–**
(Presenting) [2018/19 c20d⁴ Mar 10] rather unfurnished mare: fourth foal: sister to a
winning pointer: dam (c107/h92) maiden chaser (stayed 25f)/winning pointer: Irish point
winner: tailed off in mares novice on chasing debut. *Paul Henderson*

TRUCKERS HIGHWAY (IRE) 10 b.g. Rudimentary (USA) – Countessdee (IRE) **c115**
(Arctic Lord) [2018/19 c118, h–: c16g⁵ c16.5g⁴ c19.9g* c20v* c20m² c19.45ᶠ c19.4d **h–**
c17.4g² Apr 13] has had breathing operation: maiden hurdler: fairly useful handicap
chaser: won at Huntingdon in November and Uttoxeter in December: stays 2½m: acts on
heavy going: wears hood/tongue tie. *John Groucott*

TRUCKERS LODGE (IRE) 7 b.g. Westerner – Galeacord (IRE) (Accordion) [2018/19 **h137**
h111p: h20.3g* h20g⁴ h20g⁴ h23.6v* h23.6s² h24.4g² h23.1s* Mar 5] point winner: useful
hurdler: won maiden at Southwell (left Tom George after) in May, handicap at Chepstow
in December and novice at Exeter (by ¾ length from Unwin Vc) in March: stays 3m: acts
well on soft/heavy going: in cheekpieces last 5 starts: races prominently. *Paul Nicholls*

TRUCKERS TANGLE (IRE) 7 b.g. Tajraasi (USA) – Lodge Tangle (IRE) (Well **c92**
Chosen) [2018/19 h–, b–: h16.5d² h15.3g⁵ c16d² c21.2g⁴ c21.4g² c19.5m² Mar 29] maiden **h88**
Irish pointer: modest maiden hurdler: similar form in chases: stays 21f: acts on good to firm
and good to soft going. *Alexandra Dunn*

TRUCKIN AWAY (IRE) 6 br.g. Getaway (GER) – Simons Girl (IRE) (Grand Plaisir **h124**
(IRE)) [2018/19 h20v* h19.8vᶠ h19.5d³ h24.3g h23.1s² Mar 5] well-made gelding: second
foal: half-brother to bumper winner/useful hurdler Western Cape (2¾m winner, by
Westerner): dam (c77/h114), winning pointer, placed up to 2½m over hurdles: third in Irish
point on debut: fairly useful form over hurdles: won maiden at Ffos Las in November: stays
23f: acts on heavy going: usually front runner/races prominently. *Philip Hobbs*

TRUE COMPANION (IRE) 6 b.g. Fast Company (IRE) – Panglossian (IRE) (Barathea **h–**
(IRE)) [2018/19 h16.7g Aug 20] fair on Flat, stays 8.5f: tailed off in maiden on hurdling
debut. *Nicky Henderson*

TRUE THOUGHTS (IRE) 4 b.g. So You Think (NZ) – True Joy (IRE) (Zilzal (USA)) **h–**
[2018/19 h16.8s h16d h16.5d h16g h19.8s h23.6d Mar 20] has had breathing operation:
modest maiden on Flat, stays 12.5f: no form over hurdles: tongue tied 4 of 6 outings.
Laura Young

TRULL LA LA 5 ch.m. Flemensfirth (USA) – Chomba Womba (IRE) (Fourstars Allstar **h108 p**
(USA)) [2018/19 h21.2d³ h19.6d* Mar 3] sturdy mare: half-sister to fairly useful 25f
hurdle winner/winning pointer As I See It (by King's Theatre) and bumper winner/fair 17f
hurdle winner Chocca Wocca (by Kayf Tara): dam (h145), bumper/2m-21f hurdle winner,
half-sister to fairly useful hurdler/smart chaser (stayed 2½m) Down In Neworleans: fair
form in mares races over hurdles, winning maiden at Huntingdon in March: should be
suited by 21f+: will go on improving. *Nicky Henderson*

TRULY AMAZING (IRE) 6 br.m. Presenting – Asian Maze (IRE) (Anshan) [2018/19 **b–**
b81: b16.7g Sep 29] modest form when sixth on debut in bumpers: regressed since.
Emma Lavelle

TRUMPS BENEFIT (IRE) 6 b.g. Beneficial – Balla Brack (IRE) (Brian Boru) [2018/19 **h75** h22.1s⁶ h20.3g³ h19.9g Sep 12] off mark in Irish points at seventh attempt: poor form over hurdles. *Peter Bowen*

TRUST ME I'M A DR (IRE) 10 b.g. Dr Massini (IRE) – Friendly Flick (IRE) (Anshan) **c–** [2018/19 c–, h94: c20.1dᵖᵘ c19.3g⁵ May 15] maiden pointer: no solid form over hurdles/in **h–** chases. *Victor Thompson*

TRUST THOMAS 11 ch.g. Erhaab (USA) – Yota (FR) (Galetto (FR)) [2018/19 c107, h–: **c102** c15.6g⁵ c17.3m² c16g³ Aug 1] good-bodied gelding: winning hurdler: fair handicap chaser **h–** nowadays: left Ann Hamilton after first start: has form at 2¾m, but races mainly around 2m: acts on heavy going: tried in headgear/tongue tie: waited with. *Philip Kirby*

TRY AGAIN (IRE) 6 b.g. Dubai Destination (USA) – Diamond Katie (IRE) (Night Shift **h122** (USA)) [2018/19 h16.5g³ h17.3g² h16.4g⁵ h16g* h16g³ h16g⁶ Feb 2] lengthy gelding: fairly useful on Flat (stays 10.5f), successful in August: fairly useful handicap hurdler: won at Navan in September and Leopardstown (novice event) in December: raced around 2m: best form on good going: has worn hood. *Paul W. Flynn, Ireland*

TRY CATCH ME (IRE) 14 b.g. Commander Collins (IRE) – Misty River (IRE) (Over **c–** The River (FR)) [2018/19 c–, h–: c16.1gᵖᵘ May 21] tall, close-coupled gelding: maiden **h–** pointer/hurdler: fair handicap chaser at best: lightly raced and no form since 2015/16: usually in headgear: tried in tongue tie. *Zoe Davison*

TRY IT SOMETIME (IRE) 11 b.g. Milan – Lead'er Inn (IRE) (Supreme Leader) **c– §** [2018/19 c70§, h–: c24.2vᵖᵘ c23.6d⁴ c26.2dᵖᵘ Mar 20] winning hurdler/chaser, no form in **h–** 2018/19: wears headgear/tongue tie: temperamental. *Sheila Lewis*

TRY IT YOU (IRE) 6 b.m. Scorpion (IRE) – Tabita (IRE) (Alzao (USA)) [2018/19 **h–** h19.3g h22dᵖᵘ Mar 5] half-sister to winners on Flat abroad by Slickly and Gold And Ivory: dam German 1m winner: failed to complete in Irish points in 2018: also no promise in novice hurdles. *Alistair Whillans*

TRYNWYN 9 b.m. Grape Tree Road – Brass Buckle (IRE) (Buckskin (FR)) [2018/19 **h–** h19.9m⁴ Aug 30] fourth foal: dam unraced: tongue tied, well beaten in novice hurdle on debut. *Maurice Barnes*

TRYSOR YNYS (IRE) 6 b.m. Beat Hollow – Brave Betsy (IRE) (Pistolet Bleu (IRE)) **h–** [2018/19 h–, b–: h15.8m h16.8s h15.8m⁵ Apr 23] little show in bumper/over hurdles. *Evan Williams*

TSUNDOKU (IRE) 8 ch.m. Medicean – Toberanthawn (IRE) (Danehill Dancer (IRE)) **h102** [2018/19 h99: h20.5s² Mar 11] fair handicap hurdler: stays 21f: acts on soft going. *Alexandra Dunn*

TUCKS BERGIN (IRE) 7 b.g. Getaway (GER) – Dr Sandra (IRE) (Dr Massini (IRE)) **h–** [2018/19 h–: h21.2mᵘʳ May 13] angular gelding: point winner: no promise in novice hurdles: tried in cheekpieces/tongue strap. *Adrian Wintle*

TUDOR CITY (IRE) 7 b.g. Yeats (IRE) – She's Our Mare (IRE) (Commanche Run) **h138** [2018/19 h16g² h16g⁵ h16g h16d² Apr 23] useful handicap hurdler: held form well in 2018/19, second at Fairyhouse (2½ lengths behind Ivanovich Gorbatov) final outing: raced around 2m: acts on heavy going: tried in cheekpieces: wears tongue tie. *A. J. Martin, Ireland*

TUDORS TREASURE 8 b.g. Dr Massini (IRE) – Rude Health (Rudimentary (USA)) **c101** [2018/19 h102: c20gᶠ c20.9gᶠ h20vᵖᵘ h21d⁴ h23.1s c19.2d* c19.2s* Apr 16] lengthy **h90** gelding: modest handicap hurdler: fair form over fences: won handicaps at Exeter in March and April: best short of 3m: acts on good to firm and heavy going: has worn cheekpieces: usually front runner/races prominently. *Robert Stephens*

TULLY EAST (IRE) 9 b.g. Shantou – Ghillie's Bay (IRE) (King's Ride) [2018/19 **c–** c140, h112: h16g c22.5d h16g h16g h21s h19dᵘʳ Apr 21] good-topped gelding: useful **h132** handicap hurdler: smart chaser: well beaten in Galway Plate in August: stays 21f: acts on heavy going: patiently ridden. *Alan Fleming, Ireland*

TULSA JACK (IRE) 10 b.g. Urban Ocean (FR) – Jessica's Pet (IRE) (King's Ride) **c95** [2018/19 c135, h118: c26m h24g⁶ h24g⁶ h24m⁵ c24s c22.2g³ c26dᵖᵘ c24.2dᵖᵘ Mar 15] **h111** rather leggy gelding: fair handicap hurdler nowadays: formerly useful handicap chaser: well below form in 2018/19, leaving Noel Meade after fourth start: stays 29f: acts on soft and good to firm going: wears blinkers: temperament under suspicion. *Alexandra Dunn*

TUNNEL CREEK 7 b.g. Tobougg (IRE) – Free Offer (Generous (IRE)) [2018/19 h101: **h72** h16.4g⁶ h21d h16.8sᵖᵘ h15.8d⁵ h16.8d Apr 23] angular gelding: developed into fair handicap hurdler in 2017/18 (for Olly Murphy): poor efforts since: stays 2½m: acts on good to soft and good to firm going: wears headgear. *Sean Conway*

TURANGA LILLY (IRE) 6 b.m. Flemensfirth (USA) – Gilah (IRE) (Saddlers' Hall **h95**
(IRE)) [2018/19 h18.8g h20.3g⁴ Jul 15] half-sister to several winners, including useful
hurdler/fairly useful chaser Ainama (2m-3m winner, by Desert Prince) and useful hurdler
Doesyourdogbite (2½m/21f winner, by Notnowcato): dam unraced: fair hurdle winner in
2017/18: below form since: stays 21f: acts on heavy going: in hood last 4 starts. *Gordon
Elliott, Ireland*

TURANGI 7 b.g. King's Theatre (IRE) – Bold Fire (Bold Edge) [2018/19 h109p: h19g⁴ **h113**
h19.9s³ h20.7dᶠ Jan 25] well-made gelding: fair form over hurdles: stayed 2½m: acted on
soft going: dead. *Philip Hobbs*

TURBAN (FR) 12 b.g. Dom Alco (FR) – Indianabelle (FR) (Useful (FR)) [2018/19 c102x, **c100**
h–: c24g⁴ c21g c19.5g* c21.6g⁴ c20g c19.7g* c21.6d⁴ c20.2g⁵ c19.7d⁶ c17.8s⁵ c20.2g⁴ **h–**
c19.5m Mar 29] sturdy gelding: winning hurdler: fair handicap chaser: won at Fontwell in
August and Plumpton in November: has won at 3¼m, but races mainly at shorter: acts on
heavy going: has worn headgear. *Paul Henderson*

TURBOTIM (IRE) 6 b.g. Arakan (USA) – Katy McKay (IRE) (Milan) [2018/19 h–, b–: **c–**
h16.2g h20.3s h23.3s c24gᵖᵘ Mar 28] has had breathing operation: poor form over hurdles: **h72**
pulled up in novice handicap on chasing debut: tried in blinkers. *Michael Scudamore*

TURNBURY 8 b.g. Azamour (IRE) – Scottish Heights (Selkirk (USA)) [2018/19 **h79**
h74: h18.7g³ h18.7g⁴ h18.7g⁴ h16g Feb 19] sturdy gelding: poor maiden hurdler: stays 19f:
acts on soft going: wears cheekpieces: tried in tongue tie: usually races close up.
Nikki Evans

TURNING GOLD 5 ch.g. Pivotal – Illusion (Anabaa (USA)) [2018/19 h117: h16vᵖᵘ **h131**
h15.5g* h16.8g Apr 17] tall gelding: useful handicap hurdler: won at Leicester (by 13
lengths from Flashing Glance) in January: raced around 2m: acts on heavy going: usually
races prominently. *Nigel Twiston-Davies*

TURNOVER (FR) 12 b.g. Turgeon (USA) – Sainte Innocence (FR) (Akarad (FR)) **c– §**
[2018/19 c23sᵖᵘ May 25] maiden pointer: shown more temperament than ability in chases:
tried in cheekpieces. *Mrs Jo Bowkett*

TURTLE CASK (IRE) 10 b.g. Turtle Island (IRE) – Sayce (IRE) (Supreme Leader) **c– §**
[2018/19 c–§, h89§: h23.3g h23.1gᵖᵘ h22.8v h23.3s h23.3v² h25.3g⁴ h25gᵖᵘ h23.3v³ Mar **h81 §**
14] strong gelding: poor handicap hurdler: no aptitude for chasing in novice handicaps:
stays 3¼m: acts on heavy going: wears headgear: unreliable. *Mike Sowersby*

TURTLE WARS (FR) 6 b.g. Turtle Bowl (IRE) – Forces Sweetheart (Allied Forces **c110**
(USA)) [2018/19 h116p: c20s⁵ c20.5gᵖᵘ c23.4d⁵ c20.2gᵖᵘ Apr 14] well-made gelding: third **h–**
in Irish point: fairly useful hurdle winner: disappointing in handicap chases: should stay
3m: acts on soft going.. *Nicky Henderson*

TWENTYONEBLACKJACK (IRE) 7 b.g. Robin des Pres (FR) – Grove Juliet (IRE) **h–**
(Moscow Society (USA)) [2018/19 h–, b–: h20gᵖᵘ h24g⁶ Oct 25] little sign of ability: tried
in blinkers. *Martin Keighley*

TWENTY TWENTY (IRE) 4 b.g. Henrythenavigator (USA) – Distinctive Look (IRE) **h111**
(Danehill (USA)) [2018/19 h17.7g* h15.9g⁶ h17.7m³ h17.7s⁴ h16s⁴ h17.7m* Mar 29]
lengthy gelding: half-brother to high-class hurdler Supasundae (2m-21f winner, by
Galileo) and fairly useful hurdler Distingo (2m winner, by Smart Strike): ran once on Flat:
fair form over hurdles: won juvenile in September and handicap in March, both at Fontwell:
likely to stay beyond 2¼m: acts on good to firm going. *Gary Moore*

TWIN STAR (IRE) 5 ch.g. Tagula (IRE) – Chronicle (Observatory (USA)) [2018/19 **h– p**
h16.3d Dec 29] leggy gelding: dam half-sister to fairly useful hurdler/fair chaser (stayed
3m) Share Option: useful on Flat, stays 13.5f: breathing problem when well held in
introductory event at Newbury on hurdling debut: open to improvement. *Noel Williams*

TWIST (IRE) 4 b.g. Invincible Spirit (IRE) – Kahira (IRE) (King's Best (USA)) [2018/19 **b57**
b14d⁵ Nov 29] well beaten in bumper: fairly useful form on Flat (stays 1¼m), winning in
December. *Nicky Henderson*

TWO FOR GOLD (IRE) 6 b.g. Gold Well – Two of Each (IRE) (Shernazar) [2018/19 **h132 p**
b108: h16.4g⁴ h21.3s* h23d* h19.8s⁴ Mar 8] tall gelding: dual bumper winner: useful form
over hurdles: won novices at Wetherby in December and Bangor in January: will stay 3m:
remains open to improvement. *Kim Bailey*

TWO HOOTS (IRE) 8 gr.g. Tikkanen (USA) – Supreme Beneficial (IRE) (Beneficial) **c87**
[2018/19 c82, h80: c15.7m² c17.8m³ c17.2g⁴ c19.4m² c21.2d⁴ c15.6g⁵ c15.7g⁵ c15.7g⁶ **h–**
c19.3s* c20.3g⁴ c16.4v² c16.4g* c19.3g² Apr 23] has had breathing operation: maiden
hurdler: modest handicap chaser: won novice events at Sedgefield in January and April: left

Jeremy Scott after fourth start: should stay 2½m: acts on good to firm and heavy going: regularly in cheekpieces: tongue tied 4 of last 5 outings: front runner/races prominently. *Joanne Foster*

TWOJAYSLAD 10 b.g. Kayf Tara – Fulwell Hill (Anshan) [2018/19 c104, h–: c26.1g^{pu} Jun 20] maiden hurdler: fair handicap chaser: stays 25f: acts on heavy going: tried in cheekpieces. *Ian Williams*   c– h–

TWO SAMS (IRE) 6 b.g. Dubai Destination (USA) – Hello Louise (IRE) (Flemensfirth (USA)) [2018/19 h21.6d h19.6v^{pu} h19.5d h19s^5 h19.8s^{pu} h19.7g^{pu} c24g Apr 13] off mark in points at second attempt: little form over hurdles/in novice handicap chase: in hood last 2 starts. *Michael Blake*   c– h77

TWO SMOKIN BARRELS 10 b.m. Kayf Tara – Coldabri (IRE) (Husyan (USA)) [2018/19 c127, h–: c28.4g^4 c23.4s^4 c25.1g^2 c24.2d Feb 15] workmanlike mare: fairly useful handicap chaser: stays 25f: acts on heavy going. *Michael Scudamore*   c123 h–

TWO SWALLOWS 9 b.m. Kayf Tara – One Gulp (Hernando (FR)) [2018/19 c125, h–: h23.3d May 5] lengthy mare: fair hurdle winner: better form over fences in 2017/18: stays 3m: acts on heavy going. *Ben Pauling*   c– h87

TWOTWOTHREE (IRE) 6 b.g. Shantou (USA) – Sibury (IRE) (Overbury (IRE)) [2018/19 b90: h15.8g h16.2g h16.7v h19.7s^5 h18.6d^3 h20.6d h19.9s^5 h16.7s^3 c16.4g^6 Apr 5] has had breathing operation: point winner: modest maiden hurdler: inadequate test in novice handicap on chasing debut (should improve): stays 2½m: acts on soft going: normally hooded: tried in tongue tie. *Oliver Greenall*   c– p h98

TWYCROSS WARRIOR 7 b.g. Cockney Rebel (IRE) – Gaelic Roulette (IRE) (Turtle Island (IRE)) [2018/19 h18.7g^{pu} h15.7d^6 Apr 9] has had breathing operation: modest maiden hurdler: unproven beyond 2m: tried in tongue tie. *Robin Dickin*   h68

TYBIELASS 4 br.f. Fight Club (GER) – Capesarah (Cape Cross (IRE)) [2018/19 b15.8v b16g b16d^4 b16.8g Apr 18] second foal: dam unraced half-sister to fairly useful hurdler/fair chaser (stayed 25f) Dream Falcon: poor form in bumpers. *Bernard Llewellyn*   b72

TYCOON PRINCE (IRE) 9 b.g. Trans Island – Downtown Train (IRE) (Glacial Storm (USA)) [2018/19 c141, h–: c16d^2 c20d^5 c17g^4 c17d c17g c16g^3 c16s^4 c17.7g^2 Mar 31] strong gelding: winning hurdler: useful chaser: best around 2m: acts on heavy going: tried in hood: usually tongue tied. *Gordon Elliott, Ireland*   c141 h–

TYNECASTLE PARK 6 b.g. Sea The Stars (IRE) – So Silk (Rainbow Quest (USA)) [2018/19 h107: h22g^3 h26g^5 h25mp^{pu} Oct 4] fair on Flat, stays 21.5f, won twice in 2019: fair maiden hurdler: probably stays 2¾m: best form on good going: tried in cheekpieces. *Robert Eddery*   h103

TYRELL (IRE) 6 b.g. Teofilo (IRE) – Sleeveless (USA) (Fusaichi Pegasus (USA)) [2018/19 h119: h24.3g^4 h19.4m^6 h21.3s h23.8g^4 Jan 7] fairly useful handicap hurdler: won at Ayr in May, then left Micky Hammond: stays 3m: acts on soft going: normally in headgear: regularly tongue tied. *Andrew Crook*   h117

TYROLEAN 6 b.g. Raven's Pass (USA) – Alessandria (Sunday Silence (USA)) [2018/19 h73p: h15.8v^{pu} Nov 11] disappointing maiden on Flat: little form over hurdles. *Dai Burchell*   h–

TZAR DE L'ELFE (FR) 9 b.g. Satri (IRE) – Rue Tournefort (FR) (Marchand de Sable (USA)) [2018/19 c103, h101: h25m^6 h23.1g c23.5v^4 c20d^2 c25.7g^2 c23.6d^2 c25.7g^2 Apr 21] sturdy gelding: fair hurdler/maiden chaser: stays 3¼m: acts on heavy going: has worn headgear/tongue tie. *Richard Rowe*   c102 h–

U

UALLRIGHTHARRY (IRE) 7 b.g. Craigsteel – Enchanted Valley (IRE) (Glacial Storm (USA)) [2018/19 h15.9s^F h20.5d h17.7s^F c19.7g^4 c26m* Mar 29] sturdy gelding: seventh foal: half-brother to fairly useful hurdler/winning pointer Bunglasha Lady (19f-25f winner, by Snurge): dam unraced half-sister to useful staying chaser Torduff Express: off mark in Irish points at fourth attempt: poor form over hurdles: fair form over fences: won handicap at Fontwell in March: stays 3¼m: acts on good to firm going. *Linda Jewell*   c100 h83

UBALTIQUE (FR) 11 b.g. Balko (FR) – Ode Antique (FR) (Subotica (FR)) [2018/19 c123§, h–§: h16.8s^3 c15.7v^{ur} c16.3d^5 c15.7d^5 Mar 6] good-topped gelding: fair handicap hurdler: fairly useful handicap chaser, below form in 2018/19: stays 19f: acts on heavy going: wears blinkers/tongue tie: races off pace: temperamental. *Donald McCain*   c108 § h103 §

UCELLO CONTI (FR) 11 b.g. Martaline – Gazelle Lulu (FR) (Altayan) [2018/19 c149, h–: c23.7g* c24d* c26.3d⁵ c21.1dᵖᵘ c24.7d* Apr 23] sturdy gelding: winning hunter hurdler: fairly useful hunter chaser nowadays: won at Thurles in January, Navan in February and Fairyhouse (in cheekpieces, by 3½ lengths from Sizing Coal) in April: stays 3¼m: acts on good to firm and heavy going: wears tongue tie. *Gordon Elliott, Ireland*
c129
h–

UDOGO 8 b.g. Lucky Story (USA) – Welanga (Dansili) [2018/19 h–: h16.8g h16g⁶ h19.2dᶠ Nov 18] fair on Flat, stayed 13f: modest maiden hurdler: stayed 19f: acted on good to soft going: in headgear last 2 starts: dead. *Brendan Powell*
h91

UEUETEOTL (FR) 11 gr.g. Tikkanen (USA) – Azturk (FR) (Baby Turk) [2018/19 c109§, h111§: c21.5d⁶ c20s³ c23.4v² c21.6d⁴ Apr 8] big gelding: fair handicap hurdler/chaser: stays 25f: acts on soft going: usually wears headgear: unreliable. *James Ewart*
c102 §
h– §

UHLAN BUTE (FR) 11 ch.g. Brier Creek (USA) – Jonquiere (FR) (Trebrook (FR)) [2018/19 c121§, h–: c23.6d c23.6g⁵ c25.6s³ c25.7s* c23s³ c23.8d² c23.8g⁴ c26d c23.8m⁴ c25.6mᵖᵘ Apr 20] workmanlike gelding: winning hurdler: fairly useful handicap chaser: won at Plumpton (veterans) in January: placed at Taunton and Ludlow (amateurs) next 2 starts: stays 3¼m: acts on good to firm and heavy going: wears headgear: unreliable. *Venetia Williams*
c129 §
h–

UISCE UR (IRE) 7 b.m. City Honours (USA) – Luna Fairy (IRE) (Kadastrof (FR)) [2018/19 h15.7d h24.1g* Apr 11] €1,200 3-y-o: second foal: dam unraced half-sister to fairly useful hurdler (stayed 3m) Our Eric: point winner: modest form over hurdles: won handicap at Wetherby in April: similar form over fences for W. J. Martin: tried in cheekpieces. *Laura Morgan*
c–
h94

UKNOWMYMEANING (IRE) 5 ch.g. Touch of Land (FR) – Lucy Lodge (IRE) (Moscow Society (USA)) [2018/19 b16.2d Mar 26] well beaten in maiden bumper. *Rebecca Menzies*
b–

ULIS DE VASSY (FR) 11 b.g. Voix du Nord (FR) – Helathou (FR) (Video Rock (FR)) [2018/19 c102§, h–: c20.5g² c20.3g³ c15.7g³ c24g⁵ c20.3g⁶ c21.2g⁴ c20.1g³ c20.3d⁴ c20.3g⁵ c20.3s Dec 16] tall gelding: winning hurdler: fair handicap chaser nowadays: stays 2½m: acts on good to firm and heavy going: wears headgear: has worn tongue tie: temperamental. *Laura Morgan*
c103 §
h–

ULTIMATUM DU ROY (FR) 11 b.g. Brier Creek (USA) – La Fleur du Roy (FR) (Sleeping Car (FR)) [2018/19 c117, h–: c24s² Mar 16] good-bodied gelding: lightly-raced hurdler: fairly useful handicap chaser: stays 3¼m: acts on heavy going: has worn cheekpieces: wears tongue tie. *Alex Hales*
c114
h–

ULTRAGOLD (FR) 11 b.g. Kapgarde (FR) – Hot d'Or (FR) (Shafoun (FR)) [2018/19 c148§, h–: h23.9d⁴ c25.9s³ c29.2g⁵ c30.2sᵖᵘ c34.3g Apr 6] sturdy gelding: lightly-raced hurdler: smart handicap chaser: added to a good record over National fences when third in Becher Chase (6 lengths behind Walk In The Mill) in December: barely stays 29f: acts on heavy going: wears tongue tie: usually front runner/races prominently. *Colin Tizzard*
c145
h97

ULUROO (FR) 7 b.g. Centennial (IRE) – Kica (FR) (Noir Et Or) [2018/19 h92: c23.4gᵘʳ h23.9g Jul 5] Irish point winner: modest form over hurdles: unseated eighth on chasing debut: will prove suited by 2¼m+. *Pauline Robson*
c– p
h–

ULVERSTON (IRE) 4 b.g. Yeats (IRE) – So Supreme (IRE) (Supreme Leader) [2018/19 b16d³ Mar 19] €35,000 3-y-o: closely related to 2 winners, including fair 2m hurdle winner Juan de Gracia (by Milan), and half-brother to fairly useful hurdler/chaser Emcon (2m-2½m winner, by Vinnie Roe) and a winning pointer by Westerner: dam (h103), bumper/2m hurdle winner, half-sister to useful hurdler/chaser (stayed 25f) Native Estates: 18/1, third in bumper at Wetherby (5 lengths behind Sheshoon Sonny). *Jennie Candlish*
b86

ULYSSES (GER) 5 b.g. Sinndar (IRE) – Ungarin (GER) (Goofalik (USA)) [2018/19 h107: h16v h19.7s h16d h21.4g³ Apr 3] good-topped gelding: fair maiden hurdler, well below form in 2018/19: stays 2½m: acts on heavy going: usually wears cheekpieces: usually races close up: has joined Dan Skelton. *Barry Brennan*
h67

UMBERLEIGH 5 b.m. Arvico (FR) – Rutland Water (IRE) (Hawk Wing (USA)) [2018/19 b15.3d Dec 26] fifth foal: half-sister to 2 winners on Flat, including 1¾m-2m winner Dew Pond (by Motivator): dam unraced: tailed off in bumper. *Philip Hobbs*
b–

UMBERTO D'OLIVATE (FR) 11 b.g. Alberto Giacometti (IRE) – Komunion (FR) (Luchiroverte (IRE)) [2018/19 c107§, h–§: c24.2g c25.7s Dec 3] lengthy gelding: maiden hurdler: one-time useful chaser, retains little ability: has worn headgear: usually races close up: temperamental. *Robert Walford*
c– §
h– §

UMBRIGADO (IRE) 5 br.g. Stowaway – Dame O'Neill (IRE) (Dr Massini (IRE)) [2018/19 b15.8g* h15.7s* h18.5d* h20g⁶ Apr 6] €37,000 3-y-o, £160,000 4-y-o: tall gelding: will make a chaser: seventh foal: half-brother to 3 winners, including bumper winner/fairly useful hurdler Templeross (21f-3m winner, by Presenting) and fair hurdler/fairly useful chaser Wolf Sword (19f-3m winner, by Flemensfirth): dam unraced sister to smart hurdler/useful chaser (best at 2m) Clopf: runner-up on debut in Irish point: won bumper at Uttoxeter (by 4½ lengths from The Macon Lugnatic) in November: useful form over hurdles: won maiden at Southwell in December and novice at Exeter in February: sixth in Mersey Novices' Hurdle at Aintree (9¾ lengths behind Reserve Tank) in April. *David Pipe* **h133 b102**

U ME AND THEM (IRE) 10 ch.g. Vertical Speed (FR) – Bodies Pride (IRE) (John French) [2018/19 c91x: c32.5g⁰ May 4] point winner: modest form only completed start in chases: usually in headgear: poor jumper. *Miss Hannah Taylor* **c– x**

UMNDENI (FR) 5 b.g. Balko (FR) – Marie Royale (FR) (Turgeon (USA)) [2018/19 b101p: h16d⁴ h16.3s⁵ h19.2d⁽ʳ⁾ h19.2s* h19.3d h21.4g² h19d* Apr 24] sturdy gelding: bumper winner: fairly useful hurdler: won maiden at Fontwell in January and novice at Taunton in April: stays 21f: acts on soft going. *Philip Hobbs* **h122**

UNAI (IRE) 4 b.g. Court Cave (IRE) – The Millers Tale (IRE) (Rashar (USA)) [2018/19 b16g³ Apr 25] €10,000 3-y-o: sixth foal: closely related to fair hurdler/fairly useful chaser Tales of Milan (2¾m-29f winner, by Milan) and half-brother to 2 winners, including modest chaser Go On Henry (2½m winner, by Golan): dam unraced half-sister to useful staying chaser Dunbrody Millar: 7/1, promise when third in bumper at Warwick (3½ lengths behind Overthetop). *Ben Pauling* **b91**

U NAME IT (IRE) 11 b.g. Gold Well – Bypharthebest (IRE) (Phardante (FR)) [2018/19 c–, h89: h21.4g⁵ h23.9g⁵ h23.9g⁴ h23.9g⁵ Aug 18] has had breathing operation: modest handicap hurdler: lightly-raced chaser: stays 3m: acts on good to soft going: wore cheekpieces in 2018/19: usually races prominently. *R. Mike Smith* **c– h92**

UN BEAU ROMAN (FR) 11 bl.g. Roman Saddle (IRE) – Koukie (FR) (Lute Antique (FR)) [2018/19 c116§, h–: c16.5g³ h15.3g⁵ c15.7d⁽ᵖᵘ⁾ c20.5d² c20.5g⁴ c21.2d³ c20.2g⁴ Apr 14] lengthy gelding: winning hurdler: fair handicap chaser: stays 2½m: acts on heavy going: usually wears hood: unreliable. *Paul Henderson* **c104 § h99**

UNBLINKING 6 b.g. Cacique (IRE) – Deliberate (King's Best (USA)) [2018/19 h103: h21g² h21d⁴ h20.5d⁵ h26s⁵ h23.5m⁶ Mar 31] angular gelding: fair handicap hurdler: won at Warwick in November: stays 21f: acts on soft going: tried in tongue tie. *Nigel Twiston-Davies* **h111**

UNCLE ALASTAIR 7 b.g. Midnight Legend – Cyd Charisse (Kayf Tara) [2018/19 h131: c20s² Nov 12] has had breathing operation: useful form over hurdles: 7/2, shaped well when second in novice at Carlisle (2 lengths behind Vinndication, clear of rest) on chasing debut: will stay further than 3m: acts on heavy going: tried in tongue tie: seemed sure to improve over fences, but wasn't seen out again. *Nicky Richards* **c142 p h–**

UNCLE BOBBY 8 ch.g. Avonbridge – Aunt Hilda (Distant Relative) [2018/19 c16.3d c16.3g⁴ c16.5d⁴ c15.9m⁴ c16.5g⁽ᵘʳ⁾ c15.2g⁽ᶠ⁾ Mar 29] modest maiden on Flat in 2013, stays 6f: modest form over fences: raced only at 2m: in hood last 2 starts: usually races freely. *Michael Easterby* **c88**

UNCLE O 5 gr.g. Fair Mix (IRE) – Clever Liz (Glacial Storm (USA)) [2018/19 b16.7m⁶ h21g⁽ᵖᵘ⁾ h21.3d h17.7v² Mar 6] £3,500 3-y-o: fifth foal: brother to a winning pointer: dam, winning pointer, half-sister to fairly useful chaser (stayed 3½m) My Flora: tailed off in bumper: modest form over hurdles: best effort when second in maiden at Fontwell. *Clare Hobson* **h91 b–**

UNCLE PERCY 7 b.g. Sir Percy – Forsythia (Most Welcome) [2018/19 h96: h19.6g May 19] workmanlike gelding: has had breathing operation: maiden hurdler: well held sole start in 2018/19: stays 2½m: acts on firm going: tried in cheekpieces/tongue tie. *Ben Pauling* **h–**

UNCLE VANNY (IRE) 4 b.g. Zoffany (IRE) – Cant Hurry Love (Desert Prince (IRE)) [2018/19 h16.2g h15.8m⁽ᵖᵘ⁾ Oct 4] no show over hurdles. *Keith Dalgleish* **h–**

UNDEFINED BEAUTY (IRE) 10 gr.m. Kayf Tara – Lorna (IRE) (Roselier (FR)) [2018/19 h17.2g⁴ h18.6g⁵ h19.2g² h20.3g⁶ h16.3g⁶ Oct 20] fair handicap hurdler: stays 2¾m: acts on heavy going: has worn headgear, including last 3 starts: sometimes in tongue tie: has joined Michael G. Kennedy. *Olly Murphy* **h103**

UNDER THE PHONE (IRE) 10 b.g. Heron Island (IRE) – Theo On The Bench (IRE)   c–
(Mister Lord (USA)) [2018/19 c107, h–: c20m h26d⁴ h25.8g h26g h25g⁶ Nov 4] sturdy   **h102**
gelding: fair handicap hurdler/chaser: stays 3¼m: acts on good to soft going: has worn
headgear, including in 2018/19: usually races close up. *Robin Dickin*

UNDER THE RED SKY (IRE) 12 ch.g. Insatiable (IRE) – Official Secret (Polish   c– §
Patriot (USA)) [2018/19 c85§: c23.8gᵖᵘ May 16] maiden chaser: stays 3m: acts on heavy
going: wears headgear: no battler. *Kenny Johnson*

UN DE SCEAUX (FR) 11 b.g. Denham Red (FR) – Hotesse de Sceaux (FR) (April   **c170**
Night (FR)) [2018/19 c169, h–: c15.5v² c20.6d⁵ Mar 14]   **h–**

The story of Un de Sceaux provides food for the optimist. When he was
purchased from France as a four-year-old, trainer Willie Mullins warned owner
Edward O'Connell that Un de Sceaux 'might only last a year or two but you'll have
some fun.' A non-thoroughbred with 'no pedigree' (his unraced grandam was by an
anglo-arab stallion), Un de Sceaux was an unprepossessing youngster who had been
passed over by several potential purchasers before Mullins took him to fulfil a long-
standing order to purchase 'a good horse for small money' for the O'Connell family.
The horse was a nervy type at home and a free-going, exuberant front runner on the
track who took so much out of himself that Mullins decided to adopt a fairly low key
approach with him early in his career. After his first two seasons at Closutton, Un
de Sceaux was still unbeaten and it was clear that he was going to last longer than
the 'year or two' predicted by his trainer. His form over hurdles reached Champion
Hurdle standard without him ever being tested against the very best hurdlers in
Britain and Ireland (he won Grade 3 and Grade 2 events at Auteuil in the spring of
his second campaign as he bypassed the festivals at Cheltenham and Punchestown).

The decision to send Un de Sceaux over fences can't have been straightforward
as he lacked the size and scope of a typical chaser and his tearaway nature must have
been a worry. Starting at 8/1-on, he fell on his eagerly awaited debut over fences in a
maiden chase at Thurles, but he never looked back after that and ended his first season
as Timeform's top-rated two-mile chaser, a rare achievement for a horse while still
a novice (he won the Arkle at both Leopardstown and the Cheltenham Festival and
the Ryanair Novices' Chase at Punchestown). Un de Sceaux's breathtaking, front-
running display in the Arkle at Cheltenham yielded a performance that had been
bettered in recent runnings of that race only by Sprinter Sacre whose resurgence the
following season saw him come up against Un de Sceaux twice. In that second
season over fences, Un de Sceaux suffered his first two defeats, in races which he
had completed, both of them at the hands of Sprinter Sacre, in the Queen Mother
Champion Chase and the Celebration Chase. Apart from a very rare below-par effort
in the latest Ryanair Chase at Cheltenham, Un de Sceaux has since been beaten

*Boylesports Champion Chase (Drogheda), Punchestown—a carbon copy of 2018 as the evergreen
Un de Sceaux is clear of odds-on stable-companion Min*

only by Fox Norton (Champion Chase at Punchestown in 2017), Balko des Flos (Ryanair Chase in 2018) and Altior (Tingle Creek Chase in the latest season) when he has completed over fences. This is the sixth essay on him in *Chasers & Hurdlers* and his career record of twenty-three wins from thirty-two starts (he joined Mullins after winning two bumpers in the French Provinces) includes ten Grade 1 victories. He has achieved Cheltenham Festival victories in the Arkle and the Ryanair, and has won four times in five appearances stretching back to 2013 at the Punchestown Festival, picking up well over £1m in prize money along the way.

The dry winter restricted the appearances of Un de Sceaux in the latest campaign but he did play his part in one of the highlights of the first part of the season when he took on Altior in the Tingle Creek Chase at Sandown. Un de Sceaux had his optimum conditions—he revels in the mud—and ran right up to his best, but, in the end, he couldn't deny Altior, despite jumping superbly and holding every chance until Altior got the better of him on the run-in to win by four lengths, the pair clear of their two rivals. Un de Sceaux wasn't seen out again until the Cheltenham Festival over three months later, when perhaps he wasn't quite at peak fitness after being kept sidelined because of the prevailing, unseasonable going conditions in Ireland. He managed only fifth to Frodon in the Ryanair Chase, a race in which he had come first and then second in the two previous years. It was a rare off-day for Un de Sceaux who is more amenable nowadays and was held up in mid-field; it is the only time in his career that he has not finished either first or second when completing (he has fallen twice in his twenty-one races over fences, thirteen of which he has won).

The large group of family members and friends who follow Un de Sceaux on the big occasions, wearing their familiar scarves in the pale blue and orange of the owner's racing colours, had their moment at the Punchestown Festival, which took place shortly after the end of the British season (which is why the performance isn't featured in the form figures at the start of this essay). The going was soft, though his trainer warned beforehand that 'the ground might be too good for him', and a return to forcing tactics produced a performance from Un de Sceaux that was almost a carbon copy of the one twelve months earlier when he had lowered the colours of his odds-on stablemate Douvan in the Boylesports Champion Chase. Another tip-top stable companion, Min, started odds on in the Champion Chase this time but Un de Sceaux, who took over in front at the second fence and really pressed on with Min from some way, continually outjumped his rival and kept on well after asserting himself between the last two to win by four lengths. The rest, headed by 20/1-shot Castlegrace Paddy, finished in another parish. Min arrived at Punchestown having run at both the Cheltenham and Aintree festivals—recording a wide margin win at the latter—and wasn't quite at his best, but the performance of the evergreen Un de Sceaux confirmed that, at the age of eleven, he is still one of the very best chasers around, as well as being one of the most popular. There are said to be no plans to retire him yet.

			Pampabird		Pampapaul
	Denham Red (FR)		(b 1979)		Wood Grouse
	(b 1992)		Nativelee		Giboulee
Un de Sceaux (FR)			(b 1982)		Native Berry
(b.g. 2008)			April Night		Kaldoun
	Hotesse de Sceaux (FR)		(gr 1986)		My Destiny
	(ch 1995)		Olympe Occitane		Diarifos
			(ch 1980)		Papakiteme

The strong, compact Un de Sceaux is not the biggest for jumping fences, being the embodiment of the proverb 'Handsome is that handsome does', and his pedigree is ordinary to say the least. His sire Denham Red died in 2014 and, although he made his mark as a juvenile hurdler in France, he never had a crop much bigger than a couple of dozen in his years at stud. The dam of Un de Sceaux, Hotesse de Sceaux, showed little or no sign of ability in eight starts on the Flat and over jumps and has bred only one other winner, the French bumper winner Olympe de Sceaux (by Diableneyev). Un de Sceaux stays twenty-one furlongs (he is fully effective at

Mr Edward O'Connell's "Un de Sceaux"

two miles) and acts on heavy going. He usually races close up or makes the running, and sometimes wears ear plugs (he did so at the latest Cheltenham Festival). As genuine a racehorse as you'll find, he has been incredibly consistent throughout his career. *W. P. Mullins, Ireland*

UNDISPUTED (IRE) 8 b.m. King's Theatre (IRE) – Gleanntan (IRE) (Lil's Boy (USA)) [2018/19 h106: h20s⁵ h20.3g⁴ h19.9g⁴ h23g⁴ Aug 15] fair handicap hurdler: runner-up 3 times in points later in season: stays 21f: acts on heavy going: has worn hood. *Noel Williams* **h100**

UNIONISTE (FR) 11 gr.g. Dom Alco (FR) – Gleep Will (FR) (Cadoudal (FR)) [2018/19 c130, h–: c25.1m² c28.4d⁴ c24s² Mar 23] tall, useful-looking gelding: winning hurdler: fairly useful chaser: second in hunter at Bangor in March: stays 3¼m: acts on heavy going: has worn cheekpieces: tried in tongue tie: usually races close up. *Paul Nicholls* **c123 h–**

UNISON (IRE) 9 b.g. Jeremy (USA) – Easter Song (USA) (Rubiano (USA)) [2018/19 h141: h16g³ h16m⁵ h15.8g³ h19.7vᵖᵘ h16g² h19d* h15.3g⁴ h20.3gᵖᵘ Apr 17] sturdy gelding: useful handicap hurdler: won at Taunton (by 5 lengths from Air Horse One) in January: stays 19f: acts on good to firm and heavy going: usually leads. *Jeremy Scott* **h141**

UNOBTAINABLE 5 b.m. Malinas (GER) – Sharwakom (IRE) (Dansili) [2018/19 b16.2g May 12] first foal: dam (b87) placed in bumpers: down the field in mares bumper. *Tony Coyle* **b–**

UNO MAS 5 b.g. Morozov (USA) – Broomhill Lady (Definite Article) [2018/19 h16s⁶ h16g⁴ h20g h16.8s h20g h20.3g⁵ h18.6g⁴ h16.8m⁴ h19.3mᵖᵘ h16g* h20v⁴ h19.7d* h24.4g² h25.3g* h23.4g* h26g* h23.4d² h16.8g* Apr 17] €1,000 3-y-o: fifth foal: half-brother to a winning pointer by Vertical Speed: dam unraced: fair/progressive handicap hurdler: won novice events at Fakenham in November, Hereford and Catterick in January, and Fakenham again in February, and conditionals/amateurs events at Warwick later in February and Cheltenham in April: left Paul Power after third start: effective at 17f to 3¼m: acts on good to firm and good to soft going: wears headgear. *Christian Williams* **h114**

UNO VALOROSO (FR) 11 b.g. Voix du Nord (FR) – Danse d'Avril (FR) (Quart de Vin (FR)) [2018/19 c112§, h85: c17.4v² c15.7v⁵ c15.9g⁴ c19.2g² c17.1d³ Apr 8] close-coupled gelding: maiden hurdler: fair handicap chaser: stays 2½m: acts on heavy going: tried in cheekpieces: untrustworthy. *Mark Walford* **c102 §** **h–**

UNOWHATIMEANHARRY 11 b.g. Sir Harry Lewis (USA) – Red Nose Lady (Teenoso (USA)) [2018/19 h154: h20g³ h24.2s* h24.4sᶠ h24d h24.7g Apr 6] **h151**

Major League Soccer, America's burgeoning professional league, has proved an increasingly popular pension plan for top footballers wanting one last big pay-day as they wind down their careers. Former England captain David Beckham, Thierry Henry and Didier Drogba are among the former Premier League stars to have enjoyed one last moment in the sun via the MLS, all of them before another England captain Wayne Rooney began his recent venture on the other side of the Atlantic. Closer to home, the Champion Stayers' Hurdle at Punchestown has, unintentionally, provided a similar service to leading jumps performers of a certain vintage in the last two years. Former Champion Hurdler Faugheen registered what might prove to be his final win at Grade 1 level when landing the Punchestown race as a ten-year-old, while the veteran Unowhatimeanharry rolled back the years to spring a surprise in the latest renewal in May. It was a second win in the race for Unowhatimeanharry and his first at Grade 1 level since landing that 2017 edition, with recent down-the-field efforts at both the Cheltenham and Aintree festivals suggesting that his best days might have been behind him. Unowhatimeanharry lined up as a largely unconsidered 16/1-shot in a ten-runner field at Punchestown. It did not look a particularly strong renewal beforehand—notable names such as Paisley Park, Supasundae, Apple's Jade and even Faugheen (who had been pulled up with a fibrillating heart at Aintree) were all missing. Unowhatimeanharry was responsible for nearly half (seven) of the sixteen graded hurdles wins achieved in total by the field going into the race. The market was headed at 9/4 by the Willie Mullins-trained Bapaume (fifth behind the same connections' Faugheen in 2018), while the next two in the betting were the smart handicappers Aux Ptits Soins (4/1) and Not Many Left (11/2). With neither Barry Geraghty (broken leg) nor Noel Fehily (retired in late-March) available, Mark Walsh stepped in, not for the first time in a big race, to don the J. P. McManus silks on Unowhatimeanharry. Well positioned

Ladbrokes Champion Stayers' Hurdle, Punchestown—Vision des Flos and the departing Not Many Left blunder their chances away at the last as Unowhatimeanharry (hoops) repeats his 2017 win at the chief expense of the Willie Mullins-trained pair Bacardys (stars) and Bapaume (No.3)

throughout, Unowhatimeanharry challenged the pace-setting Killultagh Vic entering the straight and already looked to have the measure of British raider Vision des Flos (bad mistake) and Not Many Left (fell) when that pair blundered away their chances at the last. Unowhatimeanharry stayed on gamely and had three lengths to spare at the line, with Bacardys swooping late to edge out his stable-companions Bapaume and Killultagh Vic for second in a bunched finish for the minor placings (Aux Ptits Soins was also a close-up fifth). The joy proved to be relatively short-lived for the winning jockey, however, as Walsh faced his own lengthy spell on the sidelines just twenty-four hours later after breaking his right leg when the McManus-owned Scoir Mear was brought down over fences.

Happily, injuries haven't been a recurring theme during the lengthy career of Unowhatimeanharry who stood plenty of racing even in his days before joining Harry Fry's yard. That stable switch did coincide with a marked upturn in fortunes, though. One bumper win was all Unowhatimeanharry had to show from nearly three years of racing with initial trainer Helen Nelmes, which included eleven unsuccessful tries over hurdles (six placed efforts during this sequence). By contrast, Unowhatimeanharry went unbeaten in five starts in his first full season for Fry, when running in the colours of the Harry Fry Racing Club, culminating with victory in the Albert Bartlett Novices' Hurdle (Spa) at the Cheltenham Festival. That unbeaten run was extended by another three wins after he had been purchased privately by McManus. Unowhatimeanharry then lined up as a 6/5-on favourite for the 2017 Stayers' Hurdle at Cheltenham where a slightly below-par effort saw him manage only third behind Nichols Canyon, though he gained revenge on that rival in a thrilling finish to the Champion Stayers' at Punchestown six weeks later, with just a head separating the pair at the line. Wins have proved harder to come by for Unowhatimeanharry in the seasons since, but he is still smart on his day and his latest Punchestown performance came after he had been sent off 4/1 second favourite for the JLT Hurdle (Long Walk) at Ascot (a race he won in 2016) just three starts earlier and, after an uncharacteristic fall there (before the race had begun in earnest), he had had a plausible excuse for a disappointing display in the latest renewal of the Stayers' at Cheltenham as he was found to have bled. His prominence in the betting at Ascot came on the back of a strong start to the campaign. After being sharpened up by a comeback third over an inadequate trip at Aintree, Unowhatimeanharry justified well-backed favouritism in the Grade 2 Long Distance Hurdle at Newbury in late-November—a race he also won in 2016 before finishing runner-up in 2017. In truth, the Long Distance Hurdle was another race which didn't look so strong as most of its recent renewals, particularly with second favourite Sam Spinner flopping badly, but Unowhatimeanharry created a good impression in first-time cheekpieces (which he wore on his remaining starts) to beat Clyne by two and a half lengths.

A leggy son of 1987 Irish Derby winner Sir Harry Lewis, Unowhatimeanharry has had his pedigree discussed in previous editions of *Chasers & Hurdlers* and there isn't a great deal to add. He remains by far the best representative of his dam, the modest winning hurdler Red Nose Lady, who proved very durable during her racing days (albeit often looking less than keen). Red Nose Lady has seen just three of her offspring reach the racecourse to date, the latest being the four-year-old Cousin Harry (by Resplendent Cee), who finished down the field in two bumpers for Philip Rothwell in the summer of 2019. Meanwhile, her most recent foal, a two-year-old by Dabbers Ridge, was sold for just €3,500 in July.

Unowhatimeanharry has been fitted with a tongue strap throughout his time with Fry, while the aforementioned cheekpieces have presumably been added to help now that he has reached veteran status. Despite his flop in the Liverpool Hurdle at Aintree (as well as finishing well held in the last two renewals of the Stayers' at

Cheltenham), Unowhatimeanharry has largely proved a model of consistency for current connections and reflects great credit on them. He has also won on all types of ground he's encountered to date (acts on heavy, yet to race on firmer than good). The decision to keep Unowhatimeanharry over hurdles probably owed more to his late start with Fry than any perceived jumping concerns about sending him chasing. His career was reportedly in doubt leading up to Punchestown—'Like all of us, he's getting older. There was a chance if today's race didn't go well it could have been his last,' explained a jubilant Fry afterwards. Now rising twelve, winning opportunities are likely to be even harder to come by should Unowhatimeanharry continue racing, though connections could always follow the ageing footballer route by exploring lucrative options on American soil. Far Hills in New Jersey stages the American Grand National in October which, despite its grandiose title, is a twenty-one furlong hurdle race. Its lavish winning prize of £200,000 was won in the latest campaign by the Gordon Elliott-trained Jury Duty—who had managed only a distant sixth behind Unowhatimeanharry in the 2017 Champion Stayers' Hurdle at Punchestown. *Harry Fry*

UN PROPHETE (FR) 8 gr.g. Carlotamix (FR) – Pollita (FR) (Nombre Premier) [2018/19 c129, h–: c17.5s^F c16d⁵ c18.8d³ c21.2g^F Feb 15] big gelding: maiden hurdler: fairly useful handicap chaser: third at Ascot (amateurs) in January: stays 19f: acts on heavy going: often let down by jumping. *Venetia Williams*   c120 x h–

UNSAFE CONDUCT 6 ch.g. Pasternak – Symbiosis (Bien Bien (USA)) [2018/19 h91: h16.8g* h18.7g⁶ h16g⁵ h15.3g h15.8d⁵ h16.3d Mar 2] workmanlike gelding: fair handicap hurdler: won at Newton Abbot early in season: unproven beyond 17f: acts on soft going: in hood last 2 starts: wears tongue tie: has joined Dave Roberts: temperamental. *Colin Tizzard*   h102 §

UN TEMPS POUR TOUT (IRE) 10 b.g. Robin des Champs (FR) – Rougedespoir (FR) (Bonnet Rouge (FR)) [2018/19 h20g⁵ c29.2g Jan 12] strong gelding: has had breathing operation: useful hurdler/high-class chaser, below form in 2018/19 after missing previous season: stays 25f: acts on heavy going: wears headgear/tongue tie. *David Pipe*   c– h–

UNTIL WINNING (FR) 11 b.g. Kapgarde (FR) – Fripperie (FR) (Bojador (FR)) [2018/19 c120, h–: c23.8g³ May 17] maiden hurdler: fairly useful handicap chaser: stayed 3m: acted on heavy going: usually raced towards rear: dead. *Tom George*   c118 h–

UNWIN VC 5 b.g. Black Sam Bellamy (IRE) – Becky B (Alflora (IRE)) [2018/19 b106p: b16.4g h23.1v³ h23.6d h23.1s² Mar 5] strong gelding: useful bumper performer: fairly useful form over hurdles: best effort when second in novice at Exeter. *Bob Buckler*   h124 b–

UNZING (FR) 11 b.g. Voix du Nord (FR) – Magik (FR) (Kadalko (FR)) [2018/19 c17.2s³ c21.4d³ Jan 17] winning hurdler: fairly useful chaser at best: stayed 2¾m: acted on heavy going: tried in cheekpieces: dead. *Charles Pogson*   c106 h–

UP FOR REVIEW (IRE) 10 br.g. Presenting – Coolsilver (IRE) (Good Thyne (USA)) [2018/19 c144, h–: c22.5d* c25s³ c25s c34.3g^{bd} Apr 6] winning hurdler: useful chaser: won novice at Killarney early in season: third in Thyestes Handicap Chase at Gowran (12¼ lengths behind Invitation Only) in January: suffered fatal injuries when brought down first in Grand National at Aintree: stayed 25f: acted on heavy going. *W. P. Mullins, Ireland*   c141 h–

UPHAM RUNNING (IRE) 11 b.g. Definite Article – Tara Brooch (IRE) (Supreme Leader) [2018/19 h76: c21.6m^{pu} c20s⁴ c21.7d⁶ c19.7s⁶ c16s³ c17.8v^{pu} Mar 6] angular gelding: has had breathing operation: poor hurdler: similar form over fences: stays 2½m: acts on heavy going: has worn headgear, including last 3 starts: in tongue tie last 2. *Kate Buckett*   c72 h–

UP HELLY AA KING 8 ch.g. And Beyond (IRE) – Gretton (Terimon) [2018/19 h95: h19.5v h21.4s^{ur} h21.4d² c20.9v* Mar 7] has had breathing operation: modest maiden hurdler: 13/2, won novice handicap at Carlisle (by 3¼ lengths from Magic of Milan) on chasing debut: stays 21f: acts on heavy going: wears tongue tie: strong traveller, has flashed tail: open to improvement over fences. *N. W. Alexander*   c99 p h93

UPPERTOWN PRINCE (IRE) 7 b.g. Strategic Prince – Tarrawarra (IRE) (Kayf Tara) [2018/19 h140: c21.5s⁴ c24.2d^F h20.5s^{pu} Mar 9] useful-looking gelding: point winner: useful hurdler: running to similar level when falling heavily 3 out in novice at Wetherby on second start in chases: stays 25f: acts on heavy going: tried in cheekpieces: usually races close up. *Donald McCain*   c138 h–

UPSILON BLEU (FR) 11 b.g. Panoramic – Glycine Bleue (FR) (Le Nain Jaune (FR)) **c134**
[2018/19 c139, h–: c22.3g³ c20.3g⁴ Jan 1] strong gelding: winning hurdler: useful handicap **h–**
chaser: third in veterans event at Kelso (3¼ lengths behind Cultram Abbey) in December:
barely stays 2¾m: acts on heavy going: tried in hood. *Pauline Robson*

UPSWING (IRE) 11 b.g. Beneficial – Native Country (IRE) (Be My Native (USA)) **c117**
[2018/19 c120x, h–: c25g⁵ c24s⁴ c23.8dᵖᵘ c26g⁴ Feb 20] strong gelding: winning hurdler: **h–**
fairly useful hunter chaser nowadays: fourth at Warwick in January: left Jonjo O'Neill after
first start: stays 27f: acts on heavy going: has worn headgear, including in 2018/19. *T. M. Frost*

UP THE DRIVE (IRE) 6 b.g. Olden Times – Black Magic Baby (IRE) (Bob Back **c–**
(USA)) [2018/19 h19.9g h15.8g h16.7g h16d c24vᵖᵘ c26.1d Feb 25] no form: tried in **h–**
tongue tie. *Dan Skelton*

UP THE NAVAN ROAD (IRE) 7 b.g. Stowaway – Tisiphone (IRE) (Exit To Nowhere **h–**
(USA)) [2018/19 h17.7gᵖᵘ Aug 23] compact gelding: placed in bumper: well held over
hurdles: in hood last 3 starts. *Michael Roberts*

UPTOWN FUNK (IRE) 5 b.g. Galileo (IRE) – All's Forgotten (USA) (Darshaan) **h118**
[2018/19 h119: h17.2m³ h22.1g² h20.2g⁵ h20s h23.8g³ Jan 1] good-topped gelding: has
had breathing operation: fairly useful handicap hurdler: second at Cartmel in July: stays
3m: acts on good to soft going: tried in tongue tie. *Keith Dalgleish*

UPTOWN HARRY (IRE) 5 b.g. Morozov (USA) – Tudor Glyn (IRE) (Flemensfirth **h117**
(USA)) [2018/19 h22.7g² h20.5d⁴ h22d² h22.7d² Apr 8] €30,000 3-y-o, £15,000 4-y-o:
third foal: half-brother to useful hurdler/chaser Dont Kick Nor Bite (19f-21f winner,
by Beneficial), stays 25f: dam unraced: off mark in points at seventh attempt: fairly useful
form over hurdles: second in handicap at Kelso in April: likely to stay 3m. *Jane Walton*

URADEL (GER) 8 b.g. Kallisto (GER) – Unavita (GER) (Vettori (IRE)) [2018/19 h129: **h136**
h22.8dᵇᵈ h16g⁵ h21s Mar 13] close-coupled gelding: useful handicap hurdler: fifth in
Ladbrokes Hurdle at Leopardstown in February: stays 21f: acts on soft going: tried in hood.
W. P. Mullins, Ireland

URBAN ARTIST 4 ch.f. Cityscape – Cill Rialaig (Environment Friend) [2018/19 b16.5d **b90**
b16.8g⁴ Apr 18] second foal: dam (b102), 1½m/13f bumper winner, also useful 1¼m-1½m
winner on Flat: fair form in bumpers: better effort when fourth in mares event at
Cheltenham: will be suited by 2½m. *Hughie Morrison*

URBANIST (IRE) 7 b.g. Black Sam Bellamy (IRE) – Sorcillera (Anziliero (GER)) **c107**
[2018/19 h20d⁴ h20g⁴ h20v² c20.3d³ c24.2s* h21.7sᵖᵘ Jan 27] €18,000 3-y-o: has had **h96**
breathing operation: first foal: dam (h109), 2m hurdle winner, also German 1¼m winner on
Flat, half-sister to Irish Grand National winner Commanche Court: modest handicap
hurdler: fair form over fences: won handicap at Exeter in January: left Shane Nolan after
second start: stays 3m: acts on heavy going: has worn headgear, including last 2 starts.
Dr Richard Newland

URBAN KODE (IRE) 11 b.g. Kodiac – Urbanize (USA) (Chester House (USA)) **h78**
[2018/19 h86: h20.2g⁶ h20.2g⁴ h20.2g⁴ h19.3g⁶ h22g³ h19.8g³ h15.6g Jan 7] poor handicap
hurdler: stays 2¾m: acts on good to firm and heavy going: wears headgear. *Lucinda Russell*

URCA DE LIMA 6 b.m. Black Sam Bellamy (IRE) – Dame Fonteyn (Suave Dancer **h83**
(USA)) [2018/19 h76: h19.5d⁵ h21.7v* h20.5d⁵ Mar 18] good-topped mare: bumper
winner: poor form over hurdles: won 2-runner novice at Fontwell in March: tried in tongue
tie. *Anthony Honeyball*

URGENT DE GREGAINE (FR) 11 b.g. Truth Or Dare – Hispanie (FR) (Bad Conduct **c142**
(USA)) [2018/19 c148, h–: c23.4sᵖᵘ c30.2s³ Mar 13] lengthy gelding: twice-raced hurdler: **h–**
useful chaser: third in Glenfarclas Chase (Cross Country) at Cheltenham (22¾ lengths
behind Tiger Roll) in March: stays 4¼m: acts on soft going: wears cheekpieces: has worn
tongue tie, including in 2018/19. *Emmanuel Clayeux, France*

URIAH HEEP (FR) 10 b.g. Danehill Dancer (IRE) – Canasita (Zafonic (USA)) [2018/19 **c–**
c–, h–: h20.2g⁴ Jun 23] sturdy gelding: poor handicap hurdler nowadays: winning chaser: **h82**
stays 2½m: acts on good to firm and good to soft going: has worn cheekpieces. *R. Mike Smith*

URTHEONETHATIWANT (IRE) 6 ch.g. Shantou (USA) – Roberta Supreme (IRE) **h93**
(Bob's Return (IRE)) [2018/19 h–: h19d⁴ h21d* h23.9d² h23.1d* Apr 9] modest handicap
hurdler: won at Kempton in January and Exeter in April: stays 3m: acts on good to soft
going: usually races towards rear. *Jeremy Scott*

Burnham Plastering & Dry Lining Limited's "Us And Them"

US AND THEM (IRE) 6 b.g. Stowaway – Manorville (IRE) (Flemensfirth (USA)) **c150**
[2018/19 h136, b92: c16d⁴ c17d* c17d² c17g² c17g² c15.9s² c15.8g² Apr 6] rather **h–**
unfurnished gelding: useful form over hurdles: smart chaser: won maiden at Navan (by 2
lengths from Duca de Thaix) in November: runner-up next 5 starts, including in Racing
Post Novices' Chase in December and Frank Ward Solicitors Arkle Novices' Chase in
February, both at Leopardstown, Arkle Chase at Cheltenham in March and Maghull
Novices' Chase at Aintree (1¾ lengths behind Ornua) in April: bred to stay at least 2½m:
acts on heavy going: in tongue tie after third start: usually races close up. *Joseph Patrick
O'Brien, Ireland*

UTILITY (GER) 8 b.g. Yeats (IRE) – Ungarin (GER) (Goofalik (USA)) [2018/19 h127: **c118 §**
c16.5gʳʳ h16g c21gᵖᵘ h17.2g⁶ h16.8g⁶ h20g⁴ c18mʳᵒ h18.7g* h21g⁶ c16.4s² c19.1g⁴ Jan 25] **h111 §**
useful-looking gelding: has had breathing operation: fair hurdler: won conditionals seller
at Stratford in November: fairly useful form over fences: left Jonjo O'Neill after sixth start:
stays 19f: acts on soft going: tried in blinkers: has worn tongue tie: one to treat with caution
(has refused to race/run out). *David Bridgwater*

UT MAJEUR AULMES (FR) 11 ch.g. Northern Park (USA) – My Wish Aulmes (FR) **c98**
(Lyphard's Wish (FR)) [2018/19 c134, h–: c16.4sᵖᵘ c16d⁴ c15.7g⁵ c17.8v⁴ Mar 16] rangy **h–**
gelding: has had breathing operation: winning hurdler: useful chaser, well below form in
2018/19: unproven beyond 2m: acts on heavy going: has worn headgear, including last 3
starts: wears tongue tie. *Victor Dartnall*

V

VADO FORTE (FR) 6 b.g. Walk In The Park (IRE) – Gloire (FR) (Sillery (USA)) **h123**
[2018/19 h127: h16d³ h16.4g h16.4vᵖᵘ Mar 16] tall gelding: fairly useful handicap hurdler:
third at Chepstow in October: stays 19f: acts on heavy going: usually wears hood. *Tom Lacey*

VALADOM (FR) 10 gr.g. Dadarissime (FR) – Laurana (FR) (Badolato (USA)) [2018/19 c116, h74: h23.9g² c26.2g⁶ h21g⁴ h23s³ c24g⁵ c21.2g² c22.4d⁴ c23.4d² c23.8g³ Apr 24] workmanlike gelding: has had breathing operation: fair maiden hurdler: fairly useful handicap chaser: runner-up 3 times in 2018/19: stays 25f: acts on good to firm and heavy going: wears headgear/tongue tie: usually leads. *Richard Hobson*
c123
h114

VALCO DE TOUZAINE (FR) 10 gr.g. Dom Alco (FR) – Narcisse de Touzaine (FR) (Roi de Rome (USA)) [2018/19 c24gᵖᵘ c16g⁴ c19.9m c20.3g Aug 19] rather leggy gelding: multiple point winner: winning hurdler: one-time useful chaser, regressed further in 2018/19: left P. M. J. Doyle after third start: best around 2½m: acts on good to firm and heavy going: has worn hood, including in 2018/19: wears tongue tie. *Christian Williams*
c103
h–

VALDAS PRINCESS 7 b.m. King's Theatre (IRE) – Valdas Queen (GER) (Platini (GER)) [2018/19 h96, b70: h20g h20.5d⁶ Jan 22] poor form over hurdles: left Oliver Sherwood after first start: tried in cheekpieces: usually races towards rear. *Olly Murphy*
h62

VALDEZ 12 ch.g. Doyen (IRE) – Skew (Niniski (USA)) [2018/19 c141, h–: c16.8gᵖᵘ c18.8s⁴ c19.9d³ c19.9g² Mar 23] good-topped gelding: winning hurdler: smart handicap chaser: second at Newbury (length behind Gala Ball) in March: stays 2½m: acts on good to firm and heavy going. *Alan King*
c145
h–

VALDIEU (FR) 6 b.g. Diamond Boy (FR) – Vamuna (FR) (Varese (FR)) [2018/19 b17.1v³ b16g² b16.5g² b16g² b16.6d* h16d* h16g h21s h16d³ Apr 7] €54,000 3-y-o: good-topped gelding: fifth foal: half-brother to useful French chaser Vauquoise (2½m/21f winner, by Ungaro): dam French 2¼m hurdle winner: won completed start in points: fairly useful bumper performer: won maiden at Down Royal in December: similar form when winning maiden at Naas on hurdling debut in January: disappointing after: wears tongue tie. *Noel Meade, Ireland*
h124
b101

VALENCE D'AUMONT (FR) 5 b.g. Sinndar (IRE) – Ice Ti (ITY) (Mtoto) [2018/19 h17.9s* h18.9s* c18.4s h17.9s* c17.4g* c19.4s³ h17.9s h16.7g h25.3d³ c20d⁵ Mar 30] lengthy gelding: once-raced on Flat: fairly useful hurdler: won handicap at Lyon Parilly in May and claimer at Auteuil in June: fair form over fences: won claimer at Dieppe in July: left Y. Fouin after seventh start: stays 19f: acts on soft going: has worn headgear. *Sue Smith*
c114
h118

VALGOR DU RONCERAY (FR) 10 gr.g. Al Namix (FR) – Malta de Ronceray (FR) (Dress Parade) [2018/19 c116x, h116: c19.2sᵖᵘ c15.7d⁴ h23.1g h20.6m⁶ Apr 21] workmanlike gelding: fairly useful hurdler/chaser, out of form in 2018/19: has worn hood/tongue tie. *Micky Hammond*
c–
h–

VALHALLA (IRE) 9 b.g. Scorpion (IRE) – Fox Theatre (IRE) (King's Theatre (IRE)) [2018/19 c130, h–: c16.3g³ c18m³ c22.4sᵖᵘ c15.5d⁴ c22.4d Mar 22] good-topped gelding: winning hurdler: fairly useful handicap chaser: third at Newton Abbot in October: stays 3¼m, effective at much shorter: acts on heavy going: wears tongue tie. *Colin Tizzard*
c123
h–

VALJAN 5 b.m. Shirocco (GER) – Miracle (Ezzoud (IRE)) [2018/19 b16.7g h16g⁴ h15.7g⁴ Aug 19] has had breathing operation: half-sister to several winners, including Champion Hurdle winner Katchit (by Kalanisi) and useful hurdler/chaser Prince Erik (2m-3m winner, by Indian Ridge): dam French 1m winner: well held in mares bumper: modest form over hurdles. *Oliver Sherwood*
h92
b–

VALKENBURG 4 b.g. Dutch Art – Balamana (FR) (Sinndar (IRE)) [2018/19 h15.6g³ h15.7g h15.7s⁶ h21.4s⁶ h24.3d³ h20.6d Mar 5] fair on Flat, stays 2¼m: modest form over hurdles: left Keith Dalgleish after fifth start: stays 3m: acts on soft going: wears headgear: temperament under suspicion (races lazily). *Harriet Bethell*
h91

VALLEYOFMILAN (IRE) 12 b.g. Milan – Ikdam Valley (IRE) (Ikdam) [2018/19 c118, h–: c25.6d³ c22.3g Dec 9] winning hurdler: fairly useful handicap chaser: stays 29f: acts on soft and good to firm going: wears cheekpieces. *Donald McCain*
c112
h–

VAL MOME (FR) 6 b.g. Turgeon (USA) – Valle Fleurie (Bonnet Rouge (FR)) [2018/19 h16.7g² h16.7g² h19.9g⁵ h16.7g* h16.2g h15.6g² h15.6g⁵ h16g⁵ Jan 12] €11,500 3-y-o: has had breathing operation: fourth foal: half-brother to French 17f-21f hurdle/chase winner Vallee En Fleur (by Trempolino): dam once-raced half-sister to triple Grand Steeple-Chase de Paris winner Mid Dancer: won Irish point on debut: tongue tied when tailed off in bumper for J. G. Cosgrave: fair hurdler: won novice at Bangor in October: unproven beyond 17f: raced only on good going: tried in tongue tie. *Donald McCain*
h112

VALNAMIXE DU MEE (FR) 10 b.g. Al Namix (FR) – Kateline du Mee (FR) (Panoramic) [2018/19 c20sᵘʳ Nov 12] maiden hurdler: modest form at best over fences, no show only outing since 2016: usually in hood. *Rebecca Menzies*
c–
h–

VALSE AU TAILLONS (FR) 6 b.m. Montmartre (FR) – Eyaelle (FR) (Green Tune (USA)) [2018/19 h18.5v³ h16.4s³ h19d⁶ Mar 11] half-sister to French 2¼m hurdle winner Diable d'Enfer (by Saint des Saints): fair on Flat in France for C. Gourdain, stays 10.5f: fair form over hurdles: best effort at 19f: acts on heavy going. *Johnny Farrelly* **h104**

VALSEUR DU GRANVAL (FR) 10 b.g. Della Francesca (USA) – La Grande Vallee (FR) (Chef de Clan (FR)) [2018/19 c129, h–: c20g c15.8g h16.2g³ c17.5s⁶ c18.2d c15.7d⁶ c15.7g³ c16d² c16m* Apr 1] tall, useful-looking gelding: modest form over hurdles: fairly useful handicap chaser: won 3-runner race at Ludlow in April: stays 2½m: acts on soft and good to firm going: in cheekpieces last 2 starts: wears tongue tie. *Tom George* **c125 h99**

VALSEUR LIDO (FR) 10 b.g. Anzillero (GER) – Libido Rock (FR) (Video Rock (FR)) [2018/19 c154, h–: c22.5d c22m² c21.5s⁶ c25s c21g c25d³ c20.6d c34.3g c29dᵖᵘ Apr 22] compact gelding: winning hurdler: useful chaser nowadays: stays 25f: acts on good to firm and heavy going: usually in cheekpieces. *Henry de Bromhead, Ireland* **c138 h–**

VALSHAN TIME (IRE) 7 b.g. Atraf – Valshan (IRE) (Anshan) [2018/19 c–: c16.5gᶠ c19.4m³ c16.5g Jul 31] has had breathing operation: placed on completed start in Irish maiden points: poor maiden chaser: in blinkers last 4 starts. *Laura Young* **c65**

VALTOR (FR) 10 b.g. Nidor (FR) – Jossca (FR) (Badolato (USA)) [2018/19 c29.8s⁶ c21.9s c23.8s* c25.3dᵖᵘ c34.3g Apr 6] well-made gelding: maiden hurdler: very smart chaser: won Silver Cup at Ascot (by 8 lengths from Jammin Masters) in December: left E. Leray after second start: stays 3¼m: acts on heavy going: tried in cheekpieces. *Nicky Henderson* **c155 h–**

VALUE AT RISK 10 b.g. Kayf Tara – Miss Orchestra (IRE) (Orchestra) [2018/19 c135§, h141§: c19.9g c21g⁵ c19.1g³ c20.2g⁵ c19.2d* c19.9d c20.5s⁶ c20.5m³ Apr 12] strong gelding: useful hurdler: useful handicap chaser: won at Market Rasen (by ½ length from Terry The Fish) in January: stays 2½m: acts on heavy going: has worn headgear: tried in tongue tie: usually races towards rear: unreliable. *Dan Skelton* **c132 § h–**

VAMANOS (IRE) 5 b.g. Fame And Glory – Bean Ki Moon (IRE) (King's Theatre (IRE)) [2018/19 b89: h16.3g⁴ h16.7v³ h19.3g³ h20.9g⁴ Mar 23] rangy gelding: fair form over hurdles. *Olly Murphy* **h110**

VANCOUVER 7 ch.g. Generous (IRE) – All Told (IRE) (Valanjou (FR)) [2018/19 h122: h20g h18.7g² h15.5g³ h20d³ h20.7d h19d* h18.7g⁶ Mar 30] lengthy gelding: fair hurdler: won seller at Taunton in February: stays 21f: acts on good to firm and good to soft going: in hood last 4 starts. *Neil Mulholland* **h114**

*Garrard Silver Cup Handicap Chase, Ascot—a breathtaking British debut by Valtor,
who storms clear under James Bowen to defy odds of 33/1*

VANDERBILT (IRE) 5 ch.g. Intense Focus (USA) – Star of The West (Galileo (IRE)) [2018/19 h16.8g³ h16m³ h16g h16g h16.5d h16.8s⁴ h15.3g h19s⁴ Mar 19] modest maiden on Flat, stays 1¼m: fair maiden hurdler: will prove best at 2m: acts on soft and good to firm going: has worn headgear. *Mark Gillard* **h103**

VANGO DE VAIGE (FR) 6 b.g. Great Pretender (IRE) – Yellow Park (FR) (Northern Park (USA)) [2018/19 h101: h23.1g³ h23.1s* h23.1s⁵ h23.1spu h24.2d⁶ Mar 22] strong gelding: fair handicap hurdler: won at Exeter in November: stays 23f: acts on soft going: usually races off pace. *Philip Hobbs* **h100**

VAN GOGH DU GRANIT (FR) 10 b.g. Saddler Maker (IRE) – Etnou (FR) (Le Pontet (FR)) [2018/19 h19.9s² c21.4v* h18.4v* c22.9s c22.9v⁴ c23.8m² c31.8m Apr 13] fair hurdler: won claimer at Auteuil in November: fairly useful chaser: won claimer at Nantes earlier in month: second in veterans handicap at Ascot in March: left J-D. Marion after fifth start: stays 3½m: acts on good to firm and heavy going: wears headgear. *David Pipe* **c126** **h109**

VANILLA BREEZE 5 b.m. Trans Island – Vanilla Delight (IRE) (Orpen (USA)) [2018/19 b16.7g b15.8g b15.7g⁵ b16.7m⁵ Aug 5] half-sister to several winners, including bumper winner Vanilla Run (by Hurricane Run) and 17f hurdle winner Van Mildert (by Observatory): dam, ran once over hurdles, 7f winner on Flat: little show in bumpers/Flat seller. *Shaun Harris* **b56**

VANITEUX (FR) 10 br.g. Voix du Nord (FR) – Expoville (FR) (Video Rock (FR)) [2018/19 c144, h–: c18g³ c20g c23.8g³ c17.1m⁵ h25m⁵ h21g Nov 18] well-made gelding: has had breathing operation: smart hurdler/very smart chaser at best, on downgrade: best up to 2½m: acts on soft and good to firm going: usually wears headgear: has worn tongue tie. *David Pipe* **c125** **h107**

VARDS 9 b.g. Tamure (IRE) – Bank On Lady (Dromod Hill) [2018/19 h16s² h16.3s h15.9s⁵ h21.4s⁵ h18.5d Mar 24] first foal: dam placed in points: won 2 of 3 starts in points: fair form over hurdles: wears hood. *Jack R. Barber* **h109**

VASCO D'YCY (FR) 10 b.g. Equerry (USA) – Ingrid des Mottes (FR) (Useful (FR)) [2018/19 c24.1d³ c20.9vur Mar 7] winning hurdler: fair maiden chaser: missed 2017/18: stays 3m: acts on heavy going. *Julia Brooke* **c101** **h–**

VAXALCO (FR) 10 gr.g. Dom Alco (FR) – Galaxie (FR) (Useful (FR)) [2018/19 c21.2d³ c23.6d² c23.6g² c24.2m² Apr 22] angular gelding: Irish point winner: maiden hurdler: fair maiden chaser: stays 3m: acts on good to firm and good to soft going: has worn headgear/tongue tie. *Neil King* **c107** **h–**

VAZIANI (FR) 5 b.g. Sinndar (IRE) – Visinova (FR) (Anabaa (USA)) [2018/19 h110: h16v h20.5s⁵ h18.5vF Dec 20] angular gelding: fair form over hurdles: should be suited by 2½m+: usually races prominently. *Robert Walford* **h106**

VEAUCE DE SIVOLA (FR) 10 b.g. Assessor (IRE) – Eva de Chalamont (FR) (Iron Duke (FR)) [2018/19 c71§, h–: h24.3d c24.1d⁴ c26.3s² c23.8s* c24.2d² Mar 26] lengthy gelding: winning hurdler: poor handicap chaser: won at Musselburgh in March: stays 3¼m: acts on heavy going: tried in cheekpieces: wears tongue tie: usually races prominently: unreliable. *Sandy Forster* **c82 §** **h–**

VEILED SECRET (IRE) 5 b.g. Teofilo (IRE) – Seven Veils (IRE) (Danehill Dancer (IRE)) [2018/19 h104: h19.6g h19.5g h21.6spu h15.8d⁶ h19.8spu h19.7g² h16.5d* Apr 4] has had breathing operation: modest handicap hurdler: won at Taunton in April: stays 2½m: acts on good to soft going: in headgear last 4 starts: wears tongue tie. *David Dennis* **h89**

VEINARD (FR) 10 ch.g. Shaanmer (IRE) – Ombline (FR) (Subotica (FR)) [2018/19 c127p, h125: c16gur h16.7m h16gF c17d⁴ c16sur c16.5d* c17s² c16.5mur c16.7g⁴ Apr 21] good-bodied gelding: fairly useful hurdler: fairly useful handicap chaser: won novice event at Ayr in February: stays 2½m: acts on heavy going: has worn hood: wears tongue tie. *Gordon Elliott, Ireland* **c129** **h–**

VELOCITY BOY (IRE) 10 b.g. Westerner – Sambre (FR) (Turgeon (USA)) [2018/19 c19.5s² c28s⁵ c29g⁶ c20d² c24spu c21.2vpu Apr 14] winning hurdler: useful handicap chaser: runner-up twice in 2018/19: stays 2¾m: acts on heavy going: tried in hood/tongue tie. *W. P. Murphy, Ireland* **c136** **h–**

VELVET MAKER (FR) 10 b.g. Policy Maker (IRE) – Evasion de L'Orne (FR) (Beyssac (FR)) [2018/19 c–, h117: c17.8g³ c17d⁵ h21.2g Nov 15] angular gelding: useful hurdler/chaser at best, has deteriorated: stays 2¼m: acts on heavy going: has worn hood: tried in tongue tie: front runner/races prominently. *David Christie, Ireland* **c94** **h–**

VELVET VOICE 5 b.m. Azamour (IRE) – Battery Power (Royal Applause) [2018/19 **h74** h19.5d[pu] h16d[pu] h16d[5] h15.8g[5] Apr 11] rather leggy mare: dam half-sister to fairly useful hurdler (stayed 19f) Crystal Pearl: modest maiden on Flat, stays 1¼m: poor form over hurdles. *Mark H. Tompkins*

VENDOR (FR) 11 gr.g. Kendor (FR) – Village Rainbow (FR) (Village Star (FR)) [2018/19 **c119 §** h16g[6] c15.2d[5] c15.7v[4] c19.4s[4] c16.3d[4] c15.2g[4] c15.9v[3] c17.2g[3] Apr 3] leggy, useful- **h–** looking gelding: has had breathing operation: winning hurdler: fairly useful maiden chaser: fourth in handicap at Haydock in December: stays easy 2½m: acts on heavy going: temperamental. *Sue Smith*

VENDREDI TROIS (FR) 10 b.g. Shaanmer (IRE) – Legende Sacree (FR) (Hawker's **c118** News (IRE)) [2018/19 c–, h102: c20g[3] c23g* c23g[2] c23.9m[3] c24.1g[3] c22.6g[2] c22.6g[3] **h–** c23.8m[2] Apr 23] narrow gelding: fair hurdler: fairly useful handicap chaser: won at Worcester in June: placed all other starts in 2018/19: stays 3¼m: acts on soft and good to firm going: wears headgear. *Emma Lavelle*

VENETIAN PROPOSAL (IRE) 5 b.m. Fast Company (IRE) – Ide Say (IRE) (Grand **h82** Lodge (USA)) [2018/19 h83: h15.9g[3] h15.9g h16.7g h15.5g[pu] h16.5g[4] h15.9s[5] h16.5d h17.7g Apr 22] poor maiden hurdler: raced around 2m: has worn headgear. *Zoe Davison*

VENGEUR DE GUYE (FR) 10 b.g. Dom Alco (FR) – Mascotte de Guye (FR) (Video **c119** Rock (FR)) [2018/19 c118§, h–: h16.2g[5] c17.1g[4] c17.4v* c16.3d[6] Jan 19] good-topped **h106** gelding: fair handicap hurdler: fairly useful handicap chaser: won at Bangor in December: stays 2½m: acts on heavy going: has worn headgear: wears tongue tie: usually races towards rear: has flattered to deceive. *Lucinda Russell*

VENTURA MAGIC 4 b.g. Mount Nelson – Elle Desert (GER) (Next Desert (IRE)) **h102** [2018/19 h16.7m[5] h15.8s[2] h16.8g[2] Aug 15] dam half-sister to useful hurdler/fairly useful chaser (stayed 25f) El Dancer: fair on Flat, stays 1½m: fair form over hurdles: best effort when second in juvenile at Uttoxeter. *Neil King*

VENTUREPREDEMENTIA 8 b.g. Indian Danehill (IRE) – Sounds Familiar (IRE) **h–** (Orchestra) [2018/19 h–: h23.3g[pu] May 12] little show in bumpers/over hurdles. *Andrew Crook*

VENUE 9 b.g. Beat Hollow – Shirley Valentine (Shirley Heights) [2018/19 h17.2d[3] h19.9g[2] **h117** Sep 12] fairly useful handicap hurdler: fit from Flat, third at Cartmel in August: probably stays 2½m: acts on soft and good to firm going: tried in tongue tie. *Donald McCain*

VERBITUDE (IRE) 4 b.g. Vocalised (USA) – Bring Back Matron (IRE) (Rock of **h88 p** Gibraltar (IRE)) [2018/19 h16d[6] h17.7v[5] h16.2g[4] Mar 26] brother to fairly useful chaser Vocaliser (2m-2¼m winner) and half-brother to fair hurdler Miracle Cure (15f winner, by Whipper): dam half-sister to useful 2m hurdle winner Fiscal Focus: lightly-raced maiden on Flat for J. S. Bolger: modest form over hurdles: open to further improvement. *Nigel Hawke*

VERDANA BLUE (IRE) 7 b.m. Getaway (GER) – Blue Gallery (IRE) (Bluebird **h159** (USA)) [2018/19 h140: h16m* h15.3g* h16.4g[4] h16g* h16.4s[5] h16m* Apr 13]

    An unusually dry winter left trainers praying for rain as ground conditions played havoc with running plans for a lot of their horses. At least those who wanted soft ground. Not all jumpers go in the mud, however, and there cannot have been many who profited from the conditions which prevailed for much of the season more than Verdana Blue who won four times on the five occasions she encountered good ground or firmer. Ironically, the only time the ground went against her was for the Champion Hurdle. She had been declared for the race in 2018 only to be withdrawn when the going was soft, but she stood her ground for the latest edition despite similar conditions and was given a sympathetic ride, never getting into the race, by Davy Russell, finishing a well-held fifth of the seven who completed.

    Verdana Blue's campaign got off to a good start with a couple of wins in the autumn, before which she had made a successful debut on the Flat at Chelmsford in September when beating four three-year-old rivals in a novice event. That set her up for an impressive win back over hurdles in a listed contest at Kempton the following month when she accounted for the previous year's winner Old Guard by seven lengths and, with fitness on her side and conditions again ideal, she followed up in the Unibet Elite Hurdle at Wincanton in November. Wincanton provides one of the sharpest tests there is for a two-mile hurdler—the Elite is actually run over not that much more than fifteen furlongs—and Verdana Blue, always going supremely well, quickly drew clear to beat her main market rivals If The Cap Fits and stable-companion We Have A Dream by two and a quarter lengths and seven. Clearly improved since being campaigned in handicaps the previous season, Verdana Blue was turned out again under a 5-lb penalty just eight days after the Elite, and was sent off the 9/2 favourite back in handicap company for the Greatwood at Cheltenham. She ran creditably but didn't have much luck in a muddling contest where the low sun meant the flights in the straight were omitted. Twice meeting trouble on the extended run from the final flight, Verdana Blue stayed on well and finished fourth, with running left in her, behind the lightly-weighted winner Nietzsche. Back on the Flat, Verdana Blue showed useful form when second in a listed race at Kempton in early-December before being returned to the same track three weeks later for much her biggest test to date in the Christmas Hurdle.

With stable-companion Buveur d'Air sent off at 4/1-on to win the race for the second year, Verdana Blue, second favourite at 11/2, looked to be running for place money in a field completed by If The Cap Fits, the Gerry Feilden winner Global Citizen and the useful handicapper Boite. But the dual Champion Hurdle winner, successful on his last eleven starts in a sequence that had begun at Aintree three seasons earlier, had an off-day under conditions which again proved ideal for Verdana Blue. Ridden by Nico de Boinville, as she had been for her earlier Kempton win (Jerry McGrath took the ride for her next two starts), Verdana Blue stalked Buveur d'Air and Barry Geraghty for much of the way, the favourite leading two out but Verdana Blue keeping on from the last to nail him on the line and win by a short head. Despite taking the scalp of the ante-post favourite, Nicky Henderson dismissed the Champion Hurdle for Verdana Blue as a waste of time ('unless they promised to give us good to firm') and all the talk afterwards concerned her Flat programme. Even the Melbourne Cup was mentioned in the longer term, but more immediately her main goal in the spring was the two-mile contest on Finals day at the All-Weather Championships at Lingfield on Good Friday. However, Verdana Blue had to miss a fast-track qualifier for that race at Kempton in February due to having to be vaccinated following the equine flu outbreak, and when she did get a run on the all-weather at Kempton later in the month, in a novice event, she suffered a shock defeat of her own at the hands of Gumball, himself a useful hurdler making his Flat debut.

Unibet Christmas Hurdle, Kempton—
Verdana Blue (far side, partly hidden) swoops late to pip the stable's number-one Buveur d'Air
(hoops); If The Cap Fits (quartered cap) and Global Citizen complete the frame

CPMS Scottish Champion Hurdle (Limited Handicap), Ayr—
a big win for 7-lb conditional Connor Brace as top-weight Verdana Blue puts up one of the best
two-mile hurdling performances of the season

With the Champion Hurdle duly proving something of a non-event for Verdana Blue, conditions were very different again a month later at Ayr for the CPMS Scottish Champion Hurdle, her new target with Lingfield off the agenda. A combination of wind and sun made for rapidly drying ground which again suited Verdana Blue perfectly and enabled her to put up a career-best effort, off a BHA mark of 154, that was both visually impressive and backed up by a particularly good timefigure. She also lowered the new course record which had been set the day before. Sent off the 4/1 favourite, Verdana Blue was set to concede weight to all thirteen of her rivals in the limited handicap, though her fourth different jockey of the season, conditional Connor Brace, took 7 lb off her back. It is rare to see good two-mile handicap hurdles won with such authority. Travelling strongly under a patient ride as usual, Verdana Blue made ground on the bridle turning for home, wasn't fluent at the first in the straight, but loomed up at the next and was produced to lead between the final two flights before quickening clear after the last. She won by seven lengths and a length and a quarter from the lightly-weighted pair Dino Velvet and Equus Amadeus. The stable's other remaining runner Brain Power was pulled up, while their third intended runner, the novice Mister Fisher, was withdrawn, one of more than a dozen non-runners on the card because of the drying ground. Verdana Blue had finished down the field in the same race twelve months earlier and she was Henderson's first winner of the Scottish Champion Hurdle since the novice River Ceiriog thirty-three years earlier. That year's Champion Hurdle runner-up Gaye Brief finished third on that occasion, but top two-mile hurdlers no longer contest the Scottish Champion Hurdle as often as they once did, and Verdana Blue put up the best performance in the race since it went to the top-class Mister Morose between his wins at Aintree and Punchestown in 2000.

			Monsun	Konigsstuhl
		Getaway (GER)	(br 1990)	Mosella
		(b 2003)	Guernica	Unfuwain
Verdana Blue (IRE)			(b 1994)	Greenvera
(b.m. 2012)			Bluebird	Storm Bird
		Blue Gallery (IRE)	(b 1984)	Ivory Dawn
		(b 2001)	Lovely Deise	Tate Gallery
			(ch 1991)	Sun On The Spey

904

The good and firmish ground at the end of the season evidently suited a couple more of the best horses sired to date by Verdana Blue's sire Getaway, as a fortnight after the Scottish Champion Hurdle Talkischeap and Getaway Trump registered a double at Sandown in the bet365 Gold Cup and a valuable novices handicap hurdle. The high-class Getaway, a son of Monsun and winner of two Group 1 contests in Germany over a mile and half, as well as the Jockey Club Stakes, when trained by Andre Fabre who initially campaigned him as a stayer, has covered huge books at Coolmore's Grange Stud and more good winners are sure to follow on from Verdana Blue and Talkischeap who are from his first crop. While Talkischeap is out of a mare by stamina influence Milan, Verdana Blue, by contrast, is out of a mare by the King's Stand winner Bluebird which readily accounts for speed being her main asset as a hurdler. Oddly, considering she's produced such a good jumper, Verdana Blue's modest dam Blue Gallery gained her only win in a six-furlong seller at Wolverhampton as a two-year-old, the only season she raced. Blue Gallery has been mated with some top jumping sires, though, resulting in two other winners, the lightly-raced hurdle/chase winner at up to nearly three miles Blues And Twos (by Presenting), who looked useful on his only completed start over fences, and Wilde Blue Yonder (by Oscar) who won a bumper and maiden hurdle for Alan King and went on to show useful form without adding to those early wins, including when fifth in the Supreme before running over fences, and was best at up to two and a half miles. If Verdana Blue's Flat career does continue to evolve alongside her hurdling—she was fourth in the Sagaro Stakes at Ascot in May—she won't be the first good dual-purpose performer in her family. Her great grandam, the twice-raced Sun On The Spey, was a sister to Spinning who won nine times on the Flat and a further five times over hurdles for owner Paul Mellon. Spinning was a dual listed winner on the Flat, successful at up to two miles, while over hurdles his biggest

Crambourne Stud's "Verdana Blue"

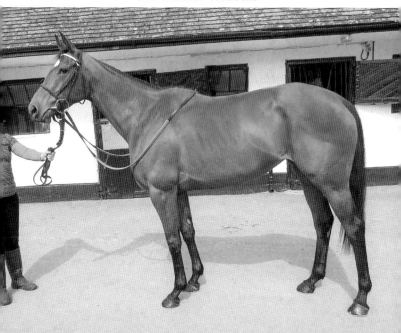

victory came in the Swinton at Haydock where he broke the course record—like Verdana Blue, Spinning was very much a 'top of the ground' performer. Verdana Blue's grandam Lovely Deise showed little in five starts at up to a mile in Ireland but produced five winners, including Dyrick Daybreak, another who operated under both codes, fairly useful both as a stayer on the Flat and at up to two and a half miles over hurdles.

The angular Verdana Blue began her career in Irish bumpers with Edmond Kent for whom she won a mares race at Killarney, and she joined Seven Barrows after being sold for £65,000 at the Cheltenham November Sales in 2016. After wins at Hereford and Taunton, she outran odds of 25/1 to finish fourth in the Dawn Run Mares' Novices' Hurdle at the Cheltenham Festival. The following season she won a good handicap at Ascot, but heavy ground scuppered her chances when she was one of the leading contenders for the Betfair Hurdle. The Melbourne Cup would now seem to be off the agenda and, assuming she's kept in training for another hurdling campaign, Verdana Blue is entitled to plenty of respect in all the top two-mile contests on condition that the ground is no softer than good, though her first win over hurdles did come on soft ground. She travels strongly and is held up to make best use of her good turn of foot. Owned by Crimbourne Stud, Verdana Blue's colours of light blue, white cross belts, red cap, will be familiar as those of the late Sir Eric Parker which were made famous by the 1991 Grand National winner Seagram and Topsham Bay who won, and was then awarded, the Whitbread Gold Cup in the following two seasons. *Nicky Henderson*

VEREINA 4 b.f. Universal (IRE) – Lady de La Vega (FR) (Kizitca (FR)) [2018/19 b14d h16d h16.7d⁶ h15.8d h19.9sᵖᵘ h21.2m h19.6d⁴ Apr 26] second foal: dam (c112/h98), 3m chase winner, half-sister to useful chaser (stayed 21f) Nadiya de La Vega: very green in bumper: poor form over hurdles: tried in cheekpieces: races off pace. *Oliver Greenall* — **h82 b–**

VERNI (FR) 10 ch.g. Sabrehill (USA) – Nobless d'Aron (FR) (Ragmar (FR)) [2018/19 c131§, h136§: c16d* May 5] useful hurdler: similar form over fences: won maiden at Uttoxeter on sole outing in 2018/19: stays 2½m: acts on heavy going: usually travels strongly: no battler. *Philip Hobbs* — **c129 § h– §**

VERSATILITY 5 b.g. Yeats (IRE) – Stravinsky Dance (Stravinsky (USA)) [2018/19 b16d b16.3d⁴ Mar 23] £25,000 3-y-o: third foal: half-brother to 11f/11½m winner Storm Force Ten (by Shirocco): dam (h137) French 2m-2¼m hurdle winner: fair form in bumpers: better effort when fourth in Goffs UK Spring Sales Bumper at Newbury. *Nicky Henderson* — **b93**

VERSIFIER 7 b.m. Yeats (IRE) – Daprika (FR) (Epervier Bleu) [2018/19 h96: h23.3m⁵ h21.7g⁶ h16.8g² h18.7g⁵ h19.7g* h17s² h20.5d² h20.5g h19.5d Mar 21] has had breathing operation: modest handicap hurdler: won mares event at Hereford in October: stays 21f: acts on heavy going: tried in cheekpieces. *Oliver Sherwood* — **h99**

VERTIGO (IRE) 7 b.g. Jeremy (USA) – Lady Coquette (SWE) (Mujadil (USA)) [2018/19 h105: c16gᵖᵘ May 16] placed completed start in Irish points: fair hurdler: pulled up in novice handicap on chasing debut: stays 21f: acts on heavy going: usually in tongue tie. *Lucinda Russell* — **c– h–**

VERY EXTRAVAGANT (IRE) 10 ch.m. Touch of Land (FR) – Raveleen Rose (IRE) (Norwich) [2018/19 c–, h–: h26.5g h26.5mᶠ h24.5gᵖᵘ h24.4g³ h24.1d³ h23.1d² h27s* h23.1g Mar 27] sturdy mare: fair handicap hurdler: won at Sedgefield in March: pulled up only chase outing: stays 27f: acts on soft going: wears cheekpieces: front runner/races prominently: has joined Robert Walford. *Neil Mulholland* — **c– h106**

VERY FIRST TIME 7 b.g. Champs Elysees – Like A Virgin (IRE) (Iron Mask (USA)) [2018/19 c130, h–: c28.4g⁵ c27.3s h25.8g⁶ c24.5s⁴ c31.9v c23.4d⁶ Apr 6] sturdy gelding: winning hurdler: useful handicap chaser, well below form in 2018/19: stays 25f: acts on heavy going: in headgear last 3 starts: usually races prominently: has joined Dan Skelton: signs of temperament. *Tim Easterby* — **c103 h–**

VERYGOODVERYGOOD (FR) 8 b.g. Yeats (IRE) – Rose d'Or (IRE) (Polish Precedent (USA)) [2018/19 c–, h116§: h19.9g h18.7m⁴ Jul 22] fairly useful hurdler, well below form in 2018/19: well held only chase outing: stays 3m: acts on good to firm and heavy going: usually wears headgear: has worn tongue tie: unreliable. *Nigel Twiston-Davies* — **c– h– §**

VERY LIVE (FR) 10 b.g. Secret Singer (FR) – Iona Will (FR) (Kadalko (FR)) [2018/19 **c95 §** c95, h–: c23.5v c19.9d^{pu} c17s* c16d c15.5d^6 Mar 8] well-made gelding: maiden hurdler: **h–** modest handicap chaser: won at Plumpton in January: stays 2½m: acts on heavy going: wears headgear/tongue tie: unreliable. *Paul Webber*

VETONCALL (IRE) 7 b.g. Well Chosen – Miss Audacious (IRE) (Supreme Leader) **c–** [2018/19 h–: c16d h20.5g h20.5s Dec 17] off mark in Irish points at fourth attempt: no form **h–** under Rules. *Alan Jones*

VEXILLUM (IRE) 10 br.g. Mujadil (USA) – Common Cause (Polish Patriot (USA)) **c85 §** [2018/19 c–, h–: h21.7g^4 h21.7m^3 h19.2g^4 h18.5d h19.6g^3 h21.4m^6 c20.2g^3 c19.5m^3 Mar **h89 §** 29] stocky gelding: modest handicap hurdler/chaser: stays 2¾m: acts on firm going: wears headgear: has worn tongue tie: often off pace: hard to win with. *Neil Mulholland*

VIA DELLE VOLTE 4 b.f. Motivator – Castellina (USA) (Danzig Connection (USA)) **h109** [2018/19 h16.6g* h16.6g^2 h15.8d h15.7d^5 h16.8g^2 Apr 18] half-sister to 3 winning hurdlers, including modest pair Castle River (2m winner, by Irish River) and Blaise Hollow (2½m winner, by Woodman): fair maiden on Flat, stays 1½m: fair form over hurdles: won maiden at Doncaster in December. *Tom Lacey*

VIA VOLUPTA 9 b.m. Kayf Tara – Via Ferrata (FR) (Nikos) [2018/19 h23g Jun 2] has **h–** had breathing operation: fair form over hurdles: last in mares handicap only start since 2015/16: should stay further than 21f: acts on soft going: wears hood. *Michael Roberts*

VIBRATO VALTAT (FR) 10 gr.g. Voix du Nord (FR) – La Tosca Valtat (FR) (Dom Alco **c–** (FR)) [2018/19 c146, h–: c20g May 27] sturdy gelding: winning hurdler: very smart chaser **h–** at best, well held sole start in 2018/19: stays 3m: acts on good to firm and heavy going: has worn headgear: wears tongue tie. *Emma Lavelle*

VICE ET VERTU (FR) 10 b.g. Network (GER) – Duchesse du Cochet (FR) (Native **c126** Guile (USA)) [2018/19 c116, h–: c23.8g* c23.8g^2 c26d c23s^6 c24.2d^5 Mar 24] tall gelding: **h–** winning hurdler: fairly useful handicap chaser: won at Ffos Las early in season: stays 3m: acts on heavy going: wears headgear: tried in tongue tie. *Henry Daly*

VICENTE (FR) 10 b.g. Dom Alco (FR) – Ireland (FR) (Kadalko (FR)) [2018/19 c151x, **c141 x** h–: c27.3g^{pu} c28.4d^3 c32.6g^F Feb 23] tall gelding: winning hurdler: smart chaser: third in **h–** minor event at Taunton (9¾ lengths behind Royal Vacation) in January: stays 4m: acts on good to firm and heavy going: usually wears headgear: often let down by jumping. *Paul Nicholls*

VICENZO MIO (FR) 9 b.g. Corri Piano (FR) – Sweet Valrose (FR) (Cadoudal (FR)) **c106 §** [2018/19 c121, h111: h16s^3 c15.5s^6 c16.4s h16s^5 c19.7d^2 c16s^6 Apr 7] well-made gelding: **h106** fair handicap hurdler/maiden chaser: stays 2¾m: acts on heavy going: wears cheekpieces/ tongue tie: best treated with caution. *Chris Gordon*

VICONTE DU NOYER (FR) 10 gr.g. Martaline – Zouk Wood (USA) (Woodman **c141 §** (USA)) [2018/19 c139, h–: h22.8g c20g^2 c21g^3 c21.4m Jul 21] lengthy, rather sparely- **h–** made gelding: has had breathing operation: winning hurdler: useful handicap chaser nowadays: stays 27f: acts on soft and good to firm going: has worn headgear, including in 2018/19: wears tongue tie: unreliable. *Colin Tizzard*

VICTARION (IRE) 7 b.g. Scorpion (IRE) – Gaye Preskina (IRE) (Presenting) [2018/19 **c100** h103: h20s^3 h20g c23.6s^5 c25.2s^F h24.2d h21.7m* Mar 29] fair form over hurdles: won **h111** handicap at Fontwell in March: similar form over fences: stays 2¾m: acts on soft and good to firm going: in cheekpieces last 4 starts. *Philip Hobbs*

VICTORIA SAYS (IRE) 7 b.m. Shantou (USA) – Ballestra (IRE) (Alflora (IRE)) **h99** [2018/19 h95: h17s^4 h20.5v^{pu} h20v^5 h24.3m Apr 12] has had breathing operation: modest handicap hurdler: stays 23f: acts on heavy going: in tongue tie last 2 starts: usually races towards rear. *Stuart Crawford, Ireland*

VICTOR LEUDORUM (IRE) 12 b.g. Wareed (IRE) – Rock Garden (IRE) (Bigstone **c–** (IRE)) [2018/19 c23.8g h26.4m^5 c27.5g^{pu} c23.8m^{pu} h23g^{pu} Jul 26] big, strong gelding: **h–** fairly useful hurdler/chaser at best: no form in 2018/19 after missing previous season: has worn cheekpieces: wears tongue tie: usually races close up. *Steve Flook*

VICTORY ECHO (IRE) 6 b.g. Cloudings (IRE) – Serendipity (IRE) (Anshan) [2018/19 **h–** h24.1g Apr 11] off mark in Irish points at fourth attempt: tailed off in novice on hurdling debut. *Maurice Barnes*

VIENNA COURT (IRE) 4 b.f. Mahler – Gales Present (IRE) (Presenting) [2018/19   **b86** b16d² b16.7d Apr 26] third foal: dam, unraced, out of half-sister to Cheltenham Gold Cup winner Denman: fair form in bumpers: better effort when second in mares event at Chepstow in March. *Nigel Twiston-Davies*

VIENS CHERCHER (IRE) 8 b.g. Milan – La Zingarella (IRE) (Phardante (FR))   **c126** [2018/19 c124, h–: c21.2d⁶ c22.6g* Mar 30] workmanlike gelding: winning hurdler: fairly   **h–** useful handicap chaser: won at Stratford in March: stays 3m: acts on good to firm and heavy going: has worn cheekpieces, including in 2018/19. *Peter Bowen*

VIEUX LILLE (IRE) 9 b.g. Robin des Champs (FR) – Park Athlete (IRE) (Supreme   **c– x** Leader) [2018/19 c114x, h–: c23.4s c30gᵘʳ c24.2dᵖᵘ c25.7gᵖᵘ Apr 7] strong gelding: has had   **h–** breathing operation: winning hurdler: useful chaser at best, no form in 2018/19: has worn headgear, including in 2018/19: in tongue tie last 3 starts: often let down by jumping. *Jamie Snowden*

VIEUX LION ROUGE (FR) 10 ch.g. Sabiango (GER) – Indecise (FR) (Cyborg (FR))   **c145** [2018/19 c140, h–: c25.9s² c29.5sᵖᵘ c28.4gᵖᵘ c34.3g Apr 6] lengthy gelding: has had   **h–** breathing operation: winning hurdler: smart handicap chaser: a regular over the Grand National fences, second in Becher Chase (4½ lengths behind Walk In The Mill) in December: stays 3½m: acts on heavy going: usually wears headgear: tongue tied in 2018/19. *David Pipe*

VIEUX MORVAN (FR) 10 bl.g. Voix du Nord (FR) – Moskoville (FR) (Kadalko (FR))   **c140** [2018/19 c143, h–: h22.4m c22.5dᵇᵈ c24sᵖᵘ c24.5g² c21g c24d Mar 10] winning hurdler in   **h–** France for G. Cherel: useful handicap chaser: second in Paddy Power Chase at Leopardstown (6½ lengths behind Auvergnat) in December: stays 3m: acts on heavy going: usually wears headgear: usually leads. *Joseph Patrick O'Brien, Ireland*

VIF ARGENT (FR) 10 b.g. Dom Alco (FR) – Formosa (FR) (Royal Charter (FR))   **c85** [2018/19 h16g³ c16.5g⁴ c20.3g³ c23m c20.3g³ h20g³ Oct 11] rather leggy gelding: poor   **h73** handicap hurdler: modest handicap chaser: stays 2¾m: acts on heavy going: has worn headgear, including last 4 starts: has worn tongue tie, including in 2018/19: usually races nearer last than first. *Dave Roberts*

VIKEKHAL (FR) 10 b.g. Khalkevi (IRE) – Gesse Parade (FR) (Dress Parade) [2018/19   **c104** c122, h–: c16m c16.5g³ c15.7g⁵ c23g Jul 4] tall gelding: winning hurdler: fair handicap   **h–** chaser nowadays: stays 25f, effective at much shorter: acts on good to firm and heavy going: has worn headgear: wears tongue tie: usually races close up. *Steve Flook*

VIKING HOARD (IRE) 5 b.g. Vale of York (IRE) – Tibouchina (IRE) (Daylami (IRE))   **h108 §** [2018/19 h17.1v h16g h20m² h22g³ h20m* h16.6gᵖᵘ h16.8m⁴ h21.5gᵖᵘ h20d h16g⁵ Mar 29] half-brother to a winning hurdler in Australia by Aussie Rules: fairly useful on Flat, stays 1¼m: fair handicap hurdler: won at Killarney (conditionals) in July: stays 2¾m: acts on good to firm going: usually wears cheekpieces: usually races off pace: temperamental. *Charles Byrnes, Ireland*

VIKING RUBY 6 ch.m. Sulamani (IRE) – Viking Torch (Loup Sauvage (USA)) [2018/19   **h–** b57: b16.5d h21.7vᵖᵘ Mar 16] little show in bumpers/novice hurdle. *Neil Mulholland*   **b–**

VILLAGE VIC (IRE) 12 b.g. Old Vic – Etoile Margot (FR) (Garde Royale) [2018/19 c–,   **c–** h–: c23.4d⁵ Mar 22] rather sparely-made gelding: has had breathing operation: winning   **h–** hurdler: very smart chaser at best, retains little ability: usually front runner/races prominently. *Philip Hobbs*

VILLIERSDORP 4 b.f. Lucarno (USA) – Ballinargh Girl (IRE) (Footstepsinthesand)   **h–** [2018/19 b14g b14.2s⁵ h15.6gᵖᵘ Jan 1] first foal: dam 5f winner: little impact in bumpers: **b59** pulled up in juvenile on hurdling debut: wears hood. *Iain Jardine*

VINCENT'S FOREVER 6 b.g. Pour Moi (IRE) – Glen Rosie (IRE) (Mujtahid (USA))   **h–** [2018/19 h–: h15.5gᵖᵘ h15.7gᵖᵘ Mar 6] sturdy gelding: has had breathing operation: fair on Flat, stays 1½m: maiden hurdler, no form since 2016/17: often in headgear: usually in tongue tie. *Sophie Leech*

VINCITORE (FR) 13 b.g. Starborough – Viva Vodka (FR) (Crystal Glitters (USA))   **c–** [2018/19 c95, h–: c32.5g May 4] leggy gelding: point winner: winning hurdler: fairly   **h–** useful chaser at best, retains little ability: has worn headgear: wears tongue tie. *Miss Sarah Rippon*

VINEGAR HILL 10 b.g. Kayf Tara – Broughton Melody (Alhijaz) [2018/19 c122, h85:   **c106 x** h23.3g³ c25g h26gᵖᵘ Apr 10] sturdy gelding: fair handicap hurdler: similar form over   **h111** fences: stays 3m: acts on heavy going: tried in visor: wears tongue tie: usually front runner/ races prominently: often let down by jumping. *Stuart Edmunds*

Moremoneythan's "Vinndication"

VINNDICATION (IRE) 6 b.g. Vinnie Roe (IRE) – Pawnee Trail (IRE) (Taipan (IRE)) **c148 p**
[2018/19 h146p, b96: c20s* c21s* c20s³ c19.8d⁵ Mar 14] lengthy gelding: bumper winner: **h–**
smart form over hurdles, won all 3 starts in 2017/18: similar form over fences: won novice
at Carlisle (by 2 lengths from Uncle Alastair) in November and Noel Novices' Chase at
Ascot (by 1½ lengths from Jerrysback) in December: third in Scilly Isles Novices' Chase
at Sandown (3¼ lengths behind Defi du Seuil): will stay at least 3m: acts on heavy going:
remains with potential as a chaser. *Kim Bailey*

VINNIE LEWIS (IRE) 8 b.g. Vinnie Roe (IRE) – Ballyann Lewis (IRE) (Sir Harry **c134**
Lewis (USA)) [2018/19 c134, h–: h24g³ h24g* h24.3v² h23.6s⁶ c24.2s² Mar 9] fairly **h116**
useful hurdler: won novice at Southwell in October: useful form over fences: second in
handicap at Sandown (3½ lengths behind Commodore) in March: stays 3½m: acts on
heavy going: front runner/races prominently. *Harry Whittington*

VINNIE RED (IRE) 10 ch.g. Vinnie Roe (IRE) – Conzara (IRE) (Mandalus) [2018/19 **c111 ?**
c23s⁴ c20g³ c23.9mᵖᵘ c20.3d⁶ c23.8dᵖᵘ c19.9d⁴ Mar 13] rangy gelding: fairly useful **h–**
hurdler/chaser at best, largely out of sorts over fences in 2018/19: left Fergal O'Brien after
third start: stays 21f: acts on good to soft going: tried in cheekpieces: has worn tongue tie.
Lady Susan Brooke

VINNIE ROUGE (IRE) 5 b.g. Vinnie Roe (IRE) – Bewildered (IRE) (Prince Sabo) **h–**
[2018/19 b17.7s h15.3g h17.7s h16.3g h16.8sᵖᵘ Apr 16] no form in bumper/over hurdles. **b–**
Neil Mulholland

VINNIE'S ICON (IRE) 5 b.m. Vinnie Roe (IRE) – Iconic Events (IRE) (Milan) **b–**
[2018/19 b16.5d⁶ Feb 28] £800 4-y-o: first foal: dam unraced half-sister to fairly useful
hurdler/smart chaser (stayed 25f) Shining Gale: placed on first of 2 starts in point bumpers:
tailed off in bumper at Taunton. *Carroll Gray*

VINNIE THE HODDIE (IRE) 5 b.g. Vinnie Roe (IRE) – Blackwater Babe (IRE) **h125**
(Arctic Lord) [2018/19 h16d³ h20m* h20.7s⁶ h20g h16.6g² h16.3d⁵ Mar 23] €45,000
3-y-o, resold €42,000 3-y-o: brother to useful hurdler/smart chaser Royal Caviar (2m-2¼m
winner) and a winning pointer, and half-brother to fairly useful hurdler/useful chaser
Above Board (19f-3m winner, by Mahler) and a winning pointer by Snurge: dam unraced:
placed in bumpers: fairly useful form over hurdles: won maiden at Gowran in October:
second in novice at Doncaster in February: left Joseph Patrick O'Brien after fourth start:
stays 2½m: acts on good to firm and good to soft going: usually races close up.
Oliver Sherwood

VINO GRIEGO (FR) 14 b.g. Kahyasi – Vie de Reine (FR) (Mansonnien (FR)) [2018/19 **c– §**
c119§, h–: c24.2v c25.6dᵖᵘ Nov 20] tall gelding: winning hurdler: smart chaser at best, no **h–**
form in 2018/19: stays 25f: acts on heavy going: has worn headgear: tried in tongue tie:
often let down by attitude. *Gary Moore*

VINO'S CHOICE (IRE) 7 b.g. Kalanisi (IRE) – Ard's Pet (IRE) (Among Men (USA)) **c89**
[2018/19 h94, b96: h16.2g⁵ c15.6m⁴ c20.1g c16g³ h15.6g³ Nov 7] modest form over **h86**
hurdles/fences: should stay 2½m: best form on good going: in hood last 2 starts: wears
tongue tie: usually races freely. *Lucinda Russell*

VINTAGE CLOUDS (IRE) 9 gr.g. Cloudings (IRE) – Rare Vintage (IRE) (Germany **c148 x**
(USA)) [2018/19 h143, h–: c25.6g* c29.5sᵖᵘ c25s² c34.3g^F c31.8m⁶ Apr 13] compact **h–**
gelding: has had breathing operation: winning hurdler: smart handicap chaser: won at
Haydock (by ½ length from Takingrisks) in November: second in Ultima Handicap Chase
at Cheltenham (1¼ lengths behind Beware The Bear) in March: stays 4m: acts on heavy
going: usually leads: often let down by jumping. *Sue Smith*

VINTAGE GLEN (IRE) 7 b.g. Ask – Rare Vintage (IRE) (Germany (USA)) [2018/19 **h–**
b69: h20.5v h16d h16d h19.7g Feb 19] well held in bumpers/over hurdles. *Rose Dobbin*

VIOGNIER 7 ch.m. Black Sam Bellamy (IRE) – Noun de La Thinte (FR) (Oblat (FR)) **h72**
[2018/19 h91, b74: h16.7m⁶ h20g⁵ Jul 26] maiden hurdler, poor form in 2018/19: stays
2½m: acts on heavy going: has worn tongue tie: has joined Stephen Michael Hanlon.
Harry Whittington

VIRAK (FR) 10 b.g. Bernebeau (FR) – Nosika d'Airy (FR) (Oblat (FR)) [2018/19 c126, **c130**
h–: c23.8m* c23.8m* Apr 23] sturdy gelding: won all 3 starts in points: winning hurdler: **h–**
fairly useful hunter chaser nowadays: won at Ascot in March and Ludlow (match) in April:
stays 3m: acts on good to firm and heavy going: has worn cheekpieces: tried in tongue tie.
Mrs Rose Loxton

VIRGILIO (FR) 10 b.g. Denham Red (FR) – Liesse de Marbeuf (FR) (Cyborg (FR)) **c155**
[2018/19 c146, h–: c25g* c26.1m* c24.2g³ c27.3gᵖᵘ Nov 17] sturdy gelding: won two races: has had **h–**
breathing operation: winning hurdler: smart handicap chaser: won at Aintree (by length
from Winter Lion) in May and Summer Cup at Uttoxeter (by 3¾ lengths from Henllan
Harri) in July: third in Charlie Hall Chase at Wetherby (5 lengths behind Definitly Red) in
November: stays 3¼m: acts on good to firm and heavy going: wears tongue tie. *Dan Skelton*

VIRGINIA CHICK (FR) 7 b.g. Nickname (FR) – Sweet Jaune (FR) (Le Nain Jaune **h123**
(FR)) [2018/19 h119: h24.2s⁴ h23.6s* h23.4s Feb 2] medium-sized gelding: fairly useful
handicap hurdler: won at Chepstow in December: stays 3m: acts on heavy going: tried in
headgear: has worn tongue tie: usually races towards rear. *Evan Williams*

VIRNON 8 b.g. Virtual – Freedom Song (Singspiel (IRE)) [2018/19 h92, h–: h15.8g **c112**
c20.3s* c19.3s² c19.2dᵖᵘ Jan 17] lengthy gelding: winning hurdler: fair handicap chaser: **h–**
won at Southwell in December: stays 2½m: acts on heavy going. *Sarah Humphrey*

VISAGE BLANC 6 b.m. Champs Elysees – Russian Empress (IRE) (Trans Island) **h94**
[2018/19 h81: h20.3g² h20.6g h19.9g⁵ h22m h18.7gᵖᵘ Sep 4] has had breathing operation:
modest maiden hurdler: stays 2½m: acts on soft going: in blinkers last 2 starts: wears
tongue tie: front runner/races prominently. *Graeme McPherson*

VISANDI (FR) 7 b.g. Azamour (IRE) – Vadaza (FR) (Zafonic (USA)) [2018/19 h20m Jun **h–**
21] maiden hurdler, well beaten sole start in 2018/19: should be suited by 2¼m+: tried in
tongue tie. *Jonjo O'Neill*

VIS A VIS 5 b.g. Dansili – Pretty Face (Rainbow Quest (USA)) [2018/19 h19.3g² h19.8s² **h117 p**
Mar 7] half-brother to fairly useful hurdler/useful chaser Fixed Rate (2m-2¾m winner, by
Oasis Dream): useful on Flat, stays 2¼m: fairly useful form when runner-up both starts
over hurdles: remains with potential. *Neil Mulholland*

VISCOUNT WILSON 4 b.g. Lethal Force (IRE) – Highland Starlight (USA) (Dixieland **h98**
Band (USA)) [2018/19 h16m⁴ h16.5g h16g h16v h19s h16d h16g² h16s² h16d h16.2gᵖᵘ

Apr 25] fair maiden on Flat, stays 1½m: modest maiden hurdler: unproven beyond 2m: acts on soft going: wears headgear/tongue tie. *Gordon Elliott, Ireland*

VISERION 7 ch.g. Tamayuz – Frivolity (Pivotal) [2018/19 h121: h16.7g h19.9g h20.9d h19.7d h23d^pu h17m Apr 20] has had breathing operation: fairly useful hurdler at best, no form in 2018/19: wears headgear. *Donald McCain* **h–**

VISIOMAN (FR) 6 b.g. Vision d'Etat (FR) – Loumie (FR) (Loup Solitaire (USA)) [2018/19 h16s² h16.5g*⁴ h16g² h16g³ h16.4g h20.2g⁵ Dec 28] good-topped gelding: half-brother to 3 winners, including fairly useful hurdler/useful chaser Nick Lost (21f-3m winner, by Nickname) and fairly useful French hurdler/chaser Policy Jumper (17f-21f winner, by Poliglote): dam (c13⅓/h132), French 15f-2½m hurdle/chase winner, also 15f winner on Flat: fair maiden hurdler: first past post in novice at Clonmel in May but later disqualified due to banned substance: stays 2½m: acts on soft going: usually races close up. *Henry de Bromhead, Ireland* **h112**

VISION CLEAR (GER) 4 b.g. Soldier Hollow – Vive Madame (GER) (Big Shuffle (USA)) [2018/19 h16.3d⁵ h15.9d² h15.9g^ur Apr 7] sturdy gelding: half-brother to a winning jumper in Slovakia by Paolini: fairly useful on Flat, stays 1½m: fair form over hurdles: best effort when second in maiden at Plumpton in March. *Gary Moore* **h112**

VISION DES FLOS (FR) 6 b.g. Balko (FR) – Marie Royale (FR) (Turgeon (USA)) [2018/19 h146: c20.9d^ur h20g² h16.4d³ h16.8s⁵ h16s² h15.3g³ h19.2d* h21s Mar 13] good sort: has had breathing operations: smart hurdler: won National Spirit Hurdle at Fontwell (by 1½ lengths from If The Cap Fits) in February: better than result when 7½ lengths sixth to Unowhatimeanharry in Champion Stayers' Hurdle at Punchestown shortly after end of British season, every chance when all but coming down last: stumbled and unseated sixth in novice at Ffos Las on chasing debut: stays 3m: acts on heavy going: wears tongue tie. *Colin Tizzard* **c– p h148**

VISION D'HONNEUR (FR) 5 b.g. Vision d'Etat (FR) – Hembra (FR) (Croco Rouge (IRE)) [2018/19 h16g⁴ h16d* h16g³ h16.4s Mar 12] tall gelding: chasing type: sixth foal: half-brother to useful hurdler/chaser Le Martalin (2m/17f winner, by Martaline), stayed 23f: dam French 1¼m winner: won 15f event on Flat in France for R. Collet: useful form over hurdles: won maiden at Punchestown in January: third in Chanelle Pharma at Leopardstown (6 lengths behind Klassical Dream) following month: held in second when fell last in minor event won by Elimay at Punchestown shortly after end of British season: should stay beyond 2m: in tongue tie last 2 starts. *Gordon Elliott, Ireland* **h137**

VISION DU PUY (FR) 4 b.f. Vision d'Etat (FR) – Fontaine Guerard (FR) (Homme de Loi (IRE)) [2018/19 h17.9g* h16.2d* Apr 26] half-sister to several winners, including fairly useful French 2¼m hurdle winner Font Froide (by Trempolino): dam French 10.5f winner: fairly useful form over hurdles: won both starts, newcomers race at Auteuil in October (for D. Bressou) and mares novice at Perth in April: remains open to progress. *Dan Skelton* **h127 p**

VIVACCIO (FR) 10 b.g. Antarctique (IRE) – Cybelle (FR) (Saint Cyrien (FR)) [2018/19 c115, h–: c16g⁴ c20d^pu c19.9d³ c19.2v² c19.9d* c20.3d⁶ Apr 26] sturdy gelding: winning hurdler: fair handicap chaser: won at Huntingdon in March: stays 2½m: acts on heavy going: tried in headgear: often let down by jumping. *Venetia Williams* **c102 x h–**

VIVA LA VEGA 5 b.m. Sulamani (IRE) – Lady de La Vega (FR) (Kizitca (FR)) [2018/19 h15.8g h16d h15.8d^F h15.5d h15.8v Mar 16] first foal: dam (c112/h98), 3m chase winner, half-sister to useful chaser (stayed 21f) Nadiya de La Vega: no form over hurdles. *Tom Gretton* **h–**

VIVALDI COLLONGES (FR) 10 b.g. Dom Alco (FR) – Diane Collonges (FR) (El Badr) [2018/19 c123+, h–: c25.8g³ c27.5d^pu Jun 8] sturdy gelding: winning hurdler: smart chaser at best, disappointing both starts in hunters in 2018/19: won twice in points later in season: stays 25f: acts on heavy going: in headgear last 3 starts: wears tongue tie. *Paul Nicholls* **c83 h–**

VIVANT 6 gr.m. Shirocco (GER) – Sisella (IRE) (Bob Back (USA)) [2018/19 h–: h20g* h20g³ h19.9g³ h23d* h21.7g* h20.1g* h24.3m^pu Apr 12] has had breathing operation: fairly useful hurdler: won maiden at Worcester in June, and handicaps at same course in August then Fontwell (mares) and Hexham in September: stays 23f: acts on good to soft going: has worn headgear, including last 3 starts: tried in tongue tie: usually leads. *Tom Lacey* **h129**

VIVA RAFA (IRE) 9 b.g. Scorpion (IRE) – Back To Stay (IRE) (Supreme Leader) [2018/19 c107, h–: c20.3g^F c20g^pu Jul 10] maiden hurdler: fair form over fences: stays 21f: acts on heavy going: has worn hood/tongue tie: often let down by jumping. *Richard Phillips* **c103 x h–**

VIVAS (FR) 8 b.g. Davidoff (GER) – Lavircas (FR) (Lavirco (GER)) [2018/19 h123: **c131** h19g⁴ c19.5s* c19.7m* c20v c19.1m* c20.5g c20.5s⁵ c21m³ c19.9m Apr 20] sturdy **h118** gelding: fairly useful handicap hurdler: useful handicap chaser: won novice events at Fontwell and Plumpton in October, and Doncaster (by 8 lengths from Dentley de Mee) in December: stays 21f: acts on soft and good to firm going: wears cheekpieces/tongue tie. *Charlie Longsdon*

VIVA VITTORIA (IRE) 5 b.m. Stowaway – La Fisarmonica (IRE) (Accordion) **h114** [2018/19 h84: h19.5s h20.5s² h21s² h20.6g* h22.8d² Mar 20] lengthy, rather unfurnished mare: fair form over hurdles: won mares handicap at Market Rasen in February: stays 23f: acts on soft going: usually travels strongly held up. *Emma Lavelle*

VIVE LE ROI (IRE) 8 b.g. Robin des Pres (FR) – Cappard View (IRE) (Rudimentary **h133** (USA)) [2018/19 h104: h16m h19.6g⁵ h15.8m³ h15.8s² h23.1g² h18.7m* h22g* h21g² h24.2s* h24dᵖᵘ h19.2d⁵ h25.8v² h24.7g Apr 6] useful-looking gelding: useful handicap hurdler: won at Stratford (conditionals seller) in September and October, and Newbury (by ½ length from Rockpoint) in November: stays 3¼m: acts on good to firm and heavy going: front runner. *Tony Carroll*

VIVRE POUR VIVRE (IRE) 6 b.g. Pour Moi (IRE) – Miss Quality (USA) (Elusive **h–** Quality (USA)) [2018/19 h21.9g⁶ Apr 21] fairly useful on Flat, stays 1¼m: tailed off in maiden on hurdling debut. *Christian Williams*

VLANNON 4 b.g. Captain Gerrard (IRE) – Attlongglast (Groom Dancer (USA)) [2018/19 **h112** h17.7m² h16m⁴ h17.7dᵖᵘ h16.3s⁴ h16g* h15.7d⁴ Jan 19] angular gelding: half-brother to very smart hurdler Mr Adjudicator (2m-2½m winner, by Camacho): modest maiden on Flat: fair form over hurdles: won juvenile at Kempton in January: unproven beyond 2m: acts on good to firm going: in visor last 4 starts. *Michael Madgwick*

VOCAL HEIR (IRE) 7 b.m. Vocalised (USA) – Heir Today (IRE) (Princely Heir (IRE)) **h85** [2018/19 h16m h16g⁵ h16g⁴ h16m h16.5s h16.3g³ h15.7g⁶ Mar 4] half-sister to fairly useful 2m hurdle winner Punch Bag (by Teofilo): modest maiden hurdler: left Stephen Michael Hanlon after sixth start: unproven beyond 2m: acts on soft going: in cheekpieces last 5 starts: tried in tongue tie. *Olly Murphy*

VOCALISER (IRE) 7 b.g. Vocalised (USA) – Bring Back Matron (IRE) (Rock of **c109** Gibraltar (IRE)) [2018/19 c119, h–: h16.4g h18.9v⁶ c16.4s⁶ c20d⁴ c19.9gᵖᵘ c16.2g⁵ c17.4g⁵ **h86** Apr 13] good-topped gelding: modest maiden hurdler: fair handicap chaser: stays 2¼m: acts on soft going: has worn headgear: tried in tongue tie. *Robin Dickin*

VODKA ALL THE WAY (IRE) 7 b.g. Oscar (IRE) – Fully Focused (IRE) (Rudimentary **c–** (USA)) [2018/19 h119: h26.5v⁶ c23.6vᵘʳ c23.4s c24.2v Mar 18] big, workmanlike gelding: **h–** fairly useful form over hurdles: disappointing in 2018/19, mainly over fences: tried in cheekpieces. *Philip Hobbs*

VOICE CONTROL (IRE) 7 gr.g. Dalakhani (IRE) – Scottish Stage (IRE) (Selkirk **h– §** (USA)) [2018/19 h16dʳʳ Jan 15] fair on Flat, stays 2m: fairly useful form when runner-up on hurdling debut in 2016/17: refused to race sole start in sphere since: one to treat with caution. *Laura Mongan*

VOIE DANS VOIE (FR) 6 br.g. Coastal Path – Peggy Pierji (FR) (Cadoudal (FR)) **c120 §** [2018/19 h120: c24.2g⁵ c22.9v⁴ c24dᶠ c24d³ c23g² c22.4d Mar 22] good-topped gelding: **h–** fairly useful maiden hurdler: similar form over fences: second in novice handicap at Taunton in February: stays 3m: acts on heavy going: in visor last 4 starts: temperamental. *Alan King*

VOILA ERIC 7 b.g. Bollin Eric – Et Voila (Alflora (IRE)) [2018/19 b15.7g³ b15.8g **h89** h23.3s⁵ h20.6g⁶ h23.1s Mar 18] runner-up in Irish maiden point: fair form in bumpers: **b87** third in maiden at Southwell: modest form over hurdles: should stay 3m. *Michael Scudamore*

VOIX D'EAU (FR) 9 b.g. Voix du Nord (FR) – Eau de Chesne (FR) (R B Chesne) **c141** [2018/19 c140, h–: c20.3g² c19.4g³ c20g³ c20m* c20s³ c20.3g* c19.9g c21.1s c20.3g⁵ **h–** c20.6d c20.5mᵘʳ Apr 12] big, lengthy gelding: winning hurdler: useful handicap chaser: won at Worcester in July and Southwell in August: left Harry Fry after sixth start: stays 21f: acts on good to firm and good to soft going: wears cheekpieces/tongue tie. *Lucinda Russell*

VOIX DU REVE (FR) 7 br.g. Voix du Nord (FR) – Pommbelle (FR) (Apple Tree **c156 +** (FR)) [2018/19 h129: h20m* h20m* h16s h16s³ c18.2d* c16.2g* c17g³ c17gᶠ **h145** c19.8dᵘʳ c20g* Apr 21]

Voix du Reve's third appearance at the Cheltenham Festival ended in pretty much the same way as his first, departing late on when looking to hold good prospects of at the very least reaching a place. He was making headway to challenge, travelling

Ryanair Gold Cup Novices' Chase, Fairyhouse—Voix du Reve gains consolation for his Cheltenham spill with a convincing victory over stable-companion Real Steel

best, in 2016 when falling at the last in the Fred Winter Juvenile Handicap and, in the latest season, he had yet to be asked for his effort when unseating Ruby Walsh at the third last (having nearly unseated him with a bad mistake at the first!) in the Golden Miller Novices' Chase (branded as the JLT). Voix du Reve's owners endured a miserable Cheltenham, as outlined in the essay on Bellshill, but at least Voix du Reve went on to provide consolation on his next outing for his unfortunate exit when winning the Grade 1 Ryanair Gold Cup at Fairyhouse's big Easter meeting.

Voix du Reve was shaded for favouritism in the Ryanair by his stablemate Real Steel who had finished sixth in the Golden Miller after stumbling badly at the seventh fence; the Golden Miller third Mengli Khan, who had a harder race at Cheltenham than either of the Mullins pair, was third favourite in the five-runner line-up at Fairyhouse. In a truly-run race, Voix du Reve was more accurate at his fences and, after travelling strongly and asserting between the last two, he went on to beat Real Steel by five and a half lengths, well on top at the finish with the pair clear. Mengli Khan came home last of four finishers—Cubomania fell fatally four out—after making the running, already weakening when bumped at the third last.

Voix du Reve's performance suggested he would have finished third at worst in the Golden Miller behind Defi du Seuil whom he met again in the Ryanair Novices' Chase, the Grade 1 two-miler for novices at the Punchestown Festival shortly after the end of the British season. Defi du Seuil finished ahead of Voix du Reve over the shorter trip at Punchestown, as did the two Closutton stable companions who accompanied Voix du Reve to post, the exciting Chacun Pour Soi, who was stepping up in class, and the Arkle Trophy winner Duc des Genievres. Voix du Reve failed to repeat his Ryanair Gold Cup effort, losing his place after a mistake at the third before being left behind from three out (eventually beaten nearly thirty lengths by the winner Chacun Pour Soi), the distance he was beaten when fourth of five finishers suggesting that a busy campaign might finally have caught up with him. Real Steel, incidentally, did his bit to uphold the Fairyhouse form when shouldering 11-10 to victory in the EMS Copiers Novices' Handicap Chase the day after Voix du Reve had run in the Ryanair Novices' Chase.

Voix du Reve had to be nursed back after a long absence following his juvenile season and he was generally below his best, following a twenty-month layoff, in the 2017/18 season, though he caught the eye on more than one occasion, including in the Coral Cup at the Cheltenham Festival where he was prominent for much of the race and right in contention on the home turn, shaping much better than his final position of fourteenth. Kept on the go over the summer, Voix du Reve picked up minor conditions events over hurdles at Killarney in May and Bellewstown in July, scoring easily both times, and he finished a good third in the valuable Listowel Handicap Hurdle in September (after a below-form effort in the

Galway Hurdle). Sent over fences at the start of October, Voix du Reve made an encouraging start with a comfortable win in a maiden chase at Galway and followed up in the Grade 2 Craddockstown Novices' Chase at Punchestown in November, giving a by now typical free-wheeling performance out in front and finding extra when challenged by Hardline and Cadmium, winning by seven lengths from the first-named. Voix du Reve showed similar form when third to Le Richebourg and Us And Them in the Grade 1 Racing Post Novices' Chase at Leopardstown's Christmas meeting, a performance he seemed set to improve upon when departing at the final fence in the Arkle over the same course on Dublin Racing Festival weekend. Voix du Reve, who again tried to make all, wasn't travelling anywhere near so well as the eventual winner Le Richebourg when he fell, but he would certainly have been involved in the finish (Us And Them was left in second by his fall).

		Valanour (b 1992)	Lomond / Vearia
	Voix du Nord (FR) (b 2001)	Dame Edith (b 1995)	Top Ville / Girl of France
Voix du Reve (FR) (br.g. 2012)		Apple Tree (ch 1989)	Bikala / Pomme Rose
	Pommbelle (FR) (b 2003)	Belle Frimousse (b 1989)	Pietru / Broukalu

The tough Voix du Reve, a neat gelding in appearance, is by Voix du Nord whose last foals (including ill-fated Champion Hurdle winner Espoir d'Allen) arrived in 2014. Among others to represent Voix du Nord in the latest season were Kemboy and Defi du Seuil who also have essays in this edition. Voix du Reve's dam Pommbelle was a winner in minor company over eleven furlongs on the Flat in France and has one other winner, the French hurdle winner at up to nineteen furlongs Pommboy (by Adieu). Voix du Reve stays two and a half miles (and is fully effective at two). He acts on good to firm going and has form on heavy. He wears a hood and is a strong traveller, usually making the running or racing close up. Although he has sometimes been let down by his jumping, he has nonetheless shown very smart form and remains open to further improvement over fences. *W. P. Mullins, Ireland*

VOLAVICIOUS 7 ch.m. Volochine (IRE) – Mrs Tweedy (IRE) (Publisher (USA)) **h–**
[2018/19 h16g Apr 26] fourth foal: dam, no form, half-sister to fairly useful cross-country chaser (stays 25f) Mtada Supreme: tailed off in maiden hurdle. *Sarah Robinson*

VOLCANIC (FR) 10 br.g. Al Namix (FR) – Queen of Rock (FR) (Video Rock (FR)) **c–**
[2018/19 c–, h116: h24.3g h22.1g² h22.1m* h22.1gF h25.4s⁶ h20.9m Sep 19] leggy **h124**
gelding: has had breathing operation: fairly useful handicap hurdler: won at Cartmel in July: winning chaser: stays easy 27f: acts on good to firm and heavy going: has worn headgear, including last 5 starts: wears tongue tie: races prominently. *Donald McCain*

VOLCANO (FR) 5 gr.g. Martaline – Lyli Rose (FR) (Lyphard's Wish (FR)) [2018/19 **h118**
b101: h16d³ h20v³ h23.3s² h22.8s⁵ h23.4g³ h19.3m² h21.9g² Apr 21] smallish gelding: bumper winner: fairly useful maiden hurdler, placed 6 of 7 starts: will be suited by 3m+: acts on good to firm and heavy going: tried in hood: has joined Sheila Lewis. *Nigel Twiston-Davies*

VOLCAN SURPRISE (FR) 11 b.g. Dom Alco (FR) – Invitee Surprise (FR) (April **c73**
Night (FR)) [2018/19 c–, h–: h24gᵖᵘ h24g h23.4g⁵ c23.9m⁶ Jun 22] neat gelding: multiple **h–**
point winner: fair maiden hurdler/chaser at best, little form in 2018/19: wears headgear. *Caroline Fryer*

VOL NOIR DE KERSER (FR) 10 b.g. Policy Maker (IRE) – Nuit de Kerser (FR) **c121**
(Dounba (FR)) [2018/19 c25.8s² c25.8s* c22.9gF c26.8s⁴ c30.2gᵘʳ c22.4s* Apr 6] rather leggy gelding: fairly useful cross-country chaser: won at Vittel in July and Nancy in April: stays 3¾m: acts on heavy going: has worn hood/tongue tie. *Patrice Quinton, France*

VOLPONE JELOIS (FR) 6 gr.g. Vol de Nuit – Jenne Jelois (FR) (My Risk (FR)) **h118**
[2018/19 h114: h15.3m³ h15.3fF² h16v⁶ h16.3d² h20.7d⁶ h19g⁶ Apr 25] fairly useful handicap hurdler: second at Newbury in January: left Paul Nicholls after second start: stays 19f: acts on firm and soft going: has worn cheekpieces, including in 2018/19. *Chris Gordon*

VOLT FACE (FR) 10 ch.g. Kapgarde (FR) – Jourenuit (FR) (Chamberlin (FR)) [2018/19 c119, h112: h19.6g h23.4v^5 c21.2d^2 c21.4d^2 c23g^4 c20s^2 c21m^5 Mar 31] rather leggy gelding: has had breathing operation: winning hurdler: fairly useful maiden chaser: runner-up 3 times in 2018/19: stays 3m: acts on good to firm and heavy going: wears headgear/tongue tie. *Paul Webber* **c115 h80**

VOLTURNUS 5 b.g. Azamour (IRE) – Daffydowndilly (Oasis Dream) [2018/19 h16g h23g^6 Sep 11] fair on Flat, stays 2m: well held in 2 maiden hurdles: wears tongue tie: has joined Oliver Sherwood. *Shaun Lycett* **h72**

VOLUNTEER 6 b.g. Aqlaam – Blaenavon (Cadeaux Genereux) [2018/19 b13.7d^2 b15.8d Mar 3] smallish gelding: sixth foal: half-brother to 3 winners, including useful hurdler Discoteca (2m-2½m winner, by Nayef) and fair hurdler Itsnowcato (2m winner, by Notnowcato): dam maiden on Flat (stayed 1¼m): fair form in bumpers: better effort when second at Huntingdon in January. *Shaun Keightley* **b88**

VOLVALIEN (FR) 10 b.g. Network (GER) – Josvalie (FR) (Panoramic) [2018/19 c116, h–: c16g^6 c17.4g* c16.4m^3 Aug 30] maiden hurdler: fairly useful handicap chaser: won at Bangor in August: stayed 2½m: acted on soft and good to firm going: sometimes in headgear, including all starts in 2018/19: wore tongue tie: front runner/raced prominently: dead. *Brian Ellison* **c120 h–**

VOODOO DOLL (IRE) 6 b.g. Getaway (GER) – Voodoo Magic (GER) (Platini (GER)) [2018/19 h103: h15.8g^{ur} h19.6g* h20g* h20m* h20.6m^3 h21.6g^3 h21.6g h15.8g^2 h21g^2 h16.4g^3 h16.3s h20.5d^5 h19g^3 h21.2g^3 h19.5d Mar 20] stocky gelding: fairly useful handicap hurdler: completed hat-trick at Bangor, Worcester and Ffos Las in June/July: stays 21f: acts on soft and good to firm going: usually wears cheekpieces. *Evan Williams* **h118**

VOSNE ROMANEE 8 ch.g. Arakan (USA) – Vento Del Oreno (FR) (Lando (GER)) [2018/19 c138, h114: c17m* c17m* c17.1m^2 c15.9d^{pu} c16.8m* c16.5m^2 c15.5g^4 Apr 27] smallish gelding: winning hurdler: smart handicap chaser: won at Stratford (twice) in July and listed event at Ascot (by 1¼ lengths from Champagne At Tara) in November: stays 2¼m: acts on soft and good to firm going: wears headgear/tongue tie: usually races off pace. *Dr Richard Newland* **c149 h–**

VOUVRAY (FR) 8 b.g. Califet (FR) – Cartzagrouas (FR) (Esprit du Nord (USA)) [2018/19 c–, h–: h25.5d^{pu} c24g^6 c29.2g^{pu} c26.2g^{pu} Apr 26] Irish point winner: no form under Rules: in cheekpieces last 2 starts. *Christian Williams* **c– h–**

VUE CAVALIERE (FR) 5 b.m. Spirit One (FR) – Grande Cavale (FR) (Ballingarry (IRE)) [2018/19 h16.9g^5 h18.4d^6 h18.9g^3 c17.9g^5 h18.5d h21.7m h19.8g^3 Apr 14] compact mare: half-sister to French 2¼m/19f chase winner Grandgarde (by Al Namix): dam, French 17f chase winner, closely related to fairly useful hurdler/useful chaser (stays 3m) Walt: made frame only Flat outing: fair handicap hurdler: fifth of 7 in 4-y-o event at Machecoul on chasing debut: left A. Lefeuvre after fourth start: stays 2¼m: acts on heavy going: in hood last 3 starts. *Suzy Smith* **c100 h102**

VYTA DU ROC (FR) 10 gr.g. Lion Noir – Dolce Vyta (FR) (Grand Tresor (FR)) [2018/19 c146, h136: c24d^{pu} c29.5s^{pu} c30.2s c28.8g^{pu} Apr 27] good-topped gelding: winning hurdler: useful handicap chaser: out of form in 2018/19: has worn headgear: tried in tongue tie. *Nicky Henderson* **c– h–**

W

WADIYATINK NOW (IRE) 6 b.m. Shantou (USA) – Simply Deep (IRE) (Simply Great (FR)) [2018/19 h16g h16d^6 h16d h16d Apr 7] sixth foal: sister to very smart hurdler/high-class chaser Ballynagour (17f-21f winner), stayed 3¼m, and half-sister to fairly useful hurdler/useful chaser Simply Wings (19f-2¾m winner, by Winged Love): dam, lightly raced, out of sister to top-class hurdler Mighty Mogul: poor form over hurdles: will stay at least 2½m. *Noel C. Kelly, Ireland* **h84**

WADSWICK COURT (IRE) 11 b.g. Court Cave (IRE) – Tarasandy (IRE) (Arapahos (FR)) [2018/19 c135, h–: c20g c17g^2 c21.2m^{ur} c21.4m^F Jul 21] winning hurdler: useful handicap chaser: stayed 3m: acted on heavy going: wore headgear/tongue tie: dead. *Peter Bowen* **c134 h–**

WAGNER KLASS (FR) 7 ch.g. Prince Kirk (FR) – Bartjack (FR) (Lost World (IRE)) [2018/19 b82: h16.2d^F h20.1g h20.1s^{pu} h19.3g^{pu} Oct 25] little show over hurdles: tried in hood. *Rebecca Menzies* **h62**

Becher Handicap Chase, Aintree—Walk In The Mill (left) stays on well under James Best to land a gamble; course-specialist Ultragold (centre) takes third as Call It Magic (right) fades into fourth

WAHWONAISA 7 b.g. Kalanisi (IRE) – Clandestine (Saddlers' Hall (IRE)) [2018/19 h–: h18.7g³ h19.6d⁶ Jan 25] rangy gelding: poor form over hurdles: stays 19f: tried in cheekpieces: usually races off pace, often freely. *David Bridgwater* **h80**

WAIHEKE 6 ch.m. Black Sam Bellamy (IRE) – Its Meant To Be (Gunner B) [2018/19 h112: h19.2g⁶ h19.8v h21.4g h19d Mar 11] sturdy mare: fair hurdler: stays 19f: acts on soft going: in cheekpieces last 2 starts: temperament under suspicion: has joined Henry Oliver. *Philip Hobbs* **h102**

WAIKIKI WAVES (FR) 6 b.g. Alexandros – Lulabelle Spar (IRE) (Milan) [2018/19 h92, b68: h21.7g⁶ h21.7m* h25.8gᵖᵘ h19.6m h21.7m⁴ h25.8g c16s* c23.5v⁶ c20.2g* c17.8m* c19.5g* Apr 24] neat gelding: modest handicap hurdler: won at Fontwell in May: good start over fences, winning handicaps at Lingfield in January, Leicester and Fontwell in March, and Fontwell again (match) in April: stays 2¾m: acts on good to firm and heavy going: has worn blinkers. *Gary Moore* **c108 h91**

WAIT FOR ME (FR) 9 b.g. Saint des Saints (FR) – Aulne River (FR) (River Mist (USA)) [2018/19 c141, h138: h22.8g⁴ h25g² h23.9d h24.2d h21.4d³ h24dᵘʳ h21.4m³ h19.8g² Apr 27] robust gelding: has had breathing operation: useful handicap hurdler: in frame 5 times in 2018/19, including when second at Sandown (length behind Colonial Dreams) in April: useful chaser: barely stays 25f: acts on good to firm and heavy going: has worn hood/tongue tie: ridden patiently: irresolute. *Philip Hobbs* **c– § h137 §**

WAITING PATIENTLY (IRE) 8 b.g. Flemensfirth (USA) – Rossavon (IRE) (Beneficial) [2018/19 c169p, h–: c24gᵘʳ c21d² c19.9d³ Apr 5] lengthy gelding: winning hurdler: high-class chaser: below best from completed starts in 2018/19, when second in Betfair Ascot Chase (17 lengths behind Cyrname) and third in Melling Chase (29 lengths behind Min) at Aintree: should stay beyond 21f: acts on soft going: tried in cheekpieces: usually travels strongly held up. *Ruth Jefferson* **c154 h–**

WAITINONASUNNYDAY (IRE) 6 gr.g. Tikkanen (USA) – Coppenagh Lady (IRE) (Tawrrific (NZ)) [2018/19 h75: h19.9m h18.5s⁶ c16d⁴ c19.4dᵖᵘ c22.7f* c22.7g* c26g* Apr 24] maiden hurdler: modest form over fences: completed hat-trick in handicaps at Leicester in February/March and Fontwell in April: stays 3¼m: acts on any going: tried in hood/tongue tie. *Michael Blake* **c85 h–**

916

WAKANDA (IRE) 10 b.g. Westerner – Chanson Indienne (FR) (Indian River (FR)) c147
[2018/19 c146, h–: h16s⁵ c24.2s⁴ c25.6d* c28.4gᵖᵘ Feb 16] sturdy gelding: fairly useful h118
handicap hurdler: smart handicap chaser: won Peter Marsh Chase at Haydock (by 1¾
lengths from Robinsfirth) in January: ran too badly to be true final start: stays 3¼m: acts on
good to firm and heavy going: tough and genuine. *Sue Smith*

WALDEN PRINCE (IRE) 12 b.g. Saffron Walden (FR) – Kahyasi Princess (IRE) c104 §
(Kahyasi) [2018/19 c100§, h–§: c16g² c16.5gᵖᵘ c16g³ c16.3m* c17.8g² Aug 23] leggy h– §
gelding: winning hurdler: fair handicap chaser: won at Newton Abbot in August: stays
2½m: acts on good to firm and heavy going: wears headgear/tongue tie: often races towards
rear: unreliable. *Sophie Leech*

WALK AWAY (IRE) 6 b.g. Black Sam Bellamy (IRE) – Pegus Love (IRE) (Executive h132 p
Perk) [2018/19 h22.5g* h24.7d⁴ Apr 5] £130,000 5-y-o: good-topped gelding: fifth foal:
half-brother to a winning pointer by Bandari: dam (b75) ran twice in bumpers: won maiden
point on debut: useful form over hurdles: won maiden at Thurles in March: did well in
circumstances when fourth in Sefton Novices' Hurdle at Aintree (12¾ lengths behind
Champ) month later: not in same form at Punchestown shortly after end of British season,
but remains with potential. *Henry de Bromhead, Ireland*

WALKERS POINT (IRE) 8 b.g. Golan (IRE) – Don't Wait (IRE) (Oscar (IRE)) h94
[2018/19 h95: h22.1g h16d² h16g³ h16.9s h16.6d⁵ Dec 26] modest maiden hurdler: stays
3m, but at least as effective at 2m: acts on soft going: has worn headgear, including last 5
starts: often tongue tied: often leads/travels strongly. *Sean McParlan, Ireland*

WALK IN MILAN (IRE) 6 b.m. Milan – Island Walk (IRE) (Bob Back (USA)) [2018/19 b–
b15.8g May 28] €12,000 3-y-o: first foal: dam lightly-raced half-sister to fairly useful
hurdler/useful chaser (stayed 29f) Sugar Baron: little show in bumper/point. *Neil King*

WALK IN THE MILL (FR) 9 b.g. Walk In The Park (IRE) – Libre Amour (FR) (Lost c140
World (IRE)) [2018/19 c140: c25g³ c25.9s* h19.5d³ h23.1s³ c34.3g⁴ Apr 6] sturdy gelding: h112
fair form over hurdles: useful handicap chaser: won Becher Chase at Aintree (by 4½
lengths from Vieux Lion Rouge) in December: creditable 16 lengths fourth of 40 to Tiger
Roll in Grand National at same course final start: barely stays 4¼m: acts on soft going:
sound jumper. *Robert Walford*

WALKONTHINICE (IRE) 6 b.g. Frozen Fire (GER) – Stroll (IRE) (Pennekamp b–
(USA)) [2018/19 b16.3s⁶ Mar 11] ran out in point on debut: in hood/tongue tie, well held
in bumper: dead. *Richard Bandey*

WALK TO FREEDOM (IRE) 9 br.g. Arcadio (GER) – Carryonharriet (IRE) (Norwich) c137
[2018/19 h20d h22.5d* h20d⁴ h24g² h24dᵖᵘ c24.7d³ Apr 22] €34,000 3-y-o: workmanlike h143
gelding: third foal: dam unraced half-sister to useful hurdler (winner up to 3m) Holland
Park and fairly useful chaser (stayed 25f) Carryonharry: useful handicap hurdler: won at
Navan in November: second at Leopardstown (½ length behind Cuneo) following month:
useful chaser: third in handicap at Fairyhouse (5½ lengths behind Sizing Rome) in April:
lacklustre effort at Punchestown shortly after end of British season: stays 25f: acts on heavy
going: wears headgear: in tongue tie after reappearance: usually races towards rear. *Mrs J.
Harrington, Ireland*

WALK WATERFORD 8 bl.g. Fair Mix (IRE) – Woore Lass (IRE) (Persian Bold) c106
[2018/19 h86: h17.2m h23g³ c21.6g* c20.9gᶠ Aug 28] workmanlike gelding: maiden h83
hurdler: fair form over fences: won novice handicap at Fontwell in August: stayed 2¾m:
acted on good to firm going: in cheekpieces last 2 starts: tried in tongue tie: dead.
Olly Murphy

WALLACE SPIRIT (FR) 6 gr.g. Le Havre (IRE) – In Love New (FR) (Perrault) [2018/19 h99 §
h114, b82: h21m³ h21.4gᵖᵘ h19g Apr 25] good-topped gelding: fair maiden hurdler: threw
race away on reappearance: tried in cheekpieces: ungenuine. *Nicky Henderson*

WALSINGHAM GRANGE (USA) 6 b.g. Paddy O'Prado (USA) – Mambo Queen c106
(USA) (Kingmambo (USA)) [2018/19 h111: c16.3g³ c15.7s c21.2d⁴ c24vᵖᵘ h16d⁶ Mar 19] h–
fair hurdler: similar form over fences: unproven beyond 17f: acts on heavy going: has worn
headgear. *Pam Sly*

WALTER ONEEIGHTONE (IRE) 7 b.g. Morozov (USA) – Matinee Show (IRE) c–
(Carroll House) [2018/19 h90: h25m⁴ h23g c25.8mᵖᵘ Jun 26] has had breathing operation: h69
modest handicap hurdler: poor efforts in 2018/19, including on chasing debut: stays 3m:
acts on soft going: has worn headgear, including last 2 starts: wears tongue tie: usually
leads. *Jonjo O'Neill*

888Sport Handicap Chase, Kempton—Double Shuffle (checked cap) is second again in this valuable event—with yet another change of sponsor—as he gives best to 14/1-shot Walt

WALT (IRE) 8 b.g. King's Theatre (IRE) – Allee Sarthoise (FR) (Pampabird) [2018/19 c123, h–: c23.8g² c23g c24.1g⁶ c21.6d⁵ c23d* c22.4d² c24g* c20.2sᵖᵘ c23.8g⁶ Apr 24] rather leggy gelding: winning hurdler: useful handicap chaser: won novice event at Taunton in December and Grade 3 at Kempton (by length from Double Shuffle) in February: stays 3m: acts on heavy going: wears headgear nowadays: in tongue tie last 5 starts. *Neil Mulholland* — **c138 h–**

WALTZ DARLING (IRE) 11 b.g. Iffraaj – Aljafliyah (Halling (USA)) [2018/19 c–, h106: h19.9m⁴ h23.3g c19.2g c24g h23.8g⁶ h23.1s² h25.3g³ Dec 28] modest handicap hurdler: winning chaser, no form over fences in 2018/19: stays 25f: acts on soft and good to firm going: wears cheekpieces. *Gillian Boanas* — **c– h89**

WANDRIN STAR (IRE) 8 b.g. Flemensfirth (IRE) – Keralba (USA) (Sheikh Albadou) [2018/19 c113, h80p: c22.5d² c24.1g* c25g⁶ c24v* c24g³ c26.7g⁵ c23.4d⁶ Mar 22] rangy gelding: once-raced hurdler: useful handicap chaser: won at Bangor in October (novice event) and December: stays 25f: acts on heavy going: wears tongue tie: races prominently. *Kim Bailey* — **c133 h–**

WAPPING (USA) 6 b.g. Smart Strike (CAN) – Exciting Times (FR) (Jeune Homme (USA)) [2018/19 h16g⁵ Mar 29] half-brother to useful 2m hurdler Stars Over The Sea (by Sea The Stars): fairly useful on Flat, stays 1½m: 20/1, some encouragement when fifth in novice at Wetherby (22½ lengths behind Denmead) on hurdling debut: entitled to progress. *Barry Brennan* — **h83 p**

WAR AT SEA (IRE) 5 gr.g. Mastercraftsman (IRE) – Swirling (IRE) (Galileo (IRE)) [2018/19 h73: h16.7g⁵ h20.6g⁶ h17g⁵ Feb 24] has had breathing operation: modest form over hurdles: left Ali Stronge after second start: often in hood: in tongue tie last 3 starts: usually races off pace. *George Bewley* — **h85**

WAR BRIGADE (FR) 5 b.g. Manduro (GER) – Adjudicate (Dansili) [2018/19 h18.6s² h16.7s* h16.5d² h16.3d⁶ Mar 2] fairly useful on Flat, stays 1m: fairly useful form over hurdles: won novice at Market Rasen in December: has worn tongue tie. *Ian Williams* — **h122**

WAR CHIEF 5 ch.g. Aqlaam – My Colleen (USA) (Discreet Cat (USA)) [2018/19 h15.8g Jan 17] fairly useful on Flat, stays 9f: in hood, well beaten in novice on hurdling debut. *Alan King* — **h–**

WAR DRUMS 5 b.g. Authorized (IRE) – Crystal Swan (IRE) (Dalakhani (IRE)) [2018/19 h16dᵖᵘ Mar 15] fair maiden on Flat, stays 1½m: pulled up in conditionals maiden on hurdling debut. *Paul Webber* — **h–**

WARENDORF (FR) 6 b.g. Speedmaster (GER) – Hyllisia (FR) (Green Tune (USA)) **h89**
[2018/19 h20.1g³ h20.1s⁵ h20.1s⁵ h20.6d Mar 5] £8,000 3-y-o: sixth foal: dam unraced:
first past post in Irish point (disqualified due to prohibited substance): modest form over
hurdles. *Stuart Coltherd*

WAR JOEY (IRE) 6 b.g. Primary (USA) – Wake Me Gently (IRE) (Be My Native **c–**
(USA)) [2018/19 h87, b–: c20.1d^pu h20.1s Oct 13] workmanlike gelding: poor maiden **h–**
hurdler: pulled up in novice on chasing debut: tried in hood: usually in tongue tie.
Ann Hamilton

WARKSBURN BOY 9 b.g. Kayf Tara – Bonchester Bridge (Shambo) [2018/19 c–, h–: **c67**
c15.6g^pu c15.6g c15.6g⁴ c21.2m⁵ Jun 29] long-backed gelding: maiden hurdler: poor **h–**
maiden chaser: tried in cheekpieces: has worn tongue tie. *Sheena Walton*

WAR LORD (GER) 4 gr.g. Jukebox Jury (IRE) – Westalin (GER) (Sternkoenig (IRE)) **b82**
[2018/19 b16.8d⁵ Mar 24] 7/1, fifth in bumper at Exeter (11 lengths behind Pileon). *Colin
Tizzard*

WARNER EDWARD (IRE) 5 br.g. Kalanisi (IRE) – Beauty Star (IRE) (Shalford (IRE)) **b–**
[2018/19 b16.2m Jun 24] failed to complete in points: well beaten in bumper. *Stuart
Crawford, Ireland*

WAR ON THE ROCKS (IRE) 10 b.g. Wareed (IRE) – Rock Garden (IRE) (Bigstone **h95**
(IRE)) [2018/19 h104: h19.9m⁴ Jul 1] bumper winner: fair maiden hurdler, lightly raced:
stays 2½m: acts on soft going. *Fergal O'Brien*

WARRATEG 9 br.g. Windsor Castle – Its Squirt (Current Edition (IRE)) [2018/19 **h–**
h21.6g^pu h23g^pu Sep 11] little show in points/over hurdles: tried in cheekpieces: dead.
Kevin Bishop

WARRIOR PRINCE 6 ch.g. Sakhee (USA) – Queen of Iceni (Erhaab (USA)) [2018/19 **h–**
h15.8g May 22] fair maiden on Flat: tailed off in maiden hurdle: dead. *Caroline Bailey*

WARRIORS TALE 10 b.g. Midnight Legend – Samandara (FR) (Kris) [2018/19 c148, **c150**
h–: c19.9g⁴ c21.1s* c24g^pu c19.9d c34.3g^pu Apr 6] workmanlike gelding: winning hurdle: **h–**
smart handicap chaser: won Grand Sefton Chase at Aintree (by 1½ lengths from Brandon
Hill) in December: stays 3m: acts on good to firm and heavy going: tried in hood: wears
tongue tie. *Paul Nicholls*

WAR SOUND 10 b.g. Kayf Tara – Come The Dawn (Gunner B) [2018/19 c136, h–: **c142**
c19.9g* c20.6d c20.6d c19.9d Mar 2] well-made gelding: winning hurdler: useful handicap **h–**
chaser: won at Aintree (by 6 lengths from King's Odyssey) in November: stays 2½m: acts
on heavy going: usually races off pace: has flattered to deceive. *Philip Hobbs*

WARTHOG (FR) 7 gr.g. Martaline – Shekira (FR) (Medaaly) [2018/19 h123: c20s* **c131**
c20.5g^pu c19.9g³ c31.7s^pu Mar 12] tall, useful-looking gelding: has had breathing operation: **h–**
maiden hurdler: useful form over fences: won novice handicap at Sandown (by 4 lengths
from Molly Carew) in December: stays 3m: acts on heavy going: tried in cheekpieces:
wears tongue tie. *David Pipe*

WASDELL 5 b.m. Black Sam Bellamy (IRE) – Lady Hight (FR) (Take Risks (FR)) **h100**
[2018/19 h16.7g⁴ h20.6g³ h19d h23.1d h20.5g^pu Apr 22] £17,000 3-y-o: second foal: dam
(h96), lightly raced (placed in bumper/only start over hurdles), sister to smart hurdler
(stayed 21f) Mister Hight: fair form over hurdles: stays 21f. *Jonjo O'Neill*

WASHED ASHORE (IRE) 8 ch.g. Presenting – Give It Time (Kayf Tara) [2018/19 **c119**
c122, h–: c29.1g^F May 8] compact gelding: winning hurdler: fairly useful handicap chaser: **h–**
probably would have won but for falling last at Fakenham, only start in 2018/19: probably
stays 29f: acts on good to soft going: usually travels strongly. *Jonjo O'Neill*

WATAR ALLSTAR (IRE) 5 ch.g. Watar (IRE) – All Star Lady (IRE) (Presenting) **b–**
[2018/19 b15.7d b15.8v Dec 21] last of 5 finishers in Irish point: no form in bumpers:
wears headgear. *Zoe Davison*

WATCHING OVER 5 b.m. Schiaparelli (GER) – Nobratinetta (FR) (Celtic Swing) **h–**
[2018/19 b15.7g⁴ b17.1d h15.7g⁵ h20.6g h19.9v^pu h20.6d^pu Apr 6] half-sister to bumper **b75**
winner Swinging Sultan (by Sulamani) and fair hurdler Vinetta (19f winner, by Grape Tree
Road): dam (b100), bumper winner, also 1½m winner on Flat, half-sister to fairly useful
hurdlers Bhutan (2m-2¼m winner) and Cloth of Gold (stayed 3m): mid-field in bumpers:
no show over hurdles: tried in cheekpieces. *Gillian Boanas*

WATCOMBE HEIGHTS (IRE) 9 b.g. Scorpion (IRE) – Golden Bay (Karinga Bay) **c133**
[2018/19 h121: h16.8g³ c21g⁶ h16.8g* c17.5s* Nov 25] lengthy, angular gelding: fairly **h125**
useful handicap hurdler: won at Exeter in November: useful form over fences: won
handicap at same course (by 3 lengths from Admiral's Secret) later in month: stayed 2¾m:
acted on good to firm and heavy going: successful with/without hood: dead. *Colin Tizzard*

WATERLOO WARRIOR (IRE) 7 b.g. Kalanisi (IRE) – Vindonissa (IRE) (Definite Article) [2018/19 h112§: h23.1m² c20g² c26mpu c26.2gF h23.1s⁴ h23.6d c24.2vpu Mar 5] good-topped gelding: has had breathing operation: fair maiden hurdler: fairly useful form over fences: won twice in points shortly after end of season: stays 3m: acts on soft and good to firm going: wears headgear: has worn tongue tie, including in 2018/19: temperamental. *Colin Tizzard* **c117 §** **h107 §**

WATER SPRITE (IRE) 8 b.m. Papal Bull – Wish Upon A Star (IRE) (Russian Revival (USA)) [2018/19 c19.5d⁵ h16.5g h19.5g³ h20.2s⁴ h20g h16g* h21g⁶ h20g h16g h20s h20d h16g Feb 24] compact mare: fairly useful handicap hurdler: won mares event at Limerick in October: similar form over fences: left Gordon Elliott after seventh start: stays 21f: acts on heavy going: tried in headgear: usually tongue tied. *Mervyn Torrens, Ireland* **c114** **h117**

WATER WAGTAIL 12 b.g. Kahyasi – Kentford Grebe (Teenoso (USA)) [2018/19 c100§, h–: c21.6d⁵ c24.2d² Apr 9] maiden hurdler: fair handicap chaser: stays 3¼m: acts on heavy going: wears headgear: untrustworthy. *Emma Lavelle* **c100 §** **h–**

WATT BRODERICK (IRE) 10 ch.g. Hawk Wing (USA) – Kingsridge (IRE) (King's Theatre (IRE)) [2018/19 h16.7g⁴ h16.3g² Aug 28] lengthy gelding: fair handicap hurdler, off 2½ years before return: stays 19f: acts on soft going: has worn cheekpieces: usually tongue tied. *Ian Williams* **h100**

WATTS AND HOPPS 7 ch.m. Recharge (IRE) – Island Hopper (Be My Native (USA)) [2018/19 b16.7g May 19] half-sister to fairly useful hurdler/useful chaser Wizards Bridge (19f-3¼m winner, by Alflora) and 2½m hurdle winner Personal Shopper (by King's Theatre): dam, unraced, out of half-sister to top-class 2m chaser Buck House: tailed off in mares bumper. *Sarah-Jayne Davies* **b–**

WAX AND WANE 4 b.g. Maxios – Moonavvara (IRE) (Sadler's Wells (USA)) [2018/19 h16d Dec 13] useful on Flat, stays 1¼m: well beaten in juvenile maiden on hurdling debut. *Tim Vaughan* **h–**

WAY BACK HOME (IRE) 4 ch.g. Power – Winged Valkyrie (IRE) (Hawk Wing (USA)) [2018/19 h16.5sur h16d³ h16v⁵ h16g³ h16g* h16d* h16d⁴ Apr 22] dam half-sister to fairly useful hurdler (17f-2½m winner) Air Supremacy: fair maiden on Flat: useful hurdler: won maiden at Fairyhouse in February and Winning Fair Juvenile Hurdle at same course (by 3½ lengths from Morosini) later in month: raced only at 2m: acts on heavy going: has worn headgear: usually tongue tied: front runner. *Padraig Roche, Ireland* **h131**

WAY OF THE WORLD (IRE) 8 b.g. Flemensfirth (USA) – Night Heron (IRE) (St Jovite (USA)) [2018/19 h86: c22.5d c20.9d⁴ h21.7g³ h23.9d³ Oct 20] poor handicap hurdler: poor form over fences: stays 3m: acts on heavy going: has worn cheekpieces. *Sheila Lewis* **c77** **h79**

WAY OUT WEST (IRE) 6 b.g. Westerner – Rose Vic (IRE) (Old Vic) [2018/19 h95, b85: h15.8g³ h15.8g⁶ h15.7g* h16g c18mpu h21.2g² h20.7d⁶ h21.4g⁴ h20.6d Feb 5] sturdy gelding: has had breathing operation: fair handicap hurdler: won at Southwell in June: pulled up in novice handicap on chasing debut: stays 21f: best form on good going: wears hood/tongue tie: has joined Robert Walford. *Charlie Longsdon* **c–** **h103**

WAZOWSKI 10 b.g. Overbury (IRE) – Malay (Karinga Bay) [2018/19 h100: h16.2g³ h20.6g⁴ h16.7g² h17.2d³ h16.2g⁴ h17.1d³ h17.1v⁶ h15.8v⁴ h16.8s* h17v² h19.6g* Apr 13] has had breathing operation: fair handicap hurdler: won at Sedgefield (walked over) in March and Bangor in April: stays 21f: acts on heavy going. *Donald McCain* **h106**

WEAKFIELD (IRE) 6 b.g. Court Cave (IRE) – Thats The Lot (IRE) (Flemensfirth (USA)) [2018/19 b17s⁶ h20.8g⁴ h20.1v⁴ h23.1d* Jan 17] £90,000 4-y-o: fourth foal: half-brother to 1m winner Sretaw (by Kalanisi): dam once-raced half-sister to dam of useful hurdler (stays 3¼m) Scotchtown: won Irish point on debut: mid-field in bumper: fair form over hurdles: won handicap at Market Rasen in January: open to further improvement. *Brian Ellison* **h111 p** **b69**

WEAPON OF CHOICE (IRE) 11 b.g. Iffraaj – Tullawadgeen (IRE) (Sinndar (IRE)) [2018/19 h98: h17.2d⁴ h15.7g⁵ h16.4m⁵ h16.8g⁵ Apr 5] modest handicap hurdler: raced around 2m: acts on good to soft going: usually in headgear/tongue tie. *Julia Brooke* **h93**

WEAPONS OUT (FR) 5 b.g. Brave Mansonnien (FR) – Scenaria (IRE) (Scenic) [2018/19 b16.7g³ b15.6g² b15.8d⁴ b13.7g⁴ Apr 12] half-brother to several winners, including useful 2m hurdle winner Doctor Deejay (by Hawk Wing): dam unraced: fair form in bumpers. *Harry Whittington* **b86**

WEATHER FRONT (USA) 6 ch.g. Stormy Atlantic (USA) – Kiswahili (Selkirk (USA)) [2018/19 h–: h17.1d² h16.2g* h16.4g* Nov 16] fairly useful on Flat, stays 1½m: similar form over hurdles: won novices at Hexham and Newcastle (11/4-on) in November. *Karen McLintock* **h117**

WEAVE SOME MAGIC 4 b.g. Cityscape – Didbrook (Alzao (USA)) [2018/19 b16s b16d Feb 25] behind in bumpers. *Tim Reed* — **b–**

WEEBILL 7 b.g. Schiaparelli (GER) – Wee Dinns (IRE) (Marju (IRE)) [2018/19 h116p, b96: h20.5g* h23.9g⁶ h20.5d³ Dec 12] fairly useful hurdler: won novice at Ayr in May: third in handicap at Leicester final start: stays 2½m: acts on heavy going: usually races towards rear. *Olly Murphy* — **h128**

WEE SAXON 10 b.g. Kayf Tara – Countess Point (Karinga Bay) [2018/19 h19.5s h20vᵁ h19.5d c24.2d c19.2vᵖᵘ Mar 5] has had breathing operation: point winner: modest form over hurdles: no show in 2 chases: should be suited by 2¾m+: acts on heavy going: sometimes in tongue tie. *Colin Tizzard* — **c–ᵁ h94**

WEE TIGER TOTS 5 b.m. Sakhee (USA) – Foxglove (Hernando (FR)) [2018/19 b16.8s⁶ h19.9v h19.8mᵖᵘ h16.8g Apr 5] closely related to useful hurdler/fair chaser Foxcub (2m-25f winner, by Bahri) and half-sister to 2 winners, including modest hurdler Ballinabearna (21f winner, by Malinas): dam French 13.5f winner: mid-field in bumper: no form over hurdles. *Iain Jardine* — **h–ᵁ b64**

WE HAVE A DREAM (FR) 5 b.g. Martaline – Sweet Dance (FR) (Kingsalsa (USA)) [2018/19 h150p: h15.3g³ h19.3g⁴ h16.8s⁴ h18.1g* h16.8d² Mar 15] very smart hurdler: won Timeform Morebattle Hurdle at Kelso (by 6 lengths from Get Out The Gate) in February: best effort when second in County Hurdle at Cheltenham (1½ lengths behind Ch'tibello) month later: should have been suited by 2½m: acted on heavy going: dead. *Nicky Henderson* — **h155**

WEIGHTFORDAVE (IRE) 7 b.g. Dark Angel (IRE) – Moon Diamond (Unfuwain (USA)) [2018/19 h16m² h15.7gᶠ h16m* h15.8g³ h16.8m² h17.7g* h16g⁵ Sep 25] has had breathing operation: brother to fair 21f hurdle winner Dark Diamond and half-brother to fair 2m hurdle winner Hippodrome (by Montjeu): modest maiden on Flat, stays 13f: fair hurdler: won maiden at Worcester in July and novice at Fontwell in September: stays 2¼m: acts on good to firm and heavy going: has worn blinkers: wears tongue tie: often travels strongly. *Dan Skelton* — **h109**

WEINBERG 4 b.g. Cityscape – Willmar (IRE) (Zafonic (USA)) [2018/19 h16.2g² h16.5g⁴ h16.3m⁴ Jul 15] lightly raced on Flat: modest form over hurdles: best effort when second in juvenile at Hexham: tried in cheekpieces. *Donald McCain* — **h98**

WELCOME BEN (IRE) 10 b.g. High Roller (IRE) – Bramble Cottage (IRE) (Eurobus) [2018/19 c110, h–: c17.1d² Apr 8] lengthy gelding: winning hurdler: fair handicap chaser: stays 2½m: acts on soft and good to firm going: has worn headgear/tongue tie: usually leads. *Jackie Stephen* — **c106 h–**

WELCOME POLLY (IRE) 7 br.m. Milan – Culmore Lady (IRE) (Insan (USA)) [2018/19 h69: h23.3g⁶ h24g h23m h20.3g Oct 10] has had breathing operation: placed only start in Irish point: poor maiden hurdler: no show over hurdles: ungenuine. *Dan Skelton* — **h68 §**

WELL ABOVE PAR (IRE) 7 b.g. Gold Well – Glynn Glory (IRE) (Presenting) [2018/19 c111, h–: c20.1s* c20.1v² c21.5d c24.1s⁴ c23.4d⁵ Apr 8] twice-raced hurdler: fairly useful handicap chaser: won at Hexham in December: stays 2½m: acts on heavy going. *Lucinda Russell* — **c117 h–**

WELLAND 6 ch.g. Beat Hollow – Circus Rose (Most Welcome) [2018/19 b16.7g³ b16d b15.8d⁵ h15.8d h16d⁵ h16.7g³ Mar 27] rather leggy gelding: fourth foal: half-brother to fairly useful chaser Popelys Gull (19f winner, by Recharge), stays 3m, and fairly useful hurdler Acertain Circus (2m-23f winner, by Definite Article), stays 2½m: dam (h128), 2m-2½m hurdle winner, half-sister to fairly useful hurdler/chaser (stayed 3¼m) Harrycone Lewis: fair form on first of 3 starts in bumpers: modest form over hurdles: best effort when third in novice at Market Rasen. *Pam Sly* — **h94 b89**

WE'LL BE THERE 10 b.m. Kayf Tara – Teachmetotango (Mister Baileys) [2018/19 h73: c25.8g³ c23.8g c25.8m c24gᵖᵘ Jul 18] has had breathing operation: maiden hurdler: poor form over fences: stays 3m: acts on heavy going: wears headgear/tongue tie. *Stuart Kittow* — **c68 h–**

WE'LLCWHATHAPPENS (IRE) 6 b.m. Court Cave (IRE) – Lost Prairie (IRE) (Be My Native (USA)) [2018/19 h20.5g³ h19.5d⁴ h20.5s⁵ h20.5g h23.9s Mar 19] €800 3-y-o, £12,000 5-y-o: neat mare: seventh foal: closely related to fairly useful chaser Final Gift (2½m-2¾m winner, by Old Vic), stayed 25f, and half-sister to winning pointers by Alderbrook and Robin des Champs: dam, unraced, out of sister to smart chaser up to 3m The Divider and half-sister to high-class staying chaser Young Hustler: won Irish point on debut: modest form over hurdles: bred to be suited by 3m+. *Richard Rowe* — **h94**

WELL JOEY (IRE) 8 b.g. Kayf Tara – Penny Queen (Nayef (USA)) [2018/19 c17d³ **c97** h16.5g c16.5g⁵ c18.2d⁶ c16.7sᵘʳ c18g⁵ c18g⁵ c24.6g c16.2g⁶ c20.1v² c20.1d* Mar 26] **h69** maiden hurdler: modest handicap chaser: won at Hexham in March: left Mrs Prunella Dobbs after ninth start: stays 2½m: acts on heavy going: has worn headgear, including in 2018/19: has worn tongue tie, including last 2 starts. *Paul Stafford, Ireland*

WELL SAID (IRE) 9 b.g. Talkin Man (CAN) – Ashpark Rose (IRE) (Roselier (FR)) **h106** [2018/19 h16g h16g⁶ h16m* h16.3mᵖᵘ Aug 2] half-brother to fair hurdlers Ballymacduff (3m winner, by Strategic Choice) and Doof (2¾m winner, by Old Vic), latter also winning pointer: dam (h91), 2m hurdle winner, half-sister to useful hurdler/chaser (2m/17f winner) Town Crier: point winner: fair form over hurdles: won maiden at Worcester in July: bred to stay at least 2½m: wears hood. *Peter Bowen*

WELLS DE LUNE (FR) 8 b.g. Irish Wells (FR) – Pepite de Lune (FR) (Mansonnien **c141** (FR)) [2018/19 c129, h–: c17.8gᵖᵘ h15.8g² h16.3m⁴ h17.2m* h17.2g* h17.2d* c17.3s* **h140** c19.4gᵖᵘ h15.9g Apr 21] good-topped gelding: useful handicap hurdler: won at Cartmel in June (amateurs), July (lady riders) and August (by 13 lengths from Lough Kent): useful handicap chaser: completed 4-timer at same course (by 12 lengths from Ifandbutwhynot) later in August: stays 21f: acts on good to firm and heavy going: has worn headgear: wears tongue tie: front runner. *Peter Bowen*

WELLS GOLD (IRE) 8 b.g. Gold Well – Exit Baby (IRE) (Exit To Nowhere (USA)) **c86** [2018/19 h83: h20.6g h21.6g³ h21.6m⁴ c21.4g⁴ c23mᵖᵘ Sep 17] Irish point winner: poor **h80** handicap hurdler: modest form on completed start in chases: stays 2¾m: acts on good to firm and good to soft going: has worn headgear, including in 2018/19. *Fergal O'Brien*

WELL SMITTEN (IRE) 7 b.g. Gold Well – The Dark One (IRE) (Mandalus) [2018/19 **c114** h110: h20.1gᵖᵘ c19.9d* c19.9gᵖᵘ c20.2f⁵ c21.2d⁴ c20.3dᵘʳ Apr 9] maiden hurdler: fair form **h–** over fences: won novice handicap at Huntingdon in December: left Warren Greatrex after first start: stays 2½m: acts on heavy going: tried in cheekpieces: usually leads. *Amy Murphy*

WELLUPTOSCRATCH (FR) 8 b.g. Irish Wells (FR) – Aulne River (FR) (River Mist **h90** (USA)) [2018/19 h97: h19.2g h25.5g² h25d³ h20.5gᵖᵘ Dec 2] lengthy gelding: modest maiden hurdler: stayed 3¼m: acted on good to soft going: tried in cheekpieces: wore tongue tie: dead. *David Arbuthnot*

WELSH DESIGNE 11 ch.g. Midnight Legend – Barton Dante (Phardante (FR)) [2018/19 **c71 x** c–, h–: c20.9g⁶ c16.5g⁵ c19.4m⁴ c17.4g⁵ c16.5g² c16g⁵ c16g⁴ Nov 5] has had breathing **h–** operation: winning pointer: twice-raced hurdler: poor maiden chaser: left Mike Hammond after sixth start: tried in visor: wears tongue tie: usually races close up: often let down by jumping. *Sarah-Jayne Davies*

WELSH RAREBIT 6 b.g. Dylan Thomas (IRE) – Chelsey Jayne (IRE) (Galileo (IRE)) **h109** [2018/19 b79: b15.7g³ h21.3d h16d³ h19.5d² h20.5s³ h16.5g h20.1g⁵ Apr 15] modest form **b80** in bumpers: fair form over hurdles: may prove best at short of 2½m: acts on good to soft going: usually leads. *Lucinda Egerton*

WELSH SAINT (FR) 5 b.g. Saint des Saints (FR) – Minirose (FR) (Mansonnien (FR)) **b105** [2018/19 b16.7s⁴ b16.6g² b16d* Mar 28] seventh foal: brother to several winners, including smart hurdler/chaser Irish Saint (2m-21f winner) and fair 2½m hurdle winner Cool Saint: dam French 2m hurdle winner: useful form in bumpers: won maiden at Warwick (by 1½ lengths from Hostile) in March. *Nicky Henderson*

WELSH'S CASTLE (IRE) 7 b.g. Mahler – Kyle Again (IRE) (Snurge) [2018/19 c26g **c–** May 4] multiple point winner: well held in hunter chasing debut. *David Kemp*

WE MOVE ON (IRE) 5 b.m. Flemensfirth (USA) – Amber Light (IRE) (Anshan) [2018/19 **b85** b16.5d² Apr 24] €20,000 3-y-o: sixth foal: half-sister to fairly useful hurdler/useful chaser Stone Hard (2m-2¼m winner, by Robin des Champs) and fair hurdler/chaser The Doorman (19f-2¾m winner, by King's Theatre): dam, winning pointer, half-sister to useful hurdler/ very smart chaser (stayed 25f) The Minack out of Irish Grand National winner Ebony Jane: 7/1, second in maiden point at Taunton (11 lengths behind Dromineer). *Tom Weston*

WEMYSS POINT 7 b.g. Champs Elysees – Wemyss Bay (Sadler's Wells (USA)) [2018/19 **h133** h114: h24.7gᵖᵘ h19.7g* h19.7g* h24s⁴ h24.4g⁴ h24.4g⁵ h21.4m⁶ Apr 13] useful handicap hurdler: won at Wetherby (twice, by 1½ lengths from Big Time Dancer second occasion) in November: stays 21f: acts on soft going: wears cheekpieces nowadays: usually leads. *Philip Kirby*

WENCESLAUS (GER) 7 b.g. Tiger Hill (IRE) – Warrior Czarina (USA) (Pleasantly **h98** Perfect (USA)) [2018/19 h99, b–: h15.9g h16.7g³ h15.9m* h15.8g* h15.5d⁵ h16g h15.8d³ Feb 17] sturdy gelding: modest handicap hurdler: won at Plumpton (novice event) in

October and Uttoxeter in November: raced mainly around 2m: acts on good to firm and good to soft going: often in cheekpieces in 2018/19. *David Bridgwater*

WENYERREADYFREDDIE (IRE) 8 ch.g. Beneficial – Ware It Vic (IRE) (Old Vic) [2018/19 c–, h103: h20g^2 c20g^2 c18.8m* c18.8g* c22.4d c20.6g^{pu} Apr 17] strong gelding: fairly useful hurdler: smart form over fences: won novice handicap (by 18 lengths from Caid du Lin) at Ascot in November (by ½ length from Kildisart), both at Ascot in November: likely to prove best up to 2½m: acts on soft and good to firm going: usually leads. *Nicky Henderson* **c145 h123**

WEST APPROACH 9 b.g. Westerner – Ardstown (Ardross) [2018/19 c142, h–: c25g^3 c20.2g^{pu} c26s^5 h24.4s^2 h24d^2 h24d h24.7g^6 c28.8g^6 Apr 27] workmanlike gelding: smart hurdler: second in Long Walk Hurdle (2 lengths behind Paisley Park) at Ascot and Cleeve Hurdle (12 lengths behind same rival) at Cheltenham: useful handicap chaser: third at Cheltenham (11¼ lengths behind Relentless Dreamer) on return: unproven beyond 25f: acts on heavy going: has worn blinkers: tried in tongue tie: temperamental. *Colin Tizzard* **c138 § h150 §**

WESTBANK (IRE) 8 b.m. Scorpion (IRE) – Gaza Strip (IRE) (Hamas (IRE)) [2018/19 h20.2g^{pu} h20.2g^3 h20.2g Sep 26] €3,800 3-y-o: fourth foal: sister to fairly useful hurdler/chaser Deadly Sting (2½m-23f winner): dam (h113) bumper/19f hurdle winner: maiden pointer: little form over hurdles: wears headgear. *Stuart Crawford, Ireland* **h58**

WESTBROOK BERTIE 4 b.g. Sixties Icon – Evanesce (Lujain (USA)) [2018/19 h16d^3 h17.7v* h15.8g^2 h17.7v^3 Feb 14] half-brother to fairly useful hurdler/chaser Alfraamsey (2m winner, by Fraam): fairly useful on Flat, barely stays 1¾m: fair form over hurdles: won juvenile maiden at Fontwell in December. *Mick Channon* **h112**

WESTBURY (IRE) 5 br.g. Westerner – Jemima Jay (IRE) (Supreme Leader) [2018/19 b15.8g* b16g^3 h19.3g^5 Nov 23] good-topped gelding: fairly useful form in bumpers: won at Huntingdon in May: well held in maiden on hurdling debut: dead. *Oliver Sherwood* **h– b99**

WEST CHINNOCK 8 ch.g. With The Flow (USA) – Roaming West (IRE) (Roi de Rome (USA)) [2018/19 h19.8g^F Mar 7] tall gelding: poor completion rate in points: tailed off when fell in maiden on hurdling debut. *Colin Tizzard* **h72**

WEST CLASS (IRE) 8 b.g. Westerner – Catch The Class (IRE) (Flemensfirth (USA)) [2018/19 c–, h98: h15.7g^6 h20.6g h15.8m h18.6m^4 h19.6g^4 h18.6g^6 Sep 29] Irish point winner: poor maiden hurdler nowadays: pulled up only chase start: stays 2½m: usually wears headgear: tried in tongue tie. *Peter Winks* **c– h73**

WEST COAST GLORY (IRE) 5 b.m. Fame And Glory – Turntofacethesun (Whipper (USA)) [2018/19 b16g^5 b15.8g^4 Apr 11] third foal: dam unraced half-sister to fair hurdler/fairly useful chaser (2m-2½m winner) Chrysander: modest form in bumpers. *Kerry Lee* **b82**

WEST COAST LASS (IRE) 6 br.m. Westerner – Afairs (IRE) (Old Vic) [2018/19 h79, b–: h16.2g^6 h20.2g^2 h20.5g^4 h15.6g^2 h16.2g^2 h18.1g h16.4m^4 h16.4s^5 h20.2g h16.2d^3 Apr 26] fair maiden hurdler: stays 2½m: best form on good going: often wears headgear: usually front runner/races prominently. *R. Mike Smith* **h103**

WEST DRIVE (IRE) 6 ch.g. Sea The Stars (IRE) – Fair Sailing (IRE) (Docksider (USA)) [2018/19 h17.7g* h15.9s^{pu} h15.9s h16.3d h19.2v^3 h17.7m^{bd} Mar 29] compact gelding: dam half-sister to useful hurdler/chaser (stayed 3¾m) Fair Question: fairly useful on Flat, stays 1¾m: fair form over hurdles: won novice at Fontwell in August: stays 19f: acts on heavy going. *Gary Moore* **h106**

WESTEND STORY (IRE) 8 b.g. Westerner – Sarahall (IRE) (Saddlers' Hall (IRE)) [2018/19 h131: h21g c19.2s^4 Dec 7] lengthy gelding: fell both starts in Irish points: useful hurdler, tired quickly on return: shaped well when fourth in novice at Exeter (9¼ lengths behind Defi du Seuil) on chasing debut: should stay at least 3m: acts on soft going: front runner/races prominently, often travels strongly: should progress over fences. *Philip Hobbs* **c137 p h–**

WESTEND THEATRE (IRE) 10 b.g. Darsi (FR) – Ballyvelig Lady (IRE) (Project Manager) [2018/19 c80, h–: h24.3d c20.5d^5 c20.1d Mar 26] maiden hurdler: poor maiden chaser: stays 3m: acts on heavy going: in cheekpieces last 2 starts. *Jane Walton* **c73 h–**

WESTERBEE (IRE) 8 b.m. Westerner – Pass The Honey (IRE) (Snurge) [2018/19 h–: h20s* h17.7g^3 h19g h19.2d Nov 18] small, angular mare: modest handicap hurdler: won mares novice at Worcester in May: stays 2½m: acts on soft going: has worn headgear: races well off pace. *Seamus Mullins* **h89**

WESTERBERRY (IRE) 7 b.m. Westerner – Casiana (GER) (Acatenango (GER)) [2018/19 h79, b–: c15.7m^F c16.1g^3 c22.5g Jun 6] has breathing operation: maiden hurdler: modest form over fences: best form at 2m. *Seamus Mullins* **c86 h–**

WESTERLY WIND (IRE) 5 b.g. Westerner – Milanella (IRE) (Milan) [2018/19 b16g^4 b16.7v h19.3s^{pu} Mar 7] modest form on first of 2 starts in bumpers: pulled up in novice on hurdling debut. *Jonjo O'Neill* **h– b79**

WESTERN AUSSIE (IRE) 6 b.g. Westerner – Squeekaussie (IRE) (Rudimentary **h110 p**
(USA)) [2018/19 h20.1g^F h21.3d^3 Jan 4] €14,000 3-y-o: second foal: half-brother to 2½m
bumper winner/winning pointer Madera Express (by Milan): dam, ran once in bumper,
half-sister to fairly useful hurdler/useful chaser Minella For Value (stays 3¼m): placed on
second of 2 starts in Irish points: fair form when third in maiden at Wetherby on completed
start over hurdles: open to improvement. *Martin Todhunter*

WESTERN BREEZE (IRE) 10 b.m. Westerner – Winsome Breeze (IRE) (Glacial **h73**
Storm (USA)) [2018/19 h19.9m h23g h23.3g^5 h23g^5 Jul 4] has had breathing operation:
poor handicap hurdler nowadays: stays 2½m: acts on heavy and good to firm going: tried
in cheekpieces. *Dan Skelton*

WESTERN CLIMATE (IRE) 10 b.g. Westerner – Jo Peeks (IRE) (Be My Native **c– §**
(USA)) [2018/19 c133, h122: h25g^{pu} h23.6s h23.6d^{pu} h23.3s^{pu} h25d^{pu} c23.6d^{pu} Mar 21] **h– §**
angular gelding: fairly useful hurdler/useful chaser at best, no form in 2018/19: has worn
headgear: ungenuine. *Tom Weston*

WESTERN DIXIE (IRE) 5 b.m. Westerner – Flame of Dixie (IRE) (Beneficial) **b–**
[2018/19 b16d b14d Dec 19] first foal: dam (h88), maiden hurdler (stayed 21f), sister to
useful hurdler/smart chaser (stayed 21f) Fiendish Flame: well held in bumpers/on
completed start on Flat (has looked temperamental). *Jennie Candlish*

WESTERN DREAM 11 b.g. Westerner – Simiola (Shaamit (IRE)) [2018/19 c–, h–: h20g **c–**
c16.5g c23m^{pu} c16g c23g^{pu} Jan 9] lengthy gelding: has had breathing operation: of no **h–**
account: left Alan Phillips after fourth start: has worn headgear, including last 4 starts: has
worn tongue tie. *Miss Hannah Taylor*

WESTERN DUKE (IRE) 5 b.g. High Chaparral (IRE) – Witch of Fife (USA) (Lear Fan **h91**
(USA)) [2018/19 h16.3d h16.8s h15.8d Feb 17] compact gelding: fairly useful on Flat,
stays 1¾m: modest form over hurdles. *Ian Williams*

WESTERNER OCEAN (IRE) 7 gr.m. Westerner – Silver Proverb (Silver Patriarch **h–**
(IRE)) [2018/19 h19s h15.3g h15.3s h19s Mar 19] fourth foal: half-sister to bumper winner
Robinsson (by Robin des Champs): dam, well held in bumpers, half-sister to useful
hurdler/chaser (23f/3m winner) Karanja: runner-up first 3 outings in Irish points: little form
over hurdles: tried in tongue tie. *Alexandra Dunn*

WESTERNER POINT (IRE) 10 b.g. Westerner – Its Only Gossip (IRE) (Lear Fan **c138**
(USA)) [2018/19 c134, h119: h16.6d^6 c19.7s* c20s* c24d^5 Apr 21] fairly useful handicap **h108**
hurdler: useful handicap chaser: won at Limerick in December and Wexford (by ½ length
from Goulane Chosen in veterans event) in March: stays 3m: acts on heavy going: tried in
hood. *Eoghan O'Grady, Ireland*

WESTERN HONOUR (IRE) 7 b.g. Westerner – Cailins Honour (IRE) (City Honours **c120**
(USA)) [2018/19 h111: h22.1g^4 h16g^2 h16d^2 h20s* h23.2g^3 h20s^5 h19.5d* h21.6v^5 c20d^4 **h119**
Apr 21] won Irish point on debut: fairly useful hurdler: won amateurs maiden at Clonmel
in December and novice at Ayr in February: 7/1, fourth in maiden at Cork (6 lengths behind
Beyond The Law) on chasing debut: left James Moffatt after first start: stays 23f: acts on
soft going: has worn cheekpieces, including last 4 starts. *Gordon Elliott, Ireland*

WESTERN JO (IRE) 11 b.g. Westerner – Jenny's Jewel (IRE) (Be My Native (USA)) **c124**
[2018/19 c126, h99: c20.6s^6 c30g^3 c23.4s^F Jan 29] sturdy gelding: winning hurdler: fairly **h–**
useful handicap chaser: stayed 3¾m: acted on heavy going: sometimes in headgear: wore
tongue tie: often led: dead. *Sam England*

WESTERN LASS (IRE) 6 br.m. Westerner – Lady Roania (IRE) (Saddlers' Hall (IRE)) **h75**
[2018/19 h91, b70: h16d h16.4v^4 Mar 16] modest form on first of 3 starts over hurdles:
bred to be suited by 2½m+. *Katie Scott*

WESTERN MILLER (IRE) 8 b.g. Westerner – Definite Miller (IRE) (Definite Article) **c125**
[2018/19 c138, h124: c19.4g^5 c18.2d^5 c20d^3 c20d^{pu} c20.2g^{pu} c19.4g^2 Apr 14] good-topped **h–**
gelding: fairly useful handicap hurdler/chaser: stays 2¾m: acts on heavy going: tried in
cheekpieces: wears tongue tie: usually front runner/races prominently. *Charlie Longsdon*

WESTERN MORNING (IRE) 6 b.g. Westerner – Gweedara (IRE) (Saddlers' Hall **c93**
(IRE)) [2018/19 h88: h20.7d^{pu} h17.7d^4 h19.6d^5 c20.2m* h20.7g c16.1d^2 c19.2d^4 c19.7g^6 **h74**
Apr 7] poor maiden hurdler: modest form over fences: won novice handicap at Leicester in
February: stayed 2½m: acted on good to firm and good to soft going: wore headgear/tongue
tie: dead. *Milton Harris*

WESTERN RULES (IRE) 9 b.g. Westerner – Ryehill Lady (IRE) (Accordion) [2018/19 **c121**
h116: c20g^{ur} h24.6v^2 c23.4s^3 c21.6g* c23.4d^3 c20d^3 c20.1d^4 Apr 26] fairly useful handicap **h120**
hurdler: similar form over fences: won 3-runner novice at Kelso in January: stays 25f: acts
on heavy going: wears cheekpieces: tried in tongue tie. *Nicky Richards*

WESTERN RYDER (IRE) 7 b.g. Westerner – Seesea (IRE) (Dr Massini (IRE)) **h142**
[2018/19 h145: h16.4g⁵ h16.8s³ h15.7s³ h15.7d³ h16.8d Mar 15] well-made gelding: useful
hurdler: fifth in Greatwood Hurdle at Cheltenham (4 lengths behind Nietzsche) in
November, and third in International Hurdle at same course (4 lengths behind Brain Power)
and Betfair Exchange Trophy at Ascot (3¼ lengths behind Mohaayed) in December: stays
2½m: acts on heavy going: in headgear last 4 starts. *Warren Greatrex*

WESTERN STORM (IRE) 7 b.g. Westerner – Torduff Storm (IRE) (Glacial Storm **h97**
(USA)) [2018/19 h19.9m⁶ h23.3g⁵ h23g² h23g² h25g h20.7gᵖᵘ Nov 13] modest maiden
hurdler: stays 23f: acts on good to firm going: often wears headgear: in tongue tie last 4
starts: usually races close up. *Richard Phillips*

WESTERN SUNRISE (IRE) 10 b.m. Westerner – Presenting Gayle (IRE) (Presenting) **c–**
[2018/19 c–, h91: h23.9d² h19.9g² h26.5g² h21.6mᶠ h26.5d* h21.6v² h27g³ h23.3d h17.7g⁶ **h106**
Apr 12] fair handicap hurdler: won at Newton Abbot in September: unseated only chase
outing: stays 3¼m: acts on good to firm and heavy going. *Johnny Farrelly*

WESTERN SUPERNOVA 5 b.m. Westerner – Supreme Nova (Supreme Leader) **h–**
[2018/19 b16.4d b16d h18.1dᶠ h16.2g Apr 15] fifth foal: half-sister to fairly useful hurdler/ **b–**
winning pointer Kid Valentine (2m-21f winner, by Scorpion) and modest chaser La
Madonnina (2¾m winner, by Milan): dam, no form in bumpers, half-sister to useful
hurdler/top-class chaser (stayed 25f) Simply Dashing: well held in bumpers/on completed
start over hurdles. *Katie Scott*

WESTERN VICTORY (IRE) 6 b.m. Westerner – Zara's Victory (IRE) (Old Vic) **h130**
[2018/19 h16s* h20d⁶ h18s² h18s² h22v⁶ h20g Apr 21] €36,000 3-y-o: sixth foal: half-
sister to useful hurdler/smart chaser Tell Us More (2m-2¼m winner, by Scorpion) and
modest hurdler/fair chaser By The Banks (2½m winner, by Alderbrook): dam, unraced, out
of half-sister to Irish Grand National winner Glebe Lad: off mark in points at second
attempt: in frame in bumpers: useful hurdler: won mares maiden at Galway in October:
second in Solerina Mares Novices' Hurdle at Fairyhouse (6 lengths behind Honeysuckle)
in January: should stay beyond 2¼m: acts on soft going: usually leads. *Colin Bowe, Ireland*

WESTERN WAVE (FR) 7 b.g. Westerner – Kaprissima (FR) (Epervier Bleu) [2018/19 **c98**
h109: c22.5dᵖᵘ c24.1g⁶ h23.6g² h24d³ h25.5v* h25.5d² h24gᶠ Mar 4] fairly useful handicap **h120**
hurdler: won at Hereford in December: modest form over fences: stayed 3¼m: acted on
heavy going: usually raced towards rear: dead. *Tom George*

WESTERN WHISKEY (IRE) 4 b.g. Ask – Westerner Hall (IRE) (Westerner) [2018/19 **b–**
b16.8s Apr 16] placed in point bumper, only sign of ability. *D. Summersby*

WESTLAND ROW (IRE) 7 br.g. Oscar (IRE) – Presenting Proform (IRE) (Presenting) **c126**
[2018/19 h22.5dᵘʳ h24s⁴ c24.6g² c24dᶠ c24.1d² Feb 25] €40,000 3-y-o: first foal: dam **h86**
(h109), bumper/point winner, ran once over hurdles (second at 2½m), half-sister to dam of
useful hurdler/chaser (stayed 23f) Loosen My Load: fairly useful hurdler, probably still
needed run completed outing in 2018/19: fairly useful form over fences: second in maiden
at Thurles and novice at Ayr: stays 25f: acts on good to soft going: wears tongue tie.
Gordon Elliott, Ireland

WEST OF THE EDGE (IRE) 11 b.g. Westerner – Bermuda Bay (IRE) (Be My Native **c119**
(USA)) [2018/19 c131, h114: h23.9v⁴ c32.4g c27.3s c32.6g Feb 23] fair handicap hurdler/ **h104**
useful handicap chaser, below best in 2018/19: stays 33f: acts on heavy going: wears
headgear. *Dr Richard Newland*

WESTSTREET (IRE) 9 b.g. Westerner – Klipperstreet (IRE) (Supreme Leader) **c122**
[2018/19 c26.1dᵖᵘ c25.7s³ c25.5s c28.8v³ c31.9v* c30.6d* Apr 26] sturdy gelding: winning **h–**
hurdler: fairly useful handicap chaser: won at Hexham in March and Perth in April: suited
by long distances: acts on heavy going: has worn headgear. *Oliver Sherwood*

WEST TO CROSSGALES (IRE) 8 b.g. Westerner – Mooreshill Bay (IRE) (Lord **h88**
America) [2018/19 h81: h20g³ h20.3g² h23.4g² h24g⁵ h24g⁶ h21.2m² Aug 30] winning
Irish pointer: modest maiden hurdler: stays 23f: acts on good to firm going: tried in hood/
tongue tie. *Charles Pogson*

WEST TORR (IRE) 8 br.g. Scorpion (IRE) – Native Craft (IRE) (Be My Native (USA)) **c–**
[2018/19 c104, h–: c24gᵖᵘ Jul 27] winning hurdler: fair form over fences, pulled up only **h–**
start in 2018/19: should be suited by further than 2½m: acts on good to firm and good to
soft going: has worn cheekpieces. *Nigel Twiston-Davies*

WEST TO THE BRIDGE (IRE) 6 b.g. Flemensfirth (USA) – Godlylady (IRE) (Old **h122**
Vic) [2018/19 b100: h16g⁵ h16v⁶ h16.3s h17s* h17.7v³ h16.3s h16.7s* h16.5g Apr 6]
good-topped gelding: has had breathing operation: fairly useful hurdler: won novices at

Aintree in December and Bangor in March: unproven beyond 17f: acts on soft going: wears hood/tongue tie. *Dan Skelton*

WEST WIZARD (FR) 10 b.g. King's Theatre (IRE) – Queen's Diamond (GER) (Konigsstuhl (GER)) [2018/19 c128, h–: c19.2g* c20.9d^{ur} c20g^2 c19.4v c21.4d^{pu} Jan 17] good sort: has had breathing operation: winning hurdler: fair handicap chaser: won at Market Rasen in September: stays 3m: acts on heavy going: has worn headgear: wears tongue tie: temperamental. *Sophie Leech* **c112 §** **h–**

WE'VE GOT PAYET 5 b.g. Authorized (IRE) – Missoula (IRE) (Kalanisi (IRE)) [2018/19 b15.8g* b16d^4 h19.9g h16m^5 h16g h16g h21.7g Apr 12] tall gelding: third foal: dam (h109), 2½m hurdle winner, also 1m-2½m winner on Flat, half-sister to fairly useful 2¼m hurdle winner Settlement Craic: won bumper at Uttoxeter in July: modest form over hurdles: left Olly Murphy after sixth start: in cheekpieces last 2 starts: usually races off pace: ungenuine. *Sophie Leech* **h95 §** **b94**

WEYBURN (IRE) 8 gr.g. September Storm (GER) – Saffron Pride (IRE) (Be My Native (USA)) [2018/19 c110, h–: c21.7g^5 c19.4m^6 Jun 21] winning hurdler: fair chaser at best, no form in 2018/19: stays easy 23f: acts on soft going: has worn headgear: wears tongue tie: temperament under suspicion. *Martin Keighley* **c–** **h–**

WHAT ABOUT BARB 4 ch.f. Excelebration (IRE) – Annie's Fortune (IRE) (Montjeu (IRE)) [2018/19 b14g b12.4s Dec 8] workmanlike filly: first foal: dam 7f winner: little show in bumpers. *Julia Feilden* **b–**

WHAT A GAME (IRE) 8 ch.g. Milan – Moscow Mo Chuisle (IRE) (Moscow Society (USA)) [2018/19 c–, h90: h22.1s h23.3g c23.4g^{pu} h23.3g Nov 9] modest hurdler at best, no form in 2018/19: little show over fences: wears blinkers: tried in tongue tie. *Tim Easterby* **c–** **h–**

WHAT A HOOT 5 b.m. Presenting – Flying Iris (IRE) (Un Desperado (FR)) [2018/19 ab16g^3 b16.5d Jan 19] seventh foal: half-sister to bumper winner Special Mate (by Generous): dam unraced sister to triple Cheltenham Gold Cup winner Best Mate: poor form in bumpers. *Emma Lavelle* **b72**

WHATAKNIGHT 10 b.g. Midnight Legend – What A Mover (Jupiter Island) [2018/19 c–, h137: h22.8g h26.5g Sep 10] good-topped gelding: useful handicap hurdler, below best in 2018/19: winning chaser but not a fluent jumper: stays 25f: acts on soft and good to firm going: wears tongue tie. *Harry Fry* **c–** **h125**

WHAT A LAUGH 14 b.g. Kayf Tara – Just For A Laugh (Idiot's Delight) [2018/19 c–, h–: c24.1g^2 c22.6m^5 c22.6m* c23g^{pu} c22.6g^2 c22.6g^6 c22.6g^2 Mar 30] sturdy gelding: maiden hurdler: fair handicap chaser: won at Stratford in July: stays 25f: acts on soft and good to firm going: usually races off pace. *Gary Hanmer* **c105** **h–**

WHAT A MUDDLE (IRE) 5 ch.g. Haafhd – Spatham Rose (Environment Friend) [2018/19 b17.7g^3 Jun 5] 14/1, green when third in bumper at Fontwell (19½ lengths behind Little Jack). *Gary Moore* **b74**

WHAT A SCORCHER 8 b.m. Authorized (IRE) – Street Fire (IRE) (Street Cry (IRE)) [2018/19 h81: h19.5s^{pu} h19.7g h20.7g Apr 22] lengthy mare: has had breathing operation: fair hurdler at best, no form in 2018/19: tried in tongue tie. *Nikki Evans* **h–**

WHATDUHAVTOGET (IRE) 7 b.m. Presenting – Smooching (IRE) (Saddlers' Hall (IRE)) [2018/19 c111, c124: c20g* c16.2d* c20d^2 c16.3g^3 Apr 18] good-topped mare: has had breathing operation: fairly useful hurdler: useful form over fences: won novices at Warwick in May, first a mares event, second a match: has won over 21f, at least as effective at 2m: acts on soft going: tried in hood: usually leads/races freely. *Dan Skelton* **c136** **h–**

WHAT HAPPENS NOW (IRE) 10 b.g. Dr Massini (IRE) – Euro Burden (IRE) (Good Thyne (USA)) [2018/19 c125, h113: c26.1g^5 c24.1g Aug 31] medium-sized gelding: fair hurdler: fairly useful handicap chaser, well below best in 2018/19: stays 25f: acts on good to firm and heavy going: tried in hood: front runner/races prominently. *Donald McCain* **c94** **h–**

WHAT LARKS (IRE) 11 b.g. Pierre – Bint Rosie (Exit To Nowhere (USA)) [2018/19 c76, h–: c24d^5 c26m^2 c24d^2 c24.2v^5 c25.2d c23.5v c24.2v c26.7g^5 c29.2g Apr 10] sturdy gelding: maiden hurdler: poor handicap chaser: stays 3¼m: acts on good to firm and heavy going: wears headgear. *Dr Jeremy Naylor* **c76** **h–**

WHATMORE 7 b.g. Schiaparelli (GER) – Polymiss (FR) (Poliglote) [2018/19 h127: h19.5d^3 h19.6d* h16.3s h16.5g h20.2d^2 Apr 26] well-made gelding: chasing type: useful handicap hurdler: won at Bangor (by 4 lengths from Ballyhill) in November: second at Perth (3 lengths behind Count Simon) final start: stays 2½m: acts on heavy going: tried in hood: front runner/races prominently. *Henry Daly* **h137**

WHATSFORUWONTGOBYU (IRE) 9 b.g. Well Chosen – Meadstown Miss (IRE)   h–
(Flemensfirth (USA)) [2018/19 h22.2m^{pu} h15.5g Dec 28] fairly useful hurdler at best, no
form in 2018/19: left A. J. Martin after first start: unproven beyond 2m: acts on heavy
going. *Jonjo O'Neill*

WHATSINTHECORNER (IRE) 7 b.g. Windsor Knot (IRE) – Caromar (IRE)   c108
(Flemensfirth (USA)) [2018/19 c19.7m c19.2g* h16g⁴ h18.8g^F c19.9g⁶ c20m^{pu} h19d h16g   h106
c21.1m⁴ c21g c16g² h19.8g² c18g* h16g² h21d² h16.9s c16.2g² h20g⁶ c16v¹⁴ Apr 14]
second foal: dam placed in point: fair maiden hurdler: fair chaser: won maiden at
Downpatrick in May and handicap at Thurles in November: effective at 2m to 3m: acts on
good to soft going: tried in hood: wears tongue tie. *John Joseph Hanlon, Ireland*

WHATSMEANTTOBE 5 b.g. Fair Mix (IRE) – Its Meant To Be (Gunner B) [2018/19   h96
h16.2g² h15.3g⁴ Jan 17] £5,000 3-y-o, £10,000 4-y-o: brother to fair chaser Todareistodo
(2m-19f winner) and half-brother to fair hurdler Waiheke (2¼m winner, by Black Sam
Bellamy): dam (b85) lightly raced in bumpers/over hurdles, half-sister to dam of very
smart chaser (stayed 3¼m) Planet of Sound: fourth on last of 3 starts in Irish points: modest
form over hurdles: better effort when second in novice at Hereford. *Philip Hobbs*

WHAT'S OCCURRING (IRE) 6 b.g. Rail Link – Lovely Origny (FR) (Robin des   h121
Champs (FR)) [2018/19 h111, b84: h16.2g* h16.3s⁵ h15.5g³ h19.4g³ h16g Apr 27]
strong gelding: fairly useful hurdler: won maiden at Hereford in October and novice there
in November: should be suited by 2½m+: acts on soft going: usually races prominently.
Oliver Sherwood

WHAT'S THE SCOOP (IRE) 9 ch.g. Presenting – Dame d'Harvard (USA) (Quest For   c–
Fame) [2018/19 c–, h106: h16g Apr 11] well-made gelding: maiden hurdler, well held only   h–
start in 2018/19: well beaten both chase outings: stays 19f: acts on heavy going: signs of
temperament. *Sue Smith*

WHATSWRONGWITHYOU (IRE) 8 ch.g. Bienamado (USA) – Greenfield Noora   c144
(IRE) (Topanoora) [2018/19 h128p: h16.3s⁶ c15.7v² c16v* c17.8d* c16.3d c15.8d Apr 4]   h122
sturdy gelding: fairly useful hurdler: useful form over fences: won 3-runner novices at Ffos
Las in January and Fontwell (by 17 lengths from Amour de Nuit) in February: stays 2¼m:
acts on heavy going: wears hood: often races freely. *Nicky Henderson*

WHATTHEBUTLERSAW (IRE) 10 br.g. Arcadio (GER) – Phar From Men (IRE)   h128
(Phardante (FR)) [2018/19 h99: h19.6g² h21.7g* h21g h19.8g² h21.4d^{pu} Dec 26] lengthy
gelding: fairly useful handicap hurdler: won at Fontwell in August: second at Wincanton in
November: stays 2¾m: acts on good to firm and heavy going: tried in tongue tie: often
races towards rear. *Dominic Ffrench Davis*

WHATZDJAZZ (IRE) 7 b.m. Yeats (IRE) – What A Mewsment (IRE) (Persian Mews)   h123
[2018/19 h126: h20g³ h20g⁶ h16g⁶ h24.5g⁴ Nov 26] useful-looking mare: fairly useful
hurdler: third in handicap at Aintree in May: stays 21f: acts on good to firm going: usually
races nearer last than first. *Dan Skelton*

WHEELBAHRI 5 b.g. Bahri (USA) – Midlem Melody (Syrtos) [2018/19 b16.2d Apr 26]   b–
well beaten in bumper. *Stuart Coltherd*

WHENHELLBROKELOOSE (IRE) 6 b.g. Black Sam Bellamy (IRE) – Star Ar Aghaidh   b68 p
(IRE) (Soviet Star (USA)) [2018/19 b16.8s Apr 16] €22,000 3-y-o: second foal: brother to
a winning pointer: dam (b81), lightly raced in bumpers, half-sister to fairly useful hurdler/
fair chaser (stayed 3m) King Ar Aghaidh out of Stayers' Hurdle winner Shuil Ar Aghaidh:
won point maiden on debut: 5/2, hampered around 2f out when seventh in maiden bumper
at Exeter (15¾ lengths behind Merchant House): should improve. *Alan King*

WHENITCOMESTOIT (IRE) 5 b.g. Arcadio (GER) – Funny Thing (IRE) (Taipan   b87
(IRE)) [2018/19 b16.2g² Sep 10] €1,500 3-y-o: fourth foal: dam (h83) runner-up over
hurdles at 2½m: 8/1, second in bumper at Perth (8 lengths behind Carrie des Champs): has
joined Ben Case. *Stuart Crawford, Ireland*

WHERE NOW (IRE) 8 b.g. Where Or When (IRE) – Exciting Prospect (IRE) (Lord   h93 §
Americo) [2018/19 h21g h19.5g⁶ h16g h20d⁴ h20.1s^{pu} h21.9v^{pu} h21.7d^{pu} Mar 9] modest
maiden hurdler: left W. J. Lanigan after fourth start: off mark in points shortly after end of
season: stays 2½m: acts on good to soft going: has worn cheekpieces: tried in tongue tie:
temperamental. *Christian Williams*

WHERE'S TOM 4 b.g. Cape Cross (IRE) – Where's Susie (Where Or When (IRE))   b93
[2018/19 b15.3g⁴ b16m⁵ b13.7m⁵ Mar 29] rather unfurnished gelding: first foal: dam
(h103), 2¼m hurdle winner, also 11.5f-2m winner on Flat: fair form in bumpers: best effort
when fifth at Kempton. *Michael Madgwick*

WHILE YOU WAIT (IRE) 10 b.g. Whipper (USA) – Azra (IRE) (Danehill (USA)) [2018/19 c–, h100: c16.1g⁵ c20g c19.4m⁴ c20g Sep 25] good-bodied gelding: fair hurdler at one time: poor maiden chaser nowadays: stays 19f: acts on soft and good to firm going: usually races towards rear. *Susan Gardner* **c76**
h–

WHIN PARK 7 b.g. Great Pretender (IRE) – Pocahontas (FR) (Nikos) [2018/19 c79p, h102: c23.6g³ c23.8g* c23.6sᶠ c21.3dᵖᵘ h19.5d Mar 21] has had breathing operation: maiden hurdler: fair form over fences: won handicap at Ludlow in October: stays 3m: acts on good to soft going: tried in blinkers/tongue tie: front runner/races prominently. *Ben Pauling* **c105**
h–

WHIPCRACKAWAY (IRE) 10 b.g. Whipper (USA) – Former Drama (USA) (Dynaformer (USA)) [2018/19 h–: h15.9dᵖᵘ Mar 18] good-topped gelding: fairly useful hurdler at best, deteriorated markedly after 2012/13: usually wore headgear: dead. *Peter Hedger* **h–**

WHISKEY CHASER (IRE) 11 br.g. Flemensfirth (USA) – Cregane Lass (IRE) (Oscar (IRE)) [2018/19 c110, h–: c23.4d⁵ c23.4d c24sᵖᵘ Mar 23] lightly-raced hurdler: fair handicap chaser, below form in 2018/19: stays 3m: raced mainly on soft/heavy going: wears headgear: usually races prominently. *Donald McCain* **c91**
h–

WHISKEY JOHN 9 b.g. Westerner – Cherry Lane (Buckley) [2018/19 h69: h22g⁶ h18.7m Jun 19] lengthy, dipped-backed gelding: maiden hurdler, no form in 2018/19: has worn cheekpieces, including last 4 starts. *Laura Young* **h–**

WHISKEY SOUR (IRE) 6 b.g. Jeremy (USA) – Swizzle Stick (IRE) (Sadler's Wells (USA)) [2018/19 h141: h16s h16.8d⁴ h16d² Apr 21] compact gelding: useful handicap hurdler: fourth in County Hurdle at Cheltenham (6 lengths behind Ch'tibello) in March: unproven beyond 17f: acts on heavy going: tried in tongue tie: usually races nearer last than first. *W. P. Mullins, Ireland* **h141**

WHISPERING AFFAIR 8 b.m. Black Sam Bellamy (IRE) – City of Angels (Woodman (USA)) [2018/19 h101: h23.1g² h23.3d⁵ h23.1s³ h20.1v⁴ h23gᶠ Apr 13] fair maiden hurdler: stays 23f: acts on soft going: has worn cheekpieces, including in 2018/19. *Ian Williams* **h106**

WHISPERINTHEBREEZE 6 gr.g. Kayf Tara – Silver Spinner (Silver Patriarch (IRE)) [2018/19 h19.3s² c18.2d⁴ c20g² c21.2g⁵ c21g² c25.5d² c21g* c31.7sᶠ c29d Apr 22] £44,000 3-y-o: compact gelding: second foal: brother to fairly useful hurdler Silver Kayf (2½m/21f winner): dam (h115), bumper/21f hurdle winner (stayed 3m), half-sister to very smart hurdler (stayed 3m) Splendid Thyne: fairly useful form over hurdles: useful chaser: won Leopardstown Handicap Chase (by 3¼ lengths from Livelovelaugh) in February: stays 25f: acts on heavy going: in cheekpieces last 5 starts: usually front runner/races prominently, often travels strongly. *Mrs J. Harrington, Ireland* **c140**
h127

WHITEABBEY (IRE) 14 b.g. Luso – Frantesa (Red Sunset) [2018/19 c26.2dᵖᵘ Apr 8] multiple point winner: maiden hurdler/chaser: tried in headgear. *Mrs R. Hewit* **c–**
h–

WHITEHOTCHILLIFILI (IRE) 5 b.m. Milan – Mhuire Na Gale (IRE) (Norwich) [2018/19 b15.7s* b16g² b16s⁴ b17d Apr 4] rather unfurnished mare: fourth foal: half-sister to fairly useful hurdler/useful chaser Wild West Wind (2½m-25f winner, by Westerner) and fairly useful hurdler/chaser Redhotfillypeppers (2¼m-2¾m winner, by Robin des Champs): dam unraced half-sister to dam of high-class staying chaser On His Own: fairly useful form in bumpers: won conditionals/amateurs contest at Southwell in December: fourth in listed mares event at Sandown (6½ lengths behind Misty Whisky) in March. *Harry Fry* **b103**

WHITE LILAC (IRE) 8 b.m. Westerner – Strawberry Lane (IRE) (Moscow Society (USA)) [2018/19 h23g⁵ h23.3d⁶ h23.1sᵖᵘ Mar 18] first foal: dam, winning pointer, half-sister to useful chaser (winner up to 2½m) Deans Road: point winner: modest maiden hurdler: stays 23f: acts on good to soft going: in cheekpieces last 3 starts. *Neil Mulholland* **h92**

WHITE MOON (GER) 7 gr.g. Sholokhov (IRE) – Westalin (GER) (Sternkoenig (IRE)) [2018/19 h127p: c20.2gᶠ c19.2s⁵ c17.5d* c24g⁴ c24d⁴ Jan 28] big gelding: has had breathing operation: fairly useful hurdle winner: useful form over fences: won maiden at Exeter in January: stays 2¾m: acts on good to soft going: wears tongue tie. *Colin Tizzard* **c136**
h–

WHITEOAK FLEUR 6 b.m. Black Sam Bellamy (IRE) – Harringay (Sir Harry Lewis (USA)) [2018/19 b86: b16.2g⁴ b17g h20.9g³ h19.9d³ h19.9v² Jan 27] fair form when in frame in bumpers/over hurdles. *Donald McCain* **h105**
b85

WHITEOAK MOLLY 5 b.m. Flemensfirth (USA) – Whiteoak (IRE) (Oscar (IRE)) [2018/19 b16.7g³ May 19] third foal: half-sister to fair hurdler Little Acorn (21f winner, by Presenting): dam (h146) bumper/2m-3m hurdle winner: 8/1, third in mares bumper at Bangor (4¾ lengths behind Kalifornia). *Donald McCain* **b88**

WHITEOAK STROLLER 6 b.m. Shirocco (GER) – Whiteoak (IRE) (Oscar (IRE)) **h71**
[2018/19 h87, b–: h15.8d⁵ h19.3g⁶ h19.9s^F h19.6d Apr 26] well-made mare: poor maiden
hurdler: usually races prominently. *Donald McCain*

WHITE VALIANT (FR) 6 gr.g. Youmzain (IRE) – Minnie's Mystery (FR) (Highest **h99**
Honor (FR)) [2018/19 h94p, b96: h17.7g⁴ h19.2s⁴ Oct 6] small, close-coupled gelding:
dual bumper winner: modest form over hurdles: tried in cheekpieces: won on Flat in Jersey
in 2019. *John Berry*

WHITLEY NEILL (IRE) 7 b.g. Shantou (USA) – Maidrin Rua (IRE) (Zaffaran (USA)) **h119**
[2018/19 h112p: h20s⁴ h18.5g³ h20g³ h23.6s⁴ h26s^pu h23.9s^ur Apr 7] has had breathing
operations: fairly useful handicap hurdler: stays 3m: acts on soft going: has worn headgear,
including last 4 starts: wears tongue tie. *David Pipe*

WHITSUNDAYS (IRE) 10 b.g. Kutub (IRE) – Urdite's Vic (IRE) (Old Vic) [2018/19 **c89 §**
c112§, h–: c20v⁴ c16.3s⁵ Jan 29] winning hurdler: fair handicap chaser, below form both **h–**
outings in 2018/19: stays 2¾m: acts on heavy going: has worn headgear, including last 3
starts: wears tongue tie: temperamental. *Donald McCain*

WHIZZ BANG 7 b.m. Schiaparelli (GER) – Whizz Back (IRE) (Bob Back (USA)) **h–**
[2018/19 h15.8g h16g Apr 26] no form over hurdles. *Polly Gundry*

WHOCALLEDMESPEEDY (IRE) 4 b.f. Rip Van Winkle (IRE) – Fig Tree Drive **b–**
(USA) (Miswaki (USA)) [2018/19 b13.7g⁵ Apr 24] €28,000 3-y-o: has had breathing
operation: half-sister to several winners, including Champion Hurdle winner Sublimity (by
Selkirk): dam 6f winner: in tongue strap, 5/1, fifth of 7 in bumper at Fontwell. *Dan Skelton*

WHOLESTONE (IRE) 8 br.g. Craigsteel – Last Theatre (IRE) (King's Theatre (IRE)) **h153**
[2018/19 h159: h20g* h24.2s⁵ h20.3d² h24d h24d⁵ h24.7g Apr 6] sturdy gelding: smart
hurdler: won minor event at Aintree (by 2¾ lengths from Vision des Flos) in November:

Simon Munir & Isaac Souede's "Wholestone"

easily best effort after when second in Relkeel Hurdle at Cheltenham (2¼ lengths behind Midnight Shadow): stays 3m: acts on soft going. *Nigel Twiston-Davies*

WHOOPSEY 4 b.f. Presenting – Whoops A Daisy (Definite Article) [2018/19 b16.5d⁴ b16.8g Apr 18] £38,000 3-y-o: second foal: sister to fairly useful hurdler Angel of Harlem (2½m/21f winner), stays 3m: dam (h131), bumper/2m-3m hurdle winner, half-sister to fairly useful hurdler/useful chaser (stayed 19f) Dick Dundee: modest form in bumpers: easily better effort when fourth in mares event at Taunton. *Henry Daly* **b82**

WHOS DE BABY (IRE) 11 gr.g. Bienamado (USA) – Beaus Rose (IRE) (Roselier (FR)) [2018/19 c96§, h–: c21.2g⁴ c21.2g³ c25.5m⁶ c21g c20.3g⁵ Aug 31] sturdy gelding: maiden hurdler: poor handicap chaser nowadays: stays 23f: acts on good to firm and heavy going: wears headgear: usually races close up: temperamental. *Sarah-Jayne Davies* **c79 §** **h–**

WHO SHOT JR (IRE) 5 b.g. Scorpion (IRE) – Ariesanne (IRE) (Primo Dominie) [2018/19 b15.3s b13.7g³ Apr 12] £17,000 3-y-o: fourth foal: half-brother to fair 2¼m hurdle winner Lake Malawi and fair hurdler/chaser Spare Brakes (2m-2¼m winner), both by Westerner: dam, 6f winner, half-sister to useful staying hurdler Paperprophet: fair form in bumpers: much better effort when third at Fontwell. *Colin Tizzard* **b85**

WHOSHOTTHESHERIFF (IRE) 5 b.g. Dylan Thomas (IRE) – Dame Foraine (FR) (Raintrap) [2018/19 b18.8d² b16d³ h16s* h16d² h19.9s* h17m* Apr 20] €100,000 3-y-o: chasing sort: seventh foal: half-brother to 3 winners, including bumper/point winner and fairly useful 2m hurdle winner Gunnery Sergeant (by Presenting) and fairly useful hurdler/chaser Damefirth (2m winner, by Flemensfirth): dam, French 17f/2¼m chase winner (also 11f winner on Flat), half-sister to useful hurdler/chaser up to 25f Celtic Son and to dam of useful hurdler/very smart staying chaser Junior: fair form in bumpers: useful form over hurdles: won novices at Ayr in January, Sedgefield in March and Carlisle (by 6 lengths from Staged Engagement) in April: left Gordon Elliott after fourth start. *Philip Kirby* **h132** **b90**

WHOSHOTWHO (IRE) 8 br.g. Beneficial – Inishbeg House (IRE) (Glacial Storm (USA)) [2018/19 h121, b91: h20.5g³ c20g² c21.4g* c21.4m* c20.2gᶠ c22.9v³ c20mᵘʳ c23d² c20.6d² Mar 20] good-topped gelding: fairly useful hurdler: useful handicap chaser: won twice at Market Rasen in July, dead-heated in novice event on second occasion: stays easy 23f: acts on good to firm and heavy going: has worn hood: usually races towards rear. *Dr Richard Newland* **c137** **h94**

WHO'S MY JOCKEY (IRE) 6 b.g. Yeats (IRE) – Scandisk (IRE) (Kenmare (FR)) [2018/19 h128: h24.7g⁴ h22g³ h24.2d h20.5s h21g³ h24.4g* h24g⁵ Apr 17] good-topped gelding: useful handicap hurdler: won at Doncaster (by 10 lengths from Faithful Mount) in March: stays 25f: acts on good to firm and good to soft going: in cheekpieces last 2 starts. *Philip Hobbs* **h139**

WHO'S THE GUV'NOR (IRE) 5 b.g. Gold Well – Clamit Brook (IRE) (Alderbrook) [2018/19 b16.7g⁶ b16.8s⁶ Mar 3] modest form on first of 2 starts in bumpers. *Micky Hammond* **b77**

WHO WHAT WHEN 4 b.f. Champs Elysees – Freya Tricks (Noverre (USA)) [2018/19 b12.6s* b16.7d* b17d Apr 4] good-topped filly: fourth foal: half-sister to 1¼m winner Roly Tricks (by Pastoral Pursuits): dam maiden (stayed 1½m): fairly useful form in bumpers: won fillies junior race at Newbury in December and listed mares event at Market Rasen (by 3¼ lengths from Mrs Hyde) in January. *Murty McGrath* **b98**

WHY LIE (IRE) 8 b.g. Zagreb (USA) – Persian Avenue (Persian Mews) [2018/19 h20g⁵ h20g⁴ h20g h15.7sᵖᵘ h21dᵖᵘ c16dꟳ h19.7g Mar 26] point winner: modest form over hurdles: fell eighth on chasing debut: best effort at 2½m: usually front runner/races prominently. *Alan Phillips* **c–** **h91**

WICKED SPICE (IRE) 10 b.g. Old Vic – Afdala (IRE) (Hernando (FR)) [2018/19 c–, h89: c23.8gᵖᵘ h23dᵖᵘ Aug 29] maiden pointer: fairly useful hurdler at best, has deteriorated markedly: winning chaser: stays 3m: acts on soft going: has worn cheekpieces. *Nicky Richards* **c–** **h–**

WICKED WILLY (IRE) 8 br.g. Arcadio (GER) – How Provincial (IRE) (Be My Native (USA)) [2018/19 c129, h–: h26.5v⁵ h24g³ h21.4g³ h25d³ h23.6d⁵ h21s* c20.1g Apr 25] compact gelding: useful handicap hurdler: won at Kempton (by 6 lengths from My Way) in March: fairly useful chaser: stays 27f: acts on soft going: wears tongue tie nowadays: usually races towards rear. *Nigel Twiston-Davies* **c–** **h130**

WICKLOW BRAVE 10 b.g. Beat Hollow – Moraine (Rainbow Quest (USA)) [2018/19   **h156 §**
h161§: h16g² h16g* h16g³ h24s^F h16.2g⁴ h20g h16d² h21s² h20d^F Apr 22] smallish, strong
gelding: very smart hurdler: 16/1-on, won 3-runner minor event at Listowel in September:
second in Coral Cup at Cheltenham (short head behind William Henry) in March and third
in Punchestown Champion Hurdle (3¾ lengths behind Buveur d'Air) shortly after end of
British season: stays 21f: acts on heavy going: has worn blinkers: usually races in rear: not
one to trust (has given trouble at start). *W. P. Mullins, Ireland*

WIG WAM WIGGLE (IRE) 7 b.g. Mahler – Last Sunrise (IRE) (Shahanndeh)   **h93**
[2018/19 h84: h24.1s⁶ h24.1d^pu h22g* h25g³ h24.1g^su Apr 11] modest handicap hurdler:
won at Newcastle (amateurs) in January: stayed 2¾m: acted on heavy going: dead.
Micky Hammond

WILBERDRAGON 9 b.g. Kayf Tara – Swaythe (USA) (Swain (IRE)) [2018/19 c122,   **c100**
h–: c21.3g c23.9m³ Apr 21] good-topped gelding: winning hurdler: fairly useful handicap   **h–**
chaser, below form both starts in 2018/19 after long absence: stays 2½m: acts on heavy
going: usually in cheekpieces nowadays: wears tongue tie: front runner/races prominently.
Charlie Longsdon

WILDE BLUE YONDER (IRE) 10 b.g. Oscar (IRE) – Blue Gallery (IRE) (Bluebird   **c133**
(USA)) [2018/19 h132: h19.6d^F c22.4d⁶ c19.9g² c23.4d⁴ Mar 22] useful-looking gelding: **h–**
useful hurdler: similar form over fences: best effort when second in novice handicap at
Haydock (1¼ lengths behind The Paddy Pie) in February: barely stays 23f: acts on good to
firm and heavy going. *Alan King*

WILDE SPIRIT (IRE) 5 b.m. Oscar (IRE) – Full of Spirit (IRE) (Exit To Nowhere   **h98**
(USA)) [2018/19 b59: h16g³ h16d³ h16.5d h20.5g⁵ Apr 22] modest form over hurdles.
Alan King

WILD EVE 5 b.m. Sulamani (IRE) – Vin Rose (Alflora (IRE)) [2018/19 b17.7g⁶   **h64**
b15.7g² b16.8g h16m h16g⁵ h24g⁵ h16s h16.7g^pu Nov 22] second foal: dam (h82),   **b74**
unreliable maiden hurdler (stayed 2½m), half-sister to useful hurdler/chaser (winner up to
21f) Twelve Roses: poor form in bumpers/over hurdles: in blinkers last 3 starts.
Mark Rimell

WILDE WATER (IRE) 5 b.g. Oscar (IRE) – Pay The Ferryman (IRE) (Supreme Leader)   **b–**
[2018/19 b16s Dec 27] tailed off in bumper. *Graeme McPherson*

WILD GYPSY BOY 4 ch.g. Intikhab (USA) – Sahabah (USA) (Swain (IRE)) [2018/19   **b76**
b16g⁵ b16.2g Apr 15] modest form on first of 2 starts in bumpers. *Micky Hammond*

WILDMOOR BOY 8 b.g. Midnight Legend – Simple Glory (IRE) (Simply Great (FR))   **c–**
[2018/19 h–: h16m c19.4m^pu h20.3g Jun 12] sturdy gelding: has had breathing operation: **h–**
fair hurdler at best: no form in 2018/19 including on chasing debut: usually wears headgear/
tongue tie. *Robin Dickin*

WILD SAM (IRE) 9 b.g. Bachelor Duke (USA) – Pure Spin (USA) (Machiavellian   **h91**
(USA)) [2018/19 h20d⁶ h24g h19d h16.4d h20.9g h20.6d³ h20.2d⁵ Apr 26] modest maiden
hurdler: left Stephen Ryan after third start: stays 21f: acts on heavy going: in headgear last
2 starts. *Iain Jardine*

WILD WEST WIND (IRE) 10 b.g. Westerner – Mhuire Na Gale (IRE) (Norwich)   **c–**
[2018/19 c142, h–: c23.6v^pu Dec 8] winning hurdler: useful chaser at best, has completely   **h–**
lost his way: stays 3¼m: acts on heavy going: wears tongue tie. *Tom George*

WILHELM VONVENSTER (FR) 5 b.g. Apsis – Princesse Gaelle (Osorio (GER))   **b82**
[2018/19 b16.4g⁴ Nov 16] €28,000 3-y-o: first foal: dam, French 17f hurdle winner, also
13f winner on Flat: 4/6, only fourth in bumper at Newcastle (7¼ lengths behind Malystic).
Nicky Richards

WILLIAM H BONNEY 8 b.g. Midnight Legend – Calamintha (Mtoto) [2018/19 h130:   **h131**
h15.7g h16.2g* h15.8d* h15.7d h16.3d Mar 22] compact gelding: has had breathing
operation: useful handicap hurdler: won at Hereford in November and Huntingdon (by
length from Great Hall) in December: unproven beyond 17f: acts on heavy going: often
travels strongly. *Alan King*

WILLIAM HENRY (IRE) 9 b.g. King's Theatre (IRE) – Cincuenta (IRE) (Bob Back   **c–**
(USA)) [2018/19 c–, h150: h21.4d^pu h21s² h24.7g⁴ Apr 6] good-topped gelding: smart   **h154**
handicap hurdler: had breathing operation before winning Coral Cup at Cheltenham (by
short head from Wicklow Brave) in March: fourth in Stayers' Hurdle (Liverpool) at Aintree

Coral Cup Handicap Hurdle, Cheltenham—William Henry (hooped cap) goes three places better than in 2018 as he storms home to pip previous Cheltenham Festival winners Wicklow Brave (star on cap) and Ballyandy (right) in the dying strides

(11½ lengths behind If The Cap Fits) 3 weeks later: lost confidence and pulled up after saddle slipped only chase outing: seems to stay 3m: acts on soft going: in cheekpieces last 5 starts. *Nicky Henderson*

WILLIAM HUNTER 7 b.g. Mawatheeq (USA) – Cosmea (Compton Place) [2018/19   **h102 §**
h105: h16.7g² h15.8g⁵ Nov 13] workmanlike gelding: has had breathing operation: fairly
useful on Flat, stays 1½m: fair maiden hurdler: unproven beyond 17f: acts on good to soft
going: has joined Nigel Twiston-Davies: weak finisher. *Alan King*

WILLIAM OF ORANGE 8 b.g. Duke of Marmalade (IRE) – Critical Acclaim (Peintre   **h126**
Celebre (USA)) [2018/19 h123: h16.2g* h15.8m⁶ h22.1g* h25.4s⁵ h23.9g⁵ h24.7g⁴ h18.9v
Dec 5] strong gelding: has had breathing operation: fairly useful handicap hurdler: won at
Kelso in May and Cartmel in July: stays 25f: acts on heavy going: wears headgear/tongue
tie: usually races nearer last than first. *Donald McCain*

WILLIAM OF WYKEHAM (IRE) 4 ch.g. Arcano (IRE) – Highland Gift (IRE)   **h95**
(Generous (IRE)) [2018/19 h16m⁶ h16.2g⁵ h16g⁵ h16gᵖᵘ Feb 9] half-brother to fairly
useful hurdler Highland Games (2½m-3m winner, by Singspiel) and fair 2m hurdle winner
Gift Voucher (by Cadeaux Genereux): well held on Flat: modest form over hurdles: wears
tongue tie. *Mark McNiff, Ireland*

WILLIE BOY (IRE) 8 b.g. Tikkanen (USA) – Pandora's Moon (IRE) (Tamayaz (CAN))   **c139**
[2018/19 c136, h–: c19.4m² c20.2gᶠ c19.4s* c24g⁴ c25sᵖᵘ c25g⁶ Apr 6] good-topped   **h–**
gelding: has had breathing operation: lightly-raced maiden hurdler: useful handicap chaser:
won at Wetherby in December: probably stays 3m: acts on soft and good to firm going: in
cheekpieces last 4 starts: usually races prominently. *Charlie Longsdon*

WILLIE BUTLER (IRE) 5 b.g. Yeats (IRE) – Belsalsa (FR) (Kingsalsa (USA))   **b93**
[2018/19 b15.8g* Apr 11] £66,000 5-y-o: fifth foal: closely related to bumper winner/
useful hurdler Mulcahys Hill (2½m winner, by Brian Boru) and half-brother to bumper
winner/fairly useful hurdler Penn Lane (21f/2¾m winner, by Scorpion): dam French 15f
hurdle winner: placed both starts in Irish points: 2/1, won maiden bumper at Huntingdon
by 1¾ lengths from Mr Perfect with bit in hand. *Neil King*

WILLIE MCLOVIN 7 b.g. Apple Tree (FR) – Kiss Me du Cochet (FR) (Orival (FR))   **h–**
[2018/19 h–, b–: h21.4mᵖᵘ h23.9dᵖᵘ Mar 11] little sign of ability, including in points.
Carroll Gray

WILL O'THE WEST (IRE) 8 b.g. Westerner – Simply Divine (IRE) (Be My Native   **c–**
(USA)) [2018/19 c118, h113: h25g² h23g² h23g³ h27m² h19.7g h23.1g h25.3d⁵ Mar 6]   **h117**
good-topped gelding: has had breathing operation: fairly useful handicap hurdler: maiden
chaser: left Henry Daly/no form after fourth start: stays 27f: acts on good to firm and heavy
going: in headgear last 3 starts: tried in tongue tie: usually races towards rear. *Laura Morgan*

932

WILLOW MAY 5 b.m. Sakhee (USA) – Cerise Bleue (FR) (Port Lyautey (FR)) [2018/19 **h–** b67: b15.3m h16.8g⁶ h19.5d h19.7g^F h18.5v h21.9v^{pu} Jan 14] poor form in bumpers, none **b70** over hurdles: tried in blinkers. *Mrs Jane Williams*

WILLSHEBETRYING 8 b.m. Act One – Precedence (IRE) (Polish Precedent (USA)) **h–** [2018/19 h82: h21.7g h21.7v h19.5d⁴ h25g^{pu} Feb 25] has had breathing operation: poor hurdler at best, no form in 2018/19: has worn headgear. *Mark Hoad*

WILLYEGOLASSIEGO 6 br.m. Kheleyf (USA) – Kryena (Kris) [2018/19 h84: **h84** h21.6m⁵ h21.6m^{pu} h21.6g² h23.3g h25g⁴ h20d⁵ h21.7g⁵ Apr 12] rather leggy mare: poor handicap hurdler: stays 2¾m: acts on good to soft going: in cheekpieces last 4 starts, in tongue tie last 5. *Neil Mulholland*

WILLY SEWELL 6 b.g. Multiplex – Cherished Love (IRE) (Tomba) [2018/19 b16.7m⁵ **b–** Jun 22] tailed off in bumper: fairly useful 8.5f winner on Flat. *Michael Appleby*

WIMPOLE 6 b.g. Zamindar (USA) – Proportional (Beat Hollow) [2018/19 b81: h15.3m **h–** h16.7g May 19] has had breathing operation: fourth in bumper on debut in 2017/18, only form: tried in tongue tie. *Michael Scudamore*

WIND OF HOPE (IRE) 10 b.g. September Storm (GER) – Ciara's Run (IRE) **c–** (Topanoora) [2018/19 c–, h95: h21.4g⁶ h20.2g⁵ May 17] lengthy gelding: multiple point **h94** winner: modest handicap hurdler: maiden chaser: stays 23f: acts on heavy going: has worn headgear, including last 5 starts: often races prominently. *Alistair Whillans*

WIND PLACE AND SHO 7 b.g. Shirocco (GER) – Coh Sho No (Old Vic) [2018/19 **h119 §** h108: h19.6g^{rr} h19.2g³ h17.7m* h19.2m² h19.7d h20d² h19.2d² h20.7d^{rr} h23.4d^{rr} Mar 4] fairly useful handicap hurdler: won at Fontwell in October: stays 2½m: wears cheekpieces: one to leave alone (has refused to race, including last 2 starts). *James Eustace*

WINDSOR AVENUE (IRE) 7 b.g. Winged Love (IRE) – Zaffarella (IRE) (Zaffaran **h131 p** (USA)) [2018/19 b104p: h17.1d² h20.1g* h22d⁴ h19.9d* h18.1d² Mar 2] point/bumper winner: useful form over hurdles: won maiden at Hexham in November and novice at Sedgefield in January: second in Premier Kelso Novices' Hurdle (4 lengths behind Rouge Vif) final start: stays 2¾m: acts on good to soft going: usually races prominently: remains with potential. *Brian Ellison*

WINDSPIEL (FR) 6 b.g. Sholokhov (IRE) – Wildlife (GER) (Waky Nao) [2018/19 h93: **c103** c16.2m³ c16.1g* c17.2g c18g² c20d⁵ c15.9m³ c15.9f^F Feb 26] good-topped gelding: **h–** maiden hurdler: fair handicap chaser: won at Towcester in May: stayed 2¼m: acted on good to firm and good to soft going: wore tongue tie: dead. *David Arbuthnot*

WINDY BOTTOM (IRE) 8 b.m. Milan – Swinley Bottom (IRE) (Woods of Windsor **h69** (USA)) [2018/19 h20.5g h21g h15.9s h20.5d h25g⁶ h23.1s h26.4g⁶ Apr 14] €1,700 3-y-o: chunky mare: has had breathing operation: second foal: dam unraced half-sister to useful staying chaser Shardam: off mark in Irish points at sixth attempt: poor maiden hurdler. *Zoe Davison*

WINGED EXPRESS (IRE) 10 b.g. Winged Love (IRE) – Zaffaran Express (IRE) **c–** (Zaffaran (USA)) [2018/19 h19s^{pu} Feb 4] fair hurdler at best, pulled up only start since **h–** 2016/17: winning chaser: usually wears headgear. *Alexandra Dunn*

WINGS OF DARKNESS (IRE) 5 b.g. Winged Love (IRE) – Night Therapy (IRE) **h–** (Mandalus) [2018/19 b–: h21g^{pu} Nov 12] good-topped gelding: has had breathing operation: no show in bumper/novice hurdle: tried in tongue tie. *Paul Webber*

WINGSOFREDEMPTION (IRE) 7 br.m. Winged Love (IRE) – Lady Oakwell (IRE) **h–** (King's Ride) [2018/19 h16.5d^F h21.4g^F Dec 6] €1,900 3-y-o: sister to fair hurdler/fairly useful chaser Posh Bird (2½m-3¾m winner) and a winning pointer, and half-sister to bumper winner/fair hurdler Ballykelly (19f winner, by Insan): dam failed to complete in points: maiden pointer: no form under Rules. *Kevin Bishop*

WINGS OF SMOKE (IRE) 14 gr.g. King's Theatre (IRE) – Grey Mo (IRE) (Roselier **c– §** (FR)) [2018/19 c107§, h–: c20.3g⁵ c20.2g Jul 26] winning hurdler: useful chaser at best, no **h–** form in 2018/19: stays 2¾m: acts on good to firm and heavy going: has worn visor: wears tongue tie: usually races in rear: weak finisher. *Tim Vaughan*

WINIDO 7 b.g. Sulamani (IRE) – Princess Claudia (IRE) (Kahyasi) [2018/19 h93: h20.3s^F **h–** Dec 4] maiden hurdler: in tongue tie last 5 starts: dead. *Tim Vaughan*

WIN MY WINGS (IRE) 6 b.m. Gold Well – Telstar (IRE) (Montelimar (USA)) [2018/19 **h114 p** h15.3g h15.8d⁶ h21.9g* Apr 21] £9,250 5-y-o: half-sister to fairly useful hurdlers/winning pointers Fairly Legal (19f winner, by Beneficial) and Star Lord (2½m-3¼m winner, by Lord Americo): dam unraced half-sister to fairly useful staying chaser On The Other Hand: off mark in Irish points at third attempt: fair form over hurdles: easily won maiden at Ffos Las in April: open to further improvement. *Christian Williams*

WINNER MASSAGOT (FR) 8 ch.g. Muhaymin (USA) – Winnor (FR) (Lesotho (USA)) [2018/19 c20g⁶ c21.4m c17.4g c16.5g⁶ c17.8g* h16g⁶ h21d² h20d* h20s Apr 20] tall, close-coupled gelding: has had breathing operation: fairly useful handicap hurdler: won at Montpelier in November: useful handicap chaser: back to form when winning easily at Fontwell in September: left Dan Skelton after sixth start: stays 21f: acts on good to soft going: has worn cheekpieces/tongue tie. *Richard L. Valentine, USA* **c129 h120**

WINNINGSEVERYTHING (IRE) 5 b.g. Flemensfirth (USA) – Baliya (IRE) (Robellino (USA)) [2018/19 b16.7g* b15.7g³ b15.8s⁴ Apr 7] €80,000 3-y-o: half-brother to several winners, including useful hurdler/chaser Edmund Kean (17f-3m winner) and useful hurdler Brave Vic (2½m winner), both by Old Vic: dam (b78), second in bumper, half-sister to useful hurdler/fair chaser (stayed 2½m) Balapour: fairly useful form in bumpers: won at Market Rasen in November. *Harry Fry* **b101**

WINNING SPARK (USA) 12 b.g. Theatrical – Spark Sept (FR) (Septieme Ciel (USA)) [2018/19 h118: h22g Oct 8] good-topped gelding: fairly useful handicap hurdler, well held only start in 2018/19: stays 2½m: acts on good to firm and heavy going: tried in tongue tie: races towards rear. *Jackie du Plessis* **h–**

WINSOME BUCKS (IRE) 9 b.g. Chevalier (IRE) – Winsome Lady (IRE) (Buckskin (FR)) [2018/19 h23gᶠ Sep 2] compact gelding: bumper winner: maiden hurdler, weakening when falling only start in 2018/19: tried in hood: wears tongue tie. *T. Hogan, Ireland* **h–**

WINSTON C (IRE) 5 b.g. Rip Van Winkle (IRE) – Pitrizza (IRE) (Machiavellian (USA)) [2018/19 h15.8d³ h15.3g* h16s* h16.2g* h16.5d⁵ Apr 5] neat gelding: fairly useful on Flat, stays 14.5f: completed hat-trick when winning maiden at Wincanton in January, novice at Sandown in February and handicap at Kelso (by nose from Champagne City) in March: will stay beyond 2m: acts on soft going: held up: has joined Jonathan Sheppard in USA. *Harry Fry* **h137**

WINTER ESCAPE (IRE) 8 b.g. Robin des Pres (FR) – Saddleeruppat (IRE) (Saddlers' Hall (IRE)) [2018/19 c89P, h–: c18.2d² c18.2s* c20s* c20d* c21g⁵ c20g³ Apr 21] lengthy gelding: winning hurdler: smart chaser: completed hat-trick when winning maiden at Galway in September, novice at Cork in November and Grade 3 novice at Punchestown (by 2¼ lengths from A Plus Tard) in January: disappointing after: stays 2½m: acts on soft going: often travels strongly. *Aidan Anthony Howard, Ireland* **c149 h–**

WINTER HOLIDAY 5 b.m. Dubai Destination (USA) – Tamara King (IRE) (Milan) [2018/19 b17.7g² Sep 9] first foal: dam winning pointer: unplaced in point: 15/8, second in mares bumper at Fontwell (7 lengths behind Cardigan Bay). *Jamie Snowden* **b78**

WINTER LION (IRE) 9 ch.g. Galileo (IRE) – Hill of Snow (Reference Point) [2018/19 c125, h–: c25g² c26.1m⁴ Jul 1] winning hurdler: fairly useful handicap chaser: stays 3¼m: acts on good to firm and heavy going: has worn headgear, including in 2018/19: wears tongue tie: often races lazily. *Fergal O'Brien* **c129 h–**

WINTER SOLDIER 9 b.g. Apple Tree (FR) – Primitive Quest (Commanche Run) [2018/19 h19d⁵ h23.6d h23.3d⁵ h23.9d⁴ c25.7gᵘʳ Apr 21] has had breathing operation: multiple point winner: bumper winner: well held over hurdles: unseated tenth on chasing debut. *Richard Mitford-Slade* **c– h–**

WINTER SOLDIER (FR) 6 b.g. Soldier Hollow – Wintersonne (GER) (Big Shuffle (USA)) [2018/19 h17d h15.3f⁵ Oct 28] runner-up only start on Flat in France: lightly-raced maiden hurdler, no form in 2018/19: left W. P. Mullins after first start: wears hood. *Robert Walford* **h–**

WINTER SPICE (IRE) 8 gr.g. Verglas (IRE) – Summer Spice (IRE) (Key of Luck (USA)) [2018/19 h16g³ h18.5g² h16.8g⁶ h18.5d³ h20g² h21.6m² h20.5g* h23.9d⁵ Nov 29] rather leggy gelding: fair handicap hurdler: won at Plumpton (amateurs) in November: stays 2¾m: acts on good to firm and good to soft going: wears hood. *Johnny Farrelly* **h109**

WINTER TIME (IRE) 7 br.g. Golan (IRE) – Winter's Folly (IRE) (Leading Counsel (USA)) [2018/19 b15.7s⁵ Dec 18] fair form when placed in bumpers in Ireland for Denis Hogan, well held only start in 2018/19. *Michael Easterby* **b–**

WINTOUR LEAP 8 b.m. Nayef (USA) – Mountain Leap (IRE) (Sadler's Wells (USA)) [2018/19 h–: h20g⁶ May 10] fair hurdler at best, well held only 2 starts in sphere since 2015/16: tried in cheekpieces. *Robert Stephens* **h–**

WISE COCO 6 b.m. Shirocco (GER) – Sensible (Almutawakel) [2018/19 b66: h20.2g⁶ h20.9g⁴ h17.1d h22g h20.1sᵖᵘ Nov 21] rather unfurnished mare: little show on Flat/over hurdles: in cheekpieces last 2 starts: tried in tongue tie. *Alistair Whillans* **h–**

WISECRACKER 6 br.g. Sageburg (IRE) – Folie Lointaine (FR) (Poliglote) [2018/19 **c83 x** h90: h16.7g^{pu} c19.7g^6 c15.7m^2 c16g^2 c16.3d^3 c16.2d^3 c17.8s^{pu} Jan 27] has had breathing **h–** operations: maiden hurdler: poor form over fences: unproven beyond 17f: acts on soft and good to firm going: has worn headgear, including last 5 starts: wears tongue tie: often let down by jumping. *Ben Case*

WISHFULL DREAMING 8 ch.g. Alflora (IRE) – Poussetiere Deux (FR) (Garde **c122** Royale) [2018/19 h115x: c20.5g^3 c17.8g^3 h15.8g^4 h17.1g h16.4g^2 h16g^2 c19.1g* c20.2f^3 **h108** c16.9s* c20.3m^5 c17.2g^2 c15.9m* Apr 20] lengthy gelding: has had breathing operation: fair handicap hurdler: fairly useful handicap chaser: won novice events at Doncaster in January, Musselburgh in March and Carlisle in April: left Olly Murphy after third start: will prove best up to 2½m: acts on firm and soft going: has worn headgear, including last 2 starts: wears tongue tie: races towards rear, often travels strongly. *Sam England*

WISHFUL TINKER (IRE) 6 br.g. Milan – Third Wish (IRE) (Second Empire (IRE)) **h–** [2018/19 h24g^{pu} Oct 25] pulled up in novice hurdle. *Dan Skelton*

WISHICOULD (IRE) 8 br.m. Asian Heights – Dark Wish (IRE) (Mister Lord (USA)) **h112** [2018/19 h25s^3 h25.5d^{pu} h25s h23.9s Apr 7] plain mare: off mark in Irish points at second attempt: fairly useful handicap hurdler, lost way in 2018/19: stays 3¼m: acts on soft going: tried in cheekpieces. *Charlie Mann*

WISH IN A WELL (IRE) 10 b.g. Gamut (IRE) – Lady Bellingham (IRE) (Montelimar **c64 x** (USA)) [2018/19 c64x, h–: c21.6d c20.9s^6 Dec 11] workmanlike gelding: maiden hurdler: **h–** poor handicap chaser nowadays: stays 21f: acts on good to firm and heavy going: wears headgear: has worn tongue tie: often let down by jumping. *Ben Case*

WISHING WELL 7 b.m. Bahri (USA) – Amourallis (IRE) (Dushyantor (USA)) [2018/19 **h–** h16.2g h16.2s h16.2g^{pu} h19.7s h20.6d^{pu} h24.1d^{pu} Mar 19] strong mare: fair on Flat, stays 2¼m: maiden hurdler, no form in 2018/19: tried in cheekpieces: often races in rear. *Micky Hammond*

WISHMOOR (IRE) 9 br.g. Winged Love (IRE) – Presentingatdawn (IRE) (Presenting) **c132** [2018/19 c20d^F c20d c19.7s h19.5d^6 c28.7d^2 c24d c24.7d Apr 22] winning hurdler: useful **h–** handicap chaser: second at Punchestown (4¼ lengths behind Dounikos) in February, standout effort in 2018/19: stays 29f: acts on heavy going: has worn headgear/tongue tie, including in 2018/19: front runner/races prominently. *Joseph Patrick O'Brien, Ireland*

WISTARI ROCKS (IRE) 10 b.g. Heron Island (IRE) – Hi Honey (IRE) (Persian Mews) **h–** [2018/19 h15.7g h15.8s Jul 29] modest hurdler at best, no form in 2018/19: raced around 2m: acts on good to firm and good to soft going. *Tim Vaughan*

WISTY (IRE) 10 gr.g. Cloudings (IRE) – Alpine Message (Tirol) [2018/19 c137, h–: **c127** c17.3g c17.3g^2 Jul 23] winning hurdler: useful handicap chaser: unproven beyond 17f: **h–** acted on soft and good to firm going: wore hood earlier in career: usually led: dead. *Martin Todhunter*

WITCHES GLEN (IRE) 7 b.m. Helissio (FR) – Native Cheer (IRE) (Be My Native **h–** (USA)) [2018/19 h20.5s^6 h15.9s^4 h16s^{pu} Mar 16] £5,000 6-y-o: half-sister to fair 2m hurdle winners Career Move (also bumper winner, by Oscar) and Cheer Up (by Rudimentary): dam, placed in 19f bumper, showed little over hurdles: placed in Irish points: no form over hurdles: tried in tongue tie. *Pat Phelan*

WITHAM 6 b.m. Beat Hollow – Wistow (Sir Harry Lewis (USA)) [2018/19 b66: h20.6d **h–** h20g^{pu} Feb 15] fourth in bumpers, best effort on debut: no form over hurdles after long absence. *Pam Sly*

WITHER OR NOT (IRE) 9 ch.g. Saffron Walden (FR) – Stage Debut (Decent Fellow) **c93** [2018/19 c25.2d^3 Mar 6] third on first of 2 starts in Irish bumpers in 2015/16: multiple point winner: 10/1, third in novice hunter at Catterick (24 lengths behind Diplomate Sivola) on chasing debut. *D. Peters*

WITHOUTDEFAVOURITE (IRE) 11 b.g. Oscar (IRE) – Camden Confusion (IRE) **c79 §** (Camden Town) [2018/19 c74§, h–: c24g^2 c24g c23g^2 c23m^3 c24g^5 Oct 18] rangy gelding: **h–** maiden hurdler: poor maiden chaser nowadays: stays 25f: acts on heavy and good to firm going: wears headgear: usually leads: temperamental. *Tim Vaughan*

WITHOUT FRONTIER (IRE) 7 b.g. Stowaway – Hollygrove Samba (IRE) **c74 §** (Accordion) [2018/19 h75§: h20g^6 c20s^5 c24d^{pu} Nov 29] poor maiden hurdler: similar **h80 §** form on first of 2 starts over fences: stays 2½m: acts on good to soft going: has worn headgear, including last 2 starts: wears tongue tie: temperamental. *Tim Vaughan*

WITH PLEASURE 6 b.g. Poet's Voice – With Fascination (USA) (Dayjur (USA)) **h94**
[2018/19 h99: h23.6g⁶ Oct 30] close-coupled gelding: fair on Flat, stays 2¼m: modest
maiden hurdler: stays 19f: acts on good to firm and heavy going: often races in rear.
John Flint

WITNESS (FR) 10 b.g. Astarabad (USA) – Belle Yepa (FR) (Mansonnien (FR)) [2018/19 **c–**
c99, h94: h22.7g h24g⁶ h20.6d⁶ h24.1d⁵ h27s² h27gᵖᵘ Apr 5] close-coupled gelding: **h88**
modest handicap hurdler: winning chaser: stays 27f: acts on heavy going: has worn
headgear: tried in tongue tie: usually races towards rear. *Micky Hammond*

WITNESS IN COURT (IRE) 12 b.g. Witness Box (USA) – Inter Alia (IRE) (Dr **c102 §**
Massini (IRE)) [2018/19 c100§, h–: c20.5m² Apr 25] tall, angular gelding: winning **h–**
hurdler: fair chaser nowadays, off 18 months before only start in 2018/19: stays 21f: acts
on good to firm and heavy going: unreliable. *Donald McCain*

WIZADORA 11 b.m. Alflora (IRE) – Moor Spring (Primitive Rising (USA)) [2018/19 c–: **c87**
c24.2d² c21.2gᵖᵘ May 28] multiple point winner: modest form when second in maiden at
Hexham, standout effort in hunter chases. *Mrs C. A. Coward*

WIZARDS BRIDGE 10 b.g. Alflora (IRE) – Island Hopper (Be My Native (USA)) **c116 §**
[2018/19 c120§, h–: h25.8m⁴ c27.7d³ c25.1gᵖᵘ c24.2d c25.7s⁵ c25.1s³ c19.4d⁵ c25.1gᵖᵘ **h– §**
Apr 3] rangy gelding: winning hurdler: fairly useful handicap chaser: third in Southern
National at Fontwell in November: stays 3½m: acts on good to firm and heavy going:
wears headgear: tried in tongue tie: temperamental. *Colin Tizzard*

WOLFCATCHER (IRE) 7 b.g. King's Best (USA) – Miss Particular (IRE) (Sadler's **c124**
Wells (USA)) [2018/19 h116: c21g* h21.6g⁶ c25g⁵ c20v⁶ c22g* c18.8d⁴ Jan 19] compact **h104**
gelding: fair handicap hurdler: fairly useful form over fences: won novice handicaps at
Newton Abbot in June and Musselburgh (3 ran) in December: stays 25f: acts on heavy
going: wears headgear/tongue tie. *Ian Williams*

WOLF OF WINDLESHAM (IRE) 7 ch.g. Mastercraftsman (IRE) – Al Amlah (USA) **h–**
(Riverman (USA)) [2018/19 h135: h22.8gᵇᵈ May 12] workmanlike gelding: useful hurdler,
lightly raced: stays 2½m: acts on soft going. *Stuart Edmunds*

WOLFSLAIR (IRE) 8 b.g. Yeats (IRE) – Hidden Reserve (IRE) (Heron Island (IRE)) **c–**
[2018/19 h100: c20.1dᵖᵘ h20.3g h22.1g Jul 23] fair hurdler at best, has lost his form (pulled **h–**
up on chasing debut): has worn headgear/tongue tie. *David Thompson*

WOLF SWORD (IRE) 10 b.g. Flemensfirth (USA) – Dame O'Neill (IRE) (Dr Massini **c–**
(IRE)) [2018/19 c123, h–: c24dᵖᵘ May 5] strong gelding: winning hurdler: fairly useful **h–**
chaser: stayed 3m: acted on good to firm and heavy going: dead. *Sue Smith*

WOLFTRAP (IRE) 10 b.g. Mountain High (IRE) – Dear Money (IRE) (Buckskin (FR)) **c–**
[2018/19 c–, h106: h16d h19.5g Apr 26] rather leggy gelding: point winner: fair hurdler at **h–**
best, well beaten both starts in 2018/19: no form in chases: has worn headgear, including
in 2018/19: tried in tongue tie. *Colin Heard*

WONDERFUL CHARM (FR) 11 b.g. Poliglote – Victoria Royale (FR) (Garde Royale) **c131 §**
[2018/19 c123§, h–: c27.7g* c27.5d³ c26g* c21.1dᵖᵘ Apr 4] rangy gelding: has had **h–**
breathing operation: winning hurdler: useful hunter chaser nowadays: won at Fontwell in
May and Doncaster (by 55 lengths) in February: stays 3½m: acts on soft going: wears
headgear/tongue tie: temperamental: usually races towards rear: dead. *Paul Nicholls*

WONDERGIRL (IRE) 5 b.m. Court Cave (IRE) – Young Elodie (FR) (Freedom Cry) **h–**
[2018/19 h15.8d h15.8m h15.8m³ Apr 23] €10,000 3-y-o: fifth foal: closely related to
bumper winner Castello Sforza (by Milan): dam (h116) 2m-2½m hurdle winner: well held
in novice hurdles. *Robin Dickin*

WONDER LAISH 7 b.g. Halling (USA) – Wonder Why (GER) (Tiger Hill (IRE)) **h142**
[2018/19 h16.3g h16d* h16g* h16g Feb 2] dam sister to useful hurdler (stayed 3m)
Whispering Hills and half-sister to useful hurdler/chaser (stayed 2¾m) Whispered Secret:
useful on Flat, stays 1¾m: useful form over hurdles: won handicaps at Navan in November
and Fairyhouse (by ½ length from Tudor City) in December: raced only at 2m: acts on
heavy going: often travels strongly. *Charles Byrnes, Ireland*

WONGA SWINGER 9 b.g. Lucky Story (USA) – Chippewa (FR) (Cricket Ball (USA)) **c59**
[2018/19 c–, h–: c15.7g³ c20g c16.3sᵖᵘ Jul 30] winning hurdler: little form in chases: stays **h–**
2¼m: acts on good to firm going: wears headgear: temperament under suspicion.
Sam Thomas

WOOD BREIZH (FR) 9 gr.g. Stormy River (FR) – Polynevees (FR) (Poliglote) **h–**
[2018/19 h109: h22.1gᵖᵘ h22.1gᵖᵘ h17.2d Aug 25] has had breathing operation: fair hurdler
at best, no form in 2018/19: has worn headgear: tried in tongue tie. *James Moffatt*

WOODBROOK BOY (IRE) 5 ch.g. Doyen (IRE) – Pohutakawa (FR) (Affirmed (USA)) [2018/19 b16.8s⁶ Apr 16] winning pointer: 5/1, sixth in maiden bumper at Exeter (11¼ lengths behind Merchant House). *John Joseph Hanlon, Ireland* **b77**

WOOD EMERY (FR) 7 b.g. Califet (FR) – Take Emery (FR) (Take Risks (FR)) [2018/19 h24sᵖᵘ h25.4m Jul 1] lengthy gelding: modest winner over hurdles, no form in 2018/19: left Alan Fleming after first start: stays 3m: acts on heavy going: has worn tongue tie. *Henry Hogarth* **h–**

WOODFIELD ROBIN (IRE) 8 ch.m. Robin des Champs (FR) – Ticket To Mars (IRE) (Sabrehill (USA)) [2018/19 h–: h20.7g h15.8dᵖᵘ Feb 6] last of 3 finishers on completed start in Irish points: no form over hurdles: wears tongue tie. *Katy Price* **h–**

WOODFLEET (IRE) 8 b.g. Fleetwood (IRE) – Norwer (IRE) (Norwich) [2018/19 c111: c25.1m* c25.1g³ Apr 14] good-topped gelding: multiple point winner: fairly useful form in hunter chases: won 4-runner event at Wincanton in May: tried in cheekpieces. *Mrs K. Bandey* **c119**

WOODFORT 7 gr.g. Dalakhani (IRE) – Akdara (IRE) (Sadler's Wells (USA)) [2018/19 h113§: h19.9g h18.7g⁵ Nov 1] well-made gelding: fourth in Irish point: bumper winner: maiden hurdler, no form in 2018/19 when tongue tied: temperamental: dead. *Dan Skelton* **h– §**

WOODLAND OPERA (IRE) 9 br.g. Robin des Champs (FR) – Opera Hat (IRE) (Strong Gale) [2018/19 c145, h–: c16g² c21g² h20m² c18.2g h19.8g* h24.4m* c20m* c24g² c16s⁵ Mar 18] useful hurdler: won minor events at Kilbeggan and Down Royal in August: smart chaser: won PWC Champion Chase at Gowran (by 10 lengths from Jury Duty) in October: second in JNwine.com Champion Chase at Down Royal (16 lengths behind Road To Respect) next time: stays 3m: acts on soft and good to firm going: wears blinkers/tongue tie: front runner/races prominently. *Mrs J. Harrington, Ireland* **c150 h141**

WOOD PIGEON (IRE) 10 b.g. Presenting – Come In Moscow (IRE) (Over The River (FR)) [2018/19 c101, h80: c21.2d² c23.6g⁴ c21.4dᵖᵘ Mar 14] has had breathing operation: maiden hurdler: fair handicap chaser: stays 25f: acts on heavy going: wears headgear: usually races close up: temperamental. *Olly Murphy* **c100 § h–**

WOODS WELL (IRE) 8 ch.g. Fleetwood (IRE) – Millbrook Marble (IRE) (Rudimentary (USA)) [2018/19 h135, h–: c22.5d* c24d c24.5g h20d c28.7d c21.3s* c21.1d⁵ c29d Apr 22] strong gelding: winning hurdler: useful chaser: won minor event at Galway in October and handicap at Leopardstown in March: stays 3m: acts on heavy going: in cheekpieces last 5 starts. *Gordon Elliott, Ireland* **c142 h–**

WOODUKHELEYFIT 5 b.g. Kheleyf (USA) – Wood Chorus (Singspiel (IRE)) [2018/19 h15.7gᵖᵘ h16.8s Apr 16] fair 7f winner on Flat at 2 yrs: no form over hurdles: in hood first start. *Emma Lavelle* **h–**

WORCESTER PEARMAIN 9 b.m. Beat All (USA) – Granoski Gala (Petoski) [2018/19 c24.2d⁴ May 5] multiple point winner: once-raced hurdler: 66/1, last of 4 finishers in maiden hunter at Hexham (7½ lengths behind Streets of Milan) on chasing debut. *A. G. Dobbin* **c83 h–**

WORKBENCH (FR) 11 b.g. Network (GER) – Danhelis (FR) (Hellios (USA)) [2018/19 c125, h114: c16m⁶ h19.9g c19.4g⁶ c22.6m c20g² c20.1g² h17.m⁴ c19.4gᵖᵘ c20.5g Nov 26] good-topped gelding: fair handicap hurdler: fairly useful handicap chaser: stays 2½m: acts on heavy going: has worn headgear, including in 2018/19: wears tongue tie. *Dan Skelton* **c121 h104**

WORK DU BRETEAU (FR) 9 ch.g. Network (GER) – Salinka (FR) (Green Tune (USA)) [2018/19 c128, h113: c23.9gᵖᵘ c24g³ May 23] has had breathing operation: winning hurdler: fairly useful handicap chaser: stays 3m: acts on good to firm and heavy going: often wears headgear: has worn tongue tie. *Dan Skelton* **c129 h–**

WORKING CLASS 5 b.g. Bahri (USA) – Louise d'Arzens (Anabaa (USA)) [2018/19 h103: h15.8g² h15.8g⁶ h16.8s h16d* h15.3g³ h15.5d³ h16s h18.6g⁴ h16m² Apr 22] workmanlike gelding: fair handicap hurdler: awarded race at Fakenham in December: may prove best around 2m: acts on good to firm and good to soft going: in tongue tie last 2 starts: often races towards rear. *Oliver Sherwood* **h111**

WORK IN PROGRESS (IRE) 9 b.g. Westerner – Parsons Term (IRE) (The Parson) [2018/19 c143, h121: c18gᵖᵘ c16.2g⁵ c19.4gᶠ Jun 9] fairly useful hurdler: useful chaser at best, no form in 2018/19: wore tongue tie: dead. *Dan Skelton* **c– h–**

WORLD PREMIER (FR) 6 gr.g. Montmartre (FR) – Kelbelange (FR) (Ganges (USA)) [2018/19 h115: h15.8g⁵ h16.2g* h15.5g³ h17.7v³ h20.7d h15.8g⁶ Apr 11] good-topped gelding: has had breathing operation: fair handicap hurdler: awarded race at Hereford in November: unproven beyond 2m: best form on good going: tried in tongue tie: often races freely: has joined N. Madden. *Ben Pauling* **h114**

WORLD WAR (IRE) 5 ch.g. Galileo (IRE) – Jacqueline Quest (IRE) (Rock of Gibraltar (IRE)) [2018/19 h16.4g h20vᵖᵘ h16g Apr 11] compact gelding: fairly useful on Flat, stays 13f: mid-field at best in novice hurdles: tried in cheekpieces/tongue tie. *Martin Keighley* **h93**

WORTHY FARM (IRE) 6 b.g. Beneficial – Muckle Flugga (IRE) (Karinga Bay) [2018/19 h113p: h26g³ h23.9d* h24g h23.5d* h25.8g Mar 23] good-topped gelding: easy winner of point: fairly useful form over hurdles: won handicaps at Taunton (novice) in November and Ascot in February: stays 3¼m: acts on good to soft going: often travels strongly. *Paul Nicholls* **h128**

WOR VERGE 6 b.g. Virtual – Hanover Gate (Motivator) [2018/19 h80, b80: h20.2g h21.2g h16.8s³ h20.1sᵖᵘ h16s h16g h20.6dᵖᵘ h16.4m Mar 22] modest maiden hurdler: tried in hood: wears tongue tie. *Susan Corbett* **h87**

WOT A SHOT (IRE) 10 b.g. Refuse To Bend (IRE) – Ashdali (IRE) (Grand Lodge (USA)) [2018/19 c–, h100: h16.2g⁶ h17.2g⁵ h16.2g³ h16.2gᵖᵘ h15.6g⁶ h16.7s⁵ h15.6g* h16.4m⁵ h16.4m Mar 22] modest handicap hurdler: won at Musselburgh in January: winning chaser: unproven beyond 2m: acts on soft and good to firm going: has worn hood: tried in tongue tie. *Nicky Richards* **c–** **h94**

WOTZIZNAME (IRE) 9 b.g. Fruits of Love (USA) – Native Beau (IRE) (Be My Native (USA)) [2018/19 c138, h–: h23.1g h24s² h24dᵖᵘ Jan 1] useful-looking gelding: useful form over hurdles: second in handicap at Southwell (½ length behind Crosspark) in December: useful chaser: stays 3¼m: acts on soft going: wears tongue tie. *Harry Fry* **c–** **h138**

WOULDUADAMANDEVEIT (IRE) 6 b.g. Stowaway – Figlette (Darshaan) [2018/19 b103: h16g h19.5v h23.1v⁶ h23.3vᵖᵘ Mar 16] compact gelding: fairly useful form in bumpers: little show over hurdles (bled final start). *Susan Gardner* **h75**

WOULD YOU BYPASS (IRE) 6 br.m. Vinnie Roe (IRE) – Academy Hall (IRE) (Saddlers' Hall (IRE)) [2018/19 h19.9v³ h19.8g³ h20.1g² Apr 15] fourth foal: dam unraced: Irish point winner: fair form over hurdles: best effort when second in mares novice at Hexham, clear of rest. *Tim Fitzgerald* **h104**

WOUNDED WARRIOR (IRE) 10 b.g. Shantou (USA) – Sparkling Sword (Broadsword (USA)) [2018/19 c136§, h–: c25g c22.5g⁶ c30.2g h19.5d³ c23.5g⁴ h22g⁵ Apr 12] tall, lengthy gelding: fairly useful form over hurdles: fairly useful chaser nowadays: best effort for a while when 22½ lengths third of 17 to Cloudy Morning in handicap at Punchestown shortly after end of British season: stays 31f: acts on heavy going: often wears headgear: usually front runner/races prominently: unreliable. *S. Curling, Ireland* **c125 §** **h119**

WRITINGSONTHEWALL (IRE) 8 ch.g. Vinnie Roe (IRE) – Saddlers Eve (IRE) (Saddlers' Hall (IRE)) [2018/19 h16d h20.5sᵖᵘ h19.5vᵖᵘ Feb 18] of no account. *Diana Grissell* **h–**

W S GILBERT 5 b.g. Librettist (USA) – Little Miss Prim (Gildoran) [2018/19 b16s b16.2s ab16s h15.8g h16.7g⁵ h19g⁶ Apr 25] close-coupled gelding: has had breathing operation: largely well held in bumpers/over hurdles: tried in hood/tongue tie. *John O'Neill* **h–** **b–**

WUFF (IRE) 11 b.g. Beneficial – Dummy Run (IRE) (Glacial Storm (USA)) [2018/19 c126§, h–: c27.5gᵖᵘ Jun 9] strong gelding: winning hurdler: useful chaser at best, has lost his way: wears cheekpieces/tongue tie: temperamental. *Tom George* **c– §** **h–**

WYE AYE 4 b.g. Shirocco (GER) – A Media Luz (FR) (Johann Quatz (FR)) [2018/19 b16d Apr 6] tailed off in bumper. *Venetia Williams* **b–**

WYFIELD ROSE 10 b.m. Kayf Tara – Miniature Rose (Anshan) [2018/19 c89§, h95§: h23.9g h25.4g h20.2g h23.9g h27m* h23.3g h25.8gᵗᵗ Oct 27] smallish, workmanlike mare: has had breathing operation: modest handicap hurdler: won at Sedgefield in September: maiden chaser: left Alistair Whillans after fourth start: stays 27f: acts on soft and good to firm going: wears headgear: tried in tongue tie: front runner/races prominently: temperamental (refused to race final start). *Dianne Sayer* **c– §** **h87 §**

WYNFORD (IRE) 6 ch.g. Dylan Thomas (IRE) – Wishing Chair (USA) (Giant's Causeway (USA)) [2018/19 h121: h19.2g² h20.6g² h24g² h23.1g* h25.4s h20g h19.9vᵖᵘ h23.1g³ h19.8g Apr 27] angular gelding: fairly useful handicap hurdler: won at Market Rasen in July: stays 3m: acts on good to firm going: has worn headgear, including in 2018/19: wears tongue tie: races off pace: temperamental. *Dan Skelton* **h128 §**

WYNN HOUSE 4 ch.f. Presenting – Glorious Twelfth (Old Vic) [2018/19 b15.8d* Mar 30] £60,000 3-y-o: second foal: dam (h112), bumper/21f hurdle winner, closely related to fairly useful hurdler/useful chaser (stays 2½m) The West's Awake, out of smart hurdler/fairly useful chaser (2m-21f winner) Bilboa: 11/1, won mares bumper at Uttoxeter (by length from The Milan Girl) on debut. *Alan King* **b93**

X

XHALE (FR) 7 br.g. Halling (USA) – Xanadu Bliss (FR) (Xaar) [2018/19 h68: h19m May 7] angular gelding: poor maiden hurdler: unproven beyond 2m: acts on good to soft going. *Ian Williams*   **h–**

XPO UNIVERSEL (FR) 10 b.g. Poliglote – Xanadu Bliss (FR) (Xaar) [2018/19 c–, h92: h17.2g² c16g⁵ c20.1g⁴ h20.2g² h17.2d* h22.1s⁶ h16.2g³ h17.1d h17.1v* h16.2g* c15.9s⁴ h17g Feb 18] fair handicap hurdler: won at Cartmel (conditionals/amateurs) in August, and Carlisle and Kelso in December: modest form over fences: stays 2½m: acts on heavy going: wears headgear/tongue tie: front runner/races prominently. *Rebecca Menzies*   **c88** **h111**

Y

YAA SALAAM (IRE) 5 ch.g. Helmet (AUS) – Ya Hajar (Lycius (USA)) [2018/19 h15.8s³ h16.7g² Mar 27] good-topped gelding: half-brother to fair 2m hurdle winner Faanan Aldaar (by Authorized): useful for Andreas Wohler on Flat, stays 9.5f: fair form over hurdles: better effort when third in novice at Ffos Las: remains with potential. *David Pipe*   **h111 p**

YALA ENKI (FR) 9 b.g. Nickname (FR) – Cadiane (FR) (Cadoudal (FR)) [2018/19 c150, h–: c24d⁴ c29.5s³ c28.4g⁵ c26.3d Mar 15] useful-looking gelding: winning hurdler: very smart handicap chaser: won at Bangor (by nose from Sir Mangan) in November: third in Welsh Grand National at Chepstow (5¼ lengths behind Elegant Escape) next time: stays 29f: acts on heavy going: tried in cheekpieces. *Venetia Williams*   **c155** **h–**

YALLA HABIBTI 6 b.m. Kayf Tara – Majeeda (IRE) (Jeremy (USA)) [2018/19 b75: b15.8m⁴ h18.7m⁵ h15.8g h15.8d⁶ h15.5d⁵ h21.2dᶠ h19.7gᵖᵘ h16gᵖᵘ Apr 10] poor form in bumpers/over hurdles. *Michael Mullineaux*   **h78** **b60**

YALLTARI 8 gr.g. Kayf Tara – Lily Grey (FR) (Kadalko (FR)) [2018/19 h125: c23.6v² c23.6s* c24.2sᶠ c23.8d³ Feb 16] rangy gelding: fairly useful hurdler: useful form over fences: won novice handicap at Chepstow in December: third in Reynoldstown Novices' Chase at Ascot (4¾ lengths behind Mister Malarky) final start: stays 3m: acts on heavy going: front runner/races prominently: remains open to improvement as a chaser. *Venetia Williams*   **c140 p** **h–**

YAMUNA RIVER 4 b.f. Foxwedge (AUS) – Harryana To (Compton Place) [2018/19 h16m⁶ h17.7d² h17.7v³ h16.8g Apr 18] fair maiden on Flat, stays 1¼m: modest form over hurdles: wears headgear: temperament under suspicion. *Chris Gordon*   **h97**

YANMARE (IRE) 9 b.g. Soapy Danger – Bell Walks Caroll (IRE) (Carroll House) [2018/19 c109, h–: c26.2gᵖᵘ c30.7sᵖᵘ Dec 7] big, workmanlike gelding: twice-raced hurdler: fair chaser at best, has lost his way: stays 31f: acts on heavy going: has worn headgear, including in 2018/19: wears tongue tie. *Nigel Twiston-Davies*   **c–** **h–**

YANWORTH 9 ch.g. Norse Dancer (IRE) – Yota (FR) (Galetto (FR)) [2018/19 c150+, h153: h24.3gᵖᵘ h24d Mar 14] compact gelding: high-class hurdler at best, no form in 2018/19: smart form but not convincing over fences: stays 25f: acts on heavy going: has worn headgear, including first start: not straightforward: has joined Enda Bolger. *Alan King*   **c–** **h–**

YASIR (USA) 11 b.g. Dynaformer (USA) – Khazayin (USA) (Bahri (USA)) [2018/19 h88§: h16s³ Mar 10] close-coupled gelding: modest handicap hurdler: stays 21f: acts on heavy going: has worn headgear: tried in tongue tie: races towards rear: moody. *Sophie Leech*   **h88 §**

YEATS BABY (IRE) 7 b.m. Yeats (IRE) – Cabo (FR) (Sagamix (FR)) [2018/19 h95: h21.5g h23.4g* h20d³ h23.8m* h24.3m* Apr 12] fair handicap hurdler: won at Fakenham in November, Musselburgh in March and Ayr in April, 2 of them mares events: left F. Flood after first start: stays 3m: acts on good to firm and good to soft going: has worn cheekpieces: tried in tongue tie. *Emmet Mullins, Ireland*   **h113**

YEAVERING BELLE 5 ch.m. Midnight Legend – Fruit Yoghurt (Hernando (FR)) [2018/19 b16g⁴ b15.7s⁴ b16.8g³ Apr 18] second foal: half-sister to useful hurdler Ronald Pump (2½m-3m winner, by Schiaparelli): dam, ran once in bumper, out of useful hurdler up to 3m Diamant Noir: third in point on debut: fairly useful form in bumpers: won mares event at Warwick in February: will be suited by at least 2½m. *Kim Bailey*   **b97**

YELLOW DOCKETS (IRE) 7 ch.m. Getaway (GER) – Soft Skin (IRE) (Rudimentary (USA)) [2018/19 b88: b16.7g⁴ h21d* h21s* Jan 21] runner-up in Irish point on debut: better effort in bumpers when third at Towcester in 2017/18: fairly useful form over hurdles: won mares novices at Warwick in December and January: will stay beyond 21f: wears hood: likely to progress further. *Nicky Henderson*   **h121 p** **b75**

YELLOW KANGAROO (IRE) 7 b.g. Aussie Rules (USA) – Sue N Win (IRE) **h72** (Beneficial) [2018/19 h57: h16.3g³ Aug 23] poor form over hurdles: best effort at 2m: tried in tongue tie. *Evan Williams*

YENSIR 6 ch.g. Sir Percy – Yensi (Doyen (IRE)) [2018/19 h15.8m³ h16g* h16.3m* **h125** h20.6g* h18.5m² Aug 6] angular gelding: fair maiden on Flat, stays 1½m: fairly useful form over hurdles: completed 4-timer in maiden at Fakenham and novices at Stratford, Market Rasen and Newton Abbot early in season: stays 21f: acts on good to firm going. *Olly Murphy*

YESANDNO (IRE) 6 b.g. Scorpion (IRE) – In Fact (IRE) (Classic Cliche (IRE)) **h–** [2018/19 b65p: h21.6d h25.5sᵖᵘ h23.1sᵖᵘ Mar 5] third when unseated last in Irish point: showed a bit in bumper: no form over hurdles. *Alan King*

YES DADDY (IRE) 11 b.g. Golan (IRE) – Hollygrove Samba (IRE) (Accordion) **c–** [2018/19 c108, h103: h21.6mᵖᵘ Aug 6] lengthy, useful-looking gelding: fair hurdler at best, **h–** has lost his way: maiden chaser: stays 2½m: acts on good to firm and good to soft going: has worn headgear, including only outing in 2018/19: in tongue tie last 4 starts. *Robert Stephens*

YES NO MAYBE SO (IRE) 5 br.g. Stowaway – Godlylady (IRE) (Old Vic) [2018/19 **b91** b16g³ b15.6g* b16.2g Jan 22] £34,000 3-y-o: fifth foal: brother to fairly useful 2¾m hurdle winner/ winning pointer Polymath and half-brother to fairly useful 17f hurdle winner West To The Bridge (by Flemensfirth): dam unraced half-sister to top-class chaser up to 3m Flemenstar: fair form in bumpers: won 4-runner event at Musselburgh in December. *Donald McCain*

YES TOM (IRE) 14 gr.g. Tikkanen (USA) – Ammieanne (IRE) (Zaffaran (USA)) **c–** [2018/19 c–, h–: h24.3g⁶ h23.9g⁶ Jul 31] lengthy gelding: maiden pointer: useful hurdler/ **h96** chaser at best, has deteriorated considerably: often wears headgear: tried in tongue tie. *Stuart Crawford, Ireland*

YORGONNAHEARMEROAR (IRE) 8 b.g. Scorpion (IRE) – Etoile Margot (FR) **c–** (Garde Royale) [2018/19 c113, h109: h19.6g c20.6s c16dᵘʳ h19.5d⁵ h20s⁶ Apr 7] fair **h97** hurdler/chaser, not at best in 2018/19: stays 19f: acts on heavy going: wears headgear. *Henry Oliver*

YORKHILL (IRE) 9 ch.g. Presenting – Lightning Breeze (IRE) (Saddlers' Hall (IRE)) **c146** [2018/19 c–, h–: h25.4s⁶ h19.4s c20g² Mar 26] rangy gelding: high-class hurdler/chaser at **h146** best, not the force of old: second in minor event over fences at Clonmel (8½ lengths behind Acapella Bourgeois) in March: stays 25f: acts on heavy going. *W. P. Mullins, Ireland*

YORKIST (IRE) 11 ch.g. Urban Ocean (FR) – Kilbarry Demon (IRE) (Bob's Return **c136** (IRE)) [2018/19 c133, h–: c15.8g* c16.3d⁴ c15.5d⁴ c15.2g³ c16d⁵ Mar 21] workmanlike **h–** gelding: has had breathing operation: winning hurdler: useful handicap chaser: won at Aintree (by 6 lengths from Theflyingportrait) in November: stays 19f: acts on heavy going: has worn headgear: has worn tongue tie, including all starts in 2018/19: usually races off pace. *Dan Skelton*

YOUGHAL BY THE SEA (IRE) 6 b.g. Milan – Down By The Sea (IRE) (Fourstars **h111** Allstar (USA)) [2018/19 h16.7m h18.8g* h16.2g* Jul 31] second foal: brother to bumper winner Cruisingdownriver: dam (b96) bumper winner: bumper winner: fair form over hurdles: won maiden at Downpatrick and novice at Perth in July: wears tongue tie. *Gordon Elliott, Ireland*

YOUKNOWELL (IRE) 6 b.m. Gold Well – Islands Sister (IRE) (Turtle Island (IRE)) **h88** [2018/19 h–: h16g h25g* h20.5d³ h23.4d⁴ Jan 1] runner-up on second of 2 starts in Irish points: modest handicap hurdler: won mares event at Plumpton in November: stays 25f: acts on good to soft going: usually races towards rear, often travels strongly. *Paul Webber*

YOU'LL DO 6 b.g. Approve (IRE) – Tentears (Cadeaux Genereux) [2018/19 h16.2m⁵ **h95 ?** h16.2g h17.2d⁵ Aug 25] modest form over hurdles: best effort when fifth in novice at Cartmel, though possibly flattered: ran out in point in early-2019: wears tongue tie. *Maurice Barnes*

YOUMZAIN STAR (FR) 4 b.g. Youmzain (IRE) – Thraya Star (FR) (Shamardal (USA)) **h–** [2018/19 h16dᵖᵘ Oct 14] fairly useful at best on Flat in France at 2 yrs: pulled up in juvenile hurdle: dead. *Jonjo O'Neill*

YOUNEVERCALL (IRE) 8 b.g. Yeats (IRE) – Afarka (IRE) (Kahyasi) [2018/19 **h153** h23.9g² h21g* h24.4s h21.5g* Apr 27] well-made gelding: smart hurdler: won handicap at Kempton (by 10 lengths from Canyon City) in November and Select Hurdle at Sandown (by 9 lengths from On The Blind Side, following breathing operation) in April: stays 3m: acts on good to soft going: in cheekpieces last 3 starts, tongue tie last 2: unsuited by left-handed tracks. *Kim Bailey*

YOUNG BULL (IRE) 5 b.g. Dubai Destination (USA) – Jane Hall (IRE) (Saddlers' Hall (IRE)) [2018/19 b15.8d³ b16v* b17g⁵ Feb 18] €20,000 3-y-o: fourth foal: brother to fairly useful 19f hurdle winner Seemingly So and half-brother to fairly useful hurdler/useful chaser Shanroe Santos (21f-3½m winner, by Definite Article): dam unraced half-sister to smart French hurdler/high-class chaser (stayed 25f) Boca Boca: runner-up on completed start in Irish points: fair form in bumpers: won at Chepstow in December: will be suited by 2½m+. *Harry Whittington* **b92**

YOUNG CHEDDAR (IRE) 12 b.m. Croco Rouge (IRE) – Sin Ceist Eile (IRE) (Simply Great (FR)) [2018/19 c93, h–: c26g^pu May 17] smallish mare: maiden pointer/hurdler: fair chaser at best, pulled up both starts in hunters: stays 3¼m: acts on heavy going: in tongue tie last 2 starts. *Georgie Howell* **c– h–**

YOUNG HURRICANE (IRE) 13 b.g. Oscar (IRE) – Georgia On My Mind (FR) (Belmez (USA)) [2018/19 c126, h–: c27.5d^pu Jun 8] multiple winning pointer: winning hurdler: fairly useful chaser at best, took no interest only start under Rules in 2018/19: stays 3½m: acts on heavy going: has worn blinkers/tongue tie: temperamental. *G. C. Brewer* **c– § h–**

YOUNG LIEUTENANT (IRE) 5 b.g. Robin des Champs (FR) – Be My Gesture (IRE) (Indian Danehill (IRE)) [2018/19 b16d⁵ b16.8s* Jan 20] £60,000 4-y-o: first foal: dam, unraced, out of sister to top-class hurdler (stayed 3m) Rhinestone Cowboy: runner-up in Irish point on debut: fair form in bumpers: won at Exeter in January. *Warren Greatrex* **b89**

YOUNG LOU 10 b.m. Kadastrof (FR) – Wanna Shout (Missed Flight) [2018/19 h93. h25m^pu May 7] modest handicap hurdler, pulled up only outing in 2018/19: stays 3¼m: acts on heavy going: usually wears headgear: has worn tongue tie: front runner/races prominently. *Robin Dickin* **h–**

YOUNGOCONNOR (IRE) 6 b.m. Kalanisi (IRE) – Strike Three (IRE) (Presenting) [2018/19 h66: c20g² c23.6g* c24.2g^F h21.2g^pu c25.3v^pu c24.2s^pu Jan 20] maiden hurdler: modest form over fences: won novice handicap at Huntingdon in May: stays 3m: best form on good going: in cheekpieces last 2 starts. *Christian Williams* **c92 h–**

YOUNG PHOENIX (IRE) 7 b.g. Robin des Pres (FR) – Lady Phoenix (IRE) (Erins Isle) [2018/19 h95, b81: h23.3d⁵ h25.8g^pu h24d h23.4d² h24.4g⁶ c19.3s^pu Jan 27] modest maiden hurdler: pulled up in novice handicap on chasing debut: stays 3¼m: acts on good to soft going: usually wears headgear. *Martin Keighley* **c– h86**

YOUNG SUNSHINE (IRE) 6 b.m. Pour Moi (IRE) – Garra Molly (Nayef (USA)) [2018/19 b64: b16m⁵ Sep 17] little show in bumpers. *Jennie Candlish* **b–**

YOUNG TED (IRE) 5 b.g. Fame And Glory – Last of Many (IRE) (Lahib (USA)) [2018/19 h16d⁴ h20d⁴ Feb 10] sixth foal: half-brother to useful hurdler Ice Cool Champs (2½m-23f winner, by Robin des Champs): dam unraced half-sister to useful hurdler/high-class chaser (stayed 33f) Shotgun Willy: bumper winner: much improved when 2 lengths second of 23 to My Sister Sarah on handicap debut at Punchestown shortly after end of British season, keeping on when bad mistake last: in hood following reappearance: capable of better again. *Noel Meade, Ireland* **h132 p**

YOUNG WOLF (IRE) 6 b.g. Vinnie Roe (IRE) – Missy O'Brien (IRE) (Supreme Leader) [2018/19 h19.9g⁴ h19.7s³ h15.7m³ h23.8m* Apr 23] third foal: brother to bumper winner/smart hurdler Neon Wolf (2m-2¼m winner) and half-brother to useful hurdler/very smart chaser Lake View Lad (2½m-3m winner, by Oscar): dam (h88) second in bumpers (including at 2½m): runner-up in bumper for Ms Margaret Mullins: fairly useful form over hurdles: won on handicap debut at Ludlow in April: stays 3m. *Jonjo O'Neill* **h122**

YOUNOSO 8 b.g. Alflora (IRE) – Teeno Nell (Teenoso (USA)) [2018/19 h–, b–: c19.4s³ c24.2s³ c20.1g* c23.8g⁴ c20.1m^pu Mar 28] no form over hurdles: poor form over fences: won handicap at Newcastle in January: stays 3m: acts on soft going: usually front runner/races prominently. *Tina Jackson* **c79 h–**

YOU'RE SO RIGHT (IRE) 6 b.g. Presenting – Miss Brandywell (IRE) (Sadler's Wells (USA)) [2018/19 h81, b78: h27g^pu Nov 8] poor form over hurdles. *Keith Dalgleish* **h–**

YOURHOLIDAYISOVER (IRE) 12 ch.g. Sulamani (IRE) – Whitehaven (Top Ville) [2018/19 c89§, h69§: c17g⁵ c16.4s² c16.3d² c16.2d⁴ c17s^F c16d⁶ c17.8v² c17.8v³ c15.7d^pu Apr 24] rather leggy gelding: winning hurdler: poor handicap chaser: left Tom Gretton after fifth start: stays 2½m: acts on heavy going: has worn headgear: wears tongue tie: irresolute. *Lady Susan Brooke* **c71 § h– §**

YOUR WAN (IRE) 6 b.m. Galileo (IRE) – Mayasta (IRE) (Bob Back (USA)) [2018/19 h88, b85: h24g⁶ May 13] modest form over hurdles: stays 3m: acts on soft going. *Jonjo O'Neill* **h91**

YOU SAY WHAT (IRE) 9 b.g. Milan – Wave Back (IRE) (Bob Back (USA)) [2018/19   **c116** c128, h–: c24.2d⁶ c30.7s³ Apr 16] workmanlike gelding: winning hurdler: fairly useful   **h–** handicap chaser: third at Exeter in April: stays 31f: acts on heavy going: wears headgear/ tongue tie. *David Pipe*

YOU TOO PET (IRE) 11 b.g. Norwich – Pollys Pet (IRE) (Little Bighorn) [2018/19   **c64** c32.5g⁵ May 4] multiple point winner: twice-raced hurdler: maiden chaser, modest at best: **h–** stays 25f: acts on heavy going: has worn cheekpieces. *D. Peters*

YOUVEBROKENMYDREAM 4 b.f. Geordieland (FR) – Mollycarrs Gambul   **h–** (General Gambul) [2018/19 b15.8v⁵ b15.8g b16.8s h15.8d Feb 6] fourth foal: half-sister to   **b–** useful hurdler/chaser Thomas Crapper (2m-3¼m winner, by Tamure): dam winning pointer: no form in bumpers/juvenile hurdle. *Bill Turner*

Z

ZABEEL STAR (IRE) 7 ch.g. Arcano (IRE) – Deep Winter (Pivotal) [2018/19 h17.1d*   **h96** h19.3g² Oct 25] fairly useful but unreliable on Flat, stays 12.5f: modest form over hurdles: won handicap at Carlisle (conditionals) in October: unproven beyond 17f: acts on good to soft going. *Karen McLintock*

ZACHARO 6 b.g. Zamindar (USA) – Winter Silence (Dansili) [2018/19 b16g h16.2g May   **h71** 17] poor form in bumper/maiden hurdle. *Andrew Hamilton*   **b–**

ZAFAR (GER) 4 b.g. Kamsin (GER) – Zambuka (FR) (Zieten (USA)) [2018/19 h16.5d²   **h110** h15.7d² h19.2d³ h15.7m Mar 31] good-topped gelding: dam half-sister to useful hurdler (stayed 3m) Jorobaden: fairly useful maiden on Flat, stays 1½m: fair form over hurdles. *Philip Hobbs*

ZAIDIYN (FR) 9 b.g. Zamindar (USA) – Zainta (IRE) (Kahyasi) [2018/19 c–, h124:   **c124** c16.5gᵘʳ Sep 2] good-topped gelding: fairly useful hurdler: failed to complete both starts in   **h–** novice chases: best around 2m: acted on heavy going: sometimes wore headgear: dead. *Sam England*

ZAKHAROVA 5 ch.m. Beat Hollow – Tcherina (IRE) (Danehill Dancer (IRE)) [2018/19   **b89** b94: ab16.3g* Jan 5] rather unfurnished mare: fair form when winning 2 of 3 starts in bumpers, landing odds in conditionals/amateurs event at Newcastle on sole appearance in 2018/19. *Laura Morgan*

ZALGARRY (FR) 12 b.g. Ballingarry (IRE) – Spleen (FR) (Sillery (USA)) [2018/19   **c–** c103, h–: c20gᵖᵘ May 10] winning hurdler: fair form first 2 starts in handicap chases in   **h–** 2017/18: stayed 3m: acted on good to firm and heavy going: tried in cheekpieces: dead. *Arthur Whitehead*

ZALIAPOUR (FR) 13 b.g. Daliapour (IRE) – Spleen (FR) (Sillery (USA)) [2018/19   **c121** c15.9v⁴ c20.2g³ Apr 14] close-coupled gelding: Flat/hurdle winner in France for C.   **h–** Gourdain: better effort over fences (fairly useful form) when third in handicap at Wincanton in April: barely stays 2½m: acts on heavy going: has worn cheekpieces. *Arthur Whitehead*

ZALVADOS (FR) 6 ch.g. Soldier of Fortune (IRE) – Zariyana (IRE) (Desert Prince   **c124** (IRE)) [2018/19 h124: h19.5d h16.8g⁴ c16.4s³ c15.7v² c16.3d² c16.5d² c19.9d c16.5g²   **h111** c20g Apr 27] rather sparely-made gelding: fairly useful handicap hurdler: similar form over fences, placed 5 of 7 outings: stays 19f: acts on heavy going: usually wears headgear/ tongue tie: held up. *Oliver Greenall*

ZAMALIGHT 5 ch.g. Zamindar (USA) – Mountain Chain (USA) (Royal Academy   **h–** (USA)) [2018/19 h–: h15.3m h15.7gᵖᵘ h16.8gᵖᵘ Aug 15] regressive maiden on Flat: no form over hurdles: left Olly Murphy after second start: tried in hood/tongue tie. *Brian Barr*

ZAMARKHAN (FR) 6 b.g. Great Journey (JPN) – Zannkiya (Sendawar (IRE)) [2018/19   **h102** h–, b–: h16.2m⁶ h16.2g h16.2g⁴ h16.2g² h15.6g Nov 7] pulled up in point: fair form over hurdles: raced around 2m: best form on good going: in hood last 3 starts. *Lucy Normile*

ZAMBINO (GER) 4 b.g. It's Gino (GER) – Zamba (GER) (Big Shuffle (USA)) [2018/19   **h–** b14.6s b13.7d h19.8sᵖᵘ h16.2g h16.8g⁶ h16g Apr 26] no form in bumpers/over hurdles: **b–** tried in tongue tie. *Milton Harris*

ZAMDY MAN 10 b.g. Authorized (IRE) – Lauderdale (GER) (Nebos (GER)) [2018/19   **c–** c–, h–: c19.2s Dec 7] strong, good-topped gelding: winning hurdler: developed into useful   **h–** novice chaser in 2016/17: well held in handicaps both starts since 13 months apart: best around 2m: acts on heavy going. *Venetia Williams*

ZAMOYSKI 9 ch.g. Dutch Art – Speech (Red Ransom (USA)) [2018/19 h104: h20.3s* h110
h19.6g³ h21s^pu h21.3g³ Apr 11] strong, compact gelding: fair handicap hurdler: won at
Southwell (amateurs) in December: probably stays 21f: acts on soft going: wears
cheekpieces: usually makes running/races prominently. *Steve Gollings*

ZAMPARELLI (IRE) 7 b.g. Mahler – Goulburn Bridge (IRE) (Rock Hopper) [2018/19 c123
c111p, h76: c19.2d* c20.9d⁵ c21.2g³ c19.9d^F c19.9g³ c23.9d* c24d c23.9m* Apr 21] h–
workmanlike gelding: has had breathing operation: maiden hurdler: fairly useful handicap
chaser: won at Market Rasen in May, March and April: stays 3m, effective at shorter: acts
on soft and good to firm going: regularly in cheekpieces: tongue tied: waited with.
Dan Skelton

ZAMPERINI (IRE) 7 ch.g. Fast Company (IRE) – Lucky Date (IRE) (Halling (USA)) h98
[2018/19 h80: h15.3g⁶ Jan 5] fair handicapper on Flat (stays 1½m): modest form over
hurdles: better effort when sixth in maiden at Wincanton on sole outing in 2018/19.
Gary Moore

ZANEVSKY 6 b.g. And Beyond (IRE) – Nevsky Bridge (Soviet Star (USA)) [2018/19 b–
ab16.3s Feb 23] well beaten in bumper. *Stella Barclay*

ZANSTRA (IRE) 9 b.g. Morozov (USA) – Enistar (IRE) (Synefos (USA)) [2018/19 c112
c109, h115: c22.5d³ May 5] lengthy gelding: fairly useful hurdler/maiden chaser: stayed h–
3m: acted on heavy going: tried in blinkers/tongue tied: dead. *Colin Tizzard*

ZANTE (FR) 7 ch.g. Zanzibari (USA) – Calling All Angels (FR) (Ange Gabriel (FR)) h86
[2018/19 h–: h17.7g⁶ h17.7v h20.5d² h21d h20.7g h15.8d⁵ Mar 13] angular gelding:
modest handicap hurdler: stays 21f: acts on good to soft going: wears cheekpieces.
Gary Moore

ZANZA (IRE) 5 b.g. Arcadio (GER) – What A Bleu (IRE) (Pistolet Bleu (IRE)) [2018/19 h133
b15.8d⁶ h16s* h16v h19d* h15.7d h16.3d* Mar 22] well-made gelding: second foal: dam b85
winning pointer: shaped well amidst greenness when sixth in maiden bumper at Ffos Las:
useful novice hurdler: won at Chepstow in November and Taunton in December, and
handicap at Newbury (in hood, by 1¾ lengths from Our Merlin) in March: stays 19f: acts
on soft going. *Philip Hobbs*

ZANZI WIN (FR) 4 b.g. Zanzibari (USA) – Go To Win (FR) (Coroner (IRE)) [2018/19 h120
h16.5d⁶ h15.8d⁴ h16d² h16.2g² h15.9g* h15.9g² Apr 22] has had breathing operation:
useful on Flat, stays 1¼m: fairly useful form over hurdles: won maiden at Plumpton in
April: will prove best around 2m: acts on good to soft going: front runner/races prominently.
Harry Whittington

ZARA HOPE (IRE) 8 b.m. Stowaway – Agua Caliente (IRE) (Old Vic) [2018/19 h19.8v c98
h21.7v⁶ c19.4g³ Apr 14] rather leggy mare: fair handicap hurdler: modest form when third h80
in novice handicap at Stratford on chasing debut: should stay beyond 21f: acts on soft
going: tried in cheekpieces. *Kerry Lee*

ZARA'S REFLECTION 6 b.m. Midnight Legend – Twoy's Reflection (Presenting) h–
[2018/19 h–, b73: h16.3g⁶ h18.7g h20g⁶ Sep 11] little form in bumpers/over hurdles: has
worn headgear, including last 3 starts: wears tongue tie. *Ben Case*

ZARIB (IRE) 8 b.g. Azamour (IRE) – Zariziyna (IRE) (Dalakhani (IRE)) [2018/19 c98, c–
h118: h24.7g Oct 28] lengthy gelding: useful hurdler/chaser at best: left Dan Skelton, h–
largely well held since 2016/17: stays easy 2½m: acts on good to firm and heavy going: has
worn headgear/tongue tie. *Dianne Sayer*

ZAROCCO 6 b.m. Shirocco (GER) – Zariyka (IRE) (Kalanisi (IRE)) [2018/19 b–: b15.8g b81
May 8] modest form in mares bumpers. *Tom Lacey*

ZARRAR (IRE) 4 b.g. Thewayyouare (USA) – Featherlight (Fantastic Light (USA)) h–
[2018/19 h16.7m⁵ Aug 5] fair on Flat, stays 1¾m: blinkered/tongue tied, well beaten in
juvenile on hurdling debut. *Brendan Powell*

ZAYFIRE ARAMIS 10 ch.g. Zafeen (FR) – Kaylifa Aramis (Kayf Tara) [2018/19 c108, c99
h–: c20g^ur c20d⁶ c19.2g³ c19.4d^pu Apr 6] lengthy, angular gelding: maiden hurdler: fair h–
handicap chaser: stays 2½m: acts on heavy going. *Michael Scudamore*

ZEBI BOY 8 b.g. Multiplex – Atlantic Jane (Tamure (IRE)) [2018/19 h–: h23.3d* h23.3g* h115
h23.3g* h24g^pu Aug 19] fairly useful handicap hurdler: landed hat-trick at Uttoxeter (first
2 novice events) early in season: should have stayed 3m: acted on good to soft going: dead.
Dan Skelton

ZEE MAN (FR) 5 b.g. Soldier of Fortune (IRE) – Sky High Flyer (Anabaa (USA)) h72
[2018/19 b85: h19.5s^pu h16.5d⁵ h15.8g h21.4g^pu h16s h20.3d Apr 24] tall, unfurnished
gelding: poor maiden hurdler on balance: tried in tongue tie. *David Dennis*

ZENAFIRE 10 b.g. Firebreak – Zen Garden (Alzao (USA)) [2018/19 h104: h19.6g⁶ Jun 5]   **h87**
compact gelding: modest handicap hurdler nowadays: should stay beyond 2m: acts on soft
going. *Sarah Hollinshead*

ZEN MASTER (IRE) 7 b.g. Shantou (USA) – Back Log (IRE) (Bob Back (USA))   **c113 x**
[2018/19 h109: h19.2g² h21.9g² c19.5s⁴ c21.2dᵘʳ c19.9dᶠ c17.8v⁴ c21.4gᶠ h20g⁴ Apr 21]   **h110**
fair handicap hurdler: similar form when fourth in novice handicap on chasing debut: let
down by jumping subsequently: stays 2¾m: acts on soft going: usually hooded. *Charlie
Mann*

ZEPHYROS BLEU (IRE) 9 b.g. Westerner – Quel Bleu (IRE) (Tel Quel (FR)) [2018/19   **c–**
c110, h–: h23.3g⁶ h20.5g⁴ h23.6vᵖᵘ h21.4gᵖᵘ Feb 27] good-topped gelding: has had   **h93**
breathing operation: disappointing maiden hurdler: winning chaser: stays 3m: acts on
heavy going: wears headgear: in tongue tie last 4 starts: usually races close up/finds little.
Dan Skelton

ZERACHIEL (IRE) 9 b.g. Winged Love (IRE) – At Dawn (IRE) (Lashkari) [2018/19   **c122**
c117, h–: c32.4gᵘʳ c27.6s² c30.7dᵖᵘ c29.2d Mar 10] sturdy gelding: maiden hurdler: fairly   **h–**
useful handicap chaser: stays 3¾m: acts on heavy going: wears headgear. *Ian Williams*

ZEROESHADESOFGREY (IRE) 10 gr.g. Portrait Gallery (IRE) – Hazy Rose (IRE)   **c111 §**
(Roselier (FR)) [2018/19 c113§, h126§: c24.2g² c24.2dᶠ Mar 15] big, workmanlike   **h– §**
gelding: has had breathing operation: won both outings in points: fairly useful hurdler/
chaser at best: runner-up on completed start in hunter chases at Fakenham in 2018/19: stays
3m: acts on heavy going: has worn headgear: tried in tongue tie: no battler. *R. Cundy*

ZERO GRAND (IRE) 8 b.g. Thousand Words – Ellistown Lady (IRE) (Red Sunset)   **c–**
[2018/19 h117: h21.6s c23.6dᵖᵘ c19.4sᵖᵘ h23.9dᵖᵘ Apr 4] sturdy gelding: has had breathing   **h101**
operation: fairly useful handicap hurdler at best: little form since reappearance in 2017/18,
including over fences (pulled up both outings): stays 3¼m: acts on heavy going: in tongue
tie last 4 starts, also in headgear last 2. *Johnny Farrelly*

ZERO TEN (IRE) 6 b.g. Shantou (USA) – Hannah Rose (IRE) (Un Desperado (FR))   **h138 p**
[2018/19 b16.6g* h16.6s* h16d* h20d² Apr 7] €34,000 3-y-o: fourth foal: half-brother to   **b103**
fair 3¼m chase winner Oriental Fixer (by Vertical Speed): dam runner-up in bumper: off
mark in maiden points at third attempt: contested maiden bumpers at Galway a year apart,
much improved when winning in July: useful form over hurdles: won maiden at Galway
(by 15 lengths) in September, novice at Leopardstown (easily) in March and minor event
at Punchestown (by 4¾ lengths from The Big Dog) shortly after end of British season: also
close second to Dommage Pour Toi in Grade 2 novice at Fairyhouse: remains with
potential. *Emmet Mullins, Ireland*

ZERO TO HERO (IRE) 4 ch.f. Arakan (USA) – Blue Daze (Danzero (AUS)) [2018/19   **b–**
b15.8d b13.7g Apr 12] £30,000 4-y-o: half-sister to several winners, including fair hurdler/
fairly useful chaser Fairyinthewind (2m winner, by Indian Haven): dam, 6f winner, out of
half-sister to smart hurdler/useful chaser (2m-2½m winner) Hasty Prince: runner-up in
Irish point on debut: failed to settle when well beaten in bumpers. *Archie Watson*

ZIGA BOY (FR) 10 gr.g. Califet (FR) – Our Ziga (FR) (Linamix (FR)) [2018/19 c26dᵖᵘ   **c–**
c26gᵖᵘ Mar 23] angular gelding: maiden hurdler: useful chaser at best: pulled up both   **h–**
outings in 2018/19 after long lay-off: stays 25f: acts on heavy going: has worn cheekpieces,
including last 3 starts. *Alan King*

ZIGGY ROSE (IRE) 5 b.m. Fame And Glory – Koko Rose (IRE) (Beneficial) [2018/19   **h–**
h19.5dᵖᵘ Oct 13] €25,000 3-y-o: fourth foal: half-sister to fairly useful hurdler Thirsty
Work (2m winner, stayed 2½m) and a winning pointer (both by Robin des Champs): dam
unraced sister to top-class hurdler/very smart chaser (stayed 3¼m) More of That: pulled up
in mares novice hurdle on debut. *Jonjo O'Neill*

ZIG ZAG (IRE) 6 b.g. Zoffany (IRE) – Le Montrachet (Nashwan (USA)) [2018/19 h122:   **h117**
h19.7g³ h19.7d⁶ h18.6s⁴ h16g* h16.4g⁴ h16.6g⁵ Mar 2] compact gelding: fairly useful
handicap hurdler: won at Wetherby in January: stays 2½m: acts on soft going: wears
cheekpieces: has worn tongue tie. *Philip Kirby*

ZILLION (IRE) 5 b.g. Zebedee – Redelusion (IRE) (Hernando (FR)) [2018/19 h–:   **h94**
h17.7g⁶ h19.5g Oct 30] fair on Flat (stays 1½m): best effort over hurdles when mid-field in
maiden at Fontwell in May: may prove best around 2m (raced too freely at 19f).
Susan Gardner

ZIZANEUR (FR) 4 b.g. Planteur (IRE) – Zitana (FR) (Zieten (USA)) [2018/19 h15.9d^{ur} **h122**
h17.4s^5 h17.4g^3 h16.9s* h17.4s^2 h16.9v^{ur} h16.9s^6 h15.8d^2 h16.3d^2 h16.4s Mar 13] rather
leggy gelding: mid-field in maiden on Flat: fairly useful juvenile hurdler: won at Dieppe in
August: left R. Chatel after first start, S. Foucher after seventh: raced around 2m: acts on
soft going. *Philip Hobbs*

ZLATAN (IRE) 6 b.g. Dark Angel (IRE) – Guard Hill (USA) (Rahy (USA)) [2018/19 **h91**
h15.9g^f Feb 25] fairly useful on Flat, stays 1¼m: weakening (having done too much too
soon) when falling 2 out in maiden won by Pentland Hills at Plumpton on hurdling debut.
Ed de Giles

ZOFFANY BAY (IRE) 5 b.g. Zoffany (IRE) – Trois Graces (USA) (Alysheba (USA)) **h121**
[2018/19 h18.5m^2 h15.9g* h16.2g^6 h16.6g^6 h15.9d^3 h15.7m^2 h16d^2 h20m^3 Apr 22] rather
leggy gelding: fairly useful on Flat, stays 1½m: fairly useful hurdler: won maiden at
Plumpton in November: best around 2m: acts on good to firm and good to soft going: front
runner/races prominently. *Ali Stronge*

ZOLFO (IRE) 7 gr.g. Cloudings (IRE) – Hardy Lamb (IRE) (Witness Box (USA)) **c103**
[2018/19 c93, h–: c20.3g* c20.3g^2 c16g^3 c20g^5 c17.4g^4 c20.3d^4 Apr 9] big, rangy gelding: **h–**
maiden hurdler: fair handicap chaser: won at Bangor on return in May: should stay beyond
2½m: acts on good to soft going: has found less than looked likely. *Jennie Candlish*

ZOLTAN VARGA 5 b.g. Sayif (IRE) – Mar Blue (FR) (Marju (IRE)) [2018/19 h91, b84: **c90**
h21m^3 h17.7m^2 c16.3s^3 c17.4g^2 Aug 20] modest maiden hurdler: placed in novice handicap **h95**
chases at Newton Abbot and Bangor: likely to prove best short of 21f: acts on soft and good
to firm going: tried in hood: normally travels strongly. *Mick Channon*

ZORLU (IRE) 6 b.g. Invincible Spirit (IRE) – Special Assignment (USA) (Lemon Drop **h–**
Kid (USA)) [2018/19 h19.7g^5 h16.2g h19.7g^5 h20v h19d Jan 19] rather leggy gelding: little
form on Flat/over hurdles: tried in blinkers. *Dai Burchell*

ZOUTOISE (FR) 4 b.f. Enrique – Belle Yepa (FR) (Mansonnien (FR)) [2018/19 b12.4g* **b91**
b16g Feb 19] half-sister to several winners, including very smart hurdler/top-class chaser
Whisper (2½m-3m winner) and smart French hurdler/fairly useful chaser Chuchoteuse
(15f-19f winner) (both by Astarabad): dam French 17f-19f hurdle winner: won junior
bumper at Wetherby on debut in January with plenty in hand: disappointing in mares event
there month later. *Tom George*

ZUBAYR (IRE) 7 b.g. Authorized (IRE) – Zaziyra (IRE) (Dalakhani (IRE)) [2018/19 **h127**
h137: h16g^4 h20g h19.8g^5 Nov 22] neat gelding: has had breathing operation: useful
handicap hurdler: stays 21f: acts on soft and good to firm going: tried in cheekpieces.
Paul Nicholls

ZULU 5 b.g. Cockney Rebel (IRE) – Pantita (Polish Precedent (USA)) [2018/19 h16.8g^{pu} **h–**
Apr 20] regressive maiden on Flat: pulled up in novice on hurdling debut. *Gail Haywood*

ZULU DAWN (IRE) 5 b.g. Fame And Glory – Maslam (IRE) (Robellino (USA)) **b92**
[2018/19 b16d^4 b16.3d^5 b16m^5 Apr 13] €38,000 3-y-o: sturdy gelding: half-brother to
several winners, including useful hurdlers/chasers Corkage (2½m-3m winner, by Second
Empire) and Holly Bush Henry (2m-25f winner, by Yeats): dam unraced: fair form in
bumpers. *Graeme McPherson*

ZULU OSCAR 10 b.g. Oscar (IRE) – Loxhill Lady (Supreme Leader) [2018/19 h108: **h94**
h21.4m^5 h23.1g Jun 5] well-made gelding: formerly useful handicap hurdler: mostly
disappointing since 2016/17: stays 2¾m: acts on soft going: tried in blinkers: has worn
tongue tie. *Jeremy Scott*

ZYON 5 gr.g. Martaline – Temptation (FR) (Lando (GER)) [2018/19 b–: b15.7m^3 Nov 3] **b90**
better effort in bumpers (fair form) 6 months apart when third at Ascot. *Paul Nicholls*

ERRATA & ADDENDA
Chasers & Hurdlers 2017/18

p6 4th line of the picture caption: Mr Patrick Mullins was Ireland's
leading amateur for the **tenth** time, **one short of** the achievement
of Mr Ted Walsh

Min p530, first line, second paragraph, Min is still waiting for his first
Grade 1 win **outside novice company**

PROMISING HORSES

Selected British- and Irish-trained horses in *Chasers & Hurdlers* thought capable of noteworthy improvement are listed under the trainers for whom they last ran.

KIM BAILEY
Alfie Corbitt (IRE) 6 b.g h95p
Espoir de Romay (FR) 5 b.g h95p
Illuminated Beauty (IRE) 6 b.m h104p
Imperial Aura (IRE) 6 b.g h123p
Mr Macho (IRE) 7 b.g h116p
Pond Road (IRE) 5 ch.g h83p b85
Robin The Raven (IRE) 7 b.g h138 c134p
Two For Gold (IRE) 6 b.g h132p
Vinndication (IRE) 6 b.g c148p

JACK R. BARBER
Darcy Ward (FR) 6 b.g h111 c126P
The Vocalist 7 b.m h113 c94p

PETER BOWEN
Bang Bang Rosie (IRE) 7 b.m h115 c106p
Fortunes Hiding (IRE) 6 b.g h100p b99
No Quarter Asked (IRE) 4 b.g h89p
Rooster Cogburn (IRE) 6 b.g h101p

MARTIN BRASSIL, IRELAND
Longhouse Poet (IRE) 5 b.g b110p

HENRY DE BROMHEAD, IRELAND
Honeysuckle 5 b.m h140p
Insult (IRE) 6 b.g h130p
Walk Away (IRE) 6 b.g h132p

CHARLES BYRNES, IRELAND
The Big Galloper (IRE) 5 ch.g h100 c102p
Thosedaysaregone (IRE) 6 b.g h121 c129p

MICK CHANNON
Glen Forsa (IRE) 7 b.g h119p c150
Hats Off To Larry 5 b.g h106p
Heydour (IRE) 6 br.g h107 c126p
Hold The Note (IRE) 5 b.g h126p b105

P. E. COLLINS, IRELAND
Staged Engagement (IRE) 6 b.g h113p b95

STUART COLTHERD
Ard Chros (IRE) 7 b.g h110p

GAVIN PATRICK CROMWELL, IRELAND
Callthebarman (IRE) 5 b.g h102 c112p

REBECCA CURTIS
Minella Bobo (IRE) 6 gr.g h118p b89

KEITH DALGLEISH
One Night In Milan (IRE) 6 b.g h121p
Raymond (IRE) 4 b.g b60p
Senor Lombardy (IRE) 6 b.g c118p

HENRY DALY
Laxey (IRE) 5 b.g h111p b78

TRISTAN DAVIDSON
Nelson Road (IRE) 6 b.g h113p

P. M. J. DOYLE, IRELAND
Kaiser Black (IRE) 8 b.g c153p

J. T. R. DREAPER, IRELAND
Sizing Rome (IRE) 7 b.g c132p

STUART EDMUNDS
Clondaw Native (IRE) 7 b.g h118 c89p

Deputy's Oscar (IRE) 6 b.m h79p b75
Maria's Benefit (IRE) 7 b.m c138p
Queenohearts (IRE) 6 ch.m h130p
Theclockisticking (IRE) 7 br.g h133 c132p

GORDON ELLIOTT, IRELAND
Andy Dufresne (IRE) 5 b.g b106P
Barra (FR) 8 b.m c130p
Battleoverdoyen (IRE) 6 b.g h142p b107
Braid Blue (IRE) 6 b.g h120p b101
Champagne Classic (IRE) 8 b.g c145p
Chosen Mate (IRE) 6 br.g h137p
Delta Work (FR) 6 br.g c163p
Festival d'Ex (FR) 4 b.g b115p
Glenloe (IRE) 8 br.g c130p
Its All Guesswork (IRE) 7 b.g h121 c125p
Make My Heart Fly (IRE) 7 b.m h124 c112p
Malone Road (IRE) 5 b.g b117p
Markhan (USA) 6 b.g h115p
Thatsy (FR) 5 gr.g b111p

BRIAN ELLISON
Weakfield (IRE) 6 b.g h111p b69
Windsor Avenue (IRE) 7 b.g h131p

SAM ENGLAND
Ask Paddy (IRE) 7 ch.g c99p
Drumochter 5 br.m h99p
Honourmission (FR) 5 b.g h85p b62
King's Coinage (IRE) 5 b.g h96p

PETER FAHEY, IRELAND
Gypsy Island (IRE) 5 b.m h105P b117

ALAN FLEMING, IRELAND
Speaker Connolly (IRE) 6 b.g c136p

HARRY FRY
Any Drama (IRE) 8 b.g c115p
Dalila du Seuil (FR) 6 gr.m c132p
Deadringerforlove 5 b.m h102p b88
Ena Baie (FR) 5 b.m h102p
Gameface (IRE) 5 b.g h65p
Ishkhara Lady 5 b.m b104p
King Roland (IRE) 5 br.g h116p
Phoenix Way (IRE) 6 b.g h119p

TOM GEORGE
Buck's Bin's (FR) 5 b.g h103p b82

NICK GIFFORD
Glen Rocco 8 ch.g c135p

CHRIS GORDON
Baddesley Prince (IRE) 5 b.g h116p
Shut The Box (IRE) 5 ch.g h106p b86

CHRIS GRANT
Theatre Legend 6 b.g h130p

WARREN GREATREX
Emitom (IRE) 5 b.g h146p b96
La Bague Au Roi (FR) 8 b.m c151p
Portrush Ted (IRE) 7 b.g h119p

OLIVER GREENALL
Absolute Jaffa 4 ch.f h96p
Blue Ballerina (IRE) 5 br.m h54p
Lucky Lover Boy (IRE) 4 b.g h129p

Mid Day Gun (IRE) 6 ch.g h90 c80p b77

JOHN HALLEY, IRELAND
Foreign Secretary 4 ch.g h120p

MRS J. HARRINGTON, IRELAND
Alletrix (IRE) 6 b.m h131 c111p
Morosini (FR) 4 b.g h127p

NICKY HENDERSON
Allart (IRE) 5 b.g b95p
Barbados Blue (IRE) 5 b.m h115p b94
Beyondthestorm (IRE) 6 b.g h86p
Champ (IRE) 7 b.g h149p
Champagne Mystery (IRE) 5 b.g h125p
Champagne Platinum (IRE) 5 gr.g h121p
Chantry House (IRE) 5 br.g b104p
Claimantakinforgan (FR) 7 b.g c139p
Daphne du Clos (FR) 6 b.m h100P
El Kaldoun (FR) 5 b.g h99p b93
Epatante (FR) 5 b.m h123p
Floressa (FR) 4 b.f h97p
Fusil Raffles (FR) 4 b.g h147p
Humphrey Bogart (IRE) 6 b.g h116p
Italian Summer 4 br.f b77p
Jen's Boy 5 b.g h89p b85
Lisheen Castle (IRE) 4 b.g h108p
Loveherandleaveher (IRE) 7 b. or br.m h108p
Mister Fisher (IRE) 5 b.g h143p
Never Adapt (FR) 4 ch.f h118p
Ok Corral (IRE) 9 b.g c148p
Pacific de Baune (FR) 6 gr.g h122 c131p
Pentland Hills (IRE) 4 b.g h146p
Pistol Whipped (IRE) 5 b.g h124p
Precious Cargo (IRE) 6 b.g h126p
Rathhill (IRE) 6 b.g h125p
Santini 7 b.g c161p
Shishkin (IRE) 5 b.g b104p
Storm of Intrigue (IRE) 7 b.g h114p
Style de Vole (FR) 4 gr.g h120p
Sunrise Ruby (IRE) 5 ch.m h116p b97
Sunshade 6 b.m h137p
Trull La La 5 ch.m h108p

PHILIP HOBBS
Defi du Seuil (FR) 6 b.g c164p
Deise Aba (IRE) 6 b.g h121p
Earth Moor (IRE) 5 ch.g h107p b97
Evidence de Thaix (FR) 5 b.m h109p
Flinck (IRE) 5 b.g h106p
I'm A Game Changer (IRE) 7 b.g h137 c127p
Mcnamaras Band (IRE) 6 b.g h120p
Musical Slave (IRE) 6 b.g h128p
Ninth Wave (IRE) 5 b.g h99 c87p b89
No Comment 8 br.g c131p
Oakley (IRE) 6 b.g h131p
Pileon (IRE) 5 b.g b99p
Smarty Wild 5 b.g h129p b70
Westend Story (IRE) 8 b.g c137p

ANTHONY HONEYBALL
Deja Vue (IRE) 5 b.m h80p
Hideaway Vic (IRE) 6 b.g h111p
Marilyn Monroe (IRE) 6 b.m b89p
Shapiro 6 b.m h108p
Sojourn (IRE) 6 b.g h110p b100

IAIN JARDINE
Tokaramore 7 b.m h105 c96p
Tomorrow's Angel 4 ch.f h100p

Tor 5 ch.g h104p

RUTH JEFFERSON
Mega Yeats (IRE) 5 br.m h125p b104
Raecius Felix (IRE) 5 ch.g h95p

MARTIN KEIGHLEY
Big Nasty 6 b.g h111p b86
Chequered View 6 b.m h100 c105p
Mister Valentine 6 b.g h88p

ALAN KING
Smith's Bay 6 b.g h106p
Timoteo (FR) 6 b.g h106 c134p
Whenhellbrokeloose 6 b.g b68p

NEIL KING
Dancing Doris 4 b.f b87p
Petite Jack 6 ch.g h97p
Third Estate (IRE) 7 b.g h112 c115p

TOM LACEY
Capac (IRE) 4 ch.g b98p
Glory And Fortune (IRE) 4 b.g b99p
Hazzaar (IRE) 5 b.g b102p
L'Incorrigible (FR) 4 b.g b102p
Sebastopol (IRE) 5 b.g h113p
Sir Egbert 6 b.g c128p

EMMA LAVELLE
De Rasher Counter 7 b.g c145p
Fontsanta (IRE) 6 b.g h124p
Freedom Run 6 ch.m h84p b82
Highly Prized 6 b. or br.g h110p
Paisley Park (IRE) 7 b.g h166p
Silent Assistant (IRE) 5 b.g h109p

CHARLIE LONGSDON
Highway Girl 6 b.m h100p
State Vision (FR) 5 b.g b73p
Stormy Milan (IRE) 6 b.g h82 c109p

MARK LOUGHNANE
Chocolate Box (IRE) 5 b.g h111p

CHARLIE MANN
Financial Conduct (IRE) 5 b.g h114p
Top Up The Fashion (IRE) 5 b.g h105p

NICKY MARTIN
The Two Amigos 7 b.g c137p

DONALD MCCAIN
Carry On 4 b.g b88p
First Account 5 b. or br.g h121p
Lord Springfield (IRE) 6 ch.g h103p
The Con Man (IRE) 6 b.g h119p
The Some Dance Kid (IRE) 6 b.g h122p

KAREN MCLINTOCK
Grey Mist 5 gr.g h110p

ERIC MCNAMARA, IRELAND
Internal Transfer 8 b.g h110 c131p

NOEL MEADE, IRELAND
Beacon Edge (IRE) 5 b.g b117p
Brace Yourself (IRE) 6 ch.g h115p
Tout Est Permis (FR) 6 gr.g c154p
Young Ted (IRE) 5 b.g h132p

GARY MOORE
Bullfrog (IRE) 6 b.m h109p
Early du Lemo (FR) 6 gr.g c136p
Episode (FR) 5 ch.m h95p
Espion de Saflo (FR) 5 b.g h117p

High Up In The Air (FR) 5 ch.g h77p
Il Re di Nessuno (FR) 4 b.g h92p

HUGHIE MORRISON
Apres Le Deluge (FR) 5 gr.g h108p
Third Wind 5 b. or br.g h132p

NEIL MULHOLLAND
Ballymilan 4 b.f b79p
Dead Right 7 b.g h120p
Deputy Jones (IRE) 6 b.m h105p
Dramatic Approach (IRE) 5 b.m b86p
Global Rhapsody (IRE) 5 b.g h80p
Golden Emblem (IRE) 5 ch.m b88p
Vis A Vis 5 b.g h117p

EMMET MULLINS, IRELAND
Zero Ten (IRE) 6 b.g h138p b103

SEAMUS MULLINS
Chesterfield (IRE) 9 ch.g h142 c138p
Lillian (IRE) 8 b. or br.m h114 c107p

W. P. MULLINS, IRELAND
Bargy Lady (IRE) 7 b.m h133 c128p
Breaken (FR) 5 b.g h134p
Burrows Saint (FR) 6 b.g c154p
Carefully Selected (IRE) 7 b.g h137p
Chacun Pour Soi (FR) 7 b.g c169p
Ciel de Neige (FR) 4 b.g h126p
Cilaos Emery (FR) 7 b.g c154p
Concertista (FR) 5 ch.m h136p
Elfile (FR) 5 b.m h135p
Klassical Dream (FR) 5 b.g h157p
Ontheropes (IRE) 5 b.g h130p b92
Real Steel (FR) 6 b.g c159p
Relegate (IRE) 6 b.m h125p
Royal Rendezvous (IRE) 7 b.g h129p b113
Shanning (FR) 6 b.m h136p
Timi Roli (FR) 7 b.g h123 c133p
Tornado Flyer (IRE) 6 b.g h141p

AMY MURPHY
Kalashnikov (IRE) 6 br.g c154p
Mercian Knight (IRE) 5 b.g b83p

OLLY MURPHY
Adjutant 4 b.g h105p
Blazer's Mill (IRE) 5 b.g b95p
Bon Calvados (FR) 5 b.g b65p
Collooney (IRE) 5 b.g h122p b100
Craigmor (IRE) 7 b.g h101 c112p
Elena Sue 6 b.m b79p
Emerald Rocket (IRE) 4 b.g h115p
Georgiator (FR) 6 b.g b91p
Monbeg Zena (IRE) 7 ch.m h113p
Nickolson (FR) 5 b.g b92p
Notre Pari (IRE) 5 b.g h110p
Peachey 5 b.g h113p b86
Smart Getaway (IRE) 7 b.m h98p b76
Time For Another (IRE) 6 ch.g h79p

DR RICHARD NEWLAND
Dashing Perk 8 b.g c126p
Rose Sea Has (FR) 4 gr.g h113 c123p

PAUL NICHOLLS
Accomplice (FR) 5 gr.g h111p
Archie Brown (IRE) 5 b.g b88p
Casko d'Airy (FR) 7 b.g h120p
Danny Kirwan (IRE) 6 b.g h133p

Danny Whizzbang (IRE) 6 b.g h128p
Dogon 4 b.g h124 c127p
Ecco 4 b.g h129p
Getaway Trump (IRE) 6 b.g h153p
Greaneteen (FR) 5 b.g h127p
Grey Getaway (IRE) 5 gr.g b65p
Highland Hunter (IRE) 6 gr.g h126p
Kapcorse (FR) 6 br.g h103 c143p
Scaramanga (IRE) 4 b.g h123p
Secret Investor 7 b.g h134+ c147p
Topofthegame (IRE) 7 ch.g c162p

FERGAL O'BRIEN
Phoenician Star (IRE) 4 ch.g h118p
Pride of Lecale 8 b.g h106p
Tequila Blaze 5 b.m b72p

JOSEPH PATRICK O'BRIEN, IRELAND
Darasso (FR) 6 br.g h155 c150p
Fakir d'Oudairies (FR) 4 b.g h143 c96P
Gardens of Babylon (IRE) 4 b.g h142p
Le Richebourg (FR) 6 br.g h130 c158p
Monarch (IRE) 6 b.g h138 c129p

JEDD O'KEEFFE
Mr Scrumpy 5 b.g h107p b100

JONJO O'NEILL
Cloth Cap (IRE) 7 b.g c134p
Cobolobo (FR) 7 br.g c129p
Flight Deck 5 b.g h96p
Generation Gap (IRE) 5 b.g h100p
Notawordofalie (IRE) 4 br.f b63p
Pagero (FR) 4 b.g h112p
Palmers Hill (IRE) 6 b.g h131p
Seaton Carew (IRE) 5 b.m b91p
Sermando (FR) 5 ch.g h106p
Tedham 5 b.g h130p
The Crafty Touch (IRE) 6 ch.m h90p

NOEL O'NEILL, IRELAND
Ministerforsport (IRE) 8 b.g c139p

HENRY OLIVER
Little Rory Mac (IRE) 5 b.g h116p

BEN PAULING
Bright Forecast (IRE) 5 b.g h146p
Chess Player (IRE) 4 ch.g b98p
The Captains Inn (IRE) 5 b.g h125p b85
Towards The Dawn 5 b.g h111p

DAVID PIPE
Delirant (FR) 6 b.g h101p
First Lord de Cuet (FR) 5 gr.g b100p
Jasmin des Bordes (FR) 5 b.g h114p b94
Moon Racer (IRE) 10 b.g h133 c124p
New Age Dawning (IRE) 5 ch.g h119p b96
Yaa Salaam (IRE) 5 ch.g h111p

JACKIE DU PLESSIS
St Erney 8 ch.g c125p

NICKY RICHARDS
Elios d'Or (FR) 5 b.g b85p
Glittering Love (IRE) 7 b.g c125p
No Regrets (IRE) 5 b.g b94p
Reivers Lad 8 b.g c133p
Uncle Alastair 7 b.g c142p

LUCINDA RUSSELL
Looks Like Murt (IRE) 6 b.g h108p b84
Mon Ami Bob 6 ch.g h88p

948

KEVIN RYAN
Erik The Red (FR) 7 b.g h105P
Susie Mac 4 ch.f b79p

JEREMY SCOTT
Hey Bud 6 b.g h119p
Orchardstown Cross (IRE) 8 b.g c122p

MICHAEL SCUDAMORE
Some Chaos (IRE) 8 b.g c140p

OLIVER SHERWOOD
Brummie Boys (IRE) 4 b.g b80p
Cilaos Glace (FR) 6 b.g h123p
Sammy Bill 6 b.g h97p
Tarada 6 br.g h123p b94

DAN SKELTON
Aggy With It (IRE) 5 b.m b92p
Amoola Gold (GER) 6 b.g h111 c125p
Annie Angel (IRE) 8 b.m c91p
Anytime Will Do (IRE) 6 b.g h131p
Bennys King (IRE) 8 b.g c141p
Betameche (FR) 8 gr.g h126p
Beyondapproach (IRE) 5 b.m h91p
Blairs Cove 7 b.g c108p
Bourbon Borderline (IRE) 5 b.g b96p
Floki 5 b.g h87p b83
Humble Hero (IRE) 5 b.g h129p
I'd Better Go Now (IRE) 6 b.g h84p
Interconnected 5 br.g h122p
Jane Lamb 6 b.m h98p
Magellan 5 b.g h101p
Marada 4 ch.f b81p
Molly The Dolly (IRE) 8 b.m c144p
No Getaway (IRE) 6 ch.g h114p
Northofthewall (IRE) 5 b.g h103p b76
Percy's Word 5 b.g h110p
Protektorat (FR) 4 b.g h122p
Sense of Adventure (IRE) 5 ch.g b85p
Shan Blue (IRE) 5 b.g h98p
Sofia's Rock (FR) 5 b.g h137p
Tigeralley 10 b.m h105 c91p
Vision du Puy (FR) 4 b.f h127p

SUZY SMITH
Debestyman (IRE) 6 b.g h113p b63
Rosy World 6 b.m h112p

JAMIE SNOWDEN
Chapmanshype (IRE) 5 b.g h103p b93

J. A. STACK, IRELAND
Carlo Biraghi (IRE) 4 ch.g h121p

JACKIE STEPHEN
Palixandre (FR) 5 b.g h88p b88
Starozov (IRE) 6 b.g h107p

ALI STRONGE
Blu Cavalier 9 b.g h134 c108p

TOM SYMONDS
Llandinabo Lad 4 ch.g b93p
Sixty's Belle 5 b.m h110p

TOM J. TAAFFE, IRELAND
Goose Man (IRE) 7 b.g h122p c140p

COLIN TIZZARD
Copperhead 5 ch.g h121p

Eldorado Allen (FR) 5 gr.g h115p
Faustinovick 5 b.g b93p
Jaytrack Parkhomes 5 b.g h80p b98
L'Air du Vent (FR) 5 b.g b101P
Lostintranslation (IRE) 7 b.g c160p
Pingshou (IRE) 9 b.g c120p
Reserve Tank (IRE) 5 b.g h150p

NIGEL TWISTON-DAVIES
Blue Flight (FR) 6 b.g h147p
Florrie Boy (IRE) 8 b.g h117 c123p
Guy (IRE) 4 ch.g b93p
Milanstorm (IRE) 6 b.g h92p

ROBERT TYNER, IRELAND
Midnight Stroll 7 b.g h134 c124p

LUCY WADHAM
Somekindofstar (IRE) 6 ch.g h91p
Trincomalee 6 b.g b84p

DONALD WHILLANS
Dali Mail (FR) 6 gr.g h124p

HARRY WHITTINGTON
Mister Coffey (FR) 4 b.g h98p
Neverbeen To Paris (IRE) 4 b.g h116p

CHRISTIAN WILLIAMS
Fifty Shades (IRE) 6 gr.g h88p c109
Win My Wings (IRE) 6 b.m h114p

EVAN WILLIAMS
Annsam 4 b.g h91p
Esprit du Large (FR) 5 b.g h120p b72
Keeping Faith (IRE) 5 br.m h92p
Mac Amara 5 b.m h94p b60
Mouseinthehouse (IRE) 5 b.g h90p
No Rematch (IRE) 5 b.g h112p b84
The Last Day (IRE) 7 b.g c132p

IAN WILLIAMS
Cracking Destiny (IRE) 6 b.g h95p c113
Monjeni 6 b.g h81p
Paddy The Chef (IRE) 4 b.g h106p
Psychedelic Rock 8 b.g h129 c133p
Speedo Boy (FR) 5 ch.g h121p
The Grand Visir 5 b.g h99p
Yellow Dockets (IRE) 7 ch.m h121p b75

MRS JANE WILLIAMS
Rococo River 5 b.g h96p

NICK WILLIAMS
Favori de Sivola (FR) 4 b.g h95p
Le Grand Rocher (FR) 3 b.g h110p
One For The Team 5 b.g h109p
Prudhomme (FR) 4 ch.g b100p
Siruh du Lac (FR) 6 b.g c147p

NOEL WILLIAMS
Another Crick 6 b.g h80 c136p
Another Drama (IRE) 7 b.g h77p
Drunken Pirate 6 b.g h101p b100

VENETIA WILLIAMS
Commodore 7 gr.g c126p
Destinee Royale (FR) 6 b.m h101p
Geordie B 6 gr.g h124p
Longhousesignora (IRE) 7 b.m h110 c101p
Yalltari 8 gr.g c140p

2018/19 IRISH STATISTICS

The following tables show the leading owners, trainers, jockeys, sires of winners and horses over jumps in Ireland during 2018/19 (April 29-May 4). The prize money statistics are in euros and have been compiled by *Timeform*. They relate to first-three prize money (prize money used to be converted to sterling at the prevailing rate at the time but that is no longer the case, though the prize money for individual races that appear in *'Selected Big Races'* has been converted to sterling).

OWNERS (1,2,3 earnings)	Horses	Wnrs	*Indiv'l Races* Won	Runs	%	*Stakes* €
1 Gigginstown House Stud	226	108	159	922	17.2	3,494,689
2 Mr John P. McManus	270	81	123	994	12.4	3,131,286
3 Mrs S. Ricci	38	15	27	92	29.3	1,410,295
4 Andrea Wylie/Graham Wylie	14	7	13	46	28.3	451,367
5 Sullivan Bloodstock Limited	18	11	18	64	28.1	399,020
6 Ann & Alan Potts Limited	21	6	10	88	11.4	344,528
7 Mrs Patricia Hunt	15	6	11	53	20.8	261,133
8 Cheveley Park Stud	10	8	13	38	34.2	254,410
9 Robcour	18	9	11	74	14.9	251,959
10 Kenneth Alexander	7	6	11	25	44.0	220,145

TRAINERS (1,2,3 earnings)	Horses	Wnrs	*Indiv'l Races* Won	Runs	%	*Stakes* €
1 W. P. Mullins	266	130	207	872	23.7	5,826,079
2 Gordon Elliott	320	120	177	1,233	14.4	3,755,131
3 Joseph Patrick O'Brien	154	65	88	609	14.4	1,770,446
4 Henry de Bromhead	152	66	98	623	15.7	1,730,685
5 Noel Meade	118	43	62	465	13.3	1,217,150
6 Mrs J. Harrington	99	34	47	424	11.1	1,188,315
7 Gavin Patrick Cromwell	69	20	32	313	10.2	419,354
8 Denis Hogan	79	14	20	354	5.6	369,561
9 Paul Nolan	53	17	20	210	9.5	350,180
10 Enda Bolger	21	8	13	75	17.3	320,680
11 Thomas Mullins	26	13	16	155	10.3	313,619
12 Peter Fahey	50	7	11	198	5.6	300,880

JOCKEYS (by winners)	1st	2nd	3rd	Unpl	Mts	%
1 P. Townend	109	81	62	224	476	22.9
2 Rachael Blackmore	90	55	68	403	616	14.6
3 Davy Russell	83	66	71	232	452	18.4
4 M. P. Walsh	67	67	52	247	433	15.5
5 Sean Flanagan	58	49	52	353	512	11.3
6 J. W. Kennedy	56	52	53	295	456	12.3
7 R. Walsh	48	26	26	65	165	29.1
8 D. E. Mullins	45	36	47	357	485	9.3
9 D. J. Mullins	42	34	28	197	301	14.0
10 Robbie Power	38	41	26	176	281	13.5
11 Mr P. W. Mullins	38	35	22	77	172	22.1
12 J. J. Slevin	27	45	34	234	340	7.9

	Races			Stakes
SIRES OF WINNERS (1,2,3 earnings)	Won	Runs	%	€
1 Presenting (by Mtoto)	45	477	9.4	989,657
2 Flemensfirth (by Alleged)	35	383	9.1	925,444
3 Beneficial (by Top Ville)	50	578	8.7	822,371
4 Milan (by Sadler's Wells)	43	482	8.9	750,626
5 Voix du Nord (by Valanour)	15	69	21.7	727,492
6 Oscar (by Sadler's Wells)	36	459	7.8	618,017
7 Westerner (by Danehill)	30	288	10.4	588,790
8 Stowaway (by Slip Anchor)	29	439	6.6	573,882
9 Network (by Monsun)	12	85	14.1	556,442
10 Saint des Saints (by Cadoudal)	12	44	27.3	507,466
11 King's Theatre (by Sadler's Wells)	25	194	12.9	500,449
12 Galileo (by Sadler's Wells)	23	144	16.0	498,837

LEADING HORSES	Won	Runs	€
1 Sharjah 6 b.g Doctor Dino–Saaryeh	3	5	322,874
2 Kemboy 7 b.g Voix du Nord–Vitora	3	3	310,248
3 Burrows Saint 6 b.g Saint des Saints–La Bombonera	3	4	304,007
4 Apple's Jade 7 b.f Saddler Maker–Apple's For Ever	4	5	257,999
5 Min 8 b.g Walk In The Park–Phemyka	2	3	190,500
6 Delta Work 6 br.g Network–Robbe	4	4	183,340
7 Le Richebourg 6 br.g Network–Fee Magic	4	6	182,827
8 Unowhatimeanharry 11 b.g Sir Harry Lewis–Red Nose Lady	1	1	176,999
9 Buveur d'Air 8 b.g Crillon–History	1	1	176,999
10 Un de Sceaux 11 b.g Denham Red–Hotesse de Sceaux	1	1	176,999
11 Clarcam 9 b.g Califet–Rose Beryl	1	1	147,500
12 Snow Falcon 9 b.g Presenting–Flocon de Neige	2	5	147,500

TIMEFORM TOP IRISH CHASERS		TIMEFORM TOP IRISH HURDLERS	
176	Kemboy	170	Espoir d'Allen
174	Al Boum Photo	162	Apple's Jade (f)
174	Min	160+	Presenting Percy
170	Un de Sceaux	159	Benie des Dieux
169p	Chacun Pour Soi	159	Samcro
167	Anibale Fly	157p	Klassical Dream
167	Tiger Roll	157+	Sharjah
165+	Presenting Percy	157	Supasundae
165	Bellshill	156	Bapaume
165	Monalee	156	Mr Adjudicator
165	Road To Respect	156$	Wicklow Brave
164	Balko des Flos	155	Darasso
163p	Delta Work	155	Petit Mouchoir
162+	Duc des Genievres	155x	Melon
162	Rathvinden	154	Faugheen
161	Alpha des Obeaux	154	Laurina (f)
161	Footpad	154	Tiger Roll
160	Ballyoisin	152	Early Doors
160	The Storyteller	152	Jezki
159p	Real Steel	151+	Saldier
159	Invitation Only	151	City Island
158p	Le Richebourg	151	Off You Go
157	A Plus Tard	151	Sire du Berlais
157	Cadmium	150	Sams Profile
156+	Voix du Reve	150	Shaneshill

SELECTED BIG RACES 2018/19

Prize money for racing abroad has been converted to £ sterling at the exchange rate current at the time of the race. The figures are correct to the nearest £.

HAYDOCK Saturday, May 12 GOOD

1 **Pertemps Network Swinton Handicap Hurdle (Gr 3) (1) (4yo+) £56,950** 1m7f144y (9)

SILVER STREAK (IRE) *EvanWilliams* 5-10-2^{132} AdamWedge	13/2		1
CHESTERFIELD (IRE) *SeamusMullins* 8-11-0^{144} DanielSansom(5)	7/1	¾	2
ASHKOUL (FR) *DanSkelton* 5-10-0 (9-10)^{130} (t) BridgetAndrews(3)	25/1	5	3
Optimus Prime (FR) *DanSkelton* 6-10-10^{140} (t) HarrySkelton	13/2	1¼	4
All Set To Go (IRE) *KevinFrost* 7-10-3^{133} AidanColeman	18/1	3¾	5
Lord Napier (IRE) *PeterBowen* 5-10-0^{130} (t) SeanBowen	25/1	1¼	6
John Constable (IRE) *EvanWilliams* 7-11-12^{156} (t) JamesBowen(3)	12/1	1¼	7
The Unit (IRE) *AlanKing* 7-10-12^{142} WayneHutchinson	12/1	9	8
Hassle (IRE) *DrRichardNewland* 9-10-0^{130} (b) SamTwiston-Davies	33/1	3¼	9
William H Bonney *AlanKing* 7-10-0 (9-13)^{130} BrendanPowell	10/1	2¼	10
Dear Sire (FR) *DonaldMcCain* 6-11-1^{145} (h) BrianHughes	33/1	½	11
Sizing Granite (IRE) *ColinTizzard* 10-10-11^{141} (t) RobbiePower	12/1	½	12
Capitaine (FR) *PaulNicholls* 6-10-7^{137} (h) HarryCobden	6/1f	10	13
Forth Bridge *CharlieLongsdon* 5-10-7^{137} JonathanBurke	20/1	18	14
Act of Valour *PaulNicholls* 4-10-1^{135} BryonyFrost(3)	13/2		F
Havana Beat (IRE) *TonyCarroll* 8-10-4^{134} JamesNixon(7)	22/1		F

Mr L. Fell 16ran 3m45.10

UTTOXETER Sunday, Jul 1 GOOD to FIRM

2 **Marston's Pedigree Summer Cup (Open Handicap Chase) (L) (1) (5yo+)** 3¼m13y (16)
£42,202

What should have been the first fence in the home straight was omitted, as was the ditch on the first circuit

VIRGILIO (FR) *DanSkelton* 9-11-12^{149} (t) HarrySkelton	8/1		1
HENLLAN HARRI (IRE) *PeterBowen* 10-10-7^{130} (b+t) SeanBowen	6/1	3¾	2
RELENTLESS DREAMER (IRE) *RebeccaCurtis* 9-10-11^{134} (s+t) AdamWedge	11/1	5	3
Winter Lion (IRE) *FergalO'Brien* 8-10-5^{128} (s+t) PaddyBrennan	7/1	3¼	4
Geordie des Champs (IRE) *RebeccaCurtis* 7-11-2^{139} NiallMadden	9/1	1½	5
Toviere (IRE) *OliverSherwood* 7-10-5^{128} ThomasGarner(3)	20/1	4½	6
Easy Street (IRE) *JonjoO'Neill* 8-10-4^{127} RichieMcLernon	25/1	4½	7
Drumlee Sunset (IRE) *TomGeorge* 8-10-13^{136} (t) JonathanBurke	16/1	2¼	8
Sporting Boy (IRE) *JohnnyFarrelly* 10-10-6^{129} (b+t) BrendanPowell	40/1	7	9
Bugsie Malone (IRE) *ChrisGordon* 8-10-0^{123} (s) HarryReed(5)	11/1	6	10
Good Man Vinnie (IRE) *PaulHenderson* 7-10-0 (9-13)^{123} SamTwiston-Davies	9/1	2	11
Beeves (IRE) *JennieCandlish* 11-11-10^{147} (v) SeanQuinlan	22/1	5	12
Ballyalton (IRE) *IanWilliams* 11-11-1^{138} (s) TomO'Brien	5/1f	12	13
Silver Man *JoHughes* 11-10-6^{129} (v) NicodeBoinville	50/1		pu
Another Hero (IRE) *JonjoO'Neill* 9-10-13^{136} AidanColeman	12/1		pu
Stellar Notion (IRE) *TomGeorge* 10-11-6^{143} (t) TomScudamore	33/1		pu
Gas Line Boy (IRE) *IanWilliams* 12-11-11^{148} (v) RobertDunne	22/1		pu
The Romford Pele (IRE) *TomGeorge* 11-11-12^{149} A.P.Heskin	14/1		pu

C J Edwards, D Futter, A H Rushworth 18ran 6m23.60

MARKET RASEN Saturday, Jul 21 GOOD to FIRM

3 **188Bet Summer Plate Handicap Chase (L) (1) (4yo+) £28,475** 2m5f89y (13)

MORE BUCK'S (IRE) *PeterBowen* 8-10-5^{127} (t) SeanBowen	6/1		1
TOO MANY DIAMONDS (IRE) *DanSkelton* 7-10-0^{122} HarrySkelton	7/1	½	2
SHANTOU VILLAGE (IRE) *NeilMulholland* 8-11-3^{139} RobertDunne	11/1	8	3
Not A Role Model (IRE) *SamThomas* 6-10-0^{122} RichardPatrick(5)	14/1	1	4
Sumkindofking (IRE) *TomGeorge* 7-10-6^{128} (t) A.P.Heskin	7/1	1¾	5
Alcala (FR) *PaulNicholls* 8-11-12^{148} (t) SamTwiston-Davies	7/1	2¼	6
Bagad Bihoue (FR) *PaulNicholls* 7-11-6^{142} NickScholfield	11/1	1¼	7
Monsieur Gibraltar (FR) *PaulNicholls* 7-10-6^{128} (t) LorcanWilliams(7)	20/1	3¾	8
Calett Mad (FR) *NigelTwiston-Davies* 6-11-7^{143} DarylJacob	5/1f	6	9
Seefood (IRE) *DrRichardNewland* 11-10-7^{129} (b) TomO'Brien	20/1	1¾	10
Days of Heaven (FR) *NickyHenderson* 8-11-9^{145} (h) NicodeBoinville	16/1	6	11
Viconte du Noyer (FR) *ColinTizzard* 9-11-5^{141} (s+t) TomScudamore	14/1	7	12
Brian Boranha (IRE) *PeterNiven* 7-10-8^{130} AidanColeman	12/1	2¼	13
Cut The Corner (IRE) *AlastairRalph* 10-11-6^{142} MrAlexEdwards(5)	25/1	1¼	14

Wadswick Court (IRE) *PeterBowen* 10-11-0[136] (b+t) JamesBowen ....25/1 F
Mickey Bowen & Regan Pallas 15ran 5m15.80

GALWAY Wednesday, Aug 1   GOOD to SOFT

4 **thetote.com Galway Plate (Handicap Chase) (Gr A) (4yo+)** £131,696   2¾m111y (14)
CLARCAM (FR) *GordonElliott* 8-10-13[147] (b+t) M.A.Enright 33/1   1
PATRICKS PARK (IRE) *W.P.Mullins* 7-10-7[141] R.Walsh 9/2f   6   2
JURY DUTY (IRE) *GordonElliott* 7-11-1[149] (t) DavyRussell ....7/1   nk   3
Snow Falcon (IRE) *NoelMeade* 8-11-0[148] SeanFlanagan 11/1   3¾   4
Sub Lieutenant (IRE) *HenrydeBromhead* 9-11-10[158] (t) D.Robinson(3) 16/1   1¼   5
Slowmotion (FR) *JosephPatrickO'Brien* 6-10-8[142] (b) BarryGeraghty 7/1   1¾   6
Lord Scoundrel (IRE) *GordonElliott* 9-10-10[144] (b+t) DonaghMeyler 33/1   4¾   7
Conrad Hastings (IRE) *HenrydeBromhead* 7-10-7[141] A.E.Lynch 40/1   3¾   8
Peregrine Run (IRE) *PeterFahey* 8-10-11[145] RogerLoughran 20/1   7½   9
Saturnas (FR) *W.P.Mullins* 7-10-8[142] D.J.Mullins ....14/1   nk 10
Rock The World (IRE) *MrsJ.Harrington* 10-10-13[147] (s+t) J.S.McGarvey 66/1   1 11
Neverushacon (IRE) *MrsJ.Harrington* 7-10-11[145] (s+t) P.D.Kennedy 20/1   3¼ 12
Calino d'Airy (FR) *HenrydeBromhead* 6-10-11[145] R.J.Cooper 12/1   3¾ 13
Kitten Rock (FR) *E.J.O'Grady* 8-10-11[145] M.P.Walsh 20/1 36 14
Devils Bride (IRE) *HenrydeBromhead* 11-10-9[143] (s+t) J.J.Slevin 33/1 31 15
Koshari (IRE) *W.P.Mullins* 6-10-13[147] D.E.Mullins ....12/1   ½ 16
Tully Lake (IRE) *AlanFleming* 8-10-12[146] DenisO'Regan 12/1 13 17
Valseur Lido (FR) *HenrydeBromhead* 9-11-5[153] RachaelBlackmore 14/1 2¾ 18
Alelchi Inois (FR) *W.P.Mullins* 10-11-1[149] (t) KatieO'Farrell(5) 50/1 11 19
De Plotting Shed (IRE) *GordonElliott* 8-10-8[142] (t) J.W.Kennedy ....16/1   F
Drumcliff (IRE) *HarryFry,GB* 7-10-8[142] (t) MissA.B.O'Connor(7) ....14/1   F
Haymount (IRE) *W.P.Mullins* 9-10-10[144] (t) P.Townend ....14/1   pu
Gigginstown House Stud 22ran 5m32.30

GALWAY Thursday, Aug 2   SOFT

5 **Guinness Galway Hurdle Handicap (Gr A) (4yo+)** £158,035   2m11y (9)
SHARJAH (FR) *W.P.Mullins* 5-11-7[146] MrP.W.Mullins 12/1   1
BLAZER (FR) *W.P.Mullins* 7-11-0[139] M.P.Walsh 12/1   3   2
LEONCAVALLO (IRE) *DrRichardNewland,GB* 5-11-1[140] (b) SamTwiston-Davies ..20/1   ½   3
Bedrock *IainJardine,GB* 5-11-5[144] (s+t) DenisO'Regan 33/1   3¼   4
Le Richebourg (FR) *JosephPatrickO'Brien* 5-11-1[140] BarryGeraghty 12/1   3½   5
Good Thyne Tara (IRE) *W.P.Mullins* 8-11-5[144] P.Townend 12/1   2   6
Whiskey Sour (IRE) *W.P.Mullins* 5-11-4[143] D.E.Mullins ....9/2f   ½   7
Ivanovich Gorbatov (IRE) *JosephPatrickO'Brien* 6-11-0[139] (b+t) J.J.Slevin ....33/1   nk   8
Davids Charm (IRE) *JohnJ.Walsh* 7-11-5[144] (h) RachaelBlackmore ....11/2   nk   9
Plinth (IRE) *JosephPatrickO'Brien* 8-10-10[135] (b+t) M.A.Enright ....33/1   hd 10
Max Dynamite (FR) *W.P.Mullins* 8-10-13[138] M.Walsh 8/1   1 11
Project Bluebook (FR) *JohnQuinn,GB* 5-10-10[135] BrianHughes 14/1   2 12
Voix du Reve (FR) *W.P.Mullins* 6-11-3[142] (t) KatieO'Farrell(5) 12/1   7½ 13
Ted Veale (IRE) *A.J.Martin* 11-10-10[135] E.O'Connell(7) 50/1   1¾ 14
Jer's Girl (IRE) *GavinPatrickCromwell* 6-11-5[144] (s) D.J.McInerney(3) 20/1   1¼ 15
Tigris River (IRE) *JosephPatrickO'Brien* 7-11-5[144] (t) J.S.McGarvey ....14/1   ½ 16
Cartwright *GordonElliott* 5-10-11[136] (b) J.W.Kennedy 10/1 19 17
Don't Touch It (IRE) *MrsJ.Harrington* 8-11-4[143] (s) DonaghMeyler 50/1 2½ 18
Monarch (IRE) *JosephPatrickO'Brien* 5-10-13[138] (t) NiallMadden 33/1 25 19
The Game Changer (IRE) *GordonElliott* 9-11-0[139] (t) DavyRussell ....25/1   pu
Mrs S. Ricci 20ran 3m45.90

GALWAY Saturday, Aug 4   GOOD to SOFT

6 **Galway Shopping Centre Handicap Hurdle (Gr B) (4yo+)** £52,678   2¾m168y (13)
LOW SUN *W.P.Mullins* 5-10-9[132] (s) KatieO'Farrell(5) 7/1   1
MINELLA AWARDS (IRE) *HarryFry,GB* 7-11-5[142] (t) DavyRussell 10/1   2½   2
SHANNING (FR) *W.P.Mullins* 5-10-3[126] R.Walsh 5/2f   6½   3
Lareena (FR) *W.P.Mullins* 5-9-10[119] M.A.Enright 16/1   8   4
Court Artist (IRE) *W.P.Mullins* 7-10-4[127] B.Hayes 40/1   6½   5
Art of Security (IRE) *NoelMeade* 8-10-8[131] SeanFlanagan 20/1   3   6
Meri Devie (FR) *W.P.Mullins* 5-11-10[147] N.M.Kelly(5) 20/1   5½   7
Oscar Knight (IRE) *ThomasMullins* 9-10-8[131] M.P.Walsh 12/1   2   8
Benkei (IRE) *HarryRogers* 8-10-9[132] (s) PhilipEnright ....22/1   nk   9
Killiney Court (IRE) *HenrydeBromhead* 7-10-3[122] (t) D.Robinson(3) 25/1 10 10
Kilcarry Bridge (IRE) *JohnPatrickRyan* 11-10-3[126] (t) DonaghMeyler 50/1 12 11
Timi Roli (FR) *W.P.Mullins* 6-10-5[128] D.E.Mullins 16/1   4 12
5 Plinth (IRE) *JosephPatrickO'Brien* 8-10-12[135] (s+t) J.S.McGarvey 33/1   7½ 13
She's a Star (IRE) *NoelMeade* 6-10-5[128] (t) JonathanMoore 33/1   6½ 14
5 Jer's Girl (IRE) *GavinPatrickCromwell* 6-11-7[144] (s) BarryGeraghty 20/1   6 15

953

	Cook Islands (IRE) *JosephPatrickO'Brien* 5-10-1^{124} (b+t) J.J.Slevin	33/1	F
	Bargy Lady (IRE) *W.P.Mullins* 6-10-9^{132} (h) D.J.Mullins	14/1	F
	Uradel (GER) *W.P.Mullins* 7-10-9^{132} P.Townend	7/2	bd
	Gran Geste (FR) *MissElizabethDoyle* 5-10-2^{125} NiallMadden	33/1	pu
	Supreme Vinnie (IRE) *MissD.M.O'Shea* 9-10-2^{125} (t) RachaelBlackmore	25/1	pu

Mrs S. Ricci 20ran 5m28.10

LISTOWEL Wednesday, Sep 12 SOFT

7 Guinness Kerry National Handicap Chase (Gr A) (4yo+) £105,357 — 3m (17)

4	SNOW FALCON (IRE) *NoelMeade* 8-11-5^{148} JonathanMoore	6/1	1
4	SATURNAS (FR) *W.P.Mullins* 7-10-13^{142} P.Townend	20/1	nk 2
	ROGUE ANGEL (IRE) *GordonElliott* 10-10-3^{132} (b+t) RachaelBlackmore	7/2f	4 3
	Dell' Arca (IRE) *DavidPipe,GB* 9-10-9^{138} (b+t) TomScudamore	20/1	½ 4
3	Shantou Village (IRE) *NeilMulholland,GB* 8-10-12^{141} (s) RobertDunne	16/1	¾ 5
	Townshend (GER) *W.P.Mullins* 7-10-11^{140} (t) D.J.Mullins	33/1	6½ 6
4	Jury Duty (IRE) *GordonElliott* 7-11-9^{152} (t) RobbiePower	8/1	12 7
5	Blazer (FR) *W.P.Mullins* 7-10-10^{139} M.P.Walsh	9/2	1¾ 8
	A Rated (IRE) *HenrydeBromhead* 7-11-0^{143} D.Robinson(3)	12/1	13 9
	Call It Magic (IRE) *RossO'Sullivan* 8-10-8^{137} (b) A.E.Lynch	20/1	5½ 10
4	Haymount (IRE) *W.P.Mullins* 9-11-1^{144} (t) D.E.Mullins	20/1	3½ 11
	Timiyan (USA) *GordonElliott* 7-10-3^{132} (t) D.J.O'Keeffe(7)	12/1	17 12
	All Hell Let Loose (IRE) *HenrydeBromhead* 9-10-3^{132} (t) MsLisaO'Neill	28/1	F
	Bishops Road (IRE) *KerryLee,GB* 10-10-10^{139} (b+t) JamieMoore	16/1	ur
	Bay of Freedom (IRE) *PeterFahey* 9-10-7^{136} (b) JonathanBurke	20/1	pu
6	Oscar Knight (IRE) *ThomasMullins* 9-10-7^{136} J.S.McGarvey	14/1	pu
	Vieux Morvan (FR) *JosephPatrickO'Brien* 9-10-9^{138} (b) ShaneShortall(3)	14/1	pu
4	Slowmotion (FR) *JosephPatrickO'Brien* 6-10-12^{141} (s) BarryGeraghty	12/1	pu

Mrs Patricia Hunt 18ran 5m55.50

LISTOWEL Thursday, Sep 13 SOFT

8 Ladbrokes Ireland Listowel Handicap Hurdle (Gr B) (5yo+) £52,678 — 2m (8)

	BALLYOISIN (IRE) *EndaBolger* 7-10-10^{131} D.J.O'Keeffe(7)	9/2	1
6	SHANNING (FR) *W.P.Mullins* 5-10-7^{128} P.Townend	5/2f	1 2
5	VOIX DU REVE (FR) *W.P.Mullins* 6-11-6^{141} (h) D.J.Mullins	14/1	2¾ 3
6	Plinth (IRE) *JosephPatrickO'Brien* 8-10-11^{132} (s+t) J.S.McGarvey	50/1	5½ 4
	Lakemilan (IRE) *TerenceO'Brien* 6-10-2^{123} (h) DenisO'Regan	16/1	hd 5
5	Davids Charm (IRE) *JohnJ.Walsh* 7-11-9^{144} A.M.McCurtin(5)	11/2	½ 6
	Political Policy (IRE) *GavinPatrickCromwell* 7-10-3^{124} (t) A.E.Lynch	50/1	½ 7
	Boot Camp (IRE) *GordonElliott* 5-10-9^{130} DavyRussell	16/1	4¾ 8
	Top Othe Ra (IRE) *ThomasMullins* 10-11-2^{137} M.A.Enright	25/1	3¼ 9
	Charlie Stout (IRE) *ShaneNolan* 7-10-6^{127} (t) P.E.Corbett(3)	16/1	hd 10
5	Ivanovich Gorbatov (IRE) *JosephPatrickO'Brien* 6-11-6^{141} (b+t) BarryGeraghty	14/1	¾ 11
	The Granson (IRE) *DenisHogan* 6-9-10^{117} MrS.Mulcahy(7)	33/1	nk 12
	Makitorix (FR) *W.P.Mullins* 5-10-9^{130} (t) D.E.Mullins	6/1	9½ 13
	On The Go Again (IRE) *MichaelMulvany* 5-11-1^{136} (t) RachaelBlackmore	7/1	2½ 14

Mr John P. McManus 14ran 3m51.70

GOWRAN Saturday, Oct 6 GOOD to FIRM

9 PWC Champion Chase (Gr 2) (5yo+) £23,495 — 2½m (14)

	WOODLAND OPERA (IRE) *MrsJ.Harrington* 8-11-8 (b+t) RobbiePower	5/1	1
7	JURY DUTY (IRE) *GordonElliott* 7-11-8 (t) KeithDonoghue	7/1	10 2
4	PEREGRINE RUN (IRE) *PeterFahey* 8-11-6 (b) RogerLoughran	11/4	5½ 3
	Ordinary World (IRE) *HenrydeBromhead* 8-11-3 B.J.Cooper	13/2	5½ 4
4	Rock The World (IRE) *MrsJ.Harrington* 10-11-3 (s+t) L.P.Dempsey	33/1	2½ 5
	A Toi Phil (FR) *GordonElliott* 8-11-8 (t) DavyRussell	15/8f	5½ 6
5	Don't Touch It (IRE) *MrsJ.Harrington* 8-11-3 (s) M.P.Walsh	12/1	16 7

Mrs T K Cooper/D Cooper/C A Waters 7ran 4m46.90

CHEPSTOW Saturday, Oct 13 GOOD to SOFT

10 Chepstow Contract Rentals 10 Year Anniversary Silver Trophy Handicap Hurdle (Gr 3) (1) (4yo+) £28,475 — 2m3f100y (11)

	GARO DE JUILLEY (FR) *SophieLeech* 6-11-2^{134} (t) PaddyBrennan	25/1	1
	POINT OF PRINCIPLE (IRE) *TimVaughan* 5-11-3^{135} AlanJohns	25/1	1¾ 2
	WHATMORE *HenryDaly* 6-11-2^{134} AndrewTinkler	16/1	1¼ 3
	Dans Le Vent (FR) *JamieSnowden* 5-11-0^{132} AidanColeman	10/1	nk 4
	Theclockisticking (IRE) *StuartEdmunds* 6-11-5^{137} CiaranGethings	9/2f	sh 5
	Captain Cattistock *PaulNicholls* 5-11-6^{138} (t) HarryCobden	7/1	nk 6
	Court Minstrel (IRE) *EvanWilliams* 11-10-13^{131} MissIsabelWilliams(7)	7/1	½ 7
	Le Patriote (FR) *DrRichardNewland* 6-11-3^{135} (s) SamTwiston-Davies	15/2	nk 8
	River Frost *AlanKing* 6-11-11^{143} BarryGeraghty	12/1	7 9

Castafiore (USA) *CharlieLongsdon* 5-10-10[128] (s+h) PaulO'Brien(5) ....50/1   sh 10
Azzerti (FR) *AlanKing* 6-11-4[136] A.P.Heskin 14/1   1¼ 11
Louis' Vac Pouch (IRE) *PhilipHobbs* 6-11-11[143] (h) MichealNolan 25/1   4½ 12
Chic Name (FR) *RichardHobson* 6-11-0[132] (h) MrTomBroughton(10) ....66/1   ½ 13
Master Dancer *TimVaughan* 7-10-12[130] (s) DavidNoonan 25/1   7 14
Sneaky Feeling (IRE) *PhilipHobbs* 6-11-0[132] RichardJohnson 11/2   19 15
Zalvados (FR) *OliverGreenall* 5-10-10[128] (t) WilliamKennedy 14/1   1¼ 16
Golden Birthday (IRE) *HarryFry* 7-11-12[144] (t) KieronEdgar(3) 33/1   40 17
Dashing Oscar (IRE) *HarryFry* 8-11-6[138] (t) NoelFehily ....20/1   pu
Mr G. Thompson 18ran 4m44.40

CHEPSTOW Sunday, Oct 14   GOOD to SOFT

11   **Fox Family Persian War Novices' Hurdle (Gr 2) (1) (4yo+)** £22,780   2m3f100y (11)
SECRET INVESTOR *PaulNicholls* 6-11-0 (t) HarryCobden 5/1   1
DOUBLE TREASURE *JamieSnowden* 7-11-0 (t) GavinSheehan 8/1   2 2
GOSHEVEN (IRE) *PhilipHobbs* 5-11-0 RichardJohnson 6/1   20 3
Minella Warrior (IRE) *KimBailey* 6-11-0 (t) DavidBass 4/1   3 4
Push The Tempo (IRE) *RobertStephens* 6-11-0 (t) TomO'Brien 10/1   10 5
Equus Millar (IRE) *NigelTwiston-Davies* 5-11-0 SamTwiston-Davies 8/1   12 6
Dorking Boy *TomLacey* 4-11-0 (t) AidanColeman 14/1   1¾ 7
Coolanly (IRE) *FergalO'Brien* 6-11-0 PaddyBrennan ....5/2f   F
Hills of Ledbury (Aga) 8ran 4m46.80

LIMERICK Sunday, Oct 14   GOOD

12   **JT McNamara Ladbrokes Munster National Handicap Chase (Gr A) (4yo+)**   3m (15)
£52,212

The final fence on the back straight was omitted due to a stricken jockey

SPIDER WEB (IRE) *ThomasMullins* 7-9-11[127] L.P.Dempsey 12/1   1
NA TRACHTALAI ABU (IRE) *J.D.Motherway* 8-9-10[122] (s+t) D.Robinson(3) ..40/1   ¾ 2
BLACK SCORPION (IRE) *EricMcNamara* 7-9-13[129] K.J.Brouder(7) 7/2f   4¾ 3
Full Cry (IRE) *HenrydeBromhead* 8-10-3[133] (s+t) H.Morgan(7) 25/1   4 4
Alpha des Obeaux (FR) *GordonElliott* 8-11-0[154] (s) DavyRussell ....5/1   nk 5
7   Rogue Angel (IRE) *GordonElliott* 10-10-5[135] (s+t) J.W.Kennedy 11/2   2½ 6
7   Timiyan (USA) *GordonElliott* 7-10-2[132] (t) M.P.Walsh 12/1   4¼ 7
Kylecrue (IRE) *JohnPatrickRyan* 11-9-10[126] (b) LiamQuinlan(7) 33/1   1¾ 8
Without Limites (FR) *MissElizabethDoyle* 6-9-12[128] A.W.Short(3) 12/1   2½ 9
Our Father (IRE) *GordonElliott* 12-10-0[130] (s+t) DenisO'Regan 8/1   17 10
Riviera Sun (IRE) *HenrydeBromhead* 9-9-10[126] (s) JonathanMoore 25/1   2¾ 11
Raz de Maree (IRE) *GavinPatrickCromwell* 13-11-0[144] G.N.Fox 25/1   9 12
Its All Guesswork (IRE) *GordonElliott* 6-10-0[130] (t) M.A.Enright ....8/1   F
Blast of Koeman (IRE) *RobertTyner* 7-10-2[132] (b+t) PhilipEnright ....10/1   F
6   Supreme Vinnie (IRE) *MissD.M.O'Shea* 9-10-3[133] (t) MrS.F.O'Keeffe ....33/1   ro
6   Kilcarry Bridge (IRE) *JohnPatrickRyan* 11-10-1[131] (t) DonaghMeyler ....25/1   pu
Mr John P. McManus 16ran 5m51.10

AINTREE Sunday, Oct 28   GOOD

13   **Monet's Garden Old Roan Limited Handicap Chase (Gr 2) (1) (4yo+)**   2m3f200y (16)
£45,016
FRODON (FR) *PaulNicholls* 6-11-10[158] (t) BryonyFrost(3) 9/2   1
JAVERT (IRE) *EmmaLavelle* 9-11-4[149] AdamWedge 6/1   1¼ 2
CLOUDY DREAM (IRE) *DonaldMcCain* 8-9-9[157] BrianHughes ....11/4f   ½ 3
Templehills (IRE) *NigelTwiston-Davies* 7-10-10[144] (h) DarylJacob 12/1   7 4
Theo (FR) *DrRichardNewland* 8-10-7[141] (h) SeanBowen ....12/1   ns 5
Flying Angel (IRE) *NigelTwiston-Davies* 7-10-10[145] SamTwiston-Davies 3/1   3¼ 6
Voix d'Eau (FR) *LucindaRussell* 8-10-13[147] (s+t) CallumBewley 40/1   8 7
Value At Risk *DanSkelton* 9-10-4[138] HarrySkelton 13/2   8 8
Mr P. J. Vogt 8ran 4m50.70

DOWN ROYAL Friday, Nov 2   GOOD

14   **WKD Hurdle (Gr 2) (5yo+)** £27,432   2m (8)
5   BEDROCK *IainJardine,GB* 5-11-5 (s+t) RachaelBlackmore 12/1   1
SAMCRO (IRE) *GordonElliott* 6-11-10 J.W.Kennedy 4/9f   1½ 2
5   SHARJAH (IRE) *W.P.Mullins* 5-11-2 R.Walsh 5/2   5 3
Schmidt (IRE) *StuartCrawford* 6-10-12 A.E.Lynch 100/1   73 4
The Risk Takers Partnership 4ran 3m43.70

ASCOT Saturday, Nov 3   GOOD to FIRM

15   **Sodexo Gold Cup Handicap Chase (Gr 3) (1) (4yo+)** £56,950   2m7f180y (20)
TRAFFIC FLUIDE (FR) *GaryMoore* 8-11-12[149] (s) JoshuaMoore 4/1   1

ART MAURESQUE (FR) *PaulNicholls* 8-11-11[148] LorcanWilliams(5) ....14/1 ½ 2
GO CONQUER (IRE) *NigelTwiston-Davies* 9-11-10[147] SamTwiston-Davies 11/4f 5 3
Adrien du Pont (FR) *PaulNicholls* 6-11-7[144] (t) HarryCobden ....13/2 ¾ 4
Kings Lad (IRE) *ColinTizzard* 11-11-1[138] (t) RichardJohnson 7/1 8 5
3 Too Many Diamonds (IRE) *DanSkelton* 7-10-12[135] HarrySkelton 18/1 16 6
2 Geordie des Champs (IRE) *RebeccaCurtis* 7-11-1[138] BarryGeraghty 3/1 5 7
   Solighoster (FR) *NeilMulholland* 6-11-0[137] RobertDunne 33/1 20 8
   Play The Ace (IRE) *PeterBowen* 9-10-11[134] (s+t) SeanBowen 18/1 36 9
Galloping On The South Downs Partnership 9ran 5m54.10

DOWN ROYAL Saturday, Nov 3   GOOD

16   **JNwine.com Champion Chase (Gr 1) (5yo+)** £74,336   3m (16)
   ROAD TO RESPECT (IRE) *NoelMeade* 7-11-10 (h) SeanFlanagan 6/4f 1
9 WOODLAND OPERA (IRE) *MrsJ.Harrington* 8-11-10 (b+t) RobbiePower 13/2 16 2
   OUTLANDER (IRE) *GordonElliott* 10-11-10 (s) J.W.Kennedy 6/1 1¾ 3
   Balko des Flos (FR) *HenrydeBromhead* 7-11-10 RachaelBlackmore 10/3 25 4
4 Sub Lieutenant (IRE) *HenrydeBromhead* 9-11-10 (t) B.J.Cooper 5/1 3 5
   Sandymount Duke (IRE) *MrsJ.Harrington* 9-11-10 (s) M.P.Walsh ....33/1 F
Gigginstown House Stud 6ran 6m01.20

17   **mycarneedsa.com Chase (Gr 2) (4yo+)** £26,106   2m3f120y (13)
   SNOW FALCON (IRE) *NoelMeade* 8-11-5 SeanFlanagan 11/4 1
7 SHATTERED LOVE (IRE) *GordonElliott* 7-11-5 (t) J.W.Kennedy 4/1 1½ 2
   MONALEE (IRE) *HenrydeBromhead* 7-11-12 NoelFehily 6/4f 5 3
9 Peregrine Run (IRE) *PeterFahey* 8-11-8 (b) RogerLoughran 8/1 5½ 4
   The Storyteller (IRE) *GordonElliott* 7-11-12 DavyRussell ....7/1 ½ 5
   Blue Empyrean (IRE) *R.K.Watson* 8-11-5 (s) AndrewRing 100/1 39 6
Mrs Patricia Hunt 6ran 4m58.40

WETHERBY Saturday, Nov 3   GOOD

18   **bet365 Charlie Hall Chase (Gr 2) (1) (5yo+)** £56,950   3m45y (19)
   DEFINITLY RED (IRE) *BrianEllison* 9-11-8 DannyCook 3/1 1
   BLACK CORTON (FR) *PaulNicholls* 7-11-3 (t) BryonyFrost 5/4f 2 2
2 VIRGILIO (FR) *DanSkelton* 9-11-4 (t) BridgetAndrews 15/2 3 3
   Double Shuffle (IRE) *TomGeorge* 8-11-0 (h) A.P.Heskin ....5/2 F
Phil & Julie Martin 4ran 5m58.50

19   **bet365 Hurdle (West Yorkshire) (Gr 2) (1) (4yo+)** £22,780   3m26y (12)
   NAUTICAL NITWIT (IRE) *PhilipKirby* 9-11-0 (s) ThomasDowson 15/2 1
   OLD GUARD *PaulNicholls* 7-11-6 BryonyFrost 15/8 1½ 2
   MONBEG THEATRE (IRE) *JamieSnowden* 9-11-0 (s+t) TomO'Brien 7/4f 6 3
   High Secret (IRE) *DanSkelton* 7-11-0 BridgetAndrews 22/1 13 4
   Keeper Hill (IRE) *WarrenGreatrex* 7-11-0 A.P.Heskin 7/2 7 5
Birrafun 2 5ran 5m43.90

CARLISLE Sunday, Nov 4   GOOD

20   **Colin Parker Memorial Intermediate Chase (L) (1) (4yo+)** £17,085   2½m (16)
   MISTER WHITAKER (IRE) *MickChannon* 6-11-6 A.P.Heskin 3/1 1
   HAPPY DIVA (IRE) *KerryLee* 7-10-9 (t) RichardPatrick 9/1 2¼ 2
   CYRNAME (FR) *PaulNicholls* 6-11-8 (h+t) HarryCobden .... evsf 2 3
   Rene's Girl (IRE) *DanSkelton* 8-10-13 HarrySkelton 4/1 8 4
   Saint Leo (FR) *SandyThomson* 5-11-2 BrianHughes 20/1 7 5
Mr T. P. Radford 5ran 5m01.20

WINCANTON Saturday, Nov 10   GOOD

21   **Jockey Club Ownership Syndicate 'Rising Stars' Novices' Chase (Gr 2)**   2½m35y (17)
   (1) (4yo+) £18,224
   BAGS GROOVE (IRE) *HarryFry* 7-11-2 (t) NoelFehily 6/5f 1
11 SECRET INVESTOR *PaulNicholls* 6-11-2 (t) HarryCobden 6/4 9 2
   THELIGNY (FR) *TimVaughan* 7-11-2 AlanJohns 14/1 21 3
   Full (FR) *NeilMulholland* 6-11-2 (b) RobertDunne 66/1 22 4
   Majestic Moll (IRE) *EmmaLavelle* 6-10-9 DarylJacob ....5/1 pu
Mr Michael Pescod 5ran 4m58.60

22   **Unibet Elite Hurdle (Gr 2) (1) (4yo+)** £34,170   1m7f65y (8)
   VERDANA BLUE (IRE) *NickyHenderson* 6-10-11 JeremiahMcGrath 5/2 1
   IF THE CAP FITS (IRE) *HarryFry* 6-11-0 NoelFehily 5/2 2¼ 2
   WE HAVE A DREAM (FR) *NickyHenderson* 4-11-3 DarylJacob 7/4f 7 3
   Redicean *AlanKing* 4-11-3 WayneHutchinson 9/1 7 4
   Smaoineamh Alainn (IRE) *RobertWalford* 6-10-7 (h) JamesBest 40/1 9 5

| | 1 | John Constable (IRE) *EvanWilliams* 7-11-0 (t) RichardJohnson | 50/1 | 1¾ | 6 |
| | | Air Horse One *HarryFry* 7-11-0 KieronEdgar | 33/1 | 19 | 7 |

Crimbourne Stud 7ran 3m31.70

23 Badger Ales Trophy Handicap Chase (L) (1) (155) (4yo+) £34,170   3m1f30y (21)

		PRESENT MAN (IRE) *PaulNicholls* 8-11-12[144] (t) BryonyFrost(3)	5/1jf		1
	3	SUMKINDOFKING (IRE) *TomGeorge* 7-10-13[131] (t) NoelFehily	10/1	2½	2
		FINGERONTHESWITCH (IRE) *NeilMulholland* 8-10-4[122] (s+t) RobertDunne	16/1	11	3
		Aunty Ann (IRE) *CharlieLongsdon* 7-10-10[128] JordanNailor(7)	16/1	2½	4
		Ramses de Teillee (FR) *DavidPipe* 6-11-9[141] (t) DavidNoonan	8/1	hd	5
		Captain Buck's (FR) *PaulNicholls* 6-10-6[124] (s+t) DarylJacob	9/1	6	6
		On Demand *ColinTizzard* 7-10-7[125] (s) WayneHutchinson	33/1	2¼	7
		Dancing Shadow (IRE) *VictorDartnall* 9-11-0[132] (b) ConorShoemark	33/1	11	8
		Allelu Alleluia (GER) *JonjoO'Neill* 7-11-5[137] (b) NickScholfield	16/1	4½	9
		Bestwork (FR) *CharlieLongsdon* 7-10-5[127] JonathanBurke	40/1	2½	10
		Sam Red (FR) *DanSkelton* 7-10-4[122] (b+t) WilliamMarshall(7)	14/1		pu
		Belmount (IRE) *NigelTwiston-Davies* 9-11-0[132] (s) JamieBargary	25/1		pu
		Bigbadjohn (IRE) *NigelTwiston-Davies* 9-11-5[137] (t) TomBellamy	7/1		pu
		Forever Field (IRE) *NickyHenderson* 8-11-5[137] JeremiahMcGrath	25/1		pu
	15	Kings Lad (IRE) *ColinTizzard* 11-11-6[138] (t) RichardJohnson	12/1		pu
		El Bandit (IRE) *PaulNicholls* 7-11-7[139] HarryCobden	5/1jf		pu

Mr & Mrs Mark Woodhouse 16ran 6m20.40

NAAS Saturday, Nov 10   GOOD to SOFT

24 Poplar Square Chase (Gr 3) (4yo+) £19,100   2m (10)

		SAINT CALVADOS (FR) *HarryWhittington,GB* 5-11-10 G.Sheehan	5/2		1
		TYCOON PRINCE (IRE) *GordonElliott* 8-11-1 (t) J.W.Kennedy	16/1	4½	2
		ARKWRIGHT (IRE) *JosephPatrickO'Brien* 8-11-1 (t) RachaelBlackmore	33/1	17	3
	17	Blue Empyrean (IRE) *R.K.Watson* 8-11-1 (s) AndrewRing	100/1		F
		Footpad (FR) *W.P.Mullins* 6-11-12 R.Walsh	4/9f		F

Kate & Andrew Brooks 5ran 4m00.40

25 Fishery Lane Hurdle (Gr 3) (4yo) £17,532   2m (8)

		ESPOIR D'ALLEN (FR) *GavinPatrickCromwell* 4-11-8 M.P.Walsh	3/1		1
		MR ADJUDICATOR *W.P.Mullins* 4-11-10 P.Townend	5/2	11	2
		MASTERMIND (IRE) *CharlesO'Brien* 4-11-3 DavyRussell	10/1	¾	3
		Grey Waters (IRE) *JosephPatrickO'Brien* 4-10-10 J.J.Slevin	25/1	2¾	4
		Conron (IRE) *MrsJ.Harrington* 4-10-13 RobbiePower	10/1	2½	5
		Saldier (FR) *W.P.Mullins* 4-11-10 R.Walsh	13/8f		F

Mr John P. McManus 6ran 3m56.30

AINTREE Saturday, Nov 10   GOOD

26 Rewards4racing Handicap Chase (2) (150) (4yo+) £49,520   2m3f200y (16)

		WAR SOUND *PhilipHobbs* 9-10-13[136] TomO'Brien	11/2		1
		KING'S ODYSSEY (IRE) *EvanWilliams* 9-11-2[139] LeightonAspell	6/1	6	2
		ROMAIN DE SENAM (FR) *PaulNicholls* 6-11-1[138] (t) LorcanWilliams(5)	10/3f	19	3
		Warriors Tale *PaulNicholls* 9-11-12[149] (t) SeanBowen	16/1	2¾	4
		Martiloo (FR) *PaulineRobson* 8-10-0[123] (t) HenryBrooke	10/1	5	5
		Mercian Prince (IRE) *AmyMurphy* 7-11-6[143] JackQuinlan	16/1	6	6
		Hell's Kitchen (IRE) *HarryFry* 7-11-8[145] (h+t) BarryGeraghty	4/1	1¾	7
		Captain Chaos (IRE) *DanSkelton* 7-10-12[135] BridgetAndrews	25/1	6	8
		Candy Burg (FR) *PeterBowen* 5-10-11[134] (t) JamesBowen	14/1		F
		Some Invitation (IRE) *DanSkelton* 7-10-10[113] (s+t) HarrySkelton	12/1		pu
		Kauto Riko (FR) *TomGretton* 7-11-0[137] A.P.Heskin	20/1		pu

The Englands and Heywoods 11ran 4m54.80

NAVAN Sunday, Nov 11   GOOD to SOFT

27 Lismullen Hurdle (Gr 2) (4yo+) £22,368   2½m (11)

		APPLE'S JADE (FR) *GordonElliott* 6-11-5 (t) J.W.Kennedy	evsf		1
		JEZKI (IRE) *MrsJ.Harrington* 10-11-8 BarryGeraghty	10/1	11	2
		CONEY ISLAND (IRE) *EdwardP.Harty* 7-11-5 M.P.Walsh	8/1	3¼	3
		Arctic Fire (IRE) *DenisW.Cullen* 9-11-5 (h) DenisO'Regan	14/1	¾	4
		Dortmund Park (FR) *GordonElliott* 5-11-9 (t) DavyRussell	6/1	5	5
		Identity Thief (IRE) *HenrydeBromhead* 8-11-12 RachaelBlackmore	7/2		pu

Gigginstown House Stud 6ran 4m50.10

28 thetote.com Fortria Chase (Gr 2) (5yo+) £24,472   2m (11)

	8	BALLYOISIN (IRE) *EndaBolger* 7-11-7 BarryGeraghty	8/13f		1
	9	ORDINARY WORLD (IRE) *HenrydeBromhead* 8-11-4 B.J.Cooper	7/2	23	2
		LISTEN DEAR (IRE) *W.P.Mullins* 8-10-11 R.Walsh	4/1	6	3

9 Rock The World (IRE) *MrsJ.Harrington* 10-11-4 (s+t) M.P.Walsh 28/1   65   4
     Mr John P. McManus 4ran 3m57.30

CLONMEL Thursday, Nov 15   GOOD

29 **Clonmel Oil Chase (Gr 2) (4yo+)** £26,314   2½m11y (12)
     KEMBOY (FR) *W.P.Mullins* 6-11-4 P.Townend 11/8f   1
  12 ALPHA DES OBEAUX (FR) *GordonElliott* 8-11-10 (s+t) J.W.Kennedy 6/4   3   2
   9 A TOI PHIL (FR) *GordonElliott* 8-11-10 (t) DavyRussell 8/1   7   3
     Rashaan (IRE) *ColinThomasKidd* 6-11-4 SeanFlanagan 8/1   11   4
     Doctor Phoenix (IRE) *GordonElliott* 10-11-8 (s+t) KeithDonoghue 16/1   7   5
     Supreme Racing/Brett Graham/Ken Sharp 5ran 5m00.10

CHELTENHAM Friday, Nov 16   GOOD

30 **Ballymore Novices' Hurdle (Hyde) (Gr 2) (1) (4yo+)** £18,006   2m5f (10)
  11 COOLANLY (IRE) *FergalO'Brien* 6-11-0 PaddyBrennan 7/2   1
     PYM (IRE) *NickyHenderson* 5-11-0 NoelFehily 9/4f   3¼   2
     PERCY VEER *EricMcNamara,Ireland* 6-11-5 AidanColeman 25/1   2   3
     Darlac (FR) *ColinTizzard* 5-11-0 RichardJohnson 5/1   2½   4
     Kapgarry (FR) *NigelTwiston-Davies* 5-11-0 SamTwiston-Davies 16/1   4½   5
     Nestor Park (FR) *BenPauling* 5-11-0 DavidBass 16/1   2   6
     Captain Peacock *OliverSherwood* 5-11-0 LeightonAspell 20/1   2¼   7
     Tricks And Trails (IRE) *AlanJones* 5-11-0 BrendanPowell 100/1   13   8
  11 Double Treasure *JamieSnowden* 7-11-0 (t) GavinSheehan ....10/3   pu
     Five Go Racing 9ran 5m08.50

CHELTENHAM Saturday, Nov 17   GOOD

31 **JCB Triumph Trial Juvenile Hurdle (Prestbury) (Gr 2) (1) (3yo)** £18,006   2m87y (8)
     QUEL DESTIN (FR) *PaulNicholls* 3-11-3 HarryCobden 10/3   1
     CRACKER FACTORY *AlanKing* 3-11-3 DarylJacob 3/1   1¼   2
     NEVER ADAPT (FR) *NickyHenderson* 3-10-10 (h) BarryGeraghty 3/1   2½   3
     Katpoli (FR) *DrRichardNewland* 3-10-12 (t) SamTwiston-Davies ....12/1   nk   4
     Needs To Be Seen (FR) *JohnRyan* 3-10-12 (b) PaddyBrennan 50/1   2½   5
     Montestrel (FR) *MrsJaneWilliams* 3-10-12 LizzieKelly 9/4f   6   6
     Martin Broughton & Friends 6ran 3m55.80

32 **betvictor.com Handicap Chase (Gr 3) (1) (4yo+)** £33,762   3m3f71y (22)
     ROCK THE KASBAH (IRE) *PhilipHobbs* 8-10-13[147] (s) RichardJohnson 9/1   1
     ROYAL VACATION (IRE) *ColinTizzard* 8-10-9[143] TomO'Brien 14/1   1¼   2
     CONEYGREE *MarkBradstock* 11-11-12[160] (t) SeanBowen 12/1   5   3
     Singlefarmpayment *TomGeorge* 8-10-12[146] (h) NoelFehily ....11/2f   nk   4
   3 Calett Mad (FR) *NigelTwiston-Davies* 6-10-7[141] (t) DarylJacob 7/1   3¼   5
     Cogry *NigelTwiston-Davies* 9-10-5[139] SamTwiston-Davies ....13/2   ½   6
     Doing Fine (IRE) *NeilMulholland* 10-10-0 (9-12)[134] (v+t) RobertDunne 16/1   4½   7
     Sharp Response (IRE) *SueSmith* 7-10-1[135] AdamWedge 14/1   8   8
     Looking Well (IRE) *NickyRichards* 7-10-1[135] BrianHughes 14/1   16   9
     Pure Vision (IRE) *AnthonyHoneyball* 7-10-0 (9-12)[134] (t) RichieMcLernon 25/1   5 10
     Mysteree (IRE) *MichaelScudamore* 10-10-2[136] (s) JamieMoore ....40/1   pu
     Daklondike (IRE) *DavidPipe* 6-10-6[140] (s+t) TomScudamore ....20/1   pu
     Vicente (FR) *PaulNicholls* 9-11-1[149] (h) HarryCobden ....13/2   pu
     Perfect Candidate (IRE) *FergalO'Brien* 11-11-2[150] PaddyBrennan ....20/1   pu
  18 Virgilio (FR) *DanSkelton* 9-11-9[157] (t) BridgetAndrews ....20/1   pu
     Mrs Diana L. Whateley 15ran 6m49.30

33 **BetVictor Gold Cup Handicap Chase (Gr 3) (1) (4yo+)** £90,032   2½m44y (16)
     BARON ALCO (FR) *GaryMoore* 7-10-11[146] JamieMoore 8/1   1
  13 FRODON (FR) *PaulNicholls* 6-11-12[161] (t) BryonyFrost 16/1   2   2
     GUITAR PETE (IRE) *NickyRichards* 8-10-2[137] BrianHughes 12/1   8   3
  20 Mister Whitaker (IRE) *MickChannon* 6-11-3[152] A.P.Heskin ....6/1f   ¾   4
     Eamon An Cnoic (IRE) *DavidPipe* 7-10-0[135] (s+t) DavidNoonan ....50/1   nk   5
  13 Javert (IRE) *EmmaLavelle* 9-11-1[150] AdamWedge 25/1   6   6
     Whoshotwho (IRE) *DrRichardNewland* 7-10-0 (9-13)[135] SeanBowen ....33/1   F
     Willie Boy (IRE) *CharlieLongsdon* 7-10-1[136] RichieMcLernon ....33/1   F
     Movewiththetimes (IRE) *PaulNicholls* 7-10-5[140] BarryGeraghty ....10/1   F
  26 Romain de Senam (FR) *PaulNicholls* 6-10-3[138] (h+t) HarryCobden ....16/1   ur
     King's Socks (FR) *DavidPipe* 6-10-4[139] (t) TomScudamore ....12/1   ur
   7 Shantou Village (IRE) *NeilMulholland* 8-10-8[143] (s+t) RobertDunne ....33/1   ur
     Kalondra (IRE) *NeilMulholland* 7-10-3[148] (t) NoelFehily ....13/2   ur
  20 Happy Diva (IRE) *KerryLee* 7-10-5[140] (t) RichardPatrick(3) ....25/1   bd
     Rather Be (IRE) *NickyHenderson* 7-11-0[149] JeremiahMcGrath ....7/1   bd
     Ballyandy *NigelTwiston-Davies* 7-10-2[137] SamTwiston-Davies ....12/1   pu

958

Splash of Ginge *NigelTwiston-Davies* 10-10-6[141] JamieBargary ....20/1   pu
West Approach *ColinTizzard* 8-10-7[142] (b) RichardJohnson ....9/1   pu
Mr John Stone 18ran 4m55.80

PUNCHESTOWN Saturday, Nov 17   GOOD

34   **Betway Craddockstown Novices' Chase (Gr 2) (4yo+)** £24,634   2m40y (12)
    8   VOIX DU REVE (IRE) *W.P.Mullins* 6-11-4 (h) P.Townend 6/4f   1
       HARDLINE (IRE) *GordonElliott* 6-11-4 (h) DavyRussell 7/4   7   2
       CADMIUM (FR) *W.P.Mullins* 6-11-7 R.Walsh 5/2   2   3
       Kildorrery (IRE) *T.M.Walsh* 5-11-4 (h) MrM.J.Stenson 33/1   6½   4
       Well Tom (IRE) *AengusKing* 6-11-4 (t) DanielHolden ....100/1   F
Andrea Wylie/Graham Wylie 5ran 4m03.60

CHELTENHAM Sunday, Nov 18   GOOD

35   **Racing Post Arkle Trophy Trial Novices' Chase (November) (Gr 2) (1)**   1m7f199y (13)
       (4yo+) £19,694
       LALOR (GER) *KayleyWoollacott* 6-11-2 RichardJohnson 11/2   1
       DYNAMITE DOLLARS (FR) *PaulNicholls* 5-11-2 HarryCobden 3/1   7   2
       CLAIMANTAKINFORGAN (FR) *NickyHenderson* 6-11-2 JeremiahMcGrath ..11/8f   4   3
       Pingshou (IRE) *ColinTizzard* 8-11-2 AidanColeman 9/1   11   4
       Defi du Seuil (FR) *PhilipHobbs* 5-11-2 BarryGeraghty 4/1   3   5
Mr D. G. Staddon 5ran 3m49.30

36   **Shloer Chase (Cheltenham) (Gr 2) (1) (4yo+)** £42,202   1m7f199y (13)
       SCEAU ROYAL (FR) *AlanKing* 6-11-3 DarylJacob 5/4f   1
       SIMPLY NED (IRE) *NickyRichards* 11-11-6 BrianHughes 28/1   2¼   2
       FOREST BIHAN (FR) *BrianEllison* 7-11-0 (s) DannyCook 16/1   12   3
       Brain Power (IRE) *NickyHenderson* 7-11-0 AidanColeman 3/1   1¼   4
       Le Prezien (FR) *PaulNicholls* 7-11-4 (t) BarryGeraghty 5/2   10   5
    1   Sizing Granite (IRE) *ColinTizzard* 10-11-0 (t) RichardJohnson 20/1   22   6
Mr Simon Munir & Mr Isaac Souede 6ran 3m47.40

37   **Unibet Greatwood Handicap Hurdle (Gr 3) (1) (4yo+)** £56,270   2m87y (5)
       Both flights in the home straight were omitted due to the low trajectory of the sun
       NIETZSCHE *BrianEllison* 5-10-0 (9-11)[126] (t) DannyMcMenamin(7) 20/1   1
    1   SILVER STREAK (IRE) *EvanWilliams* 5-11-5[145] AdamWedge ....12/1   nk   2
   19   OLD GUARD (FR) *PaulNicholls* 7-11-12[152] (s) LorcanWilliams(5) 16/1   2¾   3
   22   Verdana Blue (IRE) *NickyHenderson* 6-11-11[151] JeremiahMcGrath .... 9/2f   ½   4
       Western Ryder (IRE) *WarrenGreatrex* 6-11-5[145] RichardJohnson ....6/1   ½   5
       Not That Fuisse (FR) *DanSkelton* 5-10-0 (9-13)[126] WilliamMarshall(10) 25/1   6   6
       Mohaayed *DanSkelton* 6-11-6[146] (t) BridgetAndrews 25/1   2¼   7
       Nube Negra (SPA) *DanSkelton* 4-10-9[135] HarrySkelton ....8/1   ¾   8
       Storm Rising (IRE) *DrRichardNewland* 5-10-11[137] (b) CharlieHammond(5) ....12/1   ½   9
       Man of Plenty *SophieLeech* 9-10-0 (9-11)[126] (s+t) SeanHoulihan(5) ....33/1   hd 10
       Charli Parcs (FR) *NickyHenderson* 5-11-5[145] BarryGeraghty 11/1   1¼ 11
       Mad Jack Mytton (IRE) *JonjoO'Neill* 6-11-4[130] AidanColeman 33/1   1¾ 12
       Equus Amadeus (IRE) *TomLacey* 5-10-6[132] MrStanSheppard(3) ....25/1   ½ 13
       Midnight Shadow *SueSmith* 5-11-1[141] DannyCook 10/1   3¼ 14
       Vado Forte (FR) *TomLacey* 5-10-3[129] RobertDunne ....16/1   ½ 15
       Caius Marcius (IRE) *NickyRichards* 7-11-2[142] (s) BrianHughes 33/1   12 16
       Deyrann de Carjac (FR) *AlanKing* 5-10-2[128] WayneHutchinson ....9/1   F
       Irish Roe (IRE) *PeterAtkinson* 7-10-13[139] (s) HenryBrooke ....25/1   F
D Gilbert, M Lawrence, A Bruce, G Wills 18ran 3m47.20

38   **Sky Bet Supreme Trial Novices' Hurdle (Sharp) (Gr 2) (1) (4yo+)** £18,006   2m87y (5)
       Both flights in the home straight were omitted due to the low trajectory of the sun
       ELIXIR DE NUTZ (FR) *ColinTizzard* 4-11-0 HarryCobden 5/1   1
       ITCHY FEET (FR) *OllyMurphy* 4-11-5 GavinSheehan 5/1   1¼   2
       SEDDON (IRE) *TomGeorge* 5-11-0 A.P.Heskin ....evsf   3   3
       Two For Gold (IRE) *KimBailey* 5-11-0 DavidBass ....8/1   sh   4
       Colonel Custard (IRE) *NickyMartin* 5-11-0 MattGriffiths 6/1   18   5
Mr Terry Warner 5ran 3m51.40

PUNCHESTOWN Sunday, Nov 18   GOOD

39   **Liam & Valerie Brennan Memorial Florida Pearl Novices' Chase (Gr 2)**   2¾m140y (12)
       (5yo+) £23,840
       SOME NECK (FR) *W.P.Mullins* 7-11-3 D.J.Mullins 7/1   1
       BLOW BY BLOW (IRE) *GordonElliott* 7-11-3 (b+t) DavyRussell ....evsf   nk   2
       NICK LOST (FR) *HenrydeBromhead* 6-11-3 RachaelBlackmore 7/2   8½   3
       Cubomania (IRE) *GordonElliott* 5-11-3 (t) M.P.Walsh 6/1   5½   4

Cap d'Aubois (FR) *AndrewMcNamara* 6-11-3 (h) RobbiePower 33/1   48 5
Orion d'Aubrelle (FR) *W.P.Mullins* 5-11-3 P.Townend ....10/1   pu
Mrs S. Ricci 6ran 5m43.40

40   **Unibet Morgiana Hurdle (Gr 1) (4yo+)** £55,357   2m40y (6)
 14 SHARJAH (FR) *W.P.Mullins* 5-11-10 P.Townend 7/2   1
      FAUGHEEN (IRE) *W.P.Mullins* 10-11-10 R.Walsh 2/5f   7½ 2
      TOMBSTONE (IRE) *GordonElliott* 8-11-10 (t) RachaelBlackmore 20/1 10 3
      Wicklow Brave *W.P.Mullins* 9-11-10 MrP.W.Mullins 8/1   2¾ 4
      Mrs S. Ricci 4ran 3m47.40

ASCOT Saturday, Nov 24   GOOD

41   **Christy 1965 Chase (Gr 2) (1) (4yo+)** £39,865   2m5f8y (17)
      POLITOLOGUE (FR) *PaulNicholls* 7-11-8 (h+t) SamTwiston-Davies 5/4f   1
      CHARBEL (IRE) *KimBailey* 7-11-1 DavidBass ....5/2   ½ 2
      GOLD PRESENT (IRE) *NickyHenderson* 8-11-5 JamesBowen 15/2 10 3
      Benatar (IRE) *GaryMoore* 6-11-4 JamieMoore 9/2   6 4
 36 Sizing Granite (IRE) *ColinTizzard* 10-11-1 (s) NoelFehily 33/1   3 5
      Hammersly Lake (FR) *CharlieLongsdon* 10-11-1 SeanBowen 16/1   4 6
      Mr J. Hales 6ran 5m12.00

42   **Coral Hurdle (Ascot) (Gr 2) (1) (4yo+)** £56,950   2m3f58y (13)
 22 IF THE CAP FITS (IRE) *HarryFry* 6-11-0 NoelFehily 4/5f   1
 37 OLD GUARD *PaulNicholls* 7-11-6 (s) BryonyFrost 7/2   1½ 2
      RAYVIN BLACK *OliverSherwood* 9-11-0 (s) ThomasGarner 66/1   3½ 3
 22 We Have A Dream (FR) *NickyHenderson* 4-11-3 BarryGeraghty 5/2   1½ 4
      Tomngerry (IRE) *BrianEllison* 8-11-0 SamTwiston-Davies 40/1 44 5
      Babbling Stream *BrianBarr* 7-11-0 (s+t) GavinSheehan 100/1 27 6
      Paul & Clare Rooney 6ran 4m38.60

43   **Gerard Bertrand Hurst Park Handicap Chase (2) (4yo+)** £78,200   2m167y (13)
      CAID DU LIN (FR) *DrRichardNewland* 6-10-11¹³⁹ (s+t) SamTwiston-Davies ...16/1   1
      SPEREDEK (FR) *NigelHawke* 7-11-9¹⁵¹ (s+t) TomCannon 12/1 1¼ 2
      MARRACUDJA (FR) *DanSkelton* 7-10-7¹³⁵ (t) BridgetAndrews 14/1   3 3
      San Benedeto (FR) *PaulNicholls* 7-11-10¹⁵² (s+t) BryonyFrost 9/1   2¾ 4
      Ozzie The Oscar (IRE) *PhilipHobbs* 7-11-12¹⁵⁴ MattGriffiths 15/2   3½ 5
      Champagne At Tara *JonjoO'Neill* 9-11-3¹⁴⁵ JamesBowen 25/1   1¾ 6
 20 Cyrname (FR) *PaulNicholls* 6-11-8¹⁵⁰ (h+t) BryonyFrost 11/4f 2½ 7
      One For Billy *DanSkelton* 6-11-3¹⁴⁵ (s) NoelFehily 14/1 3½ 8
      Theinval (FR) *NickyHenderson* 8-11-8¹⁵⁰ (s) JeremiahMcGrath 16/1 1¼ 9
      Modus *PaulNicholls* 8-11-8¹⁵⁰ BarryGeraghty 6/1 27 10
      Gardefort (FR) *VenetiaWilliams* 9-11-1¹⁴³ GavinSheehan 11/1 25 11
      Duke of Navan (FR) *NickyRichards* 10-11-5¹⁴⁷ PaddyBrennan ....12/1   pu
      Valdez *AlanKing* 11-11-5¹⁴⁷ WayneHutchinson ....16/1   pu
      Foxtrot Racing 13ran 4m04.10

HAYDOCK Saturday, Nov 24   GOOD

44   **Betfair Exchange Stayers' Handicap Hurdle (Gr 3) (1) (4yo+)** £56,950   3m58y (12)
      PAISLEY PARK (IRE) *EmmaLavelle* 6-11-12¹⁴⁷ AidanColeman 4/1   1
      SHADES OF MIDNIGHT *SandyThomson* 8-11-2¹³⁷ (s+t) BrianHughes ....20/1   ½ 2
      FIRST ASSIGNMENT (IRE) *IanWilliams* 5-11-0¹³⁵ TomO'Brien 11/10f 1¼ 3
      Folsom Blue (IRE) *GordonElliott,Ireland* 11-10-11¹³² (s+t) RichardJohnson 11/1 20 4
      Theo's Charm (IRE) *NickGifford* 8-11-0¹³⁵ (s) NoelFehily 12/1 10 5
      Milrow (IRE) *SophieLeech* 5-10-4¹²⁵ (t) SeanHoulihan(5) 50/1   5 6
 10 Captain Cattistock *PaulNicholls* 5-11-3¹³⁸ (t) HarryCobden ....7/2   F
      Mr Andrew Gemmell 7ran 5m44.30

45   **Betfair Chase (Lancashire) (Gr 1) (1) (5yo+)** £112,540   3m1f125y (19)
      BRISTOL DE MAI (FR) *NigelTwiston-Davies* 7-11-7 DarylJacob 13/2   1
      NATIVE RIVER (IRE) *ColinTizzard* 8-11-7 (s) RichardJohnson 5/2   4 2
      THISTLECRACK *ColinTizzard* 10-11-7 TomScudamore 10/1 1¾ 3
      Clan des Obeaux (FR) *PaulNicholls* 6-11-7 HarryCobden 11/1   3 4
      Might Bite (IRE) *NickyHenderson* 9-11-7 NicodeBoinville ....evsf 20 5
      Mr Simon Munir & Mr Isaac Souede 5ran 6m28.70

NAVAN Sunday, Nov 25   GOOD to SOFT

46   **Ladbrokes Troytown Handicap Chase (Gr B) (150) (4yo+)** £52,678   3m (17)
      TOUT EST PERMIS (FR) *NoelMeade* 5-10-12¹³⁸ SeanFlanagan 9/1   1
      MR DIABLO (IRE) *J.P.Dempsey* 9-10-7¹³³ (t) D.J.Mullins 50/1 4½ 2
      MAGIC OF LIGHT (IRE) *MrsJ.Harrington* 7-10-10¹³⁶ (s) RobbiePower 20/1 6½ 3
      Grand Partner (IRE) *ThomasMullins* 10-9-11¹²³ A.E.Lynch 20/1 3¾ 4

Out Sam *GordonElliott* 9-11-0[140] (v+t) DavyRussell 9/1   4¾ 5
Mine Now (IRE) *PeterFahey* 10-10-2[138] RogerLoughran 20/1   4¾ 6
Eight Till Late (IRE) *FrancisCasey* 10-10-8[134] (s) ConorOrr(7) ....20/1   sh 7
12 Kylecrue (IRE) *JohnPatrickRyan* 11-9-13[125] (b) D.E.Mullins 50/1   3½ 8
Swingbridge (IRE) *GordonElliott* 10-9-12[124] (b+t) M.A.Enright 33/1   7 9
Dounikos (FR) *GordonElliott* 7-11-10[150] L.A.McKenna(7) 14/1   8 10
Woods Well (IRE) *GordonElliott* 7-10-12[138] DonaghMeyler ....11/1   hd 11
Space Cadet (IRE) *GordonElliott* 8-10-9[135] B.J.Cooper 20/1   4¼ 12
Young Turk (FR) *JosephPatrickO'Brien* 7-10-2[128] (t) MsLisaO'Neill 16/1   1½ 13
12 Na Trachtalai Abu (IRE) *J.D.Motherway* 8-10-3[129] (s+t) D.Robinson(3) ....20/1   sh 14
General Principle (IRE) *GordonElliott* 9-11-4[144] (t) KeithDonoghue ....25/1   hd 15
Poormans Hill (IRE) *GordonElliott* 7-10-3[129] (s) AndrewRing 33/1   2 16
12 Rogue Angel (IRE) *GordonElliott* 10-10-12[138] (b+t) P.Townend ....14/1   nk 17
12 Raz de Maree (FR) *GavinPatrickCromwell* 13-11-0[140] G.N.Fox 33/1   26 18
Neddyvaughan (IRE) *PadraigRoche* 7-10-0[122] (b) R.C.Colgan ....28/1   pu
12 Our Father (IRE) *GordonElliott* 12-10-3[129] (b+t) B.Hayes ....33/1   pu
12 Timiyan (USA) *GordonElliott* 7-10-4[130] (t) M.P.Walsh ....20/1   pu
Mınella Beau (IRE) *W.P.Mullins* 7-10-6[132] R.Walsh ....8/1   pu
12 Spider Web (IRE) *ThomasMullins* 7-10-9[135] L.P.Dempsey ....7/1f   pu
24 Arkwrisht (FR) *JosephPatrickO'Brien* 8-10-11[137] (t) RachaelBlackmore ....12/1   pu
Squouateur (FR) *GordonElliott* 7-10-12[138] (t) BarryGeraghty ....12/1   pu
Gigginstown House Stud 25ran 6m11.40

NEWBURY Friday, Nov 30   Chase course: GOOD to SOFT, Hurdles course: SOFT

47 **Ladbrokes Novices' Chase (Berkshire) (Gr 2) (1) (4yo+)** £22,780   2m3f187y (16)
LA BAGUE AU ROI (FR) *WarrenGreatrex* 7-10-8 RichardJohnson 5/4f   1
TALKISCHEAP (IRE) *AlanKing* 6-11-1 WayneHutchinson 10/1   7 2
LOSTINTRANSLATION (IRE) *ColinTizzard* 6-11-1 RobbiePower 13/8   6 3
Spiritofthegames (IRE) *DanSkelton* 6-11-6 HarrySkelton 9/2   8 4
Mrs Julien Turner & Mr Andrew Merriam 4ran 4m57.60

48 **Ladbrokes Long Distance Hurdle (Gr 2) (1) (4yo+)** £28,475   3m52y (12)
UNOWHATIMEANHARRY *HarryFry* 10-11-0 (s+t) BarryGeraghty 11/4f   1
CLYNE *EvanWilliams* 8-11-0 AdamWedge 14/1   2½ 2
THE MIGHTY DON (IRE) *NickGifford* 6-11-0 LeightonAspell 16/1   2 3
19 Monbeg Theatre (IRE) *JamieSnowden* 9-11-0 (s+t) PageFuller 33/1   16 4
Wholestone (IRE) *NigelTwiston-Davies* 7-11-8 DarylJacob 10/3   3½ 5
Momella (IRE) *HarryFry* 6-10-7 (t) NoelFehily ....4/1   F
Sam Spinner *JeddO'Keeffe* 6-11-6 JoeColliver ....3/1   ur
Mr John P. McManus 7ran 5m54.30

NEWBURY Saturday, Dec 1   SOFT

49 **Ladbrokes John Francome Novices' Chase (Gr 2) (1) (4yo+)** £22,780   2m7f86y (18)
SANTINI *NickyHenderson* 6-11-2 NicodeBoinville 11/8f   1
ROCKY'S TREASURE (IRE) *KimBailey* 7-11-2 DavidBass 17/2   4 2
LE BREUIL (FR) *BenPauling* 6-11-2 DarylJacob 10/1   3¾ 3
Skipthecuddles (IRE) *GraemeMcPherson* 7-11-2 (s) AdamWedge 50/1   6 4
Mr Big Shot *DavidPipe* 7-11-2 TomScudamore 9/2   3¾ 5
Kilbricken Storm (IRE) *ColinTizzard* 7-11-2 (t) HarryCobden 5/2   80 6
This Is It (IRE) *NickMitchell* 6-11-2 TomBellamy ....100/1   ur
Mr & Mrs R. Kelvin-Hughes 7ran 5m56.10

50 **Ladbrokes Intermediate Hurdle (Limited Handicap) (Gerry Feilden) (L) (1)**   2m69y (8)
(155) (4yo+) £28,475
GLOBAL CITIZEN (IRE) *BenPauling* 6-11-10[146] DavidBass 5/1   1
LISP (IRE) *AlanKing* 4-11-1[137] WayneHutchinson ....8/1   ½ 2
MONT DES AVALOIRS (FR) *PaulNicholls* 5-11-3[139] HarryCobden ......9/2   sh 3
Ballymoy (IRE) *NigelTwiston-Davies* 5-11-6[142] DarylJacob 10/3f   4½ 4
What's Occurring (IRE) *OliverSherwood* 5-10-7[129] AidanColeman 16/1   1¼ 5
Whatswrongwithyou (IRE) *NickyHenderson* 7-11-3[139] (h) NicodeBoinville ...5/1   9 6
10 Whatmore *HenryDaly* 6-11-6[142] AndrewTinkler 9/1   2 7
Voodoo Doll (IRE) *EvanWilliams* 5-10-4[126] (s) MissIsabelWilliams(7) 12/1   7 8
Gumball (FR) *PhilipHobbs* 4-11-8[144] RichardJohnson 16/1   24 9
The Megsons 9ran 3m57.00

51 **Ladbrokes Trophy Chase (Handicap) (Gr 3) (1) (4yo+)** £142,375   3m1f214y (21)
SIZING TENNESSEE (IRE) *ColinTizzard* 10-11-3[148] TomScudamore 12/1   1
ELEGANT ESCAPE (IRE) *ColinTizzard* 6-11-10[155] HarryCobden 4/1   10 2
DINGO DOLLAR (IRE) *AlanKing* 6-11-3[148] (s) WayneHutchinson 10/1   7 3
Beware The Bear (IRE) *NickyHenderson* 8-11-3[148] (s) JeremiahMcGrath ...14/1   15 4

33　West Approach *ColinTizzard* 8-10-11[142] AdamWedge ....25/1　　7　5
　　Ms Parfois (IRE) *AnthonyHoneyball* 7-11-1[146] (t) AidanColeman ....8/1　　1¼　6
　　Allysson Monterg (FR) *RichardHobson* 8-10-13[144] (t) JamesBowen ....50/1　13　7
13　Flying Angel (IRE) *NigelTwiston-Davies* 7-10-11[142] (v) TomBellamy ....18/1　　4　8
　　The Young Master *NeilMulholland* 9-10-8[139] (s) MrSamWaley-Cohen(3) ....15/2　　pu
　　Thomas Patrick (IRE) *TomLacey* 6-11-3[148] RichardJohnson ....3/1f　　pu
　　American (FR) *HarryFry* 8-11-9[154] MissA.B.O'Connor(5) ....15/2　　pu
18　Black Corton (FR) *PaulNicholls* 7-11-12[157] (t) BryonyFrost ....12/1　　pu
　　Ann & Alan Potts Limited 12ran 6m36.60

　　NEWCASTLE Saturday, Dec 1　GOOD to SOFT
52　**BetVictor 'Fighting Fifth' Hurdle (Gr 1) (1) (4yo+)** £61,897　　　　　　2m98y (9)
　　BUVEUR D'AIR (FR) *NickyHenderson* 7-11-7 BarryGeraghty ....11/8　　　1
14　SAMCRO (IRE) *GordonElliott,Ireland* 6-11-7 J.W.Kennedy ....6/5f　　8　2
　　VISION DES FLOS (FR) *ColinTizzard* 5-11-7 (t) RobbiePower ....14/1　13　3
　　Summerville Boy (IRE) *TomGeorge* 6-11-7 NoelFehily ....6/1　　1¼　4
　　Bleu Et Rouge (IRE) *BenHaslam* 7-11-7 WilliamKennedy ....100/1　　　F
　　Mr John P. McManus 5ran 3m57.71

53　**BetVictor Rehearsal Handicap Chase (L) (1) (4yo+)** £39,865　　　　2m7f91y (19)
　　LAKE VIEW LAD (IRE) *N.W.Alexander* 8-10-13[139] HenryBrooke ....8/1　　　1
26　CAPTAIN CHAOS (IRE) *DanSkelton* 7-10-4[130] (b) HarrySkelton ....13/2　2¾　2
　　OTAGO TRAIL (IRE) *VenetiaWilliams* 10-11-12[152] CharlieDeutsch ....11/1　　¾　3
32　Sharp Response (IRE) *SueSmith* 7-10-7[133] DannyCook ....10/1　　½　4
　　Ballydine (IRE) *CharlieLongsdon* 8-10-8[134] JonathanBurke ....13/2　　6　5
　　Testify (IRE) *DonaldMcCain* 7-11-5[145] (t) WilliamKennedy ....12/1　29　6
　　Baywing (IRE) *NickyRichards* 9-11-9[149] RyanDay(3) ....16/1　1¼　7
15　Solighoster (FR) *NeilMulholland* 6-10-7[133] NoelFehily ....25/1　　　F
　　Big River (IRE) *LucindaRussell* 8-11-2[142] (t) BlairCampbell(5) ....5/1f　　　F
　　Ami Desbois (FR) *GraemeMcPherson* 8-10-7[133] (t) KielanWoods ....11/1　　ur
7　Bishops Road (IRE) *KerryLee* 10-10-11[137] (b+t) RobbiePower ....6/1　　ur
13　Templehills (IRE) *NigelTwiston-Davies* 7-11-3[143] (h) J.W.Kennedy ....16/1　　pu
　　Mr Trevor Hemmings 12ran 6m06.60

　　FAIRYHOUSE Sunday, Dec 2　GOOD
54　**baroneracing.com Royal Bond Novices' Hurdle (Gr 1) (4yo+)** £49,820　　　2m (9)
　　QUICK GRABIM (IRE) *W.P.Mullins* 6-11-10 R.Walsh .... evsf　　　1
　　TRIPLICATE (IRE) *JosephPatrickO'Brien* 5-11-10 (t) M.P.Walsh ....5/1　3¾　2
　　ARAMON (GER) *W.P.Mullins* 5-11-10 P.Townend ....4/1　3¼　3
　　Commander of Fleet (IRE) *GordonElliott* 4-11-10 DavyRussell ....3/1　1¼　4
　　Geraldine Worcester 4ran 3m56.80

55　**baroneracing.com Drinmore Novices' Chase (Gr 1) (4yo+)** £47,400　　　2½m (14)
　　DELTA WORK (IRE) *GordonElliott* 5-11-10 (h+t) DavyRussell ....10/3　　　1
5　LE RICHEBOURG (FR) *JosephPatrickO'Brien* 5-11-10 BarryGeraghty ....11/4f　½　2
　　JETZ (IRE) *Mrs.J.Harrington* 6-11-10 (h) RobbiePower ....9/1　　8　3
34　Cadmium (FR) *W.P.Mullins* 6-11-10 P.Townend ....7/1　　4　4
　　Discorama (FR) *PaulNolan* 6-11-10 B.J.Cooper ....6/1　　4　5
　　Mind's Eye (IRE) *HenrydeBromhead* 6-11-10 RachaelBlackmore ....8/1　24　6
39　Blow By Blow (IRE) *GordonElliott* 7-11-10 (v+t) J.W.Kennedy ....8/1　15　7
　　Dawn Shadow (IRE) *Mrs.D.A.Love* 6-11-3 M.P.Walsh ....33/1　　　F
39　Cubomania (IRE) *GordonElliott* 5-11-10 (t) KeithDonoghue ....50/1　　　F
　　High Nellie (IRE) *MichaelJ.Bowe* 8-11-3 B.Hayes ....100/1　　pu
29　Rashaan (IRE) *ColinThomasKidd* 6-11-10 (s) SeanFlanagan ....33/1　　rr
　　Gigginstown House Stud 11ran 4m58.90

56　**baroneracing.com Hatton's Grace Hurdle (Gr 1) (4yo+)** £65,847　　　2½m (10)
27　APPLE'S JADE (FR) *GordonElliott* 6-11-3 (t) J.W.Kennedy ....4/6f　　　1
　　SUPASUNDAE (IRE) *Mrs.J.Harrington* 8-11-10 RobbiePower ....9/2　20　2
　　LIMINI (IRE) *W.P.Mullins* 7-11-3 R.Walsh ....11/2　　2　3
　　Bapaume (FR) *W.P.Mullins* 5-11-10 P.Townend ....14/1　1½　4
　　Early Doors (FR) *JosephPatrickO'Brien* 5-11-10 M.P.Walsh ....20/1　1¾　5
　　Farclas (FR) *GordonElliott* 4-11-6 (t) DavyRussell ....16/1　　1　6
40　Wicklow Brave *W.P.Mullins* 9-11-10 MrP.W.Mullins ....33/1　13　7
　　Shaneshill (IRE) *W.P.Mullins* 9-11-10 D.J.Mullins ....33/1　7½　8
27　Dortmund Park (FR) *GordonElliott* 5-11-10 (t) RachaelBlackmore ....20/1　nk　9
　　Gigginstown House Stud 9ran 4m49.80

57　**Download The App baroneracing.com Handicap Hurdle (Gr A) (4yo+)** £52,678　2m (10)
　　WONDER LAISH *CharlesByrnes* 6-10-10[136] DavyRussell ....10/3f　　　1
　　TUDOR CITY (IRE) *A.J.Martin* 6-10-3[129] (t) R.C.Colgan ....12/1　½　2

SAGLAWY (FR) *W.P.Mullins* 4-11-1^{144} R.Walsh ... 14/1 ¾ 3
Hearts Are Trumps (IRE) *DesmondMcDonogh* 5-10-10^{136} M.P.Walsh ... 12/1 hd 4
Tornado Watch (IRE) *EmmetMullins* 9-9-11^{123} ConorOrr(7) ... 9/1 2¼ 5
Sapphire Lady (IRE) *W.P.Mullins* 6-10-2^{128} D.E.Mullins ... 25/1 ½ 6
Cut The Mustard (FR) *W.P.Mullins* 6-9-13^{125} B.Hayes ... 33/1 1½ 7
Off You Go (IRE) *CharlesByrnes* 5-11-3^{143} L.P.Gilligan(7) ... 9/2 1¾ 8
Stooshie (IRE) *GordonElliott* 5-10-2^{128} J.W.Kennedy ... 28/1 1 9
27 Jezki (IRE) *MrsJ.Harrington* 10-11-10^{150} BarryGeraghty ... 14/1 1½ 10
8 Plinth (IRE) *JosephPatrickO'Brien* 8-10-7^{133} (b+t) J.J.Slevin ... 20/1 1 11
8 Davids Charm (IRE) *JohnJ.Walsh* 7-11-4^{144} RachaelBlackmore ... 14/1 ½ 12
Stratum *W.P.Mullins* 5-11-2^{142} (h) P.Townend ... 12/1 hd 13
Tara Dylan (IRE) *ThomasMullins* 6-9-10^{122} (t) JonathanMoore ... 50/1 ½ 14
The Holy One (IRE) *MrsJ.Harrington* 5-9-11^{123} MrS.F.O'Keeffe(7) ... 14/1 1 15
Morga (IRE) *DesmondMcDonogh* 8-10-5^{131} SeanFlanagan ... 40/1 1¾ 16
40 Tombstone (IRE) *GordonElliott* 8-11-3^{143} (t) MrJ.Williams(7) ... 25/1 sh 17
Brex Drago (ITY) *GavinPatrickCromwell* 6-10-2^{128} J.B.Kane(5) ... 25/1 sh 18
7 Blazer (FR) *W.P.Mullins* 7-11-4^{144} J.S.McGarvey ... 16/1 ¾ 19
8 Ivanovich Gorbatov (IRE) *JosephPatrickO'Brien* 6-10-12^{138} (t) M.A.Enright ... 22/1 17 20
Causey Arch (IRE) *W.P.Mullins* 5-10-4^{130} D.J.Mullins ... 16/1 pu
Martin White 21ran 4m00.80

SANDOWN Friday, Dec 7 HEAVY

58 Ballymore Winter Novices' Hurdle (Gr 2) (1) (4yo+) £17,085 2m3f173y (9)

ALSA MIX (FR) *AlanKing* 6-10-7 (h) WayneHutchinson ... 12/1 1
30 DARLAC (FR) *ColinTizzard* 5-11-0 RobbiePower ... 8/1 3½ 2
MERCY MERCY ME *FergalO'Brien* 6-11-0 PaddyBrennan ... 7/1 10 3
Quoi de Neuf (FR) *EvanWilliams* 4-11-0 AdamWedge ... 12/1 5 4
Trio For Rio (IRE) *WarrenGreatrex* 5-11-0 GavinSheehan ... 14/1 10 5
My Way (FR) *PaulNicholls* 4-11-0 (t) A.P.Heskin ... 4/1 2½ 6
Truckin Away (IRE) *PhilipHobbs* 5-11-0 MichealNolan ... 10/3jf F
Amateur (IRE) *JohnFlint* 5-11-0 BrendanPowell ... 66/1 pu
Another Go (IRE) *RalphSmith* 5-11-0 TomBellamy ... 200/1 pu
Down The Highway (IRE) *EmmaLavelle* 5-11-0 AidanColeman ... 10/3jf pu
Mrs June Watts 10ran 5m23.90

AINTREE Saturday, Dec 8 SOFT

59 Becher Handicap Chase (Gr 3) (1) (6yo+) £84,195 3m1f188y (21)

WALK IN THE MILL (FR) *RobertWalford* 8-10-3^{137} JamesBest ... 10/1 1
VIEUX LION ROUGE (FR) *DavidPipe* 9-10-12^{146} (s+t) TomScudamore ... 11/1 4½ 2
ULTRAGOLD (FR) *ColinTizzard* 10-11-0^{148} (t) TomO'Brien ... 12/1 1½ 3
7 Call It Magic (IRE) *RossO'Sullivan,Ireland* 8-10-1^{135} (b) MarkEnright ... 14/1 1¾ 4
Federici *DonaldMcCain* 9-10-0 (9-10)^{134} (s) BrianHughes ... 33/1 2½ 5
Missed Approach (IRE) *WarrenGreatrex* 8-10-12^{146} (b) MrSamWaley-Cohen(3) . 12/1 12 6
Just A Par (IRE) *JamesMoffatt* 11-10-12^{146} (b) SeanQuinlan ... 50/1 13 7
23 Present Man (IRE) *PaulNicholls* 8-11-3^{151} (t) BryonyFrost ... 11/1 2¼ 8
Noble Endeavor (IRE) *GordonElliott,Ireland* 9-11-4^{152} KeithDonoghue ... 14/1 3½ 9
Crosshue Boy (IRE) *SeanThomasDoyle,Ireland* 8-10-10^{144} (t) D.J.Mullins ... 12/1 6 10
Blaklion *NigelTwiston-Davies* 9-11-10^{158} SamTwiston-Davies ... 9/2f 15 11
Dare To Endeavour *PatrickGriffin,Ireland* 11-10-0 (8-11)^{134} (t) A.W.Short(3) ... 66/1 4½ 12
Fine Theatre (IRE) *PaulNolan,Ireland* 8-10-0 (9-12)^{134} (b+t) JonathanBurke ... 14/1 F
Highland Lodge (IRE) *JamesMoffatt* 12-10-1^{135} (s) HenryBrooke ... 16/1 F
Ballyoptic (IRE) *NigelTwiston-Davies* 8-11-7^{155} TomBellamy ... 15/2 F
Regal Flow *BobBuckler* 11-10-6^{140} JamesBowen ... 20/1 ur
Mustmeetalady (IRE) *JonjoO'Neill* 8-10-0 (9-10)^{134} RichieMcLernon ... 40/1 pu
Don Poli (IRE) *GordonElliott,Ireland* 9-11-12^{160} J.W.Kennedy ... 10/1 pu
Baroness Harding 18ran 6m52.60

60 Betway Many Clouds Chase (Gr 2) (1) (4yo+) £33,762 3m210y (19)

18 DEFINITLY RED (IRE) *BrianEllison* 9-11-6 DannyCook ... 1/2f 1
18 DOUBLE SHUFFLE (IRE) *TomGeorge* 8-11-0 (h) JonathanBurke ... 11/4 4½ 2
ACDC (IRE) *ChrisGrant* 8-11-0 (h+t) LiamQuinlan ... 28/1 34 3
One For Arthur (IRE) *LucindaRussell* 9-11-0 (t) TomScudamore ... 8/1 ur
Phil & Julie Martin 4ran 6m46.50

61 Betway Grand Sefton Handicap Chase (2) (6yo+) £49,520 2m5f19y (18)

26 WARRIORS TALE *PaulNicholls* 9-11-12^{147} (t) SeanBowen ... 15/2 1
BRANDON HILL (IRE) *TomGeorge* 10-10-9^{130} PaddyBrennan ... 11/1 1½ 2
KILCREA VALE (IRE) *NickyHenderson* 8-11-0^{135} JeremiahMcGrath ... 9/2cf ¾ 3
Tiquer (FR) *AlanJones* 10-10-9^{130} TomO'Brien ... 40/1 7 4
Forest des Aigles (FR) *LucindaRussell* 7-10-13^{134} (t) HenryBrooke ... 13/2 ¾ 5

Crievehill (IRE) *NigelTwiston-Davies* 6-11-11[146] SamTwiston-Davies ....8/1 nk 6
13 Voix d'Eau (FR) *LucindaRussell* 8-11-10[145] (s+t) CallumBewley 50/1 9 7
Shanahan's Turn (FR) *ColinTizzard* 10-11-0[135] (t) TomScudamore 9/2cf 20 8
Captain Redbeard (IRE) *StuartColthred* 9-11-9[144] SamColtherd(5) 7/1 21 9
Catamaran du Seuil (FR) *DrRichardNewland* 6-11-7[142] (b) BrianHughes ....9/2cf F
3 More Buck's (IRE) *PeterBowen* 8-11-2[137] (t) JamesBowen ....40/1 pu
Mr Trevor Hemmings 11ran 5m41.10

SANDOWN Saturday, Dec 8   Race 62: SOFT, Remainder: HEAVY

62 **randoxhealth.com Henry VIII Novices' Chase (Gr 1) (1) (4yo+)** £30,948   1m7f119y (13)
35 DYNAMITE DOLLARS (FR) *PaulNicholls* 5-11-2 HarryCobden 9/2 1
ORNUA (IRE) *HenrydeBromhead,Ireland* 7-11-2 DylanRobinson 9/1 1¾ 2
35 LALOR (GER) *KayleyWoollacott* 6-11-2 RichardJohnson 8/11f 10 3
Highway One O One (IRE) *ChrisGordon* 6-11-2 TomCannon 9/1 2½ 4
35 Pingshou (IRE) *ColinTizzard* 8-11-2 AidanColeman 12/1 9 5
Diakali (FR) *GaryMoore* 9-11-2 (b) JoshuaMoore ....11/1 pu
Mr Michael Geoghegan 6ran 4m00.00

63 **Jumeirah Hotels And Resorts December Handicap Hurdle (L) (1) (4yo+)**   1m7f216y (8)
£39,389
37 MAN OF PLENTY *SophieLeech* 9-10-7[123] (s+t) SeanHoulihan(5) 8/1 1
NELSON'S TOUCH *SeamusMullins* 5-10-7[123] DarylJacob 11/2 7 2
TOTTERDOWN *RichardPhillips* 7-11-9[139] (h) DanielHiskett(5) 7/1 7 3
Ardmayle (IRE) *AliStronge* 6-10-5[121] GavinSheehan 16/1 5 4
Friday Night Light (FR) *DavidPipe* 5-10-9[125] (s+t) AidanColeman 10/1 8 5
I'm A Game Changer (IRE) *PhilipHobbs* 6-11-9[139] RichardJohnson 8/1 11 6
Eragon de Chanay (FR) *GaryMoore* 4-11-7[137] (v) NiallHoulihan(10) 6/1 10 7
Timoteo (FR) *AlanKing* 5-10-9[125] TomCannon 50/1 6 8
Thounder (FR) *GaryMoore* 4-10-2[118] JamieMoore ....16/1 pu
Apple's Shakira (FR) *NickyHenderson* 4-11-12[142] (h) BarryGeraghty ....5/2f pu
Mr G. Thompson 10ran 4m14.80

64 **Betfair Tingle Creek Chase (Gr 1) (1) (4yo+)** £84,405   1m7f119y (13)
ALTIOR (IRE) *NickyHenderson* 8-11-7 NicodeBoinville 8/13f 1
UN DE SCEAUX (FR) *W.P.Mullins,Ireland* 10-11-7 R.Walsh 7/2 4 2
24 SAINT CALVADOS (FR) *HarryWhittington* 5-11-7 GavinSheehan 8/1 15 3
36 Sceau Royal (FR) *AlanKing* 6-11-7 DarylJacob 11/2 5 4
Mrs Patricia Pugh 4ran 4m04.10

CORK Sunday, Dec 9   HEAVY

65 **Kerry Group Hilly Way Chase (Gr 2) (5yo+)** £31,891   2m160y (12)
CASTLEGRACE PADDY (IRE) *P.A.Fahy* 7-11-4 P.Townend 13/2 1
29 DOCTOR PHOENIX (IRE) *GordonElliott* 10-11-7 (s+t) M.A.Enright 9/1 16 2
SPECIAL TIARA (IRE) *HenrydeBromhead* 8-11-4 B.J.Cooper 8/1 4½ 3
Three Stars (IRE) *HenrydeBromhead* 8-11-4 (s) J.J.Slevin ....25/1 hd 4
Sumos Novios (IRE) *W.J.Burke* 10-11-7 RobbiePower 25/1 2½ 5
Anibale Fly (IRE) *A.J.Martin* 8-11-4 (t) BarryGeraghty ....16/1 nk 6
29 A Toi Phil (FR) *GordonElliott* 8-11-10 (t) KeithDonoghue 10/1 3½ 7
Great Field (FR) *W.P.Mullins* 7-11-10 J.S.McGarvey ....4/7f F
Clipper Logistics Group Ltd 8ran 4m21.60

HUNTINGDON Sunday, Dec 9   GOOD to SOFT

66 **Tattersalls Ireland Edredon Bleu Chase (Peterborough) (Gr 2) (1) (4yo+)**   2m3f189y (16)
£37,018
41 CHARBEL (IRE) *KimBailey* 7-11-0 (s) NoelFehily 13/8f 1
GOD'S OWN (IRE) *TomGeorge* 10-11-6 PaddyBrennan 6/1 8 2
TEA FOR TWO *MrsJaneWilliams* 9-11-0 LizzieKelly 13/2 4 3
Josses Hill (IRE) *NickyHenderson* 10-11-0 (s) NicodeBoinville ....9/1 ¾ 4
41 Hammersly Lake (FR) *CharlieLongsdon* 10-11-0 JonathanBurke 25/1 8 5
43 San Benedeto (FR) *PaulNicholls* 7-11-0 (t) BryonyFrost ....17/2 nk 6
20 Rene's Girl (IRE) *DanSkelton* 8-10-11 (t) HarrySkelton 12/1 2¾ 7
15 Art Mauresque (FR) *PaulNicholls* 8-11-0 HarryCobden 15/2 20 8
Beggar's Wishes (IRE) *PeterBowen* 7-11-0 (b+t) SeanBowen 25/1 22 9
Mrs Julie Martin and David R. Martin 9ran 4m52.40

PUNCHESTOWN Sunday, Dec 9   GOOD to SOFT

67 **John Durkan Memorial Punchestown Chase (Gr 1) (5yo+)** £45,946   2½m40y (15)
MIN (FR) *W.P.Mullins* 7-11-10 R.Walsh .... evsf 1
17 SHATTERED LOVE (IRE) *GordonElliott* 7-11-3 (t) J.W.Kennedy 5/2 1½ 2
16 BALKO DES FLOS (FR) *HenrydeBromhead* 7-11-10 RachaelBlackmore 5/1 2½ 3

17 The Storyteller (IRE) *GordonElliott* 7-11-10 DavyRussell ....10/1　hd　4
　　Edwulf *JosephPatrickO'Brien* 9-11-10 (t) MrD.O'Connor ....14/1　31　5
　　Mrs S. Ricci 5ran 5m17.70

CHELTENHAM Friday, Dec 14　GOOD
68 **CF Roberts 25 Years of Sponsorship Handicap Chase (Gr 3) (1) (4yo+)** £33,762　3¼m (21)
32 COGRY *NigelTwiston-Davies* 9-10-12[139] (s) SamTwiston-Davies ....9/1　　　1
32 SINGLEFARMPAYMENT *TomGeorge* 8-11-5[146] (h) NoelFehily ....5/1　hd　2
　　ROLLING DYLAN (IRE) *PhilipHobbs* 7-10-13[140] (s) TomO'Brien ....16/1　nk　3
　　Theatre Territory (IRE) *WarrenGreatrex* 8-10-5[132] (s) MrSamWaley-Cohen(3) ... 7/2f　15　4
32 Doing Fine (IRE) *NeilMulholland* 10-10-5[132] (s+t) RobertDunne ....12/1　¾　5
32 Rock The Kasbah (IRE) *PhilipHobbs* 8-11-12[153] (s) RichardJohnson ....4/1　7　6
　　Coo Star Sivola (FR) *NickWilliams* 6-11-6[147] LizzieKelly(3) ....5/1　44　7
　　Kerrow (IRE) *AlanKing* 8-10-8[135] WayneHutchinson ....10/1　pu
23 El Bandit (IRE) *PaulNicholls* 7-10-12[139] HarryCobden ....9/1　pu
　　Graham and Alison Jelley 9ran 6m35.80

CHELTENHAM Saturday, Dec 15　Races 69: GOOD to SOFT, Remainder: SOFT
69 **Caspian Caviar Gold Cup Handicap Chase (Gr 3) (1) (4yo+)** £74,035　2½m127y (17)
33 FRODON (FR) *PaulNicholls* 6-11-12[164] (t) BryonyFrost ....7/1　　　1
　　CEPAGE (FR) *VenetiaWilliams* 6-10-5[143] CharlieDeutsch ....12/1　1¼　2
33 GUITAR PETE (IRE) *NickyRichards* 8-10-0 (9-13)[138] RyanDay ....13/2　15　3
33 Baron Alco (FR) *GaryMoore* 7-11-0[152] JamieMoore ....5/1　2¼　4
33 Rather Be (IRE) *NickyHenderson* 7-10-11[149] JeremiahMcGrath ....7/2f　3¼　5
　　Mr Medic *RobertWalford* 7-10-5[143] JamesBest ....12/1　¾　6
　　Foxtail Hill (IRE) *NigelTwiston-Davies* 9-10-0 (9-13)[138] SamTwiston-Davies ...14/1　5　7
61 Catamaran du Seuil (FR) *DrRichardNewland* 6-10-4[142] (b) CharlieHammond(5) .20/1　½　8
　　Casablanca Mix (FR) *NickyHenderson* 6-10-5[143] NicodeBoinville ....14/1　3¾　9
26 War Sound *PhilipHobbs* 9-10-8[146] RichardJohnson ....7/1　¾　10
33 Romain de Senam (FR) *PaulNicholls* 6-10-0 (9-13)[138] (h+t) SeanBowen ....12/1　pu
　　Cobra de Mai (FR) *DanSkelton* 6-10-5[143] (s+t) HarrySkelton ....20/1　pu
　　Mr P. J. Vogt 12ran 5m12.10

70 **Albert Bartlett Novices' Hurdle (Bristol) (Gr 2) (1) (4yo+)** £18,006　2m7f213y (12)
　　ROCKPOINT *ColinTizzard* 5-10-12 TomScudamore ....11/2　　　1
　　LISNAGAR OSCAR (IRE) *RebeccaCurtis* 5-10-12 JeremiahMcGrath ....8/1　2¾　2
　　ROCCO (IRE) *NigelTwiston-Davies* 5-10-12 SamTwiston-Davies ....12/1　3　3
　　Supremely Lucky (IRE) *DanSkelton* 6-10-12 HarrySkelton ....6/1　½　4
　　Doux Pretender (FR) *NickyHenderson* 5-11-1 NoelFehily ....11/4　¾　5
　　Aye Aye Charlie *FergalO'Brien* 6-10-12 (s) PaddyBrennan ....15/8f　12　6
　　Lough Derg Diamond (IRE) *ColinTizzard* 5-10-12 RobbiePower ....50/1　33　7
　　Three Bullet Gate (IRE) *RobinDickin* 5-10-12 CharliePoste ....66/1　3½　8
　　John and Heather Snook 8ran 6m12.00

71 **Unibet International Hurdle (Gr 2) (1) (4yo+)** £78,778　2m179y (8)
36 BRAIN POWER (IRE) *NickyHenderson* 7-11-0 (s) NicodeBoinville ....7/1　　　1
37 SILVER STREAK (IRE) *EvanWilliams* 5-11-4 BarryGeraghty ....9/2　1¾　2
37 WESTERN RYDER (IRE) *WarrenGreatrex* 6-11-0 (s) RichardJohnson ....4/1f　2¼　3
42 We Have A Dream (FR) *NickyHenderson* 4-11-3 DarylJacob ....13/2　1½　4
52 Vision des Flos (FR) *ColinTizzard* 5-11-2 (s) RobbiePower ....9/2　1¼　5
42 Old Guard *PaulNicholls* 7-11-6 (s) BryonyFrost ....11/1　1¾　6
52 Summerville Boy (IRE) *TomGeorge* 6-11-3 NoelFehily ....9/2　14　7
　　The New One (IRE) *NigelTwiston-Davies* 10-11-6 (v) SamTwiston-Davies ....14/1　pu
　　Mr Michael Buckley 8ran 4m05.30

DONCASTER Saturday, Dec 15　GOOD
72 **bet365 December Novices' Chase (Gr 2) (1) (4yo+)** £22,780　2m7f214y (18)
49 ROCKY'S TREASURE (IRE) *KimBailey* 7-11-1 DavidBass ....11/8f　　1
10 THECLOCKISTICKING (IRE) *StuartEdmunds* 6-11-1 CiaranGethings ....8/1　17　2
　　COUP DE PINCEAU (FR) *PaulNicholls* 6-11-4 HarryCobden ....9/2　1¾　3
　　King of Realms (IRE) *IanWilliams* 6-11-1 TomO'Brien ....7/4　30　4
　　Mr J. Perriss 4ran 5m53.00

73 **bet365 Summit Juvenile Hurdle (Gr 2) (1) (3yo)** £28,135　2m128y (8)
31 QUEL DESTIN (FR) *PaulNicholls* 3-11-3 HarryCobden ....8/11f　　1
　　ELYSEES (FR) *AlanKing* 3-10-12 TomBellamy ....15/2　nk　2
　　OI THE CLUBB OI'S *IanWilliams* 3-10-12 TomO'Brien ....16/1　2　3
　　Capone (GER) *CharlieMann* 3-10-12 BrianHughes ....25/1　10　4
31 Cracker Factory *AlanKing* 3-11-3 WayneHutchinson ....9/4　13　5
　　Martin Broughton & Friends 5ran 3m56.10

NAVAN Sunday, Dec 16   GOOD to SOFT

74   **Navan Novices' Hurdle (Gr 2) (4yo+)** £22,590   2½m (11)

EASY GAME (FR) *W.P.Mullins* 4-11-2 R.Walsh	4/1		1
GETAREASON (IRE) *W.P.Mullins* 5-11-3 P.Townend	10/1	2	2
DEFI BLEU (FR) *GordonElliott* 5-11-3 DavyRussell	3/1f	4¼	3
Rhinestone (IRE) *JosephPatrickO'Brien* 5-11-3 (t) M.P.Walsh	5/1	7½	4
Choungaya (FR) *JosephPatrickO'Brien* 5-11-3 (t) RachaelBlackmore	10/1	2½	5
Western Victory (IRE) *ColinBowe* 5-10-10 SeanFlanagan	25/1	2½	6
Monbeg Worldwide (IRE) *GordonElliott* 6-11-3 J.W.Kennedy	10/1	½	7
Satoshi (IRE) *GordonElliott* 4-10-13 BarryGeraghty	20/1	4	8
Magnium (IRE) *MrsJ.Harrington* 5-11-3 RobbiePower	4/1	1¼	9

Wicklow Bloodstock Ireland Ltd 9ran 4m58.70

ASCOT Friday, Dec 21   SOFT

75   **Sky Bet Supreme Trial Novices' Hurdle (Kennel Gate) (Gr 2) (1) (4yo+)**   1m7f152y (4)
£19,932

	ANGELS BREATH (IRE) *NickyHenderson* 4-11-0 NicodeBoinville	6/4f		1
	DANNY KIRWAN (IRE) *PaulNicholls* 5-11-0 HarryCobden	6/1	4½	2
38	SEDDON (IRE) *TomGeorge* 5-11-0 PaddyBrennan	11/4	3½	3
	Thistle Do Nicely (IRE) *JamieSnowden* 4-11-0 AidanColeman	14/1	4½	4
	Champagne Court (IRE) *JeremyScott* 5-11-0 NickScholfield	6/1	3¼	5
	Garbanzo (IRE) *DrRichardNewland* 4-11-0 SamTwiston-Davies	33/1	12	6
	Encore Champs (IRE) *WarrenGreatrex* 4-11-0 GavinSheehan	16/1	1	7
	Sunday At Augusta (IRE) *RichardRowe* 5-11-0 AndrewGlassonbury	100/1	8	8
	Eclair d'Ainay (FR) *DanSkelton* 4-11-0 HarrySkelton	20/1	17	9

Walters Plant Hire & Ronnie Bartlett 9ran 3m50.90

76   **Noel Novices' Chase (Gr 2) (1) (4yo+)** £19,932   2m5f8y (17)

VINNDICATION (IRE) *KimBailey* 5-11-0 DavidBass	8/13f		1
JERRYSBACK (IRE) *PhilipHobbs* 6-11-0 BarryGeraghty	6/1	1½	2
LIL ROCKERFELLER (USA) *NeilKing* 7-11-3 (s) WayneHutchinson	4/1	8	3
Count Meribel *NigelTwiston-Davies* 6-11-3 MarkGrant	7/1	13	4

Moremoneythan 4ran 5m27.60

ASCOT Saturday, Dec 22   SOFT

77   **JLT Hurdle (Long Walk) (Gr 1) (1) (4yo+)** £56,950   3m97y (12)

44	PAISLEY PARK (IRE) *EmmaLavelle* 6-11-7 AidanColeman	8/1		1
51	WEST APPROACH *ColinTizzard* 8-11-7 HarryCobden	40/1	2	2
51	TOP NOTCH (FR) *NickyHenderson* 7-11-7 JamesBowen	10/1	3¾	3
48	The Mighty Don (IRE) *NickGifford* 6-11-7 RichardJohnson	16/1	1¾	4
	Soul Emotion (FR) *NickyHenderson* 5-11-7 NicodeBoinville	9/1	nk	5
10	Garo de Juilley (FR) *SophieLeech* 6-11-7 (t) JonathanBurke	100/1	5	6
	Call Me Lord (FR) *NickyHenderson* 5-11-7 DarylJacob	7/2f	6	7
	Younevercall (IRE) *KimBailey* 7-11-7 (s+t) DavidBass	20/1	2	8
	Agrapart (FR) *NickWilliams* 7-11-7 LizzieKelly	7/1	23	9
48	Unowhatimeanharry *HarryFry* 10-11-7 (s+t) BarryGeraghty	4/1		F
48	Sam Spinner *JeddO'Keeffe* 6-11-7 (s) JoeColliver	9/2		ur

Mr Andrew Gemmell 11ran 6m04.40

78   **Garrard Silver Cup Handicap Chase (L) (1) (4yo+)** £56,950   2m7f180y (20)

	VALTOR (FR) *NickyHenderson* 9-11-3[148] JamesBowen	33/1		1
41	JAMMIN MASTERS (IRE) *WarrenGreatrex* 7-10-5[136] GavinSheehan	7/1	8	2
41	BENATAR (IRE) *GaryMoore* 6-11-4[149] JamieMoore	8/1	½	3
53	Solighoster (FR) *NeilMulholland* 6-10-2[133] RobertDunne	50/1	7	4
	The Last Samuri (IRE) *HarryFry* 10-11-12[157] NoelFehily	15/2	3½	5
	Favorito Buck's (IRE) *PaulNicholls* 6-10-4[135] (s) HarryCobden	7/1	2¼	6
51	Flying Angel (IRE) *NigelTwiston-Davies* 7-11-1[146] (v) TomBellamy	16/1	nk	7
51	Thomas Patrick (IRE) *TomLacey* 6-11-3[148] RichardJohnson	11/2f	8	8
41	Gold Present (IRE) *NickyHenderson* 8-11-7[152] NicodeBoinville	6/1	7	9
	Minella Daddy (IRE) *PeterBowen* 8-10-5[136] (s) SeanBowen	12/1	ns	10
53	Otago Trail (IRE) *VenetiaWilliams* 10-11-9[154] CharlieDeutsch	7/1	15	11
	Full Glass (FR) *AlanKing* 5-10-11[142] DarylJacob	9/1		pu

Mr Simon Munir & Mr Isaac Souede 12ran 6m02.50

79   **Betfair Exchange Trophy (Handicap Hurdle) (Gr 3) (1) (4yo+)** £85,425   1m7f152y (8)

37	MOHAAYED *DanSkelton* 6-11-0[145] (s+t) HarrySkelton	16/1		1
50	LISP (IRE) *AlanKing* 4-11-5[140] WayneHutchinson	13/2	2¼	2
71	WESTERN RYDER (IRE) *WarrenGreatrex* 6-11-10[145] (s) RichardJohnson	7/1	1	3
	Grand Sancy (FR) *PaulNicholls* 4-11-1[136] (h) LorcanWilliams(5)	14/1	2¾	4
	Mr Antolini (IRE) *NigelTwiston-Davies* 8-11-6[141] JamieBargary	12/1	1½	5

966

1	Lord Napier (IRE) *PeterBowen* 5-10-9[130] (t) SeanBowen	28/1	1¼	6
57	Tornado Watch (IRE) *EmmetMullins,Ireland* 9-10-12[133] D.J.Mullins	8/1	2	7
	Flying Tiger (IRE) *NickWilliams* 5-10-12[133] ChesterWilliams(7)	16/1	nk	8
	Court Royale (IRE) *EvanWilliams* 5-10-4[125] AdamWedge	33/1	¾	9
	Fidux (FR) *AlanKing* 5-11-10[145] TomCannon	20/1	5	10
	Fiesole *OllyMurphy* 6-10-12[133] AidanColeman	20/1	1½	11
	Not Never *GaryMoore* 6-10-7[128] JamieMoore	14/1	¾	12
	Jolly's Cracked It (FR) *HarryFry* 9-11-12[147] NoelFehily	12/1	1¼	13
50	Mont des Avaloirs (FR) *PaulNicholls* 5-11-7[142] HarryCobden	5/1f	¾	14
63	Friday Night Light (FR) *DavidPipe* 5-10-1[122] (b+t) DavidNoonan	20/1	½	15
63	Man of Plenty *SophieLeech* 9-10-11[132] (s+t) SeanHoulihan(5)	33/1	1¼	16
37	Nietzsche *BrianEllison* 5-10-11[132] (t) DannyMcMenamin(7)	16/1	¾	17
	Forecast *MartinKeighley* 6-10-6[127] (h+t) TomBellamy	33/1	2	18
	Cyrus Darius *ColinTizzard* 9-11-11[146] BarryGeraghty	16/1	13	19
	First Figaro (GER) *VenetiaWilliams* 8-10-6[127] CharlieDeutsch	25/1	12	20
	Chatez (IRE) *AlanKing* 7-10-0 (9-13)[121] BrendanPowell	20/1	15	21

Mrs June Watts 21ran 3m48.60

KEMPTON Wednesday, Dec 26 GOOD

80 **32Red Kauto Star Novices' Chase (Gr 1) (1) (4yo+)** £56,950   3m (18)

47	LA BAGUE AU ROI (FR) *WarrenGreatrex* 7-11-0 RichardJohnson	8/1		1
	TOPOFTHEGAME (IRE) *PaulNicholls* 6-11-7 (t) HarryCobden	5/1	1½	2
49	SANTINI *NickyHenderson* 6-11-7 NicodeBoinville	11/10f	2	3
	Red Indian *KellyMorgan* 6-11-7 RossChapman	25/1	11	4
21	Bags Groove (IRE) *HarryFry* 7-11-7 (t) NoelFehily	9/2	22	5
	The Worlds End (IRE) *TomGeorge* 7-11-7 GavinSheehan	6/1	6	6
	No Hassle Hoff (IRE) *DanSkelton* 6-11-7 DarylJacob	50/1		ur

Mrs Julien Turner & Mr Andrew Merriam 7ran 6m00.00

81 **Unibet Christmas Hurdle (Gr 1) (1) (4yo+)** £74,035   2m (8)

37	VERDANA BLUE (IRE) *NickyHenderson* 6-11-0 NicodeBoinville	11/2		1
52	BUVEUR D'AIR (FR) *NickyHenderson* 7-11-7 BarryGeraghty	1/4f	sh	2
42	IF THE CAP FITS (IRE) *HarryFry* 6-11-7 NoelFehily	7/1	6	3
50	Global Citizen (IRE) *BenPauling* 6-11-7 DavidBass	11/1	7	4
	Boite (IRE) *WarrenGreatrex* 8-11-7 GavinSheehan	66/1	7	5

Crimbourne Stud 5ran 3m46.60

82 **32Red King George VI Chase (Gr 1) (1) (4yo+)** £142,375   3m (18)

45	CLAN DES OBEAUX (FR) *PaulNicholls* 6-11-10 HarryCobden	12/1		1
45	THISTLECRACK *ColinTizzard* 10-11-10 TomScudamore	15/2	1½	2
45	NATIVE RIVER (IRE) *ColinTizzard* 8-11-10 (s) RichardJohnson	9/2	12	3
41	Politologue (FR) *PaulNicholls* 7-11-10 (h+t) SamTwiston-Davies	5/1	4½	4
60	Double Shuffle (IRE) *TomGeorge* 8-11-10 (h) JonathanBurke	40/1	13	5
66	Tea For Two *MrsJaneWilliams* 9-11-10 LizzieKelly	33/1	2	6
45	Might Bite (IRE) *NickyHenderson* 9-11-10 NicodeBoinville	3/1f	3¾	7
45	Bristol de Mai (FR) *NigelTwiston-Davies* 7-11-10 DarylJacob	8/1		F
32	Coneygree *MarkBradstock* 11-11-10 (t) SeanBowen	20/1		ur
	Waiting Patiently (IRE) *RuthJefferson* 7-11-10 BrianHughes	4/1		ur

Mr&Mrs P.K.Barber,G.Mason,Sir A Ferguson 10ran 5m59.70

LEOPARDSTOWN Wednesday, Dec 26 GOOD

83 **Knight Frank Juvenile Hurdle (Gr 2) (3yo)** £26,576   2m (8)

	ROCKY BLUE (IRE) *ThomasMullins* 3-10-12 D.J.Mullins	14/1		1
	CHIEF JUSTICE *GordonElliott* 3-11-1 (t) DavyRussell	4/1	3¼	2
	GOT TRUMPED *Mrs.J.Harrington* 3-10-12 B.Hayes	14/1	½	3
	La Sorelita (FR) *W.P.Mullins* 3-10-5 P.Townend	3/1jf	2½	4
	Filon d'Oudairies (FR) *JosephPatrickO'Brien* 3-10-12 M.P.Walsh	20/1	8½	5
	Flat To The Max (FR) *GordonElliott* 3-10-12 (b) RachaelBlackmore	20/1	4½	6
	Maze Runner (IRE) *W.P.Mullins* 3-10-12 D.E.Mullins	10/1	ns	7
	Smiling Eliza (IRE) *GordonElliott* 3-10-5 M.A.Enright	33/1	hd	8
	Coko Beach (FR) *GordonElliott* 3-10-12 J.W.Kennedy	6/1	1½	9
	Marmalade N Toast (IRE) *PatrickJ.Flynn* 3-10-12 J.P.Dempsey	33/1	29	10
	Coeur Sublime (IRE) *GordonElliott* 3-10-12 B.J.Cooper	3/1jf		

Mr Rory F. Larkin 11ran 3m57.00

84 **Racing Post Novices' Chase (Gr 1) (4yo+)** £53,153   2m1f (11)

55	LE RICHEBOURG (FR) *JosephPatrickO'Brien* 5-11-12 M.P.Walsh	3/1		1
	US AND THEM (IRE) *JosephPatrickO'Brien* 5-11-12 (t) ShaneShortall	16/1	4½	2
34	VOIX DU REVE (FR) *W.P.Mullins* 6-11-12 (h) P.Townend	9/4	nk	3
	Mengli Khan (IRE) *GordonElliott* 5-11-12 (t) DavyRussell	7/4f	1½	4

55 Mind's Eye (IRE) *HenrydeBromhead* 6-11-12 (t) RachaelBlackmore 12/1   6½ 5
    Ellie Mac (IRE) *HenrydeBromhead* 5-11-5 D.J.Mullins 12/1   4 6
    Mr John P. McManus 6ran 4m03.10

LIMERICK Wednesday, Dec 26   SOFT

85   **Matchbook Betting Exchange Novices' Chase (Gr 1) (4yo+) £53,153**   2m3f160y (14)
34 HARDLINE (IRE) *GordonElliott* 6-11-10 (h) KeithDonoghue 9/2   1
    GETABIRD (IRE) *W.P.Mullins* 6-11-10 R.Walsh .... 8/15f   ½ 2
    RIDERS ONTHE STORM (IRE) *TomJ.Taaffe* 5-11-10 J.J.Slevin 25/1   21 3
55 Jetz (IRE) *Mrs.J.Harrington* 6-11-10 (h) RobbiePower 4/1   4½ 4
    Beyond The Law (IRE) *M.F.Morris* 6-11-10 AndrewRing 33/1   10 5
    Game of War (IRE) *HenrydeBromhead* 6-11-10 DonaghMeyler 28/1   22 6
    Majurca (FR) *JosephPatrickO'Brien* 4-11-3 J.S.McGarvey .... 28/1   F
    Gigginstown House Stud 7ran 4m59.90

WETHERBY Wednesday, Dec 26   SOFT

86   **racingtv.com Rowland Meyrick Handicap Chase (Gr 3) (1) (4yo+) £25,628**   3m45y (19)
53 LAKE VIEW LAD (IRE) *N.W.Alexander* 8-11-10[147] HenryBrooke 5/1   1
53 CAPTAIN CHAOS (IRE) *DanSkelton* 7-10-10[133] (b) HarrySkelton 7/2f   4 2
    TAKINGRISKS (IRE) *NickyRichards* 9-10-9[132] DannyMcMenamin(7) 5/1   7 3
    Wakanda (IRE) *SueSmith* 9-11-10[147] DannyCook .... 11/2   ns 4
    Crosspark *CarolineBailey* 9-10-13[136] RobertDunne 9/2   15 5
61 Crievehill (IRE) *NigelTwiston-Davies* 6-11-8[145] JamieBargary 14/1   13 6
51 Allysson Monterg (FR) *RichardHobson* 8-11-5[142] (t) AdamNicol .... 11/2   pu
53 Baywing (IRE) *NickyRichards* 9-11-12[149] RyanDay .... 16/1   pu
    Mr Trevor Hemmings 8ran 6m25.90

CHEPSTOW Thursday, Dec 27   SOFT

87   **Coral Finale Juvenile Hurdle (Gr 1) (1) (3yo) £37,017**   2m11y (8)
73 QUEL DESTIN (FR) *PaulNicholls* 3-11-0 SamTwiston-Davies 7/4   1
    ADJALI (GER) *NickyHenderson* 3-11-0 DarylJacob .... 4/6f   nk 2
    ARVERNE (FR) *A.Lacombe,France* 3-11-0 AidanColeman 10/1   22 3
    Tazka (FR) *GaryMoore* 3-10-7 JamieMoore 25/1   11 4
    De Bruyne Horse *BrendanPowell* 3-11-0 (t) BrendanPowell 66/1   98 5
    Martin Broughton & Friends 5ran 4m02.90

88   **Coral Welsh Grand National Handicap Chase (Gr 3) (1) (4yo+) £85,425**   3m5f110y (22)
51 ELEGANT ESCAPE (IRE) *ColinTizzard* 6-11-8[151] TomO'Brien 3/1f   1
23 RAMSES DE TEILLEE (FR) *DavidPipe* 6-11-1[144] (t) DavidNoonan 10/1   1¼ 2
    YALA ENKI (FR) *VenetiaWilliams* 8-11-11[154] CharlieDeutsch 12/1   4 3
    Rons Dream *PeterBowen* 8-10-10[139] SeanBowen 16/1   11 4
46 Raz de Maree (FR) *GavinPatrickCromwell,Ireland* 13-10-13[142] ConorOrr(5) 25/1   5
59 Ballyoptic (IRE) *NigelTwiston-Davies* 8-11-12[155] (t) TomBellamy 20/1   2¼ 6
    Dawson City *PollyGundry* 9-10-4[133] JamesBest 16/1   1 7
44 Folsom Blue (IRE) *GordonElliott,Ireland* 11-11-2[145] (s+t) MrJ.J.Codd 7/1   3¼ 8
32 Mysteree (IRE) *MichaelScudamore* 10-10-4[133] (s) BrendanPowell .... 50/1   sh 9
59 Regal Flow *BobBuckler* 11-10-11[140] SeanHoulahan(5) 33/1   18 10
    Holly Bush Henry (IRE) *PhilMiddleton* 7-10-4[133] (s) JamesBowen .... 25/1   pu
    Jennys Surprise (IRE) *FergalO'Brien* 10-10-5[134] PaddyBrennan .... 25/1   pu
    Kansas City Chief (IRE) *NeilMulholland* 9-10-6[135] (s) RobertDunne .... 25/1   pu
    Lieutenant Colonel *SophieLeech* 9-10-8[137] (t) MichealNolan .... 100/1   pu
    Looksnowtlikebrian (IRE) *TimVaughan* 7-10-9[138] AlanJohns .... 12/1   pu
    Final Nudge (IRE) *DavidDennis* 9-10-9[138] SamTwiston-Davies .... 12/1   pu
    Baie des Iles (FR) *RossO'Sullivan,Ireland* 7-11-1[144] (s) MarkEnright .... 20/1   pu
    Vintage Clouds (IRE) *SueSmith* 8-11-3[146] DannyCook .... 8/1   pu
59 Vieux Lion Rouge (FR) *DavidPipe* 9-11-3[146] (b+t) TomScudamore .... 12/1   pu
    Vyta du Roc (FR) *NickyHenderson* 9-11-4[147] (s) DarylJacob .... 33/1   pu
    Mr J. P. Romans 20ran 7m48.90

KEMPTON Thursday, Dec 27   GOOD

89   **32Red.com Wayward Lad Novices' Chase (Gr 2) (1) (4yo+) £22,780**   2m (12)
62 DYNAMITE DOLLARS (FR) *PaulNicholls* 5-11-7 HarryCobden 3/1   1
    KALASHNIKOV (IRE) *AmyMurphy* 5-11-2 JackQuinlan 4/6f   1¼ 2
62 HIGHWAY ONE O ONE (IRE) *ChrisGordon* 6-11-5 TomCannon 14/1   28 3
    Hope's Wishes *BarryBrennan* 8-10-9 DavidBass 150/1   16 4
    Maria's Benefit (IRE) *StuartEdmunds* 6-11-0 CiaranGethings .... 4/1   ur
    Mr Michael Geoghegan 5ran 3m52.00

90   **Unibet Desert Orchid Chase (Gr 2) (1) (4yo+) £56,950**   2m (12)
64 ALTIOR (IRE) *NickyHenderson* 8-11-6 NicodeBoinville 1/8f   1

DIEGO DU CHARMIL (FR) *PaulNicholls* 6-11-3 (t) HarryCobden 11/1   19 2

65	SPECIAL TIARA *HenrydeBromhead,Ireland* 11-11-0 NoelFehily 8/1	5	3
43	Speredek (FR) *NigelHawke* 7-11-0 (s+t) TomCannon 9/1	29	4
62	Diakali (FR) *GaryMoore* 9-11-0 (b) JoshuaMoore 33/1	25	5

Mrs Patricia Pugh 5ran 3m51.00

LEOPARDSTOWN Thursday, Dec 27   GOOD

91   Paddy's Rewards Club 'Sugar Paddy' Chase (Gr 1) (5yo+) £66,440   2m1f (11)

36	SIMPLY NED (IRE) *NickyRichards,GB* 11-11-12 M.P.Walsh 16/1		1
24	FOOTPAD (FR) *W.P.Mullins* 6-11-12 R.Walsh .... evsf	½	2
28	ORDINARY WORLD (IRE) *HenrydeBromhead* 8-11-12 RachaelBlackmore 25/1	4¾	3
65	Castlegrace Paddy (IRE) *P.A.Fahy* 7-11-12 DavyRussell 8/1	hd	4
28	Ballyoisin (IRE) *EndaBolger* 7-11-12 BarryGeraghty 11/4	4	5
65	Doctor Phoenix (IRE) *GordonElliott* 10-11-12 (s+t) J.W.Kennedy 33/1	6	6
65	Great Field (FR) *W.P.Mullins* 7-11-12 J.S.McGarvey 5/1		F

David & Nicky Robinson 7ran 4m02.40

92   Paddy Power Future Champions Novices' Hurdle (Gr 1) (4yo+) £53,153   2m (8)

54	ARAMON (GER) *W.P.Mullins* 5-11-10 R.Walsh 6/1		1
	SANCTA SIMONA (IRE) *W.P.Mullins* 5-11-3 (t) BarryGeraghty 5/2	10	2
	TINTANGLE (IRE) *GordonElliott* 5-11-3 J.W.Kennedy 16/1	3	3
54	Triplicate (IRE) *JosephPatrickO'Brien* 5-11-10 (t) M.P.Walsh 9/4f	6½	4
	Daly Tiger (FR) *NoelMeade* 5-11-10 SeanFlanagan 7/2	3¼	5
	Due Reward (IRE) *HenrydeBromhead* 5-11-10 RachaelBlackmore 8/1	20	6

Supreme Horse Racing Club & M. Songer 6ran 3m55.40

93   Paddy Power Chase (Handicap) (Gr B) (150) (5yo+) £99,099   3m100y (17)

	AUVERGNAT (FR) *EndaBolger* 8-10-5[131] (b) D.J.McInerney(3) 28/1		1
7	VIEUX MORVAN (FR) *JosephPatrickO'Brien* 9-10-11[137] (b) J.J.Slevin 33/1	6½	2
	FITZHENRY (IRE) *PaulNolan* 6-10-7[133] (s) P.D.Kennedy 25/1	2½	3
	Solomn Grundy (IRE) *HenrydeBromhead* 8-10-3[129] H.Morgan(7) 6/1	½	4
	Any Second Now (IRE) *T.M.Walsh* 6-10-1[141] (b) M.P.Walsh 5/1f	nk	5
57	Blazer (FR) *W.P.Mullins* 7-10-13[139] J.S.McGarvey 16/1	hd	6
46	Dounikos (FR) *GordonElliott* 7-11-9[149] C.Brassil(5) 33/1	3½	7
46	Rogue Angel (IRE) *GordonElliott* 10-10-11[137] (b+t) J.W.Kennedy 28/1	¾	8
46	General Principle (IRE) *GordonElliott* 9-11-4[144] (t) MsLisaO'Neill 33/1	2	9
	Scoir Mear (IRE) *ThomasMullins* 8-10-4[130] C.D.Maxwell 20/1	2¾	10
	Timeforwest (IRE) *PeterFahey* 6-10-3[129] (s) M.J.Bolger 33/1	3	11
	Carlingford Lough (IRE) *JohnE.Kiely* 12-11-4[144] BarryGeraghty 22/1	6	12
39	Orion d'Aubrelle (FR) *W.P.Mullins* 5-10-9[135] (s) MrR.Deegan(5) 40/1	1¾	13
46	Woods Well (IRE) *GordonElliott* 7-10-12[138] B.Hayes 33/1	27	14
	Polidam (FR) *W.P.Mullins* 9-11-5[145] (h) P.Townend 20/1	1½	15
	De Name Escapes Me (IRE) *NoelMeade* 8-10-7[133] (t) NiallMadden 13/2	1¼	16
	Pairofbrowneyes (IRE) *W.P.Mullins* 9-11-7[147] D.E.Mullins 16/1	2½	17
	Borice (FR) *GordonElliott* 7-10-11[137] DavyRussell 12/1	nk	18
46	Arkwrisht (IRE) *JosephPatrickO'Brien* 8-10-11[137] (t) RachaelBlackmore 25/1	41	19
12	Black Scorpion (IRE) *EricMcNamara* 7-10-5[131] SeanFlanagan 14/1		F
	Goose Man (IRE) *TomJ.Taaffe* 6-10-8[134] LiamMcKenna(7) 22/1		F
46	Squouateur (FR) *GordonElliott* 7-10-12[138] (b+t) DonaghMeyler 20/1		F
	Snugsborough Benny (IRE) *LiamP.Cusack* 8-10-10[136] DenisO'Regan 12/1		ur
	Jett (IRE) *MrsJ.Harrington* 7-11-6[146] MrS.F.O'Keeffe(7) 25/1		ur
46	Minella Beau (IRE) *W.P.Mullins* 7-10-6[132] D.J.Mullins 33/1		pu
	Drumconnor Lad (IRE) *A.P.Keatley* 8-10-7[133] (b+t) R.C.Colgan 50/1		pu
	Livelovelaugh (IRE) *W.P.Mullins* 8-10-11[137] R.Walsh 9/1		pu

Mr John P. McManus 27ran 6m05.90

LEOPARDSTOWN Friday, Dec 28   GOOD

94   Squared Financial Christmas Hurdle (Gr 1) (4yo+) £53,636   3m (12)

56	APPLE'S JADE (FR) *GordonElliott* 6-11-3 (t) J.W.Kennedy 8/13f		1
56	EARLY DOORS (FR) *JosephPatrickO'Brien* 5-11-10 M.P.Walsh 22/1	26	2
56	BAPAUME (FR) *W.P.Mullins* 5-11-10 NoelFehily 8/1	3¼	3
57	Jezki (IRE) *MrsJ.Harrington* 10-11-10 (b) BarryGeraghty 25/1	6½	4
56	Shaneshill (IRE) *W.P.Mullins* 9-11-10 D.J.Mullins 33/1	27	5
	Cracking Smart (IRE) *GordonElliott* 6-11-10 (s+t) DavyRussell 10/1	40	6
40	Faugheen (IRE) *W.P.Mullins* 10-11-10 R.Walsh 7/2		F

Gigginstown House Stud 7ran 6m01.60

95   Savills Chase (Gr 1) (5yo+) £93,863   3m (17)

29	KEMBOY (FR) *W.P.Mullins* 6-11-10 D.J.Mullins 8/1		1
17	MONALEE (IRE) *HenrydeBromhead* 7-11-10 NoelFehily 11/2	7½	2

16 ROAD TO RESPECT (IRE) *NoelMeade* 7-11-10 (h) SeanFlanagan .... 9/4f   hd   3
   Bellshill (IRE) *W.P.Mullins* 8-11-10 R.Walsh 8/1   1¼   4
16 Outlander (IRE) *GordonElliott* 10-11-10 (s) M.A.Enright ....25/1   ¾   5
67 The Storyteller (IRE) *GordonElliott* 7-11-10 DavyRussell ....20/1   nk   6
27 Coney Island (IRE) *EdwardP.Harty* 7-11-10 M.P.Walsh 14/1   5½   7
67 Edwulf *JosephPatrickO'Brien* 9-11-10 (t) MrD.O'Connor 25/1   1½   8
67 Balko des Flos (FR) *HenrydeBromhead* 7-11-10 RachaelBlackmore 8/1   9½   9
67 Shattered Love (IRE) *GordonElliott* 7-11-3 (t) J.W.Kennedy 6/1   7½ 10
   Disko (FR) *NoelMeade* 7-11-10 RobbiePower ....14/1   F
   Supreme H R C, B T Graham & K Sharp 11ran 6m06.10

LEOPARDSTOWN Saturday, Dec 29 GOOD

96 Neville Hotels Novices' Chase (Gr 1) (4yo+) £53,636   3m (17)
55 DELTA WORK (FR) *GordonElliott* 5-11-10 (h+t) DavyRussell 8/15f   1
   MORTAL (IRE) *JosephPatrickO'Brien* 6-11-10 (t) M.P.Walsh 7/1   8   2
55 BLOW BY BLOW (IRE) *GordonElliott* 7-11-10 (b+t) J.W.Kennedy 10/1   10   3
   Moonshine Bay (IRE) *MrsJ.Harrington* 5-11-10 RobbiePower ....14/1   ¾   4
   Judgement Day (IRE) *HenrydeBromhead* 6-11-10 (s) RachaelBlackmore ....10/1   nk   5
39 Nick Lost (IRE) *HenrydeBromhead* 6-11-10 D.Robinson 14/1   20   6
   Ben Dundee (IRE) *GordonElliott* 6-11-10 (t) M.A.Enright ....16/1   F
   Gigginstown House Stud 7ran 6m02.90

97 Ryanair Hurdle (December) (Gr 1) (4yo+) £67,044   2m (8)
40 SHARJAH (FR) *W.P.Mullins* 5-11-10 MrP.W.Mullins 6/1   1
56 SUPASUNDAE (IRE) *MrsJ.Harrington* 8-11-10 RobbiePower 7/2   3¾   2
57 TOMBSTONE (IRE) *GordonElliott* 8-11-10 (t) DavyRussell 66/1   1¾   3
   Melon *W.P.Mullins* 6-11-10 R.Walsh 7/2   2   4
52 Samcro (IRE) *GordonElliott* 6-11-10 J.W.Kennedy ....6/4f   nk   5
   Petit Mouchoir (FR) *HenrydeBromhead* 7-11-10 RachaelBlackmore 7/1   1¼   6
   Mrs S. Ricci 6ran 3m55.30

LIMERICK Saturday, Dec 29 SOFT

98 Sky Sports Racing Launching January 1st Novices' Hurdle (Gr 2) (4yo+) £26,818 3m (15)
   DERRINROSS (IRE) *J.P.Dempsey* 7-11-6 (t) L.P.Dempsey 7/2   1
74 DEFI BLEU (FR) *GordonElliott* 5-11-3 DenisO'Regan ....11/4   ¾   2
   PLEASURE DOME *W.P.Mullins* 5-10-10 D.E.Mullins ....8/1   ¾   3
   Cap York (FR) *NoelMeade* 6-11-3 SeanFlanagan 12/1   3   4
74 Monbeg Worldwide (IRE) *GordonElliott* 6-11-3 DonaghMeyler 16/1   2¾   5
   Dorrells Pierji (FR) *W.P.Mullins* 5-11-3 P.Townend ....6/4f   ½   6
   Mrs M Furlong, Ex's D Dempsey/J Dempsey 6ran 6m23.30

NEWBURY Saturday, Dec 29 GOOD to SOFT

99 Betway Challow Novices' Hurdle (Gr 1) (4yo+) £25,628   2½m118y (10)
   CHAMP (IRE) *NickyHenderson* 6-11-7 BarryGeraghty .... evsf   1
   GETAWAY TRUMP (IRE) *PaulNicholls* 5-11-7 HarryCobden 10/1   2½   2
   KATESON *TomLacey* 5-11-7 TomScudamore ....9/2   ¾   3
   Brewin'upastorm (IRE) *OllyMurphy* 5-11-7 RichardJohnson ....9/2   ¾   4
30 Coolanly (IRE) *FergalO'Brien* 6-11-7 PaddyBrennan 16/1   12   5
58 Alsa Mix (FR) *AlanKing* 6-11-0 (h) WayneHutchinson 12/1   7   6
30 Nestor Park (FR) *BenPauling* 5-11-7 NicodeBoinville 28/1   7   7
   Mr John P. McManus 7ran 5m09.70

DONCASTER Saturday, Dec 29 GOOD

100 Mansionbet Yorkshire Silver Vase Mares' Chase (L) (1) (4yo+) £42,202   2½m115y (16)
   LADY BUTTONS *PhilipKirby* 8-11-0 AdamNicol .... evsf   1
66 RENE'S GIRL (IRE) *DanSkelton* 8-11-2 (t) HarrySkelton 9/2   3¾   2
   DRINKS INTERVAL *ColinTizzard* 6-10-12 (t) TomO'Brien 11/4   35   3
   Atlanta Ablaze *HenryDaly* 7-11-0 AndrewTinkler ....8/1   ur
   Sister Sibyl (IRE) *HughieMorrison* 7-10-12 NoelFehily ....14/1   pu
   Mrs Jayne Sivills 5ran 5m02.90

CHELTENHAM Tuesday, Jan 1 GOOD to SOFT

101 BetBright Dipper Novices' Chase (Gr 2) (1) (5yo+) £19,694   2½m127y (17)
47 LOSTINTRANSLATION (IRE) *ColinTizzard* 7-11-0 RobbiePower 3/1   1   1
35 DEFI DU SEUIL (FR) *PhilipHobbs* 6-11-3 BarryGeraghty 5/2   1¼   2
   BLACK OP (IRE) *TomGeorge* 8-11-0 (t) NoelFehily 3/1   6   3
   On The Blind Side (IRE) *NickyHenderson* 7-11-0 NicodeBoinville 9/4f   78   4
   Taylor & O'Dwyer 4ran 5m10.90

970

102 Download The BetBright App Handicap Chase (Gr 3) (1) (5yo+) £42,202 2½m127y (17)

	ASO (FR) *VenetiaWilliams* 9-11-12[158] CharlieDeutsch	3/1f	1
33	HAPPY DIVA (IRE) *KerryLee* 8-10-8[140] (t) RichardPatrick(3)	8/1	2 2
	BALLYHILL (FR) *NigelTwiston-Davies* 8-10-12[144] SamTwiston-Davies	7/1	2¾ 3
	Born Survivor (IRE) *DanSkelton* 8-10-11[143] HarrySkelton	7/2	18 4
69	Foxtail Hill (IRE) *NigelTwiston-Davies* 10-10-3[135] JamieBargary	11/1	2¼ 5
	Dustin des Mottes (FR) *DrRichardNewland* 6-10-1[133] CharlieHammond(5)	5/1	10 6
	Divine Spear (IRE) *NickyHenderson* 8-10-9[141] NicodeBoinville	9/2	pu

The Bellamy Partnership 7ran 5m10.20

103 Dornan Engineering Relkeel Hurdle (Gr 2) (1) (5yo+) £28,135 2½m56y (10)

37	MIDNIGHT SHADOW *SueSmith* 6-11-6 DannyCook	8/1	1
48	WHOLESTONE (IRE) *NigelTwiston-Davies* 8-11-6 DarylJacob	6/4f	2¼ 2
71	OLD GUARD *PaulNicholls* 8-11-6 (s) HarryCobden	7/2	½ 3
	Thomas Campbell *NickyHenderson* 7-11-4 (s) JamesBowen	8/1	4 4
48	Clyne *EvanWilliams* 9-11-0 AdamWedge	9/2	¾ 5
79	Cyrus Darius *ColinTizzard* 10-11-0 (t) RobbiePower	14/1	33 6

Mrs Aafke Clarke 6ran 4m59.00

SANDOWN Saturday, Jan 5   Chase course: GOOD to SOFT, Hurdles course: SOFT

104 Unibet Tolworth Novices' Hurdle (Gr 1) (1) (4yo+) £28,475 1m7f216y (8)

38	ELIXIR DE NUTZ (FR) *ColinTizzard* 5-11-7 TomO'Brien	3/1	1
79	GRAND SANCY (FR) *PaulNicholls* 5-11-7 (h) SamTwiston-Davies	4/1	½ 2
	SOUTHFIELD STONE *PaulNicholls* 6-11-7 HarryCobden	6/1	3¼ 3
	Rathhill *NickyHenderson* 6-11-7 BarryGeraghty	6/5f	8 4
58	Mercy Mercy Me *FergalO'Brien* 7-11-7 PaddyBrennan	14/1	5 5

Mr Terry Warner 5ran 4m05.20

105 Unibet Veterans' Handicap Chase (Series Final) (2) (10yo+) £61,900 3m37y (22)

	HOUBLON DES OBEAUX (FR) *VenetiaWilliams* 12-11-3[135] CharlieDeutsch	7/1	1
	THEATRE GUIDE (IRE) *ColinTizzard* 12-11-5[137] (b+t) PaddyBrennan	14/1	15 2
	ON TOUR (IRE) *EvanWilliams* 11-11-3[135] MitchellBastyan(5)	12/1	4½ 3
	Rock Gone (IRE) *DrRichardNewland* 11-11-3[135] SamTwiston-Davies	13/2	1 4
	Loose Chips *CharlieLongsdon* 13-11-6[138] (b) PaulO'Brien(3)	14/1	2¼ 5
	Exitas (IRE) *PhilMiddleton* 11-11-12[144] MrTommieM.O'Brien(5)	20/1	2¼ 6
	Halo Moon *NeilMulholland* 11-10-5[123] (s) RobertDunne	25/1	10 7
	Le Reve (IRE) *LucyWadham* 11-11-3[135] (s) DarylJacob	10/1	3½ 8
	Band of Blood (IRE) *DrRichardNewland* 11-10-12[130] (t) TomO'Brien	14/1	3 9
	Rathlin Rose (IRE) *DavidPipe* 11-10-12[130] (b) TomScudamore	6/1f	14 10
	Buywise (IRE) *EvanWilliams* 12-11-6[138] AdamWedge	25/1	F
	Cultram Abbey *NickyRichards* 12-10-13[131] RyanDay	12/1	pu
	Pete The Feat (IRE) *CharlieLongsdon* 15-11-0[132] (t) JonathanBurke	20/1	pu
	Tenor Nivernais (FR) *VenetiaWilliams* 12-10-0[132] (s) AidanColeman	11/1	pu
2	Henllan Harri (IRE) *PeterBowen* 11-11-2[134] (b+t) SeanBowen	12/1	pu
23	Kings Lad (IRE) *ColinTizzard* 12-11-4[136] (t) HarryCobden	16/1	pu
53	Bishops Road (IRE) *KerryLee* 11-11-5[137] (b+t) JamieMoore	20/1	pu

Julian Blackwell & Mrs Angus Maclay 17ran 6m23.30

NAAS Sunday, Jan 6   GOOD to SOFT

106 Lawlor's of Naas Novices' Hurdle (Gr 1) (5yo+) £47,837 2½m (11)

	BATTLEOVERDOYEN (IRE) *GordonElliott* 6-11-10 J.W.Kennedy	2/1f	1
	SAMS PROFILE *M.F.Morris* 5-11-7 B.J.Cooper	16/1	2¾ 2
74	GETAREASON (IRE) *W.P.Mullins* 6-11-10 NoelFehily	12/1	2 3
74	Magnium (IRE) *Mrs.J.Harrington* 6-11-10 RobbiePower	16/1	1 4
	Lone Wolf (IRE) *JosephPatrickO'Brien* 6-11-10 (t) M.P.Walsh	10/1	2 5
	First Approach (IRE) *NoelMeade* 6-11-10 SeanFlanagan	33/1	¾ 6
	Come To Me (FR) *W.P.Mullins* 7-11-10 P.Townend	4/1	32 7
	Tornado Flyer (IRE) *W.P.Mullins* 6-11-10 R.Walsh	9/4	pu

Gigginstown House Stud 8ran 4m40.30

WARWICK Saturday, Jan 12   GOOD

107 Ballymore Leamington Novices' Hurdle (Gr 2) (1) (5yo+) £19,932 2m5f (11)

	BEAKSTOWN (IRE) *DanSkelton* 6-11-0 (t) HarrySkelton	6/1	1
	STONEY MOUNTAIN (IRE) *HenryDaly* 6-11-0 SamTwiston-Davies	3/1	3¾ 2
	FINAWN BAWN (IRE) *OllyMurphy* 6-11-0 AidanColeman	14/1	1½ 3
70	Rockpoint *ColinTizzard* 6-11-5 TomScudamore	12/1	4½ 4
75	Champagne Court (IRE) *JeremyScott* 6-11-0 NickScholfield	12/1	6 5
	Tidal Flow *PhilipHobbs* 6-11-0 RichardJohnson	11/10f	20 6

Bryan Drew 6ran 4m50.70

108 McCoy Contractors Civil Engineering Classic Handicap Chase (Gr 3) (1) 3m5f54y (22)
(5yo+) £42,712

	IMPULSIVE STAR (IRE) *NeilMulholland* 9-10-1[133] (s) MrSamWaley-Cohen(3) .8/1		1
32	CALETT MAD (FR) *NigelTwiston-Davies* 7-10-13[145] (t) JamesBowen 7/1	3¼	2
86	CROSSPARK *CarolineBailey* 9-10-3[135] HarrySkelton 9/1	2¼	3
	Carole's Destrier *NeilMulholland* 11-10-6[138] (s) RobertDunne 12/1	3¼	4
59	Ultragold (FR) *ColinTizzard* 11-11-2[148] (t) RichardJohnson 25/1	6	5
	Step Back (IRE) *MarkBradstock* 9-11-3[149] (s) DavidBass 6/1	13	6
	Ibis du Rheu (FR) *PaulNicholls* 8-11-0[146] (t) HarryCobden 7/1	10	7
	Milansbar (IRE) *NeilKing* 12-10-8[140] (b) MissGinaAndrews(3) 16/1	½	8
	Duel At Dawn (IRE) *AlexHales* 9-10-5[137] (s) KielanWoods 7/1	½	9
68	Cogry *NigelTwiston-Davies* 10-10-10[142] (s) SamTwiston-Davies 9/2f	1¼	10
	Sizing Codelco (IRE) *ColinTizzard* 10-11-10[156] AidanColeman 33/1	8	11
	Un Temps Pour Tout (IRE) *DavidPipe* 10-11-12[158] (b+t) TomScudamore ...16/1	2½	12

Robert Waley-Cohen & Men Holding 12ran 7m16.50

FAIRYHOUSE Saturday, Jan 12 GOOD to SOFT

109 BetVictor Dan Moore Memorial Handicap Chase (Gr A) (4yo+) £53,153   2m1f (12)

	DUCA DE THAIX (FR) *GordonElliott* 6-11-1[143] (s+t) DavyRussell 3/1f		1
55	CUBOMANIA (IRE) *GordonElliott* 6-10-11[139] (t) RobbiePower 7/1	½	2
93	BLAZER (FR) *W.P.Mullins* 8-10-11[139] M.P.Walsh 7/2	¾	3
34	Kildorrery (IRE) *T.M.Walsh* 6-10-4[132] (h) R.Walsh 9/2	8	4
	Bel Ami de Sivola (FR) *NoelMeade* 8-10-7[135] (t) SeanFlanagan 10/1	½	5
46	Kylecrue (IRE) *JohnPatrickRyan* 12-10-3[131] (b) DonaghMeyler 25/1	3	6
65	Three Stars (IRE) *HenrydeBromhead* 9-10-12[140] (s) J.J.Slevin 8/1	2¼	7
24	Tycoon Prince (IRE) *GordonElliott* 9-11-0[142] (t) J.W.Kennedy 16/1	6	8
	Avenir d'Une Vie (FR) *HenrydeBromhead* 9-10-10[138] RachaelBlackmore ...12/1	6	9
65	A Toi Phil (FR) *GordonElliott* 9-11-10[152] (t) AndrewRing 25/1	pu

Gigginstown House Stud 10ran 4m17.50

PUNCHESTOWN Sunday, Jan 13 GOOD to SOFT

110 Total Event Rental Novices' Chase (Gr 3) (5yo+) £23,654   2½m (13)

	WINTER ESCAPE (IRE) *AidanAnthonyHoward* 8-11-8 M.P.Walsh 12/1		1
	A PLUS TARD (FR) *HenrydeBromhead* 5-10-8 RachaelBlackmore 5/4f	2¼	2
85	JETZ (IRE) *MrsJ.Harrington* 7-11-1 RobbiePower 7/2	13	3
	Gun Digger (IRE) *GordonElliott* 7-11-1 (s) J.W.Kennedy 9/2	16	4
85	Beyond The Law (IRE) *M.F.Morris* 7-11-1 AndrewRing 33/1	1¼	5
96	Ben Dundee (IRE) *GordonElliott* 7-11-1 (t) L.P.Dempsey 6/1	8½	6
	Poli Roi (FR) *GordonElliott* 7-11-1 (s+t) M.A.Enright 28/1	pu

Mr John P. McManus 7ran 5m09.10

111 Sky Bet Moscow Flyer Novices' Hurdle (Gr 2) (5yo+) £23,654   2m (9)

	FELIX DESJY (FR) *GordonElliott* 6-11-2 SeanFlanagan 11/4		1
	JETEZ (IRE) *MrsJ.Harrington* 6-11-2 RobbiePower 4/1	5	2
	HARRIE (FR) *W.P.Mullins* 7-11-2 R.Walsh 9/2	13	3
	Swordsman (IRE) *GordonElliott* 5-11-0 J.W.Kennedy 13/2	7	4
	Buildmeupbuttercup *W.P.Mullins* 5-10-7 P.Townend 9/4f	5	5
	Jan Maat (GER) *HenrydeBromhead* 6-11-2 RachaelBlackmore 25/1	32	6

Gigginstown House Stud 6ran 3m55.10

ASCOT Saturday, Jan 19 GOOD to SOFT

112 OLBG.com Mares' Hurdle (Warfield) (Gr 2) (4yo+) £28,475   2m7f118y (11)

46	MAGIC OF LIGHT (IRE) *MrsJ.Harrington,Ireland* 8-11-0 (s) RobbiePower .. 15/8f		1
	JESTER JET *TomLacey* 9-11-4 RobertDunne 8/1	3¼	2
	IF YOU SAY RUN (IRE) *PaulNicholls* 7-11-0 (t) HarryCobden 5/2	1¼	3
	Petticoat Tails *WarrenGreatrex* 7-11-0 (s) GavinSheehan 7/1	nk	4
	Culture de Sivola (FR) *NickWilliams* 7-11-0 LizzieKelly 4/1	5	5
	Shimmer's Rock (IRE) *P.E.Collins,Ireland* 7-11-0 JonathanBurke 66/1	pu

Ann & Alan Potts Limited 6ran 5m56.70

113 Bet365 Handicap Chase (2) (5yo+) £46,920   2m5f8y (17)

43	CYRNAME (FR) *PaulNicholls* 7-11-10[150] (t) HarryCobden 4/1		1
	DOITFORTHEVILLAGE (IRE) *PaulHenderson* 10-11-0[140] (t) PaddyBrennan ..14/1	21	2
102	HAPPY DIVA (IRE) *KerryLee* 8-11-2[142] (t) RichardPatrick(3) 7/1	½	3
33	Mister Whitaker (IRE) *MickChannon* 7-11-12[152] JonathanBurke 11/2	4	4
78	Flying Angel (IRE) *NigelTwiston-Davies* 8-11-5[145] (v+t) TomBellamy 12/1	10	5
69	Mr Medic *RobertWalford* 8-11-3[143] JamesBest 11/2	9	6
78	Benatar (IRE) *GaryMoore* 7-11-9[149] JamieMoore 7/2f	15	7
	Quite By Chance *ColinTizzard* 10-10-9[135] (t) RobbiePower 20/1	1	8
	Get On The Yager *DanSkelton* 9-10-10[136] BridgetAndrews 50/1	nk	9

972

66 San Benedeto (FR) *PaulNicholls* 8-11-10[150] (s+t) LorcanWilliams(5) ....12/1   nk 10
      Mrs Johnny de la Hey 10ran 5m13.70

114 Matchbook Clarence House Chase (Gr 1) (1) (5yo+) £85,425   2m167y (13)
90 ALTIOR (IRE) *NickyHenderson* 9-11-7 NicodeBoinville 1/10f   1
      FOX NORTON (FR) *ColinTizzard* 9-11-7 RobbiePower 10/1   7 2
90 DIEGO DU CHARMIL (FR) *PaulNicholls* 7-11-7 (t) HarryCobden 16/1   34 3
      Mrs Patricia Pugh 3ran 4m06.90

HAYDOCK Saturday, Jan 19 GOOD to SOFT
115 Patrick Coyne Memorial Altcar Novices' Chase (Gr 2) (1) (5yo+) £18,224   2m3f203y (15)
10 CASTAFIORE (USA) *CharlieLongsdon* 6-10-7 (s) PaulO'Brien 28/1   1
76 JERRYSBACK (IRE) *PhilipHobbs* 7-11-0 BarryGeraghty 6/4f   5 2
      CRUCIAL ROLE *DanSkelton* 7-11-0 HarrySkelton 2/1   9 3
49 Le Breuil (FR) *BenPauling* 7-11-0 DarylJacob ....3/1   hd 4
      Slate House (IRE) *ColinTizzard* 7-11-0 (t) TomScudamore 10/1   84 5
      Slater Stockwood Nicholson Partnership 5ran 5m08.10

116 Sky Bet Supreme Trial Rossington Main Novices' Hurdle (Gr 2) (1) (4yo+)   1m7f144y (9)
      £17,085
      MISTER FISHER (IRE) *NickyHenderson* 5-11-7 JamesBowen ....evsf   1
      BRIGHT FORECAST (IRE) *BenPauling* 5-11-4 DavidBass 2/1   2½ 2
      MURATELLO (FR) *NigelTwiston-Davies* 5-11-4 DarylJacob 8/1   3 3
      Esprit du Large (FR) *EvanWilliams* 5-11-4 AdamWedge 8/1   3½ 4
30 Tricks And Trails (IRE) *AlanJones* 6-11-4 TomO'Brien 125/1   23 5
      Idee de Garde (FR) *DanSkelton* 6-11-4 (t) HarrySkelton 20/1   11 6
      James and Jean Potter 6ran 3m47.00

117 The New One Unibet Hurdle (Champion Hurdle Trial) (Gr 2) (1) (4yo+)   1m7f144y (9)
      £42,712
81 GLOBAL CITIZEN (IRE) *BenPauling* 7-11-8 DavidBass 3/1   1
71 SILVER STREAK (IRE) *EvanWilliams* 6-11-8 AdamWedge 5/2jf   3 2
79 WESTERN RYDER (IRE) *WarrenGreatrex* 7-11-4 (s) RichardJohnson 5/2jf   9 3
79 Mohaayed *DanSkelton* 7-11-8 (s+t) HarrySkelton 4/1   10 4
62 Pingshou (IRE) *ColinTizzard* 9-11-4 TomScudamore 14/1   3¾ 5
      The Megsons 5ran 3m44.30

118 Peter Marsh Chase (Limited Handicap) (Gr 2) (1) (5yo+) £42,712   3m1f125y (19)
86 WAKANDA (IRE) *SueSmith* 10-10-10[146] DannyCook 6/1   1
      ROBINSFIRTH (IRE) *ColinTizzard* 10-10-10[146] (t) RichardJohnson 7/1   1¼ 2
53 BALLYDINE (IRE) *CharlieLongsdon* 9-10-4 (9-13)[140] (s+t) JamesBowen 13/2   2½ 3
      Ballyarthur (IRE) *NigelTwiston-Davies* 9-10-4 (10-1)[140] (t) JamieBargary ....16/1   sh 4
      Red Infantry (IRE) *IanWilliams* 9-10-6[142] (v) TomO'Brien 7/1   1¾ 5
61 Captain Redbeard (IRE) *StuartColtherd* 10-10-8[144] SamColtherd(5) 15/2   2¾ 6
78 Otago Trail (IRE) *VenetiaWilliams* 11-11-3[153] HughNugent(7) 7/1   17 7
      Three Musketeers (IRE) *DanSkelton* 9-10-4 (t) HarrySkelton 9/1   10 8
32 Daklondike (IRE) *DavidPipe* 7-10-9[145] (v) TomScudamore ....4/1f   ur
60 One For Arthur (IRE) *LucindaRussell* 10-11-4[154] (t) DerekFox ....25/1   ur
      Chase The Spud *FergalO'Brien* 11-10-7[143] AdamWedge ....40/1   pu
      Mrs M. B. Scholey 11ran 6m49.00

THURLES Sunday, Jan 20 GOOD
119 Horse & Jockey Hotel Chase (Gr 2) (6yo+) £23,495   2½m118y (10)
      The fence before the home straight was omitted due to the low trajectory of the sun
46 TOUT EST PERMIS (FR) *NoelMeade* 6-11-3 SeanFlanagan 13/8f   1
16 SUB LIEUTENANT (IRE) *HenrydeBromhead* 10-11-6 (s+t) J.J.Slevin ....6/1   sh 2
      TOTAL RECALL (IRE) *W.P.Mullins* 10-11-3 R.Walsh 15/8   9½ 3
93 Jett (IRE) *MrsJ.Harrington* 8-11-3 (s) RobbiePower 9/1   2¾ 4
109 A Toi Phil (FR) *GordonElliott* 9-11-8 (t) J.W.Kennedy ....16/1   ¾ 5
91 Doctor Phoenix (IRE) *GordonElliott* 11-11-6 (s+t) DavyRussell 12/1   4½ 6
      Amaulino (IRE) *R.K.Watson* 6-11-3 AndrewRing 200/1   16 7
      Gigginstown House Stud 7ran 4m57.10

120 Order of St George Coolmore National Hunt Sires Irish European   2½m118y (10)
      Breeders Fund Mares Novices' Chase (Gr 2) (5yo+) £30,530
      The fence before the home straight was omitted due to the low trajectory of the sun
      CAMELIA DE COTTE (FR) *W.P.Mullins* 7-11-3 (h) P.Townend 11/10f   1
25 GREY WATERS (IRE) *JosephPatrickO'Brien* 5-10-7 J.J.Slevin 16/1   20 2
84 ELLIE MAC (IRE) *HenrydeBromhead* 6-11-0 RobbiePower 9/2   2½ 3
      Oh Me Oh My (IRE) *MsM.Flynn* 8-11-0 PhilipEnright ....40/1   ¾ 4

```
   6  Meri Devie (FR) PaulNolan 6-11-0 B.J.Cooper ..........................................4/1        5½   5
      Nellie Pledge (IRE) PaulJohnGilligan 7-11-0 L.P.Gilligan ..................14/1             F
      Tell Me Annie (IRE) DeclanQueally 10-11-0 A.E.Lynch .......................7/1             pu
      Mrs S. Ricci 7ran 4m57.90
```

GOWRAN Thursday, Jan 24 SOFT

121 John Mulhern Galmoy Hurdle (Gr 2) (5yo+) £23,289   3m (13)

```
      PRESENTING PERCY PatrickG.Kelly 8-11-8 (t) DavyRussell ....................9/4f            1
   94 BAPAUME (FR) W.P.Mullins 6-11-8 P.Townend .....................................11/2       1¼   2
      KILLULTAGH VIC (IRE) W.P.Mullins 10-11-3 D.J.Mullins ..................10/1              hd   3
   56 Limini (IRE) W.P.Mullins 8-10-10 RachaelBlackmore ...........................6/1          ¾   4
      Darasso (FR) JosephPatrickO'Brien 6-11-3 M.P.Walsh ..........................9/2            7   5
      Prince of Scars (IRE) GordonElliott 9-11-3 SeanFlanagan ...................50/1           16   6
      Bleu Berry (FR) W.P.Mullins 8-11-3 B.Hayes .......................................20/1     13   7
      Mala Beach (IRE) GordonElliott 11-11-3 DenisO'Regan ......................28/1            5½   8
      Coquin Mans (FR) W.P.Mullins 7-11-8 (h) R.Walsh ..............................7/1         15   9
   59 Don Poli (IRE) GordonElliott 10-11-3 J.W.Kennedy .............................33/1               pu
   94 Shaneshill (IRE) W.P.Mullins 10-11-3 D.E.Mullins ..............................16/1               pu
      Philip J. Reynolds 11ran 6m22.80
```

122 Goffs Thyestes Handicap Chase (Gr A) (5yo+) £51,754   3m1f (17)

```
      INVITATION ONLY (IRE) W.P.Mullins 8-11-6¹⁵² R.Walsh .....................4/1f            1
   29 ALPHA DES OBEAUX (FR) GordonElliott 9-11-9¹⁵⁵ (b+t) MrR.James(7) ........20/1           1¼   2
      UP FOR REVIEW (IRE) W.P.Mullins 10-11-0¹⁴⁶ P.Townend ....................10/1           11   3
   46 Out Sam GordonElliott 10-10-8¹⁴⁰ (t) M.P.Walsh ................................20/1         ½   4
   93 General Principle (IRE) GordonElliott 10-10-11¹⁴³ (t) J.W.Kennedy ........12/1           10   5
      Mall Dini (IRE) PatrickG.Kelly 9-11-3¹⁴⁹ (t) MrP.W.Mullins ..................11/1          hd   6
   93 Polidam (FR) W.P.Mullins 10-10-12¹⁴⁴ (h) KatieO'Farrell(5) ..................28/1          hd   7
   46 Mr Diablo (IRE) J.P.Dempsey 10-10-5¹³⁷ (t) L.P.Dempsey ...................8/1             ½   8
   93 Borice (FR) GordonElliott 8-10-5¹³⁷ (t) DenisO'Regan .........................10/1           9   9
      Bellow Mome (FR) W.P.Mullins 8-10-5¹³⁷ B.Hayes ............................33/1           11  10
      Pleasant Company (IRE) W.P.Mullins 11-11-8¹⁵⁴ (h) D.J.Mullins .........25/1             3½  11
   4  Valseur Lido (FR) HenrydeBromhead 10-11-1¹⁴⁷ (s) RachaelBlackmore ......25/1             2  12
   93 Pairofbrowneyes (IRE) W.P.Mullins 10-11-1¹⁴⁷ BarryGeraghty ...............16/1           5½  13
      Monbeg Notorious (IRE) GordonElliott 8-11-6¹⁵² (v) DavyRussell ..........8/1            45  14
   39 Some Neck (FR) W.P.Mullins 8-10-13¹⁴⁵ MrR.Deegan(5) .....................15/2            F
   93 Dounikos (FR) GordonElliott 8-11-2¹⁴⁸ SeanFlanagan .........................12/1          F
      Isleofhopendreams W.P.Mullins 12-10-12¹⁴⁴ D.E.Mullins .....................18/1           pu
   65 Sumos Novios (IRE) W.J.Burke 11-11-3¹⁴⁹ RobbiePower .....................22/1          pu
      Andrea Wylie/Graham Wylie 18ran 6m28.50
```

CHELTENHAM Saturday, Jan 26 GOOD to SOFT

123 JCB Triumph Trial Juvenile Hurdle (Finesse) (Gr 2) (1) (4yo) £18,006   2m179y (8)

```
      FAKIR D'OUDAIRIES (FR) JosephPatrickO'Brien,Ireland 4-11-0 J.J.Slevin .....4/1           1
      FINE BRUNELLO (FR) JosephPatrickO'Brien,Ireland 4-11-0 BarryGeraghty ..25/1            13   2
   87 ADJALI (GER) NickyHenderson 4-11-5 DarylJacob ............................5/4f          3½   3
      Our Power (IRE) AlanKing 4-11-0 TomCannon ...................................7/1          1¾   4
      Protektorat (FR) DanSkelton 4-11-0 HarrySkelton ...............................12/1          4   5
      Nelson River TonyCarroll 4-11-3 HarryBannister ................................13/2         19   6
      Pagero (FR) JonjoO'Neill 4-11-0 RichieMcLernon .............................33/1           8   7
      Fukuto (FR) DavidBridgwater 4-11-0 TomScudamore ........................100/1           3¼   8
      Dogon PaulNicholls 4-11-0 BryonyFrost ...........................................12/1          pu
      M L Bloodstock 9ran 4m06.30
```

**124 Spectra Cyber Security Solutions Trophy Handicap Chase (Gr 3) (1)   2½m127y (17)
      (5yo+) £42,202**

```
      SIRUH DU LAC (FR) NickWilliams 6-10-9¹³⁴ LizzieKelly(3) .....................6/1           1
      JANIKA (FR) NickyHenderson 6-11-11¹⁵⁰ DarylJacob ..........................5/2f          hd   2
  102 BALLYHILL (FR) NigelTwiston-Davies 8-11-5¹⁴⁴ JordanNailor(7) ...........7/1            9   3
      The Kings Writ (IRE) KayleyWoollacott 8-10-6¹³¹ JamesBest ...............10/1           7   4
      Brelan d'As (FR) PaulNicholls 8-10-11¹³⁶ (h+t) BarryGeraghty ..............9/1          2½   5
      Activial (FR) TomGeorge 9-11-12¹⁵¹ TomScudamore .......................8/1            ¾   6
   61 Forest des Aigles (FR) LucindaRussell 8-10-8¹³³ (t) DerekFox ..............14/1         3¾   7
   69 War Sound PhilipHobbs 10-11-6¹⁴⁵ RichardJohnson ..........................8/1            2   8
      Oldgrangewood DanSkelton 8-11-6¹⁴⁵ (t) HarrySkelton ......................20/1          7   9
      Sizing Platinum (IRE) ColinTizzard 11-11-10¹⁴⁹ (t) RobbiePower ...........40/1         46  10
      Casse Tete (FR) GaryMoore 7-10-9¹³⁴ JoshuaMoore ..........................16/1           pu
      John White & Anne Underhill 11ran 5m17.10
```

125 BetBright Trial Cotswold Chase (Gr 2) (1) (5yo+) £56,270 3m1f56y (21)

69	FRODON (FR) *PaulNicholls* 7-11-6 (t) BryonyFrost 9/4		1
88	ELEGANT ESCAPE (IRE) *ColinTizzard* 7-11-4 TomO'Brien 2/1f	¾	2
	TERREFORT (FR) *NickyHenderson* 6-11-3 DarylJacob 4/1	2¼	3
86	Allysson Monterg (FR) *RichardHobson* 9-11-0 (s+t) JonathanBurke 40/1	15	4
	Minella Rocco (IRE) *JonjoO'Neill* 8-11-0 (t) RichieMcLernon 11/1	26	5
78	Valtor (FR) *NickyHenderson* 10-11-4 JamesBowen 6/1		pu

Mr P. J. Vogt 6ran 6m35.60

126 Ballymore Classic Novices' Hurdle (Gr 2) (1) (4yo+) £18,006 2½m56y (10)

	BIRCHDALE (IRE) *NickyHenderson* 5-11-5 BarryGeraghty 2/1		1
	BUSTER VALENTINE (IRE) *RuthJefferson* 6-11-5 LeightonAspell 16/1	18	2
	JARVEYS PLATE (IRE) *FergalO'Brien* 6-11-10 PaddyBrennan 5/2	½	3
	The Wolf (FR) *WarrenGreatrex* 5-11-5 DarylJacob 40/1	10	4
99	Brewin'upastorm (IRE) *OllyMurphy* 6-11-5 RichardJohnson 6/4f		F

Mr John P. McManus 5ran 5m04.80

127 galliardhomes.com Cleeve Hurdle (Gr 2) (1) (5yo+) £33,762 2m7f213y (12)

77	PAISLEY PARK (IRE) *EmmaLavelle* 7-11-6 AidanColeman 10/3f		1
77	WEST APPROACH *ColinTizzard* 9-11-0 TomScudamore 20/1	12	2
101	BLACK OP (IRE) *TomGeorge* 8-11-3 (t) NoelFehily 11/2	2	3
77	Sam Spinner *JeddO'Keeffe* 7-11-6 (t) JoeColliver 11/1	10	4
76	Lil Rockerfeller (USA) *NeilKing* 8-11-6 (s) BryonyFrost 20/1	2¾	5
70	Aye Aye Charlie *FergalO'Brien* 7-11-0 (t) PaddyBrennan 40/1	1¾	6
	Aux Ptits Soins (FR) *DanSkelton* 9-11-0 HarrySkelton 9/2	2¼	7
77	Unowhatimeanharry *HarryFry* 11-11-6 (s+t) BarryGeraghty 11/1	ns	8
103	Wholestone (IRE) *NigelTwiston-Davies* 8-11-6 DarylJacob 8/1	8	9
77	The Mighty Don (IRE) *NickGifford* 7-11-0 (s) LeightonAspell 16/1	14	10
103	Midnight Shadow *SueSmith* 6-11-6 DannyCook 17/2	ds	11
77	Agrapart (FR) *NickWilliams* 8-11-6 LizzieKelly 25/1		pu

Mr Andrew Gemmell 12ran 5m58.80

DONCASTER Saturday, Jan 26 GOOD

128 Napoleons Casino & Restaurant Owlerton Sheffield Lightning Novices' 2m78y (12)
Chase (Gr 2) (1) (5yo+) £19,932

89	DYNAMITE DOLLARS (FR) *PaulNicholls* 6-11-5 HarryCobden 1/4f		1
	BALLYWOOD (FR) *AlanKing* 5-10-11 WayneHutchinson 4/1	3½	2
	RAVENHILL ROAD (IRE) *BrianEllison* 8-11-0 (s) BrianHughes 14/1	19	3
	Shady Oaks (IRE) *CharlesPogson* 6-11-0 CharlieHammond 66/1	36	4

Mr Michael Geoghegan 4ran 3m58.60

129 Albert Bartlett River Don Novices' Hurdle (Gr 2) (1) £17,085 3m84y (11)

	NADAITAK *BenPauling* 5-10-12 (s) NicodeBoinville 12/1		1
	TRUCKERS LODGE (IRE) *PaulNicholls* 7-10-12 (s) HarryCobden 6/4jf	22	2
	COMMODORE BARRY (IRE) *KimBailey* 6-10-12 (t) DavidBass 6/4jf	2¼	3
	Bailarico (IRE) *WarrenGreatrex* 6-10-12 (s) GavinSheehan 7/2	sh	4

The Megsons 4ran 5m54.10

130 OLBG.com Yorkshire Rose Mares' Hurdle (Gr 2) (1) (4yo+) £28,475 2m128y (8)

100	LADY BUTTONS *PhilipKirby* 9-11-4 ThomasDowson ....evsf		1
	INDEFATIGABLE (IRE) *PaulWebber* 6-11-0 GavinSheehan 11/2	nk	2
37	IRISH ROE (IRE) *PeterAtkinson* 8-11-0 HenryBrooke 3/1	3	3
	Chica Buena (IRE) *KeithDalgleish* 4-10-5 BrianHughes 9/2	15	4
	Indian Opera *IainJardine* 7-11-0 RossChapman 40/1	11	5
	Cold Fusion (IRE) *DaiWilliams* 6-11-0 ShaneQuinlan 250/1	44	6

Mrs Jayne Sivills 6ran 3m56.90

131 Sky Bet Handicap Chase (L) (1) (5yo+) £56,950 2m7f214y (18)

15	GO CONQUER (IRE) *NigelTwiston-Davies* 10-11-10[151] (t) TomBellamy 8/1		1
	MONBEG RIVER (IRE) *MartinTodhunter* 10-10-6[133] SeanQuinlan 25/1	6	2
	CALIPTO (IRE) *VenetiaWilliams* 9-11-2[143] CharlieDeutsch 10/1	5	3
33	Willie Boy (IRE) *CharlieLongsdon* 8-11-4[145] (t) GavinSheehan 8/1	1¾	4
66	Art Mauresque (FR) *PaulNicholls* 9-11-11[152] HarryCobden 10/1	2	5
51	Dingo Dollar (IRE) *AlanKing* 7-11-7[148] (s) WayneHutchinson 3/1f	9	6
59	Federici *DonaldMcCain* 10-10-3[130] (b) BrianHughes 12/1	12	7
3	Brian Boranha (IRE) *PeterNiven* 8-10-12[139] HenryBrooke 16/1	1¼	8
	O O Seven (IRE) *NickyHenderson* 9-11-11[152] NicodeBoinville 19	19	9
105	On Tour (IRE) *EvanWilliams* 11-10-6[133] MitchellBastyan(5) 14/1		pu
61	Warriors Tale *PaulNicholls* 10-11-12[153] (t) SeanBowen 14/1		pu

Paul & Clare Rooney 11ran 5m54.80

975

NAAS Sunday, Jan 27   GOOD to SOFT

132 Limestone Lad Hurdle (Gr 3) (5yo+) £17,380   2m (8)

25	ESPOIR D'ALLEN (FR) *GavinPatrickCromwell* 5-11-8 BarryGeraghty	4/9f	1
56	WICKLOW BRAVE *W.P.Mullins* 10-11-1 R.Walsh	9/2	2½ 2
97	TOMBSTONE (IRE) *GordonElliott* 9-11-1 (t) J.W.Kennedy	6/1	3¼ 3
	Forge Meadow (IRE) *MrsJ.Harrington* 7-11-1 RobbiePower	9/1	1¼ 4
	Jarob *GearoidO'Loughlin* 12-11-1 M.A.Enright	66/1	nk 5

Mr John P. McManus 5ran 3m52.30

LEOPARDSTOWN Saturday, Feb 2   GOOD

133 Nathaniel Lacy & Partners Solicitors '€50,000 Cheltenham Bonus For   2¾m (10)
Stable Staff' Novices' Hurdle (Gr 1) (5yo+) £64,692

The final flight was omitted on both circuits due to the low trajectory of the sun

54	COMMANDER OF FLEET (IRE) *GordonElliott* 5-11-8 J.W.Kennedy	13/2	1
74	RHINESTONE (IRE) *JosephPatrickO'Brien* 6-11-10 (t) M.P.Walsh	10/1	½ 2
	GALLANT JOHN JOE (IRE) *OliverMcKiernan* 6-11-10 B.Browne	33/1	6 3
106	First Approach (IRE) *NoelMeade* 6-11-10 (s) SeanFlanagan	50/1	hd 4
	Relegate (IRE) *W.P.Mullins* 6-11-3 R.Walsh	4/1f	hd 5
74	Choungaya (IRE) *JosephPatrickO'Brien* 6-11-10 (t) J.J.Slevin	33/1	11 6
106	Getareason (IRE) *W.P.Mullins* 6-11-10 (h) B.Hayes	16/1	½ 7
98	Dorrells Pierji (FR) *W.P.Mullins* 6-11-10 DenisO'Regan	20/1	2½ 8
	The Big Dog (IRE) *PeterFahey* 6-11-10 D.J.Mullins	13/2	14 9
	Dunvegan (FR) *P.A.Fahy* 6-11-10 A.E.Lynch	7/1	18 10
98	Defi Bleu (FR) *GordonElliott* 6-11-10 DavyRussell	7/1	¾ 11
106	Magnium (IRE) *MrsJ.Harrington* 6-11-10 RobbiePower	12/1	18 12
	Embrun Mitja (FR) *HenrydeBromhead* 6-11-3 RachaelBlackmore	33/1	4¼ 13
	Salsaretta (FR) *W.P.Mullins* 6-11-3 MrP.W.Mullins	9/1	ur
	Malinas Jack *HenrydeBromhead* 5-11-8 B.J.Cooper	40/1	pu
106	Come To Me (FR) *W.P.Mullins* 7-11-10 (h) P.Townend	11/1	pu

Gigginstown House Stud 16ran 5m19.40

134 BHP Insurance Irish Champion Hurdle (Gr 1) (4yo+) £87,500   2m (6)

The final flight was omitted on both circuits due to the low trajectory of the sun

94	APPLE'S JADE (FR) *GordonElliott* 7-11-3 (t) J.W.Kennedy	8/11f	1
97	SUPASUNDAE *MrsJ.Harrington* 9-11-10 RobbiePower	4/1	16 2
97	PETIT MOUCHOIR (FR) *HenrydeBromhead* 8-11-10 RachaelBlackmore	12/1	5 3
97	Melon *W.P.Mullins* 7-11-10 R.Walsh	4/1	¾ 4
56	Farclas (FR) *GordonElliott* 5-11-9 (s+t) SeanFlanagan	25/1	3½ 5
132	Tombstone (IRE) *GordonElliott* 9-11-10 (t) DavyRussell	66/1	64 6

Gigginstown House Stud 6ran 3m43.20

135 Ladbrokes Hurdle (Extended Handicap) (Gr B) (150) (4yo+) £64,692   2m (6)

The final flight was omitted on both circuits due to the low trajectory of the sun

57	OFF YOU GO (IRE) *CharlesByrnes* 5-11-5¹⁴³ M.P.Walsh	8/1	1
94	JEZKI (IRE) *MrsJ.Harrington* 11-11-7¹⁴⁵ (s) D.J.O'Keeffe(7)	16/1	1 2
57	IVANOVICH GORBATOV (IRE) *JosephPatrickO'Brien* 7-10-10¹³⁴ (b+t)	16/1	½ 3
	J.J.Slevin		
	Eclair de Beaufeu (FR) *GordonElliott* 5-10-5¹²⁹ J.W.Kennedy	7/1	1½ 4
6	Uradel (GER) *W.P.Mullins* 8-10-8¹³² R.Walsh	9/2f	1½ 5
	Try Again (IRE) *PaulW.Flynn* 6-9-10¹²⁰ M.A.Enright	10/1	1¾ 6
92	Due Reward (IRE) *HenrydeBromhead* 6-10-8¹³² RachaelBlackmore	20/1	½ 7
57	Tudor City (IRE) *A.J.Martin* 7-10-9¹³³ (t) DenisO'Regan	12/1	½ 8
	Free Ranger (IRE) *NoelMeade* 5-9-10¹²⁰ (b+t) JonathanMoore	33/1	nk 9
	Hearts Are Trumps (IRE) *DesmondMcDonogh* 6-11-0¹³⁸ L.P.Dempsey	14/1	½ 10
4	Tully East (IRE) *AlanFleming* 9-10-12¹³⁶ DonaghMeyler	33/1	¾ 11
5	Cartwright *GordonElliott* 6-10-11¹³⁵ (b) B.J.Cooper	20/1	½ 12
109	Blazer (FR) *W.P.Mullins* 8-11-5¹⁴³ J.S.McGarvey	25/1	2½ 13
	Campeador (FR) *GordonElliott* 7-11-10¹⁴⁸ (h) KeithDonoghue	25/1	hd 14
111	Jetez (IRE) *MrsJ.Harrington* 6-10-12¹³⁶ RobbiePower	13/2	6½ 15
	Mitchouka (FR) *GordonElliott* 5-10-12¹³⁶ K.Brogan(7)	40/1	2 16
57	Wonder Laish *CharlesByrnes* 7-11-6¹⁴⁴ DavyRussell	7/1	2¾ 17
	Sayar (IRE) *W.P.Mullins* 6-10-12¹³⁶ P.Townend	16/1	nk 18
	Twobeelucky *HenrydeBromhead* 6-10-12¹³⁶ A.E.Lynch	50/1	2¼ 19

Mr John P. McManus 19ran 3m48.20

136 Matheson (C & G) I.N.H. Flat (Gr 2) (4, 5, 6 and 7yo) £45,285   2m

	ENVOI ALLEN (FR) *GordonElliott* 5-11-13 MrJ.J.Codd	4/6f	1
	METICULOUS (IRE) *JosephPatrickO'Brien* 5-11-10 (t) MrB.O'Neill	20/1	1¼ 2
	EMBITTERED (IRE) *JosephPatrickO'Brien* 5-11-10 (h+t) MrT.Hamilton	10/1	1¾ 3

Beacon Edge (IRE) *NoelMeade* 5-11-10 MrM.J.O'Hare ....25/1 nk 4
Mt Leinster (IRE) *W.P.Mullins* 5-11-10 (h) MrP.W.Mullins 8/1 4¼ 5
Run Wild Fred (IRE) *GordonElliott* 5-11-10 MrD.G.Lavery 16/1 9½ 6
Ash Hill (IRE) *JosephPatrickO'Brien* 5-11-10 (h) MrD.O'Connor 20/1 2¾ 7
Neptune (IRE) *D.K.Weld* 5-11-10 (b) MrFinianMaguire 8/1 7½ 8
Ebadali (IRE) *DenisHogan* 4-10-7 MrH.C.Swan 100/1 31 9
Abacadabras (FR) *GordonElliott* 5-11-10 MsLisaO'Neill ....10/1 ro
Cheveley Park Stud 10ran 3m44.90

137 Ladbrokes Dublin Chase (Gr 1) (5yo+) £72,367   2m1f (9)
The final fence in the home straight was omitted due to the low trajectory of the sun
67 MIN (FR) *W.P.Mullins* 8-11-10 R.Walsh 4/9f 1
91 ORDINARY WORLD (IRE) *HenrydeBromhead* 9-11-10 RachaelBlackmore 12/1 6 2
64 SAINT CALVADOS (FR) *HarryWhittington,GB* 6-11-10 G.Sheehan 4/1 6 3
91 Castlegrace Paddy (IRE) *P.A.Fahy* 8-11-10 A.E.Lynch ....9/1 F
90 Special Tiara *HenrydeBromhead* 12-11-10 RobbiePower ....14/1 pu
Mrs S. Ricci 5ran 3m58.70

138 Frank Ward Solicitors Arkle Novices' Chase (Gr 1) (5yo+) £67,982   2m1f (9)
The penultimate fence in the home straight was omitted due to the low trajectory of the sun
84 LE RICHEBOURG (FR) *JosephPatrickO'Brien* 6-11-10 M.P.Walsh 11/10f 1
84 US AND THEM (IRE) *JosephPatrickO'Brien* 6-11-10 (t) J.J.Slevin 11/1 7 2
84 MENGLI KHAN (IRE) *GordonElliott* 6-11-10 (t) J.W.Kennedy 5/1 13 3
109 Duca de Thaix (FR) *GordonElliott* 6-11-10 (s+t) DavyRussell 8/1 1½ 4
Knocknanuss (IRE) *GaryMoore,GB* 9-11-10 JamieMoore ....11/2 F
Voix du Reve (FR) *W.P.Mullins* 7-11-10 (h) P.Townend ....6/1 F
Mr John P. McManus 6ran 3m58.30

139 Goffs Handicap Chase (Gr B) (150) (5yo+) £45,285   2m1f (9)
The penultimate fence in the home straight was omitted due to the low trajectory of the sun
QUAMINO (GER) *PaulNolan* 6-11-1[132] (t) B.J.Cooper 14/1 1
DAKOTA MOIRETTE (FR) *GordonElliott* 6-10-8[125] (s) J.W.Kennedy ....11/1 ½ 2
43 DUKE OF NAVAN (IRE) *NickyRichards,GB* 11-11-10[141] RyanDay 20/1 1¼ 3
R'evelyn Pleasure (IRE) *SeanO.O'Brien* 7-10-10[127] DonaghMeyler 8/1 2¼ 4
Mind's Eye (IRE) *HenrydeBromhead* 7-11-7[138] RachaelBlackmore ....5/1 hd 5
109 Kildorrery (IRE) *T.M.Walsh* 6-11-2[133] (h) R.Walsh ....6/1 hd 6
Moon Over Germany (IRE) *HenrydeBromhead* 8-11-4[135] RobbiePower ...10/3f 1¾ 7
4 De Plotting Shed (IRE) *GordonElliott* 9-11-9[140] (b+t) KeithDonoghue 20/1 14 8
Lake Takapuna (IRE) *D.K.Weld* 8-10-11[128] (v) D.J.Mullins ....5/1 hd 9
Tycoon Prince (IRE) *GordonElliott* 9-11-10[141] (t) C.Brassil(5) 33/1 2½ 10
109 Kylecrue (IRE) *JohnPatrickRyan* 12-10-8[125] (b) LiamQuinlan(7) 25/1 4¾ 11
Tisamystery (IRE) *HenrydeBromhead* 11-10-11[128] (s) DanielHolden(7) .....14/1 sh 12
Presenting Mahler (IRE) *JohnPatrickRyan* 9-9-10[113] M.A.Enright 40/1 8½ 13
109 Three Stars (IRE) *HenrydeBromhead* 9-11-7[138] (b) J.J.Slevin 14/1 5½ 14
Manverton Limited 14ran 4m03.90

SANDOWN Saturday, Feb 2   SOFT
140 888Sport Contenders Hurdle (L) (1) (4yo+) £17,085   1m7f216y (8)
81 BUVEUR D'AIR (FR) *NickyHenderson* 8-11-6 BarryGeraghty 1/5f 1
71 VISION DES FLOS (FR) *ColinTizzard* 6-11-2 (t) HarryCobden 4/1 2 2
ROKSANA (IRE) *DanSkelton* 7-10-10 HarrySkelton 10/1 9 3
42 Rayvin Black *OliverSherwood* 10-11-0 (s) ThomasGarner 20/1 53 4
De Dollar Man (IRE) *EvanWilliams* 8-11-0 LeightonAspell ....40/1 pu
Mr John P. McManus 5ran 4m08.20

141 888Sport Scilly Isles Novices' Chase (Gr 1) (1) (5yo+) £31,322   2½m10y (17)
101 DEFI DU SEUIL (FR) *PhilipHobbs* 6-11-4 BarryGeraghty 7/2 1
101 LOSTINTRANSLATION (IRE) *ColinTizzard* 7-11-4 RichardJohnson ....2/1 ¾ 2
76 VINNDICATION (IRE) *KimBailey* 6-11-4 DavidBass 11/8f 2½ 3
Mulcahys Hill (IRE) *WarrenGreatrex* 7-11-4 (s) WayneHutchinson 14/1 24 4
Dell Oro (FR) *GaryMoore* 6-11-4 JoshuaMoore ....16/1 pu
Mr John P. McManus 5ran 5m12.00

142 888Sport Heroes Handicap Hurdle (Gr 3) (1) (4yo+) £56,270   2m7f98y (12)
79 LORD NAPIER (IRE) *PeterBowen* 6-10-8[134] (t) SeanBowen 8/1 1
COOLE CODY (IRE) *MichaelBlake* 8-10-11[137] (t) NickScholfield 33/1 9 2
FLEMCARA (IRE) *EmmaLavelle* 7-10-6[132] (t) AidanColeman 16/1 1¼ 3
88 Folsom Blue (IRE) *GordonElliott,Ireland* 12-10-4[130] (b+t) RichardJohnson 7/1 1¼ 4
Casko d'Airy (FR) *PaulNicholls* 7-10-1[127] (t) HarryCobden ....4/1jf nk 5
79 Man of Plenty *SophieLeech* 10-10-5[131] (s+t) ConnorBrace(7) ....40/1 ½ 6

977

```
 50  Ballymoy (IRE) NigelTwiston-Davies 6-11-12¹⁵² DarylJacob ............................. 4/1jf     ¾    7
     Eminent Poet VenetiaWilliams 8-11-3¹⁴³ CharlieDeutsch .................................16/1        7    8
     The Hollow Ginge (IRE) NigelTwiston-Davies 6-10-6¹³² JamieBargary .............20/1        9    9
     Padleyourowncanoe ColinTizzard 5-11-2¹⁴² HarryKimber(10) ........................16/1      5   10
     Virginia Chick (FR) EvanWilliams 7-10-5¹³¹ MissIsabelWilliams(7) ..................14/1      ns  11
 19  Keeper Hill (IRE) WarrenGreatrex 8-11-4¹⁴⁴ HarryTeal(5) ...............................16/1     1   12
     Lungarno Palace (USA) FergalO'Brien 8-10-1¹²⁷ (s+t) AlainCawley ..............25/1    11   13
     Mr Clarkson (IRE) DavidPipe 7-10-2¹²⁸ (s) DavidNoonan .............................33/1      pu
 79  Mr Antolini (IRE) NigelTwiston-Davies 9-11-0¹⁴⁰ SamTwiston-Davies ...............10/1      pu
     Brio Conti (FR) PaulNicholls 8-11-3¹⁴³ BryonyFrost ...................................16/1      pu
     Mr F. Lloyd 16ran 6m08.10
```

LEOPARDSTOWN Sunday, Feb 3   GOOD

143 Irish Stallion Farms European Breeders Fund Paddy Mullins Mares Handicap   2¼m (9)
Hurdle (Gr B) (4yo+) £45,285
```
     SASSY DIVA (IRE) ShaneCrawley 8-10-7¹¹⁶ (t) DonaghMeyler .....................10/3f           1
 57  CUT THE MUSTARD (FR) W.P.Mullins 7-11-5¹²⁸ (h) R.Walsh ......................5/1      2    2
     AGUSTA GOLD (IRE) MsMargaretMullins 6-10-9¹¹⁸ D.E.Mullins ...................7/1      ½    3
     Alletrix (IRE) MrsJ.Harrington 6-11-7¹³⁰ (h) RobbiePower .............................11/1      ¾    4
 83  Smiling Eliza (IRE) GordonElliott 4-9-10 (9-6)¹¹⁵ (s) M.A.Enright ..................25/1      8    5
     One First Cut (IRE) MissElizabethDoyle 7-10-5¹¹⁵ SeanFlanagan .................22/1      ½    6
     Hidden Dilemma (IRE) StuartCrawford 6-10-4¹¹⁴ J.J.Slevin ..........................11/1      ½    7
     High School Days (USA) HenrydeBromhead 6-11-10¹³³ H.Morgan(7) ...........50/1      4    8
     Countess Cathleen (IRE) DenisHickey 8-10-7¹¹⁶ JonathanMoore ...............16/1      3    9
     Court Maid (IRE) ThomasMullins 6-11-1¹²⁴ D.J.Mullins ..............................6/1     11   10
     Clementina (FR) A.J.Martin 6-10-7¹¹⁶ (t) E.O'Connell(5) ..........................12/1     3¾   11
 57  Sapphire Lady (IRE) W.P.Mullins 7-11-6¹²⁹ P.Townend .............................9/1     15  12
 57  Morga (IRE) DesmondMcDonogh 9-11-6¹²⁹ D.J.O'Keeffe(7) .......................33/1      1   13
     Cristal Icon (IRE) ThomasMullins 5-10-6¹¹⁶ (t) C.D.Maxwell .......................50/1      pu
     Shane Crawley 14ran 4m19.60
```

144 Tattersalls Ireland Spring Juvenile Hurdle (Gr 1) (4yo) £64,692   2m (8)
```
     SIR EREC (IRE) JosephPatrickO'Brien 4-11-0 M.P.Walsh ............................ 13/8f          1
     GARDENS OF BABYLON (IRE) JosephPatrickO'Brien 4-11-0 (t) BarryGeraghty .5/1      6    2
     SURIN (FR) GordonElliott 4-10-7 J.W.Kennedy ......................................7/1      ½    3
     Tiger Tap Tap (GER) W.P.Mullins 4-11-0 R.Walsh ...................................2/1     1¾   4
 83  Chief Justice GordonElliott 4-11-0 (t) DavyRussell ..................................12/1     1½   5
 83  Got Trumped MrsJ.Harrington 4-11-0 RobbiePower ...............................20/1     1¼   6
     Parisian (IRE) E.J.O'Grady 4-11-0 (s) PhilipEnright ..................................66/1     88   7
     Mr John P. McManus 7ran 3m52.00
```

145 Chanelle Pharma Novices' Hurdle (Brave Inca) (Gr 1) (5yo+) £64,692   2m (8)
```
     KLASSICAL DREAM (FR) W.P.Mullins 5-11-9 R.Walsh ............................. 9/4f           1
 92  ARAMON (GER) W.P.Mullins 6-11-10 P.Townend .................................5/2      hd   2
     VISION D'HONNEUR (FR) GordonElliott 5-11-9 J.W.Kennedy ....................3/1      6    3
     Dancing On My Own (IRE) HenrydeBromhead 5-11-9 RachaelBlackmore ........20/1     1¼   4
 92  Triplicate (IRE) JosephPatrickO'Brien 6-11-10 (t) BarryGeraghty ....................7/1      9    5
     Entoucas (FR) JosephPatrickO'Brien 5-11-9 (h+t) M.P.Walsh ..................10/1     14   6
     Valdieu (FR) NoelMeade 6-11-10 (t) SeanFlanagan ................................12/1      ½    7
     Mrs Joanne Coleman 7ran 3m49.10
```

146 William Fry Handicap Hurdle (Gr B) (150) (4yo+) £45,285   3m (12)
```
     DALLAS DES PICTONS (FR) GordonElliott 6-10-12¹³⁰ J.W.Kennedy ...........7/2jf           1
     CALIE DU MESNIL (FR) W.P.Mullins 7-10-9¹²⁷ P.Townend .....................8/1      nk   2
     JIMMY BREEKIE (IRE) StuartCrawford 6-10-7¹²⁵ (t) P.E.Corbett(3) .............12/1      2    3
     Mon Lino (FR) PaulNolan 7-10-9¹²⁷ NiallMadden ...................................50/1      ½    4
     Cuneo (FR) HenrydeBromhead 7-11-11¹³³ RachaelBlackmore .................7/2jf      ½    5
  7  Oscar Knight (IRE) ThomasMullins 10-10-12¹³⁰ M.P.Walsh ....................10/1     1¼   6
 98  Pleasure Dome W.P.Mullins 6-10-12¹³⁰ R.Walsh ................................4/1     6½   7
     Salty Boy (IRE) MsMargaretMullins 6-11-2¹³⁴ D.E.Mullins ........................8/1     1¼   8
  5  Tigris River (IRE) JosephPatrickO'Brien 8-11-7¹³⁹ (b+t) BarryGeraghty ........20/1     nk   9
     The Gatechecker (IRE) M.Hourigan 9-10-1¹¹⁹ (b) D.J.O'Keeffe(7) ..........16/1     1½  10
     Nobody Home (IRE) EdwardCawley 9-10-7¹²⁵ (h) B.Hayes .....................28/1     21  11
  8  Boot Camp (IRE) GordonElliott 6-10-9¹²⁷ (h) M.A.Enright ......................25/1     3¾  12
     Gigginstown House Stud 12ran 6m04.20
```

147 Flogas Novices' Chase (Scalp) (Gr 1) (5yo+) £64,692   2m5f(14)
```
 80  LA BAGUE AU ROI (FR) WarrenGreatrex,GB 8-11-3 RichardJohnson ..........10/11f           1
     KAISER BLACK (IRE) P.M.J.Doyle 8-11-10 (t) JackDoyle ........................33/1     1¼   2
 85  HARDLINE (IRE) GordonElliott 7-11-10 (h) J.W.Kennedy .......................7/2      4¼   3
110  Jetz (IRE) MrsJ.Harrington 7-11-10 RobbiePower ...............................14/1     3½   4
```

110 Winter Escape (IRE) *AidanAnthonyHoward* 8-11-10 M.P.Walsh ....9/2   ½ 5
96 Mortal (IRE) *JosephPatrickO'Brien* 7-11-10 (t) RachaelBlackmore 7/1   1¼ 6
    Mrs Julien Turner & Mr Andrew Merriam 6ran 5m25.80

148 Unibet Irish Gold Cup (Gr 1) (5yo+) £117,435   3m (17)
95 BELLSHILL (IRE) *W.P.Mullins* 9-11-10 R.Walsh 2/1   1
95 ROAD TO RESPECT (IRE) *NoelMeade* 8-11-10 SeanFlanagan ....5/6f   sh 2
95 THE STORYTELLER (IRE) *GordonElliott* 8-11-10 DavyRussell 8/1   7½ 3
95 Outlander (IRE) *GordonElliott* 11-11-10 (s) J.W.Kennedy 9/1   37 4
    Andrea Wylie/Graham Wylie 4ran 6m04.90

149 Abbey International Leopardstown Handicap Chase (Gr A) (5yo+) £64,692   2m5f (14)
    WHISPERINTHEBREEZE (IRE) *MrsJ.Harrington* 6-10-1[130] (s) P.D.Kennedy 7/1   1
93 LIVELOVELAUGH (IRE) *W.P.Mullins* 9-10-7[136] R.Walsh 8/1   3¾ 2
    SPEAKER CONNOLLY (IRE) *AlanFleming* 6-10-1[130] DonaghMeyler 7/1   2½ 3
55 Cadmium (FR) *W.P.Mullins* 7-11-4[147] P.Townend 5/1f   3¾ 4
109 Cubomania (IRE) *GordonElliott* 6-10-13[142] (s) J.W.Kennedy ....8/1   hd 5
    Landofhopeandglory (IRE) *JosephPatrickO'Brien* 6-10-1[130] (s+t) L.P.Dempsey .13/2   6½ 6
119 Doctor Phoenix (IRE) *GordonElliott* 11-11-7[150] (s+t) KeithDonoghue 40/1   3¼ 7
93 Vieux Morvan (FR) *JosephPatrickO'Brien* 10-10-12[141] (b) J.J.Slevin 8/1   6 8
122 Valseur Lido (FR) *HenrydeBromhead* 10-11-3[146] (s) RachaelBlackmore 25/1   4½ 9
    Last Goodbye (IRE) *MissElizabethDoyle* 8-11-3[146] (b+t) A.W.Short(3) 20/1   8 10
    Gusty Rocky (IRE) *PatrickJ.Flynn* 10-10-2[131] (t) D.E.Mullins 33/1   11 11
93 Black Scorpion (IRE) *EricMcNamara* 8-10-2[131] D.J.Mullins ....8/1   pu
109 Bel Ami de Sivola (FR) *NoelMeade* 8-10-5[134] (t) SeanFlanagan ....16/1   pu
    Ann & Alan Potts Limited 13ran 5m16.40

150 Coolmore N.H. Sires Irish European Breeders Fund Mares I.N.H. Flat (Deep Run) (Gr 2) (4, 5, 6 and 7yo) £45,285   2m
    SANTA ROSSA (IRE) *DermotAnthonyMcLoughlin* 5-11-5 MrFinianMaguire 3/1   1
    BIGBADANDBEAUTIFUL (IRE) *GordonElliott* 5-11-1 MrJ.J.Codd 8/1   3¼ 2
    JEREMYS FLAME (IRE) *GavinPatrickCromwell* 5-11-5 (h) MrM.J.O'Hare .....11/2   ½ 3
    Botani (FR) *W.P.Mullins* 5-11-1 MrD.O'Connor 12/1   1¾ 4
    Two Shoe Tom (IRE) *PeterFahey* 5-11-1 MrD.G.Lavery ....3/1   ¾ 5
    Heaven Help Us (IRE) *PaulHennessy* 5-11-5 MrN.T.Prendergast 25/1   5 6
    Rebel Og (IRE) *W.P.Mullins* 6-11-6 MrP.W.Mullins 5/2f   26 7
    Oh So Frisky (FR) *MrsLornaFowler* 6-11-2 (h+t) MrT.Hamilton 100/1   33 8
    Mrs P. J. Conway 8ran 3m46.20

    PUNCHESTOWN Sunday, Feb 10   GOOD to SOFT
151 Boylesports Grand National Trial Handicap Chase (Gr B) (5yo+) £51,754   3½m150y (20)
122 DOUNIKOS (IRE) *GordonElliott* 8-11-0[147] DavyRussell 12/1   1
    WISHMOOR (IRE) *JosephPatrickO'Brien* 9-9-11[130] AndrewRing 20/1   4¼ 2
122 GENERAL PRINCIPLE (IRE) *GordonElliott* 10-10-9[142] (t) J.W.Kennedy .....10/1   ½ 3
93 Fitzhenry (IRE) *PaulNolan* 7-10-2[135] (b) M.P.Walsh 6/1   7 4
93 Solomn Grundy (IRE) *HenrydeBromhead* 9-10-3[136] TomScudamore 11/2   4¾ 5
122 Some Neck (FR) *W.P.Mullins* 8-10-12[145] R.Walsh ....9/2f   ¾ 6
    Kilkishen (IRE) *JohnJosephHanlon* 9-9-10[129] (s) SeanBowen ....8/1   ½ 7
    Youcantcallherthat (IRE) *DenisHogan* 8-10-10[143] D.G.Hogan 25/1   11 8
    Dinnie's Vinnie (IRE) *J.P.Dempsey* 11-9-10[129] L.P.Dempsey 25/1   13 9
122 Monbeg Notorious (IRE) *GordonElliott* 8-11-5[152] (v) KeithDonoghue 20/1   27 10
93 Woods Well (IRE) *GordonElliott* 8-10-4[137] (s) DenisO'Regan 25/1   32 11
93 Arkwright (FR) *JosephPatrickO'Brien* 9-10-3[136] RachaelBlackmore ....20/1   ur
    Agent Boru (IRE) *T.Gibney* 8-9-10[129] JonathanMoore ....10/1   pu
93 Orion d'Aubrelle (FR) *W.P.Mullins* 6-10-1[134] (s) P.Townend ....16/1   pu
46 Space Cadet (IRE) *GordonElliott* 9-10-1[134] M.A.Enright ....20/1   pu
122 Isleofhopendreams (IRE) *W.P.Mullins* 8-10-9[142] D.J.Mullins ....12/1   pu
    Gigginstown House Stud 16ran 7m36.00

    SANDOWN Friday, Feb 15   Chase course: GOOD to SOFT, Hurdles course: SOFT
152 Agetur UK Kingmaker Novices' Chase (Gr 2) (1) (5yo+) £18,224   1m7f119y (13)
    GLEN FORSA (IRE) *MickChannon* 7-11-0 JonathanBurke 7/2   1
89 KALASHNIKOV (IRE) *AmyMurphy* 6-11-0 JackQuinlan 1/4f   19 2
141 DELL ORO (FR) *GaryMoore* 6-11-0 JoshuaMoore 14/1   45 3
    Mr T. P. Radford 3ran 4m00.60

153 Weatherbys TBA Jane Seymour Mares' Novices' Hurdle (Gr 2) (1) (4yo+) £17,085   2m3f173y (9)
    QUEENOHEARTS (IRE) *StuartEdmunds* 6-11-7 CiaranGethings 13/8f   1
    DANSE IDOL (IRE) *PaulNicholls* 6-11-2 HarryCobden 5/2   2¼ 2

PAPAGANA *OliverSherwood* 6-11-2 LeightonAspell ....8/1 ¾ 3
Duhallow Gesture (IRE) *AnthonyHoneyball* 7-11-2 AidanColeman 5/1 16 4
Liberty Bella *BrianEckley* 5-11-2 JackQuinlan 6/1 2¾ 5
Rosy World *SuzySmith* 6-11-2 MichealNolan 40/1 17 6
The Sherington Partnership 6ran 5m11.60

ASCOT Saturday, Feb 16   GOOD to SOFT

154 Sodexo Reynoldstown Novices' Chase (Gr 2) (1) (5yo+) £22,780   2m7f180y (20)
     MISTER MALARKY *ColinTizzard* 6-11-0 RobbiePower 7/2 1
     NOW MCGINTY (IRE) *StuartEdmunds* 8-11-0 (s) RichardJohnson 11/4 1½ 2
     YALLTARI *VenetiaWilliams* 8-11-0 CharlieDeutsch 11/2 3¼ 3
  72 Coup de Pinceau (FR) *PaulNicholls* 7-11-3 HarryCobden 13/2 11 4
     Top Ville Ben (IRE) *PhilipKirby* 7-11-0 (h) SeanQuinlan 11/5f 1 5
     Wendy & Malcolm Hezel 5ran 6m01.30

155 Keltbray Swinley Chase (Limited Handicap) (L) (1) (5yo+) £42,712   2m7f180y (20)
 131 CALIPTO (FR) *VenetiaWilliams* 9-10-8¹⁴³ CharlieDeutsch 15/2 1
  51 BLACK CORTON (FR) *PaulNicholls* 8-11-6¹⁵⁵ (t) BryonyFrost 9/4f 2¼ 2
     REGAL ENCORE (IRE) *AnthonyHoneyball* 11-11-3¹⁵² RichieMcLernon 14/1 7 3
  86 Crievehill (IRE) *NigelTwiston-Davies* 7-10-8¹⁴³ SamTwiston-Davies 14/1 3 4
     Smooth Stepper *AlexHales* 10-10-9¹⁴⁴ WayneHutchinson 33/1 11 5
     Reikers Island (IRE) *PhilipHobbs* 6-10-5¹⁴⁰ RichardJohnson 11/4 2 6
 131 Art Mauresque (FR) *PaulNicholls* 9-11-1¹⁵⁰ LorcanWilliams(5) ....8/1 F
  82 Coneygree *MarkBradstock* 12-11-10¹⁵⁹ (t) NicodeBoinville ....5/1 pu
     Lady Bolton 8ran 5m59.60

156 Betfair Denman Chase (Gr 2) (1) (5yo+) £28,475   2m7f180y (20)
  82 CLAN DES OBEAUX (FR) *PaulNicholls* 7-11-6 HarryCobden 2/5f 1
 125 TERREFORT (FR) *NickyHenderson* 5-11-6 NicodeBoinville 5/2 11 2
 124 BALLYHILL (FR) *NigelTwiston-Davies* 8-11-4 SamTwiston-Davies 25/1 25 3
  78 Thomas Patrick (IRE) *TomLacey* 7-11-4 RichardJohnson 14/1 3¼ 4
     Mr&Mrs P.K.Barber,G.Mason,Sir A Ferguson 4ran 5m58.60

157 Betfair Hurdle (Handicap) (Gr 3) (1) (4yo+) £47,829   1m7f152y (8)
     AL DANCER (FR) *NigelTwiston-Davies* 6-11-8¹⁴¹ (h) SamTwiston-Davies 5/2f 1
     MAGIC DANCER *KerryLee* 7-10-6¹²⁵ RichardPatrick(3) 20/1 3¾ 2
     BLU CAVALIER *AliStronge* 9-11-7¹⁴⁰ JonjoO'NeillJr.(5) 100/1 2½ 3
  99 Getaway Trump (IRE) *PaulNicholls* 6-11-9¹⁴² HarryCobden ....4/1 ½ 4
     Ar Mest (FR) *GaryMoore* 6-10-7¹²⁶ JamieMoore ....10/1 ¾ 5
  37 Equus Amadeus (IRE) *TomLacey* 6-11-4¹³⁷ StanSheppard(3) 33/1 4 6
  79 Mont des Avaloirs (FR) *PaulNicholls* 6-11-9¹⁴² LorcanWilliams(5) 7/1 3½ 7
  79 Lisp (IRE) *AlanKing* 5-11-12¹⁴⁵ WayneHutchinson ....13/2 nk 8
     Didtheyleaveuoutto (IRE) *NickGifford* 6-11-6¹³⁹ WilliamKennedy 9/1 1¾ 9
   1 William H Bonney *AlanKing* 8-11-0¹³³ TomCannon 25/1 1½ 10
     Nordic Combined (IRE) *DavidPipe* 5-11-0¹³³ (v) BryonyFrost 16/1 10 11
     Distingo (IRE) *GaryMoore* 6-11-2¹³⁵ JoshuaMoore ....50/1 hd 12
     Zanza (IRE) *PhilipHobbs* 5-11-2¹³⁵ RichardJohnson 14/1 2 13
  63 Nelson's Touch *SeamusMullins* 6-10-6¹²⁵ JeremiahMcGrath ....66/1 ¾ 14
     Walters Plant Hire Ltd 14ran 3m45.30

158 Betfair Ascot Chase (Gr 1) (1) (5yo+) £85,425   2m5f8y (17)
 113 CYRNAME (FR) *PaulNicholls* 7-11-7 (t) HarryCobden 3/1 1
  82 WAITING PATIENTLY (IRE) *RuthJefferson* 8-11-7 BrianHughes 11/8f 17 2
 114 FOX NORTON (FR) *ColinTizzard* 9-11-7 RobbiePower 6/1 1¼ 3
  82 Politologue (FR) *PaulNicholls* 8-11-7 (t) SamTwiston-Davies 4/1 2 4
  66 Charbel (IRE) *KimBailey* 8-11-7 (s) DavidBass 25/1 1¾ 5
 102 Aso (FR) *VenetiaWilliams* 9-11-7 CharlieDeutsch 12/1 7 6
     Mrs Johnny de la Hey 6ran 5m10.50

GOWRAN Saturday, Feb 16   GOOD to SOFT

159 Red Mills Chase (Gr 2) (5yo+) £32,921   2½m (14)
  95 MONALEE (IRE) *HenrydeBromhead* 8-11-10 RachaelBlackmore ....evsf 1
  65 ANIBALE FLY (FR) *A.J.Martin* 9-11-3 (t) BarryGeraghty 13/2 2 2
  95 EDWULF *JosephPatrickO'Brien* 10-11-10 (t) MrD.O'Connor 14/1 25 3
 121 Killultagh Vic (IRE) *W.P.Mullins* 10-11-3 R.Walsh ....6/4 ns 4
     Mr Barry Maloney 4ran 5m03.80

HAYDOCK Saturday, Feb 16   GOOD

160 William Hill Rendlesham Hurdle (Gr 2) (1) (4yo+) £22,780   3m58y (12)
  44 SHADES OF MIDNIGHT *SandyThomson* 9-11-2 (s+t) HenryBrooke 11/2 1
 112 PETTICOAT TAILS *WarrenGreatrex* 7-10-9 (s) GavinSheehan 8/1 8 2

KILCOOLEY (IRE) *NickyRichards* 10-11-2 RyanDay ....13/2   nk 3
103 Clyne *EvanWilliams* 9-11-2 LeightonAspell ....3/1   hd 4
 88 Donna's Diamond (IRE) *ChrisGrant* 10-11-8 CallumBewley 33/1   37 5
142 Man of Plenty *SophieLeech* 10-11-6 (s+t) PaddyBrennan ....50/1   nk 6
     Yanworth *AlanKing* 9-11-2 AidanColeman ....11/8f   pu
The Potassium Partnership 7ran 6m04.40

161 William Hill Grand National Trial Handicap Chase (Gr 3) (1) (5yo+)   3½m97y (22)
£56,950
118 ROBINSFIRTH (IRE) *ColinTizzard* 10-11-4[148] (t) SeanBowen 8/1   1
 88 RAMSES DE TEILLEE (FR) *DavidPipe* 7-11-5[149] (t) DavidNoonan ....8/1   ¾ 2
     CHEF D'OEUVRE (FR) *SamEngland* 8-10-0 (9-11)[130] JonathanEngland 12/1 1¼ 3
 32 Royal Vacation (IRE) *ColinTizzard* 9-11-8[152] (b) PaddyBrennan 10/1 28 4
 88 Yala Enki (FR) *VenetiaWilliams* 9-11-12[156] HughNugent(7) 6/1f 16 5
105 Bishops Road (IRE) *KerryLee* 11-10-7[137] (b) MitchellBastyan(5) ....33/1   ¾ 6
118 Ballyarthur (IRE) *NigelTwiston-Davies* 9-10-10[140] (t) JamieBargary ....28/1   F
     The Two Amigos *NickyMartin* 7-10-12[142] MattGriffiths ....7/1   F
     Pobbles Bay (IRE) *EvanWilliams* 9-10-2[132] LeightonAspell ....10/1   ur
     Ah Littleluck (IRE) *T.Gibney,Ireland* 9-10-5[135] (t) D.J.Mullins ....20/1   ur
118 Red Infantry (IRE) *IanWilliams* 9-10-12[142] (p) TomO'Brien ....14/1   ur
108 Carole's Destrier *NeilMulholland* 11-10-8[138] (s) AidanColeman ....20/1   pu
 88 Vieux Lion Rouge (FR) *DavidPipe* 10-11-2[146] (s+t) TomScudamore ....9/1   pu
118 Wakanda (IRE) *SueSmith* 10-11-6[150] DannyCook ....12/1   pu
 88 Ballyoptic (IRE) *NigelTwiston-Davies* 9-11-11[155] (t) TomBellamy ....12/1   pu
Christine Knowles & Wendy Carter 15ran 7m29.80

162 Albert Bartlett Prestige Novices' Hurdle (Gr 2) (1) (5yo+) £16,938   3m58y (12)
 70 LISNAGAR OSCAR (IRE) *RebeccaCurtis* 6-10-12 SeanBowen 6/1   1
     ASK BEN (IRE) *GraemeMcPherson* 6-11-1 KielanWoods 10/1 10 2
107 STONEY MOUNTAIN (IRE) *HenryDaly* 6-10-12 AndrewTinkler 6/1   4 3
     Star of Lanka (IRE) *WarrenGreatrex* 5-10-12 GavinSheehan 16/1 1¼ 4
     Highland Hunter (IRE) *LucindaRussell* 6-10-12 DerekFox 14/1 3¼ 5
107 Rockpoint *ColinTizzard* 6-11-3 DavidNoonan ....22/1   nk 6
 99 Kateson *TomLacey* 6-10-12 TomScudamore 5/4f   3 7
     Admiral Barratry (FR) *LucyWadham* 6-10-12 AidanColeman ....33/1   ns 8
 58 Truckin Away (IRE) *PhilipHobbs* 6-10-12 TomO'Brien 11/1 18 9
Racing for Fun 9ran 6m06.50

WINCANTON Saturday, Feb 16   GOOD
163 Betway Kingwell Hurdle (Gr 2) (1) (4yo+) £34,170   1m7f65y (8)
104 GRAND SANCY (FR) *PaulNicholls* 5-11-4 (h) HarrySkelton 4/1   1
 64 SCEAU ROYAL (FR) *AlanKing* 7-11-2 DarylJacob ....11/10f   ¾ 2
140 VISION DES FLOS (FR) *ColinTizzard* 6-11-4 (t) JamesBowen ....11/4   ½ 3
     Unison (IRE) *JeremyScott* 9-11-2 RexDingle 9/1 3½ 4
 79 Jolly's Cracked It (FR) *HarryFry* 10-11-2 JonathanBurke 12/1 10 5
Martin Broughton Racing Partners 5ran 3m37.00

NAVAN Sunday, Feb 17   GOOD to SOFT
164 Ladbrokes Ireland Boyne Hurdle (Gr 2) (5yo+) £23,289   2m5f (12)
     TIGER ROLL (IRE) *GordonElliott* 9-11-3 (b+t) KeithDonoghue 25/1   1
135 OFF YOU GO (IRE) *CharlesByrnes* 6-11-3 M.P.Walsh 7/4   4 2
 94 CRACKING SMART (FR) *GordonElliott* 7-11-3 (s+t) J.W.Kennedy 11/2 2¼ 3
     Bachasson (FR) *W.P.Mullins* 8-11-3 R.Walsh 5/4f 2½ 4
121 Coquin Mans (FR) *W.P.Mullins* 7-11-8 (h) P.Townend 8/1 9½ 5
     Bless The Wings (IRE) *GordonElliott* 14-11-3 (s) DenisO'Regan 66/1   9 6
Gigginstown House Stud 6ran 5m26.20

165 Ladbrokes Acca Boosty Ten Up Novices' Chase (Gr 2) (5yo+) £23,289   3m (17)
     CHRIS'S DREAM (IRE) *HenrydeBromhead* 7-11-3 RachaelBlackmore 5/2   1
     CHAMPAGNE CLASSIC (IRE) *GordonElliott* 8-11-3 J.W.Kennedy ....5/4f   ½ 2
 93 ANY SECOND NOW (IRE) *T.M.Walsh* 7-11-3 (b) M.P.Walsh 7/2 3½ 3
 96 Moonshine Bay (IRE) *MrsJ.Harrington* 6-11-3 RobbiePower 14/1   2 4
151 Agent Boru (IRE) *T.Gibney* 8-11-3 D.J.Mullins 50/1 44 5
 96 Blow By Blow (IRE) *GordonElliott* 8-11-3 (b+t) KeithDonoghue 8/1 35 6
Robcour 6ran 6m16.60

KEMPTON Saturday, Feb 23   Chase course: GOOD, Hurdles course: GOOD to FIRM
166 888Sport Pendil Novices' Chase (Gr 2) (1) (5yo+) £18,224   2½m110y (16)
 80 BAGS GROOVE (IRE) *HarryFry* 8-11-5 (t) NoelFehily 7/4   1
115 CASTAFIORE (USA) *CharlieLongsdon* 6-10-12 (s) PaulO'Brien 10/1 1½ 2

GOOD MAN PAT (IRE) *AlanKing* 6-11-0 WayneHutchinson 5/1   3¾   3
21   Secret Investor *PaulNicholls* 7-11-0 (t) HarryCobden 11/10f   1¾   4
Mr Michael Pescod 4ran 5m02.20

167   **888Sport Take 'Em On Adonis Juvenile Hurdle (Gr 2) (1) (4yo)** £17,085   2m (8)
   FUSIL RAFFLES (FR) *NickyHenderson* 4-10-12 DarylJacob 4/1f   1
   BEAT THE JUDGE (FR) *GaryMoore* 4-11-1 JoshuaMoore 10/1   9   2
   PRAECEPS (IRE) *AlanKing* 4-10-12 WayneHutchinson 14/1   2½   3
   Red Force One *PaulNicholls* 4-10-12 NoelFehily 7/1   2   4
   Petit Palais *TomGeorge* 4-10-12 JonathanBurke 9/2   4½   5
   Ecco *PaulNicholls* 4-10-12 HarryCobden 7/1   1¾   6
123   Protektorat (FR) *DanSkelton* 4-10-12 HarrySkelton 9/1   8   7
   Rose Sea Has (FR) *DrRichardNewland* 4-10-12 SamTwiston-Davies 14/1   1   8
   Deadline Diva *PaulNicholls* 4-10-5 (t) PaddyBrennan 25/1   2¼   9
   Giving Glances *AlanKing* 4-10-10 TomCannon 8/1   21   10
123   Pagero (FR) *JonjoO'Neill* 4-10-12 BarryGeraghty 22/1   3   11
31   Needs To Be Seen (FR) *JohnRyan* 4-10-12 JackQuinlan ....40/1   pu
Mr Simon Munir & Mr Isaac Souede 12ran 3m42.80

168   **Sky Bet Dovecote Novices' Hurdle (Gr 2) (1) (4yo+)** £17,085   2m (8)
104   SOUTHFIELD STONE *PaulNicholls* 6-11-2 HarryCobden 6/1   1
75   ANGELS BREATH (IRE) *NickyHenderson* 5-11-7 NicodeBoinville ....8/11f   ¾   2
   NORMAL NORMAN *JohnRyan* 5-11-2 PaddyBrennan 40/1   18   3
   Brecon Hill (IRE) *SarahHumphrey* 6-11-2 (t) DarylJacob 25/1   8   4
   Scarlet Dragon *AlanKing* 6-11-2 WayneHutchinson ....7/2   nk   5
   I K Brunel *OllyMurphy* 5-11-2 BarryGeraghty 20/1   28   6
   Tokay Dokey (IRE) *DanSkelton* 5-11-2 HarrySkelton ....14/1   F
Mrs Angela Hart & Mrs Angela Yeoman 7ran 3m41.50

169   **888Sport Handicap Chase (Gr 3) (1) (5yo+)** £56,950   3m (18)
   WALT (IRE) *NeilMulholland* 8-10-6[134] (v+t) SamTwiston-Davies 14/1   1
82   DOUBLE SHUFFLE (IRE) *TomGeorge* 9-11-12[154] (h) JonathanBurke 11/1   1   2
15   ADRIEN DU PONT (FR) *PaulNicholls* 7-11-9[151] (t) HarryCobden 11/2   4   3
69   Romain de Senam (FR) *PaulNicholls* 7-10-9[137] (h+t) HarrySkelton ....8/1   ½   4
47   Talkischeap (IRE) *AlanKing* 7-11-3[145] WayneHutchinson 4/1jf   3¾   5
   Glen Rocco *NickGifford* 8-10-9[137] LeightonAspell 4/1jf   1   6
43   Modus *PaulNicholls* 9-11-6[148] BarryGeraghty 12/1   8   7
   Didero Vallis (FR) *VenetiaWilliams* 6-10-8[136] CharlieDeutsch 16/1   2½   8
69   Rather Be (IRE) *NickyHenderson* 8-11-6[148] JeremiahMcGrath 13/2   1½   9
69   Catamaran du Seuil (FR) *DrRichardNewland* 7-10-13[141] (b) CharlieHammond(5) ...20/1   12   10
Mr Phil Simmonds 10ran 5m58.70

FONTWELL Sunday, Feb 24   GOOD to SOFT
170   **Netbet Casino National Spirit Hurdle (Gr 2) (1) (4yo+)** £45,560   2m3f49y (10)
163   VISION DES FLOS (FR) *ColinTizzard* 6-11-5 (t) TomScudamore 7/2   1
81   IF THE CAP FITS (IRE) *HarryFry* 7-11-9 NoelFehily 13/8f   1½   2
127   LIL ROCKERFELLER (USA) *NeilKing* 8-11-9 (b) BryonyFrost 8/1   2¼   3
103   Old Guard *PaulNicholls* 8-11-9 (s) HarryCobden 7/1   13   4
   Vive Le Roi (IRE) *TonyCarroll* 8-11-3 HarryBannister 66/1   8   5
142   Ballymoy (IRE) *NigelTwiston-Davies* 6-11-7 DarylJacob 3/1   15   6
Ann & Alan Potts Limited 6ran 4m49.30

NAAS Sunday, Feb 24   GOOD
171   **Paddy Power Onside App Novices' Hurdle (Gr 2) (4yo+)** £25,069   2m (8)
   CHOSEN MATE (IRE) *GordonElliott* 6-11-4 DavyRussell 9/10f   1
   HANNON (IRE) *JohnMcConnell* 4-10-4 (t) DavidNoonan ....10/1   ns   2
   MILAN NATIVE (IRE) *GordonElliott* 6-11-4 RachaelBlackmore 6/1   3½   3
8   Political Policy (IRE) *GavinPatrickCromwell* 5-11-4 (t) G.N.Fox 25/1   2¼   4
135   Jetez (IRE) *Mrs.J.Harrington* 6-11-4 RobbiePower ....3/1   F
   Prince d'Aubrelle (FR) *W.P.Mullins* 9-11-4 P.Townend ....8/1   pu
The Northern Four Racing Partnership 6ran 3m48.80

KELSO Saturday, Mar 2   GOOD to SOFT
172   **Edinburgh Gin Premier Kelso Novices' Hurdle (Gr 2) (1) (4yo+)** £28,475   2¼m25y (10)
   ROUGE VIF (FR) *HarryWhittington* 5-11-1 (h) GavinSheehan 7/2   1
   WINDSOR AVENUE (IRE) *BrianEllison* 7-11-1 BrianHughes 4/1   4   2
   ELVIS MAIL (FR) *N.W.Alexander* 5-11-1 (h) LucyAlexander ....28/1   sh   3
157   Getaway Trump (IRE) *PaulNicholls* 6-11-1 HarryCobden 8/11f   10   4
   Strong Glance *FergalO'Brien* 6-11-1 AlainCawley 33/1   3¼   5

Get Out The Gate (IRE) *JimGoldie* 6-11-1 CallumBewley ....25/1   sh 6
Kate & Andrew Brooks 6ran 4m27.70

173 **William Hill Grimthorpe Handicap Chase (2) (5yo+) £34,408**   3¼m1y (19)

       CHIDSWELL (IRE) *NickyRichards* 10-10-4[127] CraigNichol 18/1   1
131 DINGO DOLLAR (IRE) *AlanKing* 7-11-11[148] (s) WayneHutchinson 3/1   9 2
131 BRIAN BORANHA (IRE) *PeterNiven* 8-11-0[137] JamesBowen 12/1   4 3
       Beau du Brizais (FR) *PhilipHobbs* 7-10-12[135] MichealNolan 16/1   4½ 4
72 Rocky's Treasure (IRE) *KimBailey* 8-11-12[149] DavidBass 2/1f   13 5
       Barney Dwan (IRE) *FergalO'Brien* 9-11-3[140] (s) SeanBowen ....5/1   ½ 6
32 Looking Well (IRE) *NickyRichards* 10-11-2[139] (s) AidanColeman ....9/2   F
       David & Nicky Robinson 7ran 6m29.50

174 **William Hill Supporting Greatwood Gold Cup Handicap Chase (Gr 3) (1)**   2m3f187y (16)
     (5yo+) £28,475

113 SAN BENEDETO (FR) *PaulNicholls* 8-11-5[147] (s+t) NickScholfield 11/1   1
       GALA BALL (IRE) *PhilipHobbs* 9-10-13[141] TomO'Brien 20/1   2¼ 2
43 VALDEZ *AlanKing* 12-11-0[142] TomCannon 16/1   2 3
33 Javert (IRE) *EmmaLavelle* 10-11-7[149] TomScudamore 8/1   2½ 4
       Dolos (FR) *PaulNicholls* 6-11-12[154] (t) LorcanWilliams(5) 5/1f   1¼ 5
102 Dustin des Mottes (FR) *DrRichardNewland* 6-10-5[133] SamTwiston-Davies 9/1   3½ 6
10 Zalvados (FR) *OliverGreenall* 6-10-0 (9-11)[128] (b+t) PaddyBrennan 20/1   7 7
26 Mercian Prince (IRE) *AmyMurphy* 8-11-7[149] JackQuinlan 16/1   8 8
13 Value At Risk *DanSkelton* 10-10-6[134] WilliamMarshall(10) ....14/1   nk 9
131 Warriors Tale *PaulNicholls* 10-11-11[153] (t) NoelFehily ....14/1   nk 10
124 War Sound *PhilipHobbs* 10-11-1[143] CiaranGethings 7/1   14 11
       Azzuri *DanSkelton* 7-10-9[137] (t) HarrySkelton 50/1   1½ 12
       Nightfly *CharlieLongsdon* 8-10-4[132] (t) JonathanBurke 20/1   11 13
113 Happy Diva (IRE) *KerryLee* 8-11-0[142] (t) RichardPatrick(3) ....11/2   ur
61 Shanahan's Turn (IRE) *ColinTizzard* 11-10-2[130] (t) BenGodfrey(7) ....33/1   ur
       Master Dee (IRE) *FergalO'Brien* 10-11-9[151] (t) BarryGeraghty ....25/1   pu
       Mr P. J. Vogt 16ran 4m55.70

175 **European Breeders' Fund Matchbook VIP 'National Hunt' Novices'**   2m3f173y (9)
     Handicap Hurdle Final (Gr 3) (1) (4, 5, 6 and 7yo) £42,202

       THIRD WIND *HughieMorrison* 5-11-5[131] TomO'Brien 9/1   1
       ONE FOR ROSIE *NigelTwiston-Davies* 6-11-12[138] SamTwiston-Davies ....12/1   sh 2
       CHAMPAGNE WELL (IRE) *FergalO'Brien* 6-11-4[130] PaddyBrennan 12/1   1½ 3
       Mill Green *NickyHenderson* 7-11-6[132] NedCurtis(3) 14/1   2¼ 4
       Southern Sam *OliverSherwood* 5-10-11[123] LeightonAspell 7/1   1 5
162 Admiral Barratry (FR) *LucyWadham* 6-11-5[131] JackQuinlan ....12/1   ¾ 6
       Trixster (IRE) *TimVaughan* 6-11-3[129] CharliePrice(7) ....14/1   nk 7
       Skandiburg (FR) *OllyMurphy* 5-10-3[125] (s) GavinSheehan 25/1   2½ 8
       Boldmere *GraemeMcPherson* 6-11-2[128] KielanWoods ....25/1   ½ 9
       On The Slopes *ChrisGordon* 5-11-4[130] TomCannon 33/1   2½ 10
       Senior Citizen *AlanKing* 6-11-3[129] WayneHutchinson 20/1   4½ 11
       Smackwater Jack (IRE) *OllyMurphy* 5-13-2[129] (s) FergusGregory(5) 16/1   2½ 12
       Before Midnight *NickyHenderson* 6-11-2[128] NicodeBoinville 8/1   1¾ 13
       Russian Hawk *ColinTizzard* 5-11-7[133] RobbiePower 6/1f   4½ 14
       Golden Whisky (IRE) *EvanWilliams* 6-10-11[123] SeanBowen 16/1   14 15
       Diomede des Mottes (FR) *DanSkelton* 6-10-11[123] HarrySkelton ....16/1   hd 16
116 Muratello (FR) *NigelTwiston-Davies* 5-11-10[136] DarylJacob 20/1   24 17
       Garrettstown (IRE) *OllyMurphy* 6-11-5[131] RichardJohnson ....10/1   pu
       Mouse Hamilton-Fairley 18ran 5m07.30

176 **Matchbook Imperial Cup Handicap Hurdle (Gr 3) (1) (4yo+) £42,202**   1m7f216y (8)

       MALAYA (FR) *PaulNicholls* 5-10-2[136] HarryCobden 7/1   1
       MONSIEUR LECOQ (FR) *MrsJaneWilliams* 5-10-1 (9-12)[135] ChesterWilliams(7) .7/2   1¼ 2
77 CALL ME LORD (FR) *NickyHenderson* 6-11-12[160] DarylJacob 3/1f   4 3
37 Storm Rising (IRE) *DrRichardNewland* 6-10-1[135] (b) CharlieHammond(5) 20/1   3¼ 4
       First Flow (IRE) *KimBailey* 7-10-10[144] DavidBass 9/1   3 5
90 Speredek (FR) *NigelHawke* 8-10-12[146] (s) TomBuckley(10) ....16/1   nk 6
       Benny's Bridge (IRE) *FergalO'Brien* 6-10-0 (9-6)[134] PaddyBrennan 8/1   3¼ 7
       Dream du Grand Val (FR) *NickyHenderson* 6-10-5[139] (h) NicodeBoinville 6/1   5 8
       Our Merlin *RobertWalford* 7-10-0 (9-7)[134] BryonyFrost 20/1   3¼ 9
       Chti Balko (FR) *DonaldMcCain* 7-10-7[141] WilliamKennedy 25/1   12 10
       Pyromaniac (IRE) *AlastairRalph* 9-10-0[134] (t) SamTwiston-Davies ....50/1   pu

63	Totterdown *RichardPhillips* 8-10-1[135] DanielHiskett(5)	....	14/1	pu
	All Yours (FR) *SeanCurran* 8-10-3[137] GavinSheehan	....	66/1	pu

Mrs Johnny de la Hey 13ran 4m01.60

NAAS Sunday, Mar 10 GOOD to SOFT

177 Toalsbet Bookmakers Leinster National Handicap Chase (Gr A) (5yo+) £51,304 3m (16)

122	PAIROFBROWNEYES (IRE) *W.P.Mullins* 10-11-0[146] P.Townend	....	12/1		1
151	ISLEOFHOPENDREAMS *W.P.Mullins* 12-10-8[140] D.E.Mullins	....	16/1	5	2
122	BELLOW MOME (FR) *W.P.Mullins* 8-10-3[135] D.J.Mullins	....	10/1	4¾	3
	The Conditional *MartinHassett* 7-9-10[128] (t) C.A.Landers(5)	....	5/1	2½	4
93	De Name Escapes Me (IRE) *NoelMeade* 9-10-0[132] (h+t) NiallMadden	....	7/1	hd	5
151	Monbeg Notorious (IRE) *GordonElliott* 8-11-5[151] (v) J.W.Kennedy	....	10/1	4½	6
93	Scoir Mear (IRE) *ThomasMullins* 9-9-10[128] D.J.O'Keeffe(7)	....	14/1	15	7
151	Youcantcallherthat (IRE) *DenisHogan* 8-10-10[142] D.G.Hogan	....	16/1	9	8
149	Vieux Morvan (FR) *JosephPatrickO'Brien* 10-10-8[140] (b) J.J.Slevin	....	11/1	15	9
151	Wishmoor (IRE) *JosephPatrickO'Brien* 9-10-1[133] RachaelBlackmore	....	9/2f	12	10
149	Last Goodbye (IRE) *MissElizabethDoyle* 8-10-12[144] (b+t) A.W.Short(3)	....	33/1	9½	11
	Killer Miller (IRE) *NoelMeade* 10-9-12[130] JonathanMoore	....	10/1		ur
	Icantsay (IRE) *JohnPatrickRyan* 9-9-13[131] PhilipEnright	....	25/1		pu
165	Blow By Blow (IRE) *GordonElliott* 8-10-10[142] (b+t) SeanFlanagan	....	10/1		pu

Fibbage Syndicate 14ran 6m30.80

CHELTENHAM Tuesday, Mar 12 SOFT

178 Sky Bet Supreme Novices' Hurdle (Gr 1) (1) (4yo+) £70,337 2m87y (8)

145	KLASSICAL DREAM (FR) *W.P.Mullins,Ireland* 5-11-7 R.Walsh	....	6/1		1
	THOMAS DARBY (IRE) *OllyMurphy* 6-11-7 RichardJohnson	....	28/1	4½	2
38	ITCHY FEET (FR) *OllyMurphy* 5-11-7 GavinSheehan	....	25/1	½	3
123	Fakir d'Oudairies (FR) *JosephPatrickO'Brien,Ireland* 4-10-13 J.J.Slevin	....	9/2jf	6	4
111	Felix Desjy (FR) *GordonElliott,Ireland* 6-11-7 SeanFlanagan	....	11/1	ns	5
145	Aramon (GER) *W.P.Mullins,Ireland* 6-11-7 P.Townend	....	8/1	hd	6
168	Angels Breath (IRE) *NickyHenderson* 5-11-7 NicodeBoinville	....	11	11	7
116	Mister Fisher (IRE) *NickyHenderson* 5-11-7 JamesBowen	....	14/1	1¼	8
145	Vision d'Honneur (FR) *GordonElliott,Ireland* 5-11-7 (t) J.W.Kennedy	....	12/1	5	9
157	Al Dancer (FR) *NigelTwiston-Davies* 6-11-7 SamTwiston-Davies	....	9/2jf	5	10
163	Grand Sancy (FR) *PaulNicholls* 5-11-7 (h) HarryCobden	....	14/1	1½	11
	The Big Bite (IRE) *TomGeorge* 6-11-7 NoelFehily	....	25/1	8	12
	The Flying Sofa (FR) *GaryMoore* 6-11-7 JamieMoore	....	125/1	6	13
	Beaufort West (IRE) *ColinTizzard* 5-11-7 RobbiePower	....	66/1		pu
	Brandon Castle *NeilKing* 7-11-7 (h+t) BryonyFrost	....	25/1		pu
168	Normal Norman *JohnRyan* 5-11-7 PaddyBrennan	....	100/1		pu

Mrs J Coleman 16ran 4m00.10

179 Racing Post Arkle Challenge Trophy Novices' Chase (Gr 1) (1) (5yo+) 1m7f199y (13)
£102,772

	DUC DES GENIEVRES (FR) *W.P.Mullins,Ireland* 6-11-4 P.Townend	....	5/1		1
138	US AND THEM (IRE) *JosephPatrickO'Brien,Ireland* 6-11-4 (t) J.J.Slevin	....	14/1	13	2
	ARTICULUM (IRE) *TerenceO'Brien,Ireland* 7-11-4 (t) D.J.Mullins	....	25/1	3¾	3
	Clondaw Castle (IRE) *TomGeorge* 7-11-4 CiaranGethings	....	33/1	2¾	4
138	Knocknanuss (IRE) *GaryMoore* 9-11-4 JamieMoore	....	33/1	5	5
	Paloma Blue (IRE) *HenrydeBromhead,Ireland* 7-11-4 RobbiePower	....	10/1	2¼	6
147	Hardline (IRE) *GordonElliott,Ireland* 7-11-4 (h) DavyRussell	....	10/3f	11	7
115	Slate House (IRE) *ColinTizzard* 7-11-4 (t) HarryCobden	....	66/1	6	8
62	Ornua (IRE) *HenrydeBromhead,Ireland* 8-11-4 RachaelBlackmore	....	14/1		F
152	Glen Forsa (IRE) *MickChannon* 7-11-4 JonathanBurke	....	9/2		ur
152	Kalashnikov (IRE) *AmyMurphy* 6-11-4 JackQuinlan	....	6/1		ur
62	Lalor (GER) *KayleyWoollacott* 7-11-4 RichardJohnson	....	13/2		pu

Sullivan Bloodstock Limited 12ran 3m58.70

180 Ultima Handicap Chase (Gr 3) (1) (5yo+) £61,897 3m1f (20)

51	BEWARE THE BEAR (IRE) *NickyHenderson* 9-11-8[151] (b) JeremiahMcGrath	..10/1		1
88	VINTAGE CLOUDS (IRE) *SueSmith* 9-11-11[154] DannyCook	....	16/1	1¼	2
86	LAKE VIEW LAD (IRE) *N.W.Alexander* 9-11-12[155] HenryBrooke	....	25/1	2	3
53	Big River (IRE) *LucindaRussell* 9-10-11[140] (t) DerekFox	....	28/1	3¼	4
113	Flying Angel (IRE) *NigelTwiston-Davies* 8-10-13[142] (v) SamTwiston-Davies	...25/1	½	5
124	Activial (FR) *TomGeorge* 9-11-8[151] TomScudamore	....	40/1	hd	6
112	Magic of Light (IRE) *Mrs.J.Harrington,Ireland* 8-11-8[151] (s) RobbiePower	....25/1	4	7
122	Up For Review (IRE) *W.P.Mullins,Ireland* 10-11-3[146] P.Townend	....	8/1cf	3¾	8
124	Oldgrangewood *DanSkelton* 8-10-11[140] (t) BridgetAndrews	....	66/1	1¾	9
59	Noble Endeavor (IRE) *GordonElliott,Ireland* 10-11-7[150] (s) DavyRussell	......14/1	ns	10
115	Crucial Role *DanSkelton* 7-11-7[150] HarrySkelton	....	16/1	4½	11

131	O O Seven (IRE) *NickyHenderson* 9-11-9[152] (b) NicodeBoinville 50/1		1	12
68	Singlefarmpayment *TomGeorge* 9-11-3[146] (h) NoelFehily 10/1		20	13
	Give Me A Copper (IRE) *PaulNicholls* 9-11-2[145] (t) HarryCobden 9/1			F
169	Catamaran du Seuil (FR) *DrRichardNewland* 7-10-11[140] (v) CharlieHammond(5)	50/1		pu
33	Shantou Village (IRE) *NeilMulholland* 9-10-13[142] (s+t) RobertDunne 40/1			pu
151	General Principle (IRE) *GordonElliott,Ireland* 10-11-1[144] (t) J.W.Kennedy 14/1			pu
131	Willie Boy (IRE) *CharlieLongsdon* 8-11-1[144] (s) JonathanBurke 50/1			pu
68	Coo Star Sivola (FR) *NickWilliams* 7-11-2[145] LizzieKelly(3) 8/1cf			pu
155	Calipto (FR) *VenetiaWilliams* 9-11-5[148] CharlieDeutsch 14/1			pu
113	Mister Whitaker (IRE) *MickChannon* 7-11-8[151] BrianHughes 8/1cf			pu
161	Royal Vacation (IRE) *ColinTizzard* 9-11-8[151] (b) AidanColeman 33/1			pu
125	Minella Rocco (IRE) *JonjoO'Neill* 9-11-9[152] (s+t) RichieMcLernon 14/1			pu
108	Sizing Codelco (IRE) *ColinTizzard* 10-11-11[154] TomO'Brien 66/1			pu

Mr G. B. Barlow 24ran 6m39.70

---

181 Unibet Champion Hurdle Challenge Trophy (Gr 1) (1) (4yo+) £253,215   2m87y (8)

132	ESPOIR D'ALLEN (FR) *GavinPatrickCromwell,Ireland* 5-11-10 M.P.Walsh 16/1			1
134	MELON *W.P.Mullins,Ireland* 7-11-10 (s) P.Townend 20/1		15	2
117	SILVER STREAK (IRE) *EvanWilliams* 6-11-10 AdamWedge 80/1		nk	3
	Laurina *W.P.Mullins,Ireland* 6-11-3 R.Walsh 5/2		1½	4
81	Verdana Blue (IRE) *NickyHenderson* 7-11-3 DavyRussell 33/1		7	5
134	Apple's Jade (FR) *GordonElliott,Ireland* 7-11-3 (t) J.W.Kennedy 7/4f		6	6
117	Global Citizen (IRE) *BenPauling* 7-11-10 DavidBass 50/1		45	7
140	Buveur d'Air (FR) *NickyHenderson* 8-11-10 BarryGeraghty 11/4			F
97	Sharjah (FR) *W.P.Mullins,Ireland* 6-11-10 MrP.W.Mullins 20/1			bd
71	Brain Power (IRE) *NickyHenderson* 8-11-10 (s) NicodeBoinville 33/1			pu

Mr John P. McManus 10ran 3m59.30

---

182 OLBG Mares' Hurdle (David Nicholson) (Gr 1) (1) (4yo+) £70,563   2m3f200y (10)

140	ROKSANA (IRE) *DanSkelton* 7-11-5 HarrySkelton 10/1			1
	STORMY IRELAND (FR) *W.P.Mullins,Ireland* 5-11-5 P.Townend 7/1		2¼	2
5	GOOD THYNE TARA *W.P.Mullins,Ireland* 9-11-5 RachaelBlackmore 25/1		2	3
130	Lady Buttons *PhilipKirby* 9-11-5 ThomasDowson 12/1		12	4
7	Slowmotion (FR) *JosephPatrickO'Brien,Ireland* 5-11-5 (b) BarryGeraghty 50/1		2½	5
	Elimay (FR) *W.P.Mullins,Ireland* 5-11-5 M.P.Walsh 16/1		2¾	6
	Cap Soleil (FR) *FergalO'Brien* 6-11-5 PaddyBrennan 20/1		hd	7
112	Jester Jet *TomLacey* 9-11-5 RobertDunne 25/1		3½	8
48	Momella (FR) *HarryFry* 7-11-5 (s) NoelFehily 20/1		8	9
143	Alletrix (IRE) *MrsJ.Harrington,Ireland* 6-11-5 (h) RobbiePower 50/1		13	10
	Benie des Dieux (FR) *W.P.Mullins,Ireland* 8-11-5 R.Walsh 10/11f			F
	Champagne Lady (IRE) *AlanFleming,Ireland* 7-11-5 (t) DonaghMeyler 100/1			F
	Lackaneen Leader (IRE) *GordonElliott,Ireland* 7-11-5 DavyRussell 50/1			pu
121	Limini (IRE) *W.P.Mullins,Ireland* 8-11-5 D.J.Mullins 9/1			pu

Mrs Sarah Faulks 14ran 5m01.10

---

183 Close Brothers Novices' Handicap Chase (L) (1) (145) (5yo+) £39,389   2½m44y (16)

110	A PLUS TARD (FR) *HenrydeBromhead,Ireland* 5-11-7[143] RachaelBlackmore 5/1f			1
	TOWER BRIDGE (IRE) *JosephPatrickO'Brien,Ireland* 6-11-7[143] (s+t) J.J.Slevin ..6/1		16	2
110	BEN DUNDEE (IRE) *GordonElliott,Ireland* 7-11-5[141] (t) KeithDonoghue 33/1		4½	3
	The Russian Doyen (IRE) *ColinTizzard* 6-11-5[141] HarryCobden 20/1		3¾	4
	Springtown Lake (IRE) *PhilipHobbs* 7-11-5[141] RichardJohnson 11/1		2¼	5
	Roaring Bull (IRE) *GordonElliott,Ireland* 6-11-4[140] (b) J.W.Kennedy 16/1		2½	6
	Shady Operator (IRE) *JosephPatrickO'Brien,Ireland* 6-11-3[139] M.P.Walsh 12/1		1¾	7
33	Movewiththetimes (IRE) *PaulNicholls* 8-11-4[140] BarryGeraghty 16/1		1	8
	Huntsman Son (IRE) *AlexHales* 9-11-4[140] (t) KielanWoods 33/1		nk	9
89	Highway One O One (IRE) *ChrisGordon* 7-11-9[145] TomCannon 14/1		11	10
80	Red Indian *KellyMorgan* 7-11-9[145] RossChapman 16/1		8	11
85	Riders Onthe Storm (IRE) *TomJ.Taaffe,Ireland* 6-11-4[140] BrianHughes 10/1			F
139	Quamino (GER) *PaulNolan,Ireland* 6-11-2[138] (t) B.J.Cooper 25/1			pu
152	Dell Oro (FR) *GaryMoore* 6-11-2[138] (s) JoshuaMoore 50/1			pu
166	Good Man Pat (IRE) *AlanKing* 6-11-3[139] WayneHutchinson 12/1			pu
151	Solomn Grundy (IRE) *HenrydeBromhead,Ireland* 9-11-3[139] P.Townend 14/1			pu
	Militarian *AndrewMartin* 9-11-5[141] MrJamesMartin(7) 50/1			pu
169	Walt (IRE) *NeilMulholland* 8-11-5[141] (v+t) SamTwiston-Davies 25/1			pu
	Lough Derg Spirit (IRE) *NickyHenderson* 7-11-6[142] (s) NicodeBoinville 12/1			pu
149	Cubomania (IRE) *GordonElliott,Ireland* 6-11-9[145] (t) DavyRussell 16/1			pu

Cheveley Park Stud 20ran 5m13.30

---

184 National Hunt Challenge Cup Amateur Riders' Novices' Chase (Gr 2) (1)   3m7f147y (25)
(5yo+) £74,125

115	LE BREUIL (FR) *BenPauling* 7-11-6 MrJ.J.Codd 14/1			1

985

	55	DISCORAMA (FR) *PaulNolan,Ireland* 6-11-6 MrBarryO'Neill	.........................9/2	½	2
	115	JERRYSBACK (IRE) *PhilipHobbs* 7-11-6 MrD.G.Lavery	..............................16/1	47	3
		Clondaw Cian (IRE) *SophieLeech* 9-11-6 (s) MrDamienSkehan	......................125/1	1	4
	100	Atlanta Ablaze *HenryDaly* 8-10-13 MrWilliamBiddick	.................................20/1		F
		Ballyward (IRE) *W.P.Mullins,Ireland* 7-11-6 MrP.W.Mullins	....................9/4f		F
	110	Beyond The Law (IRE) *M.F.Morris,Ireland* 7-11-6 (h+t) MrJ.C.Barry	..............66/1		F
	110	Gun Digger (IRE) *GordonElliott,Ireland* 7-11-6 (s+t) MsL.O'Neill	................25/1		F
		Johanos (FR) *NigelHawke* 8-11-6 MrKierenBuckley	...................................100/1		F
		Just Your Type (IRE) *CharlieLongsdon* 7-11-6 (s) MrRobertJames	.................50/1		F
	141	Mulcahys Hill (IRE) *WarrenGreatrex* 7-11-6 (s) MrN.McParlan	...................40/1		F
	149	Whisperinthebreeze *Mrs.J.Harrington,Ireland* 6-11-6 (s) MrFinianMaguire	.....20/1		F
	49	Skipthecuddles (IRE) *GraemeMcPherson* 8-11-6 (s) MissLillyPinchin	............40/1		ur
		Chef des Obeaux (FR) *NickyHenderson* 7-11-6 (s) MrM.J.O'Hare	...................9/1		pu
	108	Impulsive Star (IRE) *NeilMulholland* 9-11-6 (s) MrSamWaley-Cohen	............16/1		pu
		Ok Corral (IRE) *NickyHenderson* 9-11-6 MrDerekO'Connor	.........................4/1		pu
		Plantagenet *SeamusMullins* 7-11-6 (s) MrMatthewFielding	........................100/1		pu
		Warthog (FR) *DavidPipe* 7-11-6 (t) MrRichardDeegan	...............................100/1		pu

Mrs Emma Palmer 18ran 8m42.80

CHELTENHAM Wednesday, Mar 13 SOFT

185 Ballymore Novices' Hurdle (Baring Bingham) (Gr 1) (1) (4yo+) £70,337   2m5f (10)

	CITY ISLAND (IRE) *MartinBrassil,Ireland* 6-11-7 (t) M.P.Walsh	..................8/1		1
99	CHAMP (IRE) *NickyHenderson* 7-11-7 BarryGeraghty	..............................9/2	2	2
116	BRIGHT FORECAST (IRE) *BenPauling* 5-11-7 NicodeBoinville	...............25/1	2¼	3
126	Brewin'upastorm (IRE) *OllyMurphy* 6-11-7 RichardJohnson	..................11/1	1½	4
106	Sams Profile *M.F.Morris,Ireland* 5-11-7 B.J.Cooper	...............................9/1	9	5
	Galvin (IRE) *GordonElliott,Ireland* 5-11-7 DavyRussell	..........................12/1	hd	6
75	Seddon (IRE) *TomGeorge* 6-11-7 NoelFehily	....33/1	11	7
74	Easy Game (FR) *W.P.Mullins,Ireland* 5-11-7 R.Walsh	.............................7/1	1	8
126	Jarveys Plate (IRE) *FergalO'Brien* 6-11-7 PaddyBrennan	........................25/1	¾	9
	Ask Dillon (IRE) *FergalO'Brien* 6-11-7 SeanBowen	...............................50/1	1¼	10
145	Valdieu (FR) *NoelMeade,Ireland* 6-11-7 (t) SeanFlanagan	.......................66/1	14	11
	Notebook (GER) *HenrydeBromhead,Ireland* 6-11-7 (t) RachaelBlackmore	......50/1	8	12
106	Battleoverdoyen (IRE) *GordonElliott,Ireland* 6-11-7 J.W.Kennedy	..............3/1f		pu
107	Beakstown (IRE) *DanSkelton* 6-11-7 (t) HarrySkelton	............................14/1		pu
	Castlebawn West (IRE) *W.P.Mullins,Ireland* 6-11-7 P.Townend	.................25/1		pu
133	Dunvegan (FR) *P.A.Fahy,Ireland* 6-11-7 D.J.Mullins	.............................33/1		pu

Mrs B. Mulryan 16ran 5m06.60

186 RSA Insurance Novices' Chase (Gr 1) (1) (5yo+) £98,472   3m80y (19)

80	TOPOFTHEGAME (IRE) *PaulNicholls* 7-11-4 (t) HarryCobden	................4/1		1
80	SANTINI *NickyHenderson* 7-11-4 NicodeBoinville	................................31/1	½	2
96	DELTA WORK (FR) *GordonElliott,Ireland* 6-11-4 (h+t) DavyRussell	..........15/8f	1¾	3
154	Mister Malarky *ColinTizzard* 6-11-4 RobbiePower	...............................20/1	16	4
147	Mortal (IRE) *JosephPatrickO'Brien,Ireland* 6-11-4 (t) RachaelBlackmore	....20/1	½	5
	Drovers Lane (IRE) *RebeccaCurtis* 7-11-4 SeanBowen	...........................20/1	2	6
76	Count Meribel *NigelTwiston-Davies* 7-11-4 MarkGrant	............................66/1	6	7
154	Now McGinty (IRE) *StuartEdmunds* 8-11-4 (s) TomO'Brien	.....................33/1	1	8
154	Top Ville Ben (IRE) *PhilipKirby* 7-11-4 (h) SeanQuinlan	.........................33/1		F
100	Drinks Interval *ColinTizzard* 7-10-11 (t) RichardJohnson	......................100/1		pu
101	On The Blind Side (IRE) *NickyHenderson* 7-11-4 (s) NoelFehily	...............14/1		pu
80	The Worlds End (IRE) *TomGeorge* 8-11-4 (s) PaddyBrennan	...................16/1		pu

Mr Chris Giles & Mr&Mrs P K Barber 12ran 6m18.30

187 Coral Cup Handicap Hurdle (Gr 3) (1) (4yo+) £56,270   2m5f (10)

	WILLIAM HENRY (IRE) *NickyHenderson* 9-11-0[151] (s) NicodeBoinville	........28/1		1
132	WICKLOW BRAVE *W.P.Mullins,Ireland* 10-11-12[153] MrP.W.Mullins	........28/1	sh	2
33	BALLYANDY *NigelTwiston-Davies* 8-11-7[148] SamTwiston-Davies	..............14/1	½	3
142	Brio Conti (FR) *PaulNicholls* 8-11-5[146] HarryCobden	..........................10/1	1½	4
	Canardier (FR) *DermotAnthonyMcLoughlin,Ireland* 7-11-0[141] (h) RobertDunne	.14/1	½	5
63	Apple's Shakira (FR) *NickyHenderson* 5-10-13[140] (h) BarryGeraghty	..........10/1	ns	6
135	Uradel (GER) *W.P.Mullins,Ireland* 8-10-10[137] R.Walsh	.......................13/2f	¾	7
121	Bleu Berry (FR) *W.P.Mullins,Ireland* 8-11-7[148] D.J.Mullins	..................25/1	2¾	8
135	Tully East (IRE) *AlanFleming,Ireland* 9-10-11[138] DonaghMeyler	.............16/1	1	9
170	Lil Rockerfeller (USA) *NeilKing* 8-11-9[150] (s) BryonyFrost	....................20/1	2½	10
164	Cracking Smart (FR) *GordonElliott,Ireland* 7-11-9[150] (s+t) J.W.Kennedy	...12/1	½	11
146	Oscar Knight (IRE) *ThomasMullins,Ireland* 10-10-6[133] M.P.Walsh	...........33/1	1	12
	Knight In Dubai (IRE) *DanSkelton* 6-10-12[139] (t) HarrySkelton	...............25/1	hd	13
	Scarpeta (FR) *W.P.Mullins,Ireland* 6-11-10[151] (s) D.E.Mullins	...............20/1	½	14
	Burbank (IRE) *NickyHenderson* 7-11-0[141] (s) JeremiahMcGrath	.............40/1	3	15

146	Calie du Mesnil (FR) *W.P.Mullins,Ireland* 7-10-8[135] (t) KatieO'Farrell(5) 25/1	1¾ 16
	Highest Sun (FR) *ColinTizzard* 5-10-12[139] TomO'Brien 16/1	4½ 17
170	Vision des Flos (FR) *ColinTizzard* 6-11-11[152] (t) RobbiePower 9/1	5 18
159	Killultagh Vic (IRE) *W.P.Mullins,Ireland* 10-11-9[150] P.Townend 16/1	25 19
	Erick Le Rouge (FR) *MrsJaneWilliams* 5-10-10[137] ChesterWilliams(7) 16/1	pu
63	Eragon de Chanay (FR) *GaryMoore* 5-10-11[138] (v) JoshuaMoore 66/1	pu
145	Dancing On My Own (IRE) *HenrydeBromhead,Ireland* 5-11-4[145]	
	RachaelBlackmore 16/1	pu
48	Monbeg Theatre (FR) *JamieSnowden* 10-11-7[148] (s+t) PageFuller(3) 66/1	pu
	Diamond Cauchois (FR) *GordonElliott,Ireland* 8-11-9[150] (t) NoelFehily 33/1	pu
134	Farclas (FR) *GordonElliott,Ireland* 5-11-10[151] (b+t) DavyRussell 16/1	pu

Walters Plant Hire Ltd 25ran 5m08.90

188	**Betway Queen Mother Champion Chase (Gr 1) (1) (5yo+)** £225,080	1m7f199y (13)
114	ALTIOR (IRE) *NickyHenderson* 9-11-10 NicodeBoinville 4/11f	1
158	POLITOLOGUE (FR) *PaulNicholls* 8-11-10 (h+t) HarryCobden 11/1	1¾ 2
163	SCEAU ROYAL (FR) *AlanKing* 7-11-10 DarylJacob 16/1	1¾ 3
26	Hell's Kitchen *HarryFry* 8-11-10 (h+t) BarryGeraghty 25/1	6 4
137	Min (FR) *W.P.Mullins,Ireland* 8-11-10 R.Walsh 7/2	1¾ 5
137	Castlegrace Paddy (IRE) *P.A.Fahy,Ireland* 8-11-10 DavyRussell 25/1	8 6
137	Saint Calvados (FR) *HarryWhittington* 6-11-10 (s) GavinSheehan 25/1	5 7
137	Ordinary World (IRE) *HenrydeBromhead,Ireland* 9-11-10 RachaelBlackmore ...33/1	10 8
66	God's Own (IRE) *TomGeorge* 11-11-10 PaddyBrennan 16/1	pu

Mrs Patricia Pugh 9ran 3m59.40

189	**Glenfarclas Chase (Cross Country) (2) (5yo+)** £40,235	3¾m37y (32)
164	TIGER ROLL (IRE) *GordonElliott,Ireland* 9-11-4 (b+t) KeithDonoghue 5/4f	1
	JOSIES ORDERS (IRE) *EndaBolger,Ireland* 11-11-4 (b) M.P.Walsh 15/2	22 2
	URGENT DE GREGAINE (FR) *EmmanuelClayeux,France* 11-11-4 (s+t)	
	FelixdeGiles 17/2	¾ 3
	Ballycasey (IRE) *W.P.Mullins,Ireland* 12-11-4 MrP.W.Mullins 33/1	2¾ 4
132	Jarob *GearoidO'Loughlin,Ireland* 12-11-4 MarkEnright 66/1	5 5
	Kingswell Theatre *MichaelScudamore* 10-11-4 (s) TomScudamore 33/1	9 6
88	Vyta du Roc (FR) *NickyHenderson* 10-11-4 DarylJacob 25/1	10 7
	Fact of The Matter (IRE) *JamieSnowden* 9-11-4 (s+t) GavinSheehan 16/1	10 8
	Aubusson (FR) *MrsJaneWilliams* 10-11-4 ChesterWilliams 100/1	sh 9
	Amazing Comedy (FR) *DavidCottin,France* 9-11-4 (b+t) JonathanPlouganou ..20/1	3¼ 10
82	Tea For Two *MrsJaneWilliams* 10-11-4 LizzieKelly 12/1	ur
93	Auvergnat (FR) *EndaBolger,Ireland* 9-11-4 (b) D.J.McInerney 9/1	pu
164	Bless The Wings (IRE) *GordonElliott,Ireland* 14-11-4 (s) DavyRussell 20/1	pu
4	Devils Bride (IRE) *HenrydeBromhead,Ireland* 12-11-4 (t) RachaelBlackmore . 100/1	pu
108	Ultragold (FR) *ColinTizzard* 11-11-4 (t) HarryCobden 14/1	pu

Gigginstown House Stud 15ran 8m28.40

190	**Boodles Juvenile Handicap Hurdle (Fred Winter) (1) (4yo)** £45,016	2m87y (8)
	BAND OF OUTLAWS (IRE) *JosephPatrickO'Brien,Ireland* 4-11-8[139] J.J.Slevin . 7/2f	1
83	COKO BEACH (FR) *GordonElliott,Ireland* 4-11-3[134] J.W.Kennedy 14/1	2 2
	CIEL DE NEIGE (FR) *W.P.Mullins,Ireland* 4-11-1[132] R.Walsh 17/2	1¾ 3
	King d'Argent (FR) *DanSkelton* 4-10-12[129] (t) HarrySkelton 25/1	2¾ 4
	Fanfan du Seuil (FR) *TomGeorge* 4-11-5[136] PaddyBrennan 12/1	nk 5
167	Praeceps (FR) *AlanKing* 4-10-12[129] (h) WayneHutchinson 16/1	½ 6
	Naturelle (FR) *AlainCouetil,France* 4-11-7[138] AlexisPoirier 20/1	4 7
144	Got Trumped *MrsJ.Harrington,Ireland* 4-11-7[138] RobbiePower 20/1	½ 8
123	Our Power (FR) *AlanKing* 4-11-4[135] TomCannon 25/1	1¼ 9
83	La Sorelita (FR) *W.P.Mullins,Ireland* 4-10-13[130] (t) P.Townend 16/1	1¼ 10
	Star Max (GER) *JosephPatrickO'Brien,Ireland* 4-11-0[131] RachaelBlackmore 8/1	½ 11
144	Chief Justice *GordonElliott,Ireland* 4-11-8[139] (t) KeithDonoghue 25/1	1 12
73	Cracker Factory *AlanKing* 4-11-8[139] (s) SamTwiston-Davies 50/1	1 13
	Prabeni *CharlieMann* 4-11-3[134] (t) JeremiahMcGrath 40/1	5 14
	Torpillo (FR) *NigelTwiston-Davies* 4-10-14[141] (h) DarylJacob 14/1	1 15
	Zizaneur (FR) *PhilipHobbs* 4-11-2[133] MrDavidMaxwell(5) 50/1	3 16
123	Fine Brunello (FR) *JosephPatrickO'Brien,Ireland* 4-11-8[139] BarryGeraghty 14/1	13 17
	Fox Pro (FR) *MrsJaneWilliams* 4-11-3[134] LizzieKelly(3) 50/1	4½ 18
	Lethal Steps *GordonFlliott,Ireland* 4-11-0[131] (s) DavyRussell 9/1	8 19
73	Oi The Clubb Oi's *IanWilliams* 4-10-13[130] TomO'Brien 33/1	pu
123	Dogon *PaulNicholls* 4-11-2[133] (t) HarryCobden 14/1	pu

Mr Justin Carthy 21ran 3m58.30

191	**Weatherbys Champion Bumper (Standard Open National Hunt Flat) (Gr 1) (1)**	2m87y
	(4, 5 and 6yo) £42,202	
136	ENVOI ALLEN (FR) *GordonElliott,Ireland* 5-11-5 MrJ.J.Codd 2/1f	1

	BLUE SARI (FR) *W.P.Mullins,Ireland* 4-10-11 BarryGeraghty	7/2	¾	2
	THYME HILL *PhilipHobbs* 5-11-5 RichardJohnson	20/1	1¾	3
136	Abacadabras (FR) *GordonElliott,Ireland* 5-11-5 MsL.O'Neill	14/1	3¼	4
	The Glancing Queen (IRE) *AlanKing* 5-10-12 WayneHutchinson	20/1	1½	5
	Sempo (IRE) *JosephPatrickO'Brien,Ireland* 5-11-5 (t) MrDerekO'Connor	12/1	½	6
	Some Detail (IRE) *NigelHawke* 5-11-5 SeanBowen	100/1	9	7
136	Meticulous (IRE) *JosephPatrickO'Brien,Ireland* 5-11-5 (t) DonnachaO'Brien	7/1	sh	8
	Ask For Glory (IRE) *PaulNicholls* 5-11-5 HarryCobden	13/2	¾	9
	Flic Ou Voyou (FR) *PaulNicholls* 5-11-5 SamTwiston-Davies	33/1	2	10
	Thor de Cerisy (FR) *MichaelScudamore* 5-11-5 (h) BrendanPowell	100/1	1¼	11
	Master Debonair *ColinTizzard* 5-11-5 RobbiePower	12/1	nk	12
	Cascova (IRE) *MartynMeade* 4-10-11 NoelFehily	66/1	¾	13
	Jelski (GER) *NigelTwiston-Davies* 5-11-5 JamieBargary	66/1	1	14

Cheveley Park Stud 14ran 3m55.60

CHELTENHAM Thursday, Mar 14 GOOD to SOFT

192 JLT Novices' Chase (Golden Miller) (Gr 1) (1) (5yo+) £88,209 — 2m3f168y (16)

141	DEFI DU SEUIL (FR) *PhilipHobbs* 6-11-4 BarryGeraghty	3/1f		1
141	LOSTINTRANSLATION (IRE) *ColinTizzard* 7-11-4 RobbiePower	4/1	2¼	2
138	MENGLI KHAN (IRE) *GordonElliott,Ireland* 6-11-4 (t) J.W.Kennedy	9/1	7	3
	Kildisart (IRE) *BenPauling* 7-11-4 DarylJacob	9/1	3	4
141	Vinndication (IRE) *KimBailey* 6-11-4 DavidBass	11/2	ns	5
	Real Steel (FR) *W.P.Mullins,Ireland* 6-11-4 P.Townend	13/2	6	6
166	Castafiore (USA) *CharlieLongsdon* 6-10-11 (s) PaulO'Brien	33/1	6	7
	Capeland (FR) *PaulNicholls* 7-11-4 (t) HarryCobden	28/1	15	8
	Pravalaguna (FR) *W.P.Mullins,Ireland* 7-10-11 D.J.Mullins	14/1	40	9
138	Voix du Reve (FR) *W.P.Mullins,Ireland* 7-11-4 (h) R.Walsh	9/1		ur

Mr John P. McManus 10ran 5m01.00

193 Pertemps Network Final Handicap Hurdle (Gr 3) (1) (5yo+) £56,270 — 2m7f213y (12)

	SIRE DU BERLAIS (FR) *GordonElliott,Ireland* 7-11-9^{145} (s+t) BarryGeraghty	4/1f		1
	TOBEFAIR *DebraHamer* 9-11-0^{136} TomBellamy	40/1	nk	2
	NOT MANY LEFT (IRE) *MrsJ.Harrington,Ireland* 6-11-5^{141} (s) M.P.Walsh	16/1	1¼	3
146	Cuneo (FR) *HenrydeBromhead,Ireland* 7-11-1^{137} RachaelBlackmore	12/1	2	4
119	A Toi Phil (FR) *GordonElliott,Ireland* 9-11-10^{146} (t) J.W.Kennedy	20/1	4½	5
72	Theclockisticking (IRE) *StuartEdmunds* 7-11-2^{138} CiaranGethings	25/1	1¼	6
	Thermistocles (IRE) *JosephPatrickO'Brien,Ireland* 7-11-1^{137} J.J.Slevin	9/1	nk	7
142	Padleyourowncanoe *ColinTizzard* 5-11-6^{142} HarryCobden	50/1	6	8
44	First Assignment (IRE) *IanWilliams* 6-11-6^{142} TomO'Brien	15/2	hd	9
142	Flemcara (IRE) *EmmaLavelle* 7-11-1^{137} (t) AidanColeman	14/1	7	10
	Black Mischief *HarryFry* 7-11-5^{141} (s+t) NoelFehily	50/1	1	11
	Samburu Shujaa (FR) *PhilipHobbs* 6-11-0^{136} RichardJohnson	17/2	½	12
	Oh Land Abloom (IRE) *NeilKing* 9-11-1^{137} (v+t) BryonyFrost	66/1	4	13
	Aaron Lad (IRE) *DrRichardNewland* 8-11-6^{142} CharlieHammond(5)	16/1	¾	14
	Boyhood (IRE) *TomGeorge* 8-11-7^{143} PaddyBrennan	25/1	3¾	15
142	Eminent Poet *VenetiaWilliams* 8-11-6^{142} CharlieDeutsch	66/1	3¼	16
142	Coole Cody (IRE) *MichaelBlake* 8-11-3^{139} (t) NickScholfield	33/1	23	17
	Aspen Colorado (IRE) *JonjoO'Neill* 7-10-12^{134} (s) JonjoO'NeillJr.(5)	33/1	3	18
	Wait For Me (FR) *PhilipHobbs* 9-11-0^{136} MichealNolan	33/1		ur
	Abolitionist (IRE) *DrRichardNewland* 11-10-12^{134} (s) SamTwiston-Davies	20/1		pu
	Notwhatiam (IRE) *DanSkelton* 9-10-13^{135} (t) HarrySkelton	16/1		pu
	Champers On Ice (IRE) *DavidPipe* 9-10-13^{135} (b) TomScudamore	10/1		pu
112	Culture de Sivola (FR) *NickWilliams* 7-11-5^{141} LizzieKelly(3)	40/1		pu
	Walk To Freedom (IRE) *MrsJ.Harrington,Ireland* 9-11-12^{148} (h+t) RobbiePower	16/1		pu

Mr John P. McManus 24ran 5m53.20

194 Ryanair Chase (Festival Trophy) (Gr 1) (1) (5yo+) £196,945 — 2½m127y (17)

125	FRODON (FR) *PaulNicholls* 7-11-10 (t) BryonyFrost	9/2		1
158	ASO (FR) *VenetiaWilliams* 9-11-10 CharlieDeutsch	33/1	1¼	2
148	ROAD TO RESPECT (IRE) *NoelMeade,Ireland* 8-11-10 SeanFlanagan	9/2	1¾	3
159	Monalee (IRE) *HenrydeBromhead,Ireland* 8-11-10 RachaelBlackmore	5/1	2¼	4
64	Un de Sceaux (FR) *W.P.Mullins,Ireland* 11-11-10 P.Townend	5/1	3¼	5
95	Coney Island (IRE) *EdwardP.Harty,Ireland* 8-11-10 (t) M.P.Walsh	25/1	5	6
95	Balko des Flos (FR) *HenrydeBromhead,Ireland* 8-11-10 DenisO'Regan	16/1	9	7
91	Footpad (FR) *W.P.Mullins,Ireland* 7-11-10 R.Walsh	7/2f	3½	8
158	Charbel (IRE) *KimBailey* 8-11-10 (s+t) DavidBass	40/1		pu
119	Sub Lieutenant (IRE) *HenrydeBromhead,Ireland* 10-11-10 (s+t) J.J.Slevin	66/1		pu
156	Terrefort (FR) *NickyHenderson* 6-11-10 DarylJacob	20/1		pu
148	The Storyteller (IRE) *GordonElliott,Ireland* 8-11-10 DavyRussell	20/1		pu

Mr P. J. Vogt 12ran 5m10.30

195 Sun Racing Stayers' Hurdle (Gr 1) (1) (4yo+) £182,877 2m7f213y (12)

127	PAISLEY PARK (IRE) *EmmaLavelle* 7-11-10 AidanColeman	11/8f		1
127	SAM SPINNER *JeddO'Keeffe* 7-11-10 (s) JoeColliver	33/1	2¾	2
94	FAUGHEEN (IRE) *W.P.Mullins,Ireland* 11-11-10 R.Walsh	4/1	4	3
121	Bapaume (FR) *W.P.Mullins,Ireland* 6-11-10 P.Townend	16/1	1¼	4
127	Wholestone (IRE) *NigelTwiston-Davies* 8-11-10 SamTwiston-Davies	33/1	11	5
	Bacardys (FR) *W.P.Mullins,Ireland* 8-11-10 MrP.W.Mullins	20/1	3½	6
134	Supasundae *MrsJ.Harrington,Ireland* 9-11-10 (t) RobbiePower	9/1	1¼	7
127	The Mighty Don (IRE) *NickGifford* 7-11-10 LeightonAspell	66/1	1¼	8
127	West Approach *ColinTizzard* 9-11-10 TomScudamore	33/1	6	9
142	Keeper Hill (IRE) *WarrenGreatrex* 8-11-10 RichardJohnson	66/1	2½	10
49	Kilbricken Storm (IRE) *ColinTizzard* 8-11-10 (t) HarryCobden	16/1	2	11
127	Black Op (IRE) *TomGeorge* 8-11-10 (t) NoelFehily	14/1	2¼	12
160	Yanworth *AlanKing* 9-11-10 (b) BarryGeraghty	33/1	½	13
134	Petit Mouchoir (FR) *HenrydeBromhead,Ireland* 8-11-10 RachaelBlackmore	25/1	¾	14
77	Top Notch (FR) *NickyHenderson* 8-11-10 DarylJacob	12/1	¾	15
160	Man of Plenty *SophieLeech* 10-11-10 (b+t) JonathanBurke	200/1	4	16
164	Coquin Mans (FR) *W.P.Mullins,Ireland* 7-11-10 D.J.Mullins	100/1	13	17
19	Nautical Nitwit (IRE) *PhilipKirby* 10-11-10 (s) ThomasDowson	100/1	15	18

Mr Andrew Gemmell 18ran 5m52.80

196 Brown Advisory & Merriebelle Stable Plate Handicap Chase (Gr 3) (1) (5yo+) £61,897 2½m127y (17)

124	SIRUH DU LAC (FR) *NickWilliams* 6-10-11[141] LizzieKelly(3)	9/2		1
124	JANIKA (FR) *NickyHenderson* 6-11-12[156] DarylJacob	3/1f	¾	2
47	SPIRITOFTHEGAMES (IRE) *DanSkelton* 7-11-3[147] (s) HarrySkelton	6/1	2¼	3
33	Eamon An Cnoic (IRE) *DavidPipe* 8-10-7[137] (s+t) TomScudamore	10/1	½	4
169	Didero Vallis (FR) *VenetiaWilliams* 6-10-5[135] CharlieDeutsch	16/1	8	5
	Bouvreuil (FR) *BenHaslam* 8-10-12[142] (h+t) RichieMcLernon	33/1	2½	6
10	Azzerti (FR) *AlanKing* 7-10-7[137] WayneHutchinson	20/1	1½	7
26	Kauto Riko (FR) *TomGretton* 8-11-1[145] DavidNoonan	66/1	3¼	8
	Some Buckle (IRE) *RichardBandey* 10-10-10[140] (t) HarryBannister	66/1	hd	9
53	Templehills (IRE) *NigelTwiston-Davies* 8-10-10[140] (h) TomBellamy	100/1	ns	10
113	Doitforthevillage (IRE) *PaulHenderson* 10-10-10[140] (t) PaddyBrennan	16/1	½	11
	Bigmartre (FR) *HarryWhittington* 8-11-0[144] (s) GavinSheehan	40/1	1¾	12
122	Polidam (FR) *W.P.Mullins,Ireland* 10-10-13[143] P.Townend	33/1	¾	13
149	Valseur Lido (FR) *HenrydeBromhead,Ireland* 10-11-1[145] (s) RachaelBlackmore	33/1	16	14
61	Voix d'Eau (FR) *LucindaRussell* 9-10-9[139] (s+t) CallumBewley	100/1	3	15
169	Modus *PaulNicholls* 9-11-3[147] BarryGeraghty	20/1	6	16
33	Splash of Ginge *NigelTwiston-Davies* 11-10-7[137] SamTwiston-Davies	25/1	12	17
26	King's Odyssey (IRE) *EvanWilliams* 10-10-7[137] AdamWedge	20/1		F
43	Gardefort (FR) *VenetiaWilliams* 8-10-7[137] HughNugent(5)	28/1		pu
53	Testify (IRE) *DonaldMcCain* 8-10-9[139] (b) WilliamKennedy	33/1		pu
33	Kalondra (IRE) *NeilMulholland* 8-11-3[147] (t) NoelFehily	12/1		pu
	River Wylde (IRE) *NickyHenderson* 8-11-6[150] NicodeBoinville	10/1		pu

John White & Anne Underhill 22ran 5m13.90

197 National Hunt Breeders Supported By Tattersalls Mares' Novices' Hurdle (Dawn Run) (Gr 2) (1) (4yo+) £50,643 2m179y (8)

	EGLANTINE DU SEUIL (FR) *W.P.Mullins,Ireland* 5-11-2 NoelFehily	50/1		1
	CONCERTISTA (FR) *W.P.Mullins,Ireland* 5-11-2 D.E.Mullins	66/1	sh	2
92	TINTANGLE (IRE) *GordonElliott,Ireland* 6-11-5 (s) J.W.Kennedy	40/1	1¾	3
	Black Tears *GordonElliott,Ireland* 5-11-2 DavyRussell	25/1	hd	4
130	Indefatigable (IRE) *PaulWebber* 6-11-2 GavinSheehan	33/1	3¼	5
	Elfile (FR) *W.P.Mullins,Ireland* 5-11-2 P.Townend	50/1	hd	6
	Presidente Line (FR) *AlainCouetil,France* 5-11-5 AlexisPoirier	100/1	3	7
	Posh Trish (IRE) *PaulNicholls* 6-11-7 HarryCobden	3/1	1	8
	Epatante (FR) *NickyHenderson* 5-11-2 (h) BarryGeraghty	15/8f	nk	9
153	Queenohearts (IRE) *StuartEdmunds* 6-11-7 CiaranGethings	10/1	hd	10
111	Buildmeupbuttercup *W.P.Mullins,Ireland* 5-11-2 BrianHayes	66/1	¾	11
143	Court Maid (IRE) *ThomasMullins,Ireland* 6-11-5 D.J.Mullins	100/1	hd	12
	My Sister Sarah (IRE) *W.P.Mullins,Ireland* 5-11-2 R.Walsh	13/2	sh	13
	Elusive Belle (IRE) *NickyHenderson* 5-11-2 (h) MrSamWaley-Cohen	20/1	10	14
	Lust For Glory (IRE) *NickyHenderson* 5-11-2 NicodeBoinville	20/1	1½	15
	Diamond Gait *KimBailey* 6-11-2 (t) DavidBass	100/1	2¼	16
	Allez Dance (FR) *W.P.Mullins,Ireland* 5-11-2 DarylJacob	40/1	2½	17
	Awayinthewest (IRE) *P.A.Fahy,Ireland* 7-11-2 JodyMcGarvey	100/1	10	18
	Sinoria (IRE) *HenrydeBromhead,Ireland* 6-11-7 RachaelBlackmore	11/1	12	19
	Dame du Soir (FR) *DavidBridgwater* 6-11-2 TomScudamore	100/1		pu
	Emily Moon (IRE) *MrsJ.Harrington,Ireland* 5-11-2 RobbiePower	25/1		pu

92	Sancta Simona (FR) *W.P.Mullins,Ireland* 6-11-7 (h+t) M.P.Walsh	20/1		pu
	Sullivan Bloodstock Limited 22ran 4m03.90			

198 Fulke Walwyn Kim Muir Challenge Cup Amateur Riders' Handicap Chase (2) 3¼m (22)
(145) (5yo+) £41,510

165	ANY SECOND NOW (IRE) *T.M.Walsh,Ireland* 7-11-11^{143} (b) MrDerekO'Connor	6/1		1
	KILFILUM CROSS (IRE) *HenryOliver* 8-11-7^{139} MrAlexEdwards	7/1	3¾	2
51	THE YOUNG MASTER *NeilMulholland* 10-11-10^{142} (s) MrSamWaley-Cohen	22/1	3½	3
155	Crievehill (IRE) *NigelTwiston-Davies* 7-11-8^{140} MrZacBaker	40/1	5	4
	No Comment *PhilipHobbs* 8-11-6^{138} (h) MrM.J.O'Hare	12/1	2¼	5
86	Captain Chaos (IRE) *DanSkelton* 8-11-3^{135} (b) MissGinaAndrews	20/1	¾	6
	Sky Pirate *JonjoO'Neill* 6-11-2^{134} MrTommieM.O'Brien	16/1	2	7
	Measureofmydreams (IRE) *GordonElliott,Ireland* 11-11-5^{137} MrJ.J.Codd	3/1f	½	8
	Touch Kick (IRE) *PaulNicholls* 8-11-1^{133} (t) MrWilliamBiddick	11/1	½	9
	Just A Sting (IRE) *HarryFry* 7-11-5^{137} MrMichaelLegg	16/1	4	10
161	Ah Littleluck (IRE) *T.Gibney,Ireland* 9-11-3^{135} (t) MrN.McParlan	50/1	5	11
149	Livelovelaugh (IRE) *W.P.Mullins,Ireland* 9-11-12^{144} MrP.W.Mullins	16/1	8	12
93	Rogue Angel (IRE) *GordonElliott,Ireland* 11-11-5^{137} (b+t) MsL.O'Neill	20/1	2¾	13
23	Sumkindofking (IRE) *TomGeorge* 8-11-5^{137} (t) MrNoelGeorge(3)	66/1	3¼	14
12	Its All Guesswork (IRE) *GordonElliott,Ireland* 7-11-1^{133} (t) MrBarryO'Neill	12/1	5	15
	Uhlan Bute (FR) *VenetiaWilliams* 11-11-1^{133} (s) MissLucyTurner(5)	50/1	1¼	16
	Treackle Tart (IRE) *CharlieLongsdon* 7-11-3^{135} MrE.P.O'Brien(3)	25/1	22	17
93	Drumconnor Lad (IRE) *A.P.Keatley,Ireland* 9-11-1^{133} (v+t) MrJ.C.Barry	100/1		F
151	Arkwrisht (FR) *JosephPatrickO'Brien,Ireland* 9-11-6^{138} (t) MrT.Hamilton	33/1		F
149	Speaker Connolly (IRE) *AlanFleming,Ireland* 6-11-7^{139} MrRichardDeegan	14/1		ur
93	Squouateur (FR) *BenHaslam* 8-11-6^{138} (t) MrH.D.Dunne	33/1		pu
32	Perfect Candidate (IRE) *FergalO'Brien* 12-11-8^{140} (s) MissBrodieHampson	25/1		pu
	Pearl Royale (IRE) *NigelHawke* 7-11-9^{141} MrKierenBuckley(7)	66/1		pu
	Mr John P. McManus 23ran 6m48.80			

CHELTENHAM Friday, Mar 15 GOOD to SOFT

199 JCB Triumph Hurdle (Gr 1) (1) (4yo) £70,337 2m179y (8)

	PENTLAND HILLS (IRE) *NickyHenderson* 4-11-0 NicodeBoinville	20/1		1
83	COEUR SUBLIME (IRE) *GordonElliott,Ireland* 4-11-0 DavyRussell	20/1	3	2
144	GARDENS OF BABYLON (IRE) *JosephPatrickO'Brien,Ireland* 4-11-0 (s+t) BarryGeraghty	9/1	3¾	3
123	Nelson River *TonyCarroll* 4-11-0 HarryBannister	66/1	3	4
87	Quel Destin (FR) *PaulNicholls* 4-11-0 HarryCobden	4/1	1	5
167	Ecco *PaulNicholls* 4-11-0 HarrySkelton	100/1	1½	6
123	Adjali (GER) *NickyHenderson* 4-11-0 DarylJacob	16/1	1½	7
	French Made (FR) *W.P.Mullins,Ireland* 4-10-7 P.Townend	40/1	1½	8
144	Tiger Tap Tap (GER) *W.P.Mullins,Ireland* 4-11-0 R.Walsh	7/1	nk	9
	Pic d'Orhy (FR) *PaulNicholls* 4-11-0 (t) SamTwiston-Davies	12/1	5	10
	Runrized (FR) *W.P.Mullins,Ireland* 4-11-0 D.J.Mullins	66/1	5	11
171	Hannon (IRE) *JohnMcConnell,Ireland* 4-11-0 (t) DavidNoonan	25/1	4½	12
	Authorizo (FR) *GordonElliott,Ireland* 4-11-0 (t) J.W.Kennedy	50/1		pu
144	Sir Erec (IRE) *JosephPatrickO'Brien,Ireland* 4-11-0 M.P.Walsh	11/10f		pu
	Owners Group 031 14ran 4m04.80			

200 Randox Health County Handicap Hurdle (Gr 3) (1) (5yo+) £56,270 2m179y (8)

	CH'TIBELLO (FR) *DanSkelton* 8-11-5^{146} HarrySkelton	12/1		1
71	WE HAVE A DREAM (FR) *NickyHenderson* 5-11-11^{152} DarylJacob	14/1	1½	2
	COUNTISTER (FR) *NickyHenderson* 7-10-6^{133} BarryGeraghty	18/1	hd	3
5	Whiskey Sour (IRE) *W.P.Mullins,Ireland* 6-11-3^{144} R.Walsh	5/1f	4½	4
157	Lisp (IRE) *AlanKing* 5-11-4^{145} WayneHutchinson	25/1	2½	5
	Sternrubin (GER) *PhilipHobbs* 8-10-13^{140} (s) MichealNolan	25/1	hd	6
117	Mohaayed *DanSkelton* 7-11-12^{153} (s+t) BridgetAndrews	40/1	sh	7
25	Mr Adjudicator *W.P.Mullins,Ireland* 5-11-8^{149} P.Townend	10/1	1	8
135	Due Reward (IRE) *HenrydeBromhead,Ireland* 6-10-9^{136} RachaelBlackmore	33/1	hd	9
176	Monsieur Lecoq (FR) *MrsJaneWilliams* 5-10-6^{133} LizzieKelly(3)	13/2	¾	10
143	Cut The Mustard (FR) *W.P.Mullins,Ireland* 7-10-10^{137} (h) NoelFehily	20/1	1¼	11
57	Brex Drago (ITY) *GavinPatrickCromwell,Ireland* 7-10-2^{129} (s) J.B.Kane(5)	66/1	1	12
75	Thistle Do Nicely (IRE) *JamieSnowden* 5-10-5^{132} GavinSheehan	28/1	nk	13
5	Leoncavallo (IRE) *DrRichardNewland* 7-11-3^{144} (b) SamTwiston-Davies	20/1	sh	14
117	Western Ryder (IRE) *WarrenGreatrex* 7-11-9^{150} (b) HarryTeal(5)	20/1	1	15
	Mister Fizz *MissImogenPickard* 11-11-3^{144} (s) LorcanWilliams(5)	100/1	½	16
1	Capitaine (FR) *PaulNicholls* 7-10-10^{137} (t) HarryCobden	12/1	1½	17
176	Storm Rising (IRE) *DrRichardNewland* 6-10-8^{135} (b) CharlieHammond(5)	33/1	8	18
	High Expectations (FR) *GordonElliott,Ireland* 8-10-6^{133} DenisO'Regan	40/1	10	19
	Crooks Peak *PhilipHobbs* 6-10-11^{138} RichardJohnson	8/1	4½	20

Chieftain's Choice (IRE) *KevinFrost* 10-10-0 (9-10)[127] (b) SamColtherd(3) ......100/1 | ½ 21
117 Pingshou (IRE) *ColinTizzard* 9-11-1[142] (b+t) RobbiePower ....33/1 | 19 22
135 Eclair de Beaufeu (FR) *GordonElliott,Ireland* 5-10-9[136] J.W.Kennedy ....8/1 | ur
135 Mitchouka (FR) *GordonElliott,Ireland* 5-11-1[142] DavyRussell ....33/1 | pu
The Can't Say No Partnership 24ran 4m05.50

201 Albert Bartlett Novices' Hurdle (Spa) (Gr 1) (1) (4yo+) £73,506   2m7f213y (12)

MINELLA INDO (IRE) *HenrydeBromhead,Ireland* 6-11-5 RachaelBlackmore ..50/1 | 1
133 COMMANDER OF FLEET (IRE) *GordonElliott,Ireland* 5-11-5 J.W.Kennedy .. 4/1f | 2 2
ALLAHO (FR) *W.P.Mullins,Ireland* 5-11-5 R.Walsh ....8/1 | 7 3
Dickie Diver (IRE) *NickyHenderson* 6-11-5 AidanColeman ....14/1 | 1¾ 4
162 Lisnagar Oscar (IRE) *RebeccaCurtis* 6-11-5 SeanBowen ....13/2 | 5 5
98 Derrinross (IRE) *J.P.Dempsey,Ireland* 8-11-5 (t) LukeDempsey ....12/1 | 7 6
133 Salsaretta (FR) *W.P.Mullins,Ireland* 6-10-12 P.Townend ....25/1 | ¾ 7
127 Aye Aye Charlie *FergalO'Brien* 7-11-5 (t) PaddyBrennan ....33/1 | 2 8
98 Cap York (FR) *NoelMeade,Ireland* 7-11-5 B.J.Cooper ....33/1 | nk 9
162 Ask Ben (IRE) *GraemeMcPherson* 6-11-5 KielanWoods ....33/1 | nk 10
133 First Approach (IRE) *NoelMeade,Ireland* 6-11-5 (s) SeanFlanagan ....25/1 | 4 11
129 Nadaitak (FR) *BenPauling* 5-11-5 (s) NicodeBoinville ....33/1 | hd 12
133 Dorrells Pierji (FR) *W.P.Mullins,Ireland* 6-11-5 NoelFehily ....25/1 | 13 13
162 Rockpoint *ColinTizzard* 6-11-5 TomScudamore ....33/1 | 7 14
99 Alsa Mix (FR) *AlanKing* 7-10-12 (h) WayneHutchinson ....100/1 | pu
126 Birchdale (IRE) *NickyHenderson* 5-11-5 BarryGeraghty ....6/1 | pu
58 Darlac (FR) *ColinTizzard* 6-11-5 (s) RobbiePower ....100/1 | pu
Dinons (FR) *GordonElliott,Ireland* 6-11-5 DavyRussell ....9/1 | pu
133 Rhinestone (IRE) *JosephPatrickO'Brien,Ireland* 6-11-5 (t) M.P.Walsh ....17/2 | pu
162 Stoney Mountain (IRE) *HenryDaly* 6-11-5 RichardJohnson ....16/1 | pu
Mr Barry Maloney 20ran 5m58.20

202 Magners Cheltenham Gold Cup Chase (Gr 1) (1) (5yo+) £351,687   3¼m70y (21)

What should have been the third last fence was omitted due to a stricken horse

AL BOUM PHOTO (FR) *W.P.Mullins,Ireland* 7-11-10 P.Townend ....12/1 | 1
159 ANIBALE FLY (FR) *A.J.Martin,Ireland* 9-11-10 (t) BarryGeraghty ....22/1 | 2½ 2
82 BRISTOL DE MAI (FR) *NigelTwiston-Davies* 8-11-10 DarylJacob ....18/1 | 3¾ 3
82 Native River (IRE) *ColinTizzard* 9-11-10 (s) RichardJohnson ....6/1 | 3 4
156 Clan des Obeaux (FR) *PaulNicholls* 7-11-10 HarryCobden ....5/1 | 1¾ 5
125 Elegant Escape (IRE) *ColinTizzard* 7-11-10 TomO'Brien ....20/1 | 15 6
161 Yala Enki (FR) *VenetiaWilliams* 9-11-10 CharlieDeutsch ....100/1 | 3½ 7
121 Presenting Percy *PatrickG.Kelly,Ireland* 8-11-10 (t) DavyRussell ....10/3f | 3½ 8
95 Shattered Love (IRE) *GordonElliott,Ireland* 8-11-3 (t) J.W.Kennedy ....20/1 | 2¾ 9
122 Invitation Only (IRE) *W.P.Mullins,Ireland* 8-11-10 MrP.W.Mullins ....33/1 | F
95 Kemboy (FR) *W.P.Mullins,Ireland* 7-11-10 D.J.Mullins ....8/1 | ur
60 Definitly Red (IRE) *BrianEllison* 10-11-10 DannyCook ....50/1 | bd
148 Bellshill (IRE) *W.P.Mullins,Ireland* 9-11-10 R.Walsh ....9/1 | pu
169 Double Shuffle (IRE) *TomGeorge* 9-11-10 (h) JonathanBurke ....100/1 | pu
82 Might Bite (IRE) *NickyHenderson* 10-11-10 NicodeBoinville ....14/1 | pu
82 Thistlecrack *ColinTizzard* 11-11-10 TomScudamore ....12/1 | pu
Mrs J. Donnelly 16ran 6m39.20

203 St James's Place Foxhunter Challenge Cup Open Hunters' Chase (2) (5yo+)   3¼m70y (22)
£26,685

HAZEL HILL (IRE) *PhilipRowley* 11-12-0 MrAlexEdwards ....7/2f | 1
SHANTOU FLYER (IRE) *RichardHobson* 9-12-0 (b+t) MrDavidMaxwell ....7/1 | 4 2
TOP WOOD (FR) *KellyMorgan* 12-12-0 (v+t) TabithaWorsley ....33/1 | 7 3
Road To Rome (IRE) *J.J.O'Shea* 9-12-0 MrSamWaley-Cohen ....7/1 | 4½ 4
Ucello Conti (FR) *GordonElliott,Ireland* 11-12-0 (t) MrJ.J.Codd ....4/1 | 8 5
Stand Up And Fight (IRE) *EndaBolger,Ireland* 7-12-0 MrDerekO'Connor ......13/2 | 2½ 6
Dont Do Mondays (IRE) *MrsLibbyLawson* 12-12-0 MrOswaldWedmore ....100/1 | 14 7
Asockastar (IRE) *DanielJohnBourne* 11-12-0 (s) MrBarryO'Neill ....66/1 | 5 8
Southfield Theatre (IRE) *MrsSaraV.Bradstock* 11-12-0 (b) MissLilyBradstock ..40/1 | 3 9
Ardkilly Witness (IRE) *MissK.L.Smith* 13-12-0 MrWilliamThirlby ....100/1 | ur
Some Are Lucky (IRE) *S.Curling,Ireland* 8-12-0 MrG.Spain ....66/1 | ur
Timewaitsfornoone (IRE) *AlanFleming,Ireland* 7-12-0 MrRichardDeegan ......40/1 | ur
Balnaslow (IRE) *GrahamMcKeever,Ireland* 12-12-0 MrP.W.Mullins ....50/1 | pu
Caid du Berlais (FR) *MrsRoseLoxton* 10-12-0 (t) MrWilliamBiddick ....7/1 | pu
Chosen Dream (IRE) *GrahamMcKeever,Ireland* 11-12-0 (t) MrM.J.O'Hare ......66/1 | pu
Coastal Tiep (FR) *StuartCrawford,Ireland* 7-12-0 (s) MrB.G.Crawford ....66/1 | pu
Cousin Pete *MrsElizabethBrown* 11-12-0 (t) MrNickPhillips ....22/1 | pu
Double Whammy *IainJardine* 13-12-0 (b) MrT.Hamilton ....66/1 | pu
7 Haymount (IRE) *T.Ellis* 10-12-0 (s+t) MissGinaAndrews ....20/1 | pu

Just Cause (IRE) *J.P.Owen* 9-12-0 MrJackAndrews ....100/1 pu
One Conemara (IRE) *MrsC.A.Coward* 11-12-0 (s) MrJohnDawson ....100/1 pu
Pacha du Polder (FR) *PaulNicholls* 12-12-0 MissHarrietTucker ....16/1 pu
Samanntom (IRE) *P.M.J.Doyle,Ireland* 11-12-0 (s+t) MissS.M.Doyle ....100/1 pu
Sybarite (FR) *MissV.Collins* 13-12-0 MissLillyPinchin ....100/1 pu
Mrs D. Williams 24ran 6m51.10

204 Johnny Henderson Grand Annual Challenge Cup Handicap Chase (Gr 3) (1) 2m62y (14)
(5yo+) £61,897

CROCO BAY (IRE) *BenCase* 12-10-12^{139} (s) KielanWoods 66/1 1
BUN DORAN (IRE) *TomGeorge* 8-11-7^{148} PaddyBrennan 11/1 1½ 2
124 BRELAN D'AS (FR) *PaulNicholls* 8-10-9^{136} (t) BryonyFrost 8/1 2½ 3
36 Forest Bihan (FR) *BrianEllison* 8-11-12^{153} (s) DannyCook 33/1 1 4
Not Another Muddle *GaryMoore* 8-10-11^{138} JamieMoore 6/1 3½ 5
13 Theo (IRE) *DrRichardNewland* 9-10-12^{139} (h) CharlieHammond(5) 33/1 1¼ 6
50 Whatswrongwithyou (IRE) *NickyHenderson* 8-11-4^{145} (h) NicodeBoinville ....8/1 nk 7
43 Marracudja (FR) *DanSkelton* 8-10-12^{139} (t) HarrySkelton 11/1 1½ 8
43 Champagne At Tara *JonjoO'Neill* 10-11-2^{143} JonjoO'NeillJr.(5) 33/1 1¼ 9
Magic Saint (FR) *PaulNicholls* 5-11-8^{149} HarryCobden 9/2f 4½ 10
36 Le Prezien (FR) *PaulNicholls* 8-11-10^{151} (t) BarryGeraghty ....8/1 nk 11
Tree of Liberty (IRE) *KerryLee* 7-11-6^{147} RichardPatrick(3) 33/1 4 12
43 Caid du Lin (FR) *DrRichardNewland* 7-11-3^{144} (s+t) SamTwiston-Davies 25/1 1½ 13
Top Gamble (IRE) *KerryLee* 11-11-2^{143} (s+t) MarkEnright 18/1 16 14
Theflyingportrait (IRE) *JennieCandlish* 10-11-3^{144} (t) SeanQuinlan 50/1 3 15
1 All Set To Go (IRE) *KevinFrost* 8-10-7^{134} (b+t) GavinSheehan ....50/1 pu
113 Mr Medic *RobertWalford* 8-11-0^{141} JamesBest ....33/1 pu
139 Mind's Eye (IRE) *HenrydeBromhead,Ireland* 7-11-1^{142} RachaelBlackmore ....7/1 pu
Gino Trail (IRE) *KerryLee* 12-11-11^{152} (s) RichardJohnson ....14/1 pu
Lady Jane Grosvenor 19ran 4m06.30

205 Martin Pipe Conditional Jockeys' Handicap Hurdle (2) (145) (4yo+) £43,330 2½m56y (10)

94 EARLY DOORS (FR) *JosephPatrickO'Brien,Ireland* 6-11-10^{145} JonjoO'NeillJr. ..5/1 1
146 DALLAS DES PICTONS (FR) *GordonElliott,Ireland* 6-11-5^{140} DonaghMeyler .. 7/2f 1¼ 2
133 DEFI BLEU (FR) *GordonElliott,Ireland* 6-11-4^{139} C.Brassil 14/1 4 3
107 Champagne Court (IRE) *JeremyScott* 6-10-5^{126} RexDingle 14/1 7 4
99 Coolanly (IRE) *FergalO'Brien* 7-11-5^{140} ConnorBrace 20/1 1¼ 5
135 Cartwright *GordonElliott,Ireland* 6-11-2^{137} (b) FergusGregory 9/1 1¾ 6
Doctor Dex (IRE) *TomGeorge* 6-10-8^{129} LorcanWilliams 33/1 1¼ 7
Discordantly (IRE) *MrsJ.Harrington,Ireland* 5-11-3^{138} ConorOrr ....25/1 hd 8
Burrows Park (FR) *VenetiaWilliams* 7-10-7^{128} HughNugent ....25/1 ¾ 9
Style de Garde (FR) *NickyHenderson* 5-11-5^{140} (h) NedCurtis ....25/1 ½ 10
30 Pym (IRE) *NickyHenderson* 6-11-3^{138} RichardPatrick 12/1 1¼ 11
142 Mr Antolini (IRE) *NigelTwiston-Davies* 9-11-5^{140} JordanNailor ....33/1 ¾ 12
Le Musee (FR) *NigelHawke* 6-10-11^{132} TomBuckley 33/1 3 13
Casa Tall (FR) *TomGeorge* 5-10-7^{128} (h) KieronEdgar 40/1 1¾ 14
Sakhee's City (FR) *PhilipKirby* 8-10-9^{130} (s) ThomasDowson 50/1 4½ 15
77 Garo de Juilley (FR) *SophieLeech* 7-11-3^{138} (t) SeanHoulihan 28/1 3¾ 16
Acapella Bourgeois (FR) *W.P.Mullins,Ireland* 9-11-9^{144} (h) R.A.Doyle 25/1 11 17
Big Time Dancer (IRE) *JennieCandlish* 6-10-13^{134} RossChapman ....33/1 sh 18
133 Getareason (IRE) *W.P.Mullins,Ireland* 6-11-5^{140} L.P.Gilligan ....9/1 ½ 19
30 Kapgarry (FR) *NigelTwiston-Davies* 6-10-6^{127} StanSheppard 66/1 3¼ 20
Daybreak Boy (IRE) *HenrydeBromhead,Ireland* 6-11-3^{138} D.J.McInerney 16/1 1½ 21
37 Not That Fuisse (FR) *DanSkelton* 6-10-10^{131} WilliamMarshall ....33/1 F
112 If You Say Run (IRE) *PaulNicholls* 7-11-6^{141} (s+t) BryonyFrost ....14/1 pu
Mount Mews (IRE) *DonaldMcCain* 8-11-2^{137} DannyMcMenamin ....33/1 rr
Mr John P. McManus 24ran 5m02.90

UTTOXETER Saturday, Mar 16 HEAVY

206 Marston's 61 Deep Midlands Grand National (Open Handicap Chase) (L) (1) 4¼m8y (25)
(5yo+) £84,405

POTTERS CORNER (IRE) *ChristianWilliams* 9-10-7^{135} (s) JamesBowen 20/1 1
51 MS PARFOIS (IRE) *AnthonyHoneyball* 8-11-4^{146} (t) AidanColeman 8/1 3 2
113 GET ON THE YAGER *DanSkelton* 9-10-5^{133} HarrySkelton 12/1 12 3
Prime Venture (IRE) *EvanWilliams* 8-10-11^{139} AdamWedge 20/1 3 4
88 Dawson City *PollyGundry* 10-10-11^{139} TomBellamy 12/1 2¼ 5
142 Folsom Blue (IRE) *GordonElliott,Ireland* 12-11-2^{144} (s+t) DavyRussell .... 6/1f ¾ 6
Back To The Thatch (IRE) *HenryDaly* 7-10-5^{133} RichardJohnson ....7/1 F
Jetstream Jack (IRE) *SophieLeech* 9-10-0 (9-12)^{128} (s) ConnorBrace(7) ....66/1 pu
151 Kilkishen (IRE) *JohnJosephHanlon,Ireland* 9-10-5^{133} (s) D.E.Mullins ....25/1 pu
161 Chef d'Oeuvre (FR) *SamEngland* 8-10-6^{134} JonathanEngland ....10/1 pu

78	Jammin Masters (IRE) *WarrenGreatrex* 8-10-9^{137} GavinSheehan	20/1		pu
108	Milansbar (IRE) *NeilKing* 12-10-9^{137} (b) BryonyFrost	13/2		pu
88	Regal Flow *BobBuckler* 12-10-9^{137} SeanHoulihan(3)	22/1		pu
88	Raz de Maree (FR) *GavinPatrickCromwell,Ireland* 14-10-9^{137} ConorOrr(5)	20/1		pu
	Arthur's Gift (IRE) *NigelTwiston-Davies* 8-10-10^{138} SamTwiston-Davies	10/1		pu
155	Smooth Stepper *AlexHales* 10-10-12^{140} CiaranGethings	50/1		pu
7	Dell' Arca (IRE) *DavidPipe* 10-10-12^{140} (b+t) TomScudamore	20/1		pu
118	Ballydine (IRE) *CharlieLongsdon* 9-10-12^{140} (s+t) SeanBowen	12/1		pu
51	American (FR) *HarryFry* 9-11-12^{154} NoelFehily	9/1		pu

All Stars Sports Racing & J Davies 19ran 9m39.70

LIMERICK Sunday, Mar 17 HEAVY

207 Charleville Cheese Irish European Breeders Fund Mares Novices' Chase (Dawn Run) (Gr 2) (5yo+) £26,495 — 2¾m120y (14)

	MOYHENNA (IRE) *DenisHogan* 7-11-0 D.G.Hogan	5/1		1
120	OH ME OH MY (IRE) *MsM.Flynn* 8-11-0 J.J.Slevin	33/1	25	2
	REDHOTFILLYPEPPERS (IRE) *W.P.Mullins* 7-11-0 P.Townend	6/5f	7½	3
	Sweet Destination (IRE) *G.Ahern* 7-11-0 (s) D.E.Mullins	50/1	31	4
55	Dawn Shadow (IRE) *MrsD.A.Love* 7-11-0 RachaelBlackmore	8/1		pu
	Missy Tata (FR) *GordonElliott* 7-11-0 DavyRussell	7/4		pu

Mr Robert Hennelly 6ran 6m01.50

NAVAN Monday, Mar 18 SOFT

208 toals.com Webster Cup Chase (Gr 2) (5yo+) £23,076 — 2m (11)

121	DARASSO (FR) *JosephPatrickO'Brien* 6-11-5 BarryGeraghty	evsf		1
149	CADMIUM (FR) *W.P.Mullins* 7-11-10 R.Walsh	2/1	2¼	2
	BALL D'ARC (FR) *GordonElliott* 8-11-8 KeithDonoghue	9/1	19	3
139	Tycoon Prince (IRE) *GordonElliott* 9-11-5 (t) DavyRussell	20/1	1½	4
16	Woodland Opera (IRE) *MrsJ.Harrington* 9-11-10 (b+t) P.Townend	4/1	20	5

Mr John P. McManus 5ran 4m07.50

NEWBURY Saturday, Mar 23 GOOD to SOFT

209 Goffs UK Spring Sale Bumper (Standard Open National Hunt Flat) (2) (4 and 5yo) £30,000 — 2m69y

	GET IN THE QUEUE *HarryFry* 5-11-10 NoelFehily	1/3f		1
	PRINCE LLYWELYN *KimBailey* 5-11-7 DavidBass	6/1	4½	2
	FUGITIVES DRIFT (IRE) *NickyHenderson* 4-10-10 NicodeBoinville	10/1	1¼	3
	Versatility *NickyHenderson* 5-11-3 JeremiahMcGrath	33/1	3½	4
	Legends Ryde *JamieSnowden* 4-10-3 GavinSheehan	14/1	¾	5
	Hotter Than Hell (FR) *AlanKing* 5-10-10 WayneHutchinson	8/1	12	6
	Donladd (IRE) *OliverSherwood* 5-11-3 LeightonAspell	50/1	16	7
	Frippon de Vaige (FR) *PaulWebber* 4-10-10 TomO'Brien	50/1	2¾	8
	Call Off The Dogs (IRE) *GaryMoore* 4-10-10 JamieMoore	33/1	sh	9
	Nye Bevan (IRE) *NigelTwiston-Davies* 4-10-10 SamTwiston-Davies	33/1	3½	10
	Magna Sam *SteveFlook* 5-11-3 CharlieTodd	100/1	1¾	11
	Ben Buie (IRE) *MartinKeighley* 5-11-3 RichardJohnson	20/1	33	12
	Dreamsundermyfeet (IRE) *MartinKeighley* 4-10-10 HarryStock	66/1	53	13

Paul & Clare Rooney 13ran 3m54.70

AINTREE Thursday, Apr 4 GOOD to SOFT

210 Devenish Manifesto Novices' Chase (Gr 1) (1) (5yo+) £56,130 — 2m3f200y (16)

179	KALASHNIKOV (IRE) *AmyMurphy* 6-11-4 JackQuinlan	4/1		1
147	LA BAGUE AU ROI (FR) *WarrenGreatrex* 8-10-11 RichardJohnson	7/4f	1¼	2
192	MENGLI KHAN (IRE) *GordonElliott,Ireland* 6-11-4 (t) J.W.Kennedy	7/1	1¾	3
166	Bags Groove (IRE) *HarryFry* 8-11-4 (t) SeanBowen	11/2	27	4
196	Spiritofthegames (IRE) *DanSkelton* 7-11-4 (s) HarrySkelton	8/1	2¾	5
179	Glen Forsa (IRE) *MickChannon* 7-11-4 JonathanBurke	11/2		pu

Mr Paul Murphy 6ran 5m05.80

211 Doom Bar Anniversary 4-Y-O Juvenile Hurdle (Gr 1) (1) (4yo) £56,130 — 2m209y (9)

199	PENTLAND HILLS (IRE) *NickyHenderson* 4-11-0 NicodeBoinville	11/4		1
178	FAKIR D'OUDAIRIES (FR) *JosephPatrickO'Brien,Ireland* 4-11-0 M.P.Walsh	5/2	nk	2
	CHRISTOPHER WOOD (IRE) *PaulNicholls* 4-11-0 HarryCobden	10/1	6	3
199	Adjali (GER) *NickyHenderson* 4-11-0 DarylJacob	14/1	nk	4
190	Band of Outlaws (IRE) *JosephPatrickO'Brien,Ireland* 4-11-0 J.J.Slevin	9/4f	4½	5
	Song For Someone (GER) *TomSymonds* 4-11-0 AidanColeman	25/1	15	6
190	Fanfan du Seuil (FR) *TomGeorge* 4-11-0 PaddyBrennan	20/1	5	7
	Statuario *PeterBowen* 4-11-0 SeanBowen	100/1	29	8
167	Beat The Judge (IRE) *GaryMoore* 4-11-0 JoshuaMoore	40/1		pu

Owners Group 031 9ran 4m14.10

212 Betway Bowl Chase (Gr 1) (1) (5yo+) £112,260   3m210y (19)

202	KEMBOY (FR) *W.P.Mullins,Ireland* 7-11-7 R.Walsh	9/4f		1
202	CLAN DES OBEAUX (FR) *PaulNicholls* 5-11-7 HarryCobden	11/4	9	2
194	BALKO DES FLOS (FR) *HenrydeBromhead,Ireland* 8-11-7 RachaelBlackmore	.20/1	hd	3
202	Bristol de Mai (FR) *NigelTwiston-Davies* 8-11-7 DarylJacob	.7/2	1	4
194	Road To Respect (IRE) *NoelMeade,Ireland* 8-11-7 SeanFlanagan	9/2	5	5
202	Elegant Escape (IRE) *ColinTizzard* 7-11-7 TomO'Brien	10/1	40	6

Supreme Racing/Brett Graham/Ken Sharp 6ran 6m35.20

213 Betway Aintree Hurdle (Gr 1) (1) (4yo+) £140,325   2½m (11)

195	SUPASUNDAE (*MrsJ.Harrington,Ireland* 9-11-7 (t) RobbiePower	15/2		1
181	BUVEUR D'AIR (FR) *NickyHenderson* 8-11-7 BarryGeraghty	5/6f	1¼	2
200	CH'TIBELLO (FR) *DanSkelton* 8-11-7 HarrySkelton	14/1	½	3
71	Summerville Boy (IRE) *TomGeorge* 7-11-7 JonathanBurke	25/1	31	4
181	Silver Streak (IRE) *EvanWilliams* 6-11-7 AdamWedge	25/1	10	5
181	Melon *W.P.Mullins,Ireland* 7-11-7 (s) P.Townend	8/1		F
195	Faugheen (IRE) *W.P.Mullins,Ireland* 11-11-7 R.Walsh	4/1		pu

Ann & Alan Potts Limited 7ran 5m09.10

214 Randox Health Foxhunters' Open Hunters' Chase (2) (6yo+) £26,685   2m5f19y (18)

203	TOP WOOD (FR) *KellyMorgan* 12-12-0 (v+t) TabithaWorsley	14/1		1
	BURNING AMBITION (IRE) *PierceMichaelPower,Ireland* 8-12-0 MrDerekO'Connor	11/2	2	2
	ROAD TO RICHES (IRE) *DavidChristie,Ireland* 12-12-0 (s+t) MrDavidMaxwell	.20/1	11	3
203	Coastal Tiep (FR) *StuartCrawford,Ireland* 7-12-0 (s) MrB.G.Crawford	50/1	4	4
203	Road To Rome (IRE) *J.J.O'Shea* 9-12-0 MrSamWaley-Cohen	11/4f	6	5
	Sir Jack Yeats (IRE) *RichardSpencer* 8-12-0 (b) MrJamesKing	16/1	9	6
	Greensalt (IRE) *W.H.Easterby* 11-12-0 (t) MrWilliamEasterby	25/1	2¼	7
	Kruzhlinin (GER) *GordonElliott,Ireland* 12-12-0 MrBarryO'Neill	12/1	23	8
203	Balnaslow (IRE) *GrahamMcKeever,Ireland* 12-12-0 (s) MrM.J.O'Hare	25/1	27	9
203	Just Cause (IRE) *J.P.Owen* 9-12-0 MrJackAndrews	100/1	8	10
	Never Complain (IRE) *MrsF.Marshall* 11-12-0 (s+t) MrCharlieMarshall	100/1	3	11
	Mr Mercurial (IRE) *WillRamsay* 11-12-0 (t) MrWillRamsay	33/1	22	12
	Mr Mix (FR) *S.C.Robinson* 8-12-0 MrStuartRobinson	20/1		ur
3	Seefood (IRE) *JustinLandy* 12-12-0 MissCharlotteCrane	16/1		ur
	Starkie *AnthonyWard-Thomas* 12-12-0 (t) MrMartinMcIntyre	100/1		ur
203	Asockastar (IRE) *DanielJohnBourne* 11-12-0 (s) MrP.W.Mullins	50/1		pu
	Bear's Affair (IRE) *PhilipRowley* 13-12-0 MrAlexEdwards	25/1		pu
	Champagne West (IRE) *T.M.Frost* 11-12-0 (s+t) MissLillyPinchin	50/1		pu
	Crazy Jack (IRE) *MrsA.R.Hewitt* 11-12-0 (s) MrGillonCrow	66/1		pu
	Dineur (FR) *MickeyBowen* 13-12-0 (t) MrPeterBryan	33/1		pu
	Gallery Exhibition (IRE) *P.W.Mason* 12-12-0 (t) MrGuyDisney	100/1		pu
	Numbercruncher (IRE) *DavidO'Brien* 12-12-0 TheoGillard	100/1		pu
	Pass The Hat *MissSarahRippon* 12-12-0 (t) MissSarahRippon	40/1		pu
	Shantou Magic (IRE) *WillRamsay* 12-12-0 MrNickPhillips	100/1		pu
	Shimla Dawn (IRE) *MrsC.Drury* 11-12-0 MissEmmaTodd	66/1		pu
203	Ucello Conti (FR) *GordonElliott,Ireland* 11-12-0 MrJ.J.Codd	4/1		pu
	Wonderful Charm (FR) *PaulNicholls* 11-12-0 (s+t) MrWilliamBiddick	16/1		pu

Mr J. R. Weatherby 27ran 5m46.00

215 Red Rum Handicap Chase (Gr 3) (1) (5yo+) £50,517   1m7f176y (12)

139	MOON OVER GERMANY (IRE) *HenrydeBromhead,Ireland* 8-10-7[136] RachaelBlackmore	11/2		1
182	LADY BUTTONS *PhilipKirby* 9-11-6[149] ThomasDowson(3)	5/1f	10	2
204	CHAMPAGNE AT TARA *JonjoO'Neill* 10-10-12[141] JonjoO'NeillJr.(3)	14/1	1¾	3
	Adrrastos (IRE) *JamieSnowden* 7-10-4[133] AidanColeman	12/1	11	4
204	Brelan d'As (FR) *PaulNicholls* 8-10-9[138] (t) BarryGeraghty	6/1	2¾	5
	Molineaux (IRE) *ColinTizzard* 8-10-4[133] SeanBowen	12/1	1½	6
204	Theflyingportrait (IRE) *JennieCandlish* 10-10-13[142] (t) SeanQuinlan	40/1	3½	7
204	Whatswrongwithyou (IRE) *NickyHenderson* 8-11-1[144] (h) NicodeBoinville	7/1	2	8
196	Eamon An Cnoic (IRE) *DavidPipe* 8-10-10[139] (s+t) TomScudamore	6/1	19	9
	Movie Legend *LucyWadham* 9-10-4[133] (s) LeightonAspell	18/1	24	10
	Cracking Find (IRE) *SueSmith* 8-10-8[137] DannyCook	16/1		F
139	R'evelyn Pleasure (IRE) *SeanO.O'Brien,Ireland* 7-10-2[131] DonaghMeyler	9/1		pu
	Demi Sang (FR) *BenHaslam* 6-10-9[138] (t) RichieMcLernon	40/1		pu

Philip J. Reynolds 13ran 4m06.30

216 Goffs UK Nickel Coin Mares' Standard Open National Hunt Flat (Gr 2) (1) (4, 5 and 6yo) £25,322   2m209y

191	THE GLANCING QUEEN (IRE) *AlanKing* 5-11-0 WayneHutchinson	5/1		1
	MINELLA MELODY (IRE) *HenrydeBromhead,Ireland* 5-11-0 MrP.W.Mullins	6/4f	2¼	2

DAYLIGHT KATIE (FR) *GordonElliott,Ireland* 6-11-0 (h) MrDavidDunsdon ...12/1 nk 3
Farne (IRE) *NeilKing* 5-11-0 AidanColeman 20/1 2½ 4
Shantewe (IRE) *JamieSnowden* 5-11-0 GavinSheehan 33/1 1¼ 5
Kissesforkatie (IRE) *JeremyScott* 5-11-0 NickScholfield 25/1 4 6
Misty Whisky *HarryFry* 5-11-0 SeanBowen 8/1 1½ 7
Emmas Joy *DanSkelton* 6-11-0 HarrySkelton ....33/1 nk 8
Whitehotchillifili (IRE) *HarryFry* 5-11-0 RichardJohnson 16/1 4½ 9
Who What When *MurtyMcGrath* 4-10-8 JoshuaMoore ....25/1 ½ 10
Hawthorn Cottage (IRE) *AmyMurphy* 6-11-0 (s) LucyK.Barry ....33/1 nk 11
Stainsby Girl *DonaldWhillans* 5-11-0 CallumWhillans 100/1 7 12
Mrs Hyde (IRE) *FergalO'Brien* 6-11-0 PaddyBrennan 20/1 1½ 13
Eyes Right *AlanKing* 4-10-8 DarylJacob ....50/1 ¾ 14
Miss Heritage (IRE) *DavidElsworth* 5-11-0 HarryCobden 12/1 2¼ 15
Timetochill (IRE) *KellyMorgan* 6-11-0 RossChapman 14/1 24 16
Dares To Dream (IRE) *PhilipKirby* 5-11-0 SeanQuinlan 80/1 11 17
Eyren (IRE) *DanSkelton* 4-10-8 BridgetAndrews 50/1 15 18
Giving Back *AlanKing* 5-11-0 TomCannon ....100/1 ½ 19
Briery Express *NoelWilliams* 6-11-0 (h) LeightonAspell 66/1 4½ 20
Dingwall, Farrell, Hornsey & Murray 20ran 4m22.00

AINTREE Friday, Apr 5 GOOD to SOFT
217 Merseyrail Handicap Hurdle (Gr 3) (1) (4yo+) £42,202 2½m (11)
118 THREE MUSKETEERS (IRE) *GordonElliott,Ireland* 9-10-5[132] (s) J.W.Kennedy ..8/1 1
10 POINT OF PRINCIPLE (IRE) *TimVaughan* 6-10-9[136] CharliePrice(7) 25/1 1¾ 2
187 CANARDIER (FR) *DermotAnthonyMcLoughlin,Ireland* 7-11-1[142] (h)
    BarryGeraghty 6/1 2¼ 3
200 Sternrubin (GER) *PhilipHobbs* 8-10-13[140] (s) RichardJohnson 16/1 4½ 4
187 Knight In Dubai (IRE) *DanSkelton* 6-10-11[138] (t) HarrySkelton ....14/1 hd 5
205 Doctor Dex (IRE) *TomGeorge* 6-10-0[127] JonathanBurke 20/1 3¾ 6
    Tedham *JonjoO'Neill* 5-10-4[131] NickScholfield 11/2f 1¼ 7
    Caltex (FR) *HenryOliver* 7-10-3[130] JeremiahMcGrath 50/1 5 8
200 Mohaayed *DanSkelton* 7-11-12[153] (s+t) BridgetAndrews 33/1 2¾ 9
116 Esprit du Large (FR) *EvanWilliams* 5-10-5[132] AdamWedge 8/1 14 10
11 Push The Tempo (IRE) *RobertStephens* 6-10-6[133] (h) TomO'Brien 40/1 11 11
205 Mount Mews (IRE) *DonaldMcCain* 8-10-10[137] BrianHughes 25/1 1½ 12
5 Project Bluebook (FR) *JohnQuinn* 6-10-8[135] M.P.Walsh ....20/1 ½ 13
175 Admiral Barratry (FR) *LucyWadham* 6-10-4[131] (s) LeightonAspell 14/1 2¼ 14
    Joke Dancer *SueSmith* 6-10-5[132] DannyCook 25/1 13 15
    Landsman (IRE) *TimVaughan* 6-10-0[127] (t) AlanJohns 33/1 8 16
200 Mister Fizz *MissImogenPickard* 11-11-0[141] (s) LeeEdwards 50/1 27 17
168 Brecon Hill (IRE) *SarahHumphrey* 6-10-5[132] (t) SeanBowen ....33/1 pu
157 Mont des Avaloirs (FR) *PaulNicholls* 6-10-12[139] LorcanWilliams(5) ....17/2 pu
    Kobrouk (FR) *NickyHenderson* 8-11-2[143] NicodeBoinville ....16/1 pu
187 Brio Conti (FR) *PaulNicholls* 8-11-7[148] HarryCobden ....7/1 pu
    Mr Frank McAleavy 21ran 4m58.40

218 Betway Top Novices' Hurdle (Gr 1) (1) (4yo+) £56,130 2m103y (9)
178 FELIX DESJY (FR) *GordonElliott,Ireland* 6-11-4 (h) J.W.Kennedy 7/2 1
178 ARAMON (GER) *W.P.Mullins,Ireland* 6-11-4 R.Walsh 3/1f 1½ 2
172 ROUGE VIF (FR) *HarryWhittington* 5-11-4 DarylJacob 9/1 7 3
178 Itchy Feet (FR) *OllyMurphy* 5-11-4 GavinSheehan ....7/2 hd 4
    Winston C (IRE) *HarryFry* 5-11-4 SeanBowen 12/1 1 5
    Precious Cargo (IRE) *NickyHenderson* 6-11-4 NicodeBoinville 4/1 4½ 6
168 Southfield Stone *PaulNicholls* 6-11-4 HarryCobden 9/1 6 7
    Gigginstown House Stud 7ran 4m02.90

219 Betway Mildmay Novices' Chase (Gr 1) (1) (5yo+) £56,130 3m210y (19)
192 LOSTINTRANSLATION (IRE) *ColinTizzard* 7-11-4 RobbiePower 3/1 1
186 TOPOFTHEGAME (IRE) *PaulNicholls* 7-11-4 (t) HarryCobden 10/11f 6 2
186 TOP VILLE BEN (IRE) *PhilipKirby* 7-11-4 (h) SeanQuinlan ....14/1 ½ 3
    Mr Whipped (IRE) *NickyHenderson* 6-11-4 (s) NicodeBoinville 11/1 7 4
165 Chris's Dream (IRE) *HenrydeBromhead,Ireland* 7-11-4 RachaelBlackmore 5/1 12 5
180 Crucial Role *DanSkelton* 7-11-4 HarrySkelton ....28/1 F
    Taylor & O'Dwyer 6ran 6m31.80

220 JLT Chase (Melling) (Gr 1) (1) (5yo+) £140,325 2m3f200y (16)
188 MIN (FR) *W.P.Mullins,Ireland* 8-11-7 R.Walsh 2/1f 1
188 POLITOLOGUE (FR) *PaulNicholls* 8-11-7 (h+t) HarryCobden 5/2 20 2
158 WAITING PATIENTLY (IRE) *RuthJefferson* 8-11-7 (s) BrianHughes 9/4 9 3
188 Hell's Kitchen *HarryFry* 8-11-7 (h+t) BarryGeraghty 14/1 10 4
188 God's Own (IRE) *TomGeorge* 11-11-7 PaddyBrennan 25/1 12 5

195 Top Notch (FR) *NickyHenderson* 8-11-7 DarylJacob ....8/1   pu
      Mrs S. Ricci 6ran 5m03.40

221 Randox Health Topham Handicap Chase (Gr 3) (1) (5yo+) £78,582   2m5f19y (18)
208 CADMIUM (FR) *W.P.Mullins,Ireland* 7-11-2[152] P.Townend 8/1   1
194 SUB LIEUTENANT (IRE) *HenrydeBromhead,Ireland* 10-11-5[155] (t)
      RachaelBlackmore 25/1   6 2
196 DOITFORTHEVILLAGE (IRE) *PaulHenderson* 10-10-4[140] (t) TomO'Brien 25/1   3¼ 3
196 Janika (FR) *NickyHenderson* 6-11-12[162] DarylJacob 9/2f   3¼ 4
151 Woods Well (IRE) *GordonElliott,Ireland* 8-10-6[142] (s) J.W.Kennedy 20/1   4 5
180 Flying Angel (IRE) *NigelTwiston-Davies* 8-10-6[142] (v) TomBellamy ....10/1   ¾ 6
174 San Benedeto (FR) *PaulNicholls* 8-11-4[154] (s+t) NickSchofield 18/1 13 7
180 O O Seven (IRE) *NickyHenderson* 9-11-1[151] (b) NicodeBoinville 20/1   3¾ 8
      Beau Bay (FR) *DrRichardNewland* 8-10-0 (9-10)[136] (h+t) CharlieDeutsch 66/1   8 9
59 Highland Lodge (IRE) *JamesMoffatt* 13-10-0 (9-13)[136] (s) HenryBrooke 50/1 1½ 10
196 Bigmartre (FR) *HarryWhittington* 8-10-6[142] (s) LeightonAspell ....40/1 hd 11
202 Double Shuffle (IRE) *TomGeorge* 9-11-8[158] JonathanBurke 33/1 1¾ 12
169 Adrien du Pont (FR) *PaulNicholls* 7-11-1[151] (t) HarryCobden ....12/1   ¾ 13
189 Fact of The Matter (IRE) *JamieSnowden* 9-10-4[140] (s+t) GavinSheehan 66/1 1¾ 14
61 Kilcrea Vale (IRE) *NickyHenderson* 9-10-0 (9-13)[136] (s) JeremiahMcGrath ...16/1   3 15
156 Ballyhill (FR) *NigelTwiston-Davies* 8-10-6[142] SamTwiston-Davies 9/1   3 16
      Henryville *PeterBowen* 11-10-0 (9-13)[136] RobertDunne 33/1 10 17
      Equus Secretus (IRE) *BenPauling* 7-10-0 (9-13)[136] JamieMoore 66/1 14 18
174 Mercian Prince (IRE) *AmyMurphy* 8-10-10[146] JackQuinlan 33/1 2¾ 19
180 Activial (FR) *TomGeorge* 9-11-0[150] TomScudamore 16/1 2½ 20
102 Divine Spear (IRE) *NickyHenderson* 8-10-0 (9-13)[136] JamesBowen ....33/1   F
      Indian Temple (IRE) *TimReed* 10-10-0[136] (s) HarryReed(3) ....50/1   F
17 Peregrine Run (IRE) *PeterFahey,Ireland* 9-11-1[151] (b) BarryGeraghty ....14/1   F
59 Call It Magic (IRE) *RossO'Sullivan,Ireland* 9-10-0 (9-13)[136] (b) MarkEnright ......6/1   ur
61 More Buck's (IRE) *PeterBowen* 9-10-0 (9-13)[136] SeanBowen ....66/1   ur
124 Forest des Aigles (FR) *LucindaRussell* 8-10-0 (9-11)[136] (t) DerekFox ....22/1   pu
196 Polidam (FR) *W.P.Mullins,Ireland* 8-10-4[140] D.J.Mullins ....25/1   pu
      Supreme Horse Racing Club/K. Sharp 27ran 5m29.30

222 Doom Bar Sefton Novices' Hurdle (Gr 1) (1) (4yo+) £56,130   3m149y (13)
185 CHAMP (IRE) *NickyHenderson* 7-11-4 M.P.Walsh 9/4f   1
      EMITOM (IRE) *WarrenGreatrex* 5-11-4 GavinSheehan 5/1   3 2
201 LISNAGAR OSCAR (IRE) *RebeccaCurtis* 6-11-4 SeanBowen 11/2   7 3
      Walk Away (IRE) *HenrydeBromhead,Ireland* 6-11-4 RobbiePower 12/1 2¾ 4
      Arthur Mac (IRE) *HenryOliver* 6-11-4 LiamHeard 50/1 3¼ 5
175 Champagne Well (IRE) *FergalO'Brien* 6-11-4 PaddyBrennan 25/1 3¾ 6
      Downtown Getaway (IRE) *NickyHenderson* 6-11-4 NicodeBoinville 8/1 19 7
      Ardlethen (IRE) *DanSkelton* 6-11-4 HarrySkelton ....16/1 hd 8
      Kingsplace (IRE) *NigelTwiston-Davies* 7-11-4 SamTwiston-Davies ....66/1   ½ 9
      Trevelyn's Corn (IRE) *PaulNicholls* 6-11-4 (t) HarryCobden 18/1 2¾ 10
205 Dallas des Pictons (FR) *GordonElliott,Ireland* 6-11-4 J.W.Kennedy 4/1   7 11
      The Captains Inn (IRE) *BenPauling* 6-11-4 DarylJacob ....33/1   pu
      Mr John P. McManus 12ran 6m17.80

223 Weatherbys Racing Bank Standard Open National Hunt Flat (Gr 2) (1)   2m209y
      (4, 5 and 6yo) £25,322
      MCFABULOUS (IRE) *PaulNicholls* 5-11-4 HarryCobden 2/1f   1
      THEBANNERKINGREBEL (IRE) *JamieSnowden* 6-11-4 GavinSheehan 14/1   1 2
150 SANTA ROSSA (IRE) *DermotAnthonyMcLoughlin,Ireland* 5-11-1
      MrFinianMaguire 3/1 2¾ 3
      Dewcup (IRE) *T.M.Walsh,Ireland* 4-10-12 R.Walsh 8/1 1½ 4
191 Master Debonair *ColinTizzard* 5-11-4 JamesBowen 8/1 10 5
      Ebony Jewel (IRE) *N.W.Alexander* 5-11-4 LucyAlexander 11/2 16 6
      The Cob (IRE) *BenPauling* 5-11-4 NicodeBoinville ....40/1   ½ 7
      Book of Invasions (IRE) *JohnRyan* 4-10-12 PaddyBrennan 40/1   9 8
      Onthefrontfoot (IRE) *DonaldMcCain* 5-11-4 BrianHughes ....33/1   ¾ 9
      Malystic *PeterNiven* 5-11-4 HenryBrooke 50/1 16 10
      Blackhillsofdakota (IRE) *JohnHalley,Ireland* 4-10-12 RachaelBlackmore 12/1 13 11
      Hazm (IRE) *TimVaughan* 4-10-12 AlanJohns ....33/1   pu
      Giraffa Racing 12ran 4m07.50

      AINTREE Saturday, Apr 6 GOOD
224 Gaskells Handicap Hurdle (Gr 3) (1) (4yo+) £42,202   3m149y (13)
127 AUX PTITS SOINS (FR) *DanSkelton* 9-11-8[149] HarrySkelton 11/1   1
      TOMMY RAPPER (IRE) *DanSkelton* 8-10-9[136] (t) BridgetAndrews 20/1 4½ 2

195 KEEPER HILL (IRE) *WarrenGreatrex* 8-11-3[144] RichardJohnson 25/1   1½ 3
187 Burbank (IRE) *NickyHenderson* 7-10-11[138] (b) JeremiahMcGrath 25/1   7   4
193 Theclocksticking (IRE) *StuartEdmunds* 7-10-10[137] CiaranGethings 12/1   5   5
    Canyon City *NeilKing* 6-10-9[136] JackQuinlan ....50/1   ¾   6
205 Coolanly (IRE) *FergalO'Brien* 7-10-13[140] PaddyBrennan ....8/1   sh 7
193 Sire du Berlais (FR) *GordonElliott,Ireland* 7-11-12[153] (s+t) JonjoO'NeillJr.(3) ... 7/2f   sh 8
201 Nadaitak *BenPauling* 5-11-0[141] (s) TomBellamy ....33/1   ½   9
205 Burrows Park (FR) *VenetiaWilliams* 7-10-9[136] CharlieDeutsch 16/1   14 10
193 Coole Cody (IRE) *MichaelBlake* 8-10-11[138] (t) HarryCobden 33/1   2½ 11
    First Drift *BenCase* 8-10-8[135] MaxKendrick(5) 50/1   3¾ 12
170 Vive Le Roi (IRE) *TonyCarroll* 8-10-9[136] HarryBannister ....50/1   ¾   13
    Gunfleet (IRE) *EmmaLavelle* 7-10-11[138] AdamWedge 40/1   1¼ 14
193 Flemcara (IRE) *EmmaLavelle* 7-10-10[137] (t) AidanColeman ....16/1   hd 15
183 Red Indian *KellyMorgan* 7-10-12[139] (s) FergusGregory(5) 16/1   4   16
    Poker Play (FR) *DavidPipe* 6-10-10[137] (t) TomScudamore 5/1   2¾ 17
    Knock House (IRE) *DonaldMcCain* 10-10-9[136] (b) HenryBrooke 80/1   59 18
    Mia's Storm (IRE) *AlanKing* 9-11-7[148] (s) WayneHutchinson 16/1   20 19
 99 Nestor Park (FR) *BenPauling* 6-10-9[136] NicodeBoinville ....11/1   pu
    Forza Milan (IRE) *JonjoO'Neill* 7-10-12[139] M.P.Walsh ....10/1   pu
    Mr J. Hales 21ran 6m00.30

225 Betway Mersey Novices' Hurdle (Gr 1) (1) (4yo+) £56,130   2½m (10)
    RESERVE TANK (IRE) *ColinTizzard* 5-11-4 RobbiePower 20/1   1
185 BREWIN'UPASTORM (IRE) *OllyMurphy* 6-11-4 RichardJohnson 10/3   3¼ 2
178 ANGELS BREATH (IRE) *NickyHenderson* 5-11-4 NicodeBoinville 11/4f   2¼ 3
175 ONE FOR ROSIE *NigelTwiston-Davies* 6-11-4 SamTwiston-Davies ....5/1   dh 3
171 Chosen Mate (IRE) *GordonElliott,Ireland* 6-11-4 DavyRussell 6/1   1¾ 5
    Umbrigado (IRE) *DavidPipe* 5-11-4 TomScudamore 10/1   2½ 6
162 Kateson *TomLacey* 6-11-4 SeanBowen 6/1   1¼ 7
178 The Big Bite (IRE) *TomGeorge* 6-11-4 CiaranGethings 25/1   6   8
 38 Colonel Custard (IRE) *NickyMartin* 6-11-4 MattGriffiths 25/1   36 9
    The Reserve Tankers 9ran 4m49.60

226 Doom Bar Maghull Novices' Chase (Gr 1) (1) (5yo+) £56,130   1m7f176y (13)
179 ORNUA (IRE) *HenrydeBromhead,Ireland* 8-11-4 DavyRussell 3/1jf   1
179 US AND THEM (IRE) *JosephPatrickO'Brien,Ireland* 6-11-4 (t) J.J.Slevin .. 3/1jf   1¾ 2
    DESTRIER (IRE) *DanSkelton* 6-11-4 HarrySkelton 7/1   1¼ 3
179 Clondaw Castle (IRE) *TomGeorge* 7-11-4 CiaranGethings 13/2   20 4
179 Knocknanuss (IRE) *GaryMoore* 9-11-4 JamieMoore ....8/1   nk 5
179 Lalor (GER) *KayleyWoollacott* 7-11-4 RichardJohnson 7/2   1   6
204 Caid du Lin (FR) *DrRichardNewland* 7-11-4 (b+t) SamTwiston-Davies 20/1   25 7
    John J Phelan/Syed Momin 7ran 3m50.80

227 Ryanair Stayers' Hurdle (Liverpool) (Gr 1) (1) (4yo+) £101,034   3m149y (13)
170 IF THE CAP FITS (IRE) *HarryFry* 7-11-7 (s) SeanBowen 7/1   1
182 ROKSANA (IRE) *DanSkelton* 7-11-0 HarrySkelton ....10/1   hd 2
181 APPLE'S JADE (FR) *GordonElliott,Ireland* 7-11-10 (t) J.W.Kennedy ....5/6f   nk 3
187 William Henry (IRE) *NickyHenderson* 9-11-7 (s) NicodeBoinville 8/1   11 4
142 Lord Napier (IRE) *PeterBowen* 6-11-7 (s+t) JamesBowen 40/1   5   5
195 West Approach *ColinTizzard* 9-11-7 TomScudamore 33/1   10 6
127 Agrapart (FR) *NickWilliams* 8-11-7 LizzieKelly 66/1   1½ 7
195 Sam Spinner *JeddO'Keeffe* 7-11-7 (s) JoeColliere 7/1   1¾ 8
186 The Worlds End (IRE) *TomGeorge* 8-11-7 PaddyBrennan 25/1   3   9
160 Clyne *EvanWilliams* 9-11-7 AdamWedge 50/1   1¾ 10
195 Wholestone (IRE) *NigelTwiston-Davies* 8-11-7 DarylJacob 16/1   1½ 11
127 Unowhatimeanharry *HarryFry* 11-11-7 (s+t) M.P.Walsh 25/1   3½ 12
195 Kilbricken Storm (IRE) *ColinTizzard* 8-11-7 (b+t) HarryCobden 25/1   2¾ 13
195 Nautical Nitwit (IRE) *PhilipKirby* 10-11-7 (s) ThomasDowson ....80/1   pu
    Sykes (IRE) *NickyMartin* 10-11-7 MattGriffiths ....40/1   pu
    Paul & Clare Rooney 15ran 5m58.70

228 Betway Handicap Chase (Gr 3) (1) (5yo+) £42,202   3m210y (19)
192 KILDISART (IRE) *BenPauling* 7-11-12[148] DarylJacob 8/1   1
186 MISTER MALARKY *ColinTizzard* 6-11-11[147] JonjoO'NeillJr.(3) 11/2   5   2
180 OLDGRANGEWOOD *DanSkelton* 8-11-1[137] (t) HarrySkelton 7/1   4   3
    Gold Opera *KeithDalgleish* 10-10-6[128] (v) CraigNichol 50/1   1   4
131 On Tour (IRE) *EvanWilliams* 11-10-8[130] AdamWedge 12/1   10 5
180 Willie Boy (IRE) *CharlieLongsdon* 8-11-6[142] (s) RobertDunne ....16/1   ½   6
196 Some Buckle (IRE) *RichardBandey* 10-11-2[138] (t) HarryBannister 33/1   3¼ 7
 68 Theatre Territory (IRE) *WarrenGreatrex* 9-10-8[130] (s) MrSamWaley-Cohen(3) .. 16/1   2¾ 8
    Polydora (IRE) *TomLacey* 7-11-1[137] TomScudamore 8/1   3½ 9

997

Debece *TimVaughan* 8-11-5[141] AlanJohns 9/2f   13 10
Clondaw Westie (IRE) *LawneyHill* 8-10-5[127] (s+t) AidanColeman ....28/1   pu

131 Federici *DonaldMcCain* 10-10-6[128] (b) HenryBrooke ....33/1   pu
119 Amaulino (FR) *R.K.Watson,Ireland* 6-10-8[130] (s+t) AndrewRing(3) ......16/1   pu
    Red Giant (IRE) *JennieCandlish* 8-10-10[132] (v) JonathanBurke ....28/1   pu
198 Touch Kick (IRE) *PaulNicholls* 8-10-11[133] (t) HarryCobden ....15/2   pu
206 Smooth Stepper *AlexHales* 10-11-2[138] WayneHutchinson ....50/1   pu
155 Reikers Island (IRE) *PhilipHobbs* 6-11-3[139] TomO'Brien ....22/1   pu
183 Springtown Lake (IRE) *PhilipHobbs* 7-11-4[140] RichardJohnson ....10/1   pu
    Mr Simon Munir & Mr Isaac Souede 18ran 6m21.20

229 Randox Health Grand National Handicap Chase (Gr 3) (1) (7yo+) £500,000 4¼m74y (29)

The first fence on the final circuit was omitted due to a stricken horse

189 TIGER ROLL (IRE) *GordonElliott,Ireland* 9-11-5[159] (b+t) DavyRussell 4/1f   1
180 MAGIC OF LIGHT (IRE) *MrsJ.Harrington,Ireland* 8-10-11[151] (s) P.D.Kennedy .66/1 2¾ 2
    RATHVINDEN (IRE) *W.P.Mullins,Ireland* 11-11-0[154] R.Walsh 8/1 2¼ 3
 59 Walk In The Mill (FR) *RobertWalford* 9-10-4[144] JamesBest 25/1   11 4
202 Anibale Fly (FR) *A.J.Martin,Ireland* 9-11-0[164] (t) MP.Walsh ....10/1   ½ 5
118 One For Arthur (IRE) *LucindaRussell* 10-11-0[154] (t) DerekFox 25/1   9 6
155 Regal Encore (IRE) *AnthonyHoneyball* 11-10-12[152] JonathanBurke 66/1 2¼ 7
180 Singlefarmpayment *TomGeorge* 9-10-6[146] (h) PaddyBrennan ....50/1   ½ 8
148 Outlander (IRE) *RichardSpencer* 11-11-4[158] JamesBowen 66/1   3 9
196 Valseur Lido (FR) *HenrydeBromhead,Ireland* 10-10-6[146] RachaelBlackmore 66/1   2 10
198 Livelovelaugh (IRE) *W.P.Mullins,Ireland* 9-10-4[144] D.J.Mullins ....25/1   hd 11
193 A Toi Phil (FR) *GordonElliott,Ireland* 9-10-11[151] (t) DenisO'Regan 50/1 1¼ 12
189 Bless The Wings (IRE) *GordonElliott,Ireland* 14-10-3[143] (s) RobertDunne 50/1 1¼ 13
189 Ultragold (FR) *ColinTizzard* 11-10-7[147] (t) TomO'Brien 50/1 3¼ 14
161 Vieux Lion Rouge (FR) *DavidPipe* 10-10-6[146] (s+t) TomScudamore 50/1 3¼ 15
118 Captain Redbeard (IRE) *StuartColtherd* 10-10-3[143] SamColtherd 66/1   11 16
206 Folsom Blue (IRE) *GordonElliott,Ireland* 12-10-4[144] (s+t) LukeDempsey 66/1   7 17
125 Valtor (FR) *NickyHenderson* 10-11-6[160] DarylJacob 66/1   16 18
121 Don Poli (IRE) *PhilipKirby* 10-11-3[157] (s) MrP.W.Mullins 66/1   41 19
180 Vintage Clouds (IRE) *SueSmith* 9-10-4[144] DannyCook ....11/1   F
180 General Principle (IRE) *GordonElliott,Ireland* 10-10-4[144] (t) J.J.Slevin ....33/1   F
 68 Rock The Kasbah (IRE) *PhilipHobbs* 9-10-13[153] (s) RichardJohnson ....16/1   F
161 Ballyoptic (IRE) *NigelTwiston-Davies* 9-11-1[155] TomBellamy ....25/1   F
  9 Jury Duty (IRE) *GordonElliott,Ireland* 8-10-11[151] (t) RobbiePower ....10/1   ur
122 Pleasant Company (IRE) *W.P.Mullins,Ireland* 11-11-1[155] P.Townend ....12/1   ur
180 Up For Review (IRE) *W.P.Mullins,Ireland* 10-10-6[146] D.E.Mullins ....33/1   bd
 59 Just A Par (IRE) *JamesMoffatt* 12-10-2[142] (b) AidanColeman ....100/1   pu
    Joe Farrell (IRE) *RebeccaCurtis* 10-10-2[142] AdamWedge ....14/1   pu
177 Blow By Blow (IRE) *GordonElliott,Ireland* 8-10-6[146] (b+t) AndrewRing ....66/1   pu
108 Step Back (IRE) *MarkBradstock* 9-10-7[147] (s) NicodeBoinville ....25/1   pu
161 Ramses de Teillee (FR) *DavidPipe* 7-10-9[149] (t) DavidNoonan ....20/1   pu
189 Tea For Two *MrsJaneWilliams* 10-10-9[149] LizzieKelly ....25/1   pu
180 Noble Endeavor (IRE) *GordonElliott,Ireland* 10-10-10[150] (s) MarkEnright ....50/1   pu
177 Monbeg Notorious (IRE) *GordonElliott,Ireland* 8-10-10[150] (v) SeanBowen ....50/1   pu
174 Warriors Tale *PaulNicholls* 10-10-13[153] (t) HarryCobden ....66/1   pu
151 Dounikos (FR) *GordonElliott,Ireland* 8-11-0[154] J.W.Kennedy ....16/1   pu
180 Minella Rocco (IRE) *JonjoO'Neill* 9-11-1[155] RichieMcLernon ....33/1   pu
180 Lake View Lad (IRE) *N.W.Alexander* 9-11-1[155] HenryBrooke ....14/1   pu
121 Mala Beach (IRE) *GordonElliott,Ireland* 11-11-2[156] MrJ.J.Codd ....33/1   pu
131 Go Conquer (IRE) *NigelTwiston-Davies* 10-11-3[157] (t) SamTwiston-Davies ....33/1   pu
    Gigginstown House Stud 40ran 9m01.50

230 Pinsent Masons Handicap Hurdle (Conditional Jockeys' And Amateur Riders') 2m103y (8)
(2) (4yo+) £30,950

190 CHIEF JUSTICE *GordonElliott,Ireland* 4-11-2[137] (t) MrJ.J.Codd 13/2   1
    THISTIMENEXTYEAR *RichardSpencer* 5-10-6[121] D.J.O'Keeffe(7) ....6/1   hd 2
 79 NIETZSCHE *BrianEllison* 6-11-3[132] (t) DannyMcMenamin(7) 20/1 2¾ 3
    Lord Yeats *JeddO'Keeffe* 6-11-3[132] ThomasDowson(3) 10/3f 1½ 4
    Flashing Glance *TomLacey* 6-11-2[131] StanSheppard(3) 10/1   2 5
    Scheu Time (IRE) *JamesA.Nash,Ireland* 6-10-9[124] (h) JonjoO'NeillJr.(3) ....6/1   ½ 6
 50 Whatmore *HenryDaly* 7-11-12[141] HarryTeal(5) 14/1   1 7
200 Chieftain's Choice (IRE) *KevinFrost* 10-10-8[123] (b) KieronEdgar 50/1 4½ 8
    West To The Bridge (IRE) *DanSkelton* 6-10-12[127] (h+t) WilliamMarshall(7) ......15/2   ¾ 9
    Prairie Town (IRE) *TonyCarroll* 8-10-0 (9-12)[115] (s) PatrickCowley(5) 25/1   1 10
    Pink Legend *VenetiaWilliams* 5-10-5[120] MissLucyTurner(7) 14/1   9 11
    Welsh Rarebit *LucindaEgerton* 6-10-3[118] AidenBlakemore(7) ....33/1   ¾ 12
    Beeno (IRE) *DianneSayer* 10-10-10[125] (h) CharlieTodd(7) 50/1   8 13

	Subcontinent (IRE) *VenetiaWilliams* 7-10-6[121] HughNugent(5)	25/1	1¾ 14
204	All Set To Go (IRE) *KevinFrost* 8-11-5[134] (t) SamColtherd(3)	33/1	8 15
	Locker Room Talk (IRE) *NigelTwiston-Davies* 6-11-1[130] (h) MrJackSavage(7)	22/1	2¼ 16
	Havana Hermano (IRE) *StuartEdmunds* 5-10-12[127] CharlieHammond(3)	28/1	F
	Always Resolute *IanWilliams* 8-10-11[126] (v) EdwardAustin(7)	25/1	ur
	Fin And Game (IRE) *DonaldMcCain* 7-10-12[127] D.J.McInerney(3)	25/1	pu
	Cheveley Park Stud 19ran 3m55.90		

FAIRYHOUSE Sunday, Apr 7   GOOD to SOFT

231   Fairyhouse Racecourse Supporting Irish Injured Jockeys Association Novices' Hurdle (Gr 2) (4yo+) £22,887 · 2m (8)

	MISTER BLUE SKY (IRE) *W.P.Mullins* 5-11-4 R.Walsh	15/8f	1
	CASH BACK (FR) *W.P.Mullins* 7-11-4 (h) D.J.Mullins	7/2	¾ 2
185	VALDIEU (FR) *NoelMeade* 6-11-4 (t) SeanFlanagan	12/1	18 3
	All For Joy (IRE) *OliverMcKiernan* 7-11-4 DenisO'Regan	11/4	nk 4
	Roll Again (IRE) *W.P.Mullins* 5-11-4 (h) D.E.Mullins	16/1	1 5
200	Eclair de Beaufeu (FR) *GordonElliott* 5-11-4 J.W.Kennedy	5/1	23 6
	Shanakiel Racing Syndicate 6ran 3m50.00		

232   Fairyhouse Easter Festival Novices' Hurdle (Gr 2) (4yo+) £21,616 · 2½m (10)

	DOMMAGE POUR TOI (FR) *HenrydeBromhead* 6-11-5 RachaelBlackmore	33/1	1
	ZERO TEN (IRE) *EmmetMullins* 6-11-5 D.J.Mullins	5/4f	¾ 2
185	EASY GAME (FR) *W.P.Mullins* 5-11-10 R.Walsh	9/2	nk 3
185	Castlebawn West (IRE) *W.P.Mullins* 6-11-5 D.E.Mullins	16/1	2¼ 4
171	Milan Native (IRE) *GordonElliott* 6 11 5 DavyRussell	9/1	nk 5
197	Court Maid (IRE) *ThomasMullins* 6-10-12 JonathanMoore	25/1	3 6
133	Gallant John Joe (IRE) *OliverMcKiernan* 6-11-8 (s) DenisO'Regan	8/1	15 7
197	Awayinthewest (IRE) *P.A.Fahy* 7-10-12 J.S.McGarvey	66/1	2¾ 8
201	Cap York (FR) *NoelMeade* 7-11-5 (s) SeanFlanagan	12/1	25 9
	Final List (IRE) *GordonElliott* 5-11-5 J.W.Kennedy	25/1	1½ 10
	Espanito Bello (FR) *AlanFleming* 5-11-5 DonaghMeyler	33/1	pu
111	Harrie (IRE) *W.P.Mullins* 7-11-5 MrP.W.Mullins	8/1	pu
	Hugh Bleahen 12ran 4m54.20		

AYR Saturday, Apr 13   GOOD to FIRM

233   J & D Pierce Novices' Championship Handicap Chase (2) (5yo+) £62,560 · 3m20y (19)

	MOLLY THE DOLLY (IRE) *DanSkelton* 8-11-9[139] HarrySkelton	5/1	1
	DANDY DAN (IRE) *KimBailey* 6-11-12[142] (s+t) DavidBass	7/2f	3¾ 2
	CLAUD AND GOLDIE (IRE) *SandyForster* 10-10-13[129] ThomasDowson(3)	14/1	6 3
198	Kilfilum Cross (IRE) *HenryOliver* 8-11-12[142] DaveCrosse	4/1	27 4
	Trongate (IRE) *IainJardine* 7-10-7[123] RossChapman	18/1	hd 5
	Onefortheroadtom *HarryFry* 6-10-8[124] (s) RichieMcLernon	7/1	F
186	Drinks Interval *ColinTizzard* 7-11-9[139] (t) SamTwiston-Davies	8/1	F
196	Azzerti (FR) *AlanKing* 7-11-6[136] WayneHutchinson	8/1	pu
108	Ibis du Rheu (FR) *PaulNicholls* 8-11-12[142] (s+t) HarryCobden	7/1	pu
	Mr Dermot Hanafin 9ran 5m55.40		

234   CPMS Scottish Champion Hurdle (Limited Handicap) (Gr 2) (1) (4yo+) £59,797 · 2m (9)

181	VERDANA BLUE (IRE) *NickyHenderson* 7-11-10[154] ConnorBrace(7)	4/1f	1
	DINO VELVET (FR) *AlanKing* 6-10-4[134] PaddyBrennan	14/1	7 2
157	EQUUS AMADEUS (IRE) *TomLacey* 6-10-5[135] (t) MrStanSheppard(3)	16/1	1¼ 3
130	Irish Roe (IRE) *PeterAtkinson* 8-10-4[134] HenryBrooke	25/1	½ 4
200	Leoncavallo (IRE) *DrRichardNewland* 7-11-0[144] (b) SamTwiston-Davies	17/2	¾ 5
37	Nube Negra (SPA) *DanSkelton* 5-10-7[137] (t) HarrySkelton	13/2	1 6
37	Caius Marcius (IRE) *NickyRichards* 8-10-10[140] (s) DannyMcMenamin(3)	25/1	3¼ 7
	Captain Moirette (IRE) *SueSmith* 7-10-4 (10-3)[134] DannyCook	20/1	1 8
172	Get Out The Gate (IRE) *JimGoldie* 6-10-4 (10-0)[134] CallumBewley	50/1	2¼ 9
	Pearl of The West (IRE) *JohnMcConnell,Ireland* 5-10-4[134] (t) SeanBowen	10/1	ns 10
22	Redicean *AlanKing* 5-11-0[144] WayneHutchinson	10/1	nk 11
176	Malaya (FR) *PaulNicholls* 5-10-12[142] HarryCobden	7/1	3¾ 12
	Anemoi (FR) *HarryWhittington* 5-10-5[135] GavinSheehan	7/1	26 13
181	Brain Power (IRE) *NickyHenderson* 8-11-9[153] (s) NicodeBoinville	11/1	pu
	Crimbourne Stud 14ran 3m39.30		

235   Jordan Electrics Ltd Future Champion Novices' Chase (Gr 2) (1) (5yo+) £25,978 · 2½m110y (18)

166	SECRET INVESTOR *PaulNicholls* 7-11-0 (t) HarryCobden	2/1f	1
10	LOUIS' VAC POUCH (IRE) *HenryOliver* 7-11-0 (h) JeremiahMcGrath	12/1	3¾ 2
	MONBEG LEGEND (IRE) *NickyHenderson* 9-11-0 NicodeBoinville	11/2	8 3
128	Ballywood (FR) *AlanKing* 5-11-0 WayneHutchinson	5/2	3½ 4

192 Castafiore (USA) *CharlieLongsdon* 6-10-12 (s) PaulO'Brien 9/1   5   5
183 Lough Derg Spirit (IRE) *NickyHenderson* 7-11-0 (s) JamesBowen 6/1   3   6
    Cool Mix *IainJardine* 7-11-3 (h) SeanQuinlan 25/1   4   7
    Hills of Ledbury (Aga) 7ran 4m56.70

236   Coral Scottish Grand National Handicap Chase (Gr 3) (1) (5yo+) £122,442   3m7f176y (27)

86	TAKINGRISKS (IRE) *NickyRichards* 10-10-1[135] (s) SeanQuinlan 25/1		1
108	CROSSPARK *CarolineBailey* 9-10-8[142] HarrySkelton 10/1	4	2
	CLOTH CAP (IRE) *JonjoO'Neill* 9-10-0[134] RichieMcLernon 9/1	ns	3
	Blue Flight (FR) *NigelTwiston-Davies* 6-11-0[148] CallumBewley 25/1	nk	4
180	Big River (IRE) *LucindaRussell* 9-10-6[140] (t) DerekFox 8/1	13	5
229	Vintage Clouds (IRE) *SueSmith* 9-11-1[149] DannyCook 5/1f	9	6
161	Red Infantry (IRE) *IanWilliams* 9-10-6[140] (s) TomO'Brien 40/1	1¼	7
10	Chic Name (FR) *RichardHobson* 7-10-0 (9-12)[134] (t) JonathanBurke 20/1	1¾	8
105	Rathlin Rose (IRE) *DavidPipe* 11-10-0 (9-13)[134] (b) TomScudamore 33/1	6	9
68	Doing Fine (IRE) *NeilMulholland* 11-10-0 (9-9)[134] (s+t) BrendanPowell 14/1	1	10
173	Beau du Brizais (FR) *PhilipHobbs* 7-10-0 (9-13)[134] JamesBest 50/1	½	11
	Van Gogh du Granit (FR) *DavidPipe* 10-10-0 (9-9)[134] (b) DavidNoonan 66/1	sh	12
173	Brian Boranha (IRE) *PeterNiven* 8-10-1[135] HenryBrooke 25/1	20	13
59	Crosshue Boy (IRE) *SeanThomasDoyle,Ireland* 9-10-8[142] (t) SeanFlanagan 7/1		F
108	Cogry *NigelTwiston-Davies* 10-10-6[140] (s) SamTwiston-Davies 16/1		ur
	Morney Wing (IRE) *CharlieMann* 10-10-0 (9-10)[134] (s+t) RexDingle(5) 40/1		pu
	Geronimo *SandyThomson* 8-10-0 (9-12)[134] RachaelMcDonald(5) 12/1		pu
60	Acdc (IRE) *ChrisGrant* 9-10-0 (9-13)[134] (h+t) PaddyBrennan 22/1		pu
173	Chidswell (IRE) *NickyRichards* 10-10-0[134] CraigNichol 16/1		pu
184	Impulsive Star (IRE) *NeilMulholland* 9-10-5[139] (s) MrSamWaley-Cohen(3) 12/1		pu
184	Skipthecuddles (IRE) *GraemeMcPherson* 8-10-6[140] (v) KielanWoods 16/1		pu
161	Carole's Destrier *NeilMulholland* 11-10-9[143] (s) RobertDunne 20/1		pu
180	Sizing Codelco (IRE) *ColinTizzard* 10-11-4[152] HarryCobden 33/1		pu
	Mr Frank Bird 23ran 8m03.10		

CHELTENHAM Wednesday, Apr 17   GOOD

237   Cure Parkinson's And Hambo Foundation Silver Trophy Chase   2½m127y (17)
(Limited Handicap) (Gr 2) (1) (5yo+) £33,762

180	MISTER WHITAKER (IRE) *MickChannon* 7-11-9[149] (s) JonathanBurke 4/1cf		1
	GOT AWAY (FR) *OliverSherwood* 6-10-11[137] (s+t) LeightonAspell 14/1	nk	2
183	HIGHWAY ONE O ONE (IRE) *ChrisGordon* 8-11-5[145] TomCannon 4/1cf	4	3
	Imperial Presence (IRE) *PhilipHobbs* 8-11-10[150] RichardJohnson 9/1	2	4
	Kings Monarch *KerryLee* 6-10-4 (10-2)[130] JamieMoore 3/1	3	5
100	Rene's Girl (IRE) *DanSkelton* 9-11-4[144] (t) HarrySkelton 4/1cf	5	6
204	Tree of Liberty (IRE) *KerryLee* 11-11-5[145] RichardPatrick(3) 16/1		ur
	Wenyerreadyfreddie (IRE) *NickyHenderson* 8-11-8[148] NicodeBoinville 6/1		pu
	Mr T. P. Radford 8ran 5m07.70		

FAIRYHOUSE Sunday, Apr 21   GOOD

238   Irish Stallion Farms European Breeders Fund Mares Novices' Hurdle   2½m (10)
Championship Final (Gr 1) (4yo+) £51,304

	HONEYSUCKLE *HenrydeBromhead* 5-11-7 RachaelBlackmore 6/4f		1
197	ELFILE (FR) *W.P.Mullins* 5-11-7 JonathanBurke 20/1	5½	2
197	EGLANTINE DU SEUIL (FR) *W.P.Mullins* 5-11-7 R.Walsh 4/1	3	3
197	Tintangle (IRE) *GordonElliott* 6-11-7 (s) J.W.Kennedy 12/1	nk	4
197	Black Tears (IRE) *GordonElliott* 5-11-7 DavyRussell 10/1	nk	5
232	Court Maid (IRE) *ThomasMullins* 6-11-7 D.J.Mullins 66/1	1¾	6
143	Sassy Diva (IRE) *ShaneCrawley* 8-11-7 (t) JonathanMoore 25/1	1½	7
187	Calie du Mesnil (FR) *W.P.Mullins* 7-11-7 (t) B.J.Cooper 33/1	¾	8
201	Salsaretta (FR) *W.P.Mullins* 6-11-7 P.Townend 8/1	7½	9
197	Buildmeupbuttercup *W.P.Mullins* 5-11-7 DenisO'Regan 28/1	14	10
	Caravation (IRE) *J.P.Dempsey* 6-11-7 L.P.Dempsey 22/1	2¾	11
197	Sancta Simona (FR) *W.P.Mullins* 6-11-7 (h+t) M.P.Walsh 25/1	¾	12
74	Western Victory (IRE) *ColinBowe* 6-11-7 SeanFlanagan 50/1	32	13
197	Emily Moon (IRE) *MrsJ.Harrington* 5-11-7 RobbiePower 25/1	18	14
	Robin de Carlow (IRE) *W.P.Mullins* 6-11-7 J.J.Slevin 16/1		F
	Moskovite (IRE) *DenisHogan* 6-11-7 D.G.Hogan 50/1		pu
	Kenneth Alexander 16ran 4m52.60		

239   Ryanair Gold Cup Novices' Chase (Gr 1) (5yo+) £53,913   2½m (16)

192	VOIX DU REVE (FR) *W.P.Mullins* 7-11-10 (h) R.Walsh 9/4		1
192	REAL STEEL (FR) *W.P.Mullins* 6-11-10 P.Townend 2/1f	5½	2
147	WINTER ESCAPE (IRE) *AidanAnthonyHoward* 8-11-10 M.P.Walsh 4/1	25	3
210	Mengli Khan (IRE) *GordonElliott* 6-11-10 (t) J.W.Kennedy 10/3	4½	4

1000

183 Cubomania (IRE) *GordonElliott* 6-11-10 (t) DavyRussell ....14/1   F
    Andrea Wylie/Graham Wylie 5ran 5m04.90

FAIRYHOUSE Monday, Apr 22   GOOD to SOFT

240 Rathbarry & Glenview Studs Juvenile Hurdle (Gr 2) (4yo) £25,652   2m (9)

199 FRENCH MADE (FR) *W.P.Mullins* 4-10-7 R.Walsh 6/1		1
199 GARDENS OF BABYLON (IRE) *JosephPatrickO'Brien* 4-11-0 (s+t) M.P.Walsh .5/2	½	2
199 COEUR SUBLIME (IRE) *GordonElliott* 4-11-0 DavyRussell 9/4f	14	3
Way Back Home (IRE) *PadraigRoche* 4-11-3 (s+t) P.Townend 10/1	5	4
190 Got Trumped *MrsJ.Harrington* 4-11-0 RobbiePower 9/1	17	5
199 Hannon (IRE) *JohnMcConnell* 4-11-0 (t) SeanFlanagan 14/1	1¾	6
199 Authorizo (FR) *GordonElliott* 4-11-0 (t) J.W.Kennedy 20/1	12	7
83 Filon d'Oudairies (FR) *JosephPatrickO'Brien* 4-11-0 (h) J.J.Slevin 25/1	14	8
190 Star Max (GER) *JosephPatrickO'Brien* 4-11-0 RachaelBlackmore 9/1	2¾	9

    Exors of the Late Mrs M. McManus 9ran 3m56.50

241 Keelings Irish Strawberry Hurdle (Gr 2) (5yo+) £35,913   2½m (10)

55 RASHAAN (IRE) *ColinVancKidd* 7-11-3 DavyRussell 16/1		1
193 NOT MANY LEFT (IRE) *MrsJ.Harrington* 6-11-3 (s) RobbiePower 11/2	1½	2
164 OFF YOU GO (IRE) *CharlesByrnes* 6-11-3 M.P.Walsh 6/4f	ns	3
195 Petit Mouchoir (FR) *HenrydeBromhead* 8-11-3 RachaelBlackmore 7/2	3½	4
134 Tombstone (IRE) *GordonElliott* 9-11-3 (t) J.W.Kennedy 14/1	17	5
Joey Sasa (IRE) *NoelMeade* 10-11-6 SeanFlanagan 20/1	13	6
187 Wicklow Brave *W.P.Mullins* 10-11-3 MrP.W.Mullins 7/2		F

    Mrs T J Kidd & Mrs R Treacy 7ran 5m03.40

242 Devenish Chase (Gr 2) (5yo+) £51,304   2½m (16)

119 JETT (IRE) *MrsJ.Harrington* 8-11-2 (s) RobbiePower 7/1		1
194 THE STORYTELLER (IRE) *GordonElliott* 8-11-10 DavyRussell 3/1	4¾	2
188 ORDINARY WORLD (IRE) *HenrydeBromhead* 9-11-2 RachaelBlackmore 3/1	15	3
17 Snow Falcon (IRE) *NoelMeade* 9-11-8 SeanFlanagan 15/8f	2½	4
149 Doctor Phoenix (IRE) *GordonElliott* 11-11-5 (s+t) J.W.Kennedy 12/1	11	5
236 Crosshue Boy (IRE) *SeanThomasDoyle* 9-11-2 (t) MrH.D.Dunne 14/1	3¾	6

    Mr G. McGrath 6ran 5m15.50

243 Boylesports Irish Grand National Chase (Extended Handicap) (Gr A) (5yo+)   3m5f (24)
    £234,783

BURROWS SAINT (FR) *W.P.Mullins* 6-10-8[144] (s) R.Walsh 6/1f		1
177 ISLEOFHOPENDREAMS *W.P.Mullins* 12-10-7[143] D.E.Mullins 20/1	1¾	2
205 ACAPELLA BOURGEOIS (FR) *W.P.Mullins* 9-11-0[150] (h) JonathanBurke 18/1	5½	3
93 Snugsborough Benny (IRE) *LiamP.Cusack* 9-10-9[145] DenisO'Regan 14/1	21	4
177 Bellow Mome (FR) *W.P.Mullins* 8-10-0[136] D.J.Mullins 25/1	2½	5
183 Roaring Bull (IRE) *GordonElliott* 6-10-2[138] (b) L.P.Dempsey 25/1	6½	6
221 Woods Well (IRE) *GordonElliott* 8-10-5[141] (s) B.J.Cooper 33/1	1	7
119 Tout Est Permis (FR) *NoelMeade* 6-11-7[157] SeanFlanagan 16/1	23	8
184 Whisperinthebreeze (IRE) *MrsJ.Harrington* 6-10-3[139] (s) P.D.Kennedy 16/1	½	9
122 Out Sam *GordonElliott* 10-10-4[140] (v+t) B.Hayes 66/1	15	10
198 Arkwrisht (FR) *JosephPatrickO'Brien* 9-9-13[135] (t) AndrewRing 50/1	½	11
229 A Toi Phil (FR) *GordonElliott* 9-11-1[151] (t) RachaelBlackmore 33/1	7	12
198 Measureofmydreams (IRE) *GordonElliott* 11-10-0[136] (s) M.A.Enright 20/1		F
C'est Jersey (IRE) *W.P.Mullins* 7-10-4[140] (h) KatieO'Farrell(5) 16/1		F
198 Any Second Now (IRE) *T.M.Walsh* 7-11-0[150] (b) M.P.Walsh 10/1		F
177 Pairofbrowneyes (IRE) *W.P.Mullins* 10-11-5[155] P.Townend 12/1		F
Kimberlite Candy (IRE) *TomLacey,GB* 7-10-0[136] RichieMcLernon 20/1		pu
183 Shady Operator (IRE) *JosephPatrickO'Brien* 6-10-0[136] J.J.Slevin 10/1		pu
Forever Gold (IRE) *EdwardCawley* 12-10-1[137] (s) A.W.Short(3) 50/1		pu
184 Gun Digger (IRE) *GordonElliott* 7-10-3[139] (s+t) J.W.Kennedy 14/1		pu
229 Blow By Blow (IRE) *GordonElliott* 8-10-5[141] (b+t) J.S.McGarvey 66/1		pu
229 Valseur Lido (FR) *HenrydeBromhead* 10-10-5[141] (s) H.Morgan(7) 40/1		pu
189 Auvergnat (FR) *EndaBolger* 9-10-7[143] (b) NiallMadden 16/1		pu
229 General Principle (IRE) *GordonElliott* 10-10-8[144] (t) DonaghMeyler 33/1		pu
229 Minella Rocco (IRE) *JonjoO'Neill,GB* 9-10-12[148] (s+t) MrD.O'Connor 28/1		pu
229 Monbeg Notorious (IRE) *GordonElliott* 8-11-0[150] (v) C.Brassil(5) 66/1		pu
202 Shattered Love (IRE) *GordonElliott* 8-11-4[154] (t) DavyRussell 11/1		pu
119 Total Recall (IRE) *W.P.Mullins* 10-11-5[155] MrP.W.Mullins 16/1		pu
229 Dounikos (FR) *GordonElliott* 8-11-6[156] KeithDonoghue 33/1		pu
229 Jury Duty (IRE) *GordonElliott* 8-11-6[156] (t) RobbiePower 11/1		pu

    Mrs S. Ricci 30ran 7m48.40

SANDOWN Saturday, Apr 27   GOOD

244 bet365 Novices' Championship Final Handicap Hurdle (2) (4yo+) £61,900   1m7f216y (8)

172 GETAWAY TRUMP (IRE) *PaulNicholls* 6-11-12[147] HarryCobden 9/2f   1
    HARAMBE *AlanKing* 6-10-12[133] WayneHutchinson 13/2   2¾ 2
    HUMBLE HERO (IRE) *DanSkelton* 5-10-6[127] (t) HarrySkelton ....6/1   hd 3
168 Scarlet Dragon *AlanKing* 6-10-11[132] (h) RichardJohnson 8/1   4 4
    Flash The Steel (IRE) *DanSkelton* 7-10-9[130] (t) BridgetAndrews ....16/1   ½ 5
    Birds of Prey (IRE) *PaulNicholls* 5-10-8[129] (t) LorcanWilliams(5) ....14/1   ½ 6
230 Lord Yeats *JeddO'Keeffe* 6-10-12[133] ThomasDowson(3) 7/1   1½ 7
    Romanor *SeamusMullins* 5-10-0[122] (h) KevinJones(3) 28/1   1 8
176 Benny's Bridge (IRE) *FergalO'Brien* 6-10-8[129] PaddyBrennan 17/2   5 9
    Cause Toujours (FR) *IanWilliams* 7-10-11[132] (t) SamTwiston-Davies ......20/1   ½ 10
    Heatstroke (IRE) *NickyHenderson* 7-10-7[128] (t) JamesBowen ....33/1   ¾ 11
 50 What's Occurring (IRE) *OliverSherwood* 6-10-5[126] LeightonAspell 22/1   6 12
    Airton *DavidPipe* 6-10-6[127] (b) TomScudamore ....25/1   ½ 13
176 Dream du Grand Val (FR) *NickyHenderson* 6-11-1[136] (h) NicodeBoinville 14/1   12 14
167 Petit Palais *TomGeorge* 4-10-2[128] JonathanBurke 16/1   44 15
    Owners Group 023 15ran 3m51.50

245 bet365 Oaksey Chase (Gr 2) (1) (5yo+) £31,322   2¾m164y (21)

155 BLACK CORTON (FR) *PaulNicholls* 8-11-3 (t) BryonyFrost 15/8f   1
 78 GOLD PRESENT (IRE) *NickyHenderson* 9-11-4 JeremiahMcGrath 10/1   11 2
221 SAN BENEDETO (IRE) *PaulNicholls* 8-11-4 (s+t) HarryCobden 5/1   5 3
 69 Cobra de Mai (FR) *DanSkelton* 7-11-0 (s+t) HarrySkelton 9/2   17 4
 66 Josses Hill (IRE) *NickyHenderson* 11-11-0 (t) NicodeBoinville 25/1   8 5
194 Charbel (IRE) *KimBailey* 8-11-6 (s) DavidBass 4/1   24 6
229 Go Conquer (IRE) *NigelTwiston-Davies* 10-11-4 (t) SamTwiston-Davies ....7/1   pu
    The Brooks Family & J. Kyle 7ran 5m39.20

246 bet365 Celebration Chase (Gr 1) (1) (5yo+) £85,425   1m7f119y (13)

188 ALTIOR (IRE) *NickyHenderson* 9-11-7 NicodeBoinville 1/6f   1
188 SCEAU ROYAL (FR) *AlanKing* 9-11-7 DarylJacob 10/3   2½ 2
220 GOD'S OWN (IRE) *TomGeorge* 11-11-7 PaddyBrennan 20/1   3 3
    Vosne Romanee *DrRichardNewland* 8-11-7 (v+t) SamTwiston-Davies 33/1   2 4
114 Diego du Charmil (FR) *PaulNicholls* 7-11-7 (t) HarryCobden 20/1   46 5
    Mrs Patricia Pugh 5ran 3m50.20

247 bet365 Gold Cup Handicap Chase (Gr 3) (1) (5yo+) £84,405   3½m166y (24)

169 TALKISCHEAP (IRE) *AlanKing* 7-10-11[145] WayneHutchinson 7/1   1
198 THE YOUNG MASTER *NeilMulholland* 10-10-8[142] (s) MrSamWaley-Cohen(7) ..8/1   10 2
229 STEP BACK (IRE) *MarkBradstock* 9-10-11[145] (s+t) NicodeBoinville 10/1   9 3
180 Give Me A Copper (IRE) *PaulNicholls* 9-10-9[143] (t) HarryCobden 7/1   10 4
 68 Rolling Dylan (IRE) *PhilipHobbs* 8-10-9[143] (s) JamesBest 16/1   1½ 5
227 West Approach *ColinTizzard* 9-10-7[141] JonjoO'NeillJr.(3) 5/1f   7 6
236 Rathlin Rose (IRE) *DavidPipe* 11-10-0 (9-13)[134] (b) TomScudamore 40/1   4½ 7
105 Le Reve (IRE) *LucyWadham* 11-10-2 (9-12)[136] (b) MaximeTissier(5) 16/1   9 8
206 Prime Venture (IRE) *EvanWilliams* 8-10-3[137] AdamWedge 20/1   4½ 9
198 Just A Sting (IRE) *HarryFry* 7-10-2[136] SeanBowen ....7/1   pu
189 Vyta du Roc (FR) *NickyHenderson* 9-10-9[143] (v) DarylJacob ....25/1   pu
229 Joe Farrell (IRE) *RebeccaCurtis* 10-10-11[145] AidanColeman ....16/1   pu
 59 Present Man (IRE) *PaulNicholls* 9-11-2[150] (t) BryonyFrost ....14/1   pu
229 Rock The Kasbah (IRE) *PhilipHobbs* 9-11-4[152] (s) RichardJohnson ....12/1   pu
180 Beware The Bear (IRE) *NickyHenderson* 9-11-12[160] (b) JeremiahMcGrath ....9/1   pu
    Mr Charles Dingwall 15ran 7m15.50

248 bet365 Select Hurdle (Gr 2) (1) (4yo+) £31,322   2m5f110y (11)

 77 YOUNEVERCALL (IRE) *KimBailey* 8-11-0 (s+t) DavidBass 9/4f   1
186 ON THE BLIND SIDE (IRE) *NickyHenderson* 7-11-3 (s) NicodeBoinville 11/4   9 2
103 THOMAS CAMPBELL *NickyHenderson* 7-11-4 (s) JamesBowen 12/1   12 3
195 Black Op (IRE) *TomGeorge* 8-11-3 (t) JonathanBurke 11/4   9 4
157 Blu Cavalier *AliStronge* 9-11-0 JonjoO'NeillJr. 20/1   6 5
224 Mia's Storm (IRE) *AlanKing* 9-10-11 (s) WayneHutchinson 6/1   4 6
140 Rayvin Black *OliverSherwood* 10-11-0 (s) LeightonAspell 40/1   42 7
    Youneverknow Partnership 7ran 5m15.20

PUNCHESTOWN Tuesday, Apr 30   SOFT

249 Herald Champion Novices' Hurdle (Gr 1) (5yo+) £51,304   2m100y (9)

178 KLASSICAL DREAM (FR) *W.P.Mullins* 5-11-12 R.Walsh 8/13f   1
218 FELIX DESJY (FR) *GordonElliott* 6-11-12 (h) J.W.Kennedy 11/2   5½ 2
231 MISTER BLUE SKY (IRE) *W.P.Mullins* 5-11-12 D.E.Mullins 16/1   11 3

1002

54 Quick Grabim (IRE) *W.P.Mullins* 7-11-12 P.Townend 7/1   3¾   4
Champagne Platinum (IRE) *NickyHenderson,GB* 5-11-12 M.P.Walsh 16/1   5   5
218 Aramon (GER) *W.P.Mullins* 6-11-12 D.J.Mullins 9/1   12   6
    Mrs Joanne Coleman 6ran 4m00.90

250 Boylesports Champion Chase (Drogheda) (Gr 1) (5yo+) £153,912   2m (11)

194 UN DE SCEAUX (FR) *W.P.Mullins* 11-11-12 P.Townend 11/4   1
220 MIN (FR) *W.P.Mullins* 8-11-12 R.Walsh 8/13f   4   2
188 CASTLEGRACE PADDY (IRE) *P.A.Fahy* 8-11-12 (t) DavyRussell 20/1   38   3
91 Great Field (FR) *W.P.Mullins* 8-11-12 J.S.McGarvey 8/1   4   4
220 Hell's Kitchen *HarryFry,GB* 8-11-12 (h+t) M.P.Walsh 20/1   5   5
242 Ordinary World (IRE) *HenrydeBromhead* 9-11-12 RachaelBlackmore 40/1   11   6
    Mr Edward O'Connell 6ran 4m09.20

251 Goffs Land Rover Bumper (4 and 5yo) £51,304   2m100y

    FESTIVAL D'EX (FR) *GordonElliott* 4-11-4 MrJ.J.Codd 9/1   1
    WHATSNOTKNOW (IRE) *M.F.Morris* 4-11-4 (h+t) MrR.P.Quinlan(3) 66/1   10   2
    PAPAL PEARL (IRE) *MrsJ.Harrington* 4-10-11 (t) MrL.J.McGuinness(7) 14/1   19   3
    Flanking Maneuver (IRE) *ColinBowe* 4-11-4 MrB.O'Neill 16/1   3¾   4
    Nelson's Point *RobertTyner* 4-11-4 MrJ.C.Barry(5) ....25/1   ¾   5
    Vital Move (IRE) *JamesJosephMangan* 4-11-4 MrJ.Hurley(7) 100/1   11   6
    Nathaniel's Dream *A.J.Martin* 4-11-4 MissM.O'Sullivan(7) 50/1   1½   7
    Elusive Rebeldom (IRE) *GordonElliott* 4-11-4 MrD.G.Lavery(3) 28/1   2   8
    Scalor (FR) *MissElizabethDoyle* 4-11-4 (h) MrFinianMaguire(3) 16/1   15   9
    Arthur Fonzarelli (IRE) *HenrydeBromhead* 4-11-4 MrD.Roche(3) ....33/1   nk   10
    Evie's Song *GordonElliott* 4-10-11 MrJ.Williams(7) 14/1   3   11
    Balkos (FR) *D.Hassett* 4-11-4 MrD.Kiely(7) 100/1   3   12
    Bulldoze (IRE) *M.F.Morris* 4-11-4 MsLisaO'Neill 20/1   12   13
    Fiston de Becon (FR) *RobertTyner* 4-11-4 MrD.O'Connor ....6/1   nk   14
    Champagne Diva (IRE) *NoelMeade* 4-10-11 MrM.J.O'Hare(3) 4/1   6½   15
    Arctic Ambition (IRE) *RobertTyner* 4-11-4 MrE.P.O'Brien(7) 25/1   22   16
    Gold Mix (FR) *S.Curling* 4-11-4 MrH.D.Dunne(5) 20/1   15   17
    Dylan Power (IRE) *EdwardP.Harty* 4-11-4 (b) MrT.Hamilton(5) 66/1   50   18
    Son of Camas (FR) *NickyHenderson,GB* 4-11-4 MrP.W.Mullins ....2/1f   ¾   19
    John F. Doyle 19ran 4m03.10

252 Dooley Insurance Group Champion Novices' Chase (Ellier) (Gr 1) (5yo+)   3m120y (17)
£53,913

186 DELTA WORK (FR) *GordonElliott* 6-11-10 (h+t) DavyRussell 13/8f   1
184 DISCORAMA (FR) *PaulNolan* 6-11-10 B.J.Cooper 12/1   12   2
183 A PLUS TARD (FR) *HenrydeBromhead* 5-11-5 RachaelBlackmore 9/4   2¼   3
186 Drovers Lane (IRE) *RebeccaCurtis,GB* 7-11-10 P.Townend 33/1   7½   4
179 Articulum (IRE) *TerenceO'Brien* 9-11-10 D.J.Mullins ....20/1   pu
219 Chris's Dream (IRE) *HenrydeBromhead* 7-11-10 RobbiePower ....12/1   pu
85 Getabird (IRE) *W.P.Mullins* 7-11-10 R.Walsh ....4/1   pu
239 Winter Escape (IRE) *AidanAnthonyHoward* 8-11-10 M.P.Walsh ....25/1   pu
    Gigginstown House Stud 8ran 6m41.60

    PUNCHESTOWN Wednesday, May 1   GOOD to SOFT

253 Connolly's Red Mills Irish European Breeders Fund Auction Hurdle Series   2½m (11)
Final (4yo+) £38,478

232 ZERO TEN (IRE) *EmmetMullins* 6-12-0 D.J.Mullins 5/4f   1
133 THE BIG DOG (IRE) *PeterFahey* 6-11-10 DavyRussell 11/4   4¾   2
    PRESENTED WELL (IRE) *HenrydeBromhead* 6-11-8 RachaelBlackmore 33/1   1¼   3
    Chavi Artist (IRE) *ThomasMullins* 6-11-10 P.Townend 33/1   1   4
    Voix des Tiep (FR) *W.P.Mullins* 7-11-12 R.Walsh 4/1   4½   5
    Mister Eddman (IRE) *OliverMcKiernan* 5-11-10 (h) B.Browne(5) 40/1   5   6
    Macgiloney (IRE) *DenisHogan* 6-11-3 (s) D.G.Hogan 50/1   1¾   7
    Whatsafellatodo (IRE) *MartinBrassil* 6-11-10 M.P.Walsh ....10/1   hd   8
57 The Holy One (IRE) *MrsJ.Harrington* 6-11-10 (s) RobbiePower 12/1   28   9
    Montagne d'Argent (IRE) *DavidHarryKelly* 5-11-5 (t) SeanFlanagan 100/1   2¾   10
    Makka Pakka (IRE) *MsMargaretMullins* 6-11-3 D.E.Mullins 66/1   8½   11
    Gigiplan Two Seven (IRE) *MartinBrassil* 8-11-5 (b+t) C.Brassil(5) 100/1   45   12
    Mrs A. F. Mee 12ran 4m57.40

254 Irish Daily Mirror Novices' Hurdle (War of Attrition) (Gr 1) (4yo+) £51,304   3m (13)

201 MINELLA INDO (IRE) *HenrydeBromhead* 6-11-10 RachaelBlackmore 5/1   1
201 ALLAHO (FR) *W.P.Mullins* 5-11-10 R.Walsh 11/4f   2   2
    CAREFULLY SELECTED (IRE) *W.P.Mullins* 7-11-10 P.Townend 9/2   1½   3
201 First Approach (IRE) *NoelMeade* 6-11-10 (s) SeanFlanagan 33/1   1½   4
    Go Another One (IRE) *JohnMcConnell* 7-11-10 (t) RichardJohnson ....18/1   ¾   5

232	Castlebawn West (IRE) *W.P.Mullins* 6-11-10 D.E.Mullins	25/1	12 6
222	Walk Away (IRE) *HenrydeBromhead* 6-11-10 RobbiePower	12/1	6½ 7
232	Cap York (FR) *NoelMeade* 7-11-10 DenisO'Regan	66/1	23 8
238	Salsaretta (FR) *W.P.Mullins* 6-11-3 (h) D.J.Mullins	33/1	pu
201	Commander of Fleet (IRE) *GordonElliott* 5-11-10 J.W.Kennedy	3/1	pu
205	Defi Bleu (FR) *GordonElliott* 6-11-10 DavyRussell	12/1	pu
	School Boy Hours (IRE) *NoelMeade* 6-11-10 M.P.Walsh	25/1	pu

Mr Barry Maloney 12ran 6m01.10

255 Coral Punchestown Gold Cup Chase (Gr 1) (5yo+) £153,912 3m120y (17)

212	KEMBOY (FR) *W.P.Mullins* 7-11-10 R.Walsh	13/8f	1
202	AL BOUM PHOTO (FR) *W.P.Mullins* 7-11-10 P.Townend	7/4	2 2
242	THE STORYTELLER (IRE) *GordonElliott* 8-11-10 DavyRussell	25/1	22 3
202	Bellshill (IRE) *W.P.Mullins* 9-11-10 D.J.Mullins	5/1	4¾ 4
202	Definitly Red (IRE) *BrianEllison,GB* 10-11-10 DannyCook	22/1	2 5
242	Snow Falcon (IRE) *NoelMeade* 9-11-10 SeanFlanagan	33/1	7 6
221	Sub Lieutenant (IRE) *HenrydeBromhead* 10-11-10 (s+t) J.W.Kennedy	33/1	11 7
194	Monalee (IRE) *HenrydeBromhead* 8-11-10 RachaelBlackmore	13/2	pu

Supreme Racing/Brett Graham/Ken Sharp 8ran 6m22.80

256 Racing Post App Champion INH Flat (Gr 1) (4, 5, 6 and 7yo) £51,304 2m70y

	COLREEVY (IRE) *W.P.Mullins* 6-11-7 MrJ.J.Codd	4/1	1
191	ABACADABRAS (FR) *GordonElliott* 5-12-0 MsLisaO'Neill	3/1f	1 2
136	BEACON EDGE (IRE) *NoelMeade* 5-12-0 MrM.J.O'Hare	7/1	¾ 3
136	Embittered (IRE) *JosephPatrickO'Brien* 5-12-0 (h+t) MrT.Hamilton	11/2	nk 4
223	Santa Rossa (IRE) *DermotAnthonyMcLoughlin* 5-11-7 MrFinianMaguire	6/1	2¾ 5
	December Second (IRE) *PhilipKirby,GB* 5-12-0 MrR.P.Quinlan	20/1	1¼ 6
136	Mt Leinster (IRE) *W.P.Mullins* 5-12-0 (h) MrP.W.Mullins	6/1	3¾ 7
	Golden Spread *W.P.Mullins* 6-12-0 MrB.O'Neill	9/1	nk 8
	House Island (IRE) *PaulWebber,GB* 5-12-0 MrD.O'Connor	33/1	3¼ 9
	Fire Away (IRE) *G.T.Hourigan* 6-12-0 (t) MrD.G.Lavery	66/1	10 10

Mrs N. Flynn 10ran 4m01.40

257 Guinness Handicap Chase (Gr A) (5yo+) £51,304 2½m (14)

221	O O SEVEN (IRE) *NickyHenderson,GB* 9-11-1[147] (b) NicodeBoinville	16/1	1
229	LIVELOVELAUGH (IRE) *W.P.Mullins* 9-10-8[140] D.J.Mullins	7/1	2½ 2
41	SIZING GRANITE (IRE) *ColinTizzard,GB* 11-10-12[144] (s+t) JonjoO'NeillJr.(3)	10/1	4¾ 3
183	Ben Dundee (IRE) *GordonElliott* 7-10-6[138] (t) DenisO'Regan	7/1	7 4
151	Fitzhenry (IRE) *PaulNolan* 7-10-3[135] (b) M.P.Walsh	8/1	¾ 5
242	Jett (IRE) *Mrs.J.Harrington* 8-11-7[153] (s) RobbiePower	9/1	2½ 6
	Goulane Chosen (IRE) *SeamusSpillane* 10-11-0[146] D.J.McInerney(3)	33/1	hd 7
	Monatomic (IRE) *GordonElliott* 6-9-12[130] L.P.Dempsey	18/1	28 8
12	Blast of Koeman (IRE) *RobertTyner* 8-11-0[132] (b+t) PhilipEnright	6/1	F
187	Oscar Knight (IRE) *ThomasMullins* 10-10-3[135] J.S.McGarvey	16/1	pu
174	War Sound *PhilipHobbs,GB* 10-10-6[138] RichardJohnson	10/1	pu
	Class Conti (FR) *W.P.Mullins* 7-11-1[147] (t) P.Townend	5/2f	pu

Mr Christopher Hanbury 12ran 5m17.60

PUNCHESTOWN Thursday, May 2   GOOD TO SOFT

258 pigsback.com Handicap Chase (Gr B) (4yo+) £33,060 2m (11)

	SNUGSBOROUGH HALL (IRE) *LiamP.Cusack* 8-10-1[127] (h) DenisO'Regan	11/4f	1
	IMPACT FACTOR (IRE) *Mrs.J.Harrington* 7-11-0[140] RobbiePower	7/2	11 2
204	CROCO BAY (IRE) *BenCase,GB* 12-11-2[142] (s+t) KielanWoods	16/1	8½ 3
215	Moon Over Germany (IRE) *HenrydeBromhead* 8-11-7[147] DavyRussell	7/2	9 4
204	Bun Doran (IRE) *TomGeorge,GB* 8-11-10[150] PaddyBrennan	8/1	¾ 5
9	Don't Touch It (IRE) *Mrs.J.Harrington* 9-11-5[145] (s) M.P.Walsh	20/1	6 6
204	Mind's Eye (IRE) *HenrydeBromhead* 7-10-13[139] (s) RachaelBlackmore	9/1	1½ 7
	Nearly Nama'd (IRE) *AugustineLeahy* 11-10-2[128] D.J.O'Keeffe(7)	40/1	sh 8
208	Tycoon Prince (IRE) *GordonElliott* 9-11-0[140] (t) J.W.Kennedy	28/1	2 9
215	Eamon An Cnoic (IRE) *DavidPipe,GB* 8-10-11[137] (s+t) TomScudamore	14/1	16 10
	Stowaway Forever (IRE) *J.P.Dempsey* 7-10-1[127] (b+t) L.P.Dempsey	20/1	F
242	Doctor Phoenix (IRE) *GordonElliott* 11-11-7[147] (s+t) KeithDonoghue	33/1	ur

Rising Sun Partnership 12ran 4m06.40

259 Ladbrokes Champion Stayers' Hurdle (Gr 1) (4yo+) £152,585 3m (13)

227	UNOWHATIMEANHARRY *HarryFry,GB* 11-11-10 (s+t) M.P.Walsh	16/1	1
195	BACARDYS (FR) *W.P.Mullins* 8-11-10 MrP.W.Mullins	8/1	3 2
195	BAPAUME (FR) *W.P.Mullins* 6-11-10 (t) P.Townend	9/4f	hd 3
187	Killultagh Vic (IRE) *W.P.Mullins* 10-11-10 (s) D.J.Mullins	16/1	½ 4
224	Aux Ptits Soins (FR) *DanSkelton,GB* 9-11-10 HarrySkelton	4/1	nk 5
187	Vision des Flos (FR) *ColinTizzard,GB* 6-11-10 (t) TomScudamore	10/1	3¾ 6

56	Dortmund Park (FR) *GordonElliott* 6-11-10 (t) DavyRussell 8/1	30	7
187	Cracking Smart (FR) *GordonElliott* 7-11-10 (s+t) J.W.Kennedy 8/1	18	8
121	Prince of Scars (IRE) *GordonElliott* 9-11-10 (s) KeithDonoghue 66/1	½	9
241	Not Many Left (IRE) *Mrs.J.Harrington* 6-11-10 (s) RobbiePower 11/2		F

Mr John P. McManus 10ran 6m01.30

260 Ryanair Novices' Chase (Colliers) (Gr 1) (5yo+) £59,482   2m (11)

	CHACUN POUR SOI (FR) *W.P.Mullins* 7-11-10 RobbiePower 3/1		1
192	DEFI DU SEUIL (FR) *PhilipHobbs,GB* 6-11-10 RichardJohnson 9/4f	4¼	2
179	DUC DES GENIEVRES (FR) *W.P.Mullins* 6-11-10 P.Townend 5/2	16	3
239	Voix du Reve (FR) *W.P.Mullins* 7-11-10 D.J.Mullins 10/1	9	4
138	Duca de Thaix (FR) *GordonElliott* 6-11-10 (s+t) J.W.Kennedy 50/1	nk	5
226	Us And Them (IRE) *JosephPatrickO'Brien* 6-11-10 (t) ShaneShortall 16/1		ur
226	Ornua (IRE) *HenrydeBromhead* 8-11-10 DavyRussell 7/1		pu

Mrs S. Ricci 7ran 4m07.30

PUNCHESTOWN Friday, May 3   GOOD to SOFT

261 EMS Copiers Novices' Handicap Chase (Punchestown) (Gr A) (5yo+) £51,724   2m5f (15)

239	REAL STEEL (IRE) *W.P.Mullins* 6-11-10[151] P.Townend 5/2f		1
179	HARDLINE (IRE) *GordonElliott* 7-11-10[151] (h) MrR.James[7] 7/1	6½	2
	POKER PARTY (FR) *HenrydeBromhead* 7-10-11[138] RachaelBlackmore 8/1	12	3
184	Beyond The Law (IRE) *M.F.Morris* 7-10-3[130] (t) PhilipEnright 12/1	1	4
147	Jetz (IRE) *Mrs.J.Harrington* 7-11-6[147] (s) RobbiePower 15/2	19	5
215	R'evelyn Pleasure (IRE) *SeanO.O'Brien* 7-10-3[130] DonaghMeyler 16/1		F
192	Pravalaguna (FR) *W.P.Mullins* 7-11-1[142] D.J.Mullins 9/1		F
177	De Name Escapes Me (IRE) *NoelMeade* 9-10-5[132] (h+t) NiallMadden 9/1		ur
235	Louis' Vac Pouch (IRE) *HenryOliver,GB* 7-11-2[143] (h) JeremiahMcGrath ...9/1		ur
177	Scoir Mear (IRE) *ThomasMullins* 9-10-8[135] M.P.Walsh 16/1		bd
198	Ah Littleluck (IRE) *T.Gibney* 9-10-3[130] (t) MrS.F.O'Keeffe(7) 20/1		pu
183	Quamino (GER) *PaulNolan* 6-10-10[137] (t) B.J.Cooper 14/1		pu

Sullivan Bloodstock Limited 12ran 5m32.10

**262 Hanlon Concrete Irish European Breeders Fund Glencarraig Lady Francis   2m5f (15)
Flood Mares Handicap Chase (Gr B) (4yo+) £38,146**

207	MOYHENNA (IRE) *DenisHogan* 7-11-4[132] D.G.Hogan 5/1		1
93	TIMEFORWEST (IRE) *PeterFahey* 7-11-6[134] D.J.O'Keeffe(7) 7/1	4½	2
	ASK SUSAN (IRE) *W.P.Mullins* 7-10-9[123] P.Townend 2/1f	10	3
	Gracemount (IRE) *SeanThomasDoyle* 8-10-4[118] MrS.F.O'Keeffe(7) 13/2	2¾	4
	Mill Quest (IRE) *GordonElliott* 9-11-2[130] (t) DavyRussell 16/1	1¾	5
	Carnspindle (IRE) *WarrenGreatrex,GB* 7-10-6[120] (s) HarryBannister 20/1	12	6
	Elusive Theatre (IRE) *PatrickGriffin* 8-10-5[119] A.W.Short(3) 50/1	nk	7
	Simple Steps (IRE) *RobertTyner* 9-9-10 (9-7)[113] PhilipEnright 33/1	9	8
	Miss Sassie (IRE) *PaulNolan* 6-10-9[123] (t) B.J.Cooper 66/1	16	9
120	Ellie Mac (IRE) *HenrydeBromhead* 6-10-11[125] (s) RachaelBlackmore 14/1		ur
120	Grey Waters (IRE) *JosephPatrickO'Brien* 5-10-1[118] (s) ShaneShortall 20/1		pu
	Teacher's Pet (IRE) *J.P.Dempsey* 8-11-0[128] (s+t) L.P.Dempsey 25/1		pu
	Synopsis *GordonElliott* 7-11-6[134] (t) J.W.Kennedy 25/1		pu
	Barra (FR) *GordonElliott* 8-11-9[137] (t) MrR.James(7) 7/1		pu
182	Slowmotion (FR) *JosephPatrickO'Brien* 7-11-10[138] (b) RobbiePower 16/1		pu

Mr Robert Hennelly 15ran 5m33.50

263 Betdaq Punchestown Champion Hurdle (Gr 1) (4yo+) £152,585   2m (9)

213	BUVEUR D'AIR (FR) *NickyHenderson,GB* 8-11-12 DavyRussell 2/1jf		1
213	SUPASUNDAE (IRE) *Mrs.J.Harrington* 9-11-12 (t) RobbiePower 9/2	2½	2
241	WICKLOW BRAVE *W.P.Mullins* 10-11-12 MrP.W.Mullins 16/1	1¼	3
241	Petit Mouchoir (FR) *HenrydeBromhead* 8-11-12 (s) B.J.Cooper 9/1	½	4
227	Apple's Jade (FR) *GordonElliott* 7-11-5 (t) J.W.Kennedy 2/1jf	½	5
213	Summerville Boy (IRE) *TomGeorge,GB* 7-11-12 JonathanBurke 33/1	1½	6
213	Melon *W.P.Mullins* 7-11-12 (s) P.Townend 5/1	4½	7

Mr John P. McManus 7ran 3m54.70

264 Alanna Homes Champion Novices' Hurdle (Tickell) (Gr 1) (4yo+) £50,862   2½m (11)

225	RESERVE TANK (IRE) *ColinTizzard,GB* 5-11-10 RobbiePower 13/2		1
185	SAMS PROFILE *M.F.Morris* 5-11-10 DavyRussell 6/1	½	2
238	EGLANTINE DU SEUIL (FR) *W.P.Mullins* 5-11-3 JonathanBurke 14/1	1¾	3
106	Tornado Flyer (FR) *W.P.Mullins* 6-11-10 P.Townend 6/1	6½	4
232	Dommage Pour Toi (FR) *HenrydeBromhead* 6-11-10 J.W.Kennedy 20/1	1¼	5
185	City Island (IRE) *MartinBrassil* 6-11-10 (t) AnnO'Connor 11/10f	2¼	6
232	Easy Game (FR) *W.P.Mullins* 5-11-10 B.Hayes 14/1	3¼	7
133	Come To Me (FR) *W.P.Mullins* 7-11-10 (h) D.E.Mullins 28/1	3¼	8
232	Gallant John Joe (IRE) *OliverMcKiernan* 6-11-10 (s) B.Browne 33/1	15	9

231	All For Joy (IRE) *OliverMcKiernan* 7-11-10 SeanFlanagan	50/1	F
	Royal Rendezvous (IRE) *W.P.Mullins* 7-11-10 (h) MrP.W.Mullins	12/1	pu
	The Reserve Tankers 11ran 4m50.60		

265 Star Best For Racing Coverage Champion Hunters Chase (4yo+) £16,293   3m120y (17)
203	CAID DU BERLAIS (FR) *MrsRoseLoxton,GB* 10-12-0 (t) MrWilliamBiddick	3/1	1
214	BURNING AMBITION (IRE) *PierceMichaelPower* 8-12-0 MrR.James(7)	4/1	28 2
	FENNO'S STORM (IRE) *DeclanQueally* 8-12-0 (v) MrD.L.Queally(3)	10/1	1½ 3
	Macs Legend (IRE) *GerardKelleher* 11-12-0 MrE.P.O'Brien(7)	50/1	19 4
	It Came To Pass (IRE) *EugeneM.O'Sullivan* 9-12-0 MissM.O'Sullivan(7)	12/1	ur
	Salsify (IRE) *RodgerSweeney* 14-12-0 MrT.Hamilton(5)	66/1	ur
214	Balnaslow (IRE) *GrahamMcKeever* 12-12-0 MissK.Ferris(7)	33/1	pu
203	Stand Up And Fight (IRE) *EndaBolger* 7-12-0 MrD.O'Connor	7/4f	pu
214	Ucello Conti (FR) *GordonElliott* 11-12-0 (s+t) MrB.O'Neill	5/1	pu
	Donlon, Doyle, MacDonald & C. Barber 9ran 6m33.80		

PUNCHESTOWN Saturday, May 4 GOOD to SOFT

266 Irish Stallion Farms European Breeders Fund Annie Power Mares Champion 2½m (11)
Hurdle (Gr 1) (4yo+) £53,448
182	BENIE DES DIEUX (FR) *W.P.Mullins* 8-11-7 P.Townend	2/5f	1
182	STORMY IRELAND (FR) *W.P.Mullins* 5-11-7 RobbiePower	7/2	9½ 2
182	GOOD THYNE TARA (FR) *W.P.Mullins* 9-11-7 D.J.Mullins	8/1	15 3
	With Discretion (IRE) *NickyHenderson,GB* 8-11-7 NicodeBoinville	16/1	20 4
238	Tintangle (IRE) *GordonElliott* 6-11-7 (s) J.W.Kennedy	16/1	pu
	Mrs S. Ricci 5ran 4m49.30		

267 AES Champion Four Year Old Hurdle (Gr 1) (4yo) £51,724   2m (9)
167	FUSIL RAFFLES (FR) *NickyHenderson,GB* 4-11-0 DarylJacob	13/8f	1
211	FAKIR D'OUDAIRIES (FR) *JosephPatrickO'Brien* 4-11-0 D.W.O'Connor	7/4	2¾ 2
240	FRENCH MADE (FR) *W.P.Mullins* 4-10-7 P.Townend	10/3	5 3
240	Way Back Home (IRE) *PadraigRoche* 4-11-0 (s+t) RobbiePower	16/1	2¾ 4
190	Coko Beach (FR) *GordonElliott* 4-11-0 DavyRussell	12/1	36 5
	Mr Simon Munir & Mr Isaac Souede 5ran 3m51.10		

268 Palmerstown House Pat Taaffe Handicap Chase (Gr B) (150) (5yo+) £31,035 3m120y (17)
	HERON HEIGHTS (IRE) *HenrydeBromhead* 10-11-6[141] (s+t) DavyRussell	12/1	1
233	ONEFORTHEROADTOM *HarryFry,GB* 6-10-1[122] (h) NiallMadden	6/1	6½ 2
46	SWINGBRIDGE (IRE) *GordonElliott* 11-10-3[124] (b+t) J.W.Kennedy	12/1	8½ 3
12	Full Cry (IRE) *HenrydeBromhead* 9-10-12[133] (s+t) H.Morgan(7)	25/1	1½ 4
243	Bellow Mome (FR) *W.P.Mullins* 8-11-1[136] P.Townend	9/2	34 5
	Young Paddymc (IRE) *T.Gibney* 7-9-13[120] D.E.Mullins	11/4f	F
257	Oscar Knight (IRE) *ThomasMullins* 10-11-0[135] J.S.McGarvey	16/1	ur
193	Walk To Freedom (IRE) *MrsJ.Harrington* 9-11-1[136] (h+t) RobbiePower	3/1	ur
243	Arkwrisht (FR) *JosephPatrickO'Brien* 9-10-12[133] (t) AndrewRing	25/1	pu
	Acting Lass (IRE) *HarryFry,GB* 8-11-9[144] (t) NicodeBoinville	8/1	pu
	Mr Barry Maloney 10ran 6m22.00		

269 Ballymore Handicap Hurdle (Gr B) (4yo+) £50,862   2½m (11)
200	MR ADJUDICATOR *W.P.Mullins* 5-11-9[149] MrP.W.Mullins	20/1	1
	CONTINGENCY *W.P.Mullins* 6-9-11[123] C.McNamara(7)	25/1	¾ 2
201	DORRELLS PIERJI (FR) *W.P.Mullins* 6-10-9[135] DarylJacob	11/1	½ 3
57	Stratum *W.P.Mullins* 6-11-2[142] (h) B.J.Cooper	12/1	2¼ 4
57	Davids Charm (IRE) *JohnJ.Walsh* 8-11-3[143] L.P.Gilligan(7)	33/1	2¾ 5
200	Cut The Mustard (FR) *W.P.Mullins* 7-10-6[132] (h) KatieO'Farrell(5)	14/1	3¼ 6
217	Canardier (FR) *DermotAnthonyMcLoughlin* 7-11-3[143] (h) SeanFlanagan	7/1jf	1½ 7
	Spades Are Trumps (IRE) *GavinPatrickCromwell* 6-10-1[127] NiallMadden	12/1	nk 8
	Take Revenge (IRE) *MartinBrassil* 7-10-9[135] (t) D.J.McInerney(3)	12/1	sh 9
195	Man of Plenty *SophieLeech,GB* 10-9-13[125] (h) JonathanMoore	20/1	1 10
	Lac Kivu (FR) *W.P.Mullins* 6-11-5[145] (t) D.E.Mullins	7/1jf	nk 11
	Swamp Fox (IRE) *JosephG.Murphy* 7-11-5[145] (b) B.Browne(5)	50/1	2¾ 12
208	Woodland Opera (IRE) *MrsJ.Harrington* 9-11-2[142] (b+t) RobbiePower	16/1	1¼ 13
149	Landofhopeandglory (IRE) *JosephPatrickO'Brien* 6-10-11[137] (b+t) L.P.Dempsey	25/1	6 14
8	Shanning (IRE) *W.P.Mullins* 6-10-10[136] B.Hayes	16/1	4½ 15
	La Tektor (FR) *A.J.Martin* 8-10-2[128] (t) DenisO'Regan	8/1	2¾ 16
	Eoline Jolie (FR) *W.P.Mullins* 5-9-10[122] (t) ShaneShortall	40/1	8 17
	Golden Spear (IRE) *A.J.Martin* 8-10-11[137] (t) E.O'Connell(5)	16/1	1½ 18
135	Jezki (IRE) *MrsJ.Harrington* 11-11-8[148] (s) ConorOrr(5)	16/1	5½ 19
205	Cartwright *GordonElliott* 6-10-8[134] (b) DavyRussell	12/1	nk 20
12	Supreme Vinnie (IRE) *MissD.M.O'Shea* 10-9-10[122] (t) PhilipEnright	50/1	4¼ 21
	Eight And Bob *W.P.Mullins* 6-10-2[128] P.Townend	16/1	pu
135	Sayar (IRE) *W.P.Mullins* 6-10-9[135] NicodeBoinville	25/1	pu

AUTEUIL Saturday, May 18   SOFT

270   Grande Course de Haies d'Auteuil (Gr 1) (5yo+) £135,776   3m1f77y

266 BENIE DES DIEUX (FR) *W.P.Mullins,Ireland* 8-10-6 P.Townend 88/10		1
DE BON COEUR (FR) *FrancoisNicolle,France* 6-10-6 KevinNabet 4/10f	6½	2
BERJOU (FR) *D.Windrif,France* 5-10-6 (s) NicolasGauffenic 26/1	1¼	3
259 Bapaume (FR) *W.P.Mullins,Ireland* 6-10-10 DavyRussell 16/1	1¾	4
Galop Marin (IRE) *D.Bressou,France* 7-10-10 MorganRegairaz 14/1	hd	5
Alex de Larredya (FR) *FrancoisNicolle,France* 9-10-10 GaetanMasure 81/10	3	6
269 Mr Adjudicator (FR) *W.P.Mullins,Ireland* 5-10-6 JamesReveley 52/1	1¼	7
Titi de Montmartre (FR) *R.Collet,France* 6-10-6 (s) LudovicPhilipperon 77/1	4½	8
Grand Depart (FR) *P.Lenogue,France* 5-10-10 (s) AdrienMerienne 108/1	5½	9
Paul's Saga (FR) *DavidCottin,France* 5-10-1 GeoffreyRe 17/1	ns	10
Yorkhill (IRE) *W.P.Mullins,Ireland* 9-10-10 D.E.Mullins 119/1	¾	11
263 Melon (FR) *W.P.Mullins,Ireland* 7-10-10 RobbiePower 54/1	4	12

Mrs S. Ricci 12ran 6m06.52

AUTEUIL Sunday, May 19   SOFT

271   Zeturf Grand Steeple-Chase de Paris (Gr 1) (5yo+) £318,103   3m5f182y

CARRIACOU (FR) *Mme I.Pacault,France* 7-10-10 DavyRussell 13/1		1
BIPOLAIRE (FR) *FrancoisNicolle,France* 8-10-10 JonathanPlouganou 42/10f	9	2
ROI MAGE (FR) *FrancoisNicolle,France* 7-10-10 GaetanMasure 21/1	10	3
Roxinela (FR) *Francois-MarieCottin,France* 6-10-6 RegisSchmidlin 48/1	¾	4
243 Burrows Saint (FR) *W.P.Mullins,Ireland* 6-10-10 P.Townend 57/10	2½	5
Sainte Turgeon (FR) *PatriceQuinton,France* 7-10-6 NathalieDesoutter 57/1	1½	6
Le Costaud (FR) *GuillaumeMacaire,France* 8-10-10 JamesReveley 13/1	1	7
243 Total Recall (IRE) *W.P.Mullins,Ireland* 10-10-10 (h) D.E.Mullins 105/1	12	8
Dalia Grandchamp (FR) *FrancoisNicolle,France* 6-10-6 DavidGallon 15/1	4	9
Storm of Saintly (FR) *GuillaumeMacaire,France* 10-10-10 BertrandLestrade 24/1	2½	10
So French (FR) *GuillaumeMacaire,France* 8-10-10 (s) JohnnyCharron 37/1	7½	11
229 Rathvinden (IRE) *W.P.Mullins,Ireland* 11-10-10 NicodeBoinville 16/1	10	12
229 Pleasant Company (FR) *W.P.Mullins,Ireland* 11-10-10 RobbiePower 54/1	7	13
243 Acapella Bourgeois (FR) *W.P.Mullins,Ireland* 9-10-10 (h) JonathanBurke 42/1	30	14
Docteur de Ballon (FR) *MlleLouisaCarberry,France* 7-10-10 FelixdeGiles 68/10		ur
Crystal Beach (FR) *M.Rolland,France* 7-10-10 LudovicPhilipperon 48/1		ur
Saint Pistol (FR) *L.Viel,France* 11-10-10 ArnaudDuchene 66/1		F
Spirit Sun (FR) *MlleA-S.Pacault,France* 5-10-6 AlaindeChitray 29/1		F
Eludy (FR) *FrancoisNicolle,France* 5-10-1 KevinNabet 27/1		F

Ecurie Mirande 19ran 7m34.49

INDEX TO SELECTED BIG RACES

1014

TIMEFORM 'TOP HORSES IN FRANCE'

Foreign challengers for the biggest prize in French jump racing, the Grand Steeple-Chase de Paris, have been sporadic in the modern era. None has been successful since Fred Winter's dramatic victory aboard the Fulke Walwyn-trained Mandarin in 1962. The Irish-trained Cheltenham Gold Cup winners of the 1970's, Captain Christy and Tied Cottage, have been among those to try their luck since, Captain Christy finishing runner-up in 1975. Prior to the latest renewal in May, only nine attempts by chasers trained in Britain or Ireland had been made this century, notably by another former Gold Cup winner Long Run, but none of those had finished in the first five. The 2019 renewal, worth the equivalent of £318,103 to the winner, was therefore notable for attracting no fewer than five Irish-trained chasers, all from the stable of Willie Mullins. Ironically, their presence, which contributed to a maximum field of twenty being declared, resulted in another intended Irish challenger, Baie des Iles, being unable to take her chance as she was one of three entries balloted out. Baie des Iles, trained by Ross O'Sullivan, had been a rare overseas winner of one of Auteuil's top chases when landing the Prix des Drags the previous summer, despite which her rating wasn't high enough to avoid elimination. Mullins' success with his hurdlers at Auteuil over the years has been well documented, while his all-out attempt to win the Grand Steeple-Chase came in a year when he had ticked off wins in two other major chases which had hitherto eluded him, the Cheltenham Gold Cup and the Irish Grand National. It was the winner of the latter contest, Burrows Saint, who fared much the best of his stable's quintet in finishing fifth. Although the least experienced chaser among them with just six starts in steeplechases beforehand, it was probably significant that two of Burrows Saint's previous runs over fences had come at Auteuil when trained in his early days by Guillaume Macaire.

In the end, nineteen faced the starter in the Grand Steeple-Chase following the late withdrawal of **Bob And Co** whose owner and amateur rider Mr David Maxwell was injured in a fall earlier on the card. Maxwell purchased the horse, now transferred to Paul Nicholls, with the aim of winning the 2020 Foxhunter. That still left eight British- or Irish-born jockeys with mounts in the Grand Steeple-Chase, three of them riding for French stables. James Reveley, who had been the first British jockey to win the Grand Steeple-Chase since Fred Winter, was bidding to win the race for the fourth year running for Macaire with **Le Costaud** after partnering **So French** to victory in 2016 and 2017 and On The Go in 2018. The latter missed the whole of the latest season, while So French contested the latest Grand Steeple-Chase as an outsider, his only victory since winning it for a second time coming in a minor event over hurdles at Fontainebleau in February. Macaire had another of his former Grand Steeple-Chase winners in the line-up, the 2014 winner **Storm of Saintly**, who had won a four-runner Prix Troytown in March.

Zeturf Grand Steeple-Chase de Paris, Auteuil—Davy Russell's first ride over fences at Auteuil is a winning one in France's biggest race over jumps aboard Carriacou (No.6). They are preceded over the riviere des tribunes by the favourite and eventual runner-up Bipolaire (No.9), with a couple of Willie Mullins' five runners Rathvinden (No.3) and Total Recall (No.15) also in shot

Prix La Haye Jousselin, Auteuil—the grey Bipolaire wins the most important chase of the autumn for the second year running ahead of Saint Goustan Blue

Le Costaud was the stable's main contender having won Italy's most valuable chase, the Gran Premio Merano (Macaire's fourth success in the race) in the autumn, and then won his first important chase at Auteuil in March when successful in the Prix Robert de Clermont-Tonnerre. Another British-born but now French-based jockey, Felix de Giles, was aboard another winner of one of the main prep races in the spring, **Docteur de Ballon**. Successful in the Prix Ingre, Docteur de Ballon is trained by Louisa Carberry, wife of Irishman Philip Carberry, who had been the first foreign jockey since Winter to win the Grand Steeple-Chase when successful with Princesse d'Anjou in 2006, a victory they repeated two years later. De Giles is also the regular partner of the smart cross-country chaser **Urgent de Gregaine** who was placed behind Tiger Roll in the Cross Country Chase at the Cheltenham Festival for the second year running.

Far from being an Auteuil regular like Reveley or de Giles, Davy Russell, the third foreign jockey riding for a French yard in the Grand Steeple-Chase, had never ridden over fences at the track. His mount **Carriacou** had a good record around Auteuil, on the other hand, winning the Group 1 Prix Maurice Gillois for four-year-olds in the autumn of 2016 and then finishing third behind So French in the following year's Grand Steeple-Chase. Carriacou was then off the track until January of the latest season when making a winning return over hurdles at Pau. He avoided the bigger prep races for the Grand Steeple-Chase but went there after winning the listed Prix William Head. In an open-looking edition of the Grand Steeple-Chase, the betting was headed by **Bipolaire**, also a leading fancy the year before when falling at the first, and the less experienced **Crystal Beach**. The latter, a half-brother to the Grande Course de Haies d'Auteuil winner Questarabad, had only made his chasing debut the previous September but had won three of his five starts over fences at Auteuil, notably when beating Le Costaud in the Prix Murat in April with Bipolaire a well-held third. Like Bipolaire, Crystal Beach lined up in the Grand Steeple-Chase after a defeat but had run creditably at the weights when third behind Docteur de Ballon and the mare **Dalia Grandchamp** in the Prix Ingre. Bipolaire was contesting his third Grand Steeple-Chase having won the Prix La Haye Jousselin for the second year running in November, while his spring campaign began with a listed win over hurdles prior to the Murat. Bipolaire and Dalia Grandchamp formed part of a four-strong challenge for trainer Francois Nicolle who ended Macaire's reign as champion trainer in 2018. Also bidding to give Nicolle a first win in the race was **Roi Mage** who had been brought down by Bipolaire the year before but had won twice since at Compiegne, including the Prix Romati just a fortnight before the Grand Steeple-Chase.

Both Crystal Beach and Docteur de Ballon unseated at the formidable rail ditch and fence five out by which time Bipolaire was to the fore with the mare **Roxinela** who made much of the running. At least half a dozen were still in contention on the home turn, Carriacou going well among them under a typically patient ride from Russell. Still on the bridle, Carriacou jumped the last upsides Bipolaire before drawing clear on the run-in to win by nine lengths. Bipolaire was in turn ten clear of stable-companion Roi Mage who passed several rivals after the last to snatch third from Roxinela, with Burrows Saint, another mare **Sainte Turgeon** (fourth two years earlier), and Le Costaud next home and clear of the rest, fourteen completing in all. Carriacou's trainer Isabelle Pacault (whose family also bred and own the horse) became the first woman to train a Grand Steeple-Chase winner, having twice saddled runners-up Venus de Mirande in 1994 and Lord Carmont in 2007. Another stable-companion, the latter's half-brother Toutancarmont, may be remembered for his dramatic exit two out when holding every chance in the 2015 Cross Country Chase at the Festival. Pacault also won the Prix des Drags in June when the mare **Jubilatoire** came out best in a three-way finish with Docteur de Ballon and **Poly Grandchamp**. Jubilatoire has now won five of her last six starts at Auteuil, having put up a smart performance in handicap company on her previous outing when winning the listed Prix Saint Sauveur by twelve lengths under top weight of 11-7.

   Saint Goustan Blue was absent from the Grand Steeple-Chase de Paris for the second year running having looked better than ever in the autumn. He took his winning run to six races, beating Roxinela and Bob And Co in the listed Prix Richard et Robert Hennessy and following up with a beating of **Milord Thomas** in the Prix Heros XII before finding only Bipolaire too good in the Prix La Haye Jousselin. Saint Goustan Blue unseated in two of his three subsequent starts over fences but ran well on the other occasion when trying to concede lots of weight to Storm of Saintly in the Troytown, his first start after leaving Macaire for Milord Thomas's trainer Dominique Bressou. Saint Goustan Blue made a successful return to hurdling in July in the listed Prix Dawn Run in which he was well treated at the weights on his chasing form. The former Grand Steeple-Chase winner Milord Thomas went on to make the frame in several more of the top chases after his second in the Heros XII (a race he'd won twice before), notably when third in the La Haye Jousselin, a race in which his form figures now read 11123. **Srelighonn** is another good chaser yet to contest a Grand Steeple-Chase but he wouldn't have been out of place in the latest line-up judged on his beating of Crystal Beach and Roi Mage in the Prix Georges Courtois in November, his only run of the season over fences. Elsewhere, **Forthing** was unbeaten in four starts at Pau over the winter (two of them over hurdles), notably when beating Sainte Turgeon to win the Grand Prix de Pau for a second time.

Prix Renaud du Vivier (Grande Course de Haies des 4 Ans), Auteuil—
Master Dino, ridden by James Reveley, ends 2018 as the top four-year-old over hurdles

Among the four-year-old chasers who turned five during the winter, the most interesting was **Master Dino** who had looked well on course for the Cheltenham Festival before sustaining an injury. He ended 2018 as the best of his generation over hurdles, completing a four-timer in the Prix Renaud du Vivier, before running out a thirty-length winner on his chasing debut at Auteuil later in November. He then became Guillaume Macaire's first runner and winner in Britain for six years when following up in impressive fashion in a novice chase at Plumpton and was cut to favourite for the Golden Miller, but suffered a hairline fracture in the process. Four of the five winners of the autumn championship chase for four-year-olds, the Prix Maurice Gillois, between 2013 and 2017 have now gone on to win the Grand Steeple-Chase later in their careers, though the latest winner, the German-bred filly **Cicalina**, also trained by Macaire, failed to make much impact subsequently back over hurdles. She beat **Epi Sacre** and **Eddy de Balme** in the Maurice Gillois, but when the first four from that race met again in the Prix Morgex, it was the Prix The Fellow winner **Cat Tiger**, fourth in the Maurice Gillois, who came out on top with Cicalina only third. Cat Tiger was another David Maxwell purchase—the amateur partnered him for the first time in the Morgex—and he too has joined Paul Nicholls.

When the Group 1 jumps races of the first half of the year were rescheduled in 2018 to bring them all together on the same weekend towards the end of May, the Grande Course de Haies d'Auteuil was run on the Sunday just after the Grand Steeple-Chase. The latest renewal of the Grande Course de Haies was switched to the Saturday instead, giving it more prominence as a worthy highlight of that day's racing. **De Bon Coeur**, who had been so impressive when winning by fifteen lengths twelve months earlier, was odds on to retain her crown in a field which featured another quintet of runners from the Mullins stable but none (for the first time since 2010) from Britain. Things had not gone entirely smoothly for De Bon Coeur since her victory in the 2018 Grande Course de Haies. A hairline fracture to a foot kept her off the track for the rest of that year, and it was not until March that she returned to action to win the Prix Hypothese for the second time, from the chaser Crystal Beach. Her only other start prior to the Grande Course de Haies came in the

Prix Leon Rambaud, Auteuil—another win for leading hurdler De Bon Coeur who lands the odds from her male rivals Berjou (right) and Galop Marin

Prix Ferdinand Dufaure, Auteuil—top four-year-old chaser Goliath du Berlais takes the open ditch ahead of runner-up Bel Apsis on his way to an impressive victory on his final start before taking up stallion duties in 2020.

Prix Leon Rambaud in April but she was less convincing in winning by just over a length from the handicapper **Berjou**. De Bon Coeur had met with her only defeat in completed starts up until then in the same race the year before when reported to be in season, and the same reason was given for her not winning with her usual authority in the latest renewal.

With De Bon Coeur missing from the top hurdles during the autumn, **Galop Marin** took full advantage in a division which lacked strength in depth. The front runner had finished behind De Bon Coeur on all three occasions they had met earlier in 2018, including when he had been beaten more than twenty lengths into fifth in the Grande Course de Haies. However, he returned an improved performer later in the year to complete a clean sweep of all four autumn group contests over hurdles for older horses at Auteuil. After the Prix de Compiegne and Prix Carmarthen, he put up a high-class effort when a fifteen-length winner of the Grand Prix d'Automne in which the mares **Miss Salsa Blue**, Dalia Grandchamp and **Titi de Montmartre** completed the frame. Conceding plenty of weight all round, Galop Marin completed his four-timer in the Prix Leon Olry-Roederer, which he had also won the year before, this time by twelve lengths from the Nick Williams-trained Le Rocher. However, after falling in the Prix Juigne on his return in the spring (a race won by stable-companion **Raffles Sun**), it was a familiar story when Galop Marin came up against De Bon Coeur again as he finished third behind her in her two starts in the spring and for the second year running finished fifth in the Grande Course de Haies.

This time De Bon Coeur met her match in the Grande Course de Haies as she had no answer after the last to another prolific mare, Benie des Dieux, who ran out the six and a half length winner and gave Mullins his fifth win in the top French hurdle. Benie des Dieux had won twice over hurdles at Auteuil at the start of her career when trained by Isabelle Gallorini. Behind De Bon Coeur, five-year-old Berjou confirmed himself a smart addition to the ranks of the top French hurdlers in third with the potential to win a good prize. Benie des Dieux's stable companion Bapaume, runner-up the year before, made the frame for the second year running in fourth under Davy Russell (his only previous ride at Auteuil had come in the same race six years earlier when second on Solwhit), while De Bon Coeur's stablemate **Alex de Larredya**, winner of a minor event over fences beforehand, completed the first six behind Galop Marin. The French hurdlers were again no match for members of another five-strong Mullins raiding party in the Prix La Barka three weeks later. Bapaume was back in a bid to win the race for the second year running but he was unable to concede weight to stablemate Mr Adjudicator who was only seventh in the Grande Course de Haies. Mullins was winning the La Barka for the fourth year running and the sixth time all told. Third in the Prix La Barka was the former top-class hurdler **Blue Dragon** who showed he was still capable of smart form and had won a minor event on his previous start. He had returned earlier in the year after an absence of almost two years since being pulled up when a beaten favourite for the second year running in the 2017 Grande Course de Haies. As for De Bon Coeur, connections felt she ran and jumped in the Grande Course de Haies as though feeling something (she lost a shoe from the foot she had injured previously), though subsequent tests failed to reveal any new problem. However, plans to run her in the Gold Cup at Royal Ascot were scrapped (she was entered despite never having run on the Flat) and her retirement to stud was announced later in the summer.

As already mentioned, before having his attentions turned to chasing, Master Dino dominated the four-year-old hurdles in the autumn as he and stable-companion **Tunis** continued their ongoing rivalry. Tunis had come out on top in most of their early encounters but he finished second to Master Dino in the Prix de Maisons-Laffitte, third in the Prix Pierre de Lassus, and was runner-up again in what turned out to be his final start in the Prix Renaud du Vivier. The Polish-bred Tunis, retired as a still entire colt, began a stallion career in the spring. **The Stomp**, a stable-companion of De Bon Coeur, ran his best race at Auteuil when third to Galop Marin in the Prix de Compiegne at Auteuil, though Enghien, before it ceased staging jumping, and Compiegne have been better hunting grounds for the prolific winner. However, he was denied a fourth consecutive win in the listed Prix de Besancon by **Corazones** and ran another good race in defeat back at Compiegne in the track's top hurdle, the Prix Leopold d'Orsetti, when conceding plenty of weight to the four-year-old **Highway To Hell** who wasn't seen out again but is now unbeaten in four starts over hurdles.

Tunis was not alone among the leading young jumpers in France in the latest season to have his racing career cut short to take up stallion duties. That was also the destiny of his year-younger stable-companion **Goliath du Berlais** who proved easily the best of his generation over fences and was beaten only once in his eight starts in chases at Auteuil. He failed to win over hurdles in his first four starts but Macaire sent him chasing at the earliest opportunity and he had already won three races before suffering his only defeat over fences, conceding 7 lb to **Polirico**, in the Prix Congress in November. But after the turn of the year, Goliath du Berlais emulated the same stable's Whetstone the year before by winning the Prix Duc d'Anjou, Prix Fleuret and Prix Jean Stern before signing off by galloping his rivals into the ground in much his most important race with his stallion career in mind, the Group 1 Prix Ferdinand Dufaure, which he won by margins of fourteen and fifteen lengths. Goliath du Berlais has the highest rating for a four-year-old chaser since 'Top Horses In France' was introduced in *Chasers & Hurdlers 2003/04*. In the short term, his departure to stud therefore deprives French jumping of its brightest young prospect, though if he's anything like as successful in his own stallion career as his sire Saint des Saints (himself a leading four-year-old over hurdles for Macaire) whom he joins at the Haras d'Etreham, he will produce plenty of good jumpers of his own.

Bel Apsis was the nearest thing to a rival to Goliath du Berlais, finishing runner-up to him in each of his last three races, while the filly **Thrilling**, a stable-companion of Goliath du Berlais, won three times at Pau during the winter before being beaten a long way in third in both the Jean Stern and Ferdinand Dufaure. **Farnice** wasn't too far behind the best of the three-year-old hurdlers in the autumn and he made a good start over fences in the spring, notably when having Thrilling back in third in the Prix La Perichole. Francois Nicolle's other runner in that contest **Royal Et Tic** had been runner-up to Goliath du Berlais in the Prix Duc d'Anjou and more recently a remote fourth in the Ferdinand Dufaure but was fatally injured in a fall at the riviere du huit. Although a smaller water jump than the better-known riviere des tribunes in front of the stands, the riviere du huit has a reputation for catching horses out and had already been earmarked for modification in the close season following an earlier fatality there in April. The riviere des tribunes can take some jumping as well though, and sadly claimed a victim among Willie Mullins' runners when veteran Isleofhopendreams, runner-up in the last two Irish Grand Nationals, came to grief in the Prix des Drags.

Prix Alain du Breil - Course de Haies de Printemps des Quatre Ans, Auteuil—
Feu Follet confirms himself the leading four-year-old over hurdles, drawing clear of Polirico
and Willie Mullins' challenger the filly French Made.

With Goliath du Berlais having left the scene, the top four-year-old chases of the autumn will be up for grabs, though Macaire may well have them covered by **Feu Follet** who so far has built his reputation as the best of the current crop of juveniles over hurdles. Feu Follet won both his starts over fences in the autumn, but with his stable-companion ruling the roost in that discipline, he was put back over hurdles in the spring when successful in three of his four starts, the Prix d'Indy, Prix Amadou and the Prix Alain du Breil. He ran out a clear-cut winner of the last-named contest after making much of the running, though a return to fences didn't quite go to plan when he was subsequently beaten at odds on by Farnice in the Prix La Perichole. Goliath du Berlais' conqueror Polirico failed to build on that win in the Prix Congress over fences, but he fared better over hurdles, winning the Prix General de Saint-Didier at Compiegne in the autumn and then chasing home Feu Follet in both the Amadou and Alain du Breil. Polirico had to settle for second again in the Prix Questarabad in June in which Francois Nicolle saddled the first three home, with the filly **L'Autonomie** coming out on top after making all the running, with **Porto Pollo** (a listed winner next time) back in third. L'Autonomie had finished only fourth in the Alain du Breil, but prior to that had inflicted Feu Follet's only defeat over hurdles in the spring when allowed to pinch an unassailable lead in the back straight in the Prix de Pepinvast.

L'Autonomie won her first two starts over hurdles before finishing third in the top three-year-old hurdle, the Prix Cambaceres, with Farnice fourth. For different reasons, neither of the first two from that race played a part in the remaining top juvenile contests. With a Group 1 in the bag, winner **Beaumec de Houelle** was another of the season's stallion recruits, replacing his own sire Martaline who was retired from stud duties at the Haras de Montaigu at the age of twenty. The Cambaceres took Beaumec de Houelle's record over hurdles to six out of seven, having beaten **Pic d'Orhy** and Farnice in the Prix Georges de Talhouet-Roy beforehand. Pic d'Orhy, who was again runner-up to Beaumec de Houelle in the Cambaceres, was probably the pick on autumn form of a strong squad of juveniles for the Nicolle stable, though he was next seen finishing down the field in the Triumph Hurdle with Paul Nicholls. Among the other good four-year-old hurdlers, **Fidele Au Poste** won twice at Compiegne but ran his best race when successfully conceding weight all round in a listed handicap on his final start at Auteuil in March. The filly **Listenmania** was narrowly beaten in both her starts in the autumn, giving weight to L'Autonomie in a listed contest and again best at the weights in a three-way finish behind **Floridee** and **Lady Ardilaun** in the Prix Bournosienne.

An important name missing from programmes after mid-September was that of Guy Cherel whose stable, one of the largest and most successful in French jumping, was disbanded following his arrest in connection with allegations of doping. That came after a series of escalating fines Cherel had incurred from France Galop over the period from 2011 to 2016 when several horses in his care had tested positive for banned substances. In each case, Cherel had apparently misjudged the length of time that medication had taken to clear the horses' systems before they could race again. After the last of those cases, involving the former smart chaser Lachlan Bridge, disqualified after winning over hurdles at Clairefontaine in the summer of 2016, Cherel served a three-month ban. One of the main beneficiaries of the dispersal of the Cherel string turned out to be Joseph O'Brien after J. P. McManus bought a batch of horses that included the likes of Fakir d'Oudairies and Darasso.

McManus is already stocking up on his next batch of juveniles and purchased a couple of three-year-olds who made promising winning debuts at Auteuil, **Mick Pastor** and **Gelboe de Chanay**. The latter, a half-sister to useful hurdler Eragon de Chanay, won the fillies' division of the listed Prix Wild Monarch for newcomers by fourteen lengths. Unlike that pair, another McManus acquisition, **Hipsters**, is due to remain in France with Guillaume Macaire for the time being, but after looking potentially the best early three-year-old after winning his first two starts, including the listed Prix Go Ahead in April, he sustained an injury early on his first start in the McManus colours when odds on for the Prix Aguado which required an operation. That contest was won by the colt **Nirvana du Berlais** (a half-brother to the one-time smart staying hurdler Aubusson), though the runner-up, Hipsters' stable-companion **For Fun**, winner of the listed Prix Stanley, came out marginally better at the weights. Nirvana du Berlais had finished second to Mick Pastor on his previous start. The top race for three-year-old fillies before Auteuil's summer break went to **Messagere** who made it two wins from two starts in the Prix Sagan. Third-placed **Aterisk** came out best at the weights under a penalty having won the listed Prix d'Iena beforehand. Runner-up **Invincible Dina** was also a listed winner beforehand, she too receiving weight from Aterisk when beating her in the Prix Girofla.

The Prix Girofla and Prix Go Ahead for three-year-olds are among nine new listed races in the French jumping programme in 2019. Further upgrades to the programme for three-year-old hurdlers will come in the autumn when three listed races are among a total of five contests during the year promoted to Group 3 level, while the Prix Bournosienne, the Group 3 for three-year-old fillies in early-November, becomes a Group 2. The upgraded races formed part of an action plan announced by France Galop in the autumn of 2018 to support and promote jumping. Other measures included improvements to the racing calendar and programme, investments in racecourse infrastructure and better promotion of jump racing with the public and prospective owners, particularly foreign investors.

Chasers (5yo+)					
160	Carriacou 7	148	Poly Grandchamp 7	142	So French 8
159	Bipolaire 8	147	Forthing 8	142	Taupin Rochelais 12
156	Saint Goustan Blue 7	147	Saint Xavier 7	142	Urgent de Gregaine 11
155	Le Costaud 8	146	Storm of Saintly 10	141	Arry 9
155	Milord Thomas 10	145	Dalia Grandchamp (f) 6	141	Capferret 7
152	Srelighonn 6	145	Epi Sacre 5	141	Corazones 7
151	Docteur de Ballon 7	145	Roxinela (f) 6	141	Eludy (f) 5
150p	Master Dino 5	144	Bob And Co 8	140	Edgeoy 5
150	Crystal Beach 7	144	Eddy de Balme 5	140	Monsamou 10
149	Cat Tiger 5	143	Paulougas 7	140	Spirit Sun 5
149	Jubilatoire (f) 6	142	Blasimon 5	139	Eni Light 5
149	Roi Mage 7	142	Cicalina (f) 5	139	My Maj 10
		142	Sainte Turgeon (f) 7	138	Celebre d'Allen 7

Chasers (4yo)

153+	Goliath du Berlais
143	Bel Apsis
140	Polirico
138	Farnice
138	Royal Et Tic
133	Feu Follet
132p	Happy Monarch
132	Fiumicino
131	Katana One
130	Figuero
130	Saint Corneille
130	Thrilling (f)
129	Kapdam
129	King Elvis
129	Porto Pollo
129	Shannon Verse (f)
128+	Dianakova (f)
128	Altus
128	Fandango
128	Fantastic Sivola
127p	*Dogon
127	Athena du Berlais (f)
126	Bi Beach
126	Notorius
126	Royale Joana Has (f)
124	Bernardo Bellotto
124	Doctor Squeeze
123p	*Rose Sea Has
123	La Barakas (f)
123	Last Sparkler
123	Maxenchop
123	Sunday A Paris
123	Twist de La Barre
122p	Fanion d'Estruval
122	Amenon
122	Full Paradayse
122	Korkouee (f)
122	La Doix (f)
122	Pariso
121	Amour du Mathan (f)
121	Bebe d'Or
121	Best Stroke
121	Ma Saone (f)
121	Montgeoffroy
120+	French Bird (f)
120	Cambiko
120	Faro des Malberaux
120	Uniketat

Hurdlers (4yo)

154+	Feu Follet
148	L'Autonomie (f)
147	Beaumec de Houelle
147	Polirico
145	*Pic d'Orhy
143p	Saint Sonnet
140	Porto Pollo
138	Fidele Au Poste
137	Listenmania (f)
137	Pat du Pont
136	Kimbola (f)

135	Always Magic
135	Byzance du Berlais (f)
135	Laterana (f)
134p	Floridee (f)
134	Fogo de Chao
134	Vanille du Berlais (f)
133	Bai de Baie
133	Lady Ardilaun (f)
132	Bel Apsis
132	Bernardo Bellotto
132	Flying Startandco
132	Powder Path
131	Farnice
130	Please God
129	Fuji Flight
129	Qeenie's Cash (f)
129	Thrilling (f)
128	Doctor Squeeze
128	Edidindo
128	Faucon du Bosc
128	Meredith (f)
128	Naturelle (f)
128	Tresor du Roume (f)
127p	Franco de Port
127p	*Vision du Puy (f)
127	Altus
127	Fandango
127	Fraca de Thaix
127	Friendly Star
127	My Way (Ger)
127	Playful Saint
126	Duc de Meran
126	Katana One
126	Otchoa Rouge
125	Arenui
125	Femme d'Action (f)
125	Fin du Match (f)
125	Full Paradyse
125	Matfog
125	Mester
125	Miss de Boulko (f)
125	Red Risk
124p	Photo Choc
124	Beau Saonois
124	Caradream (f)
124	Cool Me Down
124	*Dogon
124	Foja (f)
124	Premiere Amie (f)
124	Saint Roi
123	Fally Jem (f)
123	Filup
123	*Laskadine (f)
122p	*Protektorat
122	Baie Boy
122	Bowler Hat
122	Dianakova (f)
122	Face Au Large
122	Father James
122	Fou du Bresil
122	King Elvis

122	Montgeoffroy
122	My Kalores
122	Rebellio
121	Amour du Mathan (f)
121	Bebe d'Or
121	Enjoy It (f)
121	Fancytastic
121	Fan de Blues
121	Fellow Mag
121	Figuero
121	Fleur Irlandaise (f)
121	Fraulein Agatha (f)
121	Hale (f)
121	Kaplina (f)
121	Lady Linda (f)
121	Lord Pit
121	Philanthrope (f)
120p	Frisson d'Estruval
120p	Thinking
120	Fabulous Dragoness (f)
120	Fighter Sport
120	Henry Brulard
120	Hurkova (f)
120	Kelmec
120	Montroty (f)
120	Sagaline (f)

Hurdlers (3yo)

141	Hipsters
140p	Mick Pastor
140	For Fun
139	Nirvana du Berlais
135p	Gelboe de Chanay (f)
135	Al Cuarto
133	Aterisk (f)
132p	Messagere (f)
132	Kick Up
131p	Mokoia
131	Riskman
130	Irresistibles
129	Invincible Dina (f)
127	Le Lude
125	Sail Away
124	King Edward
123	Golden Park (f)
123	Misterenrique
122p	Galia Grandchamp (f)
122p	Kool Has
122	Jimble Moon
122	Kerfany
122	Line Brazil (f)
122	L'Ouragan
122	Rhodier
121	La Cafe Ine (f)
121	Rocknicara (f)
120p	Botox Has
120	Autour de Minuit
120	Falstaff
120	Grakownia (f)
120	Joshua Dream
120	Marchand de Venise

NB Ratings relate to performances between July 1st 2018 and July 2nd 2019 (which takes into account the postponed Auteuil meeting on the latter date). Horses marked with an * were trained in France for only part of the season; horses which were originally trained in France but subsequently showed much better form in Britain/Ireland are not included in the above lists.

INDEX TO PHOTOGRAPHS
PORTRAITS & SNAPSHOTS

RACE PHOTOGRAPHS

Devenish Manifesto Novices' Chase (Aintree)	*Ed Byrne*	463
Dooley Insurance Group Champion Novices' Chase (Ellier) (Punchestown)	*Peter Mooney*	271
Doom Bar Anniversary 4-Y-O Juvenile Hurdle (Aintree)	*George Selwyn*	661
Doom Bar Maghull Novices' Chase (Aintree)	*John Grossick*	640
Doom Bar Sefton Novices' Hurdle (Aintree)	*Bill Selwyn*	196
Dornen Engineering Relkeel Hurdle (Cheltenham)	*Francesca Altoft*	563
Download The BetBright App Handicap Chase (Cheltenham)	*Francesca Altoft*	87
EBF TBA Mares' National Hunt Novices' Hurdle Final (Limited Handicap) (Newbury)	*Ed Byrne*	69
888Sport Handicap Chase (Kempton)	*Ed Byrne*	918
888Sport Heroes Handicap Hurdle (Sandown)	*Francesca Altoft*	528
888Sport Pendil Novices' Chase (Kempton)	*Ed Byrne*	96
888Sport Scilly Isles Novices' Chase (Sandown)	*Francesca Altoft*	263
888Sport Take 'Em On Adonis Juvenile Hurdle (Kempton)	*Ed Byrne*	373
EMS Copiers Novices' Handicap Chase (Punchestown) (Punchestown)	*Peter Mooney*	699
European Breeders' Fund Matchbook VIP 'National Hunt' Novices' Handicap Hurdle Final (Sandown)	*George Selwyn*	849
Flogas Novices' Chase (Scalp) (Leopardstown)	*Healy Racing*	490
Follow At The Races on Twitter Novices' Chase (Plumpton)	*Bill Selwyn*	553
Frank Ward Solicitors Novices' Chase (Leopardstown)	*Peter Mooney*	514
Fulke Walwyn Kim Muir Challenge Cup Amateur Riders' Handicap Chase (Cheltenham)	*Caroline Norris*	70
galliardhomes.com Cleeve Hurdle (Cheltenham)	*George Selwyn*	651
Garrard Silver Cup Handicap Chase (Ascot)	*Francesca Altoft*	900
Glenfarclas Chase (Cross Country) (Cheltenham)	*Caroline Norris*	857
Goffs Thyestes Handicap Chase (Gowran Park)	*Caroline Norris*	442
Goffs UK Nickel Coin Mares' Standard Open National Hunt Flat (Aintree)	*Bill Selwyn*	839
Goffs UK Spring Sale Bumper (Newbury)	*Bill Selwyn*	385
Grande Course de Haies d'Auteuil (Auteuil)	*Bertrand*	122
Guinness Galway Hurdle Handicap (Galway)	*Caroline Norris*	759
Guinness Handicap Chase (Punchestown)	*Caroline Norris*	639
Guinness Kerry National Handicap Chase (Listowel)	*Caroline Norris*	789
Irish Daily Mirror Novices' Hurdle (War of Attrition) (Punchestown)	*Peter Mooney*	570
Irish Stallions Farm EBF Mares' Novices' Hurdle Championship Final (Fairyhouse)	*Peter Mooney*	424
J & D Pierce Novices' Champion Handicap Chase (Ayr)	*John Grossick*	589
JCB Triumph Hurdle (Cheltenham)	*John Crofts*	660
JCB Triumph Trial Juvenile Hurdle (Finesse) (Cheltenham)	*Francesca Altoft*	342
JLT Chase (Melling) (Aintree)	*Bill Selwyn*	575
JLT Hurdle (Long Walk) (Ascot)	*George Selwyn*	650
JLT Novices' Chase (Golden Miller) (Cheltenham)	*John Crofts*	264
JNwine.com Champion Chase (Down Royal)	*Caroline Norris*	712
John Durkan Memorial Punchestown Chase (Punchestown)	*Peter Mooney*	573
John Mulhern Galmoy Hurdle (Gowran Park)	*Peter Mooney*	681
Johnny Henderson Grand Annual Challenge Cup Handicap Chase (Cheltenham)	*George Selwyn*	242
Keltbray Swinley Chase (Limited Handicap) (Ascot)	*Francesca Altoft*	175
Knight Frank Juvenile Hurdle (Leopardstown)	*Caroline Norris*	718
Ladbrokes Champion Stayers' Hurdle (Punchestown)	*Caroline Norris*	894
Ladbrokes Dublin Chase (Leopardstown)	*Caroline Norris*	574
Ladbrokes Hurdle (Extended Handicap) (Leopardstown)	*Healy Racing*	631
Ladbrokes In Memory of Tara Von Ihering Handicap Chase (Newbury)	*George Selwyn*	494
Ladbrokes Ireland Boyne Hurdle (Navan)	*Caroline Norris*	855
Ladbrokes John Francome Novices' Chase (Newbury)	*Ed Byrne*	742
Ladbrokes Trophy Chase (Handicap) (Newbury)	*Ed Byrne*	783
Lawlor's of Naas Novices' Hurdle (Naas)	*Caroline Norris*	110
Magners Cheltenham Gold Cup (Cheltenham)	*Ed Byrne*	42

Magners Cheltenham Gold Cup (Cheltenham)	*George Selwyn*	43
Marston's 61 Deep Midlands Grand National (Open Handicap Chase) (Uttoxeter)	*Steve Davies*	676
Martin Pipe Conditional Jockeys' Handicap Hurdle (Cheltenham)	*Francesca Altoft*	306
Matchbook Clarence House Chase (Ascot)	*Ed Byrne*	57
Matchbook Holloway's Handicap Hurdle (Ascot)	*Ed Byrne*	102
Matchbook Imperial Cup Handicap Hurdle (Sandown)	*Francesca Altoft*	546
McCoy Contractors Civil Engineering Classic Handicap Chase (Warwick)	*Bill Selwyn*	437
Napoleons Casino & Restaurant Owlerton Sheffield Lightning Novices' Chase (Doncaster)	*Martin Lynch*	304
National Hunt Breeders Supported By Tattersalls Mares' Novices' Hurdle (Dawn Run) (Cheltenham)	*Ed Byrne*	313
National Hunt Challenge Cup Amateur Riders' Novices' Chase (Cheltenham)	*Ed Byrne*	507
Navan Novices' Hurdle (Navan)	*Caroline Norris*	309
1974 Grand National (Becher's) (Aintree)	*Ed Byrne*	859
OLBG Mares' Hurdle (David Nicholson) (Cheltenham)	*Peter Mooney*	722
OLBG.com Mares' Hurdle (Warfield) (Ascot)	*Ed Byrne*	540
OLBG.com Yorkshire Rose Mares' Hurdle (Doncaster)	*Martin Lynch*	495
Paddy Power Chase (Leopardstown)	*Peter Mooney*	91
Paddy Power Future Champions Novices' Hurdle (Leopardstown)	*Peter Mooney*	78
Paddy's Rewards Club 'Sugar Paddy' Chase (Leopardstown)	*Peter Mooney*	773
Palmerstown House Pat Taaffe Handicap Chase (Punchestown)	*Caroline Norris*	417
Pertemps Network Final Handicap Hurdle (Cheltenham)	*Francesca Altoft*	775
Pertemps Network Swinton Handicap Hurdle (Haydock)	*John Grossick*	770
Poplar Square Chase (Naas)	*Caroline Norris*	735
Prix La Barka Hurdle (Auteuil)	*Bertrand*	601
Racing Post App Champion INH Flat (Punchestown)	*Peter Mooney*	228
Racing Post Arkle Challenge Trophy Novices' Chase (Cheltenham)	*John Crofts*	297
Racing Post Arkle Trophy Trial Novices' Chase (November) (Cheltenham)	*John Crofts*	498
Racing Post Novices' Chase (Leopardstown)	*Peter Mooney*	513
randoxhealth.com Henry VIII Novices' Chase (Sandown)	*Ed Byrne*	303
Randox Health County Handicap Hurdle (Cheltenham)	*Ed Byrne*	207
Randox Health Foxhunters' Chase (Aintree)	*Bill Selwyn*	878
Randox Health Grand National Handicap Chase (Aintree)	*George Selwyn*	858
Randox Health Grand National Handicap Chase (Aintree)	*George Selwyn*	859
Randox Health Grand National Handicap Chase (Aintree)	*George Selwyn*	861
Randox Health Grand National Handicap Chase (Aintree)	*Bill Selwyn*	862
Randox Health Grand National Handicap Chase (Aintree)	*Bill Selwyn*	863
Randox Health Grand National Handicap Chase (Aintree)	*George Selwyn*	864
Randox Health Topham Handicap Chase (Aintree)	*George Selwyn*	172
Red Mills Chase (Gowran Park)	*Peter Mooney*	589
Red Rum Handicap Chase (Aintree)	*Martin Lynch*	594
RSA Insurance Novices' Chase (Cheltenham)	*John Crofts*	875
Ryanair Chase (Festival Trophy) (Cheltenham)	*Ed Byrne*	369
Ryanair Gold Cup Novices' Chase (Fairyhouse)	*Peter Mooney*	913
Ryanair Hurdle (Leopardstown)	*Caroline Norris*	760
Ryanair Novices' Chase (Punchestown)	*Peter Mooney*	191
Ryanair Stayers' Hurdle (Liverpool) (Aintree)	*George Selwyn*	431
Ryanair Stayers' Hurdle (Liverpool) (Aintree)	*George Selwyn*	432
Savills Chase (Leopardstown)	*Peter Mooney*	469
Shloer Chase (Cheltenham)	*John Crofts*	745
Sky Bet Handicap Chase (Doncaster)	*Martin Lynch*	392
Sky Bet Supreme Novices' Hurdle (Cheltenham)	*Bill Selwyn*	483
Sky Bet Supreme Trial Rossington Main Novices' Hurdle (Haydock)	*Martin Lynch*	581
Sodexo Gold Cup Handicap Chase (Ascot)	*Ed Byrne*	881
Sodexo Reynoldstown Novices' Chase (Ascot)	*Bill Selwyn*	582
Squared Financial Christmas Hurdle (Leopardstown)	*Peter Mooney*	74
St James's Place Foxhunter Challenge Cup (Cheltenham)	*George Selwyn*	413

ADDITIONAL PHOTOGRAPHS

The following photos appear in the Introduction:- Tiger Roll at the last in the Grand National (taken by Bill Selwyn), Poethlyn, the best steeplechaser in the war years (W. A. Rouch), *The Sporting Life* ambulance appeal (British Library), Michael O'Leary (Peter Mooney), Altior's nineteenth consecutive win (Ed Byrne), the victories of Frodon and Paisley Park provide a 'golden hour' for Cheltenham (Bill Selwyn/Peter Mooney), Paul Nicholls (Bill Selwyn), Dorothy Paget leads in Insurance (Miralgo Publications Archive), Cheltenham Gold Cup runners at the second last (George Selwyn), Ruby Walsh retires (Bill Selwyn/Caroline Norris), Richard Johnson and Harry Cobden (both Bill Selwyn).

Timeform Champions of 2018/19:- Altior (taken by Ed Byrne)

Credits for the photographs in 'Top Horses In France' are as follows:-
Grand Steeple-Chase de Paris, Prix La Haye Jousselin, Prix Renaud du Vivier, Prix Leon Rombard, Prix Ferdinand Dufaure, Prix Alain du Breil (all taken by Bertrand)

BIG RACE WINNERS

The record, dating back to the 1992/3 season (earlier results can be found in *Chasers & Hurdlers 1991/92* and preceding editions), includes the Timeform Rating recorded by the winner in the race (not its Timeform Annual Rating), the weight carried (usually preceded by age), starting price, trainer, jockey and number of runners. Race conditions, distances and sponsors' names in the race titles are for the 2018/19 runnings. An asterisk prior to a horse's name denotes that it was awarded the race.

Britain

BetVictor GOLD CUP HANDICAP CHASE (Gr 3) (Cheltenham 2½m44y)

1992	153	Tipping Tim 7-10-10: 11/2	N A Twiston-Davies	C Llewellyn	16
1993	160	Bradbury Star 8-11-8: 13/2	J T Gifford	D Murphy	15
1994	172	Bradbury Star 9-11-11: 5/1	J T Gifford	P Hide[3]	14
1995	164	Dublin Flyer 9-11-8: 4/1	T A Forster	B Powell	12
1996	154	Challenger du Luc 6-10-2: 7/1	M C Pipe	R Dunwoody	12
1997	159	Senor El Betrutti 8-10-0: 33/1	Mrs S Nock	J Osborne	9
1998	158	Cyfor Malta 5-11-3: 3/1	M C Pipe	A P McCoy	12
1999	152	The Outback Way 9-10-0: 9/1	Miss V Williams	N Williamson	14
2000	157	Lady Cricket 6-10-13: 5/1	M C Pipe	A P McCoy	15
2001	158	Shooting Light 8-11-3: 9/4	M C Pipe	A P McCoy	14
2002	166	Cyfor Malta 9-11-9: 16/1	M C Pipe	B J Geraghty	15
2003	161	Fondmort 7-10-13: 3/1	N J Henderson	M A Fitzgerald	9
2004	152	Celestial Gold 6-10-2: 12/1	M C Pipe	T J Murphy	14
2005	159	Our Vic 7-11-7: 9/2	M C Pipe	T J Murphy	18
2006	145	Exotic Dancer 6-11-2: 16/1	J O'Neill	A P McCoy	16
2007	149	L'Antartique 7-10-13: 13/2	F Murphy	G Lee	20
2008	153	Imperial Commander 7-10-7: 13/2	N A Twiston-Davies	P J Brennan	19
2009	155	Tranquil Sea 7-10-13: 11/2	E J O'Grady	A J McNamara	16
2010	153	Little Josh 8-10-5: 20/1	N A Twiston-Davies	S Twiston-Davies[3]	18
2011	160	Great Endeavour 7-10-3: 8/1	David Pipe	Timmy Murphy	20
2012	169	Al Ferof 7-11-8: 8/1	Paul Nicholls	R Walsh	18
2013	146	Johns Spirit 6-10-2: 7/1	Jonjo O'Neill	Richie McLernon	20
2014	147	Caid du Berlais 5-10-13: 10/1	Paul Nicholls	Sam Twiston-Davies	18
2015	149	Annacotty 7-11-0: 12/1	Alan King	Ian Popham	20
2016	158	Taquin du Seuil 9-11-11: 8/1	Jonjo O'Neill	Aidan Coleman	17
2017	137	Splash of Ginge 9-10-6: 25/1	Nigel Twiston-Davies	Tom Bellamy	17
2018	152	Baron Alco 7-10-11: 8/1	Gary Moore	Jamie Moore	18

UNIBET GREATWOOD HANDICAP HURDLE (Gr 3)
(Cheltenham 2m87y; listed prior to 2004)

1992	130	Valfinet 5-10-9: 7/2	M C Pipe	P Scudamore	9
1993	144	Leotard 6-12-0: 3/1	O Sherwood	J Osborne	7
1994	156	Atours 6-11-5: 3/1	D R C Elsworth	P Holley	10
1995	135	Lonesome Train 6-9-9: 33/1	C Weedon	B Fenton[5]	15
1996	146	Space Trucker 5-11-11: 7/1	Mrs J Harrington (Ir)	J Osborne	9
1997	139	Mr Percy 6-10-9: 14/1	J T Gifford	P Hide	17
1998	155	Grey Shot 6-11-5: 11/4	I A Balding	J Osborne	16
1999	132	Rodock 5-10-0: 11/4	M C Pipe	A P McCoy	13
2000	139	Hulysse Royal 5-10-0: 9/1	O Sherwood	J A McCarthy	12
2001	140	Westender 5-10-13: 11/8	M C Pipe	A P McCoy	13
2002	166	Rooster Booster 8-11-12: 7/1	P J Hobbs	S Durack	11
2003	147	Rigmarole 5-11-2: 33/1	P F Nicholls	R Walsh	10
2004	148	Accordion Etoile 5-10-6: 10/3	Paul Nolan (Ir)	J Cullen	9
2005	146	Lingo 6-10-6: 5/1	J O'Neill	A P McCoy	19
2006	160	Detroit City 4-11-12: 6/5	P J Hobbs	R Johnson	9
2007	145	Sizing Europe 5-11-6: 5/1	H de Bromhead (Ir)	T J Murphy	19
2008	129	Numide 5-10-3: 5/1	G L Moore	J Moore	12
2009	154	Khyber Kim 7-11-9: 9/1	N A Twiston-Davies	P J Brennan	15
2010	160	Menorah 5-11-12: 6/1	P J Hobbs	R Johnson	17

2011	158	Brampour 4-11-4: 12/1	Paul Nicholls	*Harry Derham[7]*	23
2012	138	Olofi 6-10-11: 8/1	Tom George	*Paddy Brennan*	18
2013	133	Dell' Arca 4-10-5: 12/1	David Pipe	*Tom Scudamore*	18
2014	151	Garde La Victoire 5-11-9: 10/1	Philip Hobbs	*Richard Johnson*	15
2015	154	Old Guard 4-11-3: 12/1	Paul Nicholls	*Harry Cobden[7]*	17
2016	144	North Hill Harvey 5-11-0: 6/1	Dan Skelton	*Harry Skelton*	16
2017	145	Elgin 5-10-8: 10/1	Alan King	*Wayne Hutchinson*	13
2018	129	Nietzsche 5-10-0: 20/1	Brian Ellison	*Danny McMenamin (7)*	18

BETFAIR CHASE (Lancashire) (Gr 1) (Haydock 3m1f125y)

2005	173	Kingscliff 8-11-8: 8/1	R H Alner	*R Walford*	7
2006	172	Kauto Star 6-11-8: 11/10	P F Nicholls	*R Walsh*	6
2007	172	Kauto Star 7-11-7: 4/5	P F Nicholls	*S Thomas*	7
2008	161	Snoopy Loopy 10-11-7: 33/1	P Bowen	*S E Durack*	6
2009	175	Kauto Star 9-11-7: 4/6	P F Nicholls	*R Walsh*	7
2010	161	Imperial Commander 9-11-7: 10/11	N A Twiston-Davies	*P Brennan*	7
2011	174	Kauto Star 11-11-7: 6/1	Paul Nicholls	*R Walsh*	6
2012	170	Silviniaco Conti 6-11-7: 7/4	Paul Nicholls	*R Walsh*	5
2013	176	Cue Card 7-11-7: 9/1	Colin Tizzard	*Joe Tizzard*	8
2014	171	Silviniaco Conti 8-11-7: 10/3	Paul Nicholls	*Noel Fehily*	9
2015	181	Cue Card 9-11-7: 7/4	Colin Tizzard	*Paddy Brennan*	5
2016	174	Cue Card 10-11-7: 15/8	Colin Tizzard	*Paddy Brennan*	6
2017	165	Bristol de Mai 6-11-7: 11/10	Nigel Twiston-Davies	*Daryl Jacob*	6
2018	169	Bristol de Mai 7-11-7: 13/2	Nigel Twiston-Davies	*Daryl Jacob*	5

LADBROKES TROPHY CHASE (HANDICAP) (Gr 3) (Newbury 3m1f214y)

1992	150	Sibton Abbey 7-10-0: 40/1	F Murphy	*A Maguire*	13
1993	151	Cogent 9-10-1: 10/1	A Turnell	*D Fortt[7]*	9
1994	144	One Man 6-10-0: 4/1	G Richards	*A Dobbin*	16
1995	160	Couldnt Be Better 8-10-8: 15/2	C P E Brooks	*D Gallagher*	11
1996	147	Coome Hill 7-10-0: 11/2	W W Dennis	*J Osborne*	11
1997	170	Suny Bay 8-11-8: 9/4	C P E Brooks	*G Bradley*	14
1998	158	Teeton Mill 9-10-5: 5/1	Miss V Williams	*N Williamson*	16
1999	148	Ever Blessed 7-10-0: 9/2	M Pitman	*T J Murphy*	13
2000	158	King's Road 7-10-7: 9/1	N A Twiston-Davies	*J Goldstein*	17
2001	153	What's Up Boys 7-10-12: 14/1	P J Hobbs	*P Flynn*	14
2002	157	*Gingembre 8-10-9: 16/1	Mrs L C Taylor	*A Thornton*	25
2003	154	Strong Flow 6-11-0: 5/1	P F Nicholls	*R Walsh*	21
2004	150	Celestial Gold 6-10-5: 9/4	M C Pipe	*T J Murphy*	14
2005	161	Trabolgan 7-11-12: 13/2	N J Henderson	*M A Fitzgerald*	19
2006	157	State of Play 6-11-4: 10/1	E Williams	*P Moloney*	16
2007	176	Denman 7-11-12: 5/1	P F Nicholls	*S Thomas*	18
2008	160	Madison du Berlais 7-11-4: 25/1	D E Pipe	*T Scudamore*	15
2009	181	Denman 9-11-12: 11/4	P F Nicholls	*R Walsh*	19
2010	163	Diamond Harry 7-10-0: 6/1	Nick Williams	*D Jacob*	18
2011	149	Carruthers 8-10-4: 10/1	Mark Bradstock	*Mattie Batchelor*	18
2012	171	Bobs Worth 7-11-6: 4/1	Nicky Henderson	*Barry Geraghty*	19
2013	157	Triolo d'Alene 6-11-1: 20/1	Nicky Henderson	*Barry Geraghty*	21
2014	159	Many Clouds 7-11-6: 8/1	Oliver Sherwood	*Leighton Aspell*	19
2015	165	Smad Place 8-11-4: 7/1	Alan King	*Wayne Hutchinson*	15
2016	162	Native River 6-11-1: 7/2	Colin Tizzard	*Richard Johnson*	19
2017	153	Total Recall 8-10-8: 9/2	W P Mullins (Ir)	*P Townend*	20
2018	157	Sizing Tennessee 10-11-3: 12/1	Colin Tizzard	*Tom Scudamore*	12

BetVictor 'FIGHTING FIFTH' HURDLE (Gr 1)
(Newcastle 2m98y; Wetherby in 2008 and Newbury in 2010; Gr 2 prior to 2004; handicap prior to 1998)

1992	135	Halkopous 6-11-0: 7/4	M H Tompkins	*S Smith Eccles*	6
1993		Abandoned			
1994	142	Batabanoo 5-11-0: 6/4	Mrs M Reveley	*P Niven*	4
1995	151	Padre Mio 7-10-10: 5/1	C P E Brooks	*R C Guest*	7
1996	151	Space Trucker 5-10-4: 5/2	Mrs J Harrington (Ir)	*J Shortt*	8
1997	141	Star Rage 7-11-2: 6/1	M Johnston	*D Gallagher*	8
1998	170	Dato Star 7-11-8: 13/8	J M Jefferson	*L Wyer*	6
1999	155	Dato Star 8-11-8: 4/9	J M Jefferson	*L Wyer*	9
2000	155	Barton 7-11-0: 8/13	T D Easterby	*A Dobbin*	6
2001	147	Landing Light 6-11-8: 4/5	N J Henderson	*J R Kavanagh*	5
2002	153	Intersky Falcon 5-11-8: 11/10	J O'Neill	*L Cooper*	6
2003	146	The French Furze 9-11-0: 25/1	N G Richards	*B Harding*	8

2004	157	Harchibald 5-11-7: 9/4	N Meade (Ir)	*P Carberry*	8
2005	150	Arcalis 5-11-7: 9/4	J H Johnson	*A Dobbin*	9
2006	150	Straw Bear 5-11-7: 1/1	N J Gifford	*A P McCoy*	9
2007	158	Harchibald 8-11-7: 4/1	N Meade (Ir)	*P Carberry*	8
2008	155	Punjabi 5-11-7: 8/11	N J Henderson	*B J Geraghty*	6
2009	160	Go Native 6-11-7: 25/1	N Meade (Ir)	*D J Condon*	7
2010	157	Peddlers Cross 5-11-7: 9/4	D McCain	*J Maguire*	5
2011	165	Overturn 7-11-7: 7/4	Donald McCain	*Jason Maguire*	5
2012	156	Countrywide Flame 4-11-7: 11/4	John Quinn	*Denis O'Regan*	4
2013	151	My Tent Or Yours 6-11-7: 8/11	Nicky Henderson	*A P McCoy*	8
2014	152	Irving 6-11-7: 6/4	Paul Nicholls	*Nick Scholfield*	6
2015	157	Identity Thief 5-11-7: 6/1	Henry de Bromhead (Ir)	*B J Cooper*	7
2016	153	Irving 8-11-7: 6/1	Paul Nicholls	*Harry Cobden*	6
2017	143	Buveur d'Air 6-11-7: 1/6	Nicky Henderson	*Barry Geraghty*	5
2018	155	Buveur d'Air 7-11-7: 11/8	Nicky Henderson	*Barry Geraghty*	5

BETFAIR TINGLE CREEK CHASE (Gr 1)
(Sandown 1m7f119y, Cheltenham 2m½f in 2000 & 2010)

1992	159	Waterloo Boy 9-12-0: 11/4	D Nicholson	*R Dunwoody*	5
1993	162	Sybillin 7-11-9: 6/1	J G FitzGerald	*P Niven*	7
1994	165	Viking Flagship 7-11-7: 9/2	D Nicholson	*A Maguire*	6
1995	159	Sound Man 7-11-7: 5/6	E J O'Grady (Ir)	*R Dunwoody*	5
1996	160	Sound Man 8-11-7: 10/11	E J O'Grady (Ir)	*R Dunwoody*	4
1997	168	Ask Tom 8-11-7: 6/1	T P Tate	*R Garritty*	7
1998	154	Direct Route 7-11-7: 7/1	J H Johnson	*N Williamson*	10
1999	167	Flagship Uberalles 5-11-7: 10/3	P F Nicholls	*J Tizzard*	6
2000	175	Flagship Uberalles 6-11-7: 3/1	N T Chance	*R Johnson*	7
2001	170	Flagship Uberalles 7-11-7: 7/2	P J Hobbs	*R Widger*	6
2002	163	Cenkos 8-11-7: 6/1	P F Nicholls	*R Walsh*	6
2003	174	Moscow Flyer 9-11-7: 6/4	Mrs J Harrington (Ir)	*B J Geraghty*	7
2004	184	Moscow Flyer 10-11-7: 2/1	Mrs J Harrington (Ir)	*B J Geraghty*	7
2005	164	Kauto Star 5-11-7: 5/2	P F Nicholls	*M A Fitzgerald*	7
2006	166	Kauto Star 6-11-7: 4/9	P F Nicholls	*R Walsh*	7
2007	157	Twist Magic 5-11-7: 5/1	P F Nicholls	*S Thomas*	8
2008	163	Master Minded 5-11-7: 4/7	P F Nicholls	*A P McCoy*	7
2009	168	Twist Magic 7-11-7: 9/4	P F Nicholls	*R Walsh*	5
2010	168	Master Minded 7-11-7: 10/11	P F Nicholls	*N Fehily*	9
2011	171	Sizing Europe 9-11-7: 11/8	H de Bromhead (Ir)	*A E Lynch*	7
2012	169	Sprinter Sacre 6-11-7: 4/11	Nicky Henderson	*Barry Geraghty*	7
2013	166	Sire de Grugy 7-11-7: 7/4	Gary Moore	*Jamie Moore*	9
2014	168	Dodging Bullets 6-11-7: 9/1	Paul Nicholls	*Sam Twiston-Davies*	10
2015	167	Sire de Grugy 9-11-7: 10/3	Gary Moore	*Jamie Moore*	7
2016	169	Un de Sceaux 8-11-7: 5/4	W P Mullins (Ir)	*R Walsh*	6
2017	164	Politologue 6-11-7: 7/2	Paul Nicholls	*Harry Cobden*	6
2018	176	Altior 8-11-7: 8/13	Nicky Henderson	*Nico de Boinville*	4

CASPIAN CAVIAR GOLD CUP (HANDICAP CHASE) (Gr 3) (Cheltenham 2½m127y)

1992	151	Another Coral 9-11-4: 11/2	D Nicholson	*R Dunwoody*	10
1993	146	Fragrant Dawn 9-10-2: 14/1	M C Pipe	*D Murphy*	11
1994	145	Dublin Flyer 8-10-2: 10/3	T A Forster	*B Powell*	11
1995		Abandoned			
1996	156	Addington Boy 8-11-10: 7/4	G Richards	*A Dobbin*	10
1997	160	Senor El Betrutti 8-11-3: 9/1	Mrs S Nock	*G Bradley*	9
1998	141	Northern Starlight 7-10-1: 15/2	M C Pipe	*A P McCoy*	13
1999	162	Legal Right 6-10-13: 6/1	J O'Neill	*R Johnson*	9
2000	139	Go Roger Go 8-11-0: 7/1	E J O'Grady (Ir)	*N Williamson*	12
2001		Abandoned			
2002	151	Fondmort 6-10-5: 5/1	N J Henderson	*M A Fitzgerald*	9
2003	144	Iris Royal 7-10-13: 7/1	N J Henderson	*M A Fitzgerald*	17
2004	143	Monkerhostin 7-10-2: 4/1	P J Hobbs	*R Johnson*	13
2005	139	Sir OJ 8-10-0: 16/1	N Meade (Ir)	*P Carberry*	16
2006	151	Exotic Dancer 6-11-4: 8/1	J O'Neill	*A Dobbin*	12
2007	155	Tamarinbleu 7-11-8: 22/1	D E Pipe	*D O'Regan*	16
2008		Abandoned			
2009	160	Poquelin 6-11-8: 7/2	P F Nicholls	*R Walsh*	17
2010	164	Poquelin 7-11-7: 16/1	P F Nicholls	*I Popham[5]*	16
2011	156	Quantitativeeasing 6-10-7: 6/1	Nicky Henderson	*Barry Geraghty*	16

2012	145	Unioniste 4-9-9: 15/2	Paul Nicholls	*Harry Derham[5]*	14
2013	137	Double Ross 7-10-8: 7/1	Nigel Twiston-Davies	*Sam Twiston-Davies*	13
2014	148	Niceonefrankie 8-11-5: 16/1	Venetia Williams	*Aidan Coleman*	12
2015	144	Village Vic 8-10-0: 8/1	Philip Hobbs	*Richard Johnson*	14
2016	146	Frodon 4-10-10: 14/1	Paul Nicholls	*Sam Twiston-Davies*	16
2017	138	Guitar Pete 7-10-5: 9/1	Nicky Richards	*Ryan Day[3]*	10
2018	167	Frodon 6-11-2: 7/1	Paul Nicholls	*Bryony Frost*	12

UNIBET INTERNATIONAL HURDLE (Gr 2)
(Cheltenham 2m179y, run at Newbury 2m½f in 2001 and at Ascot 2m in 2008)

1992	164	Halkopous 6-11-2: 8/1	M H Tompkins	*A Maguire*	6
1993	169	Staunch Friend 5-11-8: 6/1	M H Tompkins	*D Murphy*	7
1994	156	Large Action 6-11-4: 8/11	O Sherwood	*J Osborne*	8
1995		Abandoned			
1996	160	Large Action 8-11-8: 5/4	O Sherwood	*J Osborne*	7
1997	155	Relkeel 8-11-0: 8/1	D Nicholson	*R Johnson*	8
1998	163	Relkeel 9-11-8: 8/1	D Nicholson	*A Maguire*	5
1999	159	Relkeel 10-11-8: 13/2	A King	*R Johnson*	7
2000	160	Geos 5-11-4: 14/1	N J Henderson	*M A Fitzgerald*	8
2001	161	Valiramix 5-11-4: 1/2	M C Pipe	*A P McCoy*	4
2002	154	Rooster Booster 8-11-4: 11/8	P J Hobbs	*R Johnson*	9
2003	149	Rigmarole 5-11-4: 25/1	P F Nicholls	*R Thornton*	8
2004	161	Back In Front 7-11-8: 5/2	E J O'Grady (Ir)	*D N Russell*	7
2005	160	Harchibald 6-11-8: 10/11	N Meade (Ir)	*P Carberry*	9
2006	157	Detroit City 4-11-4: 4/6	P J Hobbs	*R Johnson*	4
2007	158	Osana 5-11-0: 7/1	D E Pipe	*P J Brennan*	8
2008	165	Binocular 4-11-4: 1/1	N J Henderson	*A P McCoy*	5
2009	161	Khyber Kim 7-11-4: 12/1	N A Twiston-Davies	*P J Brennan*	7
2010	157	Menorah 5-11-4: 7/4	P J Hobbs	*R Johnson*	9
2011	164	Grandouet 4-11-4: 5/2	Nicky Henderson	*Barry Geraghty*	8
2012	163	Zarkandar 5-11-4: 6/5	Paul Nicholls	*R Walsh*	7
2013	153	The New One 5-11-8: 2/5	Nigel Twiston-Davies	*Sam Twiston-Davies*	7
2014	159	The New One 6-11-8: 4/7	Nigel Twiston-Davies	*Sam Twiston-Davies*	8
2015	154	Old Guard 4-11-4: 7/1	Paul Nicholls	*Sam Twiston-Davies*	6
2016	158	The New One 8-11-8: 13/8	Nigel Twiston-Davies	*Richard Johnson*	6
2017	152	My Tent Or Yours 10-11-0: 5/1	Nicky Henderson	*Barry Geraghty*	7
2018	147	Brain Power 7-11-0: 7/1	Nicky Henderson	*Nico de Boinville*	8

JLT HURDLE (Long Walk) (Gr 1)
(Ascot 3m97y; Windsor in 2004, Chepstow in 2005 & Newbury in 2009 & 2010)

1992	156	Vagog 7-11-7: 15/2	M C Pipe	*M Foster*	9
1993	152	Sweet Duke 5-11-7: 7/2	N Twiston-Davies	*C Llewellyn*	9
1994	159	Hebridean 7-11-7: 10/3	D Nicholson	*A Maguire*	8
1995	153	Silver Wedge 4-11-7: 7/1	S Sherwood	*J Osborne*	11
1996	152	Ocean Hawk 4-11-7: 7/1	N A Twiston-Davies	*C Llewellyn*	6
1997	168	Paddy's Return 5-11-7: 8/1	F Murphy	*N Williamson*	7
1998	165	Princeful 7-11-7: 11/4	Mrs J Pitman	*R Dunwoody*	11
1999	164	Anzum 8-11-7: 4/1	A King	*R Johnson*	6
2000	172	Baracouda 5-11-7: 11/4	F Doumen (Fr)	*T Doumen*	9
2001	161	Baracouda 6-11-7: 2/5	F Doumen (Fr)	*T Doumen*	5
2002	167	Deano's Beeno 10-11-7: 14/1	M C Pipe	*A P McCoy*	8
2003	169	Baracouda 8-11-7: 2/7	F Doumen (Fr)	*T Doumen*	6
2004	156	Baracouda 9-11-7: 8/13	F Doumen (Fr)	*A P McCoy*	8
2005	157	My Way de Solzen 5-11-7: 12/1	A King	*R Thornton*	8
2006	161	Mighty Man 6-11-7: 8/11	H D Daly	*R Johnson*	9
2007	153	Lough Derg 7-11-7: 14/1	D E Pipe	*T Scudamore*	9
2008	161	Punchestowns 5-11-7: 3/1	N J Henderson	*B J Geraghty*	11
2009	165	Big Buck's 6-11-7: 1/2	P F Nicholls	*R Walsh*	8
2010	156	Big Buck's 7-11-7: 2/13	Paul Nichols	*A P McCoy*	6
2011	152	Big Buck's 8-11-7: 3/10	Paul Nicholls	*R Walsh*	7
2012	162	Reve de Sivola 7-11-7: 9/2	Nick Williams	*Richard Johnson*	8
2013	162	Reve de Sivola 8-11-7: 9/4	Nick Williams	*Richard Johnson*	7
2014	159	Reve de Sivola 9-11-7: 3/2	Nick Williams	*Daryl Jacob*	5
2015	168	Thistlecrack 7-11-7: 2/1	Colin Tizzard	*Tom Scudamore*	8
2016	155	Unowhatimeanharry 8-11-7: 6/5	Harry Fry	*Barry Geraghty*	11
2017	158	Sam Spinner 5-11-7: 9/2	Jedd O'Keeffe	*Joe Colliver*	8
2018	148	Paisley Park 6-11-7: 8/1	Emma Lavelle	*Aidan Coleman*	11

BETFAIR EXCHANGE TROPHY (HANDICAP HURDLE) (Gr 3)

(Ascot 1m7f152y; Sandown in 2005 & 2006 (Jan), Listed until 2012)

2001	142	Marble Arch 5-10-11: 7/1	H Morrison	N Williamson	16
2002	139	Chauvinist 7-10-0: 15/2	N J Henderson	N Williamson	20
2003	138	Thesis 5-11-2: 33/1	Miss V Williams	B J Crowley	17
2004	141	Tamarinbleu 5-10-11: 14/1	M C Pipe	A P McCoy	23
2005	136	Desert Air 7-10-9: 25/1	M C Pipe	T Scudamore	20
2006	142	Acambo 5-11-9: 7/1	D E Pipe	T J Murphy	20
2007	133	Jack The Giant 5-11-0: 9/4	N J Henderson	M A Fitzgerald	17
2008	154	Sentry Duty 6-11-9: 12/1	N J Henderson	B J Geraghty	21
2009		Abandoned			
2010		Abandoned			
2011	135	Raya Star 5-10-1: 12/1	Alan King	Wayne Hutchinson	16
2012	150	Cause of Causes 4-10-13: 25/1	Gordon Elliott (Ir)	Davy Condon	21
2013	139	Willow's Saviour 6-10-5: 10/1	Dan Skelton	Harry Skelton	20
2014	150	Bayan 5-11-5: 14/1	Gordon Elliott (Ir)	Davy Condon	18
2015	145	Jolly's Cracked It 6-11-3: 7/1	Harry Fry	Noel Fehily	21
	138	Sternrubin 4-10-10: 9/1	Philip Hobbs	Richard Johnson	21
2016	158	Brain Power 5-11-11: 12/1	Nicky Henderson	D J Mullins	19
2017	139	Hunters Call 7-10-3: 9/1	Olly Murphy	J W Kennedy	17
2018	147	Mohaayed 6-11-10: 16/1	Dan Skelton	Harry Skelton	21

CORAL WELSH GRAND NATIONAL HANDICAP CHASE (Gr 3)

(Chepstow 3m5f110y, Newbury in 1994, scheduled races in December 2010, 2012, 2015 and 2017 were also postponed until January of the following year)

1992	155	Run For Free 8-10-9: 11/4	M C Pipe	M Perrett	11
1993	126	Riverside Boy 10-10-0: 6/4	M C Pipe	R Dunwoody	8
1994	168	Master Oats 8-11-6: 5/2	K C Bailey	N Williamson	8
1995		Abandoned			
1996		Abandoned			
1997	146	Earth Summit 9-10-13: 25/1	N A Twiston-Davies	T Jenks	14
1998	139	Kendal Cavalier 8-10-0: 14/1	N J Hawke	B Fenton	14
1999	136	Edmond 7-10-0: 4/1	H D Daly	R Johnson	16
2000	149	Jocks Cross 9-10-4: 14/1	Miss V Williams	B J Crowley[3]	19
2001	140	Supreme Glory 8-10-0: 10/1	P G Murphy	L Aspell	13
2002	137	Mini Sensation 9-10-4: 8/1	J O'Neill	A Dobbin	16
2003	157	Bindaree 9-10-9: 10/1	N A Twiston-Davies	C Llewellyn	14
2004	135	Silver Birch 7-10-5: 10/3	P F Nicholls	R Walsh	17
2005	138	L'Aventure 6-10-4: 14/1	P F Nicholls	L Aspell	18
2006	159	Halcon Genelardais 6-11-3: 7/1	A King	W Hutchinson	18
2007	144	Miko de Beauchene 7-10-5: 13/2	R H Alner	A Thornton	18
2008	158	Notre Pere 7-11-0: 16/1	J Dreaper (Ir)	A E Lynch	20
2009	152	Dream Alliance 8-10-8: 20/1	P J Hobbs	T J O'Brien	18
2010	155	Synchronised 8-11-6: 5/1	Jonjo O'Neill	A P McCoy	18
2011	141	Le Beau Bai 8-10-1: 10/1	Richard Lee	Charlie Poste	20
2012	137	Monbeg Dude 8-10-1: 10/1	Michael Scudamore	P Carberry	17
2013	139	Mountainous 8-10-0: 20/1	Richard Lee	Paul Moloney	20
2014	136	Emperor's Choice 7-10-8: 9/1	Venetia Williams	Aidan Coleman	19
2015	139	Mountainous 11-10-6: 9/1	Kerry Lee	Jamie Moore	20
2016	162	Native River 6-11-12: 11/4	Colin Tizzard	Richard Johnson	20
2017	144	Raz de Maree 13-11-1: 16/1	Gavin P Cromwell (Ir)	James Bowen[5]	20
2018	156	Elegant Escape 6-11-8: 3/1	Colin Tizzard	Tom O'Brien	20

UNIBET CHRISTMAS HURDLE (Gr 1) (Kempton 2m, Sandown 2005)

1992	170	Mighty Mogul 5-11-7: 3/1	D Nicholson	R Dunwoody	8
1993	155	Muse 6-11-7: 3/1	D R C Elsworth	M Richards	5
1994	158	Absalom's Lady 6-11-2: 9/2	D R C Elsworth	P Holley	6
1995		Abandoned			
1996		Abandoned			
1997	153	Kerawi 4-11-7: 4/1	N A Twiston-Davies	C Llewellyn	5
1998	165	French Holly 7-11-7: 5/2	F Murphy	A Thornton	5
1999	168	Dato Star 8-11-7: 11/8	J M Jefferson	L Wyer	4
2000	144	Geos 5-11-7: 9/4	N J Henderson	M A Fitzgerald	7
2001	153	Landing Light 6-11-7: 5/4	N J Henderson	M A Fitzgerald	5
2002	158	Intersky Falcon 5-11-7: 1/1	J O'Neill	C F Swan	6
2003	157	Intersky Falcon 6-11-7: 11/4	J O'Neill	L Cooper	6
2004	160	Harchibald 5-11-7: 8/11	N Meade (Ir)	P Carberry	7

2005	152	Feathard Lady 5-11-0: 6/4	C A Murphy (Ir)	*R Walsh*	7
2006	155	Jazz Messenger 6-11-7: 10/1	N Meade (Ir)	*N P Madden*	7
2007	153	Straw Bear 6-11-7: 9/2	N J Gifford	*A P McCoy*	6
2008	152	Harchibald 9-11-7: 7/1	N Meade (Ir)	*P Carberry*	7
2009	153	Go Native 6-11-7: 5/2	N Meade (Ir)	*D J Condon*	7
2010	163	Binocular 7-11-7: 13/8	Nicky Henderson	*A P McCoy*	6
2011	164	Binocular 7-11-7: 5/4	Nicky Henderson	*A P McCoy*	5
2012	158	Darlan 5-11-7: 3/1	Nicky Henderson	*A P McCoy*	7
2013	170	My Tent Or Yours 6-11-7: 11/8	Nicky Henderson	*A P McCoy*	6
2014	171	Faugheen 6-11-7: 4/11	W P Mullins (Ir)	*R Walsh*	6
2015	167	Faugheen 7-11-7: 1/4	W P Mullins (Ir)	*R Walsh*	5
2016	164	Yanworth 6-11-7: 5/4	Alan King	*Barry Geraghty*	5
2017	153	Buveur d'Air 6-11-7: 2/11	Nicky Henderson	*Barry Geraghty*	4
2018	152	Verdana Blue 6-11-0: 11/2	Nicky Henderson	*Nico de Boinville*	5

32Red KING GEORGE VI CHASE (Gr 1) (Kempton 3m, Sandown 1996 (Jan) and 2005)

1992	161	The Fellow 7-11-10: 1/1	F Doumen (Fr)	*A Kondrat*	8
1993	167	Barton Bank 7-11-10: 9/2	D Nicholson	*A Maguire*	10
1994	158	Algan 6-11-10: 16/1	F Doumen (Fr)	*P Chevalier*	9
1996	179	One Man 8-11-10: 11/4	G Richards	*R Dunwoody*	11
1996	176	One Man 8-11-10: 8/13	G Richards	*R Dunwoody*	5
1997	167	See More Business 7-11-10: 10/1	P F Nicholls	*A Thornton*	8
1998	173	Teeton Mill 9-11-10: 7/2	Miss V Williams	*N Williamson*	9
1999	182	See More Business 9-11-10: 5/2	P F Nicholls	*M A Fitzgerald*	9
2000	180	First Gold 7-11-10: 5/2	F Doumen (Fr)	*T Doumen*	9
2001	172	Florida Pearl 9-11-10: 8/1	W P Mullins (Ir)	*A Maguire*	8
2002	170	Best Mate 7-11-10: 11/8	Miss H C Knight	*A P McCoy*	10
2003	167	Edredon Bleu 11-11-10: 25/1	Miss H C Knight	*J Culloty*	12
2004	171	Kicking King 6-11-10: 3/1	T J Taaffe (Ir)	*B J Geraghty*	13
2005	167	Kicking King 7-11-10: 11/8	T J Taaffe (Ir)	*B J Geraghty*	9
2006	174	Kauto Star 6-11-10: 8/13	P F Nicholls	*R Walsh*	9
2007	176	Kauto Star 7-11-10: 4/6	P F Nicholls	*R Walsh*	7
2008	173	Kauto Star 8-11-10: 10/11	P F Nicholls	*R Walsh*	10
2009	188	Kauto Star 9-11-10: 8/13	P F Nicholls	*R Walsh*	13
2010	178	Long Run 6-11-10: 9/2	Nicky Henderson	*Mr S Waley-Cohen*	9
2011	179	Kauto Star 11-11-10: 3/1	Paul Nicholls	*R Walsh*	7
2012	166	Long Run 7-11-10: 15/8	Nicky Henderson	*Mr S Waley-Cohen*	9
2013	176	Silviniaco Conti 7-11-10: 7/2	Paul Nicholls	*Noel Fehily*	9
2014	172	Silviniaco Conti 8-11-10: 15/8	Paul Nicholls	*Noel Fehily*	10
2015	181	Cue Card 9-11-10: 9/2	Colin Tizzard	*Paddy Brennan*	9
2016	174	Thistlecrack 8-11-10: 11/10	Colin Tizzard	*Tom Scudamore*	5
2017	163	Might Bite 8-11-10: 6/4	Nicky Henderson	*Nico de Boinville*	8
2018	165	Clan des Obeaux 6-11-10: 12/1	Paul Nicholls	*Harry Cobden*	10

MATCHBOOK CLARENCE HOUSE CHASE (Gr 1)

(Ascot 2m167y, except Warwick in 1994, Kempton in 1997, 1999 and replacement race in 2003, Cheltenham in 2005, 2013 and 2017; Sandown in 2006 and 2007; Gr 2 Handicap prior to 2008)

1993	156	Sybillin 7-10-10: 9/2	J G FitzGerald	*M Dwyer*	11
1994	151	Viking Flagship 7-10-10: 3/1	D Nicholson	*R Dunwoody*	4
1995	160	Martha's Son 8-10-9: 3/1	T A Forster	*R Farrant*	8
1996	145	Big Matt 8-10-4: 8/1	N J Henderson	*M Fitzgerald*	11
1997	157	Ask Tom 8-10-10: 9/4	T P Tate	*R Garrity*	8
1998	155	Jeffell 8-10-11: 13/2	A L T Moore (Ir)	*C O'Dwyer*	9
1999	153	Call Equiname 9-11-3: 15/2	P F Nicholls	*R Thornton*	7
2000	161	Nordance Prince 9-10-0: 13/8	Miss V Williams	*A P McCoy*	10
2001	160	Function Dream 9-10-11: 2/1	Mrs M Reveley	*A Ross3*	10
2002	136	Turgeonev 7-10-4: 9/2	T D Easterby	*R McGrath*	8
2003	153	Young Devereaux 10-10-4: 9/2	P F Nicholls	*R Walsh*	8
2004	163	Isio 8-10-5: 4/1	N J Henderson	*M A Fitzgerald*	13
2005	179	Well Chief 6-11-10: 5/1	M C Pipe	*T J Murphy*	10
2006	145	Tysou 9-11-2: 10/1	N J Henderson	*M A Fitzgerald*	10
2007		Abandoned (replaced by substitute event of lower value)			
2008	161	Tamarinbleu 8-11-7: 12/1	D E Pipe	*T Scudamore*	6
2009	167	Master Minded 6-11-7: 1/4	P F Nicholls	*R Walsh*	5
2010	168	Twist Magic 8-11-7: 11/8	P F Nicholls	*R Walsh*	7
2011	168	Master Minded 8-11-7: 4/7	Paul Nicholls	*A P McCoy*	9
2012	165	Somersby 8-11-7: 9/2	Henrietta Knight	*Dominic Elsworth*	8

1037

2013	171	Sprinter Sacre 7-11-7: 1/5	Nicky Henderson	*Barry Geraghty*	7
2014	172	Sire de Grugy 8-11-7: 5/4	Gary Moore	*Jamie Moore*	7
2015	167	Dodging Bullets 7-11-7: 7/2	Paul Nicholls	*Noel Fehily*	5
2016	174	Un de Sceaux 8-11-7: 1/2	W P Mullins (Ir)	*R Walsh*	5
2017	167	Un de Sceaux 9-11-7: 1/2	W P Mullins (Ir)	*R Walsh*	7
2018	164	Un de Sceaux 10-11-7: 4/9	W P Mullins (Ir)	*P Townend*	5
2019	173	Altior 9-11-7: 1/10	Nicky Henderson	*Nico de Boinville*	3

BETFAIR HURDLE (HANDICAP) (Gr 3) (Newbury 2m69y, Ascot 1m7f152y in 2019)

1993	147	King Credo 8-10-0: 10/1	S Woodman	*A Maguire*	16
1994	149	Large Action 6-10-8: 9/2	O Sherwood	*J Osborne*	11
1995	160	Mysilv 5-10-8: 9/4	C R Egerton	*J Osborne*	8
1996	148	Squire Silk 7-10-12: 13/2	A Turnell	*P Carberry*	18
1997	151	Make A Stand 6-11-7: 6/1	M C Pipe	*C Maude*	18
1998	145	Sharpical 6-11-1: 10/1	N J Henderson	*M A Fitzgerald*	14
1999	142	Decoupage 7-11-0: 6/1	C R Egerton	*J A McCarthy*	18
2000	155	Geos 5-11-3: 15/2	N J Henderson	*M A Fitzgerald*	17
2001	145	Landing Light 6-10-2: 4/1	N J Henderson	*M A Fitzgerald*	20
2002	157	Copeland 7-11-7: 13/2	M C Pipe	*A P McCoy*	16
2003	138	Spirit Leader 7-10-0: 14/1	Mrs J Harrington (Ir)	*N Williamson*	27
2004	149	Geos 9-10-9: 16/1	N J Henderson	*M Foley*	25
2005	152	Essex 5-11-6: 4/1	M J P O'Brien (Ir)	*B J Geraghty*	25
2006		Abandoned			
2007	132	Heathcote 5-10-6: 50/1	G L Moore	*J E Moore*	20
2008	131	Wingman 6-10-0: 14/1	G L Moore	*J E Moore*	24
2009		Abandoned			
2010	144	Get Me Out of Here 6-10-6: 6/1	J O'Neill	*A P McCoy*	23
2011	136	Recession Proof 5-10-8: 12/1	John Quinn	*Dougie Costello*	15
2012	159	Zarkandar 5-11-1: 11/4	Paul Nicholls	*R Walsh*	20
2013	162	My Tent Or Yours 6-11-2: 5/1	Nicky Henderson	*A P McCoy*	21
2014	142	Splash of Ginge 6-10-3: 33/1	Nigel Twiston-Davies	*Ryan Hatch[7]*	20
2015	139	Violet Dancer 5-10-9: 20/1	Gary Moore	*Joshua Moore*	23
2016	144	Agrapart 5-10-10: 16/1	Nick Williams	*Lizzie Kelly[5]*	22
2017	145	Ballyandy 6-11-1: 3/1	Nigel Twiston-Davies	*Sam Twiston-Davies*	16
2018	152	Kalashnikov 5-11-5: 8/1	Amy Murphy	*Jack Quinlan*	24
2019	144	Al Dancer 6-11-8: 5/2	Nigel Twiston-Davies	*Sam Twiston-Davies*	14

BETFAIR ASCOT CHASE (Gr 1)
(Ascot 2m5f8y, 2m3½f prior to 2005, 2m3f in 2007, Lingfield 2m4½f in 2005 and 2006)

1995	158	Martha's Son 8-11-7: 1/1	T A Forster	*R Farrant*	6
1996	155	Sound Man 8-11-7: 1/2	E O'Grady (Ir)	*R Dunwoody*	5
1997	171	Strong Promise 6-11-7: 10/1	G A Hubbard	*N Williamson*	4
1998	176	One Man 10-11-7: 7/4	G Richards	*A Dobbin*	3
1999	156	Teeton Mill 10-11-7: 6/4	Miss V Williams	*N Williamson*	7
2000	155	Rockforce 8-11-7: 2/1	P F Nicholls	*J Tizzard*	5
2001	163	Tiutchev 8-11-7: 11/8	N J Henderson	*M A Fitzgerald*	4
2002	148	Tresor de Mai 8-11-7: 9/2	M C Pipe	*A P McCoy*	5
2003	162	Tiutchev 10-11-7: 15/8	M C Pipe	*A P McCoy*	7
2004	161	Hand Inn Hand 8-11-7: 15/2	H D Daly	*M Bradburne*	7
2005	154	It Takes Time 11-11-7: 14/1	M C Pipe	*J E Moore*	7
2006	156	Our Vic 8-11-7: 2/1	M C Pipe	*T J Murphy*	7
2007	158	Monet's Garden 9-11-7: 11/10	N G Richards	*A Dobbin*	7
2008	168	Kauto Star 8-11-7: 4/11	P F Nicholls	*R Walsh*	9
2009	166	Voy Por Ustedes 8-11-7: 6/5	A King	*R Thornton*	4
2010	153	Monet's Garden 12-11-7: 11/2	N G Richards	*B J Geraghty*	6
2011	167	Riverside Theatre 7-11-7: 11/10	Nicky Henderson	*Barry Geraghty*	7
2012	170	Riverside Theatre 8-11-7: 13/8	Nicky Henderson	*Barry Geraghty*	8
2013	167	Cue Card 7-11-7: 15/8	Colin Tizzard	*Joe Tizzard*	6
2014	175	Captain Chris 10-11-7: 8/11	Philip Hobbs	*Richard Johnson*	8
2015	166	Balder Succes 7-11-7: 4/1	Alan King	*Wayne Hutchinson*	5
2016	169	Silviniaco Conti 10-11-7: 2/1	Paul Nicholls	*Noel Fehily*	8
2017	174	Cue Card 11-11-7: 4/9	Colin Tizzard	*Paddy Brennan*	6
2018	168	Waiting Patiently 7-11-7: 2/1	Ruth Jefferson	*Brian Hughes*	7
2019	173	Cyrname 7-11-7: 3/1	Paul Nicholls	*Harry Cobden*	6

SKY BET SUPREME NOVICES' HURDLE (Gr 1) (Cheltenham 2m87y)

| 1993 | 150 | Montelado 6-11-8: 5/1 | P Flynn (Ir) | *C F Swan* | 15 |
| 1994 | 144 | Arctic Kinsman 6-11-8: 50/1 | N A Twiston-Davies | *C Llewellyn* | 18 |

1995	137	Tourist Attraction 6-11-3: 25/1	W P Mullins (Ir)	*M Dwyer*	20
1996	143	Indefence 5-11-8: 25/1	Mrs J Pitman	*W Marston*	27
1997	138	Shadow Leader 6-11-8: 5/1	C R Egerton	*J Osborne*	16
1998	144	French Ballerina 5-11-3: 10/1	P J Flynn (Ir)	*G Bradley*	30
1999	162	Hors La Loi III 4-11-0: 9/2	M C Pipe	*A P McCoy*	20
2000	143	Sausalito Bay 6-11-8: 14/1	N Meade (Ir)	*P Carberry*	15
2001		Abandoned			
2002	138	Like-A-Butterfly 8-11-3: 7/4	C Roche (Ir)	*C F Swan*	28
2003	151	Back In Front 6-11-8: 3/1	E J O'Grady (Ir)	*N Williamson*	19
2004	147	Brave Inca 6-11-7: 7/2	C A Murphy (Ir)	*B M Cash*	19
2005	144	Arcalis 5-11-7: 20/1	J H Johnson	*G Lee*	20
2006	142	Noland 5-11-7: 6/1	P F Nicholls	*R Walsh*	20
2007	145	Ebaziyan 6-11-7: 40/1	W P Mullins (Ir)	*D J Condon*	22
2008	149	Captain Cee Bee 7-11-7: 17/2	E P Harty (Ir)	*R Thornton*	22
2009	145	Go Native 6-11-7: 12/1	N Meade (Ir)	*P Carberry*	20
2010	145	Menorah 5-11-7: 12/1	P J Hobbs	*R Johnson*	18
2011	158	Al Ferof 6-11-7: 10/1	Paul Nicholls	*R Walsh*	15
2012	149	Cinders And Ashes 5-11-7: 10/1	Donald McCain	*Jason Maguire*	19
2013	165	Champagne Fever 6-11-7: 5/1	W P Mullins (Ir)	*R Walsh*	12
2014	154	Vautour 5-11-7: 7/2	W P Mullins (Ir)	*R Walsh*	18
2015	168	Douvan 5-11-7: 2/1	W P Mullins (Ir)	*R Walsh*	12
2016	164	Altior 6-11-7: 4/1	Nicky Henderson	*Nico de Boinville*	14
2017	153	Labaik 6-11-7: 25/1	Gordon Elliott (Ir)	*J W Kennedy*	14
2018	156	Summerville Boy 6-11-7: 9/1	Tom George	*Noel Fehily*	19
2019	152	Klassical Dream 5-11-7: 6/1	W P Mullins (Ir)	*Ruby Walsh*	16

RACING POST ARKLE CHALLENGE TROPHY NOVICES' CHASE (Gr 1)

(Cheltenham 1m7f199y)

1993	158	Travado 7-11-8: 5/1	N J Henderson	*J Osborne*	8
1994	146	Nakir 6-11-8: 9/1	S Christian	*J Osborne*	10
1995	147	Klairon Davis 6-11-8: 7/2	A L T Moore (Ir)	*F Woods*	11
1996	153	Ventana Canyon 7-11-8: 7/1	E J O'Grady (Ir)	*R Dunwoody*	16
1997	146	Or Royal 6-11-8: 11/2	M C Pipe	*A P McCoy*	9
1998	137	Champleve 5-11-0: 13/2	M C Pipe	*A P McCoy*	16
1999	153	Flagship Uberalles 5-11-0: 11/1	P F Nicholls	*J Tizzard*	14
2000	152	Tiutchev 7-11-8: 8/1	N J Henderson	*M A Fitzgerald*	12
2001		Abandoned			
2002	159	Moscow Flyer 8-11-8: 11/2	Mrs J Harrington (Ir)	*B J Geraghty*	12
2003	158	Azertyuiop 6-11-8: 5/4	P F Nicholls	*R Walsh*	9
2004	146	Well Chief 5-11-3: 9/1	M C Pipe	*A P McCoy*	16
2005	150	Contraband 7-11-7: 7/1	M C Pipe	*T J Murphy*	19
2006	151	Voy Por Ustedes 5-11-2: 15/2	A King	*R Thornton*	14
2007	157	My Way de Solzen 7-11-7: 7/2	A King	*R Thornton*	13
2008	160	Tidal Bay 7-11-7: 6/1	J H Johnson	*D O'Regan*	14
2009	151	Forpadydeplasterer 7-11-7: 8/1	T Cooper (Ir)	*B J Geraghty*	17
2010	154	Sizing Europe 8-11-7: 6/1	H de Bromhead (Ir)	*A E Lynch*	12
2011	156	Captain Chris 7-11-7: 6/1	Philip Hobbs	*Richard Johnson*	10
2012	160	Sprinter Sacre 6-11-7: 8/11	Nicky Henderson	*Barry Geraghty*	6
2013	160	Simonsig 7-11-7: 8/15	Nicky Henderson	*Barry Geraghty*	7
2014	157	Western Warhorse 6-11-4: 33/1	David Pipe	*Tom Scudamore*	9
2015	169	Un de Sceaux 7-11-4: 4/6	W P Mullins (Ir)	*R Walsh*	11
2016	168	Douvan 6-11-4: 1/4	W P Mullins (Ir)	*R Walsh*	7
2017	161	Altior 7-11-4: 1/4	Nicky Henderson	*Nico de Boinville*	9
2018	174	Footpad 6-11-4: 5/6	W P Mullins (Ir)	*R Walsh*	5
2019	162	Duc des Genievres 6-11-4: 5/1	W P Mullins (Ir)	*Paul Townend*	12

UNIBET CHAMPION HURDLE CHALLENGE TROPHY (Gr 1) (Cheltenham 2m87y)

1993	164	Granville Again 7-12-0: 13/2	M C Pipe	*P Scudamore*	18
1994	166	Flakey Dove 8-11-9: 9/1	R J Price	*M Dwyer*	15
1995	174	Alderbrook 6-12-0: 11/2	K C Bailey	*N Williamson*	14
1996	170	Collier Bay 6-12-0: 9/1	J A B Old	*G Bradley*	16
1997	165	Make A Stand 6-12-0: 7/1	M C Pipe	*A P McCoy*	17
1998	172	Istabraq 6-12-0: 3/1	A P O'Brien (Ir)	*C F Swan*	18
1999	161	Istabraq 7-12-0: 4/9	A P O'Brien (Ir)	*C F Swan*	14
2000	163	Istabraq 8-12-0: 8/15	A P O'Brien (Ir)	*C F Swan*	12
2001		Abandoned			
2002	161	Hors La Loi III 7-12-0: 10/1	J R Fanshawe	*D Gallagher*	15

2003	170	Rooster Booster 9-12-0: 9/2	P J Hobbs	*R Johnson*	17
2004	165	Hardy Eustace 7-11-10: 33/1	D T Hughes (Ir)	*C O'Dwyer*	14
2005	164	Hardy Eustace 8-11-10: 7/2	D T Hughes (Ir)	*C O'Dwyer*	14
2006	167	Brave Inca 8-11-10: 7/4	C A Murphy (Ir)	*A P McCoy*	18
2007	162	Sublimity 7-11-10: 16/1	J G Carr (Ir)	*P Carberry*	10
2008	163	Katchit 5-11-10: 10/1	A King	*R Thornton*	15
2009	164	Punjabi 6-11-10: 22/1	N J Henderson	*B J Geraghty*	23
2010	167	Binocular 6-11-10: 9/1	N J Henderson	*A P McCoy*	12
2011	168	Hurricane Fly 7-11-10: 11/4	W P Mullins (Ir)	*R Walsh*	11
2012	171	Rock On Ruby 7-11-10: 11/1	Paul Nicholls	*Noel Fehily*	10
2013	170	Hurricane Fly 9-11-10: 13/8	W P Mullins (Ir)	*R Walsh*	9
2014	170	Jezki 6-11-10: 9/1	Mrs John Harrington (Ir)	*Barry Geraghty*	9
2015	170	Faugheen 7-11-10: 4/5	W P Mullins (Ir)	*R Walsh*	8
2016	163	Annie Power 8-11-3: 5/2	W P Mullins (Ir)	*R Walsh*	12
2017	170	Buveur d'Air 6-11-10: 5/1	Nicky Henderson	*Noel Fehily*	11
2018	167	Buveur d'Air 7-11-10: 4/6	Nicky Henderson	*Barry Geraghty*	11
2019	170	Espoir d'Allen 5-11-10: 16/1	Gavin Cromwell (Ir)	*Mark Walsh*	10

OLBG MARES' HURDLE (David Nicholson) (Gr 1) (Cheltenham 2m3f200y, Gr 2 prior to 2015)

2008	137	Whiteoak 5-11-0: 20/1	D McCain Jnr	*J Maguire*	13
2009	152	Quevega 5-11-3: 2/1	W P Mullins (Ir)	*R Walsh*	21
2010	148	Quevega 6-11-5: 6/4	W P Mullins (Ir)	*R Walsh*	17
2011	146	Quevega 7-11-5: 5/6	W P Mullins (Ir)	*R Walsh*	14
2012	137	Quevega 8-11-5: 4/7	W P Mullins (Ir)	*R Walsh*	19
2013	142	Quevega 9-11-5: 8/11	W P Mullins (Ir)	*R Walsh*	19
2014	139	Quevega 10-11-5: 8/11	W P Mullins (Ir)	*R Walsh*	16
2015	146	Glens Melody 7-11-5: 6/1	W P Mullins (Ir)	*P Townend*	15
2016	139	Vroum Vroum Mag 7-11-5: 4/6	W P Mullins (Ir)	*R Walsh*	19
2017	147	Apple's Jade 5-11-5: 7/2	Gordon Elliott (Ir)	*B J Cooper*	17
2018	143	Benie des Dieux 7-11-5: 9/2	W P Mullins (Ir)	*R Walsh*	9
2019	143	Roksana 7-11-5: 10/1	Dan Skelton	*Harry Skelton*	14

BALLYMORE NOVICES' HURDLE (Baring Bingham) (Gr 1) (Cheltenham 2m5f)

1993	134	Gaelstrom 6-11-2: 16/1	N A Twiston-Davies	*C Llewellyn*	19
1994	138	Danoli 6-11-7: 7/4	T Foley (Ir)	*C F Swan*	23
1995	142	Putty Road 5-11-7: 7/1	D Nicholson	*N Williamson*	21
1996	142	Urubande 6-11-7: 8/1	A P O'Brien (Ir)	*C F Swan*	24
1997	144	Istabraq 5-11-7: 6/5	A P O'Brien (Ir)	*C F Swan*	17
1998	151	French Holly 7-11-7: 2/1	F Murphy	*A Thornton*	18
1999	153	Barton 6-11-7: 2/1	T D Easterby	*L Wyer*	18
2000	149	Monsignor 6-11-7: 5/4	M Pitman	*N Williamson*	14
2001		Abandoned			
2002	148	Galileo 6-11-7: 12/1	T R George	*J M Maguire*	27
2003	147	Hardy Eustace 6-11-7: 6/1	D T Hughes (Ir)	*K A Kelly*	19
2004	147	Fundamentalist 6-11-7: 12/1	N A Twiston-Davies	*C Llewellyn*	15
2005	147	No Refuge 5-11-7: 17/2	J H Johnson	*G Lee*	20
2006	146	Nicanor 5-11-7: 17/2	N Meade (Ir)	*P Carberry*	15
2007	147	Massini's Maguire 6-11-7: 20/1	P J Hobbs	*R Johnson*	15
2008	146	Fiveforthree 6-11-7: 7/1	W P Mullins (Ir)	*R Walsh*	15
2009	151	Mikael d'Haguenet 5-11-7: 5/2	W P Mullins (Ir)	*R Walsh*	14
2010	147	Peddlers Cross 5-11-7: 7/1	D McCain Jnr	*J Maguire*	17
2011	149	First Lieutenant 6-11-7: 7/1	M F Morris (Ir)	*Davy Russell*	12
2012	157	Simonsig 6-11-7: 2/1	Nicky Henderson	*Barry Geraghty*	17
2013	155	The New One 5-11-7: 7/2	Nigel Twiston-Davies	*Sam Twiston-Davies*	8
2014	155	Faugheen 6-11-7: 6/4	W P Mullins (Ir)	*R Walsh*	15
2015	154	Windsor Park 6-11-7: 9/2	D K Weld (Ir)	*D Russell*	10
2016	156	Yorkhill 6-11-7: 3/1	W P Mullins (Ir)	*R Walsh*	11
2017	151	Willoughby Court 6-11-7: 14/1	Ben Pauling	*David Bass*	15
2018	155	Samcro 6-11-7: 8/11	Gordon Elliott (Ir)	*J W Kennedy*	14
2019	151	City Island 6-11-7: 8/1	Martin Brassil (Ir)	*Mark Walsh*	16

RSA INSURANCE NOVICES' CHASE (Gr 1) (Cheltenham 3m80y)

1993	136	Young Hustler 6-11-4: 9/4	N A Twiston-Davies	*P Scudamore*	8
1994	148	Monsieur Le Cure 8-11-4: 15/2	J A C Edwards	*P Niven*	18
1995	159	Brief Gale 8-10-13: 13/2	J T Gifford	*P Hide*	13
1996	146	Nahthen Lad 7-11-4: 7/1	Mrs J Pitman	*W Marston*	12
1997	150	Hanakham 8-11-4: 13/2	R J Hodges	*R Dunwoody*	14
1998	169	Florida Pearl 6-11-4: 11/8	W P Mullins (Ir)	*R Dunwoody*	10

1999	161	Looks Like Trouble 7-11-4: 16/1	N T Chance	P Carberry	14
2000	152	Lord Noelie 7-11-4: 9/2	Miss H C Knight	J Culloty	9
2001		Abandoned			
2002	153	Hussard Collonges 7-11-4: 33/1	P Beaumont	R Garritty	19
2003	150	One Knight 7-11-4: 15/2	P J Hobbs	R Johnson	9
2004	149	Rule Supreme 8-11-4: 25/1	W P Mullins (Ir)	D J Casey	10
2005	156	Trabolgan 7-11-4: 5/1	N J Henderson	M A Fitzgerald	9
2006	145	Star de Mohaison 5-10-8: 14/1	P F Nicholls	B J Geraghty	15
2007	156	Denman 7-11-4: 6/5	P F Nicholls	R Walsh	17
2008	148	Albertas Run 7-11-4: 4/1	J O'Neill	A P McCoy	11
2009	158	Cooldine 7-11-4: 9/4	W P Mullins (Ir)	R Walsh	15
2010	152	Weapon's Amnesty 7-11-4: 10/1	C Byrnes (Ir)	D N Russell	9
2011	147	Bostons Angel 7-11-4: 16/1	Mrs J Harrington (Ir)	Robbie Power	12
2012	159	Bobs Worth 7-11-4: 9/2	Nicky Henderson	Barry Geraghty	9
2013	149	Lord Windermere 7-11-4: 8/1	J H Culloty (Ir)	Davy Russell	11
2014	152	O'Faolains Boy 7-11-4: 12/1	Rebecca Curtis	Barry Geraghty	15
2015	161	Don Poli 6-11-4: 13/8	W P Mullins (Ir)	Bryan J Cooper	8
2016	150	Blaklion 7-11-4: 8/1	Nigel Twiston-Davies	Ryan Hatch	8
2017	166	Might Bite 8-11-4: 7/2	Nicky Henderson	Nico de Boinville	12
2018	164	Presenting Percy 7-11-4: 5/2	Patrick G Kelly (Ir)	Davy Russell	10
2019	162	Topofthegame 7-11-4: 4/1	Paul Nicholls	Harry Cobden	12

BETWAY QUEEN MOTHER CHAMPION CHASE (Gr 1) (Cheltenham 1m7f199y)

1993	148	Deep Sensation 8-12-0: 11/1	J T Gifford	D Murphy	9
1994	166	Viking Flagship 7-12-0: 4/1	D Nicholson	A Maguire	8
1995	169	Viking Flagship 8-12-0: 5/2	D Nicholson	C F Swan	10
1996	172	Klairon Davis 7-12-0: 9/1	A L T Moore (Ir)	F Woods	7
1997	171	Martha's Son 10-12-0: 9/1	T A Forster	R Farrant	6
1998	163	One Man 10-12-0: 7/2	G Richards	B Harding	8
1999	164	Call Equiname 9-12-0: 7/2	P F Nicholls	M A Fitzgerald	13
2000	167	Edredon Bleu 8-12-0: 7/2	Miss H C Knight	A P McCoy	9
2001		Abandoned			
2002	166	Flagship Uberalles 8-12-0: 7/4	P J Hobbs	R Johnson	12
2003	167	Moscow Flyer 9-12-0: 7/4	Mrs J Harrington (Ir)	B J Geraghty	11
2004	172	Azertyuiop 7-11-10: 15/8	P F Nicholls	R Walsh	8
2005	181	Moscow Flyer 11-11-10: 6/4	Mrs J Harrington (Ir)	B J Geraghty	8
2006	165	Newmill 8-11-10: 16/1	J J Murphy (Ir)	A J McNamara	12
2007	160	Voy Por Ustedes 6-11-10: 5/1	A King	R Thornton	10
2008	179	Master Minded 5-11-10: 3/1	P F Nicholls	R Walsh	8
2009	164	Master Minded 6-11-10: 4/11	P F Nicholls	R Walsh	12
2010	169	Big Zeb 9-11-10: 10/1	C A Murphy (Ir)	B J Geraghty	9
2011	171	Sizing Europe 9-11-10: 10/1	H de Bromhead (Ir)	A E Lynch	11
2012	174	Finian's Rainbow 9-11-10: 4/1	Nicky Henderson	Barry Geraghty	8
2013	192	Sprinter Sacre 7-11-10: 1/4	Nicky Henderson	Barry Geraghty	7
2014	167	Sire de Grugy 8-11-10: 11/4	Gary Moore	Jamie Moore	11
2015	167	Dodging Bullets 7-11-10: 9/2	Paul Nicholls	Sam Twiston-Davies	9
2016	176	Sprinter Sacre 10-11-10: 5/1	Nicky Henderson	Nico de Boinville	10
2017	166	Special Tiara 10-11-10: 11/1	Henry de Bromhead (Ir)	Noel Fehily	10
2018	179	Altior 8-11-10: 1/1	Nicky Henderson	Nico de Boinville	9
2019	169	Altior 9-11-10: 4/11	Nicky Henderson	Nico de Boinville	9

WEATHERBYS CHAMPION BUMPER (STANDARD OPEN NATIONAL HUNT FLAT) (Gr 1)
(Cheltenham 2m87y)

1993	109	Rhythm Section 4-10-11: 16/1	H Scott (Ir)	P Carberry	24
1994	121	Mucklemeg 6-11-5: 7/2	E O'Grady (Ir)	C F Swan	25
1995	120	Dato Star 4-10-12: 7/2	J M Jefferson	M Dwyer	21
1996	122	Wither Or Which 5-11-6: 11/4	W P Mullins (Ir)	W Mullins	24
1997	124	Florida Pearl 5-11-6: 6/1	W P Mullins (Ir)	R Dunwoody	25
1998	126	Alexander Banquet 5-11-6: 9/1	W P Mullins (Ir)	Mr R Walsh	25
1999	122	Monsignor 5-11-6: 50/1	M Pitman	B Powell	25
2000	122	Joe Cullen 5-11-6: 14/1	W P Mullins (Ir)	C F Swan	17
2001		Abandoned			
2002	123	Pizarro 5-11-6: 14/1	E J O'Grady (Ir)	J P Spencer	23
2003	119	Liberman 5-11-6: 2/1	M C Pipe	A P McCoy	25
2004	118	Total Enjoyment 5-10-2: 7/1	T Cooper (Ir)	J Culloty	24
2005	123	Missed That 6-11-5: 7/2	W P Mullins (Ir)	R Walsh	24
2006	121	Hairy Molly 6-11-5: 33/1	J Crowley (Ir)	P Carberry	23

1041

2007	122	Cork All Star 5-11-5: 11/2	Mrs J Harrington (Ir)	*B J Geraghty*	24
2008	125	Cousin Vinny 5-11-5: 12/1	W P Mullins (Ir)	*Mr P W Mullins*	23
2009	129	Dunguib 6-11-5: 9/2	P Fenton (Ir)	*Mr B T O'Connell*	24
2010	132	Cue Card 4-10-12: 40/1	C L Tizzard	*J Tizzard*	24
2011	128	Cheltenian 5-11-5: 14/1	Philip Hobbs	*Richard Johnson*	24
2012	127	Champagne Fever 5-11-5: 16/1	W P Mullins (Ir)	*Mr P W Mullins*	20
2013	130	Briar Hill 5-11-5: 25/1	W P Mullins (Ir)	*R Walsh*	23
2014	123	Silver Concorde 6-11-5: 16/1	D K Weld (Ir)	*Mr R P McNamara*	22
2015	122	Moon Racer 6-11-5: 9/2	David Pipe	*Tom Scudamore*	23
2016	123	Ballyandy 5-11-5: 5/1	Nigel Twiston-Davies	*Sam Twiston-Davies*	23
2017	115	Fayonagh 6-10-12: 7/1	Gordon Elliott (Ir)	*Mr J J Codd*	22
2018	116	Relegate 5-10-12: 25/1	W P Mullins (Ir)	*Ms K Walsh*	23
2019	125	Envoi Allen 5-11-5: 2/1	Gordon Elliott (Ir)	*Mr J. J. Codd*	14

RYANAIR CHASE (Festival Trophy) (Gr 1) (Cheltenham 2½m127y, Gr 2 before 2008)

2005	160	Thisthatandtother 9-11-3: 9/2	P F Nicholls	*R Walsh*	12
2006	158	Fondmort 10-11-0: 10/3	N J Henderson	*M A Fitzgerald*	11
2007	157	Taranis 6-11-0: 9/2	P F Nicholls	*R Walsh*	9
2008	163	Our Vic 10-11-10: 4/1	D E Pipe	*T J Murphy*	9
2009	162	Imperial Commander 8-11-10: 6/1	N A Twiston-Davies	*P J Brennan*	10
2010	165	Albertas Run 9-11-10: 14/1	J O'Neill	*A P McCoy*	13
2011	165	Albertas Run 10-11-10: 6/1	Jonjo O'Neill	*A P McCoy*	11
2012	168	Riverside Theatre 8-11-10: 7/2	Nicky Henderson	*Barry Geraghty*	12
2013	175	Cue Card 7-11-10: 7/2	Colin Tizzard	*Joe Tizzard*	8
2014	163	Dynaste 8-11-10: 3/1	David Pipe	*Tom Scudamore*	11
2015	168	Uxizandre 7-11-10: 16/1	Alan King	*A P McCoy*	14
2016	180	Vautour 7-11-10: 1/1	W P Mullins (Ir)	*R Walsh*	15
2017	169	Un de Sceaux 9-11-10: 7/4	W P Mullins (Ir)	*R Walsh*	8
2018	166	Balko des Flos 7-11-10: 8/1	Henry de Bromhead (Ir)	*Davy Russell*	6
2019	167	Frodon 7-11-10: 9/2	Paul Nicholls	*Bryony Frost*	12

JLT NOVICES' CHASE (Golden Miller) (Gr 1, Gr 2 until 2013) (Cheltenham 2m3f168y)

2011	151	Noble Prince 7-11-4: 4/1	Paul Nolan (Ir)	*A P McCoy*	11
2012	160	Sir des Champs 6-11-4: 3/1	W P Mullins (Ir)	*Davy Russell*	10
2013	153	Benefficient 7-11-4: 20/1	A J Martin (Ir)	*Bryan Cooper*	13
2014	154	Taquin du Seuil 7-11-4: 7/1	Jonjo O'Neill	*A P McCoy*	12
2015	171	Vautour 6-11-4: 6/4	W P Mullins (Ir)	*R Walsh*	8
2016	154	Black Hercules 7-11-4: 4/1	W P Mullins (Ir)	*R Walsh*	9
2017	160	Yorkhill 7-11-4: 6/4	W P Mullins (Ir)	*R Walsh*	8
2018	154	Shattered Love 7-10-11: 4/1	Gordon Elliott (Ir)	*J W Kennedy*	9
2019	161	Defi du Seuil 6-11-4: 3/1	Philip Hobbs	*Barry Geraghty*	10

SUN RACING STAYERS' HURDLE (Gr 1) (Cheltenham 2m7f213y, 3m½f before 2002)

1993	157	Shuil Ar Aghaidh 7-11-5: 20/1	P Kiely (Ir)	*C F Swan*	12
1994	157	*Balasani 8-11-10: 9/2	M C Pipe	*M Perrett*	14
1995	167	Dorans Pride 6-11-10: 11/4	M Hourigan (Ir)	*J P Broderick*	11
1996	158	Cyborgo 6-11-10: 8/1	M C Pipe	*D Bridgwater*	19
1997	164	Karshi 7-11-10: 20/1	Miss H C Knight	*J Osborne*	17
1998	161	Princeful 7-11-10: 16/1	Mrs J Pitman	*R Farrant*	9
1999	162	Anzum 8-11-10: 40/1	D Nicholson	*R Johnson*	12
2000	161	Bacchanal 6-11-10: 11/2	N J Henderson	*M A Fitzgerald*	10
2001		Abandoned			
2002	164	Baracouda 7-11-10: 13/8	F Doumen (Fr)	*T Doumen*	16
2003	173	Baracouda 8-11-10: 9/4	F Doumen (Fr)	*T Doumen*	11
2004	172	Iris's Gift 7-11-10: 9/2	J O'Neill	*B J Geraghty*	10
2005	162	Inglis Drever 6-11-10: 5/1	J H Johnson	*G Lee*	12
2006	163	My Way de Solzen 6-11-10: 8/1	A King	*R Thornton*	20
2007	164	Inglis Drever 8-11-10: 5/1	J H Johnson	*P J Brennan*	14
2008	169	Inglis Drever 9-11-10: 11/8	J H Johnson	*D O'Regan*	17
2009	172	Big Buck's 6-11-10: 6/1	P F Nicholls	*R Walsh*	14
2010	169	Big Buck's 7-11-10: 5/6	P F Nicholls	*R Walsh*	14
2011	162	Big Buck's 8-11-10: 10/11	Paul Nicholls	*R Walsh*	13
2012	168	Big Buck's 9-11-10: 5/6	Paul Nicholls	*R Walsh*	11
2013	162	Solwhit 9-11-10: 17/2	Charles Byrnes (Ir)	*Paul Carberry*	13
2014	167	More of That 6-11-10: 15/2	Jonjo O'Neill	*Barry Geraghty*	10
2015	164	Cole Harden 6-11-10: 14/1	Warren Greatrex	*Gavin Sheehan*	16
2016	169	Thistlecrack 8-11-10: 1/1	Colin Tizzard	*Tom Scudamore*	12
2017	163	Nichols Canyon 7-11-10: 10/1	W P Mullins (Ir)	*R Walsh*	12

| 2018 | 164 | Penhill 7-11-10: 12/1 | W P Mullins (Ir) | *P Townend* | 15 |
| 2019 | 161 | Paisley Park 7-11-10: 11/8 | Emma Lavelle | *Aidan Coleman* | 18 |

JCB TRIUMPH HURDLE (4-y-o) (Gr 1) (Cheltenham 2m179y)

1993	133	Shawiya 10-9: 12/1	M O'Brien (Ir)	*C F Swan*	25
1994	133	Mysilv 10-9: 2/1	D Nicholson	*A Maguire*	28
1995	143	Kissair 11-0: 16/1	M C Pipe	*J Lower*	26
1996	144	Paddy's Return 11-0: 10/1	F Murphy	*R Dunwoody*	29
1997	130	Commanche Court 11-0: 9/1	T M Walsh (Ir)	*N Williamson*	28
1998	145	Upgrade 11-0: 14/1	N A Twiston-Davies	*C Llewellyn*	25
1999	151	Katarino 11-0: 11/4	N J Henderson	*M A Fitzgerald*	23
2000	135	Snow Drop 10-9: 7/1	F Doumen (Fr)	*T Doumen*	28
2001		Abandoned			
2002	147	Scolardy 11-0: 16/1	W P Mullins (Ir)	*C F Swan*	28
2003	134	Spectroscope 11-0: 20/1	J O'Neill	*B J Geraghty*	27
2004	134	Made In Japan 11-0: 20/1	P J Hobbs	*R Johnson*	23
2005	144	Penzance 11-0: 9/1	A King	*R Thornton*	23
2006	140	Detroit City 11-0: 7/2	P J Hobbs	*R Johnson*	17
2007	151	Katchit 11-0: 11/2	A King	*R Thornton*	23
2008	141	Celestial Halo 11-0: 5/1	P F Nicholls	*R Walsh*	14
2009	149	Zaynar 11-0: 11/2	N J Henderson	*B J Geraghty*	18
2010	145	Soldatino 11-0: 6/1	N J Henderson	*B J Geraghty*	17
2011	152	Zarkandar 11-0: 13/2	Paul Nicholls	*Daryl Jacob*	23
2012	147	Countrywide Flame 11-0: 33/1	John Quinn	*Dougie Costello*	20
2013	160	Our Conor 11-0: 4/1	D T Hughes (Ir)	*Bryan Cooper*	17
2014	150	Tiger Roll 11-0: 10/1	Gordon Elliott (Ir)	*Davy Russell*	15
2015	164	Peace And Co 11-0: 2/1	Nicky Henderson	*Barry Geraghty*	16
2016	156	Ivanovich Gorbatov 11-0: 9/2	Aidan O'Brien (Ir)	*Barry Geraghty*	15
2017	146	Defi du Seuil 11-0: 5/2	Philip Hobbs	*Richard Johnson*	15
2018	149	Farclas 11-0: 9/1	Gordon Elliott (Ir)	*J W Kennedy*	9
2019	145	Pentland Hills 4-11-0: 20/1	Nicky Henderson	*Nico de Boinville*	14

ALBERT BARTLETT NOVICES' HURDLE (Spa) (Gr 1)
(Cheltenham 2m7f213y, Gr 2 before 2008)

2005	139	Moulin Riche 5-11-7: 9/1	F Doumen (Fr)	*R Thornton*	18
2006	142	Black Jack Ketchum 7-11-7: 1/1	J O'Neill	*A P McCoy*	19
2007	147	Wichita Lineman 6-11-7: 11/8	J O'Neill	*A P McCoy*	20
2008	144	Nenuphar Collonges 7-11-7: 9/1	A King	*R Thornton*	18
2009	147	Weapon's Amnesty 6-11-7: 8/1	C Byrnes (Ir)	*D N Russell*	17
2010	147	Berties Dream 7-11-7: 33/1	P J Gilligan (Ir)	*A E Lynch*	19
2011	152	Bobs Worth 6-11-7: 15/8	Nicky Henderson	*Barry Geraghty*	18
2012	150	Brindisi Breeze 6-11-7: 7/1	Lucinda Russell	*Campbell Gillies*	20
2013	150	At Fishers Cross 6-11-7: 11/8	Rebecca Curtis	*A P McCoy*	13
2014	146	Very Wood 6-11-7: 33/1	Noel Meade (Ir)	*P Carberry*	18
2015	145	Martello Tower 7-11-7: 14/1	Mrs Margaret Mullins (Ir)	*A P Heskin*	19
2016	145	Unowhatimeanharry 8-11-5: 11/1	Harry Fry	*Noel Fehily*	19
2017	152	Penhill 6-11-5: 16/1	W P Mullins (Ir)	*P Townend*	15
2018	151	Kilbricken Storm 7-11-5: 33/1	Colin Tizzard	*Harry Cobden*	20
2019	147	Minella Indo 6-11-5: 50/1	Henry de Bromhead (Ir)	*Rachael Blackmore*	20

MAGNERS CHELTENHAM GOLD CUP CHASE (Gr 1) (Cheltenham 3¼m70y)

1993	174	Jodami 8-12-0: 8/1	P Beaumont	*M Dwyer*	16
1994	171	The Fellow 9-12-0: 7/1	F Doumen (Fr)	*A Kondrat*	15
1995	183	Master Oats 9-12-0: 10/3	K C Bailey	*N Williamson*	15
1996	178	Imperial Call 7-12-0: 9/2	F Sutherland (Ir)	*C O'Dwyer*	10
1997	169	Mr Mulligan 9-12-0: 20/1	N T Chance	*A P McCoy*	14
1998	173	Cool Dawn 10-12-0: 25/1	R H Alner	*A Thornton*	17
1999	173	See More Business 9-12-0: 16/1	P F Nicholls	*M A Fitzgerald*	12
2000	176	Looks Like Trouble 8-12-0: 9/2	N T Chance	*R Johnson*	12
2001		Abandoned			
2002	173	Best Mate 7-12-0: 7/1	Miss H C Knight	*J Culloty*	18
2003	174	Best Mate 8-12-0: 13/8	Miss H C Knight	*J Culloty*	15
2004	169	Best Mate 9-11-10: 8/11	Miss H C Knight	*J Culloty*	10
2005	167	Kicking King 7-11-10: 4/1	T J Taaffe (Ir)	*B J Geraghty*	15
2006	169	War of Attrition 7-11-10: 15/2	M F Morris (Ir)	*C O'Dwyer*	22
2007	165	Kauto Star 7-11-10: 5/4	P F Nicholls	*R Walsh*	18
2008	176	Denman 8-11-10: 9/4	P F Nicholls	*S Thomas*	12
2009	184	Kauto Star 9-11-10: 7/4	P F Nicholls	*R Walsh*	16

2010	182	Imperial Commander 9-11-10: 7/1	N A Twiston-Davies	*P J Brennan*	11
2011	176	Long Run 6-11-10: 7/2	Nicky Henderson	*Mr S Waley-Cohen*	13
2012	167	Synchronised 9-11-10: 8/1	Jonjo O'Neill	*A P McCoy*	14
2013	179	Bobs Worth 8-11-10: 11/4	Nicky Henderson	*Barry Geraghty*	9
2014	161	Lord Windermere 8-11-10: 20/1	J H Culloty (Ir)	*Davy Russell*	13
2015	170	Coneygree 8-11-10: 7/1	Mark Bradstock	*Nico de Boinville*	16
2016	181	Don Cossack 9-11-10: 9/4	Gordon Elliott (Ir)	*B J Cooper*	9
2017	169	Sizing John 7-11-10: 7/1	Mrs J Harrington (Ir)	*Robbie Power*	13
2018	172	Native River 8-11-10: 5/1	Colin Tizzard	*Richard Johnson*	15
2019	169	Al Boum Photo 7-11-10: 12/1	W P Mullins (Ir)	*Paul Townend*	16

DEVENISH MANIFESTO NOVICES' CHASE (Gr 1) (Aintree 2m3f200y, Gr 2 prior to 2012)

2009	154	Tartak 6-11-4: 11/2	T R George	*P J Brennan*	8
2010	151	Mad Max 8-11-4: 4/1	N J Henderson	*B J Geraghty*	6
2011	151	Wishfull Thinking 8-11-4: 9/4	Philip Hobbs	*Richard Johnson*	7
2012	159	Menorah 7-11-4: 3/1	Philip Hobbs	*Richard Johnson*	5
2013	145	Captain Conan 6-11-4: 6/5	Nicky Henderson	*Barry Geraghty*	7
2014	153	Uxizandre 6-11-4: 11/4	Alan King	*A P McCoy*	5
2015	152	Clarcam 5-11-4: 5/1	Gordon Elliott (Ir)	*R Walsh*	6
2016	156	Arzal 6-11-4: 4/1	Harry Whittingham	*Gavin Sheehan*	8
2017	154	Flying Angel 6-11-4: 5/1	Nigel Twiston-Davies	*Noel Fehily*	6
2018	148	Finian's Oscar 6-11-4: 5/2	Colin Tizzard	*Robbie Power*	6
2019	152	Kalashnikov 6-11-4: 4/1	Amy Murphy	*Jack Quinlan*	6

RYANAIR STAYERS HURDLE (Liverpool) (Gr 1)
(Aintree 3m149y, Ascot 3m before 2004, Gr 2 prior to 2010)

1993	161	Sweet Duke 6-11-3: 5/1	N A Twiston-Davies	*C Llewellyn*	7
1994	167	Sweet Glow 7-11-7: 9/2	M C Pipe	*R Dunwoody*	12
1995	148	Cab On Target 9-11-7: 11/8	Mrs M Reveley	*P Niven*	6
1996	163	Pleasure Shared 8-11-10: 6/1	P J Hobbs	*W Marston*	7
1997	123	Trainglot 10-11-10: 1/2	J G FitzGerald	*R Dunwoody*	5
1998	160	Marello 7-11-5: 11/4	Mrs M Reveley	*P Niven*	7
1999	160	Galant Moss 5-11-3: 1/1	M C Pipe	*A P McCoy*	5
2000	160	Teaatral 6-11-7: 4/1	C R Egerton	*D Gallagher*	10
2001	147	Maid Equal 10-10-12: 14/1	M C Pipe	*Mr T Scudamore*	8
2002	149	Spendid 10-11-2: 2/1	A King	*W Marston*	7
2003	154	Deano's Beeno 11-11-10: 5/4	M C Pipe	*A P McCoy*	7
2004	153	Iris's Gift 7-11-10: 4/7	J O'Neill	*B J Geraghty*	8
2005	160	Monet's Garden 7-11-10: 11/2	N G Richards	*A Dobbin*	9
2006	166	Mighty Man 6-11-6: 11/4	H D Daly	*R Johnson*	12
2007	162	Mighty Man 7-11-10: 15/8	H D Daly	*R Johnson*	6
2008	157	Blazing Bailey 6-11-10: 5/1	A King	*R Thornton*	11
2009	173	Big Buck's 6-11-10: 5/6	P F Nicholls	*R Walsh*	10
2010	168	Big Buck's 7-11-7: 3/10	P F Nicholls	*R Walsh*	7
2011	166	Big Buck's 8-11-7: 4/6	Paul Nicholls	*R Walsh*	11
2012	169	Big Buck's 9-11-7: 2/9	Paul Nicholls	*R Walsh*	8
2013	158	Solwhit 9-11-7: 9/4	Charles Byrnes (Ir)	*Paul Carberry*	13
2014	158	Whisper 6-11-7: 4/1	Nicky Henderson	*Barry Geraghty*	7
2015	163	Whisper 7-11-7: 5/1	Nicky Henderson	*Nico de Boinville*	9
2016	162	Thistlecrack 8-11-7: 2/7	Colin Tizzard	*Tom Scudamore*	6
2017	155	Yanworth 7-11-7: 9/4	Alan King	*Barry Geraghty*	11
2018	161	Identity Thief 8-11-7: 14/1	Henry de Bromhead (Ir)	*Sean Flanagan*	10
2019	156	If The Cap Fits 7-11-7: 7/1	Harry Fry	*Sean Bowen*	15

BETWAY BOWL CHASE (Gr 1) (Aintree 3m210y, Gr 2 prior to 2010)

1993	165	Docklands Express 11-11-5: 6/4	K C Bailey	*J Osborne*	4
1994	159	Docklands Express 12-11-5: 5/2	K C Bailey	*R Dunwoody*	4
1995	170	Merry Gale 7-11-9: 5/2	J T R Dreaper (Ir)	*G Bradley*	6
1996	161	Scotton Banks 7-11-5: 9/2	T D Easterby	*L Wyer*	6
1997	162	Barton Bank 11-11-5: 10/3	D Nicholson	*D Walsh*	5
1998	171	Escartefigue 6-11-13: 11/2	D Nicholson	*R Johnson*	8
1999	155	Macgeorge 9-11-5: 11/1	R Lee	*A Maguire*	5
2000	179	See More Business 10-12-0: 5/4	P F Nicholls	*M A Fitzgerald*	4
2001	172	First Gold 8-12-0: 7/4	F Doumen (Fr)	*T Doumen*	7
2002	168	Florida Pearl 10-11-12: 5/2	W P Mullins (Ir)	*B J Geraghty*	6
2003	171	First Gold 10-11-2: 14/1	F Doumen (Fr)	*T Doumen*	7
2004	168	Tiutchev 11-11-12: 11/2	M C Pipe	*A P McCoy*	8
2005	168	Grey Abbey 11-11-12: 7/2	J H Johnson	*G Lee*	8

2006	166	Celestial Gold 8-11-8: 8/1	M C Pipe	*T J Murphy*	9
2007	175	Exotic Dancer 7-11-12: 6/4	J O'Neill	*A P McCoy*	5
2008	170	Our Vic 10-11-10: 9/1	D E Pipe	*T J Murphy*	5
2009	170	Madison du Berlais 8-11-10: 12/1	D E Pipe	*T Scudamore*	10
2010	160	What A Friend 7-11-7: 5/2	P F Nicholls	*R Walsh*	5
2011	164	Nacarat 10-11-7: 7/2	Tom George	*Paddy Brennan*	6
2012	163	Follow The Plan 9-11-7: 50/1	Oliver McKiernan (Ir)	*Tom Doyle*	11
2013	170	First Lieutenant 8-11-7: 7/2	M F Morris (Ir)	*Bryan Cooper*	8
2014	165	Silviniaco Conti 8-11-7: 9/4	Paul Nicholls	*Noel Fehily*	6
2015	165	Silviniaco Conti 9-11-7: 7/4	Paul Nicholls	*Noel Fehily*	7
2016	181	Cue Card 10-11-7: 6/5	Colin Tizzard	*Paddy Brennan*	9
2017	166	Tea For Two 8-11-7: 10/1	Nick Williams	*Lizzie Kelly*	7
2018	171	Might Bite 9-11-7: 4/5	Nicky Henderson	*Nico de Boinville*	8
2019	170	Kemboy 7-11-7: 9/4	W P Mullins (Ir)	*Ruby Walsh*	6

DOOM BAR ANNIVERSARY 4-Y-O JUVENILE HURDLE (Gr 1) (Aintree 2m209y)

1993	132	Titled Dancer 10-9: 9/2	J Coogan (Ir)	*J Shortt*	8
1994	135	Tropical Lake 10-9: 10/1	M Hourigan (Ir)	*K O'Brien*	12
1995	139	Stompin 11-0: 9/1	Miss H C Knight	*J Osborne*	18
1996	139	Zabadi 11-0: 8/1	D Nicholson	*A P McCoy*	11
1997	134	Quakers Field 11-0: 8/1	G L Moore	*D Gallagher*	12
1998	149	Deep Water 11-0: 8/1	M D Hammond	*R Garritty*	14
1999	147	Hors La Loi III 11-4: 8/15	M C Pipe	*A P McCoy*	6
2000	139	Lord Brex 11-0: 15/2	P J Hobbs	*R Johnson*	12
2001	154	Bilboa 10-13: 7/4	F Doumen (Fr)	*T Doumen*	14
2002	137	Quazar 11-4: 16/1	J O'Neill	*A Dobbin*	17
2003	133	Le Duc 11-0: 33/1	P F Nicholls	*R Walsh*	19
2004	131	Al Eile 11-0: 25/1	J Queally (Ir)	*T J Murphy*	18
2005	141	Faasel 11-0: 11/4	N G Richards	*A Dobbin*	12
2006	144	Detroit City 11-0: 3/1	P J Hobbs	*R Johnson*	13
2007	147	Katchit 11-0: 1/1	A King	*R Thornton*	12
2008	151	Binocular 11-0: 11/8	N J Henderson	*A P McCoy*	10
2009	154	Walkon 11-0: 2/1	A King	*R Thornton*	13
2010	136	Orsippus 11-0: 40/1	Michael Smith	*D J Condon*	11
2011	145	Zarkandar 11-0: 4/6	Paul Nicholls	*R Walsh*	9
2012	148	Grumeti 11-0: 11/4	Alan King	*Robert Thornton*	11
2013	139	L'Unique 10-7: 10/1	Alan King	*Wayne Hutchinson*	10
2014	144	Guitar Pete 11-0: 13/2	D T Hughes (Ir)	*Paul Carberry*	15
2015	145	All Yours 11-0: 16/1	Paul Nicholls	*Sam Twiston-Davies*	10
2016	157	Apple's Jade 10-7: 3/1	W P Mullins (Ir)	*B J Cooper*	9
2017	141	Defi du Seuil 11-0: 4/11	Philip Hobbs	*Barry Geraghty*	8
2018	150	We Have A Dream 11-0: 2/1	Nicky Henderson	*Daryl Jacob*	10
2019	138	Pentland Hills 11-0: 11/4	Nicky Henderson	*Nico de Boinville*	9

BETWAY MILDMAY NOVICES' CHASE (Gr 1) (Aintree 3m210y, Gr 2 prior to 2014)

1993	148	Cab On Target 7-11-3: 15/8	Mrs M Reveley	*P Niven*	5
1994	156	Monsieur Le Cure 8-11-9: 7/4	J A C Edwards	*P Niven*	6
1995	145	Banjo 5-11-0: 6/4	M C Pipe	*R Dunwoody*	4
1996	145	Addington Boy 8-11-10: 7/2	G Richards	*B Harding*	7
1997	143	Cyborgo 7-11-4: 13/8	M C Pipe	*R Dunwoody*	7
1998	146	Boss Doyle 6-11-7: 5/4	M F Morris (Ir)	*A P McCoy*	8
1999	140	Spendid 7-11-9: 10/3	D Nicholson	*R Johnson*	7
2000	147	High Game 6-11-4: 9/1	S E H Sherwood	*N Williamson*	8
2001	?	Whats Up Boys 7-11-4: 12/1	P J Hobbs	*R Johnson*	7
2002	154	Barton 9-11-9: 3/1	T D Easterby	*A Dobbin*	9
2003	142	Irish Hussar 7-11-2: 3/1	N J Henderson	*M A Fitzgerald*	9
2004	138	Simply Supreme 7-11-2: 13/2	Mrs S J Smith	*R McGrath*	11
2005	134	Like-A-Butterfly 11-11-2: 6/1	C Roche (Ir)	*A P McCoy*	10
2006	149	Star de Mohaison 5-11-0: 11/4	P F Nicholls	*B J Geraghty*	15
2007	149	Aces Four 8-11-5: 5/2	F Murphy	*G Lee*	10
2008	147	Big Buck's 5-11-3: 11/4	P F Nicholls	*R Walsh*	8
2009	146	Killyglen 7-11-3: 7/1	J H Johnson	*D O'Regan*	9
2010	139	Burton Port 6-11-4: 9/2	N J Henderson	*B J Geraghty*	10
2011	142	Quito de La Roque 7-11-4: 6/1	Colm Murphy (Ir)	*Davy Russell*	8
2012	158	Silviniaco Conti 6-11-4: 7/4	Paul Nicholls	*R Walsh*	5
2013	153	Dynaste 7-11-4: 9/4	David Pipe	*Tom Scudamore*	6
2014	158	Holywell 7-11-4: 7/2	Jonjo O'Neill	*A P McCoy*	6

2015	161	Saphir du Rheu 6-11-4: 13/8	Paul Nicholls	*Sam Twiston-Davies*	9
2016	152	Native River 6-11-4: 11/2	Colin Tizzard	*Richard Johnson*	8
2017	161	Might Bite 8-11-4: 8/13	Nicky Henderson	*Nico de Boinville*	5
2018	156	Terrefort 5-11-4: 3/1	Nicky Henderson	*Daryl Jacob*	9
2019	154	Lostintranslation 7-11-4: 3/1	Colin Tizzard	*Robbie Power*	6

DOOM BAR SEFTON NOVICES' HURDLE (Gr 1) (Aintree 3m149y)

1993	136	Cardinal Red 6-11-4: 4/1	Mrs F Walwyn	*B de Haan*	6
1994	136	Corner Boy 7-11-4: 10/1	D Nicholson	*A Maguire*	11
1995	135	Morgans Harbour 9-11-4: 6/1	Mrs M Reveley	*P Niven*	15
1996	146	Pleasure Shared 8-11-6: 14/1	P J Hobbs	*P Carberry*	16
1997	140	Forest Ivory 6-11-4: 11/2	D Nicholson	*R Johnson*	12
1998	145	Unsinkable Boxer 9-11-4: 10/11	M C Pipe	*A P McCoy*	12
1999	141	King's Road 6-11-4: 3/1	N A Twiston-Davies	*C Llewellyn*	15
2000	148	Sackville 7-11-4: 12/1	Ms F M Crowley (Ir)	*B J Geraghty*	17
2001	140	Garruth 7-11-4: 16/1	T D Easterby	*R Garritty*	13
2002	139	Stromness 5-11-4: 8/1	A King	*R Thornton*	15
2003	159	Iris's Gift 6-11-4: 10/11	J O'Neill	*B J Geraghty*	9
2004	140	Accipiter 5-11-4: 14/1	G B Balding	*T Best*	13
2005	142	Asian Maze 6-10-11: 7/1	T Mullins (Ir)	*R Walsh*	17
2006	151	Black Jack Ketchum 7-11-4: 8/13	J O'Neill	*A P McCoy*	11
2007	150	Chief Dan George 7-11-4: 20/1	J Moffatt	*M A Fitzgerald*	10
2008	146	Pettifour 6-11-4: 16/1	N A Twiston-Davies	*P J Brennan*	13
2009	143	Ogee 6-11-4: 25/1	Mrs P Robeson	*J A McCarthy*	15
2010	144	Wayward Prince 6-11-4: 9/1	I Williams	*D Costello*	14
2011	139	Saint Are 5-11-4: 33/1	Tim Vaughan	*Richard Johnson*	19
2012	149	Lovcen 7-11-4: 8/1	Alan King	*Robert Thornton*	19
2013	147	At Fishers Cross 6-11-4: 11/8	Rebecca Curtis	*A P McCoy*	9
2014	153	Beat That 6-11-4: 6/1	Nicky Henderson	*Barry Geraghty*	18
2015	149	Thistlecrack 7-11-4: 25/1	Colin Tizzard	*Tom Scudamore*	16
2016	146	Ballyoptic 6-11-4: 9/1	Nigel Twiston-Davies	*Ryan Hatch*	15
2017	146	The Worlds End 6-11-4: 3/1	Tom George	*A P Heskin*	11
2018	150	Santini 6-11-4: 6/4	Nicky Henderson	*Nico de Boinville*	13
2019	145	Champ 7-11-4: 9/4	Nicky Henderson	*Mark Walsh*	12

JLT CHASE (Melling) (Gr 1) (Aintree 2m3f200y)

1993	148	Deep Sensation 8-11-10: 7/4	J T Gifford	*D Murphy*	4
1994	161	Katabatic 11-11-10: 14/1	J T Gifford	*S McNeill*	5
1995	164	Viking Flagship 8-11-10: 5/2	D Nicholson	*A Maguire*	6
1996	172	Viking Flagship 9-11-10: 5/2	D Nicholson	*A P McCoy*	4
1997	177	Martha's Son 11-11-10: 5/2	T A Forster	*C Llewellyn*	4
1998	155	Opera Hat 10-11-5: 10/1	J R H Fowler (Ir)	*C O'Dwyer*	5
1999	166	Direct Route 8-11-10: 7/2	J H Johnson	*N Williamson*	6
2000	160	Direct Route 9-11-10: 11/8	J H Johnson	*N Williamson*	5
2001	167	Fadalko 8-11-10: 9/2	P F Nicholls	*R Walsh*	7
2002	158	Native Upmanship 9-11-10: 10/3	A L T Moore (Ir)	*C O'Dwyer*	8
2003	168	Native Upmanship 10-11-10: 5/4	A L T Moore (Ir)	*C O'Dwyer*	6
2004	170	Moscow Flyer 10-11-10: 1/1	Mrs J Harrington (Ir)	*B J Geraghty*	7
2005	176	Moscow Flyer 11-11-10: 4/9	Mrs J Harrington (Ir)	*B J Geraghty*	6
2006	156	Hi Cloy 9-11-10: 14/1	M Hourigan (Ir)	*A J McNamara*	11
2007	160	Monet's Garden 9-11-10: 4/1	N G Richards	*A Dobbin*	6
2008	170	Voy Por Ustedes 7-11-10: 5/1	A King	*R Thornton*	6
2009	163	Voy Por Ustedes 8-11-10: 11/8	A King	*R Thornton*	10
2010	165	Albertas Run 9-11-10: 8/1	J O'Neill	*A P McCoy*	11
2011	170	Master Minded 8-11-10: 11/2	Paul Nicholls	*R Walsh*	10
2012	170	Finian's Rainbow 9-11-10: 13/8	Nicky Henderson	*Barry Geraghty*	8
2013	180	Sprinter Sacre 7-11-10: 1/3	Nicky Henderson	*Barry Geraghty*	6
2014	159	Boston Bob 9-11-10: 5/1	W P Mullins (Ir)	*Paul Townend*	10
2015	180	Don Cossack 8-11-10: 3/1	Gordon Elliott (Ir)	*A P McCoy*	10
2016	168	God's Own 8-11-10: 10/1	Tom George	*Paddy Brennan*	6
2017	170	Fox Norton 7-11-7: 4/1	Colin Tizzard	*Robbie Power*	9
2018	166	Politologue 7-11-7: 11/1	Paul Nicholls	*Sam Twiston-Davies*	6
2019	174	Min 8-11-7: 2/1	W P Mullins (Ir)	*Ruby Walsh*	6

BETWAY TOP NOVICES' HURDLE (Gr 1) (Aintree 2m103y)

1993	140	Roll A Dollar 7-11-6: 9/4	D R C Elsworth	*P Holley*	9
1994	141	Jazilah 6-11-6: 7/4	R Akehurst	*G McCourt*	8
1995	128	Sweet Mignonette 7-10-11: 4/1	Mrs M Reveley	*P Niven*	15

1996	132	Tragic Hero 4-10-8: 20/1	M C Pipe	*J Lower*	15
1997	131	Midnight Legend 6-11-0: 11/2	D Nicholson	*R Johnson*	9
1998	137	Fataliste 4-10-12: 7/2	M C Pipe	*A P McCoy*	10
1999	142	Joe Mac 5-11-8: 6/4	C Roche (Ir)	*C O'Dwyer*	9
2000	139	Phardante Flyer 6-11-10: 5/1	P J Hobbs	*R Johnson*	13
2001	133	Ilico II 5-11-5: 16/1	P J Hobbs	*A Maguire*	15
2002	144	In Contrast 6-11-5: 5/2	P J Hobbs	*R Johnson*	11
2003	132	Limerick Boy 5-11-0: 5/1	Miss S Williams	*A Dobbin*	12
2004	138	Royal Shakespeare 5-11-3: 25/1	S Gollings	*R Thornton*	12
2005	138	Mighty Man 5-11-0: 3/1	H D Daly	*R Johnson*	7
2006	147	Straw Bear 5-11-3: 2/1	N J Gifford	*A P McCoy*	16
2007	146	Blythe Knight 7-11-0: 14/1	J J Quinn	*A P McCoy*	8
2008	149	Pierrot Lunaire 4-10-8: 5/1	P F Nicholls	*R Walsh*	14
2009	140	El Dancer 5-11-0: 14/1	Mrs L Wadham	*D Elsworth*	11
2010	143	General Miller 5-11-4: 7/1	N J Henderson	*B J Geraghty*	9
2011	143	Topolski 5-11-4: 11/2	David Arbuthnot	*Daryl Jacob*	13
2012	146	Darlan 5-11-4: 7/4	Nicky Henderson	*A P McCoy*	12
2013	159	My Tent Or Yours 6-11-4: 4/11	Nicky Henderson	*A P McCoy*	4
2014	149	Josses Hill 6-11-4: 6/4	Nicky Henderson	*Barry Geraghty*	10
2015	159	Cyrus Darius 6-11-4: 8/1	Malcolm Jefferson	*Brian Hughes*	11
2016	151	Buveur d'Air 5-11-4: 11/4	Nicky Henderson	*Noel Fehily*	11
2017	140	Pingshou 7-11-4: 16/1	Colin Tizzard	*Robbie Power*	9
2018	147	Lalor 6-11-4: 14/1	Kayley Woollacott	*Richard Johnson*	13
2019	159	Felix Desjy 6-11-4: 7/2	Gordon Elliott (Ir)	*Jack Kennedy*	7

BETWAY AINTREE HURDLE (Gr 1) (Aintree 2½m)

1993	169	Morley Street 9-11-7: 6/1	G B Balding	*G Bradley*	6
1994	172	Danoli 6-11-7: 9/2	T Foley (Ir)	*C F Swan*	8
1995	167	Danoli 7-11-7: 2/1	T Foley (Ir)	*C F Swan*	6
1996	169	Urubande 6-11-7: 10/3	A P O'Brien (Ir)	*C F Swan*	8
1997	162	Bimsey 7-11-7: 14/1	R Akehurst	*M Fitzgerald*	7
1998	168	Pridwell 8-11-7: 6/1	M C Pipe	*A P McCoy*	6
1999	170	Istabraq 7-11-7: 1/2	A P O'Brien (Ir)	*C F Swan*	7
2000	159	Mister Morose 10-11-7: 16/1	N A Twiston-Davies	*C Llewellyn*	10
2001	157	Barton 8-11-7: 9/1	T D Easterby	*A Dobbin*	8
2002	156	Ilnamar 6-11-7: 9/1	M C Pipe	*R Walsh*	14
2003	159	Sacundai 6-11-7: 9/1	E J O'Grady (Ir)	*R Walsh*	11
2004	159	Rhinestone Cowboy 8-11-7: 5/2	J O'Neill	*Mr J P Magnier*	11
2005	159	Al Eile 5-11-7: 11/1	J Queally (Ir)	*T J Murphy*	9
2006	162	Asian Maze 7-11-0: 4/1	T Mullins (Ir)	*R Walsh*	9
2007	159	Al Eile 7-11-7: 12/1	J Queally (Ir)	*T J Murphy*	11
2008	157	Al Eile 8-11-7: 11/4	J Queally (Ir)	*T J Murphy*	9
2009	160	Solwhit 5-11-7: 6/1	C Byrnes (Ir)	*D N Russell*	16
2010	157	Khyber Kim 8-11-7: 7/2	N A Twiston-Davies	*P J Brennan*	7
2011	162	Oscar Whisky 6-11-7: 6/1	Nicky Henderson	*Barry Geraghty*	8
2012	163	Oscar Whisky 7-11-7: 9/4	Nicky Henderson	*Barry Geraghty*	5
2013	160	Zarkandar 6-11-7: 11/2	Paul Nicholls	*R Walsh*	9
2014	159	The New One 6-11-7: 4/9	Nigel Twiston-Davies	*Sam Twiston-Davies*	6
2015	167	Jezki 7-11-7: 3/1	Mrs J Harrington (Ir)	*A P McCoy*	6
2016	170	Annie Power 8-11-0: 4/9	W P Mullins (Ir)	*R Walsh*	6
2017	170	Buveur d'Air 6-11-7: 4/9	Nicky Henderson	*Barry Geraghty*	6
2018	163	L'Ami Serge 8-11-7: 5/1	Nicky Henderson	*Daryl Jacob*	9
2019	157	Supasundae 9-11-7: 15/2	Mrs J. Harrington (Ir)	*Robbie Power*	7

DOOM BAR MAGHULL NOVICES' CHASE (Gr 1) (Aintree 1m7f176y)

1993	135	Valiant Boy 7-11-10: 12/1	S Kettlewell	*R Garritty*	7
1994	136	Nakir 6-11-10: 6/5	S Christian	*J Osborne*	6
1995	144	Morceli 7-11-3: 11/4	J H Johnson	*N Williamson*	7
1996	135	Ask Tom 7-11-4: 10/1	T P Tate	*P Niven*	10
1997	145	Squire Silk 8-11-4: 2/1	A Turnell	*J Osborne*	6
1998	140	Direct Route 7-11-4: 9/2	J H Johnson	*P Carberry*	6
1999	141	Flagship Uberalles 5-10-11: 5/2	P F Nicholls	*J Tizzard*	7
2000	146	Cenkos 6-11-4: 5/2	O Sherwood	*D J Casey*	6
2001	139	Ballinclay King 7-11-4: 6/1	F Murphy	*A Maguire*	7
2002	144	Armaturk 5-11-4: 5/2	P F Nicholls	*T J Murphy*	5
2003	156	Le Roi Miguel 5-11-4: 9/4	P F Nicholls	*R Walsh*	5
2004	140	Well Chief 5-11-4: 15/8	M C Pipe	*A P McCoy*	10

2005	154	Ashley Brook 7-11-4: 3/1	K Bishop	*P J Brennan*	10
2006	155	Foreman 8-11-4: 4/1	T Doumen (Fr)	*A P McCoy*	7
2007	147	Twist Magic 5-11-1: 9/4	P F Nicholls	*R Walsh*	6
2008	151	Tidal Bay 7-11-4: 6/4	J H Johnson	*D O'Regan*	8
2009	152	Kalahari King 8-11-4: 9/4	F Murphy	*G Lee*	6
2010	153	Tataniano 6-11-4: 10/3	P F Nicholls	*R Walsh*	10
2011	150	Finian's Rainbow 8-11-4: 10/11	Nicky Henderson	*Barry Geraghty*	7
2012	160	Sprinter Sacre 6-11-4: 1/7	Nicky Henderson	*Barry Geraghty*	4
2013	152	Special Tiara 6-11-4: 28/1	H de Bromhead (Ir)	*Bryan Cooper*	6
2014	158	Balder Succes 6-11-4: 7/2	Alan King	*Wayne Hutchinson*	7
2015	155	Sizing Granite 7-11-4: 9/2	Henry de Bromhead (Ir)	*J J Burke*	6
2016	180	Douvan 6-11-4: 2/13	W P Mullins (Ir)	*P Townend*	5
2017	161	San Benedeto 6-11-4: 4/1	Paul Nicholls	*Nick Scholfield*	5
2018	155	Diego du Charmil 6-11-4: 5/1	Paul Nicholls	*Harry Cobden*	6
2019	151	Ornua 8-11-4: 3/1	Henry de Bromhead (Ir)	*Davy Russell*	7

RANDOX HEALTH GRAND NATIONAL HANDICAP CHASE (Gr 3)

(Aintree 4¼m74y, 4m3½f 2013-15, 4½m before 2013)

1993		Void			
1994	159	Miinnehoma 11-10-8: 16/1	M C Pipe	*R Dunwoody*	36
1995	161	Royal Athlete 12-10-6: 40/1	Mrs J Pitman	*J Titley*	35
1996	157	Rough Quest 10-10-7: 7/1	T Casey	*M Fitzgerald*	27
1997	160	Lord Gyllene 9-10-0: 14/1	S A Brookshaw	*A Dobbin*	36
1998	156	Earth Summit 10-10-5: 7/1	N A Twiston-Davies	*C Llewellyn*	37
1999	152	Bobbyjo 9-10-0: 10/1	T Carberry (Ir)	*P Carberry*	32
2000	154	Papillon 9-10-12: 10/1	T M Walsh (Ir)	*R Walsh*	40
2001	?	Red Marauder 11-10-11: 33/1	N B Mason	*Richard Guest*	40
2002	146	Bindaree 8-10-4: 20/1	N A Twiston-Davies	*J Culloty*	40
2003	146	Monty's Pass 10-10-7: 16/1	J J Mangan (Ir)	*B J Geraghty*	40
2004	146	Amberleigh House 12-10-10: 16/1	D McCain	*G Lee*	39
2005	157	Hedgehunter 9-11-1: 7/1	W P Mullins (Ir)	*R Walsh*	40
2006	149	Numbersixvalverde 10-10-8: 11/1	M Brassil (Ir)	*N P Madden*	40
2007	147	Silver Birch 10-10-6: 33/1	G Elliott (Ir)	*R M Power*	40
2008	155	Comply Or Die 9-10-9: 7/1	D E Pipe	*T J Murphy*	40
2009	159	Mon Mome 9-11-0: 100/1	Miss V Williams	*L Treadwell*	40
2010	162	Don't Push It 10-11-5: 10/1	J O'Neill	*A P McCoy*	40
2011	159	Ballabriggs 10-11-0: 14/1	Donald McCain	*Jason Maguire*	40
2012	166	Neptune Collonges 11-11-6: 33/1	Paul Nicholls	*Daryl Jacob*	40
2013	145	Auroras Encore 11-10-3: 66/1	Sue Smith	*Ryan Mania*	40
2014	151	Pineau de Re 11-10-6: 25/1	Dr Richard Newland	*Leighton Aspell*	40
2015	168	Many Clouds 8-11-9: 25/1	Oliver Sherwood	*Leighton Aspell*	39
2016	156	Rule The World 9-10-7: 33/1	M F Morris (Ir)	*David Mullins*	39
2017	157	One For Arthur 8-10-11: 14/1	Lucinda Russell	*Derek Fox*	40
2018	155	Tiger Roll 8-10-13: 10/1	Gordon Elliott (Ir)	*Davy Russell*	38
2019	165	Tiger Roll 9-11-5: 4/1	Gordon Elliott (Ir)	*Davy Russell*	40

CORAL SCOTTISH GRAND NATIONAL HANDICAP CHASE (Gr 3)

(Ayr 3m7f176y, run over 4m1f until 2006)

1993	153	Run For Free 9-11-10: 6/1	M C Pipe	*M Perrett*	21
1994	134	Earth Summit 6-10-0: 16/1	N A Twiston-Davies	*D Bridgwater*	22
1995	144	Willsford 12-10-12: 16/1	Mrs J Pitman	*R Farrant*	22
1996	142	Moorcroft Boy 11-10-2: 20/1	D Nicholson	*M Dwyer*	20
1997	152	Belmont King 9-11-10: 16/1	P F Nicholls	*A P McCoy*	17
1998	137	Baronet 8-10-0: 7/1	D Nicholson	*A Maguire*	18
1999	153	Young Kenny 8-11-10: 5/2	P Beaumont	*B Powell*	15
2000	150	Paris Pike 8-11-0: 5/1	F Murphy	*A Maguire*	18
2001	150	Gingembre 7-11-2: 12/1	Mrs L C Taylor	*A Thornton*	30
2002	145	Take Control 8-10-6: 20/1	M C Pipe	*R Walsh*	18
2003	146	Ryalux 10-10-5: 15/2	A Crook	*R McGrath*	19
2004	159	Grey Abbey 10-11-12: 12/1	J H Johnson	*G Lee*	28
2005	138	Joes Edge 8-9-11: 20/1	F Murphy	*K Mercer[1]*	20
2006	141	Run For Paddy 10-10-2: 33/1	C Llewellyn	*C Llewellyn*	30
2007	138	Hot Weld 8-9-9: 14/1	F Murphy	*P J McDonald[8]*	23
2008	149	Iris de Balme 8-9-7: 66/1	S Curran	*Mr C Huxley[7]*	24
2009	141	Hello Bud 11-10-9: 12/1	N A Twiston-Davies	*P J Brennan*	17
2010	138	Merigo 9-10-0: 18/1	A Parker	*T J Murphy*	30
2011	149	Beshabar 9-10-4: 15/2	Tim Vaughan	*Richard Johnson*	28

2012	142	Merigo 11-10-2: 15/2	Andrew Parker	*Timmy Murphy*	24
2013	148	Godsmejudge 7-11-3: 12/1	Alan King	*Wayne Hutchinson*	24
2014	144	Al Co 9-10-0: 40/1	Peter Bowen	*Jamie Moore*	29
2015	142	Wayward Prince 11-10-1: 25/1	Hilary Parrott	*Robert Dunne*	29
2016	152	Vicente 7-11-3: 14/1	Paul Nicholls	*Sam Twiston-Davies*	28
2017	151	Vicente 8-11-10: 9/1	Paul Nicholls	*Sam Twiston-Davies*	30
2018	140	Joe Farrell 9-10-6: 33/1	Rebecca Curtis	*Adam Wedge*	29
2019	137	Takingrisks 10-10-1: 25/1	Nicky Richards	*Sean Quinlan*	23

bet365 CELEBRATION CHASE (Gr 1) (Sandown 1m7f119y; Grade 2 until 2013)

2002	160	Cenkos 8-11-6: 8/1	P F Nicholls	*B J Geraghty*	5
2003	158	Seebald 8-11-6: 11/8	M C Pipe	*A P McCoy*	5
2004	163	Cenkos 10-11-10: 9/2	P F Nicholls	*B J Geraghty*	11
2005	164	Well Chief 6-11-10: 9/4	M C Pipe	*T J Murphy*	9
2006	153	River City 9-11-6: 9/1	N T Chance	*T Doyle*	4
2007	149	Dempsey 9-11-6: 5/4	C Llewellyn	*T J Murphy*	8
2008	157	Andreas 8-11-2: 9/2	P F Nicholls	*R Walsh*	11
2009	158	Twist Magic 7-11-6: 7/2	P F Nicholls	*R Walsh*	7
2010	151	I'm So Lucky 8-11-2: 9/1	D E Pipe	*T Scudamore*	8
2011	154	French Opera 8-11-2: 2/1	Nicky Henderson	*A P McCoy*	6
2012	169	Sanctuaire 6-11-2: 9/2	Paul Nicholls	*Daryl Jacob*	8
2013	166	Sire de Grugy 7-11-2: 6/1	Gary Moore	*Jamie Moore*	10
2014	158	Sire de Grugy 8-11-7: 2/7	Gary Moore	*Jamie Moore*	6
2015	167	Special Tiara 8-11-7: 3/1	Henry de Bromhead (Ir)	*Noel Fehily*	7
2016	179	Sprinter Sacre 10-11-7: 11/10	Nicky Henderson	*Nico de Boinville*	6
2017	175	Altior 7-11-7: 30/100	Nicky Henderson	*Nico de Boinville*	4
2018	162	Altior 8-11-7: 2/11	Nicky Henderson	*Nico de Boinville*	6
2019	158	Altior 9-11-7: 1/6	Nicky Henderson	*Nico de Boinville*	5

bet365 GOLD CUP HANDICAP CHASE (Gr 3) (Sandown 3½m166y)

1993	152	*Topsham Bay 10-10-1: 10/1	D H Barons	*R Dunwoody*	13
1994	148	Ushers Island 8-10-0: 25/1	J H Johnston	*C F Swan*	12
1995	156	Cache Fleur 9-10-1: 10/1	M C Pipe	*R Dunwoody*	14
1996	166	Life of A Lord 10-11-10: 12/1	A P O'Brien (Ir)	*C F Swan*	17
1997	139	Harwell Lad 8-10-0: 14/1	R H Alner	*Mr R Nuttall*	9
1998	155	Call It A Day 8-10-10: 8/1	D Nicholson	*A Maguire*	19
1999	144	Eulogy 9-10-0: 14/1	R Rowe	*B Fenton*	19
2000	168	Beau 7-10-9: 6/1	N A Twiston-Davies	*C Llewellyn*	20
2001	149	Ad Hoc 7-10-4: 14/1	P F Nicholls	*R Walsh*	25
2002	155	Bounce Back 6-10-9: 14/1	M C Pipe	*A P McCoy*	20
2003	156	Ad Hoc 9-10-7: 7/1	P F Nicholls	*R Walsh*	16
2004	147	Puntal 8-11-4: 25/1	M C Pipe	*D J Howard[3]*	18
2005	134	Jack High 10-10-0: 16/1	T M Walsh (Ir)	*G Cotter*	19
2006	159	Lacdoudal 7-11-5: 10/1	P J Hobbs	*R Johnson*	18
2007	141	Hot Weld 8-10-0: 6/1	F Murphy	*G Lee*	10
2008	154	Monkerhostin 10-10-13: 25/1	P J Hobbs	*R Johnson*	19
2009	137	Hennessy 10-10-7: 13/2	C Llewellyn	*A P McCoy*	14
2010	149	Church Island 11-10-5: 20/1	M Hourigan (Ir)	*A P Heskin[7]*	19
2011	141	Poker de Sivola 8-10-12: 11/1	Ferdy Murphy	*Timmy Murphy*	18
2012	165	Tidal Bay 11-11-12: 9/1	Paul Nicholls	*Daryl Jacob*	19
2013	138	Quentin Collonges 9-10-12: 14/1	Henry Daly	*Andrew Tinkler*	19
2014	152	Hadrian's Approach 7-11-0: 10/1	Nicky Henderson	*Barry Geraghty*	19
2015	142	Just A Par 8-10-3: 14/1	Paul Nicholls	*Sean Bowen[3]*	20
2016	152	The Young Master 7-11-1: 8/1	Neil Mulholland	*Mr S Waley-Cohen[3]*	20
2017	127	Henllan Harri 9-10-0: 40/1	Peter Bowen	*Sean Bowen*	13
2018	146	Step Back 8-10-0: 7/1	Mark Bradstock	*Jamie Moore*	20
2019	155	Talkischeap 7-10-11: 7/1	Alan King	*Wayne Hutchinson*	15

Ireland

---

thetote.com GALWAY PLATE (HANDICAP CHASE) (Galway 2¾m111y)

1993	153	General Idea 8-12-0: 9/2	D K Weld	*A Maguire*	21
1994	123	Feathered Gale 7-9-11: 8/1	A L T Moore	*F Woods*	22
1995	156	Life of A Lord 9-11-8: 12/1	A P O'Brien	*T Horgan*	21
1996	171	Life of A Lord 10 12-0: 9/2	A P O'Brien	*C F Swan*	17

1997	128	Stroll Home 7-9-12: 11/2	J J Mangan	*P Carberry*	22
1998	142	Amlah 6-9-13: 16/1	P J Hobbs (GB)	*B Powell*	22
1999	149	Moscow Express 7-11-4: 4/1	Miss F M Crowley	*R Walsh*	21
2000	118	Dovaly 7-9-13: 20/1	M J P O'Brien	*T P Rudd*	22
2001	132	Grimes 8-10-1: 4/1	C Roche	*C O'Dwyer*	14
2002	120	Rockholm Boy 9-10-5: 20/1	M Hourigan	*K Hadnett[5]*	22
2003	130	Nearly A Moose 7-10-1: 25/1	P Mullins	*R M Power[3]*	22
2004	130	Ansar 8-10-12: 10/1	D K Weld	*D J Casey*	22
2005	143	Ansar 9-11-11: 10/1	D K Weld	*D F O'Regan[3]*	22
2006	135	Far From Trouble 7-10-4: 8/1	C Roche	*R Loughran*	22
2007	136	Sir Frederick 7-9-10: 12/1	W J Burke	*K T Coleman[3]*	22
2008	153	Oslot 6-10-13: 11/4	P F Nicholls (GB)	*R Walsh*	22
2009	142	Ballyholland 8-10-9: 16/1	C A McBratney	*A J McNamara*	20
2010	143	Finger Onthe Pulse 9-10-12: 22/1	T J Taaffe	*A P McCoy*	22
2011	151	Blazing Tempo 7-10-4: 5/1	W P Mullins	*Paul Townend*	22
2012	145	Bob Lingo 10-10-13: 16/1	Thomas Mullins	*Mark Walsh*	20
2013	141	Carlingford Lough 7-10-7: 7/2	John E Kiely	*A P McCoy*	22
2014	161	Road To Riches 7-11-4: 14/1	Noel Meade	*Shane Shortall[7]*	22
2015	149	Shanahan's Turn 7-10-10: 16/1	Henry de Bromhead	*J J Burke*	22
2016	150	Lord Scoundrel 7-10-7: 10/1	Gordon Elliott	*Donagh Meyler[5]*	22
2017	153	Balko des Flos 6-10-10: 6/1	Henry de Bromhead	*Davy Russell*	22
2018	153	Clarcam 8-10-3: 33/1	Gordon Elliott	*Mark Enright*	22

GUINNESS GALWAY HURDLE HANDICAP (Galway 2m11y)

1993	?	Camden Buzz 5-10-12: 4/1	P Mullins	*C F Swan*	22
1994	128	Oh So Grumpy 6-10-9: 7/1	Mrs J Harrington	*M Dwyer*	27
1995	130	No Tag 7-10-11: 11/2	P G Kelly	*J Titley*	23
1996	127	Mystical City 6-10-1: 20/1	W P Mullins	*D Casey*	21
1997	150	Toast The Spreece 5-10-9: 12/1	A P O'Brien	*A P McCoy*	20
1998	130	Black Queen 7-10-2: 10/1	J E Kiely	*J Barry*	24
1999	152	Quinze 6-11-12: 11/1	P Hughes	*R Dunwoody*	25
2000	137	Perugino Diamond 4-9-8: 14/1	S O'Farrell	*J Culloty*	20
2001	136	Ansar 5-9-9: 6/1	D K Weld	*P Carberry*	20
2002	131	Say Again 6-10-7: 16/1	P Nolan	*J L Cullen*	24
2003	120	Sabadilla 9-9-7: 14/1	P M Verling	*P M Verling*	24
2004	129	Cloone River 8-10-7: 7/2	P Nolan	*J Cullen*	24
2005	128	More Rainbows 5-9-10: 33/1	N Meade	*N P Madden*	17
2006	132	Cuan Na Grai 5-10-9: 7/1	P Nolan	*P W Flood*	20
2007	143	Farmer Brown 6-10-11: 9/2	P Hughes	*D N Russell*	20
2008	131	Indian Pace 7-9-10: 7/1	J E Kiely	*P Townend[8]*	20
2009	152	Bahrain Storm 6-10-12: 20/1	P J Flynn	*S J Gray[5]*	20
2010	161	Overturn 6-11-6: 6/1	Donald McCain (GB)	*Graham Lee*	19
2011	146	Moon Dice 6-10-0: 20/1	Paul Flynn	*Tom Doyle*	20
2012	156	Rebel Fitz 7-11-5: 11/2	Michael Winters	*Davy Russell*	20
2013	145	Missunited 6-10-8: 7/1	Michael Winters	*Robbie Power*	20
2014	142	Thomas Edison 7-10-6: 7/2	A J Martin	*A P McCoy*	20
2015	143	Quick Jack 6-10-4: 9/2	A J Martin	*Denis O'Regan*	20
2016	145	Clondaw Warrior 9-11-5: 9/2	W P Mullins	*R Walsh*	20
2017	144	Tigris River 6-10-9: 5/1	Joseph Patrick O'Brien	*Barry Geraghty*	20
2018	149	Sharjah 5-11-7: 12/1	W P Mullins	*Mr P W Mullins*	20

JNwine.com CHAMPION CHASE (Gr 1) (Down Royal 3m, Gr 1 from 2002)

1999	164	Florida Pearl 7-11-10: 11/10	W P Mullins	*P Carberry*	6
2000	156	Looks Like Trouble 8-11-10: 5/4	N T Chance (GB)	*R Johnson*	5
2001	143	Foxchapel King 8-11-3: 4/1	M F Morris	*D J Casey*	7
2002	144	More Than A Stroll 10-11-10: 20/1	A L T Moore	*C O'Dwyer*	7
2003	143	Glenelly Gale 9-11-10: 7/1	A L T Moore	*C O'Dwyer*	4
2004	171	Beef Or Salmon 8-11-10: 1/1	M Hourigan	*T J Murphy*	8
2005		Abandoned			
2006	155	Beef Or Salmon 10-11-10: 11/4	M Hourigan	*A J McNamara*	7
2007	146	Taranis 6-11-10: 10/11	P F Nicholls (GB)	*R Walsh*	6
2008	149	Kauto Star 8-11-10: 2/5	P F Nicholls (GB)	*R Walsh*	5
2009	164	The Listener 11-11-10: 7/1	N Mitchell	*A J McNamara*	8
2010	162	Kauto Star 10-11-10: 4/7	Paul Nicholls (GB)	*R Walsh*	7
2011	161	Quito de La Roque 7-11-10: 11/4	Colm A Murphy	*Davy Russell*	7
2012	160	Kauto Stone 6-11-10: 4/1	Paul Nicholls (GB)	*Daryl Jacob*	8
2013	159	Roi du Mee 8-11-10: 12/1	Gordon Elliott	*Bryan Cooper*	6

2014	167	Road To Riches 7-11-10: 9/2	Noel Meade	*Paul Carberry*	8
2015	173	Don Cossack 8-11-10: 2/11	Gordon Elliott	*B J Cooper*	4
2016	168	Valseur Lido 7-11-10: 2/1	Henry de Bromhead	*R Walsh*	7
2017	164	Outlander 9-11-10: 16/1	Gordon Elliott	*J W Kennedy*	8
2018	164	Road To Respect 7-11-10: 6/4	Noel Meade	*Sean Flanagan*	6

baroneracing.com HATTON'S GRACE HURDLE (Gr 1) (Fairyhouse 2½m)

1994	162	Danoli 6-12-0: 4/6	T Foley	*C F Swan*	7
1995	140	Dorans Pride 6-12-0: 1/5	M Hourigan	*J Broderick*	3
1996	160	Large Action 8-12-0: 9/4	O Sherwood (GB)	*J Osborne*	8
1997	136	Istabraq 5-12-0: 1/3	A P O'Brien	*C F Swan*	5
1998	151	Istabraq 6-12-0: 1/5	A P O'Brien	*C F Swan*	6
1999	177	Limestone Lad 7-11-9: 13/2	J Bowe	*S M McGovern*	5
2000	161	Youlneverwalkalone 6-11-12: 5/4	C Roche	*C O'Dwyer*	7
2001	167	Limestone Lad 9-11-12: 9/4	J Bowe	*P Carberry*	7
2002	152	Limestone Lad 10-11-12: 8/15	J Bowe	*B J Geraghty*	5
2003	138	Solerina 6-11-7: 7/4	J Bowe	*G T Hutchinson*	10
2004	157	Solerina 7-11-7: 4/5	J Bowe	*G T Hutchinson*	5
2005	158	Solerina 8-11-7: 6/4	J Bowe	*G T Hutchinson*	5
2006	153	Brave Inca 8-11-12: 10/3	C A Murphy	*A P McCoy*	5
2007	152	Aitmatov 6-11-10: 2/1	N Meade	*P Carberry*	8
2008	156	Catch Me 6-11-10: 7/4	E J O'Grady	*A J McNamara*	8
2009	140	Oscar Dan Dan 7-11-10: 11/2	T Mullins	*D N Russell*	7
2010	155	Hurricane Fly 6-11-10: 11/4	W P Mullins	*Paul Townend*	11
2011	149	Voler La Vedette 7-11-3: 7/4	Colm A Murphy	*A E Lynch*	4
2012	158	Zaidpour 6-11-10: 7/4	W P Mullins	*R Walsh*	5
2013	160	Jezki 5-11-10: 4/6	Mrs John Harrington	*A P McCoy*	5
2014	148	Lieutenant Colonel 5-11-10: 7/2	Ms Sandra Hughes	*Bryan J Cooper*	5
2015	155	Arctic Fire 6-11-10: 4/5	W P Mullins	*R Walsh*	7
2016	158	Apple's Jade 4-10-13: 4/1	Gordon Elliott	*B J Cooper*	7
2017	156	Apple's Jade 5-11-3: 1/1	Gordon Elliott	*J W Kennedy*	7
2018	160	Apple's Jade 6-11-3: 4/6	Gordon Elliott	*Jack Kennedy*	9

JOHN DURKAN MEMORIAL PUNCHESTOWN CHASE (Gr 1)
(Punchestown 2½m40y, run at Fairyhouse in 1997 and 2010)

1992	143	Gold Options 10-11-4: 10/1	P McCreery	*M Dwyer*	9
1993	141	Cahervillahow 9-11-4: 3/1	M F Morris	*N Williamson*	11
1994	166	Merry Gale 6-12-0: 9/4	J Dreaper	*K O'Brien*	5
1995	161	Merry Gale 7-12-0: 6/4	J Dreaper	*R Dunwoody*	7
1996	152	Royal Mountbrowne 8-11-8: 7/1	A P O'Brien	*C F Swan*	6
1997	171	Dorans Pride 8-12-0: 2/5	M Hourigan	*R Dunwoody*	5
1998	153	Imperial Call 9-12-0: 13/8	R Hurley	*P Carberry*	8
1999	152	Buck Rogers 10-11-8: 16/1	V Bowens	*K Whelan*	8
2000	157	Native Upmanship 7-11-12: 9/10	A L T Moore	*C O'Dwyer*	4
2001	163	Florida Pearl 9-11-12: 5/1	W P Mullins	*P Carberry*	4
2002	168	Native Upmanship 9-11-12: 5/4	A L T Moore	*C O'Dwyer*	5
2003	167	Beef Or Salmon 7-11-12: 4/5	M Hourigan	*T J Murphy*	7
2004	165	Kicking King 6-11-12: 2/1	T J Taaffe	*B J Geraghty*	6
2005	153	Hi Cloy 8-11-12: 7/1	M Hourigan	*A J McNamara*	8
2006	149	In Compliance 6-11-12: 5/1	M J P O'Brien	*B J Geraghty*	8
2007	166	The Listener 8-11-10: 1/1	R H Alner (GB)	*D A Jacob*	10
2008	165	Noland 7-11-10: 9/4	P F Nicholls (GB)	*S Thomas*	8
2009	154	Joncol 6-11-10: 9/4	P Nolan	*A P Cawley*	9
2010	157	Tranquil Sea 8-11-10: 5/2	E J O'Grady	*Andrew J McNamara*	8
2011	162	Rubi Light 6-11-10: 5/2	Robert Hennessy	*A E Lynch*	7
2012	174	Flemenstar 7-11-10: 1/1	Peter Casey	*A E Lynch*	3
2013	162	Arvika Ligeonniere 8-11-10: 4/7	W P Mullins	*R Walsh*	3
2014	160	Don Cossack 7-11-10: 13/8	Gordon Elliott	*Brian O'Connell*	6
2015	175	Djakadam 6-11-10: 7/4	W P Mullins	*R Walsh*	7
2016	169	Djakadam 7-11-10: 4/5	W P Mullins	*R Walsh*	5
2017	169	Sizing John 7-11-10: 2/1	Mrs J Harrington	*Robbie Power*	6
2018	163	Min 7-11-10: 1/1	W P Mullins	*Ruby Walsh*	5

PADDY'S REWARDS CLUB 'SUGAR PADDY' CHASE (Gr 1)
(Leopardstown 2m1f, 2¼m 1996-1997, handicap prior to 1999, Grade 1 from 2004)

| 1992 | 117 | Saraemma 6-10-2: 5/1 | J H Scott | *C F Swan* | 9 |
| 1993 | ? | Lasata 8-10-12: 6/1 | M F Morris | *C O'Dwyer* | 9 |

1994	139	Brockley Court 7-11-2: 7/2	Mrs J Harrington	C F Swan	9
1995		Abandoned			
1996	155	Merry Gale 8-10-13: 5/4	J T R Dreaper	R Dunwoody	5
1997	108	MacAllister 7-9-13: 7/1	V Bowens	B Bowens[1]	4
1998	143	Papillon 7-10-11: 11/4	T M Walsh	R Walsh	4
1999	139	Merry Gale 11-11-5: 8/1	J T R Dreaper	P Moloney	10
2000	142	Papillon 9-12-0: 8/1	T M Walsh	R Walsh	4
2001	146	Knife Edge 6-12-0: 1/1	M J P O'Brien	T P Rudd	8
2002	151	Moscow Flyer 8-11-12: 4/9	Mrs J Harrington	B J Geraghty	6
2003	157	Moscow Flyer 9-11-12: 2/7	Mrs J Harrington	B J Geraghty	6
2004	153	Central House 7-11-12: 9/2	D T Hughes	P Carberry	4
2005	155	Hi Cloy 8-11-12: 8/1	M Hourigan	A J McNamara	5
2006	154	Nickname 7-11-12: 5/2	M Brassil	N P Madden	6
2007	153	Mansony 8-11-12: 2/1	A L T Moore	D N Russell	6
2008	155	Big Zeb 7-11-12: 5/1	C A Murphy	M M O'Connor	7
2009	160	Golden Silver 7-11-12: 5/2	W P Mullins	P Townend	7
2010	158	Big Zeb 9-11-12: 1/1	Colm A Murphy	Barry Geraghty	4
2011	159	Big Zeb 10-11-12: 7/10	Colm A Murphy	Robbie Power	5
2012	164	Sizing Europe 10-11-12: 1/3	H de Bromhead	A E Lynch	5
2013	162	Benefficient 7-11-12: 9/1	A J Martin	Bryan Cooper	7
2014	161	Twinlight 7-11-12: 16/1	W P Mullins	R Walsh	9
2015	160	Flemenstar 8-11-12: 16/1	Anthony Curran	A E Lynch	6
2016	182	Douvan 6-11-12: 1/8	W P Mullins	R Walsh	5
2017	157	*Simply Ned 10-11-12: 16/1	Nicky Richards (GB)	M P Walsh	6
2018	162	Simply Ned 11-11-12: 16/1	Nicky Richards (GB)	Mark Walsh	7

PADDY POWER CHASE (EXTENDED HANDICAP) (Leopardstown 3m100y)

1996	137	New Co 8-10-6: 11/4	M F Morris	C O'Dwyer	17
1997	140	Time For A Run 10-11-1: 12/1	E J O'Grady	Mr P Fenton	21
1998	142	Calling Wild 8-11-3: 8/1	P F Nicholls (GB)	J Tizzard	26
1999	135	Inis Cara 7-10-8: 11/1	M Hourigan	R P McNally[5]	20
2000	116	Call Me Dara 7-9-4: 33/1	R Tyner	N P Mulholland[1]	23
2001	112	I Can Imagine 6-9-2: 12/1	R Tyner	J P Elliott[5]	23
2002	115	Coq Hardi Diamond 8-9-11: 14/1	N Meade	G T Hutchinson[3]	21
2003	122	World Wide Web 7-10-1: 8/1	J O'Neill (GB)	L Cooper	28
2004	129	Keepatem 8-10-8: 7/2	M F Morris	C O'Dwyer	30
2005	123	Black Apalachi 6-10-5: 25/1	P J Rothwell	J L Cullen	26
2006	147	Cane Brake 7-11-3: 14/1	T J Taaffe	A B Joyce[7]	28
2007	125	Newbay Prop 8-9-10: 14/1	A J Martin	R Geraghty	29
2008	141	Wheresben 9-10-7: 33/1	S Fahey	Mr J A Fahey[7]	28
2009	138	Oscar Time 8-10-3: 10/1	M M Lynch	R M Power	28
2010	153	Majestic Concorde 7-11-9: 33/1	D K Weld	Mr R P McNamara	28
2011	132	Cross Appeal 5-10-4: 7/1	Noel Meade	Paul Carberry	26
2012	144	Colbert Station 8-10-11: 5/1	T M Walsh	A P McCoy	28
2013	130	Rockyaboya 9-10-3: 7/1	W P Mullins	R Walsh	28
2014	141	Living Next Door 8-10-9: 20/1	A J Martin	Denis O'Regan	26
2015	142	Minella Foru 6-10-8: 7/1	Edward Harty	Barry Geraghty	28
2016	158	Noble Endeavor 7-11-3: 6/1	Gordon Elliott	Davy Russell	28
2017	161	Anibale Fly 7-11-8: 14/1	A J Martin	Donagh Meyler	28
2018	140	Auvergnat 8-10-5: 28/1	Enda Bolger	D J McInerney (3)	27

SAVILLS CHASE (Gr 1) (Leopardstown 3m, Gr 2 prior to 2002)

1992	153	General Idea 7-11-11: 9/4	D K Weld	B Sheridan	10
1993	150	Deep Bramble 6-11-11: 4/1	M Hourigan	P Niven	9
1994	151	Commercial Artist 8-12-0: 9/1	V Bowens	G Bradley	5
1995		Abandoned			
1996	149	Johnny Setaside 7-12-0: 2/1	N Meade	R Dunwoody	7
1997	170	Imperial Call 8-12-0: 4/7	F Sutherland	C O'Dwyer	4
1998	?	Dorans Pride 9-12-0: 4/1	M Hourigan	P Carberry	6
1999	157	Rince Ri 6-12-0: 9/2	T M Walsh	C O'Dwyer	6
2000	162	Rince Ri 7-12-0: 5/1	T M Walsh	R Walsh	7
2001	164	Foxchapel King 8-12-0: 9/2	M F Morris	D J Casey	8
2002	156	Beef Or Salmon 6-11-9: 5/1	M Hourigan	T J Murphy	7
2003	171	Best Mate 8-11-12: 8/11	Miss H C Knight	J Culloty	8
2004	171	Beef Or Salmon 8-11-12: 9/4	M Hourigan	P Carberry	6
2005	169	Beef Or Salmon 9-11-12: 9/10	M Hourigan	P Carberry	5
2006	164	The Listener 7-11-10: 7/1	R H Alner	D Jacob	6

2007	162	Denman 7-11-10: 4/9	P F Nicholls (GB)	*R Walsh*	6
2008	168	Exotic Dancer 8-11-10: 4/1	J O'Neill (GB)	*A P McCoy*	9
2009	158	What A Friend 6-11-10: 11/2	P F Nicholls (GB)	*S Thomas*	11
2010	164	Pandorama 7-11-10: 7/2	Noel Meade	*Paul Carberry*	12
2011	165	Synchronised 8-11-10: 8/1	Jonjo O'Neill (GB)	*A P McCoy*	9
2012	170	Tidal Bay 11-11-10: 9/2	Paul Nicholls (GB)	*R Walsh*	9
2013	163	Bobs Worth 8-11-10: 11/4	Nicky Henderson (GB)	*Barry Geraghty*	9
2014	161	Road To Riches 7-11-10: 4/1	Noel Meade	*Bryan J Cooper*	9
2015	160	Don Poli 6-11-10: 4/6	W P Mullins	*B J Cooper*	6
2016	165	Outlander 8-11-10: 11/1	Gordon Elliott	*J W Kennedy*	13
2017	161	Road To Respect 6-11-10: 8/1	Noel Meade	*Sean Flanagan*	12
2018	168	Kemboy 6-11-10: 8/1	W P Mullins	*D J Mullins*	11

RYANAIR HURDLE (Gr 1) (Leopardstown 2m, Grade 1 in 1993 and from 2002)

1992	140	Novello Allegro 4-11-2: 6/1	N Meade	*C F Swan*	7
1993	150	Fortune And Fame 6-12-0: 2/1	D K Weld	*B Sheridan*	7
1994	145	Boro Eight 8-11-7: 11/10	P Mullins	*T P Treacy*	4
1995	140	Kharasar 5-11-7: 10/1	A Mullins	*M Dwyer*	10
1996	144	Theatreworld 4-11-2: 2/1	A P O'Brien	*C F Swan*	6
1997	136	Istabraq 5-12-0: 1/6	A P O'Brien	*C F Swan*	5
1998	150	Istabraq 6-12-0: 1/10	A P O'Brien	*C F Swan*	3
1999	161	Istabraq 7-12-0: 1/8	A P O'Brien	*C F Swan*	6
2000	161	Moscow Flyer 6-12-0: 5/1	Mrs J Harrington	*B J Geraghty*	7
2001	157	Istabraq 9-11-12: 4/11	A P O'Brien	*C F Swan*	6
2002	158	Liss A Paoraigh 7-11-7: 11/10	J E Kiely	*B J Geraghty*	5
2003	146	Golden Cross 4-11-7: 66/1	M Halford	*A P Lane*	7
2004	163	Macs Joy 5-11-12: 7/1	Mrs J Harrington	*B J Geraghty*	6
2005	163	Brave Inca 7-11-12: 9/4	C A Murphy	*A P McCoy*	5
2006	160	Brave Inca 8-11-12: 6/4	C A Murphy	*R Walsh*	4
2007	157	Al Eile 7-11-10: 9/2	J Queally	*T J Murphy*	6
2008	158	Sublimity 8-11-10: 3/1	R A Hennessy	*P A Carberry*	9
2009	159	Solwhit 5-11-10: 8/11	C Byrnes	*D N Russell*	6
2010	159	Hurricane Fly 6-11-10: 8/11	W P Mullins	*Paul Townend*	5
2011	153	Unaccompanied 4-11-0: 10/3	D K Weld	*Paul Townend*	7
2012	169	Hurricane Fly 8-11-10: 1/5	W P Mullins	*R Walsh*	5
2013	168	Hurricane Fly 9-11-10: 11/10	W P Mullins	*R Walsh*	5
2014	157	Hurricane Fly 10-11-10: 5/6	W P Mullins	*R Walsh*	7
2015	159	Nicholas Canyon 5-11-10: 2/5	W P Mullins	*R Walsh*	4
2016	162	Petit Mouchoir 5-11-10: 6/1	Henry de Bromhead	*B J Cooper*	5
2017	159	Mick Jazz 6-11-10: 14/1	Gordon Elliott	*Davy Russell*	5
2018	154	Sharjah 5-11-10: 6/1	W P Mullins	*Mr P W Mullins*	6

BHP INSURANCE IRISH CHAMPION HURDLE (Gr 1)

(Leopardstown 2m, run at Fairyhouse 1995)

1993	144	Royal Derbi 8-11-10: 14/1	N A Callaghan (GB)	*D Murphy*	11
1994	166	Fortune And Fame 7-11-10: 4/5	D K Weld	*A Maguire*	7
1995	144	Fortune And Fame 8-11-10: 1/2	D K Weld	*M Dwyer*	5
1996	160	Collier Bay 6-11-10: 5/1	J A B Old (GB)	*J Osborne*	11
1997	150	Cockney Lad 8-11-10: 10/1	N Meade	*R Hughes*	7
1998	150	Istabraq 6-11-10: 4/11	A P O'Brien	*C F Swan*	7
1999	165	Istabraq 7-11-10: 8/15	A P O'Brien	*C F Swan*	6
2000	160	Istabraq 8-11-10: 2/9	A P O'Brien	*C F Swan*	6
2001	160	Istabraq 9-11-10: 4/11	A P O'Brien	*C F Swan*	7
2002	143	Ned Kelly 6-11-10: 11/8	E J O'Grady	*N Williamson*	8
2003	152	Like-A-Butterfly 9-11-5: 6/4	C Roche	*C F Swan*	5
2004	150	Foreman 6-11-10: 8/1	T Doumen (Fr)	*T Doumen*	8
2005	160	Macs Joy 6-11-10: 11/8	Mrs J Harrington	*B J Geraghty*	6
2006	160	Brave Inca 8-11-10: 6/5	C A Murphy	*A P McCoy*	7
2007	161	Hardy Eustace 10-11-10: 9/1	D T Hughes	*C O'Dwyer*	8
2008	160	Sizing Europe 6-11-10: 10/3	H de Bromhead	*A J McNamara*	6
2009	155	Brave Inca 11-11-10: 11/4	C A Murphy	*R Walsh*	9
2010	162	Solwhit 6-11-10: 5/6	C Byrnes	*D N Russell*	7
2011	169	Hurricane Fly 7-11-10: 4/9	W P Mullins	*Paul Townend*	5
2012	168	Hurricane Fly 8-11-10: 4/5	W P Mullins	*R Walsh*	5
2013	169	Hurricane Fly 9-11-10: 1/6	W P Mullins	*R Walsh*	5
2014	163	Hurricane Fly 10-11-10: 4/7	W P Mullins	*R Walsh*	4
2015	16/	Hurricane Fly 11-11-10: 11/10	W P Mullins	*R Walsh*	6

2016	176	Faugheen 8-11-10: 3/10	W P Mullins	R Walsh	5
2017	162	Petit Mouchoir 6-11-10: 9/10	Henry de Bromhead	D J Mullins	4
2018	162	Supasundae 8-11-10: 8/1	Mrs J Harrington	Robbie Power	8
2019	162	Apple's Jade 7-11-3: 8/11	Gordon Elliott	Jack Kennedy	6

UNIBET IRISH GOLD CUP (Gr 1) (Leopardstown 3m)

1993	161	Jodami 8-12-0: 11/8	P Beaumont (GB)	M Dwyer	7
1994	160	Jodami 9-12-0: 5/4	P Beaumont (GB)	M Dwyer	6
1995	162	Jodami 10-12-0: 13/8	P Beaumont (GB)	M Dwyer	6
1996	176	Imperial Call 7-12-0: 4/1	F Sutherland	C O'Dwyer	8
1997	168	Danoli 9-12-0: 6/1	T Foley	T Treacy	8
1998	165	Dorans Pride 9-12-0: 6/4	M Hourigan	R Dunwoody	8
1999	166	Florida Pearl 7-12-0: 8/15	W P Mullins	R Dunwoody	7
2000	170	Florida Pearl 8-12-0: 8/11	W P Mullins	P Carberry	7
2001	169	Florida Pearl 9-12-0: 5/4	W P Mullins	R Johnson	7
2002	167	Alexander Banquet 9-12-0: 3/1	W P Mullins	B J Geraghty	5
2003	159	Beef Or Salmon 7-12-0: 1/1	M Hourigan	T J Murphy	5
2004	166	Florida Pearl 12-11-12: 5/1	W P Mullins	R Johnson	7
2005	167	Rule Supreme 9-11-12: 11/2	W P Mullins	D J Casey	7
2006	160	Beef Or Salmon 10-11-12: 2/5	M Hourigan	P Carberry	7
2007	167	Beef Or Salmon 11-11-12: 11/4	M Hourigan	A J McNamara	5
2008	157	The Listener 9-11-10: 2/1	R H Alner (GB)	D A Jacob	8
2009	168	Neptune Collonges 8-11-10: 8/13	P F Nicholls (GB)	R Walsh	6
2010	159	Joncol 7-11-10: 9/4	P Nolan	A P Cawley	7
2011	159	Kempes 8-11-10: 5/1	W P Mullins	D J Casey	9
2012	156	Quel Esprit 8-11-10: 5/4	W P Mullins	R Walsh	7
2013	167	Sir des Champs 7-11-10: 11/8	W P Mullins	Davy Russell	4
2014	161	Last Instalment 9-11-10: 8/1	Philip Fenton	Brian O'Connell	7
2015	161	Carlingford Lough 9-11-10: 4/1	John E Kiely	A P McCoy	8
2016	167	Carlingford Lough 10-11-10: 20/1	John E Kiely	Barry Geraghty	10
2017	164	Sizing John 7-11-10: 100/30	Mrs J Harrington	Robbie Power	7
2018	161	Edwulf 9-11-10: 33/1	Joseph Patrick O'Brien	Mr D O'Connor	10
2019	165	Bellshill 9-11-10: 2/1	W P Mullins	Ruby Walsh	4

BOYLESPORTS IRISH GRAND NATIONAL CHASE (EXTENDED HANDICAP)
(Fairyhouse 3m5f)

1993	142	Ebony Jane 8-10-7: 6/1	F Flood	C F Swan	27
1994	148	Son of War 7-10-10: 12/1	P McCreery	F Woods	18
1995	169	Flashing Steel 10-12-0: 9/1	J Mulhern	J Osborne	18
1996	145	Feathered Gale 9-10-0: 8/1	A L T Moore	F Woods	17
1997	142	Mudahim 11-10-3: 13/2	Mrs J Pitman (GB)	J Titley	20
1998	143	Bobbyjo 8-11-3: 8/1	T Carberry	P Carberry	22
1999	138	Glebe Lad 7-10-0: 8/1	M J P O'Brien	T P Rudd	18
2000	150	Commanche Court 7-11-4: 14/1	T M Walsh	R Walsh	24
2001	140	Davids Lad 7-10-0: 10/1	A J Martin	T J Murphy	19
2002	138	The Bunny Boiler 8-9-9: 12/1	N Meade	R Geraghty[5]	17
2003	137	Timbera 9-10-12: 11/1	D T Hughes	J Culloty	21
2004	129	Granit d'Estruval 10-10-0: 33/1	F Murphy (GB)	B Harding	28
2005	129	Numbersixvalverde 9-10-1: 9/1	M Brassil	R Walsh	26
2006	134	Point Barrow 8-10-8: 20/1	P Hughes	P A Carberry	26
2007	140	Butler's Cabin 7-10-4: 14/1	J O'Neill (GB)	A P McCoy	29
2008	140	Hear The Echo 7-10-0: 33/1	M F Morris	P W Flood	23
2009	147	Niche Market 8-10-5: 33/1	R H Buckler (GB)	H Skelton[3]	28
2010	142	Bluesea Cracker 8-10-4: 25/1	J Motherway	A J McNamara	26
2011	139	Organisedconfusion 6-9-13: 12/1	A L T Moore	Miss N Carberry	25
2012	141	Lion Na Bearnai 10-10-8: 33/1	Thomas Gibney	A P Thornton[3]	29
2013	135	Liberty Counsel 10-9-5: 50/1	Mrs D A Love	Ben Dalton[5]	28
2014	148	Shutthefrontdoor 7-10-13: 8/1	Jonjo O'Neill (GB)	Barry Geraghty	26
2015	143	Thunder And Roses 7-10-6: 20/1	Ms Sandra Hughes	Ms K Walsh	28
2016	145	Rogue Angel 8-10-9: 16/1	M F Morris	G N Fox[3]	27
2017	167	Our Duke 7-11-4: 9/2	Mrs J Harrington	Robbie Power	28
2018	142	General Principle 9-10-0: 20/1	Gordon Elliott	J J Slevin	28
2019	154	Burrows Saint 6-10-8: 6/1	W P Mullins	Ruby Walsh	30

BOYLESPORTS CHAMPION CHASE (Drogheda) (Gr 1)
(Punchestown 2m, handicap before 1999, run at Fairyhouse, 2m100y in 2001)

| 1993 | 144 | Viking Flagship 6-10-7: 5/4 | D Nicholson (GB) | R Dunwoody | 8 |